THE
MAXWELL
LEADERSHIP
BIBLE

NAME

GIVEN BY

DATE

OCCASION

NEW INTERNATIONAL VERSION

THE
MAXWELL
LEADERSHIP
BIBLE

John C. Maxwell
Tim Elmore

Executive Editors

THOMAS NELSON
Since 1798

NASHVILLE   DALLAS   MEXICO CITY   RIO DE JANEIRO

TABLE OF CONTENTS

THE OLD TESTAMENT

THE NEW TESTAMENT

Where do most people go to learn leadership? The answer to that question today is that they search many places. Some examine the world of politics. Others seek models in the entertainment industry. Many look to the world of business. Most people seem to look to successful CEOs, management consultants, and theoreticians with Ph.D.s to learn about leadership.

But the truth is, the best source of leadership teaching today is the same as it has been for thousands of years. If you want to learn leadership, go to the greatest Book on leadership ever written—the Bible.

You are holding in your hands a tool that has the potential to change your life and the course of your development as a spiritual leader. It is a Bible that draws out the leadership principles that have been woven into it by the One who invented leadership. Who could possibly teach us more about leadership than God himself?

With so many different Bibles to choose from on the shelves of bookstores today, why would anyone take the time and energy to create a Leadership Bible?

▋ The Crying Need of the Church Today Is Leadership

The most critical problem facing the church today is the leadership vacuum that grew during the twentieth century. Church expert and statistician George Barna asserts, "Leadership remains one of the glaring needs of the church. People are often willing to follow God's vision, but too frequently they have no exposure to either vision or true leadership." Just a few years ago, Barna penned some sobering conclusions based on his research: "After fifteen years of digging into the world around me, I have reached several conclusions regarding the future of the Christian church in America. The central conclusion is that the American church is dying due to lack of strong leadership. In this time of unprecedented opportunity and plentiful resources, the church is actually losing influence. The primary reason is the lack of leadership . . . Nothing is more important than leadership."

Christ left his church on earth to do work that has an eternal impact. If the local church isn't well led, then the bride of Christ suffers, and she will not be able fulfill her mission for this generation.

▋ God Himself Calls Us to Leadership

God is the Ultimate Leader, and he calls every believer to lead others. God could have arranged his creation any number of ways. He chose to create human beings who possess spirits and the capacity to relate to him and follow him, yet who are not forced to do so. When mankind fell into sin, God could have easily executed a plan of redemption that did not include sinful people in the process. But he has called us to participate and to lead others as we follow him. He makes that clear from the beginning: "Let us make mankind in our image, in our likeness, so that they may rule . . ." (Ge 1:26).

I wholeheartedly believe that everything rises and falls on leadership. By that I mean that, more than anything else, the leadership of any group or organization will determine its success or failure. You can see the impact of leadership frequently in the Bible. In ancient Israel, when God's people had a good king, all was well with the nation. When they had a bad king, things went poorly for everyone. That's why Scripture teaches that without a vision people perish (see Pr 29:18).

The call to leadership is a consistent pattern in the Bible. When God decided to raise up a nation of his own, he didn't call upon the masses. He called out one leader—Abraham. When he wanted to deliver his people out of Egypt, he didn't guide them as a group. He raised up a leader to do it—Moses. When it came time for the people to cross into the promised land, they followed one man—Joshua. Every time God desires to do something great, he calls a leader to step forward. Today he still calls leaders to step forward for every great work.

▌ Believers Often Misunderstand the True Nature of Leadership

Somewhere along the way, countless Christians became convinced that if they were going to follow Christ, they must become sheepish, quiet, and withdrawn. The problem is that they have confused meekness with weakness. As Christians we recognize our own weaknesses, but that is when God's strength is perfected in us (see 2Co 12:9). What God desires is that we display a broken boldness.

A follower of God should be a leader of people. That's more than just being "boss" or having a leadership position. And it certainly doesn't mean being pushy or in control. Jesus taught that it means serving others (see Mt 20:25–28). While there is a gift of leadership (according to Romans 12:8), you need not possess that gift to exert your influence in a Christlike way. Leadership is influence—nothing more, nothing less. If you are being salt and light as Jesus commanded, then you have begun to obey God's call to leadership.

▌ All Believers Can Further Their Potential with Leadership

One of the most important leadership lessons I teach—it's the first law in The 21 Irrefutable Laws of Leadership—is the Law of the Lid, which states, "Leadership ability determines a person's level of effectiveness." That is key when working with others. Greater than resources, talent, money, or intelligence, leadership makes the difference when it comes to making an impact. Consequently, my goal in creating this Leadership Bible is to enable you to raise the "lid" on your own effectiveness. I want you to reach your potential in Christ! To become more Christlike, you need to think and act more like a leader. You must become a person of influence.

▌ Good Leadership Is the Best Means for Leaving a Lasting Legacy

We live in an age of tolerance, where protecting feelings is more highly valued than proclaiming the truth. People look with suspicion upon anyone who desires to influence others to embrace their beliefs. I want to encourage you to buck popular opinion. As Thomas Jefferson proclaimed, "In matters of fashion, swim with the current. In matters of conscience, stand like a rock."

I want to challenge you to become a dedicated student of leadership—if you aren't already one. Becoming a good leader may not guarantee that you will be able to leave a spiritual legacy for future generations, but it certainly provides you the greatest opportunity to do so.

The Law of Legacy states, "True success is measured by succession." A legacy that does not include people has no eternal value. That is why leadership is critical. Make it your aim to practice transformational leadership, where people's lives are changed from the inside out. That kind of leadership is based on character, conviction, and Christlikeness. In other words, transformational leadership follows the pattern laid down in Scripture.

The need of the hour is great. That is why I have dedicated my life to teaching leadership in the church. And I will continue to do so until God calls me home. My hope is that this Leadership Bible will be of great value and assistance to you. In addition to God's Word, which is more precious than riches, it contains leadership truths, principles, and examples which I have drawn from the Scriptures and attempted to make accessible through case studies, profiles, outlines, and lessons. Study from it, use it in your prayer times, teach from it, and use it as a reference tool as you face leadership challenges at home, in the marketplace, and at church.

My prayer is that you will be transformed by spending time with the men and women God has used as leaders to change the world for millennia. And if you are transformed as a leader, then you won't be able to keep from influencing your world.

Dr. John C. Maxwell

GOD HAS ALREADY CALLED *YOU* TO LEAD

Leadership is for everyone! How can I make such a bold claim? Because every person who accepts Christ is called to influence others. Everyone. Leadership is not just for a select few.

Years ago in his book *Spiritual Leadership*, J. Oswald Sanders gave the best definition of leadership I've ever read. He simply stated, "Leadership is influence." I have embraced that definition and taught it to thousands and thousands over the years. If you are a follower of Christ, then you recognize that you are called to influence others. Jesus said it this way: "You are the salt of the earth . . . You are the light of the world . . . Let your light shine before others, that they may see your good deeds and glorify your Father in heaven" (Mt 5:13–16).

It doesn't matter if you are a CEO or a stay-at-home mom; if you call yourself a Christian, then you are called to influence others. That's why it's important for you to learn to become a better leader—whether you are the parent in a family, the pastor of a church, the president of a company, or a potential leader for the next generation.

The problem is that, if you are like most people, you may not wake up in the morning, look in the mirror and say, "Now, there's a godly, effective leader if I ever saw one." Today most people don't believe they can make a positive impact on the world they live in. Even most pastors feel this way. In 1997 the Barna Research Group reported that 95 percent of American pastors said they don't believe they have the spiritual gift of leadership. Nor do they feel they have been adequately prepared for the task of leadership.

The truth is that few people are naturals when it comes to leading others. But everyone has potential. I believe you can become a better leader, regardless of your age, gender, marital status, or profession.

Sociologists say that even introverted people will influence an average of 10,000 people in their lifetime. Just think about that! Someone who's not even trying to lead others will impact many. Just think about what one person can do if he or she is intentional about leading—as Jesus directed us to be. What kind of impact potential has God put inside of you?

I want you to see yourself as a leader. I want you to learn from the best leaders who ever lived—the men and women in the Bible. No matter how strong or weak your leadership is—whether you are a "4" or a "9"—I want you to improve and reach your leadership potential for the glory of God.

Your friend,
John C. Maxwell

PREFACE

The goal of the New International Version (NIV) is to enable English-speaking people from around the world to read and hear God's eternal Word in their own language. Our work as translators is motivated by our conviction that the Bible is God's Word in written form. We believe that the Bible contains the divine answer to the deepest needs of humanity, sheds unique light on our path in a dark world and sets forth the way to our eternal well-being. Out of these deep convictions, we have sought to recreate as far as possible the experience of the original audience—blending transparency to the original text with accessibility for the millions of English speakers around the world. We have prioritized accuracy, clarity and literary quality with the goal of creating a translation suitable for public and private reading, evangelism, teaching, preaching, memorizing and liturgical use. We have also sought to preserve a measure of continuity with the long tradition of translating the Scriptures into English.

The complete NIV Bible was first published in 1978. It was a completely new translation made by over a hundred scholars working directly from the best available Hebrew, Aramaic and Greek texts. The translators came from the United States, Great Britain, Canada, Australia and New Zealand, giving the translation an international scope. They were from many denominations and churches—including Anglican, Assemblies of God, Baptist, Brethren, Christian Reformed, Church of Christ, Evangelical Covenant, Evangelical Free, Lutheran, Mennonite, Methodist, Nazarene, Presbyterian, Wesleyan and others. This breadth of denominational and theological perspective helped to safeguard the translation from sectarian bias. For these reasons, and by the grace of God, the NIV has gained a wide readership in all parts of the English-speaking world.

The work of translating the Bible is never finished. As good as they are, English translations must be regularly updated so that they will continue to communicate accurately the meaning of God's Word. Updates are needed in order to reflect the latest developments in our understanding of the biblical world and its languages and to keep pace with changes in English usage. Recognizing, then, that the NIV would retain its ability to communicate God's Word accurately only if it were regularly updated, the original translators established The Committee on Bible Translation (CBT). The committee is a self-perpetuating group of biblical scholars charged with keeping abreast of advances in biblical scholarship and changes in English and issuing periodic updates to the NIV. CBT is an independent, self-governing body and has sole responsibility for the NIV text. The committee mirrors the original group of translators in its diverse international and denominational makeup and in its unifying commitment to the Bible as God's inspired Word.

In obedience to its mandate, the committee has issued periodic updates to the NIV. An initial revision was released in 1984. A more thorough revision process was completed in 2005, resulting in the separately published Today's New International Version (TNIV). The updated NIV you now have in your hands builds on both the original NIV and the TNIV and represents the latest effort of the committee to articulate God's unchanging Word in the way the original authors might have said it had they been speaking in English to the global English-speaking audience today.

The first concern of the translators has continued to be the accuracy of the translation and its faithfulness to the intended meaning of the biblical writers. This has moved the translators to go beyond a formal word-for-word rendering of the original texts. Because thought patterns and syntax differ from language to language, accurate communication of the meaning of the biblical authors demands constant regard for varied contextual uses of words and idioms and for frequent modifications in sentence structures.

As an aid to the reader, sectional headings

have been inserted. They are not to be regarded as part of the biblical text and are not intended for oral reading. It is the committee's hope that these headings may prove more helpful to the reader than the traditional chapter divisions, which were introduced long after the Bible was written.

For the Old Testament the standard Hebrew text, the Masoretic Text as published in the latest edition of *Biblia Hebraica,* has been used throughout. The Masoretic Text tradition contains marginal notations that offer variant readings. These have sometimes been followed instead of the text itself. Because such instances involve variants within the Masoretic tradition, they have not been indicated in the textual notes. In a few cases, words in the basic consonantal text have been divided differently than in the Masoretic Text. Such cases are usually indicated in the textual footnotes. The Dead Sea Scrolls contain biblical texts that represent an earlier stage of the transmission of the Hebrew text. They have been consulted, as have been the Samaritan Pentateuch and the ancient scribal traditions concerning deliberate textual changes. The translators also consulted the more important early versions—the Greek Septuagint, Aquila, Symmachus and Theodotion, the Latin Vulgate, the Syriac Peshitta, the Aramaic Targums and, for the Psalms, the *Juxta Hebraica* of Jerome. Readings from these versions, the Dead Sea Scrolls and the scribal traditions were occasionally followed where the Masoretic Text seemed doubtful and where accepted principles of textual criticism showed that one or more of these textual witnesses appeared to provide the correct reading. In rare cases, the committee has emended the Hebrew text where it appears to have become corrupted at an even earlier stage of its transmission. These departures from the Masoretic Text are also indicated in the textual footnotes. Sometimes the vowel indicators (which are later additions to the basic consonantal text) found in the Masoretic Text did not, in the judgment of the committee, represent the correct vowels for the original text. Accordingly, some words have been read with a different set of vowels. These instances are usually not indicated in the footnotes.

The Greek text used in translating the New Testament is an eclectic one, based on the latest editions of the Nestle-Aland/United Bible Societies' Greek New Testament. The committee has made its choices among the variant readings in accordance with widely accepted principles of New Testament textual criticism. Footnotes call attention to places where uncertainty remains.

The New Testament authors, writing in Greek, often quote the Old Testament from its ancient Greek version, the Septuagint. This is one reason why some of the Old Testament quotations in the NIV New Testament are not identical to the corresponding passages in the NIV Old Testament. Such quotations in the New Testament are indicated with the footnote "(see Septuagint)."

Other footnotes in this version are of several kinds, most of which need no explanation. Those giving alternative translations begin with "Or" and generally introduce the alternative with the last word preceding it in the text, except when it is a single-word alternative. When poetry is quoted in a footnote, a slash mark indicates a line division.

It should be noted that references to diseases, minerals, flora and fauna, architectural details, clothing, jewelry, musical instruments and other articles cannot always be identified with precision. Also, linear measurements and measures of capacity can only be approximated (see the Table of Weights and Measures). Although *Selah,* used mainly in the Psalms, is probably a musical term, its meaning is uncertain. Since it may interrupt reading and distract the reader, this word has not been kept in the English text, but every occurrence has been signaled by a footnote.

One of the main reasons the task of Bible translation is never finished is the change in our own language, English. Although a basic core of the language remains relatively stable, many diverse and complex linguistic factors continue to bring about subtle shifts in the meanings and/or connotations of even old, well-established words and phrases. One of the shifts that creates particular challenges to writers and translators alike is the manner in which gender is presented. The original NIV (1978) was published in a time when "a man" would naturally be understood, in many contexts, to be referring to a person, whether male or female. But most English speakers today tend to hear a distinctly male connotation in this word. In recognition of this change in English, this edition of the NIV, along with almost all other recent English translations, substitutes other expressions when the original text intends to refer generically to men and women equally. Thus, for instance, the NIV (1984) rendering of 1 Corinthians 8:3, "But the man who loves God is known by God" becomes in this edition "But whoever loves God is known by God." On the other hand, "man" and "mankind," as ways of denoting the human race, are still widely used. This edition of the NIV therefore continues to use these words, along with other expressions, in this way.

A related shift in English creates a greater challenge for modern translations: the move away from using the third-person masculine singular pronouns—"he/him/his"—to refer to men and women equally. This usage does persist at a low level in some forms of English, and this revision therefore occasionally uses these pronouns in a generic sense. But the tendency, recognized in day-to-day usage and confirmed by extensive research, is away from the generic use of "he," "him" and "his." In recognition of this shift in language and in an effort to translate into the "common" English that people are actually using, this revision of the NIV generally uses other constructions when the biblical text is plainly addressed to men and women equally. The reader will frequently encounter a "they," "them" or "their" to express a generic singular idea. Thus, for instance, Mark 8:36 reads: "What good is it for someone to gain the whole world, yet forfeit their soul?" This generic use of the "indefinite" or "singular" "they/them/their" has a venerable place in English idiom and has quickly become established as standard English, spoken and written, all over the world. Where an individual emphasis is deemed to be present, "anyone" or "everyone" or some other equivalent is generally used as the antecedent of such pronouns.

Sometimes the chapter and/or verse numbering in English translations of the Old Testament differs from that found in published Hebrew texts. This is particularly the case in the Psalms, where the traditional titles are often included in the Hebrew verse numbering. Such differences are indicated in the footnotes at the bottom of the page. In the New Testament, verse numbers that marked off portions of the traditional English text not supported by the best Greek manuscripts now appear in brackets, with a footnote indicating the text that has been omitted (see, for example, Matthew 17:[21]).

Mark 16:9–20 and John 7:53—8:11, although long accorded virtually equal status with the rest of the Gospels in which they stand, have a very questionable—and confused—standing in the textual history of the New Testament, as noted in the bracketed annotations with which they are set off. A different typeface has been chosen for these passages to indicate even more clearly their uncertain status.

Basic formatting of the text, such as lining the poetry, paragraphing (both prose and poetry), setting up of (administrative-like) lists, indenting letters and lengthy prayers within narratives and the insertion of sectional headings, has been the work of the committee. However, the choice between single-column and double-column formats has been left to the publishers. Also the issuing of "red-letter" editions is a publisher's choice—one the committee does not endorse.

The committee has again been reminded that every human effort is flawed—including this revision of the NIV. We trust, however, that many will find in it an improved representation of the Word of God, through which they hear his call to faith in our Lord Jesus Christ and to service in his kingdom. We offer this version of the Bible to him in whose name and for whose glory it has been made.

The Committee on Bible Translation
September 2010

THE
OLD TESTAMENT

The
Old Testament

INTRODUCTION TO
GENESIS

Genesis, the book of beginnings, overflows with leadership lessons. It profiles some of the greatest leaders in the Bible—but everything begins with God, the Ultimate Leader. After creating the universe and the planet on which we live, he handed leadership of the earth over to humankind (1:26).

You and I were created to lead and to rule. Sin marred our ability to lead, however, and Genesis introduces the story of God's plan to redeem sinfully independent people from the bondage of following their fallen nature. Isn't most of history the story of conflict among people trying to lead and rule one another, independent of God's direction? That's why Genesis often gives accounts of men and women trying to sort out whether to lead or follow, obey or rebel, serve God or live for themselves.

Because God designed people to lead—to "rule over" the earth (1:26, 28)—we know that we possess a ruling capacity. But as sinful beings, we tend to go our own way instead of following God's leadership.

Genesis 6 tells us that humankind became so wicked and self-serving that God determined to start over. God flooded the earth, sparing the family of only one man, Noah. After the flood the earth began to repopulate itself, and people learned to cooperate with one another—but still they failed to follow God. The tower of Babel (11:1–9) provides a major symbol of humankind's arrogance. The people had a clear vision and strong leadership, but they rebelled against God. That is why God confused their speech and inaugurated a new leadership plan for them. He divided the people into language groups, then later chose one of those groups—the Hebrews—as his very own, to set an example for others.

God's Role in Genesis

God wanted his creation to begin well. He communicated his vision for the world to Adam, to Noah, to Abraham, then to Isaac and Jacob. Like all good leaders, God took initiative. Yet he never forced his leadership on anyone. Each time his people failed, he laid out his plan, then selected those he would invite to take appropriate action. He relentlessly pursued his plan of redeeming men and women from their failures, even as he maintained a relationship with them.

Leaders in Genesis

Adam, Noah, Abraham, Isaac, Jacob, Joseph, Potiphar, Pharaoh

Other People of Influence in Genesis

Eve, the builders of the tower of Babel, Sarah, Lot, Rebekah, Laban, Esau, Potiphar's wife

Lessons in Leadership

- God created humankind to lead and rule, but only within the context of his leadership.
- Leaders must learn to adjust their plans while holding tenaciously to the vision.
- Everyone leads and follows someone.
- No one can lead well without following well.
- Individuals must see the benefits of the vision before they will commit to it.

God's leadership of the Hebrews began just before his eternal covenant with Abram (later renamed Abraham) and continued with the patriarchs: Isaac, Jacob and Joseph. The leadership lessons they learned fill the final 38 chapters of Genesis. God intended not only for them to remain pure for him, but also to lead other nations back to God by modeling a lifestyle that would attract followers.

■ To win trust, leaders must exhibit both character and competence.

LEADERSHIP HIGHLIGHTS IN GENESIS

The Beginning

1 In the beginning God created the heavens and the earth. ²Now the earth was formless and empty, darkness was over the surface of the deep, and the Spirit of God was hovering over the waters.

³And God said, "Let there be light," and there was light. ⁴God saw that the light was good, and he separated the light from the darkness. ⁵God called the light "day," and the darkness he called "night." And there was evening, and there was morning—the first day.

⁶And God said, "Let there be a vault between the waters to separate water from water." ⁷So God made the vault and separated the water under the vault from the water above it. And it was so. ⁸God called the vault "sky." And there was evening, and there was morning—the second day.

⁹And God said, "Let the water under the sky be gathered to one place, and let dry ground appear." And it was so. ¹⁰God called the dry ground "land," and the gathered waters he called "seas." And God saw that it was good.

¹¹Then God said, "Let the land produce vegetation: seed-bearing plants and trees on the land that bear fruit with seed in it, according to their various kinds." And it was so. ¹²The land produced vegetation: plants bearing seed according to their kinds and trees bearing fruit with seed in it according to their kinds. And God saw that it was good. ¹³And there was evening, and there was morning—the third day.

¹⁴And God said, "Let there be lights in the vault of the sky to separate the day from the night, and let them serve as signs to mark sacred times, and days and years, ¹⁵and let them be lights in the vault of the sky to give light on the earth." And it was so. ¹⁶God made two great lights—the greater light to govern the day and the lesser light to govern the night. He also made the stars. ¹⁷God set them in the vault of the sky to give light on the earth, ¹⁸to govern the day and the night, and to separate light from darkness. And God saw that it was good. ¹⁹And there was evening, and there was morning—the fourth day.

²⁰And God said, "Let the water teem with living creatures, and let birds fly above the earth across the vault of the sky." ²¹So God created the great creatures of the sea and every living thing with which the water teems and that moves about in it, according to their kinds, and every winged bird according to its kind. And God saw that it was good. ²²God blessed them and said, "Be fruitful and increase in number and fill the water in the seas, and let the birds increase on the earth." ²³And there was evening, and there was morning—the fifth day.

²⁴And God said, "Let the land produce living creatures according to their kinds: the livestock, the creatures that move along the ground, and the wild animals, each according to its kind." And it was so. ²⁵God made the wild animals according to their kinds, the livestock according to their kinds, and all the creatures that move along the ground according to their kinds. And God saw that it was good.

²⁶Then God said, "Let us make mankind in our image, in our likeness, so that they may rule over the fish in the sea and the birds in the sky, over the livestock and all

---

Creation:
The Ultimate Leader Initiates

Genesis 1:1—2:25

Have you ever recognized God as the Ultimate Leader? Not only did he create the universe, redeem humankind, innovate with entrepreneurial energy, and act as a maverick—he also leads.

Although God could have ruled and redeemed planet earth on his own, he chose to include mortals in his plans. Think about it! He could have limited his creation to animals of instinct—but he didn't. He created human beings with a will of their own, men and women who must choose to follow his leadership according to his plan. God always brings others with him.

As the Ultimate Leader, God always initiates. He initiated the creation of the universe. He initiated the birth of our species. And he initiated the redemption process, extending himself to us so that we might be saved.

As you read the Scripture, watch how often God demonstrates his magnificent leadership. Truly he is the Ultimate Leader!

the wild animals,[a] and over all the creatures that move along the ground."

27 So God created mankind in his own image,
    in the image of God he created them;
    male and female he created them.

28 God blessed them and said to them, "Be fruitful and increase in number; fill the earth and subdue it. Rule over the fish in the sea and the birds in the sky and over every living creature that moves on the ground."

29 Then God said, "I give you every seed-bearing plant on the face of the whole earth and every tree that has fruit with seed in it. They will be yours for food. 30 And to all the beasts of the earth and all the birds in the sky and all the creatures that move along the ground — everything that has the breath of life in it — I give every green plant for food." And it was so.

31 God saw all that he had made, and it was very good. And there was evening, and there was morning — the sixth day.

2 Thus the heavens and the earth were completed in all their vast array.

2 By the seventh day God had finished the work he had been doing; so on the seventh day he rested from all his work. 3 Then God blessed the seventh day and made it holy, because on it he rested from all the work of creating that he had done.

Adam and Eve

4 This is the account of the heavens and the earth when they were created, when the LORD God made the earth and the heavens.

5 Now no shrub had yet appeared on the earth[b] and no plant had yet sprung up, for the LORD God had not sent rain on the earth and there was no one to work the ground, 6 but streams[c] came up from the earth and watered the whole surface of the ground. 7 Then the LORD God formed a man[d] from the dust of the ground and breathed into his nostrils the breath of life, and the man became a living being.

8 Now the LORD God had planted a garden in the east, in Eden; and there he put the man he had formed. 9 The LORD God made all kinds of trees grow out of the ground — trees that were pleasing to the eye and good for food. In the

---

[a] 26 Probable reading of the original Hebrew text (see Syriac); Masoretic Text the earth   [b] 5 Or land; also in verse 6
[c] 6 Or mist   [d] 7 The Hebrew for man (adam) sounds like and may be related to the Hebrew for ground (adamah); it is also the name Adam (see verse 20).

Born to Lead!

Genesis 1:26–31

You and I were born to lead. Take a look at five observations based on Genesis 1:26–31 that suggest our God-given leadership potential:

1. **Being made in God's image means we were created to lead (v. 26).** After God says, "Let us make mankind in our image," he says, "so that they may rule." One way we reflect God's image is by leading.

2. **God commanded both male and female to rule (v. 27).** Both men and women have been given the ability and authority to lead. Leadership is not gender specific.

3. **We are to rule over the earth, but not necessarily over each other (v. 28).** We were not directed to rule each other, but over the earth's creatures. History is largely the story of how men and women have perverted their God-given roles by trying to rule each other.

4. **All of us are to serve one another in the areas of our gifting and purpose (vv. 29, 30).** God created everything for a purpose. Our general purpose is to lead, but each of us should ask God, "Lord, what's my specific purpose?"

5. **Each person's leadership is best exercised in his or her area of giftedness (v. 31).** When we discover our gifts, we will naturally lead in those areas where we are most productive, intuitive, comfortable, influential and satisfied.

21 QUALITIES

Genesis 2:15–17; 3:1–6

IN GENESIS 3 we see a leader who failed in an area crucial to all leaders: communication. By failing to communicate effectively with his wife, Adam botched his role as the first spiritual leader of the human race.

God clearly told Adam that a certain tree was off-limits. "You are free to eat from any tree in the garden," God told him, "but you must not eat from the tree of the knowledge of good and evil, for when you eat from it you will certainly die." (Ge 2:16, 17). At the time Adam received this command, Eve was not present; according to Genesis 2, she had not yet been created. Consequently, it was up to Adam to pass along what God had said.

So why didn't Adam clearly communicate God's instructions to Eve? Why the breakdown in the line of communication? Certainly Eve did not completely understand what would happen if she ate the forbidden fruit. Consider her muddled response to the serpent: "God did say, 'You must not eat fruit from the tree that is in the middle of the garden, and you must not touch it, or you will die'" (Ge 3:3). Eve added the phrases, "and you must not touch it," and "or you will die." God never said any such thing. So where did she get her faulty information?

Maybe the "telephone game" can give us a clue. Have you ever played it? Everyone sits in a circle. One person whispers a message into the ear of an adjacent player, who whispers the words to the next person, and so it continues down the line. When the last person to play whispers the phrase into the ear of the one who began the game, a great distortion in the message is often revealed.

Five Reasons for Adam's Faulty Communication

Adam's communication to Eve went similarly astray. His message broke down for five basic reasons:

1. He ignored some details in the message he was supposed to communicate.
2. He allowed Eve's voice to influence him more than God's voice.
3. He failed to hold himself accountable for his communication.
4. He forgot what God had said about the consequences of disobedience.
5. He did not take responsibility for the results of his faulty communication.

Let's learn from Adam's mistake. You may be a good speaker—but are you a good communicator? Do you pay close attention to what God tells you? Do you give appropriate attention to detail? When you lead, do you make sure your audience gets the message? And do you take responsibility for what God has entrusted to you?

For a positive example of communication, see p. 326.

middle of the garden were the tree of life and the tree of the knowledge of good and evil.

[10] A river watering the garden flowed from Eden; from there it was separated into four headwaters. [11] The name of the first is the Pishon; it winds through the entire land of Havilah, where there is gold. [12] (The gold of that land is good; aromatic resin[a] and onyx are also there.) [13] The name of the second river is the Gihon; it winds through the entire land of Cush.[b] [14] The name of the third river is the Tigris; it runs along the east side of Ashur. And the fourth river is the Euphrates.

[15] The LORD God took the man and put him in the Garden of Eden to work it and take care of it. [16] And the LORD God commanded the man, "You are free to eat from any tree in the garden; [17] but you must not eat from the tree of the knowledge of good and evil, for when you eat from it you will certainly die."

[18] The LORD God said, "It is not good for the man to be alone. I will make a helper suitable for him."

[19] Now the LORD God had formed out of the ground all the wild animals and all the birds in the sky. He brought them to the man to see what he would name them; and whatever the man called each living creature, that was its name. [20] So the man gave names to all the livestock, the birds in the sky and all the wild animals.

But for Adam[c] no suitable helper was found. [21] So the LORD God caused the man to fall into a deep sleep; and while he was sleeping, he took one of the man's ribs[d] and then closed up the place with flesh. [22] Then the LORD God made a woman from the rib[e] he had taken out of the man, and he brought her to the man.

[23] The man said,

"This is now bone of my bones
    and flesh of my flesh;
she shall be called 'woman,'
    for she was taken out of man."

[24] That is why a man leaves his father and mother and is united to his wife, and they become one flesh.

[25] Adam and his wife were both naked, and they felt no shame.

The Fall

3 Now the serpent was more crafty than any of the wild animals the LORD God had made. He said to the woman, "Did God really say, 'You must not eat from any tree in the garden'?"

[2] The woman said to the serpent, "We may eat fruit from the trees in the garden, [3] but God did say, 'You must not eat fruit from the tree that is in the middle of the garden, and you must not touch it, or you will die.'"

[4] "You will not certainly die," the serpent said to the woman. [5] "For God knows that when you eat from it your eyes will be opened, and you will be like God, knowing good and evil."

[6] When the woman saw that the fruit of the tree was good for food and pleasing to the eye, and also desirable for gaining wisdom, she took some and ate it. She also gave some to her husband, who was with her, and he ate it. [7] Then the eyes of both of them were opened, and they realized they were naked; so they sewed fig leaves together and made coverings for themselves.

[8] Then the man and his wife heard the sound of the LORD God as he was walking in the garden in the cool of the day, and they hid from the LORD God among the trees of the garden. [9] But the LORD God called to the man, "Where are you?"

[10] He answered, "I heard you in the garden, and I was afraid because I was naked; so I hid."

[11] And he said, "Who told you that you were naked? Have you eaten from the tree that I commanded you not to eat from?"

[12] The man said, "The woman you put here with me — she gave me some fruit from the tree, and I ate it."

[13] Then the LORD God said to the woman, "What is this you have done?"

The woman said, "The serpent deceived me, and I ate."

[14] So the LORD God said to the serpent, "Because you have done this,

---

[a] 12 Or good; pearls   [b] 13 Possibly southeast Mesopotamia
[c] 20 Or the man   [d] 21 Or took part of the man's side
[e] 22 Or part

The Law of Influence: Eve the Negative Influencer

Genesis 3:4–6

Regardless of their titles, real leaders influence others. The story of Eve demonstrates the impact of *negative* influence. Although God commissioned Adam as her spiritual leader, Eve usurped the role of influencer. Adam followed his wife rather than God, and together they led humankind into sin.

"Cursed are you above all livestock
    and all wild animals!
You will crawl on your belly
    and you will eat dust
    all the days of your life.
¹⁵ And I will put enmity
    between you and the woman,
    and between your offspring[a] and hers;
he will crush[b] your head,
    and you will strike his heel."

¹⁶ To the woman he said,

"I will make your pains in childbearing very
    severe;
    with painful labor you will give birth to
    children.
Your desire will be for your husband,
    and he will rule over you."

¹⁷ To Adam he said, "Because you listened to
your wife and ate fruit from the tree about which
I commanded you, 'You must not eat from it,'

"Cursed is the ground because of you;
    through painful toil you will eat food
        from it
    all the days of your life.
¹⁸ It will produce thorns and thistles for you,
    and you will eat the plants of the field.
¹⁹ By the sweat of your brow
    you will eat your food
until you return to the ground,
    since from it you were taken;

for dust you are
    and to dust you will return."

²⁰ Adam[c] named his wife Eve,[d] because she
would become the mother of all the living.
²¹ The LORD God made garments of skin for
Adam and his wife and clothed them. ²² And the
LORD God said, "The man has now become like
one of us, knowing good and evil. He must not
be allowed to reach out his hand and take also
from the tree of life and eat, and live forever."
²³ So the LORD God banished him from the Garden of Eden to work the ground from which he
had been taken. ²⁴ After he drove the man out,
he placed on the east side[e] of the Garden of Eden
cherubim and a flaming sword flashing back
and forth to guard the way to the tree of life.

Cain and Abel

4 Adam[c] made love to his wife Eve, and she
    became pregnant and gave birth to Cain.[f]
She said, "With the help of the LORD I have
brought forth[g] a man." ²Later she gave birth to
his brother Abel.

Now Abel kept flocks, and Cain worked the
soil. ³In the course of time Cain brought some
of the fruits of the soil as an offering to the
LORD. ⁴And Abel also brought an offering — fat

---

[a] 15 Or seed   [b] 15 Or strike   [c] 20,1 Or The man
[d] 20 Eve probably means living.   [e] 24 Or placed in front
[f] 1 Cain sounds like the Hebrew for brought forth or acquired.
[g] 1 Or have acquired

ADAM

First Leader to Drop the Ball
Genesis 3:6–19

PROFILE in leadership

At the moment he received God's mandate to rule over the earth, Adam became the
first spiritual leader in human history. Initially, this meant overseeing the garden
and providing direction to his family. Adam was to be a good steward over his resources
and relationships. Unfortunately, he failed on both counts.

When Eve brought the forbidden fruit to Adam, he mismanaged God's creation by eating it. Adam also mismanaged his wife by remaining passive when he should have taken
a stand, thus allowing both Eve and himself to fall morally. When God confronted him
with his sin, he blamed others: "The woman you put here with me—she gave me some
fruit from the tree, and I ate it."

Spiritual leadership isn't complex; it simply requires a willingness to take responsibility. Sadly, many spiritual leaders continue to duplicate Adam's mistake by shirking their
responsibilities at home, in the neighborhood, on the job, and in the church. They forget
that while Adam's failure started at home, in just a short time it damaged all his relationships, spoiled the beautiful place he lived, and ultimately devastated the entire world.
And the whole mess can be traced back to one spineless refusal to lead.

portions from some of the firstborn of his flock. The LORD looked with favor on Abel and his offering, [5]but on Cain and his offering he did not look with favor. So Cain was very angry, and his face was downcast.

[6]Then the LORD said to Cain, "Why are you angry? Why is your face downcast? [7]If you do what is right, will you not be accepted? But if you do not do what is right, sin is crouching at your door; it desires to have you, but you must rule over it."

[8]Now Cain said to his brother Abel, "Let's go out to the field."[a] While they were in the field, Cain attacked his brother Abel and killed him.

[9]Then the LORD said to Cain, "Where is your brother Abel?"

"I don't know," he replied. "Am I my brother's keeper?"

[10]The LORD said, "What have you done? Listen! Your brother's blood cries out to me from the ground. [11]Now you are under a curse and driven from the ground, which opened its mouth to receive your brother's blood from your hand. [12]When you work the ground, it will no longer yield its crops for you. You will be a restless wanderer on the earth."

[13]Cain said to the LORD, "My punishment is more than I can bear. [14]Today you are driving me from the land, and I will be hidden from your presence; I will be a restless wanderer on the earth, and whoever finds me will kill me."

[15]But the LORD said to him, "Not so[b]; anyone who kills Cain will suffer vengeance seven times over." Then the LORD put a mark on Cain so that no one who found him would kill him. [16]So Cain went out from the LORD's presence and lived in the land of Nod,[c] east of Eden.

[17]Cain made love to his wife, and she became pregnant and gave birth to Enoch. Cain was then building a city, and he named it after his son Enoch. [18]To Enoch was born Irad, and Irad was the father of Mehujael, and Mehujael was the father of Methushael, and Methushael was the father of Lamech.

[19]Lamech married two women, one named Adah and the other Zillah. [20]Adah gave birth to Jabal; he was the father of those who live in tents and raise livestock. [21]His brother's name was Jubal; he was the father of all who play stringed instruments and pipes. [22]Zillah also had a son, Tubal-Cain, who forged all kinds of tools out of[d] bronze and iron. Tubal-Cain's sister was Naamah.

[23]Lamech said to his wives,

"Adah and Zillah, listen to me;
    wives of Lamech, hear my words.
I have killed a man for wounding me,
    a young man for injuring me.

---

[a] 8 Samaritan Pentateuch, Septuagint, Vulgate and Syriac; Masoretic Text does not have *"Let's go out to the field."*
[b] 15 Septuagint, Vulgate and Syriac; Hebrew *Very well*
[c] 16 *Nod* means *wandering* (see verses 12 and 14).   [d] 22 Or *who instructed all who work in*

A Leader Who Learned from Failure
Genesis 4:1—5:5

PROFILE
in leadership

God created Eve to fill an unmet need in Adam's otherwise perfect world. She entered a land free of pain, heartache, and sin, but her fluctuating emotions made obedience a struggle. Eventually she influenced Adam to join her in sin. Their choice to follow Satan rather than God brought devastating consequences that continue to plague us even today.

Eve exchanged a life without pain for a hostile and even brutal environment. Yet her subsequent life demonstrated an ability to recover from failure and move forward. She restored her relationship with God, and when her firstborn child arrived, she acknowledged her dependence on God. While Scripture does not comment on her parenting skills, it does indicate that Cain developed a resentful and jealous spirit. As a result, Eve became the first mother to endure the heartache of a murdered child.

Eve did not use her pain as an excuse to reject God or question him, as she had in the garden. Nor did she allow a root of bitterness to spring up. When God gave her Seth, she expressed gratitude for this new life. Ultimately, Eve came to represent a strong leader willing to accept the consequences of her choices and learn from her mistakes.

[24] If Cain is avenged seven times,
　　then Lamech seventy-seven times."

[25] Adam made love to his wife again, and she gave birth to a son and named him Seth,[a] saying, "God has granted me another child in place of Abel, since Cain killed him." [26] Seth also had a son, and he named him Enosh.

At that time people began to call on[b] the name of the LORD.

From Adam to Noah

5 This is the written account of Adam's family line.

When God created mankind, he made them in the likeness of God. [2] He created them male and female and blessed them. And he named them "Mankind"[c] when they were created.

[3] When Adam had lived 130 years, he had a son in his own likeness, in his own image; and he named him Seth. [4] After Seth was born, Adam lived 800 years and had other sons and daughters. [5] Altogether, Adam lived a total of 930 years, and then he died.

[6] When Seth had lived 105 years, he became the father[d] of Enosh. [7] After he became the father of Enosh, Seth lived 807 years and had other sons and daughters. [8] Altogether, Seth lived a total of 912 years, and then he died.

[9] When Enosh had lived 90 years, he became the father of Kenan. [10] After he became the father of Kenan, Enosh lived 815 years and had other sons and daughters. [11] Altogether, Enosh lived a total of 905 years, and then he died.

[12] When Kenan had lived 70 years, he became the father of Mahalalel. [13] After he became the father of Mahalalel, Kenan lived 840 years and had other sons and daughters. [14] Altogether, Kenan lived a total of 910 years, and then he died.

[15] When Mahalalel had lived 65 years, he became the father of Jared. [16] After he became the father of Jared, Mahalalel lived 830 years and had other sons and daughters. [17] Altogether, Mahalalel lived a total of 895 years, and then he died.

[18] When Jared had lived 162 years, he became the father of Enoch. [19] After he became the father of Enoch, Jared lived 800 years and had other sons and daughters. [20] Altogether, Jared lived a total of 962 years, and then he died.

[21] When Enoch had lived 65 years, he became the father of Methuselah. [22] After he became the father of Methuselah, Enoch walked faithfully with God 300 years and had other sons and daughters. [23] Altogether, Enoch lived a total of 365

years. [24] Enoch walked faithfully with God; then he was no more, because God took him away.

[25] When Methuselah had lived 187 years, he became the father of Lamech. [26] After he became the father of Lamech, Methuselah lived 782 years and had other sons and daughters. [27] Altogether, Methuselah lived a total of 969 years, and then he died.

[28] When Lamech had lived 182 years, he had a son. [29] He named him Noah[e] and said, "He will comfort us in the labor and painful toil of our hands caused by the ground the LORD has cursed." [30] After Noah was born, Lamech lived 595 years and had other sons and daughters. [31] Altogether, Lamech lived a total of 777 years, and then he died.

[32] After Noah was 500 years old, he became the father of Shem, Ham and Japheth.

Wickedness in the World

6 When human beings began to increase in number on the earth and daughters were born to them, [2] the sons of God saw that the daughters of humans were beautiful, and they married any of them they chose. [3] Then the LORD said, "My Spirit will not contend with[f] humans forever, for they are mortal[g]; their days will be a hundred and twenty years."

[4] The Nephilim were on the earth in those days—and also afterward—when the sons of God went to the daughters of humans and had children by them. They were the heroes of old, men of renown.

[5] The LORD saw how great the wickedness of the human race had become on the earth, and that every inclination of the thoughts of the human heart was only evil all the time. [6] The LORD regretted that he had made human beings on the earth, and his heart was deeply troubled. [7] So the LORD said, "I will wipe from the face of the earth the human race I have created—and with them the animals, the birds and the creatures that move along the ground—for I regret that I have made them." [8] But Noah found favor in the eyes of the LORD.

Noah and the Flood

[9] This is the account of Noah and his family.

Noah was a righteous man, blameless among the people of his time, and he walked faithfully

---

[a] 25 *Seth* probably means *granted.*　　[b] 26 Or *to proclaim*
[c] 2 Hebrew *adam*　　[d] 6 *Father* may mean *ancestor*; also in verses 7-26.　　[e] 29 *Noah* sounds like the Hebrew for *comfort.*
[f] 3 Or *My spirit will not remain in*　　[g] 3 Or *corrupt*

with God. [10]Noah had three sons: Shem, Ham and Japheth.

[11]Now the earth was corrupt in God's sight and was full of violence. [12]God saw how corrupt the earth had become, for all the people on earth had corrupted their ways. [13]So God said to Noah, "I am going to put an end to all people, for the earth is filled with violence because of them. I am surely going to destroy both them and the earth. [14]So make yourself an ark of cypress[a] wood; make rooms in it and coat it with pitch inside and out. [15]This is how you are to build it: The ark is to be three hundred cubits long, fifty cubits wide and thirty cubits high.[b] [16]Make a roof for it, leaving below the roof an opening one cubit[c] high all around.[d] Put a door in the side of the ark and make lower, middle and upper decks. [17]I am going to bring floodwaters on the earth to destroy all life under the heavens, every creature that has the breath of life in it. Everything on earth will perish. [18]But I will establish my covenant with you, and you will enter the ark—you and your sons and your wife and your sons' wives with you. [19]You are to bring into the ark two of all living creatures, male and female, to keep them alive with you. [20]Two of every kind of bird, of every kind of animal and of every kind of creature that moves along the ground will come to you to be kept alive. [21]You are to take every kind of food that is to be eaten and store it away as food for you and for them."

[22]Noah did everything just as God commanded him.

7 The LORD then said to Noah, "Go into the ark, you and your whole family, because I have found you righteous in this generation. [2]Take with you seven pairs of every kind of clean animal, a male and its mate, and one pair of every kind of unclean animal, a male and its mate, [3]and also seven pairs of every kind of bird, male and female, to keep their various kinds alive throughout the earth. [4]Seven days from now I will send rain on the earth for forty days and forty nights, and I will wipe from the face of the earth every living creature I have made."

[5]And Noah did all that the LORD commanded him.

[6]Noah was six hundred years old when the floodwaters came on the earth. [7]And Noah and

---

[a] 14 The meaning of the Hebrew for this word is uncertain.
[b] 15 That is, about 450 feet long, 75 feet wide and 45 feet high or about 135 meters long, 23 meters wide and 14 meters high
[c] 16 That is, about 18 inches or about 45 centimeters
[d] 16 The meaning of the Hebrew for this clause is uncertain.

NOAH

PROFILE in leadership

A Man of Righteousness
Genesis 6:8–18

There's something about righteousness—the kind of morally virtuous lifestyle powered from above—that qualifies a person to lead God's people. Noah, the man God chose to rescue the human race from extinction, demonstrated just this kind of righteousness.

Humankind had grown so evil that God pledged to destroy it and all living things on earth (Ge 6:7). But the Lord's pronouncement of judgment didn't come without hope; God had charged righteous Noah to help save a remnant.

God didn't choose Noah randomly. He knows whom he can count on to get things done—and it's not necessarily the one with the most skill, talent, or social standing. Rather, it's the one who daily walks with him, the one who hears his voice and follows his lead. Noah was just such a man.

No doubt Noah had his own weaknesses and frailties. But he walked with God, and it was that close walk that made him righteous before the Lord (Ge 6:9). Noah's righteousness qualified him to be used by God to help save the human race from annihilation, and in the bargain kept him and his loved ones from certain death.

Noah still stands as an example of the kind of person God wants to use. God hasn't changed, and even now he looks for righteous leaders who can help him change the world.

his sons and his wife and his sons' wives entered the ark to escape the waters of the flood. ⁸Pairs of clean and unclean animals, of birds and of all creatures that move along the ground, ⁹male and female, came to Noah and entered the ark, as God had commanded Noah. ¹⁰And after the seven days the floodwaters came on the earth.

¹¹In the six hundredth year of Noah's life, on the seventeenth day of the second month—on that day all the springs of the great deep burst forth, and the floodgates of the heavens were opened. ¹²And rain fell on the earth forty days and forty nights.

¹³On that very day Noah and his sons, Shem, Ham and Japheth, together with his wife and the wives of his three sons, entered the ark. ¹⁴They had with them every wild animal according to its kind, all livestock according to their kinds, every creature that moves along the ground according to its kind and every bird according to its kind, everything with wings. ¹⁵Pairs of all creatures that have the breath of life in them came to Noah and entered the ark. ¹⁶The animals going in were male and female of every living thing, as God had commanded Noah. Then the LORD shut him in.

¹⁷For forty days the flood kept coming on the earth, and as the waters increased they lifted the ark high above the earth. ¹⁸The waters rose and increased greatly on the earth, and the ark floated on the surface of the water. ¹⁹They rose greatly on the earth, and all the high mountains under the entire heavens were covered. ²⁰The waters rose and covered the mountains to a depth of more than fifteen cubits.ᵃ,ᵇ ²¹Every living thing that moved on land perished—birds, livestock, wild animals, all the creatures that swarm over the earth, and all mankind. ²²Everything on dry land that had the breath of life in its nostrils died. ²³Every living thing on the face of the earth was wiped out; people and animals and the creatures that move along the ground and the birds were wiped from the earth. Only Noah was left, and those with him in the ark.

²⁴The waters flooded the earth for a hundred and fifty days.

8 But God remembered Noah and all the wild animals and the livestock that were with him in the ark, and he sent a wind over the earth, and the waters receded. ²Now the springs of the deep and the floodgates of the heavens had been closed, and the rain had stopped falling from the sky. ³The water receded steadily from the earth. At the end of the hundred and fifty days

The Law of Sacrifice: God and Noah

Genesis 6:17–18; 8:21–22

Some of the saddest words in Scripture occur in Genesis 6:6: "The LORD regretted that he had made human beings on the earth, and his heart was deeply troubled." It saddened God that every human being except for Noah's immediate family would have to be destroyed. He loved the men and women whom he had created to be like him, those who were to rule the earth and reflect his glory.

God determined to start again, even without a guarantee that the survivors and their descendants would do a better job of following him. God made a covenant with Noah, giving up his right to ever again flood the earth to cleanse it of sinful humanity. Noah gave up everything he had accumulated in his long life in order to start over. *Sacrifice always precedes success.* They had to give up to go up.

the water had gone down, ⁴and on the seventeenth day of the seventh month the ark came to rest on the mountains of Ararat. ⁵The waters continued to recede until the tenth month, and on the first day of the tenth month the tops of the mountains became visible.

⁶After forty days Noah opened a window he had made in the ark ⁷and sent out a raven, and it kept flying back and forth until the water had dried up from the earth. ⁸Then he sent out a dove to see if the water had receded from the surface of the ground. ⁹But the dove could find nowhere to perch because there was water over all the surface of the earth; so it returned to Noah in the ark. He reached out his hand and took the dove and brought it back to himself in the ark. ¹⁰He waited seven more days and again sent out the dove from the ark. ¹¹When the dove returned to him in the evening, there in its beak was a freshly plucked olive leaf! Then Noah knew that the water had receded from the earth. ¹²He waited seven more days and sent the dove out again, but this time it did not return to him.

¹³By the first day of the first month of Noah's

ᵃ 20 That is, about 23 feet or about 6.8 meters   ᵇ 20 Or rose more than fifteen cubits, and the mountains were covered

six hundred and first year, the water had dried up from the earth. Noah then removed the covering from the ark and saw that the surface of the ground was dry. [14]By the twenty-seventh day of the second month the earth was completely dry.

[15]Then God said to Noah, [16]"Come out of the ark, you and your wife and your sons and their wives. [17]Bring out every kind of living creature that is with you—the birds, the animals, and all the creatures that move along the ground—so they can multiply on the earth and be fruitful and increase in number on it."

[18]So Noah came out, together with his sons and his wife and his sons' wives. [19]All the animals and all the creatures that move along the ground and all the birds—everything that moves on land—came out of the ark, one kind after another.

[20]Then Noah built an altar to the LORD and, taking some of all the clean animals and clean birds, he sacrificed burnt offerings on it. [21]The LORD smelled the pleasing aroma and said in his heart: "Never again will I curse the ground because of humans, even though[a] every inclination of the human heart is evil from childhood. And never again will I destroy all living creatures, as I have done.

[22]"As long as the earth endures,
　seedtime and harvest,
　cold and heat,
　summer and winter,
　day and night
　will never cease."

God's Covenant With Noah

9 Then God blessed Noah and his sons, saying to them, "Be fruitful and increase in number and fill the earth. [2]The fear and dread of you will fall on all the beasts of the earth, and on all the birds in the sky, on every creature that moves along the ground, and on all the fish in the sea; they are given into your hands. [3]Everything that lives and moves about will be food for you. Just as I gave you the green plants, I now give you everything.

[4]"But you must not eat meat that has its lifeblood still in it. [5]And for your lifeblood I will surely demand an accounting. I will demand an accounting from every animal. And from each human being, too, I will demand an accounting for the life of another human being.

[6]"Whoever sheds human blood,
　by humans shall their blood be shed;

for in the image of God
　has God made mankind.

[7]As for you, be fruitful and increase in number; multiply on the earth and increase upon it."

[8]Then God said to Noah and to his sons with him: [9]"I now establish my covenant with you and with your descendants after you [10]and with every living creature that was with you—the birds, the livestock and all the wild animals, all those that came out of the ark with you—every living creature on earth. [11]I establish my covenant with you: Never again will all life be destroyed by the waters of a flood; never again will there be a flood to destroy the earth."

[12]And God said, "This is the sign of the covenant I am making between me and you and every living creature with you, a covenant for all generations to come: [13]I have set my rainbow in the clouds, and it will be the sign of the covenant between me and the earth. [14]Whenever I bring clouds over the earth and the rainbow appears in the clouds, [15]I will remember my covenant between me and you and all living creatures of every kind. Never again will the waters become a flood to destroy all life. [16]Whenever the rainbow appears in the clouds, I will see it and remember the everlasting covenant between God and all living creatures of every kind on the earth."

[17]So God said to Noah, "This is the sign of the covenant I have established between me and all life on the earth."

The Sons of Noah

[18]The sons of Noah who came out of the ark were Shem, Ham and Japheth. (Ham was the father of Canaan.) [19]These were the three sons of Noah, and from them came the people who were scattered over the whole earth.

[20]Noah, a man of the soil, proceeded[b] to plant a vineyard. [21]When he drank some of its wine, he became drunk and lay uncovered inside his tent. [22]Ham, the father of Canaan, saw his father naked and told his two brothers outside. [23]But Shem and Japheth took a garment and laid it across their shoulders; then they walked in backward and covered their father's naked body. Their faces were turned the other way so that they would not see their father naked.

[24]When Noah awoke from his wine and found out what his youngest son had done to him, [25]he said,

---

[a] 21 Or humans, for　[b] 20 Or soil, was the first

"Cursed be Canaan!
  The lowest of slaves
  will he be to his brothers."

²⁶He also said,

"Praise be to the Lord, the God of Shem!
  May Canaan be the slave of Shem.
²⁷May God extend Japheth's[a] territory;
  may Japheth live in the tents of Shem,
  and may Canaan be the slave of Japheth."

²⁸After the flood Noah lived 350 years. ²⁹Noah lived a total of 950 years, and then he died.

The Table of Nations

10 This is the account of Shem, Ham and Japheth, Noah's sons, who themselves had sons after the flood.

The Japhethites

²The sons[b] of Japheth:
  Gomer, Magog, Madai, Javan, Tubal, Meshek and Tiras.
³The sons of Gomer:
  Ashkenaz, Riphath and Togarmah.
⁴The sons of Javan:
  Elishah, Tarshish, the Kittites and the Rodanites.[c] ⁵(From these the maritime peoples spread out into their territories by their clans within their nations, each with its own language.)

The Hamites

⁶The sons of Ham:
  Cush, Egypt, Put and Canaan.
⁷The sons of Cush:
  Seba, Havilah, Sabtah, Raamah and Sabteka.
  The sons of Raamah:
  Sheba and Dedan.

⁸Cush was the father[d] of Nimrod, who became a mighty warrior on the earth. ⁹He was a mighty hunter before the Lord; that is why it is said, "Like Nimrod, a mighty hunter before the Lord." ¹⁰The first centers of his kingdom were Babylon, Uruk, Akkad and Kalneh, in[e] Shinar.[f] ¹¹From that land he went to Assyria, where he built Nineveh, Rehoboth Ir,[g] Calah ¹²and Resen, which is between Nineveh and Calah—which is the great city.

¹³Egypt was the father of
  the Ludites, Anamites, Lehabites, Naphtuhites, ¹⁴Pathrusites, Kasluhites (from whom the Philistines came) and Caphtorites.
¹⁵Canaan was the father of
  Sidon his firstborn,[h] and of the Hittites, ¹⁶Jebusites, Amorites, Girgashites, ¹⁷Hivites, Arkites, Sinites, ¹⁸Arvadites, Zemarites and Hamathites.

Later the Canaanite clans scattered ¹⁹and the borders of Canaan reached from Sidon toward Gerar as far as Gaza, and then toward Sodom, Gomorrah, Admah and Zeboyim, as far as Lasha.
²⁰These are the sons of Ham by their clans and languages, in their territories and nations.

The Semites

²¹Sons were also born to Shem, whose older brother was[i] Japheth; Shem was the ancestor of all the sons of Eber.

²²The sons of Shem:
  Elam, Ashur, Arphaxad, Lud and Aram.
²³The sons of Aram:
  Uz, Hul, Gether and Meshek.[j]
²⁴Arphaxad was the father of[k] Shelah,
  and Shelah the father of Eber.
²⁵Two sons were born to Eber:
  One was named Peleg,[l] because in his time the earth was divided; his brother was named Joktan.
²⁶Joktan was the father of
  Almodad, Sheleph, Hazarmaveth, Jerah, ²⁷Hadoram, Uzal, Diklah, ²⁸Obal, Abimael, Sheba, ²⁹Ophir, Havilah and Jobab. All these were sons of Joktan.

³⁰The region where they lived stretched from Mesha toward Sephar, in the eastern hill country.
³¹These are the sons of Shem by their clans and languages, in their territories and nations.

³²These are the clans of Noah's sons, according to their lines of descent, within their nations. From these the nations spread out over the earth after the flood.

---

a 27 Japheth *sounds like the Hebrew for* extend.   *b 2* Sons *may mean* descendants *or* successors *or* nations; *also in verses 3, 4, 6, 7, 20-23, 29 and 31.*   *c 4* Some manuscripts of the Masoretic Text and Samaritan Pentateuch (see also Septuagint and 1 Chron. 1:7); most manuscripts of the Masoretic Text Dodanites   *d 8* Father *may mean* ancestor *or* predecessor *or* founder; *also in verses 13, 15, 24 and 26.*   *e 10* Or Uruk and Akkad—all of them in   *f 10* That is, Babylonia   *g 11* Or Nineveh with its city squares   *h 15* Or of the Sidonians, the foremost   *i 21* Or Shem, the older brother of   *j 23* See Septuagint and 1 Chron. 1:17; Hebrew Mash.   *k 24* Hebrew; Septuagint father of Cainan, and Cainan was the father of   *l 25* Peleg *means division.*

The Tower of Babel

11 Now the whole world had one language and a common speech. [2]As people moved eastward,[a] they found a plain in Shinar[b] and settled there.

[3]They said to each other, "Come, let's make bricks and bake them thoroughly." They used brick instead of stone, and tar for mortar. [4]Then they said, "Come, let us build ourselves a city, with a tower that reaches to the heavens, so that we may make a name for ourselves; otherwise we will be scattered over the face of the whole earth."

[5]But the LORD came down to see the city and the tower the people were building. [6]The LORD said, "If as one people speaking the same language they have begun to do this, then nothing they plan to do will be impossible for them. [7]Come, let us go down and confuse their language so they will not understand each other."

[8]So the LORD scattered them from there over all the earth, and they stopped building the city. [9]That is why it was called Babel[c]— because there the LORD confused the language of the whole world. From there the LORD scattered them over the face of the whole earth.

From Shem to Abram

[10]This is the account of Shem's family line.

Two years after the flood, when Shem was 100 years old, he became the father[d] of Arphaxad. [11]And after he became the father of Arphaxad, Shem lived 500 years and had other sons and daughters.

[12]When Arphaxad had lived 35 years, he became the father of Shelah. [13]And after he became the father of Shelah, Arphaxad lived 403 years and had other sons and daughters.[e]

[14]When Shelah had lived 30 years, he became the father of Eber. [15]And after he became the father of Eber, Shelah lived 403 years and had other sons and daughters.

[16]When Eber had lived 34 years, he became the father of Peleg. [17]And after he became the father of Peleg, Eber lived 430 years and had other sons and daughters.

[18]When Peleg had lived 30 years, he became the father of Reu. [19]And after he became the father of Reu, Peleg lived 209 years and had other sons and daughters.

[20]When Reu had lived 32 years, he became the father of Serug. [21]And after he became the father of Serug, Reu lived 207 years and had other sons and daughters.

[22]When Serug had lived 30 years, he became the father of Nahor. [23]And after he became the father of Nahor, Serug lived 200 years and had other sons and daughters.

[24]When Nahor had lived 29 years, he became the father of Terah. [25]And after he became the father of Terah, Nahor lived 119 years and had other sons and daughters.

[26]After Terah had lived 70 years, he became the father of Abram, Nahor and Haran.

Abram's Family

[27]This is the account of Terah's family line.

Terah became the father of Abram, Nahor and Haran. And Haran became the father of Lot. [28]While his father Terah was still alive, Haran died in Ur of the Chaldeans, in the land of his birth. [29]Abram and Nahor both married. The name of Abram's wife was Sarai, and the name of Nahor's wife was Milkah; she was the daughter of Haran, the father of both Milkah and Iskah. [30]Now Sarai was childless because she was not able to conceive.

[31]Terah took his son Abram, his grandson Lot son of Haran, and his daughter-in-law Sarai, the wife of his son Abram, and together they set out from Ur of the Chaldeans to go to Canaan. But when they came to Harran, they settled there. [32]Terah lived 205 years, and he died in Harran.

---

[a] 2 Or *from the east*; or *in the east*　　[b] 2 That is, Babylonia
[c] 9 That is, Babylon; *Babel* sounds like the Hebrew for *confused.*　　[d] 10 *Father* may mean *ancestor*; also in verses 11-25.　　[e] 12,13 Hebrew; Septuagint (see also Luke 3:35, 36 and note at Gen. 10:24) *35 years, he became the father of Cainan.* [13]*And after he became the father of Cainan, Arphaxad lived 430 years and had other sons and daughters, and then he died. When Cainan had lived 130 years, he became the father of Shelah. And after he became the father of Shelah, Cainan lived 330 years and had other sons and daughters*

The Law of the Big Mo: The Tower of Babel

Genesis 11:4

Momentum is a leader's best friend. Unity of vision, language, and effort among the people of Babel provided tremendous momentum. Unfortunately, they used the Big Mo to go their own direction. As a result, God halted their momentum by confusing their language and scattering them to the four winds.

The Call of Abram

12 The LORD had said to Abram, "Go from your country, your people and your father's household to the land I will show you.

2 "I will make you into a great nation,
　　and I will bless you;
　I will make your name great,
　　and you will be a blessing.*a*
3 I will bless those who bless you,
　　and whoever curses you I will curse;
　and all peoples on earth
　　will be blessed through you."*b*

4 So Abram went, as the LORD had told him; and Lot went with him. Abram was seventy-five years old when he set out from Harran. 5 He took his wife Sarai, his nephew Lot, all the possessions they had accumulated and the people they had acquired in Harran, and they set out for the land of Canaan, and they arrived there.

6 Abram traveled through the land as far as the site of the great tree of Moreh at Shechem. At that time the Canaanites were in the land. 7 The LORD appeared to Abram and said, "To your offspring*c* I will give this land." So he built an altar there to the LORD, who had appeared to him.

8 From there he went on toward the hills east of Bethel and pitched his tent, with Bethel on the west and Ai on the east. There he built an altar to the LORD and called on the name of the LORD. 9 Then Abram set out and continued toward the Negev.

Abram in Egypt

10 Now there was a famine in the land, and Abram went down to Egypt to live there for a while because the famine was severe. 11 As he was about to enter Egypt, he said to his wife Sarai, "I know what a beautiful woman you are. 12 When the Egyptians see you, they will say, 'This is his wife.' Then they will kill me but will let you live. 13 Say you are my sister, so that I will be treated well for your sake and my life will be spared because of you."

14 When Abram came to Egypt, the Egyptians saw that Sarai was a very beautiful woman. 15 And when Pharaoh's officials saw her, they praised her to Pharaoh, and she was taken into his palace. 16 He treated Abram well for her sake, and Abram acquired sheep and cattle, male and female donkeys, male and female servants, and camels.

17 But the LORD inflicted serious diseases on Pharaoh and his household because of Abram's

---

The Law of Connection: God and Abram

Genesis 12:1–7

At first glance, the incident at the tower of Babel looks like an angry God bent on punishing the people for disobedience. But it was much more than that; actually, God was implementing a plan called "divide and conquer." In Genesis 11, the Lord divided the people into many language groups. In Genesis 12, he chose one of those groups and made a covenant with one of their members. God spoke to Abram and promised to bless him, and through him to bless the entire human race. Because of that covenant, Abram became the father of the Hebrew nation.

It's important to observe how God proposed his plan. He told Abram that he would bless him, along with his cattle, land, family and name. God spoke to Abram heart to heart, revealing to him the blessings he would enjoy through the covenant. And Abram was no dummy: He took God up on the proposed deal.

While Abram might have chosen to obey God simply because he is God, the Lord made the effort to connect with Abram first. He touched Abram's heart before asking for his hand.

---

wife Sarai. 18 So Pharaoh summoned Abram. "What have you done to me?" he said. "Why didn't you tell me she was your wife? 19 Why did you say, 'She is my sister,' so that I took her to be my wife? Now then, here is your wife. Take her and go!" 20 Then Pharaoh gave orders about Abram to his men, and they sent him on his way, with his wife and everything he had.

Abram and Lot Separate

13 So Abram went up from Egypt to the Negev, with his wife and everything he had, and Lot went with him. 2 Abram had become very wealthy in livestock and in silver and gold.

3 From the Negev he went from place to place until he came to Bethel, to the place between Bethel and Ai where his tent had been earlier 4 and where he had first built an altar. There Abram called on the name of the LORD.

---

a 2 Or *be seen as blessed*　*b 3* Or *earth / will use your name in blessings* (see 48:20)　*c 7* Or *seed*

21 QUALITIES

VISION Abraham Seizes What He Sees

Genesis 12:1—22:4

WHILE FOLLOWERS may obsess on the challenges immediately before them, leaders see the future from a distance. They dream dreams not only about what can happen now, but also about what could happen in the next year, the next decade, even the next generation.

When God told Abraham to leave the comfort of his home in Harran, his relatives, and everything familiar, so that he might start fresh in another land (Ge 12), Abraham caught a vision. God gave Abraham the hope of fathering a great nation; in fact, God said he would become the father of many nations! Abraham felt compelled to follow this great vision, even when he had nothing else to rely on.

Lessons from Abraham on Vision

By observing Abraham in Genesis 12–22, we can learn the criteria for a God-given vision. A vision must:

1. **Begin with God's priorities (Ge 12:1, 2).** God initiated the vision, not Abraham. When leaders start with God's vision, they can more easily maintain direction and keep their motives pure.

2. **Connect with the leader's identity (Ge 15:2–4).** The vision Abraham received fit him and Sarah exactly; it matched the needs and desires of this barren couple. Even better, its fulfillment would serve others.

3. **Include others (Ge 12:2–3).** A vision from God always involves and blesses others. The Lord told Abraham he would be blessed in order to bless many nations, which is precisely what happened through the birth of Christ many generations later.

4. **Be bigger than the leader (Ge 17:1–8).** While Abraham wanted to father an heir, God wanted him to father *nations*. That hope went far beyond Abraham's wildest dreams (and his own capabilities). Such a huge vision would take more than a lifetime to fulfill.

5. **Connect with the leader's deepest convictions (Ge 18:9–12).** The vision that captured Abraham's heart mirrored his strongest values, including his desire for family and land.

6. **Be tangible and easily communicated (Ge 15:5).** God gave Abraham a tangible picture of the vision: Look at the sands on the shore, he said, and at the stars in the sky. These objects served as visual aids to help Abraham embrace and fulfill the vision.

7. **Have eternal value (Ge 17:19–20).** Abraham's vision went far beyond his life on earth and included more than wealth and fame. His vision would affect the eternal destiny of millions.

For a negative example of vision, see p. 32.

⁵Now Lot, who was moving about with Abram, also had flocks and herds and tents. ⁶But the land could not support them while they stayed together, for their possessions were so great that they were not able to stay together. ⁷And quarreling arose between Abram's herders and Lot's. The Canaanites and Perizzites were also living in the land at that time.

⁸So Abram said to Lot, "Let's not have any quarreling between you and me, or between your herders and mine, for we are close relatives. ⁹Is not the whole land before you? Let's part company. If you go to the left, I'll go to the right; if you go to the right, I'll go to the left."

¹⁰Lot looked around and saw that the whole plain of the Jordan toward Zoar was well watered, like the garden of the LORD, like the land of Egypt. (This was before the LORD destroyed Sodom and Gomorrah.) ¹¹So Lot chose for himself the whole plain of the Jordan and set out toward the east. The two men parted company: ¹²Abram lived in the land of Canaan, while Lot lived among the cities of the plain and pitched his tents near Sodom. ¹³Now the people of Sodom were wicked and were sinning greatly against the LORD.

¹⁴The LORD said to Abram after Lot had parted from him, "Look around from where you are, to the north and south, to the east and west. ¹⁵All the land that you see I will give to you and your offspring[a] forever. ¹⁶I will make your offspring like the dust of the earth, so that if anyone could count the dust, then your offspring could be counted. ¹⁷Go, walk through the length and breadth of the land, for I am giving it to you."

¹⁸So Abram went to live near the great trees of Mamre at Hebron, where he pitched his tents. There he built an altar to the LORD.

Abram Rescues Lot

14 At the time when Amraphel was king of Shinar,[b] Arioch king of Ellasar, Kedorlaomer king of Elam and Tidal king of Goyim, ²these kings went to war against Bera king of Sodom, Birsha king of Gomorrah, Shinab king of Admah, Shemeber king of Zeboyim, and the king of Bela (that is, Zoar). ³All these latter kings joined forces in the Valley of Siddim (that is, the Dead Sea Valley). ⁴For twelve years they had been subject to Kedorlaomer, but in the thirteenth year they rebelled.

⁵In the fourteenth year, Kedorlaomer and the kings allied with him went out and defeated the Rephaites in Ashteroth Karnaim, the Zuzites in Ham, the Emites in Shaveh Kiriathaim ⁶and the Horites in the hill country of Seir, as far as El

---

[a] 15 Or *seed*; also in verse 16   [b] 1 That is, Babylonia; also in verse 9

ABRAHAM

A Leader Who Went the Distance
Genesis 12:1—25:11

PROFILE in leadership

When Jews in New Testament days spoke of their heritage and spiritual legacy, they claimed Abraham as their father (Jn 8:33,39). Why did they give him the title "father," a term of respect synonymous with leadership? Because Abraham went the distance.

Genesis 11:31 tells us that Abraham's father, Terah, set out for Canaan from Ur of the Chaldeans long before Abraham made a similar trip. But for some reason, Terah stopped in Harran and never continued his journey. Did Terah receive an original call from God to move to the promised land—but neglect to follow through? We'll never know.

We do know that Abraham never made such a mistake. Although he made other leadership errors, Abraham always seemed to follow through on his commitments. When God called him to depart to an unknown land, he went the distance. When enemies abducted Lot and his goods, Abraham pursued the kidnappers and subdued them (Ge 14:14–16). When commanded to circumcise the males of his household, Abraham did it "on that very day" (17:23). And when God asked Abraham to take his beloved son, Isaac, to Mount Moriah and sacrifice him there, Abraham followed through to the last detail. Only a last-second angelic intervention spared the young man's life (22:1–19). No wonder that God, the Ultimate Leader, called Abraham "my friend" (Isa 41:8)!

The Law of Addition: Abraham Takes the High Road

Genesis 13:7–15

Abraham and Lot had reached an impasse. Both had so many possessions that a conflict arose among their herders (Ge 13:7). There wasn't enough space for all of them to remain in the same area. It would have been easy for both of these men to be overtaken with greed, and it would have been even easier for Abraham to insist on getting his own way. After all, he was the one who started the journey with God; Lot was invited later.

Abraham, however, practiced the Law of Addition by serving his nephew. He allowed Lot to choose which piece of land he wanted. Abraham would take whichever real estate Lot didn't take. He served generously and sacrificially, giving up what could have been his for the sake of someone else. Abraham could do this because:

He valued his relationships more than his possessions (v. 8).
He recognized that he already had more land than he or Lot needed (v. 9).
He knew that God was in control and would do him justice in the end (vv. 12–15).

This is a great example of a leader taking the high road. Those who do this believe life is too short to keep score. These "high road" leaders realize that God is better at providing for them than they are for themselves. Lot's decision took him to Sodom, a place where he and his family experienced a bitter life. Abraham heard from the Lord and received a bountiful promise.

Paran near the desert. ⁷Then they turned back and went to En Mishpat (that is, Kadesh), and they conquered the whole territory of the Amalekites, as well as the Amorites who were living in Hazezon Tamar.

⁸Then the king of Sodom, the king of Gomorrah, the king of Admah, the king of Zeboyim and the king of Bela (that is, Zoar) marched out and drew up their battle lines in the Valley of Siddim ⁹against Kedorlaomer king of Elam, Tidal king of Goyim, Amraphel king of Shinar and Arioch king of Ellasar—four kings against five. ¹⁰Now the Valley of Siddim was full of tar pits, and when the kings of Sodom and Gomorrah fled, some of the men fell into them and the rest fled to the hills. ¹¹The four kings seized all the goods of Sodom and Gomorrah and all their food; then they went away. ¹²They also carried off Abram's nephew Lot and his possessions, since he was living in Sodom.

¹³A man who had escaped came and reported this to Abram the Hebrew. Now Abram was living near the great trees of Mamre the Amorite, a brother*a* of Eshkol and Aner, all of whom were allied with Abram. ¹⁴When Abram heard that his relative had been taken captive, he called out the 318 trained men born in his household and went in pursuit as far as Dan. ¹⁵During the night Abram divided his men to attack them and he routed them, pursuing them as far as Hobah, north of Damascus. ¹⁶He recovered all the goods and brought back his relative Lot and his possessions, together with the women and the other people.

¹⁷After Abram returned from defeating Kedorlaomer and the kings allied with him, the king of Sodom came out to meet him in the Valley of Shaveh (that is, the King's Valley).

¹⁸Then Melchizedek king of Salem brought out bread and wine. He was priest of God Most High, ¹⁹and he blessed Abram, saying,

"Blessed be Abram by God Most High,
   Creator of heaven and earth.
²⁰And praise be to God Most High,
   who delivered your enemies into your
     hand."

Then Abram gave him a tenth of everything.
²¹The king of Sodom said to Abram, "Give me the people and keep the goods for yourself."

²²But Abram said to the king of Sodom, "With raised hand I have sworn an oath to the LORD, God Most High, Creator of heaven and earth, ²³that I will accept nothing belonging to you, not even a thread or the strap of a sandal, so that you will never be able to say, 'I made Abram rich.' ²⁴I will accept nothing but what my men have eaten and the share that belongs to the men who went with me—to Aner, Eshkol and Mamre. Let them have their share."

a 13 Or *a relative*; or *an ally*

The LORD's Covenant With Abram

15 After this, the word of the LORD came to Abram in a vision:

"Do not be afraid, Abram.
    I am your shield,[a]
    your very great reward.[b]"

[2] But Abram said, "Sovereign LORD, what can you give me since I remain childless and the one who will inherit[c] my estate is Eliezer of Damascus?" [3] And Abram said, "You have given me no children; so a servant in my household will be my heir."

[4] Then the word of the LORD came to him: "This man will not be your heir, but a son who is your own flesh and blood will be your heir." [5] He took him outside and said, "Look up at the sky and count the stars — if indeed you can count them." Then he said to him, "So shall your offspring[d] be."

[6] Abram believed the LORD, and he credited it to him as righteousness.

[7] He also said to him, "I am the LORD, who brought you out of Ur of the Chaldeans to give you this land to take possession of it."

[8] But Abram said, "Sovereign LORD, how can I know that I will gain possession of it?"

[9] So the LORD said to him, "Bring me a heifer, a goat and a ram, each three years old, along with a dove and a young pigeon."

[10] Abram brought all these to him, cut them in two and arranged the halves opposite each other; the birds, however, he did not cut in half. [11] Then birds of prey came down on the carcasses, but Abram drove them away.

[12] As the sun was setting, Abram fell into a deep sleep, and a thick and dreadful darkness came over him. [13] Then the LORD said to him, "Know for certain that for four hundred years your descendants will be strangers in a country not their own and that they will be enslaved and mistreated there. [14] But I will punish the nation they serve as slaves, and afterward they will come out with great possessions. [15] You, however, will go to your ancestors in peace and be buried at a good old age. [16] In the fourth generation your descendants will come back here, for the sin of the Amorites has not yet reached its full measure."

[17] When the sun had set and darkness had fallen, a smoking firepot with a blazing torch appeared and passed between the pieces. [18] On that day the LORD made a covenant with Abram and said, "To your descendants I give this land, from the Wadi[e] of Egypt to the great river, the Euphrates — [19] the land of the Kenizzites, Kadmonites, [20] Hittites, Perizzites, Rephaites, [21] Amorites, Canaanites, Girgashites and Jebusites."

Hagar and Ishmael

16 Now Sarai, Abram's wife, had borne him no children. But she had an Egyptian slave named Hagar; [2] so she said to Abram, "The LORD has kept me from having children. Go, sleep with my slave; perhaps I can build a family through her."

Abram agreed to what Sarai said. [3] So after Abram had been living in Canaan ten years, Sarai his wife took her Egyptian slave Hagar and gave her to her husband to be his wife. [4] He slept with Hagar, and she conceived.

When she knew she was pregnant, she began to despise her mistress. [5] Then Sarai said to Abram, "You are responsible for the wrong I am suffering. I put my slave in your arms, and now that she knows she is pregnant, she despises me. May the LORD judge between you and me."

[6] "Your slave is in your hands," Abram said. "Do with her whatever you think best." Then Sarai mistreated Hagar; so she fled from her.

[7] The angel of the LORD found Hagar near a spring in the desert; it was the spring that is beside the road to Shur. [8] And he said, "Hagar, slave of Sarai, where have you come from, and where are you going?"

"I'm running away from my mistress Sarai," she answered.

[9] Then the angel of the LORD told her, "Go back to your mistress and submit to her." [10] The angel added, "I will increase your descendants so much that they will be too numerous to count."

[11] The angel of the LORD also said to her:

"You are now pregnant
    and you will give birth to a son.
You shall name him Ishmael,[f]
    for the LORD has heard of your misery.
[12] He will be a wild donkey of a man;
    his hand will be against everyone
    and everyone's hand against him,
and he will live in hostility
    toward[g] all his brothers."

[13] She gave this name to the LORD who spoke to her: "You are the God who sees me," for she

---

[a] 1 Or sovereign   [b] 1 Or shield; / your reward will be very great   [c] 2 The meaning of the Hebrew for this phrase is uncertain.   [d] 5 Or seed   [e] 18 Or river   [f] 11 Ishmael means God hears.   [g] 12 Or live to the east / of

21 QUALITIES

THOSE WHO master problem solving—one of the 21 Indispensable Qualities of a Leader—find that it's one of the fastest ways to gain leadership in any group. Anyone who can solve problems will never lack influence.

But the influence gained isn't always positive.

Consider the case of Sarah. God told her husband, Abraham, that his offspring would grow as numerous as the sands of the seashore and the stars in the sky. But there was a problem: Sarah was barren and past the age of childbearing. As the years passed, God's promise didn't appear any closer to fulfillment.

Sarah faced a problem and felt compelled to solve it. Lacking the patience to trust God to keep his promise, Sarah looked to her own methods. After waiting more than a decade for a son, she felt she had waited long enough and unwisely attempted to fulfill God's will in her way, through an Egyptian servant named Hagar.

Sarah's solution, however, gave her no peace. When Hagar became pregnant by Abraham and bore a son named Ishmael, Sarah despised both Hagar and her new-born son. Hagar had done what she was asked, but satisfaction eluded Sarah.

Control Freak!

The true problem facing Sarah was not a need for offspring, but her own impatience. Sarah wanted *control*—something that has afflicted many leaders throughout history. Instead of trusting God, Sarah tried to make the promise come true by using her own methods and according to her own timetable. She depended upon her own strength when she should have leaned on almighty God. She illustrates what happens when an insecure leader tries to work independently of God. Insecure leaders:

1. Believe God is inattentive, absent, or even against them.
2. Allow their circumstances to determine their understanding of God's character.
3. See life through a perspective of scarcity rather than abundance.
4. Become self-seeking and manipulative.
5. Feel intimidated and deal with others through intimidation.
6. Resent the success of others and angrily turn on them.
7. Think that if one person succeeds, someone else must lose.
8. Blame others for their dilemmas.
9. See themselves as martyrs.
10. Conclude that attempts at control seem more logical than trusting God.

Do you identify with Sarah? Do you struggle with a desire to control problems rather than doing things God's way? If so, ask God to reveal how he would have you deal with your problems in a way that honors him.

For a positive example of problem solving, see p. 1463.

said, "I have now seen^a the One who sees me."
¹⁴That is why the well was called Beer Lahai
Roi^b; it is still there, between Kadesh and Bered.
¹⁵So Hagar bore Abram a son, and Abram
gave the name Ishmael to the son she had borne.
¹⁶Abram was eighty-six years old when Hagar
bore him Ishmael.

The Covenant of Circumcision

17 When Abram was ninety-nine years old,
the LORD appeared to him and said, "I am
God Almighty^c; walk before me faithfully and
be blameless. ²Then I will make my covenant
between me and you and will greatly increase
your numbers."

³Abram fell facedown, and God said to him,
⁴"As for me, this is my covenant with you: You
will be the father of many nations. ⁵No longer
will you be called Abram^d; your name will be
Abraham,^e for I have made you a father of many
nations. ⁶I will make you very fruitful; I will
make nations of you, and kings will come from
you. ⁷I will establish my covenant as an everlasting covenant between me and you and your descendants after you for the generations to come,
to be your God and the God of your descendants
after you. ⁸The whole land of Canaan, where
you now reside as a foreigner, I will give as an
everlasting possession to you and your descendants after you; and I will be their God."

⁹Then God said to Abraham, "As for you,
you must keep my covenant, you and your descendants after you for the generations to come.
¹⁰This is my covenant with you and your de-
scendants after you, the covenant you are to
keep: Every male among you shall be circum-
cised. ¹¹You are to undergo circumcision, and it
will be the sign of the covenant between me and
you. ¹²For the generations to come every male
among you who is eight days old must be circumcised, including those born in your household or bought with money from a foreigner —
those who are not your offspring. ¹³Whether
born in your household or bought with your
money, they must be circumcised. My covenant
in your flesh is to be an everlasting covenant.
¹⁴Any uncircumcised male, who has not been
circumcised in the flesh, will be cut off from his
people; he has broken my covenant."

¹⁵God also said to Abraham, "As for Sarai
your wife, you are no longer to call her Sarai; her
name will be Sarah. ¹⁶I will bless her and will
surely give you a son by her. I will bless her so
that she will be the mother of nations; kings of
peoples will come from her."

¹⁷Abraham fell facedown; he laughed and
said to himself, "Will a son be born to a man a
hundred years old? Will Sarah bear a child at the
age of ninety?" ¹⁸And Abraham said to God, "If
only Ishmael might live under your blessing!"

¹⁹Then God said, "Yes, but your wife Sarah
will bear you a son, and you will call him Isaac.^f
I will establish my covenant with him as an everlasting covenant for his descendants after him.
²⁰And as for Ishmael, I have heard you: I will
surely bless him; I will make him fruitful and
will greatly increase his numbers. He will be the
father of twelve rulers, and I will make him into
a great nation. ²¹But my covenant I will establish
with Isaac, whom Sarah will bear to you by this
time next year." ²²When he had finished speaking with Abraham, God went up from him.

²³On that very day Abraham took his son
Ishmael and all those born in his household or
bought with his money, every male in his household, and circumcised them, as God told him.
²⁴Abraham was ninety-nine years old when he
was circumcised, ²⁵and his son Ishmael was
thirteen; ²⁶Abraham and his son Ishmael were
both circumcised on that very day. ²⁷And every
male in Abraham's household, including those
born in his household or bought from a foreigner, was circumcised with him.

The Three Visitors

18 The LORD appeared to Abraham near the
great trees of Mamre while he was sitting
at the entrance to his tent in the heat of the day.
²Abraham looked up and saw three men stand-
ing nearby. When he saw them, he hurried from
the entrance of his tent to meet them and bowed
low to the ground.

³He said, "If I have found favor in your eyes,
my lord,^g do not pass your servant by. ⁴Let a little water be brought, and then you may all wash
your feet and rest under this tree. ⁵Let me get
you something to eat, so you can be refreshed
and then go on your way — now that you have
come to your servant."

"Very well," they answered, "do as you say."

⁶So Abraham hurried into the tent to Sarah.
"Quick," he said, "get three seahs^h of the finest
flour and knead it and bake some bread."

⁷Then he ran to the herd and selected a choice,

---

^a 13 Or seen the back of   ^b 14 Beer Lahai Roi means well of
the Living One who sees me.   ^c 1 Hebrew El-Shaddai
^d 5 Abram means exalted father.   ^e 5 Abraham probably
means father of many.   ^f 19 Isaac means he laughs.
^g 3 Or eyes, Lord   ^h 6 That is, probably about 36 pounds or
about 16 kilograms

tender calf and gave it to a servant, who hurried to prepare it. ⁸He then brought some curds and milk and the calf that had been prepared, and set these before them. While they ate, he stood near them under a tree.

⁹"Where is your wife Sarah?" they asked him.

"There, in the tent," he said.

¹⁰Then one of them said, "I will surely return to you about this time next year, and Sarah your wife will have a son."

Now Sarah was listening at the entrance to the tent, which was behind him. ¹¹Abraham and Sarah were already very old, and Sarah was past the age of childbearing. ¹²So Sarah laughed to herself as she thought, "After I am worn out and my lord is old, will I now have this pleasure?"

¹³Then the LORD said to Abraham, "Why did Sarah laugh and say, 'Will I really have a child, now that I am old?' ¹⁴Is anything too hard for the LORD? I will return to you at the appointed time next year, and Sarah will have a son."

¹⁵Sarah was afraid, so she lied and said, "I did not laugh."

But he said, "Yes, you did laugh."

Abraham Pleads for Sodom

¹⁶When the men got up to leave, they looked down toward Sodom, and Abraham walked along with them to see them on their way. ¹⁷Then the LORD said, "Shall I hide from Abraham what

I am about to do? ¹⁸Abraham will surely become a great and powerful nation, and all nations on earth will be blessed through him.ᵃ ¹⁹For I have chosen him, so that he will direct his children and his household after him to keep the way of the LORD by doing what is right and just, so that the LORD will bring about for Abraham what he has promised him."

²⁰Then the LORD said, "The outcry against Sodom and Gomorrah is so great and their sin so grievous ²¹that I will go down and see if what they have done is as bad as the outcry that has reached me. If not, I will know."

²²The men turned away and went toward Sodom, but Abraham remained standing before the LORD.ᵇ ²³Then Abraham approached him and said: "Will you sweep away the righteous with the wicked? ²⁴What if there are fifty righteous people in the city? Will you really sweep it away and not spareᶜ the place for the sake of the fifty righteous people in it? ²⁵Far be it from you to do such a thing—to kill the righteous with the wicked, treating the righteous and the wicked alike. Far be it from you! Will not the Judge of all the earth do right?"

²⁶The LORD said, "If I find fifty righteous

ᵃ 18 Or will use his name in blessings (see 48:20)
ᵇ 22 Masoretic Text; an ancient Hebrew scribal tradition but the LORD remained standing before Abraham   ᶜ 24 Or forgive; also in verse 26

people in the city of Sodom, I will spare the whole place for their sake."

²⁷Then Abraham spoke up again: "Now that I have been so bold as to speak to the Lord, though I am nothing but dust and ashes, ²⁸what if the number of the righteous is five less than fifty? Will you destroy the whole city for lack of five people?"

"If I find forty-five there," he said, "I will not destroy it."

²⁹Once again he spoke to him, "What if only forty are found there?"

He said, "For the sake of forty, I will not do it."

³⁰Then he said, "May the Lord not be angry, but let me speak. What if only thirty can be found there?"

He answered, "I will not do it if I find thirty there."

³¹Abraham said, "Now that I have been so bold as to speak to the Lord, what if only twenty can be found there?"

He said, "For the sake of twenty, I will not destroy it."

³²Then he said, "May the Lord not be angry, but let me speak just once more. What if only ten can be found there?"

He answered, "For the sake of ten, I will not destroy it."

³³When the LORD had finished speaking with Abraham, he left, and Abraham returned home.

Sodom and Gomorrah Destroyed

19 The two angels arrived at Sodom in the evening, and Lot was sitting in the gateway of the city. When he saw them, he got up to meet them and bowed down with his face to the ground. ²"My lords," he said, "please turn aside to your servant's house. You can wash your feet and spend the night and then go on your way early in the morning."

"No," they answered, "we will spend the night in the square."

³But he insisted so strongly that they did go with him and entered his house. He prepared a meal for them, baking bread without yeast, and they ate. ⁴Before they had gone to bed, all the men from every part of the city of Sodom — both young and old — surrounded the house. ⁵They called to Lot, "Where are the men who came to you tonight? Bring them out to us so that we can have sex with them."

⁶Lot went outside to meet them and shut the door behind him ⁷and said, "No, my friends. Don't do this wicked thing. ⁸Look, I have two daughters who have never slept with a man. Let

---

Negotiation: Abraham Takes a Stand with God

Genesis 18:16–33

In Genesis 18:16–33, Abraham does something incredible. When God revealed that he planned to destroy the cities of Sodom and Gomorrah, Abraham confronted God, knowing that his nephew lived in Sodom and believing that God would never destroy the righteous citizens there. So he took a stand, as all good leaders are able to do, and negotiated how many people it would take for God to withhold his punishment. Abraham wasn't afraid to use his resolve and his insight to ensure the safety of his family.

---

me bring them out to you, and you can do what you like with them. But don't do anything to these men, for they have come under the protection of my roof."

⁹"Get out of our way," they replied. "This fellow came here as a foreigner, and now he wants to play the judge! We'll treat you worse than them." They kept bringing pressure on Lot and moved forward to break down the door.

¹⁰But the men inside reached out and pulled Lot back into the house and shut the door. ¹¹Then they struck the men who were at the door of the house, young and old, with blindness so that they could not find the door.

¹²The two men said to Lot, "Do you have anyone else here — sons-in-law, sons or daughters, or anyone else in the city who belongs to you? Get them out of here, ¹³because we are going to destroy this place. The outcry to the LORD against its people is so great that he has sent us to destroy it."

¹⁴So Lot went out and spoke to his sons-in-law, who were pledged to marry^a his daughters. He said, "Hurry and get out of this place, because the LORD is about to destroy the city!" But his sons-in-law thought he was joking.

¹⁵With the coming of dawn, the angels urged Lot, saying, "Hurry! Take your wife and your two daughters who are here, or you will be swept away when the city is punished."

¹⁶When he hesitated, the men grasped his hand and the hands of his wife and of his two daughters and led them safely out of the city,

a 14 Or were married to

for the LORD was merciful to them. ¹⁷As soon as they had brought them out, one of them said, "Flee for your lives! Don't look back, and don't stop anywhere in the plain! Flee to the mountains or you will be swept away!"

¹⁸But Lot said to them, "No, my lords,^a please! ¹⁹Your^b servant has found favor in your^b eyes, and you^b have shown great kindness to me in sparing my life. But I can't flee to the mountains; this disaster will overtake me, and I'll die. ²⁰Look, here is a town near enough to run to, and it is small. Let me flee to it — it is very small, isn't it? Then my life will be spared."

²¹He said to him, "Very well, I will grant this request too; I will not overthrow the town you speak of. ²²But flee there quickly, because I cannot do anything until you reach it." (That is why the town was called Zoar.^c)

²³By the time Lot reached Zoar, the sun had risen over the land. ²⁴Then the LORD rained down burning sulfur on Sodom and Gomorrah — from the LORD out of the heavens. ²⁵Thus he overthrew those cities and the entire plain, destroying all those living in the cities — and also the vegetation in the land. ²⁶But Lot's wife looked back, and she became a pillar of salt.

²⁷Early the next morning Abraham got up and returned to the place where he had stood before the LORD. ²⁸He looked down toward Sodom and Gomorrah, toward all the land of the plain, and he saw dense smoke rising from the land, like smoke from a furnace.

²⁹So when God destroyed the cities of the plain, he remembered Abraham, and he brought Lot out of the catastrophe that overthrew the cities where Lot had lived.

Lot and His Daughters

³⁰Lot and his two daughters left Zoar and settled in the mountains, for he was afraid to stay in Zoar. He and his two daughters lived in a cave. ³¹One day the older daughter said to the younger, "Our father is old, and there is no man around here to give us children — as is the custom all over the earth. ³²Let's get our father to drink wine and then sleep with him and preserve our family line through our father."

³³That night they got their father to drink wine, and the older daughter went in and slept with him. He was not aware of it when she lay down or when she got up.

³⁴The next day the older daughter said to the younger, "Last night I slept with my father. Let's get him to drink wine again tonight, and you go in and sleep with him so we can preserve our

family line through our father." ³⁵So they got their father to drink wine that night also, and the younger daughter went in and slept with him. Again he was not aware of it when she lay down or when she got up.

³⁶So both of Lot's daughters became pregnant by their father. ³⁷The older daughter had a son, and she named him Moab^d; he is the father of the Moabites of today. ³⁸The younger daughter also had a son, and she named him Ben-Ammi^e; he is the father of the Ammonites^f of today.

Abraham and Abimelek

20 Now Abraham moved on from there into the region of the Negev and lived between Kadesh and Shur. For a while he stayed in Gerar, ²and there Abraham said of his wife Sarah, "She is my sister." Then Abimelek king of Gerar sent for Sarah and took her.

³But God came to Abimelek in a dream one night and said to him, "You are as good as dead because of the woman you have taken; she is a married woman."

⁴Now Abimelek had not gone near her, so he said, "Lord, will you destroy an innocent nation? ⁵Did he not say to me, 'She is my sister,' and didn't she also say, 'He is my brother'? I have done this with a clear conscience and clean hands."

⁶Then God said to him in the dream, "Yes, I know you did this with a clear conscience, and so I have kept you from sinning against me. That is why I did not let you touch her. ⁷Now return the man's wife, for he is a prophet, and he will pray for you and you will live. But if you do not return her, you may be sure that you and all who belong to you will die."

⁸Early the next morning Abimelek summoned all his officials, and when he told them all that had happened, they were very much afraid. ⁹Then Abimelek called Abraham in and said, "What have you done to us? How have I wronged you that you have brought such great guilt upon me and my kingdom? You have done things to me that should never be done." ¹⁰And Abimelek asked Abraham, "What was your reason for doing this?"

¹¹Abraham replied, "I said to myself, 'There is surely no fear of God in this place, and they will kill me because of my wife.' ¹²Besides, she really is my sister, the daughter of my father

---

^a 18 Or No, Lord; or No, my lord   ^b 19 The Hebrew is singular.   ^c 22 Zoar means small.   ^d 37 Moab sounds like the Hebrew for from father.   ^e 38 Ben-Ammi means son of my father's people.   ^f 38 Hebrew Bene-Ammon

though not of my mother; and she became my wife. [13]And when God had me wander from my father's household, I said to her, 'This is how you can show your love to me: Everywhere we go, say of me, "He is my brother." ' "

[14]Then Abimelek brought sheep and cattle and male and female slaves and gave them to Abraham, and he returned Sarah his wife to him. [15]And Abimelek said, "My land is before you; live wherever you like."

[16]To Sarah he said, "I am giving your brother a thousand shekels[a] of silver. This is to cover the offense against you before all who are with you; you are completely vindicated."

[17]Then Abraham prayed to God, and God healed Abimelek, his wife and his female slaves so they could have children again, [18]for the LORD had kept all the women in Abimelek's household from conceiving because of Abraham's wife Sarah.

The Birth of Isaac

21 Now the LORD was gracious to Sarah as he had said, and the LORD did for Sarah what he had promised. [2]Sarah became pregnant and bore a son to Abraham in his old age, at the very time God had promised him. [3]Abraham gave the name Isaac[b] to the son Sarah bore him. [4]When his son Isaac was eight days old, Abraham circumcised him, as God commanded him. [5]Abraham was a hundred years old when his son Isaac was born to him.

[6]Sarah said, "God has brought me laughter, and everyone who hears about this will laugh with me." [7]And she added, "Who would have said to Abraham that Sarah would nurse children? Yet I have borne him a son in his old age."

Hagar and Ishmael Sent Away

[8]The child grew and was weaned, and on the day Isaac was weaned Abraham held a great feast. [9]But Sarah saw that the son whom Hagar the Egyptian had borne to Abraham was mocking, [10]and she said to Abraham, "Get rid of that slave woman and her son, for that woman's son will never share in the inheritance with my son Isaac."

[11]The matter distressed Abraham greatly because it concerned his son. [12]But God said to him, "Do not be so distressed about the boy and your slave woman. Listen to whatever Sarah tells you, because it is through Isaac that your offspring[c] will be reckoned. [13]I will make the son of the slave into a nation also, because he is your offspring."

[14]Early the next morning Abraham took some food and a skin of water and gave them to Hagar. He set them on her shoulders and then sent her off with the boy. She went on her way and wandered in the Desert of Beersheba.

[15]When the water in the skin was gone, she put the boy under one of the bushes. [16]Then she went off and sat down about a bowshot away, for she thought, "I cannot watch the boy die." And as she sat there, she[d] began to sob.

[17]God heard the boy crying, and the angel of God called to Hagar from heaven and said to her, "What is the matter, Hagar? Do not be afraid; God has heard the boy crying as he lies there. [18]Lift the boy up and take him by the hand, for I will make him into a great nation."

[19]Then God opened her eyes and she saw a well of water. So she went and filled the skin with water and gave the boy a drink. [20]God was with the boy as he grew up. He lived in the desert and became an archer. [21]While he was living in the Desert of Paran, his mother got a wife for him from Egypt.

The Treaty at Beersheba

[22]At that time Abimelek and Phicol the commander of his forces said to Abraham, "God is with you in everything you do. [23]Now swear to me here before God that you will not deal falsely with me or my children or my descendants. Show to me and the country where you now reside as a foreigner the same kindness I have shown to you."

[24]Abraham said, "I swear it."

[25]Then Abraham complained to Abimelek about a well of water that Abimelek's servants had seized. [26]But Abimelek said, "I don't know who has done this. You did not tell me, and I heard about it only today."

[27]So Abraham brought sheep and cattle and gave them to Abimelek, and the two men made a treaty. [28]Abraham set apart seven ewe lambs from the flock, [29]and Abimelek asked Abraham, "What is the meaning of these seven ewe lambs you have set apart by themselves?"

[30]He replied, "Accept these seven lambs from my hand as a witness that I dug this well."

[31]So that place was called Beersheba,[e] because the two men swore an oath there.

[32]After the treaty had been made at Beersheba, Abimelek and Phicol the commander of his

---

[a] 16 That is, about 25 pounds or about 12 kilograms
[b] 3 Isaac means he laughs.   [c] 12 Or seed   [d] 16 Hebrew; Septuagint the child   [e] 31 Beersheba can mean well of seven and well of the oath.

forces returned to the land of the Philistines. ³³Abraham planted a tamarisk tree in Beersheba, and there he called on the name of the LORD, the Eternal God. ³⁴And Abraham stayed in the land of the Philistines for a long time.

Abraham Tested

22 Some time later God tested Abraham. He said to him, "Abraham!"

"Here I am," he replied.

²Then God said, "Take your son, your only son, whom you love — Isaac — and go to the region of Moriah. Sacrifice him there as a burnt offering on a mountain I will show you."

³Early the next morning Abraham got up and loaded his donkey. He took with him two of his servants and his son Isaac. When he had cut enough wood for the burnt offering, he set out for the place God had told him about. ⁴On the third day Abraham looked up and saw the place in the distance. ⁵He said to his servants, "Stay here with the donkey while I and the boy go over there. We will worship and then we will come back to you."

⁶Abraham took the wood for the burnt offering and placed it on his son Isaac, and he himself carried the fire and the knife. As the two of them went on together, ⁷Isaac spoke up and said to his father Abraham, "Father?"

"Yes, my son?" Abraham replied.

"The fire and wood are here," Isaac said, "but where is the lamb for the burnt offering?"

⁸Abraham answered, "God himself will provide the lamb for the burnt offering, my son." And the two of them went on together.

⁹When they reached the place God had told him about, Abraham built an altar there and arranged the wood on it. He bound his son Isaac and laid him on the altar, on top of the wood. ¹⁰Then he reached out his hand and took the knife to slay his son. ¹¹But the angel of the LORD called out to him from heaven, "Abraham! Abraham!"

"Here I am," he replied.

¹²"Do not lay a hand on the boy," he said. "Do not do anything to him. Now I know that you fear God, because you have not withheld from me your son, your only son."

¹³Abraham looked up and there in a thicket he saw a ram[a] caught by its horns. He went over and took the ram and sacrificed it as a burnt offering instead of his son. ¹⁴So Abraham called that place The LORD Will Provide. And to this day it is said, "On the mountain of the LORD it will be provided."

¹⁵The angel of the LORD called to Abraham from heaven a second time ¹⁶and said, "I swear by myself, declares the LORD, that because you have done this and have not withheld your son, your only son, ¹⁷I will surely bless you and make your descendants as numerous as the stars in the sky and as the sand on the seashore. Your descendants will take possession of the cities of their enemies, ¹⁸and through your offspring[b] all nations on earth will be blessed,[c] because you have obeyed me."

¹⁹Then Abraham returned to his servants, and they set off together for Beersheba. And Abraham stayed in Beersheba.

---

[a] 13 Many manuscripts of the Masoretic Text, Samaritan Pentateuch, Septuagint and Syriac; most manuscripts of the Masoretic Text *a ram behind him* [b] 18 Or *seed* [c] 18 Or *and all nations on earth will use the name of your offspring in blessings* (see 48:20)

The Law of Sacrifice: Abraham Pays a Price

Genesis 22:1–18

Did you know that God provides tests as measures of progress and as proving grounds for every person he calls to lead? Genesis 22 begins with a divine test. God calls Abraham to climb Mount Moriah and sacrifice his beloved son. If Abraham would resolve to give up Isaac, God knew he would be willing to do anything asked of him—and therefore would be a perfect candidate to become the father of the Hebrew people.

Leadership tests differ from one another, but all have a few things in common:

1. **Leaders get tested at each stage of growth.**
2. **The leader's goal is to pass the test.**
3. **Testing always precedes promotion.**
4. **Self-promotion or promotion by others can never replace divine promotion.**
5. **Promotion requires sacrifice.**

While Abraham's trial foreshadowed what God intended to do with his one and only Son thousands of years later, it also provided a leadership test.

Nahor's Sons

20Some time later Abraham was told, "Milkah is also a mother; she has borne sons to your brother Nahor: 21Uz the firstborn, Buz his brother, Kemuel (the father of Aram), 22Kesed, Hazo, Pildash, Jidlaph and Bethuel." 23Bethuel became the father of Rebekah. Milkah bore these eight sons to Abraham's brother Nahor. 24His concubine, whose name was Reumah, also had sons: Tebah, Gaham, Tahash and Maakah.

The Death of Sarah

23 Sarah lived to be a hundred and twenty-seven years old. 2She died at Kiriath Arba (that is, Hebron) in the land of Canaan, and Abraham went to mourn for Sarah and to weep over her.

3Then Abraham rose from beside his dead wife and spoke to the Hittites.a He said, 4"I am a foreigner and stranger among you. Sell me some property for a burial site here so I can bury my dead."

5The Hittites replied to Abraham, 6"Sir, listen to us. You are a mighty prince among us. Bury your dead in the choicest of our tombs. None of us will refuse you his tomb for burying your dead."

7Then Abraham rose and bowed down before the people of the land, the Hittites. 8He said to them, "If you are willing to let me bury my dead, then listen to me and intercede with Ephron son of Zohar on my behalf 9so he will sell me the cave of Machpelah, which belongs to him and is at the end of his field. Ask him to sell it to me for the full price as a burial site among you."

10Ephron the Hittite was sitting among his people and he replied to Abraham in the hearing of all the Hittites who had come to the gate of his city. 11"No, my lord," he said. "Listen to me; I giveb you the field, and I giveb you the cave that is in it. I giveb it to you in the presence of my people. Bury your dead."

12Again Abraham bowed down before the people of the land 13and he said to Ephron in their hearing, "Listen to me, if you will. I will pay the price of the field. Accept it from me so I can bury my dead there."

14Ephron answered Abraham, 15"Listen to me, my lord; the land is worth four hundred shekelsc of silver, but what is that between you and me? Bury your dead."

16Abraham agreed to Ephron's terms and weighed out for him the price he had named in the hearing of the Hittites: four hundred shekels of silver, according to the weight current among the merchants.

17So Ephron's field in Machpelah near Mamre—both the field and the cave in it, and all the trees within the borders of the field—was deeded 18to Abraham as his property in the presence of all the Hittites who had come to the gate of the city. 19Afterward Abraham buried his wife Sarah in the cave in the field of Machpelah near Mamre (which is at Hebron) in the land of Canaan. 20So the field and the cave in it were deeded to Abraham by the Hittites as a burial site.

Isaac and Rebekah

24 Abraham was now very old, and the LORD had blessed him in every way. 2He said to the senior servant in his household, the one in charge of all that he had, "Put your hand under my thigh. 3I want you to swear by the LORD, the God of heaven and the God of earth, that you will not get a wife for my son from the daughters of the Canaanites, among whom I am living, 4but will go to my country and my own relatives and get a wife for my son Isaac."

5The servant asked him, "What if the woman is unwilling to come back with me to this land? Shall I then take your son back to the country you came from?"

6"Make sure that you do not take my son back there," Abraham said. 7"The LORD, the God of heaven, who brought me out of my father's household and my native land and who spoke to me and promised me on oath, saying, 'To your offspringd I will give this land'—he will send his angel before you so that you can get a wife for my son from there. 8If the woman is unwilling to come back with you, then you will be released from this oath of mine. Only do not take my son back there." 9So the servant put his hand under the thigh of his master Abraham and swore an oath to him concerning this matter.

10Then the servant left, taking with him ten of his master's camels loaded with all kinds of good things from his master. He set out for Aram Naharaime and made his way to the town of Nahor. 11He had the camels kneel down near the well outside the town; it was toward evening, the time the women go out to draw water.

12Then he prayed, "LORD, God of my master Abraham, make me successful today, and show

---

a 3 Or the descendants of Heth; also in verses 5, 7, 10, 16, 18 and 20   b 11 Or sell   c 15 That is, about 10 pounds or about 4.6 kilograms   d 7 Or seed   e 10 That is, Northwest Mesopotamia

kindness to my master Abraham. [13]See, I am standing beside this spring, and the daughters of the townspeople are coming out to draw water. [14]May it be that when I say to a young woman, 'Please let down your jar that I may have a drink,' and she says, 'Drink, and I'll water your camels too'—let her be the one you have chosen for your servant Isaac. By this I will know that you have shown kindness to my master."

[15]Before he had finished praying, Rebekah came out with her jar on her shoulder. She was the daughter of Bethuel son of Milkah, who was the wife of Abraham's brother Nahor. [16]The woman was very beautiful, a virgin; no man had ever slept with her. She went down to the spring, filled her jar and came up again.

[17]The servant hurried to meet her and said, "Please give me a little water from your jar."

[18]"Drink, my lord," she said, and quickly lowered the jar to her hands and gave him a drink.

[19]After she had given him a drink, she said, "I'll draw water for your camels too, until they have had enough to drink." [20]So she quickly emptied her jar into the trough, ran back to the well to draw more water, and drew enough for all his camels. [21]Without saying a word, the man watched her closely to learn whether or not the LORD had made his journey successful.

[22]When the camels had finished drinking, the man took out a gold nose ring weighing a beka[a] and two gold bracelets weighing ten shekels.[b] [23]Then he asked, "Whose daughter are you? Please tell me, is there room in your father's house for us to spend the night?"

[24]She answered him, "I am the daughter of Bethuel, the son that Milkah bore to Nahor." [25]And she added, "We have plenty of straw and fodder, as well as room for you to spend the night."

[26]Then the man bowed down and worshiped the LORD, [27]saying, "Praise be to the LORD, the God of my master Abraham, who has not abandoned his kindness and faithfulness to my master. As for me, the LORD has led me on the journey to the house of my master's relatives."

[28]The young woman ran and told her mother's household about these things. [29]Now Rebekah had a brother named Laban, and he hurried out to the man at the spring. [30]As soon as he had seen the nose ring, and the bracelets on his sister's arms, and had heard Rebekah tell what the man said to her, he went out to the man and found him standing by the camels near the spring. [31]"Come, you who are blessed by the LORD," he said. "Why are you standing out here? I have prepared the house and a place for the camels."

[32]So the man went to the house, and the camels were unloaded. Straw and fodder were brought for the camels, and water for him and his men to wash their feet. [33]Then food was set before him, but he said, "I will not eat until I have told you what I have to say."

"Then tell us," Laban said.

[34]So he said, "I am Abraham's servant. [35]The LORD has blessed my master abundantly, and he has become wealthy. He has given him sheep and cattle, silver and gold, male and female servants, and camels and donkeys. [36]My master's wife Sarah has borne him a son in her old age, and he has given him everything he owns. [37]And my master made me swear an oath, and said, 'You must not get a wife for my son from the daughters of the Canaanites, in whose land I live, [38]but go to my father's family and to my own clan, and get a wife for my son.'

[39]"Then I asked my master, 'What if the woman will not come back with me?'

[40]"He replied, 'The LORD, before whom I have walked faithfully, will send his angel with you and make your journey a success, so that you can get a wife for my son from my own clan and from my father's family. [41]You will be released from my oath if, when you go to my clan, they refuse to give her to you—then you will be released from my oath.'

[42]"When I came to the spring today, I said, 'LORD, God of my master Abraham, if you will, please grant success to the journey on which I have come. [43]See, I am standing beside this spring. If a young woman comes out to draw water and I say to her, "Please let me drink a little water from your jar," [44]and if she says to me, "Drink, and I'll draw water for your camels too," let her be the one the LORD has chosen for my master's son.'

[45]"Before I finished praying in my heart, Rebekah came out, with her jar on her shoulder. She went down to the spring and drew water, and I said to her, 'Please give me a drink.'

[46]"She quickly lowered her jar from her shoulder and said, 'Drink, and I'll water your camels too.' So I drank, and she watered the camels also.

[47]"I asked her, 'Whose daughter are you?'

"She said, 'The daughter of Bethuel son of Nahor, whom Milkah bore to him.'

"Then I put the ring in her nose and the bracelets on her arms, [48]and I bowed down and worshiped the LORD. I praised the LORD, the

---

[a] 22 That is, about 1/5 ounce or about 5.7 grams   [b] 22 That is, about 4 ounces or about 115 grams

God of my master Abraham, who had led me on the right road to get the granddaughter of my master's brother for his son. ⁴⁹Now if you will show kindness and faithfulness to my master, tell me; and if not, tell me, so I may know which way to turn."

⁵⁰Laban and Bethuel answered, "This is from the LORD; we can say nothing to you one way or the other. ⁵¹Here is Rebekah; take her and go, and let her become the wife of your master's son, as the LORD has directed."

⁵²When Abraham's servant heard what they said, he bowed down to the ground before the LORD. ⁵³Then the servant brought out gold and silver jewelry and articles of clothing and gave them to Rebekah; he also gave costly gifts to her brother and to her mother. ⁵⁴Then he and the men who were with him ate and drank and spent the night there.

When they got up the next morning, he said, "Send me on my way to my master."

⁵⁵But her brother and her mother replied, "Let the young woman remain with us ten days or so; then you^a may go."

⁵⁶But he said to them, "Do not detain me, now that the LORD has granted success to my journey. Send me on my way so I may go to my master."

⁵⁷Then they said, "Let's call the young woman and ask her about it." ⁵⁸So they called Rebekah and asked her, "Will you go with this man?"

"I will go," she said.

⁵⁹So they sent their sister Rebekah on her way, along with her nurse and Abraham's servant and his men. ⁶⁰And they blessed Rebekah and said to her,

"Our sister, may you increase
    to thousands upon thousands;
may your offspring possess
    the cities of their enemies."

⁶¹Then Rebekah and her attendants got ready and mounted the camels and went back with the man. So the servant took Rebekah and left.

⁶²Now Isaac had come from Beer Lahai Roi, for he was living in the Negev. ⁶³He went out to the field one evening to meditate,^b and as he looked up, he saw camels approaching. ⁶⁴Rebekah also looked up and saw Isaac. She got down from her camel ⁶⁵and asked the servant, "Who is that man in the field coming to meet us?"

"He is my master," the servant answered. So she took her veil and covered herself.

⁶⁶Then the servant told Isaac all he had done. ⁶⁷Isaac brought her into the tent of his mother Sarah, and he married Rebekah. So she became his wife, and he loved her; and Isaac was comforted after his mother's death.

The Death of Abraham

25 Abraham had taken another wife, whose name was Keturah. ²She bore him Zimran, Jokshan, Medan, Midian, Ishbak and Shuah. ³Jokshan was the father of Sheba and Dedan; the descendants of Dedan were the Ashurites, the Letushites and the Leummites. ⁴The sons of Midian were Ephah, Epher, Hanok, Abida and Eldaah. All these were descendants of Keturah.

⁵Abraham left everything he owned to Isaac. ⁶But while he was still living, he gave gifts to the sons of his concubines and sent them away from his son Isaac to the land of the east.

⁷Abraham lived a hundred and seventy-five years. ⁸Then Abraham breathed his last and died at a good old age, an old man and full of years; and he was gathered to his people. ⁹His sons Isaac and Ishmael buried him in the cave of Machpelah near Mamre, in the field of Ephron son of Zohar the Hittite, ¹⁰the field Abraham had bought from the Hittites.^c There Abraham was buried with his wife Sarah. ¹¹After Abraham's death, God blessed his son Isaac, who then lived near Beer Lahai Roi.

Ishmael's Sons

¹²This is the account of the family line of Abraham's son Ishmael, whom Sarah's slave, Hagar the Egyptian, bore to Abraham.

¹³These are the names of the sons of Ishmael, listed in the order of their birth: Nebaioth the firstborn of Ishmael, Kedar, Adbeel, Mibsam, ¹⁴Mishma, Dumah, Massa, ¹⁵Hadad, Tema, Jetur, Naphish and Kedemah. ¹⁶These were the sons of Ishmael, and these are the names of the twelve tribal rulers according to their settlements and camps. ¹⁷Ishmael lived a hundred and thirty-seven years. He breathed his last and died, and he was gathered to his people. ¹⁸His descendants settled in the area from Havilah to Shur, near the eastern border of Egypt, as you go toward Ashur. And they lived in hostility toward^d all the tribes related to them.

Jacob and Esau

¹⁹This is the account of the family line of Abraham's son Isaac.

---

^a 55 Or she   ^b 63 The meaning of the Hebrew for this word is uncertain.   ^c 10 Or the descendants of Heth   ^d 18 Or lived to the east of

Abraham became the father of Isaac, [20]and Isaac was forty years old when he married Rebekah daughter of Bethuel the Aramean from Paddan Aram[a] and sister of Laban the Aramean.

[21]Isaac prayed to the LORD on behalf of his wife, because she was childless. The LORD answered his prayer, and his wife Rebekah became pregnant. [22]The babies jostled each other within her, and she said, "Why is this happening to me?" So she went to inquire of the LORD.

[23]The LORD said to her,

"Two nations are in your womb,
    and two peoples from within you will be
        separated;
one people will be stronger than the other,
    and the older will serve the younger."

[24]When the time came for her to give birth, there were twin boys in her womb. [25]The first to come out was red, and his whole body was like a hairy garment; so they named him Esau.[b] [26]After this, his brother came out, with his hand grasping Esau's heel; so he was named Jacob.[c] Isaac was sixty years old when Rebekah gave birth to them.

[27]The boys grew up, and Esau became a skillful hunter, a man of the open country, while Jacob was content to stay at home among the tents.

[28]Isaac, who had a taste for wild game, loved Esau, but Rebekah loved Jacob.

[29]Once when Jacob was cooking some stew, Esau came in from the open country, famished. [30]He said to Jacob, "Quick, let me have some of that red stew! I'm famished!" (That is why he was also called Edom.[d])

[31]Jacob replied, "First sell me your birthright."

[32]"Look, I am about to die," Esau said. "What good is the birthright to me?"

[33]But Jacob said, "Swear to me first." So he swore an oath to him, selling his birthright to Jacob.

[34]Then Jacob gave Esau some bread and some lentil stew. He ate and drank, and then got up and left.

So Esau despised his birthright.

Isaac and Abimelek

26 Now there was a famine in the land— besides the previous famine in Abraham's time—and Isaac went to Abimelek king of the Philistines in Gerar. [2]The LORD appeared to Isaac and said, "Do not go down to Egypt; live in the land where I tell you to live. [3]Stay in this

---

[a] 20 That is, Northwest Mesopotamia   [b] 25 Esau may mean hairy.   [c] 26 Jacob means he grasps the heel, a Hebrew idiom for he deceives.   [d] 30 Edom means red.

JACOB

A Leader Made Usable Through Brokenness
Genesis 25:26—32:32

PROFILE in leadership

Natural leaders have it easy, right? Not always. Even leaders gifted with tremendous natural leadership can have a very difficult time, especially with issues of character. That was true for Jacob. From the very beginning he wielded great influence. No matter what he did or where he went, he stirred things up. He captured the heart of his mother and the birthright of his brother, turning Isaac's household upside down. He had a similar impact on the household of Laban. Over time, his leadership created great prosperity. And it was his sons who founded the twelve tribes of the Hebrew nation.

Wealthy, strong, influential and blessed with a large family, Jacob seemed to have everything. But a leader who goes his own way and seeks to benefit only himself cannot be an effective instrument in God's hands. God had to break Jacob to make him useful. In the breaking process, Jacob—the deceiving "heel-catcher"—became Israel, a "prince with God" (according to some translators; others interpret Israel to mean "he struggles with God"), who purposed to serve God rather than himself.

Natural leaders often need to be broken. Consider your natural ability to lead a gift from God, but your character a gift to present back to God. Remember: Every time you stand up under the weight of adversity, you are being prepared, as Jacob was, to better serve God and lead people.

Influence: Jacob Cons Esau, Rebekah Deceives Isaac

Genesis 25:29–34; 27:1–30

Influence can be both positive and negative. The Bible tells us that Jacob influenced the birthright away from his brother Esau, the oldest son. A little later, Rebekah helped Jacob to influence the best blessing out of his father, a boon intended for his brother. It took *influence* to bring both events to pass. A person can wield influence in many ways. Consider seven such methods, beginning with the worst:

1. **Force:** the use of physical strength to influence others.
2. **Intimidation:** bullying others verbally or emotionally to get them to act against their will.
3. **Manipulation:** coercing others to act, sometimes against their will.
4. **Exchange:** giving something in order to receive from others (I scratch your back; you scratch mine).
5. **Persuasion:** the use of verbal skills to move someone to action.
6. **Motivation:** energizing others so that they want to act.
7. **Honor:** communicating esteem to others by serving them, thus inspiring them to act.

land for a while, and I will be with you and will bless you. For to you and your descendants I will give all these lands and will confirm the oath I swore to your father Abraham. ⁴I will make your descendants as numerous as the stars in the sky and will give them all these lands, and through your offspring*ᵃ* all nations on earth will be blessed,*ᵇ* ⁵because Abraham obeyed me and did everything I required of him, keeping my commands, my decrees and my instructions." ⁶So Isaac stayed in Gerar.

⁷When the men of that place asked him about his wife, he said, "She is my sister," because he was afraid to say, "She is my wife." He thought, "The men of this place might kill me on account of Rebekah, because she is beautiful."

⁸When Isaac had been there a long time, Abimelek king of the Philistines looked down from a window and saw Isaac caressing his wife Rebekah. ⁹So Abimelek summoned Isaac and said, "She is really your wife! Why did you say, 'She is my sister'?"

Isaac answered him, "Because I thought I might lose my life on account of her."

¹⁰Then Abimelek said, "What is this you have done to us? One of the men might well have slept with your wife, and you would have brought guilt upon us."

¹¹So Abimelek gave orders to all the people: "Anyone who harms this man or his wife shall surely be put to death."

¹²Isaac planted crops in that land and the same year reaped a hundredfold, because the LORD blessed him. ¹³The man became rich, and his wealth continued to grow until he became very wealthy. ¹⁴He had so many flocks and herds and servants that the Philistines envied him. ¹⁵So all the wells that his father's servants had dug in the time of his father Abraham, the Philistines stopped up, filling them with earth.

¹⁶Then Abimelek said to Isaac, "Move away from us; you have become too powerful for us."

¹⁷So Isaac moved away from there and encamped in the Valley of Gerar, where he settled. ¹⁸Isaac reopened the wells that had been dug in the time of his father Abraham, which the Philistines had stopped up after Abraham died, and he gave them the same names his father had given them.

¹⁹Isaac's servants dug in the valley and discovered a well of fresh water there. ²⁰But the herders of Gerar quarreled with those of Isaac and said, "The water is ours!" So he named the well Esek,*ᶜ* because they disputed with him. ²¹Then they dug another well, but they quarreled over that one also; so he named it Sitnah.*ᵈ* ²²He moved on from there and dug another well, and no one quarreled over it. He named it Rehoboth,*ᵉ* saying, "Now the LORD has given us room and we will flourish in the land."

²³From there he went up to Beersheba. ²⁴That night the LORD appeared to him and said, "I am the God of your father Abraham. Do not be

---

ᵃ 4 Or seed   ᵇ 4 Or and all nations on earth will use the name of your offspring in blessings (see 48:20)   ᶜ 20 Esek means dispute.   ᵈ 21 Sitnah means opposition.   ᵉ 22 Rehoboth means room.

VISION   Esau Fails to See the Big Picture

Genesis 25:29–34; 32:3–23; 33:1–20

IN ESAU the Bible paints a powerful picture of a leader without vision. While the eyes of some folks may be larger than their stomachs, in this case the problem was exactly the opposite.

Isaac and Rebekah's firstborn son, Esau, loved the great outdoors from very early in life. He became a skillful hunter, growing strong and resourceful and as rugged as they come. But he lived so completely in the present, depending solely on his own strength and resources, that he repeatedly failed to clearly see the future.

Esau succumbed to the kind of temptations that still entice leaders today. Take a look at six characteristics of Esau's nearsightedness and see whether any of them might trouble you:

1. Esau focused solely on the here and now, convinced that tomorrow never comes.
2. Esau relied on his natural gifts and on his birth order rather than on God's plan.
3. Esau's shortsightedness prompted him to give up the ultimate to get the immediate (a single meal).
4. Esau, favored by his father, may have thought that Isaac's love would bail him out of any poor decision he might make.
5. Esau's limited vision caused him to marry a Hittite, a choice which grieved his parents.
6. Esau's clouded vision blinded him from the deception of his brother Jacob.

In a legacy symbolic of his life, Esau's descendants became the enemies of Israel. Whenever you see the word *Edom* or read of Israel's clashes with the Edomites in Scripture, think of Esau, for it is through him that these persistent opponents of Israel came into existence. The animosity between these two ancient peoples can be seen even in the Psalms: "Remember, LORD, what the Edomites did on the day Jerusalem fell. 'Tear it down,' they cried, 'tear it down to its foundations!'" (Ps 137:7).

Today we remember Esau as a self-centered man with faulty vision. Hebrews 12:15–16 tells us to examine ourselves, so that "no one is sexually immoral, or is godless like Esau, who for a single meal sold his inheritance rights as the oldest son."

And yet God extends his grace! Before Esau died, he showed that he had matured. Genesis 32 and 33 describe a fearful meeting between Esau and his estranged brother. When the pair finally meet after years of separation, Esau embraces the deceiver Jacob and forgives him on the spot. Could it be that before he closed his eyes for the last time, Esau finally saw with clear vision? Perhaps. But imagine what *might have been* had he developed that vision sooner!

For a positive example of vision, see p. 16.

afraid, for I am with you; I will bless you and will increase the number of your descendants for the sake of my servant Abraham."

²⁵Isaac built an altar there and called on the name of the LORD. There he pitched his tent, and there his servants dug a well.

²⁶Meanwhile, Abimelek had come to him from Gerar, with Ahuzzath his personal adviser and Phicol the commander of his forces. ²⁷Isaac asked them, "Why have you come to me, since you were hostile to me and sent me away?"

²⁸They answered, "We saw clearly that the LORD was with you; so we said, 'There ought to be a sworn agreement between us' — between us and you. Let us make a treaty with you ²⁹that you will do us no harm, just as we did not harm you but always treated you well and sent you away peacefully. And now you are blessed by the LORD."

³⁰Isaac then made a feast for them, and they ate and drank. ³¹Early the next morning the men swore an oath to each other. Then Isaac sent them on their way, and they went away peacefully.

³²That day Isaac's servants came and told him about the well they had dug. They said, "We've found water!" ³³He called it Shibah,ᵃ and to this day the name of the town has been Beersheba.ᵇ

Jacob Takes Esau's Blessing

³⁴When Esau was forty years old, he married Judith daughter of Beeri the Hittite, and also Basemath daughter of Elon the Hittite. ³⁵They were a source of grief to Isaac and Rebekah.

27 When Isaac was old and his eyes were so weak that he could no longer see, he called for Esau his older son and said to him, "My son."

"Here I am," he answered.

²Isaac said, "I am now an old man and don't know the day of my death. ³Now then, get your equipment — your quiver and bow — and go out to the open country to hunt some wild game for me. ⁴Prepare me the kind of tasty food I like and bring it to me to eat, so that I may give you my blessing before I die."

⁵Now Rebekah was listening as Isaac spoke to his son Esau. When Esau left for the open country to hunt game and bring it back, ⁶Rebekah said to her son Jacob, "Look, I overheard your father say to your brother Esau, ⁷'Bring me some game and prepare me some tasty food to eat, so that I may give you my blessing in the presence of the LORD before I die.' ⁸Now, my son, listen carefully and do what I tell you: ⁹Go out to the flock and bring me two choice young goats, so I

can prepare some tasty food for your father, just the way he likes it. ¹⁰Then take it to your father to eat, so that he may give you his blessing before he dies."

¹¹Jacob said to Rebekah his mother, "But my brother Esau is a hairy man while I have smooth skin. ¹²What if my father touches me? I would appear to be tricking him and would bring down a curse on myself rather than a blessing."

¹³His mother said to him, "My son, let the curse fall on me. Just do what I say; go and get them for me."

¹⁴So he went and got them and brought them to his mother, and she prepared some tasty food, just the way his father liked it. ¹⁵Then Rebekah took the best clothes of Esau her older son, which she had in the house, and put them on her younger son Jacob. ¹⁶She also covered his hands and the smooth part of his neck with the goatskins. ¹⁷Then she handed to her son Jacob the tasty food and the bread she had made.

¹⁸He went to his father and said, "My father."

"Yes, my son," he answered. "Who is it?"

¹⁹Jacob said to his father, "I am Esau your firstborn. I have done as you told me. Please sit up and eat some of my game, so that you may give me your blessing."

²⁰Isaac asked his son, "How did you find it so quickly, my son?"

"The LORD your God gave me success," he replied.

²¹Then Isaac said to Jacob, "Come near so I can touch you, my son, to know whether you really are my son Esau or not."

²²Jacob went close to his father Isaac, who touched him and said, "The voice is the voice of Jacob, but the hands are the hands of Esau." ²³He did not recognize him, for his hands were hairy like those of his brother Esau; so he proceeded to bless him. ²⁴"Are you really my son Esau?" he asked.

"I am," he replied.

²⁵Then he said, "My son, bring me some of your game to eat, so that I may give you my blessing."

Jacob brought it to him and he ate; and he brought some wine and he drank. ²⁶Then his father Isaac said to him, "Come here, my son, and kiss me."

²⁷So he went to him and kissed him. When Isaac caught the smell of his clothes, he blessed him and said,

---

ᵃ 33 *Shibah* can mean *oath* or *seven.*   ᵇ 33 *Beersheba* can mean *well of the oath* and *well of seven.*

"Ah, the smell of my son
  is like the smell of a field
  that the LORD has blessed.
28 May God give you heaven's dew
  and earth's richness—
  an abundance of grain and new wine.
29 May nations serve you
  and peoples bow down to you.
Be lord over your brothers,
  and may the sons of your mother bow
    down to you.
May those who curse you be cursed
  and those who bless you be blessed."

30 After Isaac finished blessing him, and Jacob had scarcely left his father's presence, his brother Esau came in from hunting. 31 He too prepared some tasty food and brought it to his father. Then he said to him, "My father, please sit up and eat some of my game, so that you may give me your blessing."

32 His father Isaac asked him, "Who are you?"

"I am your son," he answered, "your firstborn, Esau."

33 Isaac trembled violently and said, "Who was it, then, that hunted game and brought it to me? I ate it just before you came and I blessed him—and indeed he will be blessed!"

34 When Esau heard his father's words, he burst out with a loud and bitter cry and said to his father, "Bless me—me too, my father!"

35 But he said, "Your brother came deceitfully and took your blessing."

36 Esau said, "Isn't he rightly named Jacob[a]? This is the second time he has taken advantage of me: He took my birthright, and now he's taken my blessing!" Then he asked, "Haven't you reserved any blessing for me?"

37 Isaac answered Esau, "I have made him lord over you and have made all his relatives his servants, and I have sustained him with grain and new wine. So what can I possibly do for you, my son?"

38 Esau said to his father, "Do you have only one blessing, my father? Bless me too, my father!" Then Esau wept aloud.

39 His father Isaac answered him,

"Your dwelling will be
  away from the earth's richness,
  away from the dew of heaven above.
40 You will live by the sword
  and you will serve your brother.
But when you grow restless,
  you will throw his yoke
  from off your neck."

41 Esau held a grudge against Jacob because of the blessing his father had given him. He said to himself, "The days of mourning for my father are near; then I will kill my brother Jacob."

42 When Rebekah was told what her older son Esau had said, she sent for her younger son Jacob and said to him, "Your brother Esau is planning to avenge himself by killing you. 43 Now then, my son, do what I say: Flee at once to my brother Laban in Harran. 44 Stay with him for a while until your brother's fury subsides. 45 When your brother is no longer angry with you and forgets what you did to him, I'll send word for you to come back from there. Why should I lose both of you in one day?"

46 Then Rebekah said to Isaac, "I'm disgusted with living because of these Hittite women. If Jacob takes a wife from among the women of this land, from Hittite women like these, my life will not be worth living."

28 So Isaac called for Jacob and blessed him. Then he commanded him: "Do not marry a Canaanite woman. 2 Go at once to Paddan Aram,[b] to the house of your mother's father Bethuel. Take a wife for yourself there, from among the daughters of Laban, your mother's brother. 3 May God Almighty[c] bless you and make you fruitful and increase your numbers until you become a community of peoples. 4 May he give you and your descendants the blessing given to Abraham, so that you may take possession of the land where you now reside as a foreigner, the land God gave to Abraham." 5 Then Isaac sent Jacob on his way, and he went to Paddan Aram, to Laban son of Bethuel the Aramean, the brother of Rebekah, who was the mother of Jacob and Esau.

6 Now Esau learned that Isaac had blessed Jacob and had sent him to Paddan Aram to take a wife from there, and that when he blessed him he commanded him, "Do not marry a Canaanite woman," 7 and that Jacob had obeyed his father and mother and had gone to Paddan Aram. 8 Esau then realized how displeasing the Canaanite women were to his father Isaac; 9 so he went to Ishmael and married Mahalath, the sister of Nebaioth and daughter of Ishmael son of Abraham, in addition to the wives he already had.

Jacob's Dream at Bethel

10 Jacob left Beersheba and set out for Harran. 11 When he reached a certain place, he stopped

---

^a 36 Jacob means he grasps the heel, a Hebrew idiom for he takes advantage of or he deceives.   ^b 2 That is, Northwest Mesopotamia; also in verses 5, 6 and 7   ^c 3 Hebrew El-Shaddai

for the night because the sun had set. Taking one of the stones there, he put it under his head and lay down to sleep. [12]He had a dream in which he saw a stairway resting on the earth, with its top reaching to heaven, and the angels of God were ascending and descending on it. [13]There above it[a] stood the LORD, and he said: "I am the LORD, the God of your father Abraham and the God of Isaac. I will give you and your descendants the land on which you are lying. [14]Your descendants will be like the dust of the earth, and you will spread out to the west and to the east, to the north and to the south. All peoples on earth will be blessed through you and your offspring.[b] [15]I am with you and will watch over you wherever you go, and I will bring you back to this land. I will not leave you until I have done what I have promised you."

[16]When Jacob awoke from his sleep, he thought, "Surely the LORD is in this place, and I was not aware of it." [17]He was afraid and said, "How awesome is this place! This is none other than the house of God; this is the gate of heaven."

[18]Early the next morning Jacob took the stone he had placed under his head and set it up as a pillar and poured oil on top of it. [19]He called that place Bethel,[c] though the city used to be called Luz.

[20]Then Jacob made a vow, saying, "If God will be with me and will watch over me on this journey I am taking and will give me food to eat and clothes to wear [21]so that I return safely to my father's household, then the LORD[d] will be my God [22]and[e] this stone that I have set up as a pillar will be God's house, and of all that you give me I will give you a tenth."

Jacob Arrives in Paddan Aram

29 Then Jacob continued on his journey and came to the land of the eastern peoples. [2]There he saw a well in the open country, with three flocks of sheep lying near it because the flocks were watered from that well. The stone over the mouth of the well was large. [3]When all the flocks were gathered there, the shepherds would roll the stone away from the well's mouth and water the sheep. Then they would return the stone to its place over the mouth of the well.

[4]Jacob asked the shepherds, "My brothers, where are you from?"

"We're from Harran," they replied.

[5]He said to them, "Do you know Laban, Nahor's grandson?"

"Yes, we know him," they answered.

[6]Then Jacob asked them, "Is he well?"

"Yes, he is," they said, "and here comes his daughter Rachel with the sheep."

[7]"Look," he said, "the sun is still high; it is not time for the flocks to be gathered. Water the sheep and take them back to pasture."

[8]"We can't," they replied, "until all the flocks are gathered and the stone has been rolled away from the mouth of the well. Then we will water the sheep."

[9]While he was still talking with them, Rachel came with her father's sheep, for she was a shepherd. [10]When Jacob saw Rachel daughter of his uncle Laban, and Laban's sheep, he went over and rolled the stone away from the mouth of the well and watered his uncle's sheep. [11]Then Jacob kissed Rachel and began to weep aloud. [12]He had told Rachel that he was a relative of her father and a son of Rebekah. So she ran and told her father.

[13]As soon as Laban heard the news about Jacob, his sister's son, he hurried to meet him. He embraced him and kissed him and brought him to his home, and there Jacob told him all these things. [14]Then Laban said to him, "You are my own flesh and blood."

Jacob Marries Leah and Rachel

After Jacob had stayed with him for a whole month, [15]Laban said to him, "Just because you are a relative of mine, should you work for me for nothing? Tell me what your wages should be."

[16]Now Laban had two daughters; the name of the older was Leah, and the name of the younger was Rachel. [17]Leah had weak[f] eyes, but Rachel had a lovely figure and was beautiful. [18]Jacob was in love with Rachel and said, "I'll work for you seven years in return for your younger daughter Rachel."

[19]Laban said, "It's better that I give her to you than to some other man. Stay here with me." [20]So Jacob served seven years to get Rachel, but they seemed like only a few days to him because of his love for her.

[21]Then Jacob said to Laban, "Give me my wife. My time is completed, and I want to make love to her."

[22]So Laban brought together all the people of the place and gave a feast. [23]But when evening came, he took his daughter Leah and brought

---

[a] 13 Or There beside him   [b] 14 Or will use your name and the name of your offspring in blessings (see 48:20)   [c] 19 Bethel means house of God.   [d] 20,21 Or Since God . . . father's household, the LORD   [e] 21,22 Or household, and the LORD will be my God, [22]then   [f] 17 Or delicate

her to Jacob, and Jacob made love to her. [24]And Laban gave his servant Zilpah to his daughter as her attendant.

[25]When morning came, there was Leah! So Jacob said to Laban, "What is this you have done to me? I served you for Rachel, didn't I? Why have you deceived me?"

[26]Laban replied, "It is not our custom here to give the younger daughter in marriage before the older one. [27]Finish this daughter's bridal week; then we will give you the younger one also, in return for another seven years of work."

[28]And Jacob did so. He finished the week with Leah, and then Laban gave him his daughter Rachel to be his wife. [29]Laban gave his servant Bilhah to his daughter Rachel as her attendant. [30]Jacob made love to Rachel also, and his love for Rachel was greater than his love for Leah. And he worked for Laban another seven years.

Jacob's Children

[31]When the LORD saw that Leah was not loved, he enabled her to conceive, but Rachel remained childless. [32]Leah became pregnant and gave birth to a son. She named him Reuben,[a] for she said, "It is because the LORD has seen my misery. Surely my husband will love me now."

Jacob, Rachel and the Law of Victory

Genesis 29:16–30

"Leaders find a way for the team to win," states the Law of Victory. That means good leaders are whatever-it-takes people. They are the "go to" guys and gals who always find a way to achieve their goals. Such a description certainly fits Jacob, the stubborn young man who fell in love with Rachel.

After requiring Jacob to work seven years for his younger daughter's hand in marriage, Laban substituted his older daughter, Leah—and Jacob didn't discover the deception until the morning after his wedding night. Some men would have battled Laban. Others might have simply walked away. Jacob fumed, but he didn't give up. He loved Rachel so deeply that he did what he had to do; he worked another seven years to get her. Jacob practiced the Law of Victory as a leader who did whatever it took to reach his goal.

[33]She conceived again, and when she gave birth to a son she said, "Because the LORD heard that I am not loved, he gave me this one too." So she named him Simeon.[b]

[34]Again she conceived, and when she gave birth to a son she said, "Now at last my husband will become attached to me, because I have borne him three sons." So he was named Levi.[c]

[35]She conceived again, and when she gave birth to a son she said, "This time I will praise the LORD." So she named him Judah.[d] Then she stopped having children.

30

When Rachel saw that she was not bearing Jacob any children, she became jealous of her sister. So she said to Jacob, "Give me children, or I'll die!"

[2]Jacob became angry with her and said, "Am I in the place of God, who has kept you from having children?"

[3]Then she said, "Here is Bilhah, my servant. Sleep with her so that she can bear children for me and I too can build a family through her."

[4]So she gave him her servant Bilhah as a wife. Jacob slept with her, [5]and she became pregnant and bore him a son. [6]Then Rachel said, "God has vindicated me; he has listened to my plea and given me a son." Because of this she named him Dan.[e]

[7]Rachel's servant Bilhah conceived again and bore Jacob a second son. [8]Then Rachel said, "I have had a great struggle with my sister, and I have won." So she named him Naphtali.[f]

[9]When Leah saw that she had stopped having children, she took her servant Zilpah and gave her to Jacob as a wife. [10]Leah's servant Zilpah bore Jacob a son. [11]Then Leah said, "What good fortune!"[g] So she named him Gad.[h]

[12]Leah's servant Zilpah bore Jacob a second son. [13]Then Leah said, "How happy I am! The women will call me happy." So she named him Asher.[i]

[14]During wheat harvest, Reuben went out into the fields and found some mandrake plants, which he brought to his mother Leah. Rachel said to Leah, "Please give me some of your son's mandrakes."

[15]But she said to her, "Wasn't it enough that

---

[a] 32 Reuben sounds like the Hebrew for he has seen my misery; the name means see, a son.　[b] 33 Simeon probably means one who hears.　[c] 34 Levi sounds like and may be derived from the Hebrew for attached.　[d] 35 Judah sounds like and may be derived from the Hebrew for praise.　[e] 6 Dan here means he has vindicated.　[f] 8 Naphtali means my struggle.　[g] 11 Or "A troop is coming!"　[h] 11 Gad can mean good fortune or a troop.　[i] 13 Asher means happy.

you took away my husband? Will you take my son's mandrakes too?"

"Very well," Rachel said, "he can sleep with you tonight in return for your son's mandrakes."

[16]So when Jacob came in from the fields that evening, Leah went out to meet him. "You must sleep with me," she said. "I have hired you with my son's mandrakes." So he slept with her that night.

[17]God listened to Leah, and she became pregnant and bore Jacob a fifth son. [18]Then Leah said, "God has rewarded me for giving my servant to my husband." So she named him Issachar.[a]

[19]Leah conceived again and bore Jacob a sixth son. [20]Then Leah said, "God has presented me with a precious gift. This time my husband will treat me with honor, because I have borne him six sons." So she named him Zebulun.[b]

[21]Some time later she gave birth to a daughter and named her Dinah.

[22]Then God remembered Rachel; he listened to her and enabled her to conceive. [23]She became pregnant and gave birth to a son and said, "God has taken away my disgrace." [24]She named him Joseph,[c] and said, "May the LORD add to me another son."

Jacob's Flocks Increase

[25]After Rachel gave birth to Joseph, Jacob said to Laban, "Send me on my way so I can go back to my own homeland. [26]Give me my wives and children, for whom I have served you, and I will be on my way. You know how much work I've done for you."

[27]But Laban said to him, "If I have found favor in your eyes, please stay. I have learned by divination that the LORD has blessed me because of you." [28]He added, "Name your wages, and I will pay them."

[29]Jacob said to him, "You know how I have worked for you and how your livestock has fared under my care. [30]The little you had before I came has increased greatly, and the LORD has blessed you wherever I have been. But now, when may I do something for my own household?"

[31]"What shall I give you?" he asked.

"Don't give me anything," Jacob replied. "But if you will do this one thing for me, I will go on tending your flocks and watching over them: [32]Let me go through all your flocks today and remove from them every speckled or spotted sheep, every dark-colored lamb and every spotted or speckled goat. They will be my wages. [33]And my honesty will testify for me in the future, whenever you check on the wages you have paid me. Any goat in my possession that is not speckled or spotted, or any lamb that is not dark-colored, will be considered stolen."

[34]"Agreed," said Laban. "Let it be as you have said." [35]That same day he removed all the male goats that were streaked or spotted, and all the speckled or spotted female goats (all that had white on them) and all the dark-colored lambs, and he placed them in the care of his sons. [36]Then he put a three-day journey between himself and Jacob, while Jacob continued to tend the rest of Laban's flocks.

[37]Jacob, however, took fresh-cut branches from poplar, almond and plane trees and made white stripes on them by peeling the bark and exposing the white inner wood of the branches. [38]Then he placed the peeled branches in all the watering troughs, so that they would be directly in front of the flocks when they came to drink. When the flocks were in heat and came to drink, [39]they mated in front of the branches. And they bore young that were streaked or speckled or spotted. [40]Jacob set apart the young of the flock by themselves, but made the rest face the streaked and dark-colored animals that belonged to Laban. Thus he made separate flocks for himself and did not put them with Laban's animals. [41]Whenever the stronger females were in heat, Jacob would place the branches in the troughs in front of the animals so they would mate near the branches, [42]but if the animals were weak, he would not place them there. So the weak animals went to Laban and the strong ones to Jacob. [43]In this way the man grew exceedingly prosperous and came to own large flocks, and female and male servants, and camels and donkeys.

Jacob Flees From Laban

31 Jacob heard that Laban's sons were saying, "Jacob has taken everything our father owned and has gained all this wealth from what belonged to our father." [2]And Jacob noticed that Laban's attitude toward him was not what it had been.

[3]Then the LORD said to Jacob, "Go back to the land of your fathers and to your relatives, and I will be with you."

[4]So Jacob sent word to Rachel and Leah to come out to the fields where his flocks were. [5]He

---

[a] 18 Issachar sounds like the Hebrew for reward.
[b] 20 Zebulun probably means honor.   [c] 24 Joseph means may he add.

said to them, "I see that your father's attitude toward me is not what it was before, but the God of my father has been with me. [6]You know that I've worked for your father with all my strength, [7]yet your father has cheated me by changing my wages ten times. However, God has not allowed him to harm me. [8]If he said, 'The speckled ones will be your wages,' then all the flocks gave birth to speckled young; and if he said, 'The streaked ones will be your wages,' then all the flocks bore streaked young. [9]So God has taken away your father's livestock and has given them to me.

[10]"In breeding season I once had a dream in which I looked up and saw that the male goats mating with the flock were streaked, speckled or spotted. [11]The angel of God said to me in the dream, 'Jacob.' I answered, 'Here I am.' [12]And he said, 'Look up and see that all the male goats mating with the flock are streaked, speckled or spotted, for I have seen all that Laban has been doing to you. [13]I am the God of Bethel, where you anointed a pillar and where you made a vow to me. Now leave this land at once and go back to your native land.'"

[14]Then Rachel and Leah replied, "Do we still have any share in the inheritance of our father's estate? [15]Does he not regard us as foreigners? Not only has he sold us, but he has used up what was paid for us. [16]Surely all the wealth that God took away from our father belongs to us and our children. So do whatever God has told you."

[17]Then Jacob put his children and his wives on camels, [18]and he drove all his livestock ahead of him, along with all the goods he had accumulated in Paddan Aram,[a] to go to his father Isaac in the land of Canaan.

[19]When Laban had gone to shear his sheep, Rachel stole her father's household gods. [20]Moreover, Jacob deceived Laban the Aramean by not telling him he was running away. [21]So he fled with all he had, crossed the Euphrates River, and headed for the hill country of Gilead.

Laban Pursues Jacob

[22]On the third day Laban was told that Jacob had fled. [23]Taking his relatives with him, he pursued Jacob for seven days and caught up with him in the hill country of Gilead. [24]Then God came to Laban the Aramean in a dream at night and said to him, "Be careful not to say anything to Jacob, either good or bad."

[25]Jacob had pitched his tent in the hill country of Gilead when Laban overtook him, and Laban and his relatives camped there too. [26]Then Laban said to Jacob, "What have you done?

You've deceived me, and you've carried off my daughters like captives in war. [27]Why did you run off secretly and deceive me? Why didn't you tell me, so I could send you away with joy and singing to the music of timbrels and harps? [28]You didn't even let me kiss my grandchildren and my daughters goodbye. You have done a foolish thing. [29]I have the power to harm you; but last night the God of your father said to me, 'Be careful not to say anything to Jacob, either good or bad.' [30]Now you have gone off because you longed to return to your father's household. But why did you steal my gods?"

[31]Jacob answered Laban, "I was afraid, because I thought you would take your daughters away from me by force. [32]But if you find anyone who has your gods, that person shall not live. In the presence of our relatives, see for yourself whether there is anything of yours here with me; and if so, take it." Now Jacob did not know that Rachel had stolen the gods.

[33]So Laban went into Jacob's tent and into Leah's tent and into the tent of the two female servants, but he found nothing. After he came out of Leah's tent, he entered Rachel's tent. [34]Now Rachel had taken the household gods and put them inside her camel's saddle and was sitting on them. Laban searched through everything in the tent but found nothing.

[35]Rachel said to her father, "Don't be angry, my lord, that I cannot stand up in your presence; I'm having my period." So he searched but could not find the household gods.

[36]Jacob was angry and took Laban to task. "What is my crime?" he asked Laban. "How have I wronged you that you hunt me down? [37]Now that you have searched through all my goods, what have you found that belongs to your household? Put it here in front of your relatives and mine, and let them judge between the two of us.

[38]"I have been with you for twenty years now. Your sheep and goats have not miscarried, nor have I eaten rams from your flocks. [39]I did not bring you animals torn by wild beasts; I bore the loss myself. And you demanded payment from me for whatever was stolen by day or night. [40]This was my situation: The heat consumed me in the daytime and the cold at night, and sleep fled from my eyes. [41]It was like this for the twenty years I was in your household. I worked for you fourteen years for your two daughters and six years for your flocks, and you changed my

---

[a] 18 That is, Northwest Mesopotamia

wages ten times. [42]If the God of my father, the God of Abraham and the Fear of Isaac, had not been with me, you would surely have sent me away empty-handed. But God has seen my hardship and the toil of my hands, and last night he rebuked you."

[43]Laban answered Jacob, "The women are my daughters, the children are my children, and the flocks are my flocks. All you see is mine. Yet what can I do today about these daughters of mine, or about the children they have borne? [44]Come now, let's make a covenant, you and I, and let it serve as a witness between us."

[45]So Jacob took a stone and set it up as a pillar. [46]He said to his relatives, "Gather some stones." So they took stones and piled them in a heap, and they ate there by the heap. [47]Laban called it Jegar Sahadutha, and Jacob called it Galeed.[a]

[48]Laban said, "This heap is a witness between you and me today." That is why it was called Galeed. [49]It was also called Mizpah,[b] because he said, "May the LORD keep watch between you and me when we are away from each other. [50]If you mistreat my daughters or if you take any wives besides my daughters, even though no one is with us, remember that God is a witness between you and me."

[51]Laban also said to Jacob, "Here is this heap, and here is this pillar I have set up between you and me. [52]This heap is a witness, and this pillar is a witness, that I will not go past this heap to your side to harm you and that you will not go past this heap and pillar to my side to harm me. [53]May the God of Abraham and the God of Nahor, the God of their father, judge between us."

So Jacob took an oath in the name of the Fear of his father Isaac. [54]He offered a sacrifice there in the hill country and invited his relatives to a meal. After they had eaten, they spent the night there.

[55]Early the next morning Laban kissed his grandchildren and his daughters and blessed them. Then he left and returned home.[c]

Jacob Prepares to Meet Esau

32[d] Jacob also went on his way, and the angels of God met him. [2]When Jacob saw them, he said, "This is the camp of God!" So he named that place Mahanaim.[e]

[3]Jacob sent messengers ahead of him to his brother Esau in the land of Seir, the country of Edom. [4]He instructed them: "This is what you are to say to my lord Esau: 'Your servant Jacob says, I have been staying with Laban and have remained there till now. [5]I have cattle and don-

keys, sheep and goats, male and female servants. Now I am sending this message to my lord, that I may find favor in your eyes.'"

[6]When the messengers returned to Jacob, they said, "We went to your brother Esau, and now he is coming to meet you, and four hundred men are with him."

[7]In great fear and distress Jacob divided the people who were with him into two groups,[f] and the flocks and herds and camels as well. [8]He thought, "If Esau comes and attacks one group,[g] the group[g] that is left may escape."

[9]Then Jacob prayed, "O God of my father Abraham, God of my father Isaac, LORD, you who said to me, 'Go back to your country and your relatives, and I will make you prosper,' [10]I am unworthy of all the kindness and faithfulness you have shown your servant. I had only my staff when I crossed this Jordan, but now I have become two camps. [11]Save me, I pray, from the hand of my brother Esau, for I am afraid he will come and attack me, and also the mothers with their children. [12]But you have said, 'I will surely make you prosper and will make your descendants like the sand of the sea, which cannot be counted.'"

[13]He spent the night there, and from what he had with him he selected a gift for his brother Esau: [14]two hundred female goats and twenty male goats, two hundred ewes and twenty rams, [15]thirty female camels with their young, forty cows and ten bulls, and twenty female donkeys and ten male donkeys. [16]He put them in the care of his servants, each herd by itself, and said to his servants, "Go ahead of me, and keep some space between the herds."

[17]He instructed the one in the lead: "When my brother Esau meets you and asks, 'Who do you belong to, and where are you going, and who owns all these animals in front of you?' [18]then you are to say, 'They belong to your servant Jacob. They are a gift sent to my lord Esau, and he is coming behind us.'"

[19]He also instructed the second, the third and all the others who followed the herds: "You are to say the same thing to Esau when you meet him. [20]And be sure to say, 'Your servant Jacob is coming behind us.'" For he thought, "I will pacify him with these gifts I am sending on ahead;

---

[a] 47 The Aramaic *Jegar Sahadutha* and the Hebrew *Galeed* both mean *witness heap.*   [b] 49 *Mizpah* means *watchtower.*   [c] 55 In Hebrew texts this verse (31:55) is numbered 32:1.   [d] In Hebrew texts 32:1-32 is numbered 32:2-33.   [e] 2 *Mahanaim* means *two camps.*   [f] 7 Or *camps*   [g] 8 Or *camp*

later, when I see him, perhaps he will receive me." [21]So Jacob's gifts went on ahead of him, but he himself spent the night in the camp.

Jacob Wrestles With God

[22]That night Jacob got up and took his two wives, his two female servants and his eleven sons and crossed the ford of the Jabbok. [23]After he had sent them across the stream, he sent over all his possessions. [24]So Jacob was left alone, and a man wrestled with him till daybreak. [25]When the man saw that he could not overpower him, he touched the socket of Jacob's hip so that his hip was wrenched as he wrestled with the man. [26]Then the man said, "Let me go, for it is daybreak."

But Jacob replied, "I will not let you go unless you bless me."

[27]The man asked him, "What is your name?"

"Jacob," he answered.

[28]Then the man said, "Your name will no longer be Jacob, but Israel,[a] because you have struggled with God and with humans and have overcome."

[29]Jacob said, "Please tell me your name."

But he replied, "Why do you ask my name?" Then he blessed him there.

[30]So Jacob called the place Peniel,[b] saying, "It is because I saw God face to face, and yet my life was spared."

[31]The sun rose above him as he passed Peniel,[c] and he was limping because of his hip. [32]Therefore to this day the Israelites do not eat the tendon attached to the socket of the hip, because the socket of Jacob's hip was touched near the tendon.

Jacob Meets Esau

33 Jacob looked up and there was Esau, coming with his four hundred men; so he divided the children among Leah, Rachel and the two female servants. [2]He put the female servants and their children in front, Leah and her children next, and Rachel and Joseph in the rear. [3]He himself went on ahead and bowed down to the ground seven times as he approached his brother.

[4]But Esau ran to meet Jacob and embraced him; he threw his arms around his neck and kissed him. And they wept. [5]Then Esau looked up and saw the women and children. "Who are these with you?" he asked.

Jacob answered, "They are the children God has graciously given your servant."

[6]Then the female servants and their children approached and bowed down. [7]Next, Leah and her children came and bowed down. Last of all came Joseph and Rachel, and they too bowed down.

[8]Esau asked, "What's the meaning of all these flocks and herds I met?"

"To find favor in your eyes, my lord," he said.

[9]But Esau said, "I already have plenty, my brother. Keep what you have for yourself."

---

[a] 28 Israel probably means he struggles with God. [b] 30 Peniel means face of God. [c] 31 Hebrew Penuel, a variant of Peniel

Jacob: Breaking Before Blessing

Genesis 32:24–32

Jacob turned a crucial corner the night he wrestled the angel of God. He broke physically when the angel dislocated his hip, but he also broke emotionally—he told the truth about his name and character. From that moment on, Jacob began to fulfill his God-ordained destiny.

All leaders, like Jacob, must "wrestle" with God in order to receive his blessing. God blessed Jacob because:

1. **Jacob was alone with God (v. 24).** All distractions had been removed.

2. **Jacob was hungry for God (v. 26).** He desperately wanted to receive what God had for him.

3. **Jacob was broken by God (vv. 25–28).** He allowed God to break him and change him.

4. **Jacob was honest with God (v. 27).** He stopped pretending in order to let God work in his life.

Have you "overcome" with God in this way? Leaders cannot do anything of significance in the kingdom of God until they humble themselves before God and seek his face. You must be broken in order to be blessed!

Commitment: Esau Releases Jacob

Genesis 33:1–4

After years of estrangement, Jacob and Esau finally met. The reunion terrified Jacob, for Esau had threatened to kill him (Ge 27:41). Yet Esau ran to his brother, embraced him, and wept—forgiving Jacob for everything. In the end, Esau's commitment to his brother overwhelmed his thirst for revenge.

¹⁰"No, please!" said Jacob. "If I have found favor in your eyes, accept this gift from me. For to see your face is like seeing the face of God, now that you have received me favorably. ¹¹Please accept the present that was brought to you, for God has been gracious to me and I have all I need." And because Jacob insisted, Esau accepted it.

¹²Then Esau said, "Let us be on our way; I'll accompany you."

¹³But Jacob said to him, "My lord knows that the children are tender and that I must care for the ewes and cows that are nursing their young. If they are driven hard just one day, all the animals will die. ¹⁴So let my lord go on ahead of his servant, while I move along slowly at the pace of the flocks and herds before me and the pace of the children, until I come to my lord in Seir."

¹⁵Esau said, "Then let me leave some of my men with you."

"But why do that?" Jacob asked. "Just let me find favor in the eyes of my lord."

¹⁶So that day Esau started on his way back to Seir. ¹⁷Jacob, however, went to Sukkoth, where he built a place for himself and made shelters for his livestock. That is why the place is called Sukkoth.ᵃ

¹⁸After Jacob came from Paddan Aram,ᵇ he arrived safely at the city of Shechem in Canaan and camped within sight of the city. ¹⁹For a hundred pieces of silver,ᶜ he bought from the sons of Hamor, the father of Shechem, the plot of ground where he pitched his tent. ²⁰There he set up an altar and called it El Elohe Israel.ᵈ

Dinah and the Shechemites

34 Now Dinah, the daughter Leah had borne to Jacob, went out to visit the women of the land. ²When Shechem son of Ha-

mor the Hivite, the ruler of that area, saw her, he took her and raped her. ³His heart was drawn to Dinah daughter of Jacob; he loved the young woman and spoke tenderly to her. ⁴And Shechem said to his father Hamor, "Get me this girl as my wife."

⁵When Jacob heard that his daughter Dinah had been defiled, his sons were in the fields with his livestock; so he did nothing about it until they came home.

⁶Then Shechem's father Hamor went out to talk with Jacob. ⁷Meanwhile, Jacob's sons had come in from the fields as soon as they heard what had happened. They were shocked and furious, because Shechem had done an outrageous thing inᵉ Israel by sleeping with Jacob's daughter—a thing that should not be done.

⁸But Hamor said to them, "My son Shechem has his heart set on your daughter. Please give her to him as his wife. ⁹Intermarry with us; give us your daughters and take our daughters for yourselves. ¹⁰You can settle among us; the land is open to you. Live in it, tradeᶠ in it, and acquire property in it."

¹¹Then Shechem said to Dinah's father and brothers, "Let me find favor in your eyes, and I will give you whatever you ask. ¹²Make the price for the bride and the gift I am to bring as great as you like, and I'll pay whatever you ask me. Only give me the young woman as my wife."

¹³Because their sister Dinah had been defiled, Jacob's sons replied deceitfully as they spoke to Shechem and his father Hamor. ¹⁴They said to them, "We can't do such a thing; we can't give our sister to a man who is not circumcised. That would be a disgrace to us. ¹⁵We will enter into an agreement with you on one condition only: that you become like us by circumcising all your males. ¹⁶Then we will give you our daughters and take your daughters for ourselves. We'll settle among you and become one people with you. ¹⁷But if you will not agree to be circumcised, we'll take our sister and go."

¹⁸Their proposal seemed good to Hamor and his son Shechem. ¹⁹The young man, who was the most honored of all his father's family, lost no time in doing what they said, because he was delighted with Jacob's daughter. ²⁰So Hamor and his son Shechem went to the gate of their

---

ᵃ 17 Sukkoth means shelters. ᵇ 18 That is, Northwest Mesopotamia ᶜ 19 Hebrew hundred kesitahs; a kesitah was a unit of money of unknown weight and value. ᵈ 20 El Elohe Israel can mean El is the God of Israel or mighty is the God of Israel. ᵉ 7 Or against ᶠ 10 Or move about freely; also in verse 21

city to speak to the men of their city. ²¹"These men are friendly toward us," they said. "Let them live in our land and trade in it; the land has plenty of room for them. We can marry their daughters and they can marry ours. ²²But the men will agree to live with us as one people only on the condition that our males be circumcised, as they themselves are. ²³Won't their livestock, their property and all their other animals become ours? So let us agree to their terms, and they will settle among us."

²⁴All the men who went out of the city gate agreed with Hamor and his son Shechem, and every male in the city was circumcised.

²⁵Three days later, while all of them were still in pain, two of Jacob's sons, Simeon and Levi, Dinah's brothers, took their swords and attacked the unsuspecting city, killing every male. ²⁶They put Hamor and his son Shechem to the sword and took Dinah from Shechem's house and left. ²⁷The sons of Jacob came upon the dead bodies and looted the city where[a] their sister had been defiled. ²⁸They seized their flocks and herds and donkeys and everything else of theirs in the city and out in the fields. ²⁹They carried off all their wealth and all their women and children, taking as plunder everything in the houses.

³⁰Then Jacob said to Simeon and Levi, "You have brought trouble on me by making me obnoxious to the Canaanites and Perizzites, the people living in this land. We are few in number, and if they join forces against me and attack me, I and my household will be destroyed."

³¹But they replied, "Should he have treated our sister like a prostitute?"

Jacob Returns to Bethel

35 Then God said to Jacob, "Go up to Bethel and settle there, and build an altar there to God, who appeared to you when you were fleeing from your brother Esau."

²So Jacob said to his household and to all who were with him, "Get rid of the foreign gods you have with you, and purify yourselves and change your clothes. ³Then come, let us go up to Bethel, where I will build an altar to God, who answered me in the day of my distress and who has been with me wherever I have gone." ⁴So they gave Jacob all the foreign gods they had and the rings in their ears, and Jacob buried them under the oak at Shechem. ⁵Then they set out, and the terror of God fell on the towns all around them so that no one pursued them.

⁶Jacob and all the people with him came to Luz (that is, Bethel) in the land of Canaan.

⁷There he built an altar, and he called the place El Bethel,[b] because it was there that God revealed himself to him when he was fleeing from his brother.

⁸Now Deborah, Rebekah's nurse, died and was buried under the oak outside Bethel. So it was named Allon Bakuth.[c]

⁹After Jacob returned from Paddan Aram,[d] God appeared to him again and blessed him. ¹⁰God said to him, "Your name is Jacob,[e] but you will no longer be called Jacob; your name will be Israel.[f]" So he named him Israel.

¹¹And God said to him, "I am God Almighty[g]; be fruitful and increase in number. A nation and a community of nations will come from you, and kings will be among your descendants. ¹²The land I gave to Abraham and Isaac I also give to you, and I will give this land to your descendants after you." ¹³Then God went up from him at the place where he had talked with him. ¹⁴Jacob set up a stone pillar at the place where God had talked with him, and he poured out a drink offering on it; he also poured oil on it. ¹⁵Jacob called the place where God had talked with him Bethel.[h]

The Deaths of Rachel and Isaac

¹⁶Then they moved on from Bethel. While they were still some distance from Ephrath, Rachel began to give birth and had great difficulty. ¹⁷And as she was having great difficulty in childbirth, the midwife said to her, "Don't despair, for you have another son." ¹⁸As she breathed her last — for she was dying — she named her son Ben-Oni.[i] But his father named him Benjamin.[j]

¹⁹So Rachel died and was buried on the way to Ephrath (that is, Bethlehem). ²⁰Over her tomb Jacob set up a pillar, and to this day that pillar marks Rachel's tomb.

²¹Israel moved on again and pitched his tent beyond Migdal Eder. ²²While Israel was living in that region, Reuben went in and slept with his father's concubine Bilhah, and Israel heard of it.

Jacob had twelve sons:
  ²³The sons of Leah:
      Reuben the firstborn of Jacob,

---

[a] 27 Or because   [b] 7 El Bethel means God of Bethel.
[c] 8 Allon Bakuth means oak of weeping.   [d] 9 That is, Northwest Mesopotamia; also in verse 26   [e] 10 Jacob means he grasps the heel, a Hebrew idiom for he deceives.   [f] 10 Israel probably means he struggles with God.   [g] 11 Hebrew El-Shaddai   [h] 15 Bethel means house of God.   [i] 18 Ben-Oni means son of my trouble.   [j] 18 Benjamin means son of my right hand.

Simeon, Levi, Judah, Issachar and Zebulun.

²⁴The sons of Rachel:

Joseph and Benjamin.

²⁵The sons of Rachel's servant Bilhah:

Dan and Naphtali.

²⁶The sons of Leah's servant Zilpah:

Gad and Asher.

These were the sons of Jacob, who were born to him in Paddan Aram.

²⁷Jacob came home to his father Isaac in Mamre, near Kiriath Arba (that is, Hebron), where Abraham and Isaac had stayed. ²⁸Isaac lived a hundred and eighty years. ²⁹Then he breathed his last and died and was gathered to his people, old and full of years. And his sons Esau and Jacob buried him.

Esau's Descendants

36 This is the account of the family line of Esau (that is, Edom).

²Esau took his wives from the women of Canaan: Adah daughter of Elon the Hittite, and Oholibamah daughter of Anah and granddaughter of Zibeon the Hivite — ³also Basemath daughter of Ishmael and sister of Nebaioth.

⁴Adah bore Eliphaz to Esau, Basemath bore Reuel, ⁵and Oholibamah bore Jeush, Jalam and Korah. These were the sons of Esau, who were born to him in Canaan.

⁶Esau took his wives and sons and daughters and all the members of his household, as well as his livestock and all his other animals and all the goods he had acquired in Canaan, and moved to a land some distance from his brother Jacob. ⁷Their possessions were too great for them to remain together; the land where they were staying could not support them both because of their livestock. ⁸So Esau (that is, Edom) settled in the hill country of Seir.

⁹This is the account of the family line of Esau the father of the Edomites in the hill country of Seir.

¹⁰These are the names of Esau's sons:

Eliphaz, the son of Esau's wife Adah, and Reuel, the son of Esau's wife Basemath.

¹¹The sons of Eliphaz:

Teman, Omar, Zepho, Gatam and Kenaz.

¹²Esau's son Eliphaz also had a concubine named Timna, who bore him Amalek.

These were grandsons of Esau's wife Adah.

¹³The sons of Reuel:

Nahath, Zerah, Shammah and Mizzah. These were grandsons of Esau's wife Basemath.

¹⁴The sons of Esau's wife Oholibamah daughter of Anah and granddaughter of Zibeon, whom she bore to Esau:

Jeush, Jalam and Korah.

¹⁵These were the chiefs among Esau's descendants:

The sons of Eliphaz the firstborn of Esau:

Chiefs Teman, Omar, Zepho, Kenaz, ¹⁶Korah,ᵃ Gatam and Amalek. These were the chiefs descended from Eliphaz in Edom; they were grandsons of Adah.

¹⁷The sons of Esau's son Reuel:

Chiefs Nahath, Zerah, Shammah and Mizzah. These were the chiefs descended from Reuel in Edom; they were grandsons of Esau's wife Basemath.

¹⁸The sons of Esau's wife Oholibamah:

Chiefs Jeush, Jalam and Korah. These were the chiefs descended from Esau's wife Oholibamah daughter of Anah.

¹⁹These were the sons of Esau (that is, Edom), and these were their chiefs.

²⁰These were the sons of Seir the Horite, who were living in the region:

Lotan, Shobal, Zibeon, Anah, ²¹Dishon, Ezer and Dishan. These sons of Seir in Edom were Horite chiefs.

²²The sons of Lotan:

Hori and Homam.ᵇ Timna was Lotan's sister.

²³The sons of Shobal:

Alvan, Manahath, Ebal, Shepho and Onam.

²⁴The sons of Zibeon:

Aiah and Anah. This is the Anah who discovered the hot springsᶜ in the desert while he was grazing the donkeys of his father Zibeon.

²⁵The children of Anah:

Dishon and Oholibamah daughter of Anah.

²⁶The sons of Dishonᵈ:

Hemdan, Eshban, Ithran and Keran.

ᵃ 16 Masoretic Text; Samaritan Pentateuch (also verse 11 and 1 Chron. 1:36) does not have *Korah*.   ᵇ 22 Hebrew *Hemam*, a variant of *Homam* (see 1 Chron. 1:39)   ᶜ 24 Vulgate; Syriac *discovered water*; the meaning of the Hebrew for this word is uncertain.   ᵈ 26 Hebrew *Dishan*, a variant of *Dishon*

²⁷The sons of Ezer:
    Bilhan, Zaavan and Akan.
²⁸The sons of Dishan:
    Uz and Aran.
²⁹These were the Horite chiefs:
    Lotan, Shobal, Zibeon, Anah, ³⁰Dishon, Ezer and Dishan. These were the Horite chiefs, according to their divisions, in the land of Seir.

The Rulers of Edom

³¹These were the kings who reigned in Edom before any Israelite king reigned:
³²Bela son of Beor became king of Edom. His city was named Dinhabah.
³³When Bela died, Jobab son of Zerah from Bozrah succeeded him as king.
³⁴When Jobab died, Husham from the land of the Temanites succeeded him as king.
³⁵When Husham died, Hadad son of Bedad, who defeated Midian in the country of Moab, succeeded him as king. His city was named Avith.
³⁶When Hadad died, Samlah from Masrekah succeeded him as king.
³⁷When Samlah died, Shaul from Rehoboth on the river succeeded him as king.
³⁸When Shaul died, Baal-Hanan son of Akbor succeeded him as king.
³⁹When Baal-Hanan son of Akbor died, Hadad[a] succeeded him as king. His city was named Pau, and his wife's name was Mehetabel daughter of Matred, the daughter of Me-Zahab.

⁴⁰These were the chiefs descended from Esau, by name, according to their clans and regions:
    Timna, Alvah, Jetheth, ⁴¹Oholibamah, Elah, Pinon, ⁴²Kenaz, Teman, Mibzar, ⁴³Magdiel and Iram. These were the chiefs of Edom, according to their settlements in the land they occupied.

This is the family line of Esau, the father of the Edomites.

Joseph's Dreams

37 Jacob lived in the land where his father had stayed, the land of Canaan.

²This is the account of Jacob's family line.

Joseph, a young man of seventeen, was tending the flocks with his brothers, the sons of Bilhah and the sons of Zilpah, his father's wives, and he brought their father a bad report about them.

³Now Israel loved Joseph more than any of his other sons, because he had been born to him in his old age; and he made an ornate[b] robe for him. ⁴When his brothers saw that their father loved him more than any of them, they hated him and could not speak a kind word to him.

⁵Joseph had a dream, and when he told it to his brothers, they hated him all the more. ⁶He said to them, "Listen to this dream I had: ⁷We were binding sheaves of grain out in the field when suddenly my sheaf rose and stood upright, while your sheaves gathered around mine and bowed down to it."

⁸His brothers said to him, "Do you intend to reign over us? Will you actually rule us?" And they hated him all the more because of his dream and what he had said.

⁹Then he had another dream, and he told it to his brothers. "Listen," he said, "I had another dream, and this time the sun and moon and eleven stars were bowing down to me."

¹⁰When he told his father as well as his brothers, his father rebuked him and said, "What is this dream you had? Will your mother and I and your brothers actually come and bow down to the ground before you?" ¹¹His brothers were jealous of him, but his father kept the matter in mind.

Joseph Sold by His Brothers

¹²Now his brothers had gone to graze their father's flocks near Shechem, ¹³and Israel said to Joseph, "As you know, your brothers are grazing the flocks near Shechem. Come, I am going to send you to them."
    "Very well," he replied.
¹⁴So he said to him, "Go and see if all is well with your brothers and with the flocks, and bring word back to me." Then he sent him off from the Valley of Hebron.
    When Joseph arrived at Shechem, ¹⁵a man found him wandering around in the fields and asked him, "What are you looking for?"
¹⁶He replied, "I'm looking for my brothers. Can you tell me where they are grazing their flocks?"
¹⁷"They have moved on from here," the man answered. "I heard them say, 'Let's go to Dothan.'"
    So Joseph went after his brothers and found

---

[a] 39 Many manuscripts of the Masoretic Text, Samaritan Pentateuch and Syriac (see also 1 Chron. 1:50); most manuscripts of the Masoretic Text *Hadar*   [b] 3 The meaning of the Hebrew for this word is uncertain; also in verses 23 and 32.

them near Dothan. [18]But they saw him in the distance, and before he reached them, they plotted to kill him.

[19]"Here comes that dreamer!" they said to each other. [20]"Come now, let's kill him and throw him into one of these cisterns and say that a ferocious animal devoured him. Then we'll see what comes of his dreams."

[21]When Reuben heard this, he tried to rescue him from their hands. "Let's not take his life," he said. [22]"Don't shed any blood. Throw him into this cistern here in the wilderness, but don't lay a hand on him." Reuben said this to rescue him from them and take him back to his father.

[23]So when Joseph came to his brothers, they stripped him of his robe — the ornate robe he was wearing — [24]and they took him and threw him into the cistern. The cistern was empty; there was no water in it.

[25]As they sat down to eat their meal, they looked up and saw a caravan of Ishmaelites coming from Gilead. Their camels were loaded with spices, balm and myrrh, and they were on their way to take them down to Egypt.

[26]Judah said to his brothers, "What will we gain if we kill our brother and cover up his blood? [27]Come, let's sell him to the Ishmaelites and not lay our hands on him; after all, he is our brother, our own flesh and blood." His brothers agreed.

[28]So when the Midianite merchants came by, his brothers pulled Joseph up out of the cistern and sold him for twenty shekels[a] of silver to the Ishmaelites, who took him to Egypt.

[29]When Reuben returned to the cistern and saw that Joseph was not there, he tore his clothes. [30]He went back to his brothers and said, "The boy isn't there! Where can I turn now?"

[31]Then they got Joseph's robe, slaughtered a goat and dipped the robe in the blood. [32]They took the ornate robe back to their father and said, "We found this. Examine it to see whether it is your son's robe."

[33]He recognized it and said, "It is my son's robe! Some ferocious animal has devoured him. Joseph has surely been torn to pieces."

[34]Then Jacob tore his clothes, put on sackcloth and mourned for his son many days. [35]All his sons and daughters came to comfort him, but he refused to be comforted. "No," he said, "I will continue to mourn until I join my son in the grave." So his father wept for him.

[36]Meanwhile, the Midianites[b] sold Joseph in Egypt to Potiphar, one of Pharaoh's officials, the captain of the guard.

Judah and Tamar

38 At that time, Judah left his brothers and went down to stay with a man of Adullam named Hirah. [2]There Judah met the

---

[a] 28 That is, about 8 ounces or about 230 grams
[b] 36 Samaritan Pentateuch, Septuagint, Vulgate and Syriac (see also verse 28); Masoretic Text *Medanites*

The Law of Intuition: Joseph Takes Effective Action in a Crisis

Genesis 37:5–36; 39:1—41:16

Problems never paralyze great leaders; they know that solutions usually exist. The Scripture shows that Joseph accomplished much because he enjoyed:

1. **A significant vision from God (37:5–6, 9–11).** As a youth, Joseph knew God had something special in mind for him.

2. **A vital relationship with God (39:2, 21, 23).** Scripture says that "the Lord was with" Joseph.

3. **A strong character developed through difficulties (39:7–8).** With each new trial, Joseph grew stronger.

4. **Practical experience gained through life (39:22).** Joseph grew in ability and experience when he took charge of the prison.

5. **A special giftedness from God (41:15–16).** Joseph's ability to interpret dreams enabled him to make a difference in many lives.

6. **A unique blessing from God (39:3–5).** Four times the Bible expresses God's blessing of Joseph with some version of "the LORD gave him success in everything he did" (Ge 39:2–3, 21, 23).

JOSEPH AND THE LAW OF PROCESS
Leadership Develops Daily, Not in a Day

Genesis 37:1—50:22

BECOMING A LEADER is a lot like investing in the stock market. If you hope to make a fortune in a day, you're doomed. It's what you do day by day, over the long haul, that matters most. If you continually develop your leadership, letting your "assets" compound over time, the inevitable result is growth.

Although some individuals have greater natural gifts than others, nearly all the skills of leadership can be learned and improved. But that process doesn't happen overnight. Leadership has so many facets: respect, experience, emotional strength, people skills, discipline, vision, momentum, timing—the list goes on. That's why leaders require so much seasoning to be effective.

The good news is that you can grow in your ability to lead. Regardless of your starting point, you can improve.

■ ■ ■ ■ ■

Joseph was a cocky kid, too arrogant for his own good. He didn't think it enough to be the favorite of his father, the child who received special treatment, the son of Jacob's old age. Joseph had to rub it in.

When God gave Joseph a dream revealing that he would one day lead his family—not only his 11 brothers, but also his parents—Joseph thoughtlessly told everyone about it. Twice. His father rebuked him. His brothers wanted revenge.

And they got it.

Early in his life, Joseph didn't know how to skillfully work with others. He lacked experience, wisdom and humility—three qualities gained only with the passage of time. Joseph's life illustrates the Law of Process. Observe how time and experience contributed to the development of Joseph's leadership skills:

PHASE ONE: I don't know what I don't know. Everyone starts out in a state of ignorance. That's where Joseph began. He didn't understand the dynamics of his family. Either he couldn't imagine how his brothers might react when he described his dream, or he didn't care. The Scripture says his brothers already hated him; when he described his dream, they hated him even more. Joseph did and said things without understanding the interpersonal issues involved. His ignorance cost him more than two decades of alienation from his family.

PHASE TWO: I know what I don't know. It took a life-changing incident to capture Joseph's attention and start him on the road to change. Thrust into slavery in Egypt, he began to learn what he didn't know. He came to understand that leadership is difficult and carries a huge weight of responsibility. Over the years, Joseph suffered betrayal and learned hard lessons in human nature, relationships and leadership. The process molded his character, granting him both patience and humility. Eventually he recognized God as his source of blessing and power.

PHASE THREE: I know and grow and it starts to show. Leaders who show great skill when opportunities arise, shine only because they've paid the price of preparation. When Pharaoh finally called Joseph, the young man performed with excellence and great wisdom. He didn't succeed because he suddenly got good at age 30; he succeeded because he paid the price for 13 years. Joseph's hard-won wisdom and discernment got him promoted to second in command of what was then the most powerful nation on earth.

PHASE FOUR: I simply go because of what I know. During seven years of plenty, Joseph executed his leadership plan with great skill. He filled the cities of Egypt with grain and prepared the country for a famine. But one can see how far his leadership had grown only by observing what he did during the lean years that followed. While he focused on feeding the people of Egypt, the strength of his leadership allowed him to feed the people of other lands as well. In the process, he brought untold money, livestock and land into his master's possession. He also fulfilled the prophecy of his teenage dreams.

Every effective leader needs time to develop, but time alone cannot make someone an effective leader. Some individuals never discover the Law of Process, never work at growth, and therefore remain at Phase One their entire lives.

Fortunately for the children of Israel, Joseph did not stop at the first stage. He grew in his journey from the pit to the palace. Yet nearly 23 years passed before he reunited with his brothers and saw his own vision fulfilled. At the end, Joseph realized that God had directed the process of his development as a leader, and that he had been groomed for a much greater purpose than he ever imagined as a cocky teenager.

By the time his father died, Joseph had learned to see things from God's perspective. When his brothers feared for their lives, Joseph calmed their nerves by saying, "Don't be afraid. Am I in the place of God? You intended to harm me, but God intended it for good to accomplish what is now being done, the saving of many lives" (Ge 50:19–20).

At last Joseph could trace God's hand over all the years of his life. And he understood the Lord's long-term plan for his people, a plan Joseph helped fulfill by growing into the leader God desired him to be.

daughter of a Canaanite man named Shua. He married her and made love to her; [3]she became pregnant and gave birth to a son, who was named Er. [4]She conceived again and gave birth to a son and named him Onan. [5]She gave birth to still another son and named him Shelah. It was at Kezib that she gave birth to him.

[6]Judah got a wife for Er, his firstborn, and her name was Tamar. [7]But Er, Judah's firstborn, was wicked in the LORD's sight; so the LORD put him to death.

[8]Then Judah said to Onan, "Sleep with your brother's wife and fulfill your duty to her as a brother-in-law to raise up offspring for your brother." [9]But Onan knew that the child would not be his; so whenever he slept with his brother's wife, he spilled his semen on the ground to keep from providing offspring for his brother. [10]What he did was wicked in the LORD's sight; so the LORD put him to death also.

[11]Judah then said to his daughter-in-law Tamar, "Live as a widow in your father's household until my son Shelah grows up." For he thought, "He may die too, just like his brothers." So Tamar went to live in her father's household.

[12]After a long time Judah's wife, the daughter of Shua, died. When Judah had recovered from his grief, he went up to Timnah, to the men who were shearing his sheep, and his friend Hirah the Adullamite went with him.

[13]When Tamar was told, "Your father-in-law is on his way to Timnah to shear his sheep," [14]she took off her widow's clothes, covered herself with a veil to disguise herself, and then sat down at the entrance to Enaim, which is on the road to Timnah. For she saw that, though Shelah had now grown up, she had not been given to him as his wife.

[15]When Judah saw her, he thought she was a prostitute, for she had covered her face. [16]Not realizing that she was his daughter-in-law, he went over to her by the roadside and said, "Come now, let me sleep with you."

"And what will you give me to sleep with you?" she asked.

[17]"I'll send you a young goat from my flock," he said.

"Will you give me something as a pledge until you send it?" she asked.

[18]He said, "What pledge should I give you?"

"Your seal and its cord, and the staff in your hand," she answered. So he gave them to her and slept with her, and she became pregnant by him. [19]After she left, she took off her veil and put on her widow's clothes again.

[20]Meanwhile Judah sent the young goat by his friend the Adullamite in order to get his pledge back from the woman, but he did not find her. [21]He asked the men who lived there, "Where is the shrine prostitute who was beside the road at Enaim?"

"There hasn't been any shrine prostitute here," they said.

[22]So he went back to Judah and said, "I didn't find her. Besides, the men who lived there said, 'There hasn't been any shrine prostitute here.'"

[23]Then Judah said, "Let her keep what she has, or we will become a laughingstock. After all, I did send her this young goat, but you didn't find her."

[24]About three months later Judah was told, "Your daughter-in-law Tamar is guilty of prostitution, and as a result she is now pregnant."

Judah said, "Bring her out and have her burned to death!"

[25]As she was being brought out, she sent a message to her father-in-law. "I am pregnant by the man who owns these," she said. And she added, "See if you recognize whose seal and cord and staff these are."

[26]Judah recognized them and said, "She is more righteous than I, since I wouldn't give her to my son Shelah." And he did not sleep with her again.

[27]When the time came for her to give birth, there were twin boys in her womb. [28]As she was giving birth, one of them put out his hand; so the midwife took a scarlet thread and tied it on his wrist and said, "This one came out first." [29]But when he drew back his hand, his brother came out, and she said, "So this is how you have broken out!" And he was named Perez.[a] [30]Then his brother, who had the scarlet thread on his wrist, came out. And he was named Zerah.[b]

Joseph and Potiphar's Wife

39 Now Joseph had been taken down to Egypt. Potiphar, an Egyptian who was one of Pharaoh's officials, the captain of the guard, bought him from the Ishmaelites who had taken him there.

[2]The LORD was with Joseph so that he prospered, and he lived in the house of his Egyptian master. [3]When his master saw that the LORD was with him and that the LORD gave him success in everything he did, [4]Joseph found favor in his eyes and became his attendant. Potiphar

---

[a] 29 Perez means breaking out. [b] 30 Zerah can mean scarlet or brightness.

put him in charge of his household, and he entrusted to his care everything he owned. [5]From the time he put him in charge of his household and of all that he owned, the LORD blessed the household of the Egyptian because of Joseph. The blessing of the LORD was on everything Potiphar had, both in the house and in the field. [6]So Potiphar left everything he had in Joseph's care; with Joseph in charge, he did not concern himself with anything except the food he ate.

Now Joseph was well-built and handsome, [7]and after a while his master's wife took notice of Joseph and said, "Come to bed with me!" [8]But he refused. "With me in charge," he told her, "my master does not concern himself with anything in the house; everything he owns he has entrusted to my care. [9]No one is greater in this house than I am. My master has withheld nothing from me except you, because you are his wife. How then could I do such a wicked thing and sin against God?" [10]And though she spoke to Joseph day after day, he refused to go to bed with her or even be with her.

[11]One day he went into the house to attend to his duties, and none of the household servants was inside. [12]She caught him by his cloak and said, "Come to bed with me!" But he left his cloak in her hand and ran out of the house.

[13]When she saw that he had left his cloak in her hand and had run out of the house, [14]she called her household servants. "Look," she said to them, "this Hebrew has been brought to us to make sport of us! He came in here to sleep with me, but I screamed. [15]When he heard me scream for help, he left his cloak beside me and ran out of the house."

[16]She kept his cloak beside her until his master came home. [17]Then she told him this story: "That Hebrew slave you brought us came to me to make sport of me. [18]But as soon as I screamed for help, he left his cloak beside me and ran out of the house."

[19]When his master heard the story his wife told him, saying, "This is how your slave treated me," he burned with anger. [20]Joseph's master took him and put him in prison, the place where the king's prisoners were confined.

But while Joseph was there in the prison, [21]the

The Law of Solid Ground: Joseph Earns Trust

Genesis 39:1—41:16

The Bible describes some dark and difficult times in Joseph's life. But it also reveals that every time he faced adversity, he used it to develop himself personally and to build trust with others. As a result, Joseph made one comeback after another and proved himself trustworthy as a leader.

Consider a few of the ways he earned trust along the way:

Adversity	Comeback
1. Sold into Egyptian slavery	1. Developed competence and organization in the palace
2. Framed as an adulterer	2. Used his ability to discern dreams and solve problems
3. Forgotten in prison	3. Displayed the wisdom to interpret Pharaoh's dream
4. Endured seven years of famine	4. Prepared to save the country and bring Pharaoh great wealth
5. Faced the return of his treacherous brothers	5. Showed patience and integrity in dealing with others

The Law of Solid Ground teaches that leadership operates on the basis of trust. How did Joseph gain trust following his bouts with adversity? He won it through regularly displaying competence and character in his connections with others. He was able to follow each setback with a comeback because he practiced the Law of Solid Ground.

were born to Joseph by Asenath daughter of Potiphera, priest of On. [51]Joseph named his firstborn Manasseh[a] and said, "It is because God has made me forget all my trouble and all my father's household." [52]The second son he named Ephraim[b] and said, "It is because God has made me fruitful in the land of my suffering."

[53]The seven years of abundance in Egypt came to an end, [54]and the seven years of famine began, just as Joseph had said. There was famine in all the other lands, but in the whole land of Egypt there was food. [55]When all Egypt began to feel the famine, the people cried to Pharaoh for food. Then Pharaoh told all the Egyptians, "Go to Joseph and do what he tells you."

[56]When the famine had spread over the whole country, Joseph opened all the storehouses and sold grain to the Egyptians, for the famine was severe throughout Egypt. [57]And all the world came to Egypt to buy grain from Joseph, because the famine was severe everywhere.

Joseph's Brothers Go to Egypt

42 When Jacob learned that there was grain in Egypt, he said to his sons, "Why do you just keep looking at each other?" [2]He continued, "I have heard that there is grain in Egypt. Go down there and buy some for us, so that we may live and not die."

[3]Then ten of Joseph's brothers went down to buy grain from Egypt. [4]But Jacob did not send Benjamin, Joseph's brother, with the others, because he was afraid that harm might come to him. [5]So Israel's sons were among those who went to buy grain, for there was famine in the land of Canaan also.

[6]Now Joseph was the governor of the land, the person who sold grain to all its people. So when Joseph's brothers arrived, they bowed down to him with their faces to the ground. [7]As soon as Joseph saw his brothers, he recognized them, but he pretended to be a stranger and spoke harshly to them. "Where do you come from?" he asked.

"From the land of Canaan," they replied, "to buy food."

[8]Although Joseph recognized his brothers, they did not recognize him. [9]Then he remembered his dreams about them and said to them, "You are spies! You have come to see where our land is unprotected."

[10]"No, my lord," they answered. "Your servants have come to buy food. [11]We are all the sons of one man. Your servants are honest men, not spies."

[12]"No!" he said to them. "You have come to see where our land is unprotected."

---

[a] 51 *Manasseh* sounds like and may be derived from the Hebrew for *forget.*   [b] 52 *Ephraim* sounds like the Hebrew for *twice fruitful.*

PHARAOH — Leading with Humility
Genesis 41:1–55

PROFILE in leadership

The Pharaoh who ruled Egypt at the time of Joseph showed remarkable wisdom and insight, as well as a heart receptive to truth. God strategically positioned this humble man as king over Egypt at a crucial time in world history.

When nightmares awakened Pharaoh, he recognized something odd was happening. As a strong leader he acknowledged his sense of unease, but as a humble leader he enlisted the advice of others. He summoned Joseph, who successfully interpreted his dreams.

Do you think Pharaoh knew his kingdom hung in the balance as he carefully processed the message God had given him? It took great wisdom and humility to designate Joseph as the point person and to give him the authority and resources necessary to survive the coming calamity. But he did it. And the people followed his leadership, carefully storing up grain during seven prophesied years of plenty. When the predicted hard times arrived, Pharaoh once more deferred to Joseph. The king of Egypt put himself and his people into the capable hands of this foreigner.

Had this Pharaoh been arrogant or intimidated by Joseph, millions would have starved. Instead, Pharaoh listened carefully, empowered Joseph to act—and in so doing, insured his own legacy as an effective leader.

[13]But they replied, "Your servants were twelve brothers, the sons of one man, who lives in the land of Canaan. The youngest is now with our father, and one is no more."

[14]Joseph said to them, "It is just as I told you: You are spies! [15]And this is how you will be tested: As surely as Pharaoh lives, you will not leave this place unless your youngest brother comes here. [16]Send one of your number to get your brother; the rest of you will be kept in prison, so that your words may be tested to see if you are telling the truth. If you are not, then as surely as Pharaoh lives, you are spies!" [17]And he put them all in custody for three days.

[18]On the third day, Joseph said to them, "Do this and you will live, for I fear God: [19]If you are honest men, let one of your brothers stay here in prison, while the rest of you go and take grain back for your starving households. [20]But you must bring your youngest brother to me, so that your words may be verified and that you may not die." This they proceeded to do.

[21]They said to one another, "Surely we are being punished because of our brother. We saw how distressed he was when he pleaded with us for his life, but we would not listen; that's why this distress has come on us."

[22]Reuben replied, "Didn't I tell you not to sin against the boy? But you wouldn't listen! Now we must give an accounting for his blood." [23]They did not realize that Joseph could understand them, since he was using an interpreter.

[24]He turned away from them and began to weep, but then came back and spoke to them again. He had Simeon taken from them and bound before their eyes.

[25]Joseph gave orders to fill their bags with grain, to put each man's silver back in his sack, and to give them provisions for their journey. After this was done for them, [26]they loaded their grain on their donkeys and left.

[27]At the place where they stopped for the night one of them opened his sack to get feed for his donkey, and he saw his silver in the mouth of his sack. [28]"My silver has been returned," he said to his brothers. "Here it is in my sack."

Their hearts sank and they turned to each other trembling and said, "What is this that God has done to us?"

[29]When they came to their father Jacob in the land of Canaan, they told him all that had happened to them. They said, [30]"The man who is lord over the land spoke harshly to us and treated us as though we were spying on the land. [31]But we said to him, 'We are honest men; we are not spies. [32]We were twelve brothers, sons of one father. One is no more, and the youngest is now with our father in Canaan.'

[33]"Then the man who is lord over the land said to us, 'This is how I will know whether you are honest men: Leave one of your brothers here with me, and take food for your starving households and go. [34]But bring your youngest brother to me so I will know that you are not spies but honest men. Then I will give your brother back to you, and you can trade[a] in the land.'"

[35]As they were emptying their sacks, there in each man's sack was his pouch of silver! When they and their father saw the money pouches, they were frightened. [36]Their father Jacob said to them, "You have deprived me of my children. Joseph is no more and Simeon is no more, and now you want to take Benjamin. Everything is against me!"

[37]Then Reuben said to his father, "You may put both of my sons to death if I do not bring him back to you. Entrust him to my care, and I will bring him back."

[38]But Jacob said, "My son will not go down there with you; his brother is dead and he is the only one left. If harm comes to him on the journey you are taking, you will bring my gray head down to the grave in sorrow."

The Second Journey to Egypt

43 Now the famine was still severe in the land. [2]So when they had eaten all the grain they had brought from Egypt, their father said to them, "Go back and buy us a little more food."

[3]But Judah said to him, "The man warned us solemnly, 'You will not see my face again unless your brother is with you.' [4]If you will send our brother along with us, we will go down and buy food for you. [5]But if you will not send him, we will not go down, because the man said to us, 'You will not see my face again unless your brother is with you.'"

[6]Israel asked, "Why did you bring this trouble on me by telling the man you had another brother?"

[7]They replied, "The man questioned us closely about ourselves and our family. 'Is your father still living?' he asked us. 'Do you have another brother?' We simply answered his questions. How were we to know he would say, 'Bring your brother down here'?"

[8]Then Judah said to Israel his father, "Send

---

[a] 34 Or *move about freely*

the boy along with me and we will go at once, so that we and you and our children may live and not die. [9]I myself will guarantee his safety; you can hold me personally responsible for him. If I do not bring him back to you and set him here before you, I will bear the blame before you all my life. [10]As it is, if we had not delayed, we could have gone and returned twice."

[11]Then their father Israel said to them, "If it must be, then do this: Put some of the best products of the land in your bags and take them down to the man as a gift—a little balm and a little honey, some spices and myrrh, some pistachio nuts and almonds. [12]Take double the amount of silver with you, for you must return the silver that was put back into the mouths of your sacks. Perhaps it was a mistake. [13]Take your brother also and go back to the man at once. [14]And may God Almighty[a] grant you mercy before the man so that he will let your other brother and Benjamin come back with you. As for me, if I am bereaved, I am bereaved."

[15]So the men took the gifts and double the amount of silver, and Benjamin also. They hurried down to Egypt and presented themselves to Joseph. [16]When Joseph saw Benjamin with them, he said to the steward of his house, "Take these men to my house, slaughter an animal and prepare a meal; they are to eat with me at noon."

[17]The man did as Joseph told him and took the men to Joseph's house. [18]Now the men were frightened when they were taken to his house. They thought, "We were brought here because of the silver that was put back into our sacks the first time. He wants to attack us and overpower us and seize us as slaves and take our donkeys."

[19]So they went up to Joseph's steward and spoke to him at the entrance to the house. [20]"We beg your pardon, our lord," they said, "we came down here the first time to buy food. [21]But at the place where we stopped for the night we opened our sacks and each of us found his silver—the exact weight—in the mouth of his sack. So we have brought it back with us. [22]We have also brought additional silver with us to buy food. We don't know who put our silver in our sacks."

[23]"It's all right," he said. "Don't be afraid. Your God, the God of your father, has given you treasure in your sacks; I received your silver." Then he brought Simeon out to them.

[24]The steward took the men into Joseph's house, gave them water to wash their feet and provided fodder for their donkeys. [25]They prepared their gifts for Joseph's arrival at noon, because they had heard that they were to eat there.

[26]When Joseph came home, they presented to him the gifts they had brought into the house, and they bowed down before him to the ground. [27]He asked them how they were, and then he said, "How is your aged father you told me about? Is he still living?"

[28]They replied, "Your servant our father is still alive and well." And they bowed down, prostrating themselves before him.

[29]As he looked about and saw his brother Benjamin, his own mother's son, he asked, "Is this your youngest brother, the one you told me about?" And he said, "God be gracious to you, my son." [30]Deeply moved at the sight of his brother, Joseph hurried out and looked for a place to weep. He went into his private room and wept there.

[31]After he had washed his face, he came out and, controlling himself, said, "Serve the food."

[32]They served him by himself, the brothers by themselves, and the Egyptians who ate with him by themselves, because Egyptians could not eat with Hebrews, for that is detestable to Egyptians. [33]The men had been seated before him in the order of their ages, from the firstborn to the youngest; and they looked at each other in astonishment. [34]When portions were served to them from Joseph's table, Benjamin's portion was five times as much as anyone else's. So they feasted and drank freely with him.

A Silver Cup in a Sack

44 Now Joseph gave these instructions to the steward of his house: "Fill the men's sacks with as much food as they can carry, and put each man's silver in the mouth of his sack. [2]Then put my cup, the silver one, in the mouth of the youngest one's sack, along with the silver for his grain." And he did as Joseph said.

[3]As morning dawned, the men were sent on their way with their donkeys. [4]They had not gone far from the city when Joseph said to his steward, "Go after those men at once, and when you catch up with them, say to them, 'Why have you repaid good with evil? [5]Isn't this the cup my master drinks from and also uses for divination? This is a wicked thing you have done.'"

[6]When he caught up with them, he repeated these words to them. [7]But they said to him, "Why does my lord say such things? Far be it from your servants to do anything like that! [8]We even brought back to you from the land of Canaan the silver we found inside the mouths of

[a] 14 Hebrew El-Shaddai

our sacks. So why would we steal silver or gold from your master's house? ⁹If any of your servants is found to have it, he will die; and the rest of us will become my lord's slaves."

¹⁰"Very well, then," he said, "let it be as you say. Whoever is found to have it will become my slave; the rest of you will be free from blame."

¹¹Each of them quickly lowered his sack to the ground and opened it. ¹²Then the steward proceeded to search, beginning with the oldest and ending with the youngest. And the cup was found in Benjamin's sack. ¹³At this, they tore their clothes. Then they all loaded their donkeys and returned to the city.

¹⁴Joseph was still in the house when Judah and his brothers came in, and they threw themselves to the ground before him. ¹⁵Joseph said to them, "What is this you have done? Don't you know that a man like me can find things out by divination?"

¹⁶"What can we say to my lord?" Judah replied. "What can we say? How can we prove our innocence? God has uncovered your servants' guilt. We are now my lord's slaves—we ourselves and the one who was found to have the cup."

¹⁷But Joseph said, "Far be it from me to do such a thing! Only the man who was found to have the cup will become my slave. The rest of you, go back to your father in peace."

¹⁸Then Judah went up to him and said: "Pardon your servant, my lord, let me speak a word to my lord. Do not be angry with your servant, though you are equal to Pharaoh himself. ¹⁹My lord asked his servants, 'Do you have a father or a brother?' ²⁰And we answered, 'We have an aged father, and there is a young son born to him in his old age. His brother is dead, and he is the only one of his mother's sons left, and his father loves him.'

²¹"Then you said to your servants, 'Bring him down to me so I can see him for myself.' ²²And we said to my lord, 'The boy cannot leave his father; if he leaves him, his father will die.' ²³But you told your servants, 'Unless your youngest brother comes down with you, you will not see my face again.' ²⁴When we went back to your servant my father, we told him what my lord had said.

²⁵"Then our father said, 'Go back and buy a little more food.' ²⁶But we said, 'We cannot go down. Only if our youngest brother is with us will we go. We cannot see the man's face unless our youngest brother is with us.'

²⁷"Your servant my father said to us, 'You know that my wife bore me two sons. ²⁸One of them went away from me, and I said, "He has surely been torn to pieces." And I have not seen him since. ²⁹If you take this one from me too and harm comes to him, you will bring my gray head down to the grave in misery.'

³⁰"So now, if the boy is not with us when I go back to your servant my father, and if my father, whose life is closely bound up with the boy's life, ³¹sees that the boy isn't there, he will die. Your servants will bring the gray head of our father down to the grave in sorrow. ³²Your servant guaranteed the boy's safety to my father. I said, 'If I do not bring him back to you, I will bear the blame before you, my father, all my life!'

³³"Now then, please let your servant remain here as my lord's slave in place of the boy, and let the boy return with his brothers. ³⁴How can I go back to my father if the boy is not with me? No! Do not let me see the misery that would come on my father."

Joseph Makes Himself Known

45 Then Joseph could no longer control himself before all his attendants, and he cried out, "Have everyone leave my presence!" So there was no one with Joseph when he made himself known to his brothers. ²And he wept so loudly that the Egyptians heard him, and Pharaoh's household heard about it.

³Joseph said to his brothers, "I am Joseph! Is my father still living?" But his brothers were not able to answer him, because they were terrified at his presence.

⁴Then Joseph said to his brothers, "Come close to me." When they had done so, he said, "I am your brother Joseph, the one you sold into Egypt! ⁵And now, do not be distressed and do not be angry with yourselves for selling me here, because it was to save lives that God sent me ahead of you. ⁶For two years now there has been famine in the land, and for the next five years there will be no plowing and reaping. ⁷But God sent me ahead of you to preserve for you a remnant on earth and to save your lives by a great deliverance.[a]

⁸"So then, it was not you who sent me here, but God. He made me father to Pharaoh, lord of his entire household and ruler of all Egypt. ⁹Now hurry back to my father and say to him, 'This is what your son Joseph says: God has made me lord of all Egypt. Come down to me; don't delay. ¹⁰You shall live in the region of Goshen and

[a] 7 Or save you as a great band of survivors

The Law of Empowerment: Joseph and His Brothers

Genesis 45:4–7

When Joseph's brothers realized that the one they had betrayed could now do with them what he pleased, they feared payback time had arrived. Instead of retaliating, however, Joseph blessed them and empowered them to complete the task that had brought them to Egypt: to secure food for their families. A careful reading of Genesis 45:4–7 reveals the qualities that made Joseph such an empowering leader:

1. **A strong sense of security.** "Come close to me" (v. 4).
2. **A strong sense of identity.** "I am your brother Joseph" (v. 4).
3. **A strong sense of empathy.** "Do not be distressed and do not be angry with yourselves" (v. 4).
4. **A strong sense of purpose.** "It was to save lives that God sent me ahead of you" (v. 5).
5. **A strong sense of perspective.** "For the next five years there will be no plowing and reaping. But God sent me ahead of you to preserve for you a remnant on earth" (vv. 6–7).

be near me — you, your children and grandchildren, your flocks and herds, and all you have. ¹¹I will provide for you there, because five years of famine are still to come. Otherwise you and your household and all who belong to you will become destitute.'

¹²"You can see for yourselves, and so can my brother Benjamin, that it is really I who am speaking to you. ¹³Tell my father about all the honor accorded me in Egypt and about everything you have seen. And bring my father down here quickly."

¹⁴Then he threw his arms around his brother Benjamin and wept, and Benjamin embraced him, weeping. ¹⁵And he kissed all his brothers and wept over them. Afterward his brothers talked with him.

¹⁶When the news reached Pharaoh's palace that Joseph's brothers had come, Pharaoh and all his officials were pleased. ¹⁷Pharaoh said to Joseph, "Tell your brothers, 'Do this: Load your animals and return to the land of Canaan, ¹⁸and bring your father and your families back to me. I will give you the best of the land of Egypt and you can enjoy the fat of the land.'

¹⁹"You are also directed to tell them, 'Do this: Take some carts from Egypt for your children and your wives, and get your father and come. ²⁰Never mind about your belongings, because the best of all Egypt will be yours.'"

²¹So the sons of Israel did this. Joseph gave them carts, as Pharaoh had commanded, and he also gave them provisions for their journey. ²²To each of them he gave new clothing, but to Benja-min he gave three hundred shekels[a] of silver and five sets of clothes. ²³And this is what he sent to his father: ten donkeys loaded with the best things of Egypt, and ten female donkeys loaded with grain and bread and other provisions for his journey. ²⁴Then he sent his brothers away, and as they were leaving he said to them, "Don't quarrel on the way!"

²⁵So they went up out of Egypt and came to their father Jacob in the land of Canaan. ²⁶They told him, "Joseph is still alive! In fact, he is ruler of all Egypt." Jacob was stunned; he did not believe them. ²⁷But when they told him everything Joseph had said to them, and when he saw the carts Joseph had sent to carry him back, the spirit of their father Jacob revived. ²⁸And Israel said, "I'm convinced! My son Joseph is still alive. I will go and see him before I die."

Jacob Goes to Egypt

46 So Israel set out with all that was his, and when he reached Beersheba, he offered sacrifices to the God of his father Isaac.

²And God spoke to Israel in a vision at night and said, "Jacob! Jacob!"

"Here I am," he replied.

³"I am God, the God of your father," he said. "Do not be afraid to go down to Egypt, for I will make you into a great nation there. ⁴I will go down to Egypt with you, and I will surely bring you back again. And Joseph's own hand will close your eyes."

---

a 22 That is, about 7 1/2 pounds or about 3.5 kilograms

[5]Then Jacob left Beersheba, and Israel's sons took their father Jacob and their children and their wives in the carts that Pharaoh had sent to transport him. [6]So Jacob and all his offspring went to Egypt, taking with them their livestock and the possessions they had acquired in Canaan. [7]Jacob brought with him to Egypt his sons and grandsons and his daughters and granddaughters—all his offspring.

[8]These are the names of the sons of Israel (Jacob and his descendants) who went to Egypt:

Reuben the firstborn of Jacob.
[9]The sons of Reuben:
    Hanok, Pallu, Hezron and Karmi.
[10]The sons of Simeon:
    Jemuel, Jamin, Ohad, Jakin, Zohar and
    Shaul the son of a Canaanite woman.
[11]The sons of Levi:
    Gershon, Kohath and Merari.
[12]The sons of Judah:
    Er, Onan, Shelah, Perez and Zerah (but
    Er and Onan had died in the land of Canaan).
    The sons of Perez:
        Hezron and Hamul.
[13]The sons of Issachar:
    Tola, Puah,[a] Jashub[b] and Shimron.
[14]The sons of Zebulun:
    Sered, Elon and Jahleel.
[15]These were the sons Leah bore to Jacob in Paddan Aram,[c] besides his daughter Dinah. These sons and daughters of his were thirty-three in all.

[16]The sons of Gad:
    Zephon,[d] Haggi, Shuni, Ezbon, Eri, Arodi and Areli.
[17]The sons of Asher:
    Imnah, Ishvah, Ishvi and Beriah.
    Their sister was Serah.
    The sons of Beriah:
        Heber and Malkiel.
[18]These were the children born to Jacob by Zilpah, whom Laban had given to his daughter Leah—sixteen in all.

[19]The sons of Jacob's wife Rachel:
    Joseph and Benjamin. [20]In Egypt, Manasseh and Ephraim were born to Joseph by Asenath daughter of Potiphera, priest of On.[e]
[21]The sons of Benjamin:
    Bela, Beker, Ashbel, Gera, Naaman, Ehi, Rosh, Muppim, Huppim and Ard.

[22]These were the sons of Rachel who were born to Jacob—fourteen in all.

[23]The son of Dan:
    Hushim.
[24]The sons of Naphtali:
    Jahziel, Guni, Jezer and Shillem.
[25]These were the sons born to Jacob by Bilhah, whom Laban had given to his daughter Rachel—seven in all.

[26]All those who went to Egypt with Jacob—those who were his direct descendants, not counting his sons' wives—numbered sixty-six persons. [27]With the two sons[f] who had been born to Joseph in Egypt, the members of Jacob's family, which went to Egypt, were seventy[g] in all.

[28]Now Jacob sent Judah ahead of him to Joseph to get directions to Goshen. When they arrived in the region of Goshen, [29]Joseph had his chariot made ready and went to Goshen to meet his father Israel. As soon as Joseph appeared before him, he threw his arms around his father[h] and wept for a long time.

[30]Israel said to Joseph, "Now I am ready to die, since I have seen for myself that you are still alive."

[31]Then Joseph said to his brothers and to his father's household, "I will go up and speak to Pharaoh and will say to him, 'My brothers and my father's household, who were living in the land of Canaan, have come to me. [32]The men are shepherds; they tend livestock, and they have brought along their flocks and herds and everything they own.' [33]When Pharaoh calls you in and asks, 'What is your occupation?' [34]you should answer, 'Your servants have tended livestock from our boyhood on, just as our fathers did.' Then you will be allowed to settle in the region of Goshen, for all shepherds are detestable to the Egyptians."

47 Joseph went and told Pharaoh, "My father and brothers, with their flocks and herds and everything they own, have come from the land of Canaan and are now in Goshen." [2]He chose five of his brothers and presented them before Pharaoh.

---

[a] 13 Samaritan Pentateuch and Syriac (see also 1 Chron. 7:1); Masoretic Text *Puvah*   [b] 13 Samaritan Pentateuch and some Septuagint manuscripts (see also Num. 26:24 and 1 Chron. 7:1); Masoretic Text *Iob*   [c] 15 That is, Northwest Mesopotamia   [d] 16 Samaritan Pentateuch and Septuagint (see also Num. 26:15); Masoretic Text *Ziphion*   [e] 20 That is, Heliopolis   [f] 27 Hebrew; Septuagint *the nine children*   [g] 27 Hebrew (see also Exodus 1:5 and note); Septuagint (see also Acts 7:14) *seventy-five*   [h] 29 Hebrew *around him*

[3]Pharaoh asked the brothers, "What is your occupation?"

"Your servants are shepherds," they replied to Pharaoh, "just as our fathers were." [4]They also said to him, "We have come to live here for a while, because the famine is severe in Canaan and your servants' flocks have no pasture. So now, please let your servants settle in Goshen."

[5]Pharaoh said to Joseph, "Your father and your brothers have come to you, [6]and the land of Egypt is before you; settle your father and your brothers in the best part of the land. Let them live in Goshen. And if you know of any among them with special ability, put them in charge of my own livestock."

[7]Then Joseph brought his father Jacob in and presented him before Pharaoh. After Jacob blessed[a] Pharaoh, [8]Pharaoh asked him, "How old are you?"

[9]And Jacob said to Pharaoh, "The years of my pilgrimage are a hundred and thirty. My years have been few and difficult, and they do not equal the years of the pilgrimage of my fathers." [10]Then Jacob blessed[b] Pharaoh and went out from his presence.

[11]So Joseph settled his father and his brothers in Egypt and gave them property in the best part of the land, the district of Rameses, as Pharaoh directed. [12]Joseph also provided his father and his brothers and all his father's household with food, according to the number of their children.

Joseph and the Famine

[13]There was no food, however, in the whole region because the famine was severe; both Egypt and Canaan wasted away because of the famine. [14]Joseph collected all the money that was to be found in Egypt and Canaan in payment for the grain they were buying, and he brought it to Pharaoh's palace. [15]When the money of the people of Egypt and Canaan was gone, all Egypt came to Joseph and said, "Give us food. Why should we die before your eyes? Our money is all gone."

[16]"Then bring your livestock," said Joseph. "I will sell you food in exchange for your livestock, since your money is gone." [17]So they brought their livestock to Joseph, and he gave them food in exchange for their horses, their sheep and goats, their cattle and donkeys. And he brought them through that year with food in exchange for all their livestock.

[18]When that year was over, they came to him the following year and said, "We cannot hide from our lord the fact that since our money is gone and our livestock belongs to you, there is nothing left for our lord except our bodies and our land. [19]Why should we perish before your eyes — we and our land as well? Buy us and our land in exchange for food, and we with our land will be in bondage to Pharaoh. Give us seed so that we may live and not die, and that the land may not become desolate."

[20]So Joseph bought all the land in Egypt for Pharaoh. The Egyptians, one and all, sold their fields, because the famine was too severe for them. The land became Pharaoh's, [21]and Joseph reduced the people to servitude,[c] from one end of Egypt to the other. [22]However, he did not buy the land of the priests, because they received a regular allotment from Pharaoh and had food enough from the allotment Pharaoh gave them. That is why they did not sell their land.

[23]Joseph said to the people, "Now that I have bought you and your land today for Pharaoh, here is seed for you so you can plant the ground. [24]But when the crop comes in, give a fifth of it to Pharaoh. The other four-fifths you may keep as seed for the fields and as food for yourselves and your households and your children."

[25]"You have saved our lives," they said. "May we find favor in the eyes of our lord; we will be in bondage to Pharaoh."

[26]So Joseph established it as a law concerning land in Egypt — still in force today — that a fifth of the produce belongs to Pharaoh. It was only the land of the priests that did not become Pharaoh's.

[27]Now the Israelites settled in Egypt in the region of Goshen. They acquired property there and were fruitful and increased greatly in number.

[28]Jacob lived in Egypt seventeen years, and the years of his life were a hundred and forty-seven. [29]When the time drew near for Israel to die, he called for his son Joseph and said to him, "If I have found favor in your eyes, put your hand under my thigh and promise that you will show me kindness and faithfulness. Do not bury me in Egypt, [30]but when I rest with my fathers, carry me out of Egypt and bury me where they are buried."

"I will do as you say," he said.

[31]"Swear to me," he said. Then Joseph swore to him, and Israel worshiped as he leaned on the top of his staff.[d]

---

[a] 7 Or *greeted*   [b] 10 Or *said farewell to*   [c] 21 Samaritan Pentateuch and Septuagint (see also Vulgate); Masoretic Text *and he moved the people into the cities*   [d] 31 Or *Israel bowed down at the head of his bed*

Manasseh and Ephraim

48 Some time later Joseph was told, "Your father is ill." So he took his two sons Manasseh and Ephraim along with him. [2]When Jacob was told, "Your son Joseph has come to you," Israel rallied his strength and sat up on the bed.

[3]Jacob said to Joseph, "God Almighty[a] appeared to me at Luz in the land of Canaan, and there he blessed me [4]and said to me, 'I am going to make you fruitful and increase your numbers. I will make you a community of peoples, and I will give this land as an everlasting possession to your descendants after you.'

[5]"Now then, your two sons born to you in Egypt before I came to you here will be reckoned as mine; Ephraim and Manasseh will be mine, just as Reuben and Simeon are mine. [6]Any children born to you after them will be yours; in the territory they inherit they will be reckoned under the names of their brothers. [7]As I was returning from Paddan,[b] to my sorrow Rachel died in the land of Canaan while we were still on the way, a little distance from Ephrath. So I buried her there beside the road to Ephrath" (that is, Bethlehem).

[8]When Israel saw the sons of Joseph, he asked, "Who are these?"

[9]"They are the sons God has given me here," Joseph said to his father.

Then Israel said, "Bring them to me so I may bless them."

[10]Now Israel's eyes were failing because of old age, and he could hardly see. So Joseph brought his sons close to him, and his father kissed them and embraced them.

[11]Israel said to Joseph, "I never expected to see your face again, and now God has allowed me to see your children too."

[12]Then Joseph removed them from Israel's knees and bowed down with his face to the ground. [13]And Joseph took both of them, Ephraim on his right toward Israel's left hand and Manasseh on his left toward Israel's right hand, and brought them close to him. [14]But Israel reached out his right hand and put it on Ephraim's head, though he was the younger, and crossing his arms, he put his left hand on Manasseh's head, even though Manasseh was the firstborn.

[15]Then he blessed Joseph and said,

"May the God before whom my fathers
    Abraham and Isaac walked faithfully,
the God who has been my shepherd
    all my life to this day,

[16]the Angel who has delivered me from all harm
    —may he bless these boys.
May they be called by my name
    and the names of my fathers Abraham
        and Isaac,
and may they increase greatly
    on the earth."

[17]When Joseph saw his father placing his right hand on Ephraim's head he was displeased; so he took hold of his father's hand to move it from Ephraim's head to Manasseh's head. [18]Joseph said to him, "No, my father, this one is the firstborn; put your right hand on his head."

[19]But his father refused and said, "I know, my son, I know. He too will become a people, and he too will become great. Nevertheless, his younger brother will be greater than he, and his descendants will become a group of nations." [20]He blessed them that day and said,

"In your[c] name will Israel pronounce this
        blessing:
    'May God make you like Ephraim and
        Manasseh.'"

So he put Ephraim ahead of Manasseh.

[21]Then Israel said to Joseph, "I am about to die, but God will be with you[d] and take you[d] back to the land of your[d] fathers. [22]And to you I give one more ridge of land[e] than to your brothers, the ridge I took from the Amorites with my sword and my bow."

Jacob Blesses His Sons

49 Then Jacob called for his sons and said: "Gather around so I can tell you what will happen to you in days to come.

[2]"Assemble and listen, sons of Jacob;
    listen to your father Israel.

[3]"Reuben, you are my firstborn,
    my might, the first sign of my strength,
    excelling in honor, excelling in power.
[4]Turbulent as the waters, you will no longer
        excel,
    for you went up onto your father's bed,
    onto my couch and defiled it.

[5]"Simeon and Levi are brothers—
    their swords[f] are weapons of violence.

---

[a] 3 Hebrew *El-Shaddai*   [b] 7 That is, Northwest Mesopotamia   [c] 20 The Hebrew is singular.   [d] 21 The Hebrew is plural.   [e] 22 The Hebrew for *ridge of land* is identical with the place name Shechem.   [f] 5 The meaning of the Hebrew for this word is uncertain.

[6] Let me not enter their council,
   let me not join their assembly,
 for they have killed men in their anger
   and hamstrung oxen as they pleased.
[7] Cursed be their anger, so fierce,
   and their fury, so cruel!
 I will scatter them in Jacob
   and disperse them in Israel.

[8] "Judah,[a] your brothers will praise you;
   your hand will be on the neck of your
     enemies;
   your father's sons will bow down to you.
[9] You are a lion's cub, Judah;
   you return from the prey, my son.
 Like a lion he crouches and lies down,
   like a lioness — who dares to rouse him?
[10] The scepter will not depart from Judah,
   nor the ruler's staff from between his
     feet,[b]
 until he to whom it belongs[c] shall come
   and the obedience of the nations shall be
     his.
[11] He will tether his donkey to a vine,
   his colt to the choicest branch;
 he will wash his garments in wine,
   his robes in the blood of grapes.
[12] His eyes will be darker than wine,
   his teeth whiter than milk.[d]

[13] "Zebulun will live by the seashore
   and become a haven for ships;
   his border will extend toward Sidon.

[14] "Issachar is a rawboned[e] donkey
   lying down among the sheep pens.[f]
[15] When he sees how good is his resting place
   and how pleasant is his land,
 he will bend his shoulder to the burden
   and submit to forced labor.

[16] "Dan[g] will provide justice for his people
   as one of the tribes of Israel.
[17] Dan will be a snake by the roadside,
   a viper along the path,
 that bites the horse's heels
   so that its rider tumbles backward.

[18] "I look for your deliverance, LORD.

[19] "Gad[h] will be attacked by a band of raiders,
   but he will attack them at their heels.

[20] "Asher's food will be rich;
   he will provide delicacies fit for a king.

[21] "Naphtali is a doe set free
   that bears beautiful fawns.[i]

[22] "Joseph is a fruitful vine,
   a fruitful vine near a spring,
   whose branches climb over a wall.[j]
[23] With bitterness archers attacked him;
   they shot at him with hostility.
[24] But his bow remained steady,
   his strong arms stayed[k] limber,
 because of the hand of the Mighty One of
     Jacob,
   because of the Shepherd, the Rock of
     Israel,
[25] because of your father's God, who helps you,
   because of the Almighty,[l] who blesses you
 with blessings of the skies above,
   blessings of the deep springs below,
   blessings of the breast and womb.
[26] Your father's blessings are greater
   than the blessings of the ancient
     mountains,
   than[m] the bounty of the age-old hills.
 Let all these rest on the head of Joseph,
   on the brow of the prince among[n] his
     brothers.

[27] "Benjamin is a ravenous wolf;
   in the morning he devours the prey,
   in the evening he divides the plunder."

[28] All these are the twelve tribes of Israel, and
this is what their father said to them when he
blessed them, giving each the blessing appropriate to him.

The Death of Jacob

[29] Then he gave them these instructions: "I
am about to be gathered to my people. Bury me
with my fathers in the cave in the field of Ephron
the Hittite, [30] the cave in the field of Machpelah,
near Mamre in Canaan, which Abraham bought
along with the field as a burial place from Ephron
the Hittite. [31] There Abraham and his wife Sarah were buried, there Isaac and his wife Rebekah
were buried, and there I buried Leah. [32] The field
and the cave in it were bought from the Hittites.[o]"

---

[a] 8 Judah sounds like and may be derived from the Hebrew for
praise.   [b] 10 Or from his descendants   [c] 10 Or to whom
tribute belongs; the meaning of the Hebrew for this phrase is
uncertain.   [d] 12 Or will be dull from wine, / his teeth white
from milk   [e] 14 Or strong   [f] 14 Or the campfires; or the
saddlebags   [g] 16 Dan here means he provides justice.
[h] 19 Gad sounds like the Hebrew for attack and also for band of
raiders.   [i] 21 Or free; / he utters beautiful words   [j] 22 Or
Joseph is a wild colt, / a wild colt near a spring, / a wild donkey
on a terraced hill   [k] 23,24 Or archers will attack . . . will
shoot . . . will remain . . . will stay   [l] 25 Hebrew Shaddai
[m] 26 Or of my progenitors, / as great as   [n] 26 Or of the one
separated from   [o] 32 Or the descendants of Heth

33When Jacob had finished giving instructions to his sons, he drew his feet up into the bed, breathed his last and was gathered to his people.

50 Joseph threw himself on his father and wept over him and kissed him. ²Then Joseph directed the physicians in his service to embalm his father Israel. So the physicians embalmed him, ³taking a full forty days, for that was the time required for embalming. And the Egyptians mourned for him seventy days.

⁴When the days of mourning had passed, Joseph said to Pharaoh's court, "If I have found favor in your eyes, speak to Pharaoh for me. Tell him, ⁵'My father made me swear an oath and said, "I am about to die; bury me in the tomb I dug for myself in the land of Canaan." Now let me go up and bury my father; then I will return.'"

⁶Pharaoh said, "Go up and bury your father, as he made you swear to do."

⁷So Joseph went up to bury his father. All Pharaoh's officials accompanied him — the dignitaries of his court and all the dignitaries of Egypt — ⁸besides all the members of Joseph's household and his brothers and those belonging to his father's household. Only their children and their flocks and herds were left in Goshen. ⁹Chariots and horsemen[a] also went up with him. It was a very large company.

¹⁰When they reached the threshing floor of Atad, near the Jordan, they lamented loudly and bitterly; and there Joseph observed a seven-day period of mourning for his father. ¹¹When the Canaanites who lived there saw the mourning at the threshing floor of Atad, they said, "The Egyptians are holding a solemn ceremony of mourning." That is why that place near the Jordan is called Abel Mizraim.[b]

¹²So Jacob's sons did as he had commanded them: ¹³They carried him to the land of Canaan and buried him in the cave in the field of Machpelah, near Mamre, which Abraham had bought along with the field as a burial place from Ephron the Hittite. ¹⁴After burying his father, Joseph returned to Egypt, together with his brothers and all the others who had gone with him to bury his father.

Joseph Reassures His Brothers

¹⁵When Joseph's brothers saw that their father was dead, they said, "What if Joseph holds a grudge against us and pays us back for all the wrongs we did to him?" ¹⁶So they sent word to Joseph, saying, "Your father left these instructions before he died: ¹⁷'This is what you are to say to Joseph: I ask you to forgive your brothers the sins and the wrongs they committed in treating you so badly.' Now please forgive the sins of the servants of the God of your father." When their message came to him, Joseph wept.

---

[a] 9 Or charioteers   [b] 11 Abel Mizraim means mourning of the Egyptians.

How Character Breeds Perspective

Genesis 50:15–21

Joseph puts his entire life in perspective in the final chapter of Genesis. During the height of a terrible famine, his brothers humbly come before him and bow down, just as he had predicted decades earlier. But instead of using his enormous power to punish them, he said, "You intended to harm me, but God intended it for good to accomplish what is now being done, the saving of many lives" (Ge 50:20).

How does one develop such a godly (and rare) perspective? What enabled Joseph to refrain from exacting the kind of vengeance most of us would be tempted to dish out in similar circumstances? One word: character. Because Joseph had spent years in God's character-building course, he could maintain a proper perspective and use his power to bless his brothers rather than curse them.

How a leader deals with the circumstances of life tells you many things about his character. Crisis doesn't necessarily make character, but it certainly does reveal it. Adversity is a crossroads that makes a person choose one of two paths: character or compromise. Every time he chooses character, he becomes stronger, even if that choice brings negative consequences. (Remember why Joseph ended up in prison?) The development of character is at the heart of our development as leaders.

If you want God's perspective on life, then make sure to develop your character. It's the only way, as Joseph reminds us.

[18]His brothers then came and threw themselves down before him. "We are your slaves," they said.

[19]But Joseph said to them, "Don't be afraid. Am I in the place of God? [20]You intended to harm me, but God intended it for good to accomplish what is now being done, the saving of many lives. [21]So then, don't be afraid. I will provide for you and your children." And he reassured them and spoke kindly to them.

The Death of Joseph

[22]Joseph stayed in Egypt, along with all his father's family. He lived a hundred and ten years [23]and saw the third generation of Ephraim's children. Also the children of Makir son of Manasseh were placed at birth on Joseph's knees.[a]

[24]Then Joseph said to his brothers, "I am about to die. But God will surely come to your aid and take you up out of this land to the land he promised on oath to Abraham, Isaac and Jacob." [25]And Joseph made the Israelites swear an oath and said, "God will surely come to your aid, and then you must carry my bones up from this place."

[26]So Joseph died at the age of a hundred and ten. And after they embalmed him, he was placed in a coffin in Egypt.

---

[a] 23 That is, were counted as his

INTRODUCTION TO
EXODUS

Examples of leadership abound in Exodus, beginning with the Lord himself. Once God established a people for his own and they pledged to follow him, he proceeded to the next stage of leadership necessary for building them into a people whose hearts beat to the same rhythm as his own.

Consider the process: God led his people through generations of slavery in Egypt and made them into a great nation. He led Moses into the wilderness to prepare and develop him as a leader. The Lord took 80 years to ready Moses for the task of guiding God's new nation out of Egypt, across the desert, and into the promised land. Over time, the Israelites became not just a handful of families, but a massive, ethnic population—large enough to frighten even the Egyptians. Moses became the first political leader of a full-fledged, Israelite nation.

In the beginning, national success looked to be just around the corner. The Hebrews had an educated leader, Moses; they had a plan; they enjoyed great organization; they had received a vision, clearly stated by God and reiterated by Moses; and they had agreed to a sharply defined goal. Nothing could derail them, right?

Wrong.

The Israelites soon lost sight of the vision. When Moses took too long to receive the "constitution" for their nation (the Ten Commandments), they fashioned a golden calf and began to worship it. When the journey grew long and uncomfortable, they began to whine, then grumble, then complain. More than once, they nearly revolted against Moses' leadership. A two-week trip through the desert ultimately took more than four decades!

God's Role in Exodus

You'd have to be blind to miss God's leadership in this book. He is there all the time, talking face-to-face with Moses and mentoring him to be the CEO of Israel. God dispenses multitudes of signs and wonders to give everyone plenty of reasons to follow, trust, and obey. He directs the nation's path through the desert, across the Red Sea, and during the 40 years of wandering, visually reminding his people of his presence and power through a cloud by day and a pillar of fire by night.

Yet it never seems to be enough for the people of Israel. They continue to doubt, delay, and defy Moses—a huge disappointment for one of the greatest leaders of all time.

Leaders in Exodus
Moses, Aaron, Pharaoh, Joshua

Other People of Influence in Exodus
Midwives, Miriam, Jochebed, Pharaoh's magicians, Jethro

Lessons in Leadership
- Leaders need time and experience to grow and prepare for leadership.
- Leading means planning: plan your work and work your plan.
- Leaders should never try to do everything all alone.

The book of Exodus records how God's people failed to cooperate, doubted the vision, disobeyed the rules, worshiped material things, forgot their goals, and soured on their leader—all of which delayed their dream by 40 years. Not only did the people doubt Moses' leadership; they also doubted God's. We can learn a great deal from the accounts in Exodus.

- Leaders must be prepared for things to go awry.
- Leaders must continually remind themselves and others of past successes.
- Leaders must repeatedly cast the vision.

LEADERSHIP HIGHLIGHTS IN EXODUS

The Israelites Oppressed

1 These are the names of the sons of Israel who went to Egypt with Jacob, each with his family: [2]Reuben, Simeon, Levi and Judah; [3]Issachar, Zebulun and Benjamin; [4]Dan and Naphtali; Gad and Asher. [5]The descendants of Jacob numbered seventy[a] in all; Joseph was already in Egypt.

[6]Now Joseph and all his brothers and all that generation died, [7]but the Israelites were exceedingly fruitful; they multiplied greatly, increased in numbers and became so numerous that the land was filled with them.

[8]Then a new king, to whom Joseph meant nothing, came to power in Egypt. [9]"Look," he said to his people, "the Israelites have become far too numerous for us. [10]Come, we must deal shrewdly with them or they will become even more numerous and, if war breaks out, will join our enemies, fight against us and leave the country."

[11]So they put slave masters over them to oppress them with forced labor, and they built Pithom and Rameses as store cities for Pharaoh. [12]But the more they were oppressed, the more they multiplied and spread; so the Egyptians came to dread the Israelites [13]and worked them ruthlessly. [14]They made their lives bitter with harsh labor in brick and mortar and with all kinds of work in the fields; in all their harsh labor the Egyptians worked them ruthlessly.

[15]The king of Egypt said to the Hebrew midwives, whose names were Shiphrah and Puah, [16]"When you are helping the Hebrew women during childbirth on the delivery stool, if you see that the baby is a boy, kill him; but if it is a girl, let her live." [17]The midwives, however, feared God and did not do what the king of Egypt had told them to do; they let the boys live. [18]Then the king of Egypt summoned the midwives and asked them, "Why have you done this? Why have you let the boys live?"

[19]The midwives answered Pharaoh, "Hebrew women are not like Egyptian women; they are vigorous and give birth before the midwives arrive."

[20]So God was kind to the midwives and the people increased and became even more numerous. [21]And because the midwives feared God, he gave them families of their own.

[22]Then Pharaoh gave this order to all his people: "Every Hebrew boy that is born you must throw into the Nile, but let every girl live."

The Birth of Moses

2 Now a man of the tribe of Levi married a Levite woman, [2]and she became pregnant and gave birth to a son. When she saw that he was a fine child, she hid him for three months. [3]But when she could hide him no longer, she got a papyrus basket[b] for him and coated it with tar and pitch. Then she placed the child in it and put it among the reeds along the bank of the Nile. [4]His sister stood at a distance to see what would happen to him.

[5]Then Pharaoh's daughter went down to the Nile to bathe, and her attendants were walking along the riverbank. She saw the basket among the reeds and sent her female slave to get it. [6]She opened it and saw the baby. He was crying, and she felt sorry for him. "This is one of the Hebrew babies," she said.

---

[a] 5 Masoretic Text (see also Gen. 46:27); Dead Sea Scrolls and Septuagint (see also Acts 7:14 and note at Gen. 46:27) *seventy-five*   [b] 3 The Hebrew can also mean *ark*, as in Gen. 6:14.

Pharaoh Violates the Laws of Connection and Empowerment

Exodus 1:8–22

The first chapter of Exodus introduces us to a man with great power, but little character or wisdom. The leader of the most powerful nation of the ancient world, this pharaoh had little in common with the confident ruler who led Egypt during Joseph's day. He constantly worried that others might usurp his power, felt his security threatened and consequently sabotaged his own leadership. Notice how he responded to the challenges he faced (along with what he should have done).

Threat	Pharaoh's Response	Right Response
Jewish population size	Oppress and force labor	Position them well
Jewish babies born	Kill all the males	Equip them to lead
Jewish complaints	Drive them harder as slaves	Lighten their loads
Racial conflict	Ruthlessly dominate them	Build relationships

⁷Then his sister asked Pharaoh's daughter, "Shall I go and get one of the Hebrew women to nurse the baby for you?"

⁸"Yes, go," she answered. So the girl went and got the baby's mother. ⁹Pharaoh's daughter said to her, "Take this baby and nurse him for me, and I will pay you." So the woman took the baby and nursed him. ¹⁰When the child grew older, she took him to Pharaoh's daughter and he became her son. She named him Moses,ᵃ saying, "I drew him out of the water."

Moses Flees to Midian

¹¹One day, after Moses had grown up, he went out to where his own people were and watched them at their hard labor. He saw an Egyptian beating a Hebrew, one of his own people. ¹²Looking this way and that and seeing no one, he killed the Egyptian and hid him in the sand. ¹³The next day he went out and saw two Hebrews fighting. He asked the one in the wrong, "Why are you hitting your fellow Hebrew?"

¹⁴The man said, "Who made you ruler and judge over us? Are you thinking of killing me as you killed the Egyptian?" Then Moses was afraid and thought, "What I did must have become known."

¹⁵When Pharaoh heard of this, he tried to kill Moses, but Moses fled from Pharaoh and went to live in Midian, where he sat down by a well. ¹⁶Now a priest of Midian had seven daughters, and they came to draw water and fill the troughs to water their father's flock. ¹⁷Some shepherds came along and drove them away, but Moses got up and came to their rescue and watered their flock.

¹⁸When the girls returned to Reuel their father, he asked them, "Why have you returned so early today?"

¹⁹They answered, "An Egyptian rescued us from the shepherds. He even drew water for us and watered the flock."

²⁰"And where is he?" Reuel asked his daughters. "Why did you leave him? Invite him to have something to eat."

²¹Moses agreed to stay with the man, who gave his daughter Zipporah to Moses in marriage. ²²Zipporah gave birth to a son, and Moses named him Gershom,ᵇ saying, "I have become a foreigner in a foreign land."

²³During that long period, the king of Egypt died. The Israelites groaned in their slavery and cried out, and their cry for help because of their slavery went up to God. ²⁴God heard

---

ᵃ 10 *Moses* sounds like the Hebrew for *draw out*.
ᵇ 22 *Gershom* sounds like the Hebrew for *a foreigner there*.

HEBREW MIDWIVES

People of Influence
Exodus 1:15–20

PROFILE
in leadership

Who changes the course of history? Kings? Potentates? Generals? The wealthy? Sure. But more often than not, it's men and women with no power and little social standing who most significantly reshape this world.

When the king of Egypt grew worried about the exploding numbers of Hebrew slaves, he summoned two midwives, Shiphrah and Puah, and instructed them to murder all Hebrew male newborns. But these midwives feared God and refused to obey such a wicked command. Despite the king's threats, they would not buckle under and continued to deliver healthy male Hebrews. Although they had no way of knowing it, their risky decision helped to spare the life of Moses, Israel's God-ordained deliverer.

In civil disobedience, Shiphrah and Puah risked their lives to protect the children God had placed in their care. Their bravery prompted God to show them kindness by blessing them with families of their own. No doubt their children and grandchildren took part in the great exodus from Egypt.

At a strategic juncture in history, these Hebrew midwives—politically powerless, socially despised, economically disadvantaged—defied the ruler of Egypt to obey the God they feared. Their perilous choice to do the right thing protected the line of Abraham through which the Messiah would come, thus fulfilling God's plan for not only the Hebrews, but for all mankind.

The Law of Process: Moses and the Test of Time

Exodus 2:1 — 4:31

How did God prepare Moses to be his man to lead the Hebrews out of Egyptian bondage? He prepared him not in a day, but over time; not through an event, but with a process. Of course, others before Moses waited years for God to fulfill his leadership development process:

- Noah—waited 120 years before the predicted rains arrived.
- Abraham—waited 25 years for a promised son.
- Joseph—waited 14 years in prison for a crime he didn't commit.
- Job—waited perhaps a lifetime, 60–70 years, for God's justice.

God prepares leaders in a Crock-Pot, not a microwave. More important than the awaited goal is the work God does in us while we wait. Waiting deepens and matures us, levels our perspective, and broadens our understanding. Tests of time determine whether we can endure seasons of seemingly unfruitful preparation, and indicate whether we can recognize and seize the opportunities that come our way.

their groaning and he remembered his covenant with Abraham, with Isaac and with Jacob. ²⁵So God looked on the Israelites and was concerned about them.

Moses and the Burning Bush

3 Now Moses was tending the flock of Jethro his father-in-law, the priest of Midian, and he led the flock to the far side of the wilderness and came to Horeb, the mountain of God. ²There the angel of the LORD appeared to him in flames of fire from within a bush. Moses saw that though the bush was on fire it did not burn up. ³So Moses thought, "I will go over and see this strange sight — why the bush does not burn up."

⁴When the LORD saw that he had gone over to look, God called to him from within the bush, "Moses! Moses!"

And Moses said, "Here I am."

⁵"Do not come any closer," God said. "Take off your sandals, for the place where you are standing is holy ground." ⁶Then he said, "I am the God of your father,^a the God of Abraham, the God of Isaac and the God of Jacob." At this, Moses hid his face, because he was afraid to look at God.

⁷The LORD said, "I have indeed seen the misery of my people in Egypt. I have heard them crying out because of their slave drivers, and I am concerned about their suffering. ⁸So I have come down to rescue them from the hand of the Egyptians and to bring them up out of that land into a good and spacious land, a land flowing with milk and honey — the home of the Canaanites, Hittites, Amorites, Perizzites, Hivites and Jebusites. ⁹And now the cry of the Israelites has reached me, and I have seen the way the Egyptians are oppressing them. ¹⁰So now, go. I am sending you to Pharaoh to bring my people the Israelites out of Egypt."

¹¹But Moses said to God, "Who am I that I should go to Pharaoh and bring the Israelites out of Egypt?"

¹²And God said, "I will be with you. And this will be the sign to you that it is I who have sent you: When you have brought the people out of Egypt, you^b will worship God on this mountain."

¹³Moses said to God, "Suppose I go to the Israelites and say to them, 'The God of your fathers has sent me to you,' and they ask me, 'What is his name?' Then what shall I tell them?"

¹⁴God said to Moses, "I AM WHO I AM.^c This is what you are to say to the Israelites: 'I AM has sent me to you.'"

¹⁵God also said to Moses, "Say to the Israelites, 'The LORD,^d the God of your fathers — the God of Abraham, the God of Isaac and the God of Jacob — has sent me to you.'

"This is my name forever,
    the name you shall call me
    from generation to generation.

¹⁶"Go, assemble the elders of Israel and say to them, 'The LORD, the God of your fathers — the God of Abraham, Isaac and Jacob — appeared to me and said: I have watched over you and have seen what has been done to you in Egypt. ¹⁷And I have promised to bring you up out of your misery in Egypt into the land of the Canaanites, Hittites, Amorites, Perizzites, Hivites and Jebusites — a land flowing with milk and honey.'

---

^a 6 Masoretic Text; Samaritan Pentateuch (see Acts 7:32) *fathers*   ^b 12 The Hebrew is plural.   ^c 14 Or *I WILL BE WHAT I WILL BE*   ^d 15 The Hebrew for LORD sounds like and may be related to the Hebrew for *I AM* in verse 14.

When God Chooses a Leader

Exodus 2:11—4:20

Moses provides a wonderful case study on how God calls a leader out of a crowd to perform an assignment.

1. God gives the leader an emotional investment in the work.
Moses "bought into" the idea of freeing the Hebrews from bondage even before God called him to the task.

2. God affirms the leader through others.
When Moses told Jethro about his encounter at the burning bush, his father-in-law affirmed him.

3. God gives the leader mentors.
Moses asked for and received help from Jethro, Aaron and others.

4. God builds on the leader's strengths, experiences and background.
God used everything in Moses' background to help him fulfill his calling: the fine education he received in Egypt; his knowledge of Pharaoh; his understanding of Egypt; and his time in the wilderness.

5. God often refines the leader's character in obscurity.
Moses received a 40-year "seminary education" in the desert.

6. God instills in the leader the value of hard work.
Moses may not have worked much in the Egyptian palace, but he learned its worth in the desert!

7. God sustains that leader with a powerful vision.
Moses caught the vision of the promised land long before the Hebrew slaves did.

8. God brings others alongside the leader to compensate for their weaknesses.
Moses enjoyed the help of Aaron as spokesman, Joshua as general, and Hur as battle supporter.

---

¹⁸"The elders of Israel will listen to you. Then you and the elders are to go to the king of Egypt and say to him, 'The LORD, the God of the Hebrews, has met with us. Let us take a three-day journey into the wilderness to offer sacrifices to the LORD our God.' ¹⁹But I know that the king of Egypt will not let you go unless a mighty hand compels him. ²⁰So I will stretch out my hand and strike the Egyptians with all the wonders that I will perform among them. After that, he will let you go.

²¹"And I will make the Egyptians favorably disposed toward this people, so that when you leave you will not go empty-handed. ²²Every woman is to ask her neighbor and any woman living in her house for articles of silver and gold and for clothing, which you will put on your sons and daughters. And so you will plunder the Egyptians."

Signs for Moses

4 Moses answered, "What if they do not believe me or listen to me and say, 'The LORD did not appear to you'?"

²Then the LORD said to him, "What is that in your hand?"

"A staff," he replied.

³The LORD said, "Throw it on the ground."

Moses threw it on the ground and it became a snake, and he ran from it. ⁴Then the LORD said to him, "Reach out your hand and take it by the tail." So Moses reached out and took hold of the snake and it turned back into a staff in his hand. ⁵"This," said the LORD, "is so that they may believe that the LORD, the God of their fathers—the God of Abraham, the God of Isaac and the God of Jacob—has appeared to you."

⁶Then the LORD said, "Put your hand inside your cloak." So Moses put his hand into his cloak, and when he took it out, the skin was leprous[a]—it had become as white as snow.

⁷"Now put it back into your cloak," he said. So Moses put his hand back into his cloak, and when he took it out, it was restored, like the rest of his flesh.

---

[a] 6 The Hebrew word for *leprous* was used for various diseases affecting the skin.

[8]Then the LORD said, "If they do not believe you or pay attention to the first sign, they may believe the second. [9]But if they do not believe these two signs or listen to you, take some water from the Nile and pour it on the dry ground. The water you take from the river will become blood on the ground."

[10]Moses said to the LORD, "Pardon your servant, Lord. I have never been eloquent, neither in the past nor since you have spoken to your servant. I am slow of speech and tongue."

[11]The LORD said to him, "Who gave human beings their mouths? Who makes them deaf or mute? Who gives them sight or makes them blind? Is it not I, the LORD? [12]Now go; I will help you speak and will teach you what to say."

[13]But Moses said, "Pardon your servant, Lord. Please send someone else."

[14]Then the LORD's anger burned against Moses and he said, "What about your brother, Aaron the Levite? I know he can speak well. He is already on his way to meet you, and he will be glad to see you. [15]You shall speak to him and put words in his mouth; I will help both of you speak and will teach you what to do. [16]He will speak to the people for you, and it will be as if he were your mouth and as if you were God to him.

[17]But take this staff in your hand so you can perform the signs with it."

Moses Returns to Egypt

[18]Then Moses went back to Jethro his father-in-law and said to him, "Let me return to my own people in Egypt to see if any of them are still alive."

Jethro said, "Go, and I wish you well."

[19]Now the LORD had said to Moses in Midian, "Go back to Egypt, for all those who wanted to kill you are dead." [20]So Moses took his wife and sons, put them on a donkey and started back to Egypt. And he took the staff of God in his hand.

[21]The LORD said to Moses, "When you return to Egypt, see that you perform before Pharaoh all the wonders I have given you the power to do. But I will harden his heart so that he will not let the people go. [22]Then say to Pharaoh, 'This is what the LORD says: Israel is my firstborn son, [23]and I told you, "Let my son go, so he may worship me." But you refused to let him go; so I will kill your firstborn son.'"

[24]At a lodging place on the way, the LORD met Moses[a] and was about to kill him. [25]But

[a] 24 Hebrew him

Moses' Life Mission and His Five Big Excuses

Exodus 3:11—4:14

Most of us can list excuses why we don't lead effectively, just as Moses did. When God called him, he instantly thought of five reasons why he couldn't lead.

Excuse One: Who Am I? (3:11). Moses struggled with his identity. He just didn't feel qualified; he thought God had picked the wrong leader.

God's response: It doesn't matter who you are. I am with you (3:12).

Excuse Two: Who Are You? (3:13). Moses felt a lack of intimacy. He didn't know God well enough to describe him to the people and lacked convictions concerning his relationship with God.

God's response: I AM WHO I AM. I AM ever present. I AM everything you need (3:14).

Excuse Three: What if they don't listen? (4:1). Moses felt intimidated. He worried about the people's reaction to him.

God's response: When I'm finished, they'll listen (4:2–9).

Excuse Four: I've never been a good speaker (4:10). Moses fretted about his inadequacies. Who would listen to him if he couldn't even speak well?

God's response: Guess who made your mouth? (4:11–12).

Excuse Five: I know you can find someone else (4:13). Moses felt inferior. He compared himself to others—even his brother—and decided that he came up short.

God's response: OK, I will let Aaron go with you . . . but I'm still calling you to go (4:14).

MOSES AND THE LAW OF SACRIFICE
A Leader Must Give Up to Go Up

Exodus 3:1—4:13

MANY LEADERS want to climb the corporate ladder, hoping that freedom and power wait at the top. They don't realize that leadership really requires sacrifice.

Leaders who want to rise must do more than take an occasional cut in pay; they have to give up their rights. That's true of every leader regardless of profession. Talk to any leader, and you will find he has made repeated sacrifices. The higher that leader has climbed, the greater the sacrifices he usually has made. Effective leaders sacrifice much that is good in order to dedicate themselves to what is best.

Leadership demands constant sacrifice. It is an ongoing process, not a onetime payment. The circumstances may change from person to person, but the principle doesn't: Leadership means sacrifice.

■　■　■　■　■

What price are you willing to pay to become a more effective leader? Many leaders keep so busy pursuing their vision and rallying their people that they give it little thought. But leadership always requires sacrifice; no one achieves success without it.

How was Moses able to give up so much and make such great sacrifices without growing bitter or resentful toward God? And what made him willing to return to Egypt as God's servant after he had enjoyed the best the country had to offer? A quick look at Moses' life shows how God molded him into an effective leader.

1. Moses was alone with God.

Had Moses stayed in Egypt, would he have listened when God called him? Who knows? But Moses' exile in Midian gave him 40 years of reflection time. When God finally appeared to him in the burning bush, Moses had grown quiet enough to hear God's voice.

Leaders in our day take too little time to get alone with God. Most seem continually on the go and rarely quiet themselves. If that description fits you, change your habits and set aside some time to be alone with God. Don't force God to send you to the desert to get your attention.

2. Moses was honest with God.

By the time Moses met God at the burning bush, no trace remained of the cockiness characteristic of his life in Egypt. He knew his weakness. When God told Moses that he would bring the people out of Egypt, the chastened man replied, "Who am I that I should go to Pharaoh and bring the Israelites out of Egypt?" (Ex 3:11). Only as an older man, humble before God, could Moses be of any use to God.

The Lord can use you, too, if you will look at yourself honestly, admit your weaknesses, and humble yourself before God.

3. Moses was hungry for God.

What does it take to make someone really hungry for God? It's different for each of us. Some desire to know God even from childhood. A personal tragedy may realign the priorities of others. And some never turn to God. For Moses, it took four decades in the wilderness.

Could Moses have given up all hope of doing something worthwhile with his life before God finally spoke to him? Probably so. A person can't be staunchly self-reliant and hungry for God at the same time.

4. Moses was broken by God.

God did not force himself or his will on Moses. God waited for Moses to willingly come to him: "When the LORD saw that he had gone over to look, God called to him from within the bush, 'Moses! Moses!'" (Ex 3:4). Once Moses had turned to God, he could be broken.

Brokenness involves two things: removing inappropriate pride and self-reliance and building healthy God-reliance. God tamed Moses' self-reliance and pride in the desert, but to create trust he had to break the man's fears. Moses dealt with different kinds of fear in his encounter with God:

■ Fears concerning himself. Moses doubted his own value (Ex 3:11). God responded by assuring Moses of his purpose.
■ Fears concerning God. Moses feared who God might be. He wanted to know his name and character (Ex 3:13). God responded by overwhelming Moses with his presence.

■ Fears concerning others. Moses then worried about how God's people would respond (Ex 4:1)—hadn't they already rejected him? God responded by demonstrating his power and commitment.
■ Fears concerning his ability. Moses doubted himself—both his speech (Ex 4:10) and ability (4:13). God responded by providing him with a partner, his brother, Aaron.

With his willfulness broken, his fears overcome, and his purpose reaffirmed, Moses finally placed himself in the hands of God.

Life is filled with trade-offs—but you can trade up only if you have something to sacrifice. Moses had to sacrifice his status and his material possessions to get prepared for his life purpose. And then to fulfill it, again he had to sacrifice. The second time he relinquished the security and safety of obscurity in the desert to return to his boyhood home.

If you desire to lead—if you hope to find and fulfill the purpose for which God created you—then you must have something to give. Keep growing and building your personal assets and hold lightly the things God gives you. And remember: You may need to sacrifice them at any time to answer his call.

Major Barriers to Successful Planning

Exodus 4:21

When Moses finally agreed to fulfill his divine assignment, he heard some unsettling news: God would harden Pharaoh's heart. The plan would work, but not right away.

Good leaders develop plans, but they also expect to make adjustments along the way. Rarely does any plan succeed without a bump or a glitch.

Zipporah took a flint knife, cut off her son's foreskin and touched Moses' feet with it.*a* "Surely you are a bridegroom of blood to me," she said. 26So the LORD let him alone. (At that time she said "bridegroom of blood," referring to circumcision.)

27The LORD said to Aaron, "Go into the wilderness to meet Moses." So he met Moses at the mountain of God and kissed him. 28Then Moses told Aaron everything the LORD had sent him to say, and also about all the signs he had commanded him to perform.

29Moses and Aaron brought together all the elders of the Israelites, 30and Aaron told them everything the LORD had said to Moses. He also performed the signs before the people, 31and they believed. And when they heard that the LORD was concerned about them and had seen their misery, they bowed down and worshiped.

Bricks Without Straw

5 Afterward Moses and Aaron went to Pharaoh and said, "This is what the LORD, the God of Israel, says: 'Let my people go, so that they may hold a festival to me in the wilderness.'"

2Pharaoh said, "Who is the LORD, that I should obey him and let Israel go? I do not know the LORD and I will not let Israel go." 3Then they said, "The God of the Hebrews has met with us. Now let us take a three-day journey into the wilderness to offer sacrifices to the LORD our God, or he may strike us with plagues or with the sword."

4But the king of Egypt said, "Moses and Aaron, why are you taking the people away from their labor? Get back to your work!" 5Then Pharaoh said, "Look, the people of the land are now numerous, and you are stopping them from working."

6That same day Pharaoh gave this order to the slave drivers and overseers in charge of the people: 7"You are no longer to supply the people with straw for making bricks; let them go and gather their own straw. 8But require them to make the same number of bricks as before; don't reduce the quota. They are lazy; that is why they are crying out, 'Let us go and sacrifice to our God.' 9Make the work harder for the people so that they keep working and pay no attention to lies."

10Then the slave drivers and the overseers went out and said to the people, "This is what Pharaoh says: 'I will not give you any more straw. 11Go and get your own straw wherever you can find it, but your work will not be reduced at all.'" 12So the people scattered all over Egypt to gather stubble to use for straw. 13The slave drivers kept pressing them, saying, "Complete the work required of you for each day, just as when you had straw." 14And Pharaoh's slave drivers beat the Israelite overseers they had appointed, demanding, "Why haven't you met your quota of bricks yesterday or today, as before?"

---

a 25 The meaning of the Hebrew for this clause is uncertain.

The Law of Navigation: Plan Ahead

Exodus 5:1

No question about it, Moses had a major challenge on his hands. Not only did he have to convince everyone—including Pharaoh—to let him lead the Hebrew slaves out of Egypt, but he had to plan the whole process. To mobilize his countrymen he first had to organize them. That required shrewd planning.

For more than 25 years the following acronym has helped leaders to think through their plans whenever a major challenge or opportunity approaches:

P—Predetermine your course of action.
L—Lay out your goals.
A—Adjust your priorities.
N—Notify key personnel.

A—Allow time for acceptance.
H—Head into action.
E—Expect problems.
A—Always point to your successes.
D—Daily review your progress.

¹⁵Then the Israelite overseers went and appealed to Pharaoh: "Why have you treated your servants this way? ¹⁶Your servants are given no straw, yet we are told, 'Make bricks!' Your servants are being beaten, but the fault is with your own people."

¹⁷Pharaoh said, "Lazy, that's what you are — lazy! That is why you keep saying, 'Let us go and sacrifice to the LORD.' ¹⁸Now get to work. You will not be given any straw, yet you must produce your full quota of bricks."

¹⁹The Israelite overseers realized they were in trouble when they were told, "You are not to reduce the number of bricks required of you for each day." ²⁰When they left Pharaoh, they found Moses and Aaron waiting to meet them, ²¹and they said, "May the LORD look on you and judge you! You have made us obnoxious to Pharaoh and his officials and have put a sword in their hand to kill us."

God Promises Deliverance

²²Moses returned to the LORD and said, "Why, Lord, why have you brought trouble on this people? Is this why you sent me? ²³Ever since I went to Pharaoh to speak in your name, he has brought trouble on this people, and you have not rescued your people at all."

6 Then the LORD said to Moses, "Now you will see what I will do to Pharaoh: Because of my mighty hand he will let them go; because of my mighty hand he will drive them out of his country."

²God also said to Moses, "I am the LORD. ³I appeared to Abraham, to Isaac and to Jacob as God Almighty,^a but by my name the LORD^b I did not make myself fully known to them. ⁴I also established my covenant with them to give them the land of Canaan, where they resided as foreigners. ⁵Moreover, I have heard the groaning of the Israelites, whom the Egyptians are enslaving, and I have remembered my covenant.

⁶"Therefore, say to the Israelites: 'I am the LORD, and I will bring you out from under the yoke of the Egyptians. I will free you from being slaves to them, and I will redeem you with an outstretched arm and with mighty acts of judgment. ⁷I will take you as my own people, and I

---

^a 3 Hebrew *El-Shaddai*   ^b 3 See note at 3:15.

The Leader's Motivation and Personal Vision

Exodus 6:2–3

God knew that Moses needed to be motivated if he were to pull off the task given to him. Exodus 6 recounts how God rekindled his vision of freeing the people from slavery. God revealed himself in a new way, telling Moses his personal name (vv. 2–3), the Hebrew word for which sounds very similar to the Hebrew for I AM. He never did that with Abraham, Isaac, or Jacob. God motivated Moses through a very personal vision.

Leaders can indeed learn from each other, but when it comes to fulfilling a vision, we all need a personal encounter with God and a personal vision that matches who we are. Leaders need a vision that is ...

1. *Personal* to who they are (it is owned by the leader).

2. *Practical* for when they live (it meets a relevant need).

3. *Possible* for what they have (it matches their gifts).

4. *Parallel* to who they are (it complements their passion and personality).

5. *Portable* for where they go (it can move with them).

6. *Powerful* for how they live (it stretches them to accomplish more than they could on their own).

7. *Profitable* for what they do (it gets results).

8. *Pleasurable* for who they are (it brings fulfillment and satisfaction).

9. *Purposeful* for why they live (it fulfills their God-given mission).

10. *Providential* for where they are heading (it provides a God-sized destiny).

will be your God. Then you will know that I am the LORD your God, who brought you out from under the yoke of the Egyptians. ⁸And I will bring you to the land I swore with uplifted hand to give to Abraham, to Isaac and to Jacob. I will give it to you as a possession. I am the LORD.'"

⁹Moses reported this to the Israelites, but they did not listen to him because of their discouragement and harsh labor.

¹⁰Then the LORD said to Moses, ¹¹"Go, tell Pharaoh king of Egypt to let the Israelites go out of his country."

¹²But Moses said to the LORD, "If the Israelites will not listen to me, why would Pharaoh listen to me, since I speak with faltering lips*a*?"

Family Record of Moses and Aaron

¹³Now the LORD spoke to Moses and Aaron about the Israelites and Pharaoh king of Egypt, and he commanded them to bring the Israelites out of Egypt.

¹⁴These were the heads of their families*b*:

The sons of Reuben the firstborn son of Israel were Hanok and Pallu, Hezron and Karmi. These were the clans of Reuben.

¹⁵The sons of Simeon were Jemuel, Jamin, Ohad, Jakin, Zohar and Shaul the son of a Canaanite woman. These were the clans of Simeon.

¹⁶These were the names of the sons of Levi according to their records: Gershon, Kohath and Merari. Levi lived 137 years.

¹⁷The sons of Gershon, by clans, were Libni and Shimei.

¹⁸The sons of Kohath were Amram, Izhar, Hebron and Uzziel. Kohath lived 133 years.

¹⁹The sons of Merari were Mahli and Mushi.

These were the clans of Levi according to their records.

²⁰Amram married his father's sister Jochebed, who bore him Aaron and Moses. Amram lived 137 years.

²¹The sons of Izhar were Korah, Nepheg and Zikri.

²²The sons of Uzziel were Mishael, Elzaphan and Sithri.

²³Aaron married Elisheba, daughter of Amminadab and sister of Nahshon, and she bore him Nadab and Abihu, Eleazar and Ithamar.

²⁴The sons of Korah were Assir, Elkanah and Abiasaph. These were the Korahite clans.

²⁵Eleazar son of Aaron married one of the daughters of Putiel, and she bore him Phinehas.

These were the heads of the Levite families, clan by clan.

²⁶It was this Aaron and Moses to whom the LORD said, "Bring the Israelites out of Egypt by their divisions." ²⁷They were the ones who spoke to Pharaoh king of Egypt about bringing the Israelites out of Egypt—this same Moses and Aaron.

Aaron to Speak for Moses

²⁸Now when the LORD spoke to Moses in Egypt, ²⁹he said to him, "I am the LORD. Tell Pharaoh king of Egypt everything I tell you."

³⁰But Moses said to the LORD, "Since I speak with faltering lips, why would Pharaoh listen to me?"

7 Then the LORD said to Moses, "See, I have made you like God to Pharaoh, and your brother Aaron will be your prophet. ²You are to say everything I command you, and your brother Aaron is to tell Pharaoh to let the Israelites go out of his country. ³But I will harden Pharaoh's heart, and though I multiply my signs and wonders in Egypt, ⁴he will not listen to you. Then I will lay my hand on Egypt and with mighty acts of judgment I will bring out my divisions, my people the Israelites. ⁵And the Egyptians will know that I am the LORD when I stretch out my hand against Egypt and bring the Israelites out of it."

⁶Moses and Aaron did just as the LORD commanded them. ⁷Moses was eighty years old and Aaron eighty-three when they spoke to Pharaoh.

Aaron's Staff Becomes a Snake

⁸The LORD said to Moses and Aaron, ⁹"When Pharaoh says to you, 'Perform a miracle,' then say to Aaron, 'Take your staff and throw it down before Pharaoh,' and it will become a snake."

¹⁰So Moses and Aaron went to Pharaoh and did just as the LORD commanded. Aaron threw his staff down in front of Pharaoh and his officials, and it became a snake. ¹¹Pharaoh then summoned wise men and sorcerers, and the Egyptian magicians also did the same things by their secret arts: ¹²Each one threw down his staff and it became a snake. But Aaron's staff swal-

---

a 12 Hebrew *I am uncircumcised of lips*; also in verse 30
b 14 The Hebrew for *families* here and in verse 25 refers to units larger than clans.

lowed up their staffs. ¹³Yet Pharaoh's heart became hard and he would not listen to them, just as the LORD had said.

The Plague of Blood

¹⁴Then the LORD said to Moses, "Pharaoh's heart is unyielding; he refuses to let the people go. ¹⁵Go to Pharaoh in the morning as he goes out to the river. Confront him on the bank of the Nile, and take in your hand the staff that was changed into a snake. ¹⁶Then say to him, 'The LORD, the God of the Hebrews, has sent me to say to you: Let my people go, so that they may worship me in the wilderness. But until now you have not listened. ¹⁷This is what the LORD says: By this you will know that I am the LORD: With the staff that is in my hand I will strike the water of the Nile, and it will be changed into blood. ¹⁸The fish in the Nile will die, and the river will stink; the Egyptians will not be able to drink its water.'"

¹⁹The LORD said to Moses, "Tell Aaron, 'Take your staff and stretch out your hand over the waters of Egypt—over the streams and canals,

over the ponds and all the reservoirs—and they will turn to blood.' Blood will be everywhere in Egypt, even in vessels^a of wood and stone."

²⁰Moses and Aaron did just as the LORD had commanded. He raised his staff in the presence of Pharaoh and his officials and struck the water of the Nile, and all the water was changed into blood. ²¹The fish in the Nile died, and the river smelled so bad that the Egyptians could not drink its water. Blood was everywhere in Egypt.

²²But the Egyptian magicians did the same things by their secret arts, and Pharaoh's heart became hard; he would not listen to Moses and Aaron, just as the LORD had said. ²³Instead, he turned and went into his palace, and did not take even this to heart. ²⁴And all the Egyptians dug along the Nile to get drinking water, because they could not drink the water of the river.

The Plague of Frogs

²⁵Seven days passed after the LORD struck the Nile. ¹Then the LORD said to Moses, "Go to Pharaoh and say to him, 'This is what the LORD says: Let my people go, so that they may worship me. ²If you refuse to let them go, I will send a plague of frogs on your whole country. ³The Nile will teem with frogs. They will come up into your palace and your bedroom and onto your bed, into the houses of your officials and on your people, and into your ovens and kneading troughs. ⁴The frogs will come up on you and your people and all your officials.'"

⁵Then the LORD said to Moses, "Tell Aaron, 'Stretch out your hand with your staff over the streams and canals and ponds, and make frogs come up on the land of Egypt.'"

⁶So Aaron stretched out his hand over the waters of Egypt, and the frogs came up and covered the land. ⁷But the magicians did the same things by their secret arts; they also made frogs come up on the land of Egypt.

⁸Pharaoh summoned Moses and Aaron and said, "Pray to the LORD to take the frogs away from me and my people, and I will let your people go to offer sacrifices to the LORD."

⁹Moses said to Pharaoh, "I leave to you the honor of setting the time for me to pray for you and your officials and your people that you and your houses may be rid of the frogs, except for those that remain in the Nile."

¹⁰"Tomorrow," Pharaoh said.

Moses replied, "It will be as you say, so that

The Law of the Inner Circle: Moses Needed Aaron

Exodus 6:26—7:20

Who wouldn't tremble at receiving a call like the one given to Moses? He quaked at the daunting task before him, and so would we. Such a challenge would require every ounce of courage we could muster.

From the very beginning, Moses' feelings of inadequacy prompted him to build an "inner circle" of close supporters. His brother, Aaron, quickly became a critical member of his team, and over time Moses assembled a unit that both shared his vision and complemented his weaknesses. Through the years Moses added to this inner circle, each time including individuals who possessed different gifts but the same vision as he.

How about you? Who sits in your inner circle? Do they share your vision? Do they have complementary gifts, useful where you need them most—or does that idea threaten you? Find yourself some Aarons, Jethros, and Joshuas, or you won't be able to accomplish all that God has for you.

---

^{a} 19 Or even on their idols ^{b} In Hebrew texts 8:1-4 is numbered 7:26-29, and 8:5-32 is numbered 8:1-28.

you may know there is no one like the LORD our God. [11] The frogs will leave you and your houses, your officials and your people; they will remain only in the Nile."

[12] After Moses and Aaron left Pharaoh, Moses cried out to the LORD about the frogs he had brought on Pharaoh. [13] And the LORD did what Moses asked. The frogs died in the houses, in the courtyards and in the fields. [14] They were piled into heaps, and the land reeked of them. [15] But when Pharaoh saw that there was relief, he hardened his heart and would not listen to Moses and Aaron, just as the LORD had said.

The Plague of Gnats

[16] Then the LORD said to Moses, "Tell Aaron, 'Stretch out your staff and strike the dust of the ground,' and throughout the land of Egypt the dust will become gnats." [17] They did this, and when Aaron stretched out his hand with the staff and struck the dust of the ground, gnats came on people and animals. All the dust throughout the land of Egypt became gnats. [18] But when the magicians tried to produce gnats by their secret arts, they could not.

Since the gnats were on people and animals everywhere, [19] the magicians said to Pharaoh, "This is the finger of God." But Pharaoh's heart was hard and he would not listen, just as the LORD had said.

The Plague of Flies

[20] Then the LORD said to Moses, "Get up early in the morning and confront Pharaoh as he goes to the river and say to him, 'This is what the LORD says: Let my people go, so that they may worship me. [21] If you do not let my people go, I will send swarms of flies on you and your officials, on your people and into your houses. The houses of the Egyptians will be full of flies; even the ground will be covered with them.

[22] "'But on that day I will deal differently with the land of Goshen, where my people live; no swarms of flies will be there, so that you will know that I, the LORD, am in this land. [23] I will make a distinction[a] between my people and your people. This sign will occur tomorrow.'"

[24] And the LORD did this. Dense swarms of flies poured into Pharaoh's palace and into the houses of his officials; throughout Egypt the land was ruined by the flies.

[25] Then Pharaoh summoned Moses and Aaron and said, "Go, sacrifice to your God here in the land."

[26] But Moses said, "That would not be right.

The sacrifices we offer the LORD our God would be detestable to the Egyptians. And if we offer sacrifices that are detestable in their eyes, will they not stone us? [27] We must take a three-day journey into the wilderness to offer sacrifices to the LORD our God, as he commands us."

[28] Pharaoh said, "I will let you go to offer sacrifices to the LORD your God in the wilderness, but you must not go very far. Now pray for me."

[29] Moses answered, "As soon as I leave you, I will pray to the LORD, and tomorrow the flies will leave Pharaoh and his officials and his people. Only let Pharaoh be sure that he does not act deceitfully again by not letting the people go to offer sacrifices to the LORD."

[30] Then Moses left Pharaoh and prayed to the LORD, [31] and the LORD did what Moses asked. The flies left Pharaoh and his officials and his people; not a fly remained. [32] But this time also Pharaoh hardened his heart and would not let the people go.

The Plague on Livestock

9 Then the LORD said to Moses, "Go to Pharaoh and say to him, 'This is what the LORD, the God of the Hebrews, says: "Let my people go, so that they may worship me." [2] If you refuse to let them go and continue to hold them back, [3] the hand of the LORD will bring a terrible plague on your livestock in the field — on your horses, donkeys and camels and on your cattle, sheep and goats. [4] But the LORD will make a distinction between the livestock of Israel and that of Egypt, so that no animal belonging to the Israelites will die.'"

[5] The LORD set a time and said, "Tomorrow the LORD will do this in the land." [6] And the next day the LORD did it: All the livestock of the Egyptians died, but not one animal belonging to the Israelites died. [7] Pharaoh investigated and found that not even one of the animals of the Israelites had died. Yet his heart was unyielding and he would not let the people go.

The Plague of Boils

[8] Then the LORD said to Moses and Aaron, "Take handfuls of soot from a furnace and have Moses toss it into the air in the presence of Pharaoh. [9] It will become fine dust over the whole land of Egypt, and festering boils will break out on people and animals throughout the land."

[10] So they took soot from a furnace and stood before Pharaoh. Moses tossed it into the air, and

---

[a] 23 Septuagint and Vulgate; Hebrew *will put a deliverance*

festering boils broke out on people and animals. [11]The magicians could not stand before Moses because of the boils that were on them and on all the Egyptians. [12]But the LORD hardened Pharaoh's heart and he would not listen to Moses and Aaron, just as the LORD had said to Moses.

The Plague of Hail

[13]Then the LORD said to Moses, "Get up early in the morning, confront Pharaoh and say to him, 'This is what the LORD, the God of the Hebrews, says: Let my people go, so that they may worship me, [14]or this time I will send the full force of my plagues against you and against your officials and your people, so you may know that there is no one like me in all the earth. [15]For by now I could have stretched out my hand and struck you and your people with a plague that would have wiped you off the earth. [16]But I have raised you up[a] for this very purpose, that I might show you my power and that my name might be proclaimed in all the earth. [17]You still set yourself against my people and will not let them go. [18]Therefore, at this time tomorrow I will send the worst hailstorm that has ever fallen on Egypt, from the day it was founded till now. [19]Give an order now to bring your livestock and everything you have in the field to a place of shelter, because the hail will fall on every person and animal that has not been brought in and is still out in the field, and they will die.'"

[20]Those officials of Pharaoh who feared the word of the LORD hurried to bring their slaves and their livestock inside. [21]But those who ignored the word of the LORD left their slaves and livestock in the field.

[22]Then the LORD said to Moses, "Stretch out your hand toward the sky so that hail will fall all over Egypt — on people and animals and on everything growing in the fields of Egypt." [23]When Moses stretched out his staff toward the sky, the LORD sent thunder and hail, and lightning flashed down to the ground. So the LORD rained hail on the land of Egypt; [24]hail fell and lightning flashed back and forth. It was the worst storm in all the land of Egypt since it had become a nation. [25]Throughout Egypt hail struck everything in the fields — both people and animals; it beat down everything growing in the fields and stripped every tree. [26]The only place it did not hail was the land of Goshen, where the Israelites were.

[27]Then Pharaoh summoned Moses and Aaron. "This time I have sinned," he said to them. "The LORD is in the right, and I and my people

---

Moses: The Plagues and the Law of Victory

Exodus 7:2—11:3

How can anyone think that Moses relished confronting Pharaoh with the plagues? While he obeyed God and warned Pharaoh of each coming judgment, he asked God to send them only to accomplish his goal. We see no pride or arrogance in him; he certainly did not summon the plagues to draw attention to himself. Moses simply called down God's judgment until Pharaoh broke and released the Hebrews.

The Law of Victory teaches that leaders find a way for the team to win. In this case, several plagues were required to convince Pharaoh to let God's people go. And how can we describe Moses' attitude during those plagues? What enabled him to win the victory he sought?

1. **He was *patient* (7:2–3).**
2. **He was *consistent* (7:4–7).**
3. **He was *discerning* (8:10–11).**
4. **He was *prayerful* (8:12).**
5. **He was *tenacious* (11:1).**
6. **He was *credible* (11:3).**

---

are in the wrong. [28]Pray to the LORD, for we have had enough thunder and hail. I will let you go; you don't have to stay any longer."

[29]Moses replied, "When I have gone out of the city, I will spread out my hands in prayer to the LORD. The thunder will stop and there will be no more hail, so you may know that the earth is the LORD's. [30]But I know that you and your officials still do not fear the LORD God." [31](The flax and barley were destroyed, since the barley had headed and the flax was in bloom. [32]The wheat and spelt, however, were not destroyed, because they ripen later.)

[33]Then Moses left Pharaoh and went out of the city. He spread out his hands toward the LORD; the thunder and hail stopped, and the rain no longer poured down on the land. [34]When Pharaoh saw that the rain and hail and thunder had stopped, he sinned again: He and his officials hardened their hearts. [35]So Pharaoh's heart was

---

[a] 16 Or *have spared you*

hard and he would not let the Israelites go, just as the LORD had said through Moses.

The Plague of Locusts

10 Then the LORD said to Moses, "Go to Pharaoh, for I have hardened his heart and the hearts of his officials so that I may perform these signs of mine among them ²that you may tell your children and grandchildren how I dealt harshly with the Egyptians and how I performed my signs among them, and that you may know that I am the LORD."

³So Moses and Aaron went to Pharaoh and said to him, "This is what the LORD, the God of the Hebrews, says: 'How long will you refuse to humble yourself before me? Let my people go, so that they may worship me. ⁴If you refuse to let them go, I will bring locusts into your country tomorrow. ⁵They will cover the face of the ground so that it cannot be seen. They will devour what little you have left after the hail, including every tree that is growing in your fields. ⁶They will fill your houses and those of all your officials and all the Egyptians — something neither your parents nor your ancestors have ever seen from the day they settled in this land till now.'" Then Moses turned and left Pharaoh.

⁷Pharaoh's officials said to him, "How long will this man be a snare to us? Let the people go, so that they may worship the LORD their God. Do you not yet realize that Egypt is ruined?"

⁸Then Moses and Aaron were brought back to Pharaoh. "Go, worship the LORD your God," he said. "But tell me who will be going."

⁹Moses answered, "We will go with our young and our old, with our sons and our daughters, and with our flocks and herds, because we are to celebrate a festival to the LORD."

¹⁰Pharaoh said, "The LORD be with you — if I let you go, along with your women and children! Clearly you are bent on evil.ᵃ ¹¹No! Have only the men go and worship the LORD, since that's what you have been asking for." Then Moses and Aaron were driven out of Pharaoh's presence.

¹²And the LORD said to Moses, "Stretch out your hand over Egypt so that locusts swarm over the land and devour everything growing in the fields, everything left by the hail."

¹³So Moses stretched out his staff over Egypt, and the LORD made an east wind blow across the land all that day and all that night. By morning the wind had brought the locusts; ¹⁴they invaded all Egypt and settled down in every area of the country in great numbers. Never before had there been such a plague of locusts, nor will there ever be again. ¹⁵They covered all the ground until it was black. They devoured all that was left after the hail — everything growing in the fields and the fruit on the trees. Nothing green remained on tree or plant in all the land of Egypt.

ᵃ 10 Or Be careful, trouble is in store for you!

PHARAOH

Attitude: My Way or the Highway
Exodus 10:1–29

PROFILE in leadership

D oes the greatness of a nation automatically make its ruler great? Pharaoh seemed to think so. Not only did Pharaoh rule with absolute power; he also displayed absolute arrogance. He thought of himself as a god and demanded that others see him the same way.

How ironic that the wealth of a nation, along with its power, came into Pharaoh's possession through the hand of the Lord's servant, Joseph (Ge 47). But years passed, and when another servant of God approached another man sitting on the throne of Egypt, an ugly confrontation erupted. Pharaoh reveals his arrogant character through his defiant response to Moses' request that he let the people go into the wilderness to worship their God: "Who is the LORD, that I should obey him and let Israel go? I do not know the LORD and I will not let Israel go" (Ex 5:2).

Pharaoh's pride led to arrogance, and his arrogance to rigidity. In time, his heart became stone-cold and hard. He could have written a song, "My Way or the Highway." Of course, the Israelites chose the highway and headed for the promised land, leaving Egypt with their pockets stuffed with Egyptian gold. And Pharaoh's way led his army straight to the bottom of the sea.

¹⁶Pharaoh quickly summoned Moses and Aaron and said, "I have sinned against the LORD your God and against you. ¹⁷Now forgive my sin once more and pray to the LORD your God to take this deadly plague away from me."

¹⁸Moses then left Pharaoh and prayed to the LORD. ¹⁹And the LORD changed the wind to a very strong west wind, which caught up the locusts and carried them into the Red Sea.[a] Not a locust was left anywhere in Egypt. ²⁰But the LORD hardened Pharaoh's heart, and he would not let the Israelites go.

The Plague of Darkness

²¹Then the LORD said to Moses, "Stretch out your hand toward the sky so that darkness spreads over Egypt — darkness that can be felt." ²²So Moses stretched out his hand toward the sky, and total darkness covered all Egypt for three days. ²³No one could see anyone else or move about for three days. Yet all the Israelites had light in the places where they lived.

²⁴Then Pharaoh summoned Moses and said, "Go, worship the LORD. Even your women and children may go with you; only leave your flocks and herds behind."

²⁵But Moses said, "You must allow us to have sacrifices and burnt offerings to present to the LORD our God. ²⁶Our livestock too must go with us; not a hoof is to be left behind. We have to use some of them in worshiping the LORD our God,

and until we get there we will not know what we are to use to worship the LORD."

²⁷But the LORD hardened Pharaoh's heart, and he was not willing to let them go. ²⁸Pharaoh said to Moses, "Get out of my sight! Make sure you do not appear before me again! The day you see my face you will die."

²⁹"Just as you say," Moses replied. "I will never appear before you again."

The Plague on the Firstborn

11 Now the LORD had said to Moses, "I will bring one more plague on Pharaoh and on Egypt. After that, he will let you go from here, and when he does, he will drive you out completely. ²Tell the people that men and women alike are to ask their neighbors for articles of silver and gold." ³(The LORD made the Egyptians favorably disposed toward the people, and Moses himself was highly regarded in Egypt by Pharaoh's officials and by the people.)

⁴So Moses said, "This is what the LORD says: 'About midnight I will go throughout Egypt. ⁵Every firstborn son in Egypt will die, from the firstborn son of Pharaoh, who sits on the throne, to the firstborn son of the female slave, who is at her hand mill, and all the firstborn of the cattle as well. ⁶There will be loud wailing throughout Egypt — worse than there has ever been or ever

---

[a] 19 Or the Sea of Reeds

MOSES

The Unexpected Leader
Exodus 11:3

PROFILE in leadership

What words come to mind when you think of great leaders? It's doubtful that "humble" appears at the top of your list—yet that is the precise word God chose to describe Moses. Numbers 12:3 declares that "Moses was a very humble man, more humble than anyone else on the face of the earth."

Moses had reasons to be humble. He certainly wasn't a natural leader. Nothing in Scripture indicates he attracted or led anyone during the first 80 years of his life. Although he was "educated in all the wisdom of the Egyptians and was powerful in speech and action" (Ac 7:22), we have no record of significant accomplishment during his first 40 years. So far as we know, his first attempt at exerting his influence to help the people resulted in the murder of an Egyptian and his flight from the country. The next 40 years Moses spent in exile in the desert of Midian, a time so uneventful that Scripture sums it up in three verses (Ex 2:21–23).

You don't have to be a "natural" to become a great leader; you simply need a heart for God and a teachable spirit. Most of the great leaders in Scripture were made, not born. Happily for us, God is still making them today. Could you be one?

will be again. [7]But among the Israelites not a dog will bark at any person or animal.' Then you will know that the LORD makes a distinction between Egypt and Israel. [8]All these officials of yours will come to me, bowing down before me and saying, 'Go, you and all the people who follow you!' After that I will leave." Then Moses, hot with anger, left Pharaoh.

[9]The LORD had said to Moses, "Pharaoh will refuse to listen to you — so that my wonders may be multiplied in Egypt." [10]Moses and Aaron performed all these wonders before Pharaoh, but the LORD hardened Pharaoh's heart, and he would not let the Israelites go out of his country.

The Passover and the Festival of Unleavened Bread

12 The LORD said to Moses and Aaron in Egypt, [2]"This month is to be for you the first month, the first month of your year. [3]Tell the whole community of Israel that on the tenth day of this month each man is to take a lamb[a] for his family, one for each household. [4]If any household is too small for a whole lamb, they must share one with their nearest neighbor, having taken into account the number of people there are. You are to determine the amount of lamb needed in accordance with what each person will eat. [5]The animals you choose must be year-old males without defect, and you may take them from the sheep or the goats. [6]Take care of them until the fourteenth day of the month, when all the members of the community of Israel must slaughter them at twilight. [7]Then they are to take some of the blood and put it on the sides and tops of the doorframes of the houses where they eat the lambs. [8]That same night they are to eat the meat roasted over the fire, along with bitter herbs, and bread made without yeast. [9]Do not eat the meat raw or boiled in water, but roast it over a fire — with the head, legs and internal organs. [10]Do not leave any of it till morning; if some is left till morning, you must burn it. [11]This is how you are to eat it: with your cloak tucked into your belt, your sandals on your feet and your staff in your hand. Eat it in haste; it is the LORD's Passover.

[12]"On that same night I will pass through Egypt and strike down every firstborn of both people and animals, and I will bring judgment on all the gods of Egypt. I am the LORD. [13]The blood will be a sign for you on the houses where you are, and when I see the blood, I will pass over you. No destructive plague will touch you when I strike Egypt.

A Leader's Communication: God Instructs His People

Exodus 12:3–23

Without the ability to communicate, a leader travels alone. No one will catch your vision unless you first transfer a picture of it into his or her heart. That's what God did when he clearly explained to the Hebrew families how they could spare the lives of their firstborn sons.

[14]"This is a day you are to commemorate; for the generations to come you shall celebrate it as a festival to the LORD — a lasting ordinance. [15]For seven days you are to eat bread made without yeast. On the first day remove the yeast from your houses, for whoever eats anything with yeast in it from the first day through the seventh must be cut off from Israel. [16]On the first day hold a sacred assembly, and another one on the seventh day. Do no work at all on these days, except to prepare food for everyone to eat; that is all you may do.

[17]"Celebrate the Festival of Unleavened Bread, because it was on this very day that I brought your divisions out of Egypt. Celebrate this day as a lasting ordinance for the generations to come. [18]In the first month you are to eat bread made without yeast, from the evening of the fourteenth day until the evening of the twenty-first day. [19]For seven days no yeast is to be found in your houses. And anyone, whether foreigner or native-born, who eats anything with yeast in it must be cut off from the community of Israel. [20]Eat nothing made with yeast. Wherever you live, you must eat unleavened bread."

[21]Then Moses summoned all the elders of Israel and said to them, "Go at once and select the animals for your families and slaughter the Passover lamb. [22]Take a bunch of hyssop, dip it into the blood in the basin and put some of the blood on the top and on both sides of the doorframe. None of you shall go out of the door of your house until morning. [23]When the LORD goes through the land to strike down the Egyptians, he will see the blood on the top and sides of the doorframe and will pass over that doorway, and he will not permit the destroyer to enter your houses and strike you down.

[24]"Obey these instructions as a lasting ordi-

---

[a] 3 The Hebrew word can mean *lamb* or *kid*; also in verse 4.

nance for you and your descendants. [25]When you enter the land that the LORD will give you as he promised, observe this ceremony. [26]And when your children ask you, 'What does this ceremony mean to you?' [27]then tell them, 'It is the Passover sacrifice to the LORD, who passed over the houses of the Israelites in Egypt and spared our homes when he struck down the Egyptians.'" Then the people bowed down and worshiped. [28]The Israelites did just what the LORD commanded Moses and Aaron.

[29]At midnight the LORD struck down all the firstborn in Egypt, from the firstborn of Pharaoh, who sat on the throne, to the firstborn of the prisoner, who was in the dungeon, and the firstborn of all the livestock as well. [30]Pharaoh and all his officials and all the Egyptians got up during the night, and there was loud wailing in Egypt, for there was not a house without someone dead.

The Exodus

[31]During the night Pharaoh summoned Moses and Aaron and said, "Up! Leave my people, you and the Israelites! Go, worship the LORD as you have requested. [32]Take your flocks and herds, as you have said, and go. And also bless me."

[33]The Egyptians urged the people to hurry and leave the country. "For otherwise," they said, "we will all die!" [34]So the people took their dough before the yeast was added, and carried it on their shoulders in kneading troughs wrapped in clothing. [35]The Israelites did as Moses instructed and asked the Egyptians for articles of silver and gold and for clothing. [36]The LORD had made the Egyptians favorably disposed toward the people, and they gave them what they asked for; so they plundered the Egyptians.

[37]The Israelites journeyed from Rameses to Sukkoth. There were about six hundred thousand men on foot, besides women and children. [38]Many other people went up with them, and also large droves of livestock, both flocks and herds. [39]With the dough the Israelites had brought from Egypt, they baked loaves of unleavened bread. The dough was without yeast because they had been driven out of Egypt and did not have time to prepare food for themselves.

[40]Now the length of time the Israelite people lived in Egypt[a] was 430 years. [41]At the end of the 430 years, to the very day, all the LORD's divisions left Egypt. [42]Because the LORD kept vigil that night to bring them out of Egypt, on this night all the Israelites are to keep vigil to honor the LORD for the generations to come.

Passover Restrictions

[43]The LORD said to Moses and Aaron, "These are the regulations for the Passover meal:

"No foreigner may eat it. [44]Any slave you have bought may eat it after you have circumcised

---

[a] 40 Masoretic Text; Samaritan Pentateuch and Septuagint *Egypt and Canaan*

Moses the 360° Leader

Exodus 12:28

The story of Moses leading the people of Israel out of Egypt is a vivid illustration of a 360° leader. He had a position, growing up in Pharaoh's palace, yet he gave it up to become a shepherd in the wilderness for 40 years. He returned with no title or position, and had to convince Pharaoh to free his entire slave population. And he had to convince the Jews that he was worth following. Moses had no experience or credibility with them. He had to depend on influencing through things other than position.

Moses leaned on other virtues:

1. **His connection with God**—The story and glory of the burning bush.

2. **His abilities and anointing**—God confirmed his words with plagues and miracles.

3. **His sacrifice**—He left his earlier position in order to fulfill a difficult calling.

4. **His wisdom**—He knew what do to and where to go as he gave instructions.

5. **His confidence**—He had convictions about his task.

6. **His humility**—He was considered the most humble leader of his time.

Equipping: God Used Aaron to Equip Moses During the Plagues

Exodus 5:1—12:37

By sending ten plagues on the people of Egypt, God accomplished many objectives at once. Not only did he secure the release of the Hebrews; he also taught the Egyptians lessons about him. Each plague spoke symbolically to the Egyptian people, establishing beyond doubt that the God of Israel was THE God. And through the plagues God also taught Moses lessons on leadership.

Because Moses resisted a return to Egypt when God called him at the burning bush (Ex 3; 4), God allowed his brother, Aaron, to accompany him. God used Aaron to equip Moses during the plagues:

- **The First Five Plagues:** Aaron used God's staff while Moses watched.
- **The Sixth Plague:** Aaron and Moses worked together to summon the plague of boils.
- **The Last Four Plagues:** Moses worked alone as Aaron watched.

From then on, Moses took the lead in everything. How often does God use willing associates to prepare his chosen leaders for success!

him, ⁴⁵but a temporary resident or a hired worker may not eat it.

⁴⁶"It must be eaten inside the house; take none of the meat outside the house. Do not break any of the bones. ⁴⁷The whole community of Israel must celebrate it.

⁴⁸"A foreigner residing among you who wants to celebrate the LORD's Passover must have all the males in his household circumcised; then he may take part like one born in the land. No uncircumcised male may eat it. ⁴⁹The same law applies both to the native-born and to the foreigner residing among you."

⁵⁰All the Israelites did just what the LORD had commanded Moses and Aaron. ⁵¹And on that very day the LORD brought the Israelites out of Egypt by their divisions.

Consecration of the Firstborn

13 The LORD said to Moses, ²"Consecrate to me every firstborn male. The first offspring of every womb among the Israelites belongs to me, whether human or animal."

³Then Moses said to the people, "Commemorate this day, the day you came out of Egypt, out of the land of slavery, because the LORD brought you out of it with a mighty hand. Eat nothing containing yeast. ⁴Today, in the month of Aviv, you are leaving. ⁵When the LORD brings you into the land of the Canaanites, Hittites, Amorites, Hivites and Jebusites—the land he swore to your ancestors to give you, a land flowing with milk and honey—you are to observe this ceremony in this month: ⁶For seven days eat bread made without yeast and on the seventh day hold a festival to the LORD. ⁷Eat unleavened bread during those seven days; nothing with yeast in it is to be seen among you, nor shall any yeast be seen anywhere within your borders. ⁸On that day tell your son, 'I do this because of what the LORD did for me when I came out of Egypt.' ⁹This observance will be for you like a sign on your hand and a reminder on your forehead that this law of the LORD is to be on your lips. For the LORD brought you out of Egypt with his mighty hand. ¹⁰You must keep this ordinance at the appointed time year after year.

¹¹"After the LORD brings you into the land of the Canaanites and gives it to you, as he promised on oath to you and your ancestors, ¹²you are to give over to the LORD the first offspring of every womb. All the firstborn males of your livestock belong to the LORD. ¹³Redeem with a lamb every firstborn donkey, but if you do not redeem it, break its neck. Redeem every firstborn among your sons.

¹⁴"In days to come, when your son asks you, 'What does this mean?' say to him, 'With a mighty hand the LORD brought us out of Egypt, out of the land of slavery. ¹⁵When Pharaoh stubbornly refused to let us go, the LORD killed the firstborn of both people and animals in Egypt. This is why I sacrifice to the LORD the first male offspring of every womb and redeem each of my firstborn sons.' ¹⁶And it will be like a sign on your hand and a symbol on your forehead that the LORD brought us out of Egypt with his mighty hand."

Crossing the Sea

¹⁷When Pharaoh let the people go, God did not lead them on the road through the Philistine country, though that was shorter. For God said, "If they face war, they might change their minds and return to Egypt." ¹⁸So God led the people around by the desert road toward the Red Sea.^a The Israelites went up out of Egypt ready for battle.

¹⁹Moses took the bones of Joseph with him because Joseph had made the Israelites swear an oath. He had said, "God will surely come to your aid, and then you must carry my bones up with you from this place."^b

²⁰After leaving Sukkoth they camped at Etham on the edge of the desert. ²¹By day the LORD went ahead of them in a pillar of cloud to guide them on their way and by night in a pillar of fire to give them light, so that they could travel by day or night. ²²Neither the pillar of cloud by day nor the pillar of fire by night left its place in front of the people.

14 Then the LORD said to Moses, ²"Tell the Israelites to turn back and encamp near Pi Hahiroth, between Migdol and the sea. They are to encamp by the sea, directly opposite Baal Zephon. ³Pharaoh will think, 'The Israelites are wandering around the land in confusion, hemmed in by the desert.' ⁴And I will harden Pharaoh's heart, and he will pursue them. But I will gain glory for myself through Pharaoh and all his army, and the Egyptians will know that I am the LORD." So the Israelites did this.

⁵When the king of Egypt was told that the people had fled, Pharaoh and his officials changed their minds about them and said, "What have we done? We have let the Israelites go and have lost their services!" ⁶So he had his chariot made ready and took his army with him. ⁷He took six hundred of the best chariots, along with all the other chariots of Egypt, with officers over all of them. ⁸The LORD hardened the heart of Pharaoh king of Egypt, so that he pursued the Israelites, who were marching out boldly. ⁹The Egyptians — all Pharaoh's horses and chariots, horsemen^c and troops — pursued the Israelites and overtook them as they camped by the sea near Pi Hahiroth, opposite Baal Zephon.

¹⁰As Pharaoh approached, the Israelites looked up, and there were the Egyptians, marching after them. They were terrified and cried out to the LORD. ¹¹They said to Moses, "Was it because there were no graves in Egypt that you brought us to the desert to die? What have you done to us by bringing us out of Egypt? ¹²Didn't we say to you in Egypt, 'Leave us alone; let us serve the Egyptians'? It would have been better for us to serve the Egyptians than to die in the desert!"

¹³Moses answered the people, "Do not be afraid. Stand firm and you will see the deliverance the LORD will bring you today. The Egyptians you see today you will never see again. ¹⁴The LORD will fight for you; you need only to be still."

¹⁵Then the LORD said to Moses, "Why are you crying out to me? Tell the Israelites to move on. ¹⁶Raise your staff and stretch out your hand over the sea to divide the water so that the Israelites can go through the sea on dry ground. ¹⁷I will harden the hearts of the Egyptians so that they will go in after them. And I will gain glory through Pharaoh and all his army, through his chariots and his horsemen. ¹⁸The Egyptians will know that I am the LORD when I gain glory through Pharaoh, his chariots and his horsemen."

¹⁹Then the angel of God, who had been traveling in front of Israel's army, withdrew and went behind them. The pillar of cloud also moved

---

^a 18 Or the Sea of Reeds   ^b 19 See Gen. 50:25.   ^c 9 Or charioteers; also in verses 17, 18, 23, 26 and 28

The Law of the Picture: Tangible Leadership with Cloud and Fire

Exodus 13:21

God's use of cloud and fire taught Israel to expect dynamic divine leadership. He would provide more than a set of rules; when the pillar halted, they were to stop. When it moved, they were to follow. God was using the Law of the Picture, providing leadership that could be seen. In a similar way, leadership today must be both definitive and dynamic. People need models and patterns they can observe and follow.

from in front and stood behind them, [20]coming between the armies of Egypt and Israel. Throughout the night the cloud brought darkness to the one side and light to the other side; so neither went near the other all night long.

[21]Then Moses stretched out his hand over the sea, and all that night the LORD drove the sea back with a strong east wind and turned it into dry land. The waters were divided, [22]and the Israelites went through the sea on dry ground, with a wall of water on their right and on their left.

[23]The Egyptians pursued them, and all Pharaoh's horses and chariots and horsemen followed them into the sea. [24]During the last watch of the night the LORD looked down from the pillar of fire and cloud at the Egyptian army and threw it into confusion. [25]He jammed[a] the wheels of their chariots so that they had difficulty driving. And the Egyptians said, "Let's get away from the Israelites! The LORD is fighting for them against Egypt."

[26]Then the LORD said to Moses, "Stretch out your hand over the sea so that the waters may flow back over the Egyptians and their chariots and horsemen." [27]Moses stretched out his hand over the sea, and at daybreak the sea went back to its place. The Egyptians were fleeing toward[b] it, and the LORD swept them into the sea. [28]The water flowed back and covered the chariots and horsemen — the entire army of Pharaoh that had followed the Israelites into the sea. Not one of them survived.

[29]But the Israelites went through the sea on dry ground, with a wall of water on their right and on their left. [30]That day the LORD saved Israel from the hands of the Egyptians, and Israel saw the Egyptians lying dead on the shore. [31]And when the Israelites saw the mighty hand of the LORD displayed against the Egyptians, the people feared the LORD and put their trust in him and in Moses his servant.

The Song of Moses and Miriam

15 Then Moses and the Israelites sang this song to the LORD:

"I will sing to the LORD,
     for he is highly exalted.
Both horse and driver
     he has hurled into the sea.

[2]"The LORD is my strength and my
          defense[c];
     he has become my salvation.
He is my God, and I will praise him,
     my father's God, and I will exalt him.

---

[a] 25 See Samaritan Pentateuch, Septuagint and Syriac; Masoretic Text removed   [b] 27 Or from   [c] 2 Or song

---

The Law of Buy-In: Moses Gains Credibility

Exodus 14:1–28

The approach of the Egyptian army terrified the Israelites, and they placed heavy pressure on Moses to handle this crisis. Moses didn't panic, since he had seen the power of God's handiwork. Instead, he exuded both poise and peace, winning for himself great credibility as a leader. Through one incident he became the nation's "go to" leader. Note what gave him credibility:

1. **He projected calm instead of craziness.**
   "Moses answered the people, 'Do not be afraid. Stand firm and you will see the deliverance the LORD will bring you today'" (Ex 14:13).

2. **He projected confidence instead of cowardice.**
   "The Egyptians you see today you will never see again" (Ex 14:13).

3. **He projected clarity instead of confusion.**
   "Then the LORD said to Moses, 'Why are you crying out to to me? Tell the Israelites to move on'" (Ex 14:15).

4. **He projected competence instead of clumsiness.**
   "Then Moses stretched out his hand over the sea, and all that night the LORD drove the sea back with a strong east wind and turned it into dry land. The waters were divided, and the Israelites went through the sea on dry ground, with a wall of water on their right and on their left" (Ex 21:21–22).

³ The Lord is a warrior;
 the Lord is his name.
⁴ Pharaoh's chariots and his army
 he has hurled into the sea.
 The best of Pharaoh's officers
 are drowned in the Red Sea.ᵃ
⁵ The deep waters have covered them;
 they sank to the depths like a stone.
⁶ Your right hand, Lord,
 was majestic in power.
 Your right hand, Lord,
 shattered the enemy.

⁷ "In the greatness of your majesty
 you threw down those who opposed you.
 You unleashed your burning anger;
 it consumed them like stubble.
⁸ By the blast of your nostrils
 the waters piled up.
 The surging waters stood up like a wall;
 the deep waters congealed in the heart of
 the sea.
⁹ The enemy boasted,
 'I will pursue, I will overtake them.
 I will divide the spoils;
 I will gorge myself on them.
 I will draw my sword
 and my hand will destroy them.'
¹⁰ But you blew with your breath,
 and the sea covered them.
 They sank like lead
 in the mighty waters.
¹¹ Who among the gods
 is like you, Lord?
 Who is like you —
 majestic in holiness,
 awesome in glory,
 working wonders?

¹² "You stretch out your right hand,
 and the earth swallows your enemies.
¹³ In your unfailing love you will lead
 the people you have redeemed.
 In your strength you will guide them
 to your holy dwelling.
¹⁴ The nations will hear and tremble;
 anguish will grip the people of Philistia.
¹⁵ The chiefs of Edom will be terrified,
 the leaders of Moab will be seized with
 trembling,
 the peopleᵇ of Canaan will melt away;
¹⁶   terror and dread will fall on them.
 By the power of your arm
 they will be as still as a stone —
 until your people pass by, Lord,
 until the people you boughtᶜ pass by.

¹⁷ You will bring them in and plant them
 on the mountain of your inheritance —
 the place, Lord, you made for your dwelling,
 the sanctuary, Lord, your hands
 established.

¹⁸ "The Lord reigns
 for ever and ever."

¹⁹ When Pharaoh's horses, chariots and horsemenᵈ went into the sea, the Lord brought the waters of the sea back over them, but the Israelites walked through the sea on dry ground. ²⁰ Then Miriam the prophet, Aaron's sister, took a timbrel in her hand, and all the women followed her, with timbrels and dancing. ²¹ Miriam sang to them:

"Sing to the Lord,
 for he is highly exalted.
 Both horse and driver
 he has hurled into the sea."

The Law of Victory: The Celebration!

Exodus 15:1–21

Leaders know the importance of identifying, celebrating, and remembering victories. After escaping Egypt, Moses led the people of Israel in a song of celebration. The Lord drowned the Egyptian army in the Red Sea, ensuring that Israel would never again have to run from Pharaoh. Celebration is often the reward for victory.

The Waters of Marah and Elim

²² Then Moses led Israel from the Red Sea and they went into the Desert of Shur. For three days they traveled in the desert without finding water. ²³ When they came to Marah, they could not drink its water because it was bitter. (That is why the place is called Marah.ᵉ) ²⁴ So the people grumbled against Moses, saying, "What are we to drink?"

²⁵ Then Moses cried out to the Lord, and the Lord showed him a piece of wood. He threw it into the water, and the water became fit to drink.

There the Lord issued a ruling and instruction for them and put them to the test. ²⁶ He said, "If you listen carefully to the Lord your

---

ᵃ 4 Or the Sea of Reeds; also in verse 22   ᵇ 15 Or rulers
ᶜ 16 Or created   ᵈ 19 Or charioteers   ᵉ 23 Marah means bitter.

God and do what is right in his eyes, if you pay attention to his commands and keep all his decrees, I will not bring on you any of the diseases I brought on the Egyptians, for I am the LORD, who heals you."

²⁷Then they came to Elim, where there were twelve springs and seventy palm trees, and they camped there near the water.

Manna and Quail

16 The whole Israelite community set out from Elim and came to the Desert of Sin, which is between Elim and Sinai, on the fifteenth day of the second month after they had come out of Egypt. ²In the desert the whole community grumbled against Moses and Aaron. ³The Israelites said to them, "If only we had died by the LORD's hand in Egypt! There we sat around pots of meat and ate all the food we wanted, but you have brought us out into this desert to starve this entire assembly to death."

⁴Then the LORD said to Moses, "I will rain down bread from heaven for you. The people are to go out each day and gather enough for that day. In this way I will test them and see whether they will follow my instructions. ⁵On the sixth day they are to prepare what they bring in, and that is to be twice as much as they gather on the other days."

⁶So Moses and Aaron said to all the Israelites, "In the evening you will know that it was the LORD who brought you out of Egypt, ⁷and in the morning you will see the glory of the LORD, because he has heard your grumbling against him. Who are we, that you should grumble against us?" ⁸Moses also said, "You will know that it was the LORD when he gives you meat to eat in the evening and all the bread you want in the morning, because he has heard your grumbling against him. Who are we? You are not grumbling against us, but against the LORD."

⁹Then Moses told Aaron, "Say to the entire Israelite community, 'Come before the LORD, for he has heard your grumbling.'"

¹⁰While Aaron was speaking to the whole Israelite community, they looked toward the desert, and there was the glory of the LORD appearing in the cloud.

¹¹The LORD said to Moses, ¹²"I have heard the grumbling of the Israelites. Tell them, 'At twilight you will eat meat, and in the morning you will be filled with bread. Then you will know that I am the LORD your God.'"

¹³That evening quail came and covered the camp, and in the morning there was a layer of dew around the camp. ¹⁴When the dew was gone, thin flakes like frost on the ground appeared on the desert floor. ¹⁵When the Israelites saw it, they said to each other, "What is it?" For they did not know what it was.

Moses said to them, "It is the bread the LORD has given you to eat. ¹⁶This is what the LORD has commanded: 'Everyone is to gather as much as they need. Take an omer^a for each person you have in your tent.'"

¹⁷The Israelites did as they were told; some gathered much, some little. ¹⁸And when they measured it by the omer, the one who gathered much did not have too much, and the one who gathered little did not have too little. Everyone had gathered just as much as they needed.

¹⁹Then Moses said to them, "No one is to keep any of it until morning."

²⁰However, some of them paid no attention to Moses; they kept part of it until morning, but it was full of maggots and began to smell. So Moses was angry with them.

²¹Each morning everyone gathered as much as they needed, and when the sun grew hot, it melted away. ²²On the sixth day, they gathered twice as much — two omers^b for each person — and the leaders of the community came and reported this to Moses. ²³He said to them, "This is what the LORD commanded: 'Tomorrow is to be a day of sabbath rest, a holy sabbath to the LORD. So bake what you want to bake and boil what you want to boil. Save whatever is left and keep it until morning.'"

²⁴So they saved it until morning, as Moses commanded, and it did not stink or get maggots in it. ²⁵"Eat it today," Moses said, "because today is a sabbath to the LORD. You will not find any of it on the ground today. ²⁶Six days you are to gather it, but on the seventh day, the Sabbath, there will not be any."

²⁷Nevertheless, some of the people went out on the seventh day to gather it, but they found none. ²⁸Then the LORD said to Moses, "How long will you^c refuse to keep my commands and my instructions? ²⁹Bear in mind that the LORD has given you the Sabbath; that is why on the sixth day he gives you bread for two days. Everyone is to stay where they are on the seventh day; no one is to go out." ³⁰So the people rested on the seventh day.

³¹The people of Israel called the bread manna.^{d}

---

^{a} 16 That is, possibly about 3 pounds or about 1.4 kilograms; also in verses 18, 32, 33 and 36 ^{b} 22 That is, possibly about 6 pounds or about 2.8 kilograms ^{c} 28 The Hebrew is plural. ^{d} 31 Manna sounds like the Hebrew for What is it? (see verse 15).

It was white like coriander seed and tasted like wafers made with honey. [32]Moses said, "This is what the LORD has commanded: 'Take an omer of manna and keep it for the generations to come, so they can see the bread I gave you to eat in the wilderness when I brought you out of Egypt.'"

[33]So Moses said to Aaron, "Take a jar and put an omer of manna in it. Then place it before the LORD to be kept for the generations to come."

[34]As the LORD commanded Moses, Aaron put the manna with the tablets of the covenant law, so that it might be preserved. [35]The Israelites ate manna forty years, until they came to a land that was settled; they ate manna until they reached the border of Canaan.

[36](An omer is one-tenth of an ephah.)

Water From the Rock

17 The whole Israelite community set out from the Desert of Sin, traveling from place to place as the LORD commanded. They camped at Rephidim, but there was no water for the people to drink. [2]So they quarreled with Moses and said, "Give us water to drink."

Moses replied, "Why do you quarrel with me? Why do you put the LORD to the test?"

[3]But the people were thirsty for water there, and they grumbled against Moses. They said, "Why did you bring us up out of Egypt to make us and our children and livestock die of thirst?"

[4]Then Moses cried out to the LORD, "What am I to do with these people? They are almost ready to stone me."

[5]The LORD answered Moses, "Go out in front of the people. Take with you some of the elders of Israel and take in your hand the staff with which you struck the Nile, and go. [6]I will stand there before you by the rock at Horeb. Strike the rock, and water will come out of it for the people to drink." So Moses did this in the sight of the elders of Israel. [7]And he called the place Massah[a] and Meribah[b] because the Israelites quarreled and because they tested the LORD saying, "Is the LORD among us or not?"

The Amalekites Defeated

[8]The Amalekites came and attacked the Israelites at Rephidim. [9]Moses said to Joshua, "Choose some of our men and go out to fight the Amalekites. Tomorrow I will stand on top of the hill with the staff of God in my hands."

[10]So Joshua fought the Amalekites as Moses had ordered, and Moses, Aaron and Hur went to the top of the hill. [11]As long as Moses held up his hands, the Israelites were winning, but

---

The Rod of God

Exodus 17:3–7

God's people received an important lesson on authority when they learned to trust God for provision. Time and again the Lord provided what they needed, thus demonstrating his right to lead them.

Moses learned to depend on God as the ultimate authority. One of the keys to Moses' greatness is the statement: "Moses cried out to the LORD" (Ex 17:4). Leaders earn their authority; few individuals just give it to someone. God earned the trust of his people and "earned" his authority through several means:

1. **Production:** He made a way for his people to cross the Red Sea safely.

2. **Protection:** He eliminated the Egyptian army in the Red Sea.

3. **Provision:** He provided manna and quail for the people to eat.

4. **Problem Solving:** He produced water from a rock.

---

whenever he lowered his hands, the Amalekites were winning. [12]When Moses' hands grew tired, they took a stone and put it under him and he sat on it. Aaron and Hur held his hands up — one on one side, one on the other — so that his hands remained steady till sunset. [13]So Joshua overcame the Amalekite army with the sword.

[14]Then the LORD said to Moses, "Write this on a scroll as something to be remembered and make sure that Joshua hears it, because I will completely blot out the name of Amalek from under heaven."

[15]Moses built an altar and called it The LORD is my Banner. [16]He said, "Because hands were lifted up against[c] the throne of the LORD,[d] the LORD will be at war against the Amalekites from generation to generation."

Jethro Visits Moses

18 Now Jethro, the priest of Midian and father-in-law of Moses, heard of everything God had done for Moses and for his people

---

[a] 7 Massah means testing.   [b] 7 Meribah means quarreling.
[c] 16 Or to   [d] 16 The meaning of the Hebrew for this clause is uncertain.

The Law of the Inner Circle: Moses Needed Help

Exodus 17:8–13

No leader can thrive without teammates, as the life of Moses illustrates. As Joshua and his troops fought the Amalekites, Moses held God's staff in his hands, assisted by Aaron and Hur, members of his inner circle. No leader should ever take the journey—or the credit—by himself.

Israel, and how the LORD had brought Israel out of Egypt.

²After Moses had sent away his wife Zipporah, his father-in-law Jethro received her ³and her two sons. One son was named Gershom,*a* for Moses said, "I have become a foreigner in a foreign land"; ⁴and the other was named Eliezer,*b* for he said, "My father's God was my helper; he saved me from the sword of Pharaoh."

⁵Jethro, Moses' father-in-law, together with Moses' sons and wife, came to him in the wilderness, where he was camped near the mountain of God. ⁶Jethro had sent word to him, "I, your father-in-law Jethro, am coming to you with your wife and her two sons."

⁷So Moses went out to meet his father-in-law and bowed down and kissed him. They greeted each other and then went into the tent. ⁸Moses told his father-in-law about everything the LORD had done to Pharaoh and the Egyptians for Israel's sake and about all the hardships they had met along the way and how the LORD had saved them.

⁹Jethro was delighted to hear about all the good things the LORD had done for Israel in rescuing them from the hand of the Egyptians. ¹⁰He said, "Praise be to the LORD, who rescued you from the hand of the Egyptians and of Pharaoh, and who rescued the people from the hand of the Egyptians. ¹¹Now I know that the LORD is greater than all other gods, for he did this to those who had treated Israel arrogantly." ¹²Then Jethro, Moses' father-in-law, brought a burnt offering and other sacrifices to God, and Aaron came with all the elders of Israel to eat a meal with Moses' father-in-law in the presence of God.

¹³The next day Moses took his seat to serve as judge for the people, and they stood around him from morning till evening. ¹⁴When his father-in-law saw all that Moses was doing for the people, he said, "What is this you are doing for the people? Why do you alone sit as judge, while all these people stand around you from morning till evening?"

¹⁵Moses answered him, "Because the people come to me to seek God's will. ¹⁶Whenever they have a dispute, it is brought to me, and I decide between the parties and inform them of God's decrees and instructions."

¹⁷Moses' father-in-law replied, "What you are doing is not good. ¹⁸You and these people who come to you will only wear yourselves out. The work is too heavy for you; you cannot handle it alone. ¹⁹Listen now to me and I will give you some advice, and may God be with you. You must be the people's representative before God and bring their disputes to him. ²⁰Teach them his decrees and instructions, and show them the way they are to live and how they are to behave. ²¹But select capable men from all the people — men who fear God, trustworthy men who hate dishonest gain — and appoint them as officials over thousands, hundreds, fifties and tens. ²²Have them serve as judges for the people at all times, but have them bring every difficult case to you; the simple cases they can decide themselves. That will make your load lighter, because they will share it with you. ²³If you do this and God so commands, you will be able to stand the strain, and all these people will go home satisfied."

²⁴Moses listened to his father-in-law and did everything he said. ²⁵He chose capable men from all Israel and made them leaders of the people, officials over thousands, hundreds, fifties and tens. ²⁶They served as judges for the people at all times. The difficult cases they brought to Moses, but the simple ones they decided themselves.

²⁷Then Moses sent his father-in-law on his way, and Jethro returned to his own country.

At Mount Sinai

19 On the first day of the third month after the Israelites left Egypt — on that very day — they came to the Desert of Sinai. ²After they set out from Rephidim, they entered the Desert of Sinai, and Israel camped there in the desert in front of the mountain. ³Then Moses went up to God, and the LORD

---

a 3 *Gershom* sounds like the Hebrew for *a foreigner there.*
b 4 *Eliezer* means *my God is helper.*

The Law of Empowerment: The Day Moses Became a Leader

Exodus 18:19–26

Something revolutionary happened after Jethro confronted Moses over his leadership methods: Moses moved from merely ministering to leading. Instead of doing all the judging himself, he released other leaders to join him and lead according to their gifts.

At this point the government of Israel grew exponentially. Empowerment was happening. Once Jethro had empowered Moses, Moses began to empower other leaders. Notice the changes Moses made in his methods. He changed his way of thinking and his way of working:

1. **He became a man of prayer (v. 19).**

2. **He committed himself to communication (v. 20).**

3. **He laid out the vision (v. 20).**

4. **He developed a plan (v. 20).**

5. **He selected and trained the leaders (v. 21).**

6. **He released them to do the work (v. 22).**

7. **He did only what they could not do (v. 22).**

What happened when Moses changed? God supplied strength for Moses, peace for the people, and empowerment for a host of new leaders (Ex 18:23).

called to him from the mountain and said, "This is what you are to say to the descendants of Jacob and what you are to tell the people of Israel: [4]'You yourselves have seen what I did to Egypt, and how I carried you on eagles' wings and brought you to myself. [5]Now if you obey me fully and keep my covenant, then out of all nations you will be my treasured possession. Although the whole earth is mine, [6]you[a] will be for me a kingdom of priests and a holy nation.' These are the words you are to speak to the Israelites."

[7]So Moses went back and summoned the elders of the people and set before them all the words the LORD had commanded him to speak. [8]The people all responded together, "We will do everything the LORD has said." So Moses brought their answer back to the LORD.

[9]The LORD said to Moses, "I am going to come to you in a dense cloud, so that the people will hear me speaking with you and will always put their trust in you." Then Moses told the LORD what the people had said.

[10]And the LORD said to Moses, "Go to the people and consecrate them today and tomorrow. Have them wash their clothes [11]and be ready by the third day, because on that day the LORD will come down on Mount Sinai in the sight of all the people. [12]Put limits for the people around the mountain and tell them, 'Be care-ful that you do not approach the mountain or touch the foot of it. Whoever touches the mountain is to be put to death. [13]They are to be stoned or shot with arrows; not a hand is to be laid on them. No person or animal shall be permitted to live.' Only when the ram's horn sounds a long blast may they approach the mountain."

[14]After Moses had gone down the mountain to the people, he consecrated them, and they washed their clothes. [15]Then he said to the people, "Prepare yourselves for the third day. Abstain from sexual relations."

[16]On the morning of the third day there was thunder and lightning, with a thick cloud over the mountain, and a very loud trumpet blast. Everyone in the camp trembled. [17]Then Moses led the people out of the camp to meet with God, and they stood at the foot of the mountain. [18]Mount Sinai was covered with smoke, because the LORD descended on it in fire. The smoke billowed up from it like smoke from a furnace, and the whole mountain[b] trembled violently. [19]As the sound of the trumpet grew louder and louder, Moses spoke and the voice of God answered him.[c]

---

[a] 5,6 Or *possession, for the whole earth is mine.* [6]*You*
[b] 18 Most Hebrew manuscripts; a few Hebrew manuscripts and Septuagint *and all the people*   [c] 19 Or *and God answered him with thunder*

JETHRO AND THE LAW OF INTUITION
Leaders Evaluate Everything with a Leadership Bias

Exodus 18:1–24

LEADERSHIP INTUITION often separates the greatest leaders from the merely good ones. Some people are born with great leadership intuition; others have to work hard to develop and hone it. But however it evolves, the result is a combination of natural ability and learned skills. This informed intuition makes crucial issues jump out at the leader, enabling him or her to get a handle on intangible factors, understand them, and work with them to accomplish leadership goals.

Successful leaders see every situation in terms of available resources: money, raw materials, technology, and, most important, people. Intuitive leaders can sense what's happening among their people and almost instantly know their hopes, fears, and concerns. Leaders also have the ability to step back from what's happening and see not only where they and their people have gone, but also where they are headed—as if they can smell change in the wind.

■　■　■　■　■

Everyone has some kind of intuition, especially in his or her area of natural giftedness. If your gift is mercy, then you can sense when someone needs comfort, and you know how to give it. If service is your gift, you instinctively know when and how to help those in need. And if you are naturally gifted at leadership, then you see everything with a leadership bias.

Moses was a good leader, not a natural one. When he met with Jethro, he hadn't led Israel for long (the Hebrew nation had just left Egypt). But over those long years in the desert, Moses' leadership improved—and so did his intuition.

Jethro, on the other hand, appears to be a natural. How do we know that? Because he looked at a situation unlike anything he had ever seen—leading more than a million disgruntled, displaced ex-slaves—and knew exactly how to handle it. That's intuition in action. Who he *was* determined what he *saw*. Jethro, the leader, saw everything with a leadership bias.

Of all the laws of leadership, the Law of Intuition is the most difficult to teach. Reading provides the best analogy for understanding intuition. Intuitive leaders "read" their people.

Jethro, the Reading Leader

Let's consider how Jethro handled Moses' situation. Like all intuitive leaders, Jethro read:

1. Situations

An intuitive leader can quickly size up a situation. Jethro watched Moses in action for a day and immediately reacted. Jethro didn't have to hire a consultant, form a committee, or do extensive research. He instantly saw a leadership problem. All leaders may not settle on a solution as quickly as Jethro did, but when they rely on their intuition, they rapidly sense that a situation needs their attention.

2. Trends

An intuitive leader sees what's happening in the present and understands where an organization is headed. Jethro could see Moses heading for trouble. He told his son-in-law, "You and these people who come to you will only wear yourselves out. The work is too heavy for you; you cannot handle it alone" (Ex 18:18).

Maybe Moses settled disputes effectively; maybe not. But even if he were able to get by with doing everything, he could never sustain it. As the population grew, his situation would worsen. Jethro knew that disaster lay ahead if Moses didn't change.

3. Resources

Intuitive leaders know how to resource their vision. They don't take anything for granted, and they maximize whatever is at hand to achieve their goals. Jethro identified Israel's greatest assets: Moses' heart, God's favor, and the people. He directed Moses to seek God's counsel, to teach the people God's laws, and to empower the people to share the burden. Jethro's plan utilized everything of value the people possessed.

4. People

Skill with people is perhaps the great-est ability of an intuitive leader. Some can understand what it takes to lead; others can actually do it. Jethro understood people and leadership well enough to know how to empower Moses' leadership, even though he had no personal experience with those who had just escaped Egypt. Jethro knew leadership had to be based on ability, not position, and he instinctively understood that the right people were present to lead thousands, hundreds, fifties, and tens. They just had to be put into place.

5. Himself

An intuitive leader reads himself. He understands his strengths, his weaknesses and his individual calling. Jethro not only read and understood Moses' leadership problem; he realized he was not the man for the job. So he read and evaluated Moses' leadership ability and planned accordingly.

Look at any leader with sharp intuition, and you will see an ability to read a leadership situation. When Nehemiah looked at the wall in Jerusalem, he knew what to do. When Joseph understood Pharaoh's dream, he knew how to prepare for the famine. Intuition, whether natural or developed intentionally, helps a *good* leader to become a *great* leader.

The Law of Connection: God's Covenant, God's Rules

Exodus 19:3–13

Have you ever noticed how God introduced the Ten Commandments? Before he spoke his laws to the people in Exodus 20, He took time to remind them of three vital truths:

1. **The love he had for them**
2. **The victories he'd won for them**
3. **The future he planned for them**

God spoke about how he intended to bless Israel as his children, and he warned them of the boundaries to keep—how to survive his fiery presence on Mount Sinai. Only then did he give them his commandments to obey. Do you see the genius of the sequence?

Leaders touch a heart before they ask for a hand. Before God demanded his people keep his rules, he reminded them of his relationship and blessings. That gave them all the incentive they needed to follow through on their commitment!

²⁰The LORD descended to the top of Mount Sinai and called Moses to the top of the mountain. So Moses went up ²¹and the LORD said to him, "Go down and warn the people so they do not force their way through to see the LORD and many of them perish. ²²Even the priests, who approach the LORD, must consecrate themselves, or the LORD will break out against them."

²³Moses said to the LORD, "The people cannot come up Mount Sinai, because you yourself warned us, 'Put limits around the mountain and set it apart as holy.'"

²⁴The LORD replied, "Go down and bring Aaron up with you. But the priests and the people must not force their way through to come up to the LORD, or he will break out against them."

²⁵So Moses went down to the people and told them.

The Ten Commandments

20 And God spoke all these words:

²"I am the LORD your God, who brought you out of Egypt, out of the land of slavery.

³"You shall have no other gods before[a] me.

⁴"You shall not make for yourself an image in the form of anything in heaven above or on the earth beneath or in the waters below. ⁵You shall not bow down to them or worship them; for I, the LORD your God, am a jealous God, punishing the children for the sin of the parents to the third and fourth generation of those who hate me, ⁶but showing love to a thousand generations of those who love me and keep my commandments.

⁷"You shall not misuse the name of the LORD your God, for the LORD will not hold anyone guiltless who misuses his name.

⁸"Remember the Sabbath day by keeping it holy. ⁹Six days you shall labor and do all your work, ¹⁰but the seventh day is a sabbath to the LORD your God. On it you shall not do any work, neither you, nor your son or daughter, nor your male or female servant, nor your animals, nor any foreigner residing in your towns. ¹¹For in six days the LORD made the heavens and the earth, the sea, and all that is in them, but he rested on the seventh day. Therefore the LORD blessed the Sabbath day and made it holy.

¹²"Honor your father and your mother, so that you may live long in the land the LORD your God is giving you.

¹³"You shall not murder.

¹⁴"You shall not commit adultery.

¹⁵"You shall not steal.

¹⁶"You shall not give false testimony against your neighbor.

¹⁷"You shall not covet your neighbor's house. You shall not covet your neighbor's wife, or his male or female servant,

[a] 3 Or besides

his ox or donkey, or anything that belongs to your neighbor."

¹⁸When the people saw the thunder and lightning and heard the trumpet and saw the mountain in smoke, they trembled with fear. They stayed at a distance ¹⁹and said to Moses, "Speak to us yourself and we will listen. But do not have God speak to us or we will die."

²⁰Moses said to the people, "Do not be afraid. God has come to test you, so that the fear of God will be with you to keep you from sinning."

²¹The people remained at a distance, while Moses approached the thick darkness where God was.

Idols and Altars

²²Then the LORD said to Moses, "Tell the Israelites this: 'You have seen for yourselves that I have spoken to you from heaven: ²³Do not make any gods to be alongside me; do not make for yourselves gods of silver or gods of gold.

²⁴"'Make an altar of earth for me and sacrifice on it your burnt offerings and fellowship offerings, your sheep and goats and your cattle. Wherever I cause my name to be honored, I will come to you and bless you. ²⁵If you make an altar of stones for me, do not build it with dressed stones, for you will defile it if you use a tool on it. ²⁶And do not go up to my altar on steps, or your private parts may be exposed.'

21 "These are the laws you are to set before them:

Hebrew Servants

²"If you buy a Hebrew servant, he is to serve you for six years. But in the seventh year, he shall go free, without paying anything. ³If he comes alone, he is to go free alone; but if he has a wife when he comes, she is to go with him. ⁴If his master gives him a wife and she bears him sons or daughters, the woman and her children shall belong to her master, and only the man shall go free.

⁵"But if the servant declares, 'I love my master and my wife and children and do not want to go free,' ⁶then his master must take him before the judges.^a He shall take him to the door or the doorpost and pierce his ear with an awl. Then he will be his servant for life.

⁷"If a man sells his daughter as a servant, she is not to go free as male servants do. ⁸If she does not please the master who has selected her for himself,^b he must let her be redeemed. He has

no right to sell her to foreigners, because he has broken faith with her. ⁹If he selects her for his son, he must grant her the rights of a daughter. ¹⁰If he marries another woman, he must not deprive the first one of her food, clothing and marital rights. ¹¹If he does not provide her with these three things, she is to go free, without any payment of money.

Personal Injuries

¹²"Anyone who strikes a person with a fatal blow is to be put to death. ¹³However, if it is not done intentionally, but God lets it happen, they are to flee to a place I will designate. ¹⁴But if anyone schemes and kills someone deliberately, that person is to be taken from my altar and put to death.

¹⁵"Anyone who attacks^c their father or mother is to be put to death.

¹⁶"Anyone who kidnaps someone is to be put to death, whether the victim has been sold or is still in the kidnapper's possession.

¹⁷"Anyone who curses their father or mother is to be put to death.

¹⁸"If people quarrel and one person hits another with a stone or with their fist^d and the victim does not die but is confined to bed, ¹⁹the one who struck the blow will not be held liable if the other can get up and walk around outside with a staff; however, the guilty party must pay the injured person for any loss of time and see that the victim is completely healed.

²⁰"Anyone who beats their male or female slave with a rod must be punished if the slave dies as a direct result, ²¹but they are not to be punished if the slave recovers after a day or two, since the slave is their property.

²²"If people are fighting and hit a pregnant woman and she gives birth prematurely^e but there is no serious injury, the offender must be fined whatever the woman's husband demands and the court allows. ²³But if there is serious injury, you are to take life for life, ²⁴eye for eye, tooth for tooth, hand for hand, foot for foot, ²⁵burn for burn, wound for wound, bruise for bruise.

²⁶"An owner who hits a male or female slave in the eye and destroys it must let the slave go free to compensate for the eye. ²⁷And an owner who knocks out the tooth of a male or female slave must let the slave go free to compensate for the tooth.

---

^a 6 Or before God   ^b 8 Or master so that he does not choose her   ^c 15 Or kills   ^d 18 Or with a tool   ^e 22 Or she has a miscarriage

[28]"If a bull gores a man or woman to death, the bull is to be stoned to death, and its meat must not be eaten. But the owner of the bull will not be held responsible. [29]If, however, the bull has had the habit of goring and the owner has been warned but has not kept it penned up and it kills a man or woman, the bull is to be stoned and its owner also is to be put to death. [30]However, if payment is demanded, the owner may redeem his life by the payment of whatever is demanded. [31]This law also applies if the bull gores a son or daughter. [32]If the bull gores a male or female slave, the owner must pay thirty shekels[a] of silver to the master of the slave, and the bull is to be stoned to death.

[33]"If anyone uncovers a pit or digs one and fails to cover it and an ox or a donkey falls into it, [34]the one who opened the pit must pay the owner for the loss and take the dead animal in exchange.

[35]"If anyone's bull injures someone else's bull and it dies, the two parties are to sell the live one and divide both the money and the dead animal equally. [36]However, if it was known that the bull had the habit of goring, yet the owner did not keep it penned up, the owner must pay, animal for animal, and take the dead animal in exchange.

Protection of Property

22[b] "Whoever steals an ox or a sheep and slaughters it or sells it must pay back five head of cattle for the ox and four sheep for the sheep.

[2]"If a thief is caught breaking in at night and is struck a fatal blow, the defender is not guilty of bloodshed; [3]but if it happens after sunrise, the defender is guilty of bloodshed.

"Anyone who steals must certainly make restitution, but if they have nothing, they must be sold to pay for their theft. [4]If the stolen animal is found alive in their possession — whether ox or donkey or sheep — they must pay back double.

[5]"If anyone grazes their livestock in a field or vineyard and lets them stray and they graze in someone else's field, the offender must make restitution from the best of their own field or vineyard.

[6]"If a fire breaks out and spreads into thornbushes so that it burns shocks of grain or standing grain or the whole field, the one who started the fire must make restitution.

[7]"If anyone gives a neighbor silver or goods for safekeeping and they are stolen from the neighbor's house, the thief, if caught, must pay back double. [8]But if the thief is not found, the owner of the house must appear before the judges, and they must[c] determine whether the owner of the house has laid hands on the other person's property. [9]In all cases of illegal possession of an ox, a donkey, a sheep, a garment, or any other lost property about which somebody says, 'This is mine,' both parties are to bring their cases before the judges.[d] The one whom the judges declare[e] guilty must pay back double to the other.

[10]"If anyone gives a donkey, an ox, a sheep or any other animal to their neighbor for safekeeping and it dies or is injured or is taken away while no one is looking, [11]the issue between them will be settled by the taking of an oath before the LORD that the neighbor did not lay hands on the other person's property. The owner is to accept this, and no restitution is required. [12]But if the animal was stolen from the neighbor, restitution must be made to the owner. [13]If it was torn to pieces by a wild animal, the neighbor shall bring in the remains as evidence and shall not be required to pay for the torn animal.

[14]"If anyone borrows an animal from their neighbor and it is injured or dies while the owner is not present, they must make restitution. [15]But if the owner is with the animal, the borrower will not have to pay. If the animal was hired, the money paid for the hire covers the loss.

Social Responsibility

[16]"If a man seduces a virgin who is not pledged to be married and sleeps with her, he must pay the bride-price, and she shall be his wife. [17]If her father absolutely refuses to give her to him, he must still pay the bride-price for virgins.

[18]"Do not allow a sorceress to live.

[19]"Anyone who has sexual relations with an animal is to be put to death.

[20]"Whoever sacrifices to any god other than the LORD must be destroyed.[f]

[21]"Do not mistreat or oppress a foreigner, for you were foreigners in Egypt.

[22]"Do not take advantage of the widow or the fatherless. [23]If you do and they cry out to me, I will certainly hear their cry. [24]My anger will be aroused, and I will kill you with the sword; your

---

[a] 32 That is, about 12 ounces or about 345 grams   [b] In Hebrew texts 22:1 is numbered 21:37, and 22:2-31 is numbered 22:1-30.   [c] 8 Or before God, and he will   [d] 9 Or before God   [e] 9 Or whom God declares   [f] 20 The Hebrew term refers to the irrevocable giving over of things or persons to the LORD, often by totally destroying them.

wives will become widows and your children fatherless.

25"If you lend money to one of my people among you who is needy, do not treat it like a business deal; charge no interest. 26If you take your neighbor's cloak as a pledge, return it by sunset, 27because that cloak is the only covering your neighbor has. What else can they sleep in? When they cry out to me, I will hear, for I am compassionate.

28"Do not blaspheme God[a] or curse the ruler of your people.

29"Do not hold back offerings from your granaries or your vats.[b]

"You must give me the firstborn of your sons. 30Do the same with your cattle and your sheep. Let them stay with their mothers for seven days, but give them to me on the eighth day.

31"You are to be my holy people. So do not eat the meat of an animal torn by wild beasts; throw it to the dogs.

Laws of Justice and Mercy

23 "Do not spread false reports. Do not help a guilty person by being a malicious witness.

2"Do not follow the crowd in doing wrong. When you give testimony in a lawsuit, do not pervert justice by siding with the crowd, 3and do not show favoritism to a poor person in a lawsuit.

4"If you come across your enemy's ox or donkey wandering off, be sure to return it. 5If you see the donkey of someone who hates you fallen down under its load, do not leave it there; be sure you help them with it.

6"Do not deny justice to your poor people in their lawsuits. 7Have nothing to do with a false charge and do not put an innocent or honest person to death, for I will not acquit the guilty.

8"Do not accept a bribe, for a bribe blinds those who see and twists the words of the innocent.

9"Do not oppress a foreigner; you yourselves know how it feels to be foreigners, because you were foreigners in Egypt.

Sabbath Laws

10"For six years you are to sow your fields and harvest the crops, 11but during the seventh year let the land lie unplowed and unused. Then the poor among your people may get food from it, and the wild animals may eat what is left. Do the same with your vineyard and your olive grove.

12"Six days do your work, but on the seventh day do not work, so that your ox and your donkey may rest, and so that the slave born in your household and the foreigner living among you may be refreshed.

13"Be careful to do everything I have said to you. Do not invoke the names of other gods; do not let them be heard on your lips.

The Three Annual Festivals

14"Three times a year you are to celebrate a festival to me.

15"Celebrate the Festival of Unleavened Bread; for seven days eat bread made without yeast, as I commanded you. Do this at the appointed time in the month of Aviv, for in that month you came out of Egypt.

"No one is to appear before me empty-handed.

16"Celebrate the Festival of Harvest with the firstfruits of the crops you sow in your field.

"Celebrate the Festival of Ingathering at the end of the year, when you gather in your crops from the field.

17"Three times a year all the men are to appear before the Sovereign LORD.

a 28 Or Do not revile the judges   b 29 The meaning of the Hebrew for this phrase is uncertain.

The Law of the Picture: God Establishes the Power of Example

Exodus 21:1—23:33

In Exodus 21–23, all sorts of laws and penalties are introduced. God's people were given instruction and clear consequences for disobedience. Why were the penalties so strict? Is God mean and fierce in the Old Testament and loving and gracious in the New Testament? We can see both sides of God in the old and the new covenants, but God laid out severe penalties because of the power of example. The people needed a picture. Once a penalty is seen, everyone is sobered by the example. God did the same thing in the New Testament when Ananias and Sapphira were punished (Ac 5:1–11). Mere "talk" would not have had the same effect on this baby nation in Exodus, nor on the baby church in Acts. Frequently people need a clear, visible demonstration in order to remember.

[18]"Do not offer the blood of a sacrifice to me along with anything containing yeast.

"The fat of my festival offerings must not be kept until morning.

[19]"Bring the best of the firstfruits of your soil to the house of the LORD your God.

"Do not cook a young goat in its mother's milk.

God's Angel to Prepare the Way

[20]"See, I am sending an angel ahead of you to guard you along the way and to bring you to the place I have prepared. [21]Pay attention to him and listen to what he says. Do not rebel against him; he will not forgive your rebellion, since my Name is in him. [22]If you listen carefully to what he says and do all that I say, I will be an enemy to your enemies and will oppose those who oppose you. [23]My angel will go ahead of you and bring you into the land of the Amorites, Hittites, Perizzites, Canaanites, Hivites and Jebusites, and I will wipe them out. [24]Do not bow down before their gods or worship them or follow their practices. You must demolish them and break their sacred stones to pieces. [25]Worship the LORD your God, and his blessing will be on your food and water. I will take away sickness from among you, [26]and none will miscarry or be barren in your land. I will give you a full life span.

[27]"I will send my terror ahead of you and throw into confusion every nation you encounter. I will make all your enemies turn their backs and run. [28]I will send the hornet ahead of you to drive the Hivites, Canaanites and Hittites out of your way. [29]But I will not drive them out in a single year, because the land would become desolate and the wild animals too numerous for you. [30]Little by little I will drive them out before you, until you have increased enough to take possession of the land.

[31]"I will establish your borders from the Red Sea[a] to the Mediterranean Sea,[b] and from the desert to the Euphrates River. I will give into your hands the people who live in the land, and you will drive them out before you. [32]Do not make a covenant with them or with their gods. [33]Do not let them live in your land or they will cause you to sin against me, because the worship of their gods will certainly be a snare to you."

The Covenant Confirmed

24 Then the LORD said to Moses, "Come up to the LORD, you and Aaron, Nadab and Abihu, and seventy of the elders of Israel. You are to worship at a distance, [2]but Moses alone is to approach the LORD; the others must not come near. And the people may not come up with him."

[3]When Moses went and told the people all the LORD's words and laws, they responded with one voice, "Everything the LORD has said we will do." [4]Moses then wrote down everything the LORD had said.

He got up early the next morning and built an altar at the foot of the mountain and set up twelve stone pillars representing the twelve tribes of Israel. [5]Then he sent young Israelite men, and they offered burnt offerings and sacrificed young bulls as fellowship offerings to the LORD. [6]Moses took half of the blood and put it in bowls, and the other half he splashed against the altar. [7]Then he took the Book of the Covenant and read it to the people. They responded, "We will do everything the LORD has said; we will obey."

[8]Moses then took the blood, sprinkled it on the people and said, "This is the blood of the covenant that the LORD has made with you in accordance with all these words."

[9]Moses and Aaron, Nadab and Abihu, and the seventy elders of Israel went up [10]and saw the God of Israel. Under his feet was something like a pavement made of lapis lazuli, as bright blue as the sky. [11]But God did not raise his hand against these leaders of the Israelites; they saw God, and they ate and drank.

[12]The LORD said to Moses, "Come up to me on the mountain and stay here, and I will give you the tablets of stone with the law and commandments I have written for their instruction."

[13]Then Moses set out with Joshua his aide, and Moses went up on the mountain of God. [14]He said to the elders, "Wait here for us until we come back to you. Aaron and Hur are with you, and anyone involved in a dispute can go to them."

[15]When Moses went up on the mountain, the cloud covered it, [16]and the glory of the LORD settled on Mount Sinai. For six days the cloud covered the mountain, and on the seventh day the LORD called to Moses from within the cloud. [17]To the Israelites the glory of the LORD looked like a consuming fire on top of the mountain. [18]Then Moses entered the cloud as he went on up the mountain. And he stayed on the mountain forty days and forty nights.

---

[a] 31 Or the Sea of Reeds   [b] 31 Hebrew to the Sea of the Philistines

The Law of Buy-In: Leading Change

Exodus 24:1–7

It was a watershed day for everyone—a whole new life had begun! The Israelites got off to a fresh start when they affirmed the covenant God had offered them.

To make it work, however, they discovered they would have to change their lifestyles and shift their paradigms—and that would take shrewd leadership. Sometimes (as in the desert) the majority even wanted to return to Egypt!

Peter Drucker helps us to learn from Moses about how to lead people into change, even in the wilderness:

Lessons from the Wilderness

1. **Magnify the plagues.** To make Pharaoh release God's people, Moses called down the plagues, and he didn't stop until the old system gave way. At this stage, problems are your friend. Don't solve them; they convince people that they need to let go of the old way.

2. **Mark the ending.** What a symbolic and memorable "boundary event" Moses had in the crossing of the Red Sea! After his people walked through the waters on dry land, there was no turning back.

3. **Deal with the "murmuring."** Don't be surprised when some lose confidence in your leadership somewhere between where they came from and where they're going. Moses heard things like, *Does our leader know the way? We've never done it this way before! What was so bad about Egypt?* In times of transition, look for opportunities to show concern for how your people feel; interact with the stragglers.

4. **Give people access to decision makers.** Thanks to Jethro, Moses appointed a new cadre of leaders to narrow the gap between the people and the decision makers. As a result, the people felt more connected.

5. **Capitalize on the creative opportunity of the wilderness.** It was in the wilderness, not the promised land, that a big innovation took place: God handed down the Ten Commandments. Some of your biggest breakthroughs will also take place in the wilderness.

6. **Resist the urge to rush ahead.** It often seems that little happens in the wilderness, but great transformation takes place there. Don't jeopardize it by hurrying ahead or removing the pain of giving birth to a new vision. Let God do his work.

7. **Understand that "wilderness leadership" is special.** Moses did not enter the promised land. His kind of leadership fit the transition time, where things seemed confusing and fluid. The nation needed Joshua to enter Canaan, because he led the military, and because a settled life required new skills. Movements and organizations don't always need a new leader, but they do require a new style of leadership once the transition is complete.

Offerings for the Tabernacle

25 The LORD said to Moses, [2]"Tell the Israelites to bring me an offering. You are to receive the offering for me from everyone whose heart prompts them to give. [3]These are the offerings you are to receive from them: gold, silver and bronze; [4]blue, purple and scarlet yarn and fine linen; goat hair; [5]ram skins dyed red and another type of durable leather[a]; acacia wood;

[6]olive oil for the light; spices for the anointing oil and for the fragrant incense; [7]and onyx stones and other gems to be mounted on the ephod and breastpiece.

[8]"Then have them make a sanctuary for me, and I will dwell among them. [9]Make this tabernacle and all its furnishings exactly like the pattern I will show you.

---

[a] 5 Possibly the hides of large aquatic mammals

The Ark

[10]"Have them make an ark[a] of acacia wood—two and a half cubits long, a cubit and a half wide, and a cubit and a half high.[b] [11]Overlay it with pure gold, both inside and out, and make a gold molding around it. [12]Cast four gold rings for it and fasten them to its four feet, with two rings on one side and two rings on the other. [13]Then make poles of acacia wood and overlay them with gold. [14]Insert the poles into the rings on the sides of the ark to carry it. [15]The poles are to remain in the rings of this ark; they are not to be removed. [16]Then put in the ark the tablets of the covenant law, which I will give you.

[17]"Make an atonement cover of pure gold—two and a half cubits long and a cubit and a half wide. [18]And make two cherubim out of hammered gold at the ends of the cover. [19]Make one cherub on one end and the second cherub on the other; make the cherubim of one piece with the cover, at the two ends. [20]The cherubim are to have their wings spread upward, overshadowing the cover with them. The cherubim are to face each other, looking toward the cover. [21]Place the cover on top of the ark and put in the ark the tablets of the covenant law that I will give you. [22]There, above the cover between the two cherubim that are over the ark of the covenant law, I will meet with you and give you all my commands for the Israelites.

The Table

[23]"Make a table of acacia wood—two cubits long, a cubit wide and a cubit and a half high.[c] [24]Overlay it with pure gold and make a gold molding around it. [25]Also make around it a rim a handbreadth[d] wide and put a gold molding on the rim. [26]Make four gold rings for the table and fasten them to the four corners, where the four legs are. [27]The rings are to be close to the rim to hold the poles used in carrying the table. [28]Make the poles of acacia wood, overlay them with gold and carry the table with them. [29]And make its plates and dishes of pure gold, as well as its pitchers and bowls for the pouring out of offerings. [30]Put the bread of the Presence on this table to be before me at all times.

The Lampstand

[31]"Make a lampstand of pure gold. Hammer out its base and shaft, and make its flowerlike cups, buds and blossoms of one piece with them. [32]Six branches are to extend from the sides of the lampstand—three on one side and three

on the other. [33]Three cups shaped like almond flowers with buds and blossoms are to be on one branch, three on the next branch, and the same for all six branches extending from the lampstand. [34]And on the lampstand there are to be four cups shaped like almond flowers with buds and blossoms. [35]One bud shall be under the first pair of branches extending from the lampstand, a second bud under the second pair, and a third bud under the third pair—six branches in all. [36]The buds and branches shall all be of one piece with the lampstand, hammered out of pure gold.

[37]"Then make its seven lamps and set them up on it so that they light the space in front of it. [38]Its wick trimmers and trays are to be of pure gold. [39]A talent[e] of pure gold is to be used for the lampstand and all these accessories. [40]See that you make them according to the pattern shown you on the mountain.

The Tabernacle

26 "Make the tabernacle with ten curtains of finely twisted linen and blue, purple and scarlet yarn, with cherubim woven into them by a skilled worker. [2]All the curtains are to be the same size—twenty-eight cubits long and four cubits wide.[f] [3]Join five of the curtains together, and do the same with the other five. [4]Make loops of blue material along the edge of the end curtain in one set, and do the same with the end curtain in the other set. [5]Make fifty loops on one curtain and fifty loops on the end curtain of the other set, with the loops opposite each other. [6]Then make fifty gold clasps and use them to fasten the curtains together so that the tabernacle is a unit.

[7]"Make curtains of goat hair for the tent over the tabernacle—eleven altogether. [8]All eleven curtains are to be the same size—thirty cubits long and four cubits wide.[g] [9]Join five of the curtains together into one set and the other six into another set. Fold the sixth curtain double at the front of the tent. [10]Make fifty loops along the edge of the end curtain in one set and also

---

[a] 10 That is, a chest   [b] 10 That is, about 3 3/4 feet long and 2 1/4 feet wide and high or about 1.1 meters long and 68 centimeters wide and high; similarly in verse 17   [c] 23 That is, about 3 feet long, 1 1/2 feet wide and 2 1/4 feet high or about 90 centimeters long, 45 centimeters wide and 68 centimeters high   [d] 25 That is, about 3 inches or about 7.5 centimeters   [e] 39 That is, about 75 pounds or about 34 kilograms   [f] 2 That is, about 42 feet long and 6 feet wide or about 13 meters long and 1.8 meters wide   [g] 8 That is, about 45 feet long and 6 feet wide or about 13.5 meters long and 1.8 meters wide

along the edge of the end curtain in the other set. [11]Then make fifty bronze clasps and put them in the loops to fasten the tent together as a unit. [12]As for the additional length of the tent curtains, the half curtain that is left over is to hang down at the rear of the tabernacle. [13]The tent curtains will be a cubit[a] longer on both sides; what is left will hang over the sides of the tabernacle so as to cover it. [14]Make for the tent a covering of ram skins dyed red, and over that a covering of the other durable leather.[b]

[15]"Make upright frames of acacia wood for the tabernacle. [16]Each frame is to be ten cubits long and a cubit and a half wide,[c] [17]with two projections set parallel to each other. Make all the frames of the tabernacle in this way. [18]Make twenty frames for the south side of the tabernacle [19]and make forty silver bases to go under them — two bases for each frame, one under each projection. [20]For the other side, the north side of the tabernacle, make twenty frames [21]and forty silver bases — two under each frame. [22]Make six frames for the far end, that is, the west end of the tabernacle, [23]and make two frames for the corners at the far end. [24]At these two corners they must be double from the bottom all the way to the top and fitted into a single ring; both shall be like that. [25]So there will be eight frames and sixteen silver bases — two under each frame.

[26]"Also make crossbars of acacia wood: five for the frames on one side of the tabernacle, [27]five for those on the other side, and five for the frames on the west, at the far end of the tabernacle. [28]The center crossbar is to extend from end to end at the middle of the frames. [29]Overlay the frames with gold and make gold rings to hold the crossbars. Also overlay the crossbars with gold.

[30]"Set up the tabernacle according to the plan shown you on the mountain.

[31]"Make a curtain of blue, purple and scarlet yarn and finely twisted linen, with cherubim woven into it by a skilled worker. [32]Hang it with gold hooks on four posts of acacia wood overlaid with gold and standing on four silver bases. [33]Hang the curtain from the clasps and place the ark of the covenant law behind the curtain. The curtain will separate the Holy Place from the Most Holy Place. [34]Put the atonement cover on the ark of the covenant law in the Most Holy Place. [35]Place the table outside the curtain on the north side of the tabernacle and put the lampstand opposite it on the south side.

[36]"For the entrance to the tent make a curtain of blue, purple and scarlet yarn and finely twist-

ed linen — the work of an embroiderer. [37]Make gold hooks for this curtain and five posts of acacia wood overlaid with gold. And cast five bronze bases for them.

The Altar of Burnt Offering

27 "Build an altar of acacia wood, three cubits[d] high; it is to be square, five cubits long and five cubits wide.[e] [2]Make a horn at each of the four corners, so that the horns and the altar are of one piece, and overlay the altar with bronze. [3]Make all its utensils of bronze — its pots to remove the ashes, and its shovels, sprinkling bowls, meat forks and firepans. [4]Make a grating for it, a bronze network, and make a bronze ring at each of the four corners of the network. [5]Put it under the ledge of the altar so that it is halfway up the altar. [6]Make poles of acacia wood for the altar and overlay them with bronze. [7]The poles are to be inserted into the rings so they will be on two sides of the altar when it is carried. [8]Make the altar hollow, out of boards. It is to be made just as you were shown on the mountain.

The Courtyard

[9]"Make a courtyard for the tabernacle. The south side shall be a hundred cubits[f] long and is to have curtains of finely twisted linen, [10]with twenty posts and twenty bronze bases and with silver hooks and bands on the posts. [11]The north side shall also be a hundred cubits long and is to have curtains, with twenty posts and twenty bronze bases and with silver hooks and bands on the posts.

[12]"The west end of the courtyard shall be fifty cubits[g] wide and have curtains, with ten posts and ten bases. [13]On the east end, toward the sunrise, the courtyard shall also be fifty cubits wide. [14]Curtains fifteen cubits[h] long are to be on one side of the entrance, with three posts and three bases, [15]and curtains fifteen cubits long are to be on the other side, with three posts and three bases.

[16]"For the entrance to the courtyard, provide a curtain twenty cubits[i] long, of blue, purple

---

[a] 13 That is, about 18 inches or about 45 centimeters
[b] 14 Possibly the hides of large aquatic mammals (see 25:5)
[c] 16 That is, about 15 feet long and 2 1/4 feet wide or about 4.5 meters long and 68 centimeters wide   [d] 1 That is, about 4 1/2 feet or about 1.4 meters   [e] 1 That is, about 7 1/2 feet or about 2.3 meters long and wide   [f] 9 That is, about 150 feet or about 45 meters; also in verse 11   [g] 12 That is, about 75 feet or about 23 meters; also in verse 13   [h] 14 That is, about 23 feet or about 6.8 meters; also in verse 15   [i] 16 That is, about 30 feet or about 9 meters

and scarlet yarn and finely twisted linen—the work of an embroiderer—with four posts and four bases. [17]All the posts around the courtyard are to have silver bands and hooks, and bronze bases. [18]The courtyard shall be a hundred cubits long and fifty cubits wide,[a] with curtains of finely twisted linen five cubits[b] high, and with bronze bases. [19]All the other articles used in the service of the tabernacle, whatever their function, including all the tent pegs for it and those for the courtyard, are to be of bronze.

Oil for the Lampstand

[20]"Command the Israelites to bring you clear oil of pressed olives for the light so that the lamps may be kept burning. [21]In the tent of meeting, outside the curtain that shields the ark of the covenant law, Aaron and his sons are to keep the lamps burning before the LORD from evening till morning. This is to be a lasting ordinance among the Israelites for the generations to come.

The Priestly Garments

28 "Have Aaron your brother brought to you from among the Israelites, along with his sons Nadab and Abihu, Eleazar and Ithamar, so they may serve me as priests. [2]Make sacred garments for your brother Aaron to give him dignity and honor. [3]Tell all the skilled workers to whom I have given wisdom in such matters that they are to make garments for Aaron, for his consecration, so he may serve me as priest. [4]These are the garments they are to make: a breastpiece, an ephod, a robe, a woven tunic, a turban and a sash. They are to make these sacred garments for your brother Aaron and his sons, so they may serve me as priests. [5]Have them use gold, and blue, purple and scarlet yarn, and fine linen.

The Ephod

[6]"Make the ephod of gold, and of blue, purple and scarlet yarn, and of finely twisted linen—the work of skilled hands. [7]It is to have two shoulder pieces attached to two of its corners, so it can be fastened. [8]Its skillfully woven waistband is to be like it—of one piece with the ephod and made with gold, and with blue, purple and scarlet yarn, and with finely twisted linen.

[9]"Take two onyx stones and engrave on them the names of the sons of Israel [10]in the order of their birth—six names on one stone and the remaining six on the other. [11]Engrave the names

of the sons of Israel on the two stones the way a gem cutter engraves a seal. Then mount the stones in gold filigree settings [12]and fasten them on the shoulder pieces of the ephod as memorial stones for the sons of Israel. Aaron is to bear the names on his shoulders as a memorial before the LORD. [13]Make gold filigree settings [14]and two braided chains of pure gold, like a rope, and attach the chains to the settings.

The Breastpiece

[15]"Fashion a breastpiece for making decisions—the work of skilled hands. Make it like the ephod: of gold, and of blue, purple and scarlet yarn, and of finely twisted linen. [16]It is to be square—a span[c] long and a span wide—and folded double. [17]Then mount four rows of precious stones on it. The first row shall be carnelian, chrysolite and beryl; [18]the second row shall be turquoise, lapis lazuli and emerald; [19]the third row shall be jacinth, agate and amethyst; [20]the fourth row shall be topaz, onyx and jasper.[d] Mount them in gold filigree settings. [21]There are to be twelve stones, one for each of the names of the sons of Israel, each engraved like a seal with the name of one of the twelve tribes.

[22]"For the breastpiece make braided chains of pure gold, like a rope. [23]Make two gold rings for it and fasten them to two corners of the breastpiece. [24]Fasten the two gold chains to the rings at the corners of the breastpiece, [25]and the other ends of the chains to the two settings, attaching them to the shoulder pieces of the ephod at the front. [26]Make two gold rings and attach them to the other two corners of the breastpiece on the inside edge next to the ephod. [27]Make two more gold rings and attach them to the bottom of the shoulder pieces on the front of the ephod, close to the seam just above the waistband of the ephod. [28]The rings of the breastpiece are to be tied to the rings of the ephod with blue cord, connecting it to the waistband, so that the breastpiece will not swing out from the ephod.

[29]"Whenever Aaron enters the Holy Place, he will bear the names of the sons of Israel over his heart on the breastpiece of decision as a continuing memorial before the LORD. [30]Also put the Urim and the Thummim in the breastpiece, so

---

[a] 18 That is, about 150 feet long and 75 feet wide or about 45 meters long and 23 meters wide   [b] 18 That is, about 7 1/2 feet or about 2.3 meters   [c] 16 That is, about 9 inches or about 23 centimeters   [d] 20 The precise identification of some of these precious stones is uncertain.

they may be over Aaron's heart whenever he enters the presence of the LORD. Thus Aaron will always bear the means of making decisions for the Israelites over his heart before the LORD.

Other Priestly Garments

[31]"Make the robe of the ephod entirely of blue cloth, [32]with an opening for the head in its center. There shall be a woven edge like a collar[a] around this opening, so that it will not tear. [33]Make pomegranates of blue, purple and scarlet yarn around the hem of the robe, with gold bells between them. [34]The gold bells and the pomegranates are to alternate around the hem of the robe. [35]Aaron must wear it when he ministers. The sound of the bells will be heard when he enters the Holy Place before the LORD and when he comes out, so that he will not die.

[36]"Make a plate of pure gold and engrave on it as on a seal: HOLY TO THE LORD. [37]Fasten a blue cord to it to attach it to the turban; it is to be on the front of the turban. [38]It will be on Aaron's forehead, and he will bear the guilt involved in the sacred gifts the Israelites consecrate, whatever their gifts may be. It will be on Aaron's forehead continually so that they will be acceptable to the LORD.

[39]"Weave the tunic of fine linen and make the turban of fine linen. The sash is to be the work of an embroiderer. [40]Make tunics, sashes and caps for Aaron's sons to give them dignity and honor. [41]After you put these clothes on your brother Aaron and his sons, anoint and ordain them. Consecrate them so they may serve me as priests.

[42]"Make linen undergarments as a covering for the body, reaching from the waist to the thigh. [43]Aaron and his sons must wear them whenever they enter the tent of meeting or approach the altar to minister in the Holy Place, so that they will not incur guilt and die.

"This is to be a lasting ordinance for Aaron and his descendants.

Consecration of the Priests

29 "This is what you are to do to consecrate them, so they may serve me as priests: Take a young bull and two rams without defect. [2]And from the finest wheat flour make round loaves without yeast, thick loaves without yeast and with olive oil mixed in, and thin loaves without yeast and brushed with olive oil. [3]Put them in a basket and present them along with the bull and the two rams. [4]Then bring Aaron and his sons to the entrance to the tent of meeting and wash them with water. [5]Take the garments and dress Aaron with the tunic, the robe of the ephod, the ephod itself and the breastpiece. Fasten the ephod on him by its skillfully woven waistband. [6]Put the turban on his head and attach the sacred emblem to the turban. [7]Take the anointing oil and anoint him by pouring it on his head. [8]Bring his sons and dress them in tunics [9]and fasten caps on them. Then tie sashes on Aaron and his sons.[b] The priesthood is theirs by a lasting ordinance.

"Then you shall ordain Aaron and his sons.

[10]"Bring the bull to the front of the tent of meeting, and Aaron and his sons shall lay their hands on its head. [11]Slaughter it in the LORD's presence at the entrance to the tent of meeting. [12]Take some of the bull's blood and put it on the horns of the altar with your finger, and pour out the rest of it at the base of the altar. [13]Then take all the fat on the internal organs, the long lobe of the liver, and both kidneys with the fat on them, and burn them on the altar. [14]But burn the bull's flesh and its hide and its intestines outside the camp. It is a sin offering.[c]

[15]"Take one of the rams, and Aaron and his sons shall lay their hands on its head. [16]Slaughter it and take the blood and splash it against the sides of the altar. [17]Cut the ram into pieces and wash the internal organs and the legs, putting them with the head and the other pieces. [18]Then burn the entire ram on the altar. It is a burnt offering to the LORD, a pleasing aroma, a food offering presented to the LORD.

[19]"Take the other ram, and Aaron and his sons shall lay their hands on its head. [20]Slaughter it, take some of its blood and put it on the lobes of the right ears of Aaron and his sons, on the thumbs of their right hands, and on the big toes of their right feet. Then splash blood against the sides of the altar. [21]And take some blood from the altar and some of the anointing oil and sprinkle it on Aaron and his garments and on his sons and their garments. Then he and his sons and their garments will be consecrated.

[22]"Take from this ram the fat, the fat tail, the fat on the internal organs, the long lobe of the liver, both kidneys with the fat on them, and the right thigh. (This is the ram for the ordination.) [23]From the basket of bread made without yeast, which is before the LORD, take one round loaf,

---

[a] 32 The meaning of the Hebrew for this word is uncertain.
[b] 9 Hebrew; Septuagint *on them*   [c] 14 Or *purification offering*; also in verse 36

one thick loaf with olive oil mixed in, and one thin loaf. ²⁴Put all these in the hands of Aaron and his sons and have them wave them before the LORD as a wave offering. ²⁵Then take them from their hands and burn them on the altar along with the burnt offering for a pleasing aroma to the LORD, a food offering presented to the LORD. ²⁶After you take the breast of the ram for Aaron's ordination, wave it before the LORD as a wave offering, and it will be your share.

²⁷"Consecrate those parts of the ordination ram that belong to Aaron and his sons: the breast that was waved and the thigh that was presented. ²⁸This is always to be the perpetual share from the Israelites for Aaron and his sons. It is the contribution the Israelites are to make to the LORD from their fellowship offerings.

²⁹"Aaron's sacred garments will belong to his descendants so that they can be anointed and ordained in them. ³⁰The son who succeeds him as priest and comes to the tent of meeting to minister in the Holy Place is to wear them seven days.

³¹"Take the ram for the ordination and cook the meat in a sacred place. ³²At the entrance to the tent of meeting, Aaron and his sons are to eat the meat of the ram and the bread that is in the basket. ³³They are to eat these offerings by which atonement was made for their ordination and consecration. But no one else may eat them, because they are sacred. ³⁴And if any of the meat of the ordination ram or any bread is left over till morning, burn it up. It must not be eaten, because it is sacred.

³⁵"Do for Aaron and his sons everything I have commanded you, taking seven days to ordain them. ³⁶Sacrifice a bull each day as a sin offering to make atonement. Purify the altar by making atonement for it, and anoint it to consecrate it. ³⁷For seven days make atonement for the altar and consecrate it. Then the altar will be most holy, and whatever touches it will be holy.

³⁸"This is what you are to offer on the altar regularly each day: two lambs a year old. ³⁹Offer one in the morning and the other at twilight. ⁴⁰With the first lamb offer a tenth of an ephah[a] of the finest flour mixed with a quarter of a hin[b] of oil from pressed olives, and a quarter of a hin of wine as a drink offering. ⁴¹Sacrifice the other lamb at twilight with the same grain offering and its drink offering as in the morning—a pleasing aroma, a food offering presented to the LORD.

⁴²"For the generations to come this burnt offering is to be made regularly at the entrance to the tent of meeting, before the LORD. There

I will meet you and speak to you; ⁴³there also I will meet with the Israelites, and the place will be consecrated by my glory.

⁴⁴"So I will consecrate the tent of meeting and the altar and will consecrate Aaron and his sons to serve me as priests. ⁴⁵Then I will dwell among the Israelites and be their God. ⁴⁶They will know that I am the LORD their God, who brought them out of Egypt so that I might dwell among them. I am the LORD their God.

The Altar of Incense

30 "Make an altar of acacia wood for burning incense. ²It is to be square, a cubit long and a cubit wide, and two cubits high[c]—its horns of one piece with it. ³Overlay the top and all the sides and the horns with pure gold, and make a gold molding around it. ⁴Make two gold rings for the altar below the molding—two on each of the opposite sides—to hold the poles used to carry it. ⁵Make the poles of acacia wood and overlay them with gold. ⁶Put the altar in front of the curtain that shields the ark of the covenant law—before the atonement cover that is over the tablets of the covenant law—where I will meet with you.

⁷"Aaron must burn fragrant incense on the altar every morning when he tends the lamps. ⁸He must burn incense again when he lights the lamps at twilight so incense will burn regularly before the LORD for the generations to come. ⁹Do not offer on this altar any other incense or any burnt offering or grain offering, and do not pour a drink offering on it. ¹⁰Once a year Aaron shall make atonement on its horns. This annual atonement must be made with the blood of the atoning sin offering[d] for the generations to come. It is most holy to the LORD."

Atonement Money

¹¹Then the LORD said to Moses, ¹²"When you take a census of the Israelites to count them, each one must pay the LORD a ransom for his life at the time he is counted. Then no plague will come on them when you number them. ¹³Each one who crosses over to those already counted is to give a half shekel,[e] according to the sanctuary shekel, which weighs twenty gerahs. This half shekel is an offering to the LORD. ¹⁴All who

[a] 40 That is, probably about 3 1/2 pounds or about 1.6 kilograms   [b] 40 That is, probably about 1 quart or about 1 liter   [c] 2 That is, about 1 1/2 feet long and wide and 3 feet high or about 45 centimeters long and wide and 90 centimeters high   [d] 10 Or purification offering   [e] 13 That is, about 1/5 ounce or about 5.8 grams; also in verse 15

cross over, those twenty years old or more, are to give an offering to the LORD. [15]The rich are not to give more than a half shekel and the poor are not to give less when you make the offering to the LORD to atone for your lives. [16]Receive the atonement money from the Israelites and use it for the service of the tent of meeting. It will be a memorial for the Israelites before the LORD, making atonement for your lives."

Basin for Washing

[17]Then the LORD said to Moses, [18]"Make a bronze basin, with its bronze stand, for washing. Place it between the tent of meeting and the altar, and put water in it. [19]Aaron and his sons are to wash their hands and feet with water from it. [20]Whenever they enter the tent of meeting, they shall wash with water so that they will not die. Also, when they approach the altar to minister by presenting a food offering to the LORD, [21]they shall wash their hands and feet so that they will not die. This is to be a lasting ordinance for Aaron and his descendants for the generations to come."

Anointing Oil

[22]Then the LORD said to Moses, [23]"Take the following fine spices: 500 shekels[a] of liquid myrrh, half as much (that is, 250 shekels) of fragrant cinnamon, 250 shekels[b] of fragrant calamus, [24]500 shekels of cassia—all according to the sanctuary shekel—and a hin[c] of olive oil. [25]Make these into a sacred anointing oil, a fragrant blend, the work of a perfumer. It will be the sacred anointing oil. [26]Then use it to anoint the tent of meeting, the ark of the covenant law, [27]the table and all its articles, the lampstand and its accessories, the altar of incense, [28]the altar of burnt offering and all its utensils, and the basin with its stand. [29]You shall consecrate them so they will be most holy, and whatever touches them will be holy.

[30]"Anoint Aaron and his sons and consecrate them so they may serve me as priests. [31]Say to the Israelites, 'This is to be my sacred anointing oil for the generations to come. [32]Do not pour it on anyone else's body and do not make any other oil using the same formula. It is sacred, and you are to consider it sacred. [33]Whoever makes perfume like it and puts it on anyone other than a priest must be cut off from their people.'"

Incense

[34]Then the LORD said to Moses, "Take fragrant spices—gum resin, onycha and galbanum—and pure frankincense, all in equal amounts, [35]and make a fragrant blend of incense, the work of a perfumer. It is to be salted and pure and sacred. [36]Grind some of it to powder and place it in front of the ark of the covenant law in the tent of meeting, where I will meet with you. It shall be most holy to you. [37]Do not make any incense with this formula for yourselves; consider it holy to the LORD. [38]Whoever makes incense like it to enjoy its fragrance must be cut off from their people."

Bezalel and Oholiab

31 Then the LORD said to Moses, [2]"See, I have chosen Bezalel son of Uri, the son of Hur, of the tribe of Judah, [3]and I have filled him with the Spirit of God, with wisdom, with understanding, with knowledge and with all kinds of skills— [4]to make artistic designs for work in gold, silver and bronze, [5]to cut and set stones, to work in wood, and to engage in all kinds of crafts. [6]Moreover, I have appointed Oholiab son of Ahisamak, of the tribe of Dan, to help him. Also I have given ability to all the skilled workers to make everything I have commanded you: [7]the tent of meeting, the ark of the covenant law with the atonement cover on it, and all the other furnishings of the tent— [8]the table and its articles, the pure gold lampstand and all its accessories, the altar of incense, [9]the altar of burnt offering and all its utensils, the basin with its stand— [10]and also the woven garments, both the sacred garments for Aaron the priest and the garments for his sons when they serve as priests, [11]and the anointing oil and fragrant incense for the Holy Place. They are to make them just as I commanded you."

The Sabbath

[12]Then the LORD said to Moses, [13]"Say to the Israelites, 'You must observe my Sabbaths. This will be a sign between me and you for the generations to come, so you may know that I am the LORD, who makes you holy.

[14]"'Observe the Sabbath, because it is holy to you. Anyone who desecrates it is to be put to death; those who do any work on that day must be cut off from their people. [15]For six days work is to be done, but the seventh day is a day of sabbath rest, holy to the LORD. Whoever does any work on the Sabbath day is to be put to death.

---

[a] 23 That is, about 12 1/2 pounds or about 5.8 kilograms; also in verse 24   [b] 23 That is, about 6 1/4 pounds or about 2.9 kilograms   [c] 24 That is, probably about 1 gallon or about 3.8 liters

[16]The Israelites are to observe the Sabbath, celebrating it for the generations to come as a lasting covenant. [17]It will be a sign between me and the Israelites forever, for in six days the LORD made the heavens and the earth, and on the seventh day he rested and was refreshed.'"

[18]When the LORD finished speaking to Moses on Mount Sinai, he gave him the two tablets of the covenant law, the tablets of stone inscribed by the finger of God.

The Golden Calf

32 When the people saw that Moses was so long in coming down from the mountain, they gathered around Aaron and said, "Come, make us gods[a] who will go before us. As for this fellow Moses who brought us up out of Egypt, we don't know what has happened to him."

[2]Aaron answered them, "Take off the gold earrings that your wives, your sons and your daughters are wearing, and bring them to me." [3]So all the people took off their earrings and brought them to Aaron. [4]He took what they handed him and made it into an idol cast in the shape of a calf, fashioning it with a tool. Then they said, "These are your gods,[b] Israel, who brought you up out of Egypt."

[5]When Aaron saw this, he built an altar in front of the calf and announced, "Tomorrow there will be a festival to the LORD." [6]So the next day the people rose early and sacrificed burnt offerings and presented fellowship offerings. Afterward they sat down to eat and drink and got up to indulge in revelry.

[7]Then the LORD said to Moses, "Go down, because your people, whom you brought up out of Egypt, have become corrupt. [8]They have been quick to turn away from what I commanded them and have made themselves an idol cast in the shape of a calf. They have bowed down to it and sacrificed to it and have said, 'These are your gods, Israel, who brought you up out of Egypt.'

[9]"I have seen these people," the LORD said to Moses, "and they are a stiff-necked people. [10]Now leave me alone so that my anger may burn against them and that I may destroy them. Then I will make you into a great nation."

[11]But Moses sought the favor of the LORD his God. "LORD," he said, "why should your anger burn against your people, whom you brought out of Egypt with great power and a mighty hand? [12]Why should the Egyptians say, 'It was with evil intent that he brought them out, to kill them in the mountains and to wipe them off the face of the earth'? Turn from your fierce anger; relent and do not bring disaster on your people. [13]Remember your servants Abraham, Isaac and Israel, to whom you swore by your own self: 'I will make your descendants as numerous as the stars in the sky and I will give your descendants all this land I promised them, and it will be their inheritance forever.'" [14]Then the LORD relented and did not bring on his people the disaster he had threatened.

[15]Moses turned and went down the mountain

---

[a] 1 Or *a god*; also in verses 23 and 31   [b] 4 Or *This is your god*; also in verse 8

The Law of Respect: Aaron Replaces Moses

Exodus 32:1–6

While Moses spoke with God on the mountain, the Israelites began to wonder just where their leader had gone. It didn't take them long to look for a new leader, at least for a season. As they gathered around Aaron to request his help in making a golden calf, they violated the first of the Ten Commandments they were about to receive.

Although Aaron's convictions lagged seriously behind those of Moses, the people begged him to take charge. Why? Probably because of the Law of Respect. Once Moses pulled his disappearing act, the people looked for the next strongest leader to take over. They did so because:

1. **People are like sheep without a shepherd.** They always need a leader; Jesus said so (Mk 6:34).

2. **People focus on immediate felt needs.** They struggle with delayed gratification.

3. **People suffer memory failure.** They always ask: What's the leader done for me lately?

4. **People are insecure.** They begin to worry without abundant signs of hope.

with the two tablets of the covenant law in his hands. They were inscribed on both sides, front and back. ¹⁶The tablets were the work of God; the writing was the writing of God, engraved on the tablets.

¹⁷When Joshua heard the noise of the people shouting, he said to Moses, "There is the sound of war in the camp."

¹⁸Moses replied:

"It is not the sound of victory,
    it is not the sound of defeat;
    it is the sound of singing that I hear."

¹⁹When Moses approached the camp and saw the calf and the dancing, his anger burned and he threw the tablets out of his hands, breaking them to pieces at the foot of the mountain. ²⁰And he took the calf the people had made and burned it in the fire; then he ground it to powder, scattered it on the water and made the Israelites drink it.

²¹He said to Aaron, "What did these people do to you, that you led them into such great sin?"

²²"Do not be angry, my lord," Aaron answered. "You know how prone these people are to evil. ²³They said to me, 'Make us gods who will go before us. As for this fellow Moses who brought us up out of Egypt, we don't know what has happened to him.' ²⁴So I told them, 'Whoever has any gold jewelry, take it off.' Then they gave me the gold, and I threw it into the fire, and out came this calf!"

²⁵Moses saw that the people were running wild and that Aaron had let them get out of control and so become a laughingstock to their enemies. ²⁶So he stood at the entrance to the camp and said, "Whoever is for the LORD, come to me." And all the Levites rallied to him.

²⁷Then he said to them, "This is what the LORD, the God of Israel, says: 'Each man strap a sword to his side. Go back and forth through the camp from one end to the other, each killing his brother and friend and neighbor.'" ²⁸The Levites did as Moses commanded, and that day about three thousand of the people died. ²⁹Then Moses said, "You have been set apart to the LORD today, for you were against your own sons and brothers, and he has blessed you this day."

³⁰The next day Moses said to the people, "You have committed a great sin. But now I will go up to the LORD; perhaps I can make atonement for your sin."

³¹So Moses went back to the LORD and said, "Oh, what a great sin these people have committed! They have made themselves gods of gold.

³²But now, please forgive their sin—but if not, then blot me out of the book you have written."

³³The LORD replied to Moses, "Whoever has sinned against me I will blot out of my book. ³⁴Now go, lead the people to the place I spoke of, and my angel will go before you. However, when the time comes for me to punish, I will punish them for their sin."

³⁵And the LORD struck the people with a plague because of what they did with the calf Aaron had made.

33

Then the LORD said to Moses, "Leave this place, you and the people you brought up out of Egypt, and go up to the land I promised on oath to Abraham, Isaac and Jacob, saying, 'I will give it to your descendants.' ²I will send an angel before you and drive out the Canaanites, Amorites, Hittites, Perizzites, Hivites and Jebusites. ³Go up to the land flowing with milk and honey. But I will not go with you, because you are a stiff-necked people and I might destroy you on the way."

⁴When the people heard these distressing words, they began to mourn and no one put on any ornaments. ⁵For the LORD had said to Moses, "Tell the Israelites, 'You are a stiff-necked people. If I were to go with you even for a moment, I might destroy you. Now take off your ornaments and I will decide what to do with you.'" ⁶So the Israelites stripped off their ornaments at Mount Horeb.

The Tent of Meeting

⁷Now Moses used to take a tent and pitch it outside the camp some distance away, calling it the "tent of meeting." Anyone inquiring of the LORD would go to the tent of meeting outside the camp. ⁸And whenever Moses went out to the tent, all the people rose and stood at the entrances to their tents, watching Moses until he entered the tent. ⁹As Moses went into the tent, the pillar of cloud would come down and stay at the entrance, while the LORD spoke with Moses. ¹⁰Whenever the people saw the pillar of cloud standing at the entrance to the tent, they all stood and worshiped, each at the entrance to their tent. ¹¹The LORD would speak to Moses face to face, as one speaks to a friend. Then Moses would return to the camp, but his young aide Joshua son of Nun did not leave the tent.

Moses and the Glory of the LORD

¹²Moses said to the LORD, "You have been telling me, 'Lead these people,' but you have not let me know whom you will send with me. You

The Law of the Picture: Moses Sets the Example for Intimacy with God

Exodus 33:7–11

Modeling provides the basis of all true leadership. Leaders must set the example for their followers. The number one management principle in the world is this: People do what people see.

Moses demonstrated this truth. The people watched him as he spent time with God, interceding for them in intimate, personal communion—and it changed them more than any sermon could have. If you want to enjoy an intimate relationship with God, as Moses did, you must practice what he did:

1. **Separate yourself regularly** (33:7). You must come apart from the crowd. The key phrase is: *outside the camp.*

2. **Seek God with all your heart** (33:7). You must pursue truth over popularity. The key phrase is: *inquiring of the LORD.*

3. **Be watched by the public** (33:8). You must be willing to take a risk, even though it feels intimidating to be watched and scrutinized. The key phrase is: *watching Moses.*

4. **Learn to listen and obey God's voice** (33:9). You must practice the patience of silence and submission. The key phrase is: *The LORD spoke with Moses.*

5. **Enter covenant partnership with God** (33:10–11). You must be faithful and committed, just as Moses was a trustworthy partner with God. The key phrase is: *The LORD would speak to Moses face to face, as one speaks to a friend.*

have said, 'I know you by name and you have found favor with me.' ¹³If you are pleased with me, teach me your ways so I may know you and continue to find favor with you. Remember that this nation is your people."

¹⁴The LORD replied, "My Presence will go with you, and I will give you rest."

¹⁵Then Moses said to him, "If your Presence does not go with us, do not send us up from here. ¹⁶How will anyone know that you are pleased with me and with your people unless you go with us? What else will distinguish me and your people from all the other people on the face of the earth?"

¹⁷And the LORD said to Moses, "I will do the very thing you have asked, because I am pleased with you and I know you by name."

¹⁸Then Moses said, "Now show me your glory."

¹⁹And the LORD said, "I will cause all my goodness to pass in front of you, and I will proclaim my name, the LORD, in your presence. I will have mercy on whom I will have mercy, and I will have compassion on whom I will have compassion. ²⁰But," he said, "you cannot see my face, for no one may see me and live."

²¹Then the LORD said, "There is a place near me where you may stand on a rock. ²²When my glory passes by, I will put you in a cleft in the rock and cover you with my hand until I have passed by. ²³Then I will remove my hand and you will see my back; but my face must not be seen."

The New Stone Tablets

34 The LORD said to Moses, "Chisel out two stone tablets like the first ones, and I will write on them the words that were on the first tablets, which you broke. ²Be ready in the morning, and then come up on Mount Sinai. Present yourself to me there on top of the mountain. ³No one is to come with you or be seen anywhere on the mountain; not even the flocks and herds may graze in front of the mountain."

⁴So Moses chiseled out two stone tablets like the first ones and went up Mount Sinai early in the morning, as the LORD had commanded him; and he carried the two stone tablets in his hands. ⁵Then the LORD came down in the cloud and stood there with him and proclaimed his name, the LORD. ⁶And he passed in front of Moses, proclaiming, "The LORD, the LORD, the compassionate and gracious God, slow to anger, abounding in love and faithfulness, ⁷maintaining love to thousands, and forgiving wickedness, rebellion and sin. Yet he does not leave

the guilty unpunished; he punishes the children and their children for the sin of the parents to the third and fourth generation."

[8]Moses bowed to the ground at once and worshiped. [9]"Lord," he said, "if I have found favor in your eyes, then let the Lord go with us. Although this is a stiff-necked people, forgive our wickedness and our sin, and take us as your inheritance."

[10]Then the LORD said: "I am making a covenant with you. Before all your people I will do wonders never before done in any nation in all the world. The people you live among will see how awesome is the work that I, the LORD, will do for you. [11]Obey what I command you today. I will drive out before you the Amorites, Canaanites, Hittites, Perizzites, Hivites and Jebusites. [12]Be careful not to make a treaty with those who live in the land where you are going, or they will be a snare among you. [13]Break down their altars, smash their sacred stones and cut down their Asherah poles.[a] [14]Do not worship any other god, for the LORD, whose name is Jealous, is a jealous God.

[15]"Be careful not to make a treaty with those who live in the land; for when they prostitute themselves to their gods and sacrifice to them, they will invite you and you will eat their sacrifices. [16]And when you choose some of their daughters as wives for your sons and those daughters prostitute themselves to their gods, they will lead your sons to do the same.

[17]"Do not make any idols.

[18]"Celebrate the Festival of Unleavened Bread. For seven days eat bread made without yeast, as I commanded you. Do this at the appointed time in the month of Aviv, for in that month you came out of Egypt.

[19]"The first offspring of every womb belongs to me, including all the firstborn males of your livestock, whether from herd or flock. [20]Redeem the firstborn donkey with a lamb, but if you do not redeem it, break its neck. Redeem all your firstborn sons.

"No one is to appear before me empty-handed.

[21]"Six days you shall labor, but on the seventh day you shall rest; even during the plowing season and harvest you must rest.

[22]"Celebrate the Festival of Weeks with the firstfruits of the wheat harvest, and the Festival of Ingathering at the turn of the year.[b] [23]Three times a year all your men are to appear before the Sovereign LORD, the God of Israel. [24]I will drive out nations before you and enlarge your territory, and no one will covet your land when you go up three times each year to appear before the LORD your God.

---

[a] 13 That is, wooden symbols of the goddess Asherah
[b] 22 That is, in the autumn

Moses Leads from His Divine Anointing

Exodus 34:5–7

After Moses shattered the first set of stone commandments, the Lord directed him to chisel out some replacements. When he brought down the new set, his face shone with the glory of God. The nature and character of God had begun to rub off on Moses. The glory took such tangible form that he had to wear a veil over his face. The Israelites sensed both God's presence in Moses' leadership and a divine anointing to lead.

Do others describe your leadership as "anointed"? What does it mean to be anointed? Here's one way to break it down. Anointed leadership is characterized by:

1. **Charisma**
   The anointed enjoy a sense of giftedness that comes from God. It seems magnetic.

2. **Character**
   People see God's nature in your leadership. They trust you.

3. **Competence**
   You have the ability to get the job done. Your leadership produces results.

4. **Conviction**
   Your leadership has backbone. You always stand for what is right.

²⁵"Do not offer the blood of a sacrifice to me along with anything containing yeast, and do not let any of the sacrifice from the Passover Festival remain until morning.

²⁶"Bring the best of the firstfruits of your soil to the house of the LORD your God.

"Do not cook a young goat in its mother's milk."

²⁷Then the LORD said to Moses, "Write down these words, for in accordance with these words I have made a covenant with you and with Israel." ²⁸Moses was there with the LORD forty days and forty nights without eating bread or drinking water. And he wrote on the tablets the words of the covenant—the Ten Commandments.

The Radiant Face of Moses

²⁹When Moses came down from Mount Sinai with the two tablets of the covenant law in his hands, he was not aware that his face was radiant because he had spoken with the LORD. ³⁰When Aaron and all the Israelites saw Moses, his face was radiant, and they were afraid to come near him. ³¹But Moses called to them; so Aaron and all the leaders of the community came back to him, and he spoke to them. ³²Afterward all the Israelites came near him, and he gave them all the commands the LORD had given him on Mount Sinai.

³³When Moses finished speaking to them, he put a veil over his face. ³⁴But whenever he entered the LORD's presence to speak with him, he removed the veil until he came out. And when he came out and told the Israelites what he had been commanded, ³⁵they saw that his face was radiant. Then Moses would put the veil back over his face until he went in to speak with the LORD.

Sabbath Regulations

35 Moses assembled the whole Israelite community and said to them, "These are the things the LORD has commanded you to do: ²For six days, work is to be done, but the seventh day shall be your holy day, a day of sabbath rest to the LORD. Whoever does any work on it is to be put to death. ³Do not light a fire in any of your dwellings on the Sabbath day."

Materials for the Tabernacle

⁴Moses said to the whole Israelite community, "This is what the LORD has commanded: ⁵From what you have, take an offering for the LORD. Everyone who is willing is to bring to the LORD an offering of gold, silver and bronze; ⁶blue, purple and scarlet yarn and fine linen; goat hair; ⁷ram skins dyed red and another type of durable leatherᵃ; acacia wood; ⁸olive oil for the light; spices for the anointing oil and for the fragrant incense; ⁹and onyx stones and other gems to be mounted on the ephod and breastpiece.

¹⁰"All who are skilled among you are to come and make everything the LORD has commanded: ¹¹the tabernacle with its tent and its covering, clasps, frames, crossbars, posts and bases; ¹²the ark with its poles and the atonement cover and the curtain that shields it; ¹³the table with its poles and all its articles and the bread of the Presence; ¹⁴the lampstand that is for light with its accessories, lamps and oil for the light; ¹⁵the altar of incense with its poles, the anointing oil and the fragrant incense; the curtain for the doorway at the entrance to the tabernacle; ¹⁶the altar of burnt offering with its bronze grating, its poles and all its utensils; the bronze basin with its stand; ¹⁷the curtains of the courtyard with its posts and bases, and the curtain for the entrance to the courtyard; ¹⁸the tent pegs for the tabernacle and for the courtyard, and their ropes; ¹⁹the woven garments worn for ministering in the sanctuary—both the sacred garments for Aaron the priest and the garments for his sons when they serve as priests."

²⁰Then the whole Israelite community withdrew from Moses' presence, ²¹and everyone who was willing and whose heart moved them came and brought an offering to the LORD for the work on the tent of meeting, for all its service, and for the sacred garments. ²²All who were willing, men and women alike, came and brought gold jewelry of all kinds: brooches, earrings, rings and ornaments. They all presented their gold as a wave offering to the LORD. ²³Everyone who had blue, purple or scarlet yarn or fine linen, or goat hair, ram skins dyed red or the other durable leather brought them. ²⁴Those presenting an offering of silver or bronze brought it as an offering to the LORD, and everyone who had acacia wood for any part of the work brought it. ²⁵Every skilled woman spun with her hands and brought what she had spun—blue, purple or scarlet yarn or fine linen. ²⁶And all the women who were willing and had the skill spun the goat hair. ²⁷The leaders brought onyx stones and other gems to be mounted on the ephod and breastpiece. ²⁸They also brought spices and olive oil for the light and for the anointing oil and for

---

ᵃ 7 Possibly the hides of large aquatic mammals; also in verse 23

the fragrant incense. ²⁹All the Israelite men and women who were willing brought to the LORD freewill offerings for all the work the LORD through Moses had commanded them to do.

Bezalel and Oholiab

³⁰Then Moses said to the Israelites, "See, the LORD has chosen Bezalel son of Uri, the son of Hur, of the tribe of Judah, ³¹and he has filled him with the Spirit of God, with wisdom, with understanding, with knowledge and with all kinds of skills — ³²to make artistic designs for work in gold, silver and bronze, ³³to cut and set stones, to work in wood and to engage in all kinds of artistic crafts. ³⁴And he has given both him and Oholiab son of Ahisamak, of the tribe of Dan, the ability to teach others. ³⁵He has filled them with skill to do all kinds of work as engravers, designers, embroiderers in blue, purple and scarlet yarn and fine linen, and weavers — all of them skilled workers and designers.

36 ¹So Bezalel, Oholiab and every skilled person to whom the LORD has given skill and ability to know how to carry out all the work of constructing the sanctuary are to do the work just as the LORD has commanded."

²Then Moses summoned Bezalel and Oholiab and every skilled person to whom the LORD had given ability and who was willing to come and do the work. ³They received from Moses all the offerings the Israelites had brought to carry out the work of constructing the sanctuary. And the people continued to bring freewill offerings morning after morning. ⁴So all the skilled workers who were doing all the work on the sanctuary left what they were doing ⁵and said to Moses, "The people are bringing more than enough for doing the work the LORD commanded to be done."

⁶Then Moses gave an order and they sent this word throughout the camp: "No man or woman is to make anything else as an offering for the sanctuary." And so the people were restrained from bringing more, ⁷because what they already had was more than enough to do all the work.

The Tabernacle

⁸All those who were skilled among the workers made the tabernacle with ten curtains of finely twisted linen and blue, purple and scarlet yarn, with cherubim woven into them by expert hands. ⁹All the curtains were the same size — twenty-eight cubits long and four cubits wide.^a ¹⁰They joined five of the curtains together and did the same with the other five. ¹¹Then

they made loops of blue material along the edge of the end curtain in one set, and the same was done with the end curtain in the other set. ¹²They also made fifty loops on one curtain and fifty loops on the end curtain of the other set, with the loops opposite each other. ¹³Then they made fifty gold clasps and used them to fasten the two sets of curtains together so that the tabernacle was a unit.

¹⁴They made curtains of goat hair for the tent over the tabernacle — eleven altogether. ¹⁵All eleven curtains were the same size — thirty cubits long and four cubits wide.^b ¹⁶They joined five of the curtains into one set and the other six into another set. ¹⁷Then they made fifty loops along the edge of the end curtain in one set and also along the edge of the end curtain in the other set. ¹⁸They made fifty bronze clasps to fasten the tent together as a unit. ¹⁹Then they made for the tent a covering of ram skins dyed red, and over that a covering of the other durable leather.^c

²⁰They made upright frames of acacia wood for the tabernacle. ²¹Each frame was ten cubits long and a cubit and a half wide,^d ²²with two projections set parallel to each other. They made all the frames of the tabernacle in this way. ²³They made twenty frames for the south side of the tabernacle ²⁴and made forty silver bases to go under them — two bases for each frame, one under each projection. ²⁵For the other side, the north side of the tabernacle, they made twenty frames ²⁶and forty silver bases — two under each frame. ²⁷They made six frames for the far end, that is, the west end of the tabernacle, ²⁸and two frames were made for the corners of the tabernacle at the far end. ²⁹At these two corners the frames were double from the bottom all the way to the top and fitted into a single ring; both were made alike. ³⁰So there were eight frames and sixteen silver bases — two under each frame.

³¹They also made crossbars of acacia wood: five for the frames on one side of the tabernacle, ³²five for those on the other side, and five for the frames on the west, at the far end of the tabernacle. ³³They made the center crossbar so that it extended from end to end at the middle of the frames. ³⁴They overlaid the frames with gold and made gold rings to hold the crossbars. They also overlaid the crossbars with gold.

---

^a 9 That is, about 42 feet long and 6 feet wide or about 13 meters long and 1.8 meters wide   ^b 15 That is, about 45 feet long and 6 feet wide or about 14 meters long and 1.8 meters wide   ^c 19 Possibly the hides of large aquatic mammals (see 35:7)   ^d 21 That is, about 15 feet long and 2 1/4 feet wide or about 4.5 meters long and 68 centimeters wide

[35] They made the curtain of blue, purple and scarlet yarn and finely twisted linen, with cherubim woven into it by a skilled worker. [36] They made four posts of acacia wood for it and overlaid them with gold. They made gold hooks for them and cast their four silver bases. [37] For the entrance to the tent they made a curtain of blue, purple and scarlet yarn and finely twisted linen — the work of an embroiderer; [38] and they made five posts with hooks for them. They overlaid the tops of the posts and their bands with gold and made their five bases of bronze.

The Ark

37 Bezalel made the ark of acacia wood — two and a half cubits long, a cubit and a half wide, and a cubit and a half high.[a] [2] He overlaid it with pure gold, both inside and out, and made a gold molding around it. [3] He cast four gold rings for it and fastened them to its four feet, with two rings on one side and two rings on the other. [4] Then he made poles of acacia wood and overlaid them with gold. [5] And he inserted the poles into the rings on the sides of the ark to carry it.

[6] He made the atonement cover of pure gold — two and a half cubits long and a cubit and a half wide. [7] Then he made two cherubim out of hammered gold at the ends of the cover. [8] He made one cherub on one end and the second cherub on the other; at the two ends he made them of one piece with the cover. [9] The cherubim had their wings spread upward, overshadowing the cover with them. The cherubim faced each other, looking toward the cover.

The Table

[10] They[b] made the table of acacia wood — two cubits long, a cubit wide and a cubit and a half high.[c] [11] Then they overlaid it with pure gold and made a gold molding around it. [12] They also made around it a rim a handbreadth[d] wide and put a gold molding on the rim. [13] They cast four gold rings for the table and fastened them to the four corners, where the four legs were. [14] The rings were put close to the rim to hold the poles used in carrying the table. [15] The poles for carrying the table were made of acacia wood and were overlaid with gold. [16] And they made from pure gold the articles for the table — its plates and dishes and bowls and its pitchers for the pouring out of drink offerings.

The Lampstand

[17] They made the lampstand of pure gold. They hammered out its base and shaft, and made its flowerlike cups, buds and blossoms of one piece with them. [18] Six branches extended from the sides of the lampstand — three on one side and three on the other. [19] Three cups shaped like almond flowers with buds and blossoms were on one branch, three on the next branch and the same for all six branches extending from the lampstand. [20] And on the lampstand were four cups shaped like almond flowers with buds and blossoms. [21] One bud was under the first pair of branches extending from the lampstand, a second bud under the second pair, and a third bud under the third pair — six branches in all. [22] The buds and the branches were all of one piece with the lampstand, hammered out of pure gold.

[23] They made its seven lamps, as well as its wick trimmers and trays, of pure gold. [24] They made the lampstand and all its accessories from one talent[e] of pure gold.

The Altar of Incense

[25] They made the altar of incense out of acacia wood. It was square, a cubit long and a cubit wide and two cubits high[f] — its horns of one piece with it. [26] They overlaid the top and all the sides and the horns with pure gold, and made a gold molding around it. [27] They made two gold rings below the molding — two on each of the opposite sides — to hold the poles used to carry it. [28] They made the poles of acacia wood and overlaid them with gold.

[29] They also made the sacred anointing oil and the pure, fragrant incense — the work of a perfumer.

The Altar of Burnt Offering

38 They[g] built the altar of burnt offering of acacia wood, three cubits[h] high; it was square, five cubits long and five cubits wide.[i] [2] They made a horn at each of the four corners, so that the horns and the altar were of one piece, and they overlaid the altar with bronze. [3] They made all its utensils of bronze — its pots, shov-

---

[a] 1 That is, about 3 3/4 feet long and 2 1/4 feet wide and high or about 1.1 meters long and 68 centimeters wide and high; similarly in verse 6　[b] 10 Or He; also in verses 11-29　[c] 10 That is, about 3 feet long, 1 1/2 feet wide and 2 1/4 feet high or about 90 centimeters long, 45 centimeters wide and 68 centimeters high　[d] 12 That is, about 3 inches or about 7.5 centimeters　[e] 24 That is, about 75 pounds or about 34 kilograms　[f] 25 That is, about 1 1/2 feet long and wide and 3 feet high or about 45 centimeters long and wide and 90 centimeters high　[g] 1 Or He; also in verses 2-9　[h] 1 That is, about 4 1/2 feet or about 1.4 meters　[i] 1 That is, about 7 1/2 feet or about 2.3 meters long and wide

els, sprinkling bowls, meat forks and firepans. [4]They made a grating for the altar, a bronze network, to be under its ledge, halfway up the altar. [5]They cast bronze rings to hold the poles for the four corners of the bronze grating. [6]They made the poles of acacia wood and overlaid them with bronze. [7]They inserted the poles into the rings so they would be on the sides of the altar for carrying it. They made it hollow, out of boards.

The Basin for Washing

[8]They made the bronze basin and its bronze stand from the mirrors of the women who served at the entrance to the tent of meeting.

The Courtyard

[9]Next they made the courtyard. The south side was a hundred cubits[a] long and had curtains of finely twisted linen, [10]with twenty posts and twenty bronze bases, and with silver hooks and bands on the posts. [11]The north side was also a hundred cubits long and had twenty posts and twenty bronze bases, with silver hooks and bands on the posts.

[12]The west end was fifty cubits[b] wide and had curtains, with ten posts and ten bases, with silver hooks and bands on the posts. [13]The east end, toward the sunrise, was also fifty cubits wide. [14]Curtains fifteen cubits[c] long were on one side of the entrance, with three posts and three bases, [15]and curtains fifteen cubits long were on the other side of the entrance to the courtyard, with three posts and three bases. [16]All the curtains around the courtyard were of finely twisted linen. [17]The bases for the posts were bronze. The hooks and bands on the posts were silver, and their tops were overlaid with silver; so all the posts of the courtyard had silver bands.

[18]The curtain for the entrance to the courtyard was made of blue, purple and scarlet yarn and finely twisted linen — the work of an embroiderer. It was twenty cubits[d] long and, like the curtains of the courtyard, five cubits[e] high, [19]with four posts and four bronze bases. Their hooks and bands were silver, and their tops were overlaid with silver. [20]All the tent pegs of the tabernacle and of the surrounding courtyard were bronze.

The Materials Used

[21]These are the amounts of the materials used for the tabernacle, the tabernacle of the covenant law, which were recorded at Moses' command by the Levites under the direction of Ithamar son of Aaron, the priest. [22](Bezalel son of Uri, the son of Hur, of the tribe of Judah, made everything the LORD commanded Moses; [23]with him was Oholiab son of Ahisamak, of the tribe of Dan — an engraver and designer, and an embroiderer in blue, purple and scarlet yarn and fine linen.) [24]The total amount of the gold from the wave offering used for all the work on the sanctuary was 29 talents and 730 shekels,[f] according to the sanctuary shekel.

[25]The silver obtained from those of the community who were counted in the census was 100 talents[g] and 1,775 shekels,[h] according to the sanctuary shekel — [26]one beka per person, that is, half a shekel,[i] according to the sanctuary shekel, from everyone who had crossed over to those counted, twenty years old or more, a total of 603,550 men. [27]The 100 talents of silver were used to cast the bases for the sanctuary and for the curtain — 100 bases from the 100 talents, one talent for each base. [28]They used the 1,775 shekels to make the hooks for the posts, to overlay the tops of the posts, and to make their bands.

[29]The bronze from the wave offering was 70 talents and 2,400 shekels.[j] [30]They used it to make the bases for the entrance to the tent of meeting, the bronze altar with its bronze grating and all its utensils, [31]the bases for the surrounding courtyard and those for its entrance and all the tent pegs for the tabernacle and those for the surrounding courtyard.

The Priestly Garments

39 From the blue, purple and scarlet yarn they made woven garments for ministering in the sanctuary. They also made sacred garments for Aaron, as the LORD commanded Moses.

The Ephod

[2]They[k] made the ephod of gold, and of blue, purple and scarlet yarn, and of finely twisted linen. [3]They hammered out thin sheets of gold and cut strands to be worked into the blue, purple

---

[a] 9 That is, about 150 feet or about 45 meters   [b] 12 That is, about 75 feet or about 23 meters   [c] 14 That is, about 22 feet or about 6.8 meters   [d] 18 That is, about 30 feet or about 9 meters   [e] 18 That is, about 7 1/2 feet or about 2.3 meters   [f] 24 The weight of the gold was a little over a ton or about 1 metric ton.   [g] 25 That is, about 3 3/4 tons or about 3.4 metric tons; also in verse 27   [h] 25 That is, about 44 pounds or about 20 kilograms; also in verse 28   [i] 26 That is, about 1/5 ounce or about 5.7 grams   [j] 29 The weight of the bronze was about 2 1/2 tons or about 2.4 metric tons.   [k] 2 Or He; also in verses 7, 8 and 22

and scarlet yarn and fine linen — the work of skilled hands. [4]They made shoulder pieces for the ephod, which were attached to two of its corners, so it could be fastened. [5]Its skillfully woven waistband was like it — of one piece with the ephod and made with gold, and with blue, purple and scarlet yarn, and with finely twisted linen, as the LORD commanded Moses.

[6]They mounted the onyx stones in gold filigree settings and engraved them like a seal with the names of the sons of Israel. [7]Then they fastened them on the shoulder pieces of the ephod as memorial stones for the sons of Israel, as the LORD commanded Moses.

The Breastpiece

[8]They fashioned the breastpiece — the work of a skilled craftsman. They made it like the ephod: of gold, and of blue, purple and scarlet yarn, and of finely twisted linen. [9]It was square — a span[a] long and a span wide — and folded double. [10]Then they mounted four rows of precious stones on it. The first row was carnelian, chrysolite and beryl; [11]the second row was turquoise, lapis lazuli and emerald; [12]the third row was jacinth, agate and amethyst; [13]the fourth row was topaz, onyx and jasper.[b] They were mounted in gold filigree settings. [14]There were twelve stones, one for each of the names of the sons of Israel, each engraved like a seal with the name of one of the twelve tribes.

[15]For the breastpiece they made braided chains of pure gold, like a rope. [16]They made two gold filigree settings and two gold rings, and fastened the rings to two of the corners of the breastpiece. [17]They fastened the two gold chains to the rings at the corners of the breastpiece, [18]and the other ends of the chains to the two settings, attaching them to the shoulder pieces of the ephod at the front. [19]They made two gold rings and attached them to the other two corners of the breastpiece on the inside edge next to the ephod. [20]Then they made two more gold rings and attached them to the bottom of the shoulder pieces on the front of the ephod, close to the seam just above the waistband of the ephod. [21]They tied the rings of the breastpiece to the rings of the ephod with blue cord, connecting it to the waistband so that the breastpiece would not swing out from the ephod — as the LORD commanded Moses.

Other Priestly Garments

[22]They made the robe of the ephod entirely of blue cloth — the work of a weaver — [23]with an opening in the center of the robe like the opening of a collar,[c] and a band around this opening, so that it would not tear. [24]They made pomegranates of blue, purple and scarlet yarn and finely twisted linen around the hem of the robe. [25]And they made bells of pure gold and attached them around the hem between the pomegranates. [26]The bells and pomegranates alternated around the hem of the robe to be worn for ministering, as the LORD commanded Moses.

[27]For Aaron and his sons, they made tunics of fine linen — the work of a weaver — [28]and the turban of fine linen, the linen caps and the undergarments of finely twisted linen. [29]The sash was made of finely twisted linen and blue, purple and scarlet yarn — the work of an embroiderer — as the LORD commanded Moses.

[30]They made the plate, the sacred emblem, out of pure gold and engraved on it, like an inscription on a seal: HOLY TO THE LORD. [31]Then they fastened a blue cord to it to attach it to the turban, as the LORD commanded Moses.

Moses Inspects the Tabernacle

[32]So all the work on the tabernacle, the tent of meeting, was completed. The Israelites did everything just as the LORD commanded Moses. [33]Then they brought the tabernacle to Moses: the tent and all its furnishings, its clasps, frames, crossbars, posts and bases; [34]the covering of ram skins dyed red and the covering of another durable leather[d] and the shielding curtain; [35]the ark of the covenant law with its poles and the atonement cover; [36]the table with all its articles and the bread of the Presence; [37]the pure gold lampstand with its row of lamps and all its accessories, and the olive oil for the light; [38]the gold altar, the anointing oil, the fragrant incense, and the curtain for the entrance to the tent; [39]the bronze altar with its bronze grating, its poles and all its utensils; the basin with its stand; [40]the curtains of the courtyard with its posts and bases, and the curtain for the entrance to the courtyard; the ropes and tent pegs for the courtyard; all the furnishings for the tabernacle, the tent of meeting; [41]and the woven garments worn for ministering in the sanctuary, both the sacred garments for Aaron the priest and the garments for his sons when serving as priests.

[42]The Israelites had done all the work just as

---

[a] 9 That is, about 9 inches or about 23 centimeters   [b] 13 The precise identification of some of these precious stones is uncertain.   [c] 23 The meaning of the Hebrew for this word is uncertain.   [d] 34 Possibly the hides of large aquatic mammals

the LORD had commanded Moses. [43]Moses inspected the work and saw that they had done it just as the LORD had commanded. So Moses blessed them.

Setting Up the Tabernacle

40 Then the LORD said to Moses: [2]"Set up the tabernacle, the tent of meeting, on the first day of the first month. [3]Place the ark of the covenant law in it and shield the ark with the curtain. [4]Bring in the table and set out what belongs on it. Then bring in the lampstand and set up its lamps. [5]Place the gold altar of incense in front of the ark of the covenant law and put the curtain at the entrance to the tabernacle.

[6]"Place the altar of burnt offering in front of the entrance to the tabernacle, the tent of meeting; [7]place the basin between the tent of meeting and the altar and put water in it. [8]Set up the courtyard around it and put the curtain at the entrance to the courtyard.

[9]"Take the anointing oil and anoint the tabernacle and everything in it; consecrate it and all its furnishings, and it will be holy. [10]Then anoint the altar of burnt offering and all its utensils; consecrate the altar, and it will be most holy. [11]Anoint the basin and its stand and consecrate them.

[12]"Bring Aaron and his sons to the entrance to the tent of meeting and wash them with water. [13]Then dress Aaron in the sacred garments, anoint him and consecrate him so he may serve me as priest. [14]Bring his sons and dress them in tunics. [15]Anoint them just as you anointed their father, so they may serve me as priests. Their anointing will be to a priesthood that will continue throughout their generations." [16]Moses did everything just as the LORD commanded him.

[17]So the tabernacle was set up on the first day of the first month in the second year. [18]When Moses set up the tabernacle, he put the bases in place, erected the frames, inserted the crossbars and set up the posts. [19]Then he spread the tent over the tabernacle and put the covering over the tent, as the LORD commanded him.

[20]He took the tablets of the covenant law and placed them in the ark, attached the poles to the ark and put the atonement cover over it. [21]Then he brought the ark into the tabernacle and hung the shielding curtain and shielded the ark of the covenant law, as the LORD commanded him.

[22]Moses placed the table in the tent of meeting on the north side of the tabernacle outside the curtain [23]and set out the bread on it before the LORD, as the LORD commanded him.

[24]He placed the lampstand in the tent of meeting opposite the table on the south side of the tabernacle [25]and set up the lamps before the LORD, as the LORD commanded him.

[26]Moses placed the gold altar in the tent of meeting in front of the curtain [27]and burned fragrant incense on it, as the LORD commanded him.

[28]Then he put up the curtain at the entrance to the tabernacle. [29]He set the altar of burnt offering near the entrance to the tabernacle, the tent of meeting, and offered on it burnt offerings and grain offerings, as the LORD commanded him.

[30]He placed the basin between the tent of meeting and the altar and put water in it for washing, [31]and Moses and Aaron and his sons used it to wash their hands and feet. [32]They washed whenever they entered the tent of meeting or approached the altar, as the LORD commanded Moses.

[33]Then Moses set up the courtyard around the tabernacle and altar and put up the curtain at the entrance to the courtyard. And so Moses finished the work.

The Glory of the LORD

[34]Then the cloud covered the tent of meeting, and the glory of the LORD filled the tabernacle. [35]Moses could not enter the tent of meeting because the cloud had settled on it, and the glory of the LORD filled the tabernacle.

[36]In all the travels of the Israelites, whenever the cloud lifted from above the tabernacle, they would set out; [37]but if the cloud did not lift, they did not set out — until the day it lifted. [38]So the cloud of the LORD was over the tabernacle by day, and fire was in the cloud by night, in the sight of all the Israelites during all their travels.

Introduction to LEVITICUS

I n Leviticus God establishes a pattern of life for both his leaders and his people. The book reminds us that leading means being an example—living a life worth imitating. It teaches us that God requires more than lip service to the cause. Our lives should reflect high values and a high standard for living visible to everyone.

Leviticus describes the beginning of a new era for the Israelites—something like what happens when a CEO establishes the policies and procedures for a brand-new organization. The Jewish nation has just gotten off the ground, like a church plant or a new business. All the employees need a system to help them get things done. They need a management-approved track to run on, which is exactly what God lays out.

The first 16 chapters teach us how to approach God, while the last 11 chapters teach us how to relate with him and each other. The book also lists blessings for obedience and consequences for disobedience.

With the ground rules in place, the nation can now move from an entrepreneurial phase to an established phase. Organizational structure enables this huge group of people called the Israelites to evolve from a *meandering crowd* into a *meaningful community*.

Scores of books have been written on the difference between leading and managing; the two functions are distinctly different. Managers may not always be leaders, but leaders must be able to manage what has begun until people and systems emerge to enable the operation to run smoothly.

God's Role in Leviticus

Once again, God takes initiative and begins laying out the rules for approaching him. Because God is holy, Israel's relationship with Yahweh could not be treated flippantly. God leads Moses and the people through the most intricate details of their relationship—from the offerings they were to offer, to the laws surrounding moral purity, to how to implement the required sacrifices. God is holy; therefore his people are to be holy.

Leadership is not some isolated category in our life. We cannot separate our lifestyle from our leadership, or vice versa. God's mega-message in this book to leaders is this: Character does count. Our personal life tremendously impacts our public leadership.

Leaders in Leviticus

Moses, Aaron, Nadab, Abihu, Ithamar

Other People of Influence in Leviticus

Eleazar

Lessons in Leadership

- Leaders must first be good followers.
- Character counts—inward purity impacts outward profession.
- Leadership must be driven by values, not public opinion.

> ■ God disciplines careless disobedience and blesses careful faithfulness.

LEADERSHIP HIGHLIGHTS IN LEVITICUS

The Burnt Offering

1 The Lord called to Moses and spoke to him from the tent of meeting. He said, ²"Speak to the Israelites and say to them: 'When anyone among you brings an offering to the Lord, bring as your offering an animal from either the herd or the flock.

³"'If the offering is a burnt offering from the herd, you are to offer a male without defect. You must present it at the entrance to the tent of meeting so that it will be acceptable to the Lord. ⁴You are to lay your hand on the head of the burnt offering, and it will be accepted on your behalf to make atonement for you. ⁵You are to slaughter the young bull before the Lord, and then Aaron's sons the priests shall bring the blood and splash it against the sides of the altar at the entrance to the tent of meeting. ⁶You are to skin the burnt offering and cut it into pieces. ⁷The sons of Aaron the priest are to put fire on the altar and arrange wood on the fire. ⁸Then Aaron's sons the priests shall arrange the pieces, including the head and the fat, on the wood that is burning on the altar. ⁹You are to wash the internal organs and the legs with water, and the priest is to burn all of it on the altar. It is a burnt offering, a food offering, an aroma pleasing to the Lord.

¹⁰"'If the offering is a burnt offering from the flock, from either the sheep or the goats, you are to offer a male without defect. ¹¹You are to slaughter it at the north side of the altar before the Lord, and Aaron's sons the priests shall splash its blood against the sides of the altar. ¹²You are to cut it into pieces, and the priest shall arrange them, including the head and the fat, on the wood that is burning on the altar. ¹³You are to wash the internal organs and the legs with water, and the priest is to bring all of them and burn them on the altar. It is a burnt offering, a food offering, an aroma pleasing to the Lord.

¹⁴"'If the offering to the Lord is a burnt offering of birds, you are to offer a dove or a young pigeon. ¹⁵The priest shall bring it to the altar, wring off the head and burn it on the altar; its blood shall be drained out on the side of the altar. ¹⁶He is to remove the crop and the feathers[a] and throw them down east of the altar where the ashes are. ¹⁷He shall tear it open by the wings, not dividing it completely, and then the priest shall burn it on the wood that is burning on the altar. It is a burnt offering, a food offering, an aroma pleasing to the Lord.

The Grain Offering

2 "'When anyone brings a grain offering to the Lord, their offering is to be of the finest flour. They are to pour olive oil on it, put incense on it ²and take it to Aaron's sons the priests. The priest shall take a handful of the flour and oil, together with all the incense, and burn this as a memorial[b] portion on the altar, a food offering, an aroma pleasing to the Lord. ³The rest of the grain offering belongs to Aaron and his sons; it is a most holy part of the food offerings presented to the Lord.

⁴"'If you bring a grain offering baked in an oven, it is to consist of the finest flour: either thick loaves made without yeast and with olive oil mixed in or thin loaves made without yeast and brushed with olive oil. ⁵If your grain offering is prepared on a griddle, it is to be made of the finest flour mixed with oil, and without yeast. ⁶Crumble it and pour oil on it; it is a grain offering. ⁷If your grain offering is cooked in a pan, it is to be made of the finest flour and some olive oil. ⁸Bring the grain offering made of these things to the Lord; present it to the priest, who shall take it to the altar. ⁹He shall take out the memorial portion from the grain offering and burn it on the altar as a food offering, an aroma pleasing to the Lord. ¹⁰The rest of the grain offering belongs to Aaron and his sons; it is a most holy part of the food offerings presented to the Lord.

¹¹"'Every grain offering you bring to the Lord must be made without yeast, for you are not to burn any yeast or honey in a food offering presented to the Lord. ¹²You may bring them to the Lord as an offering of the firstfruits, but they are not to be offered on the altar as a pleasing aroma. ¹³Season all your grain offerings with salt. Do not leave the salt of the covenant of your God out of your grain offerings; add salt to all your offerings.

¹⁴"'If you bring a grain offering of firstfruits to the Lord, offer crushed heads of new grain roasted in the fire. ¹⁵Put oil and incense on it; it is a grain offering. ¹⁶The priest shall burn the memorial portion of the crushed grain and the oil, together with all the incense, as a food offering presented to the Lord.

The Fellowship Offering

3 "'If your offering is a fellowship offering, and you offer an animal from the herd, whether male or female, you are to present be-

---

[a] 16 Or crop with its contents; the meaning of the Hebrew for this word is uncertain.   [b] 2 Or representative; also in verses 9 and 16

fore the LORD an animal without defect. [2]You are to lay your hand on the head of your offering and slaughter it at the entrance to the tent of meeting. Then Aaron's sons the priests shall splash the blood against the sides of the altar. [3]From the fellowship offering you are to bring a food offering to the LORD: the internal organs and all the fat that is connected to them, [4]both kidneys with the fat on them near the loins, and the long lobe of the liver, which you will remove with the kidneys. [5]Then Aaron's sons are to burn it on the altar on top of the burnt offering that is lying on the burning wood; it is a food offering, an aroma pleasing to the LORD.

[6]"'If you offer an animal from the flock as a fellowship offering to the LORD, you are to offer a male or female without defect. [7]If you offer a lamb, you are to present it before the LORD, [8]lay your hand on its head and slaughter it in front of the tent of meeting. Then Aaron's sons shall splash its blood against the sides of the altar. [9]From the fellowship offering you are to bring a food offering to the LORD: its fat, the entire fat tail cut off close to the backbone, the internal organs and all the fat that is connected to them, [10]both kidneys with the fat on them near the loins, and the long lobe of the liver, which you will remove with the kidneys. [11]The priest shall burn them on the altar as a food offering presented to the LORD.

[12]"'If your offering is a goat, you are to present it before the LORD, [13]lay your hand on its head and slaughter it in front of the tent of meeting. Then Aaron's sons shall splash its blood against the sides of the altar. [14]From what you offer you are to present this food offering to the LORD: the internal organs and all the fat that is connected to them, [15]both kidneys with the fat on them near the loins, and the long lobe of the liver, which you will remove with the kidneys. [16]The priest shall burn them on the altar as a food offering, a pleasing aroma. All the fat is the LORD's.

[17]"'This is a lasting ordinance for the generations to come, wherever you live: You must not eat any fat or any blood.'"

The Sin Offering

4 The LORD said to Moses, [2]"Say to the Israelites: 'When anyone sins unintentionally and does what is forbidden in any of the LORD's commands—

The Law of Sacrifice: We Must Give Up to Get It Right

Leviticus 1:1—6:30

Have you ever stopped to think that the "laws of sacrifice" in the book of Leviticus illustrate the leadership principle we call the Law of Sacrifice? God lays out specific instructions regarding how his people are to offer sacrifices acceptable to him. He makes it abundantly clear that they must give up certain things in order to get right with him—and getting right with him is crucial in light of the big picture.

Cain and Abel made the first offerings recorded in the Bible. The early leaders of the Old Testament made sacrifices to God wherever they settled. Abraham, Isaac and Jacob built sacrificial altars. Noah offered sacrifices of thanksgiving after the flood. What did all these sacrifices mean, and how can a leader today apply the purposes of these sacrifices?

Offerings	Meaning	Leader's Application
Burnt Offering	Purging of sinful acts by the worshipper	A leader must pursue moral purity.
Grain Offering	Giving the best from a person's property	A leader must offer excellent effort and service.
Peace Offering	Expressed praise to God and fellowship with others	A leader must commit to prioritize relationships.
Sin (Guilt) Offering	To atone for sin when restitution was impossible	A leader must request forgiveness when wrong.
Trespass Offering	Made for unintentional or lesser offenses	A leader must desire to maintain communication/momentum.

3"'If the anointed priest sins, bringing guilt on the people, he must bring to the LORD a young bull without defect as a sin offering[a] for the sin he has committed. 4He is to present the bull at the entrance to the tent of meeting before the LORD. He is to lay his hand on its head and slaughter it there before the LORD. 5Then the anointed priest shall take some of the bull's blood and carry it into the tent of meeting. 6He is to dip his finger into the blood and sprinkle some of it seven times before the LORD, in front of the curtain of the sanctuary. 7The priest shall then put some of the blood on the horns of the altar of fragrant incense that is before the LORD in the tent of meeting. The rest of the bull's blood he shall pour out at the base of the altar of burnt offering at the entrance to the tent of meeting. 8He shall remove all the fat from the bull of the sin offering—all the fat that is connected to the internal organs, 9both kidneys with the fat on them near the loins, and the long lobe of the liver, which he will remove with the kidneys— 10just as the fat is removed from the ox[b] sacrificed as a fellowship offering. Then the priest shall burn them on the altar of burnt offering. 11But the hide of the bull and all its flesh, as well as the head and legs, the internal organs and the intestines— 12that is, all the rest of the bull—he must take outside the camp to a place ceremonially clean, where the ashes are thrown, and burn it there in a wood fire on the ash heap.

13"'If the whole Israelite community sins unintentionally and does what is forbidden in any of the LORD's commands, even though the community is unaware of the matter, when they realize their guilt 14and the sin they committed becomes known, the assembly must bring a young bull as a sin offering and present it before the tent of meeting. 15The elders of the community are to lay their hands on the bull's head before the LORD, and the bull shall be slaughtered before the LORD. 16Then the anointed priest is to take some of the bull's blood into the tent of meeting. 17He shall dip his finger into the blood and sprinkle it before the LORD seven times in front of the curtain. 18He is to put some of the blood on the horns of the altar that is before the LORD in the tent of meeting. The rest of the blood he shall pour out at the base of the altar of burnt offering at the entrance to the tent of meeting. 19He shall remove all the fat from it and burn it on the altar, 20and do with this bull just as he did with the bull for the sin offering. In this way the priest will make atonement

for the community, and they will be forgiven. 21Then he shall take the bull outside the camp and burn it as he burned the first bull. This is the sin offering for the community.

22"'When a leader sins unintentionally and does what is forbidden in any of the commands of the LORD his God, when he realizes his guilt 23and the sin he has committed becomes known, he must bring as his offering a male goat without defect. 24He is to lay his hand on the goat's head and slaughter it at the place where the burnt offering is slaughtered before the LORD. It is a sin offering. 25Then the priest shall take some of the blood of the sin offering with his finger and put it on the horns of the altar of burnt offering and pour out the rest of the blood at the base of the altar. 26He shall burn all the fat on the altar as he burned the fat of the fellowship offering. In this way the priest will make atonement for the leader's sin, and he will be forgiven.

27"'If any member of the community sins unintentionally and does what is forbidden in any of the LORD's commands, when they realize their guilt 28and the sin they have committed becomes known, they must bring as their offering for the sin they committed a female goat without defect. 29They are to lay their hand on the head of the sin offering and slaughter it at the place of the burnt offering. 30Then the priest is to take some of the blood with his finger and put it on the horns of the altar of burnt offering and pour out the rest of the blood at the base of the altar. 31They shall remove all the fat, just as the fat is removed from the fellowship offering, and the priest shall burn it on the altar as an aroma pleasing to the LORD. In this way the priest will make atonement for them, and they will be forgiven.

32"'If someone brings a lamb as their sin offering, they are to bring a female without defect. 33They are to lay their hand on its head and slaughter it for a sin offering at the place where the burnt offering is slaughtered. 34Then the priest shall take some of the blood of the sin offering with his finger and put it on the horns of the altar of burnt offering and pour out the rest of the blood at the base of the altar. 35They shall remove all the fat, just as the fat is removed from the lamb of the fellowship offering, and the priest shall burn it on the altar on top of the food offerings presented to the LORD. In this way the

---

[a] 3 Or purification offering; here and throughout this chapter
[b] 10 The Hebrew word can refer to either male or female.

priest will make atonement for them for the sin they have committed, and they will be forgiven.

5 "'If anyone sins because they do not speak up when they hear a public charge to testify regarding something they have seen or learned about, they will be held responsible.

[2] "'If anyone becomes aware that they are guilty—if they unwittingly touch anything ceremonially unclean (whether the carcass of an unclean animal, wild or domestic, or of any unclean creature that moves along the ground) and they are unaware that they have become unclean, but then they come to realize their guilt; [3] or if they touch human uncleanness (anything that would make them unclean) even though they are unaware of it, but then they learn of it and realize their guilt; [4] or if anyone thoughtlessly takes an oath to do anything, whether good or evil (in any matter one might carelessly swear about) even though they are unaware of it, but then they learn of it and realize their guilt— [5] when anyone becomes aware that they are guilty in any of these matters, they must confess in what way they have sinned. [6] As a penalty for the sin they have committed, they must bring to the LORD a female lamb or goat from the flock as a sin offering[a]; and the priest shall make atonement for them for their sin.

[7] "'Anyone who cannot afford a lamb is to bring two doves or two young pigeons to the LORD as a penalty for their sin—one for a sin offering and the other for a burnt offering. [8] They are to bring them to the priest, who shall first offer the one for the sin offering. He is to wring its head from its neck, not dividing it completely, [9] and is to splash some of the blood of the sin offering against the side of the altar; the rest of the blood must be drained out at the base of the altar. It is a sin offering. [10] The priest shall then offer the other as a burnt offering in the prescribed way and make atonement for them for the sin they have committed, and they will be forgiven.

[11] "'If, however, they cannot afford two doves or two young pigeons, they are to bring as an offering for their sin a tenth of an ephah[b] of the finest flour for a sin offering. They must not put

---

[a] 6 Or *purification offering*; here and throughout this chapter
[b] 11 That is, probably about 3 1/2 pounds or about 1.6 kilograms

---

Planning: The Sacrifices Were Plans to Solve Problems

Leviticus 1:1—6:30

The fastest way to gain leadership is to solve problems. When Adam and Eve first sinned, it was God who initiated a plan for animal sacrifices to atone for sin. God saw the problem and God solved it. The Levitical directions for sacrifices were simply plans to solve sure-to-occur problems. Consider the biblical importance of planning:

1. **God did it.**
   "Have you not heard? Long ago I ordained it. In days of old I planned it; now I have brought it to pass" (Isa 37:26).

2. **Noah did it.**
   Noah received explicit instructions to build the ark. He finished its construction in 120 years, exactly as God told him. And the well-built ship withstood months of flooding.

3. **Nehemiah did it.**
   Nehemiah developed long-range plans to rebuild the wall of Jerusalem. He visualized the project, then planned for its construction. Israelites completed the work in 52 days.

4. **David did it.**
   David made long-range plans to build the temple. God did not allow him to build it, but David did all the planning and secured the construction materials to get the job done.

5. **Jesus told parables about it.**
   Jesus often spoke about the necessity of planning (Mt 7:24–27; Lk 14:28–32; 16:1–8).

How well do you plan? Remember, tomorrow's production begins with today's preparation.

olive oil or incense on it, because it is a sin offering. [12]They are to bring it to the priest, who shall take a handful of it as a memorial[a] portion and burn it on the altar on top of the food offerings presented to the LORD. It is a sin offering. [13]In this way the priest will make atonement for them for any of these sins they have committed, and they will be forgiven. The rest of the offering will belong to the priest, as in the case of the grain offering.'"

The Guilt Offering

[14]The LORD said to Moses: [15]"When anyone is unfaithful to the LORD by sinning unintentionally in regard to any of the LORD's holy things, they are to bring to the LORD as a penalty a ram from the flock, one without defect and of the proper value in silver, according to the sanctuary shekel.[b] It is a guilt offering. [16]They must make restitution for what they have failed to do in regard to the holy things, pay an additional penalty of a fifth of its value and give it all to the priest. The priest will make atonement for them with the ram as a guilt offering, and they will be forgiven.

[17]"If anyone sins and does what is forbidden in any of the LORD's commands, even though they do not know it, they are guilty and will be held responsible. [18]They are to bring to the priest as a guilt offering a ram from the flock, one without defect and of the proper value. In this way the priest will make atonement for them for the wrong they have committed unintentionally, and they will be forgiven. [19]It is a guilt offering; they have been guilty of[c] wrongdoing against the LORD."

6[d] The LORD said to Moses: [2]"If anyone sins and is unfaithful to the LORD by deceiving a neighbor about something entrusted to them or left in their care or about something stolen, or if they cheat their neighbor, [3]or if they find lost property and lie about it, or if they swear falsely about any such sin that people may commit— [4]when they sin in any of these ways and realize their guilt, they must return what they have stolen or taken by extortion, or what was entrusted to them, or the lost property they found, [5]or whatever it was they swore falsely about. They must make restitution in full, add a fifth of the value to it and give it all to the owner on the day they present their guilt offering. [6]And as a penalty they must bring to the priest, that is, to the LORD, their guilt offering, a ram from the flock, one without defect and of the proper value. [7]In this way the priest will make atonement for them before the LORD, and they will be forgiven for any of the things they did that made them guilty."

The Burnt Offering

[8]The LORD said to Moses: [9]"Give Aaron and his sons this command: 'These are the regulations for the burnt offering: The burnt offering is to remain on the altar hearth throughout the night, till morning, and the fire must be kept burning on the altar. [10]The priest shall then put on his linen clothes, with linen undergarments next to his body, and shall remove the ashes of the burnt offering that the fire has consumed on the altar and place them beside the altar. [11]Then he is to take off these clothes and put on others, and carry the ashes outside the camp to a place that is ceremonially clean. [12]The fire on the altar must be kept burning; it must not go out. Every morning the priest is to add firewood and arrange the burnt offering on the fire and burn the fat of the fellowship offerings on it. [13]The fire must be kept burning on the altar continuously; it must not go out.

The Grain Offering

[14]"'These are the regulations for the grain offering: Aaron's sons are to bring it before the LORD, in front of the altar. [15]The priest is to take a handful of the finest flour and some olive oil, together with all the incense on the grain offering, and burn the memorial[a] portion on the altar as an aroma pleasing to the LORD. [16]Aaron and his sons shall eat the rest of it, but it is to be eaten without yeast in the sanctuary area; they are to eat it in the courtyard of the tent of meeting. [17]It must not be baked with yeast; I have given it as their share of the food offerings presented to me. Like the sin offering[e] and the guilt offering, it is most holy. [18]Any male descendant of Aaron may eat it. For all generations to come it is his perpetual share of the food offerings presented to the LORD. Whatever touches them will become holy.[f]'"

[19]The LORD also said to Moses, [20]"This is the offering Aaron and his sons are to bring to the LORD on the day he[g] is anointed: a tenth of an ephah[h] of the finest flour as a regular grain offering, half of it in the morning and half in the

---

[a] 12,15 Or representative   [b] 15 That is, about 2/5 ounce or about 12 grams   [c] 19 Or offering; atonement has been made for their   [d] In Hebrew texts 6:1-7 is numbered 5:20-26, and 6:8-30 is numbered 6:1-23.   [e] 17 Or purification offering; also in verses 25 and 30   [f] 18 Or Whoever touches them must be holy; similarly in verse 27   [g] 20 Or each   [h] 20 That is, probably about 3 1/2 pounds or about 1.6 kilograms

The Law of the Picture: Israel Models Leadership for the Nations

Leviticus 6:1—10:20

"**E**xample is not the main thing influencing others," said Albert Schweitzer. "It is the only thing."

Leviticus 6–10 gives detailed instructions about how leaders are to implement sacrifices, how they are to be publicly ordained, and how they are to live a life of total obedience. Why all the fuss? Because example is the most important tool a leader possesses. People do what people see. Note a few of the areas God's priests and leaders were to model:

1. **Moral and ethical lifestyle**
2. **Proper appearance**
3. **Pure conscience**
4. **Excellence in fulfilling duties**
5. **Healthy relationships and restitution**
6. **Establishing proper priorities**
7. **Maintaining regulations and guidelines**
8. **Initiating forgiveness and atonement**

Once Israel's leaders had established model lifestyles, God called the entire nation to set an example for the rest of the world. The Hebrews were to model godly behavior for other nations!

evening. ²¹It must be prepared with oil on a griddle; bring it well-mixed and present the grain offering broken*ᵃ* in pieces as an aroma pleasing to the LORD. ²²The son who is to succeed him as anointed priest shall prepare it. It is the LORD's perpetual share and is to be burned completely. ²³Every grain offering of a priest shall be burned completely; it must not be eaten."

The Sin Offering

²⁴The LORD said to Moses, ²⁵"Say to Aaron and his sons: 'These are the regulations for the sin offering: The sin offering is to be slaughtered before the LORD in the place the burnt offering is slaughtered; it is most holy. ²⁶The priest who offers it shall eat it; it is to be eaten in the sanc-

tuary area, in the courtyard of the tent of meeting. ²⁷Whatever touches any of the flesh will become holy, and if any of the blood is spattered on a garment, you must wash it in the sanctuary area. ²⁸The clay pot the meat is cooked in must be broken; but if it is cooked in a bronze pot, the pot is to be scoured and rinsed with water. ²⁹Any male in a priest's family may eat it; it is most holy. ³⁰But any sin offering whose blood is brought into the tent of meeting to make atonement in the Holy Place must not be eaten; it must be burned up.

The Guilt Offering

7 "'These are the regulations for the guilt offering, which is most holy: ²The guilt offering is to be slaughtered in the place where the burnt offering is slaughtered, and its blood is to be splashed against the sides of the altar. ³All its fat shall be offered: the fat tail and the fat that covers the internal organs, ⁴both kidneys with the fat on them near the loins, and the long lobe of the liver, which is to be removed with the kidneys. ⁵The priest shall burn them on the altar as a food offering presented to the LORD. It is a guilt offering. ⁶Any male in a priest's family may eat it, but it must be eaten in the sanctuary area; it is most holy.

⁷"'The same law applies to both the sin offering*ᵇ* and the guilt offering: They belong to the priest who makes atonement with them. ⁸The priest who offers a burnt offering for anyone may keep its hide for himself. ⁹Every grain offering baked in an oven or cooked in a pan or on a griddle belongs to the priest who offers it, ¹⁰and every grain offering, whether mixed with olive oil or dry, belongs equally to all the sons of Aaron.

The Fellowship Offering

¹¹"'These are the regulations for the fellowship offering anyone may present to the LORD:
¹²"'If they offer it as an expression of thankfulness, then along with this thank offering they are to offer thick loaves made without yeast and with olive oil mixed in, thin loaves made without yeast and brushed with oil, and thick loaves of the finest flour well-kneaded and with oil mixed in. ¹³Along with their fellowship offering of thanksgiving they are to present an offering with thick loaves of bread made with yeast. ¹⁴They are to bring one of each kind as an offering, a contribution to the LORD; it belongs to the

ᵃ 21 The meaning of the Hebrew for this word is uncertain.
ᵇ 7 Or *purification offering*; also in verse 37

priest who splashes the blood of the fellowship offering against the altar. ¹⁵The meat of their fellowship offering of thanksgiving must be eaten on the day it is offered; they must leave none of it till morning.

¹⁶"'If, however, their offering is the result of a vow or is a freewill offering, the sacrifice shall be eaten on the day they offer it, but anything left over may be eaten on the next day. ¹⁷Any meat of the sacrifice left over till the third day must be burned up. ¹⁸If any meat of the fellowship offering is eaten on the third day, the one who offered it will not be accepted. It will not be reckoned to their credit, for it has become impure; the person who eats any of it will be held responsible.

¹⁹"'Meat that touches anything ceremonially unclean must not be eaten; it must be burned up. As for other meat, anyone ceremonially clean may eat it. ²⁰But if anyone who is unclean eats any meat of the fellowship offering belonging to the LORD, they must be cut off from their people. ²¹Anyone who touches something unclean—whether human uncleanness or an unclean animal or any unclean creature that moves along the ground^a—and then eats any of the meat of the fellowship offering belonging to the LORD must be cut off from their people.'"

Eating Fat and Blood Forbidden

²²The LORD said to Moses, ²³"Say to the Israelites: 'Do not eat any of the fat of cattle, sheep or goats. ²⁴The fat of an animal found dead or torn by wild animals may be used for any other purpose, but you must not eat it. ²⁵Anyone who eats the fat of an animal from which a food offering may be^b presented to the LORD must be cut off from their people. ²⁶And wherever you live, you must not eat the blood of any bird or animal. ²⁷Anyone who eats blood must be cut off from their people.'"

The Priests' Share

²⁸The LORD said to Moses, ²⁹"Say to the Israelites: 'Anyone who brings a fellowship offering to the LORD is to bring part of it as their sacrifice to the LORD. ³⁰With their own hands they are to present the food offering to the LORD; they are to bring the fat, together with the breast, and wave the breast before the LORD as a wave offering. ³¹The priest shall burn the fat on the altar, but the breast belongs to Aaron and his sons. ³²You are to give the right thigh of your fellowship offerings to the priest as a contribution. ³³The son of Aaron who offers the blood and the fat of the fellowship offering shall have the right thigh as his share. ³⁴From the fellowship offerings of the Israelites, I have taken the breast that is waved and the thigh that is presented and have given

^a 21 A few Hebrew manuscripts, Samaritan Pentateuch, Syriac and Targum (see 5:2); most Hebrew manuscripts *any unclean, detestable thing*   ^b 25 Or *offering is*

AARON | The Cost and Expectation of Leadership
Leviticus 7:33–35

PROFILE in leadership

Aaron, like many leaders throughout history, received a divine calling. God chose Aaron and his sons to serve as Israel's priests and charged them with carrying out rituals and sacrifices on behalf of all Israelites. Scripture gives meticulous detail to their ordination and calling. Their conduct was to be beyond reproach—and God made it crystal clear that failure to uphold his established guidelines would result in death.

Numerous accounts in the book of Leviticus demonstrate the high cost and expectation that goes with a holy calling to leadership positions. As the high priest, Aaron was the only one authorized to enter the Most Holy Place and appear before the very presence of God. The Lord set Aaron apart for his holy work.

Despite his high calling, Aaron struggled with his authority and later caved in to the depraved wishes of the people. He failed at a crucial juncture and led Israel in a pagan worship service, an abomination that led to the deaths of many Israelites. Aaron had been set apart for God's service, but he chose to live and lead otherwise.

The failure of a leader usually results in consequences far more grave than the fall of a non-leader. On the day Aaron failed, "about three thousand of the people died" (Ex 32:28). When leaders fail, followers pay the price.

them to Aaron the priest and his sons as their perpetual share from the Israelites.'"

³⁵This is the portion of the food offerings presented to the LORD that were allotted to Aaron and his sons on the day they were presented to serve the LORD as priests. ³⁶On the day they were anointed, the LORD commanded that the Israelites give this to them as their perpetual share for the generations to come.

³⁷These, then, are the regulations for the burnt offering, the grain offering, the sin offering, the guilt offering, the ordination offering and the fellowship offering, ³⁸which the LORD gave Moses at Mount Sinai in the Desert of Sinai on the day he commanded the Israelites to bring their offerings to the LORD.

The Ordination of Aaron and His Sons

8 The LORD said to Moses, ²"Bring Aaron and his sons, their garments, the anointing oil, the bull for the sin offering,^a the two rams and the basket containing bread made without yeast, ³and gather the entire assembly at the entrance to the tent of meeting." ⁴Moses did as the LORD commanded him, and the assembly gathered at the entrance to the tent of meeting.

⁵Moses said to the assembly, "This is what the LORD has commanded to be done." ⁶Then Moses brought Aaron and his sons forward and washed them with water. ⁷He put the tunic on Aaron, tied the sash around him, clothed him with the robe and put the ephod on him. He also fastened the ephod with a decorative waistband, which he tied around him. ⁸He placed the breastpiece on him and put the Urim and Thummim in the breastpiece. ⁹Then he placed the turban on Aaron's head and set the gold plate, the sacred emblem, on the front of it, as the LORD commanded Moses.

¹⁰Then Moses took the anointing oil and anointed the tabernacle and everything in it, and so consecrated them. ¹¹He sprinkled some of the oil on the altar seven times, anointing the altar and all its utensils and the basin with its stand, to consecrate them. ¹²He poured some of the anointing oil on Aaron's head and anointed him to consecrate him. ¹³Then he brought Aaron's sons forward, put tunics on them, tied sashes around them and fastened caps on them, as the LORD commanded Moses.

¹⁴He then presented the bull for the sin offering, and Aaron and his sons laid their hands on its head. ¹⁵Moses slaughtered the bull and took some of the blood, and with his finger he put it

on all the horns of the altar to purify the altar. He poured out the rest of the blood at the base of the altar. So he consecrated it to make atonement for it. ¹⁶Moses also took all the fat around the internal organs, the long lobe of the liver, and both kidneys and their fat, and burned it on the altar. ¹⁷But the bull with its hide and its flesh and its intestines he burned up outside the camp, as the LORD commanded Moses.

¹⁸He then presented the ram for the burnt offering, and Aaron and his sons laid their hands on its head. ¹⁹Then Moses slaughtered the ram and splashed the blood against the sides of the altar. ²⁰He cut the ram into pieces and burned the head, the pieces and the fat. ²¹He washed the internal organs and the legs with water and burned the whole ram on the altar. It was a burnt offering, a pleasing aroma, a food offering presented to the LORD, as the LORD commanded Moses.

²²He then presented the other ram, the ram for the ordination, and Aaron and his sons laid their hands on its head. ²³Moses slaughtered the ram and took some of its blood and put it on the lobe of Aaron's right ear, on the thumb of his right hand and on the big toe of his right foot. ²⁴Moses also brought Aaron's sons forward and put some of the blood on the lobes of their right ears, on the thumbs of their right hands and on the big toes of their right feet. Then he splashed blood against the sides of the altar. ²⁵After that, he took the fat, the fat tail, all the fat around the internal organs, the long lobe of the liver, both kidneys and their fat and the right thigh. ²⁶And from the basket of bread made without yeast, which was before the LORD, he took one thick loaf, one thick loaf with olive oil mixed in, and one thin loaf, and he put these on the fat portions and on the right thigh. ²⁷He put all these in the hands of Aaron and his sons, and they waved them before the LORD as a wave offering. ²⁸Then Moses took them from their hands and burned them on the altar on top of the burnt offering as an ordination offering, a pleasing aroma, a food offering presented to the LORD. ²⁹Moses also took the breast, which was his share of the ordination ram, and waved it before the LORD as a wave offering, as the LORD commanded Moses.

³⁰Then Moses took some of the anointing oil and some of the blood from the altar and sprinkled them on Aaron and his garments and on his sons and their garments. So he consecrated

---

^a 2 Or *purification offering*; also in verse 14

Aaron and his garments and his sons and their garments. ³¹Moses then said to Aaron and his sons, "Cook the meat at the entrance to the tent of meeting and eat it there with the bread from the basket of ordination offerings, as I was commanded: 'Aaron and his sons are to eat it.' ³²Then burn up the rest of the meat and the bread. ³³Do not leave the entrance to the tent of meeting for seven days, until the days of your ordination are completed, for your ordination will last seven days. ³⁴What has been done today was commanded by the LORD to make atonement for you. ³⁵You must stay at the entrance to the tent of meeting day and night for seven days and do what the LORD requires, so you will not die; for that is what I have been commanded."

³⁶So Aaron and his sons did everything the LORD commanded through Moses.

The Priests Begin Their Ministry

9 On the eighth day Moses summoned Aaron and his sons and the elders of Israel. ²He said to Aaron, "Take a bull calf for your sin offering[a] and a ram for your burnt offering, both without defect, and present them before the

---

[a] 2 Or *purification offering*; here and throughout this chapter

---

Aaron: God's Call, People's Confirmation

Leviticus 8:1–36

Aaron receives his ordination to the priesthood in Leviticus 8. By that time the people already recognized him as a leader, but now God gives him his divine calling. The Lord instructs Aaron to wear certain garments and accessories as an outward symbol of an inward call.

For the godly leader, the call of God becomes a personal foundation for ministry, a point of revelation. One dare not enter a spiritual position without a divine calling. God's call is the first step for anyone who desires a spiritual leadership position.

The Call

Every call has two components: inward and outward. God's hand on the person provides the inward component. Through it the person recognizes that he or she is supposed to occupy a leadership position. And the outward component? This comes when others confirm that God's hand does indeed rest on the person. Only God anoints a person to lead and minister; at best, organizations merely recognize and agree with his anointing. A spiritual leader's authority comes from God, not men.

The word "authorize" is derived from a Latin word which means "to increase or to grow." Frank Damazio reminds us that the word "authorize" suggests the spiritual meanings of: a builder of spiritual buildings; a creator of spiritual families; a doer of spiritual deeds; an author of spiritual writings; a teacher of spiritual knowledge; a spiritual advisor of actions; a promoter of spiritual plans; a supporter of spiritual laws; a spiritual leader in public life; a model of spiritual conduct; a spiritual guardian of women and minors; and a champion of other's spiritual welfare.

Your Response

A few signs often accompany God's call of a person into vocational ministry. Romans 1:14–16 suggests some of these signs:

1. **"I am eager"** (a sense of passion and urgency about reaching people)
2. **"I am obligated"** (a feeling that one cannot do anything else vocationally)
3. **"I am not ashamed"** (a conviction to do what others may think illogical)

The Ordination

The word "ordain" comes from a Latin word that means to "set in order, to arrange, appoint or regulate." To ordain someone means to officially appoint that person to an office and to regulate his or her ministry activities. True ordination does not precede ministry; it follows it. Only after a person exercises obvious spiritual influence, enabled by the Holy Spirit, is that individual ready to be ordained by humans. God calls, and the people confirm the call through ordination.

LORD. ³Then say to the Israelites: 'Take a male goat for a sin offering, a calf and a lamb — both a year old and without defect — for a burnt offering, ⁴and an ox[a] and a ram for a fellowship offering to sacrifice before the LORD, together with a grain offering mixed with olive oil. For today the LORD will appear to you.'"

⁵They took the things Moses commanded to the front of the tent of meeting, and the entire assembly came near and stood before the LORD. ⁶Then Moses said, "This is what the LORD has commanded you to do, so that the glory of the LORD may appear to you."

⁷Moses said to Aaron, "Come to the altar and sacrifice your sin offering and your burnt offering and make atonement for yourself and the people; sacrifice the offering that is for the people and make atonement for them, as the LORD has commanded."

⁸So Aaron came to the altar and slaughtered the calf as a sin offering for himself. ⁹His sons brought the blood to him, and he dipped his finger into the blood and put it on the horns of the altar; the rest of the blood he poured out at the base of the altar. ¹⁰On the altar he burned the fat, the kidneys and the long lobe of the liver from the sin offering, as the LORD commanded Moses; ¹¹the flesh and the hide he burned up outside the camp.

¹²Then he slaughtered the burnt offering. His sons handed him the blood, and he splashed it against the sides of the altar. ¹³They handed him the burnt offering piece by piece, including the head, and he burned them on the altar. ¹⁴He washed the internal organs and the legs and burned them on top of the burnt offering on the altar.

¹⁵Aaron then brought the offering that was for the people. He took the goat for the people's sin offering and slaughtered it and offered it for a sin offering as he did with the first one. ¹⁶He brought the burnt offering and offered it in the prescribed way. ¹⁷He also brought the grain offering, took a handful of it and burned it on the altar in addition to the morning's burnt offering.

¹⁸He slaughtered the ox and the ram as the fellowship offering for the people. His sons handed him the blood, and he splashed it against the sides of the altar. ¹⁹But the fat portions of the ox and the ram — the fat tail, the layer of fat, the kidneys and the long lobe of the liver — ²⁰these they laid on the breasts, and then Aaron burned the fat on the altar. ²¹Aaron waved the breasts and the right thigh before the LORD as a wave offering, as Moses commanded.

²²Then Aaron lifted his hands toward the people and blessed them. And having sacrificed the sin offering, the burnt offering and the fellowship offering, he stepped down.

²³Moses and Aaron then went into the tent of meeting. When they came out, they blessed the people; and the glory of the LORD appeared to all the people. ²⁴Fire came out from the presence of the LORD and consumed the burnt offering and the fat portions on the altar. And when all the people saw it, they shouted for joy and fell facedown.

The Death of Nadab and Abihu

10 Aaron's sons Nadab and Abihu took their censers, put fire in them and added incense; and they offered unauthorized fire before the LORD, contrary to his command. ²So fire came out from the presence of the LORD and consumed them, and they died before the LORD. ³Moses then said to Aaron, "This is what the LORD spoke of when he said:

"'Among those who approach me
   I will be proved holy;
in the sight of all the people
   I will be honored.'"

Aaron remained silent.

⁴Moses summoned Mishael and Elzaphan, sons of Aaron's uncle Uzziel, and said to them, "Come here; carry your cousins outside the camp, away from the front of the sanctuary." ⁵So they came and carried them, still in their tunics, outside the camp, as Moses ordered.

⁶Then Moses said to Aaron and his sons Eleazar and Ithamar, "Do not let your hair become unkempt[b] and do not tear your clothes, or you will die and the LORD will be angry with the whole community. But your relatives, all the Israelites, may mourn for those the LORD has destroyed by fire. ⁷Do not leave the entrance to the tent of meeting or you will die, because the LORD's anointing oil is on you." So they did as Moses said.

⁸Then the LORD said to Aaron, ⁹"You and your sons are not to drink wine or other fermented drink whenever you go into the tent of meeting, or you will die. This is a lasting ordinance for the generations to come, ¹⁰so that you can distinguish between the holy and the common, between the unclean and the clean, ¹¹and so you can teach the Israelites all the decrees the LORD has given them through Moses."

---

[a] 4 The Hebrew word can refer to either male or female; also in verses 18 and 19.   [b] 6 Or *Do not uncover your heads*

Nadab and Abihu Break the Law of Solid Ground

Leviticus 10:1–2

God does not take it lightly when the leaders he calls disregard his commandments. When Nadab and Abihu broke God's laws, they never recovered. God executed them on the spot.

Sounds harsh, you say? Consider this. Any movement in its infant stages must set a standard or pattern of operations. If God allowed compromise at the beginning, things would surely grow worse. The same principle came into play in the new church when God took the lives of Ananias and Sapphira (Ac 5:1–11).

Nadab and Abihu broke the Law of Solid Ground. As holy priests and trusted leaders, they were supposed to model obedience for the people. God could not permit them even the slightest renegade move, the smallest maverick act, for that would give permission for others to compromise as well. What was the sin of these leaders?

1. *Independence:* They acted presumptuously, apart from God's leadership.
2. *Impatience:* They failed to wait on the Lord for direction.
3. *Ignorance:* They moved without knowledge of what God wanted.
4. *Illegality:* They acted contrary to God's command.
5. *Impulsivity:* They did what they wanted, driven by ego, not submission.
6. *Insensitivity:* They paid no attention to God's instruction.

[12]Moses said to Aaron and his remaining sons, Eleazar and Ithamar, "Take the grain offering left over from the food offerings prepared without yeast and presented to the LORD and eat it beside the altar, for it is most holy. [13]Eat it in the sanctuary area, because it is your share and your sons' share of the food offerings presented to the LORD; for so I have been commanded. [14]But you and your sons and your daughters may eat the breast that was waved and the thigh that was presented. Eat them in a ceremonially clean place; they have been given to you and your children as your share of the Israelites' fellowship offerings. [15]The thigh that was presented and the breast that was waved must be brought with the fat portions of the food offerings, to be waved before the LORD as a wave offering. This will be the perpetual share for you and your children, as the LORD has commanded."

[16]When Moses inquired about the goat of the sin offering[a] and found that it had been burned up, he was angry with Eleazar and Ithamar, Aaron's remaining sons, and asked, [17]"Why didn't you eat the sin offering in the sanctuary area? It is most holy; it was given to you to take away the guilt of the community by making atonement for them before the LORD. [18]Since its blood was not taken into the Holy Place, you should have eaten the goat in the sanctuary area, as I commanded."

[19]Aaron replied to Moses, "Today they sacrificed their sin offering and their burnt offering before the LORD, but such things as this have happened to me. Would the LORD have been pleased if I had eaten the sin offering today?" [20]When Moses heard this, he was satisfied.

Clean and Unclean Food

11 The LORD said to Moses and Aaron, [2]"Say to the Israelites: 'Of all the animals that live on land, these are the ones you may eat: [3]You may eat any animal that has a divided hoof and that chews the cud.

[4]"There are some that only chew the cud or only have a divided hoof, but you must not eat them. The camel, though it chews the cud, does not have a divided hoof; it is ceremonially unclean for you. [5]The hyrax, though it chews the cud, does not have a divided hoof; it is unclean for you. [6]The rabbit, though it chews the cud, does not have a divided hoof; it is unclean for you. [7]And the pig, though it has a divided hoof, does not chew the cud; it is unclean for you. [8]You must not eat their meat or touch their carcasses; they are unclean for you.

[9]"Of all the creatures living in the water of the seas and the streams you may eat any that have fins and scales. [10]But all creatures in the seas or streams that do not have fins and scales — whether among all the swarming things or among all the other living creatures in the water — you are to regard as unclean. [11]And since you are to regard them as unclean, you must not eat their meat; you must regard their carcasses as unclean. [12]Anything living in the

---

[a] 16 Or *purification offering*; also in verses 17 and 19

water that does not have fins and scales is to be regarded as unclean by you.

13 "'These are the birds you are to regard as unclean and not eat because they are unclean: the eagle,[a] the vulture, the black vulture, 14the red kite, any kind of black kite, 15any kind of raven, 16the horned owl, the screech owl, the gull, any kind of hawk, 17the little owl, the cormorant, the great owl, 18the white owl, the desert owl, the osprey, 19the stork, any kind of heron, the hoopoe and the bat.

20 "'All flying insects that walk on all fours are to be regarded as unclean by you. 21There are, however, some flying insects that walk on all fours that you may eat: those that have jointed legs for hopping on the ground. 22Of these you may eat any kind of locust, katydid, cricket or grasshopper. 23But all other flying insects that have four legs you are to regard as unclean.

24 "'You will make yourselves unclean by these; whoever touches their carcasses will be unclean till evening. 25Whoever picks up one of their carcasses must wash their clothes, and they will be unclean till evening.

26 "'Every animal that does not have a divided hoof or that does not chew the cud is unclean for you; whoever touches the carcass of any of them will be unclean. 27Of all the animals that walk on all fours, those that walk on their paws are unclean for you; whoever touches their carcasses will be unclean till evening. 28Anyone who picks up their carcasses must wash their clothes, and they will be unclean till evening. These animals are unclean for you.

29 "'Of the animals that move along the ground, these are unclean for you: the weasel, the rat, any kind of great lizard, 30the gecko, the monitor lizard, the wall lizard, the skink and the chameleon. 31Of all those that move along the ground, these are unclean for you. Whoever touches them when they are dead will be unclean till evening. 32When one of them dies and falls on something, that article, whatever its use, will be unclean, whether it is made of wood, cloth, hide or sackcloth. Put it in water; it will be unclean till evening, and then it will be clean. 33If one of them falls into a clay pot, everything in it will be unclean, and you must break the pot. 34Any food you are allowed to eat that has come into contact with water from any such pot is unclean, and any liquid that is drunk from such a pot is unclean. 35Anything that one of their carcasses falls on becomes unclean; an oven or cooking pot must be broken up. They are unclean, and you are to regard them as un-

clean. 36A spring, however, or a cistern for collecting water remains clean, but anyone who touches one of these carcasses is unclean. 37If a carcass falls on any seeds that are to be planted, they remain clean. 38But if water has been put on the seed and a carcass falls on it, it is unclean for you.

39 "'If an animal that you are allowed to eat dies, anyone who touches its carcass will be unclean till evening. 40Anyone who eats some of its carcass must wash their clothes, and they will be unclean till evening. Anyone who picks up the carcass must wash their clothes, and they will be unclean till evening.

41 "'Every creature that moves along the ground is to be regarded as unclean; it is not to be eaten. 42You are not to eat any creature that moves along the ground, whether it moves on its belly or walks on all fours or on many feet; it is unclean. 43Do not defile yourselves by any of these creatures. Do not make yourselves unclean by means of them or be made unclean by them. 44I am the LORD your God; consecrate yourselves and be holy, because I am holy. Do not make yourselves unclean by any creature that moves along the ground. 45I am the LORD, who brought you up out of Egypt to be your God; therefore be holy, because I am holy.

46 "'These are the regulations concerning animals, birds, every living thing that moves about in the water and every creature that moves along the ground. 47You must distinguish between the unclean and the clean, between living creatures that may be eaten and those that may not be eaten.'"

Purification After Childbirth

12 The LORD said to Moses, 2"Say to the Israelites: 'A woman who becomes pregnant and gives birth to a son will be ceremonially unclean for seven days, just as she is unclean during her monthly period. 3On the eighth day the boy is to be circumcised. 4Then the woman must wait thirty-three days to be purified from her bleeding. She must not touch anything sacred or go to the sanctuary until the days of her purification are over. 5If she gives birth to a daughter, for two weeks the woman will be unclean, as during her period. Then she must wait sixty-six days to be purified from her bleeding.

6 "'When the days of her purification for a son or daughter are over, she is to bring to the priest

[a] 13 The precise identification of some of the birds, insects and animals in this chapter is uncertain.

at the entrance to the tent of meeting a year-old lamb for a burnt offering and a young pigeon or a dove for a sin offering.[a] [7]He shall offer them before the LORD to make atonement for her, and then she will be ceremonially clean from her flow of blood.

"'These are the regulations for the woman who gives birth to a boy or a girl. [8]But if she cannot afford a lamb, she is to bring two doves or two young pigeons, one for a burnt offering and the other for a sin offering. In this way the priest will make atonement for her, and she will be clean.'"

Character: God's Call Must Be Taken Seriously

Leviticus 10:1—12:8

God takes seriously the issue of character. We see his concern repeatedly in Leviticus, from the sin of Aaron's sons to his detailed instructions about clean and unclean food to the purification of a woman after childbirth.

While today we recognize some obvious medical and biological reasons for his precise directions, we can assume God intended through these texts to teach his leaders and his people an important lesson: Put "being" before "doing." Get *yourself* right before you work on anything else.

Far too often we jump to mechanics, methods and techniques. We put style ahead of substance. We focus on charisma but neglect character. The following axioms beckon us to put our character first:

1. **We are given our gifts, but we must develop our character.**
2. **Our character earns the trust of others.**
3. **Only good character gives lasting success with people.**
4. **Sound character communicates credibility and consistency.**
5. **Our gifts can take us further than our character can sustain us.**
6. **Our character colors our perspective.**
7. **Ability may get you to the top, but it takes character to keep you there.**
8. **We cannot rise above the limitations of our character.**

Regulations About Defiling Skin Diseases

13 The LORD said to Moses and Aaron, [2]"When anyone has a swelling or a rash or a shiny spot on their skin that may be a defiling skin disease,[b] they must be brought to Aaron the priest or to one of his sons[c] who is a priest. [3]The priest is to examine the sore on the skin, and if the hair in the sore has turned white and the sore appears to be more than skin deep, it is a defiling skin disease. When the priest examines that person, he shall pronounce them ceremonially unclean. [4]If the shiny spot on the skin is white but does not appear to be more than skin deep and the hair in it has not turned white, the priest is to isolate the affected person for seven days. [5]On the seventh day the priest is to examine them, and if he sees that the sore is unchanged and has not spread in the skin, he is to isolate them for another seven days. [6]On the seventh day the priest is to examine them again, and if the sore has faded and has not spread in the skin, the priest shall pronounce them clean; it is only a rash. They must wash their clothes, and they will be clean. [7]But if the rash does spread in their skin after they have shown themselves to the priest to be pronounced clean, they must appear before the priest again. [8]The priest is to examine that person, and if the rash has spread in the skin, he shall pronounce them unclean; it is a defiling skin disease.

[9]"When anyone has a defiling skin disease, they must be brought to the priest. [10]The priest is to examine them, and if there is a white swelling in the skin that has turned the hair white and if there is raw flesh in the swelling, [11]it is a chronic skin disease and the priest shall pronounce them unclean. He is not to isolate them, because they are already unclean.

[12]"If the disease breaks out all over their skin and, so far as the priest can see, it covers all the skin of the affected person from head to foot, [13]the priest is to examine them, and if the disease has covered their whole body, he shall pronounce them clean. Since it has all turned white, they are clean. [14]But whenever raw flesh appears on them, they will be unclean. [15]When the priest sees the raw flesh, he shall pronounce them unclean. The raw flesh is unclean; they have a defiling disease. [16]If the raw flesh changes and turns white, they must go to the priest. [17]The

---

[a] 6 Or *purification offering*; also in verse 8   [b] 2 The Hebrew word for *defiling skin disease*, traditionally translated "leprosy," was used for various diseases affecting the skin; here and throughout verses 3-46.   [c] 2 Or *descendants*

priest is to examine them, and if the sores have turned white, the priest shall pronounce the affected person clean; then they will be clean.

[18]"When someone has a boil on their skin and it heals, [19]and in the place where the boil was, a white swelling or reddish-white spot appears, they must present themselves to the priest. [20]The priest is to examine it, and if it appears to be more than skin deep and the hair in it has turned white, the priest shall pronounce that person unclean. It is a defiling skin disease that has broken out where the boil was. [21]But if, when the priest examines it, there is no white hair in it and it is not more than skin deep and has faded, then the priest is to isolate them for seven days. [22]If it is spreading in the skin, the priest shall pronounce them unclean; it is a defiling disease. [23]But if the spot is unchanged and has not spread, it is only a scar from the boil, and the priest shall pronounce them clean.

[24]"When someone has a burn on their skin and a reddish-white or white spot appears in the raw flesh of the burn, [25]the priest is to examine the spot, and if the hair in it has turned white, and it appears to be more than skin deep, it is a defiling disease that has broken out in the burn. The priest shall pronounce them unclean; it is a defiling skin disease. [26]But if the priest examines it and there is no white hair in the spot and if it is not more than skin deep and has faded, then the priest is to isolate them for seven days. [27]On the seventh day the priest is to examine that person, and if it is spreading in the skin, the priest shall pronounce them unclean; it is a defiling skin disease. [28]If, however, the spot is unchanged and has not spread in the skin but has faded, it is a swelling from the burn, and the priest shall pronounce them clean; it is only a scar from the burn.

[29]"If a man or woman has a sore on their head or chin, [30]the priest is to examine the sore, and if it appears to be more than skin deep and the hair in it is yellow and thin, the priest shall pronounce them unclean; it is a defiling skin disease on the head or chin. [31]But if, when the priest examines the sore, it does not seem to be more than skin deep and there is no black hair in it, then the priest is to isolate the affected person for seven days. [32]On the seventh day the priest is to examine the sore, and if it has not spread and there is no yellow hair in it and it does not appear to be more than skin deep, [33]then the man or woman must shave themselves, except for the affected area, and the priest is to keep them isolated another seven days. [34]On the seventh day the priest is to examine the sore, and if

it has not spread in the skin and appears to be no more than skin deep, the priest shall pronounce them clean. They must wash their clothes, and they will be clean. [35]But if the sore does spread in the skin after they are pronounced clean, [36]the priest is to examine them, and if he finds that the sore has spread in the skin, he does not need to look for yellow hair; they are unclean. [37]If, however, the sore is unchanged so far as the priest can see, and if black hair has grown in it, the affected person is healed. They are clean, and the priest shall pronounce them clean.

[38]"When a man or woman has white spots on the skin, [39]the priest is to examine them, and if the spots are dull white, it is a harmless rash that has broken out on the skin; they are clean.

[40]"A man who has lost his hair and is bald is clean. [41]If he has lost his hair from the front of his scalp and has a bald forehead, he is clean. [42]But if he has a reddish-white sore on his bald head or forehead, it is a defiling disease breaking out on his head or forehead. [43]The priest is to examine him, and if the swollen sore on his head or forehead is reddish-white like a defiling skin disease, [44]the man is diseased and is unclean. The priest shall pronounce him unclean because of the sore on his head.

[45]"Anyone with such a defiling disease must wear torn clothes, let their hair be unkempt,[a] cover the lower part of their face and cry out, 'Unclean! Unclean!' [46]As long as they have the disease they remain unclean. They must live alone; they must live outside the camp.

Regulations About Defiling Molds

[47]"As for any fabric that is spoiled with a defiling mold — any woolen or linen clothing, [48]any woven or knitted material of linen or wool, any leather or anything made of leather — [49]if the affected area in the fabric, the leather, the woven or knitted material, or any leather article, is greenish or reddish, it is a defiling mold and must be shown to the priest. [50]The priest is to examine the affected area and isolate the article for seven days. [51]On the seventh day he is to examine it, and if the mold has spread in the fabric, the woven or knitted material, or the leather, whatever its use, it is a persistent defiling mold; the article is unclean. [52]He must burn the fabric, the woven or knitted material of wool or linen, or any leather article that has been spoiled; because the defiling mold is persistent, the article must be burned.

---

[a] 45 Or clothes, uncover their head

⁵³"But if, when the priest examines it, the mold has not spread in the fabric, the woven or knitted material, or the leather article, ⁵⁴he shall order that the spoiled article be washed. Then he is to isolate it for another seven days. ⁵⁵After the article has been washed, the priest is to examine it again, and if the mold has not changed its appearance, even though it has not spread, it is unclean. Burn it, no matter which side of the fabric has been spoiled. ⁵⁶If, when the priest examines it, the mold has faded after the article has been washed, he is to tear the spoiled part out of the fabric, the leather, or the woven or knitted material. ⁵⁷But if it reappears in the fabric, in the woven or knitted material, or in the leather article, it is a spreading mold; whatever has the mold must be burned. ⁵⁸Any fabric, woven or knitted material, or any leather article that has been washed and is rid of the mold, must be washed again. Then it will be clean."

⁵⁹These are the regulations concerning defiling molds in woolen or linen clothing, woven or knitted material, or any leather article, for pronouncing them clean or unclean.

Cleansing From Defiling Skin Diseases

14 The LORD said to Moses, ²"These are the regulations for any diseased person at the time of their ceremonial cleansing, when they are brought to the priest: ³The priest is to go outside the camp and examine them. If they have been healed of their defiling skin disease,ᵃ ⁴the priest shall order that two live clean birds and some cedar wood, scarlet yarn and hyssop be brought for the person to be cleansed. ⁵Then the priest shall order that one of the birds be killed over fresh water in a clay pot. ⁶He is then to take the live bird and dip it, together with the cedar wood, the scarlet yarn and the hyssop, into the blood of the bird that was killed over the fresh water. ⁷Seven times he shall sprinkle the one to be cleansed of the defiling disease, and then pronounce them clean. After that, he is to release the live bird in the open fields.

⁸"The person to be cleansed must wash their clothes, shave off all their hair and bathe with water; then they will be ceremonially clean. After this they may come into the camp, but they must stay outside their tent for seven days. ⁹On the seventh day they must shave off all their hair; they must shave their head, their beard, their eyebrows and the rest of their hair. They must wash their clothes and bathe themselves with water, and they will be clean.

¹⁰"On the eighth day they must bring two male lambs and one ewe lamb a year old, each without defect, along with three-tenths of an ephahᵇ of the finest flour mixed with olive oil for a grain offering, and one logᶜ of oil. ¹¹The priest who pronounces them clean shall present both the one to be cleansed and their offerings before the LORD at the entrance to the tent of meeting.

¹²"Then the priest is to take one of the male lambs and offer it as a guilt offering, along with the log of oil; he shall wave them before the LORD as a wave offering. ¹³He is to slaughter the lamb in the sanctuary area where the sin offeringᵈ and the burnt offering are slaughtered. Like the sin offering, the guilt offering belongs to the priest; it is most holy. ¹⁴The priest is to take some of the blood of the guilt offering and put it on the lobe of the right ear of the one to be cleansed, on the thumb of their right hand and on the big toe of their right foot. ¹⁵The priest shall then take some of the log of oil, pour it in the palm of his own left hand, ¹⁶dip his right forefinger into the oil in his palm, and with his finger sprinkle some of it before the LORD seven times. ¹⁷The priest is to put some of the oil remaining in his palm on the lobe of the right ear of the one to be cleansed, on the thumb of their right hand and on the big toe of their right foot, on top of the blood of the guilt offering. ¹⁸The rest of the oil in his palm the priest shall put on the head of the one to be cleansed and make atonement for them before the LORD.

¹⁹"Then the priest is to sacrifice the sin offering and make atonement for the one to be cleansed from their uncleanness. After that, the priest shall slaughter the burnt offering ²⁰and offer it on the altar, together with the grain offering, and make atonement for them, and they will be clean.

²¹"If, however, they are poor and cannot afford these, they must take one male lamb as a guilt offering to be waved to make atonement for them, together with a tenth of an ephahᵉ of the finest flour mixed with olive oil for a grain offering, a log of oil, ²²and two doves or two young pigeons, such as they can afford, one for a sin offering and the other for a burnt offering.

²³"On the eighth day they must bring them

ᵃ *3* The Hebrew word for *defiling skin disease*, traditionally translated "leprosy," was used for various diseases affecting the skin; also in verses 7, 32, 54 and 57.   ᵇ *10* That is, probably about 11 pounds or about 5 kilograms   ᶜ *10* That is, about 1/3 quart or about 0.3 liter; also in verses 12, 15, 21 and 24
ᵈ *13* Or *purification offering*; also in verses 19, 22 and 31
ᵉ *21* That is, probably about 3 1/2 pounds or about 1.6 kilograms

for their cleansing to the priest at the entrance to the tent of meeting, before the LORD. ²⁴The priest is to take the lamb for the guilt offering, together with the log of oil, and wave them before the LORD as a wave offering. ²⁵He shall slaughter the lamb for the guilt offering and take some of its blood and put it on the lobe of the right ear of the one to be cleansed, on the thumb of their right hand and on the big toe of their right foot. ²⁶The priest is to pour some of the oil into the palm of his own left hand, ²⁷and with his right forefinger sprinkle some of the oil from his palm seven times before the LORD. ²⁸Some of the oil in his palm he is to put on the same places he put the blood of the guilt offering—on the lobe of the right ear of the one to be cleansed, on the thumb of their right hand and on the big toe of their right foot. ²⁹The rest of the oil in his palm the priest shall put on the head of the one to be cleansed, to make atonement for them before the LORD. ³⁰Then he shall sacrifice the doves or the young pigeons, such as the person can afford, ³¹one as a sin offering and the other as a burnt offering, together with the grain offering. In this way the priest will make atonement before the LORD on behalf of the one to be cleansed."

³²These are the regulations for anyone who has a defiling skin disease and who cannot afford the regular offerings for their cleansing.

Cleansing From Defiling Molds

³³The LORD said to Moses and Aaron, ³⁴"When you enter the land of Canaan, which I am giving you as your possession, and I put a spreading mold in a house in that land, ³⁵the owner of the house must go and tell the priest, 'I have seen something that looks like a defiling mold in my house.' ³⁶The priest is to order the house to be emptied before he goes in to examine the mold, so that nothing in the house will be pronounced unclean. After this the priest is to go in and inspect the house. ³⁷He is to examine the mold on the walls, and if it has greenish or reddish depressions that appear to be deeper than the surface of the wall, ³⁸the priest shall go out the doorway of the house and close it up for seven days. ³⁹On the seventh day the priest shall return to inspect the house. If the mold has spread on the walls, ⁴⁰he is to order that the contaminated stones be torn out and thrown into an unclean place outside the town. ⁴¹He must have all the inside walls of the house scraped and the material that is scraped off dumped into an unclean place outside the town. ⁴²Then they

are to take other stones to replace these and take new clay and plaster the house.

⁴³"If the defiling mold reappears in the house after the stones have been torn out and the house scraped and plastered, ⁴⁴the priest is to go and examine it and, if the mold has spread in the house, it is a persistent defiling mold; the house is unclean. ⁴⁵It must be torn down—its stones, timbers and all the plaster—and taken out of the town to an unclean place.

⁴⁶"Anyone who goes into the house while it is closed up will be unclean till evening. ⁴⁷Anyone who sleeps or eats in the house must wash their clothes.

⁴⁸"But if the priest comes to examine it and the mold has not spread after the house has been plastered, he shall pronounce the house clean, because the defiling mold is gone. ⁴⁹To purify the house he is to take two birds and some cedar wood, scarlet yarn and hyssop. ⁵⁰He shall kill one of the birds over fresh water in a clay pot. ⁵¹Then he is to take the cedar wood, the hyssop, the scarlet yarn and the live bird, dip them into the blood of the dead bird and the fresh water, and sprinkle the house seven times. ⁵²He shall purify the house with the bird's blood, the fresh water, the live bird, the cedar wood, the hyssop and the scarlet yarn. ⁵³Then he is to release the live bird in the open fields outside the town. In this way he will make atonement for the house, and it will be clean."

⁵⁴These are the regulations for any defiling skin disease, for a sore, ⁵⁵for defiling molds in fabric or in a house, ⁵⁶and for a swelling, a rash or a shiny spot, ⁵⁷to determine when something is clean or unclean.

These are the regulations for defiling skin diseases and defiling molds.

Discharges Causing Uncleanness

15 The LORD said to Moses and Aaron, ²"Speak to the Israelites and say to them: 'When any man has an unusual bodily discharge, such a discharge is unclean. ³Whether it continues flowing from his body or is blocked, it will make him unclean. This is how his discharge will bring about uncleanness:

⁴"'Any bed the man with a discharge lies on will be unclean, and anything he sits on will be unclean. ⁵Anyone who touches his bed must wash their clothes and bathe with water, and they will be unclean till evening. ⁶Whoever sits on anything that the man with a discharge sat on must wash their clothes and bathe with water, and they will be unclean till evening.

7"'Whoever touches the man who has a discharge must wash their clothes and bathe with water, and they will be unclean till evening.

8"'If the man with the discharge spits on anyone who is clean, they must wash their clothes and bathe with water, and they will be unclean till evening.

9"'Everything the man sits on when riding will be unclean, 10and whoever touches any of the things that were under him will be unclean till evening; whoever picks up those things must wash their clothes and bathe with water, and they will be unclean till evening.

11"'Anyone the man with a discharge touches without rinsing his hands with water must wash their clothes and bathe with water, and they will be unclean till evening.

12"'A clay pot that the man touches must be broken, and any wooden article is to be rinsed with water.

13"'When a man is cleansed from his discharge, he is to count off seven days for his ceremonial cleansing; he must wash his clothes and bathe himself with fresh water, and he will be clean. 14On the eighth day he must take two doves or two young pigeons and come before the LORD to the entrance to the tent of meeting and give them to the priest. 15The priest is to sacrifice them, the one for a sin offering[a] and the other for a burnt offering. In this way he will make atonement before the LORD for the man because of his discharge.

16"'When a man has an emission of semen, he must bathe his whole body with water, and he will be unclean till evening. 17Any clothing or leather that has semen on it must be washed with water, and it will be unclean till evening. 18When a man has sexual relations with a woman and there is an emission of semen, both of them must bathe with water, and they will be unclean till evening.

19"'When a woman has her regular flow of blood, the impurity of her monthly period will last seven days, and anyone who touches her will be unclean till evening.

20"'Anything she lies on during her period will be unclean, and anything she sits on will be unclean. 21Anyone who touches her bed will be unclean; they must wash their clothes and bathe with water, and they will be unclean till evening. 22Anyone who touches anything she sits on will be unclean; they must wash their clothes and bathe with water, and they will be unclean till evening. 23Whether it is the bed or anything she was sitting on, when anyone touches it, they will be unclean till evening.

24"'If a man has sexual relations with her and her monthly flow touches him, he will be un-

---

[a] 15 Or purification offering; also in verse 30

MOSES — God's Problem Solver
Leviticus 15:1–33

PROFILE in leadership

Have you noticed that rules, regulations and laws often bring out the human tendency to ask, "But why?"

Sometimes the Lord gives the reasons behind his laws, as he does near the end of Leviticus 15. Here God says he gave the people various ceremonial laws in order to "keep the Israelites separate from things that make them unclean, so they will not die in their uncleanness for defiling my dwelling place, which is among them" (Lev 15:31).

It may seem odd to us that God demonstrated such concern over personal cleanliness, but could it be that God knows something we don't? If Moses harped on one thing, it was this: Be sure to obey your God (whether you understand the *why* or not).

Many of our problems arise from ignoring God's Word when we don't think its instructions make sense. Moses tells us the rules and regulations God gave to his people not only kept them clean—make that *holy*—before him, but they also protected them from discomfort, sickness and untimely death.

In some ways, the law can be seen as God solving a problem before it ever occurs. Moses reminds us that God always knows what is best—best for us and best for our relationship with him.

clean for seven days; any bed he lies on will be unclean.

²⁵"'When a woman has a discharge of blood for many days at a time other than her monthly period or has a discharge that continues beyond her period, she will be unclean as long as she has the discharge, just as in the days of her period. ²⁶Any bed she lies on while her discharge continues will be unclean, as is her bed during her monthly period, and anything she sits on will be unclean, as during her period. ²⁷Anyone who touches them will be unclean; they must wash their clothes and bathe with water, and they will be unclean till evening.

²⁸"'When she is cleansed from her discharge, she must count off seven days, and after that she will be ceremonially clean. ²⁹On the eighth day she must take two doves or two young pigeons and bring them to the priest at the entrance to the tent of meeting. ³⁰The priest is to sacrifice one for a sin offering and the other for a burnt offering. In this way he will make atonement for her before the LORD for the uncleanness of her discharge.

³¹"'You must keep the Israelites separate from things that make them unclean, so they will not die in their uncleanness for defiling my dwelling place,^a which is among them.'"

³²These are the regulations for a man with a discharge, for anyone made unclean by an emission of semen, ³³for a woman in her monthly period, for a man or a woman with a discharge, and for a man who has sexual relations with a woman who is ceremonially unclean.

The Day of Atonement

16 The LORD spoke to Moses after the death of the two sons of Aaron who died when they approached the LORD. ²The LORD said to Moses: "Tell your brother Aaron that he is not to come whenever he chooses into the Most Holy Place behind the curtain in front of the atonement cover on the ark, or else he will die. For I will appear in the cloud over the atonement cover.

³"This is how Aaron is to enter the Most Holy Place: He must first bring a young bull for a sin offering^b and a ram for a burnt offering. ⁴He is to put on the sacred linen tunic, with linen undergarments next to his body; he is to tie the linen sash around him and put on the linen turban. These are sacred garments; so he must bathe himself with water before he puts them on. ⁵From the Israelite community he is to take two male goats for a sin offering and a ram for a burnt offering.

⁶"Aaron is to offer the bull for his own sin of-

fering to make atonement for himself and his household. ⁷Then he is to take the two goats and present them before the LORD at the entrance to the tent of meeting. ⁸He is to cast lots for the two goats — one lot for the LORD and the other for the scapegoat.^c ⁹Aaron shall bring the goat whose lot falls to the LORD and sacrifice it for a sin offering. ¹⁰But the goat chosen by lot as the scapegoat shall be presented alive before the LORD to be used for making atonement by sending it into the wilderness as a scapegoat.

¹¹"Aaron shall bring the bull for his own sin offering to make atonement for himself and his household, and he is to slaughter the bull for his own sin offering. ¹²He is to take a censer full of burning coals from the altar before the LORD and two handfuls of finely ground fragrant incense and take them behind the curtain. ¹³He is to put the incense on the fire before the LORD, and the smoke of the incense will conceal the atonement cover above the tablets of the covenant law, so that he will not die. ¹⁴He is to take some of the bull's blood and with his finger sprinkle it on the front of the atonement cover; then he shall sprinkle some of it with his finger seven times before the atonement cover.

¹⁵"He shall then slaughter the goat for the sin offering for the people and take its blood behind the curtain and do with it as he did with the bull's blood: He shall sprinkle it on the atonement cover and in front of it. ¹⁶In this way he will make atonement for the Most Holy Place because of the uncleanness and rebellion of the Israelites, whatever their sins have been. He is to do the same for the tent of meeting, which is among them in the midst of their uncleanness. ¹⁷No one is to be in the tent of meeting from the time Aaron goes in to make atonement in the Most Holy Place until he comes out, having made atonement for himself, his household and the whole community of Israel.

¹⁸"Then he shall come out to the altar that is before the LORD and make atonement for it. He shall take some of the bull's blood and some of the goat's blood and put it on all the horns of the altar. ¹⁹He shall sprinkle some of the blood on it with his finger seven times to cleanse it and to consecrate it from the uncleanness of the Israelites.

²⁰"When Aaron has finished making atonement for the Most Holy Place, the tent of meeting and the altar, he shall bring forward the live goat.

---

^a 31 Or *my tabernacle*   ^b 3 Or *purification offering*; here and throughout this chapter   ^c 8 The meaning of the Hebrew for this word is uncertain; also in verses 10 and 26.

²¹He is to lay both hands on the head of the live goat and confess over it all the wickedness and rebellion of the Israelites—all their sins—and put them on the goat's head. He shall send the goat away into the wilderness in the care of someone appointed for the task. ²²The goat will carry on itself all their sins to a remote place; and the man shall release it in the wilderness.

²³"Then Aaron is to go into the tent of meeting and take off the linen garments he put on before he entered the Most Holy Place, and he is to leave them there. ²⁴He shall bathe himself with water in the sanctuary area and put on his regular garments. Then he shall come out and sacrifice the burnt offering for himself and the burnt offering for the people, to make atonement for himself and for the people. ²⁵He shall also burn the fat of the sin offering on the altar.

²⁶"The man who releases the goat as a scapegoat must wash his clothes and bathe himself with water; afterward he may come into the camp. ²⁷The bull and the goat for the sin offerings, whose blood was brought into the Most Holy Place to make atonement, must be taken outside the camp; their hides, flesh and intestines are to be burned up. ²⁸The man who burns them must wash his clothes and bathe himself with water; afterward he may come into the camp.

²⁹"This is to be a lasting ordinance for you: On the tenth day of the seventh month you must deny yourselves[a] and not do any work—whether native-born or a foreigner residing among you— ³⁰because on this day atonement will be made for you, to cleanse you. Then, before the LORD, you will be clean from all your sins. ³¹It is a day of sabbath rest, and you must deny yourselves; it is a lasting ordinance. ³²The priest who is anointed and ordained to succeed his father as high priest is to make atonement. He is to put on the sacred linen garments ³³and make atonement for the Most Holy Place, for the tent of meeting and the altar, and for the priests and all the members of the community.

³⁴"This is to be a lasting ordinance for you: Atonement is to be made once a year for all the sins of the Israelites."

And it was done, as the LORD commanded Moses.

Eating Blood Forbidden

17 The LORD said to Moses, ²"Speak to Aaron and his sons and to all the Israelites and say to them: 'This is what the LORD has commanded: ³Any Israelite who sacrifices an ox,[b] a lamb or a goat in the camp or outside of it ⁴instead of bringing it to the entrance to the tent of meeting to present it as an offering to the LORD in front of the tabernacle of the LORD—that person shall be considered guilty of bloodshed; they have shed blood and must be cut off from their people. ⁵This is so the Israelites will bring to the LORD the sacrifices they are now making in the open fields. They must bring them to the priest, that is, to the LORD, at the entrance to the tent of meeting and sacrifice them as fellowship offerings. ⁶The priest is to splash the blood against the altar of the LORD at the entrance to the tent of meeting and burn the fat as an aroma pleasing to the LORD. ⁷They must no longer offer any of their sacrifices to the goat idols[c] to whom they prostitute themselves. This is to be a lasting ordinance for them and for the generations to come.'

⁸"Say to them: 'Any Israelite or any foreigner residing among them who offers a burnt offering or sacrifice ⁹and does not bring it to the entrance to the tent of meeting to sacrifice it to the LORD must be cut off from the people of Israel.

¹⁰"'I will set my face against any Israelite or any foreigner residing among them who eats blood, and I will cut them off from the people. ¹¹For the life of a creature is in the blood, and I have given it to you to make atonement for yourselves on the altar; it is the blood that makes atonement for one's life.[d] ¹²Therefore I say to the Israelites, "None of you may eat blood, nor may any foreigner residing among you eat blood."

¹³"'Any Israelite or any foreigner residing among you who hunts any animal or bird that may be eaten must drain out the blood and cover it with earth, ¹⁴because the life of every creature is its blood. That is why I have said to the Israelites, "You must not eat the blood of any creature, because the life of every creature is its blood; anyone who eats it must be cut off."

¹⁵"'Anyone, whether native-born or foreigner, who eats anything found dead or torn by wild animals must wash their clothes and bathe with water, and they will be ceremonially unclean till evening; then they will be clean. ¹⁶But if they do not wash their clothes and bathe themselves, they will be held responsible.'"

Unlawful Sexual Relations

18 The LORD said to Moses, ²"Speak to the Israelites and say to them: 'I am the LORD your God. ³You must not do as they do

---

[a] 29 Or *must fast*; also in verse 31   [b] 3 The Hebrew word can refer to either male or female.   [c] 7 Or *the demons*   [d] 11 Or *atonement by the life in the blood*

in Egypt, where you used to live, and you must not do as they do in the land of Canaan, where I am bringing you. Do not follow their practices. [4]You must obey my laws and be careful to follow my decrees. I am the LORD your God. [5]Keep my decrees and laws, for the person who obeys them will live by them. I am the LORD.

[6] "'No one is to approach any close relative to have sexual relations. I am the LORD.

[7] "'Do not dishonor your father by having sexual relations with your mother. She is your mother; do not have relations with her.

[8] "'Do not have sexual relations with your father's wife; that would dishonor your father.

[9] "'Do not have sexual relations with your sister, either your father's daughter or your mother's daughter, whether she was born in the same home or elsewhere.

[10] "'Do not have sexual relations with your son's daughter or your daughter's daughter; that would dishonor you.

[11] "'Do not have sexual relations with the daughter of your father's wife, born to your father; she is your sister.

[12] "'Do not have sexual relations with your father's sister; she is your father's close relative.

[13] "'Do not have sexual relations with your mother's sister, because she is your mother's close relative.

[14] "'Do not dishonor your father's brother by approaching his wife to have sexual relations; she is your aunt.

[15] "'Do not have sexual relations with your daughter-in-law. She is your son's wife; do not have relations with her.

[16] "'Do not have sexual relations with your brother's wife; that would dishonor your brother.

[17] "'Do not have sexual relations with both a woman and her daughter. Do not have sexual relations with either her son's daughter or her daughter's daughter; they are her close relatives. That is wickedness.

[18] "'Do not take your wife's sister as a rival wife and have sexual relations with her while your wife is living.

[19] "'Do not approach a woman to have sexual relations during the uncleanness of her monthly period.

[20] "'Do not have sexual relations with your neighbor's wife and defile yourself with her.

[21] "'Do not give any of your children to be sacrificed to Molek, for you must not profane the name of your God. I am the LORD.

[22] "'Do not have sexual relations with a man as one does with a woman; that is detestable.

[23] "'Do not have sexual relations with an animal and defile yourself with it. A woman must not present herself to an animal to have sexual relations with it; that is a perversion.

[24] "'Do not defile yourselves in any of these ways, because this is how the nations that I am going to drive out before you became defiled. [25]Even the land was defiled; so I punished it for its sin, and the land vomited out its inhabitants. [26]But you must keep my decrees and my laws. The native-born and the foreigners residing among you must not do any of these detestable things, [27]for all these things were done by the people who lived in the land before you, and the land became defiled. [28]And if you defile the land, it will vomit you out as it vomited out the nations that were before you.

[29] "'Everyone who does any of these detestable things—such persons must be cut off from their people. [30]Keep my requirements and do not follow any of the detestable customs that were practiced before you came and do not defile yourselves with them. I am the LORD your God.'"

Various Laws

19 The LORD said to Moses, [2]"Speak to the entire assembly of Israel and say to them: 'Be holy because I, the LORD your God, am holy.

[3] "'Each of you must respect your mother and father, and you must observe my Sabbaths. I am the LORD your God.

[4] "'Do not turn to idols or make metal gods for yourselves. I am the LORD your God.

[5] "'When you sacrifice a fellowship offering to the LORD, sacrifice it in such a way that it will be accepted on your behalf. [6]It shall be eaten on the day you sacrifice it or on the next day; anything left over until the third day must be burned up. [7]If any of it is eaten on the third day, it is impure and will not be accepted. [8]Whoever eats it will be held responsible because they have desecrated what is holy to the LORD; they must be cut off from their people.

[9] "'When you reap the harvest of your land, do not reap to the very edges of your field or gather the gleanings of your harvest. [10]Do not go over your vineyard a second time or pick up the grapes that have fallen. Leave them for the poor and the foreigner. I am the LORD your God.

[11] "'Do not steal.

"'Do not lie.

"'Do not deceive one another.

[12] "'Do not swear falsely by my name and so profane the name of your God. I am the LORD.

[13] "'Do not defraud or rob your neighbor.

" 'Do not hold back the wages of a hired worker overnight.

¹⁴" 'Do not curse the deaf or put a stumbling block in front of the blind, but fear your God. I am the LORD.

¹⁵" 'Do not pervert justice; do not show partiality to the poor or favoritism to the great, but judge your neighbor fairly.

¹⁶" 'Do not go about spreading slander among your people.

" 'Do not do anything that endangers your neighbor's life. I am the LORD.

¹⁷" 'Do not hate a fellow Israelite in your heart. Rebuke your neighbor frankly so you will not share in their guilt.

¹⁸" 'Do not seek revenge or bear a grudge against anyone among your people, but love your neighbor as yourself. I am the LORD.

¹⁹" 'Keep my decrees.

" 'Do not mate different kinds of animals.

" 'Do not plant your field with two kinds of seed.

" 'Do not wear clothing woven of two kinds of material.

²⁰" 'If a man sleeps with a female slave who is promised to another man but who has not been ransomed or given her freedom, there must be due punishment.ᵃ Yet they are not to be put to death, because she had not been freed. ²¹The man, however, must bring a ram to the entrance to the tent of meeting for a guilt offering to the LORD. ²²With the ram of the guilt offering the priest is to make atonement for him before the LORD for the sin he has committed, and his sin will be forgiven.

²³" 'When you enter the land and plant any kind of fruit tree, regard its fruit as forbidden.ᵇ For three years you are to consider it forbiddenᵇ; it must not be eaten. ²⁴In the fourth year all its fruit will be holy, an offering of praise to the LORD. ²⁵But in the fifth year you may eat its fruit. In this way your harvest will be increased. I am the LORD your God.

²⁶" 'Do not eat any meat with the blood still in it.

" 'Do not practice divination or seek omens.

²⁷" 'Do not cut the hair at the sides of your head or clip off the edges of your beard.

²⁸" 'Do not cut your bodies for the dead or put tattoo marks on yourselves. I am the LORD.

²⁹" 'Do not degrade your daughter by making her a prostitute, or the land will turn to prostitution and be filled with wickedness.

³⁰" 'Observe my Sabbaths and have reverence for my sanctuary. I am the LORD.

³¹" 'Do not turn to mediums or seek out spiritists, for you will be defiled by them. I am the LORD your God.

³²" 'Stand up in the presence of the aged, show respect for the elderly and revere your God. I am the LORD.

³³" 'When a foreigner resides among you in your land, do not mistreat them. ³⁴The foreigner residing among you must be treated as your native-born. Love them as yourself, for you were foreigners in Egypt. I am the LORD your God.

³⁵" 'Do not use dishonest standards when measuring length, weight or quantity. ³⁶Use honest scales and honest weights, an honest ephahᶜ and an honest hin.ᵈ I am the LORD your God, who brought you out of Egypt.

³⁷" 'Keep all my decrees and all my laws and follow them. I am the LORD.' "

Punishments for Sin

20 The LORD said to Moses, ²"Say to the Israelites: 'Any Israelite or any foreigner residing in Israel who sacrifices any of his children to Molek is to be put to death. The members of the community are to stone him. ³I myself will set my face against him and will cut him off from his people; for by sacrificing his children to Molek, he has defiled my sanctuary and profaned my holy name. ⁴If the members of the community close their eyes when that man sacrifices one of his children to Molek and if they fail to put him to death, ⁵I myself will set my face against him and his family and will cut them off from their people together with all who follow him in prostituting themselves to Molek.

⁶" 'I will set my face against anyone who turns to mediums and spiritists to prostitute themselves by following them, and I will cut them off from their people.

⁷" 'Consecrate yourselves and be holy, because I am the LORD your God. ⁸Keep my decrees and follow them. I am the LORD, who makes you holy.

⁹" 'Anyone who curses their father or mother is to be put to death. Because they have cursed their father or mother, their blood will be on their own head.

¹⁰" 'If a man commits adultery with another man's wife—with the wife of his neighbor—

ᵃ 20 Or *be an inquiry*   ᵇ 23 Hebrew *uncircumcised*
ᶜ 36 An ephah was a dry measure having the capacity of about 3/5 of a bushel or about 22 liters.   ᵈ 36 A hin was a liquid measure having the capacity of about 1 gallon or about 3.8 liters.

Israel: Raising a Higher Standard

Leviticus 18:1—21:24

God calls his people to live at a standard higher than the unbelievers who surround them. In Leviticus 18–20, God reviews his higher standards regarding relationships, religion and the rights and responsibilities of community members. In the subsequent chapter, he reviews an even higher standard for Israel's leaders, the priests.

Why these higher standards? God intended Israel to be a light and a standard for the rest of the world, and Israel's leaders to be a light and a standard for the Jewish nation. God expects the same of us today. Why must we be faithful in keeping a higher standard than the rest of the world?

1. **To be like God.**
2. **To qualify us for ministry.**
3. **To guarantee God's blessing on our life.**
4. **To prepare us for leadership tomorrow.**
5. **To receive God's reward for faithfulness.**

And what characterizes those who choose to pursue life at God's higher standard?

1. **They adopt godly values.**
2. **They care for the interests of others.**
3. **They live with integrity.**
4. **They keep their word.**
5. **They develop their gifts and potential.**
6. **They manage time and money well.**
7. **They pass on to others what they have received.**

---

both the adulterer and the adulteress are to be put to death.

[11] "If a man has sexual relations with his father's wife, he has dishonored his father. Both the man and the woman are to be put to death; their blood will be on their own heads.

[12] "If a man has sexual relations with his daughter-in-law, both of them are to be put to death. What they have done is a perversion; their blood will be on their own heads.

[13] "If a man has sexual relations with a man as one does with a woman, both of them have done what is detestable. They are to be put to death; their blood will be on their own heads.

[14] "If a man marries both a woman and her mother, it is wicked. Both he and they must be burned in the fire, so that no wickedness will be among you.

[15] "If a man has sexual relations with an animal, he is to be put to death, and you must kill the animal.

[16] "If a woman approaches an animal to have sexual relations with it, kill both the woman and the animal. They are to be put to death; their blood will be on their own heads.

[17] "If a man marries his sister, the daughter of either his father or his mother, and they have sexual relations, it is a disgrace. They are to be publicly removed from their people. He has dishonored his sister and will be held responsible.

[18] "If a man has sexual relations with a woman during her monthly period, he has exposed the source of her flow, and she has also uncovered it. Both of them are to be cut off from their people.

[19] "Do not have sexual relations with the sister of either your mother or your father, for that would dishonor a close relative; both of you would be held responsible.

[20] "If a man has sexual relations with his aunt, he has dishonored his uncle. They will be held responsible; they will die childless.

[21] "If a man marries his brother's wife, it is an act of impurity; he has dishonored his brother. They will be childless.

[22] "Keep all my decrees and laws and follow them, so that the land where I am bringing you to live may not vomit you out. [23]You must not live according to the customs of the nations I am going to drive out before you. Because they did all these things, I abhorred them. [24]But I said to you, "You will possess their land; I will give it to

you as an inheritance, a land flowing with milk and honey." I am the LORD your God, who has set you apart from the nations.

²⁵"'You must therefore make a distinction between clean and unclean animals and between unclean and clean birds. Do not defile yourselves by any animal or bird or anything that moves along the ground — those that I have set apart as unclean for you. ²⁶You are to be holy to me because I, the LORD, am holy, and I have set you apart from the nations to be my own.

²⁷"'A man or woman who is a medium or spiritist among you must be put to death. You are to stone them; their blood will be on their own heads.'"

Rules for Priests

21 The LORD said to Moses, "Speak to the priests, the sons of Aaron, and say to them: 'A priest must not make himself ceremonially unclean for any of his people who die, ²except for a close relative, such as his mother or father, his son or daughter, his brother, ³or an unmarried sister who is dependent on him since she has no husband — for her he may make himself unclean. ⁴He must not make himself unclean for people related to him by marriage,ᵃ and so defile himself.

⁵"'Priests must not shave their heads or shave off the edges of their beards or cut their bodies. ⁶They must be holy to their God and must not profane the name of their God. Because they present the food offerings to the LORD, the food of their God, they are to be holy.

⁷"'They must not marry women defiled by prostitution or divorced from their husbands, because priests are holy to their God. ⁸Regard them as holy, because they offer up the food of your God. Consider them holy, because I the LORD am holy — I who make you holy.

⁹"'If a priest's daughter defiles herself by becoming a prostitute, she disgraces her father; she must be burned in the fire.

¹⁰"'The high priest, the one among his brothers who has had the anointing oil poured on his head and who has been ordained to wear the priestly garments, must not let his hair become unkemptᵇ or tear his clothes. ¹¹He must not enter a place where there is a dead body. He must not make himself unclean, even for his father or mother, ¹²nor leave the sanctuary of his God or desecrate it, because he has been dedicated by the anointing oil of his God. I am the LORD.

¹³"'The woman he marries must be a virgin. ¹⁴He must not marry a widow, a divorced wom-

an, or a woman defiled by prostitution, but only a virgin from his own people, ¹⁵so that he will not defile his offspring among his people. I am the LORD, who makes him holy.'"

¹⁶The LORD said to Moses, ¹⁷"Say to Aaron: 'For the generations to come none of your descendants who has a defect may come near to offer the food of his God. ¹⁸No man who has any defect may come near: no man who is blind or lame, disfigured or deformed; ¹⁹no man with a crippled foot or hand, ²⁰or who is a hunchback or a dwarf, or who has any eye defect, or who has festering or running sores or damaged testicles. ²¹No descendant of Aaron the priest who has any defect is to come near to present the food offerings to the LORD. He has a defect; he must not come near to offer the food of his God. ²²He may eat the most holy food of his God, as well as the holy food; ²³yet because of his defect, he must not go near the curtain or approach the altar, and so desecrate my sanctuary. I am the LORD, who makes them holy.'"

²⁴So Moses told this to Aaron and his sons and to all the Israelites.

22 The LORD said to Moses, ²"Tell Aaron and his sons to treat with respect the sacred offerings the Israelites consecrate to me, so they will not profane my holy name. I am the LORD.

³"Say to them: 'For the generations to come, if any of your descendants is ceremonially unclean and yet comes near the sacred offerings that the Israelites consecrate to the LORD, that person must be cut off from my presence. I am the LORD.

⁴"'If a descendant of Aaron has a defiling skin diseaseᶜ or a bodily discharge, he may not eat the sacred offerings until he is cleansed. He will also be unclean if he touches something defiled by a corpse or by anyone who has an emission of semen, ⁵or if he touches any crawling thing that makes him unclean, or any person who makes him unclean, whatever the uncleanness may be. ⁶The one who touches any such thing will be unclean till evening. He must not eat any of the sacred offerings unless he has bathed himself with water. ⁷When the sun goes down, he will be clean, and after that he may eat the sacred offerings, for they are his food. ⁸He must not eat anything found dead or torn by wild animals, and so become unclean through it. I am the LORD.

ᵃ 4 Or *unclean as a leader among his people*   ᵇ 10 Or *not uncover his head*   ᶜ 4 The Hebrew word for *defiling skin disease*, traditionally translated "leprosy," was used for various diseases affecting the skin.

⁹"'The priests are to perform my service in such a way that they do not become guilty and die for treating it with contempt. I am the LORD, who makes them holy.

¹⁰"'No one outside a priest's family may eat the sacred offering, nor may the guest of a priest or his hired worker eat it. ¹¹But if a priest buys a slave with money, or if slaves are born in his household, they may eat his food. ¹²If a priest's daughter marries anyone other than a priest, she may not eat any of the sacred contributions. ¹³But if a priest's daughter becomes a widow or is divorced, yet has no children, and she returns to live in her father's household as in her youth, she may eat her father's food. No unauthorized person, however, may eat it.

¹⁴"'Anyone who eats a sacred offering by mistake must make restitution to the priest for the offering and add a fifth of the value to it. ¹⁵The priests must not desecrate the sacred offerings the Israelites present to the LORD ¹⁶by allowing them to eat the sacred offerings and so bring upon them guilt requiring payment. I am the LORD, who makes them holy.'"

Unacceptable Sacrifices

¹⁷The LORD said to Moses, ¹⁸"Speak to Aaron and his sons and to all the Israelites and say to them: 'If any of you—whether an Israelite or a foreigner residing in Israel—presents a gift for a burnt offering to the LORD, either to fulfill a vow or as a freewill offering, ¹⁹you must present a male without defect from the cattle, sheep or goats in order that it may be accepted on your behalf. ²⁰Do not bring anything with a defect, because it will not be accepted on your behalf. ²¹When anyone brings from the herd or flock a fellowship offering to the LORD to fulfill a special vow or as a freewill offering, it must be without defect or blemish to be acceptable. ²²Do not offer to the LORD the blind, the injured or the maimed, or anything with warts or festering or running sores. Do not place any of these on the altar as a food offering presented to the LORD. ²³You may, however, present as a freewill offering an oxᵃ or a sheep that is deformed or stunted, but it will not be accepted in fulfillment of a vow. ²⁴You must not offer to the LORD an animal whose testicles are bruised, crushed, torn or cut. You must not do this in your own land, ²⁵and you must not accept such animals from the hand of a foreigner and offer them as the food of your God. They will not be accepted on your behalf, because they are deformed and have defects.'"

²⁶The LORD said to Moses, ²⁷"When a calf, a lamb or a goat is born, it is to remain with its mother for seven days. From the eighth day on, it will be acceptable as a food offering presented to the LORD. ²⁸Do not slaughter a cow or a sheep and its young on the same day.

²⁹"When you sacrifice a thank offering to the LORD, sacrifice it in such a way that it will be accepted on your behalf. ³⁰It must be eaten that same day; leave none of it till morning. I am the LORD.

³¹"Keep my commands and follow them. I am the LORD. ³²Do not profane my holy name, for I must be acknowledged as holy by the Israelites. I am the LORD, who made you holy ³³and who brought you out of Egypt to be your God. I am the LORD."

The Appointed Festivals

23 The LORD said to Moses, ²"Speak to the Israelites and say to them: 'These are my appointed festivals, the appointed festivals of the LORD, which you are to proclaim as sacred assemblies.

The Sabbath

³"'There are six days when you may work, but the seventh day is a day of sabbath rest, a day of sacred assembly. You are not to do any work; wherever you live, it is a sabbath to the LORD.

The Passover and the Festival of Unleavened Bread

⁴"'These are the LORD's appointed festivals, the sacred assemblies you are to proclaim at their appointed times: ⁵The LORD's Passover begins at twilight on the fourteenth day of the first month. ⁶On the fifteenth day of that month the LORD's Festival of Unleavened Bread begins; for seven days you must eat bread made without yeast. ⁷On the first day hold a sacred assembly and do no regular work. ⁸For seven days present a food offering to the LORD. And on the seventh day hold a sacred assembly and do no regular work.'"

Offering the Firstfruits

⁹The LORD said to Moses, ¹⁰"Speak to the Israelites and say to them: 'When you enter the land I am going to give you and you reap its harvest, bring to the priest a sheaf of the first grain you harvest. ¹¹He is to wave the sheaf before the LORD so it will be accepted on your behalf; the priest is to wave it on the day after the Sabbath.

ᵃ 23 The Hebrew word can refer to either male or female.

¹²On the day you wave the sheaf, you must sacrifice as a burnt offering to the LORD a lamb a year old without defect, ¹³together with its grain offering of two-tenths of an ephah*a* of the finest flour mixed with olive oil — a food offering presented to the LORD, a pleasing aroma — and its drink offering of a quarter of a hin*b* of wine. ¹⁴You must not eat any bread, or roasted or new grain, until the very day you bring this offering to your God. This is to be a lasting ordinance for the generations to come, wherever you live.

The Festival of Weeks

¹⁵ 'From the day after the Sabbath, the day you brought the sheaf of the wave offering, count off seven full weeks. ¹⁶Count off fifty days up to the day after the seventh Sabbath, and then present an offering of new grain to the LORD. ¹⁷From wherever you live, bring two loaves made of two-tenths of an ephah of the finest flour, baked with yeast, as a wave offering of firstfruits to the LORD. ¹⁸Present with this bread seven male lambs, each a year old and without defect, one young bull and two rams. They will be a burnt offering to the LORD, together with their grain offerings and drink offerings — a food offering, an aroma pleasing to the LORD. ¹⁹Then sacrifice one male goat for a sin offering*c* and two lambs, each a year old, for a fellowship offering. ²⁰The priest is to wave the two lambs before the LORD as a wave offering, together with the bread of the firstfruits. They are a sacred offering to the LORD for the priest. ²¹On that same day you are to proclaim a sacred assembly and do no regular work. This is to be a lasting ordinance for the generations to come, wherever you live.

²² 'When you reap the harvest of your land, do not reap to the very edges of your field or gather the gleanings of your harvest. Leave them for the poor and for the foreigner residing among you. I am the LORD your God.'"

The Festival of Trumpets

²³The LORD said to Moses, ²⁴"Say to the Israelites: 'On the first day of the seventh month you are to have a day of sabbath rest, a sacred assembly commemorated with trumpet blasts. ²⁵Do no regular work, but present a food offering to the LORD.'"

The Day of Atonement

²⁶The LORD said to Moses, ²⁷"The tenth day of this seventh month is the Day of Atonement. Hold a sacred assembly and deny yourselves,*d*

and present a food offering to the LORD. ²⁸Do not do any work on that day, because it is the Day of Atonement, when atonement is made for you before the LORD your God. ²⁹Those who do not deny themselves on that day must be cut off from their people. ³⁰I will destroy from among their people anyone who does any work on that day. ³¹You shall do no work at all. This is to be a lasting ordinance for the generations to come, wherever you live. ³²It is a day of sabbath rest for you, and you must deny yourselves. From the evening of the ninth day of the month until the following evening you are to observe your sabbath."

The Festival of Tabernacles

³³The LORD said to Moses, ³⁴"Say to the Israelites: 'On the fifteenth day of the seventh month the LORD's Festival of Tabernacles begins, and it lasts for seven days. ³⁵The first day is a sacred assembly; do no regular work. ³⁶For seven days present food offerings to the LORD, and on the eighth day hold a sacred assembly and present a food offering to the LORD. It is the closing special assembly; do no regular work.

³⁷('"These are the LORD's appointed festivals, which you are to proclaim as sacred assemblies for bringing food offerings to the LORD — the burnt offerings and grain offerings, sacrifices and drink offerings required for each day. ³⁸These offerings are in addition to those for the LORD's Sabbaths and*e* in addition to your gifts and whatever you have vowed and all the freewill offerings you give to the LORD.)

³⁹ 'So beginning with the fifteenth day of the seventh month, after you have gathered the crops of the land, celebrate the festival to the LORD for seven days; the first day is a day of sabbath rest, and the eighth day also is a day of sabbath rest. ⁴⁰On the first day you are to take branches from luxuriant trees — from palms, willows and other leafy trees — and rejoice before the LORD your God for seven days. ⁴¹Celebrate this as a festival to the LORD for seven days each year. This is to be a lasting ordinance for the generations to come; celebrate it in the seventh month. ⁴²Live in temporary shelters for seven days: All native-born Israelites are to live in such shelters ⁴³so your descendants will know that I had the Israelites live in temporary shel-

---

a 13 That is, probably about 7 pounds or about 3.2 kilograms; also in verse 17   *b* 13 That is, about 1 quart or about 1 liter   *c* 19 Or *purification offering*   *d* 27 Or *and fast*; similarly in verses 29 and 32   *e* 38 Or *These festivals are in addition to the LORD's Sabbaths, and these offerings are*

ters when I brought them out of Egypt. I am the LORD your God.'"

[44]So Moses announced to the Israelites the appointed festivals of the LORD.

Olive Oil and Bread Set Before the LORD

24 The LORD said to Moses, [2]"Command the Israelites to bring you clear oil of pressed olives for the light so that the lamps may be kept burning continually. [3]Outside the curtain that shields the ark of the covenant law in the tent of meeting, Aaron is to tend the lamps before the LORD from evening till morning, continually. This is to be a lasting ordinance for the generations to come. [4]The lamps on the pure gold lampstand before the LORD must be tended continually.

[5]"Take the finest flour and bake twelve loaves of bread, using two-tenths of an ephah[a] for each loaf. [6]Arrange them in two stacks, six in each stack, on the table of pure gold before the LORD. [7]By each stack put some pure incense as a memorial[b] portion to represent the bread and to be a food offering presented to the LORD. [8]This bread is to be set out before the LORD regularly, Sabbath after Sabbath, on behalf of the Israelites, as a lasting covenant. [9]It belongs to Aaron and his sons, who are to eat it in the sanctuary area, because it is a most holy part of their perpetual share of the food offerings presented to the LORD."

A Blasphemer Put to Death

[10]Now the son of an Israelite mother and an Egyptian father went out among the Israelites, and a fight broke out in the camp between him and an Israelite. [11]The son of the Israelite woman blasphemed the Name with a curse; so they brought him to Moses. (His mother's name was Shelomith, the daughter of Dibri the Danite.) [12]They put him in custody until the will of the LORD should be made clear to them.

[13]Then the LORD said to Moses: [14]"Take the blasphemer outside the camp. All those who heard him are to lay their hands on his head, and the entire assembly is to stone him. [15]Say to the Israelites: 'Anyone who curses their God will be held responsible; [16]anyone who blasphemes the name of the LORD is to be put to death. The entire assembly must stone them. Whether foreigner or native-born, when they blaspheme the Name they are to be put to death.

[17]"'Anyone who takes the life of a human being is to be put to death. [18]Anyone who takes the life of someone's animal must make resti-

tution—life for life. [19]Anyone who injures their neighbor is to be injured in the same manner: [20]fracture for fracture, eye for eye, tooth for tooth. The one who has inflicted the injury must suffer the same injury. [21]Whoever kills an animal must make restitution, but whoever kills a human being is to be put to death. [22]You are to have the same law for the foreigner and the native-born. I am the LORD your God.'"

[23]Then Moses spoke to the Israelites, and they took the blasphemer outside the camp and stoned him. The Israelites did as the LORD commanded Moses.

The Sabbath Year

25 The LORD said to Moses at Mount Sinai, [2]"Speak to the Israelites and say to them: 'When you enter the land I am going to give you, the land itself must observe a sabbath to the LORD. [3]For six years sow your fields, and for six years prune your vineyards and gather their crops. [4]But in the seventh year the land is to have a year of sabbath rest, a sabbath to the LORD. Do not sow your fields or prune your vineyards. [5]Do not reap what grows of itself or harvest the grapes of your untended vines. The land is to have a year of rest. [6]Whatever the land yields during the sabbath year will be food for you—for yourself, your male and female servants, and the hired worker and temporary resident who live among you, [7]as well as for your livestock and the wild animals in your land. Whatever the land produces may be eaten.

The Year of Jubilee

[8]"'Count off seven sabbath years—seven times seven years—so that the seven sabbath years amount to a period of forty-nine years. [9]Then have the trumpet sounded everywhere on the tenth day of the seventh month; on the Day of Atonement sound the trumpet throughout your land. [10]Consecrate the fiftieth year and proclaim liberty throughout the land to all its inhabitants. It shall be a jubilee for you; each of you is to return to your family property and to your own clan. [11]The fiftieth year shall be a jubilee for you; do not sow and do not reap what grows of itself or harvest the untended vines. [12]For it is a jubilee and is to be holy for you; eat only what is taken directly from the fields.

[13]"'In this Year of Jubilee everyone is to return to their own property.

---

[a] 5 That is, probably about 7 pounds or about 3.2 kilograms
[b] 7 Or representative

¹⁴"'If you sell land to any of your own people or buy land from them, do not take advantage of each other. ¹⁵You are to buy from your own people on the basis of the number of years since the Jubilee. And they are to sell to you on the basis of the number of years left for harvesting crops. ¹⁶When the years are many, you are to increase the price, and when the years are few, you are to decrease the price, because what is really being sold to you is the number of crops. ¹⁷Do not take advantage of each other, but fear your God. I am the LORD your God.

¹⁸"'Follow my decrees and be careful to obey my laws, and you will live safely in the land. ¹⁹Then the land will yield its fruit, and you will eat your fill and live there in safety. ²⁰You may ask, "What will we eat in the seventh year if we do not plant or harvest our crops?" ²¹I will send you such a blessing in the sixth year that the land will yield enough for three years. ²²While you plant during the eighth year, you will eat from the old crop and will continue to eat from it until the harvest of the ninth year comes in.

²³"'The land must not be sold permanently, because the land is mine and you reside in my land as foreigners and strangers. ²⁴Throughout the land that you hold as a possession, you must provide for the redemption of the land.

²⁵"'If one of your fellow Israelites becomes poor and sells some of their property, their nearest relative is to come and redeem what they have sold. ²⁶If, however, there is no one to redeem it for them but later on they prosper and acquire sufficient means to redeem it themselves, ²⁷they are to determine the value for the years since they sold it and refund the balance to the one to whom they sold it; they can then go back to their own property. ²⁸But if they do not acquire the means to repay, what was sold will remain in the possession of the buyer until the Year of Jubilee. It will be returned in the Jubilee, and they can then go back to their property.

²⁹"'Anyone who sells a house in a walled city retains the right of redemption a full year after its sale. During that time the seller may redeem it. ³⁰If it is not redeemed before a full year has passed, the house in the walled city shall belong permanently to the buyer and the buyer's descendants. It is not to be returned in the Jubilee. ³¹But houses in villages without walls around them are to be considered as belonging to the open country. They can be redeemed, and they are to be returned in the Jubilee.

³²"'The Levites always have the right to redeem their houses in the Levitical towns, which they possess. ³³So the property of the Levites is redeemable — that is, a house sold in any town they hold — and is to be returned in the Jubilee, because the houses in the towns of the Levites are their property among the Israelites. ³⁴But the pastureland belonging to their towns must not be sold; it is their permanent possession.

³⁵"'If any of your fellow Israelites become poor and are unable to support themselves among you, help them as you would a foreigner and stranger, so they can continue to live among you. ³⁶Do not take interest or any profit from them, but fear your God, so that they may continue to live among you. ³⁷You must not lend them money at interest or sell them food at a profit. ³⁸I am the LORD your God, who brought you out of Egypt to give you the land of Canaan and to be your God.

³⁹"'If any of your fellow Israelites become poor and sell themselves to you, do not make them work as slaves. ⁴⁰They are to be treated as hired workers or temporary residents among you; they are to work for you until the Year of Jubilee. ⁴¹Then they and their children are to be released, and they will go back to their own clans and to the property of their ancestors. ⁴²Because the Israelites are my servants, whom I brought out of Egypt, they must not be sold as slaves. ⁴³Do not rule over them ruthlessly, but fear your God.

⁴⁴"'Your male and female slaves are to come from the nations around you; from them you may buy slaves. ⁴⁵You may also buy some of the temporary residents living among you and members of their clans born in your country, and they will become your property. ⁴⁶You can bequeath them to your children as inherited property and can make them slaves for life, but you must not rule over your fellow Israelites ruthlessly.

⁴⁷"'If a foreigner residing among you becomes rich and any of your fellow Israelites become poor and sell themselves to the foreigner or to a member of the foreigner's clan, ⁴⁸they retain the right of redemption after they have sold themselves. One of their relatives may redeem them: ⁴⁹An uncle or a cousin or any blood relative in their clan may redeem them. Or if they prosper, they may redeem themselves. ⁵⁰They and their buyer are to count the time from the year they sold themselves up to the Year of Jubilee. The price for their release is to be based on the rate paid to a hired worker for that number of years. ⁵¹If many years remain, they must pay for their redemption a larger share of the price

The Year of Jubilee: A Time to Rest and Sharpen the Ax

Leviticus 25:1-55

Ever hear of the sabbath year or the Year of Jubilee? Those are the delightful topics of Leviticus 25. The first occurred every seven years, while the second was to take place every fifty years.

These special years called for special behavior. God's people were to stop their usual labor, alter their daily routines, and change their normal existence. Consider a few lessons leaders can learn from these special sabbaths:

1. **They gave the people a time of rest** (v. 5). God said these special years were seasons for resting the land and their lives.

2. **They gave the people an opportunity for redemption** (vv. 10, 24). Every Israelite could return to ancestral lands and redeem them, just as God did with them.

3. **They gave the people time for reflection** (v. 12). The Jubilee Year was to be holy, recognized as a gift from the Lord.

4. **They gave the people time for reward and repair** (vv. 18–19). As a reward for obedience, God would supply abundant food and time to sharpen the ax.

5. **They gave the people time for relationships** (vv. 35–46). Everyone was to prioritize people over material gain.

6. **They gave the people a time to refocus** (v. 55). God reminds his people that they are his servants and he is their Lord.

paid for them. ⁵²If only a few years remain until the Year of Jubilee, they are to compute that and pay for their redemption accordingly. ⁵³They are to be treated as workers hired from year to year; you must see to it that those to whom they owe service do not rule over them ruthlessly.

⁵⁴"Even if someone is not redeemed in any of these ways, they and their children are to be released in the Year of Jubilee, ⁵⁵for the Israelites belong to me as servants. They are my servants, whom I brought out of Egypt. I am the LORD your God.

Reward for Obedience

26 "'Do not make idols or set up an image or a sacred stone for yourselves, and do not place a carved stone in your land to bow down before it. I am the LORD your God.

²"'Observe my Sabbaths and have reverence for my sanctuary. I am the LORD.

³"'If you follow my decrees and are careful to obey my commands, ⁴I will send you rain in its season, and the ground will yield its crops and the trees their fruit. ⁵Your threshing will continue until grape harvest and the grape harvest will continue until planting, and you will eat all the food you want and live in safety in your land.

⁶"'I will grant peace in the land, and you will lie down and no one will make you afraid. I will remove wild beasts from the land, and the sword will not pass through your country. ⁷You will pursue your enemies, and they will fall by the sword before you. ⁸Five of you will chase a hundred, and a hundred of you will chase ten thousand, and your enemies will fall by the sword before you.

⁹"'I will look on you with favor and make you fruitful and increase your numbers, and I will keep my covenant with you. ¹⁰You will still be eating last year's harvest when you will have to move it out to make room for the new. ¹¹I will put my dwelling place[a] among you, and I will not abhor you. ¹²I will walk among you and be your God, and you will be my people. ¹³I am the LORD your God, who brought you out of Egypt so that you would no longer be slaves to the Egyptians; I broke the bars of your yoke and enabled you to walk with heads held high.

Punishment for Disobedience

¹⁴"'But if you will not listen to me and carry out all these commands, ¹⁵and if you reject my decrees and abhor my laws and fail to carry out all my commands and so violate my covenant,

---

a 11 Or my tabernacle

[16]then I will do this to you: I will bring on you sudden terror, wasting diseases and fever that will destroy your sight and sap your strength. You will plant seed in vain, because your enemies will eat it. [17]I will set my face against you so that you will be defeated by your enemies; those who hate you will rule over you, and you will flee even when no one is pursuing you.

[18]" 'If after all this you will not listen to me, I will punish you for your sins seven times over. [19]I will break down your stubborn pride and make the sky above you like iron and the ground beneath you like bronze. [20]Your strength will be spent in vain, because your soil will not yield its crops, nor will the trees of your land yield their fruit.

[21]" 'If you remain hostile toward me and refuse to listen to me, I will multiply your afflictions seven times over, as your sins deserve. [22]I will send wild animals against you, and they will rob you of your children, destroy your cattle and make you so few in number that your roads will be deserted.

[23]" 'If in spite of these things you do not accept my correction but continue to be hostile toward me, [24]I myself will be hostile toward you and will afflict you for your sins seven times over. [25]And I will bring the sword on you to avenge the breaking of the covenant. When you withdraw into your cities, I will send a plague among you, and you will be given into enemy hands. [26]When I cut off your supply of bread, ten women will be able to bake your bread in one oven, and they will dole out the bread by weight. You will eat, but you will not be satisfied.

[27]" 'If in spite of this you still do not listen to me but continue to be hostile toward me, [28]then in my anger I will be hostile toward you, and I myself will punish you for your sins seven times over. [29]You will eat the flesh of your sons and the flesh of your daughters. [30]I will destroy your high places, cut down your incense altars and pile your dead bodies[a] on the lifeless forms of your idols, and I will abhor you. [31]I will turn your cities into ruins and lay waste your sanctuaries, and I will take no delight in the pleasing aroma of your offerings. [32]I myself will lay waste the land, so that your enemies who live there will be appalled. [33]I will scatter you among the nations and will draw out my sword and pursue you. Your land will be laid waste, and your cities will lie in ruins. [34]Then the land will enjoy its sabbath years all the time that it lies desolate and you are in the country of your enemies; then the land will rest and enjoy its sabbaths. [35]All the time that it lies desolate, the land will have the rest it did not have during the sabbaths you lived in it.

[36]" 'As for those of you who are left, I will make their hearts so fearful in the lands of their enemies that the sound of a windblown leaf will put them to flight. They will run as though fleeing from the sword, and they will fall, even though no one is pursuing them. [37]They will stumble over one another as though fleeing from the sword, even though no one is pursuing them. So you will not be able to stand before your enemies. [38]You will perish among the nations; the land of your enemies will devour you. [39]Those of you who are left will waste away in the lands of their enemies because of their sins; also because of their ancestors' sins they will waste away.

[40]" 'But if they will confess their sins and the

---

[a] 30 Or your funeral offerings

Sowing and Reaping: Decisions and Consequences

Leviticus 26:3-39

Leadership, like life, is the sum total of the decisions we make.

Every decision has consequences. We decide how we will respond to people. We decide how large to make a budget for promotion and marketing. We decide whom to hire. We decide which values are worth going to the mat for.

Toward the end of Leviticus, God lists the blessings he offers to those who obey him and the punishment they'll receive for disobedience. God, the Ultimate Leader, clearly outlines the consequences for his people's choices.

Leaders who fail to make good decisions . . .

1. **Lack commitment.**
2. **Suffer from a scattered focus.**
3. **Look for excuses.**
4. **Forget the big picture.**
5. **Go public with private thoughts.**
6. **Adopt the motto, "That's good enough."**
7. **Don't take God's direction seriously.**
8. **Behave inconsistently.**
9. **Create poor relationships.**
10. **Avoid change.**

sins of their ancestors—their unfaithfulness and their hostility toward me, [41]which made me hostile toward them so that I sent them into the land of their enemies—then when their uncircumcised hearts are humbled and they pay for their sin, [42]I will remember my covenant with Jacob and my covenant with Isaac and my covenant with Abraham, and I will remember the land. [43]For the land will be deserted by them and will enjoy its sabbaths while it lies desolate without them. They will pay for their sins because they rejected my laws and abhorred my decrees. [44]Yet in spite of this, when they are in the land of their enemies, I will not reject them or abhor them so as to destroy them completely, breaking my covenant with them. I am the LORD their God. [45]But for their sake I will remember the covenant with their ancestors whom I brought out of Egypt in the sight of the nations to be their God. I am the LORD.'"

[46]These are the decrees, the laws and the regulations that the LORD established at Mount Sinai between himself and the Israelites through Moses.

Redeeming What Is the LORD's

27 The LORD said to Moses, [2]"Speak to the Israelites and say to them: 'If anyone makes a special vow to dedicate a person to the LORD by giving the equivalent value, [3]set the value of a male between the ages of twenty and sixty at fifty shekels[a] of silver, according to the sanctuary shekel[b]; [4]for a female, set her value at thirty shekels[c]; [5]for a person between the ages of five and twenty, set the value of a male at twenty shekels[d] and of a female at ten shekels[e]; [6]for a person between one month and five years, set the value of a male at five shekels[f] of silver and that of a female at three shekels[g] of silver; [7]for a person sixty years old or more, set the value of a male at fifteen shekels[h] and of a female at ten shekels. [8]If anyone making the vow is too poor to pay the specified amount, the person being dedicated is to be presented to the priest, who will set the value according to what the one making the vow can afford.

[9]"'If what they vowed is an animal that is acceptable as an offering to the LORD, such an animal given to the LORD becomes holy. [10]They must not exchange it or substitute a good one for a bad one, or a bad one for a good one; if they should substitute one animal for another, both it and the substitute become holy. [11]If what they vowed is a ceremonially unclean animal—one that is not acceptable as an offering

to the LORD—the animal must be presented to the priest, [12]who will judge its quality as good or bad. Whatever value the priest then sets, that is what it will be. [13]If the owner wishes to redeem the animal, a fifth must be added to its value.

[14]"'If anyone dedicates their house as something holy to the LORD, the priest will judge its quality as good or bad. Whatever value the priest then sets, so it will remain. [15]If the one who dedicates their house wishes to redeem it, they must add a fifth to its value, and the house will again become theirs.

[16]"'If anyone dedicates to the LORD part of their family land, its value is to be set according to the amount of seed required for it—fifty shekels of silver to a homer[i] of barley seed. [17]If they dedicate a field during the Year of Jubilee, the value that has been set remains. [18]But if they dedicate a field after the Jubilee, the priest will determine the value according to the number of years that remain until the next Year of Jubilee, and its set value will be reduced. [19]If the one who dedicates the field wishes to redeem it, they must add a fifth to its value, and the field will again become theirs. [20]If, however, they do not redeem the field, or if they have sold it to someone else, it can never be redeemed. [21]When the field is released in the Jubilee, it will become holy, like a field devoted to the LORD; it will become priestly property.

[22]"'If anyone dedicates to the LORD a field they have bought, which is not part of their family land, [23]the priest will determine its value up to the Year of Jubilee, and the owner must pay its value on that day as something holy to the LORD. [24]In the Year of Jubilee the field will revert to the person from whom it was bought, the one whose land it was. [25]Every value is to be set according to the sanctuary shekel, twenty gerahs to the shekel.

[26]"'No one, however, may dedicate the firstborn of an animal, since the firstborn already belongs to the LORD; whether an ox[j] or a sheep, it is the LORD's. [27]If it is one of the unclean animals, it may be bought back at its set value,

---

[a] 3 That is, about 1 1/4 pounds or about 575 grams; also in verse 16   [b] 3 That is, about 2/5 ounce or about 12 grams; also in verse 25   [c] 4 That is, about 12 ounces or about 345 grams   [d] 5 That is, about 8 ounces or about 230 grams   [e] 5 That is, about 4 ounces or about 115 grams; also in verse 7   [f] 6 That is, about 2 ounces or about 58 grams   [g] 6 That is, about 1 1/4 ounces or about 35 grams   [h] 7 That is, about 6 ounces or about 175 grams   [i] 16 That is, probably about 300 pounds or about 135 kilograms   [j] 26 The Hebrew word can refer to either male or female.

adding a fifth of the value to it. If it is not redeemed, it is to be sold at its set value.

28 "But nothing that a person owns and devotes[a] to the LORD — whether a human being or an animal or family land — may be sold or redeemed; everything so devoted is most holy to the LORD.

29 "No person devoted to destruction[b] may be ransomed; they are to be put to death.

30 "A tithe of everything from the land, whether grain from the soil or fruit from the trees, belongs to the LORD; it is holy to the LORD. 31 Whoever would redeem any of their tithe must add a fifth of the value to it. 32 Every tithe of the herd and flock — every tenth animal that passes under the shepherd's rod — will be holy to the LORD. 33 No one may pick out the good from the bad or make any substitution. If anyone does make a substitution, both the animal and its substitute become holy and cannot be redeemed.'"

34 These are the commands the LORD gave Moses at Mount Sinai for the Israelites.

---

a 28 The Hebrew term refers to the irrevocable giving over of things or persons to the LORD.   b 29 The Hebrew term refers to the irrevocable giving over of things or persons to the LORD, often by totally destroying them.

The Census

1 The LORD spoke to Moses in the tent of meeting in the Desert of Sinai on the first day of the second month of the second year after the Israelites came out of Egypt. He said: ²"Take a census of the whole Israelite community by their clans and families, listing every man by name, one by one. ³You and Aaron are to count according to their divisions all the men in Israel who are twenty years old or more and able to serve in the army. ⁴One man from each tribe, each of them the head of his family, is to help you. ⁵These are the names of the men who are to assist you:

> from Reuben, Elizur son of Shedeur;
> ⁶from Simeon, Shelumiel son of Zurishaddai;
> ⁷from Judah, Nahshon son of Amminadab;
> ⁸from Issachar, Nethanel son of Zuar;
> ⁹from Zebulun, Eliab son of Helon;
> ¹⁰from the sons of Joseph:
> > from Ephraim, Elishama son of Ammihud;
> > from Manasseh, Gamaliel son of Pedahzur;
> ¹¹from Benjamin, Abidan son of Gideoni;
> ¹²from Dan, Ahiezer son of Ammishaddai;
> ¹³from Asher, Pagiel son of Okran;
> ¹⁴from Gad, Eliasaph son of Deuel;
> ¹⁵from Naphtali, Ahira son of Enan."

¹⁶These were the men appointed from the community, the leaders of their ancestral tribes. They were the heads of the clans of Israel.

¹⁷Moses and Aaron took these men whose names had been specified, ¹⁸and they called the whole community together on the first day of the second month. The people registered their ancestry by their clans and families, and the men twenty years old or more were listed by name, one by one, ¹⁹as the LORD commanded Moses. And so he counted them in the Desert of Sinai:

²⁰From the descendants of Reuben the firstborn son of Israel:

> All the men twenty years old or more who were able to serve in the army were listed by name, one by one, according to the records of their clans and families. ²¹The number from the tribe of Reuben was 46,500.

²²From the descendants of Simeon:

> All the men twenty years old or more who were able to serve in the army were counted and listed by name, one by one, according to the records of their clans and families. ²³The number from the tribe of Simeon was 59,300.

²⁴From the descendants of Gad:

> All the men twenty years old or more who were able to serve in the army were listed by name, according to the records of their clans and families. ²⁵The number from the tribe of Gad was 45,650.

²⁶From the descendants of Judah:

> All the men twenty years old or more who were able to serve in the army were listed by name, according to the records of their clans and families. ²⁷The number from the tribe of Judah was 74,600.

²⁸From the descendants of Issachar:

> All the men twenty years old or more who were able to serve in the army were listed by name, according to the records of their clans and families. ²⁹The number from the tribe of Issachar was 54,400.

³⁰From the descendants of Zebulun:

> All the men twenty years old or more who were able to serve in the army were listed by name, according to the records of their clans and families. ³¹The number from the tribe of Zebulun was 57,400.

³²From the sons of Joseph:

From the descendants of Ephraim:

> All the men twenty years old or more who were able to serve in the army were listed by name, according to the records of their clans and families. ³³The number from the tribe of Ephraim was 40,500.

³⁴From the descendants of Manasseh:

> All the men twenty years old or more who were able to serve in the army were listed by name, according to the records of their clans and families. ³⁵The number from the tribe of Manasseh was 32,200.

³⁶From the descendants of Benjamin:

> All the men twenty years old or more who were able to serve in the army were listed by name, according to the records of their clans and families. ³⁷The number from the tribe of Benjamin was 35,400.

³⁸From the descendants of Dan:

All the men twenty years old or more who were able to serve in the army were listed by name, according to the records of their clans and families. ³⁹The number from the tribe of Dan was 62,700.

⁴⁰From the descendants of Asher:

All the men twenty years old or more who were able to serve in the army were listed by name, according to the records of their clans and families. ⁴¹The number from the tribe of Asher was 41,500.

⁴²From the descendants of Naphtali:

All the men twenty years old or more who were able to serve in the army were listed by name, according to the records of their clans and families. ⁴³The number from the tribe of Naphtali was 53,400.

⁴⁴These were the men counted by Moses and Aaron and the twelve leaders of Israel, each one representing his family. ⁴⁵All the Israelites twenty years old or more who were able to serve in Israel's army were counted according to their families. ⁴⁶The total number was 603,550.

⁴⁷The ancestral tribe of the Levites, however, was not counted along with the others. ⁴⁸The LORD had said to Moses: ⁴⁹"You must not count the tribe of Levi or include them in the census of the other Israelites. ⁵⁰Instead, appoint the Levites to be in charge of the tabernacle of the covenant law — over all its furnishings and everything belonging to it. They are to carry the tabernacle and all its furnishings; they are to take care of it and encamp around it. ⁵¹Whenever the tabernacle is to move, the Levites are to take it down, and whenever the tabernacle is to be set up, the Levites shall do it. Anyone else who approaches it is to be put to death. ⁵²The Israelites are to set up their tents by divisions, each of them in their own camp under their standard. ⁵³The Levites, however, are to set up their tents around the tabernacle of the covenant law so that my wrath will not fall on the Israelite community. The Levites are to be responsible for the care of the tabernacle of the covenant law."

⁵⁴The Israelites did all this just as the LORD commanded Moses.

The Arrangement of the Tribal Camps

2 The LORD said to Moses and Aaron: ²"The Israelites are to camp around the tent of meeting some distance from it, each of them under their standard and holding the banners of their family."

³On the east, toward the sunrise, the divisions of the camp of Judah are to encamp under their standard. The leader of the people of Judah is Nahshon son of Amminadab. ⁴His division numbers 74,600.

⁵The tribe of Issachar will camp next to them. The leader of the people of Issachar is Nethanel son of Zuar. ⁶His division numbers 54,400.

⁷The tribe of Zebulun will be next. The leader of the people of Zebulun is Eliab son of Helon. ⁸His division numbers 57,400.

⁹All the men assigned to the camp of Judah, according to their divisions, number 186,400. They will set out first.

¹⁰On the south will be the divisions of the camp of Reuben under their standard. The leader of the people of Reuben is Elizur son of Shedeur. ¹¹His division numbers 46,500.

¹²The tribe of Simeon will camp next to them. The leader of the people of Simeon is Shelumiel son of Zurishaddai. ¹³His division numbers 59,300.

¹⁴The tribe of Gad will be next. The leader of the people of Gad is Eliasaph son of Deuel.^a ¹⁵His division numbers 45,650.

¹⁶All the men assigned to the camp of Reuben, according to their divisions, number 151,450. They will set out second.

¹⁷Then the tent of meeting and the camp of the Levites will set out in the middle of

---

First-Generation Census: Sizing Up the Resources

Numbers 1:1–54

Can you imagine the mammoth job of counting the wandering tribes of Israel? That's exactly what Moses and Aaron did. Israel's leaders broke down the huge assignment into many smaller elements, using the tribes, clans and families already in place in Hebrew culture. Good leaders organize chaos.

---

^a 14 Many manuscripts of the Masoretic Text, Samaritan Pentateuch and Vulgate (see also 1:14); most manuscripts of the Masoretic Text *Reuel*

the camps. They will set out in the same order as they encamp, each in their own place under their standard.

18On the west will be the divisions of the camp of Ephraim under their standard. The leader of the people of Ephraim is Elishama son of Ammihud. 19His division numbers 40,500.
20The tribe of Manasseh will be next to them. The leader of the people of Manasseh is Gamaliel son of Pedahzur. 21His division numbers 32,200.
22The tribe of Benjamin will be next. The leader of the people of Benjamin is Abidan son of Gideoni. 23His division numbers 35,400.
24All the men assigned to the camp of Ephraim, according to their divisions, number 108,100. They will set out third.

25On the north will be the divisions of the camp of Dan under their standard. The leader of the people of Dan is Ahiezer son of Ammishaddai. 26His division numbers 62,700.
27The tribe of Asher will camp next to them. The leader of the people of Asher is Pagiel son of Okran. 28His division numbers 41,500.
29The tribe of Naphtali will be next. The leader of the people of Naphtali is Ahira son of Enan. 30His division numbers 53,400.
31All the men assigned to the camp of Dan number 157,600. They will set out last, under their standards.

32These are the Israelites, counted according to their families. All the men in the camps, by their divisions, number 603,550. 33The Levites, however, were not counted along with the other Israelites, as the LORD commanded Moses.

34So the Israelites did everything the LORD commanded Moses; that is the way they encamped under their standards, and that is the

The Law of Navigation: Planning and Structure

Numbers 2:1–34

As a good leader, Moses methodically arranged the tribal camps in the wilderness. He set the tent of meeting in the center and arranged the priests around its four sides. Then he symmetrically distributed the twelve tribes around the priests and Levites, with three tribes on each of the four sides.
We would do well to plan and organize as Moses did.

1. *Plan to plan.* Give time for planning and organizing.
2. *Determine your primary purpose.* What's the big picture? What are you trying to do?
3. *Assess the situation.* Understand where you sit before trying to develop a strategy.
4. *Prioritize the needs.* Make sure the team agrees on the most important goals.
5. *Ask the right questions.* Ask about market, leadership, revenue, reporting, evaluation.
6. *Set specific goals.* Write goals that are realistic, measurable, convictional.
7. *Clarify and communicate.* Communication links planning and implementation.
8. *Identify possible obstacles.* Mentally walk through all you are trying to pull off.
9. *Have an open system approach to your planning.* Be sympathetic to your environment.
10. *Schedule everything you can.* Get things on the calendar and set deadlines.
11. *Budget everything you can.* Determine both the costs and due dates of projects.
12. *Monitor and correct.* Progress is like a canoe trip; constantly adjust your course.
13. *Study the results.* Evaluation prevents stagnation and exaggeration.

Remember, anyone can steer the ship, but it takes a leader to chart the course

way they set out, each of them with their clan and family.

The Levites

3 This is the account of the family of Aaron and Moses at the time the LORD spoke to Moses at Mount Sinai.

[2]The names of the sons of Aaron were Nadab the firstborn and Abihu, Eleazar and Ithamar. [3]Those were the names of Aaron's sons, the anointed priests, who were ordained to serve as priests. [4]Nadab and Abihu, however, died before the LORD when they made an offering with unauthorized fire before him in the Desert of Sinai. They had no sons, so Eleazar and Ithamar served as priests during the lifetime of their father Aaron.

[5]The LORD said to Moses, [6]"Bring the tribe of Levi and present them to Aaron the priest to assist him. [7]They are to perform duties for him and for the whole community at the tent of meeting by doing the work of the tabernacle. [8]They are to take care of all the furnishings of the tent of meeting, fulfilling the obligations of the Israelites by doing the work of the tabernacle. [9]Give the Levites to Aaron and his sons; they are the Israelites who are to be given wholly to him.[a] [10]Appoint Aaron and his sons to serve as priests; anyone else who approaches the sanctuary is to be put to death."

[11]The LORD also said to Moses, [12]"I have taken the Levites from among the Israelites in place of the first male offspring of every Israelite woman. The Levites are mine, [13]for all the firstborn are mine. When I struck down all the firstborn in Egypt, I set apart for myself every firstborn in Israel, whether human or animal. They are to be mine. I am the LORD."

[14]The LORD said to Moses in the Desert of Sinai, [15]"Count the Levites by their families and clans. Count every male a month old or more." [16]So Moses counted them, as he was commanded by the word of the LORD.

[17]These were the names of the sons of Levi:

Gershon, Kohath and Merari.

[18]These were the names of the Gershonite clans:

Libni and Shimei.

[19]The Kohathite clans:

Amram, Izhar, Hebron and Uzziel.

[20]The Merarite clans:

Mahli and Mushi.

These were the Levite clans, according to their families.

[21]To Gershon belonged the clans of the Libnites and Shimeites; these were the Gershonite clans. [22]The number of all the males a month old or more who were counted was 7,500. [23]The Gershonite clans were to camp on the west, behind the tabernacle. [24]The leader of the families of the Gershonites was Eliasaph son of Lael. [25]At the tent of meeting the Gershonites were responsible for the care of the tabernacle and tent, its coverings, the curtain at the entrance to the tent of meeting, [26]the curtains of the courtyard, the curtain at the entrance to the courtyard surrounding the tabernacle and altar, and the ropes — and everything related to their use.

[27]To Kohath belonged the clans of the Amramites, Izharites, Hebronites and Uzzielites; these were the Kohathite clans. [28]The number of all the males a month old or more was 8,600.[b] The Kohathites were responsible for the care of the sanctuary. [29]The Kohathite clans were to camp on the south side of the tabernacle. [30]The leader of the families of the Kohathite clans was Elizaphan son of Uzziel. [31]They were responsible for the care of the ark, the table, the lampstand, the altars, the articles of the sanctuary used in ministering, the curtain, and everything related to their use. [32]The chief leader of the Levites was Eleazar son of Aaron, the priest. He was appointed over those who were responsible for the care of the sanctuary.

[33]To Merari belonged the clans of the Mahlites and the Mushites; these were the Merarite clans. [34]The number of all the males a month old or more who were counted was 6,200. [35]The leader of the families of the Merarite clans was Zuriel son of Abihail; they were to camp on the north side of the tabernacle. [36]The Merarites were appointed to take care of the frames of the tabernacle, its crossbars, posts, bases, all its equipment, and everything related to their use, [37]as well as the posts of the surrounding courtyard with their bases, tent pegs and ropes.

[38]Moses and Aaron and his sons were to camp to the east of the tabernacle, toward the sunrise, in front of the tent of meeting. They were responsible for the care of the sanctuary

---

[a] 9 Most manuscripts of the Masoretic Text; some manuscripts of the Masoretic Text, Samaritan Pentateuch and Septuagint (see also 8:16) to me　　[b] 28 Hebrew; some Septuagint manuscripts 8,300

on behalf of the Israelites. Anyone else who approached the sanctuary was to be put to death.

[39]The total number of Levites counted at the LORD's command by Moses and Aaron according to their clans, including every male a month old or more, was 22,000.

[40]The LORD said to Moses, "Count all the firstborn Israelite males who are a month old or more and make a list of their names. [41]Take the Levites for me in place of all the firstborn of the Israelites, and the livestock of the Levites in place of all the firstborn of the livestock of the Israelites. I am the LORD."

[42]So Moses counted all the firstborn of the Israelites, as the LORD commanded him. [43]The total number of firstborn males a month old or more, listed by name, was 22,273.

[44]The LORD also said to Moses, [45]"Take the Levites in place of all the firstborn of Israel, and the livestock of the Levites in place of their livestock. The Levites are to be mine. I am the LORD. [46]To redeem the 273 firstborn Israelites who exceed the number of the Levites, [47]collect five shekels[a] for each one, according to the sanctuary shekel, which weighs twenty gerahs. [48]Give the money for the redemption of the additional Israelites to Aaron and his sons."

[49]So Moses collected the redemption money from those who exceeded the number redeemed by the Levites. [50]From the firstborn of the Israelites he collected silver weighing 1,365 shekels,[b] according to the sanctuary shekel. [51]Moses gave the redemption money to Aaron and his sons, as he was commanded by the word of the LORD.

The Kohathites

4 The LORD said to Moses and Aaron: [2]"Take a census of the Kohathite branch of the Levites by their clans and families. [3]Count all the men from thirty to fifty years of age who come to serve in the work at the tent of meeting.

[4]"This is the work of the Kohathites at the tent of meeting: the care of the most holy things. [5]When the camp is to move, Aaron and his sons are to go in and take down the shielding curtain and put it over the ark of the covenant law. [6]Then they are to cover the curtain with a durable leather,[c] spread a cloth of solid blue over that and put the poles in place.

[7]"Over the table of the Presence they are to spread a blue cloth and put on it the plates, dishes and bowls, and the jars for drink offerings; the bread that is continually there is to remain

on it. [8]They are to spread a scarlet cloth over them, cover that with the durable leather and put the poles in place.

[9]"They are to take a blue cloth and cover the lampstand that is for light, together with its lamps, its wick trimmers and trays, and all its jars for the olive oil used to supply it. [10]Then they are to wrap it and all its accessories in a covering of the durable leather and put it on a carrying frame.

[11]"Over the gold altar they are to spread a blue cloth and cover that with the durable leather and put the poles in place.

[12]"They are to take all the articles used for ministering in the sanctuary, wrap them in a blue cloth, cover that with the durable leather and put them on a carrying frame.

[13]"They are to remove the ashes from the bronze altar and spread a purple cloth over it. [14]Then they are to place on it all the utensils used for ministering at the altar, including the firepans, meat forks, shovels and sprinkling bowls. Over it they are to spread a covering of the durable leather and put the poles in place.

[15]"After Aaron and his sons have finished covering the holy furnishings and all the holy articles, and when the camp is ready to move, only then are the Kohathites to come and do the carrying. But they must not touch the holy things or they will die. The Kohathites are to carry those things that are in the tent of meeting.

[16]"Eleazar son of Aaron, the priest, is to have charge of the oil for the light, the fragrant incense, the regular grain offering and the anointing oil. He is to be in charge of the entire tabernacle and everything in it, including its holy furnishings and articles."

[17]The LORD said to Moses and Aaron, [18]"See that the Kohathite tribal clans are not destroyed from among the Levites. [19]So that they may live and not die when they come near the most holy things, do this for them: Aaron and his sons are to go into the sanctuary and assign to each man his work and what he is to carry. [20]But the Kohathites must not go in to look at the holy things, even for a moment, or they will die."

The Gershonites

[21]The LORD said to Moses, [22]"Take a census also of the Gershonites by their families and

---

[a] 47 That is, about 2 ounces or about 58 grams   [b] 50 That is, about 35 pounds or about 16 kilograms   [c] 6 Possibly the hides of large aquatic mammals; also in verses 8, 10, 11, 12, 14 and 25

clans. ²³Count all the men from thirty to fifty years of age who come to serve in the work at the tent of meeting.

²⁴"This is the service of the Gershonite clans in their carrying and their other work: ²⁵They are to carry the curtains of the tabernacle, that is, the tent of meeting, its covering and its outer covering of durable leather, the curtains for the entrance to the tent of meeting, ²⁶the curtains of the courtyard surrounding the tabernacle and altar, the curtain for the entrance to the courtyard, the ropes and all the equipment used in the service of the tent. The Gershonites are to do all that needs to be done with these things. ²⁷All their service, whether carrying or doing other work, is to be done under the direction of Aaron and his sons. You shall assign to them as their responsibility all they are to carry. ²⁸This is the service of the Gershonite clans at the tent of meeting. Their duties are to be under the direction of Ithamar son of Aaron, the priest.

The Merarites

²⁹"Count the Merarites by their clans and families. ³⁰Count all the men from thirty to fifty years of age who come to serve in the work at the tent of meeting. ³¹As part of all their service at the tent, they are to carry the frames of the tabernacle, its crossbars, posts and bases, ³²as well as the posts of the surrounding courtyard with their bases, tent pegs, ropes, all their equipment and everything related to their use. Assign to each man the specific things he is to carry. ³³This is the service of the Merarite clans as they work at the tent of meeting under the direction of Ithamar son of Aaron, the priest."

The Numbering of the Levite Clans

³⁴Moses, Aaron and the leaders of the community counted the Kohathites by their clans and families. ³⁵All the men from thirty to fifty years of age who came to serve in the work at the tent of meeting, ³⁶counted by clans, were 2,750. ³⁷This was the total of all those in the Kohathite clans who served at the tent of meeting. Moses and Aaron counted them according to the LORD's command through Moses.

³⁸The Gershonites were counted by their clans and families. ³⁹All the men from thirty to fifty years of age who came to serve in the work at the tent of meeting, ⁴⁰counted by their clans and families, were 2,630. ⁴¹This was the total of those in the Gershonite clans who served at the tent of meeting. Moses and Aaron counted them according to the LORD's command.

⁴²The Merarites were counted by their clans and families. ⁴³All the men from thirty to fifty years of age who came to serve in the work at the tent of meeting, ⁴⁴counted by their clans, were 3,200. ⁴⁵This was the total of those in the Merarite clans. Moses and Aaron counted them according to the LORD's command through Moses.

⁴⁶So Moses, Aaron and the leaders of Israel counted all the Levites by their clans and families. ⁴⁷All the men from thirty to fifty years of age who came to do the work of serving and carrying the tent of meeting ⁴⁸numbered 8,580. ⁴⁹At the LORD's command through Moses, each was assigned his work and told what to carry.

Thus they were counted, as the LORD commanded Moses.

The Purity of the Camp

5 The LORD said to Moses, ²"Command the Israelites to send away from the camp anyone who has a defiling skin disease[a] or a discharge of any kind, or who is ceremonially unclean because of a dead body. ³Send away male and female alike; send them outside the camp so they will not defile their camp, where I dwell among them." ⁴The Israelites did so; they sent them outside the camp. They did just as the LORD had instructed Moses.

Restitution for Wrongs

⁵The LORD said to Moses, ⁶"Say to the Israelites: 'Any man or woman who wrongs another in any way[b] and so is unfaithful to the LORD is guilty ⁷and must confess the sin they have committed. They must make full restitution for the wrong they have done, add a fifth of the value to it and give it all to the person they have wronged. ⁸But if that person has no close relative to whom restitution can be made for the wrong, the restitution belongs to the LORD and must be given to the priest, along with the ram with which atonement is made for the wrongdoer. ⁹All the sacred contributions the Israelites bring to a priest will belong to him. ¹⁰Sacred things belong to their owners, but what they give to the priest will belong to the priest.'"

The Test for an Unfaithful Wife

¹¹Then the LORD said to Moses, ¹²"Speak to the Israelites and say to them: 'If a man's wife

---

^a 2 The Hebrew word for *defiling skin disease*, traditionally translated "leprosy," was used for various diseases affecting the skin.   ^b 6 Or *woman who commits any wrong common to mankind*

goes astray and is unfaithful to him [13]so that another man has sexual relations with her, and this is hidden from her husband and her impurity is undetected (since there is no witness against her and she has not been caught in the act), [14]and if feelings of jealousy come over her husband and he suspects his wife and she is impure—or if he is jealous and suspects her even though she is not impure— [15]then he is to take his wife to the priest. He must also take an offering of a tenth of an ephah[a] of barley flour on her behalf. He must not pour olive oil on it or put incense on it, because it is a grain offering for jealousy, a reminder-offering to draw attention to wrongdoing.

[16]"'The priest shall bring her and have her stand before the LORD. [17]Then he shall take some holy water in a clay jar and put some dust from the tabernacle floor into the water. [18]After the priest has had the woman stand before the LORD, he shall loosen her hair and place in her hands the reminder-offering, the grain offering for jealousy, while he himself holds the bitter water that brings a curse. [19]Then the priest shall put the woman under oath and say to her, "If no other man has had sexual relations with you and you have not gone astray and become impure while married to your husband, may this bitter water that brings a curse not harm you. [20]But if you have gone astray while married to your husband and you have made yourself impure by having sexual relations with a man other than your husband"— [21]here the priest is to put the woman under this curse— "may the LORD cause you to become a curse[b] among your people when he makes your womb miscarry and your abdomen swell. [22]May this water that brings a curse enter your body so that your abdomen swells or your womb miscarries."

"'Then the woman is to say, "Amen. So be it."

[23]"'The priest is to write these curses on a scroll and then wash them off into the bitter water. [24]He shall make the woman drink the bitter water that brings a curse, and this water that brings a curse and causes bitter suffering will enter her. [25]The priest is to take from her hands the grain offering for jealousy, wave it before the LORD and bring it to the altar. [26]The priest is then to take a handful of the grain offering as a memorial[c] offering and burn it on the altar; after that, he is to have the woman drink the water. [27]If she has made herself impure and been unfaithful to her husband, this will be the result: When she is made to drink the water that brings a curse and causes bitter suffering, it will enter her, her abdomen will swell and her womb will

miscarry, and she will become a curse. [28]If, however, the woman has not made herself impure, but is clean, she will be cleared of guilt and will be able to have children.

[29]"'This, then, is the law of jealousy when a woman goes astray and makes herself impure while married to her husband, [30]or when feelings of jealousy come over a man because he suspects his wife. The priest is to have her stand before the LORD and is to apply this entire law to her. [31]The husband will be innocent of any wrongdoing, but the woman will bear the consequences of her sin.'"

The Nazirite

6 The LORD said to Moses, [2]"Speak to the Israelites and say to them: 'If a man or woman wants to make a special vow, a vow of dedication to the LORD as a Nazirite, [3]they must abstain from wine and other fermented drink and must not drink vinegar made from wine or other fermented drink. They must not drink grape juice or eat grapes or raisins. [4]As long as they remain under their Nazirite vow, they must not eat anything that comes from the grapevine, not even the seeds or skins.

[5]"'During the entire period of their Nazirite vow, no razor may be used on their head. They must be holy until the period of their dedication to the LORD is over; they must let their hair grow long.

[6]"'Throughout the period of their dedication to the LORD, the Nazirite must not go near a dead body. [7]Even if their own father or mother or brother or sister dies, they must not make themselves ceremonially unclean on account of them, because the symbol of their dedication to God is on their head. [8]Throughout the period of their dedication, they are consecrated to the LORD.

[9]"'If someone dies suddenly in the Nazirite's presence, thus defiling the hair that symbolizes their dedication, they must shave their head on the seventh day—the day of their cleansing. [10]Then on the eighth day they must bring two doves or two young pigeons to the priest at the entrance to the tent of meeting. [11]The priest is to offer one as a sin offering[d] and the other as a burnt offering to make atonement for the Nazirite because they sinned by being in the

---

[a] 15 That is, probably about 3 1/2 pounds or about 1.6 kilograms   [b] 21 That is, may he cause your name to be used in cursing (see Jer. 29:22); or, may others see that you are cursed; similarly in verse 27.   [c] 26 Or *representative*
[d] 11 Or *purification offering*; also in verses 14 and 16

presence of the dead body. That same day they are to consecrate their head again. [12]They must rededicate themselves to the LORD for the same period of dedication and must bring a year-old male lamb as a guilt offering. The previous days do not count, because they became defiled during their period of dedication.

[13]"'Now this is the law of the Nazirite when the period of their dedication is over. They are to be brought to the entrance to the tent of meeting. [14]There they are to present their offerings to the LORD: a year-old male lamb without defect for a burnt offering, a year-old ewe lamb without defect for a sin offering, a ram without defect for a fellowship offering, [15]together with their grain offerings and drink offerings, and a basket of bread made with the finest flour and without yeast — thick loaves with olive oil mixed in, and thin loaves brushed with olive oil.

[16]"'The priest is to present all these before the LORD and make the sin offering and the burnt offering. [17]He is to present the basket of unleavened bread and is to sacrifice the ram as a fellowship offering to the LORD, together with its grain offering and drink offering.

[18]"'Then at the entrance to the tent of meeting, the Nazirite must shave off the hair that symbolizes their dedication. They are to take the hair and put it in the fire that is under the sacrifice of the fellowship offering.

[19]"'After the Nazirite has shaved off the hair that symbolizes their dedication, the priest is to place in their hands a boiled shoulder of the ram, and one thick loaf and one thin loaf from the basket, both made without yeast. [20]The priest shall then wave these before the LORD as a wave offering; they are holy and belong to the priest, together with the breast that was waved and the thigh that was presented. After that, the Nazirite may drink wine.

[21]"'This is the law of the Nazirite who vows offerings to the LORD in accordance with their dedication, in addition to whatever else they can afford. They must fulfill the vows they have made, according to the law of the Nazirite.'"

The Priestly Blessing

[22]The LORD said to Moses, [23]"Tell Aaron and his sons, 'This is how you are to bless the Israelites. Say to them:

[24]"'"The LORD bless you
        and keep you;
[25]the LORD make his face shine on you
        and be gracious to you;
[26]the LORD turn his face toward you
        and give you peace."'

[27]"So they will put my name on the Israelites, and I will bless them."

Offerings at the Dedication of the Tabernacle

7 When Moses finished setting up the tabernacle, he anointed and consecrated it and all its furnishings. He also anointed and consecrated the altar and all its utensils. [2]Then the leaders of Israel, the heads of families who were the tribal leaders in charge of those who were counted, made offerings. [3]They brought as their gifts before the LORD six covered carts and twelve oxen — an ox from each leader and a cart from every two. These they presented before the tabernacle.

The Law of Sacrifice: Nazirites Give Up to Go Up

Numbers 6:1–21

Through the vow of the Nazirite, God provided a way for both men and women to specially consecrate themselves to the Lord for a special time and purpose. Leaders such as Samson (and perhaps Samuel) made this vow, committing to abstain from wine and strong drink, to leave their hair uncut, and to avoid contact with a corpse. They gave up certain rights or options in order to live at a higher standard—in other words, they practiced the Law of Sacrifice. They did so not to stand in judgment of others, but to discipline themselves against the temptations of the day.

How can today's leaders apply the principle behind the Nazirite vow?

Discipline	Application
Abstinence from wine/strong drink	Indulgence: discipline to prevent addiction
Uncut hair	Image: refuse to allow fashion to lead you
Avoid defilement from corpse	Integrity: stay pure; pursue a holy standard

[4]The LORD said to Moses, [5]"Accept these from them, that they may be used in the work at the tent of meeting. Give them to the Levites as each man's work requires."

[6]So Moses took the carts and oxen and gave them to the Levites. [7]He gave two carts and four oxen to the Gershonites, as their work required, [8]and he gave four carts and eight oxen to the Merarites, as their work required. They were all under the direction of Ithamar son of Aaron, the priest. [9]But Moses did not give any to the Kohathites, because they were to carry on their shoulders the holy things, for which they were responsible.

[10]When the altar was anointed, the leaders brought their offerings for its dedication and presented them before the altar. [11]For the LORD had said to Moses, "Each day one leader is to bring his offering for the dedication of the altar."

[12]The one who brought his offering on the first day was Nahshon son of Amminadab of the tribe of Judah.

[13]His offering was one silver plate weighing a hundred and thirty shekels[a] and one silver sprinkling bowl weighing seventy shekels,[b] both according to the sanctuary shekel, each filled with the finest flour mixed with olive oil as a grain offering; [14]one gold dish weighing ten shekels,[c] filled with incense; [15]one young bull, one ram and one male lamb a year old for a burnt offering; [16]one male goat for a sin offering[d]; [17]and two oxen, five rams, five male goats and five male lambs a year old to be sacrificed as a fellowship offering. This was the offering of Nahshon son of Amminadab.

[18]On the second day Nethanel son of Zuar, the leader of Issachar, brought his offering.

[19]The offering he brought was one silver plate weighing a hundred and thirty shekels and one silver sprinkling bowl weighing seventy shekels, both according to the sanctuary shekel, each filled with the finest flour mixed with olive oil as a grain offering; [20]one gold dish weighing ten shekels, filled with incense; [21]one young bull, one ram and one male lamb a year old for a burnt offering; [22]one male goat for a sin offering; [23]and two oxen, five rams, five male goats and five male lambs a year old to be sacrificed as a fellowship offering. This was the offering of Nethanel son of Zuar.

[24]On the third day, Eliab son of Helon, the leader of the people of Zebulun, brought his offering.

[25]His offering was one silver plate weighing a hundred and thirty shekels and one silver sprinkling bowl weighing seventy shekels, both according to the sanctuary shekel, each filled with the finest flour mixed with olive oil as a grain offering; [26]one gold dish weighing ten shekels, filled with incense; [27]one young bull, one ram and one male lamb a year old for a burnt offering; [28]one male goat for a sin offering; [29]and two oxen, five rams, five male goats and five male lambs a year old to be sacrificed as a fellowship offering. This was the offering of Eliab son of Helon.

[30]On the fourth day Elizur son of Shedeur, the leader of the people of Reuben, brought his offering.

[31]His offering was one silver plate weighing a hundred and thirty shekels and one silver sprinkling bowl weighing seventy shekels, both according to the sanctuary shekel, each filled with the finest flour mixed with olive oil as a grain offering; [32]one gold dish weighing ten shekels, filled with incense; [33]one young bull, one ram and one male lamb a year old for a burnt offering; [34]one male goat for a sin offering; [35]and two oxen, five rams, five male goats and five male lambs a year old to be sacrificed as a fellowship offering. This was the offering of Elizur son of Shedeur.

[36]On the fifth day Shelumiel son of Zurishaddai, the leader of the people of Simeon, brought his offering.

[37]His offering was one silver plate weighing a hundred and thirty shekels and one silver sprinkling bowl weighing seventy shekels, both according to the sanctuary shekel, each filled with the finest flour mixed with olive oil as a grain offering; [38]one gold dish weighing ten shekels, filled with incense; [39]one young bull, one ram and one male lamb a year old for a burnt offering; [40]one male goat for a sin offering; [41]and two oxen, five rams, five male goats

---

[a] 13 That is, about 3 1/4 pounds or about 1.5 kilograms; also elsewhere in this chapter   [b] 13 That is, about 1 3/4 pounds or about 800 grams; also elsewhere in this chapter   [c] 14 That is, about 4 ounces or about 115 grams; also elsewhere in this chapter   [d] 16 Or purification offering; also elsewhere in this chapter

and five male lambs a year old to be sacrificed as a fellowship offering. This was the offering of Shelumiel son of Zurishaddai.

⁴²On the sixth day Eliasaph son of Deuel, the leader of the people of Gad, brought his offering. ⁴³His offering was one silver plate weighing a hundred and thirty shekels and one silver sprinkling bowl weighing seventy shekels, both according to the sanctuary shekel, each filled with the finest flour mixed with olive oil as a grain offering; ⁴⁴one gold dish weighing ten shekels, filled with incense; ⁴⁵one young bull, one ram and one male lamb a year old for a burnt offering; ⁴⁶one male goat for a sin offering; ⁴⁷and two oxen, five rams, five male goats and five male lambs a year old to be sacrificed as a fellowship offering. This was the offering of Eliasaph son of Deuel.

⁴⁸On the seventh day Elishama son of Ammihud, the leader of the people of Ephraim, brought his offering. ⁴⁹His offering was one silver plate weighing a hundred and thirty shekels and one silver sprinkling bowl weighing seventy shekels, both according to the sanctuary shekel, each filled with the finest flour mixed with olive oil as a grain offering; ⁵⁰one gold dish weighing ten shekels, filled with incense; ⁵¹one young bull, one ram and one male lamb a year old for a burnt offering; ⁵²one male goat for a sin offering; ⁵³and two oxen, five rams, five male goats and five male lambs a year old to be sacrificed as a fellowship offering. This was the offering of Elishama son of Ammihud.

⁵⁴On the eighth day Gamaliel son of Pedahzur, the leader of the people of Manasseh, brought his offering. ⁵⁵His offering was one silver plate weighing a hundred and thirty shekels and one silver sprinkling bowl weighing seventy shekels, both according to the sanctuary shekel, each filled with the finest flour mixed with olive oil as a grain offering; ⁵⁶one gold dish weighing ten shekels, filled with incense; ⁵⁷one young bull, one ram and one male lamb a year old for a burnt offering; ⁵⁸one male goat for a sin offering; ⁵⁹and two oxen, five rams, five male goats and five male lambs a year old to be sacrificed as a fellowship offering. This was the offering of Gamaliel son of Pedahzur.

⁶⁰On the ninth day Abidan son of Gideoni, the leader of the people of Benjamin, brought his offering. ⁶¹His offering was one silver plate weighing a hundred and thirty shekels and one silver sprinkling bowl weighing seventy shekels, both according to the sanctuary shekel, each filled with the finest flour mixed with olive oil as a grain offering; ⁶²one gold dish weighing ten shekels, filled with incense; ⁶³one young bull, one ram and one male lamb a year old for a burnt offering; ⁶⁴one male goat for a sin offering; ⁶⁵and two oxen, five rams, five male goats and five male lambs a year old to be sacrificed as a fellowship offering. This was the offering of Abidan son of Gideoni.

⁶⁶On the tenth day Ahiezer son of Ammishaddai, the leader of the people of Dan, brought his offering. ⁶⁷His offering was one silver plate weighing a hundred and thirty shekels and one silver sprinkling bowl weighing seventy shekels, both according to the sanctuary shekel, each filled with the finest flour mixed with olive oil as a grain offering; ⁶⁸one gold dish weighing ten shekels, filled with incense; ⁶⁹one young bull, one ram and one male lamb a year old for a burnt offering; ⁷⁰one male goat for a sin offering; ⁷¹and two oxen, five rams, five male goats and five male lambs a year old to be sacrificed as a fellowship offering. This was the offering of Ahiezer son of Ammishaddai.

⁷²On the eleventh day Pagiel son of Okran, the leader of the people of Asher, brought his offering. ⁷³His offering was one silver plate weighing a hundred and thirty shekels and one silver sprinkling bowl weighing seventy shekels, both according to the sanctuary shekel, each filled with the finest flour mixed with olive oil as a grain offering; ⁷⁴one gold dish weighing ten shekels, filled with incense; ⁷⁵one young bull, one ram and one male lamb a year old for a burnt offering; ⁷⁶one male goat for a sin offering; ⁷⁷and two oxen, five rams, five male goats and five male lambs a year old to be sacrificed as a fellowship offering. This was the offering of Pagiel son of Okran.

⁷⁸On the twelfth day Ahira son of Enan, the leader of the people of Naphtali, brought his offering.

79His offering was one silver plate weighing a hundred and thirty shekels and one silver sprinkling bowl weighing seventy shekels, both according to the sanctuary shekel, each filled with the finest flour mixed with olive oil as a grain offering; 80one gold dish weighing ten shekels, filled with incense; 81one young bull, one ram and one male lamb a year old for a burnt offering; 82one male goat for a sin offering; 83and two oxen, five rams, five male goats and five male lambs a year old to be sacrificed as a fellowship offering. This was the offering of Ahira son of Enan.

84These were the offerings of the Israelite leaders for the dedication of the altar when it was anointed: twelve silver plates, twelve silver sprinkling bowls and twelve gold dishes. 85Each silver plate weighed a hundred and thirty shekels, and each sprinkling bowl seventy shekels. Altogether, the silver dishes weighed two thousand four hundred shekels,a according to the sanctuary shekel. 86The twelve gold dishes filled with incense weighed ten shekels each, according to the sanctuary shekel. Altogether, the gold dishes weighed a hundred and twenty shekels.b 87The total number of animals for the burnt offering came to twelve young bulls, twelve rams and twelve male lambs a year old, together with their grain offering. Twelve male goats were used for the sin offering. 88The total number of animals for the sacrifice of the fellowship offering came to twenty-four oxen, sixty rams, sixty male goats and sixty male lambs a year old. These were the offerings for the dedication of the altar after it was anointed.

89When Moses entered the tent of meeting to speak with the Lord, he heard the voice speaking to him from between the two cherubim above the atonement cover on the ark of the covenant law. In this way the Lord spoke to him.

Setting Up the Lamps

8 The Lord said to Moses, 2"Speak to Aaron and say to him, 'When you set up the lamps, see that all seven light up the area in front of the lampstand.'"

3Aaron did so; he set up the lamps so that they faced forward on the lampstand, just as the Lord commanded Moses. 4This is how the lampstand was made: It was made of hammered gold—from its base to its blossoms. The lampstand was made exactly like the pattern the Lord had shown Moses.

The Setting Apart of the Levites

5The Lord said to Moses: 6"Take the Levites from among all the Israelites and make them ceremonially clean. 7To purify them, do this: Sprinkle the water of cleansing on them; then have them shave their whole bodies and wash their clothes. And so they will purify themselves. 8Have them take a young bull with its grain offering of the finest flour mixed with olive oil; then you are to take a second young bull for a sin offering.c 9Bring the Levites to the front of the tent of meeting and assemble the whole Israelite community. 10You are to bring the Levites before the Lord, and the Israelites are to lay their hands on them. 11Aaron is to present the Levites before the Lord as a wave offering from the Israelites, so that they may be ready to do the work of the Lord.

12"Then the Levites are to lay their hands on the heads of the bulls, using one for a sin offering to the Lord and the other for a burnt offering, to make atonement for the Levites. 13Have the Levites stand in front of Aaron and his sons and then present them as a wave offering to the Lord. 14In this way you are to set the Levites apart from the other Israelites, and the Levites will be mine.

15"After you have purified the Levites and presented them as a wave offering, they are to come to do their work at the tent of meeting. 16They are the Israelites who are to be given wholly to me. I have taken them as my own in place of the firstborn, the first male offspring from every Israelite woman. 17Every firstborn male in Israel, whether human or animal, is mine. When I struck down all the firstborn in Egypt, I set them apart for myself. 18And I have taken the Levites in place of all the firstborn sons in Israel. 19From among all the Israelites, I have given the Levites as gifts to Aaron and his sons to do the work at the tent of meeting on behalf of the Israelites and to make atonement for them so that no plague will strike the Israelites when they go near the sanctuary."

20Moses, Aaron and the whole Israelite community did with the Levites just as the Lord commanded Moses. 21The Levites purified themselves and washed their clothes. Then Aaron presented them as a wave offering before the Lord and made atonement for them to purify them. 22After that, the Levites came to do their

---

a 85 That is, about 60 pounds or about 28 kilograms
b 86 That is, about 3 pounds or about 1.4 kilograms   c 8 Or purification offering; also in verse 12

work at the tent of meeting under the supervision of Aaron and his sons. They did with the Levites just as the LORD commanded Moses.

²³The LORD said to Moses, ²⁴"This applies to the Levites: Men twenty-five years old or more shall come to take part in the work at the tent of meeting, ²⁵but at the age of fifty, they must retire from their regular service and work no longer. ²⁶They may assist their brothers in performing their duties at the tent of meeting, but they themselves must not do the work. This, then, is how you are to assign the responsibilities of the Levites."

The Passover

9 The LORD spoke to Moses in the Desert of Sinai in the first month of the second year after they came out of Egypt. He said, ²"Have the Israelites celebrate the Passover at the appointed time. ³Celebrate it at the appointed time, at twilight on the fourteenth day of this month, in accordance with all its rules and regulations."

⁴So Moses told the Israelites to celebrate the Passover, ⁵and they did so in the Desert of Sinai at twilight on the fourteenth day of the first month. The Israelites did everything just as the LORD commanded Moses.

⁶But some of them could not celebrate the Passover on that day because they were ceremonially unclean on account of a dead body. So they came to Moses and Aaron that same day ⁷and said to Moses, "We have become unclean because of a dead body, but why should we be kept from presenting the LORD's offering with the other Israelites at the appointed time?"

⁸Moses answered them, "Wait until I find out what the LORD commands concerning you."

⁹Then the LORD said to Moses, ¹⁰"Tell the Israelites: 'When any of you or your descendants are unclean because of a dead body or are away on a journey, they are still to celebrate the LORD's Passover, ¹¹but they are to do it on the fourteenth day of the second month at twilight. They are to eat the lamb, together with unleavened bread and bitter herbs. ¹²They must not leave any of it till morning or break any of its bones. When they celebrate the Passover, they must follow all the regulations. ¹³But if anyone who is ceremonially clean and not on a journey fails to celebrate the Passover, they must be cut off from their people for not presenting the LORD's offering at the appointed time. They will bear the consequences of their sin.

¹⁴"'A foreigner residing among you is also

The Law of Timing: God's Dynamic Leadership

Numbers 9:15–23

God's people had no way of knowing whether they would camp in a specific location for a few days or a few years. They couldn't slip into a rut and trust in a schedule; they had to remain flexible. They learned to trust God, their Ultimate Leader.

---

to celebrate the LORD's Passover in accordance with its rules and regulations. You must have the same regulations for both the foreigner and the native-born.'"

The Cloud Above the Tabernacle

¹⁵On the day the tabernacle, the tent of the covenant law, was set up, the cloud covered it. From evening till morning the cloud above the tabernacle looked like fire. ¹⁶That is how it continued to be; the cloud covered it, and at night it looked like fire. ¹⁷Whenever the cloud lifted from above the tent, the Israelites set out; wherever the cloud settled, the Israelites encamped. ¹⁸At the LORD's command the Israelites set out, and at his command they encamped. As long as the cloud stayed over the tabernacle, they remained in camp. ¹⁹When the cloud remained over the tabernacle a long time, the Israelites obeyed the LORD's order and did not set out. ²⁰Sometimes the cloud was over the tabernacle only a few days; at the LORD's command they would encamp, and then at his command they would set out. ²¹Sometimes the cloud stayed only from evening till morning, and when it lifted in the morning, they set out. Whether by day or by night, whenever the cloud lifted, they set out. ²²Whether the cloud stayed over the tabernacle for two days or a month or a year, the Israelites would remain in camp and not set out; but when it lifted, they would set out. ²³At the LORD's command they encamped, and at the LORD's command they set out. They obeyed the LORD's order, in accordance with his command through Moses.

The Silver Trumpets

10 The LORD said to Moses: ²"Make two trumpets of hammered silver, and use them for calling the community together and for having the camps set out. [3]When both are sounded, the whole community is to assemble before you at the entrance to the tent of meeting. [4]If only one is sounded, the leaders — the heads of the clans of Israel — are to assemble before you. [5]When a trumpet blast is sounded, the tribes camping on the east are to set out. [6]At the sounding of a second blast, the camps on the south are to set out. The blast will be the signal for setting out. [7]To gather the assembly, blow the trumpets, but not with the signal for setting out.

[8]"The sons of Aaron, the priests, are to blow the trumpets. This is to be a lasting ordinance for you and the generations to come. [9]When you go into battle in your own land against an enemy who is oppressing you, sound a blast on the trumpets. Then you will be remembered by the LORD your God and rescued from your enemies. [10]Also at your times of rejoicing — your appointed festivals and New Moon feasts — you are to sound the trumpets over your burnt offerings and fellowship offerings, and they will be a memorial for you before your God. I am the LORD your God."

The Israelites Leave Sinai

[11]On the twentieth day of the second month of the second year, the cloud lifted from above the tabernacle of the covenant law. [12]Then the Israelites set out from the Desert of Sinai and traveled from place to place until the cloud came to rest in the Desert of Paran. [13]They set out, this first time, at the LORD's command through Moses.

[14]The divisions of the camp of Judah went first, under their standard. Nahshon son of Amminadab was in command. [15]Nethanel son of Zuar was over the division of the tribe of Issachar, [16]and Eliab son of Helon was over the division of the tribe of Zebulun. [17]Then the tabernacle was taken down, and the Gershonites and Merarites, who carried it, set out.

[18]The divisions of the camp of Reuben went next, under their standard. Elizur son of Shedeur was in command. [19]Shelumiel son of Zurishaddai was over the division of the tribe of Simeon, [20]and Eliasaph son of Deuel was over the division of the tribe of Gad. [21]Then the Kohathites set out, carrying the holy things. The tabernacle was to be set up before they arrived.

[22]The divisions of the camp of Ephraim went next, under their standard. Elishama son of Ammihud was in command. [23]Gamaliel son of Pedahzur was over the division of the tribe

of Manasseh, [24]and Abidan son of Gideoni was over the division of the tribe of Benjamin.

[25]Finally, as the rear guard for all the units, the divisions of the camp of Dan set out under their standard. Ahiezer son of Ammishaddai was in command. [26]Pagiel son of Okran was over the division of the tribe of Asher, [27]and Ahira son of Enan was over the division of the tribe of Naphtali. [28]This was the order of march for the Israelite divisions as they set out.

[29]Now Moses said to Hobab son of Reuel the Midianite, Moses' father-in-law, "We are setting out for the place about which the LORD said, 'I will give it to you.' Come with us and we will treat you well, for the LORD has promised good things to Israel."

[30]He answered, "No, I will not go; I am going back to my own land and my own people."

[31]But Moses said, "Please do not leave us. You know where we should camp in the wilderness, and you can be our eyes. [32]If you come with us, we will share with you whatever good things the LORD gives us."

[33]So they set out from the mountain of the LORD and traveled for three days. The ark of the covenant of the LORD went before them during those three days to find them a place to rest. [34]The cloud of the LORD was over them by day when they set out from the camp.

[35]Whenever the ark set out, Moses said,

> "Rise up, LORD!
> May your enemies be scattered;
> may your foes flee before you."

[36]Whenever it came to rest, he said,

> "Return, LORD,
> to the countless thousands of Israel."

Fire From the LORD

11 Now the people complained about their hardships in the hearing of the LORD, and when he heard them his anger was aroused. Then fire from the LORD burned among them and consumed some of the outskirts of the camp. [2]When the people cried out to Moses, he prayed to the LORD and the fire died down. [3]So that place was called Taberah,[a] because fire from the LORD had burned among them.

Quail From the LORD

[4]The rabble with them began to crave other food, and again the Israelites started wailing

---

[a] 3 *Taberah* means *burning.*

and said, "If only we had meat to eat! ⁵We remember the fish we ate in Egypt at no cost — also the cucumbers, melons, leeks, onions and garlic. ⁶But now we have lost our appetite; we never see anything but this manna!"

⁷The manna was like coriander seed and looked like resin. ⁸The people went around gathering it, and then ground it in a hand mill or crushed it in a mortar. They cooked it in a pot or made it into loaves. And it tasted like something made with olive oil. ⁹When the dew settled on the camp at night, the manna also came down.

¹⁰Moses heard the people of every family wailing at the entrance to their tents. The LORD became exceedingly angry, and Moses was troubled. ¹¹He asked the LORD, "Why have you brought this trouble on your servant? What have I done to displease you that you put the burden of all these people on me? ¹²Did I conceive all these people? Did I give them birth? Why do you tell me to carry them in my arms, as a nurse carries an infant, to the land you promised on oath to their ancestors? ¹³Where can I get meat for all these people? They keep wailing to me, 'Give us meat to eat!' ¹⁴I cannot carry all these people by myself; the burden is too heavy for me. ¹⁵If this is how you are going to treat me, please go ahead and kill me — if I have found favor in your eyes — and do not let me face my own ruin."

¹⁶The LORD said to Moses: "Bring me seventy of Israel's elders who are known to you as leaders and officials among the people. Have them come to the tent of meeting, that they may stand there with you. ¹⁷I will come down and speak with you there, and I will take some of the power of the Spirit that is on you and put it on them. They will share the burden of the people with you so that you will not have to carry it alone.

¹⁸"Tell the people: 'Consecrate yourselves in preparation for tomorrow, when you will eat meat. The LORD heard you when you wailed, "If only we had meat to eat! We were better off in Egypt!" Now the LORD will give you meat, and you will eat it. ¹⁹You will not eat it for just one day, or two days, or five, ten or twenty days, ²⁰but for a whole month — until it comes out of your nostrils and you loathe it — because you have rejected the LORD, who is among you, and have wailed before him, saying, "Why did we ever leave Egypt?"'"

²¹But Moses said, "Here I am among six hundred thousand men on foot, and you say, 'I will give them meat to eat for a whole month!' ²²Would they have enough if flocks and herds were slaughtered for them? Would they have enough if all the fish in the sea were caught for them?"

²³The LORD answered Moses, "Is the LORD's arm too short? Now you will see whether or not what I say will come true for you."

²⁴So Moses went out and told the people what

THE SEVENTY ELDERS

Sharing the Burden of God's Anointed
Numbers 11:11–17

PROFILE
in leadership

We don't know a lot about the seventy elders Moses called to aid him. Scripture does not name them, nor even mention which tribes they represent. What we do know is that they were officers and elders of the people; perhaps all or most were among the rulers of thousands, hundreds, fifties, and tens selected in Exodus 18:25. More than likely they were older men who had gained influence and respect among the people.

The Old Testament mentions the seventy elders only twice, both times to witness God's presence, power and glory (Ex 24). But the second time the elders are called, God expands their role. This time they are not only to witness, but to participate—thus revealing something remarkable about how God works with leaders. "I will take some of the power of the Spirit that is on you," God told Moses, "and put it on them. They will share the burden of the people with you so that you will not have to carry it alone" (Nu 11:17).

When a leader called by God has a burden that becomes too great, God provides help . . . if the leader will ask for it. Not only will the Lord provide helpers to share the load; he will anoint them with his power, just as he did the seventy elders of Israel.

The Law of Empowerment: What Do Potential Leaders Need?

Numbers 11:16-30

Often pastors in traditional churches ask, "Is it really my job to equip people to serve and lead? Am I not merely to be a shepherd and teach the people on Sunday?"

This question demonstrates how our culture has blinded us to the biblical call for leaders to equip other leaders. Numbers 11 demonstrates that equipping laypeople to lead and serve is God's idea, not man's. Leaders are to identify, prepare, and release teams to work.

God left no doubt about how Moses was to train the seventy leaders he had selected. In Numbers 11:16-30 we see the answer to the question: What do potential leaders need? God says:

1. *They need authority* (v. 16, "Have them come . . . that they may stand there with you").

2. *They need anointing* (v. 17, "I will take some of the power of the Spirit . . . and put it on them").

3. *They need ownership of the vision* (v. 17, "the power of the Spirit that is on you . . . on them").

4. *They need responsibility* (v. 17, "They will share the burden of the people with you").

5. *They need specific ministry roles* (v. 24, "had them stand around the tent").

6. *They need to express their gifts* (v. 25, "When the Spirit rested on them, they prophesied").

7. *They need a secure shepherd who will release them to succeed* (vv. 26–30, Moses).

the LORD had said. He brought together seventy of their elders and had them stand around the tent. 25Then the LORD came down in the cloud and spoke with him, and he took some of the power of the Spirit that was on him and put it on the seventy elders. When the Spirit rested on them, they prophesied—but did not do so again.

26However, two men, whose names were Eldad and Medad, had remained in the camp. They were listed among the elders, but did not go out to the tent. Yet the Spirit also rested on them, and they prophesied in the camp. 27A young man ran and told Moses, "Eldad and Medad are prophesying in the camp."

28Joshua son of Nun, who had been Moses' aide since youth, spoke up and said, "Moses, my lord, stop them!"

29But Moses replied, "Are you jealous for my sake? I wish that all the LORD's people were prophets and that the LORD would put his Spirit on them!" 30Then Moses and the elders of Israel returned to the camp.

31Now a wind went out from the LORD and drove quail in from the sea. It scattered them up to two cubits[a] deep all around the camp, as far as a day's walk in any direction. 32All that day and night and all the next day the people went out and gathered quail. No one gathered less than ten homers.[b] Then they spread them

out all around the camp. 33But while the meat was still between their teeth and before it could be consumed, the anger of the LORD burned against the people, and he struck them with a severe plague. 34Therefore the place was named Kibroth Hattaavah,[c] because there they buried the people who had craved other food.

35From Kibroth Hattaavah the people traveled to Hazeroth and stayed there.

Miriam and Aaron Oppose Moses

12 Miriam and Aaron began to talk against Moses because of his Cushite wife, for he had married a Cushite. 2"Has the LORD spoken only through Moses?" they asked. "Hasn't he also spoken through us?" And the LORD heard this.

3(Now Moses was a very humble man, more humble than anyone else on the face of the earth.)

4At once the LORD said to Moses, Aaron and Miriam, "Come out to the tent of meeting, all three of you." So the three of them went out. 5Then the LORD came down in a pillar of cloud; he stood at the entrance to the tent and summoned Aaron and Miriam. When the two of

---

[a] 31 That is, about 3 feet or about 90 centimeters   [b] 32 That is, possibly about 1 3/4 tons or about 1.6 metric tons   [c] 34 Kibroth Hattaavah means graves of craving.

them stepped forward, ⁶he said, "Listen to my words:

"When there is a prophet among you,
I, the LORD, reveal myself to them in visions,
I speak to them in dreams.
⁷But this is not true of my servant Moses;
he is faithful in all my house.
⁸With him I speak face to face,
clearly and not in riddles;
he sees the form of the LORD.
Why then were you not afraid
to speak against my servant Moses?"

⁹The anger of the LORD burned against them, and he left them.

¹⁰When the cloud lifted from above the tent, Miriam's skin was leprous[a] — it became as white as snow. Aaron turned toward her and saw that she had a defiling skin disease, ¹¹and he said to Moses, "Please, my lord, I ask you not to hold against us the sin we have so foolishly committed. ¹²Do not let her be like a stillborn infant coming from its mother's womb with its flesh half eaten away."

¹³So Moses cried out to the LORD, "Please, God, heal her!"

¹⁴The LORD replied to Moses, "If her father had spit in her face, would she not have been in disgrace for seven days? Confine her outside the camp for seven days; after that she can be brought back." ¹⁵So Miriam was confined outside the camp for seven days, and the people did not move on till she was brought back.

[a] 10 The Hebrew for *leprous* was used for various diseases affecting the skin.

Leadership: Criticism and Confrontation Come with the Territory

Numbers 12:3–14

Leaders can bank on two truths. First, they will be criticized. Second, criticism always changes the leader. Unhappy people tend to attack the point person. Moses' own family criticized him. Notice what God and Moses teach us on how to handle criticism:

1. *Maintain your humility* (v. 3).
2. *Face the criticism squarely* (v. 4).
3. *Be specific about the issue* (vv. 5–8).
4. *Lay out consequences* (vv. 9–10).
5. *Pray for the criticizers* (vv. 12–13).
6. *Restore them when appropriate* (v. 14).

Beyond that, consider ten ways leaders should handle criticism:

1. *Understand the difference between constructive and destructive criticism* (who benefits?).
2. *Don't take yourself too seriously* (but take your God very seriously).
3. *Look beyond the criticism to see the critic* (do you respect him? what's her need?).
4. *Guard your own attitude toward the critic* (don't get defensive; stay objective).
5. *Recognize that good people get criticized* (don't beat yourself up).
6. *Keep yourself physically and spiritually in shape* (weariness distorts our perspective).
7. *Don't see only the critic; see the crowd* (is the criticism widespread?).
8. *Wait for time to prove the critic wrong* (be mature enough to be patient).
9. *Associate with people of faith* (spend your optional time with optimists).
10. *Concentrate on your mission; change your mistakes* (focus on the big picture).

16After that, the people left Hazeroth and encamped in the Desert of Paran.

Exploring Canaan

13 The LORD said to Moses, 2"Send some men to explore the land of Canaan, which I am giving to the Israelites. From each ancestral tribe send one of its leaders."

3So at the LORD's command Moses sent them out from the Desert of Paran. All of them were leaders of the Israelites. 4These are their names:

from the tribe of Reuben, Shammua son of Zakkur;

5from the tribe of Simeon, Shaphat son of Hori;

6from the tribe of Judah, Caleb son of Jephunneh;

7from the tribe of Issachar, Igal son of Joseph;

8from the tribe of Ephraim, Hoshea son of Nun;

9from the tribe of Benjamin, Palti son of Raphu;

10from the tribe of Zebulun, Gaddiel son of Sodi;

11from the tribe of Manasseh (a tribe of Joseph), Gaddi son of Susi;

12from the tribe of Dan, Ammiel son of Gemalli;

13from the tribe of Asher, Sethur son of Michael;

14from the tribe of Naphtali, Nahbi son of Vophsi;

15from the tribe of Gad, Geuel son of Maki.

16These are the names of the men Moses sent to explore the land. (Moses gave Hoshea son of Nun the name Joshua.)

17When Moses sent them to explore Canaan, he said, "Go up through the Negev and on into the hill country. 18See what the land is like and whether the people who live there are strong or weak, few or many. 19What kind of land do they live in? Is it good or bad? What kind of towns do they live in? Are they unwalled or fortified? 20How is the soil? Is it fertile or poor? Are there trees in it or not? Do your best to bring back some of the fruit of the land." (It was the season for the first ripe grapes.)

21So they went up and explored the land from the Desert of Zin as far as Rehob, toward Lebo Hamath. 22They went up through the Negev and came to Hebron, where Ahiman, Sheshai and Talmai, the descendants of Anak, lived. (Hebron had been built seven years before Zoan in Egypt.) 23When they reached the Valley of Eshkol,[a] they cut off a branch bearing a single cluster of grapes. Two of them carried it on a pole between them, along with some pomegranates and figs. 24That place was called the Valley of Eshkol because of the cluster of grapes the Israelites cut off there. 25At the end of forty days they returned from exploring the land.

Report on the Exploration

26They came back to Moses and Aaron and the whole Israelite community at Kadesh in the Desert of Paran. There they reported to them and to the whole assembly and showed them the fruit of the land. 27They gave Moses this account: "We went into the land to which you sent us, and it does flow with milk and honey! Here is its fruit. 28But the people who live there are powerful, and the cities are fortified and very large. We even saw descendants of Anak there. 29The Amalekites live in the Negev; the Hittites, Jebusites and Amorites live in the hill country; and the Canaanites live near the sea and along the Jordan."

30Then Caleb silenced the people before Moses and said, "We should go up and take possession of the land, for we can certainly do it."

31But the men who had gone up with him said, "We can't attack those people; they are stronger than we are." 32And they spread among the Israelites a bad report about the land they had explored. They said, "The land we explored devours those living in it. All the people we saw there are of great size. 33We saw the Nephilim there (the descendants of Anak come from the Nephilim). We seemed like grasshoppers in our own eyes, and we looked the same to them."

The People Rebel

14 That night all the members of the community raised their voices and wept aloud. 2All the Israelites grumbled against Moses and Aaron, and the whole assembly said to them, "If only we had died in Egypt! Or in this wilderness! 3Why is the LORD bringing us to this land only to let us fall by the sword? Our wives and children will be taken as plunder. Wouldn't it be better for us to go back to Egypt?" 4And they said to each other, "We should choose a leader and go back to Egypt."

5Then Moses and Aaron fell facedown in front of the whole Israelite assembly gathered there. 6Joshua son of Nun and Caleb son of

---

a 23 Eshkol means cluster; also in verse 24.

21 QUALITIES

POSITIVE ATTITUDE   The Ten Spies vs. the Two Spies

Numbers 13:1—14:10

AS ISRAEL approached the Jordan River, Moses sent out twelve spies to investigate the promised land. One spy from each of the twelve tribes of Israel entered Canaan, explored the land and returned with a report. All twelve had the same external experiences, but the internal conclusions of ten differed markedly from the other two. Joshua and Caleb filed the minority report, but they happened to be right. What could account for these differing opinions?

Similarities

1. **All twelve spies were leaders in their tribes (13:2).**
2. **All twelve spies received the same promise (13:2).**
3. **All twelve spies received the same opportunities (13:2).**

Differences

MAJORITY REPORT

1. **Ten said "no"**
2. **Misunderstood their mission**
3. **Saw God in light of their circumstances**

MINORITY REPORT

1. **Two said "go"**
2. **Understood their mission**
3. **Saw circumstances in light of their God**

After their return, ten of the spies displayed a horrible attitude about the whole endeavor. It's not hard to see why. You can't find God anywhere in their report; they don't mention his name even once. Their sour disposition, pessimistic perspective and negative report spread like a plague throughout the Israelite camp. "It was, indeed, a land flowing with milk and honey—but there were giants in the land!" they declared. "There is no way we can enter and possess it."

Although Joshua and Caleb took the very same trip and saw the same things witnessed by the other ten spies, they returned with an enthusiastic, positive report. They never doubted the Israelites could take the land. They based their glowing report on God's track record with the nation through the desert. They freely admitted the obstacles, but knew nothing could stand in the way of God. They came back saying, "Yes, there are giants in the land, but they're midgets compared with our God. We can take them and the land! And by the way, Canaan really does flow with milk and honey."

The Major Difference: Attitude!

The only difference between those who delivered the majority and minority reports was internal. Their differing reports reflected contrary attitudes toward the land, the divine promises, the people in Canaan, the work involved, the Lord, and themselves. Consider the attitudes of the majority:

1. Disobeyed God
2. Believed the land had no future
3. Displayed cowardice based on fear
4. Utterly ignored God in their report
5. Suffered from a grasshopper complex

The result? These ten naysayers spread anxiety throughout Israel's camp. Their rotten attitudes infected the whole congregation until the spiritual contagion could not be contained. Notice who got blamed for the nation's negative response: "Our brothers have made our hearts melt in fear. They say, 'The people are stronger and taller than we are'" (Dt 1:28). Through a negative majority report, this ancient commission deprived nearly two million people of their inheritance in Canaan. Through their poisonous influence, the Israelites were driven back into the wilderness to die, and God delayed in fulfilling his purpose for his chosen people for 40 frustrating years.

If only they had listened to the minority! Consider their vastly better attitude:

1. Obeyed God
2. Insisted they should enter and possess the land
3. Displayed courage rooted in faith
4. Felt calm assurance
5. Saw themselves in relationship to God

The result? Caleb and Joshua stayed alive for a new era, while the other ten spies perished in the wilderness along with the rest of the adults of that unbelieving generation.

Attitude Axioms

Attitude makes all the difference. The development of a positive attitude is the first conscious step toward becoming an effective leader. Successful leadership cannot be constructed without this crucial building block. Check out the following attitude axioms suggested by the words and actions of Joshua and Caleb:

1. *Our attitude determines our approach to life.*
2. *Our attitude determines our relationships with people.*
3. *Our attitude is often the only difference between success and failure.*
4. *Our attitude at the beginning of a task will affect its outcome more than anything else.*
5. *Our attitude can turn problems into blessings.*
6. *Our attitude can give us an uncommonly positive perspective.*
7. *Our attitude is not automatically good just because we belong to God.*

Jephunneh, who were among those who had explored the land, tore their clothes [7]and said to the entire Israelite assembly, "The land we passed through and explored is exceedingly good. [8]If the LORD is pleased with us, he will lead us into that land, a land flowing with milk and honey, and will give it to us. [9]Only do not rebel against the LORD. And do not be afraid of the people of the land, because we will devour them. Their protection is gone, but the LORD is with us. Do not be afraid of them."

[10]But the whole assembly talked about stoning them. Then the glory of the LORD appeared at the tent of meeting to all the Israelites. [11]The LORD said to Moses, "How long will these people treat me with contempt? How long will they refuse to believe in me, in spite of all the signs I have performed among them? [12]I will strike them down with a plague and destroy them, but I will make you into a nation greater and stronger than they."

[13]Moses said to the LORD, "Then the Egyptians will hear about it! By your power you brought these people up from among them. [14]And they will tell the inhabitants of this land about it. They have already heard that you, LORD, are with these people and that you, LORD, have been seen face to face, that your cloud stays over them, and that you go before them in a pillar of cloud by day and a pillar of fire by night. [15]If you put all these people to death, leaving none alive, the nations who have heard this report about you will say, [16]'The LORD was not able to bring these people into the land he promised them on oath, so he slaughtered them in the wilderness.'

[17]"Now may the Lord's strength be displayed, just as you have declared: [18]'The LORD is slow to anger, abounding in love and forgiving sin and rebellion. Yet he does not leave the guilty unpunished; he punishes the children for the sin of the parents to the third and fourth generation.' [19]In accordance with your great love, forgive the sin of these people, just as you have pardoned them from the time they left Egypt until now."

[20]The LORD replied, "I have forgiven them, as you asked. [21]Nevertheless, as surely as I live and as surely as the glory of the LORD fills the whole earth, [22]not one of those who saw my glory and the signs I performed in Egypt and in the wilderness but who disobeyed me and tested me ten times— [23]not one of them will ever see the land I promised on oath to their ancestors. No one who has treated me with contempt will ever see it. [24]But because my servant Caleb has a

different spirit and follows me wholeheartedly, I will bring him into the land he went to, and his descendants will inherit it. [25]Since the Amalekites and the Canaanites are living in the valleys, turn back tomorrow and set out toward the desert along the route to the Red Sea.[a]"

[26]The LORD said to Moses and Aaron: [27]"How long will this wicked community grumble against me? I have heard the complaints of these grumbling Israelites. [28]So tell them, 'As surely as I live, declares the LORD, I will do to you the very thing I heard you say: [29]In this wilderness your bodies will fall—every one of you twenty years old or more who was counted in the census and who has grumbled against me. [30]Not one of you will enter the land I swore with uplifted hand to make your home, except Caleb son of Jephunneh and Joshua son of Nun. [31]As for your children that you said would be taken as plunder, I will bring them in to enjoy the land you have rejected. [32]But as for you, your bodies will fall in this wilderness. [33]Your children will be shepherds here for forty years, suffering for your unfaithfulness, until the last of your bodies lies in the wilderness. [34]For forty years—one year for each of the forty days you explored the land—you will suffer for your sins and know what it is like to have me against you.' [35]I, the LORD, have spoken, and I will surely do these things to this whole wicked community, which has banded together against me. They will meet their end in this wilderness; here they will die."

[36]So the men Moses had sent to explore the land, who returned and made the whole community grumble against him by spreading a bad report about it— [37]these men who were responsible for spreading the bad report about the land were struck down and died of a plague before the LORD. [38]Of the men who went to explore the land, only Joshua son of Nun and Caleb son of Jephunneh survived.

[39]When Moses reported this to all the Israelites, they mourned bitterly. [40]Early the next morning they set out for the highest point in the hill country, saying, "Now we are ready to go up to the land the LORD promised. Surely we have sinned!"

[41]But Moses said, "Why are you disobeying the LORD's command? This will not succeed! [42]Do not go up, because the LORD is not with you. You will be defeated by your enemies, [43]for the Amalekites and the Canaanites will face you there. Because you have turned away from the

---

[a] 25 Or the Sea of Reeds

LORD, he will not be with you and you will fall by the sword."

⁴⁴Nevertheless, in their presumption they went up toward the highest point in the hill country, though neither Moses nor the ark of the LORD's covenant moved from the camp. ⁴⁵Then the Amalekites and the Canaanites who lived in that hill country came down and attacked them and beat them down all the way to Hormah.

Supplementary Offerings

15 The LORD said to Moses, ²"Speak to the Israelites and say to them: 'After you enter the land I am giving you as a home ³and you present to the LORD food offerings from the herd or the flock, as an aroma pleasing to the LORD — whether burnt offerings or sacrifices, for special vows or freewill offerings or festival offerings — ⁴then the person who brings an offering shall present to the LORD a grain offering of a tenth of an ephah*ᵃ* of the finest flour mixed with a quarter of a hin*ᵇ* of olive oil, ⁵With each lamb for the burnt offering or the sacrifice, prepare a quarter of a hin of wine as a drink offering.

⁶"With a ram prepare a grain offering of two-tenths of an ephah*ᶜ* of the finest flour mixed with a third of a hin*ᵈ* of olive oil, ⁷and a third of a hin of wine as a drink offering. Offer it as an aroma pleasing to the LORD.

⁸"When you prepare a young bull as a burnt offering or sacrifice, for a special vow or a fellowship offering to the LORD, ⁹bring with the bull a grain offering of three-tenths of an ephah*ᵉ* of the finest flour mixed with half a hin*ᶠ* of olive oil, ¹⁰and also bring half a hin of wine as a drink offering. This will be a food offering, an aroma pleasing to the LORD. ¹¹Each bull or ram, each lamb or young goat, is to be prepared in this manner. ¹²Do this for each one, for as many as you prepare.

¹³"Everyone who is native-born must do these things in this way when they present a food offering as an aroma pleasing to the LORD. ¹⁴For the generations to come, whenever a foreigner or anyone else living among you presents a food offering as an aroma pleasing to the LORD, they must do exactly as you do. ¹⁵The community is to have the same rules for you and for the foreigner residing among you; this is a lasting ordinance for the generations to come. You and the foreigner shall be the same before the LORD: ¹⁶The same laws and regulations will apply both to you and to the foreigner residing among you.'"

¹⁷The LORD said to Moses, ¹⁸"Speak to the Is-

raelites and say to them: 'When you enter the land to which I am taking you ¹⁹and you eat the food of the land, present a portion as an offering to the LORD. ²⁰Present a loaf from the first of your ground meal and present it as an offering from the threshing floor. ²¹Throughout the generations to come you are to give this offering to the LORD from the first of your ground meal.

Offerings for Unintentional Sins

²²"Now if you as a community unintentionally fail to keep any of these commands the LORD gave Moses — ²³any of the LORD's commands to you through him, from the day the LORD gave them and continuing through the generations to come — ²⁴and if this is done unintentionally without the community being aware of it, then the whole community is to offer a young bull for a burnt offering as an aroma pleasing to the LORD, along with its prescribed grain offering and drink offering, and a male goat for a sin offering.*ᵍ* ²⁵The priest is to make atonement for the whole Israelite community, and they will be forgiven, for it was not intentional and they have presented to the LORD for their wrong a food offering and a sin offering. ²⁶The whole Israelite community and the foreigners residing among them will be forgiven, because all the people were involved in the unintentional wrong.

²⁷"But if just one person sins unintentionally, that person must bring a year-old female goat for a sin offering. ²⁸The priest is to make atonement before the LORD for the one who erred by sinning unintentionally, and when atonement has been made, that person will be forgiven. ²⁹One and the same law applies to everyone who sins unintentionally, whether a native-born Israelite or a foreigner residing among you.

³⁰"But anyone who sins defiantly, whether native-born or foreigner, blasphemes the LORD and must be cut off from the people of Israel. ³¹Because they have despised the LORD's word and broken his commands, they must surely be cut off; their guilt remains on them.'"

The Sabbath-Breaker Put to Death

³²While the Israelites were in the wilderness, a man was found gathering wood on the

---

ᵃ 4 That is, probably about 3 1/2 pounds or about 1.6 kilograms
ᵇ 4 That is, about 1 quart or about 1 liter; also in verse 5
ᶜ 6 That is, probably about 7 pounds or about 3.2 kilograms
ᵈ 6 That is, about 1 1/3 quarts or about 1.3 liters; also in verse 7
ᵉ 9 That is, probably about 11 pounds or about 5 kilograms
ᶠ 9 That is, about 2 quarts or about 1.9 liters; also in verse 10
ᵍ 24 Or *purification offering*; also in verses 25 and 27

21 LAWS

JOSHUA AND THE LAW OF INFLUENCE
How Did the General Expand His Reach?

Numbers 14:6–9

AMONG THE TWELVE spies who scouted out Canaan, only Joshua and Caleb believed that the Israelites could take the land. Joshua urged the people to move forward, but his influence alone couldn't sway them. At this juncture of his life, Joshua had not matured into a place of great influence. Even though he was right, he couldn't persuade the people to follow. They didn't look to him; they followed the other ten spies.

Joshua's success would eventually grow in proportion to his leadership, but he needed time to deepen his influence. Moses personally mentored him, and eventually Joshua became the obvious leader to take the Israelites into the promised land.

The Nature of Leadership

1. Leadership is influence.

The true measure of leadership is influence—nothing more, nothing less. Joshua came face-to-face with the true nature of leadership when he failed to influence the people to follow his lead. His position as tribal leader did nothing to help him influence others.

2. Leaders do not possess influence in every area.

Those selected to spy out the promised land were "leaders" (Nu 13:2). That means Joshua was a leader with some influence, but his influence apparently didn't outweigh that of the other 11 leaders.

3. Our influence is either positive or negative.

If all twelve spies had given a good report of the promised land, the people of Israel likely would have obeyed God and crossed into the land. But influence is a two-edged sword; it cuts both positively and negatively. The ten unfaithful tribal leaders used their influence to lead the people astray—a disaster for those leaders and for all of their followers.

4. Faithful leaders use their influence to add value.

Influencers who lead out of a desire to advance their own agendas manipulate the people for their own gain. That's what the other ten spies did. Their fear prompted them to use their influence to frighten Israel. They lied, claiming the land "devours those living in it" (Nu 13:32). On the other hand, Joshua and Caleb desired to motivate their countrymen to do what would benefit everyone—always the agenda of great leaders.

5. With influence comes responsibility.

Maybe the ten unfaithful tribal leaders didn't want to start a rebellion, yet that's what they did. Following their negative report, the people sought to depose Moses and Aaron and return to Egypt. As a result, those ten leaders died of plague, and all of their followers died in the desert.

Joshua's Growing Influence

Many individuals who at first seem ineffective as leaders give up. Fortunately for the nation of Israel, Joshua did not fit that mold. He determined to become a better leader. Despite his setback, Joshua continued to be faithful to God and to learn as much as he could from Moses.

1. Joshua's influence grew because of his relationship with Moses (Dt 31:1–8, 23).

Through Moses' mentorship, Joshua not only polished his skills, but the people accepted him as their leader. The Bible says that as Israel prepared to enter the promised land, "Moses summoned Joshua and said to him in the presence of all Israel, 'Be strong and courageous, for you must go with this people into the land that the LORD swore to their ancestors to give them, and you must divide it among them as their inheritance'" (Dt 31:7). In such a way Moses imparted authority to Joshua.

2. Joshua's influence grew with time and maturity (Nu 14:1–10; Jos 18:1–10).

Joshua gave basically the same speech in Numbers 14 that he delivered in Joshua 18. The difference? The second time, a mature Joshua spoke to a new generation. The people had seen his leadership skills in action, and his track record as a leader gave them the confidence to follow his directions.

3. Joshua's influence grew because of timing (Jos 1:16–18).

Sometimes a leader wields little influence until his followers want to go somewhere. Only when the Jews tired of wandering in the desert did they heed the words of Joshua. In Numbers 14, the people responded to Joshua's first exhortation to go in and take the land by loudly suggesting that he be stoned. In Joshua 1, they responded by saying, "Whatever you have commanded us we will do, and wherever you send us we will go" (v. 16).

4. Joshua's influence grew because he possessed patience and integrity (Jos 1:5–9).

Joshua continued to grow patiently even after the people rejected his words in Numbers 14. While neither he nor Caleb died in the wilderness, as did all those who rebelled against God, nevertheless they both were forced to wander in the desert for 40 years through no fault of their own. Such an "unfair" turn of events could have turned Joshua into an angry, melancholy, disgruntled and cynical man. Yet he became none of those things. Throughout the long wilderness journey, he continued to display great consistency and credibility—until at last the people were finally ready to follow.

5. Joshua's influence grew because he was right (Jos 23:1–11).

From the beginning, Joshua tried to do the right thing. He attempted to lead the people in the right direction. After the exodus from Egypt, most of Israel considered his words foolhardy and rash—yet Joshua's words stood the test of time. His message never changed, and eventually everyone saw that he was right.

Leadership is all about influence, and Joshua demonstrates that influence comes down to character and conviction.

Sabbath day. [33]Those who found him gathering wood brought him to Moses and Aaron and the whole assembly, [34]and they kept him in custody, because it was not clear what should be done to him. [35]Then the LORD said to Moses, "The man must die. The whole assembly must stone him outside the camp." [36]So the assembly took him outside the camp and stoned him to death, as the LORD commanded Moses.

Tassels on Garments

[37]The LORD said to Moses, [38]"Speak to the Israelites and say to them: 'Throughout the generations to come you are to make tassels on the corners of your garments, with a blue cord on each tassel. [39]You will have these tassels to look at and so you will remember all the commands of the LORD, that you may obey them and not prostitute yourselves by chasing after the lusts of your own hearts and eyes. [40]Then you will remember to obey all my commands and will be consecrated to your God. [41]I am the LORD your God, who brought you out of Egypt to be your God. I am the LORD your God.'"

Korah, Dathan and Abiram

16 Korah son of Izhar, the son of Kohath, the son of Levi, and certain Reubenites—Dathan and Abiram, sons of Eliab, and On son of Peleth—became insolent[a] [2]and rose up against Moses. With them were 250 Israelite men, well-known community leaders who had been appointed members of the council. [3]They came as a group to oppose Moses and Aaron and said to them, "You have gone too far! The whole community is holy, every one of them, and the LORD is with them. Why then do you set yourselves above the LORD's assembly?"

[4]When Moses heard this, he fell facedown. [5]Then he said to Korah and all his followers: "In the morning the LORD will show who belongs to him and who is holy, and he will have that person come near him. The man he chooses he will cause to come near him. [6]You, Korah, and all your followers are to do this: Take censers [7]and tomorrow put burning coals and incense in them before the LORD. The man the LORD chooses will be the one who is holy. You Levites have gone too far!"

[8]Moses also said to Korah, "Now listen, you Levites! [9]Isn't it enough for you that the God of Israel has separated you from the rest of the Israelite community and brought you near himself to do the work at the LORD's tabernacle and to stand before the community and minister to them? [10]He has brought you and all your fellow Levites near himself, but now you are trying to get the priesthood too. [11]It is against the LORD

---

[a] 1 Or Peleth—took men

KORAH

An Illegitimate Desire for More
Numbers 16:1–11

Korah, a talented but insolent Levite, had been set apart to serve in Israel's worship of the living God. His important position gave him both prestige and respect within the nation. Yet he rebelled against both Moses and the Lord, thus illustrating the tragic flaw of many leaders—a desire for power and authority beyond what God has ordained.

Korah's gifted leadership and persuasive speaking abilities earned him the backing of 250 other leaders. Yet his desire for more led to the demise of his followers and their families. Leaders with rebellious hearts always wreak havoc in the lives of those unwise enough to follow them.

Godly leaders must be willing to submit themselves to those in leadership above them. Many who hold leadership positions based on their strength, acumen, and personality find this difficult to accept. Yet willing subordination at one point may very well qualify a person for greater leadership responsibilities down the road.

The Scripture makes it clear that God places people in authority, and it is dangerous to oppose God's anointed. Korah did just that in a classic act of rebellion, and God had to remove him and his followers in order to keep the spiritual plague away from the rest of the nation.

PROFILE in leadership

that you and all your followers have banded together. Who is Aaron that you should grumble against him?"

[12]Then Moses summoned Dathan and Abiram, the sons of Eliab. But they said, "We will not come! [13]Isn't it enough that you have brought us up out of a land flowing with milk and honey to kill us in the wilderness? And now you also want to lord it over us! [14]Moreover, you haven't brought us into a land flowing with milk and honey or given us an inheritance of fields and vineyards. Do you want to treat these men like slaves[a]? No, we will not come!"

[15]Then Moses became very angry and said to the LORD, "Do not accept their offering. I have not taken so much as a donkey from them, nor have I wronged any of them."

[16]Moses said to Korah, "You and all your followers are to appear before the LORD tomorrow—you and they and Aaron. [17]Each man is to take his censer and put incense in it—250 censers in all—and present it before the LORD. You and Aaron are to present your censers also." [18]So each of them took his censer, put burning coals and incense in it, and stood with Moses and Aaron at the entrance to the tent of meeting. [19]When Korah had gathered all his followers in opposition to them at the entrance to the tent of meeting, the glory of the LORD appeared to the entire assembly. [20]The LORD said to Moses and Aaron, [21]"Separate yourselves from this assembly so I can put an end to them at once."

[22]But Moses and Aaron fell facedown and cried out, "O God, the God who gives breath to all living things, will you be angry with the entire assembly when only one man sins?"

[23]Then the LORD said to Moses, [24]"Say to the assembly, 'Move away from the tents of Korah, Dathan and Abiram.'"

[25]Moses got up and went to Dathan and Abiram, and the elders of Israel followed him. [26]He warned the assembly, "Move back from the tents of these wicked men! Do not touch anything belonging to them, or you will be swept away because of all their sins." [27]So they moved away from the tents of Korah, Dathan and Abiram. Dathan and Abiram had come out and were standing with their wives, children and little ones at the entrances to their tents.

[28]Then Moses said, "This is how you will know that the LORD has sent me to do all these things and that it was not my idea: [29]If these men die a natural death and suffer the fate of all mankind, then the LORD has not sent me. [30]But if the LORD brings about something totally new, and the earth opens its mouth and swallows

---

[a] 14 Or to deceive these men; Hebrew Will you gouge out the eyes of these men

Self-Appointed Leadership: Moses Defuses Korah's Rebellion

Numbers 16:1–33

Two kinds of false leaders emerge within organizations: man-appointed leaders and self-appointed leaders.

Balaam was a false leader of the first kind. Balak persuaded him to do something that God rejected, and the Lord rebuked Balaam for his arrogance. We read his story in Numbers 22–24.

Korah was a false leader of the second kind. Author Frank Damazio writes: "A self-appointed leader takes upon himself the authority and responsibility of a spiritual office to which he has not been divinely called." Korah blatantly and arrogantly rebelled against Moses. In self-will and presumption, Korah followed a process of self-appointment common to many who illegitimately pursue power:

1. **He caused others to rise up against existing leadership** (16:2).

2. **He publicly criticized and questioned existing leadership** (16:3).

3. **He accused leadership of what he himself was guilty of** (16:3).

4. **He despised as too little the position he had been given—he wanted more** (16:10).

5. **He continued to murmur, complain, and create a negative atmosphere** (16:11).

Unsurprisingly, God always rejects false leadership. He rebuked Balaam, and he put Korah to death. Such leadership lessons might seem harsh, but they last.

them, with everything that belongs to them, and they go down alive into the realm of the dead, then you will know that these men have treated the LORD with contempt."

31As soon as he finished saying all this, the ground under them split apart 32and the earth opened its mouth and swallowed them and their households, and all those associated with Korah, together with their possessions. 33They went down alive into the realm of the dead, with everything they owned; the earth closed over them, and they perished and were gone from the community. 34At their cries, all the Israelites around them fled, shouting, "The earth is going to swallow us too!"

35And fire came out from the LORD and consumed the 250 men who were offering the incense.

36The LORD said to Moses, 37"Tell Eleazar son of Aaron, the priest, to remove the censers from the charred remains and scatter the coals some distance away, for the censers are holy— 38the censers of the men who sinned at the cost of their lives. Hammer the censers into sheets to overlay the altar, for they were presented before the LORD and have become holy. Let them be a sign to the Israelites."

39So Eleazar the priest collected the bronze censers brought by those who had been burned to death, and he had them hammered out to overlay the altar, 40as the LORD directed him through Moses. This was to remind the Israelites that no one except a descendant of Aaron should come to burn incense before the LORD, or he would become like Korah and his followers.

41The next day the whole Israelite community grumbled against Moses and Aaron. "You have killed the LORD's people," they said.

42But when the assembly gathered in opposition to Moses and Aaron and turned toward the tent of meeting, suddenly the cloud covered it and the glory of the LORD appeared. 43Then Moses and Aaron went to the front of the tent of meeting, 44and the LORD said to Moses, 45"Get away from this assembly so I can put an end to them at once." And they fell facedown.

46Then Moses said to Aaron, "Take your censer and put incense in it, along with burning coals from the altar, and hurry to the assembly to make atonement for them. Wrath has come out from the LORD; the plague has started." 47So Aaron did as Moses said, and ran into the midst of the assembly. The plague had already started among the people, but Aaron offered the in-

cense and made atonement for them. 48He stood between the living and the dead, and the plague stopped. 49But 14,700 people died from the plague, in addition to those who had died because of Korah. 50Then Aaron returned to Moses at the entrance to the tent of meeting, for the plague had stopped.[a]

The Budding of Aaron's Staff

17[b] The LORD said to Moses, 2"Speak to the Israelites and get twelve staffs from them, one from the leader of each of their ancestral tribes. Write the name of each man on his staff. 3On the staff of Levi write Aaron's name, for there must be one staff for the head of each ancestral tribe. 4Place them in the tent of meeting in front of the ark of the covenant law, where I meet with you. 5The staff belonging to the man I choose will sprout, and I will rid myself of this constant grumbling against you by the Israelites."

6So Moses spoke to the Israelites, and their leaders gave him twelve staffs, one for the leader of each of their ancestral tribes, and Aaron's staff was among them. 7Moses placed the staffs before the LORD in the tent of the covenant law.

8The next day Moses entered the tent and saw that Aaron's staff, which represented the tribe of Levi, had not only sprouted but had budded, blossomed and produced almonds. 9Then Moses brought out all the staffs from the LORD's presence to all the Israelites. They looked at them, and each of the leaders took his own staff.

10The LORD said to Moses, "Put back Aaron's staff in front of the ark of the covenant law, to be kept as a sign to the rebellious. This will put an

---

[a] 50 In Hebrew texts 16:36-50 is numbered 17:1-15.   [b] In Hebrew texts 17:1-13 is numbered 17:16-28.

God Resolves Leadership Issue to Dissolve Grumbling Issue

Numbers 17:1–10

To resolve a grumbling issue among the people, God reiterated his calling of the leaders. Everything rises and falls with leadership. Once the leadership issue is addressed, the organization can move forward. Establish the leader and you establish the organization.

end to their grumbling against me, so that they will not die." ¹¹Moses did just as the LORD commanded him.

¹²The Israelites said to Moses, "We will die! We are lost, we are all lost! ¹³Anyone who even comes near the tabernacle of the LORD will die. Are we all going to die?"

Duties of Priests and Levites

18 The LORD said to Aaron, "You, your sons and your family are to bear the responsibility for offenses connected with the sanctuary, and you and your sons alone are to bear the responsibility for offenses connected with the priesthood. ²Bring your fellow Levites from your ancestral tribe to join you and assist you when you and your sons minister before the tent of the covenant law. ³They are to be responsible to you and are to perform all the duties of the tent, but they must not go near the furnishings of the sanctuary or the altar. Otherwise both they and you will die. ⁴They are to join you and be responsible for the care of the tent of meeting—all the work at the tent—and no one else may come near where you are.

⁵"You are to be responsible for the care of the sanctuary and the altar, so that my wrath will not fall on the Israelites again. ⁶I myself have selected your fellow Levites from among the Israelites as a gift to you, dedicated to the LORD to do the work at the tent of meeting. ⁷But only you and your sons may serve as priests in connection with everything at the altar and inside the curtain. I am giving you the service of the priesthood as a gift. Anyone else who comes near the sanctuary is to be put to death."

Offerings for Priests and Levites

⁸Then the LORD said to Aaron, "I myself have put you in charge of the offerings presented to me; all the holy offerings the Israelites give me I give to you and your sons as your portion, your perpetual share. ⁹You are to have the part of the most holy offerings that is kept from the fire. From all the gifts they bring me as most holy offerings, whether grain or sin*a* or guilt offerings, that part belongs to you and your sons. ¹⁰Eat it as something most holy; every male shall eat it. You must regard it as holy.

¹¹"This also is yours: whatever is set aside from the gifts of all the wave offerings of the Israelites. I give this to you and your sons and daughters as your perpetual share. Everyone in your household who is ceremonially clean may eat it.

¹²"I give you all the finest olive oil and all the finest new wine and grain they give the LORD as the firstfruits of their harvest. ¹³All the land's firstfruits that they bring to the LORD will be yours. Everyone in your household who is ceremonially clean may eat it.

¹⁴"Everything in Israel that is devoted*b* to the LORD is yours. ¹⁵The first offspring of every womb, both human and animal, that is offered to the LORD is yours. But you must redeem every firstborn son and every firstborn male of unclean animals. ¹⁶When they are a month old, you must redeem them at the redemption price set at five shekels*c* of silver, according to the sanctuary shekel, which weighs twenty gerahs.

¹⁷"But you must not redeem the firstborn of a cow, a sheep or a goat; they are holy. Splash their blood against the altar and burn their fat as a food offering, an aroma pleasing to the LORD. ¹⁸Their meat is to be yours, just as the breast of the wave offering and the right thigh are yours. ¹⁹Whatever is set aside from the holy offerings the Israelites present to the LORD I give to you and your sons and daughters as your perpetual share. It is an everlasting covenant of salt before the LORD for both you and your offspring."

²⁰The LORD said to Aaron, "You will have no inheritance in their land, nor will you have any share among them; I am your share and your inheritance among the Israelites.

²¹"I give to the Levites all the tithes in Israel as their inheritance in return for the work they do while serving at the tent of meeting. ²²From now on the Israelites must not go near the tent of meeting, or they will bear the consequences of their sin and will die. ²³It is the Levites who are to do the work at the tent of meeting and bear the responsibility for any offenses they commit against it. This is a lasting ordinance for the generations to come. They will receive no inheritance among the Israelites. ²⁴Instead, I give to the Levites as their inheritance the tithes that the Israelites present as an offering to the LORD. That is why I said concerning them: 'They will have no inheritance among the Israelites.'"

²⁵The LORD said to Moses, ²⁶"Speak to the Levites and say to them: 'When you receive from the Israelites the tithe I give you as your inheritance, you must present a tenth of that tithe as the LORD's offering. ²⁷Your offering will be reckoned to you as grain from the threshing floor or

---
a 9 Or *purification*   *b 14* The Hebrew term refers to the irrevocable giving over of things or persons to the LORD.
c 16 That is, about 2 ounces or about 58 grams

Lame Leadership Awards

Numbers 12–24

The book of Numbers offers several "lame leadership" illustrations. Consider just a few acts of indiscretion, foolishness, lack of judgment, poor choices and just plain old sin:

1. **Korah** (Nu 16) Korah recruited two buddies and 250 henchmen to stage an insurrection against Moses. Result? The earth swallowed them up.

2. **The prophet Balaam** (Nu 22–24) King Balak paid Balaam to put a curse on Israel. God interceded, even to the point of giving Balaam's donkey a human voice to reason with him. Result? God rebuked Balaam.

3. **Balak** (Nu 22–24) King Balak thought he could buy his way into success. He paid Balaam to curse God's people, hoping his plan could override God's sovereignty. Result? It didn't.

4. **Miriam and Aaron** (Nu 12) Moses' own sister and brother decided they wanted a bigger piece of the power. Result? Miriam got a case of leprosy, and both got a bigger piece of humble pie.

5. **The ten fearful spies** (Nu 13; 14) These men led their clans. They had witnessed God's provision. Yet they turned chicken at the edge of the promised land. Result? They destroyed the faith of the people.

6. **Moses** (Nu 20) Even Moses had bad days. Once, in a fit of anger, he disobeyed God and struck a rock twice. Result? He forfeited his right to enter Canaan.

---

juice from the winepress. ²⁸In this way you also will present an offering to the LORD from all the tithes you receive from the Israelites. From these tithes you must give the LORD's portion to Aaron the priest. ²⁹You must present as the LORD's portion the best and holiest part of everything given to you.'

³⁰"Say to the Levites: 'When you present the best part, it will be reckoned to you as the product of the threshing floor or the winepress. ³¹You and your households may eat the rest of it anywhere, for it is your wages for your work at the tent of meeting. ³²By presenting the best part of it you will not be guilty in this matter; then you will not defile the holy offerings of the Israelites, and you will not die.'"

The Water of Cleansing

19 The LORD said to Moses and Aaron: ²"This is a requirement of the law that the LORD has commanded: Tell the Israelites to bring you a red heifer without defect or blemish and that has never been under a yoke. ³Give it to Eleazar the priest; it is to be taken outside the camp and slaughtered in his presence. ⁴Then Eleazar the priest is to take some of its blood on his finger and sprinkle it seven times toward the front of the tent of meeting. ⁵While he watches, the heifer is to be burned — its hide, flesh, blood and intestines. ⁶The priest is to take some cedar wood, hyssop and scarlet wool and throw them onto the burning heifer. ⁷After that, the priest must wash his clothes and bathe himself with water. He may then come into the camp, but he will be ceremonially unclean till evening. ⁸The man who burns it must also wash his clothes and bathe with water, and he too will be unclean till evening.

⁹"A man who is clean shall gather up the ashes of the heifer and put them in a ceremonially clean place outside the camp. They are to be kept by the Israelite community for use in the water of cleansing; it is for purification from sin. ¹⁰The man who gathers up the ashes of the heifer must also wash his clothes, and he too will be unclean till evening. This will be a lasting ordinance both for the Israelites and for the foreigners residing among them.

¹¹"Whoever touches a human corpse will be unclean for seven days. ¹²They must purify themselves with the water on the third day and on the seventh day; then they will be clean. But if they do not purify themselves on the third and seventh days, they will not be clean. ¹³If they fail to purify themselves after touching a human corpse, they defile the LORD's tabernacle. They must be cut off from Israel. Because the water of cleansing has not been sprinkled on them,

they are unclean; their uncleanness remains on them.

14"This is the law that applies when a person dies in a tent: Anyone who enters the tent and anyone who is in it will be unclean for seven days, 15and every open container without a lid fastened on it will be unclean.

16"Anyone out in the open who touches someone who has been killed with a sword or someone who has died a natural death, or anyone who touches a human bone or a grave, will be unclean for seven days.

17"For the unclean person, put some ashes from the burned purification offering into a jar and pour fresh water over them. 18Then a man who is ceremonially clean is to take some hyssop, dip it in the water and sprinkle the tent and all the furnishings and the people who were there. He must also sprinkle anyone who has touched a human bone or a grave or anyone who has been killed or anyone who has died a natural death. 19The man who is clean is to sprinkle those who are unclean on the third and seventh days, and on the seventh day he is to purify them. Those who are being cleansed must wash their clothes and bathe with water, and that evening they will be clean. 20But if those who are unclean do not purify themselves, they must be cut off from the community, because they have defiled the sanctuary of the LORD. The water of cleansing has not been sprinkled on them, and they are unclean. 21This is a lasting ordinance for them.

"The man who sprinkles the water of cleansing must also wash his clothes, and anyone who touches the water of cleansing will be unclean till evening. 22Anything that an unclean person touches becomes unclean, and anyone who touches it becomes unclean till evening."

Water From the Rock

20 In the first month the whole Israelite community arrived at the Desert of Zin, and they stayed at Kadesh. There Miriam died and was buried.

2Now there was no water for the community, and the people gathered in opposition to Moses and Aaron. 3They quarreled with Moses and said, "If only we had died when our brothers fell dead before the LORD! 4Why did you bring the LORD's community into this wilderness, that we and our livestock should die here? 5Why did you bring us up out of Egypt to this terrible place? It has no grain or figs, grapevines or pomegranates. And there is no water to drink!"

6Moses and Aaron went from the assembly to the entrance to the tent of meeting and fell facedown, and the glory of the LORD appeared to them. 7The LORD said to Moses, 8"Take the staff, and you and your brother Aaron gather the assembly together. Speak to that rock before their eyes and it will pour out its water. You will bring water out of the rock for the community so they and their livestock can drink."

9So Moses took the staff from the LORD's presence, just as he commanded him. 10He and Aaron gathered the assembly together in front of the rock and Moses said to them, "Listen, you rebels, must we bring you water out of this rock?" 11Then Moses raised his arm and struck the rock twice with his staff. Water gushed out, and the community and their livestock drank.

12But the LORD said to Moses and Aaron, "Because you did not trust in me enough to honor me as holy in the sight of the Israelites, you will not bring this community into the land I give them."

The Four Spiritual Flaws of a Leader

Numbers 20:10–12

Moses' disobedience by the rock reminds us of the human flaws that bedevil us all:

- Reacting instead of leading (v. 10)
- Presuming that what worked before will work again (v. 11)
- Compromising our obedience to God so we'll look better (v. 11)
- Failing to trust God to complete what he began (v. 12)

13These were the waters of Meribah,ᵃ where the Israelites quarreled with the LORD and where he was proved holy among them.

Edom Denies Israel Passage

14Moses sent messengers from Kadesh to the king of Edom, saying:

"This is what your brother Israel says: You know about all the hardships that have come on us. 15Our ancestors went down into Egypt, and we lived there many years. The Egyptians mistreated us and

---

ᵃ 13 *Meribah* means *quarreling.*

Leadership: Are You Proactive or Reactive?

Numbers 20:2–13

We learn something invaluable about leadership at the expense of Moses in Numbers 20. By this point Moses felt unendurably weary of the complaining, the stagnation and the lack of progress among the people. He was running on empty. And in his weakened condition he made a decision that cost him his future.

Directed by God to speak to a rock in order to get water for the nation, in anger he struck it (as he had earlier). He reacted in fury rather than obeying with poise, and for his disobedience he was barred from entering the promised land. This sad incident teaches us at least two lessons.

First, never make a major decision during an emotionally low time. Make decisions in the peak times, not the valley times.

The right time to make a decision

The wrong time to make a decision

Second, choose to be proactive, not reactive, in your leadership. Don't let your mandate come from the grumbling of the crowd. Get your cues from God and the mission he has given you. Ask yourself these questions:

1. **Am I a reactor or a creator when I lead?**
2. **Do I play defense or offense when I lead?**
3. **Am I a people-pleaser or a God-pleaser when I lead?**
4. **Do I boss my calendar, or does someone else choose where I give my time?**

our ancestors, ¹⁶but when we cried out to the LORD, he heard our cry and sent an angel and brought us out of Egypt.

"Now we are here at Kadesh, a town on the edge of your territory. ¹⁷Please let us pass through your country. We will not go through any field or vineyard, or drink water from any well. We will travel along the King's Highway and not turn to the right or to the left until we have passed through your territory."

¹⁸But Edom answered:

"You may not pass through here; if you try, we will march out and attack you with the sword."

¹⁹The Israelites replied:

"We will go along the main road, and if we or our livestock drink any of your water, we will pay for it. We only want to pass through on foot — nothing else."

²⁰Again they answered:

"You may not pass through."

Then Edom came out against them with a large and powerful army. ²¹Since Edom refused to let them go through their territory, Israel turned away from them.

The Death of Aaron

²²The whole Israelite community set out from Kadesh and came to Mount Hor. ²³At Mount Hor, near the border of Edom, the LORD said to Moses and Aaron, ²⁴"Aaron will be gathered to his people. He will not enter the land I give the Israelites, because both of you rebelled against my command at the waters of Meribah. ²⁵Get Aaron and his son Eleazar and take them up Mount Hor. ²⁶Remove Aaron's garments and put them on his son Eleazar, for Aaron will be gathered to his people; he will die there."

²⁷Moses did as the LORD commanded: They went up Mount Hor in the sight of the whole

community. ²⁸Moses removed Aaron's garments and put them on his son Eleazar. And Aaron died there on top of the mountain. Then Moses and Eleazar came down from the mountain, ²⁹and when the whole community learned that Aaron had died, all the Israelites mourned for him thirty days.

Arad Destroyed

21 When the Canaanite king of Arad, who lived in the Negev, heard that Israel was coming along the road to Atharim, he attacked the Israelites and captured some of them. ²Then Israel made this vow to the LORD: "If you will deliver these people into our hands, we will totally destroy[a] their cities." ³The LORD listened to Israel's plea and gave the Canaanites over to them. They completely destroyed them and their towns; so the place was named Hormah.[b]

The Bronze Snake

⁴They traveled from Mount Hor along the route to the Red Sea,[c] to go around Edom. But the people grew impatient on the way; ⁵they spoke against God and against Moses, and said, "Why have you brought us up out of Egypt to die in the wilderness? There is no bread! There is no water! And we detest this miserable food!"

⁶Then the LORD sent venomous snakes among them; they bit the people and many Israelites died. ⁷The people came to Moses and said, "We sinned when we spoke against the LORD and against you. Pray that the LORD will take the snakes away from us." So Moses prayed for the people.

⁸The LORD said to Moses, "Make a snake and put it up on a pole; anyone who is bitten can look at it and live." ⁹So Moses made a bronze snake and put it up on a pole. Then when anyone was bitten by a snake and looked at the bronze snake, they lived.

The Journey to Moab

¹⁰The Israelites moved on and camped at Oboth. ¹¹Then they set out from Oboth and camped in Iye Abarim, in the wilderness that faces Moab toward the sunrise. ¹²From there they moved on and camped in the Zered Valley. ¹³They set out from there and camped alongside the Arnon, which is in the wilderness extending into Amorite territory. The Arnon is the border of Moab, between Moab and the Amorites. ¹⁴That is why the Book of the Wars of the LORD says:

"... Zahab[d] in Suphah and the ravines,
　　the Arnon ¹⁵and[e] the slopes of the ravines

that lead to the settlement of Ar
　　and lie along the border of Moab."

¹⁶From there they continued on to Beer, the well where the LORD said to Moses, "Gather the people together and I will give them water."

¹⁷Then Israel sang this song:

"Spring up, O well!
　　Sing about it,
¹⁸about the well that the princes dug,
　　that the nobles of the people sank—
　　the nobles with scepters and staffs."

Then they went from the wilderness to Mattanah, ¹⁹from Mattanah to Nahaliel, from Nahaliel to Bamoth, ²⁰and from Bamoth to the valley in Moab where the top of Pisgah overlooks the wasteland.

Defeat of Sihon and Og

²¹Israel sent messengers to say to Sihon king of the Amorites:

²²"Let us pass through your country. We will not turn aside into any field or vineyard, or drink water from any well. We will travel along the King's Highway until we have passed through your territory."

²³But Sihon would not let Israel pass through his territory. He mustered his entire army and marched out into the wilderness against Israel. When he reached Jahaz, he fought with Israel. ²⁴Israel, however, put him to the sword and took over his land from the Arnon to the Jabbok, but only as far as the Ammonites, because their border was fortified. ²⁵Israel captured all the cities of the Amorites and occupied them, including Heshbon and all its surrounding settlements. ²⁶Heshbon was the city of Sihon king of the Amorites, who had fought against the former king of Moab and had taken from him all his land as far as the Arnon.

²⁷That is why the poets say:

"Come to Heshbon and let it be rebuilt;
　　let Sihon's city be restored.

²⁸"Fire went out from Heshbon,
　　a blaze from the city of Sihon.
It consumed Ar of Moab,
　　the citizens of Arnon's heights.

---

[a] 2 The Hebrew term refers to the irrevocable giving over of things or persons to the LORD, often by totally destroying them; also in verse 3.　[b] 3 *Hormah* means *destruction*.　[c] 4 Or *the Sea of Reeds*　[d] 14 Septuagint; Hebrew *Waheb*　[e] 14,15 Or "*I have been given from Suphah and the ravines / of the Arnon* ¹⁵*to*

²⁹Woe to you, Moab!
  You are destroyed, people of Chemosh!
He has given up his sons as fugitives
  and his daughters as captives
  to Sihon king of the Amorites.

³⁰"But we have overthrown them;
  Heshbon's dominion has been destroyed
    all the way to Dibon.
We have demolished them as far as Nophah,
  which extends to Medeba."

³¹So Israel settled in the land of the Amorites.

³²After Moses had sent spies to Jazer, the Israelites captured its surrounding settlements and drove out the Amorites who were there. ³³Then they turned and went up along the road toward Bashan, and Og king of Bashan and his whole army marched out to meet them in battle at Edrei.

³⁴The LORD said to Moses, "Do not be afraid of him, for I have delivered him into your hands, along with his whole army and his land. Do to him what you did to Sihon king of the Amorites, who reigned in Heshbon."

³⁵So they struck him down, together with his sons and his whole army, leaving them no survivors. And they took possession of his land.

Balak Summons Balaam

22 Then the Israelites traveled to the plains of Moab and camped along the Jordan across from Jericho.

²Now Balak son of Zippor saw all that Israel had done to the Amorites, ³and Moab was terrified because there were so many people. Indeed, Moab was filled with dread because of the Israelites.

⁴The Moabites said to the elders of Midian, "This horde is going to lick up everything around us, as an ox licks up the grass of the field."

So Balak son of Zippor, who was king of Moab at that time, ⁵sent messengers to summon Balaam son of Beor, who was at Pethor, near the Euphrates River, in his native land. Balak said:

"A people has come out of Egypt; they cover the face of the land and have settled next to me. ⁶Now come and put a curse on these people, because they are too powerful for me. Perhaps then I will be able to defeat them and drive them out of the land. For I know that whoever you bless is blessed, and whoever you curse is cursed."

⁷The elders of Moab and Midian left, taking with them the fee for divination. When they came to Balaam, they told him what Balak had said.

⁸"Spend the night here," Balaam said to them, "and I will report back to you with the answer the LORD gives me." So the Moabite officials stayed with him.

⁹God came to Balaam and asked, "Who are these men with you?"

¹⁰Balaam said to God, "Balak son of Zippor, king of Moab, sent me this message: ¹¹'A people that has come out of Egypt covers the face of the land. Now come and put a curse on them for me. Perhaps then I will be able to fight them and drive them away.'"

¹²But God said to Balaam, "Do not go with them. You must not put a curse on those people, because they are blessed."

¹³The next morning Balaam got up and said to Balak's officials, "Go back to your own country, for the LORD has refused to let me go with you."

¹⁴So the Moabite officials returned to Balak and said, "Balaam refused to come with us."

¹⁵Then Balak sent other officials, more numerous and more distinguished than the first. ¹⁶They came to Balaam and said:

"This is what Balak son of Zippor says: Do not let anything keep you from coming to me, ¹⁷because I will reward you handsomely and do whatever you say. Come and put a curse on these people for me."

¹⁸But Balaam answered them, "Even if Balak gave me all the silver and gold in his palace, I could not do anything great or small to go beyond the command of the LORD my God. ¹⁹Now spend the night here so that I can find out what else the LORD will tell me."

²⁰That night God came to Balaam and said, "Since these men have come to summon you, go with them, but do only what I tell you."

Balaam Fails to Observe the Law of Buy-In

Numbers 22:5—24:25

King Balak was a strong leader with a wrong vision. Balaam was a weaker leader, but had the right vision. The two blended like oil and water. Optimally, the right leader must be in place, with right vision. People buy in to the leader before they buy in to the vision.

Balaam's Donkey

[21]Balaam got up in the morning, saddled his donkey and went with the Moabite officials. [22]But God was very angry when he went, and the angel of the LORD stood in the road to oppose him. Balaam was riding on his donkey, and his two servants were with him. [23]When the donkey saw the angel of the LORD standing in the road with a drawn sword in his hand, it turned off the road into a field. Balaam beat it to get it back on the road.

[24]Then the angel of the LORD stood in a narrow path through the vineyards, with walls on both sides. [25]When the donkey saw the angel of the LORD, it pressed close to the wall, crushing Balaam's foot against it. So he beat the donkey again.

[26]Then the angel of the LORD moved on ahead and stood in a narrow place where there was no room to turn, either to the right or to the left. [27]When the donkey saw the angel of the LORD, it lay down under Balaam, and he was angry and beat it with his staff. [28]Then the LORD opened the donkey's mouth, and it said to Balaam, "What have I done to you to make you beat me these three times?"

[29]Balaam answered the donkey, "You have made a fool of me! If only I had a sword in my hand, I would kill you right now."

[30]The donkey said to Balaam, "Am I not your own donkey, which you have always ridden, to this day? Have I been in the habit of doing this to you?"

"No," he said.

[31]Then the LORD opened Balaam's eyes, and he saw the angel of the LORD standing in the road with his sword drawn. So he bowed low and fell facedown.

[32]The angel of the LORD asked him, "Why have you beaten your donkey these three times? I have come here to oppose you because your path is a reckless one before me.[a] [33]The donkey saw me and turned away from me these three times. If it had not turned away, I would certainly have killed you by now, but I would have spared it."

[34]Balaam said to the angel of the LORD, "I have sinned. I did not realize you were standing in the road to oppose me. Now if you are displeased, I will go back."

[35]The angel of the LORD said to Balaam, "Go with the men, but speak only what I tell you." So Balaam went with Balak's officials.

[36]When Balak heard that Balaam was coming, he went out to meet him at the Moabite town on the Arnon border, at the edge of his territory. [37]Balak said to Balaam, "Did I not send you an urgent summons? Why didn't you come to me? Am I really not able to reward you?"

---

[a] 32 The meaning of the Hebrew for this clause is uncertain.

BALAAM

Good but Not Godly
Numbers 22:5—24:25

One good trait does not a godly leader make—a maxim proven by the life of Balaam. In one way, this Midianite sorcerer demonstrated good leadership. When Balak, king of Midian, tried to hire Balaam to curse the Israelites, the prophet declared he could speak only what God told him. In the end, Balaam blessed Israel three times (Nu 24:10).

Yet the balance of Scripture denounces Balaam. Joshua 13:22 tells us he practiced divination, an activity condemned by Leviticus 19:26. Both Deuteronomy 23:5 and Joshua 24:9 strongly imply that Balaam asked God for permission to curse Israel. And the New Testament uses Balaam as an example of those who "have left the straight way and wandered off" and says, "he was rebuked for his wrongdoing" (2Pe 2:15–16). Although God would not allow Balaam to curse Israel, apparently the sorcerer suggested a way for Balak to remove God's blessing on the Jewish people. Balaam "taught Balak to entice the Israelites to sin so that they ate food sacrificed to idols and committed sexual immorality" (Rev 2:14; see Nu 25:1–3).

Balaam finally met his demise when, by God's command, the Israelites killed him along with all the other male Midianites (Nu 31:8). And so this diviner died at the hands of the people he tried to curse.

38"Well, I have come to you now," Balaam replied. "But I can't say whatever I please. I must speak only what God puts in my mouth."

39Then Balaam went with Balak to Kiriath Huzoth. 40Balak sacrificed cattle and sheep, and gave some to Balaam and the officials who were with him. 41The next morning Balak took Balaam up to Bamoth Baal, and from there he could see the outskirts of the Israelite camp.

Balaam's First Message

23 Balaam said, "Build me seven altars here, and prepare seven bulls and seven rams for me." 2Balak did as Balaam said, and the two of them offered a bull and a ram on each altar.

3Then Balaam said to Balak, "Stay here beside your offering while I go aside. Perhaps the LORD will come to meet with me. Whatever he reveals to me I will tell you." Then he went off to a barren height.

4God met with him, and Balaam said, "I have prepared seven altars, and on each altar I have offered a bull and a ram."

5The LORD put a word in Balaam's mouth and said, "Go back to Balak and give him this word."

6So he went back to him and found him standing beside his offering, with all the Moabite officials. 7Then Balaam spoke his message:

"Balak brought me from Aram,
    the king of Moab from the eastern
        mountains.
'Come,' he said, 'curse Jacob for me;
    come, denounce Israel.'
8How can I curse
    those whom God has not cursed?
How can I denounce
    those whom the LORD has not
        denounced?
9From the rocky peaks I see them,
    from the heights I view them.
I see a people who live apart
    and do not consider themselves one of the
        nations.
10Who can count the dust of Jacob
    or number even a fourth of Israel?
Let me die the death of the righteous,
    and may my final end be like theirs!"

11Balak said to Balaam, "What have you done to me? I brought you to curse my enemies, but you have done nothing but bless them!"

12He answered, "Must I not speak what the LORD puts in my mouth?"

Balaam's Second Message

13Then Balak said to him, "Come with me to another place where you can see them; you will not see them all but only the outskirts of their camp. And from there, curse them for me." 14So he took him to the field of Zophim on the top of Pisgah, and there he built seven altars and offered a bull and a ram on each altar.

15Balaam said to Balak, "Stay here beside your offering while I meet with him over there."

16The LORD met with Balaam and put a word in his mouth and said, "Go back to Balak and give him this word."

17So he went to him and found him standing beside his offering, with the Moabite officials. Balak asked him, "What did the LORD say?"

18Then he spoke his message:

Balaam's Hollow, Man-Appointed Leadership

Numbers 22:14—24:25

Man-appointed leaders often claim to receive a call from God, but their authority actually derives from human sources and not from the Lord. Eventually the truth becomes clear to everyone.

In Numbers 22–24 we see an example of a man-appointed leader. Balaam son of Beor tried to curse Israel for profit, but the Lord would not allow it. How can one discern man-appointed leadership?

1. **It issues from human ingenuity rather than God's anointing (22:14–16).**

2. **It often reveals self-serving motives (22:17).**

3. **It devises plans that oppose what God is doing (22:22).**

4. **It blinds the leader to God's intentions (22:23–30).**

5. **Its goals eventually fail because they oppose the work of God (23:1—24:25).**

DISCERNMENT   Balaam Just Didn't Get It

Numbers 22:21–35

BALAAM HAS borne the brunt of many a joke. Here was a prophet who so lacked discernment that it took a donkey to sense the presence of a threatening angel and to bring the terrible danger to his attention.

Balaam lacked both discernment and intuition about what was happening around him. Note the following observations about Balaam's error:

1. Balaam angered God because he disobeyed what he knew to be right (v. 22).

2. It took the angel of the Lord standing in the way to stop Balaam (v. 23).

3. The seer could not discern the angel's blockade (v. 23).

4. Balaam's own agenda so consumed him that he whipped his donkey for responding to the angel (v. 25).

5. God enabled the donkey to speak when Balaam still didn't perceive his danger (v. 28).

6. The donkey discerned more than Balaam and interpreted reality for him (vv. 28–30).

7. It took a divine miracle for Balaam's eyes to be opened (v. 31).

No leader can long enjoy success without developing a healthy sense of discernment. Lack of discernment nearly got Balaam killed. He did not discern the Lord's presence, and he confessed his lack of discern-ment (Nu 22:34). God said the prophet would surely have been killed had it not been for his discerning donkey (22:33). When he finally realized his peril, Balaam had to feel both ashamed and embarrassed. It is one thing to lack discernment; it is another for your donkey to possess more of it than you do!

Unfortunately, many leaders today suffer exactly this plight. Many factors conspire to keep us from discerning the needs of the moment. Consider some common factors:

1. An unrelenting schedule leaves no room for listening.

2. An important agenda fosters a stubborn heart rather than a sensitive one.

3. A type-A temperament makes it difficult to slow down and discern.

4. A strong task orientation leaves little time for people or spontaneity.

5. We desire to solve spiritual and emotional problems with external answers.

Do you want to hone your leadership skills? Then make it a priority to pray for greater discernment. Listen for and interpret the root causes of the challenges you face. Consider your gut reaction to others, but also tap your mind. Discernment takes both godly intuition and intellect.

For a positive example of discernment, see p. 382.

"Arise, Balak, and listen;
    hear me, son of Zippor.
¹⁹God is not human, that he should lie,
    not a human being, that he should change
        his mind.
Does he speak and then not act?
Does he promise and not fulfill?
²⁰I have received a command to bless;
    he has blessed, and I cannot change it.

²¹"No misfortune is seen in Jacob,
    no misery observed*a* in Israel.
The LORD their God is with them;
    the shout of the King is among them.
²²God brought them out of Egypt;
    they have the strength of a wild ox.
²³There is no divination against*b* Jacob,
    no evil omens against*b* Israel.
It will now be said of Jacob
    and of Israel, 'See what God has done!'
²⁴The people rise like a lioness;
    they rouse themselves like a lion
that does not rest till it devours its prey
    and drinks the blood of its victims."

²⁵Then Balak said to Balaam, "Neither curse them at all nor bless them at all!"
²⁶Balaam answered, "Did I not tell you I must do whatever the LORD says?"

Balaam's Third Message

²⁷Then Balak said to Balaam, "Come, let me take you to another place. Perhaps it will please God to let you curse them for me from there." ²⁸And Balak took Balaam to the top of Peor, overlooking the wasteland. ²⁹Balaam said, "Build me seven altars here, and prepare seven bulls and seven rams for me." ³⁰Balak did as Balaam had said, and offered a bull and a ram on each altar.

24 Now when Balaam saw that it pleased the LORD to bless Israel, he did not resort to divination as at other times, but turned his face toward the wilderness. ²When Balaam looked out and saw Israel encamped tribe by tribe, the Spirit of God came on him ³and he spoke his message:

"The prophecy of Balaam son of Beor,
    the prophecy of one whose eye sees clearly,
⁴the prophecy of one who hears the words of
        God,
    who sees a vision from the Almighty,*c*
    who falls prostrate, and whose eyes are
        opened:

⁵"How beautiful are your tents, Jacob,
    your dwelling places, Israel!

⁶"Like valleys they spread out,
    like gardens beside a river,
like aloes planted by the LORD,
    like cedars beside the waters.
⁷Water will flow from their buckets;
    their seed will have abundant water.

"Their king will be greater than Agag;
    their kingdom will be exalted.

⁸"God brought them out of Egypt;
    they have the strength of a wild ox.
They devour hostile nations
    and break their bones in pieces;
    with their arrows they pierce them.
⁹Like a lion they crouch and lie down,
    like a lioness—who dares to rouse them?

"May those who bless you be blessed
    and those who curse you be cursed!"

¹⁰Then Balak's anger burned against Balaam. He struck his hands together and said to him, "I summoned you to curse my enemies, but you have blessed them these three times. ¹¹Now leave at once and go home! I said I would reward you handsomely, but the LORD has kept you from being rewarded."
¹²Balaam answered Balak, "Did I not tell the messengers you sent me, ¹³'Even if Balak gave me all the silver and gold in his palace, I could not do anything of my own accord, good or bad, to go beyond the command of the LORD—and I must say only what the LORD says'? ¹⁴Now I am going back to my people, but come, let me warn you of what this people will do to your people in days to come."

Balaam's Fourth Message

¹⁵Then he spoke his message:

"The prophecy of Balaam son of Beor,
    the prophecy of one whose eye sees
        clearly,
¹⁶the prophecy of one who hears the words of
        God,
    who has knowledge from the Most High,
    who sees a vision from the Almighty,
    who falls prostrate, and whose eyes are
        opened:

¹⁷"I see him, but not now;
    I behold him, but not near.
A star will come out of Jacob;
    a scepter will rise out of Israel.

a 21 Or He has not looked on Jacob's offenses / or on the wrongs found   b 23 Or in   c 4 Hebrew Shaddai; also in verse 16

He will crush the foreheads of Moab,
the skulls[a] of[b] all the people of Sheth.[c]
[18] Edom will be conquered;
Seir, his enemy, will be conquered,
but Israel will grow strong.
[19] A ruler will come out of Jacob
and destroy the survivors of the city.”

Balaam's Fifth Message

[20] Then Balaam saw Amalek and spoke his message:

“Amalek was first among the nations,
but their end will be utter destruction.”

Balaam's Sixth Message

[21] Then he saw the Kenites and spoke his message:

“Your dwelling place is secure,
your nest is set in a rock;
[22] yet you Kenites will be destroyed
when Ashur takes you captive.”

Balaam's Seventh Message

[23] Then he spoke his message:

“Alas! Who can live when God does this?[d]
[24]   Ships will come from the shores of
Cyprus;
they will subdue Ashur and Eber,
but they too will come to ruin.”

[25] Then Balaam got up and returned home, and Balak went his own way.

Moab Seduces Israel

25 While Israel was staying in Shittim, the men began to indulge in sexual immorality with Moabite women, [2] who invited them to the sacrifices to their gods. The people ate the sacrificial meal and bowed down before these gods. [3] So Israel yoked themselves to the Baal of Peor. And the LORD's anger burned against them.

[4] The LORD said to Moses, “Take all the leaders of these people, kill them and expose them in broad daylight before the LORD, so that the LORD's fierce anger may turn away from Israel.”

[5] So Moses said to Israel's judges, “Each of you must put to death those of your people who have yoked themselves to the Baal of Peor.”

[6] Then an Israelite man brought into the camp a Midianite woman right before the eyes of Moses and the whole assembly of Israel while they were weeping at the entrance to the tent of meeting. [7] When Phinehas son of Eleazar, the son of

Aaron, the priest, saw this, he left the assembly, took a spear in his hand [8] and followed the Israelite into the tent. He drove the spear into both of them, right through the Israelite man and into the woman's stomach. Then the plague against the Israelites was stopped; [9] but those who died in the plague numbered 24,000.

[10] The LORD said to Moses, [11] “Phinehas son of Eleazar, the son of Aaron, the priest, has turned my anger away from the Israelites. Since he was as zealous for my honor among them as I am, I did not put an end to them in my zeal. [12] Therefore tell him I am making my covenant of peace with him. [13] He and his descendants will have a covenant of a lasting priesthood, because he was zealous for the honor of his God and made atonement for the Israelites.”

[14] The name of the Israelite who was killed with the Midianite woman was Zimri son of Salu, the leader of a Simeonite family. [15] And the name of the Midianite woman who was put to death was Kozbi daughter of Zur, a tribal chief of a Midianite family.

[16] The LORD said to Moses, [17] “Treat the Midianites as enemies and kill them. [18] They treated you as enemies when they deceived you in the Peor incident involving their sister Kozbi, the daughter of a Midianite leader, the woman who was killed when the plague came as a result of that incident.”

The Second Census

26 After the plague the LORD said to Moses and Eleazar son of Aaron, the priest, [2] “Take a census of the whole Israelite community by families — all those twenty years old or more who are able to serve in the army of Israel.” [3] So on the plains of Moab by the Jordan across from Jericho, Moses and Eleazar the priest spoke with them and said, [4] “Take a census of the men twenty years old or more, as the LORD commanded Moses.”

These were the Israelites who came out of Egypt:

[5] The descendants of Reuben, the firstborn son of Israel, were:

through Hanok, the Hanokite clan;
through Pallu, the Palluite clan;

---

[a] 17 Samaritan Pentateuch (see also Jer. 48:45); the meaning of the word in the Masoretic Text is uncertain.   [b] 17 Or possibly *Moab, / batter*   [c] 17 Or *all the noisy boasters*
[d] 23 Masoretic Text; with a different word division of the Hebrew *The people from the islands will gather from the north.*

[6]through Hezron, the Hezronite clan;
through Karmi, the Karmite clan.
[7]These were the clans of Reuben; those numbered were 43,730.

[8]The son of Pallu was Eliab, [9]and the sons of Eliab were Nemuel, Dathan and Abiram. The same Dathan and Abiram were the community officials who rebelled against Moses and Aaron and were among Korah's followers when they rebelled against the LORD. [10]The earth opened its mouth and swallowed them along with Korah, whose followers died when the fire devoured the 250 men. And they served as a warning sign. [11]The line of Korah, however, did not die out.

[12]The descendants of Simeon by their clans were:
through Nemuel, the Nemuelite clan;
through Jamin, the Jaminite clan;
through Jakin, the Jakinite clan;
[13]through Zerah, the Zerahite clan;
through Shaul, the Shaulite clan.
[14]These were the clans of Simeon; those numbered were 22,200.

[15]The descendants of Gad by their clans were:
through Zephon, the Zephonite clan;
through Haggi, the Haggite clan;
through Shuni, the Shunite clan;
[16]through Ozni, the Oznite clan;
through Eri, the Erite clan;
[17]through Arodi,[a] the Arodite clan;
through Areli, the Arelite clan.
[18]These were the clans of Gad; those numbered were 40,500.

[19]Er and Onan were sons of Judah, but they died in Canaan. [20]The descendants of Judah by their clans were:
through Shelah, the Shelanite clan;
through Perez, the Perezite clan;
through Zerah, the Zerahite clan.
[21]The descendants of Perez were:
through Hezron, the Hezronite clan;
through Hamul, the Hamulite clan.
[22]These were the clans of Judah; those numbered were 76,500.

[23]The descendants of Issachar by their clans were:
through Tola, the Tolaite clan;
through Puah, the Puite[b] clan;
[24]through Jashub, the Jashubite clan;
through Shimron, the Shimronite clan.
[25]These were the clans of Issachar; those numbered were 64,300.

[26]The descendants of Zebulun by their clans were:
through Sered, the Seredite clan;
through Elon, the Elonite clan;
through Jahleel, the Jahleelite clan.
[27]These were the clans of Zebulun; those numbered were 60,500.

[28]The descendants of Joseph by their clans through Manasseh and Ephraim were:

[29]The descendants of Manasseh:
through Makir, the Makirite clan (Makir was the father of Gilead);
through Gilead, the Gileadite clan.
[30]These were the descendants of Gilead:
through Iezer, the Iezerite clan;
through Helek, the Helekite clan;
[31]through Asriel, the Asrielite clan;
through Shechem, the Shechemite clan;
[32]through Shemida, the Shemidaite clan;
through Hepher, the Hepherite clan.
[33](Zelophehad son of Hepher had no sons; he had only daughters, whose names were Mahlah, Noah, Hoglah, Milkah and Tirzah.)
[34]These were the clans of Manasseh; those numbered were 52,700.

[35]These were the descendants of Ephraim by their clans:
through Shuthelah, the Shuthelahite clan;
through Beker, the Bekerite clan;
through Tahan, the Tahanite clan.
[36]These were the descendants of Shuthelah:
through Eran, the Eranite clan.
[37]These were the clans of Ephraim; those numbered were 32,500.

These were the descendants of Joseph by their clans.

[38]The descendants of Benjamin by their clans were:
through Bela, the Belaite clan;
through Ashbel, the Ashbelite clan;
through Ahiram, the Ahiramite clan;
[39]through Shupham,[c] the Shuphamite clan;
through Hupham, the Huphamite clan.
[40]The descendants of Bela through Ard and Naaman were:

---

[a] 17 Samaritan Pentateuch and Syriac (see also Gen. 46:16); Masoretic Text *Arod*   [b] 23 Samaritan Pentateuch, Septuagint, Vulgate and Syriac (see also 1 Chron. 7:1); Masoretic Text *through Puvah, the Punite*   [c] 39 A few manuscripts of the Masoretic Text, Samaritan Pentateuch, Vulgate and Syriac (see also Septuagint); most manuscripts of the Masoretic Text *Shephupham*

through Ard,[a] the Ardite clan;
through Naaman, the Naamite clan.
41 These were the clans of Benjamin; those numbered were 45,600.

42 These were the descendants of Dan by their clans:
through Shuham, the Shuhamite clan.
These were the clans of Dan: 43 All of them were Shuhamite clans; and those numbered were 64,400.

44 The descendants of Asher by their clans were:
through Imnah, the Imnite clan;
through Ishvi, the Ishvite clan;
through Beriah, the Beriite clan;
45 and through the descendants of Beriah:
through Heber, the Heberite clan;
through Malkiel, the Malkielite clan.
46 (Asher had a daughter named Serah.)
47 These were the clans of Asher; those numbered were 53,400.

48 The descendants of Naphtali by their clans were:
through Jahzeel, the Jahzeelite clan;
through Guni, the Gunite clan;
49 through Jezer, the Jezerite clan;
through Shillem, the Shillemite clan.
50 These were the clans of Naphtali; those numbered were 45,400.

51 The total number of the men of Israel was 601,730.

52 The LORD said to Moses, 53 "The land is to be allotted to them as an inheritance based on the number of names. 54 To a larger group give a larger inheritance, and to a smaller group a smaller one; each is to receive its inheritance according to the number of those listed. 55 Be sure that the land is distributed by lot. What each group inherits will be according to the names for its ancestral tribe. 56 Each inheritance is to be distributed by lot among the larger and smaller groups."

57 These were the Levites who were counted by their clans:
through Gershon, the Gershonite clan;
through Kohath, the Kohathite clan;
through Merari, the Merarite clan.
58 These also were Levite clans:
the Libnite clan,
the Hebronite clan,
the Mahlite clan,
the Mushite clan,

the Korahite clan.
(Kohath was the forefather of Amram; 59 the name of Amram's wife was Jochebed, a descendant of Levi, who was born to the Levites[b] in Egypt. To Amram she bore Aaron, Moses and their sister Miriam. 60 Aaron was the father of Nadab and Abihu, Eleazar and Ithamar. 61 But Nadab and Abihu died when they made an offering before the LORD with unauthorized fire.)

62 All the male Levites a month old or more numbered 23,000. They were not counted along with the other Israelites because they received no inheritance among them.

63 These are the ones counted by Moses and Eleazar the priest when they counted the Israelites on the plains of Moab by the Jordan across from Jericho. 64 Not one of them was among those counted by Moses and Aaron the priest when they counted the Israelites in the Desert of Sinai. 65 For the LORD had told those Israelites they would surely die in the wilderness, and not one of them was left except Caleb son of Jephunneh and Joshua son of Nun.

Round Two of the Census: Evaluating What Remains

Numbers 26:1–63

As a new generation of Hebrews matured into adulthood, Moses took a second census to size up the Israelite community. At the right time, such an evaluation can be extremely helpful. Leaders must know what resources they have before they develop their plans and design their strategies.

Zelophehad's Daughters

27 The daughters of Zelophehad son of Hepher, the son of Gilead, the son of Makir, the son of Manasseh, belonged to the clans of Manasseh son of Joseph. The names of the daughters were Mahlah, Noah, Hoglah, Milkah and Tirzah. They came forward 2 and stood before Moses, Eleazar the priest, the leaders and the whole assembly at the entrance to the tent of meeting and said, 3 "Our father died in the

---

[a] 40 Samaritan Pentateuch and Vulgate (see also Septuagint); Masoretic Text does not have through Ard.   [b] 59 Or Jochebed, a daughter of Levi, who was born to Levi

wilderness. He was not among Korah's followers, who banded together against the Lord, but he died for his own sin and left no sons. [4]Why should our father's name disappear from his clan because he had no son? Give us property among our father's relatives."

[5]So Moses brought their case before the Lord, [6]and the Lord said to him, [7]"What Zelophehad's daughters are saying is right. You must certainly give them property as an inheritance among their father's relatives and give their father's inheritance to them.

[8]"Say to the Israelites, 'If a man dies and leaves no son, give his inheritance to his daughter. [9]If he has no daughter, give his inheritance to his brothers. [10]If he has no brothers, give his inheritance to his father's brothers. [11]If his father had no brothers, give his inheritance to the nearest relative in his clan, that he may possess it. This is to have the force of law for the Israelites, as the Lord commanded Moses.'"

Joshua to Succeed Moses

[12]Then the Lord said to Moses, "Go up this mountain in the Abarim Range and see the land I have given the Israelites. [13]After you have seen it, you too will be gathered to your people, as your brother Aaron was, [14]for when the community rebelled at the waters in the Desert of Zin, both of you disobeyed my command to honor me as holy before their eyes." (These were the waters of Meribah Kadesh, in the Desert of Zin.)

[15]Moses said to the Lord, [16]"May the Lord, the God who gives breath to all living things, appoint someone over this community [17]to go out and come in before them, one who will lead them out and bring them in, so the Lord's people will not be like sheep without a shepherd."

[18]So the Lord said to Moses, "Take Joshua son of Nun, a man in whom is the spirit of leadership,[a] and lay your hand on him. [19]Have him stand before Eleazar the priest and the entire assembly and commission him in their presence. [20]Give him some of your authority so the whole Israelite community will obey him. [21]He is to stand before Eleazar the priest, who will obtain decisions for him by inquiring of the Urim before the Lord. At his command he and the entire community of the Israelites will go out, and at his command they will come in."

[22]Moses did as the Lord commanded him. He took Joshua and had him stand before Eleazar the priest and the whole assembly. [23]Then he laid his hands on him and commissioned him, as the Lord instructed through Moses.

Daily Offerings

28 The Lord said to Moses, [2]"Give this command to the Israelites and say to them: 'Make sure that you present to me at the appointed time my food offerings, as an aroma pleasing to me.' [3]Say to them: 'This is the food offering you are to present to the Lord: two lambs a year old without defect, as a regular burnt offering each day. [4]Offer one lamb in the morning and the other at twilight, [5]together with a grain offering of a tenth of an ephah[b] of the finest flour mixed with a quarter of a hin[c] of oil from pressed olives. [6]This is the regular burnt offering instituted at Mount Sinai as a pleasing aroma, a food offering presented to the Lord. [7]The accompanying drink offering is to be a quarter of a hin of fermented drink with each lamb. Pour out the drink offering to the Lord at the sanctuary. [8]Offer the second lamb at twilight, along with the same kind of grain offering and drink offering that you offer in the morning. This is a food offering, an aroma pleasing to the Lord.

Sabbath Offerings

[9]"'On the Sabbath day, make an offering of two lambs a year old without defect, together with its drink offering and a grain offering of two-tenths of an ephah[d] of the finest flour mixed with olive oil. [10]This is the burnt offering for every Sabbath, in addition to the regular burnt offering and its drink offering.

Monthly Offerings

[11]"'On the first of every month, present to the Lord a burnt offering of two young bulls, one ram and seven male lambs a year old, all without defect. [12]With each bull there is to be a grain offering of three-tenths of an ephah[e] of the finest flour mixed with oil; with the ram, a grain offering of two-tenths of an ephah of the finest flour mixed with oil; [13]and with each lamb, a grain offering of a tenth of an ephah of the finest flour mixed with oil. This is for a burnt offering, a pleasing aroma, a food offering presented to the Lord. [14]With each bull there is to be a drink offering of half a hin[f] of wine; with the ram, a third of a hin[g]; and with each lamb, a quarter of

---

[a] 18 Or *the Spirit*   [b] 5 That is, probably about 3 1/2 pounds or about 1.6 kilograms; also in verses 13, 21 and 29   [c] 5 That is, about 1 quart or about 1 liter; also in verses 7 and 14
[d] 9 That is, probably about 7 pounds or about 3.2 kilograms; also in verses 12, 20 and 28   [e] 12 That is, probably about 11 pounds or about 5 kilograms; also in verses 20 and 28
[f] 14 That is, about 2 quarts or about 1.9 liters   [g] 14 That is, about 1 1/3 quarts or about 1.3 liters

A Leader's Legacy

Numbers 27:18–23

Of all the wonderful ways Moses expressed his leadership, the most strategic had to be his training of Joshua, who was destined to become the key element of Moses' legacy.

Joshua became the leader who would complete the task of leading the people into the promised land. This successful handoff resulted from Moses' example and equipping and from Joshua's hunger and giftedness. Moses passed along his authority, abilities and anointing to Joshua. He gave Joshua his time, his insight, a learning environment, an opportunity to prove himself, and a strong belief in his future. Because Moses spent the time necessary to equip Joshua, his dream of Israel entering the promised land came to pass even though he did not personally see it happen.

Notice the ways in which Moses passed along his legacy:

1. Moses **empowered** Joshua and gave him **authority** (Nu 27:20). When the time came, Moses laid his hands on Joshua and publicly commissioned him. He gave Joshua part of his authority (Nu 27:15–23). Joshua received positive recognition, a leader's approval and acceptance, and Moses' expression of faith in him. After Moses died, no one questioned Joshua's leadership.

2. Moses gave Joshua **experience** and opportunities for **application** (Nu 27:21–22). Joshua's apprenticeship went beyond the merely cerebral or passive. Moses and Joshua did more than talk over coffee; the apprenticeship involved hands-on experience. Moses shared his life and his responsibilities with Joshua by allowing him to prove his leadership as a spy, as a military commander, and as his personal assistant.

3. Moses gave Joshua **encouragement** and **affirmation** (Nu 27:23). Moses repeatedly affirmed his young protégé by taking him along on excursions exclusive of anyone else. They shared a unique intimacy, almost startling considering the difference in their ages. Moses encouraged his apprentice both through his words and his time.

a hin. This is the monthly burnt offering to be made at each new moon during the year. ¹⁵Besides the regular burnt offering with its drink offering, one male goat is to be presented to the LORD as a sin offering.ᵃ

The Passover

¹⁶"'On the fourteenth day of the first month the LORD's Passover is to be held. ¹⁷On the fifteenth day of this month there is to be a festival; for seven days eat bread made without yeast. ¹⁸On the first day hold a sacred assembly and do no regular work. ¹⁹Present to the LORD a food offering consisting of a burnt offering of two young bulls, one ram and seven male lambs a year old, all without defect. ²⁰With each bull offer a grain offering of three-tenths of an ephah of the finest flour mixed with oil; with the ram, two-tenths; ²¹and with each of the seven lambs, one-tenth. ²²Include one male goat as a sin offering to make atonement for you. ²³Offer these in addition to the regular morning burnt offering. ²⁴In this way present the food offering every day for seven days

as an aroma pleasing to the LORD; it is to be offered in addition to the regular burnt offering and its drink offering. ²⁵On the seventh day hold a sacred assembly and do no regular work.

The Festival of Weeks

²⁶"'On the day of firstfruits, when you present to the LORD an offering of new grain during the Festival of Weeks, hold a sacred assembly and do no regular work. ²⁷Present a burnt offering of two young bulls, one ram and seven male lambs a year old as an aroma pleasing to the LORD. ²⁸With each bull there is to be a grain offering of three-tenths of an ephah of the finest flour mixed with oil; with the ram, two-tenths; ²⁹and with each of the seven lambs, one-tenth. ³⁰Include one male goat to make atonement for you. ³¹Offer these together with their drink offerings, in addition to the regular burnt offering and its grain offering. Be sure the animals are without defect.

ᵃ 15 Or purification offering; also in verse 22

The Festival of Trumpets

29 "'On the first day of the seventh month hold a sacred assembly and do no regular work. It is a day for you to sound the trumpets. [2]As an aroma pleasing to the LORD, offer a burnt offering of one young bull, one ram and seven male lambs a year old, all without defect. [3]With the bull offer a grain offering of three-tenths of an ephah[a] of the finest flour mixed with olive oil; with the ram, two-tenths[b]; [4]and with each of the seven lambs, one-tenth.[c] [5]Include one male goat as a sin offering[d] to make atonement for you. [6]These are in addition to the monthly and daily burnt offerings with their grain offerings and drink offerings as specified. They are food offerings presented to the LORD, a pleasing aroma.

The Day of Atonement

[7]"'On the tenth day of this seventh month hold a sacred assembly. You must deny yourselves[e] and do no work. [8]Present as an aroma pleasing to the LORD a burnt offering of one young bull, one ram and seven male lambs a year old, all without defect. [9]With the bull offer a grain offering of three-tenths of an ephah of the finest flour mixed with oil; with the ram, two-tenths; [10]and with each of the seven lambs, one-tenth. [11]Include one male goat as a sin offering, in addition to the sin offering for atonement and the regular burnt offering with its grain offering, and their drink offerings.

The Festival of Tabernacles

[12]"'On the fifteenth day of the seventh month, hold a sacred assembly and do no regular work. Celebrate a festival to the LORD for seven days. [13]Present as an aroma pleasing to the LORD a food offering consisting of a burnt offering of thirteen young bulls, two rams and fourteen male lambs a year old, all without defect. [14]With each of the thirteen bulls offer a grain offering of three-tenths of an ephah of the finest flour mixed with oil; with each of the two rams, two-tenths; [15]and with each of the fourteen lambs, one-tenth. [16]Include one male goat as a sin offering, in addition to the regular burnt offering with its grain offering and drink offering.

[17]"'On the second day offer twelve young bulls, two rams and fourteen male lambs a year old, all without defect. [18]With the bulls, rams and lambs, offer their grain offerings and drink offerings according to the number specified. [19]Include one male goat as a sin offering, in addition to the regular burnt offering with its grain offering, and their drink offerings.

[20]"'On the third day offer eleven bulls, two rams and fourteen male lambs a year old, all without defect. [21]With the bulls, rams and lambs, offer their grain offerings and drink offerings according to the number specified. [22]Include one male goat as a sin offering, in addition to the regular burnt offering with its grain offering and drink offering.

[23]"'On the fourth day offer ten bulls, two rams and fourteen male lambs a year old, all without defect. [24]With the bulls, rams and lambs, offer their grain offerings and drink offerings according to the number specified. [25]Include one male goat as a sin offering, in addition to the regular burnt offering with its grain offering and drink offering.

[26]"'On the fifth day offer nine bulls, two rams and fourteen male lambs a year old, all without defect. [27]With the bulls, rams and lambs, offer their grain offerings and drink offerings according to the number specified. [28]Include one male goat as a sin offering, in addition to the regular burnt offering with its grain offering and drink offering.

[29]"'On the sixth day offer eight bulls, two rams and fourteen male lambs a year old, all without defect. [30]With the bulls, rams and lambs, offer their grain offerings and drink offerings according to the number specified. [31]Include one male goat as a sin offering, in addition to the regular burnt offering with its grain offering and drink offering.

[32]"'On the seventh day offer seven bulls, two rams and fourteen male lambs a year old, all without defect. [33]With the bulls, rams and lambs, offer their grain offerings and drink offerings according to the number specified. [34]Include one male goat as a sin offering, in addition to the regular burnt offering with its grain offering and drink offering.

[35]"'On the eighth day hold a closing special assembly and do no regular work. [36]Present as an aroma pleasing to the LORD a food offering consisting of a burnt offering of one bull, one ram and seven male lambs a year old, all without defect. [37]With the bull, the ram and the lambs, offer their grain offerings and drink offerings according to the number specified. [38]Include one male goat as a sin offering, in addition

---

[a] 3 That is, probably about 11 pounds or about 5 kilograms; also in verses 9 and 14   [b] 3 That is, probably about 7 pounds or about 3.2 kilograms; also in verses 9 and 14   [c] 4 That is, probably about 3 1/2 pounds or about 1.6 kilograms; also in verses 10 and 15   [d] 5 Or *purification offering*; also elsewhere in this chapter   [e] 7 Or *must fast*

to the regular burnt offering with its grain offering and drink offering.

[39] "'In addition to what you vow and your freewill offerings, offer these to the LORD at your appointed festivals: your burnt offerings, grain offerings, drink offerings and fellowship offerings.'"

[40] Moses told the Israelites all that the LORD commanded him.[a]

Vows

30[b] Moses said to the heads of the tribes of Israel: "This is what the LORD commands: [2] When a man makes a vow to the LORD or takes an oath to obligate himself by a pledge, he must not break his word but must do everything he said.

[3] "When a young woman still living in her father's household makes a vow to the LORD or obligates herself by a pledge [4] and her father hears about her vow or pledge but says nothing to her, then all her vows and every pledge by which she obligated herself will stand. [5] But if her father forbids her when he hears about it, none of her vows or the pledges by which she obligated herself will stand; the LORD will release her because her father has forbidden her.

[6] "If she marries after she makes a vow or after her lips utter a rash promise by which she obligates herself [7] and her husband hears about it but says nothing to her, then her vows or the pledges by which she obligated herself will stand. [8] But if her husband forbids her when he hears about it, he nullifies the vow that obligates her or the rash promise by which she obligates herself, and the LORD will release her.

[9] "Any vow or obligation taken by a widow or divorced woman will be binding on her.

[10] "If a woman living with her husband makes a vow or obligates herself by a pledge under oath [11] and her husband hears about it but says nothing to her and does not forbid her, then all her vows or the pledges by which she obligated herself will stand. [12] But if her husband nullifies them when he hears about them, then none of the vows or pledges that came from her lips will stand. Her husband has nullified them, and the LORD will release her. [13] Her husband may confirm or nullify any vow she makes or any sworn pledge to deny herself.[c] [14] But if her husband says nothing to her about it from day to day, then he confirms all her vows or the pledges binding on her. He confirms them by saying nothing to her when he hears about them. [15] If, however, he nullifies them some time after he hears about

them, then he must bear the consequences of her wrongdoing."

[16] These are the regulations the LORD gave Moses concerning relationships between a man and his wife, and between a father and his young daughter still living at home.

Vengeance on the Midianites

31 The LORD said to Moses, [2] "Take vengeance on the Midianites for the Israelites. After that, you will be gathered to your people."

[3] So Moses said to the people, "Arm some of your men to go to war against the Midianites so that they may carry out the LORD's vengeance on them. [4] Send into battle a thousand men from each of the tribes of Israel." [5] So twelve thousand men armed for battle, a thousand from each tribe, were supplied from the clans of Israel. [6] Moses sent them into battle, a thousand from each tribe, along with Phinehas son of Eleazar, the priest, who took with him articles from the sanctuary and the trumpets for signaling.

[7] They fought against Midian, as the LORD commanded Moses, and killed every man. [8] Among their victims were Evi, Rekem, Zur, Hur and Reba — the five kings of Midian. They also killed Balaam son of Beor with the sword. [9] The Israelites captured the Midianite women and children and took all the Midianite herds, flocks and goods as plunder. [10] They burned all the towns where the Midianites had settled, as well as all their camps. [11] They took all the plunder and spoils, including the people and animals, [12] and brought the captives, spoils and plunder to Moses and Eleazar the priest and the Israelite assembly at their camp on the plains of Moab, by the Jordan across from Jericho.

[13] Moses, Eleazar the priest and all the leaders of the community went to meet them outside the camp. [14] Moses was angry with the officers of the army — the commanders of thousands and commanders of hundreds — who returned from the battle.

[15] "Have you allowed all the women to live?" he asked them. [16] "They were the ones who followed Balaam's advice and enticed the Israelites to be unfaithful to the LORD in the Peor incident, so that a plague struck the LORD's people. [17] Now kill all the boys. And kill every woman who has slept with a man, [18] but save for yourselves every girl who has never slept with a man. [19] "Anyone who has killed someone or touched

---

[a] 40 In Hebrew texts this verse (29:40) is numbered 30:1.   [b] In Hebrew texts 30:1-16 is numbered 30:2-17.   [c] 13 Or to fast

someone who was killed must stay outside the camp seven days. On the third and seventh days you must purify yourselves and your captives. ²⁰Purify every garment as well as everything made of leather, goat hair or wood."

²¹Then Eleazar the priest said to the soldiers who had gone into battle, "This is what is required by the law that the LORD gave Moses: ²²Gold, silver, bronze, iron, tin, lead ²³and anything else that can withstand fire must be put through the fire, and then it will be clean. But it must also be purified with the water of cleansing. And whatever cannot withstand fire must be put through that water. ²⁴On the seventh day wash your clothes and you will be clean. Then you may come into the camp."

Dividing the Spoils

²⁵The LORD said to Moses, ²⁶"You and Eleazar the priest and the family heads of the community are to count all the people and animals that were captured. ²⁷Divide the spoils equally between the soldiers who took part in the battle and the rest of the community. ²⁸From the soldiers who fought in the battle, set apart as tribute for the LORD one out of every five hundred, whether people, cattle, donkeys or sheep. ²⁹Take this tribute from their half share and give it to Eleazar the priest as the LORD's part. ³⁰From the Israelites' half, select one out of every fifty, whether people, cattle, donkeys, sheep or other animals. Give them to the Levites, who are responsible for the care of the LORD's tabernacle." ³¹So Moses and Eleazar the priest did as the LORD commanded Moses.

³²The plunder remaining from the spoils that the soldiers took was 675,000 sheep, ³³72,000 cattle, ³⁴61,000 donkeys ³⁵and 32,000 women who had never slept with a man. ³⁶The half share of those who fought in the battle was:

    337,500 sheep, ³⁷of which the tribute for
        the LORD was 675;
    ³⁸36,000 cattle, of which the tribute for the
        LORD was 72;
    ³⁹30,500 donkeys, of which the tribute for
        the LORD was 61;
    ⁴⁰16,000 people, of whom the tribute for the
        LORD was 32.

⁴¹Moses gave the tribute to Eleazar the priest as the LORD's part, as the LORD commanded Moses.

⁴²The half belonging to the Israelites, which Moses set apart from that of the fighting men—

⁴³the community's half—was 337,500 sheep, ⁴⁴36,000 cattle, ⁴⁵30,500 donkeys ⁴⁶and 16,000 people. ⁴⁷From the Israelites' half, Moses selected one out of every fifty people and animals, as the LORD commanded him, and gave them to the Levites, who were responsible for the care of the LORD's tabernacle.

⁴⁸Then the officers who were over the units of the army—the commanders of thousands and commanders of hundreds—went to Moses ⁴⁹and said to him, "Your servants have counted the soldiers under our command, and not one is missing. ⁵⁰So we have brought as an offering to the LORD the gold articles each of us acquired— armlets, bracelets, signet rings, earrings and necklaces—to make atonement for ourselves before the LORD."

⁵¹Moses and Eleazar the priest accepted from them the gold—all the crafted articles. ⁵²All the gold from the commanders of thousands and commanders of hundreds that Moses and Eleazar presented as a gift to the LORD weighed 16,750 shekels.ᵃ ⁵³Each soldier had taken plunder for himself. ⁵⁴Moses and Eleazar the priest accepted the gold from the commanders of thousands and commanders of hundreds and brought it into the tent of meeting as a memorial for the Israelites before the LORD.

The Transjordan Tribes

32 The Reubenites and Gadites, who had very large herds and flocks, saw that the lands of Jazer and Gilead were suitable for livestock. ²So they came to Moses and Eleazar the priest and to the leaders of the community, and said, ³"Ataroth, Dibon, Jazer, Nimrah, Heshbon, Elealeh, Sebam, Nebo and Beon— ⁴the land the LORD subdued before the people of Israel—are suitable for livestock, and your servants have livestock. ⁵If we have found favor in your eyes," they said, "let this land be given to your servants as our possession. Do not make us cross the Jordan."

⁶Moses said to the Gadites and Reubenites, "Should your fellow Israelites go to war while you sit here? ⁷Why do you discourage the Israelites from crossing over into the land the LORD has given them? ⁸This is what your fathers did when I sent them from Kadesh Barnea to look over the land. ⁹After they went up to the Valley of Eshkol and viewed the land, they discouraged the Israelites from entering the land the LORD had given them. ¹⁰The LORD's anger was

---

ᵃ 52 That is, about 420 pounds or about 190 kilograms

aroused that day and he swore this oath: [11]'Because they have not followed me wholeheartedly, not one of those who were twenty years old or more when they came up out of Egypt will see the land I promised on oath to Abraham, Isaac and Jacob— [12]not one except Caleb son of Jephunneh the Kenizzite and Joshua son of Nun, for they followed the LORD wholeheartedly.' [13]The LORD's anger burned against Israel and he made them wander in the wilderness forty years, until the whole generation of those who had done evil in his sight was gone.

[14]"And here you are, a brood of sinners, standing in the place of your fathers and making the LORD even more angry with Israel. [15]If you turn away from following him, he will again leave all this people in the wilderness, and you will be the cause of their destruction."

[16]Then they came up to him and said, "We would like to build pens here for our livestock and cities for our women and children. [17]But we will arm ourselves for battle[a] and go ahead of the Israelites until we have brought them to their place. Meanwhile our women and children will live in fortified cities, for protection from the inhabitants of the land. [18]We will not return to our homes until each of the Israelites has received their inheritance. [19]We will not receive any inheritance with them on the other side of the Jordan, because our inheritance has come to us on the east side of the Jordan."

[20]Then Moses said to them, "If you will do this—if you will arm yourselves before the LORD for battle [21]and if all of you who are armed cross over the Jordan before the LORD until he has driven his enemies out before him — [22]then when the land is subdued before the LORD, you may return and be free from your obligation to the LORD and to Israel. And this land will be your possession before the LORD.

[23]"But if you fail to do this, you will be sinning against the LORD; and you may be sure that your sin will find you out. [24]Build cities for your women and children, and pens for your flocks, but do what you have promised."

[25]The Gadites and Reubenites said to Moses, "We your servants will do as our lord commands. [26]Our children and wives, our flocks and herds will remain here in the cities of Gilead. [27]But your servants, every man who is armed for battle, will cross over to fight before the LORD, just as our lord says."

[28]Then Moses gave orders about them to Eleazar the priest and Joshua son of Nun and to the family heads of the Israelite tribes. [29]He said to them, "If the Gadites and Reubenites, every man armed for battle, cross over the Jordan with you before the LORD, then when the land is subdued before you, you must give them the land of Gilead as their possession. [30]But if they do not cross over with you armed, they must accept their possession with you in Canaan."

[31]The Gadites and Reubenites answered, "Your servants will do what the LORD has said. [32]We will cross over before the LORD into Canaan armed, but the property we inherit will be on this side of the Jordan."

[33]Then Moses gave to the Gadites, the Reubenites and the half-tribe of Manasseh son of Joseph the kingdom of Sihon king of the Amorites and the kingdom of Og king of Bashan — the whole land with its cities and the territory around them.

[34]The Gadites built up Dibon, Ataroth, Aroer, [35]Atroth Shophan, Jazer, Jogbehah, [36]Beth Nimrah and Beth Haran as fortified cities, and built pens for their flocks. [37]And the Reubenites rebuilt Heshbon, Elealeh and Kiriathaim, [38]as well as Nebo and Baal Meon (these names were changed) and Sibmah. They gave names to the cities they rebuilt.

[39]The descendants of Makir son of Manasseh went to Gilead, captured it and drove out the Amorites who were there. [40]So Moses gave Gilead to the Makirites, the descendants of Manasseh, and they settled there. [41]Jair, a descendant of Manasseh, captured their settlements and called them Havvoth Jair.[b] [42]And Nobah captured Kenath and its surrounding settlements and called it Nobah after himself.

Stages in Israel's Journey

33 Here are the stages in the journey of the Israelites when they came out of Egypt by divisions under the leadership of Moses and Aaron. [2]At the LORD's command Moses recorded the stages in their journey. This is their journey by stages:

[3]The Israelites set out from Rameses on the fifteenth day of the first month, the day after the Passover. They marched out defiantly in full view of all the Egyptians, [4]who were burying all their firstborn, whom the LORD had struck down among them; for the LORD had brought judgment on their gods.

[a] 17 Septuagint; Hebrew *will be quick to arm ourselves*
[b] 41 Or *them the settlements of Jair*

⁵The Israelites left Rameses and camped at Sukkoth.

⁶They left Sukkoth and camped at Etham, on the edge of the desert.

⁷They left Etham, turned back to Pi Hahiroth, to the east of Baal Zephon, and camped near Migdol.

⁸They left Pi Hahiroth[a] and passed through the sea into the desert, and when they had traveled for three days in the Desert of Etham, they camped at Marah.

⁹They left Marah and went to Elim, where there were twelve springs and seventy palm trees, and they camped there.

¹⁰They left Elim and camped by the Red Sea.[b]

¹¹They left the Red Sea and camped in the Desert of Sin.

¹²They left the Desert of Sin and camped at Dophkah.

¹³They left Dophkah and camped at Alush.

¹⁴They left Alush and camped at Rephidim, where there was no water for the people to drink.

¹⁵They left Rephidim and camped in the Desert of Sinai.

¹⁶They left the Desert of Sinai and camped at Kibroth Hattaavah.

¹⁷They left Kibroth Hattaavah and camped at Hazeroth.

¹⁸They left Hazeroth and camped at Rithmah.

¹⁹They left Rithmah and camped at Rimmon Perez.

²⁰They left Rimmon Perez and camped at Libnah.

²¹They left Libnah and camped at Rissah.

²²They left Rissah and camped at Kehelathah.

²³They left Kehelathah and camped at Mount Shepher.

²⁴They left Mount Shepher and camped at Haradah.

²⁵They left Haradah and camped at Makheloth.

²⁶They left Makheloth and camped at Tahath.

²⁷They left Tahath and camped at Terah.

²⁸They left Terah and camped at Mithkah.

²⁹They left Mithkah and camped at Hashmonah.

³⁰They left Hashmonah and camped at Moseroth.

³¹They left Moseroth and camped at Bene Jaakan.

³²They left Bene Jaakan and camped at Hor Haggidgad.

³³They left Hor Haggidgad and camped at Jotbathah.

³⁴They left Jotbathah and camped at Abronah.

³⁵They left Abronah and camped at Ezion Geber.

³⁶They left Ezion Geber and camped at Kadesh, in the Desert of Zin.

³⁷They left Kadesh and camped at Mount Hor, on the border of Edom. ³⁸At the LORD's command Aaron the priest went up Mount Hor, where he died on the first day of the fifth month of the fortieth year after the Israelites came out of Egypt. ³⁹Aaron was a hundred and twenty-three years old when he died on Mount Hor.

⁴⁰The Canaanite king of Arad, who lived in the Negev of Canaan, heard that the Israelites were coming.

⁴¹They left Mount Hor and camped at Zalmonah.

⁴²They left Zalmonah and camped at Punon.

⁴³They left Punon and camped at Oboth.

⁴⁴They left Oboth and camped at Iye Abarim, on the border of Moab.

⁴⁵They left Iye Abarim and camped at Dibon Gad.

⁴⁶They left Dibon Gad and camped at Almon Diblathaim.

⁴⁷They left Almon Diblathaim and camped in the mountains of Abarim, near Nebo.

⁴⁸They left the mountains of Abarim and camped on the plains of Moab by the Jordan across from Jericho. ⁴⁹There on the plains of Moab they camped along the Jordan from Beth Jeshimoth to Abel Shittim.

⁵⁰On the plains of Moab by the Jordan across from Jericho the LORD said to Moses, ⁵¹"Speak to the Israelites and say to them: 'When you cross the Jordan into Canaan, ⁵²drive out all the inhabitants of the land before you. Destroy all their carved images and their cast idols, and

---

a 8 Many manuscripts of the Masoretic Text, Samaritan Pentateuch and Vulgate; most manuscripts of the Masoretic Text *left from before Hahiroth*   *b 10* Or *the Sea of Reeds*; also in verse 11

21 QUALITIES

Numbers 33:1–49

WE MUST travel on the inside before we can travel on the outside, because the journey of growth and success is first an internal one. The first person you lead is you—and you can't lead effectively without self-discipline.

If only the Israelites had remembered this lesson! Numbers 33 provides a review of the entire exodus journey, from Egypt to Jordan. And, boy, was it ever a journey! Tons of manna. Far too much grumbling. And it lasted 40 years.

Why didn't the Israelites get to the promised land more quickly? Not because it lay so far away; they could have made the trip in two weeks. The real reason boils down to preparation. The people simply weren't ready for God's blessing until 40 years after they began their trip.

How about you? How is your self-discipline? Plato said, "The first and best victory is to conquer self." If you want to be a leader with self-discipline, follow these action points:

1. Develop and follow your priorities. All leaders are pressed for time, but the successful ones have a plan. If you can determine what's really a priority and release yourself from everything else, it will be much easier to follow through on what's important. That's the essence of self-discipline.

2. Make a disciplined lifestyle your goal. To be successful, self-discipline can't be a onetime event. It has to become a lifestyle. One of the best ways to nurture such a lifestyle is to develop systems and routines, especially in areas crucial to your long-term growth and success. Once you have them, put them to use every day for the rest of your life.

3. Challenge your excuses. Challenge and eliminate any tendency you may have to make excuses. If you can name several reasons why you can't be self-disciplined, realize that they are really just barriers to your success—all of which need to be challenged if you want to go to the next level.

4. Remove rewards until you finish the job. If you lack self-discipline, you may be in the habit of enjoying dessert before eating your vegetables. Mike Delaney offered good counsel: He said that businesses need to differentiate between their shirkers and their workers, because if they reward both the same, they'll soon find they have a lot more of the former than the latter!

5. Stay focused on results. Anytime you concentrate on the difficulty of the work instead of its results, you're likely to become discouraged. The next time you're facing a must-do task and you're thinking of doing what's convenient instead of paying the price, change your focus. Count the benefits of doing what's right, and then dive in.

For a negative example of self-discipline, see p. 298.

demolish all their high places. ⁵³Take possession of the land and settle in it, for I have given you the land to possess. ⁵⁴Distribute the land by lot, according to your clans. To a larger group give a larger inheritance, and to a smaller group a smaller one. Whatever falls to them by lot will be theirs. Distribute it according to your ancestral tribes.

⁵⁵"But if you do not drive out the inhabitants of the land, those you allow to remain will become barbs in your eyes and thorns in your sides. They will give you trouble in the land where you will live. ⁵⁶And then I will do to you what I plan to do to them.'"

Boundaries of Canaan

34 The LORD said to Moses, ²"Command the Israelites and say to them: 'When you enter Canaan, the land that will be allotted to you as an inheritance is to have these boundaries:

³"'Your southern side will include some of the Desert of Zin along the border of Edom. Your southern boundary will start in the east from the southern end of the Dead Sea, ⁴cross south of Scorpion Pass, continue on to Zin and go south of Kadesh Barnea. Then it will go to Hazar Addar and over to Azmon, ⁵where it will turn, join the Wadi of Egypt and end at the Mediterranean Sea.

⁶"'Your western boundary will be the coast of the Mediterranean Sea. This will be your boundary on the west.

⁷"'For your northern boundary, run a line from the Mediterranean Sea to Mount Hor ⁸and from Mount Hor to Lebo Hamath. Then the boundary will go to Zedad, ⁹continue to Ziphron and end at Hazar Enan. This will be your boundary on the north.

¹⁰"'For your eastern boundary, run a line from Hazar Enan to Shepham. ¹¹The boundary will go down from Shepham to Riblah on the east side of Ain and continue along the slopes east of the Sea of Galilee.ᵃ ¹²Then the boundary will go down along the Jordan and end at the Dead Sea.

"'This will be your land, with its boundaries on every side.'"

¹³Moses commanded the Israelites: "Assign this land by lot as an inheritance. The LORD has ordered that it be given to the nine and a half tribes, ¹⁴because the families of the tribe of Reuben, the tribe of Gad and the half-tribe of Manasseh have received their inheritance. ¹⁵These two and a half tribes have received their inheri-

tance east of the Jordan across from Jericho, toward the sunrise."

¹⁶The LORD said to Moses, ¹⁷"These are the names of the men who are to assign the land for you as an inheritance: Eleazar the priest and Joshua son of Nun. ¹⁸And appoint one leader from each tribe to help assign the land. ¹⁹These are their names:

Caleb son of Jephunneh,
    from the tribe of Judah;
²⁰Shemuel son of Ammihud,
    from the tribe of Simeon;
²¹Elidad son of Kislon,
    from the tribe of Benjamin;
²²Bukki son of Jogli,
    the leader from the tribe of Dan;
²³Hanniel son of Ephod,
    the leader from the tribe of Manasseh
    son of Joseph;
²⁴Kemuel son of Shiphtan,
    the leader from the tribe of Ephraim son
    of Joseph;
²⁵Elizaphan son of Parnak,
    the leader from the tribe of Zebulun;
²⁶Paltiel son of Azzan,
    the leader from the tribe of Issachar;
²⁷Ahihud son of Shelomi,
    the leader from the tribe of Asher;
²⁸Pedahel son of Ammihud,
    the leader from the tribe of Naphtali."

²⁹These are the men the LORD commanded to assign the inheritance to the Israelites in the land of Canaan.

Towns for the Levites

35 On the plains of Moab by the Jordan across from Jericho, the LORD said to Moses, ²"Command the Israelites to give the Levites towns to live in from the inheritance the Israelites will possess. And give them pasturelands around the towns. ³Then they will have towns to live in and pasturelands for the cattle they own and all their other animals.

⁴"The pasturelands around the towns that you give the Levites will extend a thousand cubitsᵇ from the town wall. ⁵Outside the town, measure two thousand cubitsᶜ on the east side, two thousand on the south side, two thousand on the west and two thousand on the north, with the town in the center. They will have this area as pastureland for the towns.

ᵃ 11 Hebrew Kinnereth   ᵇ 4 That is, about 1,500 feet or about 450 meters   ᶜ 5 That is, about 3,000 feet or about 900 meters

Cities of Refuge

⁶"Six of the towns you give the Levites will be cities of refuge, to which a person who has killed someone may flee. In addition, give them forty-two other towns. ⁷In all you must give the Levites forty-eight towns, together with their pasturelands. ⁸The towns you give the Levites from the land the Israelites possess are to be given in proportion to the inheritance of each tribe: Take many towns from a tribe that has many, but few from one that has few."

⁹Then the LORD said to Moses: ¹⁰"Speak to the Israelites and say to them: 'When you cross the Jordan into Canaan, ¹¹select some towns to be your cities of refuge, to which a person who has killed someone accidentally may flee. ¹²They will be places of refuge from the avenger, so that anyone accused of murder may not die before they stand trial before the assembly. ¹³These six towns you give will be your cities of refuge. ¹⁴Give three on this side of the Jordan and three in Canaan as cities of refuge. ¹⁵These six towns will be a place of refuge for Israelites and for foreigners residing among them, so that anyone who has killed another accidentally can flee there.

¹⁶"'If anyone strikes someone a fatal blow with an iron object, that person is a murderer; the murderer is to be put to death. ¹⁷Or if anyone is holding a stone and strikes someone a fatal blow with it, that person is a murderer; the murderer is to be put to death. ¹⁸Or if anyone is holding a wooden object and strikes someone a fatal blow with it, that person is a murderer; the murderer is to be put to death. ¹⁹The avenger of blood shall put the murderer to death; when the avenger comes upon the murderer, the avenger shall put the murderer to death. ²⁰If anyone with malice aforethought shoves another or throws something at them intentionally so that they die ²¹or if out of enmity one person hits another with their fist so that the other dies, that person is to be put to death; that person is a murderer. The avenger of blood shall put the murderer to death when they meet.

²²"'But if without enmity someone suddenly pushes another or throws something at them unintentionally ²³or, without seeing them, drops on them a stone heavy enough to kill them, and they die, then since that other person was not an enemy and no harm was intended, ²⁴the assembly must judge between the accused and the avenger of blood according to these regulations. ²⁵The assembly must protect the one accused of murder from the avenger of blood and send the accused back to the city of refuge to which they fled. The accused must stay there until the death of the high priest, who was anointed with the holy oil.

²⁶"'But if the accused ever goes outside the limits of the city of refuge to which they fled ²⁷and the avenger of blood finds them outside the city, the avenger of blood may kill the accused without being guilty of murder. ²⁸The accused must stay in the city of refuge until the death of the high priest; only after the death of the high priest may they return to their own property.

²⁹"'This is to have the force of law for you throughout the generations to come, wherever you live.

³⁰"'Anyone who kills a person is to be put to death as a murderer only on the testimony of witnesses. But no one is to be put to death on the testimony of only one witness.

³¹"'Do not accept a ransom for the life of a murderer, who deserves to die. They are to be put to death.

³²"'Do not accept a ransom for anyone who has fled to a city of refuge and so allow them to go back and live on their own land before the death of the high priest.

³³"'Do not pollute the land where you are. Bloodshed pollutes the land, and atonement cannot be made for the land on which blood has been shed, except by the blood of the one who shed it. ³⁴Do not defile the land where you live and where I dwell, for I, the LORD, dwell among the Israelites.'"

Inheritance of Zelophehad's Daughters

36 The family heads of the clan of Gilead son of Makir, the son of Manasseh, who were from the clans of the descendants of Joseph, came and spoke before Moses and the leaders, the heads of the Israelite families. ²They said, "When the LORD commanded my lord to give the land as an inheritance to the Israelites by lot, he ordered you to give the inheritance of our brother Zelophehad to his daughters. ³Now suppose they marry men from other Israelite tribes; then their inheritance will be taken from our ancestral inheritance and added to that of the tribe they marry into. And so part of the inheritance allotted to us will be taken away. ⁴When the Year of Jubilee for the Israelites comes, their inheritance will be added to that of the tribe into which they marry, and their property will be taken from the tribal inheritance of our ancestors."

[5]Then at the LORD's command Moses gave this order to the Israelites: "What the tribe of the descendants of Joseph is saying is right. [6]This is what the LORD commands for Zelophehad's daughters: They may marry anyone they please as long as they marry within their father's tribal clan. [7]No inheritance in Israel is to pass from one tribe to another, for every Israelite shall keep the tribal inheritance of their ancestors. [8]Every daughter who inherits land in any Israelite tribe must marry someone in her father's tribal clan, so that every Israelite will possess the inheritance of their ancestors. [9]No inheritance may pass from one tribe to another, for each Israelite tribe is to keep the land it inherits."

[10]So Zelophehad's daughters did as the LORD commanded Moses. [11]Zelophehad's daughters—Mahlah, Tirzah, Hoglah, Milkah and Noah—married their cousins on their father's side. [12]They married within the clans of the descendants of Manasseh son of Joseph, and their inheritance remained in their father's tribe and clan.

[13]These are the commands and regulations the LORD gave through Moses to the Israelites on the plains of Moab by the Jordan across from Jericho.

INTRODUCTION TO DEUTERONOMY

Consider Deuteronomy a stand-alone book on leadership.

It is more, of course, but Deuteronomy is largely the story of a leader, Moses, who challenges a new generation to embrace and implement a God-given vision for the promised land. Early on, Moses says, "Enter and possess the land the LORD promised on oath to your ancestors" (8:1).

The book tells the story of a leader yearning to finish the work he had begun. Moses casts the vision over and over, hoping his people would catch sight of the total picture—namely, that God did not want merely to free them from slavery in Egypt, but to deliver them into the promised land. Hear a key verse in Deuteronomy: "He brought us out from there to bring us in and give us the land he promised on oath to our ancestors" (6:23).

Deuteronomy begins with Moses recounting all that had happened to the nation. He reminds the people how God had chosen key leaders and placed them over each of the tribes; how he had patiently endured their strife and complaints through 40 years of wandering in the wilderness; how God had led them in conquest over their enemies; and how he had repeated the Ten Commandments to them. Now it was time for this new generation to affirm God's laws, just as their parents had. Although Moses lost his chance to enter the land with them, he patiently interceded for this new generation, trying to lead them into the obedient state that would enable them to inherit the land and finish the conquest.

Deuteronomy consists chiefly of three visionary messages Moses delivered to all Israel, just before he died. His words lead the people to a crossroads at which they

God's Role in Deuteronomy

God promised to Abraham, Isaac and Jacob that he would make them into a great nation. God uses Moses to fulfill that promise. The events recounted in this book fulfill the original promise to build the descendants of Abraham into a nation of people more numerous than the stars in the sky (Ge 12:2–3; Dt 1:10). God leads Moses, who in turn leads the people to the border of the promised land.

Like a brilliant military commander addressing his troops, God displays powerful leadership by steadying his people and readying them for the conquest. He casts vision, providing fresh perspective, provision, purpose and principles to guide the Israelites. In the very first chapter of the book, God prepares his children to:

1. See the land (*vision*, 1:6–8).
2. Share the load (*delegation*, 1:9–14).
3. Select the leaders (*leadership*, 1:15).
4. Structure the leadership (*organization*, 1:16–18).

Leaders in Deuteronomy

Moses, Joshua

Other People of Influence in Deuteronomy

Canaanites, Hittites, Girgashites, Amorites, Perizzites, Hivites, Jebusites must decide their future. Like any good leader, Moses can see the options before the nation and he spells them out in his closing years. It's remarkable how this man, who claimed not to be a good communicator (Ex 4:10), now casts a clear vision for thousands of Israelites about to end their wandering in the desert! Moses dies at the end of the book, but not before preparing an apprentice, Joshua, to take over and finish the journey into Canaan.

Lessons in Leadership

- Develop your core values and beliefs before taking new territory.
- Leadership must be proactive, not reactive.
- Activity does not equal accomplishment.
- Leaders must share the benefits of buying into the vision.
- Leaders must constantly remind the people of the vision.
- One person with courage makes a majority.
- The leader must first intercede for the people.
- Leaders must provide for the future, even when they don't get to experience it.

LEADERSHIP HIGHLIGHTS IN DEUTERONOMY

The Command to Leave Horeb

1 These are the words Moses spoke to all Israel in the wilderness east of the Jordan — that is, in the Arabah — opposite Suph, between Paran and Tophel, Laban, Hazeroth and Dizahab. [2](It takes eleven days to go from Horeb to Kadesh Barnea by the Mount Seir road.)

[3]In the fortieth year, on the first day of the eleventh month, Moses proclaimed to the Israelites all that the LORD had commanded him concerning them. [4]This was after he had defeated Sihon king of the Amorites, who reigned in Heshbon, and at Edrei had defeated Og king of Bashan, who reigned in Ashtaroth.

[5]East of the Jordan in the territory of Moab, Moses began to expound this law, saying:

[6]The LORD our God said to us at Horeb, "You have stayed long enough at this mountain. [7]Break camp and advance into the hill country of the Amorites; go to all the neighboring peoples in the Arabah, in the mountains, in the western foothills, in the Negev and along the coast, to the land of the Canaanites and to Lebanon, as far as the great river, the Euphrates. [8]See, I have given you this land. Go in and take possession of the land the LORD swore he would give to your fathers — to Abraham, Isaac and Jacob — and to their descendants after them."

The Appointment of Leaders

[9]At that time I said to you, "You are too heavy a burden for me to carry alone. [10]The LORD your God has increased your numbers so that today you are as numerous as the stars in the sky. [11]May the LORD, the God of your ancestors, increase you a thousand times and bless you as he has promised! [12]But how can I bear your problems and your burdens and your disputes all by myself? [13]Choose some wise, understanding and respected men from each of your tribes, and I will set them over you."

[14]You answered me, "What you propose to do is good."

[15]So I took the leading men of your tribes, wise and respected men, and appointed them to have authority over you — as commanders of thousands, of hundreds, of fifties and of tens and as tribal officials. [16]And I charged your judges at that time, "Hear the disputes between your people and judge fairly, whether the case is between two Israelites or between an Israelite and a foreigner residing among you. [17]Do not show partiality in judging; hear both small and great alike. Do not be afraid of anyone, for judgment belongs to God. Bring me any case too hard for you, and I will hear it." [18]And at that time I told you everything you were to do.

The Law of the Inner Circle

Deuteronomy 1:6–18

The people closest to us determine our level of success. Moses learned this lesson in the wilderness and so implemented a plan to put competent, godly leaders next to him.

When ministers decide to be leaders, they cross a very important line. They no longer judge themselves solely by what they can do themselves; their value depends mainly on what they can get done through others. Moses teaches us that leaders must:

1. **See the Land: Vision (vv. 6–8)**
   Moses saw and reminded everyone of the Lord's faithfulness. God would fulfill his promise. Moses could clearly see the outcome, and he motivated others by his vision.

2. **Share the Load: Delegation (vv. 9–12)**
   Moses chose to set his ego aside and share his leadership responsibilities with others. He would give them both the responsibility and authority to do the work; the task now became a team effort.

3. **Select the Leaders: Leadership (vv. 13–15)**
   Moses chose his inner circle from among the spiritually qualified, approved, and appointed according to their abilities.

4. **Structure the Leadership: Organization (vv. 16–18)**
   Moses established a system in which the leaders were to listen fairly, minister boldly, make decisions based on principle, and refer the most difficult cases to him.

Spies Sent Out

[19]Then, as the LORD our God commanded us, we set out from Horeb and went toward the hill country of the Amorites through all that vast and dreadful wilderness that you have seen, and so we reached Kadesh Barnea. [20]Then I said to you, "You have reached the hill country of the Amorites, which the LORD our God is giving us. [21]See, the LORD your God has given you the land. Go up and take possession of it as the LORD, the God of your ancestors, told you. Do not be afraid; do not be discouraged."

[22]Then all of you came to me and said, "Let us send men ahead to spy out the land for us and bring back a report about the route we are to take and the towns we will come to."

[23]The idea seemed good to me; so I selected twelve of you, one man from each tribe. [24]They left and went up into the hill country, and came to the Valley of Eshkol and explored it. [25]Taking with them some of the fruit of the land, they brought it down to us and reported, "It is a good land that the LORD our God is giving us."

Rebellion Against the LORD

[26]But you were unwilling to go up; you rebelled against the command of the LORD your God. [27]You grumbled in your tents and said, "The LORD hates us; so he brought us out of Egypt to deliver us into the hands of the Amorites to destroy us. [28]Where can we go? Our brothers have made our hearts melt in fear. They say, 'The people are stronger and taller than we are; the cities are large, with walls up to the sky. We even saw the Anakites there.'"

[29]Then I said to you, "Do not be terrified; do not be afraid of them. [30]The LORD your God, who is going before you, will fight for you, as he did for you in Egypt, before your very eyes, [31]and in the wilderness. There you saw how the LORD your God carried you, as a father carries his son, all the way you went until you reached this place."

[32]In spite of this, you did not trust in the LORD your God, [33]who went ahead of you on your journey, in fire by night and in a cloud by day, to search out places for you to camp and to show you the way you should go.

[34]When the LORD heard what you said, he was angry and solemnly swore: [35]"No one from this evil generation shall see the good land I swore to give your ancestors, [36]except Caleb son of Jephunneh. He will see it, and I will give him and his descendants the land he set his feet on, because he followed the LORD wholeheartedly."

[37]Because of you the LORD became angry with me also and said, "You shall not enter it, either. [38]But your assistant, Joshua son of Nun, will enter it. Encourage him, because he will lead Israel to inherit it. [39]And the little ones that you said would be taken captive, your children who do not yet know good from bad — they will enter the land. I will give it to them and they will take possession of it. [40]But as for you, turn around and set out toward the desert along the route to the Red Sea.[a]"

[41]Then you replied, "We have sinned against the LORD. We will go up and fight, as the LORD our God commanded us." So every one of you put on his weapons, thinking it easy to go up into the hill country.

[42]But the LORD said to me, "Tell them, 'Do not go up and fight, because I will not be with you. You will be defeated by your enemies.'"

[43]So I told you, but you would not listen. You rebelled against the LORD's command and in your arrogance you marched up into the hill country. [44]The Amorites who lived in those hills came out against you; they chased you like a swarm of bees and beat you down from Seir all the way to Hormah. [45]You came back and wept before the LORD, but he paid no attention to your weeping and turned a deaf ear to you. [46]And so you stayed in Kadesh many days — all the time you spent there.

Wanderings in the Wilderness

2 Then we turned back and set out toward the wilderness along the route to the Red Sea,[a] as the LORD had directed me. For a long time we made our way around the hill country of Seir.

[2]Then the LORD said to me, [3]"You have made your way around this hill country long enough; now turn north. [4]Give the people these orders: 'You are about to pass through the territory of your relatives the descendants of Esau, who live in Seir. They will be afraid of you, but be very careful. [5]Do not provoke them to war, for I will not give you any of their land, not even enough to put your foot on. I have given Esau the hill country of Seir as his own. [6]You are to pay them in silver for the food you eat and the water you drink.'"

[7]The LORD your God has blessed you in all the work of your hands. He has watched over your journey through this vast wilderness. These forty years the LORD your God has been with you, and you have not lacked anything.

---

[a] 40,1 Or the Sea of Reeds

[8]So we went on past our relatives the descendants of Esau, who live in Seir. We turned from the Arabah road, which comes up from Elath and Ezion Geber, and traveled along the desert road of Moab.

[9]Then the LORD said to me, "Do not harass the Moabites or provoke them to war, for I will not give you any part of their land. I have given Ar to the descendants of Lot as a possession."

[10](The Emites used to live there—a people strong and numerous, and as tall as the Anakites. [11]Like the Anakites, they too were considered Rephaites, but the Moabites called them Emites. [12]Horites used to live in Seir, but the descendants of Esau drove them out. They destroyed the Horites from before them and settled in their place, just as Israel did in the land the LORD gave them as their possession.)

[13]And the LORD said, "Now get up and cross the Zered Valley." So we crossed the valley.

[14]Thirty-eight years passed from the time we left Kadesh Barnea until we crossed the Zered Valley. By then, that entire generation of fighting men had perished from the camp, as the LORD had sworn to them. [15]The LORD's hand was against them until he had completely eliminated them from the camp.

[16]Now when the last of these fighting men among the people had died, [17]the LORD said to me, [18]"Today you are to pass by the region of Moab at Ar. [19]When you come to the Ammonites, do not harass them or provoke them to war, for I will not give you possession of any land belonging to the Ammonites. I have given it as a possession to the descendants of Lot."

[20](That too was considered a land of the Rephaites, who used to live there; but the Ammonites called them Zamzummites. [21]They were a people strong and numerous, and as tall as the Anakites. The LORD destroyed them from before the Ammonites, who drove them out and settled in their place. [22]The LORD had done the same for the descendants of Esau, who lived in Seir, when he destroyed the Horites from before them. They drove them out and have lived in their place to this day. [23]And as for the Avvites who lived in villages as far as Gaza, the Caphtorites coming out from Caphtor[a] destroyed them and settled in their place.)

Defeat of Sihon King of Heshbon

[24]"Set out now and cross the Arnon Gorge. See, I have given into your hand Sihon the Amorite, king of Heshbon, and his country. Begin to take possession of it and engage him in battle. [25]This very day I will begin to put the terror and fear of you on all the nations under heaven. They will hear reports of you and will tremble and be in anguish because of you."

[26]From the Desert of Kedemoth I sent messengers to Sihon king of Heshbon offering peace and saying, [27]"Let us pass through your country. We will stay on the main road; we will not turn aside to the right or to the left. [28]Sell us food to eat and water to drink for their price in silver. Only let us pass through on foot— [29]as the descendants of Esau, who live in Seir, and the Moabites, who live in Ar, did for us—until we cross the Jordan into the land the LORD our God is giving us." [30]But Sihon king of Heshbon refused to let us pass through. For the LORD your God had made his spirit stubborn and his heart obstinate in order to give him into your hands, as he has now done.

[31]The LORD said to me, "See, I have begun to deliver Sihon and his country over to you. Now begin to conquer and possess his land."

[32]When Sihon and all his army came out to meet us in battle at Jahaz, [33]the LORD our God delivered him over to us and we struck him down, together with his sons and his whole army. [34]At that time we took all his towns and completely destroyed[b] them—men, women and children. We left no survivors. [35]But the livestock and the plunder from the towns we had captured we carried off for ourselves. [36]From Aroer on the rim of the Arnon Gorge, and from the town in the gorge, even as far as Gilead, not one town was too strong for us. The LORD our God gave us all of them. [37]But in accordance with the command of the LORD our God, you did not encroach on any of the land of the Ammonites, neither the land along the course of the Jabbok nor that around the towns in the hills.

Defeat of Og King of Bashan

3 Next we turned and went up along the road toward Bashan, and Og king of Bashan with his whole army marched out to meet us in battle at Edrei. [2]The LORD said to me, "Do not be afraid of him, for I have delivered him into your hands, along with his whole army and his land. Do to him what you did to Sihon king of the Amorites, who reigned in Heshbon."

[3]So the LORD our God also gave into our hands Og king of Bashan and all his army. We

---

[a] 23 That is, Crete   [b] 34 The Hebrew term refers to the irrevocable giving over of things or persons to the LORD, often by totally destroying them.

struck them down, leaving no survivors. ⁴At that time we took all his cities. There was not one of the sixty cities that we did not take from them—the whole region of Argob, Og's kingdom in Bashan. ⁵All these cities were fortified with high walls and with gates and bars, and there were also a great many unwalled villages. ⁶We completely destroyed*a* them, as we had done with Sihon king of Heshbon, destroying*a* every city—men, women and children. ⁷But all the livestock and the plunder from their cities we carried off for ourselves.

The Law of the Big Mo

Deuteronomy 3:4

Momentum is a leader's best friend. After defeating the Amorites, the Israelites came to Bashan. God told them to attack. Having tasted military victory already, they didn't hesitate, and once again they triumphed. This led to the defeat of 60 cities in the region. Success breeds success.

⁸So at that time we took from these two kings of the Amorites the territory east of the Jordan, from the Arnon Gorge as far as Mount Hermon. ⁹(Hermon is called Sirion by the Sidonians; the Amorites call it Senir.) ¹⁰We took all the towns on the plateau, and all Gilead, and all Bashan as far as Salekah and Edrei, towns of Og's kingdom in Bashan. ¹¹(Og king of Bashan was the last of the Rephaites. His bed was decorated with iron and was more than nine cubits long and four cubits wide.*b* It is still in Rabbah of the Ammonites.)

Division of the Land

¹²Of the land that we took over at that time, I gave the Reubenites and the Gadites the territory north of Aroer by the Arnon Gorge, including half the hill country of Gilead, together with its towns. ¹³The rest of Gilead and also all of Bashan, the kingdom of Og, I gave to the half-tribe of Manasseh. (The whole region of Argob in Bashan used to be known as a land of the Rephaites. ¹⁴Jair, a descendant of Manasseh, took the whole region of Argob as far as the border of the Geshurites and the Maakathites; it was named after him, so that to this day Bashan is called Havvoth Jair.*c*) ¹⁵And I gave Gilead to Makir. ¹⁶But to the Reubenites and the Gadites I gave

the territory extending from Gilead down to the Arnon Gorge (the middle of the gorge being the border) and out to the Jabbok River, which is the border of the Ammonites. ¹⁷Its western border was the Jordan in the Arabah, from Kinnereth to the Sea of the Arabah (that is, the Dead Sea), below the slopes of Pisgah.

¹⁸I commanded you at that time: "The LORD your God has given you this land to take possession of it. But all your able-bodied men, armed for battle, must cross over ahead of the other Israelites. ¹⁹However, your wives, your children and your livestock (I know you have much livestock) may stay in the towns I have given you, ²⁰until the LORD gives rest to your fellow Israelites as he has to you, and they too have taken over the land that the LORD your God is giving them across the Jordan. After that, each of you may go back to the possession I have given you."

Moses Forbidden to Cross the Jordan

²¹At that time I commanded Joshua: "You have seen with your own eyes all that the LORD your God has done to these two kings. The LORD will do the same to all the kingdoms over there where you are going. ²²Do not be afraid of them; the LORD your God himself will fight for you."

²³At that time I pleaded with the LORD: ²⁴"Sovereign LORD, you have begun to show to your servant your greatness and your strong hand. For what god is there in heaven or on earth who can do the deeds and mighty works you do? ²⁵Let me go over and see the good land beyond the Jordan—that fine hill country and Lebanon."

²⁶But because of you the LORD was angry with me and would not listen to me. "That is enough," the LORD said. "Do not speak to me anymore about this matter. ²⁷Go up to the top of Pisgah and look west and north and south and east. Look at the land with your own eyes, since you are not going to cross this Jordan. ²⁸But commission Joshua, and encourage and strengthen him, for he will lead this people across and will cause them to inherit the land that you will see." ²⁹So we stayed in the valley near Beth Peor.

Obedience Commanded

4 Now, Israel, hear the decrees and laws I am about to teach you. Follow them so that you may live and may go in and take possession of

---

a 6 The Hebrew term refers to the irrevocable giving over of things or persons to the LORD, often by totally destroying them. *b 11* That is, about 14 feet long and 6 feet wide or about 4 meters long and 1.8 meters wide   *c 14* Or *called the settlements of Jair*

the land the LORD, the God of your ancestors, is giving you. [2]Do not add to what I command you and do not subtract from it, but keep the commands of the LORD your God that I give you.

[3]You saw with your own eyes what the LORD did at Baal Peor. The LORD your God destroyed from among you everyone who followed the Baal of Peor, [4]but all of you who held fast to the LORD your God are still alive today.

[5]See, I have taught you decrees and laws as the LORD my God commanded me, so that you may follow them in the land you are entering to take possession of it. [6]Observe them carefully, for this will show your wisdom and understanding to the nations, who will hear about all these decrees and say, "Surely this great nation is a wise and understanding people." [7]What other nation is so great as to have their gods near them the way the LORD our God is near us whenever we pray to him? [8]And what other nation is so great as to have such righteous decrees and laws as this body of laws I am setting before you today?

[9]Only be careful, and watch yourselves closely so that you do not forget the things your eyes have seen or let them fade from your heart as long as you live. Teach them to your children and to their children after them. [10]Remember the day you stood before the LORD your God at Horeb, when he said to me, "Assemble the people before me to hear my words so that they may learn to revere me as long as they live in the land and may teach them to their children." [11]You came near and stood at the foot of the mountain while it blazed with fire to the very heavens, with black clouds and deep darkness. [12]Then the LORD spoke to you out of the fire. You heard the sound of words but saw no form; there was only a voice. [13]He declared to you his covenant, the Ten Commandments, which he commanded you to follow and then wrote them on two stone tablets. [14]And the LORD directed me at that time to teach you the decrees and laws you are to follow in the land that you are crossing the Jordan to possess.

Idolatry Forbidden

[15]You saw no form of any kind the day the LORD spoke to you at Horeb out of the fire. Therefore watch yourselves very carefully, [16]so that you do not become corrupt and make for yourselves an idol, an image of any shape, whether formed like a man or a woman, [17]or like any animal on earth or any bird that flies in the air, [18]or like any creature that moves along the ground or any fish in the waters below. [19]And

when you look up to the sky and see the sun, the moon and the stars — all the heavenly array — do not be enticed into bowing down to them and worshiping things the LORD your God has apportioned to all the nations under heaven. [20]But as for you, the LORD took you and brought you out of the iron-smelting furnace, out of Egypt, to be the people of his inheritance, as you now are.

[21]The LORD was angry with me because of you, and he solemnly swore that I would not cross the Jordan and enter the good land the LORD your God is giving you as your inheritance. [22]I will die in this land; I will not cross the Jordan; but you are about to cross over and take possession of that good land. [23]Be careful not to forget the covenant of the LORD your God that he made with you; do not make for yourselves an idol in the form of anything the LORD your God has forbidden. [24]For the LORD your God is a consuming fire, a jealous God.

[25]After you have had children and grandchildren and have lived in the land a long time — if you then become corrupt and make any kind of idol, doing evil in the eyes of the LORD your God and arousing his anger, [26]I call the heavens and the earth as witnesses against you this day that you will quickly perish from the land that you are crossing the Jordan to possess. You will not live there long but will certainly be destroyed. [27]The LORD will scatter you among the peoples, and only a few of you will survive among the nations to which the LORD will drive you. [28]There you will worship man-made gods of wood and stone, which cannot see or hear or eat or smell. [29]But if from there you seek the LORD your God, you will find him if you seek him with all your heart and with all your soul. [30]When you are in distress and all these things have happened to you, then in later days you will return to the LORD your God and obey him. [31]For the LORD your God is a merciful God; he will not abandon or destroy you or forget the covenant with your ancestors, which he confirmed to them by oath.

The LORD Is God

[32]Ask now about the former days, long before your time, from the day God created human beings on the earth; ask from one end of the heavens to the other. Has anything so great as this ever happened, or has anything like it ever been heard of? [33]Has any other people heard the voice of God[a] speaking out of fire, as you have, and

---

[a] 33 Or of a god

lived? ³⁴Has any god ever tried to take for himself one nation out of another nation, by testings, by signs and wonders, by war, by a mighty hand and an outstretched arm, or by great and awesome deeds, like all the things the LORD your God did for you in Egypt before your very eyes?

³⁵You were shown these things so that you might know that the LORD is God; besides him there is no other. ³⁶From heaven he made you hear his voice to discipline you. On earth he showed you his great fire, and you heard his words from out of the fire. ³⁷Because he loved your ancestors and chose their descendants after them, he brought you out of Egypt by his Presence and his great strength, ³⁸to drive out before you nations greater and stronger than you and to bring you into their land to give it to you for your inheritance, as it is today.

³⁹Acknowledge and take to heart this day that the LORD is God in heaven above and on the earth below. There is no other. ⁴⁰Keep his decrees and commands, which I am giving you today, so that it may go well with you and your children after you and that you may live long in the land the LORD your God gives you for all time.

Purpose and Passion

Deuteronomy 4:32–40

Moses' speech encourages the people to realize their purpose and calling. This great leader reminds his countrymen of God's faithful provision and imparts to them a sense of destiny.

When leaders project passion for their vision, they create an atmosphere of expectancy among the people. Moses often created at least three such atmospheres for the Jews:

1. **A Sense of Destiny**
   Moses communicated a sense of God's call on Israel's future, a future they were destined to fulfill.

2. **A Sense of Family**
   Moses convinced the people they would enter the land together; cooperatively they could accomplish the vision.

3. **A Militant Spirit**
   Moses called the Israelites to do whatever it took to enter the land; they needed to pay the price to get the job done.

Cities of Refuge

⁴¹Then Moses set aside three cities east of the Jordan, ⁴²to which anyone who had killed a person could flee if they had unintentionally killed a neighbor without malice aforethought. They could flee into one of these cities and save their life. ⁴³The cities were these: Bezer in the wilderness plateau, for the Reubenites; Ramoth in Gilead, for the Gadites; and Golan in Bashan, for the Manassites.

Introduction to the Law

⁴⁴This is the law Moses set before the Israelites. ⁴⁵These are the stipulations, decrees and laws Moses gave them when they came out of Egypt ⁴⁶and were in the valley near Beth Peor east of the Jordan, in the land of Sihon king of the Amorites, who reigned in Heshbon and was defeated by Moses and the Israelites as they came out of Egypt. ⁴⁷They took possession of his land and the land of Og king of Bashan, the two Amorite kings east of the Jordan. ⁴⁸This land extended from Aroer on the rim of the Arnon Gorge to Mount Sirion*a* (that is, Hermon), ⁴⁹and included all the Arabah east of the Jordan, as far as the Dead Sea,*b* below the slopes of Pisgah.

The Ten Commandments

5 Moses summoned all Israel and said:
Hear, Israel, the decrees and laws I declare in your hearing today. Learn them and be sure to follow them. ²The LORD our God made a covenant with us at Horeb. ³It was not with our ancestors*c* that the LORD made this covenant, but with us, with all of us who are alive here today. ⁴The LORD spoke to you face to face out of the fire on the mountain. ⁵(At that time I stood between the LORD and you to declare to you the word of the LORD, because you were afraid of the fire and did not go up the mountain.) And he said:

⁶"I am the LORD your God, who brought you out of Egypt, out of the land of slavery.

⁷"You shall have no other gods before*d* me.

⁸"You shall not make for yourself an image in the form of anything in heaven above or on the earth beneath or in the waters below. ⁹You shall not bow down to them or worship them; for I, the LORD your God, am a jealous

a 48 Syriac (see also 3:9); Hebrew *Siyon*　　*b 49* Hebrew *the Sea of the Arabah*　　*c 3* Or *not only with our parents*　　*d 7* Or *besides*

God, punishing the children for the sin of the parents to the third and fourth generation of those who hate me, [10]but showing love to a thousand generations of those who love me and keep my commandments.

[11]"You shall not misuse the name of the LORD your God, for the LORD will not hold anyone guiltless who misuses his name.

[12]"Observe the Sabbath day by keeping it holy, as the LORD your God has commanded you. [13]Six days you shall labor and do all your work, [14]but the seventh day is a sabbath to the LORD your God. On it you shall not do any work, neither you, nor your son or daughter, nor your male or female servant, nor your ox, your donkey or any of your animals, nor any foreigner residing in your towns, so that your male and female servants may rest, as you do. [15]Remember that you were slaves in Egypt and that the LORD your God brought you out of there with a mighty hand and an outstretched arm. Therefore the LORD your God has commanded you to observe the Sabbath day.

[16]"Honor your father and your mother, as the LORD your God has commanded you, so that you may live long and that it may go well with you in the land the LORD your God is giving you.

[17]"You shall not murder.

[18]"You shall not commit adultery.

[19]"You shall not steal.

[20]"You shall not give false testimony against your neighbor.

[21]"You shall not covet your neighbor's wife. You shall not set your desire on your neighbor's house or land, his male or female servant, his ox or donkey, or anything that belongs to your neighbor."

[22]These are the commandments the LORD proclaimed in a loud voice to your whole assembly there on the mountain from out of the fire, the cloud and the deep darkness; and he added nothing more. Then he wrote them on two stone tablets and gave them to me.

[23]When you heard the voice out of the darkness, while the mountain was ablaze with fire, all the leaders of your tribes and your elders

---

Character and Convictions: Foundational for Leaders

Deuteronomy 5:1–22

To ensure this new generation entered the promised land with solid moral guidelines, Moses repeats the commands he gave earlier in Exodus 20. Former general Norman Schwarzkopf put it this way: "Leadership is a potent combination of character and strategy. But if you must be without one, be without strategy."

---

came to me. [24]And you said, "The LORD our God has shown us his glory and his majesty, and we have heard his voice from the fire. Today we have seen that a person can live even if God speaks with them. [25]But now, why should we die? This great fire will consume us, and we will die if we hear the voice of the LORD our God any longer. [26]For what mortal has ever heard the voice of the living God speaking out of fire, as we have, and survived? [27]Go near and listen to all that the LORD our God says. Then tell us whatever the LORD our God tells you. We will listen and obey."

[28]The LORD heard you when you spoke to me, and the LORD said to me, "I have heard what this people said to you. Everything they said was good. [29]Oh, that their hearts would be inclined to fear me and keep all my commands always, so that it might go well with them and their children forever!

[30]"Go, tell them to return to their tents. [31]But you stay here with me so that I may give you all the commands, decrees and laws you are to teach them to follow in the land I am giving them to possess."

[32]So be careful to do what the LORD your God has commanded you; do not turn aside to the right or to the left. [33]Walk in obedience to all that the LORD your God has commanded you, so that you may live and prosper and prolong your days in the land that you will possess.

Love the LORD Your God

6 These are the commands, decrees and laws the LORD your God directed me to teach you to observe in the land that you are crossing the Jordan to possess, [2]so that you, your children and their children after them may fear the LORD your God as long as you live by keeping all

his decrees and commands that I give you, and so that you may enjoy long life. ³Hear, Israel, and be careful to obey so that it may go well with you and that you may increase greatly in a land flowing with milk and honey, just as the LORD, the God of your ancestors, promised you.

⁴Hear, O Israel: The LORD our God, the LORD is one.ᵃ ⁵Love the LORD your God with all your heart and with all your soul and with all your strength. ⁶These commandments that I give you today are to be on your hearts. ⁷Impress them on your children. Talk about them when you sit at home and when you walk along the road, when you lie down and when you get up. ⁸Tie them as symbols on your hands and bind them on your foreheads. ⁹Write them on the doorframes of your houses and on your gates.

¹⁰When the LORD your God brings you into the land he swore to your fathers, to Abraham, Isaac and Jacob, to give you — a land with large, flourishing cities you did not build, ¹¹houses filled with all kinds of good things you did not provide, wells you did not dig, and vineyards and olive groves you did not plant — then when you eat and are satisfied, ¹²be careful that you do not forget the LORD, who brought you out of Egypt, out of the land of slavery.

¹³Fear the LORD your God, serve him only and take your oaths in his name. ¹⁴Do not follow other gods, the gods of the peoples around you; ¹⁵for the LORD your God, who is among you, is a jealous God and his anger will burn against you, and he will destroy you from the face of the land. ¹⁶Do not put the LORD your God to the test as you did at Massah. ¹⁷Be sure to keep the commands of the LORD your God and the stipulations and decrees he has given you. ¹⁸Do what is right and good in the LORD's sight, so that it may go well with you and you may go in and take over the good land the LORD promised on oath to your ancestors, ¹⁹thrusting out all your enemies before you, as the LORD said.

²⁰In the future, when your son asks you, "What is the meaning of the stipulations, decrees and laws the LORD our God has commanded you?" ²¹tell him: "We were slaves of Pharaoh in Egypt, but the LORD brought us out of Egypt with a mighty hand. ²²Before our eyes the LORD sent signs and wonders — great and terrible — on Egypt and Pharaoh and his whole household. ²³But he brought us out from there to bring us in and give us the land he promised on oath to our ancestors. ²⁴The LORD commanded us to obey all these decrees and to fear the LORD our God, so that we might always prosper and be kept alive, as is the case today. ²⁵And if we are careful to obey all this law before the LORD our God, as he has commanded us, that will be our righteousness."

ᵃ 4 Or *The LORD our God is one LORD*; or *The LORD is our God, the LORD is one*; or *The LORD is our God, the LORD alone*

The Law of Priorities: Pass Them On!

Deuteronomy 6:4–9

An old phrase says, "The leader's job is to keep the main thing, the main thing." Moses attempts to do this in Deuteronomy 6 by reminding the Israelites that their existence revolves around loving God. He also tells family leaders how to transfer truth to their children. Reggie Joiner notes the principles Moses develops:

1. **Relationship comes before rules** (v. 5).

2. **Truth must be in you before it can be in them** (v. 6).

3. **Each day offers natural opportunities for teaching** (v. 7).
   a. When you sit at home: meal time
   b. When you walk along the road: drive time
   c. When you lie down: bedtime
   d. When you get up: get-ready time

4. **Repetition is the teacher's best friend** (vv. 8–9).

Make use of all of these opportunities. Decide on issues you can discuss and ask questions of each other. Pray about your priorities together.

Driving Out the Nations

7 When the LORD your God brings you into the land you are entering to possess and drives out before you many nations — the Hittites, Girgashites, Amorites, Canaanites, Perizzites, Hivites and Jebusites, seven nations larger and stronger than you — [2]and when the LORD your God has delivered them over to you and you have defeated them, then you must destroy them totally.[a] Make no treaty with them, and show them no mercy. [3]Do not intermarry with them. Do not give your daughters to their sons or take their daughters for your sons, [4]for they will turn your children away from following me to serve other gods, and the LORD's anger will burn against you and will quickly destroy you. [5]This is what you are to do to them: Break down their altars, smash their sacred stones, cut down their Asherah poles[b] and burn their idols in the fire. [6]For you are a people holy to the LORD your God. The LORD your God has chosen you out of all the peoples on the face of the earth to be his people, his treasured possession.

[7]The LORD did not set his affection on you and choose you because you were more numerous than other peoples, for you were the fewest of all peoples. [8]But it was because the LORD loved you and kept the oath he swore to your ancestors that he brought you out with a mighty hand and redeemed you from the land of slavery, from the power of Pharaoh king of Egypt. [9]Know therefore that the LORD your God is God; he is the faithful God, keeping his covenant of love to a thousand generations of those who love him and keep his commandments. [10]But

those who hate him he will repay to their
face by destruction;
he will not be slow to repay to their face
those who hate him.

[11]Therefore, take care to follow the commands, decrees and laws I give you today.

[12]If you pay attention to these laws and are careful to follow them, then the LORD your God will keep his covenant of love with you, as he swore to your ancestors. [13]He will love you and bless you and increase your numbers. He will bless the fruit of your womb, the crops of your land — your grain, new wine and olive oil — the calves of your herds and the lambs of your flocks in the land he swore to your ancestors to give you. [14]You will be blessed more than any other people; none of your men or women will be childless, nor will any of your livestock be without young. [15]The LORD will keep you free

---

The Commitment of a Leader

Deuteronomy 7:7–9

Good leaders model commitment before they ask anyone else to do so. God promises to keep his commitment to his people for "a thousand generations" (Dt 7:9). He reminds them that he didn't free them because they deserved it or because they were the largest nation on earth, but because he loved them.

---

from every disease. He will not inflict on you the horrible diseases you knew in Egypt, but he will inflict them on all who hate you. [16]You must destroy all the peoples the LORD your God gives over to you. Do not look on them with pity and do not serve their gods, for that will be a snare to you.

[17]You may say to yourselves, "These nations are stronger than we are. How can we drive them out?" [18]But do not be afraid of them; remember well what the LORD your God did to Pharaoh and to all Egypt. [19]You saw with your own eyes the great trials, the signs and wonders, the mighty hand and outstretched arm, with which the LORD your God brought you out. The LORD your God will do the same to all the peoples you now fear. [20]Moreover, the LORD your God will send the hornet among them until even the survivors who hide from you have perished. [21]Do not be terrified by them, for the LORD your God, who is among you, is a great and awesome God. [22]The LORD your God will drive out those nations before you, little by little. You will not be allowed to eliminate them all at once, or the wild animals will multiply around you. [23]But the LORD your God will deliver them over to you, throwing them into great confusion until they are destroyed. [24]He will give their kings into your hand, and you will wipe out their names from under heaven. No one will be able to stand up against you; you will destroy them. [25]The images of their gods you are to burn in the fire. Do not covet the silver and gold on them, and do not take it for yourselves, or you will be ensnared by it, for it is detestable to the LORD your God. [26]Do not bring a detestable

---

[a] 2 The Hebrew term refers to the irrevocable giving over of things or persons to the LORD, often by totally destroying them; also in verse 26.   [b] 5 That is, wooden symbols of the goddess Asherah; here and elsewhere in Deuteronomy

The Anointing of a Leader: Its Requirements and Results

Deuteronomy 7:11–13

The Old Testament consistently speaks of leaders "anointed" by God. Moses was the first such leader in Israel. The anointing represents God's intimate presence and enabling power.

But what determines God's anointing on a person? No doubt, God is sovereign and chooses to place his hand on some and not on others. But while God anoints, Frank Damazio reminds us of some human criteria for anointing. A leader must . . .

1. **Obey and teach the people to obey God's Word (Dt 7:11–13).**
2. **Desire and pursue the outpouring of the Spirit (Dt 11:13–14).**
3. **Actively build up the "house" of the Lord (Hag 1:7–11).**
4. **Recognize God is the source of his blessing and authority (Hos 2:8–9).**
5. **Use his influence for the Lord and not for selfish or evil reasons (Hos 2:8–9).**
6. **Avoid glorifying the anointing more than God himself (Hos 2:8–9).**
7. **Give himself freely to the work of the Lord (Ex 35:20–29).**
8. **Appreciate and guard the anointing (Nu 4:9, 16).**

thing into your house or you, like it, will be set apart for destruction. Regard it as vile and utterly detest it, for it is set apart for destruction.

Do Not Forget the LORD

8 Be careful to follow every command I am giving you today, so that you may live and increase and may enter and possess the land the LORD promised on oath to your ancestors. ²Remember how the LORD your God led you all the way in the wilderness these forty years, to humble and test you in order to know what was in your heart, whether or not you would keep his commands. ³He humbled you, causing you to hunger and then feeding you with manna, which neither you nor your ancestors had known, to teach you that man does not live on bread alone but on every word that comes from the mouth of the LORD. ⁴Your clothes did not wear out and your feet did not swell during these forty years. ⁵Know then in your heart that as a man disciplines his son, so the LORD your God disciplines you.

⁶Observe the commands of the LORD your God, walking in obedience to him and revering him. ⁷For the LORD your God is bringing you into a good land—a land with brooks, streams, and deep springs gushing out into the valleys and hills; ⁸a land with wheat and barley, vines and fig trees, pomegranates, olive oil and honey; ⁹a land where bread will not be scarce and

you will lack nothing; a land where the rocks are iron and you can dig copper out of the hills.

¹⁰When you have eaten and are satisfied, praise the LORD your God for the good land he has given you. ¹¹Be careful that you do not forget the LORD your God, failing to observe his commands, his laws and his decrees that I am giving you this day. ¹²Otherwise, when you eat and are satisfied, when you build fine houses and settle down, ¹³and when your herds and flocks grow large and your silver and gold increase and all you have is multiplied, ¹⁴then your heart will become proud and you will forget the LORD your God, who brought you out of Egypt, out of the land of slavery. ¹⁵He led you through the vast and dreadful wilderness, that thirsty and waterless land, with its venomous snakes and scorpions. He brought you water out of hard rock. ¹⁶He gave you manna to eat in the wilderness, something your ancestors had never known, to humble and test you so that in the end it might go well with you. ¹⁷You may say to yourself, "My power and the strength of my hands have produced this wealth for me." ¹⁸But remember the LORD your God, for it is he who gives you the ability to produce wealth, and so confirms his covenant, which he swore to your ancestors, as it is today.

¹⁹If you ever forget the LORD your God and follow other gods and worship and bow down to them, I testify against you today that you will surely be destroyed. ²⁰Like the nations the LORD

destroyed before you, so you will be destroyed for not obeying the LORD your God.

Not Because of Israel's Righteousness

9 Hear, Israel: You are now about to cross the Jordan to go in and dispossess nations greater and stronger than you, with large cities that have walls up to the sky. ²The people are strong and tall—Anakites! You know about them and have heard it said: "Who can stand up against the Anakites?" ³But be assured today that the LORD your God is the one who goes across ahead of you like a devouring fire. He will destroy them; he will subdue them before you. And you will drive them out and annihilate them quickly, as the LORD has promised you.

⁴After the LORD your God has driven them out before you, do not say to yourself, "The LORD has brought me here to take possession of this land because of my righteousness." No, it is on account of the wickedness of these nations that the LORD is going to drive them out before you. ⁵It is not because of your righteousness or your integrity that you are going in to take possession of their land; but on account of the wick-

---

Humble Leaders Alone Receive God's Grace

Deuteronomy 8:1–20

We all need occasional reminders that it is God who gives his people any power and position they may come to enjoy. God commands his people to remember his blessings in both bad times (Dt 8:1–10) and good times (8:11–20).

Because that's true, humility is the only appropriate posture—for leaders as well as followers. God constantly reminds leaders of . . .

- The privilege of being a chosen people— God will lead and provide for us.
- The price of being a chosen people—we must rely on his provision, not our own.

It's easy for leaders to succumb to the conceit that they pulled off some victory or objective. Instead, they should acknowledge that the success came to them as an under shepherd from the Master Shepherd. God shows favor to the humble, but opposes the proud (Jas 4:6). This is the only way to cooperate with the Lord.

---

edness of these nations, the LORD your God will drive them out before you, to accomplish what he swore to your fathers, to Abraham, Isaac and Jacob. ⁶Understand, then, that it is not because of your righteousness that the LORD your God is giving you this good land to possess, for you are a stiff-necked people.

The Golden Calf

⁷Remember this and never forget how you aroused the anger of the LORD your God in the wilderness. From the day you left Egypt until you arrived here, you have been rebellious against the LORD. ⁸At Horeb you aroused the LORD's wrath so that he was angry enough to destroy you. ⁹When I went up on the mountain to receive the tablets of stone, the tablets of the covenant that the LORD had made with you, I stayed on the mountain forty days and forty nights; I ate no bread and drank no water. ¹⁰The LORD gave me two stone tablets inscribed by the finger of God. On them were all the commandments the LORD proclaimed to you on the mountain out of the fire, on the day of the assembly.

¹¹At the end of the forty days and forty nights, the LORD gave me the two stone tablets, the tablets of the covenant. ¹²Then the LORD told me, "Go down from here at once, because your people whom you brought out of Egypt have become corrupt. They have turned away quickly from what I commanded them and have made an idol for themselves."

¹³And the LORD said to me, "I have seen this people, and they are a stiff-necked people indeed! ¹⁴Let me alone, so that I may destroy them and blot out their name from under heaven. And I will make you into a nation stronger and more numerous than they."

¹⁵So I turned and went down from the mountain while it was ablaze with fire. And the two tablets of the covenant were in my hands. ¹⁶When I looked, I saw that you had sinned against the LORD your God; you had made for yourselves an idol cast in the shape of a calf. You had turned aside quickly from the way that the LORD had commanded you. ¹⁷So I took the two tablets and threw them out of my hands, breaking them to pieces before your eyes.

¹⁸Then once again I fell prostrate before the LORD for forty days and forty nights; I ate no bread and drank no water, because of all the sin you had committed, doing what was evil in the LORD's sight and so arousing his anger. ¹⁹I feared the anger and wrath of the LORD, for he was angry enough with you to destroy you. But again the

LORD listened to me. [20]And the LORD was angry enough with Aaron to destroy him, but at that time I prayed for Aaron too. [21]Also I took that sinful thing of yours, the calf you had made, and burned it in the fire. Then I crushed it and ground it to powder as fine as dust and threw the dust into a stream that flowed down the mountain.

[22]You also made the LORD angry at Taberah, at Massah and at Kibroth Hattaavah.

[23]And when the LORD sent you out from Kadesh Barnea, he said, "Go up and take possession of the land I have given you." But you rebelled against the command of the LORD your God. You did not trust him or obey him. [24]You have been rebellious against the LORD ever since I have known you.

[25]I lay prostrate before the LORD those forty days and forty nights because the LORD had said he would destroy you. [26]I prayed to the LORD and said, "Sovereign LORD, do not destroy your people, your own inheritance that you redeemed by your great power and brought out of Egypt with a mighty hand. [27]Remember your servants Abraham, Isaac and Jacob. Overlook the stubbornness of this people, their wickedness and their sin. [28]Otherwise, the country from which you brought us will say, 'Because the LORD was not able to take them into the land he had promised them, and because he hated them, he brought them out to put them to death in the wilderness.' [29]But they are your people, your inheritance that you brought out by your great power and your outstretched arm."

Tablets Like the First Ones

10 At that time the LORD said to me, "Chisel out two stone tablets like the first ones and come up to me on the mountain. Also make a wooden ark.[a] [2]I will write on the tablets the words that were on the first tablets, which you broke. Then you are to put them in the ark."

[3]So I made the ark out of acacia wood and chiseled out two stone tablets like the first ones, and I went up on the mountain with the two tablets in my hands. [4]The LORD wrote on these tablets what he had written before, the Ten Commandments he had proclaimed to you on the mountain, out of the fire, on the day of the assembly. And the LORD gave them to me. [5]Then I came back down the mountain and put the tablets in the ark I had made, as the LORD commanded me, and they are there now.

[6](The Israelites traveled from the wells of Bene Jaakan to Moserah. There Aaron died and was buried, and Eleazar his son succeeded him as priest. [7]From there they traveled to Gudgodah and on to Jotbathah, a land with streams of water. [8]At that time the LORD set apart the tribe of Levi to carry the ark of the covenant of the LORD, to stand before the LORD to minister and to pronounce blessings in his name, as they still do today. [9]That is why the Levites have no share or inheritance among their fellow Israelites; the LORD is their inheritance, as the LORD your God told them.)

[10]Now I had stayed on the mountain forty days and forty nights, as I did the first time, and the LORD listened to me at this time also. It was not his will to destroy you. [11]"Go," the LORD said to me, "and lead the people on their way, so that they may enter and possess the land I swore to their ancestors to give them."

Fear the LORD

[12]And now, Israel, what does the LORD your God ask of you but to fear the LORD your God, to walk in obedience to him, to love him, to serve the LORD your God with all your heart and with all your soul, [13]and to observe the LORD's commands and decrees that I am giving you today for your own good?

[14]To the LORD your God belong the heavens, even the highest heavens, the earth and everything in it. [15]Yet the LORD set his affection on your ancestors and loved them, and he chose you, their descendants, above all the nations—as it is today. [16]Circumcise your hearts, therefore, and do not be stiff-necked any longer. [17]For the LORD your God is God of gods and Lord of lords, the great God, mighty and awesome, who shows no partiality and accepts no bribes. [18]He defends the cause of the fatherless and the widow, and loves the foreigner residing among you, giving them food and clothing. [19]And you are to love those who are foreigners, for you yourselves were foreigners in Egypt. [20]Fear the LORD your God and serve him. Hold fast to him and take your oaths in his name. [21]He is the one you praise; he is your God, who performed for you those great and awesome wonders you saw with your own eyes. [22]Your ancestors who went down into Egypt were seventy in all, and now the LORD your God has made you as numerous as the stars in the sky.

Love and Obey the LORD

11 Love the LORD your God and keep his requirements, his decrees, his laws and his commands always. [2]Remember today that your

---

[a] 1 That is, a chest

children were not the ones who saw and experienced the discipline of the LORD your God: his majesty, his mighty hand, his outstretched arm; [3]the signs he performed and the things he did in the heart of Egypt, both to Pharaoh king of Egypt and to his whole country; [4]what he did to the Egyptian army, to its horses and chariots, how he overwhelmed them with the waters of the Red Sea[a] as they were pursuing you, and how the LORD brought lasting ruin on them. [5]It was not your children who saw what he did for you in the wilderness until you arrived at this place, [6]and what he did to Dathan and Abiram, sons of Eliab the Reubenite, when the earth opened its mouth right in the middle of all Israel and swallowed them up with their households, their tents and every living thing that belonged to them. [7]But it was your own eyes that saw all these great things the LORD has done.

[8]Observe therefore all the commands I am giving you today, so that you may have the strength to go in and take over the land that you are crossing the Jordan to possess, [9]and so that you may live long in the land the LORD swore to your ancestors to give to them and their descendants, a land flowing with milk and honey. [10]The land you are entering to take over is not like the land of Egypt, from which you have come, where you planted your seed and irrigated it by foot as in a vegetable garden. [11]But the land you are crossing the Jordan to take possession of is a land of mountains and valleys that drinks rain from heaven. [12]It is a land the LORD your God cares for; the eyes of the LORD your God

are continually on it from the beginning of the year to its end.

[13]So if you faithfully obey the commands I am giving you today—to love the LORD your God and to serve him with all your heart and with all your soul— [14]then I will send rain on your land in its season, both autumn and spring rains, so that you may gather in your grain, new wine and olive oil. [15]I will provide grass in the fields for your cattle, and you will eat and be satisfied.

[16]Be careful, or you will be enticed to turn away and worship other gods and bow down to them. [17]Then the LORD's anger will burn against you, and he will shut up the heavens so that it will not rain and the ground will yield no produce, and you will soon perish from the good land the LORD is giving you. [18]Fix these words of mine in your hearts and minds; tie them as symbols on your hands and bind them on your foreheads. [19]Teach them to your children, talking about them when you sit at home and when you walk along the road, when you lie down and when you get up. [20]Write them on the doorframes of your houses and on your gates, [21]so that your days and the days of your children may be many in the land the LORD swore to give your ancestors, as many as the days that the heavens are above the earth.

[22]If you carefully observe all these commands I am giving you to follow—to love the LORD your God, to walk in obedience to him and to

[a] 4 Or the Sea of Reeds

The Law of Connection: God Touches Their Hearts First

Deuteronomy 10:1—11:25

As the Ultimate Leader, God directs his people to obey him. But he doesn't simply demand obedience without giving sufficient reason. The Lord provides a good rationale for his people to obey him. He reminds them that he first touched and blessed them—now, the only proper response is loving obedience. God's people were to follow his leadership because of:

1. **Personal Relationship (10:12–22)**
   God communicated his powerful nature, yet personal love for the descendants of Abraham.

2. **Past Record (11:1–7)**
   God reminded the people of the miracles he performed to rescue them from Egypt.

3. **Promised Results (11:8–17)**
   God predicted continued blessings if the Israelites would remain faithful.

4. **Powerful Redemption (11:18–25)**
   God underscored his plan to bless Hebrew families and possessions.

hold fast to him— [23]then the LORD will drive out all these nations before you, and you will dispossess nations larger and stronger than you. [24]Every place where you set your foot will be yours: Your territory will extend from the desert to Lebanon, and from the Euphrates River to the Mediterranean Sea. [25]No one will be able to stand against you. The LORD your God, as he promised you, will put the terror and fear of you on the whole land, wherever you go.

[26]See, I am setting before you today a blessing and a curse— [27]the blessing if you obey the commands of the LORD your God that I am giving you today; [28]the curse if you disobey the commands of the LORD your God and turn from the way that I command you today by following other gods, which you have not known. [29]When the LORD your God has brought you into the land you are entering to possess, you are to proclaim on Mount Gerizim the blessings, and on Mount Ebal the curses. [30]As you know, these mountains are across the Jordan, westward, toward the setting sun, near the great trees of Moreh, in the territory of those Canaanites living in the Arabah in the vicinity of Gilgal. [31]You are about to cross the Jordan to enter and take possession of the land the LORD your God is giving you. When you have taken it over and are living there, [32]be sure that you obey all the decrees and laws I am setting before you today.

The One Place of Worship

12 These are the decrees and laws you must be careful to follow in the land that the LORD, the God of your ancestors, has given you to possess—as long as you live in the land. [2]Destroy completely all the places on the high mountains, on the hills and under every spreading tree, where the nations you are dispossessing worship their gods. [3]Break down their altars, smash their sacred stones and burn their Asherah poles in the fire; cut down the idols of their gods and wipe out their names from those places.

[4]You must not worship the LORD your God in their way. [5]But you are to seek the place the LORD your God will choose from among all your tribes to put his Name there for his dwelling. To that place you must go; [6]there bring your burnt offerings and sacrifices, your tithes and special gifts, what you have vowed to give and your freewill offerings, and the firstborn of your herds and flocks. [7]There, in the presence of the LORD your God, you and your families shall eat and shall rejoice in everything you have put your hand to, because the LORD your God has blessed you.

[8]You are not to do as we do here today, everyone doing as they see fit, [9]since you have not yet reached the resting place and the inheritance the LORD your God is giving you. [10]But you will cross the Jordan and settle in the land the LORD your God is giving you as an inheritance, and he will give you rest from all your enemies around you so that you will live in safety. [11]Then to the place the LORD your God will choose as a dwelling for his Name—there you are to bring everything I command you: your burnt offerings and sacrifices, your tithes and special gifts, and all the choice possessions you have vowed to the LORD. [12]And there rejoice before the LORD your God—you, your sons and daughters, your male and female servants, and the Levites from your towns who have no allotment or inheritance of their own. [13]Be careful not to sacrifice your burnt offerings anywhere you please. [14]Offer them only at the place the LORD will choose in one of your tribes, and there observe everything I command you.

[15]Nevertheless, you may slaughter your animals in any of your towns and eat as much of the meat as you want, as if it were gazelle or deer, according to the blessing the LORD your God gives you. Both the ceremonially unclean and the clean may eat it. [16]But you must not eat the blood; pour it out on the ground like water. [17]You must not eat in your own towns the tithe of your grain and new wine and olive oil, or the firstborn of your herds and flocks, or whatever you have vowed to give, or your freewill offerings or special gifts. [18]Instead, you are to eat them in the presence of the LORD your God at the place the LORD your God will choose—you, your sons and daughters, your male and female servants, and the Levites from your towns—and you are to rejoice before the LORD your God in everything you put your hand to. [19]Be careful not to neglect the Levites as long as you live in your land.

[20]When the LORD your God has enlarged your territory as he promised you, and you crave meat and say, "I would like some meat," then you may eat as much of it as you want. [21]If the place where the LORD your God chooses to put his Name is too far away from you, you may slaughter animals from the herds and flocks the LORD has given you, as I have commanded you, and in your own towns you may eat as much of them as you want. [22]Eat them as you would gazelle or deer. Both the ceremonially unclean and

the clean may eat. [23]But be sure you do not eat the blood, because the blood is the life, and you must not eat the life with the meat. [24]You must not eat the blood; pour it out on the ground like water. [25]Do not eat it, so that it may go well with you and your children after you, because you will be doing what is right in the eyes of the LORD.

[26]But take your consecrated things and whatever you have vowed to give, and go to the place the LORD will choose. [27]Present your burnt offerings on the altar of the LORD your God, both the meat and the blood. The blood of your sacrifices must be poured beside the altar of the LORD your God, but you may eat the meat. [28]Be careful to obey all these regulations I am giving you, so that it may always go well with you and your children after you, because you will be doing what is good and right in the eyes of the LORD your God.

[29]The LORD your God will cut off before you the nations you are about to invade and dispossess. But when you have driven them out and settled in their land, [30]and after they have been destroyed before you, be careful not to be ensnared by inquiring about their gods, saying, "How do these nations serve their gods? We will do the same." [31]You must not worship the LORD your God in their way, because in worshiping their gods, they do all kinds of detestable things the LORD hates. They even burn their sons and daughters in the fire as sacrifices to their gods.

[32]See that you do all I command you; do not add to it or take away from it.[a]

Worshiping Other Gods

13 [b] If a prophet, or one who foretells by dreams, appears among you and announces to you a sign or wonder, [2]and if the sign or wonder spoken of takes place, and the prophet says, "Let us follow other gods" (gods you have not known) "and let us worship them," [3]you must not listen to the words of that prophet or dreamer. The LORD your God is testing you to find out whether you love him with all your heart and with all your soul. [4]It is the LORD your God you must follow, and him you must revere. Keep his commands and obey him; serve him and hold fast to him. [5]That prophet or dreamer must be put to death for inciting rebellion against the LORD your God, who brought you out of Egypt and redeemed you from the land of slavery. That prophet or dreamer tried to turn you from the way the LORD your God com-

manded you to follow. You must purge the evil from among you.

[6]If your very own brother, or your son or daughter, or the wife you love, or your closest friend secretly entices you, saying, "Let us go and worship other gods" (gods that neither you nor your ancestors have known, [7]gods of the peoples around you, whether near or far, from one end of the land to the other), [8]do not yield to them or listen to them. Show them no pity. Do not spare them or shield them. [9]You must certainly put them to death. Your hand must be the first in putting them to death, and then the hands of all the people. [10]Stone them to death, because they tried to turn you away from the LORD your God, who brought you out of Egypt, out of the land of slavery. [11]Then all Israel will hear and be afraid, and no one among you will do such an evil thing again.

[12]If you hear it said about one of the towns the LORD your God is giving you to live in [13]that troublemakers have arisen among you and have led the people of their town astray, saying, "Let us go and worship other gods" (gods you have not known), [14]then you must inquire, probe and investigate it thoroughly. And if it is true and it has been proved that this detestable thing has been done among you, [15]you must certainly put to the sword all who live in that town. You must destroy it completely,[c] both its people and its livestock. [16]You are to gather all the plunder of the town into the middle of the public square and completely burn the town and all its plunder as a whole burnt offering to the LORD your God. That town is to remain a ruin forever, never to be rebuilt, [17]and none of the condemned things[c] are to be found in your hands. Then the LORD will turn from his fierce anger, will show you mercy, and will have compassion on you. He will increase your numbers, as he promised on oath to your ancestors — [18]because you obey the LORD your God by keeping all his commands that I am giving you today and doing what is right in his eyes.

Clean and Unclean Food

14 You are the children of the LORD your God. Do not cut yourselves or shave the front of your heads for the dead, [2]for you are a people holy to the LORD your God. Out of all the

---

[a] 32 In Hebrew texts this verse (12:32) is numbered 13:1.
[b] In Hebrew texts 13:1-18 is numbered 13:2-19.   [c] 15,17 The Hebrew term refers to the irrevocable giving over of things or persons to the LORD, often by totally destroying them.

peoples on the face of the earth, the LORD has chosen you to be his treasured possession.

³Do not eat any detestable thing. ⁴These are the animals you may eat: the ox, the sheep, the goat, ⁵the deer, the gazelle, the roe deer, the wild goat, the ibex, the antelope and the mountain sheep.ᵃ ⁶You may eat any animal that has a divided hoof and that chews the cud. ⁷However, of those that chew the cud or that have a divided hoof you may not eat the camel, the rabbit or the hyrax. Although they chew the cud, they do not have a divided hoof; they are ceremonially unclean for you. ⁸The pig is also unclean; although it has a divided hoof, it does not chew the cud. You are not to eat their meat or touch their carcasses.

⁹Of all the creatures living in the water, you may eat any that has fins and scales. ¹⁰But anything that does not have fins and scales you may not eat; for you it is unclean.

¹¹You may eat any clean bird. ¹²But these you may not eat: the eagle, the vulture, the black vulture, ¹³the red kite, the black kite, any kind of falcon, ¹⁴any kind of raven, ¹⁵the horned owl, the screech owl, the gull, any kind of hawk, ¹⁶the little owl, the great owl, the white owl, ¹⁷the desert owl, the osprey, the cormorant, ¹⁸the stork, any kind of heron, the hoopoe and the bat.

¹⁹All flying insects are unclean to you; do not eat them. ²⁰But any winged creature that is clean you may eat.

²¹Do not eat anything you find already dead. You may give it to the foreigner residing in any of your towns, and they may eat it, or you may sell it to any other foreigner. But you are a people holy to the LORD your God.

Do not cook a young goat in its mother's milk.

Tithes

²²Be sure to set aside a tenth of all that your fields produce each year. ²³Eat the tithe of your grain, new wine and olive oil, and the firstborn of your herds and flocks in the presence of the LORD your God at the place he will choose as a dwelling for his Name, so that you may learn to revere the LORD your God always. ²⁴But if that place is too distant and you have been blessed by the LORD your God and cannot carry your tithe (because the place where the LORD will choose to put his Name is so far away), ²⁵then exchange your tithe for silver, and take the silver with you and go to the place the LORD your God will choose. ²⁶Use the silver to buy whatever you like: cattle, sheep, wine or other fermented drink, or anything you wish. Then you and your household shall eat there in the presence of the LORD your God and rejoice. ²⁷And do not neglect the Levites living in your towns, for they have no allotment or inheritance of their own.

²⁸At the end of every three years, bring all the tithes of that year's produce and store it in your towns, ²⁹so that the Levites (who have no allotment or inheritance of their own) and the foreigners, the fatherless and the widows who live in your towns may come and eat and be sat-

---

ᵃ 5 The precise identification of some of the birds and animals in this chapter is uncertain.

Generosity: A Candle Loses Nothing by Lighting Another

Deuteronomy 14:27—15:18

If great leaders err, they do so on the side of generosity. They are givers, not takers. They feel motivated to:

1. **Serve others**—to help them grow and thrive.

2. **Solve problems**—that prevent potential from being reached.

3. **Save causes**—that benefit mankind.

God instructs his leaders and the entire nation of Israel to imitate his generosity and grace. At the end of every seventh year, every Israelite was to cancel all debts owed by fellow citizens. If they would indeed cancel debts, model graciousness and forgiveness, and care for the poor, He would favor their land with abundant crops and freedom from invasion. Imagine! They simply needed to trust that God was in control and let him worry about rain and sun and fruitful harvest times.

God's instruction here provides us with a reminder of the nature of true leadership. We don't keep score with people; we just keep on giving.

isfied, and so that the LORD your God may bless you in all the work of your hands.

The Year for Canceling Debts

15 At the end of every seven years you must cancel debts. [2]This is how it is to be done: Every creditor shall cancel any loan they have made to a fellow Israelite. They shall not require payment from anyone among their own people, because the LORD's time for canceling debts has been proclaimed. [3]You may require payment from a foreigner, but you must cancel any debt your fellow Israelite owes you. [4]However, there need be no poor people among you, for in the land the LORD your God is giving you to possess as your inheritance, he will richly bless you, [5]if only you fully obey the LORD your God and are careful to follow all these commands I am giving you today. [6]For the LORD your God will bless you as he has promised, and you will lend to many nations but will borrow from none. You will rule over many nations but none will rule over you.

[7]If anyone is poor among your fellow Israelites in any of the towns of the land the LORD your God is giving you, do not be hardhearted or tightfisted toward them. [8]Rather, be openhanded and freely lend them whatever they need. [9]Be careful not to harbor this wicked thought: "The seventh year, the year for canceling debts, is near," so that you do not show ill will toward the needy among your fellow Israelites and give them nothing. They may then appeal to the LORD against you, and you will be found guilty of sin. [10]Give generously to them and do so without a grudging heart; then because of this the LORD your God will bless you in all your work and in everything you put your hand to. [11]There will always be poor people in the land. Therefore I command you to be openhanded toward your fellow Israelites who are poor and needy in your land.

Freeing Servants

[12]If any of your people — Hebrew men or women — sell themselves to you and serve you six years, in the seventh year you must let them go free. [13]And when you release them, do not send them away empty-handed. [14]Supply them liberally from your flock, your threshing floor and your winepress. Give to them as the LORD your God has blessed you. [15]Remember that you were slaves in Egypt and the LORD your God redeemed you. That is why I give you this command today.

[16]But if your servant says to you, "I do not want to leave you," because he loves you and your family and is well off with you, [17]then take an awl and push it through his earlobe into the door, and he will become your servant for life. Do the same for your female servant.

[18]Do not consider it a hardship to set your

Servanthood: A Word Study and Word Picture

Deuteronomy 15:12–18

The Old Testament uses several Hebrew terms that we translate as "servant," each one presenting a slightly different picture of the heart of a servant. What can a leader learn from these terms? Plenty. Remember, Jesus forever linked leadership with servanthood (Mt 20:25–28). Let's take a moment to discover what we might learn about servant leadership from some of these ancient Hebrew words:

1. **Ebed:** a love-slave or servant. This term describes someone who is at the complete disposal of another (Dt 15:12–18). Likewise, leaders must be at the disposal of the Lord and their people.

2. **Abad:** one who gives up personal rights in order to work in the fields or tabernacle (Nu 18:7, 23). In a similar way, leaders must sacrifice their rights and stay surrendered to the cause.

3. **Sakyir:** a hired servant who works for pay, by day or by year (Lev 25:39–42). A leader must avoid the perspective of a "paid professional." Remember the lesson of John 10:12–13?

4. **Sharath:** someone who will perform menial tasks to accomplish an overall goal (Ex 28:35–43). Leaders must do whatever it takes to serve the mission.

Leaders must never forget that God calls them to serve. If our Lord could wash his disciples' feet as a lowly *sharath*, then how could we frown at becoming an *ebed*?

servant free, because their service to you these six years has been worth twice as much as that of a hired hand. And the Lord your God will bless you in everything you do.

The Firstborn Animals

¹⁹Set apart for the Lord your God every firstborn male of your herds and flocks. Do not put the firstborn of your cows to work, and do not shear the firstborn of your sheep. ²⁰Each year you and your family are to eat them in the presence of the Lord your God at the place he will choose. ²¹If an animal has a defect, is lame or blind, or has any serious flaw, you must not sacrifice it to the Lord your God. ²²You are to eat it in your own towns. Both the ceremonially unclean and the clean may eat it, as if it were gazelle or deer. ²³But you must not eat the blood; pour it out on the ground like water.

The Passover

16 Observe the month of Aviv and celebrate the Passover of the Lord your God, because in the month of Aviv he brought you out of Egypt by night. ²Sacrifice as the Passover to the Lord your God an animal from your flock or herd at the place the Lord will choose as a dwelling for his Name. ³Do not eat it with bread made with yeast, but for seven days eat unleavened bread, the bread of affliction, because you left Egypt in haste—so that all the days of your life you may remember the time of your departure from Egypt. ⁴Let no yeast be found in your possession in all your land for seven days. Do not let any of the meat you sacrifice on the evening of the first day remain until morning.

⁵You must not sacrifice the Passover in any town the Lord your God gives you ⁶except in the place he will choose as a dwelling for his Name. There you must sacrifice the Passover in the evening, when the sun goes down, on the anniversary*a* of your departure from Egypt. ⁷Roast it and eat it at the place the Lord your God will choose. Then in the morning return to your tents. ⁸For six days eat unleavened bread and on the seventh day hold an assembly to the Lord your God and do no work.

The Festival of Weeks

⁹Count off seven weeks from the time you begin to put the sickle to the standing grain. ¹⁰Then celebrate the Festival of Weeks to the Lord your God by giving a freewill offering in proportion to the blessings the Lord your God has given you. ¹¹And rejoice before the Lord

your God at the place he will choose as a dwelling for his Name—you, your sons and daughters, your male and female servants, the Levites in your towns, and the foreigners, the fatherless and the widows living among you. ¹²Remember that you were slaves in Egypt, and follow carefully these decrees.

The Festival of Tabernacles

¹³Celebrate the Festival of Tabernacles for seven days after you have gathered the produce of your threshing floor and your winepress. ¹⁴Be joyful at your festival—you, your sons and daughters, your male and female servants, and the Levites, the foreigners, the fatherless and the widows who live in your towns. ¹⁵For seven days celebrate the festival to the Lord your God at the place the Lord will choose. For the Lord your God will bless you in all your harvest and in all the work of your hands, and your joy will be complete.

¹⁶Three times a year all your men must appear before the Lord your God at the place he will choose: at the Festival of Unleavened Bread, the Festival of Weeks and the Festival of Tabernacles. No one should appear before the Lord empty-handed: ¹⁷Each of you must bring a gift in proportion to the way the Lord your God has blessed you.

Judges

¹⁸Appoint judges and officials for each of your tribes in every town the Lord your God is giving you, and they shall judge the people fairly. ¹⁹Do not pervert justice or show partiality. Do not accept a bribe, for a bribe blinds the eyes of the wise and twists the words of the innocent. ²⁰Follow justice and justice alone, so that you may live and possess the land the Lord your God is giving you.

Worshiping Other Gods

²¹Do not set up any wooden Asherah pole beside the altar you build to the Lord your God, ²²and do not erect a sacred stone, for these the Lord your God hates.

17 Do not sacrifice to the Lord your God an ox or a sheep that has any defect or flaw in it, for that would be detestable to him.

²If a man or woman living among you in one of the towns the Lord gives you is found doing evil in the eyes of the Lord your God in violation of his covenant, ³and contrary to my com-

a 6 Or down, at the time of day

mand has worshiped other gods, bowing down to them or to the sun or the moon or the stars in the sky, ⁴and this has been brought to your attention, then you must investigate it thoroughly. If it is true and it has been proved that this detestable thing has been done in Israel, ⁵take the man or woman who has done this evil deed to your city gate and stone that person to death. ⁶On the testimony of two or three witnesses a person is to be put to death, but no one is to be put to death on the testimony of only one witness. ⁷The hands of the witnesses must be the first in putting that person to death, and then the hands of all the people. You must purge the evil from among you.

Law Courts

⁸If cases come before your courts that are too difficult for you to judge — whether bloodshed, lawsuits or assaults — take them to the place the LORD your God will choose. ⁹Go to the Levitical priests and to the judge who is in office at that time. Inquire of them and they will give you the verdict. ¹⁰You must act according to the decisions they give you at the place the LORD will choose. Be careful to do everything they instruct you to do. ¹¹Act according to whatever they teach you and the decisions they give you. Do not turn aside from what they tell you, to the right or to the left. ¹²Anyone who shows contempt for the judge or for the priest who stands ministering there to the LORD your God is to be put to death. You must purge the evil from Israel. ¹³All the people will hear and be afraid, and will not be contemptuous again.

The King

¹⁴When you enter the land the LORD your God is giving you and have taken possession of it and settled in it, and you say, "Let us set a king over us like all the nations around us," ¹⁵be sure to appoint over you a king the LORD your God chooses. He must be from among your fellow Israelites. Do not place a foreigner over you, one who is not an Israelite. ¹⁶The king, moreover, must not acquire great numbers of horses for himself or make the people return to Egypt to get more of them, for the LORD has told you, "You are not to go back that way again." ¹⁷He must not take many wives, or his heart will be led astray. He must not accumulate large amounts of silver and gold.

¹⁸When he takes the throne of his kingdom, he is to write for himself on a scroll a copy of this law, taken from that of the Levitical priests.

¹⁹It is to be with him, and he is to read it all the days of his life so that he may learn to revere the LORD his God and follow carefully all the words of this law and these decrees ²⁰and not consider himself better than his fellow Israelites and turn from the law to the right or to the left. Then he and his descendants will reign a long time over his kingdom in Israel.

Offerings for Priests and Levites

18 The Levitical priests — indeed, the whole tribe of Levi — are to have no allotment or inheritance with Israel. They shall live on the food offerings presented to the LORD, for that is their inheritance. ²They shall have no inheritance among their fellow Israelites; the LORD is their inheritance, as he promised them.

³This is the share due the priests from the people who sacrifice a bull or a sheep: the shoulder, the internal organs and the meat from the head. ⁴You are to give them the firstfruits of your grain, new wine and olive oil, and the first wool from the shearing of your sheep, ⁵for the LORD your God has chosen them and their descendants out of all your tribes to stand and minister in the LORD's name always.

⁶If a Levite moves from one of your towns anywhere in Israel where he is living, and comes in all earnestness to the place the LORD will choose, ⁷he may minister in the name of the LORD his God like all his fellow Levites who serve there in the presence of the LORD. ⁸He is to share equally in their benefits, even though he has received money from the sale of family possessions.

Occult Practices

⁹When you enter the land the LORD your God is giving you, do not learn to imitate the detestable ways of the nations there. ¹⁰Let no one be found among you who sacrifices their son or daughter in the fire, who practices divination or sorcery, interprets omens, engages in witchcraft, ¹¹or casts spells, or who is a medium or spiritist or who consults the dead. ¹²Anyone who does these things is detestable to the LORD; because of these same detestable practices the LORD your God will drive out those nations before you. ¹³You must be blameless before the LORD your God.

The Prophet

¹⁴The nations you will dispossess listen to those who practice sorcery or divination. But as for you, the LORD your God has not permitted

you to do so. [15]The LORD your God will raise up for you a prophet like me from among you, from your fellow Israelites. You must listen to him. [16]For this is what you asked of the LORD your God at Horeb on the day of the assembly when you said, "Let us not hear the voice of the LORD our God nor see this great fire anymore, or we will die."

[17]The LORD said to me: "What they say is good. [18]I will raise up for them a prophet like you from among their fellow Israelites, and I will put my words in his mouth. He will tell them everything I command him. [19]I myself will call to account anyone who does not listen to my words that the prophet speaks in my name. [20]But a prophet who presumes to speak in my name anything I have not commanded, or a prophet who speaks in the name of other gods, is to be put to death."

[21]You may say to yourselves, "How can we know when a message has not been spoken by the LORD?" [22]If what a prophet proclaims in the name of the LORD does not take place or come true, that is a message the LORD has not spoken. That prophet has spoken presumptuously, so do not be alarmed.

Cities of Refuge

19 When the LORD your God has destroyed the nations whose land he is giving you, and when you have driven them out and settled in their towns and houses, [2]then set aside for yourselves three cities in the land the LORD your God is giving you to possess. [3]Determine the distances involved and divide into three parts the land the LORD your God is giving you as an inheritance, so that a person who kills someone may flee for refuge to one of these cities.

[4]This is the rule concerning anyone who kills a person and flees there for safety — anyone who kills a neighbor unintentionally, without malice aforethought. [5]For instance, a man may go into the forest with his neighbor to cut wood, and as he swings his ax to fell a tree, the head may fly off and hit his neighbor and kill him. That man may flee to one of these cities and save his life. [6]Otherwise, the avenger of blood might pursue him in a rage, overtake him if the distance is too great, and kill him even though he is not deserving of death, since he did it to his neighbor without malice aforethought. [7]This is why I command you to set aside for yourselves three cities.

[8]If the LORD your God enlarges your territory, as he promised on oath to your ancestors, and gives you the whole land he promised them, [9]because you carefully follow all these laws I command you today — to love the LORD your God and to walk always in obedience to him — then you are to set aside three more cities. [10]Do this so that innocent blood will not be shed in your land, which the LORD your God is giving you as your inheritance, and so that you will not be guilty of bloodshed.

[11]But if out of hate someone lies in wait, assaults and kills a neighbor, and then flees to one of these cities, [12]the killer shall be sent for by the town elders, be brought back from the city, and be handed over to the avenger of blood to die. [13]Show no pity. You must purge from Israel the guilt of shedding innocent blood, so that it may go well with you.

[14]Do not move your neighbor's boundary stone set up by your predecessors in the inheritance you receive in the land the LORD your God is giving you to possess.

Witnesses

[15]One witness is not enough to convict anyone accused of any crime or offense they may have committed. A matter must be established by the testimony of two or three witnesses.

[16]If a malicious witness takes the stand to accuse someone of a crime, [17]the two people involved in the dispute must stand in the presence of the LORD before the priests and the judges who are in office at the time. [18]The judges must make a thorough investigation, and if the witness proves to be a liar, giving false testimony against a fellow Israelite, [19]then do to the false witness as that witness intended to do to the other party. You must purge the evil from among you. [20]The rest of the people will hear of this and be afraid, and never again will such an evil thing be done among you. [21]Show no pity: life for life, eye for eye, tooth for tooth, hand for hand, foot for foot.

Going to War

20 When you go to war against your enemies and see horses and chariots and an army greater than yours, do not be afraid of them, because the LORD your God, who brought you up out of Egypt, will be with you. [2]When you are about to go into battle, the priest shall come forward and address the army. [3]He shall say: "Hear, Israel: Today you are going into battle against your enemies. Do not be fainthearted or afraid; do not panic or be terrified by them. [4]For the LORD your God is the one who goes

The Law of Navigation: Moses Provides Future Direction
Deuteronomy 16:1—25:19

Much as America's forefathers assembled the U.S. Constitution, Moses furnished clear guidelines for his nation's future. One chief difference: Israel was to live under a theocracy, not a democracy. The nation was to be lovingly ruled by God, not by the whims of the people. Ponder the genius behind the structure and navigation Moses offers in these chapters:

Leadership Action
1. Established seven annual feasts
2. Males to worship at central location
3. Appointed judges for each tribe
4. Shared civil duties with the community
5. Communicated criteria for top leaders
6. Organized offerings for priests/Levites
7. Established cities of refuge
8. Set boundaries for national defense
9. Addressed crimes and moral failure
10. Tithing to the Lord

Purpose
1. Reminded people of the big picture
2. Provided context for participation
3. Furnished leadership at a local level
4. Created value of justice and social order
5. Cast vision for leadership with integrity
6. Prioritized holy living and godly priorities
7. Esteemed the qualities of mercy and grace
8. Taught Israel to trust God, not themselves
9. Set consequences prior to criminal acts
10. Taught stewardship as a top priority

with you to fight for you against your enemies to give you victory."

[5]The officers shall say to the army: "Has anyone built a new house and not yet begun to live in it? Let him go home, or he may die in battle and someone else may begin to live in it. [6]Has anyone planted a vineyard and not begun to enjoy it? Let him go home, or he may die in battle and someone else enjoy it. [7]Has anyone become pledged to a woman and not married her? Let him go home, or he may die in battle and someone else marry her." [8]Then the officers shall add, "Is anyone afraid or fainthearted? Let him go home so that his fellow soldiers will not become disheartened too." [9]When the officers have finished speaking to the army, they shall appoint commanders over it.

[10]When you march up to attack a city, make its people an offer of peace. [11]If they accept and open their gates, all the people in it shall be subject to forced labor and shall work for you. [12]If they refuse to make peace and they engage you in battle, lay siege to that city. [13]When the LORD your God delivers it into your hand, put to the sword all the men in it. [14]As for the women, the children, the livestock and everything else in the city, you may take these as plunder for yourselves. And you may use the plunder the LORD your God gives you from your enemies. [15]This is how you are to treat all the cities that are at a distance from you and do not belong to the nations nearby.

[16]However, in the cities of the nations the LORD your God is giving you as an inheritance, do not leave alive anything that breathes. [17]Completely destroy[a] them — the Hittites, Amorites, Canaanites, Perizzites, Hivites and Jebusites — as the LORD your God has commanded you. [18]Otherwise, they will teach you to follow all the detestable things they do in worshiping their gods, and you will sin against the LORD your God.

[19]When you lay siege to a city for a long time, fighting against it to capture it, do not destroy its trees by putting an ax to them, because you can eat their fruit. Do not cut them down. Are the trees people, that you should besiege them?[b] [20]However, you may cut down trees that you know are not fruit trees and use them to build siege works until the city at war with you falls.

Atonement for an Unsolved Murder

21 If someone is found slain, lying in a field in the land the LORD your God is giving you to possess, and it is not known who the killer was, [2]your elders and judges shall go out and measure the distance from the body to the neighboring towns. [3]Then the elders of the town nearest the body shall take a heifer that has

[a] 17 The Hebrew term refers to the irrevocable giving over of things or persons to the LORD, often by totally destroying them.
[b] 19 Or down to use in the siege, for the fruit trees are for the benefit of people.

never been worked and has never worn a yoke [4]and lead it down to a valley that has not been plowed or planted and where there is a flowing stream. There in the valley they are to break the heifer's neck. [5]The Levitical priests shall step forward, for the LORD your God has chosen them to minister and to pronounce blessings in the name of the LORD and to decide all cases of dispute and assault. [6]Then all the elders of the town nearest the body shall wash their hands over the heifer whose neck was broken in the valley, [7]and they shall declare: "Our hands did not shed this blood, nor did our eyes see it done. [8]Accept this atonement for your people Israel, whom you have redeemed, LORD, and do not hold your people guilty of the blood of an innocent person." Then the bloodshed will be atoned for, [9]and you will have purged from yourselves the guilt of shedding innocent blood, since you have done what is right in the eyes of the LORD.

Marrying a Captive Woman

[10]When you go to war against your enemies and the LORD your God delivers them into your hands and you take captives, [11]if you notice among the captives a beautiful woman and are attracted to her, you may take her as your wife. [12]Bring her into your home and have her shave her head, trim her nails [13]and put aside the clothes she was wearing when captured. After she has lived in your house and mourned her father and mother for a full month, then you may go to her and be her husband and she shall be your wife. [14]If you are not pleased with her, let her go wherever she wishes. You must not sell her or treat her as a slave, since you have dishonored her.

The Right of the Firstborn

[15]If a man has two wives, and he loves one but not the other, and both bear him sons but the firstborn is the son of the wife he does not love, [16]when he wills his property to his sons, he must not give the rights of the firstborn to the son of the wife he loves in preference to his actual firstborn, the son of the wife he does not love. [17]He must acknowledge the son of his unloved wife as the firstborn by giving him a double share of all he has. That son is the first sign of his father's strength. The right of the firstborn belongs to him.

A Rebellious Son

[18]If someone has a stubborn and rebellious son who does not obey his father and mother and will not listen to them when they discipline him, [19]his father and mother shall take hold of him and bring him to the elders at the gate of his town. [20]They shall say to the elders, "This son of ours is stubborn and rebellious. He will not obey

MOSES — PROFILE in leadership

The Confidence of God's Presence

Deuteronomy 20:1–20

It's always a good idea to have a battle plan if you intend to lead an army into war. Moses possessed a devastating plan for the army of Israel, a set of instructions that came straight from the top—the very top.

Imagine the confidence a field commander could instill in his troops knowing that he could not lose. Yet that was just the kind of guarantee God gave Moses and the people of Israel.

How astonishing this must have seemed! For at the time God issued his battle plans, the Hebrews hadn't even settled in their own land, let alone set up a line of defense. Furthermore, the Lord guaranteed his people that they would face military forces far more formidable than their own. Yet God assured them they had nothing to fear—as long as they remembered that he would remain with them always, as he had since the day they left Egypt.

Leaders today can bank on the same promise that gave Moses such courage: "For the LORD your God is the one who goes with you to fight for you against your enemies to give you victory" (Dt 20:4; cf. Heb 13:5–6). And so God gives us the same word he gave to Moses: "Do not be afraid" (Dt 20:1).

us. He is a glutton and a drunkard." 21Then all the men of his town are to stone him to death. You must purge the evil from among you. All Israel will hear of it and be afraid.

Various Laws

22If someone guilty of a capital offense is put to death and their body is exposed on a pole, 23you must not leave the body hanging on the pole overnight. Be sure to bury it that same day, because anyone who is hung on a pole is under God's curse. You must not desecrate the land the LORD your God is giving you as an inheritance.

22 If you see your fellow Israelite's ox or sheep straying, do not ignore it but be sure to take it back to its owner. 2If they do not live near you or if you do not know who owns it, take it home with you and keep it until they come looking for it. Then give it back. 3Do the same if you find their donkey or cloak or anything else they have lost. Do not ignore it.

4If you see your fellow Israelite's donkey or ox fallen on the road, do not ignore it. Help the owner get it to its feet.

5A woman must not wear men's clothing, nor a man wear women's clothing, for the LORD your God detests anyone who does this.

6If you come across a bird's nest beside the road, either in a tree or on the ground, and the mother is sitting on the young or on the eggs, do not take the mother with the young. 7You may take the young, but be sure to let the mother go, so that it may go well with you and you may have a long life.

8When you build a new house, make a parapet around your roof so that you may not bring the guilt of bloodshed on your house if someone falls from the roof.

9Do not plant two kinds of seed in your vineyard; if you do, not only the crops you plant but also the fruit of the vineyard will be defiled.*a*

10Do not plow with an ox and a donkey yoked together.

11Do not wear clothes of wool and linen woven together.

12Make tassels on the four corners of the cloak you wear.

Marriage Violations

13If a man takes a wife and, after sleeping with her, dislikes her 14and slanders her and gives her a bad name, saying, "I married this woman, but when I approached her, I did not find proof of her virginity," 15then the young woman's father and mother shall bring to the town elders at the gate proof that she was a virgin. 16Her father will say to the elders, "I gave my daughter in marriage to this man, but he dislikes her. 17Now he has slandered her and said, 'I did not find your daughter to be a virgin.' But here is the proof of my daughter's virginity." Then her parents shall display the cloth before the elders of the town, 18and the elders shall take the man and punish him. 19They shall fine him a hundred shekels*b* of silver and give them to the young woman's father, because this man has given an Israelite virgin a bad name. She shall continue to be his wife; he must not divorce her as long as he lives.

20If, however, the charge is true and no proof of the young woman's virginity can be found, 21she shall be brought to the door of her father's house and there the men of her town shall stone her to death. She has done an outrageous thing in Israel by being promiscuous while still in her father's house. You must purge the evil from among you.

22If a man is found sleeping with another man's wife, both the man who slept with her and the woman must die. You must purge the evil from Israel.

23If a man happens to meet in a town a virgin pledged to be married and he sleeps with her, 24you shall take both of them to the gate of that town and stone them to death — the young woman because she was in a town and did not scream for help, and the man because he violated another man's wife. You must purge the evil from among you.

25But if out in the country a man happens to meet a young woman pledged to be married and rapes her, only the man who has done this shall die. 26Do nothing to the woman; she has committed no sin deserving death. This case is like that of someone who attacks and murders a neighbor, 27for the man found the young woman out in the country, and though the betrothed woman screamed, there was no one to rescue her.

28If a man happens to meet a virgin who is not pledged to be married and rapes her and they are discovered, 29he shall pay her father fifty shekels*c* of silver. He must marry the young woman, for he has violated her. He can never divorce her as long as he lives.

30A man is not to marry his father's wife; he must not dishonor his father's bed.*d*

---

a 9 Or *be forfeited to the sanctuary*   *b 19* That is, about 2 1/2 pounds or about 1.2 kilograms   *c 29* That is, about 1 1/4 pounds or about 575 grams   *d 30* In Hebrew texts this verse (22:30) is numbered 23:1.

Exclusion From the Assembly

23 ^a No one who has been emasculated by crushing or cutting may enter the assembly of the LORD.

²No one born of a forbidden marriage^b nor any of their descendants may enter the assembly of the LORD, not even in the tenth generation.

³No Ammonite or Moabite or any of their descendants may enter the assembly of the LORD, not even in the tenth generation. ⁴For they did not come to meet you with bread and water on your way when you came out of Egypt, and they hired Balaam son of Beor from Pethor in Aram Naharaim^c to pronounce a curse on you. ⁵However, the LORD your God would not listen to Balaam but turned the curse into a blessing for you, because the LORD your God loves you. ⁶Do not seek a treaty of friendship with them as long as you live.

⁷Do not despise an Edomite, for the Edomites are related to you. Do not despise an Egyptian, because you resided as foreigners in their country. ⁸The third generation of children born to them may enter the assembly of the LORD.

Uncleanness in the Camp

⁹When you are encamped against your enemies, keep away from everything impure. ¹⁰If one of your men is unclean because of a nocturnal emission, he is to go outside the camp and stay there. ¹¹But as evening approaches he is to wash himself, and at sunset he may return to the camp.

¹²Designate a place outside the camp where you can go to relieve yourself. ¹³As part of your equipment have something to dig with, and when you relieve yourself, dig a hole and cover up your excrement. ¹⁴For the LORD your God moves about in your camp to protect you and to deliver your enemies to you. Your camp must be holy, so that he will not see among you anything indecent and turn away from you.

Miscellaneous Laws

¹⁵If a slave has taken refuge with you, do not hand them over to their master. ¹⁶Let them live among you wherever they like and in whatever town they choose. Do not oppress them.

¹⁷No Israelite man or woman is to become a shrine prostitute. ¹⁸You must not bring the earnings of a female prostitute or of a male prostitute^d into the house of the LORD your God to pay any vow, because the LORD your God detests them both.

¹⁹Do not charge a fellow Israelite interest, whether on money or food or anything else that may earn interest. ²⁰You may charge a foreigner interest, but not a fellow Israelite, so that the LORD your God may bless you in everything you put your hand to in the land you are entering to possess.

²¹If you make a vow to the LORD your God, do not be slow to pay it, for the LORD your God will certainly demand it of you and you will be guilty of sin. ²²But if you refrain from making a vow, you will not be guilty. ²³Whatever your lips utter you must be sure to do, because you made your vow freely to the LORD your God with your own mouth.

²⁴If you enter your neighbor's vineyard, you may eat all the grapes you want, but do not put any in your basket. ²⁵If you enter your neighbor's grainfield, you may pick kernels with your hands, but you must not put a sickle to their standing grain.

24 If a man marries a woman who becomes displeasing to him because he finds something indecent about her, and he writes her a certificate of divorce, gives it to her and sends her from his house, ²and if after she leaves his house she becomes the wife of another man, ³and her second husband dislikes her and writes her a certificate of divorce, gives it to her and sends her from his house, or if he dies, ⁴then her first husband, who divorced her, is not allowed to marry her again after she has been defiled. That would be detestable in the eyes of the LORD. Do not bring sin upon the land the LORD your God is giving you as an inheritance.

⁵If a man has recently married, he must not be sent to war or have any other duty laid on him. For one year he is to be free to stay at home and bring happiness to the wife he has married.

⁶Do not take a pair of millstones — not even the upper one — as security for a debt, because that would be taking a person's livelihood as security.

⁷If someone is caught kidnapping a fellow Israelite and treating or selling them as a slave, the kidnapper must die. You must purge the evil from among you.

⁸In cases of defiling skin diseases,^e be very careful to do exactly as the Levitical priests instruct you. You must follow carefully what I

---

^a In Hebrew texts 23:1-25 is numbered 23:2-26.   ^b 2 Or *one of illegitimate birth*   ^c 4 That is, Northwest Mesopotamia   ^d 18 Hebrew *of a dog*   ^e 8 The Hebrew word for *defiling skin diseases*, traditionally translated "leprosy," was used for various diseases affecting the skin.

have commanded them. ⁹Remember what the LORD your God did to Miriam along the way after you came out of Egypt.

¹⁰When you make a loan of any kind to your neighbor, do not go into their house to get what is offered to you as a pledge. ¹¹Stay outside and let the neighbor to whom you are making the loan bring the pledge out to you. ¹²If the neighbor is poor, do not go to sleep with their pledge in your possession. ¹³Return their cloak by sunset so that your neighbor may sleep in it. Then they will thank you, and it will be regarded as a righteous act in the sight of the LORD your God.

¹⁴Do not take advantage of a hired worker who is poor and needy, whether that worker is a fellow Israelite or a foreigner residing in one of your towns. ¹⁵Pay them their wages each day before sunset, because they are poor and are counting on it. Otherwise they may cry to the LORD against you, and you will be guilty of sin.

¹⁶Parents are not to be put to death for their children, nor children put to death for their parents; each will die for their own sin.

¹⁷Do not deprive the foreigner or the fatherless of justice, or take the cloak of the widow as a pledge. ¹⁸Remember that you were slaves in Egypt and the LORD your God redeemed you from there. That is why I command you to do this.

¹⁹When you are harvesting in your field and you overlook a sheaf, do not go back to get it. Leave it for the foreigner, the fatherless and the widow, so that the LORD your God may bless you in all the work of your hands. ²⁰When you beat the olives from your trees, do not go over the branches a second time. Leave what remains for the foreigner, the fatherless and the widow. ²¹When you harvest the grapes in your vineyard, do not go over the vines again. Leave what remains for the foreigner, the fatherless and the widow. ²²Remember that you were slaves in Egypt. That is why I command you to do this.

25 When people have a dispute, they are to take it to court and the judges will decide the case, acquitting the innocent and condemning the guilty. ²If the guilty person deserves to be beaten, the judge shall make them lie down and have them flogged in his presence with the number of lashes the crime deserves, ³but the judge must not impose more than forty lashes. If the guilty party is flogged more than that, your fellow Israelite will be degraded in your eyes.

⁴Do not muzzle an ox while it is treading out the grain.

⁵If brothers are living together and one of them dies without a son, his widow must not marry outside the family. Her husband's brother shall take her and marry her and fulfill the duty of a brother-in-law to her. ⁶The first son she bears shall carry on the name of the dead brother so that his name will not be blotted out from Israel.

⁷However, if a man does not want to marry his brother's wife, she shall go to the elders at the town gate and say, "My husband's brother refuses to carry on his brother's name in Israel. He will not fulfill the duty of a brother-in-law to me." ⁸Then the elders of his town shall summon him and talk to him. If he persists in saying, "I do not want to marry her," ⁹his brother's widow shall go up to him in the presence of the elders, take off one of his sandals, spit in his face and say, "This is what is done to the man who will not build up his brother's family line." ¹⁰That man's line shall be known in Israel as The Family of the Unsandaled.

¹¹If two men are fighting and the wife of one of them comes to rescue her husband from his assailant, and she reaches out and seizes him by his private parts, ¹²you shall cut off her hand. Show her no pity.

¹³Do not have two differing weights in your bag—one heavy, one light. ¹⁴Do not have two differing measures in your house—one large, one small. ¹⁵You must have accurate and honest weights and measures, so that you may live long in the land the LORD your God is giving you. ¹⁶For the LORD your God detests anyone who does these things, anyone who deals dishonestly.

¹⁷Remember what the Amalekites did to you along the way when you came out of Egypt. ¹⁸When you were weary and worn out, they met you on your journey and attacked all who were lagging behind; they had no fear of God. ¹⁹When the LORD your God gives you rest from all the enemies around you in the land he is giving you to possess as an inheritance, you shall blot out the name of Amalek from under heaven. Do not forget!

Firstfruits and Tithes

26 When you have entered the land the LORD your God is giving you as an inheritance and have taken possession of it and settled in it, ²take some of the firstfruits of all that you produce from the soil of the land the LORD your God is giving you and put them in a basket. Then go to the place the LORD your God will choose as a dwelling for his Name ³and say to the priest in office at the time, "I declare today to the LORD your God that I have come to the land the LORD swore to our ancestors to give us." ⁴The priest shall take the basket from your hands and set it down in front of the altar of the LORD your God. ⁵Then you shall declare before the LORD your God: "My father was a wandering Aramean, and he went down into Egypt with a few people and lived there and became a great nation, powerful and numerous. ⁶But the Egyptians mistreated us and made us suffer, subjecting us to harsh labor. ⁷Then we cried out to the LORD, the God of our ancestors, and the LORD heard our voice and saw our misery, toil and oppression. ⁸So the LORD brought us out of Egypt with a mighty hand and an outstretched arm, with great terror and with signs and wonders. ⁹He brought us to this place and gave us this land, a land flowing with milk and honey; ¹⁰and now I bring the firstfruits of the soil that you, LORD, have given me." Place the basket before the LORD your God and bow down before him. ¹¹Then you and the Levites and the foreigners residing among you shall rejoice in all the good things the LORD your God has given to you and your household.

¹²When you have finished setting aside a tenth of all your produce in the third year, the year of the tithe, you shall give it to the Levite, the foreigner, the fatherless and the widow, so that they may eat in your towns and be satisfied. ¹³Then say to the LORD your God: "I have removed from my house the sacred portion and have given it to the Levite, the foreigner, the fatherless and the widow, according to all you commanded. I have not turned aside from your commands nor have I forgotten any of them. ¹⁴I have not eaten any of the sacred portion while I was in mourning, nor have I removed any of it while I was unclean, nor have I offered any of it to the dead. I have obeyed the LORD my God; I have done everything you commanded me. ¹⁵Look down from heaven, your holy dwelling place, and bless your people Israel and the land you have given us as you promised on oath to our ancestors, a land flowing with milk and honey."

Follow the LORD's Commands

¹⁶The LORD your God commands you this day to follow these decrees and laws; carefully observe them with all your heart and with all your soul. ¹⁷You have declared this day that the LORD is your God and that you will walk in obedience to him, that you will keep his decrees, commands and laws — that you will listen to him. ¹⁸And the LORD has declared this day that you are his people, his treasured possession as he promised, and that you are to keep all his

commands. ¹⁹He has declared that he will set you in praise, fame and honor high above all the nations he has made and that you will be a people holy to the LORD your God, as he promised.

The Altar on Mount Ebal

27 Moses and the elders of Israel commanded the people: "Keep all these commands that I give you today. ²When you have crossed the Jordan into the land the LORD your God is giving you, set up some large stones and coat them with plaster. ³Write on them all the words of this law when you have crossed over to enter the land the LORD your God is giving you, a land flowing with milk and honey, just as the LORD, the God of your ancestors, promised you. ⁴And when you have crossed the Jordan, set up these stones on Mount Ebal, as I command you today, and coat them with plaster. ⁵Build there an altar to the LORD your God, an altar of stones. Do not use any iron tool on them. ⁶Build the altar of the LORD your God with fieldstones and offer burnt offerings on it to the LORD your God. ⁷Sacrifice fellowship offerings there, eating them and rejoicing in the presence of the LORD your God. ⁸And you shall write very clearly all the words of this law on these stones you have set up."

Curses From Mount Ebal

⁹Then Moses and the Levitical priests said to all Israel, "Be silent, Israel, and listen! You have now become the people of the LORD your God. ¹⁰Obey the LORD your God and follow his commands and decrees that I give you today."

¹¹On the same day Moses commanded the people:

¹²When you have crossed the Jordan, these tribes shall stand on Mount Gerizim to bless the people: Simeon, Levi, Judah, Issachar, Joseph and Benjamin. ¹³And these tribes shall stand on Mount Ebal to pronounce curses: Reuben, Gad, Asher, Zebulun, Dan and Naphtali.

¹⁴The Levites shall recite to all the people of Israel in a loud voice:

¹⁵"Cursed is anyone who makes an idol — a thing detestable to the LORD, the work of skilled hands — and sets it up in secret."

Then all the people shall say,

"Amen!"

¹⁶"Cursed is anyone who dishonors their father or mother."

Then all the people shall say,

"Amen!"

¹⁷"Cursed is anyone who moves their neighbor's boundary stone."

Then all the people shall say, "Amen!"

¹⁸"Cursed is anyone who leads the blind astray on the road."

Then all the people shall say, "Amen!"

¹⁹"Cursed is anyone who withholds justice from the foreigner, the fatherless or the widow."

Then all the people shall say, "Amen!"

²⁰"Cursed is anyone who sleeps with his father's wife, for he dishonors his father's bed."

Then all the people shall say, "Amen!"

²¹"Cursed is anyone who has sexual relations with any animal."

Then all the people shall say, "Amen!"

²²"Cursed is anyone who sleeps with his sister, the daughter of his father or the daughter of his mother."

Then all the people shall say, "Amen!"

²³"Cursed is anyone who sleeps with his mother-in-law."

Then all the people shall say, "Amen!"

²⁴"Cursed is anyone who kills their neighbor secretly."

Then all the people shall say, "Amen!"

²⁵"Cursed is anyone who accepts a bribe to kill an innocent person."

Then all the people shall say, "Amen!"

²⁶"Cursed is anyone who does not uphold the words of this law by carrying them out."

Then all the people shall say, "Amen!"

Blessings for Obedience

28 If you fully obey the LORD your God and carefully follow all his commands I give you today, the LORD your God will set you high above all the nations on earth. ²All these blessings will come on you and accompany you if you obey the LORD your God:

³You will be blessed in the city and blessed in the country.

⁴The fruit of your womb will be blessed, and the crops of your land and the young of your livestock—the calves of your herds and the lambs of your flocks.

⁵Your basket and your kneading trough will be blessed.

⁶You will be blessed when you come in and blessed when you go out.

⁷The LORD will grant that the enemies who rise up against you will be defeated before you. They will come at you from one direction but flee from you in seven.

⁸The LORD will send a blessing on your barns and on everything you put your hand to. The LORD your God will bless you in the land he is giving you.

⁹The LORD will establish you as his holy people, as he promised you on oath, if you keep the commands of the LORD your God and walk in obedience to him. ¹⁰Then all the peoples on earth will see that you are called by the name of the LORD, and they will fear you. ¹¹The LORD will grant you abundant prosperity—in the fruit of your womb, the young of your livestock and the crops of your ground—in the land he swore to your ancestors to give you.

¹²The LORD will open the heavens, the storehouse of his bounty, to send rain on your land in season and to bless all the work of your hands. You will lend to many nations but will borrow from none. ¹³The LORD will make you the head, not the tail. If you pay attention to the commands of the LORD your God that I give you this day and carefully follow them, you will always be at the top, never at the bottom. ¹⁴Do not turn aside from any of the commands I give you today, to the right or to the left, following other gods and serving them.

Curses for Disobedience

¹⁵However, if you do not obey the LORD your God and do not carefully follow all his commands and decrees I am giving you today, all these curses will come on you and overtake you:

¹⁶You will be cursed in the city and cursed in the country.

¹⁷Your basket and your kneading trough will be cursed.

¹⁸The fruit of your womb will be cursed, and the crops of your land, and the calves of your herds and the lambs of your flocks.

¹⁹You will be cursed when you come in and cursed when you go out.

²⁰The LORD will send on you curses, confusion and rebuke in everything you put your hand to, until you are destroyed and come to sudden ruin because of the evil you have done in forsaking him.[a] ²¹The LORD will plague you with diseases until he has destroyed you from the land you are entering to possess. ²²The LORD will strike you with wasting disease, with fever and inflammation, with scorching heat and drought, with blight and mildew, which will plague you until you perish. ²³The sky over your head will be bronze, the ground beneath you iron. ²⁴The LORD will turn the rain of your country into dust and powder; it will come down from the skies until you are destroyed.

²⁵The LORD will cause you to be defeated before your enemies. You will come at them from one direction but flee from them in seven, and you will become a thing of horror to all the kingdoms on earth. ²⁶Your carcasses will be food for all the birds and the wild animals, and there will be no one to frighten them away. ²⁷The LORD will afflict you with the boils of Egypt and with tumors, festering sores and the itch, from which you cannot be cured. ²⁸The LORD will afflict you with madness, blindness and confusion of mind. ²⁹At midday you will grope about like a blind person in the dark. You will be unsuccessful in everything you do; day after day you will be oppressed and robbed, with no one to rescue you.

³⁰You will be pledged to be married to a woman, but another will take her and rape her. You will build a house, but you will not live in it. You will plant a vineyard, but you will not even begin to enjoy its fruit. ³¹Your ox will be slaughtered before your eyes, but you will eat none of it. Your donkey will be forcibly taken from you and will not be returned. Your sheep will be given to your enemies, and no one will rescue them. ³²Your sons and daughters will be given to another nation, and you will wear out your eyes watching for them day after day, powerless to lift a hand. ³³A people that you do not know will eat what your land and labor produce, and you will have nothing but cruel oppression all your days. ³⁴The sights you see will drive you mad. ³⁵The LORD will afflict your knees and legs with painful boils that cannot be cured, spreading from the soles of your feet to the top of your head.

³⁶The LORD will drive you and the king you set over you to a nation unknown to you or your ancestors. There you will worship other gods, gods of wood and stone. ³⁷You will become a thing of horror, a byword and an object of ridicule among all the peoples where the LORD will drive you.

³⁸You will sow much seed in the field but you will harvest little, because locusts will devour it. ³⁹You will plant vineyards and cultivate them but you will not drink the wine or gather the grapes, because worms will eat them. ⁴⁰You will have olive trees throughout your country but you will not use the oil, because the olives will drop off. ⁴¹You will have sons and daughters but you will not keep them, because they will go into captivity. ⁴²Swarms of locusts will take over all your trees and the crops of your land.

⁴³The foreigners who reside among you will rise above you higher and higher, but you will sink lower and lower. ⁴⁴They will lend to you, but you will not lend to them. They will be the head, but you will be the tail.

⁴⁵All these curses will come on you. They will pursue you and overtake you until you are destroyed, because you did not obey the LORD your God and observe the commands and decrees he gave you. ⁴⁶They will be a sign and a wonder to you and your descendants forever. ⁴⁷Because you did not serve the LORD your God joyfully and gladly in the time of prosperity, ⁴⁸therefore in hunger and thirst, in nakedness and dire poverty, you will serve the enemies the LORD sends against you. He will put an iron yoke on your neck until he has destroyed you.

⁴⁹The LORD will bring a nation against you from far away, from the ends of the earth, like an eagle swooping down, a nation whose language you will not understand, ⁵⁰a fierce-looking nation without respect for the old or pity for the young. ⁵¹They will devour the young of your livestock and the crops of your land until you are destroyed. They will leave you no grain, new wine or olive oil, nor any calves of your herds or lambs of your flocks until you are ruined. ⁵²They will lay siege to all the cities throughout your land until the high fortified walls in which you trust fall down. They will besiege all the cities throughout the land the LORD your God is giving you.

⁵³Because of the suffering your enemy will inflict on you during the siege, you will eat the fruit of the womb, the flesh of the sons and daughters the LORD your God has given you. ⁵⁴Even the most gentle and sensitive man among you will have no compassion on his own brother or the wife he loves or his surviving children, ⁵⁵and he will not give to one of them any of the flesh of

_____
[a] 20 Hebrew me

Double Vision: Moses Enables People to See the Future from Two Angles

Deuteronomy 27:1—28:68

Most of the Israelites preparing to enter the promised land had grown up in the wilderness and had never seen the miracles in Egypt. Moses recognized that this new generation needed fresh inspiration, and so cast a vision of their future. Moses knew that their prosperity depended far more on a healthy spiritual condition than on military prowess. He therefore exhorted them to grow in their knowledge of the Lord, to trust his holy nature, and to obey his commands.

The vision Moses cast that day looked quite different from anything most leaders have communicated since then: he cast vision for what life would look like if the people obeyed God fully. He told them they would enjoy blessings and fruit beyond what they needed. They would receive favor from neighboring peoples and enjoy great prosperity. They would grow healthy and strong.

But Moses also cast vision for how life would turn out if they failed to obey. Not many leaders do this! From then on, the people could see clearly the blessings of obedience and the curses of disobedience. Moses graphically described both in his speech.

That's the power of vision, from two angles. Such a vision helps people sort out what they will do, because they can think with the end in mind.

---

his children that he is eating. It will be all he has left because of the suffering your enemy will inflict on you during the siege of all your cities. ⁵⁶The most gentle and sensitive woman among you — so sensitive and gentle that she would not venture to touch the ground with the sole of her foot — will begrudge the husband she loves and her own son or daughter ⁵⁷the afterbirth from her womb and the children she bears. For in her dire need she intends to eat them secretly because of the suffering your enemy will inflict on you during the siege of your cities.

⁵⁸If you do not carefully follow all the words of this law, which are written in this book, and do not revere this glorious and awesome name — the LORD your God — ⁵⁹the LORD will send fearful plagues on you and your descendants, harsh and prolonged disasters, and severe and lingering illnesses. ⁶⁰He will bring on you all the diseases of Egypt that you dreaded, and they will cling to you. ⁶¹The LORD will also bring on you every kind of sickness and disaster not recorded in this Book of the Law, until you are destroyed. ⁶²You who were as numerous as the stars in the sky will be left but few in number, because you did not obey the LORD your God. ⁶³Just as it pleased the LORD to make you prosper and increase in number, so it will please him to ruin and destroy you. You will be uprooted from the land you are entering to possess.

⁶⁴Then the LORD will scatter you among all nations, from one end of the earth to the other.

There you will worship other gods — gods of wood and stone, which neither you nor your ancestors have known. ⁶⁵Among those nations you will find no repose, no resting place for the sole of your foot. There the LORD will give you an anxious mind, eyes weary with longing, and a despairing heart. ⁶⁶You will live in constant suspense, filled with dread both night and day, never sure of your life. ⁶⁷In the morning you will say, "If only it were evening!" and in the evening, "If only it were morning!" — because of the terror that will fill your hearts and the sights that your eyes will see. ⁶⁸The LORD will send you back in ships to Egypt on a journey I said you should never make again. There you will offer yourselves for sale to your enemies as male and female slaves, but no one will buy you.

Renewal of the Covenant

29 ᵃ These are the terms of the covenant the LORD commanded Moses to make with the Israelites in Moab, in addition to the covenant he had made with them at Horeb.

²Moses summoned all the Israelites and said to them:

Your eyes have seen all that the LORD did in Egypt to Pharaoh, to all his officials and to all his land. ³With your own eyes you saw those great trials, those signs and great wonders.

ᵃ In Hebrew texts 29:1 is numbered 28:69, and 29:2-29 is numbered 29:1-28.

4But to this day the LORD has not given you a mind that understands or eyes that see or ears that hear. 5Yet the LORD says, "During the forty years that I led you through the wilderness, your clothes did not wear out, nor did the sandals on your feet. 6You ate no bread and drank no wine or other fermented drink. I did this so that you might know that I am the LORD your God."

7When you reached this place, Sihon king of Heshbon and Og king of Bashan came out to fight against us, but we defeated them. 8We took their land and gave it as an inheritance to the Reubenites, the Gadites and the half-tribe of Manasseh.

9Carefully follow the terms of this covenant, so that you may prosper in everything you do. 10All of you are standing today in the presence of the LORD your God—your leaders and chief men, your elders and officials, and all the other men of Israel, 11together with your children and your wives, and the foreigners living in your camps who chop your wood and carry your water. 12You are standing here in order to enter into a covenant with the LORD your God, a covenant the LORD is making with you this day and sealing with an oath, 13to confirm you this day as his people, that he may be your God as he promised you and as he swore to your fathers, Abraham, Isaac and Jacob. 14I am making this covenant, with its oath, not only with you 15who are standing here with us today in the presence of the LORD our God but also with those who are not here today.

16You yourselves know how we lived in Egypt and how we passed through the countries on the way here. 17You saw among them their detestable images and idols of wood and stone, of silver and gold. 18Make sure there is no man or woman, clan or tribe among you today whose heart turns away from the LORD our God to go and worship the gods of those nations; make sure there is no root among you that produces such bitter poison.

19When such a person hears the words of this oath and they invoke a blessing on themselves, thinking, "I will be safe, even though I persist in going my own way," they will bring disaster on the watered land as well as the dry. 20The LORD will never be willing to forgive them; his wrath and zeal will burn against them. All the curses written in this book will fall on them, and the LORD will blot out their names from under heaven. 21The LORD will single them out from all the tribes of Israel for disaster, according to all the curses of the covenant written in this Book of the Law.

22Your children who follow you in later generations and foreigners who come from distant lands will see the calamities that have fallen on the land and the diseases with which the LORD has afflicted it. 23The whole land will be a burning waste of salt and sulfur—nothing planted, nothing sprouting, no vegetation growing on it. It will be like the destruction of Sodom and Gomorrah, Admah and Zeboyim, which the LORD overthrew in fierce anger. 24All the nations will ask: "Why has the LORD done this to this land? Why this fierce, burning anger?"

25And the answer will be: "It is because this people abandoned the covenant of the LORD, the God of their ancestors, the covenant he made with them when he brought them out of Egypt. 26They went off and worshiped other gods and bowed down to them, gods they did not know, gods he had not given them. 27Therefore the LORD's anger burned against this land, so that he brought on it all the curses written in this book. 28In furious anger and in great wrath the LORD uprooted them from their land and thrust them into another land, as it is now."

29The secret things belong to the LORD our God, but the things revealed belong to us and to our children forever, that we may follow all the words of this law.

Prosperity After Turning to the LORD

30 When all these blessings and curses I have set before you come on you and you take them to heart wherever the LORD your God disperses you among the nations, 2and when you and your children return to the LORD your God and obey him with all your heart and with all your soul according to everything I command you today, 3then the LORD your God will restore your fortunes[a] and have compassion on you and gather you again from all the nations where he scattered you. 4Even if you have been banished to the most distant land under the heavens, from there the LORD your God will gather you and bring you back. 5He will bring you to the land that belonged to your ancestors, and you will take possession of it. He will make you more prosperous and numerous than your ancestors. 6The LORD your God will circumcise your hearts and the hearts of your descendants, so that you may love him with all your heart and with all your soul, and live. 7The LORD your God will put all these curses on your enemies who hate and persecute you. 8You will again

a 3 Or will bring you back from captivity

obey the LORD and follow all his commands I am giving you today. [9]Then the LORD your God will make you most prosperous in all the work of your hands and in the fruit of your womb, the young of your livestock and the crops of your land. The LORD will again delight in you and make you prosperous, just as he delighted in your ancestors, [10]if you obey the LORD your God and keep his commands and decrees that are written in this Book of the Law and turn to the LORD your God with all your heart and with all your soul.

The Offer of Life or Death

[11]Now what I am commanding you today is not too difficult for you or beyond your reach. [12]It is not up in heaven, so that you have to ask, "Who will ascend into heaven to get it and proclaim it to us so we may obey it?" [13]Nor is it beyond the sea, so that you have to ask, "Who will cross the sea to get it and proclaim it to us so we may obey it?" [14]No, the word is very near you; it is in your mouth and in your heart so you may obey it.

[15]See, I set before you today life and prosperity, death and destruction. [16]For I command you today to love the LORD your God, to walk in obedience to him, and to keep his commands, decrees and laws; then you will live and increase, and the LORD your God will bless you in the land you are entering to possess.

[17]But if your heart turns away and you are not obedient, and if you are drawn away to bow down to other gods and worship them, [18]I declare to you this day that you will certainly be destroyed. You will not live long in the land you are crossing the Jordan to enter and possess.

[19]This day I call the heavens and the earth as witnesses against you that I have set before you life and death, blessings and curses. Now choose life, so that you and your children may live [20]and that you may love the LORD your God, listen to his voice, and hold fast to him. For the LORD is your life, and he will give you many years in the land he swore to give to your fathers, Abraham, Isaac and Jacob.

Joshua to Succeed Moses

31 Then Moses went out and spoke these words to all Israel: [2]"I am now a hundred and twenty years old and I am no longer able to lead you. The LORD has said to me, 'You shall not cross the Jordan.' [3]The LORD your God himself will cross over ahead of you. He will destroy these nations before you, and you will take pos-

session of their land. Joshua also will cross over ahead of you, as the LORD said. [4]And the LORD will do to them what he did to Sihon and Og, the kings of the Amorites, whom he destroyed along with their land. [5]The LORD will deliver them to you, and you must do to them all that I have commanded you. [6]Be strong and courageous. Do not be afraid or terrified because of them, for the LORD your God goes with you; he will never leave you nor forsake you."

[7]Then Moses summoned Joshua and said to him in the presence of all Israel, "Be strong and courageous, for you must go with this people into the land that the LORD swore to their ancestors to give them, and you must divide it among them as their inheritance. [8]The LORD himself goes before you and will be with you; he will never leave you nor forsake you. Do not be afraid; do not be discouraged."

Public Reading of the Law

[9]So Moses wrote down this law and gave it to the Levitical priests, who carried the ark of the covenant of the LORD, and to all the elders of Israel. [10]Then Moses commanded them: "At the end of every seven years, in the year for canceling debts, during the Festival of Tabernacles, [11]when all Israel comes to appear before the LORD your God at the place he will choose, you shall read this law before them in their hearing. [12]Assemble the people—men, women and children, and the foreigners residing in your towns—so they can listen and learn to fear the LORD your God and follow carefully all the words of this law. [13]Their children, who do not know this law, must hear it and learn to fear the LORD your God as long as you live in the land you are crossing the Jordan to possess."

Israel's Rebellion Predicted

[14]The LORD said to Moses, "Now the day of your death is near. Call Joshua and present yourselves at the tent of meeting, where I will commission him." So Moses and Joshua came and presented themselves at the tent of meeting. [15]Then the LORD appeared at the tent in a pillar of cloud, and the cloud stood over the entrance to the tent. [16]And the LORD said to Moses: "You are going to rest with your ancestors, and these people will soon prostitute themselves to the foreign gods of the land they are entering. They will forsake me and break the covenant I made with them. [17]And in that day I will become angry with them and forsake them; I will hide my face from them, and they will be

The Law of Legacy: Success Without a Successor Means Failure

Deuteronomy 31:1–13

Just before he died, Moses formally presented his successor, Joshua, to the people. Moses had been mentoring him for years in preparation for this day. Knowing that he would not be able to enter the promised land himself, he realized he had to equip the next leader to finish what he had started. Note what Moses did for Joshua:

1. **He convinced the people that the new must replace the old (vv. 1–2).**
2. **He reminded them of God's commitment to fulfill his promise (v. 3).**
3. **He endorsed the new leader and passed on his authority to Joshua (vv. 3–5).**
4. **He forecasted victory under Joshua and cited his track record (vv. 3–6).**
5. **He commissioned Joshua with the task of leading the people into the land (vv. 7–8).**
6. **He directed Joshua to read God's Word repeatedly (vv. 9–13).**

destroyed. Many disasters and calamities will come on them, and in that day they will ask, 'Have not these disasters come on us because our God is not with us?' ¹⁸And I will certainly hide my face in that day because of all their wickedness in turning to other gods.

¹⁹"Now write down this song and teach it to the Israelites and have them sing it, so that it may be a witness for me against them. ²⁰When I have brought them into the land flowing with milk and honey, the land I promised on oath to their ancestors, and when they eat their fill and thrive, they will turn to other gods and worship them, rejecting me and breaking my covenant. ²¹And when many disasters and calamities come on them, this song will testify against them, because it will not be forgotten by their descendants. I know what they are disposed to do, even before I bring them into the land I promised them on oath." ²²So Moses wrote down this song that day and taught it to the Israelites.

²³The LORD gave this command to Joshua son of Nun: "Be strong and courageous, for you will bring the Israelites into the land I promised them on oath, and I myself will be with you."

²⁴After Moses finished writing in a book the words of this law from beginning to end, ²⁵he gave this command to the Levites who carried the ark of the covenant of the LORD: ²⁶"Take this Book of the Law and place it beside the ark of the covenant of the LORD your God. There it will remain as a witness against you. ²⁷For I know how rebellious and stiff-necked you are. If you have

been rebellious against the LORD while I am still alive and with you, how much more will you rebel after I die! ²⁸Assemble before me all the elders of your tribes and all your officials, so that I can speak these words in their hearing and call the heavens and the earth to testify against them. ²⁹For I know that after my death you are sure to become utterly corrupt and to turn from the way I have commanded you. In days to come, disaster will fall on you because you will do evil in the sight of the LORD and arouse his anger by what your hands have made."

The Song of Moses

³⁰And Moses recited the words of this song from beginning to end in the hearing of the whole assembly of Israel:

32 Listen, you heavens, and I will speak;
hear, you earth, the words of my mouth.
²Let my teaching fall like rain
and my words descend like dew,
like showers on new grass,
like abundant rain on tender plants.

³I will proclaim the name of the LORD.
Oh, praise the greatness of our God!
⁴He is the Rock, his works are perfect,
and all his ways are just.
A faithful God who does no wrong,
upright and just is he.

⁵They are corrupt and not his children;
to their shame they are a warped and
crooked generation.

⁶ Is this the way you repay the LORD,
　　you foolish and unwise people?
　Is he not your Father, your Creator,ᵃ
　　who made you and formed you?

⁷ Remember the days of old;
　　consider the generations long past.
　Ask your father and he will tell you,
　　your elders, and they will explain to you.
⁸ When the Most High gave the nations their
　　　inheritance,
　　when he divided all mankind,
　he set up boundaries for the peoples
　　according to the number of the sons of
　　　Israel.ᵇ
⁹ For the LORD's portion is his people,
　　Jacob his allotted inheritance.

¹⁰ In a desert land he found him,
　　in a barren and howling waste.
　He shielded him and cared for him;
　　he guarded him as the apple of his eye,
¹¹ like an eagle that stirs up its nest
　　and hovers over its young,
　that spreads its wings to catch them
　　and carries them aloft.
¹² The LORD alone led him;
　　no foreign god was with him.

¹³ He made him ride on the heights of the
　　　land
　　and fed him with the fruit of the fields.
　He nourished him with honey from the
　　　rock,
　　and with oil from the flinty crag,
¹⁴ with curds and milk from herd and flock
　　and with fattened lambs and goats,
　with choice rams of Bashan
　　and the finest kernels of wheat.
　You drank the foaming blood of the grape.

¹⁵ Jeshurunᶜ grew fat and kicked;
　　filled with food, they became heavy and
　　　sleek.
　They abandoned the God who made them
　　and rejected the Rock their Savior.
¹⁶ They made him jealous with their foreign
　　　gods
　　and angered him with their detestable
　　　idols.
¹⁷ They sacrificed to false gods, which are not
　　　God —
　　gods they had not known,
　　gods that recently appeared,
　　gods your ancestors did not fear.
¹⁸ You deserted the Rock, who fathered you;
　　you forgot the God who gave you birth.

¹⁹ The LORD saw this and rejected them
　　because he was angered by his sons and
　　　daughters.
²⁰ "I will hide my face from them," he said,
　　"and see what their end will be;
　for they are a perverse generation,
　　children who are unfaithful.
²¹ They made me jealous by what is no god
　　and angered me with their worthless idols.
　I will make them envious by those who are
　　　not a people;
　I will make them angry by a nation that
　　has no understanding.
²² For a fire will be kindled by my wrath,
　　one that burns down to the realm of the
　　　dead below.
　It will devour the earth and its harvests
　　and set afire the foundations of the
　　　mountains.

²³ "I will heap calamities on them
　　and spend my arrows against them.
²⁴ I will send wasting famine against them,
　　consuming pestilence and deadly plague;
　I will send against them the fangs of wild
　　　beasts,
　　the venom of vipers that glide in the dust.
²⁵ In the street the sword will make them
　　　childless;
　　in their homes terror will reign.
　The young men and young women will
　　　perish,
　　the infants and those with gray hair.
²⁶ I said I would scatter them
　　and erase their name from human
　　　memory,
²⁷ but I dreaded the taunt of the enemy,
　　lest the adversary misunderstand
　and say, 'Our hand has triumphed;
　　the LORD has not done all this.'"

²⁸ They are a nation without sense,
　　there is no discernment in them.
²⁹ If only they were wise and would understand
　　　this
　　and discern what their end will be!
³⁰ How could one man chase a thousand,
　　or two put ten thousand to flight,
　unless their Rock had sold them,
　　unless the LORD had given them up?
³¹ For their rock is not like our Rock,
　　as even our enemies concede.

ᵃ 6 Or *Father, who bought you*　　ᵇ 8 Masoretic Text; Dead Sea
Scrolls (see also Septuagint) *sons of God*　　ᶜ 15 *Jeshurun*
means *the upright one*, that is, Israel.

³²Their vine comes from the vine of Sodom
   and from the fields of Gomorrah.
Their grapes are filled with poison,
   and their clusters with bitterness.
³³Their wine is the venom of serpents,
   the deadly poison of cobras.

³⁴"Have I not kept this in reserve
   and sealed it in my vaults?
³⁵It is mine to avenge; I will repay.
   In due time their foot will slip;
their day of disaster is near
   and their doom rushes upon them."

³⁶The Lᴏʀᴅ will vindicate his people
   and relent concerning his servants
when he sees their strength is gone
   and no one is left, slave or free.ᵃ
³⁷He will say: "Now where are their gods,
   the rock they took refuge in,
³⁸the gods who ate the fat of their sacrifices
   and drank the wine of their drink
      offerings?
Let them rise up to help you!
   Let them give you shelter!

³⁹"See now that I myself am he!
   There is no god besides me.
I put to death and I bring to life,
   I have wounded and I will heal,
   and no one can deliver out of my hand.
⁴⁰I lift my hand to heaven and solemnly swear:
   As surely as I live forever,
⁴¹when I sharpen my flashing sword
   and my hand grasps it in judgment,
I will take vengeance on my adversaries
   and repay those who hate me.
⁴²I will make my arrows drunk with blood,
   while my sword devours flesh:
the blood of the slain and the captives,
   the heads of the enemy leaders."

⁴³Rejoice, you nations, with his people,ᵇ,ᶜ
   for he will avenge the blood of his
      servants;
he will take vengeance on his enemies
   and make atonement for his land and
      people.

⁴⁴Moses came with Joshuaᵈ son of Nun and
spoke all the words of this song in the hearing of
the people. ⁴⁵When Moses finished reciting all
these words to all Israel, ⁴⁶he said to them, "Take
to heart all the words I have solemnly declared
to you this day, so that you may command your
children to obey carefully all the words of this
law. ⁴⁷They are not just idle words for you—

they are your life. By them you will live long in
the land you are crossing the Jordan to possess."

Moses to Die on Mount Nebo

⁴⁸On that same day the Lᴏʀᴅ told Moses,
⁴⁹"Go up into the Abarim Range to Mount Nebo
in Moab, across from Jericho, and view Canaan,
the land I am giving the Israelites as their own
possession. ⁵⁰There on the mountain that you
have climbed you will die and be gathered to
your people, just as your brother Aaron died
on Mount Hor and was gathered to his people.
⁵¹This is because both of you broke faith with
me in the presence of the Israelites at the waters of Meribah Kadesh in the Desert of Zin and
because you did not uphold my holiness among
the Israelites. ⁵²Therefore, you will see the land
only from a distance; you will not enter the land
I am giving to the people of Israel."

Moses Blesses the Tribes

33 This is the blessing that Moses the man
of God pronounced on the Israelites before his death. ²He said:

"The Lᴏʀᴅ came from Sinai
   and dawned over them from Seir;
   he shone forth from Mount Paran.
He came withᵉ myriads of holy ones
   from the south, from his mountain
      slopes.ᶠ
³Surely it is you who love the people;
   all the holy ones are in your hand.
At your feet they all bow down,
   and from you receive instruction,
⁴the law that Moses gave us,
   the possession of the assembly of Jacob.
⁵He was king over Jeshurunᵍ
   when the leaders of the people assembled,
   along with the tribes of Israel.

⁶"Let Reuben live and not die,
   norʰ his people be few."

⁷And this he said about Judah:

"Hear, Lᴏʀᴅ, the cry of Judah;
   bring him to his people.
With his own hands he defends his cause.
   Oh, be his help against his foes!"

ᵃ 36 Or and they are without a ruler or leader   ᵇ 43 Or Make
his people rejoice, you nations   ᶜ 43 Masoretic Text; Dead Sea
Scrolls (see also Septuagint) people, / and let all the angels
worship him, /   ᵈ 44 Hebrew Hoshea, a variant of Joshua
ᵉ 2 Or from   ᶠ 2 The meaning of the Hebrew for this phrase
is uncertain.   ᵍ 5 Jeshurun means the upright one, that is,
Israel; also in verse 26.   ʰ 6 Or but let

[8] About Levi he said:

"Your Thummim and Urim belong
   to your faithful servant.
You tested him at Massah;
   you contended with him at the waters of
     Meribah.
[9] He said of his father and mother,
   'I have no regard for them.'
He did not recognize his brothers
   or acknowledge his own children,
but he watched over your word
   and guarded your covenant.
[10] He teaches your precepts to Jacob
   and your law to Israel.
He offers incense before you
   and whole burnt offerings on your altar.
[11] Bless all his skills, LORD,
   and be pleased with the work of his hands.
Strike down those who rise against him,
   his foes till they rise no more."

[12] About Benjamin he said:

"Let the beloved of the LORD rest secure in
     him,
   for he shields him all day long,
   and the one the LORD loves rests between
     his shoulders."

[13] About Joseph he said:

"May the LORD bless his land
   with the precious dew from heaven above
   and with the deep waters that lie below;
[14] with the best the sun brings forth
   and the finest the moon can yield;
[15] with the choicest gifts of the ancient
     mountains
   and the fruitfulness of the everlasting hills;
[16] with the best gifts of the earth and its
     fullness
   and the favor of him who dwelt in the
     burning bush.
Let all these rest on the head of Joseph,
   on the brow of the prince among[a] his
     brothers.
[17] In majesty he is like a firstborn bull;
   his horns are the horns of a wild ox.
With them he will gore the nations,
   even those at the ends of the earth.
Such are the ten thousands of Ephraim;
   such are the thousands of Manasseh."

[18] About Zebulun he said:

"Rejoice, Zebulun, in your going out,
   and you, Issachar, in your tents.

[19] They will summon peoples to the mountain
   and there offer the sacrifices of the
     righteous;
they will feast on the abundance of the seas,
   on the treasures hidden in the sand."

[20] About Gad he said:

"Blessed is he who enlarges Gad's domain!
   Gad lives there like a lion,
   tearing at arm or head.
[21] He chose the best land for himself;
   the leader's portion was kept for him.
When the heads of the people assembled,
   he carried out the LORD's righteous will,
   and his judgments concerning Israel."

[22] About Dan he said:

"Dan is a lion's cub,
   springing out of Bashan."

[23] About Naphtali he said:

"Naphtali is abounding with the favor of the
     LORD
   and is full of his blessing;
   he will inherit southward to the lake."

[24] About Asher he said:

"Most blessed of sons is Asher;
   let him be favored by his brothers,
   and let him bathe his feet in oil.
[25] The bolts of your gates will be iron and
     bronze,
   and your strength will equal your days.

[26] "There is no one like the God of Jeshurun,
   who rides across the heavens to help you
   and on the clouds in his majesty.
[27] The eternal God is your refuge,
   and underneath are the everlasting arms.
He will drive out your enemies before you,
   saying, 'Destroy them!'
[28] So Israel will live in safety;
   Jacob will dwell[b] secure
in a land of grain and new wine,
   where the heavens drop dew.
[29] Blessed are you, Israel!
   Who is like you,
   a people saved by the LORD?
He is your shield and helper
   and your glorious sword.
Your enemies will cower before you,
   and you will tread on their heights."

---

[a] 16 Or of the one separated from   [b] 28 Septuagint; Hebrew
Jacob's spring is

The Death of Moses

34 Then Moses climbed Mount Nebo from the plains of Moab to the top of Pisgah, across from Jericho. There the LORD showed him the whole land—from Gilead to Dan, [2]all of Naphtali, the territory of Ephraim and Manasseh, all the land of Judah as far as the Mediterranean Sea, [3]the Negev and the whole region from the Valley of Jericho, the City of Palms, as far as Zoar. [4]Then the LORD said to him, "This is the land I promised on oath to Abraham, Isaac and Jacob when I said, 'I will give it to your descendants.' I have let you see it with your eyes, but you will not cross over into it."

[5]And Moses the servant of the LORD died there in Moab, as the LORD had said. [6]He buried him[a] in Moab, in the valley opposite Beth Peor, but to this day no one knows where his grave is. [7]Moses was a hundred and twenty years old when he died, yet his eyes were not weak nor his strength gone. [8]The Israelites grieved for Moses in the plains of Moab thirty days, until the time of weeping and mourning was over.

[9]Now Joshua son of Nun was filled with the spirit[b] of wisdom because Moses had laid his hands on him. So the Israelites listened to him and did what the LORD had commanded Moses.

[10]Since then, no prophet has risen in Israel like Moses, whom the LORD knew face to face, [11]who did all those signs and wonders the LORD sent him to do in Egypt—to Pharaoh and to all his officials and to his whole land. [12]For no one has ever shown the mighty power or performed the awesome deeds that Moses did in the sight of all Israel.

---

[a] 6 Or *He was buried*   [b] 9 Or *Spirit*

INTRODUCTION TO JOSHUA

Joshua represents and encourages every second-generation leader. He didn't establish the free nation of Israel—Moses did. But Joshua succeeded Moses respectfully and naturally upon the latter's death. He finished the work Moses could not complete and led the people of Israel to victory in the promised land. Joshua challenges us to lay hold of God's promises and walk in his victory despite adversity. We learn a number of valuable lessons from this leader.

First, Joshua remained submissive to the divine chain of care. He never once attempted to displace Moses' leadership, even when Moses had grown old and could no longer do what Joshua could do. Joshua waited until his time came, just as David waited for King Saul to leave the scene. Saul was killed and then David became king.

Second, Joshua learned to "let Moses die" and to be strong and courageous in his own style of leadership. At the onset of the book, God commands Joshua to take courage. "Moses my servant is dead," God says to him. "Now then, you and all these people, get ready to cross the Jordan River into the land I am about to give to them—to the Israelites" (1:2). Joshua was a military leader, different from Moses' diplomatic or reform leadership style. Somewhere, Joshua must have decided not to imitate Moses' style, but to be himself. The timing could not have been more perfect. Joshua entered leadership in a season when Israel needed military leadership, not diplomatic leadership.

Third, as a leader Joshua did "whatever it took." He practiced the Law of Victory as much as anyone in his day—perhaps as much as anyone described in the Bible. His no-nonsense leadership style drove him to pay

God's Role in Joshua

During Moses' day, God played the role of a patient father, waiting for a new generation to mature so he could lead them into the promised land. By the time Joshua takes over, God speaks in a straightforward manner to Israel's commanding officer. He has grown weary of his people's disobedience, hesitance and complaints. He challenges Joshua not to swerve to the right or to the left, but to do all that he commands. Joshua must compromise nothing, but fulfill everything.

Clearly, we see the Lord lead in a new and appropriate style for the times. His people were entering a season in which they needed to act as a military unit, so both God and Joshua provide direction in a military style.

Leaders in Joshua
Joshua, Caleb, Achan

Other People of Influence in Joshua
Rahab, Eleazar the priest, the Gibeonites

Lessons in Leadership
- Difficult times demand a different style of leadership.
- Good leaders help their people remember past blessings and divine victories.
- Leaders must be willing to take risks and pay the price; courage elicits commitment.

whatever price seemed necessary to get the job done. He courageously took risks. He often questioned the people, asking things like, "How long will you wait before you begin to take possession of the land that the LORD, the God of your ancestors, has given you?" (18:3). He simply couldn't understand why they hesitated. Why didn't they just take the land God had promised them?

This book is all about Israel moving in and settling the promised land. Although it took the Israelites many years (and 21 full chapters) to do it, they finally possess all the real estate God had given them. And Joshua led the charge the whole way.

- Compromise on your methods, but never on your convictions or principles.
- Leaders cannot afford to be indecisive; they must give clear and specific directions.
- God will work on behalf of leaders who surrender their hearts completely to him.
- Good leaders do whatever it takes to get the job done.

LEADERSHIP HIGHLIGHTS IN JOSHUA

Joshua Installed as Leader

1 After the death of Moses the servant of the LORD, the LORD said to Joshua son of Nun, Moses' aide: [2]"Moses my servant is dead. Now then, you and all these people, get ready to cross the Jordan River into the land I am about to give to them—to the Israelites. [3]I will give you every place where you set your foot, as I promised Moses. [4]Your territory will extend from the desert to Lebanon, and from the great river, the Euphrates—all the Hittite country—to the Mediterranean Sea in the west. [5]No one will be able to stand against you all the days of your life. As I was with Moses, so I will be with you; I will never leave you nor forsake you. [6]Be strong and courageous, because you will lead these people to inherit the land I swore to their ancestors to give them.

[7]"Be strong and very courageous. Be careful to obey all the law my servant Moses gave you; do not turn from it to the right or to the left, that you may be successful wherever you go. [8]Keep this Book of the Law always on your lips; meditate on it day and night, so that you may be careful to do everything written in it. Then you will be prosperous and successful. [9]Have I not commanded you? Be strong and courageous. Do not be afraid; do not be discouraged, for the LORD your God will be with you wherever you go."

[10]So Joshua ordered the officers of the people: [11]"Go through the camp and tell the people, 'Get your provisions ready. Three days from now you will cross the Jordan here to go in and take possession of the land the LORD your God is giving you for your own.'"

[12]But to the Reubenites, the Gadites and the half-tribe of Manasseh, Joshua said, [13]"Remember the command that Moses the servant of the LORD gave you after he said, 'The LORD your God will give you rest by giving you this land.' [14]Your wives, your children and your livestock may stay in the land that Moses gave you east of the Jordan, but all your fighting men, ready for battle, must cross over ahead of your fellow Israelites. You are to help them [15]until the LORD gives them rest, as he has done for you, and until they too have taken possession of the land the LORD your God is giving them. After that, you may go back and occupy your own land, which Moses the servant of the LORD gave you east of the Jordan toward the sunrise."

[16]Then they answered Joshua, "Whatever you have commanded us we will do, and wherever you send us we will go. [17]Just as we fully obeyed Moses, so we will obey you. Only may the LORD your God be with you as he was with Moses. [18]Whoever rebels against your word and does not obey it, whatever you may command them, will be put to death. Only be strong and courageous!"

Rahab and the Spies

2 Then Joshua son of Nun secretly sent two spies from Shittim. "Go, look over the land," he said, "especially Jericho." So they went and

The Law of Timing: Joshua Begins with a Divine Call and Charge

Joshua 1:1–9

Consider this: It took 40 years for Joshua's leadership style to match the need of the moment. Moses led diplomatically. He sat and judged the people patiently as they grumbled through long years in the desert. By the time the Israelites reached Canaan, fierce enemies awaited them—and they needed a much more confrontational leader, a military man skilled in war. Enter Joshua. Note the differences between Moses and Joshua and see how timing can dictate appropriate leadership styles:

Moses	Joshua
1. Led through 40 years of desert travel	1. Led through 30 years of conquering Canaan
2. Was a political, diplomatic leader	2. Was a military, in-your-face leader
3. Patiently listened to complaints	3. Confronted laziness and fear of the enemy
4. Led people as a peacemaking shepherd	4. Led people as a tough commander
5. Provided water from a rock when the people got thirsty	5. Told the people to dig their own wells when they got thirsty

entered the house of a prostitute named Rahab and stayed there.

[2]The king of Jericho was told, "Look, some of the Israelites have come here tonight to spy out the land." [3]So the king of Jericho sent this message to Rahab: "Bring out the men who came to you and entered your house, because they have come to spy out the whole land."

[4]But the woman had taken the two men and hidden them. She said, "Yes, the men came to me, but I did not know where they had come from. [5]At dusk, when it was time to close the city gate, they left. I don't know which way they went. Go after them quickly. You may catch up with them." [6](But she had taken them up to the roof and hidden them under the stalks of flax she had laid out on the roof.) [7]So the men set out in pursuit of the spies on the road that leads to the fords of the Jordan, and as soon as the pursuers had gone out, the gate was shut.

[8]Before the spies lay down for the night, she went up on the roof [9]and said to them, "I know that the LORD has given you this land and that a great fear of you has fallen on us, so that all who live in this country are melting in fear because of you. [10]We have heard how the LORD dried up the water of the Red Sea[a] for you when you came out of Egypt, and what you did to Sihon and Og, the two kings of the Amorites east of the Jordan, whom you completely destroyed.[b] [11]When we heard of it, our hearts melted in fear and everyone's courage failed because of you, for the LORD your God is God in heaven above and on the earth below.

[12]"Now then, please swear to me by the LORD that you will show kindness to my family, because I have shown kindness to you. Give me a sure sign [13]that you will spare the lives of my father and mother, my brothers and sisters, and all who belong to them — and that you will save us from death."

[14]"Our lives for your lives!" the men assured her. "If you don't tell what we are doing, we will treat you kindly and faithfully when the LORD gives us the land."

[15]So she let them down by a rope through the window, for the house she lived in was part of the city wall. [16]She said to them, "Go to the hills so the pursuers will not find you. Hide yourselves there three days until they return, and then go on your way."

[17]Now the men had said to her, "This oath you made us swear will not be binding on us [18]unless, when we enter the land, you have tied this scarlet cord in the window through which you let us down, and unless you have brought your father

and mother, your brothers and all your family into your house. [19]If any of them go outside your house into the street, their blood will be on their own heads; we will not be responsible. As for those who are in the house with you, their blood will be on our head if a hand is laid on them. [20]But if you tell what we are doing, we will be released from the oath you made us swear."

[21]"Agreed," she replied. "Let it be as you say."

So she sent them away, and they departed. And she tied the scarlet cord in the window.

[22]When they left, they went into the hills and stayed there three days, until the pursuers had searched all along the road and returned without finding them. [23]Then the two men started back. They went down out of the hills, forded the river and came to Joshua son of Nun and told him everything that had happened to them.

---

[a] 10 Or *the Sea of Reeds*   [b] 10 The Hebrew term refers to the irrevocable giving over of things or persons to the LORD, often by totally destroying them.

The Law of Influence: God Uses Rahab

Joshua 2:1–21

The story of Rahab proves that God will use anybody. This woman worked as a prostitute in Jericho as the Israelites approached the city. Although the Hebrew spies needed someone to help them scope out the best approach to conquering the city, there seemed little logical reason why Rahab should have been considered for the role:

1. **She occupied no position and held no official title in the city.**

2. **The Israelites looked upon women as lower-class citizens.**

3. **As a prostitute, she held an even lower social rank than the average woman.**

But because leadership depends less on titles than it does on influence, God chose Rahab. She helped the spies by her quick wisdom, gutsy style, and clever plan. By doing so she saved not only her own life, but aided in accomplishing the purposes of God in Jericho. The name "Rahab" even occupies an honored place in the Hall of Faith (Heb 11:31).

²⁴They said to Joshua, "The LORD has surely given the whole land into our hands; all the people are melting in fear because of us."

Crossing the Jordan

3 Early in the morning Joshua and all the Israelites set out from Shittim and went to the Jordan, where they camped before crossing over. ²After three days the officers went throughout the camp, ³giving orders to the people: "When you see the ark of the covenant of the LORD your God, and the Levitical priests carrying it, you are to move out from your positions and follow it. ⁴Then you will know which way to go, since you have never been this way before. But keep a distance of about two thousand cubits*a* between you and the ark; do not go near it."

⁵Joshua told the people, "Consecrate yourselves, for tomorrow the LORD will do amazing things among you."

⁶Joshua said to the priests, "Take up the ark of the covenant and pass on ahead of the people." So they took it up and went ahead of them.

⁷And the LORD said to Joshua, "Today I will begin to exalt you in the eyes of all Israel, so they may know that I am with you as I was with Moses. ⁸Tell the priests who carry the ark of the covenant: 'When you reach the edge of the Jordan's waters, go and stand in the river.'"

⁹Joshua said to the Israelites, "Come here and listen to the words of the LORD your God. ¹⁰This is how you will know that the living God is among you and that he will certainly drive out before you the Canaanites, Hittites, Hivites, Perizzites, Girgashites, Amorites and Jebusites. ¹¹See, the ark of the covenant of the Lord of all the earth will go into the Jordan ahead of you. ¹²Now then, choose twelve men from the tribes of Israel, one from each tribe. ¹³And as soon as the priests who carry the ark of the LORD — the Lord of all the earth — set foot in the Jordan, its waters flowing downstream will be cut off and stand up in a heap."

¹⁴So when the people broke camp to cross the Jordan, the priests carrying the ark of the covenant went ahead of them. ¹⁵Now the Jordan is at flood stage all during harvest. Yet as soon as the priests who carried the ark reached the Jordan and their feet touched the water's edge, ¹⁶the water from upstream stopped flowing. It piled up in a heap a great distance away, at a town called Adam in the vicinity of Zarethan, while the water flowing down to the Sea of the Arabah (that is, the Dead Sea) was completely cut off. So the people crossed over opposite Jericho. ¹⁷The priests who carried the ark of the covenant of the LORD stopped in the middle of

---

a 4 That is, about 3,000 feet or about 900 meters

RAHAB

An Unusual Woman of Faith
Joshua 2:1–21; 6:22–25

PROFILE in leadership

God uses individuals of all temperaments and backgrounds to accomplish his purposes—even prostitutes.

God strategically positioned Rahab, whom the Bible calls a "prostitute" (Jos 2:1), in a home built into the wall of Jericho. When two Hebrew spies came to her for aid, she displayed a clear understanding of spiritual issues. She described how the dread of Israel had overwhelmed her people. She acknowledged that the land belonged to the Israelites and therefore willingly risked her life to hide Joshua's spies (2:4–11). Rahab leveraged her hospitality on behalf of her parents, siblings, and their extended families, begging the spies to spare the lives of all who belonged to her (2:12–13). They agreed.

Rahab was a woman of her word. Although she could have tipped off her king to the whereabouts of the hiding Israelites, she sent Israel's enemies on a wild goose chase. Why? Because she really believed that God was about to hand her city over to the Hebrews. Even prostitutes can exhibit saving faith (Heb 11:31).

Wise leaders remember that God sees the human heart; while many would never trust a woman with a personal history like that of Rahab, God selected her. Because Rahab faithfully served God, her family lived and was adopted into Hebrew society—and she became an ancestor of the Lord Jesus himself (Mt 1:5).

the Jordan and stood on dry ground, while all Israel passed by until the whole nation had completed the crossing on dry ground.

4 When the whole nation had finished crossing the Jordan, the LORD said to Joshua, ²"Choose twelve men from among the people, one from each tribe, ³and tell them to take up twelve stones from the middle of the Jordan, from right where the priests are standing, and carry them over with you and put them down at the place where you stay tonight."

⁴So Joshua called together the twelve men he had appointed from the Israelites, one from each tribe, ⁵and said to them, "Go over before the ark of the LORD your God into the middle of the Jordan. Each of you is to take up a stone on his shoulder, according to the number of the tribes of the Israelites, ⁶to serve as a sign among you. In the future, when your children ask you, 'What do these stones mean?' ⁷tell them that the flow of the Jordan was cut off before the ark of the covenant of the LORD. When it crossed the Jordan, the waters of the Jordan were cut off. These stones are to be a memorial to the people of Israel forever."

⁸So the Israelites did as Joshua commanded them. They took twelve stones from the middle of the Jordan, according to the number of the tribes of the Israelites, as the LORD had told Joshua; and they carried them over with them to their camp, where they put them down. ⁹Joshua set up the twelve stones that had been*a* in the middle of the Jordan at the spot where the priests who carried the ark of the covenant had stood. And they are there to this day.

¹⁰Now the priests who carried the ark remained standing in the middle of the Jordan until everything the LORD had commanded Joshua was done by the people, just as Moses had directed Joshua. The people hurried over, ¹¹and as soon as all of them had crossed, the ark of the LORD and the priests came to the other side while the people watched. ¹²The men of Reuben, Gad and the half-tribe of Manasseh crossed over, ready for battle, in front of the Israelites, as Moses had directed them. ¹³About forty thousand armed for battle crossed over before the LORD to the plains of Jericho for war.

¹⁴That day the LORD exalted Joshua in the sight of all Israel; and they stood in awe of him all the days of his life, just as they had stood in awe of Moses.

¹⁵Then the LORD said to Joshua, ¹⁶"Command the priests carrying the ark of the covenant law to come up out of the Jordan."

Communication: Joshua Gives Handles to Remember God's Work

Joshua 4:1–9

Effective leaders look for ways to use the successes of today to empower their people for the challenges of tomorrow. Joshua did exactly that.

Although God would work a miracle to allow the people to cross the Jordan on dry ground, Joshua knew that only those who saw the incident would remember it—and he wanted to leave a legacy for the next generation, born long after the miracle occurred. Joshua wanted to find a way to communicate God's greatness to the children of Israel yet-to-be-born.

To accomplish his goal, Joshua devised a plan called "Stones of Remembrance." He directed that 12 stones be taken from the middle of the dry riverbed—one for each of the 12 tribes who crossed the river—and be piled in a monument on shore. Thereafter, whenever Israel's children or grandchildren asked, "What do those stones mean?" the people would have an opportunity to recast God's vision and recount God's victories. The stones served as "handles" to communicate what God had done.

Good leaders always provide "handles" to enable their people to grab hold of the vision. Effective leaders find a way to communicate future vision and past victories, because their people need to be constantly reminded of both.

¹⁷So Joshua commanded the priests, "Come up out of the Jordan."

¹⁸And the priests came up out of the river carrying the ark of the covenant of the LORD. No sooner had they set their feet on the dry ground than the waters of the Jordan returned to their place and ran at flood stage as before.

¹⁹On the tenth day of the first month the people went up from the Jordan and camped at Gilgal on the eastern border of Jericho. ²⁰And Joshua set up at Gilgal the twelve stones they had taken out of the Jordan. ²¹He said to the Israelites, "In the future when your descendants ask their parents, 'What do these stones mean?'

a 9 Or Joshua also set up twelve stones

²²tell them, 'Israel crossed the Jordan on dry ground.' ²³For the LORD your God dried up the Jordan before you until you had crossed over. The LORD your God did to the Jordan what he had done to the Red Sea*a* when he dried it up before us until we had crossed over. ²⁴He did this so that all the peoples of the earth might know that the hand of the LORD is powerful and so that you might always fear the LORD your God."

5 Now when all the Amorite kings west of the Jordan and all the Canaanite kings along the coast heard how the LORD had dried up the Jordan before the Israelites until they*b* had crossed over, their hearts melted in fear and they no longer had the courage to face the Israelites.

Circumcision and Passover at Gilgal

²At that time the LORD said to Joshua, "Make flint knives and circumcise the Israelites again." ³So Joshua made flint knives and circumcised the Israelites at Gibeath Haaraloth.*c*

⁴Now this is why he did so: All those who came out of Egypt—all the men of military age—died in the wilderness on the way after leaving Egypt. ⁵All the people that came out had been circumcised, but all the people born in the wilderness during the journey from Egypt had not. ⁶The Israelites had moved about in the wilderness forty years until all the men who were of military age when they left Egypt had died, since they had not obeyed the LORD. For the LORD had sworn to them that they would not see the land he had solemnly promised their ancestors to give us, a land flowing with milk and honey. ⁷So he raised up their sons in their place, and these were the ones Joshua circumcised. They were still uncircumcised because they had not been circumcised on the way. ⁸And after the whole nation had been circumcised, they remained where they were in camp until they were healed.

⁹Then the LORD said to Joshua, "Today I have rolled away the reproach of Egypt from you." So the place has been called Gilgal*d* to this day.

¹⁰On the evening of the fourteenth day of the month, while camped at Gilgal on the plains of Jericho, the Israelites celebrated the Passover. ¹¹The day after the Passover, that very day, they ate some of the produce of the land: unleavened bread and roasted grain. ¹²The manna stopped the day after*e* they ate this food from the land; there was no longer any manna for the Israelites, but that year they ate the produce of Canaan.

The Fall of Jericho

¹³Now when Joshua was near Jericho, he looked up and saw a man standing in front of him with a drawn sword in his hand. Joshua

---

a 23 Or the Sea of Reeds   b 1 Another textual tradition we   c 3 Gibeath Haaraloth means the hill of foreskins.   d 9 Gilgal sounds like the Hebrew for roll.   e 12 Or the day

JOSHUA — A Leader's Obedience Sets the Pace
PROFILE in leadership
Joshua 5:13–15

Look at every phase of Joshua's life, and you see a man who gave himself wholeheartedly to completing whatever task was assigned to him.

The first time Joshua appears in Scripture, we see him immediately obeying the instruction of Moses (Ex 17:9–10). Thereafter Joshua took on the role of Moses' assistant. Joshua again displayed his obedience when he agreed to spy out the promised land. Upon his return from the reconnaissance mission, he and Caleb, alone among the spies, were ready to obey God and enter Canaan. Forty years later when Moses handed the reins of power to his protégé, Joshua again obeyed the call (Jos 1:5–11).

In the end, the people of Israel followed Joshua's example and did what God asked of them—and as a result inherited the land God had promised. Scripture says that "Israel served the LORD throughout the lifetime of Joshua" (Jos 24:31). When the people followed Joshua's lifelong example of obedience, they prospered.

By the time of his death, Joshua was known simply as "the servant of the LORD" (Jdg 2:7–8). That is high praise! While today we consider Joshua an exceptional leader, nowhere does Scripture describe him as a man of extraordinary might, intellect, or talent. What made him extraordinary was his obedience. And when you're a servant of the Lord, that's all you really need.

went up to him and asked, "Are you for us or for our enemies?"

[14]"Neither," he replied, "but as commander of the army of the LORD I have now come." Then Joshua fell facedown to the ground in reverence, and asked him, "What message does my Lord[a] have for his servant?"

[15]The commander of the LORD's army replied, "Take off your sandals, for the place where you are standing is holy." And Joshua did so.

6 Now the gates of Jericho were securely barred because of the Israelites. No one went out and no one came in.

[2]Then the LORD said to Joshua, "See, I have delivered Jericho into your hands, along with its king and its fighting men. [3]March around the city once with all the armed men. Do this for six days. [4]Have seven priests carry trumpets of rams' horns in front of the ark. On the seventh day, march around the city seven times, with the priests blowing the trumpets. [5]When you hear them sound a long blast on the trumpets, have the whole army give a loud shout; then the wall of the city will collapse and the army will go up, everyone straight in."

[6]So Joshua son of Nun called the priests and said to them, "Take up the ark of the covenant of the LORD and have seven priests carry trumpets in front of it." [7]And he ordered the army, "Advance! March around the city, with an armed guard going ahead of the ark of the LORD."

[8]When Joshua had spoken to the people, the seven priests carrying the seven trumpets before the LORD went forward, blowing their trumpets, and the ark of the LORD's covenant followed them. [9]The armed guard marched ahead of the priests who blew the trumpets, and the rear guard followed the ark. All this time the trumpets were sounding. [10]But Joshua had commanded the army, "Do not give a war cry, do not raise your voices, do not say a word until the day I tell you to shout. Then shout!" [11]So he had the ark of the LORD carried around the city, circling it once. Then the army returned to camp and spent the night there.

[12]Joshua got up early the next morning and the priests took up the ark of the LORD. [13]The seven priests carrying the seven trumpets went forward, marching before the ark of the LORD and blowing the trumpets. The armed men went ahead of them and the rear guard followed the ark of the LORD, while the trumpets kept sounding. [14]So on the second day they marched around the city once and returned to the camp. They did this for six days.

[15]On the seventh day, they got up at daybreak and marched around the city seven times in the same manner, except that on that day they circled the city seven times. [16]The seventh time around, when the priests sounded the trumpet blast, Joshua commanded the army, "Shout! For the LORD has given you the city! [17]The city and all that is in it are to be devoted[b] to the LORD. Only Rahab the prostitute and all who are with her in her house shall be spared, because she hid the spies we sent. [18]But keep away from the devoted things, so that you will not bring about your own destruction by taking any of them. Otherwise you will make the camp of Israel liable to destruction and bring trouble on it. [19]All the silver and gold and the articles of bronze and iron are sacred to the LORD and must go into his treasury."

[20]When the trumpets sounded, the army shouted, and at the sound of the trumpet, when the men gave a loud shout, the wall collapsed; so everyone charged straight in, and they took the city. [21]They devoted the city to the LORD and destroyed with the sword every living thing in it—men and women, young and old, cattle, sheep and donkeys.

[22]Joshua said to the two men who had spied out the land, "Go into the prostitute's house and bring her out and all who belong to her, in accordance with your oath to her." [23]So the young men who had done the spying went in and brought out Rahab, her father and mother, her brothers and sisters and all who belonged to her. They brought out her entire family and put them in a place outside the camp of Israel.

[24]Then they burned the whole city and everything in it, but they put the silver and gold and the articles of bronze and iron into the treasury of the LORD's house. [25]But Joshua spared Rahab the prostitute, with her family and all who belonged to her, because she hid the men Joshua had sent as spies to Jericho—and she lives among the Israelites to this day.

[26]At that time Joshua pronounced this solemn oath: "Cursed before the LORD is the one who undertakes to rebuild this city, Jericho:

"At the cost of his firstborn son
    he will lay its foundations;
at the cost of his youngest
    he will set up its gates."

---

[a] 14 Or *lord*   [b] 17 The Hebrew term refers to the irrevocable giving over of things or persons to the LORD, often by totally destroying them; also in verses 18 and 21.

brought this trouble on us? The LORD will bring trouble on you today."

Then all Israel stoned him, and after they had stoned the rest, they burned them. [26]Over Achan they heaped up a large pile of rocks, which remains to this day. Then the LORD turned from his fierce anger. Therefore that place has been called the Valley of Achor[a] ever since.

Ai Destroyed

8 Then the LORD said to Joshua, "Do not be afraid; do not be discouraged. Take the whole army with you, and go up and attack Ai. For I have delivered into your hands the king of Ai, his people, his city and his land. [2]You shall do to Ai and its king as you did to Jericho and its king, except that you may carry off their plunder and livestock for yourselves. Set an ambush behind the city."

[3]So Joshua and the whole army moved out to attack Ai. He chose thirty thousand of his best fighting men and sent them out at night [4]with these orders: "Listen carefully. You are to set an ambush behind the city. Don't go very far from it. All of you be on the alert. [5]I and all those with me will advance on the city, and when the men come out against us, as they did before, we will flee from them. [6]They will pursue us until we have lured them away from the city, for they will say, 'They are running away from us as they did before.' So when we flee from them, [7]you are to rise up from ambush and take the city. The LORD your God will give it into your hand. [8]When you have taken the city, set it on fire. Do what the LORD has commanded. See to it; you have my orders."

[9]Then Joshua sent them off, and they went to the place of ambush and lay in wait between Bethel and Ai, to the west of Ai—but Joshua spent that night with the people.

[10]Early the next morning Joshua mustered his army, and he and the leaders of Israel marched before them to Ai. [11]The entire force that was with him marched up and approached the city and arrived in front of it. They set up camp north of Ai, with the valley between them and the city. [12]Joshua had taken about five thousand men and set them in ambush between Bethel and Ai, to the west of the city. [13]So the soldiers took up their positions—with the main camp to the north of the city and the ambush to the west of it. That night Joshua went into the valley.

[14]When the king of Ai saw this, he and all the men of the city hurried out early in the morning to meet Israel in battle at a certain place over-

---

Convictions: Leaders Don't Allow Compromise to Dilute the Cause

Joshua 7:1—8:29

A little city with a short name caused huge problems for the Israelites.

Spies sent out to check out the village of Ai considered it an easy target; its defeat would not even require the whole army, they said. How wrong they were! The contingent dispatched against Ai quickly retreated after suffering frightening losses. What could have happened?

Joshua soon discovered that sin in his camp had caused the debacle. One of his soldiers, Achan, had kept for himself some of the spoils of war, despite God's prohibition against doing so. After a short time of confusion, Joshua dealt decisively with Achan, executing him at the command of God. Joshua would not and could not allow compromise to derail the destiny of his people. Due to his courage and convictions, the next time Israel launched an attack on Ai, the tiny city with the short name presented little problem.

---

looking the Arabah. But he did not know that an ambush had been set against him behind the city. [15]Joshua and all Israel let themselves be driven back before them, and they fled toward the wilderness. [16]All the men of Ai were called to pursue them, and they pursued Joshua and were lured away from the city. [17]Not a man remained in Ai or Bethel who did not go after Israel. They left the city open and went in pursuit of Israel.

[18]Then the LORD said to Joshua, "Hold out toward Ai the javelin that is in your hand, for into your hand I will deliver the city." So Joshua held out toward the city the javelin that was in his hand. [19]As soon as he did this, the men in the ambush rose quickly from their position and rushed forward. They entered the city and captured it and quickly set it on fire.

[20]The men of Ai looked back and saw the smoke of the city rising up into the sky, but they had no chance to escape in any direction; the Israelites who had been fleeing toward the

---

[a] 26 Achor means trouble.

wilderness had turned back against their pursuers. [21]For when Joshua and all Israel saw that the ambush had taken the city and that smoke was going up from it, they turned around and attacked the men of Ai. [22]Those in the ambush also came out of the city against them, so that they were caught in the middle, with Israelites on both sides. Israel cut them down, leaving them neither survivors nor fugitives. [23]But they took the king of Ai alive and brought him to Joshua.

[24]When Israel had finished killing all the men of Ai in the fields and in the wilderness where they had chased them, and when every one of them had been put to the sword, all the Israelites returned to Ai and killed those who were in it. [25]Twelve thousand men and women fell that day—all the people of Ai. [26]For Joshua did not draw back the hand that held out his javelin until he had destroyed[a] all who lived in Ai. [27]But Israel did carry off for themselves the livestock and plunder of this city, as the LORD had instructed Joshua.

[28]So Joshua burned Ai[b] and made it a permanent heap of ruins, a desolate place to this day. [29]He impaled the body of the king of Ai on a pole and left it there until evening. At sunset, Joshua ordered them to take the body from the pole and throw it down at the entrance of the city gate. And they raised a large pile of rocks over it, which remains to this day.

The Covenant Renewed at Mount Ebal

[30]Then Joshua built on Mount Ebal an altar to the LORD, the God of Israel, [31]as Moses the servant of the LORD had commanded the Israelites. He built it according to what is written in the Book of the Law of Moses—an altar of uncut stones, on which no iron tool had been used. On it they offered to the LORD burnt offerings and sacrificed fellowship offerings. [32]There, in the presence of the Israelites, Joshua wrote on stones a copy of the law of Moses. [33]All the Israelites, with their elders, officials and judges, were standing on both sides of the ark of the covenant of the LORD, facing the Levitical priests who carried it. Both the foreigners living among them and the native-born were there. Half of the people stood in front of Mount Gerizim and half of them in front of Mount Ebal, as Moses the servant of the LORD had formerly commanded when he gave instructions to bless the people of Israel.

[34]Afterward, Joshua read all the words of the law—the blessings and the curses—just as it is

The Law of Navigation: Joshua Balances Faith and Planning

Joshua 8:1–29

When does human planning get in the way of trusting God for results? Or conversely, when does faith become presumption, expecting God to do for us what we must grab hold of ourselves? All Christian leaders must learn the proper balance between divine faith and human preparation.

Joshua demonstrates a beautiful balance as he prepares a second attack on the city of Ai. He begins by asking the Lord whether his army should attack, and if so, when. God ordered the attack and instructed Joshua to set an ambush, but gave no further details. Joshua planned the particulars of the campaign, each step under the inspiration of the Holy Spirit. He divided his troops into two divisions and told one to stage an attack on the city. The other group was to wait in ambush until the men of Ai came out. As the men of Ai chased their attackers, the ambush could close in and allow the Israelites to set the city afire. The plan worked perfectly. When the men of Ai saw the smoke rising above their homes, they lost heart and quickly fell in battle to Israel.

Do you see the synthesis of divine guidance and human strategy? Joshua placed his faith in God for the results, but did not hesitate to lay wise plans and execute them.

written in the Book of the Law. [35]There was not a word of all that Moses had commanded that Joshua did not read to the whole assembly of Israel, including the women and children, and the foreigners who lived among them.

The Gibeonite Deception

9 Now when all the kings west of the Jordan heard about these things—the kings in the hill country, in the western foothills, and along the entire coast of the Mediterranean Sea as far as Lebanon (the kings of the Hittites, Amorites,

---

[a] 26 The Hebrew term refers to the irrevocable giving over of things or persons to the LORD, often by totally destroying them.
[b] 28 Ai means the ruin.

Canaanites, Perizzites, Hivites and Jebusites) — [2]they came together to wage war against Joshua and Israel.

[3]However, when the people of Gibeon heard what Joshua had done to Jericho and Ai, [4]they resorted to a ruse: They went as a delegation whose donkeys were loaded[a] with worn-out sacks and old wineskins, cracked and mended. [5]They put worn and patched sandals on their feet and wore old clothes. All the bread of their food supply was dry and moldy. [6]Then they went to Joshua in the camp at Gilgal and said to him and the Israelites, "We have come from a distant country; make a treaty with us."

[7]The Israelites said to the Hivites, "But perhaps you live near us, so how can we make a treaty with you?"

[8]"We are your servants," they said to Joshua.

But Joshua asked, "Who are you and where do you come from?"

[9]They answered: "Your servants have come from a very distant country because of the fame of the LORD your God. For we have heard reports of him: all that he did in Egypt, [10]and all that he did to the two kings of the Amorites east of the Jordan — Sihon king of Heshbon, and Og king of Bashan, who reigned in Ashtaroth. [11]And our elders and all those living in our country said to us, 'Take provisions for your journey; go and meet them and say to them, "We are your servants; make a treaty with us."' [12]This bread of ours was warm when we packed it at home on the day we left to come to you. But now see how dry and moldy it is. [13]And these wineskins that we filled were new, but see how cracked they are. And our clothes and sandals are worn out by the very long journey."

[14]The Israelites sampled their provisions but did not inquire of the LORD. [15]Then Joshua made a treaty of peace with them to let them live, and the leaders of the assembly ratified it by oath.

[16]Three days after they made the treaty with the Gibeonites, the Israelites heard that they were neighbors, living near them. [17]So the Israelites set out and on the third day came to their cities: Gibeon, Kephirah, Beeroth and Kiriath Jearim. [18]But the Israelites did not attack them, because the leaders of the assembly had sworn an oath to them by the LORD, the God of Israel.

The whole assembly grumbled against the leaders, [19]but all the leaders answered, "We have given them our oath by the LORD, the God of Israel, and we cannot touch them now. [20]This is what we will do to them: We will let them live, so

that God's wrath will not fall on us for breaking the oath we swore to them." [21]They continued, "Let them live, but let them be woodcutters and water carriers in the service of the whole assembly." So the leaders' promise to them was kept.

[22]Then Joshua summoned the Gibeonites and said, "Why did you deceive us by saying, 'We live a long way from you,' while actually you live near us? [23]You are now under a curse: You will never be released from service as woodcutters and water carriers for the house of my God."

[24]They answered Joshua, "Your servants were clearly told how the LORD your God had commanded his servant Moses to give you the whole land and to wipe out all its inhabitants from before you. So we feared for our lives because of you, and that is why we did this. [25]We are now in your hands. Do to us whatever seems good and right to you."

[26]So Joshua saved them from the Israelites, and they did not kill them. [27]That day he made the Gibeonites woodcutters and water carriers for the assembly, to provide for the needs of the altar of the LORD at the place the LORD would choose. And that is what they are to this day.

Negotiation and Compromise

Joshua 9:1–27

When Israel negotiated with the Gibeonites and ignored God's order to destroy the city, they allowed compromise to jeopardize their mission. While negotiation is not wrong in itself, leaders must never negotiate their convictions, direct orders, or core values. When we start negotiating these, we compromise our mission.

The Sun Stands Still

10 Now Adoni-Zedek king of Jerusalem heard that Joshua had taken Ai and totally destroyed[b] it, doing to Ai and its king as he had done to Jericho and its king, and that the people of Gibeon had made a treaty of peace with Israel and had become their allies. [2]He and his people were very much alarmed at this,

---

[a] 4 Most Hebrew manuscripts; some Hebrew manuscripts, Vulgate and Syriac (see also Septuagint) *They prepared provisions and loaded their donkeys*   [b] 1 The Hebrew term refers to the irrevocable giving over of things or persons to the LORD, often by totally destroying them; also in verses 28, 35, 37, 39 and 40.

because Gibeon was an important city, like one of the royal cities; it was larger than Ai, and all its men were good fighters. ³So Adoni-Zedek king of Jerusalem appealed to Hoham king of Hebron, Piram king of Jarmuth, Japhia king of Lachish and Debir king of Eglon. ⁴"Come up and help me attack Gibeon," he said, "because it has made peace with Joshua and the Israelites."

⁵Then the five kings of the Amorites — the kings of Jerusalem, Hebron, Jarmuth, Lachish and Eglon — joined forces. They moved up with all their troops and took up positions against Gibeon and attacked it.

⁶The Gibeonites then sent word to Joshua in the camp at Gilgal: "Do not abandon your servants. Come up to us quickly and save us! Help us, because all the Amorite kings from the hill country have joined forces against us."

⁷So Joshua marched up from Gilgal with his entire army, including all the best fighting men. ⁸The LORD said to Joshua, "Do not be afraid of them; I have given them into your hand. Not one of them will be able to withstand you."

⁹After an all-night march from Gilgal, Joshua took them by surprise. ¹⁰The LORD threw them into confusion before Israel, so Joshua and the Israelites defeated them completely at Gibeon. Israel pursued them along the road going up to Beth Horon and cut them down all the way to Azekah and Makkedah. ¹¹As they fled before Israel on the road down from Beth Horon to Azekah, the LORD hurled large hailstones down on them, and more of them died from the hail than were killed by the swords of the Israelites.

¹²On the day the LORD gave the Amorites over to Israel, Joshua said to the LORD in the presence of Israel:

> "Sun, stand still over Gibeon,
>   and you, moon, over the Valley of
>   Aijalon."
> ¹³So the sun stood still,
>   and the moon stopped,
>   till the nation avenged itself on[a] its
>   enemies,

as it is written in the Book of Jashar.

The sun stopped in the middle of the sky and delayed going down about a full day. ¹⁴There has never been a day like it before or since, a day when the LORD listened to a human being. Surely the LORD was fighting for Israel!

¹⁵Then Joshua returned with all Israel to the camp at Gilgal.

The Law of the Picture: Joshua's Integrity with the Gibeonites

Joshua 10:1-15

Joshua compromised his leadership when he made a treaty with the Gibeonites, but once he made a covenant with them, he knew it was his duty to defend them. Integrity means that you keep your oath "even when it hurts" regardless of the cost (see Ps 15:4).

Why is this so vital? It all comes down to the Law of the Picture.

1. **People do what people see. If Joshua failed in his integrity, it would haunt him later.**

2. **People follow if they trust. If Joshua failed in his integrity, few would trust him later.**

3. **People return what they've received. Joshua was more likely to receive loyalty from the Gibeonites if he demonstrated loyalty to them when it was costly to do so.**

Five Amorite Kings Killed

¹⁶Now the five kings had fled and hidden in the cave at Makkedah. ¹⁷When Joshua was told that the five kings had been found hiding in the cave at Makkedah, ¹⁸he said, "Roll large rocks up to the mouth of the cave, and post some men there to guard it. ¹⁹But don't stop; pursue your enemies! Attack them from the rear and don't let them reach their cities, for the LORD your God has given them into your hand."

²⁰So Joshua and the Israelites defeated them completely, but a few survivors managed to reach their fortified cities. ²¹The whole army then returned safely to Joshua in the camp at Makkedah, and no one uttered a word against the Israelites.

²²Joshua said, "Open the mouth of the cave and bring those five kings out to me." ²³So they brought the five kings out of the cave — the kings of Jerusalem, Hebron, Jarmuth, Lachish and Eglon. ²⁴When they had brought these kings to Joshua, he summoned all the men of

---

[a] 13 Or *nation triumphed over*

Israel and said to the army commanders who had come with him, "Come here and put your feet on the necks of these kings." So they came forward and placed their feet on their necks.

²⁵Joshua said to them, "Do not be afraid; do not be discouraged. Be strong and courageous. This is what the LORD will do to all the enemies you are going to fight." ²⁶Then Joshua put the kings to death and exposed their bodies on five poles, and they were left hanging on the poles until evening.

²⁷At sunset Joshua gave the order and they took them down from the poles and threw them into the cave where they had been hiding. At the mouth of the cave they placed large rocks, which are there to this day.

Southern Cities Conquered

²⁸That day Joshua took Makkedah. He put the city and its king to the sword and totally destroyed everyone in it. He left no survivors. And he did to the king of Makkedah as he had done to the king of Jericho.

²⁹Then Joshua and all Israel with him moved on from Makkedah to Libnah and attacked it. ³⁰The LORD also gave that city and its king into Israel's hand. The city and everyone in it Joshua put to the sword. He left no survivors there. And he did to its king as he had done to the king of Jericho.

³¹Then Joshua and all Israel with him moved on from Libnah to Lachish; he took up positions against it and attacked it. ³²The LORD gave Lachish into Israel's hands, and Joshua took it on the second day. The city and everyone in it he put to the sword, just as he had done to Libnah. ³³Meanwhile, Horam king of Gezer had come up to help Lachish, but Joshua defeated him and his army—until no survivors were left.

³⁴Then Joshua and all Israel with him moved on from Lachish to Eglon; they took up positions against it and attacked it. ³⁵They captured it that same day and put it to the sword and totally destroyed everyone in it, just as they had done to Lachish.

³⁶Then Joshua and all Israel with him went up from Eglon to Hebron and attacked it. ³⁷They took the city and put it to the sword, together with its king, its villages and everyone in it. They left no survivors. Just as at Eglon, they totally destroyed it and everyone in it.

³⁸Then Joshua and all Israel with him turned around and attacked Debir. ³⁹They took the city, its king and its villages, and put them to

Joshua and the Law of the Big Mo

Joshua 10:1–43

Not only did Joshua lack momentum at the beginning of his campaign; he actually faced several barriers to it. Consider his precarious situation:

1. **Israel had just lost its founding leader.**
2. **Joshua had to follow this hero and revered leader.**
3. **The Israelites had not realized their dream in 40 years.**
4. **In front of Israel stood a flooding river and countless walled cities.**

So what can a leader without momentum do? The answer: Learn from Joshua.

1. **Emphasize that moving forward simply reflects obedience to God.**
2. **Speak of past conquests under God's direction.**
3. **Get the people to quickly put some "wins" under their belt.**
4. **Underscore your own faith in what God has promised.**
5. **Model courage for everyone.**
6. **Erect memorials to recall God's pattern of faithfulness.**

By chapter 10, Joshua is enjoying the Law of the Big Mo. Israel won victory after victory—and each one made the next one easier to visualize and embrace.

the sword. Everyone in it they totally destroyed. They left no survivors. They did to Debir and its king as they had done to Libnah and its king and to Hebron.

⁴⁰So Joshua subdued the whole region, including the hill country, the Negev, the western foothills and the mountain slopes, together with all their kings. He left no survivors. He totally destroyed all who breathed, just as the LORD, the God of Israel, had commanded. ⁴¹Joshua subdued them from Kadesh Barnea to Gaza and from the whole region of Goshen to Gibeon. ⁴²All these kings and their lands Joshua conquered in one campaign, because the LORD, the God of Israel, fought for Israel.

⁴³Then Joshua returned with all Israel to the camp at Gilgal.

Northern Kings Defeated

11 When Jabin king of Hazor heard of this, he sent word to Jobab king of Madon, to the kings of Shimron and Akshaph, ²and to the northern kings who were in the mountains, in the Arabah south of Kinnereth, in the western foothills and in Naphoth Dor on the west; ³to the Canaanites in the east and west; to the Amorites, Hittites, Perizzites and Jebusites in the hill country; and to the Hivites below Hermon in the region of Mizpah. ⁴They came out with all their troops and a large number of horses and chariots—a huge army, as numerous as the sand on the seashore. ⁵All these kings joined forces and made camp together at the Waters of Merom to fight against Israel.

⁶The LORD said to Joshua, "Do not be afraid of them, because by this time tomorrow I will hand all of them, slain, over to Israel. You are to hamstring their horses and burn their chariots."

⁷So Joshua and his whole army came against them suddenly at the Waters of Merom and attacked them, ⁸and the LORD gave them into the hand of Israel. They defeated them and pursued them all the way to Greater Sidon, to Misrephoth Maim, and to the Valley of Mizpah on the east, until no survivors were left. ⁹Joshua did to them as the LORD had directed: He hamstrung their horses and burned their chariots.

¹⁰At that time Joshua turned back and captured Hazor and put its king to the sword. (Hazor had been the head of all these kingdoms.) ¹¹Everyone in it they put to the sword. They totally destroyed*ᵃ* them, not sparing anyone that breathed, and he burned Hazor itself.

¹²Joshua took all these royal cities and their kings and put them to the sword. He totally de-

stroyed them, as Moses the servant of the LORD had commanded. ¹³Yet Israel did not burn any of the cities built on their mounds—except Hazor, which Joshua burned. ¹⁴The Israelites carried off for themselves all the plunder and livestock of these cities, but all the people they put to the sword until they completely destroyed them, not sparing anyone that breathed. ¹⁵As the LORD commanded his servant Moses, so Moses commanded Joshua, and Joshua did it; he left nothing undone of all that the LORD commanded Moses.

¹⁶So Joshua took this entire land: the hill country, all the Negev, the whole region of Goshen, the western foothills, the Arabah and the mountains of Israel with their foothills, ¹⁷from Mount Halak, which rises toward Seir, to Baal Gad in the Valley of Lebanon below Mount Hermon. He captured all their kings and put them to death. ¹⁸Joshua waged war against all these kings for a long time. ¹⁹Except for the Hivites living in Gibeon, not one city made a treaty of peace with the Israelites, who took them all in battle. ²⁰For it was the LORD himself who hardened their hearts to wage war against Israel, so that he might destroy them totally, exterminating them without mercy, as the LORD had commanded Moses.

²¹At that time Joshua went and destroyed the Anakites from the hill country: from Hebron, Debir and Anab, from all the hill country of Judah, and from all the hill country of Israel. Joshua totally destroyed them and their towns. ²²No Anakites were left in Israelite territory; only in Gaza, Gath and Ashdod did any survive.

²³So Joshua took the entire land, just as the LORD had directed Moses, and he gave it as an inheritance to Israel according to their tribal divisions. Then the land had rest from war.

List of Defeated Kings

12 These are the kings of the land whom the Israelites had defeated and whose territory they took over east of the Jordan, from the Arnon Gorge to Mount Hermon, including all the eastern side of the Arabah:

²Sihon king of the Amorites, who reigned in Heshbon.

He ruled from Aroer on the rim of the Arnon Gorge—from the middle of the gorge—to the Jabbok River, which is the

---

ᵃ 11 The Hebrew term refers to the irrevocable giving over of things or persons to the LORD, often by totally destroying them; also in verses 12, 20 and 21.

border of the Ammonites. This included half of Gilead. ³He also ruled over the eastern Arabah from the Sea of Galilee[a] to the Sea of the Arabah (that is, the Dead Sea), to Beth Jeshimoth, and then southward below the slopes of Pisgah.

⁴And the territory of Og king of Bashan, one of the last of the Rephaites, who reigned in Ashtaroth and Edrei.

⁵He ruled over Mount Hermon, Salekah, all of Bashan to the border of the people of Geshur and Maakah, and half of Gilead to the border of Sihon king of Heshbon.

⁶Moses, the servant of the LORD, and the Israelites conquered them. And Moses the servant of the LORD gave their land to the Reubenites, the Gadites and the half-tribe of Manasseh to be their possession.

⁷Here is a list of the kings of the land that Joshua and the Israelites conquered on the west side of the Jordan, from Baal Gad in the Valley of Lebanon to Mount Halak, which rises toward Seir. Joshua gave their lands as an inheritance to the tribes of Israel according to their tribal divisions. ⁸The lands included the hill country, the western foothills, the Arabah, the mountain slopes, the wilderness and the Negev. These were the lands of the Hittites, Amorites, Canaanites, Perizzites, Hivites and Jebusites. These were the kings:

⁹the king of Jericho   one
  the king of Ai (near Bethel)   one
¹⁰the king of Jerusalem   one
  the king of Hebron   one
¹¹the king of Jarmuth   one
  the king of Lachish   one
¹²the king of Eglon   one
  the king of Gezer   one
¹³the king of Debir   one
  the king of Geder   one
¹⁴the king of Hormah   one
  the king of Arad   one
¹⁵the king of Libnah   one
  the king of Adullam   one
¹⁶the king of Makkedah   one
  the king of Bethel   one
¹⁷the king of Tappuah   one
  the king of Hepher   one
¹⁸the king of Aphek   one
  the king of Lasharon   one
¹⁹the king of Madon   one
  the king of Hazor   one

²⁰the king of Shimron Meron   one
  the king of Akshaph   one
²¹the king of Taanach   one
  the king of Megiddo   one
²²the king of Kedesh   one
  the king of Jokneam in Carmel   one
²³the king of Dor (in Naphoth Dor)   one
  the king of Goyim in Gilgal   one
²⁴the king of Tirzah   one
          thirty-one kings in all.

Land Still to Be Taken

13 When Joshua had grown old, the LORD said to him, "You are now very old, and there are still very large areas of land to be taken over.

²"This is the land that remains: all the regions of the Philistines and Geshurites, ³from the Shihor River on the east of Egypt to the territory of Ekron on the north, all of it counted as Canaanite though held by the five Philistine rulers in Gaza, Ashdod, Ashkelon, Gath and Ekron; the territory of the Avvites ⁴on the south; all the land of the Canaanites, from Arah of the Sidonians as far as Aphek and the border of the Amorites; ⁵the area of Byblos; and all Lebanon to the east, from Baal Gad below Mount Hermon to Lebo Hamath.

⁶"As for all the inhabitants of the mountain regions from Lebanon to Misrephoth Maim, that is, all the Sidonians, I myself will drive them out before the Israelites. Be sure to allocate this land to Israel for an inheritance, as I have instructed you, ⁷and divide it as an inheritance among the nine tribes and half of the tribe of Manasseh."

Division of the Land East of the Jordan

⁸The other half of Manasseh,[b] the Reubenites and the Gadites had received the inheritance that Moses had given them east of the Jordan, as he, the servant of the LORD, had assigned it to them.

⁹It extended from Aroer on the rim of the Arnon Gorge, and from the town in the middle of the gorge, and included the whole plateau of Medeba as far as Dibon, ¹⁰and all the towns of Sihon king of the Amorites, who ruled in Heshbon, out

---

[a] 3 Hebrew *Kinnereth*   [b] 8 Hebrew *With it* (that is, with the other half of Manasseh)

COMPETENCE Joshua Got the Job Done

Joshua 11:16–23

COMPETENCE RARELY happens overnight. Even the great Joshua had to be prepared over many years to handle the enormous task given him. By the time he died, competence could have been his middle name. Consider this:

1. **God used Joshua over two generations.**

2. **God trusted Joshua to lead the military campaigns from the wilderness into Canaan.**

3. **God called Joshua to spy out the promised land.**

4. **God allowed Joshua to accompany Moses up Mount Sinai.**

5. **God replaced Moses with Joshua when it came time to lead the people into Canaan.**

Ponder the effort God invested in this young leader to make him competent:

1. **He was a warrior (Ex 17:9–11).** Joshua was born to be a warrior. His first opportunity at leadership came as a military leader. God was preparing him for a much larger role, but it all began here.

2. **He was a spokesman (Ex 17:14).** Joshua received a prophetic word from the Lord concerning his life-time ministry, illustrating how God works in each of us. First, we receive a personal word from the Lord; then we become bearers of his word to others.

3. **He was a servant (Ex 24:13).** Joshua was first known as Moses' "aide." No one called him a servant of Yahweh until the time of the conquest. He proved his willingness to serve before asking anyone to serve him. Each of us must undergo the same process.

4. **He was a faithful coworker (Ex 32:17).** Moses took Joshua with him to meet with God on Mount Sinai, but when ordered to stop, Joshua halted halfway up. He experienced no glory, no cloud, no voice, and no presence, yet he remained faithful to the big picture.

5. **He was an apprentice of Moses and God (Ex 33:11).** For 40 years, Joshua served as an understudy. His competence grew from Moses' tutoring and his own observations. He would not leave Moses' tent because he wanted to get everything he could from his mentor.

6. **He was a zealot (Nu 11:29).** One day when God's presence came down upon the camp and two men began

to prophesy, Joshua grew concerned. He forbade them to continue, but Moses said to him, "I wish that all the LORD's people were prophets." Joshua's passion later became an asset as it combined with experience.

7. He was a transformed leader (Nu 13:16). Moses gave the name Joshua to the young man formerly called Hoshea. With that name change came a transformation in identity and character. Joshua became a man ready to delegate, organize, and lead the nation of Israel.

For a negative example of competence, turn to p. 1230.

Confidence and Decisiveness: Joshua Distributes the Land

Joshua 13:1–21:45

The time came when Joshua finally felt ready to divide the land God had promised to Abraham hundreds of years earlier. His leadership faced a crucial test when he saw that he needed to exhort the hesitant Jews to occupy their land. "How long will you wait before you begin to take possession of the land that the LORD, the God of your ancestors, has given you?" he scolded the faltering tribes (Jos 18:3). Joshua's courage left an unmistakable mark on the hearts of his countrymen and reminded them that they were to fulfill the expectation of God. Notice how Joshua led the people in his later years, when decisiveness became especially crucial:

1. **Evaluation (13:1—14:5).** Joshua developed a clear picture of the land remaining to be conquered.

2. **Imitation (14:6-15).** Joshua blessed Caleb and pointed to him as a model of attitude and determination.

3. **Communication (15:1—17:18).** Joshua clearly articulated the boundaries of each tribe's land and what they needed to do.

4. **Exhortation (18:1-4).** Joshua challenged the tribes of Israel to take the land God had promised them.

5. **Investigation (18:4-10).** Joshua appointed teams to survey the scope of the remaining land and report back to him.

6. **Determination (18:11—19:51).** Once he received the commissioned report, Joshua determined who should get what land.

to the border of the Ammonites. [11]It also included Gilead, the territory of the people of Geshur and Maakah, all of Mount Hermon and all Bashan as far as Salekah — [12]that is, the whole kingdom of Og in Bashan, who had reigned in Ashtaroth and Edrei. (He was the last of the Rephaites.) Moses had defeated them and taken over their land. [13]But the Israelites did not drive out the people of Geshur and Maakah, so they continue to live among the Israelites to this day.

[14]But to the tribe of Levi he gave no inheritance, since the food offerings presented to the LORD, the God of Israel, are their inheritance, as he promised them.

[15]This is what Moses had given to the tribe of Reuben, according to its clans:

[16]The territory from Aroer on the rim of the Arnon Gorge, and from the town in the middle of the gorge, and the whole plateau past Medeba [17]to Heshbon and all its towns on the plateau, including Dibon, Bamoth Baal, Beth Baal Meon, [18]Jahaz, Kedemoth, Mephaath, [19]Kiriathaim, Sibmah, Zereth Shahar on the hill in the valley, [20]Beth Peor, the slopes of Pisgah, and Beth Jeshimoth — [21]all the towns on the plateau and the entire realm of Sihon king of the Amorites, who ruled at Heshbon. Moses had defeated him and the Midianite chiefs, Evi, Rekem, Zur, Hur and Reba — princes allied with Sihon — who lived in that country. [22]In addition to those slain in battle, the Israelites had put to the sword Balaam son of Beor, who practiced divination. [23]The boundary of the Reubenites was the bank of the Jordan. These towns and their villages were the inheritance of the Reubenites, according to their clans.

[24]This is what Moses had given to the tribe of Gad, according to its clans:

[25]The territory of Jazer, all the towns of Gilead and half the Ammonite country as far as Aroer, near Rabbah; [26]and from Heshbon to Ramath Mizpah and Betonim, and from Mahanaim to the territory of Debir; [27]and in the valley, Beth Haram, Beth Nimrah, Sukkoth and Zaphon with the rest of the realm of Sihon king of Heshbon (the east side of the Jordan, the territory up

Confidence and Decisiveness: Joshua Distributes the Land

Joshua 13:1—19:51

The time came when Joshua finally felt ready to divide the land God had promised to Abraham hundreds of years earlier. His leadership faced a crucial test when he saw that he needed to exhort the hesitant Jews to occupy their land. "How long will you wait before you begin to take possession of the land that the LORD, the God of your ancestors, has given you?" he scolded the faltering tribes (Jos 18:3).

Joshua's courage left an unmistakable mark on the hearts of his countrymen and reminded them that they were to fulfill the expectations of God. Notice how Joshua led the people in his later years, when decisiveness became especially crucial:

1. **Evaluation** (13:1—14:5). Joshua developed a clear picture of the land remaining to be conquered.
2. **Imitation** (14:6–15). Joshua blessed Caleb and pointed to him as a model of attitude and determination.
3. **Communication** (15:1—17:18). Joshua clearly articulated the boundaries of each tribe's land and what they needed to do.
4. **Exhortation** (18:1–4). Joshua challenged the tribes of Israel to take the land God had promised them.
5. **Investigation** (18:4–10). Joshua appointed teams to survey the scope of the remaining land and report back to him.
6. **Determination** (18:11—19:51). Once he received the commissioned report, Joshua determined who should get what land.

to the end of the Sea of Galilee^a). [28]These towns and their villages were the inheritance of the Gadites, according to their clans.

[29]This is what Moses had given to the half-tribe of Manasseh, that is, to half the family of the descendants of Manasseh, according to its clans:

[30]The territory extending from Mahanaim and including all of Bashan, the entire realm of Og king of Bashan—all the settlements of Jair in Bashan, sixty towns, [31]half of Gilead, and Ashtaroth and Edrei (the royal cities of Og in Bashan). This was for the descendants of Makir son of Manasseh—for half of the sons of Makir, according to their clans.

[32]This is the inheritance Moses had given when he was in the plains of Moab across the Jordan east of Jericho. [33]But to the tribe of Levi, Moses had given no inheritance; the LORD, the God of Israel, is their inheritance, as he promised them.

Division of the Land West of the Jordan

14 Now these are the areas the Israelites received as an inheritance in the land of Canaan, which Eleazar the priest, Joshua son of Nun and the heads of the tribal clans of Israel allotted to them. [2]Their inheritances were assigned by lot to the nine and a half tribes, as the LORD had commanded through Moses. [3]Moses had granted the two and a half tribes their inheritance east of the Jordan but had not granted the Levites an inheritance among the rest, [4]for Joseph's descendants had become two tribes—Manasseh and Ephraim. The Levites received no share of the land but only towns to live in, with pasturelands for their flocks and herds. [5]So the Israelites divided the land, just as the LORD had commanded Moses.

Allotment for Caleb

[6]Now the people of Judah approached Joshua at Gilgal, and Caleb son of Jephunneh the Kenizzite said to him, "You know what the LORD said to Moses the man of God at Kadesh Barnea about you and me. [7]I was forty years old when Moses the servant of the LORD sent me from Kadesh Barnea to explore the land. And I brought him back a report according to my convictions, [8]but my fellow Israelites who went up with me made the hearts of the people melt in fear. I, however, followed the LORD my God wholeheartedly. [9]So on that day Moses swore to me, 'The land on which your feet have walked will be your inheritance and that of your children forever, because you have followed the LORD my God wholeheartedly.'^b

[10]"Now then, just as the LORD promised, he has kept me alive for forty-five years since the time he said this to Moses, while Israel moved about in the wilderness. So here I am today, eighty-five years old! [11]I am still as strong today as the day Moses sent me out; I'm just as vigorous to go out to battle now as I was then. [12]Now give me this hill country that the LORD promised me that day. You yourself heard then that the Anakites were there and their cities were large and fortified, but, the LORD helping me, I will drive them out just as he said."

[13]Then Joshua blessed Caleb son of Jephunneh and gave him Hebron as his inheritance. [14]So Hebron has belonged to Caleb son of Jephunneh the Kenizzite ever since, because he followed the LORD, the God of Israel, wholeheartedly. [15](Hebron used to be called

---

^a 27 Hebrew *Kinnereth*   ^b 9 Deut. 1:36

Caleb: God Uses Leaders Regardless of Age or Ability

Joshua 14:6–15

If you led an army working to conquer hostile territory, and you needed to defeat a community of giants, whom would you send to do the job? Probably not an 85-year-old man—yet that's exactly who topped Joshua's list. Why?

Because that man was Caleb.

Scripture does not indicate that Caleb was a great warrior. But it clearly shows he possessed great faith and passion, qualities that serve leaders today as well as they did in Joshua's day. Author and professor J. Robert Clinton has observed that while effective pastors and church leaders across the nation possess a wide variety of gifts and abilities, almost all of them possess the gift of faith.

Caleb teaches us that leadership has less to do with age than it does with attitude. It's not a matter of position, but of disposition. Growing older does not have to mean growing ineffective. With the power of God and the confidence of Caleb, we can overcome even giants.

Kiriath Arba after Arba, who was the greatest man among the Anakites.)

Then the land had rest from war.

Allotment for Judah

15 The allotment for the tribe of Judah, according to its clans, extended down to the territory of Edom, to the Desert of Zin in the extreme south.

[2] Their southern boundary started from the bay at the southern end of the Dead Sea, [3] crossed south of Scorpion Pass, continued on to Zin and went over to the south of Kadesh Barnea. Then it ran past Hezron up to Addar and curved around to Karka. [4] It then passed along to Azmon and joined the Wadi of Egypt, ending at the Mediterranean Sea. This is their[a] southern boundary.

[5] The eastern boundary is the Dead Sea as far as the mouth of the Jordan.

The northern boundary started from the bay of the sea at the mouth of the Jordan, [6] went up to Beth Hoglah and continued north of Beth Arabah to the Stone of Bohan son of Reuben. [7] The boundary then went up to Debir from the Valley of Achor and turned north to Gilgal, which faces the Pass of Adummim south of the gorge.

It continued along to the waters of En Shemesh and came out at En Rogel. [8] Then it ran up the Valley of Ben Hinnom along the southern slope of the Jebusite city (that is, Jerusalem). From there it climbed to the top of the hill west of the Hinnom Valley at the northern end of the Valley of Rephaim. [9] From the hilltop the boundary headed toward the spring of the waters of Nephtoah, came out at the towns of Mount Ephron and went down toward Baalah (that is, Kiriath Jearim). [10] Then it curved westward from Baalah to Mount Seir, ran along the northern slope of Mount Jearim (that is, Kesalon), continued down to Beth Shemesh and crossed to Timnah. [11] It went to the northern slope of Ekron, turned toward Shikkeron, passed along to Mount Baalah and reached Jabneel. The boundary ended at the sea.

[12] The western boundary is the coastline of the Mediterranean Sea.

These are the boundaries around the people of Judah by their clans.

[13] In accordance with the LORD's command to him, Joshua gave to Caleb son of Jephunneh a portion in Judah — Kiriath Arba, that is, He-

---

[a] 4 Septuagint; Hebrew *your*

CALEB — Owner of a Brave Heart
Joshua 14:10–12

PROFILE in leadership

The entire Old Testament proclaims God's desire for a pure nation of Israel. Why, then, would the Lord honor Caleb the Kenizzite, a man descended not from Israel, but from his brother Esau?

The answer can be found not in Caleb's blood, but in his heart.

When Caleb and Joshua returned from spying out the promised land (Nu 13), the first person to speak up for God wasn't Joshua—the man who one day would lead the nation—but Caleb. After quieting the people, he declared, "We should go up and take possession of the land, for we can certainly do it" (Nu 13:30).

Forty-five years later, Caleb still possessed extraordinary amounts of courage and devotion to God. "Here I am today, eighty-five years old!" he declared. "I am still as strong today as the day Moses sent me out . . . Now give me this hill country" (Jos 14:10–12).

Joshua obviously recognized Caleb's courage and devotion, because he blessed him and declared that Caleb had "followed the LORD, the God of Israel, wholeheartedly" (Jos 14:14). With a word, Joshua made Hebron Caleb's inheritance and fulfilled Moses' promise that God would someday reward him with the land he had walked as a spy all those years before. Caleb courageously fought the intimidating descendants of Anak and captured Hebron, their mountain home.

bron. (Arba was the forefather of Anak.) [14]From Hebron Caleb drove out the three Anakites — Sheshai, Ahiman and Talmai, the sons of Anak. [15]From there he marched against the people living in Debir (formerly called Kiriath Sepher). [16]And Caleb said, "I will give my daughter Aksah in marriage to the man who attacks and captures Kiriath Sepher." [17]Othniel son of Kenaz, Caleb's brother, took it; so Caleb gave his daughter Aksah to him in marriage.

[18]One day when she came to Othniel, she urged him[a] to ask her father for a field. When she got off her donkey, Caleb asked her, "What can I do for you?"

[19]She replied, "Do me a special favor. Since you have given me land in the Negev, give me also springs of water." So Caleb gave her the upper and lower springs.

[20]This is the inheritance of the tribe of Judah, according to its clans:

[21]The southernmost towns of the tribe of Judah in the Negev toward the boundary of Edom were:

Kabzeel, Eder, Jagur, [22]Kinah, Dimonah, Adadah, [23]Kedesh, Hazor, Ithnan, [24]Ziph, Telem, Bealoth, [25]Hazor Hadattah, Kerioth Hezron (that is, Hazor), [26]Amam, Shema, Moladah, [27]Hazar Gaddah, Heshmon, Beth Pelet, [28]Hazar Shual, Beersheba, Biziothiah, [29]Baalah, Iyim, Ezem, [30]Eltolad, Kesil, Hormah, [31]Ziklag, Madmannah, Sansannah, [32]Lebaoth, Shilhim, Ain and Rimmon — a total of twenty-nine towns and their villages.

[33]In the western foothills:

Eshtaol, Zorah, Ashnah, [34]Zanoah, En Gannim, Tappuah, Enam, [35]Jarmuth, Adullam, Sokoh, Azekah, [36]Shaaraim, Adithaim and Gederah (or Gederothaim)[b] — fourteen towns and their villages.

[37]Zenan, Hadashah, Migdal Gad, [38]Dilean, Mizpah, Joktheel, [39]Lachish, Bozkath, Eglon, [40]Kabbon, Lahmas, Kitlish, [41]Gederoth, Beth Dagon, Naamah and Makkedah — sixteen towns and their villages.

[42]Libnah, Ether, Ashan, [43]Iphtah, Ashnah, Nezib, [44]Keilah, Akzib and Mareshah — nine towns and their villages.

[45]Ekron, with its surrounding settlements and villages; [46]west of Ekron, all that were in the vicinity of Ashdod, together with their villages; [47]Ashdod, its surrounding settlements and villages; and Gaza, its settlements and villages, as far as the Wadi of Egypt and the coastline of the Mediterranean Sea.

[48]In the hill country:

Shamir, Jattir, Sokoh, [49]Dannah, Kiriath Sannah (that is, Debir), [50]Anab, Eshtemoh, Anim, [51]Goshen, Holon and Giloh — eleven towns and their villages.

[52]Arab, Dumah, Eshan, [53]Janim, Beth Tappuah, Aphekah, [54]Humtah, Kiriath Arba (that is, Hebron) and Zior — nine towns and their villages.

[55]Maon, Carmel, Ziph, Juttah, [56]Jezreel, Jokdeam, Zanoah, [57]Kain, Gibeah and Timnah — ten towns and their villages.

[58]Halhul, Beth Zur, Gedor, [59]Maarath, Beth Anoth and Eltekon — six towns and their villages.[c]

[60]Kiriath Baal (that is, Kiriath Jearim) and Rabbah — two towns and their villages.

[61]In the wilderness:

Beth Arabah, Middin, Sekakah, [62]Nibshan, the City of Salt and En Gedi — six towns and their villages.

[63]Judah could not dislodge the Jebusites, who were living in Jerusalem; to this day the Jebusites live there with the people of Judah.

Allotment for Ephraim and Manasseh

16 The allotment for Joseph began at the Jordan, east of the springs of Jericho, and went up from there through the desert into the hill country of Bethel. [2]It went on from Bethel (that is, Luz),[d] crossed over to the territory of the Arkites in Ataroth, [3]descended westward to the territory of the Japhletites as far as the region of Lower Beth Horon and on to Gezer, ending at the Mediterranean Sea.

[4]So Manasseh and Ephraim, the descendants of Joseph, received their inheritance.

[5]This was the territory of Ephraim, according to its clans:

The boundary of their inheritance went from Ataroth Addar in the east to Upper Beth Horon [6]and continued to the Mediterranean Sea. From Mikmethath on the

---

[a] 18 Hebrew and some Septuagint manuscripts; other Septuagint manuscripts (see also note at Judges 1:14) *Othniel, he urged her*   [b] 36 Or *Gederah and Gederothaim*
[c] 59 The Septuagint adds another district of eleven towns, including Tekoa and Ephrathah (Bethlehem).
[d] 2 Septuagint; Hebrew *Bethel to Luz*

north it curved eastward to Taanath Shiloh, passing by it to Janoah on the east. ⁷Then it went down from Janoah to Ataroth and Naarah, touched Jericho and came out at the Jordan. ⁸From Tappuah the border went west to the Kanah Ravine and ended at the Mediterranean Sea. This was the inheritance of the tribe of the Ephraimites, according to its clans. ⁹It also included all the towns and their villages that were set aside for the Ephraimites within the inheritance of the Manassites.

¹⁰They did not dislodge the Canaanites living in Gezer; to this day the Canaanites live among the people of Ephraim but are required to do forced labor.

17 This was the allotment for the tribe of Manasseh as Joseph's firstborn, that is, for Makir, Manasseh's firstborn. Makir was the ancestor of the Gileadites, who had received Gilead and Bashan because the Makirites were great soldiers. ²So this allotment was for the rest of the people of Manasseh—the clans of Abiezer, Helek, Asriel, Shechem, Hepher and Shemida. These are the other male descendants of Manasseh son of Joseph by their clans.

³Now Zelophehad son of Hepher, the son of Gilead, the son of Makir, the son of Manasseh, had no sons but only daughters, whose names were Mahlah, Noah, Hoglah, Milkah and Tirzah. ⁴They went to Eleazar the priest, Joshua son of Nun, and the leaders and said, "The LORD commanded Moses to give us an inheritance among our relatives." So Joshua gave them an inheritance along with the brothers of their father, according to the LORD's command. ⁵Manasseh's share consisted of ten tracts of land besides Gilead and Bashan east of the Jordan, ⁶because the daughters of the tribe of Manasseh received an inheritance among the sons. The land of Gilead belonged to the rest of the descendants of Manasseh.

⁷The territory of Manasseh extended from Asher to Mikmethath east of Shechem. The boundary ran southward from there to include the people living at En Tappuah. ⁸(Manasseh had the land of Tappuah, but Tappuah itself, on the boundary of Manasseh, belonged to the Ephraimites.) ⁹Then the boundary continued south to the Kanah Ravine. There were towns belonging to Ephraim lying among the towns of Manasseh, but the boundary of Manasseh was the northern side of the ravine and ended at the Mediterranean Sea. ¹⁰On the south the land belonged to Ephraim, on the north to Manasseh. The territory of Manasseh reached the Mediterranean Sea and bordered Asher on the north and Issachar on the east.

¹¹Within Issachar and Asher, Manasseh also had Beth Shan, Ibleam and the people of Dor, Endor, Taanach and Megiddo, together with their surrounding settlements (the third in the list is Naphoth*ᵃ*). ¹²Yet the Manassites were not able to occupy these towns, for the Canaanites were determined to live in that region. ¹³However, when the Israelites grew stronger, they subjected the Canaanites to forced labor but did not drive them out completely.

¹⁴The people of Joseph said to Joshua, "Why have you given us only one allotment and one portion for an inheritance? We are a numerous people, and the LORD has blessed us abundantly."

¹⁵"If you are so numerous," Joshua answered, "and if the hill country of Ephraim is too small for you, go up into the forest and clear land for yourselves there in the land of the Perizzites and Rephaites."

¹⁶The people of Joseph replied, "The hill country is not enough for us, and all the Canaanites who live in the plain have chariots fitted with iron, both those in Beth Shan and its settlements and those in the Valley of Jezreel."

¹⁷But Joshua said to the tribes of Joseph—to Ephraim and Manasseh—"You are numerous and very powerful. You will have not only one allotment ¹⁸but the forested hill country as well. Clear it, and its farthest limits will be yours; though the Canaanites have chariots fitted with iron and though they are strong, you can drive them out."

Division of the Rest of the Land

18 The whole assembly of the Israelites gathered at Shiloh and set up the tent of meeting there. The country was brought under their control, ²but there were still seven Israelite tribes who had not yet received their inheritance.

³So Joshua said to the Israelites: "How long will you wait before you begin to take possession of the land that the LORD, the God of your ancestors, has given you? ⁴Appoint three men from each tribe. I will send them out to make a survey of the land and to write a description of it, according to the inheritance of each. Then they

---

ᵃ 11 That is, Naphoth Dor

will return to me. [5]You are to divide the land into seven parts. Judah is to remain in its territory on the south and the tribes of Joseph in their territory on the north. [6]After you have written descriptions of the seven parts of the land, bring them here to me and I will cast lots for you in the presence of the LORD our God. [7]The Levites, however, do not get a portion among you, because the priestly service of the LORD is their inheritance. And Gad, Reuben and the half-tribe of Manasseh have already received their inheritance on the east side of the Jordan. Moses the servant of the LORD gave it to them."

[8]As the men started on their way to map out the land, Joshua instructed them, "Go and make a survey of the land and write a description of it. Then return to me, and I will cast lots for you here at Shiloh in the presence of the LORD." [9]So the men left and went through the land. They wrote its description on a scroll, town by town, in seven parts, and returned to Joshua in the camp at Shiloh. [10]Joshua then cast lots for them in Shiloh in the presence of the LORD, and there he distributed the land to the Israelites according to their tribal divisions.

Allotment for Benjamin

[11]The first lot came up for the tribe of Benjamin according to its clans. Their allotted territory lay between the tribes of Judah and Joseph:

[12]On the north side their boundary began at the Jordan, passed the northern slope of Jericho and headed west into the hill country, coming out at the wilderness of Beth Aven. [13]From there it crossed to the south slope of Luz (that is, Bethel) and went down to Ataroth Addar on the hill south of Lower Beth Horon.

[14]From the hill facing Beth Horon on the south the boundary turned south along the western side and came out at Kiriath Baal (that is, Kiriath Jearim), a town of the people of Judah. This was the western side.

[15]The southern side began at the outskirts of Kiriath Jearim on the west, and the boundary came out at the spring of the waters of Nephtoah. [16]The boundary went down to the foot of the hill facing the Valley of Ben Hinnom, north of the Valley of Rephaim. It continued down the Hinnom Valley along the southern slope of the Jebusite city and so to En Rogel. [17]It then curved north, went to En Shemesh, continued to Geliloth, which faces the Pass of Adummim, and ran down to the Stone of Bohan son of Reuben. [18]It continued to the northern slope of Beth Arabah[a] and on down into the Arabah. [19]It then went to the northern slope of Beth Hoglah and came out at the northern bay of the Dead Sea, at the mouth of the Jordan in the south. This was the southern boundary.

[20]The Jordan formed the boundary on the eastern side.

These were the boundaries that marked out the inheritance of the clans of Benjamin on all sides.

[21]The tribe of Benjamin, according to its clans, had the following towns:

Jericho, Beth Hoglah, Emek Keziz, [22]Beth Arabah, Zemaraim, Bethel, [23]Avvim, Parah, Ophrah, [24]Kephar Ammoni, Ophni and Geba—twelve towns and their villages.

[25]Gibeon, Ramah, Beeroth, [26]Mizpah, Kephirah, Mozah, [27]Rekem, Irpeel, Taralah, [28]Zelah, Haeleph, the Jebusite city (that is, Jerusalem), Gibeah and Kiriath—fourteen towns and their villages.

This was the inheritance of Benjamin for its clans.

Allotment for Simeon

19 The second lot came out for the tribe of Simeon according to its clans. Their inheritance lay within the territory of Judah. [2]It included:

Beersheba (or Sheba),[b] Moladah, [3]Hazar Shual, Balah, Ezem, [4]Eltolad, Bethul, Hormah, [5]Ziklag, Beth Markaboth, Hazar Susah, [6]Beth Lebaoth and Sharuhen—thirteen towns and their villages;

[7]Ain, Rimmon, Ether and Ashan—four towns and their villages— [8]and all the villages around these towns as far as Baalath Beer (Ramah in the Negev).

This was the inheritance of the tribe of the Simeonites, according to its clans. [9]The inheritance of the Simeonites was taken from the share of Judah, because Judah's portion was more than they needed. So the Simeonites received their inheritance within the territory of Judah.

Allotment for Zebulun

[10]The third lot came up for Zebulun according to its clans:

The boundary of their inheritance went as far as Sarid. [11]Going west it ran to Maralah, touched Dabbesheth, and extended

---

[a] 18 Septuagint; Hebrew *slope facing the Arabah*   [b] 2 Or *Beersheba, Sheba*; 1 Chron. 4:28 does not have *Sheba*.

to the ravine near Jokneam. [12]It turned east from Sarid toward the sunrise to the territory of Kisloth Tabor and went on to Daberath and up to Japhia. [13]Then it continued eastward to Gath Hepher and Eth Kazin; it came out at Rimmon and turned toward Neah. [14]There the boundary went around on the north to Hannathon and ended at the Valley of Iphtah El. [15]Included were Kattath, Nahalal, Shimron, Idalah and Bethlehem. There were twelve towns and their villages.

[16]These towns and their villages were the inheritance of Zebulun, according to its clans.

Allotment for Issachar

[17]The fourth lot came out for Issachar according to its clans. [18]Their territory included:

Jezreel, Kesulloth, Shunem, [19]Haphara-im, Shion, Anaharath, [20]Rabbith, Kishion, Ebez, [21]Remeth, En Gannim, En Haddah and Beth Pazzez. [22]The boundary touched Tabor, Shahazumah and Beth Shemesh, and ended at the Jordan. There were sixteen towns and their villages.

[23]These towns and their villages were the inheritance of the tribe of Issachar, according to its clans.

Allotment for Asher

[24]The fifth lot came out for the tribe of Asher according to its clans. [25]Their territory included:

Helkath, Hali, Beten, Akshaph, [26]Allammelek, Amad and Mishal. On the west the boundary touched Carmel and Shihor Libnath. [27]It then turned east toward Beth Dagon, touched Zebulun and the Valley of Iphtah El, and went north to Beth Emek and Neiel, passing Kabul on the left. [28]It went to Abdon,[a] Rehob, Hammon and Kanah, as far as Greater Sidon. [29]The boundary then turned back toward Ramah and went to the fortified city of Tyre, turned toward Hosah and came out at the Mediterranean Sea in the region of Akzib, [30]Ummah, Aphek and Rehob. There were twenty-two towns and their villages.

[31]These towns and their villages were the inheritance of the tribe of Asher, according to its clans.

Allotment for Naphtali

[32]The sixth lot came out for Naphtali according to its clans:

[33]Their boundary went from Heleph and the large tree in Zaanannim, pass-ing Adami Nekeb and Jabneel to Lakkum and ending at the Jordan. [34]The boundary ran west through Aznoth Tabor and came out at Hukkok. It touched Zebulun on the south, Asher on the west and the Jordan[b] on the east. [35]The fortified towns were Ziddim, Zer, Hammath, Rakkath, Kinnereth, [36]Adamah, Ramah, Hazor, [37]Kedesh, Edrei, En Hazor, [38]Iron, Migdal El, Horem, Beth Anath and Beth Shemesh. There were nineteen towns and their villages.

[39]These towns and their villages were the inheritance of the tribe of Naphtali, according to its clans.

Allotment for Dan

[40]The seventh lot came out for the tribe of Dan according to its clans. [41]The territory of their inheritance included:

Zorah, Eshtaol, Ir Shemesh, [42]Shaalabbin, Aijalon, Ithlah, [43]Elon, Timnah, Ekron, [44]Eltekeh, Gibbethon, Baalath, [45]Jehud, Bene Berak, Gath Rimmon, [46]Me Jarkon and Rakkon, with the area facing Joppa.

[47](When the territory of the Danites was lost to them, they went up and attacked Leshem, took it, put it to the sword and occupied it. They settled in Leshem and named it Dan after their ancestor.)

[48]These towns and their villages were the inheritance of the tribe of Dan, according to its clans.

Allotment for Joshua

[49]When they had finished dividing the land into its allotted portions, the Israelites gave Joshua son of Nun an inheritance among them, [50]as the LORD had commanded. They gave him the town he asked for — Timnath Serah[c] in the hill country of Ephraim. And he built up the town and settled there.

[51]These are the territories that Eleazar the priest, Joshua son of Nun and the heads of the tribal clans of Israel assigned by lot at Shiloh in the presence of the LORD at the entrance to the tent of meeting. And so they finished dividing the land.

Cities of Refuge

20 Then the LORD said to Joshua: [2]"Tell the Israelites to designate the cities of refuge, as I instructed you through Moses, [3]so that any-

---

[a] 28 Some Hebrew manuscripts (see also 21:30); most Hebrew manuscripts *Ebron*   [b] 34 Septuagint; Hebrew *west, and Judah, the Jordan,*   [c] 50 Also known as *Timnath Heres* (see Judges 2:9)

one who kills a person accidentally and unintentionally may flee there and find protection from the avenger of blood. [4]When they flee to one of these cities, they are to stand in the entrance of the city gate and state their case before the elders of that city. Then the elders are to admit the fugitive into their city and provide a place to live among them. [5]If the avenger of blood comes in pursuit, the elders must not surrender the fugitive, because the fugitive killed their neighbor unintentionally and without malice aforethought. [6]They are to stay in that city until they have stood trial before the assembly and until the death of the high priest who is serving at that time. Then they may go back to their own home in the town from which they fled."

[7]So they set apart Kedesh in Galilee in the hill country of Naphtali, Shechem in the hill country of Ephraim, and Kiriath Arba (that is, Hebron) in the hill country of Judah. [8]East of the Jordan (on the other side from Jericho) they designated Bezer in the wilderness on the plateau in the tribe of Reuben, Ramoth in Gilead in the tribe of Gad, and Golan in Bashan in the tribe of Manasseh. [9]Any of the Israelites or any foreigner residing among them who killed someone accidentally could flee to these designated cities and not be killed by the avenger of blood prior to standing trial before the assembly.

Towns for the Levites

21 Now the family heads of the Levites approached Eleazar the priest, Joshua son of Nun, and the heads of the other tribal families of Israel [2]at Shiloh in Canaan and said to them, "The LORD commanded through Moses that you give us towns to live in, with pasturelands for our livestock." [3]So, as the LORD had commanded, the Israelites gave the Levites the following towns and pasturelands out of their own inheritance:

[4]The first lot came out for the Kohathites, according to their clans. The Levites who were descendants of Aaron the priest were allotted thirteen towns from the tribes of Judah, Simeon and Benjamin. [5]The rest of Kohath's descendants were allotted ten towns from the clans of the tribes of Ephraim, Dan and half of Manasseh.

[6]The descendants of Gershon were allotted thirteen towns from the clans of the tribes of Issachar, Asher, Naphtali and the half-tribe of Manasseh in Bashan.

[7]The descendants of Merari, according to their clans, received twelve towns from the tribes of Reuben, Gad and Zebulun.

[8]So the Israelites allotted to the Levites these towns and their pasturelands, as the LORD had commanded through Moses.

[9]From the tribes of Judah and Simeon they allotted the following towns by name [10](these towns were assigned to the descendants of Aaron who were from the Kohathite clans of the Levites, because the first lot fell to them):

[11]They gave them Kiriath Arba (that is, Hebron), with its surrounding pastureland, in the hill country of Judah. (Arba was the forefather of Anak.) [12]But the fields and villages around the city they had given to Caleb son of Jephunneh as his possession.

[13]So to the descendants of Aaron the priest they gave Hebron (a city of refuge for one accused of murder), Libnah, [14]Jattir, Eshtemoa, [15]Holon, Debir, [16]Ain, Juttah and Beth Shemesh, together with their pasturelands—nine towns from these two tribes.

[17]And from the tribe of Benjamin they gave them Gibeon, Geba, [18]Anathoth and Almon, together with their pasturelands—four towns.

[19]The total number of towns for the priests, the descendants of Aaron, came to thirteen, together with their pasturelands.

[20]The rest of the Kohathite clans of the Levites were allotted towns from the tribe of Ephraim:

[21]In the hill country of Ephraim they were given Shechem (a city of refuge for one accused of murder) and Gezer, [22]Kibzaim and Beth Horon, together with their pasturelands—four towns.

[23]Also from the tribe of Dan they received Eltekeh, Gibbethon, [24]Aijalon and Gath Rimmon, together with their pasturelands—four towns.

[25]From half the tribe of Manasseh they received Taanach and Gath Rimmon, together with their pasturelands—two towns.

[26]All these ten towns and their pasturelands were given to the rest of the Kohathite clans.

[27]The Levite clans of the Gershonites were given:

from the half-tribe of Manasseh,
Golan in Bashan (a city of refuge for one accused of murder) and Be Eshterah, together with their pasturelands—two towns;

28from the tribe of Issachar,
  Kishion, Daberath, 29Jarmuth and En Gannim, together with their pasturelands—
  four towns;
30from the tribe of Asher,
  Mishal, Abdon, 31Helkath and Rehob, together with their pasturelands—four
  towns;
32from the tribe of Naphtali,
  Kedesh in Galilee (a city of refuge for
  one accused of murder), Hammoth Dor
  and Kartan, together with their pasturelands—three towns.
33The total number of towns of the Gershonite clans came to thirteen, together with their pasturelands.

34The Merarite clans (the rest of the Levites) were given:
  from the tribe of Zebulun,
  Jokneam, Kartah, 35Dimnah and Nahalal,
  together with their pasturelands—four
  towns;
36from the tribe of Reuben,
  Bezer, Jahaz, 37Kedemoth and Mephaath,
  together with their pasturelands—four
  towns;
38from the tribe of Gad,
  Ramoth in Gilead (a city of refuge for one
  accused of murder), Mahanaim, 39Hesh-
  bon and Jazer, together with their pasturelands—four towns in all.
40The total number of towns allotted to the Merarite clans, who were the rest of the Levites, came to twelve.

41The towns of the Levites in the territory held by the Israelites were forty-eight in all, together with their pasturelands. 42Each of these towns had pasturelands surrounding it; this was true for all these towns.

43So the Lord gave Israel all the land he had sworn to give their ancestors, and they took possession of it and settled there. 44The Lord gave them rest on every side, just as he had sworn to their ancestors. Not one of their enemies withstood them; the Lord gave all their enemies into their hands. 45Not one of all the Lord's good promises to Israel failed; every one was fulfilled.

Eastern Tribes Return Home

22 Then Joshua summoned the Reubenites, the Gadites and the half-tribe of Manasseh 2and said to them, "You have done all that Moses the servant of the Lord commanded, and you have obeyed me in everything I command-

ed. 3For a long time now—to this very day—you have not deserted your fellow Israelites but have carried out the mission the Lord your God gave you. 4Now that the Lord your God has given them rest as he promised, return to your homes in the land that Moses the servant of the Lord gave you on the other side of the Jordan. 5But be very careful to keep the commandment and the law that Moses the servant of the Lord gave you: to love the Lord your God, to walk in obedience to him, to keep his commands, to hold fast to him and to serve him with all your heart and with all your soul."

6Then Joshua blessed them and sent them away, and they went to their homes. 7(To the half-tribe of Manasseh Moses had given land in Bashan, and to the other half of the tribe Joshua gave land on the west side of the Jordan along with their fellow Israelites.) When Joshua sent them home, he blessed them, 8saying, "Return to your homes with your great wealth—with large herds of livestock, with silver, gold, bronze and iron, and a great quantity of clothing—and divide the plunder from your enemies with your fellow Israelites."

9So the Reubenites, the Gadites and the half-tribe of Manasseh left the Israelites at Shiloh in Canaan to return to Gilead, their own land, which they had acquired in accordance with the command of the Lord through Moses.

10When they came to Geliloth near the Jordan in the land of Canaan, the Reubenites, the Gadites and the half-tribe of Manasseh built an imposing altar there by the Jordan. 11And when the Israelites heard that they had built the altar on the border of Canaan at Geliloth near the Jordan on the Israelite side, 12the whole assembly of Israel gathered at Shiloh to go to war against them.

13So the Israelites sent Phinehas son of Eleazar, the priest, to the land of Gilead—to Reuben, Gad and the half-tribe of Manasseh. 14With him they sent ten of the chief men, one from each of the tribes of Israel, each the head of a family division among the Israelite clans.

15When they went to Gilead—to Reuben, Gad and the half-tribe of Manasseh—they said to them: 16"The whole assembly of the Lord says: 'How could you break faith with the God of Israel like this? How could you turn away from the Lord and build yourselves an altar in rebellion against him now? 17Was not the sin of Peor enough for us? Up to this very day we have not cleansed ourselves from that sin, even though a plague fell on the community of the

LORD! [18]And are you now turning away from the LORD?

"'If you rebel against the LORD today, tomorrow he will be angry with the whole community of Israel. [19]If the land you possess is defiled, come over to the LORD's land, where the LORD's tabernacle stands, and share the land with us. But do not rebel against the LORD or against us by building an altar for yourselves, other than the altar of the LORD our God. [20]When Achan son of Zerah was unfaithful in regard to the devoted things,[a] did not wrath come on the whole community of Israel? He was not the only one who died for his sin.'"

[21]Then Reuben, Gad and the half-tribe of Manasseh replied to the heads of the clans of Israel: [22]"The Mighty One, God, the LORD! The Mighty One, God, the LORD! He knows! And let Israel know! If this has been in rebellion or disobedience to the LORD, do not spare us this day. [23]If we have built our own altar to turn away from the LORD and to offer burnt offerings and grain offerings, or to sacrifice fellowship offerings on it, may the LORD himself call us to account.

[24]"No! We did it for fear that some day your descendants might say to ours, 'What do you have to do with the LORD, the God of Israel? [25]The LORD has made the Jordan a boundary between us and you — you Reubenites and Gadites! You have no share in the LORD.' So your descendants might cause ours to stop fearing the LORD.

[26]"That is why we said, 'Let us get ready and build an altar — but not for burnt offerings or sacrifices.' [27]On the contrary, it is to be a witness between us and you and the generations that follow, that we will worship the LORD at his sanctuary with our burnt offerings, sacrifices and fellowship offerings. Then in the future your descendants will not be able to say to ours, 'You have no share in the LORD.'

[28]"And we said, 'If they ever say this to us, or to our descendants, we will answer: Look at the replica of the LORD's altar, which our ancestors built, not for burnt offerings and sacrifices, but as a witness between us and you.'

[29]"Far be it from us to rebel against the LORD and turn away from him today by building an altar for burnt offerings, grain offerings and sacrifices, other than the altar of the LORD our God that stands before his tabernacle."

[30]When Phinehas the priest and the leaders of the community — the heads of the clans of the Israelites — heard what Reuben, Gad and Manasseh had to say, they were pleased. [31]And Phinehas son of Eleazar, the priest, said to Reuben, Gad and Manasseh, "Today we know that the LORD is with us, because you have not been unfaithful to the LORD in this matter. Now you have rescued the Israelites from the LORD's hand."

[32]Then Phinehas son of Eleazar, the priest, and the leaders returned to Canaan from their meeting with the Reubenites and Gadites in Gilead and reported to the Israelites. [33]They were glad to hear the report and praised God. And they talked no more about going to war against them to devastate the country where the Reubenites and the Gadites lived.

[34]And the Reubenites and the Gadites gave the altar this name: A Witness Between Us — that the LORD is God.

Joshua's Farewell to the Leaders

23 After a long time had passed and the LORD had given Israel rest from all their enemies around them, Joshua, by then a very old man, [2]summoned all Israel — their elders, leaders, judges and officials — and said to them: "I am very old. [3]You yourselves have seen everything the LORD your God has done to all these nations for your sake; it was the LORD your God who fought for you. [4]Remember how I have allotted as an inheritance for your tribes all the land of the nations that remain — the nations I conquered — between the Jordan and the Mediterranean Sea in the west. [5]The LORD your God himself will push them out for your sake. He will drive them out before you, and you will take

---

[a] 20 The Hebrew term refers to the irrevocable giving over of things or persons to the LORD, often by totally destroying them.

The Law of Magnetism: Joshua Says Good-bye with Convictions

Joshua 23:1—24:28

Joshua's farewell speech urged Israel to stay passionately committed to God. Joshua reminded the people of God's faithfulness, warned them against disobedience and concluded, "But as for me and my household, we will serve the LORD" (Jos 24:15). Everyone followed Joshua's convictions during his lifetime, for he made them both attractive and magnetic.

possession of their land, as the LORD your God promised you.

6"Be very strong; be careful to obey all that is written in the Book of the Law of Moses, without turning aside to the right or to the left. 7Do not associate with these nations that remain among you; do not invoke the names of their gods or swear by them. You must not serve them or bow down to them. 8But you are to hold fast to the LORD your God, as you have until now.

9"The LORD has driven out before you great and powerful nations; to this day no one has been able to withstand you. 10One of you routs a thousand, because the LORD your God fights for you, just as he promised. 11So be very careful to love the LORD your God.

12"But if you turn away and ally yourselves with the survivors of these nations that remain among you and if you intermarry with them and associate with them, 13then you may be sure that the LORD your God will no longer drive out these nations before you. Instead, they will become snares and traps for you, whips on your backs and thorns in your eyes, until you perish from this good land, which the LORD your God has given you.

14"Now I am about to go the way of all the earth. You know with all your heart and soul that not one of all the good promises the LORD your God gave you has failed. Every promise has been fulfilled; not one has failed. 15But just as all the good things the LORD your God has promised you have come to you, so he will bring on you all the evil things he has threatened, until the LORD your God has destroyed you from this good land he has given you. 16If you violate the covenant of the LORD your God, which he commanded you, and go and serve other gods and bow down to them, the LORD's anger will burn against you, and you will quickly perish from the good land he has given you."

The Covenant Renewed at Shechem

24 Then Joshua assembled all the tribes of Israel at Shechem. He summoned the elders, leaders, judges and officials of Israel, and they presented themselves before God.

2Joshua said to all the people, "This is what the LORD, the God of Israel, says: 'Long ago your ancestors, including Terah the father of Abraham and Nahor, lived beyond the Euphrates River and worshiped other gods. 3But I took your father Abraham from the land beyond the Euphrates and led him throughout Canaan and gave him many descendants. I gave him Isaac, 4and to Isaac I gave Jacob and Esau. I assigned

the hill country of Seir to Esau, but Jacob and his family went down to Egypt.

5"'Then I sent Moses and Aaron, and I afflicted the Egyptians by what I did there, and I brought you out. 6When I brought your people out of Egypt, you came to the sea, and the Egyptians pursued them with chariots and horsemen[a] as far as the Red Sea.[b] 7But they cried to the LORD for help, and he put darkness between you and the Egyptians; he brought the sea over them and covered them. You saw with your own eyes what I did to the Egyptians. Then you lived in the wilderness for a long time.

8"'I brought you to the land of the Amorites who lived east of the Jordan. They fought against you, but I gave them into your hands. I destroyed them from before you, and you took possession of their land. 9When Balak son of Zippor, the king of Moab, prepared to fight against Israel, he sent for Balaam son of Beor to put a curse on you. 10But I would not listen to Balaam, so he blessed you again and again, and I delivered you out of his hand.

11"'Then you crossed the Jordan and came to Jericho. The citizens of Jericho fought against you, as did also the Amorites, Perizzites, Canaanites, Hittites, Girgashites, Hivites and Jebusites, but I gave them into your hands. 12I sent the hornet ahead of you, which drove them out before you—also the two Amorite kings. You did not do it with your own sword and bow. 13So I gave you a land on which you did not toil and cities you did not build; and you live in them and eat from vineyards and olive groves that you did not plant.'

14"Now fear the LORD and serve him with all faithfulness. Throw away the gods your ancestors worshiped beyond the Euphrates River and in Egypt, and serve the LORD. 15But if serving the LORD seems undesirable to you, then choose for yourselves this day whom you will serve, whether the gods your ancestors served beyond the Euphrates, or the gods of the Amorites, in whose land you are living. But as for me and my household, we will serve the LORD."

16Then the people answered, "Far be it from us to forsake the LORD to serve other gods! 17It was the LORD our God himself who brought us and our parents up out of Egypt, from that land of slavery, and performed those great signs before our eyes. He protected us on our entire journey and among all the nations through which we traveled. 18And the LORD drove out before us all the nations, including the Amo-

---

a 6 Or charioteers   b 6 Or the Sea of Reeds

rites, who lived in the land. We too will serve the LORD, because he is our God."

¹⁹Joshua said to the people, "You are not able to serve the LORD. He is a holy God; he is a jealous God. He will not forgive your rebellion and your sins. ²⁰If you forsake the LORD and serve foreign gods, he will turn and bring disaster on you and make an end of you, after he has been good to you."

²¹But the people said to Joshua, "No! We will serve the LORD."

²²Then Joshua said, "You are witnesses against yourselves that you have chosen to serve the LORD."

"Yes, we are witnesses," they replied.

²³"Now then," said Joshua, "throw away the foreign gods that are among you and yield your hearts to the LORD, the God of Israel."

²⁴And the people said to Joshua, "We will serve the LORD our God and obey him."

²⁵On that day Joshua made a covenant for the people, and there at Shechem he reaffirmed for them decrees and laws. ²⁶And Joshua recorded these things in the Book of the Law of God. Then he took a large stone and set it up there under the oak near the holy place of the LORD.

²⁷"See!" he said to all the people. "This stone will be a witness against us. It has heard all the words the LORD has said to us. It will be a witness against you if you are untrue to your God."

The Joshua Problem: He Failed to Give the Gift Moses Gave Him
Joshua 24:29

Joshua's leadership failed at only one major point: He left no "Joshua" to follow him, as he had followed Moses. Joshua did not reproduce his leadership in someone else. Consequently, the book of Judges records a time of anarchy, when "everyone did as they saw fit" (Jdg 21:25).

²⁸Then Joshua dismissed the people, each to their own inheritance.

Buried in the Promised Land

²⁹After these things, Joshua son of Nun, the servant of the LORD, died at the age of a hundred and ten. ³⁰And they buried him in the land of his inheritance, at Timnath Serah[a] in the hill country of Ephraim, north of Mount Gaash.

³¹Israel served the LORD throughout the lifetime of Joshua and of the elders who outlived him and who had experienced everything the LORD had done for Israel.

[a] 30 Also known as Timnath Heres (see Judges 2:9)

Joshua: Picture of a Faithful Leader
Joshua 24:29–31

Joshua provides a superb example of a leader whose faithfulness prompted God to raise him up. Over the three divisions of his life (40 years in Egypt; 40 years in the wilderness; and 30 years in Canaan), God gradually moved this trustworthy man into leadership.

Note the signs of his faithfulness: **Obedience** (Ex 17:8–16; Nu 32:10–12); **Servanthood** (Ex 24:13; Jos 11:15); **Loyalty** (Ex 33:11; Nu 11:24–30); **Courage** (Nu 13:8, 16, 25–30; 14:5–10); **Promotion** (Nu 27:15–23); **Responsibility** (Dt 31:7–8); **Power** (Dt 34:9); **Credibility** (Dt 34:9). Joshua's faithfulness challenges us even today to lead as he did:

1. **Live *ahead* of your contemporaries.** Joshua spied out the same land at the same time as the other 10 spies, but he and Caleb returned with a different report. He lived ahead of his time.

2. **Live *above* your circumstances.** Joshua faced several challenges: He followed Moses; he had to conquer mighty Jericho; he had to cross the Jordan with more than one million people. But he did it.

3. **Live *deeper* than your calamities.** When Israel began to make progress in taking the promised land, some disobeyed God and brought defeat on the nation. Joshua overcame it all.

4. **Live *beyond* your capabilities.** Joshua's dream, his determination, and his ability to develop his leadership skills enabled him to soar beyond his own personal gifts.

32And Joseph's bones, which the Israelites had brought up from Egypt, were buried at Shechem in the tract of land that Jacob bought for a hundred pieces of silver[a] from the sons of Hamor, the father of Shechem. This became the inheritance of Joseph's descendants.

33And Eleazar son of Aaron died and was buried at Gibeah, which had been allotted to his son Phinehas in the hill country of Ephraim.

[a] 32 Hebrew *hundred kesitahs*; a kesitah was a unit of money of unknown weight and value.

INTRODUCTION TO JUDGES

Responsible for the Nation of Israel

Judges receives its name from the leaders who assumed responsibility for the nation of Israel from the time of Joshua until the beginning of the monarchy, a period of about 200 years. The term "judge" meant civil magistrate or governor or head of state, clearly a political term for leader.

During the times of the judges, public opinion leaned heavily against a monarchy. Only external pressures applied by prospective invaders eventually prompted the people to demand a king (1Sa 8). At the time of the judges, God himself reigned as Israel's King, while the judges served as under-shepherds.

Under Joshua's leadership, Israel defeated anyone who stood in her way and occupied the land God had promised the nation decades before. After Joshua died, however, the tribes ran into trouble trying to consolidate their inheritance. Turmoil reigned in the Holy Land. The Philistines pushed in from the Mediterranean Coast, establishing a stranglehold on the region until the time of King David. Other ethnic groups, such as the Midianites, attacked the eastern bank of Israel.

The scattered tribes had grown divided and weak. They lacked a strong leader who could cast a national vision. The last and most famous verse in the book speaks volumes: "In those days Israel had no king; everyone did as they saw fit" (Jdg 21:25).

Still, God always raises up a leader for the hour—the theme of this book. Whenever suffering grew terrible and the people cried out in despair, God called forth a judge (or deliverer) to throw off the oppressor's yoke. Sometimes these judges were good and noble men like Gideon

God's Role in Judges

God's role during this period of history cannot be over-emphasized. The people relished their conquest of Canaan, but waffled between freedom and chaos. They turned away from God, then turned back to him for help when oppressed—a pattern often repeated. Yet God always raised up a leader for the hour. Only God ruled as Israel's King, and only he could raise up human leaders to serve under him.

Leaders in Judges

Othniel, Ehud, Shamgar, Deborah, Gideon, Abimelek, Tola, Jair, Jephthah, Ibzan, Elon, Abdon, Samson

Other People of Influence in Judges

Barak, Jael, the Midianites, the Amalekites, the Philistines, the Ammonites, Micah

Lessons in Leadership

- Leaders who compromise their values eventually compromise their goals.
- It takes strong, spiritual leadership to engineer a turnaround in God's kingdom.
- Leaders should lead from their area of giftedness and strength.
- The one with the plan and insight is the one with the power and influence.

or Samuel; at other times erratic and unstable men like Samson rose to the fore.

In any case, the message rings clear: God raises up the weak and unlikely to confound the strong and sensible. Deborah, a woman, led in a time when men were considered the superior gender; Gideon, the runt of the litter in the smallest of the tribes in Israel, rose to greatness in his time; and the strong man Samson ruled for a short while until his inability to control his own appetites led to an impetuous end.

The ultimate lesson here? People need leaders. Jesus echoed this truth when he described the people of Israel as "sheep without a shepherd" (Mt 9:36). Chaos reigns whenever humankind does whatever they see "fit." Civilized life becomes impossible when every man has "his own way." We always need healthy, spiritual leaders, and this book illustrates that truth as vividly as any other.

- Leaders must learn to lead themselves before leading others.
- People first buy into the leader before they buy into the cause.
- God will often raise up the most unlikely leader to accomplish his purposes.

LEADERSHIP HIGHLIGHTS IN JUDGES

Israel Fights the Remaining Canaanites

1 After the death of Joshua, the Israelites asked the LORD, "Who of us is to go up first to fight against the Canaanites?"

²The LORD answered, "Judah shall go up; I have given the land into their hands."

³The men of Judah then said to the Simeonites their fellow Israelites, "Come up with us into the territory allotted to us, to fight against the Canaanites. We in turn will go with you into yours." So the Simeonites went with them.

⁴When Judah attacked, the LORD gave the Canaanites and Perizzites into their hands, and they struck down ten thousand men at Bezek. ⁵It was there that they found Adoni-Bezek and fought against him, putting to rout the Canaanites and Perizzites. ⁶Adoni-Bezek fled, but they chased him and caught him, and cut off his thumbs and big toes.

⁷Then Adoni-Bezek said, "Seventy kings with their thumbs and big toes cut off have picked up scraps under my table. Now God has paid me back for what I did to them." They brought him to Jerusalem, and he died there.

⁸The men of Judah attacked Jerusalem also and took it. They put the city to the sword and set it on fire.

⁹After that, Judah went down to fight against the Canaanites living in the hill country, the Negev and the western foothills. ¹⁰They advanced against the Canaanites living in Hebron (formerly called Kiriath Arba) and defeated Sheshai, Ahiman and Talmai. ¹¹From there they advanced against the people living in Debir (formerly called Kiriath Sepher).

¹²And Caleb said, "I will give my daughter Aksah in marriage to the man who attacks and captures Kiriath Sepher." ¹³Othniel son of Kenaz, Caleb's younger brother, took it; so Caleb gave his daughter Aksah to him in marriage.

¹⁴One day when she came to Othniel, she urged him[a] to ask her father for a field. When she got off her donkey, Caleb asked her, "What can I do for you?"

¹⁵She replied, "Do me a special favor. Since you have given me land in the Negev, give me also springs of water." So Caleb gave her the upper and lower springs.

¹⁶The descendants of Moses' father-in-law, the Kenite, went up from the City of Palms[b] with the people of Judah to live among the inhabitants of the Desert of Judah in the Negev near Arad.

¹⁷Then the men of Judah went with the Simeonites their fellow Israelites and attacked the Canaanites living in Zephath, and they totally destroyed[c] the city. Therefore it was called Hormah.[d] ¹⁸Judah also took[e] Gaza, Ashkelon and Ekron—each city with its territory.

¹⁹The LORD was with the men of Judah. They took possession of the hill country, but they were unable to drive the people from the plains, because they had chariots fitted with iron. ²⁰As Moses had promised, Hebron was given to Caleb, who drove from it the three sons of Anak. ²¹The Benjamites, however, did not drive out the Jebusites, who were living in Jerusalem; to this day the Jebusites live there with the Benjamites.

²²Now the tribes of Joseph attacked Bethel, and the LORD was with them. ²³When they sent men to spy out Bethel (formerly called Luz), ²⁴the spies saw a man coming out of the city and they said to him, "Show us how to get into the city and we will see that you are treated well." ²⁵So he showed them, and they put the city to the sword but spared the man and his whole family. ²⁶He then went to the land of the Hittites, where he built a city and called it Luz, which is its name to this day.

²⁷But Manasseh did not drive out the people of Beth Shan or Taanach or Dor or Ibleam or Megiddo and their surrounding settlements, for the Canaanites were determined to live in that land. ²⁸When Israel became strong, they pressed the Canaanites into forced labor but never drove them out completely. ²⁹Nor did Ephraim drive out the Canaanites living in Gezer, but the Canaanites continued to live there among them. ³⁰Neither did Zebulun drive out the Canaanites living in Kitron or Nahalol, so these Canaanites lived among them, but Zebulun did subject them to forced labor. ³¹Nor did Asher drive out those living in Akko or Sidon or Ahlab or Akzib or Helbah or Aphek or Rehob. ³²The Asherites lived among the Canaanite inhabitants of the land because they did not drive them out. ³³Neither did Naphtali drive out those living in Beth Shemesh or Beth Anath; but the Naphtalites too lived among the Canaanite inhabitants of the land, and those living in Beth Shemesh and Beth Anath became forced laborers for them. ³⁴The Amorites confined the Danites to the hill country, not allowing them to

---

[a] 14 Hebrew; Septuagint and Vulgate *Othniel, he urged her*   [b] 16 That is, Jericho   [c] 17 The Hebrew term refers to the irrevocable giving over of things or persons to the LORD, often by totally destroying them.   [d] 17 *Hormah* means *destruction.*   [e] 18 Hebrew; Septuagint *Judah did not take*

Compromising Values Leads to Compromising Goals

Judges 1:21–36

Soon after Joshua died, it became clear how much Israel had failed to fulfill God's calling. The people failed to subdue Canaan, and the book of Judges reveals a Hebrew nation pressed on the west from the Philistines and on the east from the Midianites. Disregarding God's directions, Israel decided to negotiate some deals and compromise with the inhabitants of Canaan. The people hoped that by doing so they could make friends and avoid confrontation.

How wrong they were!

The Scripture outlines how various tribes failed to drive their enemies out of the land. Compromising their values led to compromising their goals, with tragic results:

Compromises	Consequences
1. Benjamin failed to drive out Jebusites	1. Mixed marriages and diluted faith
2. Manasseh failed to drive out Canaanites	2. Spiritual apathy
3. Ephraim failed to drive out Canaanites	3. Spiritual division
4. Zebulun failed to drive out those in Kitron	4. Tribal strife
5. Dan failed to drive out Amorites	5. Defeat and lack of protection
6. Asher failed to drive out those in Akko	6. Inhabitants became a snare
7. Asher failed to drive out Canaanites	7. Failure to live in the land God had planned
8. Naphtali failed to drive out Beth Shemesh	for them

come down into the plain. [35] And the Amorites were determined also to hold out in Mount Heres, Aijalon and Shaalbim, but when the power of the tribes of Joseph increased, they too were pressed into forced labor. [36] The boundary of the Amorites was from Scorpion Pass to Sela and beyond.

The Angel of the Lord at Bokim

2 The angel of the Lord went up from Gilgal to Bokim and said, "I brought you up out of Egypt and led you into the land I swore to give to your ancestors. I said, 'I will never break my covenant with you, [2] and you shall not make a covenant with the people of this land, but you shall break down their altars.' Yet you have disobeyed me. Why have you done this? [3] And I have also said, 'I will not drive them out before you; they will become traps for you, and their gods will become snares to you.'"

[4] When the angel of the Lord had spoken these things to all the Israelites, the people wept aloud, [5] and they called that place Bokim.[a] There they offered sacrifices to the Lord.

Disobedience and Defeat

[6] After Joshua had dismissed the Israelites, they went to take possession of the land, each to their own inheritance. [7] The people served the Lord throughout the lifetime of Joshua and of the elders who outlived him and who had seen all the great things the Lord had done for Israel.

[8] Joshua son of Nun, the servant of the Lord, died at the age of a hundred and ten. [9] And they buried him in the land of his inheritance, at Timnath Heres[b] in the hill country of Ephraim, north of Mount Gaash.

[10] After that whole generation had been gathered to their ancestors, another generation grew up who knew neither the Lord nor what he had done for Israel. [11] Then the Israelites did evil in the eyes of the Lord and served the Baals. [12] They forsook the Lord, the God of their ancestors, who had brought them out of Egypt. They followed and worshiped various gods of the peoples around them. They aroused the Lord's anger [13] because they forsook him and served Baal and the Ashtoreths. [14] In his anger against Israel the Lord gave them into the hands of raiders who plundered them. He sold them into the hands of their enemies all around, whom they were no longer able to resist. [15] Whenever Israel went out to fight, the hand of the Lord was against them to defeat them, just as he had sworn to them. They were in great distress. [16] Then the Lord raised up judges,[c] who saved

[a] 5 Bokim means weepers.   [b] 9 Also known as Timnath Serah (see Joshua 19:50 and 24:30)   [c] 16 Or leaders; similarly in verses 17-19

them out of the hands of these raiders. [17]Yet they would not listen to their judges but prostituted themselves to other gods and worshiped them. They quickly turned from the ways of their ancestors, who had been obedient to the LORD's commands. [18]Whenever the LORD raised up a judge for them, he was with the judge and saved them out of the hands of their enemies as long as the judge lived; for the LORD relented because of their groaning under those who oppressed and afflicted them. [19]But when the judge died, the people returned to ways even more corrupt than those of their ancestors, following other gods and serving and worshiping them. They refused to give up their evil practices and stubborn ways.

[20]Therefore the LORD was very angry with Israel and said, "Because this nation has violated the covenant I ordained for their ancestors and has not listened to me, [21]I will no longer drive out before them any of the nations Joshua left when he died. [22]I will use them to test Israel and see whether they will keep the way of the LORD and walk in it as their ancestors did." [23]The LORD had allowed those nations to remain; he did not drive them out at once by giving them into the hands of Joshua.

3 These are the nations the LORD left to test all those Israelites who had not experienced any of the wars in Canaan [2](he did this only to teach warfare to the descendants of the Israelites who had not had previous battle experience): [3]the five rulers of the Philistines, all the Canaanites, the Sidonians, and the Hivites living in the Lebanon mountains from Mount Baal Hermon to Lebo Hamath. [4]They were left to test the Israelites to see whether they would obey the LORD's commands, which he had given their ancestors through Moses.

[5]The Israelites lived among the Canaanites, Hittites, Amorites, Perizzites, Hivites and Jebusites. [6]They took their daughters in marriage and gave their own daughters to their sons, and served their gods.

Othniel

[7]The Israelites did evil in the eyes of the LORD; they forgot the LORD their God and served the Baals and the Asherahs. [8]The anger of the LORD burned against Israel so that he sold them into

Organizational Cycle:
Understanding the Pattern of People

Judges 2:1–6

Leaders must understand how people think and behave. The book of Judges provides a vivid biography of leaders, followers and human nature, and describes a cycle repeated even today. Note the distinct patterns that recur repeatedly in this book:

Rebellion
When things go well, people drop their guard. They relax and pay less attention to details. Peacetime brings a greater chance of rebellion than wartime. In prosperous times, fallen people naturally express their bent toward independence and rebellion.

Repression
Repression follows rebellion. Whether God sends an enemy or the people cause their own misery, they endure hardship, calamity, invasion or natural disaster. Poor life choices result in retribution.

Repentance
Extreme hardships often trigger community-wide repentance. The repression serves as a wake-up call. Individuals begin to refocus on what is really important and purify their motives and behavior. Organizations cut budgets, downsize, and check egos.

Restoration
Purification leads to restoration. People regain the blessings they once had or acquire what had been intended for them. When they begin to obey God, peace returns to the land once more. And the cycle of fallen human behavior has run its full course.

the hands of Cushan-Rishathaim king of Aram Naharaim,[a] to whom the Israelites were subject for eight years. [9]But when they cried out to the LORD, he raised up for them a deliverer, Othniel son of Kenaz, Caleb's younger brother, who saved them. [10]The Spirit of the LORD came on him, so that he became Israel's judge[b] and went to war. The LORD gave Cushan-Rishathaim king of Aram into the hands of Othniel, who overpowered him. [11]So the land had peace for forty years, until Othniel son of Kenaz died.

Ehud

[12]Again the Israelites did evil in the eyes of the LORD, and because they did this evil the LORD gave Eglon king of Moab power over Israel. [13]Getting the Ammonites and Amalekites to join him, Eglon came and attacked Israel, and they took possession of the City of Palms.[c] [14]The Israelites were subject to Eglon king of Moab for eighteen years.

[15]Again the Israelites cried out to the LORD, and he gave them a deliverer — Ehud, a left-handed man, the son of Gera the Benjamite. The Israelites sent him with tribute to Eglon king of Moab. [16]Now Ehud had made a double-edged sword about a cubit[d] long, which he strapped to his right thigh under his clothing. [17]He presented the tribute to Eglon king of Moab, who was a very fat man. [18]After Ehud had presented the tribute, he sent on their way those who had carried it. [19]But on reaching the stone images near Gilgal he himself went back to Eglon and said, "Your Majesty, I have a secret message for you."

The king said to his attendants, "Leave us!" And they all left.

[20]Ehud then approached him while he was sitting alone in the upper room of his palace[e] and said, "I have a message from God for you." As the king rose from his seat, [21]Ehud reached with his left hand, drew the sword from his right thigh and plunged it into the king's belly. [22]Even the handle sank in after the blade, and his bowels discharged. Ehud did not pull the sword out, and the fat closed in over it. [23]Then Ehud went out to the porch[f]; he shut the doors of the upper room behind him and locked them.

[24]After he had gone, the servants came and found the doors of the upper room locked. They said, "He must be relieving himself in the inner room of the palace." [25]They waited to the point of embarrassment, but when he did not open the doors of the room, they took a key and unlocked them. There they saw their lord fallen to the floor, dead.

The Law of Victory: Three Leaders Find a Way to Deliver Israel

Judges 3:1–33

True leaders always find a way to help the team win.

Othniel found his people surrounded by enemies from Mesopotamia. He stepped forward, led the armies of Israel against the pagan king, and prevailed. His victory led to 40 years of peace.

Later, Moab formed an alliance with the Ammonites and Amalekites and attacked Israel. The Hebrews suffered defeat and served these enemies for 18 years. When the people cried out to the Lord, Ehud stepped forward and led them to victory. This peace lasted for 80 years.

A third judge, Shamgar, personally struck down 600 Philistines and rallied his people over Philistia. True leadership starts when a person . . .

- **Perceives a need** (spots a specific problem).
- **Possesses a gift** (has the competence to address the need).
- **Parades a passion** (casts vision for a passion to act).
- **Persuades a people** (attracts others to join the cause).
- **Pursues a purpose** (employs measures to accomplish the desired goal).

---

[26]While they waited, Ehud got away. He passed by the stone images and escaped to Seirah. [27]When he arrived there, he blew a trumpet in the hill country of Ephraim, and the Israelites went down with him from the hills, with him leading them.

[28]"Follow me," he ordered, "for the LORD has given Moab, your enemy, into your hands." So they followed him down and took possession of the fords of the Jordan that led to Moab; they allowed no one to cross over. [29]At that time they

---

[a] 8 That is, Northwest Mesopotamia   [b] 10 Or leader
[c] 13 That is, Jericho   [d] 16 That is, about 18 inches or about 45 centimeters   [e] 20 The meaning of the Hebrew for this word is uncertain; also in verse 24.   [f] 23 The meaning of the Hebrew for this word is uncertain.

struck down about ten thousand Moabites, all vigorous and strong; not one escaped. ³⁰That day Moab was made subject to Israel, and the land had peace for eighty years.

Shamgar

³¹After Ehud came Shamgar son of Anath, who struck down six hundred Philistines with an oxgoad. He too saved Israel.

Deborah

4 Again the Israelites did evil in the eyes of the Lord, now that Ehud was dead. ²So the Lord sold them into the hands of Jabin king of Canaan, who reigned in Hazor. Sisera, the commander of his army, was based in Harosheth Haggoyim. ³Because he had nine hundred chariots fitted with iron and had cruelly oppressed the Israelites for twenty years, they cried to the Lord for help.

⁴Now Deborah, a prophet, the wife of Lappidoth, was leading*a* Israel at that time. ⁵She held court under the Palm of Deborah between Ramah and Bethel in the hill country of Ephraim, and the Israelites went up to her to have their disputes decided. ⁶She sent for Barak son of Abinoam from Kedesh in Naphtali and said to him, "The Lord, the God of Israel, commands you: 'Go, take with you ten thousand men of Naphtali and Zebulun and lead them up to Mount Tabor. ⁷I will lead Sisera, the commander of Jabin's army, with his chariots and his troops to the Kishon River and give him into your hands.'"

⁸Barak said to her, "If you go with me, I will go; but if you don't go with me, I won't go."

⁹"Certainly I will go with you," said Deborah. "But because of the course you are taking, the honor will not be yours, for the Lord will deliver Sisera into the hands of a woman." So Deborah went with Barak to Kedesh. ¹⁰There Barak summoned Zebulun and Naphtali, and ten thousand men went up under his command. Deborah also went up with him.

¹¹Now Heber the Kenite had left the other Kenites, the descendants of Hobab, Moses' brother-in-law,*b* and pitched his tent by the great tree in Zaanannim near Kedesh.

¹²When they told Sisera that Barak son of Abinoam had gone up to Mount Tabor, ¹³Sisera summoned from Harosheth Haggoyim to the Kishon River all his men and his nine hundred chariots fitted with iron.

¹⁴Then Deborah said to Barak, "Go! This is the day the Lord has given Sisera into your hands. Has not the Lord gone ahead of you?" So Barak went down Mount Tabor, with ten thousand men following him. ¹⁵At Barak's advance, the Lord routed Sisera and all his chariots and army by the sword, and Sisera got down from his chariot and fled on foot.

¹⁶Barak pursued the chariots and army as far as Harosheth Haggoyim, and all Sisera's troops fell by the sword; not a man was left. ¹⁷Sisera, meanwhile, fled on foot to the tent of Jael, the wife of Heber the Kenite, because there was an alliance between Jabin king of Hazor and the family of Heber the Kenite.

¹⁸Jael went out to meet Sisera and said to him, "Come, my lord, come right in. Don't be afraid." So he entered her tent, and she covered him with a blanket.

¹⁹"I'm thirsty," he said. "Please give me some water." She opened a skin of milk, gave him a drink, and covered him up.

²⁰"Stand in the doorway of the tent," he told her. "If someone comes by and asks you, 'Is anyone in there?' say 'No.'"

²¹But Jael, Heber's wife, picked up a tent peg and a hammer and went quietly to him while he lay fast asleep, exhausted. She drove the peg through his temple into the ground, and he died.

²²Just then Barak came by in pursuit of Sisera, and Jael went out to meet him. "Come," she said, "I will show you the man you're looking for." So he went in with her, and there lay Sisera with the tent peg through his temple—dead.

²³On that day God subdued Jabin king of Canaan before the Israelites. ²⁴And the hand of the Israelites pressed harder and harder against Jabin king of Canaan until they destroyed him.

The Song of Deborah

5 On that day Deborah and Barak son of Abinoam sang this song:

²"When the princes in Israel take the lead,
   when the people willingly offer
      themselves—
   praise the Lord!

³"Hear this, you kings! Listen, you rulers!
   I, even I, will sing to*c* the Lord;
   I will praise the Lord, the God of Israel,
      in song.

⁴"When you, Lord, went out from Seir,
   when you marched from the land of Edom,
   the earth shook, the heavens poured,
      the clouds poured down water.

---

a 4 Traditionally *judging*   *b* 11 Or *father-in-law*   *c* 3 Or *of*

DEBORAH AND THE LAW OF RESPECT
People Naturally Follow Leaders Stronger Than Themselves

Judges 4:1–16

PEOPLE FOLLOW those whose leadership they respect. The less skilled follow the more highly skilled. In general, followers seek those who are better leaders than themselves.

The more leadership ability a person has, the more quickly he recognizes leadership—or its lack—in others. When groups of people get together for the first time, take a look at what happens. Leaders in the group immediately take charge. They think about the direction they desire to go and whom they want to take with them. At first, individuals may make tentative moves in several directions, but after they get to know one another, it doesn't take long for them to recognize the strongest leaders and to follow them.

■   ■   ■   ■   ■

Deborah's leadership gifts commanded the respect of both men and women, even though few women in her day rose to leadership positions. Even Barak, the military commander of the northern tribes of Israel, sought her help.

Take a look at the process any leader (including Deborah) must go through, a process summarized by the word R-E-S-P-E-C-T.

Respect yourself and those with whom you work.

Gaining the respect of others always begins with respecting yourself and your associates. Deborah did this, and people from all over Israel came to her to settle their disputes. If you desire to win the respect of others, first demonstrate a healthy respect for yourself and for your associates.

Exceed the expectations of others.

Few observers might have expected Deborah to change the way the Israelites lived. Yet she raised the standard of living for the common person and returned the nation to peace. Leaders who earn the respect of others go the extra mile, fight to achieve victory, and take others with them.

Stand firm on your convictions.

It must have taken strong convictions for Deborah to summon Barak and command him to fight. Even when Barak doubted the campaign, she did not waver, and proved her convictions by agreeing to accompany Barak to the battle. Followers respect a leader with conviction and a willingness to join the journey.

Possess uncommon security and maturity.

Deborah never tried to take credit for Israel's victory, but recognized those who helped the nation win. Respected leaders don't grab all the credit for themselves. They give as much as they can to others.

Experience personal success.

Leaders cannot help others enjoy success unless they have succeeded themselves. Deborah already had succeeded as a prophetess and a judge before she asked the people to fight.

Contribute to the success of others.

Deborah did everything right in calling the people to battle. She gave them a commander and the resources they needed. She also gave them the word of the Lord that they would win. Under her guidance, "the hand of the Israelites pressed harder and harder against Jabin king of Canaan until they destroyed him" (Jdg 4:24).

Think ahead of others.

Deborah didn't simply tell Barak to fight; she furnished a plan for his attack. Then she accompanied Barak to the battle. The result: overwhelming victory. How could the people not respect a leader of such strategy and vision?

In general, leaders exercise their authority on one of five levels:

1. Position

Titles or job descriptions provide the lowest level of leadership. People follow these leaders only because they have to. That's where Deborah began—as a prophetess. But leadership that stays on this level becomes weaker, not stronger. Leaders who want others to follow simply because they are "the boss" soon lose respect.

2. Permission

As followers grow to like and trust a leader, they begin to follow because they want to. People came to Deborah, seeking out her influence. But not even positive relationships, by themselves, can create lasting leadership.

3. Production

At this level, influence grows and respect increases because of what the leader and the people accomplish together. People begin to follow because of what the leader has done for the team or organization. Deborah's success as a judge benefited all the people. If you reach this level, you and your team can achieve many of your goals. But to experience life-changing impact and lasting success, you must make the leap to the next level.

4. People Development

The highest calling of any leader is to help other leaders reach their potential. Deborah helped Barak achieve his God-given purpose. Leaders who move to this level change their focus from inspiring and leading followers to developing and leading other leaders.

5. Personhood

Leaders who spend their lives developing individuals and organizations make such an incredible impact for so long that people follow because of who the leader is. Deborah's description as a "mother in Israel" seems to indicate she achieved the personhood level of leadership. Leaders cannot scheme to reach level 5; they arrive at this plateau only through time and God's grace.

[5] The mountains quaked before the LORD, the
One of Sinai,
before the LORD, the God of Israel.

[6] "In the days of Shamgar son of Anath,
in the days of Jael, the highways were
abandoned;
travelers took to winding paths.
[7] Villagers in Israel would not fight;
they held back until I, Deborah, arose,
until I arose, a mother in Israel.
[8] God chose new leaders
when war came to the city gates,
but not a shield or spear was seen
among forty thousand in Israel.
[9] My heart is with Israel's princes,
with the willing volunteers among the
people.
Praise the LORD!

[10] "You who ride on white donkeys,
sitting on your saddle blankets,
and you who walk along the road,
consider [11] the voice of the singers[a] at the
watering places.
They recite the victories of the LORD,
the victories of his villagers in Israel.

"Then the people of the LORD
went down to the city gates.
[12] 'Wake up, wake up, Deborah!
Wake up, wake up, break out in song!
Arise, Barak!
Take captive your captives, son of
Abinoam.'

[13] "The remnant of the nobles came down;
the people of the LORD came down to me
against the mighty.
[14] Some came from Ephraim, whose roots were
in Amalek;
Benjamin was with the people who
followed you.
From Makir captains came down,
from Zebulun those who bear a
commander's[a] staff.
[15] The princes of Issachar were with Deborah;
yes, Issachar was with Barak,
sent under his command into the valley.
In the districts of Reuben
there was much searching of heart.
[16] Why did you stay among the sheep pens[b]
to hear the whistling for the flocks?
In the districts of Reuben
there was much searching of heart.
[17] Gilead stayed beyond the Jordan.
And Dan, why did he linger by the ships?

Asher remained on the coast
and stayed in his coves.
[18] The people of Zebulun risked their very
lives;
so did Naphtali on the terraced fields.

[19] "Kings came, they fought,
the kings of Canaan fought.
At Taanach, by the waters of Megiddo,
they took no plunder of silver.
[20] From the heavens the stars fought,
from their courses they fought against
Sisera.
[21] The river Kishon swept them away,
the age-old river, the river Kishon.
March on, my soul; be strong!
[22] Then thundered the horses' hooves —
galloping, galloping go his mighty steeds.
[23] 'Curse Meroz,' said the angel of the LORD.
'Curse its people bitterly,
because they did not come to help the LORD,
to help the LORD against the mighty.'

[24] "Most blessed of women be Jael,
the wife of Heber the Kenite,
most blessed of tent-dwelling women.
[25] He asked for water, and she gave him milk;
in a bowl fit for nobles she brought him
curdled milk.
[26] Her hand reached for the tent peg,
her right hand for the workman's
hammer.
She struck Sisera, she crushed his head,
she shattered and pierced his temple.
[27] At her feet he sank,
he fell; there he lay.
At her feet he sank, he fell;
where he sank, there he fell — dead.
[28] "Through the window peered Sisera's
mother;
behind the lattice she cried out,
'Why is his chariot so long in coming?
Why is the clatter of his chariots delayed?'
[29] The wisest of her ladies answer her;
indeed, she keeps saying to herself,
[30] 'Are they not finding and dividing the
spoils:
a woman or two for each man,
colorful garments as plunder for Sisera,
colorful garments embroidered,
highly embroidered garments for my neck —
all this as plunder?'

---

[a] 11,14 The meaning of the Hebrew for this word is uncertain.
[b] 16 Or the campfires; or the saddlebags

31 "So may all your enemies perish, LORD!
    But may all who love you be like the sun
    when it rises in its strength."

Then the land had peace forty years.

Gideon

6 The Israelites did evil in the eyes of the
LORD, and for seven years he gave them into
the hands of the Midianites. ²Because the power
of Midian was so oppressive, the Israelites prepared shelters for themselves in mountain clefts,
caves and strongholds. ³Whenever the Israelites
planted their crops, the Midianites, Amalekites
and other eastern peoples invaded the country. ⁴They camped on the land and ruined the
crops all the way to Gaza and did not spare a
living thing for Israel, neither sheep nor cattle
nor donkeys. ⁵They came up with their livestock and their tents like swarms of locusts. It
was impossible to count them or their camels;
they invaded the land to ravage it. ⁶Midian so
impoverished the Israelites that they cried out
to the LORD for help.

⁷When the Israelites cried out to the LORD
because of Midian, ⁸he sent them a prophet,
who said, "This is what the LORD, the God of
Israel, says: I brought you up out of Egypt, out of
the land of slavery. ⁹I rescued you from the hand
of the Egyptians. And I delivered you from the
hand of all your oppressors; I drove them out
before you and gave you their land. ¹⁰I said to
you, 'I am the LORD your God; do not worship
the gods of the Amorites, in whose land you
live.' But you have not listened to me."

¹¹The angel of the LORD came and sat down
under the oak in Ophrah that belonged to Joash the Abiezrite, where his son Gideon was
threshing wheat in a winepress to keep it from
the Midianites. ¹²When the angel of the LORD
appeared to Gideon, he said, "The LORD is with
you, mighty warrior."

¹³"Pardon me, my lord," Gideon replied, "but
if the LORD is with us, why has all this happened
to us? Where are all his wonders that our ancestors told us about when they said, 'Did not
the LORD bring us up out of Egypt?' But now the
LORD has abandoned us and given us into the
hand of Midian."

¹⁴The LORD turned to him and said, "Go in
the strength you have and save Israel out of Midian's hand. Am I not sending you?"

¹⁵"Pardon me, my lord," Gideon replied, "but
how can I save Israel? My clan is the weakest in
Manasseh, and I am the least in my family."

¹⁶The LORD answered, "I will be with you,
and you will strike down all the Midianites,
leaving none alive."

¹⁷Gideon replied, "If now I have found favor
in your eyes, give me a sign that it is really you
talking to me. ¹⁸Please do not go away until I
come back and bring my offering and set it before you."

And the LORD said, "I will wait until you return."

¹⁹Gideon went inside, prepared a young goat,
and from an ephah^a of flour he made bread
without yeast. Putting the meat in a basket and
its broth in a pot, he brought them out and offered them to him under the oak.

²⁰The angel of God said to him, "Take the
meat and the unleavened bread, place them on
this rock, and pour out the broth." And Gideon did so. ²¹Then the angel of the LORD touched
the meat and the unleavened bread with the
tip of the staff that was in his hand. Fire flared
from the rock, consuming the meat and the
bread. And the angel of the LORD disappeared.
²²When Gideon realized that it was the angel of
the LORD, he exclaimed, "Alas, Sovereign LORD!
I have seen the angel of the LORD face to face!"

²³But the LORD said to him, "Peace! Do not be
afraid. You are not going to die."

²⁴So Gideon built an altar to the LORD there
and called it The LORD Is Peace. To this day it
stands in Ophrah of the Abiezrites.

²⁵That same night the LORD said to him,
"Take the second bull from your father's herd,
the one seven years old.^{b} Tear down your father's
altar to Baal and cut down the Asherah pole^c beside it. ²⁶Then build a proper kind of^d altar to the
LORD your God on the top of this height. Using
the wood of the Asherah pole that you cut down,
offer the second^e bull as a burnt offering."

²⁷So Gideon took ten of his servants and did
as the LORD told him. But because he was afraid
of his family and the townspeople, he did it at
night rather than in the daytime.

²⁸In the morning when the people of the town
got up, there was Baal's altar, demolished, with
the Asherah pole beside it cut down and the second bull sacrificed on the newly built altar!

²⁹They asked each other, "Who did this?"

When they carefully investigated, they were
told, "Gideon son of Joash did it."

---

^{a} 19 That is, probably about 36 pounds or about 16 kilograms
^{b} 25 Or *Take a full-grown, mature bull from your father's herd*
^{c} 25 That is, a wooden symbol of the goddess Asherah; also in
verses 26, 28 and 30 ^{d} 26 Or *build with layers of stone an*
^{e} 26 Or *full-grown*; also in verse 28

GIDEON AND THE LAW OF BUY-IN
People Buy In to the Leader, Then the Vision

Judges 6:11—8:35

AT LEADERSHIP seminars I field a lot of questions about vision. Invariably someone will come up to me during a break, give me a brief description of an evolving vision, and ask, "Do you think my people will buy in to my vision?" I always respond the same way: "First tell me this—do your people buy in to *you*?"

Many believe that if the cause is good enough, people will automatically buy in to it and follow. But that's not how leadership works. People don't at first follow worthy causes; they follow worthy leaders who promote worthwhile causes. People buy in to the leader first, then the leader's vision. Listeners filter every message through the messenger who delivers it. You cannot separate the leader from the cause he promotes. It's not an either/or proposition; the two always go together.

■　　■　　■　　■　　■

Who would have picked Gideon as a leader? Certainly not Gideon; he didn't even see himself as a leader. "Pardon me, my lord, but how can I save Israel?" asked Gideon of the angel who told him that God wanted to use him to defeat the Midianites. "My clan is the weakest in Manasseh, and I am the least in my family" (Jdg 6:15).

Despite Gideon's doubts, God used him. The people rallied around Gideon, and he led Israel to the most lopsided victory in the nation's history.

The Anatomy of Buy-In

Gideon progressed from being an obscure member of a minor clan to a leader of the northern tribes. He grew as a leader through several stages:

1. *Started at home (character)*
   A good leader first proves himself to those closest to him. Gideon started with 10 household servants. With their help, he destroyed an altar of Baal, built a new altar to God, and offered the sacrifice requested by God.

2. *Won a key influencer (charisma)*
   The men of Ophrah grew furious with Gideon when they discovered he had destroyed Baal's altar. "Bring out your son," they ordered his father, Joash. "He must die" (Jdg 6:30). Yet Gideon won over a powerful ally in his father. Joash stood up for his son and spared Gideon's life.

3. *Broadened his circle (credibility)*
   Gideon won over his city by winning the influence of Joash, then quickly won the allegiance of the Abiezrites (the people of his region), along with tribes beyond his borders: Asher, Zebulun and Naphtali. Even the people of Ephraim joined him. Once a core group of people buy in to your leadership, it's possible to broaden your circle of influence.

4. *Moved at the right time (culmination)*
So many people bought into Gideon's leadership that God had to send a bunch of them home (Jdg 7:2). God reduced the number of Gideon's followers to 300. Yet when they fought under Gideon's leadership, they won a great victory—and God received the glory.

Seven Assets Followers Want in a Leader

People always ask, "Why should I follow you?" Leaders must understand that they themselves go on display before they ever get the chance to display their vision. Once followers gain confidence in the leader, they will feel confident about the vision. Note seven qualities that attract people to a leader:

1. *Calling*
Few things are as compelling as a leader's clear calling. Beforehand, Gideon had lived in fear, doubted himself, and asked for multiple signs to confirm his mission. But once he embraced his calling, passion and boldness filled his heart.

2. *Insight*
People respect a leader with insight, wisdom to see the issues, and vision to see what lies ahead. God gave Gideon insight into the weak hearts of the Midianites. By the time Gideon called his men to battle, he understood that God had assured their victory.

3. *Charisma*
People flock to leaders who make them feel good about themselves. When Gideon invited the people of Ephraim to join in pursuing the Midianites, they reacted angrily.

But Gideon helped them see the significance of their role by reminding them that they had captured and killed the Midianite leaders (Jdg 8:1–30).

4. *Talent*
Look no further than the entertainment industry for evidence that followers swarm around talent. While we don't know much about Gideon's natural abilities, the angel called him a "mighty warrior" and instructed him to "go in the strength you have" (Jdg 6:12, 14). More than likely, Gideon possessed both physical strength and courage.

5. *Ability*
People feel a natural attraction to someone who can get things done. Gideon didn't attempt to get the Ephraimites on board until he had proven his ability.

6. *Communication Skills*
A leader who cannot communicate his calling and vision has trouble getting anyone to buy in to his leadership. Whenever Gideon spoke to his people, they understood him and eagerly followed.

7. *Character*
It takes character to win and maintain trust. Gideon started out strong, standing up when others wouldn't. He displayed courage in the face of incredible odds. But in the end, a flaw in his character betrayed both him and the people. After his victories, Gideon created an idol and erected it in Ophrah: "All Israel prostituted themselves by worshiping it there, and it became a snare to Gideon and his family" (Jdg 8:27).

³⁰The people of the town demanded of Joash, "Bring out your son. He must die, because he has broken down Baal's altar and cut down the Asherah pole beside it."

³¹But Joash replied to the hostile crowd around him, "Are you going to plead Baal's cause? Are you trying to save him? Whoever fights for him shall be put to death by morning! If Baal really is a god, he can defend himself when someone breaks down his altar." ³²So because Gideon broke down Baal's altar, they gave him the name Jerub-Baal[a] that day, saying, "Let Baal contend with him."

³³Now all the Midianites, Amalekites and other eastern peoples joined forces and crossed over the Jordan and camped in the Valley of Jezreel. ³⁴Then the Spirit of the LORD came on Gideon, and he blew a trumpet, summoning the Abiezrites to follow him. ³⁵He sent messengers throughout Manasseh, calling them to arms, and also into Asher, Zebulun and Naphtali, so that they too went up to meet them.

³⁶Gideon said to God, "If you will save Israel by my hand as you have promised— ³⁷look, I will place a wool fleece on the threshing floor. If there is dew only on the fleece and all the ground is dry, then I will know that you will save Israel by my hand, as you said." ³⁸And that is what happened. Gideon rose early the next day; he squeezed the fleece and wrung out the dew—a bowlful of water.

³⁹Then Gideon said to God, "Do not be an-gry with me. Let me make just one more request. Allow me one more test with the fleece, but this time make the fleece dry and let the ground be covered with dew." ⁴⁰That night God did so. Only the fleece was dry; all the ground was covered with dew.

Gideon Defeats the Midianites

7 Early in the morning, Jerub-Baal (that is, Gideon) and all his men camped at the spring of Harod. The camp of Midian was north of them in the valley near the hill of Moreh. ²The LORD said to Gideon, "You have too many men. I cannot deliver Midian into their hands, or Israel would boast against me, 'My own strength has saved me.' ³Now announce to the army, 'Anyone who trembles with fear may turn back and leave Mount Gilead.'" So twenty-two thousand men left, while ten thousand remained.

⁴But the LORD said to Gideon, "There are still too many men. Take them down to the water, and I will thin them out for you there. If I say, 'This one shall go with you,' he shall go; but if I say, 'This one shall not go with you,' he shall not go."

⁵So Gideon took the men down to the water. There the LORD told him, "Separate those who lap the water with their tongues as a dog laps from those who kneel down to drink." ⁶Three hundred of them drank from cupped hands,

---

[a] 32 Jerub-Baal probably means let Baal contend.

Lessons from Gideon About Choosing Leaders

Judges 7:1-25

Can you imagine having Gideon's problem? He attracted too many volunteers!
To make sure that God would get the glory for the coming victory, God led Gideon in an exercise to eliminate those who would hinder and choose those who would help Israel's cause. Note the lessons we learn from this effective leader:

1. **A committed leader always attracts many people.**

2. **God wants the credit for our victories.**

3. **Early fallout always occurs before a battle begins (their choice).**

4. **Later fallout often occurs before the battle begins (God's choice).**

5. **God doesn't choose the way we choose.**

6. **God wants *quality* of leaders, not necessarily *quantity*.**

7. **A few committed leaders with a strategy will bring victory.**

8. **When a few triumph, the masses rally.**

lapping like dogs. All the rest got down on their knees to drink.

[7]The LORD said to Gideon, "With the three hundred men that lapped I will save you and give the Midianites into your hands. Let all the others go home." [8]So Gideon sent the rest of the Israelites home but kept the three hundred, who took over the provisions and trumpets of the others.

Now the camp of Midian lay below him in the valley. [9]During that night the LORD said to Gideon, "Get up, go down against the camp, because I am going to give it into your hands. [10]If you are afraid to attack, go down to the camp with your servant Purah [11]and listen to what they are saying. Afterward, you will be encouraged to attack the camp." So he and Purah his servant went down to the outposts of the camp. [12]The Midianites, the Amalekites and all the other eastern peoples had settled in the valley, thick as locusts. Their camels could no more be counted than the sand on the seashore.

[13]Gideon arrived just as a man was telling a friend his dream. "I had a dream," he was saying. "A round loaf of barley bread came tumbling into the Midianite camp. It struck the tent with such force that the tent overturned and collapsed."

[14]His friend responded, "This can be nothing other than the sword of Gideon son of Joash, the Israelite. God has given the Midianites and the whole camp into his hands."

[15]When Gideon heard the dream and its interpretation, he bowed down and worshiped. He returned to the camp of Israel and called out, "Get up! The LORD has given the Midianite camp into your hands." [16]Dividing the three hundred men into three companies, he placed trumpets and empty jars in the hands of all of them, with torches inside.

[17]"Watch me," he told them. "Follow my lead. When I get to the edge of the camp, do exactly as I do. [18]When I and all who are with me blow our trumpets, then from all around the camp blow yours and shout, 'For the LORD and for Gideon.'"

[19]Gideon and the hundred men with him reached the edge of the camp at the beginning of the middle watch, just after they had changed the guard. They blew their trumpets and broke the jars that were in their hands. [20]The three companies blew the trumpets and smashed the jars. Grasping the torches in their left hands and holding in their right hands the trumpets they were to blow, they shouted, "A sword for the LORD and for Gideon!" [21]While each man held

Why Does God Choose Unlikely Leaders?

Judges 7:16–25

Why does God often choose unlikely leaders? Consider the following reasons:

1. **To catch the attention of the world**
2. **To bring honor to himself**
3. **To keep the message simple**
4. **To prompt reliance upon him, not people**
5. **To fill us with his power**

his position around the camp, all the Midianites ran, crying out as they fled.

[22]When the three hundred trumpets sounded, the LORD caused the men throughout the camp to turn on each other with their swords. The army fled to Beth Shittah toward Zererah as far as the border of Abel Meholah near Tabbath. [23]Israelites from Naphtali, Asher and all Manasseh were called out, and they pursued the Midianites. [24]Gideon sent messengers throughout the hill country of Ephraim, saying, "Come down against the Midianites and seize the waters of the Jordan ahead of them as far as Beth Barah."

So all the men of Ephraim were called out and they seized the waters of the Jordan as far as Beth Barah. [25]They also captured two of the Midianite leaders, Oreb and Zeeb. They killed Oreb at the rock of Oreb, and Zeeb at the winepress of Zeeb. They pursued the Midianites and brought the heads of Oreb and Zeeb to Gideon, who was by the Jordan.

Zebah and Zalmunna

8 Now the Ephraimites asked Gideon, "Why have you treated us like this? Why didn't you call us when you went to fight Midian?" And they challenged him vigorously.

[2]But he answered them, "What have I accomplished compared to you? Aren't the gleanings of Ephraim's grapes better than the full grape harvest of Abiezer? [3]God gave Oreb and Zeeb, the Midianite leaders, into your hands. What was I able to do compared to you?" At this, their resentment against him subsided.

[4]Gideon and his three hundred men, exhausted yet keeping up the pursuit, came to

the Jordan and crossed it. ⁵He said to the men of Sukkoth, "Give my troops some bread; they are worn out, and I am still pursuing Zebah and Zalmunna, the kings of Midian."

⁶But the officials of Sukkoth said, "Do you already have the hands of Zebah and Zalmunna in your possession? Why should we give bread to your troops?"

⁷Then Gideon replied, "Just for that, when the LORD has given Zebah and Zalmunna into my hand, I will tear your flesh with desert thorns and briers."

⁸From there he went up to Peniel[a] and made the same request of them, but they answered as the men of Sukkoth had. ⁹So he said to the men of Peniel, "When I return in triumph, I will tear down this tower."

¹⁰Now Zebah and Zalmunna were in Karkor with a force of about fifteen thousand men, all that were left of the armies of the eastern peoples; a hundred and twenty thousand swordsmen had fallen. ¹¹Gideon went up by the route of the nomads east of Nobah and Jogbehah and attacked the unsuspecting army. ¹²Zebah and Zalmunna, the two kings of Midian, fled, but he pursued them and captured them, routing their entire army.

¹³Gideon son of Joash then returned from the battle by the Pass of Heres. ¹⁴He caught a young man of Sukkoth and questioned him, and the young man wrote down for him the names of the seventy-seven officials of Sukkoth, the elders of the town. ¹⁵Then Gideon came and said to the men of Sukkoth, "Here are Zebah and Zalmunna, about whom you taunted me by saying, 'Do you already have the hands of Zebah and Zalmunna in your possession? Why should we give bread to your exhausted men?'" ¹⁶He took the elders of the town and taught the men of Sukkoth a lesson by punishing them with desert thorns and briers. ¹⁷He also pulled down the tower of Peniel and killed the men of the town.

¹⁸Then he asked Zebah and Zalmunna, "What kind of men did you kill at Tabor?"

"Men like you," they answered, "each one with the bearing of a prince."

¹⁹Gideon replied, "Those were my brothers, the sons of my own mother. As surely as the LORD lives, if you had spared their lives, I would not kill you." ²⁰Turning to Jether, his oldest son, he said, "Kill them!" But Jether did not draw his sword, because he was only a boy and was afraid.

²¹Zebah and Zalmunna said, "Come, do it yourself. 'As is the man, so is his strength.'" So Gideon stepped forward and killed them, and took the ornaments off their camels' necks.

Gideon's Ephod

²²The Israelites said to Gideon, "Rule over us—you, your son and your grandson—because you have saved us from the hand of Midian."

²³But Gideon told them, "I will not rule over you, nor will my son rule over you. The LORD will rule over you." ²⁴And he said, "I do have one request, that each of you give me an earring from your share of the plunder." (It was the custom of the Ishmaelites to wear gold earrings.)

²⁵They answered, "We'll be glad to give them." So they spread out a garment, and each of them threw a ring from his plunder onto it. ²⁶The weight of the gold rings he asked for came to seventeen hundred shekels,[b] not counting the ornaments, the pendants and the purple garments worn by the kings of Midian or the chains that were on their camels' necks. ²⁷Gideon made the gold into an ephod, which he placed in Ophrah, his town. All Israel prostituted themselves by worshiping it there, and it became a snare to Gideon and his family.

Gideon's Death

²⁸Thus Midian was subdued before the Israelites and did not raise its head again. During Gideon's lifetime, the land had peace forty years.

²⁹Jerub-Baal son of Joash went back home to live. ³⁰He had seventy sons of his own, for he had many wives. ³¹His concubine, who lived in Shechem, also bore him a son, whom he named Abimelek. ³²Gideon son of Joash died at a good old age and was buried in the tomb of his father Joash in Ophrah of the Abiezrites.

³³No sooner had Gideon died than the Israelites again prostituted themselves to the Baals. They set up Baal-Berith as their god ³⁴and did not remember the LORD their God, who had rescued them from the hands of all their enemies on every side. ³⁵They also failed to show any loyalty to the family of Jerub-Baal (that is, Gideon) in spite of all the good things he had done for them.

Abimelek

9 Abimelek son of Jerub-Baal went to his mother's brothers in Shechem and said to them and to all his mother's clan, ²"Ask all the citizens of Shechem, 'Which is better for you: to have all seventy of Jerub-Baal's sons rule over you, or just one man?' Remember, I am your flesh and blood."

---

[a] 8 Hebrew *Penuel*, a variant of *Peniel*; also in verses 9 and 17
[b] 26 That is, about 43 pounds or about 20 kilograms

³When the brothers repeated all this to the citizens of Shechem, they were inclined to follow Abimelek, for they said, "He is related to us." ⁴They gave him seventy shekels*ᵃ* of silver from the temple of Baal-Berith, and Abimelek used it to hire reckless scoundrels, who became his followers. ⁵He went to his father's home in Ophrah and on one stone murdered his seventy brothers, the sons of Jerub-Baal. But Jotham, the youngest son of Jerub-Baal, escaped by hiding. ⁶Then all the citizens of Shechem and Beth Millo gathered beside the great tree at the pillar in Shechem to crown Abimelek king.

⁷When Jotham was told about this, he climbed up on the top of Mount Gerizim and shouted to them, "Listen to me, citizens of Shechem, so that God may listen to you. ⁸One day the trees went out to anoint a king for themselves. They said to the olive tree, 'Be our king.'

⁹"But the olive tree answered, 'Should I give up my oil, by which both gods and humans are honored, to hold sway over the trees?'

¹⁰"Next, the trees said to the fig tree, 'Come and be our king.'

¹¹"But the fig tree replied, 'Should I give up my fruit, so good and sweet, to hold sway over the trees?'

¹²"Then the trees said to the vine, 'Come and be our king.'

¹³"But the vine answered, 'Should I give up my wine, which cheers both gods and humans, to hold sway over the trees?'

¹⁴"Finally all the trees said to the thornbush, 'Come and be our king.'

¹⁵"The thornbush said to the trees, 'If you really want to anoint me king over you, come and take refuge in my shade; but if not, then let fire come out of the thornbush and consume the cedars of Lebanon!'

¹⁶"Have you acted honorably and in good faith by making Abimelek king? Have you been fair to Jerub-Baal and his family? Have you treated him as he deserves? ¹⁷Remember that my father fought for you and risked his life to rescue you from the hand of Midian. ¹⁸But today you have revolted against my father's family. You have murdered his seventy sons on a single stone and have made Abimelek, the son of his female slave, king over the citizens of Shechem because he is related to you. ¹⁹So have you acted honorably and in good faith toward Jerub-Baal and his family today? If you have, may Abimelek be your joy, and may you be his, too! ²⁰But if you have not, let fire come out from Abimelek and consume you, the citizens of Shechem and Beth Millo, and let fire come out from you, the citizens of Shechem and Beth Millo, and consume Abimelek!"

²¹Then Jotham fled, escaping to Beer, and he lived there because he was afraid of his brother Abimelek.

²²After Abimelek had governed Israel three years, ²³God stirred up animosity between Abimelek and the citizens of Shechem so that they acted treacherously against Abimelek. ²⁴God did this in order that the crime against Jerub-Baal's seventy sons, the shedding of their blood, might be avenged on their brother Abimelek and on the citizens of Shechem, who had helped him murder his brothers. ²⁵In opposition to him these citizens of Shechem set men on the hilltops to ambush and rob everyone who passed by, and this was reported to Abimelek.

²⁶Now Gaal son of Ebed moved with his clan into Shechem, and its citizens put their confidence in him. ²⁷After they had gone out into the fields and gathered the grapes and trodden them, they held a festival in the temple of their god. While they were eating and drinking, they cursed Abimelek. ²⁸Then Gaal son of Ebed said, "Who is Abimelek, and why should we Shechemites be subject to him? Isn't he Jerub-Baal's son, and isn't Zebul his deputy? Serve the family of Hamor, Shechem's father! Why should we serve Abimelek? ²⁹If only this people were under my command! Then I would get rid of him. I would say to Abimelek, 'Call out your whole army!'"*ᵇ*

The Law of Addition: Jotham's Leadership Parable

Judges 9:7–15

Many in our world think the leader must be the biggest, strongest, and most intimidating person in the room. Yet the Bible tells us godly leaders are motivated by service, not power. Jotham used vivid imagery to describe his brother's hollow leadership of Shechem, and warned that Abimelek's power-hungry leadership would bring disaster. The Law of Addition reminds us that leaders add value to others by serving them, not by lording it over them.

ᵃ 4 That is, about 1 3/4 pounds or about 800 grams
ᵇ 29 Septuagint; Hebrew *him.*" Then he said to Abimelek, "*Call out your whole army!*"

30When Zebul the governor of the city heard what Gaal son of Ebed said, he was very angry. 31Under cover he sent messengers to Abimelek, saying, "Gaal son of Ebed and his clan have come to Shechem and are stirring up the city against you. 32Now then, during the night you and your men should come and lie in wait in the fields. 33In the morning at sunrise, advance against the city. When Gaal and his men come out against you, seize the opportunity to attack them."

34So Abimelek and all his troops set out by night and took up concealed positions near Shechem in four companies. 35Now Gaal son of Ebed had gone out and was standing at the entrance of the city gate just as Abimelek and his troops came out from their hiding place.

36When Gaal saw them, he said to Zebul, "Look, people are coming down from the tops of the mountains!"

Zebul replied, "You mistake the shadows of the mountains for men."

37But Gaal spoke up again: "Look, people are coming down from the central hill,a and a company is coming from the direction of the diviners' tree."

38Then Zebul said to him, "Where is your big talk now, you who said, 'Who is Abimelek that we should be subject to him?' Aren't these the men you ridiculed? Go out and fight them!"

39So Gaal led outb the citizens of Shechem and fought Abimelek. 40Abimelek chased him all the way to the entrance of the gate, and many were killed as they fled. 41Then Abimelek stayed in Arumah, and Zebul drove Gaal and his clan out of Shechem.

42The next day the people of Shechem went out to the fields, and this was reported to Abimelek. 43So he took his men, divided them into three companies and set an ambush in the fields. When he saw the people coming out of the city, he rose to attack them. 44Abimelek and the companies with him rushed forward to a position at the entrance of the city gate. Then two companies attacked those in the fields and struck them down. 45All that day Abimelek pressed his attack against the city until he had captured it and killed its people. Then he destroyed the city and scattered salt over it.

46On hearing this, the citizens in the tower of Shechem went into the stronghold of the temple of El-Berith. 47When Abimelek heard that they had assembled there, 48he and all his men went up Mount Zalmon. He took an ax and cut off some branches, which he lifted to his shoulders. He ordered the men with him, "Quick! Do what you have seen me do!" 49So all the men cut branches and followed Abimelek. They piled them against the stronghold and set it on fire

a 37 The Hebrew for this phrase means the navel of the earth.
b 39 Or Gaal went out in the sight of

ABIMELEK — A Picture of Self-Promotion
Judges 9:1–57

PROFILE in leadership

At first glance, Abimelek might seem like an ideal candidate for leadership. A gifted communicator and skilled tactician, he set his heart on becoming the ruler of his people. He had a passion to lead.

But passion does not mean fitness.

From the time his father Gideon passed away, ambitious Abimelek kept his eye on the throne of Israel. He effectively used his oratorical abilities to gain power, yet never sought God's view of his career choice. Abimelek hired "reckless scoundrels" (Jdg 9:4) to enforce his will. In his first act as king, he murdered 70 potential rivals—his own brothers, all of whom died on a single stone (9:5). From that point on, God determined to judge both Abimelek and his supporters. The man's arrogance, disobedience, dishonesty and self-will all should have disqualified him to lead God's people, yet he reigned over the men of Shechem for three years (9:22). In the end, this self-promoting power-seeker and his cronies all died under the terrifying frown of God (9:56–57).

Self-promotion may "work" in the short run, but over the long haul God makes sure that it fails. Godly leaders must remind themselves of the Lord's instruction: "Humble yourselves, therefore, under God's mighty hand, that he may lift you up in due time" (1Pe 5:6).

with the people still inside. So all the people in the tower of Shechem, about a thousand men and women, also died.

⁵⁰Next Abimelek went to Thebez and besieged it and captured it. ⁵¹Inside the city, however, was a strong tower, to which all the men and women — all the people of the city — had fled. They had locked themselves in and climbed up on the tower roof. ⁵²Abimelek went to the tower and attacked it. But as he approached the entrance to the tower to set it on fire, ⁵³a woman dropped an upper millstone on his head and cracked his skull.

⁵⁴Hurriedly he called to his armor-bearer, "Draw your sword and kill me, so that they can't say, 'A woman killed him.'" So his servant ran him through, and he died. ⁵⁵When the Israelites saw that Abimelek was dead, they went home.

⁵⁶Thus God repaid the wickedness that Abimelek had done to his father by murdering his seventy brothers. ⁵⁷God also made the people of Shechem pay for all their wickedness. The curse of Jotham son of Jerub-Baal came on them.

Tola

10 After the time of Abimelek, a man of Issachar named Tola son of Puah, the son of Dodo, rose to save Israel. He lived in Shamir, in the hill country of Ephraim. ²He led[a] Israel twenty-three years; then he died, and was buried in Shamir.

Jair

³He was followed by Jair of Gilead, who led Israel twenty-two years. ⁴He had thirty sons, who rode thirty donkeys. They controlled thirty towns in Gilead, which to this day are called Havvoth Jair.[b] ⁵When Jair died, he was buried in Kamon.

Jephthah

⁶Again the Israelites did evil in the eyes of the LORD. They served the Baals and the Ashtoreths, and the gods of Aram, the gods of Sidon, the gods of Moab, the gods of the Ammonites and the gods of the Philistines. And because the Israelites forsook the LORD and no longer served him, ⁷he became angry with them. He sold them into the hands of the Philistines and the Ammonites, ⁸who that year shattered and crushed them. For eighteen years they oppressed all the Israelites on the east side of the Jordan in Gilead, the land of the Amorites. ⁹The Ammonites also crossed the Jordan to fight against Judah, Benjamin and Ephraim; Israel was in great distress. ¹⁰Then the Israelites cried out to the LORD, "We have sinned against you, forsaking our God and serving the Baals."

¹¹The LORD replied, "When the Egyptians, the Amorites, the Ammonites, the Philistines, ¹²the Sidonians, the Amalekites and the Maonites[c] oppressed you and you cried to me for help, did I not save you from their hands? ¹³But you have forsaken me and served other gods, so I will no longer save you. ¹⁴Go and cry out to the gods you have chosen. Let them save you when you are in trouble!"

¹⁵But the Israelites said to the LORD, "We have sinned. Do with us whatever you think best, but please rescue us now." ¹⁶Then they got rid of the foreign gods among them and served the LORD. And he could bear Israel's misery no longer.

¹⁷When the Ammonites were called to arms and camped in Gilead, the Israelites assembled and camped at Mizpah. ¹⁸The leaders of the

---

[a] 2 Traditionally judged; also in verse 3   [b] 4 Or called the settlements of Jair   [c] 12 Hebrew; some Septuagint manuscripts Midianites

The Law of Legacy: Tola and Jair's Influence Dies with Them

Judges 10:1–6

Tola and Jair did a fair job of leading the Hebrew people, but Israel immediately did evil upon their deaths, serving the gods of Baal. So what kind of leadership did this pair really exert?

If our leadership leaves no legacy, is it complete? If the people revert to sinful patterns after we depart the scene, have we not failed to practice the Law of Legacy? Remember . . .

- The acid test of our leadership takes place after we are gone.
- Success without a successor is a failure.
- The issue isn't, *Can I change them while I'm here?* but, *Can I do it after I'm gone?*
- Reputation is what people think of us now; legacy is what they think of us long after we are gone.

people of Gilead said to each other, "Whoever will take the lead in attacking the Ammonites will be head over all who live in Gilead."

11 Jephthah the Gileadite was a mighty warrior. His father was Gilead; his mother was a prostitute. ²Gilead's wife also bore him sons, and when they were grown up, they drove Jephthah away. "You are not going to get any inheritance in our family," they said, "because you are the son of another woman." ³So Jephthah fled from his brothers and settled in the land of Tob, where a gang of scoundrels gathered around him and followed him.

⁴Some time later, when the Ammonites were fighting against Israel, ⁵the elders of Gilead went to get Jephthah from the land of Tob. ⁶"Come," they said, "be our commander, so we can fight the Ammonites."

⁷Jephthah said to them, "Didn't you hate me and drive me from my father's house? Why do you come to me now, when you're in trouble?"

⁸The elders of Gilead said to him, "Nevertheless, we are turning to you now; come with us to fight the Ammonites, and you will be head over all of us who live in Gilead."

⁹Jephthah answered, "Suppose you take me back to fight the Ammonites and the LORD gives them to me — will I really be your head?"

¹⁰The elders of Gilead replied, "The LORD is our witness; we will certainly do as you say." ¹¹So Jephthah went with the elders of Gilead, and the people made him head and commander over them. And he repeated all his words before the LORD in Mizpah.

¹²Then Jephthah sent messengers to the Ammonite king with the question: "What do you have against me that you have attacked my country?"

¹³The king of the Ammonites answered Jephthah's messengers, "When Israel came up out of Egypt, they took away my land from the Arnon to the Jabbok, all the way to the Jordan. Now give it back peaceably."

¹⁴Jephthah sent back messengers to the Ammonite king, ¹⁵saying:

"This is what Jephthah says: Israel did not take the land of Moab or the land of the Ammonites. ¹⁶But when they came up out of Egypt, Israel went through the wilderness to the Red Sea[a] and on to Kadesh. ¹⁷Then Israel sent messengers to the king of Edom, saying, 'Give us permission to go through your country,' but the king of Edom would not listen. They sent also to

a 16 Or the Sea of Reeds

JEPHTHAH — Makes a Poor Leadership Choice
Judges 11:1–31

PROFILE in leadership

Jephthah, the ninth judge of Israel, may have been "a mighty warrior," but he also began life as the son of a prostitute (Jdg 11:1). We learn some crucial leadership lessons from his life:

1. **Even unlikely candidates can become influential leaders (vv. 1–3).**
2. **People follow leaders because they possess a relevant gift (vv. 4–6).**
3. **Good leaders inquire about the request and result desired (vv. 7–11).**
4. **Effective leaders negotiate win/win agreements whenever possible (vv. 12–28).**

Ironically, although Jephthah modeled these lessons, he made a tragic choice just before conquering the Ammonites. He impetuously vowed to sacrifice to the Lord "whatever comes out of the door of my house to meet me" (Jdg 11:31). Sadly, his only child came out to greet him after his victory, and his hasty vow cost him a beloved daughter. Jephthah teaches us that:

1. **Even the brightest of leaders can be overcome by their will or emotions.**
2. **Decisions and commitments should not be made in a vacuum.**
3. **Leaders must weigh what they are willing to sacrifice, up front.**
4. **Good leaders follow through on their commitments, whatever the cost.**

the king of Moab, and he refused. So Israel stayed at Kadesh.

18"Next they traveled through the wilderness, skirted the lands of Edom and Moab, passed along the eastern side of the country of Moab, and camped on the other side of the Arnon. They did not enter the territory of Moab, for the Arnon was its border.

19"Then Israel sent messengers to Sihon king of the Amorites, who ruled in Heshbon, and said to him, 'Let us pass through your country to our own place.' 20Sihon, however, did not trust Israel[a] to pass through his territory. He mustered all his troops and encamped at Jahaz and fought with Israel.

21"Then the LORD, the God of Israel, gave Sihon and his whole army into Israel's hands, and they defeated them. Israel took over all the land of the Amorites who lived in that country, 22capturing all of it from the Arnon to the Jabbok and from the desert to the Jordan.

23"Now since the LORD, the God of Israel, has driven the Amorites out before his people Israel, what right have you to take it over? 24Will you not take what your god Chemosh gives you? Likewise, whatever the LORD our God has given us, we will possess. 25Are you any better than Balak son of Zippor, king of Moab? Did he ever quarrel with Israel or fight with them? 26For three hundred years Israel occupied Heshbon, Aroer, the surrounding settlements and all the towns along the Arnon. Why didn't you retake them during that time? 27I have not wronged you, but you are doing me wrong by waging war against me. Let the LORD, the Judge, decide the dispute this day between the Israelites and the Ammonites."

28The king of Ammon, however, paid no attention to the message Jephthah sent him.

29Then the Spirit of the LORD came on Jephthah. He crossed Gilead and Manasseh, passed through Mizpah of Gilead, and from there he advanced against the Ammonites. 30And Jephthah made a vow to the LORD: "If you give the Ammonites into my hands, 31whatever comes out of the door of my house to meet me when I return in triumph from the Ammonites will be the LORD's, and I will sacrifice it as a burnt offering."

32Then Jephthah went over to fight the Ammonites, and the LORD gave them into his hands. 33He devastated twenty towns from Aroer to the vicinity of Minnith, as far as Abel Keramim. Thus Israel subdued Ammon.

34When Jephthah returned to his home in Mizpah, who should come out to meet him but his daughter, dancing to the sound of timbrels! She was an only child. Except for her he had neither son nor daughter. 35When he saw her, he tore his clothes and cried, "Oh no, my daughter! You have brought me down and I am devastated. I have made a vow to the LORD that I cannot break."

36"My father," she replied, "you have given your word to the LORD. Do to me just as you promised, now that the LORD has avenged you of your enemies, the Ammonites. 37But grant me this one request," she said. "Give me two months to roam the hills and weep with my friends, because I will never marry."

38"You may go," he said. And he let her go for two months. She and her friends went into the hills and wept because she would never marry. 39After the two months, she returned to her father, and he did to her as he had vowed. And she was a virgin.

From this comes the Israelite tradition 40that each year the young women of Israel go out for four days to commemorate the daughter of Jephthah the Gileadite.

Jephthah and Ephraim

12 The Ephraimite forces were called out, and they crossed over to Zaphon. They said to Jephthah, "Why did you go to fight the Ammonites without calling us to go with you? We're going to burn down your house over your head."

2Jephthah answered, "I and my people were engaged in a great struggle with the Ammonites, and although I called, you didn't save me out of their hands. 3When I saw that you wouldn't help, I took my life in my hands and crossed over to fight the Ammonites, and the LORD gave me the victory over them. Now why have you come up today to fight me?"

4Jephthah then called together the men of Gilead and fought against Ephraim. The Gileadites struck them down because the Ephraimites had said, "You Gileadites are renegades from Ephraim and Manasseh." 5The Gileadites captured the fords of the Jordan leading to Ephraim, and

---

a 20 Or *however, would not make an agreement for Israel*

whenever a survivor of Ephraim said, "Let me cross over," the men of Gilead asked him, "Are you an Ephraimite?" If he replied, "No," [6]they said, "All right, say 'Shibboleth.'" If he said, "Sibboleth," because he could not pronounce the word correctly, they seized him and killed him at the fords of the Jordan. Forty-two thousand Ephraimites were killed at that time.

[7]Jephthah led[a] Israel six years. Then Jephthah the Gileadite died and was buried in a town in Gilead.

Ibzan, Elon and Abdon

[8]After him, Ibzan of Bethlehem led Israel. [9]He had thirty sons and thirty daughters. He gave his daughters away in marriage to those outside his clan, and for his sons he brought in thirty young women as wives from outside his clan. Ibzan led Israel seven years. [10]Then Ibzan died and was buried in Bethlehem.

[11]After him, Elon the Zebulunite led Israel ten years. [12]Then Elon died and was buried in Aijalon in the land of Zebulun.

[13]After him, Abdon son of Hillel, from Pirathon, led Israel. [14]He had forty sons and thirty grandsons, who rode on seventy donkeys. He led Israel eight years. [15]Then Abdon son of Hillel died and was buried at Pirathon in Ephraim, in the hill country of the Amalekites.

The Birth of Samson

13 Again the Israelites did evil in the eyes of the LORD, so the LORD delivered them into the hands of the Philistines for forty years.

[2]A certain man of Zorah, named Manoah, from the clan of the Danites, had a wife who was childless, unable to give birth. [3]The angel of the LORD appeared to her and said, "You are barren and childless, but you are going to become pregnant and give birth to a son. [4]Now see to it that you drink no wine or other fermented drink and that you do not eat anything unclean. [5]You will become pregnant and have a son whose head is never to be touched by a razor because the boy is to be a Nazirite, dedicated to God from the womb. He will take the lead in delivering Israel from the hands of the Philistines."

[6]Then the woman went to her husband and told him, "A man of God came to me. He looked like an angel of God, very awesome. I didn't ask him where he came from, and he didn't tell me his name. [7]But he said to me, 'You will become pregnant and have a son. Now then, drink no wine or other fermented drink and do not eat anything unclean, because the boy will be a

The Law of Influence: Judges with Short-Lived Influence

Judges 12:8–15

The three leaders who followed Jephthah—Ibzan, Elon and Abdon—had many sons and daughters and ruled for a total of 25 years. We don't know much about them, except that they cared more for the honor of their own names than that of Yahweh. The subsequent chapter begins by saying that once they were gone, Israel immediately did evil in God's sight (Jdg 13:1). The influence of those judges died when they did. But why? Two reasons become obvious: diminishing vision and growing pride.

When a leader's vision shrinks, so does his or her influence. The smaller the vision, the smaller the influence. These leaders attempted no great things for God because they saw no great things from God. Therefore the record of each of them ends with a mere, he "died and was buried." How sad.

The story grows even sadder when you realize that the shrunken vision of these leaders encompassed only how to further their own names. Even though these leaders trusted God in the beginning, they eventually took their eyes off of him and believed their own press reports.

It has been well said that the measure of spiritual maturity is the length of time a person can wait between achieving ministry success and being recognized for it. The moment we seek self-promotion, we forget about seeking God.

Nazirite of God from the womb until the day of his death.'"

[8]Then Manoah prayed to the LORD: "Pardon your servant, Lord. I beg you to let the man of God you sent to us come again to teach us how to bring up the boy who is to be born."

[9]God heard Manoah, and the angel of God came again to the woman while she was out in the field; but her husband Manoah was not with her. [10]The woman hurried to tell her husband, "He's here! The man who appeared to me the other day!"

[11]Manoah got up and followed his wife.

---

[a] 7 Traditionally *judged*; also in verses 8-14

When he came to the man, he said, "Are you the man who talked to my wife?"

"I am," he said.

[12]So Manoah asked him, "When your words are fulfilled, what is to be the rule that governs the boy's life and work?"

[13]The angel of the LORD answered, "Your wife must do all that I have told her. [14]She must not eat anything that comes from the grapevine, nor drink any wine or other fermented drink nor eat anything unclean. She must do everything I have commanded her."

[15]Manoah said to the angel of the LORD, "We would like you to stay until we prepare a young goat for you."

[16]The angel of the LORD replied, "Even though you detain me, I will not eat any of your food. But if you prepare a burnt offering, offer it to the LORD." (Manoah did not realize that it was the angel of the LORD.)

[17]Then Manoah inquired of the angel of the LORD, "What is your name, so that we may honor you when your word comes true?"

[18]He replied, "Why do you ask my name? It is beyond understanding.[a]" [19]Then Manoah took a young goat, together with the grain offering, and sacrificed it on a rock to the LORD. And the LORD did an amazing thing while Manoah and his wife watched: [20]As the flame blazed up from the altar toward heaven, the angel of the LORD ascended in the flame. Seeing this, Manoah and his wife fell with their faces to the ground. [21]When the angel of the LORD did not show himself again to Manoah and his wife, Manoah realized that it was the angel of the LORD.

[22]"We are doomed to die!" he said to his wife. "We have seen God!"

[23]But his wife answered, "If the LORD had

---

[a] 18 Or is wonderful

The Cry for Leadership: Judges Who Failed to Finish Well

Judges 6:11—8:32; 14:1—16:27

Why do so few leaders in the Bible finish well? More than two-thirds of biblical leaders finish poorly. Consider, for example, the two most famous judges in the book of Judges: Gideon and Samson.

Gideon

Early Career (Jdg 6:11—7:25)
1. Chosen by God
2. Hated idols
3. Had an angelic vision
4. Destroyed idols
5. Great deliverer

Later Career (Jdg 8:1–32)
1. Rejected by God
2. Made an idol
3. Caused Israel to sin
4. Became a stumbling stone
5. His good ruined by his evil

Samson

Early Career (Jdg 14:1—16:19)
1. Dedicated to God
2. Great warrior
3. Exceedingly strong
4. Killed thousands of soldiers
5. Man of faith
6. Killed a lion
7. Broke strong bands
8. Carried off the gates of Gaza

Later Career (Jdg 16:20–27)
1. Lost dedication to God
2. Deceived by a woman
3. Had eyes burned out
4. Imprisoned; hair shaved
5. Left by the Lord
6. Mocked and ridiculed
7. Never fulfilled potential
8. Lost his anointing

Many leaders fail toward the end of their life because:
1. they somehow dilute the original vision that drove them;
2. their success distorts them; and
3. their weaknesses go unaddressed.

Don't let this happen to you. While a good start helps, a good finish is up to you.

meant to kill us, he would not have accepted a burnt offering and grain offering from our hands, nor shown us all these things or now told us this."

²⁴The woman gave birth to a boy and named him Samson. He grew and the LORD blessed him, ²⁵and the Spirit of the LORD began to stir him while he was in Mahaneh Dan, between Zorah and Eshtaol.

Samson's Marriage

14 Samson went down to Timnah and saw there a young Philistine woman. ²When he returned, he said to his father and mother, "I have seen a Philistine woman in Timnah; now get her for me as my wife."

³His father and mother replied, "Isn't there an acceptable woman among your relatives or among all our people? Must you go to the uncircumcised Philistines to get a wife?"

But Samson said to his father, "Get her for me. She's the right one for me." ⁴(His parents did not know that this was from the LORD, who was seeking an occasion to confront the Philistines; for at that time they were ruling over Israel.)

⁵Samson went down to Timnah together with his father and mother. As they approached the vineyards of Timnah, suddenly a young lion came roaring toward him. ⁶The Spirit of the LORD came powerfully upon him so that he tore the lion apart with his bare hands as he might have torn a young goat. But he told neither his father nor his mother what he had done. ⁷Then he went down and talked with the woman, and he liked her.

⁸Some time later, when he went back to marry her, he turned aside to look at the lion's carcass, and in it he saw a swarm of bees and some honey. ⁹He scooped out the honey with his hands and ate as he went along. When he rejoined his parents, he gave them some, and they too ate it. But he did not tell them that he had taken the honey from the lion's carcass.

¹⁰Now his father went down to see the woman. And there Samson held a feast, as was customary for young men. ¹¹When the people saw him, they chose thirty men to be his companions.

¹²"Let me tell you a riddle," Samson said to them. "If you can give me the answer within the seven days of the feast, I will give you thirty linen garments and thirty sets of clothes. ¹³If you can't tell me the answer, you must give me thirty linen garments and thirty sets of clothes."

"Tell us your riddle," they said. "Let's hear it."

¹⁴He replied,

"Out of the eater, something to eat;
　out of the strong, something sweet."

For three days they could not give the answer.

¹⁵On the fourth*ᵃ* day, they said to Samson's wife, "Coax your husband into explaining the riddle for us, or we will burn you and your father's household to death. Did you invite us here to steal our property?"

¹⁶Then Samson's wife threw herself on him, sobbing, "You hate me! You don't really love me. You've given my people a riddle, but you haven't told me the answer."

"I haven't even explained it to my father or mother," he replied, "so why should I explain it to you?" ¹⁷She cried the whole seven days of the feast. So on the seventh day he finally told her, because she continued to press him. She in turn explained the riddle to her people.

¹⁸Before sunset on the seventh day the men of the town said to him,

"What is sweeter than honey?
　What is stronger than a lion?"

Samson said to them,

"If you had not plowed with my heifer,
　you would not have solved my riddle."

¹⁹Then the Spirit of the LORD came powerfully upon him. He went down to Ashkelon, struck down thirty of their men, stripped them of everything and gave their clothes to those who had explained the riddle. Burning with anger, he returned to his father's home. ²⁰And Samson's wife was given to one of his companions who had attended him at the feast.

Samson's Vengeance on the Philistines

15 Later on, at the time of wheat harvest, Samson took a young goat and went to visit his wife. He said, "I'm going to my wife's room." But her father would not let him go in.

²"I was so sure you hated her," he said, "that I gave her to your companion. Isn't her younger sister more attractive? Take her instead."

³Samson said to them, "This time I have a right to get even with the Philistines; I will really harm them." ⁴So he went out and caught three hundred foxes and tied them tail to tail in pairs. He then fastened a torch to every pair of tails, ⁵lit the torches and let the foxes loose in the standing grain of the Philistines. He burned up

ᵃ 15 Some Septuagint manuscripts and Syriac; Hebrew seventh the shocks and standing grain, together with the vineyards and olive groves.

⁶When the Philistines asked, "Who did this?" they were told, "Samson, the Timnite's son-in-law, because his wife was given to his companion."

So the Philistines went up and burned her and her father to death. ⁷Samson said to them, "Since you've acted like this, I swear that I won't stop until I get my revenge on you." ⁸He attacked them viciously and slaughtered many of them. Then he went down and stayed in a cave in the rock of Etam.

⁹The Philistines went up and camped in Judah, spreading out near Lehi. ¹⁰The people of Judah asked, "Why have you come to fight us?"

"We have come to take Samson prisoner," they answered, "to do to him as he did to us."

¹¹Then three thousand men from Judah went down to the cave in the rock of Etam and said to Samson, "Don't you realize that the Philistines are rulers over us? What have you done to us?"

He answered, "I merely did to them what they did to me."

¹²They said to him, "We've come to tie you up and hand you over to the Philistines."

Samson said, "Swear to me that you won't kill me yourselves."

¹³"Agreed," they answered. "We will only tie you up and hand you over to them. We will not kill you." So they bound him with two new ropes and led him up from the rock. ¹⁴As he approached Lehi, the Philistines came toward him shouting. The Spirit of the LORD came powerfully upon him. The ropes on his arms became like charred flax, and the bindings dropped from his hands. ¹⁵Finding a fresh jawbone of a donkey, he grabbed it and struck down a thousand men.

¹⁶Then Samson said,

"With a donkey's jawbone
  I have made donkeys of them.ᵃ
With a donkey's jawbone
  I have killed a thousand men."

¹⁷When he finished speaking, he threw away the jawbone; and the place was called Ramath Lehi.ᵇ

¹⁸Because he was very thirsty, he cried out to the LORD, "You have given your servant this great victory. Must I now die of thirst and fall into the hands of the uncircumcised?" ¹⁹Then God opened up the hollow place in Lehi, and water came out of it. When Samson drank, his strength returned and he revived. So the spring was called En Hakkore,ᶜ and it is still there in Lehi.

²⁰Samson ledᵈ Israel for twenty years in the days of the Philistines.

Samson and Delilah

16 One day Samson went to Gaza, where he saw a prostitute. He went in to spend the night with her. ²The people of Gaza were told, "Samson is here!" So they surrounded the place and lay in wait for him all night at the city gate. They made no move during the night, saying, "At dawn we'll kill him."

³But Samson lay there only until the middle of the night. Then he got up and took hold of the doors of the city gate, together with the two posts, and tore them loose, bar and all. He lifted them to his shoulders and carried them to the top of the hill that faces Hebron.

⁴Some time later, he fell in love with a woman in the Valley of Sorek whose name was Delilah. ⁵The rulers of the Philistines went to her and said, "See if you can lure him into showing you the secret of his great strength and how we can overpower him so we may tie him up and subdue him. Each one of us will give you eleven hundred shekelsᵉ of silver."

⁶So Delilah said to Samson, "Tell me the secret of your great strength and how you can be tied up and subdued."

⁷Samson answered her, "If anyone ties me with seven fresh bowstrings that have not been dried, I'll become as weak as any other man."

⁸Then the rulers of the Philistines brought her seven fresh bowstrings that had not been dried, and she tied him with them. ⁹With men hidden in the room, she called to him, "Samson, the Philistines are upon you!" But he snapped the bowstrings as easily as a piece of string snaps when it comes close to a flame. So the secret of his strength was not discovered.

¹⁰Then Delilah said to Samson, "You have made a fool of me; you lied to me. Come now, tell me how you can be tied."

¹¹He said, "If anyone ties me securely with new ropes that have never been used, I'll become as weak as any other man."

¹²So Delilah took new ropes and tied him with them. Then, with men hidden in the room, she called to him, "Samson, the Philistines are upon you!" But he snapped the ropes off his arms as if they were threads.

ᵃ 16 Or *made a heap or two*; the Hebrew for *donkey* sounds like the Hebrew for *heap*.   ᵇ 17 *Ramath Lehi* means *jawbone hill*.
ᶜ 19 *En Hakkore* means *caller's spring*.   ᵈ 20 Traditionally *judged*   ᵉ 5 That is, about 28 pounds or about 13 kilograms

SAMSON AND THE LAW OF SOLID GROUND
Trust Is the Foundation of Leadership

Judges 13:24—16:31

A LEADER'S HISTORY of successes and failures makes or breaks his credibility. It's a little like earning and spending pocket change. Each time you make a good leadership decision, it puts change into your pocket. Each time you make a poor one, you have to pay out some of your change. Every leader has a certain amount of change in his pocket when he starts in a new leadership position. From then on, he either builds up his change or pays it out.

To build trust, a leader must exemplify three qualities: competence, connection and character. People will forgive occasional mistakes based on ability, especially if they can see that you're still growing as a leader. But they won't trust someone who slips in character. In that area, even occasional lapses are lethal. No leader can break trust with his people and expect to keep influencing them. Trust makes leadership possible.

■　■　■　■　■

By all accounts, Samson could have become one of Israel's greatest leaders, yet he turned out to be one of the worst. How could someone with such a strong start finish so poorly?

Samson learned the hard way that trust provides the foundation for all genuine leadership. This impetuous, volatile, lustful, moody, emotional, and unpredictable man provides a very good example of a very bad leader. Since no one could trust him, none followed his leadership.

Signs of Leaders in Trouble

Leaders who erode the solid ground of trustworthy leadership usually exhibit one or more of the following signs. Leaders in trouble . . .

1. **Fail to address glaring character weaknesses.**
   Samson struggled with sexual impurity. He asked for a pagan wife, slept with prostitutes, and ultimately Delilah destroyed him. Any time a leader neglects to repair his character flaws, they worsen.

2. **Count on deception to safeguard themselves.**
   People who flirt with disobedience often deceive others to protect themselves. Samson liked using riddles to outwit others. He didn't tell the whole truth, which later led to distrust and betrayal.

3. **Act impulsively.**
   Time after time, Samson displayed his impetuosity. He chose his wife rashly. He made wagers without thinking. And more than once his impulsive spirit led him into a bloody battle. A leader who cannot control his temper endangers both himself and others.

4. **Are overcome by an area of weakness.**
   Sin eventually consumes anyone who gives it free rein. Samson met

his match in Delilah. The deceiver was deceived; the seducer, seduced. He lost a dangerous game and it cost him everything.

5. *Misuse their God-given gifts.* Samson possessed immense strength and godly anointing, but he took both for granted. Many times Samson exploited his God-given gift, intended for the deliverance of his people, for personal revenge. When a leader misuses God's gifts, serious consequences inevitably follow.

When Leaders Lose Their Teachability

Samson's self-centered, undisciplined, and arrogant nature made him unteachable. What happens when leaders lose their teachability?

1. *They lean on their own strength and understanding.* Unteachable leaders lose touch with God and his people. They lean on their strength and do not seek guidance from God or others. Samson repeatedly used brute force and violence to cope with difficulties. When embarrassed at his wedding feast, he killed 30 men. When the men of Judah turned him over to Philistia, he bludgeoned to death 1,000 men. When caught with a prostitute, he ripped apart the city gates of Gaza. Samson didn't take the advice of his parents, never took advice from his people, and didn't look to God for guidance. Worse still, Samson never acknowledged God as the source of his strength. He went from a man of anointing to a man of arrogance.

2. *They fail to learn from their mistakes.* A person's life runs uphill or down-

hill, depending on whether he fails forward or backward. It's a mistake only if you don't learn from it. Samson's life reveals no record of improvement, only a downward spiral. For leaders to learn from their mistakes, they must be . . .

■ Big enough to admit mistakes. Samson blamed everyone else for his problems. He never once admitted his sin or humbled himself before God.

■ Smart enough to profit from them. It's one thing to know you're wrong; it's another to figure out why you erred.

■ Strong enough to correct them. If you can't implement necessary changes, you can't improve yourself or your situation.

3. *They react rather than lead.* While good leaders are proactive, unteachable people almost exclusively react. When Samson saw the daughter of Timnah, he immediately asked for her in marriage. When his wife married his best man, he burned down the Philistines' fields. Samson reacted right up to his death—and left his people groaning under Philistine oppression.

4. *They are easily defeated.* Unteachable people always lose. Even great talent (like Samson's) can take a person only so far. Samson's character flaw, left unrepaired because of an unteachable spirit, led to moral erosion and unchecked sin—and that led to his destruction.

Who knows what might have happened had Samson ever humbly connected with God or sought the guidance and accountability of his people?

¹³Delilah then said to Samson, "All this time you have been making a fool of me and lying to me. Tell me how you can be tied."

He replied, "If you weave the seven braids of my head into the fabric on the loom and tighten it with the pin, I'll become as weak as any other man." So while he was sleeping, Delilah took the seven braids of his head, wove them into the fabric ¹⁴and[a] tightened it with the pin.

Again she called to him, "Samson, the Philistines are upon you!" He awoke from his sleep and pulled up the pin and the loom, with the fabric.

¹⁵Then she said to him, "How can you say, 'I love you,' when you won't confide in me? This is the third time you have made a fool of me and haven't told me the secret of your great strength." ¹⁶With such nagging she prodded him day after day until he was sick to death of it.

¹⁷So he told her everything. "No razor has ever been used on my head," he said, "because I have been a Nazirite dedicated to God from my mother's womb. If my head were shaved, my strength would leave me, and I would become as weak as any other man."

¹⁸When Delilah saw that he had told her everything, she sent word to the rulers of the Philistines, "Come back once more; he has told me everything." So the rulers of the Philistines returned with the silver in their hands. ¹⁹After putting him to sleep on her lap, she called for someone to shave off the seven braids of his hair, and so began to subdue him.[b] And his strength left him.

²⁰Then she called, "Samson, the Philistines are upon you!"

He awoke from his sleep and thought, "I'll go out as before and shake myself free." But he did not know that the LORD had left him.

²¹Then the Philistines seized him, gouged out his eyes and took him down to Gaza. Binding him with bronze shackles, they set him to grinding grain in the prison. ²²But the hair on his head began to grow again after it had been shaved.

The Death of Samson

²³Now the rulers of the Philistines assembled to offer a great sacrifice to Dagon their god and to celebrate, saying, "Our god has delivered Samson, our enemy, into our hands."

²⁴When the people saw him, they praised their god, saying,

"Our god has delivered our enemy
   into our hands,

the one who laid waste our land
   and multiplied our slain."

²⁵While they were in high spirits, they shouted, "Bring out Samson to entertain us." So they called Samson out of the prison, and he performed for them.

When they stood him among the pillars, ²⁶Samson said to the servant who held his hand, "Put me where I can feel the pillars that support the temple, so that I may lean against them." ²⁷Now the temple was crowded with men and women; all the rulers of the Philistines were there, and on the roof were about three thousand men and women watching Samson perform. ²⁸Then Samson prayed to the LORD, "Sovereign LORD, remember me. Please, God, strengthen me just once more, and let me with one blow get revenge on the Philistines for my two eyes." ²⁹Then Samson reached toward the two central pillars on which the temple stood. Bracing himself against them, his right hand on the one and his left hand on the other, ³⁰Samson said, "Let me die with the Philistines!" Then he pushed with all his might, and down came the temple on the rulers and all the people in it. Thus he killed many more when he died than while he lived.

³¹Then his brothers and his father's whole family went down to get him. They brought him back and buried him between Zorah and Eshtaol in the tomb of Manoah his father. He had led[c] Israel twenty years.

Micah's Idols

17 Now a man named Micah from the hill country of Ephraim ²said to his mother, "The eleven hundred shekels[d] of silver that were taken from you and about which I heard you utter a curse—I have that silver with me; I took it."

Then his mother said, "The LORD bless you, my son!"

³When he returned the eleven hundred shekels of silver to his mother, she said, "I solemnly consecrate my silver to the LORD for my son to make an image overlaid with silver. I will give it back to you."

⁴So after he returned the silver to his mother, she took two hundred shekels[e] of silver and gave

---

[a] 13,14 Some Septuagint manuscripts; Hebrew *replied, "I can if you weave the seven braids of my head into the fabric on the loom."* ¹⁴*So she*   [b] 19 Hebrew; some Septuagint manuscripts *and he began to weaken*   [c] 31 Traditionally *judged*   [d] 2 That is, about 28 pounds or about 13 kilograms   [e] 4 That is, about 5 pounds or about 2.3 kilograms

them to a silversmith, who used them to make the idol. And it was put in Micah's house.

⁵Now this man Micah had a shrine, and he made an ephod and some household gods and installed one of his sons as his priest. ⁶In those days Israel had no king; everyone did as they saw fit.

⁷A young Levite from Bethlehem in Judah, who had been living within the clan of Judah, ⁸left that town in search of some other place to stay. On his way[a] he came to Micah's house in the hill country of Ephraim.

⁹Micah asked him, "Where are you from?"

"I'm a Levite from Bethlehem in Judah," he said, "and I'm looking for a place to stay."

¹⁰Then Micah said to him, "Live with me and be my father and priest, and I'll give you ten shekels[b] of silver a year, your clothes and your food." ¹¹So the Levite agreed to live with him, and the young man became like one of his sons to him. ¹²Then Micah installed the Levite, and the young man became his priest and lived in his house. ¹³And Micah said, "Now I know that the LORD will be good to me, since this Levite has become my priest."

The Danites Settle in Laish

18 In those days Israel had no king.

And in those days the tribe of the Danites was seeking a place of their own where they might settle, because they had not yet come into an inheritance among the tribes of Israel. ²So the Danites sent five of their leading men from Zorah and Eshtaol to spy out the land and explore it. These men represented all the Danites. They told them, "Go, explore the land."

So they entered the hill country of Ephraim and came to the house of Micah, where they spent the night. ³When they were near Micah's house, they recognized the voice of the young Levite; so they turned in there and asked him, "Who brought you here? What are you doing in this place? Why are you here?"

⁴He told them what Micah had done for him, and said, "He has hired me and I am his priest."

⁵Then they said to him, "Please inquire of God to learn whether our journey will be successful."

⁶The priest answered them, "Go in peace. Your journey has the LORD's approval."

⁷So the five men left and came to Laish, where they saw that the people were living in safety, like the Sidonians, at peace and secure. And since their land lacked nothing, they were prosperous.[c] Also, they lived a long way from the Sidonians and had no relationship with anyone else.[d]

⁸When they returned to Zorah and Eshtaol, their fellow Danites asked them, "How did you find things?"

⁹They answered, "Come on, let's attack them! We have seen the land, and it is very good. Aren't you going to do something? Don't hesitate to go there and take it over. ¹⁰When you get there, you will find an unsuspecting people and a spacious land that God has put into your hands, a land that lacks nothing whatever."

¹¹Then six hundred men of the Danites, armed for battle, set out from Zorah and Eshtaol. ¹²On their way they set up camp near Kiriath Jearim in Judah. This is why the place west of Kiriath Jearim is called Mahaneh Dan[e] to this day. ¹³From there they went on to the hill country of Ephraim and came to Micah's house.

¹⁴Then the five men who had spied out the land of Laish said to their fellow Danites, "Do you know that one of these houses has an ephod, some household gods and an image overlaid with silver? Now you know what to do." ¹⁵So they turned in there and went to the house of the young Levite at Micah's place and greeted him. ¹⁶The six hundred Danites, armed for battle, stood at the entrance of the gate. ¹⁷The five men who had spied out the land went inside and took the idol, the ephod and the household gods while the priest and the six hundred armed men stood at the entrance of the gate.

¹⁸When the five men went into Micah's house and took the idol, the ephod and the household gods, the priest said to them, "What are you doing?"

¹⁹They answered him, "Be quiet! Don't say a word. Come with us, and be our father and priest. Isn't it better that you serve a tribe and clan in Israel as priest rather than just one man's household?" ²⁰The priest was very pleased. He took the ephod, the household gods and the idol and went along with the people. ²¹Putting their little children, their livestock and their possessions in front of them, they turned away and left.

²²When they had gone some distance from Micah's house, the men who lived near Micah were called together and overtook the Danites. ²³As they shouted after them, the Danites

---

[a] 8 Or To carry on his profession   [b] 10 That is, about 4 ounces or about 115 grams   [c] 7 The meaning of the Hebrew for this clause is uncertain.   [d] 7 Hebrew; some Septuagint manuscripts with the Arameans   [e] 12 Mahaneh Dan means Dan's camp.

21 QUALITIES

SELF-DISCIPLINE   Samson Had It, Then Lost It

Judges 16:1–20

WE MUST DETERMINE to lead our own lives well, before expecting anyone else to follow.

Samson seemed to begin his leadership journey as a very disciplined man. He could delay some gratification (although he always struggled with a weakness for women) and kept his Nazirite vow. As he grew older, it was as though he left the foundation of self-discipline and lustfully consumed whatever he wanted: food, women, drink, Philistines.

Discipline does not automatically make someone a leader, but no one can long remain a leader without it. More government leaders have failed from poor discipline than poor policies. More pastors have failed due to bad discipline than bad theology. More business leaders have sabotaged their careers from lack of discipline than by lack of cash flow.

Consider the following list of disciplines that followers want in a leader:

1. They want to see *character* in their leader.

2. They want to observe *competence* in their leader.

3. They want to witness *compassion* in their leader.

4. They want to sense *commitment* in their leader.

5. They want to feel *connection* to their leader.

6. They want to make a *contribution* with their leader.

7. They want to see *contrition* in their leader.

8. They want to join a *cause* with their leader.

9. They want to observe *consistency* in their leader.

10. They want to feel *confidence* in their leader.

11. They want to sense *courage* from their leader.

12. They want to spot *convictions* in their leader.

How to Build Convictions in Your Life

How does a leader become disciplined? Scores of books try to answer that question, but let's underscore here the spiritual dimension of discipline. Spiritual discipline begins when a leader develops personal convictions, those principles we live and die for—the values that guide our life. This is our starting point. Convictions come when . . .

1. We have studied and learned what God's Word says on a given issue.

2. We choose to apply and obey the Word of God in everyday life.

3. We have exposed ourselves to a need.

4. We meditate on specific truths over a period of six months to a year.

5. We have decided what is worth living and dying for.

6. We associate with people who possess convictions in the same areas.

7. We settle an issue before we are forced to do so.

Why not make a list now of those principles you most believe in? Then ask yourself: *Am I disciplined in those areas?* If not, begin to build convictions there first!

For a positive example of self-discipline, see p. 195.

turned and said to Micah, "What's the matter with you that you called out your men to fight?"

²⁴He replied, "You took the gods I made, and my priest, and went away. What else do I have? How can you ask, 'What's the matter with you?' "

²⁵The Danites answered, "Don't argue with us, or some of the men may get angry and attack you, and you and your family will lose your lives." ²⁶So the Danites went their way, and Micah, seeing that they were too strong for him, turned around and went back home.

²⁷Then they took what Micah had made, and his priest, and went on to Laish, against a people at peace and secure. They attacked them with the sword and burned down their city. ²⁸There was no one to rescue them because they lived a long way from Sidon and had no relationship with anyone else. The city was in a valley near Beth Rehob.

The Danites rebuilt the city and settled there. ²⁹They named it Dan after their ancestor Dan, who was born to Israel—though the city used to be called Laish. ³⁰There the Danites set up for themselves the idol, and Jonathan son of Gershom, the son of Moses,ᵃ and his sons were priests for the tribe of Dan until the time of the captivity of the land. ³¹They continued to use the idol Micah had made, all the time the house of God was in Shiloh.

A Levite and His Concubine

19 In those days Israel had no king.
Now a Levite who lived in a remote area in the hill country of Ephraim took a concubine from Bethlehem in Judah. ²But she was unfaithful to him. She left him and went back to her parents' home in Bethlehem, Judah. After she had been there four months, ³her husband went to her to persuade her to return. He had with him his servant and two donkeys. She took him into her parents' home, and when her father saw him, he gladly welcomed him. ⁴His father-in-law, the woman's father, prevailed on him to stay; so he remained with him three days, eating and drinking, and sleeping there.

⁵On the fourth day they got up early and he prepared to leave, but the woman's father said to his son-in-law, "Refresh yourself with something to eat; then you can go." ⁶So the two of them sat down to eat and drink together. Afterward the woman's father said, "Please stay tonight and enjoy yourself." ⁷And when the man got up to go, his father-in-law persuaded him, so he stayed there that night. ⁸On the morning of the fifth day, when he rose to go, the woman's

father said, "Refresh yourself. Wait till afternoon!" So the two of them ate together.

⁹Then when the man, with his concubine and his servant, got up to leave, his father-in-law, the woman's father, said, "Now look, it's almost evening. Spend the night here; the day is nearly over. Stay and enjoy yourself. Early tomorrow morning you can get up and be on your way home." ¹⁰But, unwilling to stay another night, the man left and went toward Jebus (that is, Jerusalem), with his two saddled donkeys and his concubine.

¹¹When they were near Jebus and the day was almost gone, the servant said to his master, "Come, let's stop at this city of the Jebusites and spend the night."

¹²His master replied, "No. We won't go into any city whose people are not Israelites. We will go on to Gibeah." ¹³He added, "Come, let's try to reach Gibeah or Ramah and spend the night in one of those places." ¹⁴So they went on, and the sun set as they neared Gibeah in Benjamin. ¹⁵There they stopped to spend the night. They went and sat in the city square, but no one took them in for the night.

¹⁶That evening an old man from the hill country of Ephraim, who was living in Gibeah (the inhabitants of the place were Benjamites), came in from his work in the fields. ¹⁷When he looked and saw the traveler in the city square, the old man asked, "Where are you going? Where did you come from?"

¹⁸He answered, "We are on our way from Bethlehem in Judah to a remote area in the hill country of Ephraim where I live. I have been to Bethlehem in Judah and now I am going to the house of the LORD.ᵇ No one has taken me in for the night. ¹⁹We have both straw and fodder for our donkeys and bread and wine for ourselves your servants—me, the woman and the young man with us. We don't need anything."

²⁰"You are welcome at my house," the old man said. "Let me supply whatever you need. Only don't spend the night in the square." ²¹So he took him into his house and fed his donkeys. After they had washed their feet, they had something to eat and drink.

²²While they were enjoying themselves, some of the wicked men of the city surrounded the house. Pounding on the door, they shouted to

ᵃ 30 Many Hebrew manuscripts, some Septuagint manuscripts and Vulgate; many other Hebrew manuscripts and some other Septuagint manuscripts *Manasseh*   ᵇ 18 Hebrew, Vulgate, Syriac and Targum; Septuagint *going home*

the old man who owned the house, "Bring out the man who came to your house so we can have sex with him."

²³The owner of the house went outside and said to them, "No, my friends, don't be so vile. Since this man is my guest, don't do this outrageous thing. ²⁴Look, here is my virgin daughter, and his concubine. I will bring them out to you now, and you can use them and do to them whatever you wish. But as for this man, don't do such an outrageous thing."

²⁵But the men would not listen to him. So the man took his concubine and sent her outside to them, and they raped her and abused her throughout the night, and at dawn they let her go. ²⁶At daybreak the woman went back to the house where her master was staying, fell down at the door and lay there until daylight.

²⁷When her master got up in the morning and opened the door of the house and stepped out to continue on his way, there lay his concubine, fallen in the doorway of the house, with her hands on the threshold. ²⁸He said to her, "Get up; let's go." But there was no answer. Then the man put her on his donkey and set out for home.

²⁹When he reached home, he took a knife and cut up his concubine, limb by limb, into twelve parts and sent them into all the areas of Israel. ³⁰Everyone who saw it was saying to one another, "Such a thing has never been seen or done, not since the day the Israelites came up out of Egypt. Just imagine! We must do something! So speak up!"

The Israelites Punish the Benjamites

20 Then all Israel from Dan to Beersheba and from the land of Gilead came together as one and assembled before the LORD in Mizpah. ²The leaders of all the people of the tribes of Israel took their places in the assembly of God's people, four hundred thousand men armed with swords. ³(The Benjamites heard that the Israelites had gone up to Mizpah.) Then the Israelites said, "Tell us how this awful thing happened."

⁴So the Levite, the husband of the murdered woman, said, "I and my concubine came to Gibeah in Benjamin to spend the night. ⁵During the night the men of Gibeah came after me and surrounded the house, intending to kill me. They raped my concubine, and she died. ⁶I took my concubine, cut her into pieces and sent one piece to each region of Israel's inheritance, because they committed this lewd and outrageous act in Israel. ⁷Now, all you Israelites, speak up and tell me what you have decided to do."

⁸All the men rose up together as one, saying, "None of us will go home. No, not one of us will return to his house. ⁹But now this is what we'll do to Gibeah: We'll go up against it in the order decided by casting lots. ¹⁰We'll take ten men out of every hundred from all the tribes of Israel, and a hundred from a thousand, and a thousand from ten thousand, to get provisions for the army. Then, when the army arrives at Gibeahᵃ in Benjamin, it can give them what they deserve for this outrageous act done in Israel." ¹¹So all the Israelites got together and united as one against the city.

¹²The tribes of Israel sent messengers throughout the tribe of Benjamin, saying, "What about this awful crime that was committed among you? ¹³Now turn those wicked men of Gibeah over to us so that we may put them to death and purge the evil from Israel."

But the Benjamites would not listen to their fellow Israelites. ¹⁴From their towns they came together at Gibeah to fight against the Israelites. ¹⁵At once the Benjamites mobilized twenty-six thousand swordsmen from their towns, in addition to seven hundred able young men from those living in Gibeah. ¹⁶Among all these soldiers there were seven hundred select troops who were left-handed, each of whom could sling a stone at a hair and not miss.

¹⁷Israel, apart from Benjamin, mustered four hundred thousand swordsmen, all of them fit for battle.

¹⁸The Israelites went up to Bethelᵇ and inquired of God. They said, "Who of us is to go up first to fight against the Benjamites?"

The LORD replied, "Judah shall go first."

¹⁹The next morning the Israelites got up and pitched camp near Gibeah. ²⁰The Israelites went out to fight the Benjamites and took up battle positions against them at Gibeah. ²¹The Benjamites came out of Gibeah and cut down twenty-two thousand Israelites on the battlefield that day. ²²But the Israelites encouraged one another and again took up their positions where they had stationed themselves the first day. ²³The Israelites went up and wept before the LORD until evening, and they inquired of the LORD. They said, "Shall we go up again to fight against the Benjamites, our fellow Israelites?"

The LORD answered, "Go up against them."

²⁴Then the Israelites drew near to Benjamin

ᵃ 10 One Hebrew manuscript; most Hebrew manuscripts *Geba*, a variant of *Gibeah*   ᵇ 18 Or *to the house of God*; also in verse 26

the second day. ²⁵This time, when the Benjamites came out from Gibeah to oppose them, they cut down another eighteen thousand Israelites, all of them armed with swords.

²⁶Then all the Israelites, the whole army, went up to Bethel, and there they sat weeping before the LORD. They fasted that day until evening and presented burnt offerings and fellowship offerings to the LORD. ²⁷And the Israelites inquired of the LORD. (In those days the ark of the covenant of God was there, ²⁸with Phinehas son of Eleazar, the son of Aaron, ministering before it.) They asked, "Shall we go up again to fight against the Benjamites, our fellow Israelites, or not?"

The LORD responded, "Go, for tomorrow I will give them into your hands."

²⁹Then Israel set an ambush around Gibeah. ³⁰They went up against the Benjamites on the third day and took up positions against Gibeah as they had done before. ³¹The Benjamites came out to meet them and were drawn away from the city. They began to inflict casualties on the Israelites as before, so that about thirty men fell in the open field and on the roads — the one leading to Bethel and the other to Gibeah. ³²While the Benjamites were saying, "We are defeating them as before," the Israelites were saying, "Let's retreat and draw them away from the city to the roads."

³³All the men of Israel moved from their places and took up positions at Baal Tamar, and the Israelite ambush charged out of its place on the west*a* of Gibeah.*b* ³⁴Then ten thousand of Israel's able young men made a frontal attack on Gibeah. The fighting was so heavy that the Benjamites did not realize how near disaster was. ³⁵The LORD defeated Benjamin before Israel, and on that day the Israelites struck down 25,100 Benjamites, all armed with swords. ³⁶Then the Benjamites saw that they were beaten.

Now the men of Israel had given way before Benjamin, because they relied on the ambush they had set near Gibeah. ³⁷Those who had been in ambush made a sudden dash into Gibeah, spread out and put the whole city to the sword. ³⁸The Israelites had arranged with the ambush that they should send up a great cloud of smoke from the city, ³⁹and then the Israelites would counterattack.

The Benjamites had begun to inflict casualties on the Israelites (about thirty), and they said, "We are defeating them as in the first battle." ⁴⁰But when the column of smoke began to rise from the city, the Benjamites turned and saw the whole city going up in smoke. ⁴¹Then the Israelites counterattacked, and the Benjamites were terrified, because they realized that disaster had come on them. ⁴²So they fled before the Israelites in the direction of the wilderness, but they could not escape the battle. And the Israelites who came out of the towns cut them down there. ⁴³They surrounded the Benjamites, chased them and easily*c* overran them in the vicinity of Gibeah on the east. ⁴⁴Eighteen thousand Benjamites fell, all of them valiant fighters. ⁴⁵As they turned and fled toward the wilderness to the rock of Rimmon, the Israelites cut down five thousand men along the roads. They kept pressing after the Benjamites as far as Gidom and struck down two thousand more.

⁴⁶On that day twenty-five thousand Benjamite swordsmen fell, all of them valiant fighters. ⁴⁷But six hundred of them turned and fled into the wilderness to the rock of Rimmon, where they stayed four months. ⁴⁸The men of Israel went back to Benjamin and put all the towns to the sword, including the animals and everything else they found. All the towns they came across they set on fire.

Wives for the Benjamites

21 The men of Israel had taken an oath at Mizpah: "Not one of us will give his daughter in marriage to a Benjamite."

²The people went to Bethel,*d* where they sat before God until evening, raising their voices and weeping bitterly. ³"LORD, God of Israel," they cried, "why has this happened to Israel? Why should one tribe be missing from Israel today?"

⁴Early the next day the people built an altar and presented burnt offerings and fellowship offerings.

⁵Then the Israelites asked, "Who from all the tribes of Israel has failed to assemble before the LORD?" For they had taken a solemn oath that anyone who failed to assemble before the LORD at Mizpah was to be put to death.

⁶Now the Israelites grieved for the tribe of Benjamin, their fellow Israelites. "Today one tribe is cut off from Israel," they said. ⁷"How can we provide wives for those who are left, since we have taken an oath by the LORD not to give them any of our daughters in marriage?" ⁸Then they

---

a 33 Some Septuagint manuscripts and Vulgate; the meaning of the Hebrew for this word is uncertain.　*b* 33 Hebrew *Geba*, a variant of *Gibeah*　*c* 43 The meaning of the Hebrew for this word is uncertain.　*d* 2 Or *to the house of God*

asked, "Which one of the tribes of Israel failed to assemble before the LORD at Mizpah?" They discovered that no one from Jabesh Gilead had come to the camp for the assembly. [9]For when they counted the people, they found that none of the people of Jabesh Gilead were there.

[10]So the assembly sent twelve thousand fighting men with instructions to go to Jabesh Gilead and put to the sword those living there, including the women and children. [11]"This is what you are to do," they said. "Kill every male and every woman who is not a virgin." [12]They found among the people living in Jabesh Gilead four hundred young women who had never slept with a man, and they took them to the camp at Shiloh in Canaan.

[13]Then the whole assembly sent an offer of peace to the Benjamites at the rock of Rimmon. [14]So the Benjamites returned at that time and were given the women of Jabesh Gilead who had been spared. But there were not enough for all of them.

[15]The people grieved for Benjamin, because the LORD had made a gap in the tribes of Israel. [16]And the elders of the assembly said, "With the women of Benjamin destroyed, how shall we provide wives for the men who are left? [17]The Benjamite survivors must have heirs," they said, "so that a tribe of Israel will not be wiped out.

[18]We can't give them our daughters as wives, since we Israelites have taken this oath: 'Cursed be anyone who gives a wife to a Benjamite.' [19]But look, there is the annual festival of the LORD in Shiloh, which lies north of Bethel, east of the road that goes from Bethel to Shechem, and south of Lebonah."

[20]So they instructed the Benjamites, saying, "Go and hide in the vineyards [21]and watch. When the young women of Shiloh come out to join in the dancing, rush from the vineyards and each of you seize one of them to be your wife. Then return to the land of Benjamin. [22]When their fathers or brothers complain to us, we will say to them, 'Do us the favor of helping them, because we did not get wives for them during the war. You will not be guilty of breaking your oath because you did not give your daughters to them.'"

[23]So that is what the Benjamites did. While the young women were dancing, each man caught one and carried her off to be his wife. Then they returned to their inheritance and rebuilt the towns and settled in them.

[24]At that time the Israelites left that place and went home to their tribes and clans, each to his own inheritance.

[25]In those days Israel had no king; everyone did as they saw fit.

INTRODUCTION TO
RUTH

God Honors Loyalty and Integrity

The book of Ruth reminds us that God honors and emphasizes the leadership qualities of loyalty and integrity.

Ruth, a Moabite woman widowed at an early age, found herself faced with the option of abandoning her widowed mother-in-law or risking life in a foreign land. She chose to stay committed to her friend and mentor, Naomi, and her uncommon decision ultimately paid off.

Ruth's commitment to stay with her mother-in-law, despite the death of her husband, revealed her remarkable character and showcased her sense of loyalty and responsibility. When she remained faithful to Naomi, demonstrated an impeccable work ethic, and maintained fidelity as she gleaned every day in a rich man's field, she set herself apart as unique.

Where did this non-Hebrew learn such character and trust in God to meet her needs? From her deceased husband? From Naomi? We do not know, but we do know that Ruth remained committed to doing the right thing, and God surprised her by meeting every need she had, and more. God provided for Ruth through Boaz, a man with similar character—and perhaps this is the most profound lesson of the book.

Ruth illustrates that when leaders focus on doing what is right, God will bless the fruit of their labors. To qualify for such a blessing means placing responsibilities before results. Character must precede conduct. Faithfulness must precede fruitfulness.

"Seek first his kingdom and his righteousness," Jesus reminds us, "and all these things will be given to you as well" (Mt 6:33). This is how God's kingdom works. Jesus

God's Role in Ruth

Why did God in his providence preserve the book of Ruth? Perhaps he did so because Ruth would take an honored place in the messianic family line. God moves throughout this book as the divine director of events—orchestrating a plan to graft young Ruth into the family tree of David and leading ultimately to Jesus.

God accomplishes his work and leadership through all the joys and tragedies of life. Famine, loneliness, death, voluntary exile and unshakable fidelity become the tools he uses to fulfill his sovereign plan. As a phenomenal leader, God brokered the resources and circumstances of this time in Israel's history to pull off what he intended.

Leaders in Ruth
Naomi, Boaz

Other People of Influence in Ruth
Ruth

Lessons in Leadership

- God rewards the integrity and loyalty of leaders.
- God will sovereignly accomplish his purposes through unlikely people.
- Leaders must place character and spiritual formation before conduct and skill formation.

taught that if you get the tree right, the fruit will be right (Mt 12:33–35). As in the book of Ruth, Jesus prioritizes *being* before *doing*.

Our leadership must flow out of our very being, a natural outgrowth of what we have incarnated. And yet most leaders struggle at exactly this point. By definition, most leaders are result-oriented. They jump immediately to the visible and the measurable, to the exterior results that people affirm. Who affirms their private, personal disciplines? Who asks about their character on Monday morning when they walk into the office? Most leaders tend to talk about the "bottom line."

Although we all agree character is paramount, it just seems too hard to track. So most people, even leaders, jump to results. For some, "the end justifies the means." God says, however, that when we work on the depth of our ministry, he'll work on its breadth.

Leaders need to read the beautiful story of Ruth, for it will remind them of two fundamental truths:

1. God does indeed reward character.
2. God will accomplish his purposes in the end—even if he has to use a Moabite woman to do it.

LEADERSHIP HIGHLIGHTS IN RUTH

RUTH: Willingly Follows Naomi (1:8–18)	page 306
BOAZ: Model of Kindness and Spiritual Leadership (2:4–17)	page 308
GENEROSITY: Boaz Doesn't Keep Score; He Just Keeps Giving (2:8—4:10)	page 309
WOMEN Who Made a Difference (4:13–17)	page 311

Naomi Loses Her Husband and Sons

1 In the days when the judges ruled,[a] there was a famine in the land. So a man from Bethlehem in Judah, together with his wife and two sons, went to live for a while in the country of Moab. [2]The man's name was Elimelek, his wife's name was Naomi, and the names of his two sons were Mahlon and Kilion. They were Ephrathites from Bethlehem, Judah. And they went to Moab and lived there.

[3]Now Elimelek, Naomi's husband, died, and she was left with her two sons. [4]They married Moabite women, one named Orpah and the other Ruth. After they had lived there about ten years, [5]both Mahlon and Kilion also died, and Naomi was left without her two sons and her husband.

Naomi and Ruth Return to Bethlehem

[6]When Naomi heard in Moab that the LORD had come to the aid of his people by providing food for them, she and her daughters-in-law prepared to return home from there. [7]With her two daughters-in-law she left the place where she had been living and set out on the road that would take them back to the land of Judah.

[8]Then Naomi said to her two daughters-in-law, "Go back, each of you, to your mother's home. May the LORD show you kindness, as you have shown kindness to your dead husbands and to me. [9]May the LORD grant that each of you will find rest in the home of another husband."

Then she kissed them goodbye and they wept aloud [10]and said to her, "We will go back with you to your people."

[11]But Naomi said, "Return home, my daughters. Why would you come with me? Am I going to have any more sons, who could become your husbands? [12]Return home, my daughters; I am too old to have another husband. Even if I thought there was still hope for me—even if I had a husband tonight and then gave birth to sons— [13]would you wait until they grew up? Would you remain unmarried for them? No, my daughters. It is more bitter for me than for you, because the LORD's hand has turned against me!"

[14]At this they wept aloud again. Then Orpah kissed her mother-in-law goodbye, but Ruth clung to her.

[15]"Look," said Naomi, "your sister-in-law is going back to her people and her gods. Go back with her."

[16]But Ruth replied, "Don't urge me to leave you or to turn back from you. Where you go I will go, and where you stay I will stay. Your people will be my people and your God my God. [17]Where you die I will die, and there I will be

[a] 1 Traditionally judged

RUTH — Willingly Follows Naomi
Ruth 1:8–18

PROFILE in leadership

The book of Ruth tells a tale of love and respect between two women from vastly different worlds.

Gentle and loving Ruth, a Moabite, cared deeply for her mother-in-law, Naomi. Ruth willingly left her comfort zone and the only world she had ever known to travel with Naomi to foreign Bethlehem. She exemplifies the strength and determination leaders must have to venture out and follow God, even if it means leaving family and friends behind.

Ruth submitted herself to the directions Naomi gave her in this new and strange culture. Her kinsman-redeemer, Boaz, eventually married her and blessed her with security and protection. But when Ruth first made the choice to follow Naomi's directions, the young Moabite had no way of knowing how it would all turn out. She simply stepped out in faith.

Naomi prayed that Ruth would become famous throughout Israel for her good deeds, and God is still answering that prayer today as millions turn to the book of Ruth for memorable lessons on love and faithfulness. As the great-grandmother of King David, the foreigner Ruth found a lasting place in the lineage of our Savior, Jesus Christ.

buried. May the LORD deal with me, be it ever so severely, if even death separates you and me." [18]When Naomi realized that Ruth was determined to go with her, she stopped urging her.

[19]So the two women went on until they came to Bethlehem. When they arrived in Bethlehem, the whole town was stirred because of them, and the women exclaimed, "Can this be Naomi?"

[20]"Don't call me Naomi,[a]" she told them. "Call me Mara,[b] because the Almighty[c] has made my life very bitter. [21]I went away full, but the LORD has brought me back empty. Why call me Naomi? The LORD has afflicted[d] me; the Almighty has brought misfortune upon me."

[22]So Naomi returned from Moab accompanied by Ruth the Moabite, her daughter-in-law, arriving in Bethlehem as the barley harvest was beginning.

Commitment Precedes Resources

Ruth 1:1–22

While every leader needs financial and human resources to reach his or her goals, commitment should always precede those resources. When a leader demonstrates a commitment to the mission and goals of the organization, the resources always follow.

In the very first chapter of the book that bears her name, Ruth chooses to stay with Naomi, her mother-in-law, even after she loses her husband. She didn't know it, but her commitment would lead to all kinds of open doors. Ruth finds work during a difficult time, makes friends in a foreign land, and eventually gains a new husband, Boaz. Most impressively, God includes her—a Moabite adopted into the family of Israel—in the line of Christ. The child she bore became part of the lineage of the Messiah!

The key? Commitment. Until a leader commits, a hesitancy lingers. But the moment that leader definitely commits, then God moves and a whole stream of events begins to flow. All manner of unforeseen incidents, meetings, persons and material assistance—which no one could ever dream up—begin to occur. And it all starts to happen the moment a leader makes a firm commitment.

Ruth Meets Boaz in the Grain Field

2 Now Naomi had a relative on her husband's side, a man of standing from the clan of Elimelek, whose name was Boaz.

[2]And Ruth the Moabite said to Naomi, "Let me go to the fields and pick up the leftover grain behind anyone in whose eyes I find favor."

Naomi said to her, "Go ahead, my daughter." [3]So she went out, entered a field and began to glean behind the harvesters. As it turned out, she was working in a field belonging to Boaz, who was from the clan of Elimelek.

[4]Just then Boaz arrived from Bethlehem and greeted the harvesters, "The LORD be with you!"

"The LORD bless you!" they answered.

[5]Boaz asked the overseer of his harvesters, "Who does that young woman belong to?"

[6]The overseer replied, "She is the Moabite who came back from Moab with Naomi. [7]She said, 'Please let me glean and gather among the sheaves behind the harvesters.' She came into the field and has remained here from morning till now, except for a short rest in the shelter."

[8]So Boaz said to Ruth, "My daughter, listen to me. Don't go and glean in another field and don't go away from here. Stay here with the women who work for me. [9]Watch the field where the men are harvesting, and follow along after the women. I have told the men not to lay a hand on you. And whenever you are thirsty, go and get a drink from the water jars the men have filled."

[10]At this, she bowed down with her face to the ground. She asked him, "Why have I found such favor in your eyes that you notice me—a foreigner?"

[11]Boaz replied, "I've been told all about what you have done for your mother-in-law since the death of your husband—how you left your father and mother and your homeland and came to live with a people you did not know before. [12]May the LORD repay you for what you have done. May you be richly rewarded by the LORD, the God of Israel, under whose wings you have come to take refuge."

[13]"May I continue to find favor in your eyes, my lord," she said. "You have put me at ease by speaking kindly to your servant—though I do not have the standing of one of your servants."

[14]At mealtime Boaz said to her, "Come over here. Have some bread and dip it in the wine vinegar."

---

[a] 20 Naomi means pleasant.   [b] 20 Mara means bitter.
[c] 20 Hebrew Shaddai; also in verse 21   [d] 21 Or has testified against

When she sat down with the harvesters, he offered her some roasted grain. She ate all she wanted and had some left over. [15] As she got up to glean, Boaz gave orders to his men, "Let her gather among the sheaves and don't reprimand her. [16] Even pull out some stalks for her from the bundles and leave them for her to pick up, and don't rebuke her."

[17] So Ruth gleaned in the field until evening. Then she threshed the barley she had gathered, and it amounted to about an ephah.[a] [18] She carried it back to town, and her mother-in-law saw how much she had gathered. Ruth also brought out and gave her what she had left over after she had eaten enough.

[19] Her mother-in-law asked her, "Where did you glean today? Where did you work? Blessed be the man who took notice of you!"

Then Ruth told her mother-in-law about the one at whose place she had been working. "The name of the man I worked with today is Boaz," she said.

[20] "The LORD bless him!" Naomi said to her daughter-in-law. "He has not stopped showing his kindness to the living and the dead." She added, "That man is our close relative; he is one of our guardian-redeemers.[b]"

[21] Then Ruth the Moabite said, "He even said to me, 'Stay with my workers until they finish harvesting all my grain.'"

[22] Naomi said to Ruth her daughter-in-law, "It will be good for you, my daughter, to go with the women who work for him, because in someone else's field you might be harmed."

[23] So Ruth stayed close to the women of Boaz to glean until the barley and wheat harvests were finished. And she lived with her mother-in-law.

Ruth and Boaz at the Threshing Floor

3 One day Ruth's mother-in-law Naomi said to her, "My daughter, I must find a home[c] for you, where you will be well provided for. [2] Now Boaz, with whose women you have worked, is a relative of ours. Tonight he will be winnowing barley on the threshing floor. [3] Wash, put on perfume, and get dressed in your best clothes. Then go down to the threshing floor, but don't let him know you are there until he has finished eating and drinking. [4] When he lies down, note the place where he is lying. Then go and

---

[a] 17 That is, probably about 30 pounds or about 13 kilograms
[b] 20 The Hebrew word for *guardian-redeemer* is a legal term for one who has the obligation to redeem a relative in serious difficulty (see Lev. 25:25-55).   [c] 1 Hebrew *find rest* (see 1:9)

BOAZ — Model of Kindness and Spiritual Leadership
Ruth 2:4–17

PROFILE in leadership

The first words we hear from an individual often make the most lasting impression on us.

The first recorded words of Boaz, a wealthy and influential landowner and farmer from Bethlehem, tell us that he loved God and wanted God's blessings on those around him—including those who worked his fields.

On the day Ruth asked to gather grain left behind by his servants, Boaz arrived at his field and greeted the harvesters with a hearty, "The LORD be with you!" (Ru 2:4).

"The LORD bless you!" the servants replied (2:4).

Why did these workers so enthusiastically respond in kind to Boaz's blessing? Apparently, they knew something about this extraordinary man, his relationship with God, and how he treated people.

We see Boaz's special nature in how he treated Ruth. When he heard the story of this poor Moabite widow, he showed her great kindness and consideration—even to the point of affording her special protection from men in the field and special permission to gather grain with his servants. He also gave her all the water she needed and later invited her to join him and his workers for lunch.

Boaz models the sort of kindness required in all godly leaders. He knew when to reach out and welcome those God brought into his circle of influence, even while remaining compassionate and caring toward his own.

21 QUALITIES

GENEROSITY
Boaz Doesn't Keep Score; He Just Keeps Giving

Ruth 2:8—4:10

LEADERS MUST be generous, predisposed to give their resources to others. They believe a candle loses nothing when it lights another.

No one models this better than Boaz, the spiritual leader who became Ruth's husband. He owned a large field, and like other landowners, employed reapers to gather his harvest. When the reapers finished, the less fortunate were allowed to "glean" in the field, taking whatever remained of the harvested crops. Ruth was one such person.

Boaz's generous spirit surfaced immediately when he saw Ruth. He asked the reapers about her identity, then expressed his generosity to her. Boaz displayed his generous leadership in several ways:

1. **He was generous with his compassion (2:8–9).** He told Ruth not to glean anywhere else; she would get all she needed from him.

2. **He was generous with his compliments (2:11–12).** He noticed her sacrifice and complimented her efforts.

3. **He was generous with his courtesy (2:14).** He invited her to join his staff for a meal, kindly serving her all she wanted.

4. **He was generous with his crops (2:15–16).** He told his reapers to put out extra bundles of grain for her to find.

5. **He was generous with his credibility (3:11–13).** He showed respect by doing what was right by her request.

6. **He was generous with his commitment (4:9–10).** He committed himself to ensuring that Ruth's former husband had offspring to carry on his name.

You can give without loving, but you cannot love without giving. Leaders who fail to display generosity should ask themselves, *Do I really love the people I lead?* When great leaders err, they always err on the side of generosity. If they err in paying salaries, they err in paying too much. If they err in firing a staff member, they err on the side of excessive emotional support, severance package, and affirmation. No leader gets ahead by mimicking Ebenezer Scrooge.

Jesus talked about this generous spirit when he said, "If anyone wants to sue you and take your shirt, hand over your coat as well. If anyone forces you to go one mile, go with them two miles" (Mt 5:40–41).

A generous spirit drove Boaz to go the second mile with Ruth, even before he suspected she might become his wife. (He assumed she would be attracted to a younger man, Ru 3:10.) Even so, Boaz gave her extra time, attention, grain, respect, favor and honor.

How about you? Who would describe your leadership as generous?

For a negative example of generosity, see p. 1295.

Courage: Ruth Steps Out and Takes a Risk

Ruth 3:1–6

Ruth took a risk in following her mother-in-law's instruction. What allows a leader to risk?
Responsibility: Sense the need to step out.
Initiative: Act even when no one else goes before.
Sacrifice: Make sacrifices to make things work.
Knowledge: Possess enough information to trust the decision.

uncover his feet and lie down. He will tell you what to do."

[5]"I will do whatever you say," Ruth answered. [6]So she went down to the threshing floor and did everything her mother-in-law told her to do.

[7]When Boaz had finished eating and drinking and was in good spirits, he went over to lie down at the far end of the grain pile. Ruth approached quietly, uncovered his feet and lay down. [8]In the middle of the night something startled the man; he turned—and there was a woman lying at his feet!

[9]"Who are you?" he asked.

"I am your servant Ruth," she said. "Spread the corner of your garment over me, since you are a guardian-redeemer[a] of our family."

[10]"The LORD bless you, my daughter," he re-

The Law of Solid Ground: Both Ruth and Boaz Benefit

Ruth 3:1–15

Naomi knew how a woman could properly communicate her interest in a man. She told Ruth to enter the room where Boaz slept, uncover his feet, and sleep there. When Boaz awoke and discovered Ruth, he immediately understood the overture. Yet his sense of integrity would not allow him to sleep with her; he was committed to sincerely practicing what he preached. Integrity is about wholeness. The person's words, thoughts and actions are whole.

The ancient Greek word for "sincere" carries this meaning. It comes from the Latin word *sincerus*, which means "sound, pure, whole," perhaps originally "of one growth," that is, "not hybrid, unmixed." Are your words, intentions and actions "of one growth," whole, unmixed? Are you a Boaz type of leader?

plied. "This kindness is greater than that which you showed earlier: You have not run after the younger men, whether rich or poor. [11]And now, my daughter, don't be afraid. I will do for you all you ask. All the people of my town know that you are a woman of noble character. [12]Although it is true that I am a guardian-redeemer of our family, there is another who is more closely related than I. [13]Stay here for the night, and in the morning if he wants to do his duty as your guardian-redeemer, good; let him redeem you. But if he is not willing, as surely as the LORD lives I will do it. Lie here until morning."

[14]So she lay at his feet until morning, but got up before anyone could be recognized; and he said, "No one must know that a woman came to the threshing floor."

[15]He also said, "Bring me the shawl you are wearing and hold it out." When she did so, he poured into it six measures of barley and placed the bundle on her. Then he[b] went back to town.

[16]When Ruth came to her mother-in-law, Naomi asked, "How did it go, my daughter?"

Then she told her everything Boaz had done for her [17]and added, "He gave me these six measures of barley, saying, 'Don't go back to your mother-in-law empty-handed.'"

[18]Then Naomi said, "Wait, my daughter, until you find out what happens. For the man will not rest until the matter is settled today."

Boaz Marries Ruth

4 Meanwhile Boaz went up to the town gate and sat down there just as the guardian-redeemer[c] he had mentioned came along. Boaz

[a] 9 The Hebrew word for *guardian-redeemer* is a legal term for one who has the obligation to redeem a relative in serious difficulty (see Lev. 25:25-55); also in verses 12 and 13.
[b] 15 Most Hebrew manuscripts; many Hebrew manuscripts, Vulgate and Syriac *she*   [c] 1 The Hebrew word for *guardian-redeemer* is a legal term for one who has the obligation to redeem a relative in serious difficulty (see Lev. 25:25-55); also in verses 3, 6, 8 and 14.

said, "Come over here, my friend, and sit down." So he went over and sat down.

[2]Boaz took ten of the elders of the town and said, "Sit here," and they did so. [3]Then he said to the guardian-redeemer, "Naomi, who has come back from Moab, is selling the piece of land that belonged to our relative Elimelek. [4]I thought I should bring the matter to your attention and suggest that you buy it in the presence of these seated here and in the presence of the elders of my people. If you will redeem it, do so. But if you[a] will not, tell me, so I will know. For no one has the right to do it except you, and I am next in line."

"I will redeem it," he said.

[5]Then Boaz said, "On the day you buy the land from Naomi, you also acquire Ruth the Moabite, the[b] dead man's widow, in order to maintain the name of the dead with his property."

[6]At this, the guardian-redeemer said, "Then I cannot redeem it because I might endanger my own estate. You redeem it yourself. I cannot do it."

[7](Now in earlier times in Israel, for the redemption and transfer of property to become final, one party took off his sandal and gave it to the other. This was the method of legalizing transactions in Israel.)

[8]So the guardian-redeemer said to Boaz, "Buy it yourself." And he removed his sandal.

[9]Then Boaz announced to the elders and all the people, "Today you are witnesses that I have bought from Naomi all the property of Elimelek, Kilion and Mahlon. [10]I have also acquired Ruth the Moabite, Mahlon's widow, as my wife, in order to maintain the name of the dead with his property, so that his name will not disappear from among his family or from his hometown. Today you are witnesses!"

[11]Then the elders and all the people at the gate said, "We are witnesses. May the LORD make the woman who is coming into your home like Rachel and Leah, who together built up the family of Israel. May you have standing in Ephrathah and be famous in Bethlehem. [12]Through the offspring the LORD gives you by this young woman, may your family be like that of Perez, whom Tamar bore to Judah."

[a] 4 Many Hebrew manuscripts, Septuagint, Vulgate and Syriac; most Hebrew manuscripts *he*   [b] 5 Vulgate and Syriac; Hebrew (see also Septuagint) *Naomi and from Ruth the Moabite, you acquire the*

Women Who Made a Difference

Ruth 4:13–17

Ruth and Naomi provide just two examples of women in Scripture who made a difference. Such heroines show up everywhere in both the Old and New Testaments. Study these ladies and be encouraged:

Abigail (1Sa 25:1–42)
Anna (Lk 2:36–38)
Deborah (Jdg 4; 5)
Dorcas (Ac 9:36–42)
Elizabeth (Lk 1:5–80)
Esther (Book of Esther)
Eunice (Ac 16:1–3; 2Ti 1:5)
Eve (Ge 2; 3; 2Co 11:3)
Hannah (1Sa 1:1—2:21)
Jochebed (Ex 2:1–11; 6:20)
Lois (2Ti 1:5)
Lydia (Ac 16:12–15, 40)
Martha (Lk 10:38–41; Jn 11)
Mary (Lk 10:38–42; Jn 12)
Mary, Jesus' mother (Mt 1; 2; Lk 1; 2)
Mary Magdalene (Mt 20:1–18; 27:56, 61)
Miriam (Ex 15:20–21)
Phoebe (Ro 16:1–2)
Priscilla (Ac 18:2, 18, 26)
Rachel (Ge 29–31)
Rahab (Jos 2; 6:17–25)
Rebekah (Ge 24; 25:20–28)
Sarah (Ge 11; 12; 16; 18)
Susanna (Lk 8:3)
Widow in temple (Mk 12:41–44)
Wife of Pilate (Mt 27:19–24)
Woman of Samaria (Jn 4)
Woman who washes Jesus' feet (Lk 7:36–50)

Boaz and Ruth Exhibit Character . . . and It Pays Off

Ruth 4:1–6

Both Ruth and Boaz wanted their relationship to go further, yet when the truth came to light, Boaz informed Ruth he must take the decision before the city leaders. Ruth submitted, never pushing her desire to be remarried. Character enables a leader to do what is right, even when it's difficult.

Naomi Gains a Son

[13]So Boaz took Ruth and she became his wife. When he made love to her, the LORD enabled her to conceive, and she gave birth to a son. [14]The women said to Naomi: "Praise be to the LORD, who this day has not left you without a guardian-redeemer. May he become famous throughout Israel! [15]He will renew your life and sustain you in your old age. For your daughter-in-law, who loves you and who is better to you than seven sons, has given him birth."

[16]Then Naomi took the child in her arms and cared for him. [17]The women living there said, "Naomi has a son!" And they named him Obed. He was the father of Jesse, the father of David.

The Genealogy of David

[18]This, then, is the family line of Perez:

Perez was the father of Hezron,
[19]Hezron the father of Ram,
Ram the father of Amminadab,
[20]Amminadab the father of Nahshon,
Nahshon the father of Salmon,[a]
[21]Salmon the father of Boaz,
Boaz the father of Obed,
[22]Obed the father of Jesse,
and Jesse the father of David.

---

[a] 20 A few Hebrew manuscripts, some Septuagint manuscripts and Vulgate (see also verse 21 and Septuagint of 1 Chron. 2:11); most Hebrew manuscripts *Salma*

INTRODUCTION TO
1 SAMUEL

Leaders with a Treasure Trove of Insight

Samuel was a leader of leaders—a chief advisor to the kings and military captains of Israel. When he spoke, everyone listened.

As the prophet of God, Samuel anointed kings; as the interpreter of the divine Word, he counseled and challenged kings. Serving as judge in the years just prior to Saul's monarchy, Samuel embodied the three great functions of prophet, priest, and king, as Jesus Christ would later.

Samuel and Saul illustrate vividly how a ministry leader and a marketplace leader might relate to one another.

The book begins with Samuel's birth and describes how Eli the priest mentored him as a young boy. The first several chapters depict his role as a judge and show how he led Israel back to God from Baal worship. As Samuel grew older, he appointed his sons to judge Israel, but these men did not "follow his ways" (8:3) and the people demanded a king. Samuel anoints Saul in chapter 9, and the king's flawed reign takes up the next 20 chapters of the book.

Saul's insecurity leads to a volatile monarchy. He projects his fears onto others, presumes upon the priestly role of Samuel, and jealously pursues David after the young man defeats Goliath. Samuel dies in chapter 25, leaving the leadership of Israel in chaos. By the end of the book, Saul lies dead in battle.

God's Role in 1 Samuel

It has been said that organizations move through at least four stages of growth.

The first is the entrepreneurial stage, where the group seeks viability (this happened for Israel under Moses). The second is the emerging stage, where the group seeks credibility (occurred under Joshua). The third is the established stage, where the group seeks stability (occurred under the judges, ending with Samuel). By this third stage, Israel had a problem. They forgot who they were!

First Samuel describes how God desperately tries calling his people back to him through the godly leadership of Samuel. But they refuse, demand a king, and crown Saul.

That leads the nation to the fourth and final stage of organizations: erosion, a stage marked by vulnerability. Unless the people can return to their roots and mission, they will crumble from within.

Leaders in 1 Samuel

Eli, Samuel, Saul, David, Jonathan

Other People of Influence in 1 Samuel

Hannah, the Philistines, the prophets, David's mighty men, Abigail, the spirit medium

Lessons in Leadership

- If your leadership doesn't work at home, don't export it.
- Trouble comes when leaders spend more time trying to keep their job than to do their job.
- Leaders must hear from God before they speak for God.

- God selects leaders based on their heart, not just their head and hands.
- Human promotion does not equal divine empowerment.

LEADERSHIP HIGHLIGHTS IN 1 SAMUEL

The Birth of Samuel

1 There was a certain man from Ramathaim, a Zuphite[a] from the hill country of Ephraim, whose name was Elkanah son of Jeroham, the son of Elihu, the son of Tohu, the son of Zuph, an Ephraimite. [2]He had two wives; one was called Hannah and the other Peninnah. Peninnah had children, but Hannah had none.

[3]Year after year this man went up from his town to worship and sacrifice to the Lord Almighty at Shiloh, where Hophni and Phinehas, the two sons of Eli, were priests of the Lord. [4]Whenever the day came for Elkanah to sacrifice, he would give portions of the meat to his wife Peninnah and to all her sons and daughters. [5]But to Hannah he gave a double portion because he loved her, and the Lord had closed her womb. [6]Because the Lord had closed Hannah's womb, her rival kept provoking her in order to irritate her. [7]This went on year after year. Whenever Hannah went up to the house of the Lord, her rival provoked her till she wept and would not eat. [8]Her husband Elkanah would say to her, "Hannah, why are you weeping? Why don't you eat? Why are you downhearted? Don't I mean more to you than ten sons?"

[9]Once when they had finished eating and drinking in Shiloh, Hannah stood up. Now Eli the priest was sitting on his chair by the doorpost of the Lord's house. [10]In her deep anguish Hannah prayed to the Lord, weeping bitterly. [11]And she made a vow, saying, "Lord Almighty, if you will only look on your servant's misery and remember me, and not forget your servant but give her a son, then I will give him to the Lord for all the days of his life, and no razor will ever be used on his head."

[12]As she kept on praying to the Lord, Eli observed her mouth. [13]Hannah was praying in her heart, and her lips were moving but her voice was not heard. Eli thought she was drunk [14]and said to her, "How long are you going to stay drunk? Put away your wine."

[15]"Not so, my lord," Hannah replied, "I am a woman who is deeply troubled. I have not been drinking wine or beer; I was pouring out my soul to the Lord. [16]Do not take your servant for a wicked woman; I have been praying here out of my great anguish and grief."

[17]Eli answered, "Go in peace, and may the God of Israel grant you what you have asked of him."

[18]She said, "May your servant find favor in your eyes." Then she went her way and ate something, and her face was no longer downcast.

---

[a] 1 See Septuagint and 1 Chron. 6:26-27,33-35; or *from Ramathaim Zuphim.*

HANNAH — The Power of Persistence
1 Samuel 1:1–28

When you think of Hannah, think of persistence and faith.

At a time in history when infertility earned a woman both scorn and ridicule, Hannah faced an added heartache: She became the object of cruel mocking by her husband's other wife.

Had you been Hannah, how would you have responded? Hannah refused to lash out at her rival, but instead took her sorrow and loss to God. She prayed earnestly to her Lord, begging him for a son. She refused to believe that her difficult situation had to remain permanent.

Hannah prayed sincerely, specifically, and sacrificially. She did not back away from her request, even when rebuked by an uncomprehending priest—and God rewarded her faith with a son, Samuel. When the time came for her to keep her word and give Samuel to the service of the Lord, she did so with a thankful heart.

Prayer changed the course of Hannah's life and impacted an entire nation. God used her son in a key role as prophet during the lifetime of King David, and his influence outlived him as he gave great impetus to the prophetic movement. God also blessed Hannah with many other children, proving once again his delight in the faith and persistence of his people.

PROFILE in leadership

[19]Early the next morning they arose and worshiped before the LORD and then went back to their home at Ramah. Elkanah made love to his wife Hannah, and the LORD remembered her. [20]So in the course of time Hannah became pregnant and gave birth to a son. She named him Samuel,[a] saying, "Because I asked the LORD for him."

Hannah Dedicates Samuel

[21]When her husband Elkanah went up with all his family to offer the annual sacrifice to the LORD and to fulfill his vow, [22]Hannah did not go. She said to her husband, "After the boy is weaned, I will take him and present him before the LORD, and he will live there always."[b]

[23]"Do what seems best to you," her husband Elkanah told her. "Stay here until you have weaned him; only may the LORD make good his[c] word." So the woman stayed at home and nursed her son until she had weaned him.

[24]After he was weaned, she took the boy with her, young as he was, along with a three-year-old bull,[d] an ephah[e] of flour and a skin of wine, and brought him to the house of the LORD at Shiloh. [25]When the bull had been sacrificed, they brought the boy to Eli, [26]and she said to him, "Pardon me, my lord. As surely as you live, I am the woman who stood here beside you praying to the LORD. [27]I prayed for this child, and the LORD has granted me what I asked of him. [28]So now I give him to the LORD. For his whole life he will be given over to the LORD." And he worshiped the LORD there.

Hannah's Prayer

2 Then Hannah prayed and said:

"My heart rejoices in the LORD;
　　in the LORD my horn[f] is lifted high.
My mouth boasts over my enemies,
　　for I delight in your deliverance.

[2]"There is no one holy like the LORD;
　　there is no one besides you;
　　there is no Rock like our God.

[3]"Do not keep talking so proudly
　　or let your mouth speak such arrogance,
for the LORD is a God who knows,
　　and by him deeds are weighed.

[4]"The bows of the warriors are broken,
　　but those who stumbled are armed with
　　　strength.

[5]Those who were full hire themselves out for
　　food,
　　but those who were hungry are hungry no
　　　more.
She who was barren has borne seven
　　children,
　　but she who has had many sons pines
　　　away.

[6]"The LORD brings death and makes alive;
　　he brings down to the grave and raises up.
[7]The LORD sends poverty and wealth;
　　he humbles and he exalts.
[8]He raises the poor from the dust
　　and lifts the needy from the ash heap;
he seats them with princes
　　and has them inherit a throne of honor.

"For the foundations of the earth are the
　　LORD'S;
　　on them he has set the world.
[9]He will guard the feet of his faithful
　　servants,
　　but the wicked will be silenced in the
　　　place of darkness.

"It is not by strength that one prevails;
[10]　those who oppose the LORD will be
　　　broken.
The Most High will thunder from heaven;
　　the LORD will judge the ends of the earth.

"He will give strength to his king
　　and exalt the horn of his anointed."

[11]Then Elkanah went home to Ramah, but the boy ministered before the LORD under Eli the priest.

Eli's Wicked Sons

[12]Eli's sons were scoundrels; they had no regard for the LORD. [13]Now it was the practice of the priests that, whenever any of the people offered a sacrifice, the priest's servant would come with a three-pronged fork in his hand while the meat was being boiled [14]and would plunge the fork into the pan or kettle or caldron or pot. Whatever the fork brought up the priest would take for himself. This is how they treated all the

---

[a] 20 Samuel sounds like the Hebrew for heard by God.
[b] 22 Masoretic Text; Dead Sea Scrolls always. I have dedicated him as a Nazirite — all the days of his life."　　[c] 23 Masoretic Text; Dead Sea Scrolls, Septuagint and Syriac your
[d] 24 Dead Sea Scrolls, Septuagint and Syriac; Masoretic Text with three bulls　　[e] 24 That is, probably about 36 pounds or about 16 kilograms　　[f] 1 Horn here symbolizes strength; also in verse 10.

Israelites who came to Shiloh. [15]But even before the fat was burned, the priest's servant would come and say to the person who was sacrificing, "Give the priest some meat to roast; he won't accept boiled meat from you, but only raw."

[16]If the person said to him, "Let the fat be burned first, and then take whatever you want," the servant would answer, "No, hand it over now; if you don't, I'll take it by force."

[17]This sin of the young men was very great in the Lord's sight, for they[a] were treating the Lord's offering with contempt.

[18]But Samuel was ministering before the Lord — a boy wearing a linen ephod. [19]Each year his mother made him a little robe and took it to him when she went up with her husband to offer the annual sacrifice. [20]Eli would bless Elkanah and his wife, saying, "May the Lord give you children by this woman to take the place of the one she prayed for and gave to[b] the Lord." Then they would go home. [21]And the Lord was gracious to Hannah; she gave birth to three sons and two daughters. Meanwhile, the boy Samuel grew up in the presence of the Lord.

[22]Now Eli, who was very old, heard about everything his sons were doing to all Israel and how they slept with the women who served at the entrance to the tent of meeting. [23]So he said to them, "Why do you do such things? I hear from all the people about these wicked deeds of yours. [24]No, my sons; the report I hear spreading among the Lord's people is not good. [25]If one person sins against another, God[c] may mediate for the offender; but if anyone sins against the Lord, who will intercede for them?" His sons, however, did not listen to their father's rebuke, for it was the Lord's will to put them to death.

[26]And the boy Samuel continued to grow in stature and in favor with the Lord and with people.

Prophecy Against the House of Eli

[27]Now a man of God came to Eli and said to him, "This is what the Lord says: 'Did I not clearly reveal myself to your ancestor's family when they were in Egypt under Pharaoh? [28]I chose your ancestor out of all the tribes of Israel to be my priest, to go up to my altar, to burn incense, and to wear an ephod in my presence. I also gave your ancestor's family all the food offerings presented by the Israelites. [29]Why do you[d] scorn my sacrifice and offering that I prescribed for my dwelling? Why do you honor your sons more than me by fattening yourselves on the choice parts of every offering made by my people Israel?'

[30]"Therefore the Lord, the God of Israel, declares: 'I promised that members of your family would minister before me forever.' But now the Lord declares: 'Far be it from me! Those who honor me I will honor, but those who despise me will be disdained. [31]The time is coming when I will cut short your strength and the strength of your priestly house, so that no one in it will reach old age, [32]and you will see distress in my dwelling. Although good will be done to Israel, no one in your family line will ever reach old age. [33]Every one of you that I do not cut off from serving at my altar I will spare only to destroy your sight and sap your strength, and all your descendants will die in the prime of life.

[34]"'And what happens to your two sons,

Eli's Leadership: Success as a Priest, Not as a Parent

1 Samuel 2:12–17, 22–36

Eli's failure to lead his family eventually led to his downfall as a religious leader. This revered judge in Israel failed to discipline his two sons and ended up rearing spiritual rebels. Eli lost his credibility, his job, and eventually his life.

The Scripture teaches that if we do not faithfully lead our own household, we lack the qualifications to lead beyond the home (1Ti 3:4–5)—in other words, if it doesn't work at home, don't export it.

How could a priest like Eli miss the mark? By making some crucial errors.

1. **Emphasis:** Eli emphasized teaching his colleagues and clients, not his family.

2. **Expectation:** Eli thought his sons would "get it" just because they lived in the house of the Lord.

3. **Example:** Eli failed to live out in his home what he taught in his work.

4. **Entanglements:** Eli got so caught up with his profession, he blinded himself to his failure.

---

[a] 17 Dead Sea Scrolls and Septuagint; Masoretic Text *people*
[b] 20 Dead Sea Scrolls; Masoretic Text *and asked from*
[c] 25 Or *the judges*   [d] 29 The Hebrew is plural.

Hophni and Phinehas, will be a sign to you —
they will both die on the same day. ³⁵I will raise
up for myself a faithful priest, who will do according to what is in my heart and mind. I will
firmly establish his priestly house, and they will
minister before my anointed one always. ³⁶Then
everyone left in your family line will come and
bow down before him for a piece of silver and
a loaf of bread and plead, "Appoint me to some
priestly office so I can have food to eat." ' "

The LORD Calls Samuel

3 The boy Samuel ministered before the LORD
under Eli. In those days the word of the
LORD was rare; there were not many visions.

²One night Eli, whose eyes were becoming so
weak that he could barely see, was lying down
in his usual place. ³The lamp of God had not
yet gone out, and Samuel was lying down in the
house of the LORD, where the ark of God was.
⁴Then the LORD called Samuel.

Samuel answered, "Here I am." ⁵And he ran
to Eli and said, "Here I am; you called me."

But Eli said, "I did not call; go back and lie
down." So he went and lay down.

⁶Again the LORD called, "Samuel!" And Samuel got up and went to Eli and said, "Here I am;
you called me."

"My son," Eli said, "I did not call; go back and
lie down."

⁷Now Samuel did not yet know the LORD: The
word of the LORD had not yet been revealed to him.

⁸A third time the LORD called, "Samuel!" And
Samuel got up and went to Eli and said, "Here I
am; you called me."

Then Eli realized that the LORD was calling
the boy. ⁹So Eli told Samuel, "Go and lie down,
and if he calls you, say, 'Speak, LORD, for your
servant is listening.' " So Samuel went and lay
down in his place.

¹⁰The LORD came and stood there, calling as
at the other times, "Samuel! Samuel!"

Then Samuel said, "Speak, for your servant is
listening."

¹¹And the LORD said to Samuel: "See, I am
about to do something in Israel that will make
the ears of everyone who hears about it tingle.
¹²At that time I will carry out against Eli everything I spoke against his family — from beginning to end. ¹³For I told him that I would judge
his family forever because of the sin he knew
about; his sons blasphemed God,ᵃ and he failed
to restrain them. ¹⁴Therefore I swore to the
house of Eli, 'The guilt of Eli's house will never
be atoned for by sacrifice or offering.' "

Samuel Learns to Listen to and Speak for God

1 Samuel 3:1–3

Samuel teaches us that we hear from God through:

- **Proper Practice:** Samuel was already obeying all he knew (v. 1).
- **Proper Position:** Samuel lay quiet and still and removed all distractions (v. 3).
- **Proper Proximity:** Samuel lived in the presence of God (v. 3).

¹⁵Samuel lay down until morning and then
opened the doors of the house of the LORD. He
was afraid to tell Eli the vision, ¹⁶but Eli called
him and said, "Samuel, my son."

Samuel answered, "Here I am."

¹⁷"What was it he said to you?" Eli asked. "Do
not hide it from me. May God deal with you, be
it ever so severely, if you hide from me anything
he told you." ¹⁸So Samuel told him everything,
hiding nothing from him. Then Eli said, "He is
the LORD; let him do what is good in his eyes."

¹⁹The LORD was with Samuel as he grew up,
and he let none of Samuel's words fall to the
ground. ²⁰And all Israel from Dan to Beersheba
recognized that Samuel was attested as a prophet of the LORD. ²¹The LORD continued to appear
at Shiloh, and there he revealed himself to Samuel through his word.

4 And Samuel's word came to all Israel.

The Philistines Capture the Ark

Now the Israelites went out to fight against
the Philistines. The Israelites camped at Ebenezer, and the Philistines at Aphek. ²The Philistines deployed their forces to meet Israel, and
as the battle spread, Israel was defeated by the
Philistines, who killed about four thousand of
them on the battlefield. ³When the soldiers returned to camp, the elders of Israel asked, "Why
did the LORD bring defeat on us today before the
Philistines? Let us bring the ark of the LORD's
covenant from Shiloh, so that he may go with us
and save us from the hand of our enemies."

⁴So the people sent men to Shiloh, and they
brought back the ark of the covenant of the LORD

ᵃ 13 An ancient Hebrew scribal tradition (see also Septuagint);
Masoretic Text *sons made themselves contemptible*

Almighty, who is enthroned between the cherubim. And Eli's two sons, Hophni and Phinehas, were there with the ark of the covenant of God.

⁵When the ark of the LORD's covenant came into the camp, all Israel raised such a great shout that the ground shook. ⁶Hearing the uproar, the Philistines asked, "What's all this shouting in the Hebrew camp?"

When they learned that the ark of the LORD had come into the camp, ⁷the Philistines were afraid. "A god has[a] come into the camp," they said. "Oh no! Nothing like this has happened before. ⁸We're doomed! Who will deliver us from the hand of these mighty gods? They are the gods who struck the Egyptians with all kinds of plagues in the wilderness. ⁹Be strong, Philistines! Be men, or you will be subject to the Hebrews, as they have been to you. Be men, and fight!"

¹⁰So the Philistines fought, and the Israelites were defeated and every man fled to his tent. The slaughter was very great; Israel lost thirty thousand foot soldiers. ¹¹The ark of God was captured, and Eli's two sons, Hophni and Phinehas, died.

Death of Eli

¹²That same day a Benjamite ran from the battle line and went to Shiloh with his clothes torn and dust on his head. ¹³When he arrived, there was Eli sitting on his chair by the side of the road, watching, because his heart feared for the ark of God. When the man entered the town and told what had happened, the whole town sent up a cry.

¹⁴Eli heard the outcry and asked, "What is the meaning of this uproar?"

The man hurried over to Eli, ¹⁵who was ninety-eight years old and whose eyes had failed so that he could not see. ¹⁶He told Eli, "I have just come from the battle line; I fled from it this very day."

Eli asked, "What happened, my son?"

¹⁷The man who brought the news replied, "Israel fled before the Philistines, and the army has suffered heavy losses. Also your two sons, Hophni and Phinehas, are dead, and the ark of God has been captured."

¹⁸When he mentioned the ark of God, Eli fell backward off his chair by the side of the gate. His neck was broken and he died, for he was an old man, and he was heavy. He had led[b] Israel forty years.

¹⁹His daughter-in-law, the wife of Phinehas, was pregnant and near the time of delivery. When she heard the news that the ark of God had been captured and that her father-in-law and her husband were dead, she went into labor and gave birth, but was overcome by her labor pains. ²⁰As she was dying, the women attending her said, "Don't despair; you have given birth to

---

[a] 7 Or "Gods have (see Septuagint)   [b] 18 Traditionally judged

SAMUEL — A Leader Who Learned to Listen
1 Samuel 3:1–21

PROFILE in leadership

All leaders need to learn to recognize the voice of God, even as young Samuel did. While he lay on the floor one night near the ark of God, the Lord called out to him, "Samuel! Samuel!" At first, Samuel heard but didn't recognize the Father's voice. He kept listening, however, and eventually he received word regarding a coming judgment against the priest Eli and his family.

Samuel spent a long and sleepless night, paralyzed with fear at the thought of repeating what God had told him. But Eli convinced Samuel it was far more dangerous to withhold the truth than to reveal what God had shown him (1Sa 3:17). So Samuel laid out the whole truth—and because of his obedience, God raised the young man up as a leader and prophet among his people (3:20).

Samuel is a great biblical example of godly leadership. He demonstrates that the man or woman who is fit to lead God's people is the one who has learned to hear his voice, heed his words, and speak his truth, no matter the earthly consequences.

God has never chosen his leaders based on their charisma or eloquence of speech. Rather, he looks for those with the courage to hear and speak exactly what he tells them.

a son." But she did not respond or pay any attention.

²¹She named the boy Ichabod,ᵃ saying, "The Glory has departed from Israel" — because of the capture of the ark of God and the deaths of her father-in-law and her husband. ²²She said, "The Glory has departed from Israel, for the ark of God has been captured."

The Ark in Ashdod and Ekron

5 After the Philistines had captured the ark of God, they took it from Ebenezer to Ashdod. ²Then they carried the ark into Dagon's temple and set it beside Dagon. ³When the people of Ashdod rose early the next day, there was Dagon, fallen on his face on the ground before the ark of the LORD! They took Dagon and put him back in his place. ⁴But the following morning when they rose, there was Dagon, fallen on his face on the ground before the ark of the LORD! His head and hands had been broken off and were lying on the threshold; only his body remained. ⁵That is why to this day neither the priests of Dagon nor any others who enter Dagon's temple at Ashdod step on the threshold.

⁶The LORD's hand was heavy on the people of Ashdod and its vicinity; he brought devastation on them and afflicted them with tumors.ᵇ ⁷When the people of Ashdod saw what was happening, they said, "The ark of the god of Israel must not stay here with us, because his hand is heavy on us and on Dagon our god." ⁸So they called together all the rulers of the Philistines and asked them, "What shall we do with the ark of the god of Israel?"

They answered, "Have the ark of the god of Israel moved to Gath." So they moved the ark of the God of Israel.

⁹But after they had moved it, the LORD's hand was against that city, throwing it into a great panic. He afflicted the people of the city, both young and old, with an outbreak of tumors.ᶜ ¹⁰So they sent the ark of God to Ekron.

As the ark of God was entering Ekron, the people of Ekron cried out, "They have brought the ark of the god of Israel around to us to kill us and our people." ¹¹So they called together all the rulers of the Philistines and said, "Send the ark of the god of Israel away; let it go back to its own place, or itᵈ will kill us and our people." For death had filled the city with panic; God's hand was very heavy on it. ¹²Those who did not die were afflicted with tumors, and the outcry of the city went up to heaven.

The Ark Returned to Israel

6 When the ark of the LORD had been in Philistine territory seven months, ²the Philistines called for the priests and the diviners and said, "What shall we do with the ark of the LORD? Tell us how we should send it back to its place."

³They answered, "If you return the ark of the god of Israel, do not send it back to him without a gift; by all means send a guilt offering to him. Then you will be healed, and you will know why his hand has not been lifted from you."

⁴The Philistines asked, "What guilt offering should we send to him?"

They replied, "Five gold tumors and five gold rats, according to the number of the Philistine rulers, because the same plague has struck both you and your rulers. ⁵Make models of the tumors and of the rats that are destroying the country, and give glory to Israel's god. Perhaps he will lift his hand from you and your gods and your land. ⁶Why do you harden your hearts as the Egyptians and Pharaoh did? When Israel's god dealt harshly with them, did they not send the Israelites out so they could go on their way?

⁷"Now then, get a new cart ready, with two cows that have calved and have never been yoked. Hitch the cows to the cart, but take their calves away and pen them up. ⁸Take the ark of the LORD and put it on the cart, and in a chest beside it put the gold objects you are sending back to him as a guilt offering. Send it on its way, ⁹but keep watching it. If it goes up to its own territory, toward Beth Shemesh, then the LORD has brought this great disaster on us. But if it does not, then we will know that it was not his hand that struck us but that it happened to us by chance."

¹⁰So they did this. They took two such cows and hitched them to the cart and penned up their calves. ¹¹They placed the ark of the LORD on the cart and along with it the chest containing the gold rats and the models of the tumors. ¹²Then the cows went straight up toward Beth Shemesh, keeping on the road and lowing all the way; they did not turn to the right or to the left. The rulers of the Philistines followed them as far as the border of Beth Shemesh.

¹³Now the people of Beth Shemesh were harvesting their wheat in the valley, and when they

---

ᵃ 21 Ichabod means no glory.   ᵇ 6 Hebrew; Septuagint and Vulgate tumors. And rats appeared in their land, and there was death and destruction throughout the city   ᶜ 9 Or with tumors in the groin (see Septuagint)   ᵈ 11 Or he

looked up and saw the ark, they rejoiced at the sight. [14]The cart came to the field of Joshua of Beth Shemesh, and there it stopped beside a large rock. The people chopped up the wood of the cart and sacrificed the cows as a burnt offering to the LORD. [15]The Levites took down the ark of the LORD, together with the chest containing the gold objects, and placed them on the large rock. On that day the people of Beth Shemesh offered burnt offerings and made sacrifices to the LORD. [16]The five rulers of the Philistines saw all this and then returned that same day to Ekron.

[17]These are the gold tumors the Philistines sent as a guilt offering to the LORD — one each for Ashdod, Gaza, Ashkelon, Gath and Ekron. [18]And the number of the gold rats was according to the number of Philistine towns belonging to the five rulers — the fortified towns with their country villages. The large rock on which the Levites set the ark of the LORD is a witness to this day in the field of Joshua of Beth Shemesh.

[19]But God struck down some of the inhabitants of Beth Shemesh, putting seventy[a] of them to death because they looked into the ark of the LORD. The people mourned because of the heavy blow the LORD had dealt them. [20]And the people of Beth Shemesh asked, "Who can stand in the presence of the LORD, this holy God? To whom will the ark go up from here?"

[21]Then they sent messengers to the people of Kiriath Jearim, saying, "The Philistines have returned the ark of the LORD. Come down and take it up to your town." [1]So the men of Kiriath Jearim came and took up the ark of the LORD. They brought it to Abinadab's house on the hill and consecrated Eleazar his son to guard the ark of the LORD. [2]The ark remained at Kiriath Jearim a long time — twenty years in all.

Samuel Subdues the Philistines at Mizpah

Then all the people of Israel turned back to the LORD. [3]So Samuel said to all the Israelites, "If you are returning to the LORD with all your hearts, then rid yourselves of the foreign gods and the Ashtoreths and commit yourselves to the LORD and serve him only, and he will deliver you out of the hand of the Philistines." [4]So the

---

[a] 19 A few Hebrew manuscripts; most Hebrew manuscripts and Septuagint 50,070

Samuel's Influence: One Person with Courage Makes a Majority

1 Samuel 7:1–17

It didn't take long for the Israelites to get a taste of the leadership of their new judge and prophet, Samuel. The prophet's influence grew daily. When the people trusted him, they were delivered from the Philistines, saw the ark returned to their land, and enjoyed peace in the land. He became by far the most influential leader of his day.

But how did he gain such influence? What made everyone listen to him? At least three indispensable qualities gained him the influence he won:

1. Competence
God blessed Samuel with many gifts. He heard from the Lord, he could see the future unfold, and he wisely knew what to do in crisis. His abilities provided one reason that everyone listened to him.

2. Character
Unlike Eli, Samuel exuded integrity and honestly faced each area of his life. People trusted him and knew that he had Israel's best interests in mind. They considered Samuel utterly trustworthy and depended upon him to intercede for them with God.

3. Connection
Samuel knew how to connect with people; he spoke their language. He expressed compassion for their predicaments and brought courage to their pursuits.

Fortunately for us, the formula for Samuel's success still works today:

Competence + Character + Connection = Influence

Israelites put away their Baals and Ashtoreths, and served the LORD only. 5Then Samuel said, "Assemble all Israel at Mizpah, and I will intercede with the LORD for you." 6When they had assembled at Mizpah, they drew water and poured it out before the LORD. On that day they fasted and there they confessed, "We have sinned against the LORD." Now Samuel was serving as leader[a] of Israel at Mizpah.

7When the Philistines heard that Israel had assembled at Mizpah, the rulers of the Philistines came up to attack them. When the Israelites heard of it, they were afraid because of the Philistines. 8They said to Samuel, "Do not stop crying out to the LORD our God for us, that he may rescue us from the hand of the Philistines." 9Then Samuel took a suckling lamb and sacrificed it as a whole burnt offering to the LORD. He cried out to the LORD on Israel's behalf, and the LORD answered him.

10While Samuel was sacrificing the burnt offering, the Philistines drew near to engage Israel in battle. But that day the LORD thundered with loud thunder against the Philistines and threw them into such a panic that they were routed before the Israelites. 11The men of Israel rushed out of Mizpah and pursued the Philistines, slaughtering them along the way to a point below Beth Kar.

12Then Samuel took a stone and set it up between Mizpah and Shen. He named it Ebenezer,[b] saying, "Thus far the LORD has helped us."

13So the Philistines were subdued and they stopped invading Israel's territory. Throughout Samuel's lifetime, the hand of the LORD was against the Philistines. 14The towns from Ekron to Gath that the Philistines had captured from Israel were restored to Israel, and Israel delivered the neighboring territory from the hands of the Philistines. And there was peace between Israel and the Amorites.

15Samuel continued as Israel's leader all the days of his life. 16From year to year he went on a circuit from Bethel to Gilgal to Mizpah, judging Israel in all those places. 17But he always went back to Ramah, where his home was, and there he also held court for Israel. And he built an altar there to the LORD.

Israel Asks for a King

8 When Samuel grew old, he appointed his sons as Israel's leaders.[c] 2The name of his firstborn was Joel and the name of his second was Abijah, and they served at Beersheba. 3But

his sons did not follow his ways. They turned aside after dishonest gain and accepted bribes and perverted justice.

4So all the elders of Israel gathered together and came to Samuel at Ramah. 5They said to him, "You are old, and your sons do not follow your ways; now appoint a king to lead[d] us, such as all the other nations have."

Human Promotion Does Not Equal a Divine Call
1 Samuel 8:4-5

Samuel's sons had neither the character nor the calling of their dad; the people wanted nothing to do with them. Their lack of credibility moved the nation to request a king! Yet a human verdict does not equal a divine calling—especially when it comes to leadership.

6But when they said, "Give us a king to lead us," this displeased Samuel; so he prayed to the LORD. 7And the LORD told him: "Listen to all that the people are saying to you; it is not you they have rejected, but they have rejected me as their king. 8As they have done from the day I brought them up out of Egypt until this day, forsaking me and serving other gods, so they are doing to you. 9Now listen to them; but warn them solemnly and let them know what the king who will reign over them will claim as his rights."

10Samuel told all the words of the LORD to the people who were asking him for a king. 11He said, "This is what the king who will reign over you will claim as his rights: He will take your sons and make them serve with his chariots and horses, and they will run in front of his chariots. 12Some he will assign to be commanders of thousands and commanders of fifties, and others to plow his ground and reap his harvest, and still others to make weapons of war and equipment for his chariots. 13He will take your daughters to be perfumers and cooks and bakers. 14He will take the best of your fields and vineyards and olive groves and give them to his attendants. 15He will take a tenth of your grain and of your vintage and give it to his officials and

a 6 Traditionally judge; also in verse 15   b 12 Ebenezer means stone of help.   c 1 Traditionally judges   d 5 Traditionally judge; also in verses 6 and 20

attendants. [16]Your male and female servants and the best of your cattle[a] and donkeys he will take for his own use. [17]He will take a tenth of your flocks, and you yourselves will become his slaves. [18]When that day comes, you will cry out for relief from the king you have chosen, but the LORD will not answer you in that day."

[19]But the people refused to listen to Samuel. "No!" they said. "We want a king over us. [20]Then we will be like all the other nations, with a king to lead us and to go out before us and fight our battles."

[21]When Samuel heard all that the people said, he repeated it before the LORD. [22]The LORD answered, "Listen to them and give them a king."

Then Samuel said to the Israelites, "Everyone go back to your own town."

Samuel Anoints Saul

9 There was a Benjamite, a man of standing, whose name was Kish son of Abiel, the son of Zeror, the son of Bekorath, the son of Aphiah of Benjamin. [2]Kish had a son named Saul, as handsome a young man as could be found anywhere in Israel, and he was a head taller than anyone else.

[3]Now the donkeys belonging to Saul's father Kish were lost, and Kish said to his son Saul, "Take one of the servants with you and go and look for the donkeys." [4]So he passed through the hill country of Ephraim and through the area around Shalisha, but they did not find them. They went on into the district of Shaalim, but the donkeys were not there. Then he passed through the territory of Benjamin, but they did not find them.

[5]When they reached the district of Zuph, Saul said to the servant who was with him, "Come, let's go back, or my father will stop thinking about the donkeys and start worrying about us."

[6]But the servant replied, "Look, in this town there is a man of God; he is highly respected, and everything he says comes true. Let's go there now. Perhaps he will tell us what way to take."

[7]Saul said to his servant, "If we go, what can we give the man? The food in our sacks is gone. We have no gift to take to the man of God. What do we have?"

[8]The servant answered him again. "Look," he said, "I have a quarter of a shekel[b] of silver. I will give it to the man of God so that he will tell us what way to take." [9](Formerly in Israel, if someone went to inquire of God, they would say,

"Come, let us go to the seer," because the prophet of today used to be called a seer.)

[10]"Good," Saul said to his servant. "Come, let's go." So they set out for the town where the man of God was.

[11]As they were going up the hill to the town, they met some young women coming out to draw water, and they asked them, "Is the seer here?"

[12]"He is," they answered. "He's ahead of you. Hurry now; he has just come to our town today, for the people have a sacrifice at the high place. [13]As soon as you enter the town, you will find him before he goes up to the high place to eat. The people will not begin eating until he comes, because he must bless the sacrifice; afterward, those who are invited will eat. Go up now; you should find him about this time."

[14]They went up to the town, and as they were entering it, there was Samuel, coming toward them on his way up to the high place.

[15]Now the day before Saul came, the LORD had revealed this to Samuel: [16]"About this time tomorrow I will send you a man from the land of Benjamin. Anoint him ruler over my people Israel; he will deliver them from the hand of the Philistines. I have looked on my people, for their cry has reached me."

[17]When Samuel caught sight of Saul, the LORD said to him, "This is the man I spoke to you about; he will govern my people."

[18]Saul approached Samuel in the gateway and asked, "Would you please tell me where the seer's house is?"

[19]"I am the seer," Samuel replied. "Go up ahead of me to the high place, for today you are to eat with me, and in the morning I will send you on your way and will tell you all that is in your heart. [20]As for the donkeys you lost three days ago, do not worry about them; they have been found. And to whom is all the desire of Israel turned, if not to you and your whole family line?"

[21]Saul answered, "But am I not a Benjamite, from the smallest tribe of Israel, and is not my clan the least of all the clans of the tribe of Benjamin? Why do you say such a thing to me?"

[22]Then Samuel brought Saul and his servant into the hall and seated them at the head of those who were invited—about thirty in number. [23]Samuel said to the cook, "Bring the piece of meat I gave you, the one I told you to lay aside."

---

[a] 16 Septuagint; Hebrew young men   [b] 8 That is, about 1/10 ounce or about 3 grams

²⁴So the cook took up the thigh with what was on it and set it in front of Saul. Samuel said, "Here is what has been kept for you. Eat, because it was set aside for you for this occasion from the time I said, 'I have invited guests.'" And Saul dined with Samuel that day.

²⁵After they came down from the high place to the town, Samuel talked with Saul on the roof of his house. ²⁶They rose about daybreak, and Samuel called to Saul on the roof, "Get ready, and I will send you on your way." When Saul got ready, he and Samuel went outside together. ²⁷As they were going down to the edge of the town, Samuel said to Saul, "Tell the servant to go on ahead of us"—and the servant did so—"but you stay here for a while, so that I may give you a message from God."

Strategic Partnerships: Ministry and Marketplace Leaders
How Saul and Samuel Partnered Together to Lead God's People
1 Samuel 9:1—15:31

The Scripture provides a marvelous picture of how pastors and business leaders can partner together to fulfill a God-given vision. First Samuel shows how God sovereignly uses both Samuel the priest (ministry leader) and Saul the king (marketplace leader).

Because he feels secure, Samuel is able to fulfill his role as spiritual leader to big and strong Saul. He finds his security in his divine call and in the One who called him, not in people. While Saul could be an intimidating, daunting leader (1Sa 9:2), Samuel does not envy Saul's role, nor can he be diverted from his work in Saul's life. Note the following observations regarding the partnership of these two in fulfilling God's plan.

1. ***Samuel could speak into Saul's life because he felt secure in his calling*** (9:17–19).
   While God told Samuel to anoint Saul as king, the prophet never considered the son of Kish to be a celebrity. Saul became king over Samuel—but Samuel never placed his security or emotional health in a mere man. With poise and confidence he said to Saul, "I am the seer." He then instructed Saul concerning the spiritual matters he would face as king.

2. ***Samuel affirmed Saul's complementary role and honored him for it*** (9:21–23).
   Although Samuel had been the visible leader in Israel, he intentionally gave away his status by publicly honoring Saul. He reserved special food for him and a special place at the table, so no one would question whom they were to follow.

3. ***Samuel took initiative and anointed Saul for the role he was to fulfill*** (10:1).
   Samuel didn't feel competition or envy over this new king; he knew that both would serve as leaders among God's people as complementary partners. As Coach Bill McCartney once said to some Promise Keeper speakers, "We are not here to compete with each other, but to complete each other."

4. ***Samuel helped Saul to receive a new heart for serving people*** (10:6–9).
   At this point Samuel had every reason to feel awkward or displaced; now Saul was doing the very thing Samuel had been gifted to do. But Samuel didn't resist helping Saul to develop into the spiritual leader God called him to be.

5. ***Samuel encouraged Saul to use his spiritual gifts*** (10:10–13).
   Samuel faithfully brought God's word to Saul. He prepared Saul to receive his spiritual gifts by explaining what would happen and when to look for it.

6. ***Samuel did not feel intimidated by or envious of Saul's conquests*** (13:8–13).
   Samuel allowed neither Saul's position as king nor his success as conqueror to move him. While Samuel affirmed the king, he also understood his role in Israel and in the king's life. Samuel confronted Saul's disobedience and clarified each of their roles.

7. ***Samuel spoke words of direction to Saul*** (15:1–3).
   Even after confronting Saul's disobedience, Samuel was able to provide direction for the king and

10 Then Samuel took a flask of olive oil and poured it on Saul's head and kissed him, saying, "Has not the LORD anointed you ruler over his inheritance?[a] 2When you leave me today, you will meet two men near Rachel's tomb, at Zelzah on the border of Benjamin. They will say to you, 'The donkeys you set out to look for have been found. And now your father has stopped

thinking about them and is worried about you. He is asking, "What shall I do about my son?"'

3"Then you will go on from there until you reach the great tree of Tabor. Three men going

---

[a] 1 Hebrew; Septuagint and Vulgate *over his people Israel? You will reign over the LORD's people and save them from the power of their enemies round about. And this will be a sign to you that the LORD has anointed you ruler over his inheritance:*

---

affirm his work on the battlefield. He didn't shrink from playing his role in Saul's life and again clarified Saul's place in the scheme of things. He furnished Saul with great confidence and support as he led the armies of Israel.

8. ***Samuel prayed and hurt for Saul when the king failed*** (15:10–11).
   Samuel grieved when God rejected the disobedient Saul. He knew that God intended great things for Saul—and the king's failure broke Samuel's heart. As Saul's spiritual leader, Samuel hurt for the king.

9. ***Samuel could confront Saul when he sinned and provide him perspective*** (15:12–23).
   Samuel felt called to continually provide the big-picture perspective to Saul and remind him of his roots, of God's call and mission. He offered an eternal perspective to the king and refused to let him try to do God's will in his own way.

10. ***Samuel possessed the spiritual credibility to call for repentance and worship from Saul*** (15:24–31).
    Samuel ministered to Saul with a beautiful combination of grace and truth. He spoke the truth in love, never out of spite or superiority. And when he returned with Saul, he did it not out of intimidation, but to leave Saul with as much dignity as possible.

What Every Pastor Should Know About These Partnerships

The Scripture illustrates the partnership role that ministry leaders and marketplace leaders can enjoy, if only they will work cooperatively.

1. *Samuel* illustrates the role of the *pastor* (the ministry leader). *Saul* illustrates the role of the *entrepreneur* (the marketplace leader).

2. The issue ministry leaders (pastors) must settle: *personal security*. The issue marketplace leaders (laymen) must settle: *personal submission*.

3. The pastor often envies the entrepreneur's *success* (the money). The entrepreneur often envies the pastor's *significance* (the mission).

4. Pastors must develop a *vision* big enough to attract entrepreneurs. Entrepreneurs must develop a *generous spirit* to enable pastors to fulfill it.

5. Pastors must include business leaders in *decisions* so they can own the ministry. Entrepreneurs must include pastors in both their *checkbook* and *calendar*.

6. Pastors must give the *church's ministry* to entrepreneurs/marketplace leaders. Entrepreneurs must give their *spiritual gifts* to the church's ministry.

7. Pastors fail in this partnership because they feel *intimidated*. Entrepreneurs fail in this partnership because they feel *independent*.

8. Pastors can offer one thing that entrepreneurs want most: *fulfillment*. Entrepreneurs can offer one thing that pastors need most: *resources*.

21 QUALITIES

COMMUNICATION
Samuel and the Importance of Clear Communication

1 Samuel 10:3—12:25

DR. J. ROBERT CLINTON did a formal study of Christian leaders and discovered that, without exception, all of them possessed word gifts: teaching, prophecy, evangelism, preaching, words of knowledge or wisdom, exhortation, etc. More than anything else, they used their gifts of communication to lead their people.

Peter Drucker, the father of American management, believes that 60 percent of all management problems result from faulty communication. Having a message doesn't matter if leaders don't communicate clearly and motivate others.

It is amazing how God wired us. We can listen to a leader flap his gums for 30 minutes, flinging thoughts and ideas about the room. He just talks, opens his mouth to make a few sounds—and yet we want to get up and pursue those ideas.

This is the power of communication. Proverbs 18:21 tells us, "The tongue has the power of life and death."

During his day, Samuel was Mr. Communication. Everyone listened to him. What kind of communicator was he? Look at the following examples:

1. **He spoke words of revelation** (7:3). His communication contained divine revelation, insights the people lacked.
2. **He spoke words of inspiration** (10:3–6). His communication inspired Saul to overcome his fears and step out.
3. **He spoke words of exhortation** (10:24). His communication encouraged the people to act and follow Saul as their new king.
4. **He spoke words of affirmation** (10:24). His communication affirmed, supported, and endorsed Saul publicly.
5. **He spoke words of information** (10:25). His communication overflowed with good content, edifying and teaching others.
6. **He spoke words of declaration** (12:20–25). His communication gave clear direction to the people and hope for their future.

How Did He Do It?

Each time Samuel spoke, he followed the rules below:

1. **Simplify the message.** He spoke forthrightly, clearly, and simply. No one wondered what he meant.
2. **See the person.** He always empathized with others. He knew his audience.
3. **Show the truth.** He demonstrated credibility with his passion and his life. He lived what he said.
4. **Seek the response.** He always spoke with a purpose. When finished, he urged the people to obey God.

For a negative example of communication, see p. 5.

up to worship God at Bethel will meet you there. One will be carrying three young goats, another three loaves of bread, and another a skin of wine. ⁴They will greet you and offer you two loaves of bread, which you will accept from them.

⁵"After that you will go to Gibeah of God, where there is a Philistine outpost. As you approach the town, you will meet a procession of prophets coming down from the high place with lyres, timbrels, pipes and harps being played before them, and they will be prophesying. ⁶The Spirit of the LORD will come powerfully upon you, and you will prophesy with them; and you will be changed into a different person. ⁷Once these signs are fulfilled, do whatever your hand finds to do, for God is with you.

⁸"Go down ahead of me to Gilgal. I will surely come down to you to sacrifice burnt offerings and fellowship offerings, but you must wait seven days until I come to you and tell you what you are to do."

Saul Made King

⁹As Saul turned to leave Samuel, God changed Saul's heart, and all these signs were fulfilled that day. ¹⁰When he and his servant arrived at Gibeah, a procession of prophets met him; the Spirit of God came powerfully upon him, and he joined in their prophesying. ¹¹When all those who had formerly known him saw him prophesying with the prophets, they asked each other, "What is this that has happened to the son of Kish? Is Saul also among the prophets?"

¹²A man who lived there answered, "And who is their father?" So it became a saying: "Is Saul also among the prophets?" ¹³After Saul stopped prophesying, he went to the high place.

¹⁴Now Saul's uncle asked him and his servant, "Where have you been?"

"Looking for the donkeys," he said. "But when we saw they were not to be found, we went to Samuel."

¹⁵Saul's uncle said, "Tell me what Samuel said to you."

¹⁶Saul replied, "He assured us that the donkeys had been found." But he did not tell his uncle what Samuel had said about the kingship.

¹⁷Samuel summoned the people of Israel to the LORD at Mizpah ¹⁸and said to them, "This is what the LORD, the God of Israel, says: 'I brought Israel up out of Egypt, and I delivered you from the power of Egypt and all the kingdoms that oppressed you.' ¹⁹But you have now rejected your God, who saves you out of all your disasters and calamities. And you have said, 'No, appoint a king over us.' So now present yourselves before the LORD by your tribes and clans."

²⁰When Samuel had all Israel come forward by tribes, the tribe of Benjamin was taken by lot. ²¹Then he brought forward the tribe of Benjamin, clan by clan, and Matri's clan was taken. Finally Saul son of Kish was taken. But when they looked for him, he was not to be found. ²²So they inquired further of the LORD, "Has the man come here yet?"

And the LORD said, "Yes, he has hidden himself among the supplies."

²³They ran and brought him out, and as he stood among the people he was a head taller than any of the others. ²⁴Samuel said to all the people, "Do you see the man the LORD has chosen? There is no one like him among all the people."

Then the people shouted, "Long live the king!"

²⁵Samuel explained to the people the rights and duties of kingship. He wrote them down on a scroll and deposited it before the LORD. Then Samuel dismissed the people to go to their own homes.

²⁶Saul also went to his home in Gibeah, accompanied by valiant men whose hearts God had touched. ²⁷But some scoundrels said, "How can this fellow save us?" They despised him and brought him no gifts. But Saul kept silent.

Saul Rescues the City of Jabesh

11 Nahash[a] the Ammonite went up and besieged Jabesh Gilead. And all the men of Jabesh said to him, "Make a treaty with us, and we will be subject to you."

²But Nahash the Ammonite replied, "I will make a treaty with you only on the condition that I gouge out the right eye of every one of you and so bring disgrace on all Israel."

³The elders of Jabesh said to him, "Give us seven days so we can send messengers throughout Israel; if no one comes to rescue us, we will surrender to you."

⁴When the messengers came to Gibeah of Saul and reported these terms to the people, they all wept aloud. ⁵Just then Saul was returning

a 1 Masoretic Text; Dead Sea Scrolls gifts. Now Nahash king of the Ammonites oppressed the Gadites and Reubenites severely. He gouged out all their right eyes and struck terror and dread in Israel. Not a man remained among the Israelites beyond the Jordan whose right eye was not gouged out by Nahash king of the Ammonites, except that seven thousand men fled from the Ammonites and entered Jabesh Gilead. About a month later, ¹Nahash

21 QUALITIES

COURAGE   The One Item Saul Forgot to Pack

1 Samuel 10:17—13:14

ALTHOUGH SAUL became king chiefly through his striking appearance, he never won the inward battles. On the outside, he was tall, good-looking and well-built (1Sa 9:2). On the inside, however, he amounted to little more than a shrimp. Observe the leadership of Saul:

1. When the time arrives to anoint Saul as king, he hides among the baggage.

2. When Samuel asks Saul to lead, he excuses himself as unable.

3. When Saul's soldiers begin to scatter, he panics and disobeys his divine orders.

4. When confronted over his sin, Saul makes excuses for himself.

5. When Saul attacks the Amalekites, he is afraid to trust God and destroy the enemy.

6. When Saul fears losing the allegiance of the people, he builds a statue of himself.

7. When the Philistines face Israel, Saul's fear prevents him from negotiating.

8. When David gains popularity, Saul's insecurity drives him to attempted murder.

Lessons from Saul

- *Courage and cowardice are both contagious.*
  When Goliath challenged Saul's men, they fled to their tents; when David's men faced vastly superior forces, they stood their ground, fought . . . and won (2Sa 23:8–12).

- *Without courage, it doesn't matter how good your intentions are.*
  Saul had good intentions when he presented burnt offerings to the Lord. But he let his fear that the people would desert him control his actions (1Sa 13:13–14).

- *Only courage allows you to do what you are afraid of doing.*
  Saul showed his lack of courage from the beginning, when he hid among the baggage to avoid becoming king (1Sa 10:22).

- *Without courage, we're slaves of our own insecurity and possessiveness.*
  King Saul momentarily repented on several occasions when confronted about his repeated attempts to kill David. But later, captive to his fears and insecurities, he always resumed his evil pursuit.

- *If the leader lacks courage, the people will lack commitment.*
  Contrary to God's command, Saul

and the people spared the best of the livestock they captured from the Amalekites. Saul let it happen because, as he admitted, "I was afraid of the men and so I gave in to them" (1Sa 15:24).

- **A leader without courage will never let go of the familiar.**
  Saul employed a medium to ask counsel of Samuel's departed spirit—in direct violation of God's law (1Sa 28:5–20). He lacked the courage to trust God to help him step into an unknown future.

- **Lack of courage will eventually sabotage a leader.**
  Saul's lack of courage eventually cost him not only the throne of Israel, but also his own life and the life of his faithful son, Jonathan (1Sa 31:1–6).

For a positive example of courage, see p. 435.

from the fields, behind his oxen, and he asked, "What is wrong with everyone? Why are they weeping?" Then they repeated to him what the men of Jabesh had said.

[6]When Saul heard their words, the Spirit of God came powerfully upon him, and he burned with anger. [7]He took a pair of oxen, cut them into pieces, and sent the pieces by messengers throughout Israel, proclaiming, "This is what will be done to the oxen of anyone who does not follow Saul and Samuel." Then the terror of the LORD fell on the people, and they came out together as one. [8]When Saul mustered them at Bezek, the men of Israel numbered three hundred thousand and those of Judah thirty thousand.

[9]They told the messengers who had come, "Say to the men of Jabesh Gilead, 'By the time the sun is hot tomorrow, you will be rescued.'" When the messengers went and reported this to the men of Jabesh, they were elated. [10]They said to the Ammonites, "Tomorrow we will surrender to you, and you can do to us whatever you like."

[11]The next day Saul separated his men into three divisions; during the last watch of the night they broke into the camp of the Ammonites and slaughtered them until the heat of the day. Those who survived were scattered, so that no two of them were left together.

Saul Confirmed as King

[12]The people then said to Samuel, "Who was it that asked, 'Shall Saul reign over us?' Turn these men over to us so that we may put them to death."

[13]But Saul said, "No one will be put to death today, for this day the LORD has rescued Israel."

[14]Then Samuel said to the people, "Come, let us go to Gilgal and there renew the kingship." [15]So all the people went to Gilgal and made Saul king in the presence of the LORD. There they sacrificed fellowship offerings before the LORD, and Saul and all the Israelites held a great celebration.

Samuel's Farewell Speech

12 Samuel said to all Israel, "I have listened to everything you said to me and have set a king over you. [2]Now you have a king as your leader. As for me, I am old and gray, and my sons are here with you. I have been your leader from my youth until this day. [3]Here I stand. Testify against me in the presence of the LORD and his anointed. Whose ox have I taken? Whose donkey have I taken? Whom have I cheated? Whom have I oppressed? From whose hand have I accepted a bribe to make me shut my eyes? If I have done any of these things, I will make it right."

[4]"You have not cheated or oppressed us," they replied. "You have not taken anything from anyone's hand."

[5]Samuel said to them, "The LORD is witness against you, and also his anointed is witness this day, that you have not found anything in my hand."

"He is witness," they said.

[6]Then Samuel said to the people, "It is the LORD who appointed Moses and Aaron and brought your ancestors up out of Egypt. [7]Now then, stand here, because I am going to confront you with evidence before the LORD as to all the righteous acts performed by the LORD for you and your ancestors.

[8]"After Jacob entered Egypt, they cried to the LORD for help, and the LORD sent Moses and Aaron, who brought your ancestors out of Egypt and settled them in this place.

[9]"But they forgot the LORD their God; so he sold them into the hand of Sisera, the commander of the army of Hazor, and into the hands of the Philistines and the king of Moab, who fought against them. [10]They cried out to the LORD and said, 'We have sinned; we have forsaken the LORD and served the Baals and the Ashtoreths. But now deliver us from the hands of our enemies, and we will serve you.' [11]Then the LORD sent Jerub-Baal,[a] Barak,[b] Jephthah and Samuel,[c] and he delivered you from the hands of your enemies all around you, so that you lived in safety.

[12]"But when you saw that Nahash king of the Ammonites was moving against you, you said to me, 'No, we want a king to rule over us' — even though the LORD your God was your king. [13]Now here is the king you have chosen, the one you asked for; see, the LORD has set a king over you. [14]If you fear the LORD and serve and obey him and do not rebel against his commands, and if both you and the king who reigns over you follow the LORD your God — good! [15]But if you do not obey the LORD, and if you rebel against his commands, his hand will be against you, as it was against your ancestors.

[16]"Now then, stand still and see this great thing the LORD is about to do before your eyes! [17]Is it not wheat harvest now? I will call on the

---

[a] 11 Also called Gideon [b] 11 Some Septuagint manuscripts and Syriac; Hebrew Bedan [c] 11 Hebrew; some Septuagint manuscripts and Syriac Samson

LORD to send thunder and rain. And you will realize what an evil thing you did in the eyes of the LORD when you asked for a king."

[18] Then Samuel called on the LORD, and that same day the LORD sent thunder and rain. So all the people stood in awe of the LORD and of Samuel.

[19] The people all said to Samuel, "Pray to the LORD your God for your servants so that we will not die, for we have added to all our other sins the evil of asking for a king."

[20] "Do not be afraid," Samuel replied. "You have done all this evil; yet do not turn away from the LORD, but serve the LORD with all your heart. [21] Do not turn away after useless idols. They can do you no good, nor can they rescue you, because they are useless. [22] For the sake of his great name the LORD will not reject his people, because the LORD was pleased to make you his own. [23] As for me, far be it from me that I should sin against the LORD by failing to pray for you. And I will teach you the way that is good and right. [24] But be sure to fear the LORD and serve him faithfully with all your heart; consider what great things he has done for you. [25] Yet if you persist in doing evil, both you and your king will perish."

Samuel Rebukes Saul

13 Saul was thirty[a] years old when he became king, and he reigned over Israel forty-[b] two years.

[2] Saul chose three thousand men from Israel; two thousand were with him at Mikmash and in the hill country of Bethel, and a thousand were with Jonathan at Gibeah in Benjamin. The rest of the men he sent back to their homes.

[3] Jonathan attacked the Philistine outpost at Geba, and the Philistines heard about it. Then Saul had the trumpet blown throughout the land and said, "Let the Hebrews hear!" [4] So all Israel heard the news: "Saul has attacked the Philistine outpost, and now Israel has become obnoxious to the Philistines." And the people were summoned to join Saul at Gilgal.

[5] The Philistines assembled to fight Israel, with three thousand[c] chariots, six thousand charioteers, and soldiers as numerous as the sand on the seashore. They went up and camped at Mikmash, east of Beth Aven. [6] When the Israelites saw that their situation was critical and that their army was hard pressed, they hid in caves and thickets, among the rocks, and in pits and cisterns. [7] Some Hebrews even crossed the Jordan to the land of Gad and Gilead.

Saul remained at Gilgal, and all the troops with him were quaking with fear. [8] He waited seven days, the time set by Samuel; but Samuel did not come to Gilgal, and Saul's men began to scatter. [9] So he said, "Bring me the burnt offering and the fellowship offerings." And Saul offered up the burnt offering. [10] Just as he finished making the offering, Samuel arrived, and Saul went out to greet him.

[11] "What have you done?" asked Samuel.

Saul replied, "When I saw that the men were scattering, and that you did not come at the set time, and that the Philistines were assembling at Mikmash, [12] I thought, 'Now the Philistines will come down against me at Gilgal, and I have not sought the LORD's favor.' So I felt compelled to offer the burnt offering."

[13] "You have done a foolish thing," Samuel said. "You have not kept the command the LORD your God gave you; if you had, he would have established your kingdom over Israel for all time. [14] But now your kingdom will not endure; the LORD has sought out a man after his own heart and appointed him ruler of his people, because you have not kept the LORD's command."

[15] Then Samuel left Gilgal[d] and went up to Gibeah in Benjamin, and Saul counted the men who were with him. They numbered about six hundred.

Israel Without Weapons

[16] Saul and his son Jonathan and the men with them were staying in Gibeah[e] in Benjamin, while the Philistines camped at Mikmash. [17] Raiding parties went out from the Philistine camp in three detachments. One turned toward Ophrah in the vicinity of Shual, [18] another toward Beth Horon, and the third toward the borderland overlooking the Valley of Zeboyim facing the wilderness.

[19] Not a blacksmith could be found in the whole land of Israel, because the Philistines had said, "Otherwise the Hebrews will make swords or spears!" [20] So all Israel went down to the Philistines to have their plow points, mattocks, axes and sickles[f] sharpened. [21] The price

---

[a] 1 A few late manuscripts of the Septuagint; Hebrew does not have *thirty*.   [b] 1 Probable reading of the original Hebrew text (see Acts 13:21); Masoretic Text does not have *forty-*.
[c] 5 Some Septuagint manuscripts and Syriac; Hebrew *thirty thousand*   [d] 15 Hebrew; Septuagint *Gilgal and went his way; the rest of the people went after Saul to meet the army, and they went out of Gilgal*   [e] 16 Two Hebrew manuscripts; most Hebrew manuscripts *Geba*, a variant of *Gibeah*
[f] 20 Septuagint; Hebrew *plow points*

Samuel: The Most Influential Leader of His Day

1 Samuel 12–13

Have you ever wondered what gave Samuel such credibility with others? When he spoke, people listened.

Few descriptions offer a greater compliment than the one given to Samuel's leadership in 1 Samuel 3:19–20: "The LORD was with Samuel as he grew up, and he let none of Samuel's words fall to the ground. And all Israel from Dan to Beersheba recognized that Samuel was attested as a prophet of the LORD."

Samuel's success began when he was just a boy, under his mentor, Eli. God spoke to Samuel during the night; then the lad spoke for God to Eli (1Sa 3:11–18). Despite the hardness of God's message to Eli, Samuel spoke the truth in love. This encounter began a long pattern for Samuel.

Soon, the Israelites sought out Samuel to speak words of direction for their future. They needed help to retrieve the ark of the covenant. They needed strategy against their enemy, the Philistines. They eventually sought his permission to crown a king, like the other nations around them.

The influence of the prophet just kept growing. It grew so vast that when King Saul failed in his leadership, Samuel removed him. Imagine, having the sole authority to kick out even the reigning king! Samuel lived long enough to give the Israelites two kings. Samuel exhorted, he affirmed, he corrected, he prophesied, he reminded, and he taught the people. When he died, all of Israel gathered to mourn his loss (25:1). Indeed, this was a man of impact!

Images of Leadership from Samuel's Life

1. Shepherd

The key descriptive word here is *relationships*. The Bible loves to describe God's leaders as shepherds. Even the Lord is described as a shepherd (Ps 23; Jn 10:11). A shepherd knows, loves, protects, and leads his sheep. Samuel drew from this imagery. He spoke out of relationship. He identified with the people and could be both tough and tender because of this relationship. People listened because of relationship.

2. Steward

The key word here is *responsibility*. A steward acts on behalf of an owner, overseeing others and managing possessions. Stewards are accountable to the owner. Jesus taught this principle in Luke 12:42–48. Samuel lived this truth as he confronted kings and peasants, as he wept over the disobedience of Israel, and as he sought guidance for his nation. He remained faithful to his calling, accountable to God, and responsible to people. That is why they listened.

3. Seer

The key word here is *revelation*. Leaders must possess a vision and communicate fresh direction to the people. Samuel, like other Old Testament prophets, brought the word of God to bear on contemporary issues. He spoke with divine conviction about past lessons, present situations, and future direction. He moved from being merely a judge to becoming a prophet, speaking with skill as a visionary leader. People listened because of his revelation.

4. Servant

The key word here is *rights*. A biblically informed leader gives up his rights instead of gaining them when he reaches the top. Leaders sacrifice for the good of the people they lead. Samuel modeled this as he interceded for Israel, as he made sacrifices on the altar on their behalf, and as he wept for their welfare. Power did not motivate him, but service. People listened because of his servant's heart.

was two-thirds of a shekel[a] for sharpening plow points and mattocks, and a third of a shekel[b] for sharpening forks and axes and for repointing goads.

[22]So on the day of the battle not a soldier with Saul and Jonathan had a sword or spear in his hand; only Saul and his son Jonathan had them.

Jonathan Attacks the Philistines

[23]Now a detachment of Philistines had gone out to the pass at Mikmash. [1]One day Jonathan son of Saul said to his young armor-bearer, "Come, let's go over to the Philistine outpost on the other side." But he did not tell his father.

[2]Saul was staying on the outskirts of Gibeah under a pomegranate tree in Migron. With him were about six hundred men, [3]among whom was Ahijah, who was wearing an ephod. He was a son of Ichabod's brother Ahitub son of Phinehas, the son of Eli, the LORD's priest in Shiloh. No one was aware that Jonathan had left.

[4]On each side of the pass that Jonathan intended to cross to reach the Philistine outpost was a cliff; one was called Bozez and the other Seneh. [5]One cliff stood to the north toward Mikmash, the other to the south toward Geba.

[6]Jonathan said to his young armor-bearer, "Come, let's go over to the outpost of those uncircumcised men. Perhaps the LORD will act in our behalf. Nothing can hinder the LORD from saving, whether by many or by few."

[7]"Do all that you have in mind," his armor-bearer said. "Go ahead; I am with you heart and soul."

[8]Jonathan said, "Come on, then; we will cross over toward them and let them see us. [9]If they say to us, 'Wait there until we come to you,' we will stay where we are and not go up to them. [10]But if they say, 'Come up to us,' we will climb up, because that will be our sign that the LORD has given them into our hands."

[11]So both of them showed themselves to the Philistine outpost. "Look!" said the Philistines. "The Hebrews are crawling out of the holes they were hiding in." [12]The men of the outpost shouted to Jonathan and his armor-bearer, "Come up to us and we'll teach you a lesson."

So Jonathan said to his armor-bearer, "Climb up after me; the LORD has given them into the hand of Israel."

[13]Jonathan climbed up, using his hands and feet, with his armor-bearer right behind him. The Philistines fell before Jonathan, and his armor-bearer followed and killed behind him. [14]In that first attack Jonathan and his armor-bearer killed some twenty men in an area of about half an acre.

Israel Routs the Philistines

[15]Then panic struck the whole army—those in the camp and field, and those in the outposts and raiding parties—and the ground shook. It was a panic sent by God.[c]

[16]Saul's lookouts at Gibeah in Benjamin saw the army melting away in all directions. [17]Then Saul said to the men who were with him, "Muster the forces and see who has left us." When they did, it was Jonathan and his armor-bearer who were not there.

[18]Saul said to Ahijah, "Bring the ark of God." (At that time it was with the Israelites.)[d] [19]While Saul was talking to the priest, the tumult in the Philistine camp increased more and more. So Saul said to the priest, "Withdraw your hand."

[20]Then Saul and all his men assembled and went to the battle. They found the Philistines in total confusion, striking each other with their swords. [21]Those Hebrews who had previously been with the Philistines and had gone up with them to their camp went over to the Israelites who were with Saul and Jonathan. [22]When all the Israelites who had hidden in the hill country of Ephraim heard that the Philistines were on the run, they joined the battle in hot pursuit. [23]So on that day the LORD saved Israel, and the battle moved on beyond Beth Aven.

Jonathan Eats Honey

[24]Now the Israelites were in distress that day, because Saul had bound the people under an oath, saying, "Cursed be anyone who eats food before evening comes, before I have avenged myself on my enemies!" So none of the troops tasted food.

[25]The entire army entered the woods, and there was honey on the ground. [26]When they went into the woods, they saw the honey oozing out; yet no one put his hand to his mouth, because they feared the oath. [27]But Jonathan had not heard that his father had bound the people with the oath, so he reached out the end of the staff that was in his hand and dipped it into the honeycomb. He raised his hand to his mouth, and his eyes brightened.[e] [28]Then one of the

---

[a] 21 That is, about 1/4 ounce or about 8 grams   [b] 21 That is, about 1/8 ounce or about 4 grams   [c] 15 Or a terrible panic   [d] 18 Hebrew; Septuagint "Bring the ephod." (At that time he wore the ephod before the Israelites.)   [e] 27 Or his strength was renewed; similarly in verse 29

soldiers told him, "Your father bound the army under a strict oath, saying, 'Cursed be anyone who eats food today!' That is why the men are faint."

29Jonathan said, "My father has made trouble for the country. See how my eyes brightened when I tasted a little of this honey. 30How much better it would have been if the men had eaten today some of the plunder they took from their enemies. Would not the slaughter of the Philistines have been even greater?"

31That day, after the Israelites had struck down the Philistines from Mikmash to Aijalon, they were exhausted. 32They pounced on the plunder and, taking sheep, cattle and calves, they butchered them on the ground and ate them, together with the blood. 33Then someone said to Saul, "Look, the men are sinning against the LORD by eating meat that has blood in it."

"You have broken faith," he said. "Roll a large stone over here at once." 34Then he said, "Go out among the men and tell them, 'Each of you bring me your cattle and sheep, and slaughter them here and eat them. Do not sin against the LORD by eating meat with blood still in it.'"

So everyone brought his ox that night and slaughtered it there. 35Then Saul built an altar to the LORD; it was the first time he had done this.

36Saul said, "Let us go down and pursue the Philistines by night and plunder them till dawn, and let us not leave one of them alive."

"Do whatever seems best to you," they replied.

But the priest said, "Let us inquire of God here."

37So Saul asked God, "Shall I go down and pursue the Philistines? Will you give them into Israel's hand?" But God did not answer him that day.

38Saul therefore said, "Come here, all you who are leaders of the army, and let us find out what sin has been committed today. 39As surely as the LORD who rescues Israel lives, even if the guilt lies with my son Jonathan, he must die." But not one of them said a word.

40Saul then said to all the Israelites, "You stand over there; I and Jonathan my son will stand over here."

"Do what seems best to you," they replied.

41Then Saul prayed to the LORD, the God of Israel, "Why have you not answered your servant today? If the fault is in me or my son Jonathan, respond with Urim, but if the men of Israel are at fault,[a] respond with Thummim." Jonathan and Saul were taken by lot, and the men were cleared. 42Saul said, "Cast the lot between me and Jonathan my son." And Jonathan was taken.

43Then Saul said to Jonathan, "Tell me what you have done."

So Jonathan told him, "I tasted a little honey with the end of my staff. And now I must die!"

44Saul said, "May God deal with me, be it ever so severely, if you do not die, Jonathan."

45But the men said to Saul, "Should Jonathan die — he who has brought about this great deliverance in Israel? Never! As surely as the LORD lives, not a hair of his head will fall to the ground, for he did this today with God's help." So the men rescued Jonathan, and he was not put to death.

46Then Saul stopped pursuing the Philistines, and they withdrew to their own land.

47After Saul had assumed rule over Israel, he fought against their enemies on every side: Moab, the Ammonites, Edom, the kings[b] of Zobah, and the Philistines. Wherever he turned, he inflicted punishment on them.[c] 48He fought valiantly and defeated the Amalekites, delivering Israel from the hands of those who had plundered them.

Saul's Family

49Saul's sons were Jonathan, Ishvi and Malki-Shua. The name of his older daughter was Merab, and that of the younger was Michal. 50His wife's name was Ahinoam daughter of Ahimaaz. The name of the commander of Saul's army was Abner son of Ner, and Ner was Saul's uncle. 51Saul's father Kish and Abner's father Ner were sons of Abiel.

52All the days of Saul there was bitter war with the Philistines, and whenever Saul saw a mighty or brave man, he took him into his service.

The LORD Rejects Saul as King

15 Samuel said to Saul, "I am the one the LORD sent to anoint you king over his people Israel; so listen now to the message from the LORD. 2This is what the LORD Almighty says: 'I will punish the Amalekites for what they did to Israel when they waylaid them as they came up from Egypt. 3Now go, attack the Amalekites and totally destroy[d] all that belongs to them. Do not spare them; put to death men and women,

---

[a] 41 Septuagint; Hebrew does not have "Why . . . at fault.
[b] 47 Masoretic Text; Dead Sea Scrolls and Septuagint king
[c] 47 Hebrew; Septuagint he was victorious　[d] 3 The Hebrew term refers to the irrevocable giving over of things or persons to the LORD, often by totally destroying them; also in verses 8, 9, 15, 18, 20 and 21.

The Law of Addition: From Serving to Leading

1 Samuel 15

God calls every leader to be a servant, but not every servant is to be a leader. So, how do we take the step to leadership?

In Hebrew, the word we translate as "leader" (*nagiyd*) comes from a root that conveys the idea of servanthood and being an example to others. The word is variously translated in Scripture as captain, ruler, prince, governor and noble.

Leader vs. King

The Hebrew term for "leader" stands in sharp contrast to the word for "king." The fairly neutral Hebrew term for "king" (*melech*) allowed for the possibility of independence, for being a maverick. Samuel warned against this very thing when the Israelites asked for a king. A *melech* might be a renegade, but a *nagiyd* was under authority, subject to a higher power and fulfilling the wishes of that higher power. Saul was a *melech*, while Samuel was a *nagiyd*.

To be a captain, ruler, prince, governor or noble of the people of God, a person must first come squarely under the authority of God. We can go no further without first understanding this element. Yet a second element is just as important. The Hebrew term *nagiyd* also means to stand boldly, to announce, to manifest—the natural outgrowth of receiving commands from God. The leader is to boldly stand and communicate God's commands with conviction.

God's leader is first to be a servant of the Lord, then an example, then a proclaimer and communicator to the people. And no one did this better than Samuel.

---

children and infants, cattle and sheep, camels and donkeys.'"

⁴So Saul summoned the men and mustered them at Telaim—two hundred thousand foot soldiers and ten thousand from Judah. ⁵Saul went to the city of Amalek and set an ambush in the ravine. ⁶Then he said to the Kenites, "Go away, leave the Amalekites so that I do not destroy you along with them; for you showed kindness to all the Israelites when they came up out of Egypt." So the Kenites moved away from the Amalekites.

⁷Then Saul attacked the Amalekites all the way from Havilah to Shur, near the eastern border of Egypt. ⁸He took Agag king of the Amalekites alive, and all his people he totally destroyed with the sword. ⁹But Saul and the army spared Agag and the best of the sheep and cattle, the fat calves*a* and lambs — everything that was good. These they were unwilling to destroy completely, but everything that was despised and weak they totally destroyed.

¹⁰Then the word of the Lord came to Samuel: ¹¹"I regret that I have made Saul king, because he has turned away from me and has not carried out my instructions." Samuel was angry, and he cried out to the Lord all that night.

¹²Early in the morning Samuel got up and went to meet Saul, but he was told, "Saul has gone to Carmel. There he has set up a monument in his own honor and has turned and gone on down to Gilgal."

¹³When Samuel reached him, Saul said, "The Lord bless you! I have carried out the Lord's instructions."

¹⁴But Samuel said, "What then is this bleating of sheep in my ears? What is this lowing of cattle that I hear?"

¹⁵Saul answered, "The soldiers brought them from the Amalekites; they spared the best of the sheep and cattle to sacrifice to the Lord your God, but we totally destroyed the rest."

¹⁶"Enough!" Samuel said to Saul. "Let me tell you what the Lord said to me last night."

"Tell me," Saul replied.

¹⁷Samuel said, "Although you were once small in your own eyes, did you not become the head of the tribes of Israel? The Lord anointed you king over Israel. ¹⁸And he sent you on a mission, saying, 'Go and completely destroy those wicked people, the Amalekites; wage war against them until you have wiped them out.' ¹⁹Why did you not obey the Lord? Why did you pounce on the plunder and do evil in the eyes of the Lord?"

---

a 9 Or *the grown bulls*; the meaning of the Hebrew for this phrase is uncertain.

20"But I did obey the Lord," Saul said. "I went on the mission the Lord assigned me. I completely destroyed the Amalekites and brought back Agag their king. **21**The soldiers took sheep and cattle from the plunder, the best of what was devoted to God, in order to sacrifice them to the Lord your God at Gilgal."

22But Samuel replied:

"Does the Lord delight in burnt offerings
    and sacrifices
as much as in obeying the Lord?
To obey is better than sacrifice,
    and to heed is better than the fat of
      rams.
23For rebellion is like the sin of divination,
    and arrogance like the evil of idolatry.
Because you have rejected the word of the
    Lord,
    he has rejected you as king."

24Then Saul said to Samuel, "I have sinned. I violated the Lord's command and your instructions. I was afraid of the men and so I gave in to them. **25**Now I beg you, forgive my sin and come back with me, so that I may worship the Lord." **26**But Samuel said to him, "I will not go back with you. You have rejected the word of the Lord, and the Lord has rejected you as king over Israel!"

27As Samuel turned to leave, Saul caught hold of the hem of his robe, and it tore. **28**Samuel said to him, "The Lord has torn the kingdom of Israel from you today and has given it to one of your neighbors—to one better than you. **29**He who is the Glory of Israel does not lie or change his mind; for he is not a human being, that he should change his mind."

30Saul replied, "I have sinned. But please honor me before the elders of my people and before Israel; come back with me, so that I may worship the Lord your God." **31**So Samuel went back with Saul, and Saul worshiped the Lord.

32Then Samuel said, "Bring me Agag king of the Amalekites."

Agag came to him in chains.[a] And he thought, "Surely the bitterness of death is past."

33But Samuel said,

"As your sword has made women childless,
    so will your mother be childless among
      women."

And Samuel put Agag to death before the Lord at Gilgal.

34Then Samuel left for Ramah, but Saul went up to his home in Gibeah of Saul. **35**Until the day Samuel died, he did not go to see Saul again, though Samuel mourned for him. And the Lord regretted that he had made Saul king over Israel.

---

[a] 32 The meaning of the Hebrew for this phrase is uncertain.

SAUL

PROFILE in leadership

Stopped Leading to Serve His Own Interests
1 Samuel 15:1–26

The Lord could not have been more specific. Speaking through the prophet Samuel, God commanded King Saul to destroy the Amalekites and everything they owned; no one and no thing was to be spared.

This was to be the supreme test of Saul's fitness to lead God's people—a test he failed miserably. Although he and his army routed the people of Amalek, he disobeyed God by sparing Agag, king of the Amalekites, and took for himself the best of their livestock.

When Samuel confronted Saul about his disobedience, he offered the lame excuse that he intended to sacrifice the livestock to the Lord. His rationalization didn't wash—not in Samuel's eyes and certainly not in God's. From that moment on, his days as king were numbered. And so ended what had looked to be a promising reign.

It is only a matter of time before a leader's heart reveals its true nature: soft and obedient toward the Lord? or hard and self-serving?

Truly godly leaders commit themselves to obeying the commands of God, whether they fully understand those commands or not. What they do know is the truth of Samuel's words: "To obey is better than sacrifice, and to heed is better than the fat of rams" (1Sa 15:22).

Samuel Anoints David

16 The LORD said to Samuel, "How long will you mourn for Saul, since I have rejected him as king over Israel? Fill your horn with oil and be on your way; I am sending you to Jesse of Bethlehem. I have chosen one of his sons to be king."

²But Samuel said, "How can I go? If Saul hears about it, he will kill me."

The LORD said, "Take a heifer with you and say, 'I have come to sacrifice to the LORD.' ³Invite Jesse to the sacrifice, and I will show you what to do. You are to anoint for me the one I indicate."

⁴Samuel did what the LORD said. When he arrived at Bethlehem, the elders of the town trembled when they met him. They asked, "Do you come in peace?"

⁵Samuel replied, "Yes, in peace; I have come to sacrifice to the LORD. Consecrate yourselves and come to the sacrifice with me." Then he consecrated Jesse and his sons and invited them to the sacrifice.

⁶When they arrived, Samuel saw Eliab and thought, "Surely the LORD's anointed stands here before the LORD."

⁷But the LORD said to Samuel, "Do not consider his appearance or his height, for I have rejected him. The LORD does not look at the things people look at. People look at the outward appearance, but the LORD looks at the heart."

⁸Then Jesse called Abinadab and had him pass in front of Samuel. But Samuel said, "The LORD has not chosen this one either." ⁹Jesse then had Shammah pass by, but Samuel said, "Nor has the LORD chosen this one." ¹⁰Jesse had seven of his sons pass before Samuel, but Samuel said to him, "The LORD has not chosen these." ¹¹So he asked Jesse, "Are these all the sons you have?"

"There is still the youngest," Jesse answered. "He is tending the sheep."

Samuel said, "Send for him; we will not sit down until he arrives."

¹²So he sent for him and had him brought in. He was glowing with health and had a fine appearance and handsome features.

Then the LORD said, "Rise and anoint him; this is the one."

¹³So Samuel took the horn of oil and anointed him in the presence of his brothers, and from that day on the Spirit of the LORD came powerfully upon David. Samuel then went to Ramah.

David in Saul's Service

¹⁴Now the Spirit of the LORD had departed from Saul, and an evil[a] spirit from the LORD tormented him.

---

[a] 14 Or *and a harmful*; similarly in verses 15, 16 and 23

DAVID
A Leader After God's Own Heart
1 Samuel 16:1–13

PROFILE in leadership

The selection of David to be Israel's king illustrates how God often disregards human customs and traditions to accomplish his purposes.

By human standards, David, as the youngest son of Jesse, appeared least likely to be considered for a leadership position. But God saw the heart of this young man and knew that his people needed a leader with a tenderness of spirit. David might have become a warrior, but gentleness was his defining trait.

David developed into a leader of courage with wisdom and strength beyond his years. He demonstrated his godly spirit through his willingness to take on Goliath while the great warriors of Israel hid in their tents (1Sa 17:40–50). David enjoyed a clear sense of dependence on God and made sure God would get the glory for any success in his life.

David began his leadership journey as low man on the totem pole. He did what was asked of him with a great attitude, having fun along the way. While his own brothers looked down on him, God lifted him up.

David's life illustrates that faithfulness in small things often results in much larger assignments and greater responsibility down the road. David loved the Lord and lived his life as a man after God's own heart (13:14).

How Do You Recognize a Leader?

1 Samuel 16:6–10

When did David first become a leader? The Bible makes it clear that the young man had become a leader long before he ever received a title.

This young leader first began to surface in 1 Samuel 16—but only God and Samuel recognized his leadership at first. Only after his great and unexpected victory over Goliath did everyone else recognize his special abilities (1Sa 17:55–58).

David's example shows that true leaders always declare themselves without making any announcements. It becomes obvious. Too often, we feel forced to pick someone to lead, whether or not he is a leader—and that's when wrong motives and false criteria emerge. What can we learn from 1 Samuel 16?

Mistakes We Make When Picking a Leader

1. **Looking at looks (vv. 6–7)**
2. **Picking from the past (vv. 6–7)**
3. **Picking from the pecking order (vv. 8–10)**
4. **Opting for age and tenure over ability (vv. 8–10)**

¹⁵Saul's attendants said to him, "See, an evil spirit from God is tormenting you. ¹⁶Let our lord command his servants here to search for someone who can play the lyre. He will play when the evil spirit from God comes on you, and you will feel better."

¹⁷So Saul said to his attendants, "Find someone who plays well and bring him to me."

¹⁸One of the servants answered, "I have seen a son of Jesse of Bethlehem who knows how to play the lyre. He is a brave man and a warrior. He speaks well and is a fine-looking man. And the LORD is with him."

¹⁹Then Saul sent messengers to Jesse and said, "Send me your son David, who is with the sheep." ²⁰So Jesse took a donkey loaded with bread, a skin of wine and a young goat and sent them with his son David to Saul.

²¹David came to Saul and entered his service. Saul liked him very much, and David became one of his armor-bearers. ²²Then Saul sent word to Jesse, saying, "Allow David to remain in my service, for I am pleased with him."

²³Whenever the spirit from God came on Saul, David would take up his lyre and play. Then relief would come to Saul; he would feel better, and the evil spirit would leave him.

David and Goliath

17 Now the Philistines gathered their forces for war and assembled at Sokoh in Judah. They pitched camp at Ephes Dammim, between Sokoh and Azekah. ²Saul and the Israelites assembled and camped in the Valley of Elah and drew up their battle line to meet the Philistines. ³The Philistines occupied one hill and the Israelites another, with the valley between them.

⁴A champion named Goliath, who was from Gath, came out of the Philistine camp. His height was six cubits and a span.ᵃ ⁵He had a bronze helmet on his head and wore a coat of scale armor of bronze weighing five thousand shekelsᵇ; ⁶on his legs he wore bronze greaves, and a bronze javelin was slung on his back. ⁷His spear shaft was like a weaver's rod, and its iron point weighed six hundred shekels.ᶜ His shield bearer went ahead of him.

⁸Goliath stood and shouted to the ranks of Israel, "Why do you come out and line up for battle? Am I not a Philistine, and are you not the servants of Saul? Choose a man and have him come down to me. ⁹If he is able to fight and kill me, we will become your subjects; but if I overcome him and kill him, you will become our subjects and serve us." ¹⁰Then the Philistine said, "This day I defy the armies of Israel! Give me a man and let us fight each other." ¹¹On hearing the Philistine's words, Saul and all the Israelites were dismayed and terrified.

¹²Now David was the son of an Ephrathite named Jesse, who was from Bethlehem in Judah.

ᵃ 4 That is, about 9 feet 9 inches or about 3 meters   ᵇ 5 That is, about 125 pounds or about 58 kilograms   ᶜ 7 That is, about 15 pounds or about 6.9 kilograms

Jesse had eight sons, and in Saul's time he was very old. [13]Jesse's three oldest sons had followed Saul to the war: The firstborn was Eliab; the second, Abinadab; and the third, Shammah. [14]David was the youngest. The three oldest followed Saul, [15]but David went back and forth from Saul to tend his father's sheep at Bethlehem.

[16]For forty days the Philistine came forward every morning and evening and took his stand.

[17]Now Jesse said to his son David, "Take this ephah[a] of roasted grain and these ten loaves of bread for your brothers and hurry to their camp. [18]Take along these ten cheeses to the commander of their unit. See how your brothers are and bring back some assurance[b] from them. [19]They are with Saul and all the men of Israel in the Valley of Elah, fighting against the Philistines."

[20]Early in the morning David left the flock in the care of a shepherd, loaded up and set out, as Jesse had directed. He reached the camp as the army was going out to its battle positions, shouting the war cry. [21]Israel and the Philistines were drawing up their lines facing each other. [22]David left his things with the keeper of supplies, ran to the battle lines and asked his brothers how they were. [23]As he was talking with them, Goliath, the Philistine champion from Gath, stepped out from his lines and shouted his usual defiance, and David heard it. [24]Whenever the Israelites saw the man, they all fled from him in great fear.

[25]Now the Israelites had been saying, "Do you see how this man keeps coming out? He comes out to defy Israel. The king will give great wealth to the man who kills him. He will also give him his daughter in marriage and will exempt his family from taxes in Israel."

[26]David asked the men standing near him, "What will be done for the man who kills this Philistine and removes this disgrace from Israel? Who is this uncircumcised Philistine that he should defy the armies of the living God?"

[27]They repeated to him what they had been saying and told him, "This is what will be done for the man who kills him."

[28]When Eliab, David's oldest brother, heard him speaking with the men, he burned with

---

[a] 17 That is, probably about 36 pounds or about 16 kilograms
[b] 18 Or some token; or some pledge of spoils

The Law of Victory: David Defeats Goliath and Everyone Wins

1 Samuel 17:19–58

Victory is always fun. No one likes to lose. But when a leader practices the Law of Victory, it impacts more than the leader. It affects everyone around the leader.

Consider David in his battle with Goliath. By practicing this law, he transformed the once-paralyzed Israelite soldiers into a force capable of defeating the "invincible" Philistine army. Here's how he did it:

1. ***His perspective differed from others.***
   He didn't see what everyone else saw, an invincible giant. He saw an opportunity.

2. ***His methods differed from others.***
   He decided to use proven weapons that he knew would work, not the conventional ones.

3. ***His conviction differed from others.***
   He recognized Goliath had no covenant with God, while he felt passionately committed to God's covenant.

4. ***His motives differed from others.***
   He heard Goliath's threats against the God of Israel and knew God could beat him.

5. ***His vision differed from others.***
   He wanted to make Yahweh known to the world as the most powerful God on earth.

6. ***His experience differed from others.***
   He brought to the battlefield past victories over a lion and bear, not months of paralyzing fear.

7. ***His attitude differed from others.***
   He saw Goliath not as a threat too big to hit, but as a target too big to miss!

anger at him and asked, "Why have you come down here? And with whom did you leave those few sheep in the wilderness? I know how conceited you are and how wicked your heart is; you came down only to watch the battle."

[29]"Now what have I done?" said David. "Can't I even speak?" [30]He then turned away to someone else and brought up the same matter, and the men answered him as before. [31]What David said was overheard and reported to Saul, and Saul sent for him.

[32]David said to Saul, "Let no one lose heart on account of this Philistine; your servant will go and fight him."

[33]Saul replied, "You are not able to go out against this Philistine and fight him; you are only a young man, and he has been a warrior from his youth."

[34]But David said to Saul, "Your servant has been keeping his father's sheep. When a lion or a bear came and carried off a sheep from the flock, [35]I went after it, struck it and rescued the sheep from its mouth. When it turned on me, I seized it by its hair, struck it and killed it. [36]Your servant has killed both the lion and the bear; this uncircumcised Philistine will be like one of them, because he has defied the armies of the living God. [37]The LORD who rescued me from the paw of the lion and the paw of the bear will rescue me from the hand of this Philistine."

Saul said to David, "Go, and the LORD be with you."

[38]Then Saul dressed David in his own tunic. He put a coat of armor on him and a bronze helmet on his head. [39]David fastened on his sword over the tunic and tried walking around, because he was not used to them.

"I cannot go in these," he said to Saul, "because I am not used to them." So he took them off. [40]Then he took his staff in his hand, chose five smooth stones from the stream, put them in the pouch of his shepherd's bag and, with his sling in his hand, approached the Philistine.

[41]Meanwhile, the Philistine, with his shield bearer in front of him, kept coming closer to David. [42]He looked David over and saw that he was little more than a boy, glowing with health and handsome, and he despised him. [43]He said to David, "Am I a dog, that you come at me with sticks?" And the Philistine cursed David by his gods. [44]"Come here," he said, "and I'll give your flesh to the birds and the wild animals!"

[45]David said to the Philistine, "You come against me with sword and spear and javelin, but I come against you in the name of the LORD

The Law of the Lid: Leadership Determined Saul and David's Success

1 Samuel 17:24–40

When Goliath taunted the armies of Israel, the frightened Hebrew soldiers forgot how to fight. They lacked a leader who could provide a strategy for success.

Saul was a very experienced soldier, but he cowered in fear with his men. David, on the other hand, sized up the situation, determined his weapon (a sling and five smooth stones) and ran toward Goliath.

Saul suffered under a lid of fear, paralyzed from leading. David labored under no such lid. Once he conquered the giant, the Israelite armies joined him to finish off the Philistines.

Almighty, the God of the armies of Israel, whom you have defied. [46]This day the LORD will deliver you into my hands, and I'll strike you down and cut off your head. This very day I will give the carcasses of the Philistine army to the birds and the wild animals, and the whole world will know that there is a God in Israel. [47]All those gathered here will know that it is not by sword or spear that the LORD saves; for the battle is the LORD's, and he will give all of you into our hands."

[48]As the Philistine moved closer to attack him, David ran quickly toward the battle line to meet him. [49]Reaching into his bag and taking out a stone, he slung it and struck the Philistine on the forehead. The stone sank into his forehead, and he fell facedown on the ground.

[50]So David triumphed over the Philistine with a sling and a stone; without a sword in his hand he struck down the Philistine and killed him.

[51]David ran and stood over him. He took hold of the Philistine's sword and drew it from the sheath. After he killed him, he cut off his head with the sword.

When the Philistines saw that their hero was dead, they turned and ran. [52]Then the men of Israel and Judah surged forward with a shout and pursued the Philistines to the entrance of Gath[a] and to the gates of Ekron. Their dead were

---

[a] 52 Some Septuagint manuscripts; Hebrew *of a valley*

strewn along the Shaaraim road to Gath and Ekron. ⁵³When the Israelites returned from chasing the Philistines, they plundered their camp.

⁵⁴David took the Philistine's head and brought it to Jerusalem; he put the Philistine's weapons in his own tent.

⁵⁵As Saul watched David going out to meet the Philistine, he said to Abner, commander of the army, "Abner, whose son is that young man?"

Abner replied, "As surely as you live, Your Majesty, I don't know."

⁵⁶The king said, "Find out whose son this young man is."

⁵⁷As soon as David returned from killing the Philistine, Abner took him and brought him before Saul, with David still holding the Philistine's head.

⁵⁸"Whose son are you, young man?" Saul asked him.

David said, "I am the son of your servant Jesse of Bethlehem."

Saul's Growing Fear of David

18 After David had finished talking with Saul, Jonathan became one in spirit with David, and he loved him as himself. ²From that day Saul kept David with him and did not let him return home to his family. ³And Jonathan made a covenant with David because he loved

him as himself. ⁴Jonathan took off the robe he was wearing and gave it to David, along with his tunic, and even his sword, his bow and his belt.

⁵Whatever mission Saul sent him on, David was so successful that Saul gave him a high rank in the army. This pleased all the troops, and Saul's officers as well.

⁶When the men were returning home after David had killed the Philistine, the women came out from all the towns of Israel to meet King Saul with singing and dancing, with joyful songs and with timbrels and lyres. ⁷As they danced, they sang:

"Saul has slain his thousands,
    and David his tens of thousands."

⁸Saul was very angry; this refrain displeased him greatly. "They have credited David with tens of thousands," he thought, "but me with only thousands. What more can he get but the kingdom?" ⁹And from that time on Saul kept a close eye on David.

¹⁰The next day an evil[a] spirit from God came forcefully on Saul. He was prophesying in his house, while David was playing the lyre, as he usually did. Saul had a spear in his hand ¹¹and he hurled it, saying to himself, "I'll pin David to the wall." But David eluded him twice.

---

a 10 Or a harmful

The Law of Empowerment: Saul Couldn't Give Away His Power

1 Samuel 18:7-29

King Saul clearly recognized David as a mighty warrior, a valuable team member, an obedient servant, a favored man and an effective leader. He also clearly saw him as a potential successor and threat.

Things didn't get better when he heard the Israelite ladies compare the two—and Saul came out second best (1Sa 18:7). Saul's insecurity and fear drove him to turn against David. Insecurity often drives a leader to do stupid and self-sabotaging things.

1. **Saul looked at David's every activity with suspicion (v. 9).**
2. **Saul hurled his spear at David to try to kill him (v. 11).**
3. **Saul feared David because God's Spirit was with him (v. 12).**
4. **Saul changed David's position to prevent them from seeing each other (v. 13).**
5. **Saul dreaded being compared to David in any way (vv. 15–16).**
6. **Saul put David in charge of 1,000 troops in hopes that the Philistines would kill him (vv. 13, 17).**
7. **Saul gave his daughter Michal to David, hoping she would be a snare to him (vv. 20–21).**
8. **Saul sponsored secrets to deceive David (v. 22).**
9. **Saul perceived himself as David's enemy (v. 29).**

[^12]Saul was afraid of David, because the LORD was with David but had departed from Saul. [^13]So he sent David away from him and gave him command over a thousand men, and David led the troops in their campaigns. [^14]In everything he did he had great success, because the LORD was with him. [^15]When Saul saw how successful he was, he was afraid of him. [^16]But all Israel and Judah loved David, because he led them in their campaigns.

[^17]Saul said to David, "Here is my older daughter Merab. I will give her to you in marriage; only serve me bravely and fight the battles of the LORD." For Saul said to himself, "I will not raise a hand against him. Let the Philistines do that!"

[^18]But David said to Saul, "Who am I, and what is my family or my clan in Israel, that I should become the king's son-in-law?" [^19]So[^a] when the time came for Merab, Saul's daughter, to be given to David, she was given in marriage to Adriel of Meholah.

[^20]Now Saul's daughter Michal was in love with David, and when they told Saul about it, he was pleased. [^21]"I will give her to him," he thought, "so that she may be a snare to him and so that the hand of the Philistines may be against him." So Saul said to David, "Now you have a second opportunity to become my son-in-law."

[^22]Then Saul ordered his attendants: "Speak to David privately and say, 'Look, the king likes you, and his attendants all love you; now become his son-in-law.'"

[^23]They repeated these words to David. But David said, "Do you think it is a small matter to become the king's son-in-law? I'm only a poor man and little known."

[^24]When Saul's servants told him what David had said, [^25]Saul replied, "Say to David, 'The king wants no other price for the bride than a hundred Philistine foreskins, to take revenge on his enemies.'" Saul's plan was to have David fall by the hands of the Philistines.

[^26]When the attendants told David these things, he was pleased to become the king's son-in-law. So before the allotted time elapsed, [^27]David took his men with him and went out and killed two hundred Philistines and brought back their foreskins. They counted out the full number to the king so that David might become the king's son-in-law. Then Saul gave him his daughter Michal in marriage.

[^28]When Saul realized that the LORD was with David and that his daughter Michal loved David, [^29]Saul became still more afraid of him, and he remained his enemy the rest of his days.

[^30]The Philistine commanders continued to go out to battle, and as often as they did, David met with more success than the rest of Saul's officers, and his name became well known.

Saul Tries to Kill David

19 Saul told his son Jonathan and all the attendants to kill David. But Jonathan had taken a great liking to David [^2]and warned him, "My father Saul is looking for a chance to kill you. Be on your guard tomorrow morning; go into hiding and stay there. [^3]I will go out and stand with my father in the field where you are. I'll speak to him about you and will tell you what I find out."

[^4]Jonathan spoke well of David to Saul his father and said to him, "Let not the king do wrong to his servant David; he has not wronged you, and what he has done has benefited you greatly. [^5]He took his life in his hands when he killed the Philistine. The LORD won a great victory for all Israel, and you saw it and were glad. Why then would you do wrong to an innocent man like David by killing him for no reason?"

[^6]Saul listened to Jonathan and took this oath: "As surely as the LORD lives, David will not be put to death."

[^7]So Jonathan called David and told him the whole conversation. He brought him to Saul, and David was with Saul as before.

[^8]Once more war broke out, and David went out and fought the Philistines. He struck them with such force that they fled before him.

[^9]But an evil[^b] spirit from the LORD came on Saul as he was sitting in his house with his spear in his hand. While David was playing the lyre, [^10]Saul tried to pin him to the wall with his spear, but David eluded him as Saul drove the spear into the wall. That night David made good his escape.

[^11]Saul sent men to David's house to watch it and to kill him in the morning. But Michal, David's wife, warned him, "If you don't run for your life tonight, tomorrow you'll be killed." [^12]So Michal let David down through a window, and he fled and escaped. [^13]Then Michal took an idol and laid it on the bed, covering it with a garment and putting some goats' hair at the head.

[^14]When Saul sent the men to capture David, Michal said, "He is ill."

[^15]Then Saul sent the men back to see David and told them, "Bring him up to me in his bed so that I may kill him." [^16]But when the men en-

---

[^a] 19 Or However,   [^b] 9 Or But a harmful

tered, there was the idol in the bed, and at the head was some goats' hair.

17 Saul said to Michal, "Why did you deceive me like this and send my enemy away so that he escaped?"

Michal told him, "He said to me, 'Let me get away. Why should I kill you?'"

18 When David had fled and made his escape, he went to Samuel at Ramah and told him all that Saul had done to him. Then he and Samuel went to Naioth and stayed there. 19 Word came to Saul: "David is in Naioth at Ramah"; 20 so he sent men to capture him. But when they saw a group of prophets prophesying, with Samuel standing there as their leader, the Spirit of God came on Saul's men, and they also prophesied. 21 Saul was told about it, and he sent more men, and they prophesied too. Saul sent men a third time, and they also prophesied. 22 Finally, he himself left for Ramah and went to the great cistern at Seku. And he asked, "Where are Samuel and David?"

"Over in Naioth at Ramah," they said.

23 So Saul went to Naioth at Ramah. But the Spirit of God came even on him, and he walked along prophesying until he came to Naioth. 24 He stripped off his garments, and he too prophesied in Samuel's presence. He lay naked all that day and all that night. This is why people say, "Is Saul also among the prophets?"

David and Jonathan

20 Then David fled from Naioth at Ramah and went to Jonathan and asked, "What have I done? What is my crime? How have I wronged your father, that he is trying to kill me?"

2 "Never!" Jonathan replied. "You are not going to die! Look, my father doesn't do anything, great or small, without letting me know. Why would he hide this from me? It isn't so!"

3 But David took an oath and said, "Your father knows very well that I have found favor in your eyes, and he has said to himself, 'Jonathan must not know this or he will be grieved.' Yet as surely as the LORD lives and as you live, there is only a step between me and death."

4 Jonathan said to David, "Whatever you want me to do, I'll do for you."

5 So David said, "Look, tomorrow is the New Moon feast, and I am supposed to dine with the king; but let me go and hide in the field until the evening of the day after tomorrow. 6 If your father misses me at all, tell him, 'David earnestly asked my permission to hurry to Bethlehem, his hometown, because an annual sacrifice is being made there for his whole clan.' 7 If he says, 'Very well,' then your servant is safe. But if he loses his temper, you can be sure that he is determined

DAVID

Partnership with Jonathan Enables Him to Endure

1 Samuel 19:1—23:18

PROFILE in leadership

No leader succeeds on his own—not even a great leader whom God called "a man after my own heart" (Ac 13:22), and "the apple of [my] eye" (Ps 17:8). Even David needed his Jonathan.

In the dark days when he scrambled from cave to cave to escape the murderous threats of King Saul, David turned to his friend, Jonathan, for strength and encouragement. At great risk to himself, Jonathan warned David and told him to hide out for a time (1Sa 19:2). Jonathan, hoping to pacify his father and reconcile the king to his friend, spoke well of David. And for a short while Saul relented, promising that David would not die by his hand.

Soon the old animosities reasserted themselves, however, and Jonathan once again risked his life to help his dear friend (20:30–33). Even though he knew that God had chosen David—and not him—to rule Israel, Jonathan remained faithful to his comrade until the very end of his life. One verse in particular describes Jonathan's invaluable ministry to David: "And Saul's son Jonathan went to David at Horesh and helped him find strength in God" (23:16).

Do you have someone who "helps you find strength in God"? All leaders need loyal friends who can help them to persevere through the tough times.

to harm me. ⁸As for you, show kindness to your servant, for you have brought him into a covenant with you before the LORD. If I am guilty, then kill me yourself! Why hand me over to your father?"

⁹"Never!" Jonathan said. "If I had the least inkling that my father was determined to harm you, wouldn't I tell you?"

¹⁰David asked, "Who will tell me if your father answers you harshly?"

¹¹"Come," Jonathan said, "let's go out into the field." So they went there together.

¹²Then Jonathan said to David, "I swear by the LORD, the God of Israel, that I will surely sound out my father by this time the day after tomorrow! If he is favorably disposed toward you, will I not send you word and let you know? ¹³But if my father intends to harm you, may the LORD deal with Jonathan, be it ever so severely, if I do not let you know and send you away in peace. May the LORD be with you as he has been with my father. ¹⁴But show me unfailing kindness like the LORD's kindness as long as I live, so that I may not be killed, ¹⁵and do not ever cut off your kindness from my family — not even when the LORD has cut off every one of David's enemies from the face of the earth."

¹⁶So Jonathan made a covenant with the house of David, saying, "May the LORD call David's enemies to account." ¹⁷And Jonathan had David reaffirm his oath out of love for him, because he loved him as he loved himself.

¹⁸Then Jonathan said to David, "Tomorrow is the New Moon feast. You will be missed, because your seat will be empty. ¹⁹The day after tomorrow, toward evening, go to the place where you hid when this trouble began, and wait by the stone Ezel. ²⁰I will shoot three arrows to the side of it, as though I were shooting at a target. ²¹Then I will send a boy and say, 'Go, find the arrows.' If I say to him, 'Look, the arrows are on this side of you; bring them here,' then come, because, as surely as the LORD lives, you are safe; there is no danger. ²²But if I say to the boy, 'Look, the arrows are beyond you,' then you must go, because the LORD has sent you away. ²³And about the matter you and I discussed — remember, the LORD is witness between you and me forever."

²⁴So David hid in the field, and when the New Moon feast came, the king sat down to eat. ²⁵He sat in his customary place by the wall, opposite Jonathan,ᵃ and Abner sat next to Saul, but David's place was empty. ²⁶Saul said nothing that day, for he thought, "Something must have hap-pened to David to make him ceremonially unclean — surely he is unclean." ²⁷But the next day, the second day of the month, David's place was empty again. Then Saul said to his son Jonathan, "Why hasn't the son of Jesse come to the meal, either yesterday or today?"

²⁸Jonathan answered, "David earnestly asked me for permission to go to Bethlehem. ²⁹He said, 'Let me go, because our family is observing a sacrifice in the town and my brother has ordered me to be there. If I have found favor in your eyes, let me get away to see my brothers.' That is why he has not come to the king's table."

³⁰Saul's anger flared up at Jonathan and he said to him, "You son of a perverse and rebellious woman! Don't I know that you have sided with the son of Jesse to your own shame and to the shame of the mother who bore you? ³¹As long as the son of Jesse lives on this earth, neither you nor your kingdom will be established. Now send someone to bring him to me, for he must die!"

³²"Why should he be put to death? What has he done?" Jonathan asked his father. ³³But Saul hurled his spear at him to kill him. Then Jonathan knew that his father intended to kill David.

³⁴Jonathan got up from the table in fierce anger; on that second day of the feast he did not eat, because he was grieved at his father's shameful treatment of David.

³⁵In the morning Jonathan went out to the field for his meeting with David. He had a small boy with him, ³⁶and he said to the boy, "Run and find the arrows I shoot." As the boy ran, he shot an arrow beyond him. ³⁷When the boy came to the place where Jonathan's arrow had fallen, Jonathan called out after him, "Isn't the arrow beyond you?" ³⁸Then he shouted, "Hurry! Go quickly! Don't stop!" The boy picked up the arrow and returned to his master. ³⁹(The boy knew nothing about all this; only Jonathan and David knew.) ⁴⁰Then Jonathan gave his weapons to the boy and said, "Go, carry them back to town."

⁴¹After the boy had gone, David got up from the south side of the stone and bowed down before Jonathan three times, with his face to the ground. Then they kissed each other and wept together — but David wept the most.

⁴²Jonathan said to David, "Go in peace, for we have sworn friendship with each other in the name of the LORD, saying, 'The LORD is witness between you and me, and between your descen-

ᵃ 25 Septuagint; Hebrew wall. Jonathan arose

The Law of Connection: Covenant Love Draws Commitment

1 Samuel 20:1–41

Although Jonathan was the royal prince, he exalted and encouraged David, knowing he risked his future throne. First Samuel 20 describes the four characteristics of their friendship. Jonathan was: available (vv. 1–4); dependable (vv. 5–17); vulnerable (vv. 18–33); and responsible (vv. 34–42). And so Jonathan won David's loyalty (v. 41).

dants and my descendants forever.'" Then David left, and Jonathan went back to the town.[a]

David at Nob

21 [b] David went to Nob, to Ahimelek the priest. Ahimelek trembled when he met him, and asked, "Why are you alone? Why is no one with you?"

²David answered Ahimelek the priest, "The king sent me on a mission and said to me, 'No one is to know anything about the mission I am sending you on.' As for my men, I have told them to meet me at a certain place. ³Now then, what do you have on hand? Give me five loaves of bread, or whatever you can find."

⁴But the priest answered David, "I don't have any ordinary bread on hand; however, there is some consecrated bread here — provided the men have kept themselves from women."

⁵David replied, "Indeed women have been kept from us, as usual whenever[c] I set out. The men's bodies are holy even on missions that are not holy. How much more so today!" ⁶So the priest gave him the consecrated bread, since there was no bread there except the bread of the Presence that had been removed from before the LORD and replaced by hot bread on the day it was taken away.

⁷Now one of Saul's servants was there that day, detained before the LORD; he was Doeg the Edomite, Saul's chief shepherd.

⁸David asked Ahimelek, "Don't you have a spear or a sword here? I haven't brought my sword or any other weapon, because the king's mission was urgent."

⁹The priest replied, "The sword of Goliath the Philistine, whom you killed in the Valley of Elah, is here; it is wrapped in a cloth behind the ephod. If you want it, take it; there is no sword here but that one."

David said, "There is none like it; give it to me."

David at Gath

¹⁰That day David fled from Saul and went to Achish king of Gath. ¹¹But the servants of Achish said to him, "Isn't this David, the king of the land? Isn't he the one they sing about in their dances:

"'Saul has slain his thousands,
    and David his tens of thousands'?"

¹²David took these words to heart and was very much afraid of Achish king of Gath. ¹³So he pretended to be insane in their presence; and while he was in their hands he acted like a madman, making marks on the doors of the gate and letting saliva run down his beard.

¹⁴Achish said to his servants, "Look at the man! He is insane! Why bring him to me? ¹⁵Am I so short of madmen that you have to bring this fellow here to carry on like this in front of me? Must this man come into my house?"

David at Adullam and Mizpah

22 David left Gath and escaped to the cave of Adullam. When his brothers and his father's household heard about it, they went down to him there. ²All those who were in distress or in debt or discontented gathered around him, and he became their commander. About four hundred men were with him.

³From there David went to Mizpah in Moab and said to the king of Moab, "Would you let my father and mother come and stay with you until I learn what God will do for me?" ⁴So he left them with the king of Moab, and they stayed with him as long as David was in the stronghold.

⁵But the prophet Gad said to David, "Do not stay in the stronghold. Go into the land of Judah." So David left and went to the forest of Hereth.

Saul Kills the Priests of Nob

⁶Now Saul heard that David and his men had been discovered. And Saul was seated, spear in hand, under the tamarisk tree on the hill at Gibeah, with all his officials standing at his side.

---

[a] 42 In Hebrew texts this sentence (20:42b) is numbered 21:1.
[b] In Hebrew texts 21:1-15 is numbered 21:2-16.   [c] 5 Or *from us in the past few days since*

⁷He said to them, "Listen, men of Benjamin! Will the son of Jesse give all of you fields and vineyards? Will he make all of you commanders of thousands and commanders of hundreds? ⁸Is that why you have all conspired against me? No one tells me when my son makes a covenant with the son of Jesse. None of you is concerned about me or tells me that my son has incited my servant to lie in wait for me, as he does today."

⁹But Doeg the Edomite, who was standing with Saul's officials, said, "I saw the son of Jesse come to Ahimelek son of Ahitub at Nob. ¹⁰Ahimelek inquired of the LORD for him; he also gave him provisions and the sword of Goliath the Philistine."

¹¹Then the king sent for the priest Ahimelek son of Ahitub and all the men of his family, who were the priests at Nob, and they all came to the king. ¹²Saul said, "Listen now, son of Ahitub."

"Yes, my lord," he answered.

¹³Saul said to him, "Why have you conspired against me, you and the son of Jesse, giving him bread and a sword and inquiring of God for him, so that he has rebelled against me and lies in wait for me, as he does today?"

¹⁴Ahimelek answered the king, "Who of all your servants is as loyal as David, the king's son-in-law, captain of your bodyguard and highly respected in your household? ¹⁵Was that day the first time I inquired of God for him? Of course not! Let not the king accuse your servant or any of his father's family, for your servant knows nothing at all about this whole affair."

¹⁶But the king said, "You will surely die, Ahimelek, you and your whole family."

¹⁷Then the king ordered the guards at his side: "Turn and kill the priests of the LORD, because they too have sided with David. They knew he was fleeing, yet they did not tell me."

But the king's officials were unwilling to raise a hand to strike the priests of the LORD.

¹⁸The king then ordered Doeg, "You turn and strike down the priests." So Doeg the Edomite turned and struck them down. That day he killed eighty-five men who wore the linen ephod. ¹⁹He also put to the sword Nob, the town of the priests, with its men and women, its children and infants, and its cattle, donkeys and sheep.

²⁰But one son of Ahimelek son of Ahitub, named Abiathar, escaped and fled to join David. ²¹He told David that Saul had killed the priests of the LORD. ²²Then David said to Abiathar, "That day, when Doeg the Edomite was there, I knew he would be sure to tell Saul. I am responsible for the death of your whole family. ²³Stay with me; don't be afraid. The man who wants to kill you is trying to kill me too. You will be safe with me."

David Saves Keilah

23 When David was told, "Look, the Philistines are fighting against Keilah and are looting the threshing floors," ²he inquired of the LORD, saying, "Shall I go and attack these Philistines?"

The LORD answered him, "Go, attack the Philistines and save Keilah."

³But David's men said to him, "Here in Judah we are afraid. How much more, then, if we go to Keilah against the Philistine forces!"

⁴Once again David inquired of the LORD, and the LORD answered him, "Go down to Keilah, for I am going to give the Philistines into your hand." ⁵So David and his men went to Keilah, fought the Philistines and carried off their livestock. He inflicted heavy losses on the Philistines and saved the people of Keilah. ⁶(Now Abiathar son of Ahimelek had brought the ephod down with him when he fled to David at Keilah.)

Saul Pursues David

⁷Saul was told that David had gone to Keilah, and he said, "God has delivered him into my hands, for David has imprisoned himself by entering a town with gates and bars." ⁸And Saul called up all his forces for battle, to go down to Keilah to besiege David and his men.

⁹When David learned that Saul was plotting against him, he said to Abiathar the priest, "Bring the ephod." ¹⁰David said, "LORD, God of Israel, your servant has heard definitely that Saul plans to come to Keilah and destroy the town on account of me. ¹¹Will the citizens of Keilah surrender me to him? Will Saul come down, as your servant has heard? LORD, God of Israel, tell your servant."

And the LORD said, "He will."

¹²Again David asked, "Will the citizens of Keilah surrender me and my men to Saul?"

And the LORD said, "They will."

¹³So David and his men, about six hundred in number, left Keilah and kept moving from place to place. When Saul was told that David had escaped from Keilah, he did not go there.

¹⁴David stayed in the wilderness strongholds and in the hills of the Desert of Ziph. Day after day Saul searched for him, but God did not give David into his hands.

¹⁵While David was at Horesh in the Desert of

The Law of Buy-In: David Draws Loyal Renegades

1 Samuel 22:1—23:29

After David fled from Saul to the cave of Adullam, 400 men sought him out to follow his leadership. The Bible describes these men as in distress, in debt, and discontented. Obviously, David had to train these "losers" if he was to create an effective army. And he did.

These men eventually became like David. Some even killed giants, as he did—a classic example of the Law of Buy-In. They first bought into David, then into his vision and leadership. Observe what David teaches us about his leadership:

1. **David attracted these men even without pursuing them.**

2. **David drew deep loyalty out of them without ever trying to get it.**

3. **David transformed these men without disenchanting them over their initial state.**

4. **David fought alongside these "losers" and turned them into winners.**

Consider the astounding exploits of some of these men. Second Samuel 23 tells us that Josheb-Basshebeth slew 800 men with a spear in one battle (v. 8); Eleazar struck down the enemy until his hand clung to his sword (vv. 9–10); Shammah defended a plot of ground against an enemy army (vv. 11–12). Three of these men snuck behind enemy lines just to get David a drink of water from a well in Bethlehem (vv. 15–17). David attracted men like him—souls in distress. He also reproduced men like him—warriors and conquerors.

Ziph, he learned that[a] Saul had come out to take his life. [16]And Saul's son Jonathan went to David at Horesh and helped him find strength in God. [17]"Don't be afraid," he said. "My father Saul will not lay a hand on you. You will be king over Israel, and I will be second to you. Even my father Saul knows this." [18]The two of them made a covenant before the LORD. Then Jonathan went home, but David remained at Horesh.

[19]The Ziphites went up to Saul at Gibeah and said, "Is not David hiding among us in the strongholds at Horesh, on the hill of Hakilah, south of Jeshimon? [20]Now, Your Majesty, come down whenever it pleases you to do so, and we will be responsible for giving him into your hands."

[21]Saul replied, "The LORD bless you for your concern for me. [22]Go and get more information. Find out where David usually goes and who has seen him there. They tell me he is very crafty. [23]Find out about all the hiding places he uses and come back to me with definite information. Then I will go with you; if he is in the area, I will track him down among all the clans of Judah."

[24]So they set out and went to Ziph ahead of Saul. Now David and his men were in the Desert of Maon, in the Arabah south of Jeshimon. [25]Saul and his men began the search, and when David was told about it, he went down to the rock and stayed in the Desert of Maon. When Saul heard this, he went into the Desert of Maon in pursuit of David.

[26]Saul was going along one side of the mountain, and David and his men were on the other side, hurrying to get away from Saul. As Saul and his forces were closing in on David and his men to capture them, [27]a messenger came to Saul, saying, "Come quickly! The Philistines are raiding the land." [28]Then Saul broke off his pursuit of David and went to meet the Philistines. That is why they call this place Sela Hammahlekoth.[b] [29]And David went up from there and lived in the strongholds of En Gedi.[c]

David Spares Saul's Life

24[d] After Saul returned from pursuing the Philistines, he was told, "David is in the Desert of En Gedi." [2]So Saul took three thousand able young men from all Israel and set out to look for David and his men near the Crags of the Wild Goats.

[3]He came to the sheep pens along the way; a cave was there, and Saul went in to relieve himself. David and his men were far back in the

---

[a] 15 Or *he was afraid because*   [b] 28 *Sela Hammahlekoth* means *rock of parting.*   [c] 29 In Hebrew texts this verse (23:29) is numbered 24:1.   [d] In Hebrew texts 24:1-22 is numbered 24:2-23.

The Law of Solid Ground: David's Respect for Saul Earns Him Trust

1 Samuel 24:1–22

Leadership operates on the basis of trust. Before David became king, he showed respect for the king who preceded him. Saul failed to practice this law, and lost his kingdom. The Bible provides a vivid contrast between Saul and David's leadership.

Saul	David
1. Self-conscious from the beginning	1. Displayed God-confidence from the beginning
2. Presumed on the priestly office	2. Didn't assume any right or privilege
3. Disobeyed God in the little things	3. Obeyed God in the little things
4. Lost integrity by covering his sin	4. Maintained integrity by respecting Saul
5. Failed to submit to God-given authority	5. Consistently submitted to authority
6. Preoccupied with his own fame	6. Desired to increase God's reputation

cave. ⁴The men said, "This is the day the LORD spoke of when he said[a] to you, 'I will give your enemy into your hands for you to deal with as you wish.'" Then David crept up unnoticed and cut off a corner of Saul's robe.

⁵Afterward, David was conscience-stricken for having cut off a corner of his robe. ⁶He said to his men, "The LORD forbid that I should do such a thing to my master, the LORD's anointed, or lay my hand on him; for he is the anointed of the LORD." ⁷With these words David sharply rebuked his men and did not allow them to attack Saul. And Saul left the cave and went his way.

⁸Then David went out of the cave and called out to Saul, "My lord the king!" When Saul looked behind him, David bowed down and prostrated himself with his face to the ground. ⁹He said to Saul, "Why do you listen when men say, 'David is bent on harming you'? ¹⁰This day you have seen with your own eyes how the LORD delivered you into my hands in the cave. Some urged me to kill you, but I spared you; I said, 'I will not lay my hand on my lord, because he is the LORD's anointed.' ¹¹See, my father, look at this piece of your robe in my hand! I cut off the corner of your robe but did not kill you. See that there is nothing in my hand to indicate that I am guilty of wrongdoing or rebellion. I have not wronged you, but you are hunting me down to take my life. ¹²May the LORD judge between you and me. And may the LORD avenge the wrongs you have done to me, but my hand will not touch you. ¹³As the old saying goes, 'From

evildoers come evil deeds,' so my hand will not touch you.

¹⁴"Against whom has the king of Israel come out? Who are you pursuing? A dead dog? A flea? ¹⁵May the LORD be our judge and decide between us. May he consider my cause and uphold it; may he vindicate me by delivering me from your hand."

¹⁶When David finished saying this, Saul asked, "Is that your voice, David my son?" And he wept aloud. ¹⁷"You are more righteous than I," he said. "You have treated me well, but I have treated you badly. ¹⁸You have just now told me about the good you did to me; the LORD delivered me into your hands, but you did not kill me. ¹⁹When a man finds his enemy, does he let him get away unharmed? May the LORD reward you well for the way you treated me today. ²⁰I know that you will surely be king and that the kingdom of Israel will be established in your hands. ²¹Now swear to me by the LORD that you will not kill off my descendants or wipe out my name from my father's family."

²²So David gave his oath to Saul. Then Saul returned home, but David and his men went up to the stronghold.

David, Nabal and Abigail

25 Now Samuel died, and all Israel assembled and mourned for him; and they buried him at his home in Ramah. Then David moved down into the Desert of Paran.[b]

---

[a] 4 Or *"Today the LORD is saying*   [b] 1 Hebrew and some Septuagint manuscripts; other Septuagint manuscripts *Maon*

²A certain man in Maon, who had property there at Carmel, was very wealthy. He had a thousand goats and three thousand sheep, which he was shearing in Carmel. ³His name was Nabal and his wife's name was Abigail. She was an intelligent and beautiful woman, but her husband was surly and mean in his dealings— he was a Calebite.

⁴While David was in the wilderness, he heard that Nabal was shearing sheep. ⁵So he sent ten young men and said to them, "Go up to Nabal at Carmel and greet him in my name. ⁶Say to him: 'Long life to you! Good health to you and your household! And good health to all that is yours!

⁷"'Now I hear that it is sheep-shearing time. When your shepherds were with us, we did not mistreat them, and the whole time they were at Carmel nothing of theirs was missing. ⁸Ask your own servants and they will tell you. Therefore be favorable toward my men, since we come at a festive time. Please give your servants and your son David whatever you can find for them.'"

⁹When David's men arrived, they gave Nabal this message in David's name. Then they waited.

¹⁰Nabal answered David's servants, "Who is this David? Who is this son of Jesse? Many servants are breaking away from their masters these days. ¹¹Why should I take my bread and water, and the meat I have slaughtered for my shearers, and give it to men coming from who knows where?"

¹²David's men turned around and went back. When they arrived, they reported every word. ¹³David said to his men, "Each of you strap on your sword!" So they did, and David strapped his on as well. About four hundred men went up with David, while two hundred stayed with the supplies.

¹⁴One of the servants told Abigail, Nabal's wife, "David sent messengers from the wilderness to give our master his greetings, but he hurled insults at them. ¹⁵Yet these men were very good to us. They did not mistreat us, and the whole time we were out in the fields near them nothing was missing. ¹⁶Night and day they were a wall around us the whole time we were herding our sheep near them. ¹⁷Now think it over and see what you can do, because disaster is hanging over our master and his whole household. He is such a wicked man that no one can talk to him."

¹⁸Abigail acted quickly. She took two hundred loaves of bread, two skins of wine, five dressed sheep, five seahs*ᵃ* of roasted grain, a hundred cakes of raisins and two hundred cakes of pressed figs, and loaded them on donkeys. ¹⁹Then she told her servants, "Go on ahead; I'll follow you." But she did not tell her husband Nabal.

ᵃ 18 That is, probably about 60 pounds or about 27 kilograms

ABIGAIL

The Law of Connection
1 Samuel 25:1–42

PROFILE in leadership

Following Samuel's death, David moved to the Desert of Paran. There he encountered shepherds tending the flocks of the wealthy Nabal—an insolent, rude, and contentious man. Nabal happened to be married to a beautiful, intelligent, and intuitive woman named Abigail, and his wise wife saved his miserable life.

When Nabal offended David, Abigail very quickly took steps to defuse a volatile situation. She gathered a great feast and went out to meet David. Abigail's decisive actions met the immediate need of feeding David's men. They also calmed David and diverted him from avenging himself. Abigail lived the Law of Connection.

Upon her return home, Abigail kept her head and chose not to deal with Nabal until he was sober. Regardless of her husband's rudeness and inappropriate behavior, Abigail responded forthrightly and respectfully. God himself later avenged David and chose to remove Nabal from the equation.

David never forgot this encounter. He knew a woman of God when he saw one, and after Nabal's death he chose Abigail to be his wife. Her patience and submission during difficult times, as well as her wisdom and problem-solving skills, prepared her to be an excellent wife for David. David valued Abigail's strength and felt greatly attracted to this highly capable female leader.

21 QUALITIES

ASK PEOPLE to name their favorite person in the Bible, and likely you'll hear the name Abigail. Due to her rare courage, common sense, and some fabulous relational skills, she single-handedly saved her family from certain destruction.

Her husband Nabal, on the other hand, almost provoked the slaughter of his whole household. Nabal's name means "fool," and he lived up to his name. A man without discernment, he selfishly refused to provide for David and his men. An enraged David gathered his troops to kill every male in Nabal's home, and he would have done it—except for Abigail. Note the following relationship lessons she teaches us:

Relationship Lessons from Abigail

1. *Risky initiative:* Abigail took the first step with David to resolve a sticky situation.
2. *Emotional security:* Abigail demonstrated inward security in her identity.
3. *Genuine humility:* Abigail submitted to David by falling at his feet and seeking his favor.
4. *Personal responsibility:* Abigail took responsibility for Nabal and explained his wicked behavior.
5. *Selfless attitude:* Abigail focused completely on David's welfare and future success.
6. *Generous spirit:* Abigail gave David and his men a choice gift for their journey.
7. *Forthright approach:* Abigail directly asked David to forgive Nabal.
8. *Quick wit:* Abigail suggested David didn't want a slaughter on his conscience.
9. *Eternal perspective:* Abigail saw David and their relationship from a divine viewpoint.
10. *Kind affirmation:* Abigail sought David's benefit and gave him encouraging words.

The Stuff Good Relationships Are Made Of

Effective leaders grow their relational skills in the following manner:

- *Have a Leader's Head: Understand People* Abigail knew how to appeal to David in order to accomplish her goal.
- *Have a Leader's Heart: Love People* Abigail assumed the role of a servant, submitting to both David and her husband. She felt secure enough to serve.
- *Have a Leader's Hand: Help People* Abigail gave David and his men what they needed. She added value to him and thereby saved the life of her family.

Nabal: The Other Shoe Drops

Nabal's wife may have excelled in relationships, but Nabal floundered. Their marriage illustrates that opposites really do attract.

As David and his men were getting ready to pass through Nabal's property, David sent a few men ahead to ask Nabal if he could spare anything: food, wool, drinks, anything—they weren't choosy. But Nabal refused to give them even the time of day. He grumbled loudly and sent them away with insults. How foolish!

Nabal should have known that David had saved his nation from Goliath and the Philistines. He should have known the prophet Samuel had anointed David to be the next king. He should have known that David had long protected Nabal's men and possessions. But if Nabal knew any of these things, they didn't matter to him. Nabal still refused to return David's favor.

So was Nabal a criminal? Did he do anything illegal or immoral? Not really. He simply sabotaged his leadership by his lack of people skills.

Nabal serves as a prototype of many pastors and leaders today. Like Nabal, we become so consumed with our own work and personal life that we neglect the only eternal resource on this earth: people. How exactly did Nabal fail to develop healthy relationship skills?

Why Did Nabal Fail?

1. Nabal grew wealthy and satisfied and didn't think he needed to build relationships (v. 2).
2. Nabal became selfish and distrustful of others; he couldn't overcome his evil temperament (v. 3).
3. Nabal neither gave nor received encouragement; he had grown numb to positive attitudes (v. 6).
4. Nabal forgot how others had blessed him in the past; he counted only his losses (vv. 7–8).
5. Nabal belittled people and forgot

their names; his insecurity prevented generosity (v. 10).
6. Nabal saw no reason to help others; he suffered from self-centered motives (v. 11).
7. Nabal wanted to build only his own "kingdom," not God's (v. 11).

Do you or someone you know suffer from similar symptoms? Relational skills are paramount in the kingdom of God. Jesus summarized the kingdom in two phrases: 1. Love God with all your heart; and 2. Love your neighbor as yourself. Our faith doesn't revolve around some sterile creed or doctrine, although creeds remain important. Faith revolves around relationships, vertical with God and horizontal with people. It's all about relationships.

Four Word Pictures

What could Nabal have done to improve his relational skills? He could have started by embracing the following word pictures:

1. *The Host:* Just as a host takes initiative and makes a guest feel comfortable in his or her home, so we are to host the relationships of our lives.
2. *The Doctor:* Just as a doctor does not give a prescription before first making a diagnosis, we are to poke and prod others with questions, so that our responses match the relevant need.
3. *The Counselor:* A good counselor actively listens. Since the number one emotional need of people today is the need to be understood, we must deepen our listening skills.
4. *The Tour Guide:* You hire a tour guide to help you reach your planned destination. God wants us to serve as spiritual "tour guides" for others, helping them to reach their potential.

20As she came riding her donkey into a mountain ravine, there were David and his men descending toward her, and she met them. 21David had just said, "It's been useless—all my watching over this fellow's property in the wilderness so that nothing of his was missing. He has paid me back evil for good. 22May God deal with David,a be it ever so severely, if by morning I leave alive one male of all who belong to him!"

23When Abigail saw David, she quickly got off her donkey and bowed down before David with her face to the ground. 24She fell at his feet and said: "Pardon your servant, my lord, and let me speak to you; hear what your servant has to say. 25Please pay no attention, my lord, to that wicked man Nabal. He is just like his name— his name means Fool, and folly goes with him. And as for me, your servant, I did not see the men my lord sent. 26And now, my lord, as surely as the LORD your God lives and as you live, since the LORD has kept you from bloodshed and from avenging yourself with your own hands, may your enemies and all who are intent on harming my lord be like Nabal. 27And let this gift, which your servant has brought to my lord, be given to the men who follow you.

28"Please forgive your servant's presumption. The LORD your God will certainly make a lasting dynasty for my lord, because you fight the LORD's battles, and no wrongdoing will be found in you as long as you live. 29Even though someone is pursuing you to take your life, the life of my lord will be bound securely in the bundle of the living by the LORD your God, but the lives of your enemies he will hurl away as from the pocket of a sling. 30When the LORD has fulfilled for my lord every good thing he promised concerning him and has appointed him ruler over Israel, 31my lord will not have on his conscience the staggering burden of needless bloodshed or of having avenged himself. And when the LORD your God has brought my lord success, remember your servant."

32David said to Abigail, "Praise be to the LORD, the God of Israel, who has sent you today to meet me. 33May you be blessed for your good judgment and for keeping me from bloodshed this day and from avenging myself with my own hands. 34Otherwise, as surely as the LORD, the God of Israel, lives, who has kept me from harming you, if you had not come quickly to meet me, not one male belonging to Nabal would have been left alive by daybreak."

35Then David accepted from her hand what she had brought him and said, "Go home in peace. I have heard your words and granted your request."

36When Abigail went to Nabal, he was in the house holding a banquet like that of a king. He was in high spirits and very drunk. So she told him nothing at all until daybreak. 37Then in the morning, when Nabal was sober, his wife told him all these things, and his heart failed him and he became like a stone. 38About ten days later, the LORD struck Nabal and he died.

39When David heard that Nabal was dead, he said, "Praise be to the LORD, who has upheld my cause against Nabal for treating me with contempt. He has kept his servant from doing wrong and has brought Nabal's wrongdoing down on his own head."

Then David sent word to Abigail, asking her to become his wife. 40His servants went to Carmel and said to Abigail, "David has sent us to you to take you to become his wife."

41She bowed down with her face to the ground and said, "I am your servant and am ready to serve you and wash the feet of my lord's servants." 42Abigail quickly got on a donkey and, attended by her five female servants, went with David's messengers and became his wife. 43David had also married Ahinoam of Jezreel, and they both were his wives. 44But Saul had given his daughter Michal, David's wife, to Paltielb son of Laish, who was from Gallim.

David Again Spares Saul's Life

26 The Ziphites went to Saul at Gibeah and said, "Is not David hiding on the hill of Hakilah, which faces Jeshimon?"

2So Saul went down to the Desert of Ziph, with his three thousand select Israelite troops, to search there for David. 3Saul made his camp beside the road on the hill of Hakilah facing Jeshimon, but David stayed in the wilderness. When he saw that Saul had followed him there, 4he sent out scouts and learned that Saul had definitely arrived.

5Then David set out and went to the place where Saul had camped. He saw where Saul and Abner son of Ner, the commander of the army, had lain down. Saul was lying inside the camp, with the army encamped around him.

6David then asked Ahimelek the Hittite and Abishai son of Zeruiah, Joab's brother, "Who will go down into the camp with me to Saul?"

"I'll go with you," said Abishai.

---

a 22 Some Septuagint manuscripts; Hebrew with David's enemies   b 44 Hebrew Palti, a variant of Paltiel

[7]So David and Abishai went to the army by night, and there was Saul, lying asleep inside the camp with his spear stuck in the ground near his head. Abner and the soldiers were lying around him.

[8]Abishai said to David, "Today God has delivered your enemy into your hands. Now let me pin him to the ground with one thrust of the spear; I won't strike him twice."

[9]But David said to Abishai, "Don't destroy him! Who can lay a hand on the LORD's anointed and be guiltless? [10]As surely as the LORD lives," he said, "the LORD himself will strike him, or his time will come and he will die, or he will go into battle and perish. [11]But the LORD forbid that I should lay a hand on the LORD's anointed. Now get the spear and water jug that are near his head, and let's go."

[12]So David took the spear and water jug near Saul's head, and they left. No one saw or knew about it, nor did anyone wake up. They were all sleeping, because the LORD had put them into a deep sleep.

[13]Then David crossed over to the other side and stood on top of the hill some distance away; there was a wide space between them. [14]He called out to the army and to Abner son of Ner, "Aren't you going to answer me, Abner?"

Abner replied, "Who are you who calls to the king?"

[15]David said, "You're a man, aren't you? And who is like you in Israel? Why didn't you guard your lord the king? Someone came to destroy your lord the king. [16]What you have done is not good. As surely as the LORD lives, you and your men must die, because you did not guard your master, the LORD's anointed. Look around you. Where are the king's spear and water jug that were near his head?"

[17]Saul recognized David's voice and said, "Is that your voice, David my son?"

David replied, "Yes it is, my lord the king." [18]And he added, "Why is my lord pursuing his servant? What have I done, and what wrong am I guilty of? [19]Now let my lord the king listen to his servant's words. If the LORD has incited you against me, then may he accept an offering. If, however, people have done it, may they be cursed before the LORD! They have driven me today from my share in the LORD's inheritance and have said, 'Go, serve other gods.' [20]Now do not let my blood fall to the ground far from the presence of the LORD. The king of Israel has come out to look for a flea — as one hunts a partridge in the mountains."

[21]Then Saul said, "I have sinned. Come back, David my son. Because you considered my life precious today, I will not try to harm you again. Surely I have acted like a fool and have been terribly wrong."

[22]"Here is the king's spear," David answered. "Let one of your young men come over and get it. [23]The LORD rewards everyone for their righteousness and faithfulness. The LORD delivered you into my hands today, but I would not lay a hand on the LORD's anointed. [24]As surely as I valued your life today, so may the LORD value my life and deliver me from all trouble."

[25]Then Saul said to David, "May you be blessed, David my son; you will do great things and surely triumph."

So David went on his way, and Saul returned home.

David Among the Philistines

27 But David thought to himself, "One of these days I will be destroyed by the hand of Saul. The best thing I can do is to escape to the land of the Philistines. Then Saul will give up searching for me anywhere in Israel, and I will slip out of his hand."

[2]So David and the six hundred men with him left and went over to Achish son of Maok king of Gath. [3]David and his men settled in Gath with Achish. Each man had his family with him, and David had his two wives: Ahinoam of Jezreel and Abigail of Carmel, the widow of Nabal. [4]When Saul was told that David had fled to Gath, he no longer searched for him.

[5]Then David said to Achish, "If I have found favor in your eyes, let a place be assigned to me in one of the country towns, that I may live there. Why should your servant live in the royal city with you?"

[6]So on that day Achish gave him Ziklag, and it has belonged to the kings of Judah ever since. [7]David lived in Philistine territory a year and four months.

[8]Now David and his men went up and raided the Geshurites, the Girzites and the Amalekites. (From ancient times these peoples had lived in the land extending to Shur and Egypt.) [9]Whenever David attacked an area, he did not leave a man or woman alive, but took sheep and cattle, donkeys and camels, and clothes. Then he returned to Achish.

[10]When Achish asked, "Where did you go raiding today?" David would say, "Against the Negev of Judah" or "Against the Negev of Jerahmeel" or "Against the Negev of the Kenites."

21 QUALITIES

LISTENING
David's Conflict Resolution Strategy Wins Saul Over

1 Samuel 26:1–25

THROUGH LISTENING, leaders earn the right to speak into the lives of their people. Because they listen, they speak with relevance. And as they listen, they display love, compassion and understanding.

David led well because he listened well. First Samuel 26 describes how he gained the opportunity to take Saul's life for the second time. David snuck up on the king while he slept. But instead of killing him, David took the king's spear and water jug and later, from a distance, confronted him with questions. David shows that a leader who listens possesses genuine love.

1. *Genuine love is not always popular—be different.* Remember David's men? Malcontents. Disgruntled. More than once they encouraged him to look out for himself and take Saul's life—but David refused. We must be careful how we interpret circumstances and whose advice we accept.

2. *Genuine love needs a clear perspective—be humble.* After David took Saul's spear and jug, he called to the king from a distance. He submitted himself and humbly asked for perspective. "What have I done?" he asked. We will never be able to love

people correctly until we see them clearly, with God's eyes.

3. *Genuine love is not defensive—be patient.* David knew God put him in this situation for a purpose and trusted him to deliver him. David offers to make a sacrifice if he has harmed Saul or done anything wrong, and he waits to hear Saul's rationale. Impatience indicates we lack trust and want our rights.

4. *Genuine love is powerful—be forgiving.* Saul later apologizes to David and admits his wrong. He promises to go home. At this point, David sits in the driver's seat; he still has Saul's spear and jug. But he returns them and forgives Saul of everything. Like David, we must trust God to make things right.

What Steps Did David Take?

Note the following steps David walked through with Saul (1Sa 26):

1. He initiated the contact with Saul and set the stage for communication (v. 14).

2. He appealed to Saul's sense of right and wrong (vv. 15–16).

3. He asked questions and listened for the king's heart's response (v. 18).

4. He asked them to listen so he could share his perspective (v. 19).

5. He determined to own up to anything he had done wrong (v. 19).

6. He submitted himself to Saul (v. 20).

7. He offered forgiveness and reconciliation as an act of trust in God (vv. 22–24).

How about you? Do you display love for others by listening? Are you a good listener?

For a negative example of listening, see p. 535.

¹¹He did not leave a man or woman alive to be brought to Gath, for he thought, "They might inform on us and say, 'This is what David did.'" And such was his practice as long as he lived in Philistine territory. ¹²Achish trusted David and said to himself, "He has become so obnoxious to his people, the Israelites, that he will be my servant for life."

28 In those days the Philistines gathered their forces to fight against Israel. Achish said to David, "You must understand that you and your men will accompany me in the army."

²David said, "Then you will see for yourself what your servant can do."

Achish replied, "Very well, I will make you my bodyguard for life."

Saul and the Medium at Endor

³Now Samuel was dead, and all Israel had mourned for him and buried him in his own town of Ramah. Saul had expelled the mediums and spiritists from the land.

⁴The Philistines assembled and came and set up camp at Shunem, while Saul gathered all Israel and set up camp at Gilboa. ⁵When Saul saw the Philistine army, he was afraid; terror filled his heart. ⁶He inquired of the LORD, but the LORD did not answer him by dreams or Urim or prophets. ⁷Saul then said to his attendants, "Find me a woman who is a medium, so I may go and inquire of her."

"There is one in Endor," they said.

⁸So Saul disguised himself, putting on other clothes, and at night he and two men went to the woman. "Consult a spirit for me," he said, "and bring up for me the one I name."

⁹But the woman said to him, "Surely you know what Saul has done. He has cut off the mediums and spiritists from the land. Why have you set a trap for my life to bring about my death?"

¹⁰Saul swore to her by the LORD, "As surely as the LORD lives, you will not be punished for this."

¹¹Then the woman asked, "Whom shall I bring up for you?"

"Bring up Samuel," he said.

¹²When the woman saw Samuel, she cried out at the top of her voice and said to Saul, "Why have you deceived me? You are Saul!"

¹³The king said to her, "Don't be afraid. What do you see?"

The woman said, "I see a ghostly figure[a] coming up out of the earth."

¹⁴"What does he look like?" he asked.

"An old man wearing a robe is coming up," she said.

Then Saul knew it was Samuel, and he bowed down and prostrated himself with his face to the ground.

¹⁵Samuel said to Saul, "Why have you disturbed me by bringing me up?"

"I am in great distress," Saul said. "The Philistines are fighting against me, and God has departed from me. He no longer answers me, either by prophets or by dreams. So I have called on you to tell me what to do."

¹⁶Samuel said, "Why do you consult me, now that the LORD has departed from you and become your enemy? ¹⁷The LORD has done what he predicted through me. The LORD has torn the kingdom out of your hands and given it to one of your neighbors—to David. ¹⁸Because you did not obey the LORD or carry out his fierce wrath against the Amalekites, the LORD has done this to you today. ¹⁹The LORD will deliver both Israel and you into the hands of the Philistines, and tomorrow you and your sons will be with me. The LORD will also give the army of Israel into the hands of the Philistines."

²⁰Immediately Saul fell full length on the ground, filled with fear because of Samuel's words. His strength was gone, for he had eaten nothing all that day and all that night.

²¹When the woman came to Saul and saw that he was greatly shaken, she said, "Look, your servant has obeyed you. I took my life in my hands and did what you told me to do. ²²Now please listen to your servant and let me give you some food so you may eat and have the strength to go on your way."

²³He refused and said, "I will not eat."

But his men joined the woman in urging him, and he listened to them. He got up from the ground and sat on the couch.

²⁴The woman had a fattened calf at the house, which she butchered at once. She took some flour, kneaded it and baked bread without yeast. ²⁵Then she set it before Saul and his men, and they ate. That same night they got up and left.

Achish Sends David Back to Ziklag

29 The Philistines gathered all their forces at Aphek, and Israel camped by the spring in Jezreel. ²As the Philistine rulers marched with their units of hundreds and thousands, David and his men were marching at the

---

a 13 Or *see spirits*; or *see gods*

rear with Achish. ³The commanders of the Philistines asked, "What about these Hebrews?"

Achish replied, "Is this not David, who was an officer of Saul king of Israel? He has already been with me for over a year, and from the day he left Saul until now, I have found no fault in him."

⁴But the Philistine commanders were angry with Achish and said, "Send the man back, that he may return to the place you assigned him. He must not go with us into battle, or he will turn against us during the fighting. How better could he regain his master's favor than by taking the heads of our own men? ⁵Isn't this the David they sang about in their dances:

"'Saul has slain his thousands,
    and David his tens of thousands'?"

⁶So Achish called David and said to him, "As surely as the LORD lives, you have been reliable, and I would be pleased to have you serve with me in the army. From the day you came to me until today, I have found no fault in you, but the rulers don't approve of you. ⁷Now turn back and go in peace; do nothing to displease the Philistine rulers."

⁸"But what have I done?" asked David. "What have you found against your servant from the day I came to you until now? Why can't I go and fight against the enemies of my lord the king?"

⁹Achish answered, "I know that you have been as pleasing in my eyes as an angel of God; nevertheless, the Philistine commanders have said, 'He must not go up with us into battle.' ¹⁰Now get up early, along with your master's servants who have come with you, and leave in the morning as soon as it is light."

¹¹So David and his men got up early in the morning to go back to the land of the Philistines, and the Philistines went up to Jezreel.

David Fails to Trust God and Visits the Carnal Corral

1 Samuel 29:1–11

Over time David grew weary of Saul's pursuit and chose to escape to the land of the Philistines. He became vague about his purpose, defensive about his leadership, and lost the trust of Israel. Even great leaders become vulnerable when they grow tired, lonely, angry, or hungry.

David Destroys the Amalekites

30 David and his men reached Ziklag on the third day. Now the Amalekites had raided the Negev and Ziklag. They had attacked Ziklag and burned it, ²and had taken captive the women and everyone else in it, both young and old. They killed none of them, but carried them off as they went on their way.

³When David and his men reached Ziklag, they found it destroyed by fire and their wives and sons and daughters taken captive. ⁴So David and his men wept aloud until they had no strength left to weep. ⁵David's two wives had been captured—Ahinoam of Jezreel and Abigail, the widow of Nabal of Carmel. ⁶David was greatly distressed because the men were talking of stoning him; each one was bitter in spirit because of his sons and daughters. But David found strength in the LORD his God.

⁷Then David said to Abiathar the priest, the son of Ahimelek, "Bring me the ephod." Abiathar brought it to him, ⁸and David inquired of the LORD, "Shall I pursue this raiding party? Will I overtake them?"

"Pursue them," he answered. "You will certainly overtake them and succeed in the rescue."

⁹David and the six hundred men with him came to the Besor Valley, where some stayed behind. ¹⁰Two hundred of them were too exhausted to cross the valley, but David and the other four hundred continued the pursuit.

¹¹They found an Egyptian in a field and brought him to David. They gave him water to drink and food to eat— ¹²part of a cake of pressed figs and two cakes of raisins. He ate and was revived, for he had not eaten any food or drunk any water for three days and three nights.

¹³David asked him, "Who do you belong to? Where do you come from?"

He said, "I am an Egyptian, the slave of an Amalekite. My master abandoned me when I became ill three days ago. ¹⁴We raided the Negev of the Kerethites, some territory belonging to Judah and the Negev of Caleb. And we burned Ziklag."

¹⁵David asked him, "Can you lead me down to this raiding party?"

He answered, "Swear to me before God that you will not kill me or hand me over to my master, and I will take you down to them."

¹⁶He led David down, and there they were, scattered over the countryside, eating, drinking and reveling because of the great amount of plunder they had taken from the land of the

SERVANTHOOD To Get Ahead, Put Others First

1 Samuel 30:17–20

DAVID ILLUSTRATES the leadership quality of servanthood in a positive way. His leadership was first and foremost about serving his team, not about his own fame or conquest. First Samuel 30 instructs us about relationships and partnerships. After conquering the Amalekites, David and his men took huge plunder. However, some of his older troops who were too tired to fight stayed back to help with supplies. It would have been easy for the troops who actually did the fighting to say: If you didn't show up to the battle, you don't get to share in the rewards! Surely some of those soldiers must have had this assumption. David resolved the conflict by calmly helping them all see that since God was the source of their victory and since those who helped with the supplies did play a role, they should all share in the plunder. David later turned this decision into a policy for Israel. Clearly, David valued every partner in the equation. His leadership was about service to others rather than accumulating wealth and power for oneself. Modeling this leadership quality did plenty of good things for David's situation as a leader.

The Results of David's Servant Leadership:

1. *It helped others see the contribution of every man's gift.*
   Even the older soldiers who remained at the camp because they were too tired to fight added some value to the entire army. They guarded the supplies. David's perspective on valuing everyone's gift and contribution kept everyone's eyes on others, on the big picture rather than getting preoccupied with one's own contribution.

2. *It reminded David's men that God was the true source of every good gift.*
   David knew that allowing everyone to celebrate the victory and share in its spoils would help his men to see that God was the true source of victory anyway. When people start keeping score on who gets what, they tend to get consumed with themselves and whether they are getting their fair share of the reward. David's servant leadership helped others see through God's eyes and trust him for their rewards in life.

3. *It promoted goodwill in potential allies, resources David enjoyed later as king.*
   The people soon recognized that if you cooperate with David, he makes sure you win in some way. This promoted partnerships and a contagious spirit of service and goodwill among David's troops. When leaders are selfish, it fosters a selfish atmosphere among everyone they lead. When leaders generously

serve, this kind of service orientation spreads through the camp.

4. It enabled David to prepare for the future by making him friends all over Israel.

When a leader serves today, it generally pays off tomorrow in relationships with others. David may not have realized it at the time, but as word spread about his generous style, his servant leadership prepared the hearts of citizens all over Israel to follow him. It won them over. Sometimes little acts of kindness—unpromoted by the leaders—spread faster than staged acts on a platform. One appears authentic while the other just looks artificial.

5. It developed a nationwide value of mutual benefit and good faith among people.

Once David became king, this same spirit of appreciation and servanthood became the norm for a season in Israel. When leaders don't selfishly grasp what they believe they deserve, it spawns a trust among those who follow. A sense of justice-for-all prevails. Instead of contagious selfishness there is contagious servanthood.

For a negative example of servanthood, see p. 1262.

Philistines and from Judah. [17]David fought them from dusk until the evening of the next day, and none of them got away, except four hundred young men who rode off on camels and fled. [18]David recovered everything the Amalekites had taken, including his two wives. [19]Nothing was missing: young or old, boy or girl, plunder or anything else they had taken. David brought everything back. [20]He took all the flocks and herds, and his men drove them ahead of the other livestock, saying, "This is David's plunder."

[21]Then David came to the two hundred men who had been too exhausted to follow him and who were left behind at the Besor Valley. They came out to meet David and the men with him. As David and his men approached, he asked them how they were. [22]But all the evil men and troublemakers among David's followers said, "Because they did not go out with us, we will not share with them the plunder we recovered. However, each man may take his wife and children and go."

[23]David replied, "No, my brothers, you must not do that with what the LORD has given us. He has protected us and delivered into our hands the raiding party that came against us. [24]Who will listen to what you say? The share of the man who stayed with the supplies is to be the same as that of him who went down to the battle. All will share alike." [25]David made this a statute and ordinance for Israel from that day to this.

[26]When David reached Ziklag, he sent some of the plunder to the elders of Judah, who were his friends, saying, "Here is a gift for you from the plunder of the LORD's enemies."

[27]David sent it to those who were in Bethel, Ramoth Negev and Jattir; [28]to those in Aroer, Siphmoth, Eshtemoa [29]and Rakal; to those in the towns of the Jerahmeelites and the Kenites; [30]to those in Hormah, Bor Ashan, Athak [31]and Hebron; and to those in all the other places where he and his men had roamed.

Saul Takes His Life

31 Now the Philistines fought against Israel; the Israelites fled before them, and many fell dead on Mount Gilboa. [2]The Philistines were in hot pursuit of Saul and his sons, and they killed his sons Jonathan, Abinadab and Malki-Shua. [3]The fighting grew fierce around Saul, and when the archers overtook him, they wounded him critically.

[4]Saul said to his armor-bearer, "Draw your sword and run me through, or these uncircumcised fellows will come and run me through and abuse me."

But his armor-bearer was terrified and would not do it; so Saul took his own sword and fell on it. [5]When the armor-bearer saw that Saul was dead, he too fell on his sword and died with him. [6]So Saul and his three sons and his armor-bearer and all his men died together that same day.

[7]When the Israelites along the valley and those across the Jordan saw that the Israelite army had fled and that Saul and his sons had died, they abandoned their towns and fled. And the Philistines came and occupied them.

[8]The next day, when the Philistines came to strip the dead, they found Saul and his three sons fallen on Mount Gilboa. [9]They cut off his head and stripped off his armor, and they sent messengers throughout the land of the Philistines to proclaim the news in the temple of their idols and among their people. [10]They put his armor in the temple of the Ashtoreths and fastened his body to the wall of Beth Shan.

[11]When the people of Jabesh Gilead heard what the Philistines had done to Saul, [12]all their valiant men marched through the night to Beth Shan. They took down the bodies of Saul and his sons from the wall of Beth Shan and went to Jabesh, where they burned them. [13]Then they took their bones and buried them under a tamarisk tree at Jabesh, and they fasted seven days.

INTRODUCTION TO
2 SAMUEL

Continuous Account of the First Kings of Israel

I n the original Hebrew manuscripts of the Old Testament, the books of 1 and 2 Samuel form a single volume. Together they give one continuous account of the first kings of Israel.

Second Samuel begins with the death of King Saul and Prince Jonathan. Although the prophet Samuel had anointed David king long before, only after this incident does he begin his monarchy. David refused to assume any royal authority until Saul, God's anointed king, had died.

A turbulent transition period brought civil war between David's military forces, led by Joab, and Saul's army, led by Abner. David's army grew steadily stronger, while Abner's weakened by the day. When Joab murdered Abner, all of Israel lost heart, and Judah and Israel finally joined as one under David's leadership.

The rest of the book tells the intriguing story of a leader every bit as human as he was noble. David quickly became a much stronger leader than Saul, due in large measure to the Law of the Lid. In addition, David practiced every one of the 21 Laws of Leadership. He developed a standing army; he established a capital where the ark of God could be housed; he laid plans to build a temple; and he conquered every army he faced. He wrote more than 100 psalms expressing his own intimacy with God. Two verses tell his story early on: "He became more and more powerful, because the LORD God Almighty was with him" (5:10), and "The LORD gave David victory wherever he went" (8:14).

Sadly, none of this kept David from indulging the baser side of his nature. Before the book is half finished, David has committed adultery with Bathsheba. When she becomes pregnant, he tries to cover up his sin and

God's Role in 2 Samuel

God intended for Israel to become a light to the nations, goading the surrounding kingdoms to jealousy over the special relationship between Israel and God. The Lord blessed the Hebrews in order that they might bless the nations of the world (Ge 12:1–3). Under David's reign, Israel comes close to God's goal. David takes a country the size of the state of New Jersey and develops it into a world-class nation. Everyone recognized the strength of Israel's leadership, economy, military force, and natural resources.

God desired to develop and maintain a close relationship with David, knowing that as the leader goes, so goes the nation. Even when David sinned, he managed to stay in touch with God.

Leaders in 2 Samuel
David, Joab, Abner, Ish-Bosheth, Absalom

Other People of Influence in 2 Samuel
Michal, Bathsheba, Nathan, Hushai

Lessons in Leadership
- Leaders mature when they allow God to break them.
- Leaders must be both tough and tender.

orders her soldier husband to the front lines to ensure his death. David never fully recovered from this sin. He neglected his family, leaving both sons and daughters to wonder how Dad could be such a great king, but such a distant father.

Despite all of this, David remains the only person in Scripture whom God calls a "man after his own heart" (1Sa 13:14). In 2 Samuel we see both the qualities of an effective leader and the quirks of an ineffective leader who loses sight of the big picture. David's life proves that every leader needs an inner circle to keep him or her in check.

- When leaders stop sacrificing, they stop succeeding.
- People do what people see.
- Leadership is about relationships—if you get along, they'll go along.
- If you won't carry the ball, you can't lead the team.
- The first person you must lead is you.
- The leader's source is God—not people, material resources or money.

LEADERSHIP HIGHLIGHTS IN 2 SAMUEL

David Hears of Saul's Death

1 After the death of Saul, David returned from striking down the Amalekites and stayed in Ziklag two days. ²On the third day a man arrived from Saul's camp with his clothes torn and dust on his head. When he came to David, he fell to the ground to pay him honor.

³"Where have you come from?" David asked him.

He answered, "I have escaped from the Israelite camp."

⁴"What happened?" David asked. "Tell me."

"The men fled from the battle," he replied. "Many of them fell and died. And Saul and his son Jonathan are dead."

⁵Then David said to the young man who brought him the report, "How do you know that Saul and his son Jonathan are dead?"

⁶"I happened to be on Mount Gilboa," the young man said, "and there was Saul, leaning on his spear, with the chariots and their drivers in hot pursuit. ⁷When he turned around and saw me, he called out to me, and I said, 'What can I do?'

⁸"He asked me, 'Who are you?'

"'An Amalekite,' I answered.

⁹"Then he said to me, 'Stand here by me and kill me! I'm in the throes of death, but I'm still alive.'

¹⁰"So I stood beside him and killed him, because I knew that after he had fallen he could not survive. And I took the crown that was on his head and the band on his arm and have brought them here to my lord."

¹¹Then David and all the men with him took hold of their clothes and tore them. ¹²They mourned and wept and fasted till evening for Saul and his son Jonathan, and for the army of the LORD and for the nation of Israel, because they had fallen by the sword.

¹³David said to the young man who brought him the report, "Where are you from?"

"I am the son of a foreigner, an Amalekite," he answered.

¹⁴David asked him, "Why weren't you afraid to lift your hand to destroy the LORD's anointed?"

¹⁵Then David called one of his men and said, "Go, strike him down!" So he struck him down, and he died. ¹⁶For David had said to him, "Your blood be on your own head. Your own mouth testified against you when you said, 'I killed the LORD's anointed.'"

David's Lament for Saul and Jonathan

¹⁷David took up this lament concerning Saul and his son Jonathan, ¹⁸and he ordered that the people of Judah be taught this lament of the bow (it is written in the Book of Jashar):

¹⁹"A gazelle[a] lies slain on your heights, Israel.
　How the mighty have fallen!

²⁰"Tell it not in Gath,
　proclaim it not in the streets of Ashkelon,
lest the daughters of the Philistines be glad,
　lest the daughters of the uncircumcised
　　rejoice.

²¹"Mountains of Gilboa,
　may you have neither dew nor rain,
　may no showers fall on your terraced
　　fields.[b]
For there the shield of the mighty was
　　despised,
　the shield of Saul — no longer rubbed with
　　oil.

²²"From the blood of the slain,
　from the flesh of the mighty,
the bow of Jonathan did not turn back,
　the sword of Saul did not return unsatisfied.

---

[a] 19 *Gazelle* here symbolizes a human dignitary.　[b] 21 Or / *nor fields that yield grain for offerings*

The Authority Test: David Submits Until the End

2 Samuel 1:17–27

When David hears that Saul and Jonathan have died in battle, he mourns deeply for his friend Jonathan. But he also weeps for Saul, the man who: (1) tried to murder him in the palace, (2) tried to get the Philistines to kill him in battle, and (3) chased him through hills and caves in order to execute him. Why honor such a man?

In David's mind, submission to authority has little to do with the person in charge. In fact, when a young Amalekite tells David that he put Saul out of his misery at the king's request, David orders his execution, saying, "Your blood be on your own head. Your own mouth testified against you when you said, 'I killed the LORD's anointed'" (2Sa 1:16).

While leaders earn their influence, God gives them their authority. We owe our submission to whatever authorities God installs, regardless of who they may be (Ro 13:1).

²³Saul and Jonathan —
    in life they were loved and admired,
    and in death they were not parted.
They were swifter than eagles,
    they were stronger than lions.

²⁴"Daughters of Israel,
    weep for Saul,
who clothed you in scarlet and finery,
    who adorned your garments with
        ornaments of gold.

²⁵"How the mighty have fallen in battle!
    Jonathan lies slain on your heights.
²⁶I grieve for you, Jonathan my brother;
    you were very dear to me.
Your love for me was wonderful,
    more wonderful than that of women.

²⁷"How the mighty have fallen!
    The weapons of war have perished!"

David Anointed King Over Judah

2 In the course of time, David inquired of the LORD. "Shall I go up to one of the towns of Judah?" he asked.

The LORD said, "Go up."

David asked, "Where shall I go?"

"To Hebron," the LORD answered.

²So David went up there with his two wives, Ahinoam of Jezreel and Abigail, the widow of Nabal of Carmel. ³David also took the men who were with him, each with his family, and they settled in Hebron and its towns. ⁴Then the men of Judah came to Hebron, and there they anointed David king over the tribe of Judah.

When David was told that it was the men from Jabesh Gilead who had buried Saul, ⁵he sent messengers to them to say to them, "The LORD bless you for showing this kindness to Saul your master by burying him. ⁶May the LORD now show you kindness and faithfulness, and I too will show you the same favor because you have done this. ⁷Now then, be strong and brave, for Saul your master is dead, and the people of Judah have anointed me king over them."

War Between the Houses of David and Saul

⁸Meanwhile, Abner son of Ner, the commander of Saul's army, had taken Ish-Bosheth son of Saul and brought him over to Mahanaim. ⁹He made him king over Gilead, Ashuri and Jezreel, and also over Ephraim, Benjamin and all Israel.

¹⁰Ish-Bosheth son of Saul was forty years old when he became king over Israel, and he reigned two years. The tribe of Judah, however, remained loyal to David. ¹¹The length of time David was king in Hebron over Judah was seven years and six months.

¹²Abner son of Ner, together with the men of Ish-Bosheth son of Saul, left Mahanaim and went to Gibeon. ¹³Joab son of Zeruiah and David's men went out and met them at the pool of Gibeon. One group sat down on one side of the pool and one group on the other side.

¹⁴Then Abner said to Joab, "Let's have some of the young men get up and fight hand to hand in front of us."

"All right, let them do it," Joab said.

¹⁵So they stood up and were counted off—

Conflict at the Top

2 Samuel 2:4–11

Saul's death led to all kinds of turmoil over who would become the next king. Despite David's anointing by Samuel, others saw a tempting opportunity to seize power.

Transitions often bring difficult times. Leaders who fail to plan for their departure invite trouble. Saul could have been a hero had he cooperated with God in preparing David to succeed him. He didn't have a more submissive staff person in his entire palace than David.

Saul suffered from an "I" problem, an oversize ego that blinded him. Saul could've helped himself had he recognized these truths:

1. **Since change makes people insecure, leaders must see ahead and prepare for them.**

2. **People can live without certainty, but not without clarity regarding future direction.**

3. **Wise choices today put "change in the pocket" of a leader regarding future choices.**

4. **Problem-solving skills and effective communication earn the leader trust and credibility.**

twelve men for Benjamin and Ish-Bosheth son of Saul, and twelve for David. ¹⁶Then each man grabbed his opponent by the head and thrust his dagger into his opponent's side, and they fell down together. So that place in Gibeon was called Helkath Hazzurim.ᵃ

¹⁷The battle that day was very fierce, and Abner and the Israelites were defeated by David's men.

¹⁸The three sons of Zeruiah were there: Joab, Abishai and Asahel. Now Asahel was as fleet-footed as a wild gazelle. ¹⁹He chased Abner, turning neither to the right nor to the left as he pursued him. ²⁰Abner looked behind him and asked, "Is that you, Asahel?"

"It is," he answered.

²¹Then Abner said to him, "Turn aside to the right or to the left; take on one of the young men and strip him of his weapons." But Asahel would not stop chasing him.

²²Again Abner warned Asahel, "Stop chasing me! Why should I strike you down? How could I look your brother Joab in the face?"

²³But Asahel refused to give up the pursuit; so Abner thrust the butt of his spear into Asahel's stomach, and the spear came out through his back. He fell there and died on the spot. And every man stopped when he came to the place where Asahel had fallen and died.

²⁴But Joab and Abishai pursued Abner, and as the sun was setting, they came to the hill of Ammah, near Giah on the way to the wasteland of Gibeon. ²⁵Then the men of Benjamin rallied behind Abner. They formed themselves into a group and took their stand on top of a hill.

²⁶Abner called out to Joab, "Must the sword devour forever? Don't you realize that this will end in bitterness? How long before you order your men to stop pursuing their fellow Israelites?"

²⁷Joab answered, "As surely as God lives, if you had not spoken, the men would have continued pursuing them until morning."

²⁸So Joab blew the trumpet, and all the troops came to a halt; they no longer pursued Israel, nor did they fight anymore.

²⁹All that night Abner and his men marched through the Arabah. They crossed the Jordan, continued through the morning hoursᵇ and came to Mahanaim.

³⁰Then Joab stopped pursuing Abner and assembled the whole army. Besides Asahel, nineteen of David's men were found missing. ³¹But David's men had killed three hundred and sixty Benjamites who were with Abner. ³²They took Asahel and buried him in his father's tomb at

Bethlehem. Then Joab and his men marched all night and arrived at Hebron by daybreak.

3 The war between the house of Saul and the house of David lasted a long time. David grew stronger and stronger, while the house of Saul grew weaker and weaker.

²Sons were born to David in Hebron:

His firstborn was Amnon the son of Ahinoam of Jezreel;
³his second, Kileab the son of Abigail the widow of Nabal of Carmel;
the third, Absalom the son of Maakah daughter of Talmai king of Geshur;
⁴the fourth, Adonijah the son of Haggith;
the fifth, Shephatiah the son of Abital;
⁵and the sixth, Ithream the son of David's wife Eglah.

These were born to David in Hebron.

Abner Goes Over to David

⁶During the war between the house of Saul and the house of David, Abner had been strengthening his own position in the house of Saul. ⁷Now Saul had had a concubine named Rizpah daughter of Aiah. And Ish-Bosheth said to Abner, "Why did you sleep with my father's concubine?"

⁸Abner was very angry because of what Ish-Bosheth said. So he answered, "Am I a dog's head—on Judah's side? This very day I am loyal to the house of your father Saul and to his family and friends. I haven't handed you over to David. Yet now you accuse me of an offense involving this woman! ⁹May God deal with Abner, be it ever so severely, if I do not do for David what the LORD promised him on oath ¹⁰and transfer the kingdom from the house of Saul and establish David's throne over Israel and Judah from Dan to Beersheba." ¹¹Ish-Bosheth did not dare to say another word to Abner, because he was afraid of him.

¹²Then Abner sent messengers on his behalf to say to David, "Whose land is it? Make an agreement with me, and I will help you bring all Israel over to you."

¹³"Good," said David. "I will make an agreement with you. But I demand one thing of you: Do not come into my presence unless you bring Michal daughter of Saul when you come to see me." ¹⁴Then David sent messengers to Ish-Bosheth son of Saul, demanding, "Give me

---

ᵃ 16 Helkath Hazzurim means field of daggers or field of hostilities.   ᵇ 29 See Septuagint; the meaning of the Hebrew for this phrase is uncertain.

my wife Michal, whom I betrothed to myself for the price of a hundred Philistine foreskins."

[15] So Ish-Bosheth gave orders and had her taken away from her husband Paltiel son of Laish. [16] Her husband, however, went with her, weeping behind her all the way to Bahurim. Then Abner said to him, "Go back home!" So he went back.

[17] Abner conferred with the elders of Israel and said, "For some time you have wanted to make David your king. [18] Now do it! For the LORD promised David, 'By my servant David I will rescue my people Israel from the hand of the Philistines and from the hand of all their enemies.'"

[19] Abner also spoke to the Benjamites in person. Then he went to Hebron to tell David everything that Israel and the whole tribe of Benjamin wanted to do. [20] When Abner, who had twenty men with him, came to David at Hebron, David prepared a feast for him and his men. [21] Then Abner said to David, "Let me go at once and assemble all Israel for my lord the king, so that they may make a covenant with you, and that you may rule over all that your heart desires." So David sent Abner away, and he went in peace.

Joab Murders Abner

[22] Just then David's men and Joab returned from a raid and brought with them a great deal of plunder. But Abner was no longer with David in Hebron, because David had sent him away, and he had gone in peace. [23] When Joab and all the soldiers with him arrived, he was told that Abner son of Ner had come to the king and that the king had sent him away and that he had gone in peace.

[24] So Joab went to the king and said, "What have you done? Look, Abner came to you. Why did you let him go? Now he is gone! [25] You know Abner son of Ner; he came to deceive you and observe your movements and find out everything you are doing."

[26] Joab then left David and sent messengers after Abner, and they brought him back from the cistern at Sirah. But David did not know it. [27] Now when Abner returned to Hebron, Joab took him aside into an inner chamber, as if to speak with him privately. And there, to avenge the blood of his brother Asahel, Joab stabbed him in the stomach, and he died.

[28] Later, when David heard about this, he said, "I and my kingdom are forever innocent before the LORD concerning the blood of Abner son of Ner. [29] May his blood fall on the head of Joab and on his whole family! May Joab's family never be without someone who has a running sore or leprosy[a] or who leans on a crutch or who falls by the sword or who lacks food."

---

[a] 29 The Hebrew for *leprosy* was used for various diseases affecting the skin.

JOAB — PROFILE in leadership

The General Who Forgot the Real Boss
2 Samuel 3:6–39

When you forget whom you serve, you quickly fall prey to the basest human instincts. And leaders are not exempt.

Joab, a nephew of King David and a successful army commander, showed great arrogance toward the king by chiding him for entering into a treaty with Abner, a former enemy. Joab basically called David a fool for allowing Abner to escape unharmed. Then he moved secretly to deal with Abner as he saw fit.

Joab plotted to kill Abner, not because he posed a threat to David's kingdom, but out of personal vengeance (2Sa 3:30). Without telling the king his plans, he sent messengers to retrieve Abner so that he could murder him in cold blood. When David heard what Joab had done, he praised the dead man, but pronounced a curse upon Joab and his family (3:28–29).

Many things can disqualify someone from godly leadership, and unrestrained vengeance is one of the most effective. God tells us that the right to avenge belongs to him (Dt 32:35). Those who cannot humble themselves to serve God and those he has raised up will eventually act out of selfish motives and hurt the kingdom.

When Joab lost sight of his true calling, he launched out to serve his own selfish interests. In the end, his actions cost him everything (1Ki 2:28–35).

³⁰(Joab and his brother Abishai murdered Abner because he had killed their brother Asahel in the battle at Gibeon.)

³¹Then David said to Joab and all the people with him, "Tear your clothes and put on sackcloth and walk in mourning in front of Abner." King David himself walked behind the bier. ³²They buried Abner in Hebron, and the king wept aloud at Abner's tomb. All the people wept also.

³³The king sang this lament for Abner:

"Should Abner have died as the lawless die?
³⁴   Your hands were not bound,
      your feet were not fettered.
You fell as one falls before the wicked."

And all the people wept over him again.

³⁵Then they all came and urged David to eat something while it was still day; but David took an oath, saying, "May God deal with me, be it ever so severely, if I taste bread or anything else before the sun sets!"

³⁶All the people took note and were pleased; indeed, everything the king did pleased them. ³⁷So on that day all the people there and all Israel knew that the king had no part in the murder of Abner son of Ner.

³⁸Then the king said to his men, "Do you not realize that a commander and a great man has fallen in Israel this day? ³⁹And today, though I am the anointed king, I am weak, and these sons of Zeruiah are too strong for me. May the LORD repay the evildoer according to his evil deeds!"

Ish-Bosheth Murdered

4 When Ish-Bosheth son of Saul heard that Abner had died in Hebron, he lost courage, and all Israel became alarmed. ²Now Saul's son had two men who were leaders of raiding bands. One was named Baanah and the other Rekab; they were sons of Rimmon the Beerothite from the tribe of Benjamin—Beeroth is considered part of Benjamin, ³because the people of Beeroth fled to Gittaim and have resided there as foreigners to this day.

⁴(Jonathan son of Saul had a son who was lame in both feet. He was five years old when the news about Saul and Jonathan came from Jezreel. His nurse picked him up and fled, but as she hurried to leave, he fell and became disabled. His name was Mephibosheth.)

⁵Now Rekab and Baanah, the sons of Rimmon the Beerothite, set out for the house of Ish-Bosheth, and they arrived there in the heat of the day while he was taking his noonday rest. ⁶They went into the inner part of the house as if to get some wheat, and they stabbed him in the

DAVID — The Heart of a Great King
2 Samuel 4:5–12

PROFILE in leadership

As a young teen anointed by the prophet Samuel to one day become king, David patiently awaited his ascent to the throne. Both his influence and his skills continued to grow as he faced many challenges, reflecting the process all leaders must undergo in the leadership journey.

David's honorable actions reveal his integrity and commitment to the legitimate holder of the throne, King Saul, "the LORD's anointed." David refused to usurp power and grew angry when overzealous partisans murdered Ish-Bosheth in a wicked effort to speed up God's timetable.

By conducting himself in such an honorable way, David modeled the Law of Solid Ground. He recognized that by manipulating his way to power he would only break trust. David clearly understood the Law of Timing; as the chosen leader, he refused to sacrifice his mission and calling on the altar of inappropriate timing.

David's greatness and influence vastly increased as those around him recognized he had committed himself to higher principles. He would not tolerate subordinates who felt free to take matters into their own hands. David sacrificed personal gain for those who sought to destroy him—a classic servant leader. He kept his heart close to God, and consequently his behavior reflected strong inner character and the utmost respect for God's timing.

stomach. Then Rekab and his brother Baanah slipped away.

[7] They had gone into the house while he was lying on the bed in his bedroom. After they stabbed and killed him, they cut off his head. Taking it with them, they traveled all night by way of the Arabah. [8] They brought the head of Ish-Bosheth to David at Hebron and said to the king, "Here is the head of Ish-Bosheth son of Saul, your enemy, who tried to kill you. This day the LORD has avenged my lord the king against Saul and his offspring."

[9] David answered Rekab and his brother Baanah, the sons of Rimmon the Beerothite, "As surely as the LORD lives, who has delivered me out of every trouble, [10] when someone told me, 'Saul is dead,' and thought he was bringing good news, I seized him and put him to death in Ziklag. That was the reward I gave him for his news! [11] How much more — when wicked men have killed an innocent man in his own house and on his own bed — should I not now demand his blood from your hand and rid the earth of you!"

[12] So David gave an order to his men, and they killed them. They cut off their hands and feet and hung the bodies by the pool in Hebron. But they took the head of Ish-Bosheth and buried it in Abner's tomb at Hebron.

David Becomes King Over Israel

5 All the tribes of Israel came to David at Hebron and said, "We are your own flesh and blood. [2] In the past, while Saul was king over us, you were the one who led Israel on their military campaigns. And the LORD said to you, 'You will shepherd my people Israel, and you will become their ruler.'"

[3] When all the elders of Israel had come to King David at Hebron, the king made a covenant with them at Hebron before the LORD, and they anointed David king over Israel.

[4] David was thirty years old when he became king, and he reigned forty years. [5] In Hebron he reigned over Judah seven years and six months, and in Jerusalem he reigned over all Israel and Judah thirty-three years.

David Conquers Jerusalem

[6] The king and his men marched to Jerusalem to attack the Jebusites, who lived there. The Jebusites said to David, "You will not get in here; even the blind and the lame can ward you off." They thought, "David cannot get in here." [7] Nevertheless, David captured the fortress of Zion — which is the City of David.

[8] On that day David had said, "Anyone who conquers the Jebusites will have to use the water shaft to reach those 'lame and blind' who are David's enemies.[a]" That is why they say, "The 'blind and lame' will not enter the palace."

[9] David then took up residence in the fortress and called it the City of David. He built up the area around it, from the terraces[b] inward. [10] And he became more and more powerful, because the LORD God Almighty was with him.

[a] 8 Or are hated by David   [b] 9 Or the Millo

The Value of Vision

2 Samuel 5:1–12

David's vision energized the Hebrew nation far beyond anything Saul had ever imagined. Notice what the vision of David did for the Israelite nation:

1. **Vision unites (vv. 1–3).**
   For the first time in years, "all the tribes" and "all the elders" came together.

2. **Vision provides a center for leadership (vv. 4–5).**
   David began his reign from Hebron, but desired to unite a divided land and lead from Jerusalem.

3. **Vision dominates inner conversation (vv. 6–8).**
   All of us indulge in "inner conversation." David's vision focused his men as they neared Jerusalem.

4. **Vision inspires greatness (vv. 9–10).**
   David's dream for Jerusalem helped him and his people realize a great goal together.

5. **Vision attracts others to the leader (vv. 11–12).**
   Once David had taken Jerusalem, others began to join the cause.

[11]Now Hiram king of Tyre sent envoys to David, along with cedar logs and carpenters and stonemasons, and they built a palace for David. [12]Then David knew that the LORD had established him as king over Israel and had exalted his kingdom for the sake of his people Israel.

[13]After he left Hebron, David took more concubines and wives in Jerusalem, and more sons and daughters were born to him. [14]These are the names of the children born to him there: Shammua, Shobab, Nathan, Solomon, [15]Ibhar, Elishua, Nepheg, Japhia, [16]Elishama, Eliada and Eliphelet.

David Defeats the Philistines

[17]When the Philistines heard that David had been anointed king over Israel, they went up in full force to search for him, but David heard about it and went down to the stronghold. [18]Now the Philistines had come and spread out in the Valley of Rephaim; [19]so David inquired of the LORD, "Shall I go and attack the Philistines? Will you deliver them into my hands?"

The LORD answered him, "Go, for I will surely deliver the Philistines into your hands."

[20]So David went to Baal Perazim, and there he defeated them. He said, "As waters break out, the LORD has broken out against my enemies before me." So that place was called Baal Perazim.[a] [21]The Philistines abandoned their idols there, and David and his men carried them off.

[22]Once more the Philistines came up and spread out in the Valley of Rephaim; [23]so David inquired of the LORD, and he answered, "Do not go straight up, but circle around behind them and attack them in front of the poplar trees. [24]As soon as you hear the sound of marching in the tops of the poplar trees, move quickly, because that will mean the LORD has gone out in front of you to strike the Philistine army." [25]So David did as the LORD commanded him, and he struck down the Philistines all the way from Gibeon[b] to Gezer.

The Ark Brought to Jerusalem

6 David again brought together all the able young men of Israel—thirty thousand. [2]He and all his men went to Baalah[c] in Judah to bring up from there the ark of God, which is called by the Name,[d] the name of the LORD Almighty, who is enthroned between the cherubim on the ark. [3]They set the ark of God on a new cart and brought it from the house of Abinadab, which was on the hill. Uzzah and Ahio, sons of Abinadab, were guiding the new cart [4]with the

---

Communication: Don't Go Until You Know

2 Samuel 5:19, 23; 7:3–16

One of the most crucial leadership questions of all has nothing to do with finding resources, attracting competent team members or setting a target date. This critical question employs four small but potent words:

"What does God say?"

David discovered the importance of this question in two quite different ways. In 2 Samuel 5, he twice hears the Philistines have gathered to attack him. Both times, he inquires of the Lord before he acts. Both times he gets divine instructions, follows them and succeeds.

Two chapters later, Nathan the prophet speaks for God before receiving divine instructions. God corrects him that night, and he is forced to return to David and amend what he has spoken.

The lesson: Don't act or speak for God until you are sure you represent him correctly. For the spiritual leader, listening always comes before speaking.

---

ark of God on it,[e] and Ahio was walking in front of it. [5]David and all Israel were celebrating with all their might before the LORD, with castanets,[f] harps, lyres, timbrels, sistrums and cymbals.

[6]When they came to the threshing floor of Nakon, Uzzah reached out and took hold of the ark of God, because the oxen stumbled. [7]The LORD's anger burned against Uzzah because of his irreverent act; therefore God struck him down, and he died there beside the ark of God.

[8]Then David was angry because the LORD's wrath had broken out against Uzzah, and to this day that place is called Perez Uzzah.[g]

[9]David was afraid of the LORD that day and said, "How can the ark of the LORD ever come to me?" [10]He was not willing to take the ark of the LORD to be with him in the City of David.

---

[a] 20 *Baal Perazim* means *the lord who breaks out.*
[b] 25 Septuagint (see also 1 Chron. 14:16); Hebrew *Geba*
[c] 2 That is, Kiriath Jearim (see 1 Chron. 13:6)   [d] 2 Hebrew; Septuagint and Vulgate do not have *the Name.*   [e] 3,4 Dead Sea Scrolls and some Septuagint manuscripts; Masoretic Text *cart* [4]*and they brought it with the ark of God from the house of Abinadab, which was on the hill*   [f] 5 Masoretic Text; Dead Sea Scrolls and Septuagint (see also 1 Chron. 13:8) *songs*   [g] 8 *Perez Uzzah* means *outbreak against Uzzah.*

21 LAWS

SAUL AND DAVID AND THE LAW OF THE LID
Leadership Ability Determines a Person's Level of Effectiveness

2 Samuel 5:1–4

SUCCESS LIES within the reach of nearly everyone. But personal success without leadership ability brings only limited effectiveness, achieving only a fraction of what might have occurred with good leadership. The higher you want to climb, the more you need leadership. The greater the impact you want to make, the greater your influence needs to be.

Leadership ability is the lid that determines a person's level of effectiveness. The lower an individual's ability to lead, the lower the lid on his potential. The higher the leadership, the greater the effectiveness. Your leadership ability—for better or for worse—always determines your effectiveness and the potential impact of your organization. To reach the highest level of effectiveness, you have to raise the lid on your leadership ability.

■ ■ ■ ■ ■

Why did Saul fail as Israel's king, while David succeeded? The answer can be found in the Law of the Lid: Leadership ability determines a person's level of effectiveness. While David lifted many lids, Saul's attitude kept the lid clamped down firmly on his leadership. Take a look at the similar paths the men traveled:

1. *Both received counsel from godly men.*
   Samuel, the last judge of Israel, anointed both men. And both received the benefit of godly counsel—Saul from Samuel, and David from Samuel and later Nathan the prophet.

2. *Both faced great challenges.*
   Every leader faces obstacles, tests and trials. Saul and David sometimes faced the same ones. Take Goliath, for example: When the huge Philistine offered to fight Israel's champion, both Saul and David heard the challenge. Saul, Israel's greatest warrior, hid in fear. But David, a mere boy, eagerly faced the challenge and won honor for God.

3. *Both had the choice to change and grow.*
   Saul and David reacted very differently when confronted with their shortcomings. When Samuel rebuked Saul for making an unauthorized burnt offering to God, the king spoke not a whisper of sorrow or repentance. Evidently Saul kept on the same course.

   David possessed an entirely different kind of heart. When Nathan confronted the king after the sordid incident with Bathsheba, David broke down and sorrowfully repented.

The Lids That Limited Saul

God removed all the external lids from Saul's life when the son of Kish ascended Israel's throne. But even without any external lids to his leadership, he still labored under several *internal* lids:

Fear: Saul began his reign by hiding among the equipment.

Impatience: Saul refused to wait for Samuel and offered an illegal sacrifice.

Denial: Saul continued as though all was well even after Samuel declared that God had rejected him as king.

Impulsiveness: Saul rashly made an oath that almost cost him the life of his son.

Deceit: Saul offered his daughter Michal to David, hoping the young man would die in battle to win her hand in marriage.

Jealousy: Saul became enraged when the people compared him to David, and from then on kept a jealous eye on the young man.

Anger: Saul repeatedly tried to kill David.

Because Saul never removed the lids from his leadership, God had to remove him from the throne of Israel.

The Lids That Did Not Limit David

David also had many lids on his life, both internal and external, but they did not stop him:

1. *His family*
   David's limitations started at home. When Samuel asked Jesse to gather all his sons so God could reveal the next king of Israel, no one thought to invite David. His brothers thought no better of him than did his father. When David visited the battlefront, they scorned him. When David spoke out against Goliath's blasphemy, his brothers insulted him and told him to go home.

2. *His leader*
   Saul continually tried to sabotage David's leadership and effective-

ness. When David offered to fight Goliath, Saul told him, "You are not able to go out against this Philistine and fight him" (1Sa 17:33). Then Saul tried to put his heavy armor on the boy—he certainly wasn't going to use it! For many years, Saul tried repeatedly to kill David.

3. *His background*
   David came from a family of poor shepherds. His father, Jesse the Bethlehemite, lacked both lofty lineage and powerful position. David wasn't even the eldest son in his family; seven older brothers all came before him.

4. *His youthfulness and inexperience*
   At the time Samuel anointed David, the boy had no experience leading anything but sheep. When he stepped forward to fight Goliath, others considered him "only a young man," and he had never fought a wartime battle. Time and again, people underestimated and disrespected him.

The One Who Lifted the Lid

Ultimately David became a great leader—yet not because he lacked limitations in life. He achieved much because he became a lid lifter.

Every leader has lids on his life; nobody is born without them. And they don't disappear when a person receives a title, achieves a position, or gets invested with power. The issue is not whether you have lids, but what you are going to do about them.

David's Intimacy with God: People-Pleasing vs. God-Pleasing

2 Samuel 6:1–23

What excitement must have filled the air the day David led the parade to bring the ark of the covenant to Jerusalem! The marching quickly turned into a celebration, for the "ark of the LORD"—the physical representation of God's presence and blessing—was returning to its rightful place.

David felt so exhilarated by the grand event that he stripped down to a "linen ephod" and danced "before the LORD with all his might," twirling and leaping with joy (2Sa 6:14). This radical display disgusted David's image-conscious wife, Michal. She turned on her husband and rebuked him for acting so unsophisticated. Mockingly she said, "How the king of Israel has distinguished himself today, going around half-naked in full view of the slave girls of his servants as any vulgar fellow would!" (6:20).

David responded by contrasting two pursuits: people-pleasing vs. God-pleasing. He told her, "It was before the LORD [that I danced] . . . I will celebrate before the LORD. I will become even more undignified than this, and I will be humiliated in my own eyes" (6:21–22).

God-pleasing leaders can learn three important things from David:

1. **Sacrifice:** David made many sacrifices en route to Jerusalem.

2. **Surrender:** David danced and shouted with reckless abandon before the Lord.

3. **Service:** David gave food generously to all in Israel.

Instead, he took it to the house of Obed-Edom the Gittite. [11]The ark of the LORD remained in the house of Obed-Edom the Gittite for three months, and the LORD blessed him and his entire household.

[12]Now King David was told, "The LORD has blessed the household of Obed-Edom and everything he has, because of the ark of God." So David went to bring up the ark of God from the house of Obed-Edom to the City of David with rejoicing. [13]When those who were carrying the ark of the LORD had taken six steps, he sacrificed a bull and a fattened calf. [14]Wearing a linen ephod, David was dancing before the LORD with all his might, [15]while he and all Israel were bringing up the ark of the LORD with shouts and the sound of trumpets.

[16]As the ark of the LORD was entering the City of David, Michal daughter of Saul watched from a window. And when she saw King David leaping and dancing before the LORD, she despised him in her heart.

[17]They brought the ark of the LORD and set it in its place inside the tent that David had pitched for it, and David sacrificed burnt offerings and fellowship offerings before the LORD. [18]After he had finished sacrificing the burnt offerings and fellowship offerings, he blessed the people in the name of the LORD Almighty. [19]Then he gave a loaf of bread, a cake of dates and a cake of raisins to each person in the whole crowd of Israelites, both men and women. And all the people went to their homes.

[20]When David returned home to bless his household, Michal daughter of Saul came out to meet him and said, "How the king of Israel has distinguished himself today, going around half-naked in full view of the slave girls of his servants as any vulgar fellow would!"

[21]David said to Michal, "It was before the LORD, who chose me rather than your father or anyone from his house when he appointed me ruler over the LORD's people Israel—I will celebrate before the LORD. [22]I will become even more undignified than this, and I will be humiliated in my own eyes. But by these slave girls you spoke of, I will be held in honor."

Michal: Obsessed with Image and Reputation

2 Samuel 6:20

David's wife, Michal, worried far more about image than authenticity. When David danced before the Lord, she felt ashamed of him. She wanted to guard her family's reputation, remain oh-so sophisticated. But when we focus on appearance rather than substance, we wind up with shallow spirits.

23And Michal daughter of Saul had no children to the day of her death.

God's Promise to David

7 After the king was settled in his palace and the LORD had given him rest from all his enemies around him, 2he said to Nathan the prophet, "Here I am, living in a house of cedar, while the ark of God remains in a tent."

3Nathan replied to the king, "Whatever you have in mind, go ahead and do it, for the LORD is with you."

4But that night the word of the LORD came to Nathan, saying:

5"Go and tell my servant David, 'This is what the LORD says: Are you the one to build me a house to dwell in? 6I have not dwelt in a house from the day I brought the Israelites up out of Egypt to this day. I have been moving from place to place with a tent as my dwelling. 7Wherever I have moved with all the Israelites, did I ever say to any of their rulers whom I commanded to shepherd my people Israel, "Why have you not built me a house of cedar?"'

8"Now then, tell my servant David, 'This is what the LORD Almighty says: I took you from the pasture, from tending the flock, and appointed you ruler over my people Israel. 9I have been with you wherever you have gone, and I have cut off all your enemies from before you. Now I will make your name great, like the names of the greatest men on earth. 10And I will provide a place for my people Israel and will plant them so that they can have a home of their own and no longer be disturbed. Wicked people will not oppress them anymore, as they did at the beginning 11and have done ever since the time I appointed leaders[a] over my people Israel. I will also give you rest from all your enemies.

"'The LORD declares to you that the LORD himself will establish a house for you: 12When your days are over and you rest with your ancestors, I will raise up your offspring to succeed you, your own flesh and blood, and I will establish his kingdom. 13He is the one who will build a house for my Name, and I will establish the throne of his kingdom forever. 14I will be his father, and he will be my son. When he does wrong, I will punish him with a rod wielded by men, with floggings inflicted by human hands. 15But my love will never be taken away from him, as I took it away from Saul, whom I removed from before you. 16Your house and your kingdom will endure forever before me[b]; your throne will be established forever.'"

17Nathan reported to David all the words of this entire revelation.

---

[a] 11 Traditionally *judges*   [b] 16 Some Hebrew manuscripts and Septuagint; most Hebrew manuscripts *you*

The Law of Intuition and Decision Making

2 Samuel 6:1—7:17

Within a few years of his ascent to the throne, David's leadership is in full swing. He begins to exercise broad decision-making skills as the king of Israel. Consider several principles we learn from David, the decision maker:

1. **Good leaders influence the decisions of others (6:1–2).**

2. **Good decision makers want God in the center of the process (6:3–5).**

3. **Good decision making respects the power of God (6:6–11).**

4. **Good decisions foster joy and celebration (6:12–15).**

5. **Good leaders place God's agenda ahead of their own (7:1–3).**

6. **Good decision makers listen to others (7:4–11).**

7. **Good leaders positively affect future generations (7:12–13).**

8. **Good decisions determine future conditions (7:14–17).**

David's Prayer

18Then King David went in and sat before the LORD, and he said:

"Who am I, Sovereign LORD, and what is my family, that you have brought me this far? 19And as if this were not enough in your sight, Sovereign LORD, you have also spoken about the future of the house of your servant — and this decree, Sovereign LORD, is for a mere human![a]

20"What more can David say to you? For you know your servant, Sovereign LORD. 21For the sake of your word and according to your will, you have done this great thing and made it known to your servant.

22"How great you are, Sovereign LORD! There is no one like you, and there is no God but you, as we have heard with our own ears. 23And who is like your people Israel — the one nation on earth that God went out to redeem as a people for himself, and to make a name for himself, and to perform great and awesome wonders by driving out nations and their gods from before your people, whom you redeemed from Egypt?[b] 24You have established your people Israel as your very own forever, and you, LORD, have become their God.

25"And now, LORD God, keep forever the promise you have made concerning your servant and his house. Do as you promised, 26so that your name will be great forever. Then people will say, 'The LORD Almighty is God over Israel!' And the house of your servant David will be established in your sight.

27"LORD Almighty, God of Israel, you have revealed this to your servant, saying, 'I will build a house for you.' So your servant has found courage to pray this prayer to you. 28Sovereign LORD, you are God! Your covenant is trustworthy, and you have promised these good things to your servant. 29Now be pleased to bless the house of your servant, that it may continue forever in your sight; for you, Sovereign LORD, have spoken, and with your blessing the house of your servant will be blessed forever."

David's Victories

8 In the course of time, David defeated the Philistines and subdued them, and he took Metheg Ammah from the control of the Philistines.

2David also defeated the Moabites. He made them lie down on the ground and measured them off with a length of cord. Every two lengths of them were put to death, and the third length was allowed to live. So the Moabites became subject to David and brought him tribute.

3Moreover, David defeated Hadadezer son of Rehob, king of Zobah, when he went to restore his monument at[c] the Euphrates River. 4David captured a thousand of his chariots, seven thousand charioteers[d] and twenty thousand foot soldiers. He hamstrung all but a hundred of the chariot horses.

5When the Arameans of Damascus came to help Hadadezer king of Zobah, David struck down twenty-two thousand of them. 6He put garrisons in the Aramean kingdom of Damascus, and the Arameans became subject to him

---

[a] 19 Or for the human race   [b] 23 See Septuagint and 1 Chron. 17:21; Hebrew wonders for your land and before your people, whom you redeemed from Egypt, from the nations and their gods.   [c] 3 Or his control along   [d] 4 Septuagint (see also Dead Sea Scrolls and 1 Chron. 18:4); Masoretic Text captured seventeen hundred of his charioteers

---

The Law of Victory and Team Building

2 Samuel 8:1—10:12

Repeatedly in 2 Samuel King David gives us good illustrations of both the Law of Victory and effective teamwork. David finds a way to help Israel conquer again and again, and he keeps the people working together to achieve new goals. What can we learn about winning teams from David?

A Winning Team . . .

1. **Starts with a plan (8:1–3).**

2. **Develops a structure (8:6, 14).**

3. **Has an anointed leader (8:6, 14).**

4. **Puts the interests of others first (8:15).**

5. **Shares responsibilities with others (8:16–18).**

6. **Helps each other out (10:9–12).**

7. **Develops winning team members (23:8–12).**

8. **Breeds loyalty (23:13–17).**

and brought tribute. The LORD gave David victory wherever he went.

[7]David took the gold shields that belonged to the officers of Hadadezer and brought them to Jerusalem. [8]From Tebah[a] and Berothai, towns that belonged to Hadadezer, King David took a great quantity of bronze.

[9]When Tou[b] king of Hamath heard that David had defeated the entire army of Hadadezer, [10]he sent his son Joram[c] to King David to greet him and congratulate him on his victory in battle over Hadadezer, who had been at war with Tou. Joram brought with him articles of silver, of gold and of bronze.

[11]King David dedicated these articles to the LORD, as he had done with the silver and gold from all the nations he had subdued: [12]Edom[d] and Moab, the Ammonites and the Philistines, and Amalek. He also dedicated the plunder taken from Hadadezer son of Rehob, king of Zobah.

[13]And David became famous after he returned from striking down eighteen thousand Edomites[e] in the Valley of Salt.

[14]He put garrisons throughout Edom, and all the Edomites became subject to David. The LORD gave David victory wherever he went.

David's Officials

[15]David reigned over all Israel, doing what was just and right for all his people. [16]Joab son of Zeruiah was over the army; Jehoshaphat son of Ahilud was recorder; [17]Zadok son of Ahitub and Ahimelek son of Abiathar were priests; Seraiah was secretary; [18]Benaiah son of Jehoiada was over the Kerethites and Pelethites; and David's sons were priests.[f]

David and Mephibosheth

9 David asked, "Is there anyone still left of the house of Saul to whom I can show kindness for Jonathan's sake?"

[2]Now there was a servant of Saul's household named Ziba. They summoned him to appear before David, and the king said to him, "Are you Ziba?"

"At your service," he replied.

[3]The king asked, "Is there no one still alive from the house of Saul to whom I can show God's kindness?"

Ziba answered the king, "There is still a son of Jonathan; he is lame in both feet."

[4]"Where is he?" the king asked.

Ziba answered, "He is at the house of Makir son of Ammiel in Lo Debar."

The Law of the Picture: David Returns a Favor

2 Samuel 9:1-13

Long after Jonathan's death, David returned a favor to his old friend through a kindness shown to Mephibosheth, Jonathan's disabled son. He restored to him all of Saul's belongings; he ordered servants to cultivate his land; and he provided food, income and a role at court. Gratitude cultivates generosity. This is the Law of the Picture in action. David did what he had seen: a meaningful favor.

---

[5]So King David had him brought from Lo Debar, from the house of Makir son of Ammiel.

[6]When Mephibosheth son of Jonathan, the son of Saul, came to David, he bowed down to pay him honor.

David said, "Mephibosheth!"

"At your service," he replied.

[7]"Don't be afraid," David said to him, "for I will surely show you kindness for the sake of your father Jonathan. I will restore to you all the land that belonged to your grandfather Saul, and you will always eat at my table."

[8]Mephibosheth bowed down and said, "What is your servant, that you should notice a dead dog like me?"

[9]Then the king summoned Ziba, Saul's steward, and said to him, "I have given your master's grandson everything that belonged to Saul and his family. [10]You and your sons and your servants are to farm the land for him and bring in the crops, so that your master's grandson may be provided for. And Mephibosheth, grandson of your master, will always eat at my table." (Now Ziba had fifteen sons and twenty servants.)

[11]Then Ziba said to the king, "Your servant will do whatever my lord the king commands his servant to do." So Mephibosheth ate at David's[g] table like one of the king's sons.

[12]Mephibosheth had a young son named

---

[a] 8 See some Septuagint manuscripts (see also 1 Chron. 18:8); Hebrew *Betah*.   [b] 9 Hebrew *Toi*, a variant of *Tou*; also in verse 10   [c] 10 A variant of *Hadoram*   [d] 12 Some Hebrew manuscripts, Septuagint and Syriac (see also 1 Chron. 18:11); most Hebrew manuscripts *Aram*   [e] 13 A few Hebrew manuscripts, Septuagint and Syriac (see also 1 Chron. 18:12); most Hebrew manuscripts *Aram* (that is, Arameans)   [f] 18 Or *were chief officials* (see Septuagint and Targum; see also 1 Chron. 18:17)   [g] 11 Septuagint; Hebrew *my*

Mika, and all the members of Ziba's household were servants of Mephibosheth. [13]And Mephibosheth lived in Jerusalem, because he always ate at the king's table; he was lame in both feet.

David Defeats the Ammonites

10 In the course of time, the king of the Ammonites died, and his son Hanun succeeded him as king. [2]David thought, "I will show kindness to Hanun son of Nahash, just as his father showed kindness to me." So David sent a delegation to express his sympathy to Hanun concerning his father.

When David's men came to the land of the Ammonites, [3]the Ammonite commanders said to Hanun their lord, "Do you think David is honoring your father by sending envoys to you to express sympathy? Hasn't David sent them to you only to explore the city and spy it out and overthrow it?" [4]So Hanun seized David's envoys, shaved off half of each man's beard, cut off their garments at the buttocks, and sent them away.

[5]When David was told about this, he sent messengers to meet the men, for they were greatly humiliated. The king said, "Stay at Jericho till your beards have grown, and then come back."

[6]When the Ammonites realized that they had become obnoxious to David, they hired twenty thousand Aramean foot soldiers from Beth Rehob and Zobah, as well as the king of Maakah with a thousand men, and also twelve thousand men from Tob.

[7]On hearing this, David sent Joab out with the entire army of fighting men. [8]The Ammonites came out and drew up in battle formation at the entrance of their city gate, while the Arameans of Zobah and Rehob and the men of Tob and Maakah were by themselves in the open country.

[9]Joab saw that there were battle lines in front of him and behind him; so he selected some of the best troops in Israel and deployed them against the Arameans. [10]He put the rest of the men under the command of Abishai his brother and deployed them against the Ammonites. [11]Joab said, "If the Arameans are too strong for me, then you are to come to my rescue; but if the Ammonites are too strong for you, then I will come to rescue you. [12]Be strong, and let us fight bravely for our people and the cities of our God. The LORD will do what is good in his sight."

[13]Then Joab and the troops with him advanced to fight the Arameans, and they fled before him. [14]When the Ammonites realized that the Arameans were fleeing, they fled before Abishai and went inside the city. So Joab returned from fighting the Ammonites and came to Jerusalem.

[15]After the Arameans saw that they had been routed by Israel, they regrouped. [16]Hadadezer had Arameans brought from beyond the Euphrates River; they went to Helam, with Shobak the commander of Hadadezer's army leading them.

[17]When David was told of this, he gathered all Israel, crossed the Jordan and went to Helam. The Arameans formed their battle lines to meet David and fought against him. [18]But they fled before Israel, and David killed seven hundred of their charioteers and forty thousand of their foot soldiers.[a] He also struck down Shobak the commander of their army, and he died there. [19]When all the kings who were vassals of Hadadezer saw that they had been routed by Israel, they made peace with the Israelites and became subject to them.

So the Arameans were afraid to help the Ammonites anymore.

David and Bathsheba

11 In the spring, at the time when kings go off to war, David sent Joab out with the king's men and the whole Israelite army. They destroyed the Ammonites and besieged Rabbah. But David remained in Jerusalem.

[2]One evening David got up from his bed and walked around on the roof of the palace. From the roof he saw a woman bathing. The woman was very beautiful, [3]and David sent someone to find out about her. The man said, "She is Bathsheba, the daughter of Eliam and the wife of Uriah the Hittite." [4]Then David sent messengers to get her. She came to him, and he slept with her. (Now she was purifying herself from her monthly uncleanness.) Then she went back home. [5]The woman conceived and sent word to David, saying, "I am pregnant."

[6]So David sent this word to Joab: "Send me Uriah the Hittite." And Joab sent him to David. [7]When Uriah came to him, David asked him how Joab was, how the soldiers were and how the war was going. [8]Then David said to Uriah, "Go down to your house and wash your feet." So Uriah left the palace, and a gift from the king was sent after him. [9]But Uriah slept at the entrance to the palace with all his master's servants and did not go down to his house.

---

[a] 18 Some Septuagint manuscripts (see also 1 Chron. 19:18); Hebrew *horsemen*

[10]David was told, "Uriah did not go home." So he asked Uriah, "Haven't you just come from a military campaign? Why didn't you go home?"

[11]Uriah said to David, "The ark and Israel and Judah are staying in tents,[a] and my commander Joab and my lord's men are camped in the open country. How could I go to my house to eat and drink and make love to my wife? As surely as you live, I will not do such a thing!"

[12]Then David said to him, "Stay here one more day, and tomorrow I will send you back." So Uriah remained in Jerusalem that day and the next. [13]At David's invitation, he ate and drank with him, and David made him drunk. But in the evening Uriah went out to sleep on his mat among his master's servants; he did not go home.

[14]In the morning David wrote a letter to Joab and sent it with Uriah. [15]In it he wrote, "Put Uriah out in front where the fighting is fiercest. Then withdraw from him so he will be struck down and die."

[16]So while Joab had the city under siege, he put Uriah at a place where he knew the strongest defenders were. [17]When the men of the city came out and fought against Joab, some of the men in David's army fell; moreover, Uriah the Hittite died.

[18]Joab sent David a full account of the battle. [19]He instructed the messenger: "When you have finished giving the king this account of the battle, [20]the king's anger may flare up, and he may ask you, 'Why did you get so close to the city to fight? Didn't you know they would shoot arrows from the wall? [21]Who killed Abimelek son of Jerub-Besheth[b]? Didn't a woman drop an upper millstone on him from the wall, so that he died in Thebez? Why did you get so close to the wall?' If he asks you this, then say to him, 'Moreover, your servant Uriah the Hittite is dead.'"

[22]The messenger set out, and when he arrived he told David everything Joab had sent him to say. [23]The messenger said to David, "The men overpowered us and came out against us in the open, but we drove them back to the entrance of the city gate. [24]Then the archers shot arrows at your servants from the wall, and some of the king's men died. Moreover, your servant Uriah the Hittite is dead."

[25]David told the messenger, "Say this to Joab: 'Don't let this upset you; the sword devours one as well as another. Press the attack against the city and destroy it.' Say this to encourage Joab."

---

[a] 11 Or staying at Sukkoth   [b] 21 Also known as Jerub-Baal (that is, Gideon)

The Law of Solid Ground: Five Expressions of Power Abuse

2 Samuel 11:1–27

Pittacus wrote, "The measure of a man is what he does with power." When David used Bathsheba for his own selfish purposes, he began a long spiral downward into deceit, adultery and murder.

Second Samuel 11 tells the story of a king who forgot that leaders wield power for one reason only: to serve. Consider the "Path to Abusive Power" in leaders:

Stage One: Surprise—"I get this?"

Stage Two: Self-Esteem—"I need this."

Stage Three: Satisfaction—"I deserve this."

Stage Four: Selfishness—"I demand this."

By watching King David weave a tangled web following his sin with Bathsheba, we notice five common abuses of power that still trip up leaders today. Calvin Miller describes them this way:

1. **Drifting away from those disciplines we still demand of our people (v. 1).**

2. **Believing that others owe us whatever use we can make of them (vv. 2–3).**

3. **Attempting to fix things up rather than make things right (v. 6).**

4. **Refusing to accept that we could be blindly out of God's will (v. 11).**

5. **Believing that people in our way are expendable (v. 14).**

26When Uriah's wife heard that her husband was dead, she mourned for him. 27After the time of mourning was over, David had her brought to his house, and she became his wife and bore him a son. But the thing David had done displeased the LORD.

Nathan Rebukes David

12 The LORD sent Nathan to David. When he came to him, he said, "There were two men in a certain town, one rich and the other poor. 2The rich man had a very large number of sheep and cattle, 3but the poor man had nothing except one little ewe lamb he had bought. He raised it, and it grew up with him and his children. It shared his food, drank from his cup and even slept in his arms. It was like a daughter to him.

4"Now a traveler came to the rich man, but the rich man refrained from taking one of his own sheep or cattle to prepare a meal for the traveler who had come to him. Instead, he took the ewe lamb that belonged to the poor man and prepared it for the one who had come to him."

5David burned with anger against the man and said to Nathan, "As surely as the LORD lives, the man who did this must die! 6He must pay for that lamb four times over, because he did such a thing and had no pity."

7Then Nathan said to David, "You are the man! This is what the LORD, the God of Israel, says: 'I anointed you king over Israel, and I delivered you from the hand of Saul. 8I gave your master's house to you, and your master's wives into your arms. I gave you all Israel and Judah. And if all this had been too little, I would have given you even more. 9Why did you despise the word of the LORD by doing what is evil in his eyes? You struck down Uriah the Hittite with the sword and took his wife to be your own. You killed him with the sword of the Ammonites. 10Now, therefore, the sword will never depart from your house, because you despised me and took the wife of Uriah the Hittite to be your own.'

11"This is what the LORD says: 'Out of your own household I am going to bring calamity on you. Before your very eyes I will take your wives and give them to one who is close to you, and he will sleep with your wives in broad daylight. 12You did it in secret, but I will do this thing in broad daylight before all Israel.'"

13Then David said to Nathan, "I have sinned against the LORD."

Nathan replied, "The LORD has taken away your sin. You are not going to die. 14But because by doing this you have shown utter contempt for[a] the LORD, the son born to you will die."

15After Nathan had gone home, the LORD struck the child that Uriah's wife had borne to David, and he became ill. 16David pleaded with God for the child. He fasted and spent the nights lying in sackcloth[b] on the ground. 17The elders of his household stood beside him to get him up from the ground, but he refused, and he would not eat any food with them.

18On the seventh day the child died. David's attendants were afraid to tell him that the child was dead, for they thought, "While the child was still living, he wouldn't listen to us when we spoke to him. How can we now tell him the child is dead? He may do something desperate."

19David noticed that his attendants were whispering among themselves, and he realized the child was dead. "Is the child dead?" he asked.

"Yes," they replied, "he is dead."

20Then David got up from the ground. After he had washed, put on lotions and changed his clothes, he went into the house of the LORD and worshiped. Then he went to his own house, and at his request they served him food, and he ate.

21His attendants asked him, "Why are you acting this way? While the child was alive, you fasted and wept, but now that the child is dead, you get up and eat!"

22He answered, "While the child was still alive, I fasted and wept. I thought, 'Who knows? The LORD may be gracious to me and let the child live.' 23But now that he is dead, why should

---

The Law of Sacrifice: Leaders Who Stop Sacrificing Stop Succeeding

2 Samuel 11:1—12:31

David is a different man in 2 Samuel 11; 12 than in 1 Samuel 11; 12. Somewhere along the way, he decided he didn't need to sacrifice in order to lead well. He no longer prepared for new challenges. When we stop growing, we stop leading. When we stop sacrificing, we stop succeeding.

---

[a] 14 An ancient Hebrew scribal tradition; Masoretic Text for the enemies of   [b] 16 Dead Sea Scrolls and Septuagint; Masoretic Text does not have in sackcloth.

The Law of the Inner Circle: Nathan Confronts David

2 Samuel 12:1–15

"Be sure your sins will find you out," we say almost flippantly, but David's life illustrates the reality of the phrase.

Nathan confronted David as part of the king's "inner circle." He had permission to speak hard truth in love, so he used a clever narrative to bring his point home. David had failed miserably. But his failure wasn't final. Look at what's needed in order to survive a major failure:

1. **An open and transparent heart**
   It's easier to tolerate mistakes admitted than mistakes denied.

2. **A spirit of forgiveness toward followers**
   A follower you treat with charity is more prone to forgive you when you are caught failing.

3. **A responsible attitude**
   A leader who owns up to his or her behavior will last longer and fare better.

4. **The ability to change**
   Leaders must demonstrate they are humble and teachable and willing to grow or change.

5. **A hunger to grow and stretch**
   Followers will stay with a leader in process if he or she is moving in the right direction.

David must have blanched when Nathan pointed a finger at him and shouted, "You are the man!" (2Sa 12:7). Yet thank God for Nathan! All leaders need a Nathan in their inner circle, and if they don't have one, they need to find one. Soon.

I go on fasting? Can I bring him back again? I will go to him, but he will not return to me."

²⁴Then David comforted his wife Bathsheba, and he went to her and made love to her. She gave birth to a son, and they named him Solomon. The LORD loved him; ²⁵and because the LORD loved him, he sent word through Nathan the prophet to name him Jedidiah.[a]

²⁶Meanwhile Joab fought against Rabbah of the Ammonites and captured the royal citadel. ²⁷Joab then sent messengers to David, saying, "I have fought against Rabbah and taken its water supply. ²⁸Now muster the rest of the troops and besiege the city and capture it. Otherwise I will take the city, and it will be named after me."

²⁹So David mustered the entire army and went to Rabbah, and attacked and captured it. ³⁰David took the crown from their king's[b] head, and it was placed on his own head. It weighed a talent[c] of gold, and it was set with precious stones. David took a great quantity of plunder from the city ³¹and brought out the people who were there, consigning them to labor with saws and with iron picks and axes, and he made them work at brickmaking.[d] David did this to all the Ammonite towns. Then he and his entire army returned to Jerusalem.

Amnon and Tamar

13 In the course of time, Amnon son of David fell in love with Tamar, the beautiful sister of Absalom son of David.

²Amnon became so obsessed with his sister Tamar that he made himself ill. She was a virgin, and it seemed impossible for him to do anything to her.

³Now Amnon had an adviser named Jonadab son of Shimeah, David's brother. Jonadab was a very shrewd man. ⁴He asked Amnon, "Why do you, the king's son, look so haggard morning after morning? Won't you tell me?"

Amnon said to him, "I'm in love with Tamar, my brother Absalom's sister."

⁵"Go to bed and pretend to be ill," Jonadab said. "When your father comes to see you, say to him, 'I would like my sister Tamar to come and give me something to eat. Let her prepare the food in my sight so I may watch her and then eat it from her hand.'"

⁶So Amnon lay down and pretended to be ill.

---

a 25 Jedidiah means *loved by the LORD.*   *b 30* Or *from Milkom's* (that is, Molek's)   *c 30* That is, about 75 pounds or about 34 kilograms   *d 31* The meaning of the Hebrew for this clause is uncertain.

SECURITY Nathan Feared No One

2 Samuel 12:1–14

SECURITY PROVIDES the foundation for strong leadership. When we feel insecure, we drift from our mission whenever trouble arises. We must feel secure, or when people stop liking us; when funding drops; when morale dips; or when others reject or criticize us—we will crumble. If we do not feel secure, fear will eventually cause us to sabotage our leadership.

Imagine what might have happened had Nathan lacked security. Consider the odds stacked against him. He knew he had to confront David in his sin, yet David had covered up everything so well; no one else knew what had happened. That meant Nathan could expect no moral support. Further, the popular David had led Israel to prominence among the nations, and most Israelites would side with David if he put up a fight. Finally, from a technical viewpoint, David hadn't done anything illegal to Uriah. He had set up the man to be killed in battle by the Ammonites, but it wasn't his spear or sword that took Uriah's life. Nathan had to feel utterly secure in his plan of attack, or it would backfire.

What enabled Nathan to demonstrate secure leadership?

1. *Nathan had God's truth behind him.* He didn't have to stand alone against David.

2. *Nathan had a relationship with David.* Their friendship created the bridge that allowed Nathan to do what God called him to do.

3. *Nathan's identity depended upon his divine call, not his popularity.* Nathan determined to speak God's truth regardless of the popular reaction.

4. *Nathan understood his personal mission.* He operated out of deep conviction.

5. *Nathan was humble and broken.* He had nothing to lose, for he had died to personal ambition.

Common Symptoms of Insecurity

The following symptoms usually indicate feelings of insecurity:

1. *Comparison*—We compare ourselves with others and keep score.

2. *Compensation*—We feel like a victim and must compensate for our losses.

3. *Competition*—We become self-consumed and try to outdo others for attention.

4. *Compulsion*—We feel driven to perform in order to gain others' approval.

5. *Condemnation*—We judge others or ourselves, resulting in self-pity or conceit.

6. *Control*—We feel we must take charge, protect our interests and manipulate.

Four Keys to Security

To reduce personal insecurities, build the following four ingredients into your life:

1. *Identity:* Establish your identity in Christ, not in performance.

2. *Brokenness:* Allow God to break you of self-sufficiency and self-promotion.

3. *Purpose:* Discover and practice your God-given purpose in life, not someone else's.

4. *Give and receive the blessing:* Learn to affirm others and receive affirmation.

For a negative example of security, see p. 1129.

21 QUALITIES

DISCERNMENT   Nathan Saw Below the Surface

2 Samuel 12:1–15

LIKE SAMUEL before him, the prophet Nathan served as a leader to the leaders. God used Nathan to correct his erring leader.

Nathan knew David had slept with another man's wife and subsequently caused the man's death. Although the king had multiple wives, he still insisted on having one more. Nathan saw a greedy and selfish heart in Israel's king. Few individuals in David's reign wielded the influence or had the guts to confront him in his sin. Once Nathan discerned what David had done, he gained an audience with the king, told him a compelling story, and with great poise dealt with the problem in a caring but firm manner.

Nathan could act as he did because of his keen, God-given discernment. He knew what had happened and what lay beneath the surface of David's wicked behavior. Discernment goes deeper than knowledge, resembling intuition. At times, discernment is a gift; at other times, it results from much experience. Discernment brings a profound perception of what is occurring, either on the outside or the inside of a person. What gave Nathan such keen discernment?

1. *He had been listening to God (v. 1).* The text says God "sent" him to David. Obviously, God had been speaking to his prophet.

2. *He knew David's circumstances (vv. 1–6).* Nathan had watched David for many years and so recognized the egregious changes when they came.

3. *He was objective in his perspective (vv. 7–8).* Nathan could speak for God and provide God's viewpoint on the king's situation.

4. *He understood the root issues (vv. 9–12).* Nathan saw more than symptoms; he saw root problems and consequences.

5. *He saw the ultimate cause and effect (v. 14).* Nathan passionately championed the name and reputation of God. He hated how the pagan nations surrounding Israel might mock the Lord should they hear of David's sin.

How Do We Grow in Our Discernment?

To improve your discernment as a leader, do the following:

1. *Learn to hear God's voice.* Get quiet and read Scripture. Reflect on the mind of God.

2. *Build problem-solving skills.* If you can see root issues of problems, you can solve those difficulties.

3. *Analyze your successes.* What worked? Can you identify the heart of the matter?

4. *Evaluate your options.* Discernment involves both your gut and your head.

5. *Expand your opportunities.* Get more experience to help you deepen your wisdom.

6. *Explore what others think.* Choose some leaders you admire and study how they think.

7. *Listen to your gut.* Most people are afraid to listen to their God-given intuition.

For a negative example of discernment, see p. 183.

When the king came to see him, Amnon said to him, "I would like my sister Tamar to come and make some special bread in my sight, so I may eat from her hand."

[7]David sent word to Tamar at the palace: "Go to the house of your brother Amnon and prepare some food for him." [8]So Tamar went to the house of her brother Amnon, who was lying down. She took some dough, kneaded it, made the bread in his sight and baked it. [9]Then she took the pan and served him the bread, but he refused to eat.

"Send everyone out of here," Amnon said. So everyone left him. [10]Then Amnon said to Tamar, "Bring the food here into my bedroom so I may eat from your hand." And Tamar took the bread she had prepared and brought it to her brother Amnon in his bedroom. [11]But when she took it to him to eat, he grabbed her and said, "Come to bed with me, my sister."

[12]"No, my brother!" she said to him. "Don't force me! Such a thing should not be done in Israel! Don't do this wicked thing. [13]What about me? Where could I get rid of my disgrace? And what about you? You would be like one of the wicked fools in Israel. Please speak to the king; he will not keep me from being married to you." [14]But he refused to listen to her, and since he was stronger than she, he raped her.

[15]Then Amnon hated her with intense hatred. In fact, he hated her more than he had loved her. Amnon said to her, "Get up and get out!"

[16]"No!" she said to him. "Sending me away would be a greater wrong than what you have already done to me."

But he refused to listen to her. [17]He called his personal servant and said, "Get this woman out of my sight and bolt the door after her." [18]So his servant put her out and bolted the door after her. She was wearing an ornate[a] robe, for this was the kind of garment the virgin daughters of the king wore. [19]Tamar put ashes on her head and tore the ornate robe she was wearing. She put her hands on her head and went away, weeping aloud as she went.

[20]Her brother Absalom said to her, "Has that Amnon, your brother, been with you? Be quiet for now, my sister; he is your brother. Don't take this thing to heart." And Tamar lived in her brother Absalom's house, a desolate woman.

[21]When King David heard all this, he was furious. [22]And Absalom never said a word to Amnon, either good or bad; he hated Amnon because he had disgraced his sister Tamar.

Absalom Kills Amnon

[23]Two years later, when Absalom's sheepshearers were at Baal Hazor near the border of Ephraim, he invited all the king's sons to come there. [24]Absalom went to the king and said, "Your servant has had shearers come. Will the king and his attendants please join me?"

[25]"No, my son," the king replied. "All of us

---

[a] 18 The meaning of the Hebrew for this word is uncertain; also in verse 19.

Responsibility: If You Won't Carry the Ball, You Can't Lead the Team

2 Samuel 13:1–39

David suffers the first of several horrible consequences of his sin with Bathsheba shortly after some military conquests. David's son Amnon rapes his half sister, Tamar. When David hears about it, he does nothing—surprising and upsetting David's son Absalom. After two years, Absalom murders Amnon. The whole mess plays out almost like a soap opera.

By this point, David's leadership has shrunk to a mere shadow of its former self. Note the changes in David's leadership:

1. **He no longer works proactively, but passively interacts with those closest to him (vv. 30–31).**

2. **He no longer expresses joy, but is full of grief and mourning (v. 31).**

3. **He no longer acts on his convictions, but buys into rationalizations about his loss (vv. 32–33, 39).**

4. **He no longer solves problems, but licks his wounds (vv. 34–36).**

5. **He no longer pursues his desires, but remains paralyzed regarding Absalom (v. 39).**

should not go; we would only be a burden to you." Although Absalom urged him, he still refused to go but gave him his blessing.

²⁶Then Absalom said, "If not, please let my brother Amnon come with us."

The king asked him, "Why should he go with you?" ²⁷But Absalom urged him, so he sent with him Amnon and the rest of the king's sons.

²⁸Absalom ordered his men, "Listen! When Amnon is in high spirits from drinking wine and I say to you, 'Strike Amnon down,' then kill him. Don't be afraid. Haven't I given you this order? Be strong and brave." ²⁹So Absalom's men did to Amnon what Absalom had ordered. Then all the king's sons got up, mounted their mules and fled.

³⁰While they were on their way, the report came to David: "Absalom has struck down all the king's sons; not one of them is left." ³¹The king stood up, tore his clothes and lay down on the ground; and all his attendants stood by with their clothes torn.

³²But Jonadab son of Shimeah, David's brother, said, "My lord should not think that they killed all the princes; only Amnon is dead. This has been Absalom's express intention ever since the day Amnon raped his sister Tamar. ³³My lord the king should not be concerned about the report that all the king's sons are dead. Only Amnon is dead."

³⁴Meanwhile, Absalom had fled.

Now the man standing watch looked up and saw many people on the road west of him, coming down the side of the hill. The watchman went and told the king, "I see men in the direction of Horonaim, on the side of the hill."[a]

³⁵Jonadab said to the king, "See, the king's sons have come; it has happened just as your servant said."

³⁶As he finished speaking, the king's sons came in, wailing loudly. The king, too, and all his attendants wept very bitterly.

³⁷Absalom fled and went to Talmai son of Ammihud, the king of Geshur. But King David mourned many days for his son.

³⁸After Absalom fled and went to Geshur, he stayed there three years. ³⁹And King David longed to go to Absalom, for he was consoled concerning Amnon's death.

Absalom Returns to Jerusalem

14 Joab son of Zeruiah knew that the king's heart longed for Absalom. ²So Joab sent someone to Tekoa and had a wise woman brought from there. He said to her, "Pretend you

are in mourning. Dress in mourning clothes, and don't use any cosmetic lotions. Act like a woman who has spent many days grieving for the dead. ³Then go to the king and speak these words to him." And Joab put the words in her mouth.

⁴When the woman from Tekoa went[b] to the king, she fell with her face to the ground to pay him honor, and she said, "Help me, Your Majesty!"

⁵The king asked her, "What is troubling you?"

She said, "I am a widow; my husband is dead. ⁶I your servant had two sons. They got into a fight with each other in the field, and no one was there to separate them. One struck the other and killed him. ⁷Now the whole clan has risen up against your servant; they say, 'Hand over the one who struck his brother down, so that we may put him to death for the life of his brother whom he killed; then we will get rid of the heir as well.' They would put out the only burning coal I have left, leaving my husband neither name nor descendant on the face of the earth."

⁸The king said to the woman, "Go home, and I will issue an order in your behalf."

⁹But the woman from Tekoa said to him, "Let my lord the king pardon me and my family, and let the king and his throne be without guilt."

¹⁰The king replied, "If anyone says anything to you, bring them to me, and they will not bother you again."

¹¹She said, "Then let the king invoke the LORD his God to prevent the avenger of blood from adding to the destruction, so that my son will not be destroyed."

"As surely as the LORD lives," he said, "not one hair of your son's head will fall to the ground."

¹²Then the woman said, "Let your servant speak a word to my lord the king."

"Speak," he replied.

¹³The woman said, "Why then have you devised a thing like this against the people of God? When the king says this, does he not convict himself, for the king has not brought back his banished son? ¹⁴Like water spilled on the ground, which cannot be recovered, so we must die. But that is not what God desires; rather, he devises ways so that a banished person does not remain banished from him.

¹⁵"And now I have come to say this to my lord the king because the people have made me

---

[a] 34 Septuagint; Hebrew does not have this sentence.
[b] 4 Many Hebrew manuscripts, Septuagint, Vulgate and Syriac; most Hebrew manuscripts *spoke*

afraid. Your servant thought, 'I will speak to the king; perhaps he will grant his servant's request. [16]Perhaps the king will agree to deliver his servant from the hand of the man who is trying to cut off both me and my son from God's inheritance.'

[17]"And now your servant says, 'May the word of my lord the king secure my inheritance, for my lord the king is like an angel of God in discerning good and evil. May the LORD your God be with you.'"

[18]Then the king said to the woman, "Don't keep from me the answer to what I am going to ask you."

"Let my lord the king speak," the woman said.

[19]The king asked, "Isn't the hand of Joab with you in all this?"

The woman answered, "As surely as you live, my lord the king, no one can turn to the right or to the left from anything my lord the king says. Yes, it was your servant Joab who instructed me to do this and who put all these words into the mouth of your servant. [20]Your servant Joab did this to change the present situation. My lord has wisdom like that of an angel of God — he knows everything that happens in the land."

[21]The king said to Joab, "Very well, I will do it. Go, bring back the young man Absalom."

[22]Joab fell with his face to the ground to pay him honor, and he blessed the king. Joab said, "Today your servant knows that he has found favor in your eyes, my lord the king, because the king has granted his servant's request."

[23]Then Joab went to Geshur and brought Absalom back to Jerusalem. [24]But the king said, "He must go to his own house; he must not see my face." So Absalom went to his own house and did not see the face of the king.

[25]In all Israel there was not a man so highly praised for his handsome appearance as Absalom. From the top of his head to the sole of his foot there was no blemish in him. [26]Whenever he cut the hair of his head — he used to cut his hair once a year because it became too heavy for him — he would weigh it, and its weight was two hundred shekels[a] by the royal standard.

[27]Three sons and a daughter were born to Absalom. His daughter's name was Tamar, and she became a beautiful woman.

[28]Absalom lived two years in Jerusalem without seeing the king's face. [29]Then Absalom sent for Joab in order to send him to the king, but Joab refused to come to him. So he sent a second time, but he refused to come. [30]Then he said to his servants, "Look, Joab's field is next to mine, and he has barley there. Go and set it on fire." So Absalom's servants set the field on fire.

[31]Then Joab did go to Absalom's house, and he said to him, "Why have your servants set my field on fire?"

[32]Absalom said to Joab, "Look, I sent word to you and said, 'Come here so I can send you to the king to ask, "Why have I come from Geshur? It would be better for me if I were still there!"' Now then, I want to see the king's face, and if I am guilty of anything, let him put me to death."

[33]So Joab went to the king and told him this. Then the king summoned Absalom, and he came in and bowed down with his face to the ground before the king. And the king kissed Absalom.

Absalom's Conspiracy

15 In the course of time, Absalom provided himself with a chariot and horses and with fifty men to run ahead of him. [2]He would get up early and stand by the side of the road leading to the city gate. Whenever anyone came with a complaint to be placed before the king for a decision, Absalom would call out to him, "What town are you from?" He would answer, "Your servant is from one of the tribes of Israel." [3]Then Absalom would say to him, "Look, your claims are valid and proper, but there is no representative of the king to hear you." [4]And Absalom would add, "If only I were appointed judge in the land! Then everyone who has a complaint or case could come to me and I would see that they receive justice."

[5]Also, whenever anyone approached him to bow down before him, Absalom would reach out his hand, take hold of him and kiss him. [6]Absalom behaved in this way toward all the Israelites who came to the king asking for justice, and so he stole the hearts of the people of Israel.

[7]At the end of four[b] years, Absalom said to the king, "Let me go to Hebron and fulfill a vow I made to the LORD. [8]While your servant was living at Geshur in Aram, I made this vow: 'If the LORD takes me back to Jerusalem, I will worship the LORD in Hebron.[c]'"

[9]The king said to him, "Go in peace." So he went to Hebron.

[10]Then Absalom sent secret messengers throughout the tribes of Israel to say, "As soon

---

[a] 26 That is, about 5 pounds or about 2.3 kilograms
[b] 7 Some Septuagint manuscripts, Syriac and Josephus; Hebrew *forty*   [c] 8 Some Septuagint manuscripts; Hebrew does not have *in Hebron.*

as you hear the sound of the trumpets, then say, 'Absalom is king in Hebron.'" [11]Two hundred men from Jerusalem had accompanied Absalom. They had been invited as guests and went quite innocently, knowing nothing about the matter. [12]While Absalom was offering sacrifices, he also sent for Ahithophel the Gilonite, David's counselor, to come from Giloh, his hometown. And so the conspiracy gained strength, and Absalom's following kept on increasing.

David Flees

[13]A messenger came and told David, "The hearts of the people of Israel are with Absalom."

[14]Then David said to all his officials who were with him in Jerusalem, "Come! We must flee, or none of us will escape from Absalom. We must leave immediately, or he will move quickly to overtake us and bring ruin on us and put the city to the sword."

[15]The king's officials answered him, "Your servants are ready to do whatever our lord the king chooses."

[16]The king set out, with his entire household following him; but he left ten concubines to take care of the palace. [17]So the king set out, with all the people following him, and they halted at the edge of the city. [18]All his men marched past him, along with all the Kerethites and Pelethites; and all the six hundred Gittites who had accompanied him from Gath marched before the king.

[19]The king said to Ittai the Gittite, "Why should you come along with us? Go back and stay with King Absalom. You are a foreigner, an exile from your homeland. [20]You came only yesterday. And today shall I make you wander about with us, when I do not know where I am going? Go back, and take your people with you. May the LORD show you kindness and faithfulness."[a]

[21]But Ittai replied to the king, "As surely as the LORD lives, and as my lord the king lives, wherever my lord the king may be, whether it means life or death, there will your servant be."

[22]David said to Ittai, "Go ahead, march on." So Ittai the Gittite marched on with all his men and the families that were with him.

[23]The whole countryside wept aloud as all the people passed by. The king also crossed the Kidron Valley, and all the people moved on toward the wilderness.

[24]Zadok was there, too, and all the Levites who were with him were carrying the ark of the covenant of God. They set down the ark of God, and Abiathar offered sacrifices until all the people had finished leaving the city.

[25]Then the king said to Zadok, "Take the ark of God back into the city. If I find favor in the LORD's eyes, he will bring me back and let

---

[a] 20 Septuagint; Hebrew *May kindness and faithfulness be with you*

The Law of Respect: Absalom Assumes Power, David Flees

2 Samuel 15:1–37

Some time after he returns to Jerusalem following the murder of his brother Amnon, Absalom rises to power and assumes a position of leadership in Israel. In the intervening years he becomes a stronger, more forceful leader than his father, David.

Despite David's natural leadership abilities, somehow he lost his conviction and resolve. Before the chapter ends, we see David running from his own son—thus reminding us of the Law of Respect. People usually follow leaders who are stronger than themselves. It's not hard to see why Absalom could rally so many Israelites to his side:

Absalom
1. Provides himself with resources and weapons
2. Speaks about justice and meeting others' needs
3. Steals the people's hearts with his charisma
4. Rallies the people behind his vision
5. Rises up in courage to lead Israel

David
1. No longer goes out to battle
2. Doesn't provide enough deputies
3. Becomes distant and out of touch with people
4. Maintains politically correct view
5. Flees in fear of Absalom

21 QUALITIES

PASSION   Absalom Ruins His Own Cause

2 Samuel 13:22—18:9

AFTER DAVID sinned with Bathsheba, the prophet Nathan warned the king that the sword would never depart from his house (2Sa 12:10). True to the prediction, David endured domestic problems from that day on—deception, adultery, incest, even murder. David never figured out how to deal with the rebellion effectively; it was as though his anointing and authority had left him.

No one saw this more clearly than his son Absalom. When Amnon raped his sister Tamar and David did nothing about it, Absalom became irate (13:22). His fury grew the longer the king delayed justice. Further, Absalom tried and failed to get an audience with his father. It was as though David had abandoned his role as spiritual leader over his family.

Finally, Absalom could take it no longer. He got everyone's attention by committing two crimes. First, he avenged his sister Tamar by murdering Amnon; for this crime his father David banished him (13:37–38). After he was permitted to return, Absalom got angry with general Joab and set his field on fire (14:30).

Despite his actions, Absalom couldn't get the fatherly attention he wanted so desperately. Past the boiling point, he used his passion to sabotage his father's leadership.

He played politics and convinced people to bring their lawsuits to him. He lobbied for support of his leadership. Finally he raised an army to rebel against the king.

In the end, Absalom died as a maverick leader whose passion went awry. As you study his story in 2 Samuel 13–18, look for those lessons about passion gone bad:

1. **Passion without perspective brings death (13:22–29).**

2. **Passion will find expression, in either healthy or unhealthy ways (14:28–30).**

3. **People follow passion over orthodoxy, even when it's unwise (15:1–12).**

4. **Leaders who follow passion defeat leaders who follow protocol (15:13–14).**

5. **Self-centered passion always skews the judgment of a leader (16:22).**

6. **Unchanneled and unbridled passion damages everyone near it (17; 18)**

7. **When passion outweighs wisdom, leaders sabotage themselves (18:9).**

The Good News

Absalom represents a leader who can't bridle his passion. When a leader embraces passion before he learns submission, trouble always follows.

Does this mean we should condemn passion? Absolutely not! Passion is one of the 21 Indispensable Qualities of a Leader. Consider the benefits of passion:

1. **Passion is the first step to achievement.**

2. **Passion increases your willpower.**

3. **Passion changes you.**

4. **Passion makes the impossible possible.**

Passion helps develop your leadership. Passion must, however, pour from the heart of a leader who is wise, accountable, submissive, and unselfish.

For a positive example of passion, see p. 1207.

me see it and his dwelling place again. [26]But if he says, 'I am not pleased with you,' then I am ready; let him do to me whatever seems good to him."

[27]The king also said to Zadok the priest, "Do you understand? Go back to the city with my blessing. Take your son Ahimaaz with you, and also Abiathar's son Jonathan. You and Abiathar return with your two sons. [28]I will wait at the fords in the wilderness until word comes from you to inform me." [29]So Zadok and Abiathar took the ark of God back to Jerusalem and stayed there.

[30]But David continued up the Mount of Olives, weeping as he went; his head was covered and he was barefoot. All the people with him covered their heads too and were weeping as they went up. [31]Now David had been told, "Ahithophel is among the conspirators with Absalom." So David prayed, "Lord, turn Ahithophel's counsel into foolishness."

[32]When David arrived at the summit, where people used to worship God, Hushai the Arkite was there to meet him, his robe torn and dust on his head. [33]David said to him, "If you go with me, you will be a burden to me. [34]But if you return to the city and say to Absalom, 'Your Majesty, I will be your servant; I was your father's servant in the past, but now I will be your servant,' then you can help me by frustrating Ahithophel's advice. [35]Won't the priests Zadok and Abiathar be there with you? Tell them anything you hear in the king's palace. [36]Their two sons, Ahimaaz son of Zadok and Jonathan son of Abiathar, are there with them. Send them to me with anything you hear."

[37]So Hushai, David's confidant, arrived at Jerusalem as Absalom was entering the city.

David and Ziba

16 When David had gone a short distance beyond the summit, there was Ziba, the steward of Mephibosheth, waiting to meet him. He had a string of donkeys saddled and loaded with two hundred loaves of bread, a hundred cakes of raisins, a hundred cakes of figs and a skin of wine.

[2]The king asked Ziba, "Why have you brought these?"

Ziba answered, "The donkeys are for the king's household to ride on, the bread and fruit are for the men to eat, and the wine is to refresh those who become exhausted in the wilderness."

[3]The king then asked, "Where is your master's grandson?"

Ziba said to him, "He is staying in Jerusalem, because he thinks, 'Today the Israelites will restore to me my grandfather's kingdom.'"

[4]Then the king said to Ziba, "All that belonged to Mephibosheth is now yours."

"I humbly bow," Ziba said. "May I find favor in your eyes, my lord the king."

Shimei Curses David

[5]As King David approached Bahurim, a man from the same clan as Saul's family came out from there. His name was Shimei son of Gera, and he cursed as he came out. [6]He pelted David and all the king's officials with stones, though all the troops and the special guard were on David's right and left. [7]As he cursed, Shimei said, "Get out, get out, you murderer, you scoundrel! [8]The Lord has repaid you for all the blood you shed in the household of Saul, in whose place you have reigned. The Lord has given the kingdom into the hands of your son Absalom. You have come to ruin because you are a murderer!"

[9]Then Abishai son of Zeruiah said to the king, "Why should this dead dog curse my lord the king? Let me go over and cut off his head."

[10]But the king said, "What does this have to do with you, you sons of Zeruiah? If he is cursing because the Lord said to him, 'Curse David,' who can ask, 'Why do you do this?'"

[11]David then said to Abishai and all his officials, "My son, my own flesh and blood, is trying to kill me. How much more, then, this Benjamite! Leave him alone; let him curse, for the Lord has told him to. [12]It may be that the Lord will look upon my misery and restore to me his covenant blessing instead of his curse today."

[13]So David and his men continued along the road while Shimei was going along the hillside opposite him, cursing as he went and throwing stones at him and showering him with dirt. [14]The king and all the people with him arrived at their destination exhausted. And there he refreshed himself.

The Advice of Ahithophel and Hushai

[15]Meanwhile, Absalom and all the men of Israel came to Jerusalem, and Ahithophel was with him. [16]Then Hushai the Arkite, David's confidant, went to Absalom and said to him, "Long live the king! Long live the king!"

[17]Absalom said to Hushai, "So this is the love you show your friend? If he's your friend, why didn't you go with him?"

[18]Hushai said to Absalom, "No, the one chosen by the Lord, by these people, and by all the

men of Israel—his I will be, and I will remain with him. [19]Furthermore, whom should I serve? Should I not serve the son? Just as I served your father, so I will serve you."

[20]Absalom said to Ahithophel, "Give us your advice. What should we do?"

[21]Ahithophel answered, "Sleep with your father's concubines whom he left to take care of the palace. Then all Israel will hear that you have made yourself obnoxious to your father, and the hands of everyone with you will be more resolute." [22]So they pitched a tent for Absalom on the roof, and he slept with his father's concubines in the sight of all Israel.

[23]Now in those days the advice Ahithophel gave was like that of one who inquires of God. That was how both David and Absalom regarded all of Ahithophel's advice.

17 Ahithophel said to Absalom, "I would[a] choose twelve thousand men and set out tonight in pursuit of David. [2]I would attack him while he is weary and weak. I would strike him with terror, and then all the people with him will flee. I would strike down only the king [3]and bring all the people back to you. The death of the man you seek will mean the return of all; all the people will be unharmed." [4]This plan seemed good to Absalom and to all the elders of Israel.

[5]But Absalom said, "Summon also Hushai the Arkite, so we can hear what he has to say as well." [6]When Hushai came to him, Absalom said, "Ahithophel has given this advice. Should we do what he says? If not, give us your opinion."

[7]Hushai replied to Absalom, "The advice Ahithophel has given is not good this time. [8]You know your father and his men; they are fighters, and as fierce as a wild bear robbed of her cubs. Besides, your father is an experienced fighter; he will not spend the night with the troops. [9]Even now, he is hidden in a cave or some other place. If he should attack your troops first,[b] whoever hears about it will say, 'There has been a slaughter among the troops who follow Absalom.' [10]Then even the bravest soldier, whose heart is like the heart of a lion, will melt with fear, for all Israel knows that your father is a fighter and that those with him are brave.

[11]"So I advise you: Let all Israel, from Dan to Beersheba—as numerous as the sand on the seashore—be gathered to you, with you yourself leading them into battle. [12]Then we will attack him wherever he may be found, and we will fall on him as dew settles on the ground. Neither he nor any of his men will be left alive. [13]If he

[a] 1 Or Let me   [b] 9 Or When some of the men fall at the first attack

ABSALOM

A Tragic Case of Leadership Gone Bad
2 Samuel 16:1—18:18

PROFILE in leadership

Study the Bible from cover to cover, and it would be hard to find a more tragic case study on leadership gone bad than the story of Absalom.

Absalom grew up as a child of privilege in the royal palace. He was charismatic, attractive, and very powerful. Eventually he used his personal magnetism and abilities to displace David, God's anointed. For all of David's strengths as a leader, he failed as a father and never helped Absalom acquire a heart for God.

Absalom's inner circle of advisors greatly influenced his treachery by giving him wicked counsel. Absalom chose to listen to their evil voices precisely because he had already allowed them to greatly influence his thinking. His misplaced passion to acquire the throne constituted an act of treason. And it should surprise no one that those who gathered around Absalom were themselves persons of evil intent who recognized opportunities—however despicable—for personal gain.

Absalom's abuse of positional power, won through great natural talents, inflicted enormous pain on many Israelites. His lack of respect for authority, combined with a lack of respect for God, led to chaos in the kingdom. One cannot help but wonder what might have happened had David shed his tears for Absalom as the boy grew up under his roof, rather than at his funeral (2Sa 18:33).

withdraws into a city, then all Israel will bring ropes to that city, and we will drag it down to the valley until not so much as a pebble is left."

[14]Absalom and all the men of Israel said, "The advice of Hushai the Arkite is better than that of Ahithophel." For the LORD had determined to frustrate the good advice of Ahithophel in order to bring disaster on Absalom.

[15]Hushai told Zadok and Abiathar, the priests, "Ahithophel has advised Absalom and the elders of Israel to do such and such, but I have advised them to do so and so. [16]Now send a message at once and tell David, 'Do not spend the night at the fords in the wilderness; cross over without fail, or the king and all the people with him will be swallowed up.'"

[17]Jonathan and Ahimaaz were staying at En Rogel. A female servant was to go and inform them, and they were to go and tell King David, for they could not risk being seen entering the city. [18]But a young man saw them and told Absalom. So the two of them left at once and went to the house of a man in Bahurim. He had a well in his courtyard, and they climbed down into it. [19]His wife took a covering and spread it out over the opening of the well and scattered grain over it. No one knew anything about it.

[20]When Absalom's men came to the woman at the house, they asked, "Where are Ahimaaz and Jonathan?"

The woman answered them, "They crossed over the brook."[a] The men searched but found no one, so they returned to Jerusalem.

[21]After they had gone, the two climbed out of the well and went to inform King David. They said to him, "Set out and cross the river at once; Ahithophel has advised such and such against you." [22]So David and all the people with him set out and crossed the Jordan. By daybreak, no one was left who had not crossed the Jordan.

[23]When Ahithophel saw that his advice had not been followed, he saddled his donkey and set out for his house in his hometown. He put his house in order and then hanged himself. So he died and was buried in his father's tomb.

Absalom's Death

[24]David went to Mahanaim, and Absalom crossed the Jordan with all the men of Israel. [25]Absalom had appointed Amasa over the army in place of Joab. Amasa was the son of Jether,[b] an Ishmaelite[c] who had married Abigail,[d] the daughter of Nahash and sister of Zeruiah the mother of Joab. [26]The Israelites and Absalom camped in the land of Gilead.

[27]When David came to Mahanaim, Shobi son of Nahash from Rabbah of the Ammonites, and Makir son of Ammiel from Lo Debar, and Barzillai the Gileadite from Rogelim [28]brought bedding and bowls and articles of pottery. They also brought wheat and barley, flour and roasted grain, beans and lentils,[e] [29]honey and curds, sheep, and cheese from cows' milk for David and his people to eat. For they said, "The people have become exhausted and hungry and thirsty in the wilderness."

18 David mustered the men who were with him and appointed over them commanders of thousands and commanders of hundreds. [2]David sent out his troops, a third under the command of Joab, a third under Joab's brother Abishai son of Zeruiah, and a third under Ittai the Gittite. The king told the troops, "I myself will surely march out with you."

[3]But the men said, "You must not go out; if we are forced to flee, they won't care about us. Even if half of us die, they won't care; but you are worth ten thousand of us.[f] It would be better now for you to give us support from the city."

[4]The king answered, "I will do whatever seems best to you."

So the king stood beside the gate while all his men marched out in units of hundreds and of thousands. [5]The king commanded Joab, Abishai and Ittai, "Be gentle with the young man Absalom for my sake." And all the troops heard the king giving orders concerning Absalom to each of the commanders.

[6]David's army marched out of the city to fight Israel, and the battle took place in the forest of Ephraim. [7]There Israel's troops were routed by David's men, and the casualties that day were great—twenty thousand men. [8]The battle spread out over the whole countryside, and the forest swallowed up more men that day than the sword.

[9]Now Absalom happened to meet David's men. He was riding his mule, and as the mule went under the thick branches of a large oak, Absalom's hair got caught in the tree. He was left hanging in midair, while the mule he was riding kept on going.

---

[a] 20 Or "They passed by the sheep pen toward the water."
[b] 25 Hebrew *Ithra*, a variant of *Jether*   [c] 25 Some Septuagint manuscripts (see also 1 Chron. 2:17); Hebrew and other Septuagint manuscripts *Israelite*   [d] 25 Hebrew *Abigal*, a variant of *Abigail*   [e] 28 Most Septuagint manuscripts and Syriac; Hebrew *lentils, and roasted grain*   [f] 3 Two Hebrew manuscripts, some Septuagint manuscripts and Vulgate; most Hebrew manuscripts *care; for now there are ten thousand like us*

[10]When one of the men saw what had happened, he told Joab, "I just saw Absalom hanging in an oak tree."

[11]Joab said to the man who had told him this, "What! You saw him? Why didn't you strike him to the ground right there? Then I would have had to give you ten shekels[a] of silver and a warrior's belt."

[12]But the man replied, "Even if a thousand shekels[b] were weighed out into my hands, I would not lay a hand on the king's son. In our hearing the king commanded you and Abishai and Ittai, 'Protect the young man Absalom for my sake.'[c] [13]And if I had put my life in jeopardy[d] — and nothing is hidden from the king — you would have kept your distance from me."

[14]Joab said, "I'm not going to wait like this for you." So he took three javelins in his hand and plunged them into Absalom's heart while Absalom was still alive in the oak tree. [15]And ten of Joab's armor-bearers surrounded Absalom, struck him and killed him.

[16]Then Joab sounded the trumpet, and the troops stopped pursuing Israel, for Joab halted them. [17]They took Absalom, threw him into a big pit in the forest and piled up a large heap of rocks over him. Meanwhile, all the Israelites fled to their homes.

[18]During his lifetime Absalom had taken a pillar and erected it in the King's Valley as a monument to himself, for he thought, "I have no son to carry on the memory of my name." He named the pillar after himself, and it is called Absalom's Monument to this day.

David Mourns

[19]Now Ahimaaz son of Zadok said, "Let me run and take the news to the king that the LORD has vindicated him by delivering him from the hand of his enemies."

[20]"You are not the one to take the news today," Joab told him. "You may take the news another time, but you must not do so today, because the king's son is dead."

[21]Then Joab said to a Cushite, "Go, tell the king what you have seen." The Cushite bowed down before Joab and ran off.

[22]Ahimaaz son of Zadok again said to Joab, "Come what may, please let me run behind the Cushite."

But Joab replied, "My son, why do you want to go? You don't have any news that will bring you a reward."

[23]He said, "Come what may, I want to run."

So Joab said, "Run!" Then Ahimaaz ran by way of the plain[e] and outran the Cushite.

[24]While David was sitting between the inner and outer gates, the watchman went up to the roof of the gateway by the wall. As he looked out, he saw a man running alone. [25]The watchman called out to the king and reported it.

The king said, "If he is alone, he must have good news." And the runner came closer and closer.

[26]Then the watchman saw another runner, and he called down to the gatekeeper, "Look, another man running alone!"

The king said, "He must be bringing good news, too."

[27]The watchman said, "It seems to me that the first one runs like Ahimaaz son of Zadok."

"He's a good man," the king said. "He comes with good news."

---

[a] 11 That is, about 4 ounces or about 115 grams   [b] 12 That is, about 25 pounds or about 12 kilograms   [c] 12 A few Hebrew manuscripts, Septuagint, Vulgate and Syriac; most Hebrew manuscripts may be translated Absalom, whoever you may be.   [d] 13 Or Otherwise, if I had acted treacherously toward him   [e] 23 That is, the plain of the Jordan

---

Brokenness: Maturity Comes When God Breaks a Leader

2 Samuel 18:19–33

The armies of Absalom and King David came to blows over who would lead Israel, and the old king reasserted his rule.

David's troops not only routed his son's armies; they also killed Absalom himself. Yet David couldn't rejoice, even though his rebellious son's death ended the war. His family had fallen far. Absalom was dead. Amnon was dead. Tamar had been raped. Many who remained had grown twisted and sick.

And David cried out in brokenness.

In this broken state, God began to restore David to the man he once was, the man after his own heart. David regained his resolve to lead his country and leave a worthwhile legacy. He crushed other revolts, killed other giants, restored Israel. In many ways, David matured to a new level as a leader through this awful season of brokenness. Broken boldness now characterized his leadership.

²⁸Then Ahimaaz called out to the king, "All is well!" He bowed down before the king with his face to the ground and said, "Praise be to the LORD your God! He has delivered up those who lifted their hands against my lord the king."

²⁹The king asked, "Is the young man Absalom safe?"

Ahimaaz answered, "I saw great confusion just as Joab was about to send the king's servant and me, your servant, but I don't know what it was."

³⁰The king said, "Stand aside and wait here." So he stepped aside and stood there.

³¹Then the Cushite arrived and said, "My lord the king, hear the good news! The LORD has vindicated you today by delivering you from the hand of all who rose up against you."

³²The king asked the Cushite, "Is the young man Absalom safe?"

The Cushite replied, "May the enemies of my lord the king and all who rise up to harm you be like that young man."

³³The king was shaken. He went up to the room over the gateway and wept. As he went, he said: "O my son Absalom! My son, my son Absalom! If only I had died instead of you—O Absalom, my son, my son!"[a]

19[b] Joab was told, "The king is weeping and mourning for Absalom." ²And for the whole army the victory that day was turned into mourning, because on that day the troops heard it said, "The king is grieving for his son." ³The men stole into the city that day as men steal in who are ashamed when they flee from battle. ⁴The king covered his face and cried aloud, "O my son Absalom! O Absalom, my son, my son!"

⁵Then Joab went into the house to the king and said, "Today you have humiliated all your men, who have just saved your life and the lives of your sons and daughters and the lives of your wives and concubines. ⁶You love those who hate you and hate those who love you. You have made it clear today that the commanders and their men mean nothing to you. I see that you would be pleased if Absalom were alive today and all of us were dead. ⁷Now go out and encourage your men. I swear by the LORD that if you don't go out, not a man will be left with you by nightfall. This will be worse for you than all the calamities that have come on you from your youth till now."

⁸So the king got up and took his seat in the gateway. When the men were told, "The king is sitting in the gateway," they all came before him.

Meanwhile, the Israelites had fled to their homes.

David Returns to Jerusalem

⁹Throughout the tribes of Israel, all the people were arguing among themselves, saying, "The king delivered us from the hand of our enemies; he is the one who rescued us from the hand of the Philistines. But now he has fled the country to escape from Absalom; ¹⁰and Absalom, whom we anointed to rule over us, has died in battle. So why do you say nothing about bringing the king back?"

¹¹King David sent this message to Zadok and Abiathar, the priests: "Ask the elders of Judah, 'Why should you be the last to bring the king back to his palace, since what is being said throughout Israel has reached the king at his quarters? ¹²You are my relatives, my own flesh and blood. So why should you be the last to bring back the king?' ¹³And say to Amasa, 'Are you not my own flesh and blood? May God deal with me, be it ever so severely, if you are not the commander of my army for life in place of Joab.'"

¹⁴He won over the hearts of the men of Judah so that they were all of one mind. They sent word to the king, "Return, you and all your men." ¹⁵Then the king returned and went as far as the Jordan.

Now the men of Judah had come to Gilgal to go out and meet the king and bring him across the Jordan. ¹⁶Shimei son of Gera, the Benjamite from Bahurim, hurried down with the men of Judah to meet King David. ¹⁷With him were a thousand Benjamites, along with Ziba, the steward of Saul's household, and his fifteen sons and twenty servants. They rushed to the Jordan, where the king was. ¹⁸They crossed at the ford to take the king's household over and to do whatever he wished.

When Shimei son of Gera crossed the Jordan, he fell prostrate before the king ¹⁹and said to him, "May my lord not hold me guilty. Do not remember how your servant did wrong on the day my lord the king left Jerusalem. May the king put it out of his mind. ²⁰For I your servant know that I have sinned, but today I have come here as the first from the tribes of Joseph to come down and meet my lord the king."

²¹Then Abishai son of Zeruiah said, "Shouldn't Shimei be put to death for this? He cursed the LORD's anointed."

---

[a] 33 In Hebrew texts this verse (18:33) is numbered 19:1.

[b] In Hebrew texts 19:1-43 is numbered 19:2-44.

²²David replied, "What does this have to do with you, you sons of Zeruiah? What right do you have to interfere? Should anyone be put to death in Israel today? Don't I know that today I am king over Israel?" ²³So the king said to Shimei, "You shall not die." And the king promised him on oath.

²⁴Mephibosheth, Saul's grandson, also went down to meet the king. He had not taken care of his feet or trimmed his mustache or washed his clothes from the day the king left until the day he returned safely. ²⁵When he came from Jerusalem to meet the king, the king asked him, "Why didn't you go with me, Mephibosheth?"

²⁶He said, "My lord the king, since I your servant am lame, I said, 'I will have my donkey saddled and will ride on it, so I can go with the king.' But Ziba my servant betrayed me. ²⁷And he has slandered your servant to my lord the king. My lord the king is like an angel of God; so do whatever you wish. ²⁸All my grandfather's descendants deserved nothing but death from my lord the king, but you gave your servant a place among those who eat at your table. So what right do I have to make any more appeals to the king?"

²⁹The king said to him, "Why say more? I order you and Ziba to divide the land."

³⁰Mephibosheth said to the king, "Let him take everything, now that my lord the king has returned home safely."

³¹Barzillai the Gileadite also came down from Rogelim to cross the Jordan with the king and to send him on his way from there. ³²Now Barzillai was very old, eighty years of age. He had provided for the king during his stay in Mahanaim, for he was a very wealthy man. ³³The king said to Barzillai, "Cross over with me and stay with me in Jerusalem, and I will provide for you."

³⁴But Barzillai answered the king, "How many more years will I live, that I should go up to Jerusalem with the king? ³⁵I am now eighty years old. Can I tell the difference between what is enjoyable and what is not? Can your servant taste what he eats and drinks? Can I still hear the voices of male and female singers? Why should your servant be an added burden to my lord the king? ³⁶Your servant will cross over the Jordan with the king for a short distance, but why should the king reward me in this way? ³⁷Let your servant return, that I may die in my own town near the tomb of my father and mother. But here is your servant Kimham. Let him cross over with my lord the king. Do for him whatever you wish."

³⁸The king said, "Kimham shall cross over with me, and I will do for him whatever you wish. And anything you desire from me I will do for you."

³⁹So all the people crossed the Jordan, and then the king crossed over. The king kissed Barzillai and bid him farewell, and Barzillai returned to his home.

⁴⁰When the king crossed over to Gilgal, Kimham crossed with him. All the troops of Judah and half the troops of Israel had taken the king over.

⁴¹Soon all the men of Israel were coming to the king and saying to him, "Why did our brothers, the men of Judah, steal the king away and bring him and his household across the Jordan, together with all his men?"

⁴²All the men of Judah answered the men of Israel, "We did this because the king is closely related to us. Why are you angry about it? Have we eaten any of the king's provisions? Have we taken anything for ourselves?"

⁴³Then the men of Israel answered the men of Judah, "We have ten shares in the king; so we have a greater claim on David than you have. Why then do you treat us with contempt? Weren't we the first to speak of bringing back our king?"

But the men of Judah pressed their claims even more forcefully than the men of Israel.

Sheba Rebels Against David

20 Now a troublemaker named Sheba son of Bikri, a Benjamite, happened to be there. He sounded the trumpet and shouted,

"We have no share in David,
    no part in Jesse's son!
Every man to his tent, Israel!"

²So all the men of Israel deserted David to follow Sheba son of Bikri. But the men of Judah stayed by their king all the way from the Jordan to Jerusalem.

³When David returned to his palace in Jerusalem, he took the ten concubines he had left to take care of the palace and put them in a house under guard. He provided for them but had no sexual relations with them. They were kept in confinement till the day of their death, living as widows.

⁴Then the king said to Amasa, "Summon the men of Judah to come to me within three days, and be here yourself." ⁵But when Amasa went to summon Judah, he took longer than the time the king had set for him.

6David said to Abishai, "Now Sheba son of Bikri will do us more harm than Absalom did. Take your master's men and pursue him, or he will find fortified cities and escape from us."[a] 7So Joab's men and the Kerethites and Pelethites and all the mighty warriors went out under the command of Abishai. They marched out from Jerusalem to pursue Sheba son of Bikri.

8While they were at the great rock in Gibeon, Amasa came to meet them. Joab was wearing his military tunic, and strapped over it at his waist was a belt with a dagger in its sheath. As he stepped forward, it dropped out of its sheath.

9Joab said to Amasa, "How are you, my brother?" Then Joab took Amasa by the beard with his right hand to kiss him. 10Amasa was not on his guard against the dagger in Joab's hand, and Joab plunged it into his belly, and his intestines spilled out on the ground. Without being stabbed again, Amasa died. Then Joab and his brother Abishai pursued Sheba son of Bikri.

11One of Joab's men stood beside Amasa and said, "Whoever favors Joab, and whoever is for David, let him follow Joab!" 12Amasa lay wallowing in his blood in the middle of the road, and the man saw that all the troops came to a halt there. When he realized that everyone who came up to Amasa stopped, he dragged him from the road into a field and threw a garment over him. 13After Amasa had been removed from the road, everyone went on with Joab to pursue Sheba son of Bikri.

14Sheba passed through all the tribes of Israel to Abel Beth Maakah and through the entire region of the Bikrites,[b] who gathered together and followed him. 15All the troops with Joab came and besieged Sheba in Abel Beth Maakah. They built a siege ramp up to the city, and it stood against the outer fortifications. While they were battering the wall to bring it down, 16a wise woman called from the city, "Listen! Listen! Tell Joab to come here so I can speak to him." 17He went toward her, and she asked, "Are you Joab?"

"I am," he answered.

She said, "Listen to what your servant has to say."

"I'm listening," he said.

18She continued, "Long ago they used to say, 'Get your answer at Abel,' and that settled it. 19We are the peaceful and faithful in Israel. You are trying to destroy a city that is a mother in Israel. Why do you want to swallow up the LORD's inheritance?"

20"Far be it from me!" Joab replied, "Far be it from me to swallow up or destroy! 21That is not the case. A man named Sheba son of Bikri, from the hill country of Ephraim, has lifted up his hand against the king, against David. Hand over this one man, and I'll withdraw from the city."

The woman said to Joab, "His head will be thrown to you from the wall."

22Then the woman went to all the people with her wise advice, and they cut off the head of Sheba son of Bikri and threw it to Joab. So he sounded the trumpet, and his men dispersed from the city, each returning to his home. And Joab went back to the king in Jerusalem.

David's Officials

23Joab was over Israel's entire army; Benaiah son of Jehoiada was over the Kerethites and Pelethites; 24Adoniram[c] was in charge of forced labor; Jehoshaphat son of Ahilud was recorder; 25Sheva was secretary; Zadok and Abiathar were priests; 26and Ira the Jairite[d] was David's priest.

The Gibeonites Avenged

21 During the reign of David, there was a famine for three successive years; so David sought the face of the LORD. The LORD said, "It is on account of Saul and his blood-stained house; it is because he put the Gibeonites to death."

2The king summoned the Gibeonites and spoke to them. (Now the Gibeonites were not a part of Israel but were survivors of the Amorites; the Israelites had sworn to spare them, but Saul in his zeal for Israel and Judah had tried to annihilate them.) 3David asked the Gibeonites, "What shall I do for you? How shall I make atonement so that you will bless the LORD's inheritance?"

4The Gibeonites answered him, "We have no right to demand silver or gold from Saul or his family, nor do we have the right to put anyone in Israel to death."

"What do you want me to do for you?" David asked.

5They answered the king, "As for the man who destroyed us and plotted against us so that we have been decimated and have no place anywhere in Israel, 6let seven of his male descendants be given to us to be killed and their bodies exposed before the LORD at Gibeah of Saul — the LORD's chosen one."

---

[a] 6 Or and do us serious injury   [b] 14 See Septuagint and Vulgate; Hebrew Berites.   [c] 24 Some Septuagint manuscripts (see also 1 Kings 4:6 and 5:14); Hebrew Adoram
[d] 26 Hebrew; some Septuagint manuscripts and Syriac (see also 23:38) Ithrite

So the king said, "I will give them to you."

[7]The king spared Mephibosheth son of Jonathan, the son of Saul, because of the oath before the LORD between David and Jonathan son of Saul. [8]But the king took Armoni and Mephibosheth, the two sons of Aiah's daughter Rizpah, whom she had borne to Saul, together with the five sons of Saul's daughter Merab,[a] whom she had borne to Adriel son of Barzillai the Meholathite. [9]He handed them over to the Gibeonites, who killed them and exposed their bodies on a hill before the LORD. All seven of them fell together; they were put to death during the first days of the harvest, just as the barley harvest was beginning.

[10]Rizpah daughter of Aiah took sackcloth and spread it out for herself on a rock. From the beginning of the harvest till the rain poured down from the heavens on the bodies, she did not let the birds touch them by day or the wild animals by night. [11]When David was told what Aiah's daughter Rizpah, Saul's concubine, had done, [12]he went and took the bones of Saul and his son Jonathan from the citizens of Jabesh Gilead. (They had stolen their bodies from the public square at Beth Shan, where the Philistines had hung them after they struck Saul down on Gilboa.) [13]David brought the bones of Saul and his son Jonathan from there, and the bones of those who had been killed and exposed were gathered up.

[14]They buried the bones of Saul and his son Jonathan in the tomb of Saul's father Kish, at Zela in Benjamin, and did everything the king commanded. After that, God answered prayer in behalf of the land.

Wars Against the Philistines

[15]Once again there was a battle between the Philistines and Israel. David went down with his men to fight against the Philistines, and he became exhausted. [16]And Ishbi-Benob, one of the descendants of Rapha, whose bronze spearhead weighed three hundred shekels[b] and who was armed with a new sword, said he would kill David. [17]But Abishai son of Zeruiah came to David's rescue; he struck the Philistine down and killed him. Then David's men swore to him, saying, "Never again will you go out with us to battle, so that the lamp of Israel will not be extinguished."

[18]In the course of time, there was another battle with the Philistines, at Gob. At that time Sibbekai the Hushathite killed Saph, one of the descendants of Rapha.

[19]In another battle with the Philistines at Gob, Elhanan son of Jair[c] the Bethlehemite

---

[a] 8 Two Hebrew manuscripts, some Septuagint manuscripts and Syriac (see also 1 Samuel 18:19); most Hebrew and Septuagint manuscripts *Michal*   [b] 16 That is, about 7 1/2 pounds or about 3.5 kilograms   [c] 19 See 1 Chron. 20:5; Hebrew *Jaare-Oregim*.

Relationships: Coping with Difficult People

2 Samuel 21:1–14

Every leader faces difficult people and draining circumstances. The following difficult personality types commonly accost leaders today:

Type	Strategy
1. *The Sherman Tank:* rides over people	1. Consider the issue; stand up if important.
2. *The Space Cadet:* lives in another world	2. Find and develop their unique gifts.
3. *The Volcano:* explosive, unpredictable	3. Remove from crowd, listen, be direct.
4. *The Thumb Sucker:* self-pity, pouts	4. Don't reward; expose them to real trouble.
5. *The Wet Blanket:* always down	5. Be honest, don't cater; don't let them lead.
6. *The Garbage Collector:* attracts the worst	6. Challenge their statements; force honesty.
7. *The User:* demands lots of time, energy	7. Set boundaries; require accountability.

The Gibeonites became one of David's difficult people. Answer the following questions about how David chose to deal with them:

1. Why did God send the famine and the Gibeonites to David (vv. 1–2)?

2. How far should the leader go to satisfy the complaints of a critic (vv. 3–4)?

3. Did David go too far in trying to appease the Gibeonites or Rizpah (vv. 5–14)?

killed the brother of[a] Goliath the Gittite, who had a spear with a shaft like a weaver's rod.

²⁰In still another battle, which took place at Gath, there was a huge man with six fingers on each hand and six toes on each foot — twenty-four in all. He also was descended from Rapha. ²¹When he taunted Israel, Jonathan son of Shimeah, David's brother, killed him.

²²These four were descendants of Rapha in Gath, and they fell at the hands of David and his men.

David's Song of Praise

22 David sang to the LORD the words of this song when the LORD delivered him from the hand of all his enemies and from the hand of Saul. ²He said:

"The LORD is my rock, my fortress and my
    deliverer;
³   my God is my rock, in whom I take
        refuge,
    my shield[b] and the horn[c] of my salvation.
    He is my stronghold, my refuge and my
        savior —
    from violent people you save me.

⁴"I called to the LORD, who is worthy of
        praise,
    and have been saved from my enemies.
⁵The waves of death swirled about me;
    the torrents of destruction overwhelmed
        me.
⁶The cords of the grave coiled around me;
    the snares of death confronted me.

⁷"In my distress I called to the LORD;
    I called out to my God.
From his temple he heard my voice;
    my cry came to his ears.
⁸The earth trembled and quaked,
    the foundations of the heavens[d] shook;
    they trembled because he was angry.
⁹Smoke rose from his nostrils;
    consuming fire came from his mouth,
    burning coals blazed out of it.
¹⁰He parted the heavens and came down;
    dark clouds were under his feet.
¹¹He mounted the cherubim and flew;
    he soared[e] on the wings of the wind.
¹²He made darkness his canopy around him —
    the dark[f] rain clouds of the sky.
¹³Out of the brightness of his presence
    bolts of lightning blazed forth.
¹⁴The LORD thundered from heaven;
    the voice of the Most High resounded.

¹⁵He shot his arrows and scattered the enemy,
    with great bolts of lightning he routed
        them.
¹⁶The valleys of the sea were exposed
    and the foundations of the earth laid bare
at the rebuke of the LORD,
    at the blast of breath from his nostrils.

¹⁷"He reached down from on high and took
        hold of me;
    he drew me out of deep waters.
¹⁸He rescued me from my powerful enemy,
    from my foes, who were too strong for me.
¹⁹They confronted me in the day of my
        disaster,
    but the LORD was my support.
²⁰He brought me out into a spacious place;
    he rescued me because he delighted in me.

²¹"The LORD has dealt with me according to
        my righteousness;
    according to the cleanness of my hands he
        has rewarded me.
²²For I have kept the ways of the LORD;
    I am not guilty of turning from my God.
²³All his laws are before me;
    I have not turned away from his decrees.
²⁴I have been blameless before him
    and have kept myself from sin.
²⁵The LORD has rewarded me according to my
        righteousness,
    according to my cleanness[g] in his sight.

²⁶"To the faithful you show yourself faithful,
    to the blameless you show yourself
        blameless,
²⁷to the pure you show yourself pure,
    but to the devious you show yourself shrewd.
²⁸You save the humble,
    but your eyes are on the haughty to bring
        them low.
²⁹You, LORD, are my lamp;
    the LORD turns my darkness into light.
³⁰With your help I can advance against a troop[h];
    with my God I can scale a wall.

³¹"As for God, his way is perfect:
    The LORD's word is flawless;
    he shields all who take refuge in him.

---

[a] 19 See 1 Chron. 20:5; Hebrew does not have the brother of.
[b] 3 Or sovereign   [c] 3 Horn here symbolizes strength.
[d] 8 Hebrew; Vulgate and Syriac (see also Psalm 18:7)
mountains   [e] 11 Many Hebrew manuscripts (see also Psalm 18:10); most Hebrew manuscripts appeared   [f] 12 Septuagint (see also Psalm 18:11); Hebrew massed   [g] 25 Hebrew; Septuagint and Vulgate (see also Psalm 18:24) to the cleanness of my hands   [h] 30 Or can run through a barricade

³²For who is God besides the LORD?
　　And who is the Rock except our God?
³³It is God who arms me with strength[a]
　　and keeps my way secure.
³⁴He makes my feet like the feet of a deer;
　　he causes me to stand on the heights.
³⁵He trains my hands for battle;
　　my arms can bend a bow of bronze.
³⁶You make your saving help my shield;
　　your help has made[b] me great.
³⁷You provide a broad path for my feet,
　　so that my ankles do not give way.

³⁸"I pursued my enemies and crushed them;
　　I did not turn back till they were
　　　　destroyed.
³⁹I crushed them completely, and they could
　　　　not rise;
　　they fell beneath my feet.
⁴⁰You armed me with strength for battle;
　　you humbled my adversaries before me.
⁴¹You made my enemies turn their backs in
　　　　flight,
　　and I destroyed my foes.
⁴²They cried for help, but there was no one to
　　　　save them —
　　to the LORD, but he did not answer.
⁴³I beat them as fine as the dust of the earth;
　　I pounded and trampled them like mud in
　　　　the streets.

⁴⁴"You have delivered me from the attacks of
　　　　the peoples;
　　you have preserved me as the head of
　　　　nations.
　　People I did not know now serve me,
⁴⁵　foreigners cower before me;
　　as soon as they hear of me, they obey me.
⁴⁶They all lose heart;
　　they come trembling[c] from their
　　　　strongholds.

⁴⁷"The LORD lives! Praise be to my Rock!
　　Exalted be my God, the Rock, my Savior!
⁴⁸He is the God who avenges me,
　　who puts the nations under me,
⁴⁹　who sets me free from my enemies.
　　You exalted me above my foes;
　　from a violent man you rescued me.
⁵⁰Therefore I will praise you, LORD, among the
　　　　nations;
　　I will sing the praises of your name.

⁵¹"He gives his king great victories;
　　he shows unfailing kindness to his
　　　　anointed,
　　to David and his descendants forever."

God Is the Source, Not People or Material Resources

2 Samuel 22:1–51; 24:1–15

Despite David's serious lapses in both judgment and godliness, he continued to seek the Lord out of the depths of his soul, from the beginning of his life to its very end.

In the twilight of his years, David sang a beautiful song declaring God as the source of his victory (2Sa 22). He declared that neither horses nor chariots could deliver him, but only the hand of the living God.

When toward the end of his reign David took a census against God's will, the Lord gave him his choice of punishment: seven years of famine; three months of fleeing from his enemies; or three days' pestilence. David chose the epidemic, saying, "I am in deep distress. Let us fall into the hands of the LORD, for his mercy is great; but do not let me fall into human hands" (2Sa 24:14).

Whether in punishment or provision, David knew that God is always the right choice. He still is.

David's Last Words

23 These are the last words of David:

　　"The inspired utterance of David son of
　　　　Jesse,
　　the utterance of the man exalted by the
　　　　Most High,
　　the man anointed by the God of Jacob,
　　　　the hero of Israel's songs:

²"The Spirit of the LORD spoke through me;
　　his word was on my tongue.
³The God of Israel spoke,
　　the Rock of Israel said to me:
'When one rules over people in
　　　　righteousness,
　　when he rules in the fear of God,
⁴he is like the light of morning at sunrise
　　on a cloudless morning,

---

[a] 33 Dead Sea Scrolls, some Septuagint manuscripts, Vulgate and Syriac (see also Psalm 18:32); Masoretic Text *who is my strong refuge*　[b] 36 Dead Sea Scrolls; Masoretic Text *shield; / you stoop down to make*　[c] 46 Some Septuagint manuscripts and Vulgate (see also Psalm 18:45); Masoretic Text *they arm themselves*

like the brightness after rain
  that brings grass from the earth.'

5 "If my house were not right with God,
    surely he would not have made with me
      an everlasting covenant,
    arranged and secured in every part;
  surely he would not bring to fruition my
      salvation
    and grant me my every desire.
6 But evil men are all to be cast aside like
      thorns,
    which are not gathered with the hand.
7 Whoever touches thorns
    uses a tool of iron or the shaft of a spear;
    they are burned up where they lie."

David's Mighty Warriors

8 These are the names of David's mighty warriors:

Josheb-Basshebeth,*a* a Tahkemonite,*b* was
chief of the Three; he raised his spear against
eight hundred men, whom he killed*c* in one encounter.

9 Next to him was Eleazar son of Dodai the
Ahohite. As one of the three mighty warriors,
he was with David when they taunted the Philistines gathered at Pas Dammim*d* for battle. Then
the Israelites retreated, 10 but Eleazar stood his
ground and struck down the Philistines till his
hand grew tired and froze to the sword. The
LORD brought about a great victory that day.
The troops returned to Eleazar, but only to strip
the dead.

11 Next to him was Shammah son of Agee the
Hararite. When the Philistines banded together
at a place where there was a field full of lentils,
Israel's troops fled from them. 12 But Shammah
took his stand in the middle of the field. He defended it and struck the Philistines down, and
the LORD brought about a great victory.

13 During harvest time, three of the thirty chief warriors came down to David at the
cave of Adullam, while a band of Philistines
was encamped in the Valley of Rephaim. 14 At
that time David was in the stronghold, and the
Philistine garrison was at Bethlehem. 15 David
longed for water and said, "Oh, that someone
would get me a drink of water from the well
near the gate of Bethlehem!" 16 So the three
mighty warriors broke through the Philistine
lines, drew water from the well near the gate
of Bethlehem and carried it back to David. But
he refused to drink it; instead, he poured it out
before the LORD. 17 "Far be it from me, LORD,

The Law of the Inner Circle

2 Samuel 23:14-17

It was just a casual remark. Not a command. Not
an order. Not even a request.

And yet the moment David's men heard their
leader mutter how he'd love to sip a cool drink
from a certain Bethlehem well, they immediately broke through enemy lines and braved
Philistine swords and spears to retrieve a cup of
the precious liquid. David had invested so much
in his inner circle that fierce loyalty was the natural result.

Such astonishing loyalty doesn't come from
a mere job description. It doesn't develop because the leader is scheduled for a promotion.
It doesn't appear on demand. Loyalty like this
comes only through modeling. David got this
kind of "second-mile" effort because he had
long modeled such loyalty for his men.

And it is that loyalty that drove him to do
what he did next. When his comrades returned
with the cup of water dripping in their hands,
David honored their sacrifice by presenting it to
the Lord rather than drinking it. "Far be it from
me, LORD, to do this!" he cried. "Is it not the blood
of men who went at the risk of their lives?" (2Sa
23:17). So David poured out the water as an offering to God.

Who wouldn't go the extra mile for a leader
like that?

to do this!" he said. "Is it not the blood of men
who went at the risk of their lives?" And David
would not drink it.

Such were the exploits of the three mighty
warriors.

18 Abishai the brother of Joab son of Zeruiah was chief of the Three.*e* He raised his spear
against three hundred men, whom he killed,
and so he became as famous as the Three. 19 Was
he not held in greater honor than the Three? He

a 8 Hebrew; some Septuagint manuscripts suggest *Ish-Bosheth*,
that is, *Esh-Baal* (see also 1 Chron. 11:11 *Jashobeam*).
b 8 Probably a variant of *Hakmonite* (see 1 Chron. 11:11)
c 8 Some Septuagint manuscripts (see also 1 Chron. 11:11);
Hebrew and other Septuagint manuscripts *Three; it was Adino
the Eznite who killed eight hundred men*   *d 9* See 1 Chron.
11:13; Hebrew *gathered there.*   *e 18* Most Hebrew
manuscripts (see also 1 Chron. 11:20); two Hebrew manuscripts
and Syriac *Thirty*

became their commander, even though he was not included among them.

[20]Benaiah son of Jehoiada, a valiant fighter from Kabzeel, performed great exploits. He struck down Moab's two mightiest warriors. He also went down into a pit on a snowy day and killed a lion. [21]And he struck down a huge Egyptian. Although the Egyptian had a spear in his hand, Benaiah went against him with a club. He snatched the spear from the Egyptian's hand and killed him with his own spear. [22]Such were the exploits of Benaiah son of Jehoiada; he too was as famous as the three mighty warriors. [23]He was held in greater honor than any of the Thirty, but he was not included among the Three. And David put him in charge of his bodyguard.

[24]Among the Thirty were:
Asahel the brother of Joab,
Elhanan son of Dodo from Bethlehem,
[25]Shammah the Harodite,
Elika the Harodite,
[26]Helez the Paltite,
Ira son of Ikkesh from Tekoa,
[27]Abiezer from Anathoth,
Sibbekai[a] the Hushathite,
[28]Zalmon the Ahohite,
Maharai the Netophathite,
[29]Heled[b] son of Baanah the Netophathite,
Ithai son of Ribai from Gibeah in Benjamin,
[30]Benaiah the Pirathonite,
Hiddai[c] from the ravines of Gaash,
[31]Abi-Albon the Arbathite,
Azmaveth the Barhumite,
[32]Eliahba the Shaalbonite,
the sons of Jashen,
Jonathan [33]son of[d] Shammah the Hararite,
Ahiam son of Sharar[e] the Hararite,
[34]Eliphelet son of Ahasbai the Maakathite,
Eliam son of Ahithophel the Gilonite,
[35]Hezro the Carmelite,
Paarai the Arbite,
[36]Igal son of Nathan from Zobah,
the son of Hagri,[f]
[37]Zelek the Ammonite,
Naharai the Beerothite, the armor-bearer of Joab son of Zeruiah,
[38]Ira the Ithrite,
Gareb the Ithrite,
[39]and Uriah the Hittite.
There were thirty-seven in all.

David Enrolls the Fighting Men

24 Again the anger of the LORD burned against Israel, and he incited David against them, saying, "Go and take a census of Israel and Judah."

[2]So the king said to Joab and the army commanders[g] with him, "Go throughout the tribes of Israel from Dan to Beersheba and enroll the fighting men, so that I may know how many there are."

[3]But Joab replied to the king, "May the LORD your God multiply the troops a hundred times over, and may the eyes of my lord the king see it. But why does my lord the king want to do such a thing?"

[4]The king's word, however, overruled Joab and the army commanders; so they left the presence of the king to enroll the fighting men of Israel.

[5]After crossing the Jordan, they camped near Aroer, south of the town in the gorge, and then went through Gad and on to Jazer. [6]They went to Gilead and the region of Tahtim Hodshi, and on to Dan Jaan and around toward Sidon. [7]Then they went toward the fortress of Tyre and all the towns of the Hivites and Canaanites. Finally, they went on to Beersheba in the Negev of Judah.

[8]After they had gone through the entire land, they came back to Jerusalem at the end of nine months and twenty days.

[9]Joab reported the number of the fighting men to the king: In Israel there were eight hundred thousand able-bodied men who could handle a sword, and in Judah five hundred thousand.

[10]David was conscience-stricken after he had counted the fighting men, and he said to the LORD, "I have sinned greatly in what I have done. Now, LORD, I beg you, take away the guilt of your servant. I have done a very foolish thing."

[11]Before David got up the next morning, the word of the LORD had come to Gad the prophet, David's seer: [12]"Go and tell David, 'This is what

a 27 Some Septuagint manuscripts (see also 21:18; 1 Chron. 11:29); Hebrew Mebunnai   b 29 Some Hebrew manuscripts and Vulgate (see also 1 Chron. 11:30); most Hebrew manuscripts Heleb   c 30 Hebrew; some Septuagint manuscripts (see also 1 Chron. 11:32) Hurai   d 33 Some Septuagint manuscripts (see also 1 Chron. 11:34); Hebrew does not have son of.   e 33 Hebrew; some Septuagint manuscripts (see also 1 Chron. 11:35) Sakar   f 36 Some Septuagint manuscripts (see also 1 Chron. 11:38); Hebrew Haggadi   g 2 Septuagint (see also verse 4 and 1 Chron. 21:2); Hebrew Joab the army commander the LORD says: I am giving you three options. Choose one of them for me to carry out against you.'"

[13] So Gad went to David and said to him, "Shall there come on you three[a] years of famine in your land? Or three months of fleeing from your enemies while they pursue you? Or three days of plague in your land? Now then, think it over and decide how I should answer the one who sent me."

[14] David said to Gad, "I am in deep distress. Let us fall into the hands of the LORD, for his mercy is great; but do not let me fall into human hands."

[15] So the LORD sent a plague on Israel from that morning until the end of the time designated, and seventy thousand of the people from Dan to Beersheba died. [16] When the angel stretched out his hand to destroy Jerusalem, the LORD relented concerning the disaster and said to the angel who was afflicting the people, "Enough! Withdraw your hand." The angel of the LORD was then at the threshing floor of Araunah the Jebusite.

[17] When David saw the angel who was striking down the people, he said to the LORD, "I have sinned; I, the shepherd,[b] have done wrong. These are but sheep. What have they done? Let your hand fall on me and my family."

David Builds an Altar

[18] On that day Gad went to David and said to him, "Go up and build an altar to the LORD on the threshing floor of Araunah the Jebusite." [19] So David went up, as the LORD had commanded through Gad. [20] When Araunah looked and saw the king and his officials coming toward him, he went out and bowed down before the king with his face to the ground.

[21] Araunah said, "Why has my lord the king come to his servant?"

"To buy your threshing floor," David answered, "so I can build an altar to the LORD, that the plague on the people may be stopped."

[22] Araunah said to David, "Let my lord the king take whatever he wishes and offer it up. Here are oxen for the burnt offering, and here are threshing sledges and ox yokes for the wood. [23] Your Majesty, Araunah[c] gives all this to the king." Araunah also said to him, "May the LORD your God accept you."

[24] But the king replied to Araunah, "No, I insist on paying you for it. I will not sacrifice to the LORD my God burnt offerings that cost me nothing."

So David bought the threshing floor and the oxen and paid fifty shekels[d] of silver for them. [25] David built an altar to the LORD there and sacrificed burnt offerings and fellowship offerings. Then the LORD answered his prayer in behalf of the land, and the plague on Israel was stopped.

---

[a] 13 Septuagint (see also 1 Chron. 21:12); Hebrew *seven*
[b] 17 Dead Sea Scrolls and Septuagint; Masoretic Text does not have *the shepherd*.   [c] 23 Some Hebrew manuscripts and Septuagint; most Hebrew manuscripts *King Araunah*
[d] 24 That is, about 1 1/4 pounds or about 575 grams

Introduction to
1 Kings

First and Second Kings give an account of the leaders who followed David: kings such as Solomon, Jeroboam and Rehoboam; prophets such as Elijah, Elisha and Micaiah. These men picture the necessity of purpose-driven leadership—leadership motivated by core values and strong convictions.

Some call purpose-driven leadership *visionary leadership.* Visionary leadership is motivated by something that not only could be done, but should be done. The leader carries a sense of moral obligation about the vision.

First Kings describes the reign of King Solomon. Despite his wisdom, he lacked focused leadership. He begins well, but by chapter 11 he becomes distracted from any moral obligation.

The book begins with a skirmish over who will succeed David as king of Israel. David selects Solomon, who takes over as the final king to reign over a united Israel. Solomon recognizes the overwhelming responsibility of his position and goes to the proper Source for wisdom. This pleases God immensely, to the point that God gives him all the necessary wisdom—and everything else he *didn't* ask for!

Yet Solomon illustrates a fundamental principle every leader must understand. While this man became the wisest human leader who ever lived and authored a number of books, the king's poor choices and failure to apply what God told him weakened his leadership.

Before Solomon left the way of God, the Lord greatly used him. Kings and queens from distant lands visited him and became acquainted with the God of Israel—precisely what God had in mind for the Jews. Israel was to

God's Role in 1 Kings

By the end of 1 Kings, the Hebrew nation lies divided, torn both by civil wars and invaders. God seeks out godly leaders like David—men who would listen to his voice and obey it.

As in so many Old Testament books, God's interaction in 1 Kings appears almost entirely limited to leaders—for if he can raise up leaders to model the life he intended for Israel, the people would almost certainly follow suit.

Leaders in 1 Kings

David, Adonijah, Solomon, Rehoboam, Jeroboam, Abijam, Asa, Jehoshaphat, Ahab, Jezebel

Other People of Influence in 1 Kings

Nathan, Ahijah, Elijah, a widow, Obadiah, Micaiah

Lessons in Leadership

- Success without a successor is a failure.
- Decision making and problem solving is the fastest way to gain influence.
- Check your motives before you lead anything.
- The issue is not prioritizing our schedule, but scheduling our priorities
- Influencing followers is addition; influencing leaders is multiplication.

become a light to the nations, and for a while its beacon of hope shone brightly.

But when Solomon began trusting his own wisdom and failed to stay focused on God, the Lord divided his kingdom and ripped it away. The nation remained split until outsiders like Assyria and Babylon conquered one kingdom, then the next. In the difficult years in between, God had to raise up prophets as his leaders and spokesmen, since the kings frequently would not listen to his voice.

- Keep first things first; distraction is the enemy of direction.
- Leaders must touch a heart before they ask for a hand.
- A divided leader eventually produces a divided nation.
- Passion and conviction mark the difference between a great leader and a mediocre one.
- Principles, not emotions, should guide your leadership.

LEADERSHIP HIGHLIGHTS IN 1 KINGS

Adonijah Sets Himself Up as King

1 When King David was very old, he could not keep warm even when they put covers over him. ²So his attendants said to him, "Let us look for a young virgin to serve the king and take care of him. She can lie beside him so that our lord the king may keep warm."

³Then they searched throughout Israel for a beautiful young woman and found Abishag, a Shunammite, and brought her to the king. ⁴The woman was very beautiful; she took care of the king and waited on him, but the king had no sexual relations with her.

⁵Now Adonijah, whose mother was Haggith, put himself forward and said, "I will be king." So he got chariots and horses*a* ready, with fifty men to run ahead of him. ⁶(His father had never rebuked him by asking, "Why do you behave as you do?" He was also very handsome and was born next after Absalom.)

⁷Adonijah conferred with Joab son of Zeruiah and with Abiathar the priest, and they gave him their support. ⁸But Zadok the priest, Benaiah son of Jehoiada, Nathan the prophet, Shimei and Rei and David's special guard did not join Adonijah.

⁹Adonijah then sacrificed sheep, cattle and fattened calves at the Stone of Zoheleth near En Rogel. He invited all his brothers, the king's sons, and all the royal officials of Judah, ¹⁰but he did not invite Nathan the prophet or Benaiah or the special guard or his brother Solomon.

¹¹Then Nathan asked Bathsheba, Solomon's mother, "Have you not heard that Adonijah, the son of Haggith, has become king, and our lord David knows nothing about it? ¹²Now then, let me advise you how you can save your own life and the life of your son Solomon. ¹³Go in to King David and say to him, 'My lord the king, did you not swear to me your servant: "Surely Solomon your son shall be king after me, and he will sit on my throne"? Why then has Adonijah become king?' ¹⁴While you are still there talking to the king, I will come in and add my word to what you have said."

¹⁵So Bathsheba went to see the aged king in his room, where Abishag the Shunammite was attending him. ¹⁶Bathsheba bowed down, prostrating herself before the king.

"What is it you want?" the king asked.

¹⁷She said to him, "My lord, you yourself swore to me your servant by the LORD your God: 'Solomon your son shall be king after me, and he will sit on my throne.' ¹⁸But now Adonijah has become king, and you, my lord the king, do not know about it. ¹⁹He has sacrificed great numbers of cattle, fattened calves, and sheep, and has invited all the king's sons, Abiathar the priest and Joab the commander of the army, but he has not invited Solomon your servant. ²⁰My lord the king, the eyes of all Israel are on you, to learn from you who will sit on the throne of my lord the king after him. ²¹Otherwise, as soon as my lord the king is laid to rest with his ancestors, I and my son Solomon will be treated as criminals."

²²While she was still speaking with the king, Nathan the prophet arrived. ²³And the king was told, "Nathan the prophet is here." So he went before the king and bowed with his face to the ground.

²⁴Nathan said, "Have you, my lord the king, declared that Adonijah shall be king after you, and that he will sit on your throne? ²⁵Today he has gone down and sacrificed great numbers of cattle, fattened calves, and sheep. He has invited all the king's sons, the commanders of the army and Abiathar the priest. Right now they are eating and drinking with him and saying, 'Long live King Adonijah!' ²⁶But me your servant, and Zadok the priest, and Benaiah son of Jehoiada, and your servant Solomon he did not invite. ²⁷Is this something my lord the king has done without letting his servants know who should sit on the throne of my lord the king after him?"

David Makes Solomon King

²⁸Then King David said, "Call in Bathsheba." So she came into the king's presence and stood before him.

²⁹The king then took an oath: "As surely as the LORD lives, who has delivered me out of every trouble, ³⁰I will surely carry out this very day what I swore to you by the LORD, the God of Israel: Solomon your son shall be king after me, and he will sit on my throne in my place."

³¹Then Bathsheba bowed down with her face to the ground, prostrating herself before the king, and said, "May my lord King David live forever!"

³²King David said, "Call in Zadok the priest, Nathan the prophet and Benaiah son of Jehoiada." When they came before the king, ³³he said to them: "Take your lord's servants with you and have Solomon my son mount my own mule and take him down to Gihon. ³⁴There have Zadok the priest and Nathan the prophet anoint him king over Israel. Blow the trumpet and shout,

a 5 Or charioteers

'Long live King Solomon!' ³⁵Then you are to go up with him, and he is to come and sit on my throne and reign in my place. I have appointed him ruler over Israel and Judah."

³⁶Benaiah son of Jehoiada answered the king, "Amen! May the LORD, the God of my lord the king, so declare it. ³⁷As the LORD was with my lord the king, so may he be with Solomon to make his throne even greater than the throne of my lord King David!"

³⁸So Zadok the priest, Nathan the prophet, Benaiah son of Jehoiada, the Kerethites and the Pelethites went down and had Solomon mount King David's mule, and they escorted him to Gihon. ³⁹Zadok the priest took the horn of oil from the sacred tent and anointed Solomon. Then they sounded the trumpet and all the people shouted, "Long live King Solomon!" ⁴⁰And all the people went up after him, playing pipes and rejoicing greatly, so that the ground shook with the sound.

⁴¹Adonijah and all the guests who were with him heard it as they were finishing their feast. On hearing the sound of the trumpet, Joab asked, "What's the meaning of all the noise in the city?"

⁴²Even as he was speaking, Jonathan son of Abiathar the priest arrived. Adonijah said, "Come in. A worthy man like you must be bringing good news."

⁴³"Not at all!" Jonathan answered. "Our lord King David has made Solomon king. ⁴⁴The king has sent with him Zadok the priest, Nathan the prophet, Benaiah son of Jehoiada, the Kerethites

and the Pelethites, and they have put him on the king's mule, ⁴⁵and Zadok the priest and Nathan the prophet have anointed him king at Gihon. From there they have gone up cheering, and the city resounds with it. That's the noise you hear. ⁴⁶Moreover, Solomon has taken his seat on the royal throne. ⁴⁷Also, the royal officials have come to congratulate our lord King David, saying, 'May your God make Solomon's name more famous than yours and his throne greater than yours!' And the king bowed in worship on his bed ⁴⁸and said, 'Praise be to the LORD, the God of Israel, who has allowed my eyes to see a successor on my throne today.'"

⁴⁹At this, all Adonijah's guests rose in alarm and dispersed. ⁵⁰But Adonijah, in fear of Solomon, went and took hold of the horns of the altar. ⁵¹Then Solomon was told, "Adonijah is afraid of King Solomon and is clinging to the horns of the altar. He says, 'Let King Solomon swear to me today that he will not put his servant to death with the sword.'"

⁵²Solomon replied, "If he shows himself to be worthy, not a hair of his head will fall to the ground; but if evil is found in him, he will die." ⁵³Then King Solomon sent men, and they brought him down from the altar. And Adonijah came and bowed down to King Solomon, and Solomon said, "Go to your home."

David's Charge to Solomon

2 When the time drew near for David to die, he gave a charge to Solomon his son.

²"I am about to go the way of all the earth,"

The Law of Legacy: David and Solomon

1 Kings 1:28–40

Two things greatly helped Solomon in his succession to the throne of Israel; both gave him the authority he required to rule. First, God chose him to be the next king. Second, David chose him as his successor.

Transitions in leadership often cause significant problems for groups and organizations. Notice what David did to smooth the transition process in his kingdom:

1. **He made a public commitment (vv. 28–30).**
2. **He brought key influencers into the process (v. 32).**
3. **He gave Solomon some of his own resources, easily recognizable to the people (v. 33).**
4. **He set up a public commissioning for Solomon (vv. 34–35).**
5. **He publicly endorsed Solomon's leadership (v. 35).**
6. **He initiated a celebration to transition the leadership to his successor (vv. 39–40).**

he said. "So be strong, act like a man, [3]and observe what the LORD your God requires: Walk in obedience to him, and keep his decrees and commands, his laws and regulations, as written in the Law of Moses. Do this so that you may prosper in all you do and wherever you go [4]and that the LORD may keep his promise to me: 'If your descendants watch how they live, and if they walk faithfully before me with all their heart and soul, you will never fail to have a successor on the throne of Israel.'

[5]"Now you yourself know what Joab son of Zeruiah did to me—what he did to the two commanders of Israel's armies, Abner son of Ner and Amasa son of Jether. He killed them, shedding their blood in peacetime as if in battle, and with that blood he stained the belt around his waist and the sandals on his feet. [6]Deal with him according to your wisdom, but do not let his gray head go down to the grave in peace.

[7]"But show kindness to the sons of Barzillai of Gilead and let them be among those who eat at your table. They stood by me when I fled from your brother Absalom.

[8]"And remember, you have with you Shimei son of Gera, the Benjamite from Bahurim, who called down bitter curses on me the day I went to Mahanaim. When he came down to meet me at the Jordan, I swore to him by the LORD: 'I will not put you to death by the sword.' [9]But now, do not consider him innocent. You are a man of wisdom; you will know what to do to him. Bring his gray head down to the grave in blood."

[10]Then David rested with his ancestors and was buried in the City of David. [11]He had reigned forty years over Israel—seven years in Hebron and thirty-three in Jerusalem. [12]So Solomon sat on the throne of his father David, and his rule was firmly established.

Solomon's Throne Established

[13]Now Adonijah, the son of Haggith, went to Bathsheba, Solomon's mother. Bathsheba asked him, "Do you come peacefully?"

He answered, "Yes, peacefully." [14]Then he added, "I have something to say to you."

"You may say it," she replied.

[15]"As you know," he said, "the kingdom was mine. All Israel looked to me as their king. But things changed, and the kingdom has gone to my brother; for it has come to him from the LORD. [16]Now I have one request to make of you. Do not refuse me."

"You may make it," she said.

[17]So he continued, "Please ask King Solomon—he will not refuse you—to give me Abishag the Shunammite as my wife."

[18]"Very well," Bathsheba replied, "I will speak to the king for you."

[19]When Bathsheba went to King Solomon to speak to him for Adonijah, the king stood up to meet her, bowed down to her and sat down on his throne. He had a throne brought for the king's mother, and she sat down at his right hand.

[20]"I have one small request to make of you," she said. "Do not refuse me."

The king replied, "Make it, my mother; I will not refuse you."

[21]So she said, "Let Abishag the Shunammite be given in marriage to your brother Adonijah."

[22]King Solomon answered his mother, "Why do you request Abishag the Shunammite for Adonijah? You might as well request the kingdom for him—after all, he is my older brother—yes, for him and for Abiathar the priest and Joab son of Zeruiah!"

[23]Then King Solomon swore by the LORD: "May God deal with me, be it ever so severely, if

The Law of the Inner Circle: Solomon Ensures Loyalty

1 Kings 2:1–46

Solomon had to make some tough but crucial leadership decisions at the beginning of his reign. First, he had to deal with men scheming for power; even his own brother, Adonijah, tried to set up his own kingdom. One by one, King Solomon discerned the loyalties of his associates, then removed all who refused to cooperate with him.

Solomon knew he could never work with renegades, no matter how influential or strategic they might seem. The young king ensured that his inner circle would include only loyal men who wanted to work with him.

David had seen these troubles brewing on the horizon. He knew he was placing his son in a precarious leadership situation, but twice he confidently declared that Solomon would know what to do (1Ki 2:6, 9). David understood that those closest to Solomon would greatly hinder or improve his level of success. Solomon understood the same thing—and wisely acted on it.

SOLOMON AND THE LAW OF THE BIG MO
Momentum Is a Leader's Best Friend

1 Kings 2:1—4:24

IT TAKES a leader to create momentum. Followers catch it. And managers are able to continue it once it has begun. But creating it requires someone who can motivate others, not one who needs to be motivated. Harry Truman once said, "If you can't stand the heat, get out of the kitchen." For leaders, that statement should be changed to read, "If you can't *make* some heat, get out of the kitchen."

All leaders face the challenge of creating change in an organization. Just as every sailor knows you can't steer a ship that isn't moving forward, strong leaders understand that to change direction, you first have to create forward progress. Without momentum, even the simplest tasks can seem insurmountable. But with momentum on your side, the future looks bright, obstacles appear small, and trouble seems temporary. With enough momentum, nearly any kind of change is possible.

■　■　■　■　■

The time of transition from one leader to another presents the most critical challenge to continuing momentum. How did Solomon so successfully take the reins from his father? Consider the following actions the young king took to ensure a smooth transition:

1. **He started with what David provided.** Solomon's father gave him everything he needed to start his reign: a stable kingdom, plentiful resources, wise counsel, and his public endorsement. David made it clear to everyone in Israel that he had chosen Solomon as king.

2. **He humbly asked for leadership wisdom above all else.** Solomon probably became king at about 18 years of age, yet despite his youth, he recognized the difficulties of leadership. He knew he needed wisdom above all else, so he asked for an understanding heart to judge God's people. That request kept his motives pure and made it possible for him to avoid momentum-breakers.

3. **He made wise decisions that won him credibility.** Solomon made several deft decisions concerning enemies to his throne. He exiled one opponent, executed two others, and put a fourth under house arrest. But even more important, he cemented his credibility with the people. The wisdom he displayed in a domestic dispute profoundly impacted the people: "When all Israel heard the verdict the king had given, they held the king in awe" (1Ki 3:28).

4. **He maintained the peace.** Solomon's bold moves against enemies within Israel maintained peace at home, thus preventing a bloody civil war. But Solomon wisely took additional

measures to keep other nations from threatening his country's progress—and therefore he "had peace on all sides" (1Ki 4:24).

5. *He surrounded himself with wise associates.* Only Solomon among the kings of Israel can challenge David as the architect of a great inner circle. Solomon kept on a few of David's trusted servants in his own administration, but not many. Most of them he nurtured himself.

What It Takes to Sustain Momentum

How does a winning team keep winning? What makes it possible for an organization to keep the momentum going? The answer is not what, but who. It takes a leader to sustain momentum, a leader who possesses . . .

1. *A willingness to accept responsibility for the organization's momentum.* Most leaders happily accept responsibility so long as an organization succeeds, but hedge when the organization starts to slip. Yet momentum—positive, negative, or nonexistent—is always the leader's responsibility. Olan Hendrix, CEO of the Leadership Resource Group, maintains that after you've led an organization for three years, every problem is your problem.

2. *A willingness to direct momentum instead of letting it direct him.* Momentum always has a direction. Most people in an organization have little impact on its momentum; it simply carries them. But leaders cannot afford to surf momentum; they must steer it. Before Solomon became king, an outstanding

military leader, David, created the nation's momentum. Yet Solomon never led an army; his goals weren't military in nature. He gave most of his attention to trade and construction—and that meant he had to change the direction of the nation's momentum.

3. *A willingness to be enthusiastic at all times.* Remain positive! Some personality types find it easy to remain enthusiastic; others don't. Reflect on the following secrets to keeping leadership positive all the time:

■ *The work I'm doing is most important.* Make sure your vision, your mission, and your actions all line up. It's easy to stay excited when what you're doing really matters.

■ *The people I work with are the best.* Place a high value on everyone you work with. Expect the best of them, and they'll give their best.

■ *The results will be positive.* For the most part, you get what you expect. Only occasionally will you be surprised—but even then, you'll just as often be surprised by better results as by worse ones.

Have you ever met a leader with a chronically negative attitude who was able to continually sustain positive momentum? Probably not.

No leader can ignore the impact of momentum. If you've got it, you and your people will be able to accomplish things you never thought possible. If you don't, the smallest tasks will seem difficult. As the leader, you must make the choice to have it.

Adonijah does not pay with his life for this request! [24]And now, as surely as the LORD lives— he who has established me securely on the throne of my father David and has founded a dynasty for me as he promised— Adonijah shall be put to death today!" [25]So King Solomon gave orders to Benaiah son of Jehoiada, and he struck down Adonijah and he died.

[26]To Abiathar the priest the king said, "Go back to your fields in Anathoth. You deserve to die, but I will not put you to death now, because you carried the ark of the Sovereign LORD before my father David and shared all my father's hardships." [27]So Solomon removed Abiathar from the priesthood of the LORD, fulfilling the word the LORD had spoken at Shiloh about the house of Eli.

[28]When the news reached Joab, who had conspired with Adonijah though not with Absalom, he fled to the tent of the LORD and took hold of the horns of the altar. [29]King Solomon was told that Joab had fled to the tent of the LORD and was beside the altar. Then Solomon ordered Benaiah son of Jehoiada, "Go, strike him down!"

[30]So Benaiah entered the tent of the LORD and said to Joab, "The king says, 'Come out!'"

But he answered, "No, I will die here."

Benaiah reported to the king, "This is how Joab answered me."

[31]Then the king commanded Benaiah, "Do as he says. Strike him down and bury him, and so clear me and my whole family of the guilt of the innocent blood that Joab shed. [32]The LORD will repay him for the blood he shed, because without my father David knowing it he attacked two men and killed them with the sword. Both of them— Abner son of Ner, commander of Israel's army, and Amasa son of Jether, commander of Judah's army—were better men and more upright than he. [33]May the guilt of their blood rest on the head of Joab and his descendants forever. But on David and his descendants, his house and his throne, may there be the LORD's peace forever."

[34]So Benaiah son of Jehoiada went up and struck down Joab and killed him, and he was buried at his home out in the country. [35]The king put Benaiah son of Jehoiada over the army in Joab's position and replaced Abiathar with Zadok the priest.

[36]Then the king sent for Shimei and said to him, "Build yourself a house in Jerusalem and live there, but do not go anywhere else. [37]The day you leave and cross the Kidron Valley, you can be sure you will die; your blood will be on your own head."

[38]Shimei answered the king, "What you say is good. Your servant will do as my lord the king has said." And Shimei stayed in Jerusalem for a long time.

[39]But three years later, two of Shimei's slaves ran off to Achish son of Maakah, king of Gath, and Shimei was told, "Your slaves are in Gath." [40]At this, he saddled his donkey and went to Achish at Gath in search of his slaves. So Shimei went away and brought the slaves back from Gath.

[41]When Solomon was told that Shimei had gone from Jerusalem to Gath and had returned, [42]the king summoned Shimei and said to him, "Did I not make you swear by the LORD and warn you, 'On the day you leave to go anywhere else, you can be sure you will die'? At that time you said to me, 'What you say is good. I will obey.' [43]Why then did you not keep your oath to the LORD and obey the command I gave you?"

[44]The king also said to Shimei, "You know in your heart all the wrong you did to my father David. Now the LORD will repay you for your wrongdoing. [45]But King Solomon will be blessed, and David's throne will remain secure before the LORD forever."

[46]Then the king gave the order to Benaiah son of Jehoiada, and he went out and struck Shimei down and he died.

The kingdom was now established in Solomon's hands.

Solomon Asks for Wisdom

3 Solomon made an alliance with Pharaoh king of Egypt and married his daughter. He brought her to the City of David until he finished building his palace and the temple of the LORD, and the wall around Jerusalem. [2]The people, however, were still sacrificing at the high places, because a temple had not yet been built for the Name of the LORD. [3]Solomon showed his love for the LORD by walking according to the instructions given him by his father David, except that he offered sacrifices and burned incense on the high places.

[4]The king went to Gibeon to offer sacrifices, for that was the most important high place, and Solomon offered a thousand burnt offerings on that altar. [5]At Gibeon the LORD appeared to Solomon during the night in a dream, and God said, "Ask for whatever you want me to give you."

[6]Solomon answered, "You have shown great kindness to your servant, my father David, because he was faithful to you and righteous and upright in heart. You have continued this great

kindness to him and have given him a son to sit on his throne this very day.

[7]"Now, LORD my God, you have made your servant king in place of my father David. But I am only a little child and do not know how to carry out my duties. [8]Your servant is here among the people you have chosen, a great people, too numerous to count or number. [9]So give your servant a discerning heart to govern your people and to distinguish between right and wrong. For who is able to govern this great people of yours?"

[10]The Lord was pleased that Solomon had asked for this. [11]So God said to him, "Since you have asked for this and not for long life or wealth for yourself, nor have asked for the death of your enemies but for discernment in administering justice, [12]I will do what you have asked. I will give you a wise and discerning heart, so that there will never have been anyone like you, nor will there ever be. [13]Moreover, I will give you what you have not asked for—both wealth and honor—so that in your lifetime you will have no equal among kings. [14]And if you walk in obedience to me and keep my decrees and commands as David your father did, I will give you a long life." [15]Then Solomon awoke—and he realized it had been a dream.

He returned to Jerusalem, stood before the ark of the Lord's covenant and sacrificed burnt offerings and fellowship offerings. Then he gave a feast for all his court.

A Wise Ruling

[16]Now two prostitutes came to the king and stood before him. [17]One of them said, "Pardon me, my lord. This woman and I live in the same house, and I had a baby while she was there with me. [18]The third day after my child was born, this woman also had a baby. We were alone; there was no one in the house but the two of us.

[19]"During the night this woman's son died because she lay on him. [20]So she got up in the middle of the night and took my son from my side while I your servant was asleep. She put him by her breast and put her dead son by my breast. [21]The next morning, I got up to nurse my son—and he was dead! But when I looked at him closely in the morning light, I saw that it wasn't the son I had borne."

[22]The other woman said, "No! The living one is my son; the dead one is yours."

But the first one insisted, "No! The dead one is yours; the living one is mine." And so they argued before the king.

[23]The king said, "This one says, 'My son is

The Law of Intuition: Solomon's Problem Solving Gave Him Influence

1 Kings 3:3–28

What would you choose if God offered to give you anything you named? King Solomon came face-to-face with that delightful dilemma when Yahweh presented the young king with his equivalent of the genie in the bottle. "Ask for whatever you want me to give you," the Lord said to Solomon one night (1Ki 3:5).

Solomon displayed a good amount of wisdom by asking for more of it to lead the people of Israel. God not only answered his request, but also gave him what he did not ask for: riches, honor, long life and conquest. Leadership wisdom allowed Solomon to:

1. **Make wise decisions for his nation.**

2. **Choose the right staff for his palace.**

3. **Judge wisely between disputing parties.**

4. **Recognize priorities and gain perspective.**

Before chapter 3 ends, Solomon has the chance to demonstrate his wisdom. Two women bring a child to him, both claiming to be the mother. Solomon tells them to cut the baby in half and let each woman have part of the child. He wisely used his knowledge of the overpowering maternal instinct to reveal the identity of the true mother.

alive and your son is dead,' while that one says, 'No! Your son is dead and mine is alive.'"

24Then the king said, "Bring me a sword." So they brought a sword for the king. 25He then gave an order: "Cut the living child in two and give half to one and half to the other."

26The woman whose son was alive was deeply moved out of love for her son and said to the king, "Please, my lord, give her the living baby! Don't kill him!"

But the other said, "Neither I nor you shall have him. Cut him in two!"

27Then the king gave his ruling: "Give the living baby to the first woman. Do not kill him; she is his mother."

28When all Israel heard the verdict the king had given, they held the king in awe, because they saw that he had wisdom from God to administer justice.

Solomon's Officials and Governors

4 So King Solomon ruled over all Israel. 2And these were his chief officials:

Azariah son of Zadok—the priest;
3Elihoreph and Ahijah, sons of Shisha—secretaries;
Jehoshaphat son of Ahilud—recorder;
4Benaiah son of Jehoiada—commander in chief;
Zadok and Abiathar—priests;
5Azariah son of Nathan—in charge of the district governors;
Zabud son of Nathan—a priest and adviser to the king;
6Ahishar—palace administrator;
Adoniram son of Abda—in charge of forced labor.

7Solomon had twelve district governors over all Israel, who supplied provisions for the king and the royal household. Each one had to provide supplies for one month in the year. 8These are their names:

Ben-Hur—in the hill country of Ephraim;
9Ben-Deker—in Makaz, Shaalbim, Beth Shemesh and Elon Bethhanan;
10Ben-Hesed—in Arubboth (Sokoh and all the land of Hepher were his);
11Ben-Abinadab—in Naphoth Dor (he was married to Taphath daughter of Solomon);
12Baana son of Ahilud—in Taanach and Megiddo, and in all of Beth Shan next to Zarethan below Jezreel, from Beth Shan to Abel Meholah across to Jokmeam;

13Ben-Geber—in Ramoth Gilead (the settlements of Jair son of Manasseh in Gilead were his, as well as the region of Argob in Bashan and its sixty large walled cities with bronze gate bars);
14Ahinadab son of Iddo—in Mahanaim;
15Ahimaaz—in Naphtali (he had married Basemath daughter of Solomon);
16Baana son of Hushai—in Asher and in Aloth;
17Jehoshaphat son of Paruah—in Issachar;
18Shimei son of Ela—in Benjamin;
19Geber son of Uri—in Gilead (the country of Sihon king of the Amorites and the country of Og king of Bashan). He was the only governor over the district.

Solomon's Daily Provisions

20The people of Judah and Israel were as numerous as the sand on the seashore; they ate, they drank and they were happy. 21And Solomon ruled over all the kingdoms from the Euphrates River to the land of the Philistines, as far as the border of Egypt. These countries brought tribute and were Solomon's subjects all his life.

22Solomon's daily provisions were thirty cors[a] of the finest flour and sixty cors[b] of meal, 23ten head of stall-fed cattle, twenty of pasture-fed cattle and a hundred sheep and goats, as well as deer, gazelles, roebucks and choice fowl. 24For he ruled over all the kingdoms west of the Euphrates River, from Tiphsah to Gaza, and had peace on all sides. 25During Solomon's lifetime Judah and Israel, from Dan to Beersheba, lived in safety, everyone under their own vine and under their own fig tree.

26Solomon had four[c] thousand stalls for chariot horses, and twelve thousand horses.[d]

27The district governors, each in his month, supplied provisions for King Solomon and all who came to the king's table. They saw to it that nothing was lacking. 28They also brought to the proper place their quotas of barley and straw for the chariot horses and the other horses.

Solomon's Wisdom

29God gave Solomon wisdom and very great insight, and a breadth of understanding as measureless as the sand on the seashore. 30Solomon's wisdom was greater than the wisdom of all the

[a] 22 That is, probably about 5 1/2 tons or about 5 metric tons
[b] 22 That is, probably about 11 tons or about 10 metric tons
[c] 26 Some Septuagint manuscripts (see also 2 Chron. 9:25); Hebrew forty   [d] 26 Or charioteers

people of the East, and greater than all the wisdom of Egypt. [31]He was wiser than anyone else, including Ethan the Ezrahite—wiser than Heman, Kalkol and Darda, the sons of Mahol. And his fame spread to all the surrounding nations. [32]He spoke three thousand proverbs and his songs numbered a thousand and five. [33]He spoke about plant life, from the cedar of Lebanon to the hyssop that grows out of walls. He also spoke about animals and birds, reptiles and fish. [34]From all nations people came to listen to Solomon's wisdom, sent by all the kings of the world, who had heard of his wisdom.[a]

Preparations for Building the Temple

5[b] When Hiram king of Tyre heard that Solomon had been anointed king to succeed his father David, he sent his envoys to Solomon, because he had always been on friendly terms with David. [2]Solomon sent back this message to Hiram:

[3]"You know that because of the wars waged against my father David from all sides, he could not build a temple for the Name of the LORD his God until the LORD put his enemies under his feet. [4]But now the LORD my God has given me rest on every side, and there is no adversary or disaster. [5]I intend, therefore, to build a temple for the Name of the LORD my God, as the LORD told my father David, when he said, 'Your son whom I will put on the throne in your place will build the temple for my Name.'

[6]"So give orders that cedars of Lebanon be cut for me. My men will work with yours, and I will pay you for your men whatever wages you set. You know that we have no one so skilled in felling timber as the Sidonians."

[7]When Hiram heard Solomon's message, he was greatly pleased and said, "Praise be to the LORD today, for he has given David a wise son to rule over this great nation."

[8]So Hiram sent word to Solomon:

"I have received the message you sent me and will do all you want in providing the cedar and juniper logs. [9]My men will haul them down from Lebanon to the Mediterranean Sea, and I will float them as rafts by sea to the place you specify. There I will

[a] 34 In Hebrew texts 4:21-34 is numbered 5:1-14.   [b] In Hebrew texts 5:1-18 is numbered 5:15-32.

SOLOMON

PROFILE in leadership

A Wise King Who Forgot the First Principle of Wisdom
1 Kings 4:29–34

For a smart guy, he sure ended up doing some dumb things.

Near the beginning of Solomon's reign, God approached the young king with a proposal: Ask me for anything you want. Much to God's delight, Solomon didn't ask for great riches, respect among world leaders, or an invincible nation. Solomon asked for wisdom, and God answered abundantly.

The Bible tells us that the Lord gave the king "wisdom and very great insight, and a breadth of understanding as measureless as the sand on the seashore," and that his wisdom exceeded that of anyone else (1Ki 4:29–31). Solomon's expansive mind explored the disciplines of botany, zoology and musicology, and pondered topics ranging from economics to communication to love.

The wisdom of King Solomon helped Israel to prosper greatly. His kingdom annually took in untold amounts of gold and silver and other precious commodities. Solomon himself amassed wealth greater than all the kings of his time (1Ki 10:23).

But by the end of his reign, this brilliant king somehow forgot the first principle of wisdom: "The fear of the LORD is the beginning of wisdom" (Ps 111:10). When Solomon was old, "his wives turned his heart after other gods, and his heart was not fully devoted to the LORD his God" (1Ki 11:4). Only wisdom energized by a vibrant walk with God makes godly leaders.

main hall of the temple extended the width of the temple, that is twenty cubits,[g] and projected ten cubits[h] from the front of the temple. [4]He made narrow windows high up in the temple walls. [5]Against the walls of the main hall and inner sanctuary he built a structure around the building, in which there were side rooms. [6]The lowest floor was five cubits[i] wide, the middle floor six cubits[j] and the third floor seven.[k] He made offset ledges around the outside of the temple so that nothing would be inserted into the temple walls.

[7]In building the temple, only blocks dressed at the quarry were used, and no hammer, chisel or any other iron tool was heard at the temple site while it was being built.

[8]The entrance to the lowest[l] floor was on the south side of the temple; a stairway led up to the middle level and from there to the third. [9]So he built the temple and completed it, roofing it with beams and cedar planks. [10]And he built the side rooms all along the temple. The height of each was five cubits, and they were attached to the temple by beams of cedar.

[11]The word of the LORD came to Solomon: [12]"As for this temple you are building, if you follow my decrees, observe my laws and keep all my commands and obey them, I will fulfill through you the promise I gave to David your father. [13]And I will live among the Israelites and will not abandon my people Israel."

[14]So Solomon built the temple and completed it. [15]He lined its interior walls with cedar boards, paneling them from the floor of the temple to the ceiling, and covered the floor of the temple with planks of juniper. [16]He partitioned off twenty cubits at the rear of the temple with cedar boards from floor to ceiling to form within the temple an inner sanctuary, the Most Holy Place. [17]The main hall in front of this room was forty cubits[m] long. [18]The inside of the temple was cedar, carved with gourds and open

---

Partnerships Allow Leaders to Achieve Far More

1 Kings 5:1–10

When Solomon began his rule, Hiram, the king of Tyre, congratulated him on his new position. Solomon capitalized on the relationship and invited Hiram to help him build the temple. Together, the two leaders achieved far more than they could have alone. That's partnership.

---

separate them and you can take them away. And you are to grant my wish by providing food for my royal household."

[10]In this way Hiram kept Solomon supplied with all the cedar and juniper logs he wanted, [11]and Solomon gave Hiram twenty thousand cors[a] of wheat as food for his household, in addition to twenty thousand baths[b,c] of pressed olive oil. Solomon continued to do this for Hiram year after year. [12]The LORD gave Solomon wisdom, just as he had promised him. There were peaceful relations between Hiram and Solomon, and the two of them made a treaty.

[13]King Solomon conscripted laborers from all Israel—thirty thousand men. [14]He sent them off to Lebanon in shifts of ten thousand a month, so that they spent one month in Lebanon and two months at home. Adoniram was in charge of the forced labor. [15]Solomon had seventy thousand carriers and eighty thousand stonecutters in the hills, [16]as well as thirty-three hundred[d] foremen who supervised the project and directed the workers. [17]At the king's command they removed from the quarry large blocks of high-grade stone to provide a foundation of dressed stone for the temple. [18]The craftsmen of Solomon and Hiram and workers from Byblos cut and prepared the timber and stone for the building of the temple.

Solomon Builds the Temple

6 In the four hundred and eightieth[e] year after the Israelites came out of Egypt, in the fourth year of Solomon's reign over Israel, in the month of Ziv, the second month, he began to build the temple of the LORD.

[2]The temple that King Solomon built for the LORD was sixty cubits long, twenty wide and thirty high.[f] [3]The portico at the front of the

---

[a] 11 That is, probably about 3,600 tons or about 3,250 metric tons   [b] 11 Septuagint (see also 2 Chron. 2:10); Hebrew *twenty cors*   [c] 11 That is, about 120,000 gallons or about 440,000 liters   [d] 16 Hebrew; some Septuagint manuscripts (see also 2 Chron. 2:2,18) *thirty-six hundred*   [e] 1 Hebrew; Septuagint *four hundred and fortieth*   [f] 2 That is, about 90 feet long, 30 feet wide and 45 feet high or about 27 meters long, 9 meters wide and 14 meters high   [g] 3 That is, about 30 feet or about 9 meters; also in verses 16 and 20   [h] 3 That is, about 15 feet or about 4.5 meters; also in verses 23-26   [i] 6 That is, about 7 1/2 feet or about 2.3 meters; also in verses 10 and 24   [j] 6 That is, about 9 feet or about 2.7 meters   [k] 6 That is, about 11 feet or about 3.2 meters   [l] 8 Septuagint; Hebrew *middle*   [m] 17 That is, about 60 feet or about 18 meters

flowers. Everything was cedar; no stone was to be seen.

[19] He prepared the inner sanctuary within the temple to set the ark of the covenant of the LORD there. [20] The inner sanctuary was twenty cubits long, twenty wide and twenty high. He overlaid the inside with pure gold, and he also overlaid the altar of cedar. [21] Solomon covered the inside of the temple with pure gold, and he extended gold chains across the front of the inner sanctuary, which was overlaid with gold. [22] So he overlaid the whole interior with gold. He also overlaid with gold the altar that belonged to the inner sanctuary.

[23] For the inner sanctuary he made a pair of cherubim out of olive wood, each ten cubits high. [24] One wing of the first cherub was five cubits long, and the other wing five cubits — ten cubits from wing tip to wing tip. [25] The second cherub also measured ten cubits, for the two cherubim were identical in size and shape. [26] The height of each cherub was ten cubits. [27] He placed the cherubim inside the innermost room of the temple, with their wings spread out. The wing of one cherub touched one wall, while the wing of the other touched the other wall, and their wings touched each other in the middle of the room. [28] He overlaid the cherubim with gold.

[29] On the walls all around the temple, in both the inner and outer rooms, he carved cherubim, palm trees and open flowers. [30] He also covered the floors of both the inner and outer rooms of the temple with gold.

[31] For the entrance to the inner sanctuary he made doors out of olive wood that were one fifth of the width of the sanctuary. [32] And on the two olive-wood doors he carved cherubim, palm trees and open flowers, and overlaid the cherubim and palm trees with hammered gold. [33] In the same way, for the entrance to the main hall he made doorframes out of olive wood that were one fourth of the width of the hall. [34] He also made two doors out of juniper wood, each having two leaves that turned in sockets. [35] He carved cherubim, palm trees and open flowers on them and overlaid them with gold hammered evenly over the carvings.

[36] And he built the inner courtyard of three courses of dressed stone and one course of trimmed cedar beams.

[37] The foundation of the temple of the LORD was laid in the fourth year, in the month of Ziv. [38] In the eleventh year in the month of Bul, the eighth month, the temple was finished in all its details according to its specifications. He had spent seven years building it.

The Difficulty of Handling Power

1 Kings 6:1–38

Solomon built the temple with excellence, sparing no expense and caring for each detail. He finished even the "invisible parts" with high quality and precision. Through his building program, Solomon became known everywhere and his power vastly increased.

And that may be the very thing that led to his later problems.

Every leader has power, gained in a variety of ways. Ponder the following "power platforms" and ask yourself: *Which ones do I use with others?*

1. **Coercive Power:** based on fear; failure to comply brings punishment
   Weakness: Volunteers cannot be forced to act.

2. **Connection Power:** based on who you know, not who you are
   Weakness: It becomes political.

3. **Charisma Power:** based on personality
   Weakness: Smiles and warm feelings cannot replace truth.

4. **Competence Power:** based on ability to get results
   Weakness: Raw ability is good, but not if it alienates or fails to empower people.

5. **Christmas Power:** based on gifts bestowed
   Weakness: People want what they don't need, and need what they don't want.

Solomon Builds His Palace

7 It took Solomon thirteen years, however, to complete the construction of his palace. [2]He built the Palace of the Forest of Lebanon a hundred cubits long, fifty wide and thirty high,[a] with four rows of cedar columns supporting trimmed cedar beams. [3]It was roofed with cedar above the beams that rested on the columns—forty-five beams, fifteen to a row. [4]Its windows were placed high in sets of three, facing each other. [5]All the doorways had rectangular frames; they were in the front part in sets of three, facing each other.[b]

[6]He made a colonnade fifty cubits long and thirty wide.[c] In front of it was a portico, and in front of that were pillars and an overhanging roof.

[7]He built the throne hall, the Hall of Justice, where he was to judge, and he covered it with cedar from floor to ceiling.[d] [8]And the palace in which he was to live, set farther back, was similar in design. Solomon also made a palace like this hall for Pharaoh's daughter, whom he had married.

[9]All these structures, from the outside to the great courtyard and from foundation to eaves, were made of blocks of high-grade stone cut to size and smoothed on their inner and outer faces. [10]The foundations were laid with large stones of good quality, some measuring ten cubits[e] and some eight.[f] [11]Above were high-grade stones, cut to size, and cedar beams. [12]The great courtyard was surrounded by a wall of three courses of dressed stone and one course of trimmed cedar beams, as was the inner courtyard of the temple of the LORD with its portico.

The Temple's Furnishings

[13]King Solomon sent to Tyre and brought Huram,[g] [14]whose mother was a widow from the tribe of Naphtali and whose father was from Tyre and a skilled craftsman in bronze. Huram was filled with wisdom, with understanding and with knowledge to do all kinds of bronze work. He came to King Solomon and did all the work assigned to him.

[15]He cast two bronze pillars, each eighteen cubits high and twelve cubits in circumference.[h] [16]He also made two capitals of cast bronze to set on the tops of the pillars; each capital was five cubits[i] high. [17]A network of interwoven chains adorned the capitals on top of the pillars, seven for each capital. [18]He made pomegranates in two rows[j] encircling each network to decorate the capitals on top of the pillars.[k] He did the same for each capital. [19]The capitals on top of the pillars in the portico were in the shape of lilies, four cubits[l] high. [20]On the capitals of both pillars, above the bowl-shaped part next to the network, were the two hundred pomegranates in rows all around. [21]He erected the pillars at the portico of the temple. The pillar to the south he named Jakin[m] and the one to the north Boaz.[n] [22]The capitals on top were in the shape of lilies. And so the work on the pillars was completed.

[23]He made the Sea of cast metal, circular in shape, measuring ten cubits from rim to rim and five cubits high. It took a line of thirty cubits[o] to measure around it. [24]Below the rim, gourds encircled it—ten to a cubit. The gourds were cast in two rows in one piece with the Sea.

[25]The Sea stood on twelve bulls, three facing north, three facing west, three facing south and three facing east. The Sea rested on top of them, and their hindquarters were toward the center. [26]It was a handbreadth[p] in thickness, and its rim was like the rim of a cup, like a lily blossom. It held two thousand baths.[q]

[27]He also made ten movable stands of bronze; each was four cubits long, four wide and three high.[r] [28]This is how the stands were made: They had side panels attached to uprights. [29]On the panels between the uprights were lions, bulls and cherubim—and on the uprights as well. Above and below the lions and bulls were wreaths of hammered work. [30]Each stand had four bronze wheels with bronze axles, and each had a basin resting on four supports, cast with wreaths on each side. [31]On the inside of the

---

[a] 2 That is, about 150 feet long, 75 feet wide and 45 feet high or about 45 meters long, 23 meters wide and 14 meters high
[b] 5 The meaning of the Hebrew for this verse is uncertain.
[c] 6 That is, about 75 feet long and 45 feet wide or about 23 meters long and 14 meters wide   [d] 7 Vulgate and Syriac; Hebrew *floor*   [e] 10 That is, about 15 feet or about 4.5 meters; also in verse 23   [f] 10 That is, about 12 feet or about 3.6 meters   [g] 13 Hebrew *Hiram*, a variant of *Huram*; also in verses 40 and 45   [h] 15 That is, about 27 feet high and 18 feet in circumference or about 8.1 meters high and 5.4 meters in circumference   [i] 16 That is, about 7 1/2 feet or about 2.3 meters; also in verse 23   [j] 18 Two Hebrew manuscripts and Septuagint; most Hebrew manuscripts *made the pillars, and there were two rows*   [k] 18 Many Hebrew manuscripts and Syriac; most Hebrew manuscripts *pomegranates*   [l] 19 That is, about 6 feet or about 1.8 meters; also in verse 38   [m] 21 *Jakin* probably means *he establishes*.   [n] 21 *Boaz* probably means *in him is strength*.   [o] 23 That is, about 45 feet or about 14 meters   [p] 26 That is, about 3 inches or about 7.5 centimeters   [q] 26 That is, about 12,000 gallons or about 44,000 liters; the Septuagint does not have this sentence.   [r] 27 That is, about 6 feet long and wide and about 4 1/2 feet high or about 1.8 meters long and wide and 1.4 meters high

stand there was an opening that had a circular frame one cubit[a] deep. This opening was round, and with its basework it measured a cubit and a half.[b] Around its opening there was engraving. The panels of the stands were square, not round. [32]The four wheels were under the panels, and the axles of the wheels were attached to the stand. The diameter of each wheel was a cubit and a half. [33]The wheels were made like chariot wheels; the axles, rims, spokes and hubs were all of cast metal.

[34]Each stand had four handles, one on each corner, projecting from the stand. [35]At the top of the stand there was a circular band half a cubit[c] deep. The supports and panels were attached to the top of the stand. [36]He engraved cherubim, lions and palm trees on the surfaces of the supports and on the panels, in every available space, with wreaths all around. [37]This is the way he made the ten stands. They were all cast in the same molds and were identical in size and shape.

[38]He then made ten bronze basins, each holding forty baths[d] and measuring four cubits across, one basin to go on each of the ten stands. [39]He placed five of the stands on the south side of the temple and five on the north. He placed the Sea on the south side, at the southeast corner of the temple. [40]He also made the pots[e] and shovels and sprinkling bowls.

So Huram finished all the work he had undertaken for King Solomon in the temple of the LORD:

[41] the two pillars;

the two bowl-shaped capitals on top of the pillars;

the two sets of network decorating the two bowl-shaped capitals on top of the pillars;

[42] the four hundred pomegranates for the two sets of network (two rows of pomegranates for each network decorating the bowl-shaped capitals on top of the pillars);

[43] the ten stands with their ten basins;

[44] the Sea and the twelve bulls under it;

[45] the pots, shovels and sprinkling bowls.

All these objects that Huram made for King Solomon for the temple of the LORD were of burnished bronze. [46]The king had them cast in clay molds in the plain of the Jordan between Sukkoth and Zarethan. [47]Solomon left all these things unweighed, because there were so many; the weight of the bronze was not determined.

[48]Solomon also made all the furnishings that were in the LORD's temple:

the golden altar;

the golden table on which was the bread of the Presence;

[49] the lampstands of pure gold (five on the right and five on the left, in front of the inner sanctuary);

the gold floral work and lamps and tongs;

[50] the pure gold basins, wick trimmers, sprinkling bowls, dishes and censers;

and the gold sockets for the doors of the innermost room, the Most Holy Place, and also for the doors of the main hall of the temple.

[51]When all the work King Solomon had done for the temple of the LORD was finished, he brought in the things his father David had dedicated — the silver and gold and the furnishings — and he placed them in the treasuries of the LORD's temple.

The Ark Brought to the Temple

8 Then King Solomon summoned into his presence at Jerusalem the elders of Israel, all the heads of the tribes and the chiefs of the Israelite families, to bring up the ark of the LORD's covenant from Zion, the City of David. [2]All the Israelites came together to King Solomon at the time of the festival in the month of Ethanim, the seventh month.

[3]When all the elders of Israel had arrived, the priests took up the ark, [4]and they brought up the ark of the LORD and the tent of meeting and all the sacred furnishings in it. The priests and Levites carried them up, [5]and King Solomon and the entire assembly of Israel that had gathered about him were before the ark, sacrificing so many sheep and cattle that they could not be recorded or counted.

[6]The priests then brought the ark of the LORD's covenant to its place in the inner sanctuary of the temple, the Most Holy Place, and put it beneath the wings of the cherubim. [7]The cherubim spread their wings over the place of the ark and overshadowed the ark and its carrying poles. [8]These poles were so long that their

---

[a] 31 That is, about 18 inches or about 45 centimeters

[b] 31 That is, about 2 1/4 feet or about 68 centimeters; also in verse 32   [c] 35 That is, about 9 inches or about 23 centimeters

[d] 38 That is, about 240 gallons or about 880 liters

[e] 40 Many Hebrew manuscripts, Septuagint, Syriac and Vulgate (see also verse 45 and 2 Chron. 4:11); many other Hebrew manuscripts basins

ends could be seen from the Holy Place in front of the inner sanctuary, but not from outside the Holy Place; and they are still there today. [9]There was nothing in the ark except the two stone tablets that Moses had placed in it at Horeb, where the LORD made a covenant with the Israelites after they came out of Egypt.

[10]When the priests withdrew from the Holy Place, the cloud filled the temple of the LORD. [11]And the priests could not perform their service because of the cloud, for the glory of the LORD filled his temple.

[12]Then Solomon said, "The LORD has said that he would dwell in a dark cloud; [13]I have indeed built a magnificent temple for you, a place for you to dwell forever."

[14]While the whole assembly of Israel was standing there, the king turned around and blessed them. [15]Then he said:

"Praise be to the LORD, the God of Israel, who with his own hand has fulfilled what he promised with his own mouth to my father David. For he said, [16]'Since the day I brought my people Israel out of Egypt, I have not chosen a city in any tribe of Israel to have a temple built so that my Name might be there, but I have chosen David to rule my people Israel.'

[17]"My father David had it in his heart to build a temple for the Name of the LORD, the God of Israel. [18]But the LORD said to my father David, 'You did well to have it in your heart to build a temple for my Name. [19]Nevertheless, you are not the one to build the temple, but your son, your own flesh and blood—he is the one who will build the temple for my Name.'

[20]"The LORD has kept the promise he made: I have succeeded David my father and now I sit on the throne of Israel, just as the LORD promised, and I have built the temple for the Name of the LORD, the God of Israel. [21]I have provided a place there for the ark, in which is the covenant of the LORD that he made with our ancestors when he brought them out of Egypt."

Solomon's Prayer of Dedication

[22]Then Solomon stood before the altar of the LORD in front of the whole assembly of Israel, spread out his hands toward heaven [23]and said:

"LORD, the God of Israel, there is no God like you in heaven above or on earth below—you who keep your covenant of love with your servants who continue wholeheartedly in your way. [24]You have kept your promise to your servant David my father; with your mouth you have promised and with your hand you have fulfilled it—as it is today.

[25]"Now LORD, the God of Israel, keep for your servant David my father the promises you made to him when you said, 'You shall never fail to have a successor to sit before me on the throne of Israel, if only your descendants are careful in all they do to walk before me faithfully as you have done.' [26]And now, God of Israel, let your word that you promised your servant David my father come true.

[27]"But will God really dwell on earth? The heavens, even the highest heaven, cannot contain you. How much less this temple I have built! [28]Yet give attention to your servant's prayer and his plea for mercy, LORD my God. Hear the cry and the prayer that your servant is praying in your presence this day. [29]May your eyes be open toward this temple night and day, this place of which you said, 'My Name shall be there,' so that you will hear the prayer your servant prays toward this place. [30]Hear the supplication of your servant and of your people Israel when they pray toward this place. Hear from heaven, your dwelling place, and when you hear, forgive.

[31]"When anyone wrongs their neighbor and is required to take an oath and they come and swear the oath before your altar in this temple, [32]then hear from heaven and act. Judge between your servants, condemning the guilty by bringing down on their heads what they have done, and vindicating the innocent by treating them in accordance with their innocence.

[33]"When your people Israel have been defeated by an enemy because they have sinned against you, and when they turn back to you and give praise to your name, praying and making supplication to you in this temple, [34]then hear from heaven and forgive the sin of your people Israel and bring them back to the land you gave to their ancestors.

[35]"When the heavens are shut up and there is no rain because your people have sinned against you, and when they pray toward this place and give praise to your name and turn from their sin because

you have afflicted them, [36]then hear from heaven and forgive the sin of your servants, your people Israel. Teach them the right way to live, and send rain on the land you gave your people for an inheritance.

[37]"When famine or plague comes to the land, or blight or mildew, locusts or grasshoppers, or when an enemy besieges them in any of their cities, whatever disaster or disease may come, [38]and when a prayer or plea is made by anyone among your people Israel—being aware of the afflictions of their own hearts, and spreading out their hands toward this temple— [39]then hear from heaven, your dwelling place. Forgive and act; deal with everyone according to all they do, since you know their hearts (for you alone know every human heart), [40]so that they will fear you all the time they live in the land you gave our ancestors.

[41]"As for the foreigner who does not belong to your people Israel but has come from a distant land because of your name— [42]for they will hear of your great name and your mighty hand and your outstretched arm—when they come and pray toward this temple, [43]then hear from heaven, your dwelling place. Do whatever the foreigner asks of you, so that all the peoples of the earth may know your name and fear you, as do your own people Israel, and may know that this house I have built bears your Name.

[44]"When your people go to war against their enemies, wherever you send them, and when they pray to the LORD toward the city you have chosen and the temple I have built for your Name, [45]then hear from heaven their prayer and their plea, and uphold their cause.

[46]"When they sin against you—for there is no one who does not sin—and you become angry with them and give them over to their enemies, who take them captive to their own lands, far away or near; [47]and if they have a change of heart in the land where they are held captive, and repent and plead with you in the land of their captors and say, 'We have sinned, we have done wrong, we have acted wickedly'; [48]and if they turn back to you with all their heart and soul in the land of their enemies who took them captive, and pray to you toward the land you gave their ancestors, toward the city you have chosen and the tem-

ple I have built for your Name; [49]then from heaven, your dwelling place, hear their prayer and their plea, and uphold their cause. [50]And forgive your people, who have sinned against you; forgive all the offenses they have committed against you, and cause their captors to show them mercy; [51]for they are your people and your inheritance, whom you brought out of Egypt, out of that iron-smelting furnace.

[52]"May your eyes be open to your servant's plea and to the plea of your people Israel, and may you listen to them whenever they cry out to you. [53]For you singled them out from all the nations of the world to be your own inheritance, just as you declared through your servant Moses when you, Sovereign LORD, brought our ancestors out of Egypt."

[54]When Solomon had finished all these prayers and supplications to the LORD, he rose from before the altar of the LORD, where he had been kneeling with his hands spread out toward heaven. [55]He stood and blessed the whole assembly of Israel in a loud voice, saying:

[56]"Praise be to the LORD, who has given rest to his people Israel just as he promised. Not one word has failed of all the good promises he gave through his servant Moses. [57]May the LORD our God be with us as he was with our ancestors; may he never leave us nor forsake us. [58]May he turn our hearts to him, to walk in obedience to him and keep the commands, decrees and laws he gave our ancestors. [59]And may these words of mine, which I have prayed before the LORD, be near to the LORD our God day and night, that he may uphold the cause of

Leaders Know Their Source and Give God Credit

1 Kings 8:12–61

After Solomon built a magnificent temple to house the ark of the covenant, he prayed a dedication prayer committing the temple to God. Despite his hard work, Solomon knew all the glory belonged to God. All leaders must recognize that lasting fruit appears only by the blessing of God.

his servant and the cause of his people Israel according to each day's need, [60]so that all the peoples of the earth may know that the LORD is God and that there is no other. [61]And may your hearts be fully committed to the LORD our God, to live by his decrees and obey his commands, as at this time."

The Dedication of the Temple

[62]Then the king and all Israel with him offered sacrifices before the LORD. [63]Solomon offered a sacrifice of fellowship offerings to the LORD: twenty-two thousand cattle and a hundred and twenty thousand sheep and goats. So the king and all the Israelites dedicated the temple of the LORD.

[64]On that same day the king consecrated the middle part of the courtyard in front of the temple of the LORD, and there he offered burnt offerings, grain offerings and the fat of the fellowship offerings, because the bronze altar that stood before the LORD was too small to hold the burnt offerings, the grain offerings and the fat of the fellowship offerings.

[65]So Solomon observed the festival at that time, and all Israel with him — a vast assembly, people from Lebo Hamath to the Wadi of Egypt. They celebrated it before the LORD our God for seven days and seven days more, fourteen days in all. [66]On the following day he sent the people away. They blessed the king and then went home, joyful and glad in heart for all the good things the LORD had done for his servant David and his people Israel.

The LORD Appears to Solomon

9 When Solomon had finished building the temple of the LORD and the royal palace, and had achieved all he had desired to do, [2]the LORD appeared to him a second time, as he had appeared to him at Gibeon. [3]The LORD said to him:

"I have heard the prayer and plea you have made before me; I have consecrated this temple, which you have built, by putting my Name there forever. My eyes and my heart will always be there.

[4]"As for you, if you walk before me faithfully with integrity of heart and uprightness, as David your father did, and do all I command and observe my decrees and laws, [5]I will establish your royal throne over Israel forever, as I promised David your father when I said, 'You shall never fail to have a successor on the throne of Israel.'

[6]"But if you[a] or your descendants turn away from me and do not observe the commands and decrees I have given you[a] and go off to serve other gods and worship them, [7]then I will cut off Israel from the land I have given them and will reject this temple I have consecrated for my Name. Israel will then become a byword and an object of ridicule among all peoples. [8]This temple will become a heap of rubble. All[b] who pass by will be appalled and will scoff and say, 'Why has the LORD done such a thing to this land and to this temple?' [9]People will answer, 'Because they have forsaken the LORD their God, who brought their ancestors out of Egypt, and have embraced other gods, worshiping and serving them — that is why the LORD brought all this disaster on them.'"

Solomon's Other Activities

[10]At the end of twenty years, during which Solomon built these two buildings — the temple of the LORD and the royal palace — [11]King Solomon gave twenty towns in Galilee to Hiram king of Tyre, because Hiram had supplied him with all the cedar and juniper and gold he wanted. [12]But when Hiram went from Tyre to see the towns that Solomon had given him, he was not pleased with them. [13]"What kind of towns are these you have given me, my brother?" he asked. And he called them the Land of Kabul,[c] a name they have to this day. [14]Now Hiram had sent to the king 120 talents[d] of gold.

[15]Here is the account of the forced labor King Solomon conscripted to build the LORD's temple, his own palace, the terraces,[e] the wall of Jerusalem, and Hazor, Megiddo and Gezer. [16](Pharaoh king of Egypt had attacked and captured Gezer. He had set it on fire. He killed its Canaanite inhabitants and then gave it as a wedding gift to his daughter, Solomon's wife. [17]And Solomon rebuilt Gezer.) He built up Lower Beth Horon, [18]Baalath, and Tadmor[f] in the desert, within his land, [19]as well as all his store cities and the towns for his chariots and for his horses[g] — whatever he desired to build in Jerusalem,

---

[a] 6 The Hebrew is plural.   [b] 8 See some Septuagint manuscripts, Old Latin, Syriac, Arabic and Targum; Hebrew *And though this temple is now imposing, all*   [c] 13 *Kabul* sounds like the Hebrew for *good-for-nothing.*   [d] 14 That is, about 4 1/2 tons or about 4 metric tons   [e] 15 Or *the Millo*; also in verse 24   [f] 18 The Hebrew may also be read *Tamar.* [g] 19 Or *charioteers*

in Lebanon and throughout all the territory he ruled.

[20]There were still people left from the Amorites, Hittites, Perizzites, Hivites and Jebusites (these peoples were not Israelites). [21]Solomon conscripted the descendants of all these peoples remaining in the land—whom the Israelites could not exterminate[a]—to serve as slave labor, as it is to this day. [22]But Solomon did not make slaves of any of the Israelites; they were his fighting men, his government officials, his officers, his captains, and the commanders of his chariots and charioteers. [23]They were also the chief officials in charge of Solomon's projects—550 officials supervising those who did the work.

[24]After Pharaoh's daughter had come up from the City of David to the palace Solomon had built for her, he constructed the terraces.

[25]Three times a year Solomon sacrificed burnt offerings and fellowship offerings on the altar he had built for the LORD, burning incense before the LORD along with them, and so fulfilled the temple obligations.

[26]King Solomon also built ships at Ezion Geber, which is near Elath in Edom, on the shore of the Red Sea.[b] [27]And Hiram sent his men—sailors who knew the sea—to serve in the fleet with Solomon's men. [28]They sailed to Ophir and brought back 420 talents[c] of gold, which they delivered to King Solomon.

The Queen of Sheba Visits Solomon

10 When the queen of Sheba heard about the fame of Solomon and his relationship to the LORD, she came to test Solomon with hard questions. [2]Arriving at Jerusalem with a very great caravan—with camels carrying spices, large quantities of gold, and precious stones—she came to Solomon and talked with him about all that she had on her mind. [3]Solomon answered all her questions; nothing was too hard for the king to explain to her. [4]When the queen of Sheba saw all the wisdom of Solomon and the palace he had built, [5]the food on his table, the seating of his officials, the attending servants in their robes, his cupbearers, and the burnt offerings he made at[d] the temple of the LORD, she was overwhelmed.

[6]She said to the king, "The report I heard in my own country about your achievements and your wisdom is true. [7]But I did not believe these things until I came and saw with my own eyes. Indeed, not even half was told me; in wisdom and wealth you have far exceeded the report I heard. [8]How happy your people must be! How happy your officials, who continually stand before you and hear your wisdom! [9]Praise be to the LORD your God, who has delighted in you and placed you on the throne of Israel. Because of the LORD's eternal love for Israel, he has made you king to maintain justice and righteousness."

[10]And she gave the king 120 talents[e] of gold, large quantities of spices, and precious stones. Never again were so many spices brought in as those the queen of Sheba gave to King Solomon.

---

[a] 21 The Hebrew term refers to the irrevocable giving over of things or persons to the LORD, often by totally destroying them.   [b] 26 Or *the Sea of Reeds*   [c] 28 That is, about 16 tons or about 14 metric tons   [d] 5 Or *the ascent by which he went up to*   [e] 10 That is, about 4 1/2 tons or about 4 metric tons

---

Play to Your Strength: The 70–25–5 Principle

1 Kings 10:1–9

Great leaders play to their strength. They don't spend vast amounts of time attempting to be a jack-of-all-trades. Instead, they deepen their ability to do what they do best, until they do it as well as anyone. Solomon certainly lived by this principle. God made him the wisest and richest king of his day (1Ki 3:12–13). Other monarchs heard of his wisdom and wealth and eagerly sought an audience with him. From all over the known world, powerful rulers from distant lands made the long trek to Israel to catch a glimpse of this young phenom. Solomon provided rich counsel and gifts to others, and quickly became known for his breadth of mind and depth of insight.

How did Solomon gain such fame? He focused on what he did best. Leaders would be wise to follow a similar pattern, called the 70–25–5 principle:

- Give 70 percent of your time to your areas of strength.
- Give 25 percent of your time to the areas you want to improve.
- Give 5 percent of your time to the areas of your weakness.

¹¹(Hiram's ships brought gold from Ophir; and from there they brought great cargoes of almugwood[a] and precious stones. ¹²The king used the almugwood to make supports[b] for the temple of the LORD and for the royal palace, and to make harps and lyres for the musicians. So much almugwood has never been imported or seen since that day.)

¹³King Solomon gave the queen of Sheba all she desired and asked for, besides what he had given her out of his royal bounty. Then she left and returned with her retinue to her own country.

Solomon's Splendor

¹⁴The weight of the gold that Solomon received yearly was 666 talents,[c] ¹⁵not including the revenues from merchants and traders and from all the Arabian kings and the governors of the territories.

¹⁶King Solomon made two hundred large shields of hammered gold; six hundred shekels[d] of gold went into each shield. ¹⁷He also made three hundred small shields of hammered gold, with three minas[e] of gold in each shield. The king put them in the Palace of the Forest of Lebanon.

¹⁸Then the king made a great throne covered with ivory and overlaid with fine gold. ¹⁹The throne had six steps, and its back had a rounded top. On both sides of the seat were armrests, with a lion standing beside each of them. ²⁰Twelve lions stood on the six steps, one at either end of each step. Nothing like it had ever been made for any other kingdom. ²¹All King Solomon's goblets were gold, and all the household articles in the Palace of the Forest of Lebanon were pure gold. Nothing was made of silver, because silver was considered of little value in Solomon's days. ²²The king had a fleet of trading ships[f] at sea along with the ships of Hiram. Once every three years it returned, carrying gold, silver and ivory, and apes and baboons.

²³King Solomon was greater in riches and wisdom than all the other kings of the earth. ²⁴The whole world sought audience with Solomon to hear the wisdom God had put in his heart. ²⁵Year after year, everyone who came brought a gift — articles of silver and gold, robes, weapons and spices, and horses and mules.

²⁶Solomon accumulated chariots and horses; he had fourteen hundred chariots and twelve thousand horses,[g] which he kept in the chariot cities and also with him in Jerusalem. ²⁷The king made silver as common in Jerusalem as

> ## The Law of Explosive Growth
> *1 Kings 10:24-25*
>
> Solomon impacted other leaders and multiplied his vision in them. To follow his example:
>
> 1. **Bring something to the table.**
> 2. **What do you contribute best to your world?**
> 3. **What do you want to accomplish?**
> 4. **How can you serve other leaders?**

stones, and cedar as plentiful as sycamore-fig trees in the foothills. ²⁸Solomon's horses were imported from Egypt and from Kue[h] — the royal merchants purchased them from Kue at the current price. ²⁹They imported a chariot from Egypt for six hundred shekels of silver, and a horse for a hundred and fifty.[i] They also exported them to all the kings of the Hittites and of the Arameans.

Solomon's Wives

11 King Solomon, however, loved many foreign women besides Pharaoh's daughter — Moabites, Ammonites, Edomites, Sidonians and Hittites. ²They were from nations about which the LORD had told the Israelites, "You must not intermarry with them, because they will surely turn your hearts after their gods." Nevertheless, Solomon held fast to them in love. ³He had seven hundred wives of royal birth and three hundred concubines, and his wives led him astray. ⁴As Solomon grew old, his wives turned his heart after other gods, and his heart was not fully devoted to the LORD his God, as the heart of David his father had been. ⁵He followed Ashtoreth the goddess of the Sidonians, and Molek the detestable god of the Ammonites. ⁶So Solomon did evil in the eyes of the LORD; he did not follow the LORD completely, as David his father had done.

---

[a] 11 Probably a variant of *algumwood*; also in verse 12
[b] 12 The meaning of the Hebrew for this word is uncertain.
[c] 14 That is, about 25 tons or about 23 metric tons   [d] 16 That is, about 15 pounds or about 6.9 kilograms; also in verse 29
[e] 17 That is, about 3 3/4 pounds or about 1.7 kilograms; or perhaps reference is to double minas, that is, about 7 1/2 pounds or about 3.5 kilograms.   [f] 22 Hebrew of *ships of Tarshish*   [g] 26 Or *charioteers*   [h] 28 Probably *Cilicia*
[i] 29 That is, about 3 3/4 pounds or about 1.7 kilograms

[7]On a hill east of Jerusalem, Solomon built a high place for Chemosh the detestable god of Moab, and for Molek the detestable god of the Ammonites. [8]He did the same for all his foreign wives, who burned incense and offered sacrifices to their gods.

[9]The LORD became angry with Solomon because his heart had turned away from the LORD, the God of Israel, who had appeared to him twice. [10]Although he had forbidden Solomon to follow other gods, Solomon did not keep the LORD's command. [11]So the LORD said to Solomon, "Since this is your attitude and you have not kept my covenant and my decrees, which I commanded you, I will most certainly tear the kingdom away from you and give it to one of your subordinates. [12]Nevertheless, for the sake of David your father, I will not do it during your lifetime. I will tear it out of the hand of your son. [13]Yet I will not tear the whole kingdom from him, but will give him one tribe for the sake of David my servant and for the sake of Jerusalem, which I have chosen."

Solomon's Adversaries

[14]Then the LORD raised up against Solomon an adversary, Hadad the Edomite, from the royal line of Edom. [15]Earlier when David was fighting with Edom, Joab the commander of the army, who had gone up to bury the dead, had struck down all the men in Edom. [16]Joab and all the Israelites stayed there for six months, until they had destroyed all the men in Edom. [17]But Hadad, still only a boy, fled to Egypt with some Edomite officials who had served his father. [18]They set out from Midian and went to Paran. Then taking people from Paran with them, they went to Egypt, to Pharaoh king of Egypt, who gave Hadad a house and land and provided him with food.

[19]Pharaoh was so pleased with Hadad that he gave him a sister of his own wife, Queen Tahpenes, in marriage. [20]The sister of Tahpenes bore him a son named Genubath, whom Tahpenes brought up in the royal palace. There Genubath lived with Pharaoh's own children.

[21]While he was in Egypt, Hadad heard that David rested with his ancestors and that Joab the commander of the army was also dead. Then Hadad said to Pharaoh, "Let me go, that I may return to my own country."

[22]"What have you lacked here that you want to go back to your own country?" Pharaoh asked.

"Nothing," Hadad replied, "but do let me go!"

[23]And God raised up against Solomon another adversary, Rezon son of Eliada, who had fled from his master, Hadadezer king of Zobah. [24]When David destroyed Zobah's army, Rezon gathered a band of men around him and became their leader; they went to Damascus, where they settled and took control. [25]Rezon was Israel's adversary as long as Solomon lived, adding to the trouble caused by Hadad. So Rezon ruled in Aram and was hostile toward Israel.

Jeroboam Rebels Against Solomon

[26]Also, Jeroboam son of Nebat rebelled against the king. He was one of Solomon's officials, an Ephraimite from Zeredah, and his mother was a widow named Zeruah.

[27]Here is the account of how he rebelled against the king: Solomon had built the terraces[a] and had filled in the gap in the wall of the city of David his father. [28]Now Jeroboam was a man of standing, and when Solomon saw how well the young man did his work, he put him in charge of the whole labor force of the tribes of Joseph.

[29]About that time Jeroboam was going out of Jerusalem, and Ahijah the prophet of Shiloh met him on the way, wearing a new cloak. The two of them were alone out in the country, [30]and Ahijah took hold of the new cloak he was wearing and tore it into twelve pieces. [31]Then he said to Jeroboam, "Take ten pieces for yourself, for this is what the LORD, the God of Israel, says: 'See, I am going to tear the kingdom out of Solomon's hand and give you ten tribes. [32]But for the sake of my servant David and the city of Jerusalem, which I have chosen out of all the tribes of Israel, he will have one tribe. [33]I will do this because they have[b] forsaken me and worshiped Ashtoreth the goddess of the Sidonians, Chemosh the god of the Moabites, and Molek the god of the Ammonites, and have not walked in obedience to me, nor done what is right in my eyes, nor kept my decrees and laws as David, Solomon's father, did.

[34]"'But I will not take the whole kingdom out of Solomon's hand; I have made him ruler all the days of his life for the sake of David my servant, whom I chose and who obeyed my commands and decrees. [35]I will take the kingdom from his son's hands and give you ten tribes. [36]I will give one tribe to his son so that David my servant may always have a lamp before me in Jerusalem,

[a] 27 Or the Millo　　[b] 33 Hebrew; Septuagint, Vulgate and Syriac because he has

the city where I chose to put my Name. ³⁷However, as for you, I will take you, and you will rule over all that your heart desires; you will be king over Israel. ³⁸If you do whatever I command you and walk in obedience to me and do what is right in my eyes by obeying my decrees and commands, as David my servant did, I will be with you. I will build you a dynasty as enduring as the one I built for David and will give Israel to you. ³⁹I will humble David's descendants because of this, but not forever.'"

⁴⁰Solomon tried to kill Jeroboam, but Jeroboam fled to Egypt, to Shishak the king, and stayed there until Solomon's death.

Solomon's Death

⁴¹As for the other events of Solomon's reign — all he did and the wisdom he displayed — are they not written in the book of the annals of Solomon? ⁴²Solomon reigned in Jerusalem over all Israel forty years. ⁴³Then he rested with his ancestors and was buried in the city of David his father. And Rehoboam his son succeeded him as king.

Israel Rebels Against Rehoboam

12 Rehoboam went to Shechem, for all Israel had gone there to make him king. ²When Jeroboam son of Nebat heard this (he was still in Egypt, where he had fled from King Solomon), he returned from*a* Egypt. ³So they sent for Jeroboam, and he and the whole assembly of Israel went to Rehoboam and said to him: ⁴"Your father put a heavy yoke on us, but now lighten the harsh labor and the heavy yoke he put on us, and we will serve you."

⁵Rehoboam answered, "Go away for three days and then come back to me." So the people went away.

⁶Then King Rehoboam consulted the elders who had served his father Solomon during his lifetime. "How would you advise me to answer these people?" he asked.

⁷They replied, "If today you will be a servant to these people and serve them and give them a favorable answer, they will always be your servants."

⁸But Rehoboam rejected the advice the elders gave him and consulted the young men who had grown up with him and were serving him. ⁹He asked them, "What is your advice? How should we answer these people who say to me, 'Lighten the yoke your father put on us'?"

¹⁰The young men who had grown up with him replied, "These people have said to you, 'Your father put a heavy yoke on us, but make our yoke lighter.' Now tell them, 'My little finger is thicker than my father's waist. ¹¹My father laid on you a heavy yoke; I will make it even heavier. My father scourged you with whips; I will scourge you with scorpions.'"

¹²Three days later Jeroboam and all the people returned to Rehoboam, as the king had said, "Come back to me in three days." ¹³The king answered the people harshly. Rejecting the advice given him by the elders, ¹⁴he followed the advice

---

a 2 Or he remained in

Distraction, the Enemy of Direction

1 Kings 11:1–43

How could the wisest man in history turn away from God? How could the leader whose gifts and focus once made him the talk of the world get distracted from his calling?

The temptations that enticed Solomon continue to attack every leader. Once we "arrive," it becomes easy to stop feeling hungry for growth and excellence. How quickly we become satisfied—and how soon we begin to spiral downward. Note how this process of decay looked for Solomon:

1. **Distractions:** He deviated from his call to lead and be a light to the nations.

2. **Adversaries:** God raised up adversaries to steer him back to his priorities and call.

3. **Self-absorption:** He became consumed with himself rather than his call.

4. **Loss of God's presence:** God withdrew his anointing.

5. **Pursuit of pleasure:** He became even more obsessed with his own pleasure.

6. **Emptiness:** He finally grew weary of his pursuits and recognized his emptiness.

of the young men and said, "My father made your yoke heavy; I will make it even heavier. My father scourged you with whips; I will scourge you with scorpions." ¹⁵So the king did not listen to the people, for this turn of events was from the LORD, to fulfill the word the LORD had spoken to Jeroboam son of Nebat through Ahijah the Shilonite.

¹⁶When all Israel saw that the king refused to listen to them, they answered the king:

"What share do we have in David,
   what part in Jesse's son?
To your tents, Israel!
Look after your own house, David!"

So the Israelites went home. ¹⁷But as for the Israelites who were living in the towns of Judah, Rehoboam still ruled over them.

¹⁸King Rehoboam sent out Adoniram,ᵃ who was in charge of forced labor, but all Israel stoned him to death. King Rehoboam, however, managed to get into his chariot and escape to Jerusalem. ¹⁹So Israel has been in rebellion against the house of David to this day.

²⁰When all the Israelites heard that Jeroboam had returned, they sent and called him to the assembly and made him king over all Israel. Only the tribe of Judah remained loyal to the house of David.

²¹When Rehoboam arrived in Jerusalem, he mustered all Judah and the tribe of Benjamin— a hundred and eighty thousand able young men— to go to war against Israel and to regain the kingdom for Rehoboam son of Solomon.

²²But this word of God came to Shemaiah the man of God: ²³"Say to Rehoboam son of Solomon king of Judah, to all Judah and Benjamin, and to the rest of the people, ²⁴'This is what the LORD says: Do not go up to fight against your brothers, the Israelites. Go home, every one of you, for this is my doing.'" So they obeyed the word of the LORD and went home again, as the LORD had ordered.

Golden Calves at Bethel and Dan

²⁵Then Jeroboam fortified Shechem in the hill country of Ephraim and lived there. From there he went out and built up Peniel.ᵇ

²⁶Jeroboam thought to himself, "The kingdom will now likely revert to the house of David. ²⁷If these people go up to offer sacrifices at the temple of the LORD in Jerusalem, they will again give their allegiance to their lord, Rehoboam king of Judah. They will kill me and return to King Rehoboam."

²⁸After seeking advice, the king made two golden calves. He said to the people, "It is too much for you to go up to Jerusalem. Here are your gods, Israel, who brought you up out of Egypt." ²⁹One he set up in Bethel, and the other in Dan. ³⁰And this thing became a sin; the people came to worship the one at Bethel and went as far as Dan to worship the other.ᶜ

³¹Jeroboam built shrines on high places and appointed priests from all sorts of people, even though they were not Levites. ³²He instituted a festival on the fifteenth day of the eighth month, like the festival held in Judah, and offered sacrifices on the altar. This he did in Bethel, sacrificing to the calves he had made. And at Bethel he also installed priests at the high places he had made. ³³On the fifteenth day of the eighth month, a month of his own choosing, he offered sacrifices on the altar he had built at Bethel. So he instituted the festival for the Israelites and went up to the altar to make offerings.

The Man of God From Judah

13 By the word of the LORD a man of God came from Judah to Bethel, as Jeroboam was standing by the altar to make an offering. ²By the word of the LORD he cried out against the altar: "Altar, altar! This is what the LORD says: 'A son named Josiah will be born to the house of David. On you he will sacrifice the priests of the high places who make offerings here, and human bones will be burned on you.'" ³That same day the man of God gave a sign: "This is the sign the LORD has declared: The altar will be split apart and the ashes on it will be poured out."

⁴When King Jeroboam heard what the man of God cried out against the altar at Bethel, he stretched out his hand from the altar and said, "Seize him!" But the hand he stretched out toward the man shriveled up, so that he could not pull it back. ⁵Also, the altar was split apart and its ashes poured out according to the sign given by the man of God by the word of the LORD.

⁶Then the king said to the man of God, "Intercede with the LORD your God and pray for me that my hand may be restored." So the man of God interceded with the LORD, and the king's hand was restored and became as it was before.

⁷The king said to the man of God, "Come

REHOBOAM AND THE LAW OF CONNECTION
Leaders Touch a Heart Before They Ask for a Hand

1 Kings 12:1–24

A LEADER can't connect with people only when he is communicating to groups; he must connect with individuals. The stronger the relationship and connection between individuals, the more likely the follower will want to help the leader. Some leaders have problems because they believe that followers must take the responsibility to connect. But successful leaders always initiate. They take the first step and then make the effort to continue building relationships.

When a leader has done the work to connect with his people, you can see it in the way the organization functions. Employees show incredible loyalty and a strong work ethic. The people aspire to the vision of the leader. The impact is incredible.

■ ■ ■ ■ ■

Connecting requires giving. The power-hungry Rehoboam wanted to flex his political muscles more than he desired to connect with his people. Rehoboam never learned the Law of Connection. If you desire to connect with others, check your motives:

1. *Get beyond yourself.* Dr. Albert Schweitzer asserted, "Whatever you have received more than others—in health, in talents, in ability, in success . . . all this you must not take to yourself as a matter of course. In gratitude for good fortune, you must render some sacrifice of your own life for another life."

Selfishness and insecurity usually lie at the heart of those who fail to get beyond themselves. Clearly, Rehoboam never got beyond himself. His bullying earned him not more respect, but contempt. To connect with people, remain others-minded and remember that leadership is a privilege.

2. *Grow beyond yourself.* Mahatma Gandhi once remarked, "The difference between what we do and what we are capable of doing would suffice to solve most of the world's problems."

Had Rehoboam gleaned from the experience of the elders, he would have discovered how little he knew about leading. But this cocky and unteachable young man missed a great opportunity for growth—and so destroyed the nation. If you want to grow beyond yourself, remain humble and teachable.

3. *Give beyond yourself.* Individuals with low self-esteem almost always focus chiefly on themselves. Conversely, a study from the University of Michigan revealed that people who regularly volunteer their time

heighten their zest for living and increase their life expectancy.

Rehoboam had no interest in what he could give; he aimed to get the maximum. Effective leaders must persistently ask themselves, "What am I doing for others?" Be a river, not a reservoir.

4. *Go beyond yourself.* "When you were born, you cried, and the world rejoiced," goes a Middle Eastern saying. "May you live your life so that when you die, the world will cry, and you will rejoice."

Every great leader has the ability to connect. If you want to be a better leader, you must learn to connect with people. Do it, and you will dramatically raise your level of leadership. Do it well, and people will follow you anywhere.

When You Connect with People

Connecting with people isn't complicated, but it takes effort. Observe how Rehoboam neglected this priority:

1. *Your people are more willing to take action when you first move them with emotion.*
Even when King Solomon's elders advised Rehoboam that he could win the people's hearts forever by lightening their workload, he turned a deaf ear. When he showed no concern for their welfare, they sought another leader who would listen.

When you remain open to your people's needs, they will remain open to your vision. When you take action to meet their needs, they will take action to fulfill your vision. Wise leaders discern and meet the needs of their people.

2. *When you give first, your people will give in return.*
Rehoboam squandered multiple opportunities to give to his people. It may seem paradoxical, but a leader gets more by giving more. When you give of your time, talent and possessions, you receive much more in return.

3. *When you connect with individuals, you gain the attention of crowds.*
Too arrogant to walk among his people, Rehoboam tried to lead Israel impersonally from behind the palace walls. While the nature of leadership often requires speaking before groups, effective leaders understand that true connection happens one-on-one.

4. *When you reach out to your people, they will reach back toward you.*
The initial confrontation between Rehoboam and his people took place when they came to him; he was so out of touch he couldn't see they were on the verge of revolting. Rehoboam was a reactive leader rather than a proactive one. When it became clear he had caused his people's displeasure, he pointed a finger at them. As a result, his kingdom ripped apart.

Whether you have just taken over a leadership position or are well established, you must connect with your people if you are to succeed. Remember, the telltale sign of a great leader is not what he has accomplished on his own, but what he has been able to accomplish through others. That happens only through connection.

home with me for a meal, and I will give you a gift."

⁸But the man of God answered the king, "Even if you were to give me half your possessions, I would not go with you, nor would I eat bread or drink water here. ⁹For I was commanded by the word of the LORD: 'You must not eat bread or drink water or return by the way you came.'" ¹⁰So he took another road and did not return by the way he had come to Bethel.

¹¹Now there was a certain old prophet living in Bethel, whose sons came and told him all that the man of God had done there that day. They also told their father what he had said to the king. ¹²Their father asked them, "Which way did he go?" And his sons showed him which road the man of God from Judah had taken. ¹³So he said to his sons, "Saddle the donkey for me." And when they had saddled the donkey for him, he mounted it ¹⁴and rode after the man of God. He found him sitting under an oak tree and asked, "Are you the man of God who came from Judah?"

"I am," he replied.

¹⁵So the prophet said to him, "Come home with me and eat."

¹⁶The man of God said, "I cannot turn back and go with you, nor can I eat bread or drink water with you in this place. ¹⁷I have been told by the word of the LORD: 'You must not eat bread or drink water there or return by the way you came.'"

¹⁸The old prophet answered, "I too am a prophet, as you are. And an angel said to me by the word of the LORD: 'Bring him back with you to your house so that he may eat bread and drink water.'" (But he was lying to him.) ¹⁹So the man of God returned with him and ate and drank in his house.

²⁰While they were sitting at the table, the word of the LORD came to the old prophet who had brought him back. ²¹He cried out to the man of God who had come from Judah, "This is what the LORD says: 'You have defied the word of the LORD and have not kept the command the LORD your God gave you. ²²You came back and ate bread and drank water in the place where he told you not to eat or drink. Therefore your body will not be buried in the tomb of your ancestors.'"

²³When the man of God had finished eating and drinking, the prophet who had brought him back saddled his donkey for him. ²⁴As he went on his way, a lion met him on the road and killed him, and his body was left lying on the road, with both the donkey and the lion standing beside it. ²⁵Some people who passed by saw

The Consequences of Compromise

1 Kings 13:11–24

An unnamed, elderly prophet illustrates both the power of a leader living by his convictions, and how compromise can steal away conviction. He triumphed when he stood, but perished when he turned back. Just so, we gain when we stand strong, but can lose it all when we slip.

the body lying there, with the lion standing beside the body, and they went and reported it in the city where the old prophet lived.

²⁶When the prophet who had brought him back from his journey heard of it, he said, "It is the man of God who defied the word of the LORD. The LORD has given him over to the lion, which has mauled him and killed him, as the word of the LORD had warned him."

²⁷The prophet said to his sons, "Saddle the donkey for me," and they did so. ²⁸Then he went out and found the body lying on the road, with the donkey and the lion standing beside it. The lion had neither eaten the body nor mauled the donkey. ²⁹So the prophet picked up the body of the man of God, laid it on the donkey, and brought it back to his own city to mourn for him and bury him. ³⁰Then he laid the body in his own tomb, and they mourned over him and said, "Alas, my brother!"

³¹After burying him, he said to his sons, "When I die, bury me in the grave where the man of God is buried; lay my bones beside his bones. ³²For the message he declared by the word of the LORD against the altar in Bethel and against all the shrines on the high places in the towns of Samaria will certainly come true."

³³Even after this, Jeroboam did not change his evil ways, but once more appointed priests for the high places from all sorts of people. Anyone who wanted to become a priest he consecrated for the high places. ³⁴This was the sin of the house of Jeroboam that led to its downfall and to its destruction from the face of the earth.

Ahijah's Prophecy Against Jeroboam

14 At that time Abijah son of Jeroboam became ill, ²and Jeroboam said to his wife, "Go, disguise yourself, so you won't be recognized as the wife of Jeroboam. Then go to Shiloh. Ahijah the prophet is there—the one who told me I would be king over this people. ³Take ten loaves of bread with you, some cakes and a jar of honey, and go to him. He will tell you what will happen to the boy." ⁴So Jeroboam's wife did what he said and went to Ahijah's house in Shiloh.

Now Ahijah could not see; his sight was gone because of his age. ⁵But the LORD had told Ahijah, "Jeroboam's wife is coming to ask you about her son, for he is ill, and you are to give her such and such an answer. When she arrives, she will pretend to be someone else."

⁶So when Ahijah heard the sound of her footsteps at the door, he said, "Come in, wife of Jeroboam. Why this pretense? I have been sent to you with bad news. ⁷Go, tell Jeroboam that this is what the LORD, the God of Israel, says: 'I raised you up from among the people and appointed you ruler over my people Israel. ⁸I tore the kingdom away from the house of David and gave it to you, but you have not been like my servant David, who kept my commands and followed me with all his heart, doing only what was right in my eyes. ⁹You have done more evil than all who lived before you. You have made for yourself other gods, idols made of metal; you have aroused my anger and turned your back on me.

¹⁰" 'Because of this, I am going to bring disaster on the house of Jeroboam. I will cut off from Jeroboam every last male in Israel—slave or free.ᵃ I will burn up the house of Jeroboam as one burns dung, until it is all gone. ¹¹Dogs will eat those belonging to Jeroboam who die in the city, and the birds will feed on those who die in the country. The LORD has spoken!'

¹²"As for you, go back home. When you set foot in your city, the boy will die. ¹³All Israel will mourn for him and bury him. He is the only one belonging to Jeroboam who will be buried, because he is the only one in the house of Jeroboam in whom the LORD, the God of Israel, has found anything good.

¹⁴"The LORD will raise up for himself a king over Israel who will cut off the family of Jeroboam. Even now this is beginning to happen.ᵇ ¹⁵And the LORD will strike Israel, so that it will be like a reed swaying in the water. He will uproot Israel from this good land that he gave to their ancestors and scatter them beyond the Euphrates River, because they aroused the LORD's anger by making Asherah poles.ᶜ ¹⁶And he will give Israel up because of the sins Jeroboam has committed and has caused Israel to commit."

¹⁷Then Jeroboam's wife got up and left and went to Tirzah. As soon as she stepped over the threshold of the house, the boy died. ¹⁸They buried him, and all Israel mourned for him, as the LORD had said through his servant the prophet Ahijah.

¹⁹The other events of Jeroboam's reign, his wars and how he ruled, are written in the book of the annals of the kings of Israel. ²⁰He reigned for twenty-two years and then rested with his ancestors. And Nadab his son succeeded him as king.

Rehoboam King of Judah

²¹Rehoboam son of Solomon was king in Judah. He was forty-one years old when he became king, and he reigned seventeen years in Jerusalem, the city the LORD had chosen out of all the tribes of Israel in which to put his Name. His mother's name was Naamah; she was an Ammonite.

²²Judah did evil in the eyes of the LORD. By the sins they committed they stirred up his jealous anger more than those who were before them had done. ²³They also set up for themselves high places, sacred stones and Asherah poles on every high hill and under every spreading tree. ²⁴There were even male shrine prostitutes in the land; the people engaged in all the detestable practices of the nations the LORD had driven out before the Israelites.

²⁵In the fifth year of King Rehoboam, Shishak king of Egypt attacked Jerusalem. ²⁶He carried off the treasures of the temple of the LORD and the treasures of the royal palace. He took everything, including all the gold shields Solomon had made. ²⁷So King Rehoboam made bronze shields to replace them and assigned these to the commanders of the guard on duty at the entrance to the royal palace. ²⁸Whenever the king went to the LORD's temple, the guards bore the shields, and afterward they returned them to the guardroom.

²⁹As for the other events of Rehoboam's reign, and all he did, are they not written in the book of the annals of the kings of Judah? ³⁰There was continual warfare between Rehoboam and Jeroboam. ³¹And Rehoboam rested with his ancestors and was buried with them in the City of David. His mother's name was Naamah; she was an Ammonite. And Abijahᵈ his son succeeded him as king.

ᵃ 10 Or Israel—every ruler or leader ᵇ 14 The meaning of the Hebrew for this sentence is uncertain. ᶜ 15 That is, wooden symbols of the goddess Asherah; here and elsewhere in 1 Kings ᵈ 31 Some Hebrew manuscripts and Septuagint (see also 2 Chron. 12:16); most Hebrew manuscripts Abijam

Abijah King of Judah

15 In the eighteenth year of the reign of Jeroboam son of Nebat, Abijah[a] became king of Judah, [2]and he reigned in Jerusalem three years. His mother's name was Maakah daughter of Abishalom.[b]

[3]He committed all the sins his father had done before him; his heart was not fully devoted to the Lord his God, as the heart of David his forefather had been. [4]Nevertheless, for David's sake the Lord his God gave him a lamp in Jerusalem by raising up a son to succeed him and by making Jerusalem strong. [5]For David had done what was right in the eyes of the Lord and had not failed to keep any of the Lord's commands all the days of his life — except in the case of Uriah the Hittite.

[6]There was war between Abijah[c] and Jeroboam throughout Abijah's lifetime. [7]As for the other events of Abijah's reign, and all he did, are they not written in the book of the annals of the kings of Judah? There was war between Abijah and Jeroboam. [8]And Abijah rested with his ancestors and was buried in the City of David. And Asa his son succeeded him as king.

Asa King of Judah

[9]In the twentieth year of Jeroboam king of Israel, Asa became king of Judah, [10]and he reigned in Jerusalem forty-one years. His grandmother's name was Maakah daughter of Abishalom.

[11]Asa did what was right in the eyes of the Lord, as his father David had done. [12]He expelled the male shrine prostitutes from the land and got rid of all the idols his ancestors had made. [13]He even deposed his grandmother Maakah from her position as queen mother, because she had made a repulsive image for the worship of Asherah. Asa cut it down and burned it in the Kidron Valley. [14]Although he did not remove the high places, Asa's heart was fully committed to the Lord all his life. [15]He brought into the temple of the Lord the silver and gold and the articles that he and his father had dedicated.

[16]There was war between Asa and Baasha king of Israel throughout their reigns. [17]Baasha king of Israel went up against Judah and fortified Ramah to prevent anyone from leaving or entering the territory of Asa king of Judah.

[18]Asa then took all the silver and gold that was left in the treasuries of the Lord's temple and of his own palace. He entrusted it to his officials and sent them to Ben-Hadad son of Tabrimmon, the son of Hezion, the king of Aram, who was ruling in Damascus. [19]"Let there be a treaty between me and you," he said, "as there was between my father and your father. See, I am sending you a gift of silver and gold. Now break your treaty with Baasha king of Israel so he will withdraw from me."

[20]Ben-Hadad agreed with King Asa and sent the commanders of his forces against the towns of Israel. He conquered Ijon, Dan, Abel Beth Maakah and all Kinnereth in addition to Naphtali. [21]When Baasha heard this, he stopped building Ramah and withdrew to Tirzah. [22]Then King Asa issued an order to all Judah — no one was exempt — and they carried away from Ramah the stones and timber Baasha had been using there. With them King Asa built up Geba in Benjamin, and also Mizpah.

[23]As for all the other events of Asa's reign, all his achievements, all he did and the cities he built, are they not written in the book of the annals of the kings of Judah? In his old age, however, his feet became diseased. [24]Then Asa rested with his ancestors and was buried with them in the city of his father David. And Jehoshaphat his son succeeded him as king.

Nadab King of Israel

[25]Nadab son of Jeroboam became king of Israel in the second year of Asa king of Judah, and he reigned over Israel two years. [26]He did evil in the eyes of the Lord, following the ways of his father and committing the same sin his father had caused Israel to commit.

[27]Baasha son of Ahijah from the tribe of Issachar plotted against him, and he struck him down at Gibbethon, a Philistine town, while Nadab and all Israel were besieging it. [28]Baasha killed Nadab in the third year of Asa king of Judah and succeeded him as king.

[29]As soon as he began to reign, he killed Jeroboam's whole family. He did not leave Jeroboam anyone that breathed, but destroyed them all, according to the word of the Lord given through his servant Ahijah the Shilonite. [30]This happened because of the sins Jeroboam had committed and had caused Israel to commit, and because he aroused the anger of the Lord, the God of Israel.

[31]As for the other events of Nadab's reign, and all he did, are they not written in the book of the

---

[a] 1 Some Hebrew manuscripts and Septuagint (see also 2 Chron. 12:16); most Hebrew manuscripts *Abijam*; also in verses 7 and 8   [b] 2 A variant of *Absalom*; also in verse 10   [c] 6 Some Hebrew manuscripts and Syriac *Abijam* (that is, Abijah); most Hebrew manuscripts *Rehoboam*

The Law of the Lid: As the Leader Goes, So Goes the Nation

1 Kings 14:1—15:34

Leadership ability is the lid on the success of a nation or organization. When Israel or Judah lived under good kings, things went well. Under bad kings, things went sour.

The heart and skill of a leader will always tremendously affect the life of the people under his direction. This is a law, both timeless and universal. See how this law played out under the Hebrew kings of the Old Testament:

Good Kings

1. **Drew loyalty from their people**
2. **Enjoyed victory over sin**
3. **Enjoyed peace within the kingdom**
4. **Were affirmed by God's prophets**
5. **Enjoyed prosperity**
6. **Opposed evil kings**

Bad Kings

1. **Drew rebellion from their people**
2. **Saw bondage to sin**
3. **Suffered turmoil within the kingdom**
4. **Were rebuked by God's prophets**
5. **Often endured natural disasters and war**
6. **Opposed good kings**

annals of the kings of Israel? [32]There was war between Asa and Baasha king of Israel throughout their reigns.

Baasha King of Israel

[33]In the third year of Asa king of Judah, Baasha son of Ahijah became king of all Israel in Tirzah, and he reigned twenty-four years. [34]He did evil in the eyes of the LORD, following the ways of Jeroboam and committing the same sin Jeroboam had caused Israel to commit.

16 Then the word of the LORD came to Jehu son of Hanani concerning Baasha: [2]"I lifted you up from the dust and appointed you ruler over my people Israel, but you followed the ways of Jeroboam and caused my people Israel to sin and to arouse my anger by their sins. [3]So I am about to wipe out Baasha and his house, and I will make your house like that of Jeroboam son of Nebat. [4]Dogs will eat those belonging to Baasha who die in the city, and birds will feed on those who die in the country."

[5]As for the other events of Baasha's reign, what he did and his achievements, are they not written in the book of the annals of the kings of Israel? [6]Baasha rested with his ancestors and was buried in Tirzah. And Elah his son succeeded him as king.

[7]Moreover, the word of the LORD came through the prophet Jehu son of Hanani to Baasha and his house, because of all the evil he had done in the eyes of the LORD, arousing his anger by the things he did, becoming like the house of Jeroboam — and also because he destroyed it.

Elah King of Israel

[8]In the twenty-sixth year of Asa king of Judah, Elah son of Baasha became king of Israel, and he reigned in Tirzah two years.

[9]Zimri, one of his officials, who had command of half his chariots, plotted against him. Elah was in Tirzah at the time, getting drunk in the home of Arza, the palace administrator at Tirzah. [10]Zimri came in, struck him down and killed him in the twenty-seventh year of Asa king of Judah. Then he succeeded him as king.

[11]As soon as he began to reign and was seated on the throne, he killed off Baasha's whole family. He did not spare a single male, whether relative or friend. [12]So Zimri destroyed the whole family of Baasha, in accordance with the word of the LORD spoken against Baasha through the prophet Jehu — [13]because of all the sins Baasha and his son Elah had committed and had caused Israel to commit, so that they aroused the anger of the LORD, the God of Israel, by their worthless idols.

[14]As for the other events of Elah's reign, and all he did, are they not written in the book of the annals of the kings of Israel?

Zimri King of Israel

[15]In the twenty-seventh year of Asa king of Judah, Zimri reigned in Tirzah seven days. The

army was encamped near Gibbethon, a Philistine town. [16]When the Israelites in the camp heard that Zimri had plotted against the king and murdered him, they proclaimed Omri, the commander of the army, king over Israel that very day there in the camp. [17]Then Omri and all the Israelites with him withdrew from Gibbethon and laid siege to Tirzah. [18]When Zimri saw that the city was taken, he went into the citadel of the royal palace and set the palace on fire around him. So he died, [19]because of the sins he had committed, doing evil in the eyes of the LORD and following the ways of Jeroboam and committing the same sin Jeroboam had caused Israel to commit.

[20]As for the other events of Zimri's reign, and the rebellion he carried out, are they not written in the book of the annals of the kings of Israel?

Omri King of Israel

[21]Then the people of Israel were split into two factions; half supported Tibni son of Ginath for king, and the other half supported Omri. [22]But Omri's followers proved stronger than those of Tibni son of Ginath. So Tibni died and Omri became king.

[23]In the thirty-first year of Asa king of Judah, Omri became king of Israel, and he reigned twelve years, six of them in Tirzah. [24]He bought the hill of Samaria from Shemer for two talents[a] of silver and built a city on the hill, calling it Samaria, after Shemer, the name of the former owner of the hill.

[25]But Omri did evil in the eyes of the LORD and sinned more than all those before him. [26]He followed completely the ways of Jeroboam son of Nebat, committing the same sin Jeroboam had caused Israel to commit, so that they aroused the anger of the LORD, the God of Israel, by their worthless idols.

[27]As for the other events of Omri's reign, what he did and the things he achieved, are they not written in the book of the annals of the kings of Israel? [28]Omri rested with his ancestors and was buried in Samaria. And Ahab his son succeeded him as king.

Ahab Becomes King of Israel

[29]In the thirty-eighth year of Asa king of Judah, Ahab son of Omri became king of Israel, and he reigned in Samaria over Israel twenty-two years. [30]Ahab son of Omri did more evil in the eyes of the LORD than any of those before him. [31]He not only considered it trivial to commit the sins of Jeroboam son of Nebat, but he also married Jezebel daughter of Ethbaal king

of the Sidonians, and began to serve Baal and worship him. [32]He set up an altar for Baal in the temple of Baal that he built in Samaria. [33]Ahab also made an Asherah pole and did more to arouse the anger of the LORD, the God of Israel, than did all the kings of Israel before him.

[34]In Ahab's time, Hiel of Bethel rebuilt Jericho. He laid its foundations at the cost of his firstborn son Abiram, and he set up its gates at the cost of his youngest son Segub, in accordance with the word of the LORD spoken by Joshua son of Nun.

Elijah Announces a Great Drought

17 Now Elijah the Tishbite, from Tishbe[b] in Gilead, said to Ahab, "As the LORD, the God of Israel, lives, whom I serve, there will be neither dew nor rain in the next few years except at my word."

Elijah Fed by Ravens

[2]Then the word of the LORD came to Elijah: [3]"Leave here, turn eastward and hide in the Kerith Ravine, east of the Jordan. [4]You will drink from the brook, and I have directed the ravens to supply you with food there."

[5]So he did what the LORD had told him. He went to the Kerith Ravine, east of the Jordan, and stayed there. [6]The ravens brought him bread and meat in the morning and bread and meat in the evening, and he drank from the brook.

Elijah and the Widow at Zarephath

[7]Some time later the brook dried up because there had been no rain in the land. [8]Then the word of the LORD came to him: [9]"Go at once to

---

[a] 24 That is, about 150 pounds or about 68 kilograms
[b] 1 Or Tishbite, of the settlers

Convictions: When God Is Behind You, One Is a Majority

1 Kings 17:1

Some consider Elijah the greatest prophet of the Old Testament. When he predicts a drought, he's not out to make a popular speech or gain friends in high places. Elijah spoke to the people when God spoke to him. God plus one equals a majority.

Zarephath in the region of Sidon and stay there. I have directed a widow there to supply you with food." [10]So he went to Zarephath. When he came to the town gate, a widow was there gathering sticks. He called to her and asked, "Would you bring me a little water in a jar so I may have a drink?" [11]As she was going to get it, he called, "And bring me, please, a piece of bread."

[12]"As surely as the LORD your God lives," she replied, "I don't have any bread — only a handful of flour in a jar and a little olive oil in a jug. I am gathering a few sticks to take home and make a meal for myself and my son, that we may eat it — and die."

[13]Elijah said to her, "Don't be afraid. Go home and do as you have said. But first make a small loaf of bread for me from what you have and bring it to me, and then make something for yourself and your son. [14]For this is what the LORD, the God of Israel, says: 'The jar of flour will not be used up and the jug of oil will not run dry until the day the LORD sends rain on the land.'"

[15]She went away and did as Elijah had told her. So there was food every day for Elijah and for the woman and her family. [16]For the jar of flour was not used up and the jug of oil did not run dry, in keeping with the word of the LORD spoken by Elijah.

[17]Some time later the son of the woman who owned the house became ill. He grew worse and worse, and finally stopped breathing. [18]She said to Elijah, "What do you have against me, man of God? Did you come to remind me of my sin and kill my son?"

[19]"Give me your son," Elijah replied. He took him from her arms, carried him to the upper room where he was staying, and laid him on his bed. [20]Then he cried out to the LORD, "LORD my God, have you brought tragedy even on this widow I am staying with, by causing her son to die?" [21]Then he stretched himself out on the boy three times and cried out to the LORD, "LORD my God, let this boy's life return to him!"

[22]The LORD heard Elijah's cry, and the boy's life returned to him, and he lived. [23]Elijah picked up the child and carried him down from the room into the house. He gave him to his mother and said, "Look, your son is alive!"

[24]Then the woman said to Elijah, "Now I know that you are a man of God and that the word of the LORD from your mouth is the truth."

Elijah and Obadiah

18 After a long time, in the third year, the word of the LORD came to Elijah: "Go and present yourself to Ahab, and I will send rain on the land." [2]So Elijah went to present himself to Ahab.

ELIJAH

Standing Alone, Speaking Truth
1 Kings 17:1—18:40

PROFILE in leadership

The prophet Elijah knew about the idolatry of Israel and the wickedness of King Ahab. He knew the time for judgment had arrived. And he also knew that drought and famine were about to devastate Israel.

He knew because he himself had announced God's judgment.

This all took place during a very sad time in the history of Israel, when the people had all but turned their backs on God and their king had sinned against the Lord openly and boldly. Elijah, consumed with holy indignation, prayed that it might not rain in Israel— and for more than three years, not a drop of rain fell. Streams dried up, crops failed, and people starved.

Later, all alone, the prophet stood on Mount Carmel among 450 prophets of Baal, giving the people visual proof of the impotence of their puny god. In a spectacular demonstration of the awesomeness of the true and living God, Elijah called fire down from heaven—and then directed the execution of Baal's priests.

Imagine the courage it took for one solitary man to pray for judgment on his own people, confront a wicked king, then stand before hundreds of false prophets and challenge their piety! Although the Lord took Elijah to heaven long ago (2Ki 2:11), this courageous prophet still proclaims today that true leadership may mean standing alone and speaking difficult truth.

21 QUALITIES

COURAGE   Elijah's Fire and Passion Attract Others

1 Kings 18:1–40

NOT ONLY did the crowds see the fire of God in Elijah, they soon saw it in his ministry—literally.

Elijah grew tired of his people's spiritual rebellion and angry with the false prophets of Baal. He confronted both forces atop Mount Carmel and there defeated the devil's henchmen, although they outnumbered him 850 to 1 (1Ki 18:19). No one had seen anything like his courage since the day David fought Goliath unremembered years before. And like the underdog David, Elijah met the enemy with passion. His eyes drank in the greatness of God, not the numbers of his enemies. This heavenly vision provided the fire that fueled his courage.

Leaders always need courage. No one who wants to bring about change can manage without courage. Courage flamed in Elijah's heart because:

1. *His resolution outweighed his reservations.*
   Although greatly outnumbered, Elijah resolved that Baal had to be confronted at any cost.

2. *His desires outweighed his desperation.*
   Although it meant risk, Elijah wanted to honor Yahweh more than anything else.

3. *His compassion outweighed his complaints.*
   Although Elijah hated the people's attitude, he wanted them to find and follow Yahweh.

Let the Fire Fall

As Elijah worshiped and prayed all alone atop the mountain, he mustered the courage to call down fire from heaven. The fire inside of him drew down the fire of God, decisively defeating Baal.

This poses a good question for leaders today. When will the "fire" come down in our leadership? According to Elijah, the fire comes . . .

1. **When we know our message is from God (v. 1).**

2. **When we stand for what is right, regardless of the cost (vv. 2–20).**

3. **When our need is the greatest (vv. 2, 5, 21–22).**

4. **When we take our message to the people (vv. 20–21).**

5. **When we bring others to a point of decision (v. 21).**

6. **When we repair and use the altar of God (vv. 23–32).**

7. **When we face circumstances that only God's fire will light (vv. 33–35).**

8. **When we publicly trust God to do what only he can do (vv. 33–37).**

9. **When we hunger for God to receive glory (vv. 36–39).**

10. **When we desire to see others return to the Lord (v. 37).**

For a negative example of courage, see p. 329.

Now the famine was severe in Samaria, ³and Ahab had summoned Obadiah, his palace administrator. (Obadiah was a devout believer in the Lord. ⁴While Jezebel was killing off the Lord's prophets, Obadiah had taken a hundred prophets and hidden them in two caves, fifty in each, and had supplied them with food and water.) ⁵Ahab had said to Obadiah, "Go through the land to all the springs and valleys. Maybe we can find some grass to keep the horses and mules alive so we will not have to kill any of our animals." ⁶So they divided the land they were to cover, Ahab going in one direction and Obadiah in another.

⁷As Obadiah was walking along, Elijah met him. Obadiah recognized him, bowed down to the ground, and said, "Is it really you, my lord Elijah?"

⁸"Yes," he replied. "Go tell your master, 'Elijah is here.'"

⁹"What have I done wrong," asked Obadiah, "that you are handing your servant over to Ahab to be put to death? ¹⁰As surely as the Lord your God lives, there is not a nation or kingdom where my master has not sent someone to look for you. And whenever a nation or kingdom claimed you were not there, he made them swear they could not find you. ¹¹But now you tell me to go to my master and say, 'Elijah is here.' ¹²I don't know where the Spirit of the Lord may carry you when I leave you. If I go and tell Ahab and he doesn't find you, he will kill me. Yet I your servant have worshiped the Lord since my youth. ¹³Haven't you heard, my lord, what I did while Jezebel was killing the prophets of the Lord? I hid a hundred of the Lord's prophets in two caves, fifty in each, and supplied them with food and water. ¹⁴And now you tell me to go to my master and say, 'Elijah is here.' He will kill me!"

¹⁵Elijah said, "As the Lord Almighty lives, whom I serve, I will surely present myself to Ahab today."

Elijah on Mount Carmel

¹⁶So Obadiah went to meet Ahab and told him, and Ahab went to meet Elijah. ¹⁷When he saw Elijah, he said to him, "Is that you, you troubler of Israel?"

¹⁸"I have not made trouble for Israel," Elijah replied. "But you and your father's family have. You have abandoned the Lord's commands and have followed the Baals. ¹⁹Now summon the people from all over Israel to meet me on Mount Carmel. And bring the four hundred and fifty prophets of Baal and the four hundred prophets of Asherah, who eat at Jezebel's table."

²⁰So Ahab sent word throughout all Israel and assembled the prophets on Mount Carmel. ²¹Elijah went before the people and said, "How long will you waver between two opinions? If the Lord is God, follow him; but if Baal is God, follow him."

But the people said nothing.

²²Then Elijah said to them, "I am the only one of the Lord's prophets left, but Baal has four hundred and fifty prophets. ²³Get two bulls for us. Let Baal's prophets choose one for themselves, and let them cut it into pieces and put it on the wood but not set fire to it. I will prepare the other bull and put it on the wood but not set fire to it. ²⁴Then you call on the name of your god, and I will call on the name of the Lord. The god who answers by fire — he is God."

Then all the people said, "What you say is good."

²⁵Elijah said to the prophets of Baal, "Choose one of the bulls and prepare it first, since there are so many of you. Call on the name of your god, but do not light the fire." ²⁶So they took the bull given them and prepared it.

Then they called on the name of Baal from morning till noon. "Baal, answer us!" they shouted. But there was no response; no one answered. And they danced around the altar they had made.

²⁷At noon Elijah began to taunt them. "Shout louder!" he said. "Surely he is a god! Perhaps he is deep in thought, or busy, or traveling. Maybe he is sleeping and must be awakened." ²⁸So they shouted louder and slashed themselves with swords and spears, as was their custom, until their blood flowed. ²⁹Midday passed, and they continued their frantic prophesying until the time for the evening sacrifice. But there was no response, no one answered, no one paid attention.

³⁰Then Elijah said to all the people, "Come here to me." They came to him, and he repaired the altar of the Lord, which had been torn down. ³¹Elijah took twelve stones, one for each of the tribes descended from Jacob, to whom the word of the Lord had come, saying, "Your name shall be Israel." ³²With the stones he built an altar in the name of the Lord, and he dug a trench around it large enough to hold two seahs*a* of seed. ³³He arranged the wood, cut the bull into pieces and laid it on the wood. Then he said to

---

a 32 That is, probably about 24 pounds or about 11 kilograms

them, "Fill four large jars with water and pour it on the offering and on the wood."

³⁴"Do it again," he said, and they did it again. "Do it a third time," he ordered, and they did it the third time. ³⁵The water ran down around the altar and even filled the trench.

³⁶At the time of sacrifice, the prophet Elijah stepped forward and prayed: "Lord, the God of Abraham, Isaac and Israel, let it be known today that you are God in Israel and that I am your servant and have done all these things at your command. ³⁷Answer me, Lord, answer me, so these people will know that you, Lord, are God, and that you are turning their hearts back again."

³⁸Then the fire of the Lord fell and burned up the sacrifice, the wood, the stones and the soil, and also licked up the water in the trench.

³⁹When all the people saw this, they fell prostrate and cried, "The Lord—he is God! The Lord—he is God!"

⁴⁰Then Elijah commanded them, "Seize the prophets of Baal. Don't let anyone get away!" They seized them, and Elijah had them brought down to the Kishon Valley and slaughtered there.

⁴¹And Elijah said to Ahab, "Go, eat and drink, for there is the sound of a heavy rain." ⁴²So Ahab went off to eat and drink, but Elijah climbed to the top of Carmel, bent down to the ground and put his face between his knees.

⁴³"Go and look toward the sea," he told his servant. And he went up and looked.

"There is nothing there," he said.

Seven times Elijah said, "Go back."

⁴⁴The seventh time the servant reported, "A cloud as small as a man's hand is rising from the sea."

So Elijah said, "Go and tell Ahab, 'Hitch up your chariot and go down before the rain stops you.'"

⁴⁵Meanwhile, the sky grew black with clouds, the wind rose, a heavy rain started falling and Ahab rode off to Jezreel. ⁴⁶The power of the Lord came on Elijah and, tucking his cloak into his belt, he ran ahead of Ahab all the way to Jezreel.

Elijah Flees to Horeb

19 Now Ahab told Jezebel everything Elijah had done and how he had killed all the prophets with the sword. ²So Jezebel sent a messenger to Elijah to say, "May the gods deal with me, be it ever so severely, if by this time tomorrow I do not make your life like that of one of them."

Elijah and the Law of Influence
1 Kings 18:27–38

When the man spoke, people jumped.

"Shout louder!" he told the false prophets; and they did (v. 27).

"Come here to me," he commanded the Israelites; and they did (v. 30).

"Fill four large jars with water and pour it on the offering and on the wood," he told some servants; and they did (v. 33).

"Do it again," he ordered; and they did (v. 34).

"Do it a third time," he said; and they did (v. 34).

But most amazing of all, by the end of the day, after all the theatrics, Elijah turned his face toward heaven and cried, "Answer me, Lord, answer me, so these people will know that you, Lord, are God, and that you are turning their hearts back again"; and God did (1Ki 18:37–38)!

Elijah had powerful influence and always got a hearing. How did the prophet gain the ear of everyone who heard his voice? We can discern a number of reasons:

1. **His courage:** He was willing to stand alone for God.

2. **His conviction:** He had a passion for what he believed.

3. **His character:** He was honest and forthright with everyone.

4. **His connection:** He magnetically drew the people to himself and to God.

5. **His credibility:** He eventually gained the people's ear because he got the results he was after.

³Elijah was afraid[a] and ran for his life. When he came to Beersheba in Judah, he left his servant there, ⁴while he himself went a day's journey into the wilderness. He came to a broom bush, sat down under it and prayed that he might die. "I have had enough, LORD," he said. "Take my life; I am no better than my ancestors." ⁵Then he lay down under the bush and fell asleep.

All at once an angel touched him and said, "Get up and eat." ⁶He looked around, and there by his head was some bread baked over hot coals, and a jar of water. He ate and drank and then lay down again.

⁷The angel of the LORD came back a second time and touched him and said, "Get up and eat, for the journey is too much for you." ⁸So he got up and ate and drank. Strengthened by that food, he traveled forty days and forty nights until he reached Horeb, the mountain of God. ⁹There he went into a cave and spent the night.

The LORD Appears to Elijah

And the word of the LORD came to him: "What are you doing here, Elijah?"

¹⁰He replied, "I have been very zealous for the LORD God Almighty. The Israelites have rejected your covenant, torn down your altars, and put your prophets to death with the sword. I am the only one left, and now they are trying to kill me too."

¹¹The LORD said, "Go out and stand on the mountain in the presence of the LORD, for the LORD is about to pass by."

Then a great and powerful wind tore the mountains apart and shattered the rocks before the LORD, but the LORD was not in the wind. After the wind there was an earthquake, but the LORD was not in the earthquake. ¹²After the earthquake came a fire, but the LORD was not in the fire. And after the fire came a gentle whisper. ¹³When Elijah heard it, he pulled his cloak over his face and went out and stood at the mouth of the cave.

Then a voice said to him, "What are you doing here, Elijah?"

¹⁴He replied, "I have been very zealous for the LORD God Almighty. The Israelites have rejected your covenant, torn down your altars, and put your prophets to death with the sword. I am the only one left, and now they are trying to kill me too."

¹⁵The LORD said to him, "Go back the way you came, and go to the Desert of Damascus.

_____
[a] 3 Or Elijah saw

Burnout: Principles, Not Emotions, Must Guide Leaders

1 Kings 19:1–3

Emotions are wonderful servants, but poor leaders.

How ironic that Elijah would flee from Jezebel! The courageous leader who successfully confronted 450 prophets of Baal and 400 prophets of Asherah turned on his heels and ran from a wicked woman who threatened his life.

How could it happen? The phenomenon of emotional burnout helps us make sense of the incident. Leaders burn out when they pay out huge emotional expenses without replenishing the inner person. Review what happened . . .

Elijah's Emotional Expense

- Predicted a drought to King Ahab
- Supernaturally receives food from a widow and the birds
- Announces the end of the drought
- Challenges the 450 prophets of Baal
- Mobilizes people to eliminate idols
- Prays down torrential rain in Judah
- Outruns the storm and Ahab's chariot
- Confronted by Jezebel; leaves his servant

Elijah's Eventual Consequence

- Isolation: he cut himself off from friends
- Paranoia: he felt totally alone in serving God; imagined everyone was trying to kill him
- Exhaustion: he felt famished and lay down
- Hiding: he got lost in a cave
- Self-pity: he complained of no reward
- Depression: he prayed that he might die
- Messiah complex: he alone remained as God's prophet
- Empty: he had no fresh word from the Lord

The Law of the Inner Circle: Development Beats Discouragement

1 Kings 19:4–10

Discouragement buries many land mines in our path: It hurts our self-image; it causes us to evade our responsibilities; it prompts us to blame others for our problems; it tempts us to blur the facts. We tend to lead according to the way we feel about ourselves.

Elijah became one discouraged leader after his confrontation with Jezebel. Emotionally drained, physically spent, full of self-pity and ready to die, he looked haggard and nearly done in. So what did God do to help the prophet through his deep discouragement? He told him to select and develop another leader, Elisha. Their relationship suggests several observations about leadership:

1. **God desires to continually raise up leaders (1Ki 19:16).**
2. **The leader finds and challenges the potential leader (1Ki 19:19–20).**
3. **The potential leader counts the cost, pays the price and follows (1Ki 19:20–21).**
4. **The potential leader stays close to and shadows the leader (2Ki 2:2–8).**
5. **The potential leader covets the power of God that he sees in the leader (2Ki 2:9–10).**
6. **The leader passes his authority to the potential leader (2Ki 2:11–13).**
7. **Others recognize the transfer of spiritual authority (2Ki 2:14–15).**

When you get there, anoint Hazael king over Aram. [16]Also, anoint Jehu son of Nimshi king over Israel, and anoint Elisha son of Shaphat from Abel Meholah to succeed you as prophet. [17]Jehu will put to death any who escape the sword of Hazael, and Elisha will put to death any who escape the sword of Jehu. [18]Yet I reserve seven thousand in Israel — all whose knees have not bowed down to Baal and whose mouths have not kissed him."

The Call of Elisha

[19]So Elijah went from there and found Elisha son of Shaphat. He was plowing with twelve yoke of oxen, and he himself was driving the twelfth pair. Elijah went up to him and threw his cloak around him. [20]Elisha then left his oxen and ran after Elijah. "Let me kiss my father and mother goodbye," he said, "and then I will come with you."

"Go back," Elijah replied. "What have I done to you?"

[21]So Elisha left him and went back. He took his yoke of oxen and slaughtered them. He burned the plowing equipment to cook the meat and gave it to the people, and they ate. Then he set out to follow Elijah and became his servant.

Ben-Hadad Attacks Samaria

20 Now Ben-Hadad king of Aram mustered his entire army. Accompanied by thirty-two kings with their horses and chariots, he went up and besieged Samaria and attacked it. [2]He sent messengers into the city to Ahab king of Israel, saying, "This is what Ben-Hadad says: [3]'Your silver and gold are mine, and the best of your wives and children are mine.'"

[4]The king of Israel answered, "Just as you say, my lord the king. I and all I have are yours."

[5]The messengers came again and said, "This is what Ben-Hadad says: 'I sent to demand your silver and gold, your wives and your children. [6]But about this time tomorrow I am going to send my officials to search your palace and the houses of your officials. They will seize everything you value and carry it away.'"

[7]The king of Israel summoned all the elders of the land and said to them, "See how this man is looking for trouble! When he sent for my wives and my children, my silver and my gold, I did not refuse him."

[8]The elders and the people all answered, "Don't listen to him or agree to his demands."

[9]So he replied to Ben-Hadad's messengers, "Tell my lord the king, 'Your servant will do all you demanded the first time, but this demand

21 QUALITIES

FEW COUPLES in Scripture look less attractive than King Ahab and Queen Jezebel. We get acquainted with their ugly style at the end of 1 Kings. Because they suffered an almost total lack of leadership charisma, they had to use manipulation, selfishness and cunning to get what they wanted.

Charisma has been defined as a magnetic personal attraction that draws others to the leader, making them feel better about themselves. Effective leaders do well to develop some level of charisma.

In Greek, the word *charisma* means "gift." God gives a degree of charisma to everyone. Leaders are to give it away to others; charismatic people are others-centered. So why did Ahab and Jezebel fail to demonstrate any charisma?

1. **They set out to selfishly build their own kingdoms (22:8).**

2. **They used people in order to get ahead; anyone was expendable (19:2).**

3. **They worried about image and lived under false pretenses (21:8–13).**

4. **They sulked and got angry when they didn't get their way (21:4).**

5. **They pretended to be someone they were not (21:25–27).**

6. **They abused the authority they had been given (21:18–19).**

Ahab and Jezebel felt no incentive to develop charisma because their position allowed them to use people. Why would they need to inspire others to cooperate with them? Wasn't their word law? Godly leaders must avoid this wicked attitude at all costs.

Roadblocks to Charisma

To build charisma, be others-minded. Leaders who think about others and their concerns before thinking of themselves quickly develop charisma.

How would you rate your own charisma? Are other people naturally attracted to you? Are you well liked? Consider the following roadblocks to charisma. Do you possess any of these?

- **Pride:** Nobody wants to follow a leader who thinks he is better than everyone else. Arrogant leaders lose the respect of others.

- **Insecurity:** If you are uncomfortable with yourself, others will be, too. Only secure leaders can provide a secure atmosphere.

- **Moodiness:** If people never know what to expect from you, they stop expecting anything. Eventually, they won't even approach you.

- **Selfishness:** People can tell if you are using them merely to reach your own goal. No healthy person stays for long in such an unhealthy environment.

- **Perfectionism:** People respect the desire for excellence, but loathe unrealistic expectations. No one wants to feel the program is more important than they are.

- **Cynicism:** People don't want to be rained on by someone who sees a cloud around every silver lining. Negative leaders repulse healthy followers.

For a positive look at charisma, see p. 1290.

I cannot meet.'" They left and took the answer back to Ben-Hadad.

[10] Then Ben-Hadad sent another message to Ahab: "May the gods deal with me, be it ever so severely, if enough dust remains in Samaria to give each of my men a handful."

[11] The king of Israel answered, "Tell him: 'One who puts on his armor should not boast like one who takes it off.'"

[12] Ben-Hadad heard this message while he and the kings were drinking in their tents,[a] and he ordered his men: "Prepare to attack." So they prepared to attack the city.

Ahab Defeats Ben-Hadad

[13] Meanwhile a prophet came to Ahab king of Israel and announced, "This is what the LORD says: 'Do you see this vast army? I will give it into your hand today, and then you will know that I am the LORD.'"

[14] "But who will do this?" asked Ahab.

The prophet replied, "This is what the LORD says: 'The junior officers under the provincial commanders will do it.'"

"And who will start the battle?" he asked.

The prophet answered, "You will."

[15] So Ahab summoned the 232 junior officers under the provincial commanders. Then he assembled the rest of the Israelites, 7,000 in all. [16] They set out at noon while Ben-Hadad and the 32 kings allied with him were in their tents getting drunk. [17] The junior officers under the provincial commanders went out first.

Now Ben-Hadad had dispatched scouts, who reported, "Men are advancing from Samaria."

[18] He said, "If they have come out for peace, take them alive; if they have come out for war, take them alive."

[19] The junior officers under the provincial commanders marched out of the city with the army behind them [20] and each one struck down his opponent. At that, the Arameans fled, with the Israelites in pursuit. But Ben-Hadad king of Aram escaped on horseback with some of his horsemen. [21] The king of Israel advanced and overpowered the horses and chariots and inflicted heavy losses on the Arameans.

[22] Afterward, the prophet came to the king of Israel and said, "Strengthen your position and see what must be done, because next spring the king of Aram will attack you again."

[23] Meanwhile, the officials of the king of Aram advised him, "Their gods are gods of the hills. That is why they were too strong for us. But if we fight them on the plains, surely we will be stronger than they. [24] Do this: Remove all the kings from their commands and replace them with other officers. [25] You must also raise an army like the one you lost—horse for horse and chariot for chariot—so we can fight Israel on the plains. Then surely we will be stronger than they." He agreed with them and acted accordingly.

[26] The next spring Ben-Hadad mustered the Arameans and went up to Aphek to fight against Israel. [27] When the Israelites were also mustered and given provisions, they marched out to meet them. The Israelites camped opposite them like two small flocks of goats, while the Arameans covered the countryside.

[28] The man of God came up and told the king of Israel, "This is what the LORD says: 'Because the Arameans think the LORD is a god of the hills and not a god of the valleys, I will deliver this vast army into your hands, and you will know that I am the LORD.'"

[29] For seven days they camped opposite each other, and on the seventh day the battle was joined. The Israelites inflicted a hundred thousand casualties on the Aramean foot soldiers in one day. [30] The rest of them escaped to the city of Aphek, where the wall collapsed on twenty-seven thousand of them. And Ben-Hadad fled to the city and hid in an inner room.

[31] His officials said to him, "Look, we have heard that the kings of Israel are merciful. Let us go to the king of Israel with sackcloth around our waists and ropes around our heads. Perhaps he will spare your life."

[32] Wearing sackcloth around their waists and ropes around their heads, they went to the king of Israel and said, "Your servant Ben-Hadad says: 'Please let me live.'"

The king answered, "Is he still alive? He is my brother."

[33] The men took this as a good sign and were quick to pick up his word. "Yes, your brother Ben-Hadad!" they said.

"Go and get him," the king said. When Ben-Hadad came out, Ahab had him come up into his chariot.

[34] "I will return the cities my father took from your father," Ben-Hadad offered. "You may set up your own market areas in Damascus, as my father did in Samaria."

Ahab said, "On the basis of a treaty I will set you free." So he made a treaty with him, and let him go.

---

[a] 12 Or in *Sukkoth*; also in verse 16

A Prophet Condemns Ahab

[35]By the word of the LORD one of the company of the prophets said to his companion, "Strike me with your weapon," but he refused.

[36]So the prophet said, "Because you have not obeyed the LORD, as soon as you leave me a lion will kill you." And after the man went away, a lion found him and killed him.

[37]The prophet found another man and said, "Strike me, please." So the man struck him and wounded him. [38]Then the prophet went and stood by the road waiting for the king. He disguised himself with his headband down over his eyes. [39]As the king passed by, the prophet called out to him, "Your servant went into the thick of the battle, and someone came to me with a captive and said, 'Guard this man. If he is missing, it will be your life for his life, or you must pay a talent[a] of silver.' [40]While your servant was busy here and there, the man disappeared."

"That is your sentence," the king of Israel said. "You have pronounced it yourself."

[41]Then the prophet quickly removed the headband from his eyes, and the king of Israel recognized him as one of the prophets. [42]He said to the king, "This is what the LORD says: 'You have set free a man I had determined should die.[b] Therefore it is your life for his life, your people for his people.'" [43]Sullen and angry, the king of Israel went to his palace in Samaria.

Naboth's Vineyard

21 Some time later there was an incident involving a vineyard belonging to Naboth the Jezreelite. The vineyard was in Jezreel, close to the palace of Ahab king of Samaria. [2]Ahab said to Naboth, "Let me have your vineyard to use for a vegetable garden, since it is close to my palace. In exchange I will give you a better vineyard or, if you prefer, I will pay you whatever it is worth."

[3]But Naboth replied, "The LORD forbid that I should give you the inheritance of my ancestors."

[4]So Ahab went home, sullen and angry because Naboth the Jezreelite had said, "I will not give you the inheritance of my ancestors." He lay on his bed sulking and refused to eat.

[5]His wife Jezebel came in and asked him, "Why are you so sullen? Why won't you eat?"

[6]He answered her, "Because I said to Naboth the Jezreelite, 'Sell me your vineyard; or if you prefer, I will give you another vineyard in its place.' But he said, 'I will not give you my vineyard.'"

[7]Jezebel his wife said, "Is this how you act as king over Israel? Get up and eat! Cheer up. I'll get you the vineyard of Naboth the Jezreelite."

[8]So she wrote letters in Ahab's name, placed his seal on them, and sent them to the elders and nobles who lived in Naboth's city with him. [9]In those letters she wrote:

"Proclaim a day of fasting and seat Naboth in a prominent place among the people. [10]But seat two scoundrels opposite him and have them bring charges that he has cursed both God and the king. Then take him out and stone him to death."

[11]So the elders and nobles who lived in Naboth's city did as Jezebel directed in the letters she had written to them. [12]They proclaimed a fast and seated Naboth in a prominent place among the people. [13]Then two scoundrels came and sat opposite him and brought charges against Naboth before the people, saying, "Naboth has cursed both God and the king." So they took him outside the city and stoned him to death. [14]Then they sent word to Jezebel: "Naboth has been stoned to death."

[15]As soon as Jezebel heard that Naboth had been stoned to death, she said to Ahab, "Get up and take possession of the vineyard of Naboth the Jezreelite that he refused to sell you. He is no longer alive, but dead." [16]When Ahab heard that Naboth was dead, he got up and went down to take possession of Naboth's vineyard.

[17]Then the word of the LORD came to Elijah the Tishbite: [18]"Go down to meet Ahab king of Israel, who rules in Samaria. He is now in Naboth's vineyard, where he has gone to take possession of it. [19]Say to him, 'This is what the LORD says: Have you not murdered a man and seized his property?' Then say to him, 'This is what the LORD says: In the place where dogs licked up Naboth's blood, dogs will lick up your blood—yes, yours!'"

[20]Ahab said to Elijah, "So you have found me, my enemy!"

"I have found you," he answered, "because you have sold yourself to do evil in the eyes of the LORD. [21]He says, 'I am going to bring disaster on you. I will wipe out your descendants and cut off from Ahab every last male in Israel—slave or free.[c] [22]I will make your house like that

---

[a] 39 That is, about 75 pounds or about 34 kilograms
[b] 42 The Hebrew term refers to the irrevocable giving over of things or persons to the LORD, often by totally destroying them.
[c] 21 Or Israel—every ruler or leader

of Jeroboam son of Nebat and that of Baasha son of Ahijah, because you have aroused my anger and have caused Israel to sin.'

²³"And also concerning Jezebel the LORD says: 'Dogs will devour Jezebel by the wall of*a* Jezreel.'

²⁴"Dogs will eat those belonging to Ahab who die in the city, and the birds will feed on those who die in the country."

²⁵(There was never anyone like Ahab, who sold himself to do evil in the eyes of the LORD, urged on by Jezebel his wife. ²⁶He behaved in the vilest manner by going after idols, like the Amorites the LORD drove out before Israel.)

²⁷When Ahab heard these words, he tore his clothes, put on sackcloth and fasted. He lay in sackcloth and went around meekly.

²⁸Then the word of the LORD came to Elijah the Tishbite: ²⁹"Have you noticed how Ahab has humbled himself before me? Because he has humbled himself, I will not bring this disaster in his day, but I will bring it on his house in the days of his son."

Micaiah Prophesies Against Ahab

22 For three years there was no war between Aram and Israel. ²But in the third year Jehoshaphat king of Judah went down to see the king of Israel. ³The king of Israel had said to his officials, "Don't you know that Ramoth Gilead belongs to us and yet we are doing nothing to retake it from the king of Aram?"

⁴So he asked Jehoshaphat, "Will you go with me to fight against Ramoth Gilead?"

Jehoshaphat replied to the king of Israel, "I am as you are, my people as your people, my horses as your horses." ⁵But Jehoshaphat also said to the king of Israel, "First seek the counsel of the LORD."

⁶So the king of Israel brought together the prophets — about four hundred men — and asked them, "Shall I go to war against Ramoth Gilead, or shall I refrain?"

"Go," they answered, "for the Lord will give it into the king's hand."

⁷But Jehoshaphat asked, "Is there no longer a prophet of the LORD here whom we can inquire of?"

⁸The king of Israel answered Jehoshaphat, "There is still one prophet through whom we can inquire of the LORD, but I hate him because he never prophesies anything good about me, but always bad. He is Micaiah son of Imlah."

"The king should not say such a thing," Jehoshaphat replied.

⁹So the king of Israel called one of his officials and said, "Bring Micaiah son of Imlah at once."

¹⁰Dressed in their royal robes, the king of Israel and Jehoshaphat king of Judah were sitting on their thrones at the threshing floor by the entrance of the gate of Samaria, with all the prophets prophesying before them. ¹¹Now Zedekiah son of Kenaanah had made iron horns and he declared, "This is what the LORD says: 'With these you will gore the Arameans until they are destroyed.'"

¹²All the other prophets were prophesying the same thing. "Attack Ramoth Gilead and be victorious," they said, "for the LORD will give it into the king's hand."

¹³The messenger who had gone to summon Micaiah said to him, "Look, the other prophets without exception are predicting success for the king. Let your word agree with theirs, and speak favorably."

¹⁴But Micaiah said, "As surely as the LORD lives, I can tell him only what the LORD tells me."

¹⁵When he arrived, the king asked him, "Micaiah, shall we go to war against Ramoth Gilead, or not?"

"Attack and be victorious," he answered, "for the LORD will give it into the king's hand."

¹⁶The king said to him, "How many times must I make you swear to tell me nothing but the truth in the name of the LORD?"

¹⁷Then Micaiah answered, "I saw all Israel scattered on the hills like sheep without a shepherd, and the LORD said, 'These people have no master. Let each one go home in peace.'"

¹⁸The king of Israel said to Jehoshaphat, "Didn't I tell you that he never prophesies anything good about me, but only bad?"

¹⁹Micaiah continued, "Therefore hear the word of the LORD: I saw the LORD sitting on his throne with all the multitudes of heaven standing around him on his right and on his left. ²⁰And the LORD said, 'Who will entice Ahab into attacking Ramoth Gilead and going to his death there?'

"One suggested this, and another that. ²¹Finally, a spirit came forward, stood before the LORD and said, 'I will entice him.'

²²"'By what means?' the LORD asked.

"'I will go out and be a deceiving spirit in the mouths of all his prophets,' he said.

"'You will succeed in enticing him,' said the LORD. 'Go and do it.'

---

a 23 Most Hebrew manuscripts; a few Hebrew manuscripts, Vulgate and Syriac (see also 2 Kings 9:26) *the plot of ground at*

²³"So now the LORD has put a deceiving spirit in the mouths of all these prophets of yours. The LORD has decreed disaster for you."

²⁴Then Zedekiah son of Kenaanah went up and slapped Micaiah in the face. "Which way did the spirit from*a* the LORD go when he went from me to speak to you?" he asked.

²⁵Micaiah replied, "You will find out on the day you go to hide in an inner room."

²⁶The king of Israel then ordered, "Take Micaiah and send him back to Amon the ruler of the city and to Joash the king's son ²⁷and say, 'This is what the king says: Put this fellow in prison and give him nothing but bread and water until I return safely.' "

²⁸Micaiah declared, "If you ever return safely, the LORD has not spoken through me." Then he added, "Mark my words, all you people!"

Ahab Killed at Ramoth Gilead

²⁹So the king of Israel and Jehoshaphat king of Judah went up to Ramoth Gilead. ³⁰The king of Israel said to Jehoshaphat, "I will enter the battle in disguise, but you wear your royal robes." So the king of Israel disguised himself and went into battle.

³¹Now the king of Aram had ordered his thirty-two chariot commanders, "Do not fight with anyone, small or great, except the king of Israel." ³²When the chariot commanders saw Jehoshaphat, they thought, "Surely this is the king of Israel." So they turned to attack him, but when Jehoshaphat cried out, ³³the chariot commanders saw that he was not the king of Israel and stopped pursuing him.

³⁴But someone drew his bow at random and hit the king of Israel between the sections of his armor. The king told his chariot driver, "Wheel around and get me out of the fighting. I've been wounded." ³⁵All day long the battle raged, and the king was propped up in his chariot facing the Arameans. The blood from his wound ran onto the floor of the chariot, and that evening he died. ³⁶As the sun was setting, a cry spread through the army: "Every man to his town. Every man to his land!"

³⁷So the king died and was brought to Samaria, and they buried him there. ³⁸They washed the chariot at a pool in Samaria (where the prostitutes bathed),*b* and the dogs licked up his blood, as the word of the LORD had declared.

³⁹As for the other events of Ahab's reign, including all he did, the palace he built and adorned with ivory, and the cities he fortified, are they not written in the book of the annals of the kings of Israel? ⁴⁰Ahab rested with his ancestors. And Ahaziah his son succeeded him as king.

Jehoshaphat King of Judah

⁴¹Jehoshaphat son of Asa became king of Judah in the fourth year of Ahab king of Israel. ⁴²Jehoshaphat was thirty-five years old when he became king, and he reigned in Jerusalem twenty-five years. His mother's name was Azubah daughter of Shilhi. ⁴³In everything he followed the ways of his father Asa and did not stray from them; he did what was right in the eyes of the LORD. The high places, however, were not removed, and the people continued to offer sacrifices and burn incense there.*c* ⁴⁴Jehoshaphat was also at peace with the king of Israel.

⁴⁵As for the other events of Jehoshaphat's reign, the things he achieved and his military exploits, are they not written in the book of the annals of the kings of Judah? ⁴⁶He rid the land of the rest of the male shrine prostitutes who remained there even after the reign of his father Asa. ⁴⁷There was then no king in Edom; a provincial governor ruled.

⁴⁸Now Jehoshaphat built a fleet of trading ships*d* to go to Ophir for gold, but they never set sail—they were wrecked at Ezion Geber. ⁴⁹At that time Ahaziah son of Ahab said to Jehoshaphat, "Let my men sail with yours," but Jehoshaphat refused.

⁵⁰Then Jehoshaphat rested with his ancestors and was buried with them in the city of David his father. And Jehoram his son succeeded him as king.

Ahaziah King of Israel

⁵¹Ahaziah son of Ahab became king of Israel in Samaria in the seventeenth year of Jehoshaphat king of Judah, and he reigned over Israel two years. ⁵²He did evil in the eyes of the LORD, because he followed the ways of his father and mother and of Jeroboam son of Nebat, who caused Israel to sin. ⁵³He served and worshiped Baal and aroused the anger of the LORD, the God of Israel, just as his father had done.

---

a 24 Or *Spirit of*   *b* 38 Or *Samaria and cleaned the weapons*
c 43 In Hebrew texts this sentence (22:43b) is numbered 22:44, and 22:44-53 is numbered 22:45-54.   *d* 48 Hebrew *of ships of Tarshish*

INTRODUCTION TO
2 KINGS

Final Days of the Divided Kingdom

The second book of the kings of Israel and Judah describes the final days of the divided kingdom before both halves fall into captivity. As much as anything, it is a story of failed leadership.

God had a difficult time finding leaders with character, competence, and compassion for the people. The people consistently reflect the deficiencies of their leaders, just as the Law of Magnetism would predict.

Many have said that leaders cannot lead others beyond where they have gone themselves. It's true. The division of Israel and Judah simply reflects the divided heart of each leader. To whom would each king show allegiance? To be sure, some good kings arise and bring about positive reform. Once they die, however, the new leaders neglect to follow through on the reforms, and the people return to their rebellion and apathy. Second Kings offers a sad commentary on the human condition. We discover far more negative than positive leadership examples in this book.

A few highlights may be noted, however. The prophets Elijah and Elisha never back off of their uncompromising message. Elijah ministers to the ruling elite of Israel, while Elisha focuses on the common people of many nations. King Hezekiah enjoys a personal renewal during his reign, then asks for his days to be lengthened so he can finish needed reforms. God lengthens his life and Hezekiah makes a difference. God also uses another good leader, the prophet Isaiah, to speak into Hezekiah's life and to carry the answer to his prayers. King Josiah goes down as one of the few good kings in Judah. He ascends to the throne at eight years of age, and before he

God's Role in 2 Kings

As he did in 1 Kings, God spends most of his time beckoning leaders to follow him. When they do so, he displays his goodness, answers their prayers, and provides for their needs.

Unfortunately, most Hebrew leaders pay little attention to him. Even when the prophets confront them, they listen only when the news tickles their fancy. Most either abandon the true God for Baal worship, or consider Yahweh a mere superstition to be held for good luck (the continuing practice of many current political leaders). Still, God chose to speak to these leaders through his prophets.

Leaders in 2 Kings

Elijah, Elisha, Joram, Ben-Hadad, Hazael, Ahaziah, Jehu, Jezebel, Ahab, Joash, Ahaz, Isaiah, Hezekiah, Josiah, Nebuchadnezzar

Other People of Influence in 2 Kings

Jehoiada, Naaman, Gehazi, the Babylonians, the Assyrians

Lessons in Leadership

- The measure of a man is what he does with power.
- Choose your mentors well and ask for what you want.
- Don't sweat the small stuff—think strategically as you make your battle plans.

dies, he leads Judah in massive repentance and reform, beginning with the renovation of the house of the Lord.

Unfortunately, these strong, healthy spiritual leaders make up the minority in 2 Kings. Most of the book chronicles the decline and fall of both Israel and Judah, beginning with their leaders. The book illustrates repeatedly that leaders never find what they are looking for when they abandon the higher cause of God for their own interests.

- Stay focused with your mission; stay flexible with your methods.
- Maintain an eternal perspective.
- If you compromise the ultimate, you'll become slave to the immediate.
- Never underestimate the power of God.
- Outward, public reform begins with inward, personal renewal.

LEADERSHIP HIGHLIGHTS IN 2 KINGS

The LORD's Judgment on Ahaziah

1 After Ahab's death, Moab rebelled against Israel. [2]Now Ahaziah had fallen through the lattice of his upper room in Samaria and injured himself. So he sent messengers, saying to them, "Go and consult Baal-Zebub, the god of Ekron, to see if I will recover from this injury."

[3]But the angel of the LORD said to Elijah the Tishbite, "Go up and meet the messengers of the king of Samaria and ask them, 'Is it because there is no God in Israel that you are going off to consult Baal-Zebub, the god of Ekron?' [4]Therefore this is what the LORD says: 'You will not leave the bed you are lying on. You will certainly die!' " So Elijah went.

[5]When the messengers returned to the king, he asked them, "Why have you come back?"

[6]"A man came to meet us," they replied. "And he said to us, 'Go back to the king who sent you and tell him, "This is what the LORD says: Is it because there is no God in Israel that you are sending messengers to consult Baal-Zebub, the god of Ekron? Therefore you will not leave the bed you are lying on. You will certainly die!" ' "

[7]The king asked them, "What kind of man was it who came to meet you and told you this?"

[8]They replied, "He had a garment of hair[a] and had a leather belt around his waist."

The king said, "That was Elijah the Tishbite."

[9]Then he sent to Elijah a captain with his company of fifty men. The captain went up to Elijah, who was sitting on the top of a hill, and said to him, "Man of God, the king says, 'Come down!' "

[10]Elijah answered the captain, "If I am a man of God, may fire come down from heaven and consume you and your fifty men!" Then fire fell from heaven and consumed the captain and his men.

[11]At this the king sent to Elijah another captain with his fifty men. The captain said to him, "Man of God, this is what the king says, 'Come down at once!' "

[12]"If I am a man of God," Elijah replied, "may fire come down from heaven and consume you and your fifty men!" Then the fire of God fell from heaven and consumed him and his fifty men.

[13]So the king sent a third captain with his fifty men. This third captain went up and fell on his knees before Elijah. "Man of God," he begged, "please have respect for my life and the lives of these fifty men, your servants! [14]See, fire has fallen from heaven and consumed the first two captains and all their men. But now have respect for my life!"

[15]The angel of the LORD said to Elijah, "Go down with him; do not be afraid of him." So Elijah got up and went down with him to the king.

[16]He told the king, "This is what the LORD says: Is it because there is no God in Israel for you to consult that you have sent messengers to consult Baal-Zebub, the god of Ekron? Because you have done this, you will never leave the bed you are lying on. You will certainly die!" [17]So he died, according to the word of the LORD that Elijah had spoken.

---

[a] 8 Or *He was a hairy man*

The Measure of a Man Is How He Handles Power

2 Kings 1:1–17

When Ahaziah, the king of Israel, injured himself in a fall, he wanted to know whether he would recover—but he inquired of the false god Baal, not of Yahweh, the God of Israel. This angered the Lord, who sent a prophecy through Elijah to the king, informing him that he would die.

The king in turn sent a captain and 50 soldiers to capture Elijah, but the prophet called down fire from heaven and killed them. After this happened a second time, a third delegation approached Elijah and begged for mercy. An angel told the prophet to go with the men and visit the king.

We can make some observations about this episode. Notice the humanity of this great prophet:

1. **Elijah possessed both spiritual authority and anxiety at the same time (vv. 13–15).**

2. **Elijah spoke harshly and with power (vv. 10, 12).**

3. **Elijah showed no respect for the authority of the king (vv. 9–14).**

4. **Elijah required an angel to appear to confirm that he should spare the soldiers and go with them to meet the king (v. 15).**

Because Ahaziah had no son, Joram[a] succeeded him as king in the second year of Jehoram son of Jehoshaphat king of Judah. [18]As for all the other events of Ahaziah's reign, and what he did, are they not written in the book of the annals of the kings of Israel?

Elijah Taken Up to Heaven

2 When the LORD was about to take Elijah up to heaven in a whirlwind, Elijah and Elisha were on their way from Gilgal. [2]Elijah said to Elisha, "Stay here; the LORD has sent me to Bethel."

But Elisha said, "As surely as the LORD lives and as you live, I will not leave you." So they went down to Bethel.

[3]The company of the prophets at Bethel came out to Elisha and asked, "Do you know that the LORD is going to take your master from you today?"

"Yes, I know," Elisha replied, "so be quiet."

[4]Then Elijah said to him, "Stay here, Elisha; the LORD has sent me to Jericho."

And he replied, "As surely as the LORD lives and as you live, I will not leave you." So they went to Jericho.

[5]The company of the prophets at Jericho went up to Elisha and asked him, "Do you know that the LORD is going to take your master from you today?"

"Yes, I know," he replied, "so be quiet."

[6]Then Elijah said to him, "Stay here; the LORD has sent me to the Jordan."

And he replied, "As surely as the LORD lives and as you live, I will not leave you." So the two of them walked on.

[7]Fifty men from the company of the prophets went and stood at a distance, facing the place where Elijah and Elisha had stopped at the Jordan. [8]Elijah took his cloak, rolled it up and struck the water with it. The water divided to the right and to the left, and the two of them crossed over on dry ground.

[9]When they had crossed, Elijah said to Elisha, "Tell me, what can I do for you before I am taken from you?"

"Let me inherit a double portion of your spirit," Elisha replied.

[10]"You have asked a difficult thing," Elijah said, "yet if you see me when I am taken from you, it will be yours — otherwise, it will not."

[11]As they were walking along and talking together, suddenly a chariot of fire and horses of fire appeared and separated the two of them, and Elijah went up to heaven in a whirlwind. [12]Elisha saw this and cried out, "My father! My father! The chariots and horsemen of Israel!" And Elisha saw him no more. Then he took hold of his garment and tore it in two.

---

[a] 17 Hebrew *Jehoram*, a variant of *Joram*

Choose Your Mentors Well: Elisha Risks the "Big Ask"

2 Kings 2:9–10

Every leader needs mentors, especially emerging leaders. After watching the great Elijah for many years, Elisha reached down and found the guts to ask Elijah for a double portion of his spirit.

God took Elisha through the preparation necessary under Elijah. The younger man waited for the right time, then made his request. The result? Scripture records that Elisha performed twice as many miracles as did his mentor. Note several principles outlined in 1 Kings 19 and 2 Kings 2 underlying his preparation:

Elisha's Preparation	Leadership Principle
1. He was anointed to replace Elijah.	1. Leaders must understand their call and role.
2. Elijah found him plowing a field.	2. Leaders must have a servant's heart.
3. Elisha touched Elijah's mantle long before he entered his ministry.	3. Leaders must wait patiently on God's perfect timing for their authority.
4. He asked to kiss his parents good-bye.	4. Leaders must respect parental authority.
5. He burned his farming tools.	5. Leaders must surrender former ambitions.
6. He stuck with Elijah wherever he went.	6. Leaders must pursue good mentors.
7. He absorbed all he could from Elijah.	7. Leaders must hunger to grow and develop.

THE LAW OF MAGNETISM
Elijah and Elisha Cut from the Same Cloth

2 Kings 2:1–15

EFFECTIVE LEADERS are always on the lookout for good people. Each of us carries around a mental list of what kind of people we would like in our organization. Believe it or not, whom you get is not determined by what you want, but by who you are. In most situations, you draw people who possess the same qualities you do.

It is possible for a leader to go out and recruit people unlike himself, but it's crucial to recognize that people who are different will not naturally be attracted to him. Their quality does not depend on a hiring process, a human resources department, or even what you consider to be the quality of your area's applicant pool. It depends on you. If you think the people you attract could be better, then it's time for you to improve yourself.

■　■　■　■　■

What enabled Elijah to draw like-minded people to his side? The answer is found in the Law of Magnetism. Who you are is who you attract.

1. *Every leader has a measure of magnetism.*

    All leaders attract others. Highly charismatic leaders often attract large numbers of followers, but even modest leaders gain a following. If they didn't, they wouldn't be leaders, would they?

2. *A leader's magnetism may impact others intellectually, emotionally, or volitionally.*

Not all leaders affect people in the same way, nor do they use the same means of influence. The greatest leaders connect on multiple levels: with followers' minds, hearts and wills.

Elijah's magnetism affected others on every level. When he defeated the false prophets of Baal, he connected with the people first by calling down fire from heaven so even confirmed skeptics saw the reality of God. But that alone was not enough. To give his message more emotional impact, Elijah drenched his sacrifice in gallons of water. When God's fire licked up the sacrifice, water and all, the people declared, "The LORD—he is God!" (1Ki 18:39). And the prophet connected on a volitional level when he cried, "Seize the prophets of Baal" (18:40) and the people obeyed.

3. *Magnetism is neither good nor bad in itself—it depends on what a leader does with it.*

Charismatic leaders come in all shapes and sizes. There are Adolf Hitlers and Mother Teresas, Ahabs and Elijahs. Magnetism is like money; it's a useful tool, neither good nor bad in itself. Elijah used his ability to attract like-minded people in order to fulfill his mission and extend his influence.

4. *Secure leaders draw both similar and complementary followers.*

All leaders tend to attract people similar to themselves in values, age, attitude, etc. Elijah's leadership attracted people who loved God and who were gifted in prophecy. But secure leaders—ones who acknowledge and accept their weaknesses as well as their strengths—also attract people with complementary abilities.

5. *A leader's magnetism never remains static.*

A leader can cultivate, shape, and mature his magnetism. Before Elijah drew crowds, he labored in obscurity, helping a widow and her son. God provided him with time to cultivate a vision for his life, to make his purpose clear, and to give him confidence. All those things increased his level of magnetism.

It's More Than Mere Chemistry

Mutual attraction is more than chemistry. At least four elements combine to make it happen:

1. *Mutual Vision*

Followers do not naturally line up with a leader whose vision they don't respect. Both Elijah and Elisha possessed a vision to serve God for the sake of Israel. When Elisha had the opportunity to share Elijah's work, he turned from his old life of farming and adopted Elijah's vision of leadership.

2. *Mutual Expectations*

Mutual expectations develop naturally from mutual vision. Both Elijah and Elisha expected to do great things for God. Elisha expected and received a double portion of the anointing on Elijah.

3. *Mutual Contribution*

Individuals follow leaders because they believe those leaders can take them where they want to go. Leaders enlist followers because they understand that followers help them to realize their vision. Each contributes something to fulfill the other's expectations. Elijah led and mentored Elisha, giving him the opportunity to learn how to be a godly leader. Elisha needed to humble himself, follow the older prophet, and learn. The arrangement made both of them better leaders.

4. *Mutual Commitment*

Without a strong mutual commitment, leaders and followers cannot achieve their mutual goals. As Elijah neared the end of his leadership, Elisha renewed his commitment to his mentor. Three times when Elijah offered to release his protégé, Elisha responded, "As surely as the LORD lives and as you live, I will not leave you" (2Ki 2:2, 4, 6). Elijah's commitment to Elisha had grown equally strong, culminating in his offer to do whatever he could for his servant—including the blessing of a double portion of his spirit.

Do You Like What You See?

What do you have to offer followers? Is the attraction mutual?

You will discover a lot about yourself by looking at the people your leadership has been attracting. What you observe may please you, but if you aren't getting the kind or the number of followers you'd like, there's good news. You need not be stuck where you are. You can grow and change in this area of your leadership.

[13]Elisha then picked up Elijah's cloak that had fallen from him and went back and stood on the bank of the Jordan. [14]He took the cloak that had fallen from Elijah and struck the water with it. "Where now is the LORD, the God of Elijah?" he asked. When he struck the water, it divided to the right and to the left, and he crossed over.

[15]The company of the prophets from Jericho, who were watching, said, "The spirit of Elijah is resting on Elisha." And they went to meet him and bowed to the ground before him. [16]"Look," they said, "we your servants have fifty able men. Let them go and look for your master. Perhaps the Spirit of the LORD has picked him up and set him down on some mountain or in some valley." "No," Elisha replied, "do not send them."

[17]But they persisted until he was too embarrassed to refuse. So he said, "Send them." And they sent fifty men, who searched for three days but did not find him. [18]When they returned to Elisha, who was staying in Jericho, he said to them, "Didn't I tell you not to go?"

Healing of the Water

[19]The people of the city said to Elisha, "Look, our lord, this town is well situated, as you can see, but the water is bad and the land is unproductive."

[20]"Bring me a new bowl," he said, "and put salt in it." So they brought it to him.

[21]Then he went out to the spring and threw the salt into it, saying, "This is what the LORD says: 'I have healed this water. Never again will it cause death or make the land unproductive.'" [22]And the water has remained pure to this day, according to the word Elisha had spoken.

Elisha Is Jeered

[23]From there Elisha went up to Bethel. As he was walking along the road, some boys came out of the town and jeered at him. "Get out of here, baldy!" they said. "Get out of here, baldy!" [24]He turned around, looked at them and called down a curse on them in the name of the LORD. Then two bears came out of the woods and mauled forty-two of the boys. [25]And he went on to Mount Carmel and from there returned to Samaria.

Moab Revolts

3 Joram[a] son of Ahab became king of Israel in Samaria in the eighteenth year of Jehoshaphat king of Judah, and he reigned twelve years. [2]He did evil in the eyes of the LORD, but not as his father and mother had done. He got rid of the sacred stone of Baal that his father had made. [3]Nevertheless he clung to the sins of Jeroboam son of Nebat, which he had caused Israel to commit; he did not turn away from them.

[4]Now Mesha king of Moab raised sheep, and he had to pay the king of Israel a tribute of a hundred thousand lambs and the wool of a hundred thousand rams. [5]But after Ahab died, the king of Moab rebelled against the king of Israel. [6]So at that time King Joram set out from Samaria and mobilized all Israel. [7]He also sent this message to Jehoshaphat king of Judah: "The king of Moab has rebelled against me. Will you go with me to fight against Moab?"

"I will go with you," he replied. "I am as you are, my people as your people, my horses as your horses."

[8]"By what route shall we attack?" he asked.

"Through the Desert of Edom," he answered.

[9]So the king of Israel set out with the king of Judah and the king of Edom. After a roundabout march of seven days, the army had no more water for themselves or for the animals with them.

[10]"What!" exclaimed the king of Israel. "Has the LORD called us three kings together only to deliver us into the hands of Moab?"

[11]But Jehoshaphat asked, "Is there no prophet of the LORD here, through whom we may inquire of the LORD?"

An officer of the king of Israel answered, "Elisha son of Shaphat is here. He used to pour water on the hands of Elijah.[b]"

[12]Jehoshaphat said, "The word of the LORD is with him." So the king of Israel and Jehoshaphat and the king of Edom went down to him.

[13]Elisha said to the king of Israel, "Why do you want to involve me? Go to the prophets of your father and the prophets of your mother."

"No," the king of Israel answered, "because it was the LORD who called us three kings together to deliver us into the hands of Moab."

[14]Elisha said, "As surely as the LORD Almighty lives, whom I serve, if I did not have respect for the presence of Jehoshaphat king of Judah, I would not pay any attention to you. [15]But now bring me a harpist."

While the harpist was playing, the hand of the LORD came on Elisha [16]and he said, "This is what the LORD says: I will fill this valley with pools of water. [17]For this is what the LORD says: You will see neither wind nor rain, yet this valley will be filled with water, and you, your cattle and your other animals will drink. [18]This is an easy thing in the eyes of the LORD; he will also deliver

---

[a] 1 Hebrew *Jehoram*, a variant of *Joram*; also in verse 6
[b] 11 That is, he was Elijah's personal servant.

Moab into your hands. ¹⁹You will overthrow every fortified city and every major town. You will cut down every good tree, stop up all the springs, and ruin every good field with stones."

²⁰The next morning, about the time for offering the sacrifice, there it was — water flowing from the direction of Edom! And the land was filled with water.

²¹Now all the Moabites had heard that the kings had come to fight against them; so every man, young and old, who could bear arms was called up and stationed on the border. ²²When

The Law of Intuition: Good Leaders Think Strategically

2 Kings 3:9–27

The kings of Judah, Israel and Edom ally themselves to fight Moab. But in the middle of the desert they make a horrifying discovery: They have run out of water! Panic strikes until they remember Elisha and his connection to the God of miracles.

Elisha responds differently to their request than they had imagined. He declares God will give them plenty of water—that was easy. But he also predicts God will give them Moab itself (2Ki 3:17–18)!

The principle is this: These kings were diverted from their big-picture mission with a logistical matter. No doubt, water was important. But God reminded them that they had asked only for the small thing, not the ultimate thing.

Years ago, *Discipleship Journal* published an article on this very lesson. Our prayers as leaders must become strategic.

- **Logistical prayer:** We pray logistically when we ask God for the small things: "Lord, help the microphones to work today as I teach."
- **Tactical prayer:** We pray tactically when we pray for more meaningful things, but still not for the ultimate: "Lord, help me to say something meaningful today to my people."
- **Strategic prayer:** We pray strategically when we pray for the ultimate purposes of God: "Lord, may you be glorified today and may you raise up disciples from this meeting."

they got up early in the morning, the sun was shining on the water. To the Moabites across the way, the water looked red — like blood. ²³"That's blood!" they said. "Those kings must have fought and slaughtered each other. Now to the plunder, Moab!"

²⁴But when the Moabites came to the camp of Israel, the Israelites rose up and fought them until they fled. And the Israelites invaded the land and slaughtered the Moabites. ²⁵They destroyed the towns, and each man threw a stone on every good field until it was covered. They stopped up all the springs and cut down every good tree. Only Kir Hareseth was left with its stones in place, but men armed with slings surrounded it and attacked it.

²⁶When the king of Moab saw that the battle had gone against him, he took with him seven hundred swordsmen to break through to the king of Edom, but they failed. ²⁷Then he took his firstborn son, who was to succeed him as king, and offered him as a sacrifice on the city wall. The fury against Israel was great; they withdrew and returned to their own land.

The Widow's Olive Oil

4 The wife of a man from the company of the prophets cried out to Elisha, "Your servant my husband is dead, and you know that he revered the LORD. But now his creditor is coming to take my two boys as his slaves."

²Elisha replied to her, "How can I help you? Tell me, what do you have in your house?"

"Your servant has nothing there at all," she said, "except a small jar of olive oil."

³Elisha said, "Go around and ask all your neighbors for empty jars. Don't ask for just a few. ⁴Then go inside and shut the door behind you and your sons. Pour oil into all the jars, and as each is filled, put it to one side."

⁵She left him and shut the door behind her and her sons. They brought the jars to her and she kept pouring. ⁶When all the jars were full, she said to her son, "Bring me another one."

But he replied, "There is not a jar left." Then the oil stopped flowing.

⁷She went and told the man of God, and he said, "Go, sell the oil and pay your debts. You and your sons can live on what is left."

The Shunammite's Son Restored to Life

⁸One day Elisha went to Shunem. And a well-to-do woman was there, who urged him to stay for a meal. So whenever he came by, he stopped there to eat. ⁹She said to her husband, "I know that this man who often comes our way is a holy

Running on Empty: Leadership and Brokenness

2 Kings 4:1–7

Did you know that emptiness can be a wonderful gift? That's the lesson a destitute woman learned from the prophet Elisha.

One day Elisha meets a woman with nothing—no husband, no income, no food, no prospects. The prophet tells her to gather what she has, and she returns with a jar of oil and several empty jars from neighbors. She begins to pour her oil into the empty jars, and she just keeps on pouring until all the jars are full. Only then does the oil in the first jar run out. Interestingly, the woman gets as much oil as she has empty jars.

There is something about "nothing" that moves God's hand. He loves leading us to empty places where we can lean on nothing except his provision. If we are not experiencing God's presence and provision, could it be that we aren't empty enough? Could we still be distracted and dependent on ourselves? This story teaches us that . . .

1. **Emptiness is a gift from the Lord.**

2. **Emptiness tells us we have a need.**

3. **It is possible that we may not be empty enough.**

4. **We must admit our emptiness.**

5. **Only God can truly fill us.**

man of God. ¹⁰Let's make a small room on the roof and put in it a bed and a table, a chair and a lamp for him. Then he can stay there whenever he comes to us."

¹¹One day when Elisha came, he went up to his room and lay down there. ¹²He said to his servant Gehazi, "Call the Shunammite." So he called her, and she stood before him. ¹³Elisha said to him, "Tell her, 'You have gone to all this trouble for us. Now what can be done for you? Can we speak on your behalf to the king or the commander of the army?'"

She replied, "I have a home among my own people."

¹⁴"What can be done for her?" Elisha asked.

Gehazi said, "She has no son, and her husband is old."

¹⁵Then Elisha said, "Call her." So he called her, and she stood in the doorway. ¹⁶"About this time next year," Elisha said, "you will hold a son in your arms."

"No, my lord!" she objected. "Please, man of God, don't mislead your servant!"

¹⁷But the woman became pregnant, and the next year about that same time she gave birth to a son, just as Elisha had told her.

¹⁸The child grew, and one day he went out to his father, who was with the reapers. ¹⁹He said to his father, "My head! My head!"

His father told a servant, "Carry him to his mother." ²⁰After the servant had lifted him up and carried him to his mother, the boy sat on her lap until noon, and then he died. ²¹She went up and laid him on the bed of the man of God, then shut the door and went out.

²²She called her husband and said, "Please send me one of the servants and a donkey so I can go to the man of God quickly and return."

²³"Why go to him today?" he asked. "It's not the New Moon or the Sabbath."

"That's all right," she said.

²⁴She saddled the donkey and said to her servant, "Lead on; don't slow down for me unless I tell you." ²⁵So she set out and came to the man of God at Mount Carmel.

When he saw her in the distance, the man of God said to his servant Gehazi, "Look! There's the Shunammite! ²⁶Run to meet her and ask her, 'Are you all right? Is your husband all right? Is your child all right?'"

"Everything is all right," she said.

²⁷When she reached the man of God at the mountain, she took hold of his feet. Gehazi came over to push her away, but the man of God said, "Leave her alone! She is in bitter distress, but the LORD has hidden it from me and has not told me why."

²⁸"Did I ask you for a son, my lord?" she said. "Didn't I tell you, 'Don't raise my hopes'?"

²⁹Elisha said to Gehazi, "Tuck your cloak into your belt, take my staff in your hand and run. Don't greet anyone you meet, and if anyone greets you, do not answer. Lay my staff on the boy's face."

³⁰But the child's mother said, "As surely as the LORD lives and as you live, I will not leave you." So he got up and followed her.

³¹Gehazi went on ahead and laid the staff on the boy's face, but there was no sound or response. So Gehazi went back to meet Elisha and told him, "The boy has not awakened."

³²When Elisha reached the house, there was

the boy lying dead on his couch. [33]He went in, shut the door on the two of them and prayed to the LORD. [34]Then he got on the bed and lay on the boy, mouth to mouth, eyes to eyes, hands to hands. As he stretched himself out on him, the boy's body grew warm. [35]Elisha turned away and walked back and forth in the room and then got on the bed and stretched out on him once more. The boy sneezed seven times and opened his eyes.

[36]Elisha summoned Gehazi and said, "Call the Shunammite." And he did. When she came, he said, "Take your son." [37]She came in, fell at his feet and bowed to the ground. Then she took her son and went out.

Death in the Pot

[38]Elisha returned to Gilgal and there was a famine in that region. While the company of the prophets was meeting with him, he said to his servant, "Put on the large pot and cook some stew for these prophets."

[39]One of them went out into the fields to gather herbs and found a wild vine and picked as many of its gourds as his garment could hold. When he returned, he cut them up into the pot of stew, though no one knew what they were. [40]The stew was poured out for the men, but as they began to eat it, they cried out, "Man of God, there is death in the pot!" And they could not eat it.

[41]Elisha said, "Get some flour." He put it into the pot and said, "Serve it to the people to eat." And there was nothing harmful in the pot.

Feeding of a Hundred

[42]A man came from Baal Shalishah, bringing the man of God twenty loaves of barley bread baked from the first ripe grain, along with some heads of new grain. "Give it to the people to eat," Elisha said.

[43]"How can I set this before a hundred men?" his servant asked.

But Elisha answered, "Give it to the people to eat. For this is what the LORD says: 'They will eat and have some left over.'" [44]Then he set it before them, and they ate and had some left over, according to the word of the LORD.

Naaman Healed of Leprosy

5 Now Naaman was commander of the army of the king of Aram. He was a great man in the sight of his master and highly regarded, because through him the LORD had given victory to Aram. He was a valiant soldier, but he had leprosy.[a]

[2]Now bands of raiders from Aram had gone out and had taken captive a young girl from

---

[a] 1 The Hebrew for leprosy was used for various diseases affecting the skin; also in verses 3, 6, 7, 11 and 27.

ELISHA

A Prophet with Heart
2 Kings 4:1–44

PROFILE in leadership

His name sounds a lot like that of his mentor, Elijah. Both prophets struggled against the idolatrous Baal cult; both wielded great influence over the leaders of their day. But they differed markedly in how they carried out their spiritual duties.

The prophet Elisha relied more on miracles than did his fiery mentor, Elijah, and a greater number of his signs and wonders demonstrated God's mercy and gentleness. The Bible says Elisha performed twice as many miracles as Elijah and more wonders than any Old Testament character other than Moses.

But while these two men differed in their methods, they pursued the same objective: to turn their people from idolatry and bring them back to the true and living God.

In a way, the differences between Elijah and Elisha reflect the complex nature of the God they served. Elijah most often proclaimed God's judgment and wrath, while Elisha tended to declare his love and grace. Together they provide a human illustration of Romans 11:22, which urges us to "consider . . . the kindness and sternness of God."

The life of Elisha demonstrates that God uses leaders of all kinds, both those who emphasize his judgment and wrath and those who draw men and women to himself through tender demonstrations of divine love and grace.

Israel, and she served Naaman's wife. ³She said to her mistress, "If only my master would see the prophet who is in Samaria! He would cure him of his leprosy."

⁴Naaman went to his master and told him what the girl from Israel had said. ⁵"By all means, go," the king of Aram replied. "I will send a letter to the king of Israel." So Naaman left, taking with him ten talents*a* of silver, six thousand shekels*b* of gold and ten sets of clothing. ⁶The letter that he took to the king of Israel read: "With this letter I am sending my servant Naaman to you so that you may cure him of his leprosy."

⁷As soon as the king of Israel read the letter, he tore his robes and said, "Am I God? Can I kill and bring back to life? Why does this fellow send someone to me to be cured of his leprosy? See how he is trying to pick a quarrel with me!"

⁸When Elisha the man of God heard that the king of Israel had torn his robes, he sent him this message: "Why have you torn your robes? Have the man come to me and he will know that there is a prophet in Israel." ⁹So Naaman went with his horses and chariots and stopped at the door of Elisha's house. ¹⁰Elisha sent a messenger to say to him, "Go, wash yourself seven times in the Jordan, and your flesh will be restored and you will be cleansed."

¹¹But Naaman went away angry and said, "I thought that he would surely come out to me and stand and call on the name of the LORD his God, wave his hand over the spot and cure me of my leprosy. ¹²Are not Abana and Pharpar, the rivers of Damascus, better than all the waters of Israel? Couldn't I wash in them and be cleansed?" So he turned and went off in a rage.

¹³Naaman's servants went to him and said, "My father, if the prophet had told you to do some great thing, would you not have done it? How much more, then, when he tells you, 'Wash and be cleansed'!" ¹⁴So he went down and dipped himself in the Jordan seven times, as the man of God had told him, and his flesh was restored and became clean like that of a young boy.

¹⁵Then Naaman and all his attendants went back to the man of God. He stood before him

---

a 5 That is, about 750 pounds or about 340 kilograms
b 5 That is, about 150 pounds or about 69 kilograms

NAAMAN

A New Lesson Learned
2 Kings 5:1–14

PROFILE in leadership

Naaman, one of the great military leaders of his time, had earned the love and respect of his king. Yet for all his strength and might, Naaman suffered from the dreaded disease of leprosy. When his king learned of a Hebrew prophet named Elisha who might be able to help, he sent Naaman off with great expectations, perhaps anticipating a grand healing in the courts of a great man.

But rather than an impressive meeting with the prophet, Naaman received instructions (by messenger) to wash seven times in the Jordan River. This enraged Naaman and he angrily refused to follow the prescription. He wasn't teachable. He struggled with pride, faulty expectations and inflexibility. Much like many leaders today . . .

1. **He wanted a quick fix.**
2. **He expected special treatment.**
3. **He held certain assumptions about a solution.**
4. **He grew angry about perceived unfair treatment.**
5. **He rejected the new solution.**

Yet as a strong leader, Naaman had surrounded himself with individuals who could speak up and disagree with him, and his inner circle provided good counsel. Naaman changed his mind, followed the prophet's directives, and was healed.

Leaders who remain teachable receive ongoing and sometimes unexpected blessings. But unteachable leaders will be left behind as our world changes and as God does new things in our culture.

and said, "Now I know that there is no God in all the world except in Israel. So please accept a gift from your servant."

[16] The prophet answered, "As surely as the LORD lives, whom I serve, I will not accept a thing." And even though Naaman urged him, he refused.

[17] "If you will not," said Naaman, "please let me, your servant, be given as much earth as a pair of mules can carry, for your servant will never again make burnt offerings and sacrifices to any other god but the LORD. [18] But may the LORD forgive your servant for this one thing: When my master enters the temple of Rimmon to bow down and he is leaning on my arm and I have to bow there also — when I bow down in the temple of Rimmon, may the LORD forgive your servant for this."

[19] "Go in peace," Elisha said.

After Naaman had traveled some distance, [20] Gehazi, the servant of Elisha the man of God, said to himself, "My master was too easy on Naaman, this Aramean, by not accepting from him what he brought. As surely as the LORD lives, I will run after him and get something from him."

[21] So Gehazi hurried after Naaman. When Naaman saw him running toward him, he got down from the chariot to meet him. "Is everything all right?" he asked.

[22] "Everything is all right," Gehazi answered. "My master sent me to say, 'Two young men from the company of the prophets have just come to me from the hill country of Ephraim. Please give them a talent[a] of silver and two sets of clothing.'"

[23] "By all means, take two talents," said Naaman. He urged Gehazi to accept them, and then tied up the two talents of silver in two bags, with two sets of clothing. He gave them to two of his servants, and they carried them ahead of Gehazi. [24] When Gehazi came to the hill, he took the things from the servants and put them away in the house. He sent the men away and they left.

[25] When he went in and stood before his master, Elisha asked him, "Where have you been, Gehazi?"

"Your servant didn't go anywhere," Gehazi answered.

[26] But Elisha said to him, "Was not my spirit with you when the man got down from his chariot to meet you? Is this the time to take money or to accept clothes — or olive groves and vineyards, or flocks and herds, or male and female slaves? [27] Naaman's leprosy will cling to you and to your descendants forever." Then Gehazi went

Accountability: Gehazi Got Some from Elisha

2 Kings 5:15–27

Elisha turned down the money and gifts Naaman offered him, but Elisha's servant, Gehazi, went after them by rationalizing his greed. Like Gehazi, we possess a boundless ability to deceive ourselves. That is why leaders need others to ask them difficult questions. We must welcome accountability partners.

from Elisha's presence and his skin was leprous — it had become as white as snow.

An Axhead Floats

6 The company of the prophets said to Elisha, "Look, the place where we meet with you is too small for us. [2] Let us go to the Jordan, where each of us can get a pole; and let us build a place there for us to meet."

And he said, "Go."

[3] Then one of them said, "Won't you please come with your servants?"

"I will," Elisha replied. [4] And he went with them.

They went to the Jordan and began to cut down trees. [5] As one of them was cutting down a tree, the iron axhead fell into the water. "Oh no, my lord!" he cried out. "It was borrowed!"

[6] The man of God asked, "Where did it fall?" When he showed him the place, Elisha cut a stick and threw it there, and made the iron float. [7] "Lift it out," he said. Then the man reached out his hand and took it.

Elisha Traps Blinded Arameans

[8] Now the king of Aram was at war with Israel. After conferring with his officers, he said, "I will set up my camp in such and such a place."

[9] The man of God sent word to the king of Israel: "Beware of passing that place, because the Arameans are going down there." [10] So the king of Israel checked on the place indicated by the man of God. Time and again Elisha warned the king, so that he was on his guard in such places.

[11] This enraged the king of Aram. He summoned his officers and demanded of them, "Tell me! Which of us is on the side of the king of Israel?"

[a] 22 That is, about 75 pounds or about 34 kilograms

Vision: Elisha Helps Others to See His Divine Perspective

2 Kings 6:8–17

How can a leader help an associate catch his vision? The story of Elisha and his servant gives us some clues.

The king of Aram had pursued Elisha into Dothan, surrounding him with an army large enough to frighten the servant. Elisha simply prayed that God would show the servant the true situation. Elisha's example reminds us of some important truths about perspective:

1. **Elisha felt unmoved by the physical realm and its opposition.**
2. **Elisha showed poise and calmly assured his servant he had nothing to fear.**
3. **Elisha communicated a vision invisible to others.**
4. **Elisha prayed that his servant would be able to see what he saw.**

Perspective separates leaders and followers more than any other characteristic. Leaders see *before* followers do; they see *beyond* what followers do; and they see *bigger* than followers do.

---

¹²"None of us, my lord the king," said one of his officers, "but Elisha, the prophet who is in Israel, tells the king of Israel the very words you speak in your bedroom."

¹³"Go, find out where he is," the king ordered, "so I can send men and capture him." The report came back: "He is in Dothan." ¹⁴Then he sent horses and chariots and a strong force there. They went by night and surrounded the city.

¹⁵When the servant of the man of God got up and went out early the next morning, an army with horses and chariots had surrounded the city. "Oh no, my lord! What shall we do?" the servant asked.

¹⁶"Don't be afraid," the prophet answered. "Those who are with us are more than those who are with them."

¹⁷And Elisha prayed, "Open his eyes, LORD, so that he may see." Then the LORD opened the servant's eyes, and he looked and saw the hills full of horses and chariots of fire all around Elisha.

¹⁸As the enemy came down toward him, Elisha prayed to the LORD, "Strike this army with blindness." So he struck them with blindness, as Elisha had asked.

¹⁹Elisha told them, "This is not the road and this is not the city. Follow me, and I will lead you to the man you are looking for." And he led them to Samaria.

²⁰After they entered the city, Elisha said, "LORD, open the eyes of these men so they can see." Then the LORD opened their eyes and they looked, and there they were, inside Samaria.

²¹When the king of Israel saw them, he asked Elisha, "Shall I kill them, my father? Shall I kill them?"

²²"Do not kill them," he answered. "Would you kill those you have captured with your own sword or bow? Set food and water before them so that they may eat and drink and then go back to their master." ²³So he prepared a great feast for them, and after they had finished eating and drinking, he sent them away, and they returned to their master. So the bands from Aram stopped raiding Israel's territory.

Famine in Besieged Samaria

²⁴Some time later, Ben-Hadad king of Aram mobilized his entire army and marched up and laid siege to Samaria. ²⁵There was a great famine in the city; the siege lasted so long that a donkey's head sold for eighty shekels[a] of silver, and a quarter of a cab[b] of seed pods[c] for five shekels.[d]

²⁶As the king of Israel was passing by on the wall, a woman cried to him, "Help me, my lord the king!"

²⁷The king replied, "If the LORD does not help you, where can I get help for you? From the threshing floor? From the winepress?" ²⁸Then he asked her, "What's the matter?"

She answered, "This woman said to me, 'Give up your son so we may eat him today, and tomorrow we'll eat my son.' ²⁹So we cooked my son and ate him. The next day I said to her, 'Give

---

a 25 That is, about 2 pounds or about 920 grams   *b 25* That is, probably about 1/4 pound or about 100 grams   *c 25* Or of *doves' dung*   *d 25* That is, about 2 ounces or about 58 grams

up your son so we may eat him,' but she had hidden him."

³⁰When the king heard the woman's words, he tore his robes. As he went along the wall, the people looked, and they saw that, under his robes, he had sackcloth on his body. ³¹He said, "May God deal with me, be it ever so severely, if the head of Elisha son of Shaphat remains on his shoulders today!"

³²Now Elisha was sitting in his house, and the elders were sitting with him. The king sent a messenger ahead, but before he arrived, Elisha said to the elders, "Don't you see how this murderer is sending someone to cut off my head? Look, when the messenger comes, shut the door and hold it shut against him. Is not the sound of his master's footsteps behind him?" ³³While he was still talking to them, the messenger came down to him.

The king said, "This disaster is from the LORD. Why should I wait for the LORD any longer?"

7 Elisha replied, "Hear the word of the LORD. This is what the LORD says: About this time tomorrow, a seah*ᵃ* of the finest flour will sell for a shekel*ᵇ* and two seahs*ᶜ* of barley for a shekel at the gate of Samaria."

²The officer on whose arm the king was leaning said to the man of God, "Look, even if the LORD should open the floodgates of the heavens, could this happen?"

"You will see it with your own eyes," answered Elisha, "but you will not eat any of it!"

The Siege Lifted

³Now there were four men with leprosy*ᵈ* at the entrance of the city gate. They said to each other, "Why stay here until we die? ⁴If we say, 'We'll go into the city'—the famine is there, and we will die. And if we stay here, we will die. So let's go over to the camp of the Arameans and surrender. If they spare us, we live; if they kill us, then we die."

⁵At dusk they got up and went to the camp of the Arameans. When they reached the edge of the camp, no one was there, ⁶for the Lord had caused the Arameans to hear the sound of chariots and horses and a great army, so that they said to one another, "Look, the king of Israel has hired the Hittite and Egyptian kings to attack us!" ⁷So they got up and fled in the dusk and abandoned their tents and their horses and donkeys. They left the camp as it was and ran for their lives.

⁸The men who had leprosy reached the edge of the camp, entered one of the tents and ate and

drank. Then they took silver, gold and clothes, and went off and hid them. They returned and entered another tent and took some things from it and hid them also.

⁹Then they said to each other, "What we're doing is not right. This is a day of good news and we are keeping it to ourselves. If we wait until daylight, punishment will overtake us. Let's go at once and report this to the royal palace."

¹⁰So they went and called out to the city gatekeepers and told them, "We went into the Aramean camp and no one was there—not a sound of anyone—only tethered horses and donkeys, and the tents left just as they were." ¹¹The gatekeepers shouted the news, and it was reported within the palace.

¹²The king got up in the night and said to his officers, "I will tell you what the Arameans have done to us. They know we are starving; so they have left the camp to hide in the countryside, thinking, 'They will surely come out, and then we will take them alive and get into the city.'"

¹³One of his officers answered, "Have some men take five of the horses that are left in the city. Their plight will be like that of all the Israelites left here—yes, they will only be like all these Israelites who are doomed. So let us send them to find out what happened."

¹⁴So they selected two chariots with their horses, and the king sent them after the Aramean army. He commanded the drivers, "Go and find out what has happened." ¹⁵They followed them as far as the Jordan, and they found the whole road strewn with the clothing and equipment the Arameans had thrown away in their headlong flight. So the messengers returned and reported to the king. ¹⁶Then the people went out and plundered the camp of the Arameans. So a seah of the finest flour sold for a shekel, and two seahs of barley sold for a shekel, as the LORD had said.

¹⁷Now the king had put the officer on whose arm he leaned in charge of the gate, and the people trampled him in the gateway, and he died, just as the man of God had foretold when the king came down to his house. ¹⁸It happened as the man of God had said to the king: "About this time tomorrow, a seah of the finest flour will sell for a shekel and two seahs of barley for a shekel at the gate of Samaria."

ᵃ 1 That is, probably about 12 pounds or about 5.5 kilograms of flour; also in verses 16 and 18   *ᵇ 1* That is, about 2/5 ounce or about 12 grams; also in verses 16 and 18   *ᶜ 1* That is, probably about 20 pounds or about 9 kilograms of barley; also in verses 16 and 18   *ᵈ 3* The Hebrew for *leprosy* was used for various diseases affecting the skin; also in verse 8.

[19]The officer had said to the man of God, "Look, even if the LORD should open the floodgates of the heavens, could this happen?" The man of God had replied, "You will see it with your own eyes, but you will not eat any of it!" [20]And that is exactly what happened to him, for the people trampled him in the gateway, and he died.

The Shunammite's Land Restored

8 Now Elisha had said to the woman whose son he had restored to life, "Go away with your family and stay for a while wherever you can, because the LORD has decreed a famine in the land that will last seven years." [2]The woman proceeded to do as the man of God said. She and her family went away and stayed in the land of the Philistines seven years.

[3]At the end of the seven years she came back from the land of the Philistines and went to appeal to the king for her house and land. [4]The king was talking to Gehazi, the servant of the man of God, and had said, "Tell me about all the great things Elisha has done." [5]Just as Gehazi was telling the king how Elisha had restored the dead to life, the woman whose son Elisha had brought back to life came to appeal to the king for her house and land.

Gehazi said, "This is the woman, my lord the king, and this is her son whom Elisha restored to life." [6]The king asked the woman about it, and she told him.

Then he assigned an official to her case and said to him, "Give back everything that belonged to her, including all the income from her land from the day she left the country until now."

Hazael Murders Ben-Hadad

[7]Elisha went to Damascus, and Ben-Hadad king of Aram was ill. When the king was told, "The man of God has come all the way up here," [8]he said to Hazael, "Take a gift with you and go to meet the man of God. Consult the LORD through him; ask him, 'Will I recover from this illness?'"

[9]Hazael went to meet Elisha, taking with him as a gift forty camel-loads of all the finest wares of Damascus. He went in and stood before him, and said, "Your son Ben-Hadad king of Aram has sent me to ask, 'Will I recover from this illness?'"

[10]Elisha answered, "Go and say to him, 'You will certainly recover.' Nevertheless,[a] the LORD has revealed to me that he will in fact die." [11]He stared at him with a fixed gaze until Hazael was embarrassed. Then the man of God began to weep.

[12]"Why is my lord weeping?" asked Hazael.

"Because I know the harm you will do to the Israelites," he answered. "You will set fire to their fortified places, kill their young men with the sword, dash their little children to the ground, and rip open their pregnant women." [13]Hazael said, "How could your servant, a mere dog, accomplish such a feat?"

"The LORD has shown me that you will become king of Aram," answered Elisha.

[14]Then Hazael left Elisha and returned to his master. When Ben-Hadad asked, "What did Elisha say to you?" Hazael replied, "He told me that you would certainly recover." [15]But the next day he took a thick cloth, soaked it in water and spread it over the king's face, so that he died. Then Hazael succeeded him as king.

The Law of Solid Ground: Hazael Breaks It and Pays

2 Kings 8:7-15

Hazael began his leadership by breaking trust with his leader, yet he never thought about the consequences of his example. How could he expect anything different from his people? Leaders who break the Law of Solid Ground may expect a haunting ripple effect.

Jehoram King of Judah

[16]In the fifth year of Joram son of Ahab king of Israel, when Jehoshaphat was king of Judah, Jehoram son of Jehoshaphat began his reign as king of Judah. [17]He was thirty-two years old when he became king, and he reigned in Jerusalem eight years. [18]He followed the ways of the kings of Israel, as the house of Ahab had done, for he married a daughter of Ahab. He did evil in the eyes of the LORD. [19]Nevertheless, for the sake of his servant David, the LORD was not willing to destroy Judah. He had promised to maintain a lamp for David and his descendants forever.

[20]In the time of Jehoram, Edom rebelled against Judah and set up its own king. [21]So Jehoram[b] went to Zair with all his chariots. The

---

[a] 10 The Hebrew may also be read Go and say, 'You will certainly not recover,' for.   [b] 21 Hebrew Joram, a variant of Jehoram; also in verses 23 and 24

Edomites surrounded him and his chariot commanders, but he rose up and broke through by night; his army, however, fled back home. [22]To this day Edom has been in rebellion against Judah. Libnah revolted at the same time.

[23]As for the other events of Jehoram's reign, and all he did, are they not written in the book of the annals of the kings of Judah? [24]Jehoram rested with his ancestors and was buried with them in the City of David. And Ahaziah his son succeeded him as king.

Ahaziah King of Judah

[25]In the twelfth year of Joram son of Ahab king of Israel, Ahaziah son of Jehoram king of Judah began to reign. [26]Ahaziah was twenty-two years old when he became king, and he reigned in Jerusalem one year. His mother's name was Athaliah, a granddaughter of Omri king of Israel. [27]He followed the ways of the house of Ahab and did evil in the eyes of the LORD, as the house of Ahab had done, for he was related by marriage to Ahab's family.

[28]Ahaziah went with Joram son of Ahab to war against Hazael king of Aram at Ramoth Gilead. The Arameans wounded Joram; [29]so King Joram returned to Jezreel to recover from the wounds the Arameans had inflicted on him at Ramoth[a] in his battle with Hazael king of Aram.

Then Ahaziah son of Jehoram king of Judah went down to Jezreel to see Joram son of Ahab, because he had been wounded.

Jehu Anointed King of Israel

9 The prophet Elisha summoned a man from the company of the prophets and said to him, "Tuck your cloak into your belt, take this flask of olive oil with you and go to Ramoth Gilead. [2]When you get there, look for Jehu son of Jehoshaphat, the son of Nimshi. Go to him, get him away from his companions and take him into an inner room. [3]Then take the flask and pour the oil on his head and declare, 'This is what the LORD says: I anoint you king over Israel.' Then open the door and run; don't delay!"

[4]So the young prophet went to Ramoth Gilead. [5]When he arrived, he found the army officers sitting together. "I have a message for you, commander," he said.

"For which of us?" asked Jehu.

"For you, commander," he replied.

[6]Jehu got up and went into the house. Then the prophet poured the oil on Jehu's head and declared, "This is what the LORD, the God of Israel, says: 'I anoint you king over the LORD's

people Israel. [7]You are to destroy the house of Ahab your master, and I will avenge the blood of my servants the prophets and the blood of all the LORD's servants shed by Jezebel. [8]The whole house of Ahab will perish. I will cut off from Ahab every last male in Israel—slave or free.[b] [9]I will make the house of Ahab like the house of Jeroboam son of Nebat and like the house of Baasha son of Ahijah. [10]As for Jezebel, dogs will devour her on the plot of ground at Jezreel, and no one will bury her.'" Then he opened the door and ran.

[11]When Jehu went out to his fellow officers, one of them asked him, "Is everything all right? Why did this maniac come to you?"

"You know the man and the sort of things he says," Jehu replied.

[12]"That's not true!" they said. "Tell us."

Jehu said, "Here is what he told me: 'This is what the LORD says: I anoint you king over Israel.'"

[13]They quickly took their cloaks and spread them under him on the bare steps. Then they blew the trumpet and shouted, "Jehu is king!"

Jehu Kills Joram and Ahaziah

[14]So Jehu son of Jehoshaphat, the son of Nimshi, conspired against Joram. (Now Joram and all Israel had been defending Ramoth Gilead against Hazael king of Aram, [15]but King Joram[c] had returned to Jezreel to recover from the wounds the Arameans had inflicted on him in the battle with Hazael king of Aram.) Jehu said, "If you desire to make me king, don't let anyone slip out of the city to go and tell the news in Jezreel." [16]Then he got into his chariot and rode to Jezreel, because Joram was resting there and Ahaziah king of Judah had gone down to see him.

[17]When the lookout standing on the tower in Jezreel saw Jehu's troops approaching, he called out, "I see some troops coming."

"Get a horseman," Joram ordered. "Send him to meet them and ask, 'Do you come in peace?'"

[18]The horseman rode off to meet Jehu and said, "This is what the king says: 'Do you come in peace?'"

"What do you have to do with peace?" Jehu replied. "Fall in behind me."

The lookout reported, "The messenger has reached them, but he isn't coming back."

---

[a] 29 Hebrew *Ramah*, a variant of *Ramoth*   [b] 8 Or *Israel— every ruler or leader*   [c] 15 Hebrew *Jehoram*, a variant of *Joram*; also in verses 17 and 21-24

¹⁹So the king sent out a second horseman. When he came to them he said, "This is what the king says: 'Do you come in peace?'"

Jehu replied, "What do you have to do with peace? Fall in behind me."

²⁰The lookout reported, "He has reached them, but he isn't coming back either. The driving is like that of Jehu son of Nimshi — he drives like a maniac."

²¹"Hitch up my chariot," Joram ordered. And when it was hitched up, Joram king of Israel and Ahaziah king of Judah rode out, each in his own chariot, to meet Jehu. They met him at the plot of ground that had belonged to Naboth the Jezreelite. ²²When Joram saw Jehu he asked, "Have you come in peace, Jehu?"

"How can there be peace," Jehu replied, "as long as all the idolatry and witchcraft of your mother Jezebel abound?"

²³Joram turned about and fled, calling out to Ahaziah, "Treachery, Ahaziah!"

²⁴Then Jehu drew his bow and shot Joram between the shoulders. The arrow pierced his heart and he slumped down in his chariot. ²⁵Jehu said to Bidkar, his chariot officer, "Pick him up and throw him on the field that belonged to Naboth the Jezreelite. Remember how you and I were riding together in chariots behind Ahab his father when the LORD spoke this prophecy against him: ²⁶'Yesterday I saw the blood of Naboth and the blood of his sons, declares the LORD, and I will surely make you pay for it on this plot of ground, declares the LORD.'ᵃ Now then, pick him up and throw him on that plot, in accordance with the word of the LORD."

²⁷When Ahaziah king of Judah saw what had happened, he fled up the road to Beth Haggan.ᵇ Jehu chased him, shouting, "Kill him too!" They wounded him in his chariot on the way up to Gur near Ibleam, but he escaped to Megiddo and died there. ²⁸His servants took him by chariot to Jerusalem and buried him with his ancestors in his tomb in the City of David. ²⁹(In the eleventh year of Joram son of Ahab, Ahaziah had become king of Judah.)

Jezebel Killed

³⁰Then Jehu went to Jezreel. When Jezebel heard about it, she put on eye makeup, arranged her hair and looked out of a window. ³¹As Jehu entered the gate, she asked, "Have you come in peace, you Zimri, you murderer of your master?"ᶜ

³²He looked up at the window and called out, "Who is on my side? Who?" Two or three eunuchs looked down at him. ³³"Throw her

down!" Jehu said. So they threw her down, and some of her blood spattered the wall and the horses as they trampled her underfoot.

³⁴Jehu went in and ate and drank. "Take care of that cursed woman," he said, "and bury her, for she was a king's daughter." ³⁵But when they went out to bury her, they found nothing except her skull, her feet and her hands. ³⁶They went back and told Jehu, who said, "This is the word of the LORD that he spoke through his servant Elijah the Tishbite: On the plot of ground at Jezreel dogs will devour Jezebel's flesh.ᵈ ³⁷Jezebel's body will be like dung on the ground in the plot at Jezreel, so that no one will be able to say, 'This is Jezebel.'"

Ahab's Family Killed

10 Now there were in Samaria seventy sons of the house of Ahab. So Jehu wrote letters and sent them to Samaria: to the officials of Jezreel,ᵉ to the elders and to the guardians of Ahab's children. He said, ²"You have your master's sons with you and you have chariots and horses, a fortified city and weapons. Now as soon as this letter reaches you, ³choose the best and most worthy of your master's sons and set him on his father's throne. Then fight for your master's house."

⁴But they were terrified and said, "If two kings could not resist him, how can we?"

⁵So the palace administrator, the city governor, the elders and the guardians sent this message to Jehu: "We are your servants and we will do anything you say. We will not appoint anyone as king; you do whatever you think best."

⁶Then Jehu wrote them a second letter, saying, "If you are on my side and will obey me, take the heads of your master's sons and come to me in Jezreel by this time tomorrow."

Now the royal princes, seventy of them, were with the leading men of the city, who were rearing them. ⁷When the letter arrived, these men took the princes and slaughtered all seventy of them. They put their heads in baskets and sent them to Jehu in Jezreel. ⁸When the messenger arrived, he told Jehu, "They have brought the heads of the princes."

Then Jehu ordered, "Put them in two piles at the entrance of the city gate until morning."

⁹The next morning Jehu went out. He stood before all the people and said, "You are inno-

---

ᵃ 26 See 1 Kings 21:19.   ᵇ 27 Or fled by way of the garden house   ᶜ 31 Or "Was there peace for Zimri, who murdered his master?"   ᵈ 36 See 1 Kings 21:23.   ᵉ 1 Hebrew; some Septuagint manuscripts and Vulgate of the city

cent. It was I who conspired against my master and killed him, but who killed all these? [10]Know, then, that not a word the LORD has spoken against the house of Ahab will fail. The LORD has done what he announced through his servant Elijah." [11]So Jehu killed everyone in Jezreel who remained of the house of Ahab, as well as all his chief men, his close friends and his priests, leaving him no survivor.

[12]Jehu then set out and went toward Samaria. At Beth Eked of the Shepherds, [13]he met some relatives of Ahaziah king of Judah and asked, "Who are you?"

They said, "We are relatives of Ahaziah, and we have come down to greet the families of the king and of the queen mother."

[14]"Take them alive!" he ordered. So they took them alive and slaughtered them by the well of Beth Eked — forty-two of them. He left no survivor.

[15]After he left there, he came upon Jehonadab son of Rekab, who was on his way to meet him. Jehu greeted him and said, "Are you in accord with me, as I am with you?"

"I am," Jehonadab answered.

"If so," said Jehu, "give me your hand." So he did, and Jehu helped him up into the chariot. [16]Jehu said, "Come with me and see my zeal for the LORD." Then he had him ride along in his chariot.

[17]When Jehu came to Samaria, he killed all who were left there of Ahab's family; he destroyed them, according to the word of the LORD spoken to Elijah.

Servants of Baal Killed

[18]Then Jehu brought all the people together and said to them, "Ahab served Baal a little; Jehu will serve him much. [19]Now summon all the prophets of Baal, all his servants and all his priests. See that no one is missing, because I am going to hold a great sacrifice for Baal. Anyone who fails to come will no longer live." But Jehu was acting deceptively in order to destroy the servants of Baal.

[20]Jehu said, "Call an assembly in honor of Baal." So they proclaimed it. [21]Then he sent word throughout Israel, and all the servants of Baal came; not one stayed away. They crowded into the temple of Baal until it was full from one end to the other. [22]And Jehu said to the keeper of the wardrobe, "Bring robes for all the servants of Baal." So he brought out robes for them.

[23]Then Jehu and Jehonadab son of Rekab went into the temple of Baal. Jehu said to the servants of Baal, "Look around and see that no one who serves the LORD is here with you — only servants of Baal." [24]So they went in to make sacrifices and burnt offerings. Now Jehu had posted eighty men outside with this warning: "If one of you lets any of the men I am placing in your hands escape, it will be your life for his life."

JEHU

Compromise Leads to Idolatry
2 Kings 10:1–36

Call him a man with a mission. Jehu not only accepted a charge from God to lead Israel as king; he also embraced divine instructions to destroy the house of Ahab and the worship of Baal. God told him not to spare anyone from Ahab's family and to eliminate all traces of Baal worship in Israel.

Jehu led brilliantly in fulfilling God's commands. He rid the nation of the family of Ahab and of the worshipers of Baal. He even laid waste to Baal's temple and everything in it. The Bible tells us that God commended Jehu for carrying out his mission, even promising him great blessing because of his obedience (2Ki 10:30).

But a problem eventually arose. While Jehu obeyed God to the last detail concerning the destruction of Ahab and the worship of Baal, he compromised his devotion to God by leaving intact some idols from Israel's past. Even after such great success, "Jehu was not careful to keep the law of the LORD, the God of Israel, with all his heart" (10:31). In time, idols of a different kind corrupted his heart.

Jehu accomplished great things for the Lord and the kingdom of Israel, but his compromise led to another vile form of idolatry. In the end, his disobedience overshadowed his accomplishments as a leader.

PROFILE in leadership

²⁵As soon as Jehu had finished making the burnt offering, he ordered the guards and officers: "Go in and kill them; let no one escape." So they cut them down with the sword. The guards and officers threw the bodies out and then entered the inner shrine of the temple of Baal. ²⁶They brought the sacred stone out of the temple of Baal and burned it. ²⁷They demolished the sacred stone of Baal and tore down the temple of Baal, and people have used it for a latrine to this day.

²⁸So Jehu destroyed Baal worship in Israel. ²⁹However, he did not turn away from the sins of Jeroboam son of Nebat, which he had caused Israel to commit — the worship of the golden calves at Bethel and Dan.

³⁰The LORD said to Jehu, "Because you have done well in accomplishing what is right in my eyes and have done to the house of Ahab all I had in mind to do, your descendants will sit on the throne of Israel to the fourth generation." ³¹Yet Jehu was not careful to keep the law of the LORD, the God of Israel, with all his heart. He did not turn away from the sins of Jeroboam, which he had caused Israel to commit.

³²In those days the LORD began to reduce the size of Israel. Hazael overpowered the Israelites throughout their territory ³³east of the Jordan in all the land of Gilead (the region of Gad, Reuben and Manasseh), from Aroer by the Arnon Gorge through Gilead to Bashan.

³⁴As for the other events of Jehu's reign, all he did, and all his achievements, are they not written in the book of the annals of the kings of Israel?

³⁵Jehu rested with his ancestors and was buried in Samaria. And Jehoahaz his son succeeded him as king. ³⁶The time that Jehu reigned over Israel in Samaria was twenty-eight years.

Athaliah and Joash

11 When Athaliah the mother of Ahaziah saw that her son was dead, she proceeded to destroy the whole royal family. ²But Jehosheba, the daughter of King Jehoram[a] and sister of Ahaziah, took Joash son of Ahaziah and stole him away from among the royal princes, who were about to be murdered. She put him and his nurse in a bedroom to hide him from Athaliah; so he was not killed. ³He remained hidden with his nurse at the temple of the LORD for six years while Athaliah ruled the land.

⁴In the seventh year Jehoiada sent for the commanders of units of a hundred, the Carites and the guards and had them brought to

him at the temple of the LORD. He made a covenant with them and put them under oath at the temple of the LORD. Then he showed them the king's son. ⁵He commanded them, saying, "This is what you are to do: You who are in the three companies that are going on duty on the Sabbath — a third of you guarding the royal palace, ⁶a third at the Sur Gate, and a third at the gate behind the guard, who take turns guarding the temple — ⁷and you who are in the other two companies that normally go off Sabbath duty are all to guard the temple for the king. ⁸Station yourselves around the king, each of you with weapon in hand. Anyone who approaches your ranks[b] is to be put to death. Stay close to the king wherever he goes."

⁹The commanders of units of a hundred did just as Jehoiada the priest ordered. Each one took his men — those who were going on duty on the Sabbath and those who were going off duty — and came to Jehoiada the priest. ¹⁰Then he gave the commanders the spears and shields that had belonged to King David and that were in the temple of the LORD. ¹¹The guards, each with weapon in hand, stationed themselves around the king — near the altar and the temple, from the south side to the north side of the temple.

¹²Jehoiada brought out the king's son and put the crown on him; he presented him with a copy of the covenant and proclaimed him king. They anointed him, and the people clapped their hands and shouted, "Long live the king!"

¹³When Athaliah heard the noise made by the guards and the people, she went to the people at the temple of the LORD. ¹⁴She looked and there was the king, standing by the pillar, as the custom was. The officers and the trumpeters were beside the king, and all the people of the land were rejoicing and blowing trumpets. Then Athaliah tore her robes and called out, "Treason! Treason!"

¹⁵Jehoiada the priest ordered the commanders of units of a hundred, who were in charge of the troops: "Bring her out between the ranks[c] and put to the sword anyone who follows her." For the priest had said, "She must not be put to death in the temple of the LORD." ¹⁶So they seized her as she reached the place where the horses enter the palace grounds, and there she was put to death.

¹⁷Jehoiada then made a covenant between the

---

[a] 2 Hebrew *Joram,* a variant of *Jehoram*   [b] 8 Or *approaches the precincts*   [c] 15 Or *out from the precincts*

LORD and the king and people that they would be the LORD's people. He also made a covenant between the king and the people. ¹⁸All the people of the land went to the temple of Baal and tore it down. They smashed the altars and idols to pieces and killed Mattan the priest of Baal in front of the altars.

Then Jehoiada the priest posted guards at the temple of the LORD. ¹⁹He took with him the commanders of hundreds, the Carites, the guards and all the people of the land, and together they brought the king down from the temple of the LORD and went into the palace, entering by way of the gate of the guards. The king then took his place on the royal throne. ²⁰All the people of the land rejoiced, and the city was calm, because Athaliah had been slain with the sword at the palace.

²¹Joash[a] was seven years old when he began to reign.[b]

Joash Repairs the Temple

12[c] In the seventh year of Jehu, Joash[d] became king, and he reigned in Jerusalem forty years. His mother's name was Zibiah; she was from Beersheba. ²Joash did what was right in the eyes of the LORD all the years Jehoiada the priest instructed him. ³The high places, however, were not removed; the people continued to offer sacrifices and burn incense there.

⁴Joash said to the priests, "Collect all the money that is brought as sacred offerings to the temple of the LORD—the money collected in the census, the money received from personal vows and the money brought voluntarily to the temple. ⁵Let every priest receive the money from one of the treasurers, then use it to repair whatever damage is found in the temple."

⁶But by the twenty-third year of King Joash the priests still had not repaired the temple. ⁷Therefore King Joash summoned Jehoiada the priest and the other priests and asked them, "Why aren't you repairing the damage done to the temple? Take no more money from your treasurers, but hand it over for repairing the temple." ⁸The priests agreed that they would not collect any more money from the people and that they would not repair the temple themselves.

⁹Jehoiada the priest took a chest and bored a hole in its lid. He placed it beside the altar, on the right side as one enters the temple of the LORD. The priests who guarded the entrance put into the chest all the money that was brought to the temple of the LORD. ¹⁰Whenever they saw that there was a large amount of money in the chest, the royal secretary and the high priest came, counted the money that had been brought into the temple of the LORD and put it into bags. ¹¹When the amount had been determined, they gave the money to the men appointed to supervise the work on the temple. With it they paid those who worked on the temple of the LORD—the carpenters and builders, ¹²the masons and stonecutters. They purchased timber and blocks of dressed stone for the repair of the temple of the LORD, and met all the other expenses of restoring the temple.

¹³The money brought into the temple was not spent for making silver basins, wick trimmers, sprinkling bowls, trumpets or any other articles of gold or silver for the temple of the LORD; ¹⁴it was paid to the workers, who used it to repair the temple. ¹⁵They did not require an accounting from those to whom they gave the money to pay the workers, because they acted with complete honesty. ¹⁶The money from the guilt offerings and sin offerings[e] was not brought into the temple of the LORD; it belonged to the priests.

The Law of Navigation: Joash Charts the Course to Repair the Temple

2 Kings 12:4–16

Joash well navigated the temple repairs, even though he had to fire the priests who oversaw the initial fund-raising efforts. Joash efficiently collected the money, cast the vision, and held the people accountable until the job was finished. Good leaders understand how to get the job done.

¹⁷About this time Hazael king of Aram went up and attacked Gath and captured it. Then he turned to attack Jerusalem. ¹⁸But Joash king of Judah took all the sacred objects dedicated by his predecessors—Jehoshaphat, Jehoram and Ahaziah, the kings of Judah—and the gifts he himself had dedicated and all the gold found in the

---

[a] 21 Hebrew *Jehoash*, a variant of *Joash*   [b] 21 In Hebrew texts this verse (11:21) is numbered 12:1.   [c] In Hebrew texts 12:1-21 is numbered 12:2-22.   [d] 1 Hebrew *Jehoash*, a variant of *Joash*; also in verses 2, 4, 6, 7 and 18   [e] 16 Or *purification offerings*

treasuries of the temple of the LORD and of the royal palace, and he sent them to Hazael king of Aram, who then withdrew from Jerusalem.

¹⁹As for the other events of the reign of Joash, and all he did, are they not written in the book of the annals of the kings of Judah? ²⁰His officials conspired against him and assassinated him at Beth Millo, on the road down to Silla. ²¹The officials who murdered him were Jozabad son of Shimeath and Jehozabad son of Shomer. He died and was buried with his ancestors in the City of David. And Amaziah his son succeeded him as king.

Jehoahaz King of Israel

13 In the twenty-third year of Joash son of Ahaziah king of Judah, Jehoahaz son of Jehu became king of Israel in Samaria, and he reigned seventeen years. ²He did evil in the eyes of the LORD by following the sins of Jeroboam son of Nebat, which he had caused Israel to commit, and he did not turn away from them. ³So the LORD's anger burned against Israel, and for a long time he kept them under the power of Hazael king of Aram and Ben-Hadad his son.

⁴Then Jehoahaz sought the LORD's favor, and the LORD listened to him, for he saw how severely the king of Aram was oppressing Israel. ⁵The LORD provided a deliverer for Israel, and they escaped from the power of Aram. So the Israelites lived in their own homes as they had before. ⁶But they did not turn away from the sins of the house of Jeroboam, which he had caused Israel to commit; they continued in them. Also, the Asherah pole*ᵃ* remained standing in Samaria.

⁷Nothing had been left of the army of Jehoahaz except fifty horsemen, ten chariots and ten thousand foot soldiers, for the king of Aram had destroyed the rest and made them like the dust at threshing time.

⁸As for the other events of the reign of Jehoahaz, all he did and his achievements, are they not written in the book of the annals of the kings of Israel? ⁹Jehoahaz rested with his ancestors and was buried in Samaria. And Jehoash*ᵇ* his son succeeded him as king.

Jehoash King of Israel

¹⁰In the thirty-seventh year of Joash king of Judah, Jehoash son of Jehoahaz became king of Israel in Samaria, and he reigned sixteen years. ¹¹He did evil in the eyes of the LORD and did not turn away from any of the sins of Jeroboam son of Nebat, which he had caused Israel to commit; he continued in them.

¹²As for the other events of the reign of Jehoash, all he did and his achievements, including his war against Amaziah king of Judah, are they not written in the book of the annals of the kings of Israel? ¹³Jehoash rested with his ancestors, and Jeroboam succeeded him on the throne. Jehoash was buried in Samaria with the kings of Israel.

¹⁴Now Elisha had been suffering from the illness from which he died. Jehoash king of Israel went down to see him and wept over him. "My father! My father!" he cried. "The chariots and horsemen of Israel!"

¹⁵Elisha said, "Get a bow and some arrows," and he did so. ¹⁶"Take the bow in your hands," he said to the king of Israel. When he had taken it, Elisha put his hands on the king's hands.

¹⁷"Open the east window," he said, and he opened it. "Shoot!" Elisha said, and he shot. "The LORD's arrow of victory, the arrow of victory over Aram!" Elisha declared. "You will completely destroy the Arameans at Aphek."

¹⁸Then he said, "Take the arrows," and the king took them. Elisha told him, "Strike the ground." He struck it three times and stopped. ¹⁹The man of God was angry with him and said, "You should have struck the ground five or six times; then you would have defeated Aram and completely destroyed it. But now you will defeat it only three times."

²⁰Elisha died and was buried.

Now Moabite raiders used to enter the country every spring. ²¹Once while some Israelites were burying a man, suddenly they saw a band of raiders; so they threw the man's body into Elisha's tomb. When the body touched Elisha's bones, the man came to life and stood up on his feet.

²²Hazael king of Aram oppressed Israel throughout the reign of Jehoahaz. ²³But the LORD was gracious to them and had compassion and showed concern for them because of his covenant with Abraham, Isaac and Jacob. To this day he has been unwilling to destroy them or banish them from his presence.

²⁴Hazael king of Aram died, and Ben-Hadad his son succeeded him as king. ²⁵Then Jehoash son of Jehoahaz recaptured from Ben-Hadad son of Hazael the towns he had taken in battle from his father Jehoahaz. Three times Jehoash defeated him, and so he recovered the Israelite towns.

ᵃ 6 That is, a wooden symbol of the goddess Asherah; here and elsewhere in 2 Kings *ᵇ 9* Hebrew *Joash,* a variant of *Jehoash;* also in verses 12-14 and 25

Amaziah King of Judah

14 In the second year of Jehoash[a] son of Jehoahaz king of Israel, Amaziah son of Joash king of Judah began to reign. [2]He was twenty-five years old when he became king, and he reigned in Jerusalem twenty-nine years. His mother's name was Jehoaddan; she was from Jerusalem. [3]He did what was right in the eyes of the LORD, but not as his father David had done. In everything he followed the example of his father Joash. [4]The high places, however, were not removed; the people continued to offer sacrifices and burn incense there.

[5]After the kingdom was firmly in his grasp, he executed the officials who had murdered his father the king. [6]Yet he did not put the children of the assassins to death, in accordance with what is written in the Book of the Law of Moses where the LORD commanded: "Parents are not to be put to death for their children, nor children put to death for their parents; each will die for their own sin."[b]

[7]He was the one who defeated ten thousand Edomites in the Valley of Salt and captured Sela in battle, calling it Joktheel, the name it has to this day.

[8]Then Amaziah sent messengers to Jehoash son of Jehoahaz, the son of Jehu, king of Israel, with the challenge: "Come, let us face each other in battle."

[9]But Jehoash king of Israel replied to Amaziah king of Judah: "A thistle in Lebanon sent a message to a cedar in Lebanon, 'Give your daughter to my son in marriage.' Then a wild beast in Lebanon came along and trampled the

---

[a] 1 Hebrew *Joash*, a variant of *Jehoash*; also in verses 13, 23 and 27 [b] 6 Deut. 24:16

The Law of the Picture: People Do What People See

2 Kings 14:1–4

The Bible provides ample confirmation of a key management principle called the Law of the Picture: People don't do what they hear; they do what they see. The example of the leader determines the experience of the people.

For the most part, God's people endured hard times during the days of the book of 2 Kings. Below is a list of kings in Judah and Israel. Only two kings on this list, Hezekiah and Josiah, wholeheartedly worshiped God. Remember: A nation's leadership determines the direction of the whole country. People do what people see.

Judah	Israel
Jehoram (2Ki 8)	Joram (2Ki 3)
Ahaziah (2Ki 8)	Jehu (2Ki 10)
Athaliah (2Ki 11)	Jehoahaz (2Ki 13)
Joash (2Ki 11)	Jehoash (2Ki 13)
Amaziah (2Ki 14)	Jeroboam II (2Ki 14)
Azariah (2Ki 15)	Zechariah (2Ki 15)
Jotham (2Ki 15)	Shallum (2Ki 15)
Ahaz (2Ki 16)	Menahem (2Ki 15)
Hezekiah (2Ki 18)	Pekahiah (2Ki 15)
Manasseh (2Ki 21)	Pekah (2Ki 15)
Amon (2Ki 21)	Hoshea (2Ki 17)
Josiah (2Ki 22)	
Jehoahaz (2Ki 23)	
Jehoiakim (2Ki 23)	
Jehoiakin (2Ki 24)	
Zedekiah (2Ki 24)	

thistle underfoot. [10]You have indeed defeated Edom and now you are arrogant. Glory in your victory, but stay at home! Why ask for trouble and cause your own downfall and that of Judah also?"

[11]Amaziah, however, would not listen, so Jehoash king of Israel attacked. He and Amaziah king of Judah faced each other at Beth Shemesh in Judah. [12]Judah was routed by Israel, and every man fled to his home. [13]Jehoash king of Israel captured Amaziah king of Judah, the son of Joash, the son of Ahaziah, at Beth Shemesh. Then Jehoash went to Jerusalem and broke down the wall of Jerusalem from the Ephraim Gate to the Corner Gate — a section about four hundred cubits long.[a] [14]He took all the gold and silver and all the articles found in the temple of the LORD and in the treasuries of the royal palace. He also took hostages and returned to Samaria.

[15]As for the other events of the reign of Jehoash, what he did and his achievements, including his war against Amaziah king of Judah, are they not written in the book of the annals of the kings of Israel? [16]Jehoash rested with his ancestors and was buried in Samaria with the kings of Israel. And Jeroboam his son succeeded him as king.

[17]Amaziah son of Joash king of Judah lived for fifteen years after the death of Jehoash son of Jehoahaz king of Israel. [18]As for the other events of Amaziah's reign, are they not written in the book of the annals of the kings of Judah?

[19]They conspired against him in Jerusalem, and he fled to Lachish, but they sent men after him to Lachish and killed him there. [20]He was brought back by horse and was buried in Jerusalem with his ancestors, in the City of David.

[21]Then all the people of Judah took Azariah,[b] who was sixteen years old, and made him king in place of his father Amaziah. [22]He was the one who rebuilt Elath and restored it to Judah after Amaziah rested with his ancestors.

Jeroboam II King of Israel

[23]In the fifteenth year of Amaziah son of Joash king of Judah, Jeroboam son of Jehoash king of Israel became king in Samaria, and he reigned forty-one years. [24]He did evil in the eyes of the LORD and did not turn away from any of the sins of Jeroboam son of Nebat, which he had caused Israel to commit. [25]He was the one who restored the boundaries of Israel from Lebo Hamath to the Dead Sea,[c] in accordance with the word of the LORD, the God of Israel, spoken through his servant Jonah son of Amittai, the prophet from Gath Hepher.

[26]The LORD had seen how bitterly everyone in Israel, whether slave or free, was suffering;[d] there was no one to help them. [27]And since the LORD had not said he would blot out the name of Israel from under heaven, he saved them by the hand of Jeroboam son of Jehoash.

[28]As for the other events of Jeroboam's reign, all he did, and his military achievements, including how he recovered for Israel both Damascus and Hamath, which had belonged to Judah, are they not written in the book of the annals of the kings of Israel? [29]Jeroboam rested with his ancestors, the kings of Israel. And Zechariah his son succeeded him as king.

Azariah King of Judah

15 In the twenty-seventh year of Jeroboam king of Israel, Azariah[e] son of Amaziah king of Judah began to reign. [2]He was sixteen years old when he became king, and he reigned in Jerusalem fifty-two years. His mother's name was Jekoliah; she was from Jerusalem. [3]He did what was right in the eyes of the LORD, just as his father Amaziah had done. [4]The high places, however, were not removed; the people continued to offer sacrifices and burn incense there.

[5]The LORD afflicted the king with leprosy[f] until the day he died, and he lived in a separate house.[g] Jotham the king's son had charge of the palace and governed the people of the land.

[6]As for the other events of Azariah's reign, and all he did, are they not written in the book of the annals of the kings of Judah? [7]Azariah rested with his ancestors and was buried near them in the City of David. And Jotham his son succeeded him as king.

Zechariah King of Israel

[8]In the thirty-eighth year of Azariah king of Judah, Zechariah son of Jeroboam became king of Israel in Samaria, and he reigned six months. [9]He did evil in the eyes of the LORD, as his predecessors had done. He did not turn away from the sins of Jeroboam son of Nebat, which he had caused Israel to commit.

[10]Shallum son of Jabesh conspired against

---

[a] 13 That is, about 600 feet or about 180 meters   [b] 21 Also called *Uzziah*   [c] 25 Hebrew *the Sea of the Arabah*
[d] 26 Or *Israel was suffering. They were without a ruler or leader, and*   [e] 1 Also called *Uzziah*; also in verses 6, 7, 8, 17, 23 and 27   [f] 5 The Hebrew for *leprosy* was used for various diseases affecting the skin.   [g] 5 Or *in a house where he was relieved of responsibilities*

Zechariah. He attacked him in front of the people,[a] assassinated him and succeeded him as king. [11]The other events of Zechariah's reign are written in the book of the annals of the kings of Israel. [12]So the word of the LORD spoken to Jehu was fulfilled: "Your descendants will sit on the throne of Israel to the fourth generation."[b]

Shallum King of Israel

[13]Shallum son of Jabesh became king in the thirty-ninth year of Uzziah king of Judah, and he reigned in Samaria one month. [14]Then Menahem son of Gadi went from Tirzah up to Samaria. He attacked Shallum son of Jabesh in Samaria, assassinated him and succeeded him as king.

[15]The other events of Shallum's reign, and the conspiracy he led, are written in the book of the annals of the kings of Israel.

[16]At that time Menahem, starting out from Tirzah, attacked Tiphsah and everyone in the city and its vicinity, because they refused to open their gates. He sacked Tiphsah and ripped open all the pregnant women.

Menahem King of Israel

[17]In the thirty-ninth year of Azariah king of Judah, Menahem son of Gadi became king of Israel, and he reigned in Samaria ten years. [18]He did evil in the eyes of the LORD. During his entire reign he did not turn away from the sins of Jeroboam son of Nebat, which he had caused Israel to commit.

[19]Then Pul[c] king of Assyria invaded the land, and Menahem gave him a thousand talents[d] of silver to gain his support and strengthen his own hold on the kingdom. [20]Menahem exacted this money from Israel. Every wealthy person had to contribute fifty shekels[e] of silver to be given to the king of Assyria. So the king of Assyria withdrew and stayed in the land no longer.

[21]As for the other events of Menahem's reign, and all he did, are they not written in the book of the annals of the kings of Israel? [22]Menahem rested with his ancestors. And Pekahiah his son succeeded him as king.

Pekahiah King of Israel

[23]In the fiftieth year of Azariah king of Judah, Pekahiah son of Menahem became king of Israel in Samaria, and he reigned two years. [24]Pekahiah did evil in the eyes of the LORD. He did not turn away from the sins of Jeroboam son of Nebat, which he had caused Israel to commit. [25]One of his chief officers, Pekah son of Rem-

aliah, conspired against him. Taking fifty men of Gilead with him, he assassinated Pekahiah, along with Argob and Arieh, in the citadel of the royal palace at Samaria. So Pekah killed Pekahiah and succeeded him as king.

[26]The other events of Pekahiah's reign, and all he did, are written in the book of the annals of the kings of Israel.

Pekah King of Israel

[27]In the fifty-second year of Azariah king of Judah, Pekah son of Remaliah became king of Israel in Samaria, and he reigned twenty years. [28]He did evil in the eyes of the LORD. He did not turn away from the sins of Jeroboam son of Nebat, which he had caused Israel to commit.

[29]In the time of Pekah king of Israel, Tiglath-Pileser king of Assyria came and took Ijon, Abel Beth Maakah, Janoah, Kedesh and Hazor. He took Gilead and Galilee, including all the land of Naphtali, and deported the people to Assyria. [30]Then Hoshea son of Elah conspired against Pekah son of Remaliah. He attacked and assassinated him, and then succeeded him as king in the twentieth year of Jotham son of Uzziah.

[31]As for the other events of Pekah's reign, and all he did, are they not written in the book of the annals of the kings of Israel?

Jotham King of Judah

[32]In the second year of Pekah son of Remaliah king of Israel, Jotham son of Uzziah king of Judah began to reign. [33]He was twenty-five years old when he became king, and he reigned in Jerusalem sixteen years. His mother's name was Jerusha daughter of Zadok. [34]He did what was right in the eyes of the LORD, just as his father Uzziah had done. [35]The high places, however, were not removed; the people continued to offer sacrifices and burn incense there. Jotham rebuilt the Upper Gate of the temple of the LORD.

[36]As for the other events of Jotham's reign, and what he did, are they not written in the book of the annals of the kings of Judah? [37](In those days the LORD began to send Rezin king of Aram and Pekah son of Remaliah against Judah.) [38]Jotham rested with his ancestors and was buried with them in the City of David, the city of his father. And Ahaz his son succeeded him as king.

---

[a] 10 Hebrew; some Septuagint manuscripts *in Ibleam*
[b] 12 2 Kings 10:30   [c] 19 Also called *Tiglath-Pileser*
[d] 19 That is, about 38 tons or about 34 metric tons
[e] 20 That is, about 1 1/4 pounds or about 575 grams

Ahaz King of Judah

16 In the seventeenth year of Pekah son of Remaliah, Ahaz son of Jotham king of Judah began to reign. [2]Ahaz was twenty years old when he became king, and he reigned in Jerusalem sixteen years. Unlike David his father, he did not do what was right in the eyes of the LORD his God. [3]He followed the ways of the kings of Israel and even sacrificed his son in the fire, engaging in the detestable practices of the nations the LORD had driven out before the Israelites. [4]He offered sacrifices and burned incense at the high places, on the hilltops and under every spreading tree.

[5]Then Rezin king of Aram and Pekah son of Remaliah king of Israel marched up to fight against Jerusalem and besieged Ahaz, but they could not overpower him. [6]At that time, Rezin king of Aram recovered Elath for Aram by driving out the people of Judah. Edomites then moved into Elath and have lived there to this day.

[7]Ahaz sent messengers to say to Tiglath-Pileser king of Assyria, "I am your servant and vassal. Come up and save me out of the hand of the king of Aram and of the king of Israel, who are attacking me." [8]And Ahaz took the silver and gold found in the temple of the LORD and in the treasuries of the royal palace and sent it as a gift to the king of Assyria. [9]The king of Assyria complied by attacking Damascus and capturing it. He deported its inhabitants to Kir and put Rezin to death.

[10]Then King Ahaz went to Damascus to meet Tiglath-Pileser king of Assyria. He saw an altar in Damascus and sent to Uriah the priest a sketch of the altar, with detailed plans for its construction. [11]So Uriah the priest built an altar in accordance with all the plans that King Ahaz had sent from Damascus and finished it before King Ahaz returned. [12]When the king came back from Damascus and saw the altar, he approached it and presented offerings[a] on it. [13]He offered up his burnt offering and grain offering, poured out his drink offering, and splashed the blood of his fellowship offerings against the altar. [14]As for the bronze altar that stood before the LORD, he brought it from the front of the temple — from between the new altar and the temple of the LORD — and put it on the north side of the new altar.

[15]King Ahaz then gave these orders to Uriah the priest: "On the large new altar, offer the morning burnt offering and the evening grain offering, the king's burnt offering and his grain offering, and the burnt offering of all the people of the land, and their grain offering and their drink offering. Splash against this altar the blood of all the burnt offerings and sacrifices. But I will use the bronze altar for seeking guidance." [16]And Uriah the priest did just as King Ahaz had ordered.

[17]King Ahaz cut off the side panels and removed the basins from the movable stands. He removed the Sea from the bronze bulls that supported it and set it on a stone base. [18]He took away the Sabbath canopy[b] that had been built at the temple and removed the royal entryway outside the temple of the LORD, in deference to the king of Assyria.

[19]As for the other events of the reign of Ahaz, and what he did, are they not written in the book of the annals of the kings of Judah? [20]Ahaz rested with his ancestors and was buried with them in the City of David. And Hezekiah his son succeeded him as king.

Hoshea Last King of Israel

17 In the twelfth year of Ahaz king of Judah, Hoshea son of Elah became king of Israel in Samaria, and he reigned nine years. [2]He did evil in the eyes of the LORD, but not like the kings of Israel who preceded him.

[3]Shalmaneser king of Assyria came up to attack Hoshea, who had been Shalmaneser's vassal and had paid him tribute. [4]But the king of Assyria discovered that Hoshea was a traitor, for he had sent envoys to So[c] king of Egypt, and he no longer paid tribute to the king of Assyria, as he had done year by year. Therefore Shalmaneser seized him and put him in prison. [5]The king of Assyria invaded the entire land, marched against Samaria and laid siege to it for three years. [6]In the ninth year of Hoshea, the king of Assyria captured Samaria and deported the Israelites to Assyria. He settled them in Halah, in Gozan on the Habor River and in the towns of the Medes.

Israel Exiled Because of Sin

[7]All this took place because the Israelites had sinned against the LORD their God, who had brought them up out of Egypt from under the power of Pharaoh king of Egypt. They worshiped other gods [8]and followed the practices of the nations the LORD had driven out before

---

[a] 12 Or and went up   [b] 18 Or the dais of his throne (see Septuagint)   [c] 4 So is probably an abbreviation for Osorkon.

them, as well as the practices that the kings of Israel had introduced. [9]The Israelites secretly did things against the LORD their God that were not right. From watchtower to fortified city they built themselves high places in all their towns. [10]They set up sacred stones and Asherah poles on every high hill and under every spreading tree. [11]At every high place they burned incense, as the nations whom the LORD had driven out before them had done. They did wicked things that aroused the LORD's anger. [12]They worshiped idols, though the LORD had said, "You shall not do this."[a] [13]The LORD warned Israel and Judah through all his prophets and seers: "Turn from your evil ways. Observe my commands and decrees, in accordance with the entire Law that I commanded your ancestors to obey and that I delivered to you through my servants the prophets."

[14]But they would not listen and were as stiff-necked as their ancestors, who did not trust in the LORD their God. [15]They rejected his decrees and the covenant he had made with their ancestors and the statutes he had warned them to keep. They followed worthless idols and themselves became worthless. They imitated the nations around them although the LORD had ordered them, "Do not do as they do."

[16]They forsook all the commands of the LORD their God and made for themselves two idols cast in the shape of calves, and an Asherah pole. They bowed down to all the starry hosts, and they worshiped Baal. [17]They sacrificed their sons and daughters in the fire. They practiced divination and sought omens and sold themselves to do evil in the eyes of the LORD, arousing his anger.

[18]So the LORD was very angry with Israel and removed them from his presence. Only the tribe of Judah was left, [19]and even Judah did not keep the commands of the LORD their God. They followed the practices Israel had introduced. [20]Therefore the LORD rejected all the people of Israel; he afflicted them and gave them into the hands of plunderers, until he thrust them from his presence.

[21]When he tore Israel away from the house of David, they made Jeroboam son of Nebat their king. Jeroboam enticed Israel away from following the LORD and caused them to commit a great sin. [22]The Israelites persisted in all the sins of Jeroboam and did not turn away from them [23]until the LORD removed them from his presence, as he had warned through all his servants the prophets. So the people of Israel were taken from their homeland into exile in Assyria, and they are still there.

Samaria Resettled

[24]The king of Assyria brought people from Babylon, Kuthah, Avva, Hamath and Sepharvaim and settled them in the towns of Samaria to replace the Israelites. They took over Samaria and lived in its towns. [25]When they first lived there, they did not worship the LORD; so he sent lions among them and they killed some of the people. [26]It was reported to the king of Assyria: "The people you deported and resettled in the towns of Samaria do not know what the god of that country requires. He has sent lions among them, which are killing them off, because the people do not know what he requires."

[27]Then the king of Assyria gave this order: "Have one of the priests you took captive from Samaria go back to live there and teach the people what the god of the land requires." [28]So one of the priests who had been exiled from Samaria came to live in Bethel and taught them how to worship the LORD.

[29]Nevertheless, each national group made its own gods in the several towns where they settled, and set them up in the shrines the people of Samaria had made at the high places. [30]The people from Babylon made Sukkoth Benoth, those from Kuthah made Nergal, and those from Hamath made Ashima; [31]the Avvites made Nibhaz and Tartak, and the Sepharvites burned their children in the fire as sacrifices to Adrammelek and Anammelek, the gods of Sepharvaim. [32]They worshiped the LORD, but they also appointed all sorts of their own people to officiate for them as priests in the shrines at the high places. [33]They worshiped the LORD, but they also served their own gods in accordance with the customs of the nations from which they had been brought.

[34]To this day they persist in their former practices. They neither worship the LORD nor adhere to the decrees and regulations, the laws and commands that the LORD gave the descendants of Jacob, whom he named Israel. [35]When the LORD made a covenant with the Israelites, he commanded them: "Do not worship any other gods or bow down to them, serve them or sacrifice to them. [36]But the LORD, who brought you up out of Egypt with mighty power and outstretched arm, is the one you must worship. To him you shall bow down and to him

[a] 12 Exodus 20:4,5

offer sacrifices. ³⁷You must always be careful to keep the decrees and regulations, the laws and commands he wrote for you. Do not worship other gods. ³⁸Do not forget the covenant I have made with you, and do not worship other gods. ³⁹Rather, worship the LORD your God; it is he who will deliver you from the hand of all your enemies."

⁴⁰They would not listen, however, but persisted in their former practices. ⁴¹Even while these people were worshiping the LORD, they were serving their idols. To this day their children and grandchildren continue to do as their ancestors did.

Hezekiah King of Judah

18 In the third year of Hoshea son of Elah king of Israel, Hezekiah son of Ahaz king of Judah began to reign. ²He was twenty-five years old when he became king, and he reigned in Jerusalem twenty-nine years. His mother's name was Abijah*a* daughter of Zechariah. ³He did what was right in the eyes of the LORD, just as his father David had done. ⁴He removed the high places, smashed the sacred stones and cut down the Asherah poles. He broke into pieces the bronze snake Moses had made, for up to that time the Israelites had been burning incense to it. (It was called Nehushtan.*b*)

⁵Hezekiah trusted in the LORD, the God of Israel. There was no one like him among all the kings of Judah, either before him or after him. ⁶He held fast to the LORD and did not stop following him; he kept the commands the LORD had given Moses. ⁷And the LORD was with him; he was successful in whatever he undertook. He rebelled against the king of Assyria and did not serve him. ⁸From watchtower to fortified city, he defeated the Philistines, as far as Gaza and its territory.

⁹In King Hezekiah's fourth year, which was the seventh year of Hoshea son of Elah king of Israel, Shalmaneser king of Assyria marched against Samaria and laid siege to it. ¹⁰At the end of three years the Assyrians took it. So Samaria was captured in Hezekiah's sixth year, which was the ninth year of Hoshea king of Israel. ¹¹The king of Assyria deported Israel to Assyria and settled them in Halah, in Gozan on the Habor River and in towns of the Medes. ¹²This happened because they had not obeyed the LORD their God, but had violated his covenant—all that Moses the servant of the LORD commanded. They neither listened to the commands nor carried them out.

¹³In the fourteenth year of King Hezekiah's reign, Sennacherib king of Assyria attacked all the fortified cities of Judah and captured them. ¹⁴So Hezekiah king of Judah sent this message to the king of Assyria at Lachish: "I have done wrong. Withdraw from me, and I will pay whatever you demand of me." The king of Assyria exacted from Hezekiah king of Judah three hundred talents*c* of silver and thirty talents*d* of gold. ¹⁵So Hezekiah gave him all the silver that was found in the temple of the LORD and in the treasuries of the royal palace.

¹⁶At this time Hezekiah king of Judah stripped off the gold with which he had covered the doors and doorposts of the temple of the LORD, and gave it to the king of Assyria.

Sennacherib Threatens Jerusalem

¹⁷The king of Assyria sent his supreme commander, his chief officer and his field commander with a large army, from Lachish to King Hezekiah at Jerusalem. They came up to Jerusalem and stopped at the aqueduct of the Upper Pool, on the road to the Washerman's Field. ¹⁸They called for the king; and Eliakim son of Hilkiah the palace administrator, Shebna the secretary, and Joah son of Asaph the recorder went out to them.

¹⁹The field commander said to them, "Tell Hezekiah:

"'This is what the great king, the king of Assyria, says: On what are you basing this confidence of yours? ²⁰You say you have the counsel and the might for war—but you speak only empty words. On whom are you depending, that you rebel against me? ²¹Look, I know you are depending on Egypt, that splintered reed of a staff, which pierces the hand of anyone who leans on it! Such is Pharaoh king of Egypt to all who depend on him. ²²But if you say to me, "We are depending on the LORD our God"—isn't he the one whose high places and altars Hezekiah removed, saying to Judah and Jerusalem, "You must worship before this altar in Jerusalem"?

²³"'Come now, make a bargain with my master, the king of Assyria: I will give you two thousand horses—if you can put riders on them! ²⁴How can you repulse

---

a 2 Hebrew *Abi*, a variant of *Abijah*   *b* 4 *Nehushtan* sounds like the Hebrew for both *bronze* and *snake*.   *c* 14 That is, about 11 tons or about 10 metric tons   *d* 14 That is, about 1 ton or about 1 metric ton

one officer of the least of my master's officials, even though you are depending on Egypt for chariots and horsemen*? [25]Furthermore, have I come to attack and destroy this place without word from the LORD? The LORD himself told me to march against this country and destroy it.'"

[26]Then Eliakim son of Hilkiah, and Shebna and Joah said to the field commander, "Please speak to your servants in Aramaic, since we understand it. Don't speak to us in Hebrew in the hearing of the people on the wall."

[27]But the commander replied, "Was it only to your master and you that my master sent me to say these things, and not to the people sitting on the wall—who, like you, will have to eat their own excrement and drink their own urine?"

[28]Then the commander stood and called out in Hebrew, "Hear the word of the great king, the king of Assyria! [29]This is what the king says: Do not let Hezekiah deceive you. He cannot deliver you from my hand. [30]Do not let Hezekiah persuade you to trust in the LORD when he says, 'The LORD will surely deliver us; this city will not be given into the hand of the king of Assyria.'

[31]"Do not listen to Hezekiah. This is what the king of Assyria says: Make peace with me and come out to me. Then each of you will eat fruit from your own vine and fig tree and drink water from your own cistern, [32]until I come and take you to a land like your own—a land of grain and new wine, a land of bread and vineyards, a land of olive trees and honey. Choose life and not death!

"Do not listen to Hezekiah, for he is misleading you when he says, 'The LORD will deliver us.' [33]Has the god of any nation ever delivered his land from the hand of the king of Assyria? [34]Where are the gods of Hamath and Arpad? Where are the gods of Sepharvaim, Hena and Ivvah? Have they rescued Samaria from my hand? [35]Who of all the gods of these countries has been able to save his land from me? How then can the LORD deliver Jerusalem from my hand?"

[36]But the people remained silent and said nothing in reply, because the king had commanded, "Do not answer him."

[37]Then Eliakim son of Hilkiah the palace administrator, Shebna the secretary, and Joah son of Asaph the recorder went to Hezekiah, with their clothes torn, and told him what the field commander had said.

Jerusalem's Deliverance Foretold

19 When King Hezekiah heard this, he tore his clothes and put on sackcloth and went into the temple of the LORD. [2]He sent Eliakim the palace administrator, Shebna the secretary and the leading priests, all wearing sackcloth, to the prophet Isaiah son of Amoz. [3]They told him, "This is what Hezekiah says: This day is a day of distress and rebuke and disgrace, as when children come to the moment of birth and there is no strength to deliver them. [4]It may be that the LORD your God will hear all the words of the field commander, whom his master, the king of Assyria, has sent to ridicule the living God, and that he will rebuke him for the words the LORD your God has heard. Therefore pray for the remnant that still survives."

[5]When King Hezekiah's officials came to Isaiah, [6]Isaiah said to them, "Tell your master, 'This is what the LORD says: Do not be afraid of what you have heard—those words with which the underlings of the king of Assyria have blasphemed me. [7]Listen! When he hears a certain report, I will make him want to return to his own country, and there I will have him cut down with the sword.'"

[8]When the field commander heard that the king of Assyria had left Lachish, he withdrew and found the king fighting against Libnah.

[9]Now Sennacherib received a report that Tirhakah, the king of Cush,^b was marching out to fight against him. So he again sent messengers to Hezekiah with this word: [10]"Say to Hezekiah king of Judah: Do not let the god you depend on deceive you when he says, 'Jerusalem will not be given into the hands of the king of Assyria.' [11]Surely you have heard what the kings of Assyria have done to all the countries, destroying them completely. And will you be delivered? [12]Did the gods of the nations that were destroyed by my predecessors deliver them—the gods of Gozan, Harran, Rezeph and the people of Eden who were in Tel Assar? [13]Where is the king of Hamath or the king of Arpad? Where are the kings of Lair, Sepharvaim, Hena and Ivvah?"

Hezekiah's Prayer

[14]Hezekiah received the letter from the messengers and read it. Then he went up to the temple of the LORD and spread it out before the LORD. [15]And Hezekiah prayed to the LORD: "LORD, the God of Israel, enthroned between the

---

^a 24 Or charioteers   ^b 9 That is, the upper Nile region

cherubim, you alone are God over all the kingdoms of the earth. You have made heaven and earth. ¹⁶Give ear, Lord, and hear; open your eyes, Lord, and see; listen to the words Sennacherib has sent to ridicule the living God.

¹⁷"It is true, Lord, that the Assyrian kings have laid waste these nations and their lands. ¹⁸They have thrown their gods into the fire and destroyed them, for they were not gods but only wood and stone, fashioned by human hands. ¹⁹Now, Lord our God, deliver us from his hand, so that all the kingdoms of the earth may know that you alone, Lord, are God."

Isaiah Prophesies Sennacherib's Fall

²⁰Then Isaiah son of Amoz sent a message to Hezekiah: "This is what the Lord, the God of Israel, says: I have heard your prayer concerning Sennacherib king of Assyria. ²¹This is the word that the Lord has spoken against him:

"'Virgin Daughter Zion
    despises you and mocks you.
Daughter Jerusalem
    tosses her head as you flee.
²²Who is it you have ridiculed and
      blasphemed?
    Against whom have you raised your voice
and lifted your eyes in pride?
    Against the Holy One of Israel!
²³By your messengers
    you have ridiculed the Lord.
And you have said,
    "With my many chariots
I have ascended the heights of the
      mountains,
    the utmost heights of Lebanon.
I have cut down its tallest cedars,
    the choicest of its junipers.
I have reached its remotest parts,
    the finest of its forests.
²⁴I have dug wells in foreign lands
    and drunk the water there.
With the soles of my feet
    I have dried up all the streams of Egypt."
²⁵"'Have you not heard?
    Long ago I ordained it.
In days of old I planned it;
    now I have brought it to pass,
that you have turned fortified cities
    into piles of stone.
²⁶Their people, drained of power,
    are dismayed and put to shame.
They are like plants in the field,
    like tender green shoots,
like grass sprouting on the roof,
    scorched before it grows up.

²⁷"'But I know where you are
    and when you come and go
    and how you rage against me.
²⁸Because you rage against me
    and because your insolence has reached
      my ears,
I will put my hook in your nose
    and my bit in your mouth,
and I will make you return
    by the way you came.'

²⁹"This will be the sign for you, Hezekiah:

"This year you will eat what grows by itself,
    and the second year what springs from
      that.
But in the third year sow and reap,
    plant vineyards and eat their fruit.
³⁰Once more a remnant of the kingdom of
      Judah
    will take root below and bear fruit
      above.
³¹For out of Jerusalem will come a remnant,
    and out of Mount Zion a band of
      survivors.

"The zeal of the Lord Almighty will accomplish this.

³²"Therefore this is what the Lord says concerning the king of Assyria:

"'He will not enter this city
    or shoot an arrow here.
He will not come before it with shield
    or build a siege ramp against it.
³³By the way that he came he will return;
    he will not enter this city,
           declares the Lord.
³⁴I will defend this city and save it,
    for my sake and for the sake of David my
      servant.'"

³⁵That night the angel of the Lord went out and put to death a hundred and eighty-five thousand in the Assyrian camp. When the people got up the next morning — there were all the dead bodies! ³⁶So Sennacherib king of Assyria broke camp and withdrew. He returned to Nineveh and stayed there.

³⁷One day, while he was worshiping in the temple of his god Nisrok, his sons Adrammelek and Sharezer killed him with the sword, and they escaped to the land of Ararat. And Esarhaddon his son succeeded him as king.

Hezekiah's Illness

20 In those days Hezekiah became ill and was at the point of death. The prophet Isaiah son of Amoz went to him and said, "This is what the LORD says: Put your house in order, because you are going to die; you will not recover."

²Hezekiah turned his face to the wall and prayed to the LORD, ³"Remember, LORD, how I have walked before you faithfully and with wholehearted devotion and have done what is good in your eyes." And Hezekiah wept bitterly.

⁴Before Isaiah had left the middle court, the word of the LORD came to him: ⁵"Go back and tell Hezekiah, the ruler of my people, 'This is what the LORD, the God of your father David, says: I have heard your prayer and seen your tears; I will heal you. On the third day from now you will go up to the temple of the LORD. ⁶I will add fifteen years to your life. And I will deliver you and this city from the hand of the king of Assyria. I will defend this city for my sake and for the sake of my servant David.'"

⁷Then Isaiah said, "Prepare a poultice of figs." They did so and applied it to the boil, and he recovered.

⁸Hezekiah had asked Isaiah, "What will be the sign that the LORD will heal me and that I will go up to the temple of the LORD on the third day from now?"

⁹Isaiah answered, "This is the LORD's sign to you that the LORD will do what he has promised: Shall the shadow go forward ten steps, or shall it go back ten steps?"

¹⁰"It is a simple matter for the shadow to go forward ten steps," said Hezekiah. "Rather, have it go back ten steps."

¹¹Then the prophet Isaiah called on the LORD, and the LORD made the shadow go back the ten steps it had gone down on the stairway of Ahaz.

Envoys From Babylon

¹²At that time Marduk-Baladan son of Baladan king of Babylon sent Hezekiah letters and a gift, because he had heard of Hezekiah's illness. ¹³Hezekiah received the envoys and showed them all that was in his storehouses — the silver, the gold, the spices and the fine olive oil — his armory and everything found among his treasures. There was nothing in his palace or in all his kingdom that Hezekiah did not show them.

¹⁴Then Isaiah the prophet went to King Hezekiah and asked, "What did those men say, and where did they come from?"

"From a distant land," Hezekiah replied. "They came from Babylon."

¹⁵The prophet asked, "What did they see in your palace?"

"They saw everything in my palace," Hezekiah said. "There is nothing among my treasures that I did not show them."

¹⁶Then Isaiah said to Hezekiah, "Hear the word of the LORD: ¹⁷The time will surely come when everything in your palace, and all that your predecessors have stored up until this day, will be carried off to Babylon. Nothing will be left, says the LORD. ¹⁸And some of your

Never Underestimate the Power of God

2 Kings 20:1–7

Hezekiah was one of only two kings in Judah who completely followed the Lord. In the days of Esarhaddon king of Assyria, Hezekiah lay on his deathbed. Isaiah the prophet had predicted the king's imminent death and told him to get his house in order.

But Hezekiah poured out his heart to the Lord and reminded God of his covenant, and how the king had faithfully led Judah. As Isaiah left the royal court, God heard Hezekiah's prayer and determined to heal him. God kept the king alive for another 15 years.

God did for the king what Hezekiah could not do for himself. Both God and Hezekiah knew their roles:

Hezekiah's Role	God's Role
1. Maintain a humble heart.	1. Demonstrate grace and power.
2. Submit to God's values.	2. Control the destiny of the land.
3. Ask God to meet needs.	3. Respond to needs of people.
4. Stay faithful to the covenant.	4. Stay faithful to the covenant.

descendants, your own flesh and blood who will be born to you, will be taken away, and they will become eunuchs in the palace of the king of Babylon."

¹⁹"The word of the LORD you have spoken is good," Hezekiah replied. For he thought, "Will there not be peace and security in my lifetime?"

²⁰As for the other events of Hezekiah's reign, all his achievements and how he made the pool and the tunnel by which he brought water into the city, are they not written in the book of the annals of the kings of Judah? ²¹Hezekiah rested with his ancestors. And Manasseh his son succeeded him as king.

Manasseh King of Judah

21 Manasseh was twelve years old when he became king, and he reigned in Jerusalem fifty-five years. His mother's name was Hephzibah. ²He did evil in the eyes of the LORD, following the detestable practices of the nations the LORD had driven out before the Israelites. ³He rebuilt the high places his father Hezekiah had destroyed; he also erected altars to Baal and made an Asherah pole, as Ahab king of Israel had done. He bowed down to all the starry hosts and worshiped them. ⁴He built altars in the temple of the LORD, of which the LORD had said, "In Jerusalem I will put my Name." ⁵In the two courts of the temple of the LORD, he built altars to all the starry hosts. ⁶He sacrificed his own son in the fire, practiced divination, sought omens, and consulted mediums and spiritists. He did much evil in the eyes of the LORD, arousing his anger.

⁷He took the carved Asherah pole he had made and put it in the temple, of which the LORD had said to David and to his son Solomon, "In this temple and in Jerusalem, which I have chosen out of all the tribes of Israel, I will put my Name forever. ⁸I will not again make the feet of the Israelites wander from the land I gave their ancestors, if only they will be careful to do everything I commanded them and will keep the whole Law that my servant Moses gave them." ⁹But the people did not listen. Manasseh led them astray, so that they did more evil than the nations the LORD had destroyed before the Israelites.

¹⁰The LORD said through his servants the prophets: ¹¹"Manasseh king of Judah has committed these detestable sins. He has done more evil than the Amorites who preceded him and has led Judah into sin with his idols. ¹²Therefore this is what the LORD, the God of Israel, says:

I am going to bring such disaster on Jerusalem and Judah that the ears of everyone who hears of it will tingle. ¹³I will stretch out over Jerusalem the measuring line used against Samaria and the plumb line used against the house of Ahab. I will wipe out Jerusalem as one wipes a dish, wiping it and turning it upside down. ¹⁴I will forsake the remnant of my inheritance and give them into the hands of enemies. They will be looted and plundered by all their enemies; ¹⁵they have done evil in my eyes and have aroused my anger from the day their ancestors came out of Egypt until this day."

¹⁶Moreover, Manasseh also shed so much innocent blood that he filled Jerusalem from end to end—besides the sin that he had caused Judah to commit, so that they did evil in the eyes of the LORD.

¹⁷As for the other events of Manasseh's reign, and all he did, including the sin he committed, are they not written in the book of the annals of the kings of Judah? ¹⁸Manasseh rested with his ancestors and was buried in his palace garden, the garden of Uzza. And Amon his son succeeded him as king.

Amon King of Judah

¹⁹Amon was twenty-two years old when he became king, and he reigned in Jerusalem two years. His mother's name was Meshullemeth daughter of Haruz; she was from Jotbah. ²⁰He did evil in the eyes of the LORD, as his father Manasseh had done. ²¹He followed completely the ways of his father, worshiping the idols his father had worshiped, and bowing down to them. ²²He forsook the LORD, the God of his ancestors, and did not walk in obedience to him.

²³Amon's officials conspired against him and assassinated the king in his palace. ²⁴Then the people of the land killed all who had plotted against King Amon, and they made Josiah his son king in his place.

²⁵As for the other events of Amon's reign, and what he did, are they not written in the book of the annals of the kings of Judah? ²⁶He was buried in his tomb in the garden of Uzza. And Josiah his son succeeded him as king.

The Book of the Law Found

22 Josiah was eight years old when he became king, and he reigned in Jerusalem thirty-one years. His mother's name was Jedidah daughter of Adaiah; she was from Bozkath. ²He did what was right in the eyes of the LORD and followed completely the ways of his father

David, not turning aside to the right or to the left.

[3] In the eighteenth year of his reign, King Josiah sent the secretary, Shaphan son of Azaliah, the son of Meshullam, to the temple of the LORD. He said: [4] "Go up to Hilkiah the high priest and have him get ready the money that has been brought into the temple of the LORD, which the doorkeepers have collected from the people. [5] Have them entrust it to the men appointed to supervise the work on the temple. And have these men pay the workers who repair the temple of the LORD— [6] the carpenters, the builders and the masons. Also have them purchase timber and dressed stone to repair the temple. [7] But they need not account for the money entrusted to them, because they are honest in their dealings."

[8] Hilkiah the high priest said to Shaphan the secretary, "I have found the Book of the Law in the temple of the LORD." He gave it to Shaphan, who read it. [9] Then Shaphan the secretary went to the king and reported to him: "Your officials have paid out the money that was in the temple of the LORD and have entrusted it to the workers and supervisors at the temple." [10] Then Shaphan the secretary informed the king, "Hilkiah the priest has given me a book." And Shaphan read from it in the presence of the king.

[11] When the king heard the words of the Book of the Law, he tore his robes. [12] He gave these orders to Hilkiah the priest, Ahikam son of Shaphan, Akbor son of Micaiah, Shaphan the secretary and Asaiah the king's attendant: [13] "Go and inquire of the LORD for me and for the people and for all Judah about what is written in this book that has been found. Great is the LORD's anger that burns against us because those who have gone before us have not obeyed the words of this book; they have not acted in accordance with all that is written there concerning us."

[14] Hilkiah the priest, Ahikam, Akbor, Shaphan and Asaiah went to speak to the prophet Huldah, who was the wife of Shallum son of Tikvah, the son of Harhas, keeper of the wardrobe. She lived in Jerusalem, in the New Quarter.

[15] She said to them, "This is what the LORD, the God of Israel, says: Tell the man who sent you to me, [16] 'This is what the LORD says: I am going to bring disaster on this place and its people, according to everything written in the book the king of Judah has read. [17] Because they have forsaken me and burned incense to other gods and aroused my anger by all the idols their hands have made,[a] my anger will burn against this place and will not be quenched.' [18] Tell the king of Judah, who sent you to inquire of the LORD, 'This is what the LORD, the God of Israel, says concerning the words you heard: [19] Because your heart was responsive and you humbled yourself before the LORD when you heard what I have spoken against this place and its people— that they would become a curse[b] and be laid waste—and because you tore your robes and wept in my presence, I also have heard you, declares the LORD. [20] Therefore I will gather you to your ancestors, and you will be buried in peace. Your eyes will not see all the disaster I am going to bring on this place.'"

So they took her answer back to the king.

Josiah Renews the Covenant

23 Then the king called together all the elders of Judah and Jerusalem. [2] He went up to the temple of the LORD with the people of Judah, the inhabitants of Jerusalem, the priests and the prophets—all the people from the least to the greatest. He read in their hearing all the words of the Book of the Covenant, which had been found in the temple of the LORD. [3] The king stood by the pillar and renewed the covenant in the presence of the LORD—to follow the LORD and keep his commands, statutes and decrees with all his heart and all his soul, thus confirming the words of the covenant written in this book. Then all the people pledged themselves to the covenant.

[4] The king ordered Hilkiah the high priest, the priests next in rank and the doorkeepers to remove from the temple of the LORD all the articles made for Baal and Asherah and all the starry hosts. He burned them outside Jerusalem in the fields of the Kidron Valley and took the ashes to Bethel. [5] He did away with the idolatrous priests appointed by the kings of Judah to burn incense on the high places of the towns of Judah and on those around Jerusalem—those who burned incense to Baal, to the sun and moon, to the constellations and to all the starry hosts. [6] He took the Asherah pole from the temple of the LORD to the Kidron Valley outside Jerusalem and burned it there. He ground it to powder and scattered the dust over the graves of the common people. [7] He also tore down the quarters of the male shrine prostitutes that were

---

[a] 17 Or *by everything they have done*   [b] 19 That is, their names would be used in cursing (see Jer. 29:22); or, others would see that they are cursed.

THE LAW OF THE PICTURE
Josiah: Outward Reform Begins with Inward Renewal

2 Kings 22:10—23:25

YOUNG KING Josiah is a classic example of the Law of the Picture. His leadership led to national reform in Israel, and he teaches us something today about how change occurs: Outward reform begins with inward renewal.

In 2 Kings 22–23 we read of Josiah's wholehearted devotion to God and his desire to lead the people well. He became king of Israel at the tender age of eight, if you can imagine that. His own spiritual passion began to influence the nation of Judah and eventually brought about public reform. We see that the leader must experience personal change before he or she can implement public change. Leaders make an impact the way an atomic bomb does: They implode before they explode. The cycle worked this way for King Josiah:

1. **Personal Renewal (inward work in the leader's own life)**
2. **Personal Change (outward expression)**
3. **Public Reform (inward work in the people's hearts)**
4. **Public Change (outward expression)**

Change From the Inside Out

Accomplishing public change begins with a leader's heart. True reformation isn't merely about behavior modification, but heart transformation. Once this young leader recognized the unhealthy state of his own life, he committed himself to repentance. He wanted to change himself. This reminds us that we must always begin our leadership journey with self-leadership. I must lead myself before I try to lead anyone else. Once Josiah's own heart changed, he couldn't keep it a secret. It flowed outward.

Further, when his own life changed, he was in position to change others. His example accelerated the public reform since everyone could see his transformed life. The change begins inside of the leader, then becomes visible outside. Next, it burns on the inside of the hearts of those who see the leader, and moves to an outward change in them as well.

When Albert Schweitzer spoke on the meaning of leadership, he said, "Example isn't the main thing in leadership. It's the only thing." While that may sound like an exaggeration, Schweitzer was simply saying that all the words you speak as a leader mean nothing if your life doesn't back it up. Hypocrisy is like a hole in your credibility pocket. If you don't support your words with your life, everything gets fuzzy, and you lose the authority you've accumulated. Former secretary of state Colin Powell said, "You can issue all the memos and give all the motivational speeches you want, but if the rest of the people in your organization don't see you putting forth your very best effort every single day, they won't either."

Through his own life, Josiah gave the people he led a picture of the change he wanted to see. He lived out the saying: Be the change you want to see in the world. This is what enabled him to bring about so much change in such a short amount of time.

Other kings had failed to reform Israel; still others took the nation in the wrong direction. It requires a leader to model the way to truly transform the followers.

Principles About the Law of the Picture:

1. *Most people are visual learners, not verbal learners.*

   Educators tell us that 89 percent of learning is visual. Most people need to see an example or a model before they really understand. What we see is what we will be. A picture really is worth a thousand words. Followers beg for leaders to "show me; don't just tell me."

2. *Good communication makes a vision clear. Good modeling makes it come alive.*

   There's no doubt that a leader's words are important. They clarify the vision we want to see come to pass. However, providing an example is so much more powerful and rare. It makes any vision come alive. People can see what is possible if they buy in to the vision.

3. *It's easier to teach what is right than to do what is right.*

   Any parent will tell you this. We always seem to find the right lectures on how our children should act. Sadly, they imitate our actions faster than they listen to our words. As leaders, we must do the difficult thing and practice what we preach.

4. *Leaders must work on themselves before they work on others.*

   This is exactly what Josiah did. First he bought in to the need for change in his own life; then he proclaimed the need for his citizens to change. The leader had to lead himself first.

5. *The most valuable gift I can give to others is a good example.*

   Leadership is more caught than taught. While every leader should become the best communicator he or she can be, communication is much more than words. Transforming communication combines clear speech and consistent modeling. There is nothing more confusing than a person who gives good advice but sets a bad example.

A survey was taken by a professional staffing corporation. They asked employees what single trait they most wanted from their supervisor. The number one trait desired in a boss was "to lead by example." The second most popular answer was: "to possess strong ethics and morals." In my opinion, these two characteristics are very similar. If you lead by example, you should be doing so with high morals and ethics. So almost all of the respondents said their biggest desire was for their bosses to have high integrity and lead by example. This just about says it all.

From reading these great chapters in 2 Kings, we don't really discover if Josiah was a masterful speaker, or if he possessed the charisma of King David before him. We do know that while he did read from the Holy Scriptures, he tended to turn some of the speaking task over to the priests at the time. It might be that he felt inadequate as a speaker because he was young and inexperienced. What we do know, however, is that his life spoke louder than any speech he could have given on public reform. His life drove the transformation home for everyone.

As we noted earlier in this book, when good kings led Israel, the people were good. When bad kings led Israel, the people went sour. Why? People do what people see. It isn't our words alone that can change others. King Josiah proclaimed the need for public reform, but his words had weight because he had experienced the change himself first. It has been said, "A pint of example is worth a gallon of advice."

in the temple of the LORD, the quarters where women did weaving for Asherah.

⁸Josiah brought all the priests from the towns of Judah and desecrated the high places, from Geba to Beersheba, where the priests had burned incense. He broke down the gateway at the entrance of the Gate of Joshua, the city governor, which was on the left of the city gate. ⁹Although the priests of the high places did not serve at the altar of the LORD in Jerusalem, they ate unleavened bread with their fellow priests.

¹⁰He desecrated Topheth, which was in the Valley of Ben Hinnom, so no one could use it to sacrifice their son or daughter in the fire to Molek. ¹¹He removed from the entrance to the temple of the LORD the horses that the kings of Judah had dedicated to the sun. They were in the court[a] near the room of an official named Nathan-Melek. Josiah then burned the chariots dedicated to the sun.

¹²He pulled down the altars the kings of Judah had erected on the roof near the upper room of Ahaz, and the altars Manasseh had built in the two courts of the temple of the LORD. He removed them from there, smashed them to pieces and threw the rubble into the Kidron Valley. ¹³The king also desecrated the high places that were east of Jerusalem on the south of the Hill of Corruption — the ones Solomon king of Israel had built for Ashtoreth the vile goddess of the Sidonians, for Chemosh the vile god of Moab, and for Molek the detestable god of the people of Ammon. ¹⁴Josiah smashed the sacred stones and cut down the Asherah poles and covered the sites with human bones.

¹⁵Even the altar at Bethel, the high place made by Jeroboam son of Nebat, who had caused Israel to sin — even that altar and high place he demolished. He burned the high place and ground it to powder, and burned the Asherah pole also. ¹⁶Then Josiah looked around, and when he saw the tombs that were there on the hillside, he had the bones removed from them and burned on the altar to defile it, in accordance with the word of the LORD proclaimed by the man of God who foretold these things.

¹⁷The king asked, "What is that tombstone I see?"

The people of the city said, "It marks the tomb of the man of God who came from Judah and pronounced against the altar of Bethel the very things you have done to it."

¹⁸"Leave it alone," he said. "Don't let anyone disturb his bones." So they spared his bones and those of the prophet who had come from Samaria.

¹⁹Just as he had done at Bethel, Josiah removed all the shrines at the high places that the

---

[a] 11 The meaning of the Hebrew for this word is uncertain.

JOSIAH

A King Who Could Do No Wrong
2 Kings 22:1—23:30

Josiah became king of Judah at age eight, following the murder of his wicked father (2Ki 21:23–26). Yet unlike his father, the Bible says Josiah "did what was right in the eyes of the LORD and followed completely the ways of his father David, not turning aside to the right or to the left" (22:2). Josiah's inner circle must have included righteous men and women—no doubt including his mother, Jedidah—who nurtured Josiah in the ways of God.

Josiah respected the role of spiritual leaders. He maintained a teachable spirit, desiring to hear the words of God. He listened to Scriptural rebuke and responded with brokenness, realizing how far from God's Law his people had strayed. Josiah's reign brought about the restoration of the temple, and his godly influence helped reduce the effects of decades of evil leadership. Josiah, God's servant, passionately pursued the things of God rather than personal prestige.

God rewarded Josiah by allowing him to live in peace. He died in battle, but never saw the devastation poised to sweep over his nation. Scripture devotes two entire chapters to his life and influence, compared with barely a sentence for the many wicked leaders. Unlike Josiah, their lives were like chaff blown away by the wind.

kings of Israel had built in the towns of Samaria and that had aroused the LORD's anger. ²⁰Josiah slaughtered all the priests of those high places on the altars and burned human bones on them. Then he went back to Jerusalem.

²¹The king gave this order to all the people: "Celebrate the Passover to the LORD your God, as it is written in this Book of the Covenant." ²²Neither in the days of the judges who led Israel nor in the days of the kings of Israel and the kings of Judah had any such Passover been observed. ²³But in the eighteenth year of King Josiah, this Passover was celebrated to the LORD in Jerusalem.

²⁴Furthermore, Josiah got rid of the mediums and spiritists, the household gods, the idols and all the other detestable things seen in Judah and Jerusalem. This he did to fulfill the requirements of the law written in the book that Hilkiah the priest had discovered in the temple of the LORD. ²⁵Neither before nor after Josiah was there a king like him who turned to the LORD as he did — with all his heart and with all his soul and with all his strength, in accordance with all the Law of Moses.

²⁶Nevertheless, the LORD did not turn away from the heat of his fierce anger, which burned against Judah because of all that Manasseh had done to arouse his anger. ²⁷So the LORD said, "I will remove Judah also from my presence as I removed Israel, and I will reject Jerusalem, the city I chose, and this temple, about which I said, 'My Name shall be there.'ᵃ"

²⁸As for the other events of Josiah's reign, and all he did, are they not written in the book of the annals of the kings of Judah?

²⁹While Josiah was king, Pharaoh Necho king of Egypt went up to the Euphrates River to help the king of Assyria. King Josiah marched out to meet him in battle, but Necho faced him and killed him at Megiddo. ³⁰Josiah's servants brought his body in a chariot from Megiddo to Jerusalem and buried him in his own tomb. And the people of the land took Jehoahaz son of Josiah and anointed him and made him king in place of his father.

Jehoahaz King of Judah

³¹Jehoahaz was twenty-three years old when he became king, and he reigned in Jerusalem three months. His mother's name was Hamutal daughter of Jeremiah; she was from Libnah. ³²He did evil in the eyes of the LORD, just as his predecessors had done. ³³Pharaoh Necho put him in chains at Riblah in the land of Hamath

so that he might not reign in Jerusalem, and he imposed on Judah a levy of a hundred talentsᵇ of silver and a talentᶜ of gold. ³⁴Pharaoh Necho made Eliakim son of Josiah king in place of his father Josiah and changed Eliakim's name to Jehoiakim. But he took Jehoahaz and carried him off to Egypt, and there he died. ³⁵Jehoiakim paid Pharaoh Necho the silver and gold he demanded. In order to do so, he taxed the land and exacted the silver and gold from the people of the land according to their assessments.

Jehoiakim King of Judah

³⁶Jehoiakim was twenty-five years old when he became king, and he reigned in Jerusalem eleven years. His mother's name was Zebidah daughter of Pedaiah; she was from Rumah. ³⁷And he did evil in the eyes of the LORD, just as his predecessors had done.

24 During Jehoiakim's reign, Nebuchadnezzar king of Babylon invaded the land, and Jehoiakim became his vassal for three years. But then he turned against Nebuchadnezzar and rebelled. ²The LORD sent Babylonian,ᵈ Aramean, Moabite and Ammonite raiders against him to destroy Judah, in accordance with the word of the LORD proclaimed by his servants the prophets. ³Surely these things happened to Judah according to the LORD's command, in order to remove them from his presence because of the sins of Manasseh and all he had done, ⁴including the shedding of innocent blood. For he had filled Jerusalem with innocent blood, and the LORD was not willing to forgive.

⁵As for the other events of Jehoiakim's reign, and all he did, are they not written in the book of the annals of the kings of Judah? ⁶Jehoiakim rested with his ancestors. And Jehoiachin his son succeeded him as king.

⁷The king of Egypt did not march out from his own country again, because the king of Babylon had taken all his territory, from the Wadi of Egypt to the Euphrates River.

Jehoiachin King of Judah

⁸Jehoiachin was eighteen years old when he became king, and he reigned in Jerusalem three months. His mother's name was Nehushta daughter of Elnathan; she was from Jerusalem. ⁹He did evil in the eyes of the LORD, just as his father had done.

ᵃ 27 1 Kings 8:29   ᵇ 33 That is, about 3 3/4 tons or about 3.4 metric tons   ᶜ 33 That is, about 75 pounds or about 34 kilograms   ᵈ 2 Or *Chaldean*

¹⁰At that time the officers of Nebuchadnezzar king of Babylon advanced on Jerusalem and laid siege to it, ¹¹and Nebuchadnezzar himself came up to the city while his officers were besieging it. ¹²Jehoiachin king of Judah, his mother, his attendants, his nobles and his officials all surrendered to him.

In the eighth year of the reign of the king of Babylon, he took Jehoiachin prisoner. ¹³As the LORD had declared, Nebuchadnezzar removed the treasures from the temple of the LORD and from the royal palace, and cut up the gold articles that Solomon king of Israel had made for the temple of the LORD. ¹⁴He carried all Jerusalem into exile: all the officers and fighting men, and all the skilled workers and artisans—a total of ten thousand. Only the poorest people of the land were left.

¹⁵Nebuchadnezzar took Jehoiachin captive to Babylon. He also took from Jerusalem to Babylon the king's mother, his wives, his officials and the prominent people of the land. ¹⁶The king of Babylon also deported to Babylon the entire force of seven thousand fighting men, strong and fit for war, and a thousand skilled workers and artisans. ¹⁷He made Mattaniah, Jehoiachin's uncle, king in his place and changed his name to Zedekiah.

Zedekiah King of Judah

¹⁸Zedekiah was twenty-one years old when he became king, and he reigned in Jerusalem eleven years. His mother's name was Hamutal daughter of Jeremiah; she was from Libnah. ¹⁹He did evil in the eyes of the LORD, just as Jehoiakim had done. ²⁰It was because of the LORD's anger that all this happened to Jerusalem and Judah, and in the end he thrust them from his presence.

The Fall of Jerusalem

Now Zedekiah rebelled against the king of Babylon.

25 So in the ninth year of Zedekiah's reign, on the tenth day of the tenth month, Nebuchadnezzar king of Babylon marched against Jerusalem with his whole army. He encamped outside the city and built siege works all around it. ²The city was kept under siege until the eleventh year of King Zedekiah.

³By the ninth day of the fourthᵃ month the famine in the city had become so severe that there was no food for the people to eat. ⁴Then the city wall was broken through, and the whole army fled at night through the gate between the two walls near the king's garden, though the

Babyloniansᵇ were surrounding the city. They fled toward the Arabah,ᶜ ⁵but the Babylonianᵈ army pursued the king and overtook him in the plains of Jericho. All his soldiers were separated from him and scattered, ⁶and he was captured.

He was taken to the king of Babylon at Riblah, where sentence was pronounced on him. ⁷They killed the sons of Zedekiah before his eyes. Then they put out his eyes, bound him with bronze shackles and took him to Babylon.

⁸On the seventh day of the fifth month, in the nineteenth year of Nebuchadnezzar king of Babylon, Nebuzaradan commander of the imperial guard, an official of the king of Babylon, came to Jerusalem. ⁹He set fire to the temple of the LORD, the royal palace and all the houses of Jerusalem. Every important building he burned down. ¹⁰The whole Babylonian army under the commander of the imperial guard broke down the walls around Jerusalem. ¹¹Nebuzaradan the commander of the guard carried into exile the people who remained in the city, along with the rest of the populace and those who had deserted to the king of Babylon. ¹²But the commander left behind some of the poorest people of the land to work the vineyards and fields.

¹³The Babylonians broke up the bronze pillars, the movable stands and the bronze Sea that were at the temple of the LORD and they carried the bronze to Babylon. ¹⁴They also took away the pots, shovels, wick trimmers, dishes and all the bronze articles used in the temple service. ¹⁵The commander of the imperial guard took away the censers and sprinkling bowls—all that were made of pure gold or silver.

¹⁶The bronze from the two pillars, the Sea and the movable stands, which Solomon had made for the temple of the LORD, was more than could be weighed. ¹⁷Each pillar was eighteen cubitsᵉ high. The bronze capital on top of one pillar was three cubitsᶠ high and was decorated with a network and pomegranates of bronze all around. The other pillar, with its network, was similar.

¹⁸The commander of the guard took as prisoners Seraiah the chief priest, Zephaniah the priest next in rank and the three doorkeepers. ¹⁹Of those still in the city, he took the officer in charge of the fighting men, and five royal advisers. He also took the secretary who was chief of-

---

ᵃ 3 Probable reading of the original Hebrew text (see Jer. 52:6); Masoretic Text does not have *fourth.*   ᵇ 4 Or *Chaldeans*; also in verses 13, 25 and 26   ᶜ 4 Or *the Jordan Valley*   ᵈ 5 Or *Chaldean*; also in verses 10 and 24   ᵉ 17 That is, about 27 feet or about 8.1 meters   ᶠ 17 That is, about 4 1/2 feet or about 1.4 meters

ficer in charge of conscripting the people of the land and sixty of the conscripts who were found in the city. [20]Nebuzaradan the commander took them all and brought them to the king of Babylon at Riblah. [21]There at Riblah, in the land of Hamath, the king had them executed.

So Judah went into captivity, away from her land.

[22]Nebuchadnezzar king of Babylon appointed Gedaliah son of Ahikam, the son of Shaphan, to be over the people he had left behind in Judah. [23]When all the army officers and their men heard that the king of Babylon had appointed Gedaliah as governor, they came to Gedaliah at Mizpah—Ishmael son of Nethaniah, Johanan son of Kareah, Seraiah son of Tanhumeth the Netophathite, Jaazaniah the son of the Maakathite, and their men. [24]Gedaliah took an oath to reassure them and their men. "Do not be afraid of the Babylonian officials," he said. "Settle down in the land and serve the king of Babylon, and it will go well with you."

[25]In the seventh month, however, Ishmael son of Nethaniah, the son of Elishama, who was of royal blood, came with ten men and assassinated Gedaliah and also the men of Judah and the Babylonians who were with him at Mizpah. [26]At this, all the people from the least to the greatest, together with the army officers, fled to Egypt for fear of the Babylonians.

Jehoiachin Released

[27]In the thirty-seventh year of the exile of Jehoiachin king of Judah, in the year Awel-Marduk became king of Babylon, he released Jehoiachin king of Judah from prison. He did this on the twenty-seventh day of the twelfth month. [28]He spoke kindly to him and gave him a seat of honor higher than those of the other kings who were with him in Babylon. [29]So Jehoiachin put aside his prison clothes and for the rest of his life ate regularly at the king's table. [30]Day by day the king gave Jehoiachin a regular allowance as long as he lived.

INTRODUCTION TO
1 CHRONICLES

The Public Office of Leaders

I f the books of Samuel and Kings teach us about the personal weaknesses of Israel's leaders, then 1 and 2 Chronicles outline the public office of those leaders and detail their leadership successes from a civil and religious point of view.

Rather than merely retelling the story of David's struggle with Saul, his sin with Bathsheba, and his rebellious household under Absalom, for example, 1 Chronicles focuses on the recovery of the ark of the covenant, the temple construction and dedication, and Israel's worship. It emphasizes God's mercy (especially in relation to David's shortcomings) and stresses the king's service to God.

The book begins with nine chapters of genealogies, thereby demonstrating the enormous value of heritage to the Jewish people. Ancestors often foreshadowed the lives of later descendants. Leaders could cite exactly their family trees; centuries later the apostle Paul spoke of being from the tribe of Benjamin, a Pharisee of the Pharisees. Following the genealogies, the text examines the leaders of Israel, beginning with King Saul. First Chronicles tells us precisely why Saul was killed and why David replaced him as king.

Immediately in David's leadership we observe the Law of the Lid, the Law of Respect, the Law of the Inner Circle, the Law of Timing, the Law of Solid Ground, the Law of Connection, the Law of Reproduction, the Law of Explosive Growth and the Law of Influence. His 40 years as king bring a series of remarkable accomplishments. He builds a standing army; defeats the inhabitants of Jerusalem and relocates his capital there; establishes national

God's Role in 1 Chronicles

In 1 Chronicles we see God as the grand Supervisor of Israel's exploits. Because the book does not delve much into the personal lives of the kings, but rather examines their public leadership, God plays the part of a divine Coach. He encourages, inspires, rewards, and disciplines his key players, so that the nation's spiritual climate can flourish.

God shows his pleasure when his leaders share his priorities, and displays great displeasure when they don't. The Lord affirmed King David and the citizens of Israel during his coronation, for example, but chastised the king when he usurped authority and called for a nationwide census. Again, we notice that God limits his dealings with the nation primarily to direct interaction with its leaders. God desired to lead the leaders and thus influence the whole country.

Leaders in 1 Chronicles
Saul, David, Nathan, Gad, Solomon

Other People of Influence in 1 Chronicles
Joab, Jashobeam, Eleazar, and the 30 leaders of David's mighty men

policy and order; and gathers the resources to build the temple (even though God will not allow him to build it himself). The book ends with David turning the kingdom over to Solomon, his son—and gaining the pledges of all his staff to faithfully serve the new king.

Lessons in Leadership

- Leadership is influence, nothing more and nothing less.
- Leaders who develop people win their fierce loyalty.
- Leaders increase their power when they share it with others.
- Effective leaders keep first things first.
- Leaders who last are marked by humility.
- Spiritual leaders trust God's mercy over man's justice.
- Healthy leaders assume responsibility for everything that happens under their watch.
- Great leaders expect to pay a price.
- Great leaders lead by example.
- Great leaders set up their successor for success.

LEADERSHIP HIGHLIGHTS IN 1 CHRONICLES

Historical Records From Adam to Abraham

To Noah's Sons

1 Adam, Seth, Enosh, [2]Kenan, Mahalalel, Jared, [3]Enoch, Methuselah, Lamech, Noah.

[4]The sons of Noah:[a]
Shem, Ham and Japheth.

The Japhethites

[5]The sons[b] of Japheth:
Gomer, Magog, Madai, Javan, Tubal, Meshek and Tiras.
[6]The sons of Gomer:
Ashkenaz, Riphath[c] and Togarmah.
[7]The sons of Javan:
Elishah, Tarshish, the Kittites and the Rodanites.

The Hamites

[8]The sons of Ham:
Cush, Egypt, Put and Canaan.
[9]The sons of Cush:
Seba, Havilah, Sabta, Raamah and Sabteka.
The sons of Raamah:
Sheba and Dedan.
[10]Cush was the father[d] of
Nimrod, who became a mighty warrior on earth.
[11]Egypt was the father of
the Ludites, Anamites, Lehabites, Naphtuhites, [12]Pathrusites, Kasluhites (from whom the Philistines came) and Caphtorites.
[13]Canaan was the father of
Sidon his firstborn,[e] and of the Hittites, [14]Jebusites, Amorites, Girgashites, [15]Hivites, Arkites, Sinites, [16]Arvadites, Zemarites and Hamathites.

The Semites

[17]The sons of Shem:
Elam, Ashur, Arphaxad, Lud and Aram.
The sons of Aram:[f]
Uz, Hul, Gether and Meshek.
[18]Arphaxad was the father of Shelah,
and Shelah the father of Eber.
[19]Two sons were born to Eber:
One was named Peleg,[g] because in his time the earth was divided; his brother was named Joktan.
[20]Joktan was the father of
Almodad, Sheleph, Hazarmaveth, Jerah, [21]Hadoram, Uzal, Diklah, [22]Obal,[h] Abimael, Sheba, [23]Ophir, Havilah and Jobab. All these were sons of Joktan.

[24]Shem, Arphaxad,[i] Shelah,
[25]Eber, Peleg, Reu,
[26]Serug, Nahor, Terah
[27]and Abram (that is, Abraham).

The Family of Abraham

[28]The sons of Abraham:
Isaac and Ishmael.

Descendants of Hagar

[29]These were their descendants:
Nebaioth the firstborn of Ishmael, Kedar, Adbeel, Mibsam, [30]Mishma, Dumah, Massa, Hadad, Tema, [31]Jetur, Naphish and Kedemah. These were the sons of Ishmael.

Descendants of Keturah

[32]The sons born to Keturah, Abraham's concubine:
Zimran, Jokshan, Medan, Midian, Ishbak and Shuah.
The sons of Jokshan:
Sheba and Dedan.
[33]The sons of Midian:
Ephah, Epher, Hanok, Abida and Eldaah.
All these were descendants of Keturah.

Descendants of Sarah

[34]Abraham was the father of Isaac.
The sons of Isaac:
Esau and Israel.

Esau's Sons

[35]The sons of Esau:
Eliphaz, Reuel, Jeush, Jalam and Korah.
[36]The sons of Eliphaz:
Teman, Omar, Zepho,[j] Gatam and Kenaz;
by Timna: Amalek.[k]

---

[a] 4 Septuagint; Hebrew does not have this line.   [b] 5 *Sons* may mean *descendants* or *successors* or *nations*; also in verses 6-9, 17 and 23.   [c] 6 Many Hebrew manuscripts and Vulgate (see also Septuagint and Gen. 10:3); most Hebrew manuscripts *Diphath*   [d] 10 *Father* may mean *ancestor* or *predecessor* or *founder*; also in verses 11, 13, 18 and 20.   [e] 13 Or *of the Sidonians, the foremost*   [f] 17 One Hebrew manuscript and some Septuagint manuscripts (see also Gen. 10:23); most Hebrew manuscripts do not have this line.   [g] 19 *Peleg* means *division.*   [h] 22 Some Hebrew manuscripts and Syriac (see also Gen. 10:28); most Hebrew manuscripts *Ebal*   [i] 24 Hebrew; some Septuagint manuscripts *Arphaxad, Cainan* (see also note at Gen. 11:10)   [j] 36 Many Hebrew manuscripts, some Septuagint manuscripts and Syriac (see also Gen. 36:11); most Hebrew manuscripts *Zephi*   [k] 36 Some Septuagint manuscripts (see also Gen. 36:12); Hebrew *Gatam, Kenaz, Timna and Amalek*

³⁷ The sons of Reuel:

Nahath, Zerah, Shammah and Mizzah.

The People of Seir in Edom

³⁸ The sons of Seir:

Lotan, Shobal, Zibeon, Anah, Dishon, Ezer and Dishan.

³⁹ The sons of Lotan:

Hori and Homam. Timna was Lotan's sister.

⁴⁰ The sons of Shobal:

Alvan,ᵃ Manahath, Ebal, Shepho and Onam.

The sons of Zibeon:

Aiah and Anah.

⁴¹ The son of Anah:

Dishon.

The sons of Dishon:

Hemdan,ᵇ Eshban, Ithran and Keran.

⁴² The sons of Ezer:

Bilhan, Zaavan and Akan.ᶜ

The sons of Dishanᵈ:

Uz and Aran.

The Rulers of Edom

⁴³ These were the kings who reigned in Edom before any Israelite king reigned:

Bela son of Beor, whose city was named Dinhabah.

⁴⁴ When Bela died, Jobab son of Zerah from Bozrah succeeded him as king.

⁴⁵ When Jobab died, Husham from the land of the Temanites succeeded him as king.

⁴⁶ When Husham died, Hadad son of Bedad, who defeated Midian in the country of Moab, succeeded him as king. His city was named Avith.

⁴⁷ When Hadad died, Samlah from Masrekah succeeded him as king.

⁴⁸ When Samlah died, Shaul from Rehoboth on the riverᵉ succeeded him as king.

⁴⁹ When Shaul died, Baal-Hanan son of Akbor succeeded him as king.

⁵⁰ When Baal-Hanan died, Hadad succeeded him as king. His city was named Pau,ᶠ and his wife's name was Mehetabel daughter of Matred, the daughter of Me-Zahab. ⁵¹ Hadad also died.

The chiefs of Edom were:

Timna, Alvah, Jetheth, ⁵²Oholibamah, Elah, Pinon, ⁵³Kenaz, Teman, Mibzar,

---

ᵃ 40 Many Hebrew manuscripts and some Septuagint manuscripts (see also Gen. 36:23); most Hebrew manuscripts *Alian*   ᵇ 41 Many Hebrew manuscripts and some Septuagint manuscripts (see also Gen. 36:26); most Hebrew manuscripts *Hamran*   ᶜ 42 Many Hebrew and Septuagint manuscripts (see also Gen. 36:27); most Hebrew manuscripts *Zaavan, Jaakan*   ᵈ 42 See Gen. 36:28; Hebrew *Dishon*, a variant of *Dishan*   ᵉ 48 Possibly the Euphrates   ᶠ 50 Many Hebrew manuscripts, some Septuagint manuscripts, Vulgate and Syriac (see also Gen. 36:39); most Hebrew manuscripts *Pai*

Genealogies: The Impact of a Leader's Heritage

1 Chronicles 1:1—9:44

The first nine chapters of 1 Chronicles furnish a genealogy of Israel's leaders—almost a third of the book! The enormous space given to these ancestral lists illustrates the vast importance of heritage to a Hebrew leader.

Such an emphasis can teach us several important lessons. Our generation and culture seem to place a much lower value on family stock and past tradition than did others in history. What do we learn from the lineages of these Jewish leaders?

1. **They remained connected to their heritage.**
2. **They saw their place in history and gained perspective from it.**
3. **They were able to honor and pay respect to their forefathers.**
4. **They saw their lineage as a family blessing and passed on this blessing.**
5. **They used their heritage to provide a sense of stability for their children.**
6. **They sensed tendencies of ancestral giftedness and calling.**
7. **They could retain their identity even when exiled to a foreign land.**

[54] Magdiel and Iram. These were the chiefs of Edom.

Israel's Sons

2 These were the sons of Israel:
Reuben, Simeon, Levi, Judah, Issachar, Zebulun, [2]Dan, Joseph, Benjamin, Naphtali, Gad and Asher.

Judah

To Hezron's Sons

[3] The sons of Judah:
Er, Onan and Shelah. These three were born to him by a Canaanite woman, the daughter of Shua. Er, Judah's firstborn, was wicked in the LORD's sight; so the LORD put him to death. [4]Judah's daughter-in-law Tamar bore Perez and Zerah to Judah. He had five sons in all.

[5] The sons of Perez:
Hezron and Hamul.

[6] The sons of Zerah:
Zimri, Ethan, Heman, Kalkol and Darda[a] — five in all.

[7] The son of Karmi:
Achar,[b] who brought trouble on Israel by violating the ban on taking devoted things.[c]

[8] The son of Ethan:
Azariah.

[9] The sons born to Hezron were:
Jerahmeel, Ram and Caleb.[d]

From Ram Son of Hezron

[10] Ram was the father of
Amminadab, and Amminadab the father of Nahshon, the leader of the people of Judah. [11]Nahshon was the father of Salmon,[e] Salmon the father of Boaz, [12]Boaz the father of Obed and Obed the father of Jesse.

[13] Jesse was the father of
Eliab his firstborn; the second son was Abinadab, the third Shimea, [14]the fourth Nethanel, the fifth Raddai, [15]the sixth Ozem and the seventh David. [16]Their sisters were Zeruiah and Abigail. Zeruiah's three sons were Abishai, Joab and Asahel. [17]Abigail was the mother of Amasa, whose father was Jether the Ishmaelite.

Caleb Son of Hezron

[18] Caleb son of Hezron had children by his wife Azubah (and by Jerioth). These were her sons: Jesher, Shobab and Ardon. [19]When Azubah died, Caleb married Ephrath, who bore him Hur. [20]Hur was the father of Uri, and Uri the father of Bezalel.

[21] Later, Hezron, when he was sixty years old, married the daughter of Makir the father of Gilead. He made love to her, and she bore him Segub. [22]Segub was the father of Jair, who controlled twenty-three towns in Gilead. [23](But Geshur and Aram captured Havvoth Jair,[f] as well as Kenath with its surrounding settlements — sixty towns.) All these were descendants of Makir the father of Gilead.

[24] After Hezron died in Caleb Ephrathah, Abijah the wife of Hezron bore him Ashhur the father[g] of Tekoa.

Jerahmeel Son of Hezron

[25] The sons of Jerahmeel the firstborn of Hezron:
Ram his firstborn, Bunah, Oren, Ozem and[h] Ahijah. [26]Jerahmeel had another wife, whose name was Atarah; she was the mother of Onam.

[27] The sons of Ram the firstborn of Jerahmeel:
Maaz, Jamin and Eker.

[28] The sons of Onam:
Shammai and Jada.

The sons of Shammai:
Nadab and Abishur.

[29] Abishur's wife was named Abihail, who bore him Ahban and Molid.

[30] The sons of Nadab:
Seled and Appaim. Seled died without children.

[31] The son of Appaim:
Ishi, who was the father of Sheshan.
Sheshan was the father of Ahlai.

[32] The sons of Jada, Shammai's brother:
Jether and Jonathan. Jether died without children.

---

[a] 6 Many Hebrew manuscripts, some Septuagint manuscripts and Syriac (see also 1 Kings 4:31); most Hebrew manuscripts *Dara*   [b] 7 *Achar* means *trouble*; *Achar* is called *Achan* in Joshua.   [c] 7 The Hebrew term refers to the irrevocable giving over of things or persons to the LORD, often by totally destroying them.   [d] 9 Hebrew *Kelubai*, a variant of *Caleb*   [e] 11 Septuagint (see also Ruth 4:21); Hebrew *Salma*   [f] 23 Or *captured the settlements of Jair*   [g] 24 *Father* may mean *civic leader* or *military leader*; also in verses 42, 45, 49-52 and possibly elsewhere.   [h] 25 Or *Oren and Ozem, by*

33 The sons of Jonathan:
    Peleth and Zaza.
    These were the descendants of Jerahmeel.
34 Sheshan had no sons — only daughters.
    He had an Egyptian servant named Jar-
    ha. 35 Sheshan gave his daughter in mar-
    riage to his servant Jarha, and she bore
    him Attai.
36 Attai was the father of Nathan,
    Nathan the father of Zabad,
37 Zabad the father of Ephlal,
    Ephlal the father of Obed,
38 Obed the father of Jehu,
    Jehu the father of Azariah,
39 Azariah the father of Helez,
    Helez the father of Eleasah,
40 Eleasah the father of Sismai,
    Sismai the father of Shallum,
41 Shallum the father of Jekamiah,
    and Jekamiah the father of Elishama.

The Clans of Caleb

42 The sons of Caleb the brother of Jerahme-
    el:
    Mesha his firstborn, who was the father
    of Ziph, and his son Mareshah,ᵃ who
    was the father of Hebron.
43 The sons of Hebron:
    Korah, Tappuah, Rekem and Shema.
44 Shema was the father of Raham, and
    Raham the father of Jorkeam. Rekem
    was the father of Shammai. 45 The son of
    Shammai was Maon, and Maon was the
    father of Beth Zur.
46 Caleb's concubine Ephah was the mother
    of Haran, Moza and Gazez. Haran was
    the father of Gazez.
47 The sons of Jahdai:
    Regem, Jotham, Geshan, Pelet, Ephah
    and Shaaph.
48 Caleb's concubine Maakah was the mother
    of Sheber and Tirhanah. 49 She also gave
    birth to Shaaph the father of Madman-
    nah and to Sheva the father of Makbe-
    nah and Gibea. Caleb's daughter was
    Aksah. 50 These were the descendants of
    Caleb.

    The sons of Hur the firstborn of Ephra-
    thah:
    Shobal the father of Kiriath Jearim,
51 Salma the father of Bethlehem, and
    Hareph the father of Beth Gader.
52 The descendants of Shobal the father of
    Kiriath Jearim were:

Haroeh, half the Manahathites, 53 and
the clans of Kiriath Jearim: the Ithrites,
Puthites, Shumathites and Mishraites.
From these descended the Zorathites
and Eshtaolites.
54 The descendants of Salma:
Bethlehem, the Netophathites, Atroth
Beth Joab, half the Manahathites, the
Zorites, 55 and the clans of scribesᵇ who
lived at Jabez: the Tirathites, Shimeath-
ites and Sucathites. These are the Kenites who came from Hammath, the father of the Rekabites.ᶜ

The Sons of David

3 These were the sons of David born to him
in Hebron:
    The firstborn was Amnon the son of
    Ahinoam of Jezreel;
    the second, Daniel the son of Abigail of
    Carmel;
2 the third, Absalom the son of Maakah
    daughter of Talmai king of Geshur;
    the fourth, Adonijah the son of Haggith;
3 the fifth, Shephatiah the son of Abital;
    and the sixth, Ithream, by his wife Eg-
    lah.
4 These six were born to David in Hebron,
    where he reigned seven years and six
    months.
David reigned in Jerusalem thirty-three years,
5 and these were the children born to him there:
    Shammua,ᵈ Shobab, Nathan and Sol-
    omon. These four were by Bathshebaᵉ
    daughter of Ammiel. 6 There were also
    Ibhar, Elishua,ᶠ Eliphelet, 7 Nogah, Ne-
    pheg, Japhia, 8 Elishama, Eliada and
    Eliphelet — nine in all. 9 All these were
    the sons of David, besides his sons by his
    concubines. And Tamar was their sister.

The Kings of Judah

10 Solomon's son was Rehoboam,
    Abijah his son,
    Asa his son,
    Jehoshaphat his son,
11 Jehoramᵍ his son,

ᵃ 42 The meaning of the Hebrew for this phrase is uncertain.
ᵇ 55 Or of the Sopherites   ᶜ 55 Or father of Beth Rekab
ᵈ 5 Hebrew Shimea, a variant of Shammua   ᵉ 5 One Hebrew
manuscript and Vulgate (see also Septuagint and 2 Samuel
11:3); most Hebrew manuscripts Bathshua   ᶠ 6 Two Hebrew
manuscripts (see also 2 Samuel 5:15 and 1 Chron. 14:5); most
Hebrew manuscripts Elishama   ᵍ 11 Hebrew Joram, a
variant of Jehoram

Ahaziah his son,
Joash his son,
[12] Amaziah his son,
Azariah his son,
Jotham his son,
[13] Ahaz his son,
Hezekiah his son,
Manasseh his son,
[14] Amon his son,
Josiah his son.
[15] The sons of Josiah:
Johanan the firstborn,
Jehoiakim the second son,
Zedekiah the third,
Shallum the fourth.
[16] The successors of Jehoiakim:
Jehoiachin[a] his son,
and Zedekiah.

The Royal Line After the Exile

[17] The descendants of Jehoiachin the captive:
Shealtiel his son, [18] Malkiram, Pedaiah, Shenazzar, Jekamiah, Hoshama and Nedabiah.
[19] The sons of Pedaiah:
Zerubbabel and Shimei.
The sons of Zerubbabel:
Meshullam and Hananiah.
Shelomith was their sister.
[20] There were also five others:
Hashubah, Ohel, Berekiah, Hasadiah and Jushab-Hesed.

[21] The descendants of Hananiah:
Pelatiah and Jeshaiah, and the sons of Rephaiah, of Arnan, of Obadiah and of Shekaniah.
[22] The descendants of Shekaniah:
Shemaiah and his sons:
Hattush, Igal, Bariah, Neariah and Shaphat — six in all.
[23] The sons of Neariah:
Elioenai, Hizkiah and Azrikam — three in all.
[24] The sons of Elioenai:
Hodaviah, Eliashib, Pelaiah, Akkub, Johanan, Delaiah and Anani — seven in all.

Other Clans of Judah

4 The descendants of Judah:
Perez, Hezron, Karmi, Hur and Shobal.
[2] Reaiah son of Shobal was the father of Jahath, and Jahath the father of Ahumai and Lahad. These were the clans of the Zorathites.
[3] These were the sons[b] of Etam:
Jezreel, Ishma and Idbash. Their sister was named Hazzelelponi. [4] Penuel was the father of Gedor, and Ezer the father of Hushah.

---

[a] 16 Hebrew *Jeconiah*, a variant of *Jehoiachin*; also in verse 17
[b] 3 Some Septuagint manuscripts (see also Vulgate); Hebrew *father*

AMNON
The High Cost of No Self-Discipline
1 Chronicles 3:1

PROFILE
in leadership

One might suppose the firstborn son of the greatest king of Israel to be almost fore-ordained to do great things for God and his people. Yet David's firstborn, Amnon, wound up as little more than a quick and sad footnote to the early chapters of 1 Chronicles.

Amnon forfeited any claim to leadership of his people because he could not control himself—specifically his fleshly lusts (2Sa 13:1–19). This lack of self-control led to the disgrace of his family, and eventually to his death at the hands of a vengeful brother (13:22–29).

Amnon's demise began the day he fixed his eyes upon his lovely half sister, Tamar, and lusted after her beauty. The Law expressly forbade this kind of union and laid out severe penalties for those who violated its provisions (Lev 18:9; 20:17). But this didn't deter Amnon, who hatched a plot to lie with his sister. Despite Tamar's horrified protests, Amnon forced himself on her and then sent her away in disgrace. When Absalom, Tamar's brother, heard what his half brother had done, he plotted revenge. At an opportune time, Absalom's men murdered Amnon and fled the scene.

A miserable, sordid story—and all because of a lack of discipline. No leader can afford to do without self-discipline. Amnon tried, and wished he hadn't.

These were the descendants of Hur, the firstborn of Ephrathah and father[a] of Bethlehem.

[5] Ashhur the father of Tekoa had two wives, Helah and Naarah.

[6] Naarah bore him Ahuzzam, Hepher, Temeni and Haahashtari. These were the descendants of Naarah.

[7] The sons of Helah:

Zereth, Zohar, Ethnan, [8] and Koz, who was the father of Anub and Hazzobebah and of the clans of Aharhel son of Harum.

[9] Jabez was more honorable than his brothers. His mother had named him Jabez,[b] saying, "I gave birth to him in pain." [10] Jabez cried out to the God of Israel, "Oh, that you would bless me and enlarge my territory! Let your hand be with me, and keep me from harm so that I will be free from pain." And God granted his request.

Jabez's Honorable Mention

1 Chronicles 4:9–10

God singled out one man from more than 600 others for special recognition in the genealogical lists of 1 Chronicles. Why did the Lord say Jabez lived above average? Because he modeled three qualities that make leaders rise to the top: (1) great ambition, (2) great faith, and (3) great prayer.

[11] Kelub, Shuhah's brother, was the father of Mehir, who was the father of Eshton. [12] Eshton was the father of Beth Rapha, Paseah and Tehinnah the father of Ir Nahash.[c] These were the men of Rekah.

[13] The sons of Kenaz:

Othniel and Seraiah.

The sons of Othniel:

Hathath and Meonothai.[d] [14] Meonothai was the father of Ophrah.

Seraiah was the father of Joab,

the father of Ge Harashim.[e] It was called this because its people were skilled workers.

[15] The sons of Caleb son of Jephunneh:

Iru, Elah and Naam.

The son of Elah:

Kenaz.

[16] The sons of Jehallelel:

Ziph, Ziphah, Tiria and Asarel.

[17] The sons of Ezrah:

Jether, Mered, Epher and Jalon. One of Mered's wives gave birth to Miriam, Shammai and Ishbah the father of Eshtemoa. [18] (His wife from the tribe of Judah gave birth to Jered the father of Gedor, Heber the father of Soko, and Jekuthiel the father of Zanoah.) These were the children of Pharaoh's daughter Bithiah, whom Mered had married.

[19] The sons of Hodiah's wife, the sister of Naham:

the father of Keilah the Garmite, and Eshtemoa the Maakathite.

[20] The sons of Shimon:

Amnon, Rinnah, Ben-Hanan and Tilon.

The descendants of Ishi:

Zoheth and Ben-Zoheth.

[21] The sons of Shelah son of Judah:

Er the father of Lekah, Laadah the father of Mareshah and the clans of the linen workers at Beth Ashbea, [22] Jokim, the men of Kozeba, and Joash and Saraph, who ruled in Moab and Jashubi Lehem. (These records are from ancient times.) [23] They were the potters who lived at Netaim and Gederah; they stayed there and worked for the king.

Simeon

[24] The descendants of Simeon:

Nemuel, Jamin, Jarib, Zerah and Shaul;

[25] Shallum was Shaul's son, Mibsam his son and Mishma his son.

[26] The descendants of Mishma:

Hammuel his son, Zakkur his son and Shimei his son.

[27] Shimei had sixteen sons and six daughters, but his brothers did not have many children; so their entire clan did not become as numerous as the people of Judah. [28] They lived in Beersheba, Moladah, Hazar Shual, [29] Bilhah, Ezem, Tolad, [30] Bethuel, Hormah, Ziklag, [31] Beth Markaboth, Hazar Susim, Beth Biri and Shaaraim. These were their towns until the reign of David. [32] Their surrounding villages were Etam, Ain, Rimmon, Token and Ashan — five towns —

---

[a] 4 *Father* may mean *civic leader* or *military leader*; also in verses 12, 14, 17, 18 and possibly elsewhere.   [b] 9 *Jabez* sounds like the Hebrew for *pain*.   [c] 12 Or *of the city of Nahash*   [d] 13 Some Septuagint manuscripts and Vulgate; Hebrew does not have *and Meonothai*.   [e] 14 *Ge Harashim* means *valley of skilled workers*.

³³and all the villages around these towns as far as Baalath.ᵃ These were their settlements. And they kept a genealogical record.

³⁴Meshobab, Jamlech, Joshah son of Amaziah, ³⁵Joel, Jehu son of Joshibiah, the son of Seraiah, the son of Asiel, ³⁶also Elioenai, Jaakobah, Jeshohaiah, Asaiah, Adiel, Jesimiel, Benaiah, ³⁷and Ziza son of Shiphi, the son of Allon, the son of Jedaiah, the son of Shimri, the son of Shemaiah.

³⁸The men listed above by name were leaders of their clans. Their families increased greatly, ³⁹and they went to the outskirts of Gedor to the east of the valley in search of pasture for their flocks. ⁴⁰They found rich, good pasture, and the land was spacious, peaceful and quiet. Some Hamites had lived there formerly.

⁴¹The men whose names were listed came in the days of Hezekiah king of Judah. They attacked the Hamites in their dwellings and also the Meunites who were there and completely destroyedᵇ them, as is evident to this day. Then they settled in their place, because there was pasture for their flocks. ⁴²And five hundred of these Simeonites, led by Pelatiah, Neariah, Rephaiah and Uzziel, the sons of Ishi, invaded the hill country of Seir. ⁴³They killed the remaining Amalekites who had escaped, and they have lived there to this day.

Reuben

5 The sons of Reuben the firstborn of Israel (he was the firstborn, but when he defiled his father's marriage bed, his rights as firstborn were given to the sons of Joseph son of Israel; so he could not be listed in the genealogical record in accordance with his birthright, ²and though Judah was the strongest of his brothers and a ruler came from him, the rights of the firstborn belonged to Joseph) — ³the sons of Reuben the firstborn of Israel:

Hanok, Pallu, Hezron and Karmi.
⁴The descendants of Joel:
Shemaiah his son, Gog his son, Shimei his son, ⁵Micah his son, Reaiah his son, Baal his son,
⁶and Beerah his son, whom Tiglath-Pileserᶜ king of Assyria took into exile. Beerah was a leader of the Reubenites.
⁷Their relatives by clans, listed according to their genealogical records:
Jeiel the chief, Zechariah, ⁸and Bela son of Azaz, the son of Shema, the son of Joel. They settled in the area from Aro-

er to Nebo and Baal Meon. ⁹To the east they occupied the land up to the edge of the desert that extends to the Euphrates River, because their livestock had increased in Gilead.

¹⁰During Saul's reign they waged war against the Hagrites, who were defeated at their hands; they occupied the dwellings of the Hagrites throughout the entire region east of Gilead.

Gad

¹¹The Gadites lived next to them in Bashan, as far as Salekah:
¹²Joel was the chief, Shapham the second, then Janai and Shaphat, in Bashan.
¹³Their relatives, by families, were:
Michael, Meshullam, Sheba, Jorai, Jakan, Zia and Eber — seven in all.
¹⁴These were the sons of Abihail son of Huri, the son of Jaroah, the son of Gilead, the son of Michael, the son of Jeshishai, the son of Jahdo, the son of Buz.
¹⁵Ahi son of Abdiel, the son of Guni, was head of their family.
¹⁶The Gadites lived in Gilead, in Bashan and its outlying villages, and on all the pasturelands of Sharon as far as they extended.

¹⁷All these were entered in the genealogical records during the reigns of Jotham king of Judah and Jeroboam king of Israel.

¹⁸The Reubenites, the Gadites and the half-tribe of Manasseh had 44,760 men ready for military service — able-bodied men who could handle shield and sword, who could use a bow, and who were trained for battle. ¹⁹They waged war against the Hagrites, Jetur, Naphish and Nodab. ²⁰They were helped in fighting them, and God delivered the Hagrites and all their allies into their hands, because they cried out to him during the battle. He answered their prayers, because they trusted in him. ²¹They seized the livestock of the Hagrites — fifty thousand camels, two hundred fifty thousand sheep and two thousand donkeys. They also took one hundred thousand people captive, ²²and many others fell slain, because the battle was God's. And they occupied the land until the exile.

ᵃ 33 Some Septuagint manuscripts (see also Joshua 19:8); Hebrew *Baal*   ᵇ 41 The Hebrew term refers to the irrevocable giving over of things or persons to the LORD, often by totally destroying them.   ᶜ 6 Hebrew *Tilgath-Pilneser*, a variant of *Tiglath-Pileser*; also in verse 26

The Half-Tribe of Manasseh

[23] The people of the half-tribe of Manasseh were numerous; they settled in the land from Bashan to Baal Hermon, that is, to Senir (Mount Hermon).

[24] These were the heads of their families: Epher, Ishi, Eliel, Azriel, Jeremiah, Hodaviah and Jahdiel. They were brave warriors, famous men, and heads of their families. [25] But they were unfaithful to the God of their ancestors and prostituted themselves to the gods of the peoples of the land, whom God had destroyed before them. [26] So the God of Israel stirred up the spirit of Pul king of Assyria (that is, Tiglath-Pileser king of Assyria), who took the Reubenites, the Gadites and the half-tribe of Manasseh into exile. He took them to Halah, Habor, Hara and the river of Gozan, where they are to this day.

Levi

6 [a] The sons of Levi:
 Gershon, Kohath and Merari.
[2] The sons of Kohath:
 Amram, Izhar, Hebron and Uzziel.
[3] The children of Amram:
 Aaron, Moses and Miriam.
 The sons of Aaron:
 Nadab, Abihu, Eleazar and Ithamar.
[4] Eleazar was the father of Phinehas,
 Phinehas the father of Abishua,
[5] Abishua the father of Bukki,
 Bukki the father of Uzzi,
[6] Uzzi the father of Zerahiah,
 Zerahiah the father of Meraioth,
[7] Meraioth the father of Amariah,
 Amariah the father of Ahitub,
[8] Ahitub the father of Zadok,
 Zadok the father of Ahimaaz,
[9] Ahimaaz the father of Azariah,
 Azariah the father of Johanan,
[10] Johanan the father of Azariah (it was he who served as priest in the temple Solomon built in Jerusalem),
[11] Azariah the father of Amariah,
 Amariah the father of Ahitub,
[12] Ahitub the father of Zadok,
 Zadok the father of Shallum,
[13] Shallum the father of Hilkiah,
 Hilkiah the father of Azariah,
[14] Azariah the father of Seraiah,
 and Seraiah the father of Jozadak. [b]
[15] Jozadak was deported when the LORD sent Judah and Jerusalem into exile by the hand of Nebuchadnezzar.

[16] The sons of Levi:
 Gershon, [c] Kohath and Merari.
[17] These are the names of the sons of Gershon:
 Libni and Shimei.
[18] The sons of Kohath:
 Amram, Izhar, Hebron and Uzziel.
[19] The sons of Merari:
 Mahli and Mushi.
 These are the clans of the Levites listed according to their fathers:
[20] Of Gershon:
 Libni his son, Jahath his son,
 Zimmah his son, [21] Joah his son,
 Iddo his son, Zerah his son
 and Jeatherai his son.
[22] The descendants of Kohath:
 Amminadab his son, Korah his son,
 Assir his son, [23] Elkanah his son,
 Ebiasaph his son, Assir his son,
[24] Tahath his son, Uriel his son,
 Uzziah his son and Shaul his son.
[25] The descendants of Elkanah:
 Amasai, Ahimoth,
[26] Elkanah his son, [d] Zophai his son,
 Nahath his son, [27] Eliab his son,
 Jeroham his son, Elkanah his son
 and Samuel his son. [e]
[28] The sons of Samuel:
 Joel [f] the firstborn
 and Abijah the second son.
[29] The descendants of Merari:
 Mahli, Libni his son,
 Shimei his son, Uzzah his son,
[30] Shimea his son, Haggiah his son
 and Asaiah his son.

The Temple Musicians

[31] These are the men David put in charge of the music in the house of the LORD after the ark came to rest there. [32] They ministered with music before the tabernacle, the tent of meeting, until Solomon built the temple of the LORD in Jerusalem. They performed their duties according to the regulations laid down for them.

---

[a] In Hebrew texts 6:1-15 is numbered 5:27-41, and 6:16-81 is numbered 6:1-66.   [b] 14 Hebrew Jehozadak, a variant of Jozadak; also in verse 15   [c] 16 Hebrew Gershom, a variant of Gershon; also in verses 17, 20, 43, 62 and 71   [d] 26 Some Hebrew manuscripts, Septuagint and Syriac; most Hebrew manuscripts Ahimoth [26] and Elkanah. The sons of Elkanah: [e] 27 Some Septuagint manuscripts (see also 1 Samuel 1:19,20 and 1 Chron. 6:33,34); Hebrew does not have and Samuel his son.   [f] 28 Some Septuagint manuscripts and Syriac (see also 1 Samuel 8:2 and 1 Chron. 6:33); Hebrew does not have Joel.

³³Here are the men who served, together with their sons:

From the Kohathites:
  Heman, the musician,
    the son of Joel, the son of Samuel,
  ³⁴the son of Elkanah, the son of Jeroham,
    the son of Eliel, the son of Toah,
  ³⁵the son of Zuph, the son of Elkanah,
    the son of Mahath, the son of Amasai,
  ³⁶the son of Elkanah, the son of Joel,
    the son of Azariah, the son of Zephaniah,
  ³⁷the son of Tahath, the son of Assir,
    the son of Ebiasaph, the son of Korah,
  ³⁸the son of Izhar, the son of Kohath,
    the son of Levi, the son of Israel;
³⁹and Heman's associate Asaph, who served at his right hand:
  Asaph son of Berekiah, the son of Shimea,
  ⁴⁰the son of Michael, the son of Baaseiah,^a
    the son of Malkijah, ⁴¹the son of Ethni,
    the son of Zerah, the son of Adaiah,
  ⁴²the son of Ethan, the son of Zimmah,
    the son of Shimei, ⁴³the son of Jahath,
    the son of Gershon, the son of Levi;
⁴⁴and from their associates, the Merarites, at his left hand:
  Ethan son of Kishi, the son of Abdi,
    the son of Malluk, ⁴⁵the son of Hashabiah,
    the son of Amaziah, the son of Hilkiah,
  ⁴⁶the son of Amzi, the son of Bani,
    the son of Shemer, ⁴⁷the son of Mahli,
    the son of Mushi, the son of Merari,
    the son of Levi.

⁴⁸Their fellow Levites were assigned to all the other duties of the tabernacle, the house of God. ⁴⁹But Aaron and his descendants were the ones who presented offerings on the altar of burnt offering and on the altar of incense in connection with all that was done in the Most Holy Place, making atonement for Israel, in accordance with all that Moses the servant of God had commanded.

⁵⁰These were the descendants of Aaron:
  Eleazar his son, Phinehas his son,
  Abishua his son, ⁵¹Bukki his son,
  Uzzi his son, Zerahiah his son,
  ⁵²Meraioth his son, Amariah his son,
  Ahitub his son, ⁵³Zadok his son
  and Ahimaaz his son.

⁵⁴These were the locations of their settlements allotted as their territory (they were assigned to the descendants of Aaron who were from the Kohathite clan, because the first lot was for them):

⁵⁵They were given Hebron in Judah with its surrounding pasturelands. ⁵⁶But the fields and villages around the city were given to Caleb son of Jephunneh.

⁵⁷So the descendants of Aaron were given Hebron (a city of refuge), and Libnah,^b Jattir, Eshtemoa, ⁵⁸Hilen, Debir, ⁵⁹Ashan, Juttah^c and Beth Shemesh, together with their pasturelands. ⁶⁰And from the tribe of Benjamin they were given Gibeon,^d Geba, Alemeth and Anathoth, together with their pasturelands.

The total number of towns distributed among the Kohathite clans came to thirteen.

⁶¹The rest of Kohath's descendants were allotted ten towns from the clans of half the tribe of Manasseh.

⁶²The descendants of Gershon, clan by clan, were allotted thirteen towns from the tribes of Issachar, Asher and Naphtali, and from the part of the tribe of Manasseh that is in Bashan.

⁶³The descendants of Merari, clan by clan, were allotted twelve towns from the tribes of Reuben, Gad and Zebulun.

⁶⁴So the Israelites gave the Levites these towns and their pasturelands. ⁶⁵From the tribes of Judah, Simeon and Benjamin they allotted the previously named towns.

⁶⁶Some of the Kohathite clans were given as their territory towns from the tribe of Ephraim.

⁶⁷In the hill country of Ephraim they were given Shechem (a city of refuge), and Gezer,^e ⁶⁸Jokmeam, Beth Horon, ⁶⁹Aijalon and Gath Rimmon, together with their pasturelands.

⁷⁰And from half the tribe of Manasseh the Israelites gave Aner and Bileam, together with their pasturelands, to the rest of the Kohathite clans.

⁷¹The Gershonites received the following:
  From the clan of the half-tribe of Manasseh they received Golan in Bashan and also Ashtaroth, together with their pasturelands;

^a 40 Most Hebrew manuscripts; some Hebrew manuscripts, one Septuagint manuscript and Syriac *Maaseiah*
^b 57 See Joshua 21:13; Hebrew *given the cities of refuge: Hebron, Libnah.*   ^c 59 Syriac (see also Septuagint and Joshua 21:16); Hebrew does not have *Juttah.*   ^d 60 See Joshua 21:17; Hebrew does not have *Gibeon.*   ^e 67 See Joshua 21:21; Hebrew *given the cities of refuge: Shechem, Gezer.*

⁷² from the tribe of Issachar
they received Kedesh, Daberath, ⁷³ Ramoth and Anem, together with their pasturelands;
⁷⁴ from the tribe of Asher
they received Mashal, Abdon, ⁷⁵ Hukok and Rehob, together with their pasturelands;
⁷⁶ and from the tribe of Naphtali
they received Kedesh in Galilee, Hammon and Kiriathaim, together with their pasturelands.

⁷⁷ The Merarites (the rest of the Levites) received the following:
From the tribe of Zebulun
they received Jokneam, Kartah,ᵃ Rimmono and Tabor, together with their pasturelands;
⁷⁸ from the tribe of Reuben across the Jordan east of Jericho
they received Bezer in the wilderness, Jahzah, ⁷⁹ Kedemoth and Mephaath, together with their pasturelands;
⁸⁰ and from the tribe of Gad
they received Ramoth in Gilead, Mahanaim, ⁸¹ Heshbon and Jazer, together with their pasturelands.

Issachar

7 The sons of Issachar:
Tola, Puah, Jashub and Shimron — four in all.
² The sons of Tola:
Uzzi, Rephaiah, Jeriel, Jahmai, Ibsam and Samuel — heads of their families. During the reign of David, the descendants of Tola listed as fighting men in their genealogy numbered 22,600.
³ The son of Uzzi:
Izrahiah.
The sons of Izrahiah:
Michael, Obadiah, Joel and Ishiah. All five of them were chiefs. ⁴ According to their family genealogy, they had 36,000 men ready for battle, for they had many wives and children.
⁵ The relatives who were fighting men belonging to all the clans of Issachar, as listed in their genealogy, were 87,000 in all.

Benjamin

⁶ Three sons of Benjamin:
Bela, Beker and Jediael.

⁷ The sons of Bela:
Ezbon, Uzzi, Uzziel, Jerimoth and Iri, heads of families — five in all. Their genealogical record listed 22,034 fighting men.
⁸ The sons of Beker:
Zemirah, Joash, Eliezer, Elioenai, Omri, Jeremoth, Abijah, Anathoth and Alemeth. All these were the sons of Beker. ⁹ Their genealogical record listed the heads of families and 20,200 fighting men.
¹⁰ The son of Jediael:
Bilhan.
The sons of Bilhan:
Jeush, Benjamin, Ehud, Kenaanah, Zethan, Tarshish and Ahishahar. ¹¹ All these sons of Jediael were heads of families. There were 17,200 fighting men ready to go out to war.
¹² The Shuppites and Huppites were the descendants of Ir, and the Hushitesᵇ the descendants of Aher.

Naphtali

¹³ The sons of Naphtali:
Jahziel, Guni, Jezer and Shillemᶜ — the descendants of Bilhah.

Manasseh

¹⁴ The descendants of Manasseh:
Asriel was his descendant through his Aramean concubine. She gave birth to Makir the father of Gilead. ¹⁵ Makir took a wife from among the Huppites and Shuppites. His sister's name was Maakah.
Another descendant was named Zelophehad, who had only daughters.
¹⁶ Makir's wife Maakah gave birth to a son and named him Peresh. His brother was named Sheresh, and his sons were Ulam and Rakem.
¹⁷ The son of Ulam:
Bedan.
These were the sons of Gilead son of Makir, the son of Manasseh. ¹⁸ His sister Hammoleketh gave birth to Ishhod, Abiezer and Mahlah.
¹⁹ The sons of Shemida were:
Ahian, Shechem, Likhi and Aniam.

ᵃ 77 See Septuagint and Joshua 21:34; Hebrew does not have *Jokneam, Kartah.*   ᵇ 12 Or *Ir. The sons of Dan: Hushim,* (see Gen. 46:23); Hebrew does not have *The sons of Dan.*
ᶜ 13 Some Hebrew and Septuagint manuscripts (see also Gen. 46:24 and Num. 26:49); most Hebrew manuscripts *Shallum*

Ephraim

20 The descendants of Ephraim:
Shuthelah, Bered his son,
Tahath his son, Eleadah his son,
Tahath his son, 21 Zabad his son
and Shuthelah his son.

Ezer and Elead were killed by the native-born men of Gath, when they went down to seize their livestock. 22 Their father Ephraim mourned for them many days, and his relatives came to comfort him. 23 Then he made love to his wife again, and she became pregnant and gave birth to a son. He named him Beriah,[a] because there had been misfortune in his family. 24 His daughter was Sheerah, who built Lower and Upper Beth Horon as well as Uzzen Sheerah.

25 Rephah was his son, Resheph his son,[b]
Telah his son, Tahan his son,
26 Ladan his son, Ammihud his son,
Elishama his son, 27 Nun his son
and Joshua his son.

28 Their lands and settlements included Bethel and its surrounding villages, Naaran to the east, Gezer and its villages to the west, and Shechem and its villages all the way to Ayyah and its villages. 29 Along the borders of Manasseh were Beth Shan, Taanach, Megiddo and Dor, together with their villages. The descendants of Joseph son of Israel lived in these towns.

Asher

30 The sons of Asher:
Imnah, Ishvah, Ishvi and Beriah. Their sister was Serah.
31 The sons of Beriah:
Heber and Malkiel, who was the father of Birzaith.
32 Heber was the father of Japhlet, Shomer and Hotham and of their sister Shua.
33 The sons of Japhlet:
Pasak, Bimhal and Ashvath.
These were Japhlet's sons.
34 The sons of Shomer:
Ahi, Rohgah,[c] Hubbah and Aram.
35 The sons of his brother Helem:
Zophah, Imna, Shelesh and Amal.
36 The sons of Zophah:
Suah, Harnepher, Shual, Beri, Imrah,
37 Bezer, Hod, Shamma, Shilshah, Ithran[d] and Beera.
38 The sons of Jether:
Jephunneh, Pispah and Ara.

39 The sons of Ulla:
Arah, Hanniel and Rizia.

40 All these were descendants of Asher—heads of families, choice men, brave warriors and outstanding leaders. The number of men ready for battle, as listed in their genealogy, was 26,000.

The Genealogy of Saul the Benjamite

8 Benjamin was the father of Bela his firstborn,
Ashbel the second son, Aharah the third,
2 Nohah the fourth and Rapha the fifth.
3 The sons of Bela were:
Addar, Gera, Abihud,[e] 4 Abishua, Naaman, Ahoah, 5 Gera, Shephuphan and Huram.
6 These were the descendants of Ehud, who were heads of families of those living in Geba and were deported to Manahath:
7 Naaman, Ahijah, and Gera, who deported them and who was the father of Uzza and Ahihud.
8 Sons were born to Shaharaim in Moab after he had divorced his wives Hushim and Baara. 9 By his wife Hodesh he had Jobab, Zibia, Mesha, Malkam, 10 Jeuz, Sakia and Mirmah. These were his sons, heads of families. 11 By Hushim he had Abitub and Elpaal.
12 The sons of Elpaal:
Eber, Misham, Shemed (who built Ono and Lod with its surrounding villages), 13 and Beriah and Shema, who were heads of families of those living in Aijalon and who drove out the inhabitants of Gath.
14 Ahio, Shashak, Jeremoth, 15 Zebadiah, Arad, Eder, 16 Michael, Ishpah and Joha were the sons of Beriah.
17 Zebadiah, Meshullam, Hizki, Heber, 18 Ishmerai, Izliah and Jobab were the sons of Elpaal.
19 Jakim, Zikri, Zabdi, 20 Elienai, Zillethai, Eliel, 21 Adaiah, Beraiah and Shimrath were the sons of Shimei.
22 Ishpan, Eber, Eliel, 23 Abdon, Zikri, Hanan, 24 Hananiah, Elam, Anthothijah, 25 Iphdeiah and Penuel were the sons of Shashak.

---

[a] 23 Beriah sounds like the Hebrew for misfortune.
[b] 25 Some Septuagint manuscripts; Hebrew does not have his son.   [c] 34 Or of his brother Shomer: Rohgah   [d] 37 Possibly a variant of Jether   [e] 3 Or Gera the father of Ehud

26Shamsherai, Shehariah, Athaliah, 27Jaare-shiah, Elijah and Zikri were the sons of Jeroham.

28All these were heads of families, chiefs as listed in their genealogy, and they lived in Jerusalem.

29Jeiel[a] the father[b] of Gibeon lived in Gibeon. His wife's name was Maakah, 30and his firstborn son was Abdon, followed by Zur, Kish, Baal, Ner,[c] Nadab, 31Gedor, Ahio, Zeker 32and Mikloth, who was the father of Shimeah. They too lived near their relatives in Jerusalem.

33Ner was the father of Kish, Kish the father of Saul, and Saul the father of Jonathan, Malki-Shua, Abinadab and Esh-Baal.[d]

34The son of Jonathan:
Merib-Baal,[e] who was the father of Micah.

35The sons of Micah:
Pithon, Melek, Tarea and Ahaz.

36Ahaz was the father of Jehoaddah, Jehoaddah was the father of Alemeth, Azmaveth and Zimri, and Zimri was the father of Moza. 37Moza was the father of Binea; Raphah was his son, Eleasah his son and Azel his son.

38Azel had six sons, and these were their names:
Azrikam, Bokeru, Ishmael, Sheariah, Obadiah and Hanan. All these were the sons of Azel.

39The sons of his brother Eshek:
Ulam his firstborn, Jeush the second son and Eliphelet the third. 40The sons of Ulam were brave warriors who could handle the bow. They had many sons and grandsons—150 in all.
All these were the descendants of Benjamin.

9 All Israel was listed in the genealogies recorded in the book of the kings of Israel and Judah. They were taken captive to Babylon because of their unfaithfulness.

The People in Jerusalem

2Now the first to resettle on their own property in their own towns were some Israelites, priests, Levites and temple servants.

3Those from Judah, from Benjamin, and from Ephraim and Manasseh who lived in Jerusalem were:

4Uthai son of Ammihud, the son of Omri, the son of Imri, the son of Bani, a descendant of Perez son of Judah.

5Of the Shelanites[f]:
Asaiah the firstborn and his sons.

6Of the Zerahites:
Jeuel.
The people from Judah numbered 690.

7Of the Benjamites:
Sallu son of Meshullam, the son of Hodaviah, the son of Hassenuah;

8Ibneiah son of Jeroham; Elah son of Uzzi, the son of Mikri; and Meshullam son of Shephatiah, the son of Reuel, the son of Ibnijah.

9The people from Benjamin, as listed in their genealogy, numbered 956. All these men were heads of their families.

10Of the priests:
Jedaiah; Jehoiarib; Jakin;

11Azariah son of Hilkiah, the son of Meshullam, the son of Zadok, the son of Meraioth, the son of Ahitub, the official in charge of the house of God;

12Adaiah son of Jeroham, the son of Pashhur, the son of Malkijah; and Maasai son of Adiel, the son of Jahzerah, the son of Meshullam, the son of Meshillemith, the son of Immer.

13The priests, who were heads of families, numbered 1,760. They were able men, responsible for ministering in the house of God.

14Of the Levites:
Shemaiah son of Hasshub, the son of Azrikam, the son of Hashabiah, a Merarite; 15Bakbakkar, Heresh, Galal and Mattaniah son of Mika, the son of Zikri, the son of Asaph; 16Obadiah son of Shemaiah, the son of Galal, the son of Jeduthun; and Berekiah son of Asa, the son of Elkanah, who lived in the villages of the Netophathites.

17The gatekeepers:
Shallum, Akkub, Talmon, Ahiman and their fellow Levites, Shallum their chief 18being stationed at the King's Gate on the east, up to the present time. These were the gatekeepers belonging to the camp of the Levites. 19Shallum son of

a 29 Some Septuagint manuscripts (see also 9:35); Hebrew does not have Jeiel.   b 29 Father may mean civic leader or military leader.   c 30 Some Septuagint manuscripts (see also 9:36); Hebrew does not have Ner.   d 33 Also known as Ish-Bosheth   e 34 Also known as Mephibosheth   f 5 See Num. 26:20; Hebrew Shilonites.

Kore, the son of Ebiasaph, the son of Korah, and his fellow gatekeepers from his family (the Korahites) were responsible for guarding the thresholds of the tent just as their ancestors had been responsible for guarding the entrance to the dwelling of the LORD. [20]In earlier times Phinehas son of Eleazar was the official in charge of the gatekeepers, and the LORD was with him. [21]Zechariah son of Meshelemiah was the gatekeeper at the entrance to the tent of meeting.

[22]Altogether, those chosen to be gatekeepers at the thresholds numbered 212. They were registered by genealogy in their villages. The gatekeepers had been assigned to their positions of trust by David and Samuel the seer. [23]They and their descendants were in charge of guarding the gates of the house of the LORD — the house called the tent of meeting. [24]The gatekeepers were on the four sides: east, west, north and south. [25]Their fellow Levites in their villages had to come from time to time and share their duties for seven-day periods. [26]But the four principal gatekeepers, who were Levites, were entrusted with the responsibility for the rooms and treasuries in the house of God. [27]They would spend the night stationed around the house of God, because they had to guard it; and they had charge of the key for opening it each morning.

[28]Some of them were in charge of the articles used in the temple service; they counted them when they were brought in and when they were taken out. [29]Others were assigned to take care of the furnishings and all the other articles of the sanctuary, as well as the special flour and wine, and the olive oil, incense and spices. [30]But some of the priests took care of mixing the spices. [31]A Levite named Mattithiah, the firstborn son of Shallum the Korahite, was entrusted with the responsibility for baking the offering bread. [32]Some of the Kohathites, their fellow Levites, were in charge of preparing for every Sabbath the bread set out on the table.

[33]Those who were musicians, heads of Levite families, stayed in the rooms of the temple and were exempt from other duties because they were responsible for the work day and night.

[34]All these were heads of Levite families, chiefs as listed in their genealogy, and they lived in Jerusalem.

The Genealogy of Saul

[35]Jeiel the father[a] of Gibeon lived in Gibeon. His wife's name was Maakah, [36]and his firstborn son was Abdon, followed by Zur, Kish, Baal, Ner, Nadab, [37]Gedor, Ahio, Zechariah and Mikloth. [38]Mikloth was the father of Shimeam. They too lived near their relatives in Jerusalem.

[39]Ner was the father of Kish, Kish the father of Saul, and Saul the father of Jonathan, Malki-Shua, Abinadab and Esh-Baal.[b]

[40]The son of Jonathan:

Merib-Baal,[c] who was the father of Micah.

[41]The sons of Micah:

Pithon, Melek, Tahrea and Ahaz.[d]

[42]Ahaz was the father of Jadah, Jadah[e] was the father of Alemeth, Azmaveth and Zimri, and Zimri was the father of Moza. [43]Moza was the father of Binea; Rephaiah was his son, Eleasah his son and Azel his son.

[44]Azel had six sons, and these were their names:

Azrikam, Bokeru, Ishmael, Sheariah, Obadiah and Hanan. These were the sons of Azel.

Saul Takes His Life

10 Now the Philistines fought against Israel; the Israelites fled before them, and many fell dead on Mount Gilboa. [2]The Philistines were in hot pursuit of Saul and his sons, and they killed his sons Jonathan, Abinadab and Malki-Shua. [3]The fighting grew fierce around Saul, and when the archers overtook him, they wounded him.

[4]Saul said to his armor-bearer, "Draw your sword and run me through, or these uncircumcised fellows will come and abuse me."

But his armor-bearer was terrified and would not do it; so Saul took his own sword and fell on it. [5]When the armor-bearer saw that Saul was dead, he too fell on his sword and died. [6]So Saul and his three sons died, and all his house died together.

[7]When all the Israelites in the valley saw that the army had fled and that Saul and his sons had died, they abandoned their towns and fled. And the Philistines came and occupied them.

[8]The next day, when the Philistines came to strip the dead, they found Saul and his sons fallen on Mount Gilboa. [9]They stripped him and took his head and his armor, and sent messen-

---

[a] 35 Father may mean civic leader or military leader.
[b] 39 Also known as Ish-Bosheth   [c] 40 Also known as Mephibosheth   [d] 41 Vulgate and Syriac (see also Septuagint and 8:35); Hebrew does not have and Ahaz.   [e] 42 Some Hebrew manuscripts and Septuagint (see also 8:36); most Hebrew manuscripts Jarah, Jarah

gers throughout the land of the Philistines to proclaim the news among their idols and their people. [10]They put his armor in the temple of their gods and hung up his head in the temple of Dagon.

[11]When all the inhabitants of Jabesh Gilead heard what the Philistines had done to Saul, [12]all their valiant men went and took the bodies of Saul and his sons and brought them to Jabesh. Then they buried their bones under the great tree in Jabesh, and they fasted seven days.

[13]Saul died because he was unfaithful to the LORD; he did not keep the word of the LORD and even consulted a medium for guidance, [14]and did not inquire of the LORD. So the LORD put him to death and turned the kingdom over to David son of Jesse.

David Becomes King Over Israel

11 All Israel came together to David at Hebron and said, "We are your own flesh and blood. [2]In the past, even while Saul was king, you were the one who led Israel on their military campaigns. And the LORD your God said to you, 'You will shepherd my people Israel, and you will become their ruler.'"

[3]When all the elders of Israel had come to King David at Hebron, he made a covenant with them at Hebron before the LORD, and they anointed David king over Israel, as the LORD had promised through Samuel.

David Conquers Jerusalem

[4]David and all the Israelites marched to Jerusalem (that is, Jebus). The Jebusites who lived there [5]said to David, "You will not get in here."

Nevertheless, David captured the fortress of Zion—which is the City of David.

[6]David had said, "Whoever leads the attack on the Jebusites will become commander-in-chief." Joab son of Zeruiah went up first, and so he received the command.

[7]David then took up residence in the fortress, and so it was called the City of David. [8]He built up the city around it, from the terraces[a] to the surrounding wall, while Joab restored the rest of the city. [9]And David became more and more powerful, because the LORD Almighty was with him.

David's Mighty Warriors

[10]These were the chiefs of David's mighty warriors—they, together with all Israel, gave his kingship strong support to extend it over the whole land, as the LORD had promised— [11]this is the list of David's mighty warriors:

Jashobeam,[b] a Hakmonite, was chief of the officers[c]; he raised his spear against three hundred men, whom he killed in one encounter.

[12]Next to him was Eleazar son of Dodai the Ahohite, one of the three mighty warriors. [13]He was with David at Pas Dammim when the Philistines gathered there for battle. At a place where there was a field full of barley, the troops fled from the Philistines. [14]But they took their stand in the middle of the field. They defended it and struck the Philistines down, and the LORD brought about a great victory.

---

[a] 8 Or the Millo   [b] 11 Possibly a variant of Jashob-Baal
[c] 11 Or Thirty; some Septuagint manuscripts Three (see also 2 Samuel 23:8)

The Law of Influence: David Led Before Saul Left Office

1 Chronicles 11:1–3

As the most influential man in the country, David was leading long before Saul lost his throne. Like it or not, position doesn't make a person a leader. Title may give someone authority, but not influence. Influence comes from the person; it must be earned. David had earned it and Saul had not. Why was this so?

1. **Unity:** David rallied the people and created unity (v. 1).

2. **Identification:** David identified with his followers as family (v. 1).

3. **Credibility:** David effectively led various military campaigns (v. 2).

4. **Anointing:** David enjoyed God's hand and power on his life (v. 2).

5. **Partnership:** David worked cooperatively with key leaders, not over them (v. 3).

The Law of Magnetism: David Attracted Loyal Risk Takers

1 Chronicles 11:10–23

The Scripture offers an impressive list of military leaders connected to David, calling them his "mighty warriors" and describing several of their incredible exploits.

Have you ever wondered how David was able to attract such a qualified and extraordinary group of leaders? The answer lies in the Law of Magnetism. Leaders attract people like themselves.

David's Qualities	Parallels from David's Men
1. Submissive and loyal to Saul	1. Submissive and loyal to David (v. 10)
2. Slew many enemy soldiers in battle	2. Slew many enemy soldiers in battle (v. 11)
3. Took a stand against the Philistines	3. Took a stand against the Philistines (v. 14)
4. Risked his life and went the extra mile	4. Risked life and went the extra mile (v. 18)
5. Killed a lion single-handedly	5. Killed a lion single-handedly (v. 22)
6. Slew a giant	6. Slew a giant (v. 23)

¹⁵Three of the thirty chiefs came down to David to the rock at the cave of Adullam, while a band of Philistines was encamped in the Valley of Rephaim. ¹⁶At that time David was in the stronghold, and the Philistine garrison was at Bethlehem. ¹⁷David longed for water and said, "Oh, that someone would get me a drink of water from the well near the gate of Bethlehem!" ¹⁸So the Three broke through the Philistine lines, drew water from the well near the gate of Bethlehem and carried it back to David. But he refused to drink it; instead, he poured it out to the LORD. ¹⁹"God forbid that I should do this!" he said. "Should I drink the blood of these men who went at the risk of their lives?" Because they risked their lives to bring it back, David would not drink it.

Such were the exploits of the three mighty warriors.

²⁰Abishai the brother of Joab was chief of the Three. He raised his spear against three hundred men, whom he killed, and so he became as famous as the Three. ²¹He was doubly honored above the Three and became their commander, even though he was not included among them.

²²Benaiah son of Jehoiada, a valiant fighter from Kabzeel, performed great exploits. He struck down Moab's two mightiest warriors. He also went down into a pit on a snowy day and killed a lion. ²³And he struck down an Egyptian who was five cubits*a* tall. Although the Egyptian had a spear like a weaver's rod in his hand, Benaiah went against him with a club. He snatched the spear from the Egyptian's hand and killed

him with his own spear. ²⁴Such were the exploits of Benaiah son of Jehoiada; he too was as famous as the three mighty warriors. ²⁵He was held in greater honor than any of the Thirty, but he was not included among the Three. And David put him in charge of his bodyguard.

²⁶The mighty warriors were:
Asahel the brother of Joab,
Elhanan son of Dodo from Bethlehem,
²⁷Shammoth the Harorite,
Helez the Pelonite,
²⁸Ira son of Ikkesh from Tekoa,
Abiezer from Anathoth,
²⁹Sibbekai the Hushathite,
Ilai the Ahohite,
³⁰Maharai the Netophathite,
Heled son of Baanah the Netophathite,
³¹Ithai son of Ribai from Gibeah in Benjamin,
Benaiah the Pirathonite,
³²Hurai from the ravines of Gaash,
Abiel the Arbathite,
³³Azmaveth the Baharumite,
Eliahba the Shaalbonite,
³⁴the sons of Hashem the Gizonite,
Jonathan son of Shagee the Hararite,
³⁵Ahiam son of Sakar the Hararite,
Eliphal son of Ur,
³⁶Hepher the Mekerathite,
Ahijah the Pelonite,
³⁷Hezro the Carmelite,
Naarai son of Ezbai,

a 23 That is, about 7 feet 6 inches or about 2.3 meters

³⁸ Joel the brother of Nathan,
   Mibhar son of Hagri,
³⁹ Zelek the Ammonite,
   Naharai the Berothite, the armor-bearer
   of Joab son of Zeruiah,
⁴⁰ Ira the Ithrite,
   Gareb the Ithrite,
⁴¹ Uriah the Hittite,
   Zabad son of Ahlai,
⁴² Adina son of Shiza the Reubenite, who
   was chief of the Reubenites, and the
   thirty with him,
⁴³ Hanan son of Maakah,
   Joshaphat the Mithnite,
⁴⁴ Uzzia the Ashterathite,
   Shama and Jeiel the sons of Hotham the
   Aroerite,
⁴⁵ Jediael son of Shimri,
   his brother Joha the Tizite,
⁴⁶ Eliel the Mahavite,
   Jeribai and Joshaviah the sons of Elna-
   am,
   Ithmah the Moabite,
⁴⁷ Eliel, Obed and Jaasiel the Mezobaite.

Warriors Join David

12 These were the men who came to David at Ziklag, while he was banished from the presence of Saul son of Kish (they were among the warriors who helped him in battle; ²they were armed with bows and were able to shoot arrows or to sling stones right-handed or left-handed; they were relatives of Saul from the tribe of Benjamin):

³ Ahiezer their chief and Joash the sons of Shemaah the Gibeathite; Jeziel and Pelet the sons of Azmaveth; Berakah, Jehu the Anathothite, ⁴and Ishmaiah the Gibeonite, a mighty warrior among the Thirty, who was a leader of the Thirty; Jeremiah, Jahaziel, Johanan, Jozabad the Gederathite,ᵃ ⁵Eluzai, Jerimoth, Bealiah, Shemariah and Shephatiah the Haruphite; ⁶Elkanah, Ishiah, Azarel, Joezer and Jashobeam the Korahites; ⁷and Joelah and Zebadiah the sons of Jeroham from Gedor.

⁸Some Gadites defected to David at his stronghold in the wilderness. They were brave warriors, ready for battle and able to handle the shield and spear. Their faces were the faces of lions, and they were as swift as gazelles in the mountains.

⁹ Ezer was the chief,
   Obadiah the second in command, Eliab
   the third,

¹⁰ Mishmannah the fourth, Jeremiah the fifth,
¹¹ Attai the sixth, Eliel the seventh,
¹² Johanan the eighth, Elzabad the ninth,
¹³ Jeremiah the tenth and Makbannai the
   eleventh.

¹⁴These Gadites were army commanders; the least was a match for a hundred, and the greatest for a thousand. ¹⁵It was they who crossed the Jordan in the first month when it was overflowing all its banks, and they put to flight everyone living in the valleys, to the east and to the west.

¹⁶Other Benjamites and some men from Judah also came to David in his stronghold. ¹⁷David went out to meet them and said to them, "If you have come to me in peace to help me, I am ready for you to join me. But if you have come to betray me to my enemies when my hands are free from violence, may the God of our ancestors see it and judge you."

¹⁸Then the Spirit came on Amasai, chief of the Thirty, and he said:

"We are yours, David!
   We are with you, son of Jesse!
Success, success to you,
   and success to those who help you,
      for your God will help you."

So David received them and made them leaders of his raiding bands.

¹⁹Some of the tribe of Manasseh defected to David when he went with the Philistines to fight against Saul. (He and his men did not help the Philistines because, after consultation, their rulers sent him away. They said, "It will cost us our heads if he deserts to his master Saul.") ²⁰When David went to Ziklag, these were the men of Manasseh who defected to him: Adnah, Jozabad, Jediael, Michael, Jozabad, Elihu and Zillethai, leaders of units of a thousand in Manasseh. ²¹They helped David against raiding bands, for all of them were brave warriors, and they were commanders in his army. ²²Day after day men came to help David, until he had a great army, like the army of God.ᵇ

Others Join David at Hebron

²³These are the numbers of the men armed for battle who came to David at Hebron to turn Saul's kingdom over to him, as the LORD had said:
   ²⁴from Judah, carrying shield and spear—
      6,800 armed for battle;

ᵃ 4 In Hebrew texts the second half of this verse (*Jeremiah . . . Gederathite*) is numbered 12:5, and 12:5-40 is numbered 12:6-41.   ᵇ 22 Or *a great and mighty army*

DAVID AND THE LAW OF THE INNER CIRCLE
A Leader's Potential Is Determined by Those Closest to Him

1 Chronicles 11:10—12:40

THERE ARE no Lone Ranger leaders. If you're alone, you're not *leading* anybody.

Think of any highly effective leader, and you will find someone surrounded by a strong inner circle.

Hire the best staff you can find, develop them as much as you can, and hand off everything you possibly can to them. When you have the right staff, potential skyrockets.

You see, every leader's potential is determined by the people closest to him. If those people are strong, then the leader can make a huge impact. If they are weak, he can't.

■ ■ ■ ■ ■

Examine the way David pulled together the core people who made him great:

1. *He started building a strong inner circle before he needed it.*
   David began building his team long before he was crowned king. First Chronicles emphasizes how many of the warriors who flocked to David were leaders (1Ch 12:14). David didn't attract just anyone; he attracted strong leaders.

2. *He attracted people with varied gifts.*
   David attracted men of diverse abilities. We read of experienced warriors with a variety of skills— ambidextrous bowmen, slingers and spearmen—many mighty men

of valor, and hundreds of captains. With the help of these men, David felt ready for anything.

3. *He engendered loyalty.*
   David's followers displayed incredible loyalty to him throughout his life. In the early days, three of his men risked their lives to get him some water from a favorite well in Bethlehem. Decades later his closest men stayed with him even when it looked as though Absalom might crush his father (2Sa 15:21). Those closest to David always seemed willing to put their lives on the line for him.

4. *He delegated responsibility based on ability.*
   David continually gave authority to others. He designated Joab as commander of the army, and he felt equally secure in giving others civil authority (1Ch 18:14–17). Of course, delegating authority always entails risk—witness Joab's unilateral decision to kill Abner (2Sa 3:22–30). But great leaders risk delegation in order to reach the highest level of leadership.

Inner-Circle Qualities

The following qualities spell out the words *inner circle*. Look for these traits in the people you depend on most:

Influential—Everything begins with influence. If you want to extend your reach, you must attract and lead other leaders. More than 1,200 leaders are mentioned in the list of warriors who came to David (1Ch 12:23–37).

Networking—*Who* people know is just as important as *what* they know. When David hid from Saul, he was able to escape with the help of those who cared about him.

Nurturing—People who care about each other take care of each other. Your inner circle should prop you up. Certainly Jonathan is the best example of a nurturer in David's life. He loved David unconditionally, encouraged him, and guarded his life.

Empowering—The members of your inner circle should enable you to achieve more than you could alone. David's mighty men empowered him to accomplish incredible things.

Resourceful—Inner-circle members should always add value. When David desired to conquer Jerusalem, he offered to make the man who led the charge chief over his army (2Sa 5:6–10)—and Joab won control of the armed forces.

Character-driven—The character of an inner-circle member matters more than any other quality. People of weak character in David's inner circle cost him dearly. But people of strong character often helped to steer him out of trouble.

Intuitive—While every person is naturally intuitive in his area of gifting, that doesn't mean everyone uses his or her intuition. As you seek members for your inner circle, rely on those who have learned to trust their instincts.

Responsible—Those closest to you should never leave you hanging. If you ask them to carry the ball, they must follow through. David's companions made his cause their own.

Competent—You can't get anything done if your people can't do their jobs. You don't need world-class performers exclusively, but all of your inner-circle people must perform with excellence. The skill of David's people helped make him great.

Loyal—Loyalty alone does not make people candidates for your inner circle, but lack of loyalty definitely disqualifies them. David's people stuck with him even to death. Don't keep anyone close to you whom you cannot trust.

Energetic—Energy covers a multitude of mistakes, for it helps a person to keep coming back, failure after failure. Without tenacity, David and his men never would have survived in the wilderness, nor would they have made the nation secure from its enemies.

Look Around!

When God wants a leader to do something of value for him, he provides that leader with the individuals to get the job done. That was true for David, and it will be true for you. All you need to do is look around.

²⁵ from Simeon, warriors ready for battle — 7,100;

²⁶ from Levi — 4,600, ²⁷ including Jehoiada, leader of the family of Aaron, with 3,700 men, ²⁸ and Zadok, a brave young warrior, with 22 officers from his family;

²⁹ from Benjamin, Saul's tribe — 3,000, most of whom had remained loyal to Saul's house until then;

³⁰ from Ephraim, brave warriors, famous in their own clans — 20,800;

³¹ from half the tribe of Manasseh, designated by name to come and make David king — 18,000;

³² from Issachar, men who understood the times and knew what Israel should do — 200 chiefs, with all their relatives under their command;

³³ from Zebulun, experienced soldiers prepared for battle with every type of weapon, to help David with undivided loyalty — 50,000;

³⁴ from Naphtali — 1,000 officers, together with 37,000 men carrying shields and spears;

³⁵ from Dan, ready for battle — 28,600;

³⁶ from Asher, experienced soldiers prepared for battle — 40,000;

³⁷ and from east of the Jordan, from Reuben, Gad and the half-tribe of Manasseh, armed with every type of weapon — 120,000.

³⁸ All these were fighting men who volunteered to serve in the ranks. They came to Hebron fully determined to make David king over all Israel. All the rest of the Israelites were also of one mind to make David king. ³⁹ The men spent three days there with David, eating and drinking, for their families had supplied provisions for them. ⁴⁰ Also, their neighbors from as far away as Issachar, Zebulun and Naphtali came bringing food on donkeys, camels, mules and oxen. There were plentiful supplies of flour, fig cakes, raisin cakes, wine, olive oil, cattle and sheep, for there was joy in Israel.

Bringing Back the Ark

13 David conferred with each of his officers, the commanders of thousands and commanders of hundreds. ² He then said to the whole assembly of Israel, "If it seems good to you and if it is the will of the LORD our God, let us send word far and wide to the rest of our people throughout the territories of Israel, and also to the priests and Levites who are with them in their towns and pasturelands, to

Leaders Reproduce Themselves: David Raised Up Leaders

1 Chronicles 12:1–38

We can conclude from the list of warriors who joined David in Ziklag that his ragtag team was diverse, loyal, and hungry for victory. So what did David do to reproduce his leadership in them?

1. **He was relational.**
   Unlike Saul, who lived in fear, David's personable and approachable manner enticed hundreds of misfit volunteers to serve him. David accepted anyone.

2. **He was resourceful.**
   David made use of every situation and got the best out of it—even in the wilderness. He resourced his team to become all they could be and enabled it to succeed.

3. **He was rewarding.**
   David quickly shared both rewards and recognition for victory. He affirmed his men and motivated them with words of encouragement and spoils from battle.

4. **He was respectable.**
   David modeled a leadership style that others wanted to imitate. Friends and foes alike respected him; people saw in David an example of good leadership.

The chronicler says simply, "All these were fighting men who volunteered to serve in the ranks. They came to Hebron fully determined to make David king over all Israel. All the rest of the Israelites were also of one mind to make David king" (1Ch 12:38). And he concludes, "There was joy in Israel" (1Ch 12:40).

The Law of Intuition: Discernment Comes Before Decision

1 Chronicles 12:32

One of the more popular passages in 1 Chronicles is found in chapter 12. The men of Issachar are there described as men who "understood the times and knew what Israel should do" (v. 32). What a description of the Law of Intuition! Before Israel made a decision, they got discernment. The sons of Issachar understood three key factors:

1. *The culture:* They understood the population and the place where they lived.

2. *The timing:* They understood the times and discerned when to move.

3. *The strategy:* They knew what Israel should do, the steps that should be taken.

How about you? Are you a man of Issachar? Do you understand your culture—its trends, its myths, its strengths, its dangers? Do you understand the age in which you're living—its tenor and general movement? And do you have a strategy to grapple with both the culture and the times?

---

come and join us. ³Let us bring the ark of our God back to us, for we did not inquire of[a] it[b] during the reign of Saul." ⁴The whole assembly agreed to do this, because it seemed right to all the people.

⁵So David assembled all Israel, from the Shihor River in Egypt to Lebo Hamath, to bring the ark of God from Kiriath Jearim. ⁶David and all Israel went to Baalah of Judah (Kiriath Jearim) to bring up from there the ark of God the LORD, who is enthroned between the cherubim—the ark that is called by the Name.

⁷They moved the ark of God from Abinadab's house on a new cart, with Uzzah and Ahio guiding it. ⁸David and all the Israelites were celebrating with all their might before God, with songs and with harps, lyres, timbrels, cymbals and trumpets.

⁹When they came to the threshing floor of Kidon, Uzzah reached out his hand to steady the ark, because the oxen stumbled. ¹⁰The LORD's

Leaders Must Be Teachable

1 Chronicles 13:5–12

David grew both angry and frightened when God struck down Uzzah during an accident involving the transport of the ark of God. Leaders must remain teachable. We must not presume we know exactly how things will play out or what tomorrow will bring. Leaders must be learners.

anger burned against Uzzah, and he struck him down because he had put his hand on the ark. So he died there before God.

¹¹Then David was angry because the LORD's wrath had broken out against Uzzah, and to this day that place is called Perez Uzzah.[c]

¹²David was afraid of God that day and asked, "How can I ever bring the ark of God to me?" ¹³He did not take the ark to be with him in the City of David. Instead, he took it to the house of Obed-Edom the Gittite. ¹⁴The ark of God remained with the family of Obed-Edom in his house for three months, and the LORD blessed his household and everything he had.

David's House and Family

14 Now Hiram king of Tyre sent messengers to David, along with cedar logs, stonemasons and carpenters to build a palace for him. ²And David knew that the LORD had established him as king over Israel and that his kingdom had been highly exalted for the sake of his people Israel.

³In Jerusalem David took more wives and became the father of more sons and daughters. ⁴These are the names of the children born to him there: Shammua, Shobab, Nathan, Solomon, ⁵Ibhar, Elishua, Elpelet, ⁶Nogah, Nepheg, Japhia, ⁷Elishama, Beeliada[d] and Eliphelet.

David Defeats the Philistines

⁸When the Philistines heard that David had been anointed king over all Israel, they went up

---

a 3 Or we neglected   *b 3 Or him*   *c 11 Perez Uzzah means outbreak against Uzzah.*   *d 7 A variant of Eliada*

in full force to search for him, but David heard about it and went out to meet them. ⁹Now the Philistines had come and raided the Valley of Rephaim; ¹⁰so David inquired of God: "Shall I go and attack the Philistines? Will you deliver them into my hands?"

The LORD answered him, "Go, I will deliver them into your hands."

¹¹So David and his men went up to Baal Perazim, and there he defeated them. He said, "As waters break out, God has broken out against my enemies by my hand." So that place was called Baal Perazim.ᵃ ¹²The Philistines had abandoned their gods there, and David gave orders to burn them in the fire.

¹³Once more the Philistines raided the valley; ¹⁴so David inquired of God again, and God answered him, "Do not go directly after them, but circle around them and attack them in front of the poplar trees. ¹⁵As soon as you hear the sound of marching in the tops of the poplar trees, move out to battle, because that will mean God has gone out in front of you to strike the Philistine army." ¹⁶So David did as God commanded him, and they struck down the Philistine army, all the way from Gibeon to Gezer.

¹⁷So David's fame spread throughout every land, and the LORD made all the nations fear him.

The Ark Brought to Jerusalem

15 After David had constructed buildings for himself in the City of David, he prepared a place for the ark of God and pitched a tent for it. ²Then David said, "No one but the Levites may carry the ark of God, because the LORD chose them to carry the ark of the LORD and to minister before him forever."

³David assembled all Israel in Jerusalem to bring up the ark of the LORD to the place he had prepared for it. ⁴He called together the descendants of Aaron and the Levites:

⁵From the descendants of Kohath,
   Uriel the leader and 120 relatives;
⁶from the descendants of Merari,
   Asaiah the leader and 220 relatives;
⁷from the descendants of Gershon,ᵇ
   Joel the leader and 130 relatives;
⁸from the descendants of Elizaphan,
   Shemaiah the leader and 200 relatives;
⁹from the descendants of Hebron,
   Eliel the leader and 80 relatives;
¹⁰from the descendants of Uzziel,
   Amminadab the leader and 112 relatives.

¹¹Then David summoned Zadok and Abiathar the priests, and Uriel, Asaiah, Joel, Shemaiah, Eliel and Amminadab the Levites. ¹²He said to them, "You are the heads of the Levitical families; you and your fellow Levites are to consecrate yourselves and bring up the ark of the LORD, the God of Israel, to the place I have prepared for it. ¹³It was because you, the Levites, did not bring it up the first time that the LORD our God broke out in anger against us. We did not inquire of him about how to do it in the prescribed way." ¹⁴So the priests and Levites consecrated themselves in order to bring up the ark of the LORD, the God of Israel. ¹⁵And the Levites carried the ark of God with the poles on their shoulders, as Moses had commanded in accordance with the word of the LORD.

¹⁶David told the leaders of the Levites to appoint their fellow Levites as musicians to make a joyful sound with musical instruments: lyres, harps and cymbals.

¹⁷So the Levites appointed Heman son of Joel; from his relatives, Asaph son of Berekiah; and from their relatives the Merarites, Ethan son of Kushaiah; ¹⁸and with them their relatives next in rank: Zechariah,ᶜ Jaaziel, Shemiramoth, Jehiel, Unni, Eliab, Benaiah, Maaseiah, Mattithiah, Eliphelehu, Mikneiah, Obed-Edom and Jeiel,ᵈ the gatekeepers.

¹⁹The musicians Heman, Asaph and Ethan were to sound the bronze cymbals; ²⁰Zechariah, Jaaziel,ᵉ Shemiramoth, Jehiel, Unni, Eliab, Maaseiah and Benaiah were to play the lyres according to alamoth,ᶠ ²¹and Mattithiah, Eliphelehu, Mikneiah, Obed-Edom, Jeiel and Azaziah were to play the harps, directing according to sheminith.ᶠ ²²Kenaniah the head Levite was in charge of the singing; that was his responsibility because he was skillful at it.

²³Berekiah and Elkanah were to be doorkeepers for the ark. ²⁴Shebaniah, Joshaphat, Nethanel, Amasai, Zechariah, Benaiah and Eliezer the priests were to blow trumpets before the ark of God. Obed-Edom and Jehiah were also to be doorkeepers for the ark.

²⁵So David and the elders of Israel and the commanders of units of a thousand went to

---

ᵃ 11 Baal Perazim means the lord who breaks out.
ᵇ 7 Hebrew Gershom, a variant of Gershon   ᶜ 18 Three
Hebrew manuscripts and most Septuagint manuscripts (see
also verse 20 and 16:5); most Hebrew manuscripts Zechariah
son and or Zechariah, Ben and   ᵈ 18 Hebrew; Septuagint
(see also verse 21) Jeiel and Azaziah   ᵉ 20 See verse 18;
Hebrew Aziel, a variant of Jaaziel   ᶠ 20,21 Probably a
musical term

bring up the ark of the covenant of the LORD from the house of Obed-Edom, with rejoicing. [26]Because God had helped the Levites who were carrying the ark of the covenant of the LORD, seven bulls and seven rams were sacrificed. [27]Now David was clothed in a robe of fine linen, as were all the Levites who were carrying the ark, and as were the musicians, and Kenaniah, who was in charge of the singing of the choirs. David also wore a linen ephod. [28]So all Israel brought up the ark of the covenant of the LORD with shouts, with the sounding of rams' horns and trumpets, and of cymbals, and the playing of lyres and harps.

[29]As the ark of the covenant of the LORD was entering the City of David, Michal daughter of Saul watched from a window. And when she saw King David dancing and celebrating, she despised him in her heart.

Ministering Before the Ark

16 They brought the ark of God and set it inside the tent that David had pitched for it, and they presented burnt offerings and fellowship offerings before God. [2]After David had finished sacrificing the burnt offerings and fellowship offerings, he blessed the people in the name of the LORD. [3]Then he gave a loaf of bread, a cake of dates and a cake of raisins to each Israelite man and woman.

[4]He appointed some of the Levites to minister before the ark of the LORD, to extol,[a] thank, and praise the LORD, the God of Israel: [5]Asaph was the chief, and next to him in rank were Zechariah, then Jaaziel,[b] Shemiramoth, Jehiel, Mattithiah, Eliab, Benaiah, Obed-Edom and Jeiel. They were to play the lyres and harps, Asaph was to sound the cymbals, [6]and Benaiah and Jahaziel the priests were to blow the trumpets regularly before the ark of the covenant of God.

[7]That day David first appointed Asaph and his associates to give praise to the LORD in this manner:

[8]Give praise to the LORD, proclaim his name;
  make known among the nations what he has done.
[9]Sing to him, sing praise to him;
  tell of all his wonderful acts.
[10]Glory in his holy name;
  let the hearts of those who seek the LORD rejoice.
[11]Look to the LORD and his strength;
  seek his face always.

[12]Remember the wonders he has done,
  his miracles, and the judgments he pronounced,
[13]you his servants, the descendants of Israel,
  his chosen ones, the children of Jacob.
[14]He is the LORD our God;
  his judgments are in all the earth.

[15]He remembers[c] his covenant forever,
  the promise he made, for a thousand generations,
[16]the covenant he made with Abraham,
  the oath he swore to Isaac.
[17]He confirmed it to Jacob as a decree,
  to Israel as an everlasting covenant:
[18]"To you I will give the land of Canaan
  as the portion you will inherit."

[19]When they were but few in number,
  few indeed, and strangers in it,
[20]they[d] wandered from nation to nation,
  from one kingdom to another.
[21]He allowed no one to oppress them;
  for their sake he rebuked kings:
[22]"Do not touch my anointed ones;
  do my prophets no harm."

[23]Sing to the LORD, all the earth;
  proclaim his salvation day after day.
[24]Declare his glory among the nations,
  his marvelous deeds among all peoples.

[25]For great is the LORD and most worthy of praise;
  he is to be feared above all gods.
[26]For all the gods of the nations are idols,
  but the LORD made the heavens.
[27]Splendor and majesty are before him;
  strength and joy are in his dwelling place.

[28]Ascribe to the LORD, all you families of nations,
  ascribe to the LORD glory and strength.
[29]Ascribe to the LORD the glory due his name;
  bring an offering and come before him.
  Worship the LORD in the splendor of his[e] holiness.
[30] Tremble before him, all the earth!
  The world is firmly established; it cannot be moved.

---

[a] 4 Or *petition*; or *invoke* [b] 5 See 15:18,20; Hebrew *Jeiel*, possibly another name for *Jaaziel*. [c] 15 Some Septuagint manuscripts (see also Psalm 105:8); Hebrew *Remember* [d] 18-20 One Hebrew manuscript, Septuagint and Vulgate (see also Psalm 105:12); most Hebrew manuscripts *inherit,* / [19]*though you are but few in number,* / *few indeed, and strangers in it."* / [20]*They* [e] 29 Or LORD *with the splendor of*

³¹ Let the heavens rejoice, let the earth be glad;
   let them say among the nations, "The
      LORD reigns!"
³² Let the sea resound, and all that is in it;
   let the fields be jubilant, and everything in
      them!
³³ Let the trees of the forest sing,
   let them sing for joy before the LORD,
      for he comes to judge the earth.

³⁴ Give thanks to the LORD, for he is good;
   his love endures forever.
³⁵ Cry out, "Save us, God our Savior;
   gather us and deliver us from the nations,
      that we may give thanks to your holy name,
      and glory in your praise."
³⁶ Praise be to the LORD, the God of Israel,
   from everlasting to everlasting.

Then all the people said "Amen" and "Praise the
LORD."

³⁷ David left Asaph and his associates before
the ark of the covenant of the LORD to minister there regularly, according to each day's requirements. ³⁸ He also left Obed-Edom and his
sixty-eight associates to minister with them.
Obed-Edom son of Jeduthun, and also Hosah,
were gatekeepers.

³⁹ David left Zadok the priest and his fellow
priests before the tabernacle of the LORD at the
high place in Gibeon ⁴⁰ to present burnt offerings to the LORD on the altar of burnt offering
regularly, morning and evening, in accordance
with everything written in the Law of the LORD,
which he had given Israel. ⁴¹ With them were Heman and Jeduthun and the rest of those chosen
and designated by name to give thanks to the
LORD, "for his love endures forever." ⁴² Heman
and Jeduthun were responsible for the sounding
of the trumpets and cymbals and for the playing
of the other instruments for sacred song. The
sons of Jeduthun were stationed at the gate.

⁴³ Then all the people left, each for their own
home, and David returned home to bless his
family.

God's Promise to David

17 After David was settled in his palace, he
said to Nathan the prophet, "Here I am,
living in a house of cedar, while the ark of the
covenant of the LORD is under a tent."

² Nathan replied to David, "Whatever you
have in mind, do it, for God is with you."

³ But that night the word of God came to Nathan, saying:

⁴ "Go and tell my servant David, 'This is
what the LORD says: You are not the one to
build me a house to dwell in. ⁵ I have not
dwelt in a house from the day I brought
Israel up out of Egypt to this day. I have
moved from one tent site to another, from
one dwelling place to another. ⁶ Wherever
I have moved with all the Israelites, did I
ever say to any of their leaders^a whom I
commanded to shepherd my people, "Why
have you not built me a house of cedar?" '

⁷ "Now then, tell my servant David, 'This
is what the LORD Almighty says: I took you
from the pasture, from tending the flock,
and appointed you ruler over my people Israel. ⁸ I have been with you wherever you
have gone, and I have cut off all your enemies from before you. Now I will make
your name like the names of the greatest
men on earth. ⁹ And I will provide a place
for my people Israel and will plant them so
that they can have a home of their own and
no longer be disturbed. Wicked people will
not oppress them anymore, as they did at
the beginning ¹⁰ and have done ever since
the time I appointed leaders over my people Israel. I will also subdue all your enemies.

"'I declare to you that the LORD will
build a house for you: ¹¹ When your days
are over and you go to be with your ancestors, I will raise up your offspring to succeed you, one of your own sons, and I will
establish his kingdom. ¹² He is the one who
will build a house for me, and I will establish his throne forever. ¹³ I will be his father,
and he will be my son. I will never take my
love away from him, as I took it away from
your predecessor. ¹⁴ I will set him over my
house and my kingdom forever; his throne
will be established forever.' "

¹⁵ Nathan reported to David all the words of
this entire revelation.

David's Prayer

¹⁶ Then King David went in and sat before the
LORD, and he said:

"Who am I, LORD God, and what is my
family, that you have brought me this far?
¹⁷ And as if this were not enough in your
sight, my God, you have spoken about the
future of the house of your servant. You,

---

^a 6 Traditionally *judges*; also in verse 10

LORD God, have looked on me as though I were the most exalted of men.

18"What more can David say to you for honoring your servant? For you know your servant, 19LORD. For the sake of your servant and according to your will, you have done this great thing and made known all these great promises.

20"There is no one like you, LORD, and there is no God but you, as we have heard with our own ears. 21And who is like your people Israel—the one nation on earth whose God went out to redeem a people for himself, and to make a name for yourself, and to perform great and awesome wonders by driving out nations from before your people, whom you redeemed from Egypt? 22You made your people Israel your very own forever, and you, LORD, have become their God.

23"And now, LORD, let the promise you have made concerning your servant and his house be established forever. Do as you promised, 24so that it will be established and that your name will be great forever. Then people will say, 'The LORD Almighty, the God over Israel, is Israel's God!' And the house of your servant David will be established before you.

25"You, my God, have revealed to your servant that you will build a house for him. So your servant has found courage to pray to you. 26You, LORD, are God! You have promised these good things to your servant. 27Now you have been pleased to bless the house of your servant, that it may continue forever in your sight; for you, LORD, have blessed it, and it will be blessed forever."

Humility: The Mark of a Leader Who Finishes Well

1 Chronicles 17:1–27

Both Nathan and David showed genuine humility. Nathan had to modify his instructions to David after he too quickly spoke for God, and David responded with grace when he learned he would not build the temple. Humility keeps leaders on track and enables them to see beyond themselves.

David's Victories

18 In the course of time, David defeated the Philistines and subdued them, and he took Gath and its surrounding villages from the control of the Philistines.

2David also defeated the Moabites, and they became subject to him and brought him tribute.

3Moreover, David defeated Hadadezer king of Zobah, in the vicinity of Hamath, when he went to set up his monument at[a] the Euphrates River. 4David captured a thousand of his chariots, seven thousand charioteers and twenty thousand foot soldiers. He hamstrung all but a hundred of the chariot horses.

5When the Arameans of Damascus came to help Hadadezer king of Zobah, David struck down twenty-two thousand of them. 6He put garrisons in the Aramean kingdom of Damascus, and the Arameans became subject to him and brought him tribute. The LORD gave David victory wherever he went.

7David took the gold shields carried by the officers of Hadadezer and brought them to Jerusalem. 8From Tebah[b] and Kun, towns that belonged to Hadadezer, David took a great quantity of bronze, which Solomon used to make the bronze Sea, the pillars and various bronze articles.

9When Tou king of Hamath heard that David had defeated the entire army of Hadadezer king of Zobah, 10he sent his son Hadoram to King David to greet him and congratulate him on his victory in battle over Hadadezer, who had been at war with Tou. Hadoram brought all kinds of articles of gold, of silver and of bronze.

11King David dedicated these articles to the LORD, as he had done with the silver and gold he had taken from all these nations: Edom and Moab, the Ammonites and the Philistines, and Amalek.

12Abishai son of Zeruiah struck down eighteen thousand Edomites in the Valley of Salt. 13He put garrisons in Edom, and all the Edomites became subject to David. The LORD gave David victory wherever he went.

David's Officials

14David reigned over all Israel, doing what was just and right for all his people. 15Joab son of Zeruiah was over the army; Jehoshaphat son of Ahilud was recorder; 16Zadok son of Ahitub and Ahimelek[c] son of Abiathar were priests;

[a] 3 Or to restore his control over [b] 8 Hebrew Tibhath, a variant of Tebah [c] 16 Some Hebrew manuscripts, Vulgate and Syriac (see also 2 Samuel 8:17); most Hebrew manuscripts Abimelek

---

Leaders Broker Human Resources

1 Chronicles 18:14–17

David understood that he was to broker human gifts and talents. As Scripture says, he did "what was just and right for all his people" (1Ch 18:14). The next verses report how the king placed individuals in appropriate tasks according to their gifts: Joab led the army; Jehoshaphat was the recorder; Shavsha served as the secretary; and so on.

Effective leaders know their primary job isn't to amass personal accomplishments, but to accomplish as much as possible through the gifts of others. How do leaders inspire their associates to such great heights?

1. *Know the keys to their heart:* What do they sing about, cry about, dream about?

2. *Know the gifts in their possession:* What do they do well that gets results?

3. *Know the opportunities in their path:* What next step fits their maturity?

Shavsha was secretary; [17]Benaiah son of Jehoiada was over the Kerethites and Pelethites; and David's sons were chief officials at the king's side.

David Defeats the Ammonites

19 In the course of time, Nahash king of the Ammonites died, and his son succeeded him as king. [2]David thought, "I will show kindness to Hanun son of Nahash, because his father showed kindness to me." So David sent a delegation to express his sympathy to Hanun concerning his father.

When David's envoys came to Hanun in the land of the Ammonites to express sympathy to him, [3]the Ammonite commanders said to Hanun, "Do you think David is honoring your father by sending envoys to you to express sympathy? Haven't his envoys come to you only to explore and spy out the country and overthrow it?" [4]So Hanun seized David's envoys, shaved them, cut off their garments at the buttocks, and sent them away.

[5]When someone came and told David about the men, he sent messengers to meet them, for they were greatly humiliated. The king said, "Stay at Jericho till your beards have grown, and then come back."

[6]When the Ammonites realized that they had become obnoxious to David, Hanun and the Ammonites sent a thousand talents[a] of silver to hire chariots and charioteers from Aram Naharaim,[b] Aram Maakah and Zobah. [7]They hired thirty-two thousand chariots and charioteers, as well as the king of Maakah with his troops, who came and camped near Medeba, while the Ammonites were mustered from their towns and moved out for battle.

[8]On hearing this, David sent Joab out with the entire army of fighting men. [9]The Ammonites came out and drew up in battle formation at the entrance to their city, while the kings who had come were by themselves in the open country.

[10]Joab saw that there were battle lines in front of him and behind him; so he selected some of the best troops in Israel and deployed them against the Arameans. [11]He put the rest of the men under the command of Abishai his brother, and they were deployed against the Ammonites. [12]Joab said, "If the Arameans are too strong for me, then you are to rescue me; but if the Ammonites are too strong for you, then I will rescue you. [13]Be strong, and let us fight bravely for our people and the cities of our God. The LORD will do what is good in his sight."

[14]Then Joab and the troops with him advanced to fight the Arameans, and they fled before him. [15]When the Ammonites realized that the Arameans were fleeing, they too fled before his brother Abishai and went inside the city. So Joab went back to Jerusalem.

[16]After the Arameans saw that they had been routed by Israel, they sent messengers and had Arameans brought from beyond the Euphrates River, with Shophak the commander of Hadadezer's army leading them. [17]When David was told of this, he gathered all Israel and crossed the Jordan; he advanced

---

[a] 6 That is, about 38 tons or about 34 metric tons   [b] 6 That is, Northwest Mesopotamia

against them and formed his battle lines opposite them. David formed his lines to meet the Arameans in battle, and they fought against him. ¹⁸But they fled before Israel, and David killed seven thousand of their charioteers and forty thousand of their foot soldiers. He also killed Shophak the commander of their army.

¹⁹When the vassals of Hadadezer saw that they had been routed by Israel, they made peace with David and became subject to him.

So the Arameans were not willing to help the Ammonites anymore.

The Capture of Rabbah

20 In the spring, at the time when kings go off to war, Joab led out the armed forces. He laid waste the land of the Ammonites and went to Rabbah and besieged it, but David remained in Jerusalem. Joab attacked Rabbah and left it in ruins. ²David took the crown from the head of their king[a] — its weight was found to be a talent[b] of gold, and it was set with precious stones — and it was placed on David's head. He took a great quantity of plunder from the city ³and brought out the people who were there, consigning them to labor with saws and with iron picks and axes. David did this to all the Ammonite towns. Then David and his entire army returned to Jerusalem.

War With the Philistines

⁴In the course of time, war broke out with the Philistines, at Gezer. At that time Sibbekai the Hushathite killed Sippai, one of the descendants of the Rephaites, and the Philistines were subjugated.

⁵In another battle with the Philistines, Elhanan son of Jair killed Lahmi the brother of Goliath the Gittite, who had a spear with a shaft like a weaver's rod.

⁶In still another battle, which took place at Gath, there was a huge man with six fingers on each hand and six toes on each foot — twenty-four in all. He also was descended from Rapha. ⁷When he taunted Israel, Jonathan son of Shimea, David's brother, killed him.

⁸These were descendants of Rapha in Gath, and they fell at the hands of David and his men.

David Counts the Fighting Men

21 Satan rose up against Israel and incited David to take a census of Israel. ²So David said to Joab and the commanders of the troops, "Go and count the Israelites from Beer-

---

The Law of the Picture: Giant Killers Grow Under David's Leadership

1 Chronicles 20:4–8

You might call it "Déjà vu all over again."

First Chronicles 20 describes David's army battling and beating Philistine giants. You can't help but recall 1 Samuel 17, when young David killed Goliath. His men had simply learned the second verse of the same song.

By this point in Israel's history, David had selected and trained giant killers just like himself — the story of the Law of the Picture. When leaders model behavior, they multiply themselves. People do what people see. Leaders can reproduce only what they have already become. We teach what we know, but we reproduce what we are. Consider the following truths:

1. *It takes one to know one.* We tend to see what we possess ourselves.

2. *It takes one to show one.* We cannot model for someone what we haven't done.

3. *It takes one to grow one.* We cannot train someone until we've done it ourselves.

---

sheba to Dan. Then report back to me so that I may know how many there are."

³But Joab replied, "May the LORD multiply his troops a hundred times over. My lord the king, are they not all my lord's subjects? Why does my lord want to do this? Why should he bring guilt on Israel?"

⁴The king's word, however, overruled Joab; so Joab left and went throughout Israel and then came back to Jerusalem. ⁵Joab reported the number of the fighting men to David: In all Israel there were one million one hundred thousand men who could handle a sword, including four hundred and seventy thousand in Judah.

⁶But Joab did not include Levi and Benjamin in the numbering, because the king's command was repulsive to him. ⁷This command was also evil in the sight of God; so he punished Israel.

⁸Then David said to God, "I have sinned

---

[a] 2 Or *of Milkom,* that is, Molek   [b] 2 That is, about 75 pounds or about 34 kilograms

greatly by doing this. Now, I beg you, take away the guilt of your servant. I have done a very foolish thing."

⁹The LORD said to Gad, David's seer, ¹⁰"Go and tell David, 'This is what the LORD says: I am giving you three options. Choose one of them for me to carry out against you.'"

¹¹So Gad went to David and said to him, "This is what the LORD says: 'Take your choice: ¹²three years of famine, three months of being swept away[a] before your enemies, with their swords overtaking you, or three days of the sword of the LORD — days of plague in the land, with the angel of the LORD ravaging every part of Israel.' Now then, decide how I should answer the one who sent me."

¹³David said to Gad, "I am in deep distress. Let me fall into the hands of the LORD, for his mercy is very great; but do not let me fall into human hands."

¹⁴So the LORD sent a plague on Israel, and seventy thousand men of Israel fell dead. ¹⁵And God sent an angel to destroy Jerusalem. But as the angel was doing so, the LORD saw it and relented concerning the disaster and said to the angel who was destroying the people, "Enough! Withdraw your hand." The angel of the LORD was then standing at the threshing floor of Araunah[b] the Jebusite.

¹⁶David looked up and saw the angel of the LORD standing between heaven and earth, with a drawn sword in his hand extended over Jerusalem. Then David and the elders, clothed in sackcloth, fell facedown.

¹⁷David said to God, "Was it not I who ordered the fighting men to be counted? I, the shepherd,[c] have sinned and done wrong. These are but sheep. What have they done? LORD my God, let your hand fall on me and my family, but do not let this plague remain on your people."

David Builds an Altar

¹⁸Then the angel of the LORD ordered Gad to tell David to go up and build an altar to the LORD on the threshing floor of Araunah the Jebusite. ¹⁹So David went up in obedience to the word that Gad had spoken in the name of the LORD.

²⁰While Araunah was threshing wheat, he turned and saw the angel; his four sons who were with him hid themselves. ²¹Then David approached, and when Araunah looked and saw him, he left the threshing floor and bowed down before David with his face to the ground.

²²David said to him, "Let me have the site of your threshing floor so I can build an altar to the LORD, that the plague on the people may be stopped. Sell it to me at the full price."

²³Araunah said to David, "Take it! Let my lord the king do whatever pleases him. Look, I will give the oxen for the burnt offerings, the threshing sledges for the wood, and the wheat for the grain offering. I will give all this."

²⁴But King David replied to Araunah, "No, I insist on paying the full price. I will not take for the LORD what is yours, or sacrifice a burnt offering that costs me nothing."

²⁵So David paid Araunah six hundred shekels[d] of gold for the site. ²⁶David built an altar to the LORD there and sacrificed burnt offerings and fellowship offerings. He called on the LORD, and the LORD answered him with fire from heaven on the altar of burnt offering.

²⁷Then the LORD spoke to the angel, and he put his sword back into its sheath. ²⁸At that time, when David saw that the LORD had answered him on the threshing floor of Araunah the Jebusite, he offered sacrifices there. ²⁹The tabernacle of the LORD, which Moses had made in the wilderness, and the altar of burnt offering were at that time on the high place at Gibeon. ³⁰But David could not go before it to inquire of God, because he was afraid of the sword of the angel of the LORD.

22 Then David said, "The house of the LORD God is to be here, and also the altar of burnt offering for Israel."

Pay the Price; Depend on God

1 Chronicles 21:1–13

David's choice to count his soldiers revealed he was beginning to place more confidence in his troops than in the power of God. Fortunately, he placed himself in the hands of the Lord when he chose his punishment—once again demonstrating the "divine dependency" that got him to the top.

---

a 12 Hebrew; Septuagint and Vulgate (see also 2 Samuel 24:13) *of fleeing*   *b 15* Hebrew *Ornan,* a variant of *Araunah*; also in verses 18-28   *c 17* Probable reading of the original Hebrew text (see 2 Samuel 24:17 and note); Masoretic Text does not have *the shepherd.*   *d 25* That is, about 15 pounds or about 6.9 kilograms

Preparations for the Temple

²So David gave orders to assemble the foreigners residing in Israel, and from among them he appointed stonecutters to prepare dressed stone for building the house of God. ³He provided a large amount of iron to make nails for the doors of the gateways and for the fittings, and more bronze than could be weighed. ⁴He also provided more cedar logs than could be counted, for the Sidonians and Tyrians had brought large numbers of them to David.

⁵David said, "My son Solomon is young and inexperienced, and the house to be built for the LORD should be of great magnificence and fame and splendor in the sight of all the nations. Therefore I will make preparations for it." So David made extensive preparations before his death.

⁶Then he called for his son Solomon and charged him to build a house for the LORD, the God of Israel. ⁷David said to Solomon: "My son, I had it in my heart to build a house for the Name of the LORD my God. ⁸But this word of the LORD came to me: 'You have shed much blood and have fought many wars. You are not to build a house for my Name, because you have shed much blood on the earth in my sight. ⁹But you will have a son who will be a man of peace and rest, and I will give him rest from all his enemies on every side. His name will be Solomon,ᵃ and I will grant Israel peace and quiet during his reign. ¹⁰He is the one who will build a house for my Name. He will be my son, and I will be his father. And I will establish the throne of his kingdom over Israel forever.'

¹¹"Now, my son, the LORD be with you, and may you have success and build the house of the LORD your God, as he said you would. ¹²May the LORD give you discretion and understanding when he puts you in command over Israel, so that you may keep the law of the LORD your God. ¹³Then you will have success if you are careful to observe the decrees and laws that the LORD gave Moses for Israel. Be strong and courageous. Do not be afraid or discouraged.

¹⁴"I have taken great pains to provide for the temple of the LORD a hundred thousand talentsᵇ of gold, a million talentsᶜ of silver, quantities of bronze and iron too great to be weighed, and wood and stone. And you may add to them. ¹⁵You have many workers: stonecutters, masons and carpenters, as well as those skilled in every kind of work ¹⁶in gold and silver, bronze and iron — craftsmen beyond number. Now begin the work, and the LORD be with you."

ᵃ 9 *Solomon* sounds like and may be derived from the Hebrew for *peace.*   ᵇ 14 That is, about 3,750 tons or about 3,400 metric tons   ᶜ 14 That is, about 37,500 tons or about 34,000 metric tons

---

DAVID | Willingness to Assume the Blame
PROFILE in leadership
1 Chronicles 21:1–17

Times of failure not only reveal a leader's true character, but also present opportunities for significant leadership lessons.

Following a major victory over the Philistines, King David made a major mistake. The king chose to listen to Satan, stopped trusting God for the defense of his nation, and undertook a census. His pride in the growth of his kingdom blinded his judgment. Had his spiritual advisors temporarily left the area? Or had David ignored their counsel? Either way, David failed miserably—as do most leaders at some point in the journey.

David's willingness to take responsibility for his foolish action demonstrated his depth of character. The king refused to project blame, even though the Scripture states that Satan provoked him. David repented and accepted punishment from the hand of God, acknowledging the mercy of God and trusting in the grace of God. Even so, David's error snuffed out the lives of 70,000 Israelites. When leaders mess up, many people suffer.

Many leaders attempt to hide failures, blame others, or run from God. Not David. He admitted his failure and repented. Although he faced many difficulties, David worked to restore his relationship with God and did whatever he could to minimize the consequences of his failure in the lives of others (1Ch 21:16–17).

Perspective and Vision: David Sees a Bigger Picture

1 Chronicles 22:1–19

David's personal vision and passion extended far beyond his own lifetime. Although he knew Solomon would build the temple, he did some long-range planning and preparation for its construction. "My son Solomon is young and inexperienced," he explained, "and the house to be built for the LORD should be of great magnificence and fame and splendor in the sight of all the nations. Therefore I will make preparations for it" (1Ch 22:5).

David appointed stone cutters, gathered cedar logs, acquired mounds of iron for the nails, and even gave Solomon a solemn charge to finish the job (22:11–19). This is the kind of thing that separates leaders from followers. Leaders see . . .

- **Beyond Others:** They look past their own future to the generations that follow.
- **Before Others:** They see what must happen long before others are ready.
- **Bigger Than Others:** They have a larger-than-usual vision of what can happen.

David not only prepared the materials for the construction of the temple and challenged his son to faithfully build the Lord's house, but he also commanded all the leaders of Israel to help Solomon complete the task. " Now devote your heart and soul to seeking the LORD your God," he told them. "Begin to build the sanctuary of the LORD God" (22:19). Worthy visions outlast those who cast them.

¹⁷Then David ordered all the leaders of Israel to help his son Solomon. ¹⁸He said to them, "Is not the LORD your God with you? And has he not granted you rest on every side? For he has given the inhabitants of the land into my hands, and the land is subject to the LORD and to his people. ¹⁹Now devote your heart and soul to seeking the LORD your God. Begin to build the sanctuary of the LORD God, so that you may bring the ark of the covenant of the LORD and the sacred articles belonging to God into the temple that will be built for the Name of the LORD."

The Levites

23 When David was old and full of years, he made his son Solomon king over Israel. ²He also gathered together all the leaders of Israel, as well as the priests and Levites. ³The Levites thirty years old or more were counted, and the total number of men was thirty-eight thousand. ⁴David said, "Of these, twenty-four thousand are to be in charge of the work of the temple of the LORD and six thousand are to be officials and judges. ⁵Four thousand are to be gatekeepers and four thousand are to praise the LORD with the musical instruments I have provided for that purpose."

⁶David separated the Levites into divisions corresponding to the sons of Levi: Gershon, Kohath and Merari.

Gershonites

⁷Belonging to the Gershonites:
Ladan and Shimei.

⁸The sons of Ladan:
Jehiel the first, Zetham and Joel — three in all.

⁹The sons of Shimei:
Shelomoth, Haziel and Haran — three in all.
These were the heads of the families of Ladan.

¹⁰And the sons of Shimei:
Jahath, Ziza,^a Jeush and Beriah.
These were the sons of Shimei — four in all.

¹¹Jahath was the first and Ziza the second, but Jeush and Beriah did not have many sons; so they were counted as one family with one assignment.

Kohathites

¹²The sons of Kohath:
Amram, Izhar, Hebron and Uzziel — four in all.

¹³The sons of Amram:
Aaron and Moses.
Aaron was set apart, he and his descendants forever, to consecrate the most

---

^a 10 One Hebrew manuscript, Septuagint and Vulgate (see also verse 11); most Hebrew manuscripts *Zina*

holy things, to offer sacrifices before the Lord, to minister before him and to pronounce blessings in his name forever. [14] The sons of Moses the man of God were counted as part of the tribe of Levi.

[15] The sons of Moses:
Gershom and Eliezer.

[16] The descendants of Gershom:
Shubael was the first.

[17] The descendants of Eliezer:
Rehabiah was the first.
Eliezer had no other sons, but the sons of Rehabiah were very numerous.

[18] The sons of Izhar:
Shelomith was the first.

[19] The sons of Hebron:
Jeriah the first, Amariah the second, Jahaziel the third and Jekameam the fourth.

[20] The sons of Uzziel:
Micah the first and Ishiah the second.

Merarites

[21] The sons of Merari:
Mahli and Mushi.
The sons of Mahli:
Eleazar and Kish.

[22] Eleazar died without having sons: he had only daughters. Their cousins, the sons of Kish, married them.

[23] The sons of Mushi:
Mahli, Eder and Jerimoth — three in all.

[24] These were the descendants of Levi by their families — the heads of families as they were registered under their names and counted individually, that is, the workers twenty years old or more who served in the temple of the Lord. [25] For David had said, "Since the Lord, the God of Israel, has granted rest to his people and has come to dwell in Jerusalem forever, [26] the Levites no longer need to carry the tabernacle or any of the articles used in its service." [27] According to the last instructions of David, the Levites were counted from those twenty years old or more.

[28] The duty of the Levites was to help Aaron's descendants in the service of the temple of the Lord: to be in charge of the courtyards, the side rooms, the purification of all sacred things and the performance of other duties at the house of God. [29] They were in charge of the bread set out on the table, the special flour for the grain offerings, the thin loaves made without yeast, the baking and the mixing, and all measurements of quantity and size. [30] They were also to stand every morning to thank and praise the Lord. They

were to do the same in the evening [31] and whenever burnt offerings were presented to the Lord on the Sabbaths, at the New Moon feasts and at the appointed festivals. They were to serve before the Lord regularly in the proper number and in the way prescribed for them.

[32] And so the Levites carried out their responsibilities for the tent of meeting, for the Holy Place and, under their relatives the descendants of Aaron, for the service of the temple of the Lord.

The Divisions of Priests

24 These were the divisions of the descendants of Aaron:

The sons of Aaron were Nadab, Abihu, Eleazar and Ithamar. [2] But Nadab and Abihu died before their father did, and they had no sons; so Eleazar and Ithamar served as the priests. [3] With the help of Zadok a descendant of Eleazar and Ahimelek a descendant of Ithamar, David separated them into divisions for their appointed order of ministering. [4] A larger number of leaders were found among Eleazar's descendants than among Ithamar's, and they were divided accordingly: sixteen heads of families from Eleazar's descendants and eight heads of families from Ithamar's descendants. [5] They divided them impartially by casting lots, for there were officials of the sanctuary and officials of God among the descendants of both Eleazar and Ithamar.

[6] The scribe Shemaiah son of Nethanel, a Levite, recorded their names in the presence of the king and of the officials: Zadok the priest, Ahimelek son of Abiathar and the heads of families of the priests and of the Levites — one family being taken from Eleazar and then one from Ithamar.

[7] The first lot fell to Jehoiarib,
the second to Jedaiah,

[8] the third to Harim,
the fourth to Seorim,

[9] the fifth to Malkijah,
the sixth to Mijamin,

[10] the seventh to Hakkoz,
the eighth to Abijah,

[11] the ninth to Jeshua,
the tenth to Shekaniah,

[12] the eleventh to Eliashib,
the twelfth to Jakim,

[13] the thirteenth to Huppah,
the fourteenth to Jeshebeab,

[14] the fifteenth to Bilgah,
the sixteenth to Immer,

¹⁵the seventeenth to Hezir,
  the eighteenth to Happizzez,
¹⁶the nineteenth to Pethahiah,
  the twentieth to Jehezkel,
¹⁷the twenty-first to Jakin,
  the twenty-second to Gamul,
¹⁸the twenty-third to Delaiah
  and the twenty-fourth to Maaziah.

¹⁹This was their appointed order of ministering when they entered the temple of the LORD, according to the regulations prescribed for them by their ancestor Aaron, as the LORD, the God of Israel, had commanded him.

The Rest of the Levites

²⁰As for the rest of the descendants of Levi:
  from the sons of Amram: Shubael;
    from the sons of Shubael: Jehdeiah.
  ²¹As for Rehabiah, from his sons:
    Ishiah was the first.
²²From the Izharites: Shelomoth;
  from the sons of Shelomoth: Jahath.
²³The sons of Hebron: Jeriah the first,ᵃ Amariah the second, Jahaziel the third and Jekameam the fourth.
²⁴The son of Uzziel: Micah;
  from the sons of Micah: Shamir.
  ²⁵The brother of Micah: Ishiah;
    from the sons of Ishiah: Zechariah.
²⁶The sons of Merari: Mahli and Mushi.
  The son of Jaaziah: Beno.
²⁷The sons of Merari:
  from Jaaziah: Beno, Shoham, Zakkur and Ibri.
²⁸From Mahli: Eleazar, who had no sons.
²⁹From Kish: the son of Kish:
  Jerahmeel.
³⁰And the sons of Mushi: Mahli, Eder and Jerimoth.

These were the Levites, according to their families. ³¹They also cast lots, just as their relatives the descendants of Aaron did, in the presence of King David and of Zadok, Ahimelek, and the heads of families of the priests and of the Levites. The families of the oldest brother were treated the same as those of the youngest.

The Musicians

25 David, together with the commanders of the army, set apart some of the sons of Asaph, Heman and Jeduthun for the ministry of prophesying, accompanied by harps, lyres and cymbals. Here is the list of the men who performed this service:

²From the sons of Asaph:
  Zakkur, Joseph, Nethaniah and Asarelah. The sons of Asaph were under the supervision of Asaph, who prophesied under the king's supervision.
³As for Jeduthun, from his sons:
  Gedaliah, Zeri, Jeshaiah, Shimei,ᵇ Hashabiah and Mattithiah, six in all, under the supervision of their father Jeduthun, who prophesied, using the harp in thanking and praising the LORD.
⁴As for Heman, from his sons:
  Bukkiah, Mattaniah, Uzziel, Shubael and Jerimoth; Hananiah, Hanani, Eliathah, Giddalti and Romamti-Ezer; Joshbekashah, Mallothi, Hothir and Mahazioth.
⁵(All these were sons of Heman the king's seer. They were given him through the promises of God to exalt him. God gave Heman fourteen sons and three daughters.)

⁶All these men were under the supervision of their father for the music of the temple of the LORD, with cymbals, lyres and harps, for the ministry at the house of God.

Asaph, Jeduthun and Heman were under the supervision of the king. ⁷Along with their relatives—all of them trained and skilled in music for the LORD—they numbered 288. ⁸Young and old alike, teacher as well as student, cast lots for their duties.

⁹The first lot, which was for Asaph, fell
    to Joseph,
  his sons and relativesᶜ   12ᵈ
  the second to Gedaliah,
    him and his relatives and sons 12
¹⁰the third to Zakkur,
  his sons and relatives   12
¹¹the fourth to Izri,ᵉ
  his sons and relatives   12
¹²the fifth to Nethaniah,
  his sons and relatives   12
¹³the sixth to Bukkiah,
  his sons and relatives   12
¹⁴the seventh to Jesarelah,ᶠ
  his sons and relatives   12

ᵃ 23 Two Hebrew manuscripts and some Septuagint manuscripts (see also 23:19); most Hebrew manuscripts *The sons of Jeriah:*   ᵇ 3 One Hebrew manuscript and some Septuagint manuscripts (see also verse 17); most Hebrew manuscripts do not have *Shimei.*   ᶜ 9 See Septuagint; Hebrew does not have *his sons and relatives.*   ᵈ 9 See the total in verse 7; Hebrew does not have *twelve.*   ᵉ 11 A variant of *Zeri*   ᶠ 14 A variant of *Asarelah*

¹⁵the eighth to Jeshaiah,
   his sons and relatives   12
¹⁶the ninth to Mattaniah,
   his sons and relatives   12
¹⁷the tenth to Shimei,
   his sons and relatives   12
¹⁸the eleventh to Azarel,ᵃ
   his sons and relatives   12
¹⁹the twelfth to Hashabiah,
   his sons and relatives   12
²⁰the thirteenth to Shubael,
   his sons and relatives   12
²¹the fourteenth to Mattithiah,
   his sons and relatives   12
²²the fifteenth to Jerimoth,
   his sons and relatives   12
²³the sixteenth to Hananiah,
   his sons and relatives   12
²⁴the seventeenth to Joshbekashah,
   his sons and relatives   12
²⁵the eighteenth to Hanani,
   his sons and relatives   12
²⁶the nineteenth to Mallothi,
   his sons and relatives   12
²⁷the twentieth to Eliathah,
   his sons and relatives   12
²⁸the twenty-first to Hothir,
   his sons and relatives   12
²⁹the twenty-second to Giddalti,
   his sons and relatives   12
³⁰the twenty-third to Mahazioth,
   his sons and relatives   12
³¹the twenty-fourth to Romamti-Ezer,
   his sons and relatives   12.

The Gatekeepers

26 The divisions of the gatekeepers:

From the Korahites: Meshelemiah son of Kore, one of the sons of Asaph.
²Meshelemiah had sons:
   Zechariah the firstborn,
   Jediael the second,
   Zebadiah the third,
   Jathniel the fourth,
³Elam the fifth,
   Jehohanan the sixth
   and Eliehoenai the seventh.
⁴Obed-Edom also had sons:
   Shemaiah the firstborn,
   Jehozabad the second,
   Joah the third,
   Sakar the fourth,
   Nethanel the fifth,
⁵Ammiel the sixth,

Issachar the seventh
and Peullethai the eighth.
(For God had blessed Obed-Edom.)

⁶Obed-Edom's son Shemaiah also had sons, who were leaders in their father's family because they were very capable men. ⁷The sons of Shemaiah: Othni, Rephael, Obed and Elzabad; his relatives Elihu and Semakiah were also able men. ⁸All these were descendants of Obed-Edom; they and their sons and their relatives were capable men with the strength to do the work—descendants of Obed-Edom, 62 in all.

⁹Meshelemiah had sons and relatives, who were able men—18 in all.

¹⁰Hosah the Merarite had sons: Shimri the first (although he was not the firstborn, his father had appointed him the first), ¹¹Hilkiah the second, Tabaliah the third and Zechariah the fourth. The sons and relatives of Hosah were 13 in all.

¹²These divisions of the gatekeepers, through their leaders, had duties for ministering in the temple of the LORD, just as their relatives had. ¹³Lots were cast for each gate, according to their families, young and old alike.

¹⁴The lot for the East Gate fell to Shelemiah.ᵇ Then lots were cast for his son Zechariah, a wise counselor, and the lot for the North Gate fell to him. ¹⁵The lot for the South Gate fell to Obed-Edom, and the lot for the storehouse fell to his sons. ¹⁶The lots for the West Gate and the Shalleketh Gate on the upper road fell to Shuppim and Hosah.

Guard was alongside of guard: ¹⁷There were six Levites a day on the east, four a day on the north, four a day on the south and two at a time at the storehouse. ¹⁸As for the courtᶜ to the west, there were four at the road and two at the courtᶜ itself.

¹⁹These were the divisions of the gatekeepers who were descendants of Korah and Merari.

The Treasurers and Other Officials

²⁰Their fellow Levites wereᵈ in charge of the treasuries of the house of God and the treasuries for the dedicated things.
²¹The descendants of Ladan, who were Gershonites through Ladan and who were heads

---

ᵃ 18 A variant of Uzziel   ᵇ 14 A variant of Meshelemiah
ᶜ 18 The meaning of the Hebrew for this word is uncertain.
ᵈ 20 Septuagint; Hebrew As for the Levites, Ahijah was

of families belonging to Ladan the Gershonite, were Jehieli, ²²the sons of Jehieli, Zetham and his brother Joel. They were in charge of the treasuries of the temple of the LORD.

²³From the Amramites, the Izharites, the Hebronites and the Uzzielites:

²⁴Shubael, a descendant of Gershom son of Moses, was the official in charge of the treasuries. ²⁵His relatives through Eliezer: Rehabiah his son, Jeshaiah his son, Joram his son, Zikri his son and Shelomith his son. ²⁶Shelomith and his relatives were in charge of all the treasuries for the things dedicated by King David, by the heads of families who were the commanders of thousands and commanders of hundreds, and by the other army commanders. ²⁷Some of the plunder taken in battle they dedicated for the repair of the temple of the LORD. ²⁸And everything dedicated by Samuel the seer and by Saul son of Kish, Abner son of Ner and Joab son of Zeruiah, and all the other dedicated things were in the care of Shelomith and his relatives.

²⁹From the Izharites: Kenaniah and his sons were assigned duties away from the temple, as officials and judges over Israel.

³⁰From the Hebronites: Hashabiah and his relatives—seventeen hundred able men—were responsible in Israel west of the Jordan for all the work of the LORD and for the king's service. ³¹As for the Hebronites, Jeriah was their chief according to the genealogical records of their families. In the fortieth year of David's reign a search was made in the records, and capable men among the Hebronites were found at Jazer in Gilead. ³²Jeriah had twenty-seven hundred relatives, who were able men and heads of families, and King David put them in charge of the Reubenites, the Gadites and the half-tribe of Manasseh for every matter pertaining to God and for the affairs of the king.

Army Divisions

27 This is the list of the Israelites—heads of families, commanders of thousands and commanders of hundreds, and their officers, who served the king in all that concerned the army divisions that were on duty month by month throughout the year. Each division consisted of 24,000 men.

²In charge of the first division, for the first month, was Jashobeam son of Zabdiel. There were 24,000 men in his division. ³He was a descendant of Perez and chief of all the army officers for the first month.

⁴In charge of the division for the second month was Dodai the Ahohite; Mikloth was the leader of his division. There were 24,000 men in his division.

⁵The third army commander, for the third month, was Benaiah son of Jehoiada the priest. He was chief and there were 24,000 men in his division. ⁶This was the Benaiah who was a mighty warrior among the Thirty and was over the Thirty. His son Ammizabad was in charge of his division.

⁷The fourth, for the fourth month, was Asahel the brother of Joab; his son Zebadiah was his successor. There were 24,000 men in his division.

⁸The fifth, for the fifth month, was the commander Shamhuth the Izrahite. There were 24,000 men in his division.

⁹The sixth, for the sixth month, was Ira the son of Ikkesh the Tekoite. There were 24,000 men in his division.

¹⁰The seventh, for the seventh month, was Helez the Pelonite, an Ephraimite. There were 24,000 men in his division.

¹¹The eighth, for the eighth month, was Sibbekai the Hushathite, a Zerahite. There were 24,000 men in his division.

¹²The ninth, for the ninth month, was Abiezer the Anathothite, a Benjamite. There were 24,000 men in his division.

¹³The tenth, for the tenth month, was Maharai the Netophathite, a Zerahite. There were 24,000 men in his division.

¹⁴The eleventh, for the eleventh month, was Benaiah the Pirathonite, an Ephraimite. There were 24,000 men in his division.

¹⁵The twelfth, for the twelfth month, was Heldai the Netophathite, from the family of Othniel. There were 24,000 men in his division.

Leaders of the Tribes

¹⁶The leaders of the tribes of Israel:

over the Reubenites: Eliezer son of Zikri;
over the Simeonites: Shephatiah son of Maakah;
¹⁷over Levi: Hashabiah son of Kemuel;
over Aaron: Zadok;
¹⁸over Judah: Elihu, a brother of David;

over Issachar: Omri son of Michael;

19 over Zebulun: Ishmaiah son of Obadiah;

over Naphtali: Jerimoth son of Azriel;

20 over the Ephraimites: Hoshea son of Azaziah;

over half the tribe of Manasseh: Joel son of Pedaiah;

21 over the half-tribe of Manasseh in Gilead: Iddo son of Zechariah;

over Benjamin: Jaasiel son of Abner;

22 over Dan: Azarel son of Jeroham.

These were the leaders of the tribes of Israel.

23 David did not take the number of the men twenty years old or less, because the LORD had promised to make Israel as numerous as the stars in the sky. 24 Joab son of Zeruiah began to count the men but did not finish. God's wrath came on Israel on account of this numbering, and the number was not entered in the book[a] of the annals of King David.

The King's Overseers

25 Azmaveth son of Adiel was in charge of the royal storehouses.

Jonathan son of Uzziah was in charge of the storehouses in the outlying districts, in the towns, the villages and the watchtowers.

26 Ezri son of Kelub was in charge of the workers who farmed the land.

27 Shimei the Ramathite was in charge of the vineyards.

Zabdi the Shiphmite was in charge of the produce of the vineyards for the wine vats.

28 Baal-Hanan the Gederite was in charge of the olive and sycamore-fig trees in the western foothills.

Joash was in charge of the supplies of olive oil.

29 Shitrai the Sharonite was in charge of the herds grazing in Sharon.

Shaphat son of Adlai was in charge of the herds in the valleys.

30 Obil the Ishmaelite was in charge of the camels.

Jehdeiah the Meronothite was in charge of the donkeys.

31 Jaziz the Hagrite was in charge of the flocks.

All these were the officials in charge of King David's property.

32 Jonathan, David's uncle, was a counselor, a man of insight and a scribe. Jehiel son of Hakmoni took care of the king's sons.

33 Ahithophel was the king's counselor.

Hushai the Arkite was the king's confidant. 34 Ahithophel was succeeded by Jehoiada son of Benaiah and by Abiathar.

Joab was the commander of the royal army.

David's Plans for the Temple

28 David summoned all the officials of Israel to assemble at Jerusalem: the officers over the tribes, the commanders of the divisions in the service of the king, the commanders of thousands and commanders of hundreds, and the officials in charge of all the property and livestock belonging to the king and his sons, together with the palace officials, the warriors and all the brave fighting men.

2 King David rose to his feet and said: "Listen to me, my fellow Israelites, my people. I had it in my heart to build a house as a place of rest for the ark of the covenant of the LORD, for the footstool of our God, and I made plans to build it. 3 But God said to me, 'You are not to build a house for my Name, because you are a warrior and have shed blood.'

4 "Yet the LORD, the God of Israel, chose me from my whole family to be king over Israel forever. He chose Judah as leader, and from the tribe of Judah he chose my family, and from my father's sons he was pleased to make me king over all Israel. 5 Of all my sons—and the LORD has given me many—he has chosen my son Solomon to sit on the throne of the kingdom of the LORD over Israel. 6 He said to me: 'Solomon your son is the one who will build my house and my courts, for I have chosen him to be my son, and I will be his father. 7 I will establish his kingdom forever if he is unswerving in carrying out my commands and laws, as is being done at this time.'

8 "So now I charge you in the sight of all Israel

Competence: David's Royal Administration

1 Chronicles 26:1—27:34

Toward the end of 1 Chronicles we see David's flow chart of army divisions, tribal officers, treasurers and royal overseers. God selected a leader with a compass in his head and a magnet in his heart. David had mastered the three P's of organization: planning, preparation and personnel.

---

[a] 24 Septuagint; Hebrew *number*

and of the assembly of the LORD, and in the hearing of our God: Be careful to follow all the commands of the LORD your God, that you may possess this good land and pass it on as an inheritance to your descendants forever.

⁹"And you, my son Solomon, acknowledge the God of your father, and serve him with wholehearted devotion and with a willing mind, for the LORD searches every heart and understands every desire and every thought. If you seek him, he will be found by you; but if you forsake him, he will reject you forever. ¹⁰Consider now, for the LORD has chosen you to build a house as the sanctuary. Be strong and do the work."

¹¹Then David gave his son Solomon the plans for the portico of the temple, its buildings, its storerooms, its upper parts, its inner rooms and the place of atonement. ¹²He gave him the plans of all that the Spirit had put in his mind for the courts of the temple of the LORD and all the surrounding rooms, for the treasuries of the temple of God and for the treasuries for the dedicated things. ¹³He gave him instructions for the divisions of the priests and Levites, and for all the work of serving in the temple of the LORD, as well as for all the articles to be used in its service. ¹⁴He designated the weight of gold for all the gold articles to be used in various kinds of service, and the weight of silver for all the silver articles to be used in various kinds of service: ¹⁵the weight of gold for the gold lampstands and their lamps, with the weight for each lampstand and its lamps; and the weight of silver for each silver lampstand and its lamps, according to the use of each lampstand; ¹⁶the weight of gold for each table for consecrated bread; the weight of silver for the silver tables; ¹⁷the weight of pure gold for the forks, sprinkling bowls and pitchers; the weight of gold for each gold dish; the weight of silver for each silver dish; ¹⁸and the weight of the refined gold for the altar of incense. He also gave him the plan for the chariot, that is, the cherubim of gold that spread their wings and overshadow the ark of the covenant of the LORD.

¹⁹"All this," David said, "I have in writing as a result of the LORD's hand on me, and he enabled me to understand all the details of the plan."

²⁰David also said to Solomon his son, "Be strong and courageous, and do the work. Do not be afraid or discouraged, for the LORD God, my God, is with you. He will not fail you or forsake you until all the work for the service of the temple of the LORD is finished. ²¹The divisions of the priests and Levites are ready for all the work

on the temple of God, and every willing person skilled in any craft will help you in all the work. The officials and all the people will obey your every command."

Gifts for Building the Temple

29 Then King David said to the whole assembly: "My son Solomon, the one whom God has chosen, is young and inexperienced. The task is great, because this palatial structure is not for man but for the LORD God. ²With all my resources I have provided for the temple of my God — gold for the gold work, silver for the silver, bronze for the bronze, iron for the iron and wood for the wood, as well as onyx for the settings, turquoise,ᵃ stones of various colors, and all kinds of fine stone and marble — all of these in large quantities. ³Besides, in my devotion to the temple of my God I now give my personal treasures of gold and silver for the temple of my God, over and above everything I have provided for this holy temple: ⁴three thousand talentsᵇ of gold (gold of Ophir) and seven thousand talentsᶜ of refined silver, for the overlaying of the walls of the buildings, ⁵for the gold work and the silver work, and for all the work to be done by the craftsmen. Now, who is willing to consecrate themselves to the LORD today?"

⁶Then the leaders of families, the officers of the tribes of Israel, the commanders of thousands and commanders of hundreds, and the officials in charge of the king's work gave willingly. ⁷They gave toward the work on the temple of God five thousand talentsᵈ and ten thousand daricsᵉ of gold, ten thousand talentsᶠ of silver, eighteen thousand talentsᵍ of bronze and a hundred thousand talentsʰ of iron. ⁸Anyone who had precious stones gave them to the treasury of the temple of the LORD in the custody of Jehiel the Gershonite. ⁹The people rejoiced at the willing response of their leaders, for they had given freely and wholeheartedly to the LORD. David the king also rejoiced greatly.

David's Prayer

¹⁰David praised the LORD in the presence of the whole assembly, saying,

---

ᵃ 2 The meaning of the Hebrew for this word is uncertain.
ᵇ 4 That is, about 110 tons or about 100 metric tons   ᶜ 4 That is, about 260 tons or about 235 metric tons   ᵈ 7 That is, about 190 tons or about 170 metric tons   ᵉ 7 That is, about 185 pounds or about 84 kilograms   ᶠ 7 That is, about 380 tons or about 340 metric tons   ᵍ 7 That is, about 675 tons or about 610 metric tons   ʰ 7 That is, about 3,800 tons or about 3,400 metric tons

The Law of Legacy: David Sets Up Solomon to Succeed

1 Chronicles 29:1–5

As his life begins ebbing away, we see David preparing his son Solomon to give oversight to the construction of the temple. The old king is determined to ensure his legacy by setting up the next leader and committing him to the care of God Almighty. Look closely at what he did:

1. **He rallied all the people together (v. 1).**

2. **He affirmed God's choice of his successor (v. 1).**

3. **He identified the great need for help (v. 1).**

4. **He reminded the people of his own commitment (v. 2).**

5. **He declared that the people were well on their way to the goal (vv. 3–5).**

6. **He asked for commitment (v. 5).**

The people loved this old king, and they knew he was not asking them to do anything he had not already demonstrated an eagerness to complete himself. Because people do what people see, David was able to motivate the Israelites to do three things:

- Sacrificially give toward the temple project
- Support Solomon and his leadership
- Rejoice in what God was doing among them

And so the book of 1 Chronicles comes to a close, saying of David, "He died at a good old age, having enjoyed long life, wealth and honor. His son Solomon succeeded him as king" (29:28).

"Praise be to you, LORD,
   the God of our father Israel,
   from everlasting to everlasting.
¹¹ Yours, LORD, is the greatness and the
     power
   and the glory and the majesty and the
     splendor,
   for everything in heaven and earth is
     yours.
Yours, LORD, is the kingdom;
   you are exalted as head over all.
¹² Wealth and honor come from you;
   you are the ruler of all things.
In your hands are strength and power
   to exalt and give strength to all.
¹³ Now, our God, we give you thanks,
   and praise your glorious name.

¹⁴"But who am I, and who are my people, that we should be able to give as generously as this? Everything comes from you, and we have given you only what comes from your hand. ¹⁵ We are foreigners and strangers in your sight, as were all our ancestors. Our days on earth are like a shadow, without hope. ¹⁶ LORD our God, all this abundance that we have provided for building you a temple for your Holy Name comes from your hand, and all of it belongs to you. ¹⁷ I know, my God, that you test the heart and are pleased with integrity. All these things I have given willingly and with honest intent. And now I have seen with joy how willingly your people who are here have given to you. ¹⁸ LORD, the God of our fathers Abraham, Isaac and Israel, keep these desires and thoughts in the hearts of your people forever, and keep their hearts loyal to you. ¹⁹ And give my son Solomon the whole-hearted devotion to keep your commands, statutes and decrees and to do everything to build the palatial structure for which I have provided."

²⁰ Then David said to the whole assembly, "Praise the LORD your God." So they all praised the LORD, the God of their fathers; they bowed down, prostrating themselves before the LORD and the king.

Solomon Acknowledged as King

²¹ The next day they made sacrifices to the LORD and presented burnt offerings to him: a thousand bulls, a thousand rams and a thousand male lambs, together with their drink offerings, and other sacrifices in abundance for all

Israel. ²²They ate and drank with great joy in the presence of the LORD that day.

Then they acknowledged Solomon son of David as king a second time, anointing him before the LORD to be ruler and Zadok to be priest. ²³So Solomon sat on the throne of the LORD as king in place of his father David. He prospered and all Israel obeyed him. ²⁴All the officers and warriors, as well as all of King David's sons, pledged their submission to King Solomon.

²⁵The LORD highly exalted Solomon in the sight of all Israel and bestowed on him royal splendor such as no king over Israel ever had before.

The Death of David

²⁶David son of Jesse was king over all Israel. ²⁷He ruled over Israel forty years — seven in Hebron and thirty-three in Jerusalem. ²⁸He died at a good old age, having enjoyed long life, wealth and honor. His son Solomon succeeded him as king.

²⁹As for the events of King David's reign, from beginning to end, they are written in the records of Samuel the seer, the records of Nathan the prophet and the records of Gad the seer, ³⁰together with the details of his reign and power, and the circumstances that surrounded him and Israel and the kingdoms of all the other lands.

INTRODUCTION TO
2 CHRONICLES

Leaders Need to Finish Well

If 2 Chronicles develops one major theme or offers one major lesson, it is this: Leaders need to finish well.

Four kings—Solomon, Asa, Uzziah and Jehoshaphat—all began their monarchies well, but failed to finish strongly. Each enjoyed both success and fame as a leader, but they let the good times get to them. Their perspective got fuzzy; they began to overestimate their own importance; they grew blind to their weaknesses and refused accountability; and they started to trust in human ingenuity rather than in God—all "alarm bells" appropriate for leaders yet today!

What accounts for these poor finishes? Second Chronicles considers the Jerusalem worship center as symbolic of God's covenant with his people (chapter 7). The temple represented his presence, his promises, his provision and his protection. Indeed, it symbolized his very person. As each leader drifted away from his calling, his worship grew cold and sterile, becoming nothing more than an item to be checked off of a "to-do" list. While God was still there, they grew emotionally absent—and eventually God's presence and blessings began to fade.

Second Chronicles delivers a sobering warning to leaders who are drifting from their passion. When our leadership activities become mere routine, we have wandered from our original call. When we become distracted by peripheral issues and deviate from the purpose that first drove us to lead, we have wandered from our original call. When we overestimate our importance and allow ourselves to become exceptions to the rules—we have wandered away from our leadership call.

God's Role in 2 Chronicles

God intended to call the Hebrew leaders into close, personal encounters with him. Josiah most clearly illustrates God's goal.

Josiah became king at eight years of age (34:1). As he grew older, God increasingly led this young man's life (34:3–7). Josiah led strongly to the very end: "Josiah removed all the detestable idols from all the territory belonging to the Israelites, and he had all who were present in Israel serve the LORD their God" (34:33).

Leaders in 2 Chronicles

Solomon, Rehoboam, Jeroboam, Abijah, Asa, Jehoshaphat, Ahab, Joram, Ahaziah, Joash, Amaziah, Uzziah, Jotham, Ahaz, Hezekiah, Manasseh, Josiah, Jehoahaz

Other People of Influence in 2 Chronicles

Rehoboam's young counselors, Shemaiah, Micaiah, Jehoiada, Oded

Lessons in Leadership

- Priorities must be in place: all's well that begins well.
- Leaders committed to excellence will excel themselves.

Second Chronicles demonstrates that leaders cannot separate their spiritual condition from their success as a leader. While intimacy with God does not automatically make anyone a great leader—plenty of deeply spiritual people do not lead well—yet one cannot be a godly leader apart from intimacy with God. Our leadership must begin with our relationship with God. Had the kings of Israel and Judah remained intimate with Yahweh, they would have avoided many of their mistakes, pride, blindness, presumption and failures. Nearly every king desired to lead his people in reform, yet most of them failed. The lesson for us? Leaders cannot execute public reform until they experience personal repentance.

- Healthy leaders seek wise counsel, even if it's not what they want to hear.
- When things go wrong, check the humility of the leader.
- God blesses his people so that they will bless the nations.
- Leaders who maintain God's rule over their life maintain their rule.
- Leaders cannot pursue power and love at the same time.
- Leaders can undo their accomplishments by failing to finish well.
- Example is the main ingredient in influencing others.
- Leaders find a way to reach the goal and enable the team to win.

LEADERSHIP HIGHLIGHTS IN 2 CHRONICLES

Solomon Asks for Wisdom

1 Solomon son of David established himself firmly over his kingdom, for the LORD his God was with him and made him exceedingly great.

[2] Then Solomon spoke to all Israel—to the commanders of thousands and commanders of hundreds, to the judges and to all the leaders in Israel, the heads of families— [3] and Solomon and the whole assembly went to the high place at Gibeon, for God's tent of meeting was there, which Moses the LORD's servant had made in the wilderness. [4] Now David had brought up the ark of God from Kiriath Jearim to the place he had prepared for it, because he had pitched a tent for it in Jerusalem. [5] But the bronze altar that Bezalel son of Uri, the son of Hur, had made was in Gibeon in front of the tabernacle of the LORD; so Solomon and the assembly inquired of him there. [6] Solomon went up to the bronze altar before the LORD in the tent of meeting and offered a thousand burnt offerings on it.

[7] That night God appeared to Solomon and said to him, "Ask for whatever you want me to give you."

[8] Solomon answered God, "You have shown great kindness to David my father and have made me king in his place. [9] Now, LORD God, let your promise to my father David be confirmed, for you have made me king over a people who are as numerous as the dust of the earth. [10] Give me wisdom and knowledge, that I may lead this people, for who is able to govern this great people of yours?"

[11] God said to Solomon, "Since this is your heart's desire and you have not asked for wealth, possessions or honor, nor for the death of your enemies, and since you have not asked for a long life but for wisdom and knowledge to govern my people over whom I have made you king, [12] therefore wisdom and knowledge will be given you. And I will also give you wealth, possessions and honor, such as no king who was before you ever had and none after you will have."

[13] Then Solomon went to Jerusalem from the high place at Gibeon, from before the tent of meeting. And he reigned over Israel.

[14] Solomon accumulated chariots and horses; he had fourteen hundred chariots and twelve thousand horses,[a] which he kept in the chariot cities and also with him in Jerusalem. [15] The king made silver and gold as common in Jerusalem as stones, and cedar as plentiful as sycamore-fig trees in the foothills. [16] Solomon's horses were imported from Egypt and from Kue[b]—the royal merchants purchased them from Kue at the current price. [17] They imported a chariot from Egypt for six hundred shekels[c] of silver, and a horse for a hundred and fifty.[d] They also exported them to all the kings of the Hittites and of the Arameans.

---

[a] 14 Or charioteers   [b] 16 Probably Cilicia   [c] 17 That is, about 15 pounds or about 6.9 kilograms   [d] 17 That is, about 3 3/4 pounds or about 1.7 kilograms

---

The Law of Priorities: Solomon Gets It All

2 Chronicles 1:3–12

Every leader must establish a list of priorities, then learn to put first things first. Second Chronicles begins with a lesson in priorities.

When Solomon became king of Israel, he was given the opportunity to ask God for anything. Instead of requesting riches or fame, he asked for wisdom to lead his people well. Good answer! God responded by rewarding him not only with the thing he asked for, but also with all the benefits he didn't request.

This incident illustrates how effective prioritizing often works. When you put first things first, you frequently gain the time for nonessentials. Solomon narrowed his wedge, and got it all. No doubt, King Solomon faced the same options we have today:

1. **Easy Things First:** He could've chosen to focus on the easy tasks ahead of him.

2. **Fun Things First:** He could've chosen to focus on riches or fame.

3. **Urgent Things First:** He could've asked for help in building the temple.

4. **Hard Things First:** He could've sought favor with those who didn't like him.

5. **First Things First:** Instead, he chose to seek wisdom so he could glorify God.

Preparations for Building the Temple

2[a] Solomon gave orders to build a temple for the Name of the LORD and a royal palace for himself. [2]He conscripted 70,000 men as carriers and 80,000 as stonecutters in the hills and 3,600 as foremen over them.

[3]Solomon sent this message to Hiram[b] king of Tyre:

"Send me cedar logs as you did for my father David when you sent him cedar to build a palace to live in. [4]Now I am about to build a temple for the Name of the LORD my God and to dedicate it to him for burning fragrant incense before him, for setting out the consecrated bread regularly, and for making burnt offerings every morning and evening and on the Sabbaths, at the New Moons and at the appointed festivals of the LORD our God. This is a lasting ordinance for Israel.

[5]"The temple I am going to build will be great, because our God is greater than all other gods. [6]But who is able to build a temple for him, since the heavens, even the highest heavens, cannot contain him? Who then am I to build a temple for him, except as a place to burn sacrifices before him?

[7]"Send me, therefore, a man skilled to work in gold and silver, bronze and iron, and in purple, crimson and blue yarn, and experienced in the art of engraving, to work in Judah and Jerusalem with my skilled workers, whom my father David provided.

[8]"Send me also cedar, juniper and algum[c] logs from Lebanon, for I know that your servants are skilled in cutting timber there. My servants will work with yours [9]to provide me with plenty of lumber, because the temple I build must be large and magnificent. [10]I will give your servants, the woodsmen who cut the timber, twenty thousand cors[d] of ground wheat, twenty thousand cors[e] of barley, twenty thousand baths[f] of wine and twenty thousand baths of olive oil."

[11]Hiram king of Tyre replied by letter to Solomon:

"Because the LORD loves his people, he has made you their king."

[12]And Hiram added:

"Praise be to the LORD, the God of Israel, who made heaven and earth! He has given King David a wise son, endowed with intelligence and discernment, who will build a temple for the LORD and a palace for himself.

[13]"I am sending you Huram-Abi, a man of great skill, [14]whose mother was from Dan and whose father was from Tyre. He is trained to work in gold and silver, bronze and iron, stone and wood, and with purple and blue and crimson yarn and fine linen. He is experienced in all kinds of engraving and can execute any design given to him. He will work with your skilled workers and with those of my lord, David your father.

[15]"Now let my lord send his servants the wheat and barley and the olive oil and wine he promised, [16]and we will cut all the logs from Lebanon that you need and will float them as rafts by sea down to Joppa. You can then take them up to Jerusalem."

[17]Solomon took a census of all the foreigners residing in Israel, after the census his father David had taken; and they were found to be 153,600. [18]He assigned 70,000 of them to be carriers and 80,000 to be stonecutters in the hills, with 3,600 foremen over them to keep the people working.

Solomon Builds the Temple

3 Then Solomon began to build the temple of the LORD in Jerusalem on Mount Moriah, where the LORD had appeared to his father David. It was on the threshing floor of Araunah[g] the Jebusite, the place provided by David. [2]He began building on the second day of the second month in the fourth year of his reign.

[3]The foundation Solomon laid for building the temple of God was sixty cubits long and twenty cubits wide[h] (using the cubit of the old standard). [4]The portico at the front of the temple was twenty cubits[i] long across the width of the building and twenty[j] cubits high.

He overlaid the inside with pure gold. [5]He

---

[a] In Hebrew texts 2:1 is numbered 1:18, and 2:2-18 is numbered 2:1-17.　　[b] 3 Hebrew Huram, a variant of Hiram; also in verses 11 and 12　　[c] 8 Probably a variant of almug　　[d] 10 That is, probably about 3,600 tons or about 3,200 metric tons of wheat　　[e] 10 That is, probably about 3,000 tons or about 2,700 metric tons of barley　　[f] 10 That is, about 120,000 gallons or about 440,000 liters　　[g] 1 Hebrew Ornan, a variant of Araunah　　[h] 3 That is, about 90 feet long and 30 feet wide or about 27 meters long and 9 meters wide　　[i] 4 That is, about 30 feet or about 9 meters; also in verses 8, 11 and 13　　[j] 4 Some Septuagint and Syriac manuscripts; Hebrew and a hundred and twenty

paneled the main hall with juniper and covered it with fine gold and decorated it with palm tree and chain designs. [6]He adorned the temple with precious stones. And the gold he used was gold of Parvaim. [7]He overlaid the ceiling beams, doorframes, walls and doors of the temple with gold, and he carved cherubim on the walls.

[8]He built the Most Holy Place, its length corresponding to the width of the temple — twenty cubits long and twenty cubits wide. He overlaid the inside with six hundred talents[a] of fine gold. [9]The gold nails weighed fifty shekels.[b] He also overlaid the upper parts with gold.

[10]For the Most Holy Place he made a pair of sculptured cherubim and overlaid them with gold. [11]The total wingspan of the cherubim was twenty cubits. One wing of the first cherub was five cubits[c] long and touched the temple wall, while its other wing, also five cubits long, touched the wing of the other cherub. [12]Similarly one wing of the second cherub was five cubits long and touched the other temple wall, and its other wing, also five cubits long, touched the wing of the first cherub. [13]The wings of these cherubim extended twenty cubits. They stood on their feet, facing the main hall.[d]

[14]He made the curtain of blue, purple and crimson yarn and fine linen, with cherubim worked into it.

[15]For the front of the temple he made two pillars, which together were thirty-five cubits[e] long, each with a capital five cubits high. [16]He made interwoven chains[f] and put them on top of the pillars. He also made a hundred pomegranates and attached them to the chains. [17]He erected the pillars in the front of the temple, one to the south and one to the north. The one to the south he named Jakin[g] and the one to the north Boaz.[h]

The Temple's Furnishings

4 He made a bronze altar twenty cubits long, twenty cubits wide and ten cubits high.[i] [2]He made the Sea of cast metal, circular in shape, measuring ten cubits from rim to rim and five cubits[j] high. It took a line of thirty cubits[k] to measure around it. [3]Below the rim, figures of bulls encircled it — ten to a cubit.[l] The bulls were cast in two rows in one piece with the Sea.

[4]The Sea stood on twelve bulls, three facing north, three facing west, three facing south and three facing east. The Sea rested on top of them, and their hindquarters were toward the center. [5]It was a handbreadth[m] in thickness, and its rim was like the rim of a cup, like a lily blossom. It held three thousand baths.[n]

[6]He then made ten basins for washing and placed five on the south side and five on the north. In them the things to be used for the burnt offerings were rinsed, but the Sea was to be used by the priests for washing.

[7]He made ten gold lampstands according to the specifications for them and placed them in the temple, five on the south side and five on the north.

[8]He made ten tables and placed them in the temple, five on the south side and five on the north. He also made a hundred gold sprinkling bowls.

[9]He made the courtyard of the priests, and the large court and the doors for the court, and overlaid the doors with bronze. [10]He placed the Sea on the south side, at the southeast corner.

[11]And Huram also made the pots and shovels and sprinkling bowls.

So Huram finished the work he had undertaken for King Solomon in the temple of God:

[12] the two pillars;

the two bowl-shaped capitals on top of the pillars;

the two sets of network decorating the two bowl-shaped capitals on top of the pillars;

[13] the four hundred pomegranates for the two sets of network (two rows of pomegranates for each network, decorating the bowl-shaped capitals on top of the pillars);

[14] the stands with their basins;

[15] the Sea and the twelve bulls under it;

[16] the pots, shovels, meat forks and all related articles.

All the objects that Huram-Abi made for King Solomon for the temple of the LORD were of polished bronze. [17]The king had them cast in

---

[a] 8 That is, about 23 tons or about 21 metric tons   [b] 9 That is, about 1 1/4 pounds or about 575 grams   [c] 11 That is, about 7 1/2 feet or about 2.3 meters; also in verse 15   [d] 13 Or facing inward   [e] 15 That is, about 53 feet or about 16 meters   [f] 16 Or possibly made chains in the inner sanctuary; the meaning of the Hebrew for this phrase is uncertain.   [g] 17 Jakin probably means he establishes.   [h] 17 Boaz probably means in him is strength.   [i] 1 That is, about 30 feet long and wide and 15 feet high or about 9 meters long and wide and 4.5 meters high   [j] 2 That is, about 7 1/2 feet or about 2.3 meters   [k] 2 That is, about 45 feet or about 14 meters   [l] 3 That is, about 18 inches or about 45 centimeters   [m] 5 That is, about 3 inches or about 7.5 centimeters   [n] 5 That is, about 18,000 gallons or about 66,000 liters

clay molds in the plain of the Jordan between Sukkoth and Zarethan.*a* ¹⁸All these things that Solomon made amounted to so much that the weight of the bronze could not be calculated.

¹⁹Solomon also made all the furnishings that were in God's temple:

the golden altar;
the tables on which was the bread of the Presence;
²⁰the lampstands of pure gold with their lamps, to burn in front of the inner sanctuary as prescribed;
²¹the gold floral work and lamps and tongs (they were solid gold);
²²the pure gold wick trimmers, sprinkling bowls, dishes and censers; and the gold doors of the temple: the inner doors to the Most Holy Place and the doors of the main hall.

5 When all the work Solomon had done for the temple of the LORD was finished, he brought in the things his father David had dedicated—the silver and gold and all the furnishings—and he placed them in the treasuries of God's temple.

The Ark Brought to the Temple

²Then Solomon summoned to Jerusalem the elders of Israel, all the heads of the tribes and the chiefs of the Israelite families, to bring up the ark of the LORD's covenant from Zion, the City of David. ³And all the Israelites came together to the king at the time of the festival in the seventh month.

⁴When all the elders of Israel had arrived, the Levites took up the ark, ⁵and they brought up the ark and the tent of meeting and all the sacred furnishings in it. The Levitical priests carried them up; ⁶and King Solomon and the entire assembly of Israel that had gathered about him were before the ark, sacrificing so many sheep and cattle that they could not be recorded or counted.

⁷The priests then brought the ark of the LORD's covenant to its place in the inner sanctuary of the temple, the Most Holy Place, and put it beneath the wings of the cherubim. ⁸The cherubim spread their wings over the place of the ark and covered the ark and its carrying poles. ⁹These poles were so long that their ends, extending from the ark, could be seen from in front of the inner sanctuary, but not from outside the Holy Place; and they are still there today. ¹⁰There was nothing in the ark except the

two tablets that Moses had placed in it at Horeb, where the LORD made a covenant with the Israelites after they came out of Egypt.

¹¹The priests then withdrew from the Holy Place. All the priests who were there had consecrated themselves, regardless of their divisions. ¹²All the Levites who were musicians—Asaph, Heman, Jeduthun and their sons and relatives—stood on the east side of the altar, dressed in fine linen and playing cymbals, harps and lyres. They were accompanied by 120 priests sounding trumpets. ¹³The trumpeters and musicians joined in unison to give praise and thanks to the LORD. Accompanied by trumpets, cymbals and other instruments, the singers raised their voices in praise to the LORD and sang:

"He is good;
    his love endures forever."

Then the temple of the LORD was filled with the cloud, ¹⁴and the priests could not perform their service because of the cloud, for the glory of the LORD filled the temple of God.

6 Then Solomon said, "The LORD has said that he would dwell in a dark cloud; ²I have built a magnificent temple for you, a place for you to dwell forever."

³While the whole assembly of Israel was standing there, the king turned around and blessed them. ⁴Then he said:

"Praise be to the LORD, the God of Israel, who with his hands has fulfilled what he promised with his mouth to my father David. For he said, ⁵'Since the day I brought my people out of Egypt, I have not chosen a city in any tribe of Israel to have a temple built so that my Name might be there, nor have I chosen anyone to be ruler over my people Israel. ⁶But now I have chosen Jerusalem for my Name to be there, and I have chosen David to rule my people Israel.'

⁷"My father David had it in his heart to build a temple for the Name of the LORD, the God of Israel. ⁸But the LORD said to my father David, 'You did well to have it in your heart to build a temple for my Name. ⁹Nevertheless, you are not the one to build the temple, but your son, your own flesh and blood—he is the one who will build the temple for my Name.'

¹⁰"The LORD has kept the promise he made. I have succeeded David my father

---

a 17 Hebrew Zeredatha, a variant of Zarethan

and now I sit on the throne of Israel, just as the LORD promised, and I have built the temple for the Name of the LORD, the God of Israel. [11]There I have placed the ark, in which is the covenant of the LORD that he made with the people of Israel."

Solomon's Prayer of Dedication

[12]Then Solomon stood before the altar of the LORD in front of the whole assembly of Israel and spread out his hands. [13]Now he had made a bronze platform, five cubits long, five cubits wide and three cubits high,[a] and had placed it in the center of the outer court. He stood on the platform and then knelt down before the whole assembly of Israel and spread out his hands toward heaven. [14]He said:

"LORD, the God of Israel, there is no God like you in heaven or on earth — you who keep your covenant of love with your servants who continue wholeheartedly in your way. [15]You have kept your promise to your servant David my father; with your mouth you have promised and with your hand you have fulfilled it — as it is today.

[16]"Now, LORD, the God of Israel, keep for your servant David my father the promises you made to him when you said, 'You shall never fail to have a successor to sit before me on the throne of Israel, if only your descendants are careful in all they do to walk before me according to my law, as you have done.' [17]And now, LORD, the God of Israel, let your word that you promised your servant David come true.

[18]"But will God really dwell on earth with humans? The heavens, even the highest heavens, cannot contain you. How much less this temple I have built! [19]Yet, LORD my God, give attention to your servant's prayer and his plea for mercy. Hear the cry and the prayer that your servant is praying in your presence. [20]May your eyes be open toward this temple day and night, this place of which you said you would put your Name there. May you hear the prayer your servant prays toward this place. [21]Hear the supplications of your servant and of your people Israel when they pray toward this place. Hear from heaven, your dwelling place; and when you hear, forgive.

[22]"When anyone wrongs their neighbor and is required to take an oath and they come and swear the oath before your al-

tar in this temple, [23]then hear from heaven and act. Judge between your servants, condemning the guilty and bringing down on their heads what they have done, and vindicating the innocent by treating them in accordance with their innocence.

[24]"When your people Israel have been defeated by an enemy because they have sinned against you and when they turn back and give praise to your name, praying and making supplication before you in this temple, [25]then hear from heaven and forgive the sin of your people Israel and bring them back to the land you gave to them and their ancestors.

[26]"When the heavens are shut up and there is no rain because your people have sinned against you, and when they pray toward this place and give praise to your name and turn from their sin because you have afflicted them, [27]then hear from heaven and forgive the sin of your servants, your people Israel. Teach them the right way to live, and send rain on the land you gave your people for an inheritance.

[28]"When famine or plague comes to the land, or blight or mildew, locusts or grasshoppers, or when enemies besiege them in any of their cities, whatever disaster or disease may come, [29]and when a prayer or plea is made by anyone among your people Israel — being aware of their afflictions and pains, and spreading out their hands toward this temple — [30]then hear from heaven, your dwelling place. Forgive, and deal with everyone according to all they do, since you know their hearts (for you alone know the human heart), [31]so that they will fear you and walk in obedience to you all the time they live in the land you gave our ancestors.

[32]"As for the foreigner who does not belong to your people Israel but has come from a distant land because of your great name and your mighty hand and your outstretched arm — when they come and pray toward this temple, [33]then hear from heaven, your dwelling place. Do whatever the foreigner asks of you, so that all the peoples of the earth may know your name and fear you, as do your own people Israel, and may know that this house I have built bears your Name.

---

[a] 13 That is, about 7 1/2 feet long and wide and 4 1/2 feet high or about 2.3 meters long and wide and 1.4 meters high

The Law of Navigation: Solomon Commits Himself to Excellence

2 Chronicles 2:1—6:42

Solomon saw to it that excellence controlled both the design and construction of the temple. He committed himself to excellence every step of the way, including hidden areas. If you were to ask him, "Why bother with the details of an area that no one would ever see? Who would know whether it was done right or not?" he would respond, "I would know and God would know."

Leaders who model a commitment to excellence reap great rewards, and their people tend to emulate that same concern. Look at how Solomon's commitment to excellence shows up:

Chapter	Subject	Commitment to Excellence
2	Preparation of temple	He offers sacrifices daily consecrating the work.
3	Design and dimensions	He specifies exact sizes and decorations in rooms.
4	Furnishings	He furnishes it with extravagant accessories.
5	The ark	He takes great care transporting the ark.
6	The dedication	He models godly motives for building a temple.

³⁴"When your people go to war against their enemies, wherever you send them, and when they pray to you toward this city you have chosen and the temple I have built for your Name, ³⁵then hear from heaven their prayer and their plea, and uphold their cause. ³⁶"When they sin against you—for there is no one who does not sin—and you become angry with them and give them over to the enemy, who takes them captive to a land far away or near; ³⁷and if they have a change of heart in the land where they are held captive, and repent and plead with you in the land of their captivity and say, 'We have sinned, we have done wrong and acted wickedly'; ³⁸and if they turn back to you with all their heart and soul in the land of their captivity where they were taken, and pray toward the land you gave their ancestors, toward the city you have chosen and toward the temple I have built for your Name; ³⁹then from heaven, your dwelling place, hear their prayer and their pleas, and uphold their cause. And forgive your people, who have sinned against you. ⁴⁰"Now, my God, may your eyes be open and your ears attentive to the prayers offered in this place.

⁴¹ "Now arise, LORD God, and come to your resting place,
    you and the ark of your might.

May your priests, LORD God, be clothed with salvation,
    may your faithful people rejoice in your goodness.
⁴² LORD God, do not reject your anointed one.
    Remember the great love promised to David your servant."

The Dedication of the Temple

7 When Solomon finished praying, fire came down from heaven and consumed the burnt offering and the sacrifices, and the glory of the LORD filled the temple. ²The priests could not enter the temple of the LORD because the glory of the LORD filled it. ³When all the Israelites saw the fire coming down and the glory of the LORD above the temple, they knelt on the pavement with their faces to the ground, and they worshiped and gave thanks to the LORD, saying,

"He is good;
    his love endures forever."

⁴Then the king and all the people offered sacrifices before the LORD. ⁵And King Solomon offered a sacrifice of twenty-two thousand head of cattle and a hundred and twenty thousand sheep and goats. So the king and all the people dedicated the temple of God. ⁶The priests took their positions, as did the Levites with the

LORD's musical instruments, which King David had made for praising the LORD and which were used when he gave thanks, saying, "His love endures forever." Opposite the Levites, the priests blew their trumpets, and all the Israelites were standing.

[7]Solomon consecrated the middle part of the courtyard in front of the temple of the LORD, and there he offered burnt offerings and the fat of the fellowship offerings, because the bronze altar he had made could not hold the burnt offerings, the grain offerings and the fat portions.

[8]So Solomon observed the festival at that time for seven days, and all Israel with him — a vast assembly, people from Lebo Hamath to the Wadi of Egypt. [9]On the eighth day they held an assembly, for they had celebrated the dedication of the altar for seven days and the festival for seven days more. [10]On the twenty-third day of the seventh month he sent the people to their homes, joyful and glad in heart for the good things the LORD had done for David and Solomon and for his people Israel.

The LORD Appears to Solomon

[11]When Solomon had finished the temple of the LORD and the royal palace, and had succeeded in carrying out all he had in mind to do in the temple of the LORD and in his own palace, [12]the LORD appeared to him at night and said:

"I have heard your prayer and have chosen this place for myself as a temple for sacrifices.

[13]"When I shut up the heavens so that there is no rain, or command locusts to devour the land or send a plague among my people, [14]if my people, who are called by my name, will humble themselves and pray and seek my face and turn from their wicked ways, then I will hear from heaven, and I will forgive their sin and will heal their land. [15]Now my eyes will be open and my ears attentive to the prayers offered in this place. [16]I have chosen and consecrated this temple so that my Name may be there forever. My eyes and my heart will always be there.

[17]"As for you, if you walk before me faithfully as David your father did, and do all I command, and observe my decrees and laws, [18]I will establish your royal throne, as I covenanted with David your father when I said, 'You shall never fail to have a successor to rule over Israel.'

[19]"But if you[a] turn away and forsake the decrees and commands I have given you[a] and go off to serve other gods and worship them, [20]then I will uproot Israel from my land, which I have given them, and will reject this temple I have consecrated for my Name. I will make it a byword and an object of ridicule among all peoples. [21]This temple will become a heap of rubble. All[b] who pass by will be appalled and say, 'Why has the LORD done such a thing to this land and to this temple?' [22]People will answer, 'Because they have forsaken the LORD, the God of their ancestors, who brought them out of Egypt, and have embraced other gods, worshiping and serving them — that is why he brought all this disaster on them.'"

Solomon's Other Activities

8 At the end of twenty years, during which Solomon built the temple of the LORD and his own palace, [2]Solomon rebuilt the villages that Hiram[c] had given him, and settled Israelites in them. [3]Solomon then went to Hamath Zobah and captured it. [4]He also built up Tadmor in the desert and all the store cities he had built in Hamath. [5]He rebuilt Upper Beth Horon and Lower Beth Horon as fortified cities, with walls and with gates and bars, [6]as well as Baalath and all his store cities, and all the cities for his chariots and for his horses[d] — whatever he desired to build in Jerusalem, in Lebanon and throughout all the territory he ruled.

[7]There were still people left from the Hittites, Amorites, Perizzites, Hivites and Jebusites (these people were not Israelites). [8]Solomon conscripted the descendants of all these people remaining in the land — whom the Israelites had not destroyed — to serve as slave labor, as it is to this day. [9]But Solomon did not make slaves of the Israelites for his work; they were his fighting men, commanders of his captains, and commanders of his chariots and charioteers. [10]They were also King Solomon's chief officials — two hundred and fifty officials supervising the men.

[11]Solomon brought Pharaoh's daughter up from the City of David to the palace he had built for her, for he said, "My wife must not live in the

---

[a] 19 The Hebrew is plural.   [b] 21 See some Septuagint manuscripts, Old Latin, Syriac, Arabic and Targum; Hebrew *And though this temple is now so imposing, all*   [c] 2 Hebrew *Huram*, a variant of *Hiram*; also in verse 18   [d] 6 Or *charioteers*

palace of David king of Israel, because the places the ark of the LORD has entered are holy."

¹²On the altar of the LORD that he had built in front of the portico, Solomon sacrificed burnt offerings to the LORD, ¹³according to the daily requirement for offerings commanded by Moses for the Sabbaths, the New Moons and the three annual festivals — the Festival of Unleavened Bread, the Festival of Weeks and the Festival of Tabernacles. ¹⁴In keeping with the ordinance of his father David, he appointed the divisions of the priests for their duties, and the Levites to lead the praise and to assist the priests according to each day's requirement. He also appointed the gatekeepers by divisions for the various gates, because this was what David the man of God had ordered. ¹⁵They did not deviate from the king's commands to the priests or to the Levites in any matter, including that of the treasuries.

¹⁶All Solomon's work was carried out, from the day the foundation of the temple of the LORD was laid until its completion. So the temple of the LORD was finished.

¹⁷Then Solomon went to Ezion Geber and Elath on the coast of Edom. ¹⁸And Hiram sent him ships commanded by his own men, sailors who knew the sea. These, with Solomon's men, sailed to Ophir and brought back four hundred and fifty talents[a] of gold, which they delivered to King Solomon.

The Queen of Sheba Visits Solomon

9 When the queen of Sheba heard of Solomon's fame, she came to Jerusalem to test him with hard questions. Arriving with a very great caravan — with camels carrying spices, large quantities of gold, and precious stones — she came to Solomon and talked with him about all she had on her mind. ²Solomon answered all her questions; nothing was too hard for him to explain to her. ³When the queen of Sheba saw the wisdom of Solomon, as well as the palace he had built, ⁴the food on his table, the seating of his officials, the attending servants in their robes, the cupbearers in their robes and the burnt offerings he made at[b] the temple of the LORD, she was overwhelmed.

⁵She said to the king, "The report I heard in my own country about your achievements and your wisdom is true. ⁶But I did not believe what they said until I came and saw with my own eyes. Indeed, not even half the greatness of your wisdom was told me; you have far exceeded the report I heard. ⁷How happy your people must be! How happy your officials, who continually stand before you and hear your wisdom! ⁸Praise be to the LORD your God, who has delighted in you and placed you on his throne as king to rule for the LORD your God. Because of the love

---

[a] 18 That is, about 17 tons or about 15 metric tons   [b] 4 Or and the ascent by which he went up to

---

SOLOMON
PROFILE in leadership

Blessed by God to Bless the Nations
2 Chronicles 9:1–23

Before he careened off course in his later years, Solomon began to fulfill God's dream of blessing the nations through the nation of Israel. When leaders from the surrounding countries heard of his great wisdom, they hopped aboard their camels and made the long trek to Jerusalem to see whether the reports could be trusted. The Queen of Sheba spoke for these wide-eyed visitors when she said, "Praise be to the LORD your God, who has delighted in you and placed you on his throne as king to rule for the LORD your God" (2Ch 9:8).

After the queen saw Solomon's splendor, he sent her away with much more than she brought (9:12). So she returned to her own land, blessed by God. Many other interested leaders visited Solomon after she left (9:23).

Centuries later, the Lord Jesus Christ would tell his followers that what they had received freely, they should freely give (Mt 10:8). Solomon had asked for godly wisdom that he might rule in a way pleasing to God. The Lord freely gave him that wisdom, so he freely shared it with others—in his words, in his music, and in his writings.

Effective, godly leadership means giving what you have so that God may be glorified in all you do. What you have freely received, freely give—and so bless others.

of your God for Israel and his desire to uphold them forever, he has made you king over them, to maintain justice and righteousness."

[9]Then she gave the king 120 talents[a] of gold, large quantities of spices, and precious stones. There had never been such spices as those the queen of Sheba gave to King Solomon.

[10](The servants of Hiram and the servants of Solomon brought gold from Ophir; they also brought algumwood[b] and precious stones. [11]The king used the algumwood to make steps for the temple of the LORD and for the royal palace, and to make harps and lyres for the musicians. Nothing like them had ever been seen in Judah.)

[12]King Solomon gave the queen of Sheba all she desired and asked for; he gave her more than she had brought to him. Then she left and returned with her retinue to her own country.

Solomon's Splendor

[13]The weight of the gold that Solomon received yearly was 666 talents,[c] [14]not including the revenues brought in by merchants and traders. Also all the kings of Arabia and the governors of the territories brought gold and silver to Solomon.

[15]King Solomon made two hundred large shields of hammered gold; six hundred shekels[d] of hammered gold went into each shield. [16]He also made three hundred small shields of hammered gold, with three hundred shekels[e] of gold in each shield. The king put them in the Palace of the Forest of Lebanon.

[17]Then the king made a great throne covered with ivory and overlaid with pure gold. [18]The throne had six steps, and a footstool of gold was attached to it. On both sides of the seat were armrests, with a lion standing beside each of them. [19]Twelve lions stood on the six steps, one at either end of each step. Nothing like it had ever been made for any other kingdom. [20]All King Solomon's goblets were gold, and all the household articles in the Palace of the Forest of Lebanon were pure gold. Nothing was made of silver, because silver was considered of little value in Solomon's day. [21]The king had a fleet of trading ships[f] manned by Hiram's[g] servants. Once every three years it returned, carrying gold, silver and ivory, and apes and baboons.

[22]King Solomon was greater in riches and wisdom than all the other kings of the earth. [23]All the kings of the earth sought audience with Solomon to hear the wisdom God had put in his heart. [24]Year after year, everyone who came brought a gift — articles of silver and gold,

and robes, weapons and spices, and horses and mules.

[25]Solomon had four thousand stalls for horses and chariots, and twelve thousand horses,[h] which he kept in the chariot cities and also with him in Jerusalem. [26]He ruled over all the kings from the Euphrates River to the land of the Philistines, as far as the border of Egypt. [27]The king made silver as common in Jerusalem as stones, and cedar as plentiful as sycamore-fig trees in the foothills. [28]Solomon's horses were imported from Egypt and from all other countries.

Solomon's Death

[29]As for the other events of Solomon's reign, from beginning to end, are they not written in the records of Nathan the prophet, in the prophecy of Ahijah the Shilonite and in the visions of Iddo the seer concerning Jeroboam son of Nebat? [30]Solomon reigned in Jerusalem over all Israel forty years. [31]Then he rested with his ancestors and was buried in the city of David his father. And Rehoboam his son succeeded him as king.

Israel Rebels Against Rehoboam

10 Rehoboam went to Shechem, for all Israel had gone there to make him king. [2]When Jeroboam son of Nebat heard this (he was in Egypt, where he had fled from King Solomon), he returned from Egypt. [3]So they sent for Jeroboam, and he and all Israel went to Rehoboam and said to him: [4]"Your father put a heavy yoke

---

[a] 9 That is, about 4 1/2 tons or about 4 metric tons
[b] 10 Probably a variant of *almugwood*   [c] 13 That is, about 25 tons or about 23 metric tons   [d] 15 That is, about 15 pounds or about 6.9 kilograms   [e] 16 That is, about 7 1/2 pounds or about 3.5 kilograms   [f] 21 Hebrew *of ships that could go to Tarshish*   [g] 21 Hebrew *Huram*, a variant of *Hiram*
[h] 25 Or *charioteers*

Rehoboam Violates the Law of Intuition and Pays

2 Chronicles 10:1–17

Rehoboam, the successor to Solomon, knew little about good leadership. Instead of sizing up his situation and culture, he went on a power trip. He failed to discern, listen or follow wise counsel from those who could help him most—and lost more than half of the kingdom.

on us, but now lighten the harsh labor and the heavy yoke he put on us, and we will serve you."

⁵Rehoboam answered, "Come back to me in three days." So the people went away.

⁶Then King Rehoboam consulted the elders who had served his father Solomon during his lifetime. "How would you advise me to answer these people?" he asked.

⁷They replied, "If you will be kind to these people and please them and give them a favorable answer, they will always be your servants."

⁸But Rehoboam rejected the advice the elders gave him and consulted the young men who had grown up with him and were serving him. ⁹He asked them, "What is your advice? How should we answer these people who say to me, 'Lighten the yoke your father put on us'?"

¹⁰The young men who had grown up with him replied, "The people have said to you, 'Your father put a heavy yoke on us, but make our yoke lighter.' Now tell them, 'My little finger is thicker than my father's waist. ¹¹My father laid on you a heavy yoke; I will make it even heavier. My father scourged you with whips; I will scourge you with scorpions.'"

¹²Three days later Jeroboam and all the people returned to Rehoboam, as the king had said, "Come back to me in three days." ¹³The king answered them harshly. Rejecting the advice of the elders, ¹⁴he followed the advice of the young men and said, "My father made your yoke heavy; I will make it even heavier. My father scourged you with whips; I will scourge you with scorpions." ¹⁵So the king did not listen to the people,

for this turn of events was from God, to fulfill the word the LORD had spoken to Jeroboam son of Nebat through Ahijah the Shilonite.

¹⁶When all Israel saw that the king refused to listen to them, they answered the king:

"What share do we have in David,
    what part in Jesse's son?
To your tents, Israel!
    Look after your own house, David!"

So all the Israelites went home. ¹⁷But as for the Israelites who were living in the towns of Judah, Rehoboam still ruled over them.

¹⁸King Rehoboam sent out Adoniram,ᵃ who was in charge of forced labor, but the Israelites stoned him to death. King Rehoboam, however, managed to get into his chariot and escape to Jerusalem. ¹⁹So Israel has been in rebellion against the house of David to this day.

11 When Rehoboam arrived in Jerusalem, he mustered Judah and Benjamin—a hundred and eighty thousand able young men—to go to war against Israel and to regain the kingdom for Rehoboam.

²But this word of the LORD came to Shemaiah the man of God: ³"Say to Rehoboam son of Solomon king of Judah and to all Israel in Judah and Benjamin, ⁴'This is what the LORD says: Do not go up to fight against your fellow Israelites. Go home, every one of you, for this is my doing.'" So they obeyed the words of the LORD and turned back from marching against Jeroboam.

ᵃ 18 Hebrew *Hadoram*, a variant of *Adoniram*

Rehoboam and the Law of the Inner Circle

2 Chronicles 10:6–8

Be careful what kind of inner circle you choose! King Rehoboam had the benefit of his father's inner circle, men who gave him wise counsel. But the foolish young king rejected their advice and instead looked for advice that agreed with his own opinion. Horrible move! He should have gone with a core team who possessed the qualities of a solid inner circle:

1. *Experience:* People who have been down the road of life and understand it.

2. *Heart for God:* People who place God first and uphold his values.

3. *Objectivity:* People who see the pros and cons of the issues.

4. *Love for people:* People who love others and value them more than things.

5. *Complementary gifts:* People who bring diverse gifts to the relationship.

6. *Loyalty to the leader:* People who truly love and are concerned for the leader.

LISTENING   Rehoboam Fails to Listen to the Right People

2 Chronicles 10:15

KING REHOBOAM'S dysfunctional leadership split the nation of Israel in two. His hunger for power, unreasonable demands, poor decision making and lack of compassion for those who worked under him all conspired to doom his leadership. But probably the root of his problem can be found in 2 Chronicles 10:15: "So the king did not listen to the people . . ."

Listening is one of the 21 Indispensable Qualities of a Leader. Leaders must listen for two reasons:

1. **to connect with others, and**
2. **to learn from others.**

President Woodrow Wilson said, "The ear of the leader must ring with the voices of the people." What's more, a good leader encourages followers to tell him what he needs to know, not what he wants to hear. Sometimes 50 percent of your leadership involves simple listening. So why did Rehoboam fail at this simple task?

1. *Narrow Vision*
    The people promised to serve him if he lightened their load; he didn't see it.
2. *Poor Decision-Making Skills*
    He wavered on what to do about their request and told them to come back later.
3. *Self-Centered Focus*
    He rejected wise counsel after deciding it didn't match his desires.
4. *Demanding and Impatient Style*
    He promised to make life tougher, not easier, for his people.

We learn from King Rehoboam the difference between "hearing" and "listening." Hearing is a function of the ears; the king heard all the spoken words. Listening, however, is a function of the will; leaders listen to connect and to learn. Rehoboam failed to do both, as he refused to listen to history, his followers, the wise counsel of his staff, and to God.

Certainly we cannot listen to everyone—far too many opposing voices and views cry out for that. So to whom should leaders be listening? Listen especially well to the following:

1. *Your Followers*
    Good leaders take the time to get a feel for each team member as a person.
2. *Your Customers*
    Good leaders make it a priority to keep in contact with those they serve.
3. *Your Competitors*
    Good leaders don't imitate the competition, but they listen in order to learn from the encounter.
4. *Your Mentors*
    No leader can afford to be without a mentor's insight.
5. *Your Inner Circle*
    Leaders must listen to those closest to them to confirm the pulse of the organization.

For a positive example of listening, see p. 354.

Rehoboam Fortifies Judah

[5]Rehoboam lived in Jerusalem and built up towns for defense in Judah: [6]Bethlehem, Etam, Tekoa, [7]Beth Zur, Soko, Adullam, [8]Gath, Mareshah, Ziph, [9]Adoraim, Lachish, Azekah, [10]Zorah, Aijalon and Hebron. These are fortified cities in Judah and Benjamin. [11]He strengthened their defenses and put commanders in them, with supplies of food, olive oil and wine. [12]He put shields and spears in all the cities, and made them very strong. So Judah and Benjamin were his.

[13]The priests and Levites from all their districts throughout Israel sided with him. [14]The Levites even abandoned their pasturelands and property and came to Judah and Jerusalem, because Jeroboam and his sons had rejected them as priests of the LORD [15]when he appointed his own priests for the high places and for the goat and calf idols he had made. [16]Those from every tribe of Israel who set their hearts on seeking the LORD, the God of Israel, followed the Levites to Jerusalem to offer sacrifices to the LORD, the God of their ancestors. [17]They strengthened the kingdom of Judah and supported Rehoboam son of Solomon three years, following the ways of David and Solomon during this time.

Rehoboam's Family

[18]Rehoboam married Mahalath, who was the daughter of David's son Jerimoth and of Abihail, the daughter of Jesse's son Eliab. [19]She bore him sons: Jeush, Shemariah and Zaham. [20]Then he married Maakah daughter of Absalom, who bore him Abijah, Attai, Ziza and Shelomith. [21]Rehoboam loved Maakah daughter of Absalom more than any of his other wives and concubines. In all, he had eighteen wives and sixty concubines, twenty-eight sons and sixty daughters.

[22]Rehoboam appointed Abijah son of Maakah as crown prince among his brothers, in order to make him king. [23]He acted wisely, dispersing some of his sons throughout the districts of Judah and Benjamin, and to all the fortified cities. He gave them abundant provisions and took many wives for them.

Shishak Attacks Jerusalem

12 After Rehoboam's position as king was established and he had become strong, he and all Israel[a] with him abandoned the law of the LORD. [2]Because they had been unfaithful to the LORD, Shishak king of Egypt attacked Jerusalem in the fifth year of King Rehoboam.

[3]With twelve hundred chariots and sixty thousand horsemen and the innumerable troops of Libyans, Sukkites and Cushites[b] that came with him from Egypt, [4]he captured the fortified cities of Judah and came as far as Jerusalem.

[5]Then the prophet Shemaiah came to Rehoboam and to the leaders of Judah who had assembled in Jerusalem for fear of Shishak, and he said to them, "This is what the LORD says, 'You have abandoned me; therefore, I now abandon you to Shishak.'"

[6]The leaders of Israel and the king humbled themselves and said, "The LORD is just."

[7]When the LORD saw that they humbled themselves, this word of the LORD came to Shemaiah: "Since they have humbled themselves, I will not destroy them but will soon give them deliverance. My wrath will not be poured out on Jerusalem through Shishak. [8]They will, however, become subject to him, so that they may learn the difference between serving me and serving the kings of other lands."

[9]When Shishak king of Egypt attacked Jerusalem, he carried off the treasures of the temple of the LORD and the treasures of the royal palace. He took everything, including the gold shields Solomon had made. [10]So King Rehoboam made bronze shields to replace them and assigned these to the commanders of the guard on duty at the entrance to the royal palace. [11]Whenever the king went to the LORD's temple, the guards went with him, bearing the shields, and afterward they returned them to the guardroom.

[12]Because Rehoboam humbled himself, the LORD's anger turned from him, and he was not totally destroyed. Indeed, there was some good in Judah.

[13]King Rehoboam established himself firmly in Jerusalem and continued as king. He was forty-one years old when he became king, and he reigned seventeen years in Jerusalem, the city the LORD had chosen out of all the tribes of Israel in which to put his Name. His mother's name was Naamah; she was an Ammonite. [14]He did evil because he had not set his heart on seeking the LORD.

[15]As for the events of Rehoboam's reign, from beginning to end, are they not written in the records of Shemaiah the prophet and of Iddo the seer that deal with genealogies? There was continual warfare between Rehoboam and Jeroboam. [16]Rehoboam rested with his ancestors

---

[a] 1 That is, Judah, as frequently in 2 Chronicles   [b] 3 That is, people from the upper Nile region

and was buried in the City of David. And Abijah his son succeeded him as king.

Abijah King of Judah

13 In the eighteenth year of the reign of Jeroboam, Abijah became king of Judah, [2]and he reigned in Jerusalem three years. His mother's name was Maakah,[a] a daughter[b] of Uriel of Gibeah.

There was war between Abijah and Jeroboam. [3]Abijah went into battle with an army of four hundred thousand able fighting men, and Jeroboam drew up a battle line against him with eight hundred thousand able troops.

[4]Abijah stood on Mount Zemaraim, in the hill country of Ephraim, and said, "Jeroboam and all Israel, listen to me! [5]Don't you know that the LORD, the God of Israel, has given the kingship of Israel to David and his descendants forever by a covenant of salt? [6]Yet Jeroboam son of Nebat, an official of Solomon son of David, rebelled against his master. [7]Some worthless scoundrels gathered around him and opposed Rehoboam son of Solomon when he was young and indecisive and not strong enough to resist them.

[8]"And now you plan to resist the kingdom of the LORD, which is in the hands of David's descendants. You are indeed a vast army and have with you the golden calves that Jeroboam made to be your gods. [9]But didn't you drive out the priests of the LORD, the sons of Aaron, and the Levites, and make priests of your own as the peoples of other lands do? Whoever comes to consecrate himself with a young bull and seven rams may become a priest of what are not gods.

[10]"As for us, the LORD is our God, and we have not forsaken him. The priests who serve the LORD are sons of Aaron, and the Levites assist them. [11]Every morning and evening they present burnt offerings and fragrant incense to the LORD. They set out the bread on the ceremonially clean table and light the lamps on the gold lampstand every evening. We are observing the requirements of the LORD our God. But you have forsaken him. [12]God is with us; he is our leader. His priests with their trumpets will sound the battle cry against you. People of Israel, do not fight against the LORD, the God of your ancestors, for you will not succeed."

[13]Now Jeroboam had sent troops around to the rear, so that while he was in front of Judah the ambush was behind them. [14]Judah turned and saw that they were being attacked at both front and rear. Then they cried out to the LORD. The priests blew their trumpets [15]and the men of Judah raised the battle cry. At the sound of their battle cry, God routed Jeroboam and all Israel before Abijah and Judah. [16]The Israelites fled before Judah, and God delivered them into their hands. [17]Abijah and his troops inflicted heavy losses on them, so that there were five hundred thousand casualties among Israel's able men. [18]The Israelites were subdued on that occasion, and the people of Judah were victorious

---

[a] 2 Most Septuagint manuscripts and Syriac (see also 11:20 and 1 Kings 15:2); Hebrew *Micaiah*   [b] 2 Or *granddaughter*

Vision: Abijah Learns the Right Vision, Gets the Right Results

2 Chronicles 13:1–18

An unusual king named Abijah reminds us that the right vision at the right time brings the right results. Abijah followed Rehoboam as king of Judah. He tried to warn the leaders of Israel (the northern kingdom) against their folly in rebelling against the Lord. He cast the vision, reminded them of their heritage and encouraged them to follow it. "God is with us," he said. "He is our leader. His priests with their trumpets will sound the battle cry against you. People of Israel, do not fight against the LORD, the God of your ancestors, for you will not succeed" (2Ch 13:12).

When king Jeroboam refused to listen, God honored Abijah and delivered him from Jeroboam's ambush. That day 500,000 enemy soldiers fell on the battlefield. Abijah's vision led to his victory. Consider this:

- The wrong vision at the wrong time = Disaster
- The wrong vision at the right time = Mistake
- The right vision at the wrong time = Blunder
- The right vision at the right time = Success

because they relied on the LORD, the God of their ancestors.

¹⁹Abijah pursued Jeroboam and took from him the towns of Bethel, Jeshanah and Ephron, with their surrounding villages. ²⁰Jeroboam did not regain power during the time of Abijah. And the LORD struck him down and he died.

²¹But Abijah grew in strength. He married fourteen wives and had twenty-two sons and sixteen daughters.

²²The other events of Abijah's reign, what he did and what he said, are written in the annotations of the prophet Iddo.

14 ^a And Abijah rested with his ancestors and was buried in the City of David. Asa his son succeeded him as king, and in his days the country was at peace for ten years.

Asa King of Judah

²Asa did what was good and right in the eyes of the LORD his God. ³He removed the foreign altars and the high places, smashed the sacred stones and cut down the Asherah poles.^b ⁴He commanded Judah to seek the LORD, the God of their ancestors, and to obey his laws and commands. ⁵He removed the high places and incense altars in every town in Judah, and the kingdom was at peace under him. ⁶He built up the fortified cities of Judah, since the land was at peace. No one was at war with him during those years, for the LORD gave him rest.

⁷"Let us build up these towns," he said to Judah, "and put walls around them, with towers, gates and bars. The land is still ours, because we have sought the LORD our God; we sought him and he has given us rest on every side." So they built and prospered.

⁸Asa had an army of three hundred thousand men from Judah, equipped with large shields and with spears, and two hundred and eighty thousand from Benjamin, armed with small shields and with bows. All these were brave fighting men.

⁹Zerah the Cushite marched out against them with an army of thousands upon thousands and three hundred chariots, and came as far as Mareshah. ¹⁰Asa went out to meet him, and they took up battle positions in the Valley of Zephathah near Mareshah.

¹¹Then Asa called to the LORD his God and said, "LORD, there is no one like you to help the powerless against the mighty. Help us, LORD our God, for we rely on you, and in your name we have come against this vast army. LORD, you are our God; do not let mere mortals prevail against you."

¹²The LORD struck down the Cushites before Asa and Judah. The Cushites fled, ¹³and Asa and his army pursued them as far as Gerar. Such a great number of Cushites fell that they could not recover; they were crushed before the LORD and his forces. The men of Judah carried off a large amount of plunder. ¹⁴They destroyed all the villages around Gerar, for the terror of the LORD had fallen on them. They looted all these villages, since there was much plunder there. ¹⁵They also attacked the camps of the herders and carried off droves of sheep and goats and camels. Then they returned to Jerusalem.

Asa's Reform

15 The Spirit of God came on Azariah son of Oded. ²He went out to meet Asa and said to him, "Listen to me, Asa and all Judah and Benjamin. The LORD is with you when you are with him. If you seek him, he will be found by you, but if you forsake him, he will forsake you. ³For a long time Israel was without the true God, without a priest to teach and without the law. ⁴But in their distress they turned to the LORD, the God of Israel, and sought him, and he was found by them. ⁵In those days it was not safe to travel about, for all the inhabitants of the lands were in great turmoil. ⁶One nation was being crushed by another and one city by another, because God was troubling them with every kind of distress. ⁷But as for you, be strong and do not give up, for your work will be rewarded."

⁸When Asa heard these words and the prophecy of Azariah son of^c Oded the prophet, he took courage. He removed the detestable idols from the whole land of Judah and Benjamin and from the towns he had captured in the hills of Ephraim. He repaired the altar of the LORD that was in front of the portico of the LORD's temple.

⁹Then he assembled all Judah and Benjamin and the people from Ephraim, Manasseh and Simeon who had settled among them, for large numbers had come over to him from Israel when they saw that the LORD his God was with him.

¹⁰They assembled at Jerusalem in the third month of the fifteenth year of Asa's reign. ¹¹At that time they sacrificed to the LORD seven hundred head of cattle and seven thousand sheep and goats from the plunder they had brought back. ¹²They entered into a covenant to seek the

---

^a In Hebrew texts 14:1 is numbered 13:23, and 14:2-15 is numbered 14:1-14.   ^b 3 That is, wooden symbols of the goddess Asherah; here and elsewhere in 2 Chronicles   ^c 8 Vulgate and Syriac (see also Septuagint and verse 1); Hebrew does not have Azariah son of.

LORD, the God of their ancestors, with all their heart and soul. [13]All who would not seek the LORD, the God of Israel, were to be put to death, whether small or great, man or woman. [14]They took an oath to the LORD with loud acclamation, with shouting and with trumpets and horns. [15]All Judah rejoiced about the oath because they had sworn it wholeheartedly. They sought God eagerly, and he was found by them. So the LORD gave them rest on every side.

[16]King Asa also deposed his grandmother Maakah from her position as queen mother, because she had made a repulsive image for the worship of Asherah. Asa cut it down, broke it up and burned it in the Kidron Valley. [17]Although he did not remove the high places from Israel, Asa's heart was fully committed to the LORD all his life. [18]He brought into the temple of God the silver and gold and the articles that he and his father had dedicated.

[19]There was no more war until the thirty-fifth year of Asa's reign.

Asa's Last Years

16 In the thirty-sixth year of Asa's reign Baasha king of Israel went up against Judah and fortified Ramah to prevent anyone from leaving or entering the territory of Asa king of Judah.

[2]Asa then took the silver and gold out of the treasuries of the LORD's temple and of his own palace and sent it to Ben-Hadad king of Aram, who was ruling in Damascus. [3]"Let there be a treaty between me and you," he said, "as there was between my father and your father. See, I am sending you silver and gold. Now break your treaty with Baasha king of Israel so he will withdraw from me."

[4]Ben-Hadad agreed with King Asa and sent the commanders of his forces against the towns of Israel. They conquered Ijon, Dan, Abel Maim[a] and all the store cities of Naphtali. [5]When Baasha heard this, he stopped building Ramah and

---

[a] 4 Also known as *Abel Beth Maakah*

ASA

PROFILE in leadership

The Difficulty of Finishing Well
2 Chronicles 15:1—16:13

King Asa is one of many Old Testament kings who failed to finish well. At the beginning of his time of leadership he discovered this timeless principle: The Lord is with you when you are with him (2Ch 15:2). Immediately after the king learned this truth from the prophet Azariah, he initiated sweeping national reforms. After several years, however, he returned to his old leadership patterns and relied on men instead of God (16:7–12). When God's prophet warned him against this pattern, he grew angry and imprisoned him. He also "brutally oppressed some of the people" (16:10). Asa eventually died, a hollow leader who failed to finish well.

Asa stands with the majority who fail to finish well. Often, the pattern of failure stems from secret sin in the leader's life. Look at how this worked with David and Solomon:

David
1. Anointed king
2. Mighty warrior
3. Musician of the Lord
4. Faithful, loyal man
5. Great leader who made preparations for the temple

Solomon
1. Anointed king
2. Humble person of prayer
3. Temple builder
4. Greatest wealth and wisdom
5. Authored proverbs and songs

Tragic Ending
1. Disloyal to his men
2. Committed adultery
3. Committed murder
4. Tried to cover his sins
5. Brought judgment on family

Tragic Ending
1. Turned his heart from God
2. Became idol worshiper
3. Bought into vain philosophy
4. Selfishly sinned against the Lord
5. Sought to kill Jeroboam

abandoned his work. ⁶Then King Asa brought all the men of Judah, and they carried away from Ramah the stones and timber Baasha had been using. With them he built up Geba and Mizpah.

⁷At that time Hanani the seer came to Asa king of Judah and said to him: "Because you relied on the king of Aram and not on the LORD your God, the army of the king of Aram has escaped from your hand. ⁸Were not the Cushites[a] and Libyans a mighty army with great numbers of chariots and horsemen[b]? Yet when you relied on the LORD, he delivered them into your hand. ⁹For the eyes of the LORD range throughout the earth to strengthen those whose hearts are fully committed to him. You have done a foolish thing, and from now on you will be at war."

¹⁰Asa was angry with the seer because of this; he was so enraged that he put him in prison. At the same time Asa brutally oppressed some of the people.

¹¹The events of Asa's reign, from beginning to end, are written in the book of the kings of Judah and Israel. ¹²In the thirty-ninth year of his reign Asa was afflicted with a disease in his feet. Though his disease was severe, even in his illness he did not seek help from the LORD, but only from the physicians. ¹³Then in the forty-first year of his reign Asa died and rested with his ancestors. ¹⁴They buried him in the tomb that he had cut out for himself in the City of David. They laid him on a bier covered with spices and various blended perfumes, and they made a huge fire in his honor.

Jehoshaphat King of Judah

17 Jehoshaphat his son succeeded him as king and strengthened himself against Israel. ²He stationed troops in all the fortified cities of Judah and put garrisons in Judah and in the towns of Ephraim that his father Asa had captured.

³The LORD was with Jehoshaphat because he followed the ways of his father David before him. He did not consult the Baals ⁴but sought the God of his father and followed his commands rather than the practices of Israel. ⁵The LORD established the kingdom under his control; and all Judah brought gifts to Jehoshaphat, so that he had great wealth and honor. ⁶His heart was devoted to the ways of the LORD; furthermore, he removed the high places and the Asherah poles from Judah.

⁷In the third year of his reign he sent his officials Ben-Hail, Obadiah, Zechariah, Nethanel and Micaiah to teach in the towns of Judah.

⁸With them were certain Levites—Shemaiah, Nethaniah, Zebadiah, Asahel, Shemiramoth, Jehonathan, Adonijah, Tobijah and Tob-Adonijah—and the priests Elishama and Jehoram. ⁹They taught throughout Judah, taking with them the Book of the Law of the LORD; they went around to all the towns of Judah and taught the people.

¹⁰The fear of the LORD fell on all the kingdoms of the lands surrounding Judah, so that they did not go to war against Jehoshaphat. ¹¹Some Philistines brought Jehoshaphat gifts and silver as tribute, and the Arabs brought him flocks: seven thousand seven hundred rams and seven thousand seven hundred goats.

¹²Jehoshaphat became more and more powerful; he built forts and store cities in Judah ¹³and had large supplies in the towns of Judah. He also kept experienced fighting men in Jerusalem. ¹⁴Their enrollment by families was as follows:

From Judah, commanders of units of 1,000:
　Adnah the commander, with 300,000 fighting men;
　¹⁵next, Jehohanan the commander, with 280,000;
　¹⁶next, Amasiah son of Zikri, who volunteered himself for the service of the LORD, with 200,000.
¹⁷From Benjamin:
　Eliada, a valiant soldier, with 200,000 men armed with bows and shields;
　¹⁸next, Jehozabad, with 180,000 men armed for battle.

¹⁹These were the men who served the king, besides those he stationed in the fortified cities throughout Judah.

Micaiah Prophesies Against Ahab

18 Now Jehoshaphat had great wealth and honor, and he allied himself with Ahab by marriage. ²Some years later he went down to see Ahab in Samaria. Ahab slaughtered many sheep and cattle for him and the people with him and urged him to attack Ramoth Gilead. ³Ahab king of Israel asked Jehoshaphat king of Judah, "Will you go with me against Ramoth Gilead?"

Jehoshaphat replied, "I am as you are, and my people as your people; we will join you in the war." ⁴But Jehoshaphat also said to the king of Israel, "First seek the counsel of the LORD."

⁵So the king of Israel brought together the

---

[a] 8 That is, people from the upper Nile region　　[b] 8 Or charioteers

prophets—four hundred men—and asked them, "Shall we go to war against Ramoth Gilead, or shall I not?"

"Go," they answered, "for God will give it into the king's hand."

⁶But Jehoshaphat asked, "Is there no longer a prophet of the Lord here whom we can inquire of?"

⁷The king of Israel answered Jehoshaphat, "There is still one prophet through whom we can inquire of the Lord, but I hate him because he never prophesies anything good about me, but always bad. He is Micaiah son of Imlah."

"The king should not say such a thing," Jehoshaphat replied.

⁸So the king of Israel called one of his officials and said, "Bring Micaiah son of Imlah at once."

⁹Dressed in their royal robes, the king of Israel and Jehoshaphat king of Judah were sitting on their thrones at the threshing floor by the entrance of the gate of Samaria, with all the prophets prophesying before them. ¹⁰Now Zedekiah son of Kenaanah had made iron horns, and he declared, "This is what the Lord says: 'With these you will gore the Arameans until they are destroyed.'"

¹¹All the other prophets were prophesying the same thing. "Attack Ramoth Gilead and be victorious," they said, "for the Lord will give it into the king's hand."

¹²The messenger who had gone to summon Micaiah said to him, "Look, the other prophets without exception are predicting success for the king. Let your word agree with theirs, and speak favorably."

¹³But Micaiah said, "As surely as the Lord lives, I can tell him only what my God says."

¹⁴When he arrived, the king asked him, "Micaiah, shall we go to war against Ramoth Gilead, or shall I not?"

"Attack and be victorious," he answered, "for they will be given into your hand."

¹⁵The king said to him, "How many times must I make you swear to tell me nothing but the truth in the name of the Lord?"

¹⁶Then Micaiah answered, "I saw all Israel scattered on the hills like sheep without a shepherd, and the Lord said, 'These people have no master. Let each one go home in peace.'"

¹⁷The king of Israel said to Jehoshaphat, "Didn't I tell you that he never prophesies anything good about me, but only bad?"

¹⁸Micaiah continued, "Therefore hear the word of the Lord: I saw the Lord sitting on his throne with all the multitudes of heaven standing on his right and on his left. ¹⁹And the Lord said, 'Who will entice Ahab king of Israel into attacking Ramoth Gilead and going to his death there?'

"One suggested this, and another that. ²⁰Finally, a spirit came forward, stood before the Lord and said, 'I will entice him.'

"'By what means?' the Lord asked.

²¹"'I will go and be a deceiving spirit in the mouths of all his prophets,' he said.

"'You will succeed in enticing him,' said the Lord. 'Go and do it.'

²²"So now the Lord has put a deceiving spirit in the mouths of these prophets of yours. The Lord has decreed disaster for you."

²³Then Zedekiah son of Kenaanah went up and slapped Micaiah in the face. "Which way did the spirit from[a] the Lord go when he went from me to speak to you?" he asked.

²⁴Micaiah replied, "You will find out on the day you go to hide in an inner room."

²⁵The king of Israel then ordered, "Take Micaiah and send him back to Amon the ruler of the city and to Joash the king's son, ²⁶and say, 'This is what the king says: Put this fellow in prison and give him nothing but bread and water until I return safely.'"

²⁷Micaiah declared, "If you ever return safely, the Lord has not spoken through me." Then he added, "Mark my words, all you people!"

Ahab Killed at Ramoth Gilead

²⁸So the king of Israel and Jehoshaphat king of Judah went up to Ramoth Gilead. ²⁹The king of Israel said to Jehoshaphat, "I will enter the battle in disguise, but you wear your royal

---

[a] 23 Or *Spirit of*

Compromise: Sometimes There's No Room for Tolerance

2 Chronicles 18:1–31

There are times when tolerance cannot be tolerated. King Jehoshaphat formed an alliance with King Ahab of Israel to fight a common enemy, failing to understand that when you partner with an immoral or deceitful leader, you are asking for trouble. Moral failure impacts every part of leadership.

robes." So the king of Israel disguised himself and went into battle.

³⁰Now the king of Aram had ordered his chariot commanders, "Do not fight with anyone, small or great, except the king of Israel." ³¹When the chariot commanders saw Jehoshaphat, they thought, "This is the king of Israel." So they turned to attack him, but Jehoshaphat cried out, and the LORD helped him. God drew them away from him, ³²for when the chariot commanders saw that he was not the king of Israel, they stopped pursuing him.

³³But someone drew his bow at random and hit the king of Israel between the breastplate and the scale armor. The king told the chariot driver, "Wheel around and get me out of the fighting. I've been wounded." ³⁴All day long the battle raged, and the king of Israel propped himself up in his chariot facing the Arameans until evening. Then at sunset he died.

19 When Jehoshaphat king of Judah returned safely to his palace in Jerusalem, ²Jehu the seer, the son of Hanani, went out to meet him and said to the king, "Should you help the wicked and love*ᵃ* those who hate the LORD? Because of this, the wrath of the LORD is on you. ³There is, however, some good in you, for you have rid the land of the Asherah poles and have set your heart on seeking God."

Jehoshaphat Appoints Judges

⁴Jehoshaphat lived in Jerusalem, and he went out again among the people from Beersheba to the hill country of Ephraim and turned them back to the LORD, the God of their ancestors. ⁵He appointed judges in the land, in each of the fortified cities of Judah. ⁶He told them, "Consider carefully what you do, because you are not judging for mere mortals but for the LORD, who is with you whenever you give a verdict. ⁷Now let the fear of the LORD be on you. Judge carefully, for with the LORD our God there is no injustice or partiality or bribery."

⁸In Jerusalem also, Jehoshaphat appointed some of the Levites, priests and heads of Israelite families to administer the law of the LORD and to settle disputes. And they lived in Jerusalem. ⁹He gave them these orders: "You must serve faithfully and wholeheartedly in the fear of the LORD. ¹⁰In every case that comes before you from your people who live in the cities — whether bloodshed or other concerns of the law, commands, decrees or regulations — you are to warn them not to sin against the LORD; otherwise his wrath will

come on you and your people. Do this, and you will not sin.

¹¹"Amariah the chief priest will be over you in any matter concerning the LORD, and Zebadiah son of Ishmael, the leader of the tribe of Judah, will be over you in any matter concerning the king, and the Levites will serve as officials before you. Act with courage, and may the LORD be with those who do well."

Jehoshaphat Defeats Moab and Ammon

20 After this, the Moabites and Ammonites with some of the Meunites*ᵇ* came to wage war against Jehoshaphat.

²Some people came and told Jehoshaphat, "A vast army is coming against you from Edom,*ᶜ* from the other side of the Dead Sea. It is already in Hazezon Tamar" (that is, En Gedi). ³Alarmed, Jehoshaphat resolved to inquire of the LORD, and he proclaimed a fast for all Judah. ⁴The people of Judah came together to seek help from the LORD; indeed, they came from every town in Judah to seek him.

⁵Then Jehoshaphat stood up in the assembly of Judah and Jerusalem at the temple of the LORD in the front of the new courtyard ⁶and said:

"LORD, the God of our ancestors, are you not the God who is in heaven? You rule over all the kingdoms of the nations. Power and might are in your hand, and no one can withstand you. ⁷Our God, did you not drive out the inhabitants of this land before your people Israel and give it forever to the descendants of Abraham your friend? ⁸They have lived in it and have built in it a sanctuary for your Name, saying, ⁹'If calamity comes upon us, whether the sword of judgment, or plague or famine, we will stand in your presence before this temple that bears your Name and will cry out to you in our distress, and you will hear us and save us.'

¹⁰"But now here are men from Ammon, Moab and Mount Seir, whose territory you would not allow Israel to invade when they came from Egypt; so they turned away from them and did not destroy them. ¹¹See how they are repaying us by coming to drive us out of the possession you gave us

---

ᵃ 2 Or *and make alliances with*   *ᵇ 1* Some Septuagint manuscripts; Hebrew *Ammonites*   *ᶜ 2* One Hebrew manuscript; most Hebrew manuscripts, Septuagint and Vulgate *Aram*

21 QUALITIES

RESPONSIBILITY   Leaders Cannot Give It Away

2 Chronicles 20:1–25

A LEADER can delegate anything except responsibility. Leaders simply cannot give it away. They can model it; they can teach it; they can share it. But in the words of President Harry Truman, the buck stops with the leader.

Responsibility—"the ability to meet obligations; the act of being accountable; a duty of trust"—is one of the 21 Indispensable Qualities of a Leader. It's the ability to make and keep commitments.

When Jehoshaphat became king of Judah, he assumed a trust. Like all kings, he was to lead the people, protect the people, and manage the resources of the nation. Second Chronicles 20 records his greatest challenge to that point in his leadership. An army from three countries laid plans to attack Judah. Reports of their activity frightened the king (2Ch 20:3). No doubt, he faced the same options we all face in a crisis: give up, back up, or stand up. At such times we find out the quality of our leadership:

1. **The dropouts:** leaders who give up and fail to take responsibility.

2. **The cop-outs:** leaders who make excuses for why they aren't responsible.

3. **The hold-outs:** leaders who waiver too long to take responsibility.

4. **The all-outs:** leaders who own the responsibility and take action.

What Steps Did Jehoshaphat Take?

Second Chronicles 20 provides us with a beautiful story of a human leader who did what was right. Consider the appropriate steps he took:

1. *He fought his fear* (vv. 2–3). Jehoshaphat was terrified, but he didn't let it paralyze him. He stayed calm enough to think.

2. *He sought the Lord* (vv. 3, 6–13). Before he did anything else, he sought perspective by praying and seeking wisdom from God.

3. *He brought the synergy* (vv. 3–4). He didn't act alone, but gathered the people to inform them of the issue.

4. *He caught the vision* (vv. 14–17). He listened to the voice of the Lord until he knew what to do.

5. *He bought the idea* (vv. 18–19). He bowed his head and began to embrace the steps he and his nation had to take.

6. *He taught the plan* (vv. 20–23). He assembled the key players and gave them instructions on what each had to do.

7. *He got the victory* (vv. 24–25). He followed through with precision and succeeded, just as God predicted.

For a negative example of responsibility, see p. 1168.

as an inheritance. ¹²Our God, will you not judge them? For we have no power to face this vast army that is attacking us. We do not know what to do, but our eyes are on you."

¹³All the men of Judah, with their wives and children and little ones, stood there before the LORD.

¹⁴Then the Spirit of the LORD came on Jahaziel son of Zechariah, the son of Benaiah, the son of Jeiel, the son of Mattaniah, a Levite and descendant of Asaph, as he stood in the assembly.

¹⁵He said: "Listen, King Jehoshaphat and all who live in Judah and Jerusalem! This is what the LORD says to you: 'Do not be afraid or discouraged because of this vast army. For the battle is not yours, but God's. ¹⁶Tomorrow march down against them. They will be climbing up by the Pass of Ziz, and you will find them at the end of the gorge in the Desert of Jeruel. ¹⁷You will not have to fight this battle. Take up your positions; stand firm and see the deliverance the LORD will give you, Judah and Jerusalem. Do not be afraid; do not be discouraged. Go out to face them tomorrow, and the LORD will be with you.'"

¹⁸Jehoshaphat bowed down with his face to the ground, and all the people of Judah and Jerusalem fell down in worship before the LORD.

¹⁹Then some Levites from the Kohathites and Korahites stood up and praised the LORD, the God of Israel, with a very loud voice.

²⁰Early in the morning they left for the Desert of Tekoa. As they set out, Jehoshaphat stood and said, "Listen to me, Judah and people of Jerusalem! Have faith in the LORD your God and you will be upheld; have faith in his prophets and you will be successful." ²¹After consulting the people, Jehoshaphat appointed men to sing to the LORD and to praise him for the splendor of his^a holiness as they went out at the head of the army, saying:

"Give thanks to the LORD,
  for his love endures forever."

²²As they began to sing and praise, the LORD set ambushes against the men of Ammon and Moab and Mount Seir who were invading Judah, and they were defeated. ²³The Ammonites and Moabites rose up against the men from Mount Seir to destroy and annihilate them. After they finished slaughtering the men from Seir, they helped to destroy one another.

²⁴When the men of Judah came to the place that overlooks the desert and looked toward the vast army, they saw only dead bodies lying on the ground; no one had escaped. ²⁵So Jehosha-

^a 21 Or him with the splendor of

JEHOSHAPHAT

Finished Poorly by Forming Destructive Alliances
2 Chronicles 20:1–37

PROFILE in leadership

King Jehoshaphat of Judah handled a major national crisis the way any great leader should: by leading his people to God in prayer.

Judah faced almost certain defeat. A great army of Moabites, Ammonites and others stood poised to attack. The badly outnumbered forces of Judah stared destruction in the face and trembled over their fate. In his most desperate hour, the king called his people from all over Judah to pray in Jerusalem for national deliverance. "We have no power to face this vast army that is attacking us," he admitted to God. "We do not know what to do, but our eyes are on you" (2Ch 20:12).

The Lord answered Jehoshaphat's prayers and miraculously delivered his people from death—and he did so without one soldier of Judah marching off to battle.

Sadly, the king did not spend all his years on the throne expressing such great faith. Late in his reign, Jehoshaphat allowed pagan influences to corrupt his people. He also made an unwise alliance with King Ahaziah of Israel, a wicked man who worshiped Baal (20:33, 35).

Jehoshaphat somehow forgot that God calls leaders not only to begin a race, but to finish it. That is the only way to stand in the winner's circle at heaven's reward ceremonies.

phat and his men went to carry off their plunder, and they found among them a great amount of equipment and clothing[a] and also articles of value — more than they could take away. There was so much plunder that it took three days to collect it. [26]On the fourth day they assembled in the Valley of Berakah, where they praised the LORD. This is why it is called the Valley of Berakah[b] to this day.

[27]Then, led by Jehoshaphat, all the men of Judah and Jerusalem returned joyfully to Jerusalem, for the LORD had given them cause to rejoice over their enemies. [28]They entered Jerusalem and went to the temple of the LORD with harps and lyres and trumpets.

[29]The fear of God came on all the surrounding kingdoms when they heard how the LORD had fought against the enemies of Israel. [30]And the kingdom of Jehoshaphat was at peace, for his God had given him rest on every side.

The End of Jehoshaphat's Reign

[31]So Jehoshaphat reigned over Judah. He was thirty-five years old when he became king of Judah, and he reigned in Jerusalem twenty-five years. His mother's name was Azubah daughter of Shilhi. [32]He followed the ways of his father Asa and did not stray from them; he did what was right in the eyes of the LORD. [33]The high places, however, were not removed, and the people still had not set their hearts on the God of their ancestors.

[34]The other events of Jehoshaphat's reign, from beginning to end, are written in the annals of Jehu son of Hanani, which are recorded in the book of the kings of Israel.

[35]Later, Jehoshaphat king of Judah made an alliance with Ahaziah king of Israel, whose ways were wicked. [36]He agreed with him to construct a fleet of trading ships.[c] After these were built at Ezion Geber, [37]Eliezer son of Dodavahu of Mareshah prophesied against Jehoshaphat, saying, "Because you have made an alliance with Ahaziah, the LORD will destroy what you have made." The ships were wrecked and were not able to set sail to trade.[d]

21 Then Jehoshaphat rested with his ancestors and was buried with them in the City of David. And Jehoram his son succeeded him as king. [2]Jehoram's brothers, the sons of Jehoshaphat, were Azariah, Jehiel, Zechariah, Azariahu, Michael and Shephatiah. All these were sons of Jehoshaphat king of Israel.[e] [3]Their father had given them many gifts of silver and gold and articles of value, as well as fortified cities in Ju-

dah, but he had given the kingdom to Jehoram because he was his firstborn son.

Jehoram King of Judah

[4]When Jehoram established himself firmly over his father's kingdom, he put all his brothers to the sword along with some of the officials of Israel. [5]Jehoram was thirty-two years old when he became king, and he reigned in Jerusalem eight years. [6]He followed the ways of the kings of Israel, as the house of Ahab had done, for he married a daughter of Ahab. He did evil in the eyes of the LORD. [7]Nevertheless, because of the covenant the LORD had made with David, the LORD was not willing to destroy the house of David. He had promised to maintain a lamp for him and his descendants forever.

[8]In the time of Jehoram, Edom rebelled against Judah and set up its own king. [9]So Jehoram went there with his officers and all his chariots. The Edomites surrounded him and his chariot commanders, but he rose up and broke through by night. [10]To this day Edom has been in rebellion against Judah.

Libnah revolted at the same time, because Jehoram had forsaken the LORD, the God of his ancestors. [11]He had also built high places on the hills of Judah and had caused the people of Jerusalem to prostitute themselves and had led Judah astray.

[12]Jehoram received a letter from Elijah the prophet, which said:

"This is what the LORD, the God of your father David, says: 'You have not followed the ways of your father Jehoshaphat or of Asa king of Judah. [13]But you have followed the ways of the kings of Israel, and you have led Judah and the people of Jerusalem to prostitute themselves, just as the house of Ahab did. You have also murdered your own brothers, members of your own family, men who were better than you. [14]So now the LORD is about to strike your people, your sons, your wives and everything that is yours, with a heavy blow. [15]You yourself will be very ill with a lingering disease of the bowels, until the disease causes your bowels to come out.'"

---

[a] 25 Some Hebrew manuscripts and Vulgate; most Hebrew manuscripts *corpses*   [b] 26 Berakah means *praise.*
[c] 36 Hebrew *of ships that could go to Tarshish*   [d] 37 Hebrew *sail for Tarshish*   [e] 2 That is, Judah, as frequently in 2 Chronicles

¹⁶The LORD aroused against Jehoram the hostility of the Philistines and of the Arabs who lived near the Cushites. ¹⁷They attacked Judah, invaded it and carried off all the goods found in the king's palace, together with his sons and wives. Not a son was left to him except Ahaziah,ᵃ the youngest.

¹⁸After all this, the LORD afflicted Jehoram with an incurable disease of the bowels. ¹⁹In the course of time, at the end of the second year, his bowels came out because of the disease, and he died in great pain. His people made no funeral fire in his honor, as they had for his predecessors.

²⁰Jehoram was thirty-two years old when he became king, and he reigned in Jerusalem eight years. He passed away, to no one's regret, and was buried in the City of David, but not in the tombs of the kings.

Ahaziah King of Judah

22 The people of Jerusalem made Ahaziah, Jehoram's youngest son, king in his place, since the raiders, who came with the Arabs into the camp, had killed all the older sons. So Ahaziah son of Jehoram king of Judah began to reign.

²Ahaziah was twenty-twoᵇ years old when he became king, and he reigned in Jerusalem one year. His mother's name was Athaliah, a granddaughter of Omri.

³He too followed the ways of the house of Ahab, for his mother encouraged him to act wickedly. ⁴He did evil in the eyes of the LORD, as the house of Ahab had done, for after his father's death they became his advisers, to his undoing. ⁵He also followed their counsel when he went with Joramᶜ son of Ahab king of Israel to wage war against Hazael king of Aram at Ramoth Gilead. The Arameans wounded Joram; ⁶so he returned to Jezreel to recover from the wounds they had inflicted on him at Ramothᵈ in his battle with Hazael king of Aram.

Then Ahaziahᵉ son of Jehoram king of Judah went down to Jezreel to see Joram son of Ahab because he had been wounded.

⁷Through Ahaziah's visit to Joram, God brought about Ahaziah's downfall. When Ahaziah arrived, he went out with Joram to meet

---

ᵃ 17 Hebrew *Jehoahaz*, a variant of *Ahaziah*   ᵇ 2 Some Septuagint manuscripts and Syriac (see also 2 Kings 8:26); Hebrew *forty-two*   ᶜ 5 Hebrew *Jehoram*, a variant of *Joram*; also in verses 6 and 7   ᵈ 6 Hebrew *Ramah*, a variant of *Ramoth*   ᵉ 6 Some Hebrew manuscripts, Septuagint, Vulgate and Syriac (see also 2 Kings 8:29); most Hebrew manuscripts *Azariah*

Servanthood: Leaders Serve Their People and Their Purpose
2 Chronicles 22:1–9

What impact can godless character have on leaders and nations? We find out in the life of King Ahaziah.

The young king and several other political and military leaders lost their lives and their positions through a self-centered pursuit of power. This chapter is a negative example of a positive truth, the Law of Addition: Leaders are to add value, not take it away. These leaders forgot that they must serve their people and their purpose. Leaders are not given authority to better themselves, to enlarge their income or social status, or to improve their standard of living. They are first and always servants of others.

This biblical idea appears throughout the Scripture, but finds special emphasis in the Gospels through the teaching of Jesus Christ. Consider what our Lord teaches us about servant leadership:

Human Economy	God's Economy
1. Pursuit of power and prestige	1. Pursuit of love and service to others
2. Improve wealth and status of the leader	2. Improve the welfare of the people
3. See others as enemies and competitors	3. See others as brothers who complement
4. Motive is to remove or kill opposition	4. Motive is to meet needs and grow the cause
5. The result: the leader is glorified	5. The result: God is glorified

Jehu son of Nimshi, whom the LORD had anointed to destroy the house of Ahab. ⁸While Jehu was executing judgment on the house of Ahab, he found the officials of Judah and the sons of Ahaziah's relatives, who had been attending Ahaziah, and he killed them. ⁹He then went in search of Ahaziah, and his men captured him while he was hiding in Samaria. He was brought to Jehu and put to death. They buried him, for they said, "He was a son of Jehoshaphat, who sought the LORD with all his heart." So there was no one in the house of Ahaziah powerful enough to retain the kingdom.

Athaliah and Joash

¹⁰When Athaliah the mother of Ahaziah saw that her son was dead, she proceeded to destroy the whole royal family of the house of Judah. ¹¹But Jehosheba,ᵃ the daughter of King Jehoram, took Joash son of Ahaziah and stole him away from among the royal princes who were about to be murdered and put him and his nurse in a bedroom. Because Jehosheba,ᵃ the daughter of King Jehoram and wife of the priest Jehoiada, was Ahaziah's sister, she hid the child from Athaliah so she could not kill him. ¹²He remained hidden with them at the temple of God for six years while Athaliah ruled the land.

23 In the seventh year Jehoiada showed his strength. He made a covenant with the commanders of units of a hundred: Aza-

riah son of Jeroham, Ishmael son of Jehohanan, Azariah son of Obed, Maaseiah son of Adaiah, and Elishaphat son of Zikri. ²They went throughout Judah and gathered the Levites and the heads of Israelite families from all the towns. When they came to Jerusalem, ³the whole assembly made a covenant with the king at the temple of God.

Jehoiada said to them, "The king's son shall reign, as the LORD promised concerning the descendants of David. ⁴Now this is what you are to do: A third of you priests and Levites who are going on duty on the Sabbath are to keep watch at the doors, ⁵a third of you at the royal palace and a third at the Foundation Gate, and all the others are to be in the courtyards of the temple of the LORD. ⁶No one is to enter the temple of the LORD except the priests and Levites on duty; they may enter because they are consecrated, but all the others are to observe the LORD's command not to enter.ᵇ ⁷The Levites are to station themselves around the king, each with weapon in hand. Anyone who enters the temple is to be put to death. Stay close to the king wherever he goes."

⁸The Levites and all the men of Judah did just as Jehoiada the priest ordered. Each one took his men — those who were going on duty on the

---

ᵃ 11 Hebrew *Jehoshabeath*, a variant of *Jehosheba*   ᵇ 6 Or *are to stand guard where the LORD has assigned them*

ATHALIAH

Pursuing Power Rather Than Love
2 Chronicles 22:10—23:15

PROFILE in leadership

Some leaders step into positions of power out of love and a sense of mission. Others seek leadership merely to gain power over others and to revel in a smug feeling of superiority. Normally it doesn't take long to determine which sort of leader you've got.

It took no time at all to decide in the case of Athaliah.

As soon as she heard that her son, King Ahaziah, had been killed by Jehu, "she proceeded to destroy the whole royal family of the house of Judah" (2Ch 22:10)—including all her grandsons. She missed only one, Joash, who escaped her murderous rampage only when a godly young woman named Jehosheba hid him in the house of God for six years. Athaliah did not care in the slightest that God had promised his people that the Messiah would come through the royal line of David.

This is a picture of a leader so thirsty for power that she would do anything to attain and hold her illegitimate title—including murdering her own kin. Athaliah ruled over Judah for seven years. In the end, the people violently removed her from power (23:12–15).

Queen Athaliah is an extreme example of a leader motivated not by love, but by power, prestige and position. It never takes long to spot the difference.

Sabbath and those who were going off duty—for Jehoiada the priest had not released any of the divisions. ⁹Then he gave the commanders of units of a hundred the spears and the large and small shields that had belonged to King David and that were in the temple of God. ¹⁰He stationed all the men, each with his weapon in his hand, around the king—near the altar and the temple, from the south side to the north side of the temple.

¹¹Jehoiada and his sons brought out the king's son and put the crown on him; they presented him with a copy of the covenant and proclaimed him king. They anointed him and shouted, "Long live the king!"

¹²When Athaliah heard the noise of the people running and cheering the king, she went to them at the temple of the LORD. ¹³She looked, and there was the king, standing by his pillar at the entrance. The officers and the trumpeters were beside the king, and all the people of the land were rejoicing and blowing trumpets, and musicians with their instruments were leading the praises. Then Athaliah tore her robes and shouted, "Treason! Treason!"

¹⁴Jehoiada the priest sent out the commanders of units of a hundred, who were in charge of the troops, and said to them: "Bring her out between the ranks[a] and put to the sword anyone who follows her." For the priest had said, "Do not put her to death at the temple of the LORD." ¹⁵So they seized her as she reached the entrance of the Horse Gate on the palace grounds, and there they put her to death.

¹⁶Jehoiada then made a covenant that he, the people and the king[b] would be the LORD's people. ¹⁷All the people went to the temple of Baal and tore it down. They smashed the altars and idols and killed Mattan the priest of Baal in front of the altars.

¹⁸Then Jehoiada placed the oversight of the temple of the LORD in the hands of the Levitical priests, to whom David had made assignments in the temple, to present the burnt offerings of the LORD as written in the Law of Moses, with rejoicing and singing, as David had ordered. ¹⁹He also stationed gatekeepers at the gates of the LORD's temple so that no one who was in any way unclean might enter.

²⁰He took with him the commanders of hundreds, the nobles, the rulers of the people and all the people of the land and brought the king down from the temple of the LORD. They went into the palace through the Upper Gate and seated the king on the royal throne. ²¹All the

people of the land rejoiced, and the city was calm, because Athaliah had been slain with the sword.

Joash Repairs the Temple

24 Joash was seven years old when he became king, and he reigned in Jerusalem forty years. His mother's name was Zibiah; she was from Beersheba. ²Joash did what was right in the eyes of the LORD all the years of Jehoiada the priest. ³Jehoiada chose two wives for him, and he had sons and daughters.

⁴Some time later Joash decided to restore the temple of the LORD. ⁵He called together the priests and Levites and said to them, "Go to the towns of Judah and collect the money due annually from all Israel, to repair the temple of your God. Do it now." But the Levites did not act at once.

⁶Therefore the king summoned Jehoiada the chief priest and said to him, "Why haven't you required the Levites to bring in from Judah and Jerusalem the tax imposed by Moses the servant of the LORD and by the assembly of Israel for the tent of the covenant law?"

⁷Now the sons of that wicked woman Athaliah had broken into the temple of God and had used even its sacred objects for the Baals.

⁸At the king's command, a chest was made and placed outside, at the gate of the temple of the LORD. ⁹A proclamation was then issued in Judah and Jerusalem that they should bring to the LORD the tax that Moses the servant of God had required of Israel in the wilderness. ¹⁰All the officials and all the people brought their contributions gladly, dropping them into the chest until it was full. ¹¹Whenever the chest was brought in by the Levites to the king's officials and they saw that there was a large amount of money, the royal secretary and the officer of the chief priest would come and empty the chest and carry it back to its place. They did this regularly and collected a great amount of money. ¹²The king and Jehoiada gave it to those who carried out the work required for the temple of the LORD. They hired masons and carpenters to restore the LORD's temple, and also workers in iron and bronze to repair the temple.

¹³The men in charge of the work were diligent, and the repairs progressed under them. They rebuilt the temple of God according to its original design and reinforced it. ¹⁴When they

---

[a] 14 Or out from the precincts   [b] 16 Or covenant between the LORD and the people and the king that they (see 2 Kings 11:17)

had finished, they brought the rest of the money to the king and Jehoiada, and with it were made articles for the LORD's temple: articles for the service and for the burnt offerings, and also dishes and other objects of gold and silver. As long as Jehoiada lived, burnt offerings were presented continually in the temple of the LORD.

¹⁵Now Jehoiada was old and full of years, and he died at the age of a hundred and thirty. ¹⁶He was buried with the kings in the City of David, because of the good he had done in Israel for God and his temple.

The Wickedness of Joash

¹⁷After the death of Jehoiada, the officials of Judah came and paid homage to the king, and he listened to them. ¹⁸They abandoned the temple of the LORD, the God of their ancestors, and worshiped Asherah poles and idols. Because of their guilt, God's anger came on Judah and Jerusalem. ¹⁹Although the LORD sent prophets to the people to bring them back to him, and though they testified against them, they would not listen.

Motives: Why You Do Determines What You Do

2 Chronicles 24:4–18

As a young man, Joash committed himself to restoring the temple. He remained true as long as the high priest Jehoiada was alive. When Jehoiada died, however, the king abandoned the temple and worshiped idols. *Why* we do something ultimately determines *what* we do.

²⁰Then the Spirit of God came on Zechariah son of Jehoiada the priest. He stood before the people and said, "This is what God says: 'Why do you disobey the LORD's commands? You will not prosper. Because you have forsaken the LORD, he has forsaken you.'"

²¹But they plotted against him, and by order of the king they stoned him to death in the courtyard of the LORD's temple. ²²King Joash did not remember the kindness Zechariah's father Jehoiada had shown him but killed his son, who said as he lay dying, "May the LORD see this and call you to account."

²³At the turn of the year,[a] the army of Aram marched against Joash; it invaded Judah and Je-

rusalem and killed all the leaders of the people. They sent all the plunder to their king in Damascus. ²⁴Although the Aramean army had come with only a few men, the LORD delivered into their hands a much larger army. Because Judah had forsaken the LORD, the God of their ancestors, judgment was executed on Joash. ²⁵When the Arameans withdrew, they left Joash severely wounded. His officials conspired against him for murdering the son of Jehoiada the priest, and they killed him in his bed. So he died and was buried in the City of David, but not in the tombs of the kings.

²⁶Those who conspired against him were Zabad,[b] son of Shimeath an Ammonite woman, and Jehozabad, son of Shimrith[c] a Moabite woman. ²⁷The account of his sons, the many prophecies about him, and the record of the restoration of the temple of God are written in the annotations on the book of the kings. And Amaziah his son succeeded him as king.

Amaziah King of Judah

25 Amaziah was twenty-five years old when he became king, and he reigned in Jerusalem twenty-nine years. His mother's name was Jehoaddan; she was from Jerusalem. ²He did what was right in the eyes of the LORD, but not wholeheartedly. ³After the kingdom was firmly in his control, he executed the officials who had murdered his father the king. ⁴Yet he did not put their children to death, but acted in accordance with what is written in the Law, in the Book of Moses, where the LORD commanded: "Parents shall not be put to death for their children, nor children be put to death for their parents; each will die for their own sin."[d]

⁵Amaziah called the people of Judah together and assigned them according to their families to commanders of thousands and commanders of hundreds for all Judah and Benjamin. He then mustered those twenty years old or more and found that there were three hundred thousand men fit for military service, able to handle the spear and shield. ⁶He also hired a hundred thousand fighting men from Israel for a hundred talents[e] of silver.

⁷But a man of God came to him and said, "Your Majesty, these troops from Israel must not march with you, for the LORD is not with Israel — not with any of the people of Ephraim.

---

[a] 23 Probably in the spring   [b] 26 A variant of *Jozabad*
[c] 26 A variant of *Shomer*   [d] 4 Deut. 24:16   [e] 6 That is, about 3 3/4 tons or about 3.4 metric tons; also in verse 9

[8]Even if you go and fight courageously in battle, God will overthrow you before the enemy, for God has the power to help or to overthrow."

[9]Amaziah asked the man of God, "But what about the hundred talents I paid for these Israelite troops?"

The man of God replied, "The LORD can give you much more than that."

[10]So Amaziah dismissed the troops who had come to him from Ephraim and sent them home. They were furious with Judah and left for home in a great rage.

[11]Amaziah then marshaled his strength and led his army to the Valley of Salt, where he killed ten thousand men of Seir. [12]The army of Judah also captured ten thousand men alive, took them to the top of a cliff and threw them down so that all were dashed to pieces.

[13]Meanwhile the troops that Amaziah had sent back and had not allowed to take part in the war raided towns belonging to Judah from Samaria to Beth Horon. They killed three thousand people and carried off great quantities of plunder.

[14]When Amaziah returned from slaughtering the Edomites, he brought back the gods of the people of Seir. He set them up as his own gods, bowed down to them and burned sacrifices to them. [15]The anger of the LORD burned against Amaziah, and he sent a prophet to him, who said, "Why do you consult this people's gods, which could not save their own people from your hand?"

[16]While he was still speaking, the king said to him, "Have we appointed you an adviser to the king? Stop! Why be struck down?"

So the prophet stopped but said, "I know that God has determined to destroy you, because you have done this and have not listened to my counsel."

[17]After Amaziah king of Judah consulted his advisers, he sent this challenge to Jehoash[a] son of Jehoahaz, the son of Jehu, king of Israel: "Come, let us face each other in battle."

[18]But Jehoash king of Israel replied to Amaziah king of Judah: "A thistle in Lebanon sent a message to a cedar in Lebanon, 'Give your daughter to my son in marriage.' Then a wild beast in Lebanon came along and trampled the thistle underfoot. [19]You say to yourself that you have defeated Edom, and now you are arrogant and proud. But stay at home! Why ask for trouble and cause your own downfall and that of Judah also?"

[20]Amaziah, however, would not listen, for God so worked that he might deliver them into the hands of Jehoash, because they sought the gods of Edom. [21]So Jehoash king of Israel attacked. He and Amaziah king of Judah faced each other at Beth Shemesh in Judah. [22]Judah was routed by Israel, and every man fled to his home. [23]Jehoash king of Israel captured Amaziah king of Judah, the son of Joash, the son of Ahaziah,[b] at Beth Shemesh. Then Jehoash brought him to Jerusalem and broke down the wall of Jerusalem from the Ephraim Gate to the Corner Gate — a section about four hundred cubits[c] long. [24]He took all the gold and silver and all the articles found in the temple of God that had been in the care of Obed-Edom, together with the palace treasures and the hostages, and returned to Samaria.

[25]Amaziah son of Joash king of Judah lived for fifteen years after the death of Jehoash son of Jehoahaz king of Israel. [26]As for the other events of Amaziah's reign, from beginning to end, are they not written in the book of the kings of Judah and Israel? [27]From the time that Amaziah turned away from following the LORD, they conspired against him in Jerusalem and he fled to Lachish, but they sent men after him to Lachish and killed him there. [28]He was brought back by horse and was buried with his ancestors in the City of Judah.[d]

Uzziah King of Judah

26 Then all the people of Judah took Uzziah,[e] who was sixteen years old, and made him king in place of his father Amaziah. [2]He was the one who rebuilt Elath and restored it to Judah after Amaziah rested with his ancestors.

[3]Uzziah was sixteen years old when he became king, and he reigned in Jerusalem fifty-two years. His mother's name was Jekoliah; she was from Jerusalem. [4]He did what was right in the eyes of the LORD, just as his father Amaziah had done. [5]He sought God during the days of Zechariah, who instructed him in the fear[f] of God. As long as he sought the LORD, God gave him success.

[6]He went to war against the Philistines and broke down the walls of Gath, Jabneh and Ashdod. He then rebuilt towns near Ashdod and

---

[a] 17 Hebrew *Joash*, a variant of *Jehoash*; also in verses 18, 21, 23 and 25   [b] 23 Hebrew *Jehoahaz*, a variant of *Ahaziah*   [c] 23 That is, about 600 feet or about 180 meters   [d] 28 Most Hebrew manuscripts; some Hebrew manuscripts, Septuagint, Vulgate and Syriac (see also 2 Kings 14:20) *David*   [e] 1 Also called *Azariah*   [f] 5 Many Hebrew manuscripts, Septuagint and Syriac; other Hebrew manuscripts *vision*

elsewhere among the Philistines. [7]God helped him against the Philistines and against the Arabs who lived in Gur Baal and against the Meunites. [8]The Ammonites brought tribute to Uzziah, and his fame spread as far as the border of Egypt, because he had become very powerful.

[9]Uzziah built towers in Jerusalem at the Corner Gate, at the Valley Gate and at the angle of the wall, and he fortified them. [10]He also built towers in the wilderness and dug many cisterns, because he had much livestock in the foothills and in the plain. He had people working his fields and vineyards in the hills and in the fertile lands, for he loved the soil.

[11]Uzziah had a well-trained army, ready to go out by divisions according to their numbers as mustered by Jeiel the secretary and Maaseiah the officer under the direction of Hananiah, one of the royal officials. [12]The total number of family leaders over the fighting men was 2,600. [13]Under their command was an army of 307,500 men trained for war, a powerful force to support the king against his enemies. [14]Uzziah provided shields, spears, helmets, coats of armor, bows and slingstones for the entire army. [15]In Jerusalem he made devices invented for use on the towers and on the corner defenses so that soldiers could shoot arrows and hurl large stones from the walls. His fame spread far and wide, for he was greatly helped until he became powerful.

[16]But after Uzziah became powerful, his pride led to his downfall. He was unfaithful to the LORD his God, and entered the temple of the LORD to burn incense on the altar of incense. [17]Azariah the priest with eighty other courageous priests of the LORD followed him in. [18]They confronted King Uzziah and said, "It is not right for you, Uzziah, to burn incense to the LORD. That is for the priests, the descendants of Aaron, who have been consecrated to burn incense. Leave the sanctuary, for you have been unfaithful; and you will not be honored by the LORD God."

[19]Uzziah, who had a censer in his hand ready to burn incense, became angry. While he was raging at the priests in their presence before the incense altar in the LORD's temple, leprosy[a] broke out on his forehead. [20]When Azariah the chief priest and all the other priests looked at him, they saw that he had leprosy on his forehead, so they hurried him out. Indeed, he himself was eager to leave, because the LORD had afflicted him.

[21]King Uzziah had leprosy until the day he

---

[a] 19 The Hebrew for *leprosy* was used for various diseases affecting the skin; also in verses 20, 21 and 23.

UZZIAH

Built His Military, Later His Own Power
2 Chronicles 26:1–23

PROFILE in leadership

The ancient kings of Israel and Judah died centuries ago, yet like all leaders, the choices they made nearly always reflected their true character. Uzziah's reign mirrored that of Asa, Josiah and Amaziah—it began very strong and ended in disgrace.

In the early years, Uzziah displayed strong, godly leadership skills. The Lord blessed him with military success. During this time, his inner circle included a godly spiritual counselor, Zechariah, who exerted significant influence for good. Uzziah sought after God, and the Lord prospered him.

As Uzziah's kingdom and wealth increased, however, he lost focus. His priorities shifted to personal success and fame rather than the things that delighted God's heart. His eyes drifted from God, and sin blinded his actions.

Like many highly successful leaders, Uzziah developed an attitude of superiority. He exhibited an astonishing lack of discernment when he usurped the priestly role by offering incense in the temple. A raw desire for power consumed his soul, and the king intentionally stepped out of his God-ordained role. As a result, Uzziah left a legacy of disgrace. The Word of God says of him: "King Uzziah had leprosy until the day he died. He lived in a separate house—leprous, and banned from the temple of the LORD" (2Ch 26:21). A sad ending to a promising start.

died. He lived in a separate house[a] — leprous, and banned from the temple of the LORD. Jotham his son had charge of the palace and governed the people of the land.

[22] The other events of Uzziah's reign, from beginning to end, are recorded by the prophet Isaiah son of Amoz. [23] Uzziah rested with his ancestors and was buried near them in a cemetery that belonged to the kings, for people said, "He had leprosy." And Jotham his son succeeded him as king.

Jotham King of Judah

27 Jotham was twenty-five years old when he became king, and he reigned in Jerusalem sixteen years. His mother's name was Jerusha daughter of Zadok. [2] He did what was right in the eyes of the LORD, just as his father Uzziah had done, but unlike him he did not enter the temple of the LORD. The people, however, continued their corrupt practices. [3] Jotham rebuilt the Upper Gate of the temple of the LORD and did extensive work on the wall at the hill of Ophel. [4] He built towns in the hill country of Judah and forts and towers in the wooded areas.

[5] Jotham waged war against the king of the Ammonites and conquered them. That year the Ammonites paid him a hundred talents[b] of silver, ten thousand cors[c] of wheat and ten thousand cors[d] of barley. The Ammonites brought him the same amount also in the second and third years.

[6] Jotham grew powerful because he walked steadfastly before the LORD his God.

[7] The other events in Jotham's reign, including all his wars and the other things he did, are written in the book of the kings of Israel and Judah. [8] He was twenty-five years old when he became king, and he reigned in Jerusalem sixteen years. [9] Jotham rested with his ancestors and was buried in the City of David. And Ahaz his son succeeded him as king.

Ahaz King of Judah

28 Ahaz was twenty years old when he became king, and he reigned in Jerusalem sixteen years. Unlike David his father, he did not do what was right in the eyes of the LORD. [2] He followed the ways of the kings of Israel and also made idols for worshiping the Baals. [3] He burned sacrifices in the Valley of Ben Hinnom and sacrificed his children in the fire, engaging in the detestable practices of the nations the LORD had driven out before the Israelites. [4] He offered sacrifices and burned incense at the high places, on the hilltops and under every spreading tree.

[5] Therefore the LORD his God delivered him into the hands of the king of Aram. The Arameans defeated him and took many of his people as prisoners and brought them to Damascus.

He was also given into the hands of the king of Israel, who inflicted heavy casualties on him. [6] In one day Pekah son of Remaliah killed a hundred and twenty thousand soldiers in Judah — because Judah had forsaken the LORD, the God of their ancestors. [7] Zikri, an Ephraimite warrior, killed Maaseiah the king's son, Azrikam the officer in charge of the palace, and Elkanah, second to the king. [8] The men of Israel took captive from their fellow Israelites who were from Judah two hundred thousand wives, sons and daughters. They also took a great deal of plunder, which they carried back to Samaria.

[9] But a prophet of the LORD named Oded was there, and he went out to meet the army when it returned to Samaria. He said to them, "Because the LORD, the God of your ancestors, was angry with Judah, he gave them into your hand. But you have slaughtered them in a rage that reaches to heaven. [10] And now you intend to make the men and women of Judah and Jerusalem your slaves. But aren't you also guilty of sins against the LORD your God? [11] Now listen to me! Send back your fellow Israelites you have taken as prisoners, for the LORD's fierce anger rests on you."

[12] Then some of the leaders in Ephraim — Azariah son of Jehohanan, Berekiah son of Meshillemoth, Jehizkiah son of Shallum, and Amasa son of Hadlai — confronted those who were arriving from the war. [13] "You must not bring those prisoners here," they said, "or we will be guilty before the LORD. Do you intend to add to our sin and guilt? For our guilt is already great, and his fierce anger rests on Israel."

[14] So the soldiers gave up the prisoners and plunder in the presence of the officials and all the assembly. [15] The men designated by name took the prisoners, and from the plunder they clothed all who were naked. They provided them with clothes and sandals, food and drink, and healing balm. All those who were weak they put on donkeys. So they took them back to their fellow Israelites at Jericho, the City of Palms, and returned to Samaria.

---

[a] 21 Or in a house where he was relieved of responsibilities
[b] 5 That is, about 3 3/4 tons or about 3.4 metric tons
[c] 5 That is, probably about 1,800 tons or about 1,600 metric tons of wheat   [d] 5 That is, probably about 1,500 tons or about 1,350 metric tons of barley

[16]At that time King Ahaz sent to the kings[a] of Assyria for help. [17]The Edomites had again come and attacked Judah and carried away prisoners, [18]while the Philistines had raided towns in the foothills and in the Negev of Judah. They captured and occupied Beth Shemesh, Aijalon and Gederoth, as well as Soko, Timnah and Gimzo, with their surrounding villages. [19]The Lord had humbled Judah because of Ahaz king of Israel,[b] for he had promoted wickedness in Judah and had been most unfaithful to the Lord. [20]Tiglath-Pileser[c] king of Assyria came to him, but he gave him trouble instead of help. [21]Ahaz took some of the things from the temple of the Lord and from the royal palace and from the officials and presented them to the king of Assyria, but that did not help him.

[22]In his time of trouble King Ahaz became even more unfaithful to the Lord. [23]He offered sacrifices to the gods of Damascus, who had defeated him; for he thought, "Since the gods of the kings of Aram have helped them, I will sacrifice to them so they will help me." But they were his downfall and the downfall of all Israel. [24]Ahaz gathered together the furnishings from the temple of God and cut them in pieces. He shut the doors of the Lord's temple and set up altars at every street corner in Jerusalem. [25]In every town in Judah he built high places to burn sacrifices to other gods and aroused the anger of the Lord, the God of his ancestors.

[26]The other events of his reign and all his ways, from beginning to end, are written in the book of the kings of Judah and Israel. [27]Ahaz rested with his ancestors and was buried in the city of Jerusalem, but he was not placed in the tombs of the kings of Israel. And Hezekiah his son succeeded him as king.

Hezekiah Purifies the Temple

29 Hezekiah was twenty-five years old when he became king, and he reigned in Jerusalem twenty-nine years. His mother's name was Abijah daughter of Zechariah. [2]He did what was right in the eyes of the Lord, just as his father David had done.

[3]In the first month of the first year of his reign, he opened the doors of the temple of the Lord and repaired them. [4]He brought in the priests and the Levites, assembled them in the square on the east side [5]and said: "Listen to me, Levites! Consecrate yourselves now and consecrate the temple of the Lord, the God of your ancestors. Remove all defilement from the sanctuary. [6]Our parents were unfaithful; they did evil in the eyes of the Lord our God and forsook him. They turned their faces away from the Lord's dwelling place and turned their backs on him. [7]They also shut the doors of the portico and put out the lamps. They did not burn incense or present any burnt offerings at the sanctuary to the God of Israel. [8]Therefore, the anger of the Lord has fallen on Judah and Jerusalem; he has made them an object of dread and horror and scorn, as you can see with your own eyes. [9]This is why our fathers have fallen by the sword and why our sons and daughters and our wives are in captivity. [10]Now I intend to make a covenant with the Lord, the God of Israel, so that his fierce anger will turn away from us. [11]My sons, do not be negligent now, for the Lord has chosen you to stand before him and serve him, to minister before him and to burn incense."

[12]Then these Levites set to work:

from the Kohathites,

> Mahath son of Amasai and Joel son of Azariah;

from the Merarites,

> Kish son of Abdi and Azariah son of Jehallel;

from the Gershonites,

> Joah son of Zimmah and Eden son of Joah;

[13]from the descendants of Elizaphan,

> Shimri and Jeiel;

from the descendants of Asaph,

> Zechariah and Mattaniah;

[14]from the descendants of Heman,

> Jehiel and Shimei;

from the descendants of Jeduthun,

> Shemaiah and Uzziel.

[15]When they had assembled their fellow Levites and consecrated themselves, they went in to purify the temple of the Lord, as the king had ordered, following the word of the Lord. [16]The priests went into the sanctuary of the Lord to purify it. They brought out to the courtyard of the Lord's temple everything unclean that they found in the temple of the Lord. The Levites took it and carried it out to the Kidron Valley. [17]They began the consecration on the first day of the first month, and by the eighth day of the month they reached the portico of the Lord. For eight more days they consecrated the temple of

---

[a] 16 Most Hebrew manuscripts; one Hebrew manuscript, Septuagint and Vulgate (see also 2 Kings 16:7) *king*
[b] 19 That is, Judah, as frequently in 2 Chronicles
[c] 20 Hebrew *Tilgath-Pilneser*, a variant of *Tiglath-Pileser*

the LORD itself, finishing on the sixteenth day of the first month.

[18]Then they went in to King Hezekiah and reported: "We have purified the entire temple of the LORD, the altar of burnt offering with all its utensils, and the table for setting out the consecrated bread, with all its articles. [19]We have prepared and consecrated all the articles that King Ahaz removed in his unfaithfulness while he was king. They are now in front of the LORD's altar."

[20]Early the next morning King Hezekiah gathered the city officials together and went up to the temple of the LORD. [21]They brought seven bulls, seven rams, seven male lambs and seven male goats as a sin offering[a] for the kingdom, for the sanctuary and for Judah. The king commanded the priests, the descendants of Aaron, to offer these on the altar of the LORD. [22]So they slaughtered the bulls, and the priests took the blood and splashed it against the altar; next they slaughtered the rams and splashed their blood against the altar; then they slaughtered the lambs and splashed their blood against the altar. [23]The goats for the sin offering were brought before the king and the assembly, and they laid their hands on them. [24]The priests then slaughtered the goats and presented their blood on the altar for a sin offering to atone for all Israel, because the king had ordered the burnt offering and the sin offering for all Israel.

[25]He stationed the Levites in the temple of the LORD with cymbals, harps and lyres in the way prescribed by David and Gad the king's seer and Nathan the prophet; this was commanded by the LORD through his prophets. [26]So the Levites stood ready with David's instruments, and the priests with their trumpets.

[27]Hezekiah gave the order to sacrifice the burnt offering on the altar. As the offering began, singing to the LORD began also, accompanied by trumpets and the instruments of David king of Israel. [28]The whole assembly bowed in worship, while the musicians played and the trumpets sounded. All this continued until the sacrifice of the burnt offering was completed.

[29]When the offerings were finished, the king and everyone present with him knelt down and worshiped. [30]King Hezekiah and his officials ordered the Levites to praise the LORD with the words of David and of Asaph the seer. So they sang praises with gladness and bowed down and worshiped.

[31]Then Hezekiah said, "You have now dedicated yourselves to the LORD. Come and bring

sacrifices and thank offerings to the temple of the LORD." So the assembly brought sacrifices and thank offerings, and all whose hearts were willing brought burnt offerings.

[32]The number of burnt offerings the assembly brought was seventy bulls, a hundred rams and two hundred male lambs—all of them for burnt offerings to the LORD. [33]The animals consecrated as sacrifices amounted to six hundred bulls and three thousand sheep and goats. [34]The priests, however, were too few to skin all the burnt offerings; so their relatives the Levites helped them until the task was finished and un-

<hr/>

[a] 21 Or *purification offering*; also in verses 23 and 24

The Law of the Picture: Leaders Are Examples, Not Exceptions

2 Chronicles 29:1–36

Far too often, leaders drift. Once they get some experience under their belt and a track record of accomplishments, they often abandon the lifestyle that helped them reach the top. They chafe under the very rules that they established or endorsed. They continue to call the people to follow them, but they see themselves as exceptions to the rules, not examples of keeping the rules.

Sadly, leaders like these forget the Law of the Picture: People do what people see. If they want to succeed, leaders must incarnate the life they desire in their followers.

Hezekiah teaches us this principle. He inherited an unholy mess left by his father, King Ahaz. He repaired the temple, restored legitimate worship, removed the idols, repented for the people, and required a change in the land. Once the population saw his example of worship, they followed suit.

Second Chronicles 29 ends with these wonderful words: "Hezekiah and all the people rejoiced at what God had brought about for his people, because it was done so quickly" (v. 36). These events took place so quickly not only because of a sovereign God who replaced Ahaz with the king's godly son, but because Hezekiah modeled the life he expected of others.

til other priests had been consecrated, for the Levites had been more conscientious in consecrating themselves than the priests had been. [35]There were burnt offerings in abundance, together with the fat of the fellowship offerings and the drink offerings that accompanied the burnt offerings.

So the service of the temple of the LORD was reestablished. [36]Hezekiah and all the people rejoiced at what God had brought about for his people, because it was done so quickly.

Hezekiah Celebrates the Passover

30 Hezekiah sent word to all Israel and Judah and also wrote letters to Ephraim and Manasseh, inviting them to come to the temple of the LORD in Jerusalem and celebrate the Passover to the LORD, the God of Israel. [2]The king and his officials and the whole assembly in Jerusalem decided to celebrate the Passover in the second month. [3]They had not been able to celebrate it at the regular time because not enough priests had consecrated themselves and the people had not assembled in Jerusalem. [4]The plan seemed right both to the king and to the whole assembly. [5]They decided to send a proclamation throughout Israel, from Beersheba to Dan, calling the people to come to Jerusalem and celebrate the Passover to the LORD, the God of Israel. It had not been celebrated in large numbers according to what was written.

[6]At the king's command, couriers went throughout Israel and Judah with letters from the king and from his officials, which read:

"People of Israel, return to the LORD, the God of Abraham, Isaac and Israel, that he may return to you who are left, who have escaped from the hand of the kings of Assyria. [7]Do not be like your parents and your fellow Israelites, who were unfaithful to the LORD, the God of their ancestors, so that he made them an object of horror, as you see. [8]Do not be stiff-necked, as your ancestors were; submit to the LORD. Come to his sanctuary, which he has consecrated forever. Serve the LORD your God, so that his fierce anger will turn away from you. [9]If you return to the LORD, then your fellow Israelites and your children will be shown compassion by their captors and will return to this land, for the LORD your God is gracious and compassionate. He will not turn his face from you if you return to him."

[10]The couriers went from town to town in Ephraim and Manasseh, as far as Zebulun, but people scorned and ridiculed them. [11]Nevertheless, some from Asher, Manasseh and Zebulun humbled themselves and went to Jerusalem. [12]Also in Judah the hand of God was on the people to give them unity of mind to carry out what the king and his officials had ordered, following the word of the LORD.

[13]A very large crowd of people assembled in Jerusalem to celebrate the Festival of Unleavened Bread in the second month. [14]They removed the altars in Jerusalem and cleared away the incense altars and threw them into the Kidron Valley.

[15]They slaughtered the Passover lamb on the fourteenth day of the second month. The priests and the Levites were ashamed and consecrated themselves and brought burnt offerings to the temple of the LORD. [16]Then they took up their regular positions as prescribed in the Law of Moses the man of God. The priests splashed against the altar the blood handed to them by the Levites. [17]Since many in the crowd had not consecrated themselves, the Levites had to kill the Passover lambs for all those who were not ceremonially clean and could not consecrate their lambs[a] to the LORD. [18]Although most of the many people who came from Ephraim, Manasseh, Issachar and Zebulun had not purified themselves, yet they ate the Passover, contrary to what was written. But Hezekiah prayed for them, saying, "May the LORD, who is good, pardon everyone [19]who sets their heart on seeking God—the LORD, the God of their ancestors—even if they are not clean according to the rules of the sanctuary." [20]And the LORD heard Hezekiah and healed the people.

[21]The Israelites who were present in Jerusalem celebrated the Festival of Unleavened Bread for seven days with great rejoicing, while the Levites and priests praised the LORD every day with resounding instruments dedicated to the LORD.[b]

[22]Hezekiah spoke encouragingly to all the Levites, who showed good understanding of the service of the LORD. For the seven days they ate their assigned portion and offered fellowship offerings and praised[c] the LORD, the God of their ancestors.

[23]The whole assembly then agreed to celebrate

---

[a] 17 Or consecrate themselves   [b] 21 Or priests sang to the LORD every day, accompanied by the LORD's instruments of praise   [c] 22 Or and confessed their sins to

the festival seven more days; so for another seven days they celebrated joyfully. ²⁴Hezekiah king of Judah provided a thousand bulls and seven thousand sheep and goats for the assembly, and the officials provided them with a thousand bulls and ten thousand sheep and goats. A great number of priests consecrated themselves. ²⁵The entire assembly of Judah rejoiced, along with the priests and Levites and all who had assembled from Israel, including the foreigners who had come from Israel and also those who resided in Judah. ²⁶There was great joy in Jerusalem, for since the days of Solomon son of David king of Israel there had been nothing like this in Jerusalem. ²⁷The priests and the Levites stood to bless the people, and God heard them, for their prayer reached heaven, his holy dwelling place.

31 When all this had ended, the Israelites who were there went out to the towns of Judah, smashed the sacred stones and cut down the Asherah poles. They destroyed the high places and the altars throughout Judah and Benjamin and in Ephraim and Manasseh. After they had destroyed all of them, the Israelites returned to their own towns and to their own property.

Contributions for Worship

²Hezekiah assigned the priests and Levites to divisions — each of them according to their duties as priests or Levites — to offer burnt offerings and fellowship offerings, to minister, to give thanks and to sing praises at the gates of the LORD's dwelling. ³The king contributed from his own possessions for the morning and evening burnt offerings and for the burnt offerings on the Sabbaths, at the New Moons and at the appointed festivals as written in the Law of the LORD. ⁴He ordered the people living in Jerusalem to give the portion due the priests and Levites so they could devote themselves to the Law of the LORD. ⁵As soon as the order went out, the Israelites generously gave the firstfruits of their grain, new wine, olive oil and honey and all that the fields produced. They brought a great amount, a tithe of everything. ⁶The people of Israel and Judah who lived in the towns of Judah also brought a tithe of their herds and flocks and a tithe of the holy things dedicated to the LORD their God, and they piled them in heaps. ⁷They began doing this in the third month and finished in the seventh month. ⁸When Hezekiah and his officials came and saw the heaps, they praised the LORD and blessed his people Israel. ⁹Hezekiah asked the priests and Levites about

the heaps; ¹⁰and Azariah the chief priest, from the family of Zadok, answered, "Since the people began to bring their contributions to the temple of the LORD, we have had enough to eat and plenty to spare, because the LORD has blessed his people, and this great amount is left over."

¹¹Hezekiah gave orders to prepare storerooms in the temple of the LORD, and this was done. ¹²Then they faithfully brought in the contributions, tithes and dedicated gifts. Konaniah, a Levite, was the overseer in charge of these things, and his brother Shimei was next in rank. ¹³Jehiel, Azaziah, Nahath, Asahel, Jerimoth, Jozabad, Eliel, Ismakiah, Mahath and Benaiah were assistants of Konaniah and Shimei his brother. All these served by appointment of King Hezekiah and Azariah the official in charge of the temple of God.

¹⁴Kore son of Imnah the Levite, keeper of the East Gate, was in charge of the freewill offerings given to God, distributing the contributions made to the LORD and also the consecrated gifts. ¹⁵Eden, Miniamin, Jeshua, Shemaiah, Amariah and Shekaniah assisted him faithfully in the towns of the priests, distributing to their fellow priests according to their divisions, old and young alike.

¹⁶In addition, they distributed to the males three years old or more whose names were in the genealogical records — all who would enter the temple of the LORD to perform the daily duties of their various tasks, according to their responsibilities and their divisions. ¹⁷And they distributed to the priests enrolled by their families in the genealogical records and likewise to the Levites twenty years old or more, according to their responsibilities and their divisions. ¹⁸They included all the little ones, the wives, and the sons and daughters of the whole community listed in these genealogical records. For they were faithful in consecrating themselves.

¹⁹As for the priests, the descendants of Aaron, who lived on the farmlands around their towns or in any other towns, men were designated by name to distribute portions to every male among them and to all who were recorded in the genealogies of the Levites.

²⁰This is what Hezekiah did throughout Judah, doing what was good and right and faithful before the LORD his God. ²¹In everything that he undertook in the service of God's temple and in obedience to the law and the commands, he sought his God and worked wholeheartedly. And so he prospered.

Commitment: Hezekiah Has What It Takes

2 Chronicles 31:20–21

The Bible describes King Hezekiah as a leader who did "what was good and right and faithful before the LORD his God. In everything that he undertook in the service of God's temple and in obedience to the law and the commands, he sought his God and worked wholeheartedly. And so he prospered" (2Ch 31:20–21).

Hezekiah paid the price to get the job done. But what is the price of commitment?

1. *Change of lifestyle:* Hezekiah couldn't live the way his father lived.
2. *Loneliness:* Hezekiah stepped out in obedience, alone at first.
3. *Faith in God:* Hezekiah believed that God would bless his efforts.
4. *Criticism:* Hezekiah weathered the harsh questions of an older generation.
5. *Hard work and money:* The king gave up time, energy, and budget to reach his goal.
6. *Daily discipline:* Hezekiah had to instill a daily regimen to bring about reform.
7. *Constant pressure:* The king endured the pressure of potential failure and misunderstanding.

Sennacherib Threatens Jerusalem

32 After all that Hezekiah had so faithfully done, Sennacherib king of Assyria came and invaded Judah. He laid siege to the fortified cities, thinking to conquer them for himself. ²When Hezekiah saw that Sennacherib had come and that he intended to wage war against Jerusalem, ³he consulted with his officials and military staff about blocking off the water from the springs outside the city, and they helped him. ⁴They gathered a large group of people who blocked all the springs and the stream that flowed through the land. "Why should the kings*a* of Assyria come and find plenty of water?" they said. ⁵Then he worked hard repairing all the broken sections of the wall and building towers on it. He built another wall outside that one and reinforced the terraces*b* of the City of David. He also made large numbers of weapons and shields.

⁶He appointed military officers over the people and assembled them before him in the square at the city gate and encouraged them with these words: ⁷"Be strong and courageous. Do not be afraid or discouraged because of the king of Assyria and the vast army with him, for there is a greater power with us than with him. ⁸With him is only the arm of flesh, but with us is the LORD our God to help us and to fight our battles." And the people gained confidence from what Hezekiah the king of Judah said.

⁹Later, when Sennacherib king of Assyria and all his forces were laying siege to Lachish, he sent his officers to Jerusalem with this message for Hezekiah king of Judah and for all the people of Judah who were there:

¹⁰"This is what Sennacherib king of Assyria says: On what are you basing your confidence, that you remain in Jerusalem under siege? ¹¹When Hezekiah says, 'The LORD our God will save us from the hand of the king of Assyria,' he is misleading you, to let you die of hunger and thirst. ¹²Did not Hezekiah himself remove this god's high places and altars, saying to Judah and Jerusalem, 'You must worship before one altar and burn sacrifices on it'?

¹³"Do you not know what I and my predecessors have done to all the peoples of the other lands? Were the gods of those nations ever able to deliver their land from my hand? ¹⁴Who of all the gods of these nations that my predecessors destroyed has been able to save his people from me? How then can your god deliver you from my hand? ¹⁵Now do not let Hezekiah deceive you and mislead you like this. Do not believe him, for no god of any nation or kingdom has been able to deliver his people from my hand or the hand of my predecessors. How much less will your god deliver you from my hand!"

---

a 4 Hebrew; Septuagint and Syriac *king*   *b 5* Or *the Millo*

¹⁶Sennacherib's officers spoke further against the LORD God and against his servant Hezekiah. ¹⁷The king also wrote letters ridiculing the LORD, the God of Israel, and saying this against him: "Just as the gods of the peoples of the other lands did not rescue their people from my hand, so the god of Hezekiah will not rescue his people from my hand." ¹⁸Then they called out in Hebrew to the people of Jerusalem who were on the wall, to terrify them and make them afraid in order to capture the city. ¹⁹They spoke about the God of Jerusalem as they did about the gods of the other peoples of the world—the work of human hands.

²⁰King Hezekiah and the prophet Isaiah son of Amoz cried out in prayer to heaven about this. ²¹And the LORD sent an angel, who annihilated all the fighting men and the commanders and officers in the camp of the Assyrian king. So he withdrew to his own land in disgrace. And when he went into the temple of his god, some of his sons, his own flesh and blood, cut him down with the sword.

²²So the LORD saved Hezekiah and the people of Jerusalem from the hand of Sennacherib king of Assyria and from the hand of all others. He took care of them*a* on every side. ²³Many brought offerings to Jerusalem for the LORD and valuable gifts for Hezekiah king of Judah. From then on he was highly regarded by all the nations.

Hezekiah's Pride, Success and Death

²⁴In those days Hezekiah became ill and was at the point of death. He prayed to the LORD, who answered him and gave him a miraculous sign. ²⁵But Hezekiah's heart was proud and he did not respond to the kindness shown him; therefore the LORD's wrath was on him and on Judah and Jerusalem. ²⁶Then Hezekiah repented of the pride of his heart, as did the people of Jerusalem; therefore the LORD's wrath did not come on them during the days of Hezekiah.

²⁷Hezekiah had very great wealth and honor, and he made treasuries for his silver and gold and for his precious stones, spices, shields and all kinds of valuables. ²⁸He also made buildings to store the harvest of grain, new wine and olive oil; and he made stalls for various kinds of cattle, and pens for the flocks. ²⁹He built villages and acquired great numbers of flocks and herds, for God had given him very great riches.

³⁰It was Hezekiah who blocked the upper outlet of the Gihon spring and channeled the water down to the west side of the City of David. He succeeded in everything he undertook. ³¹But

when envoys were sent by the rulers of Babylon to ask him about the miraculous sign that had occurred in the land, God left him to test him and to know everything that was in his heart.

³²The other events of Hezekiah's reign and his acts of devotion are written in the vision of the prophet Isaiah son of Amoz in the book of the kings of Judah and Israel. ³³Hezekiah rested with his ancestors and was buried on the hill where the tombs of David's descendants are. All Judah and the people of Jerusalem honored him when he died. And Manasseh his son succeeded him as king.

Manasseh King of Judah

33 Manasseh was twelve years old when he became king, and he reigned in Jerusalem fifty-five years. ²He did evil in the eyes of the LORD, following the detestable practices of the nations the LORD had driven out before the Israelites. ³He rebuilt the high places his father Hezekiah had demolished; he also erected altars to the Baals and made Asherah poles. He bowed down to all the starry hosts and worshiped them. ⁴He built altars in the temple of the LORD, of which the LORD had said, "My Name will remain in Jerusalem forever." ⁵In both courts of the temple of the LORD, he built altars to all the starry hosts. ⁶He sacrificed his children in the fire in the Valley of Ben Hinnom, practiced divination and witchcraft, sought omens, and consulted mediums and spiritists. He did much evil in the eyes of the LORD, arousing his anger.

⁷He took the image he had made and put it in God's temple, of which God had said to David and to his son Solomon, "In this temple and in Jerusalem, which I have chosen out of all the tribes of Israel, I will put my Name forever. ⁸I will not again make the feet of the Israelites leave the land I assigned to your ancestors, if only they will be careful to do everything I commanded them concerning all the laws, decrees and regulations given through Moses." ⁹But Manasseh led Judah and the people of Jerusalem astray, so that they did more evil than the nations the LORD had destroyed before the Israelites.

¹⁰The LORD spoke to Manasseh and his people, but they paid no attention. ¹¹So the LORD brought against them the army commanders of the king of Assyria, who took Manasseh prisoner, put a hook in his nose, bound him with bronze shackles and took him to Babylon. ¹²In his distress he sought the favor of the LORD his

a 22 Hebrew; Septuagint and Vulgate *He gave them rest*

God and humbled himself greatly before the God of his ancestors. [13]And when he prayed to him, the LORD was moved by his entreaty and listened to his plea; so he brought him back to Jerusalem and to his kingdom. Then Manasseh knew that the LORD is God.

[14]Afterward he rebuilt the outer wall of the City of David, west of the Gihon spring in the valley, as far as the entrance of the Fish Gate and encircling the hill of Ophel; he also made it much higher. He stationed military commanders in all the fortified cities in Judah.

[15]He got rid of the foreign gods and removed the image from the temple of the LORD, as well as all the altars he had built on the temple hill and in Jerusalem; and he threw them out of the city. [16]Then he restored the altar of the LORD and sacrificed fellowship offerings and thank offerings on it, and told Judah to serve the LORD, the God of Israel. [17]The people, however, continued to sacrifice at the high places, but only to the LORD their God.

[18]The other events of Manasseh's reign, including his prayer to his God and the words the seers spoke to him in the name of the LORD, the God of Israel, are written in the annals of the kings of Israel.[a] [19]His prayer and how God was moved by his entreaty, as well as all his sins and unfaithfulness, and the sites where he built high places and set up Asherah poles and idols before he humbled himself—all these are written in the records of the seers.[b] [20]Manasseh rested with his ancestors and was buried in his palace. And Amon his son succeeded him as king.

Amon King of Judah

[21]Amon was twenty-two years old when he became king, and he reigned in Jerusalem two years. [22]He did evil in the eyes of the LORD, as his father Manasseh had done. Amon worshiped and offered sacrifices to all the idols Manasseh had made. [23]But unlike his father Manasseh, he did not humble himself before the LORD; Amon increased his guilt.

[24]Amon's officials conspired against him and assassinated him in his palace. [25]Then the people of the land killed all who had plotted against King Amon, and they made Josiah his son king in his place.

Josiah's Reforms

34 Josiah was eight years old when he became king, and he reigned in Jerusalem thirty-one years. [2]He did what was right in the eyes of the LORD and followed the ways of his father David, not turning aside to the right or to the left.

[3]In the eighth year of his reign, while he was still young, he began to seek the God of his father David. In his twelfth year he began to purge Judah and Jerusalem of high places, Asherah poles and idols. [4]Under his direction the altars of the Baals were torn down; he cut to pieces the incense altars that were above them, and smashed the Asherah poles and the idols. These he broke to pieces and scattered over the graves of those who had sacrificed to them. [5]He burned the bones of the priests on their altars, and so he purged Judah and Jerusalem. [6]In the towns of Manasseh, Ephraim and Simeon, as far as Naphtali, and in the ruins around them, [7]he tore down the altars and the Asherah poles and crushed the idols to powder and cut to pieces all the incense altars throughout Israel. Then he went back to Jerusalem.

[8]In the eighteenth year of Josiah's reign, to purify the land and the temple, he sent Shaphan son of Azaliah and Maaseiah the ruler of the city, with Joah son of Joahaz, the recorder, to repair the temple of the LORD his God.

[9]They went to Hilkiah the high priest and gave him the money that had been brought into the temple of God, which the Levites who were the gatekeepers had collected from the people of Manasseh, Ephraim and the entire remnant of Israel and from all the people of Judah and Benjamin and the inhabitants of Jerusalem. [10]Then they entrusted it to the men appointed to supervise the work on the LORD's temple. These men paid the workers who repaired and restored the temple. [11]They also gave money to the carpenters and builders to purchase dressed stone, and timber for joists and beams for the buildings that the kings of Judah had allowed to fall into ruin.

[12]The workers labored faithfully. Over them to direct them were Jahath and Obadiah, Levites descended from Merari, and Zechariah and Meshullam, descended from Kohath. The Levites—all who were skilled in playing musical instruments— [13]had charge of the laborers and supervised all the workers from job to job. Some of the Levites were secretaries, scribes and gatekeepers.

The Book of the Law Found

[14]While they were bringing out the money that had been taken into the temple of the LORD,

---

[a] 18 That is, Judah, as frequently in 2 Chronicles
[b] 19 One Hebrew manuscript and Septuagint; most Hebrew manuscripts of Hozai

Hilkiah the priest found the Book of the Law of the LORD that had been given through Moses. [15]Hilkiah said to Shaphan the secretary, "I have found the Book of the Law in the temple of the LORD." He gave it to Shaphan.

[16]Then Shaphan took the book to the king and reported to him: "Your officials are doing everything that has been committed to them. [17]They have paid out the money that was in the temple of the LORD and have entrusted it to the supervisors and workers." [18]Then Shaphan the secretary informed the king, "Hilkiah the priest has given me a book." And Shaphan read from it in the presence of the king.

[19]When the king heard the words of the Law, he tore his robes. [20]He gave these orders to Hilkiah, Ahikam son of Shaphan, Abdon son of Micah,[a] Shaphan the secretary and Asaiah the king's attendant: [21]"Go and inquire of the LORD for me and for the remnant in Israel and Judah about what is written in this book that has been found. Great is the LORD's anger that is poured out on us because those who have gone before us have not kept the word of the LORD; they have not acted in accordance with all that is written in this book."

[22]Hilkiah and those the king had sent with him[b] went to speak to the prophet Huldah, who was the wife of Shallum son of Tokhath,[c] the son of Hasrah,[d] keeper of the wardrobe. She lived in Jerusalem, in the New Quarter.

[23]She said to them, "This is what the LORD, the God of Israel, says: Tell the man who sent you to me, [24]'This is what the LORD says: I am going to bring disaster on this place and its people—all the curses written in the book that has been read in the presence of the king of Judah. [25]Because they have forsaken me and burned incense to other gods and aroused my anger by all that their hands have made,[e] my anger will be poured out on this place and will not be quenched.' [26]Tell the king of Judah, who sent you to inquire of the LORD, 'This is what the LORD, the God of Israel, says concerning the words you heard: [27]Because your heart was responsive and you humbled yourself before God when you heard what he spoke against this place and its people, and because you humbled yourself before me and tore your robes and wept in my presence, I have heard you, declares the LORD. [28]Now I will gather you to your ancestors, and you will be buried in peace. Your eyes will not see all the disaster I am going to bring on this place and on those who live here.'"

So they took her answer back to the king.

[29]Then the king called together all the elders

---

[a] 20 Also called *Akbor son of Micaiah*   [b] 22 One Hebrew manuscript, Vulgate and Syriac; most Hebrew manuscripts do not have *had sent with him.*   [c] 22 Also called *Tikvah*   [d] 22 Also called *Harhas*   [e] 25 Or *by everything they have done*

JOSIAH

Personal Repentance Precedes Public Reform
2 Chronicles 34:3–33

PROFILE in leadership

As the leader goes, so go the people. Over and over in the history of Israel, we see that pattern repeated—for both evil and good.

When young King Josiah heard the words of God's long-forgotten law, sorrow gripped his heart (2Ch 34:8, 15, 19–21). He tore his clothes in repentance and directed several godly men to petition the Lord to see what he needed to do.

For years already Josiah had busied himself doing everything he could to purify the kingdom from idolatry. He had ordered images of Baal, altars to false gods, and other religious shrines destroyed. He even burned the bones of deceased pagan priests over their altars. And then he turned his attention toward purifying and renovating the temple.

God saw the repentant heart of Judah's king and told Josiah that he would withhold his wrath against the people until after Josiah had died. The genuine repentance of this godly leader led to changes in behavior among the people of Judah. They, too, renewed their covenant with the God of their ancestors. And for the rest of Josiah's life, the people stayed devoted to the Lord and his law.

Such is the power of a leader modeling godliness. As the leader goes, so go the people—for good or for evil.

of Judah and Jerusalem. [30]He went up to the temple of the LORD with the people of Judah, the inhabitants of Jerusalem, the priests and the Levites—all the people from the least to the greatest. He read in their hearing all the words of the Book of the Covenant, which had been found in the temple of the LORD. [31]The king stood by his pillar and renewed the covenant in the presence of the LORD—to follow the LORD and keep his commands, statutes and decrees with all his heart and all his soul, and to obey the words of the covenant written in this book.

[32]Then he had everyone in Jerusalem and Benjamin pledge themselves to it; the people of Jerusalem did this in accordance with the covenant of God, the God of their ancestors.

[33]Josiah removed all the detestable idols from all the territory belonging to the Israelites, and he had all who were present in Israel serve the LORD their God. As long as he lived, they did not fail to follow the LORD, the God of their ancestors.

Josiah Celebrates the Passover

35 Josiah celebrated the Passover to the LORD in Jerusalem, and the Passover lamb was slaughtered on the fourteenth day of the first month. [2]He appointed the priests to their duties and encouraged them in the service of the LORD's temple. [3]He said to the Levites, who instructed all Israel and who had been consecrated to the LORD: "Put the sacred ark in the temple that Solomon son of David king of Israel built. It is not to be carried about on your shoulders. Now serve the LORD your God and his people Israel. [4]Prepare yourselves by families in your divisions, according to the instructions written by David king of Israel and by his son Solomon.

[5]"Stand in the holy place with a group of Levites for each subdivision of the families of your fellow Israelites, the lay people. [6]Slaughter the Passover lambs, consecrate yourselves and prepare the lambs for your fellow Israelites, doing what the LORD commanded through Moses."

[7]Josiah provided for all the lay people who were there a total of thirty thousand lambs and goats for the Passover offerings, and also three thousand cattle—all from the king's own possessions.

[8]His officials also contributed voluntarily to the people and the priests and Levites. Hilkiah, Zechariah and Jehiel, the officials in charge of God's temple, gave the priests twenty-six hundred Passover offerings and three hundred cat-

tle. [9]Also Konaniah along with Shemaiah and Nethanel, his brothers, and Hashabiah, Jeiel and Jozabad, the leaders of the Levites, provided five thousand Passover offerings and five hundred head of cattle for the Levites.

[10]The service was arranged and the priests stood in their places with the Levites in their divisions as the king had ordered. [11]The Passover lambs were slaughtered, and the priests splashed against the altar the blood handed to them, while the Levites skinned the animals. [12]They set aside the burnt offerings to give them to the subdivisions of the families of the people to offer to the LORD, as it is written in the Book of Moses. They did the same with the cattle. [13]They roasted the Passover animals over the fire as prescribed, and boiled the holy offerings in pots, caldrons and pans and served them quickly to all the people. [14]After this, they made preparations for themselves and for the priests, because the priests, the descendants of Aaron, were sacrificing the burnt offerings and the fat portions until nightfall. So the Levites made preparations for themselves and for the Aaronic priests.

[15]The musicians, the descendants of Asaph, were in the places prescribed by David, Asaph, Heman and Jeduthun the king's seer. The gatekeepers at each gate did not need to leave their posts, because their fellow Levites made the preparations for them.

[16]So at that time the entire service of the LORD was carried out for the celebration of the Passover and the offering of burnt offerings on the altar of the LORD, as King Josiah had ordered. [17]The Israelites who were present celebrated the Passover at that time and observed the Festival of Unleavened Bread for seven days. [18]The Passover had not been observed like this in Israel since the days of the prophet Samuel; and none of the kings of Israel had ever celebrated such a Passover as did Josiah, with the priests, the Levites and all Judah and Israel who were there with the people of Jerusalem. [19]This Passover was celebrated in the eighteenth year of Josiah's reign.

The Death of Josiah

[20]After all this, when Josiah had set the temple in order, Necho king of Egypt went up to fight at Carchemish on the Euphrates, and Josiah marched out to meet him in battle. [21]But Necho sent messengers to him, saying, "What quarrel is there, king of Judah, between you and me? It is not you I am attacking at this time, but the house with which I am at war. God has told

21 LAWS

JOSIAH AND THE LAW OF VICTORY
Leaders Find a Way for the Team to Win

2 Chronicles 34:3—35:19

HAVE YOU ever thought about what separates the leaders who achieve victory from those who suffer defeat? What does it take to be a winner? Victorious leaders share an inability to accept defeat. The alternative to winning seems totally unacceptable to them, so they figure out what must be done to achieve victory, and then they go after it with everything at their disposal.

Leaders who practice the Law of Victory believe that anything less than success is unacceptable. And they have no Plan B. That keeps them fighting.

■   ■   ■   ■   ■

Winning is an inside job. The team that achieves victory is the one that first wins its internal battles. And the first one to face and win these internal battles is the leader.

Achieving a Personal Victory

How does a leader seek victory over self? Consider how Josiah conquered himself:

1. *He remained open and teachable.*
   Leaders who remain willing to learn and open to change put themselves in a position to win. Josiah demonstrated that kind of openness and teachability. As a 16-year-old, instead of trying to convince everyone that he knew it all, he humbled himself. He departed from the ways of his arrogant father and sought God.

2. *He removed obstacles carried forward from the past.*
   All leaders have to deal with baggage. One way or another, a leader has to win battles involving past problems. For Josiah, a major battle involved idol worship, a problem since the time of King Solomon. He courageously swept the country clean of idols. As you seek victory in your organization, you must face and overcome problems from the past. They may be ineffective traditions, incompetent players who need to be released, errors in judgment, or unrepented-of sins. Whatever they are, you must find the courage to face and resolve them.

3. *He realized what he needed to give and gave it.*
   Victory always carries a personal cost. For Josiah, that meant repairing the temple and reinstating the Passover. Out of his own holdings, he gave 30,000 lambs and young goats and 3,000 cattle to be sacrificed (2Ch 35:7, 18).

4. *He recognized the key to victory.*
   Every leader must find the key to victory. For Josiah, that key was repentance. After the Book of the Law was discovered and read, he genuinely repented of his own sins and of those of his people, then prompted his countrymen to follow

his lead. Every leadership situation contains a key to victory. If you are the leader, you must find that key and turn it.

5. *He retained a personal commitment to succeed.*
   People never become more committed than their leader. Josiah's personal commitment inspired the people to be faithful despite their evil desires and history (2Ch 34:31). If members of an organization discover they have greater commitment than their leaders, they will find another organization with another leader.

Helping Others Break Through for Victory

If you're fighting the necessary inside battles, you are putting yourself in the best place to lead your team to victory. But that may not be enough. For your organization to reach the next level, your people need their own breakthroughs. Here's a good way to help them achieve their own triumphs:

1. *Understand breakthrough timing.*
   There are three prime times for leading people to a breakthrough. People are ripe for a change when . . .
   - they hurt enough that they need a breakthrough.
   - they learn enough that they want a breakthrough.
   - they receive enough that they are able to break through.
   Provide your people with learning opportunities, give them resources and encouragement, and pay attention to where they are mentally, spiritually, and emotionally. Then, when they're ready, give a little nudge to help them over the hump.

2. *Pray for a breakthrough.*
   The best thing you can do for your people is to pray for them. The eminent evangelist John Wesley observed, "God does nothing but in answer to prayer." Ask God for a breakthrough. Then ask God to help you do your part, to reveal to the people their part, and to fulfill His part.

3. *Become a breakthrough person.*
   If you show what it means to be a breakthrough person, your people will value breakthroughs. Most breakthrough people exhibit these qualities.
   - *Vulnerability:* They realize they aren't perfect, they can't do it all, and they need God to make up the difference.
   - *Humility:* They're not out to prove anything and they don't care who gets the credit. They're glad to share the spotlight with others.
   - *Transparency:* They live their lives as open books. They admit where they're coming short as well as where God is working in their lives.

4. *Find breakthrough leaders.*
   Gathering strong leaders adept at breakthroughs can make a difference in your organization. It's like having a team of breakthrough catalysts working alongside you.

If you want a winning team, you must have winning players. The best way to do that is to create breakthroughs. If you can become a breakthrough person who leads a team of breakthrough leaders who oversee an organization filled with breakthrough people, then victory becomes almost inevitable.

me to hurry; so stop opposing God, who is with me, or he will destroy you."

²²Josiah, however, would not turn away from him, but disguised himself to engage him in battle. He would not listen to what Necho had said at God's command but went to fight him on the plain of Megiddo.

²³Archers shot King Josiah, and he told his officers, "Take me away; I am badly wounded." ²⁴So they took him out of his chariot, put him in his other chariot and brought him to Jerusalem, where he died. He was buried in the tombs of his ancestors, and all Judah and Jerusalem mourned for him.

²⁵Jeremiah composed laments for Josiah, and to this day all the male and female singers commemorate Josiah in the laments. These became a tradition in Israel and are written in the Laments.

²⁶The other events of Josiah's reign and his acts of devotion in accordance with what is written in the Law of the LORD— ²⁷all the events, from beginning to end, are written in the book **36** of the kings of Israel and Judah. ¹And the people of the land took Jehoahaz son of Josiah and made him king in Jerusalem in place of his father.

Jehoahaz King of Judah

²Jehoahaz*ᵃ* was twenty-three years old when he became king, and he reigned in Jerusalem three months. ³The king of Egypt dethroned him in Jerusalem and imposed on Judah a levy of a hundred talents*ᵇ* of silver and a talent*ᶜ* of gold. ⁴The king of Egypt made Eliakim, a brother of Jehoahaz, king over Judah and Jerusalem and changed Eliakim's name to Jehoiakim. But Necho took Eliakim's brother Jehoahaz and carried him off to Egypt.

Jehoiakim King of Judah

⁵Jehoiakim was twenty-five years old when he became king, and he reigned in Jerusalem eleven years. He did evil in the eyes of the LORD his God. ⁶Nebuchadnezzar king of Babylon attacked him and bound him with bronze shackles to take him to Babylon. ⁷Nebuchadnezzar also took to Babylon articles from the temple of the LORD and put them in his temple*ᵈ* there.

⁸The other events of Jehoiakim's reign, the detestable things he did and all that was found against him, are written in the book of the kings of Israel and Judah. And Jehoiachin his son succeeded him as king.

Jehoiachin King of Judah

⁹Jehoiachin was eighteen*ᵉ* years old when he became king, and he reigned in Jerusalem three months and ten days. He did evil in the eyes of the LORD. ¹⁰In the spring, King Nebuchadnezzar sent for him and brought him to Babylon, together with articles of value from the temple of the LORD, and he made Jehoiachin's uncle,*ᶠ* Zedekiah, king over Judah and Jerusalem.

Zedekiah King of Judah

¹¹Zedekiah was twenty-one years old when he became king, and he reigned in Jerusalem eleven years. ¹²He did evil in the eyes of the LORD his God and did not humble himself before Jeremiah the prophet, who spoke the word of the LORD. ¹³He also rebelled against King Nebuchadnezzar, who had made him take an oath in God's name. He became stiff-necked and hardened his heart and would not turn to the LORD, the God of Israel. ¹⁴Furthermore, all the leaders of the priests and the people became more and more unfaithful, following all the detestable practices of the nations and defiling the temple of the LORD, which he had consecrated in Jerusalem.

The Fall of Jerusalem

¹⁵The LORD, the God of their ancestors, sent word to them through his messengers again and again, because he had pity on his people and on his dwelling place. ¹⁶But they mocked God's messengers, despised his words and scoffed at his prophets until the wrath of the LORD was aroused against his people and there was no remedy. ¹⁷He brought up against them the king of the Babylonians,*ᵍ* who killed their young men with the sword in the sanctuary, and did not spare young men or young women, the elderly or the infirm. God gave them all into the hands of Nebuchadnezzar. ¹⁸He carried to Babylon all the articles from the temple of God, both large and small, and the treasures of the LORD's temple and the treasures of the king and his officials. ¹⁹They set fire to God's temple and broke down the wall of Jerusalem; they burned all the palaces and destroyed everything of value there.

²⁰He carried into exile to Babylon the remnant, who escaped from the sword, and they

ᵃ 2 Hebrew *Joahaz,* a variant of *Jehoahaz;* also in verse 4
ᵇ 3 That is, about 3 3/4 tons or about 3.4 metric tons
ᶜ 3 That is, about 75 pounds or about 34 kilograms   *ᵈ* 7 Or *palace*   *ᵉ* 9 One Hebrew manuscript, some Septuagint manuscripts and Syriac (see also 2 Kings 24:8); most Hebrew manuscripts *eight*   *ᶠ* 10 Hebrew *brother,* that is, relative (see 2 Kings 24:17)   *ᵍ* 17 Or *Chaldeans*

became servants to him and his successors until the kingdom of Persia came to power. [21]The land enjoyed its sabbath rests; all the time of its desolation it rested, until the seventy years were completed in fulfillment of the word of the LORD spoken by Jeremiah.

[22]In the first year of Cyrus king of Persia, in order to fulfill the word of the LORD spoken by Jeremiah, the LORD moved the heart of Cyrus king of Persia to make a proclamation throughout his realm and also to put it in writing:

[23]"This is what Cyrus king of Persia says:

"'The LORD, the God of heaven, has given me all the kingdoms of the earth and he has appointed me to build a temple for him at Jerusalem in Judah. Any of his people among you may go up, and may the LORD their God be with them.'"

The Jews Return from Babylonian Captivity to Israel

The scribe Ezra and the cupbearer-turned-building-contractor Nehemiah both led the Jews in their return from Babylonian captivity to Israel. Their leadership roles complemented one another.

Nehemiah restored the people's hope as he enabled them to rebuild the Jerusalem wall in record time. Ezra restored their faith as he enabled them to become "people of the Book" once more. Ezra helped supervise the reconstruction of the Jerusalem temple in anticipation of the restoration of Israel's true worship.

While Zerubbabel led the first group of Jews back to Jerusalem to rebuild the temple, Ezra led a second group. God had commissioned him to rebuild the temple worship. Both men had to endure tremendous discouragement, yet overcame long odds to reach their goals. Both displayed tenacious leadership.

Like some other Old Testament leaders, Ezra might be considered a "teaching leader" who led mostly with his word gifts. He organized and directed and provided vision for the people. He shepherded those who were prone to wander. But more than anything, he used his teaching gift to lead the people back to where they belonged spiritually.

Ezra not only spoke, he wrote. Many believe that he wrote four biblical books: 1 and 2 Chronicles, Ezra and Nehemiah. He also delivered sermons that communicated God's dream of gathering his people to himself again in the Holy City.

His leadership skills appear throughout this book. Perhaps we could best describe him in four words:

God's Role in Ezra

The book of Ezra records the fulfillment of God's promise through Jeremiah to bring the Israelites back to their land after 70 years of captivity.

God provided direction to a variety of leaders. First, he led the leaders of Persia. God softened the hearts of Cyrus, Darius and Artaxerxes to let the Jews return to Jerusalem and rebuild their lives, both physically and spiritually. Second, he directed Ezra, Zerubbabel and Nehemiah as they led the Jews in their return to faith in God. More than any other man, Ezra shaped the returning Jews into the spiritual leaders God intended for them to be. Through the protection of the three Persian kings and the leadership of such great and godly Jews as Zerubbabel, Joshua, Haggai, Zechariah and Ezra, the people completed the second temple, and true worship at last returned to Jerusalem.

Leaders in Ezra

Darius, Cyrus, Artaxerxes, Ezra, Zerubbabel

Other People of Influence in Ezra

Zechariah, Haggai

Lessons in Leadership

■ God's leadership may seem subtle or absent, but he steadily finishes the work he starts.

1. *Pioneer:* Ezra blazed the trail and helped the Jews restart their temple worship.

2. *Model:* Ezra committed himself first to study God's Word, then to practice it, then to communicate it to the rest of Israel.

3. *Catalyst:* Ezra's courage and decisiveness in the face of opposition prompted the Jews to finish the work they had started.

4. *Teacher:* Ezra put into understandable words the very thoughts of God.

- Both courage and fear are contagious.
- In times of conflict, leaders must act decisively.
- If workers are to give their perspiration, leaders must give them inspiration.
- Most people need a catalyst before they'll do anything risky.
- Incarnational leadership studies the truth, practices the truth, then teaches the truth.

LEADERSHIP HIGHLIGHTS IN EZRA

Cyrus Helps the Exiles to Return

1 In the first year of Cyrus king of Persia, in order to fulfill the word of the Lord spoken by Jeremiah, the Lord moved the heart of Cyrus king of Persia to make a proclamation throughout his realm and also to put it in writing:

[2]"This is what Cyrus king of Persia says:

"'The Lord, the God of heaven, has given me all the kingdoms of the earth and he has appointed me to build a temple for him at Jerusalem in Judah. [3]Any of his people among you may go up to Jerusalem in Judah and build the temple of the Lord, the God of Israel, the God who is in Jerusalem, and may their God be with them. [4]And in any locality where survivors may now be living, the people are to provide them with silver and gold, with goods and livestock, and with freewill offerings for the temple of God in Jerusalem.'"

[5]Then the family heads of Judah and Benjamin, and the priests and Levites—everyone whose heart God had moved—prepared to go up and build the house of the Lord in Jerusalem. [6]All their neighbors assisted them with articles of silver and gold, with goods and livestock, and with valuable gifts, in addition to all the freewill offerings.

[7]Moreover, King Cyrus brought out the articles belonging to the temple of the Lord, which Nebuchadnezzar had carried away from Jerusalem and had placed in the temple of his god.[a] [8]Cyrus king of Persia had them brought by Mithredath the treasurer, who counted them out to Sheshbazzar the prince of Judah.

[9]This was the inventory:

gold dishes	30
silver dishes	1,000
silver pans[b]	29
[10] gold bowls	30
matching silver bowls	410
other articles	1,000

[11]In all, there were 5,400 articles of gold and of silver. Sheshbazzar brought all these along with the exiles when they came up from Babylon to Jerusalem.

The List of the Exiles Who Returned

2 Now these are the people of the province who came up from the captivity of the exiles, whom Nebuchadnezzar king of Babylon had taken captive to Babylon (they returned to Jerusalem and Judah, each to their own town,

[2]in company with Zerubbabel, Joshua, Nehemiah, Seraiah, Reelaiah, Mordecai, Bilshan, Mispar, Bigvai, Rehum and Baanah):

The list of the men of the people of Israel:

[3] the descendants of Parosh	2,172
[4] of Shephatiah	372
[5] of Arah	775
[6] of Pahath-Moab (through the line of Jeshua and Joab)	2,812
[7] of Elam	1,254
[8] of Zattu	945
[9] of Zakkai	760
[10] of Bani	642
[11] of Bebai	623
[12] of Azgad	1,222
[13] of Adonikam	666
[14] of Bigvai	2,056
[15] of Adin	454
[16] of Ater (through Hezekiah)	98
[17] of Bezai	323
[18] of Jorah	112
[19] of Hashum	223
[20] of Gibbar	95
[21] the men of Bethlehem	123
[22] of Netophah	56
[23] of Anathoth	128
[24] of Azmaveth	42
[25] of Kiriath Jearim,[c] Kephirah and Beeroth	743
[26] of Ramah and Geba	621
[27] of Mikmash	122
[28] of Bethel and Ai	223
[29] of Nebo	52
[30] of Magbish	156
[31] of the other Elam	1,254
[32] of Harim	320
[33] of Lod, Hadid and Ono	725
[34] of Jericho	345
[35] of Senaah	3,630

[36]The priests:

the descendants of Jedaiah (through the family of Jeshua)	973
[37] of Immer	1,052
[38] of Pashhur	1,247
[39] of Harim	1,017

[40]The Levites:

the descendants of Jeshua and Kadmiel (of the line of Hodaviah)	74

---

[a] 7 Or gods   [b] 9 The meaning of the Hebrew for this word is uncertain.   [c] 25 See Septuagint (see also Neh. 7:29); Hebrew Kiriath Arim.

The Law of Connection: Cyrus Rules People by Relating to Them

Ezra 1:1–7

Unlike King Rehoboam, the Persian king Cyrus was able to connect with God's people. He first displayed mercy and then identified with the values and heart of his people. This allowed him to strengthen his reign

What enabled King Cyrus to connect with the people? Ezra tells us he practiced . . .

1. *Humility:* He realized his power came from God and should honor God (v. 2).

2. *Responsibility:* He felt strongly he should build a place of worship for the Jews (v. 2).

3. *Empowerment:* He allowed those who had a heart to build to fulfill their call (v. 3).

4. *Resources:* He issued a decree to support the builders (v. 4).

5. *Stewardship:* He managed people's gifts, enabling them to play to their strengths (v. 5).

6. *Priorities:* He valued what was most important to the people (v. 7).

It was no accident that Cyrus arose to help Israel. Many years before these events transpired, God predicted through the prophet Isaiah that Cyrus would "subdue nations before him and strip kings of their armor." He declared, "For the sake of Jacob my servant, of Israel my chosen, I summon you by name, and bestow on you a title of honor, though you do not acknowledge me. I am the LORD, and there is no other; apart from me there is no God" (Isa 45:1, 4–5).

---

41 The musicians:

the descendants of Asaph   128

42 The gatekeepers of the temple:

the descendants of
Shallum, Ater, Talmon,
Akkub, Hatita and Shobai   139

43 The temple servants:

the descendants of
Ziha, Hasupha, Tabbaoth,
44 Keros, Siaha, Padon,
45 Lebanah, Hagabah, Akkub,
46 Hagab, Shalmai, Hanan,
47 Giddel, Gahar, Reaiah,
48 Rezin, Nekoda, Gazzam,
49 Uzza, Paseah, Besai,
50 Asnah, Meunim, Nephusim,
51 Bakbuk, Hakupha, Harhur,
52 Bazluth, Mehida, Harsha,
53 Barkos, Sisera, Temah,
54 Neziah and Hatipha

55 The descendants of the servants of Solomon:

the descendants of
Sotai, Hassophereth, Peruda,

56 Jaala, Darkon, Giddel,
57 Shephatiah, Hattil,
Pokereth-Hazzebaim and Ami

58 The temple servants and the
descendants of the servants of
Solomon   392

59 The following came up from the towns of Tel Melah, Tel Harsha, Kerub, Addon and Immer, but they could not show that their families were descended from Israel:

60 The descendants of
Delaiah, Tobiah and Nekoda   652

61 And from among the priests:

The descendants of
Hobaiah, Hakkoz and Barzillai (a man who had married a daughter of Barzillai the Gileadite and was called by that name).

62 These searched for their family records, but they could not find them and so were excluded from the priesthood as unclean. 63 The governor ordered them not to eat any of the most sacred food until there was a priest ministering with the Urim and Thummim.

⁶⁴The whole company numbered 42,360, ⁶⁵besides their 7,337 male and female slaves; and they also had 200 male and female singers. ⁶⁶They had 736 horses, 245 mules, ⁶⁷435 camels and 6,720 donkeys.

⁶⁸When they arrived at the house of the LORD in Jerusalem, some of the heads of the families gave freewill offerings toward the rebuilding of the house of God on its site. ⁶⁹According to their ability they gave to the treasury for this work 61,000 darics[a] of gold, 5,000 minas[b] of silver and 100 priestly garments.

⁷⁰The priests, the Levites, the musicians, the gatekeepers and the temple servants settled in their own towns, along with some of the other people, and the rest of the Israelites settled in their towns.

Rebuilding the Altar

3 When the seventh month came and the Israelites had settled in their towns, the people assembled together as one in Jerusalem. ²Then Joshua son of Jozadak and his fellow priests and Zerubbabel son of Shealtiel and his associates began to build the altar of the God of Israel to sacrifice burnt offerings on it, in accordance with what is written in the Law of Moses the man of God. ³Despite their fear of the peoples around them, they built the altar on its foundation and sacrificed burnt offerings on it to the LORD, both the morning and evening sacrifices. ⁴Then in accordance with what is written, they celebrated the Festival of Tabernacles with the required number of burnt offerings prescribed for each day. ⁵After that, they presented the regular burnt offerings, the New Moon sacrifices and the sacrifices for all the appointed sacred festivals of the LORD, as well as those brought as freewill offerings to the LORD. ⁶On the first day of the seventh month they began to offer burnt offerings to the LORD, though the foundation of the LORD's temple had not yet been laid.

Rebuilding the Temple

⁷Then they gave money to the masons and carpenters, and gave food and drink and olive oil to the people of Sidon and Tyre, so that they would bring cedar logs by sea from Lebanon to Joppa, as authorized by Cyrus king of Persia.

⁸In the second month of the second year after their arrival at the house of God in Jerusalem, Zerubbabel son of Shealtiel, Joshua son of Jozadak and the rest of the people (the priests and the Levites and all who had returned from the

Courage: People Need Permission to Take Risks
Ezra 3:7

Most people need permission to take a risk. By issuing his proclamation, King Cyrus modeled another leadership principle.

Cyrus issued a decree to all the Jews that they could return to their homeland and begin life again there. You might think that every Jew would jump at this opportunity to leave a land of captivity and go home, but out of a population of hundreds of thousands of Jews (in 538 BC), only 49,897 responded to the offer. The ones who did return gave up a life of comfort and familiarity to pursue a life of rebuilding.

A risk like this is tough for most people. Usually, a leader must step forward and give men and women permission to take a risk, step out, and make sacrifices. Most people generally take the path of least resistance and migrate toward comfort zones. This is why leaders must both model courage and call forth courage from others.

captivity to Jerusalem) began the work. They appointed Levites twenty years old and older to supervise the building of the house of the LORD. ⁹Joshua and his sons and brothers and Kadmiel and his sons (descendants of Hodaviah[c]) and the sons of Henadad and their sons and brothers—all Levites—joined together in supervising those working on the house of God.

¹⁰When the builders laid the foundation of the temple of the LORD, the priests in their vestments and with trumpets, and the Levites (the sons of Asaph) with cymbals, took their places to praise the LORD, as prescribed by David king of Israel. ¹¹With praise and thanksgiving they sang to the LORD:

"He is good;
  his love toward Israel endures forever."

And all the people gave a great shout of praise to the LORD, because the foundation of the house of the LORD was laid. ¹²But many of the older priests and Levites and family heads, who had seen the former temple, wept aloud when they saw the

---
[a] 69 That is, about 1,100 pounds or about 500 kilograms
[b] 69 That is, about 3 tons or about 2.8 metric tons
[c] 9 Hebrew *Yehudah*, a variant of *Hodaviah*

foundation of this temple being laid, while many others shouted for joy. ¹³No one could distinguish the sound of the shouts of joy from the sound of weeping, because the people made so much noise. And the sound was heard far away.

Opposition to the Rebuilding

4 When the enemies of Judah and Benjamin heard that the exiles were building a temple for the LORD, the God of Israel, ²they came to Zerubbabel and to the heads of the families and said, "Let us help you build because, like you, we seek your God and have been sacrificing to him since the time of Esarhaddon king of Assyria, who brought us here."

³But Zerubbabel, Joshua and the rest of the heads of the families of Israel answered, "You have no part with us in building a temple to our God. We alone will build it for the LORD, the God of Israel, as King Cyrus, the king of Persia, commanded us."

Discernment: Zerubbabel Reads the People, Then Acts

Ezra 4:1–3

Leaders must practice discernment. Relationships can get messy; people often harbor personal agendas and attempt to mask their true motives or to make them sound more noble than they really are.

Such was the case when a group of outsiders approached Zerubbabel and offered to help. "Let us help you build because, like you, we seek your God and have been sacrificing to him since the time of Esarhaddon king of Assyria, who brought us here," they said (Ezr 4:2). Zerubbabel sized them up and read the situation perfectly. He quickly recognized these folks had really arrived only to discourage and poison the minds of the builders. His relational discernment kept these negative influences from infiltrating the flock.

Leaders must read the people, then lead the people. They must understand the timing, the people, the situation and the priorities, then act accordingly. Their action depends upon how they read these factors. Discernment always precedes decision. Analysis always precedes action.

---

⁴Then the peoples around them set out to discourage the people of Judah and make them afraid to go on building.[a] ⁵They bribed officials to work against them and frustrate their plans during the entire reign of Cyrus king of Persia and down to the reign of Darius king of Persia.

Later Opposition Under Xerxes and Artaxerxes

⁶At the beginning of the reign of Xerxes,[b] they lodged an accusation against the people of Judah and Jerusalem.

⁷And in the days of Artaxerxes king of Persia, Bishlam, Mithredath, Tabeel and the rest of his associates wrote a letter to Artaxerxes. The letter was written in Aramaic script and in the Aramaic language.[c,d]

⁸Rehum the commanding officer and Shimshai the secretary wrote a letter against Jerusalem to Artaxerxes the king as follows:

⁹Rehum the commanding officer and Shimshai the secretary, together with the rest of their associates—the judges, officials and administrators over the people from Persia, Uruk and Babylon, the Elamites of Susa, ¹⁰and the other people whom the great and honorable Ashurbanipal deported and settled in the city of Samaria and elsewhere in Trans-Euphrates.

¹¹(This is a copy of the letter they sent him.)

To King Artaxerxes,

From your servants in Trans-Euphrates:

¹²The king should know that the people who came up to us from you have gone to Jerusalem and are rebuilding that rebellious and wicked city. They are restoring the walls and repairing the foundations.

¹³Furthermore, the king should know that if this city is built and its walls are restored, no more taxes, tribute or duty will be paid, and eventually the royal revenues will suffer.[e] ¹⁴Now since we are under obligation to the palace and it is not proper for us to see the king dishonored, we are sending this message to inform the king, ¹⁵so that a search may be made in the archives of your predecessors. In these records you will find that this city is a rebellious city, troublesome to kings and provinces, a

---

[a] 4 Or and troubled them as they built   [b] 6 Hebrew Ahasuerus   [c] 7 Or written in Aramaic and translated
[d] 7 The text of 4:8–6:18 is in Aramaic.   [e] 13 The meaning of the Aramaic for this clause is uncertain.

place with a long history of sedition. That is why this city was destroyed. [16]We inform the king that if this city is built and its walls are restored, you will be left with nothing in Trans-Euphrates.

[17]The king sent this reply:

To Rehum the commanding officer, Shimshai the secretary and the rest of their associates living in Samaria and elsewhere in Trans-Euphrates:

Greetings.

[18]The letter you sent us has been read and translated in my presence. [19]I issued an order and a search was made, and it was found that this city has a long history of revolt against kings and has been a place of rebellion and sedition. [20]Jerusalem has had powerful kings ruling over the whole of Trans-Euphrates, and taxes, tribute and duty were paid to them. [21]Now issue an order to these men to stop work, so that this city will not be rebuilt until I so order. [22]Be careful not to neglect this matter. Why let this threat grow, to the detriment of the royal interests?

[23]As soon as the copy of the letter of King Artaxerxes was read to Rehum and Shimshai the secretary and their associates, they went immediately to the Jews in Jerusalem and compelled them by force to stop.

[24]Thus the work on the house of God in Jerusalem came to a standstill until the second year of the reign of Darius king of Persia.

Tattenai's Letter to Darius

5 Now Haggai the prophet and Zechariah the prophet, a descendant of Iddo, prophesied to the Jews in Judah and Jerusalem in the name of the God of Israel, who was over them. [2]Then Zerubbabel son of Shealtiel and Joshua son of Jozadak set to work to rebuild the house of God in Jerusalem. And the prophets of God were with them, supporting them.

[3]At that time Tattenai, governor of Trans-Euphrates, and Shethar-Bozenai and their associates went to them and asked, "Who authorized you to rebuild this temple and to finish it?" [4]They[a] also asked, "What are the names of those who are constructing this building?" [5]But the eye of their God was watching over the elders of the Jews, and they were not stopped until

a report could go to Darius and his written reply be received.

[6]This is a copy of the letter that Tattenai, governor of Trans-Euphrates, and Shethar-Bozenai and their associates, the officials of Trans-Euphrates, sent to King Darius. [7]The report they sent him read as follows:

To King Darius:

Cordial greetings.

[8]The king should know that we went to the district of Judah, to the temple of the great God. The people are building it with large stones and placing the timbers in the walls. The work is being carried on with diligence and is making rapid progress under their direction.

[9]We questioned the elders and asked them, "Who authorized you to rebuild this temple and to finish it?" [10]We also asked them their names, so that we could write down the names of their leaders for your information.

[11]This is the answer they gave us:

"We are the servants of the God of heaven and earth, and we are rebuilding the temple that was built many years ago, one that a great king of Israel built and finished. [12]But because our ancestors angered the God of heaven, he gave them into the hands of Nebuchadnezzar the Chaldean, king of Babylon, who destroyed this temple and deported the people to Babylon.

[13]"However, in the first year of Cyrus king of Babylon, King Cyrus issued a decree to rebuild this house of God. [14]He even removed from the temple[b] of Babylon the gold and silver articles of the house of God, which Nebuchadnezzar had taken from the temple in Jerusalem and brought to the temple[b] in Babylon. Then King Cyrus gave them to a man named Sheshbazzar, whom he had appointed governor, [15]and he told him, 'Take these articles and go and deposit them in the temple in Jerusalem. And rebuild the house of God on its site.'

[16]"So this Sheshbazzar came and laid the foundations of the house of God in Jerusalem. From that day to the present it has been under construction but is not yet finished."

[17]Now if it pleases the king, let a search be made in the royal archives of Babylon to

---

a 4 See Septuagint; Aramaic We.   b 14 Or palace

see if King Cyrus did in fact issue a decree to rebuild this house of God in Jerusalem. Then let the king send us his decision in this matter.

The Decree of Darius

6 King Darius then issued an order, and they searched in the archives stored in the treasury at Babylon. ²A scroll was found in the citadel of Ecbatana in the province of Media, and this was written on it:

Memorandum:

³In the first year of King Cyrus, the king issued a decree concerning the temple of God in Jerusalem:

Let the temple be rebuilt as a place to present sacrifices, and let its foundations be laid. It is to be sixty cubits*a* high and sixty cubits wide, ⁴with three courses of large stones and one of timbers. The costs are to be paid by the royal treasury. ⁵Also, the gold and silver articles of the house of God, which Nebuchadnezzar took from the temple in Jerusalem and brought to Babylon, are to be returned to their places in the temple in Jerusalem; they are to be deposited in the house of God.

⁶Now then, Tattenai, governor of Trans-Euphrates, and Shethar-Bozenai and you other officials of that province, stay away from there. ⁷Do not interfere with the work on this temple of God. Let the governor of the Jews and the Jewish elders rebuild this house of God on its site.

⁸Moreover, I hereby decree what you are to do for these elders of the Jews in the construction of this house of God:

Their expenses are to be fully paid out of the royal treasury, from the revenues of Trans-Euphrates, so that the work will not stop. ⁹Whatever is needed — young bulls, rams, male lambs for burnt offerings to the God of heaven, and wheat, salt, wine and olive oil, as requested by the priests in Jerusalem — must be given them daily without fail, ¹⁰so that they may offer sacrifices pleasing to the God of heaven and pray for the well-being of the king and his sons. ¹¹Furthermore, I decree that if anyone defies this edict, a beam is to be pulled from their house and they are to be impaled on it. And for this crime their house is to be made a pile of rubble. ¹²May God, who has caused his Name to dwell there, overthrow any king or people who lifts a hand to change this decree or to destroy this temple in Jerusalem.

I Darius have decreed it. Let it be carried out with diligence.

Completion and Dedication of the Temple

¹³Then, because of the decree King Darius had sent, Tattenai, governor of Trans-Euphrates, and Shethar-Bozenai and their associates carried it out with diligence. ¹⁴So the elders of the Jews continued to build and prosper under the preaching of Haggai the prophet and Zechariah, a descendant of Iddo. They finished building the temple according to the command of the God of Israel and the decrees of Cyrus, Darius and Artaxerxes, kings of Persia. ¹⁵The temple was completed on the third day of the month Adar, in the sixth year of the reign of King Darius.

¹⁶Then the people of Israel — the priests, the Levites and the rest of the exiles — celebrated the dedication of the house of God with joy. ¹⁷For the dedication of this house of God they offered a hundred bulls, two hundred rams, four hundred male lambs and, as a sin offering*b* for all Israel, twelve male goats, one for each of the tribes of Israel. ¹⁸And they installed the priests in their divisions and the Levites in their groups for the service of God at Jerusalem, according to what is written in the Book of Moses.

The Passover

¹⁹On the fourteenth day of the first month, the exiles celebrated the Passover. ²⁰The priests

---

a 3 That is, about 90 feet or about 27 meters   *b* 17 Or *purification offering*

Zechariah Learns Motivation Comes Before Mobilization

Ezra 6:14

Opposition and conflict delayed temple construction for 14 years. Only the leadership of Haggai and Zechariah motivated the people to finish what they had begun. Leaders make sure the team follows through on what it begins. Through the influence of these two prophets, construction was completed in 516 BC.

and Levites had purified themselves and were all ceremonially clean. The Levites slaughtered the Passover lamb for all the exiles, for their relatives the priests and for themselves. [21]So the Israelites who had returned from the exile ate it, together with all who had separated themselves from the unclean practices of their Gentile neighbors in order to seek the LORD, the God of Israel. [22]For seven days they celebrated with joy the Festival of Unleavened Bread, because the LORD had filled them with joy by changing the attitude of the king of Assyria so that he assisted them in the work on the house of God, the God of Israel.

Ezra Comes to Jerusalem

7 After these things, during the reign of Artaxerxes king of Persia, Ezra son of Seraiah, the son of Azariah, the son of Hilkiah, [2]the son of Shallum, the son of Zadok, the son of Ahitub, [3]the son of Amariah, the son of Azariah, the son of Meraioth, [4]the son of Zerahiah, the son of Uzzi, the son of Bukki, [5]the son of Abishua, the son of Phinehas, the son of Eleazar, the son of Aaron the chief priest— [6]this Ezra came up from Babylon. He was a teacher well versed in the Law of Moses, which the LORD, the God of Israel, had given. The king had granted him everything he asked, for the hand of the LORD his God was on him. [7]Some of the Israelites, including priests, Levites, musicians, gatekeepers and temple servants, also came up to Jerusalem in the seventh year of King Artaxerxes.

[8]Ezra arrived in Jerusalem in the fifth month of the seventh year of the king. [9]He had begun his journey from Babylon on the first day of the first month, and he arrived in Jerusalem on the first day of the fifth month, for the gracious hand of his God was on him. [10]For Ezra had devoted himself to the study and observance of the Law of the LORD, and to teaching its decrees and laws in Israel.

King Artaxerxes' Letter to Ezra

[11]This is a copy of the letter King Artaxerxes had given to Ezra the priest, a teacher of the Law, a man learned in matters concerning the commands and decrees of the LORD for Israel:

[12]Artaxerxes, king of kings,

To Ezra the priest, teacher of the Law of the God of heaven:

Greetings.

[13]Now I decree that any of the Israelites in my kingdom, including priests and Levites, who volunteer to go to Jerusalem with you, may go. [14]You are sent by the king and his seven advisers to inquire about Judah and Jerusalem with regard

EZRA

Many Years of Doing the Right Thing

Ezra 7:6–10

PROFILE in leadership

Even at a young age, Ezra diligently studied and learned to become a scholar. He won the respect of many, including the political leader of the land of his exile, King Artaxerxes. Although Ezra's passion and vision centered on Jerusalem, he clearly kept himself busy doing God's work while in exile. He established his connections and influence over time—a necessary step if the dream of restoring Jerusalem were to be fulfilled.

As a result of many years of consistently doing the right thing, the king finally trusted Ezra with great power and resources, acknowledging his character qualities in writing. He provided all that Ezra needed to get the job done.

Ezra led many Israelites back to Jerusalem during this time of restoration. As a spiritual leader, Ezra had prepared, studied, and connected with many ordinary Jews, and his pronounced influence prompted many to follow him to Jerusalem. Ezra did not utilize his power, intellect and influence for personal gain, but rather to restore Jerusalem.

When Ezra arrived in Jerusalem and found that a remnant of Jews had disobeyed God and polluted the bloodlines of his people, he did not shrink from making the tough call (Ezr 9; 10). Throughout his life, Ezra exercised the very best leadership qualities with both passion and zeal, which God utilized to fulfill his call.

Ezra: Being Before Doing

Ezra 7:10

On the basis of King Artaxerxes' decree, Ezra traveled from Babylon to Jerusalem (Ezr 7:1–10). As a priest, he felt committed to establishing spiritual priorities among the people, especially as it pertained to their new temple. One verse reflects the heart of a leader fully committed to his God: "For Ezra had devoted himself to the study and observance of the Law of the LORD, and to teaching its decrees and laws in Israel" (7:10). Do you see the order of priorities in his leadership?

1. *Learn it:* Ezra studied and discovered the truth himself.

2. *Live it:* Ezra practiced and applied what he had learned.

3. *Loan it:* Ezra passed on to others what he had already embraced.

Successful leaders must learn to follow Ezra's model. Dwight L. Moody suggested the greatest tragedy of his day was that Christian leaders attempted to traffic in unlived truth. It is our tragedy as well. We cannot give away what we don't incarnate. We must import truth before we export truth. God wants to construct our "being" before our "doing."

to the Law of your God, which is in your hand. [15]Moreover, you are to take with you the silver and gold that the king and his advisers have freely given to the God of Israel, whose dwelling is in Jerusalem, [16]together with all the silver and gold you may obtain from the province of Babylon, as well as the freewill offerings of the people and priests for the temple of their God in Jerusalem. [17]With this money be sure to buy bulls, rams and male lambs, together with their grain offerings and drink offerings, and sacrifice them on the altar of the temple of your God in Jerusalem.

[18]You and your fellow Israelites may then do whatever seems best with the rest of the silver and gold, in accordance with the will of your God. [19]Deliver to the God of Jerusalem all the articles entrusted to you for worship in the temple of your God. [20]And anything else needed for the temple of your God that you are responsible to supply, you may provide from the royal treasury.

[21]Now I, King Artaxerxes, decree that all the treasurers of Trans-Euphrates are to provide with diligence whatever Ezra the priest, the teacher of the Law of the God of heaven, may ask of you — [22]up to a hundred talents[a] of silver, a hundred cors[b] of wheat, a hundred baths[c] of wine, a hundred baths[c] of olive oil, and salt without limit. [23]Whatever the God of heaven has pre-

scribed, let it be done with diligence for the temple of the God of heaven. Why should his wrath fall on the realm of the king and of his sons? [24]You are also to know that you have no authority to impose taxes, tribute or duty on any of the priests, Levites, musicians, gatekeepers, temple servants or other workers at this house of God.

[25]And you, Ezra, in accordance with the wisdom of your God, which you possess, appoint magistrates and judges to administer justice to all the people of Trans-Euphrates — all who know the laws of your God. And you are to teach any who do not know them. [26]Whoever does not obey the law of your God and the law of the king must surely be punished by death, banishment, confiscation of property, or imprisonment.[d]

[27]Praise be to the LORD, the God of our ancestors, who has put it into the king's heart to bring honor to the house of the LORD in Jerusalem in this way, [28]and who has extended his good favor to me before the king and his advisers and all the king's powerful officials. Because the hand of the LORD my God was on me, I took courage and gathered leaders from Israel to go up with me.

---

[a] 22 That is, about 3 3/4 tons or about 3.4 metric tons
[b] 22 That is, probably about 18 tons or about 16 metric tons
[c] 22 That is, about 600 gallons or about 2,200 liters
[d] 26 The text of 7:12-26 is in Aramaic.

List of the Family Heads Returning With Ezra

8 These are the family heads and those registered with them who came up with me from Babylon during the reign of King Artaxerxes:

[2] of the descendants of Phinehas, Gershom;
of the descendants of Ithamar, Daniel;
of the descendants of David, Hattush [3] of
the descendants of Shekaniah;

of the descendants of Parosh, Zechariah,
and with him were registered 150 men;

[4] of the descendants of Pahath-Moab, Eliehoenai son of Zerahiah, and with him
200 men;

[5] of the descendants of Zattu,[a] Shekaniah
son of Jahaziel, and with him 300 men;

[6] of the descendants of Adin, Ebed son of
Jonathan, and with him 50 men;

[7] of the descendants of Elam, Jeshaiah son of
Athaliah, and with him 70 men;

[8] of the descendants of Shephatiah, Zebadiah son of Michael, and with him 80
men;

[9] of the descendants of Joab, Obadiah son of
Jehiel, and with him 218 men;

[10] of the descendants of Bani,[b] Shelomith son
of Josiphiah, and with him 160 men;

[11] of the descendants of Bebai, Zechariah son
of Bebai, and with him 28 men;

[12] of the descendants of Azgad, Johanan son
of Hakkatan, and with him 110 men;

[13] of the descendants of Adonikam, the last
ones, whose names were Eliphelet, Jeuel
and Shemaiah, and with them 60 men;

[14] of the descendants of Bigvai, Uthai and
Zakkur, and with them 70 men.

The Return to Jerusalem

[15] I assembled them at the canal that flows toward Ahava, and we camped there three days. When I checked among the people and the priests, I found no Levites there. [16] So I summoned Eliezer, Ariel, Shemaiah, Elnathan, Jarib, Elnathan, Nathan, Zechariah and Meshullam, who were leaders, and Joiarib and Elnathan, who were men of learning, [17] and I ordered them to go to Iddo, the leader in Kasiphia. I told him what to say to Iddo and his fellow Levites, the temple servants in Kasiphia, so that they might bring attendants to us for the house of our God. [18] Because the gracious hand of our God was on us, they brought us Sherebiah, a capable man, from the descendants of Mahli son of Levi, the son of Israel, and Sherebiah's sons and broth-

ers, 18 in all; [19] and Hashabiah, together with Jeshaiah from the descendants of Merari, and his brothers and nephews, 20 in all. [20] They also brought 220 of the temple servants — a body that David and the officials had established to assist the Levites. All were registered by name.

[21] There, by the Ahava Canal, I proclaimed a fast, so that we might humble ourselves before our God and ask him for a safe journey for us and our children, with all our possessions. [22] I was ashamed to ask the king for soldiers and horsemen to protect us from enemies on the road, because we had told the king, "The gracious hand of our God is on everyone who looks to him, but his great anger is against all who forsake him." [23] So we fasted and petitioned our God about this, and he answered our prayer.

[24] Then I set apart twelve of the leading priests, namely, Sherebiah, Hashabiah and ten of their brothers, [25] and I weighed out to them the offering of silver and gold and the articles that the king, his advisers, his officials and all Israel present there had donated for the house of our God. [26] I weighed out to them 650 talents[c] of silver, silver articles weighing 100 talents,[d] 100 talents[d] of gold, [27] 20 bowls of gold valued at 1,000 darics,[e] and two fine articles of polished bronze, as precious as gold.

[28] I said to them, "You as well as these articles are consecrated to the LORD. The silver and gold are a freewill offering to the LORD, the God of your ancestors. [29] Guard them carefully until you weigh them out in the chambers of the house of the LORD in Jerusalem before the leading priests and the Levites and the family heads of Israel." [30] Then the priests and Levites received the silver and gold and sacred articles that had been weighed out to be taken to the house of our God in Jerusalem.

[31] On the twelfth day of the first month we set out from the Ahava Canal to go to Jerusalem. The hand of our God was on us, and he protected us from enemies and bandits along the way. [32] So we arrived in Jerusalem, where we rested three days.

[33] On the fourth day, in the house of our God, we weighed out the silver and gold and the sacred articles into the hands of Meremoth son of Uriah, the priest. Eleazar son of Phinehas was

---

a 5 Some Septuagint manuscripts (also 1 Esdras 8:32); Hebrew does not have *Zattu.*   *b 10* Some Septuagint manuscripts (also 1 Esdras 8:36); Hebrew does not have *Bani.*   *c 26* That is, about 24 tons or about 22 metric tons   *d 26* That is, about 3 3/4 tons or about 3.4 metric tons   *e 27* That is, about 19 pounds or about 8.4 kilograms

with him, and so were the Levites Jozabad son of Jeshua and Noadiah son of Binnui. ³⁴Everything was accounted for by number and weight, and the entire weight was recorded at that time.

³⁵Then the exiles who had returned from captivity sacrificed burnt offerings to the God of Israel: twelve bulls for all Israel, ninety-six rams, seventy-seven male lambs and, as a sin offering,ᵃ twelve male goats. All this was a burnt offering to the LORD. ³⁶They also delivered the king's orders to the royal satraps and to the governors of Trans-Euphrates, who then gave assistance to the people and to the house of God.

Ezra's Prayer About Intermarriage

9 After these things had been done, the leaders came to me and said, "The people of Israel, including the priests and the Levites, have not kept themselves separate from the neighboring peoples with their detestable practices, like those of the Canaanites, Hittites, Perizzites, Jebusites, Ammonites, Moabites, Egyptians and Amorites. ²They have taken some of their daughters as wives for themselves and their sons, and have mingled the holy race with the peoples around them. And the leaders and officials have led the way in this unfaithfulness."

³When I heard this, I tore my tunic and cloak, pulled hair from my head and beard and sat down appalled. ⁴Then everyone who trembled at the words of the God of Israel gathered around me because of this unfaithfulness of the exiles. And I sat there appalled until the evening sacrifice.

⁵Then, at the evening sacrifice, I rose from my self-abasement, with my tunic and cloak torn, and fell on my knees with my hands spread out to the LORD my God ⁶and prayed:

"I am too ashamed and disgraced, my God, to lift up my face to you, because our sins are higher than our heads and our guilt has reached to the heavens. ⁷From the days of our ancestors until now, our guilt has been great. Because of our sins, we and our kings and our priests have been subjected to the sword and captivity, to pillage and humiliation at the hand of foreign kings, as it is today.

⁸"But now, for a brief moment, the LORD our God has been gracious in leaving us a remnant and giving us a firm placeᵇ in his sanctuary, and so our God gives light to our eyes and a little relief in our bondage. ⁹Though we are slaves, our God has not

forsaken us in our bondage. He has shown us kindness in the sight of the kings of Persia: He has granted us new life to rebuild the house of our God and repair its ruins, and he has given us a wall of protection in Judah and Jerusalem.

¹⁰"But now, our God, what can we say after this? For we have forsaken the commands ¹¹you gave through your servants the prophets when you said: 'The land you are entering to possess is a land polluted by the corruption of its peoples. By their detestable practices they have filled it with their impurity from one end to the other. ¹²Therefore, do not give your daughters in marriage to their sons or take their daughters for your sons. Do not seek a treaty of friendship with them at any time, that you may be strong and eat the good things of the land and leave it to your children as an everlasting inheritance.'

¹³"What has happened to us is a result of our evil deeds and our great guilt, and yet, our God, you have punished us less than our sins deserved and have given us a remnant like this. ¹⁴Shall we then break your commands again and intermarry with the peoples who commit such detestable practices? Would you not be angry enough with us to destroy us, leaving us no remnant or survivor? ¹⁵LORD, the God of Israel, you are righteous! We are left this day as a remnant. Here we are before you in our guilt, though because of it not one of us can stand in your presence."

The People's Confession of Sin

10 While Ezra was praying and confessing, weeping and throwing himself down before the house of God, a large crowd of Israelites—men, women and children—gathered around him. They too wept bitterly. ²Then Shekaniah son of Jehiel, one of the descendants of Elam, said to Ezra, "We have been unfaithful to our God by marrying foreign women from the peoples around us. But in spite of this, there is still hope for Israel. ³Now let us make a covenant before our God to send away all these women and their children, in accordance with the counsel of my lord and of those who fear the commands of our God. Let it be done according to the Law. ⁴Rise up; this matter is in your hands. We will support you, so take courage and do it."

ᵃ 35 Or *purification offering*   ᵇ 8 Or *a foothold*

[5]So Ezra rose up and put the leading priests and Levites and all Israel under oath to do what had been suggested. And they took the oath. [6]Then Ezra withdrew from before the house of God and went to the room of Jehohanan son of Eliashib. While he was there, he ate no food and drank no water, because he continued to mourn over the unfaithfulness of the exiles.

[7]A proclamation was then issued throughout Judah and Jerusalem for all the exiles to assemble in Jerusalem. [8]Anyone who failed to appear within three days would forfeit all his property, in accordance with the decision of the officials and elders, and would himself be expelled from the assembly of the exiles.

[9]Within the three days, all the men of Judah and Benjamin had gathered in Jerusalem. And on the twentieth day of the ninth month, all the people were sitting in the square before the house of God, greatly distressed by the occasion and because of the rain. [10]Then Ezra the priest stood up and said to them, "You have been unfaithful; you have married foreign women, adding to Israel's guilt. [11]Now honor[a] the LORD, the God of your ancestors, and do his will. Separate yourselves from the peoples around you and from your foreign wives."

[12]The whole assembly responded with a loud voice: "You are right! We must do as you say. [13]But there are many people here and it is the rainy season; so we cannot stand outside. Besides, this matter cannot be taken care of in a day or two, because we have sinned greatly in this thing. [14]Let our officials act for the whole assembly. Then let everyone in our towns who has married a foreign woman come at a set time, along with the elders and judges of each town, until the fierce anger of our God in this matter is turned away from us." [15]Only Jonathan son of Asahel and Jahzeiah son of Tikvah, supported by Meshullam and Shabbethai the Levite, opposed this.

[16]So the exiles did as was proposed. Ezra the priest selected men who were family heads, one from each family division, and all of them designated by name. On the first day of the tenth month they sat down to investigate the cases, [17]and by the first day of the first month they finished dealing with all the men who had married foreign women.

Those Guilty of Intermarriage

[18]Among the descendants of the priests, the following had married foreign women:

From the descendants of Joshua son of Jozadak, and his brothers: Maaseiah, Eliezer, Jarib and Gedaliah. [19](They all gave their hands in pledge to put away their wives, and for their guilt they each presented a ram from the flock as a guilt offering.)

[20]From the descendants of Immer:

[a] 11 Or *Now make confession to*

Ezra Shows Us the Law of the Picture

Ezra 9:1 — 10:44

Like all great leaders, we see Ezra demonstrating the number one management principle in the world, the Law of the Picture: People do what people see. When Ezra heard of the sin and compromise of the Israelites, he mourned and fasted. He then took logical steps to bring about change. The steps he took are transferable, and led to the repentance of a nation. Ponder the sequence of events in this example of pure leadership:

1. **He felt genuine remorse over national sin (10:6).**

2. **He issued a proclamation for the Jews to gather in Jerusalem (10:7).**

3. **He spoke clearly and directly concerning the issue (10:10).**

4. **He challenged the people to repent and change (10:11).**

5. **He accepted a plan for leaders to meet with the transgressors (10:13–17).**

6. **He started with the leaders who failed, then moved to the people (10:18–24).**

7. **He brought about public repentance and reformation (10:25–44).**

Hanani and Zebadiah.

²¹From the descendants of Harim:
Maaseiah, Elijah, Shemaiah, Jehiel and Uzziah.

²²From the descendants of Pashhur:
Elioenai, Maaseiah, Ishmael, Nethanel, Jozabad and Elasah.

²³Among the Levites:

Jozabad, Shimei, Kelaiah (that is, Kelita), Pethahiah, Judah and Eliezer.

²⁴From the musicians:
Eliashib.

From the gatekeepers:
Shallum, Telem and Uri.

²⁵And among the other Israelites:

From the descendants of Parosh:
Ramiah, Izziah, Malkijah, Mijamin, Eleazar, Malkijah and Benaiah.

²⁶From the descendants of Elam:
Mattaniah, Zechariah, Jehiel, Abdi, Jeremoth and Elijah.

²⁷From the descendants of Zattu:
Elioenai, Eliashib, Mattaniah, Jeremoth, Zabad and Aziza.

²⁸From the descendants of Bebai:
Jehohanan, Hananiah, Zabbai and Athlai.

²⁹From the descendants of Bani:

Meshullam, Malluk, Adaiah, Jashub, Sheal and Jeremoth.

³⁰From the descendants of Pahath-Moab:
Adna, Kelal, Benaiah, Maaseiah, Mattaniah, Bezalel, Binnui and Manasseh.

³¹From the descendants of Harim:
Eliezer, Ishijah, Malkijah, Shemaiah, Shimeon, ³²Benjamin, Malluk and Shemariah.

³³From the descendants of Hashum:
Mattenai, Mattattah, Zabad, Eliphelet, Jeremai, Manasseh and Shimei.

³⁴From the descendants of Bani:
Maadai, Amram, Uel, ³⁵Benaiah, Bedeiah, Keluhi, ³⁶Vaniah, Meremoth, Eliashib, ³⁷Mattaniah, Mattenai and Jaasu.

³⁸From the descendants of Binnui:^a
Shimei, ³⁹Shelemiah, Nathan, Adaiah, ⁴⁰Maknadebai, Shashai, Sharai, ⁴¹Azarel, Shelemiah, Shemariah, ⁴²Shallum, Amariah and Joseph.

⁴³From the descendants of Nebo:
Jeiel, Mattithiah, Zabad, Zebina, Jaddai, Joel and Benaiah.

⁴⁴All these had married foreign women, and some of them had children by these wives.^b

---

^a 37,38 See Septuagint (also 1 Esdras 9:34); Hebrew *Jaasu* ³⁸*and Bani and Binnui,*   ^b 44 Or *and they sent them away with their children*

INTRODUCTION TO
NEHEMIAH

In a Nutshell—a Classic Case Study in Leadership

The man saw a need, rose up, captured a vision, laid a plan, and mobilized others to join him in his cause. In a nutshell, that's the story of Nehemiah, a classic case study in leadership.

In fact, one distinctive of Nehemiah is that no overt miracles occur in the book. Nobody is healed or raised from the dead. God simply answers prayer by providing a leader with favor, strength and wisdom. Then the work of God is fleshed out in the day-to-day grind of committed workers under one man's gifted leadership—ordinary people enjoying God's blessing as they follow a gifted leader. If you want a study in the fundamentals of leadership, this book is a good place to begin.

A contemporary of Ezra, Nehemiah served as cupbearer for King Artaxerxes. He instinctively understood the laws of navigation, connection, timing, buy-in, priorities, the "big mo," and victory; you see them all in action in these few chapters.

One day Nehemiah heard that the walls surrounding Jerusalem lay in ruins, a disgrace to the Hebrews. Other nations mocked them. This terrible news burdened Nehemiah, and he knew something had to be done. Once he decided to take on the rebuilding project, the walls that for years had been nothing but rubble were completed in just 52 days.

Nehemiah stationed workers in logical positions, and they all labored successfully until they finished the work. Yet it took a coach for them to work as a team. Israel had never lacked for workers; what the nation needed was a leader to chart the course and set the people in motion. Zerubbabel had led the way to restore Jerusalem's temple;

God's Role in Nehemiah

God works behind the scenes to set up Nehemiah's success. He influences the influencers.

When Nehemiah began to weep and pray over the disgrace of Jerusalem's ruins, God furnished him with the vision to rebuild the wall. Then God provided favor as Nehemiah sought permission from the king to leave his post and return to Jerusalem to inspect the city. Through the wealth of the Persian Empire, God even supplied the resources Nehemiah would need for rebuilding the wall.

While this book provides extremely pragmatic lessons in sound leadership principles, God remains clearly visible from the beginning. Before he did anything else, Nehemiah took time to pray. Each step of the way, Nehemiah sought the Lord for direction. As the walls rose, so did the hopes of the Jews living in Jerusalem. They saw the rebuilt walls as a symbol that God had not abandoned them and was ready to restore their lives.

Leaders in Nehemiah

Nehemiah, King Artaxerxes, the leaders of each family

Other People of Influence in Nehemiah

Sanballat, Tobiah, Geshem

Ezra led the way to restore Jerusalem's worship. Now, a new leader was needed to restore Jerusalem's walls.

Under Nehemiah's leadership, the Jews received a permit for the rebuilding job, gathered the resources, identified workers' gifts, assigned positions, overcame criticism, and labored until the walls stood firm and tall once more. And it all happened in record time.

Lessons in Leadership

- You cannot separate good leadership from clear vision.
- Lasting leaders feel the burden of a need before they receive the vision to meet it.
- Leaders act from a deep sense of responsibility.
- The greater the preparation, the easier the motivation.
- Leaders are more fulfilled by empowering others than by doing the work themselves.

LEADERSHIP HIGHLIGHTS IN NEHEMIAH

Nehemiah's Prayer

1 The words of Nehemiah son of Hakaliah:

In the month of Kislev in the twentieth year, while I was in the citadel of Susa, ²Hanani, one of my brothers, came from Judah with some other men, and I questioned them about the Jewish remnant that had survived the exile, and also about Jerusalem.

³They said to me, "Those who survived the exile and are back in the province are in great trouble and disgrace. The wall of Jerusalem is broken down, and its gates have been burned with fire."

⁴When I heard these things, I sat down and wept. For some days I mourned and fasted and prayed before the God of heaven. ⁵Then I said:

"Lord, the God of heaven, the great and awesome God, who keeps his covenant of love with those who love him and keep his commandments, ⁶let your ear be attentive and your eyes open to hear the prayer your servant is praying before you day and night for your servants, the people of Israel. I confess the sins we Israelites, including myself and my father's family, have committed against you. ⁷We have acted very wickedly toward you. We have not obeyed the commands, decrees and laws you gave your servant Moses.

⁸"Remember the instruction you gave your servant Moses, saying, 'If you are unfaithful, I will scatter you among the nations, ⁹but if you return to me and obey my commands, then even if your exiled people are at the farthest horizon, I will gather them from there and bring them to the place I have chosen as a dwelling for my Name.'

¹⁰"They are your servants and your people, whom you redeemed by your great strength and your mighty hand. ¹¹Lord, let your ear be attentive to the prayer of this your servant and to the prayer of your servants who delight in revering your name. Give your servant success today by granting him favor in the presence of this man."

I was cupbearer to the king.

Artaxerxes Sends Nehemiah to Jerusalem

2 In the month of Nisan in the twentieth year of King Artaxerxes, when wine was brought for him, I took the wine and gave it to the king. I had not been sad in his presence before, ²so the king asked me, "Why does your face look so sad when you are not ill? This can be nothing but sadness of heart."

I was very much afraid, ³but I said to the king, "May the king live forever! Why should my face not look sad when the city where my ancestors are buried lies in ruins, and its gates have been destroyed by fire?"

⁴The king said to me, "What is it you want?"

Then I prayed to the God of heaven, ⁵and I answered the king, "If it pleases the king and if your servant has found favor in his sight, let him send me to the city in Judah where my ancestors are buried so that I can rebuild it."

⁶Then the king, with the queen sitting beside him, asked me, "How long will your journey

Nehemiah Prays First!

Nehemiah 1:4

When Nehemiah heard that the walls of Jerusalem lay in ruins, that its charred gates sat rotting, and that the Jewish survivors lived in distress and reproach, he did what every great leader must do: He fasted and prayed.

Something powerful happens when a leader prays and stands in the gap for his people. Intercession must always be a primary role for a leader. The apostle Peter once declared his top two leadership priorities: prayer and the ministry of God's Word (Ac 6:4). A leader's prayer accomplishes four things:

1. **Prayer internalizes the burden, deepening our ownership of a need.**

2. **Prayer insists that we quiet our hearts and wait, slowing us down to receive from God.**

3. **Prayer infuses the vision, enabling us to see what God wants to do.**

4. **Prayer initiates the vision's fulfillment, acting as a catalyst for us to act.**

21 QUALITIES

INITIATIVE Nehemiah Takes the Lead

Nehemiah 1:4—2:8

NEHEMIAH MIGHT have served as the poster boy for the philosophy, "You never have to recover from a good start." He powerfully illustrates the role of initiative in a leader's life.

This godly leader took initiative in praying for Jerusalem's problem, in planning the rebuilding project, in persuading the people to act, and in pursuing the product they all wanted. And he did it in that order. His initiative showed great insight.

Nehemiah couldn't imagine sitting still when he heard the walls of Jerusalem lay in shambles. He had to act. Of all the things a leader should fear, complacency ought to head the list.

But what enables good leaders to initiate? Nehemiah demonstrates that leaders know something in their heart or in their gut that prompts them to move. They don't know everything, but they know enough to act. Nehemiah had insight into the following areas:

1. *He knew how long the project would take* (2:6).
   Nehemiah gave King Artaxerxes a definite time period for his absence.

2. *He knew how to get there* (2:7).
   Nehemiah asked for letters of permission to pass through the provinces beyond the river to Judah.

3. *He knew what he would need to get the job done* (2:8).
   Nehemiah requested timbers from

Asaph to make beams and gates for the wall.

4. *He knew that God's hand was upon him* (2:8).
   Nehemiah got all that he requested because the hand of God rested on him.

Qualities of Initiators

Nehemiah displayed the qualities that make for initiative in leaders:

1. *They know what they want.*
   Desire is the starting point of all achievement. Nehemiah knew that he wanted that wall up.

2. *They push themselves to act.*
   At first, Nehemiah acted alone. He pushed to get the facts that would move others.

3. *They take more risks.*
   Nehemiah took some major risks as he got permission to go, to get wood, and to survey the job.

4. *They make more mistakes.*
   Nehemiah wasn't afraid to mobilize men who weren't professional contractors or soldiers to build and fight.

5. *They go with their gut.*
   What Nehemiah lacked in experience, he made up for with the passion of his heart.

For a negative example of initiative, see p. 1066.

The Law of Timing: Nehemiah Chose the Moment to See the King

Nehemiah 2:1–5

Good leaders understand that timing is everything. Nehemiah spoke to the king about Jerusalem, but not until four months after he first heard about its broken wall. He began praying about the ruined wall in December, but not until April did he approach the king about rebuilding them. What was he waiting on?

No one knows for sure, but Nehemiah might well have been waiting on . . .

1. **His ownership of the burden and vision.**
2. **A foundation of prayer to be laid.**
3. **His own readiness with a plan.**
4. **The king's mental and emotional mood.**
5. **The season when he could move quickly.**
6. **A trust to deepen between him and the king.**

few others. I had not told anyone what my God had put in my heart to do for Jerusalem. There were no mounts with me except the one I was riding on.

[13]By night I went out through the Valley Gate toward the Jackal[a] Well and the Dung Gate, examining the walls of Jerusalem, which had been broken down, and its gates, which had been destroyed by fire. [14]Then I moved on toward the Fountain Gate and the King's Pool, but there was not enough room for my mount to get through; [15]so I went up the valley by night, examining the wall. Finally, I turned back and reentered through the Valley Gate. [16]The officials did not know where I had gone or what I was doing, because as yet I had said nothing to the Jews or the priests or nobles or officials or any others who would be doing the work.

[17]Then I said to them, "You see the trouble we are in: Jerusalem lies in ruins, and its gates have been burned with fire. Come, let us rebuild the wall of Jerusalem, and we will no longer be in disgrace." [18]I also told them about the gracious hand of my God on me and what the king had said to me.

They replied, "Let us start rebuilding." So they began this good work.

[19]But when Sanballat the Horonite, Tobiah the Ammonite official and Geshem the Arab heard about it, they mocked and ridiculed us. "What is this you are doing?" they asked. "Are you rebelling against the king?"

[20]I answered them by saying, "The God of heaven will give us success. We his servants will start rebuilding, but as for you, you have no share in Jerusalem or any claim or historic right to it."

Builders of the Wall

3 Eliashib the high priest and his fellow priests went to work and rebuilt the Sheep Gate. They dedicated it and set its doors in place, building as far as the Tower of the Hundred, which they dedicated, and as far as the Tower of Hananel. [2]The men of Jericho built the adjoining section, and Zakkur son of Imri built next to them.

[3]The Fish Gate was rebuilt by the sons of Hassenaah. They laid its beams and put its doors and bolts and bars in place. [4]Meremoth son of Uriah, the son of Hakkoz, repaired the next section. Next to him Meshullam son of Berekiah,

take, and when will you get back?" It pleased the king to send me; so I set a time.

[7]I also said to him, "If it pleases the king, may I have letters to the governors of Trans-Euphrates, so that they will provide me safe-conduct until I arrive in Judah? [8]And may I have a letter to Asaph, keeper of the royal park, so he will give me timber to make beams for the gates of the citadel by the temple and for the city wall and for the residence I will occupy?" And because the gracious hand of my God was on me, the king granted my requests. [9]So I went to the governors of Trans-Euphrates and gave them the king's letters. The king had also sent army officers and cavalry with me.

[10]When Sanballat the Horonite and Tobiah the Ammonite official heard about this, they were very much disturbed that someone had come to promote the welfare of the Israelites.

Nehemiah Inspects Jerusalem's Walls

[11]I went to Jerusalem, and after staying there three days [12]I set out during the night with a

---

[a] 13 Or Serpent or Fig

585 feet or about 450 meters

The Law of Buy-In: Nehemiah Shares the Why Before the What

Nehemiah 2:5–17

Nehemiah takes three days to size things up in Jerusalem before he speaks to the Jews, the officials, the priests and the nobles. When he does speak, he practices the Law of Buy-In. He knows his countrymen would have to buy in to *him* before they would buy in to his *plan*.

Notice how this man declares the *why* before he explains the *what*. He provides the following reasons to get his colleagues to buy in to his vision for rebuilding the wall:

1. **He had committed himself to oversee the project (2:5).**

2. **Asaph had approved timber for the beams and gates (2:8).**

3. **The situation was a reproach to Israel (2:17).**

4. **The ruined walls could not protect any of them (2:17).**

5. **God's hand was on him and had given him favor (2:18).**

6. **King Artaxerxes had given him permission to come and rebuild (2:18).**

the son of Meshezabel, made repairs, and next to him Zadok son of Baana also made repairs. [5]The next section was repaired by the men of Tekoa, but their nobles would not put their shoulders to the work under their supervisors.[a]

[6]The Jeshanah[b] Gate was repaired by Joiada son of Paseah and Meshullam son of Besodeiah. They laid its beams and put its doors with their bolts and bars in place. [7]Next to them, repairs were made by men from Gibeon and Mizpah — Melatiah of Gibeon and Jadon of Meronoth — places under the authority of the governor of Trans-Euphrates. [8]Uzziel son of Harhaiah, one of the goldsmiths, repaired the next section; and

The Law of Connection: Nehemiah's Construction Follows Connection

Nehemiah 2:17–18

Nehemiah connected with the hearts of his volunteers before asking them to sacrifice their time and energy. He appealed to their sense of dignity, identity and responsibility. The wall went up in record time because he won the hearts of the builders prior to winning the hands of the builders.

Hananiah, one of the perfume-makers, made repairs next to that. They restored Jerusalem as far as the Broad Wall. [9]Rephaiah son of Hur, ruler of a half-district of Jerusalem, repaired the next section. [10]Adjoining this, Jedaiah son of Harumaph made repairs opposite his house, and Hattush son of Hashabneiah made repairs next to him. [11]Malkijah son of Harim and Hasshub son of Pahath-Moab repaired another section and the Tower of the Ovens. [12]Shallum son of Hallohesh, ruler of a half-district of Jerusalem, repaired the next section with the help of his daughters.

[13]The Valley Gate was repaired by Hanun and the residents of Zanoah. They rebuilt it and put its doors with their bolts and bars in place. They also repaired a thousand cubits[c] of the wall as far as the Dung Gate.

[14]The Dung Gate was repaired by Malkijah son of Rekab, ruler of the district of Beth Hakkerem. He rebuilt it and put its doors with their bolts and bars in place.

[15]The Fountain Gate was repaired by Shallun son of Kol-Hozeh, ruler of the district of Mizpah. He rebuilt it, roofing it over and putting its doors and bolts and bars in place. He also repaired the wall of the Pool of Siloam,[d]

---

[a] 5 Or *their Lord* or *the governor*   [b] 6 Or *Old*   [c] 13 That is, about 1,500 feet or about 450 meters   [d] 15 Hebrew *Shelah*, a variant of *Shiloah*, that is, Siloam

NEHEMIAH AND THE LAW OF NAVIGATION   Anyone Can Steer the Ship, but It Takes a Leader to Chart the Course

Nehemiah 1:1—3:32

LEADERS WHO navigate do even more than control the direction in which they and their people travel. They see the whole trip in their minds before they leave the dock. They have a vision for their destination, they understand what it will take to get there, they know who they'll need on the team to be successful, and they recognize the obstacles long before they appear on the horizon.

Sometimes it's difficult balancing optimism and realism, intuition and planning, faith and fact. But that's what it takes to be effective as a navigating leader.

Above everything else, the secret to the Law of Navigation is preparation. When you prepare well, you convey confidence and trust to the people. It's not the size of the project that determines its acceptance, support and success. It's the size of the leader. Leaders who are good navigators are capable of taking their people just about anywhere.

■ ■ ■ ■ ■

It seems remarkable, but Nehemiah could see both the problem and the solution even though he had never visited Jerusalem. That's an incredible characteristic of all great leaders: They have uncommon vision. And that's why they can navigate groups of people.

A leader sees . . .

■ *Farther than others see.* Nehemiah was able to see the problem even

though he lived hundreds of miles away from Jerusalem. And he could picture the solution in his head.

■ *More than others see.* Nehemiah knew that the wall could and should be rebuilt, and he knew what it would take to do it. Before he left Shushan, he asked the king to provide him with letters allowing him to gather materials and granting him safe passage to Judah.

■ *Before others see.* None of Jerusalem's neighbors wanted to see the Jews rebuild their wall, and several enemy leaders conspired against Nehemiah and the people. But Nehemiah saw the danger and planned accordingly; he refused to give in to enemy plots. And when the people sensed danger, he formulated strategies to defend the city and keep the people working at the same time.

The Jews needed only 52 days to rebuild a city wall that had lain in ruins for more than 120 years. And they were able to do it because they had a great leader to navigate for them.

Nehemiah knew his purpose, made his plans, and led the people through the process. His is truly one of the most remarkable stories of leadership ever recorded.

Nehemiah's Navigation

Before the building process could begin,

Nehemiah spent time getting himself and his people ready.

1. **He identified with the problem** (1:2–4). Nehemiah first inquired about the status of the Jews and the wall around Jerusalem. When he heard that the wall remained a rubble and that God's name was being mocked, he wept. The people's problem became his problem and his burden to bear.

2. **He spent time in prayer** (1:4–11). Almost immediately Nehemiah went to his knees to pray. He confessed his wrongdoing and that of the people and he interceded for them. Then he asked for God's favor. No doubt he got the vision and plan to rebuild the wall during his time of connection with God.

3. **He approached the key influencers** (2:1–9). In any leadership endeavor, key people of influence can make or break the whole undertaking. In this case, it was the Persian king Artaxerxes. From him, Nehemiah received not only permission to rebuild the wall, but also resources and support. Nehemiah undoubtedly also selected and approached other key people to take with him.

4. **He assessed the situation** (2:11–15). When he finally arrived in Jerusalem, Nehemiah surveyed firsthand the challenge facing him. He did it quietly, at night, personally assessing the damage and planning the project without interference or unwanted advice.

5. **He met with the people and cast the vision** (2:16–17). We don't know exactly how Nehemiah approached the people or with whom he met first, but we do know he spoke with the Jews, the priests, the nobles, the officials, and the people who did the work. He described his vision for rebuilding the wall and the spiritual ramifications of the project.

6. **He encouraged them with past successes** (2:18). With a task as daunting as the rebuilding of the wall, Nehemiah knew he needed to encourage the people. So he "told them about the gracious hand of [his] God . . . and what the king had said to [him]" (2:18).

7. **He received buy-in from the people** (2:18). Two short sentences record the turning point for the whole rebuilding process: "They replied, 'Let us start rebuilding.' So they began this good work" (2:18). The people had bought in. They dedicated themselves to Nehemiah's leadership and vision.

8. **He organized the people and got them working** (3:1–32). The people didn't work haphazardly. Nehemiah organized them by family and set them to work according to planned priorities, beginning with the city's gates.

Nehemiah put a lot of work into realizing his vision. Without his great leadership and careful planning, the wall may never have been built.

by the King's Garden, as far as the steps going down from the City of David. [16]Beyond him, Nehemiah son of Azbuk, ruler of a half-district of Beth Zur, made repairs up to a point opposite the tombs[a] of David, as far as the artificial pool and the House of the Heroes.

[17]Next to him, the repairs were made by the Levites under Rehum son of Bani. Beside him, Hashabiah, ruler of half the district of Keilah, carried out repairs for his district. [18]Next to him, the repairs were made by their fellow Levites under Binnui[b] son of Henadad, ruler of the other half-district of Keilah. [19]Next to him, Ezer son of Jeshua, ruler of Mizpah, repaired another section, from a point facing the ascent to the armory as far as the angle of the wall. [20]Next to him, Baruch son of Zabbai zealously repaired another section, from the angle to the entrance of the house of Eliashib the high priest. [21]Next to him, Meremoth son of Uriah, the son of Hakkoz, repaired another section, from the entrance of Eliashib's house to the end of it.

[22]The repairs next to him were made by the priests from the surrounding region. [23]Beyond them, Benjamin and Hasshub made repairs in front of their house; and next to them, Azariah son of Maaseiah, the son of Ananiah, made repairs beside his house. [24]Next to him, Binnui son of Henadad repaired another section, from Azariah's house to the angle and the corner,

[25]and Palal son of Uzai worked opposite the angle and the tower projecting from the upper palace near the court of the guard. Next to him, Pedaiah son of Parosh [26]and the temple servants living on the hill of Ophel made repairs up to a point opposite the Water Gate toward the east and the projecting tower. [27]Next to them, the men of Tekoa repaired another section, from the great projecting tower to the wall of Ophel.

[28]Above the Horse Gate, the priests made repairs, each in front of his own house. [29]Next to them, Zadok son of Immer made repairs opposite his house. Next to him, Shemaiah son of Shekaniah, the guard at the East Gate, made repairs. [30]Next to him, Hananiah son of Shelemiah, and Hanun, the sixth son of Zalaph, repaired another section. Next to them, Meshullam son of Berekiah made repairs opposite his living quarters. [31]Next to him, Malkijah, one of the goldsmiths, made repairs as far as the house of the temple servants and the merchants, opposite the Inspection Gate, and as far as the room above the corner; [32]and between the room above the corner and the Sheep Gate the goldsmiths and merchants made repairs.

---

a 16 Hebrew; Septuagint, some Vulgate manuscripts and Syriac *tomb*   *b 18* Two Hebrew manuscripts and Syriac (see also Septuagint and verse 24); most Hebrew manuscripts *Bavvai*

The Law of Priorities: Nehemiah Wisely Uses His Resources

Nehemiah 3:1–32

Thomas Jefferson once said, "No duty the executive has to perform is so trying as to put the right man in the right place." Shortly after his arrival in Jerusalem, we see Nehemiah busily at work putting the right men in the right places.

The text lists specific men as the builders of specific gates. Why? Nehemiah has placed them in stations according to their natural gifts and interests and has them build the portion of the wall right in front of their homes. Talk about self-motivation!

Nehemiah recognized the principles that make organizations progress:

1. **Motivation without organization equals frustration.**

2. **The strongest organizations are the simplest.**

3. **Leaders love everybody, but move with the movers.**

4. **Good organizations establish clear lines of authority.**

5. **People do what you inspect, not what you expect.**

6. **Leaders provide a supportive climate of trust and teamwork.**

7. **Successful organizations recognize and reward effort.**

Opposition to the Rebuilding

4[a] When Sanballat heard that we were rebuilding the wall, he became angry and was greatly incensed. He ridiculed the Jews, [2]and in the presence of his associates and the army of Samaria, he said, "What are those feeble Jews doing? Will they restore their wall? Will they offer sacrifices? Will they finish in a day? Can they bring the stones back to life from those heaps of rubble — burned as they are?"

[3]Tobiah the Ammonite, who was at his side, said, "What they are building — even a fox climbing up on it would break down their wall of stones!"

[4]Hear us, our God, for we are despised. Turn their insults back on their own heads. Give them over as plunder in a land of captivity. [5]Do not cover up their guilt or blot out their sins from your sight, for they have thrown insults in the face of[b] the builders.

[6]So we rebuilt the wall till all of it reached half its height, for the people worked with all their heart.

[7]But when Sanballat, Tobiah, the Arabs, the Ammonites and the people of Ashdod heard that the repairs to Jerusalem's walls had gone ahead and that the gaps were being closed, they were very angry. [8]They all plotted together to come and fight against Jerusalem and stir up trouble against it. [9]But we prayed to our God and posted a guard day and night to meet this threat.

[10]Meanwhile, the people in Judah said, "The strength of the laborers is giving out, and there is so much rubble that we cannot rebuild the wall."

[11]Also our enemies said, "Before they know it or see us, we will be right there among them and will kill them and put an end to the work."

[12]Then the Jews who lived near them came and told us ten times over, "Wherever you turn, they will attack us."

[13]Therefore I stationed some of the people behind the lowest points of the wall at the exposed places, posting them by families, with their swords, spears and bows. [14]After I looked things over, I stood up and said to the nobles, the officials and the rest of the people, "Don't be afraid of them. Remember the Lord, who is great and awesome, and fight for your families, your sons and your daughters, your wives and your homes."

[15]When our enemies heard that we were aware of their plot and that God had frustrated it, we all returned to the wall, each to our own work.

[16]From that day on, half of my men did the work, while the other half were equipped with spears, shields, bows and armor. The officers

---

[a] In Hebrew texts 4:1-6 is numbered 3:33-38, and 4:7-23 is numbered 4:1-17.   [b] 5 Or *have aroused your anger before*

The Law of the Big Mo: Nehemiah's Best Friend

Nehemiah 4:9–20

Momentum is a leader's best friend. When leaders lack momentum, they appear worse than they really are. When they have momentum, they appear better than they really are.

Nehemiah saw his momentum grind to a halt when opponents ridiculed and mocked the wall rebuilding project. Workers became discouraged. After prayer and a word of encouragement from their leader, the work continued, and momentum kicked in once more. Nehemiah regained momentum by these actions:

1. **He prayed for the work and the workers (4:9–10).**

2. **He created a plan to address the problems (4:12–13).**

3. **He called for the best out of his workers (4:14).**

4. **He reminded them of God's help in their divine mission (4:14).**

5. **He provided a new strategy for victory (4:16).**

6. **He furnished new tools (weapons) for the workers (4:16–17).**

7. **He rallied the people to support each other (4:19–20).**

Commitment: How to Beat Your Problems

Nehemiah 4:1—5:13

One of the great tests of leadership is how you handle opposition. Nehemiah faced the usual tactics of the opposition: ridicule (Ne 4:1–3); resistance (4:7–8); and rumor (4:11–12). Nehemiah modeled the right response to all three of these challenges. He . . .

1. **Relied on God (4:4–5).**
2. **Respected the opposition (4:9).**
3. **Reinforced his weak points (4:13).**
4. **Reassured the people (4:14).**
5. **Refused to quit (4:15).**
6. **Renewed the people's strength continually (4:16–23).**

While Nehemiah 4 concerns problems from without, chapter 5 deals with problems from within—disputes about food, property and taxes.

Persistence is the ultimate gauge of our leadership; the secret is to outlast our critics. Nehemiah taught us this lesson by staying committed to his ultimate calling.

posted themselves behind all the people of Judah [17]who were building the wall. Those who carried materials did their work with one hand and held a weapon in the other, [18]and each of the builders wore his sword at his side as he worked. But the man who sounded the trumpet stayed with me.

[19]Then I said to the nobles, the officials and the rest of the people, "The work is extensive and spread out, and we are widely separated from each other along the wall. [20]Wherever you hear the sound of the trumpet, join us there. Our God will fight for us!"

[21]So we continued the work with half the men holding spears, from the first light of dawn till the stars came out. [22]At that time I also said to the people, "Have every man and his helper stay inside Jerusalem at night, so they can serve us as guards by night and as workers by day." [23]Neither I nor my brothers nor my men nor the guards with me took off our clothes; each had his weapon, even when he went for water.[a]

Nehemiah Helps the Poor

5 Now the men and their wives raised a great outcry against their fellow Jews. [2]Some were saying, "We and our sons and daughters are numerous; in order for us to eat and stay alive, we must get grain."

[3]Others were saying, "We are mortgaging our fields, our vineyards and our homes to get grain during the famine."

[4]Still others were saying, "We have had to borrow money to pay the king's tax on our fields and vineyards. [5]Although we are of the same flesh and blood as our fellow Jews and though our children are as good as theirs, yet we have to subject our sons and daughters to slavery. Some of our daughters have already been enslaved, but we are powerless, because our fields and our vineyards belong to others."

[6]When I heard their outcry and these charges, I was very angry. [7]I pondered them in my mind and then accused the nobles and officials. I told them, "You are charging your own people interest!" So I called together a large meeting to deal with them [8]and said: "As far as possible, we have bought back our fellow Jews who were sold to the Gentiles. Now you are selling your own people, only for them to be sold back to us!" They kept quiet, because they could find nothing to say.

[9]So I continued, "What you are doing is not right. Shouldn't you walk in the fear of our God to avoid the reproach of our Gentile enemies? [10]I and my brothers and my men are also lending the people money and grain. But let us stop charging interest! [11]Give back to them immediately their fields, vineyards, olive groves and houses, and also the interest you are charging them — one percent of the money, grain, new wine and olive oil."

---

[a] 23 The meaning of the Hebrew for this clause is uncertain.

¹²"We will give it back," they said. "And we will not demand anything more from them. We will do as you say."

Then I summoned the priests and made the nobles and officials take an oath to do what they had promised. ¹³I also shook out the folds of my robe and said, "In this way may God shake out of his house and possessions anyone who does not keep this promise. So may such a person be shaken out and emptied!"

At this the whole assembly said, "Amen," and praised the LORD. And the people did as they had promised.

¹⁴Moreover, from the twentieth year of King Artaxerxes, when I was appointed to be their governor in the land of Judah, until his thirty-second year—twelve years—neither I nor my brothers ate the food allotted to the governor. ¹⁵But the earlier governors—those preceding me—placed a heavy burden on the people and took forty shekels[a] of silver from them in addition to food and wine. Their assistants also lorded it over the people. But out of reverence for God I did not act like that. ¹⁶Instead, I devoted myself to the work on this wall. All my men were assembled there for the work; we[b] did not acquire any land.

¹⁷Furthermore, a hundred and fifty Jews and officials ate at my table, as well as those who came to us from the surrounding nations. ¹⁸Each day one ox, six choice sheep and some poultry were prepared for me, and every ten days an abundant supply of wine of all kinds. In spite of all this, I never demanded the food allot- ted to the governor, because the demands were heavy on these people.

¹⁹Remember me with favor, my God, for all I have done for these people.

Further Opposition to the Rebuilding

6 When word came to Sanballat, Tobiah, Geshem the Arab and the rest of our enemies that I had rebuilt the wall and not a gap was left in it—though up to that time I had not set the doors in the gates— ²Sanballat and Geshem sent me this message: "Come, let us meet together in one of the villages[c] on the plain of Ono."

But they were scheming to harm me; ³so I sent messengers to them with this reply: "I am carrying on a great project and cannot go down. Why should the work stop while I leave it and go down to you?" ⁴Four times they sent me the same message, and each time I gave them the same answer.

⁵Then, the fifth time, Sanballat sent his aide to me with the same message, and in his hand was an unsealed letter ⁶in which was written:

> "It is reported among the nations—and Geshem[d] says it is true—that you and the Jews are plotting to revolt, and therefore you are building the wall. Moreover, according to these reports you are about to

---

[a] 15 That is, about 1 pound or about 460 grams   [b] 16 Most Hebrew manuscripts; some Hebrew manuscripts, Septuagint, Vulgate and Syriac *I*   [c] 2 Or *in Kephirim*   [d] 6 Hebrew *Gashmu,* a variant of *Geshem*

The Law of Victory: Nehemiah Finishes the Wall in Record Time

Nehemiah 5:14—6:9

Nehemiah did nearly everything right as a leader. He never distanced himself from his people by eating from the governor's allowance; he didn't levy heavy taxes; he stayed committed to hands-on construction; and he refused to buy real estate, unlike previous governors (Ne 5:14–19).

As the wall neared completion, Sanballat and Tobiah invited Nehemiah to come down from his work for a chat. He responded, "I am carrying on a great project and cannot go down. Why should the work stop while I leave it and go down to you?" (Ne 6:3). Before long the wall was completed, finished in record time. We can learn at least four significant leadership lessons from studying Nehemiah's leadership:

1. **The quickest way to stop a great work is to stop a great leader.**

2. **Problems and projects seem to go together.**

3. **The tide turns once the project is successful.**

4. **A successful project will bring glory to God.**

become their king ⁷and have even appointed prophets to make this proclamation about you in Jerusalem: 'There is a king in Judah!' Now this report will get back to the king; so come, let us meet together."

⁸I sent him this reply: "Nothing like what you are saying is happening; you are just making it up out of your head."

⁹They were all trying to frighten us, thinking, "Their hands will get too weak for the work, and it will not be completed."

But I prayed, "Now strengthen my hands."

¹⁰One day I went to the house of Shemaiah son of Delaiah, the son of Mehetabel, who was shut in at his home. He said, "Let us meet in the house of God, inside the temple, and let us close the temple doors, because men are coming to kill you—by night they are coming to kill you."

¹¹But I said, "Should a man like me run away? Or should someone like me go into the temple to save his life? I will not go!" ¹²I realized that God had not sent him, but that he had prophesied against me because Tobiah and Sanballat had hired him. ¹³He had been hired to intimidate me so that I would commit a sin by doing

this, and then they would give me a bad name to discredit me.

¹⁴Remember Tobiah and Sanballat, my God, because of what they have done; remember also the prophet Noadiah and how she and the rest of the prophets have been trying to intimidate me. ¹⁵So the wall was completed on the twenty-fifth of Elul, in fifty-two days.

Opposition to the Completed Wall

¹⁶When all our enemies heard about this, all the surrounding nations were afraid and lost their self-confidence, because they realized that this work had been done with the help of our God.

¹⁷Also, in those days the nobles of Judah were sending many letters to Tobiah, and replies from Tobiah kept coming to them. ¹⁸For many in Judah were under oath to him, since he was son-in-law to Shekaniah son of Arah, and his son Jehohanan had married the daughter of Meshullam son of Berekiah. ¹⁹Moreover, they kept reporting to me his good deeds and then telling him what I said. And Tobiah sent letters to intimidate me.

SANBALLAT — The Great Distracter
Nehemiah 4:1–23; 6:1–19

Nehemiah had to contend with the same kind of pest that plagues most true leaders today: distracters who torment and do everything possible to interfere in the work of the kingdom. Sanballat played this distracting role in the life of Nehemiah.

Soon after the wall around Jerusalem started going up, word reached Sanballat of the construction. He knew that the repair of the wall and the restoration of Jerusalem would bring a major shift in commerce and political power. Sanballat liked the status quo and had a vested interest in Jerusalem remaining in disrepair, so he set about his distracting work.

Sanballat first tried to stop the work by mocking and ridiculing the Jews. When that didn't work, this evil but resourceful leader adjusted his strategies. He shifted his tactics to fear, entrapment and political maneuvering.

The contrast between Nehemiah and Sanballat could hardly be more pronounced. Nehemiah's leadership and character countered every assault of Sanballat and provided the impetus for his godly vision to be completed.

Contemporary leaders can learn several valuable lessons from studying Sanballat's assaults, threats and schemes:

- Expect distracters.
- Don't give them the time of day.
- Trust God to protect you and your reputation.
- Keep your hands to the plow and don't look back.

PROFILE in leadership

Commitment: Four Characteristics of Those Who Complete a Task

Nehemiah 6:15–16

Commitment comes before anything else in a leader's life. Because Nehemiah had it and drew it out of others, the people finished the wall in 52 days, despite many adversities. Their great accomplishment so thrilled Nehemiah that he wrote, "When all our enemies heard about this, all the surrounding nations were afraid and lost their self-confidence, because they realized that this work had been done with the help of our God" (Ne 6:16).

Leaders who complete a task possess at least four characteristics:

1. **A compelling purpose: They make a great commitment to a great cause.**

2. **A clear perspective: They don't let fear cloud their view of the future.**

3. **A continual prayer: They pray about everything and gain God's favor.**

4. **A courageous persistence: They move ahead despite the odds.**

7 After the wall had been rebuilt and I had set the doors in place, the gatekeepers, the musicians and the Levites were appointed. ²I put in charge of Jerusalem my brother Hanani, along with Hananiah the commander of the citadel, because he was a man of integrity and feared God more than most people do. ³I said to them, "The gates of Jerusalem are not to be opened until the sun is hot. While the gatekeepers are still on duty, have them shut the doors and bar them. Also appoint residents of Jerusalem as guards, some at their posts and some near their own houses."

The List of the Exiles Who Returned

⁴Now the city was large and spacious, but there were few people in it, and the houses had not yet been rebuilt. ⁵So my God put it into my heart to assemble the nobles, the officials and the common people for registration by families. I found the genealogical record of those who had been the first to return. This is what I found written there:

⁶These are the people of the province who came up from the captivity of the exiles whom Nebuchadnezzar king of Babylon had taken captive (they returned to Jerusalem and Judah, each to his own town, ⁷in company with Zerubbabel, Joshua, Nehemiah, Azariah, Raamiah, Nahamani, Mordecai, Bilshan, Mispereth, Bigvai, Nehum and Baanah):

The list of the men of Israel:

⁸the descendants of Parosh	2,172
⁹of Shephatiah	372
¹⁰of Arah	652
¹¹of Pahath-Moab (through the line of Jeshua and Joab)	2,818
¹²of Elam	1,254
¹³of Zattu	845
¹⁴of Zakkai	760
¹⁵of Binnui	648
¹⁶of Bebai	628
¹⁷of Azgad	2,322
¹⁸of Adonikam	667
¹⁹of Bigvai	2,067
²⁰of Adin	655
²¹of Ater (through Hezekiah)	98
²²of Hashum	328
²³of Bezai	324
²⁴of Hariph	112
²⁵of Gibeon	95
²⁶the men of Bethlehem and Netophah	188
²⁷of Anathoth	128
²⁸of Beth Azmaveth	42
²⁹of Kiriath Jearim, Kephirah and Beeroth	743
³⁰of Ramah and Geba	621
³¹of Mikmash	122
³²of Bethel and Ai	123
³³of the other Nebo	52
³⁴of the other Elam	1,254
³⁵of Harim	320

Changing with the Times
Nehemiah 7:1-2

Two emotions usually follow a great achievement: first, a sigh of relief and celebration; and second, a sense of . . . *now what?*

How we handle achievement tells us a lot about our character. The period following a success can become a dangerous time. Sometimes we feel tempted toward complacency, especially if we lack another goal. We can become satisfied and let down our guard. Momentum leaks.

The moment of victory is a crucial time for any organization. The leader must be able to change—or face a transitional problem. The transitional problem occurs when the leader does not know how to grow with the organization. Nehemiah's life illustrates the problem:

Two Types of Leadership Seasons

1. Catalyst: Gets it going
2. Designer: Thinks it up
3. Motivator: Encourages
4. Entrepreneur: Relies on self

1. Consolidator: Keeps it going
2. Developer: Follows it up
3. Manager: Organizes
4. Executive: Relies on others

---

³⁶ of Jericho — 345
³⁷ of Lod, Hadid and Ono — 721
³⁸ of Senaah — 3,930

³⁹ The priests:

the descendants of Jedaiah
(through the family of Jeshua) — 973
⁴⁰ of Immer — 1,052
⁴¹ of Pashhur — 1,247
⁴² of Harim — 1,017

⁴³ The Levites:

the descendants of Jeshua (through
Kadmiel through the line of
Hodaviah) — 74

⁴⁴ The musicians:

the descendants of Asaph — 148

⁴⁵ The gatekeepers:

the descendants of
Shallum, Ater, Talmon, Akkub,
Hatita and Shobai — 138

⁴⁶ The temple servants:

the descendants of
Ziha, Hasupha, Tabbaoth,
⁴⁷ Keros, Sia, Padon,
⁴⁸ Lebana, Hagaba, Shalmai,
⁴⁹ Hanan, Giddel, Gahar,
⁵⁰ Reaiah, Rezin, Nekoda,
⁵¹ Gazzam, Uzza, Paseah,

⁵² Besai, Meunim, Nephusim,
⁵³ Bakbuk, Hakupha, Harhur,
⁵⁴ Bazluth, Mehida, Harsha,
⁵⁵ Barkos, Sisera, Temah,
⁵⁶ Neziah and Hatipha

⁵⁷ The descendants of the servants of Solomon:

the descendants of
Sotai, Sophereth, Perida,
⁵⁸ Jaala, Darkon, Giddel,
⁵⁹ Shephatiah, Hattil,
Pokereth-Hazzebaim and Amon

⁶⁰ The temple servants and the
descendants of the servants of
Solomon — 392

⁶¹ The following came up from the towns of Tel Melah, Tel Harsha, Kerub, Addon and Immer, but they could not show that their families were descended from Israel:

⁶² the descendants of
Delaiah, Tobiah and Nekoda — 642

⁶³ And from among the priests:

the descendants of
Hobaiah, Hakkoz and Barzillai (a man who had married a daughter of Barzillai the Gileadite and was called by that name).

⁶⁴ These searched for their family records, but they could not find them and so

were excluded from the priesthood as unclean. ⁶⁵The governor, therefore, ordered them not to eat any of the most sacred food until there should be a priest ministering with the Urim and Thummim.

⁶⁶The whole company numbered 42,360, ⁶⁷besides their 7,337 male and female slaves; and they also had 245 male and female singers. ⁶⁸There were 736 horses, 245 mules,ᵃ ⁶⁹435 camels and 6,720 donkeys.

⁷⁰Some of the heads of the families contributed to the work. The governor gave to the treasury 1,000 daricsᵇ of gold, 50 bowls and 530 garments for priests. ⁷¹Some of the heads of the families gave to the treasury for the work 20,000 daricsᶜ of gold and 2,200 minasᵈ of silver. ⁷²The total given by the rest of the people was 20,000 darics of gold, 2,000 minasᵉ of silver and 67 garments for priests.

⁷³The priests, the Levites, the gatekeepers, the musicians and the temple servants, along with certain of the people and the rest of the Israelites, settled in their own towns.

Ezra Reads the Law

When the seventh month came and the Israelites had settled in their towns, ¹all the people came together as one in the square before the Water Gate. They told Ezra the teacher of the Law to bring out the Book of the Law of Moses, which the LORD had commanded for Israel.

²So on the first day of the seventh month Ezra the priest brought the Law before the assembly, which was made up of men and women and all who were able to understand. ³He read it aloud from daybreak till noon as he faced the square before the Water Gate in the presence of the men, women and others who could understand. And all the people listened attentively to the Book of the Law.

⁴Ezra the teacher of the Law stood on a high wooden platform built for the occasion. Beside him on his right stood Mattithiah, Shema, Anaiah, Uriah, Hilkiah and Maaseiah; and on his left were Pedaiah, Mishael, Malkijah, Hashum, Hashbaddanah, Zechariah and Meshullam.

⁵Ezra opened the book. All the people could see him because he was standing above them; and as he opened it, the people all stood up. ⁶Ezra praised the LORD, the great God; and all the people lifted their hands and responded, "Amen! Amen!" Then they bowed down and worshiped the LORD with their faces to the ground.

⁷The Levites—Jeshua, Bani, Sherebiah, Jamin, Akkub, Shabbethai, Hodiah, Maaseiah, Kelita, Azariah, Jozabad, Hanan and Pelaiah—instructed the people in the Law while the people were standing there. ⁸They read from the Book of the Law of God, making it clearᶠ and giving the meaning so that the people understood what was being read.

⁹Then Nehemiah the governor, Ezra the priest and teacher of the Law, and the Levites who were instructing the people said to them all, "This day is holy to the LORD your God. Do not mourn or weep." For all the people had been weeping as they listened to the words of the Law.

¹⁰Nehemiah said, "Go and enjoy choice food and sweet drinks, and send some to those who have nothing prepared. This day is holy to our Lord. Do not grieve, for the joy of the LORD is your strength."

¹¹The Levites calmed all the people, saying, "Be still, for this is a holy day. Do not grieve."

¹²Then all the people went away to eat and drink, to send portions of food and to celebrate with great joy, because they now understood the words that had been made known to them.

¹³On the second day of the month, the heads of all the families, along with the priests and the Levites, gathered around Ezra the teacher to give attention to the words of the Law. ¹⁴They found written in the Law, which the LORD had commanded through Moses, that the Israelites were to live in temporary shelters during the festival of the seventh month ¹⁵and that they should proclaim this word and spread it throughout

---

ᵃ 68 Some Hebrew manuscripts (see also Ezra 2:66); most Hebrew manuscripts do not have this verse.   ᵇ 70 That is, about 19 pounds or about 8.4 kilograms   ᶜ 71 That is, about 375 pounds or about 170 kilograms; also in verse 72   ᵈ 71 That is, about 1 1/3 tons or about 1.2 metric tons   ᵉ 72 That is, about 1 1/4 tons or about 1.1 metric tons   ᶠ 8 Or God, translating it

The Practical Leader

Nehemiah 8:8

Nehemiah and Ezra both wanted the rebuilt wall to symbolize rebuilt spiritual lives. "They read from the Book of the Law of God, making it clear and giving the meaning so that the people understood what was being read" (Ne 8:8). These leaders wanted their people to understand and apply what they heard.

their towns and in Jerusalem: "Go out into the hill country and bring back branches from olive and wild olive trees, and from myrtles, palms and shade trees, to make temporary shelters" — as it is written.[a]

[16] So the people went out and brought back branches and built themselves temporary shelters on their own roofs, in their courtyards, in the courts of the house of God and in the square by the Water Gate and the one by the Gate of Ephraim. [17] The whole company that had returned from exile built temporary shelters and lived in them. From the days of Joshua son of Nun until that day, the Israelites had not celebrated it like this. And their joy was very great.

[18] Day after day, from the first day to the last, Ezra read from the Book of the Law of God. They celebrated the festival for seven days, and on the eighth day, in accordance with the regulation, there was an assembly.

The Israelites Confess Their Sins

9 On the twenty-fourth day of the same month, the Israelites gathered together, fasting and wearing sackcloth and putting dust on their heads. [2] Those of Israelite descent had separated themselves from all foreigners. They stood in their places and confessed their sins and the sins of their ancestors. [3] They stood where they were and read from the Book of the Law of the LORD their God for a quarter of the day, and spent another quarter in confession and in worshiping the LORD their God. [4] Standing on the stairs of the Levites were Jeshua, Bani, Kadmiel, Shebaniah, Bunni, Sherebiah, Bani and Kenani. They cried out with loud voices to the LORD their God. [5] And the Levites — Jeshua, Kadmiel, Bani, Hashabneiah, Sherebiah, Hodiah, Shebaniah and Pethahiah — said: "Stand up and praise the LORD your God, who is from everlasting to everlasting.[b]"

"Blessed be your glorious name, and may it be exalted above all blessing and praise. [6] You alone are the LORD. You made the heavens, even the highest heavens, and all their starry host, the earth and all that is on it, the seas and all that is in them. You give life to everything, and the multitudes of heaven worship you.

[7] "You are the LORD God, who chose Abram and brought him out of Ur of the Chaldeans and named him Abraham. [8] You found his heart faithful to you, and you made a covenant with him to give to his descendants the land of the Canaanites, Hittites, Amorites, Perizzites, Jebusites and Girgashites. You have kept your promise because you are righteous.

[9] "You saw the suffering of our ancestors in Egypt; you heard their cry at the Red Sea.[c] [10] You sent signs and wonders against Pharaoh, against all his officials and all the people of his land, for you knew how arrogantly the Egyptians treated them. You made a name for yourself, which remains to this day. [11] You divided the sea before them, so that they passed through it on dry ground, but you hurled their pursuers into the depths, like a stone into mighty waters. [12] By day you led them with a pillar of cloud, and by night with a pillar of fire to give them light on the way they were to take.

[13] "You came down on Mount Sinai; you spoke to them from heaven. You gave them regulations and laws that are just and right, and decrees and commands that are good. [14] You made known to them your holy Sabbath and gave them commands, decrees and laws through your servant Moses. [15] In their hunger you gave them bread from heaven and in their thirst you brought them water from the rock; you told them to go in and take possession of the land you had sworn with uplifted hand to give them.

[16] "But they, our ancestors, became arrogant and stiff-necked, and they did not obey your commands. [17] They refused to listen and failed to remember the miracles you performed among them. They became stiff-necked and in their rebellion appointed a leader in order to return to their slavery. But you are a forgiving God, gracious and compassionate, slow to anger and abounding in love. Therefore you did not desert them, [18] even when they cast for themselves an image of a calf and said, 'This is your god, who brought you up out of Egypt,' or when they committed awful blasphemies.

[19] "Because of your great compassion you did not abandon them in the wilderness. By day the pillar of cloud did not fail to guide them on their path, nor the pillar of fire by night to shine on the way they were to take. [20] You gave your good Spir-

---

[a] 15 See Lev. 23:37-40.   [b] 5 Or God for ever and ever
[c] 9 Or the Sea of Reeds

it to instruct them. You did not withhold your manna from their mouths, and you gave them water for their thirst. [21]For forty years you sustained them in the wilderness; they lacked nothing, their clothes did not wear out nor did their feet become swollen.

[22]"You gave them kingdoms and nations, allotting to them even the remotest frontiers. They took over the country of Sihon[a] king of Heshbon and the country of Og king of Bashan. [23]You made their children as numerous as the stars in the sky, and you brought them into the land that you told their parents to enter and possess. [24]Their children went in and took possession of the land. You subdued before them the Canaanites, who lived in the land; you gave the Canaanites into their hands, along with their kings and the peoples of the land, to deal with them as they pleased. [25]They captured fortified cities and fertile land; they took possession of houses filled with all kinds of good things, wells already dug, vineyards, olive groves and fruit trees in abundance. They ate to the full and were well-nourished; they reveled in your great goodness.

[26]"But they were disobedient and rebelled against you; they turned their backs on your law. They killed your prophets, who had warned them in order to turn them back to you; they committed awful blasphemies. [27]So you delivered them into the hands of their enemies, who oppressed them. But when they were oppressed they cried out to you. From heaven you heard them, and in your great compassion you gave them deliverers, who rescued them from the hand of their enemies.

[28]"But as soon as they were at rest, they again did what was evil in your sight. Then you abandoned them to the hand of their enemies so that they ruled over them. And when they cried out to you again, you heard from heaven, and in your compassion you delivered them time after time.

[29]"You warned them in order to turn them back to your law, but they became arrogant and disobeyed your commands. They sinned against your ordinances, of which you said, 'The person who obeys them will live by them.' Stubbornly they turned their backs on you, became stiff-necked and refused to listen. [30]For

many years you were patient with them. By your Spirit you warned them through your prophets. Yet they paid no attention, so you gave them into the hands of the neighboring peoples. [31]But in your great mercy you did not put an end to them or abandon them, for you are a gracious and merciful God.

[32]"Now therefore, our God, the great God, mighty and awesome, who keeps his covenant of love, do not let all this hardship seem trifling in your eyes — the hardship that has come on us, on our kings and leaders, on our priests and prophets, on our ancestors and all your people, from the days of the kings of Assyria until today. [33]In all that has happened to us, you have remained righteous; you have acted faithfully, while we acted wickedly. [34]Our kings, our leaders, our priests and our ancestors did not follow your law; they did not pay attention to your commands or the statutes you warned them to keep. [35]Even while they were in their kingdom, enjoying your great goodness to them in the spacious and fertile land you gave them, they did not serve you or turn from their evil ways.

[36]"But see, we are slaves today, slaves in the land you gave our ancestors so they could eat its fruit and the other good things it produces. [37]Because of our sins, its abundant harvest goes to the kings you have placed over us. They rule over our bodies and our cattle as they please. We are in great distress.

The Agreement of the People

[38]"In view of all this, we are making a binding agreement, putting it in writing, and our leaders, our Levites and our priests are affixing their seals to it."[b]

10[c] Those who sealed it were:

Nehemiah the governor, the son of Hakaliah.

Zedekiah, [2]Seraiah, Azariah, Jeremiah, [3]Pashhur, Amariah, Malkijah, [4]Hattush, Shebaniah, Malluk,

---

[a] 22 One Hebrew manuscript and Septuagint; most Hebrew manuscripts *Sihon, that is, the country of the*   [b] 38 In Hebrew texts this verse (9:38) is numbered 10:1.   [c] In Hebrew texts 10:1-39 is numbered 10:2-40.

5 Harim, Meremoth, Obadiah,
6 Daniel, Ginnethon, Baruch,
7 Meshullam, Abijah, Mijamin,
8 Maaziah, Bilgai and Shemaiah.
These were the priests.

9 The Levites:

Jeshua son of Azaniah, Binnui of the sons
of Henadad, Kadmiel,
10 and their associates: Shebaniah,
Hodiah, Kelita, Pelaiah, Hanan,
11 Mika, Rehob, Hashabiah,
12 Zakkur, Sherebiah, Shebaniah,
13 Hodiah, Bani and Beninu.

14 The leaders of the people:

Parosh, Pahath-Moab, Elam, Zattu, Bani,
15 Bunni, Azgad, Bebai,
16 Adonijah, Bigvai, Adin,
17 Ater, Hezekiah, Azzur,
18 Hodiah, Hashum, Bezai,
19 Hariph, Anathoth, Nebai,
20 Magpiash, Meshullam, Hezir,
21 Meshezabel, Zadok, Jaddua,
22 Pelatiah, Hanan, Anaiah,
23 Hoshea, Hananiah, Hasshub,
24 Hallohesh, Pilha, Shobek,
25 Rehum, Hashabnah, Maaseiah,
26 Ahiah, Hanan, Anan,
27 Malluk, Harim and Baanah.

28 "The rest of the people — priests, Levites, gatekeepers, musicians, temple servants and all who separated themselves from the neighboring peoples for the sake of the Law of God, together with their wives and all their sons and daughters who are able to understand — 29 all these now join their fellow Israelites the nobles, and bind themselves with a curse and an oath to follow the Law of God given through Moses the servant of God and to obey carefully all the commands, regulations and decrees of the LORD our Lord.

30 "We promise not to give our daughters in marriage to the peoples around us or take their daughters for our sons.

31 "When the neighboring peoples bring merchandise or grain to sell on the Sabbath, we will not buy from them on the Sabbath or on any holy day. Every seventh year we will forgo working the land and will cancel all debts.

32 "We assume the responsibility for carrying out the commands to give a third of a shekel*a* each year for the service of the house of our God: 33 for the bread set out on the table; for the regular grain offerings and burnt offerings; for the offerings

---

a 32 That is, about 1/8 ounce or about 4 grams

NEHEMIAH

Committed to the Way of God
Nehemiah 10:1–29

PROFILE in leadership

Nehemiah and the rest of Israel's leaders well understood the gravity of entering into covenants, making promises, and signing contracts. So can there be any doubt that a reverent hush fell over them when they determined together to sign a covenant with the true and living God?

After Nehemiah had led his countrymen through a time of confession and repentance, the governor decided it was time to commit themselves to obey the laws and commands that God had given Israel so long before. It was time to commit their hearts to the Lord himself.

Nehemiah made sure the people did not sign this agreement lightly. Following the example of Moses centuries earlier, he urged the people to swear an oath to God, accepting both blessings for obedience and curses for rebellion. They promised to faithfully adhere to every word of God's Law and not deviate from it in any way (Ne 10:29).

As governor and top leader of his people, Nehemiah signed the document first. In doing so, he showed his commitment to sticking with the agreement and set an example for the rest of the leadership and the nation. As always, he acted as a "leader's leader."

When leaders step forward the way Nehemiah did, they make possible a climate for renewal and revival. Even today we rightly look to him as an example of true leadership.

on the Sabbaths, at the New Moon feasts and at the appointed festivals; for the holy offerings; for sin offerings[a] to make atonement for Israel; and for all the duties of the house of our God.

[34]"We — the priests, the Levites and the people — have cast lots to determine when each of our families is to bring to the house of our God at set times each year a contribution of wood to burn on the altar of the LORD our God, as it is written in the Law.

[35]"We also assume responsibility for bringing to the house of the LORD each year the firstfruits of our crops and of every fruit tree.

[36]"As it is also written in the Law, we will bring the firstborn of our sons and of our cattle, of our herds and of our flocks to the house of our God, to the priests ministering there.

[37]"Moreover, we will bring to the storerooms of the house of our God, to the priests, the first of our ground meal, of our grain offerings, of the fruit of all our trees and of our new wine and olive oil. And we will bring a tithe of our crops to the Levites, for it is the Levites who collect the tithes in all the towns where we work. [38]A priest descended from Aaron is to accompany the Levites when they receive the tithes, and the Levites are to bring a tenth of the tithes up to the house of our God, to the storerooms of the treasury. [39]The people of Israel, including the Levites, are to bring their contributions of grain, new wine and olive oil to the storerooms, where the articles for the sanctuary and for the ministering priests, the gatekeepers and the musicians are also kept.

"We will not neglect the house of our God."

The New Residents of Jerusalem

11 Now the leaders of the people settled in Jerusalem. The rest of the people cast lots to bring one out of every ten of them to live in Jerusalem, the holy city, while the remaining nine were to stay in their own towns. [2]The people commended all who volunteered to live in Jerusalem.

[3]These are the provincial leaders who settled in Jerusalem (now some Israelites, priests, Levites, temple servants and descendants of Solomon's servants lived in the towns of Judah, each on their own property in the various towns,

[4]while other people from both Judah and Benjamin lived in Jerusalem):

From the descendants of Judah:

Athaiah son of Uzziah, the son of Zechariah, the son of Amariah, the son of Shephatiah, the son of Mahalalel, a descendant of Perez; [5]and Maaseiah son of Baruch, the son of Kol-Hozeh, the son of Hazaiah, the son of Adaiah, the son of Joiarib, the son of Zechariah, a descendant of Shelah. [6]The descendants of Perez who lived in Jerusalem totaled 468 men of standing.

[7]From the descendants of Benjamin:

Sallu son of Meshullam, the son of Joed, the son of Pedaiah, the son of Kolaiah, the son of Maaseiah, the son of Ithiel, the son of Jeshaiah, [8]and his followers, Gabbai and Sallai — 928 men. [9]Joel son of Zikri was their chief officer, and Judah son of Hassenuah was over the New Quarter of the city.

[10]From the priests:

Jedaiah; the son of Joiarib; Jakin; [11]Seraiah son of Hilkiah, the son of Meshullam, the son of Zadok, the son of Meraioth, the son of Ahitub, the official in charge of the house of God, [12]and their associates, who carried on work for the temple — 822 men; Adaiah son of Jeroham, the son of Pelaliah, the son of Amzi, the son of Zechariah, the son of Pashhur, the son of Malkijah, [13]and his associates, who were heads of families — 242 men; Amashsai son of Azarel, the son of Ahzai, the son of Meshillemoth, the son of Immer, [14]and his[b] associates, who were men of standing — 128. Their chief officer was Zabdiel son of Haggedolim.

[15]From the Levites:

Shemaiah son of Hasshub, the son of Azrikam, the son of Hashabiah, the son of Bunni; [16]Shabbethai and Jozabad, two of the heads of the Levites, who had charge of the outside work of the house of God; [17]Mattaniah son of Mika, the son of Zabdi, the son of Asaph, the director who led in thanksgiving and prayer; Bakbukiah, second among his associates; and Abda son of Shammua, the son of Galal, the son of

---

[a] 33 Or purification offerings   [b] 14 Most Septuagint manuscripts; Hebrew their

Jeduthun. [18]The Levites in the holy city totaled 284.

[19]The gatekeepers:

Akkub, Talmon and their associates, who kept watch at the gates — 172 men.

[20]The rest of the Israelites, with the priests and Levites, were in all the towns of Judah, each on their ancestral property.

[21]The temple servants lived on the hill of Ophel, and Ziha and Gishpa were in charge of them.

[22]The chief officer of the Levites in Jerusalem was Uzzi son of Bani, the son of Hashabiah, the son of Mattaniah, the son of Mika. Uzzi was one of Asaph's descendants, who were the musicians responsible for the service of the house of God. [23]The musicians were under the king's orders, which regulated their daily activity.

[24]Pethahiah son of Meshezabel, one of the descendants of Zerah son of Judah, was the king's agent in all affairs relating to the people.

[25]As for the villages with their fields, some of the people of Judah lived in Kiriath Arba and its surrounding settlements, in Dibon and its settlements, in Jekabzeel and its villages, [26]in Jeshua, in Moladah, in Beth Pelet, [27]in Hazar Shual, in Beersheba and its settlements, [28]in Ziklag, in Mekonah and its settlements, [29]in En Rimmon, in Zorah, in Jarmuth, [30]Zanoah, Adullam and their villages, in Lachish and its fields, and in Azekah and its settlements. So they were living all the way from Beersheba to the Valley of Hinnom.

[31]The descendants of the Benjamites from Geba lived in Mikmash, Aija, Bethel and its settlements, [32]in Anathoth, Nob and Ananiah, [33]in Hazor, Ramah and Gittaim, [34]in Hadid, Zeboim and Neballat, [35]in Lod and Ono, and in Ge Harashim.

[36]Some of the divisions of the Levites of Judah settled in Benjamin.

Priests and Levites

12 These were the priests and Levites who returned with Zerubbabel son of Shealtiel and with Joshua:

Seraiah, Jeremiah, Ezra,
[2]Amariah, Malluk, Hattush,
[3]Shekaniah, Rehum, Meremoth,
[4]Iddo, Ginnethon,[a] Abijah,
[5]Mijamin,[b] Moadiah, Bilgah,
[6]Shemaiah, Joiarib, Jedaiah,
[7]Sallu, Amok, Hilkiah and Jedaiah.

These were the leaders of the priests and their associates in the days of Joshua.

[8]The Levites were Jeshua, Binnui, Kadmiel, Sherebiah, Judah, and also Mattaniah, who, together with his associates, was in charge of the songs of thanksgiving. [9]Bakbukiah and Unni, their associates, stood opposite them in the services.

[10]Joshua was the father of Joiakim, Joiakim the father of Eliashib, Eliashib the father of Joiada, [11]Joiada the father of Jonathan, and Jonathan the father of Jaddua.

[12]In the days of Joiakim, these were the heads of the priestly families:

of Seraiah's family, Meraiah;
of Jeremiah's, Hananiah;
[13]of Ezra's, Meshullam;
of Amariah's, Jehohanan;
[14]of Malluk's, Jonathan;
of Shekaniah's,[c] Joseph;
[15]of Harim's, Adna;
of Meremoth's,[d] Helkai;
[16]of Iddo's, Zechariah;
of Ginnethon's, Meshullam;
[17]of Abijah's, Zikri;
of Miniamin's and of Moadiah's, Piltai;
[18]of Bilgah's, Shammua;
of Shemaiah's, Jehonathan;
[19]of Joiarib's, Mattenai;
of Jedaiah's, Uzzi;
[20]of Sallu's, Kallai;
of Amok's, Eber;
[21]of Hilkiah's, Hashabiah;
of Jedaiah's, Nethanel.

[22]The family heads of the Levites in the days of Eliashib, Joiada, Johanan and Jaddua, as well as those of the priests, were recorded in the reign of Darius the Persian. [23]The family heads among the descendants of Levi up to the time of Johanan son of Eliashib were recorded in the book of the annals. [24]And the leaders of the Levites were Hashabiah, Sherebiah, Jeshua son of Kadmiel, and their associates, who stood opposite them to give praise and thanksgiving, one section responding to the other, as prescribed by David the man of God.

[25]Mattaniah, Bakbukiah, Obadiah, Meshullam, Talmon and Akkub were gatekeepers who guarded the storerooms at the gates. [26]They

---

[a] 4 Many Hebrew manuscripts and Vulgate (see also verse 16); most Hebrew manuscripts *Ginnethoi*   [b] 5 A variant of *Miniamin*   [c] 14 Very many Hebrew manuscripts, some Septuagint manuscripts and Syriac (see also verse 3); most Hebrew manuscripts *Shebaniah's*   [d] 15 Some Septuagint manuscripts (see also verse 3); Hebrew *Meraioth's*

served in the days of Joiakim son of Joshua, the son of Jozadak, and in the days of Nehemiah the governor and of Ezra the priest, the teacher of the Law.

Dedication of the Wall of Jerusalem

²⁷At the dedication of the wall of Jerusalem, the Levites were sought out from where they lived and were brought to Jerusalem to celebrate joyfully the dedication with songs of thanksgiving and with the music of cymbals, harps and lyres. ²⁸The musicians also were brought together from the region around Jerusalem — from the villages of the Netophathites, ²⁹from Beth Gilgal, and from the area of Geba and Azmaveth, for the musicians had built villages for themselves around Jerusalem. ³⁰When the priests and Levites had purified themselves ceremonially, they purified the people, the gates and the wall.

³¹I had the leaders of Judah go up on top of^a the wall. I also assigned two large choirs to give thanks. One was to proceed on top of^b the wall to the right, toward the Dung Gate. ³²Hoshaiah and half the leaders of Judah followed them, ³³along with Azariah, Ezra, Meshullam, ³⁴Judah, Benjamin, Shemaiah, Jeremiah, ³⁵as well as some priests with trumpets, and also Zechariah son of Jonathan, the son of Shemaiah, the son of Mattaniah, the son of Micaiah, the son of Zakkur, the son of Asaph, ³⁶and his associates — Shemaiah, Azarel, Milalai, Gilalai, Maai, Nethanel, Judah and Hanani — with musical instruments prescribed by David the man of God. Ezra the teacher of the Law led the procession. ³⁷At the Fountain Gate they continued directly up the steps of the City of David on the ascent to the wall and passed above the site of David's palace to the Water Gate on the east.

³⁸The second choir proceeded in the opposite direction. I followed them on top of^c the wall, together with half the people — past the Tower of the Ovens to the Broad Wall, ³⁹over the Gate of Ephraim, the Jeshanah^d Gate, the Fish Gate, the Tower of Hananel and the Tower of the Hundred, as far as the Sheep Gate. At the Gate of the Guard they stopped.

⁴⁰The two choirs that gave thanks then took their places in the house of God; so did I, together with half the officials, ⁴¹as well as the priests — Eliakim, Maaseiah, Miniamin, Micaiah, Elioenai, Zechariah and Hananiah with their trumpets — ⁴²and also Maaseiah, Shemaiah, Eleazar, Uzzi, Jehohanan, Malkijah, Elam and Ezer. The choirs sang under the direction of Jezrahiah. ⁴³And on that day they offered

great sacrifices, rejoicing because God had given them great joy. The women and children also rejoiced. The sound of rejoicing in Jerusalem could be heard far away.

⁴⁴At that time men were appointed to be in charge of the storerooms for the contributions, firstfruits and tithes. From the fields around the towns they were to bring into the storerooms the portions required by the Law for the priests and the Levites, for Judah was pleased with the ministering priests and Levites. ⁴⁵They performed the service of their God and the service of purification, as did also the musicians and gatekeepers, according to the commands of David and his son Solomon. ⁴⁶For long ago, in the days of David and Asaph, there had been directors for the musicians and for the songs of praise and thanksgiving to God. ⁴⁷So in the days of Zerubbabel and of Nehemiah, all Israel contributed the daily portions for the musicians and the gatekeepers. They also set aside the portion for the other Levites, and the Levites set aside the portion for the descendants of Aaron.

Nehemiah's Final Reforms

13 On that day the Book of Moses was read aloud in the hearing of the people and there it was found written that no Ammonite or Moabite should ever be admitted into the assembly of God, ²because they had not met the Israelites with food and water but had hired Balaam to call a curse down on them. (Our God, however, turned the curse into a blessing.) ³When the people heard this law, they excluded from Israel all who were of foreign descent.

⁴Before this, Eliashib the priest had been put in charge of the storerooms of the house of our God. He was closely associated with Tobiah, ⁵and he had provided him with a large room formerly used to store the grain offerings and incense and temple articles, and also the tithes of grain, new wine and olive oil prescribed for the Levites, musicians and gatekeepers, as well as the contributions for the priests.

⁶But while all this was going on, I was not in Jerusalem, for in the thirty-second year of Artaxerxes king of Babylon I had returned to the king. Some time later I asked his permission ⁷and came back to Jerusalem. Here I learned about the evil thing Eliashib had done in providing Tobiah a room in the courts of the house of God. ⁸I was greatly displeased and threw all

---

^a 31 Or go alongside   ^b 31 Or proceed alongside   ^c 38 Or them alongside   ^d 39 Or Old

Tobiah's household goods out of the room. [9]I gave orders to purify the rooms, and then I put back into them the equipment of the house of God, with the grain offerings and the incense.

[10]I also learned that the portions assigned to the Levites had not been given to them, and that all the Levites and musicians responsible for the service had gone back to their own fields. [11]So I rebuked the officials and asked them, "Why is the house of God neglected?" Then I called them together and stationed them at their posts.

[12]All Judah brought the tithes of grain, new wine and olive oil into the storerooms. [13]I put Shelemiah the priest, Zadok the scribe, and a Levite named Pedaiah in charge of the storerooms and made Hanan son of Zakkur, the son of Mattaniah, their assistant, because they were considered trustworthy. They were made responsible for distributing the supplies to their fellow Levites.

[14]Remember me for this, my God, and do not blot out what I have so faithfully done for the house of my God and its services.

[15]In those days I saw people in Judah treading winepresses on the Sabbath and bringing in grain and loading it on donkeys, together with wine, grapes, figs and all other kinds of loads. And they were bringing all this into Jerusalem on the Sabbath. Therefore I warned them against selling food on that day. [16]People

from Tyre who lived in Jerusalem were bringing in fish and all kinds of merchandise and selling them in Jerusalem on the Sabbath to the people of Judah. [17]I rebuked the nobles of Judah and said to them, "What is this wicked thing you are doing — desecrating the Sabbath day? [18]Didn't your ancestors do the same things, so that our God brought all this calamity on us and on this city? Now you are stirring up more wrath against Israel by desecrating the Sabbath."

[19]When evening shadows fell on the gates of Jerusalem before the Sabbath, I ordered the doors to be shut and not opened until the Sabbath was over. I stationed some of my own men at the gates so that no load could be brought in on the Sabbath day. [20]Once or twice the merchants and sellers of all kinds of goods spent the night outside Jerusalem. [21]But I warned them and said, "Why do you spend the night by the wall? If you do this again, I will arrest you." From that time on they no longer came on the Sabbath. [22]Then I commanded the Levites to purify themselves and go and guard the gates in order to keep the Sabbath day holy.

Remember me for this also, my God, and show mercy to me according to your great love.

[23]Moreover, in those days I saw men of Judah who had married women from Ashdod, Ammon and Moab. [24]Half of their children spoke

The Law of Legacy: There Is No Success Without a Successor

Nehemiah 13:1–31

Even after Nehemiah returned to King Artaxerxes, he felt the necessity to follow up on the work in Jerusalem. When he returned to visit the walled city, he learned the people already had compromised God's statutes—and he knew he had to do something to ensure the success of the last several months of labor.

Nehemiah learned that when the leader is away, the people tend to stray. Consider the following problems he encountered:

1. **Compromising companionship (vv. 1–9)**

2. **Financial fiasco (vv. 10–14)**

3. **Secularized Sabbath (vv. 15–22)**

4. **Domestic disobedience (vv. 23–31)**

When Nehemiah failed to develop a strong inner circle and reproduce his vision in a team of leaders, everyone drifted. He witnessed firsthand the second law of thermodynamics: Things don't wind up; they wind down, unless energy is applied. A sound legacy develops only when a team has been trained and positioned to carry on.

the language of Ashdod or the language of one of the other peoples, and did not know how to speak the language of Judah. 25I rebuked them and called curses down on them. I beat some of the men and pulled out their hair. I made them take an oath in God's name and said: "You are not to give your daughters in marriage to their sons, nor are you to take their daughters in marriage for your sons or for yourselves. 26Was it not because of marriages like these that Solomon king of Israel sinned? Among the many nations there was no king like him. He was loved by his God, and God made him king over all Israel, but even he was led into sin by foreign women. 27Must we hear now that you too are doing all this terrible wickedness and are being unfaithful to our God by marrying foreign women?"

28One of the sons of Joiada son of Eliashib the high priest was son-in-law to Sanballat the Horonite. And I drove him away from me.

29Remember them, my God, because they defiled the priestly office and the covenant of the priesthood and of the Levites.

30So I purified the priests and the Levites of everything foreign, and assigned them duties, each to his own task. 31I also made provision for contributions of wood at designated times, and for the firstfruits.

Remember me with favor, my God.

The Law of Empowerment: Nehemiah Develops Others to Carry On

Nehemiah 13:13

Once the work was finished, Nehemiah chose to return to King Artaxerxes. But he recognized that he must appoint and equip others to lead the Jews in Jerusalem. Nehemiah wasn't satisfied with a one-time victory. For the work to go on, he knew he had to empower others to lead. He had to give his power away. And he did. Once he did, he felt his work was done and he could return to the king as he had promised.

As Nehemiah draws to a close, we observe numerous lessons throughout the story. It is one grand narrative on leadership. Consider the following list called "Ten Things I Know About Leadership." Not surprisingly, Nehemiah models every one of these truths:

1. **Leadership is influence (2:5–8, 16–18).**

2. **Everything rises and falls on leadership (4:9–15).**

3. **Leadership must be in the hands of few, ministry in the hands of many (5:1–7).**

4. **Leadership takes responsibility for every area of the task (6:1–14).**

5. **The most important ingredient in leadership is credibility/integrity (5:14–19).**

6. **Leaders possess tremendous faith in people (3:1–32).**

7. **Leadership can be taught (4:21–23).**

8. **Great leaders are effective communicators of vision (2:17–18).**

9. **Problem solving is the quickest way to gain leadership (4:7–23).**

10. **Great leadership is always assisted by other people (3:1–32; 13:13).**

INTRODUCTION TO ESTHER

The Story of a Woman—Beautiful Inside and Out

While leadership principles can be found throughout the Scriptures, they are not taught systematically—just as no single doctrine is taught systematically through the 66 books of the Bible. Instead, God chooses to teach these principles experientially, through the lives of ordinary persons in history. That is precisely how leadership shows up in the book of Esther.

If you look closely, you can spot a divine pattern. God always takes the initiative in executing his plan. Then he looks for a person who will submit to him, makes that individual aware of a need, and the need quickly becomes the personal burden of the person God has chosen. Ultimately, the individual embraces God's plan and feels morally compelled to act on it. The vision becomes his or her possession. Finally, the person calls others to join the cause, often at great personal risk.

The book of Esther tells the story of a woman who is beautiful both inside and out. Mordecai, an older cousin, takes her under his wing in her early years; in a sense, he becomes her mentor. As a gorgeous young Jewish woman, Esther is chosen to replace Queen Vashti as the consort of King Xerxes. She marries into the royal family and over the years deepens her influence.

Somewhere in the midst of her reign, a man named Haman feels snubbed by Mordecai and responds by making plans to exterminate the Jewish people. When Mordecai learns of the plot, he returns to his protégée, Queen Esther, and tries to convince her that she must stop this genocidal plan. After a moment of indecision, she agrees to take the enormous risk. Her courageous initiative, quick wit, charm and poise in this desperate

God's Role in Esther

Esther is one of only two books in Scripture where the name of God does not appear even once (the Song of Songs is the other). Why this amazing omission? Some have conjectured that the writer simply could not risk open worship of God. Whatever the reason, it doesn't really matter. While we may not see God's face anywhere in the book, we see his hand everywhere.

God's work can be clearly seen through his inner prompting of three leaders: Mordecai, King Xerxes and Esther. In this great book, God's providence and Esther's preparation meet. We see this in Mordecai's phrase: "And who knows but that you have come to your royal position for such a time as this?" (4:14).

The word "providence" comes from two root words: *pro*, meaning "before," and *video*, meaning "to see." God sees beforehand and orchestrates events to accomplish his purposes. First, God took Queen Vashti off the throne. Then, he gave the throne to Esther. Finally, he put the right people in the right places.

Leaders in Esther

King Xerxes, Mordecai, Haman, Esther

Other People of Influence in Esther

Hathach

the king. ³Let the king appoint commissioners in every province of his realm to bring all these beautiful young women into the harem at the citadel of Susa. Let them be placed under the care of Hegai, the king's eunuch, who is in charge of the women; and let beauty treatments be given to them. ⁴Then let the young woman who pleases the king be queen instead of Vashti." This advice appealed to the king, and he followed it.

⁵Now there was in the citadel of Susa a Jew of the tribe of Benjamin, named Mordecai son of Jair, the son of Shimei, the son of Kish, ⁶who had been carried into exile from Jerusalem by Nebuchadnezzar king of Babylon, among those taken captive with Jehoiachin[a] king of Judah. ⁷Mordecai had a cousin named Hadassah, whom he had brought up because she had neither father nor mother. This young woman, who was also known as Esther, had a lovely figure and was beautiful. Mordecai had taken her as his own daughter when her father and mother died.

⁸When the king's order and edict had been proclaimed, many young women were brought to the citadel of Susa and put under the care of Hegai. Esther also was taken to the king's palace and entrusted to Hegai, who had charge of the harem. ⁹She pleased him and won his favor. Immediately he provided her with her beauty treatments and special food. He assigned to her seven female attendants selected from the king's palace and moved her and her attendants into the best place in the harem.

¹⁰Esther had not revealed her nationality and family background, because Mordecai had forbidden her to do so. ¹¹Every day he walked back and forth near the courtyard of the harem to find out how Esther was and what was happening to her.

¹²Before a young woman's turn came to go in to King Xerxes, she had to complete twelve months of beauty treatments prescribed for the women, six months with oil of myrrh and six with perfumes and cosmetics. ¹³And this is how she would go to the king: Anything she wanted was given her to take with her from the harem to the king's palace. ¹⁴In the evening she would go there and in the morning return to another part of the harem to the care of Shaashgaz, the king's eunuch who was in charge of the concubines. She would not return to the king unless he was pleased with her and summoned her by name.

¹⁵When the turn came for Esther (the young woman Mordecai had adopted, the daughter of his uncle Abihail) to go to the king, she asked for nothing other than what Hegai, the king's eunuch who was in charge of the harem, suggested. And Esther won the favor of everyone who saw her. ¹⁶She was taken to King Xerxes in the royal residence in the tenth month, the month of Tebeth, in the seventh year of his reign.

¹⁷Now the king was attracted to Esther more than to any of the other women, and she won

---

[a] 6 Hebrew *Jeconiah*, a variant of *Jehoiachin*

ESTHER

Protector of the Messianic Line
Esther 2:1–17

By risking her life after rising to prominence, Esther, the captive Jewish orphan, protected the lineage of the coming Messiah. Her gift of intuition and exquisite sense of timing energized her leadership. Through the whole ordeal she remained humbly committed to her people and used her influence to save them all.

Through her kindness and gracious spirit, Esther found favor with the eunuch in charge of the candidates for queen. He rewarded her with a position of prominence and high visibility. During this time, Esther remained close to her foster father, Mordecai. She maintained a teachable spirit and did not lose sight of her origins. Thanks to these godly qualities, Mordecai was able to guide Esther through many potential land mines.

One sees the true nature of Esther's heart following her selection as queen. Here was a former peasant girl who easily could have gotten caught up in the pageantry and fame of royalty. Instead, Esther constantly reminded herself that she had received a God-given status for a reason. Her servant heart enabled her to risk her life for others. She had earned the trust of the king, used her intuition well, and really did come to the kingdom "for such a time as this" (Est 4:14).

PROFILE in leadership

his favor and approval more than any of the other virgins. So he set a royal crown on her head and made her queen instead of Vashti. [18]And the king gave a great banquet, Esther's banquet, for all his nobles and officials. He proclaimed a holiday throughout the provinces and distributed gifts with royal liberality.

Mordecai Uncovers a Conspiracy

[19]When the virgins were assembled a second time, Mordecai was sitting at the king's gate. [20]But Esther had kept secret her family background and nationality just as Mordecai had told her to do, for she continued to follow Mordecai's instructions as she had done when he was bringing her up.

[21]During the time Mordecai was sitting at the king's gate, Bigthana[a] and Teresh, two of the king's officers who guarded the doorway, became angry and conspired to assassinate King Xerxes. [22]But Mordecai found out about the plot and told Queen Esther, who in turn reported it to the king, giving credit to Mordecai. [23]And when the report was investigated and found to be true, the two officials were impaled on poles. All this was recorded in the book of the annals in the presence of the king.

Haman's Plot to Destroy the Jews

3 After these events, King Xerxes honored Haman son of Hammedatha, the Agagite, elevating him and giving him a seat of honor higher than that of all the other nobles. [2]All the royal officials at the king's gate knelt down and paid honor to Haman, for the king had commanded this concerning him. But Mordecai would not kneel down or pay him honor.

[3]Then the royal officials at the king's gate asked Mordecai, "Why do you disobey the king's command?" [4]Day after day they spoke to him but he refused to comply. Therefore they told Haman about it to see whether Mordecai's behavior would be tolerated, for he had told them he was a Jew.

[5]When Haman saw that Mordecai would not kneel down or pay him honor, he was enraged. [6]Yet having learned who Mordecai's people were, he scorned the idea of killing only Mordecai. Instead Haman looked for a way to destroy all Mordecai's people, the Jews, throughout the whole kingdom of Xerxes.

[7]In the twelfth year of King Xerxes, in the first month, the month of Nisan, the *pur* (that is, the lot) was cast in the presence of Haman to select a day and month. And the lot fell on[b] the twelfth month, the month of Adar.

[8]Then Haman said to King Xerxes, "There is a certain people dispersed among the peoples in all the provinces of your kingdom who keep themselves separate. Their customs are different from those of all other people, and they do not obey the king's laws; it is not in the king's best interest to tolerate them. [9]If it pleases the king,

---

a 21 Hebrew *Bigthan*, a variant of *Bigthana*   *b 7* Septuagint; Hebrew does not have *And the lot fell on*.

The Law of Respect: Esther Stays Accountable to Mordecai

Esther 2:20–22

Esther was a beautiful young Jew being reared by her older cousin, Mordecai, in the days of the Persian captivity. When Esther found favor with the king and was chosen to become his next queen, the choice surprised both her and Mordecai. She would now hold a significant place of influence in the empire, even as a Jewish captive!

Because she had learned well the Law of Respect, she remained accountable to Mordecai's leadership and mentoring even after she moved into the palace. She listened and followed his counsel about concealing her identity as a Jew. His advice paid off, and the king selected her to be the queen of Persia.

What allowed Mordecai to continue to be a persuasive mentor in Esther's life, even though she became rich, famous, and influential? We see four reasons in chapter two:

1. *Relationship:* He had raised her and known her for years.

2. *Wisdom:* He intuitively knew what she should do when campaigning to be queen.

3. *Concern:* Every day he paced in front of Esther's court out of love and concern.

4. *Courage:* He informed Esther when he discovered a plot against the king.

let a decree be issued to destroy them, and I will give ten thousand talents[a] of silver to the king's administrators for the royal treasury."

[10]So the king took his signet ring from his finger and gave it to Haman son of Hammedatha, the Agagite, the enemy of the Jews. [11]"Keep the money," the king said to Haman, "and do with the people as you please."

[12]Then on the thirteenth day of the first month the royal secretaries were summoned. They wrote out in the script of each province and in the language of each people all Haman's orders to the king's satraps, the governors of the various provinces and the nobles of the various peoples. These were written in the name of King Xerxes himself and sealed with his own ring. [13]Dispatches were sent by couriers to all the king's provinces with the order to destroy, kill and annihilate all the Jews—young and old, women and children—on a single day, the thirteenth day of the twelfth month, the month of Adar, and to plunder their goods. [14]A copy of the text of the edict was to be issued as law in every province and made known to the people of every nationality so they would be ready for that day.

[15]The couriers went out, spurred on by the king's command, and the edict was issued in the citadel of Susa. The king and Haman sat down to drink, but the city of Susa was bewildered.

Mordecai Persuades Esther to Help

4 When Mordecai learned of all that had been done, he tore his clothes, put on sackcloth and ashes, and went out into the city, wailing loudly and bitterly. [2]But he went only as far as the king's gate, because no one clothed in sackcloth was allowed to enter it. [3]In every province to which the edict and order of the king came, there was great mourning among the Jews, with fasting, weeping and wailing. Many lay in sackcloth and ashes.

[4]When Esther's eunuchs and female attendants came and told her about Mordecai, she was in great distress. She sent clothes for him to put on instead of his sackcloth, but he would not accept them. [5]Then Esther summoned Hathak, one of the king's eunuchs assigned to attend her, and ordered him to find out what was troubling Mordecai and why.

[6]So Hathak went out to Mordecai in the open square of the city in front of the king's gate. [7]Mordecai told him everything that had happened to him, including the exact amount of money Haman had promised to pay into the royal treasury for the destruction of the Jews. [8]He also gave him a copy of the text of the edict for their annihilation, which had been published

---

[a] 9 That is, about 375 tons or about 340 metric tons

MORDECAI

Refusing the Smallest Compromise
Esther 3:1–6

Being God's kind of leader means refusing even the smallest compromise in what you believe. Mordecai was that kind of leader.

Mordecai wasn't going to bend—not one bit—when Haman, the newly appointed prime minister of Persia, demanded a show of reverence bordering on worship (Est 3:2). When the palace officials asked Mordecai why he refused to reverence the prime minister, he told them he was a Jew. And what difference did that make? The Lord Himself had said, "You shall have no other gods before me . . . You shall not bow down to them or worship them" (Ex 20:3, 5). Day after day these men tried to "talk some sense" into Mordecai; didn't Haman have the authority to execute him for his insolence?

Haman, in his arrogance and pride, decided not to challenge Mordecai directly, but to wipe out his whole race. In a plot eerily similar to the one carried out many centuries later in Nazi Germany, Haman decreed that Mordecai's people, the Jews, should be exterminated.

Mordecai, of course, paled at the news. Still, he held steadfastly to his refusal to dishonor his God by bowing before a mere man. In the end, through a twist utterly characteristic of the Lord, God honored Mordecai and exalted him before the very people who had begged him to compromise his principles.

PROFILE in leadership

21 LAWS

ESTHER AND THE LAW OF TIMING
When to Lead Is As Important As What to Do and Where to Go

Esther 4:6–17

WHEN THE RIGHT leader and the right moment come together, incredible things happen. Winston Churchill described it like this: "There comes a special moment in everyone's life, a moment for which that person was born. That special opportunity, when he seizes it, will fulfill his mission—a mission for which he is uniquely qualified. In that moment he finds greatness. It is his finest hour."

Reading a situation and knowing what to do are not enough to make you succeed in leadership. Only the right action at the right time will bring success. Anything else exacts a high price.

■   ■   ■   ■   ■

To be an effective leader, you must overcome whatever keeps you from moving forward. Like Esther, you must learn that if you don't seize the moment . . .

1. *Your fate will be like that of the rest of the crowd.*
   Sometimes it's easy to buy in to the notion that we are special and won't have to take the risks of earlier generations. But that is a myth. If we don't take risks, we can never expect to rise to the occasion. Mordecai reminded Esther that even though she was queen, she would fare no better than the rest of the Jews if she didn't talk to the king.

2. *God will replace you with someone else.*
   Mordecai motivated Esther by reminding her that God would accomplish his purposes even if she sat on the sidelines. It's not necessarily the giftedness of the leader that prompts God's blessing; it's more often the leader's willingness to move when and where he indicates.

3. *You could lose more than an opportunity.*
   Mordecai reminded Esther that if she sat back and did nothing, she could lose more than a chance to do the right thing—she could lose her life. Although doing the right thing at the right time can seem risky, in the long run, leaders incur a greater risk by not taking action.

4. *You could miss out on your mission in life.*
   Mordecai speculated that if Esther failed to act on behalf of her people, she might miss out on God's purpose for her life. You will never accomplish your mission by remaining idle. What paralyzes you? Fear? Image? Regardless of what keeps you from pursuing an opportunity, you will succeed only by making one timely decision after another. There is no such thing as zero risk in leadership. But when you determine to seize a ripe opportunity despite the risk, you build momentum.

The Test of Timing

Make sure that each decision you make stands the test of timing. To help determine if it's the right time to seize an opportunity, consider the following:

1. **The Needs Around You**
   When you keep a finger on the pulse of your people's basic needs, you will always find opportune times to lead.

   Esther understood the needs of her people. She understood not only what they needed, but also what they needed *from her*. Get in touch with your people's needs. Then make a point to continually ask: What is their mood? What do they desire to accomplish? What do they need from me, their leader?

2. **The Opportunities Before You**
   You find ripe opportunities only by looking for them.

   Early in Esther's leadership, Mordecai did much of the "spotting." He let her know each time he discerned a small window of opportunity. Esther learned from Mordecai's insight, and later discerned the opportune time to inform the king of Mordecai's actions. When you take the time to spot golden opportunities, they start to stick out.

3. **The Influencers Behind You**
   Esther came to value Mordecai's opinion so much that she made sure he remained by her side throughout her reign. Before you make an important decision, ask your key influencers what they are feeling. Do they see the same opportunity you do? Are they discerning the same timing? When trying to discern the right time to take action, you must get feedback from your key people.

4. **The Successes Under You**
   Experience provides practical advice, so take a minute to recall your successes. Have you done anything like this before? Is it reasonable to expect the same outcome from this decision?

   Mordecai had to convince Esther about the right time to approach the king. Success in that incident gave her confidence for the future. Before long, Esther had gained so much influence with the king that he was asking her for advice.

5. **The Courage Within You**
   Leadership requires courage—the courage to risk, to reach, and to put yourself on the line to seize an opportunity. The word *courage* comes from a French word that means "heart." Taking advantage of an opportunity at the right time requires heart.

   Esther demonstrated tremendous courage, time after time. It took great heart to stand before the king. Fear tried to get her to back down—and fear will also try to get the better of you. But good leaders understand that ripe opportunities never come without fear. So they move forward despite a moment of hesitation.

in Susa, to show to Esther and explain it to her, and he told him to instruct her to go into the king's presence to beg for mercy and plead with him for her people.

[9]Hathak went back and reported to Esther what Mordecai had said. [10]Then she instructed him to say to Mordecai, [11]"All the king's officials and the people of the royal provinces know that for any man or woman who approaches the king in the inner court without being summoned the king has but one law: that they be put to death unless the king extends the gold scepter to them and spares their lives. But thirty days have passed since I was called to go to the king."

[12]When Esther's words were reported to Mordecai, [13]he sent back this answer: "Do not think that because you are in the king's house you alone of all the Jews will escape. [14]For if you remain silent at this time, relief and deliverance for the Jews will arise from another place, but you and your father's family will perish. And who knows but that you have come to your royal position for such a time as this?"

The Law of Sacrifice: Esther Is Willing to Give Her Life for the People

Esther 4:11–16

After Mordecai confronts Esther about risking her life for her people, she makes a commitment to approach the king uninvited—even though such an appearance invited death (Est 4:11). Esther says simply, "I will go to the king, even though it is against the law. And if I perish, I perish" (4:16). She took the step; she informed the king; she changed his mind; she saved the day.

Such is the life of a leader who practices the Law of Sacrifice. A leader must be willing to give up to go up.

Of course, leaders do this only when their cause becomes more important than their life. Jesus called his staff to deny themselves, take up their cross, and follow him (Mt 16:24). He told them that those who saved their lives would lose them. Esther put the cause of her people above her instinct for self-preservation—and not only lived, but enabled many others to live as well.

[15]Then Esther sent this reply to Mordecai: [16]"Go, gather together all the Jews who are in Susa, and fast for me. Do not eat or drink for three days, night or day. I and my attendants will fast as you do. When this is done, I will go to the king, even though it is against the law. And if I perish, I perish."

[17]So Mordecai went away and carried out all of Esther's instructions.

Esther's Request to the King

5 On the third day Esther put on her royal robes and stood in the inner court of the palace, in front of the king's hall. The king was sitting on his royal throne in the hall, facing the entrance. [2]When he saw Queen Esther standing in the court, he was pleased with her and held out to her the gold scepter that was in his hand. So Esther approached and touched the tip of the scepter.

[3]Then the king asked, "What is it, Queen Esther? What is your request? Even up to half the kingdom, it will be given you."

[4]"If it pleases the king," replied Esther, "let the king, together with Haman, come today to a banquet I have prepared for him."

[5]"Bring Haman at once," the king said, "so that we may do what Esther asks."

So the king and Haman went to the banquet Esther had prepared. [6]As they were drinking wine, the king again asked Esther, "Now what is your petition? It will be given you. And what is your request? Even up to half the kingdom, it will be granted."

[7]Esther replied, "My petition and my request is this: [8]If the king regards me with favor and if it pleases the king to grant my petition and fulfill my request, let the king and Haman come tomorrow to the banquet I will prepare for them. Then I will answer the king's question."

Haman's Rage Against Mordecai

[9]Haman went out that day happy and in high spirits. But when he saw Mordecai at the king's gate and observed that he neither rose nor showed fear in his presence, he was filled with rage against Mordecai. [10]Nevertheless, Haman restrained himself and went home.

Calling together his friends and Zeresh, his wife, [11]Haman boasted to them about his vast wealth, his many sons, and all the ways the king had honored him and how he had elevated him above the other nobles and officials. [12]"And that's not all," Haman added. "I'm the only person Queen Esther invited to accompany the king to the banquet she gave. And she has invited me along with the king tomorrow. [13]But all this gives me no satisfaction as long as I see that Jew Mordecai sitting at the king's gate."

[14]His wife Zeresh and all his friends said to him, "Have a pole set up, reaching to a height of fifty cubits,[a] and ask the king in the morning to have Mordecai impaled on it. Then go with the king to the banquet and enjoy yourself." This suggestion delighted Haman, and he had the pole set up.

Mordecai Honored

6 That night the king could not sleep; so he ordered the book of the chronicles, the record of his reign, to be brought in and read to him. [2]It was found recorded there that Mordecai had exposed Bigthana and Teresh, two of the king's officers who guarded the doorway, who had conspired to assassinate King Xerxes.

[3]"What honor and recognition has Mordecai received for this?" the king asked.

"Nothing has been done for him," his attendants answered.

[4]The king said, "Who is in the court?" Now Haman had just entered the outer court of the palace to speak to the king about impaling Mordecai on the pole he had set up for him.

[5]His attendants answered, "Haman is standing in the court."

"Bring him in," the king ordered.

[6]When Haman entered, the king asked him, "What should be done for the man the king delights to honor?"

Now Haman thought to himself, "Who is there that the king would rather honor than me?" [7]So he answered the king, "For the man the king delights to honor, [8]have them bring a royal robe the king has worn and a horse the king has ridden, one with a royal crest placed on its head. [9]Then let the robe and horse be entrusted to one of the king's most noble princes. Let them robe the man the king delights to honor, and lead him on the horse through the city streets, proclaiming before him, 'This is what is done for the man the king delights to honor!' "

[10]"Go at once," the king commanded Haman. "Get the robe and the horse and do just as you have suggested for Mordecai the Jew, who sits at the king's gate. Do not neglect anything you have recommended."

[11]So Haman got the robe and the horse. He robed Mordecai, and led him on horseback through the city streets, proclaiming before him, "This is what is done for the man the king delights to honor!"

[12]Afterward Mordecai returned to the king's gate. But Haman rushed home, with his head covered in grief, [13]and told Zeresh his wife and all his friends everything that had happened to him.

His advisers and his wife Zeresh said to him, "Since Mordecai, before whom your downfall has started, is of Jewish origin, you cannot stand against him—you will surely come to ruin!" [14]While they were still talking with him, the king's eunuchs arrived and hurried Haman away to the banquet Esther had prepared.

Haman Impaled

7 So the king and Haman went to Queen Esther's banquet, [2]and as they were drinking wine on the second day, the king again asked, "Queen Esther, what is your petition? It will be given you. What is your request? Even up to half the kingdom, it will be granted."

[3]Then Queen Esther answered, "If I have found favor with you, Your Majesty, and if it pleases you, grant me my life—this is my petition. And spare my people—this is my request. [4]For I and my people have been sold to be destroyed, killed and annihilated. If we had merely been sold as male and female slaves, I would have kept quiet, because no such distress would justify disturbing the king.[b]"

[5]King Xerxes asked Queen Esther, "Who is he? Where is he—the man who has dared to do such a thing?"

[6]Esther said, "An adversary and enemy! This vile Haman!"

Then Haman was terrified before the king and queen. [7]The king got up in a rage, left his wine and went out into the palace garden. But Haman, realizing that the king had already decided his fate, stayed behind to beg Queen Esther for his life.

[8]Just as the king returned from the palace garden to the banquet hall, Haman was falling on the couch where Esther was reclining.

The king exclaimed, "Will he even molest the queen while she is with me in the house?"

As soon as the word left the king's mouth, they covered Haman's face. [9]Then Harbona, one of the eunuchs attending the king, said, "A pole reaching to a height of fifty cubits[a] stands

---

[a] 14,9 That is, about 75 feet or about 23 meters   [b] 4 Or quiet, but the compensation our adversary offers cannot be compared with the loss the king would suffer

by Haman's house. He had it set up for Mordecai, who spoke up to help the king."

The king said, "Impale him on it!" [10]So they impaled Haman on the pole he had set up for Mordecai. Then the king's fury subsided.

The Law of Solid Ground: God, Esther and Haman

Esther 7:1–10

God, Esther and Haman each play a leading role in the book of Esther. God is the Leader in control; Esther is the leader under control; and Haman is the leader out of control. Consider each one.

God: The Leader in Control
1. He took Queen Vashti off the throne.
2. He gave Esther the throne.
3. He used Mordecai to supply information.
4. He put everyone in place before the crisis.

Esther: The Leader Under Control
1. Her position didn't steal her compassion.
2. She felt limited in what she could do.
3. She knew her place in the organization.
4. She felt the need to fast and pray.
5. She depended on the prayers of others.
6. She was willing to take a risk and obey.
7. She didn't take advantage of generosity.
8. She recognized the importance of timing.

Haman: The Leader Out of Control
1. He misunderstood the times.
2. He lost joy over little problems.
3. He needed friends to build his self-image.
4. His greed and ambition made him unhappy.
5. He listened to the wrong people.
6. He thought too highly of himself.
7. He set himself up for a fall.
8. He reaped what he sowed.

The King's Edict in Behalf of the Jews

8 That same day King Xerxes gave Queen Esther the estate of Haman, the enemy of the Jews. And Mordecai came into the presence of the king, for Esther had told how he was related to her. [2]The king took off his signet ring, which he had reclaimed from Haman, and presented it to Mordecai. And Esther appointed him over Haman's estate.

[3]Esther again pleaded with the king, falling at his feet and weeping. She begged him to put an end to the evil plan of Haman the Agagite, which he had devised against the Jews. [4]Then the king extended the gold scepter to Esther and she arose and stood before him.

[5]"If it pleases the king," she said, "and if he regards me with favor and thinks it the right thing to do, and if he is pleased with me, let an order be written overruling the dispatches that Haman son of Hammedatha, the Agagite, devised and wrote to destroy the Jews in all the king's provinces. [6]For how can I bear to see disaster fall on my people? How can I bear to see the destruction of my family?"

[7]King Xerxes replied to Queen Esther and to Mordecai the Jew, "Because Haman attacked the Jews, I have given his estate to Esther, and they have impaled him on the pole he set up. [8]Now write another decree in the king's name in behalf of the Jews as seems best to you, and seal it with the king's signet ring—for no document written in the king's name and sealed with his ring can be revoked."

[9]At once the royal secretaries were summoned—on the twenty-third day of the third month, the month of Sivan. They wrote out all Mordecai's orders to the Jews, and to the satraps, governors and nobles of the 127 provinces stretching from India to Cush.[a] These orders were written in the script of each province and the language of each people and also to the Jews in their own script and language. [10]Mordecai wrote in the name of King Xerxes, sealed the dispatches with the king's signet ring, and sent them by mounted couriers, who rode fast horses especially bred for the king.

[11]The king's edict granted the Jews in every city the right to assemble and protect themselves; to destroy, kill and annihilate the armed men of any nationality or province who might attack them and their women and children,[b] and to plunder the property of their enemies.

---

[a] 9 That is, the upper Nile region   [b] 11 Or province, together with their women and children, who might attack them;

The Law of Solid Ground: Mordecai Gets a Reward

Esther 8:1–2

Twice Mordecai protected the king from destructive leaders, and twice he was rewarded. He reaped the benefits of a track record that showed him to be a leader who could be trusted. He demonstrates that a leader cannot be successful unless other people want him to be.

[12]The day appointed for the Jews to do this in all the provinces of King Xerxes was the thirteenth day of the twelfth month, the month of Adar. [13]A copy of the text of the edict was to be issued as law in every province and made known to the people of every nationality so that the Jews would be ready on that day to avenge themselves on their enemies.

[14]The couriers, riding the royal horses, went out, spurred on by the king's command, and the edict was issued in the citadel of Susa.

The Triumph of the Jews

[15]When Mordecai left the king's presence, he was wearing royal garments of blue and white, a large crown of gold and a purple robe of fine linen. And the city of Susa held a joyous celebration. [16]For the Jews it was a time of happiness and joy, gladness and honor. [17]In every province and in every city to which the edict of the king came, there was joy and gladness among the Jews, with feasting and celebrating. And many people of other nationalities became Jews because fear of the Jews had seized them.

9 On the thirteenth day of the twelfth month, the month of Adar, the edict commanded by the king was to be carried out. On this day the enemies of the Jews had hoped to overpower them, but now the tables were turned and the Jews got the upper hand over those who hated them. [2]The Jews assembled in their cities in all the provinces of King Xerxes to attack those determined to destroy them. No one could stand against them, because the people of all the other nationalities were afraid of them. [3]And all the nobles of the provinces, the satraps, the governors and the king's administrators helped the Jews, because fear of Mordecai had seized them. [4]Mordecai was prominent in the palace; his rep-

utation spread throughout the provinces, and he became more and more powerful.

[5]The Jews struck down all their enemies with the sword, killing and destroying them, and they did what they pleased to those who hated them. [6]In the citadel of Susa, the Jews killed and destroyed five hundred men. [7]They also killed Parshandatha, Dalphon, Aspatha, [8]Poratha, Adalia, Aridatha, [9]Parmashta, Arisai, Aridai and Vaizatha, [10]the ten sons of Haman son of Hammedatha, the enemy of the Jews. But they did not lay their hands on the plunder.

[11]The number of those killed in the citadel of Susa was reported to the king that same day. [12]The king said to Queen Esther, "The Jews have killed and destroyed five hundred men and the ten sons of Haman in the citadel of Susa. What have they done in the rest of the king's provinces? Now what is your petition? It will be given you. What is your request? It will also be granted."

[13]"If it pleases the king," Esther answered, "give the Jews in Susa permission to carry out this day's edict tomorrow also, and let Haman's ten sons be impaled on poles."

[14]So the king commanded that this be done. An edict was issued in Susa, and they impaled the ten sons of Haman. [15]The Jews in Susa came together on the fourteenth day of the month of Adar, and they put to death in Susa three hundred men, but they did not lay their hands on the plunder.

[16]Meanwhile, the remainder of the Jews who were in the king's provinces also assembled to protect themselves and get relief from their enemies. They killed seventy-five thousand of them but did not lay their hands on the plunder. [17]This happened on the thirteenth day of the month of Adar, and on the fourteenth they rested and made it a day of feasting and joy.

[18]The Jews in Susa, however, had assembled on the thirteenth and fourteenth, and then on the fifteenth they rested and made it a day of feasting and joy.

[19]That is why rural Jews — those living in villages — observe the fourteenth of the month of Adar as a day of joy and feasting, a day for giving presents to each other.

Purim Established

[20]Mordecai recorded these events, and he sent letters to all the Jews throughout the provinces of King Xerxes, near and far, [21]to have them celebrate annually the fourteenth and fifteenth days of the month of Adar [22]as the time when

the Jews got relief from their enemies, and as the month when their sorrow was turned into joy and their mourning into a day of celebration. He wrote them to observe the days as days of feasting and joy and giving presents of food to one another and gifts to the poor.

23So the Jews agreed to continue the celebration they had begun, doing what Mordecai had written to them. 24For Haman son of Hammedatha, the Agagite, the enemy of all the Jews, had plotted against the Jews to destroy them and had cast the *pur* (that is, the lot) for their ruin and destruction. 25But when the plot came to the king's attention,[a] he issued written orders that the evil scheme Haman had devised against the Jews should come back onto his own head, and that he and his sons should be impaled on poles. 26(Therefore these days were called Purim, from the word *pur*.) Because of everything written in this letter and because of what they had seen and what had happened to them, 27the Jews took it on themselves to establish the custom that they and their descendants and all who join them should without fail observe these two days every year, in the way prescribed and at the time appointed. 28These days should be remembered and observed in every generation by every family, and in every province and in every city. And these days of Purim should never fail to be celebrated by the Jews — nor should the memory of these days die out among their descendants.

29So Queen Esther, daughter of Abihail, along with Mordecai the Jew, wrote with full authority to confirm this second letter concerning Purim. 30And Mordecai sent letters to all the Jews in the 127 provinces of Xerxes' kingdom — words of goodwill and assurance — 31to establish these days of Purim at their designated times, as Mordecai the Jew and Queen Esther had decreed for them, and as they had established for themselves and their descendants in regard to their times of fasting and lamentation. 32Esther's decree confirmed these regulations about Purim, and it was written down in the records.

The Greatness of Mordecai

10 King Xerxes imposed tribute throughout the empire, to its distant shores. 2And all his acts of power and might, together with a full account of the greatness of Mordecai, whom the king had promoted, are they not written in the book of the annals of the kings of Media and Persia? 3Mordecai the Jew was second in rank to King Xerxes, preeminent among the Jews, and held in high esteem by his many fellow Jews, because he worked for the good of his people and spoke up for the welfare of all the Jews.

---

a 25 Or *when Esther came before the king*

INTRODUCTION TO JOB

Job's 42 chapters describe one man's hellish loss of nearly everything he holds dear, including his ten children. The book begins by describing Job as blameless and upright, a man who shuns evil. His reputation for integrity makes him a strong leader within his family and community. He has amassed a considerable fortune and demonstrates great wisdom in his business and community affairs. It would be difficult to imagine a better leadership model than Job—discerning, industrious, devoted to God and family, successful, and well-thought-of by his colleagues.

And that is exactly what makes his story so troubling. In no time at all, he loses it all. Through no fault of his own, he must deal with tragedy in its deepest forms. Yet how he deals with it provides a beautiful case study in character, integrity, credibility, patience and poise.

First, Job maintains perspective. Immediately after hearing the first round of tragic news, he falls to the ground and worships (1:20). He knows that unless he consciously remains subject to God's authority, he will react with bitterness and rancor. He maintains a big-picture perspective.

Next, Job does some soul searching. He looks within and asks whether anything needs correction—something only a secure person can do.

Third, Job begins to ask questions of God and others. Yet even in his complaints, he never abandons his commitment to God or his core values.

Finally, Job determines to continue trusting the process. At one point he declares, "Though he slay me, yet will I hope in him" (13:15). Job decides to await God's response; he will continue to rely on divine insight.

God's Role in Job

God plays the part of the C.E.O. who finds himself needing to cast the vision to those who have lost sight of it. In the same way that a supervisor must repeatedly communicate the "big picture" to employees who see things only from their departmental perspective, God shows up at the end of the book to correct all five speakers. He asks, "Where were you when I laid the earth's foundation?" (38:4). God plays the leader's role, providing perspective for the characters in the story.

Leaders in Job
Job

Other People of Influence in Job
Eliphaz, Bildad, Zophar, Elihu

Lessons in Leadership
- Mature leaders maintain perspective, especially when things don't go according to plan.
- Good leaders remain teachable and choose their counselors wisely.
- Integrity and character are the foundations for leadership.
- Never pretend or presume to have all the answers.
- We can live without having all the answers.
- Effective leaders can adjust when things go wrong.

Yet that is not the end of his sad story. To compound his dilemma, four "friends" approach Job to offer their counsel. They offer several explanations for why all of this is happening, centering around the theme, "You must have sinned."

The majority of the book features three cycles of debate between Eliphaz, Bildad, Zophar (and Elihu) on one side, and Job on the other. After Job's "friends" present their futile arguments, God steps in with a series of probing questions. Job realizes his presumption and sincerely repents. He acknowledges that God is God and that he has no right to second-guess the Omniscient One. Then, as a leader who always takes the "high road," Job prays for his four friends that God would show them mercy for their foolish words.

LEADERSHIP HIGHLIGHTS IN JOB

Prologue

1 In the land of Uz there lived a man whose name was Job. This man was blameless and upright; he feared God and shunned evil. [2]He had seven sons and three daughters, [3]and he owned seven thousand sheep, three thousand camels, five hundred yoke of oxen and five hundred donkeys, and had a large number of servants. He was the greatest man among all the people of the East.

[4]His sons used to hold feasts in their homes on their birthdays, and they would invite their three sisters to eat and drink with them. [5]When a period of feasting had run its course, Job would make arrangements for them to be purified. Early in the morning he would sacrifice a burnt offering for each of them, thinking, "Perhaps my children have sinned and cursed God in their hearts." This was Job's regular custom.

[6]One day the angels[a] came to present themselves before the LORD, and Satan[b] also came with them. [7]The LORD said to Satan, "Where have you come from?"

Satan answered the LORD, "From roaming throughout the earth, going back and forth on it."

[8]Then the LORD said to Satan, "Have you considered my servant Job? There is no one on earth like him; he is blameless and upright, a man who fears God and shuns evil."

[9]"Does Job fear God for nothing?" Satan replied. [10]"Have you not put a hedge around him and his household and everything he has? You have blessed the work of his hands, so that his flocks and herds are spread throughout the land. [11]But now stretch out your hand and strike everything he has, and he will surely curse you to your face."

[12]The LORD said to Satan, "Very well, then, everything he has is in your power, but on the man himself do not lay a finger."

Then Satan went out from the presence of the LORD.

[13]One day when Job's sons and daughters were feasting and drinking wine at the oldest brother's house, [14]a messenger came to Job and said, "The oxen were plowing and the donkeys were grazing nearby, [15]and the Sabeans attacked and made off with them. They put the servants to the sword, and I am the only one who has escaped to tell you!"

[16]While he was still speaking, another messenger came and said, "The fire of God fell from the heavens and burned up the sheep and the servants, and I am the only one who has escaped to tell you!"

[17]While he was still speaking, another messenger came and said, "The Chaldeans formed three raiding parties and swept down on your

---

[a] 6 Hebrew the sons of God   [b] 6 Hebrew satan means adversary.

Self-Discipline: Job Maintains Perspective

Job 1:1–22

All hell broke loose. The man lost almost everything: His livestock, his land, his home, and even his children.

Job was a disciplined person, however. He lived his life from his character, not his emotions. Consequently, Job maintained perspective when terrible tragedy struck him: "At this, Job got up, tore his robe, and shaved his head. Then he fell to the ground in worship" (Job 1:20). The Scripture later tells us that in all the crises he faced, Job never sinned against God with his words (2:10). He maintained his sense of integrity all the way through his ordeal.

Wow! What discipline! Job modeled a valuable leadership posture for us. Note the sequence of remarkable events in his life:

1. **Worship:** Job worshiped and articulated God's sovereignty in his life.

2. **Perspective:** Worship enabled Job to capture God's perspective and power.

3. **Humility:** Perspective allowed Job to see his limited knowledge.

4. **Teachability:** Humility caused Job to hunger and seek God's insight.

5. **Victory:** Teachability ultimately led Job to gain victory over his losses.

camels and made off with them. They put the servants to the sword, and I am the only one who has escaped to tell you!"

¹⁸While he was still speaking, yet another messenger came and said, "Your sons and daughters were feasting and drinking wine at the oldest brother's house, ¹⁹when suddenly a mighty wind swept in from the desert and struck the four corners of the house. It collapsed on them and they are dead, and I am the only one who has escaped to tell you!"

²⁰At this, Job got up and tore his robe and shaved his head. Then he fell to the ground in worship ²¹and said:

"Naked I came from my mother's womb,
    and naked I will depart.ᵃ
The Lord gave and the Lord has taken
    away;
    may the name of the Lord be praised."

²²In all this, Job did not sin by charging God with wrongdoing.

2 On another day the angelsᵇ came to present themselves before the Lord, and Satan also came with them to present himself before him. ²And the Lord said to Satan, "Where have you come from?"

Satan answered the Lord, "From roaming throughout the earth, going back and forth on it."

³Then the Lord said to Satan, "Have you considered my servant Job? There is no one on earth like him; he is blameless and upright, a man who fears God and shuns evil. And he still maintains his integrity, though you incited me against him to ruin him without any reason."

⁴"Skin for skin!" Satan replied. "A man will give all he has for his own life. ⁵But now stretch out your hand and strike his flesh and bones, and he will surely curse you to your face."

⁶The Lord said to Satan, "Very well, then, he is in your hands; but you must spare his life."

⁷So Satan went out from the presence of the Lord and afflicted Job with painful sores from the soles of his feet to the crown of his head. ⁸Then Job took a piece of broken pottery and scraped himself with it as he sat among the ashes.

⁹His wife said to him, "Are you still maintaining your integrity? Curse God and die!"

¹⁰He replied, "You are talking like a foolishᶜ woman. Shall we accept good from God, and not trouble?"

In all this, Job did not sin in what he said.

¹¹When Job's three friends, Eliphaz the Temanite, Bildad the Shuhite and Zophar the Na-

amathite, heard about all the troubles that had come upon him, they set out from their homes and met together by agreement to go and sympathize with him and comfort him. ¹²When they saw him from a distance, they could hardly recognize him; they began to weep aloud, and they tore their robes and sprinkled dust on their heads. ¹³Then they sat on the ground with him for seven days and seven nights. No one said a word to him, because they saw how great his suffering was.

Job Speaks

3 After this, Job opened his mouth and cursed the day of his birth. ²He said:

³"May the day of my birth perish,
    and the night that said, 'A boy is conceived!'

ᵃ 21 Or *will return there*   ᵇ 1 Hebrew *the sons of God*
ᶜ 10 The Hebrew word rendered *foolish* denotes moral deficiency.

Listening: To Connect with Job, His Friends Listen for a Week

Job 2:11–13

When Job's friends hear about his catastrophe, they want to help. By this time, boils have broken out all over Job's body, and his friends don't even recognize him. They feel his pain and are horrified to see a friend in such need. Mercifully, they keep their mouths shut for one whole week (if only they had continued their silence!). They sit with their friend and listen.

Somehow these friends realized an important truth: People don't lose intimacy when they stop talking, but when they stop listening. Leaders seldom realize how much their listening empowers the other person. Because they are leaders, the sheer act of listening speaks volumes that even a great speech can't communicate. Listening . . .

- Communicates the value of the other person and his or her thoughts.
- Communicates love and understanding and care for their needs.
- Communicates a desire to grow, learn, and remain teachable.

⁴That day — may it turn to darkness;
  may God above not care about it;
  may no light shine on it.
⁵May gloom and utter darkness claim it once
    more;
  may a cloud settle over it;
  may blackness overwhelm it.
⁶That night — may thick darkness seize it;
  may it not be included among the days of
    the year
  nor be entered in any of the months.
⁷May that night be barren;
  may no shout of joy be heard in it.
⁸May those who curse days*ᵃ* curse that day,
  those who are ready to rouse Leviathan.
⁹May its morning stars become dark;
  may it wait for daylight in vain
  and not see the first rays of dawn,
¹⁰for it did not shut the doors of the womb
    on me
  to hide trouble from my eyes.

¹¹"Why did I not perish at birth,
  and die as I came from the womb?
¹²Why were there knees to receive me
  and breasts that I might be nursed?
¹³For now I would be lying down in peace;
  I would be asleep and at rest
¹⁴with kings and rulers of the earth,
  who built for themselves places now lying
    in ruins,
¹⁵with princes who had gold,
  who filled their houses with silver.
¹⁶Or why was I not hidden away in the ground
    like a stillborn child,
  like an infant who never saw the light of
    day?
¹⁷There the wicked cease from turmoil,
  and there the weary are at rest.
¹⁸Captives also enjoy their ease;
  they no longer hear the slave driver's
    shout.
¹⁹The small and the great are there,
  and the slaves are freed from their owners.

²⁰"Why is light given to those in misery,
  and life to the bitter of soul,
²¹to those who long for death that does not
    come,
  who search for it more than for hidden
    treasure,
²²who are filled with gladness
  and rejoice when they reach the grave?
²³Why is life given to a man
  whose way is hidden,
  whom God has hedged in?

²⁴For sighing has become my daily food;
  my groans pour out like water.
²⁵What I feared has come upon me;
  what I dreaded has happened to me.
²⁶I have no peace, no quietness;
  I have no rest, but only turmoil."

Eliphaz

4 Then Eliphaz the Temanite replied:

²"If someone ventures a word with you, will
    you be impatient?
  But who can keep from speaking?
³Think how you have instructed many,
  how you have strengthened feeble hands.
⁴Your words have supported those who
    stumbled;
  you have strengthened faltering knees.
⁵But now trouble comes to you, and you are
    discouraged;
  it strikes you, and you are dismayed.
⁶Should not your piety be your confidence
  and your blameless ways your hope?

⁷"Consider now: Who, being innocent, has
    ever perished?
  Where were the upright ever destroyed?
⁸As I have observed, those who plow evil
  and those who sow trouble reap it.
⁹At the breath of God they perish;
  at the blast of his anger they are no more.
¹⁰The lions may roar and growl,
  yet the teeth of the great lions are
    broken.
¹¹The lion perishes for lack of prey,
  and the cubs of the lioness are scattered.

¹²"A word was secretly brought to me,
  my ears caught a whisper of it.
¹³Amid disquieting dreams in the night,
  when deep sleep falls on people,
¹⁴fear and trembling seized me
  and made all my bones shake.
¹⁵A spirit glided past my face,
  and the hair on my body stood on end.
¹⁶It stopped,
  but I could not tell what it was.
A form stood before my eyes,
  and I heard a hushed voice:
¹⁷'Can a mortal be more righteous than God?
  Can even a strong man be more pure than
    his Maker?
¹⁸If God places no trust in his servants,
  if he charges his angels with error,

ᵃ 8 Or curse the sea

¹⁹ how much more those who live in houses of
     clay,
    whose foundations are in the dust,
    who are crushed more readily than a moth!
²⁰ Between dawn and dusk they are broken to
     pieces;
    unnoticed, they perish forever.
²¹ Are not the cords of their tent pulled up,
    so that they die without wisdom?'

5 "Call if you will, but who will answer you?
    To which of the holy ones will you turn?
² Resentment kills a fool,
    and envy slays the simple.
³ I myself have seen a fool taking root,
    but suddenly his house was cursed.
⁴ His children are far from safety,
    crushed in court without a defender.
⁵ The hungry consume his harvest,
    taking it even from among thorns,
    and the thirsty pant after his wealth.
⁶ For hardship does not spring from the soil,
    nor does trouble sprout from the ground.
⁷ Yet man is born to trouble
    as surely as sparks fly upward.

⁸ "But if I were you, I would appeal to God;
    I would lay my cause before him.
⁹ He performs wonders that cannot be
     fathomed,
    miracles that cannot be counted.
¹⁰ He provides rain for the earth;
    he sends water on the countryside.
¹¹ The lowly he sets on high,
    and those who mourn are lifted to safety.
¹² He thwarts the plans of the crafty,
    so that their hands achieve no success.
¹³ He catches the wise in their craftiness,
    and the schemes of the wily are swept
     away.
¹⁴ Darkness comes upon them in the daytime;
    at noon they grope as in the night.
¹⁵ He saves the needy from the sword in their
     mouth;
    he saves them from the clutches of the
     powerful.
¹⁶ So the poor have hope,
    and injustice shuts its mouth.

¹⁷ "Blessed is the one whom God corrects;
    so do not despise the discipline of the
     Almighty.[a]
¹⁸ For he wounds, but he also binds up;
    he injures, but his hands also heal.
¹⁹ From six calamities he will rescue you;
    in seven no harm will touch you.

²⁰ In famine he will deliver you from death,
    and in battle from the stroke of the sword.
²¹ You will be protected from the lash of the
     tongue,
    and need not fear when destruction
     comes.
²² You will laugh at destruction and famine,
    and need not fear the wild animals.
²³ For you will have a covenant with the stones
     of the field,
    and the wild animals will be at peace with
     you.
²⁴ You will know that your tent is secure;
    you will take stock of your property and
     find nothing missing.
²⁵ You will know that your children will be
     many,
    and your descendants like the grass of the
     earth.
²⁶ You will come to the grave in full vigor,
    like sheaves gathered in season.

²⁷ "We have examined this, and it is true.
    So hear it and apply it to yourself."

Job

6 Then Job replied:

² "If only my anguish could be weighed
    and all my misery be placed on the scales!
³ It would surely outweigh the sand of the
     seas—
    no wonder my words have been
     impetuous.
⁴ The arrows of the Almighty are in me,
    my spirit drinks in their poison;
    God's terrors are marshaled against me.
⁵ Does a wild donkey bray when it has grass,
    or an ox bellow when it has fodder?
⁶ Is tasteless food eaten without salt,
    or is there flavor in the sap of the
     mallow[b]?
⁷ I refuse to touch it;
    such food makes me ill.

⁸ "Oh, that I might have my request,
    that God would grant what I hope for,
⁹ that God would be willing to crush me,
    to let loose his hand and cut off my life!
¹⁰ Then I would still have this consolation—
    my joy in unrelenting pain—
    that I had not denied the words of the
     Holy One.

---

[a] 17 Hebrew *Shaddai*; here and throughout Job   [b] 6 The
meaning of the Hebrew for this phrase is uncertain.

11 "What strength do I have, that I should still hope?
What prospects, that I should be patient?
12 Do I have the strength of stone?
Is my flesh bronze?
13 Do I have any power to help myself,
now that success has been driven from me?

14 "Anyone who withholds kindness from a friend
forsakes the fear of the Almighty.
15 But my brothers are as undependable as intermittent streams,
as the streams that overflow
16 when darkened by thawing ice
and swollen with melting snow,
17 but that stop flowing in the dry season,
and in the heat vanish from their channels.
18 Caravans turn aside from their routes;
they go off into the wasteland and perish.
19 The caravans of Tema look for water,
the traveling merchants of Sheba look in hope.
20 They are distressed, because they had been confident;
they arrive there, only to be disappointed.
21 Now you too have proved to be of no help;
you see something dreadful and are afraid.
22 Have I ever said, 'Give something on my behalf,
pay a ransom for me from your wealth,
23 deliver me from the hand of the enemy,
rescue me from the clutches of the ruthless'?

24 "Teach me, and I will be quiet;
show me where I have been wrong.
25 How painful are honest words!
But what do your arguments prove?
26 Do you mean to correct what I say,
and treat my desperate words as wind?
27 You would even cast lots for the fatherless
and barter away your friend.

28 "But now be so kind as to look at me.
Would I lie to your face?
29 Relent, do not be unjust;
reconsider, for my integrity is at stake.[a]
30 Is there any wickedness on my lips?
Can my mouth not discern malice?

7 "Do not mortals have hard service on earth?
Are not their days like those of hired laborers?

2 Like a slave longing for the evening shadows,
or a hired laborer waiting to be paid,
3 so I have been allotted months of futility,
and nights of misery have been assigned to me.
4 When I lie down I think, 'How long before I get up?'
The night drags on, and I toss and turn until dawn.
5 My body is clothed with worms and scabs,
my skin is broken and festering.

6 "My days are swifter than a weaver's shuttle,
and they come to an end without hope.
7 Remember, O God, that my life is but a breath;
my eyes will never see happiness again.
8 The eye that now sees me will see me no longer;
you will look for me, but I will be no more.
9 As a cloud vanishes and is gone,
so one who goes down to the grave does not return.
10 He will never come to his house again;
his place will know him no more.

11 "Therefore I will not keep silent;
I will speak out in the anguish of my spirit,
I will complain in the bitterness of my soul.
12 Am I the sea, or the monster of the deep,
that you put me under guard?
13 When I think my bed will comfort me
and my couch will ease my complaint,
14 even then you frighten me with dreams
and terrify me with visions,
15 so that I prefer strangling and death,
rather than this body of mine.
16 I despise my life; I would not live forever.
Let me alone; my days have no meaning.

17 "What is mankind that you make so much of them,
that you give them so much attention,
18 that you examine them every morning
and test them every moment?
19 Will you never look away from me,
or let me alone even for an instant?
20 If I have sinned, what have I done to you,
you who see everything we do?

---

[a] 29 Or *my righteousness still stands*

Integrity: Job Challenges His Friends to Identify His Flaws

Job 6:1—7:21

All of Job's friends posed a theory about his troubles, but Job simply asked them to survey his life and point out any place where he lacked integrity. He felt so certain of the blamelessness of his heart that he invited the scrutiny of his peers. Only a leader with strong character and a strong sense of security can do that!

C. S. Lewis calls this quality, "Leaders with chests." Lewis likened the properly ordered soul to the human body: the head (reason) must rule the belly (the sensual appetites) through the chest (character and spirit). The chest is the indispensable liaison between reason and the appetites. Without a strong "chest," men would succumb to excuses, relativism and compromise. Lewis called those with no character or integrity, "men without chests."

What enabled Job to possess such integrity as a leader?

1. *Strong Security:* He felt emotionally secure enough to take criticism.

2. *Clear Conscience:* He kept a clear and sensitive conscience regarding sin.

3. *Pure Motives:* He refused to entertain self-indulgent motives.

4. *Solid Character:* He was committed to doing the right thing at any cost.

Why have you made me your target?
Have I become a burden to you?[a]
21 Why do you not pardon my offenses
and forgive my sins?
For I will soon lie down in the dust;
you will search for me, but I will be no
more."

Bildad

8 Then Bildad the Shuhite replied:

2 "How long will you say such things?
Your words are a blustering wind.
3 Does God pervert justice?
Does the Almighty pervert what is right?
4 When your children sinned against him,
he gave them over to the penalty of their
sin.
5 But if you will seek God earnestly
and plead with the Almighty,
6 if you are pure and upright,
even now he will rouse himself on your
behalf
and restore you to your prosperous state.
7 Your beginnings will seem humble,
so prosperous will your future be.

8 "Ask the former generation
and find out what their ancestors learned,
9 for we were born only yesterday and know
nothing,
and our days on earth are but a shadow.

10 Will they not instruct you and tell you?
Will they not bring forth words from their
understanding?
11 Can papyrus grow tall where there is no marsh?
Can reeds thrive without water?
12 While still growing and uncut,
they wither more quickly than grass.
13 Such is the destiny of all who forget God;
so perishes the hope of the godless.
14 What they trust in is fragile[b];
what they rely on is a spider's web.
15 They lean on the web, but it gives way;
they cling to it, but it does not hold.
16 They are like a well-watered plant in the
sunshine,
spreading its shoots over the garden;
17 it entwines its roots around a pile of rocks
and looks for a place among the stones.
18 But when it is torn from its spot,
that place disowns it and says, 'I never saw
you.'
19 Surely its life withers away,
and[c] from the soil other plants grow.

20 "Surely God does not reject one who is
blameless
or strengthen the hands of evildoers.

---

[a] 20 A few manuscripts of the Masoretic Text, an ancient Hebrew scribal tradition and Septuagint; most manuscripts of the Masoretic Text *I have become a burden to myself.*
[b] 14 The meaning of the Hebrew for this word is uncertain.
[c] 19 Or *Surely all the joy it has / is that*

²¹ He will yet fill your mouth with laughter
and your lips with shouts of joy.
²² Your enemies will be clothed in shame,
and the tents of the wicked will be no
more."

Job

9 Then Job replied:

² "Indeed, I know that this is true.
But how can mere mortals prove their
innocence before God?
³ Though they wished to dispute with him,
they could not answer him one time out of
a thousand.
⁴ His wisdom is profound, his power is vast.
Who has resisted him and come out
unscathed?
⁵ He moves mountains without their knowing
it
and overturns them in his anger.
⁶ He shakes the earth from its place
and makes its pillars tremble.
⁷ He speaks to the sun and it does not shine;
he seals off the light of the stars.
⁸ He alone stretches out the heavens
and treads on the waves of the sea.
⁹ He is the Maker of the Bear[a] and Orion,
the Pleiades and the constellations of the
south.
¹⁰ He performs wonders that cannot be
fathomed,
miracles that cannot be counted.
¹¹ When he passes me, I cannot see him;
when he goes by, I cannot perceive him.
¹² If he snatches away, who can stop him?
Who can say to him, 'What are you
doing?'
¹³ God does not restrain his anger;
even the cohorts of Rahab cowered at his
feet.

¹⁴ "How then can I dispute with him?
How can I find words to argue with him?
¹⁵ Though I were innocent, I could not answer
him;
I could only plead with my Judge for
mercy.
¹⁶ Even if I summoned him and he responded,
I do not believe he would give me a
hearing.
¹⁷ He would crush me with a storm
and multiply my wounds for no reason.
¹⁸ He would not let me catch my breath
but would overwhelm me with misery.

¹⁹ If it is a matter of strength, he is mighty!
And if it is a matter of justice, who can
challenge him[b]?
²⁰ Even if I were innocent, my mouth would
condemn me;
if I were blameless, it would pronounce
me guilty.

²¹ "Although I am blameless,
I have no concern for myself;
I despise my own life.
²² It is all the same; that is why I say,
'He destroys both the blameless and the
wicked.'
²³ When a scourge brings sudden death,
he mocks the despair of the innocent.
²⁴ When a land falls into the hands of the
wicked,
he blindfolds its judges.
If it is not he, then who is it?

²⁵ "My days are swifter than a runner;
they fly away without a glimpse of joy.
²⁶ They skim past like boats of papyrus,
like eagles swooping down on their prey.
²⁷ If I say, 'I will forget my complaint,
I will change my expression, and smile,'
²⁸ I still dread all my sufferings,
for I know you will not hold me innocent.
²⁹ Since I am already found guilty,
why should I struggle in vain?
³⁰ Even if I washed myself with soap
and my hands with cleansing powder,
³¹ you would plunge me into a slime pit
so that even my clothes would detest me.

³² "He is not a mere mortal like me that I might
answer him,
that we might confront each other in court.
³³ If only there were someone to mediate
between us,
someone to bring us together,
³⁴ someone to remove God's rod from me,
so that his terror would frighten me no
more.
³⁵ Then I would speak up without fear of him,
but as it now stands with me, I cannot.

10 "I loathe my very life;
therefore I will give free rein to my
complaint
and speak out in the bitterness of my soul.
² I say to God: Do not declare me guilty,
but tell me what charges you have against
me.

---

[a] 9 Or of Leo   [b] 19 See Septuagint; Hebrew me.

³ Does it please you to oppress me,
  to spurn the work of your hands,
  while you smile on the plans of the
    wicked?
⁴ Do you have eyes of flesh?
  Do you see as a mortal sees?
⁵ Are your days like those of a mortal
  or your years like those of a strong man,
⁶ that you must search out my faults
  and probe after my sin —
⁷ though you know that I am not guilty
  and that no one can rescue me from your
    hand?

⁸ "Your hands shaped me and made me.
  Will you now turn and destroy me?
⁹ Remember that you molded me like clay.
  Will you now turn me to dust again?
¹⁰ Did you not pour me out like milk
  and curdle me like cheese,
¹¹ clothe me with skin and flesh
  and knit me together with bones and
    sinews?
¹² You gave me life and showed me kindness,
  and in your providence watched over my
    spirit.

¹³ "But this is what you concealed in your
    heart,
  and I know that this was in your mind:
¹⁴ If I sinned, you would be watching me
  and would not let my offense go
    unpunished.
¹⁵ If I am guilty — woe to me!
  Even if I am innocent, I cannot lift my
    head,
  for I am full of shame
  and drowned in[a] my affliction.
¹⁶ If I hold my head high, you stalk me like a
    lion
  and again display your awesome power
    against me.
¹⁷ You bring new witnesses against me
  and increase your anger toward me;
  your forces come against me wave upon
    wave.

¹⁸ "Why then did you bring me out of the
    womb?
  I wish I had died before any eye saw me.
¹⁹ If only I had never come into being,
  or had been carried straight from the
    womb to the grave!
²⁰ Are not my few days almost over?
  Turn away from me so I can have a
    moment's joy

²¹ before I go to the place of no return,
  to the land of gloom and utter darkness,
²² to the land of deepest night,
  of utter darkness and disorder,
  where even the light is like darkness."

Zophar

11 Then Zophar the Naamathite replied:

² "Are all these words to go unanswered?
  Is this talker to be vindicated?
³ Will your idle talk reduce others to silence?
  Will no one rebuke you when you mock?
⁴ You say to God, 'My beliefs are flawless
  and I am pure in your sight.'
⁵ Oh, how I wish that God would speak,
  that he would open his lips against you
⁶ and disclose to you the secrets of wisdom,
  for true wisdom has two sides.
  Know this: God has even forgotten some
    of your sin.

⁷ "Can you fathom the mysteries of God?
  Can you probe the limits of the Almighty?
⁸ They are higher than the heavens above —
  what can you do?
  They are deeper than the depths below —
  what can you know?
⁹ Their measure is longer than the earth
  and wider than the sea.

¹⁰ "If he comes along and confines you in
    prison
  and convenes a court, who can oppose him?
¹¹ Surely he recognizes deceivers;
  and when he sees evil, does he not take
    note?
¹² But the witless can no more become wise
  than a wild donkey's colt can be born
    human.[b]

¹³ "Yet if you devote your heart to him
  and stretch out your hands to him,
¹⁴ if you put away the sin that is in your hand
  and allow no evil to dwell in your tent,
¹⁵ then, free of fault, you will lift up your face;
  you will stand firm and without fear.
¹⁶ You will surely forget your trouble,
  recalling it only as waters gone by.
¹⁷ Life will be brighter than noonday,
  and darkness will become like morning.
¹⁸ You will be secure, because there is hope;
  you will look about you and take your rest
    in safety.

---

a 15 Or *and aware of*   *b* 12 Or *wild donkey can be born tame*

¹⁹ You will lie down, with no one to make you afraid,
and many will court your favor.
²⁰ But the eyes of the wicked will fail,
and escape will elude them;
their hope will become a dying gasp."

Job

12 Then Job replied:

² "Doubtless you are the only people who matter,
and wisdom will die with you!
³ But I have a mind as well as you;
I am not inferior to you.
Who does not know all these things?

⁴ "I have become a laughingstock to my friends,
though I called on God and he answered—
a mere laughingstock, though righteous and blameless!
⁵ Those who are at ease have contempt for misfortune
as the fate of those whose feet are slipping.
⁶ The tents of marauders are undisturbed,
and those who provoke God are secure—
those God has in his hand.ᵃ

⁷ "But ask the animals, and they will teach you,
or the birds in the sky, and they will tell you;
⁸ or speak to the earth, and it will teach you,
or let the fish in the sea inform you.
⁹ Which of all these does not know
that the hand of the LORD has done this?
¹⁰ In his hand is the life of every creature
and the breath of all mankind.
¹¹ Does not the ear test words
as the tongue tastes food?
¹² Is not wisdom found among the aged?
Does not long life bring understanding?

¹³ "To God belong wisdom and power;
counsel and understanding are his.
¹⁴ What he tears down cannot be rebuilt;
those he imprisons cannot be released.
¹⁵ If he holds back the waters, there is drought;
if he lets them loose, they devastate the land.
¹⁶ To him belong strength and insight;
both deceived and deceiver are his.

¹⁷ He leads rulers away stripped
and makes fools of judges.
¹⁸ He takes off the shackles put on by kings
and ties a loinclothᵇ around their waist.
¹⁹ He leads priests away stripped
and overthrows officials long established.
²⁰ He silences the lips of trusted advisers
and takes away the discernment of elders.
²¹ He pours contempt on nobles
and disarms the mighty.
²² He reveals the deep things of darkness
and brings utter darkness into the light.
²³ He makes nations great, and destroys them;
he enlarges nations, and disperses them.
²⁴ He deprives the leaders of the earth of their reason;
he makes them wander in a trackless waste.
²⁵ They grope in darkness with no light;
he makes them stagger like drunkards.

13 "My eyes have seen all this,
my ears have heard and understood it.
² What you know, I also know;
I am not inferior to you.
³ But I desire to speak to the Almighty
and to argue my case with God.
⁴ You, however, smear me with lies;
you are worthless physicians, all of you!
⁵ If only you would be altogether silent!
For you, that would be wisdom.
⁶ Hear now my argument;
listen to the pleas of my lips.
⁷ Will you speak wickedly on God's behalf?
Will you speak deceitfully for him?
⁸ Will you show him partiality?
Will you argue the case for God?
⁹ Would it turn out well if he examined you?
Could you deceive him as you might deceive a mortal?
¹⁰ He would surely call you to account
if you secretly showed partiality.
¹¹ Would not his splendor terrify you?
Would not the dread of him fall on you?
¹² Your maxims are proverbs of ashes;
your defenses are defenses of clay.
¹³ "Keep silent and let me speak;
then let come to me what may.
¹⁴ Why do I put myself in jeopardy
and take my life in my hands?

ᵃ 6 Or *those whose god is in their own hand*   ᵇ 18 Or *shackles of kings / and ties a belt*

¹⁵ Though he slay me, yet will I hope in him;
　　I will surely*ª* defend my ways to his face.
¹⁶ Indeed, this will turn out for my deliverance,
　　for no godless person would dare come
　　　before him!
¹⁷ Listen carefully to what I say;
　　let my words ring in your ears.
¹⁸ Now that I have prepared my case,
　　I know I will be vindicated.
¹⁹ Can anyone bring charges against me?
　　If so, I will be silent and die.

²⁰ "Only grant me these two things, God,
　　and then I will not hide from you:
²¹ Withdraw your hand far from me,
　　and stop frightening me with your terrors.
²² Then summon me and I will answer,
　　or let me speak, and you reply to me.
²³ How many wrongs and sins have I committed?
　　Show me my offense and my sin.
²⁴ Why do you hide your face
　　and consider me your enemy?
²⁵ Will you torment a windblown leaf?
　　Will you chase after dry chaff?

Commitment: Job Stays Steady at All Costs

Job 13:15

The statement confounds nominal Christians, yet it is exactly the kind of affirmation that God uses to build his kingdom in the darkest places on earth. "Though he slay me," Job says, "yet will I hope in him" (Job 13:15).

Statements like this shake the very gates of hell. What can stop a leader who has made this kind of commitment? Not pain. Not death. Not hardship.

Why has terrorism, for instance, become such an international problem? Because terrorists already have given up their lives for their cause. They will drive a truck full of explosives into enemy headquarters because they no longer hold their lives dear.

This is where Job finally ended up—willing to give up his life for God. Only in that position do we find complete liberation—free from any temptation, threat, bribe, sin, or enticement. When we can say, with the apostle Paul, that we have already died (Gal 2:20), then we will have reached the place where God can really use us.

²⁶ For you write down bitter things against me
　　and make me reap the sins of my youth.
²⁷ You fasten my feet in shackles;
　　you keep close watch on all my paths
　　by putting marks on the soles of my feet.

²⁸ "So man wastes away like something rotten,
　　like a garment eaten by moths.

14 "Mortals, born of woman,
　　are of few days and full of trouble.
² They spring up like flowers and wither away;
　　like fleeting shadows, they do not endure.
³ Do you fix your eye on them?
　　Will you bring them*ᵇ* before you for
　　　judgment?
⁴ Who can bring what is pure from the impure?
　　No one!
⁵ A person's days are determined;
　　you have decreed the number of his
　　　months
　　and have set limits he cannot exceed.
⁶ So look away from him and let him alone,
　　till he has put in his time like a hired
　　　laborer.

⁷ "At least there is hope for a tree:
　　If it is cut down, it will sprout again,
　　and its new shoots will not fail.
⁸ Its roots may grow old in the ground
　　and its stump die in the soil,
⁹ yet at the scent of water it will bud
　　and put forth shoots like a plant.
¹⁰ But a man dies and is laid low;
　　he breathes his last and is no more.
¹¹ As the water of a lake dries up
　　or a riverbed becomes parched and dry,
¹² so he lies down and does not rise;
　　till the heavens are no more, people will
　　　not awake
　　or be roused from their sleep.

¹³ "If only you would hide me in the grave
　　and conceal me till your anger has
　　　passed!
　　If only you would set me a time
　　and then remember me!
¹⁴ If someone dies, will they live again?
　　All the days of my hard service
　　I will wait for my renewal*ᶜ* to come.
¹⁵ You will call and I will answer you;
　　you will long for the creature your hands
　　　have made.

ª 15 Or *He will surely slay me; I have no hope — / yet I will*　ᵇ 3 Septuagint, Vulgate and Syriac; Hebrew *me*　ᶜ 14 Or *release*

¹⁶Surely then you will count my steps
but not keep track of my sin.
¹⁷My offenses will be sealed up in a bag;
you will cover over my sin.

¹⁸"But as a mountain erodes and crumbles
and as a rock is moved from its place,
¹⁹as water wears away stones
and torrents wash away the soil,
so you destroy a person's hope.
²⁰You overpower them once for all, and they are gone;
you change their countenance and send them away.
²¹If their children are honored, they do not know it;
if their offspring are brought low, they do not see it.
²²They feel but the pain of their own bodies
and mourn only for themselves."

Eliphaz

15 Then Eliphaz the Temanite replied:

²"Would a wise person answer with empty notions
or fill their belly with the hot east wind?
³Would they argue with useless words,
with speeches that have no value?
⁴But you even undermine piety
and hinder devotion to God.

⁵Your sin prompts your mouth;
you adopt the tongue of the crafty.
⁶Your own mouth condemns you, not mine;
your own lips testify against you.

⁷"Are you the first man ever born?
Were you brought forth before the hills?
⁸Do you listen in on God's council?
Do you have a monopoly on wisdom?
⁹What do you know that we do not know?
What insights do you have that we do not have?
¹⁰The gray-haired and the aged are on our side,
men even older than your father.
¹¹Are God's consolations not enough for you,
words spoken gently to you?
¹²Why has your heart carried you away,
and why do your eyes flash,
¹³so that you vent your rage against God
and pour out such words from your mouth?

¹⁴"What are mortals, that they could be pure,
or those born of woman, that they could be righteous?
¹⁵If God places no trust in his holy ones,
if even the heavens are not pure in his eyes,
¹⁶how much less mortals, who are vile and corrupt,
who drink up evil like water!

JOB PROFILE in leadership

Puzzled, Not Unbelieving
Job 13:20—14:22

God doesn't mind questions; it's doubt that he hates.

For many wearying hours, the three friends of Job—Eliphaz, Bildad and Zophar—accused Job of all kinds of evil. They spoke the kind of foolish words that the healthy and ill-informed often speak to those in pain.

O, how Job wanted to take his case to the Lord himself! "Why did I not perish at birth?" he asked the Lord. "Will you never look away from me, or let me alone even for an instant?" (Job 3:11; 7:19).

Job's words reflect the kind of torment we would expect from a godly man in deep pain. But God says nothing. Only at the end of the book does God at last break his silence. And while he answers not one of Job's questions, neither does he chastise him for asking them. God rebukes Job for only one thing: doubting his righteous character (40:8).

Leaders must never be afraid to ask hard questions of God, but neither must they demand that he answer. And no matter how dark our circumstances may grow, we must resist the temptation to doubt God's holy nature. When we, like Job, through trembling lips confess the awesome majesty of God, we may at last be ready for the awesome blessing of God.

17 "Listen to me and I will explain to you;
   let me tell you what I have seen,
18 what the wise have declared,
   hiding nothing received from their
      ancestors
19 (to whom alone the land was given
   when no foreigners moved among them):
20 All his days the wicked man suffers torment,
   the ruthless man through all the years
      stored up for him.
21 Terrifying sounds fill his ears;
   when all seems well, marauders attack
      him.
22 He despairs of escaping the realm of
      darkness;
   he is marked for the sword.
23 He wanders about for food like a vulture;
   he knows the day of darkness is at hand.
24 Distress and anguish fill him with terror;
   troubles overwhelm him, like a king
      poised to attack,
25 because he shakes his fist at God
   and vaunts himself against the Almighty,
26 defiantly charging against him
   with a thick, strong shield.

27 "Though his face is covered with fat
   and his waist bulges with flesh,
28 he will inhabit ruined towns
   and houses where no one lives,
   houses crumbling to rubble.

29 He will no longer be rich and his wealth will
      not endure,
   nor will his possessions spread over the
      land.
30 He will not escape the darkness;
   a flame will wither his shoots,
   and the breath of God's mouth will carry
      him away.
31 Let him not deceive himself by trusting what
      is worthless,
   for he will get nothing in return.
32 Before his time he will wither,
   and his branches will not flourish.
33 He will be like a vine stripped of its unripe
      grapes,
   like an olive tree shedding its blossoms.
34 For the company of the godless will be
      barren,
   and fire will consume the tents of those
      who love bribes.
35 They conceive trouble and give birth to evil;
   their womb fashions deceit."

Job

16

Then Job replied:

2 "I have heard many things like these;
   you are miserable comforters, all of you!
3 Will your long-winded speeches never end?
   What ails you that you keep on arguing?

Job's Friends Fail at the Law of Connection

Job 16:2

Eliphaz, Bildad and Zophar accused Job of acting foolishly, of speaking wrongly, of leading wickedly. But they never got their message across for two reasons: First, they didn't have all the facts; and second, they didn't practice the Law of Connection.

Many leaders are tempted to make the same mistakes. We voice our opinions even though we remain ignorant of important information and lack any heart connection to our audience. Job called his friends, "miserable comforters." Every good communicator seeks first to understand before being understood. Note how they differ from public speakers:

Public Speaker	Communicator
1. Seeks to be understood and liked	1. Seeks to understand and connect
2. Asks: What do I have?	2. Asks: What do they need?
3. Focuses on techniques	3. Focuses on atmosphere
4. Is self-conscious	4. Is audience-oriented
5. Wants to complete the speech	5. Wants to complete the people
6. Content-oriented	6. Change-oriented

⁴I also could speak like you,
    if you were in my place;
  I could make fine speeches against you
    and shake my head at you.
⁵But my mouth would encourage you;
    comfort from my lips would bring you
      relief.

⁶"Yet if I speak, my pain is not relieved;
    and if I refrain, it does not go away.
⁷Surely, God, you have worn me out;
    you have devastated my entire
      household.
⁸You have shriveled me up—and it has
      become a witness;
    my gauntness rises up and testifies
      against me.
⁹God assails me and tears me in his anger
      and gnashes his teeth at me;
    my opponent fastens on me his piercing
      eyes.
¹⁰People open their mouths to jeer at me;
    they strike my cheek in scorn
    and unite together against me.
¹¹God has turned me over to the ungodly
    and thrown me into the clutches of the
      wicked.
¹²All was well with me, but he shattered me;
    he seized me by the neck and crushed me.
  He has made me his target;
¹³   his archers surround me.
  Without pity, he pierces my kidneys
    and spills my gall on the ground.
¹⁴Again and again he bursts upon me;
    he rushes at me like a warrior.

¹⁵"I have sewed sackcloth over my skin
    and buried my brow in the dust.
¹⁶My face is red with weeping,
    dark shadows ring my eyes;
¹⁷yet my hands have been free of violence
    and my prayer is pure.

¹⁸"Earth, do not cover my blood;
    may my cry never be laid to rest!
¹⁹Even now my witness is in heaven;
    my advocate is on high.
²⁰My intercessor is my friend[a]
    as my eyes pour out tears to God;
²¹on behalf of a man he pleads with God
    as one pleads for a friend.

²²"Only a few years will pass
    before I take the path of no return.

17 ¹My spirit is broken,
    my days are cut short,
    the grave awaits me.

²Surely mockers surround me;
    my eyes must dwell on their hostility.

³"Give me, O God, the pledge you demand.
    Who else will put up security for me?
⁴You have closed their minds to
      understanding;
    therefore you will not let them triumph.
⁵If anyone denounces their friends for
      reward,
    the eyes of their children will fail.

⁶"God has made me a byword to everyone,
    a man in whose face people spit.
⁷My eyes have grown dim with grief;
    my whole frame is but a shadow.
⁸The upright are appalled at this;
    the innocent are aroused against the
      ungodly.
⁹Nevertheless, the righteous will hold to their
      ways,
    and those with clean hands will grow
      stronger.

¹⁰"But come on, all of you, try again!
    I will not find a wise man among you.
¹¹My days have passed, my plans are shattered.
    Yet the desires of my heart
¹²turn night into day;
    in the face of the darkness light is near.
¹³If the only home I hope for is the grave,
    if I spread out my bed in the realm of
      darkness,
¹⁴if I say to corruption, 'You are my father,'
    and to the worm, 'My mother' or 'My
      sister,'
¹⁵where then is my hope—
    who can see any hope for me?
¹⁶Will it go down to the gates of death?
    Will we descend together into the dust?"

Bildad

18 Then Bildad the Shuhite replied:

²"When will you end these speeches?
    Be sensible, and then we can talk.
³Why are we regarded as cattle
    and considered stupid in your sight?
⁴You who tear yourself to pieces in your
      anger,
    is the earth to be abandoned for your
      sake?
  Or must the rocks be moved from their
      place?

---

[a] 20 Or *My friends treat me with scorn*

5 "The lamp of a wicked man is snuffed out;
    the flame of his fire stops burning.
6 The light in his tent becomes dark;
    the lamp beside him goes out.
7 The vigor of his step is weakened;
    his own schemes throw him down.
8 His feet thrust him into a net;
    he wanders into its mesh.
9 A trap seizes him by the heel;
    a snare holds him fast.
10 A noose is hidden for him on the ground;
    a trap lies in his path.
11 Terrors startle him on every side
    and dog his every step.
12 Calamity is hungry for him;
    disaster is ready for him when he falls.
13 It eats away parts of his skin;
    death's firstborn devours his limbs.
14 He is torn from the security of his tent
    and marched off to the king of terrors.
15 Fire resides*a* in his tent;
    burning sulfur is scattered over his
      dwelling.
16 His roots dry up below
    and his branches wither above.
17 The memory of him perishes from the earth;
    he has no name in the land.
18 He is driven from light into the realm of
      darkness
    and is banished from the world.
19 He has no offspring or descendants among
      his people,
    no survivor where once he lived.
20 People of the west are appalled at his fate;
    those of the east are seized with horror.
21 Surely such is the dwelling of an evil man;
    such is the place of one who does not
      know God."

Job

19

Then Job replied:

2 "How long will you torment me
    and crush me with words?
3 Ten times now you have reproached me;
    shamelessly you attack me.
4 If it is true that I have gone astray,
    my error remains my concern alone.
5 If indeed you would exalt yourselves above me
    and use my humiliation against me,
6 then know that God has wronged me
    and drawn his net around me.

7 "Though I cry, 'Violence!' I get no response;
    though I call for help, there is no justice.

8 He has blocked my way so I cannot pass;
    he has shrouded my paths in darkness.
9 He has stripped me of my honor
    and removed the crown from my head.
10 He tears me down on every side till I am
      gone;
    he uproots my hope like a tree.
11 His anger burns against me;
    he counts me among his enemies.
12 His troops advance in force;
    they build a siege ramp against me
    and encamp around my tent.

13 "He has alienated my family from me;
    my acquaintances are completely
      estranged from me.
14 My relatives have gone away;
    my closest friends have forgotten me.
15 My guests and my female servants count me
      a foreigner;
    they look on me as on a stranger.
16 I summon my servant, but he does not
      answer,
    though I beg him with my own mouth.
17 My breath is offensive to my wife;
    I am loathsome to my own family.
18 Even the little boys scorn me;
    when I appear, they ridicule me.
19 All my intimate friends detest me;
    those I love have turned against me.
20 I am nothing but skin and bones;
    I have escaped only by the skin of my
      teeth.*b*

21 "Have pity on me, my friends, have pity,
    for the hand of God has struck me.
22 Why do you pursue me as God does?
    Will you never get enough of my flesh?

23 "Oh, that my words were recorded,
    that they were written on a scroll,
24 that they were inscribed with an iron tool
      on*c* lead,
    or engraved in rock forever!
25 I know that my redeemer*d* lives,
    and that in the end he will stand on the
      earth.*e*
26 And after my skin has been destroyed,
    yet*f* in*g* my flesh I will see God;
27 I myself will see him
    with my own eyes — I, and not another.
    How my heart yearns within me!

---

a 15 Or *Nothing he had remains*   *b* 20 Or *only by my gums*
c 24 Or *and*   *d* 25 Or *vindicator*   *e* 25 Or *on my grave*
f 26 Or *And after I awake, / though this body has been
destroyed, / then*   *g* 26 Or *destroyed, / apart from*

Vision: Job's Perspective Separates Him from the Others

Job 19:25–27

The first difference separating leaders from followers is perspective. Both can have character and integrity; both can love others; both can obey God. But leaders think differently than followers.

Job and his friends held profoundly different perspectives. Throughout the book, Job maintains an eternal perspective. "I know that my redeemer lives, and that in the end he will stand on the earth," he says (Job 19:25). In the following two verses he continues to cast vision for the reality of life beyond the grave. Unlike his wife, who told him to curse God and die; unlike his friends, who told him none of this would have happened had he just lived better—Job saw beyond the superficial to the eternal. What enabled Job to see what God saw?

1. *He renewed his perspective:* **He clung to the justice and character of God.**

2. *He released his past:* **He was willing to let go of what he had lost.**

3. *He remembered his purpose:* **He realized that he existed only to glorify God.**

---

28 "If you say, 'How we will hound him,
    since the root of the trouble lies in him,'*a*'
29 you should fear the sword yourselves;
    for wrath will bring punishment by the
        sword,
    and then you will know that there is
        judgment.*b*"

Zophar

20 Then Zophar the Naamathite replied:

2 "My troubled thoughts prompt me to answer
    because I am greatly disturbed.
3 I hear a rebuke that dishonors me,
    and my understanding inspires me to
        reply.
4 "Surely you know how it has been from of old,
    ever since mankind*c* was placed on the
        earth,
5 that the mirth of the wicked is brief,
    the joy of the godless lasts but a moment.
6 Though the pride of the godless person
        reaches to the heavens
    and his head touches the clouds,
7 he will perish forever, like his own dung;
    those who have seen him will say, 'Where
        is he?'
8 Like a dream he flies away, no more to be
        found,
    banished like a vision of the night.
9 The eye that saw him will not see him again;
    his place will look on him no more.
10 His children must make amends to the poor;
    his own hands must give back his wealth.

11 The youthful vigor that fills his bones
    will lie with him in the dust.
12 "Though evil is sweet in his mouth
    and he hides it under his tongue,
13 though he cannot bear to let it go
    and lets it linger in his mouth,
14 yet his food will turn sour in his stomach;
    it will become the venom of serpents
        within him.
15 He will spit out the riches he swallowed;
    God will make his stomach vomit them up.
16 He will suck the poison of serpents;
    the fangs of an adder will kill him.
17 He will not enjoy the streams,
    the rivers flowing with honey and cream.
18 What he toiled for he must give back
        uneaten;
    he will not enjoy the profit from his
        trading.
19 For he has oppressed the poor and left them
        destitute;
    he has seized houses he did not build.
20 "Surely he will have no respite from his
        craving;
    he cannot save himself by his treasure.
21 Nothing is left for him to devour;
    his prosperity will not endure.
22 In the midst of his plenty, distress will
        overtake him;
    the full force of misery will come upon
        him.

---

a 28 Many Hebrew manuscripts, Septuagint and Vulgate; most Hebrew manuscripts *me*   *b* 29 Or *sword, / that you may come to know the Almighty*   *c* 4 Or *Adam*

²³ When he has filled his belly,
　　God will vent his burning anger against
　　　him
　　and rain down his blows on him.
²⁴ Though he flees from an iron weapon,
　　a bronze-tipped arrow pierces him.
²⁵ He pulls it out of his back,
　　the gleaming point out of his liver.
　　Terrors will come over him;
²⁶ 　total darkness lies in wait for his treasures.
　　A fire unfanned will consume him
　　and devour what is left in his tent.
²⁷ The heavens will expose his guilt;
　　the earth will rise up against him.
²⁸ A flood will carry off his house,
　　rushing waters*ᵃ* on the day of God's
　　　wrath.
²⁹ Such is the fate God allots the wicked,
　　the heritage appointed for them by God."

Job

21

Then Job replied:

² "Listen carefully to my words;
　　let this be the consolation you give me.
³ Bear with me while I speak,
　　and after I have spoken, mock on.

⁴ "Is my complaint directed to a human
　　　being?
　　Why should I not be impatient?
⁵ Look at me and be appalled;
　　clap your hand over your mouth.
⁶ When I think about this, I am terrified;
　　trembling seizes my body.
⁷ Why do the wicked live on,
　　growing old and increasing in power?
⁸ They see their children established around
　　　them,
　　their offspring before their eyes.
⁹ Their homes are safe and free from fear;
　　the rod of God is not on them.
¹⁰ Their bulls never fail to breed;
　　their cows calve and do not miscarry.
¹¹ They send forth their children as a flock;
　　their little ones dance about.
¹² They sing to the music of timbrel and lyre;
　　they make merry to the sound of the pipe.
¹³ They spend their years in prosperity
　　and go down to the grave in peace.*ᵇ*
¹⁴ Yet they say to God, 'Leave us alone!
　　We have no desire to know your ways.
¹⁵ Who is the Almighty, that we should serve
　　　him?
　　What would we gain by praying to him?'

¹⁶ But their prosperity is not in their own
　　　hands,
　　so I stand aloof from the plans of the
　　　wicked.

¹⁷ "Yet how often is the lamp of the wicked
　　　snuffed out?
　　How often does calamity come upon them,
　　the fate God allots in his anger?
¹⁸ How often are they like straw before the
　　　wind,
　　like chaff swept away by a gale?
¹⁹ It is said, 'God stores up the punishment of
　　　the wicked for their children.'
　　Let him repay the wicked, so that they
　　　themselves will experience it!
²⁰ Let their own eyes see their destruction;
　　let them drink the cup of the wrath of the
　　　Almighty.
²¹ For what do they care about the families they
　　　leave behind
　　when their allotted months come to an
　　　end?

²² "Can anyone teach knowledge to God,
　　since he judges even the highest?
²³ One person dies in full vigor,
　　completely secure and at ease,
²⁴ well nourished in body,*ᶜ*
　　bones rich with marrow.
²⁵ Another dies in bitterness of soul,
　　never having enjoyed anything good.
²⁶ Side by side they lie in the dust,
　　and worms cover them both.

²⁷ "I know full well what you are thinking,
　　the schemes by which you would wrong me.
²⁸ You say, 'Where now is the house of the
　　　great,
　　the tents where the wicked lived?'
²⁹ Have you never questioned those who travel?
　　Have you paid no regard to their
　　　accounts —
³⁰ that the wicked are spared from the day of
　　　calamity,
　　that they are delivered from*ᵈ* the day of
　　　wrath?
³¹ Who denounces their conduct to their face?
　　Who repays them for what they have
　　　done?
³² They are carried to the grave,
　　and watch is kept over their tombs.

ᵃ 28 Or The possessions in his house will be carried off, / washed away   *ᵇ 13 Or in an instant*   *ᶜ 24 The meaning of the Hebrew for this word is uncertain.*   *ᵈ 30 Or wicked are reserved for the day of calamity, / that they are brought forth to*

³³ The soil in the valley is sweet to them;
　　everyone follows after them,
　　and a countless throng goes[a] before them.

³⁴ "So how can you console me with your
　　nonsense?
　　Nothing is left of your answers but
　　falsehood!"

Eliphaz

22

Then Eliphaz the Temanite replied:

² "Can a man be of benefit to God?
　　Can even a wise person benefit him?
³ What pleasure would it give the Almighty if
　　you were righteous?
　　What would he gain if your ways were
　　blameless?

⁴ "Is it for your piety that he rebukes you
　　and brings charges against you?
⁵ Is not your wickedness great?
　　Are not your sins endless?
⁶ You demanded security from your relatives
　　for no reason;
　　you stripped people of their clothing,
　　leaving them naked.
⁷ You gave no water to the weary
　　and you withheld food from the hungry,
⁸ though you were a powerful man, owning
　　land—
　　an honored man, living on it.
⁹ And you sent widows away empty-handed
　　and broke the strength of the fatherless.
¹⁰ That is why snares are all around you,
　　why sudden peril terrifies you,
¹¹ why it is so dark you cannot see,
　　and why a flood of water covers you.

¹² "Is not God in the heights of heaven?
　　And see how lofty are the highest stars!
¹³ Yet you say, 'What does God know?
　　Does he judge through such darkness?
¹⁴ Thick clouds veil him, so he does not see us
　　as he goes about in the vaulted heavens.'
¹⁵ Will you keep to the old path
　　that the wicked have trod?
¹⁶ They were carried off before their time,
　　their foundations washed away by a
　　flood.
¹⁷ They said to God, 'Leave us alone!
　　What can the Almighty do to us?'
¹⁸ Yet it was he who filled their houses with
　　good things,
　　so I stand aloof from the plans of the
　　wicked.

¹⁹ The righteous see their ruin and rejoice;
　　the innocent mock them, saying,
²⁰ 'Surely our foes are destroyed,
　　and fire devours their wealth.'

²¹ "Submit to God and be at peace with him;
　　in this way prosperity will come to you.
²² Accept instruction from his mouth
　　and lay up his words in your heart.
²³ If you return to the Almighty, you will be
　　restored:
　　If you remove wickedness far from your
　　tent
²⁴ and assign your nuggets to the dust,
　　your gold of Ophir to the rocks in the
　　ravines,
²⁵ then the Almighty will be your gold,
　　the choicest silver for you.
²⁶ Surely then you will find delight in the
　　Almighty
　　and will lift up your face to God.
²⁷ You will pray to him, and he will hear you,
　　and you will fulfill your vows.
²⁸ What you decide on will be done,
　　and light will shine on your ways.
²⁹ When people are brought low and you say,
　　'Lift them up!'
　　then he will save the downcast.
³⁰ He will deliver even one who is not innocent,
　　who will be delivered through the
　　cleanness of your hands."

Job

23

Then Job replied:

² "Even today my complaint is bitter;
　　his hand[b] is heavy in spite of[c] my
　　groaning.
³ If only I knew where to find him;
　　if only I could go to his dwelling!
⁴ I would state my case before him
　　and fill my mouth with arguments.
⁵ I would find out what he would answer me,
　　and consider what he would say to me.
⁶ Would he vigorously oppose me?
　　No, he would not press charges against me.
⁷ There the upright can establish their
　　innocence before him,
　　and there I would be delivered forever
　　from my judge.

⁸ "But if I go to the east, he is not there;
　　if I go to the west, I do not find him.

ᵃ 33 Or *them, / as a countless throng went*　　ᵇ 2 Septuagint
and Syriac; Hebrew / *the hand on me*　　ᶜ 2 Or *heavy on me in*

⁹When he is at work in the north, I do not see
  him;
    when he turns to the south, I catch no
      glimpse of him.
¹⁰But he knows the way that I take;
    when he has tested me, I will come forth
      as gold.
¹¹My feet have closely followed his steps;
    I have kept to his way without turning
      aside.
¹²I have not departed from the commands of
  his lips;
    I have treasured the words of his mouth
      more than my daily bread.

¹³"But he stands alone, and who can oppose
  him?
    He does whatever he pleases.
¹⁴He carries out his decree against me,
    and many such plans he still has in store.
¹⁵That is why I am terrified before him;
    when I think of all this, I fear him.
¹⁶God has made my heart faint;
    the Almighty has terrified me.
¹⁷Yet I am not silenced by the darkness,
    by the thick darkness that covers my face.

24 "Why does the Almighty not set times
      for judgment?
    Why must those who know him look in
      vain for such days?
²There are those who move boundary
    stones;
    they pasture flocks they have stolen.
³They drive away the orphan's donkey
    and take the widow's ox in pledge.
⁴They thrust the needy from the path
    and force all the poor of the land into
      hiding.
⁵Like wild donkeys in the desert,
    the poor go about their labor of foraging
      food;
    the wasteland provides food for their
      children.
⁶They gather fodder in the fields
    and glean in the vineyards of the wicked.
⁷Lacking clothes, they spend the night naked;
    they have nothing to cover themselves in
      the cold.
⁸They are drenched by mountain rains
    and hug the rocks for lack of shelter.
⁹The fatherless child is snatched from the
    breast;
    the infant of the poor is seized for a debt.
¹⁰Lacking clothes, they go about naked;
    they carry the sheaves, but still go hungry.

¹¹They crush olives among the terraces[a];
    they tread the winepresses, yet suffer
      thirst.
¹²The groans of the dying rise from the city,
    and the souls of the wounded cry out for
      help.
    But God charges no one with wrongdoing.

¹³"There are those who rebel against the light,
    who do not know its ways
    or stay in its paths.
¹⁴When daylight is gone, the murderer
      rises up,
    kills the poor and needy,
    and in the night steals forth like a thief.
¹⁵The eye of the adulterer watches for dusk;
    he thinks, 'No eye will see me,'
    and he keeps his face concealed.
¹⁶In the dark, thieves break into houses,
    but by day they shut themselves in;
    they want nothing to do with the light.
¹⁷For all of them, midnight is their morning;
    they make friends with the terrors of
      darkness.

¹⁸"Yet they are foam on the surface of the
      water;
    their portion of the land is cursed,
    so that no one goes to the vineyards.
¹⁹As heat and drought snatch away the melted
      snow,
    so the grave snatches away those who have
      sinned.
²⁰The womb forgets them,
    the worm feasts on them;
    the wicked are no longer remembered
    but are broken like a tree.
²¹They prey on the barren and childless
      woman,
    and to the widow they show no kindness.
²²But God drags away the mighty by his
      power;
    though they become established, they
      have no assurance of life.
²³He may let them rest in a feeling of security,
    but his eyes are on their ways.
²⁴For a little while they are exalted, and then
      they are gone;
    they are brought low and gathered up like
      all others;
    they are cut off like heads of grain.

²⁵"If this is not so, who can prove me false
    and reduce my words to nothing?"

ᵃ 11 The meaning of the Hebrew for this word is uncertain.

Bildad

25

Then Bildad the Shuhite replied:

2 "Dominion and awe belong to God;
    he establishes order in the heights of
    heaven.
3 Can his forces be numbered?
    On whom does his light not rise?
4 How then can a mortal be righteous before
    God?
    How can one born of woman be pure?
5 If even the moon is not bright
    and the stars are not pure in his eyes,
6 how much less a mortal, who is but a
    maggot —
    a human being, who is only a worm!"

Job

26

Then Job replied:

2 "How you have helped the powerless!
    How you have saved the arm that is
    feeble!
3 What advice you have offered to one without
    wisdom!
    And what great insight you have
    displayed!
4 Who has helped you utter these words?
    And whose spirit spoke from your mouth?

5 "The dead are in deep anguish,
    those beneath the waters and all that live
    in them.
6 The realm of the dead is naked before God;
    Destruction[a] lies uncovered.
7 He spreads out the northern skies over
    empty space;
    he suspends the earth over nothing.
8 He wraps up the waters in his clouds,
    yet the clouds do not burst under their
    weight.
9 He covers the face of the full moon,
    spreading his clouds over it.
10 He marks out the horizon on the face of the
    waters
    for a boundary between light and
    darkness.
11 The pillars of the heavens quake,
    aghast at his rebuke.
12 By his power he churned up the sea;
    by his wisdom he cut Rahab to pieces.
13 By his breath the skies became fair;
    his hand pierced the gliding serpent.
14 And these are but the outer fringe of his
    works;
    how faint the whisper we hear of him!
    Who then can understand the thunder of
    his power?"

---

a 6 Hebrew *Abaddon*

JOB'S FRIENDS

Misguided Companions Who Meant Well

Job 24:25

PROFILE in leadership

At a time when Job most needed the love and encouragement of his friends, he received only their condemnation, torment and wrath. Eliphaz argued from experience, Bildad from tradition and Zophar from legalism, and as is often the case, many of their arguments contained elements of truth. These three friends could have become major obstacles—lids—in Job's life. And yet he did not allow that to happen.

Job's friends believed he must have behaved treacherously to meet with such awful tragedy. Would God treat a good friend like this? They accused him of many specific sins, adding their names to a long list of amateur theologians who assume that people in pain have done something to deserve their suffering. While that may indeed be the case (see Jn 5:14), it is not universally so.

False accusation can debilitate the falsely accused. At the most vulnerable time of his life, Job's friends continued to slander him—yet he continued to depend on God. He fought hard against depression and discouragement. In the midst of great pain and loss, Job demonstrated solid character and great strength; nothing was able to destroy his faith in God. In the end, truth prevailed and God blessed Job greatly. Job's story reminds us that all leaders must filter the counsel of their inner circle through the truth of God's Word.

Job's Final Word to His Friends

27

And Job continued his discourse:

[2] "As surely as God lives, who has denied me
      justice,
   the Almighty, who has made my life bitter,
[3] as long as I have life within me,
   the breath of God in my nostrils,
[4] my lips will not say anything wicked,
   and my tongue will not utter lies.
[5] I will never admit you are in the right;
   till I die, I will not deny my integrity.
[6] I will maintain my innocence and never let
      go of it;
   my conscience will not reproach me as
      long as I live.

[7] "May my enemy be like the wicked,
   my adversary like the unjust!
[8] For what hope have the godless when they
      are cut off,
   when God takes away their life?
[9] Does God listen to their cry
   when distress comes upon them?
[10] Will they find delight in the Almighty?
   Will they call on God at all times?

[11] "I will teach you about the power of God;
   the ways of the Almighty I will not
      conceal.
[12] You have all seen this yourselves.
   Why then this meaningless talk?

[13] "Here is the fate God allots to the wicked,
   the heritage a ruthless man receives from
      the Almighty:
[14] However many his children, their fate is the
      sword;
   his offspring will never have enough
      to eat.
[15] The plague will bury those who survive him,
   and their widows will not weep for them.
[16] Though he heaps up silver like dust
   and clothes like piles of clay,
[17] what he lays up the righteous will wear,
   and the innocent will divide his silver.
[18] The house he builds is like a moth's cocoon,
   like a hut made by a watchman.
[19] He lies down wealthy, but will do so no
      more;
   when he opens his eyes, all is gone.
[20] Terrors overtake him like a flood;
   a tempest snatches him away in the night.
[21] The east wind carries him off, and he is
      gone;
   it sweeps him out of his place.

[22] It hurls itself against him without mercy
   as he flees headlong from its power.
[23] It claps its hands in derision
   and hisses him out of his place."

Interlude: Where Wisdom Is Found

28

There is a mine for silver
and a place where gold is refined.

[2] Iron is taken from the earth,
   and copper is smelted from ore.
[3] Mortals put an end to the darkness;
   they search out the farthest recesses
      for ore in the blackest darkness.
[4] Far from human dwellings they cut a shaft,
   in places untouched by human feet;
   far from other people they dangle and
      sway.
[5] The earth, from which food comes,
   is transformed below as by fire;
[6] lapis lazuli comes from its rocks,
   and its dust contains nuggets of gold.
[7] No bird of prey knows that hidden path,
   no falcon's eye has seen it.
[8] Proud beasts do not set foot on it,
   and no lion prowls there.
[9] People assault the flinty rock with their
      hands
   and lay bare the roots of the mountains.
[10] They tunnel through the rock;
   their eyes see all its treasures.
[11] They search[a] the sources of the rivers
   and bring hidden things to light.

[12] But where can wisdom be found?
   Where does understanding dwell?
[13] No mortal comprehends its worth;
   it cannot be found in the land of the
      living.
[14] The deep says, "It is not in me";
   the sea says, "It is not with me."
[15] It cannot be bought with the finest gold,
   nor can its price be weighed out in silver.
[16] It cannot be bought with the gold of Ophir,
   with precious onyx or lapis lazuli.
[17] Neither gold nor crystal can compare
      with it,
   nor can it be had for jewels of gold.
[18] Coral and jasper are not worthy of mention;
   the price of wisdom is beyond rubies.
[19] The topaz of Cush cannot compare with it;
   it cannot be bought with pure gold.

[20] Where then does wisdom come from?
   Where does understanding dwell?

---

[a] 11 Septuagint, Aquila and Vulgate; Hebrew *They dam up*

21 It is hidden from the eyes of every living
thing,
　concealed even from the birds in the sky.
22 Destruction[a] and Death say,
　"Only a rumor of it has reached our ears."
23 God understands the way to it
　and he alone knows where it dwells,
24 for he views the ends of the earth
　and sees everything under the heavens.
25 When he established the force of the wind
　and measured out the waters,
26 when he made a decree for the rain
　and a path for the thunderstorm,
27 then he looked at wisdom and appraised it;
　he confirmed it and tested it.
28 And he said to the human race,
　"The fear of the Lord — that is wisdom,
　and to shun evil is understanding."

Job's Final Defense

29 Job continued his discourse:

2 "How I long for the months gone by,
　for the days when God watched over me,
3 when his lamp shone on my head
　and by his light I walked through
　darkness!
4 Oh, for the days when I was in my prime,
　when God's intimate friendship blessed
　my house,
5 when the Almighty was still with me
　and my children were around me,
6 when my path was drenched with cream
　and the rock poured out for me streams of
　olive oil.

7 "When I went to the gate of the city
　and took my seat in the public square,
8 the young men saw me and stepped aside
　and the old men rose to their feet;
9 the chief men refrained from speaking
　and covered their mouths with their
　hands;
10 the voices of the nobles were hushed,
　and their tongues stuck to the roof of their
　mouths.
11 Whoever heard me spoke well of me,
　and those who saw me commended me,
12 because I rescued the poor who cried for
　help,
　and the fatherless who had none to assist
　them.
13 The one who was dying blessed me;
　I made the widow's heart sing.
14 I put on righteousness as my clothing;
　justice was my robe and my turban.
15 I was eyes to the blind
　and feet to the lame.
16 I was a father to the needy;
　I took up the case of the stranger.
17 I broke the fangs of the wicked
　and snatched the victims from their teeth.

18 "I thought, 'I will die in my own house,
　my days as numerous as the grains of sand.
19 My roots will reach to the water,
　and the dew will lie all night on my
　branches.
20 My glory will not fade;
　the bow will be ever new in my hand.'

---

[a] 22 Hebrew *Abaddon*

Wisdom: Job Recognizes His Source of Wisdom and Seeks It

Job 28:23–28

Despite his confusion and pain, Job makes it clear that he looks to God alone for wisdom. He understands that he cannot lead himself, much less his family, without God as his never-ending source of perspective and understanding. Job has heard from his friends and knows their theories ring hollow. The best they can muster is the wisdom of men; Job will not be satisfied until he has the wisdom of God.

The third chapter of James distinguishes between these two radically different sources of wisdom:

Wisdom from Below	Wisdom from Above
1. Works temporarily in a few situations	1. Is universal and timeless, yet eternally relevant
2. Seems logical for the moment	2. Often seems illogical or even backwards
3. Limited in scope	3. Always big picture and unlimited in scope
4. Competitive: it is win/lose	4. Complementary: it is win/win

21 "People listened to me expectantly,
     waiting in silence for my counsel.
22 After I had spoken, they spoke no more;
     my words fell gently on their ears.
23 They waited for me as for showers
     and drank in my words as the spring rain.
24 When I smiled at them, they scarcely
         believed it;
     the light of my face was precious to them.[a]
25 I chose the way for them and sat as their
         chief;
     I dwelt as a king among his troops;
     I was like one who comforts mourners.

30 "But now they mock me,
       men younger than I,
   whose fathers I would have disdained
     to put with my sheep dogs.
2 Of what use was the strength of their hands
         to me,
     since their vigor had gone from them?
3 Haggard from want and hunger,
     they roamed[b] the parched land
   in desolate wastelands at night.
4 In the brush they gathered salt herbs,
     and their food[c] was the root of the broom
         bush.
5 They were banished from human society,
     shouted at as if they were thieves.
6 They were forced to live in the dry stream
         beds,
     among the rocks and in holes in the
         ground.
7 They brayed among the bushes
     and huddled in the undergrowth.
8 A base and nameless brood,
     they were driven out of the land.

9 "And now those young men mock me in song;
     I have become a byword among them.
10 They detest me and keep their distance;
     they do not hesitate to spit in my face.
11 Now that God has unstrung my bow and
         afflicted me,
     they throw off restraint in my presence.
12 On my right the tribe[d] attacks;
     they lay snares for my feet,
     they build their siege ramps against me.
13 They break up my road;
     they succeed in destroying me.
   'No one can help him,' they say.
14 They advance as through a gaping breach;
     amid the ruins they come rolling in.
15 Terrors overwhelm me;
     my dignity is driven away as by the wind,
     my safety vanishes like a cloud.

16 "And now my life ebbs away;
     days of suffering grip me.
17 Night pierces my bones;
     my gnawing pains never rest.
18 In his great power God becomes like
         clothing to me[e];
     he binds me like the neck of my garment.
19 He throws me into the mud,
     and I am reduced to dust and ashes.

20 "I cry out to you, God, but you do not
         answer;
     I stand up, but you merely look at me.
21 You turn on me ruthlessly;
     with the might of your hand you attack me.
22 You snatch me up and drive me before the
         wind;
     you toss me about in the storm.
23 I know you will bring me down to death,
     to the place appointed for all the living.

24 "Surely no one lays a hand on a broken man
     when he cries for help in his distress.
25 Have I not wept for those in trouble?
     Has not my soul grieved for the poor?
26 Yet when I hoped for good, evil came;
     when I looked for light, then came
         darkness.
27 The churning inside me never stops;
     days of suffering confront me.
28 I go about blackened, but not by the sun;
     I stand up in the assembly and cry for help.
29 I have become a brother of jackals,
     a companion of owls.
30 My skin grows black and peels;
     my body burns with fever.
31 My lyre is tuned to mourning,
     and my pipe to the sound of wailing.

31 "I made a covenant with my eyes
       not to look lustfully at a young woman.
2 For what is our lot from God above,
     our heritage from the Almighty on high?
3 Is it not ruin for the wicked,
     disaster for those who do wrong?
4 Does he not see my ways
     and count my every step?
5 "If I have walked with falsehood
     or my foot has hurried after deceit—
6 let God weigh me in honest scales
     and he will know that I am blameless—

---

a 24 The meaning of the Hebrew for this clause is uncertain.
b 3 Or gnawed   c 4 Or fuel   d 12 The meaning of the
Hebrew for this word is uncertain.   e 18 Hebrew; Septuagint
power he grasps my clothing

7 if my steps have turned from the path,
  if my heart has been led by my eyes,
  or if my hands have been defiled,
8 then may others eat what I have sown,
  and may my crops be uprooted.

9 "If my heart has been enticed by a woman,
  or if I have lurked at my neighbor's door,
10 then may my wife grind another man's
    grain,
  and may other men sleep with her.
11 For that would have been wicked,
  a sin to be judged.
12 It is a fire that burns to Destruction[a];
  it would have uprooted my harvest.

13 "If I have denied justice to any of my servants,
  whether male or female,
  when they had a grievance against me,
14 what will I do when God confronts me?
  What will I answer when called to account?
15 Did not he who made me in the womb make
    them?
  Did not the same one form us both within
    our mothers?

16 "If I have denied the desires of the poor
  or let the eyes of the widow grow weary,
17 if I have kept my bread to myself,
  not sharing it with the fatherless —
18 but from my youth I reared them as a father
    would,
  and from my birth I guided the widow —

19 if I have seen anyone perishing for lack of
    clothing,
  or the needy without garments,
20 and their hearts did not bless me
  for warming them with the fleece from
    my sheep,
21 if I have raised my hand against the
    fatherless,
  knowing that I had influence in court,
22 then let my arm fall from the shoulder,
  let it be broken off at the joint.
23 For I dreaded destruction from God,
  and for fear of his splendor I could not do
    such things.

24 "If I have put my trust in gold
  or said to pure gold, 'You are my security,'
25 if I have rejoiced over my great wealth,
  the fortune my hands had gained,
26 if I have regarded the sun in its radiance
  or the moon moving in splendor,
27 so that my heart was secretly enticed
  and my hand offered them a kiss of
    homage,
28 then these also would be sins to be judged,
  for I would have been unfaithful to God
    on high.

29 "If I have rejoiced at my enemy's misfortune
  or gloated over the trouble that came to
    him —

---

[a] 12 Hebrew *Abaddon*

Character and Consistency: Job Affirms His Promise

Job 31:1–40

One of the beautiful facets of the book of Job is that it displays how a man can be very human, and yet very heavenly at the same time.

Job feels all the emotions of a man who has endured great loss. He becomes angry, depressed, and anxious, and declares his feelings openly. At the same time, he never drifts from his strong character; he remains consistent through everything. The moment it appears he will curse God and give up on him, he affirms his promise to be faithful even when he doesn't understand what is happening. Job pledges to maintain his integrity despite his circumstances.

Such a commitment is a crucial key to leadership. Here's why:

1. **Leaders must be visionary, but they cannot see everything in the future.**

2. **Instead of pretending to be in control, leaders must model being under control.**

3. **Leaders must model humanity and identify with the limitations of followers.**

4. **Leaders must model an anchored life, living from character, not emotions.**

5. **While leaders don't know what tomorrow holds, they do know who holds tomorrow.**

³⁰ I have not allowed my mouth to sin
     by invoking a curse against their life —
³¹ if those of my household have never said,
     'Who has not been filled with Job's
         meat?' —
³² but no stranger had to spend the night in the
         street,
     for my door was always open to the
         traveler —
³³ if I have concealed my sin as people do,ᵃ
     by hiding my guilt in my heart
³⁴ because I so feared the crowd
     and so dreaded the contempt of the clans
     that I kept silent and would not go
         outside —

³⁵ ("Oh, that I had someone to hear me!
     I sign now my defense — let the Almighty
         answer me;
     let my accuser put his indictment in
         writing.
³⁶ Surely I would wear it on my shoulder,
     I would put it on like a crown.
³⁷ I would give him an account of my every
         step;
     I would present it to him as to a ruler.) —

³⁸ "if my land cries out against me
     and all its furrows are wet with tears,
³⁹ if I have devoured its yield without
         payment
     or broken the spirit of its tenants,
⁴⁰ then let briers come up instead of wheat
     and stinkweed instead of barley."

The words of Job are ended.

Elihu

32 So these three men stopped answering Job, because he was righteous in his own eyes. ²But Elihu son of Barakel the Buzite, of the family of Ram, became very angry with Job for justifying himself rather than God. ³He was also angry with the three friends, because they had found no way to refute Job, and yet had condemned him.ᵇ ⁴Now Elihu had waited before speaking to Job because they were older than he. ⁵But when he saw that the three men had nothing more to say, his anger was aroused.

⁶So Elihu son of Barakel the Buzite said:

"I am young in years,
     and you are old;
that is why I was fearful,
     not daring to tell you what I know.
⁷ I thought, 'Age should speak;
     advanced years should teach wisdom.'

⁸ But it is the spiritᶜ in a person,
     the breath of the Almighty, that gives
         them understanding.
⁹ It is not only the oldᵈ who are wise,
     not only the aged who understand what is
         right.
¹⁰ "Therefore I say: Listen to me;
     I too will tell you what I know.
¹¹ I waited while you spoke,
     I listened to your reasoning;
while you were searching for words,
¹²   I gave you my full attention.
But not one of you has proved Job wrong;
     none of you has answered his
         arguments.
¹³ Do not say, 'We have found wisdom;
     let God, not a man, refute him.'
¹⁴ But Job has not marshaled his words
         against me,
     and I will not answer him with your
         arguments.

¹⁵ "They are dismayed and have no more to
         say;
     words have failed them.
¹⁶ Must I wait, now that they are silent,
     now that they stand there with no reply?
¹⁷ I too will have my say;
     I too will tell what I know.
¹⁸ For I am full of words,
     and the spirit within me compels me;
¹⁹ inside I am like bottled-up wine,
     like new wineskins ready to burst.
²⁰ I must speak and find relief;
     I must open my lips and reply.
²¹ I will show no partiality,
     nor will I flatter anyone;
²² for if I were skilled in flattery,
     my Maker would soon take me away.

33 "But now, Job, listen to my words;
     pay attention to everything I say.
² I am about to open my mouth;
     my words are on the tip of my tongue.
³ My words come from an upright heart;
     my lips sincerely speak what I know.
⁴ The Spirit of God has made me;
     the breath of the Almighty gives me life.
⁵ Answer me then, if you can;
     stand up and argue your case before me.
⁶ I am the same as you in God's sight;
     I too am a piece of clay.

ᵃ 33 Or *as Adam did*   ᵇ 3 Masoretic Text; an ancient Hebrew scribal tradition *Job, and so had condemned God*   ᶜ 8 Or *Spirit*; also in verse 18   ᵈ 9 Or *many*; or *great*

⁷No fear of me should alarm you,
  nor should my hand be heavy on you.

⁸"But you have said in my hearing—
  I heard the very words—
⁹'I am pure, I have done no wrong;
  I am clean and free from sin.
¹⁰Yet God has found fault with me;
  he considers me his enemy.
¹¹He fastens my feet in shackles;
  he keeps close watch on all my paths.'

¹²"But I tell you, in this you are not right,
  for God is greater than any mortal.
¹³Why do you complain to him
  that he responds to no one's words*a*?
¹⁴For God does speak—now one way, now
    another—
  though no one perceives it.
¹⁵In a dream, in a vision of the night,
  when deep sleep falls on people
  as they slumber in their beds,
¹⁶he may speak in their ears
  and terrify them with warnings,
¹⁷to turn them from wrongdoing
  and keep them from pride,
¹⁸to preserve them from the pit,
  their lives from perishing by the sword.*b*

¹⁹"Or someone may be chastened on a bed of
    pain
  with constant distress in their bones,
²⁰so that their body finds food repulsive
  and their soul loathes the choicest meal.
²¹Their flesh wastes away to nothing,
  and their bones, once hidden, now stick out.
²²They draw near to the pit,
  and their life to the messengers of death.*c*
²³Yet if there is an angel at their side,
  a messenger, one out of a thousand,
  sent to tell them how to be upright,
²⁴and he is gracious to that person and says
    to God,
  'Spare them from going down to the pit;
  I have found a ransom for them—
²⁵let their flesh be renewed like a child's;
  let them be restored as in the days of their
    youth'—
²⁶then that person can pray to God and find
    favor with him,
  they will see God's face and shout for joy;
  he will restore them to full well-being.
²⁷And they will go to others and say,
  'I have sinned, I have perverted what is
    right,
  but I did not get what I deserved.

²⁸God has delivered me from going down to
    the pit,
  and I shall live to enjoy the light of life.'
²⁹"God does all these things to a person—
  twice, even three times—
³⁰to turn them back from the pit,
  that the light of life may shine on them.
³¹"Pay attention, Job, and listen to me;
  be silent, and I will speak.
³²If you have anything to say, answer me;
  speak up, for I want to vindicate you.
³³But if not, then listen to me;
  be silent, and I will teach you wisdom."

34 Then Elihu said:

²"Hear my words, you wise men;
  listen to me, you men of learning.
³For the ear tests words
  as the tongue tastes food.
⁴Let us discern for ourselves what is right;
  let us learn together what is good.

⁵"Job says, 'I am innocent,
  but God denies me justice.
⁶Although I am right,
  I am considered a liar;
  although I am guiltless,
  his arrow inflicts an incurable wound.'
⁷Is there anyone like Job,
  who drinks scorn like water?
⁸He keeps company with evildoers;
  he associates with the wicked.
⁹For he says, 'There is no profit
  in trying to please God.'

¹⁰"So listen to me, you men of understanding.
  Far be it from God to do evil,
  from the Almighty to do wrong.
¹¹He repays everyone for what they have done;
  he brings on them what their conduct
    deserves.
¹²It is unthinkable that God would do wrong,
  that the Almighty would pervert justice.
¹³Who appointed him over the earth?
  Who put him in charge of the whole
    world?
¹⁴If it were his intention
  and he withdrew his spirit*d* and breath,
¹⁵all humanity would perish together
  and mankind would return to the dust.

---

a 13 Or *that he does not answer for any of his actions*
b 18 Or *from crossing the river*   *c* 22 Or *to the place of the*
dead   *d* 14 Or *Spirit*

16 "If you have understanding, hear this;
    listen to what I say.
17 Can someone who hates justice govern?
    Will you condemn the just and mighty
        One?
18 Is he not the One who says to kings, 'You are
        worthless,'
    and to nobles, 'You are wicked,'
19 who shows no partiality to princes
    and does not favor the rich over the poor,
    for they are all the work of his hands?
20 They die in an instant, in the middle of the
        night;
    the people are shaken and they pass
        away;
    the mighty are removed without human
        hand.

21 "His eyes are on the ways of mortals;
    he sees their every step.
22 There is no deep shadow, no utter darkness,
    where evildoers can hide.
23 God has no need to examine people further,
    that they should come before him for
        judgment.
24 Without inquiry he shatters the mighty
    and sets up others in their place.
25 Because he takes note of their deeds,
    he overthrows them in the night and they
        are crushed.
26 He punishes them for their wickedness
    where everyone can see them,
27 because they turned from following him
    and had no regard for any of his ways.
28 They caused the cry of the poor to come
        before him,
    so that he heard the cry of the needy.
29 But if he remains silent, who can condemn
        him?
    If he hides his face, who can see him?
    Yet he is over individual and nation alike,
30   to keep the godless from ruling,
    from laying snares for the people.

31 "Suppose someone says to God,
    'I am guilty but will offend no more.
32 Teach me what I cannot see;
    if I have done wrong, I will not do so
        again.'
33 Should God then reward you on your terms,
    when you refuse to repent?
    You must decide, not I;
    so tell me what you know.

34 "Men of understanding declare,
    wise men who hear me say to me,

35 'Job speaks without knowledge;
    his words lack insight.'
36 Oh, that Job might be tested to the utmost
    for answering like a wicked man!
37 To his sin he adds rebellion;
    scornfully he claps his hands among us
    and multiplies his words against God."

35 Then Elihu said:

2 "Do you think this is just?
    You say, 'I am in the right, not God.'
3 Yet you ask him, 'What profit is it to me,[a]
    and what do I gain by not sinning?'

4 "I would like to reply to you
    and to your friends with you.
5 Look up at the heavens and see;
    gaze at the clouds so high above you.
6 If you sin, how does that affect him?
    If your sins are many, what does that do to
        him?
7 If you are righteous, what do you give to
        him,
    or what does he receive from your hand?
8 Your wickedness only affects humans like
        yourself,
    and your righteousness only other people.

9 "People cry out under a load of oppression;
    they plead for relief from the arm of the
        powerful.
10 But no one says, 'Where is God my Maker,
    who gives songs in the night,
11 who teaches us more than he teaches[b] the
        beasts of the earth
    and makes us wiser than[c] the birds in the
        sky?'
12 He does not answer when people cry out
    because of the arrogance of the wicked.
13 Indeed, God does not listen to their empty
        plea;
    the Almighty pays no attention to it.
14 How much less, then, will he listen
    when you say that you do not see him,
    that your case is before him
    and you must wait for him,
15 and further, that his anger never punishes
    and he does not take the least notice of
        wickedness.[d]
16 So Job opens his mouth with empty talk;
    without knowledge he multiplies words."

---

[a] 3 Or you   [b] 10,11 Or night, / [11]who teaches us by
[c] 11 Or us wise by   [d] 15 Symmachus, Theodotion and
Vulgate; the meaning of the Hebrew for this word is uncertain.

36

Elihu continued:

2 "Bear with me a little longer and I will show
you
that there is more to be said in God's behalf.
3 I get my knowledge from afar;
I will ascribe justice to my Maker.
4 Be assured that my words are not false;
one who has perfect knowledge is with you.

5 "God is mighty, but despises no one;
he is mighty, and firm in his purpose.
6 He does not keep the wicked alive
but gives the afflicted their rights.
7 He does not take his eyes off the righteous;
he enthrones them with kings
and exalts them forever.
8 But if people are bound in chains,
held fast by cords of affliction,
9 he tells them what they have done —
that they have sinned arrogantly.
10 He makes them listen to correction
and commands them to repent of their
evil.
11 If they obey and serve him,
they will spend the rest of their days in
prosperity
and their years in contentment.
12 But if they do not listen,
they will perish by the sword[a]
and die without knowledge.

13 "The godless in heart harbor resentment;
even when he fetters them, they do not cry
for help.
14 They die in their youth,
among male prostitutes of the shrines.
15 But those who suffer he delivers in their
suffering;
he speaks to them in their affliction.

16 "He is wooing you from the jaws of distress
to a spacious place free from restriction,
to the comfort of your table laden with
choice food.
17 But now you are laden with the judgment
due the wicked;
judgment and justice have taken hold of
you.
18 Be careful that no one entices you by riches;
do not let a large bribe turn you aside.
19 Would your wealth or even all your mighty
efforts
sustain you so you would not be in distress?
20 Do not long for the night,
to drag people away from their homes.[b]

21 Beware of turning to evil,
which you seem to prefer to affliction.

22 "God is exalted in his power.
Who is a teacher like him?
23 Who has prescribed his ways for him,
or said to him, 'You have done wrong'?
24 Remember to extol his work,
which people have praised in song.
25 All humanity has seen it;
mortals gaze on it from afar.
26 How great is God — beyond our
understanding!
The number of his years is past finding out.

27 "He draws up the drops of water,
which distill as rain to the streams[c];
28 the clouds pour down their moisture
and abundant showers fall on mankind.
29 Who can understand how he spreads out the
clouds,
how he thunders from his pavilion?
30 See how he scatters his lightning about him,
bathing the depths of the sea.
31 This is the way he governs[d] the nations
and provides food in abundance.
32 He fills his hands with lightning
and commands it to strike its mark.
33 His thunder announces the coming storm;
even the cattle make known its approach.[e]

37

"At this my heart pounds
and leaps from its place.
2 Listen! Listen to the roar of his voice,
to the rumbling that comes from his mouth.
3 He unleashes his lightning beneath the
whole heaven
and sends it to the ends of the earth.
4 After that comes the sound of his roar;
he thunders with his majestic voice.
When his voice resounds,
he holds nothing back.
5 God's voice thunders in marvelous ways;
he does great things beyond our
understanding.
6 He says to the snow, 'Fall on the earth,'
and to the rain shower, 'Be a mighty
downpour.'
7 So that everyone he has made may know his
work,
he stops all people from their labor.[f]

---

[a] 12 Or will cross the river   [b] 20 The meaning of the Hebrew
for verses 18-20 is uncertain.   [c] 27 Or distill from the mist as
rain   [d] 31 Or nourishes   [e] 33 Or announces his coming —
/ the One zealous against evil   [f] 7 Or work, / he fills all people
with fear by his power

8 The animals take cover;
    they remain in their dens.
9 The tempest comes out from its chamber,
    the cold from the driving winds.
10 The breath of God produces ice,
    and the broad waters become frozen.
11 He loads the clouds with moisture;
    he scatters his lightning through them.
12 At his direction they swirl around
    over the face of the whole earth
    to do whatever he commands them.
13 He brings the clouds to punish people,
    or to water his earth and show his love.

14 "Listen to this, Job;
    stop and consider God's wonders.
15 Do you know how God controls the clouds
    and makes his lightning flash?
16 Do you know how the clouds hang poised,
    those wonders of him who has perfect
        knowledge?
17 You who swelter in your clothes
    when the land lies hushed under the south
        wind,
18 can you join him in spreading out the
        skies,
    hard as a mirror of cast bronze?

19 "Tell us what we should say to him;
    we cannot draw up our case because of
        our darkness.
20 Should he be told that I want to speak?
    Would anyone ask to be swallowed up?
21 Now no one can look at the sun,
    bright as it is in the skies
    after the wind has swept them clean.
22 Out of the north he comes in golden
        splendor;
    God comes in awesome majesty.
23 The Almighty is beyond our reach and
        exalted in power;
    in his justice and great righteousness, he
        does not oppress.
24 Therefore, people revere him,
    for does he not have regard for all the wise
        in heart?ª"

The Lord Speaks

38 Then the Lord spoke to Job out of the
    storm. He said:

2 "Who is this that obscures my plans
    with words without knowledge?
3 Brace yourself like a man;
    I will question you,
    and you shall answer me.

4 "Where were you when I laid the earth's
        foundation?
    Tell me, if you understand.
5 Who marked off its dimensions? Surely you
        know!
    Who stretched a measuring line
        across it?
6 On what were its footings set,
    or who laid its cornerstone—
7 while the morning stars sang together
    and all the angelsᵇ shouted for joy?

8 "Who shut up the sea behind doors
    when it burst forth from the womb,
9 when I made the clouds its garment
    and wrapped it in thick darkness,

ª 24 Or for he does not have regard for any who think they are
wise.   ᵇ 7 Hebrew the sons of God

God Rebukes Men for Questioning His Justice

Job 38:1–7

When God finally enters the scene in Job 38, he brings justice and perspective with him. He rebukes Eliphaz, Bildad and Zophar for projecting their opinions as though they represented the mind of God (a danger every spiritual leader faces!). Before God is finished, he poses his own question: Where were you when I created the world?

Many leaders feel a great temptation to pretend they know everything that's coming down the pike. They feel an unreasonable need to project self-confidence, not realizing that people soon recognize their pretension. Leaders often fail to understand that people do not need a leader to have every answer.

Consider this: Individuals can live without certainty from a leader, but not without clarity. Leaders must be genuine with their people. Unless a word has come to us directly from the mouth of the Lord, we cannot know what is coming in the future. Don't speak with certainty on an issue of which you are unsure! Yet when you do speak, speak with clarity, even if your words paint only a small part of the whole picture. Your people do not need certainty on every issue, but they do need clarity on every issue. It is clarity that helps organizations to progress.

¹⁰when I fixed limits for it
  and set its doors and bars in place,
¹¹when I said, 'This far you may come and no
    farther;
  here is where your proud waves halt'?

¹²"Have you ever given orders to the
    morning,
  or shown the dawn its place,
¹³that it might take the earth by the edges
  and shake the wicked out of it?
¹⁴The earth takes shape like clay under a seal;
  its features stand out like those of a
    garment.
¹⁵The wicked are denied their light,
  and their upraised arm is broken.

¹⁶"Have you journeyed to the springs of
    the sea
  or walked in the recesses of the deep?
¹⁷Have the gates of death been shown to you?
  Have you seen the gates of the deepest
    darkness?
¹⁸Have you comprehended the vast expanses
    of the earth?
  Tell me, if you know all this.

¹⁹"What is the way to the abode of light?
  And where does darkness reside?
²⁰Can you take them to their places?
  Do you know the paths to their
    dwellings?
²¹Surely you know, for you were already born!
  You have lived so many years!

²²"Have you entered the storehouses of the
    snow
  or seen the storehouses of the hail,
²³which I reserve for times of trouble,
  for days of war and battle?
²⁴What is the way to the place where the
    lightning is dispersed,
  or the place where the east winds are
    scattered over the earth?
²⁵Who cuts a channel for the torrents of rain,
  and a path for the thunderstorm,
²⁶to water a land where no one lives,
  an uninhabited desert,
²⁷to satisfy a desolate wasteland
  and make it sprout with grass?
²⁸Does the rain have a father?
  Who fathers the drops of dew?
²⁹From whose womb comes the ice?
  Who gives birth to the frost from the
    heavens
³⁰when the waters become hard as stone,
  when the surface of the deep is frozen?

³¹"Can you bind the chains*ᵃ* of the Pleiades?
  Can you loosen Orion's belt?
³²Can you bring forth the constellations in
    their seasons*ᵇ*
  or lead out the Bear*ᶜ* with its cubs?
³³Do you know the laws of the heavens?
  Can you set up God's*ᵈ* dominion over the
    earth?

³⁴"Can you raise your voice to the clouds
  and cover yourself with a flood of water?
³⁵Do you send the lightning bolts on their
    way?
  Do they report to you, 'Here we are'?
³⁶Who gives the ibis wisdom*ᵉ*
  or gives the rooster understanding?*ᶠ*
³⁷Who has the wisdom to count the clouds?
  Who can tip over the water jars of the
    heavens
³⁸when the dust becomes hard
  and the clods of earth stick together?

³⁹"Do you hunt the prey for the lioness
  and satisfy the hunger of the lions
⁴⁰when they crouch in their dens
  or lie in wait in a thicket?
⁴¹Who provides food for the raven
  when its young cry out to God
  and wander about for lack of food?

39 "Do you know when the mountain goats
    give birth?
  Do you watch when the doe bears her
    fawn?
²Do you count the months till they bear?
  Do you know the time they give birth?
³They crouch down and bring forth their
    young;
  their labor pains are ended.
⁴Their young thrive and grow strong in the
    wilds;
  they leave and do not return.

⁵"Who let the wild donkey go free?
  Who untied its ropes?
⁶I gave it the wasteland as its home,
  the salt flats as its habitat.
⁷It laughs at the commotion in the town;
  it does not hear a driver's shout.
⁸It ranges the hills for its pasture
  and searches for any green thing.

ᵃ 31 Septuagint; Hebrew *beauty*   *ᵇ 32* Or *the morning star in
its season*   *ᶜ 32* Or *out Leo*   *ᵈ 33* Or *their*   *ᵉ 36* That is,
wisdom about the flooding of the Nile   *ᶠ 36* That is,
understanding of when to crow; the meaning of the Hebrew for
this verse is uncertain.

9 "Will the wild ox consent to serve you?
     Will it stay by your manger at night?
10 Can you hold it to the furrow with a
         harness?
     Will it till the valleys behind you?
11 Will you rely on it for its great strength?
     Will you leave your heavy work to it?
12 Can you trust it to haul in your grain
     and bring it to your threshing floor?

13 "The wings of the ostrich flap joyfully,
     though they cannot compare
     with the wings and feathers of the stork.
14 She lays her eggs on the ground
     and lets them warm in the sand,
15 unmindful that a foot may crush them,
     that some wild animal may trample
         them.
16 She treats her young harshly, as if they were
         not hers;
     she cares not that her labor was in vain,
17 for God did not endow her with wisdom
     or give her a share of good sense.
18 Yet when she spreads her feathers to run,
     she laughs at horse and rider.

19 "Do you give the horse its strength
     or clothe its neck with a flowing mane?
20 Do you make it leap like a locust,
     striking terror with its proud snorting?
21 It paws fiercely, rejoicing in its strength,
     and charges into the fray.
22 It laughs at fear, afraid of nothing;
     it does not shy away from the sword.
23 The quiver rattles against its side,
     along with the flashing spear and lance.
24 In frenzied excitement it eats up the
         ground;
     it cannot stand still when the trumpet
         sounds.
25 At the blast of the trumpet it snorts, 'Aha!'
     It catches the scent of battle from afar,
     the shout of commanders and the
         battle cry.

26 "Does the hawk take flight by your
         wisdom
     and spread its wings toward the south?
27 Does the eagle soar at your command
     and build its nest on high?
28 It dwells on a cliff and stays there at night;
     a rocky crag is its stronghold.
29 From there it looks for food;
     its eyes detect it from afar.
30 Its young ones feast on blood,
     and where the slain are, there it is."

40

The LORD said to Job:

2 "Will the one who contends with the
         Almighty correct him?
     Let him who accuses God answer him!"

3 Then Job answered the LORD:

4 "I am unworthy—how can I reply to you?
     I put my hand over my mouth.
5 I spoke once, but I have no answer—
     twice, but I will say no more."

6 Then the LORD spoke to Job out of the storm:

7 "Brace yourself like a man;
     I will question you,
     and you shall answer me.

8 "Would you discredit my justice?
     Would you condemn me to justify
         yourself?
9 Do you have an arm like God's,
     and can your voice thunder like his?
10 Then adorn yourself with glory and
         splendor,
     and clothe yourself in honor and majesty.
11 Unleash the fury of your wrath,
     look at all who are proud and bring them
         low,
12 look at all who are proud and humble them,
     crush the wicked where they stand.
13 Bury them all in the dust together;
     shroud their faces in the grave.
14 Then I myself will admit to you
     that your own right hand can save you.

15 "Look at Behemoth,
     which I made along with you
     and which feeds on grass like an ox.
16 What strength it has in its loins,
     what power in the muscles of its belly!
17 Its tail sways like a cedar;
     the sinews of its thighs are close-knit.
18 Its bones are tubes of bronze,
     its limbs like rods of iron.
19 It ranks first among the works of God,
     yet its Maker can approach it with his
         sword.
20 The hills bring it their produce,
     and all the wild animals play nearby.
21 Under the lotus plants it lies,
     hidden among the reeds in the marsh.
22 The lotuses conceal it in their shadow;
     the poplars by the stream surround it.
23 A raging river does not alarm it;
     it is secure, though the Jordan should
         surge against its mouth.

Humility: Like All Good Leaders, Job Acknowledges His Weakness

Job 40:3–5; 42:1–6

When God confronts Job with his power and majesty, Job responds with absolute humility (Job 40:3–5). The chastened man doesn't try to defend himself or rationalize his feelings. He confesses his humanity, then shuts his mouth.

And still God is not finished with his awesome lesson.

Even after Job acknowledges his insignificance and presumption, God delivers a second speech, graphically describing his power to control everything. He glories in the might of Behemoth and the ferocity of Leviathan, and asks Job if he dare go near either one. This time Job responds with deep repentance (42:1–6), clearly marking the difference between his friends and him.

Good leaders feel secure enough to repent when wrong. They don't have to project their self-worth, defend their every move, or make excuses for their failures. In the end, God rebuked Job's friends and rewarded Job—but not until the end.

[24] Can anyone capture it by the eyes,
  or trap it and pierce its nose?

41 [a] "Can you pull in Leviathan with a fishhook
  or tie down its tongue with a rope?
[2] Can you put a cord through its nose
  or pierce its jaw with a hook?
[3] Will it keep begging you for mercy?
  Will it speak to you with gentle words?
[4] Will it make an agreement with you
  for you to take it as your slave for life?
[5] Can you make a pet of it like a bird
  or put it on a leash for the young women
    in your house?
[6] Will traders barter for it?
  Will they divide it up among the merchants?
[7] Can you fill its hide with harpoons
  or its head with fishing spears?
[8] If you lay a hand on it,
  you will remember the struggle and never
    do it again!

[9] Any hope of subduing it is false;
  the mere sight of it is overpowering.
[10] No one is fierce enough to rouse it.
  Who then is able to stand against me?
[11] Who has a claim against me that I must pay?
  Everything under heaven belongs to me.

[12] "I will not fail to speak of Leviathan's limbs,
  its strength and its graceful form.
[13] Who can strip off its outer coat?
  Who can penetrate its double coat of
    armor[b]?
[14] Who dares open the doors of its mouth,
  ringed about with fearsome teeth?
[15] Its back has[c] rows of shields
  tightly sealed together;
[16] each is so close to the next
  that no air can pass between.
[17] They are joined fast to one another;
  they cling together and cannot be
    parted.
[18] Its snorting throws out flashes of light;
  its eyes are like the rays of dawn.
[19] Flames stream from its mouth;
  sparks of fire shoot out.
[20] Smoke pours from its nostrils
  as from a boiling pot over burning reeds.
[21] Its breath sets coals ablaze,
  and flames dart from its mouth.
[22] Strength resides in its neck;
  dismay goes before it.
[23] The folds of its flesh are tightly joined;
  they are firm and immovable.
[24] Its chest is hard as rock,
  hard as a lower millstone.
[25] When it rises up, the mighty are terrified;
  they retreat before its thrashing.
[26] The sword that reaches it has no effect,
  nor does the spear or the dart or the
    javelin.
[27] Iron it treats like straw
  and bronze like rotten wood.
[28] Arrows do not make it flee;
  slingstones are like chaff to it.
[29] A club seems to it but a piece of straw;
  it laughs at the rattling of the lance.
[30] Its undersides are jagged potsherds,
  leaving a trail in the mud like a threshing
    sledge.
[31] It makes the depths churn like a boiling
    caldron
  and stirs up the sea like a pot of ointment.

---

[a] In Hebrew texts 41:1-8 is numbered 40:25-32, and 41:9-34 is numbered 41:1-26.   [b] 13 Septuagint; Hebrew *double bridle*
[c] 15 Or *Its pride is its*

³²It leaves a glistening wake behind it;
  one would think the deep had white hair.
³³Nothing on earth is its equal—
  a creature without fear.
³⁴It looks down on all that are haughty;
  it is king over all that are proud."

Job

42

Then Job replied to the LORD:

²"I know that you can do all things;
  no purpose of yours can be thwarted.
³You asked, 'Who is this that obscures my
    plans without knowledge?'
  Surely I spoke of things I did not
    understand,
  things too wonderful for me to know.

⁴"You said, 'Listen now, and I will speak;
  I will question you,
  and you shall answer me.'
⁵My ears had heard of you
  but now my eyes have seen you.
⁶Therefore I despise myself
  and repent in dust and ashes."

Epilogue

⁷After the LORD had said these things to Job, he said to Eliphaz the Temanite, "I am angry with you and your two friends, because you have not spoken the truth about me, as my servant Job has. ⁸So now take seven bulls and seven rams and go to my servant Job and sacrifice a burnt offering for yourselves. My servant Job will pray for you, and I will accept his prayer and not deal with you according to your folly. You have not spoken the truth about me, as my servant Job has." ⁹So Eliphaz the Temanite, Bildad the Shuhite and Zophar the Naamathite did what the LORD told them; and the LORD accepted Job's prayer.

¹⁰After Job had prayed for his friends, the LORD restored his fortunes and gave him twice as much as he had before. ¹¹All his brothers and sisters and everyone who had known him before came and ate with him in his house. They comforted and consoled him over all the trouble the LORD had brought on him, and each one gave him a piece of silver[a] and a gold ring.

¹²The LORD blessed the latter part of Job's life more than the former part. He had fourteen thousand sheep, six thousand camels, a thousand yoke of oxen and a thousand donkeys. ¹³And he also had seven sons and three daughters. ¹⁴The first daughter he named Jemimah, the second Keziah and the third Keren-Happuch. ¹⁵Nowhere in all the land were there found women as beautiful as Job's daughters, and their father granted them an inheritance along with their brothers.

¹⁶After this, Job lived a hundred and forty years; he saw his children and their children to the fourth generation. ¹⁷And so Job died, an old man and full of years.

---

[a] 11 Hebrew *him a kesitah*; a kesitah was a unit of money of unknown weight and value.

Relationships: Job Takes the High Road

Job 42:10

After enduring nearly 40 chapters of criticism and condemnation from Eliphaz, Bildad and Zophar, Job has the opportunity to get even. God announces his displeasure with them, apparently giving Job a wonderful chance to say, "I told you so." Instead, Job prays for his foolish friends.

Like all great leaders, Job refused to take vengeance or hold grudges. Instead, he took the high road. He forgave his friends, interceded for them, and sent them on their way. Remind yourself of the differences between the low road and the high road:

Low Road	High Road
1. Revenge and retaliation when wronged	1. Unconditional love and forgiveness
2. Plays the same game as others	2. Refuses to play games; lives by principles
3. Guided by emotions; is up and down	3. Guided by character and values
4. Reactive: lives no better than anyone else	4. Proactive: lives above merely human standards

INTRODUCTION TO
PSALMS

B ible readers through the ages have flocked to the book of Psalms. Its poetic words reflect the entire range of human emotions. The various writers of the psalms aim to express their deepest feelings and longings—as well as the truth of God's wisdom.

These ancient Hebrew songs contribute to our understanding of leadership in both definitive and dynamic ways. They are *definitive* because they contain God's thoughts and values; they help leaders to understand how God thinks, what he values, and how he might respond to a leader's circumstances. They are *dynamic* because they explore the ups and downs of a leader's humanity. David, who wrote the majority of the psalms, expressed every emotion he felt as a leader, from the joy of God's victories, to deep contrition for his sin and shortcomings, anger over national injustice and lack of vision, and sadness over his weakness and lack of understanding.

Several writers contributed over many years to the collection we know as the Psalms. David, Asaph, the sons of Korah, Solomon, Moses, Heman, Ethan and a handful of anonymous authors all made unique contributions to this amazing "hymnal of Israel." We learn at least two great leadership lessons from them:

1. Leaders remain human.
2. Leadership is relationships.

Leadership always concerns more than cold, sterile strategy or achievement of goals. It demands that leaders shepherd others, exhort them, and build internal motivation in the hearts of their followers. David, especially,

God's Role in Psalms

Can anyone doubt that Psalm 23 would win a contest for "Most Popular Psalm"? It portrays the Lord not as the omnipotent Creator, not as the brilliant Strategist or the mighty Captain, but as a loving Shepherd who leads and guides his people with a rod and a staff.

David worked as a shepherd in his youth and later, as king, tapped the lessons he had learned in the fields. The psalms picture the intimate nature of God's relationship to his people.

Leaders in Psalms

David, Asaph, Solomon, the sons of Korah, Moses, Heman, Ethan

Other People of Influence in Psalms

The enemies of Israel, the wicked, the people of Israel

Lessons in Leadership

- Leaders never lose their humanity; they hurt when their people hurt.
- Leaders must be guided by principles and values worth dying for.
- Leaders gain credibility through their own vulnerability and transparency.
- Leaders take refuge in the Lord and allow him to fight battles through them.
- Leaders must be honest about their emotions.

speaks continually about his relationships—both his vertical relationship with God and his horizontal relationships with people. The people loved him because of his competency and compassion.

- Leaders recognize that the good in their lives comes from above.
- A leader's highest aim should be to honor and glorify God.
- The primary difference between a follower and a leader is perspective.

LEADERSHIP HIGHLIGHTS IN PSALMS

Several writers contributed over many years to the collection we know as the Psalms: David, Asaph, the sons of Korah, Solomon, Moses, Heman, Ethan and a handful of anonymous authors all made unique contributions to this amazing "hymnal of Israel". We learn at least two great leadership lessons from them.

1. Leaders remain human.
2. Leadership is relationships.

Leadership always concerns more than cold, sterile strategy or achievement of goals. It demands that leaders shepherd others, exhort them, and build internal motivation in the hearts of their followers. David, especially

BOOK I

Psalms 1–41

PSALM 1

[1] Blessed is the one
who does not walk in step with the wicked
or stand in the way that sinners take
or sit in the company of mockers,
[2] but whose delight is in the law of the LORD,
and who meditates on his law day and
night.
[3] That person is like a tree planted by streams
of water,
which yields its fruit in season
and whose leaf does not wither —
whatever they do prospers.

[4] Not so the wicked!
They are like chaff
that the wind blows away.
[5] Therefore the wicked will not stand in the
judgment,
nor sinners in the assembly of the
righteous.

[6] For the LORD watches over the way of the
righteous,
but the way of the wicked leads to
destruction.

PSALM 2

[1] Why do the nations conspire[a]
and the peoples plot in vain?
[2] The kings of the earth rise up
and the rulers band together
against the LORD and against his
anointed, saying,
[3] "Let us break their chains
and throw off their shackles."

[4] The One enthroned in heaven laughs;
the Lord scoffs at them.
[5] He rebukes them in his anger
and terrifies them in his wrath, saying,
[6] "I have installed my king
on Zion, my holy mountain."

[7] I will proclaim the LORD's decree:

He said to me, "You are my son;
today I have become your father.
[8] Ask me,
and I will make the nations your
inheritance,
the ends of the earth your possession.

The Law of the Inner Circle: Be Careful Where You Get Your Counsel

Psalm 1:1–3

The brilliant first psalm contrasts the righteous and the wicked. Leaders, take note, for the difference between the two seems to be where they get their counsel! Observe how a foolish leader can be led astray by a corrupt inner circle:

1. **The leader begins to browse for the wrong counsel (v. 1).**

2. **The leader begins to listen to the wrong voices (v. 1).**

3. **The leader joins the wrong inner circle (v. 1).**

Psalm 1:2 tells us that a wise leader meditates on God's Word day and night. To meditate means to examine, to experience, and to evaluate. Note the results of receiving counsel from the right inner circle:

1. **Stability (v. 3)**

2. **Inward nourishment and refreshment (v. 3)**

3. **Fruitfulness and productivity (v. 3)**

4. **Strength and durability (v. 3)**

5. **Success (v. 3)**

---

[9] You will break them with a rod of
iron[b];
you will dash them to pieces like
pottery."

[10] Therefore, you kings, be wise;
be warned, you rulers of the earth.
[11] Serve the LORD with fear
and celebrate his rule with trembling.
[12] Kiss his son, or he will be angry
and your way will lead to your
destruction,
for his wrath can flare up in a moment.
Blessed are all who take refuge in him.

---

[a] 1 Hebrew; Septuagint rage   [b] 9 Or will rule them with an
iron scepter (see Septuagint and Syriac)

PSALM 3[a]

*A psalm of David. When he fled from
his son Absalom.*

1 Lord, how many are my foes!
  How many rise up against me!
2 Many are saying of me,
  "God will not deliver him."[b]

3 But you, Lord, are a shield around me,
  my glory, the One who lifts my head
  high.
4 I call out to the Lord,
  and he answers me from his holy
  mountain.

5 I lie down and sleep;
  I wake again, because the Lord sustains
  me.
6 I will not fear though tens of thousands
  assail me on every side.

7 Arise, Lord!
  Deliver me, my God!
  Strike all my enemies on the jaw;
  break the teeth of the wicked.

8 From the Lord comes deliverance.
  May your blessing be on your people.

PSALM 4[c]

*For the director of music. With stringed instruments.
A psalm of David.*

1 Answer me when I call to you,
  my righteous God.
  Give me relief from my distress;
  have mercy on me and hear my prayer.

2 How long will you people turn my glory into
  shame?
  How long will you love delusions and seek
  false gods[d]?[e]
3 Know that the Lord has set apart his faithful
  servant for himself;
  the Lord hears when I call to him.

4 Tremble and[f] do not sin;
  when you are on your beds,
  search your hearts and be silent.
5 Offer the sacrifices of the righteous
  and trust in the Lord.

6 Many, Lord, are asking, "Who will bring us
  prosperity?"
  Let the light of your face shine on us.
7 Fill my heart with joy
  when their grain and new wine abound.

8 In peace I will lie down and sleep,
  for you alone, Lord,
  make me dwell in safety.

PSALM 5[g]

*For the director of music. For pipes.
A psalm of David.*

1 Listen to my words, Lord,
  consider my lament.
2 Hear my cry for help,
  my King and my God,
  for to you I pray.

3 In the morning, Lord, you hear my voice;
  in the morning I lay my requests before
  you
  and wait expectantly.
4 For you are not a God who is pleased with
  wickedness;
  with you, evil people are not welcome.
5 The arrogant cannot stand
  in your presence.
  You hate all who do wrong;
6   you destroy those who tell lies.
  The bloodthirsty and deceitful
  you, Lord, detest.
7 But I, by your great love,
  can come into your house;
  in reverence I bow down
  toward your holy temple.

8 Lead me, Lord, in your righteousness
  because of my enemies—
  make your way straight before me.
9 Not a word from their mouth can be
  trusted;
  their heart is filled with malice.
  Their throat is an open grave;
  with their tongues they tell lies.
10 Declare them guilty, O God!
  Let their intrigues be their downfall.
  Banish them for their many sins,
  for they have rebelled against you.
11 But let all who take refuge in you be glad;
  let them ever sing for joy.
  Spread your protection over them,
  that those who love your name may
  rejoice in you.

---

[a] In Hebrew texts 3:1-8 is numbered 3:2-9.   [b] 2 The Hebrew
has *Selah* (a word of uncertain meaning) here and at the end of
verses 4 and 8.   [c] In Hebrew texts 4:1-8 is numbered 4:2-9.
[d] 2 Or *seek lies*   [e] 2 The Hebrew has *Selah* (a word of
uncertain meaning) here and at the end of verse 4.   [f] 4 Or *In
your anger* (see Septuagint)   [g] In Hebrew texts 5:1-12 is
numbered 5:2-13.

¹² Surely, Lord, you bless the righteous;
you surround them with your favor as
with a shield.

PSALM 6 [a]

For the director of music. With stringed instruments.
According to *sheminith*.[b] A psalm of David.

¹ Lord, do not rebuke me in your anger
or discipline me in your wrath.
² Have mercy on me, Lord, for I am faint;
heal me, Lord, for my bones are in
agony.
³ My soul is in deep anguish.
How long, Lord, how long?

⁴ Turn, Lord, and deliver me;
save me because of your unfailing love.
⁵ Among the dead no one proclaims your
name.
Who praises you from the grave?

⁶ I am worn out from my groaning.

All night long I flood my bed with weeping
and drench my couch with tears.
⁷ My eyes grow weak with sorrow;
they fail because of all my foes.

⁸ Away from me, all you who do evil,
for the Lord has heard my weeping.
⁹ The Lord has heard my cry for mercy;
the Lord accepts my prayer.
¹⁰ All my enemies will be overwhelmed with
shame and anguish;
they will turn back and suddenly be put to
shame.

PSALM 7 [c]

A *shiggaion*[d] of David, which he sang to the Lord
concerning Cush, a Benjamite.

¹ Lord my God, I take refuge in you;
save and deliver me from all who pursue
me,
² or they will tear me apart like a lion
and rip me to pieces with no one to
rescue me.

³ Lord my God, if I have done this
and there is guilt on my hands —
⁴ if I have repaid my ally with evil
or without cause have robbed my foe —
⁵ then let my enemy pursue and overtake
me;
let him trample my life to the ground
and make me sleep in the dust.[e]

The Leader's Humanity: Don't Hide It

Psalm 6:1–10

David was a "man after [God's] own heart" (Ac 13:22), but he never hesitated to reveal his emotions or his weakness. Even as king of Israel, he declared his fears, his anxieties and his ambitions. Good leaders know how to balance transparency with being an example. Good leaders feel secure enough to be vulnerable.

⁶ Arise, Lord, in your anger;
rise up against the rage of my enemies.
Awake, my God; decree justice.
⁷ Let the assembled peoples gather around
you,
while you sit enthroned over them on
high.
⁸ Let the Lord judge the peoples.
Vindicate me, Lord, according to my
righteousness,
according to my integrity, O Most High.
⁹ Bring to an end the violence of the wicked
and make the righteous secure —
you, the righteous God
who probes minds and hearts.

¹⁰ My shield[f] is God Most High,
who saves the upright in heart.
¹¹ God is a righteous judge,
a God who displays his wrath every day.
¹² If he does not relent,
he[g] will sharpen his sword;
he will bend and string his bow.
¹³ He has prepared his deadly weapons;
he makes ready his flaming arrows.

¹⁴ Whoever is pregnant with evil
conceives trouble and gives birth to
disillusionment.
¹⁵ Whoever digs a hole and scoops it out
falls into the pit they have made.
¹⁶ The trouble they cause recoils on them;
their violence comes down on their own
heads.

[a] In Hebrew texts 6:1-10 is numbered 6:2-11.   [b] Title: Probably a musical term   [c] In Hebrew texts 7:1-17 is numbered 7:2-18.   [d] Title: Probably a literary or musical term   [e] 5 The Hebrew has *Selah* (a word of uncertain meaning) here.   [f] 10 Or *sovereign*   [g] 12 Or *If anyone does not repent, / God*

17 I will give thanks to the LORD because of his righteousness;
I will sing the praises of the name of the LORD Most High.

PSALM 8[a]

For the director of music. According to *gittith*.[b] A psalm of David.

1 LORD, our Lord,
how majestic is your name in all the earth!

You have set your glory
in the heavens.
2 Through the praise of children and infants
you have established a stronghold against your enemies,
to silence the foe and the avenger.
3 When I consider your heavens,
the work of your fingers,
the moon and the stars,
which you have set in place,
4 what is mankind that you are mindful of them,
human beings that you care for them?[c]

5 You have made them[d] a little lower than the angels[e]
and crowned them[d] with glory and honor.
6 You made them rulers over the works of your hands;
you put everything under their[f] feet:

7 all flocks and herds,
and the animals of the wild,
8 the birds in the sky,
and the fish in the sea,
all that swim the paths of the seas.

9 LORD, our Lord,
how majestic is your name in all the earth!

PSALM 9[g,h]

For the director of music. To the tune of "The Death of the Son." A psalm of David.

1 I will give thanks to you, LORD, with all my heart;
I will tell of all your wonderful deeds.
2 I will be glad and rejoice in you;
I will sing the praises of your name,
O Most High.

3 My enemies turn back;
they stumble and perish before you.
4 For you have upheld my right and my cause,
sitting enthroned as the righteous judge.

---

[a] In Hebrew texts 8:1-9 is numbered 8:2-10.   [b] Title: Probably a musical term   [c] 4 Or *what is a human being that you are mindful of him, / a son of man that you care for him?*   [d] 5 Or *him*   [e] 5 Or *than God*   [f] 6 Or *made him ruler . . . ; / . . . his*   [g] Psalms 9 and 10 may originally have been a single acrostic poem in which alternating lines began with the successive letters of the Hebrew alphabet. In the Septuagint they constitute one psalm.   [h] In Hebrew texts 9:1-20 is numbered 9:2-21.

Identity: A Balanced Perspective of God's Role and the Leader's Role

Psalm 8:3–9

Have you ever asked, "When does a leader's confidence become arrogance? How self-assured should I be as a leader? What does humility look like in a leader's life?"

Psalm 8 answers those questions. This passage shows leaders how to balance their identity with their self-esteem. Consider how David perceives his identity and maintains both confidence and humility:

1. **David sees clearly his own weakness and humanity (vv. 3–4).**
   David begins by asking a question: "Why does God even give any thought to me?" he realizes that in the sweep of the galaxy, man accounts for only a very small part. Remembering this helps us to remain humble.

2. **David sees his God-given position and privileges (vv. 5–8).**
   David knows that God has made humankind a little lower than himself. The Lord put men and women in charge of the whole earth and gave them authority over creation.

3. **David sees a balance by giving all the glory to God (v. 9).**
   David closes the psalm the way he began. He magnifies the Lord and gives him the credit for the good that has come from his life and leadership.

5 You have rebuked the nations and destroyed the wicked;
  you have blotted out their name for ever and ever.
6 Endless ruin has overtaken my enemies, you have uprooted their cities;
  even the memory of them has perished.

7 The LORD reigns forever;
  he has established his throne for judgment.
8 He rules the world in righteousness
  and judges the peoples with equity.
9 The LORD is a refuge for the oppressed,
  a stronghold in times of trouble.
10 Those who know your name trust in you,
  for you, LORD, have never forsaken those who seek you.

11 Sing the praises of the LORD, enthroned in Zion;
  proclaim among the nations what he has done.
12 For he who avenges blood remembers;
  he does not ignore the cries of the afflicted.

13 LORD, see how my enemies persecute me!
  Have mercy and lift me up from the gates of death,
14 that I may declare your praises
  in the gates of Daughter Zion,
  and there rejoice in your salvation.

15 The nations have fallen into the pit they have dug;
  their feet are caught in the net they have hidden.
16 The LORD is known by his acts of justice;
  the wicked are ensnared by the work of their hands.*a*
17 The wicked go down to the realm of the dead,
  all the nations that forget God.
18 But God will never forget the needy;
  the hope of the afflicted will never perish.

19 Arise, LORD, do not let mortals triumph;
  let the nations be judged in your presence.
20 Strike them with terror, LORD;
  let the nations know they are only mortal.

PSALM 10*b*

1 Why, LORD, do you stand far off?
  Why do you hide yourself in times of trouble?

2 In his arrogance the wicked man hunts down the weak,
  who are caught in the schemes he devises.
3 He boasts about the cravings of his heart;
  he blesses the greedy and reviles the LORD.
4 In his pride the wicked man does not seek him;
  in all his thoughts there is no room for God.
5 His ways are always prosperous;
  your laws are rejected by*c* him;
  he sneers at all his enemies.
6 He says to himself, "Nothing will ever shake me."
  He swears, "No one will ever do me harm."

7 His mouth is full of lies and threats;
  trouble and evil are under his tongue.
8 He lies in wait near the villages;
  from ambush he murders the innocent.
  His eyes watch in secret for his victims;
9   like a lion in cover he lies in wait.
  He lies in wait to catch the helpless;
  he catches the helpless and drags them off in his net.
10 His victims are crushed, they collapse;
  they fall under his strength.
11 He says to himself, "God will never notice;
  he covers his face and never sees."

12 Arise, LORD! Lift up your hand, O God.
  Do not forget the helpless.
13 Why does the wicked man revile God?
  Why does he say to himself,
  "He won't call me to account"?
14 But you, God, see the trouble of the afflicted;
  you consider their grief and take it in hand.
  The victims commit themselves to you;
  you are the helper of the fatherless.
15 Break the arm of the wicked man;
  call the evildoer to account for his wickedness
  that would not otherwise be found out.
16 The LORD is King for ever and ever;
  the nations will perish from his land.

---

a 16 The Hebrew has *Higgaion* and *Selah* (words of uncertain meaning) here; *Selah* occurs also at the end of verse 20. *b* Psalms 9 and 10 may originally have been a single acrostic poem in which alternating lines began with the successive letters of the Hebrew alphabet. In the Septuagint they constitute one psalm. *c* 5 See Septuagint; Hebrew / *they are haughty, and your laws are far from*

17 You, LORD, hear the desire of the afflicted;
　　you encourage them, and you listen to
　　　their cry,
18 defending the fatherless and the oppressed,
　　so that mere earthly mortals
　　will never again strike terror.

PSALM 11

For the director of music. Of David.

1 In the LORD I take refuge.
　　How then can you say to me:
　　"Flee like a bird to your mountain.
2 For look, the wicked bend their bows;
　　they set their arrows against the strings
　to shoot from the shadows
　　at the upright in heart.
3 When the foundations are being destroyed,
　　what can the righteous do?"

4 The LORD is in his holy temple;
　　the LORD is on his heavenly throne.
　He observes everyone on earth;
　　his eyes examine them.
5 The LORD examines the righteous,
　　but the wicked, those who love violence,
　　he hates with a passion.
6 On the wicked he will rain
　　fiery coals and burning sulfur;
　　a scorching wind will be their lot.

7 For the LORD is righteous,
　　he loves justice;
　　the upright will see his face.

PSALM 12 [a]

For the director of music. According to *sheminith.* [b]
A psalm of David.

1 Help, LORD, for no one is faithful anymore;
　　those who are loyal have vanished from
　　　the human race.
2 Everyone lies to their neighbor;
　　they flatter with their lips
　　but harbor deception in their hearts.

3 May the LORD silence all flattering lips
　　and every boastful tongue —
4 those who say,
　　"By our tongues we will prevail;
　　our own lips will defend us — who is lord
　　　over us?"

5 "Because the poor are plundered and the
　　　needy groan,
　　I will now arise," says the LORD.

"I will protect them from those who
　　malign them."
6 And the words of the LORD are flawless,
　　like silver purified in a crucible,
　　like gold [c] refined seven times.

7 You, LORD, will keep the needy safe
　　and will protect us forever from the wicked,
8 who freely strut about
　　when what is vile is honored by the
　　　human race.

PSALM 13 [d]

For the director of music. A psalm of David.

1 How long, LORD? Will you forget me forever?
　　How long will you hide your face from
　　　me?
2 How long must I wrestle with my thoughts
　　and day after day have sorrow in my
　　　heart?
　　How long will my enemy triumph over me?

3 Look on me and answer, LORD my God.
　　Give light to my eyes, or I will sleep in
　　　death,
4 and my enemy will say, "I have overcome
　　　him,"
　　and my foes will rejoice when I fall.

5 But I trust in your unfailing love;
　　my heart rejoices in your salvation.
6 I will sing the LORD's praise,
　　for he has been good to me.

PSALM 14

For the director of music. Of David.

1 The fool [e] says in his heart,
　　"There is no God."
　They are corrupt, their deeds are vile;
　　there is no one who does good.

2 The LORD looks down from heaven
　　on all mankind
　to see if there are any who understand,
　　any who seek God.
3 All have turned away, all have become
　　　corrupt;
　　there is no one who does good,
　　not even one.

---

[a] In Hebrew texts 12:1-8 is numbered 12:2-9.　　[b] Title:
Probably a musical term　　[c] 6 Probable reading of the
original Hebrew text; Masoretic Text *earth*　　[d] In Hebrew
texts 13:1-6 is numbered 13:2-6.　　[e] 1 The Hebrew words
rendered *fool* in Psalms denote one who is morally deficient.

⁴Do all these evildoers know nothing?

They devour my people as though eating
        bread;
    they never call on the LORD.
⁵But there they are, overwhelmed with
        dread,
    for God is present in the company of the
        righteous.
⁶You evildoers frustrate the plans of the poor,
    but the LORD is their refuge.

⁷Oh, that salvation for Israel would come out
        of Zion!
    When the LORD restores his people,
    let Jacob rejoice and Israel be glad!

PSALM 15

A psalm of David.

¹LORD, who may dwell in your sacred tent?
    Who may live on your holy mountain?

²The one whose walk is blameless,
    who does what is righteous,
    who speaks the truth from their heart;
³whose tongue utters no slander,
    who does no wrong to a neighbor,
    and casts no slur on others;
⁴who despises a vile person
    but honors those who fear the LORD;
who keeps an oath even when it hurts,
    and does not change their mind;
⁵who lends money to the poor without
        interest;
    who does not accept a bribe against the
        innocent.

Whoever does these things
    will never be shaken.

PSALM 16

A *miktam*ᵃ of David.

¹Keep me safe, my God,
    for in you I take refuge.

²I say to the LORD, "You are my Lord;
    apart from you I have no good thing."
³I say of the holy people who are in the land,
    "They are the noble ones in whom is all
        my delight."
⁴Those who run after other gods will suffer
        more and more.
    I will not pour out libations of blood to
        such gods
    or take up their names on my lips.

Value-Driven Leadership

Psalm 15:1–5

What qualities should every leader possess?
Psalm 15 furnishes us with a list of many of
the necessary traits.

David describes a righteous man who walks
in integrity and gains not only the respect of
others, but also an audience with God (Ps 15:1–
2). He demonstrates why predetermined values
and ethics, not expediency, must drive our leadership. How does David picture a godly leader?
The leader . . .

- **possesses integrity (v. 2)**
- **does what is right (v. 2)**
- **is honest and trustworthy (v. 2)**
- **does not gossip (v. 3)**
- **does not listen to gossip (v. 3)**
- **does no harm to others (v. 3)**
- **speaks out against wrong (v. 4)**
- **honors others who walk in truth (v. 4)**
- **keeps their word even when it costs
  them (v. 4)**
- **isn't greedy to gain at the expense of
  others (v. 5)**
- **takes no bribes against anyone (v. 5)**
- **is strong and stable (v. 5)**

---

⁵LORD, you alone are my portion and my cup;
    you make my lot secure.
⁶The boundary lines have fallen for me in
        pleasant places;
    surely I have a delightful inheritance.
⁷I will praise the LORD, who counsels me;
    even at night my heart instructs me.
⁸I keep my eyes always on the LORD.
    With him at my right hand, I will not be
        shaken.

⁹Therefore my heart is glad and my tongue
        rejoices;
    my body also will rest secure,
¹⁰because you will not abandon me to the
        realm of the dead,
    nor will you let your faithfulᵇ one see
        decay.
¹¹You make known to me the path of life;
    you will fill me with joy in your presence,
    with eternal pleasures at your right hand.

ᵃ Title: Probably a literary or musical term   ᵇ 10 Or *holy*

PSALM 17

A prayer of David.

[1] Hear me, LORD, my plea is just;
  listen to my cry.
Hear my prayer—
  it does not rise from deceitful lips.
[2] Let my vindication come from you;
  may your eyes see what is right.

[3] Though you probe my heart,
    though you examine me at night and
      test me,
  you will find that I have planned no evil;
    my mouth has not transgressed.
[4] Though people tried to bribe me,
    I have kept myself from the ways of the
      violent
    through what your lips have commanded.
[5] My steps have held to your paths;
  my feet have not stumbled.

[6] I call on you, my God, for you will answer
    me;
  turn your ear to me and hear my prayer.
[7] Show me the wonders of your great love,
  you who save by your right hand
    those who take refuge in you from their
      foes.
[8] Keep me as the apple of your eye;
  hide me in the shadow of your wings
[9] from the wicked who are out to destroy me,
  from my mortal enemies who surround me.

[10] They close up their callous hearts,
  and their mouths speak with arrogance.
[11] They have tracked me down, they now
    surround me,
  with eyes alert, to throw me to the
    ground.
[12] They are like a lion hungry for prey,
  like a fierce lion crouching in cover.

[13] Rise up, LORD, confront them, bring them
    down;
  with your sword rescue me from the
    wicked.
[14] By your hand save me from such people,
    LORD,
  from those of this world whose reward is
    in this life.
May what you have stored up for the wicked
    fill their bellies;
  may their children gorge themselves on it,
  and may there be leftovers for their little
    ones.

[15] As for me, I will be vindicated and will see
    your face;
  when I awake, I will be satisfied with
    seeing your likeness.

PSALM 18[a]

For the director of music. Of David the servant of the
LORD. He sang to the LORD the words of this song
when the LORD delivered him from the hand of all his
enemies and from the hand of Saul. He said:

[1] I love you, LORD, my strength.

[2] The LORD is my rock, my fortress and my
    deliverer;
  my God is my rock, in whom I take
    refuge,
  my shield[b] and the horn[c] of my salvation,
    my stronghold.

[3] I called to the LORD, who is worthy of praise,
  and I have been saved from my enemies.
[4] The cords of death entangled me;
  the torrents of destruction overwhelmed
    me.
[5] The cords of the grave coiled around me;
  the snares of death confronted me.
[6] In my distress I called to the LORD;
  I cried to my God for help.
From his temple he heard my voice;
  my cry came before him, into his ears.
[7] The earth trembled and quaked,
  and the foundations of the mountains
    shook;
  they trembled because he was angry.
[8] Smoke rose from his nostrils;
  consuming fire came from his mouth,
  burning coals blazed out of it.
[9] He parted the heavens and came down;
  dark clouds were under his feet.
[10] He mounted the cherubim and flew;
  he soared on the wings of the wind.
[11] He made darkness his covering, his canopy
    around him—
  the dark rain clouds of the sky.
[12] Out of the brightness of his presence clouds
    advanced,
  with hailstones and bolts of lightning.
[13] The LORD thundered from heaven;
  the voice of the Most High resounded.[d]

---

[a] In Hebrew texts 18:1-50 is numbered 18:2-51.   [b] 2 Or
sovereign   [c] 2 Horn here symbolizes strength.   [d] 13 Some
Hebrew manuscripts and Septuagint (see also 2 Samuel 22:14);
most Hebrew manuscripts resounded, / amid hailstones and
bolts of lightning

14 He shot his arrows and scattered the enemy,
with great bolts of lightning he routed
them.
15 The valleys of the sea were exposed
and the foundations of the earth laid
bare
at your rebuke, LORD,
at the blast of breath from your nostrils.

16 He reached down from on high and took
hold of me;
he drew me out of deep waters.
17 He rescued me from my powerful enemy,
from my foes, who were too strong for me.
18 They confronted me in the day of my
disaster,
but the LORD was my support.
19 He brought me out into a spacious place;
he rescued me because he delighted in me.

20 The LORD has dealt with me according to my
righteousness;
according to the cleanness of my hands he
has rewarded me.
21 For I have kept the ways of the LORD;
I am not guilty of turning from my God.
22 All his laws are before me;
I have not turned away from his decrees.
23 I have been blameless before him
and have kept myself from sin.

24 The LORD has rewarded me according to my
righteousness,
according to the cleanness of my hands in
his sight.
25 To the faithful you show yourself faithful,
to the blameless you show yourself
blameless,
26 to the pure you show yourself pure,
but to the devious you show yourself
shrewd.
27 You save the humble
but bring low those whose eyes are haughty.
28 You, LORD, keep my lamp burning;
my God turns my darkness into light.
29 With your help I can advance against a
troop*a*;
with my God I can scale a wall.
30 As for God, his way is perfect:
The LORD's word is flawless;
he shields all who take refuge in him.
31 For who is God besides the LORD?
And who is the Rock except our God?
32 It is God who arms me with strength
and keeps my way secure.
33 He makes my feet like the feet of a deer;
he causes me to stand on the heights.

a 29 Or can run through a barricade

God: An Absolute Leader in a Relative World

Psalm 18:1–34

God is an absolute in a relative world. So how can leaders learn to rely on him? Psalm 18 gives some answers.

David not only models what it means to be a leader, but also how to lean completely on the God who transcends the universe and judges it. Human leaders can find refuge in God's absolute leadership for two reasons:

1. **The Lord is a mighty Protector.**

2. **The Lord is an effective Equipper.**

Psalm 18:1–29 describes the tangible benefits of living according to this truth. When leaders adopt it, they can perform beyond their abilities. Why? Because God enables them to do so. The psalmist declares that God "teaches" or "trains" their hands for battle (18:34). Leaders are to emulate both roles, in addition to several others pictured throughout the psalms:

1. **The leader as a king (20:9)**

2. **The leader as a shepherd (23:1)**

3. **The leader as a guide/counselor (48:14)**

4. **The leader as a disciplinarian (50:16–21)**

5. **The leader as a provider (72:6)**

6. **The leader as a creator/innovator (95:5)**

7. **The leader as a worker/producer (107:37)**

³⁴He trains my hands for battle;
  my arms can bend a bow of bronze.
³⁵You make your saving help my shield,
  and your right hand sustains me;
  your help has made me great.
³⁶You provide a broad path for my feet,
  so that my ankles do not give way.

³⁷I pursued my enemies and overtook them;
  I did not turn back till they were
    destroyed.
³⁸I crushed them so that they could not rise;
  they fell beneath my feet.
³⁹You armed me with strength for battle;
  you humbled my adversaries before me.
⁴⁰You made my enemies turn their backs in
    flight,
  and I destroyed my foes.
⁴¹They cried for help, but there was no one to
    save them —
  to the LORD, but he did not answer.
⁴²I beat them as fine as windblown dust;
  I trampled them[a] like mud in the streets.
⁴³You have delivered me from the attacks of
    the people;
  you have made me the head of nations.
  People I did not know now serve me,
⁴⁴ foreigners cower before me;
  as soon as they hear of me, they obey me.
⁴⁵They all lose heart;
  they come trembling from their
    strongholds.

⁴⁶The LORD lives! Praise be to my Rock!
  Exalted be God my Savior!

⁴⁷He is the God who avenges me,
  who subdues nations under me,
⁴⁸ who saves me from my enemies.
  You exalted me above my foes;
  from a violent man you rescued me.
⁴⁹Therefore I will praise you, LORD, among the
    nations;
  I will sing the praises of your name.

⁵⁰He gives his king great victories;
  he shows unfailing love to his anointed,
  to David and to his descendants forever.

PSALM 19[b]

For the director of music. A psalm of David.

¹The heavens declare the glory of God;
  the skies proclaim the work of his hands.
²Day after day they pour forth speech;
  night after night they reveal knowledge.
³They have no speech, they use no words;
  no sound is heard from them.
⁴Yet their voice[c] goes out into all the earth,
  their words to the ends of the world.
  In the heavens God has pitched a tent for the
    sun.
⁵ It is like a bridegroom coming out of his
    chamber,
  like a champion rejoicing to run his
    course.

---

[a] 42 Many Hebrew manuscripts, Septuagint, Syriac and Targum (see also 2 Samuel 22:43); Masoretic Text *I poured them out*   [b] In Hebrew texts 19:1-14 is numbered 19:2-15.   [c] 4 Septuagint, Jerome and Syriac; Hebrew *measuring line*

Leaders Communicate

Psalm 19:1–14

God is not only the Ultimate Leader, but the Ultimate Communicator. The creation declares God's power and glory (Ps 19:1–6). The Law declares God's wisdom and will (19:7–14). God precisely reveals his message to his followers through both. Three simple verses (19:7–9) declare the results of this ultimate communication:

God's Revelation	Description	The Results
1. His Law	1. Perfect	1. Restores the soul
2. Testimony	2. Sure	2. Makes us wise
3. Statutes	3. Right	3. Gives joy to the heart
4. Commandments	4. Pure	4. Enlightens our perception
5. Fear and reverence	5. Clean	5. Endures forever
6. Judgments	6. True	6. Completely right

⁶It rises at one end of the heavens
    and makes its circuit to the other;
    nothing is deprived of its warmth.

⁷The law of the LORD is perfect,
    refreshing the soul.
The statutes of the LORD are trustworthy,
    making wise the simple.
⁸The precepts of the LORD are right,
    giving joy to the heart.
The commands of the LORD are radiant,
    giving light to the eyes.
⁹The fear of the LORD is pure,
    enduring forever.
The decrees of the LORD are firm,
    and all of them are righteous.

¹⁰They are more precious than gold,
    than much pure gold;
they are sweeter than honey,
    than honey from the honeycomb.
¹¹By them your servant is warned;
    in keeping them there is great reward.
¹²But who can discern their own errors?
    Forgive my hidden faults.
¹³Keep your servant also from willful sins;
    may they not rule over me.
Then I will be blameless,
    innocent of great transgression.

¹⁴May these words of my mouth and this
    meditation of my heart
be pleasing in your sight,
    LORD, my Rock and my Redeemer.

PSALM 20[a]

For the director of music. A psalm of David.

¹May the LORD answer you when you are in
    distress;
may the name of the God of Jacob protect
    you.
²May he send you help from the sanctuary
    and grant you support from Zion.
³May he remember all your sacrifices
    and accept your burnt offerings.[b]
⁴May he give you the desire of your heart
    and make all your plans succeed.
⁵May we shout for joy over your victory
    and lift up our banners in the name of
    our God.

May the LORD grant all your requests.

⁶Now this I know:
    The LORD gives victory to his
    anointed.

He answers him from his heavenly
    sanctuary
    with the victorious power of his right
    hand.
⁷Some trust in chariots and some in horses,
    but we trust in the name of the LORD our
    God.
⁸They are brought to their knees and fall,
    but we rise up and stand firm.
⁹LORD, give victory to the king!
    Answer us when we call!

PSALM 21[c]

For the director of music. A psalm of David.

¹The king rejoices in your strength, LORD.
    How great is his joy in the victories you
    give!

²You have granted him his heart's desire
    and have not withheld the request of his
    lips.[b]
³You came to greet him with rich blessings
    and placed a crown of pure gold on his
    head.
⁴He asked you for life, and you gave it to
    him—
    length of days, for ever and ever.
⁵Through the victories you gave, his glory is
    great;
    you have bestowed on him splendor and
    majesty.
⁶Surely you have granted him unending
    blessings
    and made him glad with the joy of your
    presence.
⁷For the king trusts in the LORD;
    through the unfailing love of the Most
    High
    he will not be shaken.

⁸Your hand will lay hold on all your enemies;
    your right hand will seize your foes.
⁹When you appear for battle,
    you will burn them up as in a blazing
    furnace.
The LORD will swallow them up in his
    wrath,
    and his fire will consume them.
¹⁰You will destroy their descendants from the
    earth,
    their posterity from mankind.

---

[a] In Hebrew texts 20:1-9 is numbered 20:2-10.   [b] 3,2 The Hebrew has *Selah* (a word of uncertain meaning) here.   [c] In Hebrew texts 21:1-13 is numbered 21:2-14.

11 Though they plot evil against you
　　and devise wicked schemes, they cannot
　　　succeed.
12 You will make them turn their backs
　　when you aim at them with drawn bow.

13 Be exalted in your strength, LORD;
　　we will sing and praise your might.

PSALM 22[a]

For the director of music. To the tune of "The Doe of
the Morning." A psalm of David.

1 My God, my God, why have you forsaken
　　me?
　　Why are you so far from saving me,
　　so far from my cries of anguish?
2 My God, I cry out by day, but you do not
　　answer,
　　by night, but I find no rest.[b]

3 Yet you are enthroned as the Holy One;
　　you are the one Israel praises.[c]
4 In you our ancestors put their trust;
　　they trusted and you delivered them.
5 To you they cried out and were saved;
　　in you they trusted and were not put to
　　　shame.

6 But I am a worm and not a man,
　　scorned by everyone, despised by the
　　　people.
7 All who see me mock me;
　　they hurl insults, shaking their heads.
8 "He trusts in the LORD," they say,
　　"let the LORD rescue him.
　Let him deliver him,
　　since he delights in him."

9 Yet you brought me out of the womb;
　　you made me trust in you, even at my
　　　mother's breast.
10 From birth I was cast on you;
　　from my mother's womb you have been
　　　my God.

11 Do not be far from me,
　　for trouble is near
　　and there is no one to help.

12 Many bulls surround me;
　　strong bulls of Bashan encircle me.
13 Roaring lions that tear their prey
　　open their mouths wide against me.
14 I am poured out like water,
　　and all my bones are out of joint.
　My heart has turned to wax;
　　it has melted within me.

15 My mouth[d] is dried up like a potsherd,
　　and my tongue sticks to the roof of my
　　　mouth;
　　you lay me in the dust of death.

16 Dogs surround me,
　　a pack of villains encircles me;
　　they pierce[e] my hands and my feet.
17 All my bones are on display;
　　people stare and gloat over me.
18 They divide my clothes among them
　　and cast lots for my garment.

19 But you, LORD, do not be far from me.
　　You are my strength; come quickly to
　　　help me.
20 Deliver me from the sword,
　　my precious life from the power of the
　　　dogs.
21 Rescue me from the mouth of the lions;
　　save me from the horns of the wild
　　　oxen.

22 I will declare your name to my people;
　　in the assembly I will praise you.
23 You who fear the LORD, praise him!
　　All you descendants of Jacob, honor
　　　him!
　　Revere him, all you descendants of
　　　Israel!
24 For he has not despised or scorned
　　the suffering of the afflicted one;
　　he has not hidden his face from him
　　but has listened to his cry for help.

25 From you comes the theme of my praise in
　　the great assembly;
　　before those who fear you[f] I will fulfill
　　　my vows.
26 The poor will eat and be satisfied;
　　those who seek the LORD will praise
　　　him—
　　may your hearts live forever!

27 All the ends of the earth
　　will remember and turn to the LORD,
　and all the families of the nations
　　will bow down before him,
28 for dominion belongs to the LORD
　　and he rules over the nations.

---

[a] In Hebrew texts 22:1-31 is numbered 22:2-32.　　[b] 2 Or night,
and am not silent　　[c] 3 Or Yet you are holy, / enthroned on the
praises of Israel　　[d] 15 Probable reading of the original
Hebrew text; Masoretic Text strength　　[e] 16 Dead Sea Scrolls
and some manuscripts of the Masoretic Text, Septuagint and
Syriac; most manuscripts of the Masoretic Text me, / like a lion
[f] 25 Hebrew him

²⁹ All the rich of the earth will feast and worship;
 all who go down to the dust will kneel
  before him —
  those who cannot keep themselves alive.
³⁰ Posterity will serve him;
 future generations will be told about the
  Lord.
³¹ They will proclaim his righteousness,
 declaring to a people yet unborn:
  He has done it!

PSALM 23

A psalm of David.

¹ The Lord is my shepherd, I lack nothing.
² He makes me lie down in green pastures,
he leads me beside quiet waters,
³ he refreshes my soul.
He guides me along the right paths
 for his name's sake.
⁴ Even though I walk
 through the darkest valley,ᵃ

I will fear no evil,
 for you are with me;
your rod and your staff,
 they comfort me.

⁵ You prepare a table before me
 in the presence of my enemies.
You anoint my head with oil;
 my cup overflows.
⁶ Surely your goodness and love will follow me
 all the days of my life,
and I will dwell in the house of the Lord
 forever.

The Leader as a Shepherd

Psalm 23:1–6

No psalm has gained more admirers than Psalm 23. In it, we learn not only about God's nature, but also about his leadership. David describes the Lord as a Shepherd, no doubt seeing him this way because of his own leadership bias. David also had been a model shepherd.

Both Old and New Testaments use the term "shepherd" to illustrate leadership. The word communicates the love, nurture, intimacy and spiritual care a godly leader provides. It involves both the rod (correction) and the staff (direction). Psalm 23 describes the Ultimate Shepherd performing several functions. The Shepherd . . .

- **provides (v. 1)**
- **gives rest (v. 2)**
- **confidently leads (v. 3)**
- **renews and restores (v. 3)**
- **guides and directs (v. 3)**
- **protects (v. 4)**
- **corrects and comforts (v. 4)**
- **feeds and anoints (v. 5)**
- **loves (v. 6)**
- **furnishes permanent shelter (v. 6)**

The Leader and Stress

Psalm 23:1–6

Have you discovered the difference between problems and facts? Problems are things we can do something about; we can solve problems. Facts are things we can do nothing about; therefore we do well not to worry about them. We apply energy only to those things we can change. We can feel peace and act with poise, because we no longer beat our heads against an unbreakable wall.

Psalm 23 reminds us of what God alone can control and what we can control. It distinguishes between problems and facts. It defines God as . . .

- **our possession (v. 1)**
- **our provision (v. 1)**
- **our peace (v. 2)**
- **our pardon (v. 3)**
- **our partner (v. 4)**
- **our preparation (v. 5)**
- **our praise (v. 5)**
- **our paradise (v. 6)**

PSALM 24

Of David. A psalm.

¹ The earth is the Lord's, and everything in it,
 the world, and all who live in it;
² for he founded it on the seas
 and established it on the waters.

³ Who may ascend the mountain of the Lord?
 Who may stand in his holy place?

ᵃ 4 Or *the valley of the shadow of death*

[4]The one who has clean hands and a pure
heart,
who does not trust in an idol
or swear by a false god.[a]

[5]They will receive blessing from the LORD
and vindication from God their Savior.
[6]Such is the generation of those who seek him,
who seek your face, God of Jacob.[b,c]

[7]Lift up your heads, you gates;
be lifted up, you ancient doors,
that the King of glory may come in.
[8]Who is this King of glory?
The LORD strong and mighty,
the LORD mighty in battle.
[9]Lift up your heads, you gates;
lift them up, you ancient doors,
that the King of glory may come in.
[10]Who is he, this King of glory?
The LORD Almighty—
he is the King of glory.

PSALM 25[d]

Of David.

[1]In you, LORD my God,
I put my trust.

[2]I trust in you;
do not let me be put to shame,
nor let my enemies triumph over me.
[3]No one who hopes in you
will ever be put to shame,
but shame will come on those
who are treacherous without cause.

[4]Show me your ways, LORD,
teach me your paths.
[5]Guide me in your truth and teach me,
for you are God my Savior,
and my hope is in you all day long.
[6]Remember, LORD, your great mercy and love,
for they are from of old.
[7]Do not remember the sins of my youth
and my rebellious ways;
according to your love remember me,
for you, LORD, are good.

[8]Good and upright is the LORD;
therefore he instructs sinners in his ways.
[9]He guides the humble in what is right
and teaches them his way.
[10]All the ways of the LORD are loving and
faithful
toward those who keep the demands of his
covenant.

[11]For the sake of your name, LORD,
forgive my iniquity, though it is great.

[12]Who, then, are those who fear the LORD?
He will instruct them in the ways they
should choose.[e]
[13]They will spend their days in prosperity,
and their descendants will inherit the land.
[14]The LORD confides in those who fear him;
he makes his covenant known to them.
[15]My eyes are ever on the LORD,
for only he will release my feet from the
snare.

[16]Turn to me and be gracious to me,
for I am lonely and afflicted.
[17]Relieve the troubles of my heart
and free me from my anguish.
[18]Look on my affliction and my distress
and take away all my sins.
[19]See how numerous are my enemies
and how fiercely they hate me!

[20]Guard my life and rescue me;
do not let me be put to shame,
for I take refuge in you.
[21]May integrity and uprightness protect me,
because my hope, LORD,[f] is in you.

[22]Deliver Israel, O God,
from all their troubles!

PSALM 26

Of David.

[1]Vindicate me, LORD,
for I have led a blameless life;
I have trusted in the LORD
and have not faltered.
[2]Test me, LORD, and try me,
examine my heart and my mind;
[3]for I have always been mindful of your
unfailing love
and have lived in reliance on your
faithfulness.

[4]I do not sit with the deceitful,
nor do I associate with hypocrites.
[5]I abhor the assembly of evildoers
and refuse to sit with the wicked.

---

[a] 4 Or *swear falsely*   [b] 6 Two Hebrew manuscripts and
Syriac (see also Septuagint); most Hebrew manuscripts *face,
Jacob*   [c] 6 The Hebrew has *Selah* (a word of uncertain
meaning) here and at the end of verse 10.   [d] This psalm is an
acrostic poem, the verses of which begin with the successive
letters of the Hebrew alphabet.   [e] 12 Or *ways he chooses*
[f] 21 Septuagint; Hebrew does not have LORD.

[6] I wash my hands in innocence,
and go about your altar, LORD,
[7] proclaiming aloud your praise
and telling of all your wonderful deeds.

[8] LORD, I love the house where you live,
the place where your glory dwells.
[9] Do not take away my soul along with sinners,
my life with those who are bloodthirsty,
[10] in whose hands are wicked schemes,
whose right hands are full of bribes.
[11] I lead a blameless life;
deliver me and be merciful to me.

[12] My feet stand on level ground;
in the great congregation I will praise the
LORD.

PSALM 27

Of David.

[1] The LORD is my light and my salvation —
whom shall I fear?
The LORD is the stronghold of my life —
of whom shall I be afraid?

[2] When the wicked advance against me
to devour[a] me,
it is my enemies and my foes
who will stumble and fall.
[3] Though an army besiege me,
my heart will not fear;
though war break out against me,
even then I will be confident.

[4] One thing I ask from the LORD,
this only do I seek:
that I may dwell in the house of the LORD
all the days of my life,
to gaze on the beauty of the LORD
and to seek him in his temple.
[5] For in the day of trouble
he will keep me safe in his dwelling;
he will hide me in the shelter of his sacred
tent
and set me high upon a rock.

[6] Then my head will be exalted
above the enemies who surround me;
at his sacred tent I will sacrifice with shouts
of joy;
I will sing and make music to the LORD.

[7] Hear my voice when I call, LORD;
be merciful to me and answer me.
[8] My heart says of you, "Seek his face!"
Your face, LORD, I will seek.

[9] Do not hide your face from me,
do not turn your servant away in anger;
you have been my helper.
Do not reject me or forsake me,
God my Savior.
[10] Though my father and mother forsake me,
the LORD will receive me.
[11] Teach me your way, LORD;
lead me in a straight path
because of my oppressors.
[12] Do not turn me over to the desire of my foes,
for false witnesses rise up against me,
spouting malicious accusations.

[13] I remain confident of this:
I will see the goodness of the LORD
in the land of the living.
[14] Wait for the LORD;
be strong and take heart
and wait for the LORD.

PSALM 28

Of David.

[1] To you, LORD, I call;
you are my Rock,
do not turn a deaf ear to me.
For if you remain silent,
I will be like those who go down to the pit.
[2] Hear my cry for mercy
as I call to you for help,
as I lift up my hands
toward your Most Holy Place.

[3] Do not drag me away with the wicked,
with those who do evil,
who speak cordially with their neighbors
but harbor malice in their hearts.
[4] Repay them for their deeds
and for their evil work;
repay them for what their hands have done
and bring back on them what they deserve.

[5] Because they have no regard for the deeds of
the LORD
and what his hands have done,
he will tear them down
and never build them up again.

[6] Praise be to the LORD,
for he has heard my cry for mercy.
[7] The LORD is my strength and my shield;
my heart trusts in him, and he helps me.
My heart leaps for joy,
and with my song I praise him.

---

[a] 2 Or slander

8 The LORD is the strength of his people,
 a fortress of salvation for his anointed one.
9 Save your people and bless your inheritance;
 be their shepherd and carry them forever.

PSALM 29

A psalm of David.

1 Ascribe to the LORD, you heavenly beings,
 ascribe to the LORD glory and strength.
2 Ascribe to the LORD the glory due his name;
 worship the LORD in the splendor of his[a]
  holiness.

3 The voice of the LORD is over the waters;
 the God of glory thunders,
 the LORD thunders over the mighty
  waters.
4 The voice of the LORD is powerful;
 the voice of the LORD is majestic.
5 The voice of the LORD breaks the cedars;
 the LORD breaks in pieces the cedars of
  Lebanon.
6 He makes Lebanon leap like a calf,
 Sirion[b] like a young wild ox.
7 The voice of the LORD strikes
 with flashes of lightning.
8 The voice of the LORD shakes the desert;
 the LORD shakes the Desert of Kadesh.
9 The voice of the LORD twists the oaks[c]
 and strips the forests bare.
And in his temple all cry, "Glory!"

10 The LORD sits enthroned over the flood;
 the LORD is enthroned as King forever.
11 The LORD gives strength to his people;
 the LORD blesses his people with peace.

PSALM 30[d]

A psalm. A song. For the dedication of the temple.[e]
Of David.

1 I will exalt you, LORD,
 for you lifted me out of the depths
 and did not let my enemies gloat over me.
2 LORD my God, I called to you for help,
 and you healed me.
3 You, LORD, brought me up from the realm of
  the dead;
 you spared me from going down to the pit.

4 Sing the praises of the LORD, you his faithful
  people;
 praise his holy name.
5 For his anger lasts only a moment,
 but his favor lasts a lifetime;

weeping may stay for the night,
 but rejoicing comes in the morning.
6 When I felt secure, I said,
 "I will never be shaken."
7 LORD, when you favored me,
 you made my royal mountain[f] stand firm;
but when you hid your face,
 I was dismayed.

8 To you, LORD, I called;
 to the Lord I cried for mercy:
9 "What is gained if I am silenced,
 if I go down to the pit?
Will the dust praise you?
 Will it proclaim your faithfulness?
10 Hear, LORD, and be merciful to me;
 LORD, be my help."

11 You turned my wailing into dancing;
 you removed my sackcloth and clothed
  me with joy,
12 that my heart may sing your praises and not
  be silent.
 LORD my God, I will praise you forever.

PSALM 31[g]

For the director of music. A psalm of David.

1 In you, LORD, I have taken refuge;
 let me never be put to shame;
 deliver me in your righteousness.
2 Turn your ear to me,
 come quickly to my rescue;
be my rock of refuge,
 a strong fortress to save me.
3 Since you are my rock and my fortress,
 for the sake of your name lead and
  guide me.
4 Keep me free from the trap that is set for me,
 for you are my refuge.
5 Into your hands I commit my spirit;
 deliver me, LORD, my faithful God.

6 I hate those who cling to worthless idols;
 as for me, I trust in the LORD.
7 I will be glad and rejoice in your love,
 for you saw my affliction
 and knew the anguish of my soul.
8 You have not given me into the hands of the
  enemy
 but have set my feet in a spacious place.

---

[a] 2 Or LORD with the splendor of [b] 6 That is, Mount
Hermon [c] 9 Or LORD makes the deer give birth [d] In
Hebrew texts 30:1-12 is numbered 30:2-13. [e] Title: Or palace
[f] 7 That is, Mount Zion [g] In Hebrew texts 31:1-24 is
numbered 31:2-25.

⁹ Be merciful to me, LORD, for I am in
    distress;
  my eyes grow weak with sorrow,
  my soul and body with grief.
¹⁰ My life is consumed by anguish
  and my years by groaning;
  my strength fails because of my affliction,ᵃ
  and my bones grow weak.
¹¹ Because of all my enemies,
  I am the utter contempt of my neighbors
and an object of dread to my closest
    friends—
  those who see me on the street flee from
    me.
¹² I am forgotten as though I were dead;
  I have become like broken pottery.
¹³ For I hear many whispering,
  "Terror on every side!"
They conspire against me
  and plot to take my life.

¹⁴ But I trust in you, LORD;
  I say, "You are my God."
¹⁵ My times are in your hands;
  deliver me from the hands of my
    enemies,
  from those who pursue me.
¹⁶ Let your face shine on your servant;
  save me in your unfailing love.
¹⁷ Let me not be put to shame, LORD,
  for I have cried out to you;
but let the wicked be put to shame
  and be silent in the realm of the dead.
¹⁸ Let their lying lips be silenced,
  for with pride and contempt
  they speak arrogantly against the
    righteous.

¹⁹ How abundant are the good things
  that you have stored up for those who
    fear you,
  that you bestow in the sight of all,
  on those who take refuge in you.
²⁰ In the shelter of your presence you hide
    them
  from all human intrigues;
you keep them safe in your dwelling
  from accusing tongues.

²¹ Praise be to the LORD,
  for he showed me the wonders of his love
  when I was in a city under siege.
²² In my alarm I said,
  "I am cut off from your sight!"
Yet you heard my cry for mercy
  when I called to you for help.

²³ Love the LORD, all his faithful people!
  The LORD preserves those who are true to
    him,
  but the proud he pays back in full.
²⁴ Be strong and take heart,
  all you who hope in the LORD.

PSALM 32

Of David. A *maskil.*ᵇ

¹ Blessed is the one
  whose transgressions are forgiven,
  whose sins are covered.
² Blessed is the one
  whose sin the LORD does not count
    against them
  and in whose spirit is no deceit.

³ When I kept silent,
  my bones wasted away
  through my groaning all day long.
⁴ For day and night
  your hand was heavy on me;
my strength was sapped
  as in the heat of summer.ᶜ

⁵ Then I acknowledged my sin to you
  and did not cover up my iniquity.
I said, "I will confess
  my transgressions to the LORD."
And you forgave
  the guilt of my sin.

⁶ Therefore let all the faithful pray to you
  while you may be found;
surely the rising of the mighty waters
  will not reach them.
⁷ You are my hiding place;
  you will protect me from trouble
  and surround me with songs of
    deliverance.

⁸ I will instruct you and teach you in the way
    you should go;
  I will counsel you with my loving eye on
    you.
⁹ Do not be like the horse or the mule,
  which have no understanding
but must be controlled by bit and bridle
  or they will not come to you.
¹⁰ Many are the woes of the wicked,
  but the LORD's unfailing love
  surrounds the one who trusts in him.

ᵃ 10 Or *guilt*   ᵇ Title: Probably a literary or musical term
ᶜ 4 The Hebrew has *Selah* (a word of uncertain meaning) here
and at the end of verses 5 and 7.

Guidance: Leaders Are Not Perfect, but Whole

Psalm 32:8

God does not expect leaders to be perfect, but to be whole. Have you appreciated the enormous difference? To have integrity means to be whole, as in a whole number (an "integer"). Despite his or her human frailties, a leader can effectively guide those who follow.

Psalm 32:8 reminds us that leaders must closely observe the flock for its needs and problems. God expects spiritual leaders to serve as guides. A guide gets a person or group safely to a planned destination. The Hebrew word for "guide" gives us several clues as to what God expects from those he uses as leaders:

1. **A guide is a spiritual head who unites and directs people in their walk with God.**

2. **A guide takes people on the straight path that leads to fellowship with God.**

3. **A guide gives accurate and godly counsel to those who need it.**

4. **A guide leads with gentleness and trustworthiness, making others feel safe.**

5. **A guide bases his or her direction on the Spirit and the Word of God.**

[11] Rejoice in the LORD and be glad, you
righteous;
sing, all you who are upright in heart!

PSALM 33

[1] Sing joyfully to the LORD, you righteous;
it is fitting for the upright to praise him.
[2] Praise the LORD with the harp;
make music to him on the ten-stringed lyre.
[3] Sing to him a new song;
play skillfully, and shout for joy.

[4] For the word of the LORD is right and true;
he is faithful in all he does.
[5] The LORD loves righteousness and justice;
the earth is full of his unfailing love.

[6] By the word of the LORD the heavens were
made,
their starry host by the breath of his mouth.
[7] He gathers the waters of the sea into jars[a];
he puts the deep into storehouses.
[8] Let all the earth fear the LORD;
let all the people of the world revere him.
[9] For he spoke, and it came to be;
he commanded, and it stood firm.

[10] The LORD foils the plans of the nations;
he thwarts the purposes of the peoples.
[11] But the plans of the LORD stand firm forever,
the purposes of his heart through all
generations.

[12] Blessed is the nation whose God is the LORD,
the people he chose for his inheritance.

[13] From heaven the LORD looks down
and sees all mankind;
[14] from his dwelling place he watches
all who live on earth —
[15] he who forms the hearts of all,
who considers everything they do.

[16] No king is saved by the size of his army;
no warrior escapes by his great strength.
[17] A horse is a vain hope for deliverance;
despite all its great strength it cannot save.
[18] But the eyes of the LORD are on those who
fear him,
on those whose hope is in his unfailing
love,
[19] to deliver them from death
and keep them alive in famine.

[20] We wait in hope for the LORD;
he is our help and our shield.
[21] In him our hearts rejoice,
for we trust in his holy name.
[22] May your unfailing love be with us, LORD,
even as we put our hope in you.

PSALM 34[b,c]

Of David. When he pretended to be insane before
Abimelek, who drove him away, and he left.

[1] I will extol the LORD at all times;
his praise will always be on my lips.

---

[a] 7 Or *sea as into a heap*   [b] This psalm is an acrostic poem,
the verses of which begin with the successive letters of the
Hebrew alphabet.   [c] In Hebrew texts 34:1-22 is numbered
34:2-23.

[2] I will glory in the LORD;
    let the afflicted hear and rejoice.
[3] Glorify the LORD with me;
    let us exalt his name together.

[4] I sought the LORD, and he answered me;
    he delivered me from all my fears.
[5] Those who look to him are radiant;
    their faces are never covered with shame.
[6] This poor man called, and the LORD heard
    him;
    he saved him out of all his troubles.
[7] The angel of the LORD encamps around
       those who fear him,
    and he delivers them.

[8] Taste and see that the LORD is good;
    blessed is the one who takes refuge in
       him.
[9] Fear the LORD, you his holy people,
    for those who fear him lack nothing.
[10] The lions may grow weak and hungry,
    but those who seek the LORD lack no good
       thing.
[11] Come, my children, listen to me;
    I will teach you the fear of the LORD.
[12] Whoever of you loves life
    and desires to see many good days,
[13] keep your tongue from evil
    and your lips from telling lies.
[14] Turn from evil and do good;
    seek peace and pursue it.

[15] The eyes of the LORD are on the righteous,
    and his ears are attentive to their cry;
[16] but the face of the LORD is against those who
       do evil,
    to blot out their name from the earth.

[17] The righteous cry out, and the LORD hears
       them;
    he delivers them from all their troubles.
[18] The LORD is close to the brokenhearted
    and saves those who are crushed in spirit.

[19] The righteous person may have many
       troubles,
    but the LORD delivers him from them all;
[20] he protects all his bones,
    not one of them will be broken.

[21] Evil will slay the wicked;
    the foes of the righteous will be
       condemned.
[22] The LORD will rescue his servants;
    no one who takes refuge in him will be
       condemned.

PSALM 35

Of David.

[1] Contend, LORD, with those who contend
       with me;
    fight against those who fight against me.
[2] Take up shield and armor;
    arise and come to my aid.
[3] Brandish spear and javelin[a]
    against those who pursue me.
Say to me,
    "I am your salvation."

[4] May those who seek my life
    be disgraced and put to shame;
may those who plot my ruin
    be turned back in dismay.
[5] May they be like chaff before the wind,
    with the angel of the LORD driving them
       away;
[6] may their path be dark and slippery,
    with the angel of the LORD pursuing them.

[7] Since they hid their net for me without cause
    and without cause dug a pit for me,
[8] may ruin overtake them by surprise—
    may the net they hid entangle them,
    may they fall into the pit, to their ruin.
[9] Then my soul will rejoice in the LORD
    and delight in his salvation.
[10] My whole being will exclaim,
    "Who is like you, LORD?
You rescue the poor from those too strong
       for them,
    the poor and needy from those who rob
       them."

[11] Ruthless witnesses come forward;
    they question me on things I know
       nothing about.
[12] They repay me evil for good
    and leave me like one bereaved.
[13] Yet when they were ill, I put on sackcloth
    and humbled myself with fasting.
When my prayers returned to me
       unanswered,
[14]   I went about mourning
    as though for my friend or brother.
I bowed my head in grief
    as though weeping for my mother.
[15] But when I stumbled, they gathered in glee;
    assailants gathered against me without my
       knowledge.
    They slandered me without ceasing.

---

[a] 3 Or *and block the way*

16 Like the ungodly they maliciously mocked;[a]
    they gnashed their teeth at me.

17 How long, Lord, will you look on?
    Rescue me from their ravages,
    my precious life from these lions.
18 I will give you thanks in the great assembly;
    among the throngs I will praise you.
19 Do not let those gloat over me
    who are my enemies without cause;
  do not let those who hate me without
      reason
    maliciously wink the eye.
20 They do not speak peaceably,
    but devise false accusations
  against those who live quietly in the land.
21 They sneer at me and say, "Aha! Aha!
    With our own eyes we have seen it."

22 Lord, you have seen this; do not be silent.
    Do not be far from me, Lord.
23 Awake, and rise to my defense!
    Contend for me, my God and Lord.
24 Vindicate me in your righteousness, Lord
    my God;
    do not let them gloat over me.
25 Do not let them think, "Aha, just what we
      wanted!"
  or say, "We have swallowed him up."

26 May all who gloat over my distress
    be put to shame and confusion;
  may all who exalt themselves over me
    be clothed with shame and disgrace.
27 May those who delight in my vindication
    shout for joy and gladness;
  may they always say, "The Lord be exalted,
    who delights in the well-being of his
      servant."

28 My tongue will proclaim your righteousness,
    your praises all day long.

PSALM 36[b]

For the director of music. Of David the servant
of the Lord.

1 I have a message from God in my heart
    concerning the sinfulness of the wicked:[c]
There is no fear of God
    before their eyes.

2 In their own eyes they flatter themselves
    too much to detect or hate their sin.
3 The words of their mouths are wicked and
      deceitful;
    they fail to act wisely or do good.

4 Even on their beds they plot evil;
    they commit themselves to a sinful course
    and do not reject what is wrong.

5 Your love, Lord, reaches to the heavens,
    your faithfulness to the skies.
6 Your righteousness is like the highest
      mountains,
    your justice like the great deep.
    You, Lord, preserve both people and
      animals.
7 How priceless is your unfailing love, O God!
    People take refuge in the shadow of your
      wings.
8 They feast on the abundance of your house;
    you give them drink from your river of
      delights.
9 For with you is the fountain of life;
    in your light we see light.

10 Continue your love to those who know you,
    your righteousness to the upright in heart.
11 May the foot of the proud not come against
      me,
    nor the hand of the wicked drive me
      away.
12 See how the evildoers lie fallen—
    thrown down, not able to rise!

PSALM 37[d]

Of David.

1 Do not fret because of those who are evil
    or be envious of those who do wrong;
2 for like the grass they will soon wither,
    like green plants they will soon die away.

3 Trust in the Lord and do good;
    dwell in the land and enjoy safe pasture.
4 Take delight in the Lord,
    and he will give you the desires of your
      heart.

5 Commit your way to the Lord;
    trust in him and he will do this:
6 He will make your righteous reward shine
    like the dawn,
    your vindication like the noonday sun.

7 Be still before the Lord
    and wait patiently for him;

---

a 16 Septuagint; Hebrew may mean *Like an ungodly circle of
mockers,*   b In Hebrew texts 36:1-12 is numbered 36:2-13.
c 1 Or *A message from God: The transgression of the wicked /
resides in their hearts.*   d This psalm is an acrostic poem, the
stanzas of which begin with the successive letters of the Hebrew
alphabet.

do not fret when people succeed in their
		ways,
	when they carry out their wicked schemes.
8 Refrain from anger and turn from wrath;
	do not fret — it leads only to evil.
9 For those who are evil will be destroyed,
	but those who hope in the LORD will
		inherit the land.

10 A little while, and the wicked will be no more;
	though you look for them, they will not
		be found.
11 But the meek will inherit the land
	and enjoy peace and prosperity.

12 The wicked plot against the righteous
	and gnash their teeth at them;
13 but the Lord laughs at the wicked,
	for he knows their day is coming.

14 The wicked draw the sword
	and bend the bow
to bring down the poor and needy,
	to slay those whose ways are upright.
15 But their swords will pierce their own
		hearts,
	and their bows will be broken.

16 Better the little that the righteous have
	than the wealth of many wicked;
17 for the power of the wicked will be broken,
	but the LORD upholds the righteous.

18 The blameless spend their days under the
		LORD's care,
	and their inheritance will endure forever.
19 In times of disaster they will not wither;
	in days of famine they will enjoy plenty.
20 But the wicked will perish:
	Though the LORD's enemies are like the
		flowers of the field,
	they will be consumed, they will go up in
		smoke.

21 The wicked borrow and do not repay,
	but the righteous give generously;
22 those the LORD blesses will inherit the
		land,
	but those he curses will be destroyed.

23 The LORD makes firm the steps
	of the one who delights in him;
24 though he may stumble, he will not fall,
	for the LORD upholds him with his hand.

25 I was young and now I am old,
	yet I have never seen the righteous
		forsaken
	or their children begging bread.
26 They are always generous and lend freely;
	their children will be a blessing.[a]

---

[a] 26 Or *freely; / the names of their children will be used in
blessings* (see Gen. 48:20); or *freely; / others will see that their
children are blessed*

The Law of Intuition: David Makes Decisions Wisely

Psalm 37:3–9

Do you ever feel as though you need a therapist? If so, then Psalm 37 is for you.
	David writes as a counselor, providing wise steps to take as you face crises and decisions. Whenever you feel the pressure of competition in the market, the compulsion to perform, or to compare your lot with other leaders, pause and remember these words. David brings eternal perspective and long-term vision that prevents mistakes in short-term decisions:

1. **Trust in the Lord and do good; do what is right despite what others do (v. 3).**
2. **Cultivate faithfulness and don't move too quickly; don't rush anything (v. 3).**
3. **Prioritize God and his values; he will reward and satisfy you in the end (v. 4).**
4. **Commit your plans to him and trust him; the results are in his hand (v. 5).**
5. **Be quiet and patient; perspective comes when we grow still and think (v. 7).**
6. **Don't fret or compare; such anxiety always gives bad motivation (v. 7).**
7. **Refuse to get angry at competition; anger does not bring the results you desire (v. 8).**
8. **Put your hope in the Lord; ultimately, he will guide and use your decision (v. 9).**

27 Turn from evil and do good;
then you will dwell in the land forever.
28 For the LORD loves the just
and will not forsake his faithful ones.

Wrongdoers will be completely destroyed[a];
the offspring of the wicked will perish.
29 The righteous will inherit the land
and dwell in it forever.

30 The mouths of the righteous utter wisdom,
and their tongues speak what is just.
31 The law of their God is in their hearts;
their feet do not slip.

32 The wicked lie in wait for the righteous,
intent on putting them to death;
33 but the LORD will not leave them in the
power of the wicked
or let them be condemned when brought
to trial.

34 Hope in the LORD
and keep his way.
He will exalt you to inherit the land;
when the wicked are destroyed, you will
see it.

35 I have seen a wicked and ruthless man
flourishing like a luxuriant native tree,
36 but he soon passed away and was no more;
though I looked for him, he could not be
found.

37 Consider the blameless, observe the upright;
a future awaits those who seek peace.[b]
38 But all sinners will be destroyed;
there will be no future[c] for the wicked.

39 The salvation of the righteous comes from
the LORD;
he is their stronghold in time of trouble.
40 The LORD helps them and delivers them;
he delivers them from the wicked and
saves them,
because they take refuge in him.

PSALM 38[d]

A psalm of David. A petition.

1 LORD, do not rebuke me in your anger
or discipline me in your wrath.
2 Your arrows have pierced me,
and your hand has come down on me.
3 Because of your wrath there is no health in
my body;
there is no soundness in my bones
because of my sin.

4 My guilt has overwhelmed me
like a burden too heavy to bear.

5 My wounds fester and are loathsome
because of my sinful folly.
6 I am bowed down and brought very low;
all day long I go about mourning.
7 My back is filled with searing pain;
there is no health in my body.
8 I am feeble and utterly crushed;
I groan in anguish of heart.

9 All my longings lie open before you,
Lord;
my sighing is not hidden from you.
10 My heart pounds, my strength fails me;
even the light has gone from my eyes.
11 My friends and companions avoid me
because of my wounds;
my neighbors stay far away.
12 Those who want to kill me set their
traps,
those who would harm me talk of my
ruin;
all day long they scheme and lie.

13 I am like the deaf, who cannot hear,
like the mute, who cannot speak;
14 I have become like one who does not hear,
whose mouth can offer no reply.
15 LORD, I wait for you;
you will answer, Lord my God.
16 For I said, "Do not let them gloat
or exalt themselves over me when my
feet slip."

17 For I am about to fall,
and my pain is ever with me.
18 I confess my iniquity;
I am troubled by my sin.
19 Many have become my enemies without
cause[e];
those who hate me without reason are
numerous.
20 Those who repay my good with evil
lodge accusations against me,
though I seek only to do what is good.

21 LORD, do not forsake me;
do not be far from me, my God.
22 Come quickly to help me,
my Lord and my Savior.

---

a 28 See Septuagint; Hebrew *They will be protected forever*
b 37 Or *upright; / those who seek peace will have posterity*
c 38 Or *posterity*   d In Hebrew texts 38:1-22 is numbered
38:2-23.   e 19 One Dead Sea Scrolls manuscript; Masoretic
Text *my vigorous enemies*

PSALM 39[a]

For the director of music. For Jeduthun.
A psalm of David.

[1] I said, "I will watch my ways
　　and keep my tongue from sin;
I will put a muzzle on my mouth
　　while in the presence of the wicked."
[2] So I remained utterly silent,
　　not even saying anything good.
But my anguish increased;
[3]　　my heart grew hot within me.
While I meditated, the fire burned;
　　then I spoke with my tongue:

[4] "Show me, LORD, my life's end
　　and the number of my days;
　　let me know how fleeting my life is.
[5] You have made my days a mere
　　　handbreadth;
　　the span of my years is as nothing before
　　　you.
Everyone is but a breath,
　　even those who seem secure.[b]

[6] "Surely everyone goes around like a mere
　　　phantom;
　　in vain they rush about, heaping up
　　　wealth
　　without knowing whose it will
　　　finally be.

[7] "But now, Lord, what do I look for?
　　My hope is in you.

[8] Save me from all my transgressions;
　　do not make me the scorn of fools.
[9] I was silent; I would not open my mouth,
　　for you are the one who has done this.
[10] Remove your scourge from me;
　　I am overcome by the blow of your hand.
[11] When you rebuke and discipline anyone for
　　　their sin,
　　you consume their wealth like a moth —
　　surely everyone is but a breath.

[12] "Hear my prayer, LORD,
　　listen to my cry for help;
　　do not be deaf to my weeping.
I dwell with you as a foreigner,
　　a stranger, as all my ancestors were.
[13] Look away from me, that I may enjoy life
　　　again
　　before I depart and am no more."

PSALM 40[c]

For the director of music. Of David. A psalm.

[1] I waited patiently for the LORD;
　　he turned to me and heard my cry.
[2] He lifted me out of the slimy pit,
　　out of the mud and mire;
　　he set my feet on a rock
　　and gave me a firm place to stand.

---

[a] In Hebrew texts 39:1-13 is numbered 39:2-14. 　　[b] 5 The Hebrew has *Selah* (a word of uncertain meaning) here and at the end of verse 11. 　　[c] In Hebrew texts 40:1-17 is numbered 40:2-18.

The Law of Timing: Leaders Value Time, They Don't Kill It

Psalm 39:4–5

Like Moses in Psalm 90, David shows his mindfulness of his brief time on earth. He asks God to help him number his days (Ps 39:4–5), which ought to be the prayer of every leader. Wise leaders work to redeem the time they have (Eph 5:16–17).

Management expert Peter Drucker identified this leadership principle: He said that good leaders need to regard first of all not their *task*, but their *time*.

A leader needs to wonder if the task is worth the time investment. What would happen if the leader wasn't the one doing it? Would there be someone else who could do it just as well, and for whom the task would be time better spent?

A good leader knows that time is like gold, and good "spending habits" are essential. It's just that in this case the units are minutes, not dollars.

If you don't know where your time goes—that's a danger signal. If you can save small bits of time and consolidate them into a chunk of time that can be spent on something worthwhile—that's like "found money."

If leaders can number their minutes and hours, "numbering their days" will be easier.

³ He put a new song in my mouth,
     a hymn of praise to our God.
Many will see and fear the LORD
     and put their trust in him.

⁴ Blessed is the one
     who trusts in the LORD,
who does not look to the proud,
     to those who turn aside to false gods.ᵃ
⁵ Many, LORD my God,
     are the wonders you have done,
     the things you planned for us.
None can compare with you;
     were I to speak and tell of your deeds,
     they would be too many to declare.

⁶ Sacrifice and offering you did not desire —
     but my ears you have openedᵇ —
     burnt offerings and sin offeringsᶜ you did
         not require.
⁷ Then I said, "Here I am, I have come —
     it is written about me in the scroll.ᵈ
⁸ I desire to do your will, my God;
     your law is within my heart."

⁹ I proclaim your saving acts in the great
         assembly;
     I do not seal my lips, LORD,
     as you know.
¹⁰ I do not hide your righteousness in my
         heart;
     I speak of your faithfulness and your
         saving help.

I do not conceal your love and your faithfulness
     from the great assembly.

¹¹ Do not withhold your mercy from me, LORD;
     may your love and faithfulness always
         protect me.
¹² For troubles without number surround me;
     my sins have overtaken me, and I cannot see.
They are more than the hairs of my head,
     and my heart fails within me.
¹³ Be pleased to save me, LORD;
     come quickly, LORD, to help me.

¹⁴ May all who want to take my life
     be put to shame and confusion;
may all who desire my ruin
     be turned back in disgrace.
¹⁵ May those who say to me, "Aha! Aha!"
     be appalled at their own shame.
¹⁶ But may all who seek you
     rejoice and be glad in you;
may those who long for your saving help
         always say,
     "The LORD is great!"

¹⁷ But as for me, I am poor and needy;
     may the Lord think of me.
You are my help and my deliverer;
     you are my God, do not delay.

ᵃ 4 Or to lies   ᵇ 6 Hebrew; some Septuagint manuscripts but
a body you have prepared for me   ᶜ 6 Or purification
offerings   ᵈ 7 Or come / with the scroll written for me

DAVID — Trusting in God Alone
Psalm 40:1–17

PROFILE in leadership

King David knew something about suffering, particularly suffering caused by his own actions. But he also knew to whom he could turn during those times of trouble. This "man after [God's] own heart" (Ac 13:22) made it a point to seek the Lord in difficult days and to make the news of God's goodness known to everyone who would listen.

David knew that God would always remain faithful to himself and to his holy nature—even when David acted unfaithfully. David knew that at just the right time, God would deliver him from despair. He knew the freedom and security that come from trusting in God alone as his deliverer.

What great comfort and joy come to us when we understand that God is rich in grace and mercy, that he not only forgives, but restores and redeems! The Lord lifts us up from our personal pits of despair and puts us in right standing with him.

David was far from a perfect man, but he understood something all godly leaders must grasp: When times of trouble arrive—even trouble we bring on ourselves—we must turn to God and wait patiently for his help. He'll never fail us. Remember these truths about the God you serve, then proclaim them to everyone who will hear.

PSALM 41[a]

For the director of music. A psalm of David.

[1] Blessed are those who have regard for the
weak;
the LORD delivers them in times of trouble.
[2] The LORD protects and preserves them —
they are counted among the blessed in the
land —
he does not give them over to the desire of
their foes.
[3] The LORD sustains them on their sickbed
and restores them from their bed of
illness.

[4] I said, "Have mercy on me, LORD;
heal me, for I have sinned against you."
[5] My enemies say of me in malice,
"When will he die and his name perish?"
[6] When one of them comes to see me,
he speaks falsely, while his heart gathers
slander;
then he goes out and spreads it around.

[7] All my enemies whisper together against me;
they imagine the worst for me, saying,
[8] "A vile disease has afflicted him;
he will never get up from the place where
he lies."
[9] Even my close friend,
someone I trusted,
one who shared my bread,
has turned[b] against me.

[10] But may you have mercy on me, LORD;
raise me up, that I may repay them.
[11] I know that you are pleased with me,
for my enemy does not triumph over me.
[12] Because of my integrity you uphold me
and set me in your presence forever.

[13] Praise be to the LORD, the God of Israel,
from everlasting to everlasting.
Amen and Amen.

BOOK II

Psalms 42 – 72

PSALM 42[c,d]

For the director of music. A maskil[e] of the Sons
of Korah.

[1] As the deer pants for streams of water,
so my soul pants for you, my God.

[2] My soul thirsts for God, for the living God.
When can I go and meet with God?
[3] My tears have been my food
day and night,
while people say to me all day long,
"Where is your God?"
[4] These things I remember
as I pour out my soul:
how I used to go to the house of God
under the protection of the Mighty One[f]
with shouts of joy and praise
among the festive throng.

[5] Why, my soul, are you downcast?
Why so disturbed within me?
Put your hope in God,
for I will yet praise him,
my Savior and my God.

[6] My soul is downcast within me;
therefore I will remember you
from the land of the Jordan,
the heights of Hermon — from Mount Mizar.
[7] Deep calls to deep
in the roar of your waterfalls;
all your waves and breakers
have swept over me.

[8] By day the LORD directs his love,
at night his song is with me —
a prayer to the God of my life.

[9] I say to God my Rock,
"Why have you forgotten me?
Why must I go about mourning,
oppressed by the enemy?"
[10] My bones suffer mortal agony
as my foes taunt me,
saying to me all day long,
"Where is your God?"

[11] Why, my soul, are you downcast?
Why so disturbed within me?
Put your hope in God,
for I will yet praise him,
my Savior and my God.

PSALM 43[c]

[1] Vindicate me, my God,
and plead my cause
against an unfaithful nation.

[a] In Hebrew texts 41:1-13 is numbered 41:2-14.   [b] 9 Hebrew
has lifted up his heel   [c] In many Hebrew manuscripts Psalms
42 and 43 constitute one psalm.   [d] In Hebrew texts 42:1-11 is
numbered 42:2-12.   [e] Title: Probably a literary or musical
term   [f] 4 See Septuagint and Syriac; the meaning of the
Hebrew for this line is uncertain.

The Law of the Picture: Leaders Can't Lead Further Than Their Own Life

Psalm 42:1–11

In Psalm 42, we see a leader who is dry and thirsty. This leader is experiencing a wilderness period, as every leader does at some point. Nothing seems to be exciting or motivating. In verses 2–4, the writer seems to be saying, "I used to lead the people in a parade to God, and now I can't even find him myself!" Fortunately, this leader recaptures his perspective in verse 5. He begins to tell himself the truth. In the final verse, he concludes that God will prevail.

What I love about this psalm is its humanity. This leader realizes that he cannot lead people any further than where he himself stands. He refuses to fake it. He doesn't want to pretend all is well. So before he attempts to lead anyone again, he cries out to God for renewal. Leaders who understand the Law of the Picture are like that:

1. **They are honest with themselves about their state.**

2. **They cry out to God for renewal.**

3. **They refuse to fake it; they want to model the truth for others.**

4. **They tell themselves the truth about the future.**

Rescue me from those who are
    deceitful and wicked.
² You are God my stronghold.
    Why have you rejected me?
Why must I go about mourning,
    oppressed by the enemy?
³ Send me your light and your faithful care,
    let them lead me;
let them bring me to your holy mountain,
    to the place where you dwell.
⁴ Then I will go to the altar of God,
    to God, my joy and my delight.
I will praise you with the lyre,
    O God, my God.

⁵ Why, my soul, are you downcast?
    Why so disturbed within me?
Put your hope in God,
    for I will yet praise him,
    my Savior and my God.

PSALM 44[a]

For the director of music. Of the Sons of Korah.
A *maskil.*[b]

¹ We have heard it with our ears, O God;
    our ancestors have told us
what you did in their days,
    in days long ago.
² With your hand you drove out the nations
    and planted our ancestors;

you crushed the peoples
    and made our ancestors flourish.
³ It was not by their sword that they won the
    land,
    nor did their arm bring them victory;
it was your right hand, your arm,
    and the light of your face, for you loved
    them.

⁴ You are my King and my God,
    who decrees[c] victories for Jacob.
⁵ Through you we push back our enemies;
    through your name we trample our foes.
⁶ I put no trust in my bow,
    my sword does not bring me victory;
⁷ but you give us victory over our enemies,
    you put our adversaries to shame.
⁸ In God we make our boast all day long,
    and we will praise your name forever.[d]

⁹ But now you have rejected and humbled us;
    you no longer go out with our armies.
¹⁰ You made us retreat before the enemy,
    and our adversaries have plundered us.
¹¹ You gave us up to be devoured like sheep
    and have scattered us among the
    nations.

---

[a] In Hebrew texts 44:1-26 is numbered 44:2-27.   [b] Title: Probably a literary or musical term   [c] 4 Septuagint, Aquila and Syriac; Hebrew *King, O God; / command*   [d] 8 The Hebrew has *Selah* (a word of uncertain meaning) here.

¹² You sold your people for a pittance,
    gaining nothing from their sale.

¹³ You have made us a reproach to our
    neighbors,
    the scorn and derision of those around us.
¹⁴ You have made us a byword among the
    nations;
    the peoples shake their heads at us.
¹⁵ I live in disgrace all day long,
    and my face is covered with shame
¹⁶ at the taunts of those who reproach and
    revile me,
    because of the enemy, who is bent on
    revenge.

¹⁷ All this came upon us,
    though we had not forgotten you;
    we had not been false to your covenant.
¹⁸ Our hearts had not turned back;
    our feet had not strayed from your path.
¹⁹ But you crushed us and made us a haunt for
    jackals;
    you covered us over with deep darkness.

²⁰ If we had forgotten the name of our God
    or spread out our hands to a foreign
    god,
²¹ would not God have discovered it,
    since he knows the secrets of the heart?
²² Yet for your sake we face death all day
    long;
    we are considered as sheep to be
    slaughtered.

²³ Awake, Lord! Why do you sleep?
    Rouse yourself! Do not reject us forever.
²⁴ Why do you hide your face
    and forget our misery and oppression?

²⁵ We are brought down to the dust;
    our bodies cling to the ground.
²⁶ Rise up and help us;
    rescue us because of your unfailing love.

PSALM 45 ᵃ

For the director of music. To the tune of "Lilies."
Of the Sons of Korah. A *maskil*.ᵇ A wedding song.

¹ My heart is stirred by a noble theme
    as I recite my verses for the king;
    my tongue is the pen of a skillful writer.

² You are the most excellent of men
    and your lips have been anointed with
    grace,
    since God has blessed you forever.

³ Gird your sword on your side, you mighty
    one;
    clothe yourself with splendor and majesty.
⁴ In your majesty ride forth victoriously
    in the cause of truth, humility and justice;
    let your right hand achieve awesome
    deeds.
⁵ Let your sharp arrows pierce the hearts of
    the king's enemies;
    let the nations fall beneath your feet.
⁶ Your throne, O God,ᶜ will last for ever and
    ever;
    a scepter of justice will be the scepter of
    your kingdom.
⁷ You love righteousness and hate wickedness;
    therefore God, your God, has set you
    above your companions
    by anointing you with the oil of joy.
⁸ All your robes are fragrant with myrrh and
    aloes and cassia;
    from palaces adorned with ivory
    the music of the strings makes you glad.
⁹ Daughters of kings are among your honored
    women;
    at your right hand is the royal bride in
    gold of Ophir.

¹⁰ Listen, daughter, and pay careful attention:
    Forget your people and your father's
    house.
¹¹ Let the king be enthralled by your beauty;
    honor him, for he is your lord.
¹² The city of Tyre will come with a gift,ᵈ
    people of wealth will seek your favor.
¹³ All glorious is the princess within her
    chamber;
    her gown is interwoven with gold.
¹⁴ In embroidered garments she is led to the
    king;
    her virgin companions follow her—
    those brought to be with her.
¹⁵ Led in with joy and gladness,
    they enter the palace of the king.

¹⁶ Your sons will take the place of your fathers;
    you will make them princes throughout
    the land.

¹⁷ I will perpetuate your memory through all
    generations;
    therefore the nations will praise you for
    ever and ever.

ᵃ In Hebrew texts 45:1-17 is numbered 45:2-18.   ᵇ Title:
Probably a literary or musical term   ᶜ 6 Here the king is
addressed as God's representative.   ᵈ 12 Or *A Tyrian robe is
among the gifts*

PSALM 46[a]

For the director of music. Of the Sons of Korah.
According to *alamoth*.[b] A song.

1 God is our refuge and strength,
    an ever-present help in trouble.
2 Therefore we will not fear, though the earth
        give way
    and the mountains fall into the heart of
        the sea,
3 though its waters roar and foam
    and the mountains quake with their
        surging.[c]

4 There is a river whose streams make glad the
        city of God,
    the holy place where the Most High dwells.
5 God is within her, she will not fall;
    God will help her at break of day.
6 Nations are in uproar, kingdoms fall;
    he lifts his voice, the earth melts.

7 The LORD Almighty is with us;
    the God of Jacob is our fortress.

8 Come and see what the LORD has done,
    the desolations he has brought on the
        earth.
9 He makes wars cease
    to the ends of the earth.
He breaks the bow and shatters the spear;
    he burns the shields[d] with fire.
10 He says, "Be still, and know that I am God;
    I will be exalted among the nations,
    I will be exalted in the earth."

11 The LORD Almighty is with us;
    the God of Jacob is our fortress.

PSALM 47[e]

For the director of music. Of the Sons of Korah.
A psalm.

1 Clap your hands, all you nations;
    shout to God with cries of joy.

2 For the LORD Most High is awesome,
    the great King over all the earth.
3 He subdued nations under us,
    peoples under our feet.
4 He chose our inheritance for us,
    the pride of Jacob, whom he loved.[f]

5 God has ascended amid shouts of joy,
    the LORD amid the sounding of trumpets.
6 Sing praises to God, sing praises;
    sing praises to our King, sing praises.

7 For God is the King of all the earth;
    sing to him a psalm of praise.
8 God reigns over the nations;
    God is seated on his holy throne.
9 The nobles of the nations assemble
    as the people of the God of Abraham,
for the kings[g] of the earth belong to God;
    he is greatly exalted.

PSALM 48[h]

A song. A psalm of the Sons of Korah.

1 Great is the LORD, and most worthy of
        praise,
    in the city of our God, his holy mountain.

2 Beautiful in its loftiness,
    the joy of the whole earth,
like the heights of Zaphon[i] is Mount Zion,
    the city of the Great King.
3 God is in her citadels;
    he has shown himself to be her fortress.

4 When the kings joined forces,
    when they advanced together,
5 they saw her and were astounded;
    they fled in terror.
6 Trembling seized them there,
    pain like that of a woman in labor.
7 You destroyed them like ships of Tarshish
    shattered by an east wind.

8 As we have heard,
    so we have seen
in the city of the LORD Almighty,
    in the city of our God:
God makes her secure
    forever.[f]

9 Within your temple, O God,
    we meditate on your unfailing love.
10 Like your name, O God,
    your praise reaches to the ends of the earth;
    your right hand is filled with
        righteousness.
11 Mount Zion rejoices,
    the villages of Judah are glad
    because of your judgments.

---

[a] In Hebrew texts 46:1-11 is numbered 46:2-12.   [b] Title:
Probably a musical term   [c] 3 The Hebrew has *Selah* (a word
of uncertain meaning) here and at the end of verses 7 and 11.
[d] 9 Or *chariots*   [e] In Hebrew texts 47:1-9 is numbered
47:2-10.   [f] 4,8 The Hebrew has *Selah* (a word of uncertain
meaning) here.   [g] 9 Or *shields*   [h] In Hebrew texts 48:1-14
is numbered 48:2-15.   [i] 2 *Zaphon* was the most sacred
mountain of the Canaanites.

¹²Walk about Zion, go around her,
    count her towers,
¹³consider well her ramparts,
    view her citadels,
that you may tell of them
    to the next generation.

¹⁴For this God is our God for ever and ever;
    he will be our guide even to the end.

PSALM 49[a]

For the director of music. Of the Sons of Korah.
A psalm.

¹Hear this, all you peoples;
    listen, all who live in this world,
²both low and high,
    rich and poor alike:
³My mouth will speak words of wisdom;
    the meditation of my heart will give you
      understanding.
⁴I will turn my ear to a proverb;
    with the harp I will expound my riddle:

⁵Why should I fear when evil days come,
    when wicked deceivers surround me —
⁶those who trust in their wealth
    and boast of their great riches?
⁷No one can redeem the life of another
    or give to God a ransom for them —
⁸the ransom for a life is costly,
    no payment is ever enough —

⁹so that they should live on forever
    and not see decay.
¹⁰For all can see that the wise die,
    that the foolish and the senseless also perish,
    leaving their wealth to others.
¹¹Their tombs will remain their houses[b]
      forever,
    their dwellings for endless generations,
    though they had[c] named lands after
      themselves.

¹²People, despite their wealth, do not endure;
    they are like the beasts that perish.

¹³This is the fate of those who trust in
      themselves,
    and of their followers, who approve their
      sayings.[d]
¹⁴They are like sheep and are destined to die;
    death will be their shepherd
    (but the upright will prevail over them in
      the morning).
    Their forms will decay in the grave,
    far from their princely mansions.
¹⁵But God will redeem me from the realm of
      the dead;
    he will surely take me to himself.

---

[a] In Hebrew texts 49:1-20 is numbered 49:2-21.
[b] 11 Septuagint and Syriac; Hebrew *In their thoughts their houses will remain*   [c] 11 Or *generations, / for they have*
[d] 13 The Hebrew has *Selah* (a word of uncertain meaning) here and at the end of verse 15.

The Law of Priorities: When Activity Becomes Achievement

Psalm 49:12–17

God encourages us to fix our eyes on the things that endure. In light of eternity, leaders cannot become consumed with the temporary. Leaders cannot allow the pursuit of wealth or power to move them (Ps 49:12–13). Only a vision that outlives them, a vision connected to eternity, will fulfill a godly leader.

In other words, we must build a legacy. What are we going to leave behind when we die? Psalm 49:17 reminds us we will take nothing with us, no matter how rich we become. So what will we leave behind that counts?

A huge difference exists between a legacy and an inheritance. Anyone can leave an inheritance. An inheritance is something you leave to your family or loved ones, and it also fades. A legacy is something you leave *in* your family and loved ones. Consider the differences between the two:

Inheritance	Legacy
1. Something tangible you give to others	1. Something tangible you place in others
2. Temporarily brings them happiness	2. Permanently transforms them
3. Eventually fades as it is spent	3. Lives on long after you die
4. Your activity may or may not pay off	4. Your activity becomes achievement

¹⁶Do not be overawed when others grow rich,
    when the splendor of their houses
        increases;
¹⁷for they will take nothing with them when
    they die,
    their splendor will not descend with them.
¹⁸Though while they live they count
    themselves blessed—
    and people praise you when you
        prosper—
¹⁹they will join those who have gone before
    them,
    who will never again see the light of life.

²⁰People who have wealth but lack
    understanding
    are like the beasts that perish.

PSALM 50

A psalm of Asaph.

¹The Mighty One, God, the LORD,
    speaks and summons the earth
    from the rising of the sun to where it sets.
²From Zion, perfect in beauty,
    God shines forth.
³Our God comes
    and will not be silent;
  a fire devours before him,
    and around him a tempest rages.
⁴He summons the heavens above,
    and the earth, that he may judge his
        people:
⁵"Gather to me this consecrated people,
    who made a covenant with me by
        sacrifice."
⁶And the heavens proclaim his righteousness,
    for he is a God of justice.^{a,b}

⁷"Listen, my people, and I will speak;
    I will testify against you, Israel:
    I am God, your God.
⁸I bring no charges against you concerning
        your sacrifices
    or concerning your burnt offerings, which
        are ever before me.
⁹I have no need of a bull from your stall
    or of goats from your pens,
¹⁰for every animal of the forest is mine,
    and the cattle on a thousand hills.
¹¹I know every bird in the mountains,
    and the insects in the fields are mine.
¹²If I were hungry I would not tell you,
    for the world is mine, and all that is in it.
¹³Do I eat the flesh of bulls
    or drink the blood of goats?

¹⁴"Sacrifice thank offerings to God,
    fulfill your vows to the Most High,
¹⁵and call on me in the day of trouble;
    I will deliver you, and you will honor me."

¹⁶But to the wicked person, God says:

"What right have you to recite my laws
    or take my covenant on your lips?
¹⁷You hate my instruction
    and cast my words behind you.
¹⁸When you see a thief, you join with him;
    you throw in your lot with adulterers.
¹⁹You use your mouth for evil
    and harness your tongue to deceit.
²⁰You sit and testify against your brother
    and slander your own mother's son.
²¹When you did these things and I kept silent,
    you thought I was exactly^c like you.
But I now arraign you
    and set my accusations before you.

²²"Consider this, you who forget God,
    or I will tear you to pieces, with no one to
        rescue you:
²³Those who sacrifice thank offerings
        honor me,
    and to the blameless^d I will show my
        salvation."

PSALM 51^e

For the director of music. A psalm of David. When
the prophet Nathan came to him after David had
committed adultery with Bathsheba.

¹Have mercy on me, O God,
    according to your unfailing love;
  according to your great compassion
    blot out my transgressions.
²Wash away all my iniquity
    and cleanse me from my sin.

³For I know my transgressions,
    and my sin is always before me.
⁴Against you, you only, have I sinned
    and done what is evil in your sight;
  so you are right in your verdict
    and justified when you judge.
⁵Surely I was sinful at birth,
    sinful from the time my mother
        conceived me.

^a 6 With a different word division of the Hebrew; Masoretic
Text *for God himself is judge*   ^b 6 The Hebrew has *Selah* (a
word of uncertain meaning) here.   ^c 21 Or *thought the 'I AM'
was*   ^d 23 Probable reading of the original Hebrew text; the
meaning of the Masoretic Text for this phrase is uncertain.
^e In Hebrew texts 51:1-19 is numbered 51:3-21.

The Law of Solid Ground: David Faces His Sin, Remains King

Psalm 51:3–4

David wrote Psalm 51 shortly after he committed adultery with Bathsheba (2Sa 11:1—12:15). When Nathan confronted him about his sin, the king fell to the floor and wept in bitter repentance. He publicly sought restoration as a king and as a spiritual man, as this great psalm demonstrates. Because of his repentant heart, God allowed him to remain in office until he died.

Why, then, are some leaders removed from office when they fail morally? Why could David remain king? The answer may lie in the Law of Solid Ground. David practiced this law and maintained his trust in God. Those who do not repent after some failure—or who do so only for public show—often lose their positions. Some sins no doubt disqualify leaders from continuing in leadership, but more fail in leadership from their deceptions than from their mistakes. History teaches that the public usually forgives a leader who owns up to his mistakes, but refuses to forgive those who remain unrepentant.

Mistakes don't have to prove fatal; we all make them. But when a leader deceives the people and loses their trust, they will no longer follow him or her.

⁶ Yet you desired faithfulness even in the
   womb;
   you taught me wisdom in that secret
      place.

⁷ Cleanse me with hyssop, and I will be clean;
   wash me, and I will be whiter than snow.
⁸ Let me hear joy and gladness;
   let the bones you have crushed rejoice.
⁹ Hide your face from my sins
   and blot out all my iniquity.

¹⁰ Create in me a pure heart, O God,
   and renew a steadfast spirit within me.
¹¹ Do not cast me from your presence
   or take your Holy Spirit from me.
¹² Restore to me the joy of your salvation
   and grant me a willing spirit, to sustain
      me.

¹³ Then I will teach transgressors your ways,
   so that sinners will turn back to you.
¹⁴ Deliver me from the guilt of bloodshed,
      O God,
   you who are God my Savior,
   and my tongue will sing of your
      righteousness.
¹⁵ Open my lips, Lord,
   and my mouth will declare your praise.
¹⁶ You do not delight in sacrifice, or I would
      bring it;
   you do not take pleasure in burnt
      offerings.
¹⁷ My sacrifice, O God, is*ᵃ* a broken spirit;
   a broken and contrite heart
   you, God, will not despise.

¹⁸ May it please you to prosper Zion,
   to build up the walls of Jerusalem.
¹⁹ Then you will delight in the sacrifices of the
      righteous,
   in burnt offerings offered whole;
   then bulls will be offered on your altar.

PSALM 52ᵇ

For the director of music. A *maskil*ᶜ of David. When Doeg the Edomite had gone to Saul and told him: "David has gone to the house of Ahimelek."

¹ Why do you boast of evil, you mighty hero?
   Why do you boast all day long,
   you who are a disgrace in the eyes of God?
² You who practice deceit,
   your tongue plots destruction;
   it is like a sharpened razor.
³ You love evil rather than good,
   falsehood rather than speaking the
      truth.ᵈ
⁴ You love every harmful word,
   you deceitful tongue!

⁵ Surely God will bring you down to
      everlasting ruin:
   He will snatch you up and pluck you from
      your tent;
   he will uproot you from the land of the
      living.
⁶ The righteous will see and fear;
   they will laugh at you, saying,
⁷ "Here now is the man
   who did not make God his stronghold

ᵃ 17 Or *The sacrifices of God are*   ᵇ In Hebrew texts 52:1-9 is numbered 52:3-11.   ᶜ Title: Probably a literary or musical term   ᵈ 3 The Hebrew has *Selah* (a word of uncertain meaning) here and at the end of verse 5.

but trusted in his great wealth
  and grew strong by destroying others!"

[8] But I am like an olive tree
  flourishing in the house of God;
I trust in God's unfailing love
  for ever and ever.
[9] For what you have done I will always praise
    you
  in the presence of your faithful people.
And I will hope in your name,
  for your name is good.

PSALM 53 [a]

For the director of music. According to *mahalath*. [b]
A *maskil* [c] of David.

[1] The fool says in his heart,
  "There is no God."
They are corrupt, and their ways are vile;
  there is no one who does good.

[2] God looks down from heaven
  on all mankind
to see if there are any who understand,
  any who seek God.
[3] Everyone has turned away, all have become
    corrupt;
  there is no one who does good,
    not even one.

[4] Do all these evildoers know nothing?

They devour my people as though eating
    bread;
  they never call on God.
[5] But there they are, overwhelmed with dread,
  where there was nothing to dread.
God scattered the bones of those who
    attacked you;
  you put them to shame, for God despised
    them.

[6] Oh, that salvation for Israel would come out
    of Zion!
  When God restores his people,
  let Jacob rejoice and Israel be glad!

PSALM 54 [d]

For the director of music. With stringed instruments.
A *maskil* [c] of David. When the Ziphites had gone to Saul
and said, "Is not David hiding among us?"

[1] Save me, O God, by your name;
  vindicate me by your might.
[2] Hear my prayer, O God;
  listen to the words of my mouth.

[3] Arrogant foes are attacking me;
  ruthless people are trying to kill me —
  people without regard for God. [e]

[4] Surely God is my help;
  the Lord is the one who sustains me.

[5] Let evil recoil on those who slander me;
  in your faithfulness destroy them.

[6] I will sacrifice a freewill offering to you;
  I will praise your name, LORD, for it is
    good.
[7] You have delivered me from all my troubles,
  and my eyes have looked in triumph on
    my foes.

PSALM 55 [f]

For the director of music. With stringed instruments.
A *maskil* [c] of David.

[1] Listen to my prayer, O God,
  do not ignore my plea;
[2] hear me and answer me.
My thoughts trouble me and I am
    distraught
[3] because of what my enemy is saying,
  because of the threats of the wicked;
for they bring down suffering on me
  and assail me in their anger.

[4] My heart is in anguish within me;
  the terrors of death have fallen on me.
[5] Fear and trembling have beset me;
  horror has overwhelmed me.
[6] I said, "Oh, that I had the wings of a dove!
  I would fly away and be at rest.
[7] I would flee far away
  and stay in the desert; [g]
[8] I would hurry to my place of shelter,
  far from the tempest and storm."

[9] Lord, confuse the wicked, confound their
    words,
  for I see violence and strife in the city.
[10] Day and night they prowl about on its
    walls;
  malice and abuse are within it.
[11] Destructive forces are at work in the city;
  threats and lies never leave its streets.

---

[a] In Hebrew texts 53:1-6 is numbered 53:2-7.   [b] Title:
Probably a musical term   [c] Title: Probably a literary or
musical term   [d] In Hebrew texts 54:1-7 is numbered 54:3-9.
[e] 3 The Hebrew has *Selah* (a word of uncertain meaning) here.
[f] In Hebrew texts 55:1-23 is numbered 55:2-24.   [g] 7 The
Hebrew has *Selah* (a word of uncertain meaning) here and in
the middle of verse 19.

¹² If an enemy were insulting me,
  I could endure it;
if a foe were rising against me,
  I could hide.
¹³ But it is you, a man like myself,
  my companion, my close friend,
¹⁴ with whom I once enjoyed sweet fellowship
  at the house of God,
as we walked about
  among the worshipers.

¹⁵ Let death take my enemies by surprise;
  let them go down alive to the realm of the
    dead,
  for evil finds lodging among them.

¹⁶ As for me, I call to God,
  and the Lord saves me.
¹⁷ Evening, morning and noon
  I cry out in distress,
  and he hears my voice.
¹⁸ He rescues me unharmed
  from the battle waged against me,
  even though many oppose me.
¹⁹ God, who is enthroned from of old,
  who does not change —
he will hear them and humble them,
  because they have no fear of God.

²⁰ My companion attacks his friends;
  he violates his covenant.
²¹ His talk is smooth as butter,
  yet war is in his heart;
his words are more soothing than oil,
  yet they are drawn swords.

²² Cast your cares on the Lord
  and he will sustain you;
he will never let
  the righteous be shaken.
²³ But you, God, will bring down the wicked
  into the pit of decay;
the bloodthirsty and deceitful
  will not live out half their days.

But as for me, I trust in you.

PSALM 56[a]

For the director of music. To the tune of "A Dove
on Distant Oaks." Of David. A *miktam*.[b] When the
  Philistines had seized him in Gath.

¹ Be merciful to me, my God,
  for my enemies are in hot pursuit;
  all day long they press their attack.
² My adversaries pursue me all day long;
  in their pride many are attacking me.

³ When I am afraid, I put my trust in you.
⁴   In God, whose word I praise —
in God I trust and am not afraid.
  What can mere mortals do to me?

⁵ All day long they twist my words;
  all their schemes are for my ruin.
⁶ They conspire, they lurk,
  they watch my steps,
  hoping to take my life.
⁷ Because of their wickedness do not[c] let them
    escape;
  in your anger, God, bring the nations down.

⁸ Record my misery;
  list my tears on your scroll[d] —
  are they not in your record?
⁹ Then my enemies will turn back
  when I call for help.
  By this I will know that God is for me.

¹⁰ In God, whose word I praise,
  in the Lord, whose word I praise —
¹¹ in God I trust and am not afraid.
  What can man do to me?

¹² I am under vows to you, my God;
  I will present my thank offerings to you.
¹³ For you have delivered me from death
  and my feet from stumbling,
that I may walk before God
  in the light of life.

PSALM 57[e]

For the director of music. To the tune of "Do Not
Destroy." Of David. A *miktam*.[b] When he had fled
  from Saul into the cave.

¹ Have mercy on me, my God, have mercy on
    me,
  for in you I take refuge.
I will take refuge in the shadow of your
    wings
  until the disaster has passed.

² I cry out to God Most High,
  to God, who vindicates me.
³ He sends from heaven and saves me,
  rebuking those who hotly pursue me —[f]
  God sends forth his love and his
    faithfulness.

^a In Hebrew texts 56:1-13 is numbered 56:2-14.   ^b Title:
Probably a literary or musical term   ^c 7 Probable reading of
the original Hebrew text; Masoretic Text does not have *do not*.
^d 8 Or *misery; / put my tears in your wineskin*   ^e In Hebrew
texts 57:1-11 is numbered 57:2-12.   ^f 3 The Hebrew has *Selah*
(a word of uncertain meaning) here and at the end of verse 6.

⁴I am in the midst of lions;
  I am forced to dwell among ravenous
    beasts—
men whose teeth are spears and arrows,
  whose tongues are sharp swords.

⁵Be exalted, O God, above the heavens;
  let your glory be over all the earth.

⁶They spread a net for my feet—
  I was bowed down in distress.
They dug a pit in my path—
  but they have fallen into it themselves.

⁷My heart, O God, is steadfast,
  my heart is steadfast;
  I will sing and make music.
⁸Awake, my soul!
  Awake, harp and lyre!
  I will awaken the dawn.

⁹I will praise you, Lord, among the nations;
  I will sing of you among the peoples.
¹⁰For great is your love, reaching to the
    heavens;
  your faithfulness reaches to the skies.

Leaders Practice Telling Themselves the Truth

Psalm 57:1–11

Psalm 57 gives us a beautiful picture of a leader in touch with his humanity. David composed it as he fled from Saul in the mountains and caves of Israel. The psalm expresses anxiety and fear, yet it ends with triumph: "Be exalted, O God, above the heavens; let your glory be over all the earth" (Ps 57:11).

Author Philip Yancey suggests that David wrote and sang the psalms as therapy for himself. Somehow, telling himself the truth enabled him to rise above his fear and see a transcendent God who remained in control.

Fortunately, few of us live with such danger. Like David, however, we all have times when nerves fail and fear creeps in. We feel surrounded by adversaries. Telling ourselves the truth, as David did, will heal and comfort us, as it did him. The truth of Psalm 57 can serve as our counselor. Successful leaders tell themselves the truth and gain perspective in the midst of volatile emotions.

¹¹Be exalted, O God, above the heavens;
  let your glory be over all the earth.

PSALM 58[a]

For the director of music. To the tune of "Do Not Destroy." Of David. A *miktam.*[b]

¹Do you rulers indeed speak justly?
  Do you judge people with equity?
²No, in your heart you devise injustice,
  and your hands mete out violence on the
    earth.

³Even from birth the wicked go astray;
  from the womb they are wayward,
    spreading lies.
⁴Their venom is like the venom of a snake,
  like that of a cobra that has stopped its
    ears,
⁵that will not heed the tune of the charmer,
  however skillful the enchanter may be.

⁶Break the teeth in their mouths, O God;
  LORD, tear out the fangs of those lions!
⁷Let them vanish like water that flows away;
  when they draw the bow, let their arrows
    fall short.
⁸May they be like a slug that melts away as it
    moves along,
  like a stillborn child that never sees the sun.

⁹Before your pots can feel the heat of the
    thorns—
  whether they be green or dry—the
    wicked will be swept away.[c]
¹⁰The righteous will be glad when they are
    avenged,
  when they dip their feet in the blood of
    the wicked.
¹¹Then people will say,
  "Surely the righteous still are rewarded;
  surely there is a God who judges the
    earth."

PSALM 59[d]

For the director of music. To the tune of "Do Not Destroy." Of David. A *miktam.*[b] When Saul had sent men to watch David's house in order to kill him.

¹Deliver me from my enemies, O God;
  be my fortress against those who are
    attacking me.

---

[a] In Hebrew texts 58:1-11 is numbered 58:2-12.   [b] Title: Probably a literary or musical term   [c] 9 The meaning of the Hebrew for this verse is uncertain.   [d] In Hebrew texts 59:1-17 is numbered 59:2-18.

² Deliver me from evildoers
　　and save me from those who are after my
　　　blood.
³ See how they lie in wait for me!
　　Fierce men conspire against me
　　for no offense or sin of mine, LORD.
⁴ I have done no wrong, yet they are ready to
　　　attack me.
　　Arise to help me; look on my plight!
⁵ You, LORD God Almighty,
　　you who are the God of Israel,
　　rouse yourself to punish all the nations;
　　show no mercy to wicked traitors.ᵃ

⁶ They return at evening,
　　snarling like dogs,
　　and prowl about the city.
⁷ See what they spew from their mouths—
　　the words from their lips are sharp as
　　　swords,
　　and they think, "Who can hear us?"
⁸ But you laugh at them, LORD;
　　you scoff at all those nations.

⁹ You are my strength, I watch for you;
　　you, God, are my fortress,
¹⁰　my God on whom I can rely.

God will go before me
　　and will let me gloat over those who
　　　slander me.
¹¹ But do not kill them, Lord our shield,ᵇ
　　or my people will forget.
In your might uproot them
　　and bring them down.
¹² For the sins of their mouths,
　　for the words of their lips,
　　let them be caught in their pride.
For the curses and lies they utter,
¹³　consume them in your wrath,
　　consume them till they are no more.
Then it will be known to the ends of the earth
　　that God rules over Jacob.

¹⁴ They return at evening,
　　snarling like dogs,
　　and prowl about the city.
¹⁵ They wander about for food
　　and howl if not satisfied.
¹⁶ But I will sing of your strength,
　　in the morning I will sing of your love;
for you are my fortress,
　　my refuge in times of trouble.

¹⁷ You are my strength, I sing praise to you;
　　you, God, are my fortress,
　　my God on whom I can rely.

PSALM 60ᶜ

For the director of music. To the tune of "The Lily
of the Covenant." A miktamᵈ of David. For teaching.
When he fought Aram Naharaimᵉ and Aram Zobah,ᶠ
and when Joab returned and struck down twelve
thousand Edomites in the Valley of Salt.

¹ You have rejected us, God, and burst
　　　upon us;
　　you have been angry—now restore us!
² You have shaken the land and torn it
　　　open;
　　mend its fractures, for it is quaking.
³ You have shown your people desperate
　　　times;
　　you have given us wine that makes us
　　　stagger.
⁴ But for those who fear you, you have raised
　　a banner
　　to be unfurled against the bow.ᵍ

⁵ Save us and help us with your right hand,
　　that those you love may be delivered.
⁶ God has spoken from his sanctuary:
　　"In triumph I will parcel out Shechem
　　and measure off the Valley of Sukkoth.
⁷ Gilead is mine, and Manasseh is mine;
　　Ephraim is my helmet,
　　Judah is my scepter.
⁸ Moab is my washbasin,
　　on Edom I toss my sandal;
　　over Philistia I shout in triumph."

⁹ Who will bring me to the fortified city?
　　Who will lead me to Edom?
¹⁰ Is it not you, God, you who have now
　　　rejected us
　　and no longer go out with our armies?
¹¹ Give us aid against the enemy,
　　for human help is worthless.
¹² With God we will gain the victory,
　　and he will trample down our enemies.

PSALM 61ʰ

For the director of music. With stringed instruments.
Of David.

¹ Hear my cry, O God;
　　listen to my prayer.

ᵃ 5 The Hebrew has Selah (a word of uncertain meaning) here
and at the end of verse 13.　　ᵇ 11 Or sovereign　　ᶜ In Hebrew
texts 60:1-12 is numbered 60:3-14.　　ᵈ Title: Probably a
literary or musical term　　ᵉ Title: That is, Arameans of
Northwest Mesopotamia　　ᶠ Title: That is, Arameans of
central Syria　　ᵍ 4 The Hebrew has Selah (a word of uncertain
meaning) here.　　ʰ In Hebrew texts 61:1-8 is numbered 61:2-9.

² From the ends of the earth I call to you,
  I call as my heart grows faint;
  lead me to the rock that is higher than I.
³ For you have been my refuge,
  a strong tower against the foe.

⁴ I long to dwell in your tent forever
  and take refuge in the shelter of your wings.[a]
⁵ For you, God, have heard my vows;
  you have given me the heritage of those
    who fear your name.

⁶ Increase the days of the king's life,
  his years for many generations.
⁷ May he be enthroned in God's presence forever;
  appoint your love and faithfulness to
    protect him.

⁸ Then I will ever sing in praise of your name
  and fulfill my vows day after day.

PSALM 62[b]

For the director of music. For Jeduthun.
A psalm of David.

¹ Truly my soul finds rest in God;
  my salvation comes from him.
² Truly he is my rock and my salvation;
  he is my fortress, I will never be shaken.

³ How long will you assault me?
  Would all of you throw me down —
  this leaning wall, this tottering fence?
⁴ Surely they intend to topple me
  from my lofty place;
  they take delight in lies.
  With their mouths they bless,
  but in their hearts they curse.[c]

⁵ Yes, my soul, find rest in God;
  my hope comes from him.
⁶ Truly he is my rock and my salvation;
  he is my fortress, I will not be shaken.
⁷ My salvation and my honor depend on God[d];
  he is my mighty rock, my refuge.
⁸ Trust in him at all times, you people;
  pour out your hearts to him,
  for God is our refuge.

⁹ Surely the lowborn are but a breath,
  the highborn are but a lie.
  If weighed on a balance, they are nothing;
  together they are only a breath.
¹⁰ Do not trust in extortion
  or put vain hope in stolen goods;
  though your riches increase,
  do not set your heart on them.

¹¹ One thing God has spoken,
  two things I have heard:
  "Power belongs to you, God,
¹² and with you, Lord, is unfailing love";
  and, "You reward everyone
    according to what they have done."

PSALM 63[e]

A psalm of David. When he was in the Desert of Judah.

¹ You, God, are my God,
  earnestly I seek you;
  I thirst for you,
  my whole being longs for you,
  in a dry and parched land
  where there is no water.

² I have seen you in the sanctuary
  and beheld your power and your glory.
³ Because your love is better than life,
  my lips will glorify you.
⁴ I will praise you as long as I live,
  and in your name I will lift up my hands.
⁵ I will be fully satisfied as with the richest of
    foods;
  with singing lips my mouth will praise
    you.

⁶ On my bed I remember you;
  I think of you through the watches of the
    night.
⁷ Because you are my help,
  I sing in the shadow of your wings.
⁸ I cling to you;
  your right hand upholds me.

⁹ Those who want to kill me will be destroyed;
  they will go down to the depths of the
    earth.
¹⁰ They will be given over to the sword
  and become food for jackals.

¹¹ But the king will rejoice in God;
  all who swear by God will glory in him,
  while the mouths of liars will be silenced.

PSALM 64[f]

For the director of music. A psalm of David.

¹ Hear me, my God, as I voice my complaint;
  protect my life from the threat of the enemy.

---

[a] 4 The Hebrew has *Selah* (a word of uncertain meaning) here.
[b] In Hebrew texts 62:1-12 is numbered 62:2-13.   [c] 4 The
Hebrew has *Selah* (a word of uncertain meaning) here and at
the end of verse 8.   [d] 7 Or / *God Most High is my salvation
and my honor*   [e] In Hebrew texts 63:1-11 is numbered
63:2-12.   [f] In Hebrew texts 64:1-10 is numbered 64:2-11.

² Hide me from the conspiracy of the
    wicked,
  from the plots of evildoers.
³ They sharpen their tongues like swords
  and aim cruel words like deadly arrows.
⁴ They shoot from ambush at the innocent;
  they shoot suddenly, without fear.

⁵ They encourage each other in evil plans,
  they talk about hiding their snares;
  they say, "Who will see it*a*?"
⁶ They plot injustice and say,
  "We have devised a perfect plan!"
  Surely the human mind and heart are
    cunning.

⁷ But God will shoot them with his arrows;
  they will suddenly be struck down.
⁸ He will turn their own tongues against
    them
  and bring them to ruin;
  all who see them will shake their heads in
    scorn.
⁹ All people will fear;
  they will proclaim the works of God
  and ponder what he has done.

¹⁰ The righteous will rejoice in the LORD
  and take refuge in him;
  all the upright in heart will glory in him!

PSALM 65 *b*

For the director of music. A psalm of David. A song.

¹ Praise awaits*c* you, our God, in Zion;
  to you our vows will be fulfilled.
² You who answer prayer,
  to you all people will come.
³ When we were overwhelmed by sins,
  you forgave*d* our transgressions.
⁴ Blessed are those you choose
  and bring near to live in your courts!
We are filled with the good things of your
    house,
  of your holy temple.

⁵ You answer us with awesome and righteous
    deeds,
  God our Savior,
the hope of all the ends of the earth
  and of the farthest seas,
⁶ who formed the mountains by your power,
  having armed yourself with strength,
⁷ who stilled the roaring of the seas,
  the roaring of their waves,
  and the turmoil of the nations.

⁸ The whole earth is filled with awe at your
    wonders;
  where morning dawns, where evening
    fades,
  you call forth songs of joy.

⁹ You care for the land and water it;
  you enrich it abundantly.
The streams of God are filled with water
  to provide the people with grain,
  for so you have ordained it.*e*
¹⁰ You drench its furrows and level its ridges;
  you soften it with showers and bless its
    crops.
¹¹ You crown the year with your bounty,
  and your carts overflow with abundance.
¹² The grasslands of the wilderness overflow;
  the hills are clothed with gladness.
¹³ The meadows are covered with flocks
  and the valleys are mantled with grain;
  they shout for joy and sing.

PSALM 66

For the director of music. A song. A psalm.

¹ Shout for joy to God, all the earth!
² ⠀⠀Sing the glory of his name;
  make his praise glorious.
³ Say to God, "How awesome are your deeds!
  So great is your power
  that your enemies cringe before you.
⁴ All the earth bows down to you;
  they sing praise to you,
  they sing the praises of your name."*f*

⁵ Come and see what God has done,
  his awesome deeds for mankind!
⁶ He turned the sea into dry land,
  they passed through the waters on
    foot —
  come, let us rejoice in him.
⁷ He rules forever by his power,
  his eyes watch the nations —
  let not the rebellious rise up against him.

⁸ Praise our God, all peoples,
  let the sound of his praise be heard;
⁹ he has preserved our lives
  and kept our feet from slipping.
¹⁰ For you, God, tested us;
  you refined us like silver.

---

a 5 Or *us*   *b* In Hebrew texts 65:1-13 is numbered 65:2-14.
c 1 Or *befits*; the meaning of the Hebrew for this word is
uncertain.   *d* 3 Or *made atonement for*   *e* 9 Or *for that is
how you prepare the land*   *f* 4 The Hebrew has *Selah* (a word
of uncertain meaning) here and at the end of verses 7 and 15.

11 You brought us into prison
    and laid burdens on our backs.
12 You let people ride over our heads;
    we went through fire and water,
    but you brought us to a place of
        abundance.

13 I will come to your temple with burnt
        offerings
    and fulfill my vows to you—
14 vows my lips promised and my mouth spoke
    when I was in trouble.
15 I will sacrifice fat animals to you
    and an offering of rams;
    I will offer bulls and goats.

16 Come and hear, all you who fear God;
    let me tell you what he has done for me.
17 I cried out to him with my mouth;
    his praise was on my tongue.
18 If I had cherished sin in my heart,
    the Lord would not have listened;
19 but God has surely listened
    and has heard my prayer.
20 Praise be to God,
    who has not rejected my prayer
    or withheld his love from me!

PSALM 67[a]

For the director of music. With stringed instruments.
A psalm. A song.

1 May God be gracious to us and bless us
    and make his face shine on us— [b]
2 so that your ways may be known on earth,
    your salvation among all nations.

3 May the peoples praise you, God;
    may all the peoples praise you.
4 May the nations be glad and sing for joy,
    for you rule the peoples with equity
    and guide the nations of the earth.
5 May the peoples praise you, God;
    may all the peoples praise you.

6 The land yields its harvest;
    God, our God, blesses us.
7 May God bless us still,
    so that all the ends of the earth will fear
        him.

PSALM 68[c]

For the director of music. Of David.
A psalm. A song.

1 May God arise, may his enemies be scattered;
    may his foes flee before him.
2 May you blow them away like smoke—
    as wax melts before the fire,
    may the wicked perish before God.
3 But may the righteous be glad
    and rejoice before God;
    may they be happy and joyful.

4 Sing to God, sing in praise of his name,
    extol him who rides on the clouds[d];
    rejoice before him—his name is the
        LORD.

---

[a] In Hebrew texts 67:1-7 is numbered 67:2-8.   [b] 1 The
Hebrew has *Selah* (a word of uncertain meaning) here and at
the end of verse 4.   [c] In Hebrew texts 68:1-35 is numbered
68:2-36.   [d] 4 Or *name, / prepare the way for him who rides
through the deserts*

The Law of Intuition: Vision for the World Drives God's Leaders

Psalm 67:1–7

God's blessings follow leaders who adopt his vision for the nations of the world.
    Psalm 67 contains both the "top line" and the "bottom line" of the covenant God invites us to enter. The top line represents God's blessings for his people; the bottom line represents the natural response to that blessing. When God blesses us, we are to turn around and bless all the unblessed nations of the earth.
    Psalm 67:1 asks God to be gracious, to bless, and to make his face to shine upon his people (the *top line* of the covenant). Verse 2 says, "That your ways may be known on earth, your salvation among all nations" (the *bottom line* of the covenant). The last two verses of the psalm reiterate the top and bottom lines.
    God blesses his people so that they can bless those who have yet to be blessed. Godly leaders feel driven by this vision. Maintenance is not the goal. Getting blessed is not the goal. The top line represents only half of the deal; the goal is to participate in the bottom line. World conquest motivates God's heart, and he accomplishes this mission through leaders who cast vision for participating in bottom-line living.

⁵A father to the fatherless, a defender of
    widows,
    is God in his holy dwelling.
⁶God sets the lonely in families,[a]
    he leads out the prisoners with singing;
    but the rebellious live in a sun-scorched
        land.

⁷When you, God, went out before your
    people,
    when you marched through the
        wilderness,[b]
⁸the earth shook, the heavens poured down
    rain,
    before God, the One of Sinai,
    before God, the God of Israel.
⁹You gave abundant showers, O God;
    you refreshed your weary inheritance.
¹⁰Your people settled in it,
    and from your bounty, God, you provided
        for the poor.

¹¹The Lord announces the word,
    and the women who proclaim it are a
        mighty throng:
¹²"Kings and armies flee in haste;
    the women at home divide the plunder.
¹³Even while you sleep among the sheep pens,[c]
    the wings of my dove are sheathed with
        silver,
    its feathers with shining gold."
¹⁴When the Almighty[d] scattered the kings in
    the land,
    it was like snow fallen on Mount Zalmon.

¹⁵Mount Bashan, majestic mountain,
    Mount Bashan, rugged mountain,
¹⁶why gaze in envy, you rugged mountain,
    at the mountain where God chooses to
        reign,
    where the Lord himself will dwell
        forever?
¹⁷The chariots of God are tens of thousands
    and thousands of thousands;
    the Lord has come from Sinai into his
        sanctuary.[e]
¹⁸When you ascended on high,
    you took many captives;
    you received gifts from people,
    even from[f] the rebellious —
    that you,[g] Lord God, might dwell there.

¹⁹Praise be to the Lord, to God our Savior,
    who daily bears our burdens.
²⁰Our God is a God who saves;
    from the Sovereign Lord comes escape
        from death.

²¹Surely God will crush the heads of his
    enemies,
    the hairy crowns of those who go on in
        their sins.
²²The Lord says, "I will bring them from
    Bashan;
    I will bring them from the depths of the
        sea,
²³that your feet may wade in the blood of your
    foes,
    while the tongues of your dogs have their
        share."

²⁴Your procession, God, has come into view,
    the procession of my God and King into
        the sanctuary.
²⁵In front are the singers, after them the
    musicians;
    with them are the young women playing
        the timbrels.
²⁶Praise God in the great congregation;
    praise the Lord in the assembly of
        Israel.
²⁷There is the little tribe of Benjamin, leading
    them,
    there the great throng of Judah's princes,
    and there the princes of Zebulun and of
        Naphtali.

²⁸Summon your power, God[h];
    show us your strength, our God, as you
        have done before.
²⁹Because of your temple at Jerusalem
    kings will bring you gifts.
³⁰Rebuke the beast among the reeds,
    the herd of bulls among the calves of the
        nations.
    Humbled, may the beast bring bars of silver.
    Scatter the nations who delight in war.
³¹Envoys will come from Egypt;
    Cush[i] will submit herself to God.

³²Sing to God, you kingdoms of the earth,
    sing praise to the Lord,
³³to him who rides across the highest heavens,
    the ancient heavens,
    who thunders with mighty voice.

---

[a] 6 Or *the desolate in a homeland*   [b] 7 The Hebrew has *Selah*
(a word of uncertain meaning) here and at the end of verses 19
and 32.   [c] 13 Or *the campfires*; or *the saddlebags*
[d] 14 Hebrew *Shaddai*   [e] 17 Probable reading of the original
Hebrew text; Masoretic Text *Lord is among them at Sinai in
holiness*   [f] 18 Or *gifts for people, / even*   [g] 18 Or *they*
[h] 28 Many Hebrew manuscripts, Septuagint and Syriac; most
Hebrew manuscripts *Your God has summoned power for you*
[i] 31 That is, the upper Nile region

34 Proclaim the power of God,
   whose majesty is over Israel,
   whose power is in the heavens.
35 You, God, are awesome in your sanctuary;
   the God of Israel gives power and strength
      to his people.

Praise be to God!

PSALM 69[a]

For the director of music. To the tune of "Lilies."
Of David.

1 Save me, O God,
   for the waters have come up to my neck.
2 I sink in the miry depths,
   where there is no foothold.
 I have come into the deep waters;
   the floods engulf me.
3 I am worn out calling for help;
   my throat is parched.
 My eyes fail,
   looking for my God.
4 Those who hate me without reason
   outnumber the hairs of my head;
 many are my enemies without cause,
   those who seek to destroy me.
 I am forced to restore
   what I did not steal.

5 You, God, know my folly;
   my guilt is not hidden from you.

6 Lord, the LORD Almighty,
   may those who hope in you
   not be disgraced because of me;
 God of Israel,
   may those who seek you
   not be put to shame because of me.
7 For I endure scorn for your sake,
   and shame covers my face.
8 I am a foreigner to my own family,
   a stranger to my own mother's children;
9 for zeal for your house consumes me,
   and the insults of those who insult you fall
      on me.
10 When I weep and fast,
   I must endure scorn;
11 when I put on sackcloth,
   people make sport of me.
12 Those who sit at the gate mock me,
   and I am the song of the drunkards.

13 But I pray to you, LORD,
   in the time of your favor;
 in your great love, O God,
   answer me with your sure salvation.

14 Rescue me from the mire,
   do not let me sink;
 deliver me from those who hate me,
   from the deep waters.
15 Do not let the floodwaters engulf me
   or the depths swallow me up
   or the pit close its mouth over me.

16 Answer me, LORD, out of the goodness of
      your love;
   in your great mercy turn to me.
17 Do not hide your face from your servant;
   answer me quickly, for I am in trouble.
18 Come near and rescue me;
   deliver me because of my foes.

19 You know how I am scorned, disgraced and
      shamed;
   all my enemies are before you.
20 Scorn has broken my heart
   and has left me helpless;
 I looked for sympathy, but there was none,
   for comforters, but I found none.
21 They put gall in my food
   and gave me vinegar for my thirst.

22 May the table set before them become a
      snare;
   may it become retribution and[b] a trap.
23 May their eyes be darkened so they cannot
      see,
   and their backs be bent forever.
24 Pour out your wrath on them;
   let your fierce anger overtake them.
25 May their place be deserted;
   let there be no one to dwell in their tents.
26 For they persecute those you wound
   and talk about the pain of those you hurt.
27 Charge them with crime upon crime;
   do not let them share in your salvation.
28 May they be blotted out of the book of life
   and not be listed with the righteous.

29 But as for me, afflicted and in pain —
   may your salvation, God, protect me.

30 I will praise God's name in song
   and glorify him with thanksgiving.
31 This will please the LORD more than an ox,
   more than a bull with its horns and
      hooves.
32 The poor will see and be glad —
   you who seek God, may your hearts live!
33 The LORD hears the needy
   and does not despise his captive people.

---

[a] In Hebrew texts 69:1-36 is numbered 69:2-37.   [b] 22 Or
snare / and their fellowship become

³⁴ Let heaven and earth praise him,
    the seas and all that move in them,
³⁵ for God will save Zion
    and rebuild the cities of Judah.
Then people will settle there and possess it;
³⁶   the children of his servants will inherit it,
    and those who love his name will dwell
      there.

PSALM 70[a]

For the director of music. Of David. A petition.

¹ Hasten, O God, to save me;
    come quickly, LORD, to help me.

² May those who want to take my life
    be put to shame and confusion;
may all who desire my ruin
    be turned back in disgrace.
³ May those who say to me, "Aha! Aha!"
    turn back because of their shame.
⁴ But may all who seek you
    rejoice and be glad in you;
may those who long for your saving help
    always say,
    "The LORD is great!"

⁵ But as for me, I am poor and needy;
    come quickly to me, O God.
You are my help and my deliverer;
    LORD, do not delay.

PSALM 71

¹ In you, LORD, I have taken refuge;
    let me never be put to shame.
² In your righteousness, rescue me and deliver
    me;
    turn your ear to me and save me.
³ Be my rock of refuge,
    to which I can always go;
give the command to save me,
    for you are my rock and my fortress.
⁴ Deliver me, my God, from the hand of the
    wicked,
    from the grasp of those who are evil and
      cruel.

⁵ For you have been my hope, Sovereign LORD,
    my confidence since my youth.
⁶ From birth I have relied on you;
    you brought me forth from my mother's
      womb.
    I will ever praise you.
⁷ I have become a sign to many;
    you are my strong refuge.

⁸ My mouth is filled with your praise,
    declaring your splendor all day long.

⁹ Do not cast me away when I am old;
    do not forsake me when my strength is
      gone.
¹⁰ For my enemies speak against me;
    those who wait to kill me conspire together.
¹¹ They say, "God has forsaken him;
    pursue him and seize him,
    for no one will rescue him."
¹² Do not be far from me, my God;
    come quickly, God, to help me.
¹³ May my accusers perish in shame;
    may those who want to harm me
    be covered with scorn and disgrace.

¹⁴ As for me, I will always have hope;
    I will praise you more and more.

¹⁵ My mouth will tell of your righteous deeds,
    of your saving acts all day long—
    though I know not how to relate them all.
¹⁶ I will come and proclaim your mighty acts,
    Sovereign LORD;
    I will proclaim your righteous deeds,
    yours alone.
¹⁷ Since my youth, God, you have taught me,
    and to this day I declare your marvelous
      deeds.
¹⁸ Even when I am old and gray,
    do not forsake me, my God,
till I declare your power to the next
      generation,
    your mighty acts to all who are to come.

¹⁹ Your righteousness, God, reaches to the
      heavens,
    you who have done great things.
    Who is like you, God?
²⁰ Though you have made me see troubles,
    many and bitter,
    you will restore my life again;
from the depths of the earth
    you will again bring me up.
²¹ You will increase my honor
    and comfort me once more.

²² I will praise you with the harp
    for your faithfulness, my God;
I will sing praise to you with the lyre,
    Holy One of Israel.
²³ My lips will shout for joy
    when I sing praise to you—
    I whom you have delivered.

---

[a] In Hebrew texts 70:1-5 is numbered 70:2-6.

24 My tongue will tell of your righteous acts
        all day long,
    for those who wanted to harm me
        have been put to shame and confusion.

PSALM 72

Of Solomon.

1 Endow the king with your justice, O God,
        the royal son with your righteousness.
2 May he judge your people in righteousness,
        your afflicted ones with justice.

3 May the mountains bring prosperity to the
        people,
    the hills the fruit of righteousness.
4 May he defend the afflicted among the
        people
    and save the children of the needy;
    may he crush the oppressor.
5 May he endure[a] as long as the sun,
    as long as the moon, through all
        generations.
6 May he be like rain falling on a mown field,
    like showers watering the earth.
7 In his days may the righteous flourish
    and prosperity abound till the moon is no
        more.

8 May he rule from sea to sea
    and from the River[b] to the ends of the
        earth.
9 May the desert tribes bow before him
    and his enemies lick the dust.
10 May the kings of Tarshish and of distant
        shores
    bring tribute to him.
    May the kings of Sheba and Seba
        present him gifts.
11 May all kings bow down to him
    and all nations serve him.

12 For he will deliver the needy who cry out,
    the afflicted who have no one to help.
13 He will take pity on the weak and the needy
    and save the needy from death.
14 He will rescue them from oppression and
        violence,
    for precious is their blood in his sight.

15 Long may he live!
    May gold from Sheba be given him.
    May people ever pray for him
        and bless him all day long.
16 May grain abound throughout the land;
    on the tops of the hills may it sway.

May the crops flourish like Lebanon
    and thrive[c] like the grass of the field.
17 May his name endure forever;
    may it continue as long as the sun.

Then all nations will be blessed through
        him,[d]
    and they will call him blessed.

18 Praise be to the LORD God, the God of Israel,
    who alone does marvelous deeds.
19 Praise be to his glorious name forever;
    may the whole earth be filled with his
        glory.
            Amen and Amen.

20 This concludes the prayers of David son of
    Jesse.

BOOK III

Psalms 73–89

PSALM 73

A psalm of Asaph.

1 Surely God is good to Israel,
    to those who are pure in heart.

2 But as for me, my feet had almost slipped;
    I had nearly lost my foothold.
3 For I envied the arrogant
    when I saw the prosperity of the wicked.

4 They have no struggles;
    their bodies are healthy and strong.[e]
5 They are free from common human
        burdens;
    they are not plagued by human ills.
6 Therefore pride is their necklace;
    they clothe themselves with violence.
7 From their callous hearts comes iniquity[f];
    their evil imaginations have no limits.
8 They scoff, and speak with malice;
    with arrogance they threaten oppression.
9 Their mouths lay claim to heaven,
    and their tongues take possession of the
        earth.

---

a 5 Septuagint; Hebrew *You will be feared*   b 8 That is, the
Euphrates   c 16 Probable reading of the original Hebrew
text; Masoretic Text *Lebanon, / from the city*   d 17 Or *will
use his name in blessings* (see Gen. 48:20)   e 4 With a
different word division of the Hebrew; Masoretic Text *struggles
at their death; / their bodies are healthy*   f 7 Syriac (see also
Septuagint); Hebrew *Their eyes bulge with fat*

¹⁰ Therefore their people turn to them
    and drink up waters in abundance.*a*
¹¹ They say, "How would God know?
    Does the Most High know anything?"

¹² This is what the wicked are like—
    always free of care, they go on amassing
      wealth.

¹³ Surely in vain I have kept my heart pure
    and have washed my hands in innocence.
¹⁴ All day long I have been afflicted,
    and every morning brings new
      punishments.

¹⁵ If I had spoken out like that,
    I would have betrayed your children.
¹⁶ When I tried to understand all this,
    it troubled me deeply
¹⁷ till I entered the sanctuary of God;
    then I understood their final destiny.

Vision: The Difference Between Followers and Leaders

Psalm 73:1–17

Vision is the friend of every leader, helping them to keep perspective and stay the course. When Asaph sees the final destiny of the wicked, he is able to endure his season of oppression. Without hope in the future, we lack power in the present.

¹⁸ Surely you place them on slippery ground;
    you cast them down to ruin.
¹⁹ How suddenly are they destroyed,
    completely swept away by terrors!
²⁰ They are like a dream when one awakes;
    when you arise, Lord,
    you will despise them as fantasies.

²¹ When my heart was grieved
    and my spirit embittered,
²² I was senseless and ignorant;
    I was a brute beast before you.

²³ Yet I am always with you;
    you hold me by my right hand.
²⁴ You guide me with your counsel,
    and afterward you will take me into glory.
²⁵ Whom have I in heaven but you?
    And earth has nothing I desire besides you.

²⁶ My flesh and my heart may fail,
    but God is the strength of my heart
    and my portion forever.

²⁷ Those who are far from you will perish;
    you destroy all who are unfaithful to you.
²⁸ But as for me, it is good to be near God.
    I have made the Sovereign Lᴏʀᴅ my
      refuge;
    I will tell of all your deeds.

PSALM 74

*A maskil*b *of Asaph.*

¹ O God, why have you rejected us forever?
    Why does your anger smolder against the
      sheep of your pasture?
² Remember the nation you purchased long
      ago,
    the people of your inheritance, whom you
      redeemed—
    Mount Zion, where you dwelt.
³ Turn your steps toward these everlasting
      ruins,
    all this destruction the enemy has brought
      on the sanctuary.

⁴ Your foes roared in the place where you met
      with us;
    they set up their standards as signs.
⁵ They behaved like men wielding axes
    to cut through a thicket of trees.
⁶ They smashed all the carved paneling
    with their axes and hatchets.
⁷ They burned your sanctuary to the ground;
    they defiled the dwelling place of your
      Name.
⁸ They said in their hearts, "We will crush
      them completely!"
    They burned every place where God was
      worshiped in the land.

⁹ We are given no signs from God;
    no prophets are left,
    and none of us knows how long this will be.
¹⁰ How long will the enemy mock you, God?
    Will the foe revile your name forever?
¹¹ Why do you hold back your hand, your right
      hand?
    Take it from the folds of your garment and
      destroy them!

¹² But God is my King from long ago;
    he brings salvation on the earth.

---

a 10 The meaning of the Hebrew for this verse is uncertain.
b Title: Probably a literary or musical term

¹³ It was you who split open the sea by your
power;
you broke the heads of the monster in the
waters.
¹⁴ It was you who crushed the heads of
Leviathan
and gave it as food to the creatures of the
desert.
¹⁵ It was you who opened up springs and
streams;
you dried up the ever-flowing rivers.
¹⁶ The day is yours, and yours also the night;
you established the sun and moon.
¹⁷ It was you who set all the boundaries of the
earth;
you made both summer and winter.

¹⁸ Remember how the enemy has mocked you,
LORD,
how foolish people have reviled your name.
¹⁹ Do not hand over the life of your dove to
wild beasts;
do not forget the lives of your afflicted
people forever.
²⁰ Have regard for your covenant,
because haunts of violence fill the dark
places of the land.
²¹ Do not let the oppressed retreat in disgrace;
may the poor and needy praise your name.
²² Rise up, O God, and defend your cause;
remember how fools mock you all day long.
²³ Do not ignore the clamor of your
adversaries,
the uproar of your enemies, which rises
continually.

PSALM 75[a]

For the director of music. To the tune of "Do Not
Destroy." A psalm of Asaph. A song.

¹ We praise you, God,
we praise you, for your Name is near;
people tell of your wonderful deeds.

² You say, "I choose the appointed time;
it is I who judge with equity.
³ When the earth and all its people quake,
it is I who hold its pillars firm.[b]
⁴ To the arrogant I say, 'Boast no more,'
and to the wicked, 'Do not lift up your
horns.[c]
⁵ Do not lift your horns against heaven;
do not speak so defiantly.'"

⁶ No one from the east or the west
or from the desert can exalt themselves.

⁷ It is God who judges:
He brings one down, he exalts another.
⁸ In the hand of the LORD is a cup
full of foaming wine mixed with spices;
he pours it out, and all the wicked of the
earth
drink it down to its very dregs.

⁹ As for me, I will declare this forever;
I will sing praise to the God of Jacob,
¹⁰ who says, "I will cut off the horns of all the
wicked,
but the horns of the righteous will be
lifted up."

PSALM 76[d]

For the director of music. With stringed instruments.
A psalm of Asaph. A song.

¹ God is renowned in Judah;
in Israel his name is great.
² His tent is in Salem,
his dwelling place in Zion.
³ There he broke the flashing arrows,
the shields and the swords, the weapons of
war.[e]

⁴ You are radiant with light,
more majestic than mountains rich with
game.
⁵ The valiant lie plundered,
they sleep their last sleep;
not one of the warriors
can lift his hands.
⁶ At your rebuke, God of Jacob,
both horse and chariot lie still.

⁷ It is you alone who are to be feared.
Who can stand before you when you are
angry?
⁸ From heaven you pronounced judgment,
and the land feared and was quiet—
⁹ when you, God, rose up to judge,
to save all the afflicted of the land.
¹⁰ Surely your wrath against mankind brings
you praise,
and the survivors of your wrath are
restrained.[f]

---

[a] In Hebrew texts 75:1-10 is numbered 75:2-11.   [b] 3 The
Hebrew has *Selah* (a word of uncertain meaning) here.
[c] 4 *Horns* here symbolize strength; also in verses 5 and 10.
[d] In Hebrew texts 76:1-12 is numbered 76:2-13.   [e] 3 The
Hebrew has *Selah* (a word of uncertain meaning) here and at
the end of verse 9.   [f] 10 Or *Surely the wrath of mankind
brings you praise, / and with the remainder of wrath you arm
yourself*

[11] Make vows to the LORD your God and fulfill
them;
let all the neighboring lands
bring gifts to the One to be feared.
[12] He breaks the spirit of rulers;
he is feared by the kings of the earth.

PSALM 77[a]

For the director of music. For Jeduthun.
Of Asaph. A psalm.

[1] I cried out to God for help;
I cried out to God to hear me.
[2] When I was in distress, I sought the Lord;
at night I stretched out untiring hands,
and I would not be comforted.

[3] I remembered you, God, and I groaned;
I meditated, and my spirit grew faint.[b]
[4] You kept my eyes from closing;
I was too troubled to speak.
[5] I thought about the former days,
the years of long ago;
[6] I remembered my songs in the night.
My heart meditated and my spirit asked:

[7] "Will the Lord reject forever?
Will he never show his favor again?
[8] Has his unfailing love vanished forever?
Has his promise failed for all time?
[9] Has God forgotten to be merciful?
Has he in anger withheld his compassion?"

[10] Then I thought, "To this I will appeal:
the years when the Most High stretched
out his right hand.
[11] I will remember the deeds of the LORD;
yes, I will remember your miracles of long
ago.
[12] I will consider all your works
and meditate on all your mighty deeds."

[13] Your ways, God, are holy.
What god is as great as our God?
[14] You are the God who performs miracles;
you display your power among the
peoples.
[15] With your mighty arm you redeemed your
people,
the descendants of Jacob and Joseph.

[16] The waters saw you, God,
the waters saw you and writhed;
the very depths were convulsed.
[17] The clouds poured down water,
the heavens resounded with thunder;
your arrows flashed back and forth.

[18] Your thunder was heard in the whirlwind,
your lightning lit up the world;
the earth trembled and quaked.
[19] Your path led through the sea,
your way through the mighty waters,
though your footprints were not seen.

[20] You led your people like a flock
by the hand of Moses and Aaron.

PSALM 78

A maskil[c] of Asaph.

[1] My people, hear my teaching;
listen to the words of my mouth.
[2] I will open my mouth with a parable;
I will utter hidden things, things from of
old —
[3] things we have heard and known,
things our ancestors have told us.
[4] We will not hide them from their
descendants;
we will tell the next generation
the praiseworthy deeds of the LORD,
his power, and the wonders he has done.
[5] He decreed statutes for Jacob
and established the law in Israel,
which he commanded our ancestors
to teach their children,
[6] so the next generation would know them,
even the children yet to be born,
and they in turn would tell their children.
[7] Then they would put their trust in God
and would not forget his deeds
but would keep his commands.
[8] They would not be like their ancestors —
a stubborn and rebellious generation,
whose hearts were not loyal to God,
whose spirits were not faithful to him.

[9] The men of Ephraim, though armed with
bows,
turned back on the day of battle;
[10] they did not keep God's covenant
and refused to live by his law.
[11] They forgot what he had done,
the wonders he had shown them.
[12] He did miracles in the sight of their
ancestors
in the land of Egypt, in the region of
Zoan.

---

[a] In Hebrew texts 77:1-20 is numbered 77:2-21.   [b] 3 The
Hebrew has *Selah* (a word of uncertain meaning) here and at
the end of verses 9 and 15.   [c] Title: Probably a literary or
musical term

¹³ He divided the sea and led them through;
    he made the water stand up like a wall.
¹⁴ He guided them with the cloud by day
    and with light from the fire all night.
¹⁵ He split the rocks in the wilderness
    and gave them water as abundant as the
       seas;
¹⁶ he brought streams out of a rocky crag
    and made water flow down like rivers.

¹⁷ But they continued to sin against him,
    rebelling in the wilderness against the
       Most High.
¹⁸ They willfully put God to the test
    by demanding the food they craved.
¹⁹ They spoke against God;
    they said, "Can God really
      spread a table in the wilderness?
²⁰ True, he struck the rock,
    and water gushed out,
    streams flowed abundantly,
  but can he also give us bread?
    Can he supply meat for his people?"
²¹ When the LORD heard them, he was furious;
    his fire broke out against Jacob,
    and his wrath rose against Israel,
²² for they did not believe in God
    or trust in his deliverance.
²³ Yet he gave a command to the skies above
    and opened the doors of the heavens;
²⁴ he rained down manna for the people to eat,
    he gave them the grain of heaven.
²⁵ Human beings ate the bread of angels;
    he sent them all the food they could eat.
²⁶ He let loose the east wind from the heavens
    and by his power made the south wind
       blow.
²⁷ He rained meat down on them like dust,
    birds like sand on the seashore.
²⁸ He made them come down inside their camp,
    all around their tents.
²⁹ They ate till they were gorged —
    he had given them what they craved.
³⁰ But before they turned from what they
      craved,
    even while the food was still in their
      mouths,
³¹ God's anger rose against them;
    he put to death the sturdiest among them,
    cutting down the young men of Israel.

³² In spite of all this, they kept on sinning;
    in spite of his wonders, they did not
      believe.
³³ So he ended their days in futility
    and their years in terror.

³⁴ Whenever God slew them, they would seek
      him;
    they eagerly turned to him again.
³⁵ They remembered that God was their Rock,
    that God Most High was their Redeemer.
³⁶ But then they would flatter him with their
      mouths,
    lying to him with their tongues;
³⁷ their hearts were not loyal to him,
    they were not faithful to his covenant.
³⁸ Yet he was merciful;
    he forgave their iniquities
    and did not destroy them.
  Time after time he restrained his anger
    and did not stir up his full wrath.
³⁹ He remembered that they were but flesh,
    a passing breeze that does not return.

⁴⁰ How often they rebelled against him in the
      wilderness
    and grieved him in the wasteland!
⁴¹ Again and again they put God to the test;
    they vexed the Holy One of Israel.
⁴² They did not remember his power —
    the day he redeemed them from the
      oppressor,
⁴³ the day he displayed his signs in Egypt,
    his wonders in the region of Zoan.
⁴⁴ He turned their river into blood;
    they could not drink from their streams.
⁴⁵ He sent swarms of flies that devoured them,
    and frogs that devastated them.
⁴⁶ He gave their crops to the grasshopper,
    their produce to the locust.
⁴⁷ He destroyed their vines with hail
    and their sycamore-figs with sleet.
⁴⁸ He gave over their cattle to the hail,
    their livestock to bolts of lightning.
⁴⁹ He unleashed against them his hot anger,
    his wrath, indignation and hostility —
    a band of destroying angels.
⁵⁰ He prepared a path for his anger;
    he did not spare them from death
    but gave them over to the plague.
⁵¹ He struck down all the firstborn of Egypt,
    the firstfruits of manhood in the tents of
      Ham.
⁵² But he brought his people out like a flock;
    he led them like sheep through the
      wilderness.
⁵³ He guided them safely, so they were unafraid;
    but the sea engulfed their enemies.
⁵⁴ And so he brought them to the border of his
      holy land,
    to the hill country his right hand had taken.

55 He drove out nations before them
and allotted their lands to them as an
inheritance;
he settled the tribes of Israel in their
homes.

56 But they put God to the test
and rebelled against the Most High;
they did not keep his statutes.
57 Like their ancestors they were disloyal and
faithless,
as unreliable as a faulty bow.
58 They angered him with their high places;
they aroused his jealousy with their
idols.
59 When God heard them, he was furious;
he rejected Israel completely.
60 He abandoned the tabernacle of Shiloh,
the tent he had set up among humans.
61 He sent the ark of his might into captivity,
his splendor into the hands of the enemy.
62 He gave his people over to the sword;
he was furious with his inheritance.
63 Fire consumed their young men,
and their young women had no wedding
songs;
64 their priests were put to the sword,
and their widows could not weep.

65 Then the Lord awoke as from sleep,
as a warrior wakes from the stupor of
wine.
66 He beat back his enemies;
he put them to everlasting shame.
67 Then he rejected the tents of Joseph,
he did not choose the tribe of Ephraim;
68 but he chose the tribe of Judah,
Mount Zion, which he loved.
69 He built his sanctuary like the heights,
like the earth that he established forever.
70 He chose David his servant
and took him from the sheep pens;
71 from tending the sheep he brought him
to be the shepherd of his people Jacob,
of Israel his inheritance.
72 And David shepherded them with integrity
of heart;
with skillful hands he led them.

PSALM 79

A psalm of Asaph.

1 O God, the nations have invaded your
inheritance;
they have defiled your holy temple,
they have reduced Jerusalem to rubble.

Skill and Competence: Eleven Keys to Excellence

Psalm 78:72

David's leadership succeeded through a two-sided coin: His hands and his heart, or outward skill and inward integrity. Every great spiritual leader must have this combination. David's excellent leadership combined both heart and art. To have one without the other leads to failure.

Consider the following list of 11 keys to excellence, aimed at helping us to develop our leadership skills today. Leaders must . . .

- **first value excellence**
- **not settle for average**
- **pay attention to detail**
- **remain committed to what really matters**
- **display integrity and sound ethics**
- **show genuine respect for others**
- **go the second mile**
- **demonstrate consistency**
- **never stop improving**
- **always give 100%**
- **make excellence a lifestyle**

2 They have left the dead bodies of your
servants
as food for the birds of the sky,
the flesh of your own people for the
animals of the wild.
3 They have poured out blood like water
all around Jerusalem,
and there is no one to bury the dead.
4 We are objects of contempt to our neighbors,
of scorn and derision to those around us.

5 How long, Lord? Will you be angry forever?
How long will your jealousy burn like fire?
6 Pour out your wrath on the nations
that do not acknowledge you,
on the kingdoms
that do not call on your name;
7 for they have devoured Jacob
and devastated his homeland.

8 Do not hold against us the sins of past
generations;
may your mercy come quickly to meet us,
for we are in desperate need.

⁹ Help us, God our Savior,
  for the glory of your name;
deliver us and forgive our sins
  for your name's sake.
¹⁰ Why should the nations say,
  "Where is their God?"

Before our eyes, make known among the
    nations
  that you avenge the outpoured blood of
    your servants.
¹¹ May the groans of the prisoners come before
    you;
  with your strong arm preserve those
    condemned to die.
¹² Pay back into the laps of our neighbors seven
    times
  the contempt they have hurled at you, Lord.
¹³ Then we your people, the sheep of your
    pasture,
  will praise you forever;
from generation to generation
  we will proclaim your praise.

PSALM 80 [a]

For the director of music. To the tune of "The Lilies of
the Covenant." Of Asaph. A psalm.

¹ Hear us, Shepherd of Israel,
  you who lead Joseph like a flock.
You who sit enthroned between the
    cherubim,
  shine forth ²before Ephraim, Benjamin
    and Manasseh.
Awaken your might;
  come and save us.

³ Restore us, O God;
  make your face shine on us,
  that we may be saved.

⁴ How long, LORD God Almighty,
  will your anger smolder
  against the prayers of your people?
⁵ You have fed them with the bread of tears;
  you have made them drink tears by the
    bowlful.
⁶ You have made us an object of derision [b] to
    our neighbors,
  and our enemies mock us.

⁷ Restore us, God Almighty;
  make your face shine on us,
  that we may be saved.

⁸ You transplanted a vine from Egypt;
  you drove out the nations and planted it.

⁹ You cleared the ground for it,
  and it took root and filled the land.
¹⁰ The mountains were covered with its shade,
  the mighty cedars with its branches.
¹¹ Its branches reached as far as the Sea, [c]
  its shoots as far as the River. [d]

¹² Why have you broken down its walls
  so that all who pass by pick its grapes?
¹³ Boars from the forest ravage it,
  and insects from the fields feed on it.
¹⁴ Return to us, God Almighty!
  Look down from heaven and see!
Watch over this vine,
¹⁵   the root your right hand has planted,
  the son [e] you have raised up for yourself.

¹⁶ Your vine is cut down, it is burned with
    fire;
  at your rebuke your people perish.
¹⁷ Let your hand rest on the man at your right
    hand,
  the son of man you have raised up for
    yourself.
¹⁸ Then we will not turn away from you;
  revive us, and we will call on your name.

¹⁹ Restore us, LORD God Almighty;
  make your face shine on us,
  that we may be saved.

PSALM 81 [f]

For the director of music. According to gittith. [g]
Of Asaph.

¹ Sing for joy to God our strength;
  shout aloud to the God of Jacob!
² Begin the music, strike the timbrel,
  play the melodious harp and lyre.

³ Sound the ram's horn at the New Moon,
  and when the moon is full, on the day of
    our festival;
⁴ this is a decree for Israel,
  an ordinance of the God of Jacob.
⁵ When God went out against Egypt,
  he established it as a statute for Joseph.

I heard an unknown voice say:

⁶ "I removed the burden from their shoulders;
  their hands were set free from the basket.

---

[a] In Hebrew texts 80:1-19 is numbered 80:2-20.   [b] 6 Probable
reading of the original Hebrew text; Masoretic Text contention
[c] 11 Probably the Mediterranean   [d] 11 That is, the
Euphrates   [e] 15 Or branch   [f] In Hebrew texts 81:1-16 is
numbered 81:2-17.   [g] Title: Probably a musical term

7 In your distress you called and I rescued you,
  I answered you out of a thundercloud;
  I tested you at the waters of Meribah.[a]
8 Hear me, my people, and I will warn you —
  if you would only listen to me, Israel!
9 You shall have no foreign god among you;
  you shall not worship any god other
    than me.
10 I am the Lord your God,
  who brought you up out of Egypt.
  Open wide your mouth and I will fill it.

11 "But my people would not listen to me;
  Israel would not submit to me.
12 So I gave them over to their stubborn hearts
  to follow their own devices.

13 "If my people would only listen to me,
  if Israel would only follow my ways,
14 how quickly I would subdue their enemies
  and turn my hand against their foes!
15 Those who hate the Lord would cringe
    before him,
  and their punishment would last forever.
16 But you would be fed with the finest of wheat;
  with honey from the rock I would satisfy
    you."

PSALM 82

A psalm of Asaph.

1 God presides in the great assembly;
  he renders judgment among the "gods":

2 "How long will you[b] defend the unjust
  and show partiality to the wicked?[a]

3 Defend the weak and the fatherless;
  uphold the cause of the poor and the
    oppressed.
4 Rescue the weak and the needy;
  deliver them from the hand of the
    wicked.

5 "The 'gods' know nothing, they understand
    nothing.
  They walk about in darkness;
  all the foundations of the earth are
    shaken.

6 "I said, 'You are "gods";
  you are all sons of the Most High.'
7 But you will die like mere mortals;
  you will fall like every other ruler."

8 Rise up, O God, judge the earth,
  for all the nations are your
    inheritance.

PSALM 83[c]

A song. A psalm of Asaph.

1 O God, do not remain silent;
  do not turn a deaf ear,
  do not stand aloof, O God.
2 See how your enemies growl,
  how your foes rear their heads.
3 With cunning they conspire against your
    people;
  they plot against those you cherish.

---

a 7,2 The Hebrew has *Selah* (a word of uncertain meaning) here.   b 2 The Hebrew is plural.   c In Hebrew texts 83:1-18 is numbered 83:2-19.

The Law of Influence: Measuring Your Leadership

Psalm 82:1–8

Many passages in Scripture declare God to be the Ultimate Judge (Pss. 7:8; 9:8; 10:18; 26:1; Pr 31:9; Isa 1:17; etc.). A judge brings justice to bear, punishing the criminal and rewarding the righteous.

But before the final day of judgment, God uses his leaders to vindicate his people and urge the wicked to repent. God has entrusted his leaders with the gospel of Jesus Christ, through which men can be delivered from final judgment. Listen to the Lord's promise to his people: "I will restore your leaders as in days of old" (Isa 1:26). Spiritual leaders are to take this task seriously and to use their influence to promote justice. This differentiates true judges from false judges:

True Judges	False Judges
1. Chosen and appointed by God (Dt 16:18)	1. Rule by their own power (Jer 5:30–31)
2. Responsible for certain areas (2Ch 19:5)	2. Lead others astray (Mic 3:5)
3. Righteous and trustworthy (Dt 16:18)	3. Irresponsible, selfish (Mic 3:1–2)

4 "Come," they say, "let us destroy them as a
        nation,
    so that Israel's name is remembered no
        more."

5 With one mind they plot together;
    they form an alliance against you —
6 the tents of Edom and the Ishmaelites,
    of Moab and the Hagrites,
7 Byblos, Ammon and Amalek,
    Philistia, with the people of Tyre.
8 Even Assyria has joined them
    to reinforce Lot's descendants.[a]

9 Do to them as you did to Midian,
    as you did to Sisera and Jabin at the river
        Kishon,
10 who perished at Endor
    and became like dung on the ground.
11 Make their nobles like Oreb and Zeeb,
    all their princes like Zebah and Zalmunna,
12 who said, "Let us take possession
    of the pasturelands of God."

13 Make them like tumbleweed, my God,
    like chaff before the wind.
14 As fire consumes the forest
    or a flame sets the mountains ablaze,
15 so pursue them with your tempest
    and terrify them with your storm.
16 Cover their faces with shame, LORD,
    so that they will seek your name.

17 May they ever be ashamed and dismayed;
    may they perish in disgrace.
18 Let them know that you, whose name is the
        LORD —
    that you alone are the Most High over all
        the earth.

PSALM 84[b]

For the director of music. According to gittith.[c]
Of the Sons of Korah. A psalm.

1 How lovely is your dwelling place,
    LORD Almighty!
2 My soul yearns, even faints,
    for the courts of the LORD;
my heart and my flesh cry out
    for the living God.
3 Even the sparrow has found a home,
    and the swallow a nest for herself,
    where she may have her young —
a place near your altar,
    LORD Almighty, my King and my God.
4 Blessed are those who dwell in your house;
    they are ever praising you.[d]

5 Blessed are those whose strength is in you,
    whose hearts are set on pilgrimage.
6 As they pass through the Valley of Baka,
    they make it a place of springs;
    the autumn rains also cover it with pools.[e]
7 They go from strength to strength,
    till each appears before God in Zion.

8 Hear my prayer, LORD God Almighty;
    listen to me, God of Jacob.
9 Look on our shield,[f] O God;
    look with favor on your anointed one.

10 Better is one day in your courts
    than a thousand elsewhere;
    I would rather be a doorkeeper in the house
        of my God
    than dwell in the tents of the wicked.
11 For the LORD God is a sun and shield;
    the LORD bestows favor and honor;
no good thing does he withhold
    from those whose walk is blameless.

12 LORD Almighty,
    blessed is the one who trusts in you.

PSALM 85[g]

For the director of music. Of the Sons of Korah.
A psalm.

1 You, LORD, showed favor to your land;
    you restored the fortunes of Jacob.
2 You forgave the iniquity of your people
    and covered all their sins.[a]
3 You set aside all your wrath
    and turned from your fierce anger.

4 Restore us again, God our Savior,
    and put away your displeasure toward us.
5 Will you be angry with us forever?
    Will you prolong your anger through all
        generations?
6 Will you not revive us again,
    that your people may rejoice in you?
7 Show us your unfailing love, LORD,
    and grant us your salvation.

8 I will listen to what God the LORD says;
    he promises peace to his people, his
        faithful servants —
    but let them not turn to folly.

---

[a] 8,2 The Hebrew has Selah (a word of uncertain meaning)
here.   [b] In Hebrew texts 84:1-12 is numbered 84:2-13.
[c] Title: Probably a musical term   [d] 4 The Hebrew has Selah
(a word of uncertain meaning) here and at the end of verse 8.
[e] 6 Or blessings   [f] 9 Or sovereign   [g] In Hebrew texts 85:1-
13 is numbered 85:2-14.

⁹Surely his salvation is near those who fear
    him,
    that his glory may dwell in our land.

¹⁰Love and faithfulness meet together;
    righteousness and peace kiss each other.
¹¹Faithfulness springs forth from the earth,
    and righteousness looks down from
    heaven.
¹²The LORD will indeed give what is good,
    and our land will yield its harvest.
¹³Righteousness goes before him
    and prepares the way for his steps.

PSALM 86

A prayer of David.

¹Hear me, LORD, and answer me,
    for I am poor and needy.
²Guard my life, for I am faithful to you;
    save your servant who trusts in you.
    You are my God; ³have mercy on me, Lord,
    for I call to you all day long.
⁴Bring joy to your servant, Lord,
    for I put my trust in you.

⁵You, Lord, are forgiving and good,
    abounding in love to all who call to you.
⁶Hear my prayer, LORD;
    listen to my cry for mercy.
⁷When I am in distress, I call to you,
    because you answer me.

⁸Among the gods there is none like you, Lord;
    no deeds can compare with yours.
⁹All the nations you have made
    will come and worship before you, Lord;
    they will bring glory to your name.
¹⁰For you are great and do marvelous deeds;
    you alone are God.

¹¹Teach me your way, LORD,
    that I may rely on your faithfulness;
    give me an undivided heart,
    that I may fear your name.
¹²I will praise you, Lord my God, with all my
    heart;
    I will glorify your name forever.
¹³For great is your love toward me;
    you have delivered me from the depths,
    from the realm of the dead.

¹⁴Arrogant foes are attacking me, O God;
    ruthless people are trying to kill me—
    they have no regard for you.
¹⁵But you, Lord, are a compassionate and
    gracious God,

slow to anger, abounding in love and
    faithfulness.
¹⁶Turn to me and have mercy on me;
    show your strength in behalf of your
    servant;
    save me, because I serve you
    just as my mother did.
¹⁷Give me a sign of your goodness,
    that my enemies may see it and be put to
    shame,
    for you, LORD, have helped me and
    comforted me.

PSALM 87

Of the Sons of Korah. A psalm. A song.

¹He has founded his city on the holy
    mountain.
²The LORD loves the gates of Zion
    more than all the other dwellings of Jacob.

³Glorious things are said of you,
    city of God:ᵃ
⁴"I will record Rahabᵇ and Babylon
    among those who acknowledge me—
    Philistia too, and Tyre, along with Cushᶜ—
    and will say, 'This one was born in
    Zion.' "ᵈ
⁵Indeed, of Zion it will be said,
    "This one and that one were born in her,
    and the Most High himself will establish
    her."
⁶The LORD will write in the register of the
    peoples:
    "This one was born in Zion."

⁷As they make music they will sing,
    "All my fountains are in you."

PSALM 88ᵉ

A song. A psalm of the Sons of Korah. For the director
of music. According to *mahalath leannoth.*ᶠ
A *maskil*ᵍ of Heman the Ezrahite.

¹LORD, you are the God who saves me;
    day and night I cry out to you.
²May my prayer come before you;
    turn your ear to my cry.

ᵃ 3 The Hebrew has *Selah* (a word of uncertain meaning) here
and at the end of verse 6.   ᵇ 4 A poetic name for Egypt
ᶜ 4 That is, the upper Nile region   ᵈ 4 Or "*I will record
concerning those who acknowledge me:* / '*This one was born in
Zion.*' / *Hear this, Rahab and Babylon,* / *and you too, Philistia,
Tyre and Cush.*"   ᵉ In Hebrew texts 88:1-18 is numbered 88:2-
19.   ᶠ Title: Possibly a tune, "The Suffering of Affliction"
ᵍ Title: Probably a literary or musical term

³I am overwhelmed with troubles
  and my life draws near to death.
⁴I am counted among those who go down to
    the pit;
  I am like one without strength.
⁵I am set apart with the dead,
  like the slain who lie in the grave,
whom you remember no more,
  who are cut off from your care.

⁶You have put me in the lowest pit,
  in the darkest depths.
⁷Your wrath lies heavily on me;
  you have overwhelmed me with all your
    waves.ᵃ
⁸You have taken from me my closest friends
  and have made me repulsive to them.
I am confined and cannot escape;
⁹   my eyes are dim with grief.

I call to you, Lord, every day;
  I spread out my hands to you.
¹⁰Do you show your wonders to the dead?
  Do their spirits rise up and praise you?
¹¹Is your love declared in the grave,
  your faithfulness in Destructionᵇ?
¹²Are your wonders known in the place of
    darkness,
  or your righteous deeds in the land of
    oblivion?

¹³But I cry to you for help, Lord;
  in the morning my prayer comes before
    you.
¹⁴Why, Lord, do you reject me
  and hide your face from me?

¹⁵From my youth I have suffered and been
    close to death;
  I have borne your terrors and am in
    despair.
¹⁶Your wrath has swept over me;
  your terrors have destroyed me.
¹⁷All day long they surround me like a flood;
  they have completely engulfed me.
¹⁸You have taken from me friend and
    neighbor —
  darkness is my closest friend.

PSALM 89ᶜ

A *maskil*ᵈ of Ethan the Ezrahite.

¹I will sing of the Lord's great love forever;
  with my mouth I will make your
    faithfulness known
    through all generations.

²I will declare that your love stands firm
    forever,
  that you have established your
    faithfulness in heaven itself.
³You said, "I have made a covenant with my
    chosen one,
  I have sworn to David my servant,
⁴'I will establish your line forever
  and make your throne firm through all
    generations.'"ᵉ

⁵The heavens praise your wonders, Lord,
  your faithfulness too, in the assembly of
    the holy ones.
⁶For who in the skies above can compare with
    the Lord?
  Who is like the Lord among the heavenly
    beings?
⁷In the council of the holy ones God is greatly
    feared;
  he is more awesome than all who
    surround him.
⁸Who is like you, Lord God Almighty?
  You, Lord, are mighty, and your
    faithfulness surrounds you.

⁹You rule over the surging sea;
  when its waves mount up, you still them.
¹⁰You crushed Rahab like one of the slain;
  with your strong arm you scattered your
    enemies.
¹¹The heavens are yours, and yours also the
    earth;
  you founded the world and all that is in it.
¹²You created the north and the south;
  Tabor and Hermon sing for joy at your
    name.
¹³Your arm is endowed with power;
  your hand is strong, your right hand
    exalted.

¹⁴Righteousness and justice are the foundation
    of your throne;
  love and faithfulness go before you.
¹⁵Blessed are those who have learned to
    acclaim you,
  who walk in the light of your presence,
    Lord.
¹⁶They rejoice in your name all day long;
  they celebrate your righteousness.

ᵃ 7 The Hebrew has *Selah* (a word of uncertain meaning) here
and at the end of verse 10.   ᵇ 11 Hebrew *Abaddon*   ᶜ In
Hebrew texts 89:1-52 is numbered 89:2-53.   ᵈ Title: Probably
a literary or musical term   ᵉ 4 The Hebrew has *Selah* (a word
of uncertain meaning) here and at the end of verses 37, 45
and 48.

¹⁷ For you are their glory and strength,
  and by your favor you exalt our horn.ᵃ
¹⁸ Indeed, our shieldᵇ belongs to the LORD,
  our king to the Holy One of Israel.

¹⁹ Once you spoke in a vision,
  to your faithful people you said:
"I have bestowed strength on a warrior;
  I have raised up a young man from among
    the people.
²⁰ I have found David my servant;
  with my sacred oil I have anointed him.
²¹ My hand will sustain him;
  surely my arm will strengthen him.
²² The enemy will not get the better of him;
  the wicked will not oppress him.
²³ I will crush his foes before him
  and strike down his adversaries.
²⁴ My faithful love will be with him,
  and through my name his hornᶜ will be
    exalted.
²⁵ I will set his hand over the sea,
  his right hand over the rivers.
²⁶ He will call out to me, 'You are my Father,
  my God, the Rock my Savior.'
²⁷ And I will appoint him to be my firstborn,
  the most exalted of the kings of the earth.
²⁸ I will maintain my love to him forever,
  and my covenant with him will never fail.
²⁹ I will establish his line forever,
  his throne as long as the heavens endure.

³⁰ "If his sons forsake my law
  and do not follow my statutes,
³¹ if they violate my decrees
  and fail to keep my commands,
³² I will punish their sin with the rod,
  their iniquity with flogging;
³³ but I will not take my love from him,
  nor will I ever betray my faithfulness.
³⁴ I will not violate my covenant
  or alter what my lips have uttered.
³⁵ Once for all, I have sworn by my holiness—
  and I will not lie to David—
³⁶ that his line will continue forever
  and his throne endure before me like the
    sun;
³⁷ it will be established forever like the moon,
  the faithful witness in the sky."

³⁸ But you have rejected, you have spurned,
  you have been very angry with your
    anointed one.
³⁹ You have renounced the covenant with your
    servant
  and have defiled his crown in the dust.

The Fruit That Comes from God's Anointing

Psalm 89:19–29

All leaders should seek the anointing of God. They need to be empowered by the hand of God, and show evidence of this by leading in a way far superior to what they could have achieved on their own.

What does God promise leaders anointed by his Spirit?

1. **God's help (v. 19)**
2. **Being called God's servant (v. 20)**
3. **God's strength (v. 21)**
4. **God's hand with them (v. 21)**
5. **Freedom from affliction (v. 22)**
6. **Freedom from deception (v. 22)**
7. **Victory over the enemy (v. 23)**
8. **God's faithfulness and kindness (v. 24)**
9. **Influence in the world (v. 25)**
10. **God's saving power (v. 26)**
11. **A Father-son relationship (v. 26)**
12. **Exaltation and authority (vv. 27–29)**
13. **Partaking of the covenant (v. 28)**
14. **Promise of descendants (v. 29)**

⁴⁰ You have broken through all his walls
  and reduced his strongholds to ruins.
⁴¹ All who pass by have plundered him;
  he has become the scorn of his
    neighbors.
⁴² You have exalted the right hand of his foes;
  you have made all his enemies rejoice.
⁴³ Indeed, you have turned back the edge of his
    sword
  and have not supported him in battle.
⁴⁴ You have put an end to his splendor
  and cast his throne to the ground.
⁴⁵ You have cut short the days of his youth;
  you have covered him with a mantle of
    shame.

ᵃ 17 *Horn* here symbolizes strong one. ᵇ 18 Or *sovereign*
ᶜ 24 *Horn* here symbolizes strength.

46 How long, Lord? Will you hide yourself
      forever?
   How long will your wrath burn like fire?
47 Remember how fleeting is my life.
   For what futility you have created all
      humanity!
48 Who can live and not see death,
   or who can escape the power of the grave?
49 Lord, where is your former great love,
   which in your faithfulness you swore to
      David?
50 Remember, Lord, how your servant has*a*
      been mocked,
   how I bear in my heart the taunts of all
      the nations,
51 the taunts with which your enemies, Lord,
   have mocked,
   with which they have mocked every step
      of your anointed one.

52 Praise be to the Lord forever!
   Amen and Amen.

BOOK IV

Psalms 90 – 106

PSALM 90

A prayer of Moses the man of God.

1 Lord, you have been our dwelling place
   throughout all generations.
2 Before the mountains were born
   or you brought forth the whole world,
   from everlasting to everlasting you are
      God.

3 You turn people back to dust,
   saying, "Return to dust, you mortals."
4 A thousand years in your sight
   are like a day that has just gone by,
   or like a watch in the night.
5 Yet you sweep people away in the sleep of
      death —
   they are like the new grass of the morning:
6 In the morning it springs up new,
   but by evening it is dry and withered.

7 We are consumed by your anger
   and terrified by your indignation.
8 You have set our iniquities before you,
   our secret sins in the light of your
      presence.
9 All our days pass away under your wrath;
   we finish our years with a moan.

10 Our days may come to seventy years,
   or eighty, if our strength endures;
   yet the best of them are but trouble and
      sorrow,
   for they quickly pass, and we fly away.
11 If only we knew the power of your anger!
   Your wrath is as great as the fear that is
      your due.
12 Teach us to number our days,
   that we may gain a heart of wisdom.
13 Relent, Lord! How long will it be?
   Have compassion on your servants.
14 Satisfy us in the morning with your
      unfailing love,
   that we may sing for joy and be glad all
      our days.
15 Make us glad for as many days as you have
      afflicted us,
   for as many years as we have seen trouble.
16 May your deeds be shown to your servants,
   your splendor to their children.

17 May the favor*b* of the Lord our God rest on us;
   establish the work of our hands for us —
   yes, establish the work of our hands.

Leaders Manage Their Time and Do More with Less

Psalm 90:12, 17

Moses had seen a generation squander 40 years in the wilderness. He believed that if leaders could only gain a keen sense of the swift passage of time, and if they would work for something significant, they could die with a great sense of satisfaction. Leaders don't kill time, they execute it.

PSALM 91

1 Whoever dwells in the shelter of the Most High
   will rest in the shadow of the Almighty.*c*
2 I will say of the Lord, "He is my refuge and
      my fortress,
   my God, in whom I trust."

3 Surely he will save you
   from the fowler's snare
   and from the deadly pestilence.

---

a 50 Or *your servants have*   *b 17* Or *beauty*   *c 1* Hebrew
Shaddai

⁴He will cover you with his feathers,
  and under his wings you will find refuge;
  his faithfulness will be your shield and
    rampart.
⁵You will not fear the terror of night,
  nor the arrow that flies by day,
⁶nor the pestilence that stalks in the darkness,
  nor the plague that destroys at midday.
⁷A thousand may fall at your side,
  ten thousand at your right hand,
  but it will not come near you.
⁸You will only observe with your eyes
  and see the punishment of the wicked.

⁹If you say, "The LORD is my refuge,"
  and you make the Most High your
    dwelling,
¹⁰no harm will overtake you,
  no disaster will come near your tent.
¹¹For he will command his angels concerning
    you
  to guard you in all your ways;
¹²they will lift you up in their hands,
  so that you will not strike your foot
    against a stone.
¹³You will tread on the lion and the cobra;
  you will trample the great lion and the
    serpent.

¹⁴"Because he[a] loves me," says the LORD, "I
    will rescue him;
  I will protect him, for he acknowledges
    my name.
¹⁵He will call on me, and I will answer him;
  I will be with him in trouble,
  I will deliver him and honor him.

¹⁶With long life I will satisfy him
  and show him my salvation."

PSALM 92[b]

A psalm. A song. For the Sabbath day.

¹It is good to praise the LORD
  and make music to your name, O Most
    High,
²proclaiming your love in the morning
  and your faithfulness at night,
³to the music of the ten-stringed lyre
  and the melody of the harp.

⁴For you make me glad by your deeds,
    LORD;
  I sing for joy at what your hands have
    done.
⁵How great are your works, LORD,
  how profound your thoughts!
⁶Senseless people do not know,
  fools do not understand,
⁷that though the wicked spring up like grass
  and all evildoers flourish,
  they will be destroyed forever.

⁸But you, LORD, are forever exalted.

⁹For surely your enemies, LORD,
  surely your enemies will perish;
  all evildoers will be scattered.
¹⁰You have exalted my horn[c] like that of a
    wild ox;
  fine oils have been poured on me.

---

[a] 14 That is, probably the king   [b] In Hebrew texts 92:1-15 is numbered 92:2-16.   [c] 10 *Horn* here symbolizes strength.

The Leader's Refuge

Psalm 91:1–16

We discover one of the most comforting chapters in the Bible in Psalm 91. It describes the security believers can enjoy through faith in God. Leaders can especially benefit from this set of promises. Study them and enjoy them:

Promise	Leader's Benefit
1. **God's presence (vv. 1–2)**	1. **It doesn't have to be lonely at the top.**
2. **God's protection (vv. 3–4)**	2. **As you take initiative and risks, God keeps you safe.**
3. **God's peace (vv. 5–6)**	3. **You don't have to feel insecure in unknown territory.**
4. **God's perspective (vv. 7–10)**	4. **God gives an eternal view of life that keeps you steady.**
5. **God's provision (vv. 11–13)**	5. **Regardless of your needs, God meets them.**
6. **God's power (vv. 14–16)**	6. **In adversity, God delivers and helps you reach your goal.**

[11] My eyes have seen the defeat of my
  adversaries;
  my ears have heard the rout of my wicked
  foes.

[12] The righteous will flourish like a palm tree,
  they will grow like a cedar of Lebanon;
[13] planted in the house of the Lord,
  they will flourish in the courts of our God.
[14] They will still bear fruit in old age,
  they will stay fresh and green,
[15] proclaiming, "The Lord is upright;
  he is my Rock, and there is no wickedness
  in him."

PSALM 93

[1] The Lord reigns, he is robed in majesty;
  the Lord is robed in majesty and armed
  with strength;
  indeed, the world is established, firm and
  secure.
[2] Your throne was established long ago;
  you are from all eternity.

[3] The seas have lifted up, Lord,
  the seas have lifted up their voice;
  the seas have lifted up their pounding
  waves.
[4] Mightier than the thunder of the great waters,
  mightier than the breakers of the sea—
  the Lord on high is mighty.

[5] Your statutes, Lord, stand firm;
  holiness adorns your house
  for endless days.

PSALM 94

[1] The Lord is a God who avenges.
  O God who avenges, shine forth.
[2] Rise up, Judge of the earth;
  pay back to the proud what they deserve.
[3] How long, Lord, will the wicked,
  how long will the wicked be jubilant?

[4] They pour out arrogant words;
  all the evildoers are full of boasting.
[5] They crush your people, Lord;
  they oppress your inheritance.
[6] They slay the widow and the foreigner;
  they murder the fatherless.
[7] They say, "The Lord does not see;
  the God of Jacob takes no notice."

[8] Take notice, you senseless ones among the
  people;
  you fools, when will you become wise?

[9] Does he who fashioned the ear not hear?
  Does he who formed the eye not see?
[10] Does he who disciplines nations not
  punish?
  Does he who teaches mankind lack
  knowledge?
[11] The Lord knows all human plans;
  he knows that they are futile.

[12] Blessed is the one you discipline, Lord,
  the one you teach from your law;
[13] you grant them relief from days of trouble,
  till a pit is dug for the wicked.
[14] For the Lord will not reject his people;
  he will never forsake his inheritance.
[15] Judgment will again be founded on
  righteousness,
  and all the upright in heart will follow it.

[16] Who will rise up for me against the wicked?
  Who will take a stand for me against
  evildoers?
[17] Unless the Lord had given me help,
  I would soon have dwelt in the silence of
  death.
[18] When I said, "My foot is slipping,"
  your unfailing love, Lord, supported me.
[19] When anxiety was great within me,
  your consolation brought me joy.

[20] Can a corrupt throne be allied with you—
  a throne that brings on misery by its
  decrees?
[21] The wicked band together against the
  righteous
  and condemn the innocent to death.
[22] But the Lord has become my fortress,
  and my God the rock in whom I take
  refuge.
[23] He will repay them for their sins
  and destroy them for their wickedness;
  the Lord our God will destroy them.

PSALM 95

[1] Come, let us sing for joy to the Lord;
  let us shout aloud to the Rock of our
  salvation.
[2] Let us come before him with thanksgiving
  and extol him with music and song.

[3] For the Lord is the great God,
  the great King above all gods.
[4] In his hand are the depths of the earth,
  and the mountain peaks belong to him.
[5] The sea is his, for he made it,
  and his hands formed the dry land.

⁶Come, let us bow down in worship,
  let us kneel before the LORD our Maker;
⁷for he is our God
  and we are the people of his pasture,
    the flock under his care.

Today, if only you would hear his voice,
⁸"Do not harden your hearts as you did at
    Meribah,ᵃ
  as you did that day at Massahᵇ in the
    wilderness,
⁹where your ancestors tested me;
  they tried me, though they had seen what
    I did.
¹⁰For forty years I was angry with that
    generation;
  I said, 'They are a people whose hearts go
    astray,
  and they have not known my ways.'
¹¹So I declared on oath in my anger,
  'They shall never enter my rest.'"

PSALM 96

¹Sing to the LORD a new song;
  sing to the LORD, all the earth.
²Sing to the LORD, praise his name;
  proclaim his salvation day after day.
³Declare his glory among the nations,
  his marvelous deeds among all peoples.

⁴For great is the LORD and most worthy of
    praise;
  he is to be feared above all gods.
⁵For all the gods of the nations are idols,
  but the LORD made the heavens.
⁶Splendor and majesty are before him;
  strength and glory are in his sanctuary.

⁷Ascribe to the LORD, all you families of nations,
  ascribe to the LORD glory and strength.
⁸Ascribe to the LORD the glory due his name;
  bring an offering and come into his
    courts.
⁹Worship the LORD in the splendor of hisᶜ
    holiness;
  tremble before him, all the earth.
¹⁰Say among the nations, "The LORD reigns."
  The world is firmly established, it cannot
    be moved;
  he will judge the peoples with equity.

¹¹Let the heavens rejoice, let the earth be glad;
  let the sea resound, and all that is in it.
¹²Let the fields be jubilant, and everything in
    them;
  let all the trees of the forest sing for joy.

¹³Let all creation rejoice before the LORD, for
    he comes,
  he comes to judge the earth.
He will judge the world in righteousness
  and the peoples in his faithfulness.

PSALM 97

¹The LORD reigns, let the earth be glad;
  let the distant shores rejoice.
²Clouds and thick darkness surround him;
  righteousness and justice are the
    foundation of his throne.
³Fire goes before him
  and consumes his foes on every side.
⁴His lightning lights up the world;
  the earth sees and trembles.
⁵The mountains melt like wax before the
    LORD,
  before the Lord of all the earth.
⁶The heavens proclaim his righteousness,
  and all peoples see his glory.

⁷All who worship images are put to shame,
  those who boast in idols—
  worship him, all you gods!

⁸Zion hears and rejoices
  and the villages of Judah are glad
  because of your judgments, LORD.
⁹For you, LORD, are the Most High over all
    the earth;
  you are exalted far above all gods.
¹⁰Let those who love the LORD hate evil,
  for he guards the lives of his faithful ones
  and delivers them from the hand of the
    wicked.
¹¹Light shinesᵈ on the righteous
  and joy on the upright in heart.
¹²Rejoice in the LORD, you who are righteous,
  and praise his holy name.

PSALM 98

A psalm.

¹Sing to the LORD a new song,
  for he has done marvelous things;
his right hand and his holy arm
  have worked salvation for him.
²The LORD has made his salvation known
  and revealed his righteousness to the
    nations.

ᵃ 8 Meribah means quarreling.   ᵇ 8 Massah means testing.
ᶜ 9 Or LORD with the splendor of   ᵈ 11 One Hebrew
manuscript and ancient versions (see also 112:4); most Hebrew
manuscripts Light is sown

³ He has remembered his love
   and his faithfulness to Israel;
all the ends of the earth have seen
   the salvation of our God.

⁴ Shout for joy to the LORD, all the earth,
   burst into jubilant song with music;
⁵ make music to the LORD with the harp,
   with the harp and the sound of singing,
⁶ with trumpets and the blast of the ram's
      horn —
   shout for joy before the LORD, the King.

⁷ Let the sea resound, and everything in it,
   the world, and all who live in it.
⁸ Let the rivers clap their hands,
   let the mountains sing together for joy;
⁹ let them sing before the LORD,
   for he comes to judge the earth.
He will judge the world in righteousness
   and the peoples with equity.

PSALM 99

¹ The LORD reigns,
   let the nations tremble;
he sits enthroned between the cherubim,
   let the earth shake.
² Great is the LORD in Zion;
   he is exalted over all the nations.
³ Let them praise your great and awesome
      name —
   he is holy.

⁴ The King is mighty, he loves justice —
   you have established equity;
in Jacob you have done
   what is just and right.
⁵ Exalt the LORD our God
   and worship at his footstool;
   he is holy.

⁶ Moses and Aaron were among his priests,
   Samuel was among those who called on
      his name;
they called on the LORD
   and he answered them.
⁷ He spoke to them from the pillar of cloud;
   they kept his statutes and the decrees he
      gave them.

⁸ LORD our God,
   you answered them;
you were to Israel a forgiving God,
   though you punished their misdeeds.ᵃ
⁹ Exalt the LORD our God
   and worship at his holy mountain,
   for the LORD our God is holy.

PSALM 100

A psalm. For giving grateful praise.

¹ Shout for joy to the LORD, all the earth.
²   Worship the LORD with gladness;
   come before him with joyful songs.
³ Know that the LORD is God.
   It is he who made us, and we are his ᵇ;
   we are his people, the sheep of his pasture.

⁴ Enter his gates with thanksgiving
   and his courts with praise;
   give thanks to him and praise his name.
⁵ For the LORD is good and his love endures
      forever;
   his faithfulness continues through all
      generations.

PSALM 101

Of David. A psalm.

¹ I will sing of your love and justice;
   to you, LORD, I will sing praise.
² I will be careful to lead a blameless life —
   when will you come to me?

I will conduct the affairs of my house
   with a blameless heart.
³ I will not look with approval
   on anything that is vile.

I hate what faithless people do;
   I will have no part in it.
⁴ The perverse of heart shall be far from me;
   I will have nothing to do with what is evil.

⁵ Whoever slanders their neighbor in secret,
   I will put to silence;
whoever has haughty eyes and a proud heart,
   I will not tolerate.

⁶ My eyes will be on the faithful in the land,
   that they may dwell with me;
the one whose walk is blameless
   will minister to me.

⁷ No one who practices deceit
   will dwell in my house;
no one who speaks falsely
   will stand in my presence.

⁸ Every morning I will put to silence
   all the wicked in the land;
I will cut off every evildoer
   from the city of the LORD.

ᵃ 8 Or *God, / an avenger of the wrongs done to them*   ᵇ 3 Or
and not we ourselves

PSALM 102 [a]

*A prayer of an afflicted person who has grown weak
and pours out a lament before the LORD.*

[1] Hear my prayer, LORD;
  let my cry for help come to you.
[2] Do not hide your face from me
  when I am in distress.
Turn your ear to me;
  when I call, answer me quickly.

[3] For my days vanish like smoke;
  my bones burn like glowing embers.
[4] My heart is blighted and withered like
  grass;
  I forget to eat my food.
[5] In my distress I groan aloud
  and am reduced to skin and bones.
[6] I am like a desert owl,
  like an owl among the ruins.
[7] I lie awake; I have become
  like a bird alone on a roof.
[8] All day long my enemies taunt me;
  those who rail against me use my name as
  a curse.
[9] For I eat ashes as my food
  and mingle my drink with tears
[10] because of your great wrath,
  for you have taken me up and thrown me
  aside.
[11] My days are like the evening shadow;
  I wither away like grass.

[12] But you, LORD, sit enthroned forever;
  your renown endures through all
  generations.
[13] You will arise and have compassion on Zion,
  for it is time to show favor to her;
  the appointed time has come.
[14] For her stones are dear to your servants;
  her very dust moves them to pity.
[15] The nations will fear the name of the LORD,
  all the kings of the earth will revere your
  glory.
[16] For the LORD will rebuild Zion
  and appear in his glory.
[17] He will respond to the prayer of the
  destitute;
  he will not despise their plea.

[18] Let this be written for a future generation,
  that a people not yet created may praise
  the LORD:
[19] "The LORD looked down from his sanctuary
  on high,
  from heaven he viewed the earth,

[20] to hear the groans of the prisoners
  and release those condemned to death."
[21] So the name of the LORD will be declared in
  Zion
  and his praise in Jerusalem
[22] when the peoples and the kingdoms
  assemble to worship the LORD.

[23] In the course of my life [b] he broke my
  strength;
  he cut short my days.
[24] So I said:
"Do not take me away, my God, in the midst
  of my days;
  your years go on through all generations.
[25] In the beginning you laid the foundations of
  the earth,
  and the heavens are the work of your
  hands.
[26] They will perish, but you remain;
  they will all wear out like a garment.
Like clothing you will change them
  and they will be discarded.
[27] But you remain the same,
  and your years will never end.
[28] The children of your servants will live in
  your presence;
  their descendants will be established
  before you."

PSALM 103

Of David.

[1] Praise the LORD, my soul;
  all my inmost being, praise his holy name.
[2] Praise the LORD, my soul,
  and forget not all his benefits—
[3] who forgives all your sins
  and heals all your diseases,
[4] who redeems your life from the pit
  and crowns you with love and
  compassion,
[5] who satisfies your desires with good things
  so that your youth is renewed like the
  eagle's.

[6] The LORD works righteousness
  and justice for all the oppressed.

[7] He made known his ways to Moses,
  his deeds to the people of Israel:
[8] The LORD is compassionate and gracious,
  slow to anger, abounding in love.

---

[a] In Hebrew texts 102:1-28 is numbered 102:2-29.   [b] 23 Or
By his power

⁹He will not always accuse,
    nor will he harbor his anger forever;
¹⁰he does not treat us as our sins deserve
    or repay us according to our iniquities.
¹¹For as high as the heavens are above the
        earth,
    so great is his love for those who fear him;
¹²as far as the east is from the west,
    so far has he removed our transgressions
        from us.

¹³As a father has compassion on his children,
    so the LORD has compassion on those who
        fear him;
¹⁴for he knows how we are formed,
    he remembers that we are dust.
¹⁵The life of mortals is like grass,
    they flourish like a flower of the field;
¹⁶the wind blows over it and it is gone,
    and its place remembers it no more.
¹⁷But from everlasting to everlasting
    the LORD's love is with those who fear him,
    and his righteousness with their children's
        children—
¹⁸with those who keep his covenant
    and remember to obey his precepts.

¹⁹The LORD has established his throne in
        heaven,
    and his kingdom rules over all.

²⁰Praise the LORD, you his angels,
    you mighty ones who do his bidding,
    who obey his word.
²¹Praise the LORD, all his heavenly hosts,
    you his servants who do his will.
²²Praise the LORD, all his works
    everywhere in his dominion.

Praise the LORD, my soul.

PSALM 104

¹Praise the LORD, my soul.

LORD my God, you are very great;
    you are clothed with splendor and majesty.

²The LORD wraps himself in light as with a
        garment;
    he stretches out the heavens like a tent
³   and lays the beams of his upper chambers
        on their waters.
He makes the clouds his chariot
    and rides on the wings of the wind.
⁴He makes winds his messengers,[a]
    flames of fire his servants.

⁵He set the earth on its foundations;
    it can never be moved.
⁶You covered it with the watery depths as
        with a garment;
    the waters stood above the mountains.
⁷But at your rebuke the waters fled,
    at the sound of your thunder they took to
        flight;
⁸they flowed over the mountains,
    they went down into the valleys,
    to the place you assigned for them.
⁹You set a boundary they cannot cross;
    never again will they cover the earth.

¹⁰He makes springs pour water into the
        ravines;
    it flows between the mountains.
¹¹They give water to all the beasts of the field;
    the wild donkeys quench their thirst.
¹²The birds of the sky nest by the waters;
    they sing among the branches.

---

[a] 4 Or *angels*

How God Raises a Leader

Psalm 103:1–5

The benefits of trusting the Lord listed in this text correspond to the stages God uses in building someone into a healthy, spiritual leader. The psalmist lists the benefits in this order:

1. **God pardons (v. 3)—Leaders must put their past shame or blame behind them.**

2. **God heals (v. 3)—They must become healthy and be liberated from old wounds.**

3. **God redeems (v. 4)—They see their abilities and personality redeemed.**

4. **God crowns (v. 4)—They are crowned with gifts and a place to serve.**

5. **God satisfies (v. 5)—They feel satisfied and fulfilled as they live out their role.**

Natural Leadership vs. Spiritual Leadership

Psalm 103:13–18

Good leaders remember where they came from and who their source is—a memory that separates spiritual leaders from natural leaders.

God leads his people more like a parent than a boss. He maintains a vision of the big picture and sticks with the right priorities. While natural leaders display obvious leadership abilities, they often drift from this style of leadership. They tend to lean more on their gifts than on God. Consider the differences between the two types of leaders:

Natural Leader	Spiritual Leader
1. Self-confident	1. Confident in God (Ps 56:9; 118:6)
2. Knows men	2. Knows God (Jn 10:14)
3. Makes own decisions	3. Seeks to find God's will (Ro 12:2; Eph 5:17)
4. Ambitious	4. Self-sacrificing (Mt 20:25–28; Lk 9:23)
5. Originates own methods	5. Finds and follows God's methods (Ps 40:8; 143:10)
6. Enjoys commanding others	6. Servant of all (Mk 10:42–45)
7. Motivated by self-interest	7. Motivated by love for God and man (1Jn 4:7–21)
8. Independent	8. God-dependent (Isa 42:1; Jn 15:5)
9. Gets power through personality	9. Empowered by the Holy Spirit (Ac 1:8)
10. Cowboy driving the herd	10. Shepherd leading the flock (1Pe 5:2–3)

¹³ He waters the mountains from his upper
        chambers;
    the land is satisfied by the fruit of his work.
¹⁴ He makes grass grow for the cattle,
    and plants for people to cultivate—
    bringing forth food from the earth:
¹⁵ wine that gladdens human hearts,
    oil to make their faces shine,
    and bread that sustains their hearts.
¹⁶ The trees of the LORD are well watered,
    the cedars of Lebanon that he planted.

Leaders Are Stewards, Not Owners

Psalm 104:1–5

The earth belongs to the Lord, not to humankind. Therefore, leaders should never act as if they own the place. While we can feel confident of our mission, we must remember we are stewards, not owners. We simply manage what he has established, based on his values and vision.

¹⁷ There the birds make their nests;
    the stork has its home in the junipers.
¹⁸ The high mountains belong to the wild
        goats;
    the crags are a refuge for the hyrax.

¹⁹ He made the moon to mark the seasons,
    and the sun knows when to go down.
²⁰ You bring darkness, it becomes night,
    and all the beasts of the forest prowl.
²¹ The lions roar for their prey
    and seek their food from God.
²² The sun rises, and they steal away;
    they return and lie down in their dens.
²³ Then people go out to their work,
    to their labor until evening.

²⁴ How many are your works, LORD!
    In wisdom you made them all;
    the earth is full of your creatures.
²⁵ There is the sea, vast and spacious,
    teeming with creatures beyond
        number—
    living things both large and small.
²⁶ There the ships go to and fro,
    and Leviathan, which you formed to
        frolic there.

27 All creatures look to you
    to give them their food at the proper
       time.
28 When you give it to them,
    they gather it up;
 when you open your hand,
    they are satisfied with good things.
29 When you hide your face,
    they are terrified;
 when you take away their breath,
    they die and return to the dust.
30 When you send your Spirit,
    they are created,
    and you renew the face of the ground.

31 May the glory of the Lord endure forever;
    may the Lord rejoice in his works —
32 he who looks at the earth, and it trembles,
    who touches the mountains, and they
       smoke.

33 I will sing to the Lord all my life;
    I will sing praise to my God as long as I
       live.
34 May my meditation be pleasing to him,
    as I rejoice in the Lord.
35 But may sinners vanish from the earth
    and the wicked be no more.

   Praise the Lord, my soul.

   Praise the Lord.[a]

PSALM 105

1 Give praise to the Lord, proclaim his name;
    make known among the nations what he
       has done.
2 Sing to him, sing praise to him;
    tell of all his wonderful acts.
3 Glory in his holy name;
    let the hearts of those who seek the Lord
       rejoice.
4 Look to the Lord and his strength;
    seek his face always.

5 Remember the wonders he has done,
    his miracles, and the judgments he
       pronounced,
6 you his servants, the descendants of
       Abraham,
    his chosen ones, the children of Jacob.
7 He is the Lord our God;
    his judgments are in all the earth.

8 He remembers his covenant forever,
    the promise he made, for a thousand
       generations,

9 the covenant he made with Abraham,
    the oath he swore to Isaac.
10 He confirmed it to Jacob as a decree,
    to Israel as an everlasting covenant:
11 "To you I will give the land of Canaan
    as the portion you will inherit."

12 When they were but few in number,
    few indeed, and strangers in it,
13 they wandered from nation to nation,
    from one kingdom to another.
14 He allowed no one to oppress them;
    for their sake he rebuked kings:
15 "Do not touch my anointed ones;
    do my prophets no harm."

16 He called down famine on the land
    and destroyed all their supplies of food;
17 and he sent a man before them —
    Joseph, sold as a slave.
18 They bruised his feet with shackles,
    his neck was put in irons,
19 till what he foretold came to pass,
    till the word of the Lord proved him true.
20 The king sent and released him,
    the ruler of peoples set him free.
21 He made him master of his household,
    ruler over all he possessed,
22 to instruct his princes as he pleased
    and teach his elders wisdom.

23 Then Israel entered Egypt;
    Jacob resided as a foreigner in the land of
       Ham.
24 The Lord made his people very fruitful;
    he made them too numerous for their
       foes,
25 whose hearts he turned to hate his people,
    to conspire against his servants.
26 He sent Moses his servant,
    and Aaron, whom he had chosen.
27 They performed his signs among them,
    his wonders in the land of Ham.
28 He sent darkness and made the land dark —
    for had they not rebelled against his
       words?
29 He turned their waters into blood,
    causing their fish to die.
30 Their land teemed with frogs,
    which went up into the bedrooms of their
       rulers.
31 He spoke, and there came swarms of flies,
    and gnats throughout their country.

___

a 35 Hebrew *Hallelu Yah*; in the Septuagint this line stands at
the beginning of Psalm 105.

³² He turned their rain into hail,
   with lightning throughout their land;
³³ he struck down their vines and fig trees
   and shattered the trees of their country.
³⁴ He spoke, and the locusts came,
   grasshoppers without number;
³⁵ they ate up every green thing in their land,
   ate up the produce of their soil.
³⁶ Then he struck down all the firstborn in
   their land,
   the firstfruits of all their manhood.
³⁷ He brought out Israel, laden with silver and
   gold,
   and from among their tribes no one
   faltered.
³⁸ Egypt was glad when they left,
   because dread of Israel had fallen on
   them.

³⁹ He spread out a cloud as a covering,
   and a fire to give light at night.
⁴⁰ They asked, and he brought them quail;
   he fed them well with the bread of heaven.
⁴¹ He opened the rock, and water gushed out;
   it flowed like a river in the desert.

⁴² For he remembered his holy promise
   given to his servant Abraham.
⁴³ He brought out his people with rejoicing,
   his chosen ones with shouts of joy;
⁴⁴ he gave them the lands of the nations,
   and they fell heir to what others had toiled
   for —
⁴⁵ that they might keep his precepts
   and observe his laws.

Praise the LORD.ᵃ

PSALM 106

¹ Praise the LORD.ᵇ

Give thanks to the LORD, for he is good;
   his love endures forever.

² Who can proclaim the mighty acts of the
   LORD
   or fully declare his praise?
³ Blessed are those who act justly,
   who always do what is right.

⁴ Remember me, LORD, when you show favor
   to your people,
   come to my aid when you save them,
⁵ that I may enjoy the prosperity of your
   chosen ones,
   that I may share in the joy of your nation
   and join your inheritance in giving praise.

⁶ We have sinned, even as our ancestors did;
   we have done wrong and acted wickedly.
⁷ When our ancestors were in Egypt,
   they gave no thought to your miracles;
   they did not remember your many
      kindnesses,
   and they rebelled by the sea, the Red Sea.ᶜ
⁸ Yet he saved them for his name's sake,
   to make his mighty power known.
⁹ He rebuked the Red Sea, and it dried up;
   he led them through the depths as
      through a desert.
¹⁰ He saved them from the hand of the foe;
   from the hand of the enemy he redeemed
      them.
¹¹ The waters covered their adversaries;
   not one of them survived.
¹² Then they believed his promises
   and sang his praise.

¹³ But they soon forgot what he had done
   and did not wait for his plan to unfold.
¹⁴ In the desert they gave in to their craving;
   in the wilderness they put God to the
      test.
¹⁵ So he gave them what they asked for,
   but sent a wasting disease among them.

¹⁶ In the camp they grew envious of Moses
   and of Aaron, who was consecrated to the
      LORD.
¹⁷ The earth opened up and swallowed
      Dathan;
   it buried the company of Abiram.
¹⁸ Fire blazed among their followers;
   a flame consumed the wicked.
¹⁹ At Horeb they made a calf
   and worshiped an idol cast from metal.
²⁰ They exchanged their glorious God
   for an image of a bull, which eats grass.
²¹ They forgot the God who saved them,
   who had done great things in Egypt,
²² miracles in the land of Ham
   and awesome deeds by the Red Sea.
²³ So he said he would destroy them —
   had not Moses, his chosen one,
   stood in the breach before him
   to keep his wrath from destroying them.

²⁴ Then they despised the pleasant land;
   they did not believe his promise.
²⁵ They grumbled in their tents
   and did not obey the LORD.

ᵃ 45 Hebrew Hallelu Yah   ᵇ 1 Hebrew Hallelu Yah; also in
verse 48   ᶜ 7 Or the Sea of Reeds; also in verses 9 and 22

26 So he swore to them with uplifted hand
    that he would make them fall in the
        wilderness,
27 make their descendants fall among the
        nations
    and scatter them throughout the lands.

28 They yoked themselves to the Baal of Peor
    and ate sacrifices offered to lifeless gods;
29 they aroused the LORD's anger by their
        wicked deeds,
    and a plague broke out among them.
30 But Phinehas stood up and intervened,
    and the plague was checked.
31 This was credited to him as righteousness
    for endless generations to come.
32 By the waters of Meribah they angered the
        LORD,
    and trouble came to Moses because of
        them;
33 for they rebelled against the Spirit of God,
    and rash words came from Moses' lips.[a]

34 They did not destroy the peoples
    as the LORD had commanded them,
35 but they mingled with the nations
    and adopted their customs.
36 They worshiped their idols,
    which became a snare to them.
37 They sacrificed their sons
    and their daughters to false gods.
38 They shed innocent blood,
    the blood of their sons and daughters,
    whom they sacrificed to the idols of Canaan,
    and the land was desecrated by their
        blood.
39 They defiled themselves by what they did;
    by their deeds they prostituted
        themselves.

40 Therefore the LORD was angry with his
        people
    and abhorred his inheritance.
41 He gave them into the hands of the nations,
    and their foes ruled over them.
42 Their enemies oppressed them
    and subjected them to their power.
43 Many times he delivered them,
    but they were bent on rebellion
    and they wasted away in their sin.
44 Yet he took note of their distress
    when he heard their cry;
45 for their sake he remembered his covenant
    and out of his great love he relented.
46 He caused all who held them captive
    to show them mercy.

47 Save us, LORD our God,
    and gather us from the nations,
    that we may give thanks to your holy name
    and glory in your praise.

48 Praise be to the LORD, the God of Israel,
    from everlasting to everlasting.

Let all the people say, "Amen!"

Praise the LORD.

BOOK V

Psalms 107 – 150

PSALM 107

1 Give thanks to the LORD, for he is good;
    his love endures forever.

2 Let the redeemed of the LORD tell their
        story—
    those he redeemed from the hand of the
        foe,
3 those he gathered from the lands,
    from east and west, from north and
        south.[b]

4 Some wandered in desert wastelands,
    finding no way to a city where they could
        settle.
5 They were hungry and thirsty,
    and their lives ebbed away.
6 Then they cried out to the LORD in their
        trouble,
    and he delivered them from their distress.
7 He led them by a straight way
    to a city where they could settle.
8 Let them give thanks to the LORD for his
        unfailing love
    and his wonderful deeds for mankind,
9 for he satisfies the thirsty
    and fills the hungry with good things.

10 Some sat in darkness, in utter darkness,
    prisoners suffering in iron chains,
11 because they rebelled against God's
        commands
    and despised the plans of the Most High.
12 So he subjected them to bitter labor;
    they stumbled, and there was no one to
        help.
13 Then they cried to the LORD in their trouble,
    and he saved them from their distress.

[a] 33 Or *against his spirit, / and rash words came from his lips*
[b] 3 Hebrew *north and the sea*

¹⁴He brought them out of darkness, the utter darkness,
and broke away their chains.
¹⁵Let them give thanks to the LORD for his unfailing love
and his wonderful deeds for mankind,
¹⁶for he breaks down gates of bronze
and cuts through bars of iron.

¹⁷Some became fools through their rebellious ways
and suffered affliction because of their iniquities.
¹⁸They loathed all food
and drew near the gates of death.
¹⁹Then they cried to the LORD in their trouble,
and he saved them from their distress.
²⁰He sent out his word and healed them;
he rescued them from the grave.
²¹Let them give thanks to the LORD for his unfailing love
and his wonderful deeds for mankind.
²²Let them sacrifice thank offerings
and tell of his works with songs of joy.

²³Some went out on the sea in ships;
they were merchants on the mighty waters.
²⁴They saw the works of the LORD,
his wonderful deeds in the deep.
²⁵For he spoke and stirred up a tempest
that lifted high the waves.
²⁶They mounted up to the heavens and went down to the depths;
in their peril their courage melted away.
²⁷They reeled and staggered like drunkards;
they were at their wits' end.
²⁸Then they cried out to the LORD in their trouble,
and he brought them out of their distress.
²⁹He stilled the storm to a whisper;
the waves of the sea[a] were hushed.
³⁰They were glad when it grew calm,
and he guided them to their desired haven.
³¹Let them give thanks to the LORD for his unfailing love
and his wonderful deeds for mankind.
³²Let them exalt him in the assembly of the people
and praise him in the council of the elders.

³³He turned rivers into a desert,
flowing springs into thirsty ground,
³⁴and fruitful land into a salt waste,
because of the wickedness of those who lived there.

³⁵He turned the desert into pools of water
and the parched ground into flowing springs;
³⁶there he brought the hungry to live,
and they founded a city where they could settle.
³⁷They sowed fields and planted vineyards
that yielded a fruitful harvest;
³⁸he blessed them, and their numbers greatly increased,
and he did not let their herds diminish.

³⁹Then their numbers decreased, and they were humbled
by oppression, calamity and sorrow;
⁴⁰he who pours contempt on nobles
made them wander in a trackless waste.
⁴¹But he lifted the needy out of their affliction
and increased their families like flocks.
⁴²The upright see and rejoice,
but all the wicked shut their mouths.

⁴³Let the one who is wise heed these things
and ponder the loving deeds of the LORD.

PSALM 108[b]

A song. A psalm of David.

¹My heart, O God, is steadfast;
I will sing and make music with all my soul.
²Awake, harp and lyre!
I will awaken the dawn.
³I will praise you, LORD, among the nations;
I will sing of you among the peoples.
⁴For great is your love, higher than the heavens;
your faithfulness reaches to the skies.
⁵Be exalted, O God, above the heavens;
let your glory be over all the earth.

⁶Save us and help us with your right hand,
that those you love may be delivered.
⁷God has spoken from his sanctuary:
"In triumph I will parcel out Shechem
and measure off the Valley of Sukkoth.
⁸Gilead is mine, Manasseh is mine;
Ephraim is my helmet,
Judah is my scepter.
⁹Moab is my washbasin,
on Edom I toss my sandal;
over Philistia I shout in triumph."

¹⁰Who will bring me to the fortified city?
Who will lead me to Edom?

---

a 29 Dead Sea Scrolls; Masoretic Text / *their waves*　　*b* In Hebrew texts 108:1-13 is numbered 108:2-14.

11 Is it not you, God, you who have rejected us
        and no longer go out with our armies?
12 Give us aid against the enemy,
        for human help is worthless.
13 With God we will gain the victory,
        and he will trample down our enemies.

PSALM 109

For the director of music. Of David. A psalm.

1 My God, whom I praise,
        do not remain silent,
2 for people who are wicked and deceitful
        have opened their mouths against me;
        they have spoken against me with lying
        tongues.
3 With words of hatred they surround me;
        they attack me without cause.
4 In return for my friendship they accuse me,
        but I am a man of prayer.
5 They repay me evil for good,
        and hatred for my friendship.

6 Appoint someone evil to oppose my enemy;
        let an accuser stand at his right hand.
7 When he is tried, let him be found guilty,
        and may his prayers condemn him.
8 May his days be few;
        may another take his place of leadership.
9 May his children be fatherless
        and his wife a widow.
10 May his children be wandering beggars;
        may they be driven[a] from their ruined
        homes.
11 May a creditor seize all he has;
        may strangers plunder the fruits of his
        labor.
12 May no one extend kindness to him
        or take pity on his fatherless children.
13 May his descendants be cut off,
        their names blotted out from the next
        generation.
14 May the iniquity of his fathers be
        remembered before the LORD;
        may the sin of his mother never be blotted
        out.
15 May their sins always remain before the
        LORD,
        that he may blot out their name from the
        earth.

16 For he never thought of doing a kindness,
        but hounded to death the poor
        and the needy and the brokenhearted.
17 He loved to pronounce a curse—
        may it come back on him.

He found no pleasure in blessing—
        may it be far from him.
18 He wore cursing as his garment;
        it entered into his body like water,
        into his bones like oil.
19 May it be like a cloak wrapped about him,
        like a belt tied forever around him.
20 May this be the LORD's payment to my
        accusers,
        to those who speak evil of me.

21 But you, Sovereign LORD,
        help me for your name's sake;
        out of the goodness of your love, deliver me.
22 For I am poor and needy,
        and my heart is wounded within me.
23 I fade away like an evening shadow;
        I am shaken off like a locust.
24 My knees give way from fasting;
        my body is thin and gaunt.
25 I am an object of scorn to my accusers;
        when they see me, they shake their heads.

26 Help me, LORD my God;
        save me according to your unfailing love.
27 Let them know that it is your hand,
        that you, LORD, have done it.
28 While they curse, may you bless;
        may those who attack me be put to shame,
        but may your servant rejoice.
29 May my accusers be clothed with disgrace
        and wrapped in shame as in a cloak.

30 With my mouth I will greatly extol the
        LORD;
        in the great throng of worshipers I will
        praise him.
31 For he stands at the right hand of the needy,
        to save their lives from those who would
        condemn them.

PSALM 110

Of David. A psalm.

1 The LORD says to my lord:[b]

"Sit at my right hand
        until I make your enemies
        a footstool for your feet."

2 The LORD will extend your mighty scepter
        from Zion, saying,
        "Rule in the midst of your enemies!"
3 Your troops will be willing
        on your day of battle.

---

a 10 Septuagint; Hebrew sought   b 1 Or Lord

Arrayed in holy splendor,
　your young men will come to you
　like dew from the morning's womb.[a]

4 The Lord has sworn
　and will not change his mind:
"You are a priest forever,
　in the order of Melchizedek."

5 The Lord is at your right hand[b];
　he will crush kings on the day of his wrath.
6 He will judge the nations, heaping up the
　dead
　and crushing the rulers of the whole earth.
7 He will drink from a brook along the way,[c]
　and so he will lift his head high.

PSALM 111[d]

1 Praise the Lord.[e]

I will extol the Lord with all my heart
　in the council of the upright and in the
　assembly.

2 Great are the works of the Lord;
　they are pondered by all who delight in
　them.
3 Glorious and majestic are his deeds,
　and his righteousness endures forever.
4 He has caused his wonders to be
　remembered;
　the Lord is gracious and compassionate.
5 He provides food for those who fear him;
　he remembers his covenant forever.

6 He has shown his people the power of his
　works,
　giving them the lands of other nations.
7 The works of his hands are faithful and just;
　all his precepts are trustworthy.
8 They are established for ever and ever,
　enacted in faithfulness and uprightness.
9 He provided redemption for his people;
　he ordained his covenant forever —
　holy and awesome is his name.

10 The fear of the Lord is the beginning of
　wisdom;
　all who follow his precepts have good
　understanding.
　To him belongs eternal praise.

PSALM 112[d]

1 Praise the Lord.[e]

Blessed are those who fear the Lord,
　who find great delight in his commands.

2 Their children will be mighty in the land;
　the generation of the upright will be
　blessed.
3 Wealth and riches are in their houses,
　and their righteousness endures forever.
4 Even in darkness light dawns for the upright,
　for those who are gracious and
　compassionate and righteous.
5 Good will come to those who are generous
　and lend freely,
　who conduct their affairs with justice.

6 Surely the righteous will never be shaken;
　they will be remembered forever.
7 They will have no fear of bad news;
　their hearts are steadfast, trusting in the
　Lord.
8 Their hearts are secure, they will have no
　fear;
　in the end they will look in triumph on
　their foes.
9 They have freely scattered their gifts to the
　poor,
　their righteousness endures forever;
　their horn[f] will be lifted high in honor.

10 The wicked will see and be vexed,
　they will gnash their teeth and waste
　away;
　the longings of the wicked will come to
　nothing.

PSALM 113

1 Praise the Lord.[g]

Praise the Lord, you his servants;
　praise the name of the Lord.
2 Let the name of the Lord be praised,
　both now and forevermore.
3 From the rising of the sun to the place where
　it sets,
　the name of the Lord is to be praised.

4 The Lord is exalted over all the nations,
　his glory above the heavens.
5 Who is like the Lord our God,
　the One who sits enthroned on high,
6 who stoops down to look
　on the heavens and the earth?

---

a 3 The meaning of the Hebrew for this sentence is uncertain.
b 5 Or My lord is at your right hand, Lord　　c 7 The meaning
of the Hebrew for this clause is uncertain.　　d This psalm is an
acrostic poem, the lines of which begin with the successive
letters of the Hebrew alphabet.　　e 1,1 Hebrew Hallelu Yah
f 9 Horn here symbolizes dignity.　　g 1 Hebrew Hallelu Yah;
also in verse 9

7 He raises the poor from the dust
  and lifts the needy from the ash heap;
8 he seats them with princes,
  with the princes of his people.
9 He settles the childless woman in her home
  as a happy mother of children.

Praise the Lord.

PSALM 114

1 When Israel came out of Egypt,
  Jacob from a people of foreign tongue,
2 Judah became God's sanctuary,
  Israel his dominion.

3 The sea looked and fled,
  the Jordan turned back;
4 the mountains leaped like rams,
  the hills like lambs.

5 Why was it, sea, that you fled?
  Why, Jordan, did you turn back?
6 Why, mountains, did you leap like rams,
  you hills, like lambs?

7 Tremble, earth, at the presence of the Lord,
  at the presence of the God of Jacob,
8 who turned the rock into a pool,
  the hard rock into springs of water.

PSALM 115

1 Not to us, Lord, not to us
  but to your name be the glory,
  because of your love and faithfulness.

2 Why do the nations say,
  "Where is their God?"
3 Our God is in heaven;
  he does whatever pleases him.
4 But their idols are silver and gold,
  made by human hands.
5 They have mouths, but cannot speak,
  eyes, but cannot see.
6 They have ears, but cannot hear,
  noses, but cannot smell.
7 They have hands, but cannot feel,
  feet, but cannot walk,
  nor can they utter a sound with their
    throats.
8 Those who make them will be like them,
  and so will all who trust in them.

9 All you Israelites, trust in the Lord —
  he is their help and shield.
10 House of Aaron, trust in the Lord —
  he is their help and shield.

11 You who fear him, trust in the Lord —
  he is their help and shield.

12 The Lord remembers us and will bless us:
  He will bless his people Israel,
  he will bless the house of Aaron,
13 he will bless those who fear the Lord —
  small and great alike.

14 May the Lord cause you to flourish,
  both you and your children.
15 May you be blessed by the Lord,
  the Maker of heaven and earth.

16 The highest heavens belong to the Lord,
  but the earth he has given to mankind.
17 It is not the dead who praise the Lord,
  those who go down to the place of silence;
18 it is we who extol the Lord,
  both now and forevermore.

Praise the Lord.[a]

PSALM 116

1 I love the Lord, for he heard my voice;
  he heard my cry for mercy.
2 Because he turned his ear to me,
  I will call on him as long as I live.

3 The cords of death entangled me,
  the anguish of the grave came over me;
  I was overcome by distress and sorrow.
4 Then I called on the name of the Lord:
  "Lord, save me!"

5 The Lord is gracious and righteous;
  our God is full of compassion.
6 The Lord protects the unwary;
  when I was brought low, he saved me.

7 Return to your rest, my soul,
  for the Lord has been good to you.

8 For you, Lord, have delivered me from
    death,
  my eyes from tears,
  my feet from stumbling,
9 that I may walk before the Lord
  in the land of the living.

10 I trusted in the Lord when I said,
  "I am greatly afflicted";
11 in my alarm I said,
  "Everyone is a liar."

12 What shall I return to the Lord
  for all his goodness to me?

---

a 18 Hebrew *Hallelu Yah*

¹³ I will lift up the cup of salvation
    and call on the name of the LORD.
¹⁴ I will fulfill my vows to the LORD
    in the presence of all his people.

¹⁵ Precious in the sight of the LORD
    is the death of his faithful servants.
¹⁶ Truly I am your servant, LORD;
    I serve you just as my mother did;
    you have freed me from my chains.

¹⁷ I will sacrifice a thank offering to you
    and call on the name of the LORD.
¹⁸ I will fulfill my vows to the LORD
    in the presence of all his people,
¹⁹ in the courts of the house of the LORD—
    in your midst, Jerusalem.

    Praise the LORD.ᵃ

PSALM 117

¹ Praise the LORD, all you nations;
    extol him, all you peoples.
² For great is his love toward us,
    and the faithfulness of the LORD endures
      forever.

    Praise the LORD.ᵃ

PSALM 118

¹ Give thanks to the LORD, for he is good;
    his love endures forever.

² Let Israel say:
    "His love endures forever."
³ Let the house of Aaron say:
    "His love endures forever."
⁴ Let those who fear the LORD say:
    "His love endures forever."

⁵ When hard pressed, I cried to the LORD;
    he brought me into a spacious place.
⁶ The LORD is with me; I will not be afraid.
    What can mere mortals do to me?
⁷ The LORD is with me; he is my helper.
    I look in triumph on my enemies.

⁸ It is better to take refuge in the LORD
    than to trust in humans.
⁹ It is better to take refuge in the LORD
    than to trust in princes.
¹⁰ All the nations surrounded me,
    but in the name of the LORD I cut them
      down.
¹¹ They surrounded me on every side,
    but in the name of the LORD I cut them
      down.

¹² They swarmed around me like bees,
    but they were consumed as quickly as
      burning thorns;
    in the name of the LORD I cut them
      down.
¹³ I was pushed back and about to fall,
    but the LORD helped me.
¹⁴ The LORD is my strength and my defenseᵇ;
    he has become my salvation.

¹⁵ Shouts of joy and victory
    resound in the tents of the righteous:
    "The LORD's right hand has done mighty
      things!
¹⁶   The LORD's right hand is lifted high;
    the LORD's right hand has done mighty
      things!"
¹⁷ I will not die but live,
    and will proclaim what the LORD has
      done.
¹⁸ The LORD has chastened me severely,
    but he has not given me over to death.
¹⁹ Open for me the gates of the righteous;
    I will enter and give thanks to the LORD.
²⁰ This is the gate of the LORD
    through which the righteous may enter.
²¹ I will give you thanks, for you answered me;
    you have become my salvation.

²² The stone the builders rejected
    has become the cornerstone;
²³ the LORD has done this,
    and it is marvelous in our eyes.
²⁴ The LORD has done it this very day;
    let us rejoice today and be glad.

²⁵ LORD, save us!
    LORD, grant us success!

²⁶ Blessed is he who comes in the name of the
      LORD.
    From the house of the LORD we bless
      you.ᶜ
²⁷ The LORD is God,
    and he has made his light shine on us.
    With boughs in hand, join in the festal
      procession
    upᵈ to the horns of the altar.

²⁸ You are my God, and I will praise you;
    you are my God, and I will exalt you.

²⁹ Give thanks to the LORD, for he is good;
    his love endures forever.

ᵃ 19,2 Hebrew *Hallelu Yah*   ᵇ 14 Or *song*   ᶜ 26 The Hebrew is plural.   ᵈ 27 Or *Bind the festal sacrifice with ropes / and take it*

PSALM 119[a]

א Aleph

¹ Blessed are those whose ways are
blameless,
who walk according to the law of the
LORD.
² Blessed are those who keep his statutes
and seek him with all their heart—
³ they do no wrong
but follow his ways.
⁴ You have laid down precepts
that are to be fully obeyed.
⁵ Oh, that my ways were steadfast
in obeying your decrees!
⁶ Then I would not be put to shame
when I consider all your commands.
⁷ I will praise you with an upright heart
as I learn your righteous laws.
⁸ I will obey your decrees;
do not utterly forsake me.

ב Beth

⁹ How can a young person stay on the path of
purity?
By living according to your word.
¹⁰ I seek you with all my heart;
do not let me stray from your commands.
¹¹ I have hidden your word in my heart
that I might not sin against you.
¹² Praise be to you, LORD;
teach me your decrees.
¹³ With my lips I recount
all the laws that come from your mouth.
¹⁴ I rejoice in following your statutes
as one rejoices in great riches.
¹⁵ I meditate on your precepts
and consider your ways.
¹⁶ I delight in your decrees;
I will not neglect your word.

ג Gimel

¹⁷ Be good to your servant while I live,
that I may obey your word.
¹⁸ Open my eyes that I may see
wonderful things in your law.
¹⁹ I am a stranger on earth;
do not hide your commands from me.
²⁰ My soul is consumed with longing
for your laws at all times.
²¹ You rebuke the arrogant, who are accursed,
those who stray from your commands.
²² Remove from me their scorn and contempt,
for I keep your statutes.

²³ Though rulers sit together and slander me,
your servant will meditate on your
decrees.
²⁴ Your statutes are my delight;
they are my counselors.

ד Daleth

²⁵ I am laid low in the dust;
preserve my life according to your word.
²⁶ I gave an account of my ways and you
answered me;
teach me your decrees.
²⁷ Cause me to understand the way of your
precepts,
that I may meditate on your wonderful
deeds.
²⁸ My soul is weary with sorrow;
strengthen me according to your word.
²⁹ Keep me from deceitful ways;
be gracious to me and teach me your
law.
³⁰ I have chosen the way of faithfulness;
I have set my heart on your laws.
³¹ I hold fast to your statutes, LORD;
do not let me be put to shame.
³² I run in the path of your commands,
for you have broadened my
understanding.

ה He

³³ Teach me, LORD, the way of your decrees,
that I may follow it to the end.[b]
³⁴ Give me understanding, so that I may keep
your law
and obey it with all my heart.
³⁵ Direct me in the path of your commands,
for there I find delight.
³⁶ Turn my heart toward your statutes
and not toward selfish gain.
³⁷ Turn my eyes away from worthless things;
preserve my life according to your
word.[c]
³⁸ Fulfill your promise to your servant,
so that you may be feared.
³⁹ Take away the disgrace I dread,
for your laws are good.
⁴⁰ How I long for your precepts!
In your righteousness preserve my life.

---

[a] This psalm is an acrostic poem, the stanzas of which begin
with successive letters of the Hebrew alphabet; moreover, the
verses of each stanza begin with the same letter of the Hebrew
alphabet.   [b] 33 Or *follow it for its reward*
[c] 37 Two manuscripts of the Masoretic Text and Dead Sea
Scrolls; most manuscripts of the Masoretic Text *life in your way*

ו Waw

⁴¹ May your unfailing love come to me, LORD,
  your salvation, according to your promise;
⁴² then I can answer anyone who taunts me,
  for I trust in your word.
⁴³ Never take your word of truth from my
    mouth,
  for I have put my hope in your laws.
⁴⁴ I will always obey your law,
  for ever and ever.
⁴⁵ I will walk about in freedom,
  for I have sought out your precepts.
⁴⁶ I will speak of your statutes before kings
  and will not be put to shame,
⁴⁷ for I delight in your commands
  because I love them.
⁴⁸ I reach out for your commands, which I love,
  that I may meditate on your decrees.

ז Zayin

⁴⁹ Remember your word to your servant,
  for you have given me hope.
⁵⁰ My comfort in my suffering is this:
  Your promise preserves my life.
⁵¹ The arrogant mock me unmercifully,
  but I do not turn from your law.
⁵² I remember, LORD, your ancient laws,
  and I find comfort in them.
⁵³ Indignation grips me because of the wicked,
  who have forsaken your law.
⁵⁴ Your decrees are the theme of my song
  wherever I lodge.
⁵⁵ In the night, LORD, I remember your name,
  that I may keep your law.
⁵⁶ This has been my practice:
  I obey your precepts.

ח Heth

⁵⁷ You are my portion, LORD;
  I have promised to obey your words.
⁵⁸ I have sought your face with all my heart;
  be gracious to me according to your
    promise.
⁵⁹ I have considered my ways
  and have turned my steps to your statutes.
⁶⁰ I will hasten and not delay
  to obey your commands.
⁶¹ Though the wicked bind me with ropes,
  I will not forget your law.
⁶² At midnight I rise to give you thanks
  for your righteous laws.
⁶³ I am a friend to all who fear you,
  to all who follow your precepts.

⁶⁴ The earth is filled with your love, LORD;
  teach me your decrees.

ט Teth

⁶⁵ Do good to your servant
  according to your word, LORD.
⁶⁶ Teach me knowledge and good judgment,
  for I trust your commands.
⁶⁷ Before I was afflicted I went astray,
  but now I obey your word.
⁶⁸ You are good, and what you do is good;
  teach me your decrees.
⁶⁹ Though the arrogant have smeared me
    with lies,
  I keep your precepts with all my heart.
⁷⁰ Their hearts are callous and unfeeling,
  but I delight in your law.
⁷¹ It was good for me to be afflicted
  so that I might learn your decrees.
⁷² The law from your mouth is more precious
    to me
  than thousands of pieces of silver and gold.

י Yodh

⁷³ Your hands made me and formed me;
  give me understanding to learn your
    commands.
⁷⁴ May those who fear you rejoice when they
    see me,
  for I have put my hope in your word.
⁷⁵ I know, LORD, that your laws are righteous,
  and that in faithfulness you have afflicted
    me.
⁷⁶ May your unfailing love be my comfort,
  according to your promise to your
    servant.
⁷⁷ Let your compassion come to me that I may
    live,
  for your law is my delight.
⁷⁸ May the arrogant be put to shame for
    wronging me without cause;
  but I will meditate on your precepts.
⁷⁹ May those who fear you turn to me,
  those who understand your statutes.
⁸⁰ May I wholeheartedly follow your decrees,
  that I may not be put to shame.

כ Kaph

⁸¹ My soul faints with longing for your
    salvation,
  but I have put my hope in your word.
⁸² My eyes fail, looking for your promise;
  I say, "When will you comfort me?"

⁸³ Though I am like a wineskin in the smoke,
I do not forget your decrees.
⁸⁴ How long must your servant wait?
When will you punish my persecutors?
⁸⁵ The arrogant dig pits to trap me,
contrary to your law.
⁸⁶ All your commands are trustworthy;
help me, for I am being persecuted
without cause.
⁸⁷ They almost wiped me from the earth,
but I have not forsaken your precepts.
⁸⁸ In your unfailing love preserve my life,
that I may obey the statutes of your mouth.

ל Lamedh

⁸⁹ Your word, LORD, is eternal;
it stands firm in the heavens.
⁹⁰ Your faithfulness continues through all
generations;
you established the earth, and it endures.
⁹¹ Your laws endure to this day,
for all things serve you.
⁹² If your law had not been my delight,
I would have perished in my affliction.
⁹³ I will never forget your precepts,
for by them you have preserved my life.
⁹⁴ Save me, for I am yours;
I have sought out your precepts.
⁹⁵ The wicked are waiting to destroy me,
but I will ponder your statutes.
⁹⁶ To all perfection I see a limit,
but your commands are boundless.

מ Mem

⁹⁷ Oh, how I love your law!
I meditate on it all day long.
⁹⁸ Your commands are always with me
and make me wiser than my enemies.
⁹⁹ I have more insight than all my teachers,
for I meditate on your statutes.
¹⁰⁰ I have more understanding than the elders,
for I obey your precepts.
¹⁰¹ I have kept my feet from every evil path
so that I might obey your word.
¹⁰² I have not departed from your laws,
for you yourself have taught me.
¹⁰³ How sweet are your words to my taste,
sweeter than honey to my mouth!
¹⁰⁴ I gain understanding from your precepts;
therefore I hate every wrong path.

נ Nun

¹⁰⁵ Your word is a lamp for my feet,
a light on my path.

¹⁰⁶ I have taken an oath and confirmed it,
that I will follow your righteous laws.
¹⁰⁷ I have suffered much;
preserve my life, LORD, according to your
word.
¹⁰⁸ Accept, LORD, the willing praise of my
mouth,
and teach me your laws.
¹⁰⁹ Though I constantly take my life in my
hands,
I will not forget your law.
¹¹⁰ The wicked have set a snare for me,
but I have not strayed from your precepts.
¹¹¹ Your statutes are my heritage forever;
they are the joy of my heart.
¹¹² My heart is set on keeping your decrees
to the very end.ᵃ

ס Samekh

¹¹³ I hate double-minded people,
but I love your law.
¹¹⁴ You are my refuge and my shield;
I have put my hope in your word.
¹¹⁵ Away from me, you evildoers,
that I may keep the commands of my God!
¹¹⁶ Sustain me, my God, according to your
promise, and I will live;
do not let my hopes be dashed.
¹¹⁷ Uphold me, and I will be delivered;
I will always have regard for your decrees.
¹¹⁸ You reject all who stray from your decrees,
for their delusions come to nothing.
¹¹⁹ All the wicked of the earth you discard like
dross;
therefore I love your statutes.
¹²⁰ My flesh trembles in fear of you;
I stand in awe of your laws.

ע Ayin

¹²¹ I have done what is righteous and just;
do not leave me to my oppressors.
¹²² Ensure your servant's well-being;
do not let the arrogant oppress me.
¹²³ My eyes fail, looking for your salvation,
looking for your righteous promise.
¹²⁴ Deal with your servant according to your
love
and teach me your decrees.
¹²⁵ I am your servant; give me discernment
that I may understand your statutes.
¹²⁶ It is time for you to act, LORD;
your law is being broken.

ᵃ 112 Or decrees / for their enduring reward

127Because I love your commands
    more than gold, more than pure gold,
128and because I consider all your precepts
    right,
    I hate every wrong path.

פ Pe

129Your statutes are wonderful;
    therefore I obey them.
130The unfolding of your words gives light;
    it gives understanding to the simple.
131I open my mouth and pant,
    longing for your commands.
132Turn to me and have mercy on me,
    as you always do to those who love your
    name.
133Direct my footsteps according to your word;
    let no sin rule over me.
134Redeem me from human oppression,
    that I may obey your precepts.
135Make your face shine on your servant
    and teach me your decrees.
136Streams of tears flow from my eyes,
    for your law is not obeyed.

צ Tsadhe

137You are righteous, LORD,
    and your laws are right.
138The statutes you have laid down are righteous;
    they are fully trustworthy.
139My zeal wears me out,
    for my enemies ignore your words.
140Your promises have been thoroughly tested,
    and your servant loves them.
141Though I am lowly and despised,
    I do not forget your precepts.
142Your righteousness is everlasting
    and your law is true.
143Trouble and distress have come upon me,
    but your commands give me delight.
144Your statutes are always righteous;
    give me understanding that I may live.

ק Qoph

145I call with all my heart; answer me, LORD,
    and I will obey your decrees.
146I call out to you; save me
    and I will keep your statutes.
147I rise before dawn and cry for help;
    I have put my hope in your word.
148My eyes stay open through the watches of
    the night,
    that I may meditate on your promises.

149Hear my voice in accordance with your
    love;
    preserve my life, LORD, according to your
    laws.
150Those who devise wicked schemes are near,
    but they are far from your law.
151Yet you are near, LORD,
    and all your commands are true.
152Long ago I learned from your statutes
    that you established them to last forever.

ר Resh

153Look on my suffering and deliver me,
    for I have not forgotten your law.
154Defend my cause and redeem me;
    preserve my life according to your
    promise.
155Salvation is far from the wicked,
    for they do not seek out your decrees.
156Your compassion, LORD, is great;
    preserve my life according to your laws.
157Many are the foes who persecute me,
    but I have not turned from your statutes.
158I look on the faithless with loathing,
    for they do not obey your word.
159See how I love your precepts;
    preserve my life, LORD, in accordance
    with your love.
160All your words are true;
    all your righteous laws are eternal.

ש Sin and Shin

161Rulers persecute me without cause,
    but my heart trembles at your word.
162I rejoice in your promise
    like one who finds great spoil.
163I hate and detest falsehood
    but I love your law.
164Seven times a day I praise you
    for your righteous laws.
165Great peace have those who love your law,
    and nothing can make them stumble.
166I wait for your salvation, LORD,
    and I follow your commands.
167I obey your statutes,
    for I love them greatly.
168I obey your precepts and your statutes,
    for all my ways are known to you.

ת Taw

169May my cry come before you, LORD;
    give me understanding according to your
    word.

Leaders Cannot Show the Way Until They Know the Way

Psalm 119:1–176

The longest psalm in the Bible is a song about the priority of the Word of God. For 176 verses, Psalm 119 holds high the words and wisdom of God and convinces us to treasure it more than anything else in life.

Why is this challenge so crucial for us? Leaders in our world face two realities:

1. **Change happens faster than ever, so leaders must remain adaptable.**

2. **We need timeless values more than ever, so leaders must remain principle-driven.**

Psalm 119 provides a roadmap for getting the wisdom, values and principles we need to lead effectively. Consider what Psalm 119 teaches about adopting God's Word as our source for leadership principles. Our leadership will . . .

- **be blessed (vv. 1–2)**
- **remain pure and ethical (vv. 9–11)**
- **be strengthened and revitalized (vv. 28, 149, 154–159)**
- **insightfully answer criticism (v. 42)**
- **enjoy liberty (v. 45)**
- **gain wise counsel when needed (v. 66)**
- **remain steady even when afflicted (vv. 67–72, 92)**
- **display more insight than our teachers (vv. 99–100)**
- **be enlightened and intuitive (vv. 105, 130)**
- **have a reliable guide even for new issues (vv. 129, 160)**
- **enjoy inward peace and poise (v. 165)**
- **get divine help (vv. 173–175)**

---

170 May my supplication come before you;
    deliver me according to your promise.
171 May my lips overflow with praise,
    for you teach me your decrees.
172 May my tongue sing of your word,
    for all your commands are righteous.
173 May your hand be ready to help me,
    for I have chosen your precepts.
174 I long for your salvation, LORD,
    and your law gives me delight.
175 Let me live that I may praise you,
    and may your laws sustain me.
176 I have strayed like a lost sheep.
    Seek your servant,
    for I have not forgotten your commands.

PSALM 120

A song of ascents.

1 I call on the LORD in my distress,
    and he answers me.
2 Save me, LORD,
    from lying lips
    and from deceitful tongues.

3 What will he do to you,
    and what more besides,
    you deceitful tongue?
4 He will punish you with a warrior's sharp
        arrows,
    with burning coals of the broom bush.

5 Woe to me that I dwell in Meshek,
    that I live among the tents of Kedar!
6 Too long have I lived
    among those who hate peace.
7 I am for peace;
    but when I speak, they are for war.

PSALM 121

A song of ascents.

1 I lift up my eyes to the mountains—
    where does my help come from?
2 My help comes from the LORD,
    the Maker of heaven and earth.

3 He will not let your foot slip—
    he who watches over you will not
        slumber;

4 indeed, he who watches over Israel
    will neither slumber nor sleep.

5 The LORD watches over you —
    the LORD is your shade at your right hand;
6 the sun will not harm you by day,
    nor the moon by night.

7 The LORD will keep you from all harm —
    he will watch over your life;
8 the LORD will watch over your coming and
    going
    both now and forevermore.

PSALM 122

A song of ascents. Of David.

1 I rejoiced with those who said to me,
    "Let us go to the house of the LORD."
2 Our feet are standing
    in your gates, Jerusalem.

3 Jerusalem is built like a city
    that is closely compacted together.
4 That is where the tribes go up —
    the tribes of the LORD —
to praise the name of the LORD
    according to the statute given to Israel.
5 There stand the thrones for judgment,
    the thrones of the house of David.

6 Pray for the peace of Jerusalem:
    "May those who love you be secure.
7 May there be peace within your walls
    and security within your citadels."
8 For the sake of my family and friends,
    I will say, "Peace be within you."
9 For the sake of the house of the LORD our God,
    I will seek your prosperity.

PSALM 123

A song of ascents.

1 I lift up my eyes to you,
    to you who sit enthroned in heaven.
2 As the eyes of slaves look to the hand of their
    master,
    as the eyes of a female slave look to the
    hand of her mistress,
so our eyes look to the LORD our God,
    till he shows us his mercy.

3 Have mercy on us, LORD, have mercy on us,
    for we have endured no end of contempt.
4 We have endured no end
    of ridicule from the arrogant,
    of contempt from the proud.

PSALM 124

A song of ascents. Of David.

1 If the LORD had not been on our side —
    let Israel say —
2 if the LORD had not been on our side
    when people attacked us,
3 they would have swallowed us alive
    when their anger flared against us;
4 the flood would have engulfed us,
    the torrent would have swept over us,
5 the raging waters
    would have swept us away.

6 Praise be to the LORD,
    who has not let us be torn by their teeth.
7 We have escaped like a bird
    from the fowler's snare;
the snare has been broken,
    and we have escaped.
8 Our help is in the name of the LORD,
    the Maker of heaven and earth.

PSALM 125

A song of ascents.

1 Those who trust in the LORD are like Mount
    Zion,
    which cannot be shaken but endures
    forever.
2 As the mountains surround Jerusalem,
    so the LORD surrounds his people
    both now and forevermore.

3 The scepter of the wicked will not remain
    over the land allotted to the righteous,
for then the righteous might use
    their hands to do evil.

4 LORD, do good to those who are good,
    to those who are upright in heart.
5 But those who turn to crooked ways
    the LORD will banish with the evildoers.

Peace be on Israel.

PSALM 126

A song of ascents.

1 When the LORD restored the fortunes of[a]
    Zion,
    we were like those who dreamed.[b]
2 Our mouths were filled with laughter,
    our tongues with songs of joy.

---

a 1 Or LORD brought back the captives to   b 1 Or those restored to health

Then it was said among the nations,
  "The LORD has done great things for
    them."
[3] The LORD has done great things for us,
  and we are filled with joy.

[4] Restore our fortunes,[a] LORD,
  like streams in the Negev.
[5] Those who sow with tears
  will reap with songs of joy.
[6] Those who go out weeping,
  carrying seed to sow,
will return with songs of joy,
  carrying sheaves with them.

PSALM 127

A song of ascents. Of Solomon.

[1] Unless the LORD builds the house,
  the builders labor in vain.
Unless the LORD watches over the city,
  the guards stand watch in vain.
[2] In vain you rise early
  and stay up late,
toiling for food to eat—
  for he grants sleep to[b] those he loves.

[3] Children are a heritage from the LORD,
  offspring a reward from him.
[4] Like arrows in the hands of a warrior
  are children born in one's youth.
[5] Blessed is the man
  whose quiver is full of them.
They will not be put to shame
  when they contend with their opponents
    in court.

PSALM 128

A song of ascents.

[1] Blessed are all who fear the LORD,
  who walk in obedience to him.
[2] You will eat the fruit of your labor;
  blessings and prosperity will be yours.
[3] Your wife will be like a fruitful vine
  within your house;
your children will be like olive shoots
  around your table.
[4] Yes, this will be the blessing
  for the man who fears the LORD.

[5] May the LORD bless you from Zion;
  may you see the prosperity of Jerusalem
  all the days of your life.
[6] May you live to see your children's
    children—
  peace be on Israel.

PSALM 129

A song of ascents.

[1] "They have greatly oppressed me from my
    youth,"
  let Israel say;
[2] "they have greatly oppressed me from my
    youth,
  but they have not gained the victory over
    me.
[3] Plowmen have plowed my back
  and made their furrows long.

---

[a] 4 Or Bring back our captives   [b] 2 Or eat — / for while they sleep he provides for

Security Is Found in the Lord, Not in Followers

Psalm 127:1

Psalm 127:1 says it all. Unless God remains at the center of your efforts, you labor in vain. Whether we lead in the military, in construction, or sit behind a desk, we cannot fight, build, or plan well enough to gain anything permanent. Smart leaders not only include God in their strategy, they place him at its center. He alone can provide leaders with security; we cannot get it from followers. Consider the following list of rules regarding security and people:

1. **People cannot provide permanent security for a leader.**

2. **Leaders should never put their emotional health in the hands of someone else.**

3. **Spiritual and emotional health requires the truth.**

4. **Leaders must remember that hurting people naturally hurt people.**

5. **Trouble arises when leaders depend on people to do what only God can do.**

⁴But the LORD is righteous;
　　he has cut me free from the cords of the
　　　wicked."

⁵May all who hate Zion
　　be turned back in shame.
⁶May they be like grass on the roof,
　　which withers before it can grow;
⁷a reaper cannot fill his hands with it,
　　nor one who gathers fill his arms.
⁸May those who pass by not say to them,
　　"The blessing of the LORD be on you;
　　we bless you in the name of the LORD."

PSALM 130

A song of ascents.

¹Out of the depths I cry to you, LORD;
²　　Lord, hear my voice.
Let your ears be attentive
　　to my cry for mercy.

³If you, LORD, kept a record of sins,
　　Lord, who could stand?
⁴But with you there is forgiveness,
　　so that we can, with reverence,
　　　serve you.

⁵I wait for the LORD, my whole being waits,
　　and in his word I put my hope.
⁶I wait for the Lord
　　more than watchmen wait for the
　　　morning,
　　more than watchmen wait for the
　　　morning.

⁷Israel, put your hope in the LORD,
　　for with the LORD is unfailing love
　　and with him is full redemption.
⁸He himself will redeem Israel
　　from all their sins.

PSALM 131

A song of ascents. Of David.

¹My heart is not proud, LORD,
　　my eyes are not haughty;
I do not concern myself with great
　　matters
　　or things too wonderful for me.
²But I have calmed and quieted myself,
　　I am like a weaned child with its
　　　mother;
　　like a weaned child I am content.

³Israel, put your hope in the LORD
　　both now and forevermore.

Balancing Childlike and Childish Styles

Psalm 131:1–3

The Christian leader is mature enough to not act childish, yet remains trusting enough to stay childlike. David describes himself as a "weaned child" (Ps 131:2)—not a helpless baby, but neither a self-sufficient maverick. He must trust his mother for help and strength. This illustrates the balance of spiritual maturity.

PSALM 132

A song of ascents.

¹LORD, remember David
　　and all his self-denial.

²He swore an oath to the LORD,
　　he made a vow to the Mighty One of
　　　Jacob:
³"I will not enter my house
　　or go to my bed,
⁴I will allow no sleep to my eyes
　　or slumber to my eyelids,
⁵till I find a place for the LORD,
　　a dwelling for the Mighty One of Jacob."

⁶We heard it in Ephrathah,
　　we came upon it in the fields of Jaar:ᵃ
⁷"Let us go to his dwelling place,
　　let us worship at his footstool, saying,
⁸'Arise, LORD, and come to your resting
　　　place,
　　you and the ark of your might.
⁹May your priests be clothed with your
　　　righteousness;
　　may your faithful people sing for joy.'"

¹⁰For the sake of your servant David,
　　do not reject your anointed one.

¹¹The LORD swore an oath to David,
　　a sure oath he will not revoke:
"One of your own descendants
　　I will place on your throne.
¹²If your sons keep my covenant
　　and the statutes I teach them,
then their sons will sit
　　on your throne for ever and ever."

ᵃ 6 Or *heard of it in Ephrathah, / we found it in the fields of Jearim.* (See 1 Chron. 13:5,6) (And no quotation marks around verses 7-9)

13 For the LORD has chosen Zion,
    he has desired it for his dwelling, saying,
14 "This is my resting place for ever and ever;
    here I will sit enthroned, for I have
       desired it.
15 I will bless her with abundant provisions;
    her poor I will satisfy with food.
16 I will clothe her priests with salvation,
    and her faithful people will ever sing for joy.
17 "Here I will make a horn[a] grow for David
    and set up a lamp for my anointed one.
18 I will clothe his enemies with shame,
    but his head will be adorned with a
       radiant crown."

PSALM 133

A song of ascents. Of David.

1 How good and pleasant it is
    when God's people live together in unity!

2 It is like precious oil poured on the head,
    running down on the beard,
running down on Aaron's beard,
    down on the collar of his robe.
3 It is as if the dew of Hermon
    were falling on Mount Zion.
For there the LORD bestows his blessing,
    even life forevermore.

PSALM 134

A song of ascents.

1 Praise the LORD, all you servants of the LORD
    who minister by night in the house of the
       LORD.
2 Lift up your hands in the sanctuary
    and praise the LORD.

3 May the LORD bless you from Zion,
    he who is the Maker of heaven and earth.

PSALM 135

1 Praise the LORD.[b]

Praise the name of the LORD;
    praise him, you servants of the LORD,
2 you who minister in the house of the LORD,
    in the courts of the house of our God.

3 Praise the LORD, for the LORD is good;
    sing praise to his name, for that is pleasant.
4 For the LORD has chosen Jacob to be his own,
    Israel to be his treasured possession.

5 I know that the LORD is great,
    that our Lord is greater than all gods.

6 The LORD does whatever pleases him,
    in the heavens and on the earth,
    in the seas and all their depths.
7 He makes clouds rise from the ends of the
       earth;
    he sends lightning with the rain
    and brings out the wind from his
       storehouses.

8 He struck down the firstborn of Egypt,
    the firstborn of people and animals.
9 He sent his signs and wonders into your
       midst, Egypt,
    against Pharaoh and all his servants.
10 He struck down many nations
    and killed mighty kings—
11 Sihon king of the Amorites,
    Og king of Bashan,
    and all the kings of Canaan—
12 and he gave their land as an inheritance,
    an inheritance to his people Israel.

13 Your name, LORD, endures forever,
    your renown, LORD, through all generations.
14 For the LORD will vindicate his people
    and have compassion on his servants.

15 The idols of the nations are silver and gold,
    made by human hands.
16 They have mouths, but cannot speak,
    eyes, but cannot see.
17 They have ears, but cannot hear,
    nor is there breath in their mouths.
18 Those who make them will be like them,
    and so will all who trust in them.

19 All you Israelites, praise the LORD;
    house of Aaron, praise the LORD;
20 house of Levi, praise the LORD;
    you who fear him, praise the LORD.
21 Praise be to the LORD from Zion,
    to him who dwells in Jerusalem.

Praise the LORD.

PSALM 136

1 Give thanks to the LORD, for he is good.
    His love endures forever.
2 Give thanks to the God of gods.
    His love endures forever.
3 Give thanks to the Lord of lords:
    His love endures forever.

4 to him who alone does great wonders,
    His love endures forever.

---

[a] 17 *Horn* here symbolizes strong one, that is, king.
[b] 1 Hebrew *Hallelu Yah*; also in verses 3 and 21

⁵who by his understanding made the heavens,
His love endures forever.
⁶who spread out the earth upon the waters,
His love endures forever.
⁷who made the great lights —
His love endures forever.
⁸the sun to govern the day,
His love endures forever.
⁹the moon and stars to govern the night;
His love endures forever.

¹⁰to him who struck down the firstborn of Egypt
His love endures forever.
¹¹and brought Israel out from among them
His love endures forever.
¹²with a mighty hand and outstretched arm;
His love endures forever.

¹³to him who divided the Red Sea*ᵃ* asunder
His love endures forever.
¹⁴and brought Israel through the midst of it,
His love endures forever.
¹⁵but swept Pharaoh and his army into the Red Sea;
His love endures forever.

¹⁶to him who led his people through the wilderness;
His love endures forever.
¹⁷to him who struck down great kings,
His love endures forever.

¹⁸and killed mighty kings —
His love endures forever.
¹⁹Sihon king of the Amorites
His love endures forever.
²⁰and Og king of Bashan —
His love endures forever.
²¹and gave their land as an inheritance,
His love endures forever.
²²an inheritance to his servant Israel.
His love endures forever.

²³He remembered us in our low estate
His love endures forever.
²⁴and freed us from our enemies.
His love endures forever.
²⁵He gives food to every creature.
His love endures forever.

²⁶Give thanks to the God of heaven.
His love endures forever.

PSALM 137

¹By the rivers of Babylon we sat and wept
when we remembered Zion.
²There on the poplars
we hung our harps,
³for there our captors asked us for songs,
our tormentors demanded songs of joy;
they said, "Sing us one of the songs of Zion!"

ᵃ 13 Or *the Sea of Reeds*; also in verse 15

Three Questions for Christian Leaders

Psalm 137:1–6

Three great issues erupt from the lyrics of this psalm: the writer dreams, the writer cries, and the writer sings.

No wonder the people wept—the Jews had been taken from Israel against their will and exiled to Babylon. No wonder they sang—they could not forget Zion, the land of their birth. No wonder they dreamed—they hoped and prayed for the day of their return home.

These issues pose great questions for every leader:

1. **What do you dream about?**
   The psalmist remembered Zion; he longed to live again in his homeland. What are the dreams of your heart? What would you do if you had no fear of failure?

2. **What do you cry about?**
   The psalmist cried about living in Babylon; he wept over the captivity of his people. What makes you cry? What burdens drive you to become passionate?

3. **What do you sing about?**
   The psalmist sang about the blessings of God; he sang his remembrances of God's justice. What do you sing about? What causes you to rejoice or express joy?

4 How can we sing the songs of the LORD
    while in a foreign land?
5 If I forget you, Jerusalem,
    may my right hand forget its skill.
6 May my tongue cling to the roof of my mouth
    if I do not remember you,
    if I do not consider Jerusalem
    my highest joy.

7 Remember, LORD, what the Edomites did
    on the day Jerusalem fell.
"Tear it down," they cried,
    "tear it down to its foundations!"
8 Daughter Babylon, doomed to destruction,
    happy is the one who repays you
    according to what you have done to us.
9 Happy is the one who seizes your infants
    and dashes them against the rocks.

PSALM 138

Of David.

1 I will praise you, LORD, with all my heart;
    before the "gods" I will sing your praise.
2 I will bow down toward your holy temple
    and will praise your name
    for your unfailing love and your
        faithfulness,
for you have so exalted your solemn decree
    that it surpasses your fame.
3 When I called, you answered me;
    you greatly emboldened me.

4 May all the kings of the earth praise you,
    LORD,
    when they hear what you have decreed.
5 May they sing of the ways of the LORD,
    for the glory of the LORD is great.

6 Though the LORD is exalted, he looks kindly
    on the lowly;
    though lofty, he sees them from afar.
7 Though I walk in the midst of trouble,
    you preserve my life.
You stretch out your hand against the anger
    of my foes;
    with your right hand you save me.
8 The LORD will vindicate me;
    your love, LORD, endures forever —
    do not abandon the works of your hands.

PSALM 139

For the director of music. Of David. A psalm.

1 You have searched me, LORD,
    and you know me.

2 You know when I sit and when I rise;
    you perceive my thoughts from afar.
3 You discern my going out and my lying
       down;
    you are familiar with all my ways.
4 Before a word is on my tongue
    you, LORD, know it completely.
5 You hem me in behind and before,
    and you lay your hand upon me.
6 Such knowledge is too wonderful for me,
    too lofty for me to attain.

7 Where can I go from your Spirit?
    Where can I flee from your presence?
8 If I go up to the heavens, you are there;
    if I make my bed in the depths, you are
       there.
9 If I rise on the wings of the dawn,
    if I settle on the far side of the sea,
10 even there your hand will guide me,
    your right hand will hold me fast.
11 If I say, "Surely the darkness will hide me
    and the light become night around me,"
12 even the darkness will not be dark to you;
    the night will shine like the day,
    for darkness is as light to you.

13 For you created my inmost being;
    you knit me together in my mother's
       womb.
14 I praise you because I am fearfully and
       wonderfully made;
    your works are wonderful,
    I know that full well.
15 My frame was not hidden from you
    when I was made in the secret place,
    when I was woven together in the depths
       of the earth.
16 Your eyes saw my unformed body;
    all the days ordained for me were written
       in your book
    before one of them came to be.
17 How precious to me are your thoughts,[a]
       God!
    How vast is the sum of them!
18 Were I to count them,
    they would outnumber the grains of
       sand —
    when I awake, I am still with you.

19 If only you, God, would slay the wicked!
    Away from me, you who are bloodthirsty!
20 They speak of you with evil intent;
    your adversaries misuse your name.

a 17 Or *How amazing are your thoughts concerning me*

A Leader's Relationship with God Shapes His or Her Perspective

Psalm 139:1–24

Talk about seeing the big picture! In this psalm David explores the depths of God's omniscience, omnipotence and omnipresence.

David's dynamic and intimate relationship with God shapes his perspective on life. The king of Israel knew he wasn't alone. He rejoiced that he could draw upon God's infinite wisdom, that he could never run from God or his justice, and that he could count on God's power whenever he needed it. The leader of Israel had a Leader himself, named Yahweh. Ponder the benefits of an intimate relationship with God as Leader:

1. **God knows our every thought, every word and every move (vv. 1–6).**

2. **God directs us, no matter where we go (vv. 7–10).**

3. **God knows no hopeless or helpless situations (vv. 11–12).**

4. **God formed every complex detail of our bodies, minds and spirits (vv. 13–16).**

5. **God constantly thinks of us and is concerned with the details of our lives (vv. 17–18).**

6. **God searches our hearts and will purify our motives (vv. 23–24).**

21 Do I not hate those who hate you, Lord,
     and abhor those who are in rebellion
          against you?
22 I have nothing but hatred for them;
     I count them my enemies.
23 Search me, God, and know my heart;
     test me and know my anxious thoughts.
24 See if there is any offensive way in me,
     and lead me in the way everlasting.

PSALM 140[a]

For the director of music. A psalm of David.

1 Rescue me, Lord, from evildoers;
     protect me from the violent,
2 who devise evil plans in their hearts
     and stir up war every day.
3 They make their tongues as sharp as a
          serpent's;
     the poison of vipers is on their lips.[b]

4 Keep me safe, Lord, from the hands of the
          wicked;
     protect me from the violent,
     who devise ways to trip my feet.
5 The arrogant have hidden a snare for me;
     they have spread out the cords of their net
     and have set traps for me along my path.

6 I say to the Lord, "You are my God."
     Hear, Lord, my cry for mercy.

7 Sovereign Lord, my strong deliverer,
     you shield my head in the day of battle.
8 Do not grant the wicked their desires, Lord;
     do not let their plans succeed.

9 Those who surround me proudly rear their
          heads;
     may the mischief of their lips engulf them.
10 May burning coals fall on them;
     may they be thrown into the fire,
     into miry pits, never to rise.
11 May slanderers not be established in the land;
     may disaster hunt down the violent.

12 I know that the Lord secures justice for the
          poor
     and upholds the cause of the needy.
13 Surely the righteous will praise your name,
     and the upright will live in your presence.

PSALM 141

A psalm of David.

1 I call to you, Lord, come quickly to me;
     hear me when I call to you.
2 May my prayer be set before you like incense;
     may the lifting up of my hands be like the
          evening sacrifice.

[a] In Hebrew texts 140:1-13 is numbered 140:2-14.   [b] 3 The
Hebrew has *Selah* (a word of uncertain meaning) here and at
the end of verses 5 and 8.

³ Set a guard over my mouth, LORD;
  keep watch over the door of my lips.
⁴ Do not let my heart be drawn to what is
    evil
  so that I take part in wicked deeds
along with those who are evildoers;
  do not let me eat their delicacies.

⁵ Let a righteous man strike me — that is a
    kindness;
  let him rebuke me — that is oil on my
    head.
My head will not refuse it,
  for my prayer will still be against the
    deeds of evildoers.

⁶ Their rulers will be thrown down from the
    cliffs,
  and the wicked will learn that my words
    were well spoken.
⁷ They will say, "As one plows and breaks up
    the earth,
  so our bones have been scattered at the
    mouth of the grave."

⁸ But my eyes are fixed on you, Sovereign
    LORD;
  in you I take refuge — do not give me over
    to death.
⁹ Keep me safe from the traps set by
    evildoers,
  from the snares they have laid for me.
¹⁰ Let the wicked fall into their own nets,
  while I pass by in safety.

PSALM 142ᵃ

A *maskil*ᵇ of David. When he was in the cave.
A prayer.

¹ I cry aloud to the LORD;
  I lift up my voice to the LORD for mercy.
² I pour out before him my complaint;
  before him I tell my trouble.

³ When my spirit grows faint within me,
  it is you who watch over my way.
In the path where I walk
  people have hidden a snare for me.
⁴ Look and see, there is no one at my right
    hand;
  no one is concerned for me.
I have no refuge;
  no one cares for my life.

⁵ I cry to you, LORD;
  I say, "You are my refuge,
  my portion in the land of the living."

⁶ Listen to my cry,
  for I am in desperate need;
rescue me from those who pursue me,
  for they are too strong for me.
⁷ Set me free from my prison,
  that I may praise your name.
Then the righteous will gather about me
  because of your goodness to me.

PSALM 143

A psalm of David.

¹ LORD, hear my prayer,
  listen to my cry for mercy;
in your faithfulness and righteousness
  come to my relief.
² Do not bring your servant into judgment,
  for no one living is righteous before you.
³ The enemy pursues me,
  he crushes me to the ground;
he makes me dwell in the darkness
  like those long dead.
⁴ So my spirit grows faint within me;
  my heart within me is dismayed.
⁵ I remember the days of long ago;
  I meditate on all your works
  and consider what your hands have
    done.
⁶ I spread out my hands to you;
  I thirst for you like a parched land.ᶜ

⁷ Answer me quickly, LORD;
  my spirit fails.
Do not hide your face from me
  or I will be like those who go down to the
    pit.
⁸ Let the morning bring me word of your
    unfailing love,
  for I have put my trust in you.
Show me the way I should go,
  for to you I entrust my life.
⁹ Rescue me from my enemies, LORD,
  for I hide myself in you.
¹⁰ Teach me to do your will,
  for you are my God;
may your good Spirit
  lead me on level ground.

¹¹ For your name's sake, LORD, preserve my
    life;
  in your righteousness, bring me out of
    trouble.

ᵃ In Hebrew texts 142:1-7 is numbered 142:2-8.   ᵇ Title:
Probably a literary or musical term   ᶜ 6 The Hebrew has
Selah (a word of uncertain meaning) here.

¹²In your unfailing love, silence my enemies;
    destroy all my foes,
    for I am your servant.

PSALM 144

Of David.

¹Praise be to the LORD my Rock,
    who trains my hands for war,
    my fingers for battle.
²He is my loving God and my fortress,
    my stronghold and my deliverer,
    my shield, in whom I take refuge,
    who subdues peoples*a* under me.

³LORD, what are human beings that you care
        for them,
    mere mortals that you think of them?
⁴They are like a breath;
    their days are like a fleeting shadow.

⁵Part your heavens, LORD, and come down;
    touch the mountains, so that they smoke.
⁶Send forth lightning and scatter the enemy;
    shoot your arrows and rout them.
⁷Reach down your hand from on high;
    deliver me and rescue me
    from the mighty waters,
    from the hands of foreigners
⁸whose mouths are full of lies,
    whose right hands are deceitful.

⁹I will sing a new song to you, my God;
    on the ten-stringed lyre I will make music
        to you,
¹⁰to the One who gives victory to kings,
    who delivers his servant David.

From the deadly sword ¹¹deliver me;
    rescue me from the hands of foreigners
whose mouths are full of lies,
    whose right hands are deceitful.

¹²Then our sons in their youth
    will be like well-nurtured plants,
and our daughters will be like pillars
    carved to adorn a palace.
¹³Our barns will be filled
    with every kind of provision.
Our sheep will increase by thousands,
    by tens of thousands in our fields;
¹⁴   our oxen will draw heavy loads.*b*
There will be no breaching of walls,
    no going into captivity,
    no cry of distress in our streets.
¹⁵Blessed is the people of whom this is true;
    blessed is the people whose God is the LORD.

PSALM 145*c*

A psalm of praise. Of David.

¹I will exalt you, my God the King;
    I will praise your name for ever and ever.
²Every day I will praise you
    and extol your name for ever and ever.

³Great is the LORD and most worthy of praise;
    his greatness no one can fathom.
⁴One generation commends your works to
        another;
    they tell of your mighty acts.
⁵They speak of the glorious splendor of your
        majesty—
    and I will meditate on your wonderful
        works.*d*
⁶They tell of the power of your awesome
        works—
    and I will proclaim your great deeds.
⁷They celebrate your abundant goodness
    and joyfully sing of your righteousness.

⁸The LORD is gracious and compassionate,
    slow to anger and rich in love.

⁹The LORD is good to all;
    he has compassion on all he has made.
¹⁰All your works praise you, LORD;
    your faithful people extol you.
¹¹They tell of the glory of your kingdom
    and speak of your might,
¹²so that all people may know of your mighty
        acts
    and the glorious splendor of your
        kingdom.
¹³Your kingdom is an everlasting kingdom,
    and your dominion endures through all
        generations.

The LORD is trustworthy in all he promises
    and faithful in all he does.*e*
¹⁴The LORD upholds all who fall
    and lifts up all who are bowed down.
¹⁵The eyes of all look to you,
    and you give them their food at the proper
        time.

---

a 2 Many manuscripts of the Masoretic Text, Dead Sea Scrolls,
Aquila, Jerome and Syriac; most manuscripts of the Masoretic
Text *subdues my people*   *b 14* Or *our chieftains will be firmly
established*   *c* This psalm is an acrostic poem, the verses of
which (including verse 13b) begin with the successive letters of
the Hebrew alphabet.   *d 5* Dead Sea Scrolls and Syriac (see
also Septuagint); Masoretic Text *On the glorious splendor of
your majesty / and on your wonderful works I will meditate*
e 13 One manuscript of the Masoretic Text, Dead Sea Scrolls
and Syriac (see also Septuagint); most manuscripts of the
Masoretic Text do not have the last two lines of verse 13.

16 You open your hand
     and satisfy the desires of every living
          thing.

17 The LORD is righteous in all his ways
     and faithful in all he does.
18 The LORD is near to all who call on him,
     to all who call on him in truth.
19 He fulfills the desires of those who fear
          him;
     he hears their cry and saves them.
20 The LORD watches over all who love him,
     but all the wicked he will destroy.

21 My mouth will speak in praise of the
          LORD.
     Let every creature praise his holy name
     for ever and ever.

PSALM 146

1 Praise the LORD.[a]

Praise the LORD, my soul.

2 I will praise the LORD all my life;
     I will sing praise to my God as long as I live.

3 Do not put your trust in princes,
     in human beings, who cannot save.
4 When their spirit departs, they return to the
          ground;
     on that very day their plans come to
          nothing.
5 Blessed are those whose help is the God of
          Jacob,
     whose hope is in the LORD their God.

6 He is the Maker of heaven and earth,
     the sea, and everything in them—
     he remains faithful forever.
7 He upholds the cause of the oppressed
     and gives food to the hungry.
   The LORD sets prisoners free,
8   the LORD gives sight to the blind,
   the LORD lifts up those who are bowed
          down,
     the LORD loves the righteous.
9 The LORD watches over the foreigner
     and sustains the fatherless and the widow,
     but he frustrates the ways of the wicked.

---

a 1 Hebrew *Hallelu Yah*; also in verse 10

Commitment Comes Before Provision

Psalm 145:8–20

If Psalm 145 communicates just one message, it is that God deserves our unconditional commitment. David praises God for his goodness and his provisions. But he also makes it clear that leaders must walk in reckless abandon to the ways of God.

Once leaders make a commitment, they find that God provides the people, resources and strategy necessary to fulfill their dream. In one sense, God enters a partnership with his leaders and promises to fulfill his role as we fulfill ours:

God's Role: Provision (vv. 8–17)

   1. **He is gracious and merciful.**

   2. **His acts are mighty.**

   3. **His kingdom is everlasting.**

   4. **His dominion endures through all generations.**

   5. **He satisfies our desires.**

   6. **He is righteous and kind in all his ways.**

Our Role: Commitment (vv. 18–20)

   1. **To those who call upon him.**

   2. **To those who fear him.**

   3. **To those who love him.**

¹⁰ The LORD reigns forever,
　　your God, O Zion, for all generations.

Praise the LORD.

PSALM 147

¹ Praise the LORD.^a

How good it is to sing praises to our God,
　　how pleasant and fitting to praise him!

² The LORD builds up Jerusalem;
　　he gathers the exiles of Israel.
³ He heals the brokenhearted
　　and binds up their wounds.
⁴ He determines the number of the stars
　　and calls them each by name.
⁵ Great is our Lord and mighty in power;
　　his understanding has no limit.
⁶ The LORD sustains the humble
　　but casts the wicked to the ground.

⁷ Sing to the LORD with grateful praise;
　　make music to our God on the harp.

⁸ He covers the sky with clouds;
　　he supplies the earth with rain
　　and makes grass grow on the hills.
⁹ He provides food for the cattle
　　and for the young ravens when they call.

¹⁰ His pleasure is not in the strength of the
　　　horse,
　　nor his delight in the legs of the warrior;
¹¹ the LORD delights in those who fear him,
　　who put their hope in his unfailing love.

¹² Extol the LORD, Jerusalem;
　　praise your God, Zion.

¹³ He strengthens the bars of your gates
　　and blesses your people within you.
¹⁴ He grants peace to your borders
　　and satisfies you with the finest of wheat.

¹⁵ He sends his command to the earth;
　　his word runs swiftly.
¹⁶ He spreads the snow like wool
　　and scatters the frost like ashes.
¹⁷ He hurls down his hail like pebbles.
　　Who can withstand his icy blast?
¹⁸ He sends his word and melts them;
　　he stirs up his breezes, and the waters flow.

¹⁹ He has revealed his word to Jacob,
　　his laws and decrees to Israel.
²⁰ He has done this for no other nation;
　　they do not know his laws.^b

Praise the LORD.

PSALM 148

¹ Praise the LORD.^c

Praise the LORD from the heavens;
　　praise him in the heights above.
² Praise him, all his angels;
　　praise him, all his heavenly hosts.
³ Praise him, sun and moon;
　　praise him, all you shining stars.
⁴ Praise him, you highest heavens
　　and you waters above the skies.

⁵ Let them praise the name of the LORD,
　　for at his command they were created,
⁶ and he established them for ever and ever—
　　he issued a decree that will never pass
　　away.

⁷ Praise the LORD from the earth,
　　you great sea creatures and all ocean
　　　depths,
⁸ lightning and hail, snow and clouds,
　　stormy winds that do his bidding,
⁹ you mountains and all hills,
　　fruit trees and all cedars,
¹⁰ wild animals and all cattle,
　　small creatures and flying birds,
¹¹ kings of the earth and all nations,
　　you princes and all rulers on earth,
¹² young men and women,
　　old men and children.

¹³ Let them praise the name of the LORD,
　　for his name alone is exalted;
　　his splendor is above the earth and the
　　　heavens.
¹⁴ And he has raised up for his people a horn,^d
　　the praise of all his faithful servants,
　　of Israel, the people close to his heart.

Praise the LORD.

PSALM 149

¹ Praise the LORD.^e

Sing to the LORD a new song,
　　his praise in the assembly of his faithful
　　people.

² Let Israel rejoice in their Maker;
　　let the people of Zion be glad in their
　　King.

^a 1 Hebrew *Hallelu Yah;* also in verse 20　　^b 20 Masoretic
Text; Dead Sea Scrolls and Septuagint *nation; / he has not made
his laws known to them*　　^c 1 Hebrew *Hallelu Yah;* also in
verse 14　　^d 14 *Horn* here symbolizes strength.
^e 1 Hebrew *Hallelu Yah;* also in verse 9

³Let them praise his name with dancing
  and make music to him with timbrel and
    harp.
⁴For the LORD takes delight in his people;
  he crowns the humble with victory.
⁵Let his faithful people rejoice in this honor
  and sing for joy on their beds.

⁶May the praise of God be in their mouths
  and a double-edged sword in their hands,
⁷to inflict vengeance on the nations
  and punishment on the peoples,
⁸to bind their kings with fetters,
  their nobles with shackles of iron,
⁹to carry out the sentence written against
    them—
  this is the glory of all his faithful people.

Praise the LORD.

PSALM 150

¹Praise the LORD.ᵃ

Praise God in his sanctuary;
  praise him in his mighty heavens.
²Praise him for his acts of power;
  praise him for his surpassing greatness.
³Praise him with the sounding of the trumpet,
  praise him with the harp and lyre,
⁴praise him with timbrel and dancing,
  praise him with the strings and pipe,
⁵praise him with the clash of cymbals,
  praise him with resounding cymbals.

⁶Let everything that has breath praise the LORD.

Praise the LORD.

ᵃ 1 Hebrew *Hallelu Yah*; also in verse 6

INTRODUCTION TO PROVERBS

Principles for Guiding One's Life

A vast amount of leadership wisdom lies within the 31 chapters of Proverbs. Its excellent principles for guiding one's life come to us in the form of poetry, like the Psalms. But where Psalms portrays the relationships and emotions of a leader, Proverbs displays the principles, values and intellect of a leader. The Law of Navigation, the Law of Solid Ground and the Law of Intuition surface repeatedly in this book.

Proverbs is all about the mind of a leader, how a leader thinks. Who would dispute that leaders think differently from followers? Good leaders see things *before* followers do; they see *beyond* what followers do; and they see *bigger* than followers do. While followers may barely feel able to see and plan beyond next week, leaders must think, envision, and plan well into the future.

Fuller Seminary professor Bobby Clinton has said, "The primary difference between a follower and a leader is perspective. The primary difference between a leader and an effective leader is better perspective." Both leaders and followers can have strong character. Both can possess warm relational skills. Both can even have a strong personality and a strong will. What separates them is how they think and perceive reality.

Because the Scripture teaches that we were all made to rule (Ge 1:26–28), everyone possesses the capacity to raise their level of leadership ability. Each of us can improve the way we influence others. We must, however, begin with our perspective—and that is what makes the book of Proverbs so profound. It is a book about improving the way we think and therefore act. It is a book about raising the "lid" on our leadership ability—first by the way we lead our own lives, then by the way we lead others.

God's Role in Proverbs

God is the ultimate source of wisdom and of life itself. He mentors leaders who seek wisdom for their decision making. Proverbs paints a picture of wisdom as a person calling out for listeners, but finding few. God is also the divine Parent disciplining his children. He furnishes words of correction and guidance, again beseeching us to listen. Finally, this book presents God as the divine Preacher or Teacher. He contrasts the diligent and the sluggard, the good and the wicked, the wise and the foolish. The axioms flow off his tongue, teaching the student how the Master thinks and acts.

Leaders in Proverbs

Solomon, wise men, Agur, Lemuel

Other People of Influence in Proverbs

The wise person, the adulterous woman, the sluggard, the wicked person, the fool

Lessons in Leadership

- Good leadership begins with good wisdom and insight.
- Competency cannot substitute for lack of character.
- Leadership development begins with "being" before "doing."
- Leaders who solve problems will never lack followers.

In this book you will encounter wisdom principles that appear so simple, yet are tremendously deep and profound. Soak in every verse through the eyes of a leader. The wisdom lies in front of every one of us, "she raises her voice in the public square," longing to be noticed (1:20–23). Embrace the disciplines and the character that Solomon suggests, and you will be on your way to transforming your leadership.

- Wisdom is available to leaders who pursue it diligently, but it is not automatic.
- Laziness can steal everything a leader has worked to achieve.
- God rewards leaders who do right.

LEADERSHIP HIGHLIGHTS IN PROVERBS

Purpose and Theme

1 The proverbs of Solomon son of David, king of Israel:

[2] for gaining wisdom and instruction;
    for understanding words of insight;
[3] for receiving instruction in prudent
    behavior,
    doing what is right and just and fair;
[4] for giving prudence to those who are
    simple,[a]
    knowledge and discretion to the young—
[5] let the wise listen and add to their learning,
    and let the discerning get guidance—
[6] for understanding proverbs and parables,
    the sayings and riddles of the wise.[b]

[7] The fear of the LORD is the beginning of
    knowledge,
    but fools[c] despise wisdom and instruction.

Prologue: Exhortations to Embrace Wisdom

Warning Against the Invitation of Sinful Men

[8] Listen, my son, to your father's instruction
    and do not forsake your mother's
    teaching.
[9] They are a garland to grace your head
    and a chain to adorn your neck.

[10] My son, if sinful men entice you,
    do not give in to them.

[11] If they say, "Come along with us;
    let's lie in wait for innocent blood,
    let's ambush some harmless soul;
[12] let's swallow them alive, like the grave,
    and whole, like those who go down to
    the pit;
[13] we will get all sorts of valuable things
    and fill our houses with plunder;
[14] cast lots with us;
    we will all share the loot"—
[15] my son, do not go along with them,
    do not set foot on their paths;
[16] for their feet rush into evil,
    they are swift to shed blood.
[17] How useless to spread a net
    where every bird can see it!
[18] These men lie in wait for their own blood;
    they ambush only themselves!
[19] Such are the paths of all who go after ill-
    gotten gain;
    it takes away the life of those who get it.

Wisdom's Rebuke

[20] Out in the open wisdom calls aloud,
    she raises her voice in the public
    square;

---

[a] 4 The Hebrew word rendered *simple* in Proverbs denotes a person who is gullible, without moral direction and inclined to evil.   [b] 6 Or *understanding a proverb, namely, a parable, / and the sayings of the wise, their riddles*   [c] 7 The Hebrew words rendered *fool* in Proverbs, and often elsewhere in the Old Testament, denote a person who is morally deficient.

Decision Making: The Fast Way to Gain Leadership

Proverbs 1:7–33

Wisdom can be a leader's best friend, especially in times of decision. Suppose you find yourself in a large committee meeting in which a crucial decision must be made. The committee reaches an impasse and everything stops. Who will become the most influential person in that room? Answer: the one with the wisdom to draw a conclusion that not only works, but which receives the blessing of that committee.

Proverbs 1 describes wisdom as a woman crying out in the streets (v. 20). What a beautiful picture! Wisdom does not hide herself, but shouts publicly! We must go out and find her and build a friendship with her. What can we learn about decision making from Proverbs 1?

1. **The foundation for every decision is to honor and revere God (v. 7).**

2. **We must build off our heritage and conscience: what values are we to embrace? (vv. 8–9).**

3. **We must avoid the counsel of the ungodly (vv. 10–19).**

4. **We must pursue wisdom. What are the facts? What are the options? (vv. 20–23).**

5. **We must move toward inward peace (vv. 32–33).**

21 on top of the wall[a] she cries out,
   at the city gate she makes her speech:

22 "How long will you who are simple love your
      simple ways?
   How long will mockers delight in mockery
      and fools hate knowledge?
23 Repent at my rebuke!
   Then I will pour out my thoughts to you,
   I will make known to you my teachings.
24 But since you refuse to listen when I call
   and no one pays attention when I stretch
      out my hand,
25 since you disregard all my advice
   and do not accept my rebuke,
26 I in turn will laugh when disaster strikes you;
   I will mock when calamity overtakes
      you —
27 when calamity overtakes you like a storm,
   when disaster sweeps over you like a
      whirlwind,
   when distress and trouble overwhelm you.

28 "Then they will call to me but I will not
      answer;
   they will look for me but will not find me,
29 since they hated knowledge
   and did not choose to fear the LORD.
30 Since they would not accept my advice
   and spurned my rebuke,

31 they will eat the fruit of their ways
   and be filled with the fruit of their schemes.
32 For the waywardness of the simple will kill
      them,
   and the complacency of fools will destroy
      them;
33 but whoever listens to me will live in safety
   and be at ease, without fear of harm."

Moral Benefits of Wisdom

2 My son, if you accept my words
   and store up my commands within you,
2 turning your ear to wisdom
   and applying your heart to
      understanding —
3 indeed, if you call out for insight
   and cry aloud for understanding,
4 and if you look for it as for silver
   and search for it as for hidden treasure,
5 then you will understand the fear of the LORD
   and find the knowledge of God.
6 For the LORD gives wisdom;
   from his mouth come knowledge and
      understanding.
7 He holds success in store for the upright,
   he is a shield to those whose walk is
      blameless,

---

[a] 21 Septuagint; Hebrew / at noisy street corners

Desire: What Separates Leaders from Followers

Proverbs 2:1–4

Good leaders seem to know what steps to take into a bright future. But what enables them to know what to do? How do they differ from followers? Proverbs 2 tells us the key difference may be desire. We all must answer three great questions in life:

1. **What do we want?**
2. **Why do we want it?**
3. **How badly do we want it?**

Consider the phrases Proverbs 2 uses to talk about the passionate search for wisdom:

- *receive* my words (v. 1)
- *treasure* my commands (v. 1)
- *incline* your ear to wisdom (v. 2)
- *apply* your heart to understanding (v. 2)
- *cry out* for discernment (v. 3)
- *lift up* your voice for understanding (v. 3)
- *seek* her as silver (v. 4)
- *search* for her as for hidden treasure (v. 4)

Good leaders hunt for wisdom as though it were diamonds and rubies. So—what are *you* searching for?

8 for he guards the course of the just
    and protects the way of his faithful ones.

9 Then you will understand what is right and just
    and fair — every good path.

10 For wisdom will enter your heart,
    and knowledge will be pleasant to your soul.

11 Discretion will protect you,
    and understanding will guard you.

12 Wisdom will save you from the ways of wicked men,
    from men whose words are perverse,

13 who have left the straight paths
    to walk in dark ways,

14 who delight in doing wrong
    and rejoice in the perverseness of evil,

15 whose paths are crooked
    and who are devious in their ways.

16 Wisdom will save you also from the adulterous woman,
    from the wayward woman with her seductive words,

17 who has left the partner of her youth
    and ignored the covenant she made before God.[a]

18 Surely her house leads down to death
    and her paths to the spirits of the dead.

19 None who go to her return
    or attain the paths of life.

20 Thus you will walk in the ways of the good
    and keep to the paths of the righteous.

21 For the upright will live in the land,
    and the blameless will remain in it;

22 but the wicked will be cut off from the land,
    and the unfaithful will be torn from it.

Wisdom Bestows Well-Being

3 My son, do not forget my teaching,
    but keep my commands in your heart,

2 for they will prolong your life many years
    and bring you peace and prosperity.

3 Let love and faithfulness never leave you;
    bind them around your neck,
    write them on the tablet of your heart.

4 Then you will win favor and a good name
    in the sight of God and man.

5 Trust in the LORD with all your heart
    and lean not on your own understanding;

6 in all your ways submit to him,
    and he will make your paths straight.[b]

7 Do not be wise in your own eyes;
    fear the LORD and shun evil.

[a] 17 Or covenant of her God   [b] 6 Or will direct your paths

---

The Irony of Spiritual Leadership: Get Understanding but Don't Lean On It

Proverbs 3:5–6

Proverbs 2 and 3 poses an apparent paradox in spiritual leadership. We are to get wisdom and understanding (2:1–5), yet we are not to lean on it apart from the Lord (3:5–6). Even good wisdom divorced from God can become a snare. So how are godly leaders to think?

1. **Godly leaders think *big*:** They realize God's vision is usually bigger than theirs.

2. **Godly leaders think *other people*:** They always include others in the mix.

3. **Godly leaders think *continually*:** They're not satisfied with today's answers.

4. **Godly leaders think *bottom line*:** They want to see results and fruit.

5. **Godly leaders think *continual growth*:** They want to keep improving.

6. **Godly leaders think *without lines*:** They let God outside of the box.

7. **Godly leaders think *victory*:** They want to see God's rule come to earth.

8. **Godly leaders think *intuitively*:** They have a sense of what will work.

9. **Godly leaders think *servanthood*:** They want to serve and add value to people.

10. **Godly leaders think *quickly*:** They evaluate quickly and see possible answers.

8 This will bring health to your body
and nourishment to your bones.

9 Honor the LORD with your wealth,
with the firstfruits of all your crops;
10 then your barns will be filled to overflowing,
and your vats will brim over with new
wine.

11 My son, do not despise the LORD's discipline,
and do not resent his rebuke,
12 because the LORD disciplines those he loves,
as a father the son he delights in.*a*

13 Blessed are those who find wisdom,
those who gain understanding,
14 for she is more profitable than silver
and yields better returns than gold.
15 She is more precious than rubies;
nothing you desire can compare with her.
16 Long life is in her right hand;
in her left hand are riches and honor.
17 Her ways are pleasant ways,
and all her paths are peace.
18 She is a tree of life to those who take hold of
her;
those who hold her fast will be blessed.

19 By wisdom the LORD laid the earth's
foundations,
by understanding he set the heavens in
place;
20 by his knowledge the watery depths were
divided,
and the clouds let drop the dew.

21 My son, do not let wisdom and
understanding out of your sight,
preserve sound judgment and discretion;
22 they will be life for you,
an ornament to grace your neck.
23 Then you will go on your way in safety,
and your foot will not stumble.
24 When you lie down, you will not be afraid;
when you lie down, your sleep will be
sweet.
25 Have no fear of sudden disaster
or of the ruin that overtakes the wicked,
26 for the LORD will be at your side
and will keep your foot from being snared.

27 Do not withhold good from those to whom it
is due,
when it is in your power to act.
28 Do not say to your neighbor,
"Come back tomorrow and I'll give it to
you" —
when you already have it with you.

29 Do not plot harm against your neighbor,
who lives trustfully near you.
30 Do not accuse anyone for no reason —
when they have done you no harm.
31 Do not envy the violent
or choose any of their ways.
32 For the LORD detests the perverse
but takes the upright into his confidence.
33 The LORD's curse is on the house of the
wicked,
but he blesses the home of the righteous.
34 He mocks proud mockers
but shows favor to the humble and
oppressed.
35 The wise inherit honor,
but fools get only shame.

Get Wisdom at Any Cost

4 Listen, my sons, to a father's instruction;
pay attention and gain understanding.
2 I give you sound learning,
so do not forsake my teaching.
3 For I too was a son to my father,
still tender, and cherished by my mother.
4 Then he taught me, and he said to me,
"Take hold of my words with all your
heart;
keep my commands, and you will live.
5 Get wisdom, get understanding;
do not forget my words or turn away from
them.
6 Do not forsake wisdom, and she will protect
you;
love her, and she will watch over you.
7 The beginning of wisdom is this: Get*b*
wisdom.
Though it cost all you have,*c* get
understanding.
8 Cherish her, and she will exalt you;
embrace her, and she will honor you.
9 She will give you a garland to grace your
head
and present you with a glorious crown."

10 Listen, my son, accept what I say,
and the years of your life will be many.
11 I instruct you in the way of wisdom
and lead you along straight paths.
12 When you walk, your steps will not be
hampered;
when you run, you will not stumble.

---

a 12 Hebrew; Septuagint *loves, / and he chastens everyone he
accepts as his child*   *b* 7 Or *Wisdom is supreme; therefore get*
c 7 Or *wisdom. / Whatever else you get*

¹³ Hold on to instruction, do not let it go;
  guard it well, for it is your life.
¹⁴ Do not set foot on the path of the wicked
  or walk in the way of evildoers.
¹⁵ Avoid it, do not travel on it;
  turn from it and go on your way.
¹⁶ For they cannot rest until they do evil;
  they are robbed of sleep till they make
    someone stumble.
¹⁷ They eat the bread of wickedness
  and drink the wine of violence.

¹⁸ The path of the righteous is like the morning
    sun,
  shining ever brighter till the full light of
    day.
¹⁹ But the way of the wicked is like deep
    darkness;
  they do not know what makes them
    stumble.

²⁰ My son, pay attention to what I say;
  turn your ear to my words.
²¹ Do not let them out of your sight,
  keep them within your heart;
²² for they are life to those who find them
  and health to one's whole body.
²³ Above all else, guard your heart,
  for everything you do flows from it.
²⁴ Keep your mouth free of perversity;
  keep corrupt talk far from your lips.
²⁵ Let your eyes look straight ahead;
  fix your gaze directly before you.
²⁶ Give careful thought to the*ᵃ* paths for your
    feet
  and be steadfast in all your ways.

²⁷ Do not turn to the right or the left;
  keep your foot from evil.

Warning Against Adultery

5 My son, pay attention to my wisdom,
  turn your ear to my words of insight,
² that you may maintain discretion
  and your lips may preserve knowledge.
³ For the lips of the adulterous woman drip
    honey,
  and her speech is smoother than oil;
⁴ but in the end she is bitter as gall,
  sharp as a double-edged sword.
⁵ Her feet go down to death;
  her steps lead straight to the grave.
⁶ She gives no thought to the way of life;
  her paths wander aimlessly, but she does
    not know it.

⁷ Now then, my sons, listen to me;
  do not turn aside from what I say.
⁸ Keep to a path far from her,
  do not go near the door of her house,
⁹ lest you lose your honor to others
  and your dignityᵇ to one who is cruel,
¹⁰ lest strangers feast on your wealth
  and your toil enrich the house of
    another.
¹¹ At the end of your life you will groan,
  when your flesh and body are spent.
¹² You will say, "How I hated discipline!
  How my heart spurned correction!
¹³ I would not obey my teachers
  or turn my ear to my instructors.

ᵃ 26 Or *Make level*   ᵇ 9 Or *years*

Principle-Centered Leadership

Proverbs 4:20–27

Leaders who last do not merely react to their culture; they base their leadership on timeless and universal principles. They remain relevant because they marry cultural context to timeless truth. Proverbs 4 encourages leaders to become principle centered. Verses 20–27 teach us that God's principles give us three crucial tools:

1. **They are a *guide*; they help us stay on the right path.**

2. **They are a *guard*; they keep our hearts and bodies protected.**

3. **They are a *gauge*; they enable us to evaluate where we are.**

These principles build our character, direct our decisions, and correct our lifestyles. Every leader ought to consume God's Word, then put the truths he or she discovers in the form of principles that can guide, guard and gauge his or her life.

SOLOMON

It Is More Blessed to Follow Good Advice Than to Give It

Proverbs 5:3–21

PROFILE in leadership

It doesn't take a leader very long to realize that it's easier to give good advice than to follow it. Solomon proves the point.

This wisest of kings didn't hold back when it came to warning his people against adultery. He tells us repeatedly and with great conviction that only fools fall into adultery. Perhaps he spoke so forcefully after pondering the fate of his own father, David, who brought on himself no end of trouble through his illicit affair with Bathsheba (2Sa 12:10). Solomon therefore counseled other men to stay at home and find contentment with "the wife of your youth" (Pr 5:18). The king knew very well the spiritual issues at stake in marriage, for he declares, "Your ways are in full view of the Lord, and he examines all your paths" (5:21).

And yet, somehow, this same leader failed to heed God's explicit warning against kings taking many wives (Dt 17:17). Solomon blatantly disobeyed this command and married *seven hundred* women. The result? "His wives turned his heart after other gods, and his heart was not fully devoted to the Lord his God" (1Ki 11:4).

Wise leaders not only give good advice; they heed it. How different the fortunes of Israel might have turned out had Solomon acted on the wisdom he so forcefully expressed to others!

Moral Failure: Disciplines Prevent Nightmares

Proverbs 5:3–23

How many leaders have ruined their lives and damaged the lives of others through immorality? Character has become a crucial issue today precisely because of the myriad leaders in the political, business, and religious worlds who have fallen morally. No doubt spiritual warfare has played a big role in the tens of thousands of leaders who have failed. They fall partly because the enemy has targeted leaders for attack.

Leaders need to remember that they influence many others beyond themselves; they never fall in a vacuum. They also need to realize that replacing fallen leaders is a slow and difficult process.

So how can we guard against falling? First, we must take care not to emphasize the gifts of a leader over his or her character. We have an unhealthy tendency to see and reward the gift more than the character, but both are to be developed. We must strike the following balance if we are to finish well:

GIFT DEPOSITED   CHARACTER BUILT

WHAT I AM	WHAT I DO	THE RESULT
Humble	Rely on God	God's Power
Visionary	Set Goals	High Morale
Convictional	Do Right	Credibility

¹⁴And I was soon in serious trouble
  in the assembly of God's people."

¹⁵Drink water from your own cistern,
  running water from your own well.
¹⁶Should your springs overflow in the streets,
  your streams of water in the public
    squares?
¹⁷Let them be yours alone,
  never to be shared with strangers.
¹⁸May your fountain be blessed,
  and may you rejoice in the wife of your
    youth.
¹⁹A loving doe, a graceful deer —
  may her breasts satisfy you always,
  may you ever be intoxicated with her love.
²⁰Why, my son, be intoxicated with another
    man's wife?
  Why embrace the bosom of a wayward
    woman?
²¹For your ways are in full view of the LORD,
  and he examines all your paths.
²²The evil deeds of the wicked ensnare them;
  the cords of their sins hold them fast.
²³For lack of discipline they will die,
  led astray by their own great folly.

Warnings Against Folly

6 My son, if you have put up security for your
    neighbor,
  if you have shaken hands in pledge for a
    stranger,
²you have been trapped by what you said,
  ensnared by the words of your mouth.

³So do this, my son, to free yourself,
  since you have fallen into your neighbor's
    hands:
  Go — to the point of exhaustion — ^a
    and give your neighbor no rest!
⁴Allow no sleep to your eyes,
  no slumber to your eyelids.
⁵Free yourself, like a gazelle from the hand of
    the hunter,
  like a bird from the snare of the fowler.

⁶Go to the ant, you sluggard;
  consider its ways and be wise!
⁷It has no commander,
  no overseer or ruler,
⁸yet it stores its provisions in summer
  and gathers its food at harvest.

⁹How long will you lie there, you sluggard?
  When will you get up from your sleep?
¹⁰A little sleep, a little slumber,
  a little folding of the hands to rest —
¹¹and poverty will come on you like a thief
  and scarcity like an armed man.

¹²A troublemaker and a villain,
  who goes about with a corrupt mouth,
¹³ who winks maliciously with his eye,
  signals with his feet
  and motions with his fingers,
¹⁴ who plots evil with deceit in his
    heart —
  he always stirs up conflict.

^a 3 Or *Go and humble yourself,*

Leadership Lessons from the Ant

Proverbs 6:6–8

Do you want to make a difference? Then pay attention to the metaphor of the ant. It's amazing that one of the smallest of God's creatures can become one of his greatest teachers. The lessons the ant teaches us can be summarized this way:

A — Attitude of Initiative
Ants don't need a commander to tell them to get started.

N — Nature of Integrity
Ants work faithfully and need no outside accountability to keep them doing right.

T — Thirst for Industry
Ants work hard and will replace their anthill when it gets ruined.

S — Source of Insight
Ants store provisions in summer.

If we consider and learn from the ways of the ant, we can grow wise.

¹⁵ Therefore disaster will overtake him in an
     instant;
     he will suddenly be destroyed — without
     remedy.

¹⁶ There are six things the LORD hates,
     seven that are detestable to him:
¹⁷   haughty eyes,
       a lying tongue,
       hands that shed innocent blood,
¹⁸   a heart that devises wicked schemes,
       feet that are quick to rush into evil,
¹⁹   a false witness who pours out lies
       and a person who stirs up conflict in
         the community.

Warning Against Adultery

²⁰ My son, keep your father's command
     and do not forsake your mother's teaching.
²¹ Bind them always on your heart;
     fasten them around your neck.
²² When you walk, they will guide you;
     when you sleep, they will watch over you;
     when you awake, they will speak to you.
²³ For this command is a lamp,
     this teaching is a light,
   and correction and instruction
     are the way to life,
²⁴ keeping you from your neighbor's wife,
     from the smooth talk of a wayward woman.

²⁵ Do not lust in your heart after her beauty
     or let her captivate you with her eyes.
²⁶ For a prostitute can be had for a loaf of
     bread,
     but another man's wife preys on your very
       life.
²⁷ Can a man scoop fire into his lap
     without his clothes being burned?
²⁸ Can a man walk on hot coals
     without his feet being scorched?
²⁹ So is he who sleeps with another man's wife;
     no one who touches her will go
       unpunished.

³⁰ People do not despise a thief if he steals
     to satisfy his hunger when he is starving.
³¹ Yet if he is caught, he must pay sevenfold,
     though it costs him all the wealth of his
       house.
³² But a man who commits adultery has no
     sense;
     whoever does so destroys himself.
³³ Blows and disgrace are his lot,
     and his shame will never be wiped away.

³⁴ For jealousy arouses a husband's fury,
     and he will show no mercy when he takes
       revenge.
³⁵ He will not accept any compensation;
     he will refuse a bribe, however great it is.

THE SLUGGARD

Worthless to the Kingdom
Proverbs 6:6, 9–11

PROFILE in leadership

King Solomon had plenty to say about the "sluggard," or the habitually lazy person. He contrasts the sluggard with the ant, who works diligently during the summer to gather enough food for the winter. In Proverbs 20:4, Solomon describes the sluggard as one who refuses to work hard during the growing season and so has nothing at harvest time. The sluggard makes only one commitment: to his leisure. He'll try any excuse to shy away from honest labor, even excusing himself through irrational claims of danger (Pr 22:13).

The sluggard in the physical sense does nothing for the world around him; he leaves it unchanged, except for pillaging some of its resources. The sluggard in the spiritual sense is little different; he leaves the world no better than he found it, and perhaps a little poorer. When leaders become lazy and lose their diligence in doing good for God, they become spiritual sluggards and worthless to the kingdom (Mt 5:13).

Wise leaders know their time is limited. They know they have no way to retrieve misused or wasted time. Jesus stressed this when he said, "As long as it is day, we must do the works of him who sent me. Night is coming, when no one can work" (Jn 9:4). Leaders in the body of Christ must remain diligent in doing good and in encouraging others to do likewise.

Warning Against the Adulterous Woman

7 My son, keep my words
and store up my commands within you.
[2] Keep my commands and you will live;
guard my teachings as the apple of your
eye.
[3] Bind them on your fingers;
write them on the tablet of your heart.
[4] Say to wisdom, "You are my sister,"
and to insight, "You are my relative."
[5] They will keep you from the adulterous
woman,
from the wayward woman with her
seductive words.

[6] At the window of my house
I looked down through the lattice.
[7] I saw among the simple,
I noticed among the young men,
a youth who had no sense.
[8] He was going down the street near her corner,
walking along in the direction of her
house
[9] at twilight, as the day was fading,
as the dark of night set in.

[10] Then out came a woman to meet him,
dressed like a prostitute and with crafty
intent.
[11] (She is unruly and defiant,
her feet never stay at home;
[12] now in the street, now in the squares,
at every corner she lurks.)
[13] She took hold of him and kissed him
and with a brazen face she said:

[14] "Today I fulfilled my vows,
and I have food from my fellowship
offering at home.
[15] So I came out to meet you;
I looked for you and have found you!
[16] I have covered my bed
with colored linens from Egypt.
[17] I have perfumed my bed
with myrrh, aloes and cinnamon.
[18] Come, let's drink deeply of love till morning;
let's enjoy ourselves with love!
[19] My husband is not at home;
he has gone on a long journey.
[20] He took his purse filled with money
and will not be home till full moon."

[21] With persuasive words she led him astray;
she seduced him with her smooth talk.
[22] All at once he followed her
like an ox going to the slaughter,

like a deer[a] stepping into a noose[b]
[23] till an arrow pierces his liver,
like a bird darting into a snare,
little knowing it will cost him his life.

[24] Now then, my sons, listen to me;
pay attention to what I say.
[25] Do not let your heart turn to her ways
or stray into her paths.
[26] Many are the victims she has brought down;
her slain are a mighty throng.
[27] Her house is a highway to the grave,
leading down to the chambers of death.

Wisdom's Call

8 Does not wisdom call out?
Does not understanding raise her voice?
[2] At the highest point along the way,
where the paths meet, she takes her stand;
[3] beside the gate leading into the city,
at the entrance, she cries aloud:
[4] "To you, O people, I call out;
I raise my voice to all mankind.
[5] You who are simple, gain prudence;
you who are foolish, set your hearts on it.[c]
[6] Listen, for I have trustworthy things to say;
I open my lips to speak what is right.
[7] My mouth speaks what is true,
for my lips detest wickedness.
[8] All the words of my mouth are just;
none of them is crooked or perverse.
[9] To the discerning all of them are right;
they are upright to those who have found
knowledge.
[10] Choose my instruction instead of silver,
knowledge rather than choice gold,
[11] for wisdom is more precious than rubies,
and nothing you desire can compare
with her.

[12] "I, wisdom, dwell together with prudence;
I possess knowledge and discretion.
[13] To fear the LORD is to hate evil;
I hate pride and arrogance,
evil behavior and perverse speech.
[14] Counsel and sound judgment are mine;
I have insight, I have power.
[15] By me kings reign
and rulers issue decrees that are just;
[16] by me princes govern,
and nobles — all who rule on earth.[d]

---

[a] 22 Syriac (see also Septuagint); Hebrew *fool* [b] 22 The
meaning of the Hebrew for this line is uncertain.
[c] 5 Septuagint; Hebrew *foolish, instruct your minds*
[d] 16 Some Hebrew manuscripts and Septuagint; other Hebrew
manuscripts *all righteous rulers*

The Law of Intuition: Wisdom Makes the Difference

Proverbs 8:15–16

Leadership begins with our thoughts even before our actions. When our mind and our attitudes are right, we position ourselves to lead well. Wisdom desires to be the best friend of any leader. Wise leaders also have discernment in relationships, a hatred for what is wrong, and influence.

17 I love those who love me,
    and those who seek me find me.
18 With me are riches and honor,
    enduring wealth and prosperity.
19 My fruit is better than fine gold;
    what I yield surpasses choice silver.
20 I walk in the way of righteousness,
    along the paths of justice,
21 bestowing a rich inheritance on those who
        love me
    and making their treasuries full.

22 "The LORD brought me forth as the first of
        his works,[a,b]
    before his deeds of old;
23 I was formed long ages ago,
    at the very beginning, when the world
        came to be.
24 When there were no watery depths, I was
        given birth,
    when there were no springs overflowing
        with water;
25 before the mountains were settled in place,
    before the hills, I was given birth,
26 before he made the world or its fields
    or any of the dust of the earth.
27 I was there when he set the heavens in place,
    when he marked out the horizon on the
        face of the deep,
28 when he established the clouds above
    and fixed securely the fountains of the
        deep,
29 when he gave the sea its boundary
    so the waters would not overstep his
        command,
    and when he marked out the foundations of
        the earth.
30   Then I was constantly[c] at his side.
    I was filled with delight day after day,
        rejoicing always in his presence,

31 rejoicing in his whole world
    and delighting in mankind.

32 "Now then, my children, listen to me;
    blessed are those who keep my ways.
33 Listen to my instruction and be wise;
    do not disregard it.
34 Blessed are those who listen to me,
    watching daily at my doors,
    waiting at my doorway.
35 For those who find me find life
    and receive favor from the LORD.
36 But those who fail to find me harm
        themselves;
    all who hate me love death."

Invitations of Wisdom and Folly

9 Wisdom has built her house;
    she has set up[d] its seven pillars.
2 She has prepared her meat and mixed her
        wine;
    she has also set her table.
3 She has sent out her servants, and she calls
    from the highest point of the city,
4   "Let all who are simple come to my
        house!"
    To those who have no sense she says,
5   "Come, eat my food
    and drink the wine I have mixed.
6 Leave your simple ways and you will live;
    walk in the way of insight."

7 Whoever corrects a mocker invites insults;
    whoever rebukes the wicked incurs abuse.
8 Do not rebuke mockers or they will hate you;
    rebuke the wise and they will love you.
9 Instruct the wise and they will be wiser still;
    teach the righteous and they will add to
        their learning.

10 The fear of the LORD is the beginning of
        wisdom,
    and knowledge of the Holy One is
        understanding.
11 For through wisdom[e] your days will be many,
    and years will be added to your life.
12 If you are wise, your wisdom will reward
        you;
    if you are a mocker, you alone will suffer.

13 Folly is an unruly woman;
    she is simple and knows nothing.

---

[a] 22 Or way; or dominion   [b] 22 Or The LORD possessed me at the beginning of his work; or The LORD brought me forth at the beginning of his work   [c] 30 Or was the artisan; or was a little child   [d] 1 Septuagint, Syriac and Targum; Hebrew has hewn out   [e] 11 Septuagint, Syriac and Targum; Hebrew me

14 She sits at the door of her house,
    on a seat at the highest point of the city,
15 calling out to those who pass by,
    who go straight on their way,
16   "Let all who are simple come to my house!"
  To those who have no sense she says,
17   "Stolen water is sweet;
    food eaten in secret is delicious!"
18 But little do they know that the dead are there,
    that her guests are deep in the realm of the dead.

Proverbs of Solomon

10

The proverbs of Solomon:

A wise son brings joy to his father,
    but a foolish son brings grief to his mother.

2 Ill-gotten treasures have no lasting value,
    but righteousness delivers from death.

3 The LORD does not let the righteous go hungry,
    but he thwarts the craving of the wicked.

4 Lazy hands make for poverty,
    but diligent hands bring wealth.

5 He who gathers crops in summer is a prudent son,
    but he who sleeps during harvest is a disgraceful son.

6 Blessings crown the head of the righteous,
    but violence overwhelms the mouth of the wicked.[a]

7 The name of the righteous is used in blessings,[b]
    but the name of the wicked will rot.

8 The wise in heart accept commands,
    but a chattering fool comes to ruin.

9 Whoever walks in integrity walks securely,
    but whoever takes crooked paths will be found out.

10 Whoever winks maliciously causes grief,
    and a chattering fool comes to ruin.

11 The mouth of the righteous is a fountain of life,
    but the mouth of the wicked conceals violence.

12 Hatred stirs up conflict,
    but love covers over all wrongs.

13 Wisdom is found on the lips of the discerning,
    but a rod is for the back of one who has no sense.

14 The wise store up knowledge,
    but the mouth of a fool invites ruin.

15 The wealth of the rich is their fortified city,
    but poverty is the ruin of the poor.

16 The wages of the righteous is life,
    but the earnings of the wicked are sin and death.

17 Whoever heeds discipline shows the way to life,
    but whoever ignores correction leads others astray.

18 Whoever conceals hatred with lying lips
    and spreads slander is a fool.

19 Sin is not ended by multiplying words,
    but the prudent hold their tongues.

20 The tongue of the righteous is choice silver,
    but the heart of the wicked is of little value.

21 The lips of the righteous nourish many,
    but fools die for lack of sense.

22 The blessing of the LORD brings wealth,
    without painful toil for it.

23 A fool finds pleasure in wicked schemes,
    but a person of understanding delights in wisdom.

24 What the wicked dread will overtake them;
    what the righteous desire will be granted.

25 When the storm has swept by, the wicked are gone,
    but the righteous stand firm forever.

26 As vinegar to the teeth and smoke to the eyes,
    so are sluggards to those who send them.

27 The fear of the LORD adds length to life,
    but the years of the wicked are cut short.

28 The prospect of the righteous is joy,
    but the hopes of the wicked come to nothing.

29 The way of the LORD is a refuge for the blameless,
    but it is the ruin of those who do evil.

---

[a] 6 Or righteous, / but the mouth of the wicked conceals violence
[b] 7 See Gen. 48:20.

The Law of Influence: Leaders Must Have a Skillful Tongue

Proverbs 10:6–32

A number of verses in Proverbs speak of the tongue and how to use it as a positive influence. Leaders who use words skillfully increase their influence. Leaders who understand the power of their words accomplish the following:

1. **They proclaim justice and are blessed (v. 6).**

2. **They speak hope for the future, becoming a fountain of life to others (v. 11).**

3. **They speak forth wisdom and save others from ruin (vv. 13–14).**

4. **They know when silence is more powerful than words (v. 19).**

5. **Their words feed and nourish many others (v. 21).**

6. **They express what is right and nurture the right in the hearts of those who follow (vv. 31–32).**

30 The righteous will never be uprooted,
but the wicked will not remain in the
land.

31 From the mouth of the righteous comes the
fruit of wisdom,
but a perverse tongue will be silenced.

32 The lips of the righteous know what finds
favor,
but the mouth of the wicked only what is
perverse.

11 The LORD detests dishonest scales,
but accurate weights find favor with
him.

2 When pride comes, then comes disgrace,
but with humility comes wisdom.

3 The integrity of the upright guides them,
but the unfaithful are destroyed by their
duplicity.

4 Wealth is worthless in the day of wrath,
but righteousness delivers from death.

5 The righteousness of the blameless makes
their paths straight,
but the wicked are brought down by their
own wickedness.

6 The righteousness of the upright delivers
them,
but the unfaithful are trapped by evil
desires.

7 Hopes placed in mortals die with them;
all the promise of[a] their power comes to
nothing.

8 The righteous person is rescued from
trouble,
and it falls on the wicked instead.

9 With their mouths the godless destroy their
neighbors,
but through knowledge the righteous
escape.

10 When the righteous prosper, the city rejoices;
when the wicked perish, there are shouts
of joy.

11 Through the blessing of the upright a city is
exalted,
but by the mouth of the wicked it is
destroyed.

12 Whoever derides their neighbor has no
sense,
but the one who has understanding holds
their tongue.

13 A gossip betrays a confidence,
but a trustworthy person keeps a secret.

14 For lack of guidance a nation falls,
but victory is won through many advisers.

15 Whoever puts up security for a stranger will
surely suffer,
but whoever refuses to shake hands in
pledge is safe.

16 A kindhearted woman gains honor,
but ruthless men gain only wealth.

---

[a] 7 Two Hebrew manuscripts; most Hebrew manuscripts,
Vulgate, Syriac and Targum *When the wicked die, their hope
perishes; / all they expected from*

17 Those who are kind benefit themselves,
    but the cruel bring ruin on themselves.

18 A wicked person earns deceptive wages,
    but the one who sows righteousness reaps
      a sure reward.

19 Truly the righteous attain life,
    but whoever pursues evil finds death.

20 The LORD detests those whose hearts are
      perverse,
    but he delights in those whose ways are
      blameless.

21 Be sure of this: The wicked will not go
      unpunished,
    but those who are righteous will go free.

22 Like a gold ring in a pig's snout
    is a beautiful woman who shows no
      discretion.

23 The desire of the righteous ends only in
      good,
    but the hope of the wicked only in wrath.

24 One person gives freely, yet gains even more;
    another withholds unduly, but comes to
      poverty.

25 A generous person will prosper;
    whoever refreshes others will be refreshed.

26 People curse the one who hoards grain,
    but they pray God's blessing on the one
      who is willing to sell.

27 Whoever seeks good finds favor,
    but evil comes to one who searches for it.

28 Those who trust in their riches will fall,
    but the righteous will thrive like a green
      leaf.

29 Whoever brings ruin on their family will
      inherit only wind,
    and the fool will be servant to the wise.

30 The fruit of the righteous is a tree of life,
    and the one who is wise saves lives.

31 If the righteous receive their due on earth,
    how much more the ungodly and the
      sinner!

12 Whoever loves discipline loves
      knowledge,
    but whoever hates correction is stupid.

2 Good people obtain favor from the LORD,
    but he condemns those who devise wicked
      schemes.

3 No one can be established through
      wickedness,
    but the righteous cannot be uprooted.

The Law of the Inner Circle: Your Advisors Will Make or Break You

Proverbs 11:14

Every leader ought to build an inner circle that adds value to him or her and to the leadership of the organization. But choose well, for the members of this inner circle will become your closest confidantes; your inner circle will make you or break you.

Proverbs 11:14 says, "For lack of guidance a nation falls, but victory is won through many advisers." So who belongs in this inner circle? Strive for the following:

1. **Creative people**
2. **Loyal people**
3. **People who share your vision**
4. **Wise and intelligent people**
5. **People with complementary gifts**
6. **People with influence**
7. **People of faith**
8. **People of integrity**

⁴A wife of noble character is her husband's
    crown,
  but a disgraceful wife is like decay in his
    bones.

⁵The plans of the righteous are just,
  but the advice of the wicked is deceitful.

⁶The words of the wicked lie in wait for
    blood,
  but the speech of the upright rescues
    them.

⁷The wicked are overthrown and are no
    more,
  but the house of the righteous stands firm.

⁸A person is praised according to their
    prudence,
  and one with a warped mind is despised.

⁹Better to be a nobody and yet have a servant
    than pretend to be somebody and have no
    food.

¹⁰The righteous care for the needs of their
    animals,
  but the kindest acts of the wicked are
    cruel.

¹¹Those who work their land will have
    abundant food,
  but those who chase fantasies have no
    sense.

¹²The wicked desire the stronghold of
    evildoers,
  but the root of the righteous endures.

¹³Evildoers are trapped by their sinful talk,
  and so the innocent escape trouble.

¹⁴From the fruit of their lips people are filled
    with good things,
  and the work of their hands brings them
    reward.

¹⁵The way of fools seems right to them,
  but the wise listen to advice.

¹⁶Fools show their annoyance at once,
  but the prudent overlook an insult.

¹⁷An honest witness tells the truth,
  but a false witness tells lies.

¹⁸The words of the reckless pierce like
    swords,
  but the tongue of the wise brings healing.

¹⁹Truthful lips endure forever,
  but a lying tongue lasts only a moment.

²⁰Deceit is in the hearts of those who plot evil,
  but those who promote peace have joy.

²¹No harm overtakes the righteous,
  but the wicked have their fill of trouble.

²²The LORD detests lying lips,
  but he delights in people who are
    trustworthy.

²³The prudent keep their knowledge to
    themselves,
  but a fool's heart blurts out folly.

²⁴Diligent hands will rule,
  but laziness ends in forced labor.

²⁵Anxiety weighs down the heart,
  but a kind word cheers it up.

²⁶The righteous choose their friends carefully,
  but the way of the wicked leads them
    astray.

²⁷The lazy do not roast[a] any game,
  but the diligent feed on the riches of the
    hunt.

²⁸In the way of righteousness there is life;
  along that path is immortality.

13 A wise son heeds his father's instruction,
  but a mocker does not respond to
    rebukes.

²From the fruit of their lips people enjoy good
    things,
  but the unfaithful have an appetite for
    violence.

³Those who guard their lips preserve their
    lives,
  but those who speak rashly will come to
    ruin.

⁴A sluggard's appetite is never filled,
  but the desires of the diligent are fully
    satisfied.

⁵The righteous hate what is false,
  but the wicked make themselves a stench
    and bring shame on themselves.

⁶Righteousness guards the person of integrity,
  but wickedness overthrows the sinner.

⁷One person pretends to be rich, yet has
    nothing;
  another pretends to be poor, yet has great
    wealth.

⁻⁻⁻⁻⁻
ᵃ 27 The meaning of the Hebrew for this word is uncertain.

8 A person's riches may ransom their life,
  but the poor cannot respond to
    threatening rebukes.

9 The light of the righteous shines brightly,
  but the lamp of the wicked is snuffed out.

10 Where there is strife, there is pride,
   but wisdom is found in those who take
     advice.

11 Dishonest money dwindles away,
   but whoever gathers money little by little
     makes it grow.

12 Hope deferred makes the heart sick,
   but a longing fulfilled is a tree of life.

13 Whoever scorns instruction will pay for it,
   but whoever respects a command is
     rewarded.

14 The teaching of the wise is a fountain of life,
   turning a person from the snares of
     death.

15 Good judgment wins favor,
   but the way of the unfaithful leads to their
     destruction.[a]

16 All who are prudent act with[b] knowledge,
   but fools expose their folly.

17 A wicked messenger falls into trouble,
   but a trustworthy envoy brings healing.

18 Whoever disregards discipline comes to
     poverty and shame,
   but whoever heeds correction is honored.

19 A longing fulfilled is sweet to the soul,
   but fools detest turning from evil.

20 Walk with the wise and become wise,
   for a companion of fools suffers harm.

Effective Leadership Invites Partnerships

Proverbs 13:20

You become like those with whom you partner. Choose your partners for many of the
same reasons a leader chooses his or her inner
circle. Choose those who add value to you and
can benefit from you. Both leaders and organizations should see improvement for having
entered into partnership.

21 Trouble pursues the sinner,
   but the righteous are rewarded with good
     things.

22 A good person leaves an inheritance for their
     children's children,
   but a sinner's wealth is stored up for the
     righteous.

23 An unplowed field produces food for the
     poor,
   but injustice sweeps it away.

24 Whoever spares the rod hates their
     children,
   but the one who loves their children is
     careful to discipline them.

25 The righteous eat to their hearts' content,
   but the stomach of the wicked goes
     hungry.

14 The wise woman builds her house,
   but with her own hands the foolish one
     tears hers down.

2 Whoever fears the LORD walks uprightly,
  but those who despise him are devious in
    their ways.

3 A fool's mouth lashes out with pride,
  but the lips of the wise protect them.

4 Where there are no oxen, the manger is
    empty,
  but from the strength of an ox come
    abundant harvests.

5 An honest witness does not deceive,
  but a false witness pours out lies.

6 The mocker seeks wisdom and finds none,
  but knowledge comes easily to the
    discerning.

7 Stay away from a fool,
  for you will not find knowledge on their
    lips.

8 The wisdom of the prudent is to give thought
    to their ways,
  but the folly of fools is deception.

9 Fools mock at making amends for sin,
  but goodwill is found among the upright.

10 Each heart knows its own bitterness,
   and no one else can share its joy.

[a] 15 Septuagint and Syriac; the meaning of the Hebrew for this phrase is uncertain.   [b] 16 Or prudent protect themselves through

11 The house of the wicked will be destroyed,
  but the tent of the upright will flourish.

12 There is a way that appears to be right,
  but in the end it leads to death.

13 Even in laughter the heart may ache,
  and rejoicing may end in grief.

14 The faithless will be fully repaid for their
    ways,
  and the good rewarded for theirs.

15 The simple believe anything,
  but the prudent give thought to their
    steps.

16 The wise fear the LORD and shun evil,
  but a fool is hotheaded and yet feels
    secure.

17 A quick-tempered person does foolish
    things,
  and the one who devises evil schemes is
    hated.

18 The simple inherit folly,
  but the prudent are crowned with
    knowledge.

19 Evildoers will bow down in the presence of
    the good,
  and the wicked at the gates of the
    righteous.

20 The poor are shunned even by their
    neighbors,
  but the rich have many friends.

21 It is a sin to despise one's neighbor,
  but blessed is the one who is kind to the
    needy.

22 Do not those who plot evil go astray?
  But those who plan what is good find[a]
    love and faithfulness.

23 All hard work brings a profit,
  but mere talk leads only to poverty.

24 The wealth of the wise is their crown,
  but the folly of fools yields folly.

25 A truthful witness saves lives,
  but a false witness is deceitful.

26 Whoever fears the LORD has a secure
    fortress,
  and for their children it will be a refuge.

27 The fear of the LORD is a fountain of life,
  turning a person from the snares of death.

28 A large population is a king's glory,
  but without subjects a prince is ruined.

29 Whoever is patient has great understanding,
  but one who is quick-tempered displays
    folly.

30 A heart at peace gives life to the body,
  but envy rots the bones.

31 Whoever oppresses the poor shows contempt
    for their Maker,
  but whoever is kind to the needy honors
    God.

32 When calamity comes, the wicked are
    brought down,
  but even in death the righteous seek
    refuge in God.

33 Wisdom reposes in the heart of the
    discerning
  and even among fools she lets herself be
    known.[b]

34 Righteousness exalts a nation,
  but sin condemns any people.

35 A king delights in a wise servant,
  but a shameful servant arouses his fury.

15 A gentle answer turns away wrath,
  but a harsh word stirs up anger.

2 The tongue of the wise adorns knowledge,
  but the mouth of the fool gushes folly.

3 The eyes of the LORD are everywhere,
  keeping watch on the wicked and the good.

4 The soothing tongue is a tree of life,
  but a perverse tongue crushes the spirit.

5 A fool spurns a parent's discipline,
  but whoever heeds correction shows
    prudence.

6 The house of the righteous contains great
    treasure,
  but the income of the wicked brings ruin.

7 The lips of the wise spread knowledge,
  but the hearts of fools are not upright.

8 The LORD detests the sacrifice of the wicked,
  but the prayer of the upright pleases him.

9 The LORD detests the way of the wicked,
  but he loves those who pursue
    righteousness.

[a] 22 Or show   [b] 33 Hebrew; Septuagint and Syriac
discerning / but in the heart of fools she is not known

Master Communication and You Manage Conflict

Proverbs 15:1–7

God rightly expects leaders to manage conflict within their organizations. But how can you best accomplish this?

A good place to start is Proverbs 15:1—yet while we often quote this verse, we seldom practice it. Sometimes only the leaders are given liberty to express anger, and sooner or later this kind of unhealthy environment comes back to haunt them. Leaders must create safe places for communication. Master communication and you manage conflict. Look at the first seven verses of Proverbs 15 and note its counsel about managing conflict:

1. **Remain calm and gentle when confronting conflict, and your example will become contagious (v. 1).**

2. **Speak wisely, making sure your information is truthful and accurate (v. 2).**

3. **Remember, God is the ultimate Judge and will execute justice (v. 3).**

4. **Use your words to foster healing; fix the problem, not the blame (v. 4).**

5. **Stay teachable; be open to correction and quick to apologize when wrong (v. 5).**

6. **Add value to everyone who contacts you, even when you disagree (v. 6).**

7. **Speak words that spread knowledge and understanding (v. 7).**

¹⁰ Stern discipline awaits anyone who leaves
    the path;
  the one who hates correction will die.

¹¹ Death and Destruction[a] lie open before the
    LORD —
  how much more do human hearts!

¹² Mockers resent correction,
  so they avoid the wise.

¹³ A happy heart makes the face cheerful,
  but heartache crushes the spirit.

¹⁴ The discerning heart seeks knowledge,
  but the mouth of a fool feeds on folly.

¹⁵ All the days of the oppressed are wretched,
  but the cheerful heart has a continual
    feast.

¹⁶ Better a little with the fear of the LORD
  than great wealth with turmoil.

¹⁷ Better a small serving of vegetables with love
  than a fattened calf with hatred.

¹⁸ A hot-tempered person stirs up conflict,
  but the one who is patient calms a quarrel.

¹⁹ The way of the sluggard is blocked with
    thorns,
  but the path of the upright is a highway.

²⁰ A wise son brings joy to his father,
  but a foolish man despises his mother.

²¹ Folly brings joy to one who has no sense,
  but whoever has understanding keeps a
    straight course.

²² Plans fail for lack of counsel,
  but with many advisers they succeed.

²³ A person finds joy in giving an apt reply —
  and how good is a timely word!

²⁴ The path of life leads upward for the prudent
  to keep them from going down to the
    realm of the dead.

²⁵ The LORD tears down the house of the proud,
  but he sets the widow's boundary stones
    in place.

²⁶ The LORD detests the thoughts of the
    wicked,
  but gracious words are pure in his sight.

²⁷ The greedy bring ruin to their households,
  but the one who hates bribes will live.

²⁸ The heart of the righteous weighs its
    answers,
  but the mouth of the wicked gushes evil.

a 11 Hebrew Abaddon

²⁹The LORD is far from the wicked,
    but he hears the prayer of the righteous.

³⁰Light in a messenger's eyes brings joy to the
    heart,
    and good news gives health to the bones.

³¹Whoever heeds life-giving correction
    will be at home among the wise.

³²Those who disregard discipline despise
    themselves,
    but the one who heeds correction gains
    understanding.

³³Wisdom's instruction is to fear the LORD,
    and humility comes before honor.

16 To humans belong the plans of the heart,
    but from the LORD comes the proper
    answer of the tongue.

²All a person's ways seem pure to them,
    but motives are weighed by the LORD.

³Commit to the LORD whatever you do,
    and he will establish your plans.

⁴The LORD works out everything to its proper
    end —
    even the wicked for a day of disaster.

⁵The LORD detests all the proud of heart.
    Be sure of this: They will not go
    unpunished.

⁶Through love and faithfulness sin is atoned
    for;
    through the fear of the LORD evil is
    avoided.

⁷When the LORD takes pleasure in anyone's
    way,
    he causes their enemies to make peace
    with them.

⁸Better a little with righteousness
    than much gain with injustice.

⁹In their hearts humans plan their course,
    but the LORD establishes their steps.

¹⁰The lips of a king speak as an oracle,
    and his mouth does not betray justice.

¹¹Honest scales and balances belong to the
    LORD;
    all the weights in the bag are of his
    making.

¹²Kings detest wrongdoing,
    for a throne is established through
    righteousness.

¹³Kings take pleasure in honest lips;
    they value the one who speaks what is
    right.

¹⁴A king's wrath is a messenger of death,
    but the wise will appease it.

The Law of Navigation

Proverbs 16:1–3

Effective leaders practice the Law of Navigation. Proverbs 16 opens with these words: "To humans belong the plans of the heart, but from the LORD comes the proper answer of the tongue. All a person's ways seem pure to them, but motives ear weighed by the LORD. Commit to the LORD whatever you do, and he will establish your plans" (vv. 1–3).

These verses teach us to:

- **check the source of our wisdom**
- **check our motives**
- **check the outcome we are pursuing**

Consider five key words to understanding how God helps leaders to navigate their way through life:

1. *Process:* God's plan usually unfolds over time. What is he revealing progressively?

2. *Purpose:* God wants to accomplish his purposes. Why were you created?

3. *Potential:* God will use your gifts and passion. Does this goal fit who you are?

4. *Prioritize:* God will ask you to adjust your time and energy. What steps must you take?

5. *Proceed:* God will eventually require you to act. When should you start?

¹⁵ When a king's face brightens, it means life;
   his favor is like a rain cloud in spring.

¹⁶ How much better to get wisdom than gold,
   to get insight rather than silver!

¹⁷ The highway of the upright avoids evil;
   those who guard their ways preserve their
   lives.

¹⁸ Pride goes before destruction,
   a haughty spirit before a fall.

¹⁹ Better to be lowly in spirit along with the
   oppressed
   than to share plunder with the proud.

²⁰ Whoever gives heed to instruction prospers,[a]
   and blessed is the one who trusts in the
   LORD.

²¹ The wise in heart are called discerning,
   and gracious words promote instruction.[b]

²² Prudence is a fountain of life to the prudent,
   but folly brings punishment to fools.

²³ The hearts of the wise make their mouths
   prudent,
   and their lips promote instruction.[c]

²⁴ Gracious words are a honeycomb,
   sweet to the soul and healing to the bones.

²⁵ There is a way that appears to be right,
   but in the end it leads to death.

²⁶ The appetite of laborers works for them;
   their hunger drives them on.

²⁷ A scoundrel plots evil,
   and on their lips it is like a scorching fire.

²⁸ A perverse person stirs up conflict,
   and a gossip separates close friends.

²⁹ A violent person entices their neighbor
   and leads them down a path that is not
   good.

³⁰ Whoever winks with their eye is plotting
   perversity;
   whoever purses their lips is bent on evil.

³¹ Gray hair is a crown of splendor;
   it is attained in the way of righteousness.

³² Better a patient person than a warrior,
   one with self-control than one who takes a
   city.

³³ The lot is cast into the lap,
   but its every decision is from the LORD.

17 Better a dry crust with peace and quiet
   than a house full of feasting, with strife.

² A prudent servant will rule over a
   disgraceful son
   and will share the inheritance as one of
   the family.

³ The crucible for silver and the furnace for
   gold,
   but the LORD tests the heart.

---

[a] 20 Or *whoever speaks prudently finds what is good*   [b] 21 Or
words make a person persuasive   [c] 23 Or *prudent / and make
their lips persuasive*

It's Not About Position, but Empowerment

Proverbs 17:2

Our influence has less to do with our position or title than it does with the life we live. It's not about position, but production. It is not the education we get, but the empowerment we give, that makes a difference to others.

The key word is *credibility*. We gain credibility when our life matches our talk and when both add value to others. In the words of Proverbs 17:2, it's better to be a wise slave than a foolish son. Answer the following vital questions:

1. *Consistency:* Are you the same person no matter who's with you?

2. *Choices:* Do you make decisions based on how they benefit *you* or *others*?

3. *Credit:* Are you quick to recognize others for their efforts when you succeed?

4. *Character:* Do you work harder at your image or your integrity?

5. *Credibility:* Have you recognized that credibility is a victory, not a gift?

⁴A wicked person listens to deceitful lips;
   a liar pays attention to a destructive
     tongue.

⁵Whoever mocks the poor shows contempt
   for their Maker;
   whoever gloats over disaster will not go
     unpunished.

⁶Children's children are a crown to the aged,
   and parents are the pride of their children.

⁷Eloquent lips are unsuited to a godless
     fool—
   how much worse lying lips to a ruler!

⁸A bribe is seen as a charm by the one who
     gives it;
   they think success will come at every turn.

⁹Whoever would foster love covers over an
     offense,
   but whoever repeats the matter separates
     close friends.

¹⁰A rebuke impresses a discerning person
   more than a hundred lashes a fool.

¹¹Evildoers foster rebellion against God;
   the messenger of death will be sent against
     them.

¹²Better to meet a bear robbed of her cubs
   than a fool bent on folly.

¹³Evil will never leave the house
   of one who pays back evil for good.

¹⁴Starting a quarrel is like breaching a dam;
   so drop the matter before a dispute breaks
     out.

¹⁵Acquitting the guilty and condemning the
     innocent—
   the Lord detests them both.

¹⁶Why should fools have money in hand to
     buy wisdom,
   when they are not able to understand it?

¹⁷A friend loves at all times,
   and a brother is born for a time of adversity.

¹⁸One who has no sense shakes hands in pledge
   and puts up security for a neighbor.

¹⁹Whoever loves a quarrel loves sin;
   whoever builds a high gate invites
     destruction.

²⁰One whose heart is corrupt does not prosper;
   one whose tongue is perverse falls into
     trouble.

²¹To have a fool for a child brings grief;
   there is no joy for the parent of a godless
     fool.

²²A cheerful heart is good medicine,
   but a crushed spirit dries up the bones.

²³The wicked accept bribes in secret
   to pervert the course of justice.

²⁴A discerning person keeps wisdom in view,
   but a fool's eyes wander to the ends of the
     earth.

²⁵A foolish son brings grief to his father
   and bitterness to the mother who bore him.

²⁶If imposing a fine on the innocent is not
     good,
   surely to flog honest officials is not right.

²⁷The one who has knowledge uses words with
     restraint,
   and whoever has understanding is even-
     tempered.

²⁸Even fools are thought wise if they keep
     silent,
   and discerning if they hold their tongues.

18 An unfriendly person pursues selfish
     ends
   and against all sound judgment starts
     quarrels.

²Fools find no pleasure in understanding
   but delight in airing their own opinions.

³When wickedness comes, so does contempt,
   and with shame comes reproach.

⁴The words of the mouth are deep waters,
   but the fountain of wisdom is a rushing
     stream.

⁵It is not good to be partial to the wicked
   and so deprive the innocent of justice.

⁶The lips of fools bring them strife,
   and their mouths invite a beating.

⁷The mouths of fools are their undoing,
   and their lips are a snare to their very
     lives.

⁸The words of a gossip are like choice morsels;
   they go down to the inmost parts.

⁹One who is slack in his work
   is brother to one who destroys.

¹⁰The name of the Lord is a fortified tower;
   the righteous run to it and are safe.

[11] The wealth of the rich is their fortified
   city;
   they imagine it a wall too high to
      scale.

[12] Before a downfall the heart is haughty,
   but humility comes before honor.

[13] To answer before listening—
   that is folly and shame.

[14] The human spirit can endure in sickness,
   but a crushed spirit who can bear?

[15] The heart of the discerning acquires
      knowledge,
   for the ears of the wise seek it out.

[16] A gift opens the way
   and ushers the giver into the presence of
      the great.

[17] In a lawsuit the first to speak seems right,
   until someone comes forward and cross-
      examines.

[18] Casting the lot settles disputes
   and keeps strong opponents apart.

[19] A brother wronged is more unyielding than
      a fortified city;
   disputes are like the barred gates of a
      citadel.

[20] From the fruit of their mouth a person's
      stomach is filled;
   with the harvest of their lips they are
      satisfied.

[21] The tongue has the power of life and
      death,
   and those who love it will eat its fruit.

[22] He who finds a wife finds what is good
   and receives favor from the LORD.

[23] The poor plead for mercy,
   but the rich answer harshly.

[24] One who has unreliable friends soon comes
      to ruin,
   but there is a friend who sticks closer than
      a brother.

19 Better the poor whose walk is blameless
   than a fool whose lips are perverse.

[2] Desire without knowledge is not good—
   how much more will hasty feet miss the
      way!

[3] A person's own folly leads to their ruin,
   yet their heart rages against the LORD.

[4] Wealth attracts many friends,
   but even the closest friend of the poor
      person deserts them.

The Law of Influence: The Evolution of Leadership

Proverbs 18:21

Few muscles in a body wield more power than the little one inside the mouth. The Bible says, "The tongue has the power of life and death, and those who love it will eat its fruit" (Pr 18:21). Leaders who understand this greatly increase their influence.

Our understanding of leadership has evolved over the last five or six decades. The way people expect leaders to lead has changed. Many have said our culture has witnessed four styles of leadership since 1950:

1. *The Military Commander:* **Leaders came out of the army and expected unquestioning obedience from subordinates. Many of our presidents had military backgrounds.**

2. *The Chief Executive Officer:* **Most leaders migrated to a different style driven by vision and shared by everyone. Yet it was still top down and possibly very narrow in scope.**

3. *The Coach:* **Leaders moved toward a coach model where they saw employees as players on a team. This produced even better results, but still limited the possibilities to the vision of the coach.**

4. *The Poet and Gardener:* **Today, leaders see the need to express the heart of the team, as a poet gives words to the heart of readers. They develop players using encouragement and direction. They recognize the power of words and use them wisely.**

⁵A false witness will not go unpunished,
  and whoever pours out lies will not go
    free.

⁶Many curry favor with a ruler,
  and everyone is the friend of one who
    gives gifts.

⁷The poor are shunned by all their relatives—
  how much more do their friends avoid
    them!
Though the poor pursue them with
    pleading,
  they are nowhere to be found.ᵃ

⁸The one who gets wisdom loves life;
  the one who cherishes understanding will
    soon prosper.

⁹A false witness will not go unpunished,
  and whoever pours out lies will perish.

¹⁰It is not fitting for a fool to live in luxury—
  how much worse for a slave to rule over
    princes!

¹¹A person's wisdom yields patience;
  it is to one's glory to overlook an offense.

¹²A king's rage is like the roar of a lion,
  but his favor is like dew on the grass.

¹³A foolish child is a father's ruin,
  and a quarrelsome wife is like
    the constant dripping of a leaky roof.

¹⁴Houses and wealth are inherited from
    parents,
  but a prudent wife is from the LORD.

¹⁵Laziness brings on deep sleep,
  and the shiftless go hungry.

¹⁶Whoever keeps commandments keeps their
    life,
  but whoever shows contempt for their
    ways will die.

¹⁷Whoever is kind to the poor lends to the
    LORD,
  and he will reward them for what they
    have done.

¹⁸Discipline your children, for in that there is
    hope;
  do not be a willing party to their death.

¹⁹A hot-tempered person must pay the
    penalty;
  rescue them, and you will have to do it
    again.

²⁰Listen to advice and accept discipline,
  and at the end you will be counted among
    the wise.

²¹Many are the plans in a person's heart,
  but it is the LORD's purpose that prevails.

²²What a person desires is unfailing loveᵇ;
  better to be poor than a liar.

²³The fear of the LORD leads to life;
  then one rests content, untouched by
    trouble.

²⁴A sluggard buries his hand in the dish;
  he will not even bring it back to his
    mouth!

²⁵Flog a mocker, and the simple will learn
    prudence;
  rebuke the discerning, and they will gain
    knowledge.

²⁶Whoever robs their father and drives out
    their mother
  is a child who brings shame and disgrace.

²⁷Stop listening to instruction, my son,
  and you will stray from the words of
    knowledge.

²⁸A corrupt witness mocks at justice,
  and the mouth of the wicked gulps down
    evil.

²⁹Penalties are prepared for mockers,
  and beatings for the backs of fools.

20 Wine is a mocker and beer a brawler;
  whoever is led astray by them is not
    wise.

²A king's wrath strikes terror like the roar of
    a lion;
  those who anger him forfeit their lives.

³It is to one's honor to avoid strife,
  but every fool is quick to quarrel.

⁴Sluggards do not plow in season;
  so at harvest time they look but find
    nothing.

⁵The purposes of a person's heart are deep
    waters,
  but one who has insight draws them out.

⁶Many claim to have unfailing love,
  but a faithful person who can find?

ᵃ 7 The meaning of the Hebrew for this sentence is uncertain.
ᵇ 22 Or *Greed is a person's shame*

7 The righteous lead blameless lives;
  blessed are their children after them.

8 When a king sits on his throne to judge,
  he winnows out all evil with his eyes.

9 Who can say, "I have kept my heart pure;
  I am clean and without sin"?

10 Differing weights and differing measures —
  the LORD detests them both.

11 Even small children are known by their
    actions,
  so is their conduct really pure and
    upright?

12 Ears that hear and eyes that see —
  the LORD has made them both.

13 Do not love sleep or you will grow poor;
  stay awake and you will have food to
    spare.

14 "It's no good, it's no good!" says the buyer —
  then goes off and boasts about the
    purchase.

15 Gold there is, and rubies in abundance,
  but lips that speak knowledge are a rare
    jewel.

16 Take the garment of one who puts up
    security for a stranger;
  hold it in pledge if it is done for an
    outsider.

17 Food gained by fraud tastes sweet,
  but one ends up with a mouth full of
    gravel.

18 Plans are established by seeking advice;
  so if you wage war, obtain guidance.

19 A gossip betrays a confidence;
  so avoid anyone who talks too much.

20 If someone curses their father or mother,
  their lamp will be snuffed out in pitch
    darkness.

21 An inheritance claimed too soon
  will not be blessed at the end.

22 Do not say, "I'll pay you back for this wrong!"
  Wait for the LORD, and he will avenge you.

23 The LORD detests differing weights,
  and dishonest scales do not please him.

24 A person's steps are directed by the LORD.
  How then can anyone understand their
    own way?

25 It is a trap to dedicate something rashly
  and only later to consider one's vows.

26 A wise king winnows out the wicked;
  he drives the threshing wheel over them.

27 The human spirit is[a] the lamp of the LORD
  that sheds light on one's inmost being.

28 Love and faithfulness keep a king safe;
  through love his throne is made secure.

29 The glory of young men is their strength,
  gray hair the splendor of the old.

30 Blows and wounds scrub away evil,
  and beatings purge the inmost being.

21 In the LORD's hand the king's heart is a
    stream of water
  that he channels toward all who please him.

2 A person may think their own ways are right,
  but the LORD weighs the heart.

3 To do what is right and just
  is more acceptable to the LORD than
    sacrifice.

4 Haughty eyes and a proud heart —
  the unplowed field of the wicked —
    produce sin.

5 The plans of the diligent lead to profit
  as surely as haste leads to poverty.

a 27 Or *A person's words are*

Leaders Know the Difference

Proverbs 21:1

Leaders can and should make their plans, but they must never forget that it is God who controls the future. "In the LORD's hand the king's heart is a stream of water that he channels toward all who please him," says Proverbs 21:1. Successful leaders remember this and therefore know the difference between being in charge and being in control.

We kid ourselves if we think we are in control. We may have charge of a group, but the best we can do is remain *under* control. God is the Ultimate Leader, and he is forever *in* control. It has been rightly said: "We don't know what the future holds, but we do know the One who holds the future."

6 A fortune made by a lying tongue
　　is a fleeting vapor and a deadly snare.[a]

7 The violence of the wicked will drag them
　　away,
　　for they refuse to do what is right.

8 The way of the guilty is devious,
　　but the conduct of the innocent is upright.

9 Better to live on a corner of the roof
　　than share a house with a quarrelsome
　　wife.

10 The wicked crave evil;
　　their neighbors get no mercy from them.

11 When a mocker is punished, the simple gain
　　wisdom;
　　by paying attention to the wise they get
　　knowledge.

12 The Righteous One[b] takes note of the house
　　of the wicked
　　and brings the wicked to ruin.

13 Whoever shuts their ears to the cry of the
　　poor
　　will also cry out and not be answered.

14 A gift given in secret soothes anger,
　　and a bribe concealed in the cloak pacifies
　　great wrath.

15 When justice is done, it brings joy to the
　　righteous
　　but terror to evildoers.

16 Whoever strays from the path of prudence
　　comes to rest in the company of the dead.

17 Whoever loves pleasure will become poor;
　　whoever loves wine and olive oil will
　　never be rich.

18 The wicked become a ransom for the
　　righteous,
　　and the unfaithful for the upright.

19 Better to live in a desert
　　than with a quarrelsome and nagging wife.

20 The wise store up choice food and olive oil,
　　but fools gulp theirs down.

21 Whoever pursues righteousness and love
　　finds life, prosperity[c] and honor.

22 One who is wise can go up against the city of
　　the mighty
　　and pull down the stronghold in which
　　they trust.

23 Those who guard their mouths and their
　　tongues
　　keep themselves from calamity.

24 The proud and arrogant person — "Mocker"
　　is his name —
　　behaves with insolent fury.

25 The craving of a sluggard will be the death
　　of him,
　　because his hands refuse to work.

26 All day long he craves for more,
　　but the righteous give without sparing.

27 The sacrifice of the wicked is detestable —
　　how much more so when brought with
　　evil intent!

28 A false witness will perish,
　　but a careful listener will testify
　　successfully.

29 The wicked put up a bold front,
　　but the upright give thought to their
　　ways.

30 There is no wisdom, no insight, no plan
　　that can succeed against the LORD.

31 The horse is made ready for the day of
　　battle,
　　but victory rests with the LORD.

22 A good name is more desirable than
　　　great riches;
　　to be esteemed is better than silver or
　　gold.

2 Rich and poor have this in common:
　　The LORD is the Maker of them all.

3 The prudent see danger and take refuge,
　　but the simple keep going and pay the
　　penalty.

4 Humility is the fear of the LORD;
　　its wages are riches and honor and life.

5 In the paths of the wicked are snares and
　　pitfalls,
　　but those who would preserve their life
　　stay far from them.

6 Start children off on the way they
　　should go,
　　and even when they are old they will
　　not turn from it.

[a] 6 Some Hebrew manuscripts, Septuagint and Vulgate; most
Hebrew manuscripts *vapor for those who seek death*　　[b] 12 Or
The righteous person　　[c] 21 Or *righteousness*

Leading Our Children

Proverbs 22:6

God calls parents to lead their children. He tells them that if they start off a child in the way they should go, when they are old they will not turn from it (Pr 22:6). And just how does a parent become a good leader for a child? Partly by focusing on three key words:

1. *Modeling:* Abraham Lincoln said, "There is but one way to train up a child in the way he should go, and that is to travel it yourself." A good example is worth a thousand sermons. What you do has more impact on your child than all the lectures you could ever give.

2. *Management:* Good management is the ability to discern the uniqueness of a child and teach him or her accordingly. We are to train up a child in the way he should go. This may mean we will have to adapt our style, depending on the child's temperament and wiring.

3. *Memories:* Parents should create memories. Why? Because memories are more important than things. Note that the verse says, "When they are old, they will not turn ..." This implies that the child retains some memories of his early experiences and embraces them later in life.

7 The rich rule over the poor,
     and the borrower is slave to the lender.

8 Whoever sows injustice reaps calamity,
     and the rod they wield in fury will be broken.

9 The generous will themselves be blessed,
     for they share their food with the poor.

10 Drive out the mocker, and out goes strife;
     quarrels and insults are ended.

11 One who loves a pure heart and who speaks with grace
     will have the king for a friend.

12 The eyes of the LORD keep watch over knowledge,
     but he frustrates the words of the unfaithful.

13 The sluggard says, "There's a lion outside!
     I'll be killed in the public square!"

14 The mouth of an adulterous woman is a deep pit;
     a man who is under the LORD's wrath falls into it.

15 Folly is bound up in the heart of a child,
     but the rod of discipline will drive it far away.

16 One who oppresses the poor to increase his wealth
     and one who gives gifts to the rich — both come to poverty.

Thirty Sayings of the Wise

Saying 1

17 Pay attention and turn your ear to the sayings of the wise;
     apply your heart to what I teach,
18 for it is pleasing when you keep them in your heart
     and have all of them ready on your lips.
19 So that your trust may be in the LORD,
     I teach you today, even you.
20 Have I not written thirty sayings for you,
     sayings of counsel and knowledge,
21 teaching you to be honest and to speak the truth,
     so that you bring back truthful reports to those you serve?

Saying 2

22 Do not exploit the poor because they are poor
     and do not crush the needy in court,
23 for the LORD will take up their case
     and will exact life for life.

Saying 3

24 Do not make friends with a hot-tempered person,
     do not associate with one easily angered,
25 or you may learn their ways
     and get yourself ensnared.

Saying 4

26 Do not be one who shakes hands in pledge
     or puts up security for debts;

27 if you lack the means to pay,
your very bed will be snatched from under
you.

Saying 5

28 Do not move an ancient boundary stone
set up by your ancestors.

Saying 6

29 Do you see someone skilled in their work?
They will serve before kings;
they will not serve before officials of low
rank.

Saying 7

23 When you sit to dine with a ruler,
note well what*a* is before you,
2 and put a knife to your throat
if you are given to gluttony.
3 Do not crave his delicacies,
for that food is deceptive.

Saying 8

4 Do not wear yourself out to get rich;
do not trust your own cleverness.
5 Cast but a glance at riches, and they are
gone,
for they will surely sprout wings
and fly off to the sky like an eagle.

Saying 9

6 Do not eat the food of a begrudging host,
do not crave his delicacies;
7 for he is the kind of person
who is always thinking about the cost.*b*

"Eat and drink," he says to you,
but his heart is not with you.
8 You will vomit up the little you have eaten
and will have wasted your compliments.

Saying 10

9 Do not speak to fools,
for they will scorn your prudent words.

Saying 11

10 Do not move an ancient boundary stone
or encroach on the fields of the
fatherless,
11 for their Defender is strong;
he will take up their case against you.

Saying 12

12 Apply your heart to instruction
and your ears to words of knowledge.

Saying 13

13 Do not withhold discipline from a child;
if you punish them with the rod, they will
not die.
14 Punish them with the rod
and save them from death.

Saying 14

15 My son, if your heart is wise,
then my heart will be glad indeed;
16 my inmost being will rejoice
when your lips speak what is right.

---

a 1 Or who   *b* 7 Or for as he thinks within himself, / so he is;
or for as he puts on a feast, / so he is

Vision: Hope for a Preferred Future

Proverbs 23:7–19

Leaders understand the importance of their minds to the future of their organizations. Consider some of the timeless principles offered in Proverbs 23 about our minds and a godly vision for tomorrow:

1. **Your thoughts determine your character (v. 7).**

2. **Be careful of your thoughts; they may break into words at any time (v. 7).**

3. **Don't waste your thoughts on those who don't hunger for them (v. 9).**

4. **The first person you lead is you, and the first organ you master is your mind (v. 12).**

5. **Don't let your mind drift away from God's truth and into vain envy (v. 17).**

6. **Stay confident that your vision will come to pass (v. 18).**

7. **Discipline your thoughts to remain steadfast in what you know is right (v. 19).**

Saying 15

17 Do not let your heart envy sinners,
  but always be zealous for the fear of the
   Lord.
18 There is surely a future hope for you,
  and your hope will not be cut off.

Saying 16

19 Listen, my son, and be wise,
  and set your heart on the right path:
20 Do not join those who drink too much wine
  or gorge themselves on meat,
21 for drunkards and gluttons become poor,
  and drowsiness clothes them in rags.

Saying 17

22 Listen to your father, who gave you life,
  and do not despise your mother when she
   is old.
23 Buy the truth and do not sell it —
  wisdom, instruction and insight as well.
24 The father of a righteous child has great joy;
  a man who fathers a wise son rejoices in
   him.
25 May your father and mother rejoice;
  may she who gave you birth be joyful!

Saying 18

26 My son, give me your heart
  and let your eyes delight in my ways,
27 for an adulterous woman is a deep pit,
  and a wayward wife is a narrow well.
28 Like a bandit she lies in wait
  and multiplies the unfaithful among men.

Saying 19

29 Who has woe? Who has sorrow?
  Who has strife? Who has complaints?
  Who has needless bruises? Who has
   bloodshot eyes?
30 Those who linger over wine,
  who go to sample bowls of mixed wine.
31 Do not gaze at wine when it is red,
  when it sparkles in the cup,
  when it goes down smoothly!
32 In the end it bites like a snake
  and poisons like a viper.
33 Your eyes will see strange sights,
  and your mind will imagine confusing
   things.
34 You will be like one sleeping on the high seas,
  lying on top of the rigging.
35 "They hit me," you will say, "but I'm not
   hurt!
  They beat me, but I don't feel it!

When will I wake up
  so I can find another drink?"

Saying 20

24 Do not envy the wicked,
  do not desire their company;
2 for their hearts plot violence,
  and their lips talk about making trouble.

Saying 21

3 By wisdom a house is built,
  and through understanding it is
   established;
4 through knowledge its rooms are filled
  with rare and beautiful treasures.

Saying 22

5 The wise prevail through great power,
  and those who have knowledge muster
   their strength.
6 Surely you need guidance to wage war,
  and victory is won through many
   advisers.

Saying 23

7 Wisdom is too high for fools;
  in the assembly at the gate they must not
   open their mouths.

Saying 24

8 Whoever plots evil
  will be known as a schemer.
9 The schemes of folly are sin,
  and people detest a mocker.

Saying 25

10 If you falter in a time of trouble,
  how small is your strength!
11 Rescue those being led away to death;
  hold back those staggering toward
   slaughter.
12 If you say, "But we knew nothing about this,"
  does not he who weighs the heart
   perceive it?
  Does not he who guards your life know it?
  Will he not repay everyone according to
   what they have done?

Saying 26

13 Eat honey, my son, for it is good;
  honey from the comb is sweet to your
   taste.
14 Know also that wisdom is like honey for you:
  If you find it, there is a future hope for you,
  and your hope will not be cut off.

Saying 27

15 Do not lurk like a thief near the house of the
    righteous,
        do not plunder their dwelling place;
16 for though the righteous fall seven times,
        they rise again,
    but the wicked stumble when calamity
        strikes.

Saying 28

17 Do not gloat when your enemy falls;
    when they stumble, do not let your heart
        rejoice,
18 or the LORD will see and disapprove
    and turn his wrath away from them.

Saying 29

19 Do not fret because of evildoers
        or be envious of the wicked,
20 for the evildoer has no future hope,
        and the lamp of the wicked will be snuffed
        out.

Saying 30

21 Fear the LORD and the king, my son,
        and do not join with rebellious officials,
22 for those two will send sudden destruction
        on them,
    and who knows what calamities they can
        bring?

Further Sayings of the Wise

23 These also are sayings of the wise:

To show partiality in judging is not good:
24 Whoever says to the guilty, "You are
        innocent,"
    will be cursed by peoples and denounced
        by nations.
25 But it will go well with those who convict the
        guilty,
    and rich blessing will come on them.

26 An honest answer
    is like a kiss on the lips.

27 Put your outdoor work in order
        and get your fields ready;
    after that, build your house.

28 Do not testify against your neighbor without
        cause—
    would you use your lips to mislead?
29 Do not say, "I'll do to them as they have done
        to me;
    I'll pay them back for what they did."

30 I went past the field of a sluggard,
    past the vineyard of someone who has no
        sense;
31 thorns had come up everywhere,
    the ground was covered with weeds,
    and the stone wall was in ruins.
32 I applied my heart to what I observed
    and learned a lesson from what I saw:
33 A little sleep, a little slumber,
    a little folding of the hands to rest—
34 and poverty will come on you like a thief
    and scarcity like an armed man.

More Proverbs of Solomon

25 These are more proverbs of Solomon,
    compiled by the men of Hezekiah king
of Judah:

2 It is the glory of God to conceal a matter;
    to search out a matter is the glory of kings.
3 As the heavens are high and the earth is
        deep,
    so the hearts of kings are unsearchable.

4 Remove the dross from the silver,
    and a silversmith can produce a vessel;
5 remove wicked officials from the king's
        presence,
    and his throne will be established through
        righteousness.

6 Do not exalt yourself in the king's presence,
    and do not claim a place among his great
        men;
7 it is better for him to say to you, "Come up
        here,"
    than for him to humiliate you before his
        nobles.

What you have seen with your eyes
8   do not bring[a] hastily to court,
for what will you do in the end
    if your neighbor puts you to shame?

9 If you take your neighbor to court,
    do not betray another's confidence,
10 or the one who hears it may shame you
    and the charge against you will stand.

11 Like apples[b] of gold in settings of silver
    is a ruling rightly given.
12 Like an earring of gold or an ornament of
        fine gold
    is the rebuke of a wise judge to a listening
        ear.

---

[a] 7,8 Or nobles / on whom you had set your eyes. / [8]Do not go
[b] 11 Or possibly apricots

13 Like a snow-cooled drink at harvest time
    is a trustworthy messenger to the one who
       sends him;
    he refreshes the spirit of his master.
14 Like clouds and wind without rain
    is one who boasts of gifts never given.

15 Through patience a ruler can be persuaded,
    and a gentle tongue can break a bone.

16 If you find honey, eat just enough —
    too much of it, and you will vomit.
17 Seldom set foot in your neighbor's house —
    too much of you, and they will hate you.

18 Like a club or a sword or a sharp arrow
    is one who gives false testimony against a
       neighbor.
19 Like a broken tooth or a lame foot
    is reliance on the unfaithful in a time of
       trouble.
20 Like one who takes away a garment on a cold
       day,
    or like vinegar poured on a wound,
    is one who sings songs to a heavy heart.

21 If your enemy is hungry, give him food to eat;
    if he is thirsty, give him water to drink.
22 In doing this, you will heap burning coals on
       his head,
    and the LORD will reward you.

23 Like a north wind that brings unexpected rain
    is a sly tongue — which provokes a
       horrified look.

24 Better to live on a corner of the roof
    than share a house with a quarrelsome
       wife.

25 Like cold water to a weary soul
    is good news from a distant land.
26 Like a muddied spring or a polluted well
    are the righteous who give way to the
       wicked.

27 It is not good to eat too much honey,
    nor is it honorable to search out matters
       that are too deep.
28 Like a city whose walls are broken through
    is a person who lacks self-control.

26 Like snow in summer or rain in harvest,
    honor is not fitting for a fool.
2 Like a fluttering sparrow or a darting
       swallow,
    an undeserved curse does not come to
       rest.
3 A whip for the horse, a bridle for the
       donkey,
    and a rod for the backs of fools!
4 Do not answer a fool according to his folly,
    or you yourself will be just like him.
5 Answer a fool according to his folly,
    or he will be wise in his own eyes.
6 Sending a message by the hands of a fool
    is like cutting off one's feet or drinking
       poison.
7 Like the useless legs of one who is lame
    is a proverb in the mouth of a fool.

Situational Leaders: Read the Need, Then Lead

Proverbs 25:21–22

Leaders need to respond to individuals based on their needs rather than their faults. Proverbs 25:21–22 encourages us to see what others need—even our enemies—and respond accordingly.

Good leaders do this well. They don't lead out of a predetermined package of behaviors, but size up every situation and discern what must happen to reach the desired goal. Like a quarterback who reads the defense, then calls an audible from the line of scrimmage, good leaders remain flexible and may change their response, based not on what a person deserves, but on what they need to succeed. Good leaders follow this path in difficult situations:

1. **They need: They aren't afraid to admit they need to listen and get understanding.**

2. **They read: They evaluate what has happened and what steps are best to take.**

3. **They feed: They communicate what they've observed to key players.**

4. **They heed: They act on the basis of their discovery, even if it means change.**

5. **They lead: They provide direction to those involved.**

⁸ Like tying a stone in a sling
   is the giving of honor to a fool.
⁹ Like a thornbush in a drunkard's hand
   is a proverb in the mouth of a fool.
¹⁰ Like an archer who wounds at random
   is one who hires a fool or any passer-by.
¹¹ As a dog returns to its vomit,
   so fools repeat their folly.
¹² Do you see a person wise in their own eyes?
   There is more hope for a fool than for
   them.

¹³ A sluggard says, "There's a lion in the road,
   a fierce lion roaming the streets!"
¹⁴ As a door turns on its hinges,
   so a sluggard turns on his bed.
¹⁵ A sluggard buries his hand in the dish;
   he is too lazy to bring it back to his mouth.
¹⁶ A sluggard is wiser in his own eyes
   than seven people who answer discreetly.

¹⁷ Like one who grabs a stray dog by the ears
   is someone who rushes into a quarrel not
   their own.

¹⁸ Like a maniac shooting
   flaming arrows of death
¹⁹ is one who deceives their neighbor
   and says, "I was only joking!"

²⁰ Without wood a fire goes out;
   without a gossip a quarrel dies down.
²¹ As charcoal to embers and as wood to fire,
   so is a quarrelsome person for kindling
   strife.
²² The words of a gossip are like choice morsels;
   they go down to the inmost parts.

²³ Like a coating of silver dross on earthenware
   are fervent[a] lips with an evil heart.
²⁴ Enemies disguise themselves with their lips,
   but in their hearts they harbor deceit.
²⁵ Though their speech is charming, do not
   believe them,
   for seven abominations fill their hearts.
²⁶ Their malice may be concealed by deception,
   but their wickedness will be exposed in
   the assembly.
²⁷ Whoever digs a pit will fall into it;
   if someone rolls a stone, it will roll back
   on them.
²⁸ A lying tongue hates those it hurts,
   and a flattering mouth works ruin.

27 Do not boast about tomorrow,
   for you do not know what a day may
   bring.

² Let someone else praise you, and not your
   own mouth;
   an outsider, and not your own lips.

³ Stone is heavy and sand a burden,
   but a fool's provocation is heavier than
   both.

⁴ Anger is cruel and fury overwhelming,
   but who can stand before jealousy?

⁵ Better is open rebuke
   than hidden love.

⁶ Wounds from a friend can be trusted,
   but an enemy multiplies kisses.

⁷ One who is full loathes honey from the
   comb,
   but to the hungry even what is bitter tastes
   sweet.

⁸ Like a bird that flees its nest
   is anyone who flees from home.

⁹ Perfume and incense bring joy to the heart,
   and the pleasantness of a friend
   springs from their heartfelt advice.

¹⁰ Do not forsake your friend or a friend of
   your family,
   and do not go to your relative's house
   when disaster strikes you —
   better a neighbor nearby than a relative
   far away.

¹¹ Be wise, my son, and bring joy to my heart;
   then I can answer anyone who treats me
   with contempt.

¹² The prudent see danger and take refuge,
   but the simple keep going and pay the
   penalty.

¹³ Take the garment of one who puts up
   security for a stranger;
   hold it in pledge if it is done for an
   outsider.

¹⁴ If anyone loudly blesses their neighbor early
   in the morning,
   it will be taken as a curse.

¹⁵ A quarrelsome wife is like the dripping
   of a leaky roof in a rainstorm;
¹⁶ restraining her is like restraining the wind
   or grasping oil with the hand.

¹⁷ As iron sharpens iron,
   so one person sharpens another.

a 23 Hebrew; Septuagint *smooth*

18 The one who guards a fig tree will eat its
        fruit,
    and whoever protects their master will be
        honored.

19 As water reflects the face,
    so one's life reflects the heart.[a]

20 Death and Destruction[b] are never satisfied,
    and neither are human eyes.

21 The crucible for silver and the furnace for
        gold,
    but people are tested by their praise.

22 Though you grind a fool in a mortar,
        grinding them like grain with a pestle,
    you will not remove their folly from them.

23 Be sure you know the condition of your
        flocks,
    give careful attention to your herds;
24 for riches do not endure forever,
    and a crown is not secure for all
        generations.
25 When the hay is removed and new growth
        appears
    and the grass from the hills is gathered in,
26 the lambs will provide you with clothing,
    and the goats with the price of a field.
27 You will have plenty of goats' milk to feed
        your family
    and to nourish your female servants.

28 The wicked flee though no one
        pursues,
    but the righteous are as bold as a lion.

2 When a country is rebellious, it has many
        rulers,
    but a ruler with discernment and
        knowledge maintains order.

3 A ruler[c] who oppresses the poor
    is like a driving rain that leaves no crops.

4 Those who forsake instruction praise the
        wicked,
    but those who heed it resist them.

5 Evildoers do not understand what is right,
    but those who seek the LORD understand
        it fully.

6 Better the poor whose walk is blameless
    than the rich whose ways are perverse.

7 A discerning son heeds instruction,
    but a companion of gluttons disgraces his
        father.

8 Whoever increases wealth by taking interest
        or profit from the poor
    amasses it for another, who will be kind to
        the poor.

a 19 Or so others reflect your heart back to you   b 20 Hebrew
Abaddon   c 3 Or A poor person

The Law of Addition: When People Are Esteemed, Relationships Are Redeemed

Proverbs 27:1–21

Leaders understand that people represent an organization's most appreciable asset. No resource is more valuable than people. Therefore, people skills represent a leader's most important attribute. Wise leaders practice the Law of Addition: Leaders add value to an organization by serving their people.

This text presents some fundamentals on relationships. It teaches that if people are esteemed, relationships are redeemed. Leaders can learn at least the following principles from this chapter:

1. **Don't brag (vv. 1–2)—Leaders understand how little they get from self-promotion.**

2. **Don't envy (v. 4)—Leaders sabotage themselves if their motive is to keep up with others.**

3. **Be forthright (vv. 5–6)—Leaders don't fear confrontation, but speak the truth in love.**

4. **Don't forsake your roots (v. 8)—Leaders understand the power of relational heritage.**

5. **Stay close (vv. 9–10)—Leaders work at maintaining relationships and meeting needs.**

6. **Add value (v. 17)—Leaders sharpen those with whom they come in contact.**

7. **Don't be moved by flattery (v. 21)—Stay humble or you will stumble.**

⁹ If anyone turns a deaf ear to my instruction,
even their prayers are detestable.

¹⁰ Whoever leads the upright along an evil
path
will fall into their own trap,
but the blameless will receive a good
inheritance.

¹¹ The rich are wise in their own eyes;
one who is poor and discerning sees how
deluded they are.

¹² When the righteous triumph, there is great
elation;
but when the wicked rise to power, people
go into hiding.

¹³ Whoever conceals their sins does not
prosper,
but the one who confesses and renounces
them finds mercy.

¹⁴ Blessed is the one who always trembles
before God,
but whoever hardens their heart falls into
trouble.

¹⁵ Like a roaring lion or a charging bear
is a wicked ruler over a helpless people.

¹⁶ A tyrannical ruler practices extortion,
but one who hates ill-gotten gain will
enjoy a long reign.

¹⁷ Anyone tormented by the guilt of murder
will seek refuge in the grave;
let no one hold them back.

¹⁸ The one whose walk is blameless is kept safe,
but the one whose ways are perverse will
fall into the pit.ᵃ

¹⁹ Those who work their land will have
abundant food,
but those who chase fantasies will have
their fill of poverty.

²⁰ A faithful person will be richly blessed,
but one eager to get rich will not go
unpunished.

²¹ To show partiality is not good —
yet a person will do wrong for a piece of
bread.

²² The stingy are eager to get rich
and are unaware that poverty awaits them.

²³ Whoever rebukes a person will in the end
gain favor

rather than one who has a flattering
tongue.

²⁴ Whoever robs their father or mother
and says, "It's not wrong,"
is partner to one who destroys.

²⁵ The greedy stir up conflict,
but those who trust in the LORD will
prosper.

²⁶ Those who trust in themselves are fools,
but those who walk in wisdom are kept
safe.

²⁷ Those who give to the poor will lack
nothing,
but those who close their eyes to them
receive many curses.

²⁸ When the wicked rise to power, people go
into hiding;
but when the wicked perish, the righteous
thrive.

29

Whoever remains stiff-necked after
many rebukes
will suddenly be destroyed — without
remedy.

² When the righteous thrive, the people
rejoice;
when the wicked rule, the people groan.

³ A man who loves wisdom brings joy to his
father,
but a companion of prostitutes squanders
his wealth.

⁴ By justice a king gives a country stability,
but those who are greedy forᵇ bribes tear it
down.

⁵ Those who flatter their neighbors
are spreading nets for their feet.

⁶ Evildoers are snared by their own sin,
but the righteous shout for joy and are
glad.

⁷ The righteous care about justice for the poor,
but the wicked have no such concern.

⁸ Mockers stir up a city,
but the wise turn away anger.

⁹ If a wise person goes to court with a fool,
the fool rages and scoffs, and there is no
peace.

ᵃ 18 Syriac (see Septuagint); Hebrew into one   ᵇ 4 Or who give

¹⁰ The bloodthirsty hate a person of integrity
and seek to kill the upright.

¹¹ Fools give full vent to their rage,
but the wise bring calm in the end.

¹² If a ruler listens to lies,
all his officials become wicked.

¹³ The poor and the oppressor have this in
common:
The LORD gives sight to the eyes of
both.

¹⁴ If a king judges the poor with fairness,
his throne will be established forever.

¹⁵ A rod and a reprimand impart wisdom,
but a child left undisciplined disgraces its
mother.

¹⁶ When the wicked thrive, so does sin,
but the righteous will see their downfall.

¹⁷ Discipline your children, and they will give
you peace;
they will bring you the delights you
desire.

¹⁸ Where there is no revelation, people cast off
restraint;
but blessed is the one who heeds wisdom's
instruction.

¹⁹ Servants cannot be corrected by mere words;
though they understand, they will not
respond.

²⁰ Do you see someone who speaks in haste?
There is more hope for a fool than for
them.

²¹ A servant pampered from youth
will turn out to be insolent.

²² An angry person stirs up conflict,
and a hot-tempered person commits many
sins.

²³ Pride brings a person low,
but the lowly in spirit gain honor.

²⁴ The accomplices of thieves are their own
enemies;
they are put under oath and dare not
testify.

²⁵ Fear of man will prove to be a snare,
but whoever trusts in the LORD is kept
safe.

²⁶ Many seek an audience with a ruler,
but it is from the LORD that one gets
justice.

²⁷ The righteous detest the dishonest;
the wicked detest the upright.

The Law of the Picture: The Leader Causes People to Thrive or Groan

Proverbs 29:2–18

People reflect their leader. We cannot expect followers to grow beyond their leader. We cannot expect followers to turn out fundamentally different from their leader. People feel attracted to leaders like them; they also reflect those who lead them. Consider what Proverbs 29 tells us about the influence of good and bad leaders:

1. **Attitudes (v. 2)**
   When good leaders rule, people rejoice; when the wicked reign, people groan.

2. **Stability (v. 4)**
   When moral leaders rule, they establish justice; compromising leaders tear things down.

3. **Compassion (v. 7)**
   Good leaders express concern for the poor; bad leaders reflect no compassion for anyone.

4. **Honesty (v. 12)**
   When leaders pay attention to lies, their staff begins to esteem the same deceptions.

5. **Vision (v. 18)**
   Solid vision keeps everyone on track; chaos reigns wherever the vision lapses.

Sayings of Agur

30 The sayings of Agur son of Jakeh — an inspired utterance.

This man's utterance to Ithiel:

"I am weary, God,
  but I can prevail.[a]
2 Surely I am only a brute, not a man;
  I do not have human understanding.
3 I have not learned wisdom,
  nor have I attained to the knowledge of
    the Holy One.
4 Who has gone up to heaven and come
    down?
  Whose hands have gathered up the wind?
Who has wrapped up the waters in a cloak?
  Who has established all the ends of the
    earth?
What is his name, and what is the name of
    his son?
  Surely you know!

5 "Every word of God is flawless;
  he is a shield to those who take refuge in
    him.
6 Do not add to his words,
  or he will rebuke you and prove you a liar.

7 "Two things I ask of you, LORD;
  do not refuse me before I die:
8 Keep falsehood and lies far from me;
  give me neither poverty nor riches,
  but give me only my daily bread.
9 Otherwise, I may have too much and disown
    you
  and say, 'Who is the LORD?'
Or I may become poor and steal,
  and so dishonor the name of my God.

10 "Do not slander a servant to their master,
  or they will curse you, and you will pay
    for it.

11 "There are those who curse their fathers
  and do not bless their mothers;
12 those who are pure in their own eyes
  and yet are not cleansed of their filth;
13 those whose eyes are ever so haughty,
  whose glances are so disdainful;
14 those whose teeth are swords
  and whose jaws are set with knives
to devour the poor from the earth
  and the needy from among mankind.

15 "The leech has two daughters.
  'Give! Give!' they cry.

"There are three things that are never satisfied,
  four that never say, 'Enough!':
16 the grave, the barren womb,
  land, which is never satisfied with water,
  and fire, which never says, 'Enough!'

17 "The eye that mocks a father,
  that scorns an aged mother,
will be pecked out by the ravens of the valley,
  will be eaten by the vultures.

18 "There are three things that are too amazing
    for me,
  four that I do not understand:
19 the way of an eagle in the sky,
  the way of a snake on a rock,
the way of a ship on the high seas,
  and the way of a man with a young woman.

20 "This is the way of an adulterous woman:
  She eats and wipes her mouth
  and says, 'I've done nothing wrong.'

21 "Under three things the earth trembles,
  under four it cannot bear up:
22 a servant who becomes king,
  a godless fool who gets plenty to eat,
23 a contemptible woman who gets married,
  and a servant who displaces her mistress.

24 "Four things on earth are small,
  yet they are extremely wise:
25 Ants are creatures of little strength,
  yet they store up their food in the summer;
26 hyraxes are creatures of little power,
  yet they make their home in the crags;
27 locusts have no king,
  yet they advance together in ranks;
28 a lizard can be caught with the hand,
  yet it is found in kings' palaces.

29 "There are three things that are stately in
    their stride,
  four that move with stately bearing:
30 a lion, mighty among beasts,
  who retreats before nothing;
31 a strutting rooster, a he-goat,
  and a king secure against revolt.[b]

32 "If you play the fool and exalt yourself,
  or if you plan evil,
  clap your hand over your mouth!
33 For as churning cream produces butter,
  and as twisting the nose produces blood,
  so stirring up anger produces strife."

---

a 1 With a different word division of the Hebrew; Masoretic Text *utterance to Ithiel, / to Ithiel and Ukal:*   *b 31* The meaning of the Hebrew for this phrase is uncertain.

Sayings of King Lemuel

31 The sayings of King Lemuel—an inspired utterance his mother taught him.

² Listen, my son! Listen, son of my womb!
  Listen, my son, the answer to my prayers!
³ Do not spend your strength[a] on women,
  your vigor on those who ruin kings.

⁴ It is not for kings, Lemuel—
  it is not for kings to drink wine,
  not for rulers to crave beer,
⁵ lest they drink and forget what has been
    decreed,
  and deprive all the oppressed of their rights.
⁶ Let beer be for those who are perishing,
  wine for those who are in anguish!
⁷ Let them drink and forget their poverty
  and remember their misery no more.

⁸ Speak up for those who cannot speak for
    themselves,
  for the rights of all who are destitute.
⁹ Speak up and judge fairly;
  defend the rights of the poor and needy.

Epilogue: The Wife of Noble Character

¹⁰[b] A wife of noble character who can find?
  She is worth far more than rubies.
¹¹ Her husband has full confidence in her
  and lacks nothing of value.
¹² She brings him good, not harm,
  all the days of her life.
¹³ She selects wool and flax
  and works with eager hands.

---

a 3 Or *wealth*   *b* 10 Verses 10-31 are an acrostic poem, the verses of which begin with the successive letters of the Hebrew alphabet.

A Woman of Influence

Proverbs 31:10–31

Proverbs 31 no doubt gets more airtime on Mother's Day than any other passage of Scripture. The majority of the proverb describes a virtuous woman who leads her home with integrity, discipline, and giftedness. This wife and mother is a leader not because she tries to be one, but because of who she is.

Her Assets
1. She is trustworthy (v. 11).
2. She is a positive influence (v. 12).
3. She is a hard worker (vv. 13–14, 19, 24–27).
4. She is a planner (vv. 21–22).
5. She is protective (v. 27).

Her Achievements
1. She meets the needs of her home (v. 15).
2. She invests for her household (v. 16).
3. She keeps herself in shape (v. 17).
4. She helps her husband become successful (v. 23).

Her Attitudes
1. Delightful (v. 13).
2. Healthy (v. 18).
3. Compassionate (v. 20).
4. Unselfish (v. 20).
5. Public (v. 25).

Her Applause
1. From her family (v. 28).
2. From her husband (vv. 28–29).
3. From God's Word (v. 30).
4. From her works (v. 31).

[14] She is like the merchant ships,
  bringing her food from afar.
[15] She gets up while it is still night;
  she provides food for her family
  and portions for her female servants.
[16] She considers a field and buys it;
  out of her earnings she plants a vineyard.
[17] She sets about her work vigorously;
  her arms are strong for her tasks.
[18] She sees that her trading is profitable,
  and her lamp does not go out at night.
[19] In her hand she holds the distaff
  and grasps the spindle with her fingers.
[20] She opens her arms to the poor
  and extends her hands to the needy.
[21] When it snows, she has no fear for her
  household;
  for all of them are clothed in scarlet.
[22] She makes coverings for her bed;
  she is clothed in fine linen and purple.
[23] Her husband is respected at the city gate,
  where he takes his seat among the elders
  of the land.
[24] She makes linen garments and sells them,
  and supplies the merchants with sashes.
[25] She is clothed with strength and dignity;
  she can laugh at the days to come.
[26] She speaks with wisdom,
  and faithful instruction is on her tongue.
[27] She watches over the affairs of her
  household
  and does not eat the bread of idleness.
[28] Her children arise and call her blessed;
  her husband also, and he praises her:
[29] "Many women do noble things,
  but you surpass them all."
[30] Charm is deceptive, and beauty is fleeting;
  but a woman who fears the LORD is to be
  praised.
[31] Honor her for all that her hands have done,
  and let her works bring her praise at the
  city gate.

INTRODUCTION TO
ECCLESIASTES

Unique Message for Leaders

Ecclesiastes, like the book of Job, presents one of the greatest challenges to understanding in the Bible. Ancient Hebrews used to debate its meaning and whether it should even be included in the canon of Scripture. Fortunately for us, by divine providence, Ecclesiastes did make it into the Bible with its unique message for leaders.

The central themes of the book focus on the meaning of life, motives for behavior, and where God fits into our personal mission—paramount issues for every leader.

Our leadership must be about something much bigger than us. If our leadership advances merely our own "kingdom," only increases the profits of our company, or only benefits ourselves—we have failed the higher call of leadership. All leadership must bring honor to God, serve and benefit others, and utilize the gifts of each team member to their fullest potential.

The tone of this book displays an overriding pessimism, as expressed through the words "under the sun" or "under the heavens." The writer explores life almost devoid of a divine perspective, lived from a selfish, humanistic worldview. He generally leaves God out of his deliberations, leaving himself with human reason alone and resulting in superficial and shallow leadership.

A second theme of the book deals with our motives. *Why* we do something ultimately determines *what* we do. The author shows from personal experience that all earthly goals and blessings, when pursued as an end in themselves, lead to dissatisfaction and emptiness.

Finally, the book answers the question, Where does God fit into our personal mission? All good leaders operate from a personal and corporate mission statement. Vision drives them. In chapter two alone, this book

God's Role in Ecclesiastes

Leaders cannot find genuine fulfillment outside of linking their lives to God's purposes for the world. As "the Teacher" explores various avenues for satisfaction—power, possessions, prestige, pleasure—he finds them hollow. God moves him along the path of discovery until he finds no real meaning to life "under the heavens," but only in relationship to God and his eternal purposes. God provides all meaning and fulfillment in this life. The author could not find anything of value apart from a life lived in obedience to God's calling.

Leaders in Ecclesiastes
"The Teacher," God

Other People of Influence in Ecclesiastes
Wise men, fools

Lessons in Leadership
- No real meaning exists apart from linking our lives to God's purpose.
- Humanism and materialism provide incomplete counsel for decision making.
- Possessions, people, pleasure, prestige and power make great servants but poor masters.

questions the materialistic mission of building buildings, making money, controlling workers, and pursuing pleasure. Of course, there's nothing wrong with buildings, money, or workers—as long as they serve only as a means to an eternal end, not an end in themselves.

Instead, leaders ought to wrestle with how they might change eternity through their leadership. After reading this book, leaders should ask themselves: "Who am I? Why am I attempting to lead others? Where am I trying to go? What values guide my life?" The final chapter reminds us that a day of reckoning awaits when God will bring all these issues to light.

- Timing is key: *When* to lead is as important as *what* to do and *where* to go.
- People are motivated by a variety of incentives.
- Divine wisdom provides direction, protection, correction and resolution.
- Leaders must invest themselves generously, knowing the payoff comes later.

LEADERSHIP HIGHLIGHTS IN ECCLESIASTES

Everything Is Meaningless

1 The words of the Teacher,[a] son of David, king in Jerusalem:

[2] "Meaningless! Meaningless!"
  says the Teacher.
"Utterly meaningless!
  Everything is meaningless."

[3] What do people gain from all their labors
  at which they toil under the sun?
[4] Generations come and generations go,
  but the earth remains forever.
[5] The sun rises and the sun sets,
  and hurries back to where it rises.
[6] The wind blows to the south
  and turns to the north;
round and round it goes,
  ever returning on its course.
[7] All streams flow into the sea,
  yet the sea is never full.
To the place the streams come from,
  there they return again.
[8] All things are wearisome,
  more than one can say.
The eye never has enough of seeing,
  nor the ear its fill of hearing.

[9] What has been will be again,
  what has been done will be done
    again;
  there is nothing new under the sun.
[10] Is there anything of which one can say,
  "Look! This is something new"?
It was here already, long ago;
  it was here before our time.
[11] No one remembers the former
    generations,
  and even those yet to come
will not be remembered
  by those who follow them.

Wisdom Is Meaningless

[12] I, the Teacher, was king over Israel in Jerusalem. [13] I applied my mind to study and to explore by wisdom all that is done under the heavens. What a heavy burden God has laid on mankind! [14] I have seen all the things that are done under the sun; all of them are meaningless, a chasing after the wind.

[15] What is crooked cannot be straightened;
  what is lacking cannot be counted.

[a] 1 Or *the leader of the assembly*; also in verses 2 and 12

Vision: If Life Has No Meaning, Leadership Has No Mission

Ecclesiastes 1:3–11

"Life is meaningless," writes Solomon. Imagine the wisest, richest, most powerful man in his time, proclaiming everything worthless! Solomon's name means "peace," but he enjoyed none of it while writing most of this book. He grew deflated, depressed, and disillusioned about life "under the sun." Here we see a leader who lost the air in his sails because he abandoned his true mission. He teaches us . . .

1. **There is no profit (vv. 3–4).**
   Life without God is an exercise in futility. Generations come and go; all we do is move things around.

2. **There is no purpose (vv. 5–7).**
   The sun rises only to set again, endlessly repeating a meaningless cycle. Wind blows, river flows, all in monotony.

3. **There is no progress (vv. 8–11).**
   There is no satisfaction; there's nothing new under the sun, nor pleasant remembrance of earlier life.

Leadership without an eternal perspective falls into the trap of meaninglessness. Leadership must work toward significant, meaningful goals. We are forced to conclude that:

1. **If nothing worthwhile exists under the sun, our only hope must lie above it.**

2. **If the man with everything investigated every visible delight and still wound up unsatisfied, then what satisfies must be invisible.**

3. **If the wisest man on earth finds no answers under heaven, then we must look to heaven itself for those answers.**

16I said to myself, "Look, I have increased in wisdom more than anyone who has ruled over Jerusalem before me; I have experienced much of wisdom and knowledge." 17Then I applied myself to the understanding of wisdom, and also of madness and folly, but I learned that this, too, is a chasing after the wind.

18 For with much wisdom comes much sorrow;
     the more knowledge, the more grief.

Pleasures Are Meaningless

2 I said to myself, "Come now, I will test you with pleasure to find out what is good." But that also proved to be meaningless. 2"Laughter," I said, "is madness. And what does pleasure accomplish?" 3I tried cheering myself with wine, and embracing folly — my mind still guiding me with wisdom. I wanted to see what was good for people to do under the heavens during the few days of their lives.

4I undertook great projects: I built houses for myself and planted vineyards. 5I made gardens and parks and planted all kinds of fruit trees in them. 6I made reservoirs to water groves of flourishing trees. 7I bought male and female slaves and had other slaves who were born in my house. I also owned more herds and flocks than anyone in Jerusalem before me. 8I amassed silver and gold for myself, and the treasure of kings and prov-

inces. I acquired male and female singers, and a harem[a] as well — the delights of a man's heart. 9I became greater by far than anyone in Jerusalem before me. In all this my wisdom stayed with me.

10 I denied myself nothing my eyes desired;
     I refused my heart no pleasure.
My heart took delight in all my labor,
     and this was the reward for all my toil.
11 Yet when I surveyed all that my hands had done
     and what I had toiled to achieve,
everything was meaningless, a chasing after the wind;
     nothing was gained under the sun.

Wisdom and Folly Are Meaningless

12 Then I turned my thoughts to consider wisdom,
     and also madness and folly.
What more can the king's successor do
     than what has already been done?
13 I saw that wisdom is better than folly,
     just as light is better than darkness.
14 The wise have eyes in their heads,
     while the fool walks in the darkness;
but I came to realize
     that the same fate overtakes them both.

---

[a] 8 The meaning of the Hebrew for this phrase is uncertain.

The Law of Priorities and the Law of Sacrifice: Things Don't Make a Leader

Ecclesiastes 2:1–26

Solomon attempted to find satisfaction in accumulating things: houses, gardens, vineyards, flocks, slaves, etc. He found all of it empty.

Many leaders succumb to the same temptation. They begin well, but once they reach their first level of goals—if they don't continue to stretch—they shrink. Their shrinking often takes the form of accumulating. Their success gains them a nice discretionary income. So they spend and gain. Spend and gain. Spend and gain. But none of this fills the void inside.

All leaders have two major voids:

1. **The God-sized vacuum inside their heart; only the Lord can fill it.**
2. **The life-sized vacuum inside their heart; only their life mission can fulfill it.**

To reach these goals, leaders must give up the pursuit of lesser things. C. S. Lewis wrote, "Indeed, if we consider the unblushing promises of reward . . . promised in the Gospels, it would seem that our Lord finds our desires, not too strong, but too weak. We are halfhearted creatures, fooling about with drink and sex and ambition when infinite joy is offered us, like an ignorant child who wants to go on making mud pies in a slum because he cannot imagine what is meant by an offer of a holiday at the sea. We are far too easily pleased."

21 QUALITIES

FOCUS   The Danger of Too Many Pursuits

Ecclesiastes 2:1–11

WE CAN LEARN from Solomon's costly mistakes. The King of Israel desperately pursued several unrelated goals in a vain attempt to satisfy himself. Ecclesiastes 2:1–11 provides a good example of a leader who didn't know how to get what he wanted.

By the time Solomon wrote these words, he had reached a high level of success—but still felt empty. He couldn't put his finger on why fulfillment continued to escape him. Because he lacked focus, he searched high and low, experimenting with all kinds of goals, yet never achieved satisfaction. Sadly, he attempted to solve an inward problem with an outward solution.

The old axiom remains true: If you chase two rabbits, both will escape. This was certainly true of Solomon's futile attempts to reach his varied goals. (He pursued eight goals in Ecclesiastes 2 alone!) So, what can we learn from this leader about focus?

1. **He pursued too many things in too short a time.**
2. **He pursued the wrong goals to reach his desired outcome.**
3. **His self-serving goals were all wrong.**
4. **He despaired because he never identified what he really wanted.**

A Checklist for Making Decisions

Solomon eventually did narrow his focus, but it took him a lifetime and an entire book to do so (see Ecc 12). He finally determined what really mattered and what he really wanted.

How about you? Have you figured out your focus? How do you make major decisions? Do you have a way of determining your focus, based on what really matters or what really counts? Consider the following checklist as you make decisions about where to invest your time and energy. When faced with a decision, ask yourself:

1. **Is this consistent with my priorities?**
2. **Is this within my area of competence?**
3. **Can someone else do it better?**
4. **What do my trusted friends say?**
5. **Do I have the time?**

When you say "yes" to an opportunity, get ready to focus. Make to-do lists. Set your priorities. Avoid clutter. Pursue excellence, but avoid perfectionism. Question everything. Work to prevent procrastination. Control interruptions and distractions. Use the calendar. Narrow your wedge—don't try to do everything. That means you'll have to say no to some good things. And how can you say no gracefully?

1. **Say no to the proposition, not to the person.**
2. **Respond in terms that convey the best interests of the person who's requesting your involvement.**
3. **Defer creatively; suggest an alternative.**

For a positive example of focus, see p. 1420.

¹⁵Then I said to myself,

"The fate of the fool will overtake me also.
    What then do I gain by being wise?"
I said to myself,
    "This too is meaningless."
¹⁶For the wise, like the fool, will not be long
        remembered;
    the days have already come when both
        have been forgotten.
Like the fool, the wise too must die!

Toil Is Meaningless

¹⁷So I hated life, because the work that is done under the sun was grievous to me. All of it is meaningless, a chasing after the wind. ¹⁸I hated all the things I had toiled for under the sun, because I must leave them to the one who comes after me. ¹⁹And who knows whether that person will be wise or foolish? Yet they will have control over all the fruit of my toil into which I have poured my effort and skill under the sun. This too is meaningless. ²⁰So my heart began to despair over all my toilsome labor under the sun. ²¹For a person may labor with wisdom, knowledge and skill, and then they must leave all they own to another who has not toiled for it. This too is meaningless and a great misfortune. ²²What do people get for all the toil and anxious striving with which they labor under the sun? ²³All their days their work is grief and pain; even at night their minds do not rest. This too is meaningless.

²⁴A person can do nothing better than to eat and drink and find satisfaction in their own toil. This too, I see, is from the hand of God, ²⁵for without him, who can eat or find enjoyment? ²⁶To the person who pleases him, God gives wisdom, knowledge and happiness, but to the sinner he gives the task of gathering and storing up wealth to hand it over to the one who pleases God. This too is meaningless, a chasing after the wind.

A Time for Everything

3 There is a time for everything,
    and a season for every activity under the
        heavens:

²   a time to be born and a time to die,
    a time to plant and a time to uproot,
³   a time to kill and a time to heal,
    a time to tear down and a time to build,
⁴   a time to weep and a time to laugh,
    a time to mourn and a time to dance,
⁵   a time to scatter stones and a time to
        gather them,
    a time to embrace and a time to refrain
        from embracing,
⁶   a time to search and a time to give up,
    a time to keep and a time to throw away,
⁷   a time to tear and a time to mend,
    a time to be silent and a time to speak,
⁸   a time to love and a time to hate,
    a time for war and a time for peace.

⁹What do workers gain from their toil? ¹⁰I have seen the burden God has laid on the human race. ¹¹He has made everything beautiful

---

The Law of Timing: There's a Season for Everything

Ecclesiastes 3:1–8

Solomon knew quite a bit about the Law of Timing. He tells us there exists an appointed time for everything under heaven. Then he lists several examples: birth, death, planting, reaping, weeping, laughing, etc.

We don't *control* the timing of most events; the best we can do is to *recognize* the timing. Ecclesiastes 3 teaches leaders several important lessons:

1. **It is our responsibility to recognize God's timing, not to change it.**

2. **It is our responsibility to accept and cooperate with God's timing.**

3. **Our alignment with God's timing makes a great difference.**

4. **God has made everything appropriate in its time.**

5. **God has put eternity in our hearts, so we must trust God to communicate his timing.**

6. **We can do nothing better during our lifetime than to rejoice and do good.**

in its time. He has also set eternity in the human heart; yet[a] no one can fathom what God has done from beginning to end. [12]I know that there is nothing better for people than to be happy and to do good while they live. [13]That each of them may eat and drink, and find satisfaction in all their toil — this is the gift of God. [14]I know that everything God does will endure forever; nothing can be added to it and nothing taken from it. God does it so that people will fear him.

[15]Whatever is has already been,
    and what will be has been before;
    and God will call the past to account.[b]

[16]And I saw something else under the sun:

In the place of judgment — wickedness was
        there,
    in the place of justice — wickedness was
        there.

[17]I said to myself,

"God will bring into judgment
    both the righteous and the wicked,
for there will be a time for every activity,
    a time to judge every deed."

[18]I also said to myself, "As for humans, God tests them so that they may see that they are like the animals. [19]Surely the fate of human beings is like that of the animals; the same fate awaits them both: As one dies, so dies the other. All have the same breath[c]; humans have no advantage over animals. Everything is meaningless. [20]All go to the same place; all come from dust, and to dust all return. [21]Who knows if the human spirit rises upward and if the spirit of the animal goes down into the earth?"

[22]So I saw that there is nothing better for a person than to enjoy their work, because that is their lot. For who can bring them to see what will happen after them?

Oppression, Toil, Friendlessness

4 Again I looked and saw all the oppression that was taking place under the sun:

I saw the tears of the oppressed —
    and they have no comforter;
power was on the side of their oppressors —
    and they have no comforter.

---

[a] 11 Or *also placed ignorance in the human heart, so that*
[b] 15 Or *God calls back the past*   [c] 19 Or *spirit*

Motivational Needs: What Every Leader Needs to Know

Ecclesiastes 4:1–8

While Ecclesiastes 4 seems to continue the theme of futility, it actually attempts to address the issue of motivation. Solomon says that he observes people in a variety of contexts, and nothing seems to satisfy them.

Where do people search for satisfaction? What do they seek in life? Note Solomon's observations about what motivates most men and women:

1. **Comfort and fulfillment (vv. 1–3)**

2. **Competition and triumph (vv. 4–6)**

3. **Consumption and greed (vv. 7–8)**

As leaders, we must understand people's motivational needs. A scholar named David McClellan identified three main motivations, or "drivers," that people exhibit in their work. According to McClellan, each person generally has a primary driver, and perhaps another driver as their backup.

One driver is achievement. Achievers like to perform, to finish a task. Getting across the goal line is what satisfies them.

Another driver is affiliation. Affiliators put emphasis on belonging to a group and relating well to others. They're "people people," and they want everybody to be happy.

The third driver is influence. Influencers seek to have power over whatever situation they're in. They like things their way. Status is important to them. For them, the name of the game is control.

To work well with others, it helps to know what motivations "make them tick."

²And I declared that the dead,
who had already died,
are happier than the living,
who are still alive.
³But better than both
is the one who has never been born,
who has not seen the evil
that is done under the sun.

⁴And I saw that all toil and all achievement spring from one person's envy of another. This too is meaningless, a chasing after the wind.

⁵Fools fold their hands
and ruin themselves.
⁶Better one handful with tranquillity
than two handfuls with toil
and chasing after the wind.

⁷Again I saw something meaningless under the sun:

⁸There was a man all alone;
he had neither son nor brother.
There was no end to his toil,
yet his eyes were not content with his wealth.
"For whom am I toiling," he asked,
"and why am I depriving myself of
enjoyment?"
This too is meaningless—
a miserable business!

⁹Two are better than one,
because they have a good return for their
labor:
¹⁰If either of them falls down,
one can help the other up.
But pity anyone who falls
and has no one to help them up.
¹¹Also, if two lie down together, they will keep
warm.
But how can one keep warm alone?
¹²Though one may be overpowered,
two can defend themselves.
A cord of three strands is not quickly broken.

Advancement Is Meaningless

¹³Better a poor but wise youth than an old but foolish king who no longer knows how to heed a warning. ¹⁴The youth may have come from prison to the kingship, or he may have been born in poverty within his kingdom. ¹⁵I saw that all who lived and walked under the sun followed the youth, the king's successor. ¹⁶There was no end to all the people who were before them. But those who came later were not pleased with the successor. This too is meaningless, a chasing after the wind.

The Rewards of Partnership

Ecclesiastes 4:9–12

Most leaders recognize they need partnerships to reach big goals. Note the rewards of a healthy partnership:

1. **Partners accomplish more (v. 9).**

2. **Partners complement each other (v. 10).**

3. **Partners supply support and warmth for each other (v. 11).**

4. **Partners give strength to each other (v. 12).**

Fulfill Your Vow to God

5 ᵃ Guard your steps when you go to the house of God. Go near to listen rather than to offer the sacrifice of fools, who do not know that they do wrong.

²Do not be quick with your mouth,
do not be hasty in your heart
to utter anything before God.
God is in heaven
and you are on earth,
so let your words be few.
³A dream comes when there are many cares,
and many words mark the speech of a
fool.

⁴When you make a vow to God, do not delay to fulfill it. He has no pleasure in fools; fulfill your vow. ⁵It is better not to make a vow than to make one and not fulfill it. ⁶Do not let your mouth lead you into sin. And do not protest to the temple messenger, "My vow was a mistake." Why should God be angry at what you say and destroy the work of your hands? ⁷Much dreaming and many words are meaningless. Therefore fear God.

Riches Are Meaningless

⁸If you see the poor oppressed in a district, and justice and rights denied, do not be surprised at such things; for one official is eyed by a higher one, and over them both are others higher still. ⁹The increase from the land is taken by all; the king himself profits from the fields.

ᵃ In Hebrew texts 5:1 is numbered 4:17, and 5:2-20 is numbered 5:1-19.

Leadership Pitfalls

Ecclesiastes 5:2–7

Do you ever make promises to God? Scripture advises caution before we commit something to God—good advice for any decision a leader must make. Solomon describes three major pitfalls lying in wait for careless leaders:

1. **Hasty Speech (vv. 2–3)**
   Leaders must listen as much as they speak. It takes more than words to fulfill dreams.

2. **Empty Promises (vv. 4–5)**
   Leaders tend to say what others want to hear. Don't promise what you can't deliver.

3. **Lame Excuses (vv. 6–7)**
   Leaders diminish their influence when they try to reverse a mistake with a lame excuse.

[10] Whoever loves money never has enough;
   whoever loves wealth is never satisfied
      with their income.
   This too is meaningless.

[11] As goods increase,
   so do those who consume them.
And what benefit are they to the owners
   except to feast their eyes on them?

[12] The sleep of a laborer is sweet,
   whether they eat little or much,
but as for the rich, their abundance
   permits them no sleep.

[13] I have seen a grievous evil under the sun:

wealth hoarded to the harm of its owners,
[14]   or wealth lost through some misfortune,
so that when they have children
   there is nothing left for them to inherit.
[15] Everyone comes naked from their mother's
      womb,
   and as everyone comes, so they depart.
They take nothing from their toil
   that they can carry in their hands.

[16] This too is a grievous evil:

As everyone comes, so they depart,
   and what do they gain,
   since they toil for the wind?
[17] All their days they eat in darkness,
   with great frustration, affliction and anger.

[18] This is what I have observed to be good: that it is appropriate for a person to eat, to drink and to find satisfaction in their toilsome labor under the sun during the few days of life God has given them — for this is their lot. [19] Moreover, when God gives someone wealth and possessions, and the ability to enjoy them, to accept their lot and be happy in their toil—this is a gift of God. [20] They seldom reflect on the days of their life, because God keeps them occupied with gladness of heart.

6 I have seen another evil under the sun, and it weighs heavily on mankind: [2] God gives some people wealth, possessions and honor, so that they lack nothing their hearts desire, but God does not grant them the ability to enjoy them, and strangers enjoy them instead. This is meaningless, a grievous evil.

[3] A man may have a hundred children and live many years; yet no matter how long he lives, if he cannot enjoy his prosperity and does not receive proper burial, I say that a stillborn child is better off than he. [4] It comes without meaning, it departs in darkness, and in darkness its name is shrouded. [5] Though it never saw the sun or knew anything, it has more rest than does that man — [6] even if he lives a thousand years twice over but fails to enjoy his prosperity. Do not all go to the same place?

[7] Everyone's toil is for their mouth,
   yet their appetite is never satisfied.
[8] What advantage have the wise over fools?
   What do the poor gain
      by knowing how to conduct themselves
         before others?
[9] Better what the eye sees
   than the roving of the appetite.
This too is meaningless,
   a chasing after the wind.

[10] Whatever exists has already been named,
   and what humanity is has been known;
no one can contend
   with someone who is stronger.

11 The more the words,
　　the less the meaning,
　　and how does that profit anyone?

12 For who knows what is good for a person in life, during the few and meaningless days they pass through like a shadow? Who can tell them what will happen under the sun after they are gone?

Wisdom

7 A good name is better than fine perfume,
　　and the day of death better than the day of
　　　birth.
2 It is better to go to a house of mourning
　　than to go to a house of feasting,
　for death is the destiny of everyone;
　　the living should take this to heart.
3 Frustration is better than laughter,
　　because a sad face is good for the heart.
4 The heart of the wise is in the house of
　　　mourning,
　　but the heart of fools is in the house of
　　　pleasure.
5 It is better to heed the rebuke of a wise person
　　than to listen to the song of fools.
6 Like the crackling of thorns under the pot,
　　so is the laughter of fools.
　　This too is meaningless.

7 Extortion turns a wise person into a fool,
　　and a bribe corrupts the heart.
8 The end of a matter is better than its beginning,
　　and patience is better than pride.
9 Do not be quickly provoked in your spirit,
　　for anger resides in the lap of fools.

10 Do not say, "Why were the old days better
　　　than these?"
　　For it is not wise to ask such questions.

11 Wisdom, like an inheritance, is a good thing
　　and benefits those who see the sun.
12 Wisdom is a shelter
　　as money is a shelter,
　but the advantage of knowledge is this:
　　Wisdom preserves those who have it.

13 Consider what God has done:

Who can straighten
　　what he has made crooked?
14 When times are good, be happy;
　　but when times are bad, consider this:
God has made the one
　　as well as the other.
Therefore, no one can discover
　　anything about their future.

15 In this meaningless life of mine I have seen both of these:

the righteous perishing in their righteousness,
　　and the wicked living long in their
　　　wickedness.
16 Do not be overrighteous,
　　neither be overwise —
　　why destroy yourself?
17 Do not be overwicked,
　　and do not be a fool —
　　why die before your time?
18 It is good to grasp the one
　　and not let go of the other.
　　Whoever fears God will avoid all extremes.[a]

19 Wisdom makes one wise person more
　　　powerful
　　than ten rulers in a city.

20 Indeed, there is no one on earth who is
　　　righteous,
　　no one who does what is right and never
　　　sins.

21 Do not pay attention to every word people say,
　　or you may hear your servant cursing
　　　you —
22 for you know in your heart
　　that many times you yourself have cursed
　　　others.

23 All this I tested by wisdom and I said,

"I am determined to be wise" —
　　but this was beyond me.
24 Whatever exists is far off and most profound —
　　who can discover it?
25 So I turned my mind to understand,
　　to investigate and to search out wisdom
　　　and the scheme of things
　and to understand the stupidity of wickedness
　　and the madness of folly.

26 I find more bitter than death
　　the woman who is a snare,
　whose heart is a trap
　　and whose hands are chains.
　The man who pleases God will escape her,
　　but the sinner she will ensnare.

27 "Look," says the Teacher,[b] "this is what I have discovered:

"Adding one thing to another to discover the
　　scheme of things —

---

[a] 18 Or will follow them both　　[b] 27 Or the leader of the assembly

28 while I was still searching
    but not finding—
I found one upright man among a thousand,
    but not one upright woman among them
    all.
29 This only have I found:
    God created mankind upright,
    but they have gone in search of many
    schemes."

8 Who is like the wise?
    Who knows the explanation of things?
A person's wisdom brightens their face
    and changes its hard appearance.

Obey the King

2 Obey the king's command, I say, because you took an oath before God. 3 Do not be in a hurry to leave the king's presence. Do not stand up for a bad cause, for he will do whatever he pleases. 4 Since a king's word is supreme, who can say to him, "What are you doing?"

5 Whoever obeys his command will come to
    no harm,
    and the wise heart will know the proper
    time and procedure.
6 For there is a proper time and procedure for
    every matter,
    though a person may be weighed down by
    misery.
7 Since no one knows the future,
    who can tell someone else what is to
    come?
8 As no one has power over the wind to
    contain it,
    so[a] no one has power over the time of
    their death.

As no one is discharged in time of war,
    so wickedness will not release those who
    practice it.

9 All this I saw, as I applied my mind to everything done under the sun. There is a time when a man lords it over others to his own[b] hurt. 10 Then too, I saw the wicked buried—those who used to come and go from the holy place and receive praise[c] in the city where they did this. This too is meaningless.

11 When the sentence for a crime is not quickly carried out, people's hearts are filled with schemes to do wrong. 12 Although a wicked person who commits a hundred crimes may live a long time, I know that it will go better with those who fear God, who are reverent before him. 13 Yet because the wicked do not fear God, it will not go well with them, and their days will not lengthen like a shadow.

14 There is something else meaningless that occurs on earth: the righteous who get what the wicked deserve, and the wicked who get what the righteous deserve. This too, I say, is meaningless. 15 So I commend the enjoyment of life, because there is nothing better for a person under the sun than to eat and drink and be glad. Then joy will accompany them in their toil all the days of the life God has given them under the sun.

16 When I applied my mind to know wisdom and to observe the labor that is done on earth—people getting no sleep day or night— 17 then I saw all that God has done. No one can comprehend what goes on under the sun. Despite all

---

[a] 8 Or over the human spirit to retain it, / and so   [b] 9 Or to their   [c] 10 Some Hebrew manuscripts and Septuagint (Aquila); most Hebrew manuscripts and are forgotten

---

Servanthood: The Quality of a Leader Who Lasts

Ecclesiastes 8:1–9

Solomon reminds us about our relationship to leaders above us. We are to submit to them, not because the person deserves it, but because the office deserves it and God decrees it.

And what about leaders in authority? Solomon also issues a warning. When leaders try to exercise authority without a servant's heart, they eventually hurt themselves. Leaders add value by serving others.

Role of the Follower

1. **Submit to God-given authority.**

2. **Trust God to accomplish his purpose.**

3. **Don't quit or become divisive.**

Role of the Leader

1. **Exercise authority with wisdom and caution.**

2. **Recognize that no human controls all of life.**

3. **Lead others by serving not bossing them.**

their efforts to search it out, no one can discover its meaning. Even if the wise claim they know, they cannot really comprehend it.

A Common Destiny for All

9 So I reflected on all this and concluded that the righteous and the wise and what they do are in God's hands, but no one knows whether love or hate awaits them. ²All share a common destiny—the righteous and the wicked, the good and the bad,[a] the clean and the unclean, those who offer sacrifices and those who do not.

As it is with the good,
    so with the sinful;
as it is with those who take oaths,
    so with those who are afraid to take them.

³This is the evil in everything that happens under the sun: The same destiny overtakes all. The hearts of people, moreover, are full of evil and there is madness in their hearts while they live, and afterward they join the dead. ⁴Anyone who is among the living has hope[b]—even a live dog is better off than a dead lion!

⁵For the living know that they will die,
    but the dead know nothing;
they have no further reward,
    and even their name is forgotten.
⁶Their love, their hate
    and their jealousy have long since vanished;
never again will they have a part
    in anything that happens under the sun.

⁷Go, eat your food with gladness, and drink your wine with a joyful heart, for God has already approved what you do. ⁸Always be clothed in white, and always anoint your head with oil. ⁹Enjoy life with your wife, whom you love, all the days of this meaningless life that God has given you under the sun—all your meaningless days. For this is your lot in life and in your toilsome labor under the sun. ¹⁰Whatever your hand finds to do, do it with all your might, for in the realm of the dead, where you are going, there is neither working nor planning nor knowledge nor wisdom.

¹¹I have seen something else under the sun:

The race is not to the swift
    or the battle to the strong,
nor does food come to the wise
    or wealth to the brilliant
    or favor to the learned;
but time and chance happen to them all.

¹²Moreover, no one knows when their hour will come:

As fish are caught in a cruel net,
    or birds are taken in a snare,
so people are trapped by evil times
    that fall unexpectedly upon them.

Wisdom Better Than Folly

¹³I also saw under the sun this example of wisdom that greatly impressed me: ¹⁴There was once a small city with only a few people in it. And a powerful king came against it, surrounded it and built huge siege works against it. ¹⁵Now there lived in that city a man poor but wise, and he saved the city by his wisdom. But nobody remembered that poor man. ¹⁶So I said, "Wisdom is better than strength." But the poor man's wisdom is despised, and his words are no longer heeded.

¹⁷The quiet words of the wise are more to be heeded
    than the shouts of a ruler of fools.
¹⁸Wisdom is better than weapons of war,
    but one sinner destroys much good.

10 As dead flies give perfume a bad smell,
    so a little folly outweighs wisdom and honor.

---

[a] 2 Septuagint (Aquila), Vulgate and Syriac; Hebrew does not have *and the bad.*   [b] 4 Or *What then is to be chosen? With all who live, there is hope*

The Law of Legacy: Your Work and Your Job

Ecclesiastes 9:7–18

Everyone on earth has a work to do, and it may be different from one's job. A job may be the task we get paid for at the moment, but a work is the task God gives us for our lives. Jobs come and go but the work remains. Your present job may be preparation for your ultimate work. This passage gives us direction for leaving the right legacy to those who come behind us.

- Work joyfully, since approval comes from God (vv. 7–9).
- Work energetically, even if the results seem uncertain (vv. 10–12).
- Work wisely, with the benefit of God's perspective (vv. 13–18).

² The heart of the wise inclines to the right,
　　but the heart of the fool to the left.
³ Even as fools walk along the road,
　　they lack sense
　　and show everyone how stupid they are.
⁴ If a ruler's anger rises against you,
　　do not leave your post;
　　calmness can lay great offenses to rest.

⁵ There is an evil I have seen under the sun,
　　the sort of error that arises from a ruler:
⁶ Fools are put in many high positions,
　　while the rich occupy the low ones.
⁷ I have seen slaves on horseback,
　　while princes go on foot like slaves.

⁸ Whoever digs a pit may fall into it;
　　whoever breaks through a wall may be
　　　　bitten by a snake.
⁹ Whoever quarries stones may be injured by
　　　　them;
　　whoever splits logs may be endangered by
　　　　them.

¹⁰ If the ax is dull
　　and its edge unsharpened,
more strength is needed,
　　but skill will bring success.

¹¹ If a snake bites before it is charmed,
　　the charmer receives no fee.

¹² Words from the mouth of the wise are gracious,
　　but fools are consumed by their own lips.
¹³ At the beginning their words are folly;
　　at the end they are wicked madness —
¹⁴ 　and fools multiply words.

No one knows what is coming —
　　who can tell someone else what will
　　　　happen after them?

¹⁵ The toil of fools wearies them;
　　they do not know the way to town.

¹⁶ Woe to the land whose king was a servant[a]
　　and whose princes feast in the morning.
¹⁷ Blessed is the land whose king is of noble
　　　　birth
　　and whose princes eat at a proper time —
　　for strength and not for drunkenness.

¹⁸ Through laziness, the rafters sag;
　　because of idle hands, the house leaks.

¹⁹ A feast is made for laughter,
　　wine makes life merry,
　　and money is the answer for everything.

²⁰ Do not revile the king even in your
　　　　thoughts,
　　or curse the rich in your bedroom,
because a bird in the sky may carry your
　　　　words,
　　and a bird on the wing may report what
　　　　you say.

Invest in Many Ventures

11 Ship your grain across the sea;
　　after many days you may receive a return.
² Invest in seven ventures, yes, in eight;
　　you do not know what disaster may come
　　　　upon the land.

[a] 16 Or *king is a child*

Generosity: Leaders Give Before They Receive

Ecclesiastes 11:1–9

Solomon knew a thing or two about wise investing. He counsels leaders to be generous, giving before they receive. And why should leaders initiate giving? Because they know they will eventually receive a hefty return. Wise leaders embrace the following truths about generosity:

1. **Givers go first (v. 1).**

2. **Givers receive a return (v. 1).**

3. **The return may not be immediate (v. 1).**

4. **Giving does not keep us from misfortune (vv. 2–3).**

5. **If you do not give, you cannot expect a return (v. 4).**

6. **The return will be in proportion to your giving (v. 6).**

7. **The motive for giving is love for God (v. 9).**

³ If clouds are full of water,
  they pour rain on the earth.
Whether a tree falls to the south or to the
    north,
  in the place where it falls, there it will lie.
⁴ Whoever watches the wind will not plant;
  whoever looks at the clouds will not reap.

⁵ As you do not know the path of the wind,
  or how the body is formed*ᵃ* in a mother's
    womb,
so you cannot understand the work of God,
  the Maker of all things.

⁶ Sow your seed in the morning,
  and at evening let your hands not be idle,
for you do not know which will succeed,
  whether this or that,
  or whether both will do equally well.

Remember Your Creator While Young

⁷ Light is sweet,
  and it pleases the eyes to see the sun.
⁸ However many years anyone may live,
  let them enjoy them all.
But let them remember the days of darkness,
  for there will be many.
  Everything to come is meaningless.

⁹ You who are young, be happy while you are
    young,
  and let your heart give you joy in the days
    of your youth.
Follow the ways of your heart
  and whatever your eyes see,

but know that for all these things
  God will bring you into judgment.
¹⁰ So then, banish anxiety from your heart
  and cast off the troubles of your body,
  for youth and vigor are meaningless.

12 Remember your Creator
  in the days of your youth,
before the days of trouble come
  and the years approach when you will say,
  "I find no pleasure in them" —
² before the sun and the light
  and the moon and the stars grow dark,
  and the clouds return after the rain;
³ when the keepers of the house tremble,
  and the strong men stoop,
when the grinders cease because they are
    few,
  and those looking through the windows
    grow dim;
⁴ when the doors to the street are closed
  and the sound of grinding fades;
when people rise up at the sound of birds,
  but all their songs grow faint;
⁵ when people are afraid of heights
  and of dangers in the streets;
when the almond tree blossoms
  and the grasshopper drags itself along
  and desire no longer is stirred.
Then people go to their eternal home
  and mourners go about the streets.

ᵃ 5 Or know how life (or the spirit) | enters the body being formed

---

Wise Words for Leaders on How to Finish Well

Ecclesiastes 12:1–14

Amazing how God can bring sunshine out of the cloudiest day, isn't it? So it is with the book of Ecclesiastes. An otherwise pessimistic and discouraging book ends, by God's grace, on a significant "up" note.

Chapter 12 concludes Solomon's meditation with some wise words that should direct every leader. They sound like the lecture of an experienced mentor attempting to counsel an emerging leader, trying to keep him or her from making some of the same mistakes he made. Consider Solomon's wisdom in this grand finale:

1. **Don't lose sight of the big picture, especially when you are young (vv. 1–4).**

2. **Do what is right before it is too late to correct yourself (vv. 5–8).**

3. **Use your words like tools to shepherd and add value to others (v. 11).**

4. **Don't try to master everything in life, just what is important (v. 12).**

5. **Trust and obey God, because he is the ultimate Judge (vv. 13–14).**

[6]Remember him — before the silver cord is
    severed,
  and the golden bowl is broken;
before the pitcher is shattered at the spring,
  and the wheel broken at the well,
[7]and the dust returns to the ground it came
    from,
  and the spirit returns to God who gave it.

[8]"Meaningless! Meaningless!" says the Teacher.[a]
  "Everything is meaningless!"

The Conclusion of the Matter

[9]Not only was the Teacher wise, but he also
imparted knowledge to the people. He pondered
and searched out and set in order many proverbs. [10]The Teacher searched to find just the right
words, and what he wrote was upright and true.

[11]The words of the wise are like goads, their
collected sayings like firmly embedded nails —
given by one shepherd.[b] [12]Be warned, my son, of
anything in addition to them.

Of making many books there is no end, and
much study wearies the body.

[13]Now all has been heard;
  here is the conclusion of the matter:
Fear God and keep his commandments,
  for this is the duty of all mankind.
[14]For God will bring every deed into
    judgment,
  including every hidden thing,
    whether it is good or evil.

---

[a] 8 Or *the leader of the assembly*; also in verses 9 and 10
[b] 11 Or *Shepherd*

INTRODUCTION TO
SONG OF SONGS

God's Love for His People

The Song of Songs stands alone among 1,005 songs that Solomon wrote (1Ki 4:32). It is called the Song of Songs because many consider it the best of his songs, the most excellent composition he ever wrote. Pious Jews read it every year on the eighth day of the Passover.

The Song proclaims a husband's love for his wife and illustrates God's love for his people, the love that Christ has for the church, his bride. It describes how a lover cherishes his beloved and how he enjoys the way she completes him.

The song implies that leaders must learn to love the people God has placed within their sphere of influence. We cannot separate leadership from relationship. This book vividly portrays the mutual love both parties have for each other, a love that drives them to appreciate each other and serve each other extravagantly. This kind of love prompts the spiritual leader and the follower to "go the extra mile" and do more than the expected. The book frequently exhibits the "and then some" principle— the lover relishes his beloved, cares for her, provides for her . . . *and then some*. Healthy, intimate relationships create this kind of generous attitude.

Far too often, leaders believe their position forces them to remain distant from their people. They imagine they must remain aloof, even a bit mysterious, living at a level unattainable by others. This is not a biblical idea. This song reveals a transparent and vulnerable spiritual leader who speaks intimately of both his strengths and his needs. He feels secure enough to quit hiding behind smokescreens, as leaders today often do. What kind of smokescreens trouble us? Consider two: "I just cannot open up with my people." "I don't have time to build

God's Role in Song of Songs

Scholars have interpreted this book in four primary ways:

1. **Allegory.** This view sees the book expressing the love of God for his chosen people. Each part of the song contains some symbolic meaning.
2. **Dramatic narrative.** The song expresses Solomon's own love affair with a Shulamite woman, whom he takes as wife to his palace in Jerusalem.
3. **Extended parable.** This view sees the song not as an allegory seeking meaning in every verse, but as a parable of Christ and his church.
4. **Literal.** This view sees Solomon celebrating the virtues of human love.

However you view the book, think of God's role as the Ultimate Leader whose love for his people motivates him to lead and to act on their behalf.

Leaders in Song of Songs
The husband (or God)

Other People of Influence in Song of Songs
The wife or the beloved (the body of Christ), the friends

relationships—I'm too busy trying to reach my goals." The lover in this song is honest enough to quit believing the kind of lies we often believe today. He wouldn't think of saying, "If my people are going to submit to me as a leader, I cannot let them get too close to me," or, "If I become vulnerable, my people won't respect me."

The Song of Songs may give you a whole new perspective on the love a spiritual leader can have for his people. You can also apply these principles to the expressive, vulnerable relationships you find in your church, office, or neighborhood.

Lessons in Leadership

- The best leaders feel motivated by love and compassion for their people.
- You cannot separate leadership from relationships.
- When leaders practice transparency, respect goes up, not down.
- Both the leader and the people need each other.
- Even the toughest of problems can be solved when relationships are managed well.

LEADERSHIP HIGHLIGHTS IN SONG OF SONGS

THE PASSIONATE, Consuming Love of God (1:1)	page 794
AFFIRMATION: Leaders Identify and Affirm Qualities in Others (1:10–15)	page 795
LEADERS HONOR THEIR TEAMS: Put 10s on Their Foreheads (4:1–16)	page 797

1 Solomon's Song of Songs.

She[a]

2 Let him kiss me with the kisses of his
　　mouth —
　for your love is more delightful than
　　wine.
3 Pleasing is the fragrance of your perfumes;
　your name is like perfume poured out.
　No wonder the young women love you!
4 Take me away with you — let us hurry!
　Let the king bring me into his chambers.

Friends

　We rejoice and delight in you[b];
　　we will praise your love more than wine.

She

　How right they are to adore you!

5 Dark am I, yet lovely,
　　daughters of Jerusalem,
　dark like the tents of Kedar,
　　like the tent curtains of Solomon.[c]
6 Do not stare at me because I am dark,
　　because I am darkened by the sun.
　My mother's sons were angry with me
　　and made me take care of the vineyards;
　　my own vineyard I had to neglect.
7 Tell me, you whom I love,
　　where you graze your flock
　and where you rest your sheep at midday.
　Why should I be like a veiled woman
　　beside the flocks of your friends?

Friends

8 If you do not know, most beautiful of
　　women,
　　follow the tracks of the sheep
　and graze your young goats
　　by the tents of the shepherds.

He

9 I liken you, my darling, to a mare
　　among Pharaoh's chariot horses.
10 Your cheeks are beautiful with earrings,
　　your neck with strings of jewels.
11 We will make you earrings of gold,
　　studded with silver.

She

12 While the king was at his table,
　　my perfume spread its fragrance.
13 My beloved is to me a sachet of myrrh
　　resting between my breasts.

14 My beloved is to me a cluster of henna blossoms
　　from the vineyards of En Gedi.

He

15 How beautiful you are, my darling!
　Oh, how beautiful!
　Your eyes are doves.

She

16 How handsome you are, my beloved!
　Oh, how charming!
　And our bed is verdant.

---

a The main male and female speakers (identified primarily on the basis of the gender of the relevant Hebrew forms) are indicated by the captions *He* and *She* respectively. The words of others are marked *Friends*. In some instances the divisions and their captions are debatable.　*b 4* The Hebrew is masculine singular.　*c 5* Or *Salma*

The Passionate, Consuming Love of God

Song of Songs 1:1

Most of the time when we use words like "passion" and "love," we speak of the affection between a man and a woman. But have you ever thought of God's love in terms of *passion*?

In the Song of Songs, we see a beautiful picture of the tender devotion that God means to be shared between a husband and wife. But we also see a picture of the love God wants his people to share with Jesus Christ.

King Solomon understood that this love was unearned and unmerited, that in many ways God poured it out on his people despite themselves. This kind of love represents an actual communion between Christ and his church. On his part, it's a love that gives all to those with nothing to give in exchange. On our part, it is the kind of love that inspires us to hunger for more of him, to thirst for him to shine out through us.

Godly leaders understand that the relationship between Christ and his people amounts to far more than some kind of religious arrangement or contractual agreement. Rather, it is a relationship of love, tenderness and passion, a relationship in which we, the bride, remain aware of our unworthiness of the bridegroom's love—yet bask in its limitless depths.

Affirmation: Leaders Identify and Affirm Qualities in Others

Song of Songs 1:10–15

Leaders whom others love and loyally follow are usually those who express appreciation to their followers. They live the principle of affirmation.

The Song of Songs reveals a spiritual leader who identifies specific qualities he appreciates about his beloved, then expresses his appreciation. This marvelous love letter shows a spiritual leader communicating love and affirmation. The follower almost always reciprocates the sentiment. Notice what Solomon and all great leaders do to encourage those in their care:

1. **Identify**—Declare what it is you appreciate. Name it.

2. **Specify**—Be as specific as you can. No generalizations about their style!

3. **Quantify**—Express how they have made a measurable difference in your life.

4. **Magnify**—Encourage your followers liberally in public, before their peers.

He

17 The beams of our house are cedars;
    our rafters are firs.

She[a]

2 I am a rose[b] of Sharon,
    a lily of the valleys.

He

2 Like a lily among thorns
    is my darling among the young women.

She

3 Like an apple[c] tree among the trees of the
       forest
    is my beloved among the young men.
I delight to sit in his shade,
    and his fruit is sweet to my taste.
4 Let him lead me to the banquet hall,
    and let his banner over me be love.
5 Strengthen me with raisins,
    refresh me with apples,
    for I am faint with love.
6 His left arm is under my head,
    and his right arm embraces me.
7 Daughters of Jerusalem, I charge you
    by the gazelles and by the does of the field:
Do not arouse or awaken love
    until it so desires.

8 Listen! My beloved!
    Look! Here he comes,
leaping across the mountains,
    bounding over the hills.
9 My beloved is like a gazelle or a young stag.
    Look! There he stands behind our wall,

gazing through the windows,
    peering through the lattice.
10 My beloved spoke and said to me,
    "Arise, my darling,
    my beautiful one, come with me.
11 See! The winter is past;
    the rains are over and gone.
12 Flowers appear on the earth;
    the season of singing has come,
the cooing of doves
    is heard in our land.
13 The fig tree forms its early fruit;
    the blossoming vines spread their
       fragrance.
Arise, come, my darling;
    my beautiful one, come with me."

He

14 My dove in the clefts of the rock,
    in the hiding places on the
       mountainside,
show me your face,
    let me hear your voice;
for your voice is sweet,
    and your face is lovely.
15 Catch for us the foxes,
    the little foxes
that ruin the vineyards,
    our vineyards that are in bloom.

She

16 My beloved is mine and I am his;
    he browses among the lilies.

[a] Or He   [b] 1 Probably a member of the crocus family
[c] 3 Or possibly *apricot*; here and elsewhere in Song of Songs

Catching the Little Foxes

Song of Songs 2:15

It's the "little foxes" that often ruin an organization—bad attitudes, lack of encouragement, no time off, impatient supervisors, or gossip. Leaders must listen for the sounds of little fox feet. Remember, it's better to build a fence at the top of the cliff than a hospital at the bottom.

¹⁷ Until the day breaks
    and the shadows flee,
turn, my beloved,
    and be like a gazelle
or like a young stag
    on the rugged hills.ᵃ

3 All night long on my bed
    I looked for the one my heart loves;
    I looked for him but did not find him.
² I will get up now and go about the city,
    through its streets and squares;
I will search for the one my heart loves.
    So I looked for him but did not find him.
³ The watchmen found me
    as they made their rounds in the city.
    "Have you seen the one my heart loves?"
⁴ Scarcely had I passed them
    when I found the one my heart loves.
I held him and would not let him go
    till I had brought him to my mother's
        house,
    to the room of the one who conceived me.
⁵ Daughters of Jerusalem, I charge you
    by the gazelles and by the does of the
        field:
Do not arouse or awaken love
    until it so desires.

⁶ Who is this coming up from the wilderness
    like a column of smoke,
perfumed with myrrh and incense
    made from all the spices of the merchant?
⁷ Look! It is Solomon's carriage,
    escorted by sixty warriors,
    the noblest of Israel,
⁸ all of them wearing the sword,
    all experienced in battle,
each with his sword at his side,
    prepared for the terrors of the night.
⁹ King Solomon made for himself the
        carriage;
    he made it of wood from Lebanon.

¹⁰ Its posts he made of silver,
    its base of gold.
Its seat was upholstered with purple,
    its interior inlaid with love.
Daughters of Jerusalem, ¹¹ come out,
    and look, you daughters of Zion.
Lookᵇ on King Solomon wearing a crown,
    the crown with which his mother crowned
        him
on the day of his wedding,
    the day his heart rejoiced.

He

4 How beautiful you are, my darling!
    Oh, how beautiful!
    Your eyes behind your veil are doves.
Your hair is like a flock of goats
    descending from the hills of Gilead.
² Your teeth are like a flock of sheep just
        shorn,
    coming up from the washing.
Each has its twin;
    not one of them is alone.
³ Your lips are like a scarlet ribbon;
    your mouth is lovely.
Your temples behind your veil
    are like the halves of a pomegranate.
⁴ Your neck is like the tower of David,
    built with courses of stoneᶜ;
on it hang a thousand shields,
    all of them shields of warriors.
⁵ Your breasts are like two fawns,
    like twin fawns of a gazelle
    that browse among the lilies.
⁶ Until the day breaks
    and the shadows flee,
I will go to the mountain of myrrh
    and to the hill of incense.
⁷ You are altogether beautiful, my darling;
    there is no flaw in you.

⁸ Come with me from Lebanon, my bride,
    come with me from Lebanon.
Descend from the crest of Amana,
    from the top of Senir, the summit of
        Hermon,
from the lions' dens
    and the mountain haunts of leopards.
⁹ You have stolen my heart, my sister, my
        bride;
    you have stolen my heart

ᵃ **17** Or *the hills of Bether*   ᵇ **10,11** Or *interior lovingly inlaid / by the daughters of Jerusalem. / ¹¹Come out, you daughters of Zion, / and look*   ᶜ **4** The meaning of the Hebrew for this phrase is uncertain.

Leaders Honor Their Teams: Put 10s on Their Foreheads

Song of Songs 4:1–16

Solomon spoke delightful words that honored and lifted up his bride. Many scholars believe this song is actually a metaphor for Christ's love for his people. The song also gives leaders a beautiful picture about how to communicate honor from the heart. How can we best communicate compliments to those we lead?

1. **Make them sincere. Be genuine and authentic about what you say.**

2. **Make them specific. Get very pointed and detailed about what you say.**

3. **Make them public. Declare these honoring words in front of others.**

4. **Make them personal. Be personal about what you say.**

Whenever I see my staff, I put an imaginary "10" on the forehead of each individual. This helps me treat each person like a 10, a high performer who makes a difference to me and the organization. Inevitably, they respond as if they *are* a 10!

If you don't already do this, why not start today? Put "10s" on the people you lead. Treat them based on their potential, not their performance. You'll be amazed how both will rise.

---

with one glance of your eyes,
　with one jewel of your necklace.
¹⁰ How delightful is your love, my sister, my
　　bride!
　How much more pleasing is your love
　　than wine,
and the fragrance of your perfume
　more than any spice!
¹¹ Your lips drop sweetness as the honeycomb,
　my bride;
　milk and honey are under your tongue.
The fragrance of your garments
　is like the fragrance of Lebanon.
¹² You are a garden locked up, my sister, my
　　bride;
　you are a spring enclosed, a sealed
　　fountain.
¹³ Your plants are an orchard of pomegranates
　with choice fruits,
　with henna and nard,
¹⁴ 　nard and saffron,
　calamus and cinnamon,
　with every kind of incense tree,
　with myrrh and aloes
　and all the finest spices.
¹⁵ You are*ᵃ* a garden fountain,
　a well of flowing water
　streaming down from Lebanon.

She

¹⁶ Awake, north wind,
　and come, south wind!

Blow on my garden,
　that its fragrance may spread everywhere.
Let my beloved come into his garden
　and taste its choice fruits.

He

5 I have come into my garden, my sister, my
　　bride;
　I have gathered my myrrh with my spice.
I have eaten my honeycomb and my honey;
　I have drunk my wine and my milk.

Friends

Eat, friends, and drink;
　drink your fill of love.

She

² I slept but my heart was awake.
　Listen! My beloved is knocking:
"Open to me, my sister, my darling,
　my dove, my flawless one.
My head is drenched with dew,
　my hair with the dampness of the night."
³ I have taken off my robe—
　must I put it on again?
I have washed my feet—
　must I soil them again?
⁴ My beloved thrust his hand through the
　　latch-opening;
　my heart began to pound for him.

ᵃ 15 Or I am (spoken by She)

Leaders Bless People

Song of Songs 4:1–16

Good leaders give the "blessing" to those they lead. In the Hebrew culture, fathers or patriarchs usually gave the blessing to their sons; rabbis and other spiritual leaders also pronounced blessings. Gary Smalley and John Trent remind us that the blessing contains five key elements:

1. *Affirming words:* **words that give hope and encouragement to the listener.**

2. *Meaningful touch:* **an embrace or a hand on a shoulder communicating care.**

3. *Expression of high value:* **a statement on the value that person adds to everyone.**

4. *Vision of a special future:* **provides word pictures that communicate potential.**

5. *Application of genuine commitment:* **do everything in your power to see that blessing comes to pass.**

---

5 I arose to open for my beloved,
    and my hands dripped with myrrh,
my fingers with flowing myrrh,
    on the handles of the bolt.
6 I opened for my beloved,
    but my beloved had left; he was gone.
    My heart sank at his departure.[a]
I looked for him but did not find him.
    I called him but he did not answer.
7 The watchmen found me
    as they made their rounds in the city.
They beat me, they bruised me;
    they took away my cloak,
    those watchmen of the walls!
8 Daughters of Jerusalem, I charge you —
    if you find my beloved,
what will you tell him?
    Tell him I am faint with love.

Friends

9 How is your beloved better than others,
    most beautiful of women?
How is your beloved better than others,
    that you so charge us?

She

10 My beloved is radiant and ruddy,
    outstanding among ten thousand.
11 His head is purest gold;
    his hair is wavy
    and black as a raven.
12 His eyes are like doves
    by the water streams,
washed in milk,
    mounted like jewels.
13 His cheeks are like beds of spice
    yielding perfume.

His lips are like lilies
    dripping with myrrh.
14 His arms are rods of gold
    set with topaz.
His body is like polished ivory
    decorated with lapis lazuli.
15 His legs are pillars of marble
    set on bases of pure gold.
His appearance is like Lebanon,
    choice as its cedars.
16 His mouth is sweetness itself;
    he is altogether lovely.
This is my beloved, this is my friend,
    daughters of Jerusalem.

Friends

6 Where has your beloved gone,
    most beautiful of women?
Which way did your beloved turn,
    that we may look for him with you?

She

2 My beloved has gone down to his garden,
    to the beds of spices,
to browse in the gardens
    and to gather lilies.
3 I am my beloved's and my beloved is mine;
    he browses among the lilies.

He

4 You are as beautiful as Tirzah, my darling,
    as lovely as Jerusalem,
    as majestic as troops with banners.
5 Turn your eyes from me;
    they overwhelm me.

---

[a] 6 Or *heart had gone out to him when he spoke*

Your hair is like a flock of goats
   descending from Gilead.
[6] Your teeth are like a flock of sheep
   coming up from the washing.
Each has its twin,
   not one of them is missing.
[7] Your temples behind your veil
   are like the halves of a pomegranate.
[8] Sixty queens there may be,
   and eighty concubines,
   and virgins beyond number;
[9] but my dove, my perfect one, is unique,
   the only daughter of her mother,
   the favorite of the one who bore her.
The young women saw her and called her
   blessed;
   the queens and concubines praised her.

Friends

[10] Who is this that appears like the dawn,
   fair as the moon, bright as the sun,
   majestic as the stars in procession?

He

[11] I went down to the grove of nut trees
   to look at the new growth in the valley,

to see if the vines had budded
   or the pomegranates were in bloom.
[12] Before I realized it,
   my desire set me among the royal chariots
     of my people.[a]

Friends

[13] Come back, come back, O Shulammite;
   come back, come back, that we may gaze
     on you!

He

Why would you gaze on the Shulammite
   as on the dance of Mahanaim?[b]

7[c] How beautiful your sandaled feet,
   O prince's daughter!
Your graceful legs are like jewels,
   the work of an artist's hands.
[2] Your navel is a rounded goblet
   that never lacks blended wine.
Your waist is a mound of wheat
   encircled by lilies.
[3] Your breasts are like two fawns,
   like twin fawns of a gazelle.
[4] Your neck is like an ivory tower.
Your eyes are the pools of Heshbon
   by the gate of Bath Rabbim.
Your nose is like the tower of Lebanon
   looking toward Damascus.
[5] Your head crowns you like Mount Carmel.
Your hair is like royal tapestry;
   the king is held captive by its tresses.
[6] How beautiful you are and how pleasing,
   my love, with your delights!
[7] Your stature is like that of the palm,
   and your breasts like clusters of fruit.
[8] I said, "I will climb the palm tree;
   I will take hold of its fruit."
May your breasts be like clusters of grapes
   on the vine,
   the fragrance of your breath like
     apples,
[9]   and your mouth like the best wine.

She

May the wine go straight to my beloved,
   flowing gently over lips and teeth.[d]
[10] I belong to my beloved,
   and his desire is for me.

---

[a] 12 Or *among the chariots of Amminadab*; or *among the chariots of the people of the prince*   [b] 13 In Hebrew texts this verse (6:13) is numbered 7:1.   [c] In Hebrew texts 7:1-13 is numbered 7:2-14.   [d] 9 Septuagint, Aquila, Vulgate and Syriac; Hebrew *lips of sleepers*

Leaders Practice Good People Skills

Song of Songs 5:1—6:13

The Song of Songs overflows with heart, describing a passionate relationship between two people who deeply love each other.

What can leaders learn from this book? Leaders must relate to their people from the soul, not merely by protocol. The best way to overcome problems is to involve your heart, not just your head.

Unfortunately, we're tempted toward another direction. When we fail at something, we tend to see why it happened and cut ourselves some slack; we may even make excuses for our mistakes. In other words, we deal with ourselves using our heart. Yet we often neglect the heart when dealing with others. We can be direct and even demanding. It really works best to switch the whole thing around. When dealing with yourself, use your head. When dealing with others, use your heart.

11 Come, my beloved, let us go to the
  countryside,
 let us spend the night in the villages.[a]
12 Let us go early to the vineyards
  to see if the vines have budded,
 if their blossoms have opened,
  and if the pomegranates are in bloom—
 there I will give you my love.
13 The mandrakes send out their fragrance,
  and at our door is every delicacy,
 both new and old,
  that I have stored up for you, my
   beloved.

8 If only you were to me like a brother,
  who was nursed at my mother's breasts!
 Then, if I found you outside,
  I would kiss you,
 and no one would despise me.
2 I would lead you
 and bring you to my mother's house—
 she who has taught me.
 I would give you spiced wine to drink,
  the nectar of my pomegranates.
3 His left arm is under my head
 and his right arm embraces me.
4 Daughters of Jerusalem, I charge you:
 Do not arouse or awaken love
 until it so desires.

Friends

5 Who is this coming up from the wilderness
 leaning on her beloved?

She

 Under the apple tree I roused you;
 there your mother conceived you,
 there she who was in labor gave you
  birth.
6 Place me like a seal over your heart,
 like a seal on your arm;
 for love is as strong as death,
 its jealousy[b] unyielding as the grave.
 It burns like blazing fire,
 like a mighty flame.[c]

7 Many waters cannot quench love;
 rivers cannot sweep it away.
 If one were to give
  all the wealth of one's house for love,
 it[d] would be utterly scorned.

Friends

8 We have a little sister,
 and her breasts are not yet grown.
 What shall we do for our sister
 on the day she is spoken for?
9 If she is a wall,
 we will build towers of silver on her.
 If she is a door,
 we will enclose her with panels of cedar.

She

10 I am a wall,
 and my breasts are like towers.
 Thus I have become in his eyes
 like one bringing contentment.
11 Solomon had a vineyard in Baal Hamon;
 he let out his vineyard to tenants.
 Each was to bring for its fruit
 a thousand shekels[e] of silver.
12 But my own vineyard is mine to give;
 the thousand shekels are for you,
  Solomon,
 and two hundred[f] are for those who tend
  its fruit.

He

13 You who dwell in the gardens
 with friends in attendance,
 let me hear your voice!

She

14 Come away, my beloved,
 and be like a gazelle
 or like a young stag
 on the spice-laden mountains.

---

[a] 11 Or *the henna bushes* [b] 6 Or *ardor* [c] 6 Or *fire, / like the very flame of the LORD* [d] 7 Or *he* [e] 11 That is, about 25 pounds or about 12 kilograms; also in verse 12 [f] 12 That is, about 5 pounds or about 2.3 kilograms

INTRODUCTION TO
ISAIAH

Consistent Lifestyle ...
Uncompromising
Convictions ...
Clear Vision

We remember Isaiah as one of the greatest prophets in Jewish history and as one of the most powerful models in the Bible. The book that bears his name describes his consistent lifestyle, his uncompromising convictions, and his clear vision that drove him to continue speaking out despite the unfaithfulness of his people.

Isaiah's lifestyle reminds us that we cannot separate a leader's words and walk. A leader must first be an example to the people. People do what people see. Isaiah led with integrity. Integrity means "oneness," the quality of purity and consistency. When we speak of the integrity of Scripture, we mean that it proclaims one consistent message. This word describes Isaiah, a man of God full of consistency.

Isaiah's convictions teach us about avoiding ungodly compromise. He and his contemporary, the prophet Micah, both raised the bar for the people by holding to God's standards with unswerving determination. While leaders must remain flexible with their methods, they cannot compromise their convictions.

Finally, Isaiah furnishes a beautiful case study of a leader who led from vision. He describes a God-given vision that drives him to fulfill his calling as a leader. He clings to it despite rejection (6:9). Throughout the book he communicates his vision to the people and warns them to repent. Before he finishes, he has influenced King Hezekiah to bring about national reforms. Through his tenacious intercession with God, Sennacherib's entire army is destroyed (2Ki 19:36–37; 2Ch 32:20–23; Isa 37:36–38).

God's Role in Isaiah

As the One who inspired both Isaiah's ministry and his writings, God again reveals himself as the Leader of leaders. We see the Lord telling Isaiah what to say to the people and warning them of the impending judgment if they fail to repent. God also gives Isaiah visions about the future. While the first 39 chapters lay out some bleak moments, the remaining 27 provide strong hope. Isaiah predicts the coming Messiah as the Ultimate Leader for the people of Israel. The Messiah embodies all the positive qualities of an effective leader.

Leaders in Isaiah

Isaiah, King Hezekiah, the Messiah

Other People of Influence in Isaiah

Kings of Judah and Israel, leaders of Assyria, Babylon, Edom, Egypt, Tyre, Cush, Philistia, Moab, Damascus (Syria), Dedan and Kedar

Lessons in Leadership

- Vision is born out of values and ethics—they must align.
- The measure of a person is what he or she does with power.
- Leaders create atmospheres and environments for growth and success.

- Ability, opportunity and desire make up the components of a call to lead.
- God reduces prideful leaders but resources humble leaders.
- Strategic planning that ignores God and the changing culture is doomed to fail.

- Insecure leaders inevitably destroy people; secure leaders develop people.
- The higher leaders climb, the fewer there are who can hold them accountable.
- God himself provides the ultimate model of servant leadership.

LEADERSHIP HIGHLIGHTS IN ISAIAH

1 The vision concerning Judah and Jerusalem that Isaiah son of Amoz saw during the reigns of Uzziah, Jotham, Ahaz and Hezekiah, kings of Judah.

A Rebellious Nation

²Hear me, you heavens! Listen, earth!
For the LORD has spoken:
"I reared children and brought them up,
but they have rebelled against me.
³The ox knows its master,
the donkey its owner's manger,
but Israel does not know,
my people do not understand."

⁴Woe to the sinful nation,
a people whose guilt is great,
a brood of evildoers,
children given to corruption!
They have forsaken the LORD;
they have spurned the Holy One of
Israel
and turned their backs on him.

⁵Why should you be beaten anymore?
Why do you persist in rebellion?
Your whole head is injured,
your whole heart afflicted.
⁶From the sole of your foot to the top of your
head
there is no soundness—
only wounds and welts
and open sores,
not cleansed or bandaged
or soothed with olive oil.

⁷Your country is desolate,
your cities burned with fire;
your fields are being stripped by foreigners
right before you,
laid waste as when overthrown by
strangers.
⁸Daughter Zion is left
like a shelter in a vineyard,
like a hut in a cucumber field,
like a city under siege.
⁹Unless the LORD Almighty
had left us some survivors,
we would have become like Sodom,
we would have been like Gomorrah.

¹⁰Hear the word of the LORD,
you rulers of Sodom;
listen to the instruction of our God,
you people of Gomorrah!
¹¹"The multitude of your sacrifices—
what are they to me?" says the LORD.
"I have more than enough of burnt offerings,
of rams and the fat of fattened animals;
I have no pleasure
in the blood of bulls and lambs and goats.
¹²When you come to appear before me,
who has asked this of you,
this trampling of my courts?
¹³Stop bringing meaningless offerings!
Your incense is detestable to me.

Growth Occurs When Vision and Values Match

Isaiah 1:10–17

God scolds the leaders of Judah and Jerusalem—even calling them rulers of Sodom and people of Gomorrah, the wicked cities he wiped out in Genesis 19—because they continued to perform religious rituals long after their hearts had grown cold and distant toward God. In other words, they continued to pursue a godly vision far from the values that birthed it. They had become empty, hollow leaders.

God resents perfunctory behavior. He doesn't want leaders who merely go through the motions. Leaders can look good while pursuing a worthwhile vision that they no longer consider valuable. Leaders find power only when . . .

1. **Their vision and values match.**
2. **Their lifestyle and lip service match.**
3. **Their conduct and character match.**
4. **Their image and integrity match.**
5. **Their promises and production match.**
6. **Their strategy and support match.**

New Moons, Sabbaths and convocations —
　　I cannot bear your worthless assemblies.
14 Your New Moon feasts and your appointed
　　　　festivals
　　I hate with all my being.
They have become a burden to me;
　　I am weary of bearing them.
15 When you spread out your hands in prayer,
　　I hide my eyes from you;
even when you offer many prayers,
　　I am not listening.

Your hands are full of blood!

16 Wash and make yourselves clean.
　　Take your evil deeds out of my sight;
　　stop doing wrong.
17 Learn to do right; seek justice.
　　Defend the oppressed.[a]
Take up the cause of the fatherless;
　　plead the case of the widow.

18 "Come now, let us settle the matter,"
　　says the LORD.
"Though your sins are like scarlet,
　　they shall be as white as snow;
though they are red as crimson,
　　they shall be like wool.
19 If you are willing and obedient,
　　you will eat the good things of the land;
20 but if you resist and rebel,
　　you will be devoured by the sword."
　　　　　　　For the mouth of the LORD
　　　　　　　　　　has spoken.

21 See how the faithful city
　　has become a prostitute!
She once was full of justice;
　　righteousness used to dwell in her —
　　but now murderers!
22 Your silver has become dross,
　　your choice wine is diluted with water.
23 Your rulers are rebels,
　　partners with thieves;
they all love bribes
　　and chase after gifts.
They do not defend the cause of the
　　　　fatherless;
　　the widow's case does not come before them.

24 Therefore the Lord, the LORD Almighty,
　　the Mighty One of Israel, declares:
"Ah! I will vent my wrath on my foes
　　and avenge myself on my enemies.
25 I will turn my hand against you;[b]
　　I will thoroughly purge away your dross
　　and remove all your impurities.

26 I will restore your leaders as in days of old,
　　your rulers as at the beginning.
Afterward you will be called
　　the City of Righteousness,
　　the Faithful City."

27 Zion will be delivered with justice,
　　her penitent ones with righteousness.
28 But rebels and sinners will both be broken,
　　and those who forsake the LORD will
　　　　perish.

29 "You will be ashamed because of the sacred
　　　　oaks
　　in which you have delighted;
you will be disgraced because of the gardens
　　that you have chosen.
30 You will be like an oak with fading leaves,
　　like a garden without water.
31 The mighty man will become tinder
　　and his work a spark;
both will burn together,
　　with no one to quench the fire."

The Mountain of the LORD

2 This is what Isaiah son of Amoz saw concerning Judah and Jerusalem:

2 In the last days

the mountain of the LORD's temple will be
　　　　established
　　as the highest of the mountains;
it will be exalted above the hills,
　　and all nations will stream to it.

3 Many peoples will come and say,

"Come, let us go up to the mountain of the
　　　　LORD,
　　to the temple of the God of Jacob.
He will teach us his ways,
　　so that we may walk in his paths."
The law will go out from Zion,
　　the word of the LORD from Jerusalem.
4 He will judge between the nations
　　and will settle disputes for many peoples.
They will beat their swords into plowshares
　　and their spears into pruning hooks.
Nation will not take up sword against
　　　　nation,
　　nor will they train for war anymore.

5 Come, descendants of Jacob,
　　let us walk in the light of the LORD.

---

[a] 17 Or justice. / Correct the oppressor　　[b] 25 That is, against
Jerusalem

The Day of the LORD

⁶ You, LORD, have abandoned your people,
    the descendants of Jacob.
They are full of superstitions from the East;
    they practice divination like the
        Philistines
    and embrace pagan customs.
⁷ Their land is full of silver and gold;
    there is no end to their treasures.
Their land is full of horses;
    there is no end to their chariots.
⁸ Their land is full of idols;
    they bow down to the work of their hands,
    to what their fingers have made.
⁹ So people will be brought low
    and everyone humbled —
    do not forgive them.ᵃ

¹⁰ Go into the rocks, hide in the ground
    from the fearful presence of the LORD
    and the splendor of his majesty!
¹¹ The eyes of the arrogant will be humbled
    and human pride brought low;
    the LORD alone will be exalted in that day.

¹² The LORD Almighty has a day in store
    for all the proud and lofty,
for all that is exalted
    (and they will be humbled),
¹³ for all the cedars of Lebanon, tall and lofty,
    and all the oaks of Bashan,
¹⁴ for all the towering mountains
    and all the high hills,
¹⁵ for every lofty tower
    and every fortified wall,
¹⁶ for every trading shipᵇ
    and every stately vessel.
¹⁷ The arrogance of man will be brought low
    and human pride humbled;
    the LORD alone will be exalted in that day,
¹⁸   and the idols will totally disappear.

¹⁹ People will flee to caves in the rocks
    and to holes in the ground
from the fearful presence of the LORD
    and the splendor of his majesty,
    when he rises to shake the earth.
²⁰ In that day people will throw away
    to the moles and bats
their idols of silver and idols of gold,
    which they made to worship.
²¹ They will flee to caverns in the rocks
    and to the overhanging crags
from the fearful presence of the LORD
    and the splendor of his majesty,
    when he rises to shake the earth.

²² Stop trusting in mere humans,
    who have but a breath in their nostrils.
    Why hold them in esteem?

Judgment on Jerusalem and Judah

3 See now, the Lord,
    the LORD Almighty,
    is about to take from Jerusalem and Judah
        both supply and support:
    all supplies of food and all supplies of water,
²   the hero and the warrior,
    the judge and the prophet,
        the diviner and the elder,
³ the captain of fifty and the man of rank,
    the counselor, skilled craftsman and
        clever enchanter.

⁴ "I will make mere youths their officials;
    children will rule over them."

Judah's Lousy Leaders: Everything Rises and Falls on Leadership

Isaiah 3:1–4

God had a strategy for judging Judah, and part of his judgment involved removing good leaders from the nation. No organization or nation can prosper without good leadership. People suffer with poor leaders at the helm. God knew the way to impact the nation was to change its leadership.

---

⁵ People will oppress each other —
    man against man, neighbor against
        neighbor.
The young will rise up against the old,
    the nobody against the honored.

⁶ A man will seize one of his brothers
    in his father's house, and say,
"You have a cloak, you be our leader;
    take charge of this heap of ruins!"
⁷ But in that day he will cry out,
    "I have no remedy.
I have no food or clothing in my house;
    do not make me the leader of the people."

⁸ Jerusalem staggers,
    Judah is falling;

ᵃ 9 Or *not raise them up*   ᵇ 16 Hebrew *every ship of Tarshish*

their words and deeds are against the Lord,
　　defying his glorious presence.
⁹ The look on their faces testifies against
　　them;
　　they parade their sin like Sodom;
　　they do not hide it.
　Woe to them!
　　They have brought disaster upon
　　　themselves.

¹⁰ Tell the righteous it will be well with them,
　　for they will enjoy the fruit of their deeds.
¹¹ Woe to the wicked!
　　Disaster is upon them!
　They will be paid back
　　for what their hands have done.

¹² Youths oppress my people,
　　women rule over them.
　My people, your guides lead you astray;
　　they turn you from the path.

¹³ The Lord takes his place in court;
　　he rises to judge the people.
¹⁴ The Lord enters into judgment
　　against the elders and leaders of his
　　　people:
　"It is you who have ruined my vineyard;
　　the plunder from the poor is in your
　　　houses.
¹⁵ What do you mean by crushing my people
　　and grinding the faces of the poor?"
　　　　　　　　　　declares the Lord,
　　　　　　　the Lord Almighty.

¹⁶ The Lord says,
　　"The women of Zion are haughty,
　walking along with outstretched necks,
　　flirting with their eyes,
　strutting along with swaying hips,
　　with ornaments jingling on their ankles.
¹⁷ Therefore the Lord will bring sores on the
　　heads of the women of Zion;
　　the Lord will make their scalps bald."

¹⁸ In that day the Lord will snatch away their
finery: the bangles and headbands and crescent
necklaces, ¹⁹ the earrings and bracelets and veils,
²⁰ the headdresses and anklets and sashes, the
perfume bottles and charms, ²¹ the signet rings
and nose rings, ²² the fine robes and the capes
and cloaks, the purses ²³ and mirrors, and the
linen garments and tiaras and shawls.

²⁴ Instead of fragrance there will be a stench;
　　instead of a sash, a rope;
　instead of well-dressed hair, baldness;
　　instead of fine clothing, sackcloth;
　　instead of beauty, branding.
²⁵ Your men will fall by the sword,
　　your warriors in battle.
²⁶ The gates of Zion will lament and mourn;
　　destitute, she will sit on the ground.

4 ¹ In that day seven women
　　will take hold of one man
　and say, "We will eat our own food
　　and provide our own clothes;
　only let us be called by your name.
　　Take away our disgrace!"

The Law of Navigation: How Leaders Lead

Isaiah 3:14–15

The more power leaders gain, the more they reveal of themselves. Power causes the heart to disclose its contents.

The leaders described in Isaiah 3 displayed their corrupt hearts the moment they won a position of authority. Good or bad, leaders determine where and when the organization goes; this is the ripple effect of the Law of Navigation. The Lord responded to these corrupt leaders by sounding judgment against them.

Leaders must consider the impact of their every move. Leaders always lead. There are no time-outs! There never comes a time when it doesn't matter what you do. Think of your leadership like a diet. Suppose you eat right in the restaurant with friends, but then go home and consume a whole strawberry cheesecake. You won't lose weight that way! What you eat eventually shows. In the same way, those you lead eventually reflect your leadership. Your navigation as a leader depends on the following:

1. **When you know where you are going, you gain *conviction*.**

2. **When you have been there before, you gain *credibility*.**

3. **When you can take someone with you, you gain *connection*.**

The Branch of the LORD

[2] In that day the Branch of the LORD will be beautiful and glorious, and the fruit of the land will be the pride and glory of the survivors in Israel. [3] Those who are left in Zion, who remain in Jerusalem, will be called holy, all who are recorded among the living in Jerusalem. [4] The Lord will wash away the filth of the women of Zion; he will cleanse the bloodstains from Jerusalem by a spirit[a] of judgment and a spirit[a] of fire. [5] Then the LORD will create over all of Mount Zion and over those who assemble there a cloud of smoke by day and a glow of flaming fire by night; over everything the glory[b] will be a canopy. [6] It will be a shelter and shade from the heat of the day, and a refuge and hiding place from the storm and rain.

The Song of the Vineyard

5 I will sing for the one I love
 a song about his vineyard:
My loved one had a vineyard
 on a fertile hillside.
[2] He dug it up and cleared it of stones
 and planted it with the choicest vines.
He built a watchtower in it
 and cut out a winepress as well.
Then he looked for a crop of good grapes,
 but it yielded only bad fruit.

[3] "Now you dwellers in Jerusalem and people of Judah,
 judge between me and my vineyard.
[4] What more could have been done for my vineyard
 than I have done for it?
When I looked for good grapes,
 why did it yield only bad?
[5] Now I will tell you
 what I am going to do to my vineyard:
I will take away its hedge,
 and it will be destroyed;
I will break down its wall,
 and it will be trampled.
[6] I will make it a wasteland,
 neither pruned nor cultivated,
 and briers and thorns will grow there.
I will command the clouds
 not to rain on it."

[7] The vineyard of the LORD Almighty
 is the nation of Israel,
and the people of Judah
 are the vines he delighted in.
And he looked for justice, but saw bloodshed;
 for righteousness, but heard cries of distress.

[a] 4 Or the Spirit   [b] 5 Or over all the glory there

The Value of Vision

Isaiah 4:2–6

Isaiah 4 illustrates how good leaders create a climate for growth based on a picture of a preferred future. A strong God-given vision drove all the worthwhile accomplishments recorded in the Bible. Consider the following examples:

Leader	Vision
1. Abraham (Ge 12)	To create a great nation of people of faith
2. Moses (Ex 3; 4)	To lead the people of Israel out of Egypt
3. Joshua (Nu 27)	To lead the people of Israel into the promised land
4. David (1Ch 22)	To build the temple in Jerusalem
5. Solomon (2Ch 28)	To complete the building of the temple
6. Nehemiah (Ne 2)	To rebuild the Jerusalem wall
7. Esther (Est 4)	To save the Jewish people from Haman
8. Zerubbabel (Hag 1)	To rebuild the temple
9. Jesus (Mt 28; Lk 15)	To seek and save the lost, and to disciple men to do the same
10. Paul (Ac 9)	To take the gospel to the Jews and Gentiles

Woes and Judgments

8 Woe to you who add house to house
    and join field to field
till no space is left
    and you live alone in the land.

9 The Lord Almighty has declared in my hearing:

"Surely the great houses will become
        desolate,
    the fine mansions left without occupants.
10 A ten-acre vineyard will produce only a
        bath[a] of wine;
    a homer[b] of seed will yield only an ephah[c]
        of grain."

11 Woe to those who rise early in the morning
        to run after their drinks,
who stay up late at night
        till they are inflamed with wine.
12 They have harps and lyres at their banquets,
        pipes and timbrels and wine,
but they have no regard for the deeds of the
        Lord,
    no respect for the work of his hands.
13 Therefore my people will go into exile
        for lack of understanding;
those of high rank will die of hunger
        and the common people will be parched
        with thirst.
14 Therefore Death expands its jaws,
        opening wide its mouth;
into it will descend their nobles and masses
        with all their brawlers and revelers.
15 So people will be brought low
        and everyone humbled,
    the eyes of the arrogant humbled.
16 But the Lord Almighty will be exalted by his
        justice,
    and the holy God will be proved holy by
        his righteous acts.
17 Then sheep will graze as in their own
        pasture;
    lambs will feed[d] among the ruins of the
        rich.

18 Woe to those who draw sin along with cords
        of deceit,
    and wickedness as with cart ropes,
19 to those who say, "Let God hurry;
        let him hasten his work
    so we may see it.
The plan of the Holy One of Israel—
        let it approach, let it come into view,
    so we may know it."

20 Woe to those who call evil good
        and good evil,
who put darkness for light
        and light for darkness,
who put bitter for sweet
        and sweet for bitter.

21 Woe to those who are wise in their own eyes
        and clever in their own sight.

22 Woe to those who are heroes at drinking
        wine
    and champions at mixing drinks,
23 who acquit the guilty for a bribe,
        but deny justice to the innocent.
24 Therefore, as tongues of fire lick up straw
        and as dry grass sinks down in the
        flames,
so their roots will decay
        and their flowers blow away like dust;
for they have rejected the law of the Lord
        Almighty
    and spurned the word of the Holy One of
        Israel.
25 Therefore the Lord's anger burns against his
        people;
    his hand is raised and he strikes them
        down.
The mountains shake,
        and the dead bodies are like refuse in the
        streets.

Yet for all this, his anger is not turned away,
        his hand is still upraised.

26 He lifts up a banner for the distant nations,
        he whistles for those at the ends of the
        earth.
Here they come,
        swiftly and speedily!
27 Not one of them grows tired or stumbles,
        not one slumbers or sleeps;
not a belt is loosened at the waist,
        not a sandal strap is broken.
28 Their arrows are sharp,
        all their bows are strung;
their horses' hooves seem like flint,
        their chariot wheels like a whirlwind.
29 Their roar is like that of the lion,
        they roar like young lions;
they growl as they seize their prey
        and carry it off with no one to rescue.

---

[a] 10 That is, about 6 gallons or about 22 liters   [b] 10 That is,
probably about 360 pounds or about 160 kilograms
[c] 10 That is, probably about 36 pounds or about 16 kilograms
[d] 17 Septuagint; Hebrew / strangers will eat

³⁰ In that day they will roar over it
   like the roaring of the sea.
And if one looks at the land,
   there is only darkness and distress;
   even the sun will be darkened by clouds.

Isaiah's Commission

6 In the year that King Uzziah died, I saw the Lord, high and exalted, seated on a throne; and the train of his robe filled the temple. ²Above him were seraphim, each with six wings: With two wings they covered their faces, with two they covered their feet, and with two they were flying. ³And they were calling to one another:

"Holy, holy, holy is the Lord Almighty;
   the whole earth is full of his glory."

⁴At the sound of their voices the doorposts and thresholds shook and the temple was filled with smoke.

⁵"Woe to me!" I cried. "I am ruined! For I am a man of unclean lips, and I live among a people of unclean lips, and my eyes have seen the King, the Lord Almighty."

⁶Then one of the seraphim flew to me with a live coal in his hand, which he had taken with tongs from the altar. ⁷With it he touched my mouth and said, "See, this has touched your lips; your guilt is taken away and your sin atoned for."

⁸Then I heard the voice of the Lord saying, "Whom shall I send? And who will go for us?"

And I said, "Here am I. Send me!"

⁹He said, "Go and tell this people:

"'Be ever hearing, but never understanding;
   be ever seeing, but never perceiving.'

¹⁰Make the heart of this people calloused;
   make their ears dull
   and close their eyes.ᵃ
Otherwise they might see with their eyes,
   hear with their ears,
   understand with their hearts,
and turn and be healed."

¹¹Then I said, "For how long, Lord?"
And he answered:

"Until the cities lie ruined
   and without inhabitant,
until the houses are left deserted
   and the fields ruined and ravaged,
¹²until the Lord has sent everyone far away
   and the land is utterly forsaken.
¹³And though a tenth remains in the land,
   it will again be laid waste.
But as the terebinth and oak
   leave stumps when they are cut down,
   so the holy seed will be the stump in the
      land."

The Sign of Immanuel

7 When Ahaz son of Jotham, the son of Uzziah, was king of Judah, King Rezin of Aram and Pekah son of Remaliah king of Israel marched up to fight against Jerusalem, but they could not overpower it.

²Now the house of David was told, "Aram has allied itself withᵇ Ephraim"; so the hearts of

---

ᵃ 9,10 Hebrew; Septuagint 'You will be ever hearing, but never understanding; / you will be ever seeing, but never perceiving.' / ¹⁰This people's heart has become calloused; / they hardly hear with their ears, / and they have closed their eyes   ᵇ 2 Or has set up camp in

---

The Call of a Leader

Isaiah 6:1–8

The first eight verses of Isaiah 6 illustrate how God calls many leaders. After Isaiah captures a vision for God, the Lord lays out a need for someone to speak for him. God has a message and is looking for a messenger. God issued a general call, for anyone, and Isaiah took it personally. He did so because of three factors that make up a divine call to lead:

1. **Opportunity: We see a specific place where we can make a difference. This has to do with timing (v. 1).**

2. **Ability: We recognize that we have the God-given gifts to do something about the need. This has to do with competence (vv. 6–7).**

3. **Desire: We want to step out and address the need; our hunger pushes us. This has to do with our passion (v. 8).**

Responding to a Divine Call

Isaiah 6:1–8

Have you ever noticed that the experience of Isaiah parallels our own process of responding to a divine call to lead?

Isaiah gets a vision of God (Isa 6:1–4), a vision of himself (6:5–7) and a vision of ministry (6:8). At least five stages in this process apply to us:

Stage One: *The Revelation of God* (vv. 1–2)
Isaiah saw the Lord in a face-to-face encounter that changed him forever.

Stage Two: *The Realization of God's Holiness* (vv. 3–4)
Isaiah experiences God as holy. Through this encounter, the Lord becomes more than an abstract idea. Isaiah learns of God's awesome personality.

Stage Three: *The Recognition of His Own Sinfulness* (v. 5)
Isaiah sees the vast distance between God and himself. He sees the infinite contrast and is broken of self.

Stage Four: *The Renewal of His Perspective* (vv. 6–7)
An angel touches the prophet, cleansing him and giving him a new outlook. He is ready to serve.

Stage Five: *The Response of His Lifestyle* (v. 8)
When God calls, Isaiah eagerly steps forward. A call is marked by a fruitful life.

Ahaz and his people were shaken, as the trees of the forest are shaken by the wind.

³Then the LORD said to Isaiah, "Go out, you and your son Shear-Jashub,[a] to meet Ahaz at the end of the aqueduct of the Upper Pool, on the road to the Launderer's Field. ⁴Say to him, 'Be careful, keep calm and don't be afraid. Do not lose heart because of these two smoldering stubs of firewood — because of the fierce anger of Rezin and Aram and of the son of Remaliah. ⁵Aram, Ephraim and Remaliah's son have plotted your ruin, saying, ⁶"Let us invade Judah; let us tear it apart and divide it among ourselves, and make the son of Tabeel king over it." ⁷Yet this is what the Sovereign LORD says:

"'It will not take place,
　　it will not happen,
⁸for the head of Aram is Damascus,
　　and the head of Damascus is only
　　　Rezin.
Within sixty-five years
　　Ephraim will be too shattered to be a
　　　people.
⁹The head of Ephraim is Samaria,
　　and the head of Samaria is only
　　　Remaliah's son.
If you do not stand firm in your faith,
　　you will not stand at all.'"

¹⁰Again the LORD spoke to Ahaz, ¹¹"Ask the LORD your God for a sign, whether in the deepest depths or in the highest heights."

¹²But Ahaz said, "I will not ask; I will not put the LORD to the test."

¹³Then Isaiah said, "Hear now, you house of David! Is it not enough to try the patience of humans? Will you try the patience of my God also? ¹⁴Therefore the Lord himself will give you[b] a sign: The virgin[c] will conceive and give birth to a son, and[d] will call him Immanuel.[e] ¹⁵He will be eating curds and honey when he knows enough to reject the wrong and choose the right, ¹⁶for before the boy knows enough to reject the wrong and choose the right, the land of the two kings you dread will be laid waste. ¹⁷The LORD will bring on you and on your people and on the house of your father a time unlike any since Ephraim broke away from Judah — he will bring the king of Assyria."

Assyria, the LORD's Instrument

¹⁸In that day the LORD will whistle for flies from the Nile delta in Egypt and for bees from

---

a 3 Shear-Jashub means a remnant will return. *b 14 The Hebrew is plural.* *c 14 Or young woman* *d 14 Masoretic Text; Dead Sea Scrolls son, and he or son, and they* *e 14 Immanuel means God with us.*

the land of Assyria. ¹⁹They will all come and settle in the steep ravines and in the crevices in the rocks, on all the thornbushes and at all the water holes. ²⁰In that day the Lord will use a razor hired from beyond the Euphrates River — the king of Assyria — to shave your head and private parts, and to cut off your beard also. ²¹In that day, a person will keep alive a young cow and two goats. ²²And because of the abundance of the milk they give, there will be curds to eat. All who remain in the land will eat curds and honey. ²³In that day, in every place where there were a thousand vines worth a thousand silver shekels,[a] there will be only briers and thorns. ²⁴Hunters will go there with bow and arrow, for the land will be covered with briers and thorns. ²⁵As for all the hills once cultivated by the hoe, you will no longer go there for fear of the briers and thorns; they will become places where cattle are turned loose and where sheep run.

Isaiah and His Children as Signs

8 The LORD said to me, "Take a large scroll and write on it with an ordinary pen: Maher-Shalal-Hash-Baz."[b] ²So I called in Uriah the priest and Zechariah son of Jeberekiah as reliable witnesses for me. ³Then I made love to the prophetess, and she conceived and gave birth to a son. And the LORD said to me, "Name him Maher-Shalal-Hash-Baz. ⁴For before the boy knows how to say 'My father' or 'My mother,' the wealth of Damascus and the plunder of Samaria will be carried off by the king of Assyria."

⁵The LORD spoke to me again:

⁶"Because this people has rejected
    the gently flowing waters of Shiloah
and rejoices over Rezin
    and the son of Remaliah,
⁷therefore the Lord is about to bring against them
    the mighty floodwaters of the Euphrates —
    the king of Assyria with all his pomp.
It will overflow all its channels,
    run over all its banks
⁸and sweep on into Judah, swirling over it,
    passing through it and reaching up to the neck.
Its outspread wings will cover the breadth of your land,
    Immanuel[c]!"

---

[a] 23 That is, about 25 pounds or about 12 kilograms
[b] 1 Maher-Shalal-Hash-Baz means quick to the plunder, swift to the spoil; also in verse 3.   [c] 8 Immanuel means God with us.

The Law of Connection: The Call Pushes Leaders to Communicate

Isaiah 7:1–17

Isaiah wants to communicate a message that begins to burn inside of him (as it did with Jeremiah). The divine message gives him an urgency to connect with others and spread God's word. God's call gives him a divine compulsion to speak and act.

A leader's sense of call provides divine energy. Ponder a few other examples of this phenomenon:

1. **Abraham was called by God through a divine visitation (Ge 12).**

2. **Joseph was called by God through a dream (Ge 37).**

3. **Moses was called by God through a voice in a burning bush (Ex 3; 4).**

4. **Aaron was called by God through his brother Moses (Ex 4).**

5. **Joshua was called by God through Moses (Ex 17).**

6. **Gideon was called by God through an angel (Jdg 6).**

7. **Samuel was called by God through God's audible voice (1Sa 3).**

8. **David was called by God through the prophet Samuel (1Sa 16).**

9. **Paul was called by God through a vision while he traveled (Ac 9).**

10. **Timothy was called by God by Paul's preaching and through his upbringing (1Ti 1; 2Ti 1; 2).**

⁹Raise the war cry,ᵃ you nations, and be
> shattered!
>> Listen, all you distant lands.
>> Prepare for battle, and be shattered!
>> Prepare for battle, and be shattered!
¹⁰Devise your strategy, but it will be thwarted;
>> propose your plan, but it will not stand,
>> for God is with us.ᵇ

¹¹This is what the LORD says to me with his strong hand upon me, warning me not to follow the way of this people:

¹²"Do not call conspiracy
>> everything this people calls a conspiracy;
> do not fear what they fear,
> and do not dread it.
¹³The LORD Almighty is the one you are to
>> regard as holy,
> he is the one you are to fear,
> he is the one you are to dread.
¹⁴He will be a holy place;
>> for both Israel and Judah he will be
> a stone that causes people to stumble
> and a rock that makes them fall.
> And for the people of Jerusalem he will be
> a trap and a snare.
¹⁵Many of them will stumble;
>> they will fall and be broken,
>> they will be snared and captured."

¹⁶Bind up this testimony of warning
>> and seal up God's instruction among my
>> disciples.
¹⁷I will wait for the LORD,
>> who is hiding his face from the
>> descendants of Jacob.
> I will put my trust in him.

¹⁸Here am I, and the children the LORD has given me. We are signs and symbols in Israel from the LORD Almighty, who dwells on Mount Zion.

The Darkness Turns to Light

¹⁹When someone tells you to consult mediums and spiritists, who whisper and mutter, should not a people inquire of their God? Why consult the dead on behalf of the living? ²⁰Consult God's instruction and the testimony of warning. If anyone does not speak according to this word, they have no light of dawn. ²¹Distressed and hungry, they will roam through the land; when they are famished, they will become enraged and, looking upward, will curse their king and their God. ²²Then they will look toward the earth and see only distress and darkness and fearful gloom, and they will be thrust into utter darkness.

9ᶜ Nevertheless, there will be no more gloom for those who were in distress. In the past he humbled the land of Zebulun and the land of Naphtali, but in the future he will honor Galilee of the nations, by the Way of the Sea, beyond the Jordan —

²The people walking in darkness
>> have seen a great light;
> on those living in the land of deep darkness
>> a light has dawned.
³You have enlarged the nation
>> and increased their joy;
> they rejoice before you
>> as people rejoice at the harvest,
> as warriors rejoice
>> when dividing the plunder.
⁴For as in the day of Midian's defeat,
>> you have shattered
> the yoke that burdens them,
>> the bar across their shoulders,
>> the rod of their oppressor.
⁵Every warrior's boot used in battle
>> and every garment rolled in blood
> will be destined for burning,
>> will be fuel for the fire.
⁶For to us a child is born,
>> to us a son is given,
>> and the government will be on his
>> shoulders.
> And he will be called
>> Wonderful Counselor, Mighty God,
>> Everlasting Father, Prince of Peace.
⁷Of the greatness of his government and peace
>> there will be no end.
> He will reign on David's throne
>> and over his kingdom,
> establishing and upholding it
>> with justice and righteousness
>> from that time on and forever.
> The zeal of the LORD Almighty
>> will accomplish this.

The LORD's Anger Against Israel

⁸The Lord has sent a message against Jacob;
>> it will fall on Israel.
⁹All the people will know it —
>> Ephraim and the inhabitants of
>> Samaria —
> who say with pride
>> and arrogance of heart,

ᵃ 9 Or *Do your worst*   ᵇ 10 Hebrew *Immanuel*   ᶜ In Hebrew texts 9:1 is numbered 8:23, and 9:2-21 is numbered 9:1-20.

10 "The bricks have fallen down,
   but we will rebuild with dressed stone;
   the fig trees have been felled,
   but we will replace them with cedars."
11 But the LORD has strengthened Rezin's foes
      against them
   and has spurred their enemies on.
12 Arameans from the east and Philistines from
      the west
   have devoured Israel with open mouth.

   Yet for all this, his anger is not turned away,
      his hand is still upraised.

13 But the people have not returned to him who
      struck them,
   nor have they sought the LORD Almighty.
14 So the LORD will cut off from Israel both
      head and tail,
   both palm branch and reed in a single
      day;
15 the elders and dignitaries are the head,
   the prophets who teach lies are the tail.
16 Those who guide this people mislead
      them,
   and those who are guided are led astray.
17 Therefore the Lord will take no pleasure
      in the young men,
   nor will he pity the fatherless and
      widows,
   for everyone is ungodly and wicked,
      every mouth speaks folly.

   Yet for all this, his anger is not turned away,
      his hand is still upraised.

18 Surely wickedness burns like a fire;
   it consumes briers and thorns,
   it sets the forest thickets ablaze,
   so that it rolls upward in a column of
      smoke.
19 By the wrath of the LORD Almighty
   the land will be scorched
   and the people will be fuel for the fire;
   they will not spare one another.
20 On the right they will devour,
   but still be hungry;
   on the left they will eat,
   but not be satisfied.
   Each will feed on the flesh of their own
      offspring[a]:
21   Manasseh will feed on Ephraim, and
         Ephraim on Manasseh;
   together they will turn against Judah.

   Yet for all this, his anger is not turned away,
      his hand is still upraised.

10 Woe to those who make unjust laws,
      to those who issue oppressive decrees,
2 to deprive the poor of their rights
   and withhold justice from the oppressed
      of my people,
   making widows their prey
   and robbing the fatherless.
3 What will you do on the day of reckoning,
   when disaster comes from afar?
   To whom will you run for help?
   Where will you leave your riches?
4 Nothing will remain but to cringe among the
      captives
   or fall among the slain.

   Yet for all this, his anger is not turned away,
      his hand is still upraised.

God's Judgment on Assyria

5 "Woe to the Assyrian, the rod of my anger,
   in whose hand is the club of my wrath!
6 I send him against a godless nation,
   I dispatch him against a people who
      anger me,
   to seize loot and snatch plunder,
   and to trample them down like mud in
      the streets.
7 But this is not what he intends,
   this is not what he has in mind;
   his purpose is to destroy,
   to put an end to many nations.
8 'Are not my commanders all kings?' he says.
9   'Has not Kalno fared like Carchemish?
   Is not Hamath like Arpad,
   and Samaria like Damascus?
10 As my hand seized the kingdoms of the idols,
   kingdoms whose images excelled those of
      Jerusalem and Samaria —
11 shall I not deal with Jerusalem and her images
   as I dealt with Samaria and her idols?'"

12 When the Lord has finished all his work against Mount Zion and Jerusalem, he will say, "I will punish the king of Assyria for the willful pride of his heart and the haughty look in his eyes. 13 For he says:

"'By the strength of my hand I have done
      this,
   and by my wisdom, because I have
      understanding.
   I removed the boundaries of nations,
   I plundered their treasures;
   like a mighty one I subdued[b] their kings.

---

[a] 20 Or arm   [b] 13 Or treasures; / I subdued the mighty,

The Benefits of Humility, the Liabilities of Pride

Isaiah 10:1-6

Beware of treating followers unjustly! God reserves a stern condemnation for oppressive leaders.

In Isaiah 10, God speaks to both Assyria and Israel to declare the benefits of humility and the liabilities of pride. Later, God even models the leadership style he wants every leader to embrace by sending the Suffering Servant. The Messiah will come to serve, not to be served (Isa 52; 53; Mk 10:45). God perfectly illustrates servant leadership. Followers come when leaders serve. Look how often God calls his leaders "servants":

1. *Abraham:* **called God's servant (Ge 26:24)**

2. *Moses:* **called God's servant (Ex 14:31)**

3. *Joshua:* **called Moses' servant (Ex 33:11)**

4. *Caleb:* **called God's servant (Nu 14:24)**

5. *Samuel:* **called God's servant (1Sa 3:9)**

6. *David:* **called Saul's servant (1Sa 29:3)**

7. *Elijah:* **called God's servant (2Ki 9:36)**

8. *Isaiah:* **called God's servant (Isa 20:3)**

¹⁴ As one reaches into a nest,
    so my hand reached for the wealth of the
       nations;
as people gather abandoned eggs,
    so I gathered all the countries;
not one flapped a wing,
    or opened its mouth to chirp.'"

¹⁵ Does the ax raise itself above the person who
       swings it,
    or the saw boast against the one who
       uses it?
As if a rod were to wield the person who lifts
       it up,
    or a club brandish the one who is not wood!
¹⁶ Therefore, the Lord, the LORD Almighty,
    will send a wasting disease upon his
       sturdy warriors;
under his pomp a fire will be kindled
    like a blazing flame.

¹⁷ The Light of Israel will become a fire,
    their Holy One a flame;
in a single day it will burn and consume
    his thorns and his briers.
¹⁸ The splendor of his forests and fertile fields
    it will completely destroy,
    as when a sick person wastes away.
¹⁹ And the remaining trees of his forests will be
       so few
    that a child could write them down.

The Remnant of Israel

²⁰ In that day the remnant of Israel,
    the survivors of Jacob,
will no longer rely on him
    who struck them down
but will truly rely on the LORD,
    the Holy One of Israel.
²¹ A remnant will return,^a a remnant of Jacob
    will return to the Mighty God.
²² Though your people be like the sand by the
       sea, Israel,
    only a remnant will return.
Destruction has been decreed,
    overwhelming and righteous.
²³ The Lord, the LORD Almighty, will carry out
    the destruction decreed upon the whole
       land.

²⁴ Therefore this is what the Lord, the LORD
Almighty, says:

"My people who live in Zion,
    do not be afraid of the Assyrians,
who beat you with a rod
    and lift up a club against you, as Egypt did.
²⁵ Very soon my anger against you will end
    and my wrath will be directed to their
       destruction."

²⁶ The LORD Almighty will lash them with a
       whip,
    as when he struck down Midian at the
       rock of Oreb;
and he will raise his staff over the waters,
    as he did in Egypt.
²⁷ In that day their burden will be lifted from
       your shoulders,
    their yoke from your neck;
the yoke will be broken
    because you have grown so fat.^b

²⁸ They enter Aiath;
    they pass through Migron;
    they store supplies at Mikmash.

---

^a 21 Hebrew *shear-jashub* (see 7:3 and note); also in verse 22
^b 27 Hebrew; Septuagint *broken / from your shoulders*

²⁹They go over the pass, and say,
  "We will camp overnight at Geba."
Ramah trembles;
  Gibeah of Saul flees.
³⁰Cry out, Daughter Gallim!
  Listen, Laishah!
  Poor Anathoth!
³¹Madmenah is in flight;
  the people of Gebim take cover.
³²This day they will halt at Nob;
  they will shake their fist
at the mount of Daughter Zion,
  at the hill of Jerusalem.

³³See, the Lord, the Lord Almighty,
  will lop off the boughs with great power.
The lofty trees will be felled,
  the tall ones will be brought low.
³⁴He will cut down the forest thickets with
    an ax;
  Lebanon will fall before the Mighty One.

The Branch From Jesse

11 A shoot will come up from the stump of
    Jesse;
  from his roots a Branch will bear fruit.
²The Spirit of the Lord will rest on him —
  the Spirit of wisdom and of
    understanding,
  the Spirit of counsel and of might,
  the Spirit of the knowledge and fear of the
    Lord —
³and he will delight in the fear of the Lord.

He will not judge by what he sees with his
    eyes,
  or decide by what he hears with his ears;
⁴but with righteousness he will judge the
    needy,
  with justice he will give decisions for the
    poor of the earth.
He will strike the earth with the rod of his
    mouth;
  with the breath of his lips he will slay the
    wicked.
⁵Righteousness will be his belt
  and faithfulness the sash around his waist.

⁶The wolf will live with the lamb,
  the leopard will lie down with the goat,
the calf and the lion and the yearlingᵃ
    together;
  and a little child will lead them.
⁷The cow will feed with the bear,
  their young will lie down together,
  and the lion will eat straw like the ox.

⁸The infant will play near the cobra's den,
  and the young child will put its hand into
    the viper's nest.
⁹They will neither harm nor destroy
  on all my holy mountain,
for the earth will be filled with the
    knowledge of the Lord
  as the waters cover the sea.

¹⁰In that day the Root of Jesse will stand as
a banner for the peoples; the nations will rally
to him, and his resting place will be glorious.
¹¹In that day the Lord will reach out his hand a
second time to reclaim the surviving remnant
of his people from Assyria, from Lower Egypt,
from Upper Egypt, from Cush,ᵇ from Elam,
from Babylonia,ᶜ from Hamath and from the islands of the Mediterranean.

¹²He will raise a banner for the nations
  and gather the exiles of Israel;
he will assemble the scattered people of Judah
  from the four quarters of the earth.
¹³Ephraim's jealousy will vanish,
  and Judah's enemiesᵈ will be destroyed;
Ephraim will not be jealous of Judah,
  nor Judah hostile toward Ephraim.
¹⁴They will swoop down on the slopes of
    Philistia to the west;
  together they will plunder the people to
    the east.
They will subdue Edom and Moab,
  and the Ammonites will be subject to
    them.
¹⁵The Lord will dry up
  the gulf of the Egyptian sea;
with a scorching wind he will sweep his hand
  over the Euphrates River.
He will break it up into seven streams
  so that anyone can cross over in sandals.
¹⁶There will be a highway for the remnant of
    his people
  that is left from Assyria,
as there was for Israel
  when they came up from Egypt.

Songs of Praise

12 In that day you will say:

"I will praise you, Lord.
  Although you were angry with me,
your anger has turned away
  and you have comforted me.

ᵃ 6 Hebrew; Septuagint *lion will feed*   ᵇ 11 That is, the upper
Nile region   ᶜ 11 Hebrew *Shinar*   ᵈ 13 Or *hostility*

² Surely God is my salvation;
    I will trust and not be afraid.
The Lord, the Lord himself, is my strength
      and my defense*ᵃ*;
    he has become my salvation."
³ With joy you will draw water
    from the wells of salvation.

⁴ In that day you will say:

"Give praise to the Lord, proclaim his
      name;
    make known among the nations what he
      has done,
    and proclaim that his name is exalted.
⁵ Sing to the Lord, for he has done glorious
      things;
    let this be known to all the world.
⁶ Shout aloud and sing for joy, people of Zion,
    for great is the Holy One of Israel among
      you."

A Prophecy Against Babylon

13 A prophecy against Babylon that Isaiah
son of Amoz saw:

² Raise a banner on a bare hilltop,
    shout to them;
beckon to them
    to enter the gates of the nobles.
³ I have commanded those I prepared for
      battle;
    I have summoned my warriors to carry
      out my wrath —
    those who rejoice in my triumph.

⁴ Listen, a noise on the mountains,
    like that of a great multitude!
Listen, an uproar among the kingdoms,
    like nations massing together!
The Lord Almighty is mustering
    an army for war.
⁵ They come from faraway lands,
    from the ends of the heavens —
the Lord and the weapons of his wrath —
    to destroy the whole country.

⁶ Wail, for the day of the Lord is near;
    it will come like destruction from the
      Almighty.*ᵇ*
⁷ Because of this, all hands will go limp,
    every heart will melt with fear.
⁸ Terror will seize them,
    pain and anguish will grip them;
    they will writhe like a woman in labor.
They will look aghast at each other,
    their faces aflame.

⁹ See, the day of the Lord is coming
    — a cruel day, with wrath and fierce
      anger —
to make the land desolate
    and destroy the sinners within it.
¹⁰ The stars of heaven and their constellations
    will not show their light.
The rising sun will be darkened
    and the moon will not give its light.
¹¹ I will punish the world for its evil,
    the wicked for their sins.
I will put an end to the arrogance of the
      haughty
    and will humble the pride of the ruthless.
¹² I will make people scarcer than pure gold,
    more rare than the gold of Ophir.
¹³ Therefore I will make the heavens tremble;
    and the earth will shake from its place
at the wrath of the Lord Almighty,
    in the day of his burning anger.

¹⁴ Like a hunted gazelle,
    like sheep without a shepherd,
they will all return to their own people,
    they will flee to their native land.
¹⁵ Whoever is captured will be thrust
      through;
    all who are caught will fall by the sword.
¹⁶ Their infants will be dashed to pieces before
      their eyes;
    their houses will be looted and their wives
      violated.

¹⁷ See, I will stir up against them the Medes,
    who do not care for silver
    and have no delight in gold.
¹⁸ Their bows will strike down the young men;
    they will have no mercy on infants,
    nor will they look with compassion on
      children.
¹⁹ Babylon, the jewel of kingdoms,
    the pride and glory of the Babylonians,*ᶜ*
will be overthrown by God
    like Sodom and Gomorrah.
²⁰ She will never be inhabited
    or lived in through all generations;
there no nomads will pitch their tents,
    there no shepherds will rest their flocks.
²¹ But desert creatures will lie there,
    jackals will fill her houses;
there the owls will dwell,
    and there the wild goats will leap about.
²² Hyenas will inhabit her strongholds,
    jackals her luxurious palaces.

ᵃ 2 Or *song*   *ᵇ* 6 Hebrew *Shaddai*   *ᶜ* 19 Or *Chaldeans*

Her time is at hand,
  and her days will not be prolonged.

14 The Lord will have compassion on
      Jacob;
  once again he will choose Israel
  and will settle them in their own land.
Foreigners will join them
  and unite with the descendants of Jacob.
² Nations will take them
  and bring them to their own place.
And Israel will take possession of the nations
  and make them male and female servants
    in the Lord's land.
They will make captives of their captors
  and rule over their oppressors.

³ On the day the Lord gives you relief from
your suffering and turmoil and from the harsh
labor forced on you, ⁴ you will take up this taunt
against the king of Babylon:

How the oppressor has come to an end!
  How his fury[a] has ended!
⁵ The Lord has broken the rod of the wicked,
  the scepter of the rulers,
⁶ which in anger struck down peoples
  with unceasing blows,
and in fury subdued nations
  with relentless aggression.
⁷ All the lands are at rest and at peace;
  they break into singing.
⁸ Even the junipers and the cedars of
    Lebanon
  gloat over you and say,
"Now that you have been laid low,
  no one comes to cut us down."

⁹ The realm of the dead below is all astir
  to meet you at your coming;
it rouses the spirits of the departed to greet
    you —
  all those who were leaders in the world;
it makes them rise from their thrones —
  all those who were kings over the nations.
¹⁰ They will all respond,
  they will say to you,
"You also have become weak, as we are;
  you have become like us."
¹¹ All your pomp has been brought down to the
    grave,
  along with the noise of your harps;
maggots are spread out beneath you
  and worms cover you.

¹² How you have fallen from heaven,
  morning star, son of the dawn!

You have been cast down to the earth,
  you who once laid low the nations!
¹³ You said in your heart,
  "I will ascend to the heavens;
I will raise my throne
  above the stars of God;
I will sit enthroned on the mount of assembly,
  on the utmost heights of Mount Zaphon.[b]
¹⁴ I will ascend above the tops of the clouds;
  I will make myself like the Most High."
¹⁵ But you are brought down to the realm of
    the dead,
  to the depths of the pit.

¹⁶ Those who see you stare at you,
  they ponder your fate:
"Is this the man who shook the earth
  and made kingdoms tremble,
¹⁷ the man who made the world a wilderness,
  who overthrew its cities
  and would not let his captives go home?"
¹⁸ All the kings of the nations lie in state,
  each in his own tomb.
¹⁹ But you are cast out of your tomb
  like a rejected branch;
you are covered with the slain,
  with those pierced by the sword,
  those who descend to the stones of the pit.
Like a corpse trampled underfoot,
²⁰   you will not join them in burial,
for you have destroyed your land
  and killed your people.

Let the offspring of the wicked
  never be mentioned again.
²¹ Prepare a place to slaughter his children
  for the sins of their ancestors;
they are not to rise to inherit the land
  and cover the earth with their cities.

²² "I will rise up against them,"
  declares the Lord Almighty.
"I will wipe out Babylon's name and
    survivors,
  her offspring and descendants,"
              declares the Lord.
²³ "I will turn her into a place for owls
  and into swampland;
I will sweep her with the broom of
    destruction,"
  declares the Lord Almighty.

---

[a] 4 Dead Sea Scrolls, Septuagint and Syriac; the meaning of the
word in the Masoretic Text is uncertain.   [b] 13 Or of the
north; Zaphon was the most sacred mountain of the
Canaanites.

A Riches to Rags Story

Isaiah 14:3–23

Proverbs 16:18 reminds us that pride comes before a fall and that a haughty spirit causes one to stumble. We see that truth in action in Isaiah 14.

While we see the immediate fulfillment of this passage in the king of Babylon, many scholars believe the text also speaks of Satan. Note the arrogant words in verses 12–17. What a sobering picture of a leader who goes astray! Both the oppressive king and Satan had one common characteristic: a lust for pride and power. Consider the devil's fall from his original place in heaven, as described in Isaiah 14, Ezekiel 28, and Revelation 12; 20:

1. **The one cast down (to the bottomless pit) (Isa 14:15; Rev 12:10; 20:3)**

2. **Full of wisdom (Eze 28:12)**

3. **Perfect in beauty (Eze 28:12)**

4. **Song leader and musician of heaven (Eze 28:13)**

5. **The anointed cherub (Eze 28:14)**

6. **One who covered the throne (Eze 28:14, 16)**

7. **Great dragon (Rev 12:9)**

8. **The serpent (Rev 12:9; 20:2)**

9. **The devil; the spirit of deception (Rev 12:9; 20:10)**

10. **Accuser of the brethren (Rev 20:10)**

24 The LORD Almighty has sworn,

"Surely, as I have planned, so it will be,
    and as I have purposed, so it will
        happen.
25 I will crush the Assyrian in my land;
    on my mountains I will trample him
        down.
His yoke will be taken from my people,
    and his burden removed from their
        shoulders."
26 This is the plan determined for the whole
        world;
    this is the hand stretched out over all
        nations.
27 For the LORD Almighty has purposed, and
        who can thwart him?
    His hand is stretched out, and who can
        turn it back?

A Prophecy Against the Philistines

28 This prophecy came in the year King Ahaz
died:

29 Do not rejoice, all you Philistines,
    that the rod that struck you is broken;

from the root of that snake will spring up a
        viper,
    its fruit will be a darting, venomous
        serpent.
30 The poorest of the poor will find pasture,
    and the needy will lie down in safety.
But your root I will destroy by famine;
    it will slay your survivors.

31 Wail, you gate! Howl, you city!
    Melt away, all you Philistines!
A cloud of smoke comes from the north,
    and there is not a straggler in its ranks.
32 What answer shall be given
    to the envoys of that nation?
"The LORD has established Zion,
    and in her his afflicted people will find
        refuge."

A Prophecy Against Moab

15 A prophecy against Moab:

Ar in Moab is ruined,
    destroyed in a night!
Kir in Moab is ruined,
    destroyed in a night!

[2] Dibon goes up to its temple,
  to its high places to weep;
Moab wails over Nebo and Medeba.
Every head is shaved
  and every beard cut off.
[3] In the streets they wear sackcloth;
  on the roofs and in the public squares
they all wail,
  prostrate with weeping.
[4] Heshbon and Elealeh cry out,
  their voices are heard all the way to
    Jahaz.
Therefore the armed men of Moab cry out,
  and their hearts are faint.

[5] My heart cries out over Moab;
  her fugitives flee as far as Zoar,
  as far as Eglath Shelishiyah.
They go up the hill to Luhith,
  weeping as they go;
on the road to Horonaim
  they lament their destruction.
[6] The waters of Nimrim are dried up
  and the grass is withered;
the vegetation is gone
  and nothing green is left.
[7] So the wealth they have acquired and
    stored up
  they carry away over the Ravine of the
    Poplars.
[8] Their outcry echoes along the border of
    Moab;
  their wailing reaches as far as Eglaim,
  their lamentation as far as Beer Elim.
[9] The waters of Dimon[a] are full of blood,
  but I will bring still more upon
    Dimon[a] —
a lion upon the fugitives of Moab
  and upon those who remain in the
    land.

16

Send lambs as tribute
  to the ruler of the land,
from Sela, across the desert,
  to the mount of Daughter Zion.
[2] Like fluttering birds
  pushed from the nest,
so are the women of Moab
  at the fords of the Arnon.

[3] "Make up your mind," Moab says.
  "Render a decision.
Make your shadow like night —
  at high noon.
Hide the fugitives,
  do not betray the refugees.

[4] Let the Moabite fugitives stay with you;
  be their shelter from the destroyer."

The oppressor will come to an end,
  and destruction will cease;
  the aggressor will vanish from the land.
[5] In love a throne will be established;
  in faithfulness a man will sit on it —
  one from the house[b] of David —
one who in judging seeks justice
  and speeds the cause of righteousness.

[6] We have heard of Moab's pride —
  how great is her arrogance! —
of her conceit, her pride and her insolence;
  but her boasts are empty.
[7] Therefore the Moabites wail,
  they wail together for Moab.
Lament and grieve
  for the raisin cakes of Kir Hareseth.
[8] The fields of Heshbon wither,
  the vines of Sibmah also.
The rulers of the nations
  have trampled down the choicest vines,
which once reached Jazer
  and spread toward the desert.
Their shoots spread out
  and went as far as the sea.[c]
[9] So I weep, as Jazer weeps,
  for the vines of Sibmah.
Heshbon and Elealeh,
  I drench you with tears!
The shouts of joy over your ripened fruit
  and over your harvests have been
    stilled.
[10] Joy and gladness are taken away from the
    orchards;
  no one sings or shouts in the vineyards;
no one treads out wine at the presses,
  for I have put an end to the shouting.
[11] My heart laments for Moab like a harp,
  my inmost being for Kir Hareseth.
[12] When Moab appears at her high place,
  she only wears herself out;
when she goes to her shrine to pray,
  it is to no avail.

[13] This is the word the LORD has already spoken concerning Moab. [14] But now the LORD says: "Within three years, as a servant bound by contract would count them, Moab's splendor and all her many people will be despised, and her survivors will be very few and feeble."

---

[a] 9 *Dimon*, a wordplay on *Dibon* (see verse 2), sounds like the Hebrew for *blood*. [b] 5 Hebrew *tent* [c] 8 Probably the Dead Sea

A Prophecy Against Damascus

17 A prophecy against Damascus:

"See, Damascus will no longer be a city
    but will become a heap of ruins.
²The cities of Aroer will be deserted
    and left to flocks, which will lie down,
    with no one to make them afraid.
³The fortified city will disappear from
        Ephraim,
    and royal power from Damascus;
the remnant of Aram will be
    like the glory of the Israelites,"
            declares the LORD Almighty.

⁴"In that day the glory of Jacob will fade;
    the fat of his body will waste away.
⁵It will be as when reapers harvest the
        standing grain,
    gathering the grain in their arms—
as when someone gleans heads of grain
    in the Valley of Rephaim.
⁶Yet some gleanings will remain,
    as when an olive tree is beaten,
leaving two or three olives on the topmost
        branches,
    four or five on the fruitful boughs,"
        declares the LORD, the God of Israel.

⁷In that day people will look to their Maker
    and turn their eyes to the Holy One of
        Israel.
⁸They will not look to the altars,
    the work of their hands,
and they will have no regard for the Asherah
        poles[a]
    and the incense altars their fingers have
        made.

⁹In that day their strong cities, which they left
because of the Israelites, will be like places abandoned to thickets and undergrowth. And all will
be desolation.

¹⁰You have forgotten God your Savior;
    you have not remembered the Rock, your
        fortress.
Therefore, though you set out the finest
        plants
    and plant imported vines,
¹¹though on the day you set them out, you
        make them grow,
    and on the morning when you plant them,
        you bring them to bud,
yet the harvest will be as nothing
    in the day of disease and incurable pain.

ᵃ 8 That is, wooden symbols of the goddess Asherah

A Leader's Heart of Love for the Unlovely
Isaiah 15:5; 16:9, 11

Someone must have forgotten to tell the prophet Isaiah that he lived in Old Testament times.

You know the picture most have of ancient Hebrew leaders-eye-for-an-eye types, angry, hair akimbo, and eager for God's righteous judgment to fall upon the pagans and the wicked. And yet, here stands Isaiah, crying out for heathen Moab and weeping for wayward Heshbon.

Isaiah demonstrates for us the attitude of a godly leader who sees approaching judgment on unbelievers. He actually *grieves* over what is coming on lost souls. While he acknowledges and even celebrates God's righteousness and sovereignty in judging those who reject him, he also proclaims that the calamity about to descend is nothing other than a terrible tragedy.

Isaiah's lament over the fate of these ancient nations reveals the attitude of a truly godly leader. While he knew those erring nations surely deserved God's judgment, he also knew that without God's grace and mercy, none of us could expect anything else.

We ought to stand in awed silence when we see the judgment of God falling on those who have forsaken his way. But we should never see his judgment as an occasion to celebrate our own righteousness. Rather, we ought to grieve for the lost and reflect deeply on the grace and mercy God has extended to us.

12 Woe to the many nations that rage —
    they rage like the raging sea!
Woe to the peoples who roar —
    they roar like the roaring of great waters!
13 Although the peoples roar like the roar of
      surging waters,
    when he rebukes them they flee far away,
driven before the wind like chaff on the hills,
    like tumbleweed before a gale.
14 In the evening, sudden terror!
    Before the morning, they are gone!
This is the portion of those who loot us,
    the lot of those who plunder us.

A Prophecy Against Cush

18 Woe to the land of whirring wings[a]
    along the rivers of Cush,[b]
2 which sends envoys by sea
    in papyrus boats over the water.

Go, swift messengers,
to a people tall and smooth-skinned,
    to a people feared far and wide,
an aggressive nation of strange speech,
    whose land is divided by rivers.

3 All you people of the world,
    you who live on the earth,
when a banner is raised on the mountains,
    you will see it,
and when a trumpet sounds,
    you will hear it.
4 This is what the LORD says to me:
    "I will remain quiet and will look on from
      my dwelling place,
like shimmering heat in the sunshine,
    like a cloud of dew in the heat of harvest."
5 For, before the harvest, when the blossom is
      gone
    and the flower becomes a ripening grape,
he will cut off the shoots with pruning
      knives,
    and cut down and take away the spreading
      branches.
6 They will all be left to the mountain birds of
      prey
    and to the wild animals;
the birds will feed on them all summer,
    the wild animals all winter.

7 At that time gifts will be brought to the
LORD Almighty

from a people tall and smooth-skinned,
    from a people feared far and wide,
an aggressive nation of strange speech,
    whose land is divided by rivers —

the gifts will be brought to Mount Zion, the
place of the Name of the LORD Almighty.

A Prophecy Against Egypt

19 A prophecy against Egypt:

See, the LORD rides on a swift cloud
    and is coming to Egypt.
The idols of Egypt tremble before him,
    and the hearts of the Egyptians melt with
      fear.

2 "I will stir up Egyptian against Egyptian —
    brother will fight against brother,
neighbor against neighbor,
    city against city,
    kingdom against kingdom.
3 The Egyptians will lose heart,
    and I will bring their plans to nothing;
they will consult the idols and the spirits of
      the dead,
    the mediums and the spiritists.
4 I will hand the Egyptians over
    to the power of a cruel master,
and a fierce king will rule over them,"
    declares the Lord, the LORD Almighty.

5 The waters of the river will dry up,
    and the riverbed will be parched and dry.
6 The canals will stink;
    the streams of Egypt will dwindle and
      dry up.
The reeds and rushes will wither,
7   also the plants along the Nile,
    at the mouth of the river.
Every sown field along the Nile
    will become parched, will blow away and
      be no more.
8 The fishermen will groan and lament,
    all who cast hooks into the Nile;
those who throw nets on the water
    will pine away.
9 Those who work with combed flax will
      despair,
    the weavers of fine linen will lose hope.
10 The workers in cloth will be dejected,
    and all the wage earners will be sick at
      heart.

11 The officials of Zoan are nothing but fools;
    the wise counselors of Pharaoh give
      senseless advice.
How can you say to Pharaoh,
    "I am one of the wise men,
    a disciple of the ancient kings"?

---

[a] 1 Or of locusts   [b] 1 That is, the upper Nile region

¹²Where are your wise men now?
Let them show you and make known
what the LORD Almighty
has planned against Egypt.
¹³The officials of Zoan have become fools,
the leaders of Memphis are deceived;
the cornerstones of her peoples
have led Egypt astray.
¹⁴The LORD has poured into them
a spirit of dizziness;
they make Egypt stagger in all that she does,
as a drunkard staggers around in his
vomit.
¹⁵There is nothing Egypt can do—
head or tail, palm branch or reed.

¹⁶In that day the Egyptians will become weaklings. They will shudder with fear at the uplifted hand that the LORD Almighty raises against them. ¹⁷And the land of Judah will bring terror to the Egyptians; everyone to whom Judah is mentioned will be terrified, because of what the LORD Almighty is planning against them.

¹⁸In that day five cities in Egypt will speak the language of Canaan and swear allegiance to the LORD Almighty. One of them will be called the City of the Sun.*ᵃ

¹⁹In that day there will be an altar to the LORD in the heart of Egypt, and a monument to the LORD at its border. ²⁰It will be a sign and witness to the LORD Almighty in the land of Egypt.

When they cry out to the LORD because of their oppressors, he will send them a savior and defender, and he will rescue them. ²¹So the LORD will make himself known to the Egyptians, and in that day they will acknowledge the LORD. They will worship with sacrifices and grain offerings; they will make vows to the LORD and keep them. ²²The LORD will strike Egypt with a plague; he will strike them and heal them. They will turn to the LORD, and he will respond to their pleas and heal them.

²³In that day there will be a highway from Egypt to Assyria. The Assyrians will go to Egypt and the Egyptians to Assyria. The Egyptians and Assyrians will worship together. ²⁴In that day Israel will be the third, along with Egypt and Assyria, a blessingᵇ on the earth. ²⁵The LORD Almighty will bless them, saying, "Blessed be Egypt my people, Assyria my handiwork, and Israel my inheritance."

A Prophecy Against Egypt and Cush

20 In the year that the supreme commander, sent by Sargon king of Assyria, came to Ashdod and attacked and captured it— ²at that time the LORD spoke through Isaiah son of Amoz.

ᵃ 18 Some manuscripts of the Masoretic Text, Dead Sea Scrolls, Symmachus and Vulgate; most manuscripts of the Masoretic Text *City of Destruction*   *ᵇ 24* Or *Assyria, whose names will be used in blessings* (see Gen. 48:20); or *Assyria, who will be seen by others as blessed*

Personal Qualifications of Leadership
Isaiah 19:11–15

What qualifies a person to be a leader? Most natural leaders don't aspire to be great *leaders*; they aspire to be great *persons*. Personal qualifications lead to leadership qualifications. When leaders lead their own lives well, others naturally want to follow.

Consider Mother Teresa of Calcutta, India. It's doubtful she ever said, "I am going to set out to be a great leader!" Yet that is what she became by determining to be the person God created her to be. She developed personal qualities that became leadership qualities.

Isaiah illustrates this from a negative viewpoint. The senseless, naïve leaders of Zoan and Noph lacked the foresight to lead others. Their incompetence prompted God to compare them with a drunken man who can't even walk straight. If we want our leadership to last, we must pay attention to four crucial elements:

1. **Character**—enables us to do what is right even when it seems difficult.

2. **Perspective**—enables us to understand what must happen to reach a goal.

3. **Courage**—enables us to initiate and take the risks to step out toward a worthy goal.

4. **Favor**—enables us to attract and empower others to join us in the cause.

He said to him, "Take off the sackcloth from your body and the sandals from your feet." And he did so, going around stripped and barefoot.

[3]Then the LORD said, "Just as my servant Isaiah has gone stripped and barefoot for three years, as a sign and portent against Egypt and Cush,[a] [4]so the king of Assyria will lead away stripped and barefoot the Egyptian captives and Cushite exiles, young and old, with buttocks bared—to Egypt's shame. [5]Those who trusted in Cush and boasted in Egypt will be dismayed and put to shame. [6]In that day the people who live on this coast will say, 'See what has happened to those we relied on, those we fled to for help and deliverance from the king of Assyria! How then can we escape?'"

A Prophecy Against Babylon

21

A prophecy against the Desert by the Sea:

Like whirlwinds sweeping through the
    southland,
  an invader comes from the desert,
  from a land of terror.
[2]A dire vision has been shown to me:
  The traitor betrays, the looter takes loot.
Elam, attack! Media, lay siege!
  I will bring to an end all the groaning she
    caused.

[3]At this my body is racked with pain,
  pangs seize me, like those of a woman in
    labor;
I am staggered by what I hear,
  I am bewildered by what I see.
[4]My heart falters,
  fear makes me tremble;
the twilight I longed for
  has become a horror to me.

[5]They set the tables,
  they spread the rugs,
  they eat, they drink!
Get up, you officers,
  oil the shields!

[6]This is what the Lord says to me:

"Go, post a lookout
  and have him report what he sees.
[7]When he sees chariots
  with teams of horses,
riders on donkeys
  or riders on camels,
let him be alert,
  fully alert."

[8]And the lookout[b] shouted,

"Day after day, my lord, I stand on the
    watchtower;
  every night I stay at my post.
[9]Look, here comes a man in a chariot
  with a team of horses.
And he gives back the answer:
  'Babylon has fallen, has fallen!
All the images of its gods
  lie shattered on the ground!'"

[10]My people who are crushed on the threshing
    floor,
  I tell you what I have heard
from the LORD Almighty,
  from the God of Israel.

A Prophecy Against Edom

[11]A prophecy against Dumah[c]:

Someone calls to me from Seir,
  "Watchman, what is left of the night?
  Watchman, what is left of the night?"
[12]The watchman replies,
  "Morning is coming, but also the night.
If you would ask, then ask;
  and come back yet again."

A Prophecy Against Arabia

[13]A prophecy against Arabia:

You caravans of Dedanites,
  who camp in the thickets of Arabia,
[14]   bring water for the thirsty;
you who live in Tema,
  bring food for the fugitives.
[15]They flee from the sword,
  from the drawn sword,
from the bent bow
  and from the heat of battle.

[16]This is what the Lord says to me: "Within one year, as a servant bound by contract would count it, all the splendor of Kedar will come to an end. [17]The survivors of the archers, the warriors of Kedar, will be few." The LORD, the God of Israel, has spoken.

A Prophecy About Jerusalem

22

A prophecy against the Valley of Vision:

What troubles you now,
  that you have all gone up on the roofs,

---

[a] 3 That is, the upper Nile region; also in verse 5   [b] 8 Dead Sea Scrolls and Syriac; Masoretic Text A lion   [c] 11 Dumah, a wordplay on Edom, means silence or stillness.

2 you town so full of commotion,
  you city of tumult and revelry?
Your slain were not killed by the sword,
  nor did they die in battle.
3 All your leaders have fled together;
  they have been captured without using the
    bow.
All you who were caught were taken prisoner
    together,
  having fled while the enemy was still far
    away.
4 Therefore I said, "Turn away from me;
  let me weep bitterly.
Do not try to console me
  over the destruction of my people."

5 The Lord, the LORD Almighty, has a day
  of tumult and trampling and terror
    in the Valley of Vision,
  a day of battering down walls
    and of crying out to the mountains.
6 Elam takes up the quiver,
  with her charioteers and horses;
Kir uncovers the shield.
7 Your choicest valleys are full of chariots,
  and horsemen are posted at the city gates.

8 The Lord stripped away the defenses of
    Judah,
  and you looked in that day
    to the weapons in the Palace of the Forest.
9 You saw that the walls of the City of David
  were broken through in many places;
you stored up water
  in the Lower Pool.
10 You counted the buildings in Jerusalem
  and tore down houses to strengthen the
    wall.
11 You built a reservoir between the two walls
  for the water of the Old Pool,
but you did not look to the One who made it,
  or have regard for the One who planned it
    long ago.

12 The Lord, the LORD Almighty,
  called you on that day
to weep and to wail,
  to tear out your hair and put on sackcloth.
13 But see, there is joy and revelry,
  slaughtering of cattle and killing of sheep,
    eating of meat and drinking of wine!
"Let us eat and drink," you say,
  "for tomorrow we die!"

14 The LORD Almighty has revealed this in my
hearing: "Till your dying day this sin will not be
atoned for," says the Lord, the LORD Almighty.

15 This is what the Lord, the LORD Almighty,
says:

"Go, say to this steward,
  to Shebna the palace administrator:
16 What are you doing here and who gave you
    permission
  to cut out a grave for yourself here,
hewing your grave on the height
  and chiseling your resting place in the rock?

17 "Beware, the LORD is about to take firm hold
    of you
  and hurl you away, you mighty man.
18 He will roll you up tightly like a ball
  and throw you into a large country.
There you will die
  and there the chariots you were so proud of
  will become a disgrace to your master's
    house.
19 I will depose you from your office,
  and you will be ousted from your position.

20 "In that day I will summon my servant, Eliakim son of Hilkiah. 21 I will clothe him with
your robe and fasten your sash around him and
hand your authority over to him. He will be a
father to those who live in Jerusalem and to the
people of Judah. 22 I will place on his shoulder
the key to the house of David; what he opens no
one can shut, and what he shuts no one can open.
23 I will drive him like a peg into a firm place; he
will become a seat[a] of honor for the house of his
father. 24 All the glory of his family will hang on
him: its offspring and offshoots — all its lesser
vessels, from the bowls to all the jars.

25 "In that day," declares the LORD Almighty,
"the peg driven into the firm place will give way;
it will be sheared off and will fall, and the load
hanging on it will be cut down." The LORD has
spoken.

A Prophecy Against Tyre

23 A prophecy against Tyre:

Wail, you ships of Tarshish!
  For Tyre is destroyed
    and left without house or harbor.
From the land of Cyprus
  word has come to them.

2 Be silent, you people of the island
  and you merchants of Sidon,
    whom the seafarers have enriched.

a 23 Or throne

³On the great waters
came the grain of the Shihor;
the harvest of the Nile[a] was the revenue of
Tyre,
and she became the marketplace of the
nations.

⁴Be ashamed, Sidon, and you fortress of the
sea,
for the sea has spoken:
"I have neither been in labor nor given birth;
I have neither reared sons nor brought up
daughters."
⁵When word comes to Egypt,
they will be in anguish at the report from
Tyre.

⁶Cross over to Tarshish;
wail, you people of the island.
⁷Is this your city of revelry,
the old, old city,
whose feet have taken her
to settle in far-off lands?
⁸Who planned this against Tyre,
the bestower of crowns,
whose merchants are princes,
whose traders are renowned in the earth?
⁹The LORD Almighty planned it,
to bring down her pride in all her splendor
and to humble all who are renowned on
the earth.

¹⁰Till[b] your land as they do along the Nile,
Daughter Tarshish,
for you no longer have a harbor.
¹¹The LORD has stretched out his hand over
the sea
and made its kingdoms tremble.
He has given an order concerning Phoenicia
that her fortresses be destroyed.
¹²He said, "No more of your reveling,
Virgin Daughter Sidon, now crushed!

"Up, cross over to Cyprus;
even there you will find no rest."
¹³Look at the land of the Babylonians,[c]
this people that is now of no account!
The Assyrians have made it
a place for desert creatures;
they raised up their siege towers,
they stripped its fortresses bare
and turned it into a ruin.

¹⁴Wail, you ships of Tarshish;
your fortress is destroyed!

¹⁵At that time Tyre will be forgotten for seventy years, the span of a king's life. But at the end of these seventy years, it will happen to Tyre as in the song of the prostitute:

¹⁶"Take up a harp, walk through the city,
you forgotten prostitute;
play the harp well, sing many a song,
so that you will be remembered."

¹⁷At the end of seventy years, the LORD will deal with Tyre. She will return to her lucrative prostitution and will ply her trade with all the kingdoms on the face of the earth. ¹⁸Yet her profit and her earnings will be set apart for the LORD; they will not be stored up or hoarded. Her profits will go to those who live before the LORD, for abundant food and fine clothes.

God's Providence: He Raises Up Leaders and Brings Them Down

Isaiah 23:1–18

The city of Tyre wielded great international influence during Isaiah's day. Its wealthy merchants created a high standard of living. But when God chose to bring them down, no one could stop him. We can position people, but only God exalts them. We can develop others, but only God raises them up.

The LORD's Devastation of the Earth

24 See, the LORD is going to lay waste the earth
and devastate it;
he will ruin its face
and scatter its inhabitants —
²it will be the same
for priest as for people,
for the master as for his servant,
for the mistress as for her servant,
for seller as for buyer,
for borrower as for lender,
for debtor as for creditor.
³The earth will be completely laid waste
and totally plundered.
The LORD has spoken this word.

a 2,3 Masoretic Text; Dead Sea Scrolls Sidon, / who cross over the sea; / your envoys ³are on the great waters. / The grain of the Shihor, / the harvest of the Nile,   b 10 Dead Sea Scrolls and some Septuagint manuscripts; Masoretic Text Go through   c 13 Or Chaldeans

⁴The earth dries up and withers,
    the world languishes and withers,
    the heavens languish with the earth.
⁵The earth is defiled by its people;
    they have disobeyed the laws,
  violated the statutes
    and broken the everlasting covenant.
⁶Therefore a curse consumes the earth;
    its people must bear their guilt.
  Therefore earth's inhabitants are burned up,
    and very few are left.
⁷The new wine dries up and the vine withers;
    all the merrymakers groan.
⁸The joyful timbrels are stilled,
    the noise of the revelers has stopped,
    the joyful harp is silent.
⁹No longer do they drink wine with a song;
    the beer is bitter to its drinkers.
¹⁰The ruined city lies desolate;
    the entrance to every house is barred.
¹¹In the streets they cry out for wine;
    all joy turns to gloom,
    all joyful sounds are banished from the
      earth.
¹²The city is left in ruins,
    its gate is battered to pieces.
¹³So will it be on the earth
    and among the nations,
  as when an olive tree is beaten,
    or as when gleanings are left after the
      grape harvest.

¹⁴They raise their voices, they shout for joy;
    from the west they acclaim the LORD's
      majesty.
¹⁵Therefore in the east give glory to the
    LORD;
    exalt the name of the LORD, the God of
      Israel,
    in the islands of the sea.
¹⁶From the ends of the earth we hear singing:
    "Glory to the Righteous One."

But I said, "I waste away, I waste away!
    Woe to me!
The treacherous betray!
    With treachery the treacherous betray!"
¹⁷Terror and pit and snare await you,
    people of the earth.
¹⁸Whoever flees at the sound of terror
    will fall into a pit;
whoever climbs out of the pit
    will be caught in a snare.

The floodgates of the heavens are opened,
    the foundations of the earth shake.

¹⁹The earth is broken up,
    the earth is split asunder,
    the earth is violently shaken.
²⁰The earth reels like a drunkard,
    it sways like a hut in the wind;
so heavy upon it is the guilt of its rebellion
    that it falls—never to rise again.

²¹In that day the LORD will punish
    the powers in the heavens above
    and the kings on the earth below.
²²They will be herded together
    like prisoners bound in a dungeon;
they will be shut up in prison
    and be punished[a] after many days.
²³The moon will be dismayed,
    the sun ashamed;
for the LORD Almighty will reign
    on Mount Zion and in Jerusalem,
    and before its elders—with great glory.

Praise to the LORD

25 LORD, you are my God;
    I will exalt you and praise your name,
for in perfect faithfulness
    you have done wonderful things,
    things planned long ago.
²You have made the city a heap of rubble,
    the fortified town a ruin,
the foreigners' stronghold a city no more;
    it will never be rebuilt.
³Therefore strong peoples will honor you;
    cities of ruthless nations will revere you.
⁴You have been a refuge for the poor,
    a refuge for the needy in their distress,
a shelter from the storm
    and a shade from the heat.
For the breath of the ruthless
    is like a storm driving against a wall
⁵   and like the heat of the desert.
You silence the uproar of foreigners;
    as heat is reduced by the shadow of a
      cloud,
    so the song of the ruthless is stilled.

⁶On this mountain the LORD Almighty will
      prepare
    a feast of rich food for all peoples,
a banquet of aged wine—
    the best of meats and the finest of wines.
⁷On this mountain he will destroy
    the shroud that enfolds all peoples,
    the sheet that covers all nations;
⁸   he will swallow up death forever.

Vision: Great Leaders Never Lose Sight of the Big Picture

Isaiah 25:1–12

Good leaders never shrink from dealing with the realities of the here and now, no matter how depressing they might be. Yet they never lose sight of the big picture and what the ultimate future looks like. While Isaiah 25 boasts a wonderful vision for the future, it comes on the heels of chapter 24, which predicts doom and gloom for the immediate future. One chapter deals with a temporary situation; the next pictures the ultimate situation. Leadership must stay in touch with both. Vision separates leaders from followers:

Followers

1. **See the here and now**
2. **Driven by the atmosphere of today**
3. **Limited perspective on their abilities**
4. **Can be diverted by today's losses**
5. **Key word: immediate**

Leaders

1. **See the ultimate goals and potential**
2. **Driven by their vision for tomorrow**
3. **Larger perspective on everyone's abilities**
4. **Stays on track by focusing on the goal**
5. **Key word: ultimate**

The Sovereign LORD will wipe away the tears
  from all faces;
he will remove his people's disgrace
  from all the earth.
                    The LORD has spoken.

[9] In that day they will say,

"Surely this is our God;
  we trusted in him, and he saved us.
This is the LORD, we trusted in him;
  let us rejoice and be glad in his salvation."

[10] The hand of the LORD will rest on this
    mountain;
  but Moab will be trampled in their land
    as straw is trampled down in the manure.
[11] They will stretch out their hands in it,
  as swimmers stretch out their hands to
    swim.
God will bring down their pride
  despite the cleverness[a] of their hands.
[12] He will bring down your high fortified walls
  and lay them low;
he will bring them down to the ground,
  to the very dust.

A Song of Praise

26 In that day this song will be sung in the
    land of Judah:

We have a strong city;
  God makes salvation
    its walls and ramparts.

[2] Open the gates
    that the righteous nation may enter,
    the nation that keeps faith.
[3] You will keep in perfect peace
    those whose minds are steadfast,
    because they trust in you.
[4] Trust in the LORD forever,
    for the LORD, the LORD himself, is the
        Rock eternal.
[5] He humbles those who dwell on high,
    he lays the lofty city low;
  he levels it to the ground
    and casts it down to the dust.
[6] Feet trample it down—
    the feet of the oppressed,
    the footsteps of the poor.

[a] 11 The meaning of the Hebrew for this word is uncertain.

Leaders Manage Stress by Managing Perspective

Isaiah 26:3–4

Those who fix their eyes on the past risk a severe collision with the future. Those who see only the future hit much too hard the speed bumps of today. Only those who fix their eyes on God can effectively negotiate the right pace of life.

7 The path of the righteous is level;
    you, the Upright One, make the way of the
        righteous smooth.
8 Yes, LORD, walking in the way of your laws,[a]
    we wait for you;
your name and renown
    are the desire of our hearts.
9 My soul yearns for you in the night;
    in the morning my spirit longs for you.
When your judgments come upon the earth,
    the people of the world learn
        righteousness.
10 But when grace is shown to the wicked,
    they do not learn righteousness;
even in a land of uprightness they go on
        doing evil
    and do not regard the majesty of the
        LORD.
11 LORD, your hand is lifted high,
    but they do not see it.
Let them see your zeal for your people and
        be put to shame;
    let the fire reserved for your enemies
        consume them.
12 LORD, you establish peace for us;
    all that we have accomplished you have
        done for us.
13 LORD our God, other lords besides you have
        ruled over us,
    but your name alone do we honor.
14 They are now dead, they live no more;
    their spirits do not rise.
You punished them and brought them to
        ruin;
    you wiped out all memory of them.
15 You have enlarged the nation, LORD;
    you have enlarged the nation.
You have gained glory for yourself;
    you have extended all the borders of the
        land.

16 LORD, they came to you in their distress;
    when you disciplined them,
    they could barely whisper a prayer.[b]
17 As a pregnant woman about to give birth
    writhes and cries out in her pain,
    so were we in your presence, LORD.
18 We were with child, we writhed in labor,
    but we gave birth to wind.
We have not brought salvation to the earth,
    and the people of the world have not come
        to life.

19 But your dead will live, LORD;
    their bodies will rise —

let those who dwell in the dust
    wake up and shout for joy —
your dew is like the dew of the morning;
    the earth will give birth to her dead.

20 Go, my people, enter your rooms
    and shut the doors behind you;
hide yourselves for a little while
    until his wrath has passed by.
21 See, the LORD is coming out of his dwelling
    to punish the people of the earth for their
        sins.
The earth will disclose the blood shed on it;
    the earth will conceal its slain no longer.

Deliverance of Israel

27 In that day,

the LORD will punish with his sword —
    his fierce, great and powerful sword —
Leviathan the gliding serpent,
    Leviathan the coiling serpent;
he will slay the monster of the sea.

2 In that day —

"Sing about a fruitful vineyard:
3   I, the LORD, watch over it;
    I water it continually.
I guard it day and night
    so that no one may harm it.
4   I am not angry.
If only there were briers and thorns
        confronting me!
    I would march against them in battle;
    I would set them all on fire.
5 Or else let them come to me for refuge;
    let them make peace with me,
    yes, let them make peace with me."

6 In days to come Jacob will take root,
    Israel will bud and blossom
    and fill all the world with fruit.

7 Has the LORD struck her
    as he struck down those who struck her?
Has she been killed
    as those were killed who killed her?
8 By warfare[c] and exile you contend with her —
    with his fierce blast he drives her out,
    as on a day the east wind blows.
9 By this, then, will Jacob's guilt be atoned for,
    and this will be the full fruit of the
        removal of his sin:

---

[a] 8 Or judgments   [b] 16 The meaning of the Hebrew for this
clause is uncertain.   [c] 8 See Septuagint; the meaning of the
Hebrew for this word is uncertain.

When he makes all the altar stones
  to be like limestone crushed to pieces,
no Asherah poles[a] or incense altars
  will be left standing.
¹⁰The fortified city stands desolate,
  an abandoned settlement, forsaken like
    the wilderness;
there the calves graze,
  there they lie down;
  they strip its branches bare.
¹¹When its twigs are dry, they are broken off
  and women come and make fires with
    them.
For this is a people without understanding;
  so their Maker has no compassion on them,
  and their Creator shows them no favor.

¹²In that day the LORD will thresh from the flowing Euphrates to the Wadi of Egypt, and you, Israel, will be gathered up one by one. ¹³And in that day a great trumpet will sound. Those who were perishing in Assyria and those who were exiled in Egypt will come and worship the LORD on the holy mountain in Jerusalem.

Woe to the Leaders of Ephraim and Judah

28 Woe to that wreath, the pride of
    Ephraim's drunkards,
to the fading flower, his glorious beauty,
set on the head of a fertile valley—
  to that city, the pride of those laid low by
    wine!
²See, the Lord has one who is powerful and
    strong.
Like a hailstorm and a destructive wind,
like a driving rain and a flooding downpour,
  he will throw it forcefully to the ground.
³That wreath, the pride of Ephraim's
    drunkards,
  will be trampled underfoot.
⁴That fading flower, his glorious beauty,
  set on the head of a fertile valley,
will be like figs ripe before harvest—
  as soon as people see them and take them
    in hand,
  they swallow them.

⁵In that day the LORD Almighty
  will be a glorious crown,
a beautiful wreath
  for the remnant of his people.
⁶He will be a spirit of justice
  to the one who sits in judgment,
a source of strength
  to those who turn back the battle at the
    gate.

⁷And these also stagger from wine
  and reel from beer:
Priests and prophets stagger from beer
  and are befuddled with wine;
they reel from beer,
  they stagger when seeing visions,
  they stumble when rendering decisions.
⁸All the tables are covered with vomit
  and there is not a spot without filth.

⁹"Who is it he is trying to teach?
  To whom is he explaining his message?
To children weaned from their milk,
  to those just taken from the breast?
¹⁰For it is:
  Do this, do that,
  a rule for this, a rule for that[b];
  a little here, a little there."

¹¹Very well then, with foreign lips and strange
    tongues
  God will speak to this people,
¹²to whom he said,
  "This is the resting place, let the weary
    rest";
and, "This is the place of repose"—
  but they would not listen.
¹³So then, the word of the LORD to them will
    become:
  Do this, do that,
  a rule for this, a rule for that;
  a little here, a little there—
so that as they go they will fall backward;
  they will be injured and snared and
    captured.

¹⁴Therefore hear the word of the LORD, you
    scoffers
  who rule this people in Jerusalem.
¹⁵You boast, "We have entered into a covenant
    with death,
  with the realm of the dead we have made
    an agreement.
When an overwhelming scourge sweeps by,
  it cannot touch us,
for we have made a lie our refuge
  and falsehood[c] our hiding place."

¹⁶So this is what the Sovereign LORD says:

"See, I lay a stone in Zion, a tested stone,
  a precious cornerstone for a sure
    foundation;

---

[a] 9 That is, wooden symbols of the goddess Asherah
[b] 10 Hebrew / sav lasav sav lasav / kav lakav kav lakav (probably meaningless sounds mimicking the prophet's words); also in verse 13   [c] 15 Or false gods

the one who relies on it
will never be stricken with panic.
17 I will make justice the measuring line
and righteousness the plumb line;
hail will sweep away your refuge, the lie,
and water will overflow your hiding place.
18 Your covenant with death will be annulled;
your agreement with the realm of the
dead will not stand.
When the overwhelming scourge sweeps by,
you will be beaten down by it.
19 As often as it comes it will carry you away;
morning after morning, by day and by
night,
it will sweep through."

The understanding of this message
will bring sheer terror.
20 The bed is too short to stretch out on,
the blanket too narrow to wrap around
you.
21 The LORD will rise up as he did at Mount
Perazim,
he will rouse himself as in the Valley of
Gibeon —
to do his work, his strange work,
and perform his task, his alien task.
22 Now stop your mocking,
or your chains will become heavier;
the Lord, the LORD Almighty, has told me
of the destruction decreed against the
whole land.

23 Listen and hear my voice;
pay attention and hear what I say.
24 When a farmer plows for planting, does he
plow continually?
Does he keep on breaking up and working
the soil?
25 When he has leveled the surface,
does he not sow caraway and scatter cumin?
Does he not plant wheat in its place,[a]
barley in its plot,[a]
and spelt in its field?
26 His God instructs him
and teaches him the right way.

27 Caraway is not threshed with a sledge,
nor is the wheel of a cart rolled over cumin;
caraway is beaten out with a rod,
and cumin with a stick.
28 Grain must be ground to make bread;
so one does not go on threshing it forever.
The wheels of a threshing cart may be rolled
over it,
but one does not use horses to grind grain.

29 All this also comes from the LORD Almighty,
whose plan is wonderful,
whose wisdom is magnificent.

Woe to David's City

29 Woe to you, Ariel, Ariel,
the city where David settled!
Add year to year
and let your cycle of festivals go on.
2 Yet I will besiege Ariel;
she will mourn and lament,
she will be to me like an altar hearth.[b]
3 I will encamp against you on all sides;
I will encircle you with towers
and set up my siege works against you.
4 Brought low, you will speak from the
ground;
your speech will mumble out of the dust.
Your voice will come ghostlike from the
earth;
out of the dust your speech will whisper.

5 But your many enemies will become like fine
dust,
the ruthless hordes like blown chaff.
Suddenly, in an instant,
6 the LORD Almighty will come
with thunder and earthquake and great
noise,
with windstorm and tempest and flames
of a devouring fire.
7 Then the hordes of all the nations that fight
against Ariel,
that attack her and her fortress and
besiege her,
will be as it is with a dream,
with a vision in the night —
8 as when a hungry person dreams of eating,
but awakens hungry still;
as when a thirsty person dreams of drinking,
but awakens faint and thirsty still.
So will it be with the hordes of all the
nations
that fight against Mount Zion.

9 Be stunned and amazed,
blind yourselves and be sightless;
be drunk, but not from wine,
stagger, but not from beer.
10 The LORD has brought over you a deep sleep:
He has sealed your eyes (the prophets);
he has covered your heads (the seers).

---

[a] 25 The meaning of the Hebrew for this word is uncertain.
[b] 2 The Hebrew for *altar hearth* sounds like the Hebrew for
Ariel.

[11]For you this whole vision is nothing but words sealed in a scroll. And if you give the scroll to someone who can read, and say, "Read this, please," they will answer, "I can't; it is sealed." [12]Or if you give the scroll to someone who cannot read, and say, "Read this, please," they will answer, "I don't know how to read."

[13]The Lord says:

"These people come near to me with their
      mouth
   and honor me with their lips,
   but their hearts are far from me.
Their worship of me
   is based on merely human rules they have
      been taught.[a]
[14]Therefore once more I will astound these
      people
   with wonder upon wonder;
the wisdom of the wise will perish,
   the intelligence of the intelligent will
      vanish."
[15]Woe to those who go to great depths
   to hide their plans from the LORD,
who do their work in darkness and think,
   "Who sees us? Who will know?"
[16]You turn things upside down,
   as if the potter were thought to be like the
      clay!
Shall what is formed say to the one who
      formed it,
   "You did not make me"?
Can the pot say to the potter,
   "You know nothing"?

[17]In a very short time, will not Lebanon be
      turned into a fertile field
   and the fertile field seem like a forest?
[18]In that day the deaf will hear the words of
      the scroll,
   and out of gloom and darkness
   the eyes of the blind will see.
[19]Once more the humble will rejoice in the
      LORD;
   the needy will rejoice in the Holy One of
      Israel.
[20]The ruthless will vanish,
   the mockers will disappear,
   and all who have an eye for evil will be cut
      down —
[21]those who with a word make someone out to
      be guilty,
   who ensnare the defender in court
   and with false testimony deprive the
      innocent of justice.

[22]Therefore this is what the LORD, who redeemed Abraham, says to the descendants of
Jacob:

"No longer will Jacob be ashamed;
   no longer will their faces grow pale.
[23]When they see among them their children,
   the work of my hands,
they will keep my name holy;
   they will acknowledge the holiness of the
      Holy One of Jacob,
   and will stand in awe of the God of Israel.
[24]Those who are wayward in spirit will gain
      understanding;
   those who complain will accept
      instruction."

Woe to the Obstinate Nation

30 "Woe to the obstinate children,"
      declares the LORD,
"to those who carry out plans that are not
      mine,
   forming an alliance, but not by my Spirit,
      heaping sin upon sin;
[2]who go down to Egypt
   without consulting me;
who look for help to Pharaoh's protection,
   to Egypt's shade for refuge.
[3]But Pharaoh's protection will be to your
      shame,
   Egypt's shade will bring you disgrace.
[4]Though they have officials in Zoan
   and their envoys have arrived in Hanes,
[5]everyone will be put to shame
   because of a people useless to them,
who bring neither help nor advantage,
   but only shame and disgrace."

[6]A prophecy concerning the animals of the
Negev:

Through a land of hardship and distress,
   of lions and lionesses,
   of adders and darting snakes,
the envoys carry their riches on donkeys'
      backs,
   their treasures on the humps of camels,
to that unprofitable nation,
[7]   to Egypt, whose help is utterly useless.
Therefore I call her
   Rahab the Do-Nothing.

[8]Go now, write it on a tablet for them,
   inscribe it on a scroll,

---

[a] 13 Hebrew; Septuagint *They worship me in vain; / their
teachings are merely human rules*

Strategic Planning: Where God Fits In

Isaiah 30:1–5

Leaders and organizations constantly make plans. This is one reason why leaders are in demand; they plan for and negotiate the future. Yet Isaiah issues a warning to every leader who develops plans without asking if they fit the mind of God.

Leaders must remember just how tentative strategic plans need to be. No one knows the future except God. Keep in mind the following equation as you plan:

Our Preparation + God's Providence = Success

Leaders must constantly ask if their plans fit God's revealed will for them and their organization. Then they must ask if their plans remain relevant to the needs of their mission, their values, their vision, and their long-range objectives. Finally, they need to ask if their plans fit the needs of their culture and time. This makes for wise leadership and strategic planning.

that for the days to come
 it may be an everlasting witness.
⁹For these are rebellious people, deceitful
   children,
 children unwilling to listen to the LORD's
   instruction.
¹⁰They say to the seers,
   "See no more visions!"
 and to the prophets,
   "Give us no more visions of what is right!
 Tell us pleasant things,
   prophesy illusions.
¹¹Leave this way,
   get off this path,
 and stop confronting us
   with the Holy One of Israel!"

¹²Therefore this is what the Holy One of Israel says:

"Because you have rejected this message,
   relied on oppression
 and depended on deceit,
¹³this sin will become for you
   like a high wall, cracked and bulging,
   that collapses suddenly, in an instant.
¹⁴It will break in pieces like pottery,
   shattered so mercilessly
 that among its pieces not a fragment will be
   found
   for taking coals from a hearth
   or scooping water out of a cistern."

¹⁵This is what the Sovereign LORD, the Holy One of Israel, says:

"In repentance and rest is your salvation,
   in quietness and trust is your strength,
 but you would have none of it.

¹⁶You said, 'No, we will flee on horses.'
   Therefore you will flee!
 You said, 'We will ride off on swift horses.'
   Therefore your pursuers will be swift!
¹⁷A thousand will flee
   at the threat of one;
 at the threat of five
   you will all flee away,
 till you are left
   like a flagstaff on a mountaintop,
   like a banner on a hill."

¹⁸Yet the LORD longs to be gracious to you;
   therefore he will rise up to show you
   compassion.
 For the LORD is a God of justice.
   Blessed are all who wait for him!

¹⁹People of Zion, who live in Jerusalem, you will weep no more. How gracious he will be when you cry for help! As soon as he hears, he will answer you. ²⁰Although the Lord gives you the bread of adversity and the water of affliction, your teachers will be hidden no more; with your own eyes you will see them. ²¹Whether you turn to the right or to the left, your ears will hear a voice behind you, saying, "This is the way; walk in it." ²²Then you will desecrate your idols overlaid with silver and your images covered with gold; you will throw them away like a menstrual cloth and say to them, "Away with you!"

²³He will also send you rain for the seed you sow in the ground, and the food that comes from the land will be rich and plentiful. In that day your cattle will graze in broad meadows. ²⁴The oxen and donkeys that work the soil will eat fodder and mash, spread out with fork and

shovel. [25]In the day of great slaughter, when the towers fall, streams of water will flow on every high mountain and every lofty hill. [26]The moon will shine like the sun, and the sunlight will be seven times brighter, like the light of seven full days, when the LORD binds up the bruises of his people and heals the wounds he inflicted.

[27]See, the Name of the LORD comes from afar,
  with burning anger and dense clouds of
    smoke;
his lips are full of wrath,
  and his tongue is a consuming fire.
[28]His breath is like a rushing torrent,
  rising up to the neck.
He shakes the nations in the sieve of
    destruction;
  he places in the jaws of the peoples
  a bit that leads them astray.
[29]And you will sing
  as on the night you celebrate a holy festival;
your hearts will rejoice
  as when people playing pipes go up
to the mountain of the LORD,
  to the Rock of Israel.
[30]The LORD will cause people to hear his
    majestic voice
  and will make them see his arm coming
    down
with raging anger and consuming fire,
  with cloudburst, thunderstorm and hail.
[31]The voice of the LORD will shatter Assyria;
  with his rod he will strike them down.
[32]Every stroke the LORD lays on them
  with his punishing club
will be to the music of timbrels and harps,
  as he fights them in battle with the blows
    of his arm.
[33]Topheth has long been prepared;
  it has been made ready for the king.
Its fire pit has been made deep and wide,
  with an abundance of fire and wood;
the breath of the LORD,
  like a stream of burning sulfur,
  sets it ablaze.

Woe to Those Who Rely on Egypt

31 Woe to those who go down to Egypt for
    help,
  who rely on horses,
who trust in the multitude of their chariots
  and in the great strength of their
    horsemen,
but do not look to the Holy One of Israel,
  or seek help from the LORD.

[2]Yet he too is wise and can bring disaster;
  he does not take back his words.
He will rise up against that wicked nation,
  against those who help evildoers.
[3]But the Egyptians are mere mortals and not
    God;
  their horses are flesh and not spirit.
When the LORD stretches out his hand,
  those who help will stumble,
  those who are helped will fall;
  all will perish together.

[4]This is what the LORD says to me:

"As a lion growls,
  a great lion over its prey—
and though a whole band of shepherds
  is called together against it,
it is not frightened by their shouts
  or disturbed by their clamor—
so the LORD Almighty will come down
  to do battle on Mount Zion and on its
    heights.
[5]Like birds hovering overhead,
  the LORD Almighty will shield Jerusalem;
he will shield it and deliver it,
  he will 'pass over' it and will rescue it."

[6]Return, you Israelites, to the One you have so greatly revolted against. [7]For in that day every one of you will reject the idols of silver and gold your sinful hands have made.

[8]"Assyria will fall by no human sword;
  a sword, not of mortals, will devour them.
They will flee before the sword
  and their young men will be put to forced
    labor.
[9]Their stronghold will fall because of terror;
  at the sight of the battle standard their
    commanders will panic,"
declares the LORD,
  whose fire is in Zion,
  whose furnace is in Jerusalem.

The Kingdom of Righteousness

32 See, a king will reign in righteousness
    and rulers will rule with justice.
[2]Each one will be like a shelter from the wind
  and a refuge from the storm,
like streams of water in the desert
  and the shadow of a great rock in a thirsty
    land.
[3]Then the eyes of those who see will no longer
    be closed,
  and the ears of those who hear will listen.

4 The fearful heart will know and understand,
　　and the stammering tongue will be fluent
　　　and clear.
5 No longer will the fool be called noble
　　nor the scoundrel be highly respected.
6 For fools speak folly,
　　their hearts are bent on evil:
　They practice ungodliness
　　and spread error concerning the LORD;
　the hungry they leave empty
　　and from the thirsty they withhold water.
7 Scoundrels use wicked methods,
　　they make up evil schemes
　to destroy the poor with lies,
　　even when the plea of the needy is just.
8 But the noble make noble plans,
　　and by noble deeds they stand.

The Women of Jerusalem

9 You women who are so complacent,
　　rise up and listen to me;
　you daughters who feel secure,
　　hear what I have to say!
10 In little more than a year
　　you who feel secure will tremble;
　the grape harvest will fail,
　　and the harvest of fruit will not come.
11 Tremble, you complacent women;
　　shudder, you daughters who feel secure!
　Strip off your fine clothes
　　and wrap yourselves in rags.
12 Beat your breasts for the pleasant fields,
　　for the fruitful vines
13 and for the land of my people,
　　a land overgrown with thorns and briers —
　yes, mourn for all houses of merriment
　　and for this city of revelry.
14 The fortress will be abandoned,
　　the noisy city deserted;
　citadel and watchtower will become a
　　wasteland forever,
　　the delight of donkeys, a pasture for
　　　flocks,
15 till the Spirit is poured on us from on high,
　　and the desert becomes a fertile field,
　　and the fertile field seems like a forest.
16 The LORD's justice will dwell in the desert,
　　his righteousness live in the fertile field.
17 The fruit of that righteousness will be peace;
　　its effect will be quietness and confidence
　　　forever.
18 My people will live in peaceful dwelling
　　　places,
　　in secure homes,
　　in undisturbed places of rest.

19 Though hail flattens the forest
　　and the city is leveled completely,
20 how blessed you will be,
　　sowing your seed by every stream,
　　and letting your cattle and donkeys range
　　　free.

Distress and Help

33 Woe to you, destroyer,
　　you who have not been destroyed!
　Woe to you, betrayer,
　　you who have not been betrayed!
　When you stop destroying,
　　you will be destroyed;
　when you stop betraying,
　　you will be betrayed.

2 LORD, be gracious to us;
　　we long for you.
　Be our strength every morning,
　　our salvation in time of distress.
3 At the uproar of your army, the peoples flee;
　　when you rise up, the nations scatter.
4 Your plunder, O nations, is harvested as by
　　　young locusts;
　　like a swarm of locusts people pounce on
　　　it.

5 The LORD is exalted, for he dwells on high;
　　he will fill Zion with his justice and
　　　righteousness.
6 He will be the sure foundation for your
　　　times,
　　a rich store of salvation and wisdom and
　　　knowledge;
　　the fear of the LORD is the key to this
　　　treasure.[a]

7 Look, their brave men cry aloud in the
　　　streets;
　　the envoys of peace weep bitterly.
8 The highways are deserted,
　　no travelers are on the roads.
　The treaty is broken,
　　its witnesses[b] are despised,
　　no one is respected.
9 The land dries up and wastes away,
　　Lebanon is ashamed and withers;
　Sharon is like the Arabah,
　　and Bashan and Carmel drop their leaves.

10 "Now will I arise," says the LORD.
　　"Now will I be exalted;
　　now will I be lifted up.

---

[a] 6 Or is a treasure from him　　[b] 8 Dead Sea Scrolls;
Masoretic Text / the cities

11 You conceive chaff,
　　you give birth to straw;
　　your breath is a fire that consumes you.
12 The peoples will be burned to ashes;
　　like cut thornbushes they will be set
　　　ablaze."

13 You who are far away, hear what I have
　　　done;
　　you who are near, acknowledge my power!
14 The sinners in Zion are terrified;
　　trembling grips the godless:
　　"Who of us can dwell with the consuming
　　　fire?
　　Who of us can dwell with everlasting
　　　burning?"
15 Those who walk righteously
　　and speak what is right,
　　who reject gain from extortion
　　　and keep their hands from accepting
　　　bribes,
　　who stop their ears against plots of murder
　　　and shut their eyes against contemplating
　　　evil —
16 they are the ones who will dwell on the
　　　heights,
　　whose refuge will be the mountain
　　　fortress.
　　Their bread will be supplied,
　　and water will not fail them.

17 Your eyes will see the king in his beauty
　　and view a land that stretches afar.

18 In your thoughts you will ponder the former
　　　terror:
　　"Where is that chief officer?
　　Where is the one who took the revenue?
　　Where is the officer in charge of the
　　　towers?"
19 You will see those arrogant people no more,
　　people whose speech is obscure,
　　whose language is strange and
　　　incomprehensible.

20 Look on Zion, the city of our festivals;
　　your eyes will see Jerusalem,
　　a peaceful abode, a tent that will not be
　　　moved;
　　its stakes will never be pulled up,
　　nor any of its ropes broken.
21 There the LORD will be our Mighty One.
　　It will be like a place of broad rivers and
　　　streams.
　　No galley with oars will ride them,
　　no mighty ship will sail them.
22 For the LORD is our judge,
　　the LORD is our lawgiver,
　　the LORD is our king;
　　it is he who will save us.

23 Your rigging hangs loose:
　　The mast is not held secure,
　　the sail is not spread.
　　Then an abundance of spoils will be
　　　divided
　　and even the lame will carry off plunder.

The Law of Solid Ground: Leaders Must Earn Trust

Isaiah 33:14–16

Who can stand up under the purification process of God? Who can remain unchanged through the fire of God?

That's the question Isaiah asks and then answers. He lays out a list of traits for the kind of people who can stand in a crisis. Ponder his description:

1. *Integrity:* The leader's life and words match (v. 15).

2. *Justice:* The leader rejects dishonest gain (v. 15).

3. *Convictions:* The leader's values won't allow him to accept bribes (v. 15).

4. *Positive focus:* The leader refuses to dwell on destructive issues (v. 15).

5. *Pure:* The leader disciplines his or her mind to remain clean and pure (v. 15).

6. *Secure:* The leader is firm, stable in his identity and source of strength (v. 16).

Characteristics like these earn the trust of others. When leaders possess them, they feel secure enough to develop others, rather than destroy them. Remember, only secure leaders empower others.

24 No one living in Zion will say, "I am ill";
    and the sins of those who dwell there will
      be forgiven.

Judgment Against the Nations

34 Come near, you nations, and listen;
    pay attention, you peoples!
Let the earth hear, and all that is in it,
    the world, and all that comes out of it!
2 The LORD is angry with all nations;
    his wrath is on all their armies.
He will totally destroy[a] them,
    he will give them over to slaughter.
3 Their slain will be thrown out,
    their dead bodies will stink;
    the mountains will be soaked with their
      blood.
4 All the stars in the sky will be dissolved
    and the heavens rolled up like a scroll;
all the starry host will fall
    like withered leaves from the vine,
    like shriveled figs from the fig tree.

5 My sword has drunk its fill in the heavens;
    see, it descends in judgment on Edom,
    the people I have totally destroyed.
6 The sword of the LORD is bathed in blood,
    it is covered with fat—
the blood of lambs and goats,
    fat from the kidneys of rams.
For the LORD has a sacrifice in Bozrah
    and a great slaughter in the land of Edom.
7 And the wild oxen will fall with them,
    the bull calves and the great bulls.
Their land will be drenched with blood,
    and the dust will be soaked with fat.

8 For the LORD has a day of vengeance,
    a year of retribution, to uphold Zion's
      cause.
9 Edom's streams will be turned into pitch,
    her dust into burning sulfur;
    her land will become blazing pitch!
10 It will not be quenched night or day;
    its smoke will rise forever.
From generation to generation it will lie
      desolate;
    no one will ever pass through it again.
11 The desert owl[b] and screech owl[b] will
      possess it;
    the great owl[b] and the raven will nest
      there.
God will stretch out over Edom
    the measuring line of chaos
    and the plumb line of desolation.

12 Her nobles will have nothing there to be
      called a kingdom,
    all her princes will vanish away.
13 Thorns will overrun her citadels,
    nettles and brambles her strongholds.
She will become a haunt for jackals,
    a home for owls.
14 Desert creatures will meet with hyenas,
    and wild goats will bleat to each other;
there the night creatures will also lie down
    and find for themselves places of rest.
15 The owl will nest there and lay eggs,
    she will hatch them, and care for her
      young
    under the shadow of her wings;
there also the falcons will gather,
    each with its mate.

16 Look in the scroll of the LORD and read:

None of these will be missing,
    not one will lack her mate.
For it is his mouth that has given the order,
    and his Spirit will gather them together.
17 He allots their portions;
    his hand distributes them by measure.
They will possess it forever
    and dwell there from generation to
      generation.

Joy of the Redeemed

35 The desert and the parched land will be
      glad;
    the wilderness will rejoice and blossom.
Like the crocus, 2 it will burst into bloom;
    it will rejoice greatly and shout for joy.
The glory of Lebanon will be given to it,
    the splendor of Carmel and Sharon;
they will see the glory of the LORD,
    the splendor of our God.

3 Strengthen the feeble hands,
    steady the knees that give way;
4 say to those with fearful hearts,
    "Be strong, do not fear;
your God will come,
    he will come with vengeance;
with divine retribution
    he will come to save you."

5 Then will the eyes of the blind be opened
    and the ears of the deaf unstopped.

---

a 2 The Hebrew term refers to the irrevocable giving over of
things or persons to the LORD, often by totally destroying them;
also in verse 5.   b 11 The precise identification of these birds
is uncertain.

⁶Then will the lame leap like a deer,
  and the mute tongue shout for joy.
Water will gush forth in the wilderness
  and streams in the desert.
⁷The burning sand will become a pool,
  the thirsty ground bubbling springs.
In the haunts where jackals once lay,
  grass and reeds and papyrus will grow.

⁸And a highway will be there;
  it will be called the Way of Holiness;
  it will be for those who walk on that Way.
The unclean will not journey on it;
  wicked fools will not go about on it.
⁹No lion will be there,
  nor any ravenous beast;
  they will not be found there.
But only the redeemed will walk there,
¹⁰ and those the Lord has rescued will return.
They will enter Zion with singing;
  everlasting joy will crown their heads.
Gladness and joy will overtake them,
  and sorrow and sighing will flee away.

Sennacherib Threatens Jerusalem

36 In the fourteenth year of King Hezekiah's reign, Sennacherib king of Assyria attacked all the fortified cities of Judah and captured them. ²Then the king of Assyria sent his field commander with a large army from Lachish to King Hezekiah at Jerusalem. When the commander stopped at the aqueduct of the Upper Pool, on the road to the Launderer's Field, ³Eliakim son of Hilkiah the palace administrator, Shebna the secretary, and Joah son of Asaph the recorder went out to him.

⁴The field commander said to them, "Tell Hezekiah:

"'This is what the great king, the king of Assyria, says: On what are you basing this confidence of yours? ⁵You say you have counsel and might for war—but you speak only empty words. On whom are you depending, that you rebel against me? ⁶Look, I know you are depending on Egypt, that splintered reed of a staff, which pierces the hand of anyone who leans on it! Such is Pharaoh king of Egypt to all who depend on him. ⁷But if you say to me, "We are depending on the Lord our God"—isn't he the one whose high places and altars Hezekiah removed, saying to Judah and Jerusalem, "You must worship before this altar"?

⁸"'Come now, make a bargain with my master, the king of Assyria: I will give you two thousand horses—if you can put riders on them! ⁹How then can you repulse one officer of the least of my master's officials, even though you are depending on Egypt for chariots and horsemen[a]? ¹⁰Furthermore, have I come to attack and destroy this land without the Lord? The Lord himself told me to march against this country and destroy it.'"

¹¹Then Eliakim, Shebna and Joah said to the field commander, "Please speak to your servants in Aramaic, since we understand it. Don't speak to us in Hebrew in the hearing of the people on the wall."

¹²But the commander replied, "Was it only to your master and you that my master sent me to say these things, and not to the people sitting on the wall—who, like you, will have to eat their own excrement and drink their own urine?"

¹³Then the commander stood and called out in Hebrew, "Hear the words of the great king, the king of Assyria! ¹⁴This is what the king says: Do not let Hezekiah deceive you. He cannot deliver you! ¹⁵Do not let Hezekiah persuade you to trust in the Lord when he says, 'The Lord will surely deliver us; this city will not be given into the hand of the king of Assyria.'

¹⁶"Do not listen to Hezekiah. This is what the king of Assyria says: Make peace with me and come out to me. Then each of you will eat fruit from your own vine and fig tree and drink water from your own cistern, ¹⁷until I come and take you to a land like your own—a land of grain and new wine, a land of bread and vineyards.

¹⁸"Do not let Hezekiah mislead you when he says, 'The Lord will deliver us.' Have the gods of any nations ever delivered their lands from the hand of the king of Assyria? ¹⁹Where are the gods of Hamath and Arpad? Where are the gods of Sepharvaim? Have they rescued Samaria from my hand? ²⁰Who of all the gods of these countries have been able to save their lands from me? How then can the Lord deliver Jerusalem from my hand?"

²¹But the people remained silent and said nothing in reply, because the king had commanded, "Do not answer him."

²²Then Eliakim son of Hilkiah the palace administrator, Shebna the secretary and Joah son of Asaph the recorder went to Hezekiah, with their clothes torn, and told him what the field commander had said.

ᵃ 9 Or *charioteers*

Jerusalem's Deliverance Foretold

37 When King Hezekiah heard this, he tore his clothes and put on sackcloth and went into the temple of the LORD. [2] He sent Eliakim the palace administrator, Shebna the secretary, and the leading priests, all wearing sackcloth, to the prophet Isaiah son of Amoz. [3] They told him, "This is what Hezekiah says: This day is a day of distress and rebuke and disgrace, as when children come to the moment of birth and there is no strength to deliver them. [4] It may be that the LORD your God will hear the words of the field commander, whom his master, the king of Assyria, has sent to ridicule the living God, and that he will rebuke him for the words the LORD your God has heard. Therefore pray for the remnant that still survives."

[5] When King Hezekiah's officials came to Isaiah, [6] Isaiah said to them, "Tell your master, 'This is what the LORD says: Do not be afraid of what you have heard—those words with which the underlings of the king of Assyria have blasphemed me. [7] Listen! When he hears a certain report, I will make him want to return to his own country, and there I will have him cut down with the sword.'"

[8] When the field commander heard that the king of Assyria had left Lachish, he withdrew and found the king fighting against Libnah.

[9] Now Sennacherib received a report that Tirhakah, the king of Cush,[a] was marching out to fight against him. When he heard it, he sent messengers to Hezekiah with this word: [10] "Say to Hezekiah king of Judah: Do not let the god you depend on deceive you when he says, 'Jerusalem will not be given into the hands of the king of Assyria.' [11] Surely you have heard what the kings of Assyria have done to all the countries, destroying them completely. And will you be delivered? [12] Did the gods of the nations that were destroyed by my predecessors deliver them—the gods of Gozan, Harran, Rezeph and the people of Eden who were in Tel Assar? [13] Where is the king of Hamath or the king of Arpad? Where are the kings of Lair, Sepharvaim, Hena and Ivvah?"

Hezekiah's Prayer

[14] Hezekiah received the letter from the messengers and read it. Then he went up to the temple of the LORD and spread it out before the LORD. [15] And Hezekiah prayed to the LORD: [16] "LORD Almighty, the God of Israel, enthroned between the cherubim, you alone are God over all the kingdoms of the earth. You have made heaven and earth. [17] Give ear, LORD, and hear; open your eyes, LORD, and see; listen to all the words Sennacherib has sent to ridicule the living God.

[18] "It is true, LORD, that the Assyrian kings have laid waste all these peoples and their lands. [19] They have thrown their gods into the fire and destroyed them, for they were not gods but only wood and stone, fashioned by human hands. [20] Now, LORD our God, deliver us from his hand, so that all the kingdoms of the earth may know that you, LORD, are the only God.[b]"

Sennacherib's Fall

[21] Then Isaiah son of Amoz sent a message to Hezekiah: "This is what the LORD, the God of Israel, says: Because you have prayed to me concerning Sennacherib king of Assyria, [22] this is the word the LORD has spoken against him:

"Virgin Daughter Zion
    despises and mocks you.
Daughter Jerusalem
    tosses her head as you flee.
[23] Who is it you have ridiculed and
    blasphemed?
    Against whom have you raised your
      voice
and lifted your eyes in pride?
    Against the Holy One of Israel!
[24] By your messengers
    you have ridiculed the Lord.
And you have said,
    'With my many chariots
I have ascended the heights of the
      mountains,
    the utmost heights of Lebanon.
I have cut down its tallest cedars,
    the choicest of its junipers.
I have reached its remotest heights,
    the finest of its forests.
[25] I have dug wells in foreign lands[c]
    and drunk the water there.
With the soles of my feet
    I have dried up all the streams of Egypt.'

[26] "Have you not heard?
    Long ago I ordained it.
In days of old I planned it;
    now I have brought it to pass,
that you have turned fortified cities
    into piles of stone.

---

[a] 9 That is, the upper Nile region   [b] 20 Dead Sea Scrolls (see also 2 Kings 19:19); Masoretic Text *you alone are the LORD*
[c] 25 Dead Sea Scrolls (see also 2 Kings 19:24); Masoretic Text does not have *in foreign lands*.

27 Their people, drained of power,
  are dismayed and put to shame.
They are like plants in the field,
  like tender green shoots,
like grass sprouting on the roof,
  scorched[a] before it grows up.

28 "But I know where you are
  and when you come and go
  and how you rage against me.
29 Because you rage against me
  and because your insolence has reached
    my ears,
I will put my hook in your nose
  and my bit in your mouth,
and I will make you return
  by the way you came.

30 "This will be the sign for you, Hezekiah:

"This year you will eat what grows by itself,
  and the second year what springs from
    that.
But in the third year sow and reap,
  plant vineyards and eat their fruit.
31 Once more a remnant of the kingdom of
    Judah
  will take root below and bear fruit above.
32 For out of Jerusalem will come a remnant,
  and out of Mount Zion a band of
    survivors.
The zeal of the LORD Almighty
  will accomplish this.

33 "Therefore this is what the LORD says concerning the king of Assyria:

"He will not enter this city
  or shoot an arrow here.
He will not come before it with shield
  or build a siege ramp against it.
34 By the way that he came he will return;
  he will not enter this city,"
                              declares the LORD.
35 "I will defend this city and save it,
  for my sake and for the sake of David my
    servant!"

36 Then the angel of the LORD went out and put to death a hundred and eighty-five thousand in the Assyrian camp. When the people got up the next morning—there were all the dead bodies! **37** So Sennacherib king of Assyria broke camp and withdrew. He returned to Nineveh and stayed there.

38 One day, while he was worshiping in the temple of his god Nisrok, his sons Adrammelek and Sharezer killed him with the sword, and

---

The Law of Navigation: The Role of Planning and Praying

Isaiah 37:1–37

King Hezekiah provides an example of a leader who does what is humanly possible, then leans on God for the outcome. God had to do what the king could not do. A place exists for both preparation and prayer. To employ only one is naïve and incomplete.

---

they escaped to the land of Ararat. And Esarhaddon his son succeeded him as king.

Hezekiah's Illness

38 In those days Hezekiah became ill and was at the point of death. The prophet Isaiah son of Amoz went to him and said, "This is what the LORD says: Put your house in order, because you are going to die; you will not recover."

2 Hezekiah turned his face to the wall and prayed to the LORD, **3** "Remember, LORD, how I have walked before you faithfully and with wholehearted devotion and have done what is good in your eyes." And Hezekiah wept bitterly.

4 Then the word of the LORD came to Isaiah: **5** "Go and tell Hezekiah, 'This is what the LORD, the God of your father David, says: I have heard your prayer and seen your tears; I will add fifteen years to your life. **6** And I will deliver you and this city from the hand of the king of Assyria. I will defend this city.

7 "This is the LORD's sign to you that the LORD will do what he has promised: **8** I will make the shadow cast by the sun go back the ten steps it has gone down on the stairway of Ahaz.'" So the sunlight went back the ten steps it had gone down.

9 A writing of Hezekiah king of Judah after his illness and recovery:

10 I said, "In the prime of my life
  must I go through the gates of death
  and be robbed of the rest of my years?"

---

[a] **27** Some manuscripts of the Masoretic Text, Dead Sea Scrolls and some Septuagint manuscripts (see also 2 Kings 19:26); most manuscripts of the Masoretic Text *roof / and terraced fields*

11 I said, "I will not again see the LORD himself
    in the land of the living;
no longer will I look on my fellow man,
    or be with those who now dwell in this
        world.
12 Like a shepherd's tent my house
    has been pulled down and taken from me.
Like a weaver I have rolled up my life,
    and he has cut me off from the loom;
    day and night you made an end of me.
13 I waited patiently till dawn,
    but like a lion he broke all my bones;
    day and night you made an end of me.
14 I cried like a swift or thrush,
    I moaned like a mourning dove.
My eyes grew weak as I looked to the
        heavens.
    I am being threatened; Lord, come to my
        aid!"

15 But what can I say?
    He has spoken to me, and he himself has
        done this.
    I will walk humbly all my years
    because of this anguish of my soul.
16 Lord, by such things people live;
    and my spirit finds life in them too.
You restored me to health
    and let me live.
17 Surely it was for my benefit
    that I suffered such anguish.

In your love you kept me
    from the pit of destruction;
you have put all my sins
    behind your back.
18 For the grave cannot praise you,
    death cannot sing your praise;
those who go down to the pit
    cannot hope for your faithfulness.
19 The living, the living — they praise you,
    as I am doing today;
parents tell their children
    about your faithfulness.

20 The LORD will save me,
    and we will sing with stringed instruments
all the days of our lives
    in the temple of the LORD.

21 Isaiah had said, "Prepare a poultice of figs
and apply it to the boil, and he will recover."
22 Hezekiah had asked, "What will be the sign
that I will go up to the temple of the LORD?"

Envoys From Babylon

39 At that time Marduk-Baladan son of
Baladan king of Babylon sent Hezekiah
letters and a gift, because he had heard of his
illness and recovery. 2 Hezekiah received the envoys gladly and showed them what was in his
storehouses — the silver, the gold, the spices,
the fine olive oil — his entire armory and ev-

HEZEKIAH

PROFILE in leadership

The Art of Thanksgiving
Isaiah 38:9–20

Nothing brings out gratefulness like a reprieve from imminent death.

When King Hezekiah of Judah, a good and godly king, heard from the prophet Isaiah that he was about to die, he immediately turned to the God he had faithfully served. He begged God for an extension of life—and the Lord granted him an additional 15 years. When Hezekiah learned that the Lord would lengthen his life, he did what any godly leader would do: He thanked and praised his God. Upon his recovery, he wrote to the Lord a poem of thanksgiving and praise for the good he had done.

As the godly king meditated on God's goodness, he realized that the Lord had used even his sickness for his good. In verse 17 he wrote, "Surely it was for my benefit that I suffered such anguish"—the same sentiment expressed many years before by his revered ancestor, David: "It was good for me to be afflicted so that I might learn your decrees" (Ps 119:71).

Hezekiah's hymn of gratitude not only thanked the Lord for sparing his life, it also expressed his commitment to "sing with stringed instruments all the days of our lives" (Isa 38:20). He realized that expressing gratitude to God ought to be more than a onetime event; it must be a lifestyle.

erything found among his treasures. There was nothing in his palace or in all his kingdom that Hezekiah did not show them.

[3] Then Isaiah the prophet went to King Hezekiah and asked, "What did those men say, and where did they come from?"

"From a distant land," Hezekiah replied. "They came to me from Babylon."

[4] The prophet asked, "What did they see in your palace?"

"They saw everything in my palace," Hezekiah said. "There is nothing among my treasures that I did not show them."

[5] Then Isaiah said to Hezekiah, "Hear the word of the LORD Almighty: [6] The time will surely come when everything in your palace, and all that your predecessors have stored up until this day, will be carried off to Babylon. Nothing will be left, says the LORD. [7] And some of your descendants, your own flesh and blood who will be born to you, will be taken away, and they will become eunuchs in the palace of the king of Babylon."

[8] "The word of the LORD you have spoken is good," Hezekiah replied. For he thought, "There will be peace and security in my lifetime."

Comfort for God's People

40 Comfort, comfort my people,
    says your God.
[2] Speak tenderly to Jerusalem,
    and proclaim to her
that her hard service has been completed,
    that her sin has been paid for,
that she has received from the LORD's hand
    double for all her sins.

[3] A voice of one calling:
"In the wilderness prepare
    the way for the LORD[a];
make straight in the desert
    a highway for our God.[b]
[4] Every valley shall be raised up,
    every mountain and hill made low;
the rough ground shall become level,
    the rugged places a plain.
[5] And the glory of the LORD will be revealed,
    and all people will see it together.
                For the mouth of the LORD
                        has spoken."

[6] A voice says, "Cry out."
    And I said, "What shall I cry?"

"All people are like grass,
    and all their faithfulness is like the
        flowers of the field.

[7] The grass withers and the flowers fall,
    because the breath of the LORD blows on
        them.
    Surely the people are grass.
[8] The grass withers and the flowers fall,
    but the word of our God endures forever."

[9] You who bring good news to Zion,
    go up on a high mountain.
You who bring good news to Jerusalem,[c]
    lift up your voice with a shout,
lift it up, do not be afraid;
    say to the towns of Judah,
    "Here is your God!"
[10] See, the Sovereign LORD comes with power,
    and he rules with a mighty arm.
See, his reward is with him,
    and his recompense accompanies him.
[11] He tends his flock like a shepherd:
    He gathers the lambs in his arms
and carries them close to his heart;
    he gently leads those that have young.

[12] Who has measured the waters in the hollow
        of his hand,
    or with the breadth of his hand marked
        off the heavens?
Who has held the dust of the earth in a
        basket,
    or weighed the mountains on the scales
    and the hills in a balance?
[13] Who can fathom the Spirit[d] of the LORD,
    or instruct the LORD as his counselor?
[14] Whom did the LORD consult to enlighten
        him,
    and who taught him the right way?
Who was it that taught him knowledge,
    or showed him the path of understanding?

[15] Surely the nations are like a drop in a bucket;
    they are regarded as dust on the scales;
he weighs the islands as though they were
    fine dust.
[16] Lebanon is not sufficient for altar fires,
    nor its animals enough for burnt
        offerings.
[17] Before him all the nations are as nothing;
    they are regarded by him as worthless
    and less than nothing.

[18] With whom, then, will you compare God?
    To what image will you liken him?

---

[a] 3 Or A voice of one calling in the wilderness: / "Prepare the way for the LORD   [b] 3 Hebrew; Septuagint make straight the paths of our God   [c] 9 Or Zion, bringer of good news, / go up on a high mountain. / Jerusalem, bringer of good news   [d] 13 Or mind

¹⁹ As for an idol, a metalworker casts it,
     and a goldsmith overlays it with gold
     and fashions silver chains for it.
²⁰ A person too poor to present such an
       offering
     selects wood that will not rot;
they look for a skilled worker
     to set up an idol that will not topple.

²¹ Do you not know?
     Have you not heard?
Has it not been told you from the beginning?
     Have you not understood since the earth
       was founded?
²² He sits enthroned above the circle of the earth,
     and its people are like grasshoppers.
He stretches out the heavens like a canopy,
     and spreads them out like a tent to live in.
²³ He brings princes to naught
     and reduces the rulers of this world to
       nothing.
²⁴ No sooner are they planted,
     no sooner are they sown,
     no sooner do they take root in the ground,
than he blows on them and they wither,
     and a whirlwind sweeps them away like
       chaff.

²⁵ "To whom will you compare me?
     Or who is my equal?" says the Holy One.
²⁶ Lift up your eyes and look to the heavens:
     Who created all these?

He who brings out the starry host one by one
     and calls forth each of them by name.
Because of his great power and mighty
       strength,
     not one of them is missing.

²⁷ Why do you complain, Jacob?
     Why do you say, Israel,
"My way is hidden from the LORD;
     my cause is disregarded by my God"?
²⁸ Do you not know?
     Have you not heard?
The LORD is the everlasting God,
     the Creator of the ends of the earth.
He will not grow tired or weary,
     and his understanding no one can fathom.
²⁹ He gives strength to the weary
     and increases the power of the weak.
³⁰ Even youths grow tired and weary,
     and young men stumble and fall;
³¹ but those who hope in the LORD
     will renew their strength.
They will soar on wings like eagles;
     they will run and not grow weary,
     they will walk and not be faint.

The Helper of Israel

41 "Be silent before me, you islands!
     Let the nations renew their strength!
Let them come forward and speak;
     let us meet together at the place of judgment.

The Model for Leadership

Isaiah 40:1–31

We must never forget that the greatest model for leadership always comes from the life of God himself. Isaiah 40 makes it clear that God, as the Ultimate Leader, models:

1. **Comfort and Security**
   God supplies comfort and cleansing to his people (vv. 1–2).

2. **Empowerment and Delegation**
   God makes the path straight for others, then has them speak his words (vv. 3–8).

3. **Shepherding and Direction**
   God proclaims good news and guides his people like a Shepherd (vv. 9–11).

4. **Power and Authority**
   No one can challenge God's strength. He is a Leader with unequaled power (vv. 12–17).

5. **Creator and Developer**
   God is the transcendent Leader who builds and develops others (vv. 21–26).

6. **Wise Counselor and Provider**
   God is the source for every need we may have (vv. 27–31).

2 "Who has stirred up one from the east,
    calling him in righteousness to his
        service[a]?
He hands nations over to him
    and subdues kings before him.
He turns them to dust with his sword,
    to windblown chaff with his bow.
3 He pursues them and moves on unscathed,
    by a path his feet have not traveled before.
4 Who has done this and carried it through,
    calling forth the generations from the
        beginning?
I, the LORD — with the first of them
    and with the last — I am he."

5 The islands have seen it and fear;
    the ends of the earth tremble.
They approach and come forward;
6   they help each other
    and say to their companions, "Be strong!"
7 The metalworker encourages the goldsmith,
    and the one who smooths with the
        hammer
    spurs on the one who strikes the anvil.
One says of the welding, "It is good."
    The other nails down the idol so it will not
        topple.

8 "But you, Israel, my servant,
    Jacob, whom I have chosen,
    you descendants of Abraham my friend,
9 I took you from the ends of the earth,
    from its farthest corners I called you.
I said, 'You are my servant';
    I have chosen you and have not rejected
        you.
10 So do not fear, for I am with you;
    do not be dismayed, for I am your God.
I will strengthen you and help you;
    I will uphold you with my righteous right
        hand.

11 "All who rage against you
    will surely be ashamed and disgraced;
those who oppose you
    will be as nothing and perish.
12 Though you search for your enemies,
    you will not find them.
Those who wage war against you
    will be as nothing at all.
13 For I am the LORD your God
    who takes hold of your right hand
and says to you, Do not fear;
    I will help you.
14 Do not be afraid, you worm Jacob,
    little Israel, do not fear,

for I myself will help you," declares the
    LORD,
    your Redeemer, the Holy One of Israel.
15 "See, I will make you into a threshing sledge,
    new and sharp, with many teeth.
You will thresh the mountains and crush
        them,
    and reduce the hills to chaff.
16 You will winnow them, the wind will pick
        them up,
    and a gale will blow them away.
But you will rejoice in the LORD
    and glory in the Holy One of Israel.

17 "The poor and needy search for water,
    but there is none;
    their tongues are parched with thirst.
But I the LORD will answer them;
    I, the God of Israel, will not forsake them.
18 I will make rivers flow on barren heights,
    and springs within the valleys.
I will turn the desert into pools of water,
    and the parched ground into springs.
19 I will put in the desert
    the cedar and the acacia, the myrtle and
        the olive.
I will set junipers in the wasteland,
    the fir and the cypress together,
20 so that people may see and know,
    may consider and understand,
that the hand of the LORD has done this,
    that the Holy One of Israel has created it.

21 "Present your case," says the LORD.
    "Set forth your arguments," says Jacob's
        King.
22 "Tell us, you idols,
    what is going to happen.
Tell us what the former things were,
    so that we may consider them
    and know their final outcome.
Or declare to us the things to come,
23   tell us what the future holds,
    so we may know that you are gods.
Do something, whether good or bad,
    so that we will be dismayed and filled
        with fear.
24 But you are less than nothing
    and your works are utterly worthless;
    whoever chooses you is detestable.

25 "I have stirred up one from the north, and he
        comes —
    one from the rising sun who calls on my
        name.

---

[a] 2 Or east, / whom victory meets at every step

He treads on rulers as if they were mortar,
as if he were a potter treading the clay.
²⁶ Who told of this from the beginning, so we
could know,
or beforehand, so we could say, 'He was
right'?
No one told of this,
no one foretold it,
no one heard any words from you.
²⁷ I was the first to tell Zion, 'Look, here they are!'
I gave to Jerusalem a messenger of good
news.
²⁸ I look but there is no one —
no one among the gods to give counsel,
no one to give answer when I ask them.
²⁹ See, they are all false!
Their deeds amount to nothing;
their images are but wind and confusion.

The Servant of the Lord

42 "Here is my servant, whom I uphold,
my chosen one in whom I delight;
I will put my Spirit on him,
and he will bring justice to the nations.
² He will not shout or cry out,
or raise his voice in the streets.
³ A bruised reed he will not break,
and a smoldering wick he will not snuff
out.
In faithfulness he will bring forth justice;
⁴   he will not falter or be discouraged
till he establishes justice on earth.
In his teaching the islands will put their
hope."

⁵ This is what God the Lord says —
the Creator of the heavens, who stretches
them out,
who spreads out the earth with all that
springs from it,
who gives breath to its people,
and life to those who walk on it:
⁶ "I, the Lord, have called you in
righteousness;
I will take hold of your hand.
I will keep you and will make you
to be a covenant for the people
and a light for the Gentiles,
⁷ to open eyes that are blind,
to free captives from prison
and to release from the dungeon those
who sit in darkness.

⁸ "I am the Lord; that is my name!
I will not yield my glory to another
or my praise to idols.

⁹ See, the former things have taken place,
and new things I declare;
before they spring into being
I announce them to you."

Song of Praise to the Lord

¹⁰ Sing to the Lord a new song,
his praise from the ends of the earth,
you who go down to the sea, and all that is
in it,
you islands, and all who live in them.
¹¹ Let the wilderness and its towns raise their
voices;
let the settlements where Kedar lives
rejoice.
Let the people of Sela sing for joy;
let them shout from the mountaintops.
¹² Let them give glory to the Lord
and proclaim his praise in the islands.
¹³ The Lord will march out like a champion,
like a warrior he will stir up his zeal;
with a shout he will raise the battle cry
and will triumph over his enemies.

¹⁴ "For a long time I have kept silent,
I have been quiet and held myself back.
But now, like a woman in childbirth,
I cry out, I gasp and pant.
¹⁵ I will lay waste the mountains and hills
and dry up all their vegetation;
I will turn rivers into islands
and dry up the pools.
¹⁶ I will lead the blind by ways they have not
known,
along unfamiliar paths I will guide them;
I will turn the darkness into light before
them
and make the rough places smooth.
These are the things I will do;
I will not forsake them.
¹⁷ But those who trust in idols,
who say to images, 'You are our gods,'
will be turned back in utter shame.

Israel Blind and Deaf

¹⁸ "Hear, you deaf;
look, you blind, and see!
¹⁹ Who is blind but my servant,
and deaf like the messenger I send?
Who is blind like the one in covenant with
me,
blind like the servant of the Lord?
²⁰ You have seen many things, but you pay no
attention;
your ears are open, but you do not listen."

21 It pleased the LORD
for the sake of his righteousness
to make his law great and glorious.
22 But this is a people plundered and looted,
all of them trapped in pits
or hidden away in prisons.
They have become plunder,
with no one to rescue them;
they have been made loot,
with no one to say, "Send them back."

23 Which of you will listen to this
or pay close attention in time to come?
24 Who handed Jacob over to become loot,
and Israel to the plunderers?
Was it not the LORD,
against whom we have sinned?
For they would not follow his ways;
they did not obey his law.
25 So he poured out on them his burning anger,
the violence of war.
It enveloped them in flames, yet they did not
understand;
it consumed them, but they did not take it
to heart.

Israel's Only Savior

43 But now, this is what the LORD says —
he who created you, Jacob,
he who formed you, Israel:
"Do not fear, for I have redeemed you;
I have summoned you by name; you are
mine.
2 When you pass through the waters,
I will be with you;
and when you pass through the rivers,
they will not sweep over you.
When you walk through the fire,
you will not be burned;
the flames will not set you ablaze.
3 For I am the LORD your God,
the Holy One of Israel, your Savior;
I give Egypt for your ransom,
Cush[a] and Seba in your stead.
4 Since you are precious and honored in my sight,
and because I love you,
I will give people in exchange for you,
nations in exchange for your life.
5 Do not be afraid, for I am with you;
I will bring your children from the east
and gather you from the west.
6 I will say to the north, 'Give them up!'
and to the south, 'Do not hold them back.'
Bring my sons from afar
and my daughters from the ends of the
earth —

The Law of Sacrifice

Isaiah 43:1–7

God, as the Ultimate Leader, consistently practices the Law of Sacrifice. Leaders will do the illogical and surrender valuable possessions in order to fulfill and capture their dream. Fortunately for us, we are God's dream. Only through the prophet Isaiah does God say directly to his people, "I love you."

7 everyone who is called by my name,
whom I created for my glory,
whom I formed and made."

8 Lead out those who have eyes but are blind,
who have ears but are deaf.
9 All the nations gather together
and the peoples assemble.
Which of their gods foretold this
and proclaimed to us the former things?
Let them bring in their witnesses to prove
they were right,
so that others may hear and say, "It is
true."
10 "You are my witnesses," declares the LORD,
"and my servant whom I have chosen,
so that you may know and believe me
and understand that I am he.
Before me no god was formed,
nor will there be one after me.
11 I, even I, am the LORD,
and apart from me there is no savior.
12 I have revealed and saved and proclaimed —
I, and not some foreign god among you.
You are my witnesses," declares the LORD,
"that I am God.
13 Yes, and from ancient days I am he.
No one can deliver out of my hand.
When I act, who can reverse it?"

God's Mercy and Israel's Unfaithfulness

14 This is what the LORD says —
your Redeemer, the Holy One of Israel:
"For your sake I will send to Babylon
and bring down as fugitives all the
Babylonians,[b]
in the ships in which they took pride.
15 I am the LORD, your Holy One,
Israel's Creator, your King."

---

[a] 3 That is, the upper Nile region   [b] 14 Or Chaldeans

16 This is what the LORD says—
    he who made a way through the sea,
    a path through the mighty waters,
17 who drew out the chariots and horses,
    the army and reinforcements together,
and they lay there, never to rise again,
    extinguished, snuffed out like a wick:
18 "Forget the former things;
    do not dwell on the past.
19 See, I am doing a new thing!
    Now it springs up; do you not perceive it?
I am making a way in the wilderness
    and streams in the wasteland.
20 The wild animals honor me,
    the jackals and the owls,
because I provide water in the wilderness
    and streams in the wasteland,
to give drink to my people, my chosen,
21   the people I formed for myself
    that they may proclaim my praise.

22 "Yet you have not called on me, Jacob,
    you have not wearied yourselves for[a] me,
    Israel.
23 You have not brought me sheep for burnt
    offerings,
    nor honored me with your sacrifices.
I have not burdened you with grain offerings
    nor wearied you with demands for
    incense.
24 You have not bought any fragrant calamus
    for me,
    or lavished on me the fat of your sacrifices.
But you have burdened me with your sins
    and wearied me with your offenses.

25 "I, even I, am he who blots out
    your transgressions, for my own sake,
    and remembers your sins no more.
26 Review the past for me,
    let us argue the matter together;
    state the case for your innocence.
27 Your first father sinned;
    those I sent to teach you rebelled against
    me.
28 So I disgraced the dignitaries of your temple;
    I consigned Jacob to destruction[b]
    and Israel to scorn.

Israel the Chosen

44 "But now listen, Jacob, my servant,
    Israel, whom I have chosen.
2 This is what the LORD says—
    he who made you, who formed you in the
    womb,
    and who will help you:

Do not be afraid, Jacob, my servant,
    Jeshurun,[c] whom I have chosen.
3 For I will pour water on the thirsty land,
    and streams on the dry ground;
I will pour out my Spirit on your offspring,
    and my blessing on your descendants.
4 They will spring up like grass in a meadow,
    like poplar trees by flowing streams.
5 Some will say, 'I belong to the LORD';
    others will call themselves by the name of
    Jacob;
still others will write on their hand, 'The
    LORD's,'
    and will take the name Israel.

The LORD, Not Idols

6 "This is what the LORD says—
    Israel's King and Redeemer, the LORD
    Almighty:
I am the first and I am the last;
    apart from me there is no God.
7 Who then is like me? Let him proclaim it.
    Let him declare and lay out before me
what has happened since I established my
    ancient people,
    and what is yet to come—
    yes, let them foretell what will come.
8 Do not tremble, do not be afraid.
    Did I not proclaim this and foretell it
    long ago?
You are my witnesses. Is there any God
    besides me?
    No, there is no other Rock; I know not
    one."

9 All who make idols are nothing,
    and the things they treasure are worthless.
Those who would speak up for them are
    blind;
    they are ignorant, to their own shame.
10 Who shapes a god and casts an idol,
    which can profit nothing?
11 People who do that will be put to shame;
    such craftsmen are only human beings.
Let them all come together and take their
    stand;
    they will be brought down to terror and
    shame.
12 The blacksmith takes a tool
    and works with it in the coals;

---

a 22 Or *Jacob; / surely you have grown weary of*   b 28 The
Hebrew term refers to the irrevocable giving over of things or
persons to the LORD, often by totally destroying them.
c 2 *Jeshurun* means *the upright one,* that is, Israel.

Revival Fire: Man-Made or God-Given?

Isaiah 44:1–8

What godly leader has no desire in their heart to see the fire of God? We all long for fire to descend from heaven to empower us to accomplish a great task. Sometimes, however, when it seems hard to wait for the "heavenly" fire, we resort to "homemade" fire. Consider four kinds of homemade fire:

1. **The fire of association:** We feel this fire when we're enjoying a revival atmosphere. It serves as a hot poker.

2. **The fire of yesterday:** This fire comes from hearing testimonies of saints who talk about the good old days.

3. **The fire of selfish desires:** This fire comes as a spark when we see how it will benefit me to serve God today.

4. **The fire of tradition:** This fire comes when we feel warm and comfortable with the way we've always done it.

So what distinguishes divine fire from man-made fire?

Man-Made Fires	God-Given Fires
1. Have a tendency to go out	1. Remain as long as our focus stays on him
2. Are not sufficient for today	2. Are more than enough to meet our needs
3. Are not contagious	3. Are contagious for those who see them

---

he shapes an idol with hammers,
    he forges it with the might of his arm.
He gets hungry and loses his strength;
    he drinks no water and grows faint.
[13] The carpenter measures with a line
    and makes an outline with a marker;
he roughs it out with chisels
    and marks it with compasses.
He shapes it in human form,
    human form in all its glory,
    that it may dwell in a shrine.
[14] He cut down cedars,
    or perhaps took a cypress or oak.
He let it grow among the trees of the forest,
    or planted a pine, and the rain made it
      grow.
[15] It is used as fuel for burning;
    some of it he takes and warms himself,
    he kindles a fire and bakes bread.
But he also fashions a god and worships it;
    he makes an idol and bows down to it.
[16] Half of the wood he burns in the fire;
    over it he prepares his meal,
    he roasts his meat and eats his fill.
He also warms himself and says,
    "Ah! I am warm; I see the fire."
[17] From the rest he makes a god, his idol;
    he bows down to it and worships.

He prays to it and says,
    "Save me! You are my god!"
[18] They know nothing, they understand
      nothing;
    their eyes are plastered over so they
      cannot see,
    and their minds closed so they cannot
      understand.
[19] No one stops to think,
    no one has the knowledge or
      understanding to say,
"Half of it I used for fuel;
    I even baked bread over its coals,
    I roasted meat and I ate.
Shall I make a detestable thing from what is
      left?
    Shall I bow down to a block of wood?"
[20] Such a person feeds on ashes; a deluded heart
      misleads him;
    he cannot save himself, or say,
    "Is not this thing in my right hand a lie?"
[21] "Remember these things, Jacob,
    for you, Israel, are my servant.
I have made you, you are my servant;
    Israel, I will not forget you.
[22] I have swept away your offenses like a cloud,
    your sins like the morning mist.

Return to me,
   for I have redeemed you."

23 Sing for joy, you heavens, for the LORD has
         done this;
   shout aloud, you earth beneath.
Burst into song, you mountains,
   you forests and all your trees,
for the LORD has redeemed Jacob,
   he displays his glory in Israel.

Jerusalem to Be Inhabited

24 "This is what the LORD says —
   your Redeemer, who formed you in the
         womb:

I am the LORD,
   the Maker of all things,
   who stretches out the heavens,
   who spreads out the earth by myself,
25 who foils the signs of false prophets
   and makes fools of diviners,
who overthrows the learning of the wise
   and turns it into nonsense,
26 who carries out the words of his servants
   and fulfills the predictions of his
         messengers,

who says of Jerusalem, 'It shall be inhabited,'
   of the towns of Judah, 'They shall be
         rebuilt,'
   and of their ruins, 'I will restore them,'
27 who says to the watery deep, 'Be dry,
   and I will dry up your streams,'
28 who says of Cyrus, 'He is my shepherd
   and will accomplish all that I please;
he will say of Jerusalem, "Let it be rebuilt,"
   and of the temple, "Let its foundations be
         laid."'

45 "This is what the LORD says to his
         anointed,
   to Cyrus, whose right hand I take hold of
to subdue nations before him
   and to strip kings of their armor,
to open doors before him
   so that gates will not be shut:
2 I will go before you
   and will level the mountains[a];
I will break down gates of bronze
   and cut through bars of iron.
3 I will give you hidden treasures,
   riches stored in secret places,
so that you may know that I am the LORD,
   the God of Israel, who summons you by
         name.

4 For the sake of Jacob my servant,
   of Israel my chosen,
I summon you by name
   and bestow on you a title of honor,
   though you do not acknowledge me.
5 I am the LORD, and there is no other;
   apart from me there is no God.
I will strengthen you,
   though you have not acknowledged me,
6 so that from the rising of the sun
   to the place of its setting
people may know there is none besides me.
   I am the LORD, and there is no other.
7 I form the light and create darkness,
   I bring prosperity and create disaster;
   I, the LORD, do all these things.

8 "You heavens above, rain down my
         righteousness;
   let the clouds shower it down.
Let the earth open wide,
   let salvation spring up,
let righteousness flourish with it;
   I, the LORD, have created it.

9 "Woe to those who quarrel with their Maker,
   those who are nothing but potsherds
   among the potsherds on the ground.
Does the clay say to the potter,
   'What are you making?'
Does your work say,
   'The potter has no hands'?
10 Woe to the one who says to a father,
   'What have you begotten?'
or to a mother,
   'What have you brought to birth?'

11 "This is what the LORD says —
   the Holy One of Israel, and its Maker:
Concerning things to come,
   do you question me about my children,
   or give me orders about the work of my
         hands?
12 It is I who made the earth
   and created mankind on it.
My own hands stretched out the heavens;
   I marshaled their starry hosts.
13 I will raise up Cyrus[b] in my righteousness:
   I will make all his ways straight.
He will rebuild my city
   and set my exiles free,
but not for a price or reward,
   says the LORD Almighty."

---

[a] 2 Dead Sea Scrolls and Septuagint; the meaning of the word
in the Masoretic Text is uncertain.   [b] 13 Hebrew him

¹⁴This is what the LORD says:

"The products of Egypt and the merchandise
    of Cush,ᵃ
  and those tall Sabeans—
they will come over to you
  and will be yours;
they will trudge behind you,
  coming over to you in chains.
They will bow down before you
  and plead with you, saying,
'Surely God is with you, and there is no
    other;
  there is no other god.'"

¹⁵Truly you are a God who has been hiding
    himself,
  the God and Savior of Israel.
¹⁶All the makers of idols will be put to shame
    and disgraced;
  they will go off into disgrace together.
¹⁷But Israel will be saved by the LORD
  with an everlasting salvation;
you will never be put to shame or disgraced,
  to ages everlasting.

¹⁸For this is what the LORD says—
  he who created the heavens,
    he is God;
he who fashioned and made the earth,
    he founded it;
he did not create it to be empty,
    but formed it to be inhabited—
he says:
"I am the LORD,
    and there is no other.
¹⁹I have not spoken in secret,
    from somewhere in a land of darkness;
I have not said to Jacob's descendants,
    'Seek me in vain.'
I, the LORD, speak the truth;
    I declare what is right.

²⁰"Gather together and come;
    assemble, you fugitives from the
      nations.
Ignorant are those who carry about idols of
      wood,
  who pray to gods that cannot save.
²¹Declare what is to be, present it—
    let them take counsel together.
Who foretold this long ago,
    who declared it from the distant past?
Was it not I, the LORD?
    And there is no God apart from me,
a righteous God and a Savior;
    there is none but me.

²²"Turn to me and be saved,
    all you ends of the earth;
  for I am God, and there is no other.
²³By myself I have sworn,
    my mouth has uttered in all integrity
    a word that will not be revoked:
Before me every knee will bow;
    by me every tongue will swear.
²⁴They will say of me, 'In the LORD alone
    are deliverance and strength.'"
All who have raged against him
    will come to him and be put to shame.
²⁵But all the descendants of Israel
    will find deliverance in the LORD
  and will make their boast in him.

Gods of Babylon

46 Bel bows down, Nebo stoops low;
    their idols are borne by beasts of
      burden.ᵇ
The images that are carried about are
      burdensome,
  a burden for the weary.
²They stoop and bow down together;
  unable to rescue the burden,
    they themselves go off into captivity.

³"Listen to me, you descendants of Jacob,
    all the remnant of the people of Israel,
you whom I have upheld since your birth,
    and have carried since you were born.
⁴Even to your old age and gray hairs
    I am he, I am he who will sustain you.
I have made you and I will carry you;
    I will sustain you and I will rescue you.

⁵"With whom will you compare me or count
      me equal?
  To whom will you liken me that we may
      be compared?
⁶Some pour out gold from their bags
    and weigh out silver on the scales;
they hire a goldsmith to make it into a god,
    and they bow down and worship it.
⁷They lift it to their shoulders and carry it;
    they set it up in its place, and there it
      stands.
From that spot it cannot move.
Even though someone cries out to it, it
      cannot answer;
  it cannot save them from their troubles.

⁸"Remember this, keep it in mind,
    take it to heart, you rebels.

ᵃ 14 That is, the upper Nile region　ᵇ 1 Or are but beasts and
cattle

⁹ Remember the former things, those of long
ago;
    I am God, and there is no other;
    I am God, and there is none like me.
¹⁰ I make known the end from the beginning,
    from ancient times, what is still to come.
I say, 'My purpose will stand,
    and I will do all that I please.'
¹¹ From the east I summon a bird of prey;
    from a far-off land, a man to fulfill my
        purpose.
What I have said, that I will bring about;
    what I have planned, that I will do.
¹² Listen to me, you stubborn-hearted,
    you who are now far from my
        righteousness.
¹³ I am bringing my righteousness near,
    it is not far away;
    and my salvation will not be delayed.
I will grant salvation to Zion,
    my splendor to Israel.

The Fall of Babylon

47 "Go down, sit in the dust,
    Virgin Daughter Babylon;
sit on the ground without a throne,
    queen city of the Babylonians.ᵃ
No more will you be called
    tender or delicate.
² Take millstones and grind flour;
    take off your veil.
Lift up your skirts, bare your legs,
    and wade through the streams.
³ Your nakedness will be exposed
    and your shame uncovered.
I will take vengeance;
    I will spare no one."

⁴ Our Redeemer — the Lᴏʀᴅ Almighty is his
    name —
    is the Holy One of Israel.

⁵ "Sit in silence, go into darkness,
    queen city of the Babylonians;
no more will you be called
    queen of kingdoms.
⁶ I was angry with my people
    and desecrated my inheritance;
I gave them into your hand,
    and you showed them no mercy.
Even on the aged
    you laid a very heavy yoke.
⁷ You said, 'I am forever —
    the eternal queen!'
But you did not consider these things
    or reflect on what might happen.

⁸ "Now then, listen, you lover of pleasure,
    lounging in your security
and saying to yourself,
    'I am, and there is none besides me.
I will never be a widow
    or suffer the loss of children.'
⁹ Both of these will overtake you
    in a moment, on a single day:
    loss of children and widowhood.
They will come upon you in full measure,
    in spite of your many sorceries
    and all your potent spells.
¹⁰ You have trusted in your wickedness
    and have said, 'No one sees me.'
Your wisdom and knowledge mislead you
    when you say to yourself,
    'I am, and there is none besides me.'
¹¹ Disaster will come upon you,
    and you will not know how to conjure it
        away.
A calamity will fall upon you
    that you cannot ward off with a ransom;
a catastrophe you cannot foresee
    will suddenly come upon you.

¹² "Keep on, then, with your magic spells
    and with your many sorceries,
    which you have labored at since childhood.
Perhaps you will succeed,
    perhaps you will cause terror.
¹³ All the counsel you have received has only
        worn you out!
Let your astrologers come forward,
those stargazers who make predictions
        month by month,
    let them save you from what is coming
        upon you.
¹⁴ Surely they are like stubble;
    the fire will burn them up.
They cannot even save themselves
    from the power of the flame.
These are not coals for warmth;
    this is not a fire to sit by.
¹⁵ That is all they are to you —
    these you have dealt with
    and labored with since childhood.
All of them go on in their error;
    there is not one that can save you.

Stubborn Israel

48 "Listen to this, you descendants of
    Jacob,
    you who are called by the name of Israel
    and come from the line of Judah,

ᵃ 1 Or *Chaldeans*; also in verse 5

you who take oaths in the name of the
    LORD
    and invoke the God of Israel —
    but not in truth or righteousness —
[2] you who call yourselves citizens of the holy
        city
    and claim to rely on the God of Israel —
    the LORD Almighty is his name:
[3] I foretold the former things long ago,
    my mouth announced them and I made
        them known;
    then suddenly I acted, and they came to
        pass.
[4] For I knew how stubborn you were;
    your neck muscles were iron,
    your forehead was bronze.
[5] Therefore I told you these things long ago;
    before they happened I announced them
        to you
    so that you could not say,
        'My images brought them about;
    my wooden image and metal god
        ordained them.'
[6] You have heard these things; look at them
        all.
    Will you not admit them?

    "From now on I will tell you of new things,
    of hidden things unknown to you.
[7] They are created now, and not long ago;
    you have not heard of them before today.
    So you cannot say,
        'Yes, I knew of them.'
[8] You have neither heard nor understood;
    from of old your ears have not been
        open.
    Well do I know how treacherous you are;
    you were called a rebel from birth.
[9] For my own name's sake I delay my wrath;
    for the sake of my praise I hold it back
        from you,
    so as not to destroy you completely.
[10] See, I have refined you, though not as
        silver;
    I have tested you in the furnace of
        affliction.
[11] For my own sake, for my own sake, I do this.
    How can I let myself be defamed?
    I will not yield my glory to another.

Israel Freed

[12] "Listen to me, Jacob,
    Israel, whom I have called:
    I am he;
    I am the first and I am the last.

[13] My own hand laid the foundations of the
        earth,
    and my right hand spread out the heavens;
    when I summon them,
    they all stand up together.

[14] "Come together, all of you, and listen:
    Which of the idols has foretold these
        things?
    The LORD's chosen ally
    will carry out his purpose against
        Babylon;
    his arm will be against the Babylonians.[a]
[15] I, even I, have spoken;
    yes, I have called him.
    I will bring him,
    and he will succeed in his mission.

[16] "Come near me and listen to this:

    "From the first announcement I have not
        spoken in secret;
    at the time it happens, I am there."

    And now the Sovereign LORD has sent me,
    endowed with his Spirit.

[17] This is what the LORD says —
    your Redeemer, the Holy One of Israel:
    "I am the LORD your God,
    who teaches you what is best for you,
    who directs you in the way you should go.
[18] If only you had paid attention to my
        commands,
    your peace would have been like a river,
    your well-being like the waves of the sea.
[19] Your descendants would have been like the
        sand,
    your children like its numberless grains;
    their name would never be blotted out
    nor destroyed from before me."

[20] Leave Babylon,
    flee from the Babylonians!
    Announce this with shouts of joy
    and proclaim it.
    Send it out to the ends of the earth;
    say, "The LORD has redeemed his servant
        Jacob."
[21] They did not thirst when he led them
        through the deserts;
    he made water flow for them from the rock;
    he split the rock
    and water gushed out.

[22] "There is no peace," says the LORD, "for the
        wicked."

---

[a] 14 Or *Chaldeans*; also in verse 20

The Servant of the LORD

49 Listen to me, you islands;
hear this, you distant nations:
Before I was born the LORD called me;
from my mother's womb he has spoken
my name.
[2] He made my mouth like a sharpened sword,
in the shadow of his hand he hid me;
he made me into a polished arrow
and concealed me in his quiver.
[3] He said to me, "You are my servant,
Israel, in whom I will display my
splendor."
[4] But I said, "I have labored in vain;
I have spent my strength for nothing at
all.
Yet what is due me is in the LORD's hand,
and my reward is with my God."

[5] And now the LORD says —
he who formed me in the womb to be his
servant
to bring Jacob back to him
and gather Israel to himself,
for I am[a] honored in the eyes of the LORD
and my God has been my strength —
[6] he says:
"It is too small a thing for you to be my
servant
to restore the tribes of Jacob
and bring back those of Israel I have kept.
I will also make you a light for the Gentiles,
that my salvation may reach to the ends of
the earth."

[7] This is what the LORD says —
the Redeemer and Holy One of Israel —
to him who was despised and abhorred by
the nation,
to the servant of rulers:
"Kings will see you and stand up,
princes will see and bow down,
because of the LORD, who is faithful,
the Holy One of Israel, who has chosen
you."

Restoration of Israel

[8] This is what the LORD says:

"In the time of my favor I will answer you,
and in the day of salvation I will help you;
I will keep you and will make you
to be a covenant for the people,
to restore the land
and to reassign its desolate inheritances,
[9] to say to the captives, 'Come out,'
and to those in darkness, 'Be free!'

"They will feed beside the roads
and find pasture on every barren hill.
[10] They will neither hunger nor thirst,
nor will the desert heat or the sun beat
down on them.
He who has compassion on them will guide
them
and lead them beside springs of water.
[11] I will turn all my mountains into roads,
and my highways will be raised up.

---

[a] 5 Or him, / but Israel would not be gathered; / yet I will be

---

The Mission and Vision of a Leader

Isaiah 49:1–3

Leaders must give their lives to causes that count. They must sense that what they do matters to God. Only then will they feel deep satisfaction for their work. Isaiah speaks some incredible words about the Messiah's mission as a Leader:

1. **He was called from his mother's womb (v. 1).**

2. **He was gifted with specific resources (v. 2).**

3. **He was protected supernaturally by God (v. 2).**

4. **He was given a particular divine mission (v. 2).**

5. **He was ordained to reflect God's glory (v. 3).**

While any leader might well covet these descriptions, only in the life of the Messiah, God's servant sent from heaven to redeem earth, were they perfectly fulfilled. Yet they serve as a model for us as we pursue our God-given mission and vision.

¹²See, they will come from afar —
    some from the north, some from the west,
    some from the region of Aswan.ᵃ"

¹³Shout for joy, you heavens;
    rejoice, you earth;
    burst into song, you mountains!
For the Lᴏʀᴅ comforts his people
    and will have compassion on his afflicted
      ones.

¹⁴But Zion said, "The Lᴏʀᴅ has forsaken me,
    the Lord has forgotten me."

¹⁵"Can a mother forget the baby at her breast
    and have no compassion on the child she
      has borne?
Though she may forget,
    I will not forget you!
¹⁶See, I have engraved you on the palms of my
      hands;
    your walls are ever before me.
¹⁷Your children hasten back,
    and those who laid you waste depart from
      you.
¹⁸Lift up your eyes and look around;
    all your children gather and come to you.
As surely as I live," declares the Lᴏʀᴅ,
    "you will wear them all as ornaments;
    you will put them on, like a bride.

¹⁹"Though you were ruined and made desolate
    and your land laid waste,
now you will be too small for your people,
    and those who devoured you will be far
      away.
²⁰The children born during your
      bereavement
    will yet say in your hearing,
'This place is too small for us;
    give us more space to live in.'
²¹Then you will say in your heart,
    'Who bore me these?
I was bereaved and barren;
    I was exiled and rejected.
Who brought these up?
I was left all alone,
    but these — where have they come from?' "

²²This is what the Sovereign Lᴏʀᴅ says:

"See, I will beckon to the nations,
    I will lift up my banner to the peoples;
they will bring your sons in their arms
    and carry your daughters on their hips.
²³Kings will be your foster fathers,
    and their queens your nursing mothers.

They will bow down before you with their
      faces to the ground;
    they will lick the dust at your feet.
Then you will know that I am the Lᴏʀᴅ;
    those who hope in me will not be
      disappointed."

²⁴Can plunder be taken from warriors,
    or captives be rescued from the fierceᵇ?

²⁵But this is what the Lᴏʀᴅ says:

"Yes, captives will be taken from warriors,
    and plunder retrieved from the fierce;
I will contend with those who contend with
      you,
    and your children I will save.
²⁶I will make your oppressors eat their own
      flesh;
    they will be drunk on their own blood, as
      with wine.
Then all mankind will know
    that I, the Lᴏʀᴅ, am your Savior,
    your Redeemer, the Mighty One of Jacob."

Israel's Sin and the Servant's Obedience

50 This is what the Lᴏʀᴅ says:

"Where is your mother's certificate of divorce
    with which I sent her away?
Or to which of my creditors
    did I sell you?
Because of your sins you were sold;
    because of your transgressions your
      mother was sent away.
²When I came, why was there no one?
    When I called, why was there no one to
      answer?
Was my arm too short to deliver you?
    Do I lack the strength to rescue you?
By a mere rebuke I dry up the sea,
    I turn rivers into a desert;
their fish rot for lack of water
    and die of thirst.
³I clothe the heavens with darkness
    and make sackcloth its covering."

⁴The Sovereign Lᴏʀᴅ has given me a well-
      instructed tongue,
    to know the word that sustains the weary.
He wakens me morning by morning,
    wakens my ear to listen like one being
      instructed.

ᵃ 12 Dead Sea Scrolls; Masoretic Text *Sinim*   ᵇ 24 Dead Sea
Scrolls, Vulgate and Syriac (see also Septuagint and verse 25);
Masoretic Text *righteous*

⁵The Sovereign LORD has opened my ears;
  I have not been rebellious,
  I have not turned away.
⁶I offered my back to those who beat me,
  my cheeks to those who pulled out my
    beard;
 I did not hide my face
  from mocking and spitting.
⁷Because the Sovereign LORD helps me,
  I will not be disgraced.
Therefore have I set my face like flint,
  and I know I will not be put to shame.
⁸He who vindicates me is near.
  Who then will bring charges against me?
  Let us face each other!
Who is my accuser?
  Let him confront me!
⁹It is the Sovereign LORD who helps me.
  Who will condemn me?
They will all wear out like a garment;
  the moths will eat them up.

¹⁰Who among you fears the LORD
  and obeys the word of his servant?
Let the one who walks in the dark,
  who has no light,
trust in the name of the LORD
  and rely on their God.
¹¹But now, all you who light fires
  and provide yourselves with flaming
    torches,
go, walk in the light of your fires
  and of the torches you have set ablaze.
This is what you shall receive from my hand:
  You will lie down in torment.

Everlasting Salvation for Zion

51 "Listen to me, you who pursue
    righteousness
  and who seek the LORD:
Look to the rock from which you were cut
  and to the quarry from which you were
    hewn;
²look to Abraham, your father,
  and to Sarah, who gave you birth.
When I called him he was only one man,
  and I blessed him and made him many.
³The LORD will surely comfort Zion
  and will look with compassion on all her
    ruins;
he will make her deserts like Eden,
  her wastelands like the garden of the
    LORD.
Joy and gladness will be found in her,
  thanksgiving and the sound of singing.

⁴"Listen to me, my people;
  hear me, my nation:
Instruction will go out from me;
  my justice will become a light to the
    nations.
⁵My righteousness draws near speedily,
  my salvation is on the way,
  and my arm will bring justice to the
    nations.
The islands will look to me
  and wait in hope for my arm.
⁶Lift up your eyes to the heavens,
  look at the earth beneath;
the heavens will vanish like smoke,
  the earth will wear out like a garment
  and its inhabitants die like flies.
But my salvation will last forever,
  my righteousness will never fail.

⁷"Hear me, you who know what is right,
  you people who have taken my instruction
    to heart:
Do not fear the reproach of mere mortals
  or be terrified by their insults.
⁸For the moth will eat them up like a
    garment;
  the worm will devour them like wool.
But my righteousness will last forever,
  my salvation through all generations."

⁹Awake, awake, arm of the LORD,
  clothe yourself with strength!
Awake, as in days gone by,
  as in generations of old.
Was it not you who cut Rahab to pieces,
  who pierced that monster through?
¹⁰Was it not you who dried up the sea,
  the waters of the great deep,
who made a road in the depths of the sea
  so that the redeemed might cross over?
¹¹Those the LORD has rescued will return.
  They will enter Zion with singing;
  everlasting joy will crown their heads.
Gladness and joy will overtake them,
  and sorrow and sighing will flee away.

¹²"I, even I, am he who comforts you.
  Who are you that you fear mere mortals,
  human beings who are but grass,
¹³that you forget the LORD your Maker,
  who stretches out the heavens
  and who lays the foundations of the
    earth,
that you live in constant terror every day
  because of the wrath of the oppressor,
  who is bent on destruction?

For where is the wrath of the oppressor?
¹⁴   The cowering prisoners will soon be set
free;
    they will not die in their dungeon,
        nor will they lack bread.
¹⁵ For I am the LORD your God,
    who stirs up the sea so that its waves
        roar—
    the LORD Almighty is his name.
¹⁶ I have put my words in your mouth
    and covered you with the shadow of my
        hand—
    I who set the heavens in place,
    who laid the foundations of the earth,
    and who say to Zion, 'You are my
        people.'"

The Cup of the LORD's Wrath

¹⁷ Awake, awake!
    Rise up, Jerusalem,
    you who have drunk from the hand of the
        LORD
        the cup of his wrath,
    you who have drained to its dregs
        the goblet that makes people stagger.
¹⁸ Among all the children she bore
        there was none to guide her;
    among all the children she reared
        there was none to take her by the hand.
¹⁹ These double calamities have come upon
        you—
    who can comfort you?—
    ruin and destruction, famine and
        sword—
    who can^a console you?
²⁰ Your children have fainted;
        they lie at every street corner,
    like antelope caught in a net.
    They are filled with the wrath of the LORD,
        with the rebuke of your God.
²¹ Therefore hear this, you afflicted one,
        made drunk, but not with wine.
²² This is what your Sovereign LORD says,
        your God, who defends his people:
    "See, I have taken out of your hand
        the cup that made you stagger;
    from that cup, the goblet of my wrath,
        you will never drink again.
²³ I will put it into the hands of your
        tormentors,
    who said to you,
        'Fall prostrate that we may walk on you.'
    And you made your back like the ground,
        like a street to be walked on."

⁵² Awake, awake, Zion,
    clothe yourself with strength!
Put on your garments of splendor,
    Jerusalem, the holy city.
The uncircumcised and defiled
    will not enter you again.
² Shake off your dust;
    rise up, sit enthroned, Jerusalem.
Free yourself from the chains on your neck,
    Daughter Zion, now a captive.

³ For this is what the LORD says:

"You were sold for nothing,
    and without money you will be redeemed."

⁴ For this is what the Sovereign LORD says:

"At first my people went down to Egypt to
        live;
    lately, Assyria has oppressed them.

⁵ "And now what do I have here?" declares the
LORD.

"For my people have been taken away for
        nothing,
    and those who rule them mock,^b"
                    declares the LORD.
"And all day long
    my name is constantly blasphemed.
⁶ Therefore my people will know my name;
    therefore in that day they will know
that it is I who foretold it.
    Yes, it is I."

⁷ How beautiful on the mountains
    are the feet of those who bring good news,
who proclaim peace,
    who bring good tidings,
    who proclaim salvation,
who say to Zion,
    "Your God reigns!"
⁸ Listen! Your watchmen lift up their voices;
    together they shout for joy.
When the LORD returns to Zion,
    they will see it with their own eyes.
⁹ Burst into songs of joy together,
    you ruins of Jerusalem,
for the LORD has comforted his people,
    he has redeemed Jerusalem.
¹⁰ The LORD will lay bare his holy arm
    in the sight of all the nations,
and all the ends of the earth will see
    the salvation of our God.

---

^a 19 Dead Sea Scrolls, Septuagint, Vulgate and Syriac;
Masoretic Text / how can I   ^b 5 Dead Sea Scrolls and
Vulgate; Masoretic Text wail

[11] Depart, depart, go out from there!
　　Touch no unclean thing!
　Come out from it and be pure,
　　you who carry the articles of the LORD's
　　　house.
[12] But you will not leave in haste
　　or go in flight;
　for the LORD will go before you,
　　the God of Israel will be your rear guard.

The Suffering and Glory of the Servant

[13] See, my servant will act wisely[a];
　　he will be raised and lifted up and highly
　　　exalted.
[14] Just as there were many who were appalled at
　　him[b] —
　his appearance was so disfigured beyond
　　that of any human being
　and his form marred beyond human
　　likeness —
[15] so he will sprinkle many nations,[c]
　　and kings will shut their mouths because
　　　of him.
　For what they were not told, they will see,
　　and what they have not heard, they will
　　　understand.

53

Who has believed our message
and to whom has the arm of the LORD
been revealed?
[2] He grew up before him like a tender shoot,
　　and like a root out of dry ground.

He had no beauty or majesty to attract us to
　　him,
　　nothing in his appearance that we should
　　　desire him.
[3] He was despised and rejected by mankind,
　　a man of suffering, and familiar with pain.
　Like one from whom people hide their faces
　　he was despised, and we held him in low
　　　esteem.
[4] Surely he took up our pain
　　and bore our suffering,
　yet we considered him punished by God,
　　stricken by him, and afflicted.
[5] But he was pierced for our transgressions,
　　he was crushed for our iniquities;
　the punishment that brought us peace was
　　on him,
　　and by his wounds we are healed.
[6] We all, like sheep, have gone astray,
　　each of us has turned to our own way;
　and the LORD has laid on him
　　the iniquity of us all.

[7] He was oppressed and afflicted,
　　yet he did not open his mouth;
　he was led like a lamb to the slaughter,
　　and as a sheep before its shearers is silent,
　　so he did not open his mouth.

---

[a] 13 Or will prosper   [b] 14 Hebrew you   [c] 15 Or so will
many nations be amazed at him (see also Septuagint)

Servant Leadership Modeled by the Messiah

Isaiah 52:13—53:12

Beyond all question, Jesus Christ modeled the Law of Sacrifice. He gave up for a time the riches of heaven in order to fulfill his divinely ordained role on earth.

Isaiah 53 describes what is often called "the exchanged life." Jesus took our sin, pain and failures so we could have his righteousness, healing and victory. While he offers this package to everyone, leaders have the opportunity to benefit from this sacrifice in a particularly tangible fashion.

Ponder for a moment what Christ gave up and what we obtain. Imagine what might happen if you were to implement the entire gift of redemption that Christ paid for on your behalf! He sacrificed greatly so that we might enjoy the following gifts:

His Sacrifice	Our Gain
1. Grief, infirmities, insecurities	1. Security and solid emotions
2. Sins and transgressions	2. Forgiveness from guilt
3. Sicknesses and diseases	3. Health and wholeness
4. Mental turmoil and pain	4. Peace of mind
5. Weaknesses	5. His strength

[8] By oppression[a] and judgment he was taken
        away.
    Yet who of his generation protested?
    For he was cut off from the land of the living;
        for the transgression of my people he was
        punished.[b]
[9] He was assigned a grave with the wicked,
        and with the rich in his death,
    though he had done no violence,
        nor was any deceit in his mouth.

[10] Yet it was the LORD's will to crush him and
        cause him to suffer,
    and though the LORD makes[c] his life an
        offering for sin,
    he will see his offspring and prolong his days,
        and the will of the LORD will prosper in
        his hand.
[11] After he has suffered,
        he will see the light of life[d] and be satisfied[e];
    by his knowledge[f] my righteous servant will
        justify many,
        and he will bear their iniquities.
[12] Therefore I will give him a portion among
        the great,[g]
    and he will divide the spoils with the
        strong,[h]
    because he poured out his life unto death,
        and was numbered with the transgressors.
    For he bore the sin of many,
        and made intercession for the
        transgressors.

The Future Glory of Zion

54 "Sing, barren woman,
        you who never bore a child;
    burst into song, shout for joy,
        you who were never in labor;
    because more are the children of the desolate
        woman
        than of her who has a husband,"
                                        says the LORD.
[2] "Enlarge the place of your tent,
        stretch your tent curtains wide,
        do not hold back;
    lengthen your cords,
        strengthen your stakes.
[3] For you will spread out to the right and to
        the left;
    your descendants will dispossess nations
        and settle in their desolate cities.

[4] "Do not be afraid; you will not be put to
        shame.
    Do not fear disgrace; you will not be
        humiliated.

    You will forget the shame of your youth
        and remember no more the reproach of
        your widowhood.
[5] For your Maker is your husband—
        the LORD Almighty is his name—
    the Holy One of Israel is your Redeemer;
        he is called the God of all the earth.
[6] The LORD will call you back
        as if you were a wife deserted and
        distressed in spirit—
    a wife who married young,
        only to be rejected," says your God.
[7] "For a brief moment I abandoned you,
        but with deep compassion I will bring you
        back.
[8] In a surge of anger
        I hid my face from you for a moment,
    but with everlasting kindness
        I will have compassion on you,"
                says the LORD your Redeemer.

[9] "To me this is like the days of Noah,
        when I swore that the waters of Noah
        would never again cover the earth.
    So now I have sworn not to be angry with you,
        never to rebuke you again.
[10] Though the mountains be shaken
        and the hills be removed,
    yet my unfailing love for you will not be
        shaken
        nor my covenant of peace be removed,"
        says the LORD, who has compassion on
        you.

[11] "Afflicted city, lashed by storms and not
        comforted,
    I will rebuild you with stones of
        turquoise,[i]
    your foundations with lapis lazuli.
[12] I will make your battlements of rubies,
        your gates of sparkling jewels,
        and all your walls of precious stones.
[13] All your children will be taught by the LORD,
        and great will be their peace.
[14] In righteousness you will be established:
    Tyranny will be far from you;
        you will have nothing to fear.

---

[a] 8 Or *From arrest*   [b] 8 Or *generation considered / that he
was cut off from the land of the living, / that he was punished for
the transgression of my people?*   [c] 10 Hebrew *though you
make*   [d] 11 Dead Sea Scrolls (see also Septuagint); Masoretic
Text does not have *the light of life.*   [e] 11 Or (with Masoretic
Text) [11] *He will see the fruit of his suffering / and will be satisfied*
[f] 11 Or *by knowledge of him*   [g] 12 Or *many*   [h] 12 Or
numerous   [i] 11 The meaning of the Hebrew for this word is
uncertain.

Terror will be far removed;
    it will not come near you.
¹⁵ If anyone does attack you, it will not be my doing;
    whoever attacks you will surrender to you.

¹⁶ "See, it is I who created the blacksmith
    who fans the coals into flame
    and forges a weapon fit for its work.
And it is I who have created the destroyer to wreak havoc;
¹⁷   no weapon forged against you will prevail,
    and you will refute every tongue that accuses you.
This is the heritage of the servants of the LORD,
    and this is their vindication from me,"
                        declares the LORD.

Invitation to the Thirsty

55 "Come, all you who are thirsty,
    come to the waters;
and you who have no money,
    come, buy and eat!
Come, buy wine and milk
    without money and without cost.
² Why spend money on what is not bread,
    and your labor on what does not satisfy?
Listen, listen to me, and eat what is good,
    and you will delight in the richest of fare.

³ Give ear and come to me;
    listen, that you may live.
I will make an everlasting covenant with you,
    my faithful love promised to David.
⁴ See, I have made him a witness to the peoples,
    a ruler and commander of the peoples.
⁵ Surely you will summon nations you know not,
    and nations you do not know will come running to you,
because of the LORD your God,
    the Holy One of Israel,
    for he has endowed you with splendor."

⁶ Seek the LORD while he may be found;
    call on him while he is near.
⁷ Let the wicked forsake their ways
    and the unrighteous their thoughts.
Let them turn to the LORD, and he will have mercy on them,
    and to our God, for he will freely pardon.

⁸ "For my thoughts are not your thoughts,
    neither are your ways my ways,"
                        declares the LORD.
⁹ "As the heavens are higher than the earth,
    so are my ways higher than your ways
    and my thoughts than your thoughts.
¹⁰ As the rain and the snow
    come down from heaven,

The Law of Victory: Leaders Communicate Until They See Results

Isaiah 55:1–11

Isaiah 55 offers the words of a great communicator. In this passage God invites everyone to participate in his offer to quench their thirst. He tries to convince his hearers that he alone can fulfill their desires and permanently meet their needs. Then he beckons them to seek him while he may be found.

Verses 10–12 contain a marvelous promise. God says that just as the rain and snow fall from the sky and do not return without watering the earth, so his Word will also accomplish the goals he sets for it. God's Word *will* bear fruit. From these three simple verses, note how God evaluates good communication:

1. **His Word will get results (v. 10).**

2. **His Word will furnish tools and resources (v. 10).**

3. **His Word will meet needs (v. 10).**

4. **His Word will perform his will (v. 11).**

5. **His Word will satisfy the soul of the hearers (v. 12).**

How about you? Can you, as a leader, make those claims? How do you evaluate your communication? What fruit does your communication produce?

and do not return to it
    without watering the earth
and making it bud and flourish,
    so that it yields seed for the sower and
        bread for the eater,
¹¹ so is my word that goes out from my mouth:
    It will not return to me empty,
but will accomplish what I desire
    and achieve the purpose for which I sent it.
¹² You will go out in joy
    and be led forth in peace;
the mountains and hills
    will burst into song before you,
and all the trees of the field
    will clap their hands.
¹³ Instead of the thornbush will grow the
        juniper,
    and instead of briers the myrtle will grow.
This will be for the LORD's renown,
    for an everlasting sign,
    that will endure forever."

Salvation for Others

56 This is what the LORD says:

"Maintain justice
    and do what is right,
for my salvation is close at hand
    and my righteousness will soon be revealed.
² Blessed is the one who does this—
    the person who holds it fast,
who keeps the Sabbath without desecrating it,
    and keeps their hands from doing any
        evil."

³ Let no foreigner who is bound to the LORD
    say,
    "The LORD will surely exclude me from
        his people."
And let no eunuch complain,
    "I am only a dry tree."

⁴ For this is what the LORD says:

"To the eunuchs who keep my Sabbaths,
    who choose what pleases me
    and hold fast to my covenant—
⁵ to them I will give within my temple and its
        walls
    a memorial and a name
    better than sons and daughters;
I will give them an everlasting name
    that will endure forever.
⁶ And foreigners who bind themselves to the
        LORD
    to minister to him,

to love the name of the LORD,
    and to be his servants,
all who keep the Sabbath without
        desecrating it
    and who hold fast to my covenant—
⁷ these I will bring to my holy mountain
    and give them joy in my house of prayer.
Their burnt offerings and sacrifices
    will be accepted on my altar;
for my house will be called
    a house of prayer for all nations."
⁸ The Sovereign LORD declares—
    he who gathers the exiles of Israel:
"I will gather still others to them
    besides those already gathered."

God's Accusation Against the Wicked

⁹ Come, all you beasts of the field,
    come and devour, all you beasts of the
        forest!
¹⁰ Israel's watchmen are blind,
    they all lack knowledge;
they are all mute dogs,
    they cannot bark;
they lie around and dream,
    they love to sleep.
¹¹ They are dogs with mighty appetites;
    they never have enough.
They are shepherds who lack understanding;
    they all turn to their own way,
    they seek their own gain.
¹² "Come," each one cries, "let me get wine!
    Let us drink our fill of beer!
And tomorrow will be like today,
    or even far better."

57 The righteous perish,
    and no one takes it to heart;
the devout are taken away,
    and no one understands
that the righteous are taken away
    to be spared from evil.
² Those who walk uprightly
    enter into peace;
    they find rest as they lie in death.

³ "But you—come here, you children of a
        sorceress,
you offspring of adulterers and
        prostitutes!
⁴ Who are you mocking?
    At whom do you sneer
    and stick out your tongue?
Are you not a brood of rebels,
    the offspring of liars?

⁵ You burn with lust among the oaks
    and under every spreading tree;
you sacrifice your children in the ravines
    and under the overhanging crags.
⁶ The idols among the smooth stones of the
        ravines are your portion;
    indeed, they are your lot.
Yes, to them you have poured out drink
        offerings
    and offered grain offerings.
    In view of all this, should I relent?
⁷ You have made your bed on a high and lofty
        hill;
    there you went up to offer your
        sacrifices.
⁸ Behind your doors and your doorposts
    you have put your pagan symbols.
Forsaking me, you uncovered your bed,
    you climbed into it and opened it wide;
you made a pact with those whose beds you
        love,
    and you looked with lust on their naked
        bodies.
⁹ You went to Molek*ᵃ* with olive oil
    and increased your perfumes.
You sent your ambassadors*ᵇ* far away;
    you descended to the very realm of the
        dead!
¹⁰ You wearied yourself by such going about,
    but you would not say, 'It is hopeless.'
You found renewal of your strength,
    and so you did not faint.

¹¹ "Whom have you so dreaded and feared
    that you have not been true to me,
and have neither remembered me
    nor taken this to heart?
Is it not because I have long been silent
    that you do not fear me?
¹² I will expose your righteousness and your
        works,
    and they will not benefit you.
¹³ When you cry out for help,
    let your collection of idols save you!
The wind will carry all of them off,
    a mere breath will blow them away.
But whoever takes refuge in me
    will inherit the land
    and possess my holy mountain."

Comfort for the Contrite

¹⁴ And it will be said:

"Build up, build up, prepare the road!
    Remove the obstacles out of the way of my
        people."

¹⁵ For this is what the high and exalted One
        says—
    he who lives forever, whose name is holy:
"I live in a high and holy place,
    but also with the one who is contrite and
        lowly in spirit,
to revive the spirit of the lowly
    and to revive the heart of the contrite.
¹⁶ I will not accuse them forever,
    nor will I always be angry,
for then they would faint away because of
        me—
    the very people I have created.
¹⁷ I was enraged by their sinful greed;
    I punished them, and hid my face in
        anger,
    yet they kept on in their willful ways.
¹⁸ I have seen their ways, but I will heal them;
    I will guide them and restore comfort to
        Israel's mourners,
¹⁹   creating praise on their lips.
Peace, peace, to those far and near,"
    says the LORD. "And I will heal them."
²⁰ But the wicked are like the tossing sea,
    which cannot rest,
    whose waves cast up mire and mud.
²¹ "There is no peace," says my God, "for the
        wicked."

True Fasting

58 "Shout it aloud, do not hold back.
        Raise your voice like a trumpet.
Declare to my people their rebellion
    and to the descendants of Jacob their sins.
² For day after day they seek me out;
    they seem eager to know my ways,
as if they were a nation that does what is
        right
    and has not forsaken the commands of its
        God.
They ask me for just decisions
    and seem eager for God to come near
        them.
³ 'Why have we fasted,' they say,
    'and you have not seen it?
Why have we humbled ourselves,
    and you have not noticed?'

"Yet on the day of your fasting, you do as you
        please
    and exploit all your workers.
⁴ Your fasting ends in quarreling and strife,
    and in striking each other with wicked
        fists.

ᵃ 9 Or *to the king*   *ᵇ* 9 Or *idols*

You cannot fast as you do today
　　and expect your voice to be heard on high.
5 Is this the kind of fast I have chosen,
　　only a day for people to humble
　　　　themselves?
　Is it only for bowing one's head like a reed
　　and for lying in sackcloth and ashes?
　Is that what you call a fast,
　　a day acceptable to the Lord?

6 "Is not this the kind of fasting I have chosen:
　to loose the chains of injustice
　　and untie the cords of the yoke,
　to set the oppressed free
　　and break every yoke?
7 Is it not to share your food with the hungry
　　and to provide the poor wanderer with
　　　　shelter —
　when you see the naked, to clothe them,
　　and not to turn away from your own flesh
　　　　and blood?
8 Then your light will break forth like the
　　　　dawn,
　　and your healing will quickly appear;
　then your righteousness[a] will go before you,
　　and the glory of the Lord will be your
　　　　rear guard.
9 Then you will call, and the Lord will
　　　　answer;
　　you will cry for help, and he will say: Here
　　　　am I.

"If you do away with the yoke of oppression,
　　with the pointing finger and malicious
　　　　talk,
10 and if you spend yourselves in behalf of the
　　　　hungry
　　and satisfy the needs of the oppressed,
　then your light will rise in the darkness,
　　and your night will become like the
　　　　noonday.
11 The Lord will guide you always;
　　he will satisfy your needs in a sun-
　　　　scorched land
　　and will strengthen your frame.
　You will be like a well-watered garden,
　　like a spring whose waters never fail.
12 Your people will rebuild the ancient ruins
　　and will raise up the age-old foundations;
　you will be called Repairer of Broken Walls,
　　Restorer of Streets with Dwellings.

13 "If you keep your feet from breaking the
　　　　Sabbath
　　and from doing as you please on my holy
　　　　day,

Leadership Must Reflect God's Values and Ethics

Isaiah 58:1-14

The practice of fasting goes much deeper than the act of going without food. God declares that he delights not merely in his people going without some daily staples, but in loosing the "chains of injustice" and undoing "the cords of the yoke" of those they have oppressed (Isa 58:6).

Leaders would do well to learn from these words. God is calling us to live from his set of values and ethics. Fasting is fine and good—and these days we don't do it enough—but to fast while continuing to harbor destructive thoughts and oppressive attitudes does not reflect godly leadership. Ethics supply the foundation for our values. Values supply the power that drives our leadership. Consider what God expects from the "fasted life":

1. **Liberate those who are oppressed (v. 6).**

2. **Share resources with the needy (v. 7).**

3. **Provide shelter to the homeless (v. 7).**

4. **Supply clothing to the naked (v. 7).**

5. **Stop accusing and judging others (v. 9).**

if you call the Sabbath a delight
　　and the Lord's holy day honorable,
and if you honor it by not going your own way
　　and not doing as you please or speaking
　　　　idle words,
14 then you will find your joy in the Lord,
　　and I will cause you to ride in triumph on
　　　　the heights of the land
　and to feast on the inheritance of your
　　　　father Jacob."
　　　　　　　　For the mouth of the Lord
　　　　　　　　　　has spoken.

Sin, Confession and Redemption

59 Surely the arm of the Lord is not too
　　　　short to save,
　　nor his ear too dull to hear.
2 But your iniquities have separated
　　you from your God;

---

a 8 Or your righteous One

your sins have hidden his face from you,
　　so that he will not hear.
[3] For your hands are stained with blood,
　　your fingers with guilt.
Your lips have spoken falsely,
　　and your tongue mutters wicked things.
[4] No one calls for justice;
　　no one pleads a case with integrity.
They rely on empty arguments, they utter
　　lies;
　　they conceive trouble and give birth to
　　　evil.
[5] They hatch the eggs of vipers
　　and spin a spider's web.
Whoever eats their eggs will die,
　　and when one is broken, an adder is
　　　hatched.
[6] Their cobwebs are useless for clothing;
　　they cannot cover themselves with what
　　　they make.
Their deeds are evil deeds,
　　and acts of violence are in their hands.
[7] Their feet rush into sin;
　　they are swift to shed innocent blood.
They pursue evil schemes;
　　acts of violence mark their ways.
[8] The way of peace they do not know;
　　there is no justice in their paths.
They have turned them into crooked roads;
　　no one who walks along them will know
　　　peace.
[9] So justice is far from us,
　　and righteousness does not reach us.
We look for light, but all is darkness;
　　for brightness, but we walk in deep
　　　shadows.
[10] Like the blind we grope along the wall,
　　feeling our way like people without eyes.
At midday we stumble as if it were twilight;
　　among the strong, we are like the dead.
[11] We all growl like bears;
　　we moan mournfully like doves.
We look for justice, but find none;
　　for deliverance, but it is far away.
[12] For our offenses are many in your sight,
　　and our sins testify against us.
Our offenses are ever with us,
　　and we acknowledge our iniquities:
[13] rebellion and treachery against the LORD,
　　turning our backs on our God,
inciting revolt and oppression,
　　uttering lies our hearts have conceived.
[14] So justice is driven back,
　　and righteousness stands at a distance;

truth has stumbled in the streets,
　　honesty cannot enter.
[15] Truth is nowhere to be found,
　　and whoever shuns evil becomes a prey.

The LORD looked and was displeased
　　that there was no justice.
[16] He saw that there was no one,
　　he was appalled that there was no one to
　　　intervene;
so his own arm achieved salvation for him,
　　and his own righteousness sustained him.
[17] He put on righteousness as his breastplate,
　　and the helmet of salvation on his head;
he put on the garments of vengeance
　　and wrapped himself in zeal as in a cloak.
[18] According to what they have done,
　　so will he repay
wrath to his enemies
　　and retribution to his foes;
　　he will repay the islands their due.
[19] From the west, people will fear the name of
　　　the LORD,
　　and from the rising of the sun, they will
　　　revere his glory.
For he will come like a pent-up flood
　　that the breath of the LORD drives
　　　along.[a]

[20] "The Redeemer will come to Zion,
　　to those in Jacob who repent of their sins,"
　　　　　　declares the LORD.

[21] "As for me, this is my covenant with them,"
says the LORD. "My Spirit, who is on you, will
not depart from you, and my words that I have
put in your mouth will always be on your lips,
on the lips of your children and on the lips of
their descendants — from this time on and forever," says the LORD.

The Glory of Zion

60 "Arise, shine, for your light has come,
　　and the glory of the LORD rises upon
　　　you.
[2] See, darkness covers the earth
　　and thick darkness is over the peoples,
but the LORD rises upon you
　　and his glory appears over you.
[3] Nations will come to your light,
　　and kings to the brightness of your dawn.

[4] "Lift up your eyes and look about you:
　　All assemble and come to you;

---

[a] 19 Or When enemies come in like a flood, / the Spirit of the
LORD will put them to flight

your sons come from afar,
    and your daughters are carried on the hip.
[5] Then you will look and be radiant,
    your heart will throb and swell with joy;
the wealth on the seas will be brought
        to you,
    to you the riches of the nations will come.
[6] Herds of camels will cover your land,
    young camels of Midian and Ephah.
And all from Sheba will come,
    bearing gold and incense
    and proclaiming the praise of the LORD.
[7] All Kedar's flocks will be gathered to you,
    the rams of Nebaioth will serve you;
they will be accepted as offerings on my
        altar,
    and I will adorn my glorious temple.

[8] "Who are these that fly along like clouds,
    like doves to their nests?
[9] Surely the islands look to me;
    in the lead are the ships of Tarshish,[a]
bringing your children from afar,
    with their silver and gold,
to the honor of the LORD your God,
    the Holy One of Israel,
    for he has endowed you with splendor.

[10] "Foreigners will rebuild your walls,
    and their kings will serve you.
Though in anger I struck you,
    in favor I will show you compassion.
[11] Your gates will always stand open,
    they will never be shut, day or night,
so that people may bring you the wealth of
        the nations —
    their kings led in triumphal procession.
[12] For the nation or kingdom that will not serve
        you will perish;
    it will be utterly ruined.

[13] "The glory of Lebanon will come to you,
    the juniper, the fir and the cypress
        together,
to adorn my sanctuary;
    and I will glorify the place for my feet.
[14] The children of your oppressors will come
        bowing before you;
    all who despise you will bow down at your
        feet
and will call you the City of the LORD,
    Zion of the Holy One of Israel.

[15] "Although you have been forsaken and
        hated,
    with no one traveling through,

I will make you the everlasting pride
    and the joy of all generations.
[16] You will drink the milk of nations
    and be nursed at royal breasts.
Then you will know that I, the LORD, am
        your Savior,
    your Redeemer, the Mighty One of Jacob.
[17] Instead of bronze I will bring you gold,
    and silver in place of iron.
Instead of wood I will bring you bronze,
    and iron in place of stones.
I will make peace your governor
    and well-being your ruler.
[18] No longer will violence be heard in your
        land,
    nor ruin or destruction within your
        borders,
but you will call your walls Salvation
    and your gates Praise.
[19] The sun will no more be your light by day,
    nor will the brightness of the moon shine
        on you,
for the LORD will be your everlasting light,
    and your God will be your glory.
[20] Your sun will never set again,
    and your moon will wane no more;
the LORD will be your everlasting light,
    and your days of sorrow will end.
[21] Then all your people will be righteous
    and they will possess the land forever.
They are the shoot I have planted,
    the work of my hands,
    for the display of my splendor.
[22] The least of you will become a thousand,
    the smallest a mighty nation.
I am the LORD;
    in its time I will do this swiftly."

The Year of the LORD's Favor

61 The Spirit of the Sovereign LORD is on
        me,
    because the LORD has anointed me
    to proclaim good news to the poor.
He has sent me to bind up the
        brokenhearted,
    to proclaim freedom for the captives
    and release from darkness for the
        prisoners,[b]
[2] to proclaim the year of the LORD's favor
    and the day of vengeance of our God,
to comfort all who mourn,
[3]   and provide for those who grieve in
        Zion —

---

[a] 9 Or *the trading ships*   [b] 1 Hebrew; Septuagint *the blind*

The Purpose of God's Anointing

Isaiah 61:1–3

What does God call his anointed Leader to do? Isaiah describes how God's Servant comes to preach good tidings to the poor, to heal the brokenhearted, to proclaim liberty to the captives, and to proclaim the acceptable year of the Lord. God is the One who anoints, who prepares his leaders for service. But what is the purpose of the anointing?

God anoints leaders to enable them to speak the supernatural words and perform the supernatural tasks he has called them to do. Consider the purposes of God's anointing, according to Isaiah:

1. **To supernaturally enable men and women to perform their ministries**
2. **To bring hope and good news to the afflicted**
3. **To heal the brokenhearted**
4. **To proclaim liberty to the captives**
5. **To set prisoners free**
6. **To proclaim the acceptable year of the Lord**
7. **To announce the day of God's vengeance and justice**
8. **To comfort all who mourn**
9. **To furnish beauty for those who have lost it**
10. **To provide happiness and a glad heart**
11. **To supply an opportunity to praise God's name**
12. **To glorify the Lord and not man**

to bestow on them a crown of beauty
  instead of ashes,
the oil of joy
  instead of mourning,
and a garment of praise
  instead of a spirit of despair.
They will be called oaks of righteousness,
  a planting of the LORD
  for the display of his splendor.

⁴They will rebuild the ancient ruins
  and restore the places long devastated;
they will renew the ruined cities
  that have been devastated for
    generations.
⁵Strangers will shepherd your flocks;
  foreigners will work your fields and
    vineyards.
⁶And you will be called priests of the LORD,
  you will be named ministers of our God.
You will feed on the wealth of nations,
  and in their riches you will boast.

⁷Instead of your shame
  you will receive a double portion,

and instead of disgrace
  you will rejoice in your inheritance.
And so you will inherit a double portion in
    your land,
  and everlasting joy will be yours.

⁸"For I, the LORD, love justice;
  I hate robbery and wrongdoing.
In my faithfulness I will reward my people
  and make an everlasting covenant with
    them.
⁹Their descendants will be known among the
    nations
  and their offspring among the peoples.
All who see them will acknowledge
  that they are a people the LORD has blessed."

¹⁰I delight greatly in the LORD;
  my soul rejoices in my God.
For he has clothed me with garments of
    salvation
  and arrayed me in a robe of his
    righteousness,
as a bridegroom adorns his head like a priest,
  and as a bride adorns herself with her jewels.

[11] For as the soil makes the sprout come up
    and a garden causes seeds to grow,
  so the Sovereign LORD will make
      righteousness
    and praise spring up before all nations.

Zion's New Name

62 For Zion's sake I will not keep silent,
    for Jerusalem's sake I will not remain
      quiet,
  till her vindication shines out like the
      dawn,
    her salvation like a blazing torch.
[2] The nations will see your vindication,
    and all kings your glory;
  you will be called by a new name
    that the mouth of the LORD will bestow.
[3] You will be a crown of splendor in the
      LORD's hand,
    a royal diadem in the hand of your God.
[4] No longer will they call you Deserted,
    or name your land Desolate.
  But you will be called Hephzibah,[a]
    and your land Beulah[b];
  for the LORD will take delight in you,
    and your land will be married.
[5] As a young man marries a young woman,
    so will your Builder marry you;
  as a bridegroom rejoices over his bride,
    so will your God rejoice over you.

[6] I have posted watchmen on your walls,
    Jerusalem;
  they will never be silent day or night.
  You who call on the LORD,
    give yourselves no rest,
[7] and give him no rest till he establishes
    Jerusalem
    and makes her the praise of the earth.

[8] The LORD has sworn by his right hand
    and by his mighty arm:
  "Never again will I give your grain
    as food for your enemies,
  and never again will foreigners drink the
      new wine
    for which you have toiled;
[9] but those who harvest it will eat it
    and praise the LORD,
  and those who gather the grapes will drink it
    in the courts of my sanctuary."

[10] Pass through, pass through the gates!
    Prepare the way for the people.
  Build up, build up the highway!
    Remove the stones.

  Raise a banner for the nations.

[11] The LORD has made proclamation
    to the ends of the earth:
  "Say to Daughter Zion,
    'See, your Savior comes!
  See, his reward is with him,
    and his recompense accompanies him.'"
[12] They will be called the Holy People,
    the Redeemed of the LORD;
  and you will be called Sought After,
    the City No Longer Deserted.

God's Day of Vengeance and Redemption

63 Who is this coming from Edom,
    from Bozrah, with his garments stained
      crimson?
  Who is this, robed in splendor,
    striding forward in the greatness of his
      strength?

  "It is I, proclaiming victory,
    mighty to save."

[2] Why are your garments red,
    like those of one treading the winepress?

[3] "I have trodden the winepress alone;
    from the nations no one was with me.
  I trampled them in my anger
    and trod them down in my wrath;
  their blood spattered my garments,
    and I stained all my clothing.
[4] It was for me the day of vengeance;
    the year for me to redeem had come.
[5] I looked, but there was no one to help,
    I was appalled that no one gave support;
  so my own arm achieved salvation for me,
    and my own wrath sustained me.
[6] I trampled the nations in my anger;
    in my wrath I made them drunk
    and poured their blood on the ground."

Praise and Prayer

[7] I will tell of the kindnesses of the LORD,
    the deeds for which he is to be praised,
    according to all the LORD has done for us—
  yes, the many good things
    he has done for Israel,
    according to his compassion and many
      kindnesses.
[8] He said, "Surely they are my people,
    children who will be true to me";
  and so he became their Savior.

---

[a] 4 *Hephzibah* means *my delight is in her.*   [b] 4 *Beulah* means
married.

9 In all their distress he too was distressed,
　　and the angel of his presence saved them.[a]
In his love and mercy he redeemed them;
　　he lifted them up and carried them
　　all the days of old.
10 Yet they rebelled
　　and grieved his Holy Spirit.
So he turned and became their enemy
　　and he himself fought against them.

11 Then his people recalled[b] the days of old,
　　the days of Moses and his people —
where is he who brought them through the
　　sea,
　　with the shepherd of his flock?
Where is he who set
　　his Holy Spirit among them,
12 who sent his glorious arm of power
　　to be at Moses' right hand,
who divided the waters before them,
　　to gain for himself everlasting renown,
13 who led them through the depths?
Like a horse in open country,
　　they did not stumble;
14 like cattle that go down to the plain,
　　they were given rest by the Spirit of the
　　LORD.
This is how you guided your people
　　to make for yourself a glorious name.

Daring Courage Comes from Deep Conviction

Isaiah 63:11–14

Isaiah recalls that Moses received his courage from his God-given convictions. Moses' relationship with God came first; next came a foundation of convictions; and finally the courage to lead others without compromise. Popularity with God controlled Moses' life, not popularity with people.

15 Look down from heaven and see,
　　from your lofty throne, holy and glorious.
Where are your zeal and your might?
　　Your tenderness and compassion are
　　withheld from us.
16 But you are our Father,
　　though Abraham does not know us
　　or Israel acknowledge us;
you, LORD, are our Father,
　　our Redeemer from of old is your name.

17 Why, LORD, do you make us wander from
　　your ways
　　and harden our hearts so we do not revere
　　you?
Return for the sake of your servants,
　　the tribes that are your inheritance.
18 For a little while your people possessed your
　　holy place,
　　but now our enemies have trampled down
　　your sanctuary.
19 We are yours from of old;
　　but you have not ruled over them,
　　they have not been called[c] by your name.

64[d] Oh, that you would rend the heavens
　　and come down,
　　that the mountains would tremble before
　　you!
2 As when fire sets twigs ablaze
　　and causes water to boil,
come down to make your name known to
　　your enemies
　　and cause the nations to quake before
　　you!
3 For when you did awesome things that we
　　did not expect,
　　you came down, and the mountains
　　trembled before you.
4 Since ancient times no one has heard,
　　no ear has perceived,
no eye has seen any God besides you,
　　who acts on behalf of those who wait for
　　him.
5 You come to the help of those who gladly do
　　right,
　　who remember your ways.
But when we continued to sin against them,
　　you were angry.
　　How then can we be saved?
6 All of us have become like one who is
　　unclean,
　　and all our righteous acts are like filthy
　　rags;
we all shrivel up like a leaf,
　　and like the wind our sins sweep us away.
7 No one calls on your name
　　or strives to lay hold of you;
for you have hidden your face from us
　　and have given us over to[e] our sins.

---

[a] 9 Or Savior 9in their distress. / It was no envoy or angel / but his own presence that saved them　　[b] 11 Or But may he recall
[c] 19 Or We are like those you have never ruled, / like those never called　　[d] In Hebrew texts 64:1 is numbered 63:19b, and 64:2-12 is numbered 64:1-11.　　[e] 7 Septuagint, Syriac and Targum; Hebrew have made us melt because of

⁸ Yet you, Lord, are our Father.
    We are the clay, you are the potter;
    we are all the work of your hand.
⁹ Do not be angry beyond measure, Lord;
    do not remember our sins forever.
  Oh, look on us, we pray,
    for we are all your people.
¹⁰ Your sacred cities have become a wasteland;
    even Zion is a wasteland, Jerusalem a
        desolation.
¹¹ Our holy and glorious temple, where our
        ancestors praised you,
    has been burned with fire,
    and all that we treasured lies in ruins.
¹² After all this, Lord, will you hold yourself
        back?
    Will you keep silent and punish us beyond
        measure?

Judgment and Salvation

65 "I revealed myself to those who did not
        ask for me;
    I was found by those who did not seek me.
  To a nation that did not call on my name,
    I said, 'Here am I, here am I.'
² All day long I have held out my hands
    to an obstinate people,
  who walk in ways not good,
    pursuing their own imaginations—
³ a people who continually provoke me
    to my very face,
  offering sacrifices in gardens
    and burning incense on altars of brick;
⁴ who sit among the graves
    and spend their nights keeping secret vigil;
  who eat the flesh of pigs,
    and whose pots hold broth of impure meat;
⁵ who say, 'Keep away; don't come near me,
    for I am too sacred for you!'
  Such people are smoke in my nostrils,
    a fire that keeps burning all day.

⁶ "See, it stands written before me:
    I will not keep silent but will pay back in
        full;
    I will pay it back into their laps—
⁷ both your sins and the sins of your
        ancestors,"
    says the Lord.
  "Because they burned sacrifices on the
        mountains
    and defied me on the hills,
  I will measure into their laps
    the full payment for their former deeds."

⁸ This is what the Lord says:

  "As when juice is still found in a cluster of
        grapes
    and people say, 'Don't destroy it,
      there is still a blessing in it,'
  so will I do in behalf of my servants;
    I will not destroy them all.
⁹ I will bring forth descendants from Jacob,
    and from Judah those who will possess
        my mountains;
  my chosen people will inherit them,
    and there will my servants live.
¹⁰ Sharon will become a pasture for flocks,
    and the Valley of Achor a resting place for
        herds,
  for my people who seek me.

¹¹ "But as for you who forsake the Lord
    and forget my holy mountain,
  who spread a table for Fortune
    and fill bowls of mixed wine for Destiny,
¹² I will destine you for the sword,
    and all of you will fall in the slaughter;
  for I called but you did not answer,
    I spoke but you did not listen.
  You did evil in my sight
    and chose what displeases me."

¹³ Therefore this is what the Sovereign Lord
says:

  "My servants will eat,
    but you will go hungry;
  my servants will drink,
    but you will go thirsty;
  my servants will rejoice,
    but you will be put to shame.
¹⁴ My servants will sing
    out of the joy of their hearts,
  but you will cry out
    from anguish of heart
    and wail in brokenness of spirit.
¹⁵ You will leave your name
    for my chosen ones to use in their curses;
  the Sovereign Lord will put you to death,
    but to his servants he will give another
        name.
¹⁶ Whoever invokes a blessing in the land
    will do so by the one true God;
  whoever takes an oath in the land
    will swear by the one true God.
  For the past troubles will be forgotten
    and hidden from my eyes.

New Heavens and a New Earth

¹⁷ "See, I will create
    new heavens and a new earth.

The former things will not be remembered,
　nor will they come to mind.
18 But be glad and rejoice forever
　in what I will create,
for I will create Jerusalem to be a delight
　and its people a joy.
19 I will rejoice over Jerusalem
　and take delight in my people;
the sound of weeping and of crying
　will be heard in it no more.

20 "Never again will there be in it
　an infant who lives but a few days,
　or an old man who does not live out his
　　years;
the one who dies at a hundred
　will be thought a mere child;
the one who fails to reach[a] a hundred
　will be considered accursed.
21 They will build houses and dwell in them;
　they will plant vineyards and eat their fruit.
22 No longer will they build houses and others
　　live in them,
　or plant and others eat.
For as the days of a tree,
　so will be the days of my people;
my chosen ones will long enjoy
　the work of their hands.
23 They will not labor in vain,
　nor will they bear children doomed to
　　misfortune;
for they will be a people blessed by the LORD,
　they and their descendants with them.
24 Before they call I will answer;
　while they are still speaking I will hear.
25 The wolf and the lamb will feed together,
　and the lion will eat straw like the ox,
　and dust will be the serpent's food.
They will neither harm nor destroy
　on all my holy mountain,"
　　　　　　　　　　says the LORD.

Judgment and Hope

66 This is what the LORD says:

"Heaven is my throne,
　and the earth is my footstool.
Where is the house you will build for me?
　Where will my resting place be?
2 Has not my hand made all these things,
　and so they came into being?"
　　　　　　　　　　declares the LORD.

"These are the ones I look on with favor:
　those who are humble and contrite in spirit,
　and who tremble at my word.

3 But whoever sacrifices a bull
　is like one who kills a person,
and whoever offers a lamb
　is like one who breaks a dog's neck;
whoever makes a grain offering
　is like one who presents pig's blood,
and whoever burns memorial incense
　is like one who worships an idol.
They have chosen their own ways,
　and they delight in their abominations;
4 so I also will choose harsh treatment for
　　them
　and will bring on them what they dread.
For when I called, no one answered,
　when I spoke, no one listened.
They did evil in my sight
　and chose what displeases me."

5 Hear the word of the LORD,
　you who tremble at his word:
"Your own people who hate you,
　and exclude you because of my name,
　　have said,
'Let the LORD be glorified,
　that we may see your joy!'
Yet they will be put to shame.
6 Hear that uproar from the city,
　hear that noise from the temple!
It is the sound of the LORD
　repaying his enemies all they deserve.

7 "Before she goes into labor,
　she gives birth;
before the pains come upon her,
　she delivers a son.
8 Who has ever heard of such things?
　Who has ever seen things like this?
Can a country be born in a day
　or a nation be brought forth in a moment?
Yet no sooner is Zion in labor
　than she gives birth to her children.
9 Do I bring to the moment of birth
　and not give delivery?" says the LORD.
"Do I close up the womb
　when I bring to delivery?" says your God.
10 "Rejoice with Jerusalem and be glad for her,
　all you who love her;
rejoice greatly with her,
　all you who mourn over her.
11 For you will nurse and be satisfied
　at her comforting breasts;
you will drink deeply
　and delight in her overflowing
　　abundance."

---

[a] 20 Or the sinner who reaches

[12]For this is what the LORD says:

"I will extend peace to her like a river,
  and the wealth of nations like a flooding
    stream;
you will nurse and be carried on her arm
  and dandled on her knees.
[13]As a mother comforts her child,
  so will I comfort you;
and you will be comforted over
    Jerusalem."

[14]When you see this, your heart will rejoice
  and you will flourish like grass;
the hand of the LORD will be made known to
    his servants,
  but his fury will be shown to his foes.
[15]See, the LORD is coming with fire,
  and his chariots are like a whirlwind;
he will bring down his anger with fury,
  and his rebuke with flames of fire.
[16]For with fire and with his sword
  the LORD will execute judgment on all
    people,
  and many will be those slain by the LORD.

[17]"Those who consecrate and purify themselves to go into the gardens, following one who
is among those who eat the flesh of pigs, rats and
other unclean things — they will meet their end
together with the one they follow," declares the
LORD.

[18]"And I, because of what they have planned
and done, am about to come[a] and gather the
people of all nations and languages, and they
will come and see my glory.

[19]"I will set a sign among them, and I will
send some of those who survive to the nations — to Tarshish, to the Libyans[b] and Lyd-
ians (famous as archers), to Tubal and Greece,
and to the distant islands that have not heard of
my fame or seen my glory. They will proclaim
my glory among the nations. [20]And they will
bring all your people, from all the nations, to
my holy mountain in Jerusalem as an offering
to the LORD — on horses, in chariots and wagons, and on mules and camels," says the LORD.
"They will bring them, as the Israelites bring
their grain offerings, to the temple of the LORD
in ceremonially clean vessels. [21]And I will select some of them also to be priests and Levites,"
says the LORD.

[22]"As the new heavens and the new earth
that I make will endure before me," declares
the LORD, "so will your name and descendants
endure. [23]From one New Moon to another and
from one Sabbath to another, all mankind will
come and bow down before me," says the LORD.
[24]"And they will go out and look on the dead
bodies of those who rebelled against me; the
worms that eat them will not die, the fire that
burns them will not be quenched, and they will
be loathsome to all mankind."

---

[a] 18 The meaning of the Hebrew for this clause is uncertain.
[b] 19 Some Septuagint manuscripts Put (Libyans); Hebrew Pul

INTRODUCTION TO JEREMIAH

A Call to Change and Repentance

Without question the prophet Jeremiah received one of the toughest assignments of any leader in the Old Testament. God called him to lead a stubborn people, then informed him that the people would not follow his lead (7:27–28).

Jeremiah was born toward the end of the reign of King Josiah, the last good king of Judah. The prophet's leadership came at a time of moral, political, and religious decline, ending in the Babylonian exile. God called Jeremiah as a youth and immediately began to prepare him to serve as a prophet to the nations. He was a priest called to prophetic service at a most unhappy time.

God directed Jeremiah to deliver a hard message, a message of critical evaluation rather than of salvation. He was to call the people to change and repentance, to raise the standard they had dropped, and to call them to recapture their values and heritage. Think of him as a new C.E.O., called in to turn around a failing organization—only Jeremiah had a country to overhaul, not a mere corporation. He couldn't fire anyone; and in fact, those he attempted to influence rejected him. Jeremiah led the Hebrews during tough times, yet he never lost his vision.

We understand Jeremiah's personality more thoroughly than any other prophet. He clung tenaciously to his assigned task through long years of rejection and persecution, and still stands as a tribute to God's grace and the mettle of a strong leader. What's more, we call Jeremiah "the weeping prophet" because he shed so many tears over the hardness of his people and the severity of their judgment.

This embattled leader embraced core convictions, yet never lost his compassion. His heart didn't grow cold

God's Role in Jeremiah

Jeremiah learned early to rely on God for sustaining grace. In chapter one, God tells him that even before his body took shape in his mother's womb, the Lord had ordained him as a prophet to the nations—to pluck up, tear down, and build again. Several times during his career, Jeremiah determined to quit, but God reminded him of the vision and strengthened him. This divine call became the very reason Jeremiah remained true to his task.

At one point, the prophet likened God's word to an inner fire that would consume him if he didn't continue to speak. Jeremiah provides an example of a leader who continued in tough times through the supernatural work of God. Divine conviction drove him, along with a divine compassion and a divine call.

Leaders in Jeremiah
Jeremiah, King Jehoiakim, Hananiah

Other People of Influence in Jeremiah
Pashhur, false prophets

Lessons in Leadership
- God's calling of a leader matches his empowerment.
- Leaders must expect criticism and sometimes must confront.

and crusty, despite the calloused hearts of his listeners. He continued to invest himself in his cause even though the people considered him a meddler and a traitor. Jewish men, nobles and kings all tried to assassinate him at one time or another. While God warned Jeremiah from the start that the masses would reject his leadership, he continued to set the pace for what was right.

- Leaders must not only endure change, but create it.
- Effective leaders identify with the sins and failures of their people.
- Leaders can be compared to both watchmen and shepherds.
- Great leaders never lose their ability to empathize.
- Successful leaders find memorable and creative ways to communicate truth.
- Leaders must cling to their God-given vision even when the people stray.

LEADERSHIP HIGHLIGHTS IN JEREMIAH

1 The words of Jeremiah son of Hilkiah, one of the priests at Anathoth in the territory of Benjamin. [2] The word of the LORD came to him in the thirteenth year of the reign of Josiah son of Amon king of Judah, [3] and through the reign of Jehoiakim son of Josiah king of Judah, down to the fifth month of the eleventh year of Zedekiah son of Josiah king of Judah, when the people of Jerusalem went into exile.

The Call of Jeremiah

[4] The word of the LORD came to me, saying,

[5] "Before I formed you in the womb I knew[a] you,
    before you were born I set you apart;
    I appointed you as a prophet to the nations."

[6] "Alas, Sovereign LORD," I said, "I do not know how to speak; I am too young."

[7] But the LORD said to me, "Do not say, 'I am too young.' You must go to everyone I send you to and say whatever I command you. [8] Do not be afraid of them, for I am with you and will rescue you," declares the LORD.

[9] Then the LORD reached out his hand and touched my mouth and said to me, "I have put my words in your mouth. [10] See, today I appoint you over nations and kingdoms to uproot and tear down, to destroy and overthrow, to build and to plant."

[11] The word of the LORD came to me: "What do you see, Jeremiah?"

"I see the branch of an almond tree," I replied.

[12] The LORD said to me, "You have seen correctly, for I am watching[b] to see that my word is fulfilled."

[13] The word of the LORD came to me again: "What do you see?"

"I see a pot that is boiling," I answered. "It is tilting toward us from the north."

[14] The LORD said to me, "From the north disaster will be poured out on all who live in the land. [15] I am about to summon all the peoples of the northern kingdoms," declares the LORD.

"Their kings will come and set up their
        thrones
    in the entrance of the gates of Jerusalem;
    they will come against all her surrounding
        walls
    and against all the towns of Judah.
[16] I will pronounce my judgments on my
        people
    because of their wickedness in forsaking me,
    in burning incense to other gods
    and in worshiping what their hands have
        made.

---

[a] 5 Or *chose*   [b] 12 The Hebrew for *watching* sounds like the Hebrew for *almond tree*.

God's Call and Empowerment Match

Jeremiah 1:4–10

Jeremiah's call to become a prophet to the nations came early in his life—and it scared him terribly. Why? He failed to see that God's call and his empowerment always match. When God calls you to do something, he always provides the empowerment to fulfill that calling.

If God calls you, heed the call. He will also give you the resources to accomplish the work. But if he hasn't called you, don't conjure up some self-appointment. If he doesn't send you, you will not ultimately succeed (Jer 23:21–32). Jeremiah received his call through a "word of the LORD," one of several Jewish leaders called this way (Jer 1:4; Eze 1:3; Hos 1:1; Joel 1:1; Jnh 1:1). Note the circumstances of God's call on Jeremiah's life given in Jeremiah 1:4–10:

- **God created Jeremiah for a purpose (v. 5).**
- **Jeremiah felt inadequate (v. 6).**
- **God wanted total control (v. 7).**
- **God gave the promise of a blessing (v. 8).**
- **God gave Jeremiah spiritual anointing (v. 9).**
- **God gave Jeremiah a difficult ministry (v. 10).**

God's call, whether from birth or otherwise (see Ac 9 for other types of calls), eventually gets confirmed when God endorses a person's vocation. They feel they can do nothing else. How about you? What are your earliest memories of the call of God on your life?

[17]"Get yourself ready! Stand up and say to them whatever I command you. Do not be terrified by them, or I will terrify you before them. [18]Today I have made you a fortified city, an iron pillar and a bronze wall to stand against the whole land — against the kings of Judah, its officials, its priests and the people of the land. [19]They will fight against you but will not overcome you, for I am with you and will rescue you," declares the LORD.

Israel Forsakes God

2 The word of the LORD came to me: [2]"Go and proclaim in the hearing of Jerusalem:

"This is what the LORD says:

"'I remember the devotion of your youth,
    how as a bride you loved me
and followed me through the wilderness,
    through a land not sown.
[3]Israel was holy to the LORD,
    the firstfruits of his harvest;
all who devoured her were held guilty,
    and disaster overtook them,'"
                          declares the LORD.

[4]Hear the word of the LORD, you descendants of Jacob,
    all you clans of Israel.

[5]This is what the LORD says:

"What fault did your ancestors find in me,
    that they strayed so far from me?
They followed worthless idols
    and became worthless themselves.
[6]They did not ask, 'Where is the LORD,
    who brought us up out of Egypt
and led us through the barren wilderness,
    through a land of deserts and ravines,
a land of drought and utter darkness,
    a land where no one travels and no one
        lives?'
[7]I brought you into a fertile land
    to eat its fruit and rich produce.
But you came and defiled my land
    and made my inheritance detestable.
[8]The priests did not ask,
    'Where is the LORD?'
Those who deal with the law did not know me;
    the leaders rebelled against me.
The prophets prophesied by Baal,
    following worthless idols.

[9]"Therefore I bring charges against you again,"
                          declares the LORD.
"And I will bring charges against your
    children's children.

The Law of Sacrifice: Jeremiah Gave Up Loads to Lead

Jeremiah 1:18–19

Leaders must practice the Law of Sacrifice. We must give up to go up. Our call to lead is no cakewalk, but calls for responsibility and sacrifice.

1. **He was called to a ministry of opposition (1:18–19).**
   Jeremiah never gained popularity. People didn't flock to hear him denounce their wickedness.

2. **He was not permitted to marry (16:1–2).**
   Jeremiah lived a life of solitude without the joys of family and loved ones.

3. **He was beaten and put into stocks (20:1–3).**
   The people responded to the prophet's message with physical punishment.

4. **He was publicly disgraced to depict the judgment of Israel (27:1–3).**
   God told Jeremiah to put bonds and stocks around his neck to illustrate the coming yoke of Babylon.

5. **He was imprisoned in a dungeon (38:1–6).**
   Jeremiah was treated worse than thieves or murderers; he almost suffocated in this dry well.

Do you suddenly feel a little better about your plight as a leader? Jeremiah faced horrible odds, yet never walked away from his message or his call from God.

Communication: Effective Leaders Use Memorable Imagery

Jeremiah 2:1–16

We increase our ability to cast vision when we improve our communication. Effective leaders find memorable ways to communicate with their people.

Jeremiah uses vivid analogies and metaphors to describe how Israel has drifted from the Lord. He uses word pictures like a bride running to and then from her husband, a man digging a cistern, and a slave who has lost his freedom.

God challenged Jeremiah to communicate with those who refused to listen to him. This likely stretched him to become an even better communicator than if he had been given an easy task. As you scan the pages of his book, notice that Jeremiah, along with other Old Testament prophets, used five tools in an attempt to drive home his message:

1. **Strong Beginning**
   Jeremiah didn't waste words as he grabbed the people's attention.

2. **Simple Language**
   Jeremiah didn't try to impress anyone with huge, theological terms.

3. **One Theme**
   Jeremiah stuck with one profound issue per message, not seventeen.

4. **Pictures**
   Jeremiah used word pictures, illustrations and object lessons to drive home his message.

5. **Emotional Ending**
   Jeremiah closed his communication with an appeal to strike both heart and head.

---

¹⁰ Cross over to the coasts of Cyprus and
        look,
    send to Kedar*a* and observe closely;
    see if there has ever been anything like
        this:
¹¹ Has a nation ever changed its gods?
    (Yet they are not gods at all.)
But my people have exchanged their glorious
        God
    for worthless idols.
¹² Be appalled at this, you heavens,
    and shudder with great horror,"
                    declares the LORD.
¹³ "My people have committed two sins:
They have forsaken me,
    the spring of living water,
and have dug their own cisterns,
    broken cisterns that cannot hold water.
¹⁴ Is Israel a servant, a slave by birth?
    Why then has he become plunder?
¹⁵ Lions have roared;
    they have growled at him.
They have laid waste his land;
    his towns are burned and deserted.
¹⁶ Also, the men of Memphis and Tahpanhes
    have cracked your skull.

¹⁷ Have you not brought this on yourselves
    by forsaking the LORD your God
    when he led you in the way?
¹⁸ Now why go to Egypt
    to drink water from the Nile*b*?
And why go to Assyria
    to drink water from the Euphrates?
¹⁹ Your wickedness will punish you;
    your backsliding will rebuke you.
Consider then and realize
    how evil and bitter it is for you
when you forsake the LORD your God
    and have no awe of me,"
                    declares the Lord,
                    the LORD Almighty.

²⁰ "Long ago you broke off your yoke
    and tore off your bonds;
    you said, 'I will not serve you!'
Indeed, on every high hill
    and under every spreading tree
    you lay down as a prostitute.
²¹ I had planted you like a choice vine
    of sound and reliable stock.

---

a 10 In the Syro-Arabian desert   *b* 18 Hebrew *Shihor*; that is, a branch of the Nile

How then did you turn against me
    into a corrupt, wild vine?
²²Although you wash yourself with soap
    and use an abundance of cleansing
        powder,
    the stain of your guilt is still before me,"
        declares the Sovereign LORD.
²³"How can you say, 'I am not defiled;
    I have not run after the Baals'?
See how you behaved in the valley;
    consider what you have done.
You are a swift she-camel
    running here and there,
²⁴a wild donkey accustomed to the desert,
    sniffing the wind in her craving—
in her heat who can restrain her?
    Any males that pursue her need not tire
        themselves;
at mating time they will find her.
²⁵Do not run until your feet are bare
    and your throat is dry.
But you said, 'It's no use!
    I love foreign gods,
    and I must go after them.'

²⁶"As a thief is disgraced when he is caught,
    so the people of Israel are disgraced—
they, their kings and their officials,
    their priests and their prophets.
²⁷They say to wood, 'You are my father,'
    and to stone, 'You gave me birth.'
They have turned their backs to me
    and not their faces;
yet when they are in trouble, they say,
    'Come and save us!'
²⁸Where then are the gods you made for
    yourselves?
Let them come if they can save you
    when you are in trouble!
For you, Judah, have as many gods
    as you have towns.

²⁹"Why do you bring charges against me?
    You have all rebelled against me,"
        declares the LORD.
³⁰"In vain I punished your people;
    they did not respond to correction.
Your sword has devoured your prophets
    like a ravenous lion.

³¹"You of this generation, consider the word
of the LORD:

"Have I been a desert to Israel
    or a land of great darkness?
Why do my people say, 'We are free to roam;
    we will come to you no more'?

³²Does a young woman forget her jewelry,
    a bride her wedding ornaments?
Yet my people have forgotten me,
    days without number.
³³How skilled you are at pursuing love!
    Even the worst of women can learn from
        your ways.
³⁴On your clothes is found
    the lifeblood of the innocent poor,
    though you did not catch them breaking in.
Yet in spite of all this
³⁵   you say, 'I am innocent;
    he is not angry with me.'
But I will pass judgment on you
    because you say, 'I have not sinned.'
³⁶Why do you go about so much,
    changing your ways?
You will be disappointed by Egypt
    as you were by Assyria.
³⁷You will also leave that place
    with your hands on your head,
for the LORD has rejected those you trust;
    you will not be helped by them.

3 "If a man divorces his wife
    and she leaves him and marries another
        man,
should he return to her again?
    Would not the land be completely defiled?
But you have lived as a prostitute with many
        lovers—
would you now return to me?"
        declares the LORD.
²"Look up to the barren heights and see.
    Is there any place where you have not been
        ravished?
By the roadside you sat waiting for lovers,
    sat like a nomad in the desert.
You have defiled the land
    with your prostitution and wickedness.
³Therefore the showers have been withheld,
    and no spring rains have fallen.
Yet you have the brazen look of a prostitute;
    you refuse to blush with shame.
⁴Have you not just called to me:
    'My Father, my friend from my youth,
⁵will you always be angry?
    Will your wrath continue forever?'
This is how you talk,
    but you do all the evil you can."

Unfaithful Israel

⁶During the reign of King Josiah, the LORD
said to me, "Have you seen what faithless Israel
has done? She has gone up on every high hill and

under every spreading tree and has committed adultery there. [7]I thought that after she had done all this she would return to me but she did not, and her unfaithful sister Judah saw it. [8]I gave faithless Israel her certificate of divorce and sent her away because of all her adulteries. Yet I saw that her unfaithful sister Judah had no fear; she also went out and committed adultery. [9]Because Israel's immorality mattered so little to her, she defiled the land and committed adultery with stone and wood. [10]In spite of all this, her unfaithful sister Judah did not return to me with all her heart, but only in pretense," declares the LORD.

[11]The LORD said to me, "Faithless Israel is more righteous than unfaithful Judah. [12]Go, proclaim this message toward the north:

"'Return, faithless Israel,' declares the LORD,
  'I will frown on you no longer,
for I am faithful,' declares the LORD,
  'I will not be angry forever.
[13]Only acknowledge your guilt—
  you have rebelled against the LORD your
    God,
you have scattered your favors to foreign
    gods
  under every spreading tree,
  and have not obeyed me,'"
                declares the LORD.

[14]"Return, faithless people," declares the LORD, "for I am your husband. I will choose you—one from a town and two from a clan—and bring you to Zion. [15]Then I will give you shepherds after my own heart, who will lead you with knowledge and understanding. [16]In those days, when your numbers have increased greatly in the land," declares the LORD, "people will no longer say, 'The ark of the covenant of the LORD.' It will never enter their minds or be remembered; it will not be missed, nor will another one be made. [17]At that time they will call Jerusalem The Throne of the LORD, and all nations will gather in Jerusalem to honor the name of the LORD. No longer will they follow the stubbornness of their evil hearts. [18]In those days the people of Judah will join the people of Israel, and together they will come from a northern land to the land I gave your ancestors as an inheritance.

[19]"I myself said,

"'How gladly would I treat you like my
    children
and give you a pleasant land,
  the most beautiful inheritance of any
    nation.'
I thought you would call me 'Father'
  and not turn away from following me.
[20]But like a woman unfaithful to her husband,
  so you, Israel, have been unfaithful
    to me,"
                declares the LORD.

God's Criteria for Leaders: Shepherds After His Heart

Jeremiah 3:15

God tells us his criteria for leadership when he promises through Jeremiah that he will give the people shepherds after his own heart—the same description given to David in the book of 1 Samuel. What does this mean? God says these shepherds are to lead his people with "knowledge and understanding."

This kind of leader doesn't develop automatically. Most seminaries still struggle with providing practical, usable tools for the men and women they are preparing for ministry. A "shepherd after God's own heart" must possess at least four skills:

1. **Attitude Skills**
   A servant's heart, both positive and persistent.

2. **People Skills**
   The ability to relate to others: communicate, delegate, motivate, confront, etc.

3. **Equipping Skills**
   The ability to train and develop others for service.

4. **Leadership Skills**
   The ability to cast vision, plan strategy, direct teams, and empower others.

²¹ A cry is heard on the barren heights,
   the weeping and pleading of the people of
     Israel,
because they have perverted their ways
   and have forgotten the LORD their God.

²² "Return, faithless people;
   I will cure you of backsliding."

"Yes, we will come to you,
   for you are the LORD our God.
²³ Surely the idolatrous commotion on the hills
   and mountains is a deception;
surely in the LORD our God
   is the salvation of Israel.
²⁴ From our youth shameful gods have consumed
   the fruits of our ancestors' labor —
their flocks and herds,
   their sons and daughters.
²⁵ Let us lie down in our shame,
   and let our disgrace cover us.
We have sinned against the LORD our God,
   both we and our ancestors;
from our youth till this day
   we have not obeyed the LORD our God."

4   "If you, Israel, will return,
     then return to me,"
                 declares the LORD.
"If you put your detestable idols out of my
     sight
   and no longer go astray,
² and if in a truthful, just and righteous way
   you swear, 'As surely as the LORD lives,'
then the nations will invoke blessings by him
   and in him they will boast."

³ This is what the LORD says to the people of
Judah and to Jerusalem:

"Break up your unplowed ground
   and do not sow among thorns.
⁴ Circumcise yourselves to the LORD,
   circumcise your hearts,
   you people of Judah and inhabitants of
     Jerusalem,
or my wrath will flare up and burn like fire
   because of the evil you have done —
burn with no one to quench it.

Disaster From the North

⁵ "Announce in Judah and proclaim in
     Jerusalem and say:
   'Sound the trumpet throughout the land!'
Cry aloud and say:
   'Gather together!
Let us flee to the fortified cities!'

⁶ Raise the signal to go to Zion!
   Flee for safety without delay!
For I am bringing disaster from the north,
   even terrible destruction."

⁷ A lion has come out of his lair;
   a destroyer of nations has set out.
He has left his place
   to lay waste your land.
Your towns will lie in ruins
   without inhabitant.
⁸ So put on sackcloth,
   lament and wail,
for the fierce anger of the LORD
   has not turned away from us.

⁹ "In that day," declares the LORD,
   "the king and the officials will lose heart,
the priests will be horrified,
   and the prophets will be appalled."

¹⁰ Then I said, "Alas, Sovereign LORD! How
completely you have deceived this people and
Jerusalem by saying, 'You will have peace,' when
the sword is at our throats!"

¹¹ At that time this people and Jerusalem
will be told, "A scorching wind from the barren heights in the desert blows toward my people, but not to winnow or cleanse; ¹²a wind
too strong for that comes from me. Now I pronounce my judgments against them."

¹³ Look! He advances like the clouds,
   his chariots come like a whirlwind,
his horses are swifter than eagles.
   Woe to us! We are ruined!
¹⁴ Jerusalem, wash the evil from your heart and
     be saved.
   How long will you harbor wicked
     thoughts?
¹⁵ A voice is announcing from Dan,
   proclaiming disaster from the hills of
     Ephraim.
¹⁶ "Tell this to the nations,
   proclaim concerning Jerusalem:
'A besieging army is coming from a distant
     land,
   raising a war cry against the cities of
     Judah.
¹⁷ They surround her like men guarding a field,
   because she has rebelled against me,'"
                 declares the LORD.
¹⁸ "Your own conduct and actions
   have brought this on you.
This is your punishment.
   How bitter it is!
   How it pierces to the heart!"

¹⁹ Oh, my anguish, my anguish!
     I writhe in pain.
Oh, the agony of my heart!
     My heart pounds within me,
     I cannot keep silent.
For I have heard the sound of the trumpet;
     I have heard the battle cry.
²⁰ Disaster follows disaster;
     the whole land lies in ruins.
In an instant my tents are destroyed,
     my shelter in a moment.
²¹ How long must I see the battle standard
     and hear the sound of the trumpet?

²² "My people are fools;
     they do not know me.
They are senseless children;
     they have no understanding.
They are skilled in doing evil;
     they know not how to do good."

²³ I looked at the earth,
     and it was formless and empty;
and at the heavens,
     and their light was gone.
²⁴ I looked at the mountains,
     and they were quaking;
     all the hills were swaying.
²⁵ I looked, and there were no people;
     every bird in the sky had flown away.
²⁶ I looked, and the fruitful land was a desert;
     all its towns lay in ruins
     before the LORD, before his fierce anger.

²⁷ This is what the LORD says:

"The whole land will be ruined,
     though I will not destroy it completely.
²⁸ Therefore the earth will mourn
     and the heavens above grow dark,

Compassion: Leaders Must Empathize with Human Flaws

Jeremiah 4:19–26

Compassion drove Jeremiah. He empathized with the flaws of his people, and even though he warned them of coming judgment, his proclamation sounded far from cold and sterile. He identified with the Israelites and anguished over their plight. This enabled him to lead over the long haul.

because I have spoken and will not relent,
     I have decided and will not turn back."

²⁹ At the sound of horsemen and archers
     every town takes to flight.
Some go into the thickets;
     some climb up among the rocks.
All the towns are deserted;
     no one lives in them.

³⁰ What are you doing, you devastated one?
     Why dress yourself in scarlet
     and put on jewels of gold?
Why highlight your eyes with makeup?
     You adorn yourself in vain.
Your lovers despise you;
     they want to kill you.

³¹ I hear a cry as of a woman in labor,
     a groan as of one bearing her first
         child —
the cry of Daughter Zion gasping for breath,
     stretching out her hands and saying,
"Alas! I am fainting;
     my life is given over to murderers."

Not One Is Upright

5 "Go up and down the streets of Jerusalem,
     look around and consider,
     search through her squares.
If you can find but one person
     who deals honestly and seeks the truth,
     I will forgive this city.
² Although they say, 'As surely as the LORD
         lives,'
     still they are swearing falsely."

³ LORD, do not your eyes look for truth?
     You struck them, but they felt no pain;
     you crushed them, but they refused
         correction.
They made their faces harder than stone
     and refused to repent.
⁴ I thought, "These are only the poor;
     they are foolish,
for they do not know the way of the LORD,
     the requirements of their God.
⁵ So I will go to the leaders
     and speak to them;
surely they know the way of the LORD,
     the requirements of their God."
But with one accord they too had broken off
         the yoke
     and torn off the bonds.
⁶ Therefore a lion from the forest will attack
         them,
     a wolf from the desert will ravage them,

a leopard will lie in wait near their towns
   to tear to pieces any who venture out,
for their rebellion is great
   and their backslidings many.

7 "Why should I forgive you?
   Your children have forsaken me
   and sworn by gods that are not gods.
I supplied all their needs,
   yet they committed adultery
   and thronged to the houses of prostitutes.
8 They are well-fed, lusty stallions,
   each neighing for another man's wife.
9 Should I not punish them for this?"
   declares the Lord.
   "Should I not avenge myself
   on such a nation as this?

10 "Go through her vineyards and ravage
     them,
   but do not destroy them completely.
Strip off her branches,
   for these people do not belong to the
     Lord.
11 The people of Israel and the people of Judah
   have been utterly unfaithful to me,"
               declares the Lord.

12 They have lied about the Lord;
   they said, "He will do nothing!
No harm will come to us;
   we will never see sword or famine.
13 The prophets are but wind
   and the word is not in them;
   so let what they say be done to them."

14 Therefore this is what the Lord God Almighty says:

"Because the people have spoken these
     words,
I will make my words in your mouth a fire
   and these people the wood it consumes.
15 People of Israel," declares the Lord,
   "I am bringing a distant nation against
     you—
an ancient and enduring nation,
   a people whose language you do not know,
   whose speech you do not understand.
16 Their quivers are like an open grave;
   all of them are mighty warriors.
17 They will devour your harvests and food,
   devour your sons and daughters;
they will devour your flocks and herds,
   devour your vines and fig trees.
With the sword they will destroy
   the fortified cities in which you trust.

18 "Yet even in those days," declares the Lord,
"I will not destroy you completely. 19 And when
the people ask, 'Why has the Lord our God
done all this to us?' you will tell them, 'As you
have forsaken me and served foreign gods in
your own land, so now you will serve foreigners
in a land not your own.'

20 "Announce this to the descendants of Jacob
   and proclaim it in Judah:
21 Hear this, you foolish and senseless people,
   who have eyes but do not see,
   who have ears but do not hear:
22 Should you not fear me?" declares the Lord.
   "Should you not tremble in my presence?
I made the sand a boundary for the sea,
   an everlasting barrier it cannot cross.
The waves may roll, but they cannot prevail;
   they may roar, but they cannot cross it.
23 But these people have stubborn and
     rebellious hearts;
   they have turned aside and gone away.
24 They do not say to themselves,
   'Let us fear the Lord our God,
who gives autumn and spring rains in
     season,
   who assures us of the regular weeks of
     harvest.'
25 Your wrongdoings have kept these away;
   your sins have deprived you of good.

26 "Among my people are the wicked
   who lie in wait like men who snare birds
   and like those who set traps to catch
     people.
27 Like cages full of birds,
   their houses are full of deceit;
they have become rich and powerful
28   and have grown fat and sleek.
Their evil deeds have no limit;
   they do not seek justice.
They do not promote the case of the
     fatherless;
   they do not defend the just cause of the
     poor.
29 Should I not punish them for this?"
   declares the Lord.
   "Should I not avenge myself
   on such a nation as this?

30 "A horrible and shocking thing
   has happened in the land:
31 The prophets prophesy lies,
   the priests rule by their own authority,
and my people love it this way.
   But what will you do in the end?

Jerusalem Under Siege

6 "Flee for safety, people of Benjamin!
   Flee from Jerusalem!
Sound the trumpet in Tekoa!
   Raise the signal over Beth Hakkerem!
For disaster looms out of the north,
   even terrible destruction.
² I will destroy Daughter Zion,
   so beautiful and delicate.
³ Shepherds with their flocks will come
               against her;
   they will pitch their tents around her,
   each tending his own portion."

⁴ "Prepare for battle against her!
   Arise, let us attack at noon!
But, alas, the daylight is fading,
   and the shadows of evening grow long.
⁵ So arise, let us attack at night
   and destroy her fortresses!"

⁶ This is what the LORD Almighty says:

"Cut down the trees
   and build siege ramps against Jerusalem.
This city must be punished;
   it is filled with oppression.
⁷ As a well pours out its water,
   so she pours out her wickedness.
Violence and destruction resound in her;
   her sickness and wounds are ever
               before me.
⁸ Take warning, Jerusalem,
   or I will turn away from you
and make your land desolate
   so no one can live in it."

⁹ This is what the LORD Almighty says:

"Let them glean the remnant of Israel
   as thoroughly as a vine;
pass your hand over the branches again,
   like one gathering grapes."

¹⁰ To whom can I speak and give warning?
   Who will listen to me?
Their ears are closed[a]
   so they cannot hear.
The word of the LORD is offensive to them;
   they find no pleasure in it.
¹¹ But I am full of the wrath of the LORD,
   and I cannot hold it in.

"Pour it out on the children in the street
   and on the young men gathered together;
both husband and wife will be caught in it,
   and the old, those weighed down with
               years.
¹² Their houses will be turned over to others,
   together with their fields and their wives,
when I stretch out my hand
   against those who live in the land,"
                              declares the LORD.
¹³ "From the least to the greatest,
   all are greedy for gain;
prophets and priests alike,
   all practice deceit.
¹⁴ They dress the wound of my people
   as though it were not serious.
'Peace, peace,' they say,
   when there is no peace.
¹⁵ Are they ashamed of their detestable
               conduct?
No, they have no shame at all;
   they do not even know how to blush.
So they will fall among the fallen;
   they will be brought down when I punish
               them,"
                              says the LORD.

¹⁶ This is what the LORD says:

"Stand at the crossroads and look;
   ask for the ancient paths,
ask where the good way is, and walk in it,
   and you will find rest for your souls.
But you said, 'We will not walk in it.'
¹⁷ I appointed watchmen over you and said,
   'Listen to the sound of the trumpet!'
But you said, 'We will not listen.'
¹⁸ Therefore hear, you nations;
   you who are witnesses,
observe what will happen to them.
¹⁹ Hear, you earth:
   I am bringing disaster on this people,
   the fruit of their schemes,
because they have not listened to my words
   and have rejected my law.
²⁰ What do I care about incense from Sheba
   or sweet calamus from a distant land?
Your burnt offerings are not acceptable;
   your sacrifices do not please me."

²¹ Therefore this is what the LORD says:

"I will put obstacles before this people.
   Parents and children alike will stumble
               over them;
neighbors and friends will perish."

²² This is what the LORD says:

"Look, an army is coming
   from the land of the north;

---

[a] 10 Hebrew *uncircumcised*

The Leader Is a Watchman Who Guards and Guides the Flock

Jeremiah 6:16–19

Jeremiah illustrates the leader's job as a watchman. God appointed watchmen over his people to sound the trumpet in times of danger and to serve as his voice.

A watchman provides an outstanding metaphor for a leader. Watchmen guard and guide those they supervise. They guard against anything that would endanger the vision. They guide those they oversee, encouraging them to continue on the path toward that vision. They watch out for danger and maintain quality control. They cry out warnings to those who drift from the vision. They commit themselves to finishing the task they began. Watchmen must possess strong moral fiber and must remain committed to a strong sense of right and wrong.

Jeremiah served well as a watchman, but he never convinced the masses to get on board with what was right. In your own leadership, where do you draw the line between doing what is right and doing what will retain followers?

a great nation is being stirred up
   from the ends of the earth.
²³ They are armed with bow and spear;
   they are cruel and show no mercy.
They sound like the roaring sea
   as they ride on their horses;
they come like men in battle formation
   to attack you, Daughter Zion."

²⁴ We have heard reports about them,
   and our hands hang limp.
Anguish has gripped us,
   pain like that of a woman in labor.
²⁵ Do not go out to the fields
   or walk on the roads,
for the enemy has a sword,
   and there is terror on every side.
²⁶ Put on sackcloth, my people,
   and roll in ashes;
mourn with bitter wailing
   as for an only son,
for suddenly the destroyer
   will come upon us.

²⁷ "I have made you a tester of metals
   and my people the ore,
that you may observe
   and test their ways.
²⁸ They are all hardened rebels,
   going about to slander.
They are bronze and iron;
   they all act corruptly.
²⁹ The bellows blow fiercely
   to burn away the lead with fire,
but the refining goes on in vain;
   the wicked are not purged out.
³⁰ They are called rejected silver,
   because the LORD has rejected them."

False Religion Worthless

7 This is the word that came to Jeremiah from the LORD: ² "Stand at the gate of the LORD's house and there proclaim this message:

" 'Hear the word of the LORD, all you people of Judah who come through these gates to worship the LORD. ³ This is what the LORD Almighty, the God of Israel, says: Reform your ways and your actions, and I will let you live in this place. ⁴ Do not trust in deceptive words and say, "This is the temple of the LORD, the temple of the LORD, the temple of the LORD!" ⁵ If you really change your ways and your actions and deal with each other justly, ⁶ if you do not oppress the foreigner, the fatherless or the widow and do not shed innocent blood in this place, and if you do not follow other gods to your own harm, ⁷ then I will let you live in this place, in the land I gave your ancestors for ever and ever. ⁸ But look, you are trusting in deceptive words that are worthless.

⁹ " 'Will you steal and murder, commit adultery and perjury,ᵃ burn incense to Baal and follow other gods you have not known, ¹⁰ and then come and stand before me in this house, which bears my Name, and say, "We are safe" — safe to do all these detestable things? ¹¹ Has this house, which bears my Name, become a den of robbers to you? But I have been watching! declares the LORD.

¹² " 'Go now to the place in Shiloh where I first made a dwelling for my Name, and see what I did to it because of the wickedness of my people Israel. ¹³ While you were doing all these things, declares the LORD, I spoke to you again and again, but you did not listen; I called you, but you did not answer. ¹⁴ Therefore, what I did to Shiloh I will now do to the house that bears my Name, the temple you trust in, the place I gave to

ᵃ 9 Or and swear by false gods

you and your ancestors. ¹⁵I will thrust you from my presence, just as I did all your fellow Israelites, the people of Ephraim.'

¹⁶"So do not pray for this people nor offer any plea or petition for them; do not plead with me, for I will not listen to you. ¹⁷Do you not see what they are doing in the towns of Judah and in the streets of Jerusalem? ¹⁸The children gather wood, the fathers light the fire, and the women knead the dough and make cakes to offer to the Queen of Heaven. They pour out drink offerings to other gods to arouse my anger. ¹⁹But am I the one they are provoking? declares the LORD. Are they not rather harming themselves, to their own shame?

²⁰"'Therefore this is what the Sovereign LORD says: My anger and my wrath will be poured out on this place — on man and beast, on the trees of the field and on the crops of your land — and it will burn and not be quenched.

²¹"'This is what the LORD Almighty, the God of Israel, says: Go ahead, add your burnt offerings to your other sacrifices and eat the meat yourselves! ²²For when I brought your ancestors out of Egypt and spoke to them, I did not just give them commands about burnt offerings and sacrifices, ²³but I gave them this command: Obey me, and I will be your God and you will be my people. Walk in obedience to all I command you, that it may go well with you. ²⁴But they did not listen or pay attention; instead, they followed the stubborn inclinations of their evil hearts. They went backward and not forward. ²⁵From the time your ancestors left Egypt until now, day after day, again and again I sent you my servants the prophets. ²⁶But they did not listen to me or pay attention. They were stiff-necked and did more evil than their ancestors.'

²⁷"When you tell them all this, they will not listen to you; when you call to them, they will not answer. ²⁸Therefore say to them, 'This is the nation that has not obeyed the LORD its God or responded to correction. Truth has perished; it has vanished from their lips.

²⁹"'Cut off your hair and throw it away; take up a lament on the barren heights, for the LORD has rejected and abandoned this generation that is under his wrath.

The Valley of Slaughter

³⁰"'The people of Judah have done evil in my eyes, declares the LORD. They have set up their detestable idols in the house that bears my Name and have defiled it. ³¹They have built the high places of Topheth in the Valley of Ben Hinnom

to burn their sons and daughters in the fire — something I did not command, nor did it enter my mind. ³²So beware, the days are coming, declares the LORD, when people will no longer call it Topheth or the Valley of Ben Hinnom, but the Valley of Slaughter, for they will bury the dead in Topheth until there is no more room. ³³Then the carcasses of this people will become food for the birds and the wild animals, and there will be no one to frighten them away. ³⁴I will bring an end to the sounds of joy and gladness and to the voices of bride and bridegroom in the towns of Judah and the streets of Jerusalem, for the land will become desolate.

8 "'At that time, declares the LORD, the bones of the kings and officials of Judah, the bones of the priests and prophets, and the bones of the people of Jerusalem will be removed from their graves. ²They will be exposed to the sun and the moon and all the stars of the heavens, which they have loved and served and which they have followed and consulted and worshiped. They will not be gathered up or buried, but will be like dung lying on the ground. ³Wherever I banish them, all the survivors of this evil nation will prefer death to life, declares the LORD Almighty.'

Sin and Punishment

⁴"Say to them, 'This is what the LORD says:

"'When people fall down, do they not get up?
    When someone turns away, do they not
        return?
⁵Why then have these people turned away?
    Why does Jerusalem always turn away?
They cling to deceit;
    they refuse to return.
⁶I have listened attentively,
    but they do not say what is right.
None of them repent of their wickedness,
    saying, "What have I done?"
Each pursues their own course
    like a horse charging into battle.
⁷Even the stork in the sky
    knows her appointed seasons,
and the dove, the swift and the thrush
    observe the time of their migration.
But my people do not know
    the requirements of the LORD.

⁸"'How can you say, "We are wise,
    for we have the law of the LORD,"
when actually the lying pen of the scribes
    has handled it falsely?
⁹The wise will be put to shame;
    they will be dismayed and trapped.

Since they have rejected the word of the
LORD,
what kind of wisdom do they have?
[10] Therefore I will give their wives to other men
and their fields to new owners.
From the least to the greatest,
all are greedy for gain;
prophets and priests alike,
all practice deceit.
[11] They dress the wound of my people
as though it were not serious.
"Peace, peace," they say,
when there is no peace.
[12] Are they ashamed of their detestable
conduct?
No, they have no shame at all;
they do not even know how to blush.
So they will fall among the fallen;
they will be brought down when they are
punished,
says the LORD.

[13] "'I will take away their harvest,
declares the LORD.
There will be no grapes on the vine.
There will be no figs on the tree,
and their leaves will wither.
What I have given them
will be taken from them.[a]'"

[14] Why are we sitting here?
Gather together!
Let us flee to the fortified cities
and perish there!
For the LORD our God has doomed us to
perish
and given us poisoned water to drink,
because we have sinned against him.
[15] We hoped for peace
but no good has come,
for a time of healing
but there is only terror.
[16] The snorting of the enemy's horses
is heard from Dan;
at the neighing of their stallions
the whole land trembles.
They have come to devour
the land and everything in it,
the city and all who live there.

[17] "See, I will send venomous snakes among you,
vipers that cannot be charmed,
and they will bite you,"
declares the LORD.

[18] You who are my Comforter[b] in sorrow,
my heart is faint within me.

---

[a] 13 The meaning of the Hebrew for this sentence is uncertain.
[b] 18 The meaning of the Hebrew for this word is uncertain.

JEREMIAH

PROFILE in leadership

Speaking Hard Truth Without Compromise

Jeremiah 8:1–13

Jeremiah did not receive a pleasant message from God to deliver to his people. The Lord ordered him to declare judgment and destruction on Judah. God told the prophet that he was about to destroy a sinful generation, a group of stubborn men and women who had turned to the basest kind of idolatry.

The Lord had patiently borne with these people. For many years he had issued stern warnings about their sin—yet they refused to surrender to him. They had grown so depraved and shameless that God told Jeremiah they could no longer even blush over their vile conduct (Jer 8:12).

The truly godly leader takes no pleasure in announcing divine judgment. It is a grievous thing to have to announce that the time for retribution has come. God himself grieves when his people's sin sinks to the point of no return. On the other hand, a truly godly leader never shrinks from confronting sin or from declaring the message of God. Effective leaders faithfully confront sin and call the sinner to repentance.

It could not have been easy for Jeremiah to communicate God's words of judgment. Neither is it easy to communicate today with people who need to be confronted over their sin. But leadership means speaking all the truth—sometimes unpleasant and painful truth—that God has entrusted to us.

¹⁹ Listen to the cry of my people
    from a land far away:
"Is the LORD not in Zion?
    Is her King no longer there?"

"Why have they aroused my anger with their
    images,
    with their worthless foreign idols?"

²⁰ "The harvest is past,
    the summer has ended,
    and we are not saved."

²¹ Since my people are crushed, I am crushed;
    I mourn, and horror grips me.
²² Is there no balm in Gilead?
    Is there no physician there?
Why then is there no healing
    for the wound of my people?

9ᵃ ¹ Oh, that my head were a spring of water
    and my eyes a fountain of tears!
I would weep day and night
    for the slain of my people.
² Oh, that I had in the desert
    a lodging place for travelers,
so that I might leave my people
    and go away from them;
for they are all adulterers,
    a crowd of unfaithful people.

³ "They make ready their tongue
    like a bow, to shoot lies;
it is not by truth
    that they triumphᵇ in the land.
They go from one sin to another;
    they do not acknowledge me,"
                declares the LORD.
⁴ "Beware of your friends;
    do not trust anyone in your clan.
For every one of them is a deceiver,ᶜ
    and every friend a slanderer.
⁵ Friend deceives friend,
    and no one speaks the truth.
They have taught their tongues to lie;
    they weary themselves with sinning.
⁶ Youᵈ live in the midst of deception;
    in their deceit they refuse to acknowledge
    me,"
                declares the LORD.

⁷ Therefore this is what the LORD Almighty
says:

"See, I will refine and test them,
    for what else can I do
because of the sin of my people?
⁸ Their tongue is a deadly arrow;
    it speaks deceitfully.

With their mouths they all speak cordially to
    their neighbors,
    but in their hearts they set traps for
    them.
⁹ Should I not punish them for this?"
    declares the LORD.
"Should I not avenge myself
    on such a nation as this?"

¹⁰ I will weep and wail for the mountains
    and take up a lament concerning the
    wilderness grasslands.
They are desolate and untraveled,
    and the lowing of cattle is not heard.
The birds have all fled
    and the animals are gone.

¹¹ "I will make Jerusalem a heap of ruins,
    a haunt of jackals;
and I will lay waste the towns of Judah
    so no one can live there."

¹² Who is wise enough to understand this? Who has been instructed by the LORD and can explain it? Why has the land been ruined and laid waste like a desert that no one can cross? ¹³ The LORD said, "It is because they have forsaken my law, which I set before them; they have not obeyed me or followed my law. ¹⁴ Instead, they have followed the stubbornness of their hearts; they have followed the Baals, as their ancestors taught them." ¹⁵ Therefore this is what the LORD Almighty, the God of Israel, says: "See, I will make this people eat bitter food and drink poisoned water. ¹⁶ I will scatter them among nations that neither they nor their ancestors have known, and I will pursue them with the sword until I have made an end of them."

¹⁷ This is what the LORD Almighty says:

"Consider now! Call for the wailing women
    to come;
    send for the most skillful of them.
¹⁸ Let them come quickly
    and wail over us
till our eyes overflow with tears
    and water streams from our eyelids.
¹⁹ The sound of wailing is heard from Zion:
    'How ruined we are!
    How great is our shame!
We must leave our land
    because our houses are in ruins.'"

ᵃ In Hebrew texts 9:1 is numbered 8:23, and 9:2-26 is numbered 9:1-25. ᵇ 3 Or lies; / they are not valiant for truth ᶜ 4 Or a deceiving Jacob ᵈ 6 That is, Jeremiah (the Hebrew is singular)

^{20}Now, you women, hear the word of the LORD;
    open your ears to the words of his mouth.
Teach your daughters how to wail;
    teach one another a lament.
^{21}Death has climbed in through our windows
    and has entered our fortresses;
it has removed the children from the streets
    and the young men from the public squares.

^{22}Say, "This is what the LORD declares:

"'Dead bodies will lie
    like dung on the open field,
like cut grain behind the reaper,
    with no one to gather them.'"

^{23}This is what the LORD says:

"Let not the wise boast of their wisdom
    or the strong boast of their strength
    or the rich boast of their riches,
^{24}but let the one who boasts boast about this:
    that they have the understanding to
        know me,
that I am the LORD, who exercises kindness,
    justice and righteousness on earth,
    for in these I delight,"
                                declares the LORD.

^{25}"The days are coming," declares the LORD,
"when I will punish all who are circumcised
only in the flesh — ^{26}Egypt, Judah, Edom, Ammon, Moab and all who live in the wilderness in
distant places.^{a} For all these nations are really
uncircumcised, and even the whole house of Israel is uncircumcised in heart."

God and Idols

10 Hear what the LORD says to you, people of
Israel. ^{2}This is what the LORD says:

"Do not learn the ways of the nations
    or be terrified by signs in the heavens,
    though the nations are terrified by them.
^{3}For the practices of the peoples are worthless;
    they cut a tree out of the forest,
    and a craftsman shapes it with his chisel.
^{4}They adorn it with silver and gold;
    they fasten it with hammer and nails
    so it will not totter.
^{5}Like a scarecrow in a cucumber field,
    their idols cannot speak;
they must be carried
    because they cannot walk.
Do not fear them;
    they can do no harm
    nor can they do any good."

^{6}No one is like you, LORD;
    you are great,
    and your name is mighty in power.
^{7}Who should not fear you,
    King of the nations?
    This is your due.
Among all the wise leaders of the nations
    and in all their kingdoms,
    there is no one like you.

^{8}They are all senseless and foolish;
    they are taught by worthless wooden idols.

---

^{a} 26 Or *wilderness and who clip the hair by their foreheads*

Priorities: Leaders Must Know What's Really Valuable

Jeremiah 9:23–24

What is our ultimate priority? What should we pursue more than anything else? What is worth boasting about? Some business leaders would answer, "Wealth and investments." Some educational or political leaders would reply, "Intelligence and strategy." Some athletic or sports leaders might respond, "Strength and speed."

But Jeremiah warns us against boasting about any of these. These are valuable resources, but not ultimate priorities. The only thing worth boasting about is a vital relationship with God. The others are merely a means to an end.

Leaders must recognize the difference between these two:

The Ultimate	**The Immediate**
1. God is the source.	1. The others are a resource.
2. He provides a life.	2. These provide a living.
3. Spiritual things are the end.	3. Material things are a means to an end.

⁹Hammered silver is brought from Tarshish
   and gold from Uphaz.
What the craftsman and goldsmith have
      made
   is then dressed in blue and purple—
   all made by skilled workers.
¹⁰But the LORD is the true God;
   he is the living God, the eternal King.
When he is angry, the earth trembles;
   the nations cannot endure his wrath.

¹¹"Tell them this: 'These gods, who did not
make the heavens and the earth, will perish
from the earth and from under the heavens.'"ᵃ

¹²But God made the earth by his power;
   he founded the world by his wisdom
   and stretched out the heavens by his
      understanding.
¹³When he thunders, the waters in the heavens
      roar;
   he makes clouds rise from the ends of the
      earth.
He sends lightning with the rain
   and brings out the wind from his
      storehouses.

¹⁴Everyone is senseless and without
      knowledge;
   every goldsmith is shamed by his idols.
The images he makes are a fraud;
   they have no breath in them.
¹⁵They are worthless, the objects of mockery;
   when their judgment comes, they will
      perish.
¹⁶He who is the Portion of Jacob is not like
      these,
   for he is the Maker of all things,
including Israel, the people of his
      inheritance—
   the LORD Almighty is his name.

Coming Destruction

¹⁷Gather up your belongings to leave the land,
   you who live under siege.
¹⁸For this is what the LORD says:
   "At this time I will hurl out
   those who live in this land;
I will bring distress on them
   so that they may be captured."

¹⁹Woe to me because of my injury!
   My wound is incurable!
Yet I said to myself,
   "This is my sickness, and I must endure it."
²⁰My tent is destroyed;
   all its ropes are snapped.

My children are gone from me and are no
      more;
   no one is left now to pitch my tent
   or to set up my shelter.
²¹The shepherds are senseless
   and do not inquire of the LORD;
so they do not prosper
   and all their flock is scattered.
²²Listen! The report is coming—
   a great commotion from the land of the
      north!
It will make the towns of Judah desolate,
   a haunt of jackals.

Jeremiah's Prayer

²³LORD, I know that people's lives are not their
      own;
   it is not for them to direct their steps.
²⁴Discipline me, LORD, but only in due
      measure—
   not in your anger,
   or you will reduce me to nothing.
²⁵Pour out your wrath on the nations
   that do not acknowledge you,
   on the peoples who do not call on your
      name.
For they have devoured Jacob;
   they have devoured him completely
   and destroyed his homeland.

The Covenant Is Broken

11 This is the word that came to Jeremiah from the LORD: ²"Listen to the terms of this covenant and tell them to the people of Judah and to those who live in Jerusalem. ³Tell them that this is what the LORD, the God of Israel, says: 'Cursed is the one who does not obey the terms of this covenant— ⁴the terms I commanded your ancestors when I brought them out of Egypt, out of the iron-smelting furnace.' I said, 'Obey me and do everything I command you, and you will be my people, and I will be your God. ⁵Then I will fulfill the oath I swore to your ancestors, to give them a land flowing with milk and honey'—the land you possess today."

I answered, "Amen, LORD."

⁶The LORD said to me, "Proclaim all these words in the towns of Judah and in the streets of Jerusalem: 'Listen to the terms of this covenant and follow them. ⁷From the time I brought your ancestors up from Egypt until today, I warned them again and again, saying, "Obey me." ⁸But they did not listen or pay attention; instead, they

---

ᵃ 11 The text of this verse is in Aramaic.

followed the stubbornness of their evil hearts. So I brought on them all the curses of the covenant I had commanded them to follow but that they did not keep.'"

⁹Then the LORD said to me, "There is a conspiracy among the people of Judah and those who live in Jerusalem. ¹⁰They have returned to the sins of their ancestors, who refused to listen to my words. They have followed other gods to serve them. Both Israel and Judah have broken the covenant I made with their ancestors. ¹¹Therefore this is what the LORD says: 'I will bring on them a disaster they cannot escape. Although they cry out to me, I will not listen to them. ¹²The towns of Judah and the people of Jerusalem will go and cry out to the gods to whom they burn incense, but they will not help them at all when disaster strikes. ¹³You, Judah, have as many gods as you have towns; and the altars you have set up to burn incense to that shameful god Baal are as many as the streets of Jerusalem.'

¹⁴"Do not pray for this people or offer any plea or petition for them, because I will not listen when they call to me in the time of their distress.

¹⁵"What is my beloved doing in my temple
    as she, with many others, works out her
        evil schemes?
Can consecrated meat avert your
        punishment?
When you engage in your wickedness,
    then you rejoice.ᵃ"

¹⁶The LORD called you a thriving olive tree
    with fruit beautiful in form.
But with the roar of a mighty storm
    he will set it on fire,
    and its branches will be broken.

¹⁷The LORD Almighty, who planted you, has decreed disaster for you, because the people of both Israel and Judah have done evil and aroused my anger by burning incense to Baal.

Plot Against Jeremiah

¹⁸Because the LORD revealed their plot to me, I knew it, for at that time he showed me what they were doing. ¹⁹I had been like a gentle lamb led to the slaughter; I did not realize that they had plotted against me, saying,

"Let us destroy the tree and its fruit;
    let us cut him off from the land of the
        living,
    that his name be remembered no more."

²⁰But you, LORD Almighty, who judge
        righteously
    and test the heart and mind,
let me see your vengeance on them,
    for to you I have committed my cause.

²¹Therefore this is what the LORD says about the people of Anathoth who are threatening to kill you, saying, "Do not prophesy in the name of the LORD or you will die by our hands"— ²²therefore this is what the LORD Almighty says: "I will punish them. Their young men will die by the sword, their sons and daughters by famine. ²³Not even a remnant will be left to them, because I will bring disaster on the people of Anathoth in the year of their punishment."

Jeremiah's Complaint

12 You are always righteous, LORD,
    when I bring a case before you.
Yet I would speak with you about your justice:
    Why does the way of the wicked prosper?
    Why do all the faithless live at ease?
²You have planted them, and they have taken
        root;
    they grow and bear fruit.
You are always on their lips
    but far from their hearts.
³Yet you know me, LORD;
    you see me and test my thoughts about
        you.
Drag them off like sheep to be butchered!
    Set them apart for the day of slaughter!
⁴How long will the land lie parched
    and the grass in every field be withered?
Because those who live in it are wicked,
    the animals and birds have perished.

ᵃ 15 Or Could consecrated meat avert your punishment? / Then you would rejoice

---

Attitude: Leaders Don't Get Lost in the Problems

Jeremiah 12:1–4

If Jeremiah complained about relatively easy days, then how could God use him in hard times? Like us, Jeremiah suffered from hardening of the attitudes. We lose perspective on what real problems look like and what God is able to do. Let's focus on his promise, not our problems.

Moreover, the people are saying,
   "He will not see what happens to us."

God's Answer

5 "If you have raced with men on foot
      and they have worn you out,
   how can you compete with horses?
   If you stumble*a* in safe country,
      how will you manage in the thickets by*b*
         the Jordan?
6 Your relatives, members of your own
         family —
      even they have betrayed you;
   they have raised a loud cry against you.
   Do not trust them,
      though they speak well of you.

7 "I will forsake my house,
      abandon my inheritance;
   I will give the one I love
      into the hands of her enemies.
8 My inheritance has become to me
      like a lion in the forest.
   She roars at me;
      therefore I hate her.
9 Has not my inheritance become to me
      like a speckled bird of prey
   that other birds of prey surround and
         attack?
   Go and gather all the wild beasts;
      bring them to devour.
10 Many shepherds will ruin my vineyard
      and trample down my field;
   they will turn my pleasant field
      into a desolate wasteland.
11 It will be made a wasteland,
      parched and desolate before me;
   the whole land will be laid waste
      because there is no one who cares.
12 Over all the barren heights in the desert
      destroyers will swarm,
   for the sword of the LORD will devour
      from one end of the land to the other;
      no one will be safe.
13 They will sow wheat but reap thorns;
      they will wear themselves out but gain
         nothing.
   They will bear the shame of their harvest
      because of the LORD's fierce anger."

14 This is what the LORD says: "As for all my wicked neighbors who seize the inheritance I gave my people Israel, I will uproot them from their lands and I will uproot the people of Judah from among them. 15 But after I uproot them, I will again have compassion and will bring each of them back to their own inheritance and their own country. 16 And if they learn well the ways of my people and swear by my name, saying, 'As surely as the LORD lives' — even as they once taught my people to swear by Baal — then they will be established among my people. 17 But if any nation does not listen, I will completely uproot and destroy it," declares the LORD.

A Linen Belt

13 This is what the LORD said to me: "Go and buy a linen belt and put it around your waist, but do not let it touch water." 2 So I bought a belt, as the LORD directed, and put it around my waist.

3 Then the word of the LORD came to me a second time: 4 "Take the belt you bought and are wearing around your waist, and go now to Perath*c* and hide it there in a crevice in the rocks." 5 So I went and hid it at Perath, as the LORD told me.

6 Many days later the LORD said to me, "Go now to Perath and get the belt I told you to hide there." 7 So I went to Perath and dug up the belt and took it from the place where I had hidden it, but now it was ruined and completely useless.

8 Then the word of the LORD came to me: 9 "This is what the LORD says: 'In the same way I will ruin the pride of Judah and the great pride of Jerusalem. 10 These wicked people, who refuse to listen to my words, who follow the stubbornness of their hearts and go after other gods to serve and worship them, will be like this belt — completely useless! 11 For as a belt is bound around the waist, so I bound all the people of Israel and all the people of Judah to me,' declares the LORD, 'to be my people for my renown and praise and honor. But they have not listened.'

Wineskins

12 "Say to them: 'This is what the LORD, the God of Israel, says: Every wineskin should be filled with wine.' And if they say to you, 'Don't we know that every wineskin should be filled with wine?' 13 then tell them, 'This is what the LORD says: I am going to fill with drunkenness all who live in this land, including the kings who sit on David's throne, the priests, the prophets and all those living in Jerusalem. 14 I will smash them one against the other, parents and children alike, declares the LORD. I will allow no pity or mercy or compassion to keep me from destroying them.'"

---

a 5 Or *you feel secure only*   *b* 5 Or *the flooding of*   *c* 4 Or possibly *to the Euphrates*; similarly in verses 5-7

The Linen Sash: An Analogy for Leaders Who Want to Be Useful

Jeremiah 13:1–11

God instructed Jeremiah to wear a linen sash for a while, then bury it. What happened? The once useful sash became useless.

Through this sash, God provides a teaching analogy for his people. The ruined piece of clothing represented the people of Israel who once served and worshiped God, but then became useless through their disobedience. Leaders have special reasons to pay close attention to this object lesson. Consider the parallels between leaders and the linen sash:

Remain useful when:

1. *They are stretched.*
   We must be stretched and challenged.

2. *They are secure.*
   We must draw our identity from God.

3. *They are solid.*
   We must possess stable values.

Become useless when:

1. *They are soiled.*
   We cannot live with sin and apathy.

2. *They are separated.*
   We cannot live as mavericks.

3. *They are shrunk.*
   We aren't useful when we think small.

Threat of Captivity

¹⁵ Hear and pay attention,
   do not be arrogant,
   for the LORD has spoken.
¹⁶ Give glory to the LORD your God
   before he brings the darkness,
before your feet stumble
   on the darkening hills.
You hope for light,
   but he will turn it to utter darkness
   and change it to deep gloom.
¹⁷ If you do not listen,
   I will weep in secret
   because of your pride;
my eyes will weep bitterly,
   overflowing with tears,
   because the LORD's flock will be taken
      captive.

¹⁸ Say to the king and to the queen mother,
   "Come down from your thrones,
for your glorious crowns
   will fall from your heads."
¹⁹ The cities in the Negev will be shut up,
   and there will be no one to open them.
All Judah will be carried into exile,
   carried completely away.

²⁰ Look up and see
   those who are coming from the north.
Where is the flock that was entrusted to you,
   the sheep of which you boasted?

²¹ What will you say when the LORD sets over
      you
   those you cultivated as your special
      allies?
Will not pain grip you
   like that of a woman in labor?
²² And if you ask yourself,
   "Why has this happened to me?" —
it is because of your many sins
   that your skirts have been torn off
   and your body mistreated.
²³ Can an Ethiopianª change his skin
   or a leopard its spots?
Neither can you do good
   who are accustomed to doing evil.

²⁴ "I will scatter you like chaff
   driven by the desert wind.
²⁵ This is your lot,
   the portion I have decreed for you,"
                                 declares the LORD,
   "because you have forgotten me
   and trusted in false gods.
²⁶ I will pull up your skirts over your face
   that your shame may be seen —
²⁷ your adulteries and lustful neighings,
   your shameless prostitution!
I have seen your detestable acts
   on the hills and in the fields.

ª 23 Hebrew *Cushite* (probably a person from the upper Nile region)

Woe to you, Jerusalem!
How long will you be unclean?"

Drought, Famine, Sword

14 This is the word of the LORD that came to Jeremiah concerning the drought:

2 "Judah mourns,
her cities languish;
they wail for the land,
and a cry goes up from Jerusalem.
3 The nobles send their servants for water;
they go to the cisterns
but find no water.
They return with their jars unfilled;
dismayed and despairing,
they cover their heads.
4 The ground is cracked
because there is no rain in the land;
the farmers are dismayed
and cover their heads.
5 Even the doe in the field
deserts her newborn fawn
because there is no grass.
6 Wild donkeys stand on the barren
heights
and pant like jackals;
their eyes fail
for lack of food."

7 Although our sins testify against us,
do something, LORD, for the sake of your
name.
For we have often rebelled;
we have sinned against you.
8 You who are the hope of Israel,
its Savior in times of distress,
why are you like a stranger in the land,
like a traveler who stays only a night?
9 Why are you like a man taken by surprise,
like a warrior powerless to save?
You are among us, LORD,
and we bear your name;
do not forsake us!

10 This is what the LORD says about this people:

"They greatly love to wander;
they do not restrain their feet.
So the LORD does not accept them;
he will now remember their
wickedness
and punish them for their sins."

11 Then the LORD said to me, "Do not pray for the well-being of this people. 12 Although they fast, I will not listen to their cry; though they offer burnt offerings and grain offerings, I will not accept them. Instead, I will destroy them with the sword, famine and plague."

13 But I said, "Alas, Sovereign LORD! The prophets keep telling them, 'You will not see the sword or suffer famine. Indeed, I will give you lasting peace in this place.'"

14 Then the LORD said to me, "The prophets are prophesying lies in my name. I have not sent them or appointed them or spoken to them. They are prophesying to you false visions, divinations, idolatries[a] and the delusions of their own minds. 15 Therefore this is what the LORD says about the prophets who are prophesying in my name: I did not send them, yet they are saying, 'No sword or famine will touch this land.' Those same prophets will perish by sword and famine. 16 And the people they are prophesying to will be thrown out into the streets of Jerusalem because of the famine and sword. There will be no one to bury them, their wives, their sons and their daughters. I will pour out on them the calamity they deserve.

17 "Speak this word to them:

"'Let my eyes overflow with tears
night and day without ceasing;
for the Virgin Daughter, my people,
has suffered a grievous wound,
a crushing blow.
18 If I go into the country,
I see those slain by the sword;
if I go into the city,
I see the ravages of famine.
Both prophet and priest
have gone to a land they know not.'"

19 Have you rejected Judah completely?
Do you despise Zion?
Why have you afflicted us
so that we cannot be healed?
We hoped for peace
but no good has come,
for a time of healing
but there is only terror.
20 We acknowledge our wickedness, LORD,
and the guilt of our ancestors;
we have indeed sinned against you.
21 For the sake of your name do not
despise us;
do not dishonor your glorious throne.
Remember your covenant with us
and do not break it.

---

a 14 Or *visions, worthless divinations*

What Happens to Leaders Who Mislead and Damage Others?

Jeremiah 14:14–16

A group of false prophets spoke about the future, as Jeremiah did, yet they proclaimed a much more positive message than his. People liked them because they spoke what they wanted to hear. Nevertheless, God told Jeremiah to continue speaking truthfully. The very drought, famine and sword the false prophets denied would soon kill them.

God reserves special judgment for leaders who speak out of turn and who give the people merely what they want to hear. Note the sharp contrast between these prophets and Jeremiah:

Jeremiah	False Leaders
1. **Spoke the truth even when it hurt**	1. **Spoke only what made people feel good**
2. **Constantly checked and purified his motives**	2. **Were motivated by selfish gain and popularity**
3. **Gave direction tied to an eternal hope**	3. **Gave direction tied to temporary pleasure**
4. **Was eventually proven right**	4. **Lost their lives because of what they said**

22 Do any of the worthless idols of the nations
    bring rain?
  Do the skies themselves send down
    showers?
No, it is you, LORD our God.
  Therefore our hope is in you,
    for you are the one who does all this.

15 Then the LORD said to me: "Even if Moses and Samuel were to stand before me, my heart would not go out to this people. Send them away from my presence! Let them go! 2And if they ask you, 'Where shall we go?' tell them, 'This is what the LORD says:

"'Those destined for death, to death;
  those for the sword, to the sword;
  those for starvation, to starvation;
  those for captivity, to captivity.'

3"I will send four kinds of destroyers against them," declares the LORD, "the sword to kill and the dogs to drag away and the birds and the wild animals to devour and destroy. 4I will make them abhorrent to all the kingdoms of the earth because of what Manasseh son of Hezekiah king of Judah did in Jerusalem.

5"Who will have pity on you, Jerusalem?
  Who will mourn for you?
  Who will stop to ask how you are?
6You have rejected me," declares the LORD.
  "You keep on backsliding.
So I will reach out and destroy you;
  I am tired of holding back.

7I will winnow them with a winnowing fork
    at the city gates of the land.
  I will bring bereavement and destruction on
    my people,
    for they have not changed their ways.
8I will make their widows more numerous
    than the sand of the sea.
  At midday I will bring a destroyer
    against the mothers of their young men;
  suddenly I will bring down on them
    anguish and terror.
9The mother of seven will grow faint
    and breathe her last.
  Her sun will set while it is still day;
    she will be disgraced and humiliated.
  I will put the survivors to the sword
    before their enemies,"
                                declares the LORD.

10 Alas, my mother, that you gave me birth,
    a man with whom the whole land strives
      and contends!
  I have neither lent nor borrowed,
    yet everyone curses me.

11The LORD said,

"Surely I will deliver you for a good
    purpose;
  surely I will make your enemies plead
    with you
  in times of disaster and times of distress.

12"Can a man break iron —
    iron from the north — or bronze?

13 "Your wealth and your treasures
    I will give as plunder, without charge,
because of all your sins
    throughout your country.
14 I will enslave you to your enemies
    in*a* a land you do not know,
for my anger will kindle a fire
    that will burn against you."

15 LORD, you understand;
    remember me and care for me.
    Avenge me on my persecutors.
You are long-suffering — do not take me
    away;
    think of how I suffer reproach for your
    sake.
16 When your words came, I ate them;
    they were my joy and my heart's delight,
for I bear your name,
    LORD God Almighty.
17 I never sat in the company of revelers,
    never made merry with them;
I sat alone because your hand was on me
    and you had filled me with indignation.
18 Why is my pain unending
    and my wound grievous and incurable?
You are to me like a deceptive brook,
    like a spring that fails.

19 Therefore this is what the LORD says:

"If you repent, I will restore you
    that you may serve me;

if you utter worthy, not worthless, words,
    you will be my spokesman.
Let this people turn to you,
    but you must not turn to them.
20 I will make you a wall to this people,
    a fortified wall of bronze;
they will fight against you
    but will not overcome you,
for I am with you
    to rescue and save you,"
                    declares the LORD.
21 "I will save you from the hands of the wicked
    and deliver you from the grasp of the
    cruel."

Day of Disaster

16 Then the word of the LORD came to me: 2 "You must not marry and have sons or daughters in this place." 3 For this is what the LORD says about the sons and daughters born in this land and about the women who are their mothers and the men who are their fathers: 4 "They will die of deadly diseases. They will not be mourned or buried but will be like dung lying on the ground. They will perish by sword and famine, and their dead bodies will become food for the birds and the wild animals."

5 For this is what the LORD says: "Do not en-

---

a 14 Some Hebrew manuscripts, Septuagint and Syriac (see also 17:4); most Hebrew manuscripts *I will cause your enemies to bring you / into*

Courage: One Person Standing with God Is Invincible

Jeremiah 15:15–21

Jeremiah asked God to remember the stand he took. This leader acted with courage when no one else seemed to be able to do so. In three short verses, we read what Jeremiah endured in his struggle to stand courageously:

    1. **He was neglected (v. 15).**

    2. **He was mistreated (v. 15).**

    3. **He was lonely (v. 17).**

    4. **He endured continual discouragement (v. 18).**

    5. **He felt let down by God (v. 18).**

In verses 19–21, God gave his prophet courage by giving him a . . .

    1. *Picture of himself*—God allowed him to stand and see a vision of Yahweh.

    2. *Picture of the people*—God confirms Jeremiah's view: The people are stubborn.

    3. *Picture of victory*—God reminds him that the Lord is greater than any circumstance.

ter a house where there is a funeral meal; do not go to mourn or show sympathy, because I have withdrawn my blessing, my love and my pity from this people," declares the LORD. ⁶"Both high and low will die in this land. They will not be buried or mourned, and no one will cut themselves or shave their head for the dead. ⁷No one will offer food to comfort those who mourn for the dead—not even for a father or a mother—nor will anyone give them a drink to console them.

⁸"And do not enter a house where there is feasting and sit down to eat and drink. ⁹For this is what the LORD Almighty, the God of Israel, says: Before your eyes and in your days I will bring an end to the sounds of joy and gladness and to the voices of bride and bridegroom in this place.

¹⁰"When you tell these people all this and they ask you, 'Why has the LORD decreed such a great disaster against us? What wrong have we done? What sin have we committed against the LORD our God?' ¹¹then say to them, 'It is because your ancestors forsook me,' declares the LORD, 'and followed other gods and served and worshiped them. They forsook me and did not keep my law. ¹²But you have behaved more wickedly than your ancestors. See how all of you are following the stubbornness of your evil hearts instead of obeying me. ¹³So I will throw you out of this land into a land neither you nor your ancestors have known, and there you will serve other gods day and night, for I will show you no favor.'

¹⁴"However, the days are coming," declares the LORD, "when it will no longer be said, 'As surely as the LORD lives, who brought the Israelites up out of Egypt,' ¹⁵but it will be said, 'As surely as the LORD lives, who brought the Israelites up out of the land of the north and out of all the countries where he had banished them.' For I will restore them to the land I gave their ancestors.

¹⁶"But now I will send for many fishermen," declares the LORD, "and they will catch them. After that I will send for many hunters, and they will hunt them down on every mountain and hill and from the crevices of the rocks. ¹⁷My eyes are on all their ways; they are not hidden from me, nor is their sin concealed from my eyes. ¹⁸I will repay them double for their wickedness and their sin, because they have defiled my land with the lifeless forms of their vile images and have filled my inheritance with their detestable idols."

¹⁹LORD, my strength and my fortress,
  my refuge in time of distress,
to you the nations will come
  from the ends of the earth and say,
"Our ancestors possessed nothing but false gods,
  worthless idols that did them no good.
²⁰Do people make their own gods?
  Yes, but they are not gods!"

²¹"Therefore I will teach them—
  this time I will teach them
  my power and might.
Then they will know
  that my name is the LORD.

17 "Judah's sin is engraved with an iron tool,
  inscribed with a flint point,
on the tablets of their hearts
  and on the horns of their altars.
²Even their children remember
  their altars and Asherah poles[a]
beside the spreading trees
  and on the high hills.
³My mountain in the land
  and your[b] wealth and all your treasures
I will give away as plunder,
  together with your high places,
  because of sin throughout your country.
⁴Through your own fault you will lose
  the inheritance I gave you.
I will enslave you to your enemies
  in a land you do not know,
for you have kindled my anger,
  and it will burn forever."

⁵This is what the LORD says:

"Cursed is the one who trusts in man,
  who draws strength from mere flesh
  and whose heart turns away from the LORD.
⁶That person will be like a bush in the wastelands;
  they will not see prosperity when it comes.
They will dwell in the parched places of the desert,
  in a salt land where no one lives.

⁷"But blessed is the one who trusts in the LORD,
  whose confidence is in him.
⁸They will be like a tree planted by the water
  that sends out its roots by the stream.

_____
[a] 2 That is, wooden symbols of the goddess Asherah
[b] 2,3 Or hills / ³and the mountains of the land. / Your

It does not fear when heat comes;
　　its leaves are always green.
It has no worries in a year of drought
　　and never fails to bear fruit."

9 The heart is deceitful above all things
　　and beyond cure.
　Who can understand it?

10 "I the LORD search the heart
　　and examine the mind,
　to reward each person according to their
　　　conduct,
　　according to what their deeds deserve."

11 Like a partridge that hatches eggs it did not
　　　lay
　　are those who gain riches by unjust means.
　When their lives are half gone, their riches
　　　will desert them,
　　and in the end they will prove to be fools.

12 A glorious throne, exalted from the
　　　beginning,
　　is the place of our sanctuary.

13 LORD, you are the hope of Israel;
　　all who forsake you will be put to shame.
　Those who turn away from you will be
　　　written in the dust
　　because they have forsaken the LORD,
　　the spring of living water.

14 Heal me, LORD, and I will be healed;
　　save me and I will be saved,
　　for you are the one I praise.

15 They keep saying to me,
　　"Where is the word of the LORD?
　　Let it now be fulfilled!"

16 I have not run away from being your shepherd;
　　you know I have not desired the day of
　　　despair.
　　What passes my lips is open before you.

17 Do not be a terror to me;
　　you are my refuge in the day of disaster.

18 Let my persecutors be put to shame,
　　but keep me from shame;
　let them be terrified,
　　but keep me from terror.
　Bring on them the day of disaster;
　　destroy them with double destruction.

Keeping the Sabbath Day Holy

19 This is what the LORD said to me: "Go and
stand at the Gate of the People,[a] through which
the kings of Judah go in and out; stand also at
all the other gates of Jerusalem. 20 Say to them,
'Hear the word of the LORD, you kings of Judah

and all people of Judah and everyone living in
Jerusalem who come through these gates. 21 This
is what the LORD says: Be careful not to carry a
load on the Sabbath day or bring it through the
gates of Jerusalem. 22 Do not bring a load out of
your houses or do any work on the Sabbath, but
keep the Sabbath day holy, as I commanded your
ancestors. 23 Yet they did not listen or pay attention; they were stiff-necked and would not listen
or respond to discipline. 24 But if you are careful
to obey me, declares the LORD, and bring no load
through the gates of this city on the Sabbath, but
keep the Sabbath day holy by not doing any work
on it, 25 then kings who sit on David's throne will
come through the gates of this city with their officials. They and their officials will come riding
in chariots and on horses, accompanied by the
men of Judah and those living in Jerusalem, and
this city will be inhabited forever. 26 People will
come from the towns of Judah and the villages
around Jerusalem, from the territory of Benjamin
and the western foothills, from the hill country
and the Negev, bringing burnt offerings and sacrifices, grain offerings and incense, and bringing
thank offerings to the house of the LORD. 27 But if
you do not obey me to keep the Sabbath day holy
by not carrying any load as you come through the
gates of Jerusalem on the Sabbath day, then I will
kindle an unquenchable fire in the gates of Jerusalem that will consume her fortresses.'"

At the Potter's House

18 This is the word that came to Jeremiah
from the LORD: 2 "Go down to the potter's
house, and there I will give you my message."
3 So I went down to the potter's house, and I saw
him working at the wheel. 4 But the pot he was
shaping from the clay was marred in his hands;
so the potter formed it into another pot, shaping
it as seemed best to him.

5 Then the word of the LORD came to me. 6 He
said, "Can I not do with you, Israel, as this potter does?" declares the LORD. "Like clay in the
hand of the potter, so are you in my hand, Israel. 7 If at any time I announce that a nation or
kingdom is to be uprooted, torn down and destroyed, 8 and if that nation I warned repents of
its evil, then I will relent and not inflict on it the
disaster I had planned. 9 And if at another time I
announce that a nation or kingdom is to be built
up and planted, 10 and if it does evil in my sight
and does not obey me, then I will reconsider the
good I had intended to do for it.

a 19 Or Army

¹¹"Now therefore say to the people of Judah and those living in Jerusalem, 'This is what the LORD says: Look! I am preparing a disaster for you and devising a plan against you. So turn from your evil ways, each one of you, and reform your ways and your actions.' ¹²But they will reply, 'It's no use. We will continue with our own plans; we will all follow the stubbornness of our evil hearts.'"

¹³Therefore this is what the LORD says:

"Inquire among the nations:
  Who has ever heard anything like this?
A most horrible thing has been done
  by Virgin Israel.
¹⁴Does the snow of Lebanon
  ever vanish from its rocky slopes?
Do its cool waters from distant sources
  ever stop flowing?ᵃ
¹⁵Yet my people have forgotten me;
  they burn incense to worthless idols,
which made them stumble in their ways,
  in the ancient paths.
They made them walk in byways,
  on roads not built up.
¹⁶Their land will be an object of horror
  and of lasting scorn;
all who pass by will be appalled
  and will shake their heads.
¹⁷Like a wind from the east,
  I will scatter them before their enemies;
I will show them my back and not my
     face
  in the day of their disaster."

¹⁸They said, "Come, let's make plans against Jeremiah; for the teaching of the law by the priest will not cease, nor will counsel from the wise, nor the word from the prophets. So come, let's attack him with our tongues and pay no attention to anything he says."

Teachability: To Keep Leading, Keep Learning

Jeremiah 18:18

If you want to keep leading, you must keep learning. Yesterday's growth cannot suffice for today. We must remain teachable and flexible. God is the Potter; we are the clay. He will do what he wishes. We must allow him to mold us in the way he desires.

¹⁹Listen to me, LORD;
  hear what my accusers are saying!
²⁰Should good be repaid with evil?
  Yet they have dug a pit for me.
Remember that I stood before you
  and spoke in their behalf
  to turn your wrath away from them.
²¹So give their children over to famine;
  hand them over to the power of the sword.
Let their wives be made childless and
     widows;
  let their men be put to death,
  their young men slain by the sword in
     battle.
²²Let a cry be heard from their houses
  when you suddenly bring invaders against
     them,
for they have dug a pit to capture me
  and have hidden snares for my feet.
²³But you, LORD, know
  all their plots to kill me.
Do not forgive their crimes
  or blot out their sins from your sight.
Let them be overthrown before you;
  deal with them in the time of your anger.

19 This is what the LORD says: "Go and buy a clay jar from a potter. Take along some of the elders of the people and of the priests ²and go out to the Valley of Ben Hinnom, near the entrance of the Potsherd Gate. There proclaim the words I tell you, ³and say, 'Hear the word of the LORD, you kings of Judah and people of Jerusalem. This is what the LORD Almighty, the God of Israel, says: Listen! I am going to bring a disaster on this place that will make the ears of everyone who hears of it tingle. ⁴For they have forsaken me and made this a place of foreign gods; they have burned incense in it to gods that neither they nor their ancestors nor the kings of Judah ever knew, and they have filled this place with the blood of the innocent. ⁵They have built the high places of Baal to burn their children in the fire as offerings to Baal—something I did not command or mention, nor did it enter my mind. ⁶So beware, the days are coming, declares the LORD, when people will no longer call this place Topheth or the Valley of Ben Hinnom, but the Valley of Slaughter.

⁷"'In this place I will ruinᵇ the plans of Judah and Jerusalem. I will make them fall by

---

ᵃ 14 The meaning of the Hebrew for this sentence is uncertain.
ᵇ 7 The Hebrew for *ruin* sounds like the Hebrew for *jar* (see verses 1 and 10).

the sword before their enemies, at the hands of those who want to kill them, and I will give their carcasses as food to the birds and the wild animals. ⁸I will devastate this city and make it an object of horror and scorn; all who pass by will be appalled and will scoff because of all its wounds. ⁹I will make them eat the flesh of their sons and daughters, and they will eat one another's flesh because their enemies will press the siege so hard against them to destroy them.'

¹⁰"Then break the jar while those who go with you are watching, ¹¹and say to them, 'This is what the LORD Almighty says: I will smash this nation and this city just as this potter's jar is smashed and cannot be repaired. They will bury the dead in Topheth until there is no more room. ¹²This is what I will do to this place and to those who live here, declares the LORD. I will make this city like Topheth. ¹³The houses in Jerusalem and those of the kings of Judah will be defiled like this place, Topheth — all the houses where they burned incense on the roofs to all the starry hosts and poured out drink offerings to other gods.'"

¹⁴Jeremiah then returned from Topheth, where the LORD had sent him to prophesy, and stood in the court of the LORD's temple and said to all the people, ¹⁵"This is what the LORD Almighty, the God of Israel, says: 'Listen! I am going to bring on this city and all the villages around it every disaster I pronounced against them, because they were stiff-necked and would not listen to my words.'"

Jeremiah and Pashhur

20 When the priest Pashhur son of Immer, the official in charge of the temple of the LORD, heard Jeremiah prophesying these things, ²he had Jeremiah the prophet beaten and put in the stocks at the Upper Gate of Benjamin at the LORD's temple. ³The next day, when Pashhur released him from the stocks, Jeremiah said to him, "The LORD's name for you is not Pashhur, but Terror on Every Side. ⁴For this is what the LORD says: 'I will make you a terror to yourself and to all your friends; with your own eyes you will see them fall by the sword of their enemies. I will give all Judah into the hands of the king of Babylon, who will carry them away to Babylon or put them to the sword. ⁵I will deliver all the wealth of this city into the hands of their enemies — all its products, all its valuables and all the treasures of the kings of Judah. They will take it away as plunder and carry it off to Babylon. ⁶And you, Pashhur, and all who live in

your house will go into exile to Babylon. There you will die and be buried, you and all your friends to whom you have prophesied lies.'"

Jeremiah's Complaint

⁷You deceived[a] me, LORD, and I was
        deceived[a];
    you overpowered me and prevailed.
I am ridiculed all day long;
    everyone mocks me.
⁸Whenever I speak, I cry out
    proclaiming violence and destruction.
So the word of the LORD has brought me
    insult and reproach all day long.
⁹But if I say, "I will not mention his word
    or speak anymore in his name,"
his word is in my heart like a fire,
    a fire shut up in my bones.
I am weary of holding it in;
    indeed, I cannot.
¹⁰I hear many whispering,
    "Terror on every side!
    Denounce him! Let's denounce him!"
All my friends
    are waiting for me to slip, saying,
"Perhaps he will be deceived;
    then we will prevail over him
    and take our revenge on him."

¹¹But the LORD is with me like a mighty
        warrior;
    so my persecutors will stumble and not
        prevail.
They will fail and be thoroughly disgraced;
    their dishonor will never be forgotten.
¹²LORD Almighty, you who examine the
        righteous
    and probe the heart and mind,
let me see your vengeance on them,
    for to you I have committed my cause.

¹³Sing to the LORD!
    Give praise to the LORD!
He rescues the life of the needy
    from the hands of the wicked.

¹⁴Cursed be the day I was born!
    May the day my mother bore me not be
        blessed!
¹⁵Cursed be the man who brought my father
        the news,
    who made him very glad, saying,
    "A child is born to you — a son!"
¹⁶May that man be like the towns
    the LORD overthrew without pity.

ᵃ 7 Or *persuaded*

Convictions: Turning Defeat into Dividends

Jeremiah 20:1–18

Every leader experiences both good and bad days. Even God's greatest leaders become discouraged. Jeremiah 20 allows us to see into the heart of a great leader. Jeremiah complains to God in the first ten verses. He praises God for his victories in the next four verses. And in the next five verses he curses the day he was born.

The key question on *your* bad day is: Are you going to give up or get up? And how *can* you get up?

1. **Rise above self-pity.** Failure is an attitude, not just an outcome.

2. **Think positively.** Success comes by going from failure to failure without losing enthusiasm.

3. **Learn from your experiences.** Failure isn't failure unless you learn nothing from it.

4. **Seek alternatives.** All successful leaders vary their approaches.

5. **Develop a sense of humor.** Laughter is the shortest distance between two people and the fastest way to get perspective.

6. **Be realistic.** The first job of the leader is to define reality.

7. **Establish new goals.** Failure is an opportunity to begin again, but more intelligently.

8. **Develop a passion.** Your own resolution to succeed counts for more than anything else.

9. **Broaden your base of support.** No single venture should support your entire emotional life.

10. **Separate your self-worth from your performance.** A positive self-image prepares you for success.

May he hear wailing in the morning,
   a battle cry at noon.
¹⁷ For he did not kill me in the womb,
   with my mother as my grave,
   her womb enlarged forever.
¹⁸ Why did I ever come out of the womb
   to see trouble and sorrow
   and to end my days in shame?

God Rejects Zedekiah's Request

21 The word came to Jeremiah from the LORD when King Zedekiah sent to him Pashhur son of Malkijah and the priest Zephaniah son of Maaseiah. They said: ²"Inquire now of the LORD for us because Nebuchadnezzar[a] king of Babylon is attacking us. Perhaps the LORD will perform wonders for us as in times past so that he will withdraw from us."

³But Jeremiah answered them, "Tell Zedekiah, ⁴'This is what the LORD, the God of Israel, says: I am about to turn against you the weapons of war that are in your hands, which you are using to fight the king of Babylon and the Babylonians[b] who are outside the wall besieging you. And I will gather them inside this city. ⁵I myself will fight against you with an outstretched

hand and a mighty arm in furious anger and in great wrath. ⁶I will strike down those who live in this city — both man and beast — and they will die of a terrible plague. ⁷After that, declares the LORD, I will give Zedekiah king of Judah, his officials and the people in this city who survive the plague, sword and famine, into the hands of Nebuchadnezzar king of Babylon and to their enemies who want to kill them. He will put them to the sword; he will show them no mercy or pity or compassion.'

⁸"Furthermore, tell the people, 'This is what the LORD says: See, I am setting before you the way of life and the way of death. ⁹Whoever stays in this city will die by the sword, famine or plague. But whoever goes out and surrenders to the Babylonians who are besieging you will live; they will escape with their lives. ¹⁰I have determined to do this city harm and not good, declares the LORD. It will be given into the hands of the king of Babylon, and he will destroy it with fire.'

---

[a] 2 Hebrew *Nebuchadrezzar*, of which *Nebuchadnezzar* is a variant; here and often in Jeremiah and Ezekiel   [b] 4 Or *Chaldeans*; also in verse 9

[11]"Moreover, say to the royal house of Judah, 'Hear the word of the LORD. [12]This is what the LORD says to you, house of David:

"'Administer justice every morning;
　　rescue from the hand of the oppressor
　　the one who has been robbed,
or my wrath will break out and burn like fire
　　because of the evil you have done—
　　burn with no one to quench it.
[13]I am against you, Jerusalem,
　　you who live above this valley
　　on the rocky plateau, declares the LORD—
you who say, "Who can come against us?
　　Who can enter our refuge?"
[14]I will punish you as your deeds deserve,
　　declares the LORD.
I will kindle a fire in your forests
　　that will consume everything around
　　　　you.'"

Judgment Against Wicked Kings

22 This is what the LORD says: "Go down to the palace of the king of Judah and proclaim this message there: [2]'Hear the word of the LORD to you, king of Judah, you who sit on David's throne—you, your officials and your people who come through these gates. [3]This is what the LORD says: Do what is just and right. Rescue from the hand of the oppressor the one who has been robbed. Do no wrong or violence to the foreigner, the fatherless or the widow, and do not shed innocent blood in this place. [4]For if you are careful to carry out these commands, then kings who sit on David's throne will come through the gates of this palace, riding in chariots and on horses, accompanied by their officials and their people. [5]But if you do not obey these commands, declares the LORD, I swear by myself that this palace will become a ruin.'"

[6]For this is what the LORD says about the palace of the king of Judah:

"Though you are like Gilead to me,
　　like the summit of Lebanon,
I will surely make you like a wasteland,
　　like towns not inhabited.
[7]I will send destroyers against you,
　　each man with his weapons,
and they will cut up your fine cedar beams
　　and throw them into the fire.

[8]"People from many nations will pass by this city and will ask one another, 'Why has the LORD done such a thing to this great city?' [9]And the answer will be: 'Because they have forsaken the covenant of the LORD their God and have worshiped and served other gods.'"

[10]Do not weep for the dead king or mourn his
　　　　loss;
rather, weep bitterly for him who is
　　　　exiled,
because he will never return
　　nor see his native land again.

[11]For this is what the LORD says about Shallum[a] son of Josiah, who succeeded his father as king of Judah but has gone from this place: "He will never return. [12]He will die in the place where they have led him captive; he will not see this land again."

[13]"Woe to him who builds his palace by
　　　　unrighteousness,
　　his upper rooms by injustice,
making his own people work for nothing,
　　not paying them for their labor.
[14]He says, 'I will build myself a great palace
　　with spacious upper rooms.'
So he makes large windows in it,
　　panels it with cedar
　　and decorates it in red.

[15]"Does it make you a king
　　to have more and more cedar?
Did not your father have food and drink?
　　He did what was right and just,
　　so all went well with him.
[16]He defended the cause of the poor and
　　　　needy,
　　and so all went well.
Is that not what it means to know me?"
　　declares the LORD.
[17]"But your eyes and your heart
　　are set only on dishonest gain,
on shedding innocent blood
　　and on oppression and extortion."

[18]Therefore this is what the LORD says about Jehoiakim son of Josiah king of Judah:

"They will not mourn for him:
　　'Alas, my brother! Alas, my sister!'
They will not mourn for him:
　　'Alas, my master! Alas, his splendor!'
[19]He will have the burial of a donkey—
　　dragged away and thrown
　　outside the gates of Jerusalem."

[20]"Go up to Lebanon and cry out,
　　let your voice be heard in Bashan,

---

[a] 11 Also called *Jehoahaz*

cry out from Abarim,
for all your allies are crushed.
²¹I warned you when you felt secure,
but you said, 'I will not listen!'
This has been your way from your youth;
you have not obeyed me.
²²The wind will drive all your shepherds away,
and your allies will go into exile.
Then you will be ashamed and disgraced
because of all your wickedness.
²³You who live in 'Lebanon,ᵃ'
who are nestled in cedar buildings,
how you will groan when pangs come upon
you,
pain like that of a woman in labor!

²⁴"As surely as I live," declares the LORD, "even if you, Jehoiachinᵇ son of Jehoiakim king of Judah, were a signet ring on my right hand, I would still pull you off. ²⁵I will deliver you into the hands of those who want to kill you, those you fear—Nebuchadnezzar king of Babylon and the Babylonians.ᶜ ²⁶I will hurl you and the mother who gave you birth into another country, where neither of you was born, and there you both will die. ²⁷You will never come back to the land you long to return to."

²⁸Is this man Jehoiachin a despised, broken pot,
an object no one wants?
Why will he and his children be hurled out,
cast into a land they do not know?
²⁹O land, land, land,
hear the word of the LORD!
³⁰This is what the LORD says:
"Record this man as if childless,
a man who will not prosper in his lifetime,
for none of his offspring will prosper,
none will sit on the throne of David
or rule anymore in Judah."

The Measure of a Man Is What He Does with Power

Jeremiah 22:6-30

Leaders who use their power or influence for personal gain offend God. Jeremiah cautions leaders who build their own "kingdoms" but fail to exhibit wisdom. He warns them against preoccupation with their own welfare rather than the people God has given them. God considers such misuse of power grounds for removal.

The Righteous Branch

23 "Woe to the shepherds who are destroying and scattering the sheep of my pasture!" declares the LORD. ²Therefore this is what the LORD, the God of Israel, says to the shepherds who tend my people: "Because you have scattered my flock and driven them away and have not bestowed care on them, I will bestow punishment on you for the evil you have done," declares the LORD. ³"I myself will gather the remnant of my flock out of all the countries where I have driven them and will bring them back to their pasture, where they will be fruitful and increase in number. ⁴I will place shepherds over them who will tend them, and they will no longer be afraid or terrified, nor will any be missing," declares the LORD.

⁵"The days are coming," declares the LORD,
"when I will raise up for Davidᵈ a
righteous Branch,
a King who will reign wisely
and do what is just and right in the land.
⁶In his days Judah will be saved
and Israel will live in safety.
This is the name by which he will be called:
The LORD Our Righteous Savior.

⁷"So then, the days are coming," declares the LORD, "when people will no longer say, 'As surely as the LORD lives, who brought the Israelites up out of Egypt,' ⁸but they will say, 'As surely as the LORD lives, who brought the descendants of Israel up out of the land of the north and out of all the countries where he had banished them.' Then they will live in their own land."

Lying Prophets

⁹Concerning the prophets:

My heart is broken within me;
all my bones tremble.
I am like a drunken man,
like a strong man overcome by wine,
because of the LORD
and his holy words.
¹⁰The land is full of adulterers;
because of the curseᵉ the land lies parched
and the pastures in the wilderness are
withered.
The prophets follow an evil course
and use their power unjustly.

ᵃ 23 That is, the palace in Jerusalem (see 1 Kings 7:2)
ᵇ 24 Hebrew Koniah, a variant of Jehoiachin; also in verse 28
ᶜ 25 Or Chaldeans   ᵈ 5 Or up from David's line   ᵉ 10 Or because of these things

11 "Both prophet and priest are godless;
　　even in my temple I find their
　　　　wickedness,"
　　　　　　　　　declares the LORD.
12 "Therefore their path will become slippery;
　　they will be banished to darkness
　　and there they will fall.
　I will bring disaster on them
　　in the year they are punished,"
　　　　　　　　　declares the LORD.

13 "Among the prophets of Samaria
　　I saw this repulsive thing:
　They prophesied by Baal
　　and led my people Israel astray.
14 And among the prophets of Jerusalem
　　I have seen something horrible:
　They commit adultery and live a lie.
　They strengthen the hands of evildoers,
　　so that not one of them turns from their
　　　wickedness.
　They are all like Sodom to me;
　　the people of Jerusalem are like
　　　Gomorrah."

15 Therefore this is what the LORD Almighty
says concerning the prophets:

"I will make them eat bitter food
　　and drink poisoned water,
because from the prophets of Jerusalem
　　ungodliness has spread throughout the
　　　land."

16 This is what the LORD Almighty says:

"Do not listen to what the prophets are
　　　prophesying to you;
　they fill you with false hopes.
They speak visions from their own
　　　minds,
　　not from the mouth of the LORD.
17 They keep saying to those who despise me,
　　'The LORD says: You will have peace.'
And to all who follow the stubbornness of
　　　their hearts
　they say, 'No harm will come to you.'
18 But which of them has stood in the council
　　　of the LORD
　　to see or to hear his word?
　Who has listened and heard his word?
19 See, the storm of the LORD
　　will burst out in wrath,
　a whirlwind swirling down
　　on the heads of the wicked.

The Changing of the Guard: When Leaders Need to Be Replaced

Jeremiah 23:1–16

God does not hesitate to remove poor or wicked leaders—and beyond their removal, God pronounces his judgment on them.

Jeremiah 23 supplies us with a good evaluation tool to recognize what God values in a leader and what constitutes grounds for dismissal and replacement. Study the characteristics of the kind of leaders God promised to replace:

1. **Leaders who destroy their people instead of developing them (v. 1)**

2. **Leaders who scatter their people instead of uniting them in a cause (v. 1)**

3. **Leaders who abandon their people in fear instead of remaining responsible (v. 4)**

4. **Leaders who act in self-serving and unjust ways instead of standing for the truth (v. 10)**

5. **Leaders who lie, as though there were no God (v. 11)**

6. **Leaders who lead their people astray instead of guiding them into security (v. 13)**

7. **Leaders who foster evil and deceit instead of integrity and honesty (v. 14)**

8. **Leaders who fill people with false hope rather than speaking God's Word (v. 16)**

God didn't merely threaten to remove bad leaders; he also promised to raise up a Righteous Branch from the line of David to replace these artificial leaders. Today we know that Righteous Branch has a beautiful name: Jesus Christ!

^{20}The anger of the LORD will not turn back
    until he fully accomplishes
    the purposes of his heart.
In days to come
    you will understand it clearly.
^{21}I did not send these prophets,
    yet they have run with their message;
I did not speak to them,
    yet they have prophesied.
^{22}But if they had stood in my council,
    they would have proclaimed my words to
      my people
and would have turned them from their evil
    ways
    and from their evil deeds.

^{23}"Am I only a God nearby,"
                    declares the LORD,
    "and not a God far away?
^{24}Who can hide in secret places
    so that I cannot see them?"
                    declares the LORD.
    "Do not I fill heaven and earth?"
                    declares the LORD.

^{25}"I have heard what the prophets say who prophesy lies in my name. They say, 'I had a dream! I had a dream!' ^{26}How long will this continue in the hearts of these lying prophets, who prophesy the delusions of their own minds? ^{27}They think the dreams they tell one another will make my people forget my name, just as their ancestors forgot my name through Baal worship. ^{28}Let the prophet who has a dream recount the dream, but let the one who has my word speak it faithfully. For what has straw to do with grain?" declares the LORD. ^{29}"Is not my word like fire," declares the LORD, "and like a hammer that breaks a rock in pieces?

^{30}"Therefore," declares the LORD, "I am against the prophets who steal from one another words supposedly from me. ^{31}Yes," declares the LORD, "I am against the prophets who wag their own tongues and yet declare, 'The LORD declares.' ^{32}Indeed, I am against those who prophesy false dreams," declares the LORD. "They tell them and lead my people astray with their reckless lies, yet I did not send or appoint them. They do not benefit these people in the least," declares the LORD.

False Prophecy

^{33}"When these people, or a prophet or a priest, ask you, 'What is the message from the LORD?' say to them, 'What message? I will forsake you, declares the LORD.' ^{34}If a prophet or a priest or anyone else claims, 'This is a message from the LORD,' I will punish them and their household. ^{35}This is what each of you keeps saying to your friends and other Israelites: 'What is the LORD's answer?' or 'What has the LORD spoken?' ^{36}But you must not mention 'a message from the LORD' again, because each one's word becomes their own message. So you distort the words of the living God, the LORD Almighty, our God. ^{37}This is what you keep saying to a prophet: 'What is the LORD's answer to you?' or 'What has the LORD spoken?' ^{38}Although you claim, 'This is a message from the LORD,' this is what the LORD says: You used the words, 'This is a message from the LORD,' even though I told you that you must not claim, 'This is a message from the LORD.' ^{39}Therefore, I will surely forget you and cast you out of my presence along with the city I gave to you and your ancestors. ^{40}I will bring on you everlasting disgrace — everlasting shame that will not be forgotten."

Vision: God-Given or Man-Made?

Jeremiah 23:13–40

How do we recognize a vision as God-given or as man-made? First, does it align with the Word of God, the nature of God, and the ways of God? Second, does it advance God's kingdom, and not necessarily the leader's? Third, does it bless other people? Finally, does the vision stand the test of time?

Two Baskets of Figs

24 After Jehoiachin^{a} son of Jehoiakim king of Judah and the officials, the skilled workers and the artisans of Judah were carried into exile from Jerusalem to Babylon by Nebuchadnezzar king of Babylon, the LORD showed me two baskets of figs placed in front of the temple of the LORD. ^{2}One basket had very good figs, like those that ripen early; the other basket had very bad figs, so bad they could not be eaten.

^{3}Then the LORD asked me, "What do you see, Jeremiah?"

"Figs," I answered. "The good ones are very good, but the bad ones are so bad they cannot be eaten."

---

^{a} *1* Hebrew *Jeconiah,* a variant of *Jehoiachin*

⁴Then the word of the LORD came to me: ⁵"This is what the LORD, the God of Israel, says: 'Like these good figs, I regard as good the exiles from Judah, whom I sent away from this place to the land of the Babylonians.ᵃ ⁶My eyes will watch over them for their good, and I will bring them back to this land. I will build them up and not tear them down; I will plant them and not uproot them. ⁷I will give them a heart to know me, that I am the LORD. They will be my people, and I will be their God, for they will return to me with all their heart.

⁸"'But like the bad figs, which are so bad they cannot be eaten,' says the LORD, 'so will I deal with Zedekiah king of Judah, his officials and the survivors from Jerusalem, whether they remain in this land or live in Egypt. ⁹I will make them abhorrent and an offense to all the kingdoms of the earth, a reproach and a byword, a curseᵇ and an object of ridicule, wherever I banish them. ¹⁰I will send the sword, famine and plague against them until they are destroyed from the land I gave to them and their ancestors.'"

Seventy Years of Captivity

25 The word came to Jeremiah concerning all the people of Judah in the fourth year of Jehoiakim son of Josiah king of Judah, which was the first year of Nebuchadnezzar king of Babylon. ²So Jeremiah the prophet said to all the people of Judah and to all those living in Jerusalem: ³For twenty-three years — from the thirteenth year of Josiah son of Amon king of Judah until this very day — the word of the LORD has come to me and I have spoken to you again and again, but you have not listened.

⁴And though the LORD has sent all his servants the prophets to you again and again, you have not listened or paid any attention. ⁵They said, "Turn now, each of you, from your evil ways and your evil practices, and you can stay in the land the LORD gave to you and your ancestors for ever and ever. ⁶Do not follow other gods to serve and worship them; do not arouse my anger with what your hands have made. Then I will not harm you."

⁷"But you did not listen to me," declares the LORD, "and you have aroused my anger with what your hands have made, and you have brought harm to yourselves."

⁸Therefore the LORD Almighty says this: "Because you have not listened to my words, ⁹I will summon all the peoples of the north and my servant Nebuchadnezzar king of Babylon," de-

clares the LORD, "and I will bring them against this land and its inhabitants and against all the surrounding nations. I will completely destroyᶜ them and make them an object of horror and scorn, and an everlasting ruin. ¹⁰I will banish from them the sounds of joy and gladness, the voices of bride and bridegroom, the sound of millstones and the light of the lamp. ¹¹This whole country will become a desolate wasteland, and these nations will serve the king of Babylon seventy years.

¹²"But when the seventy years are fulfilled, I will punish the king of Babylon and his nation, the land of the Babylonians,ᵃ for their guilt," declares the LORD, "and will make it desolate forever. ¹³I will bring on that land all the things I have spoken against it, all that are written in this book and prophesied by Jeremiah against all the nations. ¹⁴They themselves will be enslaved by many nations and great kings; I will repay them according to their deeds and the work of their hands."

The Cup of God's Wrath

¹⁵This is what the LORD, the God of Israel, said to me: "Take from my hand this cup filled with the wine of my wrath and make all the nations to whom I send you drink it. ¹⁶When they drink it, they will stagger and go mad because of the sword I will send among them."

¹⁷So I took the cup from the LORD's hand and made all the nations to whom he sent me drink it: ¹⁸Jerusalem and the towns of Judah, its kings and officials, to make them a ruin and an object of horror and scorn, a curseᵈ — as they are today; ¹⁹Pharaoh king of Egypt, his attendants, his officials and all his people, ²⁰and all the foreign people there; all the kings of Uz; all the kings of the Philistines (those of Ashkelon, Gaza, Ekron, and the people left at Ashdod); ²¹Edom, Moab and Ammon; ²²all the kings of Tyre and Sidon; the kings of the coastlands across the sea; ²³Dedan, Tema, Buz and all who are in distant placesᵉ; ²⁴all the kings of Arabia and all the kings of the foreign people who live in the wilderness; ²⁵all the kings of Zimri, Elam and Media; ²⁶and all the kings of the north, near and far, one after the other — all the kingdoms on the face of

---

ᵃ 5,12 Or *Chaldeans*   ᵇ 9 That is, their names will be used in cursing (see 29:22); or, others will see that they are cursed.
ᶜ 9 The Hebrew term refers to the irrevocable giving over of things or persons to the LORD, often by totally destroying them.
ᵈ 18 That is, their names to be used in cursing (see 29:22); or, to be seen by others as cursed   ᵉ 23 Or *who clip the hair by their foreheads*

the earth. And after all of them, the king of She-shak[a] will drink it too.

[27]"Then tell them, 'This is what the LORD Almighty, the God of Israel, says: Drink, get drunk and vomit, and fall to rise no more because of the sword I will send among you.' [28]But if they refuse to take the cup from your hand and drink, tell them, 'This is what the LORD Almighty says: You must drink it! [29]See, I am beginning to bring disaster on the city that bears my Name, and will you indeed go unpunished? You will not go unpunished, for I am calling down a sword on all who live on the earth, declares the LORD Almighty.'

[30]"Now prophesy all these words against them and say to them:

"'The LORD will roar from on high;
    he will thunder from his holy dwelling
    and roar mightily against his land.
He will shout like those who tread the
    grapes,
    shout against all who live on the earth.
[31]The tumult will resound to the ends of the
    earth,
    for the LORD will bring charges against
    the nations;
he will bring judgment on all mankind
    and put the wicked to the sword,'"
                  declares the LORD.

[32]This is what the LORD Almighty says:

"Look! Disaster is spreading
    from nation to nation;
a mighty storm is rising
    from the ends of the earth."

[33]At that time those slain by the LORD will be everywhere—from one end of the earth to the other. They will not be mourned or gathered up or buried, but will be like dung lying on the ground.

[34]Weep and wail, you shepherds;
    roll in the dust, you leaders of the flock.
For your time to be slaughtered has come;
    you will fall like the best of the rams.[b]
[35]The shepherds will have nowhere to flee,
    the leaders of the flock no place to escape.
[36]Hear the cry of the shepherds,
    the wailing of the leaders of the flock,
    for the LORD is destroying their pasture.
[37]The peaceful meadows will be laid waste
    because of the fierce anger of the LORD.
[38]Like a lion he will leave his lair,
    and their land will become desolate

because of the sword[c] of the oppressor
    and because of the LORD's fierce anger.

Jeremiah Threatened With Death

26 Early in the reign of Jehoiakim son of Josiah king of Judah, this word came from the LORD: [2]"This is what the LORD says: Stand in the courtyard of the LORD's house and speak to all the people of the towns of Judah who come to worship in the house of the LORD. Tell them everything I command you; do not omit a word. [3]Perhaps they will listen and each will turn from their evil ways. Then I will relent and not inflict on them the disaster I was planning because of the evil they have done. [4]Say to them, 'This is what the LORD says: If you do not listen to me and follow my law, which I have set before you, [5]and if you do not listen to the words of my servants the prophets, whom I have sent to you again and again (though you have not listened), [6]then I will make this house like Shiloh and this city a curse[d] among all the nations of the earth.'"

[7]The priests, the prophets and all the people heard Jeremiah speak these words in the house of the LORD. [8]But as soon as Jeremiah finished telling all the people everything the LORD had commanded him to say, the priests, the prophets and all the people seized him and said, "You must die! [9]Why do you prophesy in the LORD's name that this house will be like Shiloh and this city will be desolate and deserted?" And all the people crowded around Jeremiah in the house of the LORD.

[10]When the officials of Judah heard about these things, they went up from the royal palace to the house of the LORD and took their places at the entrance of the New Gate of the LORD's house. [11]Then the priests and the prophets said to the officials and all the people, "This man should be sentenced to death because he has prophesied against this city. You have heard it with your own ears!"

[12]Then Jeremiah said to all the officials and all the people: "The LORD sent me to prophesy against this house and this city all the things you have heard. [13]Now reform your ways and your actions and obey the LORD your God. Then the LORD will relent and not bring the disaster he

---

[a] 26 *Sheshak* is a cryptogram for Babylon.   [b] 34 Septuagint; Hebrew *fall and be shattered like fine pottery*   [c] 38 Some Hebrew manuscripts and Septuagint (see also 46:16 and 50:16); most Hebrew manuscripts *anger*   [d] 6 That is, its name will be used in cursing (see 29:22); or, others will see that it is cursed.

has pronounced against you. ¹⁴As for me, I am in your hands; do with me whatever you think is good and right. ¹⁵Be assured, however, that if you put me to death, you will bring the guilt of innocent blood on yourselves and on this city and on those who live in it, for in truth the LORD has sent me to you to speak all these words in your hearing."

¹⁶Then the officials and all the people said to the priests and the prophets, "This man should not be sentenced to death! He has spoken to us in the name of the LORD our God."

¹⁷Some of the elders of the land stepped forward and said to the entire assembly of people, ¹⁸"Micah of Moresheth prophesied in the days of Hezekiah king of Judah. He told all the people of Judah, 'This is what the LORD Almighty says:

"'Zion will be plowed like a field,
　　Jerusalem will become a heap of rubble,
　　the temple hill a mound overgrown with
　　　　thickets.'ᵃ

¹⁹"Did Hezekiah king of Judah or anyone else in Judah put him to death? Did not Hezekiah fear the LORD and seek his favor? And did not the LORD relent, so that he did not bring the disaster he pronounced against them? We are about to bring a terrible disaster on ourselves!"

²⁰(Now Uriah son of Shemaiah from Kiriath Jearim was another man who prophesied in the name of the LORD; he prophesied the same things against this city and this land as Jeremiah did. ²¹When King Jehoiakim and all his officers and officials heard his words, the king was determined to put him to death. But Uriah heard of it and fled in fear to Egypt. ²²King Jehoiakim,

however, sent Elnathan son of Akbor to Egypt, along with some other men. ²³They brought Uriah out of Egypt and took him to King Jehoiakim, who had him struck down with a sword and his body thrown into the burial place of the common people.)

²⁴Furthermore, Ahikam son of Shaphan supported Jeremiah, and so he was not handed over to the people to be put to death.

Judah to Serve Nebuchadnezzar

27 Early in the reign of Zedekiahᵇ son of Josiah king of Judah, this word came to Jeremiah from the LORD: ²This is what the LORD said to me: "Make a yoke out of straps and crossbars and put it on your neck. ³Then send word to the kings of Edom, Moab, Ammon, Tyre and Sidon through the envoys who have come to Jerusalem to Zedekiah king of Judah. ⁴Give them a message for their masters and say, 'This is what the LORD Almighty, the God of Israel, says: "Tell this to your masters: ⁵With my great power and outstretched arm I made the earth and its people and the animals that are on it, and I give it to anyone I please. ⁶Now I will give all your countries into the hands of my servant Nebuchadnezzar king of Babylon; I will make even the wild animals subject to him. ⁷All nations will serve him and his son and his grandson until the time for his land comes; then many nations and great kings will subjugate him.

ᵃ 18 Micah 3:12　　ᵇ 1 A few Hebrew manuscripts and Syriac (see also 27:3,12 and 28:1); most Hebrew manuscripts *Jehoiakim* (Most Septuagint manuscripts do not have this verse.)

God Uses the Unrighteous Leader to Prune the Righteous

Jeremiah 27:1–8

While God never ordains false leaders, he may use wicked leaders—even self-appointed ones—to perform his purposes.

What an irony! God warns against false leaders and simultaneously uses an evil king (the Babylonian Nebuchadnezzar) to prune the people he calls his own. Jeremiah 27 helps us to see an important truth regarding how God carries out his will in history:

1. **His Moral Will**
   God instructs us to lead with a heart of integrity. We must not lead without his approval. But it is our choice. We learn this lesson from the false prophets of Jeremiah's day.

2. **His Sovereign Will**
   God may choose to use any leader to accomplish his purposes. It is God's choice. We learn this lesson from King Nebuchadnezzar of Babylon.

8"'"If, however, any nation or kingdom will not serve Nebuchadnezzar king of Babylon or bow its neck under his yoke, I will punish that nation with the sword, famine and plague, declares the LORD, until I destroy it by his hand. 9So do not listen to your prophets, your diviners, your interpreters of dreams, your mediums or your sorcerers who tell you, 'You will not serve the king of Babylon.' 10They prophesy lies to you that will only serve to remove you far from your lands; I will banish you and you will perish. 11But if any nation will bow its neck under the yoke of the king of Babylon and serve him, I will let that nation remain in its own land to till it and to live there, declares the LORD.'"'

12I gave the same message to Zedekiah king of Judah. I said, "Bow your neck under the yoke of the king of Babylon; serve him and his people, and you will live. 13Why will you and your people die by the sword, famine and plague with which the LORD has threatened any nation that will not serve the king of Babylon? 14Do not listen to the words of the prophets who say to you, 'You will not serve the king of Babylon,' for they are prophesying lies to you. 15'I have not sent them,' declares the LORD. 'They are prophesying lies in my name. Therefore, I will banish you and you will perish, both you and the prophets who prophesy to you.'"

16Then I said to the priests and all these people, "This is what the LORD says: Do not listen to the prophets who say, 'Very soon now the articles from the LORD's house will be brought back from Babylon.' They are prophesying lies to you. 17Do not listen to them. Serve the king of Babylon, and you will live. Why should this city become a ruin? 18If they are prophets and have the word of the LORD, let them plead with the LORD Almighty that the articles remaining in the house of the LORD and in the palace of the king of Judah and in Jerusalem not be taken to Babylon. 19For this is what the LORD Almighty says about the pillars, the bronze Sea, the movable stands and the other articles that are left in this city, 20which Nebuchadnezzar king of Babylon did not take away when he carried Jehoiachin*a* son of Jehoiakim king of Judah into exile from Jerusalem to Babylon, along with all the nobles of Judah and Jerusalem— 21yes, this is what the LORD Almighty, the God of Israel, says about the things that are left in the house of the LORD and in the palace of the king of Judah and in Jerusalem: 22"They will be taken to Babylon and there they will remain until the day I come for them,' declares the LORD.

'Then I will bring them back and restore them to this place.'"

The False Prophet Hananiah

28 In the fifth month of that same year, the fourth year, early in the reign of Zedekiah king of Judah, the prophet Hananiah son of Azzur, who was from Gibeon, said to me in the house of the LORD in the presence of the priests and all the people: 2"This is what the LORD Almighty, the God of Israel, says: 'I will break the yoke of the king of Babylon. 3Within two years I will bring back to this place all the articles of the LORD's house that Nebuchadnezzar king of Babylon removed from here and took to Babylon. 4I will also bring back to this place Jehoiachin*a* son of Jehoiakim king of Judah and all the other exiles from Judah who went to Babylon,' declares the LORD, 'for I will break the yoke of the king of Babylon.'"

5Then the prophet Jeremiah replied to the prophet Hananiah before the priests and all the people who were standing in the house of the LORD. 6He said, "Amen! May the LORD do so! May the LORD fulfill the words you have prophesied by bringing the articles of the LORD's house and all the exiles back to this place from Babylon. 7Nevertheless, listen to what I have to say in your hearing and in the hearing of all the people: 8From early times the prophets who preceded you and me have prophesied war, disaster and plague against many countries and great kingdoms. 9But the prophet who prophesies peace will be recognized as one truly sent by the LORD only if his prediction comes true."

10Then the prophet Hananiah took the yoke off the neck of the prophet Jeremiah and broke it, 11and he said before all the people, "This is what the LORD says: 'In the same way I will break the yoke of Nebuchadnezzar king of Babylon off the neck of all the nations within two years.'" At this, the prophet Jeremiah went on his way.

12After the prophet Hananiah had broken the yoke off the neck of the prophet Jeremiah, the word of the LORD came to Jeremiah: 13"Go and tell Hananiah, 'This is what the LORD says: You have broken a wooden yoke, but in its place you will get a yoke of iron. 14This is what the LORD Almighty, the God of Israel, says: I will put an iron yoke on the necks of all these nations to make them serve Nebuchadnezzar king of Babylon, and they will serve him. I will even give him control over the wild animals.'"

---

a 20,4 Hebrew *Jeconiah*, a variant of *Jehoiachin*

[15]Then the prophet Jeremiah said to Hananiah the prophet, "Listen, Hananiah! The LORD has not sent you, yet you have persuaded this nation to trust in lies. [16]Therefore this is what the LORD says: 'I am about to remove you from the face of the earth. This very year you are going to die, because you have preached rebellion against the LORD.'"

[17]In the seventh month of that same year, Hananiah the prophet died.

A Letter to the Exiles

29 This is the text of the letter that the prophet Jeremiah sent from Jerusalem to the surviving elders among the exiles and to the priests, the prophets and all the other people Nebuchadnezzar had carried into exile from Jerusalem to Babylon. [2](This was after King Jehoiachin[a] and the queen mother, the court officials and the leaders of Judah and Jerusalem, the skilled workers and the artisans had gone into exile from Jerusalem.) [3]He entrusted the letter to Elasah son of Shaphan and to Gemariah son of Hilkiah, whom Zedekiah king of Judah sent to King Nebuchadnezzar in Babylon. It said:

[4]This is what the LORD Almighty, the God of Israel, says to all those I carried into exile from Jerusalem to Babylon: [5]"Build houses and settle down; plant gardens and eat what they produce. [6]Marry and have sons and daughters; find wives for your sons and give your daughters in marriage, so that they too may have sons and daughters. Increase in number there; do not decrease. [7]Also, seek the peace and prosperity of the city to which I have carried you into exile. Pray to the LORD for it, because if it prospers, you too will prosper." [8]Yes, this is what the LORD Almighty, the God of Israel, says: "Do not let the prophets and diviners among you deceive you. Do not listen to the dreams you encourage them to have. [9]They are prophesying lies to you in my name. I have not sent them," declares the LORD.

[10]This is what the LORD says: "When seventy years are completed for Babylon, I will come to you and fulfill my good promise to bring you back to this place. [11]For I know the plans I have for you," declares the LORD, "plans to prosper you and not to harm you, plans to give you hope and a future. [12]Then you will call on me and come and pray to me, and I will listen to you. [13]You will seek me and find me when you seek me with all your heart. [14]I will be found by you," declares the LORD, "and will bring you back from captivity.[b] I will gather you from all the nations and places where I have banished you," declares the LORD, "and will bring you back to the place from which I carried you into exile."

Rewards: Leaders with Integrity Can Remain Optimistic

Jeremiah 29:11–14

Even in Israel's darkest hour, God assured the people of his plans to prosper them and give them a hopeful future. Just so, even when we don't see immediate results, we can remain assured of God's ultimate blessing and benefit. The fruit may not come immediately, but it will come ultimately.

[15]You may say, "The LORD has raised up prophets for us in Babylon," [16]but this is what the LORD says about the king who sits on David's throne and all the people who remain in this city, your fellow citizens who did not go with you into exile— [17]yes, this is what the LORD Almighty says: "I will send the sword, famine and plague against them and I will make them like figs that are so bad they cannot be eaten. [18]I will pursue them with the sword, famine and plague and will make them abhorrent to all the kingdoms of the earth, a curse[c] and an object of horror, of scorn and reproach, among all the nations where I drive them. [19]For they have not listened to my words," declares the LORD, "words that I sent to them again and again by my servants the prophets. And you exiles have not listened either," declares the LORD.

[20]Therefore, hear the word of the LORD, all you exiles whom I have sent away from Jerusalem to Babylon. [21]This is what the LORD Almighty, the God of Israel, says about Ahab son of Kolaiah and Zedekiah son of Maaseiah, who are prophesying lies

---

[a] 2 Hebrew *Jeconiah*, a variant of *Jehoiachin*   [b] 14 Or will restore your fortunes   [c] 18 That is, their names will be used in cursing (see verse 22); or, others will see that they are cursed.

to you in my name: "I will deliver them into the hands of Nebuchadnezzar king of Babylon, and he will put them to death before your very eyes. [22]Because of them, all the exiles from Judah who are in Babylon will use this curse: 'May the LORD treat you like Zedekiah and Ahab, whom the king of Babylon burned in the fire.' [23]For they have done outrageous things in Israel; they have committed adultery with their neighbors' wives, and in my name they have uttered lies — which I did not authorize. I know it and am a witness to it," declares the LORD.

Message to Shemaiah

[24]Tell Shemaiah the Nehelamite, [25]"This is what the LORD Almighty, the God of Israel, says: You sent letters in your own name to all the people in Jerusalem, to the priest Zephaniah son of Maaseiah, and to all the other priests. You said to Zephaniah, [26]"The LORD has appointed you priest in place of Jehoiada to be in charge of the house of the LORD; you should put any maniac who acts like a prophet into the stocks and neck-irons. [27]So why have you not reprimanded Jeremiah from Anathoth, who poses as a prophet among you? [28]He has sent this message to us in Babylon: It will be a long time. Therefore build houses and settle down; plant gardens and eat what they produce.'"

[29]Zephaniah the priest, however, read the letter to Jeremiah the prophet. [30]Then the word of the LORD came to Jeremiah: [31]"Send this message to all the exiles: 'This is what the LORD says about Shemaiah the Nehelamite: Because Shemaiah has prophesied to you, even though I did not send him, and has persuaded you to trust in lies, [32]this is what the LORD says: I will surely punish Shemaiah the Nehelamite and his descendants. He will have no one left among this people, nor will he see the good things I will do for my people, declares the LORD, because he has preached rebellion against me.'"

Restoration of Israel

30 This is the word that came to Jeremiah from the LORD: [2]"This is what the LORD, the God of Israel, says: 'Write in a book all the words I have spoken to you. [3]The days are coming,' declares the LORD, 'when I will bring my people Israel and Judah back from captivity[a] and restore them to the land I gave their ancestors to possess,' says the LORD."

[4]These are the words the LORD spoke con-

cerning Israel and Judah: [5]"This is what the LORD says:

"'Cries of fear are heard —
  terror, not peace.
[6]Ask and see:
  Can a man bear children?
Then why do I see every strong man
  with his hands on his stomach like a
    woman in labor,
  every face turned deathly pale?
[7]How awful that day will be!
  No other will be like it.
It will be a time of trouble for Jacob,
  but he will be saved out of it.

[8]"'In that day,' declares the LORD Almighty,
  'I will break the yoke off their necks
and will tear off their bonds;
  no longer will foreigners enslave them.
[9]Instead, they will serve the LORD their God
  and David their king,
  whom I will raise up for them.

[10]"'So do not be afraid, Jacob my servant;
  do not be dismayed, Israel,'
                    declares the LORD.
'I will surely save you out of a distant place,
  your descendants from the land of their
    exile.
Jacob will again have peace and security,
  and no one will make him afraid.
[11]I am with you and will save you,'
  declares the LORD.
'Though I completely destroy all the nations
  among which I scatter you,
  I will not completely destroy you.
I will discipline you but only in due measure;
  I will not let you go entirely unpunished.'

[12]"This is what the LORD says:

"'Your wound is incurable,
  your injury beyond healing.
[13]There is no one to plead your cause,
  no remedy for your sore,
  no healing for you.
[14]All your allies have forgotten you;
  they care nothing for you.
I have struck you as an enemy would
  and punished you as would the cruel,
because your guilt is so great
  and your sins so many.
[15]Why do you cry out over your wound,
  your pain that has no cure?

---

[a] 3 Or will restore the fortunes of my people Israel and Judah

Because of your great guilt and many sins
  I have done these things to you.

16 "'But all who devour you will be devoured;
  all your enemies will go into exile.
Those who plunder you will be plundered;
  all who make spoil of you I will despoil.
17 But I will restore you to health
  and heal your wounds,'
                                    declares the LORD,
'because you are called an outcast,
  Zion for whom no one cares.'

18 "This is what the LORD says:

"'I will restore the fortunes of Jacob's tents
  and have compassion on his dwellings;
the city will be rebuilt on her ruins,
  and the palace will stand in its proper
    place.
19 From them will come songs of thanksgiving
  and the sound of rejoicing.
I will add to their numbers,
  and they will not be decreased;
I will bring them honor,
  and they will not be disdained.
20 Their children will be as in days of old,
  and their community will be established
    before me;
I will punish all who oppress them.
21 Their leader will be one of their own;
  their ruler will arise from among them.
I will bring him near and he will come close
    to me—
  for who is he who will devote himself
to be close to me?'
                                    declares the LORD.
22 "'So you will be my people,
  and I will be your God.'"

23 See, the storm of the LORD
  will burst out in wrath,
a driving wind swirling down
  on the heads of the wicked.
24 The fierce anger of the LORD will not turn
    back
  until he fully accomplishes
    the purposes of his heart.
In days to come
  you will understand this.

31 "At that time," declares the LORD, "I will be the God of all the families of Israel, and they will be my people."
2 This is what the LORD says:

"The people who survive the sword
  will find favor in the wilderness;
  I will come to give rest to Israel."

3 The LORD appeared to us in the past,[a] saying:

"I have loved you with an everlasting love;
  I have drawn you with unfailing kindness.
4 I will build you up again,
  and you, Virgin Israel, will be rebuilt.
Again you will take up your timbrels
  and go out to dance with the joyful.
5 Again you will plant vineyards
  on the hills of Samaria;
the farmers will plant them
  and enjoy their fruit.
6 There will be a day when watchmen cry out
  on the hills of Ephraim,
'Come, let us go up to Zion,
  to the LORD our God.'"

---

[a] 3 Or LORD has appeared to us from afar

God Punishes with Bad Leaders, Rewards with Good Ones

Jeremiah 30:10–22

Jeremiah declares that God's way of punishing his people is to give them bad leaders (Jer 30:10–11), while the Lord's way of rewarding them is to give them good leaders (30:21–22). Everything rises and falls on leadership. As the leader goes, so go the people. Why is this true?

1. **Because leaders represent the people they oversee.**
2. **Because people reflect the leader they follow.**
3. **Because leaders are usually the most influential individuals among the people.**
4. **Because when God starts a movement, he uses one person to spearhead it.**
5. **Because people are like sheep and look to leaders for models.**

[7]This is what the LORD says:

"Sing with joy for Jacob;
  shout for the foremost of the nations.
Make your praises heard, and say,
  'LORD, save your people,
  the remnant of Israel.'
[8]See, I will bring them from the land of the
    north
  and gather them from the ends of the
    earth.
Among them will be the blind and the lame,
  expectant mothers and women in labor;
  a great throng will return.
[9]They will come with weeping;
  they will pray as I bring them back.
I will lead them beside streams of water
  on a level path where they will not
    stumble,
because I am Israel's father,
  and Ephraim is my firstborn son.

[10]"Hear the word of the LORD, you nations;
  proclaim it in distant coastlands:
'He who scattered Israel will gather them
  and will watch over his flock like a
    shepherd.'
[11]For the LORD will deliver Jacob
  and redeem them from the hand of those
    stronger than they.
[12]They will come and shout for joy on the
    heights of Zion;
  they will rejoice in the bounty of the
    LORD—
the grain, the new wine and the olive oil,
  the young of the flocks and herds.
They will be like a well-watered garden,
  and they will sorrow no more.
[13]Then young women will dance and be glad,
  young men and old as well.
I will turn their mourning into gladness;
  I will give them comfort and joy instead of
    sorrow.
[14]I will satisfy the priests with abundance,
  and my people will be filled with my
    bounty,"
                declares the LORD.

[15]This is what the LORD says:

"A voice is heard in Ramah,
  mourning and great weeping,
Rachel weeping for her children
  and refusing to be comforted,
  because they are no more."

[16]This is what the LORD says:

"Restrain your voice from weeping
  and your eyes from tears,
for your work will be rewarded,"
                declares the LORD.
"They will return from the land of the
    enemy.
[17]So there is hope for your descendants,"
                declares the LORD.
"Your children will return to their own
    land.

[18]"I have surely heard Ephraim's moaning:
'You disciplined me like an unruly calf,
  and I have been disciplined.
Restore me, and I will return,
  because you are the LORD my God.
[19]After I strayed,
  I repented;
after I came to understand,
  I beat my breast.
I was ashamed and humiliated
  because I bore the disgrace of my youth.'
[20]Is not Ephraim my dear son,
  the child in whom I delight?
Though I often speak against him,
  I still remember him.
Therefore my heart yearns for him;
  I have great compassion for him,"
                declares the LORD.

[21]"Set up road signs;
  put up guideposts.
Take note of the highway,
  the road that you take.
Return, Virgin Israel,
  return to your towns.
[22]How long will you wander,
  unfaithful Daughter Israel?
The LORD will create a new thing on earth—
  the woman will return to[a] the man."

[23]This is what the LORD Almighty, the God of Israel, says: "When I bring them back from captivity,[b] the people in the land of Judah and in its towns will once again use these words: 'The LORD bless you, you prosperous city, you sacred mountain.' [24]People will live together in Judah and all its towns—farmers and those who move about with their flocks. [25]I will refresh the weary and satisfy the faint."

[26]At this I awoke and looked around. My sleep had been pleasant to me.

[27]"The days are coming," declares the LORD, "when I will plant the kingdoms of Israel and Judah with the offspring of people and of animals.

---

[a] 22 Or will protect   [b] 23 Or I restore their fortunes

28Just as I watched over them to uproot and tear down, and to overthrow, destroy and bring disaster, so I will watch over them to build and to plant," declares the LORD. 29"In those days people will no longer say,

'The parents have eaten sour grapes,
    and the children's teeth are set on edge.'

30Instead, everyone will die for their own sin; whoever eats sour grapes — their own teeth will be set on edge.

31 "The days are coming," declares the LORD,
    "when I will make a new covenant
with the people of Israel
    and with the people of Judah.
32 It will not be like the covenant
    I made with their ancestors
when I took them by the hand
    to lead them out of Egypt,
because they broke my covenant,
    though I was a husband to*a* them,*b*"
                        declares the LORD.
33 "This is the covenant I will make with the
                people of Israel
    after that time," declares the LORD.
"I will put my law in their minds
    and write it on their hearts.
I will be their God,
    and they will be my people.
34 No longer will they teach their neighbor,
    or say to one another, 'Know the LORD,'
because they will all know me,
    from the least of them to the greatest,"
                        declares the LORD.
"For I will forgive their wickedness
    and will remember their sins no more."

35This is what the LORD says,

he who appoints the sun
    to shine by day,
who decrees the moon and stars
    to shine by night,
who stirs up the sea
    so that its waves roar —
    the LORD Almighty is his name:
36 "Only if these decrees vanish from my sight,"
                declares the LORD,
"will Israel ever cease
    being a nation before me."

37This is what the LORD says:

"Only if the heavens above can be measured
    and the foundations of the earth below be
                searched out

will I reject all the descendants of Israel
    because of all they have done,"
                        declares the LORD.

38"The days are coming," declares the LORD, "when this city will be rebuilt for me from the Tower of Hananel to the Corner Gate. 39The measuring line will stretch from there straight to the hill of Gareb and then turn to Goah. 40The whole valley where dead bodies and ashes are thrown, and all the terraces out to the Kidron Valley on the east as far as the corner of the Horse Gate, will be holy to the LORD. The city will never again be uprooted or demolished."

Jeremiah Buys a Field

32 This is the word that came to Jeremiah from the LORD in the tenth year of Zedekiah king of Judah, which was the eighteenth year of Nebuchadnezzar. 2The army of the king of Babylon was then besieging Jerusalem, and Jeremiah the prophet was confined in the courtyard of the guard in the royal palace of Judah.

3Now Zedekiah king of Judah had imprisoned him there, saying, "Why do you prophesy as you do? You say, 'This is what the LORD says: I am about to give this city into the hands of the king of Babylon, and he will capture it. 4Zedekiah king of Judah will not escape the Babylonians*c* but will certainly be given into the hands of the king of Babylon, and will speak with him face to face and see him with his own eyes. 5He will take Zedekiah to Babylon, where he will remain until I deal with him, declares the LORD. If you fight against the Babylonians, you will not succeed.'"

6Jeremiah said, "The word of the LORD came to me: 7Hanamel son of Shallum your uncle is going to come to you and say, 'Buy my field at Anathoth, because as nearest relative it is your right and duty to buy it.'

8"Then, just as the LORD had said, my cousin Hanamel came to me in the courtyard of the guard and said, 'Buy my field at Anathoth in the territory of Benjamin. Since it is your right to redeem it and possess it, buy it for yourself.'

"I knew that this was the word of the LORD; 9so I bought the field at Anathoth from my cousin Hanamel and weighed out for him seventeen shekels*d* of silver. 10I signed and sealed the deed, had it witnessed, and weighed out the silver on

---

a 32 Hebrew; Septuagint and Syriac / and I turned away from *b* 32 Or was their master *c* 4 Or Chaldeans; also in verses 5, 24, 25, 28, 29 and 43 *d* 9 That is, about 7 ounces or about 200 grams

the scales. ¹¹I took the deed of purchase — the sealed copy containing the terms and conditions, as well as the unsealed copy — ¹²and I gave this deed to Baruch son of Neriah, the son of Mahseiah, in the presence of my cousin Hanamel and of the witnesses who had signed the deed and of all the Jews sitting in the courtyard of the guard.

¹³"In their presence I gave Baruch these instructions: ¹⁴"This is what the Lord Almighty, the God of Israel, says: Take these documents, both the sealed and unsealed copies of the deed of purchase, and put them in a clay jar so they will last a long time. ¹⁵For this is what the Lord Almighty, the God of Israel, says: Houses, fields and vineyards will again be bought in this land.'

¹⁶"After I had given the deed of purchase to Baruch son of Neriah, I prayed to the Lord:

¹⁷"Ah, Sovereign Lord, you have made the heavens and the earth by your great power and outstretched arm. Nothing is too hard for you. ¹⁸You show love to thousands but bring the punishment for the parents' sins into the laps of their children after them. Great and mighty God, whose name is the Lord Almighty, ¹⁹great are your purposes and mighty are your deeds. Your eyes are open to the ways of all mankind; you reward each person according to their conduct and as their deeds deserve. ²⁰You performed signs and wonders in Egypt and have continued them to this day, in Israel and among all mankind, and have gained the renown that is still yours. ²¹You brought your people Israel out of Egypt with signs and wonders, by a mighty hand and an outstretched arm and with great terror. ²²You gave them this land you had sworn to give their ancestors, a land flowing with milk and honey. ²³They came in and took possession of it, but they did not obey you or follow your law; they did not do what you commanded them to do. So you brought all this disaster on them.

²⁴"See how the siege ramps are built up to take the city. Because of the sword, famine and plague, the city will be given into the hands of the Babylonians who are attacking it. What you said has happened, as you now see. ²⁵And though the city will be given into the hands of the Babylonians, you, Sovereign Lord, say to me, 'Buy the field with silver and have the transaction witnessed.'"

²⁶Then the word of the Lord came to Jeremiah: ²⁷"I am the Lord, the God of all mankind. Is anything too hard for me? ²⁸Therefore this is what the Lord says: I am about to give this city into the hands of the Babylonians and to Nebuchadnezzar king of Babylon, who will capture it. ²⁹The Babylonians who are attacking this city will come in and set it on fire; they will burn it down, along with the houses where the people aroused my anger by burning incense on the roofs to Baal and by pouring out drink offerings to other gods.

³⁰"The people of Israel and Judah have done nothing but evil in my sight from their youth; indeed, the people of Israel have done nothing but arouse my anger with what their hands have made, declares the Lord. ³¹From the day it was built until now, this city has so aroused my anger and wrath that I must remove it from my sight. ³²The people of Israel and Judah have provoked me by all the evil they have done — they, their kings and officials, their priests and prophets, the people of Judah and those living in Jerusalem. ³³They turned their backs to me and not their faces; though I taught them again and again, they would not listen or respond to discipline. ³⁴They set up their vile images in the house that bears my Name and defiled it. ³⁵They built high places for Baal in the Valley of Ben Hinnom to sacrifice their sons and daughters to Molek, though I never commanded — nor did it enter my mind — that they should do such a detestable thing and so make Judah sin.

³⁶"You are saying about this city, 'By the sword, famine and plague it will be given into the hands of the king of Babylon'; but this is what the Lord, the God of Israel, says: ³⁷I will surely gather them from all the lands where I banish them in my furious anger and great wrath; I will bring them back to this place and let them live in safety. ³⁸They will be my people, and I will be their God. ³⁹I will give them singleness of heart and action, so that they will always fear me and that all will then go well for them and for their children after them. ⁴⁰I will make an everlasting covenant with them: I will never stop doing good to them, and I will inspire them to fear me, so that they will never turn away from me. ⁴¹I will rejoice in doing them good and will assuredly plant them in this land with all my heart and soul.

⁴²"This is what the Lord says: As I have brought all this great calamity on this people, so I will give them all the prosperity I have promised them. ⁴³Once more fields will be bought

in this land of which you say, 'It is a desolate waste, without people or animals, for it has been given into the hands of the Babylonians.' [44]Fields will be bought for silver, and deeds will be signed, sealed and witnessed in the territory of Benjamin, in the villages around Jerusalem, in the towns of Judah and in the towns of the hill country, of the western foothills and of the Negev, because I will restore their fortunes,[a] declares the LORD."

Promise of Restoration

33 While Jeremiah was still confined in the courtyard of the guard, the word of the LORD came to him a second time: [2]"This is what the LORD says, he who made the earth, the LORD who formed it and established it — the LORD is his name: [3]'Call to me and I will answer you and tell you great and unsearchable things you do not know.' [4]For this is what the LORD, the God of Israel, says about the houses in this city and the royal palaces of Judah that have been torn down to be used against the siege ramps and the sword [5]in the fight with the Babylonians[b]: 'They will be filled with the dead bodies of the people I will slay in my anger and wrath. I will hide my face from this city because of all its wickedness.

[6]"'Nevertheless, I will bring health and healing to it; I will heal my people and will let them enjoy abundant peace and security. [7]I will bring Judah and Israel back from captivity[c] and will rebuild them as they were before. [8]I will cleanse them from all the sin they have committed against me and will forgive all their sins of rebellion against me. [9]Then this city will bring me renown, joy, praise and honor before all nations on earth that hear of all the good things I do for it; and they will be in awe and will tremble at the abundant prosperity and peace I provide for it.'

[10]"This is what the LORD says: 'You say about this place, "It is a desolate waste, without people or animals." Yet in the towns of Judah and the streets of Jerusalem that are deserted, inhabited by neither people nor animals, there will be heard once more [11]the sounds of joy and gladness, the voices of bride and bridegroom, and the voices of those who bring thank offerings to the house of the LORD, saying,

"Give thanks to the LORD Almighty,
    for the LORD is good;
    his love endures forever."

For I will restore the fortunes of the land as they were before,' says the LORD. [12]"This is what the LORD Almighty says: 'In

this place, desolate and without people or animals — in all its towns there will again be pastures for shepherds to rest their flocks. [13]In the towns of the hill country, of the western foothills and of the Negev, in the territory of Benjamin, in the villages around Jerusalem and in the towns of Judah, flocks will again pass under the hand of the one who counts them,' says the LORD.

[14]"'The days are coming,' declares the LORD, 'when I will fulfill the good promise I made to the people of Israel and Judah.

[15]"'In those days and at that time
    I will make a righteous Branch sprout
        from David's line;
    he will do what is just and right in the
        land.
[16]In those days Judah will be saved
    and Jerusalem will live in safety.
This is the name by which it[d] will be called:
    The LORD Our Righteous Savior.'

[17]For this is what the LORD says: 'David will never fail to have a man to sit on the throne of Israel, [18]nor will the Levitical priests ever fail to have a man to stand before me continually to offer burnt offerings, to burn grain offerings and to present sacrifices.'"

[19]The word of the LORD came to Jeremiah: [20]"This is what the LORD says: 'If you can break my covenant with the day and my covenant with the night, so that day and night no longer come at their appointed time, [21]then my covenant with David my servant — and my covenant with the Levites who are priests ministering before me — can be broken and David will no longer have a descendant to reign on his throne. [22]I will make the descendants of David my servant and the Levites who minister before me as countless as the stars in the sky and as measureless as the sand on the seashore.'"

[23]The word of the LORD came to Jeremiah: [24]"Have you not noticed that these people are saying, 'The LORD has rejected the two kingdoms[e] he chose'? So they despise my people and no longer regard them as a nation. [25]This is what the LORD says: 'If I have not made my covenant with day and night and established the laws of heaven and earth, [26]then I will reject the descendants of Jacob and David my servant and will not choose one of his sons to rule over the

descendants of Abraham, Isaac and Jacob. For I will restore their fortunes[a] and have compassion on them.'"

Warning to Zedekiah

34 While Nebuchadnezzar king of Babylon and all his army and all the kingdoms and peoples in the empire he ruled were fighting against Jerusalem and all its surrounding towns, this word came to Jeremiah from the LORD: 2"This is what the LORD, the God of Israel, says: Go to Zedekiah king of Judah and tell him, 'This is what the LORD says: I am about to give this city into the hands of the king of Babylon, and he will burn it down. 3You will not escape from his grasp but will surely be captured and given into his hands. You will see the king of Babylon with your own eyes, and he will speak with you face to face. And you will go to Babylon.

4"'Yet hear the LORD's promise to you, Zedekiah king of Judah. This is what the LORD says concerning you: You will not die by the sword; 5you will die peacefully. As people made a funeral fire in honor of your predecessors, the kings who ruled before you, so they will make a fire in your honor and lament, "Alas, master!" I myself make this promise, declares the LORD.'"

6Then Jeremiah the prophet told all this to Zedekiah king of Judah, in Jerusalem, 7while the army of the king of Babylon was fighting against Jerusalem and the other cities of Judah that were still holding out—Lachish and Azekah. These were the only fortified cities left in Judah.

Freedom for Slaves

8The word came to Jeremiah from the LORD after King Zedekiah had made a covenant with all the people in Jerusalem to proclaim freedom for the slaves. 9Everyone was to free their Hebrew slaves, both male and female; no one was to hold a fellow Hebrew in bondage. 10So all the officials and people who entered into this covenant agreed that they would free their male and female slaves and no longer hold them in bondage. They agreed, and set them free. 11But afterward they changed their minds and took back the slaves they had freed and enslaved them again.

12Then the word of the LORD came to Jeremiah: 13"This is what the LORD, the God of Israel, says: I made a covenant with your ancestors when I brought them out of Egypt, out of the land of slavery. I said, 14'Every seventh year each of you must free any fellow Hebrews who have sold themselves to you. After they have served

you six years, you must let them go free.'[b] Your ancestors, however, did not listen to me or pay attention to me. 15Recently you repented and did what is right in my sight: Each of you proclaimed freedom to your own people. You even made a covenant before me in the house that bears my Name. 16But now you have turned around and profaned my name; each of you has taken back the male and female slaves you had set free to go where they wished. You have forced them to become your slaves again.

17"Therefore this is what the LORD says: You have not obeyed me; you have not proclaimed freedom to your own people. So I now proclaim 'freedom' for you, declares the LORD—'freedom' to fall by the sword, plague and famine. I will make you abhorrent to all the kingdoms of the earth. 18Those who have violated my covenant and have not fulfilled the terms of the covenant they made before me, I will treat like the calf they cut in two and then walked between its pieces. 19The leaders of Judah and Jerusalem, the court officials, the priests and all the people of the land who walked between the pieces of the calf, 20I will deliver into the hands of their enemies who want to kill them. Their dead bodies will become food for the birds and the wild animals.

21"I will deliver Zedekiah king of Judah and his officials into the hands of their enemies who want to kill them, to the army of the king of Babylon, which has withdrawn from you. 22I am going to give the order, declares the LORD, and I will bring them back to this city. They will fight against it, take it and burn it down. And I will lay waste the towns of Judah so no one can live there."

The Rekabites

35 This is the word that came to Jeremiah from the LORD during the reign of Jehoiakim son of Josiah king of Judah: 2"Go to the Rekabite family and invite them to come to one of the side rooms of the house of the LORD and give them wine to drink."

3So I went to get Jaazaniah son of Jeremiah, the son of Habazziniah, and his brothers and all his sons—the whole family of the Rekabites. 4I brought them into the house of the LORD, into the room of the sons of Hanan son of Igdaliah the man of God. It was next to the room of the officials, which was over that of Maaseiah son of Shallum the doorkeeper. 5Then I set bowls full

---

[a] 26 Or will bring them back from captivity   [b] 14 Deut. 15:12

of wine and some cups before the Rekabites and said to them, "Drink some wine."

[6]But they replied, "We do not drink wine, because our forefather Jehonadab[a] son of Rekab gave us this command: 'Neither you nor your descendants must ever drink wine. [7]Also you must never build houses, sow seed or plant vineyards; you must never have any of these things, but must always live in tents. Then you will live a long time in the land where you are nomads.' [8]We have obeyed everything our forefather Jehonadab son of Rekab commanded us. Neither we nor our wives nor our sons and daughters have ever drunk wine [9]or built houses to live in or had vineyards, fields or crops. [10]We have lived in tents and have fully obeyed everything our forefather Jehonadab commanded us. [11]But when Nebuchadnezzar king of Babylon invaded this land, we said, 'Come, we must go to Jerusalem to escape the Babylonian[b] and Aramean armies.' So we have remained in Jerusalem."

[12]Then the word of the LORD came to Jeremiah, saying: [13]"This is what the LORD Almighty, the God of Israel, says: Go and tell the people of Judah and those living in Jerusalem, 'Will you not learn a lesson and obey my words?' declares the LORD. [14]'Jehonadab son of Rekab ordered his descendants not to drink wine and this command has been kept. To this day they do not drink wine, because they obey their forefather's command. But I have spoken to you again and again, yet you have not obeyed me. [15]Again and again I sent all my servants the prophets to you. They said, "Each of you must turn from your wicked ways and reform your actions; do not follow other gods to serve them. Then you will live in the land I have given to you and your ancestors." But you have not paid attention or listened to me. [16]The descendants of Jehonadab son of Rekab have carried out the command their forefather gave them, but these people have not obeyed me.'

[17]"Therefore this is what the LORD God Almighty, the God of Israel, says: 'Listen! I am going to bring on Judah and on everyone living in Jerusalem every disaster I pronounced against them. I spoke to them, but they did not listen; I called to them, but they did not answer.'"

[18]Then Jeremiah said to the family of the Rekabites, "This is what the LORD Almighty, the God of Israel, says: 'You have obeyed the command of your forefather Jehonadab and have followed all his instructions and have done everything he ordered.' [19]Therefore this is what the LORD Almighty, the God of Israel, says: 'Je-

honadab son of Rekab will never fail to have a descendant to serve me.'"

Jehoiakim Burns Jeremiah's Scroll

36 In the fourth year of Jehoiakim son of Josiah king of Judah, this word came to Jeremiah from the LORD: [2]"Take a scroll and write on it all the words I have spoken to you concerning Israel, Judah and all the other nations from the time I began speaking to you in the reign of Josiah till now. [3]Perhaps when the people of Judah hear about every disaster I plan to inflict on them, they will each turn from their wicked ways; then I will forgive their wickedness and their sin."

[4]So Jeremiah called Baruch son of Neriah, and while Jeremiah dictated all the words the LORD had spoken to him, Baruch wrote them on the scroll. [5]Then Jeremiah told Baruch, "I am restricted; I am not allowed to go to the LORD's temple. [6]So you go to the house of the LORD on a day of fasting and read to the people from the scroll the words of the LORD that you wrote as I dictated. Read them to all the people of Judah who come in from their towns. [7]Perhaps they will bring their petition before the LORD and will each turn from their wicked ways, for the anger and wrath pronounced against this people by the LORD are great."

[8]Baruch son of Neriah did everything Jeremiah the prophet told him to do; at the LORD's temple he read the words of the LORD from the scroll. [9]In the ninth month of the fifth year of Jehoiakim son of Josiah king of Judah, a time of fasting before the LORD was proclaimed for all the people in Jerusalem and those who had come from the towns of Judah. [10]From the room of Gemariah son of Shaphan the secretary, which was in the upper courtyard at the entrance of the New Gate of the temple, Baruch read to all the people at the LORD's temple the words of Jeremiah from the scroll.

[11]When Micaiah son of Gemariah, the son of Shaphan, heard all the words of the LORD from the scroll, [12]he went down to the secretary's room in the royal palace, where all the officials were sitting: Elishama the secretary, Delaiah son of Shemaiah, Elnathan son of Akbor, Gemariah son of Shaphan, Zedekiah son of Hananiah, and all the other officials. [13]After Micaiah told them everything he had heard Baruch read to the people from the scroll, [14]all the officials sent Jehudi

---

[a] 6 Hebrew *Jonadab*, a variant of *Jehonadab*; here and often in this chapter   [b] 11 Or *Chaldean*

son of Nethaniah, the son of Shelemiah, the son of Cushi, to say to Baruch, "Bring the scroll from which you have read to the people and come." So Baruch son of Neriah went to them with the scroll in his hand. [15]They said to him, "Sit down, please, and read it to us."

So Baruch read it to them. [16]When they heard all these words, they looked at each other in fear and said to Baruch, "We must report all these words to the king." [17]Then they asked Baruch, "Tell us, how did you come to write all this? Did Jeremiah dictate it?"

[18]"Yes," Baruch replied, "he dictated all these words to me, and I wrote them in ink on the scroll."

[19]Then the officials said to Baruch, "You and Jeremiah, go and hide. Don't let anyone know where you are."

[20]After they put the scroll in the room of Elishama the secretary, they went to the king in the courtyard and reported everything to him. [21]The king sent Jehudi to get the scroll, and Jehudi brought it from the room of Elishama the secretary and read it to the king and all the officials standing beside him. [22]It was the ninth month and the king was sitting in the winter apartment, with a fire burning in the firepot in front of him. [23]Whenever Jehudi had read three or four columns of the scroll, the king cut them off with a scribe's knife and threw them into the firepot, until the entire scroll was burned in the fire. [24]The king and all his attendants who heard all these words showed no fear, nor did they tear their clothes. [25]Even though Elnathan, Delaiah and Gemariah urged the king not to burn the scroll, he would not listen to them. [26]Instead, the king commanded Jerahmeel, a son of the king, Seraiah son of Azriel and Shelemiah son of Abdeel to arrest Baruch the scribe and Jeremiah the prophet. But the LORD had hidden them.

[27]After the king burned the scroll containing the words that Baruch had written at Jeremiah's dictation, the word of the LORD came to Jeremiah: [28]"Take another scroll and write on it all the words that were on the first scroll, which Jehoiakim king of Judah burned up. [29]Also tell Jehoiakim king of Judah, 'This is what the LORD says: You burned that scroll and said, "Why did you write on it that the king of Babylon would certainly come and destroy this land and wipe from it both man and beast?" [30]Therefore this is what the LORD says about Jehoiakim king of Judah: He will have no one to sit on the throne of David; his body will be thrown out and exposed to the heat by day and the frost by night. [31]I will punish him and his children and his attendants for their wickedness; I will bring on them and those living in Jerusalem and the people of Judah every disaster I pronounced against them, because they have not listened.'"

[32]So Jeremiah took another scroll and gave it to the scribe Baruch son of Neriah, and as Jeremiah dictated, Baruch wrote on it all the words of the scroll that Jehoiakim king of Judah had burned in the fire. And many similar words were added to them.

Jeremiah in Prison

37 Zedekiah son of Josiah was made king of Judah by Nebuchadnezzar king of Babylon; he reigned in place of Jehoiachin[a] son of Jehoiakim. [2]Neither he nor his attendants nor the people of the land paid any attention to the words the LORD had spoken through Jeremiah the prophet.

[3]King Zedekiah, however, sent Jehukal son of Shelemiah with the priest Zephaniah son of Maaseiah to Jeremiah the prophet with this message: "Please pray to the LORD our God for us."

[4]Now Jeremiah was free to come and go among the people, for he had not yet been put in prison. [5]Pharaoh's army had marched out of Egypt, and when the Babylonians[b] who were besieging Jerusalem heard the report about them, they withdrew from Jerusalem.

[6]Then the word of the LORD came to Jeremiah the prophet: [7]"This is what the LORD, the God of Israel, says: Tell the king of Judah, who sent you to inquire of me, 'Pharaoh's army, which has marched out to support you, will go back to its own land, to Egypt. [8]Then the Babylonians will return and attack this city; they will capture it and burn it down.'

[9]"This is what the LORD says: Do not deceive yourselves, thinking, 'The Babylonians will surely leave us.' They will not! [10]Even if you were to defeat the entire Babylonian[c] army that is attacking you and only wounded men were left in their tents, they would come out and burn this city down."

[11]After the Babylonian army had withdrawn from Jerusalem because of Pharaoh's army, [12]Jeremiah started to leave the city to go to the territory of Benjamin to get his share of the property among the people there. [13]But when he reached the Benjamin Gate, the captain of the

---

[a] 1 Hebrew *Koniah*, a variant of *Jehoiachin*   [b] 5 Or *Chaldeans*; also in verses 8, 9, 13 and 14   [c] 10 Or *Chaldean*; also in verse 11

guard, whose name was Irijah son of Shelemiah, the son of Hananiah, arrested him and said, "You are deserting to the Babylonians!"

¹⁴"That's not true!" Jeremiah said. "I am not deserting to the Babylonians." But Irijah would not listen to him; instead, he arrested Jeremiah and brought him to the officials. ¹⁵They were angry with Jeremiah and had him beaten and imprisoned in the house of Jonathan the secretary, which they had made into a prison.

¹⁶Jeremiah was put into a vaulted cell in a dungeon, where he remained a long time. ¹⁷Then King Zedekiah sent for him and had him brought to the palace, where he asked him privately, "Is there any word from the LORD?"

"Yes," Jeremiah replied, "you will be delivered into the hands of the king of Babylon."

¹⁸Then Jeremiah said to King Zedekiah, "What crime have I committed against you or your attendants or this people, that you have put me in prison? ¹⁹Where are your prophets who prophesied to you, 'The king of Babylon will not attack you or this land'? ²⁰But now, my lord the king, please listen. Let me bring my petition before you: Do not send me back to the house of Jonathan the secretary, or I will die there."

²¹King Zedekiah then gave orders for Jeremiah to be placed in the courtyard of the guard and given a loaf of bread from the street of the bakers each day until all the bread in the city was gone. So Jeremiah remained in the courtyard of the guard.

Jeremiah Thrown Into a Cistern

38 Shephatiah son of Mattan, Gedaliah son of Pashhur, Jehukal[a] son of Shelemiah, and Pashhur son of Malkijah heard what Jeremiah was telling all the people when he said, ²"This is what the LORD says: 'Whoever stays in this city will die by the sword, famine or plague, but whoever goes over to the Babylonians[b] will live. They will escape with their lives; they will live.' ³And this is what the LORD says: 'This city will certainly be given into the hands of the army of the king of Babylon, who will capture it.'"

⁴Then the officials said to the king, "This man should be put to death. He is discouraging the soldiers who are left in this city, as well as all the people, by the things he is saying to them. This man is not seeking the good of these people but their ruin."

⁵"He is in your hands," King Zedekiah answered. "The king can do nothing to oppose you."

⁶So they took Jeremiah and put him into the cistern of Malkijah, the king's son, which was in the courtyard of the guard. They lowered Jeremiah by ropes into the cistern; it had no water in it, only mud, and Jeremiah sank down into the mud.

⁷But Ebed-Melek, a Cushite,[c] an official[d] in the royal palace, heard that they had put Jeremiah into the cistern. While the king was sitting in the Benjamin Gate, ⁸Ebed-Melek went out of the palace and said to him, ⁹"My lord the king, these men have acted wickedly in all they have done to Jeremiah the prophet. They have thrown him into a cistern, where he will starve to death when there is no longer any bread in the city."

¹⁰Then the king commanded Ebed-Melek the Cushite, "Take thirty men from here with you and lift Jeremiah the prophet out of the cistern before he dies."

---

[a] 1 Hebrew *Jukal*, a variant of *Jehukal*;   [b] 2 Or *Chaldeans*; also in verses 18, 19 and 23   [c] 7 Probably from the upper Nile region   [d] 7 Or *a eunuch*

Responsibility: Like It or Not, the Buck Stops with the Leader

Jeremiah 38:1–6

Power abuse occurs not only when evil leaders act out of selfishness, but when good leaders neglect to do what they should. In this case, King Zedekiah delegated an undesirable task to someone else, declaring himself powerless to act. The king lacked the courage to use his power to protect God's prophet.

Jeremiah, on the other hand, remained responsible to a call he didn't like. He proclaimed destruction against his own people, naming Babylon as the executioner. Imagine that you were an evangelist standing in church today, declaring that God was raising up the communists to punish America. You declare that God cares nothing for the Declaration of Independence or the Constitution; in fact, the things we emphasize offend God. If you try to stop speaking this message, you feel disobedient. The word burns inside you and you must speak. So you pursue responsibility, not popularity.

Such was the man and the message of Jeremiah.

[11] So Ebed-Melek took the men with him and went to a room under the treasury in the palace. He took some old rags and worn-out clothes from there and let them down with ropes to Jeremiah in the cistern. [12] Ebed-Melek the Cushite said to Jeremiah, "Put these old rags and worn-out clothes under your arms to pad the ropes." Jeremiah did so, [13] and they pulled him up with the ropes and lifted him out of the cistern. And Jeremiah remained in the courtyard of the guard.

Zedekiah Questions Jeremiah Again

[14] Then King Zedekiah sent for Jeremiah the prophet and had him brought to the third entrance to the temple of the LORD. "I am going to ask you something," the king said to Jeremiah. "Do not hide anything from me."

[15] Jeremiah said to Zedekiah, "If I give you an answer, will you not kill me? Even if I did give you counsel, you would not listen to me."

[16] But King Zedekiah swore this oath secretly to Jeremiah: "As surely as the LORD lives, who has given us breath, I will neither kill you nor hand you over to those who want to kill you."

[17] Then Jeremiah said to Zedekiah, "This is what the LORD God Almighty, the God of Israel, says: 'If you surrender to the officers of the king of Babylon, your life will be spared and this city will not be burned down; you and your family will live. [18] But if you will not surrender to the officers of the king of Babylon, this city will be given into the hands of the Babylonians and they will burn it down; you yourself will not escape from them.'"

[19] King Zedekiah said to Jeremiah, "I am afraid of the Jews who have gone over to the Babylonians, for the Babylonians may hand me over to them and they will mistreat me."

[20] "They will not hand you over," Jeremiah replied. "Obey the LORD by doing what I tell you. Then it will go well with you, and your life will be spared. [21] But if you refuse to surrender, this is what the LORD has revealed to me: [22] All the women left in the palace of the king of Judah will be brought out to the officials of the king of Babylon. Those women will say to you:

"'They misled you and overcame you —
    those trusted friends of yours.
Your feet are sunk in the mud;
    your friends have deserted you.'

[23] "All your wives and children will be brought out to the Babylonians. You yourself will not escape from their hands but will be cap- tured by the king of Babylon; and this city will[a] be burned down."

[24] Then Zedekiah said to Jeremiah, "Do not let anyone know about this conversation, or you may die. [25] If the officials hear that I talked with you, and they come to you and say, 'Tell us what you said to the king and what the king said to you; do not hide it from us or we will kill you,' [26] then tell them, 'I was pleading with the king not to send me back to Jonathan's house to die there.'"

[27] All the officials did come to Jeremiah and question him, and he told them everything the king had ordered him to say. So they said no more to him, for no one had heard his conversation with the king.

[28] And Jeremiah remained in the courtyard of the guard until the day Jerusalem was captured.

The Fall of Jerusalem

39 This is how Jerusalem was taken: [1] In the ninth year of Zedekiah king of Judah, in the tenth month, Nebuchadnezzar king of Babylon marched against Jerusalem with his whole army and laid siege to it. [2] And on the ninth day of the fourth month of Zedekiah's eleventh year, the city wall was broken through. [3] Then all the officials of the king of Babylon came and took seats in the Middle Gate: Nergal-Sharezer of Samgar, Nebo-Sarsekim a chief officer, Nergal-Sharezer a high official and all the other officials of the king of Babylon. [4] When Zedekiah king of Judah and all the soldiers saw them, they fled; they left the city at night by way of the king's garden, through the gate between the two walls, and headed toward the Arabah.[b]

[5] But the Babylonian[c] army pursued them and overtook Zedekiah in the plains of Jericho. They captured him and took him to Nebuchadnezzar king of Babylon at Riblah in the land of Hamath, where he pronounced sentence on him. [6] There at Riblah the king of Babylon slaughtered the sons of Zedekiah before his eyes and also killed all the nobles of Judah. [7] Then he put out Zedekiah's eyes and bound him with bronze shackles to take him to Babylon.

[8] The Babylonians[d] set fire to the royal palace and the houses of the people and broke down the walls of Jerusalem. [9] Nebuzaradan commander of the imperial guard carried into exile to Babylon the people who remained in the city, along with those who had gone over to him, and the rest of the people. [10] But Nebuzaradan the

---

[a] 23 Or and you will cause this city to   [b] 4 Or the Jordan Valley   [c] 5 Or Chaldean   [d] 8 Or Chaldeans

commander of the guard left behind in the land of Judah some of the poor people, who owned nothing; and at that time he gave them vineyards and fields.

¹¹Now Nebuchadnezzar king of Babylon had given these orders about Jeremiah through Nebuzaradan commander of the imperial guard: ¹²"Take him and look after him; don't harm him but do for him whatever he asks." ¹³So Nebuzaradan the commander of the guard, Nebushazban a chief officer, Nergal-Sharezer a high official and all the other officers of the king of Babylon ¹⁴sent and had Jeremiah taken out of the courtyard of the guard. They turned him over to Gedaliah son of Ahikam, the son of Shaphan, to take him back to his home. So he remained among his own people.

¹⁵While Jeremiah had been confined in the courtyard of the guard, the word of the LORD came to him: ¹⁶"Go and tell Ebed-Melek the Cushite, 'This is what the LORD Almighty, the God of Israel, says: I am about to fulfill my words against this city—words concerning disaster, not prosperity. At that time they will be fulfilled before your eyes. ¹⁷But I will rescue you on that day, declares the LORD; you will not be given into the hands of those you fear. ¹⁸I will save you; you will not fall by the sword but will escape with your life, because you trust in me, declares the LORD.'"

Jeremiah Freed

40 The word came to Jeremiah from the LORD after Nebuzaradan commander of the imperial guard had released him at Ramah. He had found Jeremiah bound in chains among all the captives from Jerusalem and Judah who were being carried into exile to Babylon. ²When the commander of the guard found Jeremiah, he said to him, "The LORD your God decreed this disaster for this place. ³And now the LORD has brought it about; he has done just as he said he would. All this happened because you people sinned against the LORD and did not obey him. ⁴But today I am freeing you from the chains on your wrists. Come with me to Babylon, if you like, and I will look after you; but if you do not want to, then don't come. Look, the whole country lies before you; go wherever you please." ⁵However, before Jeremiah turned to go,ᵃ Nebuzaradan added, "Go back to Gedaliah son of Ahikam, the son of Shaphan, whom the king of Babylon has appointed over the towns of Judah, and live with him among the people, or go anywhere else you please."

Then the commander gave him provisions and a present and let him go. ⁶So Jeremiah went to Gedaliah son of Ahikam at Mizpah and

ᵃ 5 Or *Jeremiah answered*

stayed with him among the people who were left behind in the land.

Gedaliah Assassinated

7When all the army officers and their men who were still in the open country heard that the king of Babylon had appointed Gedaliah son of Ahikam as governor over the land and had put him in charge of the men, women and children who were the poorest in the land and who had not been carried into exile to Babylon, 8they came to Gedaliah at Mizpah — Ishmael son of Nethaniah, Johanan and Jonathan the sons of Kareah, Seraiah son of Tanhumeth, the sons of Ephai the Netophathite, and Jaazaniah[a] the son of the Maakathite, and their men. 9Gedaliah son of Ahikam, the son of Shaphan, took an oath to reassure them and their men. "Do not be afraid to serve the Babylonians,[b]" he said. "Settle down in the land and serve the king of Babylon, and it will go well with you. 10I myself will stay at Mizpah to represent you before the Babylonians who come to us, but you are to harvest the wine, summer fruit and olive oil, and put them in your storage jars, and live in the towns you have taken over."

11When all the Jews in Moab, Ammon, Edom and all the other countries heard that the king of Babylon had left a remnant in Judah and had appointed Gedaliah son of Ahikam, the son of Shaphan, as governor over them, 12they all came back to the land of Judah, to Gedaliah at Mizpah, from all the countries where they had been scattered. And they harvested an abundance of wine and summer fruit.

13Johanan son of Kareah and all the army officers still in the open country came to Gedaliah at Mizpah 14and said to him, "Don't you know that Baalis king of the Ammonites has sent Ishmael son of Nethaniah to take your life?" But Gedaliah son of Ahikam did not believe them.

15Then Johanan son of Kareah said privately to Gedaliah in Mizpah, "Let me go and kill Ishmael son of Nethaniah, and no one will know it. Why should he take your life and cause all the Jews who are gathered around you to be scattered and the remnant of Judah to perish?"

16But Gedaliah son of Ahikam said to Johanan son of Kareah, "Don't do such a thing! What you are saying about Ishmael is not true."

41 In the seventh month Ishmael son of Nethaniah, the son of Elishama, who was of royal blood and had been one of the king's

a 8 Hebrew Jezaniah, a variant of Jaazaniah   b 9 Or Chaldeans; also in verse 10

Gedaliah's Poor Decision-Making Skills Lead to Disaster
Jeremiah 40:5—41:2

The Babylonians appointed Gedaliah the governor of Judah and put him in charge of the poor who had not been taken into exile. But the man failed to develop good decision-making skills. In fact, he made one disastrous decision because he neglected to process available information. A man named Ishmael eventually assassinated him, preventing him from ever reaching his potential as a leader.

What could Gedaliah have done to better approach the decisions before him?

1. **Maintain a vision of the big picture.**
2. **Gather all the information possible.**
3. **Listen to those closest to the situation.**
4. **Narrow the best options.**
5. **Imagine the outcome of each option.**
6. **Note the moral and spiritual ramifications to the decision.**
7. **Make choices based on the following criteria:**
   a. **Which best reflects the mind of God?**
   b. **Which benefits the whole of the people?**
   c. **Which aligns itself with the mission you are to accomplish?**

officers, came with ten men to Gedaliah son of Ahikam at Mizpah. While they were eating together there, [2]Ishmael son of Nethaniah and the ten men who were with him got up and struck down Gedaliah son of Ahikam, the son of Shaphan, with the sword, killing the one whom the king of Babylon had appointed as governor over the land. [3]Ishmael also killed all the men of Judah who were with Gedaliah at Mizpah, as well as the Babylonian[a] soldiers who were there.

[4]The day after Gedaliah's assassination, before anyone knew about it, [5]eighty men who had shaved off their beards, torn their clothes and cut themselves came from Shechem, Shiloh and Samaria, bringing grain offerings and incense with them to the house of the LORD. [6]Ishmael son of Nethaniah went out from Mizpah to meet them, weeping as he went. When he met them, he said, "Come to Gedaliah son of Ahikam." [7]When they went into the city, Ishmael son of Nethaniah and the men who were with him slaughtered them and threw them into a cistern. [8]But ten of them said to Ishmael, "Don't kill us! We have wheat and barley, olive oil and honey, hidden in a field." So he let them alone and did not kill them with the others. [9]Now the cistern where he threw all the bodies of the men he had killed along with Gedaliah was the one King Asa had made as part of his defense against Baasha king of Israel. Ishmael son of Nethaniah filled it with the dead.

[10]Ishmael made captives of all the rest of the people who were in Mizpah—the king's daughters along with all the others who were left there, over whom Nebuzaradan commander of the imperial guard had appointed Gedaliah son of Ahikam. Ishmael son of Nethaniah took them captive and set out to cross over to the Ammonites.

[11]When Johanan son of Kareah and all the army officers who were with him heard about all the crimes Ishmael son of Nethaniah had committed, [12]they took all their men and went to fight Ishmael son of Nethaniah. They caught up with him near the great pool in Gibeon. [13]When all the people Ishmael had with him saw Johanan son of Kareah and the army officers who were with him, they were glad. [14]All the people Ishmael had taken captive at Mizpah turned and went over to Johanan son of Kareah. [15]But Ishmael son of Nethaniah and eight of his men escaped from Johanan and fled to the Ammonites.

Flight to Egypt

[16]Then Johanan son of Kareah and all the army officers who were with him led away all the people of Mizpah who had survived, whom Johanan had recovered from Ishmael son of Nethaniah after Ishmael had assassinated Gedaliah son of Ahikam—the soldiers, women, children and court officials he had recovered from Gibeon. [17]And they went on, stopping at Geruth Kimham near Bethlehem on their way to Egypt [18]to escape the Babylonians.[b] They were afraid of them because Ishmael son of Nethaniah had killed Gedaliah son of Ahikam, whom the king of Babylon had appointed as governor over the land.

42 Then all the army officers, including Johanan son of Kareah and Jezaniah[c] son of Hoshaiah, and all the people from the least to the greatest approached [2]Jeremiah the prophet and said to him, "Please hear our petition and pray to the LORD your God for this entire remnant. For as you now see, though we were once many, now only a few are left. [3]Pray that the LORD your God will tell us where we should go and what we should do."

[4]"I have heard you," replied Jeremiah the prophet. "I will certainly pray to the LORD your God as you have requested; I will tell you everything the LORD says and will keep nothing back from you."

[5]Then they said to Jeremiah, "May the LORD be a true and faithful witness against us if we do not act in accordance with everything the LORD your God sends you to tell us. [6]Whether it is favorable or unfavorable, we will obey the LORD our God, to whom we are sending you, so that it will go well with us, for we will obey the LORD our God."

[7]Ten days later the word of the LORD came to Jeremiah. [8]So he called together Johanan son of Kareah and all the army officers who were with him and all the people from the least to the greatest. [9]He said to them, "This is what the LORD, the God of Israel, to whom you sent me to present your petition, says: [10]'If you stay in this land, I will build you up and not tear you down; I will plant you and not uproot you, for I have relented concerning the disaster I have inflicted on you. [11]Do not be afraid of the king of Babylon, whom you now fear. Do not be afraid of him, declares the LORD, for I am with you and will save you and deliver you from his hands. [12]I will show you compassion so that he will have compassion on you and restore you to your land.'

---

[a] 3 Or Chaldean　　[b] 18 Or Chaldeans　　[c] 1 Hebrew; Septuagint (see also 43:2) Azariah

¹³"However, if you say, 'We will not stay in this land,' and so disobey the LORD your God, ¹⁴and if you say, 'No, we will go and live in Egypt, where we will not see war or hear the trumpet or be hungry for bread,' ¹⁵then hear the word of the LORD, you remnant of Judah. This is what the LORD Almighty, the God of Israel, says: 'If you are determined to go to Egypt and you do go to settle there, ¹⁶then the sword you fear will overtake you there, and the famine you dread will follow you into Egypt, and there you will die. ¹⁷Indeed, all who are determined to go to Egypt to settle there will die by the sword, famine and plague; not one of them will survive or escape the disaster I will bring on them.' ¹⁸This is what the LORD Almighty, the God of Israel, says: 'As my anger and wrath have been poured out on those who lived in Jerusalem, so will my wrath be poured out on you when you go to Egypt. You will be a curse*ᵃ* and an object of horror, a curse*ᵃ* and an object of reproach; you will never see this place again.'

¹⁹"Remnant of Judah, the LORD has told you, 'Do not go to Egypt.' Be sure of this: I warn you today ²⁰that you made a fatal mistake when you sent me to the LORD your God and said, 'Pray to the LORD our God for us; tell us everything he says and we will do it.' ²¹I have told you to-day, but you still have not obeyed the LORD your God in all he sent me to tell you. ²²So now, be sure of this: You will die by the sword, famine and plague in the place where you want to go to settle."

43 When Jeremiah had finished telling the people all the words of the LORD their God — everything the LORD had sent him to tell them — ²Azariah son of Hoshaiah and Johanan son of Kareah and all the arrogant men said to Jeremiah, "You are lying! The LORD our God has not sent you to say, 'You must not go to Egypt to settle there.' ³But Baruch son of Neriah is inciting you against us to hand us over to the Babylonians,*ᵇ* so they may kill us or carry us into exile to Babylon."

⁴So Johanan son of Kareah and all the army officers and all the people disobeyed the LORD's command to stay in the land of Judah. ⁵Instead, Johanan son of Kareah and all the army officers led away all the remnant of Judah who had come back to live in the land of Judah from all the nations where they had been scattered. ⁶They also led away all those whom Nebuzaradan commander of the imperial guard had left with

---

ᵃ 18 That is, your name will be used in cursing (see 29:22); or, others will see that you are cursed.   *ᵇ 3* Or *Chaldeans*

Jeremiah Makes a Tough Call

Jeremiah 42:1— 43:13

Most leaders don't look forward to making tough calls. Jeremiah had to make a tough call when his people rejected God's solution to a dilemma. Jeremiah had to remind them of their disobedience and explain the consequences of their choice (Jer 42:19–22).

Many leaders fail because of an inability to make tough decisions. Consider some guidelines for making a tough call:

1. **Accept tough calls as a requirement of leadership.**
2. **Do your homework. Research can make or break a decision.**
3. **Set a deadline.**
4. **Make sure the timing is right.**
5. **Seek counsel from the right people.**
6. **Make your decisions on the principles and values you believe in.**
7. **Develop systems that enable you to make the tough call.**
8. **Understand the emotional expense of making the tough call.**
9. **Recognize your part and God's part.**
10. **Pray for discernment and courage.**

Gedaliah son of Ahikam, the son of Shaphan — the men, the women, the children and the king's daughters. And they took Jeremiah the prophet and Baruch son of Neriah along with them. ⁷So they entered Egypt in disobedience to the LORD and went as far as Tahpanhes.

⁸In Tahpanhes the word of the LORD came to Jeremiah: ⁹"While the Jews are watching, take some large stones with you and bury them in clay in the brick pavement at the entrance to Pharaoh's palace in Tahpanhes. ¹⁰Then say to them, 'This is what the LORD Almighty, the God of Israel, says: I will send for my servant Nebuchadnezzar king of Babylon, and I will set his throne over these stones I have buried here; he will spread his royal canopy above them. ¹¹He will come and attack Egypt, bringing death to those destined for death, captivity to those destined for captivity, and the sword to those destined for the sword. ¹²He will set fire to the temples of the gods of Egypt; he will burn their temples and take their gods captive. As a shep-

herd picks his garment clean of lice, so he will pick Egypt clean and depart. ¹³There in the temple of the sun*a* in Egypt he will demolish the sacred pillars and will burn down the temples of the gods of Egypt.'"

Disaster Because of Idolatry

44 This word came to Jeremiah concerning all the Jews living in Lower Egypt — in Migdol, Tahpanhes and Memphis — and in Upper Egypt: ²"This is what the LORD Almighty, the God of Israel, says: You saw the great disaster I brought on Jerusalem and on all the towns of Judah. Today they lie deserted and in ruins ³because of the evil they have done. They aroused my anger by burning incense to and worshiping other gods that neither they nor you nor your ancestors ever knew. ⁴Again and again I sent my servants the prophets, who said, 'Do not do this detestable thing that I hate!' ⁵But they did not

---

a 13 Or *in Heliopolis*

Communication: Jeremiah Uses Word Pictures

Jeremiah 43:8–13

Jeremiah led the people primarily through his word gifts. He expressed his leadership using gifts of prophecy, teaching and exhortation. Through wise use of these gifts, he became a master communicator.

His book features at least 12 metaphors, or word pictures, that he used to communicate God's message to God's people. Effective leaders find similar analogies and object lessons to make their point. Study and learn from Jeremiah, a master communicator.

Jeremiah's twelve object lessons:

1. **The almond branch (1:11–12)**
2. **The boiling pot (1:13–19)**
3. **The ruined linen belt (13:1–11)**
4. **The wineskins (13:12–14)**
5. **The drought (14:1–9)**
6. **The partridge (17:9–11)**
7. **The potter and the clay (18:1–17)**
8. **The broken jar (19:1–13)**
9. **Two baskets of figs (24:1–10)**
10. **The crossbars and yokes (27:1–11)**
11. **The command to buy a field (32:6–25)**
12. **The parable of the stones (43:8–13)**

listen or pay attention; they did not turn from their wickedness or stop burning incense to other gods. [6]Therefore, my fierce anger was poured out; it raged against the towns of Judah and the streets of Jerusalem and made them the desolate ruins they are today.

[7]"Now this is what the LORD God Almighty, the God of Israel, says: Why bring such great disaster on yourselves by cutting off from Judah the men and women, the children and infants, and so leave yourselves without a remnant? [8]Why arouse my anger with what your hands have made, burning incense to other gods in Egypt, where you have come to live? You will destroy yourselves and make yourselves a curse[a] and an object of reproach among all the nations on earth. [9]Have you forgotten the wickedness committed by your ancestors and by the kings and queens of Judah and the wickedness committed by you and your wives in the land of Judah and the streets of Jerusalem? [10]To this day they have not humbled themselves or shown reverence, nor have they followed my law and the decrees I set before you and your ancestors.

[11]"Therefore this is what the LORD Almighty, the God of Israel, says: I am determined to bring disaster on you and to destroy all Judah. [12]I will take away the remnant of Judah who were determined to go to Egypt to settle there. They will all perish in Egypt; they will fall by the sword or die from famine. From the least to the greatest, they will die by sword or famine. They will become a curse and an object of horror, a curse and an object of reproach. [13]I will punish those who live in Egypt with the sword, famine and plague, as I punished Jerusalem. [14]None of the remnant of Judah who have gone to live in Egypt will escape or survive to return to the land of Judah, to which they long to return and live; none will return except a few fugitives."

[15]Then all the men who knew that their wives were burning incense to other gods, along with all the women who were present—a large assembly—and all the people living in Lower and Upper Egypt, said to Jeremiah, [16]"We will not listen to the message you have spoken to us in the name of the LORD! [17]We will certainly do everything we said we would: We will burn incense to the Queen of Heaven and will pour out drink offerings to her just as we and our ancestors, our kings and our officials did in the towns of Judah and in the streets of Jerusalem. At that time we had plenty of food and were well off and suffered no harm. [18]But ever since we stopped burning incense to the Queen of Heaven and pouring out drink offerings to her, we have had nothing and have been perishing by sword and famine."

[19]The women added, "When we burned incense to the Queen of Heaven and poured out drink offerings to her, did not our husbands know that we were making cakes impressed with her image and pouring out drink offerings to her?"

[20]Then Jeremiah said to all the people, both men and women, who were answering him, [21]"Did not the LORD remember and call to mind the incense burned in the towns of Judah and the streets of Jerusalem by you and your ancestors, your kings and your officials and the people of the land? [22]When the LORD could no longer endure your wicked actions and the detestable things you did, your land became a curse and a desolate waste without inhabitants, as it is today. [23]Because you have burned incense and have sinned against the LORD and have not obeyed him or followed his law or his decrees or his stipulations, this disaster has come upon you, as you now see."

[24]Then Jeremiah said to all the people, including the women, "Hear the word of the LORD, all you people of Judah in Egypt. [25]This is what the LORD Almighty, the God of Israel, says: You and your wives have done what you said you would do when you promised, 'We will certainly carry out the vows we made to burn incense and pour out drink offerings to the Queen of Heaven.'

"Go ahead then, do what you promised! Keep your vows! [26]But hear the word of the LORD, all you Jews living in Egypt: 'I swear by my great name,' says the LORD, 'that no one from Judah living anywhere in Egypt will ever again invoke my name or swear, "As surely as the Sovereign LORD lives." [27]For I am watching over them for harm, not for good; the Jews in Egypt will perish by sword and famine until they are all destroyed. [28]Those who escape the sword and return to the land of Judah from Egypt will be very few. Then the whole remnant of Judah who came to live in Egypt will know whose word will stand—mine or theirs.

[29]"This will be the sign to you that I will punish you in this place,' declares the LORD, 'so that you will know that my threats of harm against you will surely stand.' [30]This is what the LORD says: 'I am going to deliver Pharaoh Hophra

---

[a] 8 That is, your name will be used in cursing (see 29:22); or, others will see that you are cursed; also in verse 12; similarly in verse 22.

king of Egypt into the hands of his enemies who want to kill him, just as I gave Zedekiah king of Judah into the hands of Nebuchadnezzar king of Babylon, the enemy who wanted to kill him.'"

A Message to Baruch

45 When Baruch son of Neriah wrote on a scroll the words Jeremiah the prophet dictated in the fourth year of Jehoiakim son of Josiah king of Judah, Jeremiah said this to Baruch: ²"This is what the LORD, the God of Israel, says to you, Baruch: ³You said, 'Woe to me! The LORD has added sorrow to my pain; I am worn out with groaning and find no rest.' ⁴But the LORD has told me to say to you, 'This is what the LORD says: I will overthrow what I have built and uproot what I have planted, throughout the earth. ⁵Should you then seek great things for yourself? Do not seek them. For I will bring disaster on all people, declares the LORD, but wherever you go I will let you escape with your life.'"

A Message About Egypt

46 This is the word of the LORD that came to Jeremiah the prophet concerning the nations:

²Concerning Egypt:

This is the message against the army of Pharaoh Necho king of Egypt, which was defeated at Carchemish on the Euphrates River by Nebuchadnezzar king of Babylon in the fourth year of Jehoiakim son of Josiah king of Judah:

³"Prepare your shields, both large and small,
    and march out for battle!
⁴Harness the horses,
    mount the steeds!
Take your positions
    with helmets on!
Polish your spears,
    put on your armor!
⁵What do I see?
    They are terrified,
they are retreating,
    their warriors are defeated.
They flee in haste
    without looking back,
    and there is terror on every side,"
                declares the LORD.
⁶"The swift cannot flee
    nor the strong escape.
In the north by the River Euphrates
    they stumble and fall.

⁷"Who is this that rises like the Nile,
    like rivers of surging waters?
⁸Egypt rises like the Nile,
    like rivers of surging waters.
She says, 'I will rise and cover the earth;
    I will destroy cities and their people.'
⁹Charge, you horses!
    Drive furiously, you charioteers!
March on, you warriors—men of Cush*a* and
    Put who carry shields,
    men of Lydia who draw the bow.
¹⁰But that day belongs to the Lord, the LORD
    Almighty—
    a day of vengeance, for vengeance on his
    foes.
The sword will devour till it is satisfied,
    till it has quenched its thirst with blood.
For the Lord, the LORD Almighty, will offer
    sacrifice
    in the land of the north by the River
    Euphrates.

¹¹"Go up to Gilead and get balm,
    Virgin Daughter Egypt.
But you try many medicines in vain;
    there is no healing for you.
¹²The nations will hear of your shame;
    your cries will fill the earth.
One warrior will stumble over another;
    both will fall down together."

¹³This is the message the LORD spoke to Jeremiah the prophet about the coming of Nebuchadnezzar king of Babylon to attack Egypt:

¹⁴"Announce this in Egypt, and proclaim it in
    Migdol;
    proclaim it also in Memphis and
    Tahpanhes:
'Take your positions and get ready,
    for the sword devours those around you.'
¹⁵Why will your warriors be laid low?
    They cannot stand, for the LORD will push
    them down.
¹⁶They will stumble repeatedly;
    they will fall over each other.
They will say, 'Get up, let us go back
    to our own people and our native lands,
    away from the sword of the oppressor.'
¹⁷There they will exclaim,
    'Pharaoh king of Egypt is only a loud noise;
    he has missed his opportunity.'

¹⁸"As surely as I live," declares the King,
    whose name is the LORD Almighty,

---

a 9 That is, the upper Nile region

"one will come who is like Tabor among the
    mountains,
    like Carmel by the sea.
¹⁹ Pack your belongings for exile,
    you who live in Egypt,
for Memphis will be laid waste
    and lie in ruins without inhabitant.

²⁰ "Egypt is a beautiful heifer,
    but a gadfly is coming
    against her from the north.
²¹ The mercenaries in her ranks
    are like fattened calves.
They too will turn and flee together,
    they will not stand their ground,
for the day of disaster is coming upon them,
    the time for them to be punished.
²² Egypt will hiss like a fleeing serpent
    as the enemy advances in force;
they will come against her with axes,
    like men who cut down trees.
²³ They will chop down her forest,"
                                    declares the LORD,
    "dense though it be.
They are more numerous than locusts,
    they cannot be counted.
²⁴ Daughter Egypt will be put to shame,
    given into the hands of the people of the
    north."

²⁵ The LORD Almighty, the God of Israel, says:
"I am about to bring punishment on Amon god
of Thebes, on Pharaoh, on Egypt and her gods
and her kings, and on those who rely on Pharaoh. ²⁶ I will give them into the hands of those
who want to kill them — Nebuchadnezzar king
of Babylon and his officers. Later, however,
Egypt will be inhabited as in times past," declares the LORD.

²⁷ "Do not be afraid, Jacob my servant;
    do not be dismayed, Israel.
I will surely save you out of a distant place,
    your descendants from the land of their
    exile.
Jacob will again have peace and security,
    and no one will make him afraid.
²⁸ Do not be afraid, Jacob my servant,
    for I am with you," declares the LORD.
"Though I completely destroy all the
    nations
    among which I scatter you,
    I will not completely destroy you.
I will discipline you but only in due
    measure;
    I will not let you go entirely unpunished."

A Message About the Philistines

47 This is the word of the LORD that came
to Jeremiah the prophet concerning the
Philistines before Pharaoh attacked Gaza:

²This is what the LORD says:

"See how the waters are rising in the north;
    they will become an overflowing torrent.
They will overflow the land and everything
    in it,
    the towns and those who live in them.
The people will cry out;
    all who dwell in the land will wail
³ at the sound of the hooves of galloping
    steeds,
    at the noise of enemy chariots
    and the rumble of their wheels.
Parents will not turn to help their children;
    their hands will hang limp.
⁴ For the day has come
    to destroy all the Philistines
and to remove all survivors
    who could help Tyre and Sidon.
The LORD is about to destroy the Philistines,
    the remnant from the coasts of Caphtor.ᵃ
⁵ Gaza will shave her head in mourning;
    Ashkelon will be silenced.
You remnant on the plain,
    how long will you cut yourselves?

⁶ " 'Alas, sword of the LORD,
    how long till you rest?
Return to your sheath;
    cease and be still.'
⁷ But how can it rest
    when the LORD has commanded it,
when he has ordered it
    to attack Ashkelon and the coast?"

A Message About Moab

48 Concerning Moab:

This is what the LORD Almighty, the God of
Israel, says:

"Woe to Nebo, for it will be ruined.
    Kiriathaim will be disgraced and
    captured;
    the strongholdᵇ will be disgraced and
    shattered.
² Moab will be praised no more;
    in Heshbonᶜ people will plot her downfall:
    'Come, let us put an end to that nation.'

ᵃ 4 That is, Crete   ᵇ 1 Or captured; / Misgab   ᶜ 2 The
Hebrew for Heshbon sounds like the Hebrew for plot.

You, the people of Madmen,[a] will also be
    silenced;
    the sword will pursue you.
3 Cries of anguish arise from Horonaim,
    cries of great havoc and destruction.
4 Moab will be broken;
    her little ones will cry out.[b]
5 They go up the hill to Luhith,
    weeping bitterly as they go;
on the road down to Horonaim
    anguished cries over the destruction are
    heard.
6 Flee! Run for your lives;
    become like a bush[c] in the desert.
7 Since you trust in your deeds and riches,
    you too will be taken captive,
and Chemosh will go into exile,
    together with his priests and officials.
8 The destroyer will come against every town,
    and not a town will escape.
The valley will be ruined
    and the plateau destroyed,
    because the LORD has spoken.
9 Put salt on Moab,
    for she will be laid waste;[d]
    her towns will become desolate,
    with no one to live in them.

10 "A curse on anyone who is lax in doing the
    LORD's work!
    A curse on anyone who keeps their sword
    from bloodshed!

11 "Moab has been at rest from youth,
    like wine left on its dregs,
not poured from one jar to another —
    she has not gone into exile.
So she tastes as she did,
    and her aroma is unchanged.
12 But days are coming,"
    declares the LORD,
    "when I will send men who pour from
        pitchers,
    and they will pour her out;
    they will empty her pitchers
    and smash her jars.
13 Then Moab will be ashamed of Chemosh,
    as Israel was ashamed
    when they trusted in Bethel.

14 "How can you say, 'We are warriors,
    men valiant in battle'?
15 Moab will be destroyed and her towns
        invaded;
    her finest young men will go down in the
        slaughter,"

declares the King, whose name is the
    LORD Almighty.
16 "The fall of Moab is at hand;
    her calamity will come quickly.
17 Mourn for her, all who live around her,
    all who know her fame;
    say, 'How broken is the mighty scepter,
    how broken the glorious staff!'

18 "Come down from your glory
    and sit on the parched ground,
    you inhabitants of Daughter Dibon,
for the one who destroys Moab
    will come up against you
    and ruin your fortified cities.
19 Stand by the road and watch,
    you who live in Aroer.
Ask the man fleeing and the woman
        escaping,
    ask them, 'What has happened?'
20 Moab is disgraced, for she is shattered.
    Wail and cry out!
Announce by the Arnon
    that Moab is destroyed.
21 Judgment has come to the plateau —
    to Holon, Jahzah and Mephaath,
22   to Dibon, Nebo and Beth Diblathaim,
23   to Kiriathaim, Beth Gamul and Beth Meon,
24   to Kerioth and Bozrah —
    to all the towns of Moab, far and near.
25 Moab's horn[e] is cut off;
    her arm is broken,"
                    declares the LORD.
26 "Make her drunk,
    for she has defied the LORD.
Let Moab wallow in her vomit;
    let her be an object of ridicule.
27 Was not Israel the object of your ridicule?
    Was she caught among thieves,
    that you shake your head in scorn
    whenever you speak of her?
28 Abandon your towns and dwell among the
        rocks,
    you who live in Moab.
Be like a dove that makes its nest
    at the mouth of a cave.

29 "We have heard of Moab's pride —
    how great is her arrogance! —
of her insolence, her pride, her conceit
    and the haughtiness of her heart.

---

[a] 2 The name of the Moabite town Madmen sounds like the
Hebrew for be silenced.   [b] 4 Hebrew; Septuagint / proclaim it
to Zoar   [c] 6 Or like Aroer   [d] 9 Or Give wings to Moab, /
for she will fly away   [e] 25 Horn here symbolizes strength.

Leadership Brings Temptations

Jeremiah 48:26–30

The nation of Moab dominated several others in her most powerful years, but God pronounced a severe judgment against her. Why? Moab's leaders, caught up in their own power, defied the Lord. Pride, conceit and arrogance began to drive her leaders.

The same danger often ruins leaders today. Several related temptations commonly lead to the destruction of contemporary leaders:

1. **Pride:** We enjoy thinking that we did it on our own.

2. **Possessions:** We pursue the perks that come with our visibility.

3. **Popularity:** We begin to believe our own press.

4. **Power:** We recognize our clout and use it to advance ourselves.

5. **Prestige:** We love the feeling of being important and irreplaceable.

6. **Pleasure:** We think we deserve special treatment not given to others.

7. **People:** We cross a line from serving others to pleasing people.

After enjoying leadership success, a sequence of events often follows:

1. **Satisfaction:** We enjoy the victory we have achieved.

2. **Indulgence:** We unconsciously feel we deserve a pleasurable reward.

3. **Compromise:** We rationalize our behavior.

4. **Denial:** We continue leading, not realizing our impure motives.

5. **Adultery:** We give ourselves to another, sexually, emotionally, or financially.

6. **Obsession:** We get trapped in a pattern that consumes us.

---

[30] I know her insolence but it is futile,"
> declares the LORD,
"and her boasts accomplish nothing.
[31] Therefore I wail over Moab,
    for all Moab I cry out,
    I moan for the people of Kir Hareseth.
[32] I weep for you, as Jazer weeps,
    you vines of Sibmah.
Your branches spread as far as the sea[a];
    they reached as far as[b] Jazer.
The destroyer has fallen
    on your ripened fruit and grapes.
[33] Joy and gladness are gone
    from the orchards and fields of Moab.
I have stopped the flow of wine from the
      presses;
    no one treads them with shouts of joy.
Although there are shouts,
    they are not shouts of joy.
[34] "The sound of their cry rises
    from Heshbon to Elealeh and Jahaz,
from Zoar as far as Horonaim and Eglath
    Shelishiyah,
    for even the waters of Nimrim are dried up.
[35] In Moab I will put an end
    to those who make offerings on the high
      places
    and burn incense to their gods,"
> declares the LORD.
[36] "So my heart laments for Moab like the
    music of a pipe;
    it laments like a pipe for the people of Kir
      Hareseth.
    The wealth they acquired is gone.
[37] Every head is shaved
    and every beard cut off;
every hand is slashed
    and every waist is covered with sackcloth.
[38] On all the roofs in Moab
    and in the public squares

---

a 32 Probably the Dead Sea   *b 32* Two Hebrew manuscripts and Septuagint; most Hebrew manuscripts *as far as the Sea of*

there is nothing but mourning,
    for I have broken Moab
    like a jar that no one wants,"
                        declares the LORD.
39 "How shattered she is! How they wail!
    How Moab turns her back in shame!
Moab has become an object of ridicule,
    an object of horror to all those around
        her."

40 This is what the LORD says:

"Look! An eagle is swooping down,
    spreading its wings over Moab.
41 Kerioth[a] will be captured
    and the strongholds taken.
In that day the hearts of Moab's warriors
    will be like the heart of a woman in labor.
42 Moab will be destroyed as a nation
    because she defied the LORD.
43 Terror and pit and snare await you,
    you people of Moab,"
                        declares the LORD.
44 "Whoever flees from the terror
    will fall into a pit,
    whoever climbs out of the pit
    will be caught in a snare;
for I will bring on Moab
    the year of her punishment,"
                        declares the LORD.

45 "In the shadow of Heshbon
    the fugitives stand helpless,
for a fire has gone out from Heshbon,
    a blaze from the midst of Sihon;
it burns the foreheads of Moab,
    the skulls of the noisy boasters.
46 Woe to you, Moab!
    The people of Chemosh are destroyed;
your sons are taken into exile
    and your daughters into captivity.

47 "Yet I will restore the fortunes of Moab
    in days to come,"
                        declares the LORD.

Here ends the judgment on Moab.

A Message About Ammon

49 Concerning the Ammonites:

This is what the LORD says:

"Has Israel no sons?
    Has Israel no heir?
Why then has Molek[b] taken possession of
        Gad?
    Why do his people live in its towns?

2 But the days are coming,"
                        declares the LORD,
"when I will sound the battle cry
    against Rabbah of the Ammonites;
it will become a mound of ruins,
    and its surrounding villages will be set on
        fire.
Then Israel will drive out
    those who drove her out,"
                        says the LORD.

3 "Wail, Heshbon, for Ai is destroyed!
    Cry out, you inhabitants of Rabbah!
Put on sackcloth and mourn;
    rush here and there inside the walls,
for Molek will go into exile,
    together with his priests and officials.
4 Why do you boast of your valleys,
    boast of your valleys so fruitful?
Unfaithful Daughter Ammon,
    you trust in your riches and say,
    'Who will attack me?'
5 I will bring terror on you
    from all those around you,"
                        declares the Lord,
                        the LORD Almighty.
"Every one of you will be driven away,
    and no one will gather the fugitives.

6 "Yet afterward, I will restore the fortunes of
        the Ammonites,"
                        declares the LORD.

A Message About Edom

7 Concerning Edom:

This is what the LORD Almighty says:

"Is there no longer wisdom in Teman?
    Has counsel perished from the prudent?
    Has their wisdom decayed?
8 Turn and flee, hide in deep caves,
    you who live in Dedan,
for I will bring disaster on Esau
    at the time when I punish him.
9 If grape pickers came to you,
    would they not leave a few grapes?
If thieves came during the night,
    would they not steal only as much as they
        wanted?
10 But I will strip Esau bare;
    I will uncover his hiding places,
    so that he cannot conceal himself.
His armed men are destroyed,
    also his allies and neighbors,
    so there is no one to say,

---

[a] 41 Or *The cities*   [b] 1 Or *their king*; also in verse 3

¹¹ 'Leave your fatherless children; I will keep
>> them alive.
>> Your widows too can depend on me.' "

¹²This is what the LORD says: "If those who do not deserve to drink the cup must drink it, why should you go unpunished? You will not go unpunished, but must drink it. ¹³I swear by myself," declares the LORD, "that Bozrah will become a ruin and a curse,^a an object of horror and reproach; and all its towns will be in ruins forever."

¹⁴I have heard a message from the LORD;
>> an envoy was sent to the nations to say,
>> "Assemble yourselves to attack it!
>> Rise up for battle!"

¹⁵ "Now I will make you small among the
>> nations,
>> despised by mankind.
¹⁶ The terror you inspire
>> and the pride of your heart have deceived
>> you,
>> you who live in the clefts of the rocks,
>> who occupy the heights of the hill.
>> Though you build your nest as high as the
>> eagle's,
>> from there I will bring you down,"
>>>> declares the LORD.

¹⁷ "Edom will become an object of horror;
>> all who pass by will be appalled and will
>> scoff
>> because of all its wounds.
¹⁸ As Sodom and Gomorrah were overthrown,
>> along with their neighboring towns,"
>>>> says the LORD,
>> "so no one will live there;
>> no people will dwell in it.

¹⁹ "Like a lion coming up from Jordan's thickets
>> to a rich pastureland,
>> I will chase Edom from its land in an instant.
>> Who is the chosen one I will appoint for
>> this?
>> Who is like me and who can challenge me?
>> And what shepherd can stand against me?"

²⁰ Therefore, hear what the LORD has planned
>> against Edom,
>> what he has purposed against those who
>> live in Teman:
>> The young of the flock will be dragged away;
>> their pasture will be appalled at their fate.
²¹ At the sound of their fall the earth will
>> tremble;
>> their cry will resound to the Red Sea.^b

²² Look! An eagle will soar and swoop down,
>> spreading its wings over Bozrah.
>> In that day the hearts of Edom's warriors
>> will be like the heart of a woman in labor.

A Message About Damascus

²³Concerning Damascus:

>> "Hamath and Arpad are dismayed,
>> for they have heard bad news.
>> They are disheartened,
>> troubled like^c the restless sea.
²⁴ Damascus has become feeble,
>> she has turned to flee
>> and panic has gripped her;
>> anguish and pain have seized her,
>> pain like that of a woman in labor.
²⁵ Why has the city of renown not been
>> abandoned,
>> the town in which I delight?
²⁶ Surely, her young men will fall in the
>> streets;
>> all her soldiers will be silenced in that
>> day,"
>>>> declares the LORD Almighty.
²⁷ "I will set fire to the walls of Damascus;
>> it will consume the fortresses of Ben-
>> Hadad."

A Message About Kedar and Hazor

²⁸Concerning Kedar and the kingdoms of Hazor, which Nebuchadnezzar king of Babylon attacked:

>> This is what the LORD says:

>> "Arise, and attack Kedar
>> and destroy the people of the East.
²⁹ Their tents and their flocks will be taken;
>> their shelters will be carried off
>> with all their goods and camels.
>> People will shout to them,
>> 'Terror on every side!'

³⁰ "Flee quickly away!
>> Stay in deep caves, you who live in Hazor,"
>>>> declares the LORD.
>> "Nebuchadnezzar king of Babylon has
>> plotted against you;
>> he has devised a plan against you.

³¹ "Arise and attack a nation at ease,
>> which lives in confidence,"
>>>> declares the LORD,

---

^a 13 That is, its name will be used in cursing (see 29:22); or, others will see that it is cursed.   ^b 21 Or the Sea of Reeds   ^c 23 Hebrew on or by

"a nation that has neither gates nor bars;
   its people live far from danger.
32 Their camels will become plunder,
   and their large herds will be spoils of war.
I will scatter to the winds those who are in
      distant places[a]
   and will bring disaster on them from
      every side,"
                              declares the LORD.
33 "Hazor will become a haunt of jackals,
   a desolate place forever.
No one will live there;
   no people will dwell in it."

A Message About Elam

34 This is the word of the LORD that came to
Jeremiah the prophet concerning Elam, early in
the reign of Zedekiah king of Judah:

35 This is what the LORD Almighty says:

"See, I will break the bow of Elam,
   the mainstay of their might.
36 I will bring against Elam the four winds
   from the four quarters of heaven;
I will scatter them to the four winds,
   and there will not be a nation
   where Elam's exiles do not go.
37 I will shatter Elam before their foes,
   before those who want to kill them;
I will bring disaster on them,
   even my fierce anger,"
                              declares the LORD.
"I will pursue them with the sword
   until I have made an end of them.
38 I will set my throne in Elam
   and destroy her king and officials,"
                              declares the LORD.

39 "Yet I will restore the fortunes of Elam
   in days to come,"
                              declares the LORD.

A Message About Babylon

50 This is the word the LORD spoke through
Jeremiah the prophet concerning Babylon and the land of the Babylonians[b]:

2 "Announce and proclaim among the
      nations,
   lift up a banner and proclaim it;
   keep nothing back, but say,
'Babylon will be captured;
   Bel will be put to shame,
   Marduk filled with terror.
Her images will be put to shame
   and her idols filled with terror.'

3 A nation from the north will attack her
   and lay waste her land.
No one will live in it;
   both people and animals will flee away.

4 "In those days, at that time,"
   declares the LORD,
"the people of Israel and the people of Judah
      together
   will go in tears to seek the LORD their
      God.
5 They will ask the way to Zion
   and turn their faces toward it.
They will come and bind themselves to the
      LORD
   in an everlasting covenant
   that will not be forgotten.

6 "My people have been lost sheep;
   their shepherds have led them astray
   and caused them to roam on the
      mountains.
They wandered over mountain and hill
   and forgot their own resting place.
7 Whoever found them devoured them;
   their enemies said, 'We are not guilty,
for they sinned against the LORD, their
      verdant pasture,
   the LORD, the hope of their ancestors.'

8 "Flee out of Babylon;
   leave the land of the Babylonians,
   and be like the goats that lead the flock.
9 For I will stir up and bring against
      Babylon
   an alliance of great nations from the land
      of the north.
They will take up their positions against her,
   and from the north she will be captured.
Their arrows will be like skilled warriors
   who do not return empty-handed.
10 So Babylonia[c] will be plundered;
   all who plunder her will have their fill,"
                              declares the LORD.

11 "Because you rejoice and are glad,
   you who pillage my inheritance,
because you frolic like a heifer threshing
      grain
   and neigh like stallions,
12 your mother will be greatly ashamed;
   she who gave you birth will be disgraced.
She will be the least of the nations —
   a wilderness, a dry land, a desert.

---

a 32 Or *who clip the hair by their foreheads*   *b 1* Or
Chaldeans; also in verses 8, 25, 35 and 45   *c 10* Or *Chaldea*

¹³Because of the LORD's anger she will not be
        inhabited
    but will be completely desolate.
All who pass Babylon will be appalled;
    they will scoff because of all her wounds.

¹⁴"Take up your positions around Babylon,
    all you who draw the bow.
Shoot at her! Spare no arrows,
    for she has sinned against the LORD.
¹⁵Shout against her on every side!
    She surrenders, her towers fall,
    her walls are torn down.
Since this is the vengeance of the LORD,
    take vengeance on her;
    do to her as she has done to others.
¹⁶Cut off from Babylon the sower,
    and the reaper with his sickle at harvest.
Because of the sword of the oppressor
    let everyone return to their own people,
    let everyone flee to their own land.

¹⁷"Israel is a scattered flock
    that lions have chased away.
The first to devour them
    was the king of Assyria;
the last to crush their bones
    was Nebuchadnezzar king of Babylon."

¹⁸Therefore this is what the LORD Almighty,
the God of Israel, says:

"I will punish the king of Babylon and his
        land
    as I punished the king of Assyria.
¹⁹But I will bring Israel back to their own
        pasture,
    and they will graze on Carmel and Bashan;
their appetite will be satisfied
    on the hills of Ephraim and Gilead.
²⁰In those days, at that time,"
        declares the LORD,
"search will be made for Israel's guilt,
    but there will be none,
and for the sins of Judah,
    but none will be found,
    for I will forgive the remnant I spare.

²¹"Attack the land of Merathaim
    and those who live in Pekod.
Pursue, kill and completely destroy[a] them,"
        declares the LORD.
    "Do everything I have commanded you.
²²The noise of battle is in the land,
    the noise of great destruction!
²³How broken and shattered
    is the hammer of the whole earth!

How desolate is Babylon
    among the nations!
²⁴I set a trap for you, Babylon,
    and you were caught before you knew it;
you were found and captured
    because you opposed the LORD.
²⁵The LORD has opened his arsenal
    and brought out the weapons of his wrath,
for the Sovereign LORD Almighty has work
        to do
    in the land of the Babylonians.
²⁶Come against her from afar.
    Break open her granaries;
    pile her up like heaps of grain.
Completely destroy her
    and leave her no remnant.
²⁷Kill all her young bulls;
    let them go down to the slaughter!
Woe to them! For their day has come,
    the time for them to be punished.
²⁸Listen to the fugitives and refugees from
        Babylon
    declaring in Zion
how the LORD our God has taken vengeance,
    vengeance for his temple.

²⁹"Summon archers against Babylon,
    all those who draw the bow.
Encamp all around her;
    let no one escape.
Repay her for her deeds;
    do to her as she has done.
For she has defied the LORD,
    the Holy One of Israel.
³⁰Therefore, her young men will fall in the
        streets;
    all her soldiers will be silenced in that day,"
        declares the LORD.
³¹"See, I am against you, you arrogant one,"
    declares the Lord, the LORD Almighty,
"for your day has come,
    the time for you to be punished.
³²The arrogant one will stumble and fall
    and no one will help her up;
I will kindle a fire in her towns
    that will consume all who are around her."

³³This is what the LORD Almighty says:

"The people of Israel are oppressed,
    and the people of Judah as well.
All their captors hold them fast,
    refusing to let them go.

ᵃ 21 The Hebrew term refers to the irrevocable giving over of
things or persons to the LORD, often by totally destroying them;
also in verse 26.

³⁴ Yet their Redeemer is strong;
	the Lord Almighty is his name.
He will vigorously defend their cause
	so that he may bring rest to their land,
	but unrest to those who live in Babylon.

³⁵ "A sword against the Babylonians!"
	declares the Lord —
	"against those who live in Babylon
	and against her officials and wise men!
³⁶ A sword against her false prophets!
	They will become fools.
A sword against her warriors!
	They will be filled with terror.
³⁷ A sword against her horses and chariots
	and all the foreigners in her ranks!
	They will become weaklings.
A sword against her treasures!
	They will be plundered.
³⁸ A drought on*ᵃ* her waters!
	They will dry up.
For it is a land of idols,
	idols that will go mad with terror.

³⁹ "So desert creatures and hyenas will live
		there,
	and there the owl will dwell.
It will never again be inhabited
	or lived in from generation to generation.
⁴⁰ As I overthrew Sodom and Gomorrah
	along with their neighboring towns,"
		declares the Lord,
	"so no one will live there;
	no people will dwell in it.

⁴¹ "Look! An army is coming from the north;
	a great nation and many kings
	are being stirred up from the ends of the
		earth.
⁴² They are armed with bows and spears;
	they are cruel and without mercy.
They sound like the roaring sea
	as they ride on their horses;
they come like men in battle formation
	to attack you, Daughter Babylon.
⁴³ The king of Babylon has heard reports about
		them,
	and his hands hang limp.
Anguish has gripped him,
	pain like that of a woman in labor.
⁴⁴ Like a lion coming up from Jordan's thickets
	to a rich pastureland,
I will chase Babylon from its land in an
		instant.
	Who is the chosen one I will appoint for
		this?

Who is like me and who can challenge me?
	And what shepherd can stand against me?"

⁴⁵ Therefore, hear what the Lord has planned
		against Babylon,
	what he has purposed against the land of
		the Babylonians:
The young of the flock will be dragged away;
	their pasture will be appalled at their fate.
⁴⁶ At the sound of Babylon's capture the earth
		will tremble;
	its cry will resound among the nations.

51 This is what the Lord says:

"See, I will stir up the spirit of a destroyer
	against Babylon and the people of Leb
		Kamai.*ᵇ*
² I will send foreigners to Babylon
	to winnow her and to devastate her land;
they will oppose her on every side
	in the day of her disaster.
³ Let not the archer string his bow,
	nor let him put on his armor.
Do not spare her young men;
	completely destroy*ᶜ* her army.
⁴ They will fall down slain in Babylon,*ᵈ*
	fatally wounded in her streets.
⁵ For Israel and Judah have not been forsaken
	by their God, the Lord Almighty,
though their land*ᵉ* is full of guilt
	before the Holy One of Israel.

⁶ "Flee from Babylon!
	Run for your lives!
	Do not be destroyed because of her sins.
It is time for the Lord's vengeance;
	he will repay her what she deserves.
⁷ Babylon was a gold cup in the Lord's hand;
	she made the whole earth drunk.
The nations drank her wine;
	therefore they have now gone mad.
⁸ Babylon will suddenly fall and be broken.
	Wail over her!
Get balm for her pain;
	perhaps she can be healed.

⁹ "'We would have healed Babylon,
	but she cannot be healed;
let us leave her and each go to our own land,
	for her judgment reaches to the skies,
	it rises as high as the heavens.'

ᵃ 38 Or *A sword against*   *ᵇ 1 Leb Kamai* is a cryptogram for
Chaldea, that is, Babylonia.   *ᶜ 3* The Hebrew term refers to
the irrevocable giving over of things or persons to the Lord,
often by totally destroying them.   *ᵈ 4* Or *Chaldea*   *ᵉ 5* Or
Almighty, / and the land of the Babylonians

10 " 'The LORD has vindicated us;
    come, let us tell in Zion
what the LORD our God has done.'

11 "Sharpen the arrows,
    take up the shields!
The LORD has stirred up the kings of the
    Medes,
    because his purpose is to destroy Babylon.
The LORD will take vengeance,
    vengeance for his temple.
12 Lift up a banner against the walls of
    Babylon!
    Reinforce the guard,
station the watchmen,
    prepare an ambush!
The LORD will carry out his purpose,
    his decree against the people of Babylon.
13 You who live by many waters
    and are rich in treasures,
your end has come,
    the time for you to be destroyed.
14 The LORD Almighty has sworn by himself:
    I will surely fill you with troops, as with a
        swarm of locusts,
    and they will shout in triumph over you.

15 "He made the earth by his power;
    he founded the world by his wisdom
    and stretched out the heavens by his
        understanding.
16 When he thunders, the waters in the heavens
        roar;
    he makes clouds rise from the ends of the
        earth.
He sends lightning with the rain
    and brings out the wind from his
        storehouses.

17 "Everyone is senseless and without
        knowledge;
    every goldsmith is shamed by his idols.
The images he makes are a fraud;
    they have no breath in them.
18 They are worthless, the objects of mockery;
    when their judgment comes, they will
        perish.
19 He who is the Portion of Jacob is not like
        these,
    for he is the Maker of all things,
including the people of his inheritance—
    the LORD Almighty is his name.

20 "You are my war club,
    my weapon for battle—
with you I shatter nations,
    with you I destroy kingdoms,

21 with you I shatter horse and rider,
    with you I shatter chariot and driver,
22 with you I shatter man and woman,
    with you I shatter old man and youth,
    with you I shatter young man and young
        woman,
23 with you I shatter shepherd and flock,
    with you I shatter farmer and oxen,
    with you I shatter governors and officials.

24 "Before your eyes I will repay Babylon and
all who live in Babylonia*a* for all the wrong they
have done in Zion," declares the LORD.

25 "I am against you, you destroying mountain,
    you who destroy the whole earth,"
                                        declares the LORD.
    "I will stretch out my hand against you,
        roll you off the cliffs,
        and make you a burned-out mountain.
26 No rock will be taken from you for a
        cornerstone,
    nor any stone for a foundation,
    for you will be desolate forever,"
                                        declares the LORD.

27 "Lift up a banner in the land!
    Blow the trumpet among the nations!
Prepare the nations for battle against her;
    summon against her these kingdoms:
    Ararat, Minni and Ashkenaz.
Appoint a commander against her;
    send up horses like a swarm of locusts.
28 Prepare the nations for battle against her—
    the kings of the Medes,
    their governors and all their officials,
    and all the countries they rule.
29 The land trembles and writhes,
    for the LORD's purposes against Babylon
        stand—
    to lay waste the land of Babylon
    so that no one will live there.
30 Babylon's warriors have stopped fighting;
    they remain in their strongholds.
Their strength is exhausted;
    they have become weaklings.
Her dwellings are set on fire;
    the bars of her gates are broken.
31 One courier follows another
    and messenger follows messenger
to announce to the king of Babylon
    that his entire city is captured,
32 the river crossings seized,
    the marshes set on fire,
    and the soldiers terrified."

---

a 24 Or *Chaldea*; also in verse 35

33This is what the LORD Almighty, the God of Israel, says:

> "Daughter Babylon is like a threshing floor
>> at the time it is trampled;
>> the time to harvest her will soon come."

34"Nebuchadnezzar king of Babylon has
>> devoured us,
> he has thrown us into confusion,
> he has made us an empty jar.
> Like a serpent he has swallowed us
> and filled his stomach with our
>> delicacies,
> and then has spewed us out.
35May the violence done to our flesh*a* be on
>> Babylon,"
> say the inhabitants of Zion.
> "May our blood be on those who live in
>> Babylonia,"
> says Jerusalem.

36Therefore this is what the LORD says:

> "See, I will defend your cause
>> and avenge you;
> I will dry up her sea
> and make her springs dry.
37Babylon will be a heap of ruins,
>> a haunt of jackals,
> an object of horror and scorn,
>> a place where no one lives.
38Her people all roar like young lions,
>> they growl like lion cubs.
39But while they are aroused,
>> I will set out a feast for them
>> and make them drunk,
> so that they shout with laughter—
> then sleep forever and not awake,"
>>>> declares the LORD.
40"I will bring them down
>> like lambs to the slaughter,
>> like rams and goats.

41"How Sheshak*b* will be captured,
>> the boast of the whole earth seized!
> How desolate Babylon will be
>> among the nations!
42The sea will rise over Babylon;
>> its roaring waves will cover her.
43Her towns will be desolate,
>> a dry and desert land,
> a land where no one lives,
>> through which no one travels.
44I will punish Bel in Babylon
>> and make him spew out what he has
>> swallowed.

> The nations will no longer stream to him.
> And the wall of Babylon will fall.

45"Come out of her, my people!
>> Run for your lives!
> Run from the fierce anger of the LORD.
46Do not lose heart or be afraid
>> when rumors are heard in the land;
> one rumor comes this year, another the next,
>> rumors of violence in the land
>> and of ruler against ruler.
47For the time will surely come
>> when I will punish the idols of Babylon;
> her whole land will be disgraced
> and her slain will all lie fallen within her.
48Then heaven and earth and all that is in them
>> will shout for joy over Babylon,
> for out of the north
>> destroyers will attack her,"
>>>> declares the LORD.

49"Babylon must fall because of Israel's slain,
>> just as the slain in all the earth
>> have fallen because of Babylon.
50You who have escaped the sword,
>> leave and do not linger!
> Remember the LORD in a distant land,
> and call to mind Jerusalem."

51"We are disgraced,
>> for we have been insulted
> and shame covers our faces,
> because foreigners have entered
> the holy places of the LORD's house."

52"But days are coming," declares the LORD,
>> "when I will punish her idols,
> and throughout her land
>> the wounded will groan.
53Even if Babylon ascends to the heavens
>> and fortifies her lofty stronghold,
> I will send destroyers against her,"
>>>> declares the LORD.

54"The sound of a cry comes from Babylon,
>> the sound of great destruction
>> from the land of the Babylonians.*c*
55The LORD will destroy Babylon;
>> he will silence her noisy din.
> Waves of enemies will rage like great waters;
>> the roar of their voices will resound.
56A destroyer will come against Babylon;
>> her warriors will be captured,
> and their bows will be broken.

---

a 35 Or *done to us and to our children*   *b 41 Sheshak* is a cryptogram for Babylon.   *c 54* Or *Chaldeans*

For the LORD is a God of retribution;
   he will repay in full.
[57] I will make her officials and wise men
    drunk,
   her governors, officers and warriors as
    well;
   they will sleep forever and not awake,"
   declares the King, whose name is the
    LORD Almighty.

[58] This is what the LORD Almighty says:

"Babylon's thick wall will be leveled
   and her high gates set on fire;
the peoples exhaust themselves for nothing,
   the nations' labor is only fuel for the
    flames."

[59] This is the message Jeremiah the prophet gave to the staff officer Seraiah son of Neriah, the son of Mahseiah, when he went to Babylon with Zedekiah king of Judah in the fourth year of his reign. [60] Jeremiah had written on a scroll about all the disasters that would come upon Babylon—all that had been recorded concerning Babylon. [61] He said to Seraiah, "When you get to Babylon, see that you read all these words aloud. [62] Then say, 'LORD, you have said you will destroy this place, so that neither people nor animals will live in it; it will be desolate forever.' [63] When you finish reading this scroll, tie a stone to it and throw it into the Euphrates. [64] Then say, 'So will Babylon sink to rise no more because of the disaster I will bring on her. And her people will fall.'"

The words of Jeremiah end here.

The Fall of Jerusalem

52 Zedekiah was twenty-one years old when he became king, and he reigned in Jerusalem eleven years. His mother's name was Hamutal daughter of Jeremiah; she was from Libnah. [2] He did evil in the eyes of the LORD, just as Jehoiakim had done. [3] It was because of the LORD's anger that all this happened to Jerusalem and Judah, and in the end he thrust them from his presence.

Now Zedekiah rebelled against the king of Babylon.

[4] So in the ninth year of Zedekiah's reign, on the tenth day of the tenth month, Nebuchadnezzar king of Babylon marched against Jerusalem with his whole army. They encamped outside the city and built siege works all around it. [5] The city was kept under siege until the eleventh year of King Zedekiah.

[6] By the ninth day of the fourth month the famine in the city had become so severe that there was no food for the people to eat. [7] Then the city wall was broken through, and the whole army fled. They left the city at night through the gate between the two walls near the king's garden, though the Babylonians[a] were surrounding the city. They fled toward the Arabah,[b] [8] but the Babylonian[c] army pursued King Zedekiah and overtook him in the plains of Jericho. All his soldiers were separated from him and scattered, [9] and he was captured.

He was taken to the king of Babylon at Riblah in the land of Hamath, where he pronounced sentence on him. [10] There at Riblah the king of Babylon killed the sons of Zedekiah before his eyes; he also killed all the officials of Judah. [11] Then he put out Zedekiah's eyes, bound him with bronze shackles and took him to Babylon, where he put him in prison till the day of his death.

[12] On the tenth day of the fifth month, in the nineteenth year of Nebuchadnezzar king of Babylon, Nebuzaradan commander of the imperial guard, who served the king of Babylon, came to Jerusalem. [13] He set fire to the temple of the LORD, the royal palace and all the houses of Jerusalem. Every important building he burned down. [14] The whole Babylonian army, under the commander of the imperial guard, broke down all the walls around Jerusalem. [15] Nebuzaradan the commander of the guard carried into exile some of the poorest people and those who remained in the city, along with the rest of the craftsmen[d] and those who had deserted to the

---

[a] 7 Or *Chaldeans*; also in verse 17   [b] 7 Or *the Jordan Valley*
[c] 8 Or *Chaldean*; also in verse 14   [d] 15 Or *the populace*

The Law of Connection: Leaders Must Achieve Reception, Not Rebellion

Jeremiah 52:1–11

God judged Zedekiah because he rebelled against the king of Babylon. Zedekiah forgot that even the leader works for someone. His rebellion led to the downfall of Jerusalem. Leaders must remember they are stewards of the people God has given them. A leader's rebellion leads to rebellion among the people.

king of Babylon. [16]But Nebuzaradan left behind the rest of the poorest people of the land to work the vineyards and fields.

[17]The Babylonians broke up the bronze pillars, the movable stands and the bronze Sea that were at the temple of the LORD and they carried all the bronze to Babylon. [18]They also took away the pots, shovels, wick trimmers, sprinkling bowls, dishes and all the bronze articles used in the temple service. [19]The commander of the imperial guard took away the basins, censers, sprinkling bowls, pots, lampstands, dishes and bowls used for drink offerings—all that were made of pure gold or silver.

[20]The bronze from the two pillars, the Sea and the twelve bronze bulls under it, and the movable stands, which King Solomon had made for the temple of the LORD, was more than could be weighed. [21]Each pillar was eighteen cubits high and twelve cubits in circumference[a]; each was four fingers thick, and hollow. [22]The bronze capital on top of one pillar was five cubits[b] high and was decorated with a network and pomegranates of bronze all around. The other pillar, with its pomegranates, was similar. [23]There were ninety-six pomegranates on the sides; the total number of pomegranates above the surrounding network was a hundred.

[24]The commander of the guard took as prisoners Seraiah the chief priest, Zephaniah the priest next in rank and the three doorkeepers. [25]Of those still in the city, he took the officer in charge of the fighting men, and seven royal advisers. He also took the secretary who was chief officer in charge of conscripting the people of the land, sixty of whom were found in the city. [26]Nebuzaradan the commander took them all and brought them to the king of Babylon at Riblah. [27]There at Riblah, in the land of Hamath, the king had them executed.

So Judah went into captivity, away from her land. [28]This is the number of the people Nebuchadnezzar carried into exile:

in the seventh year, 3,023 Jews;
[29]in Nebuchadnezzar's eighteenth year,
832 people from Jerusalem;
[30]in his twenty-third year,
745 Jews taken into exile by Nebuzaradan the commander of the imperial guard.
There were 4,600 people in all.

Jehoiachin Released

[31]In the thirty-seventh year of the exile of Jehoiachin king of Judah, in the year Awel-Marduk became king of Babylon, on the twenty-fifth day of the twelfth month, he released Jehoiachin king of Judah and freed him from prison. [32]He spoke kindly to him and gave him a seat of honor higher than those of the other kings who were with him in Babylon. [33]So Jehoiachin put aside his prison clothes and for the rest of his life ate regularly at the king's table. [34]Day by day the king of Babylon gave Jehoiachin a regular allowance as long as he lived, till the day of his death.

---

[a] 21 That is, about 27 feet high and 18 feet in circumference or about 8.1 meters high and 5.4 meters in circumference
[b] 22 That is, about 7 1/2 feet or about 2.3 meters

INTRODUCTION TO
LAMENTATIONS

Reflecting the Heart of a Leader

The prophet Jeremiah wrote the passionate little book of Lamentations after the Babylonians captured and destroyed Jerusalem. It is a deeply personal work, displaying the raw emotions of the prophet in response to the brutalization of Judah. Although he had predicted his people's exile and rebuked them for their unrepentant hearts, he deeply felt their pain and hurt when foreigners killed many of them and forced most of the others into exile in a pagan land.

This book feels like the book of Psalms, full of emotion and reflecting the heart of a leader who desires the best for the people he once influenced. At the same time, it captures the mind of a leader who never waivers from his convictions, even when he must stand by them all alone. Midway through the book, Jeremiah reminds the people that repentance is all God requires and that he renews his mercies every morning (3:22–23).

Jeremiah is rightly called the "weeping prophet," and Lamentations summarizes his cry for the people. We learn again that a leader cannot divorce himself or herself from the people he or she leads. Good leaders model both the heart and the behavior they want others to embrace. Someone once said, "Don't get too far out in front of your people or they will mistake you for the enemy." While standards must be upheld, the leader cannot hold those standards in some cold, distant fashion, unfeeling of the peopleheart.

Good leaders are more than entrepreneurs. Entrepreneurs can act alone, but leaders cannot. By definition, they have followers whom they always want to take with them. Jeremiah knew what was best for the people, but he did not force them to cooperate. He pled with them

God's Role in Lamentations

God must play the disciplinarian in this book. He informed Jeremiah that unless the Jews repented, they would fall into captivity. God continued to remind Jeremiah of his divine standards and imperatives: repentance and obedience.

At the same time, God communicates his mercy and is seen as the Lord who weeps over the state of his people. How difficult it must be for God! He foreknows the decline of his people and how simple it would be for them to avoid disaster, yet he chooses to wait for their decision and repentance, like a parent who awaits a prodigal's return. This book is not merely about Jeremiah's lament, but God's as well.

Leaders in Lamentations
Jeremiah, Zedekiah

Other People of Influence in Lamentations
Babylonians

Lessons in Leadership
- God must break leaders over a need before they can implement a vision for that need.
- In tough spots, the person who leads best maintains compassion for the followers.

to obey, but they refused. As a result, he lamented their apathy and their wasted potential.

As you read this book, allow the emotions of this "weeping prophet" to penetrate your own heart. Do you care for the people you lead to this degree? Are you as concerned for the "one lost sheep" who fails to take the journey, as you are for the 99 who go? Do you really love the people you lead? Perhaps Jeremiah can mentor us.

- Even the most noble endeavors fail with immoral leadership.
- Good leaders provide justice, but never without mercy on those who repent.

LEADERSHIP HIGHLIGHTS IN LAMENTATIONS

1 [a] How deserted lies the city,
      once so full of people!
  How like a widow is she,
      who once was great among the
          nations!
  She who was queen among the provinces
      has now become a slave.

2 Bitterly she weeps at night,
      tears are on her cheeks.
  Among all her lovers
      there is no one to comfort her.
  All her friends have betrayed her;
      they have become her enemies.

3 After affliction and harsh labor,
      Judah has gone into exile.
  She dwells among the nations;
      she finds no resting place.
  All who pursue her have overtaken her
      in the midst of her distress.

4 The roads to Zion mourn,
      for no one comes to her appointed
          festivals.
  All her gateways are desolate,
      her priests groan,
  her young women grieve,
      and she is in bitter anguish.

5 Her foes have become her masters;
      her enemies are at ease.

The LORD has brought her grief
    because of her many sins.
Her children have gone into exile,
    captive before the foe.

6 All the splendor has departed
    from Daughter Zion.
Her princes are like deer
    that find no pasture;
in weakness they have fled
    before the pursuer.

7 In the days of her affliction and wandering
    Jerusalem remembers all the treasures
    that were hers in days of old.
When her people fell into enemy hands,
    there was no one to help her.
Her enemies looked at her
    and laughed at her destruction.

8 Jerusalem has sinned greatly
    and so has become unclean.
All who honored her despise her,
    for they have all seen her naked;
she herself groans
    and turns away.

9 Her filthiness clung to her skirts;
    she did not consider her future.

[a] This chapter is an acrostic poem, the verses of which begin
with the successive letters of the Hebrew alphabet.

We Sustain God's Conquest When We Maintain Our Character

Lamentations 1:7-8

God had given his people so many possessions. For centuries they had enjoyed conquest of the promised land. Now they lost everything—and all because they had sinned greatly.

Great conquests must be supported by great character. Whatever gains leaders make, they can lose in a heartbeat, unless they simultaneously develop the character to support those gains. Over the last 20 years we have watched many leaders fall morally. Generally speaking, their charisma (gifts) exceeded their character (moral infrastructure). The gift grew bigger than the person.

It has been said, "Nothing is so hard to gain, and so easy to lose, as a good reputation." Leaders must recognize how fleeting is their fame or popularity. Instead, they must give themselves to constructing their character. Only then will they keep the gains God gives them through their leadership.

We usually recognize . . .	We should equally recognize . . .
1. Talents and gifts.	1. Solid character and integrity.
2. The superb product.	2. The process that develops on the way.
3. Excellence in performance.	3. Excellence in discipline.
4. External appearances.	4. Internal stability and obedience.

Her fall was astounding;
    there was none to comfort her.
"Look, Lord, on my affliction,
    for the enemy has triumphed."

10 The enemy laid hands
    on all her treasures;
she saw pagan nations
    enter her sanctuary —
those you had forbidden
    to enter your assembly.

11 All her people groan
    as they search for bread;
they barter their treasures for food
    to keep themselves alive.
"Look, Lord, and consider,
    for I am despised."

12 "Is it nothing to you, all you who pass by?
    Look around and see.
Is any suffering like my suffering
    that was inflicted on me,
that the Lord brought on me
    in the day of his fierce anger?

13 "From on high he sent fire,
    sent it down into my bones.
He spread a net for my feet
    and turned me back.
He made me desolate,
    faint all the day long.

14 "My sins have been bound into a yoke[a];
    by his hands they were woven together.
They have been hung on my neck,
    and the Lord has sapped my strength.
He has given me into the hands
    of those I cannot withstand.

15 "The Lord has rejected
    all the warriors in my midst;
he has summoned an army against me
    to[b] crush my young men.
In his winepress the Lord has trampled
    Virgin Daughter Judah.

16 "This is why I weep
    and my eyes overflow with tears.
No one is near to comfort me,
    no one to restore my spirit.
My children are destitute
    because the enemy has prevailed."

17 Zion stretches out her hands,
    but there is no one to comfort her.
The Lord has decreed for Jacob
    that his neighbors become his foes;

Jerusalem has become
    an unclean thing among them.

18 "The Lord is righteous,
    yet I rebelled against his command.
Listen, all you peoples;
    look on my suffering.
My young men and young women
    have gone into exile.

19 "I called to my allies
    but they betrayed me.
My priests and my elders
    perished in the city
while they searched for food
    to keep themselves alive.

20 "See, Lord, how distressed I am!
    I am in torment within,
and in my heart I am disturbed,
    for I have been most rebellious.
Outside, the sword bereaves;
    inside, there is only death.

21 "People have heard my groaning,
    but there is no one to comfort me.
All my enemies have heard of my distress;
    they rejoice at what you have done.
May you bring the day you have
    announced
so they may become like me.

22 "Let all their wickedness come before you;
    deal with them
as you have dealt with me
    because of all my sins.
My groans are many
    and my heart is faint."

2[c] How the Lord has covered Daughter
    Zion
        with the cloud of his anger[d]!
He has hurled down the splendor of Israel
    from heaven to earth;
he has not remembered his footstool
    in the day of his anger.

2 Without pity the Lord has swallowed up
    all the dwellings of Jacob;
in his wrath he has torn down
    the strongholds of Daughter Judah.

---

[a] 14 Most Hebrew manuscripts; many Hebrew manuscripts
and Septuagint *He kept watch over my sins*   [b] 15 *Or has set a
time for me / when he will*   [c] This chapter is an acrostic poem,
the verses of which begin with the successive letters of the
Hebrew alphabet.   [d] 1 *Or How the Lord in his anger / has
treated Daughter Zion with contempt*

He has brought her kingdom and its princes
  down to the ground in dishonor.

³ In fierce anger he has cut off
  every horn^a,b of Israel.
He has withdrawn his right hand
  at the approach of the enemy.
He has burned in Jacob like a flaming fire
  that consumes everything around it.

⁴ Like an enemy he has strung his bow;
  his right hand is ready.
Like a foe he has slain
  all who were pleasing to the eye;
he has poured out his wrath like fire
  on the tent of Daughter Zion.

⁵ The Lord is like an enemy;
  he has swallowed up Israel.
He has swallowed up all her palaces
  and destroyed her strongholds.
He has multiplied mourning and
      lamentation
  for Daughter Judah.

⁶ He has laid waste his dwelling like a
      garden;
  he has destroyed his place of meeting.
The LORD has made Zion forget
  her appointed festivals and her Sabbaths;
in his fierce anger he has spurned
  both king and priest.

⁷ The Lord has rejected his altar
  and abandoned his sanctuary.
He has given the walls of her palaces
  into the hands of the enemy;
they have raised a shout in the house of the
      LORD
  as on the day of an appointed festival.

⁸ The LORD determined to tear down
  the wall around Daughter Zion.
He stretched out a measuring line
  and did not withhold his hand from
      destroying.
He made ramparts and walls lament;
  together they wasted away.

⁹ Her gates have sunk into the ground;
  their bars he has broken and destroyed.
Her king and her princes are exiled among
      the nations,
  the law is no more,
and her prophets no longer find
  visions from the LORD.

¹⁰ The elders of Daughter Zion
  sit on the ground in silence;

they have sprinkled dust on their heads
  and put on sackcloth.
The young women of Jerusalem
  have bowed their heads to the ground.

¹¹ My eyes fail from weeping,
  I am in torment within;
my heart is poured out on the ground
  because my people are destroyed,
because children and infants faint
  in the streets of the city.

¹² They say to their mothers,
  "Where is bread and wine?"
as they faint like the wounded
  in the streets of the city,
as their lives ebb away
  in their mothers' arms.

¹³ What can I say for you?
  With what can I compare you,
  Daughter Jerusalem?
To what can I liken you,
  that I may comfort you,
  Virgin Daughter Zion?
Your wound is as deep as the sea.
  Who can heal you?

¹⁴ The visions of your prophets
  were false and worthless;
they did not expose your sin
  to ward off your captivity.
The prophecies they gave you
  were false and misleading.

¹⁵ All who pass your way
  clap their hands at you;
they scoff and shake their heads
  at Daughter Jerusalem:
"Is this the city that was called
  the perfection of beauty,
  the joy of the whole earth?"

¹⁶ All your enemies open their mouths
  wide against you;
they scoff and gnash their teeth
  and say, "We have swallowed her up.
This is the day we have waited for;
  we have lived to see it."

¹⁷ The LORD has done what he planned;
  he has fulfilled his word,
  which he decreed long ago.
He has overthrown you without pity,
  he has let the enemy gloat over you,
  he has exalted the horn^b of your foes.

ª 3 Or off / all the strength; or every king   ᵇ 3,17 Horn here
symbolizes strength.

¹⁸ The hearts of the people
　　cry out to the Lord.
You walls of Daughter Zion,
　　let your tears flow like a river
　　　day and night;
give yourself no relief,
　　your eyes no rest.

¹⁹ Arise, cry out in the night,
　　as the watches of the night begin;
pour out your heart like water
　　in the presence of the Lord.
Lift up your hands to him
　　for the lives of your children,
who faint from hunger
　　at every street corner.

²⁰ "Look, LORD, and consider:
　　Whom have you ever treated like this?
Should women eat their offspring,
　　the children they have cared for?
Should priest and prophet be killed
　　in the sanctuary of the Lord?

²¹ "Young and old lie together
　　in the dust of the streets;
my young men and young women
　　have fallen by the sword.
You have slain them in the day of your
　　　anger;
　　you have slaughtered them without pity.

²² "As you summon to a feast day,
　　so you summoned against me terrors on
　　　every side.
In the day of the LORD's anger
　　no one escaped or survived;
those I cared for and reared
　　my enemy has destroyed."

3 ^{*a*} I am the man who has seen affliction
　　by the rod of the LORD's wrath.
² He has driven me away and made me walk
　　in darkness rather than light;
³ indeed, he has turned his hand against me
　　again and again, all day long.

⁴ He has made my skin and my flesh grow old
　　and has broken my bones.
⁵ He has besieged me and surrounded me
　　with bitterness and hardship.
⁶ He has made me dwell in darkness
　　like those long dead.

⁷ He has walled me in so I cannot escape;
　　he has weighed me down with chains.
⁸ Even when I call out or cry for help,
　　he shuts out my prayer.

Compassion for a Need Brings Commitment to a Vision

Lamentations 2:20

Although for many years Jeremiah had predicted the captivity of his rebellious people, he weeps when his prophecy comes true. In Lamentations 2:20 he begs the Lord to stop the punishment. He asks for pity.

This dialogue between Jeremiah and God about the Hebrews offers a rare glimpse into the heart-shaping work God did in Jeremiah, the leader. While the prophet has a passion for righteousness and justice, at the same time he has compassion for the very people who so anger him. Like Moses, Jeremiah often displayed one face to the people—usually judgment and threats—but another to God in prayer. He begged Yahweh not to abandon his people. Compassion enabled Jeremiah to remain committed to the vision that one day God would restore his people.

This is what makes a godly leader great: clear and firm leadership, yet a compassionate heart as an intercessor. Reggie McNeal writes, "One mark of genuine spiritual greatness is compassion for one's tormentors."

Leaders must first feel burdened for the people's needs; only then will they commit themselves to a vision of their deliverance. Jeremiah's compassion kept him in the game when it would have been easier to walk away. He teaches us that while people may reject your messages and oppose your arguments, they remain helpless against your prayers.

---

⁹ He has barred my way with blocks of stone;
　　he has made my paths crooked.

¹⁰ Like a bear lying in wait,
　　like a lion in hiding,
¹¹ he dragged me from the path and mangled me
　　and left me without help.
¹² He drew his bow
　　and made me the target for his arrows.

---

^{*a*} This chapter is an acrostic poem; the verses of each stanza begin with the successive letters of the Hebrew alphabet, and the verses within each stanza begin with the same letter.

¹³He pierced my heart
    with arrows from his quiver.
¹⁴I became the laughingstock of all my people;
    they mock me in song all day long.
¹⁵He has filled me with bitter herbs
    and given me gall to drink.

¹⁶He has broken my teeth with gravel;
    he has trampled me in the dust.
¹⁷I have been deprived of peace;
    I have forgotten what prosperity is.
¹⁸So I say, "My splendor is gone
    and all that I had hoped from the LORD."

¹⁹I remember my affliction and my
       wandering,
    the bitterness and the gall.
²⁰I well remember them,
    and my soul is downcast within me.
²¹Yet this I call to mind
    and therefore I have hope:

²²Because of the LORD's great love we are not
       consumed,
    for his compassions never fail.
²³They are new every morning;
    great is your faithfulness.
²⁴I say to myself, "The LORD is my portion;
    therefore I will wait for him."

²⁵The LORD is good to those whose hope is in
       him,
    to the one who seeks him;
²⁶it is good to wait quietly
    for the salvation of the LORD.
²⁷It is good for a man to bear the yoke
    while he is young.

²⁸Let him sit alone in silence,
    for the LORD has laid it on him.
²⁹Let him bury his face in the dust —
    there may yet be hope.
³⁰Let him offer his cheek to one who would
       strike him,
    and let him be filled with disgrace.

³¹For no one is cast off
    by the Lord forever.
³²Though he brings grief, he will show
       compassion,
    so great is his unfailing love.
³³For he does not willingly bring affliction
    or grief to anyone.

³⁴To crush underfoot
    all prisoners in the land,
³⁵to deny people their rights
    before the Most High,

³⁶to deprive them of justice —
    would not the Lord see such things?
³⁷Who can speak and have it happen
    if the Lord has not decreed it?
³⁸Is it not from the mouth of the Most High
    that both calamities and good things come?
³⁹Why should the living complain
    when punished for their sins?

⁴⁰Let us examine our ways and test them,
    and let us return to the LORD.
⁴¹Let us lift up our hearts and our hands
    to God in heaven, and say:
⁴²"We have sinned and rebelled
    and you have not forgiven.

⁴³"You have covered yourself with anger and
       pursued us;
    you have slain without pity.
⁴⁴You have covered yourself with a cloud
    so that no prayer can get through.
⁴⁵You have made us scum and refuse
    among the nations.

⁴⁶"All our enemies have opened their mouths
    wide against us.
⁴⁷We have suffered terror and pitfalls,
    ruin and destruction."
⁴⁸Streams of tears flow from my eyes
    because my people are destroyed.

⁴⁹My eyes will flow unceasingly,
    without relief,
⁵⁰until the LORD looks down
    from heaven and sees.
⁵¹What I see brings grief to my soul
    because of all the women of my city.
⁵²Those who were my enemies without cause
    hunted me like a bird.

God Is Ultimately in Control and Will Mercifully Act for His People

Lamentations 3:21–36

Jeremiah the leader wisely remains fixed on a vision of God's sovereignty: God is more powerful than the Babylonians. He focuses on God's nature: God is full of mercy and compassion. He dwells on his vision of God's plans: God will deliver his people and give them a hopeful future.

⁵³ They tried to end my life in a pit
    and threw stones at me;
⁵⁴ the waters closed over my head,
    and I thought I was about to perish.

⁵⁵ I called on your name, LORD,
    from the depths of the pit.
⁵⁶ You heard my plea: "Do not close your ears
    to my cry for relief."
⁵⁷ You came near when I called you,
    and you said, "Do not fear."

⁵⁸ You, Lord, took up my case;
    you redeemed my life.
⁵⁹ LORD, you have seen the wrong done to me.
    Uphold my cause!
⁶⁰ You have seen the depth of their vengeance,
    all their plots against me.

⁶¹ LORD, you have heard their insults,
    all their plots against me —
⁶² what my enemies whisper and mutter
    against me all day long.
⁶³ Look at them! Sitting or standing,
    they mock me in their songs.

⁶⁴ Pay them back what they deserve, LORD,
    for what their hands have done.
⁶⁵ Put a veil over their hearts,
    and may your curse be on them!

⁶⁶ Pursue them in anger and destroy them
    from under the heavens of the LORD.

4 ᵃ How the gold has lost its luster,
    the fine gold become dull!
The sacred gems are scattered
    at every street corner.

² How the precious children of Zion,
    once worth their weight in gold,
are now considered as pots of clay,
    the work of a potter's hands!

³ Even jackals offer their breasts
    to nurse their young,
but my people have become heartless
    like ostriches in the desert.

⁴ Because of thirst the infant's tongue
    sticks to the roof of its mouth;
the children beg for bread,
    but no one gives it to them.

⁵ Those who once ate delicacies
    are destitute in the streets.
Those brought up in royal purple
    now lie on ash heaps.

ᵃ This chapter is an acrostic poem, the verses of which begin with the successive letters of the Hebrew alphabet.

JEREMIAH

PROFILE in leadership

Hope in the Midst of Calamity
Lamentations 3:1–66

As Jeremiah trudged through his ruined city, he smelled destruction everywhere. He knew the invading Babylonians had devastated Jerusalem because the people of Judah had forsaken their God. The Lord's people had brought this misery on themselves—yet his heart still broke.

For two whole chapters Jeremiah laments the calamity. He recognizes the chastening hand of God, for he says, "Is it not from the mouth of the Most High that both calamities and good things come?" (La 3:38). Right in the middle of his dirge he pauses to express one of the most hopeful pronouncements in the Old Testament: "Because of the LORD's great love we are not consumed, for his compassions never fail. They are new every morning; great is your faithfulness" (3:22–23).

In the midst of the carnage, in the midst of his own wailing, the prophet finds hope in knowing that God still reigns. He knows that restoration and repentance can occur. God's anger will not burn against his people forever. And so Jeremiah can continue. Oh, there will still be tears—the last two chapters of Lamentations again play the mournful sounds of a funeral march. Yet because God lives, hope lives!

Effective leaders bank on hope, even in the face of God's judgment. They know that, for those who call on the name of the Lord Jesus Christ, restoration and redemption can indeed follow destruction.

⁶ The punishment of my people
    is greater than that of Sodom,
which was overthrown in a moment
    without a hand turned to help her.

⁷ Their princes were brighter than snow
    and whiter than milk,
their bodies more ruddy than rubies,
    their appearance like lapis lazuli.

⁸ But now they are blacker than soot;
    they are not recognized in the streets.
Their skin has shriveled on their bones;
    it has become as dry as a stick.

⁹ Those killed by the sword are better off
    than those who die of famine;
racked with hunger, they waste away
    for lack of food from the field.

¹⁰ With their own hands compassionate women
    have cooked their own children,
who became their food
    when my people were destroyed.

¹¹ The LORD has given full vent to his wrath;
    he has poured out his fierce anger.
He kindled a fire in Zion
    that consumed her foundations.

¹² The kings of the earth did not believe,
    nor did any of the peoples of the world,
that enemies and foes could enter
    the gates of Jerusalem.

¹³ But it happened because of the sins of her
    prophets
    and the iniquities of her priests,
who shed within her
    the blood of the righteous.

¹⁴ Now they grope through the streets
    as if they were blind.
They are so defiled with blood
    that no one dares to touch their
    garments.

¹⁵ "Go away! You are unclean!" people cry to
    them.
    "Away! Away! Don't touch us!"
When they flee and wander about,
    people among the nations say,
    "They can stay here no longer."

¹⁶ The LORD himself has scattered them;
    he no longer watches over them.
The priests are shown no honor,
    the elders no favor.

¹⁷ Moreover, our eyes failed,
    looking in vain for help;
from our towers we watched
    for a nation that could not save us.

The Principle of Rewards

Lamentations 4:6–8

You might call it the principle of rewards: What gets rewarded gets done. Good leaders recognize how to attach both rewards and consequences to team members' performance. Any system of rewards should prioritize the most important conduct, then reward it publicly. In addition, the system ought to prioritize the non-negotiable negatives, because they damage the team. A price should be attached to these, as well.

Jeremiah gives us a snapshot of how God did this with his people. He says the consequences for their sin exceeded that of Sodom, for while that ancient city vanished in a moment, Judah's punishment dragged on and on.

How do we communicate rewards to our people? To what do we pay attention? Do our people know what is important? When team members don't produce the results the leader desires, usually just a few reasons explain why:

1. **They are not sure what to do.**

2. **They don't know what to do first.**

3. **They don't know how to do it.**

4. **The reward system does not align with the group goals.**

5. **The leader presents unnecessary obstacles.**

¹⁸People stalked us at every step,
  so we could not walk in our streets.
Our end was near, our days were numbered,
  for our end had come.

¹⁹Our pursuers were swifter
  than eagles in the sky;
they chased us over the mountains
  and lay in wait for us in the desert.

²⁰The LORD's anointed, our very life breath,
  was caught in their traps.
We thought that under his shadow
  we would live among the nations.

²¹Rejoice and be glad, Daughter Edom,
  you who live in the land of Uz.
But to you also the cup will be passed;
  you will be drunk and stripped naked.

²²Your punishment will end, Daughter Zion;
  he will not prolong your exile.
But he will punish your sin, Daughter
  Edom,
  and expose your wickedness.

5 Remember, LORD, what has happened to us;
  look, and see our disgrace.
²Our inheritance has been turned over to
  strangers,
  our homes to foreigners.
³We have become fatherless,
  our mothers are widows.
⁴We must buy the water we drink;
  our wood can be had only at a price.
⁵Those who pursue us are at our heels;
  we are weary and find no rest.
⁶We submitted to Egypt and Assyria
  to get enough bread.
⁷Our ancestors sinned and are no more,
  and we bear their punishment.
⁸Slaves rule over us,
  and there is no one to free us from their
  hands.
⁹We get our bread at the risk of our lives
  because of the sword in the desert.

Successful Leaders Depend on God

Lamentations 5:14–19

Successful leaders depend not on their own wit and wisdom, but on God. Jeremiah confesses both the sin of the people and that God reigns forever and will ultimately restore what has been lost. Leaders act according to their gifts and calling, but trust God to bring about the desired results.

¹⁰Our skin is hot as an oven,
  feverish from hunger.
¹¹Women have been violated in Zion,
  and virgins in the towns of Judah.
¹²Princes have been hung up by their hands;
  elders are shown no respect.
¹³Young men toil at the millstones;
  boys stagger under loads of wood.
¹⁴The elders are gone from the city gate;
  the young men have stopped their music.
¹⁵Joy is gone from our hearts;
  our dancing has turned to mourning.
¹⁶The crown has fallen from our head.
  Woe to us, for we have sinned!
¹⁷Because of this our hearts are faint,
  because of these things our eyes grow dim
¹⁸for Mount Zion, which lies desolate,
  with jackals prowling over it.

¹⁹You, LORD, reign forever;
  your throne endures from generation to
  generation.
²⁰Why do you always forget us?
  Why do you forsake us so long?
²¹Restore us to yourself, LORD, that we may
  return;
  renew our days as of old
²²unless you have utterly rejected us
  and are angry with us beyond measure.

INTRODUCTION TO
EZEKIEL

A Leader with Backbone and Conviction

God raised up Ezekiel to serve as a prophet during a most difficult time in Israel's history. He provides a tremendous illustration of a leader with backbone and conviction.

From the beginning, God warned Ezekiel that he would speak to a stubborn group. He faced opposition at almost every turn—a level of opposition that might cause many leaders to reevaluate their position and move on. Ezekiel chose to remain and stay true to his convictions. Appropriately enough, the name of this strong prophet means "God strengthens."

Ezekiel demonstrates for us three leadership skills. First, a leader can lead off of vision, even in tough times. Second, a leader can stay true to core values, even in tough times. Third, a leader can compel people to grapple even with hard truth.

Ezekiel clearly led out of vision. God consistently provided him with unusual visions that drove him to speak in unusual ways. From hands and scrolls descending from heaven, to four abominations committed in the temple, to vines, eagles, lions, dry bones, and fires, Ezekiel trafficked in strange but memorable pictures. These pictures often arrived with a divine interpretation and instructions on how he was to communicate God's Word to the people. Ezekiel closely followed the leadership axiom on vision: See it clearly, show it creatively, and say it constantly.

Ezekiel managed to stay true to his convictions and core values despite the people's response. God said from the beginning: "And whether they listen or fail to listen —for they are a rebellious people—they will know that a prophet has been among them. And you, son of man,

God's Role in Ezekiel

God described Ezekiel as a watchman. He called the prophet to warn the Jews of impending danger if they did not repent. Like a watchman who sees an invading army *en route*, he admonishes the people to get ready or be destroyed. God describes himself to Ezekiel as the One who supplies the right words. God is the Director of this great drama that Ezekiel acts out. He is the Writer of the script Ezekiel is to read to the people. And he is the Author who closes the curtain when the play ends—a finale in the form of the invading Babylonian army—when it's too late for the people to discover the play is no mere act.

Leaders in Ezekiel
Ezekiel

Other People of Influence in Ezekiel
Pelatiah, Jaazaniah, Nebuchadnezzar, Pharaoh

Lessons in Leadership

- One leader with courage is a majority.
- Effective leaders communicate creatively and unforgettably.
- Leaders are stewards of the people and of the resources they oversee.
- We must lead ourselves before we lead anyone else.

do not be afraid of them or their words . . . or be terrified by them, though they are a rebellious people. You must speak my words to them, whether they listen or fail to listen, for they are rebellious. But you, son of man, listen to what I say to you. Do not rebel like that rebellious people; open your mouth and eat what I give you" (2:5–8).

Ezekiel compelled the people to hear him and wrestle with the pressing issues. He was an extremely creative communicator, often using visual aids or dramatically acting out his message. He quickly obeyed the Lord's instructions, even when many of the symbolic actions God called him to enact looked difficult or embarrassing. His dynamic ministry won the respect, attention and admiration of Judah's elders. But while they listened to him, they refused to act on what he said. This disappointed Ezekiel, for no one took greater pains to cast a vision to his own generation than he did.

- A leader stands between God's goals and the people's problems.
- Often, a leader takes his or her first step alone.

LEADERSHIP HIGHLIGHTS IN EZEKIEL

COMMUNICATING Vision (1:1–3)	page 949
ADAPTABILITY: Effective Leaders Adapt to Changing Needs (3:8–9)	page 952
EZEKIEL: Zealous for the Name of the Lord (6:7, 10, 13–14)	page 954
DISCERNMENT: Leaders Assess Situations, Then Respond (18:1–32)	page 966
THE POSITION OF A LEADER: Standing in the Gap (22:24–31)	page 971
LEADERS Are to Relate as Shepherds to People (34:11–24)	page 985

Ezekiel's Inaugural Vision

1 In my thirtieth year, in the fourth month on the fifth day, while I was among the exiles by the Kebar River, the heavens were opened and I saw visions of God.

[2] On the fifth of the month — it was the fifth year of the exile of King Jehoiachin — [3] the word of the LORD came to Ezekiel the priest, the son of Buzi, by the Kebar River in the land of the Babylonians.[a] There the hand of the LORD was on him.

[4] I looked, and I saw a windstorm coming out of the north — an immense cloud with flashing lightning and surrounded by brilliant light. The center of the fire looked like glowing metal, [5] and in the fire was what looked like four living creatures. In appearance their form was human, [6] but each of them had four faces and four wings. [7] Their legs were straight; their feet were like those of a calf and gleamed like burnished bronze. [8] Under their wings on their four sides they had human hands. All four of them had faces and wings, [9] and the wings of one touched the wings of another. Each one went straight ahead; they did not turn as they moved.

[10] Their faces looked like this: Each of the four had the face of a human being, and on the right side each had the face of a lion, and on the left side the face of an ox; each also had the face of an eagle. [11] Such were their faces. They each had two wings spreading out upward, each wing touching that of the creature on either side; and each had two other wings covering its body. [12] Each one went straight ahead. Wherever the spirit would go, they would go, without turning as they went. [13] The appearance of the living creatures was like burning coals of fire or like torches. Fire moved back and forth among the creatures; it was bright, and lightning flashed out of it. [14] The creatures sped back and forth like flashes of lightning.

[15] As I looked at the living creatures, I saw a wheel on the ground beside each creature with its four faces. [16] This was the appearance and structure of the wheels: They sparkled like topaz, and all four looked alike. Each appeared to be made like a wheel intersecting a wheel. [17] As they moved, they would go in any one of the four directions the creatures faced; the wheels did not change direction as the creatures went. [18] Their rims were high and awesome, and all four rims were full of eyes all around.

[19] When the living creatures moved, the wheels beside them moved; and when the living

_____
[a] 3 Or *Chaldeans*

Communicating Vision

Ezekiel 1:1–3

Like Jeremiah, Ezekiel knew how to communicate a message so that every listener understood and knew what to do. This is the mark of a successful communicator. Note how he communicated:

1. **His vision was memorable; his words inventive.**
   God instructed the prophet how to cast his vision. He is told to use object lessons, using materials like a brick, an iron plate, his own body, ropes, ingredients for bread, human dung, and cow manure. God's instructions seemed so radical that even Ezekiel felt repulsed by them. Yet no one would ever forget the lessons.

2. **His vision was measurable; his words insightful.**
   Ezekiel spoke specifically about future events. He gave no fuzzy, ambiguous word about how God wanted the people to follow, should they decide to cooperate. He delivered a compelling and detailed word about how long Israel had drifted from God, the siege of Jerusalem, how long the exile would last, and what conditions would be like when God brought about his long-threatened punishment.

3. **His vision was motivational; his words gave incentive.**
   Ezekiel didn't talk merely to pronounce judgment. He wanted to compel the Israelites to repent and return to God. He discussed how defiling life would be under a foreign leader and the horror of submitting to a power that didn't understand them. He gave them a reason to act.

creatures rose from the ground, the wheels also rose. ²⁰Wherever the spirit would go, they would go, and the wheels would rise along with them, because the spirit of the living creatures was in the wheels. ²¹When the creatures moved, they also moved; when the creatures stood still, they also stood still; and when the creatures rose from the ground, the wheels rose along with them, because the spirit of the living creatures was in the wheels.

²²Spread out above the heads of the living creatures was what looked something like a vault, sparkling like crystal, and awesome. ²³Under the vault their wings were stretched out one toward the other, and each had two wings covering its body. ²⁴When the creatures moved, I heard the sound of their wings, like the roar of rushing waters, like the voice of the Almighty,ᵃ like the tumult of an army. When they stood still, they lowered their wings.

²⁵Then there came a voice from above the vault over their heads as they stood with lowered wings. ²⁶Above the vault over their heads was what looked like a throne of lapis lazuli, and high above on the throne was a figure like that of a man. ²⁷I saw that from what appeared to be his waist up he looked like glowing metal, as if full of fire, and that from there down he looked like fire; and brilliant light surrounded him. ²⁸Like the appearance of a rainbow in the clouds on a rainy day, so was the radiance around him.

This was the appearance of the likeness of the glory of the LORD. When I saw it, I fell facedown, and I heard the voice of one speaking.

Ezekiel's Call to Be a Prophet

2 He said to me, "Son of man,ᵇ stand up on your feet and I will speak to you." ²As he spoke, the Spirit came into me and raised me to my feet, and I heard him speaking to me.

³He said: "Son of man, I am sending you to the Israelites, to a rebellious nation that has rebelled against me; they and their ancestors have been in revolt against me to this very day. ⁴The people to whom I am sending you are obstinate and stubborn. Say to them, 'This is what the Sovereign LORD says.' ⁵And whether they listen

---

ᵃ 24 Hebrew *Shaddai*   ᵇ 1 The Hebrew phrase *ben adam* means *human being*. The phrase *son of man* is retained as a form of address here and throughout Ezekiel because of its possible association with "Son of Man" in the New Testament.

Vision: You Can Seize Only What You Can See

Ezekiel 1:4–28

This great book begins with a vision. Ezekiel receives a revelation from God of four angelic figures. In this vision, God calls the prophet to be his spokesman and watchman to the Hebrew exiles. This vision is the first of four in the book:

1. **The vision of the four angels (Eze 1–3)**
2. **The vision of glory and godlessness (Eze 8–11)**
3. **The vision of the burning vine (Eze 15)**
4. **The vision of the dry bones (Eze 37)**

Ezekiel describes this first vision in vivid detail. Like all effective leaders, he spoke as clearly as possible. A pastor once said, "If it's fuzzy in the pulpit, it's foggy in the pew."

Ezekiel provided vision by way of analogies, then applied those visions. He communicated a picture (Eze 1), then communicated his point (Eze 2). Divine visions always help a leader and the people move in the right direction. A divine vision also seems to include these components:

1. *A clear mental image:* It serves as a sort of blueprint inside of us.
2. *A positive change:* It serves to improve present conditions.
3. *A future focus:* It furnishes insight and direction for the unseen future.
4. *A gift from God:* It is divinely inspired, not humanly manipulated.
5. *A chosen people and time:* It is for a select leader and group at a given time.

The Necessity of a Call in Tough Times

Ezekiel 2:1–10

God described not only what he wanted Ezekiel to do, but also the conditions in which he would serve. God told him he was sending him to a rebellious people who acted like stubborn children. Yet he was to continue speaking whether they listened or not (Eze 2:7). God's call didn't depend on the people's response. Ezekiel had to stand strong even when the people ignored him.

God has Ezekiel eat a scroll (representing the divine words he is to speak), inscribed both on the front and the back, leaving him no room to change or add to the message he is to speak (2:10). Ezekiel had to stay honest and true to those words.

This presents a challenge to leaders. What role does God play and what role do we play? Are leaders never permitted to speak from their own mind and emotions? Consider the roles of both God and people:

God's Role

1. He calls us into service.

2. He gives us gifts and graces.

3. He provides words of direction.

4. He supplies a compelling fire inside us.

5. He controls the outcome.

The Human Role

1. People confirm our call.

2. People cooperate with their gifts.

3. We use our mind and emotions.

4. Others recognize and respect the fire.

5. We are to be faithful to the end.

---

or fail to listen — for they are a rebellious people — they will know that a prophet has been among them. ⁶And you, son of man, do not be afraid of them or their words. Do not be afraid, though briers and thorns are all around you and you live among scorpions. Do not be afraid of what they say or be terrified by them, though they are a rebellious people. ⁷You must speak my words to them, whether they listen or fail to listen, for they are rebellious. ⁸But you, son of man, listen to what I say to you. Do not rebel like that rebellious people; open your mouth and eat what I give you."

⁹Then I looked, and I saw a hand stretched out to me. In it was a scroll, ¹⁰which he unrolled before me. On both sides of it were written words of lament and mourning and woe.

3 And he said to me, "Son of man, eat what is before you, eat this scroll; then go and speak to the people of Israel." ²So I opened my mouth, and he gave me the scroll to eat.

³Then he said to me, "Son of man, eat this scroll I am giving you and fill your stomach with it." So I ate it, and it tasted as sweet as honey in my mouth.

⁴He then said to me: "Son of man, go now to the people of Israel and speak my words to them. ⁵You are not being sent to a people of obscure speech and strange language, but to the people of Israel — ⁶not to many peoples of obscure

speech and strange language, whose words you cannot understand. Surely if I had sent you to them, they would have listened to you. ⁷But the people of Israel are not willing to listen to you because they are not willing to listen to me, for all the Israelites are hardened and obstinate. ⁸But I will make you as unyielding and hardened as they are. ⁹I will make your forehead like the hardest stone, harder than flint. Do not be afraid of them or terrified by them, though they are a rebellious people."

¹⁰And he said to me, "Son of man, listen carefully and take to heart all the words I speak to you. ¹¹Go now to your people in exile and speak to them. Say to them, 'This is what the Sovereign LORD says,' whether they listen or fail to listen."

¹²Then the Spirit lifted me up, and I heard behind me a loud rumbling sound as the glory of the LORD rose from the place where it was standing.ᵃ ¹³It was the sound of the wings of the living creatures brushing against each other and the sound of the wheels beside them, a loud rumbling sound. ¹⁴The Spirit then lifted me up and took me away, and I went in bitterness and in the anger of my spirit, with the strong hand of the LORD on me. ¹⁵I came to the exiles who lived at Tel Aviv near the Kebar River. And

---

ᵃ 12 Probable reading of the original Hebrew text; Masoretic Text *sound — may the glory of the LORD be praised from his place*

Adaptability: Effective Leaders Adapt to Changing Needs

Ezekiel 3:8–9

Because Israel acted like a stubborn mule and would not listen to the prophet's words, Ezekiel had to adapt to the needs of his audience. God spoke these words to him: "I will make you as unyielding and hardened as they are. I will make your forehead like the hardest stone, harder than flint. Do not be afraid of them or terrified by them, though they are a rebellious people" (Eze 3:8–9).

Effective leaders allow God to shape them into the kind of people they need to be for each situation they encounter. They don't get stuck on one method or mode of operation. When approaching a new and different context, leaders should read . . .

1. **Situations:** Do my circumstances tell me it is time to move forward?
2. **People:** Are the people ready and willing to make a move?
3. **Timing:** Is this the right time to make a move?
4. **Staff:** Does my team have the gifts and the influence to lead the way?
5. **Opportunity:** Do we have the opportunity to be successful if we move?
6. **Resources:** Do we possess the resources to move now?
7. **Themselves:** Am I the right person to lead the way?

there, where they were living, I sat among them for seven days — deeply distressed.

Ezekiel's Task as Watchman

[16] At the end of seven days the word of the LORD came to me: [17]"Son of man, I have made you a watchman for the people of Israel; so hear the word I speak and give them warning from me. [18]When I say to a wicked person, 'You will surely die,' and you do not warn them or speak out to dissuade them from their evil ways in order to save their life, that wicked person will die for[a] their sin, and I will hold you accountable for their blood. [19]But if you do warn the wicked person and they do not turn from their wickedness or from their evil ways, they will die for their sin; but you will have saved yourself.

[20]"Again, when a righteous person turns from their righteousness and does evil, and I put a stumbling block before them, they will die. Since you did not warn them, they will die for their sin. The righteous things that person did will not be remembered, and I will hold you accountable for their blood. [21]But if you do warn the righteous person not to sin and they do not sin, they will surely live because they took warning, and you will have saved yourself."

[22]The hand of the LORD was on me there, and he said to me, "Get up and go out to the plain, and there I will speak to you." [23]So I got up and went out to the plain. And the glory of the LORD was standing there, like the glory I had seen by the Kebar River, and I fell facedown.

[24]Then the Spirit came into me and raised me to my feet. He spoke to me and said: "Go, shut yourself inside your house. [25]And you, son of man, they will tie with ropes; you will be bound so that you cannot go out among the people. [26]I will make your tongue stick to the roof of your mouth so that you will be silent and unable to rebuke them, for they are a rebellious people. [27]But when I speak to you, I will open your mouth and you shall say to them, 'This is what the Sovereign LORD says.' Whoever will listen let them listen, and whoever will refuse let them refuse; for they are a rebellious people.

Siege of Jerusalem Symbolized

4 "Now, son of man, take a block of clay, put it in front of you and draw the city of Jerusalem on it. [2]Then lay siege to it: Erect siege works against it, build a ramp up to it, set up camps against it and put battering rams around it. [3]Then take an iron pan, place it as an iron wall between you and the city and turn your face toward it. It will be under siege, and you shall besiege it. This will be a sign to the people of Israel.

[4]"Then lie on your left side and put the sin of

---

[a] 18 Or *in*; also in verses 19 and 20

the people of Israel upon yourself.[a] You are to bear their sin for the number of days you lie on your side. [5]I have assigned you the same number of days as the years of their sin. So for 390 days you will bear the sin of the people of Israel.

[6]"After you have finished this, lie down again, this time on your right side, and bear the sin of the people of Judah. I have assigned you 40 days, a day for each year. [7]Turn your face toward the siege of Jerusalem and with bared arm prophesy against her. [8]I will tie you up with ropes so that you cannot turn from one side to the other until you have finished the days of your siege.

[9]"Take wheat and barley, beans and lentils, millet and spelt; put them in a storage jar and use them to make bread for yourself. You are to eat it during the 390 days you lie on your side. [10]Weigh out twenty shekels[b] of food to eat each day and eat it at set times. [11]Also measure out a sixth of a hin[c] of water and drink it at set times. [12]Eat the food as you would a loaf of barley bread; bake it in the sight of the people, using human excrement for fuel." [13]The LORD said, "In this way the people of Israel will eat defiled food among the nations where I will drive them."

[14]Then I said, "Not so, Sovereign LORD! I have never defiled myself. From my youth until now I have never eaten anything found dead or torn by wild animals. No impure meat has ever entered my mouth."

[15]"Very well," he said, "I will let you bake your bread over cow dung instead of human excrement."

[16]He then said to me: "Son of man, I am about to cut off the food supply in Jerusalem. The people will eat rationed food in anxiety and drink rationed water in despair, [17]for food and water will be scarce. They will be appalled at the sight of each other and will waste away because of[d] their sin.

God's Razor of Judgment

5 "Now, son of man, take a sharp sword and use it as a barber's razor to shave your head and your beard. Then take a set of scales and divide up the hair. [2]When the days of your siege come to an end, burn a third of the hair inside the city. Take a third and strike it with the sword all around the city. And scatter a third to the wind. For I will pursue them with drawn sword. [3]But take a few hairs and tuck them away in the folds of your garment. [4]Again, take a few of these and throw them into the fire and burn them up. A fire will spread from there to all Israel.

[5]"This is what the Sovereign LORD says: This is Jerusalem, which I have set in the center of the nations, with countries all around her. [6]Yet in her wickedness she has rebelled against my laws and decrees more than the nations and countries around her. She has rejected my laws and has not followed my decrees.

[7]"Therefore this is what the Sovereign LORD says: You have been more unruly than the nations around you and have not followed my decrees or kept my laws. You have not even[e] conformed to the standards of the nations around you.

[8]"Therefore this is what the Sovereign LORD says: I myself am against you, Jerusalem, and I will inflict punishment on you in the sight of the nations. [9]Because of all your detestable idols, I will do to you what I have never done before and will never do again. [10]Therefore in your midst parents will eat their children, and children will eat their parents. I will inflict punishment on you and will scatter all your survivors to the winds. [11]Therefore as surely as I live, declares the Sovereign LORD, because you have defiled my sanctuary with all your vile images and detestable practices, I myself will shave you; I will not look on you with pity or spare you. [12]A third of your people will die of the plague or perish by famine inside you; a third will fall by the sword outside your walls; and a third I will scatter to the winds and pursue with drawn sword.

[13]"Then my anger will cease and my wrath against them will subside, and I will be avenged. And when I have spent my wrath on them, they will know that I the LORD have spoken in my zeal.

[14]"I will make you a ruin and a reproach among the nations around you, in the sight of all who pass by. [15]You will be a reproach and a taunt, a warning and an object of horror to the nations around you when I inflict punishment on you in anger and in wrath and with stinging rebuke. I the LORD have spoken. [16]When I shoot at you with my deadly and destructive arrows of famine, I will shoot to destroy you. I will bring more and more famine upon you and cut off your supply of food. [17]I will send famine and wild beasts against you, and they will leave you childless. Plague and bloodshed will sweep through you, and I will bring the sword against you. I the LORD have spoken."

---

[a] 4 Or *upon your side*   [b] 10 That is, about 8 ounces or about 230 grams   [c] 11 That is, about 2/3 quart or about 0.6 liter   [d] 17 Or *away in*   [e] 7 Most Hebrew manuscripts; some Hebrew manuscripts and Syriac *You have*

Doom for the Mountains of Israel

6 The word of the LORD came to me: [2]"Son of man, set your face against the mountains of Israel; prophesy against them [3]and say: 'You mountains of Israel, hear the word of the Sovereign LORD. This is what the Sovereign LORD says to the mountains and hills, to the ravines and valleys: I am about to bring a sword against you, and I will destroy your high places. [4]Your altars will be demolished and your incense altars will be smashed; and I will slay your people in front of your idols. [5]I will lay the dead bodies of the Israelites in front of their idols, and I will scatter your bones around your altars. [6]Wherever you live, the towns will be laid waste and the high places demolished, so that your altars will be laid waste and devastated, your idols smashed and ruined, your incense altars broken down, and what you have made wiped out. [7]Your people will fall slain among you, and you will know that I am the LORD.

[8]"But I will spare some, for some of you will escape the sword when you are scattered among the lands and nations. [9]Then in the nations where they have been carried captive, those who escape will remember me—how I have been grieved by their adulterous hearts, which have turned away from me, and by their eyes, which have lusted after their idols. They will loathe themselves for the evil they have done and for all their detestable practices. [10]And they will know that I am the LORD; I did not threaten in vain to bring this calamity on them.

[11]"This is what the Sovereign LORD says: Strike your hands together and stamp your feet and cry out "Alas!" because of all the wicked and detestable practices of the people of Israel, for they will fall by the sword, famine and plague. [12]One who is far away will die of the plague, and one who is near will fall by the sword, and anyone who survives and is spared will die of famine. So will I pour out my wrath on them. [13]And they will know that I am the LORD, when their people lie slain among their idols around their altars, on every high hill and on all the mountaintops, under every spreading tree and every leafy oak—places where they offered fragrant incense to all their idols. [14]And I will stretch out my hand against them and make the land a desolate waste from the desert to Diblah[a]—wherever they live. Then they will know that I am the LORD.'"

The End Has Come

7 The word of the LORD came to me: [2]"Son of man, this is what the Sovereign LORD says to the land of Israel:

---

[a] 14 Most Hebrew manuscripts; a few Hebrew manuscripts *Riblah*

EZEKIEL

Zealous for the Name of the Lord

Ezekiel 6:7, 10, 13–14

PROFILE in leadership

Like many other prophets, Ezekiel warned his people of coming destruction should they refuse to abandon their sin. Yet more than any other prophet, Ezekiel wedded his announcements of judgment to a deep concern that the people see God's hand in the devastation. At least 43 times the prophet attaches to his fearsome prophecies some form of the phrase, "And they will know that I am the LORD."

Ezekiel felt a burning desire, not only to communicate to his people the seriousness of their sin, but also that God stood at the center of all that was about to happen—God, and not fate or bad luck or poor military strategy. The prophet possessed a profound zeal to relate almighty God to every area of their lives. And he wanted the scattered remnant to remember their unbreakable connection to the Lord.

Ezekiel's passion for the name of God should drive home in the heart of every leader the seriousness of the sin of idolatry. God spoke with awesome solemnity when he forbade the Israelites from worshiping anyone or anything other than him (Ex 20:3). Wise leaders always keep in mind that God requires not only that we have no gods *before* him, but that we have no other gods *beside* him. No one long escapes who treats his name with contempt. Not then, and not today.

" 'The end! The end has come
  upon the four corners of the land!
3 The end is now upon you,
  and I will unleash my anger against you.
I will judge you according to your conduct
  and repay you for all your detestable
    practices.
4 I will not look on you with pity;
  I will not spare you.
I will surely repay you for your conduct
  and for the detestable practices among
    you.

" 'Then you will know that I am the LORD.'

5 "This is what the Sovereign LORD says:

" 'Disaster! Unheard-of*a* disaster!
  See, it comes!
6 The end has come!
  The end has come!
It has roused itself against you.
  See, it comes!
7 Doom has come upon you,
  upon you who dwell in the land.
The time has come! The day is near!
  There is panic, not joy, on the mountains.
8 I am about to pour out my wrath on you
  and spend my anger against you.
I will judge you according to your conduct
  and repay you for all your detestable
    practices.
9 I will not look on you with pity;
  I will not spare you.
I will repay you for your conduct
  and for the detestable practices among
    you.

" 'Then you will know that it is I the LORD who
strikes you.

10 " 'See, the day!
  See, it comes!
Doom has burst forth,
  the rod has budded,
  arrogance has blossomed!
11 Violence has arisen,*b*
  a rod to punish the wicked.
None of the people will be left,
  none of that crowd—
none of their wealth,
  nothing of value.
12 The time has come!
  The day has arrived!
Let not the buyer rejoice
  nor the seller grieve,
  for my wrath is on the whole crowd.

13 The seller will not recover
  the property that was sold—
  as long as both buyer and seller live.
For the vision concerning the whole crowd
  will not be reversed.
Because of their sins, not one of them
  will preserve their life.

14 " 'They have blown the trumpet,
  they have made all things ready,
but no one will go into battle,
  for my wrath is on the whole crowd.
15 Outside is the sword;
  inside are plague and famine.
Those in the country
  will die by the sword;
those in the city
  will be devoured by famine and plague.
16 The fugitives who escape
  will flee to the mountains.
Like doves of the valleys,
  they will all moan,
  each for their own sins.
17 Every hand will go limp;
  every leg will be wet with urine.
18 They will put on sackcloth
  and be clothed with terror.
Every face will be covered with shame,
  and every head will be shaved.

19 " 'They will throw their silver into the streets,
  and their gold will be treated as a thing
    unclean.
Their silver and gold
  will not be able to deliver them
  in the day of the LORD's wrath.
It will not satisfy their hunger
  or fill their stomachs,
  for it has caused them to stumble into sin.
20 They took pride in their beautiful jewelry
  and used it to make their detestable idols.
They made it into vile images;
  therefore I will make it a thing unclean for
    them.
21 I will give their wealth as plunder to
    foreigners
  and as loot to the wicked of the earth,
  who will defile it.
22 I will turn my face away from the people,
  and robbers will desecrate the place I
    treasure.
They will enter it
  and will defile it.

---

a 5 Most Hebrew manuscripts; some Hebrew manuscripts and
Syriac *Disaster after*   *b* 11 Or *The violent one has become*

²³"'Prepare chains!
     For the land is full of bloodshed,
        and the city is full of violence.
²⁴I will bring the most wicked of nations
        to take possession of their houses.
  I will put an end to the pride of the mighty,
        and their sanctuaries will be desecrated.
²⁵When terror comes,
     they will seek peace in vain.
²⁶Calamity upon calamity will come,
     and rumor upon rumor.
  They will go searching for a vision from the
        prophet,
     priestly instruction in the law will cease,
     the counsel of the elders will come to an
        end.
²⁷The king will mourn,
     the prince will be clothed with despair,
     and the hands of the people of the land
        will tremble.
  I will deal with them according to their
        conduct,
     and by their own standards I will judge
        them.

  "'Then they will know that I am the LORD.'"

Idolatry in the Temple

8 In the sixth year, in the sixth month on the
   fifth day, while I was sitting in my house
and the elders of Judah were sitting before me,
the hand of the Sovereign LORD came on me
there. ²I looked, and I saw a figure like that of
a man.ᵃ From what appeared to be his waist
down he was like fire, and from there up his appearance was as bright as glowing metal. ³He
stretched out what looked like a hand and took
me by the hair of my head. The Spirit lifted me
up between earth and heaven and in visions of
God he took me to Jerusalem, to the entrance of
the north gate of the inner court, where the idol
that provokes to jealousy stood. ⁴And there before me was the glory of the God of Israel, as in
the vision I had seen in the plain.

⁵Then he said to me, "Son of man, look toward the north." So I looked, and in the entrance north of the gate of the altar I saw this
idol of jealousy.

⁶And he said to me, "Son of man, do you see
what they are doing—the utterly detestable
things the Israelites are doing here, things that
will drive me far from my sanctuary? But you
will see things that are even more detestable."

⁷Then he brought me to the entrance to the
court. I looked, and I saw a hole in the wall. ⁸He

said to me, "Son of man, now dig into the wall."
So I dug into the wall and saw a doorway there.

⁹And he said to me, "Go in and see the wicked
and detestable things they are doing here." ¹⁰So
I went in and looked, and I saw portrayed all
over the walls all kinds of crawling things and
unclean animals and all the idols of Israel. ¹¹In
front of them stood seventy elders of Israel, and
Jaazaniah son of Shaphan was standing among
them. Each had a censer in his hand, and a fragrant cloud of incense was rising.

¹²He said to me, "Son of man, have you seen
what the elders of Israel are doing in the darkness, each at the shrine of his own idol? They say,
'The LORD does not see us; the LORD has forsaken
the land.'" ¹³Again, he said, "You will see them
doing things that are even more detestable."

The Law of Solid Ground: Leaders Pay for Conduct No One Sees

Ezekiel 8:12–13

When leaders believe they can do whatever
they want in private even if it contradicts
what they do in public, they violate their calling.
Leaders who last commit themselves to personal integrity, even when no one is watching,
because they know it will pay off in public, when
many may be watching.

---

¹⁴Then he brought me to the entrance of the
north gate of the house of the LORD, and I saw
women sitting there, mourning the god Tam-
muz. ¹⁵He said to me, "Do you see this, son of
man? You will see things that are even more detestable than this."

¹⁶He then brought me into the inner court of
the house of the LORD, and there at the entrance
to the temple, between the portico and the altar,
were about twenty-five men. With their backs
toward the temple of the LORD and their faces
toward the east, they were bowing down to the
sun in the east.

¹⁷He said to me, "Have you seen this, son of
man? Is it a trivial matter for the people of Judah
to do the detestable things they are doing here?
Must they also fill the land with violence and
continually arouse my anger? Look at them put-

ᵃ 2 Or *saw a fiery figure*

ting the branch to their nose! ¹⁸Therefore I will deal with them in anger; I will not look on them with pity or spare them. Although they shout in my ears, I will not listen to them."

Judgment on the Idolaters

9 Then I heard him call out in a loud voice, "Bring near those who are appointed to execute judgment on the city, each with a weapon in his hand." ²And I saw six men coming from the direction of the upper gate, which faces north, each with a deadly weapon in his hand. With them was a man clothed in linen who had a writing kit at his side. They came in and stood beside the bronze altar.

³Now the glory of the God of Israel went up from above the cherubim, where it had been, and moved to the threshold of the temple. Then the Lord called to the man clothed in linen who had the writing kit at his side ⁴and said to him, "Go throughout the city of Jerusalem and put a mark on the foreheads of those who grieve and lament over all the detestable things that are done in it."

⁵As I listened, he said to the others, "Follow him through the city and kill, without showing pity or compassion. ⁶Slaughter the old men, the young men and women, the mothers and children, but do not touch anyone who has the mark. Begin at my sanctuary." So they began with the old men who were in front of the temple.

⁷Then he said to them, "Defile the temple and fill the courts with the slain. Go!" So they went out and began killing throughout the city. ⁸While they were killing and I was left alone, I fell facedown, crying out, "Alas, Sovereign Lord! Are you going to destroy the entire remnant of Israel in this outpouring of your wrath on Jerusalem?"

⁹He answered me, "The sin of the people of Israel and Judah is exceedingly great; the land is full of bloodshed and the city is full of injustice. They say, 'The Lord has forsaken the land; the Lord does not see.' ¹⁰So I will not look on them with pity or spare them, but I will bring down on their own heads what they have done."

¹¹Then the man in linen with the writing kit at his side brought back word, saying, "I have done as you commanded."

God's Glory Departs From the Temple

10 I looked, and I saw the likeness of a throne of lapis lazuli above the vault that was over the heads of the cherubim. ²The Lord said to the man clothed in linen, "Go in among

the wheels beneath the cherubim. Fill your hands with burning coals from among the cherubim and scatter them over the city." And as I watched, he went in.

³Now the cherubim were standing on the south side of the temple when the man went in, and a cloud filled the inner court. ⁴Then the glory of the Lord rose from above the cherubim and moved to the threshold of the temple. The cloud filled the temple, and the court was full of the radiance of the glory of the Lord. ⁵The sound of the wings of the cherubim could be heard as far away as the outer court, like the voice of God Almighty*ᵃ* when he speaks.

⁶When the Lord commanded the man in linen, "Take fire from among the wheels, from among the cherubim," the man went in and stood beside a wheel. ⁷Then one of the cherubim reached out his hand to the fire that was among them. He took up some of it and put it into the hands of the man in linen, who took it and went out. ⁸(Under the wings of the cherubim could be seen what looked like human hands.)

⁹I looked, and I saw beside the cherubim four wheels, one beside each of the cherubim; the wheels sparkled like topaz. ¹⁰As for their appearance, the four of them looked alike; each was like a wheel intersecting a wheel. ¹¹As they moved, they would go in any one of the four directions the cherubim faced; the wheels did not turn about*ᵇ* as the cherubim went. The cherubim went in whatever direction the head faced, without turning as they went. ¹²Their entire bodies, including their backs, their hands and their wings, were completely full of eyes, as were their four wheels. ¹³I heard the wheels being called "the whirling wheels." ¹⁴Each of the cherubim had four faces: One face was that of a cherub, the second the face of a human being, the third the face of a lion, and the fourth the face of an eagle.

¹⁵Then the cherubim rose upward. These were the living creatures I had seen by the Kebar River. ¹⁶When the cherubim moved, the wheels beside them moved; and when the cherubim spread their wings to rise from the ground, the wheels did not leave their side. ¹⁷When the cherubim stood still, they also stood still; and when the cherubim rose, they rose with them, because the spirit of the living creatures was in them.

¹⁸Then the glory of the Lord departed from over the threshold of the temple and stopped above the cherubim. ¹⁹While I watched, the

---

ᵃ 5 Hebrew *El-Shaddai*   *ᵇ 11* Or *aside*

cherubim spread their wings and rose from the ground, and as they went, the wheels went with them. They stopped at the entrance of the east gate of the LORD's house, and the glory of the God of Israel was above them.

20These were the living creatures I had seen beneath the God of Israel by the Kebar River, and I realized that they were cherubim. 21Each had four faces and four wings, and under their wings was what looked like human hands. 22Their faces had the same appearance as those I had seen by the Kebar River. Each one went straight ahead.

God's Sure Judgment on Jerusalem

11 Then the Spirit lifted me up and brought me to the gate of the house of the LORD that faces east. There at the entrance of the gate were twenty-five men, and I saw among them Jaazaniah son of Azzur and Pelatiah son of Benaiah, leaders of the people. 2The LORD said to me, "Son of man, these are the men who are plotting evil and giving wicked advice in this city. 3They say, 'Haven't our houses been recently rebuilt? This city is a pot, and we are the meat in it.' 4Therefore prophesy against them; prophesy, son of man."

5Then the Spirit of the LORD came on me, and he told me to say: "This is what the LORD says: That is what you are saying, you leaders in Israel, but I know what is going through your mind. 6You have killed many people in this city and filled its streets with the dead.

7"Therefore this is what the Sovereign LORD says: The bodies you have thrown there are the meat and this city is the pot, but I will drive you out of it. 8You fear the sword, and the sword is what I will bring against you, declares the Sovereign LORD. 9I will drive you out of the city and deliver you into the hands of foreigners and inflict punishment on you. 10You will fall by the sword, and I will execute judgment on you at the borders of Israel. Then you will know that I am the LORD. 11This city will not be a pot for you, nor will you be the meat in it; I will execute judgment on you at the borders of Israel. 12And you will know that I am the LORD, for you have not followed my decrees or kept my laws but have conformed to the standards of the nations around you."

13Now as I was prophesying, Pelatiah son of Benaiah died. Then I fell facedown and cried out in a loud voice, "Alas, Sovereign LORD! Will you completely destroy the remnant of Israel?"

God Looks at the Leader's Heart

Ezekiel 11:1–13

When God measures the greatness of a leader, he puts his tape measure around the heart, not the head. Ezekiel 11 echoes the message we learn from King David in 1 Samuel 16. When God punishes evil leaders, their followers also get punished. We may conclude from this that no nation rises above its leadership.

What can we learn from these failed leaders? The chief lesson lies in their hearts. God desires that leaders first develop the following heart characteristics:

1. **Healthy personal security**
2. **Strong Biblical identity**
3. **Growing intimacy with him**
4. **Consistent personal disciplines**
5. **Pure motives and ambitions**
6. **Biblical values and priorities**
7. **Humble servant's heart**
8. **Healthy community relationships**
9. **Principle-centered decisions**
10. **Compassionate love for people**

The Promise of Israel's Return

[14]The word of the LORD came to me: [15]"Son of man, the people of Jerusalem have said of your fellow exiles and all the other Israelites, 'They are far away from the LORD; this land was given to us as our possession.'

[16]"Therefore say: 'This is what the Sovereign LORD says: Although I sent them far away among the nations and scattered them among the countries, yet for a little while I have been a sanctuary for them in the countries where they have gone.'

[17]"Therefore say: 'This is what the Sovereign LORD says: I will gather you from the nations and bring you back from the countries where you have been scattered, and I will give you back the land of Israel again.'

[18]"They will return to it and remove all its vile images and detestable idols. [19]I will give them an undivided heart and put a new spirit in them; I will remove from them their heart of stone and give them a heart of flesh. [20]Then they will follow my decrees and be careful to keep my laws. They will be my people, and I will be their God. [21]But as for those whose hearts are devoted to their vile images and detestable idols, I will bring down on their own heads what they have done, declares the Sovereign LORD."

[22]Then the cherubim, with the wheels beside them, spread their wings, and the glory of the God of Israel was above them. [23]The glory of the LORD went up from within the city and stopped above the mountain east of it. [24]The Spirit lifted me up and brought me to the exiles in Babylonia[a] in the vision given by the Spirit of God. Then the vision I had seen went up from me, [25]and I told the exiles everything the LORD had shown me.

The Exile Symbolized

12 The word of the LORD came to me: [2]"Son of man, you are living among a rebellious people. They have eyes to see but do not see and ears to hear but do not hear, for they are a rebellious people.

[3]"Therefore, son of man, pack your belongings for exile and in the daytime, as they watch, set out and go from where you are to another place. Perhaps they will understand, though they are a rebellious people. [4]During the daytime, while they watch, bring out your belongings packed for exile. Then in the evening, while they are watching, go out like those who go into exile. [5]While they watch, dig through the wall and take your belongings out through it. [6]Put

them on your shoulder as they are watching and carry them out at dusk. Cover your face so that you cannot see the land, for I have made you a sign to the Israelites."

[7]So I did as I was commanded. During the day I brought out my things packed for exile. Then in the evening I dug through the wall with my hands. I took my belongings out at dusk, carrying them on my shoulders while they watched.

[8]In the morning the word of the LORD came to me: [9]"Son of man, did not the Israelites, that rebellious people, ask you, 'What are you doing?'

[10]"Say to them, 'This is what the Sovereign LORD says: This prophecy concerns the prince in Jerusalem and all the Israelites who are there.' [11]Say to them, 'I am a sign to you.'

"As I have done, so it will be done to them. They will go into exile as captives.

[12]"The prince among them will put his things on his shoulder at dusk and leave, and a hole will be dug in the wall for him to go through. He will cover his face so that he cannot see the land. [13]I will spread my net for him, and he will be caught in my snare; I will bring him to Babylonia, the land of the Chaldeans, but he will not see it, and there he will die. [14]I will scatter to the winds all those around him—his staff and all his troops—and I will pursue them with drawn sword.

[15]"They will know that I am the LORD, when I disperse them among the nations and scatter them through the countries. [16]But I will spare a few of them from the sword, famine and plague, so that in the nations where they go they may acknowledge all their detestable practices. Then they will know that I am the LORD."

[17]The word of the LORD came to me: [18]"Son of man, tremble as you eat your food, and shudder in fear as you drink your water. [19]Say to the people of the land: 'This is what the Sovereign LORD says about those living in Jerusalem and in the land of Israel: They will eat their food in anxiety and drink their water in despair, for their land will be stripped of everything in it because of the violence of all who live there. [20]The inhabited towns will be laid waste and the land will be desolate. Then you will know that I am the LORD.'"

There Will Be No Delay

[21]The word of the LORD came to me: [22]"Son of man, what is this proverb you have in the land of Israel: 'The days go by and every vision comes to

---

[a] 24 Or *Chaldea*

nothing'? ²³Say to them, 'This is what the Sovereign LORD says: I am going to put an end to this proverb, and they will no longer quote it in Israel.' Say to them, 'The days are near when every vision will be fulfilled. ²⁴For there will be no more false visions or flattering divinations among the people of Israel. ²⁵But I the LORD will speak what I will, and it shall be fulfilled without delay. For in your days, you rebellious people, I will fulfill whatever I say, declares the Sovereign LORD.'"

²⁶The word of the LORD came to me: ²⁷"Son of man, the Israelites are saying, 'The vision he sees is for many years from now, and he prophesies about the distant future.'

²⁸"Therefore say to them, 'This is what the Sovereign LORD says: None of my words will be delayed any longer; whatever I say will be fulfilled, declares the Sovereign LORD.'"

False Prophets Condemned

13 The word of the LORD came to me: ²"Son of man, prophesy against the prophets of Israel who are now prophesying. Say to those who prophesy out of their own imagination: 'Hear the word of the LORD! ³This is what the Sovereign LORD says: Woe to the foolish*a* prophets who follow their own spirit and have seen nothing! ⁴Your prophets, Israel, are like jackals among ruins. ⁵You have not gone up to the breaches in the wall to repair it for the people of Israel so that it will stand firm in the battle

on the day of the LORD. ⁶Their visions are false and their divinations a lie. Even though the LORD has not sent them, they say, "The LORD declares," and expect him to fulfill their words. ⁷Have you not seen false visions and uttered lying divinations when you say, "The LORD declares," though I have not spoken?

⁸"'Therefore this is what the Sovereign LORD says: Because of your false words and lying visions, I am against you, declares the Sovereign LORD. ⁹My hand will be against the prophets who see false visions and utter lying divinations. They will not belong to the council of my people or be listed in the records of Israel, nor will they enter the land of Israel. Then you will know that I am the Sovereign LORD.

¹⁰"'Because they lead my people astray, saying, "Peace," when there is no peace, and because, when a flimsy wall is built, they cover it with whitewash, ¹¹therefore tell those who cover it with whitewash that it is going to fall. Rain will come in torrents, and I will send hailstones hurtling down, and violent winds will burst forth. ¹²When the wall collapses, will people not ask you, "Where is the whitewash you covered it with?"

¹³"'Therefore this is what the Sovereign LORD says: In my wrath I will unleash a violent wind, and in my anger hailstones and torrents of rain will fall with destructive fury. ¹⁴I will tear down the wall you have covered with whitewash and

---

a 3 Or wicked

Vision: A Revelation Without Action Fades

Ezekiel 12:1–28

God told Ezekiel to pack up his belongings and symbolically act out the exile awaiting the Jews, once again using creative means to communicate vision.

In Ezekiel 12:21–28 God speaks of the powerlessness of visions unless someone puts feet to them. Visions lose their strength without action to support them. Good leaders always share both the vision and the steps to its implementation.

Yet the first step always must be to catch the God-given vision. Consider one process to go through as you attempt to catch God's vision for the people:

1. *Look within you:* What do you feel?

2. *Look behind you:* What have you learned?

3. *Look around you:* What is happening to others?

4. *Look ahead of you:* What is the big picture?

5. *Look above you:* What does God expect of you?

6. *Look beside you:* What resources are available to you?

will level it to the ground so that its foundation will be laid bare. When it[a] falls, you will be destroyed in it; and you will know that I am the LORD. [15]So I will pour out my wrath against the wall and against those who covered it with whitewash. I will say to you, "The wall is gone and so are those who whitewashed it, [16]those prophets of Israel who prophesied to Jerusalem and saw visions of peace for her when there was no peace, declares the Sovereign LORD."'

[17]"Now, son of man, set your face against the daughters of your people who prophesy out of their own imagination. Prophesy against them [18]and say, 'This is what the Sovereign LORD says: Woe to the women who sew magic charms on all their wrists and make veils of various lengths for their heads in order to ensnare people. Will you ensnare the lives of my people but preserve your own? [19]You have profaned me among my people for a few handfuls of barley and scraps of bread. By lying to my people, who listen to lies, you have killed those who should not have died and have spared those who should not live.

[20]"'Therefore this is what the Sovereign LORD says: I am against your magic charms with which you ensnare people like birds and I will tear them from your arms; I will set free the people that you ensnare like birds. [21]I will tear off your veils and save my people from your hands, and they will no longer fall prey to your power. Then you will know that I am the LORD. [22]Because you disheartened the righteous with your lies, when I had brought them no grief, and because you encouraged the wicked not to turn from their evil ways and so save their lives, [23]therefore you will no longer see false visions or practice divination. I will save my people from your hands. And then you will know that I am the LORD.'"

Idolaters Condemned

14 Some of the elders of Israel came to me and sat down in front of me. [2]Then the word of the LORD came to me: [3]"Son of man, these men have set up idols in their hearts and put wicked stumbling blocks before their faces. Should I let them inquire of me at all? [4]Therefore speak to them and tell them, 'This is what the Sovereign LORD says: When any of the Israelites set up idols in their hearts and put a wicked stumbling block before their faces and then go to a prophet, I the LORD will answer them myself in keeping with their great idolatry. [5]I will do this to recapture the hearts of the people of Israel, who have all deserted me for their idols.'

[6]"Therefore say to the people of Israel, 'This is what the Sovereign LORD says: Repent! Turn from your idols and renounce all your detestable practices!

[7]"'When any of the Israelites or any foreigner residing in Israel separate themselves from me and set up idols in their hearts and put a wicked stumbling block before their faces and then go to a prophet to inquire of me, I the LORD will answer them myself. [8]I will set my face against them and make them an example and a byword. I will remove them from my people. Then you will know that I am the LORD.

[9]"'And if the prophet is enticed to utter a prophecy, I the LORD have enticed that prophet, and I will stretch out my hand against him and destroy him from among my people Israel. [10]They will bear their guilt—the prophet will be as guilty as the one who consults him. [11]Then the people of Israel will no longer stray from me, nor will they defile themselves anymore with all their sins. They will be my people, and I will be their God, declares the Sovereign LORD.'"

Jerusalem's Judgment Inescapable

[12]The word of the LORD came to me: [13]"Son of man, if a country sins against me by being unfaithful and I stretch out my hand against it to cut off its food supply and send famine upon it and kill its people and their animals, [14]even if these three men—Noah, Daniel[b] and Job—were in it, they could save only themselves by their righteousness, declares the Sovereign LORD.

[15]"Or if I send wild beasts through that country and they leave it childless and it becomes

---

[a] 14 Or the city   [b] 14 Or Danel, a man of renown in ancient literature; also in verse 20

The Law of Influence: Even the Best Leaders Can't Force Action

Ezekiel 14:12–14

Even the best leaders cannot force followers to act. God says even three of his choice servants—Noah, Daniel and Job—could not save rebellious Judah. All three were full of integrity, character and discipline, totally competent and responsible to do the right thing. Yet God says even they could save only themselves.

desolate so that no one can pass through it because of the beasts, ¹⁶as surely as I live, declares the Sovereign LORD, even if these three men were in it, they could not save their own sons or daughters. They alone would be saved, but the land would be desolate.

¹⁷"Or if I bring a sword against that country and say, 'Let the sword pass throughout the land,' and I kill its people and their animals, ¹⁸as surely as I live, declares the Sovereign LORD, even if these three men were in it, they could not save their own sons or daughters. They alone would be saved.

¹⁹"Or if I send a plague into that land and pour out my wrath on it through bloodshed, killing its people and their animals, ²⁰as surely as I live, declares the Sovereign LORD, even if Noah, Daniel and Job were in it, they could save neither son nor daughter. They would save only themselves by their righteousness.

²¹"For this is what the Sovereign LORD says: How much worse will it be when I send against Jerusalem my four dreadful judgments — sword and famine and wild beasts and plague — to kill its men and their animals! ²²Yet there will be some survivors — sons and daughters who will be brought out of it. They will come to you, and when you see their conduct and their actions, you will be consoled regarding the disaster I have brought on Jerusalem — every disaster I have brought on it. ²³You will be consoled when you see their conduct and their actions, for you will know that I have done nothing in it without cause, declares the Sovereign LORD."

Jerusalem as a Useless Vine

15 The word of the LORD came to me: ²"Son of man, how is the wood of a vine different from that of a branch from any of the trees in the forest? ³Is wood ever taken from it to make anything useful? Do they make pegs from it to hang things on? ⁴And after it is thrown on the fire as fuel and the fire burns both ends and chars the middle, is it then useful for anything? ⁵If it was not useful for anything when it was whole, how much less can it be made into something useful when the fire has burned it and it is charred?

⁶"Therefore this is what the Sovereign LORD says: As I have given the wood of the vine among the trees of the forest as fuel for the fire, so will I treat the people living in Jerusalem. ⁷I will set my face against them. Although they have come out of the fire, the fire will yet consume them. And when I set my face against them, you will

know that I am the LORD. ⁸I will make the land desolate because they have been unfaithful, declares the Sovereign LORD."

Jerusalem as an Adulterous Wife

16 The word of the LORD came to me: ²"Son of man, confront Jerusalem with her detestable practices ³and say, 'This is what the Sovereign LORD says to Jerusalem: Your ancestry and birth were in the land of the Canaanites; your father was an Amorite and your mother a Hittite. ⁴On the day you were born your cord was not cut, nor were you washed with water to make you clean, nor were you rubbed with salt or wrapped in cloths. ⁵No one looked on you with pity or had compassion enough to do any of these things for you. Rather, you were thrown out into the open field, for on the day you were born you were despised.

⁶"'Then I passed by and saw you kicking about in your blood, and as you lay there in your blood I said to you, "Live!"ᵃ ⁷I made you grow like a plant of the field. You grew and developed and entered puberty. Your breasts had formed and your hair had grown, yet you were stark naked.

⁸"'Later I passed by, and when I looked at you and saw that you were old enough for love, I spread the corner of my garment over you and covered your naked body. I gave you my solemn oath and entered into a covenant with you, declares the Sovereign LORD, and you became mine.

⁹"'I bathed you with water and washed the blood from you and put ointments on you. ¹⁰I clothed you with an embroidered dress and put sandals of fine leather on you. I dressed you in fine linen and covered you with costly garments. ¹¹I adorned you with jewelry: I put bracelets on your arms and a necklace around your neck, ¹²and I put a ring on your nose, earrings on your ears and a beautiful crown on your head. ¹³So you were adorned with gold and silver; your clothes were of fine linen and costly fabric and embroidered cloth. Your food was honey, olive oil and the finest flour. You became very beautiful and rose to be a queen. ¹⁴And your fame spread among the nations on account of your beauty, because the splendor I had given you made your beauty perfect, declares the Sovereign LORD.

ᵃ 6 A few Hebrew manuscripts, Septuagint and Syriac; most Hebrew manuscripts repeat *and as you lay there in your blood I said to you, "Live!"*

15 " 'But you trusted in your beauty and used your fame to become a prostitute. You lavished your favors on anyone who passed by and your beauty became his. 16You took some of your garments to make gaudy high places, where you carried on your prostitution. You went to him, and he possessed your beauty.[a] 17You also took the fine jewelry I gave you, the jewelry made of my gold and silver, and you made for yourself male idols and engaged in prostitution with them. 18And you took your embroidered clothes to put on them, and you offered my oil and incense before them. 19Also the food I provided for you—the flour, olive oil and honey I gave you to eat—you offered as fragrant incense before them. That is what happened, declares the Sovereign LORD.

20 " 'And you took your sons and daughters whom you bore to me and sacrificed them as food to the idols. Was your prostitution not enough? 21You slaughtered my children and sacrificed them to the idols. 22In all your detestable practices and your prostitution you did not remember the days of your youth, when you were naked and bare, kicking about in your blood.

23 " 'Woe! Woe to you, declares the Sovereign LORD. In addition to all your other wickedness, 24you built a mound for yourself and made a lofty shrine in every public square. 25At every street corner you built your lofty shrines and degraded your beauty, spreading your legs with increasing promiscuity to anyone who passed by. 26You engaged in prostitution with the Egyptians, your neighbors with large genitals, and aroused my anger with your increasing promiscuity. 27So I stretched out my hand against you and reduced your territory; I gave you over to the greed of your enemies, the daughters of the Philistines, who were shocked by your lewd conduct. 28You engaged in prostitution with the Assyrians too, because you were insatiable; and even after that, you still were not satisfied. 29Then you increased your promiscuity to include Babylonia,[b] a land of merchants, but even with this you were not satisfied.

30 " 'I am filled with fury against you,[c] declares the Sovereign LORD, when you do all these things, acting like a brazen prostitute! 31When you built your mounds at every street corner and made your lofty shrines in every public square, you were unlike a prostitute, because you scorned payment.

32 " 'You adulterous wife! You prefer strangers to your own husband! 33All prostitutes receive gifts, but you give gifts to all your lovers, bribing

---

The Law of Magnetism: God's People Become Like Pagan Leaders

Ezekiel 16:23–29

We attract who we are, not who we want. Consider the following:

1. **Attraction: We tend to attract those similar to us.**

2. **Reflection: We tend to reflect those who lead or follow us.**

3. **Repercussion: We tend to face similar consequences as those who are like us.**

---

them to come to you from everywhere for your illicit favors. 34So in your prostitution you are the opposite of others; no one runs after you for your favors. You are the very opposite, for you give payment and none is given to you.

35 " 'Therefore, you prostitute, hear the word of the LORD! 36This is what the Sovereign LORD says: Because you poured out your lust and exposed your naked body in your promiscuity with your lovers, and because of all your detestable idols, and because you gave them your children's blood, 37therefore I am going to gather all your lovers, with whom you found pleasure, those you loved as well as those you hated. I will gather them against you from all around and will strip you in front of them, and they will see you stark naked. 38I will sentence you to the punishment of women who commit adultery and who shed blood; I will bring on you the blood vengeance of my wrath and jealous anger. 39Then I will deliver you into the hands of your lovers, and they will tear down your mounds and destroy your lofty shrines. They will strip you of your clothes and take your fine jewelry and leave you stark naked. 40They will bring a mob against you, who will stone you and hack you to pieces with their swords. 41They will burn down your houses and inflict punishment on you in the sight of many women. I will put a stop to your prostitution, and you will no longer pay your lovers. 42Then my wrath against you will subside and my jealous anger will turn away from you; I will be calm and no longer angry.

---

[a] 16 The meaning of the Hebrew for this sentence is uncertain.
[b] 29 Or *Chaldea*   [c] 30 Or *How feverish is your heart,*

43" 'Because you did not remember the days of your youth but enraged me with all these things, I will surely bring down on your head what you have done, declares the Sovereign LORD. Did you not add lewdness to all your other detestable practices?

44" 'Everyone who quotes proverbs will quote this proverb about you: "Like mother, like daughter." 45You are a true daughter of your mother, who despised her husband and her children; and you are a true sister of your sisters, who despised their husbands and their children. Your mother was a Hittite and your father an Amorite. 46Your older sister was Samaria, who lived to the north of you with her daughters; and your younger sister, who lived to the south of you with her daughters, was Sodom. 47You not only followed their ways and copied their detestable practices, but in all your ways you soon became more depraved than they. 48As surely as I live, declares the Sovereign LORD, your sister Sodom and her daughters never did what you and your daughters have done.

49" 'Now this was the sin of your sister Sodom: She and her daughters were arrogant, overfed and unconcerned; they did not help the poor and needy. 50They were haughty and did detestable things before me. Therefore I did away with them as you have seen. 51Samaria did not commit half the sins you did. You have done more detestable things than they, and have made your sisters seem righteous by all these things you have done. 52Bear your disgrace, for you have furnished some justification for your sisters. Because your sins were more vile than theirs, they appear more righteous than you. So then, be ashamed and bear your disgrace, for you have made your sisters appear righteous.

53" 'However, I will restore the fortunes of Sodom and her daughters and of Samaria and her daughters, and your fortunes along with them, 54so that you may bear your disgrace and be ashamed of all you have done in giving them comfort. 55And your sisters, Sodom with her daughters and Samaria with her daughters, will return to what they were before; and you and your daughters will return to what you were before. 56You would not even mention your sister Sodom in the day of your pride, 57before your wickedness was uncovered. Even so, you are now scorned by the daughters of Edom[a] and all her neighbors and the daughters of the Philistines — all those around you who despise you. 58You will bear the consequences of your lewdness and your detestable practices, declares the LORD.

59" 'This is what the Sovereign LORD says: I will deal with you as you deserve, because you have despised my oath by breaking the covenant. 60Yet I will remember the covenant I made with you in the days of your youth, and I will establish an everlasting covenant with you. 61Then you will remember your ways and be ashamed when you receive your sisters, both those who are older than you and those who are younger. I will give them to you as daughters, but not on the basis of my covenant with you. 62So I will establish my covenant with you, and you will know that I am the LORD. 63Then, when I make atonement for you for all you have done, you will remember and be ashamed and never again open your mouth because of your humiliation, declares the Sovereign LORD.' "

Two Eagles and a Vine

17 The word of the LORD came to me: 2"Son of man, set forth an allegory and tell it to the Israelites as a parable. 3Say to them, 'This is what the Sovereign LORD says: A great eagle with powerful wings, long feathers and full plumage of varied colors came to Lebanon. Taking hold of the top of a cedar, 4he broke off its topmost shoot and carried it away to a land of merchants, where he planted it in a city of traders.

5" 'He took one of the seedlings of the land and put it in fertile soil. He planted it like a willow by abundant water, 6and it sprouted and became a low, spreading vine. Its branches turned toward him, but its roots remained under it. So it became a vine and produced branches and put out leafy boughs.

7" 'But there was another great eagle with powerful wings and full plumage. The vine now sent out its roots toward him from the plot where it was planted and stretched out its branches to him for water. 8It had been planted in good soil by abundant water so that it would produce branches, bear fruit and become a splendid vine.'

9"Say to them, 'This is what the Sovereign LORD says: Will it thrive? Will it not be uprooted and stripped of its fruit so that it withers? All its new growth will wither. It will not take a strong arm or many people to pull it up by the roots. 10It has been planted, but will it thrive? Will it not wither completely when the east wind strikes it — wither away in the plot where it grew?' "

---

[a] 57 Many Hebrew manuscripts and Syriac; most Hebrew manuscripts, Septuagint and Vulgate *Aram*

¹¹Then the word of the Lord came to me: ¹²"Say to this rebellious people, 'Do you not know what these things mean?' Say to them: 'The king of Babylon went to Jerusalem and carried off her king and her nobles, bringing them back with him to Babylon. ¹³Then he took a member of the royal family and made a treaty with him, putting him under oath. He also carried away the leading men of the land, ¹⁴so that the kingdom would be brought low, unable to rise again, surviving only by keeping his treaty. ¹⁵But the king rebelled against him by sending his envoys to Egypt to get horses and a large army. Will he succeed? Will he who does such things escape? Will he break the treaty and yet escape?

¹⁶" 'As surely as I live, declares the Sovereign Lord, he shall die in Babylon, in the land of the king who put him on the throne, whose oath he despised and whose treaty he broke. ¹⁷Pharaoh with his mighty army and great horde will be of no help to him in war, when ramps are built and siege works erected to destroy many lives. ¹⁸He despised the oath by breaking the covenant. Because he had given his hand in pledge and yet did all these things, he shall not escape.

¹⁹" 'Therefore this is what the Sovereign Lord says: As surely as I live, I will repay him for despising my oath and breaking my covenant. ²⁰I will spread my net for him, and he will be caught in my snare. I will bring him to Babylon and execute judgment on him there because he was unfaithful to me. ²¹All his choice troops will fall by the sword, and the survivors will be scattered to the winds. Then you will know that I the Lord have spoken.

²²" 'This is what the Sovereign Lord says: I myself will take a shoot from the very top of a cedar and plant it; I will break off a tender sprig from its topmost shoots and plant it on a high and lofty mountain. ²³On the mountain heights of Israel I will plant it; it will produce branches and bear fruit and become a splendid cedar. Birds of every kind will nest in it; they will find shelter in the shade of its branches. ²⁴All the trees of the forest will know that I the Lord bring down the tall tree and make the low tree grow tall. I dry up the green tree and make the dry tree flourish.

" 'I the Lord have spoken, and I will do it.' "

The One Who Sins Will Die

18 The word of the Lord came to me: ²"What do you people mean by quoting this proverb about the land of Israel:

" 'The parents eat sour grapes,
    and the children's teeth are set on edge'?

³"As surely as I live, declares the Sovereign Lord, you will no longer quote this proverb in Israel. ⁴For everyone belongs to me, the parent as well as the child—both alike belong to me. The one who sins is the one who will die.

⁵"Suppose there is a righteous man
    who does what is just and right.
⁶He does not eat at the mountain shrines
    or look to the idols of Israel.
He does not defile his neighbor's wife
    or have sexual relations with a woman
        during her period.
⁷He does not oppress anyone,
    but returns what he took in pledge for a loan.
He does not commit robbery
    but gives his food to the hungry
    and provides clothing for the naked.
⁸He does not lend to them at interest
    or take a profit from them.
He withholds his hand from doing wrong
    and judges fairly between two parties.
⁹He follows my decrees
    and faithfully keeps my laws.
That man is righteous;
    he will surely live,
            declares the Sovereign Lord.

¹⁰"Suppose he has a violent son, who sheds blood or does any of these other things[a] ¹¹(though the father has done none of them):

"He eats at the mountain shrines.
He defiles his neighbor's wife.
¹²He oppresses the poor and needy.
He commits robbery.
He does not return what he took in pledge.
He looks to the idols.
He does detestable things.
¹³He lends at interest and takes a profit.

Will such a man live? He will not! Because he has done all these detestable things, he is to be put to death; his blood will be on his own head.

¹⁴"But suppose this son has a son who sees all the sins his father commits, and though he sees them, he does not do such things:

¹⁵"He does not eat at the mountain shrines
    or look to the idols of Israel.
He does not defile his neighbor's wife.
¹⁶He does not oppress anyone
    or require a pledge for a loan.

---

^a 10 Or *things to a brother*

He does not commit robbery
but gives his food to the hungry
and provides clothing for the naked.
[17] He withholds his hand from mistreating the
poor
and takes no interest or profit from them.
He keeps my laws and follows my decrees.

He will not die for his father's sin; he will surely
live. [18] But his father will die for his own sin, because he practiced extortion, robbed his brother
and did what was wrong among his people.

[19] "Yet you ask, 'Why does the son not share
the guilt of his father?' Since the son has done
what is just and right and has been careful to
keep all my decrees, he will surely live. [20] The
one who sins is the one who will die. The child
will not share the guilt of the parent, nor will
the parent share the guilt of the child. The righteousness of the righteous will be credited to
them, and the wickedness of the wicked will be
charged against them.

[21] "But if a wicked person turns away from
all the sins they have committed and keeps all
my decrees and does what is just and right, that
person will surely live; they will not die. [22] None
of the offenses they have committed will be remembered against them. Because of the righteous things they have done, they will live. [23] Do
I take any pleasure in the death of the wicked?

declares the Sovereign LORD. Rather, am I not
pleased when they turn from their ways and
live?

[24] "But if a righteous person turns from their
righteousness and commits sin and does the
same detestable things the wicked person does,
will they live? None of the righteous things that
person has done will be remembered. Because
of the unfaithfulness they are guilty of and because of the sins they have committed, they will
die.

[25] "Yet you say, 'The way of the Lord is not just.'
Hear, you Israelites: Is my way unjust? Is it not
your ways that are unjust? [26] If a righteous person
turns from their righteousness and commits sin,
they will die for it; because of the sin they have
committed they will die. [27] But if a wicked person
turns away from the wickedness they have committed and does what is just and right, they will
save their life. [28] Because they consider all the offenses they have committed and turn away from
them, that person will surely live; they will not
die. [29] Yet the Israelites say, 'The way of the Lord
is not just.' Are my ways unjust, people of Israel?
Is it not your ways that are unjust?

[30] "Therefore, you Israelites, I will judge each
of you according to your own ways, declares the
Sovereign LORD. Repent! Turn away from all
your offenses; then sin will not be your down-

Discernment: Leaders Assess Situations, Then Respond

Ezekiel 18:1–32

God handles each circumstance based on his assessment of the individual situation. In Ezekiel 18 God
reminds us to use discernment in each situation we face. Don't package everyone together, but size
everyone up, one at a time. Respond correctly to each situation.

Consider a few rules of thumb to increase your leadership discernment:

1. **Analyze past successes.**
   **Try to identify the root issues of problems you have already solved. What patterns do you
   see? What enabled you to succeed?**

2. **Assess each person based on their particular situation.**
   **Don't fall into such a rut that you begin to stereotype everyone. Let each team member be an
   individual and discern what is right for him or her, without the baggage of others.**

3. **Listen to your gut.**
   **Try to recall times when your intuition "spoke" to you correctly. Get data, but go beyond
   mere information to your heart's sense of the right thing.**

4. **Learn from wise leaders.**
   **What great leaders do you admire? Study and read the lives of other leaders with gifting
   similar to yours and discover how they think and make decisions.**

fall. ³¹Rid yourselves of all the offenses you have committed, and get a new heart and a new spirit. Why will you die, people of Israel? ³²For I take no pleasure in the death of anyone, declares the Sovereign LORD. Repent and live!

A Lament Over Israel's Princes

19 "Take up a lament concerning the princes of Israel ²and say:

"'What a lioness was your mother
among the lions!
She lay down among them
and reared her cubs.
³She brought up one of her cubs,
and he became a strong lion.
He learned to tear the prey
and he became a man-eater.
⁴The nations heard about him,
and he was trapped in their pit.
They led him with hooks
to the land of Egypt.

⁵"'When she saw her hope unfulfilled,
her expectation gone,
she took another of her cubs
and made him a strong lion.
⁶He prowled among the lions,
for he was now a strong lion.
He learned to tear the prey
and he became a man-eater.
⁷He broke down[a] their strongholds
and devastated their towns.
The land and all who were in it
were terrified by his roaring.
⁸Then the nations came against him,
those from regions round about.
They spread their net for him,
and he was trapped in their pit.
⁹With hooks they pulled him into a cage
and brought him to the king of Babylon.
They put him in prison,
so his roar was heard no longer
on the mountains of Israel.

¹⁰"'Your mother was like a vine in your
vineyard[b]
planted by the water;
it was fruitful and full of branches
because of abundant water.
¹¹Its branches were strong,
fit for a ruler's scepter.
It towered high
above the thick foliage,
conspicuous for its height
and for its many branches.

¹²But it was uprooted in fury
and thrown to the ground.
The east wind made it shrivel,
it was stripped of its fruit;
its strong branches withered
and fire consumed them.
¹³Now it is planted in the desert,
in a dry and thirsty land.
¹⁴Fire spread from one of its main[c] branches
and consumed its fruit.
No strong branch is left on it
fit for a ruler's scepter.'

"This is a lament and is to be used as a lament."

Discipline: If Leaders Can't Rule Themselves, They Can't Rule Others

Ezekiel 19:1–14

There is no leadership without self-discipline. Since the "princes" of Ezekiel 19 lacked the discipline to lead their own lives well, they also failed to lead anyone else well. Leaders must first lead themselves and earn the right to attract followers. The best leader serves as a model for others.

Rebellious Israel Purged

20 In the seventh year, in the fifth month on the tenth day, some of the elders of Israel came to inquire of the LORD, and they sat down in front of me.

²Then the word of the LORD came to me: ³"Son of man, speak to the elders of Israel and say to them, 'This is what the Sovereign LORD says: Have you come to inquire of me? As surely as I live, I will not let you inquire of me, declares the Sovereign LORD.'

⁴"Will you judge them? Will you judge them, son of man? Then confront them with the detestable practices of their ancestors ⁵and say to them: 'This is what the Sovereign LORD says: On the day I chose Israel, I swore with uplifted hand to the descendants of Jacob and revealed myself to them in Egypt. With uplifted hand I said to them, "I am the LORD your God." ⁶On that day

---

[a] 7 Targum (see Septuagint); Hebrew *He knew*
[b] 10 Two Hebrew manuscripts; most Hebrew manuscripts *your blood*   [c] 14 Or *from under its*

I swore to them that I would bring them out of Egypt into a land I had searched out for them, a land flowing with milk and honey, the most beautiful of all lands. ⁷And I said to them, "Each of you, get rid of the vile images you have set your eyes on, and do not defile yourselves with the idols of Egypt. I am the LORD your God."

⁸"'But they rebelled against me and would not listen to me; they did not get rid of the vile images they had set their eyes on, nor did they forsake the idols of Egypt. So I said I would pour out my wrath on them and spend my anger against them in Egypt. ⁹But for the sake of my name, I brought them out of Egypt. I did it to keep my name from being profaned in the eyes of the nations among whom they lived and in whose sight I had revealed myself to the Israelites. ¹⁰Therefore I led them out of Egypt and brought them into the wilderness. ¹¹I gave them my decrees and made known to them my laws, by which the person who obeys them will live. ¹²Also I gave them my Sabbaths as a sign between us, so they would know that I the LORD made them holy.

¹³"'Yet the people of Israel rebelled against me in the wilderness. They did not follow my decrees but rejected my laws — by which the person who obeys them will live — and they utterly desecrated my Sabbaths. So I said I would pour out my wrath on them and destroy them in the wilderness. ¹⁴But for the sake of my name I did what would keep it from being profaned in the eyes of the nations in whose sight I had brought them out. ¹⁵Also with uplifted hand I swore to them in the wilderness that I would not bring them into the land I had given them — a land flowing with milk and honey, the most beautiful of all lands — ¹⁶because they rejected my laws and did not follow my decrees and desecrated my Sabbaths. For their hearts were devoted to their idols. ¹⁷Yet I looked on them with pity and did not destroy them or put an end to them in the wilderness. ¹⁸I said to their children in the wilderness, "Do not follow the statutes of your parents or keep their laws or defile yourselves with their idols. ¹⁹I am the LORD your God; follow my decrees and be careful to keep my laws. ²⁰Keep my Sabbaths holy, that they may be a sign between us. Then you will know that I am the LORD your God."

²¹"'But the children rebelled against me: They did not follow my decrees, they were not careful to keep my laws, of which I said, "The person who obeys them will live by them," and they desecrated my Sabbaths. So I said I would pour out my wrath on them and spend my anger against them in the wilderness. ²²But I withheld my hand, and for the sake of my name I did what would keep it from being profaned in the eyes of the nations in whose sight I had brought them out. ²³Also with uplifted hand I swore to them in the wilderness that I would disperse them among the nations and scatter them through the countries, ²⁴because they had not obeyed my laws but had rejected my decrees and desecrated my Sabbaths, and their eyes lusted after their parents' idols. ²⁵So I gave them other statutes that were not good and laws through which they could not live; ²⁶I defiled them through their gifts — the sacrifice of every firstborn — that I might fill them with horror so they would know that I am the LORD.'

²⁷"Therefore, son of man, speak to the people of Israel and say to them, 'This is what the Sovereign LORD says: In this also your ancestors blasphemed me by being unfaithful to me: ²⁸When I brought them into the land I had sworn to give them and they saw any high hill or any leafy tree, there they offered their sacrifices, made offerings that aroused my anger, presented their fragrant incense and poured out their drink offerings. ²⁹Then I said to them: What is this high place you go to?'" (It is called Bamah[a] to this day.)

Rebellious Israel Renewed

³⁰"Therefore say to the Israelites: 'This is what the Sovereign LORD says: Will you defile yourselves the way your ancestors did and lust after their vile images? ³¹When you offer your gifts — the sacrifice of your children in the fire — you continue to defile yourselves with all your idols to this day. Am I to let you inquire of me, you Israelites? As surely as I live, declares the Sovereign LORD, I will not let you inquire of me.

³²"'You say, "We want to be like the nations, like the peoples of the world, who serve wood and stone." But what you have in mind will never happen. ³³As surely as I live, declares the Sovereign LORD, I will reign over you with a mighty hand and an outstretched arm and with outpoured wrath. ³⁴I will bring you from the nations and gather you from the countries where you have been scattered — with a mighty hand and an outstretched arm and with outpoured wrath. ³⁵I will bring you into the wilderness of the nations and there, face to face, I will execute judgment upon you. ³⁶As I judged your ancestors in the wilderness of the land of Egypt, so I will judge you, declares the Sovereign LORD. ³⁷I

---

[a] 29 *Bamah* means *high place.*

will take note of you as you pass under my rod, and I will bring you into the bond of the covenant. [38]I will purge you of those who revolt and rebel against me. Although I will bring them out of the land where they are living, yet they will not enter the land of Israel. Then you will know that I am the LORD.

[39]"'As for you, people of Israel, this is what the Sovereign LORD says: Go and serve your idols, every one of you! But afterward you will surely listen to me and no longer profane my holy name with your gifts and idols. [40]For on my holy mountain, the high mountain of Israel, declares the Sovereign LORD, there in the land all the people of Israel will serve me, and there I will accept them. There I will require your offerings and your choice gifts,[a] along with all your holy sacrifices. [41]I will accept you as fragrant incense when I bring you out from the nations and gather you from the countries where you have been scattered, and I will be proved holy through you in the sight of the nations. [42]Then you will know that I am the LORD, when I bring you into the land of Israel, the land I had sworn with uplifted hand to give to your ancestors. [43]There you will remember your conduct and all the actions by which you have defiled yourselves, and you will loathe yourselves for all the evil you have done. [44]You will know that I am the LORD, when I deal with you for my name's sake and not according to your evil ways and your corrupt practices, you people of Israel, declares the Sovereign LORD.'"

Prophecy Against the South

[45]The word of the LORD came to me: [46]"Son of man, set your face toward the south; preach against the south and prophesy against the forest of the southland. [47]Say to the southern forest: 'Hear the word of the LORD. This is what the Sovereign LORD says: I am about to set fire to you, and it will consume all your trees, both green and dry. The blazing flame will not be quenched, and every face from south to north will be scorched by it. [48]Everyone will see that I the LORD have kindled it; it will not be quenched.'"

[49]Then I said, "Sovereign LORD, they are saying of me, 'Isn't he just telling parables?'"[b]

Babylon as God's Sword of Judgment

21[c] The word of the LORD came to me: [2]"Son of man, set your face against Jerusalem and preach against the sanctuary. Prophesy against the land of Israel [3]and say to her: 'This is what the LORD says: I am against you. I will draw my sword from its sheath and cut off from you both the righteous and the wicked. [4]Because I am going to cut off the righteous and the wicked, my sword will be unsheathed against everyone from south to north. [5]Then all people will know that I the LORD have drawn my sword from its sheath; it will not return again.'

[6]"Therefore groan, son of man! Groan before them with broken heart and bitter grief. [7]And when they ask you, 'Why are you groaning?' you shall say, 'Because of the news that is coming. Every heart will melt with fear and every hand go limp; every spirit will become faint and every leg will be wet with urine.' It is coming! It will surely take place, declares the Sovereign LORD."

[8]The word of the LORD came to me: [9]"Son of man, prophesy and say, 'This is what the Lord says:

"'A sword, a sword,
    sharpened and polished—
[10]sharpened for the slaughter,
    polished to flash like lightning!

"'Shall we rejoice in the scepter of my royal son? The sword despises every such stick.

[11]"'The sword is appointed to be polished,
    to be grasped with the hand;
it is sharpened and polished,
    made ready for the hand of the slayer.
[12]Cry out and wail, son of man,
    for it is against my people;
    it is against all the princes of Israel.
They are thrown to the sword
    along with my people.
Therefore beat your breast.

[13]"'Testing will surely come. And what if even the scepter, which the sword despises, does not continue? declares the Sovereign LORD.'

[14]"So then, son of man, prophesy
    and strike your hands together.
Let the sword strike twice,
    even three times.
It is a sword for slaughter—
    a sword for great slaughter,
    closing in on them from every side.
[15]So that hearts may melt with fear
    and the fallen be many,
I have stationed the sword for slaughter[d]
    at all their gates.

---

[a] 40 Or *and the gifts of your firstfruits*   [b] 49 In Hebrew texts 20:45-49 is numbered 21:1-5.   [c] In Hebrew texts 21:1-32 is numbered 21:6-37.   [d] 15 Septuagint; the meaning of the Hebrew for this word is uncertain.

Look! It is forged to strike like lightning,
    it is grasped for slaughter.
[16] Slash to the right, you sword,
    then to the left,
    wherever your blade is turned.
[17] I too will strike my hands together,
    and my wrath will subside.
I the LORD have spoken."

[18] The word of the LORD came to me: [19] "Son of man, mark out two roads for the sword of the king of Babylon to take, both starting from the same country. Make a signpost where the road branches off to the city. [20] Mark out one road for the sword to come against Rabbah of the Ammonites and another against Judah and fortified Jerusalem. [21] For the king of Babylon will stop at the fork in the road, at the junction of the two roads, to seek an omen: He will cast lots with arrows, he will consult his idols, he will examine the liver. [22] Into his right hand will come the lot for Jerusalem, where he is to set up battering rams, to give the command to slaughter, to sound the battle cry, to set battering rams against the gates, to build a ramp and to erect siege works. [23] It will seem like a false omen to those who have sworn allegiance to him, but he will remind them of their guilt and take them captive.

[24] "Therefore this is what the Sovereign LORD says: 'Because you people have brought to mind your guilt by your open rebellion, revealing your sins in all that you do — because you have done this, you will be taken captive.

[25] "'You profane and wicked prince of Israel, whose day has come, whose time of punishment has reached its climax, [26] this is what the Sovereign LORD says: Take off the turban, remove the crown. It will not be as it was: The lowly will be exalted and the exalted will be brought low. [27] A ruin! A ruin! I will make it a ruin! The crown will not be restored until he to whom it rightfully belongs shall come; to him I will give it.'

[28] "And you, son of man, prophesy and say, 'This is what the Sovereign LORD says about the Ammonites and their insults:

"'A sword, a sword,
    drawn for the slaughter,
polished to consume
    and to flash like lightning!
[29] Despite false visions concerning you
    and lying divinations about you,
it will be laid on the necks
    of the wicked who are to be slain,

whose day has come,
    whose time of punishment has reached its
    climax.
[30] "'Let the sword return to its sheath.
    In the place where you were created,
in the land of your ancestry,
    I will judge you.
[31] I will pour out my wrath on you
    and breathe out my fiery anger against
    you;
I will deliver you into the hands of brutal
    men,
    men skilled in destruction.
[32] You will be fuel for the fire,
    your blood will be shed in your land,
you will be remembered no more;
    for I the LORD have spoken.'"

Judgment on Jerusalem's Sins

22 The word of the LORD came to me:

[2] "Son of man, will you judge her? Will you judge this city of bloodshed? Then confront her with all her detestable practices [3] and say: 'This is what the Sovereign LORD says: You city that brings on herself doom by shedding blood in her midst and defiles herself by making idols, [4] you have become guilty because of the blood you have shed and have become defiled by the idols you have made. You have brought your days to a close, and the end of your years has come. Therefore I will make you an object of scorn to the nations and a laughingstock to all the countries. [5] Those who are near and those who are far away will mock you, you infamous city, full of turmoil.

[6] "'See how each of the princes of Israel who are in you uses his power to shed blood. [7] In you they have treated father and mother with contempt; in you they have oppressed the foreigner and mistreated the fatherless and the widow. [8] You have despised my holy things and desecrated my Sabbaths. [9] In you are slanderers who are bent on shedding blood; in you are those who eat at the mountain shrines and commit lewd acts. [10] In you are those who dishonor their father's bed; in you are those who violate women during their period, when they are ceremonially unclean. [11] In you one man commits a detestable offense with his neighbor's wife, another shamefully defiles his daughter-in-law, and another violates his sister, his own father's daughter. [12] In you are people who accept bribes to shed blood; you take interest and make a profit from the poor. You extort unjust gain from your neigh-

bors. And you have forgotten me, declares the Sovereign LORD.

13"'I will surely strike my hands together at the unjust gain you have made and at the blood you have shed in your midst. 14Will your courage endure or your hands be strong in the day I deal with you? I the LORD have spoken, and I will do it. 15I will disperse you among the nations and scatter you through the countries; and I will put an end to your uncleanness. 16When you have been defiled[a] in the eyes of the nations, you will know that I am the LORD.'"

17Then the word of the LORD came to me: 18"Son of man, the people of Israel have become dross to me; all of them are the copper, tin, iron and lead left inside a furnace. They are but the dross of silver. 19Therefore this is what the Sovereign LORD says: 'Because you have all become dross, I will gather you into Jerusalem. 20As silver, copper, iron, lead and tin are gathered into a furnace to be melted with a fiery blast, so will I gather you in my anger and my wrath and put you inside the city and melt you. 21I will gather you and I will blow on you with my fiery wrath, and you will be melted inside her. 22As silver is melted in a furnace, so you will be melted inside her, and you will know that I the LORD have poured out my wrath on you.'"

23Again the word of the LORD came to me: 24"Son of man, say to the land, 'You are a land that has not been cleansed or rained on in the day of wrath.' 25There is a conspiracy of her princes[b] within her like a roaring lion tearing its prey; they devour people, take treasures and precious things and make many widows within her. 26Her priests do violence to my law and profane my holy things; they do not distinguish between the holy and the common; they teach that there is no difference between the unclean and the clean; and they shut their eyes to the keeping of my Sabbaths, so that I am profaned among them. 27Her officials within her are like wolves tearing their prey; they shed blood and kill people to make unjust gain. 28Her prophets whitewash these deeds for them by false visions and lying divinations. They say, 'This is what the Sovereign LORD says' — when the LORD has not spoken. 29The people of the land practice extortion and commit robbery; they oppress the poor and needy and mistreat the foreigner, denying them justice.

30"I looked for someone among them who would build up the wall and stand before me in

---

[a] 16 Or *When I have allotted you your inheritance*
[b] 25 Septuagint; Hebrew *prophets*

The Position of a Leader: Standing in the Gap

Ezekiel 22:24–31

God contrasts the poor leader with the godly leader in Ezekiel 22. The poor leader oppresses and destroys his or her followers, while the godly leader "stands in the gap" on behalf of the land and the people (v. 30). These leaders represent God to the people, and represent the people to God. They serve as "middlemen," serving God and serving the needs of the people. This text describes ten traits of the leader God affirms:

1. **Consecration: They set themselves apart and remain committed to their call.**
2. **Discipline: They do what is right even when it is difficult.**
3. **Servanthood: They model a selfless life, lived for the benefit of others.**
4. **Vision: They see what God sees and live off the power of potential.**
5. **Compassion: Love for their cause and their people moves them to action.**
6. **Trustworthiness: They keep their word regardless of what others do.**
7. **Decisiveness: They make good decisions in a timely manner.**
8. **Wisdom: They think like God thinks and avoid impetuous moves.**
9. **Courage: They take risks for what is right.**
10. **Passion: They demonstrate enthusiasm for their divine calling.**

What Does God Look for in a Leader?

Ezekiel 22:30

This single verse contains a good description of the kind of leader God looks for. Take a look at what God was seeking in Ezekiel's day:

1. **A man:** God wasn't looking for a large committee, but a single person.

2. **Among them:** This person would relate best to people within his own culture.

3. **A builder of walls:** He must be constructive and hard working.

4. **Stand in the gap:** He must bridge the gap between people and God.

5. **On behalf of the land:** He carries a burden and vision for where he lives.

the gap on behalf of the land so I would not have to destroy it, but I found no one. ³¹So I will pour out my wrath on them and consume them with my fiery anger, bringing down on their own heads all they have done, declares the Sovereign LORD."

Two Adulterous Sisters

23 The word of the LORD came to me: ²"Son of man, there were two women, daughters of the same mother. ³They became prostitutes in Egypt, engaging in prostitution from their youth. In that land their breasts were fondled and their virgin bosoms caressed. ⁴The older was named Oholah, and her sister was Oholibah. They were mine and gave birth to sons and daughters. Oholah is Samaria, and Oholibah is Jerusalem.

⁵"Oholah engaged in prostitution while she was still mine; and she lusted after her lovers, the Assyrians — warriors ⁶clothed in blue, governors and commanders, all of them handsome young men, and mounted horsemen. ⁷She gave herself as a prostitute to all the elite of the Assyrians and defiled herself with all the idols of everyone she lusted after. ⁸She did not give up the prostitution she began in Egypt, when during her youth men slept with her, caressed her virgin bosom and poured out their lust on her.

⁹"Therefore I delivered her into the hands of her lovers, the Assyrians, for whom she lusted. ¹⁰They stripped her naked, took away her sons and daughters and killed her with the sword. She became a byword among women, and punishment was inflicted on her.

¹¹"Her sister Oholibah saw this, yet in her lust and prostitution she was more depraved than her sister. ¹²She too lusted after the Assyrians — governors and commanders, warriors in full

dress, mounted horsemen, all handsome young men. ¹³I saw that she too defiled herself; both of them went the same way.

¹⁴"But she carried her prostitution still further. She saw men portrayed on a wall, figures of Chaldeans[a] portrayed in red, ¹⁵with belts around their waists and flowing turbans on their heads; all of them looked like Babylonian chariot officers, natives of Chaldea.[b] ¹⁶As soon as she saw them, she lusted after them and sent messengers to them in Chaldea. ¹⁷Then the Babylonians came to her, to the bed of love, and in their lust they defiled her. After she had been defiled by them, she turned away from them in disgust. ¹⁸When she carried on her prostitution openly and exposed her naked body, I turned away from her in disgust, just as I had turned away from her sister. ¹⁹Yet she became more and more promiscuous as she recalled the days of her youth, when she was a prostitute in Egypt. ²⁰There she lusted after her lovers, whose genitals were like those of donkeys and whose emission was like that of horses. ²¹So you longed for the lewdness of your youth, when in Egypt your bosom was caressed and your young breasts fondled.[c]

²²"Therefore, Oholibah, this is what the Sovereign LORD says: I will stir up your lovers against you, those you turned away from in disgust, and I will bring them against you from every side — ²³the Babylonians and all the Chaldeans, the men of Pekod and Shoa and Koa, and all the Assyrians with them, handsome young men, all of them governors and commanders, chariot officers and men of high rank, all mounted on

---

a 14 Or *Babylonians*   *b 15* Or *Babylonia*; also in verse 16
c 21 Syriac (see also verse 3); Hebrew *caressed because of your young breasts*

horses. [24]They will come against you with weapons,[a] chariots and wagons and with a throng of people; they will take up positions against you on every side with large and small shields and with helmets. I will turn you over to them for punishment, and they will punish you according to their standards. [25]I will direct my jealous anger against you, and they will deal with you in fury. They will cut off your noses and your ears, and those of you who are left will fall by the sword. They will take away your sons and daughters, and those of you who are left will be consumed by fire. [26]They will also strip you of your clothes and take your fine jewelry. [27]So I will put a stop to the lewdness and prostitution you began in Egypt. You will not look on these things with longing or remember Egypt anymore.

[28]"For this is what the Sovereign Lord says: I am about to deliver you into the hands of those you hate, to those you turned away from in disgust. [29]They will deal with you in hatred and take away everything you have worked for. They will leave you stark naked, and the shame of your prostitution will be exposed. Your lewdness and promiscuity [30]have brought this on you, because you lusted after the nations and defiled yourself with their idols. [31]You have gone the way of your sister; so I will put her cup into your hand.

[32]"This is what the Sovereign Lord says:

"You will drink your sister's cup,
    a cup large and deep;
it will bring scorn and derision,
    for it holds so much.
[33]You will be filled with drunkenness and sorrow,
    the cup of ruin and desolation,
    the cup of your sister Samaria.
[34]You will drink it and drain it dry
    and chew on its pieces—
    and you will tear your breasts.

I have spoken, declares the Sovereign Lord.

[35]"Therefore this is what the Sovereign Lord says: Since you have forgotten me and turned your back on me, you must bear the consequences of your lewdness and prostitution."

[36]The Lord said to me: "Son of man, will you judge Oholah and Oholibah? Then confront them with their detestable practices, [37]for they have committed adultery and blood is on their hands. They committed adultery with their idols; they even sacrificed their children, whom they bore to me, as food for them. [38]They have also done this to me: At that same time they defiled my sanctuary and desecrated my Sabbaths. [39]On the very day they sacrificed their children to their idols, they entered my sanctuary and desecrated it. That is what they did in my house.

[40]"They even sent messengers for men who came from far away, and when they arrived you bathed yourself for them, applied eye makeup and put on your jewelry. [41]You sat on an elegant

---

[a] 24 The meaning of the Hebrew for this word is uncertain.

Confrontation: It Comes with the Territory

Ezekiel 23:36–39

God told Ezekiel to confront his people using colorful and striking imagery. "Oholah" and "Oholibah" are symbolic names for sinful Israel and Judah. God describes the sins they have committed and demands that Ezekiel confront the people with their rebellion.

At times a leader must confront sinful or destructive behavior in the ranks. No healthy leader enjoys confrontation, but no healthy leader avoids it, either. What can we learn from God and Ezekiel about confrontation?

1. *Be compassionate.* Ezekiel hurt as he recalled the sins of Israel.

2. *Be forthright.* Ezekiel spoke honestly and directly to the issues.

3. *Be specific.* Ezekiel didn't drop hints, but gave specifics about the problem.

4. *Be clear.* Ezekiel spoke simply about the consequences of such behavior.

5. *Be redemptive.* Ezekiel communicated for the purpose of restoring the people.

6. *Be hopeful.* Ezekiel ended with words of hope for the future.

couch, with a table spread before it on which you had placed the incense and olive oil that belonged to me.

⁴²"The noise of a carefree crowd was around her; drunkards were brought from the desert along with men from the rabble, and they put bracelets on the wrists of the woman and her sister and beautiful crowns on their heads. ⁴³Then I said about the one worn out by adultery, 'Now let them use her as a prostitute, for that is all she is.' ⁴⁴And they slept with her. As men sleep with a prostitute, so they slept with those lewd women, Oholah and Oholibah. ⁴⁵But righteous judges will sentence them to the punishment of women who commit adultery and shed blood, because they are adulterous and blood is on their hands.

⁴⁶"This is what the Sovereign LORD says: Bring a mob against them and give them over to terror and plunder. ⁴⁷The mob will stone them and cut them down with their swords; they will kill their sons and daughters and burn down their houses.

⁴⁸"So I will put an end to lewdness in the land, that all women may take warning and not imitate you. ⁴⁹You will suffer the penalty for your lewdness and bear the consequences of your sins of idolatry. Then you will know that I am the Sovereign LORD."

Jerusalem as a Cooking Pot

24 In the ninth year, in the tenth month on the tenth day, the word of the LORD came to me: ²"Son of man, record this date, this very date, because the king of Babylon has laid siege to Jerusalem this very day. ³Tell this rebellious people a parable and say to them: 'This is what the Sovereign LORD says:

"'Put on the cooking pot; put it on
   and pour water into it.
⁴Put into it the pieces of meat,
   all the choice pieces — the leg and the
      shoulder.
Fill it with the best of these bones;
⁵   take the pick of the flock.
Pile wood beneath it for the bones;
   bring it to a boil
and cook the bones in it.

⁶"'For this is what the Sovereign LORD says:

"'Woe to the city of bloodshed,
   to the pot now encrusted,
   whose deposit will not go away!
Take the meat out piece by piece
   in whatever order it comes.

⁷"'For the blood she shed is in her midst:
   She poured it on the bare rock;
she did not pour it on the ground,
   where the dust would cover it.
⁸To stir up wrath and take revenge
   I put her blood on the bare rock,
   so that it would not be covered.

⁹"'Therefore this is what the Sovereign LORD says:

"'Woe to the city of bloodshed!
   I, too, will pile the wood high.
¹⁰So heap on the wood
   and kindle the fire.
Cook the meat well,
   mixing in the spices;
   and let the bones be charred.
¹¹Then set the empty pot on the coals
   till it becomes hot and its copper glows,
so that its impurities may be melted
   and its deposit burned away.
¹²It has frustrated all efforts;
   its heavy deposit has not been removed,
   not even by fire.

¹³"'Now your impurity is lewdness. Because I tried to cleanse you but you would not be cleansed from your impurity, you will not be clean again until my wrath against you has subsided.

¹⁴"'I the LORD have spoken. The time has come for me to act. I will not hold back; I will not have pity, nor will I relent. You will be judged according to your conduct and your actions, declares the Sovereign LORD.'"

Ezekiel's Wife Dies

¹⁵The word of the LORD came to me: ¹⁶"Son of man, with one blow I am about to take away from you the delight of your eyes. Yet do not lament or weep or shed any tears. ¹⁷Groan quietly; do not mourn for the dead. Keep your turban fastened and your sandals on your feet; do not cover your mustache and beard or eat the customary food of mourners."

¹⁸So I spoke to the people in the morning, and in the evening my wife died. The next morning I did as I had been commanded.

¹⁹Then the people asked me, "Won't you tell us what these things have to do with us? Why are you acting like this?"

²⁰So I said to them, "The word of the LORD came to me: ²¹Say to the people of Israel, 'This is what the Sovereign LORD says: I am about to desecrate my sanctuary — the stronghold in which

you take pride, the delight of your eyes, the object of your affection. The sons and daughters you left behind will fall by the sword. [22]And you will do as I have done. You will not cover your mustache and beard or eat the customary food of mourners. [23]You will keep your turbans on your heads and your sandals on your feet. You will not mourn or weep but will waste away because of[a] your sins and groan among yourselves. [24]Ezekiel will be a sign to you; you will do just as he has done. When this happens, you will know that I am the Sovereign Lord.'

[25]"And you, son of man, on the day I take away their stronghold, their joy and glory, the delight of their eyes, their heart's desire, and their sons and daughters as well — [26]on that day a fugitive will come to tell you the news. [27]At that time your mouth will be opened; you will speak with him and will no longer be silent. So you will be a sign to them, and they will know that I am the Lord."

A Prophecy Against Ammon

25 The word of the Lord came to me: [2]"Son of man, set your face against the Ammonites and prophesy against them. [3]Say to them, 'Hear the word of the Sovereign Lord. This is what the Sovereign Lord says: Because you said "Aha!" over my sanctuary when it was desecrated and over the land of Israel when it was laid waste and over the people of Judah when they went into exile, [4]therefore I am going to give you to the people of the East as a possession. They will set up their camps and pitch their tents among you; they will eat your fruit and drink your milk. [5]I will turn Rabbah into a pasture for camels and Ammon into a resting place for sheep. Then you will know that I am the Lord. [6]For this is what the Sovereign Lord says: Because you have clapped your hands and stamped your feet, rejoicing with all the malice of your heart against the land of Israel, [7]therefore I will stretch out my hand against you and give you as plunder to the nations. I will wipe you out from among the nations and exterminate you from the countries. I will destroy you, and you will know that I am the Lord.'"

A Prophecy Against Moab

[8]"This is what the Sovereign Lord says: 'Because Moab and Seir said, "Look, Judah has become like all the other nations," [9]therefore I will expose the flank of Moab, beginning at its frontier towns — Beth Jeshimoth, Baal Meon and Kiriathaim — the glory of that land. [10]I will give

Moab along with the Ammonites to the people of the East as a possession, so that the Ammonites will not be remembered among the nations; [11]and I will inflict punishment on Moab. Then they will know that I am the Lord.'"

A Prophecy Against Edom

[12]"This is what the Sovereign Lord says: 'Because Edom took revenge on Judah and became very guilty by doing so, [13]therefore this is what the Sovereign Lord says: I will stretch out my hand against Edom and kill both man and beast. I will lay it waste, and from Teman to Dedan they will fall by the sword. [14]I will take vengeance on Edom by the hand of my people Israel, and they will deal with Edom in accordance with my anger and my wrath; they will know my vengeance, declares the Sovereign Lord.'"

A Prophecy Against Philistia

[15]"This is what the Sovereign Lord says: 'Because the Philistines acted in vengeance and took revenge with malice in their hearts, and with ancient hostility sought to destroy Judah, [16]therefore this is what the Sovereign Lord says: I am about to stretch out my hand against the Philistines, and I will wipe out the Kerethites and destroy those remaining along the coast. [17]I will carry out great vengeance on them and punish them in my wrath. Then they will know that I am the Lord, when I take vengeance on them.'"

A Prophecy Against Tyre

26 In the eleventh month of the twelfth[b] year, on the first day of the month, the word of the Lord came to me: [2]"Son of man, because Tyre has said of Jerusalem, 'Aha! The gate to the nations is broken, and its doors have swung open to me; now that she lies in ruins I will prosper,' [3]therefore this is what the Sovereign Lord says: I am against you, Tyre, and I will bring many nations against you, like the sea casting up its waves. [4]They will destroy the walls of Tyre and pull down her towers; I will scrape away her rubble and make her a bare rock. [5]Out in the sea she will become a place to spread fishnets, for I have spoken, declares the Sovereign Lord. She will become plunder for the nations, [6]and her settlements on the mainland will be ravaged by the sword. Then they will know that I am the Lord.

[a] 23 Or away in   [b] 1 Probable reading of the original Hebrew text; Masoretic Text does not have month of the twelfth.

[7]"For this is what the Sovereign LORD says: From the north I am going to bring against Tyre Nebuchadnezzar[a] king of Babylon, king of kings, with horses and chariots, with horsemen and a great army. [8]He will ravage your settlements on the mainland with the sword; he will set up siege works against you, build a ramp up to your walls and raise his shields against you. [9]He will direct the blows of his battering rams against your walls and demolish your towers with his weapons. [10]His horses will be so many that they will cover you with dust. Your walls will tremble at the noise of the warhorses, wagons and chariots when he enters your gates as men enter a city whose walls have been broken through. [11]The hooves of his horses will trample all your streets; he will kill your people with the sword, and your strong pillars will fall to the ground. [12]They will plunder your wealth and loot your merchandise; they will break down your walls and demolish your fine houses and throw your stones, timber and rubble into the sea. [13]I will put an end to your noisy songs, and the music of your harps will be heard no more. [14]I will make you a bare rock, and you will become a place to spread fishnets. You will never be rebuilt, for I the LORD have spoken, declares the Sovereign LORD.

[15]"This is what the Sovereign LORD says to Tyre: Will not the coastlands tremble at the sound of your fall, when the wounded groan and the slaughter takes place in you? [16]Then all the princes of the coast will step down from their thrones and lay aside their robes and take off their embroidered garments. Clothed with terror, they will sit on the ground, trembling every moment, appalled at you. [17]Then they will take up a lament concerning you and say to you:

> "'How you are destroyed, city of renown,
>   peopled by men of the sea!
> You were a power on the seas,
>   you and your citizens;
> you put your terror
>   on all who lived there.
> [18]Now the coastlands tremble
>   on the day of your fall;
> the islands in the sea
>   are terrified at your collapse.'

[19]"This is what the Sovereign LORD says: When I make you a desolate city, like cities no longer inhabited, and when I bring the ocean depths over you and its vast waters cover you, [20]then I will bring you down with those who go down to the pit, to the people of long ago. I will make you dwell in the earth below, as in ancient ruins, with those who go down to the pit, and you will not return or take your place[b] in the land of the living. [21]I will bring you to a horrible end and you will be no more. You will be sought, but you will never again be found, declares the Sovereign LORD."

A Lament Over Tyre

27 The word of the LORD came to me: [2]"Son of man, take up a lament concerning Tyre. [3]Say to Tyre, situated at the gateway to the sea, merchant of peoples on many coasts, 'This is what the Sovereign LORD says:

> "'You say, Tyre,
>   "I am perfect in beauty."
> [4]Your domain was on the high seas;
>   your builders brought your beauty to
>   perfection.
> [5]They made all your timbers
>   of juniper from Senir[c];
> they took a cedar from Lebanon
>   to make a mast for you.
> [6]Of oaks from Bashan
>   they made your oars;
> of cypress wood[d] from the coasts of Cyprus
>   they made your deck, adorned with ivory.
> [7]Fine embroidered linen from Egypt was your
>   sail
>   and served as your banner;
> your awnings were of blue and purple
>   from the coasts of Elishah.
> [8]Men of Sidon and Arvad were your oarsmen;
>   your skilled men, Tyre, were aboard as
>   your sailors.
> [9]Veteran craftsmen of Byblos were on board
>   as shipwrights to caulk your seams.
> All the ships of the sea and their sailors
>   came alongside to trade for your wares.

> [10]"'Men of Persia, Lydia and Put
>   served as soldiers in your army.
> They hung their shields and helmets on your
>   walls,
>   bringing you splendor.
> [11]Men of Arvad and Helek
>   guarded your walls on every side;
> men of Gammad
>   were in your towers.
> They hung their shields around your walls;
>   they brought your beauty to perfection.

---

[a] 7 Hebrew *Nebuchadrezzar*, of which *Nebuchadnezzar* is a variant; here and often in Ezekiel and Jeremiah
[b] 20 Septuagint; Hebrew *return, and I will give glory*
[c] 5 That is, Mount Hermon   [d] 6 Targum; the Masoretic Text has a different division of the consonants.

¹²"'Tarshish did business with you because of your great wealth of goods; they exchanged silver, iron, tin and lead for your merchandise.

¹³"'Greece, Tubal and Meshek did business with you; they traded human beings and articles of bronze for your wares.

¹⁴"'Men of Beth Togarmah exchanged chariot horses, cavalry horses and mules for your merchandise.

¹⁵"'The men of Rhodes[a] traded with you, and many coastlands were your customers; they paid you with ivory tusks and ebony.

¹⁶"'Aram[b] did business with you because of your many products; they exchanged turquoise, purple fabric, embroidered work, fine linen, coral and rubies for your merchandise.

¹⁷"'Judah and Israel traded with you; they exchanged wheat from Minnith and confections,[c] honey, olive oil and balm for your wares.

¹⁸"'Damascus did business with you because of your many products and great wealth of goods. They offered wine from Helbon, wool from Zahar ¹⁹and casks of wine from Izal in exchange for your wares: wrought iron, cassia and calamus.

²⁰"'Dedan traded in saddle blankets with you.

²¹"'Arabia and all the princes of Kedar were your customers; they did business with you in lambs, rams and goats.

²²"'The merchants of Sheba and Raamah traded with you; for your merchandise they exchanged the finest of all kinds of spices and precious stones, and gold.

²³"'Harran, Kanneh and Eden and merchants of Sheba, Ashur and Kilmad traded with you. ²⁴In your marketplace they traded with you beautiful garments, blue fabric, embroidered work and multicolored rugs with cords twisted and tightly knotted.

²⁵"'The ships of Tarshish serve
    as carriers for your wares.
You are filled with heavy cargo
    as you sail the sea.
²⁶Your oarsmen take you
    out to the high seas.
But the east wind will break you to pieces
    far out at sea.
²⁷Your wealth, merchandise and wares,
    your mariners, sailors and shipwrights,
your merchants and all your soldiers,
    and everyone else on board
will sink into the heart of the sea
    on the day of your shipwreck.

²⁸The shorelands will quake
    when your sailors cry out.
²⁹All who handle the oars
    will abandon their ships;
the mariners and all the sailors
    will stand on the shore.
³⁰They will raise their voice
    and cry bitterly over you;
they will sprinkle dust on their heads
    and roll in ashes.
³¹They will shave their heads because of you
    and will put on sackcloth.
They will weep over you with anguish of
        soul
    and with bitter mourning.
³²As they wail and mourn over you,
    they will take up a lament concerning you:
"Who was ever silenced like Tyre,
    surrounded by the sea?"
³³When your merchandise went out on the seas,
    you satisfied many nations;
with your great wealth and your wares
    you enriched the kings of the earth.
³⁴Now you are shattered by the sea
    in the depths of the waters;
your wares and all your company
    have gone down with you.
³⁵All who live in the coastlands
    are appalled at you;
their kings shudder with horror
    and their faces are distorted with fear.
³⁶The merchants among the nations scoff at
        you;
    you have come to a horrible end
    and will be no more.'"

A Prophecy Against the King of Tyre

28 The word of the LORD came to me: ²"Son of man, say to the ruler of Tyre, 'This is what the Sovereign LORD says:

"'In the pride of your heart
    you say, "I am a god;
I sit on the throne of a god
    in the heart of the seas."
But you are a mere mortal and not a god,
    though you think you are as wise as a god.
³Are you wiser than Daniel[d]?
    Is no secret hidden from you?
⁴By your wisdom and understanding
    you have gained wealth for yourself

---

[a] 15 Septuagint; Hebrew *Dedan*   [b] 16 Most Hebrew manuscripts; some Hebrew manuscripts and Syriac *Edom*
[c] 17 The meaning of the Hebrew for this word is uncertain.
[d] 3 Or *Danel*, a man of renown in ancient literature

and amassed gold and silver
    in your treasuries.
[5] By your great skill in trading
    you have increased your wealth,
and because of your wealth
    your heart has grown proud.

[6] "'Therefore this is what the Sovereign LORD
says:

    "'Because you think you are wise,
        as wise as a god,
[7] I am going to bring foreigners against you,
        the most ruthless of nations;
they will draw their swords against your
        beauty and wisdom
    and pierce your shining splendor.
[8] They will bring you down to the pit,
    and you will die a violent death
    in the heart of the seas.
[9] Will you then say, "I am a god,"
    in the presence of those who kill you?
You will be but a mortal, not a god,
    in the hands of those who slay you.
[10] You will die the death of the uncircumcised
    at the hands of foreigners.

I have spoken, declares the Sovereign LORD.'"

[11] The word of the LORD came to me: [12] "Son
of man, take up a lament concerning the king of
Tyre and say to him: 'This is what the Sovereign
LORD says:

    "'You were the seal of perfection,
        full of wisdom and perfect in beauty.
[13] You were in Eden,
        the garden of God;

every precious stone adorned you:
    carnelian, chrysolite and emerald,
    topaz, onyx and jasper,
    lapis lazuli, turquoise and beryl.[a]
Your settings and mountings[b] were made of
        gold;
    on the day you were created they were
        prepared.
[14] You were anointed as a guardian cherub,
    for so I ordained you.
You were on the holy mount of God;
    you walked among the fiery stones.
[15] You were blameless in your ways
    from the day you were created
    till wickedness was found in you.
[16] Through your widespread trade
    you were filled with violence,
    and you sinned.
So I drove you in disgrace from the mount of
        God,
    and I expelled you, guardian cherub,
    from among the fiery stones.
[17] Your heart became proud
    on account of your beauty,
and you corrupted your wisdom
    because of your splendor.
So I threw you to the earth;
    I made a spectacle of you before kings.
[18] By your many sins and dishonest trade
    you have desecrated your sanctuaries.
So I made a fire come out from you,
    and it consumed you,

---

[a] 13 The precise identification of some of these precious stones
is uncertain.   [b] 13 The meaning of the Hebrew for this
phrase is uncertain.

Ezekiel Speaks with Courage

Ezekiel 28:1–19

Ezekiel could speak hard truth to the king of Tyre because God had deposited in him a . . .

1. **Dream:** He saw what God saw—a preferred future with just leaders.

2. **Desire:** He had a desire to see change and to be part of the solution.

3. **Decisiveness:** He recognized what needed to be done and he chose to step in.

4. **Daring:** His courage to act outweighed his fear of the king.

5. **Dedication:** He remained committed to fulfilling his call, whatever the cost.

6. **Direction:** He had a clear plan for change.

7. **Dependence on God:** He relied on God to do what only he could do.

and I reduced you to ashes on the ground
　in the sight of all who were watching.
[19] All the nations who knew you
　are appalled at you;
you have come to a horrible end
　and will be no more.'"

A Prophecy Against Sidon

[20] The word of the LORD came to me: [21] "Son of man, set your face against Sidon; prophesy against her [22] and say: 'This is what the Sovereign LORD says:

"'I am against you, Sidon,
　and among you I will display my glory.
You will know that I am the LORD,
　when I inflict punishment on you
　and within you am proved to be holy.
[23] I will send a plague upon you
　and make blood flow in your streets.
The slain will fall within you,
　with the sword against you on every side.
Then you will know that I am the LORD.

[24] "'No longer will the people of Israel have malicious neighbors who are painful briers and sharp thorns. Then they will know that I am the Sovereign LORD.

[25] "'This is what the Sovereign LORD says: When I gather the people of Israel from the nations where they have been scattered, I will be proved holy through them in the sight of the nations. Then they will live in their own land, which I gave to my servant Jacob. [26] They will live there in safety and will build houses and plant vineyards; they will live in safety when I inflict punishment on all their neighbors who maligned them. Then they will know that I am the LORD their God.'"

A Prophecy Against Egypt
Judgment on Pharaoh

29 In the tenth year, in the tenth month on the twelfth day, the word of the LORD came to me: [2] "Son of man, set your face against Pharaoh king of Egypt and prophesy against him and against all Egypt. [3] Speak to him and say: 'This is what the Sovereign LORD says:

"'I am against you, Pharaoh king of Egypt,
　you great monster lying among your streams.
You say, "The Nile belongs to me;
　I made it for myself."
[4] But I will put hooks in your jaws
　and make the fish of your streams stick to
　　your scales.

I will pull you out from among your streams,
　with all the fish sticking to your scales.
[5] I will leave you in the desert,
　you and all the fish of your streams.
You will fall on the open field
　and not be gathered or picked up.
I will give you as food
　to the beasts of the earth and the birds of
　　the sky.

[6] Then all who live in Egypt will know that I am the LORD.

"'You have been a staff of reed for the people of Israel. [7] When they grasped you with their hands, you splintered and you tore open their shoulders; when they leaned on you, you broke and their backs were wrenched.[a]

[8] "'Therefore this is what the Sovereign LORD says: I will bring a sword against you and kill both man and beast. [9] Egypt will become a desolate wasteland. Then they will know that I am the LORD.

"'Because you said, "The Nile is mine; I made it," [10] therefore I am against you and against your streams, and I will make the land of Egypt a ruin and a desolate waste from Migdol to Aswan, as far as the border of Cush.[b] [11] The foot of neither man nor beast will pass through it; no one will live there for forty years. [12] I will make the land of Egypt desolate among devastated lands, and her cities will lie desolate forty years among ruined cities. And I will disperse the Egyptians among the nations and scatter them through the countries.

[13] "'Yet this is what the Sovereign LORD says: At the end of forty years I will gather the Egyptians from the nations where they were scattered. [14] I will bring them back from captivity and return them to Upper Egypt, the land of their ancestry. There they will be a lowly kingdom. [15] It will be the lowliest of kingdoms and will never again exalt itself above the other nations. I will make it so weak that it will never again rule over the nations. [16] Egypt will no longer be a source of confidence for the people of Israel but will be a reminder of their sin in turning to her for help. Then they will know that I am the Sovereign LORD.'"

Nebuchadnezzar's Reward

[17] In the twenty-seventh year, in the first month on the first day, the word of the LORD

---

[a] 7 Syriac (see also Septuagint and Vulgate); Hebrew *and you caused their backs to stand*　　[b] 10 That is, the upper Nile region

came to me: [18]"Son of man, Nebuchadnezzar king of Babylon drove his army in a hard campaign against Tyre; every head was rubbed bare and every shoulder made raw. Yet he and his army got no reward from the campaign he led against Tyre. [19]Therefore this is what the Sovereign LORD says: I am going to give Egypt to Nebuchadnezzar king of Babylon, and he will carry off its wealth. He will loot and plunder the land as pay for his army. [20]I have given him Egypt as a reward for his efforts because he and his army did it for me, declares the Sovereign LORD. [21]"On that day I will make a horn[a] grow for the Israelites, and I will open your mouth among them. Then they will know that I am the LORD."

A Lament Over Egypt

30 The word of the LORD came to me: [2]"Son of man, prophesy and say: 'This is what the Sovereign LORD says:

"'Wail and say,
    "Alas for that day!"
[3]For the day is near,
    the day of the LORD is near—
a day of clouds,
    a time of doom for the nations.
[4]A sword will come against Egypt,
    and anguish will come upon Cush.[b]
When the slain fall in Egypt,
    her wealth will be carried away
    and her foundations torn down.

[5]Cush and Libya, Lydia and all Arabia, Kub and the people of the covenant land will fall by the sword along with Egypt.

[6]"'This is what the LORD says:

"'The allies of Egypt will fall
    and her proud strength will fail.
From Migdol to Aswan
    they will fall by the sword within her,
        declares the Sovereign LORD.
[7]"'They will be desolate
    among desolate lands,
and their cities will lie
    among ruined cities.
[8]Then they will know that I am the LORD,
    when I set fire to Egypt
    and all her helpers are crushed.

[9]"'On that day messengers will go out from me in ships to frighten Cush out of her complacency. Anguish will take hold of them on the day of Egypt's doom, for it is sure to come.

[10]"'This is what the Sovereign LORD says:

"'I will put an end to the hordes of Egypt
    by the hand of Nebuchadnezzar king of
        Babylon.
[11]He and his army—the most ruthless of
        nations—
    will be brought in to destroy the land.
They will draw their swords against Egypt
    and fill the land with the slain.
[12]I will dry up the waters of the Nile
    and sell the land to an evil nation;
by the hand of foreigners
    I will lay waste the land and everything in
        it.

I the LORD have spoken.

[13]"'This is what the Sovereign LORD says:

"'I will destroy the idols
    and put an end to the images in Memphis.
No longer will there be a prince in Egypt,
    and I will spread fear throughout the land.
[14]I will lay waste Upper Egypt,
    set fire to Zoan
    and inflict punishment on Thebes.
[15]I will pour out my wrath on Pelusium,
    the stronghold of Egypt,
    and wipe out the hordes of Thebes.
[16]I will set fire to Egypt;
    Pelusium will writhe in agony.
Thebes will be taken by storm;
    Memphis will be in constant distress.
[17]The young men of Heliopolis and Bubastis
    will fall by the sword,
    and the cities themselves will go into
        captivity.
[18]Dark will be the day at Tahpanhes
    when I break the yoke of Egypt;
    there her proud strength will come to an
        end.
She will be covered with clouds,
    and her villages will go into captivity.
[19]So I will inflict punishment on Egypt,
    and they will know that I am the LORD.'"

Pharaoh's Arms Are Broken

[20]In the eleventh year, in the first month on the seventh day, the word of the LORD came to me: [21]"Son of man, I have broken the arm of Pharaoh king of Egypt. It has not been bound up to be healed or put in a splint so that it may become strong enough to hold a sword. [22]Therefore this is what the Sovereign LORD says: I am against Pharaoh king of Egypt. I will break both

---

[a] 21 *Horn* here symbolizes strength.   [b] 4 That is, the upper Nile region; also in verses 5 and 9

his arms, the good arm as well as the broken one, and make the sword fall from his hand. ²³I will disperse the Egyptians among the nations and scatter them through the countries. ²⁴I will strengthen the arms of the king of Babylon and put my sword in his hand, but I will break the arms of Pharaoh, and he will groan before him like a mortally wounded man. ²⁵I will strengthen the arms of the king of Babylon, but the arms of Pharaoh will fall limp. Then they will know that I am the LORD, when I put my sword into the hand of the king of Babylon and he brandishes it against Egypt. ²⁶I will disperse the Egyptians among the nations and scatter them through the countries. Then they will know that I am the LORD."

God Is the One Who Raises Up and Removes Leaders

Ezekiel 30:20-26

It is God who raises up leaders and who removes them from office; our job is to submit to his bidding. Leaders commonly misunderstand this truth. God says that whether leaders are good or evil, he ultimately is the One who puts them there—and he will remove them.

Pharaoh as a Felled Cedar of Lebanon

31 In the eleventh year, in the third month on the first day, the word of the LORD came to me: ²"Son of man, say to Pharaoh king of Egypt and to his hordes:

"'Who can be compared with you in majesty?
³ Consider Assyria, once a cedar in Lebanon,
    with beautiful branches overshadowing
        the forest;
    it towered on high,
        its top above the thick foliage.
⁴ The waters nourished it,
        deep springs made it grow tall;
    their streams flowed
        all around its base
    and sent their channels
        to all the trees of the field.
⁵ So it towered higher
        than all the trees of the field;
    its boughs increased
        and its branches grew long,
        spreading because of abundant waters.

⁶ All the birds of the sky
        nested in its boughs,
    all the animals of the wild
        gave birth under its branches;
    all the great nations
        lived in its shade.
⁷ It was majestic in beauty,
        with its spreading boughs,
    for its roots went down
        to abundant waters.
⁸ The cedars in the garden of God
        could not rival it,
    nor could the junipers
        equal its boughs,
    nor could the plane trees
        compare with its branches—
    no tree in the garden of God
        could match its beauty.
⁹ I made it beautiful
        with abundant branches,
    the envy of all the trees of Eden
        in the garden of God.

¹⁰ "'Therefore this is what the Sovereign LORD says: Because the great cedar towered over the thick foliage, and because it was proud of its height, ¹¹I gave it into the hands of the ruler of the nations, for him to deal with according to its wickedness. I cast it aside, ¹²and the most ruthless of foreign nations cut it down and left it. Its boughs fell on the mountains and in all the valleys; its branches lay broken in all the ravines of the land. All the nations of the earth came out from under its shade and left it. ¹³All the birds settled on the fallen tree, and all the wild animals lived among its branches. ¹⁴Therefore no other trees by the waters are ever to tower proudly on high, lifting their tops above the thick foliage. No other trees so well-watered are ever to reach such a height; they are all destined for death, for the earth below, among mortals who go down to the realm of the dead.

¹⁵ "'This is what the Sovereign LORD says: On the day it was brought down to the realm of the dead I covered the deep springs with mourning for it; I held back its streams, and its abundant waters were restrained. Because of it I clothed Lebanon with gloom, and all the trees of the field withered away. ¹⁶I made the nations tremble at the sound of its fall when I brought it down to the realm of the dead to be with those who go down to the pit. Then all the trees of Eden, the choicest and best of Lebanon, the well-watered trees, were consoled in the earth below. ¹⁷They too, like the great cedar, had gone down to the

realm of the dead, to those killed by the sword, along with the armed men who lived in its shade among the nations.

¹⁸"'Which of the trees of Eden can be compared with you in splendor and majesty? Yet you, too, will be brought down with the trees of Eden to the earth below; you will lie among the uncircumcised, with those killed by the sword.

"'This is Pharaoh and all his hordes, declares the Sovereign LORD.'"

A Lament Over Pharaoh

32 In the twelfth year, in the twelfth month on the first day, the word of the LORD came to me: ²"Son of man, take up a lament concerning Pharaoh king of Egypt and say to him:

"'You are like a lion among the nations;
    you are like a monster in the seas
thrashing about in your streams,
    churning the water with your feet
    and muddying the streams.

³"'This is what the Sovereign LORD says:

"'With a great throng of people
    I will cast my net over you,
    and they will haul you up in my net.
⁴I will throw you on the land
    and hurl you on the open field.
I will let all the birds of the sky settle on you
    and all the animals of the wild gorge
        themselves on you.
⁵I will spread your flesh on the mountains
    and fill the valleys with your remains.
⁶I will drench the land with your flowing
        blood
    all the way to the mountains,
    and the ravines will be filled with your
        flesh.
⁷When I snuff you out, I will cover the heavens
    and darken their stars;
I will cover the sun with a cloud,
    and the moon will not give its light.
⁸All the shining lights in the heavens
    I will darken over you;
I will bring darkness over your land,
        declares the Sovereign LORD.
⁹I will trouble the hearts of many peoples
    when I bring about your destruction
        among the nations,
    among^a lands you have not known.
¹⁰I will cause many peoples to be appalled at you,
    and their kings will shudder with horror
        because of you
    when I brandish my sword before them.

On the day of your downfall
    each of them will tremble
    every moment for his life.

¹¹"'For this is what the Sovereign LORD says:

"'The sword of the king of Babylon
    will come against you.
¹²I will cause your hordes to fall
    by the swords of mighty men—
    the most ruthless of all nations.
They will shatter the pride of Egypt,
    and all her hordes will be overthrown.
¹³I will destroy all her cattle
    from beside abundant waters
no longer to be stirred by the foot of man
    or muddied by the hooves of cattle.
¹⁴Then I will let her waters settle
    and make her streams flow like oil,
        declares the Sovereign LORD.
¹⁵When I make Egypt desolate
    and strip the land of everything in it,
when I strike down all who live there,
    then they will know that I am the LORD.'

¹⁶"This is the lament they will chant for her. The daughters of the nations will chant it; for Egypt and all her hordes they will chant it, declares the Sovereign LORD."

Egypt's Descent Into the Realm of the Dead

¹⁷In the twelfth year, on the fifteenth day of the month, the word of the LORD came to me: ¹⁸"Son of man, wail for the hordes of Egypt and consign to the earth below both her and the daughters of mighty nations, along with those who go down to the pit. ¹⁹Say to them, 'Are you more favored than others? Go down and be laid among the uncircumcised.' ²⁰They will fall among those killed by the sword. The sword is drawn; let her be dragged off with all her hordes. ²¹From within the realm of the dead the mighty leaders will say of Egypt and her allies, 'They have come down and they lie with the uncircumcised, with those killed by the sword.'

²²"Assyria is there with her whole army; she is surrounded by the graves of all her slain, all who have fallen by the sword. ²³Their graves are in the depths of the pit and her army lies around her grave. All who had spread terror in the land of the living are slain, fallen by the sword.

²⁴"Elam is there, with all her hordes around her grave. All of them are slain, fallen by the sword. All who had spread terror in the land

---

^{a} 9 Hebrew; Septuagint *bring you into captivity among the nations, / to*

of the living went down uncircumcised to the earth below. They bear their shame with those who go down to the pit. ²⁵A bed is made for her among the slain, with all her hordes around her grave. All of them are uncircumcised, killed by the sword. Because their terror had spread in the land of the living, they bear their shame with those who go down to the pit; they are laid among the slain.

²⁶"Meshek and Tubal are there, with all their hordes around their graves. All of them are uncircumcised, killed by the sword because they spread their terror in the land of the living. ²⁷But they do not lie with the fallen warriors of old,ᵃ who went down to the realm of the dead with their weapons of war — their swords placed under their heads and their shieldsᵇ resting on their bones — though these warriors also had terrorized the land of the living.

²⁸"You too, Pharaoh, will be broken and will lie among the uncircumcised, with those killed by the sword.

²⁹"Edom is there, her kings and all her princes; despite their power, they are laid with those killed by the sword. They lie with the uncircumcised, with those who go down to the pit.

³⁰"All the princes of the north and all the Sidonians are there; they went down with the slain in disgrace despite the terror caused by their power. They lie uncircumcised with those killed by the sword and bear their shame with those who go down to the pit.

³¹"Pharaoh — he and all his army — will see them and he will be consoled for all his hordes that were killed by the sword, declares the Sovereign LORD. ³²Although I had him spread terror in the land of the living, Pharaoh and all his hordes will be laid among the uncircumcised, with those killed by the sword, declares the Sovereign LORD."

Renewal of Ezekiel's Call as Watchman

33 The word of the LORD came to me: ²"Son of man, speak to your people and say to them: 'When I bring the sword against a land, and the people of the land choose one of their men and make him their watchman, ³and he sees the sword coming against the land and blows the trumpet to warn the people, ⁴then if anyone hears the trumpet but does not heed the warning and the sword comes and takes their life, their blood will be on their own head. ⁵Since they heard the sound of the trumpet but did not heed the warning, their blood will be on their own head. If they had heeded the warning, they

---

Watchmen: All Leaders Are Stewards of Their God-Given Resources

Ezekiel 33:1–6

If a leader sees calamity approaching and sounds the trumpet to warn the people, he has done his work. If the watchman fails to warn the people of approaching disaster, God will hold the watchman accountable for the lives lost—a sobering truth about the awesome responsibility of leadership.

---

would have saved themselves. ⁶But if the watchman sees the sword coming and does not blow the trumpet to warn the people and the sword comes and takes someone's life, that person's life will be taken because of their sin, but I will hold the watchman accountable for their blood.'

⁷"Son of man, I have made you a watchman for the people of Israel; so hear the word I speak and give them warning from me. ⁸When I say to the wicked, 'You wicked person, you will surely die,' and you do not speak out to dissuade them from their ways, that wicked person will die forᶜ their sin, and I will hold you accountable for their blood. ⁹But if you do warn the wicked person to turn from their ways and they do not do so, they will die for their sin, though you yourself will be saved.

¹⁰"Son of man, say to the Israelites, 'This is what you are saying: "Our offenses and sins weigh us down, and we are wasting away because ofᵈ them. How then can we live?"' ¹¹Say to them, 'As surely as I live, declares the Sovereign LORD, I take no pleasure in the death of the wicked, but rather that they turn from their ways and live. Turn! Turn from your evil ways! Why will you die, people of Israel?'

¹²"Therefore, son of man, say to your people, 'If someone who is righteous disobeys, that person's former righteousness will count for nothing. And if someone who is wicked repents, that person's former wickedness will not bring condemnation. The righteous person who sins will not be allowed to live even though they were formerly righteous.' ¹³If I tell a righteous person

---

ᵃ 27 Septuagint; Hebrew *warriors who were uncircumcised*   ᵇ 27 Probable reading of the original Hebrew text; Masoretic Text *punishment*   ᶜ 8 Or *in;* also in verse 9   ᵈ 10 Or *away in*

that they will surely live, but then they trust in their righteousness and do evil, none of the righteous things that person has done will be remembered; they will die for the evil they have done. [14]And if I say to a wicked person, 'You will surely die,' but they then turn away from their sin and do what is just and right— [15]if they give back what they took in pledge for a loan, return what they have stolen, follow the decrees that give life, and do no evil— that person will surely live; they will not die. [16]None of the sins that person has committed will be remembered against them. They have done what is just and right; they will surely live.

[17]"Yet your people say, 'The way of the Lord is not just.' But it is their way that is not just. [18]If a righteous person turns from their righteousness and does evil, they will die for it. [19]And if a wicked person turns away from their wickedness and does what is just and right, they will live by doing so. [20]Yet you Israelites say, 'The way of the Lord is not just.' But I will judge each of you according to your own ways."

Jerusalem's Fall Explained

[21]In the twelfth year of our exile, in the tenth month on the fifth day, a man who had escaped from Jerusalem came to me and said, "The city has fallen!" [22]Now the evening before the man arrived, the hand of the LORD was on me, and he opened my mouth before the man came to me in the morning. So my mouth was opened and I was no longer silent.

[23]Then the word of the LORD came to me: [24]"Son of man, the people living in those ruins in the land of Israel are saying, 'Abraham was only one man, yet he possessed the land. But we are many; surely the land has been given to us as our possession.' [25]Therefore say to them, 'This is what the Sovereign LORD says: Since you eat meat with the blood still in it and look to your idols and shed blood, should you then possess the land? [26]You rely on your sword, you do detestable things, and each of you defiles his neighbor's wife. Should you then possess the land?'

[27]"Say this to them: 'This is what the Sovereign LORD says: As surely as I live, those who are left in the ruins will fall by the sword, those out in the country I will give to the wild animals to be devoured, and those in strongholds and caves will die of a plague. [28]I will make the land a desolate waste, and her proud strength will come to an end, and the mountains of Israel will become desolate so that no one will cross them. [29]Then they will know that I am the LORD, when I have made the land a desolate waste because of all the detestable things they have done.'

[30]"As for you, son of man, your people are talking together about you by the walls and at the doors of the houses, saying to each other, 'Come and hear the message that has come from the LORD.' [31]My people come to you, as they usually do, and sit before you to hear your words, but they do not put them into practice. Their mouths speak of love, but their hearts are greedy for unjust gain. [32]Indeed, to them you are nothing more than one who sings love songs with a beautiful voice and plays an instrument well, for they hear your words but do not put them into practice.

[33]"When all this comes true— and it surely will— then they will know that a prophet has been among them."

The LORD Will Be Israel's Shepherd

34 The word of the LORD came to me: [2]"Son of man, prophesy against the shepherds of Israel; prophesy and say to them: 'This is what the Sovereign LORD says: Woe to you shepherds of Israel who only take care of yourselves! Should not shepherds take care of the flock? [3]You eat the curds, clothe yourselves with the wool and slaughter the choice animals, but you do not take care of the flock. [4]You have not strengthened the weak or healed the sick or bound up the injured. You have not brought back the strays or searched for the lost. You have ruled them harshly and brutally. [5]So they were scattered because there was no shepherd, and when they were scattered they became food for all the wild animals. [6]My sheep wandered over all the mountains and on every high hill. They were scattered over the whole earth, and no one searched or looked for them.

[7]"'Therefore, you shepherds, hear the word of the LORD: [8]As surely as I live, declares the Sovereign LORD, because my flock lacks a shepherd and so has been plundered and has become food for all the wild animals, and because my shepherds did not search for my flock but cared for themselves rather than for my flock, [9]therefore, you shepherds, hear the word of the LORD: [10]This is what the Sovereign LORD says: I am against the shepherds and will hold them accountable for my flock. I will remove them from tending the flock so that the shepherds can no longer feed themselves. I will rescue my flock from their mouths, and it will no longer be food for them.

[11]"'For this is what the Sovereign LORD says: I myself will search for my sheep and look after

them. [12]As a shepherd looks after his scattered flock when he is with them, so will I look after my sheep. I will rescue them from all the places where they were scattered on a day of clouds and darkness. [13]I will bring them out from the nations and gather them from the countries, and I will bring them into their own land. I will pasture them on the mountains of Israel, in the ravines and in all the settlements in the land. [14]I will tend them in a good pasture, and the mountain heights of Israel will be their grazing land. There they will lie down in good grazing land, and there they will feed in a rich pasture on the mountains of Israel. [15]I myself will tend my sheep and have them lie down, declares the Sovereign LORD. [16]I will search for the lost and bring back the strays. I will bind up the injured and strengthen the weak, but the sleek and the strong I will destroy. I will shepherd the flock with justice.

[17]"'As for you, my flock, this is what the Sovereign LORD says: I will judge between one sheep and another, and between rams and goats. [18]Is it not enough for you to feed on the good pasture? Must you also trample the rest of your pasture with your feet? Is it not enough for you to drink clear water? Must you also muddy the rest with

your feet? [19]Must my flock feed on what you have trampled and drink what you have muddied with your feet?

[20]"'Therefore this is what the Sovereign LORD says to them: See, I myself will judge between the fat sheep and the lean sheep. [21]Because you shove with flank and shoulder, butting all the weak sheep with your horns until you have driven them away, [22]I will save my flock, and they will no longer be plundered. I will judge between one sheep and another. [23]I will place over them one shepherd, my servant David, and he will tend them; he will tend them and be their shepherd. [24]I the LORD will be their God, and my servant David will be prince among them. I the LORD have spoken.

[25]"'I will make a covenant of peace with them and rid the land of savage beasts so that they may live in the wilderness and sleep in the forests in safety. [26]I will make them and the places surrounding my hill a blessing.[a] I will send down showers in season; there will be showers

---

[a] 26 Or I will cause them and the places surrounding my hill to be named in blessings (see Gen. 48:20); or I will cause them and the places surrounding my hill to be seen as blessed

---

Leaders Are to Relate as Shepherds to People

Ezekiel 34:11–24

The Lord of ancient Israel was the Great Shepherd to his flock, Israel. He calls all spiritual leaders to view their role in the same way. The word picture of the shepherd enables us to see what kind of relational skills and attitudes we are to build into our leadership. Ezekiel 34 describes how the shepherd cares for his flock. The shepherd . . .

1. **Searches out the lost sheep (vv. 11–16).**
2. **Delivers the captive sheep (v. 12).**
3. **Gathers the dispersed sheep (v. 13).**
4. **Feeds the hungry sheep (v. 13).**
5. **Rests the weary sheep (v. 15).**
6. **Binds up the hurt sheep (v. 16).**
7. **Strengthens the weak sheep (v. 16).**
8. **Protects the vulnerable sheep (vv. 17–22).**
9. **Equips the needy sheep (v. 23).**
10. **Directs all the sheep (v. 24).**

You may want to compare this text to Psalm 23, another picture of the leader as a shepherd. In that psalm God is the Shepherd, providing guidance, restoration, preparation, resources, comfort and anointing for his sheep.

of blessing. ²⁷The trees will yield their fruit and the ground will yield its crops; the people will be secure in their land. They will know that I am the LORD, when I break the bars of their yoke and rescue them from the hands of those who enslaved them. ²⁸They will no longer be plundered by the nations, nor will wild animals devour them. They will live in safety, and no one will make them afraid. ²⁹I will provide for them a land renowned for its crops, and they will no longer be victims of famine in the land or bear the scorn of the nations. ³⁰Then they will know that I, the LORD their God, am with them and that they, the Israelites, are my people, declares the Sovereign LORD. ³¹You are my sheep, the sheep of my pasture, and I am your God, declares the Sovereign LORD.'"

A Prophecy Against Edom

35 The word of the LORD came to me: ²"Son of man, set your face against Mount Seir; prophesy against it ³and say: 'This is what the Sovereign LORD says: I am against you, Mount Seir, and I will stretch out my hand against you and make you a desolate waste. ⁴I will turn your towns into ruins and you will be desolate. Then you will know that I am the LORD.

⁵"'Because you harbored an ancient hostility and delivered the Israelites over to the sword at the time of their calamity, the time their punishment reached its climax, ⁶therefore as surely as I live, declares the Sovereign LORD, I will give you over to bloodshed and it will pursue you. Since you did not hate bloodshed, bloodshed will pursue you. ⁷I will make Mount Seir a desolate waste and cut off from it all who come and go. ⁸I will fill your mountains with the slain; those killed by the sword will fall on your hills and in your valleys and in all your ravines. ⁹I will make you desolate forever; your towns will not be inhabited. Then you will know that I am the LORD.

¹⁰"'Because you have said, "These two nations and countries will be ours and we will take possession of them," even though I the LORD was there, ¹¹therefore as surely as I live, declares the Sovereign LORD, I will treat you in accordance with the anger and jealousy you showed in your hatred of them and I will make myself known among them when I judge you. ¹²Then you will know that I the LORD have heard all the contemptible things you have said against the mountains of Israel. You said, "They have been laid waste and have been given over to us to devour." ¹³You boasted against me and spoke against me

without restraint, and I heard it. ¹⁴This is what the Sovereign LORD says: While the whole earth rejoices, I will make you desolate. ¹⁵Because you rejoiced when the inheritance of Israel became desolate, that is how I will treat you. You will be desolate, Mount Seir, you and all of Edom. Then they will know that I am the LORD.'"

Hope for the Mountains of Israel

36 "Son of man, prophesy to the mountains of Israel and say, 'Mountains of Israel, hear the word of the LORD. ²This is what the Sovereign LORD says: The enemy said of you, "Aha! The ancient heights have become our possession."' ³Therefore prophesy and say, 'This is what the Sovereign LORD says: Because they ravaged and crushed you from every side so that you became the possession of the rest of the nations and the object of people's malicious talk and slander, ⁴therefore, mountains of Israel, hear the word of the Sovereign LORD: This is what the Sovereign LORD says to the mountains and hills, to the ravines and valleys, to the desolate ruins and the deserted towns that have been plundered and ridiculed by the rest of the nations around you— ⁵this is what the Sovereign LORD says: In my burning zeal I have spoken against the rest of the nations, and against all Edom, for with glee and with malice in their hearts they made my land their own possession so that they might plunder its pastureland.' ⁶Therefore prophesy concerning the land of Israel and say to the mountains and hills, to the ravines and valleys: 'This is what the Sovereign LORD says: I speak in my jealous wrath because you have suffered the scorn of the nations. ⁷Therefore this is what the Sovereign LORD says: I swear with uplifted hand that the nations around you will also suffer scorn.

⁸"'But you, mountains of Israel, will produce branches and fruit for my people Israel, for they will soon come home. ⁹I am concerned for you and will look on you with favor; you will be plowed and sown, ¹⁰and I will cause many people to live on you—yes, all of Israel. The towns will be inhabited and the ruins rebuilt. ¹¹I will increase the number of people and animals living on you, and they will be fruitful and become numerous. I will settle people on you as in the past and will make you prosper more than before. Then you will know that I am the LORD. ¹²I will cause people, my people Israel, to live on you. They will possess you, and you will be their inheritance; you will never again deprive them of their children.

¹³"'This is what the Sovereign LORD says: Be-

cause some say to you, "You devour people and deprive your nation of its children," [14]therefore you will no longer devour people or make your nation childless, declares the Sovereign LORD. [15]No longer will I make you hear the taunts of the nations, and no longer will you suffer the scorn of the peoples or cause your nation to fall, declares the Sovereign LORD.'"

Israel's Restoration Assured

[16]Again the word of the LORD came to me: [17]"Son of man, when the people of Israel were living in their own land, they defiled it by their conduct and their actions. Their conduct was like a woman's monthly uncleanness in my sight. [18]So I poured out my wrath on them because they had shed blood in the land and because they had defiled it with their idols. [19]I dispersed them among the nations, and they were scattered through the countries; I judged them according to their conduct and their actions. [20]And wherever they went among the nations they profaned my holy name, for it was said of them, 'These are the LORD's people, and yet they had to leave his land.' [21]I had concern for my holy name, which the people of Israel profaned among the nations where they had gone.

[22]"Therefore say to the Israelites, 'This is what the Sovereign LORD says: It is not for your sake, people of Israel, that I am going to do these things, but for the sake of my holy name, which you have profaned among the nations where you have gone. [23]I will show the holiness of my great name, which has been profaned among the nations, the name you have profaned among them. Then the nations will know that I am the LORD, declares the Sovereign LORD, when I am proved holy through you before their eyes.

[24]"'For I will take you out of the nations; I will gather you from all the countries and bring you back into your own land. [25]I will sprinkle clean water on you, and you will be clean; I will cleanse you from all your impurities and from all your idols. [26]I will give you a new heart and put a new spirit in you; I will remove from you your heart of stone and give you a heart of flesh. [27]And I will put my Spirit in you and move you to follow my decrees and be careful to keep my laws. [28]Then you will live in the land I gave your ancestors; you will be my people, and I will be your God. [29]I will save you from all your uncleanness. I will call for the grain and make it plentiful and will not bring famine upon you. [30]I will increase the fruit of the trees and the crops of the field, so that you will no longer suffer

disgrace among the nations because of famine. [31]Then you will remember your evil ways and wicked deeds, and you will loathe yourselves for your sins and detestable practices. [32]I want you to know that I am not doing this for your sake, declares the Sovereign LORD. Be ashamed and disgraced for your conduct, people of Israel!

[33]"'This is what the Sovereign LORD says: On the day I cleanse you from all your sins, I will resettle your towns, and the ruins will be rebuilt. [34]The desolate land will be cultivated instead of lying desolate in the sight of all who pass through it. [35]They will say, "This land that was laid waste has become like the garden of Eden; the cities that were lying in ruins, desolate and destroyed, are now fortified and inhabited." [36]Then the nations around you that remain will know that I the LORD have rebuilt what was destroyed and have replanted what was desolate. I the LORD have spoken, and I will do it.'

[37]"This is what the Sovereign LORD says: Once again I will yield to Israel's plea and do this for them: I will make their people as numerous as sheep, [38]as numerous as the flocks for offerings at Jerusalem during her appointed festivals. So will the ruined cities be filled with flocks of people. Then they will know that I am the LORD."

The Valley of Dry Bones

37 The hand of the LORD was on me, and he brought me out by the Spirit of the LORD and set me in the middle of a valley; it was full of bones. [2]He led me back and forth among them, and I saw a great many bones on the floor of the valley, bones that were very dry. [3]He asked me, "Son of man, can these bones live?"

I said, "Sovereign LORD, you alone know."

[4]Then he said to me, "Prophesy to these bones and say to them, 'Dry bones, hear the word of the LORD! [5]This is what the Sovereign LORD says to these bones: I will make breath[a] enter you, and you will come to life. [6]I will attach tendons to you and make flesh come upon you and cover you with skin; I will put breath in you, and you will come to life. Then you will know that I am the LORD.'"

[7]So I prophesied as I was commanded. And as I was prophesying, there was a noise, a rattling sound, and the bones came together, bone to bone. [8]I looked, and tendons and flesh appeared on them and skin covered them, but there was no breath in them.

---

[a] 5 The Hebrew for this word can also mean *wind* or *spirit* (see verses 6-14).

[9]Then he said to me, "Prophesy to the breath; prophesy, son of man, and say to it, 'This is what the Sovereign LORD says: Come, breath, from the four winds and breathe into these slain, that they may live.'" [10]So I prophesied as he commanded me, and breath entered them; they came to life and stood up on their feet—a vast army.

[11]Then he said to me: "Son of man, these bones are the people of Israel. They say, 'Our bones are dried up and our hope is gone; we are cut off.' [12]Therefore prophesy and say to them: 'This is what the Sovereign LORD says: My people, I am going to open your graves and bring you up from them; I will bring you back to the land of Israel. [13]Then you, my people, will know that I am the LORD, when I open your graves and bring you up from them. [14]I will put my Spirit in you and you will live, and I will settle you in your own land. Then you will know that I the LORD have spoken, and I have done it, declares the LORD.'"

One Nation Under One King

[15]The word of the LORD came to me: [16]"Son of man, take a stick of wood and write on it, 'Belonging to Judah and the Israelites associated with him.' Then take another stick of wood, and write on it, 'Belonging to Joseph (that is, to Ephraim) and all the Israelites associated with him.' [17]Join them together into one stick so that they will become one in your hand.

[18]"When your people ask you, 'Won't you tell us what you mean by this?' [19]say to them, 'This is what the Sovereign LORD says: I am going to take the stick of Joseph—which is in Ephraim's hand—and of the Israelite tribes associated with him, and join it to Judah's stick. I will make them into a single stick of wood, and they will become one in my hand.' [20]Hold before their eyes the sticks you have written on [21]and say to them, 'This is what the Sovereign LORD says: I will take the Israelites out of the nations where they have gone. I will gather them from all around and bring them back into their own land. [22]I will make them one nation in the land, on the mountains of Israel. There will be one king over all of them and they will never again be two nations or be divided into two kingdoms. [23]They will no longer defile themselves with their idols and vile images or with any of their offenses, for I will save them from all their sinful backsliding,[a] and I will cleanse them. They will be my people, and I will be their God.

[24]"'My servant David will be king over them,

and they will all have one shepherd. They will follow my laws and be careful to keep my decrees. [25]They will live in the land I gave to my servant Jacob, the land where your ancestors lived. They and their children and their children's children will live there forever, and David my servant will be their prince forever. [26]I will make a covenant of peace with them; it will be an everlasting covenant. I will establish them and increase their numbers, and I will put my sanctuary among them forever. [27]My dwelling place will be with them; I will be their God, and they will be my people. [28]Then the nations will know that I the LORD make Israel holy, when my sanctuary is among them forever.'"

The LORD's Great Victory Over the Nations

38 The word of the LORD came to me: [2]"Son of man, set your face against Gog, of the land of Magog, the chief prince of[b] Meshek and Tubal; prophesy against him [3]and say: 'This is what the Sovereign LORD says: I am against you, Gog, chief prince of[c] Meshek and Tubal. [4]I will turn you around, put hooks in your jaws and bring you out with your whole army— your horses, your horsemen fully armed, and a great horde with large and small shields, all of them brandishing their swords. [5]Persia, Cush[d] and Put will be with them, all with shields and helmets, [6]also Gomer with all its troops, and Beth Togarmah from the far north with all its troops—the many nations with you.

[7]"'Get ready; be prepared, you and all the hordes gathered about you, and take command of them. [8]After many days you will be called to arms. In future years you will invade a land that has recovered from war, whose people were gathered from many nations to the mountains of Israel, which had long been desolate. They had been brought out from the nations, and now all of them live in safety. [9]You and all your troops and the many nations with you will go up, advancing like a storm; you will be like a cloud covering the land.

[10]"'This is what the Sovereign LORD says: On that day thoughts will come into your mind and you will devise an evil scheme. [11]You will say, "I will invade a land of unwalled villages; I will attack a peaceful and unsuspecting people—all of them living without walls and without gates and bars. [12]I will plunder and loot and turn my

---

[a] 23 Many Hebrew manuscripts (see also Septuagint); most Hebrew manuscripts *all their dwelling places where they sinned*
[b] 2 Or *the prince of Rosh,*   [c] 3 Or *Gog, prince of Rosh,*
[d] 5 That is, the upper Nile region

hand against the resettled ruins and the people gathered from the nations, rich in livestock and goods, living at the center of the land.*a* 13Sheba and Dedan and the merchants of Tarshish and all her villages*b* will say to you, "Have you come to plunder? Have you gathered your hordes to loot, to carry off silver and gold, to take away livestock and goods and to seize much plunder?"'

14"Therefore, son of man, prophesy and say to Gog: 'This is what the Sovereign LORD says: In that day, when my people Israel are living in safety, will you not take notice of it? 15You will come from your place in the far north, you and many nations with you, all of them riding on horses, a great horde, a mighty army. 16You will advance against my people Israel like a cloud that covers the land. In days to come, Gog, I will bring you against my land, so that the nations may know me when I am proved holy through you before their eyes.

17"'This is what the Sovereign LORD says: You are the one I spoke of in former days by my servants the prophets of Israel. At that time they prophesied for years that I would bring you against them. 18This is what will happen in that day: When Gog attacks the land of Israel, my hot anger will be aroused, declares the Sovereign LORD. 19In my zeal and fiery wrath I declare that at that time there shall be a great earthquake in the land of Israel. 20The fish in the sea, the birds in the sky, the beasts of the field, every creature that moves along the ground, and all the people on the face of the earth will tremble at my presence. The mountains will be overturned, the cliffs will crumble and every wall will fall to the ground. 21I will summon a sword against Gog on all my mountains, declares the Sovereign LORD. Every man's sword will be against his brother. 22I will execute judgment on him with plague and bloodshed; I will pour down torrents of rain, hailstones and burning sulfur on him and on his troops and on the many nations with him. 23And so I will show my greatness and my holiness, and I will make myself known in the sight of many nations. Then they will know that I am the LORD.'

39 "Son of man, prophesy against Gog and say: 'This is what the Sovereign LORD says: I am against you, Gog, chief prince of*c* Meshek and Tubal. 2I will turn you around and drag you along. I will bring you from the far north and send you against the mountains of Israel. 3Then I will strike your bow from your left hand and make your arrows drop from your right hand. 4On the mountains of Israel you will fall, you and all your troops and the nations with you. I will give you as food to all kinds of carrion birds and to the wild animals. 5You will fall in the open field, for I have spoken, declares the Sovereign LORD. 6I will send fire on Magog and on those who live in safety in the coastlands, and they will know that I am the LORD.

7"'I will make known my holy name among my people Israel. I will no longer let my holy name be profaned, and the nations will know that I the LORD am the Holy One in Israel. 8It is coming! It will surely take place, declares the Sovereign LORD. This is the day I have spoken of.

9"'Then those who live in the towns of Israel will go out and use the weapons for fuel and burn them up — the small and large shields, the bows and arrows, the war clubs and spears. For seven years they will use them for fuel. 10They will not need to gather wood from the fields or cut it from the forests, because they will use the weapons for fuel. And they will plunder those who plundered them and loot those who looted them, declares the Sovereign LORD.

11"'On that day I will give Gog a burial place in Israel, in the valley of those who travel east of the Sea. It will block the way of travelers, because Gog and all his hordes will be buried there. So it will be called the Valley of Hamon Gog.*d*

12"'For seven months the Israelites will be burying them in order to cleanse the land. 13All the people of the land will bury them, and the day I display my glory will be a memorable day for them, declares the Sovereign LORD. 14People will be continually employed in cleansing the land. They will spread out across the land and, along with others, they will bury any bodies that are lying on the ground.

"'After the seven months they will carry out a more detailed search. 15As they go through the land, anyone who sees a human bone will leave a marker beside it until the gravediggers bury it in the Valley of Hamon Gog, 16near a town called Hamonah.*e* And so they will cleanse the land.'

17"Son of man, this is what the Sovereign LORD says: Call out to every kind of bird and all the wild animals: 'Assemble and come together from all around to the sacrifice I am preparing for you, the great sacrifice on the mountains of Israel. There you will eat flesh and

---

a 12 The Hebrew for this phrase means *the navel of the earth.*
b 13 Or *her strong lions*   *c 1* Or *Gog, prince of Rosh,*
d 11 Hamon Gog means *hordes of Gog.*   *e 16 Hamonah* means *horde.*

drink blood. [18]You will eat the flesh of mighty men and drink the blood of the princes of the earth as if they were rams and lambs, goats and bulls — all of them fattened animals from Bashan. [19]At the sacrifice I am preparing for you, you will eat fat till you are glutted and drink blood till you are drunk. [20]At my table you will eat your fill of horses and riders, mighty men and soldiers of every kind,' declares the Sovereign LORD.

[21]"I will display my glory among the nations, and all the nations will see the punishment I inflict and the hand I lay on them. [22]From that day forward the people of Israel will know that I am the LORD their God. [23]And the nations will know that the people of Israel went into exile for their sin, because they were unfaithful to me. So I hid my face from them and handed them over to their enemies, and they all fell by the sword. [24]I dealt with them according to their uncleanness and their offenses, and I hid my face from them.

[25]"Therefore this is what the Sovereign LORD says: I will now restore the fortunes of Jacob[a] and will have compassion on all the people of Israel, and I will be zealous for my holy name. [26]They will forget their shame and all the unfaithfulness they showed toward me when they lived in safety in their land with no one to make them afraid. [27]When I have brought them back from the nations and have gathered them from the countries of their enemies, I will be proved holy through them in the sight of many nations. [28]Then they will know that I am the LORD their God, for though I sent them into exile among the nations, I will gather them to their own land, not leaving any behind. [29]I will no longer hide my face from them, for I will pour out my Spirit on the people of Israel, declares the Sovereign LORD."

The Temple Area Restored

40 In the twenty-fifth year of our exile, at the beginning of the year, on the tenth of the month, in the fourteenth year after the fall of the city — on that very day the hand of the LORD was on me and he took me there. [2]In visions of God he took me to the land of Israel and set me on a very high mountain, on whose south side were some buildings that looked like a city. [3]He took me there, and I saw a man whose appearance was like bronze; he was standing in the gateway with a linen cord and a measuring rod in his hand. [4]The man said to me, "Son of man, look carefully and listen closely and pay atten-

tion to everything I am going to show you, for that is why you have been brought here. Tell the people of Israel everything you see."

The East Gate to the Outer Court

[5]I saw a wall completely surrounding the temple area. The length of the measuring rod in the man's hand was six long cubits,[b] each of which was a cubit and a handbreadth. He measured the wall; it was one measuring rod thick and one rod high.

[6]Then he went to the east gate. He climbed its steps and measured the threshold of the gate; it was one rod deep. [7]The alcoves for the guards were one rod long and one rod wide, and the projecting walls between the alcoves were five cubits[c] thick. And the threshold of the gate next to the portico facing the temple was one rod deep.

[8]Then he measured the portico of the gateway; [9]it[d] was eight cubits[e] deep and its jambs were two cubits[f] thick. The portico of the gateway faced the temple.

[10]Inside the east gate were three alcoves on each side; the three had the same measurements, and the faces of the projecting walls on each side had the same measurements. [11]Then he measured the width of the entrance of the gateway; it was ten cubits and its length was thirteen cubits.[g] [12]In front of each alcove was a wall one cubit high, and the alcoves were six cubits square. [13]Then he measured the gateway from the top of the rear wall of one alcove to the top of the opposite one; the distance was twenty-five cubits[h] from one parapet opening to the opposite one. [14]He measured along the faces of the projecting walls all around the inside of the gateway — sixty cubits.[i] The measurement was up to the portico[j] facing the courtyard.[k] [15]The distance from the entrance of the gateway to the far end of its portico was fifty

[a] 25 Or *now bring Jacob back from captivity*   [b] 5 That is, about 11 feet or about 3.2 meters; also in verse 12. The long cubit of about 21 inches or about 53 centimeters is the basic unit of measurement of length throughout chapters 40 – 48.
[c] 7 That is, about 8 3/4 feet or about 2.7 meters; also in verse 48
[d] 8,9 Many Hebrew manuscripts, Septuagint, Vulgate and Syriac; most Hebrew manuscripts *gateway facing the temple; it was one rod deep.* [9]*Then he measured the portico of the gateway; it*   [e] 9 That is, about 14 feet or about 4.2 meters   [f] 9 That is, about 3 1/2 feet or about 1 meter   [g] 11 That is, about 18 feet wide and 23 feet long or about 5.3 meters wide and 6.9 meters long   [h] 13 That is, about 44 feet or about 13 meters; also in verses 21, 25, 29, 30, 33 and 36   [i] 14 That is, about 105 feet or about 32 meters   [j] 14 Septuagint; Hebrew *projecting wall*   [k] 14 The meaning of the Hebrew for this verse is uncertain.

cubits.*a* *16*The alcoves and the projecting walls inside the gateway were surmounted by narrow parapet openings all around, as was the portico; the openings all around faced inward. The faces of the projecting walls were decorated with palm trees.

The Outer Court

*17*Then he brought me into the outer court. There I saw some rooms and a pavement that had been constructed all around the court; there were thirty rooms along the pavement. *18*It abutted the sides of the gateways and was as wide as they were long; this was the lower pavement. *19*Then he measured the distance from the inside of the lower gateway to the outside of the inner court; it was a hundred cubits*b* on the east side as well as on the north.

The North Gate

*20*Then he measured the length and width of the north gate, leading into the outer court. *21*Its alcoves — three on each side — its projecting walls and its portico had the same measurements as those of the first gateway. It was fifty cubits long and twenty-five cubits wide. *22*Its openings, its portico and its palm tree decorations had the same measurements as those of the gate facing east. Seven steps led up to it, with its portico opposite them. *23*There was a gate to the inner court facing the north gate, just as there was on the east. He measured from one gate to the opposite one; it was a hundred cubits.

The South Gate

*24*Then he led me to the south side and I saw the south gate. He measured its jambs and its portico, and they had the same measurements as the others. *25*The gateway and its portico had narrow openings all around, like the openings of the others. It was fifty cubits long and twenty-five cubits wide. *26*Seven steps led up to it, with its portico opposite them; it had palm tree decorations on the faces of the projecting walls on each side. *27*The inner court also had a gate facing south, and he measured from this gate to the outer gate on the south side; it was a hundred cubits.

The Gates to the Inner Court

*28*Then he brought me into the inner court through the south gate, and he measured the south gate; it had the same measurements as the others. *29*Its alcoves, its projecting walls and its portico had the same measurements as the oth-

ers. The gateway and its portico had openings all around. It was fifty cubits long and twenty-five cubits wide. *30*(The porticoes of the gateways around the inner court were twenty-five cubits wide and five cubits deep.) *31*Its portico faced the outer court; palm trees decorated its jambs, and eight steps led up to it.

*32*Then he brought me to the inner court on the east side, and he measured the gateway; it had the same measurements as the others. *33*Its alcoves, its projecting walls and its portico had the same measurements as the others. The gateway and its portico had openings all around. It was fifty cubits long and twenty-five cubits wide. *34*Its portico faced the outer court; palm trees decorated the jambs on either side, and eight steps led up to it.

*35*Then he brought me to the north gate and measured it. It had the same measurements as the others, *36*as did its alcoves, its projecting walls and its portico, and it had openings all around. It was fifty cubits long and twenty-five cubits wide. *37*Its portico*c* faced the outer court; palm trees decorated the jambs on either side, and eight steps led up to it.

The Rooms for Preparing Sacrifices

*38*A room with a doorway was by the portico in each of the inner gateways, where the burnt offerings were washed. *39*In the portico of the gateway were two tables on each side, on which the burnt offerings, sin offerings*d* and guilt offerings were slaughtered. *40*By the outside wall of the portico of the gateway, near the steps at the entrance of the north gateway were two tables, and on the other side of the steps were two tables. *41*So there were four tables on one side of the gateway and four on the other — eight tables in all — on which the sacrifices were slaughtered. *42*There were also four tables of dressed stone for the burnt offerings, each a cubit and a half long, a cubit and a half wide and a cubit high.*e* On them were placed the utensils for slaughtering the burnt offerings and the other sacrifices. *43*And double-pronged hooks, each a handbreadth*f* long, were attached to the wall all around. The tables were for the flesh of the offerings.

---

a 15 That is, about 88 feet or about 27 meters; also in verses 21, 25, 29, 33 and 36   *b* 19 That is, about 175 feet or about 53 meters; also in verses 23, 27 and 47   *c* 37 Septuagint (see also verses 31 and 34); Hebrew *jambs*   *d* 39 Or *purification offerings*   *e* 42 That is, about 2 2/3 feet long and wide and 21 inches high or about 80 centimeters long and wide and 53 centimeters high   *f* 43 That is, about 3 1/2 inches or about 9 centimeters

The Rooms for the Priests

[44]Outside the inner gate, within the inner court, were two rooms, one[a] at the side of the north gate and facing south, and another at the side of the south[b] gate and facing north. [45]He said to me, "The room facing south is for the priests who guard the temple, [46]and the room facing north is for the priests who guard the altar. These are the sons of Zadok, who are the only Levites who may draw near to the LORD to minister before him."

[47]Then he measured the court: It was square—a hundred cubits long and a hundred cubits wide. And the altar was in front of the temple.

The New Temple

[48]He brought me to the portico of the temple and measured the jambs of the portico; they were five cubits wide on either side. The width of the entrance was fourteen cubits[c] and its projecting walls were[d] three cubits[e] wide on either side. [49]The portico was twenty cubits[f] wide, and twelve[g] cubits[h] from front to back. It was reached by a flight of stairs,[i] and there were pillars on each side of the jambs.

41 Then the man brought me to the main hall and measured the jambs; the width of the jambs was six cubits[j] on each side.[k] [2]The entrance was ten cubits[l] wide, and the projecting walls on each side of it were five cubits[m] wide. He also measured the main hall; it was forty cubits long and twenty cubits wide.[n]

[3]Then he went into the inner sanctuary and measured the jambs of the entrance; each was two cubits[o] wide. The entrance was six cubits wide, and the projecting walls on each side of it were seven cubits[p] wide. [4]And he measured the length of the inner sanctuary; it was twenty cubits, and its width was twenty cubits across the end of the main hall. He said to me, "This is the Most Holy Place."

[5]Then he measured the wall of the temple; it was six cubits thick, and each side room around the temple was four cubits[q] wide. [6]The side rooms were on three levels, one above another, thirty on each level. There were ledges all around the wall of the temple to serve as supports for the side rooms, so that the supports were not inserted into the wall of the temple. [7]The side rooms all around the temple were wider at each successive level. The structure surrounding the temple was built in ascending stages, so that the rooms widened as one went upward. A stairway went up from the lowest floor to the top floor through the middle floor.

[8]I saw that the temple had a raised base all around it, forming the foundation of the side rooms. It was the length of the rod, six long cubits. [9]The outer wall of the side rooms was five cubits thick. The open area between the side rooms of the temple [10]and the priests' rooms was twenty cubits wide all around the temple. [11]There were entrances to the side rooms from the open area, one on the north and another on the south; and the base adjoining the open area was five cubits wide all around.

[12]The building facing the temple courtyard on the west side was seventy cubits[r] wide. The wall of the building was five cubits thick all around, and its length was ninety cubits.[s]

[13]Then he measured the temple; it was a hundred cubits[t] long, and the temple courtyard and the building with its walls were also a hundred cubits long. [14]The width of the temple courtyard on the east, including the front of the temple, was a hundred cubits.

[15]Then he measured the length of the building facing the courtyard at the rear of the temple, including its galleries on each side; it was a hundred cubits.

The main hall, the inner sanctuary and the portico facing the court, [16]as well as the thresholds and the narrow windows and galleries around the three of them—everything beyond and including the threshold was covered with wood. The floor, the wall up to the windows, and the windows were covered. [17]In the space above the outside of the entrance to the inner sanctuary and on the walls at regular intervals all around the inner and outer sanctuary [18]were carved cherubim and palm trees. Palm trees

---

[a] 44 Septuagint; Hebrew *were rooms for singers, which were*
[b] 44 Septuagint; Hebrew *east*   [c] 48 That is, about 25 feet or about 7.4 meters   [d] 48 Septuagint; Hebrew *entrance was*
[e] 48 That is, about 5 1/4 feet or about 1.6 meters   [f] 49 That is, about 35 feet or about 11 meters   [g] 49 Septuagint; Hebrew *eleven*   [h] 49 That is, about 21 feet or about 6.4 meters
[i] 49 Hebrew; Septuagint *Ten steps led up to it*   [j] 1 That is, about 11 feet or about 3.2 meters; also in verses 3, 5 and 8
[k] 1 One Hebrew manuscript and Septuagint; most Hebrew manuscripts *side, the width of the tent*   [l] 2 That is, about 18 feet or about 5.3 meters   [m] 2 That is, about 8 3/4 feet or about 2.7 meters; also in verses 9, 11 and 12   [n] 2 That is, about 70 feet long and 35 feet wide or about 21 meters long and 11 meters wide   [o] 3 That is, about 3 1/2 feet or about 1.1 meters; also in verse 22   [p] 3 That is, about 12 feet or about 3.7 meters   [q] 5 That is, about 7 feet or about 2.1 meters
[r] 12 That is, about 123 feet or about 37 meters   [s] 12 That is, about 158 feet or about 48 meters   [t] 13 That is, about 175 feet or about 53 meters; also in verses 14 and 15

alternated with cherubim. Each cherub had two faces: [19]the face of a human being toward the palm tree on one side and the face of a lion toward the palm tree on the other. They were carved all around the whole temple. [20]From the floor to the area above the entrance, cherubim and palm trees were carved on the wall of the main hall.

[21]The main hall had a rectangular doorframe, and the one at the front of the Most Holy Place was similar. [22]There was a wooden altar three cubits[a] high and two cubits square[b]; its corners, its base[c] and its sides were of wood. The man said to me, "This is the table that is before the LORD." [23]Both the main hall and the Most Holy Place had double doors. [24]Each door had two leaves — two hinged leaves for each door. [25]And on the doors of the main hall were carved cherubim and palm trees like those carved on the walls, and there was a wooden overhang on the front of the portico. [26]On the sidewalls of the portico were narrow windows with palm trees carved on each side. The side rooms of the temple also had overhangs.

The Rooms for the Priests

42 Then the man led me northward into the outer court and brought me to the rooms opposite the temple courtyard and opposite the outer wall on the north side. [2]The building whose door faced north was a hundred cubits long and fifty cubits wide.[d] [3]Both in the section twenty cubits[e] from the inner court and in the section opposite the pavement of the outer court, gallery faced gallery at the three levels. [4]In front of the rooms was an inner passageway ten cubits wide and a hundred cubits[f] long.[g] Their doors were on the north. [5]Now the upper rooms were narrower, for the galleries took more space from them than from the rooms on the lower and middle floors of the building. [6]The rooms on the top floor had no pillars, as the courts had; so they were smaller in floor space than those on the lower and middle floors. [7]There was an outer wall parallel to the rooms and the outer court; it extended in front of the rooms for fifty cubits. [8]While the row of rooms on the side next to the outer court was fifty cubits long, the row on the side nearest the sanctuary was a hundred cubits long. [9]The lower rooms had an entrance on the east side as one enters them from the outer court.

[10]On the south side[h] along the length of the wall of the outer court, adjoining the temple courtyard and opposite the outer wall, were rooms [11]with a passageway in front of them. These were like the rooms on the north; they had the same length and width, with similar exits and dimensions. Similar to the doorways on the north [12]were the doorways of the rooms on the south. There was a doorway at the beginning of the passageway that was parallel to the corresponding wall extending eastward, by which one enters the rooms.

[13]Then he said to me, "The north and south rooms facing the temple courtyard are the priests' rooms, where the priests who approach the LORD will eat the most holy offerings. There they will put the most holy offerings — the grain offerings, the sin offerings[i] and the guilt offerings — for the place is holy. [14]Once the priests enter the holy precincts, they are not to go into the outer court until they leave behind the garments in which they minister, for these are holy. They are to put on other clothes before they go near the places that are for the people."

[15]When he had finished measuring what was inside the temple area, he led me out by the east gate and measured the area all around: [16]He measured the east side with the measuring rod; it was five hundred cubits.[j,k] [17]He measured the north side; it was five hundred cubits[l] by the measuring rod. [18]He measured the south side; it was five hundred cubits by the measuring rod. [19]Then he turned to the west side and measured; it was five hundred cubits by the measuring rod. [20]So he measured the area on all four sides. It had a wall around it, five hundred cubits long and five hundred cubits wide, to separate the holy from the common.

God's Glory Returns to the Temple

43 Then the man brought me to the gate facing east, [2]and I saw the glory of the God of Israel coming from the east. His voice was like the roar of rushing waters, and the land was radiant with his glory. [3]The vision I saw was like the vision I had seen when he[m] came to

---

[a] 22 That is, about 5 1/4 feet or about 1.5 meters
[b] 22 Septuagint; Hebrew *long*   [c] 22 Septuagint; Hebrew *length*   [d] 2 That is, about 175 feet long and 88 feet wide or about 53 meters long and 27 meters wide   [e] 3 That is, about 35 feet or about 11 meters   [f] 4 Septuagint and Syriac; Hebrew *and one cubit*   [g] 4 That is, about 18 feet wide and 175 feet long or about 5.3 meters wide and 53 meters long
[h] 10 Septuagint; Hebrew *Eastward*   [i] 13 Or *purification offerings*   [j] 16 See Septuagint of verse 17; Hebrew *rods*; also in verses 18 and 19.   [k] 16 Five hundred cubits equal about 875 feet or about 265 meters; also in verses 17, 18 and 19.
[l] 17 Septuagint; Hebrew *rods*   [m] 3 Some Hebrew manuscripts and Vulgate; most Hebrew manuscripts *I*

destroy the city and like the visions I had seen by the Kebar River, and I fell facedown. [4]The glory of the LORD entered the temple through the gate facing east. [5]Then the Spirit lifted me up and brought me into the inner court, and the glory of the LORD filled the temple.

[6]While the man was standing beside me, I heard someone speaking to me from inside the temple. [7]He said: "Son of man, this is the place of my throne and the place for the soles of my feet. This is where I will live among the Israelites forever. The people of Israel will never again defile my holy name — neither they nor their kings — by their prostitution and the funeral offerings[a] for their kings at their death.[b] [8]When they placed their threshold next to my threshold and their doorposts beside my doorposts, with only a wall between me and them, they defiled my holy name by their detestable practices. So I destroyed them in my anger. [9]Now let them put away from me their prostitution and the funeral offerings for their kings, and I will live among them forever.

[10]"Son of man, describe the temple to the people of Israel, that they may be ashamed of their sins. Let them consider its perfection, [11]and if they are ashamed of all they have done, make known to them the design of the temple — its arrangement, its exits and entrances — its whole design and all its regulations[c] and laws. Write these down before them so that they may be faithful to its design and follow all its regulations.

[12]"This is the law of the temple: All the surrounding area on top of the mountain will be most holy. Such is the law of the temple.

The Great Altar Restored

[13]"These are the measurements of the altar in long cubits,[d] that cubit being a cubit and a handbreadth: Its gutter is a cubit deep and a cubit wide, with a rim of one span[e] around the edge. And this is the height of the altar: [14]From the gutter on the ground up to the lower ledge that goes around the altar it is two cubits high, and the ledge is a cubit wide.[f] From this lower ledge to the upper ledge that goes around the altar it is four cubits high, and that ledge is also a cubit wide.[g] [15]Above that, the altar hearth is four cubits high, and four horns project upward from the hearth. [16]The altar hearth is square, twelve cubits[h] long and twelve cubits wide. [17]The upper ledge also is square, fourteen cubits[i] long and fourteen cubits wide. All around the altar is a gutter of one cubit with a rim of half a cubit.[e] The steps of the altar face east."

[18]Then he said to me, "Son of man, this is what the Sovereign LORD says: These will be the regulations for sacrificing burnt offerings and splashing blood against the altar when it is built: [19]You are to give a young bull as a sin offering[j] to the Levitical priests of the family of Zadok, who come near to minister before me, declares the Sovereign LORD. [20]You are to take some of its blood and put it on the four horns of the altar and on the four corners of the upper ledge and all around the rim, and so purify the altar and make atonement for it. [21]You are to take the bull for the sin offering and burn it in the designated part of the temple area outside the sanctuary.

[22]"On the second day you are to offer a male goat without defect for a sin offering, and the altar is to be purified as it was purified with the bull. [23]When you have finished purifying it, you are to offer a young bull and a ram from the flock, both without defect. [24]You are to offer them before the LORD, and the priests are to sprinkle salt on them and sacrifice them as a burnt offering to the LORD.

[25]"For seven days you are to provide a male goat daily for a sin offering; you are also to provide a young bull and a ram from the flock, both without defect. [26]For seven days they are to make atonement for the altar and cleanse it; thus they will dedicate it. [27]At the end of these days, from the eighth day on, the priests are to present your burnt offerings and fellowship offerings on the altar. Then I will accept you, declares the Sovereign LORD."

The Priesthood Restored

44 Then the man brought me back to the outer gate of the sanctuary, the one facing east, and it was shut. [2]The LORD said to me, "This gate is to remain shut. It must not be opened; no one may enter through it. It is to remain shut because the LORD, the God of Israel, has entered through it. [3]The prince himself is

---

[a] 7 Or *the memorial monuments*; also in verse 9　　[b] 7 Or *their high places*　　[c] 11 Some Hebrew manuscripts and Septuagint; most Hebrew manuscripts *regulations and its whole design*
[d] 13 That is, about 21 inches or about 53 centimeters; also in verses 14 and 17. The long cubit is the basic unit for linear measurement throughout Ezekiel 40 – 48.　　[e] 13,17 That is, about 11 inches or about 27 centimeters　　[f] 14 That is, about 3 1/2 feet high and 1 3/4 feet wide or about 105 centimeters high and 53 centimeters wide　　[g] 14 That is, about 7 feet high and 1 3/4 feet wide or about 2.1 meters high and 53 centimeters wide　　[h] 16 That is, about 21 feet or about 6.4 meters
[i] 17 That is, about 25 feet or about 7.4 meters　　[j] 19 Or *purification offering*; also in verses 21, 22 and 25

the only one who may sit inside the gateway to eat in the presence of the LORD. He is to enter by way of the portico of the gateway and go out the same way."

⁴Then the man brought me by way of the north gate to the front of the temple. I looked and saw the glory of the LORD filling the temple of the LORD, and I fell facedown.

⁵The LORD said to me, "Son of man, look carefully, listen closely and give attention to everything I tell you concerning all the regulations and instructions regarding the temple of the LORD. Give attention to the entrance to the temple and all the exits of the sanctuary. ⁶Say to rebellious Israel, 'This is what the Sovereign LORD says: Enough of your detestable practices, people of Israel! ⁷In addition to all your other detestable practices, you brought foreigners uncircumcised in heart and flesh into my sanctuary, desecrating my temple while you offered me food, fat and blood, and you broke my covenant. ⁸Instead of carrying out your duty in regard to my holy things, you put others in charge of my sanctuary. ⁹This is what the Sovereign LORD says: No foreigner uncircumcised in heart and flesh is to enter my sanctuary, not even the foreigners who live among the Israelites.

¹⁰"The Levites who went far from me when Israel went astray and who wandered from me after their idols must bear the consequences of their sin. ¹¹They may serve in my sanctuary, having charge of the gates of the temple and serving in it; they may slaughter the burnt offerings and sacrifices for the people and stand before the people and serve them. ¹²But because they served them in the presence of their idols and made the people of Israel fall into sin, therefore I have sworn with uplifted hand that they must bear the consequences of their sin, declares the Sovereign LORD. ¹³They are not to come near to serve me as priests or come near any of my holy things or my most holy offerings; they must bear the shame of their detestable practices. ¹⁴And I will appoint them to guard the temple for all the work that is to be done in it.

¹⁵"But the Levitical priests, who are descendants of Zadok and who guarded my sanctuary when the Israelites went astray from me, are to come near to minister before me; they are to stand before me to offer sacrifices of fat and blood, declares the Sovereign LORD. ¹⁶They alone are to enter my sanctuary; they alone are to come near my table to minister before me and serve me as guards.

¹⁷"When they enter the gates of the inner court, they are to wear linen clothes; they must not wear any woolen garment while ministering at the gates of the inner court or inside the temple. ¹⁸They are to wear linen turbans on their heads and linen undergarments around their waists. They must not wear anything that makes them perspire. ¹⁹When they go out into the outer court where the people are, they are to take off the clothes they have been ministering in and are to leave them in the sacred rooms, and put on other clothes, so that the people are not consecrated through contact with their garments.

²⁰"They must not shave their heads or let their hair grow long, but they are to keep the hair of their heads trimmed. ²¹No priest is to drink wine when he enters the inner court. ²²They must not marry widows or divorced women; they may marry only virgins of Israelite descent or widows of priests. ²³They are to teach my people the difference between the holy and the common and show them how to distinguish between the unclean and the clean.

²⁴"In any dispute, the priests are to serve as judges and decide it according to my ordinances. They are to keep my laws and my decrees for all my appointed festivals, and they are to keep my Sabbaths holy.

²⁵"A priest must not defile himself by going near a dead person; however, if the dead person was his father or mother, son or daughter, brother or unmarried sister, then he may defile himself. ²⁶After he is cleansed, he must wait seven days. ²⁷On the day he goes into the inner court of the sanctuary to minister in the sanctuary, he

Great Leaders See the Big Picture and the Little Process

Ezekiel 40:1—44:31

God, the Ultimate Leader, never loses sight of the whole, but never ignores details, either. What does God communicate in these chapters?

1. **I care about the details.**

2. **No one is unimportant.**

3. **We have a bigger purpose for what we do.**

4. **The labor of each individual has meaning.**

is to offer a sin offering[a] for himself, declares the Sovereign LORD.

28"'I am to be the only inheritance the priests have. You are to give them no possession in Israel; I will be their possession. 29They will eat the grain offerings, the sin offerings and the guilt offerings; and everything in Israel devoted[b] to the LORD will belong to them. 30The best of all the firstfruits and of all your special gifts will belong to the priests. You are to give them the first portion of your ground meal so that a blessing may rest on your household. 31The priests must not eat anything, whether bird or animal, found dead or torn by wild animals.

Israel Fully Restored

45 "'When you allot the land as an inheritance, you are to present to the LORD a portion of the land as a sacred district, 25,000 cubits[c] long and 20,000[d] cubits[e] wide; the entire area will be holy. 2Of this, a section 500 cubits[f] square is to be for the sanctuary, with 50 cubits[g] around it for open land. 3In the sacred district, measure off a section 25,000 cubits long and 10,000 cubits[h] wide. In it will be the sanctuary, the Most Holy Place. 4It will be the sacred portion of the land for the priests, who minister in the sanctuary and who draw near to minister before the LORD. It will be a place for their houses as well as a holy place for the sanctuary. 5An area 25,000 cubits long and 10,000 cubits wide will belong to the Levites, who serve in the temple, as their possession for towns to live in.[i]

6"'You are to give the city as its property an area 5,000 cubits[j] wide and 25,000 cubits long, adjoining the sacred portion; it will belong to all Israel.

7"'The prince will have the land bordering each side of the area formed by the sacred district and the property of the city. It will extend westward from the west side and eastward from the east side, running lengthwise from the western to the eastern border parallel to one of the tribal portions. 8This land will be his possession in Israel. And my princes will no longer oppress my people but will allow the people of Israel to possess the land according to their tribes.

9"'This is what the Sovereign LORD says: You have gone far enough, princes of Israel! Give up your violence and oppression and do what is just and right. Stop dispossessing my people, declares the Sovereign LORD. 10You are to use accurate scales, an accurate ephah[k] and an accurate bath.[l] 11The ephah and the bath are to be the same size, the bath containing a tenth of

a homer and the ephah a tenth of a homer; the homer is to be the standard measure for both. 12The shekel[m] is to consist of twenty gerahs. Twenty shekels plus twenty-five shekels plus fifteen shekels equal one mina.[n]

13"'This is the special gift you are to offer: a sixth of an ephah[o] from each homer of wheat and a sixth of an ephah[p] from each homer of barley. 14The prescribed portion of olive oil, measured by the bath, is a tenth of a bath[q] from each cor (which consists of ten baths or one homer, for ten baths are equivalent to a homer). 15Also one sheep is to be taken from every flock of two hundred from the well-watered pastures of Israel. These will be used for the grain offerings, burnt offerings and fellowship offerings to make atonement for the people, declares the Sovereign LORD. 16All the people of the land will be required to give this special offering to the prince in Israel. 17It will be the duty of the prince to provide the burnt offerings, grain offerings and drink offerings at the festivals, the New Moons and the Sabbaths—at all the appointed festivals of Israel. He will provide the sin offerings,[r] grain offerings, burnt offerings and fellowship offerings to make atonement for the Israelites.

18"'This is what the Sovereign LORD says: In the first month on the first day you are to take a young bull without defect and purify the sanctuary. 19The priest is to take some of the blood of the sin offering and put it on the doorposts of the temple, on the four corners of the upper ledge of the altar and on the gateposts of the inner court. 20You are to do the same on the seventh day of the month for anyone who sins

---

a 27 Or purification offering; also in verse 29   b 29 The Hebrew term refers to the irrevocable giving over of things or persons to the LORD.   c 1 That is, about 8 miles or about 13 kilometers; also in verses 3, 5 and 6   d 1 Septuagint (see also verses 3 and 5 and 48:9); Hebrew 10,000   e 1 That is, about 6 1/2 miles or about 11 kilometers   f 2 That is, about 875 feet or about 265 meters   g 2 That is, about 88 feet or about 27 meters   h 3 That is, about 3 1/3 miles or about 5.3 kilometers; also in verse 5   i 5 Septuagint; Hebrew temple; they will have as their possession 20 rooms   j 6 That is, about 1 2/3 miles or about 2.7 kilometers   k 10 An ephah was a dry measure having the capacity of about 3/5 bushel or about 22 liters.   l 10 A bath was a liquid measure equaling about 6 gallons or about 22 liters.   m 12 A shekel weighed about 2/5 ounce or about 12 grams.   n 12 That is, 60 shekels; the common mina was 50 shekels. Sixty shekels were about 1 1/2 pounds or about 690 grams.   o 13 That is, probably about 6 pounds or about 2.7 kilograms   p 13 That is, probably about 5 pounds or about 2.3 kilograms   q 14 That is, about 2 1/2 quarts or about 2.2 liters   r 17 Or purification offerings; also in verses 19, 22, 23 and 25

unintentionally or through ignorance; so you are to make atonement for the temple.

²¹ "'In the first month on the fourteenth day you are to observe the Passover, a festival lasting seven days, during which you shall eat bread made without yeast. ²²On that day the prince is to provide a bull as a sin offering for himself and for all the people of the land. ²³Every day during the seven days of the festival he is to provide seven bulls and seven rams without defect as a burnt offering to the LORD, and a male goat for a sin offering. ²⁴He is to provide as a grain offering an ephah for each bull and an ephah for each ram, along with a hin^a of olive oil for each ephah.

²⁵ "'During the seven days of the festival, which begins in the seventh month on the fifteenth day, he is to make the same provision for sin offerings, burnt offerings, grain offerings and oil.

46

"'This is what the Sovereign LORD says: The gate of the inner court facing east is to be shut on the six working days, but on the Sabbath day and on the day of the New Moon it is to be opened. ²The prince is to enter from the outside through the portico of the gateway and stand by the gatepost. The priests are to sacrifice his burnt offering and his fellowship offerings. He is to bow down in worship at the threshold of the gateway and then go out, but the gate will not be shut until evening. ³On the Sabbaths and New Moons the people of the land are to worship in the presence of the LORD at the entrance of that gateway. ⁴The burnt offering the prince brings to the LORD on the Sabbath day is to be six male lambs and a ram, all without defect. ⁵The grain offering given with the ram is to be an ephah,^{b} and the grain offering with the lambs is to be as much as he pleases, along with a hin^c of olive oil for each ephah. ⁶On the day of the New Moon he is to offer a young bull, six lambs and a ram, all without defect. ⁷He is to provide as a grain offering one ephah with the bull, one ephah with the ram, and with the lambs as much as he wants to give, along with a hin of oil for each ephah. ⁸When the prince enters, he is to go in through the portico of the gateway, and he is to come out the same way.

⁹ "'When the people of the land come before the LORD at the appointed festivals, whoever enters by the north gate to worship is to go out the south gate; and whoever enters by the south gate is to go out the north gate. No one is to return through the gate by which they entered, but each is to go out the opposite gate. ¹⁰The prince is to

be among them, going in when they go in and going out when they go out. ¹¹At the feasts and the appointed festivals, the grain offering is to be an ephah with a bull, an ephah with a ram, and with the lambs as much as he pleases, along with a hin of oil for each ephah.

¹² "'When the prince provides a freewill offering to the LORD — whether a burnt offering or fellowship offerings — the gate facing east is to be opened for him. He shall offer his burnt offering or his fellowship offerings as he does on the Sabbath day. Then he shall go out, and after he has gone out, the gate will be shut.

¹³ "'Every day you are to provide a year-old lamb without defect for a burnt offering to the LORD; morning by morning you shall provide it. ¹⁴You are also to provide with it morning by morning a grain offering, consisting of a sixth of an ephah^d with a third of a hin^e of oil to moisten the flour. The presenting of this grain offering to the LORD is a lasting ordinance. ¹⁵So the lamb and the grain offering and the oil shall be provided morning by morning for a regular burnt offering.

¹⁶ "'This is what the Sovereign LORD says: If the prince makes a gift from his inheritance to one of his sons, it will also belong to his descendants; it is to be their property by inheritance. ¹⁷If, however, he makes a gift from his inheritance to one of his servants, the servant may keep it until the year of freedom; then it will revert to the prince. His inheritance belongs to his sons only; it is theirs. ¹⁸The prince must not take any of the inheritance of the people, driving them off their property. He is to give his sons their inheritance out of his own property, so that not one of my people will be separated from their property.'"

¹⁹Then the man brought me through the entrance at the side of the gate to the sacred rooms facing north, which belonged to the priests, and showed me a place at the western end. ²⁰He said to me, "This is the place where the priests are to cook the guilt offering and the sin offering^f and bake the grain offering, to avoid bringing them into the outer court and consecrating the people."

²¹He then brought me to the outer court and led me around to its four corners, and I saw in

---

^{a} 24 That is, about 1 gallon or about 3.8 liters ^{b} 5 That is, probably about 35 pounds or about 16 kilograms; also in verses 7 and 11 ^{c} 5 That is, about 1 gallon or about 3.8 liters; also in verses 7 and 11 ^{d} 14 That is, probably about 6 pounds or about 2.7 kilograms ^{e} 14 That is, about 1 1/2 quarts or about 1.3 liters ^{f} 20 Or purification offering

each corner another court. ²²In the four corners of the outer court were enclosed[a] courts, forty cubits long and thirty cubits wide;[b] each of the courts in the four corners was the same size. ²³Around the inside of each of the four courts was a ledge of stone, with places for fire built all around under the ledge. ²⁴He said to me, "These are the kitchens where those who minister at the temple are to cook the sacrifices of the people."

The River From the Temple

47 The man brought me back to the entrance to the temple, and I saw water coming out from under the threshold of the temple toward the east (for the temple faced east). The water was coming down from under the south side of the temple, south of the altar. ²He then brought me out through the north gate and led me around the outside to the outer gate facing east, and the water was trickling from the south side.

³As the man went eastward with a measuring line in his hand, he measured off a thousand cubits[c] and then led me through water that was ankle-deep. ⁴He measured off another thousand cubits and led me through water that was knee-deep. He measured off another thousand and led me through water that was up to the waist. ⁵He measured off another thousand, but now it was a river that I could not cross, because the water had risen and was deep enough to swim in — a river that no one could cross. ⁶He asked me, "Son of man, do you see this?"

Then he led me back to the bank of the river. ⁷When I arrived there, I saw a great number of trees on each side of the river. ⁸He said to me, "This water flows toward the eastern region and goes down into the Arabah,[d] where it enters the Dead Sea. When it empties into the sea, the salty water there becomes fresh. ⁹Swarms of living creatures will live wherever the river flows. There will be large numbers of fish, because this water flows there and makes the salt water fresh; so where the river flows everything will live. ¹⁰Fishermen will stand along the shore; from En Gedi to En Eglaim there will be places for spreading nets. The fish will be of many kinds — like the fish of the Mediterranean Sea. ¹¹But the swamps and marshes will not become fresh; they will be left for salt. ¹²Fruit trees of all kinds will grow on both banks of the river. Their leaves will not wither, nor will their fruit fail. Every month they will bear fruit, because the water from the sanctuary flows to them.

Their fruit will serve for food and their leaves for healing."

The Boundaries of the Land

¹³This is what the Sovereign LORD says: "These are the boundaries of the land that you will divide among the twelve tribes of Israel as their inheritance, with two portions for Joseph. ¹⁴You are to divide it equally among them. Because I swore with uplifted hand to give it to your ancestors, this land will become your inheritance.

¹⁵"This is to be the boundary of the land:

"On the north side it will run from the Mediterranean Sea by the Hethlon road past Lebo Hamath to Zedad, ¹⁶Berothah[e] and Sibraim (which lies on the border between Damascus and Hamath), as far as Hazer Hattikon, which is on the border of Hauran. ¹⁷The boundary will extend from the sea to Hazar Enan,[f] along the northern border of Damascus, with the border of Hamath to the north. This will be the northern boundary.

¹⁸"On the east side the boundary will run between Hauran and Damascus, along the Jordan between Gilead and the land of Israel, to the Dead Sea and as far as Tamar.[g] This will be the eastern boundary.

¹⁹"On the south side it will run from Tamar as far as the waters of Meribah Kadesh, then along the Wadi of Egypt to the Mediterranean Sea. This will be the southern boundary.

²⁰"On the west side, the Mediterranean Sea will be the boundary to a point opposite Lebo Hamath. This will be the western boundary.

²¹"You are to distribute this land among yourselves according to the tribes of Israel. ²²You are to allot it as an inheritance for yourselves and for the foreigners residing among you and who have children. You are to consider them as native-born Israelites; along with you they are to be allotted an inheritance among the tribes of Israel. ²³In whatever tribe a foreigner resides, there you are to give them their inheritance," declares the Sovereign LORD.

---

[a] 22 The meaning of the Hebrew for this word is uncertain.   [b] 22 That is, about 70 feet long and 53 feet wide or about 21 meters long and 16 meters wide   [c] 3 That is, about 1,700 feet or about 530 meters   [d] 8 Or *the Jordan Valley*   [e] 15,16 See Septuagint and 48:1; Hebrew *road to go into Zedad,* ¹⁶*Hamath, Berothah.*   [f] 17 Hebrew *Enon,* a variant of *Enan*   [g] 18 See Syriac; Hebrew *Israel. You will measure to the Dead Sea.*

The Division of the Land

48 "These are the tribes, listed by name: At the northern frontier, Dan will have one portion; it will follow the Hethlon road to Lebo Hamath; Hazar Enan and the northern border of Damascus next to Hamath will be part of its border from the east side to the west side.

2"Asher will have one portion; it will border the territory of Dan from east to west.

3"Naphtali will have one portion; it will border the territory of Asher from east to west.

4"Manasseh will have one portion; it will border the territory of Naphtali from east to west.

5"Ephraim will have one portion; it will border the territory of Manasseh from east to west.

6"Reuben will have one portion; it will border the territory of Ephraim from east to west.

7"Judah will have one portion; it will border the territory of Reuben from east to west.

8"Bordering the territory of Judah from east to west will be the portion you are to present as a special gift. It will be 25,000 cubits*a* wide, and its length from east to west will equal one of the tribal portions; the sanctuary will be in the center of it.

9"The special portion you are to offer to the LORD will be 25,000 cubits long and 10,000 cubits*b* wide. 10This will be the sacred portion for the priests. It will be 25,000 cubits long on the north side, 10,000 cubits wide on the west side, 10,000 cubits wide on the east side and 25,000 cubits long on the south side. In the center of it will be the sanctuary of the LORD. 11This will be for the consecrated priests, the Zadokites, who were faithful in serving me and did not go astray as the Levites did when the Israelites went astray. 12It will be a special gift to them from the sacred portion of the land, a most holy portion, bordering the territory of the Levites.

13"Alongside the territory of the priests, the Levites will have an allotment 25,000 cubits long and 10,000 cubits wide. Its total length will be 25,000 cubits and its width 10,000 cubits. 14They must not sell or exchange any of it. This is the best of the land and must not pass into other hands, because it is holy to the LORD.

15"The remaining area, 5,000 cubits*c* wide and 25,000 cubits long, will be for the common use of the city, for houses and for pastureland. The city will be in the center of it 16and will have these measurements: the north side 4,500 cubits,*d* the south side 4,500 cubits, the east side 4,500 cubits, and the west side 4,500 cubits. 17The pastureland for the city will be 250 cubits*e*

on the north, 250 cubits on the south, 250 cubits on the east, and 250 cubits on the west. 18What remains of the area, bordering on the sacred portion and running the length of it, will be 10,000 cubits on the east side and 10,000 cubits on the west side. Its produce will supply food for the workers of the city. 19The workers from the city who farm it will come from all the tribes of Israel. 20The entire portion will be a square, 25,000 cubits on each side. As a special gift you will set aside the sacred portion, along with the property of the city.

21"What remains on both sides of the area formed by the sacred portion and the property of the city will belong to the prince. It will extend eastward from the 25,000 cubits of the sacred portion to the eastern border, and westward from the 25,000 cubits to the western border. Both these areas running the length of the tribal portions will belong to the prince, and the sacred portion with the temple sanctuary will be in the center of them. 22So the property of the Levites and the property of the city will lie in the center of the area that belongs to the prince. The area belonging to the prince will lie between the border of Judah and the border of Benjamin.

23"As for the rest of the tribes: Benjamin will have one portion; it will extend from the east side to the west side.

24"Simeon will have one portion; it will border the territory of Benjamin from east to west.

25"Issachar will have one portion; it will border the territory of Simeon from east to west.

26"Zebulun will have one portion; it will border the territory of Issachar from east to west.

27"Gad will have one portion; it will border the territory of Zebulun from east to west.

28"The southern boundary of Gad will run south from Tamar to the waters of Meribah Kadesh, then along the Wadi of Egypt to the Mediterranean Sea.

29"This is the land you are to allot as an inheritance to the tribes of Israel, and these will be their portions," declares the Sovereign LORD.

The Gates of the New City

30"These will be the exits of the city: Beginning on the north side, which is 4,500 cubits long, 31the gates of the city will be named after

---

a 8 That is, about 8 miles or about 13 kilometers; also in verses 9, 10, 13, 15, 20 and 21   *b 9* That is, about 3 1/3 miles or about 5.3 kilometers; also in verses 10, 13 and 18   *c 15* That is, about 1 2/3 miles or about 2.7 kilometers   *d 16* That is, about 1 1/2 miles or about 2.4 kilometers; also in verses 30, 32, 33 and 34   *e 17* That is, about 440 feet or about 135 meters

the tribes of Israel. The three gates on the north side will be the gate of Reuben, the gate of Judah and the gate of Levi.

³²"On the east side, which is 4,500 cubits long, will be three gates: the gate of Joseph, the gate of Benjamin and the gate of Dan.

³³"On the south side, which measures 4,500 cubits, will be three gates: the gate of Simeon, the gate of Issachar and the gate of Zebulun.

³⁴"On the west side, which is 4,500 cubits long, will be three gates: the gate of Gad, the gate of Asher and the gate of Naphtali.

³⁵"The distance all around will be 18,000 cubits.[a]

"And the name of the city from that time on will be:

THE LORD IS THERE."

---

[a] 35 That is, about 6 miles or about 9.5 kilometers

INTRODUCTION TO DANIEL

Faith and Leadership in Action

The exemplary personal character of Daniel makes him a favorite Bible personality for many. He is one of only a handful of men in the Bible about whom God says nothing negative. Although he shared the human nature of all other biblical leaders, he seems to rise above the others because of a combination of qualities:

- **Character**—He displays character by refusing to do wrong before foreign kings.
- **Competence**—Kings offer to pay him for his ability to interpret dreams.
- **Convictions**—He refuses to eat the king's meat or drink his wine.
- **Courage**—He faces the lions' den without flinching.
- **Charisma**—He is so winsome that royalty wants him to play key roles in government.
- **Commitment**—He remains committed to his God despite pressure to compromise.
- **Compassion**—He never loses his love for others, even in an enemy culture.

In the early chapters of the book, we see Daniel and his Hebrew friends in action as they live out their faith and leadership in a foreign land. Daniel stands up to King Nebuchadnezzar and requests that he and his friends be allowed to eat something other than what fills the plates of the other young men in the palace. He negotiates terms and ends up stronger and healthier for his decision. This catches the attention of the Babylonian officials and Daniel becomes a man of influence, even as a youth. Soon, he is interpreting dreams for the king, offering wise counsel

God's Role in Daniel

Old Testament leaders succeeded as long as they stayed intimately connected to God. Daniel proves this pattern. God continually blessed Daniel with wisdom, skills and favor, as long as Daniel maintained his character and courage.

God led Daniel faithfully from the time he was a young boy. By the time of the Babylonian captivity, Daniel and his friends had followed Yahweh for years. They continued this lifestyle as adults, and God not only blessed them but bailed them out of dangerous and even deadly situations.

The book of Daniel serves as a powerful illustration of what can happen when God and a healthy, spiritual leader cooperate to reach their world.

Leaders in Daniel

Daniel, Nebuchadnezzar, Darius, Belshazzar

Other People of Influence in Daniel

Shadrach, Meshach, Abednego, the king's officials

Lessons in Leadership

- Leaders must first possess godly qualities before they develop skills.
- Commitment precedes everything—resources will follow a leader's resolve.

to officials, and demonstrating a commitment to his faith rare for anyone, young or old.

Before he is through, Daniel has left a legacy stretching over the reigns of three kings, both Babylonian and Persian. He was a leader who lived the life God meant him to live. As he aged, he moved from interpreter of dreams to a dreamer himself—providing prophetic insight into the end times. He delivered his deep and complex words from a pure heart, showing himself to be a man who loved God, lived his faith, and wanted to influence many others to embrace Yahweh. As you read the book, watch for Daniel, Shadrach, Meshach and Abednego to demonstrate leadership powerful enough to influence entire people groups to follow.

- Leaders must often stand alone as they begin their journey.
- To identify the leader in a group, look for the one to whom everyone listens.
- A gift may take a leader to the top, but humility enables him to endure.
- Spiritual leaders talk to God about people before talking to people about God.
- Godly leaders do not pursue their own fame, but are out to make God famous.

LEADERSHIP HIGHLIGHTS IN DANIEL

Daniel's Training in Babylon

1 In the third year of the reign of Jehoiakim king of Judah, Nebuchadnezzar king of Babylon came to Jerusalem and besieged it. ²And the Lord delivered Jehoiakim king of Judah into his hand, along with some of the articles from the temple of God. These he carried off to the temple of his god in Babylonia*a* and put in the treasure house of his god.

³Then the king ordered Ashpenaz, chief of his court officials, to bring into the king's service some of the Israelites from the royal family and the nobility — ⁴young men without any physical defect, handsome, showing aptitude for every kind of learning, well informed, quick to understand, and qualified to serve in the king's palace. He was to teach them the language and literature of the Babylonians.*b* ⁵The king assigned them a daily amount of food and wine from the king's table. They were to be trained for three years, and after that they were to enter the king's service.

⁶Among those who were chosen were some from Judah: Daniel, Hananiah, Mishael and Azariah. ⁷The chief official gave them new names: to Daniel, the name Belteshazzar; to Hananiah, Shadrach; to Mishael, Meshach; and to Azariah, Abednego.

⁸But Daniel resolved not to defile himself with the royal food and wine, and he asked the chief official for permission not to defile himself this way. ⁹Now God had caused the official to show favor and compassion to Daniel, ¹⁰but the official told Daniel, "I am afraid of my lord the king, who has assigned your*c* food and drink. Why should he see you looking worse than the other young men your age? The king would then have my head because of you."

¹¹Daniel then said to the guard whom the chief official had appointed over Daniel, Hananiah, Mishael and Azariah, ¹²"Please test your servants for ten days: Give us nothing but vegetables to eat and water to drink. ¹³Then compare our appearance with that of the young men who eat the royal food, and treat your servants

---

a 2 Hebrew *Shinar*   *b 4* Or *Chaldeans*   *c 10* The Hebrew for *your* and *you* in this verse is plural.

Leadership Qualifications: Prerequisite for Responsibility

Daniel 1:4–19

The victorious Babylonians took Daniel and other sharp, young Hebrews to their king, who wanted to groom them as leaders. What qualities did the king seek? Take a look and see if you would like to have such emerging leaders working alongside of you!

1. **Young (v. 4).** They were youths, still young enough to be trained.

2. **Sharp looking (v. 4).** They were well-groomed and well-dressed.

3. **Intelligent (v. 4).** They had good minds and could process information quickly.

4. **Diverse skills (v. 4).** They displayed a variety of skills.

5. **Competent (v. 4).** They showed wisdom in using their skills to achieve results.

6. **Servant's heart (v. 4).** They served others however they might be needed.

7. **Teachable (vv. 4–5).** They were able and hungry to learn new concepts.

8. **Convictional (v. 8).** They possessed inward strength and values.

9. **Favor with people (v. 9).** They enjoyed influence with others.

10. **Submissive (v. 12).** They willingly became team players.

11. **Relational (v. 12).** They had good people skills and charisma.

12. **Well-informed (v. 17).** They possessed knowledge in a variety of areas.

13. **Gifted (v. 17).** They had valuable abilities obvious to others.

14. **Excellence (v. 19).** They were men of excellence and high standards.

in accordance with what you see." [14]So he agreed to this and tested them for ten days.

[15]At the end of the ten days they looked healthier and better nourished than any of the young men who ate the royal food. [16]So the guard took away their choice food and the wine they were to drink and gave them vegetables instead.

[17]To these four young men God gave knowledge and understanding of all kinds of literature and learning. And Daniel could understand visions and dreams of all kinds.

[18]At the end of the time set by the king to bring them into his service, the chief official presented them to Nebuchadnezzar. [19]The king talked with them, and he found none equal to Daniel, Hananiah, Mishael and Azariah; so they entered the king's service. [20]In every matter of wisdom and understanding about which the king questioned them, he found them ten times better than all the magicians and enchanters in his whole kingdom.

[21]And Daniel remained there until the first year of King Cyrus.

Nebuchadnezzar's Dream

2 In the second year of his reign, Nebuchadnezzar had dreams; his mind was troubled and he could not sleep. [2]So the king summoned the magicians, enchanters, sorcerers and astrologers[a] to tell him what he had dreamed. When they came in and stood before the king, [3]he said to them, "I have had a dream that troubles me and I want to know what it means.[b]"

[4]Then the astrologers answered the king,[c] "May the king live forever! Tell your servants the dream, and we will interpret it."

[5]The king replied to the astrologers, "This is what I have firmly decided: If you do not tell me what my dream was and interpret it, I will have you cut into pieces and your houses turned into piles of rubble. [6]But if you tell me the dream and explain it, you will receive from me gifts and rewards and great honor. So tell me the dream and interpret it for me."

[7]Once more they replied, "Let the king tell his servants the dream, and we will interpret it."

[8]Then the king answered, "I am certain that you are trying to gain time, because you realize that this is what I have firmly decided: [9]If you do not tell me the dream, there is only one penalty for you. You have conspired to tell me misleading and wicked things, hoping the situation will change. So then, tell me the dream, and I will know that you can interpret it for me."

[10]The astrologers answered the king, "There is no one on earth who can do what the king asks! No king, however great and mighty, has ever asked such a thing of any magician or enchanter or astrologer. [11]What the king asks is too difficult. No one can reveal it to the king except the gods, and they do not live among humans."

[12]This made the king so angry and furious that he ordered the execution of all the wise men of Babylon. [13]So the decree was issued to put the wise men to death, and men were sent to look for Daniel and his friends to put them to death.

[14]When Arioch, the commander of the king's guard, had gone out to put to death the wise men of Babylon, Daniel spoke to him with wisdom and tact. [15]He asked the king's officer, "Why did the king issue such a harsh decree?" Arioch then explained the matter to Daniel. [16]At this, Daniel went in to the king and asked for time, so that he might interpret the dream for him.

[17]Then Daniel returned to his house and explained the matter to his friends Hananiah, Mishael and Azariah. [18]He urged them to plead for mercy from the God of heaven concerning this mystery, so that he and his friends might not be executed with the rest of the wise men of Babylon. [19]During the night the mystery was revealed to Daniel in a vision. Then Daniel praised the God of heaven [20]and said:

"Praise be to the name of God for ever and
        ever;
    wisdom and power are his.
[21]He changes times and seasons;
    he deposes kings and raises up others.
He gives wisdom to the wise
    and knowledge to the discerning.
[22]He reveals deep and hidden things;
    he knows what lies in darkness,
    and light dwells with him.
[23]I thank and praise you, God of my ancestors:
    You have given me wisdom and power,
you have made known to me what we asked
        of you,
    you have made known to us the dream of
        the king."

Daniel Interprets the Dream

[24]Then Daniel went to Arioch, whom the king had appointed to execute the wise men of

---

[a] 2 Or *Chaldeans*; also in verses 4, 5 and 10   [b] 3 Or *was*
[c] 4 At this point the Hebrew text has *in Aramaic*, indicating that the text from here through the end of chapter 7 is in Aramaic.

Babylon, and said to him, "Do not execute the wise men of Babylon. Take me to the king, and I will interpret his dream for him."

²⁵Arioch took Daniel to the king at once and said, "I have found a man among the exiles from Judah who can tell the king what his dream means."

²⁶The king asked Daniel (also called Belteshazzar), "Are you able to tell me what I saw in my dream and interpret it?"

²⁷Daniel replied, "No wise man, enchanter, magician or diviner can explain to the king the mystery he has asked about, ²⁸but there is a God in heaven who reveals mysteries. He has shown King Nebuchadnezzar what will happen in days to come. Your dream and the visions that passed through your mind as you were lying in bed are these:

²⁹"As Your Majesty was lying there, your mind turned to things to come, and the revealer of mysteries showed you what is going to happen. ³⁰As for me, this mystery has been revealed to me, not because I have greater wisdom than anyone else alive, but so that Your Majesty may know the interpretation and that you may understand what went through your mind.

³¹"Your Majesty looked, and there before you stood a large statue—an enormous, dazzling statue, awesome in appearance. ³²The head of the statue was made of pure gold, its chest and arms of silver, its belly and thighs of bronze, ³³its legs of iron, its feet partly of iron and partly of baked clay. ³⁴While you were watching, a rock was cut out, but not by human hands. It struck the statue on its feet of iron and clay and smashed them. ³⁵Then the iron, the clay, the bronze, the silver and the gold were all broken to pieces and became like chaff on a threshing floor in the summer. The wind swept them away without leaving a trace. But the rock that struck the statue became a huge mountain and filled the whole earth.

³⁶"This was the dream, and now we will interpret it to the king. ³⁷Your Majesty, you are the king of kings. The God of heaven has given you dominion and power and might and glory; ³⁸in your hands he has placed all mankind and the beasts of the field and the birds in the sky. Wherever they live, he has made you ruler over them all. You are that head of gold.

³⁹"After you, another kingdom will arise, inferior to yours. Next, a third kingdom, one of bronze, will rule over the whole earth. ⁴⁰Finally, there will be a fourth kingdom, strong as iron— for iron breaks and smashes everything—and as iron breaks things to pieces, so it will crush and break all the others. ⁴¹Just as you saw that the feet and toes were partly of baked clay and partly of iron, so this will be a divided kingdom; yet it will have some of the strength of iron in it, even as you saw iron mixed with clay. ⁴²As the toes were partly iron and partly clay, so this kingdom will be partly strong and partly brittle. ⁴³And just as you saw the iron mixed with baked clay, so the people will be a mixture and will not remain united, any more than iron mixes with clay.

⁴⁴"In the time of those kings, the God of heaven will set up a kingdom that will never be destroyed, nor will it be left to another people. It will crush all those kingdoms and bring them to an end, but it will itself endure forever. ⁴⁵This is the meaning of the vision of the rock cut out of a mountain, but not by human hands—a rock that broke the iron, the bronze, the clay, the silver and the gold to pieces.

"The great God has shown the king what will take place in the future. The dream is true and its interpretation is trustworthy."

⁴⁶Then King Nebuchadnezzar fell prostrate before Daniel and paid him honor and ordered that an offering and incense be presented to him. ⁴⁷The king said to Daniel, "Surely your God is the God of gods and the Lord of kings and a revealer of mysteries, for you were able to reveal this mystery."

⁴⁸Then the king placed Daniel in a high position and lavished many gifts on him. He made him ruler over the entire province of Babylon and placed him in charge of all its wise men. ⁴⁹Moreover, at Daniel's request the king appointed Shadrach, Meshach and Abednego administrators over the province of Babylon, while Daniel himself remained at the royal court.

Nebuchadnezzar and Daniel: A Contrast in Pride and Humility

Daniel 2:1-28

When the magicians of Babylon fail to interpret a troubling dream, Nebuchadnezzar threatens to kill them all. He embodies pride and arrogance. Contrast him with Daniel, who steps forward to interpret the dream, yet refuses to accept personal glory. Instead, he honors the God of heaven.

21 QUALITIES

CHARACTER   Daniel Had What It Took!

Daniel 2:48

DOES THE PRIVATE life of a leader truly impact his or her public life? No question about it. Daniel illustrates why character plays such a vital role.

Daniel could have tried merely to survive his experience as a captive in a foreign land. Instead, he never left his disciplined life of character and personal commitment. Ponder the character he displayed during his times of testing under the kings of Babylon:

1. **His Diet: He wouldn't compromise on ritually unclean foods, but ate only vegetables.**

2. **His Motives: He didn't take credit for interpreting dreams, but glorified God instead.**

3. **His Honesty: He spoke the truth to authorities, regardless of its unpopularity.**

4. **His Disciplines: He continued praying daily, even though it might cost him his life.**

5. **His Integrity: He had no interest in bribes or payoffs.**

6. **His Convictions: He stayed committed to his friends and beliefs even as he rose through the ranks.**

How a leader deals with the circumstances of life tells you many things about his character. Crisis doesn't necessarily *make* character, but it certainly does *reveal* it. Adversity makes a person choose one of two paths: character or compromise. Every time a leader chooses character, he grows stronger.

Character is the foundation on which a leader builds his or her life. It all begins with character, because leadership operates on the basis of trust. People will follow a leader only so far as they trust him or her. Character communicates credibility, harnesses respect, creates consistency and earns trust.

Every leader must know the following about character:

1. **Character is more than talk.**
   Anyone can say that he has integrity, but action is the real indicator of character. Your character determines who you are and what you do. That's why you can never separate a leader's character from his actions. If a leader's actions and intentions continually work against each other, look to his character to find out why.

2. **Talent is a gift, but character is a choice.**
   We have no control over a lot of things in life. We don't get to choose our parents or the circumstances of our birth and upbringing. But we do choose our character. We create it each time we make choices.

3. Character brings lasting success with people.

True leadership always involves others. Followers do not trust leaders whose character they know to be flawed, and they will not continue to follow them.

4. Leaders cannot rise above the limitations of their character.

Character will either limit or support a leader, depending on its strength. It will always determine whether a leader finishes well.

For a negative example of character, see p. 1312.

The Image of Gold and the Blazing Furnace

3 King Nebuchadnezzar made an image of gold, sixty cubits high and six cubits wide,[a] and set it up on the plain of Dura in the province of Babylon. [2]He then summoned the satraps, prefects, governors, advisers, treasurers, judges, magistrates and all the other provincial officials to come to the dedication of the image he had set up. [3]So the satraps, prefects, governors, advisers, treasurers, judges, magistrates and all the other provincial officials assembled for the dedication of the image that King Nebuchadnezzar had set up, and they stood before it.

[4]Then the herald loudly proclaimed, "Nations and peoples of every language, this is what you are commanded to do: [5]As soon as you hear the sound of the horn, flute, zither, lyre, harp, pipe and all kinds of music, you must fall down and worship the image of gold that King Nebuchadnezzar has set up. [6]Whoever does not fall down and worship will immediately be thrown into a blazing furnace."

[7]Therefore, as soon as they heard the sound of the horn, flute, zither, lyre, harp and all kinds of music, all the nations and peoples of every language fell down and worshiped the image of gold that King Nebuchadnezzar had set up.

[8]At this time some astrologers[b] came forward and denounced the Jews. [9]They said to King Nebuchadnezzar, "May the king live forever! [10]Your Majesty has issued a decree that everyone who hears the sound of the horn, flute, zither, lyre, harp, pipe and all kinds of music must fall down and worship the image of gold, [11]and that whoever does not fall down and worship will be thrown into a blazing furnace. [12]But there are some Jews whom you have set over the affairs of the province of Babylon—Shadrach, Meshach and Abednego—who pay no attention to you, Your Majesty. They neither serve your gods nor worship the image of gold you have set up."

[13]Furious with rage, Nebuchadnezzar summoned Shadrach, Meshach and Abednego. So these men were brought before the king, [14]and Nebuchadnezzar said to them, "Is it true, Shadrach, Meshach and Abednego, that you do not serve my gods or worship the image of gold I have set up? [15]Now when you hear the sound of the horn, flute, zither, lyre, harp, pipe and all kinds of music, if you are ready to fall down and worship the image I made, very good. But if you do not worship it, you will be thrown immediately into a blazing furnace. Then what god will be able to rescue you from my hand?"

[16]Shadrach, Meshach and Abednego replied to him, "King Nebuchadnezzar, we do not need to defend ourselves before you in this matter. [17]If we are thrown into the blazing furnace, the

---

[a] 1 That is, about 90 feet high and 9 feet wide or about 27 meters high and 2.7 meters wide   [b] 8 Or *Chaldeans*

Commitment: When a Leader Has Resolve, Resources Follow

Daniel 3:1–18

When the three friends of Daniel refused to worship a statue Nebuchadnezzar had made, they told the king that they expected their God to deliver them. Immediately afterwards they made a bold statement of commitment: "But even if he does not, we want you to know, Your Majesty, that we will not serve your gods or worship the image of gold you have set up" (Da 3:18). The second statement did not dilute the first, but simply declared the men's resolve.

Once we make a commitment, the resources follow—but they seldom follow until we declare our commitment. From this text we learn the following about developing commitment:

1. **It usually begins with a struggle.**

2. **It seldom surrounds abilities or gifts.**

3. **It is the result of choice, not condition.**

4. **It is fostered when we settle the issue before it arises.**

5. **It is enhanced by deep trust in God.**

6. **It lasts when we remain single-minded.**

God we serve is able to deliver us from it, and he will deliver us[a] from Your Majesty's hand. [18]But even if he does not, we want you to know, Your Majesty, that we will not serve your gods or worship the image of gold you have set up."

[19]Then Nebuchadnezzar was furious with Shadrach, Meshach and Abednego, and his attitude toward them changed. He ordered the furnace heated seven times hotter than usual [20]and commanded some of the strongest soldiers in his army to tie up Shadrach, Meshach and Abednego and throw them into the blazing furnace. [21]So these men, wearing their robes, trousers, turbans and other clothes, were bound and thrown into the blazing furnace. [22]The king's command was so urgent and the furnace so hot that the flames of the fire killed the soldiers who took up Shadrach, Meshach and Abednego, [23]and these three men, firmly tied, fell into the blazing furnace.

[24]Then King Nebuchadnezzar leaped to his feet in amazement and asked his advisers, "Weren't there three men that we tied up and threw into the fire?"

They replied, "Certainly, Your Majesty."

[25]He said, "Look! I see four men walking around in the fire, unbound and unharmed, and the fourth looks like a son of the gods."

[26]Nebuchadnezzar then approached the opening of the blazing furnace and shouted, "Shadrach, Meshach and Abednego, servants of the Most High God, come out! Come here!"

So Shadrach, Meshach and Abednego came out of the fire, [27]and the satraps, prefects, governors and royal advisers crowded around them. They saw that the fire had not harmed their bodies, nor was a hair of their heads singed; their robes were not scorched, and there was no smell of fire on them.

[28]Then Nebuchadnezzar said, "Praise be to the God of Shadrach, Meshach and Abednego, who has sent his angel and rescued his servants! They trusted in him and defied the king's command and were willing to give up their lives rather than serve or worship any god except their own God. [29]Therefore I decree that the people of any nation or language who say anything against the God of Shadrach, Meshach and Abednego be cut into pieces and their houses be

---

[a] 17 Or *If the God we serve is able to deliver us, then he will deliver us from the blazing furnace and*

NEBUCHADNEZZAR

Face-to-Face with the Majesty of God
Daniel 3:1–30

PROFILE in leadership

While King Nebuchadnezzar provides a great example of a leader with seriously misplaced passion, he provides an even better example of what happens when a man comes face-to-face with the majesty of the living God.

Nebuchadnezzar, full of pride, created a 90-foot-high golden "god" whom all of his subjects were ordered to worship. It must have been a magnificent sight, gleaming brightly and all alone in the glare of the hot Mesopotamian sun.

But it was *just* a statue.

Nebuchadnezzar, a leader of great passion, threatened to kill anyone who disobeyed his orders. When three of God's servants refused to bow down, the king flew into a rage and ordered them burned alive. On that day, the king saw up close the infinite difference between the God of Israel and the idol he had set up. Before the king's bedazzled eyes, God performed a great miracle that left Nebuchadnezzar and the other witnesses gaping in awe.

The king would never be the same. He turned from his idol to the God whose people he had once persecuted. He praised the Lord and demanded that his subjects worship him alone.

Godly leaders should ask the Lord to show them regular glimpses of his power and glory. When he does that, it becomes much easier to direct our passion toward serving the one, true God.

turned into piles of rubble, for no other god can save in this way."

30 Then the king promoted Shadrach, Meshach and Abednego in the province of Babylon.

Nebuchadnezzar's Dream of a Tree

4 [a] King Nebuchadnezzar,

To the nations and peoples of every language, who live in all the earth:

May you prosper greatly!

2 It is my pleasure to tell you about the miraculous signs and wonders that the Most High God has performed for me.

3 How great are his signs,
   how mighty his wonders!
His kingdom is an eternal kingdom;
   his dominion endures from
      generation to generation.

4 I, Nebuchadnezzar, was at home in my palace, contented and prosperous. 5 I had a dream that made me afraid. As I was lying in bed, the images and visions that passed through my mind terrified me. 6 So

I commanded that all the wise men of Babylon be brought before me to interpret the dream for me. 7 When the magicians, enchanters, astrologers[b] and diviners came, I told them the dream, but they could not interpret it for me. 8 Finally, Daniel came into my presence and I told him the dream. (He is called Belteshazzar, after the name of my god, and the spirit of the holy gods is in him.)

9 I said, "Belteshazzar, chief of the magicians, I know that the spirit of the holy gods is in you, and no mystery is too difficult for you. Here is my dream; interpret it for me. 10 These are the visions I saw while lying in bed: I looked, and there before me stood a tree in the middle of the land. Its height was enormous. 11 The tree grew large and strong and its top touched the sky; it was visible to the ends of the earth. 12 Its leaves were beautiful, its fruit abundant, and on it was food for all. Under it the wild animals found shelter, and the

---

[a] In Aramaic texts 4:1-3 is numbered 3:31-33, and 4:4-37 is numbered 4:1-34.   [b] 7 Or *Chaldeans*

Competence: People Come to See a Gift in Action

Daniel 4:8

Although Nebuchadnezzar pays lip service to the Most High God after seeing him in action, he still thinks too highly of himself. So God gives him a vision about how he will be humbled. Once again, Daniel is called upon to interpret a dream, since all recognize him as the only one with the ability to explain such visions.

When a leader operates in the area of his or her gift, people *will* watch and listen. Competence is a key attribute for every leader. Without even knowing it, followers ask four questions of every leader:

1. **Knowledge: Does the leader know where he is going?**

2. **Desire: Do I want to go where the leader is going?**

3. **Ability: Can the leader get me there?**

4. **Trust: Do I trust this leader?**

Because Daniel could answer "yes" to each of these questions, he entered each challenge primed to succeed. He enjoyed peace, not panic; faith, not fear; and commitment, not compromise.

Every leader must ask, "What is my gift? What do I offer that people need? What unique contribution do I make that makes people want to follow me?"

---

birds lived in its branches; from it every creature was fed.

¹³"In the visions I saw while lying in bed, I looked, and there before me was a holy one, a messenger,ᵃ coming down from heaven. ¹⁴He called in a loud voice: 'Cut down the tree and trim off its branches; strip off its leaves and scatter its fruit. Let the animals flee from under it and the birds from its branches. ¹⁵But let the stump and its roots, bound with iron and bronze, remain in the ground, in the grass of the field.

"'Let him be drenched with the dew of heaven, and let him live with the animals among the plants of the earth. ¹⁶Let his mind be changed from that of a man and let him be given the mind of an animal, till seven timesᵇ pass by for him.

¹⁷"'The decision is announced by messengers, the holy ones declare the verdict, so that the living may know that the Most High is sovereign over all kingdoms on earth and gives them to anyone he wishes and sets over them the lowliest of people.'

¹⁸"This is the dream that I, King Nebuchadnezzar, had. Now, Belteshazzar, tell me what it means, for none of the wise men in my kingdom can interpret it for me. But you can, because the spirit of the holy gods is in you."

Daniel Interprets the Dream

¹⁹Then Daniel (also called Belteshazzar) was greatly perplexed for a time, and his thoughts terrified him. So the king said, "Belteshazzar, do not let the dream or its meaning alarm you."

Belteshazzar answered, "My lord, if only the dream applied to your enemies and its meaning to your adversaries! ²⁰The tree you saw, which grew large and strong, with its top touching the sky, visible to the whole earth, ²¹with beautiful leaves and abundant fruit, providing food for all, giving shelter to the wild animals, and having nesting places in its branches for the birds — ²²Your Majesty, you are that tree! You have become great and strong; your greatness has grown until it reaches the sky, and your dominion extends to distant parts of the earth.

²³"Your Majesty saw a holy one, a messenger, coming down from heaven and saying, 'Cut down the tree and destroy it, but leave the stump, bound with iron and bronze, in the grass of the field, while its roots remain in the ground. Let him be drenched with the dew of heaven; let him live with the wild animals, until seven times pass by for him.'

ᵃ 13 Or *watchman*; also in verses 17 and 23   ᵇ 16 Or *years*; also in verses 23, 25 and 32

24"This is the interpretation, Your Majesty, and this is the decree the Most High has issued against my lord the king: 25You will be driven away from people and will live with the wild animals; you will eat grass like the ox and be drenched with the dew of heaven. Seven times will pass by for you until you acknowledge that the Most High is sovereign over all kingdoms on earth and gives them to anyone he wishes. 26The command to leave the stump of the tree with its roots means that your kingdom will be restored to you when you acknowledge that Heaven rules. 27Therefore, Your Majesty, be pleased to accept my advice: Renounce your sins by doing what is right, and your wickedness by being kind to the oppressed. It may be that then your prosperity will continue."

The Dream Is Fulfilled

28All this happened to King Nebuchadnezzar. 29Twelve months later, as the king was walking on the roof of the royal palace of Babylon, 30he said, "Is not this the great Babylon I have built as the royal residence, by my mighty power and for the glory of my majesty?"

31Even as the words were on his lips, a voice came from heaven, "This is what is decreed for you, King Nebuchadnezzar: Your royal authority has been taken from you. 32You will be driven away from people and will live with the wild animals; you will eat grass like the ox. Seven times will pass by for you until you acknowledge that the Most High is sovereign over all kingdoms on earth and gives them to anyone he wishes."

33Immediately what had been said about Nebuchadnezzar was fulfilled. He was driven away from people and ate grass like the ox. His body was drenched with the dew of heaven until his hair grew like the feathers of an eagle and his nails like the claws of a bird.

34At the end of that time, I, Nebuchadnezzar, raised my eyes toward heaven, and my sanity was restored. Then I praised the Most High; I honored and glorified him who lives forever.

His dominion is an eternal dominion;
   his kingdom endures from generation to generation.

35All the peoples of the earth
   are regarded as nothing.
He does as he pleases
   with the powers of heaven
   and the peoples of the earth.
No one can hold back his hand
   or say to him: "What have you done?"

36At the same time that my sanity was restored, my honor and splendor were returned to me for the glory of my kingdom. My advisers and nobles sought me out, and I was restored to my throne and became even greater than before. 37Now I, Nebuchadnezzar, praise and exalt and glorify the King of heaven, because everything he does is right and all his ways are just. And those who walk in pride he is able to humble.

The Writing on the Wall

5 King Belshazzar gave a great banquet for a thousand of his nobles and drank wine with them. 2While Belshazzar was drinking his wine, he gave orders to bring in the gold and silver goblets that Nebuchadnezzar his father[a] had taken from the temple in Jerusalem, so that the king and his nobles, his wives and his concubines might drink from them. 3So they brought in the gold goblets that had been taken from the temple of God in Jerusalem, and the king and his nobles, his wives and his concubines drank from them. 4As they drank the wine, they praised the gods of gold and silver, of bronze, iron, wood and stone.

5Suddenly the fingers of a human hand appeared and wrote on the plaster of the wall, near the lampstand in the royal palace. The king watched the hand as it wrote. 6His face turned pale and he was so frightened that his legs became weak and his knees were knocking.

7The king summoned the enchanters, astrologers[b] and diviners. Then he said to these wise men of Babylon, "Whoever reads this writing and tells me what it means will be clothed in purple and have a gold chain placed around his neck, and he will be made the third highest ruler in the kingdom."

8Then all the king's wise men came in, but they could not read the writing or tell the king what it meant. 9So King Belshazzar became even more terrified and his face grew more pale. His nobles were baffled.

---

[a] 2 Or *ancestor;* or *predecessor;* also in verses 11, 13 and 18
[b] 7 Or *Chaldeans;* also in verse 11

21 QUALITIES

TEACHABILITY The King Is Slow to Learn

Daniel 4:1–37

KING NEBUCHADNEZZAR proved himself to be one of the most arrogant leaders in history, so self-centered and prideful that God dealt with him in a most unusual way.

God gave the king a vision of a huge tree, chopped down by an angel. The tree represented *him*. God removed him from his position and drove him into the wilderness to live like an animal. His hair and fingernails grew long; he ate the same diet as the beasts of the field; he dwelt in caves and dirt shelters. And he stayed out there until he fully recognized God as the supreme Ruler of the world. He had to learn submission, relinquish control and power, and become teachable.

Fortunately, God's discipline worked. Once the king returned to the palace, he became a different man. He no longer laid claim to sovereignty or wisdom. He perceived his greatness as God-given (Da 4:36). He sought to honor God rather than himself as the source of every good thing (4:37). Notice how Nebuchadnezzar developed a teachable spirit:

1. **Grateful Words**
   The king expressed appreciation and blessing for God's grace and mercy.
2. **Hungry Mind**
   The king possessed a passion and hunger for personal growth.
3. **Big-picture Perspective**
   The king saw things from a new, larger viewpoint.
4. **Dissatisfaction with the Present**
   The king did not feel content with the status quo or mediocrity.
5. **Humble Heart**
   The king expressed humility regarding his own importance and power.
6. **Magnetic Spirit**
   The king began once more to attract nobles and counselors.

How about you? Are you a teachable leader? Do you want to dictate the people or circumstances from whom you will learn, or will you learn from anyone? Consider a few steps to improve your teachability:

1. *Don't believe your own press.*
   The greatest enemy of tomorrow's success is today's. Don't get distracted by your achievements.
2. *Observe how you react to mistakes.*
   Do you admit them when you make them? Do you apologize or get defensive? Get honest about your needs.
3. *Try something new.*
   When was the last time you did something for the first time? Challenges change us for the better and keep us learning.
4. *Grow in the area of your strength.*
   Read books on leadership and in your area of giftedness. Don't be satisfied with where you are today. Keep stretching.

For a positive example of teachability, see p. 1323.

[10]The queen,[a] hearing the voices of the king and his nobles, came into the banquet hall. "May the king live forever!" she said. "Don't be alarmed! Don't look so pale! [11]There is a man in your kingdom who has the spirit of the holy gods in him. In the time of your father he was found to have insight and intelligence and wisdom like that of the gods. Your father, King Nebuchadnezzar, appointed him chief of the magicians, enchanters, astrologers and diviners. [12]He did this because Daniel, whom the king called Belteshazzar, was found to have a keen mind and knowledge and understanding, and also the ability to interpret dreams, explain riddles and solve difficult problems. Call for Daniel, and he will tell you what the writing means."

[13]So Daniel was brought before the king, and the king said to him, "Are you Daniel, one of the exiles my father the king brought from Judah? [14]I have heard that the spirit of the gods is in you and that you have insight, intelligence and outstanding wisdom. [15]The wise men and enchanters were brought before me to read this writing and tell me what it means, but they could not explain it. [16]Now I have heard that you are able to give interpretations and to solve difficult problems. If you can read this writing and tell me what it means, you will be clothed in purple and have a gold chain placed around your neck, and you will be made the third highest ruler in the kingdom."

[17]Then Daniel answered the king, "You may keep your gifts for yourself and give your rewards to someone else. Nevertheless, I will read the writing for the king and tell him what it means.

[18]"Your Majesty, the Most High God gave your father Nebuchadnezzar sovereignty and

---

[a] 10 Or queen mother

The Law of Influence: When Daniel Spoke, People Listened

Daniel 5:13–14

Despite the fact that Daniel was a refugee in a foreign land, he had influence. At times, he had no position or title, but when Daniel spoke, everyone listened. Why? People listened to Daniel for the following reasons:

1. **Relationships: People listen to us because of who we know.**
   Daniel had a reputation for knowing the God of Israel.

2. **Sacrifice: People listen to us because of what we have suffered.**
   Daniel gave up his right to eat the king's food.

3. **Character: People listen to us because of our integrity.**
   Daniel remained blameless and trustworthy even when he had to rebuke kings.

4. **Relevance: People listen to us because we identify with their needs.**
   Daniel lived with the Babylonians and identified with their struggles and lifestyle.

5. **Insight: People listen to us because of what we know.**
   Daniel could interpret dreams and visions that confused everyone else.

6. **Vulnerability: People listen to us because we are genuinely transparent.**
   Daniel's life was an open book.

7. **Experience: People listen to us because we've succeeded in the past.**
   Daniel's credibility came from years of living well.

8. **Humility: People listen to us when we incarnate meekness.**
   Daniel served and submitted to authorities, unless they broke a higher law.

9. **Competence: People listen to us because of our abilities and expertise.**
   Daniel did many things better than anyone else.

10. **Courage: People listen to us because we demonstrate conviction.**
    Daniel was no one's puppet and showed he would die for his convictions.

greatness and glory and splendor. [19]Because of the high position he gave him, all the nations and peoples of every language dreaded and feared him. Those the king wanted to put to death, he put to death; those he wanted to spare, he spared; those he wanted to promote, he promoted; and those he wanted to humble, he humbled. [20]But when his heart became arrogant and hardened with pride, he was deposed from his royal throne and stripped of his glory. [21]He was driven away from people and given the mind of an animal; he lived with the wild donkeys and ate grass like the ox; and his body was drenched with the dew of heaven, until he acknowledged that the Most High God is sovereign over all kingdoms on earth and sets over them anyone he wishes.

[22]"But you, Belshazzar, his son,[a] have not humbled yourself, though you knew all this. [23]Instead, you have set yourself up against the Lord of heaven. You had the goblets from his temple brought to you, and you and your nobles, your wives and your concubines drank wine from them. You praised the gods of silver and gold, of bronze, iron, wood and stone, which cannot see or hear or understand. But you did not honor the God who holds in his hand your life and all your ways. [24]Therefore he sent the hand that wrote the inscription.

[25]"This is the inscription that was written:

MENE, MENE, TEKEL, PARSIN

[26]"Here is what these words mean:

Mene[b]: God has numbered the days of your reign and brought it to an end.
[27] *Tekel*[c]: You have been weighed on the scales and found wanting.
[28] *Peres*[d]: Your kingdom is divided and given to the Medes and Persians."

[29]Then at Belshazzar's command, Daniel was clothed in purple, a gold chain was placed around his neck, and he was proclaimed the third highest ruler in the kingdom.

[30]That very night Belshazzar, king of the Babylonians,[e] was slain, [31]and Darius the Mede took over the kingdom, at the age of sixty-two.[f]

Daniel in the Den of Lions

6[g] It pleased Darius to appoint 120 satraps to rule throughout the kingdom, [2]with three administrators over them, one of whom was Daniel. The satraps were made accountable to them so that the king might not suffer loss.

[3]Now Daniel so distinguished himself among the administrators and the satraps by his exceptional qualities that the king planned to set him over the whole kingdom. [4]At this, the administrators and the satraps tried to find grounds for charges against Daniel in his conduct of government affairs, but they were unable to do so. They could find no corruption in him, because he was trustworthy and neither corrupt nor negligent. [5]Finally these men said, "We will never find any basis for charges against this man Daniel unless it has something to do with the law of his God."

[6]So these administrators and satraps went as a group to the king and said: "May King Darius live forever! [7]The royal administrators, prefects, satraps, advisers and governors have all agreed that the king should issue an edict and enforce the decree that anyone who prays to any god or human being during the next thirty days, except to you, Your Majesty, shall be thrown into the lions' den. [8]Now, Your Majesty, issue the decree and put it in writing so that it cannot be altered—in accordance with the law of the Medes and Persians, which cannot be repealed." [9]So King Darius put the decree in writing.

[10]Now when Daniel learned that the decree had been published, he went home to his upstairs room where the windows opened toward Jerusalem. Three times a day he got down on his knees and prayed, giving thanks to his God, just as he had done before. [11]Then these men went as a group and found Daniel praying and asking God for help. [12]So they went to the king and spoke to him about his royal decree: "Did you not publish a decree that during the next thirty days anyone who prays to any god or human being except to you, Your Majesty, would be thrown into the lions' den?"

The king answered, "The decree stands—in accordance with the law of the Medes and Persians, which cannot be repealed."

[13]Then they said to the king, "Daniel, who is one of the exiles from Judah, pays no attention to you, Your Majesty, or to the decree you put in writing. He still prays three times a day." [14]When the king heard this, he was greatly distressed; he was determined to rescue Daniel and made every effort until sundown to save him.

---

[a] 22 Or *descendant*; or *successor*   [b] 26 *Mene* can mean *numbered* or *mina* (a unit of money).   [c] 27 *Tekel* can mean *weighed* or *shekel*.   [d] 28 *Peres* (the singular of *Parsin*) can mean *divided* or *Persia* or *a half mina* or *a half shekel*.   [e] 30 Or *Chaldeans*   [f] 31 In Aramaic texts this verse (5:31) is numbered 6:1.   [g] In Aramaic texts 6:1-28 is numbered 6:2-29.

Decision Making: Choices Confirm or Compromise Values

Daniel 6:1–10

One day Daniel had to decide whether he would submit to an ungodly law, or stick with his convictions. He chose his life principles. He likely followed in the footsteps of other strong leaders of the Old Testament:

1. **Weigh out the options in front of you.**

2. **Ask if those choices force you to compromise personal values.**

3. **Seek wise counsel.**

4. **Count the cost.**

5. **Decide based on principles.**

6. **Act on your decision swiftly and firmly.**

Someone once said, "If you take so much time making a decision that it is too late to act, then you might as well have whittled a stick." This happens too often among contemporary leaders. They desire to do right, but by waiting to survey the pulse of their people, they paralyze the organization. Some leaders are so indecisive, their favorite color is plaid. Daniel maintained a set of values and principles that enabled him to make decisions quickly and confidently.

15Then the men went as a group to King Darius and said to him, "Remember, Your Majesty, that according to the law of the Medes and Persians no decree or edict that the king issues can be changed."

16So the king gave the order, and they brought Daniel and threw him into the lions' den. The king said to Daniel, "May your God, whom you serve continually, rescue you!"

17A stone was brought and placed over the mouth of the den, and the king sealed it with his own signet ring and with the rings of his nobles, so that Daniel's situation might not be changed. 18Then the king returned to his palace and spent the night without eating and without any entertainment being brought to him. And he could not sleep.

19At the first light of dawn, the king got up and hurried to the lions' den. 20When he came near the den, he called to Daniel in an anguished voice, "Daniel, servant of the living God, has your God, whom you serve continually, been able to rescue you from the lions?"

21Daniel answered, "May the king live forever! 22My God sent his angel, and he shut the mouths of the lions. They have not hurt me, because I was found innocent in his sight. Nor have I ever done any wrong before you, Your Majesty."

23The king was overjoyed and gave orders

to lift Daniel out of the den. And when Daniel was lifted from the den, no wound was found on him, because he had trusted in his God.

24At the king's command, the men who had falsely accused Daniel were brought in and thrown into the lions' den, along with their wives and children. And before they reached the floor of the den, the lions overpowered them and crushed all their bones.

25Then King Darius wrote to all the nations and peoples of every language in all the earth:

"May you prosper greatly!

26"I issue a decree that in every part of my kingdom people must fear and reverence the God of Daniel.

"For he is the living God
 and he endures forever;
his kingdom will not be destroyed,
 his dominion will never end.
27 He rescues and he saves;
 he performs signs and wonders
 in the heavens and on the earth.
He has rescued Daniel
 from the power of the lions."

28So Daniel prospered during the reign of Darius and the reign of Cyrus*a* the Persian.

a 28 Or *Darius, that is, the reign of Cyrus*

Daniel's Dream of Four Beasts

7 In the first year of Belshazzar king of Babylon, Daniel had a dream, and visions passed through his mind as he was lying in bed. He wrote down the substance of his dream.

[2] Daniel said: "In my vision at night I looked, and there before me were the four winds of heaven churning up the great sea. [3] Four great beasts, each different from the others, came up out of the sea.

[4] "The first was like a lion, and it had the wings of an eagle. I watched until its wings were torn off and it was lifted from the ground so that it stood on two feet like a human being, and the mind of a human was given to it.

[5] "And there before me was a second beast, which looked like a bear. It was raised up on one of its sides, and it had three ribs in its mouth between its teeth. It was told, 'Get up and eat your fill of flesh!'

[6] "After that, I looked, and there before me was another beast, one that looked like a leopard. And on its back it had four wings like those of a bird. This beast had four heads, and it was given authority to rule.

[7] "After that, in my vision at night I looked, and there before me was a fourth beast—terrifying and frightening and very powerful. It had large iron teeth; it crushed and devoured its victims and trampled underfoot whatever was left. It was different from all the former beasts, and it had ten horns.

[8] "While I was thinking about the horns, there before me was another horn, a little one, which came up among them; and three of the first horns were uprooted before it. This horn had eyes like the eyes of a human being and a mouth that spoke boastfully.

[9] "As I looked,

"thrones were set in place,
    and the Ancient of Days took his seat.
His clothing was as white as snow;
    the hair of his head was white like wool.
His throne was flaming with fire,
    and its wheels were all ablaze.
[10] A river of fire was flowing,
    coming out from before him.
Thousands upon thousands attended him;
    ten thousand times ten thousand stood
        before him.
The court was seated,
    and the books were opened.

[11] "Then I continued to watch because of the boastful words the horn was speaking. I kept looking until the beast was slain and its body destroyed and thrown into the blazing fire. [12] (The other beasts had been stripped of their authority, but were allowed to live for a period of time.)

[13] "In my vision at night I looked, and there before me was one like a son of man,[a] coming with the clouds of heaven. He approached the Ancient of Days and was led into his presence. [14] He was given authority, glory and sovereign power; all nations and peoples of every language worshiped him. His dominion is an everlasting dominion that will not pass away, and his kingdom is one that will never be destroyed.

The Interpretation of the Dream

[15] "I, Daniel, was troubled in spirit, and the visions that passed through my mind disturbed me. [16] I approached one of those standing there and asked him the meaning of all this.

"So he told me and gave me the interpretation of these things: [17] 'The four great beasts are four kings that will rise from the earth. [18] But the holy people of the Most High will receive the kingdom and will possess it forever—yes, for ever and ever.'

[19] "Then I wanted to know the meaning of the fourth beast, which was different from all the others and most terrifying, with its iron teeth and bronze claws—the beast that crushed and devoured its victims and trampled underfoot whatever was left. [20] I also wanted to know about the ten horns on its head and about the other horn that came up, before which three of them fell—the horn that looked more imposing than the others and that had eyes and a mouth that spoke boastfully. [21] As I watched, this horn was waging war against the holy people and defeating them, [22] until the Ancient of Days came and pronounced judgment in favor of the holy people of the Most High, and the time came when they possessed the kingdom.

[23] "He gave me this explanation: 'The fourth beast is a fourth kingdom that will appear on earth. It will be different from all the other kingdoms and will devour the whole earth, trampling it down and crushing it. [24] The ten horns are ten kings who will come from this kingdom. After them another king will arise, different from the earlier ones; he will subdue three kings. [25] He will speak against the Most High

---

[a] 13 The Aramaic phrase *bar enash* means *human being*. The phrase *son of man* is retained here because of its use in the New Testament as a title of Jesus, probably based largely on this verse.

The Role of Praying and Planning in Leadership

Daniel 7:1—12:13

God controls the future. Therefore, we should never plan without praying. If God isn't in our plans, we waste our time. At the same time, we should respond to the guidance God gives us. Once we get confirmation and peace from God, we should act accordingly. Obedience is a reflection of faith.

and oppress his holy people and try to change the set times and the laws. The holy people will be delivered into his hands for a time, times and half a time.*a*

26 " 'But the court will sit, and his power will be taken away and completely destroyed forever. 27 Then the sovereignty, power and greatness of all the kingdoms under heaven will be handed over to the holy people of the Most High. His kingdom will be an everlasting kingdom, and all rulers will worship and obey him.'

28 "This is the end of the matter. I, Daniel, was deeply troubled by my thoughts, and my face turned pale, but I kept the matter to myself."

Daniel's Vision of a Ram and a Goat

8 In the third year of King Belshazzar's reign, I, Daniel, had a vision, after the one that had already appeared to me. 2 In my vision I saw myself in the citadel of Susa in the province of Elam; in the vision I was beside the Ulai Canal. 3 I looked up, and there before me was a ram with two horns, standing beside the canal, and the horns were long. One of the horns was longer than the other but grew up later. 4 I watched the ram as it charged toward the west and the north and the south. No animal could stand against it, and none could rescue from its power. It did as it pleased and became great.

5 As I was thinking about this, suddenly a goat with a prominent horn between its eyes came from the west, crossing the whole earth without touching the ground. 6 It came toward the two-horned ram I had seen standing beside the canal and charged at it in great rage. 7 I saw it attack the ram furiously, striking the ram and shattering its two horns. The ram was powerless to stand against it; the goat knocked it to the ground and trampled on it, and none could res-

cue the ram from its power. 8 The goat became very great, but at the height of its power the large horn was broken off, and in its place four prominent horns grew up toward the four winds of heaven.

9 Out of one of them came another horn, which started small but grew in power to the south and to the east and toward the Beautiful Land. 10 It grew until it reached the host of the heavens, and it threw some of the starry host down to the earth and trampled on them. 11 It set itself up to be as great as the commander of the army of the LORD; it took away the daily sacrifice from the LORD, and his sanctuary was thrown down. 12 Because of rebellion, the LORD's people*b* and the daily sacrifice were given over to it. It prospered in everything it did, and truth was thrown to the ground.

13 Then I heard a holy one speaking, and another holy one said to him, "How long will it take for the vision to be fulfilled — the vision concerning the daily sacrifice, the rebellion that causes desolation, the surrender of the sanctuary and the trampling underfoot of the LORD's people?"

14 He said to me, "It will take 2,300 evenings and mornings; then the sanctuary will be reconsecrated."

The Interpretation of the Vision

15 While I, Daniel, was watching the vision and trying to understand it, there before me stood one who looked like a man. 16 And I heard a man's voice from the Ulai calling, "Gabriel, tell this man the meaning of the vision."

17 As he came near the place where I was standing, I was terrified and fell prostrate. "Son of man,"*c* he said to me, "understand that the vision concerns the time of the end."

18 While he was speaking to me, I was in a deep sleep, with my face to the ground. Then he touched me and raised me to my feet.

19 He said: "I am going to tell you what will happen later in the time of wrath, because the vision concerns the appointed time of the end.*d* 20 The two-horned ram that you saw represents the kings of Media and Persia. 21 The shaggy goat is the king of Greece, and the large horn between its eyes is the first king. 22 The four horns

a 25 Or *for a year, two years and half a year*   *b 12* Or *rebellion, the armies*   *c 17* The Hebrew phrase *ben adam* means *human being.* The phrase *son of man* is retained as a form of address here because of its possible association with "Son of Man" in the New Testament.   *d 19* Or *because the end will be at the appointed time*

that replaced the one that was broken off represent four kingdoms that will emerge from his nation but will not have the same power.

²³"In the latter part of their reign, when rebels have become completely wicked, a fierce-looking king, a master of intrigue, will arise. ²⁴He will become very strong, but not by his own power. He will cause astounding devastation and will succeed in whatever he does. He will destroy those who are mighty, the holy people. ²⁵He will cause deceit to prosper, and he will consider himself superior. When they feel secure, he will destroy many and take his stand against the Prince of princes. Yet he will be destroyed, but not by human power.

²⁶"The vision of the evenings and mornings that has been given you is true, but seal up the vision, for it concerns the distant future."

²⁷I, Daniel, was worn out. I lay exhausted for several days. Then I got up and went about the king's business. I was appalled by the vision; it was beyond understanding.

Daniel's Prayer

9 In the first year of Darius son of Xerxes*ᵃ* (a Mede by descent), who was made ruler over the Babylonian*ᵇ* kingdom — ²in the first year of his reign, I, Daniel, understood from the Scriptures, according to the word of the LORD given to Jeremiah the prophet, that the desolation of Jerusalem would last seventy years. ³So I turned

to the Lord God and pleaded with him in prayer and petition, in fasting, and in sackcloth and ashes.

⁴I prayed to the LORD my God and confessed:

"Lord, the great and awesome God, who keeps his covenant of love with those who love him and keep his commandments, ⁵we have sinned and done wrong. We have been wicked and have rebelled; we have turned away from your commands and laws. ⁶We have not listened to your servants the prophets, who spoke in your name to our kings, our princes and our ancestors, and to all the people of the land.

⁷"Lord, you are righteous, but this day we are covered with shame — the people of Judah and the inhabitants of Jerusalem and all Israel, both near and far, in all the countries where you have scattered us because of our unfaithfulness to you. ⁸We and our kings, our princes and our ancestors are covered with shame, LORD, because we have sinned against you. ⁹The Lord our God is merciful and forgiving, even though we have rebelled against him; ¹⁰we have not obeyed the LORD our God or kept the laws he gave us through his servants the prophets. ¹¹All Israel has transgressed your law and turned away, refusing to obey you.

ᵃ 1 Hebrew *Ahasuerus*   ᵇ 1 Or *Chaldean*

DANIEL — A Man Who Sought Understanding
Daniel 8:15, 17, 27

PROFILE in leadership

The prophet Daniel, like any godly leader, craved insight from the Lord. But Daniel wanted more than to receive a vision from God; he wanted God to explain the vision. The Lord obliged, but also showed Daniel the price attached to such a privilege.

Do you realize the cost of receiving a genuine vision from the Lord? After Daniel received this prophecy, he fainted, lay sick in bed for days, felt great astonishment over what he had seen, yet still didn't fully understand it (Da 8:27). And during the vision itself, he felt great fear (8:17). It is no trifling matter to receive a genuine word from God!

By the time of this vision, Daniel was an old man. He had served three pagan kings and had accumulated enormous experience. He constantly studied the Scripture. Yet he realized he still had to work to gain an accurate understanding of what God told him. After he received this vision, he tells us that he was "trying to understand it" (8:15).

It is not enough for leaders to know the Word of God or to know the prophecies contained in that Word. They must seek to understand how that Word applies to them and to their followers. And they must never take for granted the enormous privilege of communicating the revelation of God.

"Therefore the curses and sworn judgments written in the Law of Moses, the servant of God, have been poured out on us, because we have sinned against you. [12]You have fulfilled the words spoken against us and against our rulers by bringing on us great disaster. Under the whole heaven nothing has ever been done like what has been done to Jerusalem. [13]Just as it is written in the Law of Moses, all this disaster has come on us, yet we have not sought the favor of the LORD our God by turning from our sins and giving attention to your truth. [14]The LORD did not hesitate to bring the disaster on us, for the LORD our God is righteous in everything he does; yet we have not obeyed him.

[15]"Now, Lord our God, who brought your people out of Egypt with a mighty hand and who made for yourself a name that endures to this day, we have sinned, we have done wrong. [16]Lord, in keeping with all your righteous acts, turn away your anger and your wrath from Jerusalem, your city, your holy hill. Our sins and the iniquities of our ancestors have made Jerusalem and your people an object of scorn to all those around us.

[17]"Now, our God, hear the prayers and petitions of your servant. For your sake, Lord, look with favor on your desolate sanctuary. [18]Give ear, our God, and hear; open your eyes and see the desolation of the city that bears your Name. We do not make requests of you because we are righteous, but because of your great mercy. [19]Lord, listen! Lord, forgive! Lord, hear and act! For your sake, my God, do not delay, because your city and your people bear your Name."

The Seventy "Sevens"

[20]While I was speaking and praying, confessing my sin and the sin of my people Israel and making my request to the LORD my God for his holy hill— [21]while I was still in prayer, Gabriel, the man I had seen in the earlier vision, came to me in swift flight about the time of the evening sacrifice. [22]He instructed me and said to me, "Daniel, I have now come to give you insight and understanding. [23]As soon as you began to pray, a word went out, which I have come to tell you, for you are highly esteemed. Therefore, consider the word and understand the vision:

[24]"Seventy 'sevens'[a] are decreed for your people and your holy city to finish[b] transgression, to put an end to sin, to atone for wickedness, to bring in everlasting righteousness, to seal up vision and prophecy and to anoint the Most Holy Place.[c]

[25]"Know and understand this: From the time the word goes out to restore and rebuild Jerusalem until the Anointed One,[d] the ruler, comes, there will be seven 'sevens,' and sixty-two 'sevens.' It will be rebuilt with streets and a trench, but in times of trouble. [26]After the sixty-two 'sevens,' the Anointed One will be put to death and will have nothing.[e] The people of the ruler who will come will destroy the city and the sanctuary. The end will come like a flood: War will continue until the end, and desolations have been decreed. [27]He will confirm a covenant with many for one 'seven.'[f] In the middle of the 'seven'[f] he will put an end to sacrifice and offering. And at the temple[g] he will set up an abomination that causes desolation, until the end that is decreed is poured out on him."[h][i]

Daniel's Vision of a Man

10 In the third year of Cyrus king of Persia, a revelation was given to Daniel (who was called Belteshazzar). Its message was true and it concerned a great war.[j] The understanding of the message came to him in a vision.

[2]At that time I, Daniel, mourned for three weeks. [3]I ate no choice food; no meat or wine touched my lips; and I used no lotions at all until the three weeks were over.

[4]On the twenty-fourth day of the first month, as I was standing on the bank of the great river, the Tigris, [5]I looked up and there before me was a man dressed in linen, with a belt of fine gold from Uphaz around his waist. [6]His body was like topaz, his face like lightning, his eyes like flaming torches, his arms and legs like the gleam of burnished bronze, and his voice like the sound of a multitude.

[7]I, Daniel, was the only one who saw the vision; those who were with me did not see it, but such terror overwhelmed them that they fled and hid themselves. [8]So I was left alone, gazing at this great vision; I had no strength left, my face turned deathly pale and I was helpless. [9]Then I

---

[a] 24 Or 'weeks'; also in verses 25 and 26   [b] 24 Or restrain
[c] 24 Or the most holy One   [d] 25 Or an anointed one; also in verse 26   [e] 26 Or death and will have no one; or death, but not for himself   [f] 27 Or 'week'   [g] 27 Septuagint and Theodotion; Hebrew wing   [h] 27 Or it   [i] 27 Or And one who causes desolation will come upon the wing of the abominable temple, until the end that is decreed is poured out on the desolated city   [j] 1 Or true and burdensome

heard him speaking, and as I listened to him, I fell into a deep sleep, my face to the ground.

[10]A hand touched me and set me trembling on my hands and knees. [11]He said, "Daniel, you who are highly esteemed, consider carefully the words I am about to speak to you, and stand up, for I have now been sent to you." And when he said this to me, I stood up trembling.

[12]Then he continued, "Do not be afraid, Daniel. Since the first day that you set your mind to gain understanding and to humble yourself before your God, your words were heard, and I have come in response to them. [13]But the prince of the Persian kingdom resisted me twenty-one days. Then Michael, one of the chief princes, came to help me, because I was detained there with the king of Persia. [14]Now I have come to explain to you what will happen to your people in the future, for the vision concerns a time yet to come."

[15]While he was saying this to me, I bowed with my face toward the ground and was speechless. [16]Then one who looked like a man[a] touched my lips, and I opened my mouth and began to speak. I said to the one standing before me, "I am overcome with anguish because of the vision, my lord, and I feel very weak. [17]How can I, your servant, talk with you, my lord? My strength is gone and I can hardly breathe."

[18]Again the one who looked like a man touched me and gave me strength. [19]"Do not be afraid, you who are highly esteemed," he said. "Peace! Be strong now; be strong."

When he spoke to me, I was strengthened and said, "Speak, my lord, since you have given me strength."

[20]So he said, "Do you know why I have come to you? Soon I will return to fight against the prince of Persia, and when I go, the prince of Greece will come; [21]but first I will tell you what is written in the Book of Truth. (No one supports me against them except Michael, your prince.

11 [1]And in the first year of Darius the Mede, I took my stand to support and protect him.)

The Kings of the South and the North

[2]"Now then, I tell you the truth: Three more kings will arise in Persia, and then a fourth, who will be far richer than all the others. When he has gained power by his wealth, he will stir up everyone against the kingdom of Greece. [3]Then a mighty king will arise, who will rule with great power and do as he pleases. [4]After he has arisen, his empire will be broken up and parceled out toward the four winds of heaven. It will not go to his descendants, nor will it have the power he exercised, because his empire will be uprooted and given to others.

[5]"The king of the South will become strong, but one of his commanders will become even

---

[a] 16 Most manuscripts of the Masoretic Text; one manuscript of the Masoretic Text, Dead Sea Scrolls and Septuagint *Then something that looked like a human hand*

Spiritual Leaders Lead God's Family and God's Army

Daniel 10:1–21

The vision Daniel receives in chapter 10 presents him with a deeper challenge than any in his past. He now learns he is engaged in spiritual warfare. In his dialogue with an angel, Daniel learns some important lessons every leader ought to master:

1. **Spiritual leaders lead not only God's family, but God's army (vv. 10–21).**

2. **Prayer ignites spiritual warfare invisible to us (vv. 10–12).**

3. **Both spiritual kingdoms seem to have princes (v. 13).**

4. **Spiritual warfare can delay victories (vv. 13–14).**

5. **We must not fear spiritual warfare (vv. 18–19).**

6. **Understanding warfare enables us to cooperate with God's purposes (vv. 20–21).**

As you seek to lead in a more strategic way, recognize that you will encounter struggles beyond mere human opposition. You must wisely face an invisible, spiritual world around you. You need both prayer and persistence.

stronger than he and will rule his own kingdom with great power. [6]After some years, they will become allies. The daughter of the king of the South will go to the king of the North to make an alliance, but she will not retain her power, and he and his power[a] will not last. In those days she will be betrayed, together with her royal escort and her father[b] and the one who supported her.

[7]"One from her family line will arise to take her place. He will attack the forces of the king of the North and enter his fortress; he will fight against them and be victorious. [8]He will also seize their gods, their metal images and their valuable articles of silver and gold and carry them off to Egypt. For some years he will leave the king of the North alone. [9]Then the king of the North will invade the realm of the king of the South but will retreat to his own country. [10]His sons will prepare for war and assemble a great army, which will sweep on like an irresistible flood and carry the battle as far as his fortress.

[11]"Then the king of the South will march out in a rage and fight against the king of the North, who will raise a large army, but it will be defeated. [12]When the army is carried off, the king of the South will be filled with pride and will slaughter many thousands, yet he will not remain triumphant. [13]For the king of the North will muster another army, larger than the first; and after several years, he will advance with a huge army fully equipped.

[14]"In those times many will rise against the king of the South. Those who are violent among your own people will rebel in fulfillment of the vision, but without success. [15]Then the king of the North will come and build up siege ramps and will capture a fortified city. The forces of the South will be powerless to resist; even their best troops will not have the strength to stand. [16]The invader will do as he pleases; no one will be able to stand against him. He will establish himself in the Beautiful Land and will have the power to destroy it. [17]He will determine to come with the might of his entire kingdom and will make an alliance with the king of the South. And he will give him a daughter in marriage in order to overthrow the kingdom, but his plans[c] will not succeed or help him. [18]Then he will turn his attention to the coastlands and will take many of them, but a commander will put an end to his insolence and will turn his insolence back on him. [19]After this, he will turn back toward the fortresses of his own country but will stumble and fall, to be seen no more. [20]"His successor will send out a tax collector

to maintain the royal splendor. In a few years, however, he will be destroyed, yet not in anger or in battle.

[21]"He will be succeeded by a contemptible person who has not been given the honor of royalty. He will invade the kingdom when its people feel secure, and he will seize it through intrigue. [22]Then an overwhelming army will be swept away before him; both it and a prince of the covenant will be destroyed. [23]After coming to an agreement with him, he will act deceitfully, and with only a few people he will rise to power. [24]When the richest provinces feel secure, he will invade them and will achieve what neither his fathers nor his forefathers did. He will distribute plunder, loot and wealth among his followers. He will plot the overthrow of fortresses—but only for a time.

[25]"With a large army he will stir up his strength and courage against the king of the South. The king of the South will wage war with a large and very powerful army, but he will not be able to stand because of the plots devised against him. [26]Those who eat from the king's provisions will try to destroy him; his army will be swept away, and many will fall in battle. [27]The two kings, with their hearts bent on evil, will sit at the same table and lie to each other, but to no avail, because an end will still come at the appointed time. [28]The king of the North will return to his own country with great wealth, but his heart will be set against the holy covenant. He will take action against it and then return to his own country.

[29]"At the appointed time he will invade the South again, but this time the outcome will be different from what it was before. [30]Ships of the western coastlands will oppose him, and he will lose heart. Then he will turn back and vent his fury against the holy covenant. He will return and show favor to those who forsake the holy covenant.

[31]"His armed forces will rise up to desecrate the temple fortress and will abolish the daily sacrifice. Then they will set up the abomination that causes desolation. [32]With flattery he will corrupt those who have violated the covenant, but the people who know their God will firmly resist him.

[33]"Those who are wise will instruct many, though for a time they will fall by the sword or be burned or captured or plundered. [34]When they fall, they will receive a little help, and many

---

[a] 6 Or *offspring*   [b] 6 Or *child* (see Vulgate and Syriac)
[c] 17 Or *but she*

who are not sincere will join them. [35]Some of the wise will stumble, so that they may be refined, purified and made spotless until the time of the end, for it will still come at the appointed time.

The King Who Exalts Himself

[36]"The king will do as he pleases. He will exalt and magnify himself above every god and will say unheard-of things against the God of gods. He will be successful until the time of wrath is completed, for what has been determined must take place. [37]He will show no regard for the gods of his ancestors or for the one desired by women, nor will he regard any god, but will exalt himself above them all. [38]Instead of them, he will honor a god of fortresses; a god unknown to his ancestors he will honor with gold and silver, with precious stones and costly gifts. [39]He will attack the mightiest fortresses with the help of a foreign god and will greatly honor those who acknowledge him. He will make them rulers over many people and will distribute the land at a price.[a]

[40]"At the time of the end the king of the South will engage him in battle, and the king of the North will storm out against him with chariots and cavalry and a great fleet of ships. He will invade many countries and sweep through them like a flood. [41]He will also invade the Beautiful Land. Many countries will fall, but Edom, Moab and the leaders of Ammon will be delivered from his hand. [42]He will extend his power over many countries; Egypt will not escape. [43]He will gain control of the treasures of gold and silver and all the riches of Egypt, with the Libyans and Cushites[b] in submission. [44]But reports from the east and the north will alarm him, and he will set out in a great rage to destroy and annihilate many. [45]He will pitch his royal tents between the seas at[c] the beautiful holy mountain. Yet he will come to his end, and no one will help him.

The End Times

12 "At that time Michael, the great prince who protects your people, will arise. There will be a time of distress such as has not happened from the beginning of nations until then. But at that time your people — everyone whose name is found written in the book — will be delivered. [2]Multitudes who sleep in the dust of the earth will awake: some to everlasting life, others to shame and everlasting contempt. [3]Those who are wise[d] will shine like the brightness of the heavens, and those who lead many to righteousness, like the stars for ever and ever. [4]But you, Daniel, roll up and seal the words of the scroll until the time of the end. Many will go here and there to increase knowledge."

[5]Then I, Daniel, looked, and there before me stood two others, one on this bank of the river and one on the opposite bank. [6]One of them said to the man clothed in linen, who was above the waters of the river, "How long will it be before these astonishing things are fulfilled?"

[7]The man clothed in linen, who was above the waters of the river, lifted his right hand and his left hand toward heaven, and I heard him swear by him who lives forever, saying, "It will be for a time, times and half a time.[e] When the power of the holy people has been finally broken, all these things will be completed."

[8]I heard, but I did not understand. So I asked, "My lord, what will the outcome of all this be?"

[9]He replied, "Go your way, Daniel, because the words are rolled up and sealed until the time of the end. [10]Many will be purified, made spotless and refined, but the wicked will continue to be wicked. None of the wicked will understand, but those who are wise will understand.

[11]"From the time that the daily sacrifice is abolished and the abomination that causes desolation is set up, there will be 1,290 days. [12]Blessed is the one who waits for and reaches the end of the 1,335 days.

[13]"As for you, go your way till the end. You will rest, and then at the end of the days you will rise to receive your allotted inheritance."

---

[a] 39 Or *land for a reward*   [b] 43 That is, people from the upper Nile region   [c] 45 Or *the sea and*   [d] 3 Or *who impart wisdom*   [e] 7 Or *a year, two years and half a year*

INTRODUCTION TO HOSEA

A Visual Demonstration of Israel's Unfaithfulness to God

Hosea, the first of the "minor prophets," led and prophesied in Israel during a season of material wealth but spiritual poverty. Because of this, God called him to do something very costly. In order to send a memorable message to the people of Israel, Hosea was to marry a prostitute—thus giving the people a visual demonstration of their unfaithfulness to Yahweh. Hosea's words were to help the people feel the grief of God, who responded to their rebellion like a husband with an adulterous wife. In the same way Gomer had betrayed Hosea, Israel had betrayed God.

Hosea vividly illustrates the Law of Sacrifice. In order to fulfill his divine calling, he had to pay a huge price. At his own expense, he married Gomer and watched her drift from her marriage time and again. We can only imagine his pain, called to live with her lies and deception, having to explain to his children that their mother would not be home that night, then watching her public humiliation as evil men auctioned off her body for the carnal delight of strangers. Certainly, when Hosea spoke to the Israelites about their spiritual state, he could do it with empathy and passion. He knew firsthand how God felt about the spiritual adultery of his chosen people.

Leadership really is about sacrifice. Many of us want the perks of leadership without the price of leadership. Yet becoming a leader isn't about gaining rights; it's about giving them up. Leaders in the business world often err in thinking that becoming a C.E.O. means more liberties with the budget, more options with their time, and more freedom with their lifestyle. From God's perspective, leadership means quite the opposite. Leaders relinquish

God's Role in Hosea

God reveals himself in this book as both a forgiving Lord and a holy Judge who requires repentance on the part of his erring people. Because he endured an adulterous bride in Israel, he called Hosea to imitate his situation—then to speak to the people about his forgiveness and judgment. God led his leader, Hosea, in an experience he would never forget. Hosea got to step into God's shoes for a season and feel what he felt. Through Hosea, God communicated both his unconditional love and his unchanging law.

Leaders in Hosea

Hosea

Other People of Influence in Hosea

Gomer

Lessons in Leadership

- Leaders must maintain poise even in the midst of unfair demands.
- The simple game plan is the best when restoring or rebuilding.
- Followers in volatile situations need consistency from leaders.
- Leaders must lead from established values and standards.
- Regardless of what the people do, leaders must model what is right.

options and remain careful to do all things for the sake of the gospel (1Co 9:19–23).

Leading people is also about more than words; it really is a lifestyle. We cannot separate our communication from our conduct. To speak with the kind of credibility and emotion he did, Hosea had to live what God was living. Hollow leadership results when we do not incarnate the values we want others to embrace. Hypocrisy replaces integrity. No one wants to follow this kind of leader. The way we talk, the way we lead, and the way we live should mesh. Just ask Hosea.

> ■ Effective leaders never lose sight of the big picture.

LEADERSHIP HIGHLIGHTS IN HOSEA

1 The word of the LORD that came to Hosea son of Beeri during the reigns of Uzziah, Jotham, Ahaz and Hezekiah, kings of Judah, and during the reign of Jeroboam son of Jehoash[a] king of Israel:

Hosea's Wife and Children

2 When the LORD began to speak through Hosea, the LORD said to him, "Go, marry a promiscuous woman and have children with her, for like an adulterous wife this land is guilty of unfaithfulness to the LORD." 3 So he married Gomer daughter of Diblaim, and she conceived and bore him a son.

4 Then the LORD said to Hosea, "Call him Jezreel, because I will soon punish the house of Jehu for the massacre at Jezreel, and I will put an end to the kingdom of Israel. 5 In that day I will break Israel's bow in the Valley of Jezreel."

6 Gomer conceived again and gave birth to a daughter. Then the LORD said to Hosea, "Call her Lo-Ruhamah (which means "not loved"), for I will no longer show love to Israel, that I should at all forgive them. 7 Yet I will show love to Judah; and I will save them — not by bow, sword or battle, or by horses and horsemen, but I, the LORD their God, will save them."

8 After she had weaned Lo-Ruhamah, Gomer had another son. 9 Then the LORD said, "Call him Lo-Ammi (which means "not my people"), for you are not my people, and I am not your God.[b]

10 "Yet the Israelites will be like the sand on the seashore, which cannot be measured or counted. In the place where it was said to them, 'You are not my people,' they will be called 'children of the living God.' 11 The people of Judah and the people of Israel will come together; they will appoint one leader and will come up out of the land, for great will be the day of Jezreel.[c]

2[d] "Say of your brothers, 'My people,' and of your sisters, 'My loved one.'

Israel Punished and Restored

2 "Rebuke your mother, rebuke her,
    for she is not my wife,
    and I am not her husband.
Let her remove the adulterous look from her face
    and the unfaithfulness from between her breasts.
3 Otherwise I will strip her naked
    and make her as bare as on the day she was born;

---

[a] 1 Hebrew *Joash*, a variant of *Jehoash*   [b] 9 Or *your I AM*   [c] 11 In Hebrew texts 1:10,11 is numbered 2:1,2.   [d] In Hebrew texts 2:1-23 is numbered 2:3-25.

The Law of Sacrifice: Hosea Marries a Harlot to Teach the Truth

Hosea 1:2

Can you imagine what Hosea must have felt when God asked him to propose to a prostitute? The Lord instructed him to marry Gomer in order to illustrate the spiritual adultery Israel had committed against God. The Hebrews had been unfaithful to God and pursued other gods, just as a harlot joins herself to several men. What a request!

Leadership is about sacrifice. It means giving up personal options in order to guide the people to where they need to go. Hosea made several sacrifices in his leadership:

1. **He was asked to marry a prostitute.**

2. **He was asked to lead in a time of rebellion.**

3. **He was given a very unpopular message.**

4. **He was told to have children despite an absentee wife.**

5. **He was committed to remain poised under harsh demands.**

6. **He was instructed to live faithfully and consistently in a volatile situation.**

Leaders lose their right to selfishness. They must take into account the lives of others when making decisions. They must say what the people *need* to hear, not merely what they *want* to hear. They must guide the people to where they *ought* to go, not necessarily where they *desire* to go. Could this explain why we have so few good leaders?

I will make her like a desert,
   turn her into a parched land,
   and slay her with thirst.
[4] I will not show my love to her children,
   because they are the children of
      adultery.
[5] Their mother has been unfaithful
   and has conceived them in disgrace.
She said, 'I will go after my lovers,
   who give me my food and my water,
   my wool and my linen, my olive oil and
      my drink.'
[6] Therefore I will block her path with
      thornbushes;
   I will wall her in so that she cannot find
      her way.
[7] She will chase after her lovers but not catch
      them;
   she will look for them but not find them.
Then she will say,
   'I will go back to my husband as at first,
   for then I was better off than now.'
[8] She has not acknowledged that I was the
      one
   who gave her the grain, the new wine
      and oil,
   who lavished on her the silver and gold —
   which they used for Baal.

[9] "Therefore I will take away my grain when
      it ripens,
   and my new wine when it is ready.

I will take back my wool and my linen,
   intended to cover her naked body.
[10] So now I will expose her lewdness
   before the eyes of her lovers;
   no one will take her out of my hands.
[11] I will stop all her celebrations:
   her yearly festivals, her New Moons,
   her Sabbath days — all her appointed
      festivals.
[12] I will ruin her vines and her fig trees,
   which she said were her pay from her
      lovers;
   I will make them a thicket,
   and wild animals will devour them.
[13] I will punish her for the days
   she burned incense to the Baals;
she decked herself with rings and jewelry,
   and went after her lovers,
   but me she forgot,"
                                                declares the LORD.

[14] "Therefore I am now going to allure her;
   I will lead her into the wilderness
   and speak tenderly to her.
[15] There I will give her back her vineyards,
   and will make the Valley of Achor[a] a door
      of hope.
There she will respond[b] as in the days of her
      youth,
   as in the day she came up out of Egypt.

---

[a] 15 Achor means trouble.   [b] 15 Or sing

HOSEA

The Cost of Leadership
Hosea 1:1—3:5

PROFILE in leadership

It can be painful to read the story of Hosea. Out of obedience to God, the prophet marries the prostitute Gomer, who refuses to change her ways for her husband or for their children. Still, Hosea tries to bring his wife back, to redeem her from the sordid life to which she so stubbornly clings.

From the human perspective, it is easy to wonder why Hosea continues to punish himself this way. Why would a man subject himself to the kind of heartache he must have felt in trying to make a faithful wife out of a prostitute? Why wouldn't he just "cut his losses" and rid himself of this wicked woman?

The quick answer is that Hosea's life did not belong to him alone. Like us, he had given his heart and soul to God. In Paul's words, "You are not your own . . . you were bought at a price" (1Co 6:19–20). Hosea realized that God had called him to become a living metaphor of the love of God for his people—and he obeyed, regardless of the personal cost.

Hosea illustrates the heartaches that may come from following the call of God. As leaders, we continue to pray for and minister to those who have strayed from the Lord—even when it hurts—knowing that God did the same for us.

16 "In that day," declares the LORD,
   "you will call me 'my husband';
   you will no longer call me 'my master.'*
17 I will remove the names of the Baals from
      her lips;
   no longer will their names be invoked.
18 In that day I will make a covenant for
      them
   with the beasts of the field, the birds in
      the sky
   and the creatures that move along the
      ground.
Bow and sword and battle
   I will abolish from the land,
   so that all may lie down in safety.
19 I will betroth you to me forever;
   I will betroth you in*b* righteousness and
      justice,
   in*b* love and compassion.
20 I will betroth you in*b* faithfulness,
   and you will acknowledge the LORD.

21 "In that day I will respond,"
   declares the LORD —
   "I will respond to the skies,
   and they will respond to the earth;
22 and the earth will respond to the grain,
   the new wine and the olive oil,
   and they will respond to Jezreel.*c*
23 I will plant her for myself in the land;
   I will show my love to the one I called
      'Not my loved one.'*d*
   I will say to those called 'Not my people,'*e*
      'You are my people';
   and they will say, 'You are my God.'"

Hosea's Reconciliation With His Wife

3 The LORD said to me, "Go, show your love
to your wife again, though she is loved by
another man and is an adulteress. Love her as
the LORD loves the Israelites, though they turn
to other gods and love the sacred raisin cakes."

2 So I bought her for fifteen shekels*f* of silver
and about a homer and a lethek*g* of barley. 3 Then
I told her, "You are to live with me many days;
you must not be a prostitute or be intimate with
any man, and I will behave the same way toward
you."

4 For the Israelites will live many days without king or prince, without sacrifice or sacred
stones, without ephod or household gods. 5 Afterward the Israelites will return and seek the
LORD their God and David their king. They will
come trembling to the LORD and to his blessings
in the last days.

The Law of Empowerment: Hosea Loves by Decision, Not Reaction

Hosea 3:1

In Hosea 3 the prophet receives one profound
command. He is told to go and reconcile with
his wife, who remains in an adulterous relationship. He is told to act, not react. He is to love
Gomer rather than take revenge.

God calls leaders to live on a higher level than
followers. We are called to respond as God did
to Israel. Although Israel had committed falsehood (Hos 4:1), prostitution (4:11), murder (5:2),
robbery (7:1) and oppression (12:7), along with
repeated spiritual adultery, God continued to
guide and empower his people.

In the final chapter, the prophet pleads with
Israel to return to the Lord (14:1), that they might
be graciously received, restored and healed
(14:2–4). Leaders can do this only when they
live and lead from principle rather than from
reaction.

The Charge Against Israel

4 Hear the word of the LORD, you Israelites,
   because the LORD has a charge to bring
   against you who live in the land:
   "There is no faithfulness, no love,
      no acknowledgment of God in the
      land.
2 There is only cursing,*h* lying and murder,
      stealing and adultery;
   they break all bounds,
      and bloodshed follows bloodshed.
3 Because of this the land dries up,
      and all who live in it waste away;
   the beasts of the field, the birds in the sky
      and the fish in the sea are swept away.

4 "But let no one bring a charge,
      let no one accuse another,
   for your people are like those
      who bring charges against a priest.

a 16 Hebrew *baal*   *b* 19,20 Or *with*   *c* 22 *Jezreel* means
God plants.   *d* 23 Hebrew *Lo-Ruhamah* (see 1:6)
e 23 Hebrew *Lo-Ammi* (see 1:9)   *f* 2 That is, about 6 ounces
or about 170 grams   *g* 2 A homer and a lethek possibly
weighed about 430 pounds or about 195 kilograms.
h 2 That is, to pronounce a curse on

5 You stumble day and night,
  and the prophets stumble with you.
So I will destroy your mother—
6   my people are destroyed from lack of
      knowledge.

"Because you have rejected knowledge,
  I also reject you as my priests;
because you have ignored the law of your
      God,
  I also will ignore your children.
7 The more priests there were,
    the more they sinned against me;
  they exchanged their glorious God[a] for
      something disgraceful.
8 They feed on the sins of my people
  and relish their wickedness.
9 And it will be: Like people, like priests.
  I will punish both of them for their ways
  and repay them for their deeds.

10 "They will eat but not have enough;
    they will engage in prostitution but not
      flourish,
because they have deserted the LORD
  to give themselves 11 to prostitution;
old wine and new wine
  take away their understanding.
12 My people consult a wooden idol,
  and a diviner's rod speaks to them.
A spirit of prostitution leads them astray;
  they are unfaithful to their God.
13 They sacrifice on the mountaintops
    and burn offerings on the hills,
under oak, poplar and terebinth,
  where the shade is pleasant.
Therefore your daughters turn to
      prostitution
  and your daughters-in-law to adultery.

14 "I will not punish your daughters
    when they turn to prostitution,
nor your daughters-in-law
  when they commit adultery,
because the men themselves consort with
      harlots
  and sacrifice with shrine prostitutes—
  a people without understanding will come
      to ruin!

15 "Though you, Israel, commit adultery,
  do not let Judah become guilty.

"Do not go to Gilgal;
  do not go up to Beth Aven.[b]
And do not swear, 'As surely as the LORD
      lives!'

16 The Israelites are stubborn,
    like a stubborn heifer.
How then can the LORD pasture them
    like lambs in a meadow?
17 Ephraim is joined to idols;
  leave him alone!
18 Even when their drinks are gone,
    they continue their prostitution;
  their rulers dearly love shameful ways.
19 A whirlwind will sweep them away,
    and their sacrifices will bring them shame.

Judgment Against Israel

5 "Hear this, you priests!
    Pay attention, you Israelites!
Listen, royal house!
    This judgment is against you:
You have been a snare at Mizpah,
    a net spread out on Tabor.
2 The rebels are knee-deep in slaughter.
    I will discipline all of them.
3 I know all about Ephraim;
    Israel is not hidden from me.
Ephraim, you have now turned to
      prostitution;
    Israel is corrupt.

4 "Their deeds do not permit them
    to return to their God.
A spirit of prostitution is in their heart;
    they do not acknowledge the LORD.
5 Israel's arrogance testifies against them;
    the Israelites, even Ephraim, stumble in
      their sin;
    Judah also stumbles with them.
6 When they go with their flocks and herds
    to seek the LORD,
they will not find him;
    he has withdrawn himself from them.
7 They are unfaithful to the LORD;
    they give birth to illegitimate children.
When they celebrate their New Moon feasts,
    he will devour[c] their fields.

8 "Sound the trumpet in Gibeah,
    the horn in Ramah.
Raise the battle cry in Beth Aven[b];
    lead on, Benjamin.
9 Ephraim will be laid waste
    on the day of reckoning.

---

[a] 7 Syriac (see also an ancient Hebrew scribal tradition);
Masoretic Text me; / I will exchange their glory   [b] 15,8 Beth
Aven means house of wickedness (a derogatory name for Bethel,
which means house of God).   [c] 7 Or Now their New Moon
feasts / will devour them and

Among the tribes of Israel
 I proclaim what is certain.
¹⁰Judah's leaders are like those
 who move boundary stones.
 I will pour out my wrath on them
 like a flood of water.
¹¹Ephraim is oppressed,
 trampled in judgment,
 intent on pursuing idols.ᵃ
¹²I am like a moth to Ephraim,
 like rot to the people of Judah.

¹³"When Ephraim saw his sickness,
 and Judah his sores,
 then Ephraim turned to Assyria,
 and sent to the great king for help.
 But he is not able to cure you,
 not able to heal your sores.
¹⁴For I will be like a lion to Ephraim,
 like a great lion to Judah.
 I will tear them to pieces and go away;
 I will carry them off, with no one to
 rescue them.
¹⁵Then I will return to my lair
 until they have borne their guilt
 and seek my face —
 in their misery
 they will earnestly seek me."

Israel Unrepentant

6 "Come, let us return to the LORD.
 He has torn us to pieces
 but he will heal us;
 he has injured us
 but he will bind up our wounds.
² After two days he will revive us;
 on the third day he will restore us,
 that we may live in his presence.
³ Let us acknowledge the LORD;
 let us press on to acknowledge him.
 As surely as the sun rises,
 he will appear;
 he will come to us like the winter rains,
 like the spring rains that water the
 earth."

⁴"What can I do with you, Ephraim?
 What can I do with you, Judah?
 Your love is like the morning mist,
 like the early dew that disappears.
⁵ Therefore I cut you in pieces with my
 prophets,
 I killed you with the words of my
 mouth —
 then my judgments go forth like the
 sun.ᵇ

The Law of Solid Ground: Leaders Who Move Boundaries

Hosea 5:10

Boundary stones were to be fixed and so bring definition to a plot of land. Israel's leaders moved what never should have been moved; they compromised values. Leaders who cannot be trusted with basic integrity will surely suffer God's anger. Every organization needs boundary stones. Leaders must establish and keep them.

---

⁶For I desire mercy, not sacrifice,
 and acknowledgment of God rather than
 burnt offerings.
⁷ As at Adam,ᶜ they have broken the
 covenant;
 they were unfaithful to me there.
⁸Gilead is a city of evildoers,
 stained with footprints of blood.
⁹ As marauders lie in ambush for a victim,
 so do bands of priests;
 they murder on the road to Shechem,
 carrying out their wicked schemes.
¹⁰I have seen a horrible thing in Israel:
 There Ephraim is given to prostitution,
 Israel is defiled.

¹¹"Also for you, Judah,
 a harvest is appointed.

"Whenever I would restore the fortunes of
 my people,

7 ¹whenever I would heal Israel,
 the sins of Ephraim are exposed
 and the crimes of Samaria revealed.
 They practice deceit,
 thieves break into houses,
 bandits rob in the streets;
² but they do not realize
 that I remember all their evil deeds.
 Their sins engulf them;
 they are always before me.

³"They delight the king with their
 wickedness,
 the princes with their lies.

ᵃ *11* The meaning of the Hebrew for this word is uncertain.
ᵇ *5* The meaning of the Hebrew for this line is uncertain.
ᶜ *7* Or *Like Adam*; or *Like human beings*

⁴They are all adulterers,
  burning like an oven
whose fire the baker need not stir
  from the kneading of the dough till it
    rises.
⁵On the day of the festival of our king
  the princes become inflamed with wine,
  and he joins hands with the mockers.
⁶Their hearts are like an oven;
  they approach him with intrigue.
Their passion smolders all night;
  in the morning it blazes like a flaming
    fire.
⁷All of them are hot as an oven;
  they devour their rulers.
All their kings fall,
  and none of them calls on me.

⁸"Ephraim mixes with the nations;
  Ephraim is a flat loaf not turned over.
⁹Foreigners sap his strength,
  but he does not realize it.
His hair is sprinkled with gray,
  but he does not notice.
¹⁰Israel's arrogance testifies against him,
  but despite all this
he does not return to the LORD his God
  or search for him.

¹¹"Ephraim is like a dove,
  easily deceived and senseless—

now calling to Egypt,
  now turning to Assyria.
¹²When they go, I will throw my net over
    them;
  I will pull them down like the birds in the
    sky.
When I hear them flocking together,
  I will catch them.
¹³Woe to them,
  because they have strayed from me!
Destruction to them,
  because they have rebelled against me!
I long to redeem them
  but they speak about me falsely.
¹⁴They do not cry out to me from their hearts
  but wail on their beds.
They slash themselves,ᵃ appealing to their
    gods
  for grain and new wine,
  but they turn away from me.
¹⁵I trained them and strengthened their
    arms,
  but they plot evil against me.
¹⁶They do not turn to the Most High;
  they are like a faulty bow.
Their leaders will fall by the sword
  because of their insolent words.

ᵃ 14 Some Hebrew manuscripts and Septuagint; most Hebrew manuscripts *They gather together*

The Art of Confrontation

Hosea 6:1—7:16

Hosea is not above speaking words of confrontation. He uses vivid imagery and colorful images to describe the evil behavior of his people. Look at his train of thought:

1. **He clarifies the desired relationship he wishes to have (6:1–3).**

2. **He defines the unacceptable behavior (6:4–5).**

3. **He highlights his values and priorities (6:6).**

4. **He lists the conduct that illustrates his point (7:1–14).**

5. **He reminds the people of their training (7:15).**

6. **He declares the consequences (7:16).**

For six more chapters Hosea continues to detail the people's unacceptable conduct. Then, in chapter 14, he offers words of restoration. All good confrontation ends in the hope of restoration. The goal is always reconciliation, not excommunication.

When team members drift from goals, leaders owe it to them and to the organization to confront or clarify the situation. This is the only way to stay on track and to maintain respect from the team. Hosea has written the book on it!

For this they will be ridiculed
in the land of Egypt.

Israel to Reap the Whirlwind

8 "Put the trumpet to your lips!
An eagle is over the house of the LORD
because the people have broken my covenant
and rebelled against my law.
[2] Israel cries out to me,
'Our God, we acknowledge you!'
[3] But Israel has rejected what is good;
an enemy will pursue him.
[4] They set up kings without my consent;
they choose princes without my approval.
With their silver and gold
they make idols for themselves
to their own destruction.
[5] Samaria, throw out your calf-idol!
My anger burns against them.
How long will they be incapable of purity?
[6] They are from Israel!
This calf—a metalworker has made it;
it is not God.
It will be broken in pieces,
that calf of Samaria.

[7] "They sow the wind
and reap the whirlwind.
The stalk has no head;
it will produce no flour.
Were it to yield grain,
foreigners would swallow it up.
[8] Israel is swallowed up;
now she is among the nations
like something no one wants.
[9] For they have gone up to Assyria
like a wild donkey wandering alone.
Ephraim has sold herself to lovers.
[10] Although they have sold themselves among
the nations,
I will now gather them together.
They will begin to waste away
under the oppression of the mighty king.

[11] "Though Ephraim built many altars for sin
offerings,
these have become altars for sinning.
[12] I wrote for them the many things of my law,
but they regarded them as something
foreign.
[13] Though they offer sacrifices as gifts to me,
and though they eat the meat,
the LORD is not pleased with them.
Now he will remember their wickedness
and punish their sins:
They will return to Egypt.

[14] Israel has forgotten their Maker
and built palaces;
Judah has fortified many towns.
But I will send fire on their cities
that will consume their fortresses."

Punishment for Israel

9 Do not rejoice, Israel;
do not be jubilant like the other
nations.
For you have been unfaithful to your God;
you love the wages of a prostitute
at every threshing floor.
[2] Threshing floors and winepresses will not
feed the people;
the new wine will fail them.
[3] They will not remain in the LORD's land;
Ephraim will return to Egypt
and eat unclean food in Assyria.
[4] They will not pour out wine offerings to the
LORD,
nor will their sacrifices please him.
Such sacrifices will be to them like the bread
of mourners;
all who eat them will be unclean.
This food will be for themselves;
it will not come into the temple of the
LORD.

[5] What will you do on the day of your
appointed festivals,
on the feast days of the LORD?
[6] Even if they escape from destruction,
Egypt will gather them,
and Memphis will bury them.
Their treasures of silver will be taken over
by briers,
and thorns will overrun their tents.
[7] The days of punishment are coming,
the days of reckoning are at hand.
Let Israel know this.
Because your sins are so many
and your hostility so great,
the prophet is considered a fool,
the inspired person a maniac.
[8] The prophet, along with my God,
is the watchman over Ephraim,[a]
yet snares await him on all his paths,
and hostility in the house of his God.
[9] They have sunk deep into corruption,
as in the days of Gibeah.
God will remember their wickedness
and punish them for their sins.

---

[a] 8 Or *The prophet is the watchman over Ephraim, / the people of my God*

10 "When I found Israel,
  it was like finding grapes in the desert;
  when I saw your ancestors,
  it was like seeing the early fruit on the
   fig tree.
 But when they came to Baal Peor,
  they consecrated themselves to that
   shameful idol
  and became as vile as the thing they
   loved.
11 Ephraim's glory will fly away like a bird —
  no birth, no pregnancy, no conception.
12 Even if they rear children,
  I will bereave them of every one.
 Woe to them
  when I turn away from them!
13 I have seen Ephraim, like Tyre,
  planted in a pleasant place.
 But Ephraim will bring out
  their children to the slayer."

14 Give them, LORD —
  what will you give them?
 Give them wombs that miscarry
  and breasts that are dry.

15 "Because of all their wickedness in Gilgal,
  I hated them there.
 Because of their sinful deeds,
  I will drive them out of my house.
 I will no longer love them;
  all their leaders are rebellious.
16 Ephraim is blighted,
  their root is withered,
  they yield no fruit.
 Even if they bear children,
  I will slay their cherished offspring."

17 My God will reject them
  because they have not obeyed him;
  they will be wanderers among the nations.

10 Israel was a spreading vine;
  he brought forth fruit for himself.
 As his fruit increased,
  he built more altars;
 as his land prospered,
  he adorned his sacred stones.
2 Their heart is deceitful,
  and now they must bear their guilt.
 The LORD will demolish their altars
  and destroy their sacred stones.

3 Then they will say, "We have no king
  because we did not revere the LORD.
 But even if we had a king,
  what could he do for us?"

Israel's Leaders Broke the Law of Solid Ground

Hosea 10:3–4

How had Israel drifted into such serious sin? Hosea's answer: Israel had no real leadership. False promises had eroded the people's confidence in their leaders. They concluded: "We have no king . . . They make many promises, take false oaths and make agreements" (Hos 10:3–4). People follow only in proportion to their trust in the leader.

4 They make many promises,
  take false oaths
  and make agreements;
 therefore lawsuits spring up
  like poisonous weeds in a plowed field.
5 The people who live in Samaria fear
  for the calf-idol of Beth Aven.[a]
 Its people will mourn over it,
  and so will its idolatrous priests,
 those who had rejoiced over its splendor,
  because it is taken from them into
   exile.
6 It will be carried to Assyria
  as tribute for the great king.
 Ephraim will be disgraced;
  Israel will be ashamed of its foreign
   alliances.
7 Samaria's king will be destroyed,
  swept away like a twig on the surface of
   the waters.
8 The high places of wickedness[b] will be
   destroyed —
  it is the sin of Israel.
 Thorns and thistles will grow up
  and cover their altars.
 Then they will say to the mountains,
   "Cover us!"
  and to the hills, "Fall on us!"

9 "Since the days of Gibeah, you have sinned,
   Israel,
  and there you have remained.[c]
 Will not war again overtake
  the evildoers in Gibeah?

---

[a] 5 *Beth Aven* means *house of wickedness* (a derogatory name for Bethel, which means *house of God*). [b] 8 Hebrew *aven*, a reference to Beth Aven (a derogatory name for Bethel); see verse 5. [c] 9 Or *there a stand was taken*

¹⁰ When I please, I will punish them;
     nations will be gathered against them
     to put them in bonds for their double sin.
¹¹ Ephraim is a trained heifer
     that loves to thresh;
so I will put a yoke
     on her fair neck.
I will drive Ephraim,
     Judah must plow,
     and Jacob must break up the ground.
¹² Sow righteousness for yourselves,
     reap the fruit of unfailing love,
and break up your unplowed ground;
     for it is time to seek the LORD,
until he comes
     and showers his righteousness on you.
¹³ But you have planted wickedness,
     you have reaped evil,
     you have eaten the fruit of deception.
Because you have depended on your own
         strength
     and on your many warriors,
¹⁴ the roar of battle will rise against your people,
     so that all your fortresses will be
         devastated —
as Shalman devastated Beth Arbel on the day
     of battle,
     when mothers were dashed to the ground
     with their children.
¹⁵ So will it happen to you, Bethel,
     because your wickedness is great.
When that day dawns,
     the king of Israel will be completely
     destroyed.

God's Love for Israel

11 "When Israel was a child, I loved him,
     and out of Egypt I called my son.
² But the more they were called,
     the more they went away from me.^a
They sacrificed to the Baals
     and they burned incense to images.
³ It was I who taught Ephraim to walk,
     taking them by the arms;
but they did not realize
     it was I who healed them.
⁴ I led them with cords of human kindness,
     with ties of love.
To them I was like one who lifts
     a little child to the cheek,
     and I bent down to feed them.

⁵ "Will they not return to Egypt
     and will not Assyria rule over them
     because they refuse to repent?

⁶ A sword will flash in their cities;
     it will devour their false prophets
     and put an end to their plans.
⁷ My people are determined to turn from me.
     Even though they call me God Most High,
     I will by no means exalt them.

⁸ "How can I give you up, Ephraim?
     How can I hand you over, Israel?
How can I treat you like Admah?
     How can I make you like Zeboyim?
My heart is changed within me;
     all my compassion is aroused.
⁹ I will not carry out my fierce anger,
     nor will I devastate Ephraim again.
For I am God, and not a man —
     the Holy One among you.
     I will not come against their cities.
¹⁰ They will follow the LORD;
     he will roar like a lion.
When he roars,
     his children will come trembling from the
         west.
¹¹ They will come from Egypt,
     trembling like sparrows,
     from Assyria, fluttering like doves.
I will settle them in their homes,"
     declares the LORD.

Israel's Sin

¹² Ephraim has surrounded me with lies,
     Israel with deceit.
And Judah is unruly against God,
     even against the faithful Holy One.^b

12^c ¹ Ephraim feeds on the wind;
     he pursues the east wind all day
     and multiplies lies and violence.
He makes a treaty with Assyria
     and sends olive oil to Egypt.
² The LORD has a charge to bring against
         Judah;
     he will punish Jacob^d according to his
         ways
     and repay him according to his deeds.
³ In the womb he grasped his brother's heel;
     as a man he struggled with God.
⁴ He struggled with the angel and overcame
         him;
     he wept and begged for his favor.
He found him at Bethel
     and talked with him there —

---

^a 2 Septuagint; Hebrew *them*   ^b 12 In Hebrew texts this verse (11:12) is numbered 12:1.   ^c In Hebrew texts 12:1-14 is numbered 12:2-15.   ^d 2 *Jacob* means *he grasps the heel*, a Hebrew idiom for *he takes advantage of* or *he deceives*.

⁵the LORD God Almighty,
   the LORD is his name!
⁶But you must return to your God;
   maintain love and justice,
   and wait for your God always.

⁷The merchant uses dishonest scales
   and loves to defraud.
⁸Ephraim boasts,
   "I am very rich; I have become wealthy.
With all my wealth they will not find in me
   any iniquity or sin."

⁹"I have been the LORD your God
   ever since you came out of Egypt;
I will make you live in tents again,
   as in the days of your appointed festivals.
¹⁰I spoke to the prophets,
   gave them many visions
   and told parables through them."

¹¹Is Gilead wicked?
   Its people are worthless!
Do they sacrifice bulls in Gilgal?
   Their altars will be like piles of stones
   on a plowed field.
¹²Jacob fled to the country of Aram*ᵃ*;
   Israel served to get a wife,
   and to pay for her he tended sheep.
¹³The LORD used a prophet to bring Israel up
   from Egypt,
   by a prophet he cared for him.
¹⁴But Ephraim has aroused his bitter anger;
   his Lord will leave on him the guilt of his
   bloodshed
   and will repay him for his contempt.

The LORD's Anger Against Israel

13 When Ephraim spoke, people trembled;
   he was exalted in Israel.
   But he became guilty of Baal worship and
   died.
²Now they sin more and more;
   they make idols for themselves from their
   silver,
cleverly fashioned images,
   all of them the work of craftsmen.
It is said of these people,
   "They offer human sacrifices!
They kiss*ᵇ* calf-idols!"
³Therefore they will be like the morning mist,
   like the early dew that disappears,
   like chaff swirling from a threshing floor,
   like smoke escaping through a window.

⁴"But I have been the LORD your God
   ever since you came out of Egypt.
You shall acknowledge no God but me,
   no Savior except me.
⁵I cared for you in the wilderness,
   in the land of burning heat.
⁶When I fed them, they were satisfied;
   when they were satisfied, they became
   proud;
   then they forgot me.
⁷So I will be like a lion to them,
   like a leopard I will lurk by the path.
⁸Like a bear robbed of her cubs,
   I will attack them and rip them open;

ᵃ 12 That is, Northwest Mesopotamia   *ᵇ 2* Or "Men who
sacrifice / kiss

Humility: No Matter Who the Leader Is—God Still Rules!

Hosea 14:1–7

One of the missing pieces in Israel's leadership was humility. They had forgotten who created their prosperity and good fortune. Hosea 11:1–4 and 12:7–9 remind the nation that God taught them and provided for them.

Leaders err when they assume they are the source of blessing. Wise leaders seek to make good decisions, but realize the outcome remains in God's hands. Leaders merely manage what God owns. Leaders are in charge, but God is in control.

Hosea 14:1–7 gives a prescription to help leaders recapture humility:

1. **Return: Do a turnaround and pursue the Lord (v. 1).**

2. **Repent: Confess specifically your self-sufficiency (v. 2).**

3. **Remember: Remind yourself that only God is in control (v. 3).**

4. **Result: Only then will God respond with blessing and restoration (vv. 4–7).**

like a lion I will devour them —
　　a wild animal will tear them apart.

[9] "You are destroyed, Israel,
　　because you are against me, against your
　　　helper.
[10] Where is your king, that he may save you?
　　Where are your rulers in all your towns,
　　of whom you said,
　　　'Give me a king and princes'?
[11] So in my anger I gave you a king,
　　and in my wrath I took him away.
[12] The guilt of Ephraim is stored up,
　　his sins are kept on record.
[13] Pains as of a woman in childbirth come
　　　to him,
　　but he is a child without wisdom;
when the time arrives,
　　he doesn't have the sense to come out of
　　　the womb.

[14] "I will deliver this people from the power of
　　　the grave;
　　I will redeem them from death.
Where, O death, are your plagues?
　　Where, O grave, is your destruction?

"I will have no compassion,
[15]　　even though he thrives among his brothers.
An east wind from the LORD will come,
　　blowing in from the desert;
his spring will fail
　　and his well dry up.
His storehouse will be plundered
　　of all its treasures.

[16] The people of Samaria must bear their guilt,
　　because they have rebelled against their
　　　God.
They will fall by the sword;
　　their little ones will be dashed to the ground,
　　their pregnant women ripped open."[a]

Repentance to Bring Blessing

14[b] Return, Israel, to the LORD your God.
　　Your sins have been your downfall!
[2] Take words with you
　　and return to the LORD.
Say to him:
　　"Forgive all our sins
and receive us graciously,
　　that we may offer the fruit of our lips.[c]
[3] Assyria cannot save us;
　　we will not mount warhorses.
We will never again say 'Our gods'
　　to what our own hands have made,
　　for in you the fatherless find compassion."

[4] "I will heal their waywardness
　　and love them freely,
　　for my anger has turned away from them.
[5] I will be like the dew to Israel;
　　he will blossom like a lily.
Like a cedar of Lebanon
　　he will send down his roots;
[6]　　his young shoots will grow.

---

[a] 16 In Hebrew texts this verse (13:16) is numbered 14:1.
[b] In Hebrew texts 14:1-9 is numbered 14:2-10.　　[c] 2 Or offer
our lips as sacrifices of bulls

Leaders Love Everyone, but Don't Drop Their Convictions

Hosea 14:9

Do leaders always love and care for people, regardless of who they are? Certainly, both God and Hosea modeled unconditional love. But does a time come when showing compassion for someone ends, or otherwise a leader violates a bedrock principle?

This is where leaders draw a line in the sand. While they are to love and care for anyone they contact, this doesn't mean they chuck their convictions. They respond with grace, but never drift from their guiding priorities and principles. We cling to convictions even in our lowest moment.

Both God and Hosea continued to act from principle. Leaders practice the Law of Empowerment by living out priorities:

Leaders are to . . .	Followers often . . .
1. Act from their principles.	1. React from their feelings.
2. Empower others even when it's difficult.	2. Withdraw in difficult times.
3. Live off of character.	3. Live off of emotions.

His splendor will be like an olive tree,
  his fragrance like a cedar of Lebanon.
[7] People will dwell again in his shade;
  they will flourish like the grain,
they will blossom like the vine —
  Israel's fame will be like the wine of
    Lebanon.
[8] Ephraim, what more have I[a] to do with idols?
  I will answer him and care for him.

I am like a flourishing juniper;
  your fruitfulness comes from me."

[9] Who is wise? Let them realize these things.
  Who is discerning? Let them understand.
The ways of the LORD are right;
  the righteous walk in them,
  but the rebellious stumble in them.

[a] 8 Or Hebrew; Septuagint *What more has Ephraim*

INTRODUCTION TO
JOEL

A God-Given Message to Judah

The prophet Joel directed his message to Judah and, more specifically, to the city of Jerusalem. Joel was an educated, well-read leader who knew not only the writings of the other prophets, but also the current events of his day. He used them all to illustrate the message God had given him.

Joel effectively used an invasion of locusts that occurred during his day as his primary word picture. He utilized this natural catastrophe to underscore his message of repentance. He spoke of the "day of the LORD" which would come much like the locusts—surprising and terrifying. He attempted to awaken the people of Judah from their spiritual apathy and disobedience and provoke them to return to the Lord.

Joel teaches us that leaders must see the future clearly and project what steps must be taken to thrive in it. Joel called the leaders of his day to sound a warning of repentance to successive generations he would never meet—a futurist in the truest sense of the word.

Second, leaders must read and interpret current events. Joel saw and explained the locusts of his day in a way that made his message vivid and memorable. He took a physical reality and capitalized on it to illustrate a spiritual reality. His mind focused on both current events and eternal outcomes.

Third, corporate or community repentance begins with the leader. People usually act *en masse* when a leader sounds the trumpet and provides an example of what must be done. This proved true in Joel's case. Joel called the priests to model repentance with sackcloth and mourning. People do what people see.

Fourth, leaders must never cry out for change with-

God's Role in Joel

God is the Ultimate Leader in control, the One who sends the locusts and the One who will come on the day of the Lord—a day far more terrifying than mere locusts. God sometimes uses the natural realm to direct us to truths in the spiritual realm. God uses the disastrous locust plague to illustrate a far greater spiritual catastrophe to come if his people refuse to return to him.

Leaders in Joel

Joel

Other People of Influence in Joel

Leaders in Jerusalem and Judah

Lessons in Leadership

- Leaders are realistic futurists—they define reality and distribute hope.
- Great leaders communicate in relevant ways, connecting the known to the unknown.
- If leaders project a problem to the people, they must propose a plan for the people.

out providing some solutions. It does little good to merely complain. Leaders must sound the alarm, but then say, "And here are some steps we can take to improve." Along with his warning of judgment, Joel talks about the promise of the Holy Spirit and the need for his filling. He spoke of the coming day of the Lord and the need to call on God for deliverance. He listed the steps of repentance the people of Judah needed to take if they were to renew themselves and find restoration in the grace of God.

LEADERSHIP HIGHLIGHTS IN JOEL

THE LAW OF INTUITION: Joel Interprets the Disaster of the Locusts (1:6–7)   **page 1040**

THE LAW OF CONNECTION: Joel Uses the Times to Say the Timeless (2:1–32)   **page 1042**

THE LAW OF NAVIGATION: Joel Declares Hope if Judah Will Respond (3:1–21)   **page 1043**

1
The word of the LORD that came to Joel son
of Pethuel.

An Invasion of Locusts

² Hear this, you elders;
  listen, all who live in the land.
Has anything like this ever happened in
    your days
  or in the days of your ancestors?
³ Tell it to your children,
  and let your children tell it to their
    children,
  and their children to the next generation.
⁴ What the locust swarm has left
  the great locusts have eaten;
what the great locusts have left
  the young locusts have eaten;
what the young locusts have left
  other locusts*a* have eaten.

⁵ Wake up, you drunkards, and weep!
  Wail, all you drinkers of wine;
wail because of the new wine,
  for it has been snatched from your lips.
⁶ A nation has invaded my land,
  a mighty army without number;
it has the teeth of a lion,
  the fangs of a lioness.

The Law of Intuition:
Joel Interprets the Disaster
of the Locusts

Joel 1:6–7

Joel provides us with an example of a leader
who rightly reads his times and culture and
interprets them for the masses. His divine intuition enables him to stay ahead of the times and
lead in a wise and discerning manner.

Intuition is like a head start in a race; you can
beat the fastest runner in the world with a big
enough head start. Joel provides this head start
to the Hebrews, then gives them a plan to respond to the coming disaster. "Declare a holy
fast; call a sacred assembly. Summon the elders
and all who live in the land to the house of the
LORD your God, and cry out to the LORD," he advises them (Joel 1:14). He helps us see that God
sometimes uses the natural realm to illustrate
realities in the spiritual realm.

---

⁷ It has laid waste my vines
  and ruined my fig trees.
It has stripped off their bark
  and thrown it away,
  leaving their branches white.

⁸ Mourn like a virgin in sackcloth
  grieving for the betrothed of her youth.
⁹ Grain offerings and drink offerings
  are cut off from the house of the LORD.
The priests are in mourning,
  those who minister before the LORD.
¹⁰ The fields are ruined,
  the ground is dried up;
the grain is destroyed,
  the new wine is dried up,
  the olive oil fails.

¹¹ Despair, you farmers,
  wail, you vine growers;
grieve for the wheat and the barley,
  because the harvest of the field is
    destroyed.
¹² The vine is dried up
  and the fig tree is withered;
the pomegranate, the palm and the apple*b*
    tree—
  all the trees of the field—are dried up.
Surely the people's joy
  is withered away.

A Call to Lamentation

¹³ Put on sackcloth, you priests, and mourn;
  wail, you who minister before the altar.
Come, spend the night in sackcloth,
  you who minister before my God;
for the grain offerings and drink offerings
  are withheld from the house of your God.
¹⁴ Declare a holy fast;
  call a sacred assembly.
Summon the elders
  and all who live in the land
to the house of the LORD your God,
  and cry out to the LORD.

¹⁵ Alas for that day!
  For the day of the LORD is near;
  it will come like destruction from the
    Almighty.*c*

¹⁶ Has not the food been cut off
  before our very eyes—
joy and gladness
  from the house of our God?

---

a 4 The precise meaning of the four Hebrew words used here
for locusts is uncertain.   *b 12* Or possibly *apricot*
c 15 Hebrew *Shaddai*

[17] The seeds are shriveled
   beneath the clods.[a]
The storehouses are in ruins,
   the granaries have been broken down,
   for the grain has dried up.
[18] How the cattle moan!
   The herds mill about
because they have no pasture;
   even the flocks of sheep are suffering.

[19] To you, LORD, I call,
   for fire has devoured the pastures in the
      wilderness
   and flames have burned up all the trees of
      the field.
[20] Even the wild animals pant for you;
   the streams of water have dried up
   and fire has devoured the pastures in the
      wilderness.

An Army of Locusts

2 Blow the trumpet in Zion;
   sound the alarm on my holy hill.

Let all who live in the land tremble,
   for the day of the LORD is coming.
It is close at hand —
[2]   a day of darkness and gloom,
   a day of clouds and blackness.
Like dawn spreading across the mountains
   a large and mighty army comes,
such as never was in ancient times
   nor ever will be in ages to come.

[3] Before them fire devours,
   behind them a flame blazes.
Before them the land is like the garden of
      Eden,
   behind them, a desert waste —
   nothing escapes them.
[4] They have the appearance of horses;
   they gallop along like cavalry.
[5] With a noise like that of chariots
   they leap over the mountaintops,
like a crackling fire consuming stubble,
   like a mighty army drawn up for battle.

[6] At the sight of them, nations are in anguish;
   every face turns pale.
[7] They charge like warriors;
   they scale walls like soldiers.
They all march in line,
   not swerving from their course.
[8] They do not jostle each other;
   each marches straight ahead.
They plunge through defenses
   without breaking ranks.

[9] They rush upon the city;
   they run along the wall.
They climb into the houses;
   like thieves they enter through the
      windows.

[10] Before them the earth shakes,
   the heavens tremble,
the sun and moon are darkened,
   and the stars no longer shine.
[11] The LORD thunders
   at the head of his army;
his forces are beyond number,
   and mighty is the army that obeys his
      command.
The day of the LORD is great;
   it is dreadful.
   Who can endure it?

Rend Your Heart

[12] "Even now," declares the LORD,
   "return to me with all your heart,
   with fasting and weeping and mourning."

[13] Rend your heart
   and not your garments.
Return to the LORD your God,
   for he is gracious and compassionate,
slow to anger and abounding in love,
   and he relents from sending calamity.
[14] Who knows? He may turn and relent
   and leave behind a blessing —
grain offerings and drink offerings
   for the LORD your God.

[15] Blow the trumpet in Zion,
   declare a holy fast,
   call a sacred assembly.
[16] Gather the people,
   consecrate the assembly;
bring together the elders,
   gather the children,
   those nursing at the breast.
Let the bridegroom leave his room
   and the bride her chamber.
[17] Let the priests, who minister before the
      LORD,
   weep between the portico and the altar.
Let them say, "Spare your people, LORD.
   Do not make your inheritance an object of
      scorn,
   a byword among the nations.
Why should they say among the peoples,
   'Where is their God?'"

---

[a] 17 The meaning of the Hebrew for this word is uncertain.

The LORD's Answer

18 Then the LORD was jealous for his land
    and took pity on his people.

19 The LORD replied[a] to them:

"I am sending you grain, new wine and olive
    oil,
    enough to satisfy you fully;
never again will I make you
    an object of scorn to the nations.

20 "I will drive the northern horde far from
    you,
    pushing it into a parched and barren
    land;
its eastern ranks will drown in the Dead Sea
    and its western ranks in the
    Mediterranean Sea.
And its stench will go up;
    its smell will rise."

Surely he has done great things!
21   Do not be afraid, land of Judah;
    be glad and rejoice.
Surely the LORD has done great things!
22   Do not be afraid, you wild animals,
    for the pastures in the wilderness are
    becoming green.
The trees are bearing their fruit;
    the fig tree and the vine yield their
    riches.
23 Be glad, people of Zion,
    rejoice in the LORD your God,
for he has given you the autumn rains
    because he is faithful.
He sends you abundant showers,
    both autumn and spring rains, as before.

24 The threshing floors will be filled with
    grain;
    the vats will overflow with new wine and
    oil.

25 "I will repay you for the years the locusts
    have eaten —
    the great locust and the young locust,
    the other locusts and the locust
    swarm[b] —
my great army that I sent among you.
26 You will have plenty to eat, until you are
    full,
    and you will praise the name of the LORD
    your God,
    who has worked wonders for you;
never again will my people be shamed.
27 Then you will know that I am in Israel,
    that I am the LORD your God,
    and that there is no other;
never again will my people be shamed.

The Day of the LORD

28 "And afterward,
    I will pour out my Spirit on all people.
Your sons and daughters will prophesy,
    your old men will dream dreams,
    your young men will see visions.
29 Even on my servants, both men and
    women,
    I will pour out my Spirit in those days.
30 I will show wonders in the heavens
    and on the earth,
    blood and fire and billows of smoke.

---

a 18,19 Or LORD will be jealous . . . / and take pity . . . / 19The
LORD will reply   b 25 The precise meaning of the four
Hebrew words used here for locusts is uncertain.

The Law of Connection: Joel Uses the Times to Say the Timeless

Joel 2:1–32

Leaders understand how to be relevant. Relevance means using temporal events to say what is timeless. The prophet uses the current events of his time to share timeless truth. Every Hebrew knew of the plague of locusts. When that subject came up, everyone paid attention. Joel grabbed their attention with a current event and used it to illustrate God's coming judgment. He and God communicated in these ways:

1. *Creatively:* They used word pictures and current events.

2. *Constantly:* They continued to speak until the people understood.

3. *Consistently:* Their messages didn't contradict each other.

³¹ The sun will be turned to darkness
    and the moon to blood
    before the coming of the great and
        dreadful day of the LORD.
³² And everyone who calls
    on the name of the LORD will be saved;
for on Mount Zion and in Jerusalem
    there will be deliverance,
    as the LORD has said,
even among the survivors
    whom the LORD calls.ᵃ

The Nations Judged

3 ᵇ "In those days and at that time,
    when I restore the fortunes of Judah and
        Jerusalem,
² I will gather all nations
    and bring them down to the Valley of
        Jehoshaphat.ᶜ
There I will put them on trial
    for what they did to my inheritance, my
        people Israel,
because they scattered my people among the
        nations
    and divided up my land.
³ They cast lots for my people
    and traded boys for prostitutes;
    they sold girls for wine to drink.

⁴"Now what have you against me, Tyre and Sidon and all you regions of Philistia? Are you repaying me for something I have done? If you are paying me back, I will swiftly and speedily return on your own heads what you have done. ⁵For you took my silver and my gold and carried off my finest treasuresᵈ to your temples. ⁶You sold the people of Judah and Jerusalem to the Greeks, that you might send them far from their homeland.

⁷"See, I am going to rouse them out of the places to which you sold them, and I will return on your own heads what you have done. ⁸I will sell your sons and daughters to the people of Judah, and they will sell them to the Sabeans, a nation far away." The LORD has spoken.

⁹ Proclaim this among the nations:
    Prepare for war!
Rouse the warriors!
    Let all the fighting men draw near and
        attack.
¹⁰ Beat your plowshares into swords
    and your pruning hooks into spears.
Let the weakling say,
    "I am strong!"
¹¹ Come quickly, all you nations from every side,
    and assemble there.

The Law of Navigation: Joel Declares Hope if Judah Will Respond

Joel 3:1–21

In the last chapter of his short book, Joel pronounces judgment on the nations. The nation of Israel could look forward to a future full of hope—if they would respond with obedience. Joel predicts that God will use them to judge the nations. The day of the Lord will bring terror to the rebellious and hope to the trusting.

The Law of Navigation forces leaders to become students of three facets of leadership: discernment, strategy and the future. They must interpret the times, see the future, and plan the steps. Joel paints pictures for the people to help them see what he sees.

Bring down your warriors, LORD!

¹² "Let the nations be roused;
    let them advance into the Valley of
        Jehoshaphat,
for there I will sit
    to judge all the nations on every side.
¹³ Swing the sickle,
    for the harvest is ripe.
Come, trample the grapes,
    for the winepress is full
    and the vats overflow—
so great is their wickedness!"

¹⁴ Multitudes, multitudes
    in the valley of decision!
For the day of the LORD is near
    in the valley of decision.
¹⁵ The sun and moon will be darkened,
    and the stars no longer shine.
¹⁶ The LORD will roar from Zion
    and thunder from Jerusalem;
    the earth and the heavens will tremble.
But the LORD will be a refuge for his people,
    a stronghold for the people of Israel.

Blessings for God's People

¹⁷ "Then you will know that I, the LORD your God,
    dwell in Zion, my holy hill.

ᵃ 32 In Hebrew texts 2:28-32 is numbered 3:1-5.   ᵇ In Hebrew texts 3:1-21 is numbered 4:1-21.   ᶜ 2 Jehoshaphat means *the LORD judges*; also in verse 12.   ᵈ 5 Or *palaces*

Jerusalem will be holy;
    never again will foreigners invade her.

18 "In that day the mountains will drip new
        wine,
    and the hills will flow with milk;
    all the ravines of Judah will run with
        water.
A fountain will flow out of the LORD's house
    and will water the valley of acacias.^a
19 But Egypt will be desolate,
    Edom a desert waste,

because of violence done to the people of
        Judah,
    in whose land they shed innocent blood.
20 Judah will be inhabited forever
    and Jerusalem through all generations.
21 Shall I leave their innocent blood
        unavenged?
    No, I will not."

The LORD dwells in Zion!

---

^a 18 Or *Valley of Shittim*

INTRODUCTION TO
AMOS

A Spiritual Plumb Line Raised

God called the fiery prophet Amos to correct the injustice of the leaders of his day in Israel, Judah and the surrounding nations. He seems an unlikely leader, called as a shepherd in the desert of Judah. As a shepherd, he supplemented his income by taking care of "sycamore-fig trees" (1:1; 7:14–15). He brought no known credentials to his prophetic work except for his divine call.

Amos first challenged the sins of the surrounding nations—something the Israelites liked. But when he turned to correct his own people, his popularity plummeted. The writings of this clear thinker show that he possessed a thorough knowledge of history and the problems of his day. He uses language rich in symbols and figures, with close attention to detail. He tries to compel the people to see the immorality and injustice of their generation and to make it right.

In Amos's day, marketplace exploitation had grown so bad that God used him to threaten the people with "fire": war, economic depression and destruction. God gives power to leaders for the provision, protection and progress of followers. Whenever leaders abuse that power, God shows his displeasure with their stewardship.

Amos also shows us that God hates injustice. While it may look as if he doesn't do anything about the outrage, he is watching and disapproves of leaders who tolerate it. Amos accused leaders of a spiritual deterioration that paralleled their material prosperity (5:12, 21). They still "went to church," yet didn't see their own hypocrisy. Amos castigated the leaders for their corruption (2:7–8) and pointed out their disregard for human rights (2:6). For about a decade, Amos became God's eyes, heart and mouthpiece to the people of Israel.

God's Role in Amos

Amos did not base his plea on the nature of man or the innate goodness of human nature. God was the standard—and he remains the same at all times and in every place. Self-interest always distorts man's perspective. Amos based his plea on the nature and righteousness of God, the "plumb line" from which every person is measured. Despite the shifting values of mankind, God never changes, nor does he grade on a curve. He is the absolute leader and controller of history and challenges leaders when they drift from his absolutes.

Leaders in Amos

Amos, Jeroboam II, Uzziah

Other People of Influence in Amos

Amaziah, the sellers in the marketplace

Lessons in Leadership

- It's easiest for leaders to drift when there is economic security.
- God gives power to leaders to help followers, not themselves.
- When an organization goes bad, leaders must own the responsibility.
- The foundation for all leadership is trust, integrity and justice.

Amos taught that leaders must lead from moral absolutes, not from convenience and expediency. Amos used a plumb line to illustrate that God's people had drifted from the revealed standard. A plumb line helped builders detect the straightness of a wall, the equivalent of a level today. Builders attached a weight to a string, then let gravity use the string to draw a straight vertical line. Amos attempted to raise a spiritual plumb line against the corruption and crookedness of his day.

> ■ Leaders must raise the standard; as the leader goes, so goes the organization.

LEADERSHIP HIGHLIGHTS IN AMOS

1 The words of Amos, one of the shepherds of Tekoa — the vision he saw concerning Israel two years before the earthquake, when Uzziah was king of Judah and Jeroboam son of Jehoash[a] was king of Israel.

²He said:

"The LORD roars from Zion
and thunders from Jerusalem;
the pastures of the shepherds dry up,
and the top of Carmel withers."

Judgment on Israel's Neighbors

³This is what the LORD says:

"For three sins of Damascus,
even for four, I will not relent.
Because she threshed Gilead
with sledges having iron teeth,
⁴I will send fire on the house of Hazael
that will consume the fortresses of Ben-
Hadad.
⁵I will break down the gate of Damascus;
I will destroy the king who is in[b] the
Valley of Aven[c]
and the one who holds the scepter in Beth
Eden.
The people of Aram will go into exile to Kir,"
says the LORD.

⁶This is what the LORD says:

"For three sins of Gaza,
even for four, I will not relent.
Because she took captive whole communities
and sold them to Edom,
⁷I will send fire on the walls of Gaza
that will consume her fortresses.

⁸I will destroy the king[d] of Ashdod
and the one who holds the scepter in
Ashkelon.
I will turn my hand against Ekron,
till the last of the Philistines are dead,"
says the Sovereign LORD.

⁹This is what the LORD says:

"For three sins of Tyre,
even for four, I will not relent.
Because she sold whole communities of
captives to Edom,
disregarding a treaty of brotherhood,
¹⁰I will send fire on the walls of Tyre
that will consume her fortresses."

¹¹This is what the LORD says:

"For three sins of Edom,
even for four, I will not relent.
Because he pursued his brother with a sword
and slaughtered the women of the land,
because his anger raged continually
and his fury flamed unchecked,
¹²I will send fire on Teman
that will consume the fortresses of Bozrah."

¹³This is what the LORD says:

"For three sins of Ammon,
even for four, I will not relent.
Because he ripped open the pregnant women
of Gilead
in order to extend his borders,

---

[a] 1 Hebrew *Joash*, a variant of *Jehoash*   [b] 5 Or *the inhabitants of*   [c] 5 *Aven* means *wickedness*.   [d] 8 Or *inhabitants*

Efficiency Minus Ethics Equals Emptiness

Amos 1:1—2:16

Leaders who fail morally do not lead anyone to a better place. The higher the leader goes, the deeper his character must develop. The larger the outward privilege, the larger the inward character must be. Character represents the inner life of a leader. God judged ancient leaders because of missing character:

1. **Damascus, Syria—because they ruthlessly butchered Gilead without just cause.**

2. **Gaza—because they made captives of free people and sold them into slavery.**

3. **Tyre—because they ignored a covenant of peace and brotherhood.**

4. **Edom—because they attacked their own family tribes and showed no compassion.**

5. **Ammon—because they murdered women in order to expand their territory.**

6. **Moab—because they displayed no respect for leadership in neighboring nations.**

¹⁴I will set fire to the walls of Rabbah
    that will consume her fortresses
amid war cries on the day of battle,
    amid violent winds on a stormy day.
¹⁵Her king[a] will go into exile,
    he and his officials together,"
                              says the LORD.

2 This is what the LORD says:

"For three sins of Moab,
    even for four, I will not relent.
Because he burned to ashes
    the bones of Edom's king,
²I will send fire on Moab
    that will consume the fortresses of Kerioth.[b]
Moab will go down in great tumult
    amid war cries and the blast of the
        trumpet.
³I will destroy her ruler
    and kill all her officials with him,"
                              says the LORD.

⁴This is what the LORD says:

"For three sins of Judah,
    even for four, I will not relent.
Because they have rejected the law of the
        LORD
    and have not kept his decrees,
because they have been led astray by false
        gods,[c]
    the gods[d] their ancestors followed,

⁵I will send fire on Judah
    that will consume the fortresses of
        Jerusalem."

Judgment on Israel

⁶This is what the LORD says:

"For three sins of Israel,
    even for four, I will not relent.
They sell the innocent for silver,
    and the needy for a pair of sandals.
⁷They trample on the heads of the poor
    as on the dust of the ground
    and deny justice to the oppressed.
Father and son use the same girl
    and so profane my holy name.
⁸They lie down beside every altar
    on garments taken in pledge.
In the house of their god
    they drink wine taken as fines.

⁹"Yet I destroyed the Amorites before
        them,
    though they were tall as the cedars
    and strong as the oaks.
I destroyed their fruit above
    and their roots below.
¹⁰I brought you up out of Egypt
    and led you forty years in the wilderness
    to give you the land of the Amorites.

---

[a] 15 Or / Molek   [b] 2 Or of her cities   [c] 4 Or by lies
[d] 4 Or lies

The Law of Solid Ground: Good Leaders Remove the Planks from Their Eyes

Amos 2:4–16

The entire first chapter of Amos and part of the second details God's judgment on Israel's neighbors. No doubt Israel enjoyed these words. They likely cheered Amos on, yelling, "Preach it, brother! Those heathen nations really need to get their act together!"

Once Amos finished with Damascus, Gaza, Tyre, Edom, Ammon and Moab, however, he directed his words closer to home—to Judah. Now his listeners probably squirmed. Finally, Amos dropped the bomb and declared judgment on Israel. Everyone grew quiet. How dare Amos lump *them* into God's judgment!

Quality leaders remain objective. They can be trusted because they see the "plank in their own eye" before trying to remove the speck from their brother's (Mt 7:3–5). When leaders fail to be objective, people begin to question whether their perspective is skewed by self-interest. Trust wanes. People trust leaders who practice the Law of Solid Ground. Such leaders fulfill three primary objectives:

1. **Protection: To make sure the people are defended from harm.**

2. **Provision: To make sure the people are resourced to do their work.**

3. **Progress: To make sure the enterprise reaches the desired destination.**

11 "I also raised up prophets from among your
      children
   and Nazirites from among your youths.
   Is this not true, people of Israel?"
                              declares the LORD.
12 "But you made the Nazirites drink wine
   and commanded the prophets not to
      prophesy.

13 "Now then, I will crush you
   as a cart crushes when loaded with grain.
14 The swift will not escape,
   the strong will not muster their strength,
   and the warrior will not save his life.
15 The archer will not stand his ground,
   the fleet-footed soldier will not get away,
   and the horseman will not save his life.
16 Even the bravest warriors
   will flee naked on that day,"
                              declares the LORD.

Witnesses Summoned Against Israel

3 Hear this word, people of Israel, the word
   the LORD has spoken against you — against
the whole family I brought up out of Egypt:

2 "You only have I chosen
   of all the families of the earth;
   therefore I will punish you
   for all your sins."

3 Do two walk together
   unless they have agreed to do so?
4 Does a lion roar in the thicket
   when it has no prey?
   Does it growl in its den
   when it has caught nothing?
5 Does a bird swoop down to a trap on the
      ground
   when no bait is there?
   Does a trap spring up from the ground
   if it has not caught anything?
6 When a trumpet sounds in a city,
   do not the people tremble?
   When disaster comes to a city,
   has not the LORD caused it?

7 Surely the Sovereign LORD does nothing
   without revealing his plan
   to his servants the prophets.

8 The lion has roared —
   who will not fear?
   The Sovereign LORD has spoken —
   who can but prophesy?

9 Proclaim to the fortresses of Ashdod
   and to the fortresses of Egypt:

The Law of the Picture: God Holds His People Accountable to Lead the World

Amos 3:1–2

God's people had wanted to live like other nations did. They failed to realize that he held them to a higher standard than other nations. God intended to guide them himself, making them a nation of leaders who could become a model for the world. It's an example of the Law of the Picture: people do what people see. God wanted Israel to be a light to the nations. They were to exemplify the life all people were to live. God's heavy judgment fell because he held his people accountable to lead the world to himself.

"Assemble yourselves on the mountains of
      Samaria;
   see the great unrest within her
   and the oppression among her people."

10 "They do not know how to do right,"
                              declares the LORD,
   "who store up in their fortresses
   what they have plundered and looted."

11 Therefore this is what the Sovereign LORD
says:

"An enemy will overrun your land,
   pull down your strongholds
   and plunder your fortresses."

12 This is what the LORD says:

"As a shepherd rescues from the lion's
      mouth
   only two leg bones or a piece of an ear,
so will the Israelites living in Samaria be
      rescued,
   with only the head of a bed
   and a piece of fabric[a] from a couch.[b]"

13 "Hear this and testify against the descendants of Jacob," declares the Lord, the LORD God Almighty.

---

[a] 12 The meaning of the Hebrew for this phrase is uncertain.
[b] 12 Or Israelites be rescued, / those who sit in Samaria / on the edge of their beds / and in Damascus on their couches.

14 "On the day I punish Israel for her sins,
   I will destroy the altars of Bethel;
the horns of the altar will be cut off
   and fall to the ground.
15 I will tear down the winter house
   along with the summer house;
the houses adorned with ivory will be
      destroyed
   and the mansions will be demolished,"
                    declares the LORD.

Israel Has Not Returned to God

4 Hear this word, you cows of Bashan on
   Mount Samaria,
you women who oppress the poor and
   crush the needy
and say to your husbands, "Bring us some
   drinks!"
2 The Sovereign LORD has sworn by his
      holiness:
   "The time will surely come
when you will be taken away with hooks,
   the last of you with fishhooks.a
3 You will each go straight out
   through breaches in the wall,
and you will be cast out toward
   Harmon,b"
                    declares the LORD.
4 "Go to Bethel and sin;
   go to Gilgal and sin yet more.

Bring your sacrifices every morning,
   your tithes every three years.c
5 Burn leavened bread as a thank offering
   and brag about your freewill
      offerings—
boast about them, you Israelites,
   for this is what you love to do,"
                    declares the Sovereign LORD.

6 "I gave you empty stomachs in every city
   and lack of bread in every town,
yet you have not returned to me,"
                    declares the LORD.

7 "I also withheld rain from you
   when the harvest was still three months
      away.
I sent rain on one town,
   but withheld it from another.
One field had rain;
   another had none and dried up.
8 People staggered from town to town for
      water
   but did not get enough to drink,
yet you have not returned to me,"
                    declares the LORD.

---

a 2 Or away in baskets, / the last of you in fish baskets
b 3 Masoretic Text; with a different word division of the
Hebrew (see Septuagint) out, you mountain of oppression
c 4 Or days

⁹"Many times I struck your gardens and
vineyards,
  destroying them with blight and mildew.
Locusts devoured your fig and olive trees,
  yet you have not returned to me,"
      declares the LORD.

¹⁰"I sent plagues among you
  as I did to Egypt.
I killed your young men with the sword,
  along with your captured horses.
I filled your nostrils with the stench of your
  camps,
  yet you have not returned to me,"
      declares the LORD.

¹¹"I overthrew some of you
  as I overthrew Sodom and Gomorrah.
You were like a burning stick snatched from
  the fire,
  yet you have not returned to me,"
      declares the LORD.

¹²"Therefore this is what I will do to you,
  Israel,
and because I will do this to you, Israel,
  prepare to meet your God."

¹³He who forms the mountains,
  who creates the wind,
and who reveals his thoughts to mankind,
who turns dawn to darkness,
  and treads on the heights of the earth —
  the LORD God Almighty is his name.

A Lament and Call to Repentance

5 Hear this word, Israel, this lament I take up
  concerning you:

²"Fallen is Virgin Israel,
  never to rise again,
deserted in her own land,
  with no one to lift her up."

³This is what the Sovereign LORD says to Israel:

"Your city that marches out a thousand
  strong
  will have only a hundred left;
your town that marches out a hundred
  strong
  will have only ten left."

⁴This is what the LORD says to Israel:

"Seek me and live;
⁵ do not seek Bethel,
do not go to Gilgal,
  do not journey to Beersheba.

For Gilgal will surely go into exile,
  and Bethel will be reduced to nothing.ᵃ"
⁶Seek the LORD and live,
  or he will sweep through the tribes of
    Joseph like a fire;
it will devour them,
  and Bethel will have no one to quench it.

⁷There are those who turn justice into
    bitterness
  and cast righteousness to the ground.

⁸He who made the Pleiades and Orion,
  who turns midnight into dawn
  and darkens day into night,
who calls for the waters of the sea
  and pours them out over the face of the
    land—
  the LORD is his name.
⁹With a blinding flash he destroys the
    stronghold
  and brings the fortified city to ruin.

¹⁰There are those who hate the one who
    upholds justice in court
  and detest the one who tells the truth.

¹¹You levy a straw tax on the poor
  and impose a tax on their grain.
Therefore, though you have built stone
    mansions,
  you will not live in them;
though you have planted lush vineyards,
  you will not drink their wine.
¹²For I know how many are your offenses
  and how great your sins.

There are those who oppress the innocent
    and take bribes
  and deprive the poor of justice in the
    courts.
¹³Therefore the prudent keep quiet in such
    times,
  for the times are evil.

¹⁴Seek good, not evil,
  that you may live.
Then the LORD God Almighty will be with
    you,
  just as you say he is.
¹⁵Hate evil, love good;
  maintain justice in the courts.
Perhaps the LORD God Almighty will have
    mercy
  on the remnant of Joseph.

ᵃ 5 Hebrew *aven*, a reference to Beth Aven (a derogatory name
for Bethel); see Hosea 4:15.

The Law of Influence: Amos Judges Leaders for Abusing Their Positions

Amos 5:7–17

Amos is sometimes called the angry prophet. Most of his words express heated emotion. He condemns leaders who fail to provide justice for their people. Amos 5:7–17 contains his lamentation and call for repentance to those who turn justice into bitterness.

When leaders act unjustly, their influence creates a ripple effect. God hates injustice, but especially among leaders whose crooked influence infects an entire nation! Note the leadership abuses in Amos's day:

1. **They abandoned morality (v. 7).**

2. **They confused values (v. 10).**

3. **They taxed the poor for selfish gain (v. 11).**

4. **They were corrupt and oppressed citizens (v. 12).**

5. **They took bribes (v. 12).**

6. **They deprived people of justice in court (v. 12).**

The scary part of this sad story is that these leaders could not see their own corruption. Amos 5:18 warns against longing for the day of the Lord, for it will be a dreadful day of judgment, not a joyful celebration.

---

¹⁶Therefore this is what the Lord, the LORD God Almighty, says:

"There will be wailing in all the streets
 and cries of anguish in every public square.
The farmers will be summoned to weep
 and the mourners to wail.
¹⁷There will be wailing in all the vineyards,
 for I will pass through your midst,"
  says the LORD.

The Day of the LORD

¹⁸Woe to you who long
 for the day of the LORD!
Why do you long for the day of the LORD?
 That day will be darkness, not light.
¹⁹It will be as though a man fled from a lion
 only to meet a bear,
as though he entered his house
 and rested his hand on the wall
 only to have a snake bite him.
²⁰Will not the day of the LORD be darkness,
  not light—
 pitch-dark, without a ray of brightness?

²¹"I hate, I despise your religious festivals;
 your assemblies are a stench to me.
²²Even though you bring me burnt offerings
 and grain offerings,
 I will not accept them.

Though you bring choice fellowship
  offerings,
 I will have no regard for them.
²³Away with the noise of your songs!
 I will not listen to the music of your harps.
²⁴But let justice roll on like a river,
 righteousness like a never-failing stream!

²⁵"Did you bring me sacrifices and offerings
 forty years in the wilderness, people of
  Israel?
²⁶You have lifted up the shrine of your king,
 the pedestal of your idols,
 the star of your god*ᵃ*—
 which you made for yourselves.
²⁷Therefore I will send you into exile beyond
  Damascus,"
 says the LORD, whose name is God
  Almighty.

Woe to the Complacent

6 Woe to you who are complacent in Zion,
 and to you who feel secure on Mount
  Samaria,
you notable men of the foremost nation,
 to whom the people of Israel come!

ᵃ 26 Or lifted up Sakkuth your king / and Kaiwan your idols, / your star-gods; Septuagint lifted up the shrine of Molek / and the star of your god Rephan, / their idols

²Go to Kalneh and look at it;
  go from there to great Hamath,
  and then go down to Gath in Philistia.
Are they better off than your two
    kingdoms?
  Is their land larger than yours?
³You put off the day of disaster
  and bring near a reign of terror.
⁴You lie on beds adorned with ivory
  and lounge on your couches.
You dine on choice lambs
  and fattened calves.
⁵You strum away on your harps like David
  and improvise on musical instruments.
⁶You drink wine by the bowlful
  and use the finest lotions,
  but you do not grieve over the ruin of
    Joseph.
⁷Therefore you will be among the first to go
    into exile;
  your feasting and lounging will end.

The LORD Abhors the Pride of Israel

⁸The Sovereign LORD has sworn by himself—
the LORD God Almighty declares:

"I abhor the pride of Jacob
  and detest his fortresses;
I will deliver up the city
  and everything in it."

⁹If ten people are left in one house, they too will die. ¹⁰And if the relative who comes to carry the bodies out of the house to burn them[a] asks anyone who might be hiding there, "Is anyone else with you?" and he says, "No," then he will go on to say, "Hush! We must not mention the name of the LORD."

¹¹For the LORD has given the command,
  and he will smash the great house into
    pieces
  and the small house into bits.

¹²Do horses run on the rocky crags?
  Does one plow the sea[b] with oxen?
But you have turned justice into poison
  and the fruit of righteousness into
    bitterness—
¹³you who rejoice in the conquest of Lo
    Debar[c]
  and say, "Did we not take Karnaim[d] by
    our own strength?"

¹⁴For the LORD God Almighty declares,
  "I will stir up a nation against you,
    Israel,

that will oppress you all the way
  from Lebo Hamath to the valley of the
    Arabah."

Locusts, Fire and a Plumb Line

7 This is what the Sovereign LORD showed me: He was preparing swarms of locusts after the king's share had been harvested and just as the late crops were coming up. ²When they had stripped the land clean, I cried out, "Sovereign LORD, forgive! How can Jacob survive? He is so small!"

³So the LORD relented.

"This will not happen," the LORD said.

⁴This is what the Sovereign LORD showed me: The Sovereign LORD was calling for judgment by fire; it dried up the great deep and devoured the land. ⁵Then I cried out, "Sovereign LORD, I beg you, stop! How can Jacob survive? He is so small!"

⁶So the LORD relented.

---

[a] 10 Or to make a funeral fire in honor of the dead
[b] 12 With a different word division of the Hebrew; Masoretic Text plow there   [c] 13 Lo Debar means nothing.
[d] 13 Karnaim means horns; horn here symbolizes strength.

Leaders Influence in the Prayer Closet

Amos 7:1-6

Amos must have felt overwhelmed: God had threatened to annihilate Israel! The prophet already had warned the people of judgment; now it had arrived. What could he do?

The only thing he could do was to beg God to forgive. Amos prayed for his people with compassion and honesty. Tiny Israel, he said, would not survive the judgment. Twice he interceded and twice God withdrew his judgment. Amos stepped in between the people and God, and negotiated their survival.

Prayer changes things. Amos shows us what to do with impossible problems. Of course, prayer doesn't take the place of solid leadership; Amos continued to perform his job of truth telling (Am 7:10–17). Yet he reminds leaders how powerful their prayers can be in the face of trouble. Sometimes we have no idea what kind of changes we orchestrate or what kind of pain we spare others by what we do in our prayer closets!

"This will not happen either," the Sovereign LORD said.

[7] This is what he showed me: The Lord was standing by a wall that had been built true to plumb,[a] with a plumb line[b] in his hand. [8] And the LORD asked me, "What do you see, Amos?"

"A plumb line," I replied.

Then the Lord said, "Look, I am setting a plumb line among my people Israel; I will spare them no longer.

[9] "The high places of Isaac will be destroyed
    and the sanctuaries of Israel will be
        ruined;
    with my sword I will rise against the
        house of Jeroboam."

Amos and Amaziah

[10] Then Amaziah the priest of Bethel sent a message to Jeroboam king of Israel: "Amos is raising a conspiracy against you in the very heart of Israel. The land cannot bear all his words. [11] For this is what Amos is saying:

" 'Jeroboam will die by the sword,
    and Israel will surely go into exile,
        away from their native land.' "

[12] Then Amaziah said to Amos, "Get out, you seer! Go back to the land of Judah. Earn your bread there and do your prophesying there. [13] Don't prophesy anymore at Bethel, because this is the king's sanctuary and the temple of the kingdom."

[14] Amos answered Amaziah, "I was neither a prophet nor the son of a prophet, but I was a shepherd, and I also took care of sycamore-fig trees. [15] But the LORD took me from tending the flock and said to me, 'Go, prophesy to my people Israel.' [16] Now then, hear the word of the LORD. You say,

" 'Do not prophesy against Israel,
    and stop preaching against the
        descendants of Isaac.'

[17] "Therefore this is what the LORD says:

" 'Your wife will become a prostitute in the
        city,
    and your sons and daughters will fall by
        the sword.
Your land will be measured and divided up,
    and you yourself will die in a pagan[c]
        country.
And Israel will surely go into exile,
    away from their native land.' "

A Basket of Ripe Fruit

[8] This is what the Sovereign LORD showed me: a basket of ripe fruit. [2] "What do you see, Amos?" he asked.

"A basket of ripe fruit," I answered.

Then the LORD said to me, "The time is ripe for my people Israel; I will spare them no longer.

[3] "In that day," declares the Sovereign LORD, "the songs in the temple will turn to wailing.[d] Many, many bodies — flung everywhere! Silence!"

[4] Hear this, you who trample the needy
    and do away with the poor of the land,

[5] saying,

"When will the New Moon be over
    that we may sell grain,
and the Sabbath be ended
    that we may market wheat?" —
skimping on the measure,
    boosting the price
    and cheating with dishonest scales,
[6] buying the poor with silver
    and the needy for a pair of sandals,
    selling even the sweepings with the wheat.

[7] The LORD has sworn by himself, the Pride of Jacob: "I will never forget anything they have done.

[8] "Will not the land tremble for this,
    and all who live in it mourn?
The whole land will rise like the Nile;
    it will be stirred up and then sink
    like the river of Egypt.

[9] "In that day," declares the Sovereign LORD,

"I will make the sun go down at noon
    and darken the earth in broad daylight.
[10] I will turn your religious festivals into
        mourning
    and all your singing into weeping.
I will make all of you wear sackcloth
    and shave your heads.
I will make that time like mourning for an
        only son
    and the end of it like a bitter day.

[11] "The days are coming," declares the
        Sovereign LORD,
"when I will send a famine through the
        land —

---

[a] 7 The meaning of the Hebrew for this phrase is uncertain.
[b] 7 The meaning of the Hebrew for this phrase is uncertain; also in verse 8.   [c] 17 Hebrew an unclean   [d] 3 Or "the temple singers will wail

not a famine of food or a thirst for water,
but a famine of hearing the words of the
LORD.
¹²People will stagger from sea to sea
and wander from north to east,
searching for the word of the LORD,
but they will not find it.

¹³"In that day

"the lovely young women and strong young
men
will faint because of thirst.
¹⁴Those who swear by the sin of Samaria—
who say, 'As surely as your god lives,
Dan,'
or, 'As surely as the god*a* of Beersheba
lives'—
they will fall, never to rise again."

Israel to Be Destroyed

9 I saw the Lord standing by the altar, and he
said:

"Strike the tops of the pillars
so that the thresholds shake.
Bring them down on the heads of all the
people;
those who are left I will kill with the
sword.
Not one will get away,
none will escape.
²Though they dig down to the depths
below,
from there my hand will take them.
Though they climb up to the heavens
above,
from there I will bring them down.
³Though they hide themselves on the top of
Carmel,
there I will hunt them down and seize
them.
Though they hide from my eyes at the
bottom of the sea,
there I will command the serpent to bite
them.
⁴Though they are driven into exile by their
enemies,
there I will command the sword to slay
them.

"I will keep my eye on them
for harm and not for good."

⁵The Lord, the LORD Almighty—
he touches the earth and it melts,
and all who live in it mourn;

the whole land rises like the Nile,
then sinks like the river of Egypt;
⁶he builds his lofty palace*b* in the heavens
and sets its foundation*c* on the earth;
he calls for the waters of the sea
and pours them out over the face of the
land—
the LORD is his name.

⁷"Are not you Israelites
the same to me as the Cushites*d*?"
declares the LORD.
"Did I not bring Israel up from Egypt,
the Philistines from Caphtor*e*
and the Arameans from Kir?

⁸"Surely the eyes of the Sovereign LORD
are on the sinful kingdom.
I will destroy it
from the face of the earth.
Yet I will not totally destroy
the descendants of Jacob,"
declares the LORD.
⁹"For I will give the command,
and I will shake the people of Israel
among all the nations
as grain is shaken in a sieve,
and not a pebble will reach the ground.
¹⁰All the sinners among my people
will die by the sword,
all those who say,
'Disaster will not overtake or meet us.'

Israel's Restoration

¹¹"In that day

"I will restore David's fallen shelter—
I will repair its broken walls
and restore its ruins—
and will rebuild it as it used to be,
¹²so that they may possess the remnant of Edom
and all the nations that bear my name,*f*"
declares the LORD, who will
do these things.

¹³"The days are coming," declares the LORD,

"when the reaper will be overtaken by the
plowman
and the planter by the one treading
grapes.

---

a 14 Hebrew *the way*   *b 6* The meaning of the Hebrew for
this phrase is uncertain.   *c 6* The meaning of the Hebrew for
this word is uncertain.   *d 7* That is, people from the upper
Nile region   *e 7* That is, Crete   *f 12* Hebrew; Septuagint
*so that the remnant of people / and all the nations that bear my
name may seek me*

New wine will drip from the mountains
   and flow from all the hills,
14 and I will bring my people Israel back
      from exile.[a]

"They will rebuild the ruined cities and live
   in them.
They will plant vineyards and drink their
   wine;

they will make gardens and eat their
   fruit.
15 I will plant Israel in their own land,
   never again to be uprooted
   from the land I have given them,"

                    says the LORD your God.

[a] 14 Or will restore the fortunes of my people Israel

Vision: Amos Finishes with a Hopeful Vision of the Future

Amos 9:11–15

The prophet followed his warnings of judgment with words of encouragement. The book concludes with Amos's vision for the future—full of hope, healing and positive change. It illustrates once again how much people need both admonishment and affirmation.

The prophets nearly always followed the same pattern to address the erring population. They pronounced judgment, then painted a picture of a preferred future in which people would repent and realign themselves with the vision. In Amos 9:11–15, Amos spoke of this better tomorrow. Look at how he put it:

1. **Leadership would be restored (v. 11).**

2. **Broken places would be repaired (v. 11).**

3. **Lost land would be replaced (v. 12).**

4. **Hope for prosperity would be renewed (vv. 13–15).**

Men and women become depressed when they hear only words of judgment. We all need some picture of how we can cooperate with God to redeem our situation.

INTRODUCTION TO
OBADIAH

No more obscure Old Testament prophet exists than Obadiah. He wrote the shortest book in the Old Testament, with just 21 verses. We know very little about the dating of the book or the author, except for his name, which means, "servant of the Lord."

We do know, however, his message. Obadiah wrote about the people of Edom, the descendants of Esau. Esau was Jacob's twin brother, an outdoorsman and a hunter whom God scolded after he succumbed to his lust for immediate gratification (Ge 25:27–34; Heb 12:16). Esau neglected his priorities and lost sight of God's eternal perspective. This inclination led to self-centered descendants, angry and arrogant people who desired vengeance over Jacob's descendants (Israel). For centuries the Edomites gloated over the misfortunes of the Jews. Obadiah targeted their selfish pride.

The prophet's timeless lesson applies to leaders universally. Obadiah declares that pride and treachery earn the reward of destruction, but humility and loyalty to God gain the Lord's blessing.

We learn from Obadiah that destructive rivalry, comparison and competition provide a horrible motivation for leadership. Those incentives so moved the Edomites that they lost perspective and sabotaged their own activities. How often does this happen to leaders today?

Second, God hates pride. He promised to humble the Edomites for their arrogant attitudes and their self-centered worldview. They thought they had achieved the success they enjoyed, but God exposed their faulty thinking. Leaders must never buy into the notion that they "did it all" themselves. The higher leaders go and

God's Role in Obadiah

God sees what goes on worldwide and stands ready to move with irresistible power. He used Obadiah to confront the pride of the Edomites as an example to leaders and nations everywhere. He will not allow arrogance to continue indefinitely. Generally, he grants a warning to leaders through a word from another leader, a failure, a broken relationship, a personal weakness, or a plan that falls through. If the leader fails to take heed, God sets the wheels of justice in motion. And he will execute his sentence through whatever means he wishes.

Leaders in Obadiah

Obadiah, Edom's leaders

Other People of Influence in Obadiah

Esau and his descendants

Lessons in Leadership

- Leaders must not violate a primary reason they have power: to protect the powerless.
- Pride clouds a leader's perspective and causes him or her to act illogically.
- One can gain power in any of three fundamental ways: intimidation, exchange, or honor.
- God judges leaders who abuse their power.

the deeper they grow, the more they become aware that God has promoted them. Their success does not deceive them. Leaders blinded by pride should be pitied. God will raise up an Obadiah to humble them and clear up the issue.

LEADERSHIP HIGHLIGHTS IN OBADIAH

GOD IS THE SOURCE for a Leader's Success (2–4)	**page 1059**
POWER ABUSE: Edom Used Its Power for Unjust Causes (8–14)	**page 1059**
THE PRINCIPLE OF THE HARVEST: Leaders Reap What They Sow (15–18)	**page 1060**

Obadiah's Vision

¹The vision of Obadiah.

This is what the Sovereign LORD says about Edom —

We have heard a message from the LORD:
    An envoy was sent to the nations to say,
"Rise, let us go against her for battle" —

²"See, I will make you small among the
        nations;
    you will be utterly despised.
³The pride of your heart has deceived you,
    you who live in the clefts of the rocks[a]
    and make your home on the heights,
you who say to yourself,
    'Who can bring me down to the
        ground?'
⁴Though you soar like the eagle
    and make your nest among the stars,
    from there I will bring you down,"
                  declares the LORD.

God Is the Source for a Leader's Success

Obadiah 2–4

We humans tend toward self-centeredness, self-promotion, self-sufficiency, self-reliance and self-righteousness. When leaders succumb to this tendency, they adversely affect their followers. While leaders may determine the course of their success, God remains the source of their success. God is the source of any gains we make.

⁵"If thieves came to you,
    if robbers in the night —
oh, what a disaster awaits you! —
    would they not steal only as much as they
        wanted?
If grape pickers came to you,
    would they not leave a few grapes?
⁶But how Esau will be ransacked,
    his hidden treasures pillaged!
⁷All your allies will force you to the border;
    your friends will deceive and overpower
        you;
    those who eat your bread will set a trap for
        you,[b]
    but you will not detect it.

⁸"In that day," declares the LORD,
    "will I not destroy the wise men of
        Edom,
    those of understanding in the mountains
        of Esau?
⁹Your warriors, Teman, will be terrified,
    and everyone in Esau's mountains
    will be cut down in the slaughter.
¹⁰Because of the violence against your brother
        Jacob,
    you will be covered with shame;
    you will be destroyed forever.
¹¹On the day you stood aloof
    while strangers carried off his wealth
  and foreigners entered his gates
    and cast lots for Jerusalem,
    you were like one of them.
¹²You should not gloat over your brother
    in the day of his misfortune,
nor rejoice over the people of Judah
    in the day of their destruction,
nor boast so much
    in the day of their trouble.
¹³You should not march through the gates of
        my people
    in the day of their disaster,
nor gloat over them in their calamity
    in the day of their disaster,
nor seize their wealth
    in the day of their disaster.
¹⁴You should not wait at the crossroads
    to cut down their fugitives,
nor hand over their survivors
    in the day of their trouble.

¹⁵"The day of the LORD is near
    for all nations.

---

[a] 3 Or *of Sela*   [b] 7 The meaning of the Hebrew for this clause is uncertain.

Power Abuse: Edom Used Its Power for Unjust Causes

Obadiah 8–14

The Edomites violated an important use of power: to protect the powerless. Even though the Edomites did not directly violate the Jews, they did stand idly by when another country abused them. When leaders have the power to do good and don't use it, God holds them equally guilty (Jas 4:17).

As you have done, it will be done to you;
your deeds will return upon your own
head.
16 Just as you drank on my holy hill,
so all the nations will drink continually;
they will drink and drink
and be as if they had never been.
17 But on Mount Zion will be deliverance;
it will be holy,
and Jacob will possess his inheritance.

The Principle of the Harvest: Leaders Reap What They Sow

Obadiah 15–18

Every leader reaps what he sows. The self-preoccupation that kept the Edomites from helping neighboring nations came back to haunt them in the day of their need. Power can be used to achieve or to intimidate; it can help others or haunt others. Edom misused its power and reaped terror and destruction.

18 Jacob will be a fire
and Joseph a flame;
Esau will be stubble,
and they will set him on fire and destroy
him.
There will be no survivors
from Esau."
         The LORD has spoken.
19 People from the Negev will occupy
the mountains of Esau,
and people from the foothills will possess
the land of the Philistines.
They will occupy the fields of Ephraim and
Samaria,
and Benjamin will possess Gilead.
20 This company of Israelite exiles who are in
Canaan
will possess the land as far as Zarephath;
the exiles from Jerusalem who are in Sepharad
will possess the towns of the Negev.
21 Deliverers will go up on[a] Mount Zion
to govern the mountains of Esau.
And the kingdom will be the LORD's.

---

[a] 21 Or *from*

INTRODUCTION TO
JONAH

W e should feel grateful that God included Jonah in the canon of Scripture. If ever God provided a picture of our human nature—our inclination to run from duty in favor of serving self—he did it through Jonah. He furnishes the perfect portrait of a reluctant leader in a needy time.

Yet he is not alone! God has called many reluctant leaders. Consider Moses, who, in Egypt, thought he could do more than he really could. God called him only after 40 years of preparation, when he thought he could do less than he really could. He expressed total reluctance as he stood before a burning bush, trying to excuse himself from leadership. Or consider Gideon, whom God called to lead an attack against the Midianites. He argued with an angel, explaining why he couldn't do it. Or consider King Saul, who stood head and shoulders above everyone else. Yet he hid among the luggage when Samuel came to anoint him king of Israel. Or consider Jeremiah, whom God called to be a prophet to the nations. This young man debated with God on the basis of his tender age, as though God had forgotten how old he was. God basically responded, "I have been preparing you since before you took shape in your mother's womb."

Jonah's reluctance didn't take the form of a debate; he simply ran in the other direction. He didn't object to his call on the basis of his inabilities, but upon the seeming irrationality of calling Nineveh to repent. Jonah saw this as an evil culture that didn't deserve a warning of impending doom. So he ran. Days later he discovered that called leaders can't outrun God. Some frightened sailors threw him overboard (at his direction), and a huge fish swallowed the sputtering prophet. Over the next

God's Role in Jonah

God once again takes the initiative in this book. The leader he chooses refuses at first to obey. God chases him down, calls upon a huge fish (perhaps a whale) to swallow him, enables him to live for three days in the belly of that creature, then orders him spit up on shore. Only then does Jonah go to Nineveh to speak. Yet even after he delivers his message, God has to take the initiative once more when Jonah reacts angrily to their repentance. God raises up a vine to give him shade, then teaches him a lesson about mercy and grace. God must work harder at getting his chosen leader into an obedient posture than he has to for the Ninevites!

Leaders in Jonah
Jonah, the king of Nineveh

Other People of Influence in Jonah
The sailors

Lessons in Leadership
- Motives are key: Why a leader does something ultimately determines what he does.
- Leaders must model what they demand from the people.
- God's mercy overcomes our reluctance, prejudice and small thinking.

three days he regained perspective while in the belly of the fish, and when God ordered the beast to spit him up on shore, the chastened prophet at last fulfilled the task God had given him.

It is interesting to note that every major player in the story—the storm, the sailors, the fish, the king, the Ninevites, the vine, the worm and the east wind—all obey God . . . except for Jonah, the leader God chose. Sometimes the leader must repent before he can call the people to do so.

Despite Jonah's disobedience, his lack of perspective, his cultural prejudice, his self-righteousness, his wrong motives, and his bad attitude, God never gave up on him. The central lesson? Sometimes God uses us, in spite of us. He even uses reluctant leaders to accomplish his gracious mission.

- We can still lead if our impulse for obedience grows stronger than our reluctance.
- Leaders lose their right to be selfish.

LEADERSHIP HIGHLIGHTS IN JONAH

JONAH: The Prophet Who Ran Down (1:1–17)	**page 1063**
THE LAW OF THE PICTURE: Leaders Must Incarnate What They Ask Others to Do (2:7–9)	**page 1064**
THE LAW OF INFLUENCE: The King Leads in Delivering Nineveh (3:6–9)	**page 1065**
INITIATIVE: One Earmark of a True Leader (2:10—3:10)	**page 1066**
MOTIVE CHECK: Why We Act Determines How We React (4:1–2)	**page 1068**

Jonah Flees From the LORD

1 The word of the LORD came to Jonah son of Amittai: ²"Go to the great city of Nineveh and preach against it, because its wickedness has come up before me."

³But Jonah ran away from the LORD and headed for Tarshish. He went down to Joppa, where he found a ship bound for that port. After paying the fare, he went aboard and sailed for Tarshish to flee from the LORD.

⁴Then the LORD sent a great wind on the sea, and such a violent storm arose that the ship threatened to break up. ⁵All the sailors were afraid and each cried out to his own god. And they threw the cargo into the sea to lighten the ship.

But Jonah had gone below deck, where he lay down and fell into a deep sleep. ⁶The captain went to him and said, "How can you sleep? Get up and call on your god! Maybe he will take notice of us so that we will not perish."

⁷Then the sailors said to each other, "Come, let us cast lots to find out who is responsible for this calamity." They cast lots and the lot fell on Jonah. ⁸So they asked him, "Tell us, who is responsible for making all this trouble for us? What kind of work do you do? Where do you come from? What is your country? From what people are you?"

⁹He answered, "I am a Hebrew and I worship the LORD, the God of heaven, who made the sea and the dry land."

¹⁰This terrified them and they asked, "What have you done?" (They knew he was running away from the LORD, because he had already told them so.)

¹¹The sea was getting rougher and rougher. So they asked him, "What should we do to you to make the sea calm down for us?"

¹²"Pick me up and throw me into the sea," he replied, "and it will become calm. I know that it is my fault that this great storm has come upon you."

¹³Instead, the men did their best to row back to land. But they could not, for the sea grew even wilder than before. ¹⁴Then they cried out to the LORD, "Please, LORD, do not let us die for taking this man's life. Do not hold us accountable for killing an innocent man, for you, LORD, have done as you pleased." ¹⁵Then they took Jonah and threw him overboard, and the raging sea grew calm. ¹⁶At this the men greatly feared the LORD, and they offered a sacrifice to the LORD and made vows to him.

Jonah's Prayer

¹⁷Now the LORD provided a huge fish to swallow Jonah, and Jonah was in the belly of the fish

---

JONAH

The Prophet Who Ran Down
Jonah 1:1–17

PROFILE in leadership

Who among us hasn't heard God telling us to do something we really didn't want to do? Sometimes it's easy to convince ourselves that we know better than God what needs to be done.

Jonah was a godly prophet, yet when God commanded him to preach repentance to the Ninevites, Jonah ran in the opposite direction. As he ran, he went nowhere but down—down to the seashore, down to the bottom of the ship, down to the water, and down into the belly of the fish. Jonah learned what can happen to the man or woman who is called to lead but who shrinks from that role of leadership.

One can only imagine the wretched conditions inside the creature God had prepared to temporarily house Jonah. But was it any worse than the situations into which we put ourselves when we run from God? Eventually the Lord will bring us to a place where we have little choice but to stop, listen, and obey.

But why wait for such an unpleasant place?

Leaders may not always understand why God wants them to do certain things, but he doesn't ask us to depend upon our own understanding or logic. Rather, he calls us to walk in obedience to his instruction. Don't make it necessary for God to introduce you to the inside of a fish!

Character: Jonah Runs from Commitment

Jonah 1:1–10

When God told Jonah to warn the people of Nineveh to repent, the prophet turned the other direction and fled. Spot someone who runs from commitment, and you'll find a person who lacks character. Many times a leader must ask his followers to make a commitment. Usually God first asks the leader to commit. At this point, the leader discovers how much he's embraced the cause. Is he cautious, curious, or committed? Jonah teaches us the consequences of avoiding God's call to commitment:

1. **We miss the privilege of partnership with God (vv. 1–3).**

2. **Our choice damages more people than we know (v. 4).**

3. **We become hardened and desensitized to the tragedies we cause (vv. 5–8).**

4. **We lose both integrity and trust (vv. 9–10).**

2 *ᵃ* three days and three nights. ¹From inside the fish Jonah prayed to the LORD his God. ²He said:

"In my distress I called to the LORD,
    and he answered me.
From deep in the realm of the dead I called
        for help,
    and you listened to my cry.
³You hurled me into the depths,
    into the very heart of the seas,
    and the currents swirled about me;
all your waves and breakers
    swept over me.
⁴I said, 'I have been banished
    from your sight;
yet I will look again
    toward your holy temple.'
⁵The engulfing waters threatened me,*ᵇ*
    the deep surrounded me;
    seaweed was wrapped around my head.
⁶To the roots of the mountains I sank down;
    the earth beneath barred me in forever.
But you, LORD my God,
    brought my life up from the pit.

⁷"When my life was ebbing away,
    I remembered you, LORD,
and my prayer rose to you,
    to your holy temple.

⁸"Those who cling to worthless idols
    turn away from God's love for them.
⁹But I, with shouts of grateful praise,
    will sacrifice to you.
What I have vowed I will make good.
    I will say, 'Salvation comes from the
        LORD.'"

The Law of the Picture: Leaders Must Incarnate What They Ask Others to Do

Jonah 2:7–9

God told Jonah to call the people of Nineveh to repent. They had lived a life of pride and selfishness, and had failed to submit to God in worship. But when Jonah ran from God, he was guilty of the same things! God humbled Jonah and gave him perspective in the belly of the fish, where the prophet got his heart right through a profound worship experience.

The leader must first incarnate the life he calls the people to live. People do what people see. Once Jonah repented, he was ready to call others to repent.

¹⁰And the LORD commanded the fish, and it vomited Jonah onto dry land.

Jonah Goes to Nineveh

3 Then the word of the LORD came to Jonah a second time: ²"Go to the great city of Nineveh and proclaim to it the message I give you."

³Jonah obeyed the word of the LORD and went to Nineveh. Now Nineveh was a very large city; it took three days to go through it. ⁴Jonah began by going a day's journey into the city,

---

ᵃ In Hebrew texts 2:1 is numbered 1:17, and 2:1-10 is numbered 2:2-11.   *ᵇ* 5 Or *waters were at my throat*

proclaiming, "Forty more days and Nineveh will be overthrown." [5]The Ninevites believed God. A fast was proclaimed, and all of them, from the greatest to the least, put on sackcloth.

[6]When Jonah's warning reached the king of Nineveh, he rose from his throne, took off his royal robes, covered himself with sackcloth and sat down in the dust. [7]This is the proclamation he issued in Nineveh:

"By the decree of the king and his nobles:

Do not let people or animals, herds or flocks, taste anything; do not let them eat or drink. [8]But let people and animals be covered with sackcloth. Let everyone call urgently on God. Let them give up their evil ways and their violence. [9]Who knows? God may yet relent and with compassion turn from his fierce anger so that we will not perish."

[10]When God saw what they did and how they turned from their evil ways, he relented and did not bring on them the destruction he had threatened.

Jonah's Anger at the LORD's Compassion

4 But to Jonah this seemed very wrong, and he became angry. [2]He prayed to the LORD, "Isn't this what I said, LORD, when I was still at home? That is what I tried to forestall by fleeing to Tarshish. I knew that you are a gracious and compassionate God, slow to anger and abounding in love, a God who relents from sending calamity. [3]Now, LORD, take away my life, for it is better for me to die than to live."

[4]But the LORD replied, "Is it right for you to be angry?"

[5]Jonah had gone out and sat down at a place east of the city. There he made himself a shelter,

God Can Use Even a Reluctant Leader

Jonah 3:1–3

We often get caught up in the story of "the big fish" and miss the story of "the big God"! The miracle of Nineveh's redemption is a story of God's pursuit of a leader who ran from a commitment. God wanted a divine partnership in which both parties committed themselves to the cause with reckless abandon.

What might have happened had Jonah failed to go? What if he had rejected God's call to commitment? What if he avoided it and God never pursued him? History might be different . . . at least for one ancient people.

Fortunately, God comes for us when we run from commitment. Most of the time he gives us a second opportunity, just as he did with Jonah. Note the stages leading up to that second chance:

1. **Recognition of failure or inability**
2. **A crisis of honest reflection**
3. **Drawing near to God for empowerment**
4. **The opportunity to recommit ourselves**

The Law of Influence: The King Leads in Delivering Nineveh

Jonah 3:6–9

When the news of Jonah's message of judgment reached the king of Nineveh, he immediately repented. He took off his royal robe, covered himself with sackcloth, and sat down in the dust. He repented for his own sin. Then he used his influence to bring about citywide revival. He issued a decree that every citizen follow his lead. When God saw his response, he had compassion on the Ninevites and did not destroy them.

In this case, the leader influenced the fate of an entire population. He did so by providing the three fundamentals every follower needs:

1. **A clear model: He repented first, setting an example (v. 6).**
2. **A clear message: He called his people to a specific action (vv. 7–8).**
3. **A clear motivation: He gave the people a reason for taking action (v. 9).**

INITIATIVE   One Earmark of a True Leader

Jonah 2:10–3:10

ONE EARMARK of a true leader is the display of initiative. By definition, leaders cannot wait for someone else to move; if they do, they are really followers, not leaders. Initiative requires an element of risk, faith and foresight. When did you last initiate something significant? If you haven't pushed yourself lately and left your comfort zone, you may need a jump start in initiative.

Why Do We Fail to Initiate?

It seems easier to run from a challenge than to step out and take a risk. When we initiate, we commit ourselves to a direction. We may feel uncertain about what the future holds. What if we change our minds? What if no one follows? What if we fail in front of our followers? We run from commitment and initiative for a variety of reasons.

Reason	Issue
1. We are afraid we'll be unable to keep the commitment.	1. Low sense of security
2. We suspect we might find "greener grass" somewhere else.	2. Paralyzed will
3. We expend time and energy only for personal gain.	3. No surrender
4. Our past makes trust difficult.	4. Emotional baggage
5. We are lazy and unmotivated.	5. Apathy and neutrality
6. We fear the risk of being rejected.	6. Poor self-esteem
7. We fear the unknown and the unfamiliar	7. Low confidence
8. We don't want to lose our freedom.	8. Entitlement philosophy
9. We fear being different from others.	9. Politically correct
10. We don't really know who we are.	10. Gifts and calling

Jonah had to learn initiative. It started with learning submission to God. Once we surrender to his call on our life and leadership, we can step out to follow him. We can take risks because our future lies in his hands. Once Jonah submitted to God's call, he saw all kinds of results. What happens when we accept God's call to initiate and commit?

1. We assume healthy personal responsibility (1:12).

2. We'll likely see many come to faith in God (1:13–16).

3. We receive a God-given time and place to gain perspective (1:17).

4. We deepen our experience of worship and prayer (2:1–9).

5. We progress toward a new level of personal freedom (2:10).

6. We enjoy partnership with God (3:1–9).

7. We gain the satisfaction of seeing changed lives (3:10).

For a positive example of initiative, see p. 583.

Motive Check: Why We Act Determines How We React

Jonah 4:1–2

Jonah felt great delight when God planned to destroy the wicked people of Nineveh, but he grew angry when they repented and God showed them compassion. He suspected God might do something just like that, and that made him even angrier. He would have preferred to see God remove the threat of Nineveh. His selfish motives led him astray.

Consequently, God gave him an object lesson. When the Lord sent a worm to eat the plant that gave Jonah shade, the prophet grew angry. God reminded him that he had no right to his anger, since he had done nothing to create the plant. Would he be angry at the death of a mere vine, but unmoved at the destruction of more than 120,000 people? Didn't the Creator have a right to restore them? Of course he did.

God gave Jonah a motive check—and us a reminder. Leaders must determine to be motivated only by what motivates God.

sat in its shade and waited to see what would happen to the city. ⁶Then the LORD God provided a leafy plant[a] and made it grow up over Jonah to give shade for his head to ease his discomfort, and Jonah was very happy about the plant. ⁷But at dawn the next day God provided a worm, which chewed the plant so that it withered. ⁸When the sun rose, God provided a scorching east wind, and the sun blazed on Jonah's head so that he grew faint. He wanted to die, and said, "It would be better for me to die than to live."

⁹But God said to Jonah, "Is it right for you to be angry about the plant?"

"It is," he said. "And I'm so angry I wish I were dead."

¹⁰But the LORD said, "You have been concerned about this plant, though you did not tend it or make it grow. It sprang up overnight and died overnight. ¹¹And should I not have concern for the great city of Nineveh, in which there are more than a hundred and twenty thousand people who cannot tell their right hand from their left — and also many animals?"

---

[a] 6 The precise identification of this plant is uncertain; also in verses 7, 9 and 10.

MICAH

What Does the Lord Require of You?

Micah's name means, "Who is like the LORD?" This is precisely the question he posed in his prophetic ministry in the middle of the eighth century BC. His life modeled one who is "like the LORD," and he called the people of Judah to this same lifestyle of divine imitation. His leadership challenged false prophets, corrupt political leaders and wayward residents of Judah to live their faith authentically.

The summary verse of his book, Micah 6:8, asks: "He has shown you, O mortal, what is good. And what does the LORD require of you? To act justly and to love mercy and to walk humbly with your God."

Micah deeply suspected the wickedness and corruption of the cities of Judah. This country prophet intuitively perceived the greed that lay behind the decisions of the priestly and political leaders of his day. He championed the cause of the poor and the oppressed and rebuked those in charge for their exploitation of others.

Micah warns leaders today about leading for personal gain rather than organizational gain. When leaders benefit from the system apart from followers—something is wrong with the leader or the system, and maybe both.

Micah also cautions leaders about doing what's right on the surface to hide a corrupt heart. Leadership cannot merely be an "outside" job; it must be an "inside" job as well. Healthy, effective leadership stems from who we are, not just what we do. Leaders can masquerade only for a while . . . before reality becomes obvious.

Finally, Micah teaches us that a leader's spiritual life must transform his or her social ethics and approach to leadership. Integrity means "oneness," the opposite of hypocrisy. One compartment of our life cannot contradict another.

God's Role in Micah

The book of Micah pictures God as the Ruler of all things. The Lord used the prophet Micah to spell out what he wanted from the Hebrews—but he also used ungodly neighbors like Assyria to punish the corrupt leaders of Israel and Judah. Micah began to connect the wickedness of Judah and the lightning raids of the Assyrians. As evil rose in Judah, military power rose in Assyria. God would sovereignly use even this to accomplish his purposes. He will use even unjust instruments to correct his own unjust people.

In addition, God assumed the role of watching over the peasants of Judah. Passing armies would often invade villages and make slaves of the residents while Judah's leaders looked the other way. God chose to use Micah to speak out against the selfishness of the nation's leaders.

Leaders in Micah

Micah, King Jotham, King Ahaz, King Hezekiah

Other People of Influence in Micah

The Assyrians, the corrupt vendors, the false prophets

Lessons in Leadership

■ Healthy leadership enables everyone to win: the leader, the follower and the organization.

- God expects leaders to guard the poor and oppressed, those without an advocate.
- Leadership is a life we live, not a show we perform.

- Values absent from the leader cannot be exported.
- Leadership plus hypocrisy equals leadership minus credibility.

LEADERSHIP HIGHLIGHTS IN MICAH

1 The word of the LORD that came to Micah of Moresheth during the reigns of Jotham, Ahaz and Hezekiah, kings of Judah — the vision he saw concerning Samaria and Jerusalem.

² Hear, you peoples, all of you,
    listen, earth and all who live in it,
that the Sovereign LORD may bear witness
        against you,
    the Lord from his holy temple.

Judgment Against Samaria and Jerusalem

³ Look! The LORD is coming from his dwelling
        place;
    he comes down and treads on the heights
        of the earth.
⁴ The mountains melt beneath him
    and the valleys split apart,
like wax before the fire,
    like water rushing down a slope.
⁵ All this is because of Jacob's transgression,
    because of the sins of the people of Israel.
What is Jacob's transgression?
    Is it not Samaria?
What is Judah's high place?
    Is it not Jerusalem?

⁶ "Therefore I will make Samaria a heap of
        rubble,
    a place for planting vineyards.
I will pour her stones into the valley
    and lay bare her foundations.
⁷ All her idols will be broken to pieces;
    all her temple gifts will be burned with fire;
    I will destroy all her images.

Since she gathered her gifts from the wages
        of prostitutes,
    as the wages of prostitutes they will again
        be used."

Weeping and Mourning

⁸ Because of this I will weep and wail;
    I will go about barefoot and naked.
I will howl like a jackal
    and moan like an owl.
⁹ For Samaria's plague is incurable;
    it has spread to Judah.
It has reached the very gate of my people,
    even to Jerusalem itself.
¹⁰ Tell it not in Gath[a];
    weep not at all.
In Beth Ophrah[b]
    roll in the dust.
¹¹ Pass by naked and in shame,
    you who live in Shaphir.[c]
Those who live in Zaanan[d]
    will not come out.
Beth Ezel is in mourning;
    it no longer protects you.
¹² Those who live in Maroth[e] writhe in
        pain,
    waiting for relief,
because disaster has come from the LORD,
    even to the gate of Jerusalem.

---

[a] 10 Gath sounds like the Hebrew for tell.   [b] 10 Beth Ophrah means house of dust.   [c] 11 Shaphir means pleasant.
[d] 11 Zaanan sounds like the Hebrew for come out.
[e] 12 Maroth sounds like the Hebrew for bitter.

Values: Leaders Know What to Cry About

Micah 1:1–9

Micah provides us with an example of a leader who knows what to cry about. While he could declare the Lord's judgment against Samaria and Jerusalem, he also wept over the punishment their citizens were to endure. They would always be the people he loved.

The more leaders mature, the more value they place on people. When all is said and done, leadership isn't about strategy, marketing, organization, efficiency, or high-quality products, but about people. Micah hurt when others hurt, even though they were in the wrong. The high value he placed on people teaches us:

1. **People are an organization's most appreciable asset.**

2. **People skills are a leader's most important asset.**

3. **If you are good with people, you can lead in a variety of contexts.**

4. **You can have people skills and not be a good leader, but you cannot be a good leader without people skills.**

13 You who live in Lachish,
    harness fast horses to the chariot.
You are where the sin of Daughter Zion
    began,
    for the transgressions of Israel were found
      in you.
14 Therefore you will give parting gifts
    to Moresheth Gath.
The town of Akzib[a] will prove deceptive
    to the kings of Israel.
15 I will bring a conqueror against you
    who live in Mareshah.[b]
The nobles of Israel
    will flee to Adullam.
16 Shave your head in mourning
    for the children in whom you delight;
make yourself as bald as the vulture,
    for they will go from you into exile.

Human Plans and God's Plans

2 Woe to those who plan iniquity,
    to those who plot evil on their beds!
At morning's light they carry it out
    because it is in their power to do it.
2 They covet fields and seize them,
    and houses, and take them.
They defraud people of their homes,
    they rob them of their inheritance.

3 Therefore, the LORD says:

"I am planning disaster against this people,
    from which you cannot save yourselves.
You will no longer walk proudly,
    for it will be a time of calamity.

4 In that day people will ridicule you;
    they will taunt you with this mournful song:
'We are utterly ruined;
    my people's possession is divided up.
He takes it from me!
    He assigns our fields to traitors.'"

5 Therefore you will have no one in the
      assembly of the LORD
to divide the land by lot.

False Prophets

6 "Do not prophesy," their prophets say.
    "Do not prophesy about these things;
    disgrace will not overtake us."
7 You descendants of Jacob, should it be said,
    "Does the LORD become[c] impatient?
    Does he do such things?"

"Do not my words do good
    to the one whose ways are upright?
8 Lately my people have risen up
    like an enemy.
You strip off the rich robe
    from those who pass by without a care,
    like men returning from battle.
9 You drive the women of my people
    from their pleasant homes.
You take away my blessing
    from their children forever.
10 Get up, go away!
    For this is not your resting place,

---

[a] 14 *Akzib* means *deception*.　　[b] 15 *Mareshah* sounds like the Hebrew for *conqueror*.　　[c] 7 Or *Is the Spirit of the LORD*

Character: Leaders Can't Give What They Don't Have

Micah 2:1–13

The wicked leaders of Micah's day led out of convenience and expediency. They did what was right by them.

The Greek word for character is often translated "image." It means a notch, indentation, a sharpening, scratching, or writing on a stone or a coin. Consequently, character historically meant a distinctive mark impressed or formed on the inside of a person by an outside force. To better understand character, take a look at some common misconceptions about it:

1. **Character is not merely how a person acts; some can masquerade poor character.**

2. **Character isn't just what a person will ideally be in the future; that's called hope.**

3. **Character is not only what others see on the outside; it begins on the inside.**

4. **Character isn't limited to wisdom in evaluating others' behavior; that's judgment.**

5. **Character isn't only about discipline; I may be disciplined in one area and not in another.**

because it is defiled,
it is ruined, beyond all remedy.
[11] If a liar and deceiver comes and says,
'I will prophesy for you plenty of wine and beer,'
that would be just the prophet for this people!

Deliverance Promised

[12] "I will surely gather all of you, Jacob;
I will surely bring together the remnant of Israel.
I will bring them together like sheep in a pen,
like a flock in its pasture;
the place will throng with people.
[13] The One who breaks open the way will go up before them;
they will break through the gate and go out.
Their King will pass through before them,
the LORD at their head."

Leaders Must Motivate, Not Manipulate

Micah 2:12–13

God pronounces judgment on the win-lose proposition of manipulation. Manipulation means moving together for my advantage; motivation means moving together for mutual advantage. God warns that plans should be laid for the benefit of the people, not the leader. And he promises to deliver his people from selfish, wicked leaders.

Leaders and Prophets Rebuked

3 Then I said,

"Listen, you leaders of Jacob,
you rulers of Israel.
Should you not embrace justice,
[2]   you who hate good and love evil;
who tear the skin from my people
and the flesh from their bones;
[3] who eat my people's flesh,
strip off their skin
and break their bones in pieces;
who chop them up like meat for the pan,
like flesh for the pot?"

[4] Then they will cry out to the LORD,
but he will not answer them.
At that time he will hide his face from them
because of the evil they have done.

[5] This is what the LORD says:

"As for the prophets
who lead my people astray,
they proclaim 'peace'
if they have something to eat,
but prepare to wage war against anyone
who refuses to feed them.
[6] Therefore night will come over you, without visions,
and darkness, without divination.
The sun will set for the prophets,
and the day will go dark for them.
[7] The seers will be ashamed
and the diviners disgraced.
They will all cover their faces
because there is no answer from God."
[8] But as for me, I am filled with power,
with the Spirit of the LORD,
and with justice and might,

The Law of Influence: Woe to Leaders Who Abuse Power

Micah 3:1–12

God pronounces a dark future for leaders who practice injustice and abuse their power to take advantage of others. God rebukes poor leaders and false prophets for their sins that impacted the entire land. God notes that these leaders had power and influence, but that they used it for their own purposes. Study the chapter to see what God hated so much about these abusive leaders:

1. **They destroyed people instead of developing them (vv. 1–3).**

2. **They misled people into confusion, instead of leading them in a cause (vv. 5–7).**

3. **They distorted justice instead of upholding justice for the common man (vv. 9–10).**

4. **They took bribes for themselves instead of taking responsibility for the people (vv. 11–12).**

to declare to Jacob his transgression,
  to Israel his sin.

⁹ Hear this, you leaders of Jacob,
  you rulers of Israel,
who despise justice
  and distort all that is right;
¹⁰ who build Zion with bloodshed,
  and Jerusalem with wickedness.
¹¹ Her leaders judge for a bribe,
  her priests teach for a price,
  and her prophets tell fortunes for
    money.
Yet they look for the LORD's support and
    say,
  "Is not the LORD among us?
  No disaster will come upon us."
¹² Therefore because of you,
  Zion will be plowed like a field,
Jerusalem will become a heap of rubble,
  the temple hill a mound overgrown with
    thickets.

The Mountain of the LORD

4 In the last days

the mountain of the LORD's temple will be
    established
  as the highest of the mountains;

it will be exalted above the hills,
  and peoples will stream to it.

² Many nations will come and say,

"Come, let us go up to the mountain of the
    LORD,
  to the temple of the God of Jacob.
He will teach us his ways,
  so that we may walk in his paths."
The law will go out from Zion,
  the word of the LORD from Jerusalem.
³ He will judge between many peoples
  and will settle disputes for strong nations
    far and wide.
They will beat their swords into
    plowshares
  and their spears into pruning hooks.
Nation will not take up sword against
    nation,
  nor will they train for war anymore.
⁴ Everyone will sit under their own vine
  and under their own fig tree,
and no one will make them afraid,
  for the LORD Almighty has spoken.
⁵ All the nations may walk
  in the name of their gods,
but we will walk in the name of the LORD
  our God for ever and ever.

Vision: Leaders See It, Say It, and Show It Before They Seize It

Micah 4:1–2

All great leaders begin their journey with a vision. People have to buy in to both the leader and the vision before they take the journey.

The prophet paints a picture of what life will be like in the future, during the last days—a glorious vision anyone could get excited about!

The "house of the LORD" was to be a strategic place (Mic 4:1), an influential place (4:2) and an equipping place (4:2). In order for Micah to succeed, he had to possess and persuade the people concerning God's vision for them. Then, he had to wait. Visions usually work like the birth of a baby; they take a long time in coming.

For any leader to successfully communicate a vision, they should know the vital signs of a successful vision:

1. **A clear picture**—the ability to see the vision.

2. **A committed people**—the ability to transmit the vision.

3. **A consistent prayer**—the ability to intercede for the vision.

4. **A constructive passion**—the ability to work toward the vision.

5. **A calm persistence**—the ability to patiently wait for the vision.

The Lord's Plan

6"In that day," declares the Lord,

"I will gather the lame;
　I will assemble the exiles
　and those I have brought to grief.
7I will make the lame my remnant,
　those driven away a strong nation.
The Lord will rule over them in Mount Zion
　from that day and forever.
8As for you, watchtower of the flock,
　stronghold[a] of Daughter Zion,
the former dominion will be restored to you;
　kingship will come to Daughter
　　Jerusalem."

9Why do you now cry aloud—
　have you no king[b]?
Has your ruler[c] perished,
　that pain seizes you like that of a woman
　　in labor?
10Writhe in agony, Daughter Zion,
　like a woman in labor,
for now you must leave the city
　to camp in the open field.
You will go to Babylon;
　there you will be rescued.
There the Lord will redeem you
　out of the hand of your enemies.

11But now many nations
　are gathered against you.
They say, "Let her be defiled,
　let our eyes gloat over Zion!"
12But they do not know
　the thoughts of the Lord;
they do not understand his plan,
　that he has gathered them like sheaves to
　　the threshing floor.
13"Rise and thresh, Daughter Zion,
　for I will give you horns of iron;
I will give you hooves of bronze,
　and you will break to pieces many nations."
You will devote their ill-gotten gains to the
　Lord,
　their wealth to the Lord of all the earth.

A Promised Ruler From Bethlehem

5[d] Marshal your troops now, city of troops,
　for a siege is laid against us.
They will strike Israel's ruler
　on the cheek with a rod.

2"But you, Bethlehem Ephrathah,
　though you are small among the clans[e] of
　　Judah,

out of you will come for me
　one who will be ruler over Israel,
whose origins are from of old,
　from ancient times."

3Therefore Israel will be abandoned
　until the time when she who is in labor
　　bears a son,
and the rest of his brothers return
　to join the Israelites.

4He will stand and shepherd his flock
　in the strength of the Lord,
　in the majesty of the name of the Lord his
　　God.
And they will live securely, for then his
　greatness
　will reach to the ends of the earth.

5And he will be our peace
　when the Assyrians invade our land
　and march through our fortresses.
We will raise against them seven shepherds,
　even eight commanders,
6who will rule[f] the land of Assyria with the
　sword,
　the land of Nimrod with drawn sword.[g]
He will deliver us from the Assyrians
　when they invade our land
　and march across our borders.

7The remnant of Jacob will be
　in the midst of many peoples
like dew from the Lord,
　like showers on the grass,
which do not wait for anyone
　or depend on man.
8The remnant of Jacob will be among the
　nations,
　in the midst of many peoples,
like a lion among the beasts of the forest,
　like a young lion among flocks of sheep,
which mauls and mangles as it goes,
　and no one can rescue.
9Your hand will be lifted up in triumph over
　your enemies,
　and all your foes will be destroyed.

10"In that day," declares the Lord,

"I will destroy your horses from among you
　and demolish your chariots.
11I will destroy the cities of your land
　and tear down all your strongholds.

---

a 8 Or hill　　b 9 Or King　　c 9 Or Ruler　　d In Hebrew
texts 5:1 is numbered 4:14, and 5:2-15 is numbered 5:1-14.
e 2 Or rulers　　f 6 Or crush　　g 6 Or Nimrod in its gates

¹² I will destroy your witchcraft
    and you will no longer cast spells.
¹³ I will destroy your idols
    and your sacred stones from among you;
you will no longer bow down
    to the work of your hands.
¹⁴ I will uproot from among you your Asherah
    poles[a]
    when I demolish your cities.
¹⁵ I will take vengeance in anger and wrath
    on the nations that have not obeyed me."

The LORD's Case Against Israel

6 Listen to what the LORD says:

"Stand up, plead my case before the mountains;
    let the hills hear what you have to say.

² "Hear, you mountains, the LORD's
        accusation;
    listen, you everlasting foundations of the
        earth.
For the LORD has a case against his people;
    he is lodging a charge against Israel.

³ "My people, what have I done to you?
    How have I burdened you? Answer me.
⁴ I brought you up out of Egypt
    and redeemed you from the land of slavery.
I sent Moses to lead you,
    also Aaron and Miriam.
⁵ My people, remember
    what Balak king of Moab plotted
    and what Balaam son of Beor answered.
Remember your journey from Shittim to
        Gilgal,
    that you may know the righteous acts of
        the LORD."

⁶ With what shall I come before the LORD
    and bow down before the exalted God?
Shall I come before him with burnt
        offerings,
    with calves a year old?
⁷ Will the LORD be pleased with thousands of
        rams,
    with ten thousand rivers of olive oil?
Shall I offer my firstborn for my
        transgression,
    the fruit of my body for the sin of my
        soul?
⁸ He has shown you, O mortal, what is good.
    And what does the LORD require of you?
To act justly and to love mercy
    and to walk humbly[b] with your God.

Israel's Guilt and Punishment

⁹ Listen! The LORD is calling to the city—
    and to fear your name is wisdom—
    "Heed the rod and the One who
        appointed it.[c]
¹⁰ Am I still to forget your ill-gotten treasures,
        you wicked house,
    and the short ephah,[d] which is accursed?
¹¹ Shall I acquit someone with dishonest
        scales,
    with a bag of false weights?
¹² Your rich people are violent;
    your inhabitants are liars
    and their tongues speak deceitfully.
¹³ Therefore, I have begun to destroy you,
    to ruin[e] you because of your sins.

---

a 14 That is, wooden symbols of the goddess Asherah   *b 8* Or
prudently   *c 9* The meaning of the Hebrew for this line is
uncertain.   *d 10* An ephah was a dry measure.   *e 13* Or
Therefore, I will make you ill and destroy you; / I will ruin

---

God Holds Leaders Responsible for Creating an Environment of Justice

Micah 6:8

Micah 6:8 declares what God expects of every one of his people, a lesson especially crucial for leaders. Why? Because God holds leaders responsible for creating healthy environments. The people learn to love justice and show mercy when their leader creates an environment for both.

The three items listed in this text define the values and character of a godly leader:

1. **Act justly: Justice and integrity rule their decisions regarding policy and program.**

2. **Love mercy: A love for people and relationship skills remain a high priority.**

3. **Walk humbly with God: A respectful relationship with God governs their strategy and lifestyle.**

¹⁴ You will eat but not be satisfied;
    your stomach will still be empty.ᵃ
You will store up but save nothing,
    because what you saveᵇ I will give to the
        sword.
¹⁵ You will plant but not harvest;
    you will press olives but not use the oil,
    you will crush grapes but not drink
        the wine.
¹⁶ You have observed the statutes of Omri
    and all the practices of Ahab's house;
    you have followed their traditions.
Therefore I will give you over to ruin
    and your people to derision;
    you will bear the scorn of the nations.ᶜ"

Israel's Misery

7 What misery is mine!
    I am like one who gathers summer fruit
    at the gleaning of the vineyard;
there is no cluster of grapes to eat,
    none of the early figs that I crave.
² The faithful have been swept from the
        land;
    not one upright person remains.

Everyone lies in wait to shed blood;
    they hunt each other with nets.
³ Both hands are skilled in doing evil;
    the ruler demands gifts,
the judge accepts bribes,
    the powerful dictate what they desire —
    they all conspire together.
⁴ The best of them is like a brier,
    the most upright worse than a thorn
        hedge.
The day God visits you has come,
    the day your watchmen sound the alarm.
    Now is the time of your confusion.
⁵ Do not trust a neighbor;
    put no confidence in a friend.
Even with the woman who lies in your
        embrace
    guard the words of your lips.
⁶ For a son dishonors his father,
    a daughter rises up against her mother,

ᵃ 14 The meaning of the Hebrew for this word is uncertain.
ᵇ 14 Or *You will press toward birth but not give birth, / and
what you bring to birth*   ᶜ 16 Septuagint; Hebrew *scorn due
my people*

Servanthood: Leaders Who Fail to Practice Servant Leadership Become Self-Serving

Micah 7:3–4

The final chapter of Micah paints a dim picture of Israel. The people couldn't be trusted, but lay in wait to use, abuse, and destroy each other.

Micah 7:3–4 tells us why this happened: poor leadership at the top. The rulers, princes and judges worked for kickbacks and bribes. They schemed how they could beat the system and better their own status. They expected the people to serve them instead of them serving the people.

The Law of Addition reminds us that leaders add value by serving others. When leaders fail to practice servant leadership, inevitably they become self-serving. Without a compelling cause to better mankind, all leaders find a cause to serve their own interests. This self-service eventually becomes a thorn in their leadership. Consider these other case studies in Scripture:

1. **With a cause, Samson won many battles; without one, he couldn't beat the temptation posed by Delilah.**

2. **With a cause, Saul conquered the kingdom; without one, he could not conquer even his own jealousy.**

3. **With a cause, David conquered Goliath; without one, he could not conquer his own lust.**

4. **With a cause, Elijah prayed down fire from heaven and beat 450 prophets of Baal; without one, he ran in fear from a solitary woman, Jezebel.**

5. **With a cause, Simon Peter preached at Pentecost and 3,000 people were saved; without one, he denied he even belonged to the crowd that followed Jesus.**

a daughter-in-law against her mother-in-law —
a man's enemies are the members of his own household.

⁷ But as for me, I watch in hope for the LORD,
I wait for God my Savior;
my God will hear me.

Israel Will Rise

⁸ Do not gloat over me, my enemy!
Though I have fallen, I will rise.
Though I sit in darkness,
the LORD will be my light.
⁹ Because I have sinned against him,
I will bear the LORD's wrath,
until he pleads my case
and upholds my cause.
He will bring me out into the light;
I will see his righteousness.
¹⁰ Then my enemy will see it
and will be covered with shame,
she who said to me,
"Where is the LORD your God?"
My eyes will see her downfall;
even now she will be trampled underfoot
like mire in the streets.

¹¹ The day for building your walls will come,
the day for extending your boundaries.
¹² In that day people will come to you
from Assyria and the cities of Egypt,
even from Egypt to the Euphrates
and from sea to sea
and from mountain to mountain.
¹³ The earth will become desolate because of its inhabitants,
as the result of their deeds.

Prayer and Praise

¹⁴ Shepherd your people with your staff,
the flock of your inheritance,
which lives by itself in a forest,
in fertile pasturelands.ᵃ
Let them feed in Bashan and Gilead
as in days long ago.

¹⁵ "As in the days when you came out of Egypt,
I will show them my wonders."

¹⁶ Nations will see and be ashamed,
deprived of all their power.
They will put their hands over their mouths
and their ears will become deaf.
¹⁷ They will lick dust like a snake,
like creatures that crawl on the ground.
They will come trembling out of their dens;
they will turn in fear to the LORD our God
and will be afraid of you.
¹⁸ Who is a God like you,
who pardons sin and forgives the transgression
of the remnant of his inheritance?
You do not stay angry forever
but delight to show mercy.
¹⁹ You will again have compassion on us;
you will tread our sins underfoot
and hurl all our iniquities into the depths of the sea.
²⁰ You will be faithful to Jacob,
and show love to Abraham,
as you pledged on oath to our ancestors
in days long ago.

ᵃ 14 Or in the middle of Carmel

INTRODUCTION TO
NAHUM

God's Fundamental Message for Every Erring Leader

The little-known prophet Nahum witnessed to the people of Judah, just as did the prophets Jeremiah, Habakkuk and Zephaniah. God instructed him to announce his judgment on the wicked city of Nineveh.

More than a century before, God had commissioned Jonah to call the people of Nineveh to repent—and they did. That generation failed to leave any legacy of humility or repentance, however, and by the seventh century BC, the nation had fallen into pitiful shape, both morally and spiritually.

Nahum sounds the alarm. In chapter one, he clearly communicates God's anger against the city of Nineveh—a declaration of judgment against wicked government and public immorality. In chapter two, he predicts Nineveh's impending doom. He prophesies it will be attacked and will fall. In chapter three, he describes in detail what this downfall will look like.

This little book packs a wallop. It contains God's fundamental message for every erring leader: No matter how much power you accumulate, it can never compensate for failure with God.

The Ninevites had it all—or so it seemed. They wielded power over many nations and arrogantly flaunted their might. But leadership success without spiritual success equals failure. Jesus asked, "What good is it for someone to gain the whole world, yet forfeit their soul?" (Mk 8:36). Put another way, professional wealth minus personal health yields bankruptcy. Organizational power is only temporary; personal power with God lasts. When leaders are right spiritually, they are able to lead *with* their soul rather than in spite of it.

In the final chapter of this book, Nahum notices a

God's Role in Nahum

God confronts and disciplines in this book. He is the divine Judge who must serve papers on Nineveh and execute justice. He used Nahum to lay out the charges against the Assyrians. God indicted them not only for the crimes they committed within their own borders, but for the cruelty they inflicted on other nations they victimized, including Israel.

God once again demonstrates that he is the ultimate power broker in the world. He builds up and tears down. He is not only the King of kings and the Lord of lords, but the Leader of leaders.

Leaders in Nahum

Nahum, the king of Nineveh

Other People of Influence in Nahum

Leaders and public officers of Nineveh

Lessons in Leadership

- Every generation must respond to God for themselves; you can't inherit salvation.
- Wicked leaders ultimately reap what they sow.
- Self-sufficiency can blind leaders from their own infirmities and weaknesses.

fatal flaw in the king of Nineveh. He had failed to reproduce leaders to shepherd the people. Even if he had been a moral man, by himself he lacked the influence to save his nation. He didn't develop healthy governmental leaders, and the nation collapsed morally (3:18).

LEADERSHIP HIGHLIGHTS IN NAHUM

GOD'S LEADERSHIP Is Like a Judge and a Father (1:2–13)	**page 1081**
THE LAW OF EMPOWERMENT: Assyria's King Failed to Develop Other Leaders and Paid for It (3:18–19)	**page 1083**

1
A prophecy concerning Nineveh. The book of the vision of Nahum the Elkoshite.

The Lord's Anger Against Nineveh

² The Lord is a jealous and avenging God;
   the Lord takes vengeance and is filled
      with wrath.
The Lord takes vengeance on his foes
   and vents his wrath against his enemies.
³ The Lord is slow to anger but great in power;
   the Lord will not leave the guilty
      unpunished.
His way is in the whirlwind and the storm,
   and clouds are the dust of his feet.
⁴ He rebukes the sea and dries it up;
   he makes all the rivers run dry.
Bashan and Carmel wither
   and the blossoms of Lebanon fade.
⁵ The mountains quake before him
   and the hills melt away.
The earth trembles at his presence,
   the world and all who live in it.
⁶ Who can withstand his indignation?
   Who can endure his fierce anger?
His wrath is poured out like fire;
   the rocks are shattered before him.

⁷ The Lord is good,
   a refuge in times of trouble.
He cares for those who trust in him,
⁸   but with an overwhelming flood
he will make an end of Nineveh;
   he will pursue his foes into the realm of
      darkness.

⁹ Whatever they plot against the Lord
   he will bring*a* to an end;
   trouble will not come a second time.
¹⁰ They will be entangled among thorns
   and drunk from their wine;
   they will be consumed like dry stubble.*b*
¹¹ From you, Nineveh, has one come forth
   who plots evil against the Lord
   and devises wicked plans.

¹² This is what the Lord says:

"Although they have allies and are numerous,
   they will be destroyed and pass away.
Although I have afflicted you, Judah,
   I will afflict you no more.
¹³ Now I will break their yoke from your neck
   and tear your shackles away."

¹⁴ The Lord has given a command concerning
      you, Nineveh:
"You will have no descendants to bear
      your name.
I will destroy the images and idols
   that are in the temple of your gods.
I will prepare your grave,
   for you are vile."

¹⁵ Look, there on the mountains,
   the feet of one who brings good news,
   who proclaims peace!
Celebrate your festivals, Judah,
   and fulfill your vows.

---

a 9 Or *What do you foes plot against the Lord? / He will bring it*
b 10 The meaning of the Hebrew for this verse is uncertain.

God's Leadership Is Like a Judge and a Father

Nahum 1:2–13

Although their ancestors had repented, the generation to which Nahum spoke failed miserably. The Ninevites that Jonah confronted returned to God, while those Nahum confronted never did. Yet in both cases, God led appropriately.

God modeled situational leadership for leaders everywhere, showing when to act as Judge and when to act as Father. These two images demonstrate a wonderful balance every leader must strike. Examine what God did in each situation:

The Leader as a Judge

1. God is jealous (v. 2).
2. God is an avenger (v. 2).
3. God is furious (v. 2).
4. God is great in power (v. 3).
5. God punishes the guilty (v. 3).

The Leader as a Father

1. God is slow to anger (v. 3).
2. God is good (v. 7).
3. God is a stronghold (v. 7).
4. God is a refuge (v. 7).
5. God is a liberator (v. 13).

No more will the wicked invade you;
  they will be completely destroyed.[a]

Nineveh to Fall

2[b] An attacker advances against you,
      Nineveh.
  Guard the fortress,
  watch the road,
  brace yourselves,
  marshal all your strength!

2 The LORD will restore the splendor of Jacob
    like the splendor of Israel,
  though destroyers have laid them waste
    and have ruined their vines.

3 The shields of the soldiers are red;
    the warriors are clad in scarlet.
  The metal on the chariots flashes
    on the day they are made ready;
    the spears of juniper are brandished.[c]

4 The chariots storm through the streets,
    rushing back and forth through the
      squares.
  They look like flaming torches;
    they dart about like lightning.

5 Nineveh summons her picked troops,
    yet they stumble on their way.
  They dash to the city wall;
    the protective shield is put in place.

6 The river gates are thrown open
    and the palace collapses.

7 It is decreed[d] that Nineveh
    be exiled and carried away.
  Her female slaves moan like doves
    and beat on their breasts.

8 Nineveh is like a pool
    whose water is draining away.
  "Stop! Stop!" they cry,
    but no one turns back.

9 Plunder the silver!
    Plunder the gold!
  The supply is endless,
    the wealth from all its treasures!

10 She is pillaged, plundered, stripped!
    Hearts melt, knees give way,
    bodies tremble, every face grows pale.

11 Where now is the lions' den,
    the place where they fed their young,
  where the lion and lioness went,
    and the cubs, with nothing to fear?

12 The lion killed enough for his cubs
    and strangled the prey for his mate,
  filling his lairs with the kill
    and his dens with the prey.

13 "I am against you,"
    declares the LORD Almighty.
  "I will burn up your chariots in smoke,
    and the sword will devour your young lions.
  I will leave you no prey on the earth.
  The voices of your messengers
    will no longer be heard."

God's Method of Discipline

Nahum 2:13

God uses many methods to discipline his
erring people—even pagan nations like
Assyria. This means, first, that no sin is more
acceptable than another. Second, God desires
to humble as well as discipline. Third, he is sovereign and will correct his people in whatever
manner he sees fit.

Woe to Nineveh

3 Woe to the city of blood,
      full of lies,
  full of plunder,
    never without victims!

2 The crack of whips,
    the clatter of wheels,
  galloping horses
    and jolting chariots!

3 Charging cavalry,
    flashing swords
    and glittering spears!
  Many casualties,
    piles of dead,
  bodies without number,
    people stumbling over the corpses —

4 all because of the wanton lust of a prostitute,
    alluring, the mistress of sorceries,
  who enslaved nations by her prostitution
    and peoples by her witchcraft.

5 "I am against you," declares the LORD
      Almighty.
  "I will lift your skirts over your face.
  I will show the nations your nakedness
    and the kingdoms your shame.

6 I will pelt you with filth,
    I will treat you with contempt
    and make you a spectacle.

---

[a] 15 In Hebrew texts this verse (1:15) is numbered 2:1.   [b] In
Hebrew texts 2:1-13 is numbered 2:2-14.   [c] 3 Hebrew;
Septuagint and Syriac *ready; / the horsemen rush to and fro.*
[d] 7 The meaning of the Hebrew for this word is uncertain.

⁷All who see you will flee from you and say,
  'Nineveh is in ruins — who will mourn
    for her?'
  Where can I find anyone to comfort
    you?"

⁸Are you better than Thebes,
  situated on the Nile,
  with water around her?
  The river was her defense,
    the waters her wall.
⁹Cush*a* and Egypt were her boundless
    strength;
  Put and Libya were among her allies.
¹⁰Yet she was taken captive
    and went into exile.
  Her infants were dashed to pieces
    at every street corner.
  Lots were cast for her nobles,
    and all her great men were put in chains.
¹¹You too will become drunk;
  you will go into hiding
  and seek refuge from the enemy.

¹²All your fortresses are like fig trees
    with their first ripe fruit;

when they are shaken,
  the figs fall into the mouth of the eater.
¹³Look at your troops —
  they are all weaklings.
  The gates of your land
    are wide open to your enemies;
  fire has consumed the bars of your
    gates.
¹⁴Draw water for the siege,
  strengthen your defenses!
  Work the clay,
    tread the mortar,
    repair the brickwork!
¹⁵There the fire will consume you;
  the sword will cut you down —
  they will devour you like a swarm of
    locusts.
  Multiply like grasshoppers,
    multiply like locusts!
¹⁶You have increased the number of your
    merchants
  till they are more numerous than the
    stars in the sky,

---

a 9 That is, the upper Nile region

The Law of Empowerment: Assyria's King Failed to Develop Other Leaders and Paid for It

Nahum 3:18–19

Through Nahum, God offers some insight as to why Nineveh failed so deeply. The prophet declared, "King of Assyria, your shepherds slumber; your nobles lie down to rest. Your people are scattered on the mountains with no one to gather them" (Na 3:18). Since the king had failed to empower other leaders, his people lay scattered like sheep without a shepherd. When we fail to develop other leaders, our leadership is limited to:

- Whatever leadership abilities we can offer
- The generation we live in
- The finite volume of gifts we possess
- The boundaries of our own wisdom
- The scope of our own influence

Because the King of Assyria had failed to develop other leaders, he had no way to change what was happening to the people of Nineveh. The population had grown too large for one man to perform a turn-around; one leader could not prevent the calamity the city had earned. Consider what happened when the king failed to practice the Law of Empowerment:

1. The local leaders grew blind and failed at their duties (v. 18).

2. The people had scattered and no one could organize them (v. 18).

3. The people had no relief or healing for their wounds (v. 19).

4. Everyone who heard of Nineveh's chaos would clap their hands and cheer (v. 19).

but like locusts they strip the land
and then fly away.
[17] Your guards are like locusts,
your officials like swarms of locusts
that settle in the walls on a cold day —
but when the sun appears they fly away,
and no one knows where.

[18] King of Assyria, your shepherds[a] slumber;
your nobles lie down to rest.

Your people are scattered on the mountains
with no one to gather them.
[19] Nothing can heal you;
your wound is fatal.
All who hear the news about you
clap their hands at your fall,
for who has not felt
your endless cruelty?

---

[a] 18 That is, rulers

INTRODUCTION TO
HABAKKUK

Leadership with No Easy Answers

God commissioned Habakkuk, a contemporary of Jeremiah and Ezekiel, to lead in troubled times. His name means "to embrace," and he earned the title by wrestling with God in the beginning of his book and by developing deep intimacy with God by the book's end.

Habakkuk could have titled his book, *Leadership with No Easy Answers*. This prophet struggled with why God allowed the people of Judah to get by with their immoral and sinful ways. He cried out to God and at first got no answer. God seemed far too tolerant for Habakkuk's tastes. Finally, God gave him a vision about his plan to rectify the situation by raising up Babylon to plunder and capture Judah in war. At this point, Habakkuk faced a whole new dilemma. Would God really use a nation even more wicked than Judah to correct Judah? This seemed preposterous to him. So he presented God with an integrity check: *Do you really know what you are doing here?* When God answered his question, he learned to trust, and ended the book with a beautiful psalm of faith.

Habakkuk teaches us to be praying leaders. The entire book is a dialogue between God and him, the only book in the Bible laid out in this way. As a prophet, Habakkuk had to *feed* the people and *lead* the people— but first, *intercede* for the people. Far too often, those of us who assume leadership positions are "doers" who forget this key role. In the New Testament, Peter said he would give himself to two priorities: the Word of God and prayer. This is the first job of a spiritual leader.

Habakkuk also teaches us that it's OK to ask God questions. We should enjoy such intimacy with God that we can candidly express our questions, concerns,

God's Role in Habakkuk

Habakkuk has to learn to follow God as the Leader. The Lord remains silent in the beginning and teaches his leader to wait. He eventually responds to Habakkuk's complaint in an unexpected fashion and teaches his leader to trust. He later confirms his sovereign control over all things and teaches his leader to rejoice, regardless of the circumstances. Habakkuk rises to a whole new level of leadership by the way God deals with him. May God do the same for each of us.

Leaders in Habakkuk

Habakkuk, the leaders of Judah, King Jehoahaz

Other People of Influence in Habakkuk

The Babylonian army

Lessons in Leadership

- Leaders must learn to wait on the Lord before they act on his Word.
- Wise leaders acknowledge their limitations and seek wise counsel from God.
- Godly leaders are not ashamed or afraid to ask detailed questions of the Lord.
- Good leaders discipline themselves to listen to the voice of God and thereby

or confusion over God's ways. When we lack answers, we ought to run to God, seeking his wisdom. Habakkuk asked detailed and specific questions. Leaders must feel secure enough to admit they don't know it all and seek insight from God.

Finally, the greatest leadership principle we learn from Habakkuk is trust. He knew he wasn't in control, any more than we are today. He waited on God. When God finally spoke, Habakkuk had to trust him; he certainly didn't understand. In essence, his closing psalm says, "Although I don't understand what is happening, and nothing is working out the way I would like it—I'll still rejoice and trust God's wisdom."

develop an intimate relationship with him.

■ Mature leaders rejoice in each circumstance, knowing who controls all things.

LEADERSHIP HIGHLIGHTS IN HABAKKUK

LISTENING: Leaders Earn Their Right to Be Heard (1:1–11)	**page 1087**
VISION: The Blueprint for Building a Bridge to the Future (2:2–3)	**page 1088**
WAITING: The Act Most Leaders Hate (2:1–20)	**page 1089**
GOD'S LEADERSHIP in the World (3:1–16)	**page 1090**
RESOURCES, Wisdom and People Follow Commitment (3:17–19)	**page 1091**

1 The prophecy that Habakkuk the prophet received.

Habakkuk's Complaint

2 How long, LORD, must I call for help,
  but you do not listen?
Or cry out to you, "Violence!"
  but you do not save?
3 Why do you make me look at injustice?
  Why do you tolerate wrongdoing?
Destruction and violence are before me;
  there is strife, and conflict abounds.
4 Therefore the law is paralyzed,
  and justice never prevails.
The wicked hem in the righteous,
  so that justice is perverted.

The LORD's Answer

5 "Look at the nations and watch—
  and be utterly amazed.
For I am going to do something in your
    days
  that you would not believe,
    even if you were told.

6 I am raising up the Babylonians,*a*
  that ruthless and impetuous people,
who sweep across the whole earth
  to seize dwellings not their own.
7 They are a feared and dreaded people;
  they are a law to themselves
  and promote their own honor.
8 Their horses are swifter than leopards,
  fiercer than wolves at dusk.
Their cavalry gallops headlong;
  their horsemen come from afar.
They fly like an eagle swooping to
    devour;
9   they all come intent on violence.
Their hordes*b* advance like a desert wind
  and gather prisoners like sand.
10 They mock kings
  and scoff at rulers.
They laugh at all fortified cities;
  by building earthen ramps they capture
    them.

---

a 6 Or *Chaldeans*   *b* 9 The meaning of the Hebrew for this word is uncertain.

Listening: Leaders Earn Their Right to Be Heard

Habakkuk 1:1–11

Habakkuk teaches us that leaders must first be listeners. In the first four verses of his book, the prophet cries out for God to answer his questions. He begs God to respond to the injustice, the violence and the perversion of his nation. He knew God was infinitely just, and he could not understand why God didn't seem interested in doing something about Judah's rebellion.

When God finally did respond, he gave Habakkuk a distasteful answer. God declared that he planned to use the Babylonians to punish Judah. He intended to use a nation more unjust than Judah to correct injustice among the Jews. That just didn't make sense to Habakkuk!

Even so, the prophet continued to listen. He wrestled with God but knew that leaders earn their right to speak by listening. When they listen, they gain something more precious than the privilege to speak:

1. **They gain insight about people.**

2. **They connect with the speaker.**

3. **They earn their right to speak.**

4. **They become relevant.**

5. **They understand the keys to the speaker's heart.**

6. **They identify.**

7. **They gain authority.**

8. **They learn.**

Remember: When you speak, nothing you say will teach you anything. Only when you listen—to God and to others—will you gain understanding.

11 Then they sweep past like the wind and go
    on —
    guilty people, whose own strength is their
      god."

Habakkuk's Second Complaint

12 LORD, are you not from everlasting?
    My God, my Holy One, you[a] will never
      die.
    You, LORD, have appointed them to execute
      judgment;
    you, my Rock, have ordained them to
      punish.
13 Your eyes are too pure to look on evil;
    you cannot tolerate wrongdoing.
    Why then do you tolerate the treacherous?
    Why are you silent while the wicked
    swallow up those more righteous than
      themselves?
14 You have made people like the fish in
      the sea,
    like the sea creatures that have no ruler.
15 The wicked foe pulls all of them up with
      hooks,
    he catches them in his net,
    he gathers them up in his dragnet;
    and so he rejoices and is glad.
16 Therefore he sacrifices to his net
    and burns incense to his dragnet,
    for by his net he lives in luxury
    and enjoys the choicest food.
17 Is he to keep on emptying his net,
    destroying nations without mercy?

2 I will stand at my watch
    and station myself on the ramparts;
I will look to see what he will say to me,
    and what answer I am to give to this
      complaint.[b]

The LORD's Answer

2 Then the LORD replied:

"Write down the revelation
    and make it plain on tablets
    so that a herald[c] may run with it.
3 For the revelation awaits an appointed
      time;
    it speaks of the end
    and will not prove false.
    Though it linger, wait for it;
    it[d] will certainly come
    and will not delay.

4 "See, the enemy is puffed up;
    his desires are not upright —

Vision: The Blueprint for Building a Bridge to the Future

Habakkuk 2:2–3

Leaders and vision go together like fire and heat; you can't separate them without destroying their essence. Through Habakkuk, God furnishes some instruction on vision for all of us. A divine vision . . .

- **should be written down (v. 2).**
- **should be distributed to people (v. 2).**
- **should be acted on (v. 2).**
- **is for a select time in the future (v. 3).**
- **motivates us toward the goal (v. 3).**
- **should not be discarded (v. 3).**
- **will not fail (v. 3).**

---

    but the righteous person will live by his
      faithfulness[e] —
5 indeed, wine betrays him;
    he is arrogant and never at rest.
Because he is as greedy as the grave
    and like death is never satisfied,
he gathers to himself all the nations
    and takes captive all the peoples.

6 "Will not all of them taunt him with ridicule
and scorn, saying,

" 'Woe to him who piles up stolen goods
    and makes himself wealthy by extortion!
    How long must this go on?'
7 Will not your creditors suddenly arise?
    Will they not wake up and make you
      tremble?
    Then you will become their prey.
8 Because you have plundered many nations,
    the peoples who are left will plunder you.
For you have shed human blood;
    you have destroyed lands and cities and
      everyone in them.

9 "Woe to him who builds his house by unjust
      gain,
    setting his nest on high
    to escape the clutches of ruin!

---

[a] 12 An ancient Hebrew scribal tradition; Masoretic Text *we*
[b] 1 Or *and what to answer when I am rebuked*   [c] 2 Or *so that whoever reads it*   [d] 3 Or *Though he linger, wait for him; / he*
[e] 4 Or *faith*

10 You have plotted the ruin of many peoples,
   shaming your own house and forfeiting
      your life.
11 The stones of the wall will cry out,
   and the beams of the woodwork will
      echo it.

12 "Woe to him who builds a city with
      bloodshed
   and establishes a town by injustice!
13 Has not the LORD Almighty determined
   that the people's labor is only fuel for the
      fire,
   that the nations exhaust themselves for
      nothing?
14 For the earth will be filled with the
      knowledge of the glory of the LORD
   as the waters cover the sea.

15 "Woe to him who gives drink to his
      neighbors,
   pouring it from the wineskin till they are
      drunk,
   so that he can gaze on their naked bodies!
16 You will be filled with shame instead of
      glory.
   Now it is your turn! Drink and let your
      nakedness be exposed*a*!
The cup from the LORD's right hand is
      coming around to you,
   and disgrace will cover your glory.
17 The violence you have done to Lebanon will
      overwhelm you,
   and your destruction of animals will
      terrify you.

For you have shed human blood;
   you have destroyed lands and cities and
      everyone in them.

18 "Of what value is an idol carved by a
      craftsman?
   Or an image that teaches lies?
For the one who makes it trusts in his own
      creation;
   he makes idols that cannot speak.
19 Woe to him who says to wood, 'Come to life!'
   Or to lifeless stone, 'Wake up!'
Can it give guidance?
   It is covered with gold and silver;
   there is no breath in it."

20 The LORD is in his holy temple;
   let all the earth be silent before him.

Habakkuk's Prayer

3 A prayer of Habakkuk the prophet. On *shig-
   ionoth.*b

2 LORD, I have heard of your fame;
   I stand in awe of your deeds, LORD.
Repeat them in our day,
   in our time make them known;
   in wrath remember mercy.

3 God came from Teman,
   the Holy One from Mount Paran.*c*

---

a 16 Masoretic Text; Dead Sea Scrolls, Aquila, Vulgate and
Syriac (see also Septuagint) *and stagger*   *b* 1 Probably a
literary or musical term   *c* 3 The Hebrew has *Selah* (a word
of uncertain meaning) here and at the middle of verse 9 and at
the end of verse 13.

Waiting: The Act Most Leaders Hate

Habakkuk 2:1–20

Habakkuk teaches us that leaders must learn to cherish the waiting time before they get their answers. In chapter one, the prophet is positioned to watch and see. In chapter two, he is positioned to stand and see. In chapter three, he is positioned to kneel and see.

God declares five "woes" to Habakkuk in the second chapter of his book, describing his intense displeasure with his people. Yet if God is sovereign, reigning over everything, then why doesn't he use his leader to bring about justice immediately? The answer appears to be this: While Habakkuk waited, God did a wonderful work in his heart. Before God leads the world, he first wants to lead his leaders. Habakkuk learned at least four lessons about God's leadership in the world:

1. **Not everything that happens conforms to God's will and wishes.**

2. **Nothing that happens gets overlooked by God.**

3. **Everything that happens will ultimately be addressed with justice.**

4. **Nothing that happens should distract us from continuing to respond faithfully.**

God's Leadership in the World

Habakkuk 3:1–16

Who can fully grasp God's method of dealing with the world around us? He truly is the Ultimate Leader who governs the affairs of mankind. Habakkuk shows how God influences the nations to perform his will. Consider his methods of influence:

1. *He sometimes exerts a restraining influence.*
Through this, he prevents people from doing what they feel naturally inclined to do.

2. *He sometimes exerts a softening influence.*
Through this, he causes them to move contrary to natural inclinations and to promote his cause.

3. *He sometimes exerts a directing influence.*
Through this, he causes good to result from the evil that others intend.

His glory covered the heavens
and his praise filled the earth.
⁴ His splendor was like the sunrise;
rays flashed from his hand,
where his power was hidden.
⁵ Plague went before him;
pestilence followed his steps.
⁶ He stood, and shook the earth;
he looked, and made the nations
tremble.
The ancient mountains crumbled
and the age-old hills collapsed —
but he marches on forever.
⁷ I saw the tents of Cushan in distress,
the dwellings of Midian in anguish.

⁸ Were you angry with the rivers, LORD?
Was your wrath against the streams?
Did you rage against the sea
when you rode your horses
and your chariots to victory?
⁹ You uncovered your bow,
you called for many arrows.
You split the earth with rivers;
10   the mountains saw you and writhed.
Torrents of water swept by;
the deep roared
and lifted its waves on high.

¹¹ Sun and moon stood still in the heavens
at the glint of your flying arrows,
at the lightning of your flashing spear.
¹² In wrath you strode through the earth
and in anger you threshed the nations.
¹³ You came out to deliver your people,
to save your anointed one.

You crushed the leader of the land of
wickedness,
you stripped him from head to foot.
¹⁴ With his own spear you pierced his head
when his warriors stormed out to scatter us,
gloating as though about to devour
the wretched who were in hiding.
¹⁵ You trampled the sea with your horses,
churning the great waters.

¹⁶ I heard and my heart pounded,
my lips quivered at the sound;
decay crept into my bones,
and my legs trembled.
Yet I will wait patiently for the day of
calamity
to come on the nation invading us.
¹⁷ Though the fig tree does not bud
and there are no grapes on the vines,

The Difference Between Leaders and Followers Is Perspective

Habakkuk 3:17–19

Once Habakkuk grasps God's leadership of the world, he can lead with confidence and poise. He once felt perplexed; now he has peace. He once felt confused; now he has contentment. He once felt fearful; now he has faith in the future God has planned. The only thing that changed? His perspective!

though the olive crop fails
   and the fields produce no food,
though there are no sheep in the pen
   and no cattle in the stalls,
[18] yet I will rejoice in the LORD,
   I will be joyful in God my Savior.

[19] The Sovereign LORD is my strength;
   he makes my feet like the feet of a deer,
   he enables me to tread on the heights.

For the director of music. On my stringed
   instruments.

Resources, Wisdom and People Follow Commitment

Habakkuk 3:17–19

The prophet concludes his book with a ringing declaration of his commitment. He recommits himself to God, to his vision, and to the destiny of his nation. Regardless of what happened, he would trust the process in which God had placed him.

This is the kind of attitude that enables leaders to "make it." Once we make this kind of commitment, all sorts of resources, wisdom and people follow. When leaders commit in this way, followers rise to the occasion despite adverse circumstances. Habakkuk teaches us the steps to this kind of commitment:

1. **Request:** Go ahead and ask for God's wisdom and will to be done.
2. **Relax:** Rest in his control; trust his power and providence.
3. **Receive:** Listen and wait for his instruction; remain open to change.
4. **Respond:** Obey whatever he commands.
5. **Rejoice:** Worship him regardless of your present circumstances.

Introduction to ZEPHANIAH

Zephaniah, a contemporary of Judah's King Josiah, represents a type of leader that every organization needs. Josiah was the godly king who, as a 20-year-old monarch, began to initiate much-needed national reforms. He restored the worship practices of old, ordered the Book of the Law to be read aloud, and required everyone to bow down and repent for their sin and spiritual drifting.

Merely external reforms, however, remain incomplete. You cannot perfume a skunk and expect to transform him. Many in Josiah's day performed the repentance rituals but continued in their secret sins. Many never acknowledged their private sinfulness, nor did they inwardly repent of their personal wickedness.

Zephaniah decided that repentance needed to go deeper than outward behavior. You might say that he practiced the Law of Intuition. He intuitively knew that real change requires more than what the leader can legislate. He sought more than external reformation—he wanted internal transformation. He knew that mere respect for the king could not produce the needed metamorphosis. The people didn't need to turn over a new leaf; they needed a new life. So the prophet took a risk and acted. He began to call the Hebrews to look at their hearts, their motives, their desires, their private lives. He meddled—but touched a chord. He spoke to issues that needed to be addressed, issues that most leaders fear to bring up.

The people of Judah respected the prophet Zephaniah. Many scholars believe that royal blood coursed through his veins, giving him direct access to the king. As such, he could have enjoyed his favored position

God's Role in Zephaniah

In Zephaniah's day, God played a key role as the broker of talents. God used King Josiah to bring about necessary legislative reforms. He called the people to corporate reform. But to transform the people, he also used Zephaniah's gift to call the people to personal reflection and repentance. If the nation were to benefit from the new legislation, each individual needed to repent of specific private sins. Change always begins in the heart of an individual. So, God raised up both a Josiah and a Zephaniah. The nation needed their complementary gifts.

Leaders in Zephaniah
Zephaniah, King Josiah

Other People of Influence in Zephaniah
Wicked people of Judah, Nebuchadnezzar

Lessons in Leadership
- God brings about change from the inside out.
- Leadership is often best exercised in teams, where complementary gifts are used.
- Leaders cannot let their safe positions keep them from risking radical obedience.
- Leaders must never shift their focus from doing their job to keeping their job.

and let well enough alone. But he refused to sit still. He wouldn't allow his power and position to water down his convictions. Instead, he leveraged his influence with King Josiah to create needed civil and religious reforms. He called a spade, a spade.

Early in Josiah's reign, Zephaniah began challenging the wicked patterns initiated under the kings Manasseh and Amon. He warned the people of impending judgment and likely played an influential role in Josiah's determination to initiate national change. Nevertheless, even though the king joined Zephaniah in the reform movement, the evil tide rolled on. This led the prophet to predict that God would use an outsider (namely Nebuchadnezzar) as the rod of his discipline. Despite this, the book ends on a note of hope as Zephaniah points to a time when all people will call on the name of the Lord.

> ■ Leaders who confront tough issues will enjoy the respect of others and the joy of corporate purity.

LEADERSHIP HIGHLIGHTS IN ZEPHANIAH

COMMUNICATION: Zephaniah Spoke with Divine Authority (1:1–18)	**page 1094**
THE LAW OF INTUITION: The Prophet Knows Change Begins Inside (2:1–3)	**page 1095**
THE LAW OF NAVIGATION: Zephaniah Gives Hope and a Plan (3:8–20)	**page 1097**

1 The word of the LORD that came to Zephaniah son of Cushi, the son of Gedaliah, the son of Amariah, the son of Hezekiah, during the reign of Josiah son of Amon king of Judah:

Judgment on the Whole Earth in the Day of the LORD

2 "I will sweep away everything
    from the face of the earth,"
                declares the LORD.
3 "I will sweep away both man and beast;
    I will sweep away the birds in the sky
    and the fish in the sea —
    and the idols that cause the wicked to
        stumble."[a]

"When I destroy all mankind
    on the face of the earth,"
                declares the LORD,
4 "I will stretch out my hand against Judah
    and against all who live in Jerusalem.
I will destroy every remnant of Baal worship
        in this place,
    the very names of the idolatrous
        priests —
5 those who bow down on the roofs
    to worship the starry host,

those who bow down and swear by the
        LORD
    and who also swear by Molek,[b]
6 those who turn back from following the
        LORD
    and neither seek the LORD nor inquire of
        him."

7 Be silent before the Sovereign LORD,
    for the day of the LORD is near.
The LORD has prepared a sacrifice;
    he has consecrated those he has invited.

8 "On the day of the LORD's sacrifice
    I will punish the officials
    and the king's sons
and all those clad
    in foreign clothes.
9 On that day I will punish
    all who avoid stepping on the threshold,[c]
    who fill the temple of their gods
        with violence and deceit.
10 "On that day,"
    declares the LORD,

---

[a] 3 The meaning of the Hebrew for this line is uncertain.
[b] 5 Hebrew *Malkam*   [c] 9 See 1 Samuel 5:5.

Communication: Zephaniah Spoke with Divine Authority

Zephaniah 1:1–18

Zephaniah spoke for God, just as other Old Testament prophets had done. This divine message required Zephaniah to possess unique qualifications, for God called him to deliver a message his audience didn't want to hear. The message wasn't fun to preach and contained difficult and even disgusting metaphors.

Nevertheless, Zephaniah communicated judgment upon the house of Judah with great authority. How could he stand strong and deliver his message with passion in the face of entrenched opposition? And how can we follow his example? Make sure you follow the pattern Zephaniah did:

1. **Believe in your God.**
   Zephaniah had to trust in God to protect and empower him to communicate the message.

2. **Believe in your message.**
   Zephaniah had to be convinced that this hard word was exactly what the people needed to hear.

3. **Believe in your cause.**
   Zephaniah had to embrace his ultimate cause.

4. **Believe in your people.**
   Zephaniah had to have hope that the people would change and buy into his message.

5. **Believe in yourself.**
   Zephaniah had to be convinced that he was the man to deliver this message.

"a cry will go up from the Fish Gate,
    wailing from the New Quarter,
    and a loud crash from the hills.
[11] Wail, you who live in the market district[a];
    all your merchants will be wiped out,
    all who trade with[b] silver will be
      destroyed.
[12] At that time I will search Jerusalem with lamps
    and punish those who are complacent,
    who are like wine left on its dregs,
who think, 'The LORD will do nothing,
    either good or bad.'
[13] Their wealth will be plundered,
    their houses demolished.
Though they build houses,
    they will not live in them;
though they plant vineyards,
    they will not drink the wine."

[14] The great day of the LORD is near —
    near and coming quickly.
The cry on the day of the LORD is bitter;
    the Mighty Warrior shouts his battle cry.
[15] That day will be a day of wrath —
    a day of distress and anguish,
      a day of trouble and ruin,
    a day of darkness and gloom,
      a day of clouds and blackness —
[16]   a day of trumpet and battle cry

against the fortified cities
    and against the corner towers.

[17] "I will bring such distress on all people
    that they will grope about like those who
      are blind,
    because they have sinned against the
      LORD.
Their blood will be poured out like dust
    and their entrails like dung.
[18] Neither their silver nor their gold
    will be able to save them
    on the day of the LORD's wrath."

In the fire of his jealousy
    the whole earth will be consumed,
for he will make a sudden end
    of all who live on the earth.

Judah and Jerusalem Judged Along With the Nations
Judah Summoned to Repent

2 Gather together, gather yourselves together,
    you shameful nation,
[2] before the decree takes effect
    and that day passes like windblown chaff,
before the LORD's fierce anger
    comes upon you,

---

[a] 11 Or the Mortar   [b] 11 Or in

The Law of Intuition: The Prophet Knows Change Begins Inside

Zephaniah 2:1–3

The prophet intuitively knows what needs to happen to change the people of Judah. Zephaniah lived during the reform of King Josiah. Even with the external reforms in worship the king initiated, Zephaniah knew more changes were required. He knew change begins with the heart. Transformation happens from the inside out.

To enhance your own leadership intuition, practice the following activities:

1. **Work in the areas of your strength.**
   We are most intuitive in the areas of our gifts and interests.

2. **Explore the opportunities in front of you.**
   Our intuition comes most alive when we size up the options near us.

3. **Discern root causes for the issues you face.**
   Work to get past superficial answers and solve root issues.

4. **Analyze past successes.**
   Study your victories and see if you find a pattern that reveals how you won them.

5. **Listen to your gut.**
   Effective leaders lead from their soul. Both your heart and your head have answers.

before the day of the LORD's wrath
  comes upon you.
[3] Seek the LORD, all you humble of the land,
  you who do what he commands.
Seek righteousness, seek humility;
  perhaps you will be sheltered
  on the day of the LORD's anger.

Philistia

[4] Gaza will be abandoned
  and Ashkelon left in ruins.
At midday Ashdod will be emptied
  and Ekron uprooted.
[5] Woe to you who live by the sea,
  you Kerethite people;
the word of the LORD is against you,
  Canaan, land of the Philistines.
He says, "I will destroy you,
  and none will be left."
[6] The land by the sea will become pastures
  having wells for shepherds
  and pens for flocks.
[7] That land will belong
  to the remnant of the people of Judah;
  there they will find pasture.
In the evening they will lie down
  in the houses of Ashkelon.
The LORD their God will care for them;
  he will restore their fortunes.[a]

Moab and Ammon

[8] "I have heard the insults of Moab
  and the taunts of the Ammonites,
who insulted my people
  and made threats against their land.
[9] Therefore, as surely as I live,"
  declares the LORD Almighty,
  the God of Israel,
"surely Moab will become like Sodom,
  the Ammonites like Gomorrah —
a place of weeds and salt pits,
  a wasteland forever.
The remnant of my people will plunder
    them;
  the survivors of my nation will inherit
    their land."

[10] This is what they will get in return for their
      pride,
  for insulting and mocking
  the people of the LORD Almighty.
[11] The LORD will be awesome to them
  when he destroys all the gods of the earth.
Distant nations will bow down to him,
  all of them in their own lands.

Cush

[12] "You Cushites,[b] too,
  will be slain by my sword."

Assyria

[13] He will stretch out his hand against the north
  and destroy Assyria,
leaving Nineveh utterly desolate
  and dry as the desert.
[14] Flocks and herds will lie down there,
  creatures of every kind.
The desert owl and the screech owl
  will roost on her columns.
Their hooting will echo through the windows,
  rubble will fill the doorways,
  the beams of cedar will be exposed.
[15] This is the city of revelry
  that lived in safety.
She said to herself,
  "I am the one! And there is none besides
    me."
What a ruin she has become,
  a lair for wild beasts!
All who pass by her scoff
  and shake their fists.

Confrontation: Zephaniah Does It and Gains Credibility

Zephaniah 2:4–15

While not everyone agreed with Zephaniah's judgment on Judah, he gained widespread credibility due to his ability to confront tough issues. He called out specific groups of people to be judged for their sins, then named their specific sins. When leaders are willing to confront difficult issues, they win the respect of others.

Jerusalem

3 Woe to the city of oppressors,
  rebellious and defiled!
[2] She obeys no one,
  she accepts no correction.
She does not trust in the LORD,
  she does not draw near to her God.
[3] Her officials within her
  are roaring lions;

---

[a] 7 Or *will bring back their captives*   [b] 12 That is, people from the upper Nile region

her rulers are evening wolves,
who leave nothing for the morning.
[4] Her prophets are unprincipled;
they are treacherous people.
Her priests profane the sanctuary
and do violence to the law.
[5] The LORD within her is righteous;
he does no wrong.
Morning by morning he dispenses his
justice,
and every new day he does not fail,
yet the unrighteous know no shame.

Jerusalem Remains Unrepentant

[6] "I have destroyed nations;
their strongholds are demolished.
I have left their streets deserted,
with no one passing through.
Their cities are laid waste;
they are deserted and empty.
[7] Of Jerusalem I thought,
'Surely you will fear me
and accept correction!'
Then her place of refuge[a] would not be
destroyed,
nor all my punishments come upon[b] her.
But they were still eager
to act corruptly in all they did.
[8] Therefore wait for me,"
declares the LORD,
"for the day I will stand up to testify.[c]
I have decided to assemble the nations,
to gather the kingdoms
and to pour out my wrath on them —
all my fierce anger.
The whole world will be consumed
by the fire of my jealous anger.

Restoration of Israel's Remnant

[9] "Then I will purify the lips of the
peoples,
that all of them may call on the name
of the LORD
and serve him shoulder to shoulder.
[10] From beyond the rivers of Cush[d]
my worshipers, my scattered people,
will bring me offerings.
[11] On that day you, Jerusalem, will not be put
to shame
for all the wrongs you have done to me,
because I will remove from you
your arrogant boasters.
Never again will you be haughty
on my holy hill.
[12] But I will leave within you
the meek and humble.
The remnant of Israel
will trust in the name of the LORD.
[13] They will do no wrong;
they will tell no lies.
A deceitful tongue
will not be found in their mouths.
They will eat and lie down
and no one will make them afraid."

[14] Sing, Daughter Zion;
shout aloud, Israel!
Be glad and rejoice with all your heart,
Daughter Jerusalem!
[15] The LORD has taken away your punishment,
he has turned back your enemy.

---

[a] 7 Or *her sanctuary*　　[b] 7 Or *all those I appointed over*
[c] 8 Septuagint and Syriac; Hebrew *will rise up to plunder*
[d] 10 That is, the upper Nile region

The Law of Navigation: Zephaniah Gives Hope and a Plan

Zephaniah 3:8–20

Regardless of the hopeless situation they had to judge, the Old Testament prophets almost always closed their writings with words of hope. Zephaniah even offers a plan for repentance and invites the people to walk in it. He navigates the path back to God, outlining it this way:

1. **Wait for God to *remove* the cancerous population (vv. 8–11).**

2. **Trust God to *restore* a remnant of humble, obedient men and women (vv. 12–13).**

3. **Look to God and *rejoice* that he has taken away your guilt (vv. 14–15).**

4. **Hope in God to *renew* your peace and strength (vv. 16–17).**

5. **Allow God to *recover* the appointed feasts and the lost people (vv. 18–20).**

The LORD, the King of Israel, is with you;
    never again will you fear any harm.
[16] On that day
    they will say to Jerusalem,
"Do not fear, Zion;
    do not let your hands hang limp.
[17] The LORD your God is with you,
    the Mighty Warrior who saves.
He will take great delight in you;
    in his love he will no longer rebuke you,
    but will rejoice over you with singing."

[18] "I will remove from you
    all who mourn over the loss of your
        appointed festivals,
    which is a burden and reproach for you.

[19] At that time I will deal
    with all who oppressed you.
I will rescue the lame;
    I will gather the exiles.
I will give them praise and honor
    in every land where they have suffered
        shame.
[20] At that time I will gather you;
    at that time I will bring you home.
I will give you honor and praise
    among all the peoples of the earth
when I restore your fortunes[a]
    before your very eyes,"

                    says the LORD.

---

[a] 20 Or I bring back your captives

INTRODUCTION TO
HAGGAI

Calling God's People Back to Their Faith and Values

The prophet Haggai teaches us about the Law of Priorities. God raised him up to address the misplaced priorities of the Hebrews under the Persian reign of Cyrus. Haggai insisted on doing the right things at the right time, for the right reasons.

Haggai became the first prophet to serve God's people when the Jews returned to their homeland after the Babylonian exile. King Cyrus conquered the Babylonians 70 years after they had taken the Jews into captivity. Cyrus allowed the Jews to return to their homeland, just as the prophets Jeremiah and Daniel had foretold. He sent them back to Israel in order to rebuild the Jerusalem temple.

Upon their arrival, they laid the foundation for the sanctuary and the work began. But soon hostile neighbors tried to stop the work. (There is a spiritual lesson in there somewhere!) Slowly, the building project ground to a halt—but outward opposition accounted for only part of the problem. An inward enemy called "indifference" posed the major threat.

Most of the workers became apathetic, even though the rebuilding project supplied the very reason for their return to Jerusalem. Before long, many began constructing their own homes and businesses and all but lost the divine vision for their presence in Zion. By the time King Darius took the throne of Persia, the temple had lain untouched for 16 years. God sent Haggai, and later Zechariah, to call the people back to their priorities. He called them back to their vision ("this is why we are here") and back to their faith and values ("we exist to glorify the Lord and make him famous").

Haggai was more than just a building supervisor; his

God's Role in Haggai

Haggai served as a mouthpiece for God, like the other prophets in the Old Testament. God was the One who called the people to recover their misplaced priorities. He found a man named Haggai who shared this passion and who would eagerly voice it. God had to deal with a people who had become spiritually lethargic, discouraged about paying a price to rebuild the temple, and disinterested in their own walk with God. God inspired Haggai to write this book as a wake-up call to draw the people back to the original purpose for their homecoming. Through this book God continues to remind leaders everywhere that we should never feel satisfied until we incarnate his priorities.

Leaders in Haggai

Haggai, Joshua, Darius, Cyrus, Zerubbabel

Other People of Influence in Haggai

Shealtiel, the priests

Lessons in Leadership

- If you forget the ultimate, you will become a slave to the immediate.
- Activity does not always mean accomplishment.
- The issue is not, "Will my calendar be full?" but, "What will fill my calendar?"

leadership addressed priorities in general. He began his message by talking about finishing the building, but then focused on the presence of God. He teaches us how our calendars and behavior reflect what is really important to us. He longed to see not only Israel, but all nations, turn to God and live out proper priorities.

- If I don't evaluate, I will stagnate.
- Priorities are a matter of both perception and practice; I must know and do them.

LEADERSHIP HIGHLIGHTS IN HAGGAI

PRIORITIES: If I Forget the Ultimate, I'll Be Enslaved to the Immediate (1:3–9)		**page 1101**
LEADERSHIP PERSPECTIVE: Keeping Your Eye on the Big Picture (2:6–9)		**page 1102**

A Call to Build the House of the Lord

1 In the second year of King Darius, on the first day of the sixth month, the word of the Lord came through the prophet Haggai to Zerubbabel son of Shealtiel, governor of Judah, and to Joshua son of Jozadak,[a] the high priest:

²This is what the Lord Almighty says: "These people say, 'The time has not yet come to rebuild the Lord's house.'"

³Then the word of the Lord came through the prophet Haggai: ⁴"Is it a time for you yourselves to be living in your paneled houses, while this house remains a ruin?"

⁵Now this is what the Lord Almighty says: "Give careful thought to your ways. ⁶You have planted much, but harvested little. You eat, but never have enough. You drink, but never have your fill. You put on clothes, but are not warm. You earn wages, only to put them in a purse with holes in it."

⁷This is what the Lord Almighty says: "Give careful thought to your ways. ⁸Go up into the mountains and bring down timber and build my house, so that I may take pleasure in it and be honored," says the Lord. ⁹"You expected much, but see, it turned out to be little. What you brought home, I blew away. Why?" declares the Lord Almighty. "Because of my house, which remains a ruin, while each of you is busy with your own house. ¹⁰Therefore, because of you the heavens have withheld their dew and the earth its crops. ¹¹I called for a drought on the fields and the mountains, on the grain, the new wine, the olive oil and everything else the ground produces, on people and livestock, and on all the labor of your hands."

¹²Then Zerubbabel son of Shealtiel, Joshua son of Jozadak, the high priest, and the whole remnant of the people obeyed the voice of the Lord their God and the message of the prophet Haggai, because the Lord their God had sent him. And the people feared the Lord.

¹³Then Haggai, the Lord's messenger, gave this message of the Lord to the people: "I am with you," declares the Lord. ¹⁴So the Lord stirred up the spirit of Zerubbabel son of Shealtiel, governor of Judah, and the spirit of Joshua son of Jozadak, the high priest, and the spirit of the whole remnant of the people. They came and began to work on the house of the Lord Almighty, their God, ¹⁵on the twenty-fourth day of the sixth month.

The Promised Glory of the New House

2 In the second year of King Darius, ¹on the twenty-first day of the seventh month, the word of the Lord came through the prophet Haggai: ²"Speak to Zerubbabel son of Shealtiel,

---

[a] 1 Hebrew *Jehozadak*, a variant of *Jozadak*; also in verses 12 and 14

Priorities: If I Forget the Ultimate, I'll Be Enslaved to the Immediate

Haggai 1:3–9

Leadership means you lose your right to be selfish. The builders in Haggai's day had left their original purpose to construct the temple and instead went to work on their own houses and businesses. It took a leader like Haggai to call them back to their purpose. Chapter one outlines what happened when they abandoned their highest priority:

1. **They failed to consider how their actions contradicted their faith (vv. 3–5).**

2. **They worked hard but saw few results (v. 6).**

3. **They spent much but received little in return (v. 6).**

4. **They felt dissatisfied in their production (vv. 7–9).**

When leaders and people fail to maintain proper priorities, disappointment always results. Remember the 80/20 Principle: With the right priorities, 20% of your effort will get you 80% of the desired results. But with the wrong priorities, 80% of your effort will get you 20% of the desired results. It is not about working harder, but smarter.

governor of Judah, to Joshua son of Jozadak,[a] the high priest, and to the remnant of the people. Ask them, 3'Who of you is left who saw this house in its former glory? How does it look to you now? Does it not seem to you like nothing? 4But now be strong, Zerubbabel,' declares the LORD. 'Be strong, Joshua son of Jozadak, the high priest. Be strong, all you people of the land,' declares the LORD, 'and work. For I am with you,' declares the LORD Almighty. 5'This is what I covenanted with you when you came out of Egypt. And my Spirit remains among you. Do not fear.'

6"This is what the LORD Almighty says: 'In a little while I will once more shake the heavens and the earth, the sea and the dry land. 7I will shake all nations, and what is desired by all nations will come, and I will fill this house with glory,' says the LORD Almighty. 8'The silver is mine and the gold is mine,' declares the LORD Almighty. 9'The glory of this present house will be greater than the glory of the former house,' says the LORD Almighty. 'And in this place I will grant peace,' declares the LORD Almighty."

Blessings for a Defiled People

10On the twenty-fourth day of the ninth month, in the second year of Darius, the word of the LORD came to the prophet Haggai: 11"This is what the LORD Almighty says: 'Ask the priests what the law says: 12If someone carries consecrated meat in the fold of their garment, and that fold touches some bread or stew, some wine, olive oil or other food, does it become consecrated?'"

The priests answered, "No."

13Then Haggai said, "If a person defiled by contact with a dead body touches one of these things, does it become defiled?"

"Yes," the priests replied, "it becomes defiled."

14Then Haggai said, "'So it is with this people and this nation in my sight,' declares the LORD. 'Whatever they do and whatever they offer there is defiled.

15"'Now give careful thought to this from this day on[b]— consider how things were before one stone was laid on another in the LORD's temple. 16When anyone came to a heap of twenty measures, there were only ten. When anyone went to a wine vat to draw fifty measures, there were only twenty. 17I struck all the work of your hands with blight, mildew and hail, yet you did not return to me,' declares the LORD. 18'From this day on, from this twenty-fourth day of the ninth month, give careful thought to the day when the foundation of the LORD's temple was laid. Give careful thought: 19Is there yet any seed left in the barn? Until now, the vine and the fig tree, the pomegranate and the olive tree have not borne fruit.

"'From this day on I will bless you.'"

Zerubbabel the LORD's Signet Ring

20The word of the LORD came to Haggai a second time on the twenty-fourth day of the month: 21"Tell Zerubbabel governor of Judah that I am

---

[a] 2 Hebrew Jehozadak, a variant of Jozadak; also in verse 4
[b] 15 Or to the days past

Leadership Perspective: Keeping Your Eye on the Big Picture

Haggai 2:6–9

Leaders must understand their priorities before they can implement them. Once they perceive what is most important, their work is half finished. It's all about perspective.

Haggai had big-picture perspective. He didn't focus on personal interests—on immediate gratification, on easy results, or on pleasing people. Instead, he put first things first.

In the second chapter of his book, the prophet addresses the complaints of the nation simply and in a straightforward manner. Haggai spoke for God and gave his countrymen the divine perspective on the challenge before them:

The People's Complaint (Haggai 1)	God's Response (Haggai 2)
1. The job is too big.	1. The job is mine; let's work together.
2. The resources are too small.	2. I am your Source; I own all the resources.
3. What we build will not be as great as the past.	3. What you build, I will fill with my glory. That's good enough!

going to shake the heavens and the earth. ²²I will overturn royal thrones and shatter the power of the foreign kingdoms. I will overthrow chariots and their drivers; horses and their riders will fall, each by the sword of his brother.

²³"'On that day,' declares the LORD Almighty, 'I will take you, my servant Zerubbabel son of Shealtiel,' declares the LORD, 'and I will make you like my signet ring, for I have chosen you,' declares the LORD Almighty."

INTRODUCTION TO
ZECHARIAH

Leadership Equals Vision and Purpose

Two leadership words come to mind in reading the book of Zechariah: *vision* and *purpose*. This prophet, whose name means "the LORD remembers," reminds the people of Israel that God does indeed remember his covenant with them and will fulfill his part of it—if the people will only perform their part.

Like Haggai, his older contemporary, Zechariah calls the people to finish the work of rebuilding the temple. He saw their lethargy as Haggai did, but instead of an angry chastisement, he encourages them by painting a mental picture of how it will impact their future. For about a dozen years the temple had lain half finished. God commissioned Zechariah to encourage its completion through use of a metaphor. The rising of the temple pictured their lives. One day the Messiah would dwell in this temple and eventually in them. So, both the temple and their lives must be given top priority. As they worked on both, they built their future.

Vision is a key word in this book. Zechariah sees eight visions between chapters one and six. But while he was a man of many visions, he kept to only one priority. All these visions call the people to repent and turn to God. Like any great leader, Zechariah knows he must cast a compelling vision for the people to act on. These pictures rock the people and serve to ignite them to finish what they had started.

Purpose is yet another key word in Zechariah. The prophet feels the need to remind the people of the higher purpose to which they had been called. Again, like all great leaders, he reminds them of the big picture. They aren't merely constructing a building; they are building their legacy. Zechariah delivers four messages in response

God's Role in Zechariah

God has a twofold role in this book. First, he uses Zechariah to speak for him about needed change. The prophet calls the people to repent and obey. He challenges and encourages them to fulfill the covenant they had entered into and expected God to fulfill. Second, God uses Zechariah to forecast the coming Messiah as the Righteous Branch, the King-Priest, the humble King, the Cornerstone, the Good Shepherd and the pierced One. By book's end, God promises to return to his people and dwell in the midst of Zion.

Leaders in Zechariah

Zechariah, Zerubbabel, Joshua, Darius

Other People of Influence in Zechariah

Heldai, Tobijah, Jedaiah

Lessons in Leadership

■ A vision should include a principle for the "head" and a picture for the "heart."

■ Encouragement is vital; you catch more bees with honey than with vinegar.

■ Where there is no hope in the future, there is no power in the present.

■ If you stop learning today, you stop leading tomorrow.

to questions about fasting. First, he rebukes the people for performing empty rituals. Next, he reminds them of past disobedience. Third, he speaks of the restoration of Israel. Finally, he points to the recovery of joy within the reign of God. In the last six chapters, he sheds light on the first and second comings of Christ—definitely a big-picture, long-term purpose. Although Zechariah lived during tough times, he kept alive an undying vision of a greater vision and purpose.

- A big vision without core values is like a winding road without guard rails.
- When communicating vision, always give the people something to act upon.

LEADERSHIP HIGHLIGHTS IN ZECHARIAH

TEACHABILITY: If We Don't Learn from History, We Will Repeat It (1:4–6)	**page 1106**
VISION: People Are Energized by a Picture of a Better Tomorrow (3:1–10)	**page 1108**
THE POWER OF A PICTURE: We Do on the Outside What We Picture Inside (5:1–11)	**page 1110**
COMMUNICATION: Without It, the Leader Travels Alone (8:1–8)	**page 1111**

A Call to Return to the LORD

1 In the eighth month of the second year of Darius, the word of the LORD came to the prophet Zechariah son of Berekiah, the son of Iddo:

2"The LORD was very angry with your ancestors. 3Therefore tell the people: This is what the LORD Almighty says: 'Return to me,' declares the LORD Almighty, 'and I will return to you,' says the LORD Almighty. 4Do not be like your ancestors, to whom the earlier prophets proclaimed: This is what the LORD Almighty says: 'Turn from your evil ways and your evil practices.' But they would not listen or pay attention to me, declares the LORD. 5Where are your ancestors now? And the prophets, do they live forever? 6But did not my words and my decrees, which I commanded my servants the prophets, overtake your ancestors?

"Then they repented and said, 'The LORD Almighty has done to us what our ways and practices deserve, just as he determined to do.'"

The Man Among the Myrtle Trees

7On the twenty-fourth day of the eleventh month, the month of Shebat, in the second year of Darius, the word of the LORD came to the prophet Zechariah son of Berekiah, the son of Iddo.

8During the night I had a vision, and there before me was a man mounted on a red horse. He was standing among the myrtle trees in a ravine. Behind him were red, brown and white horses.

9I asked, "What are these, my lord?"

The angel who was talking with me answered, "I will show you what they are."

10Then the man standing among the myrtle trees explained, "They are the ones the LORD has sent to go throughout the earth."

11And they reported to the angel of the LORD who was standing among the myrtle trees, "We have gone throughout the earth and found the whole world at rest and in peace."

12Then the angel of the LORD said, "LORD Almighty, how long will you withhold mercy from Jerusalem and from the towns of Judah, which you have been angry with these seventy years?" 13So the LORD spoke kind and comforting words to the angel who talked with me.

14Then the angel who was speaking to me said, "Proclaim this word: This is what the LORD Almighty says: 'I am very jealous for Jerusalem and Zion, 15and I am very angry with the nations that feel secure. I was only a little angry, but they went too far with the punishment.'

16"Therefore this is what the LORD says: 'I will return to Jerusalem with mercy, and there my house will be rebuilt. And the measuring line will be stretched out over Jerusalem,' declares the LORD Almighty.

17"Proclaim further: This is what the LORD Almighty says: 'My towns will again overflow with prosperity, and the LORD will again comfort Zion and choose Jerusalem.'"

Teachability: If We Don't Learn from History, We Will Repeat It

Zechariah 1:4–6

Good leaders are continual learners. We must keep learning or we will stop leading. We cannot afford to stagnate, for our world and our people are changing too quickly. New insights and new opportunities appear all the time.

Zechariah needed to learn from the past. His Hebrew forefathers had failed to follow Yahweh. God warned Zechariah to take heed and not follow in their footsteps. God told him to learn from . . .

1. **The past—Israel's previous years were to warn future generations.**

2. **The prophets—These men of God spoke God's word and cautioned Israel to listen.**

3. **The people—The people repeatedly failed to repent and felt miserable.**

4. **The problems—Trials served to punish the people for disobedience.**

5. **The present—Zechariah found himself in a similar predicament.**

6. **The principles of God—God's truth cried out to Zechariah's generation.**

Four Horns and Four Craftsmen

[18]Then I looked up, and there before me were four horns. [19]I asked the angel who was speaking to me, "What are these?"

He answered me, "These are the horns that scattered Judah, Israel and Jerusalem."

[20]Then the LORD showed me four craftsmen. [21]I asked, "What are these coming to do?"

He answered, "These are the horns that scattered Judah so that no one could raise their head, but the craftsmen have come to terrify them and throw down these horns of the nations who lifted up their horns against the land of Judah to scatter its people."[a]

A Man With a Measuring Line

2[b] Then I looked up, and there before me was a man with a measuring line in his hand. [2]I asked, "Where are you going?"

He answered me, "To measure Jerusalem, to find out how wide and how long it is."

[3]While the angel who was speaking to me was leaving, another angel came to meet him [4]and said to him: "Run, tell that young man, 'Jerusalem will be a city without walls because of the great number of people and animals in it. [5]And I myself will be a wall of fire around it,' declares the LORD, 'and I will be its glory within.'

[6]"Come! Come! Flee from the land of the north," declares the LORD, "for I have scattered you to the four winds of heaven," declares the LORD.

[7]"Come, Zion! Escape, you who live in Daughter Babylon!" [8]For this is what the LORD Almighty says: "After the Glorious One has sent me against the nations that have plundered you — for whoever touches you touches the apple of his eye — [9]I will surely raise my hand against them so that their slaves will plunder them.[c] Then you will know that the LORD Almighty has sent me.

[10]"Shout and be glad, Daughter Zion. For I am coming, and I will live among you," declares the LORD. [11]"Many nations will be joined with the LORD in that day and will become my people. I will live among you and you will know that the LORD Almighty has sent me to you. [12]The LORD will inherit Judah as his portion in the holy land and will again choose Jerusalem. [13]Be still before the LORD, all mankind, because he has roused himself from his holy dwelling."

Clean Garments for the High Priest

3 Then he showed me Joshua the high priest standing before the angel of the LORD, and Satan[d] standing at his right side to accuse him. [2]The LORD said to Satan, "The LORD rebuke you, Satan! The LORD, who has chosen Jerusalem, rebuke you! Is not this man a burning stick snatched from the fire?"

---

[a] 21 In Hebrew texts 1:18-21 is numbered 2:1-4.   [b] In Hebrew texts 2:1-13 is numbered 2:5-17.   [c] 8,9 Or says after . . . eye: [9]"I . . . plunder them."   [d] 1 Hebrew satan means adversary.

The Law of Connection: Encouragement Is the Oxygen of the Soul

Zechariah 2:3–13

Through a vision, Zechariah tries to encourage the people concerning their future. God plans to gather them again and expand their population. God promises to bless his people in the following areas:

1. **More people (v. 4)**

2. **More livestock (v. 4)**

3. **Divine protection (v. 5)**

4. **Deliverance from enemies (v. 9)**

5. **Conversions of other ethnic groups (v. 11)**

6. **The return of the favor of God on his people (v. 12)**

Leaders know that encouragement is the oxygen of the soul. Notice that Zechariah's encouragement was: 1. specific; 2. personal; 3. public; 4. detailed; 5. hopeful; 6. sincere; and 7. centered around results only God could pull off. Leaders who encourage always draw more from their people than those who don't.

³Now Joshua was dressed in filthy clothes as he stood before the angel. ⁴The angel said to those who were standing before him, "Take off his filthy clothes."

Then he said to Joshua, "See, I have taken away your sin, and I will put fine garments on you."

⁵Then I said, "Put a clean turban on his head." So they put a clean turban on his head and clothed him, while the angel of the LORD stood by.

⁶The angel of the LORD gave this charge to Joshua: ⁷"This is what the LORD Almighty says: 'If you will walk in obedience to me and keep my requirements, then you will govern my house and have charge of my courts, and I will give you a place among these standing here.

⁸"'Listen, High Priest Joshua, you and your associates seated before you, who are men symbolic of things to come: I am going to bring my servant, the Branch. ⁹See, the stone I have set in front of Joshua! There are seven eyes[a] on that one stone, and I will engrave an inscription on it,' says the LORD Almighty, 'and I will remove the sin of this land in a single day.

¹⁰"'In that day each of you will invite your neighbor to sit under your vine and fig tree,' declares the LORD Almighty."

The Gold Lampstand and the Two Olive Trees

4 Then the angel who talked with me returned and woke me up, like someone awakened from sleep. ²He asked me, "What do you see?"

I answered, "I see a solid gold lampstand with a bowl at the top and seven lamps on it, with seven channels to the lamps. ³Also there are two olive trees by it, one on the right of the bowl and the other on its left."

⁴I asked the angel who talked with me, "What are these, my lord?"

⁵He answered, "Do you not know what these are?"

"No, my lord," I replied.

⁶So he said to me, "This is the word of the LORD to Zerubbabel: 'Not by might nor by power, but by my Spirit,' says the LORD Almighty.

⁷"What are you, mighty mountain? Before Zerubbabel you will become level ground. Then he will bring out the capstone to shouts of 'God bless it! God bless it!'"

⁸Then the word of the LORD came to me: ⁹"The hands of Zerubbabel have laid the foundation of this temple; his hands will also complete it. Then you will know that the LORD Almighty has sent me to you.

¹⁰"Who dares despise the day of small things,

---

[a] 9 Or facets

Vision: People Are Energized by a Picture of a Better Tomorrow

Zechariah 3:1–10

Vision is an essential part of healthy leadership. Good leaders feel moved by God-given dreams and visions regarding the future. Zechariah illustrates the power of vision by describing eight visions in the first six chapters of his book:

1. **The vision of the horses (1:7–17)**

2. **The vision of the horns and craftsmen (1:18–21)**

3. **The vision of the measure (2:1–13)**

4. **The vision of Joshua (3:1–10)**

5. **The vision of the lampstand and olive trees (4:1–14)**

6. **The vision of the flying scroll (5:1–4)**

7. **The vision of the basket (5:5–11)**

8. **The vision of the chariots and horses (6:1–8)**

When was the last time you were moved by a God-given vision? Is your leadership driven by the power of a vision? How have you communicated your vision to others?

The God Factor: Leaders Must Lean on Someone Bigger

Zechariah 4:6–9

God reminds the people through Zechariah that they would succeed, not because of their own might and power, but because of his Spirit. *He* would be the Source of their victory.

Secure leaders do not feel put off by this truth; they aren't interested in monopolizing the credit. They welcome God's intervention and direct their followers to seek it. Every great leader yearns for God's partnership. We are wise when, from the beginning, we welcome God's direction and strength as we enter a new project. Consider what Zechariah wants to teach us:

1. **Great works are done by God's divine hands (v. 6).**

2. **The foundation of these works are human; the Lord works through people (v. 9).**

3. **Great works are done by God's Spirit, through us, to glorify him (v. 9).**

since the seven eyes of the LORD that range throughout the earth will rejoice when they see the chosen capstone*a* in the hand of Zerubbabel?"

[11] Then I asked the angel, "What are these two olive trees on the right and the left of the lampstand?"

[12] Again I asked him, "What are these two olive branches beside the two gold pipes that pour out golden oil?"

[13] He replied, "Do you not know what these are?"

"No, my lord," I said.

[14] So he said, "These are the two who are anointed to*b* serve the Lord of all the earth."

The Flying Scroll

5 I looked again, and there before me was a flying scroll.

[2] He asked me, "What do you see?"

I answered, "I see a flying scroll, twenty cubits long and ten cubits wide.*c*"

[3] And he said, "This is the curse that is going out over the whole land; for according to what it says on one side, every thief will be banished, and according to what it says on the other, everyone who swears falsely will be banished. [4] The LORD Almighty declares, 'I will send it out, and it will enter the house of the thief and the house of anyone who swears falsely by my name. It will remain in that house and destroy it completely, both its timbers and its stones.'"

The Woman in a Basket

[5] Then the angel who was speaking to me came forward and said to me, "Look up and see what is appearing."

[6] I asked, "What is it?"

He replied, "It is a basket." And he added, "This is the iniquity*d* of the people throughout the land."

[7] Then the cover of lead was raised, and there in the basket sat a woman! [8] He said, "This is wickedness," and he pushed her back into the basket and pushed its lead cover down on it.

[9] Then I looked up — and there before me were two women, with the wind in their wings! They had wings like those of a stork, and they lifted up the basket between heaven and earth.

[10] "Where are they taking the basket?" I asked the angel who was speaking to me.

[11] He replied, "To the country of Babylonia*e* to build a house for it. When the house is ready, the basket will be set there in its place."

Four Chariots

6 I looked up again, and there before me were four chariots coming out from between two mountains — mountains of bronze. [2] The first chariot had red horses, the second black, [3] the third white, and the fourth dappled — all of them powerful. [4] I asked the angel who was speaking to me, "What are these, my lord?"

[5] The angel answered me, "These are the four spirits*f* of heaven, going out from standing in the presence of the Lord of the whole world. [6] The one with the black horses is going toward the north country, the one with the white horses toward the west,*g* and the one with the dappled horses toward the south."

[7] When the powerful horses went out, they were straining to go throughout the earth. And he said, "Go throughout the earth!" So they went throughout the earth.

[8] Then he called to me, "Look, those going

---

a 10 Or *the plumb line*   *b* 14 Or *two who bring oil and*
c 2 That is, about 30 feet long and 15 feet wide or about 9 meters long and 4.5 meters wide   *d* 6 Or *appearance*   *e* 11 Hebrew *Shinar*   *f* 5 Or *winds*   *g* 6 Or *horses after them*

The Power of a Picture: We Do on the Outside What We Picture Inside

Zechariah 5:1–11

Zechariah knew how to paint vivid pictures in the minds of his people. He did so because he knew people think in images. In chapter five, he describes a vision of a flying scroll declaring a curse on everyone who steals or swears. Then he tells of another vision concerning a basket. Two women flew, carrying it through the air to Shinar, where a "house" would be built for it.

These kinds of portraits capture our imaginations and make God's thoughts memorable. Because the prophet's chief concern was to prepare the land for the coming Messiah, he relayed several images about Christ. Zechariah foretold of Christ more than any other Old Testament prophet. Consider how he did it:

Christ Is Seen As:

1. **Servant and Branch (3:8)**

2. **Priest (6:13)**

3. **Just and Lowly King (9:9)**

4. **Shepherd (9:16; 13:7)**

5. **Firstborn Son (12:10)**

6. **Fountain (13:1)**

How do you communicate vision? Do people remember your words? Do you paint pictures inside of them?

toward the north country have given my Spirit*a* rest in the land of the north."

A Crown for Joshua

⁹The word of the LORD came to me: ¹⁰"Take silver and gold from the exiles Heldai, Tobijah and Jedaiah, who have arrived from Babylon. Go the same day to the house of Josiah son of Zephaniah. ¹¹Take the silver and gold and make a crown, and set it on the head of the high priest, Joshua son of Jozadak.*b* ¹²Tell him this is what the LORD Almighty says: 'Here is the man whose name is the Branch, and he will branch out from his place and build the temple of the LORD. ¹³It is he who will build the temple of the LORD, and he will be clothed with majesty and will sit and rule on his throne. And he*c* will be a priest on his throne. And there will be harmony between the two.' ¹⁴The crown will be given to Heldai,*d* Tobijah, Jedaiah and Hen*e* son of Zephaniah as a memorial in the temple of the LORD. ¹⁵Those who are far away will come and help to build the temple of the LORD, and you will know that the LORD Almighty has sent me to you. This will happen if you diligently obey the LORD your God."

Justice and Mercy, Not Fasting

7 In the fourth year of King Darius, the word of the LORD came to Zechariah on the fourth day of the ninth month, the month of Kislev. ²The people of Bethel had sent Sharezer and Regem-Melek, together with their men, to entreat the LORD ³by asking the priests of the house of the LORD Almighty and the prophets, "Should I mourn and fast in the fifth month, as I have done for so many years?"

⁴Then the word of the LORD Almighty came to me: ⁵"Ask all the people of the land and the priests, 'When you fasted and mourned in the fifth and seventh months for the past seventy years, was it really for me that you fasted? ⁶And when you were eating and drinking, were you not just feasting for yourselves? ⁷Are these not the words the LORD proclaimed through the earlier prophets when Jerusalem and its surrounding towns were at rest and prosperous, and the Negev and the western foothills were settled?'"

⁸And the word of the LORD came again to

a 8 Or *spirit*   *b* 11 Hebrew *Jehozadak*, a variant of *Jozadak*
c 13 Or *there*   *d* 14 Syriac; Hebrew *Helem*   *e* 14 Or *and the gracious one, the*

Zechariah: [9]"This is what the LORD Almighty said: 'Administer true justice; show mercy and compassion to one another. [10]Do not oppress the widow or the fatherless, the foreigner or the poor. Do not plot evil against each other.'

[11]"But they refused to pay attention; stubbornly they turned their backs and covered their ears. [12]They made their hearts as hard as flint and would not listen to the law or to the words that the LORD Almighty had sent by his Spirit through the earlier prophets. So the LORD Almighty was very angry.

[13]"'When I called, they did not listen; so when they called, I would not listen,' says the LORD Almighty. [14]'I scattered them with a whirlwind among all the nations, where they were strangers. The land they left behind them was so desolate that no one traveled through it. This is how they made the pleasant land desolate.'"

The LORD Promises to Bless Jerusalem

8 The word of the LORD Almighty came to me.

[2]This is what the LORD Almighty says: "I am very jealous for Zion; I am burning with jealousy for her."

[3]This is what the LORD says: "I will return to Zion and dwell in Jerusalem. Then Jerusalem will be called the Faithful City, and the mountain of the LORD Almighty will be called the Holy Mountain."

[4]This is what the LORD Almighty says: "Once again men and women of ripe old age will sit in the streets of Jerusalem, each of them with cane in hand because of their age. [5]The city streets will be filled with boys and girls playing there."

[6]This is what the LORD Almighty says: "It may seem marvelous to the remnant of this people at that time, but will it seem marvelous to me?" declares the LORD Almighty.

[7]This is what the LORD Almighty says: "I will save my people from the countries of the east and the west. [8]I will bring them back to live in Jerusalem; they will be my people, and I will be faithful and righteous to them as their God."

[9]This is what the LORD Almighty says: "Now hear these words, 'Let your hands be strong so

---

Discernment: Zechariah Knew the Issue Was Justice, Not Fasting

Zechariah 7:1–10

God questions the motives behind our behavior. While the Jews had fasted and feasted at appropriate times, Zechariah declared their spiritual rituals meant little unless accompanied by justice. When leaders discern people and relationships, they get a head start in providing relevant help to those who need it.

Communication: Without It, the Leader Travels Alone

Zechariah 8:1–8

Israel struggled morally and needed immediate discipline during the dark days of Zechariah's ministry. Yet before the end of his prophecy, Zechariah offers the hope of a better tomorrow, even if in the distant future. He gives the people a specific hope, just as in Zechariah 3:4–5, where he promises Joshua would be cleansed, clothed and crowned.

Successful leaders know how to empower their people through effective communication. They also know what to communicate that will encourage their people. Note the clear distinctions:

Poor Communicators Offer:	Good Communicators Offer:
1. *Hoops* People grow discouraged by all they must do to "make progress."	1. *Hope* People are encouraged by a picture of a better and brighter tomorrow.
2. *Hype* People may get excited, but they have nothing tangible to grasp and apply when it's over.	2. *Help* People receive practical help as the leader offers steps to take.

that the temple may be built.' This is also what the prophets said who were present when the foundation was laid for the house of the LORD Almighty. ¹⁰Before that time there were no wages for people or hire for animals. No one could go about their business safely because of their enemies, since I had turned everyone against their neighbor. ¹¹But now I will not deal with the remnant of this people as I did in the past," declares the LORD Almighty.

¹²"The seed will grow well, the vine will yield its fruit, the ground will produce its crops, and the heavens will drop their dew. I will give all these things as an inheritance to the remnant of this people. ¹³Just as you, Judah and Israel, have been a curse*a* among the nations, so I will save you, and you will be a blessing.*b* Do not be afraid, but let your hands be strong."

¹⁴This is what the LORD Almighty says: "Just as I had determined to bring disaster on you and showed no pity when your ancestors angered me," says the LORD Almighty, ¹⁵"so now I have determined to do good again to Jerusalem and Judah. Do not be afraid. ¹⁶These are the things you are to do: Speak the truth to each other, and render true and sound judgment in your courts; ¹⁷do not plot evil against each other, and do not love to swear falsely. I hate all this," declares the LORD.

¹⁸The word of the LORD Almighty came to me. ¹⁹This is what the LORD Almighty says: "The fasts of the fourth, fifth, seventh and tenth months will become joyful and glad occasions and happy festivals for Judah. Therefore love truth and peace."

²⁰This is what the LORD Almighty says: "Many peoples and the inhabitants of many cities will yet come, ²¹and the inhabitants of one city will go to another and say, 'Let us go at once to entreat the LORD and seek the LORD Almighty. I myself am going.' ²²And many peoples and powerful nations will come to Jerusalem to seek the LORD Almighty and to entreat him."

²³This is what the LORD Almighty says: "In those days ten people from all languages and nations will take firm hold of one Jew by the hem of his robe and say, 'Let us go with you, because we have heard that God is with you.'"

Judgment on Israel's Enemies

9 A prophecy:

The word of the LORD is against the land of Hadrak
   and will come to rest on Damascus—

for the eyes of all people and all the tribes of Israel
   are on the LORD—*c*
²and on Hamath too, which borders on it,
   and on Tyre and Sidon, though they are
      very skillful.
³Tyre has built herself a stronghold;
   she has heaped up silver like dust,
   and gold like the dirt of the streets.
⁴But the Lord will take away her possessions
   and destroy her power on the sea,
   and she will be consumed by fire.
⁵Ashkelon will see it and fear;
   Gaza will writhe in agony,
   and Ekron too, for her hope will wither.
  Gaza will lose her king
   and Ashkelon will be deserted.
⁶A mongrel people will occupy Ashdod,
   and I will put an end to the pride of the
      Philistines.
⁷I will take the blood from their mouths,
   the forbidden food from between their
      teeth.
  Those who are left will belong to our God
   and become a clan in Judah,
   and Ekron will be like the Jebusites.
⁸But I will encamp at my temple
   to guard it against marauding forces.
  Never again will an oppressor overrun my
      people,
   for now I am keeping watch.

The Coming of Zion's King

⁹Rejoice greatly, Daughter Zion!
   Shout, Daughter Jerusalem!
See, your king comes to you,
   righteous and victorious,
lowly and riding on a donkey,
   on a colt, the foal of a donkey.
¹⁰I will take away the chariots from Ephraim
   and the warhorses from Jerusalem,
   and the battle bow will be broken.
He will proclaim peace to the nations.
   His rule will extend from sea to sea
   and from the River*d* to the ends of the earth.
¹¹As for you, because of the blood of my
      covenant with you,
   I will free your prisoners from the
      waterless pit.

---

a 13 That is, your name has been used in cursing (see Jer. 29:22); or, you have been regarded as under a curse.   *b* 13 Or *and your name will be used in blessings* (see Gen. 48:20); or *and you will be seen as blessed*   *c* 1 Or *Damascus. / For the eye of the* LORD *is on all people, / as well as on the tribes of Israel,*   *d* 10 That is, the Euphrates

¹²Return to your fortress, you prisoners of
hope;
    even now I announce that I will restore
        twice as much to you.
¹³I will bend Judah as I bend my bow
    and fill it with Ephraim.
I will rouse your sons, Zion,
    against your sons, Greece,
    and make you like a warrior's sword.

The LORD Will Appear

¹⁴Then the LORD will appear over them;
    his arrow will flash like lightning.
The Sovereign LORD will sound the
        trumpet;
    he will march in the storms of the south,
¹⁵   and the LORD Almighty will shield them.
They will destroy
    and overcome with slingstones.
They will drink and roar as with wine;
    they will be full like a bowl
    used for sprinkling^a the corners of the
        altar.
¹⁶The LORD their God will save his people on
        that day
    as a shepherd saves his flock.
They will sparkle in his land
    like jewels in a crown.
¹⁷How attractive and beautiful they will be!
    Grain will make the young men thrive,
    and new wine the young women.

The LORD Will Care for Judah

10 Ask the LORD for rain in the springtime;
    it is the LORD who sends the
        thunderstorms.
He gives showers of rain to all people,
    and plants of the field to everyone.
²The idols speak deceitfully,
    diviners see visions that lie;
they tell dreams that are false,
    they give comfort in vain.
Therefore the people wander like sheep
    oppressed for lack of a shepherd.

³"My anger burns against the shepherds,
    and I will punish the leaders;
for the LORD Almighty will care
    for his flock, the people of Judah,
    and make them like a proud horse in
        battle.
⁴From Judah will come the cornerstone,
    from him the tent peg,
from him the battle bow,
    from him every ruler.

Commitment: It Comes Before Authority and Responsibility

Zechariah 10:1–3

Few things present more danger than an uncommitted leader. While followers may often remain uncommitted, they usually wield limited influence. Leaders, however, impact everyone who follows. When they remain uncommitted, they not only fail their organizations and God, but they model failure for others.

---

⁵Together they^b will be like warriors in battle
    trampling their enemy into the mud of the
        streets.
They will fight because the LORD is with
        them,
    and they will put the enemy horsemen to
        shame.

⁶"I will strengthen Judah
    and save the tribes of Joseph.
I will restore them
    because I have compassion on them.
They will be as though
    I had not rejected them,
for I am the LORD their God
    and I will answer them.
⁷The Ephraimites will become like warriors,
    and their hearts will be glad as with wine.
Their children will see it and be joyful;
    their hearts will rejoice in the LORD.
⁸I will signal for them
    and gather them in.
Surely I will redeem them;
    they will be as numerous as before.
⁹Though I scatter them among the peoples,
    yet in distant lands they will remember me.
They and their children will survive,
    and they will return.
¹⁰I will bring them back from Egypt
    and gather them from Assyria.
I will bring them to Gilead and Lebanon,
    and there will not be room enough for
        them.
¹¹They will pass through the sea of trouble;
    the surging sea will be subdued
    and all the depths of the Nile will dry up.

---

^a 15 Or bowl, / like   ^b 4,5 Or ruler, all of them together. / ⁵They

Assyria's pride will be brought down
  and Egypt's scepter will pass away.
¹²I will strengthen them in the LORD
  and in his name they will live securely,"
                        declares the LORD.

11

Open your doors, Lebanon,
  so that fire may devour your cedars!
²Wail, you juniper, for the cedar has fallen;
  the stately trees are ruined!
Wail, oaks of Bashan;
  the dense forest has been cut down!
³Listen to the wail of the shepherds;
  their rich pastures are destroyed!
Listen to the roar of the lions;
  the lush thicket of the Jordan is ruined!

Two Shepherds

⁴This is what the LORD my God says: "Shepherd the flock marked for slaughter. ⁵Their buyers slaughter them and go unpunished. Those who sell them say, 'Praise the LORD, I am rich!' Their own shepherds do not spare them. ⁶For I will no longer have pity on the people of the land," declares the LORD. "I will give everyone into the hands of their neighbors and their king. They will devastate the land, and I will not rescue anyone from their hands."

⁷So I shepherded the flock marked for slaughter, particularly the oppressed of the flock. Then I took two staffs and called one Favor and the other Union, and I shepherded the flock. ⁸In one month I got rid of the three shepherds.

The flock detested me, and I grew weary of them ⁹and said, "I will not be your shepherd. Let the dying die, and the perishing perish. Let those who are left eat one another's flesh."

¹⁰Then I took my staff called Favor and broke it, revoking the covenant I had made with all the nations. ¹¹It was revoked on that day, and so the oppressed of the flock who were watching me knew it was the word of the LORD.

¹²I told them, "If you think it best, give me my pay; but if not, keep it." So they paid me thirty pieces of silver.

¹³And the LORD said to me, "Throw it to the potter"—the handsome price at which they valued me! So I took the thirty pieces of silver and threw them to the potter at the house of the LORD.

¹⁴Then I broke my second staff called Union, breaking the family bond between Judah and Israel.

¹⁵Then the LORD said to me, "Take again the equipment of a foolish shepherd. ¹⁶For I am going to raise up a shepherd over the land who will not care for the lost, or seek the young, or heal the injured, or feed the healthy, but will eat the meat of the choice sheep, tearing off their hooves.

¹⁷"Woe to the worthless shepherd,
  who deserts the flock!
May the sword strike his arm and his right
    eye!
May his arm be completely withered,
  his right eye totally blinded!"

Jerusalem's Enemies to Be Destroyed

12

A prophecy: The word of the LORD concerning Israel.

The LORD, who stretches out the heavens, who lays the foundation of the earth, and who forms the human spirit within a person, declares: ²"I am going to make Jerusalem a cup that sends all the surrounding peoples reeling. Judah will be besieged as well as Jerusalem. ³On that day, when all the nations of the earth are gathered against her, I will make Jerusalem an immovable rock for all the nations. All who try to move it will injure themselves. ⁴On that day I will strike every horse with panic and its rider with madness," declares the LORD. "I will keep a watchful eye over Judah, but I will blind all the horses of the nations. ⁵Then the clans of Judah will say in their hearts, 'The people of Jerusalem are strong, because the LORD Almighty is their God.'

⁶"On that day I will make the clans of Judah like a firepot in a woodpile, like a flaming torch among sheaves. They will consume all the surrounding peoples right and left, but Jerusalem will remain intact in her place.

⁷"The LORD will save the dwellings of Judah first, so that the honor of the house of David and of Jerusalem's inhabitants may not be greater than that of Judah. ⁸On that day the LORD will shield those who live in Jerusalem, so that the feeblest among them will be like David, and the house of David will be like God, like the angel of the LORD going before them. ⁹On that day I will set out to destroy all the nations that attack Jerusalem.

Mourning for the One They Pierced

¹⁰"And I will pour out on the house of David and the inhabitants of Jerusalem a spirit[a] of grace and supplication. They will look on[b] me,

---

a 10 Or *the Spirit*   *b 10* Or *to*

the one they have pierced, and they will mourn for him as one mourns for an only child, and grieve bitterly for him as one grieves for a first-born son. ¹¹On that day the weeping in Jerusalem will be as great as the weeping of Hadad Rimmon in the plain of Megiddo. ¹²The land will mourn, each clan by itself, with their wives by themselves: the clan of the house of David and their wives, the clan of the house of Nathan and their wives, ¹³the clan of the house of Levi and their wives, the clan of Shimei and their wives, ¹⁴and all the rest of the clans and their wives.

Cleansing From Sin

13 "On that day a fountain will be opened to the house of David and the inhabitants of Jerusalem, to cleanse them from sin and impurity.

²"On that day, I will banish the names of the idols from the land, and they will be remembered no more," declares the LORD Almighty. "I will remove both the prophets and the spirit of impurity from the land. ³And if anyone still prophesies, their father and mother, to whom they were born, will say to them, 'You must die, because you have told lies in the LORD's name.' Then their own parents will stab the one who prophesies.

⁴"On that day every prophet will be ashamed of their prophetic vision. They will not put on a prophet's garment of hair in order to deceive. ⁵Each will say, 'I am not a prophet. I am a farmer; the land has been my livelihood since my youth.ᵃ' ⁶If someone asks, 'What are these wounds on your bodyᵇ?' they will answer, 'The wounds I was given at the house of my friends.'

The Shepherd Struck, the Sheep Scattered

⁷"Awake, sword, against my shepherd,
    against the man who is close to me!"
        declares the LORD Almighty.
"Strike the shepherd,
    and the sheep will be scattered,
    and I will turn my hand against the little
        ones.
⁸In the whole land," declares the LORD,
    "two-thirds will be struck down and
        perish;
    yet one-third will be left in it.
⁹This third I will put into the fire;
    I will refine them like silver
    and test them like gold.
They will call on my name
    and I will answer them;

I will say, 'They are my people,'
    and they will say, 'The LORD is our God.'"

The LORD Comes and Reigns

14 A day of the LORD is coming, Jerusalem, when your possessions will be plundered and divided up within your very walls. ²I will gather all the nations to Jerusalem to fight against it; the city will be captured, the houses ransacked, and the women raped. Half of the city will go into exile, but the rest of the people will not be taken from the city. ³Then the LORD will go out and fight against those nations, as he fights on a day of battle. ⁴On that day his feet will stand on the Mount of Olives, east of Jerusalem, and the Mount of Olives will be split in two from east to west, forming a great valley, with half of the mountain moving north and half moving south. ⁵You will flee by my mountain valley, for it will extend to Azel. You will flee as you fled from the earthquakeᶜ in the days of Uzziah king of Judah. Then the LORD my God will come, and all the holy ones with him.

⁶On that day there will be neither sunlight nor cold, frosty darkness. ⁷It will be a unique day — a day known only to the LORD — with no distinction between day and night. When evening comes, there will be light.

⁸On that day living water will flow out from Jerusalem, half of it east to the Dead Sea and half of it west to the Mediterranean Sea, in summer and in winter.

⁹The LORD will be king over the whole earth. On that day there will be one LORD, and his name the only name.

¹⁰The whole land, from Geba to Rimmon, south of Jerusalem, will become like the Arabah. But Jerusalem will be raised up high from the Benjamin Gate to the site of the First Gate, to the Corner Gate, and from the Tower of Hananel to the royal winepresses, and will remain in its place. ¹¹It will be inhabited; never again will it be destroyed. Jerusalem will be secure.

¹²This is the plague with which the LORD will strike all the nations that fought against Jerusalem: Their flesh will rot while they are still standing on their feet, their eyes will rot in their sockets, and their tongues will rot in their mouths. ¹³On that day people will be stricken by the LORD with great panic. They will seize each

---

ᵃ 5 Or farmer; a man sold me in my youth   ᵇ 6 Or wounds between your hands   ᶜ 5 Or ⁵My mountain valley will be blocked and will extend to Azel. It will be blocked as it was blocked because of the earthquake

other by the hand and attack one another. [14]Judah too will fight at Jerusalem. The wealth of all the surrounding nations will be collected — great quantities of gold and silver and clothing. [15]A similar plague will strike the horses and mules, the camels and donkeys, and all the animals in those camps.

[16]Then the survivors from all the nations that have attacked Jerusalem will go up year after year to worship the King, the LORD Almighty, and to celebrate the Festival of Tabernacles. [17]If any of the peoples of the earth do not go up to Jerusalem to worship the King, the LORD Almighty, they will have no rain. [18]If the Egyptian people do not go up and take part, they will have no rain. The LORD[a] will bring on them the plague he inflicts on the nations that do not go up to celebrate the Festival of Tabernacles. [19]This will be the punishment of Egypt and the punishment of all the nations that do not go up to celebrate the Festival of Tabernacles.

[20]On that day HOLY TO THE LORD will be inscribed on the bells of the horses, and the cooking pots in the LORD's house will be like the sacred bowls in front of the altar. [21]Every pot in Jerusalem and Judah will be holy to the LORD Almighty, and all who come to sacrifice will take some of the pots and cook in them. And on that day there will no longer be a Canaanite[b] in the house of the LORD Almighty.

[a] 18 Or part, then the LORD   [b] 21 Or merchant

The Law of Victory: Leaders Know What It Takes to Win in the End

Zechariah 14:16–21

It is appropriate that the final chapter of Zechariah declares God's ultimate victory. No one practices the Law of Victory quite like the Lord himself! In this case, God predicts victory and gives the people direction on how to live, motivation to persist, and hope for a better tomorrow.

Introduction to
MALACHI

Malachi, the final book of the Old Testament, was written by a prophet who served during Nehemiah's day—a period in the Jewish people's history characterized by corrupt priests, wicked practices, compromising leaders and a false sense of security in their status with God. Malachi calls God's people to authenticity. More than that, however, he calls God's leaders to lead from relationship rather than mere position.

The name Malachi means "Messenger of Yahweh"— and no further messenger from God came until John the Baptist arrived centuries later in the New Testament era. Malachi uses an easy-to-follow question-and-answer format to address specific issues such as divorce, infidelity, mixed marriages, hypocrisy, tithing, false worship, complacency and arrogance. This divine dialogue contrasts God's perspective with the people's perspective. It illustrates not only the difference between the eternal God and finite man, but serves as a metaphor for the gap between the perspective of a leader and a follower. The spiritual leader maintains the eternal and ultimate viewpoint, while the follower may see only the immediate and the temporal.

The book supplies leaders with a wonderful case study in communication. Without communication, we travel alone. Malachi uses a heartfelt appeal featuring not only passion for repentance, but also compassion and understanding for the people's point of view. Six times Malachi does the "point-counterpoint" debate, where he speaks for the listener and identifies their apathetic attitude. He can hear them arguing, "Oh, come now—it's not that bad!" In response he lays out an explicit, persuasive argument for why it really *is* that bad!

God's Role in Malachi
God uses the book of Malachi to communicate to his people that while he understands their vantage point, he does not change his own or grade on a curve. God uses Malachi's series of questions and answers to expose the people's underlying motives, their negative attitudes and their selfish ways. The book concerns itself with the heart of God's followers. These people had become consumed with outward appearances rather than inward purity and submission. God wants obedience from our hearts, not just our hands. His leadership raises the bar once again on what it means to follow with our whole heart.

Leaders in Malachi
Malachi, Persian governors

Other People of Influence in Malachi
The priests and religious leaders

Lessons in Leadership
- Effective leaders seek to understand before they seek to be understood.
- Great leaders are great communicators.
- Complete obedience involves inward submission, not mere outward service.
- Strong leaders raise the bar and challenge people to reach it.

Four hundred years of divine silence follow the book of Malachi, as God refuses to speak to his people through a prophet. Malachi becomes his last word until the new covenant arrives, calling for authentic faith and genuine leadership integrity from priests and governors alike.

- Effective leaders know what they stand for and what they won't stand for.
- Healthy leaders compromise on methods but never on principles.

LEADERSHIP HIGHLIGHTS IN MALACHI

1

A prophecy: The word of the LORD to Israel through Malachi.[a]

Israel Doubts God's Love

2"I have loved you," says the LORD.

"But you ask, 'How have you loved us?'

"Was not Esau Jacob's brother?" declares the LORD. "Yet I have loved Jacob, 3but Esau I have hated, and I have turned his hill country into a wasteland and left his inheritance to the desert jackals."

4Edom may say, "Though we have been crushed, we will rebuild the ruins."

But this is what the LORD Almighty says: "They may build, but I will demolish. They will be called the Wicked Land, a people always under the wrath of the LORD. 5You will see it with your own eyes and say, 'Great is the LORD— even beyond the borders of Israel!'

Breaking Covenant Through Blemished Sacrifices

6"A son honors his father, and a slave his master. If I am a father, where is the honor due me?

If I am a master, where is the respect due me?" says the LORD Almighty.

"It is you priests who show contempt for my name.

"But you ask, 'How have we shown contempt for your name?'

7"By offering defiled food on my altar.

"But you ask, 'How have we defiled you?'

"By saying that the LORD's table is contemptible. 8When you offer blind animals for sacrifice, is that not wrong? When you sacrifice lame or diseased animals, is that not wrong? Try offering them to your governor! Would he be pleased with you? Would he accept you?" says the LORD Almighty.

9"Now plead with God to be gracious to us. With such offerings from your hands, will he accept you?"—says the LORD Almighty.

10"Oh, that one of you would shut the temple doors, so that you would not light useless fires

---

[a] 1 Malachi means my messenger.

The Law of Connection: Malachi Touches the Heart First

Malachi 1:2–14

Malachi begins his book by practicing the Law of Connection. Prior to any declarations of judgment, Malachi speaks words of compassion, straight from the heart of God (Mal 1:2–5). The Lord reviews how much he loves the people, how he has chosen them and privileged them above the Edomites. Only then does he begin to address their need for improvement (1:6–14). He makes both his love and his correction very specific:

Affirmation	Admonition
1. I have loved you (v. 2).	1. Where is my honor? (v. 6).
2. I have chosen you (v. 2).	2. You defiled my altar (vv. 7–8).
3. I will defeat your enemies (vv. 3–4).	3. You act like my enemy (v. 10).
4. I will be magnified worldwide (v. 5).	4. You've profaned my name (v. 12).

Effective leaders connect before they correct. They earn their right to change the life of their followers by first affirming their identity and relationship to the leader. How do we do this? Consider the following simple process:

1. Look for the good first.

2. Identify what you can affirm.

3. Be specific about your encouragement.

4. Note what needs to be changed.

5. Challenge the person to grow through change.

6. Tell them why the change is important.

7. Express confidence that they can do it.

Excellence: Leaders Don't Just Set Goals, They Set Standards

Malachi 1:7–8

If we give our best for our people, how much more should we pursue excellence with God! Good leaders don't settle for less than excellence. They don't merely set goals, they set standards that raise the bar for everyone. Malachi insists that these standards begin with our spiritual life.

on my altar! I am not pleased with you," says the LORD Almighty, "and I will accept no offering from your hands. ¹¹My name will be great among the nations, from where the sun rises to where it sets. In every place incense and pure offerings will be brought to me, because my name will be great among the nations," says the LORD Almighty.

¹²"But you profane it by saying, 'The Lord's table is defiled,' and, 'Its food is contemptible.' ¹³And you say, 'What a burden!' and you sniff at it contemptuously," says the LORD Almighty.

"When you bring injured, lame or diseased animals and offer them as sacrifices, should I accept them from your hands?" says the LORD. ¹⁴"Cursed is the cheat who has an acceptable

male in his flock and vows to give it, but then sacrifices a blemished animal to the Lord. For I am a great king," says the LORD Almighty, "and my name is to be feared among the nations.

Additional Warning to the Priests

2 "And now, you priests, this warning is for you. ²If you do not listen, and if you do not resolve to honor my name," says the LORD Almighty, "I will send a curse on you, and I will curse your blessings. Yes, I have already cursed them, because you have not resolved to honor me.

³"Because of you I will rebuke your descendants[a]; I will smear on your faces the dung from your festival sacrifices, and you will be carried off with it. ⁴And you will know that I have sent you this warning so that my covenant with Levi may continue," says the LORD Almighty. ⁵"My covenant was with him, a covenant of life and peace, and I gave them to him; this called for reverence and he revered me and stood in awe of my name. ⁶True instruction was in his mouth and nothing false was found on his lips. He walked with me in peace and uprightness, and turned many from sin.

⁷"For the lips of a priest ought to preserve knowledge, because he is the messenger of the LORD Almighty and people seek instruction from his mouth. ⁸But you have turned from the way and by your teaching have caused many to stum-

---

[a] 3 Or will blight your grain

The Law of the Picture: Demonstration Precedes Imitation

Malachi 2:7–9

The priests and other leaders of Malachi's day failed to walk their talk. The second chapter of Malachi brims with accusations against their hypocrisy: treachery in the home, profanity in the sanctuary, mixed marriages, rampant divorce, and false teaching (Mal 2:10–17).

God expects leaders to incarnate the life their followers should live. Successful leaders know they must first demonstrate the desired lifestyle. People do what people see. Leaders are models before they are ministers, mentors, or managers.

Notice what happened when Israel's leaders failed to live model lives:

1. **They failed to preserve truth for the people (v. 7).**

2. **They diluted the people's appetite for growth and instruction (v. 7).**

3. **They caused many to stumble due to their poor example (v. 8).**

4. **They corrupted the covenant God made with them (v. 8).**

5. **They lost their credibility (v. 9).**

ble; you have violated the covenant with Levi," says the LORD Almighty. [9]"So I have caused you to be despised and humiliated before all the people, because you have not followed my ways but have shown partiality in matters of the law."

Breaking Covenant Through Divorce

[10]Do we not all have one Father[a]? Did not one God create us? Why do we profane the covenant of our ancestors by being unfaithful to one another?

[11]Judah has been unfaithful. A detestable thing has been committed in Israel and in Jerusalem: Judah has desecrated the sanctuary the LORD loves by marrying women who worship a foreign god. [12]As for the man who does this, whoever he may be, may the LORD remove him from the tents of Jacob[b] — even though he brings an offering to the LORD Almighty.

[13]Another thing you do: You flood the LORD's altar with tears. You weep and wail because he no longer looks with favor on your offerings or accepts them with pleasure from your hands. [14]You ask, "Why?" It is because the LORD is the witness between you and the wife of your youth. You have been unfaithful to her, though she is your partner, the wife of your marriage covenant.

[15]Has not the one God made you? You belong to him in body and spirit. And what does the one God seek? Godly offspring.[c] So be on your guard, and do not be unfaithful to the wife of your youth.

[16]"The man who hates and divorces his wife," says the LORD, the God of Israel, "does violence to the one he should protect,"[d] says the LORD Almighty.

So be on your guard, and do not be unfaithful.

Breaking Covenant Through Injustice

[17]You have wearied the LORD with your words.

"How have we wearied him?" you ask.

By saying, "All who do evil are good in the eyes of the LORD, and he is pleased with them" or "Where is the God of justice?"

3 "I will send my messenger, who will prepare the way before me. Then suddenly the Lord you are seeking will come to his temple; the messenger of the covenant, whom you desire, will come," says the LORD Almighty.

[2]But who can endure the day of his coming? Who can stand when he appears? For he will be like a refiner's fire or a launderer's soap. [3]He will sit as a refiner and purifier of silver; he will

purify the Levites and refine them like gold and silver. Then the LORD will have men who will bring offerings in righteousness, [4]and the offerings of Judah and Jerusalem will be acceptable to the LORD, as in days gone by, as in former years.

[5]"So I will come to put you on trial. I will be quick to testify against sorcerers, adulterers and perjurers, against those who defraud laborers of their wages, who oppress the widows and the fatherless, and deprive the foreigners among you of justice, but do not fear me," says the LORD Almighty.

Breaking Covenant by Withholding Tithes

[6]"I the LORD do not change. So you, the descendants of Jacob, are not destroyed. [7]Ever since the time of your ancestors you have turned away from my decrees and have not kept them. Return to me, and I will return to you," says the LORD Almighty.

"But you ask, 'How are we to return?'

[8]"Will a mere mortal rob God? Yet you rob me.

"But you ask, 'How are we robbing you?'

"In tithes and offerings. [9]You are under a curse — your whole nation — because you are robbing me. [10]Bring the whole tithe into the storehouse, that there may be food in my house. Test me in this," says the LORD Almighty, "and see if I will not throw open the floodgates of heaven and pour out so much blessing that there will not be room enough to store it. [11]I

---

[a] 10 Or father   [b] 12 Or [12]May the LORD remove from the tents of Jacob anyone who gives testimony in behalf of the man who does this   [c] 15 The meaning of the Hebrew for the first part of this verse is uncertain.   [d] 16 Or "I hate divorce," says the LORD, the God of Israel, "because the man who divorces his wife covers his garment with violence,"

Stewardship: Leaders Are Only Stewards of What God Owns

Malachi 3:8–12

We are stewards of what God owns, nothing more. God promises that if we practice good stewardship, he will bless us greatly. But if we disobey, he will allow the devourer to destroy what we produce. Leaders especially must remember that we do not own anything; we only manage God's resources.

will prevent pests from devouring your crops, and the vines in your fields will not drop their fruit before it is ripe," says the LORD Almighty. [12]"Then all the nations will call you blessed, for yours will be a delightful land," says the LORD Almighty.

Israel Speaks Arrogantly Against God

[13]"You have spoken arrogantly against me," says the LORD.

"Yet you ask, 'What have we said against you?'

[14]"You have said, 'It is futile to serve God. What do we gain by carrying out his requirements and going about like mourners before the LORD Almighty? [15]But now we call the arrogant blessed. Certainly evildoers prosper, and even when they put God to the test, they get away with it.'"

The Faithful Remnant

[16]Then those who feared the LORD talked with each other, and the LORD listened and heard. A scroll of remembrance was written in his presence concerning those who feared the LORD and honored his name.

[17]"On the day when I act," says the LORD Almighty, "they will be my treasured possession. I will spare them, just as a father has compassion and spares his son who serves him. [18]And you will again see the distinction between the righteous and the wicked, between those who serve God and those who do not.

Judgment and Covenant Renewal

4 [a] "Surely the day is coming; it will burn like a furnace. All the arrogant and every evildoer will be stubble, and the day that is coming will set them on fire," says the LORD Almighty. "Not a root or a branch will be left to them. [2]But for you who revere my name, the sun of righteousness will rise with healing in its rays. And you will go out and frolic like well-fed calves. [3]Then you will trample on the wicked; they will be ashes under the soles of your feet on the day when I act," says the LORD Almighty.

[4]"Remember the law of my servant Moses, the decrees and laws I gave him at Horeb for all Israel.

[5]"See, I will send the prophet Elijah to you before that great and dreadful day of the LORD comes. [6]He will turn the hearts of the parents to their children, and the hearts of the children to their parents; or else I will come and strike the land with total destruction."

[a] In Hebrew texts 4:1-6 is numbered 3:19-24.

The Law of Timing: God Knows When and How to Move

Malachi 4:5

God is a master at timing. Like any good leader, he knows when to move and how to prepare the people for his moves.

Malachi predicts a day when God will bring justice to everyone and burn away the evil, like chaff burning away from the wheat. God promises to send Elijah the prophet before this terrible day of the Lord. Like so many prophecies, this scripture has two fulfillments. The first came after Jesus was born in Bethlehem; as the Elijah figure, John the Baptist prepared the way. The ultimate fulfillment of this passage will occur in the last days, when God will send another Elijah figure to prepare the way for his second coming.

God practices the Law of Timing, making sure everything is in order when he makes his move. This word from Malachi is the last word God gave before coming in the person of Jesus.

THE NEW TESTAMENT

INTRODUCTION TO MATTHEW

Jesus as the Long-Awaited Messiah

Matthew is the first of four books in the New Testament that depict the Ultimate Leader, Jesus Christ. Matthew describes Jesus as the long-awaited Messiah for the Jews, the fulfillment of so much Old Testament prophecy. Every Jew knew that when the Messiah came, he would right the wrongs in Israel and somehow restore the nation to her rightful place.

Of course, Jesus fulfilled these expectations in a far different manner than what most people expected. He *did* fulfill Old Testament prophecy, but most Jews missed the part about the suffering Messiah (Isa 53). He *did* make things right, but he worked on the spiritual dimension of the nation's life rather than the political aspect. He concerned himself more with cleansing them and making them whole than with helping them gain economic freedom from Rome. He brought about change from the inside out, rather than by some legislative act or military revolution.

Jesus' leadership differs from all others. He doesn't merely reform—he transforms. He knew that if he got the people's spirit right, the rest would follow. Jesus was a uniquely different leader, an "upside-down" leader who reversed the values and conduct of nearly every other leader of his day.

Matthew shows Jesus practicing every one of the 21 Laws of Leadership, incarnating everything that makes for successful, transformational leadership. And this was only the beginning!

Try to read Matthew's stories with fresh eyes. See Jesus not only as a wonderful Savior and Redeemer, but as the greatest Leader who ever walked the earth. When

God's Role in Matthew

This book assumes a unique role among the four Gospels. Matthew wrote to the Jews, who needed to be convinced from Scripture that Jesus was who he claimed to be. Jesus worked not only to ensure that he did indeed fulfill Old Testament prophecies, but that he performed sufficient miracles to demonstrate his compassion and credibility as Messiah. Once God confirmed his word with signs following, the writing came easy.

God guided Matthew to include dozens of Old Testament scriptures, confirming each with an act or statement from Jesus. We see God acting well in advance to map out details and fulfill future prophetic statements.

Leaders in Matthew

Jesus, John the Baptist, Pilate, Herod, the centurion

Other People of Influence in Matthew

The zealots, the twelve disciples, the scribes and Pharisees

Lessons in Leadership

- The fastest way to gain leadership is to solve problems.
- Leaders go where the people are.
- Leaders first instill new values into their team.

you have begun to see him this way, jot down how he led others. Note his unusual style, his unorthodox methods and strategy, his unshakable commitment to his mission and values. What a Leader!

- Leaders never misrepresent their product or service.
- Leaders don't allow rejection to change their opinion of themselves.
- Leaders know they have something the people need.
- Leaders are motivated by a love for people and a desire to serve.
- Leaders are on a mission and never drift from it.

LEADERSHIP HIGHLIGHTS IN MATTHEW

The Genealogy of Jesus the Messiah

1 This is the genealogy[a] of Jesus the Messiah[b] the son of David, the son of Abraham:

[2] Abraham was the father of Isaac,
Isaac the father of Jacob,
Jacob the father of Judah and his brothers,
[3] Judah the father of Perez and Zerah, whose mother was Tamar,
Perez the father of Hezron,
Hezron the father of Ram,
[4] Ram the father of Amminadab,
Amminadab the father of Nahshon,
Nahshon the father of Salmon,
[5] Salmon the father of Boaz, whose mother was Rahab,
Boaz the father of Obed, whose mother was Ruth,
Obed the father of Jesse,
[6] and Jesse the father of King David.

David was the father of Solomon, whose mother had been Uriah's wife,
[7] Solomon the father of Rehoboam,
Rehoboam the father of Abijah,
Abijah the father of Asa,
[8] Asa the father of Jehoshaphat,
Jehoshaphat the father of Jehoram,
Jehoram the father of Uzziah,
[9] Uzziah the father of Jotham,
Jotham the father of Ahaz,
Ahaz the father of Hezekiah,
[10] Hezekiah the father of Manasseh,
Manasseh the father of Amon,
Amon the father of Josiah,
[11] and Josiah the father of Jeconiah[c] and his brothers at the time of the exile to Babylon.

[12] After the exile to Babylon:
Jeconiah was the father of Shealtiel,
Shealtiel the father of Zerubbabel,
[13] Zerubbabel the father of Abihud,
Abihud the father of Eliakim,
Eliakim the father of Azor,
[14] Azor the father of Zadok,
Zadok the father of Akim,
Akim the father of Elihud,
[15] Elihud the father of Eleazar,
Eleazar the father of Matthan,
Matthan the father of Jacob,
[16] and Jacob the father of Joseph, the husband of Mary, and Mary was the mother of Jesus who is called the Messiah.

Planning: God Uses Long-Range Planning to Prepare the World
Matthew 1:1–17

Matthew provides an exhaustive list of Jesus' ancestors, beginning with Abraham. This genealogy demonstrates God's long-range plan to save the human race. He made sure to cover every step and prepare every person to participate in the line of Christ. Effective leaders lay plans with the end in mind.

[17] Thus there were fourteen generations in all from Abraham to David, fourteen from David to the exile to Babylon, and fourteen from the exile to the Messiah.

Joseph Accepts Jesus as His Son

[18] This is how the birth of Jesus the Messiah came about[d]: His mother Mary was pledged to be married to Joseph, but before they came together, she was found to be pregnant through the Holy Spirit. [19] Because Joseph her husband was faithful to the law, and yet[e] did not want to expose her to public disgrace, he had in mind to divorce her quietly.

[20] But after he had considered this, an angel of the Lord appeared to him in a dream and said, "Joseph son of David, do not be afraid to take Mary home as your wife, because what is conceived in her is from the Holy Spirit. [21] She will give birth to a son, and you are to give him the name Jesus,[f] because he will save his people from their sins."

[22] All this took place to fulfill what the Lord had said through the prophet: [23] "The virgin will conceive and give birth to a son, and they will call him Immanuel"[g] (which means "God with us").

[24] When Joseph woke up, he did what the angel of the Lord had commanded him and took Mary home as his wife. [25] But he did not consummate their marriage until she gave birth to a son. And he gave him the name Jesus.

---

[a] 1 Or *is an account of the origin*   [b] 1 Or *Jesus Christ. Messiah* (Hebrew) and *Christ* (Greek) both mean *Anointed One*; also in verse 18.   [c] 11 That is, Jehoiachin; also in verse 12   [d] 18 Or *The origin of Jesus the Messiah was like this*   [e] 19 Or *was a righteous man and*   [f] 21 *Jesus* is the Greek form of *Joshua*, which means *the LORD saves*.   [g] 23 Isaiah 7:14

The Magi Visit the Messiah

2 After Jesus was born in Bethlehem in Judea, during the time of King Herod, Magi[a] from the east came to Jerusalem [2]and asked, "Where is the one who has been born king of the Jews? We saw his star when it rose and have come to worship him."

[3]When King Herod heard this he was disturbed, and all Jerusalem with him. [4]When he had called together all the people's chief priests and teachers of the law, he asked them where the Messiah was to be born. [5]"In Bethlehem in Judea," they replied, "for this is what the prophet has written:

[6]"'But you, Bethlehem, in the land of Judah,
    are by no means least among the rulers of
        Judah;
for out of you will come a ruler
    who will shepherd my people Israel.'[b]"

[7]Then Herod called the Magi secretly and found out from them the exact time the star had appeared. [8]He sent them to Bethlehem and said, "Go and search carefully for the child. As soon as you find him, report to me, so that I too may go and worship him."

[9]After they had heard the king, they went on their way, and the star they had seen when it rose went ahead of them until it stopped over the place where the child was. [10]When they saw the star, they were overjoyed. [11]On coming to the house, they saw the child with his mother Mary, and they bowed down and worshiped him. Then they opened their treasures and presented him with gifts of gold, frankincense and myrrh. [12]And having been warned in a dream not to go back to Herod, they returned to their country by another route.

The Escape to Egypt

[13]When they had gone, an angel of the Lord appeared to Joseph in a dream. "Get up," he said, "take the child and his mother and escape to Egypt. Stay there until I tell you, for Herod is going to search for the child to kill him."

[14]So he got up, took the child and his mother during the night and left for Egypt, [15]where he stayed until the death of Herod. And so was fulfilled what the Lord had said through the prophet: "Out of Egypt I called my son."[c]

[16]When Herod realized that he had been outwitted by the Magi, he was furious, and he gave orders to kill all the boys in Bethlehem and its vicinity who were two years old and under, in accordance with the time he had learned from the Magi. [17]Then what was said through the prophet Jeremiah was fulfilled:

[18]"A voice is heard in Ramah,
    weeping and great mourning,
Rachel weeping for her children
    and refusing to be comforted,
    because they are no more."[d]

The Return to Nazareth

[19]After Herod died, an angel of the Lord appeared in a dream to Joseph in Egypt [20]and said, "Get up, take the child and his mother and go to the land of Israel, for those who were trying to take the child's life are dead."

[21]So he got up, took the child and his mother and went to the land of Israel. [22]But when he heard that Archelaus was reigning in Judea in place of his father Herod, he was afraid to go there. Having been warned in a dream, he withdrew to the district of Galilee, [23]and he went and

---

[a] 1 Traditionally wise men   [b] 6 Micah 5:2,4
[c] 15 Hosea 11:1   [d] 18 Jer. 31:15

The Law of Empowerment: Herod Abused Power Instead of Sharing It

Matthew 2:3–18

King Herod failed to empower anyone; in fact, he drained power from people in a continual grab for power. Check out the ugly symptoms we see in his leadership that every one of us should avoid:

1. He felt disturbed and threatened when he learned of a coming king (v. 3).
2. He leveraged his power against any possible competitor (v. 4).
3. He used people to serve his own purposes (vv. 7–8).
4. He lied in order to project the right image (v. 8).
5. He reacted with fury when he didn't get his way (v. 16).
6. He concerned himself only with his own benefit (v. 16).
7. He sought to destroy any potential threat to his leadership (vv. 16–18).

SECURITY Herod Felt the Threat of Competition

Matthew 2:1–18

THE TREMENDOUS insecurity of King Herod became apparent when strangers announced Jesus' birth. Upon hearing the news, Herod grew angry, impatient, self-consumed, and disturbed—all signs of an insecure leader. Insecure leaders share several common traits:

1. They don't provide security for others.
2. They take more than they give.
3. They continually limit their best people.
4. They continually limit or sabotage their organization's success.
5. They spend more energy trying to keep their job than to do their job.

Effective leadership begins with an emotionally and spiritually healthy leader. Why is this true? Why must we focus on our personal security? Consider several reasons:

1. Leadership must flow out of "being," not merely "doing."
2. Strong character is necessary to sustain strong conduct.
3. Insecure leaders cause their organizations to plateau.
4. Personal security provides the infrastructure to support leaders in adversity.
5. Insecure leaders will never empower and develop secure followers.
6. Inward strength provides the only hope of finishing well.

Most of us struggle with feelings of insecurity. Leadership roles, however, work like a magnifying glass on our personal insecurity, blowing everything out of proportion because we know everyone is watching. We tend to react by trying to cover up our flaws, rather than being honest. This is yet another reason why leaders must commit to laying a foundation of strong personal security.

None of us ever grow beyond four fundamental human needs:

1. *A Sense of Worth*—if missing, we feel inferior.
2. *A Sense of Belonging*—if missing, we feel insecure.
3. *A Sense of Purpose*—if missing, we feel illegitimate.
4. *A Sense of Competence*—if missing, we feel inadequate.

How, then, should we respond to these crucial issues?

1. Leaders should settle this issue with God before they reach positions of influence.
2. Our personal worth and security must come from our "secret history" with God.
3. We should never place our emotional health in the hands of another.
4. We must release people from the expectation that they will meet our basic needs.

We become healthy leaders only when we don't expect others to meet the needs that only God can meet.

For a positive example of security, see p. 381.

lived in a town called Nazareth. So was fulfilled what was said through the prophets, that he would be called a Nazarene.

John the Baptist Prepares the Way

3 In those days John the Baptist came, preaching in the wilderness of Judea [2]and saying, "Repent, for the kingdom of heaven has come near." [3]This is he who was spoken of through the prophet Isaiah:

"A voice of one calling in the wilderness,
    'Prepare the way for the Lord,
       make straight paths for him.'"[a]

[4]John's clothes were made of camel's hair, and he had a leather belt around his waist. His food was locusts and wild honey. [5]People went out to him from Jerusalem and all Judea and the whole region of the Jordan. [6]Confessing their sins, they were baptized by him in the Jordan River.

[7]But when he saw many of the Pharisees and Sadducees coming to where he was baptizing, he said to them: "You brood of vipers! Who warned you to flee from the coming wrath? [8]Produce fruit in keeping with repentance. [9]And do not think you can say to yourselves, 'We have Abraham as our father.' I tell you that out of these stones God can raise up children for Abraham. [10]The ax is already at the root of the trees, and every tree that does not produce good fruit will be cut down and thrown into the fire.

[11]"I baptize you with[b] water for repentance. But after me comes one who is more powerful than I, whose sandals I am not worthy to carry. He will baptize you with[b] the Holy Spirit and fire. [12]His winnowing fork is in his hand, and he will clear his threshing floor, gathering his wheat into the barn and burning up the chaff with unquenchable fire."

The Baptism of Jesus

[13]Then Jesus came from Galilee to the Jordan to be baptized by John. [14]But John tried to deter him, saying, "I need to be baptized by you, and do you come to me?"

[15]Jesus replied, "Let it be so now; it is proper for us to do this to fulfill all righteousness." Then John consented.

---

[a] 3 Isaiah 40:3   [b] 11 Or *in*

Courage: John Demonstrates Courageous Leadership

Matthew 3:1–10

John the Baptist, the cousin of Jesus, paved the way for Christ. John prepared the people for Jesus' ministry with a unique ministry of his own, courageously calling people to repent and live out what they claimed to believe.

John confronted Pharisees, common people who lived hypocritically, and even King Herod himself. Note how his courageous leadership demonstrated itself:

1. John preached a clear message; the Pharisees, a complex one (vv. 1–3).

2. John cared more about his integrity than about his image (vv. 4–6).

3. John had stronger convictions than his critics (vv. 7–10).

How did John become so courageous? What helped him build his courage?

1. *His mission was deliberate:* His job was to prepare for the coming of the Lord.

2. *His message was decisive:* He said, "Repent, for the kingdom of heaven has come near" (Mt 3:2).

3. *His motive was direct:* He had Elijah's voice, crying in the wilderness.

4. *His manner was different:* His clothes came from camel hair; he ate locusts.

5. *His principles were deep:* He believed people must exhibit the fruit of repentance.

6. *His method was daring:* He directed people to confess their sins and be baptized.

7. *His mind was discerning:* He perceived the pretenses of the Pharisees.

8. *His ministry was developing:* He drew people from all over Judea.

The Law of Respect: John Submits to Jesus' Leadership

Matthew 3:11–14

Even though John the Baptist possessed the strongest voice of his day, when Jesus stepped forward, he willingly submitted to his authority. He even predicted Christ's coming. He knew his role was to prepare everyone for the Messiah. He laid his ego aside and humbly fulfilled his calling. He acknowledged the One who was greater than he and publicly said to Jesus: "I need to be baptized by you" (Mt 3:14).

Healthy leaders remain in touch with their own influence and wield it without reservation. Yet they never allow ego to drive them. They yield to stronger leaders when they appear, because the cause is more important than personal popularity.

¹⁶As soon as Jesus was baptized, he went up out of the water. At that moment heaven was opened, and he saw the Spirit of God descending like a dove and alighting on him. ¹⁷And a voice from heaven said, "This is my Son, whom I love; with him I am well pleased."

Jesus Is Tested in the Wilderness

4 Then Jesus was led by the Spirit into the wilderness to be tempted[a] by the devil. ²After fasting forty days and forty nights, he was hungry. ³The tempter came to him and said, "If you are the Son of God, tell these stones to become bread."

⁴Jesus answered, "It is written: 'Man shall not live on bread alone, but on every word that comes from the mouth of God.'[b]"

⁵Then the devil took him to the holy city and had him stand on the highest point of the temple. ⁶"If you are the Son of God," he said, "throw yourself down. For it is written:

" 'He will command his angels concerning you,
    and they will lift you up in their hands,
    so that you will not strike your foot
        against a stone.'[c]"

⁷Jesus answered him, "It is also written: 'Do not put the Lord your God to the test.'[d]"

⁸Again, the devil took him to a very high mountain and showed him all the kingdoms of the world and their splendor. ⁹"All this I will give you," he said, "if you will bow down and worship me."

¹⁰Jesus said to him, "Away from me, Satan! For it is written: 'Worship the Lord your God, and serve him only.'[e]"

¹¹Then the devil left him, and angels came and attended him.

Jesus Begins to Preach

¹²When Jesus heard that John had been put in prison, he withdrew to Galilee. ¹³Leaving Nazareth, he went and lived in Capernaum, which was by the lake in the area of Zebulun and Naphtali— ¹⁴to fulfill what was said through the prophet Isaiah:

¹⁵"Land of Zebulun and land of Naphtali,
    the Way of the Sea, beyond the Jordan,
    Galilee of the Gentiles—
¹⁶the people living in darkness
    have seen a great light;
on those living in the land of the shadow of
        death
    a light has dawned."[f]

¹⁷From that time on Jesus began to preach, "Repent, for the kingdom of heaven has come near."

Jesus Calls His First Disciples

¹⁸As Jesus was walking beside the Sea of Galilee, he saw two brothers, Simon called Peter and his brother Andrew. They were casting a net into the lake, for they were fishermen. ¹⁹"Come, follow me," Jesus said, "and I will send you out to fish for people." ²⁰At once they left their nets and followed him.

²¹Going on from there, he saw two other brothers, James son of Zebedee and his brother John. They were in a boat with their father Zebedee, preparing their nets. Jesus called them, ²²and immediately they left the boat and their father and followed him.

Jesus Heals the Sick

²³Jesus went throughout Galilee, teaching in their synagogues, proclaiming the good news of the kingdom, and healing every disease and sickness among the people. ²⁴News about him

---

[a] 1 The Greek for *tempted* can also mean *tested*.
[b] 4 Deut. 8:3   [c] 6 Psalm 91:11,12   [d] 7 Deut. 6:16
[e] 10 Deut. 6:13   [f] 16 Isaiah 9:1,2

The Law of Sacrifice: Quality Leaders Are Prepared in the Wilderness

Matthew 4:1–11

The Holy Spirit led Jesus out into the wilderness right after his baptism by John, reminding us that at least part of his preparation for ministry came from a wilderness experience.

Does this sound familiar? Quality leaders can almost always point to a wilderness experience as part of their leadership preparation. During this time, our motives get purified, our backbone solidifies, and our calling gets clarified.

The devil tempted Jesus for 40 days in the wilderness—a screening process to see what Jesus would give up and how he would trust God to provide. In his book, *In the Name of Jesus*, Henry Nouwen reminds us that the three temptations of Jesus correspond to three temptations leaders face today:

1. *The temptation to be self-sufficient* (vv. 2–4)
   Jesus didn't become controlling, even with his legitimate needs. He trusted God.

2. *The temptation to be spectacular* (vv. 5–7)
   Jesus refused to become a stunt man. He didn't perform in order to become a celebrity.

3. *The temptation to be powerful* (vv. 8–10)
   Jesus wouldn't take a shortcut to gain power or worship.

How do you deal with the temptations of leadership? Study Jesus' method for combating these familiar temptations of legitimate needs, gifting and fame. Jesus provides our standard for defeating temptation. He never lost.

---

spread all over Syria, and people brought to him all who were ill with various diseases, those suffering severe pain, the demon-possessed, those having seizures, and the paralyzed; and he healed them. [25]Large crowds from Galilee, the Decapolis,[a] Jerusalem, Judea and the region across the Jordan followed him.

Introduction to the Sermon on the Mount

5 Now when Jesus saw the crowds, he went up on a mountainside and sat down. His disciples came to him, [2]and he began to teach them.

The Beatitudes

He said:

[3]"Blessed are the poor in spirit,
for theirs is the kingdom of heaven.
[4]Blessed are those who mourn,
for they will be comforted.
[5]Blessed are the meek,
for they will inherit the earth.
[6]Blessed are those who hunger and thirst for righteousness,
for they will be filled.
[7]Blessed are the merciful,
for they will be shown mercy.

[8]Blessed are the pure in heart,
for they will see God.
[9]Blessed are the peacemakers,
for they will be called children of God.
[10]Blessed are those who are persecuted because of righteousness,
for theirs is the kingdom of heaven.

[11]"Blessed are you when people insult you, persecute you and falsely say all kinds of evil against you because of me. [12]Rejoice and be glad, because great is your reward in heaven, for in the same way they persecuted the prophets who were before you.

Salt and Light

[13]"You are the salt of the earth. But if the salt loses its saltiness, how can it be made salty again? It is no longer good for anything, except to be thrown out and trampled underfoot.

[14]"You are the light of the world. A town built on a hill cannot be hidden. [15]Neither do people light a lamp and put it under a bowl. Instead they put it on its stand, and it gives light to everyone in the house. [16]In the same way, let your

---

[a] 25 That is, the Ten Cities

light shine before others, that they may see your good deeds and glorify your Father in heaven.

The Fulfillment of the Law

17"Do not think that I have come to abolish the Law or the Prophets; I have not come to abolish them but to fulfill them. 18For truly I tell you, until heaven and earth disappear, not the smallest letter, not the least stroke of a pen, will by any means disappear from the Law until everything is accomplished. 19Therefore anyone who sets aside one of the least of these commands and teaches others accordingly will be called least in the kingdom of heaven, but whoever practices and teaches these commands will be called great in the kingdom of heaven. 20For I tell you that unless your righteousness surpasses that of the Pharisees and the teachers of the law, you will certainly not enter the kingdom of heaven.

Murder

21"You have heard that it was said to the people long ago, 'You shall not murder,*a* and anyone who murders will be subject to judgment.' 22But I tell you that anyone who is angry with a brother or sister*b,c* will be subject to judgment. Again, anyone who says to a brother or sister, 'Raca,'*d* is answerable to the court. And anyone who says, 'You fool!' will be in danger of the fire of hell.

23"Therefore, if you are offering your gift at the altar and there remember that your brother or sister has something against you, 24leave your gift there in front of the altar. First go and be reconciled to them; then come and offer your gift.

25"Settle matters quickly with your adversary who is taking you to court. Do it while you are still together on the way, or your adversary may hand you over to the judge, and the judge may hand you over to the officer, and you may be thrown into prison. 26Truly I tell you, you will not get out until you have paid the last penny.

Adultery

27"You have heard that it was said, 'You shall not commit adultery.'*e* 28But I tell you that anyone who looks at a woman lustfully has already committed adultery with her in his heart. 29If your right eye causes you to stumble, gouge it

---

a 21 Exodus 20:13   *b* 22 The Greek word for *brother or sister* (*adelphos*) refers here to a fellow disciple, whether man or woman; also in verse 23.   *c* 22 Some manuscripts *brother or sister without cause*   *d* 22 An Aramaic term of contempt   *e* 27 Exodus 20:14

The Law of Legacy: Jesus Raised Up Leaders

Matthew 4:12–25

As Jesus began his public ministry, he preached (Mt 4:12–17), then passed yet another test of leadership: He called other leaders to join him (4:18–22). These twelve men he called disciples. Immediately he began developing them into future leaders for the church.

Jesus passed the acid test of leadership: *Could he reproduce his leadership in someone else?* At the same time he chose three fishermen, he cast vision for spiritual reproduction: "Follow me," he said, "and I will send you out to fish for people" (4:19). Clearly, he called these men to become leaders as well.

What do we learn about Jesus' selection and development of leaders?

1. *He found them in the course of his everyday world* (v. 18).
   Jesus was walking by the Sea of Galilee and spotted men close to him.

2. *He handpicked them* (v. 19).
   Jesus didn't hold a popularity vote; he chose the ones he knew were right.

3. *He called them to become leaders* (v. 19).
   Jesus called them not only to follow him, but to influence others.

4. *He used language they understood* (v. 19).
   Jesus plainly challenged them to catch men instead of fish.

5. *He took them on a journey and demonstrated leadership* (vv. 23–25).
   Jesus modeled leadership as he traveled through Judea.

out and throw it away. It is better for you to lose one part of your body than for your whole body to be thrown into hell. [30]And if your right hand causes you to stumble, cut it off and throw it away. It is better for you to lose one part of your body than for your whole body to go into hell.

Divorce

[31]"It has been said, 'Anyone who divorces his wife must give her a certificate of divorce.'[a] [32]But I tell you that anyone who divorces his wife, except for sexual immorality, makes her the victim of adultery, and anyone who marries a divorced woman commits adultery.

Oaths

[33]"Again, you have heard that it was said to the people long ago, 'Do not break your oath, but fulfill to the Lord the vows you have made.' [34]But I tell you, do not swear an oath at all: either by heaven, for it is God's throne; [35]or by the earth, for it is his footstool; or by Jerusalem, for it is the city of the Great King. [36]And do not swear by your head, for you cannot make even one hair white or black. [37]All you need to say is simply 'Yes' or 'No'; anything beyond this comes from the evil one.[b]

Eye for Eye

[38]"You have heard that it was said, 'Eye for eye, and tooth for tooth.'[c] [39]But I tell you, do not resist an evil person. If anyone slaps you on the right cheek, turn to them the other cheek also. [40]And if anyone wants to sue you and take your shirt, hand over your coat as well. [41]If anyone forces you to go one mile, go with them two miles. [42]Give to the one who asks you, and do not turn away from the one who wants to borrow from you.

Love for Enemies

[43]"You have heard that it was said, 'Love your neighbor[d] and hate your enemy.' [44]But I tell you, love your enemies and pray for those who persecute you, [45]that you may be children of your Father in heaven. He causes his sun to rise on the evil and the good, and sends rain on the righteous and the unrighteous. [46]If you love those who love you, what reward will you get? Are not even the tax collectors doing that? [47]And if you greet only your own people, what are you doing more than others? Do not even pagans do that? [48]Be perfect, therefore, as your heavenly Father is perfect.

Giving to the Needy

6 "Be careful not to practice your righteousness in front of others to be seen by them. If you do, you will have no reward from your Father in heaven.

[2]"So when you give to the needy, do not announce it with trumpets, as the hypocrites do in the synagogues and on the streets, to be honored by others. Truly I tell you, they have received

---

[a] 31 Deut. 24:1   [b] 37 Or from evil   [c] 38 Exodus 21:24; Lev. 24:20; Deut. 19:21   [d] 43 Lev. 19:18

Followers of God Are to Be Leaders of Men and Live at a Higher Level

Matthew 5:1–48

Between the "seed" of leadership planted in the early stages and the fruit of leadership that comes with maturity, every leader goes through two major phases: the call and the preparation.

During the preparation season, all leaders get tested to live at a higher level than others. No one responded better than Jesus.

Jesus calls his people to live at a higher level than the rest of the world. His call brings many other tests along the way, for tests always follow the call in order to prepare leaders for the role they are to play.

The Call		The Preparation	
The Seed of Leadership	The Beginning of Leadership	The Tests of Leadership	The Fulfillment of Leadership

During the middle two stages, emerging leaders experiment to discover their strengths and weaknesses. To reach their potential, however, leaders must pass many tests. Ask yourself: Do I measure up to living at a higher level?

their reward in full. ³But when you give to the needy, do not let your left hand know what your right hand is doing, ⁴so that your giving may be in secret. Then your Father, who sees what is done in secret, will reward you.

Prayer

⁵"And when you pray, do not be like the hypocrites, for they love to pray standing in the synagogues and on the street corners to be seen by others. Truly I tell you, they have received their reward in full. ⁶But when you pray, go into your room, close the door and pray to your Father, who is unseen. Then your Father, who sees what is done in secret, will reward you. ⁷And when you pray, do not keep on babbling like pagans, for they think they will be heard because of their many words. ⁸Do not be like them, for your Father knows what you need before you ask him.

⁹"This, then, is how you should pray:

"'Our Father in heaven,
hallowed be your name,
¹⁰your kingdom come,
your will be done,
    on earth as it is in heaven.
¹¹Give us today our daily bread.
¹²And forgive us our debts,
    as we also have forgiven our debtors.
¹³And lead us not into temptation,ᵃ
    but deliver us from the evil one.ᵇ'

¹⁴For if you forgive other people when they sin against you, your heavenly Father will also forgive you. ¹⁵But if you do not forgive others their sins, your Father will not forgive your sins.

Fasting

¹⁶"When you fast, do not look somber as the hypocrites do, for they disfigure their faces to show others they are fasting. Truly I tell you, they have received their reward in full. ¹⁷But when you fast, put oil on your head and wash your face, ¹⁸so that it will not be obvious to others that you are fasting, but only to your Father, who is unseen; and your Father, who sees what is done in secret, will reward you.

Treasures in Heaven

¹⁹"Do not store up for yourselves treasures on earth, where moths and vermin destroy, and where thieves break in and steal. ²⁰But store up for yourselves treasures in heaven, where moths and vermin do not destroy, and where thieves do not break in and steal. ²¹For where your treasure is, there your heart will be also.

²²"The eye is the lamp of the body. If your eyes are healthy,ᶜ your whole body will be full of light. ²³But if your eyes are unhealthy,ᵈ your whole body will be full of darkness. If then the light within you is darkness, how great is that darkness!

²⁴"No one can serve two masters. Either you will hate the one and love the other, or you will be devoted to the one and despise the other. You cannot serve both God and money.

Do Not Worry

²⁵"Therefore I tell you, do not worry about your life, what you will eat or drink; or about your body, what you will wear. Is not life more than food, and the body more than clothes? ²⁶Look at the birds of the air; they do not sow or reap or store away in barns, and yet your heavenly Father feeds them. Are you not much more

---

ᵃ 13 The Greek for *temptation* can also mean *testing*.
ᵇ 13 Or *from evil*; some late manuscripts *one, / for yours is the kingdom and the power and the glory forever. Amen.*
ᶜ 22 The Greek for *healthy* here implies *generous.*   ᵈ 23 The Greek for *unhealthy* here implies *stingy.*

Leadership Development Begins with an Attitude Adjustment

Matthew 5:1—7:29

Jesus' most famous message, the Sermon on the Mount, focused on the hearts of his listeners. He targeted his disciples as the audience (Mt 5:1–2) and proceeded to preach what we now call the "Beatitudes." He called his men to be different, to see the world from God's perspective, to relate to people in a supernatural fashion.

Jesus demonstrated that leadership development begins with shaping the perspective of the listener. Jesus challenged the normal human perspective on . . .

- spiritual poverty and success
- sadness and mourning
- meekness and gentleness
- passion and hunger
- mercy and compassion
- purity and integrity
- peacemaking and revenge
- persecution and adversity

Motive Check: Leaders Must Do the Right Thing for the Right Reason

Matthew 6:1–34

Leaders can so easily get caught up in doing things for image sake—after all, so many people are watching.

Jesus warns us about facades and hypocrisy. He means this text for everyone, with crucial application to leaders. Our Lord speaks about doing things to be seen by men rather than to please God (Mt 6:1). Jesus wants to build strong convictions in his followers. He wants to produce God-pleasers (1Th 4:1), not people-pleasers (Col 3:22). In this text, Jesus covers our motives for:

- doing good (v. 1)
- giving to charity (vv. 2–4)
- prayer (vv. 5–15)
- fasting (vv. 16–18)
- priorities and values (vv. 19–24)
- work and worry (vv. 25–34)

valuable than they? [27]Can any one of you by worrying add a single hour to your life[a]?

[28]"And why do you worry about clothes? See how the flowers of the field grow. They do not labor or spin. [29]Yet I tell you that not even Solomon in all his splendor was dressed like one of these. [30]If that is how God clothes the grass of the field, which is here today and tomorrow is thrown into the fire, will he not much more clothe you — you of little faith? [31]So do not worry, saying, 'What shall we eat?' or 'What shall we drink?' or 'What shall we wear?' [32]For the pagans run after all these things, and your heavenly Father knows that you need them. [33]But seek first his kingdom and his righteousness, and all these things will be given to you as well. [34]Therefore do not worry about tomorrow, for tomorrow will worry about itself. Each day has enough trouble of its own.

Judging Others

7 "Do not judge, or you too will be judged. [2]For in the same way you judge others, you will be judged, and with the measure you use, it will be measured to you.

[3]"Why do you look at the speck of sawdust in your brother's eye and pay no attention to the plank in your own eye? [4]How can you say to your brother, 'Let me take the speck out of your eye,' when all the time there is a plank in your own eye? [5]You hypocrite, first take the plank out of your own eye, and then you will see clearly to remove the speck from your brother's eye.

[6]"Do not give dogs what is sacred; do not throw your pearls to pigs. If you do, they may trample them under their feet, and turn and tear you to pieces.

Ask, Seek, Knock

[7]"Ask and it will be given to you; seek and you will find; knock and the door will be opened to you. [8]For everyone who asks receives; the one who seeks finds; and to the one who knocks, the door will be opened.

[9]"Which of you, if your son asks for bread, will give him a stone? [10]Or if he asks for a fish, will give him a snake? [11]If you, then, though you are evil, know how to give good gifts to your children, how much more will your Father in heaven give good gifts to those who ask him! [12]So in everything, do to others what you would have them do to you, for this sums up the Law and the Prophets.

The Narrow and Wide Gates

[13]"Enter through the narrow gate. For wide is the gate and broad is the road that leads to destruction, and many enter through it. [14]But small is the gate and narrow the road that leads to life, and only a few find it.

True and False Prophets

[15]"Watch out for false prophets. They come to you in sheep's clothing, but inwardly they are ferocious wolves. [16]By their fruit you will recognize them. Do people pick grapes from thornbushes, or figs from thistles? [17]Likewise, every good tree bears good fruit, but a bad tree bears bad fruit. [18]A good tree cannot bear bad fruit, and a bad tree cannot bear good fruit. [19]Every tree that does not bear good fruit is cut down and thrown into the fire. [20]Thus, by their fruit you will recognize them.

True and False Disciples

[21]"Not everyone who says to me, 'Lord, Lord,' will enter the kingdom of heaven, but only the one who does the will of my Father who is in

---

[a] 27 Or *single cubit to your height*

heaven. [22]Many will say to me on that day, 'Lord, Lord, did we not prophesy in your name and in your name drive out demons and in your name perform many miracles?' [23]Then I will tell them plainly, 'I never knew you. Away from me, you evildoers!'

The Wise and Foolish Builders

[24]"Therefore everyone who hears these words of mine and puts them into practice is like a wise man who built his house on the rock. [25]The rain came down, the streams rose, and the winds blew and beat against that house; yet it did not fall, because it had its foundation on the rock. [26]But everyone who hears these words of mine and does not put them into practice is like a foolish man who built his house on sand.

The First Task of a Leader Is to Define Core Values

Matthew 6:1—7:27

In the first sermon recorded in his Gospel, Matthew spotlights Jesus' major emphasis on values. Jesus knew his first task was to provide a set of core values for his men. Note Jesus' list of core values:

1. Do the right things for the right reasons (6:1–8, 16–18).
2. Pray God's agenda, not your own (6:9–13).
3. Relationships will make or break you (6:14–15).
4. Prioritize eternal things, not temporal things (6:19–24).
5. Don't sweat the small stuff (6:25–31, 34).
6. God's kingdom is paramount; seek it first (6:32–33).
7. Judge yourself before you judge others (7:1–6).
8. If you need something, ask; if you have something, give it (7:7–12).
9. Stay true to your convictions; don't wander from the narrow path (7:13–20).
10. Obedience to God is the only sure foundation for life (7:21–27).

If you're still not convinced that Jesus gives a list of core values here, look at Matthew 7:12, where he summarizes the law in a single statement.

---

[27]The rain came down, the streams rose, and the winds blew and beat against that house, and it fell with a great crash."

[28]When Jesus had finished saying these things, the crowds were amazed at his teaching, [29]because he taught as one who had authority, and not as their teachers of the law.

Jesus Heals a Man With Leprosy

8 When Jesus came down from the mountainside, large crowds followed him. [2]A man with leprosy[a] came and knelt before him and said, "Lord, if you are willing, you can make me clean."

[3]Jesus reached out his hand and touched the man. "I am willing," he said. "Be clean!" Immediately he was cleansed of his leprosy. [4]Then Jesus said to him, "See that you don't tell anyone. But go, show yourself to the priest and offer the gift Moses commanded, as a testimony to them."

The Faith of the Centurion

[5]When Jesus had entered Capernaum, a centurion came to him, asking for help. [6]"Lord," he said, "my servant lies at home paralyzed, suffering terribly."

[7]Jesus said to him, "Shall I come and heal him?"

[8]The centurion replied, "Lord, I do not deserve to have you come under my roof. But just say the word, and my servant will be healed. [9]For I myself am a man under authority, with soldiers under me. I tell this one, 'Go,' and he goes; and that one, 'Come,' and he comes. I say to my servant, 'Do this,' and he does it."

[10]When Jesus heard this, he was amazed and said to those following him, "Truly I tell you, I have not found anyone in Israel with such great faith. [11]I say to you that many will come from the east and the west, and will take their places at the feast with Abraham, Isaac and Jacob in the kingdom of heaven. [12]But the subjects of the kingdom will be thrown outside, into the darkness, where there will be weeping and gnashing of teeth."

[13]Then Jesus said to the centurion, "Go! Let it be done just as you believed it would." And his servant was healed at that moment.

Jesus Heals Many

[14]When Jesus came into Peter's house, he saw Peter's mother-in-law lying in bed with a fever.

---

[a] 2 The Greek word traditionally translated *leprosy* was used for various diseases affecting the skin.

The Centurion Teaches a Lesson on Authority

Matthew 8:5–13

The centurion who asked Jesus to heal his servant clearly understood authority. In the same way that he commanded soldiers under his charge, he knew Jesus could command diseases. When leaders possess authority, their words carry weight. How much weight do your words carry? Who listens to you?

---

[15]He touched her hand and the fever left her, and she got up and began to wait on him.

[16]When evening came, many who were demon-possessed were brought to him, and he drove out the spirits with a word and healed all the sick. [17]This was to fulfill what was spoken through the prophet Isaiah:

"He took up our infirmities
    and bore our diseases."[a]

The Cost of Following Jesus

[18]When Jesus saw the crowd around him, he gave orders to cross to the other side of the lake. [19]Then a teacher of the law came to him and said, "Teacher, I will follow you wherever you go."

[20]Jesus replied, "Foxes have dens and birds have nests, but the Son of Man has no place to lay his head."

[21]Another disciple said to him, "Lord, first let me go and bury my father."

[22]But Jesus told him, "Follow me, and let the dead bury their own dead."

Jesus Calms the Storm

[23]Then he got into the boat and his disciples followed him. [24]Suddenly a furious storm came up on the lake, so that the waves swept over the boat. But Jesus was sleeping. [25]The disciples went and woke him, saying, "Lord, save us! We're going to drown!"

[26]He replied, "You of little faith, why are you so afraid?" Then he got up and rebuked the winds and the waves, and it was completely calm.

[27]The men were amazed and asked, "What kind of man is this? Even the winds and the waves obey him!"

Jesus Restores Two Demon-Possessed Men

[28]When he arrived at the other side in the region of the Gadarenes,[b] two demon-possessed men coming from the tombs met him. They were so violent that no one could pass that way. [29]"What do you want with us, Son of God?" they shouted. "Have you come here to torture us before the appointed time?"

[30]Some distance from them a large herd of pigs was feeding. [31]The demons begged Jesus, "If you drive us out, send us into the herd of pigs."

[32]He said to them, "Go!" So they came out and went into the pigs, and the whole herd rushed down the steep bank into the lake and died in the water. [33]Those tending the pigs ran off, went into the town and reported all this, including what had happened to the demon-possessed

---

[a] 17 Isaiah 53:4 (see Septuagint)   [b] 28 Some manuscripts *Gergesenes*; other manuscripts *Gerasenes*

Commitment: What All Leaders Must Demonstrate and Draw

Matthew 8:18–34

Jesus issues tough challenges to potential followers about what it means to follow him. He questions his disciples' wavering faith when they fear a storm. It is as if he were screening his audience and testing their level of commitment to him and to the kingdom.

Jesus never begged anyone to follow him. In fact, he often sifted through his followers to see what they were made of and where they stood. No good leader is afraid to do this. Look at how Jesus did it:

1. Jesus' **clarification** of our commitment (vv. 18–22)
   When he saw the crowd, he knew it was time to clarify the cost of following him.

2. Jesus' **credibility** for our commitment (vv. 23–27)
   After the clarification, he demonstrated good reason to follow him by his miracles.

3. Jesus' **challenge** for our commitment (vv. 28–34)
   In Gadara, he divided the cautious, the curious and the committed.

men. [34]Then the whole town went out to meet Jesus. And when they saw him, they pleaded with him to leave their region.

Jesus Forgives and Heals a Paralyzed Man

9 Jesus stepped into a boat, crossed over and came to his own town. [2]Some men brought to him a paralyzed man, lying on a mat. When Jesus saw their faith, he said to the man, "Take heart, son; your sins are forgiven."

[3]At this, some of the teachers of the law said to themselves, "This fellow is blaspheming!"

[4]Knowing their thoughts, Jesus said, "Why do you entertain evil thoughts in your hearts? [5]Which is easier: to say, 'Your sins are forgiven,' or to say, 'Get up and walk'? [6]But I want you to know that the Son of Man has authority on earth to forgive sins." So he said to the paralyzed man, "Get up, take your mat and go home." [7]Then the man got up and went home. [8]When the crowd saw this, they were filled with awe; and they praised God, who had given such authority to man.

The Calling of Matthew

[9]As Jesus went on from there, he saw a man named Matthew sitting at the tax collector's booth. "Follow me," he told him, and Matthew got up and followed him.

[10]While Jesus was having dinner at Matthew's house, many tax collectors and sinners came and ate with him and his disciples. [11]When the Pharisees saw this, they asked his disciples, "Why does your teacher eat with tax collectors and sinners?"

[12]On hearing this, Jesus said, "It is not the healthy who need a doctor, but the sick. [13]But go and learn what this means: 'I desire mercy, not sacrifice.'[a] For I have not come to call the righteous, but sinners."

Jesus Questioned About Fasting

[14]Then John's disciples came and asked him, "How is it that we and the Pharisees fast often, but your disciples do not fast?"

[15]Jesus answered, "How can the guests of the bridegroom mourn while he is with them? The time will come when the bridegroom will be taken from them; then they will fast.

[16]"No one sews a patch of unshrunk cloth on an old garment, for the patch will pull away from the garment, making the tear worse. [17]Neither do people pour new wine into old wineskins. If they do, the skins will burst; the wine will run out and the wineskins will be ruined. No, they pour new wine into new wineskins, and both are preserved."

Jesus Raises a Dead Girl and Heals a Sick Woman

[18]While he was saying this, a synagogue leader came and knelt before him and said, "My daughter has just died. But come and put your hand on her, and she will live." [19]Jesus got up and went with him, and so did his disciples.

[20]Just then a woman who had been subject to bleeding for twelve years came up behind him and touched the edge of his cloak. [21]She said to herself, "If I only touch his cloak, I will be healed."

[22]Jesus turned and saw her. "Take heart, daughter," he said, "your faith has healed you." And the woman was healed at that moment.

[23]When Jesus entered the synagogue leader's house and saw the noisy crowd and people playing pipes, [24]he said, "Go away. The girl is not dead but asleep." But they laughed at him. [25]After the crowd had been put outside, he went in and took the girl by the hand, and she got up. [26]News of this spread through all that region.

---

[a] 13. Hosea 6:6

The Law of Intuition: Jesus' Diagnosis and Prescription

Matthew 9:35–38

The Ultimate Leader teaches us about the divine order of capturing and casting a vision. Leaders often err by flitting from vision to vision. Why? Because they fail to take the time to become burdened over a need. Burden always comes first; then vision. Consider the order we see in Jesus' leadership:

1. *He sought a need:* As Jesus traveled the villages, he saw their needs (vv. 35–36).

2. *He bought a burden:* He diagnosed the problem: "I need more workers" (v. 37).

3. *He caught a vision:* He gave a prescription for the burden (v. 38).

Leaders remain relevant only as they meet real needs. Consequently, we must pause long enough to observe needs, then feel the tug of a burden. Finally, we must catch a vision that will address the burden.

Jesus Heals the Blind and the Mute

27 As Jesus went on from there, two blind men followed him, calling out, "Have mercy on us, Son of David!"

28 When he had gone indoors, the blind men came to him, and he asked them, "Do you believe that I am able to do this?"

"Yes, Lord," they replied.

29 Then he touched their eyes and said, "According to your faith let it be done to you"; 30 and their sight was restored. Jesus warned them sternly, "See that no one knows about this." 31 But they went out and spread the news about him all over that region.

32 While they were going out, a man who was demon-possessed and could not talk was brought to Jesus. 33 And when the demon was driven out, the man who had been mute spoke. The crowd was amazed and said, "Nothing like this has ever been seen in Israel."

34 But the Pharisees said, "It is by the prince of demons that he drives out demons."

The Workers Are Few

35 Jesus went through all the towns and villages, teaching in their synagogues, proclaiming the good news of the kingdom and healing every disease and sickness. 36 When he saw the crowds, he had compassion on them, because they were harassed and helpless, like sheep without a shepherd. 37 Then he said to his disciples, "The harvest is plentiful but the workers are few. 38 Ask the Lord of the harvest, therefore, to send out workers into his harvest field."

Jesus Sends Out the Twelve

10 Jesus called his twelve disciples to him and gave them authority to drive out impure spirits and to heal every disease and sickness.

2 These are the names of the twelve apostles: first, Simon (who is called Peter) and his brother Andrew; James son of Zebedee, and his brother John; 3 Philip and Bartholomew; Thomas and Matthew the tax collector; James son of Alphaeus, and Thaddaeus; 4 Simon the Zealot and Judas Iscariot, who betrayed him.

5 These twelve Jesus sent out with the following instructions: "Do not go among the Gentiles or enter any town of the Samaritans. 6 Go rather to the lost sheep of Israel. 7 As you go, proclaim this message: 'The kingdom of heaven has come

Vision: The Process Toward Fulfilling a God-Given Vision

Matthew 9:35—10:5

Jesus teaches us the process of fulfilling a God-given vision. Study this passage and watch for these steps:

1. *Take initiative to obey.* Get active in service.
   "Jesus went through all the towns and villages" (9:35).

2. *Communicate the truth you have already.*
   "... teaching in their synagogues [and] proclaiming the good news of the kingdom" (9:35).

3. *Observe and understand the reality of human conditions.*
   "When he saw the crowds" (9:36).

4. *Allow God to burden you with a specific need.*
   "He had compassion on them, because they were ... like sheep without a shepherd" (9:36).

5. *See a divine diagnosis.* What is the issue to be resolved?
   "The harvest is plentiful but the workers are few" (9:37).

6. *Pray to determine what action could meet that need.*
   "Ask the Lord of the harvest, therefore, to send out workers into his harvest field" (9:38).

7. *Choose a team and empower them for partnership.*
   "Jesus called his twelve disciples to him and gave them authority" (10:1).

8. *Take immediate action toward the fulfillment of the vision.*
   "These twelve Jesus sent out" (10:5).

near.' [8]Heal the sick, raise the dead, cleanse those who have leprosy,[a] drive out demons. Freely you have received; freely give.

[9]"Do not get any gold or silver or copper to take with you in your belts — [10]no bag for the journey or extra shirt or sandals or a staff, for the worker is worth his keep. [11]Whatever town or village you enter, search there for some worthy person and stay at their house until you leave. [12]As you enter the home, give it your greeting. [13]If the home is deserving, let your peace rest on it; if it is not, let your peace return to you. [14]If anyone will not welcome you or listen to your words, leave that home or town and shake the dust off your feet. [15]Truly I tell you, it will be more bearable for Sodom and Gomorrah on the day of judgment than for that town.

[16]"I am sending you out like sheep among wolves. Therefore be as shrewd as snakes and as innocent as doves. [17]Be on your guard; you will be handed over to the local councils and be flogged in the synagogues. [18]On my ac-count you will be brought before governors and kings as witnesses to them and to the Gentiles. [19]But when they arrest you, do not worry about what to say or how to say it. At that time you will be given what to say, [20]for it will not be you speaking, but the Spirit of your Father speaking through you.

[21]"Brother will betray brother to death, and a father his child; children will rebel against their parents and have them put to death. [22]You will be hated by everyone because of me, but the one who stands firm to the end will be saved. [23]When you are persecuted in one place, flee to another. Truly I tell you, you will not finish going through the towns of Israel before the Son of Man comes.

[24]"The student is not above the teacher, nor a servant above his master. [25]It is enough for students to be like their teachers, and servants like

---

[a] 8 The Greek word traditionally translated *leprosy* was used for various diseases affecting the skin.

The Law of Empowerment: Jesus Gave Power Away . . . and Multiplied His Influence

Matthew 10:1–15

Effective leadership attracts and brokers the talents of others. Leaders must develop others to reach their potential. No one did this better than Jesus.

In Matthew 10 we see the results of Jesus' vision for more workers (9:37–38). Even though he has not finished training his disciples, he sends them out to exercise their gifts.

So it is with our people. At some point we need to end the lecture and send them out to try what they have learned. Consider how Jesus empowered his twelve-man staff:

1. *A personal call* (vv. 1–4)
   Jesus selected them and called them by name.

2. *A direct commission* (v. 5)
   After instructing them, he sent them out.

3. *A central objective* (vv. 5–6)
   He told them to go to the Hebrews, not the Gentiles.

4. *A clear message* (v. 7)
   He gave them the specific message.

5. *Practical credentials* (v. 8)
   He equipped them to gain credibility by giving them tools to confirm their message.

6. *Confidence for provision* (vv. 9–10)
   He instilled confidence and gave them a plan to acquire needed resources.

7. *Solid convictions* (vv. 11–15)
   He furnished convictions on how they were to act with both friends and critics.

Mentoring: Jesus Prepares Leaders for the Future

Matthew 10:16–33

Jesus not only sends out his twelve disciples to serve, but he reminds them that he intends to reproduce his own leadership in them. As part of the preparation process, he instructs them on what is coming:

1. He challenges them to be wise but innocent (v. 16).

2. He warns them about future hardships (vv. 17–18).

3. He instructs them on how to handle these hardships (vv. 19–20).

4. He predicts their personal anguish (vv. 21–22).

5. He gives them hope and assurance of ultimate victory (v. 23).

Jesus also clarifies the meaning of discipleship. He continues to prepare his men for any contingency. From the perspective of an equipper, consider what Jesus teaches trainers and trainees about leadership development:

1. Trainees should submit to the authority of the trainer (v. 24).

2. Trainees must recognize that trainers can reproduce only what they are (v. 25).

3. Trainees are to emulate their master (v. 25).

4. Trainees must trust God to care for their needs (vv. 26–31).

5. Trainees are to be loyal (vv. 32–33).

---

their masters. If the head of the house has been called Beelzebul, how much more the members of his household!

26 "So do not be afraid of them, for there is nothing concealed that will not be disclosed, or hidden that will not be made known. 27 What I tell you in the dark, speak in the daylight; what is whispered in your ear, proclaim from the roofs. 28 Do not be afraid of those who kill the body but cannot kill the soul. Rather, be afraid of the One who can destroy both soul and body in hell. 29 Are not two sparrows sold for a penny? Yet not one of them will fall to the ground outside your Father's care.*ᵃ* 30 And even the very hairs of your head are all numbered. 31 So don't be afraid; you are worth more than many sparrows.

32 "Whoever acknowledges me before others, I will also acknowledge before my Father in heaven. 33 But whoever disowns me before others, I will disown before my Father in heaven.

34 "Do not suppose that I have come to bring peace to the earth. I did not come to bring peace, but a sword. 35 For I have come to turn

"'a man against his father,
    a daughter against her mother,
a daughter-in-law against her mother-in-
        law—

36   a man's enemies will be the members of
        his own household.'*ᵇ*

37 "Anyone who loves their father or mother more than me is not worthy of me; anyone who loves their son or daughter more than me is not worthy of me. 38 Whoever does not take up their cross and follow me is not worthy of me. 39 Whoever finds their life will lose it, and whoever loses their life for my sake will find it.

40 "Anyone who welcomes you welcomes me, and anyone who welcomes me welcomes the one who sent me. 41 Whoever welcomes a prophet as a prophet will receive a prophet's reward, and whoever welcomes a righteous person as a righteous person will receive a righteous person's reward. 42 And if anyone gives even a cup of cold water to one of these little ones who is my disciple, truly I tell you, that person will certainly not lose their reward."

Jesus and John the Baptist

11 After Jesus had finished instructing his twelve disciples, he went on from there to teach and preach in the towns of Galilee.*ᶜ*

ᵃ 29 Or *will*; or *knowledge*   *ᵇ 36* Micah 7:6   *ᶜ 1* Greek *in their towns*

[2]When John, who was in prison, heard about the deeds of the Messiah, he sent his disciples [3]to ask him, "Are you the one who is to come, or should we expect someone else?"

[4]Jesus replied, "Go back and report to John what you hear and see: [5]The blind receive sight, the lame walk, those who have leprosy[a] are cleansed, the deaf hear, the dead are raised, and the good news is proclaimed to the poor. [6]Blessed is anyone who does not stumble on account of me."

[7]As John's disciples were leaving, Jesus began to speak to the crowd about John: "What did you go out into the wilderness to see? A reed swayed by the wind? [8]If not, what did you go out to see? A man dressed in fine clothes? No, those who wear fine clothes are in kings' palaces. [9]Then what did you go out to see? A prophet? Yes, I tell you, and more than a prophet. [10]This is the one about whom it is written:

> "'I will send my messenger ahead of you,
>   who will prepare your way before you.'[b]

[11]Truly I tell you, among those born of women there has not risen anyone greater than John the Baptist; yet whoever is least in the kingdom of heaven is greater than he. [12]From the days of John the Baptist until now, the kingdom of heaven has been subjected to violence,[c] and violent people have been raiding it. [13]For all the Prophets and the Law prophesied until John. [14]And if you are willing to accept it, he is the Elijah who was to come. [15]Whoever has ears, let them hear.

[16]"To what can I compare this generation? They are like children sitting in the marketplaces and calling out to others:

[17]"'We played the pipe for you,
    and you did not dance;
we sang a dirge,
    and you did not mourn.'

[18]For John came neither eating nor drinking, and they say, 'He has a demon.' [19]The Son of Man came eating and drinking, and they say, 'Here is a glutton and a drunkard, a friend of tax collectors and sinners.' But wisdom is proved right by her deeds."

Woe on Unrepentant Towns

[20]Then Jesus began to denounce the towns in which most of his miracles had been performed, because they did not repent. [21]"Woe to you, Chorazin! Woe to you, Bethsaida! For if the miracles that were performed in you had been performed in Tyre and Sidon, they would have repented long ago in sackcloth and ashes. [22]But I tell you, it will be more bearable for Tyre and Sidon on the day of judgment than for you. [23]And you, Capernaum, will you be lifted to the heavens? No, you will go down to Hades.[d] For if the miracles that were performed in you had been performed in Sodom, it would have remained to this day. [24]But I tell you that it will be more bearable for Sodom on the day of judgment than for you."

The Father Revealed in the Son

[25]At that time Jesus said, "I praise you, Father, Lord of heaven and earth, because you have hidden these things from the wise and learned, and revealed them to little children. [26]Yes, Father, for this is what you were pleased to do.

[27]"All things have been committed to me by my Father. No one knows the Son except the Father, and no one knows the Father except the Son and those to whom the Son chooses to reveal him.

[28]"Come to me, all you who are weary and burdened, and I will give you rest. [29]Take my yoke upon you and learn from me, for I am gentle and humble in heart, and you will find rest for your souls. [30]For my yoke is easy and my burden is light."

Jesus Is Lord of the Sabbath

12 At that time Jesus went through the grainfields on the Sabbath. His disciples were hungry and began to pick some heads of

---

The Law of the Inner Circle: John Feels the Vacuum of Isolation

Matthew 11:2–3

When John loses his inner circle of disciples, his empty emotional tank prompts him to question Jesus' identity and credentials. Leaders need a close team of associates who allow the leader to vent, and who lend support through speaking words of truth. Do you have an inner circle?

---

[a] 5 The Greek word traditionally translated *leprosy* was used for various diseases affecting the skin.   [b] 10 Mal. 3:1
[c] 12 Or *been forcefully advancing*   [d] 23 That is, the realm of the dead

The Law of Empowerment: Jesus Touches Hearts First

Matthew 11:28–30

Although Jesus puts his early disciples to work, he knows he has to touch their hearts before he asks for their hands. So he promises to give them rest.

The word "rest" refers to an inward holiday—not a cessation of activity, but a whole new energy and motive. Many of us are more active on vacation than at work; what changes is our reason for activity. We feel energized on vacation because we want to do certain things. Jesus describes a new relationship that changes us on the inside. Note what he promises to give us:

1. *Rest:* an inward rest, free from anxieties (v. 28)

2. *Framework:* a yoke, by which we are guided by a stronger partner (v. 29)

3. *Gentle and humble leadership:* an understanding leader who meets our needs (v. 29)

4. *A manageable load:* a system and workload that fits who we are (v. 30)

grain and eat them. ²When the Pharisees saw this, they said to him, "Look! Your disciples are doing what is unlawful on the Sabbath."

³He answered, "Haven't you read what David did when he and his companions were hungry? ⁴He entered the house of God, and he and his companions ate the consecrated bread — which was not lawful for them to do, but only for the priests. ⁵Or haven't you read in the Law that the priests on Sabbath duty in the temple desecrate the Sabbath and yet are innocent? ⁶I tell you that something greater than the temple is here. ⁷If you had known what these words mean, 'I desire mercy, not sacrifice,'ᵃ you would not have condemned the innocent. ⁸For the Son of Man is Lord of the Sabbath."

⁹Going on from that place, he went into their synagogue, ¹⁰and a man with a shriveled hand was there. Looking for a reason to bring charges against Jesus, they asked him, "Is it lawful to heal on the Sabbath?"

¹¹He said to them, "If any of you has a sheep and it falls into a pit on the Sabbath, will you not take hold of it and lift it out? ¹²How much more valuable is a person than a sheep! Therefore it is lawful to do good on the Sabbath."

¹³Then he said to the man, "Stretch out your hand." So he stretched it out and it was completely restored, just as sound as the other. ¹⁴But the Pharisees went out and plotted how they might kill Jesus.

God's Chosen Servant

¹⁵Aware of this, Jesus withdrew from that place. A large crowd followed him, and he healed all who were ill. ¹⁶He warned them not to tell others about him. ¹⁷This was to fulfill what was spoken through the prophet Isaiah:

¹⁸"Here is my servant whom I have chosen,
   the one I love, in whom I delight;
 I will put my Spirit on him,
   and he will proclaim justice to the nations.
¹⁹He will not quarrel or cry out;
   no one will hear his voice in the streets.
²⁰A bruised reed he will not break,
   and a smoldering wick he will not snuff
     out,
 till he has brought justice through to victory.
²¹   In his name the nations will put their
     hope."ᵇ

Jesus and Beelzebul

²²Then they brought him a demon-possessed man who was blind and mute, and Jesus healed him, so that he could both talk and see. ²³All the people were astonished and said, "Could this be the Son of David?"

²⁴But when the Pharisees heard this, they said, "It is only by Beelzebul, the prince of demons, that this fellow drives out demons."

²⁵Jesus knew their thoughts and said to them, "Every kingdom divided against itself will be ruined, and every city or household divided against itself will not stand. ²⁶If Satan drives out Satan, he is divided against himself. How then can his kingdom stand? ²⁷And if I drive out demons by Beelzebul, by whom do your people drive them out? So then, they will be your judges. ²⁸But if it is by the Spirit of God that I drive out demons, then the kingdom of God has come upon you.

²⁹"Or again, how can anyone enter a strong man's house and carry off his possessions unless he first ties up the strong man? Then he can plunder his house.

³⁰"Whoever is not with me is against me, and whoever does not gather with me scatters. ³¹And

ᵃ 7 Hosea 6:6   ᵇ 21 Isaiah 42:1-4

so I tell you, every kind of sin and slander can be forgiven, but blasphemy against the Spirit will not be forgiven. ³²Anyone who speaks a word against the Son of Man will be forgiven, but anyone who speaks against the Holy Spirit will not be forgiven, either in this age or in the age to come.

³³"Make a tree good and its fruit will be good, or make a tree bad and its fruit will be bad, for a tree is recognized by its fruit. ³⁴You brood of vipers, how can you who are evil say anything good? For the mouth speaks what the heart is full of. ³⁵A good man brings good things out of the good stored up in him, and an evil man brings evil things out of the evil stored up in him. ³⁶But I tell you that everyone will have to give account on the day of judgment for every empty word they have spoken. ³⁷For by your words you will be acquitted, and by your words you will be condemned."

The Sign of Jonah

³⁸Then some of the Pharisees and teachers of the law said to him, "Teacher, we want to see a sign from you."

Communication: Words Carry a Thought and Shape a Destiny

Matthew 12:33–37

Jesus teaches us the centrality of communication. Like an echo of Proverbs 18:21, the Ultimate Leader helps us see that words carry the power of life and death:

1. Words transmit power (vv. 33–37).

2. Words reveal our character (vv. 33–35).

3. Words determine our reward and judgment (vv. 36–37).

4. Words produce fruit (vv. 33, 35–36).

5. Words shape our destiny (v. 37).

Leaders must never forget the power of their words. God shaped the universe with his words (Ge 1; 2). He sustains his creation with his Word (Heb 1:3). He even performs miracles through the use of words (Ro 4:17). What's more, God designed us to accomplish things by the wise use of our words.

³⁹He answered, "A wicked and adulterous generation asks for a sign! But none will be given it except the sign of the prophet Jonah. ⁴⁰For as Jonah was three days and three nights in the belly of a huge fish, so the Son of Man will be three days and three nights in the heart of the earth. ⁴¹The men of Nineveh will stand up at the judgment with this generation and condemn it; for they repented at the preaching of Jonah, and now something greater than Jonah is here. ⁴²The Queen of the South will rise at the judgment with this generation and condemn it; for she came from the ends of the earth to listen to Solomon's wisdom, and now something greater than Solomon is here.

⁴³"When an impure spirit comes out of a person, it goes through arid places seeking rest and does not find it. ⁴⁴Then it says, 'I will return to the house I left.' When it arrives, it finds the house unoccupied, swept clean and put in order. ⁴⁵Then it goes and takes with it seven other spirits more wicked than itself, and they go in and live there. And the final condition of that person is worse than the first. That is how it will be with this wicked generation."

Jesus' Mother and Brothers

⁴⁶While Jesus was still talking to the crowd, his mother and brothers stood outside, wanting to speak to him. ⁴⁷Someone told him, "Your mother and brothers are standing outside, wanting to speak to you."

⁴⁸He replied to him, "Who is my mother, and who are my brothers?" ⁴⁹Pointing to his disciples, he said, "Here are my mother and my brothers. ⁵⁰For whoever does the will of my Father in heaven is my brother and sister and mother."

The Parable of the Sower

13 That same day Jesus went out of the house and sat by the lake. ²Such large crowds gathered around him that he got into a boat and sat in it, while all the people stood on the shore. ³Then he told them many things in parables, saying: "A farmer went out to sow his seed. ⁴As he was scattering the seed, some fell along the path, and the birds came and ate it up. ⁵Some fell on rocky places, where it did not have much soil. It sprang up quickly, because the soil was shallow. ⁶But when the sun came up, the plants were scorched, and they withered because they had no root. ⁷Other seed fell among thorns, which grew up and choked the plants. ⁸Still other seed fell on good soil, where it produced a crop—a hundred, sixty or thirty times what was sown. [9]Whoever has ears, let them hear."

[10]The disciples came to him and asked, "Why do you speak to the people in parables?"

[11]He replied, "Because the knowledge of the secrets of the kingdom of heaven has been given to you, but not to them. [12]Whoever has will be given more, and they will have an abundance. Whoever does not have, even what they have will be taken from them. [13]This is why I speak to them in parables:

"Though seeing, they do not see;
   though hearing, they do not hear or
     understand.

[14]In them is fulfilled the prophecy of Isaiah:

"'You will be ever hearing but never
   understanding;
you will be ever seeing but never
   perceiving.
[15]For this people's heart has become
   calloused;
they hardly hear with their ears,
   and they have closed their eyes.
Otherwise they might see with their eyes,
   hear with their ears,
   understand with their hearts
and turn, and I would heal them.'[a]

[16]But blessed are your eyes because they see, and your ears because they hear. [17]For truly I tell you, many prophets and righteous people longed to see what you see but did not see it, and to hear what you hear but did not hear it.

[18]"Listen then to what the parable of the sower means: [19]When anyone hears the message about the kingdom and does not understand it, the evil one comes and snatches away what was sown in their heart. This is the seed sown along the path. [20]The seed falling on rocky ground refers to someone who hears the word and at once receives it with joy. [21]But since they have no root, they last only a short time. When trouble or persecution comes because of the word, they quickly fall away. [22]The seed falling among the thorns refers to someone who hears the word, but the worries of this life and the deceitfulness of wealth choke the word, making it unfruitful. [23]But the seed falling on good soil refers to someone who hears the word and understands it. This is the one who produces a crop, yielding a hundred, sixty or thirty times what was sown."

The Parable of the Weeds

[24]Jesus told them another parable: "The kingdom of heaven is like a man who sowed good seed in his field. [25]But while everyone was sleeping, his enemy came and sowed weeds among the wheat, and went away. [26]When the wheat sprouted and formed heads, then the weeds also appeared.

[27]"The owner's servants came to him and said, 'Sir, didn't you sow good seed in your field? Where then did the weeds come from?'

[28]"'An enemy did this,' he replied.

"The servants asked him, 'Do you want us to go and pull them up?'

[29]"'No,' he answered, 'because while you are pulling the weeds, you may uproot the wheat with them. [30]Let both grow together until the harvest. At that time I will tell the harvesters: First collect the weeds and tie them in bundles to be burned; then gather the wheat and bring it into my barn.'"

The Parables of the Mustard Seed and the Yeast

[31]He told them another parable: "The kingdom of heaven is like a mustard seed, which a man took and planted in his field. [32]Though it is the smallest of all seeds, yet when it grows, it is the largest of garden plants and becomes a tree, so that the birds come and perch in its branches."

[33]He told them still another parable: "The kingdom of heaven is like yeast that a woman took and mixed into about sixty pounds[b] of flour until it worked all through the dough."

[34]Jesus spoke all these things to the crowd in parables; he did not say anything to them without using a parable. [35]So was fulfilled what was spoken through the prophet:

"I will open my mouth in parables,
   I will utter things hidden since the
     creation of the world."[c]

The Parable of the Weeds Explained

[36]Then he left the crowd and went into the house. His disciples came to him and said, "Explain to us the parable of the weeds in the field."

[37]He answered, "The one who sowed the good seed is the Son of Man. [38]The field is the world, and the good seed stands for the people of the kingdom. The weeds are the people of the evil one, [39]and the enemy who sows them is the dev-

---

[a] 15 Isaiah 6:9,10 (see Septuagint)   [b] 33 Or about 27 kilograms   [c] 35 Psalm 78:2

il. The harvest is the end of the age, and the harvesters are angels.

[40]"As the weeds are pulled up and burned in the fire, so it will be at the end of the age. [41]The Son of Man will send out his angels, and they will weed out of his kingdom everything that causes sin and all who do evil. [42]They will throw them into the blazing furnace, where there will be weeping and gnashing of teeth. [43]Then the righteous will shine like the sun in the kingdom of their Father. Whoever has ears, let them hear.

The Parables of the Hidden Treasure and the Pearl

[44]"The kingdom of heaven is like treasure hidden in a field. When a man found it, he hid it again, and then in his joy went and sold all he had and bought that field.

[45]"Again, the kingdom of heaven is like a merchant looking for fine pearls. [46]When he found one of great value, he went away and sold everything he had and bought it.

The Parable of the Net

[47]"Once again, the kingdom of heaven is like a net that was let down into the lake and caught all kinds of fish. [48]When it was full, the fishermen pulled it up on the shore. Then they sat down and collected the good fish in baskets, but threw the bad away. [49]This is how it will be at the end of the age. The angels will come and separate the wicked from the righteous [50]and throw them into the blazing furnace, where there will be weeping and gnashing of teeth.

[51]"Have you understood all these things?" Jesus asked.

"Yes," they replied.

[52]He said to them, "Therefore every teacher of the law who has become a disciple in the kingdom of heaven is like the owner of a house who brings out of his storeroom new treasures as well as old."

A Prophet Without Honor

[53]When Jesus had finished these parables, he moved on from there. [54]Coming to his hometown, he began teaching the people in their synagogue, and they were amazed. "Where did this man get this wisdom and these miraculous powers?" they asked. [55]"Isn't this the carpenter's son? Isn't his mother's name Mary, and aren't his brothers James, Joseph, Simon and Judas? [56]Aren't all his sisters with us? Where then did this man get all these things?" [57]And they took offense at him.

But Jesus said to them, "A prophet is not without honor except in his own town and in his own home."

[58]And he did not do many miracles there because of their lack of faith.

JESUS PROFILE in leadership

An Unwavering Commitment to Speak the Truth

Matthew 12:22—13:53

The apostle Matthew knew Jesus—after all, he had accepted Christ's invitation to leave his life as a tax collector to follow him. But the Savior's commitment to speaking truth must have amazed even Matthew.

In a single day, Jesus chided the religious leaders for their insistence on seeing signs; he told his own mother that his true family consisted of all those who obey God; then he told a great crowd of people some revolutionary ideas about the kingdom of God.

This tax-collector-turned-disciple recognized Jesus as the kind of leader who spoke the Word of God with great conviction and authority, but who also spoke in such a way that only those who truly desired to know the truth could discern his meaning. He recognized Christ as the kind of leader who didn't necessarily say what the people *wanted* to hear, but one who always said what they *needed* to hear.

Not everyone who heard Jesus' words understood and applied them. Some eagerly received his truth, while the hearts of others had grown too hard to hear him.

As it was then, so it is today. Nevertheless, it is not the leader's job to prepare human hearts to receive God's truth. Rather, it is his or her responsibility to speak that same truth with all the authority he has given his servants.

Communicating Vision: Jesus Defined a Mission Larger Than Life

Matthew 13:3–58

Matthew 13 contains some of Jesus' simplest but most profound parables in the Bible. Jesus is a Master at communicating vision. His simple stories illustrate the kingdom of heaven. Jesus teaches us some fundamentals about communicating a vision:

1. *Simplify the message* (vv. 3, 10–13). Make it clear, repeat it often, focus on the familiar.

2. *See the person* (vv. 1–2, 9). Know the audience and its needs; don't try to impress.

3. *Seize the moment* (vv. 2, 14–17). Recognize teachable moments and receptivity.

4. *Show the truth* (v. 54). Be sure your life lends credibility to your words.

5. *See the response* (v. 51). Evaluate to ensure the audience understands and can respond to you.

John the Baptist Beheaded

14 At that time Herod the tetrarch heard the reports about Jesus, [2]and he said to his attendants, "This is John the Baptist; he has risen from the dead! That is why miraculous powers are at work in him."

[3]Now Herod had arrested John and bound him and put him in prison because of Herodias, his brother Philip's wife, [4]for John had been saying to him: "It is not lawful for you to have her." [5]Herod wanted to kill John, but he was afraid of the people, because they considered John a prophet.

[6]On Herod's birthday the daughter of Herodias danced for the guests and pleased Herod so much [7]that he promised with an oath to give her whatever she asked. [8]Prompted by her mother, she said, "Give me here on a platter the head of John the Baptist." [9]The king was distressed, but because of his oaths and his dinner guests, he ordered that her request be granted [10]and had John beheaded in the prison. [11]His head was brought in on a platter and given to the girl, who carried it to her mother. [12]John's disciples came

and took his body and buried it. Then they went and told Jesus.

Jesus Feeds the Five Thousand

[13]When Jesus heard what had happened, he withdrew by boat privately to a solitary place. Hearing of this, the crowds followed him on foot from the towns. [14]When Jesus landed and saw a large crowd, he had compassion on them and healed their sick.

[15]As evening approached, the disciples came to him and said, "This is a remote place, and it's already getting late. Send the crowds away, so they can go to the villages and buy themselves some food."

[16]Jesus replied, "They do not need to go away. You give them something to eat."

[17]"We have here only five loaves of bread and two fish," they answered.

[18]"Bring them here to me," he said. [19]And he directed the people to sit down on the grass. Taking the five loaves and the two fish and looking up to heaven, he gave thanks and broke the loaves. Then he gave them to the disciples, and the disciples gave them to the people. [20]They all ate and were satisfied, and the disciples picked up twelve basketfuls of broken pieces that were left over. [21]The number of those who ate was about five thousand men, besides women and children.

Jesus Walks on the Water

[22]Immediately Jesus made the disciples get into the boat and go on ahead of him to the other side, while he dismissed the crowd. [23]After he had dismissed them, he went up on a mountainside by himself to pray. Later that night, he was there alone, [24]and the boat was already a considerable distance from land, buffeted by the waves because the wind was against it.

[25]Shortly before dawn Jesus went out to them, walking on the lake. [26]When the disciples saw him walking on the lake, they were terrified. "It's a ghost," they said, and cried out in fear.

[27]But Jesus immediately said to them: "Take courage! It is I. Don't be afraid."

[28]"Lord, if it's you," Peter replied, "tell me to come to you on the water."

[29]"Come," he said.

Then Peter got down out of the boat, walked on the water and came toward Jesus. [30]But when he saw the wind, he was afraid and, beginning to sink, cried out, "Lord, save me!"

[31]Immediately Jesus reached out his hand and caught him. "You of little faith," he said, "why did you doubt?"

³²And when they climbed into the boat, the wind died down. ³³Then those who were in the boat worshiped him, saying, "Truly you are the Son of God."

³⁴When they had crossed over, they landed at Gennesaret. ³⁵And when the men of that place recognized Jesus, they sent word to all the surrounding country. People brought all their sick to him ³⁶and begged him to let the sick just touch the edge of his cloak, and all who touched it were healed.

That Which Defiles

15 Then some Pharisees and teachers of the law came to Jesus from Jerusalem and asked, ²"Why do your disciples break the tradition of the elders? They don't wash their hands before they eat!"

³Jesus replied, "And why do you break the command of God for the sake of your tradition? ⁴For God said, 'Honor your father and mother'[a] and 'Anyone who curses their father or mother is to be put to death.'[b] ⁵But you say that if anyone declares that what might have been used to help their father or mother is 'devoted to God,' ⁶they are not to 'honor their father or mother' with it. Thus you nullify the word of God for the sake of your tradition. ⁷You hypocrites! Isaiah was right when he prophesied about you:

⁸" 'These people honor me with their lips,
   but their hearts are far from me.
⁹They worship me in vain;
   their teachings are merely human rules.'[c]"

¹⁰Jesus called the crowd to him and said, "Listen and understand. ¹¹What goes into someone's mouth does not defile them, but what comes out of their mouth, that is what defiles them."

¹²Then the disciples came to him and asked, "Do you know that the Pharisees were offended when they heard this?"

¹³He replied, "Every plant that my heavenly Father has not planted will be pulled up by the roots. ¹⁴Leave them; they are blind guides.[d] If the blind lead the blind, both will fall into a pit."

¹⁵Peter said, "Explain the parable to us."

¹⁶"Are you still so dull?" Jesus asked them. ¹⁷"Don't you see that whatever enters the mouth goes into the stomach and then out of the body? ¹⁸But the things that come out of a person's mouth come from the heart, and these defile them. ¹⁹For out of the heart come evil thoughts — murder, adultery, sexual immorality, theft, false testimony, slander. ²⁰These are what defile a person; but eating with unwashed hands does not defile them."

The Faith of a Canaanite Woman

²¹Leaving that place, Jesus withdrew to the region of Tyre and Sidon. ²²A Canaanite woman from that vicinity came to him, crying out, "Lord, Son of David, have mercy on me! My daughter is demon-possessed and suffering terribly."

²³Jesus did not answer a word. So his disciples came to him and urged him, "Send her away, for she keeps crying out after us."

²⁴He answered, "I was sent only to the lost sheep of Israel."

²⁵The woman came and knelt before him. "Lord, help me!" she said.

²⁶He replied, "It is not right to take the children's bread and toss it to the dogs."

²⁷"Yes it is, Lord," she said. "Even the dogs eat the crumbs that fall from their master's table."

The Law of Addition: Jesus Faced Difficulty by Putting Others First

Matthew 14:1–14

When Jesus hears about John's execution, he withdraws to be alone. John is his cousin and the only one who seems to understand Jesus' mission. Now he is gone. Jesus wants some quiet time to grieve and gain perspective. But does he get it? Not a chance. When the multitudes learn of his presence, they seek him out, thinking only of their own needs.

This is often the lot of the leader. Jesus would have been justified in saying: "Can't you see I need some time away from all of you?" But he didn't. Instead, he responded by being "other-centered." The key was to focus on adding value to others: the Law of Addition. So Jesus felt compassion for the crowds and began to heal their sick.

One of the greatest remedies for our own suffering is serving others. Servant-leadership becomes a solution for both the one serving and the one being served.

---

[a] 4 Exodus 20:12; Deut. 5:16   [b] 4 Exodus 21:17; Lev. 20:9
[c] 9 Isaiah 29:13   [d] 14 Some manuscripts *blind guides of the blind*

²⁸Then Jesus said to her, "Woman, you have great faith! Your request is granted." And her daughter was healed at that moment.

Jesus Feeds the Four Thousand

²⁹Jesus left there and went along the Sea of Galilee. Then he went up on a mountainside and sat down. ³⁰Great crowds came to him, bringing the lame, the blind, the crippled, the mute and many others, and laid them at his feet; and he healed them. ³¹The people were amazed when they saw the mute speaking, the crippled made well, the lame walking and the blind seeing. And they praised the God of Israel.

³²Jesus called his disciples to him and said, "I have compassion for these people; they have already been with me three days and have nothing to eat. I do not want to send them away hungry, or they may collapse on the way."

³³His disciples answered, "Where could we get enough bread in this remote place to feed such a crowd?"

³⁴"How many loaves do you have?" Jesus asked.

"Seven," they replied, "and a few small fish."

³⁵He told the crowd to sit down on the ground. ³⁶Then he took the seven loaves and the fish, and when he had given thanks, he broke them and gave them to the disciples, and they in turn to the people. ³⁷They all ate and were satisfied. Afterward the disciples picked up seven basketfuls of broken pieces that were left over. ³⁸The number of those who ate was four thousand men, besides women and children. ³⁹After

Jesus had sent the crowd away, he got into the boat and went to the vicinity of Magadan.

The Demand for a Sign

16 The Pharisees and Sadducees came to Jesus and tested him by asking him to show them a sign from heaven.

²He replied, "When evening comes, you say, 'It will be fair weather, for the sky is red,' ³and in the morning, 'Today it will be stormy, for the sky is red and overcast.' You know how to interpret the appearance of the sky, but you cannot interpret the signs of the times.ᵃ ⁴A wicked and adulterous generation looks for a sign, but none will be given it except the sign of Jonah." Jesus then left them and went away.

The Yeast of the Pharisees and Sadducees

⁵When they went across the lake, the disciples forgot to take bread. ⁶"Be careful," Jesus said to them. "Be on your guard against the yeast of the Pharisees and Sadducees."

⁷They discussed this among themselves and said, "It is because we didn't bring any bread."

⁸Aware of their discussion, Jesus asked, "You of little faith, why are you talking among yourselves about having no bread? ⁹Do you still not understand? Don't you remember the five loaves for the five thousand, and how many basketfuls you gathered? ¹⁰Or the seven loaves for the four thousand, and how many basketfuls you gathered? ¹¹How is it you don't understand that I was not talking to you about bread? But be on your guard against the yeast of the Pharisees and Sadducees." ¹²Then they understood that he was not telling them to guard against the yeast used in bread, but against the teaching of the Pharisees and Sadducees.

Peter Declares That Jesus Is the Messiah

¹³When Jesus came to the region of Caesarea Philippi, he asked his disciples, "Who do people say the Son of Man is?"

¹⁴They replied, "Some say John the Baptist; others say Elijah; and still others, Jeremiah or one of the prophets."

¹⁵"But what about you?" he asked. "Who do you say I am?"

¹⁶Simon Peter answered, "You are the Messiah, the Son of the living God."

¹⁷Jesus replied, "Blessed are you, Simon son of Jonah, for this was not revealed to you by flesh

---

Problem Solving: The Fastest Way to Gain Leadership

Matthew 15:29–39

Jesus deepened his credibility by solving the problem of a hungry crowd:

1. He identified the problem and informed his team (v. 32).

2. He instructed them to brainstorm the solution (vv. 33–34).

3. He invited them into the problem-solving process (vv. 35–36).

4. He included them in the solution (vv. 35–38).

ᵃ 2,3 Some early manuscripts do not have *When evening comes . . . of the times.*

Peter's Charisma Compels Others to Affirm His Lead

Matthew 16:13–20

In a decisive conversation, Jesus asks Simon Peter about his identity: "Who do you say I am?" (Mt 16:15). Peter doesn't hesitate; he confesses Christ as Lord. Jesus then affirms his confession and declares that on the rock of that confession he will build his church (16:18). Jesus promises divine authority to Peter (16:19)—and during the infancy of the church, Peter did indeed lead in Jerusalem.

Peter was loaded with charisma and attracted others to follow him. As a disciple, he became a leader among leaders. What gave Peter this charisma that sparked others to affirm his leadership? From the four Gospels, we can surmise the answer:

1. *His Personality*
   Peter seemed to possess a sanguine/choleric temperament. Usually he was the first to speak.

2. *His Purpose*
   Peter embraced his mission as quickly as any of the twelve. He was the first to act.

3. *His People Skills*
   Peter was drawn to people. He acted like a magnet that either attracted or repelled others.

4. *His Passion*
   Peter had a fire inside. He wanted to please God and make a difference.

and blood, but by my Father in heaven. [18]And I tell you that you are Peter,[a] and on this rock I will build my church, and the gates of Hades[b] will not overcome it. [19]I will give you the keys of the kingdom of heaven; whatever you bind on earth will be[c] bound in heaven, and whatever you loose on earth will be[c] loosed in heaven." [20]Then he ordered his disciples not to tell anyone that he was the Messiah.

Jesus Predicts His Death

[21]From that time on Jesus began to explain to his disciples that he must go to Jerusalem and suffer many things at the hands of the elders, the chief priests and the teachers of the law, and that he must be killed and on the third day be raised to life.

[22]Peter took him aside and began to rebuke him. "Never, Lord!" he said. "This shall never happen to you!"

[23]Jesus turned and said to Peter, "Get behind me, Satan! You are a stumbling block to me; you do not have in mind the concerns of God, but merely human concerns."

[24]Then Jesus said to his disciples, "Whoever wants to be my disciple must deny themselves and take up their cross and follow me. [25]For whoever wants to save their life[d] will lose it, but whoever loses their life for me will find it. [26]What good will it be for someone to gain the whole world, yet forfeit their soul? Or what can anyone give in exchange for their soul? [27]For the Son of Man is going to come in his Father's glory with his angels, and then he will reward each person according to what they have done.

[28]"Truly I tell you, some who are standing here will not taste death before they see the Son of Man coming in his kingdom."

The Transfiguration

17 After six days Jesus took with him Peter, James and John the brother of James, and led them up a high mountain by themselves. [2]There he was transfigured before them. His face shone like the sun, and his clothes became as white as the light. [3]Just then there appeared before them Moses and Elijah, talking with Jesus.

[4]Peter said to Jesus, "Lord, it is good for us to be here. If you wish, I will put up three shelters — one for you, one for Moses and one for Elijah."

[5]While he was still speaking, a bright cloud covered them, and a voice from the cloud said, "This is my Son, whom I love; with him I am well pleased. Listen to him!"

[6]When the disciples heard this, they fell facedown to the ground, terrified. [7]But Jesus came and touched them. "Get up," he said. "Don't be

---

[a] 18 The Greek word for *Peter* means *rock.*   [b] 18 That is, the realm of the dead   [c] 19 Or *will have been*   [d] 25 The Greek word means either *life* or *soul;* also in verse 26.

afraid." ⁸When they looked up, they saw no one except Jesus.

⁹As they were coming down the mountain, Jesus instructed them, "Don't tell anyone what you have seen, until the Son of Man has been raised from the dead."

¹⁰The disciples asked him, "Why then do the teachers of the law say that Elijah must come first?"

¹¹Jesus replied, "To be sure, Elijah comes and will restore all things. ¹²But I tell you, Elijah has already come, and they did not recognize him, but have done to him everything they wished. In the same way the Son of Man is going to suffer at their hands." ¹³Then the disciples understood that he was talking to them about John the Baptist.

Jesus Heals a Demon-Possessed Boy

¹⁴When they came to the crowd, a man approached Jesus and knelt before him. ¹⁵"Lord, have mercy on my son," he said. "He has seizures and is suffering greatly. He often falls into the fire or into the water. ¹⁶I brought him to your disciples, but they could not heal him."

¹⁷"You unbelieving and perverse generation," Jesus replied, "how long shall I stay with you? How long shall I put up with you? Bring the boy here to me." ¹⁸Jesus rebuked the demon, and it came out of the boy, and he was healed at that moment.

¹⁹Then the disciples came to Jesus in private and asked, "Why couldn't we drive it out?"

²⁰He replied, "Because you have so little faith. Truly I tell you, if you have faith as small as a mustard seed, you can say to this mountain, 'Move from here to there,' and it will move. Nothing will be impossible for you." [21]*a*

Jesus Predicts His Death a Second Time

²²When they came together in Galilee, he said to them, "The Son of Man is going to be delivered into the hands of men. ²³They will kill him, and on the third day he will be raised to life." And the disciples were filled with grief.

The Temple Tax

²⁴After Jesus and his disciples arrived in Capernaum, the collectors of the two-drachma temple tax came to Peter and asked, "Doesn't your teacher pay the temple tax?"

²⁵"Yes, he does," he replied.

When Peter came into the house, Jesus was the first to speak. "What do you think, Simon?" he asked. "From whom do the kings of the earth collect duty and taxes — from their own children or from others?"

Mentoring: Jesus Assesses and Holds His Disciples Accountable

Matthew 17:14–21

Following Jesus' transfiguration, he comes down from the mountain to find nine of his disciples attempting to cast a demon out of a boy. At that moment, he again becomes a mentor for his men. He commits himself to the training of the Twelve, believing every exposure they get becomes an opportunity to learn. Review the story and see what we learn from Jesus, the leadership Mentor:

1. He feels angry that his disciples can't do the job (v. 17).

2. He assumes responsibility to model for them what they should do (v. 18).

3. He evaluates their performance and assesses why they failed (vv. 19–21).

4. He affirms the truth and holds them accountable to embrace it (v. 20–21).

Jesus' methods include four elements: instruction; demonstration; experience; and assessment. He teaches them, shows them, allows them to try it themselves, and then processes what happened. Jesus is the master Mentor in developing leaders.

---

²⁶"From others," Peter answered.

"Then the children are exempt," Jesus said to him. ²⁷"But so that we may not cause offense, go to the lake and throw out your line. Take the first fish you catch; open its mouth and you will find a four-drachma coin. Take it and give it to them for my tax and yours."

The Greatest in the Kingdom of Heaven

18 At that time the disciples came to Jesus and asked, "Who, then, is the greatest in the kingdom of heaven?"

²He called a little child to him, and placed the child among them. ³And he said: "Truly I tell you, unless you change and become like little children, you will never enter the kingdom of

---

a 21 Some manuscripts include here words similar to Mark 9:29.

heaven. [4]Therefore, whoever takes the lowly position of this child is the greatest in the kingdom of heaven. [5]And whoever welcomes one such child in my name welcomes me.

Causing to Stumble

[6]"If anyone causes one of these little ones — those who believe in me — to stumble, it would be better for them to have a large millstone hung around their neck and to be drowned in the depths of the sea. [7]Woe to the world because of the things that cause people to stumble! Such things must come, but woe to the person through whom they come! [8]If your hand or your foot causes you to stumble, cut it off and throw it away. It is better for you to enter life maimed or crippled than to have two hands or two feet and be thrown into eternal fire. [9]And if your eye causes you to stumble, gouge it out and throw it away. It is better for you to enter life with one eye than to have two eyes and be thrown into the fire of hell.

The Parable of the Wandering Sheep

[10]"See that you do not despise one of these little ones. For I tell you that their angels in heaven always see the face of my Father in heaven. [11]a

[12]"What do you think? If a man owns a hundred sheep, and one of them wanders away, will he not leave the ninety-nine on the hills and go to look for the one that wandered off? [13]And if he finds it, truly I tell you, he is happier about that one sheep than about the ninety-nine that did not wander off. [14]In the same way your Father in heaven is not willing that any of these little ones should perish.

Dealing With Sin in the Church

[15]"If your brother or sister[b] sins,[c] go and point out their fault, just between the two of you. If they listen to you, you have won them over. [16]But if they will not listen, take one or two others along, so that 'every matter may be established by the testimony of two or three witnesses.'[d] [17]If they still refuse to listen, tell it to the church; and if they refuse to listen even to the church, treat them as you would a pagan or a tax collector.

[18]"Truly I tell you, whatever you bind on earth

---

[a] 11 Some manuscripts include here the words of Luke 19:10.
[b] 15 The Greek word for *brother or sister* (*adelphos*) refers here to a fellow disciple, whether man or woman; also in verses 21 and 35.   [c] 15 Some manuscripts *sins against you*
[d] 16 Deut. 19:15

Conflict Resolution: Jesus Taught How to Manage Conflict

Matthew 18:15–20

There may be no clearer passage in the Gospels on conflict resolution than Matthew 18. While Jesus spoke about addressing sin in the church, his words suggest broader principles.

According to Jesus, addressing conflict and healing offenses should be a priority for us. He even instructs us to postpone our worship if we remember an unresolved offense (Mt 5:23–24).

Conflicts *will* arise in any organization. Humans disagree because they are wired differently and have different agendas. Note what Jesus taught about organizational conflict when someone has clearly done wrong:

1. Initiate the contact (v. 15).

2. Confront the person in private (v. 15).

3. If no resolution comes, meet again with one or two more people (v. 16).

4. Confirm the facts in the meeting and work toward a solution (v. 16).

5. If no resolution comes, bring the issue before the church or organization (v. 17).

6. Agree upon the truth and the appropriate options for the offender (v. 17).

7. If no resolution comes, release the offender from the church or organization (v. 17).

Behind this process lies the authority Jesus has given to church leaders (Mt 18:18–20). We must act wisely, because we have God-given authority (18:18), because God will confirm and support the decisions made in harmony (18:19), and because he is present when we gather in his name (18:20).

will be[a] bound in heaven, and whatever you loose on earth will be[a] loosed in heaven.

[19]"Again, truly I tell you that if two of you on earth agree about anything they ask for, it will be done for them by my Father in heaven. [20]For where two or three gather in my name, there am I with them."

The Parable of the Unmerciful Servant

[21]Then Peter came to Jesus and asked, "Lord, how many times shall I forgive my brother or sister who sins against me? Up to seven times?"

[22]Jesus answered, "I tell you, not seven times, but seventy-seven times.[b]

[23]"Therefore, the kingdom of heaven is like a king who wanted to settle accounts with his servants. [24]As he began the settlement, a man who owed him ten thousand bags of gold[c] was brought to him. [25]Since he was not able to pay, the master ordered that he and his wife and his children and all that he had be sold to repay the debt.

[26]"At this the servant fell on his knees before him. 'Be patient with me,' he begged, 'and I will pay back everything.' [27]The servant's master took pity on him, canceled the debt and let him go.

[28]"But when that servant went out, he found one of his fellow servants who owed him a hundred silver coins.[d] He grabbed him and began to choke him. 'Pay back what you owe me!' he demanded.

[29]"His fellow servant fell to his knees and begged him, 'Be patient with me, and I will pay it back.'

[30]"But he refused. Instead, he went off and had the man thrown into prison until he could pay the debt. [31]When the other servants saw what had happened, they were outraged and went and told their master everything that had happened.

[32]"Then the master called the servant in. 'You wicked servant,' he said, 'I canceled all that debt of yours because you begged me to. [33]Shouldn't you have had mercy on your fellow servant just as I had on you?' [34]In anger his master handed him over to the jailers to be tortured, until he should pay back all he owed.

[35]"This is how my heavenly Father will treat each of you unless you forgive your brother or sister from your heart."

Divorce

19 When Jesus had finished saying these things, he left Galilee and went into the region of Judea to the other side of the Jordan. [2]Large crowds followed him, and he healed them there.

[3]Some Pharisees came to him to test him. They asked, "Is it lawful for a man to divorce his wife for any and every reason?"

[4]"Haven't you read," he replied, "that at the beginning the Creator 'made them male and female,'[e] [5]and said, 'For this reason a man will leave his father and mother and be united to his wife, and the two will become one flesh'[f]? [6]So they are no longer two, but one flesh. Therefore what God has joined together, let no one separate."

[7]"Why then," they asked, "did Moses command that a man give his wife a certificate of divorce and send her away?"

[8]Jesus replied, "Moses permitted you to divorce your wives because your hearts were hard. But it was not this way from the beginning. [9]I tell you that anyone who divorces his wife, except for sexual immorality, and marries another woman commits adultery."

[10]The disciples said to him, "If this is the situation between a husband and wife, it is better not to marry."

[11]Jesus replied, "Not everyone can accept this word, but only those to whom it has been given. [12]For there are eunuchs who were born that way, and there are eunuchs who have been made eunuchs by others—and there are those who choose to live like eunuchs for the sake of the kingdom of heaven. The one who can accept this should accept it."

The Little Children and Jesus

[13]Then people brought little children to Jesus for him to place his hands on them and pray for them. But the disciples rebuked them.

[14]Jesus said, "Let the little children come to me, and do not hinder them, for the kingdom of heaven belongs to such as these." [15]When he had placed his hands on them, he went on from there.

The Rich and the Kingdom of God

[16]Just then a man came up to Jesus and asked, "Teacher, what good thing must I do to get eternal life?"

[17]"Why do you ask me about what is good?" Jesus replied. "There is only One who is good.

---

[a] 18 Or *will have been*   [b] 22 Or *seventy times seven*
[c] 24 Greek *ten thousand talents*; a talent was worth about 20 years of a day laborer's wages.   [d] 28 Greek *a hundred denarii*; a denarius was the usual daily wage of a day laborer (see 20:2).   [e] 4 Gen. 1:27   [f] 5 Gen. 2:24

If you want to enter life, keep the commandments." ¹⁸"Which ones?" he inquired.

Jesus replied, " 'You shall not murder, you shall not commit adultery, you shall not steal, you shall not give false testimony, ¹⁹honor your father and mother,'ᵃ and 'love your neighbor as yourself.'ᵇ"

²⁰"All these I have kept," the young man said. "What do I still lack?"

²¹Jesus answered, "If you want to be perfect, go, sell your possessions and give to the poor, and you will have treasure in heaven. Then come, follow me."

²²When the young man heard this, he went away sad, because he had great wealth.

²³Then Jesus said to his disciples, "Truly I tell you, it is hard for someone who is rich to enter the kingdom of heaven. ²⁴Again I tell you, it is easier for a camel to go through the eye of a needle than for someone who is rich to enter the kingdom of God."

²⁵When the disciples heard this, they were greatly astonished and asked, "Who then can be saved?"

²⁶Jesus looked at them and said, "With man this is impossible, but with God all things are possible."

²⁷Peter answered him, "We have left everything to follow you! What then will there be for us?"

²⁸Jesus said to them, "Truly I tell you, at the renewal of all things, when the Son of Man sits on his glorious throne, you who have followed me will also sit on twelve thrones, judging the twelve tribes of Israel. ²⁹And everyone who has left houses or brothers or sisters or father or mother or wifeᶜ or children or fields for my sake will receive a hundred times as much and will

Discernment: Jesus and the Rich Young Ruler

Matthew 19:16–26

Jesus cut through the periphery to get to the real issues. Discerning that a young man had failed to "have no other gods before [him]" (Ex 20:3), Jesus tells him to sell everything, give it to the poor, and follow him. The man walks away, unable to take the step that would free him from bondage.

inherit eternal life. ³⁰But many who are first will be last, and many who are last will be first.

The Parable of the Workers in the Vineyard

20 "For the kingdom of heaven is like a landowner who went out early in the morning to hire workers for his vineyard. ²He agreed to pay them a denariusᵈ for the day and sent them into his vineyard.

³"About nine in the morning he went out and saw others standing in the marketplace doing nothing. ⁴He told them, 'You also go and work in my vineyard, and I will pay you whatever is right.' ⁵So they went.

"He went out again about noon and about three in the afternoon and did the same thing. ⁶About five in the afternoon he went out and found still others standing around. He asked them, 'Why have you been standing here all day long doing nothing?'

⁷"'Because no one has hired us,' they answered.

"He said to them, 'You also go and work in my vineyard.'

⁸"When evening came, the owner of the vineyard said to his foreman, 'Call the workers and pay them their wages, beginning with the last ones hired and going on to the first.'

⁹"The workers who were hired about five in the afternoon came and each received a denarius. ¹⁰So when those came who were hired first, they expected to receive more. But each one of them also received a denarius. ¹¹When they received it, they began to grumble against the landowner. ¹²'These who were hired last worked only one hour,' they said, 'and you have made them equal to us who have borne the burden of the work and the heat of the day.'

¹³"But he answered one of them, 'I am not being unfair to you, friend. Didn't you agree to work for a denarius? ¹⁴Take your pay and go. I want to give the one who was hired last the same as I gave you. ¹⁵Don't I have the right to do what I want with my own money? Or are you envious because I am generous?'

¹⁶"So the last will be first, and the first will be last."

Jesus Predicts His Death a Third Time

¹⁷Now Jesus was going up to Jerusalem. On the way, he took the Twelve aside and said to

---

ᵃ 19 Exodus 20:12-16; Deut. 5:16-20   ᵇ 19 Lev. 19:18
ᶜ 29 Some manuscripts do not have or wife.   ᵈ 2 A denarius was the usual daily wage of a day laborer.

Attitude: Leaders Must Focus on God's Ability, Not Their Own

Matthew 20:1–16

Leaders should often read this story. It describes God's grace, illustrated by a landowner and his vineyard workers. The workers show us how leaders look when they take their eyes off God and focus on themselves. Through this parable Jesus attempts to correct wrong attitudes. He is trying to address:

1. *Self-absorption*
   We grumble and complain about inequities. We focus more on our work than God's.

2. *Comparison*
   We ignore God's grace, remaining preoccupied with the status of others.

3. *Presumption*
   We assume too much when it comes to rewards, forgetting that every blessing is a gift.

4. *Distortion*
   When we judge others as unworthy, we misunderstand that the entire kingdom is built on grace.

them, 18"We are going up to Jerusalem, and the Son of Man will be delivered over to the chief priests and the teachers of the law. They will condemn him to death 19and will hand him over to the Gentiles to be mocked and flogged and crucified. On the third day he will be raised to life!"

A Mother's Request

20Then the mother of Zebedee's sons came to Jesus with her sons and, kneeling down, asked a favor of him.

21"What is it you want?" he asked.

She said, "Grant that one of these two sons of mine may sit at your right and the other at your left in your kingdom."

22"You don't know what you are asking," Jesus said to them. "Can you drink the cup I am going to drink?"

"We can," they answered.

23Jesus said to them, "You will indeed drink from my cup, but to sit at my right or left is not for me to grant. These places belong to those for whom they have been prepared by my Father."

24When the ten heard about this, they were indignant with the two brothers. 25Jesus called them together and said, "You know that the rulers of the Gentiles lord it over them, and their high officials exercise authority over them. 26Not so with you. Instead, whoever wants to become great among you must be your servant, 27and whoever wants to be first must be your slave— 28just as the Son of Man did not come to be served, but to serve, and to give his life as a ransom for many."

Two Blind Men Receive Sight

29As Jesus and his disciples were leaving Jericho, a large crowd followed him. 30Two blind men were sitting by the roadside, and when they heard that Jesus was going by, they shouted, "Lord, Son of David, have mercy on us!"

31The crowd rebuked them and told them to be quiet, but they shouted all the louder, "Lord, Son of David, have mercy on us!"

32Jesus stopped and called them. "What do you want me to do for you?" he asked.

33"Lord," they answered, "we want our sight."

34Jesus had compassion on them and touched their eyes. Immediately they received their sight and followed him.

Jesus Comes to Jerusalem as King

21 As they approached Jerusalem and came to Bethphage on the Mount of Olives, Jesus sent two disciples, 2saying to them, "Go to the village ahead of you, and at once you will find a donkey tied there, with her colt by her. Untie them and bring them to me. 3If anyone says anything to you, say that the Lord needs them, and he will send them right away."

4This took place to fulfill what was spoken through the prophet:

5"Say to Daughter Zion,
    'See, your king comes to you,
gentle and riding on a donkey,
    and on a colt, the foal of a donkey.'"*a*

6The disciples went and did as Jesus had instructed them. 7They brought the donkey and the colt and placed their cloaks on them for Jesus to sit on. 8A very large crowd spread their cloaks on the road, while others cut branches

a 5 Zech. 9:9

Servanthood: Jesus Teaches That We Lead by Serving and Serve by Leading

Matthew 20:25–28

As Jesus makes his way toward Jerusalem to be executed, the mother of James and John requests that her sons be given a preferred seat, next to Jesus, in the kingdom of heaven. Both the disciples and their families have become preoccupied with status rather than serving. They have missed the whole point of Jesus' leadership.

Jesus tells them plainly that his style of leadership stands in stark contrast to the world's. He teaches that the greatest must be the servant. Leadership is about adding value, not getting perks (the Law of Addition). As responsibilities increase, rights decrease. Consider a "leadership pyramid" based on this principle:

RIGHTS

Opportunities and Responsibilities

RESPONSIBILITIES

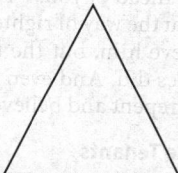

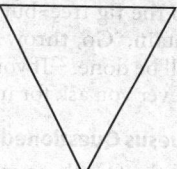

Rights DECREASE as you
climb toward leadership
in the church

Responsibilities INCREASE as you
climb toward leadership
in the church

Options and Rights

If this pyramid represents your life and the base represents the beginning of your leadership journey, your range of options is widest at the beginning. The younger you are, the more liberties you have with your time, vocabulary, money, etc. But as you grow into leadership, you deliberately surrender those rights and options. Servants push for no options and assume no rights.

---

from the trees and spread them on the road. [9]The crowds that went ahead of him and those that followed shouted,

"Hosanna[a] to the Son of David!"

"Blessed is he who comes in the name of the Lord!"[b]

"Hosanna[a] in the highest heaven!"

[10]When Jesus entered Jerusalem, the whole city was stirred and asked, "Who is this?"

[11]The crowds answered, "This is Jesus, the prophet from Nazareth in Galilee."

Jesus at the Temple

[12]Jesus entered the temple courts and drove out all who were buying and selling there. He overturned the tables of the money changers and the benches of those selling doves. [13]"It is written," he said to them, "'My house will be called a house of prayer,'[c] but you are making it 'a den of robbers.'[d]"

[14]The blind and the lame came to him at the temple, and he healed them. [15]But when the chief priests and the teachers of the law saw the wonderful things he did and the children shouting in the temple courts, "Hosanna to the Son of David," they were indignant.

[16]"Do you hear what these children are saying?" they asked him.

"Yes," replied Jesus, "have you never read,

---

[a] 9 A Hebrew expression meaning "Save!" which became an exclamation of praise; also in verse 15   [b] 9 Psalm 118:25,26   [c] 13 Isaiah 56:7   [d] 13 Jer. 7:11

" 'From the lips of children and infants
    you, Lord, have called forth your
      praise'[a]?"

¹⁷And he left them and went out of the city to Bethany, where he spent the night.

Jesus Curses a Fig Tree

¹⁸Early in the morning, as Jesus was on his way back to the city, he was hungry. ¹⁹Seeing a fig tree by the road, he went up to it but found nothing on it except leaves. Then he said to it, "May you never bear fruit again!" Immediately the tree withered.

²⁰When the disciples saw this, they were amazed. "How did the fig tree wither so quickly?" they asked.

²¹Jesus replied, "Truly I tell you, if you have faith and do not doubt, not only can you do what was done to the fig tree, but also you can say to this mountain, 'Go, throw yourself into the sea,' and it will be done. ²²If you believe, you will receive whatever you ask for in prayer."

The Authority of Jesus Questioned

²³Jesus entered the temple courts, and, while he was teaching, the chief priests and the elders of the people came to him. "By what authority are you doing these things?" they asked. "And who gave you this authority?"

²⁴Jesus replied, "I will also ask you one question. If you answer me, I will tell you by what authority I am doing these things. ²⁵John's baptism—where did it come from? Was it from heaven, or of human origin?"

They discussed it among themselves and said, "If we say, 'From heaven,' he will ask, 'Then why didn't you believe him?' ²⁶But if we say, 'Of human origin'—we are afraid of the people, for they all hold that John was a prophet."

Communication: The Test of a Hostile Crowd

Matthew 21:23–27

The religious leaders challenged Jesus' authority when he entered the temple. He responded by using the best tool a leader has when facing such antagonism: He answered their question with a question. Handling people who don't want to travel with you is the acid test of a leader's poise.

²⁷So they answered Jesus, "We don't know."

Then he said, "Neither will I tell you by what authority I am doing these things.

The Parable of the Two Sons

²⁸"What do you think? There was a man who had two sons. He went to the first and said, 'Son, go and work today in the vineyard.'

²⁹" 'I will not,' he answered, but later he changed his mind and went.

³⁰"Then the father went to the other son and said the same thing. He answered, 'I will, sir,' but he did not go.

³¹"Which of the two did what his father wanted?"

"The first," they answered.

Jesus said to them, "Truly I tell you, the tax collectors and the prostitutes are entering the kingdom of God ahead of you. ³²For John came to you to show you the way of righteousness, and you did not believe him, but the tax collectors and the prostitutes did. And even after you saw this, you did not repent and believe him.

The Parable of the Tenants

³³"Listen to another parable: There was a landowner who planted a vineyard. He put a wall around it, dug a winepress in it and built a watchtower. Then he rented the vineyard to some farmers and moved to another place. ³⁴When the harvest time approached, he sent his servants to the tenants to collect his fruit.

³⁵"The tenants seized his servants; they beat one, killed another, and stoned a third. ³⁶Then he sent other servants to them, more than the first time, and the tenants treated them the same way. ³⁷Last of all, he sent his son to them. 'They will respect my son,' he said.

³⁸"But when the tenants saw the son, they said to each other, 'This is the heir. Come, let's kill him and take his inheritance.' ³⁹So they took him and threw him out of the vineyard and killed him.

⁴⁰"Therefore, when the owner of the vineyard comes, what will he do to those tenants?"

⁴¹"He will bring those wretches to a wretched end," they replied, "and he will rent the vineyard to other tenants, who will give him his share of the crop at harvest time."

⁴²Jesus said to them, "Have you never read in the Scriptures:

" 'The stone the builders rejected
    has become the cornerstone;

---

[a] 16 Psalm 8:2 (see Septuagint)

the Lord has done this,
and it is marvelous in our eyes'[a]?

43"Therefore I tell you that the kingdom of God will be taken away from you and given to a people who will produce its fruit. 44Anyone who falls on this stone will be broken to pieces; anyone on whom it falls will be crushed."[b]

45When the chief priests and the Pharisees heard Jesus' parables, they knew he was talking about them. 46They looked for a way to arrest him, but they were afraid of the crowd because the people held that he was a prophet.

The Parable of the Wedding Banquet

22 Jesus spoke to them again in parables, saying: 2"The kingdom of heaven is like a king who prepared a wedding banquet for his son. 3He sent his servants to those who had been invited to the banquet to tell them to come, but they refused to come.

4"Then he sent some more servants and said, 'Tell those who have been invited that I have prepared my dinner: My oxen and fattened cattle have been butchered, and everything is ready. Come to the wedding banquet.'

5"But they paid no attention and went off — one to his field, another to his business. 6The rest seized his servants, mistreated them and killed them. 7The king was enraged. He sent his army and destroyed those murderers and burned their city.

8"Then he said to his servants, 'The wedding banquet is ready, but those I invited did not deserve to come. 9So go to the street corners and invite to the banquet anyone you find.' 10So the servants went out into the streets and gathered all the people they could find, the bad as well as the good, and the wedding hall was filled with guests.

11"But when the king came in to see the guests, he noticed a man there who was not wearing wedding clothes. 12He asked, 'How did you get in here without wedding clothes, friend?' The man was speechless.

13"Then the king told the attendants, 'Tie him hand and foot, and throw him outside, into the darkness, where there will be weeping and gnashing of teeth.'

14"For many are invited, but few are chosen."

Paying the Imperial Tax to Caesar

15Then the Pharisees went out and laid plans to trap him in his words. 16They sent their disciples to him along with the Herodians. "Teach-

er," they said, "we know that you are a man of integrity and that you teach the way of God in accordance with the truth. You aren't swayed by others, because you pay no attention to who they are. 17Tell us then, what is your opinion? Is it right to pay the imperial tax[c] to Caesar or not?"

18But Jesus, knowing their evil intent, said, "You hypocrites, why are you trying to trap me? 19Show me the coin used for paying the tax." They brought him a denarius, 20and he asked them, "Whose image is this? And whose inscription?"

21"Caesar's," they replied.

Then he said to them, "So give back to Caesar what is Caesar's, and to God what is God's."

22When they heard this, they were amazed. So they left him and went away.

Marriage at the Resurrection

23That same day the Sadducees, who say there is no resurrection, came to him with a question. 24"Teacher," they said, "Moses told us that if a man dies without having children, his brother must marry the widow and raise up offspring for him. 25Now there were seven brothers among us. The first one married and died, and since he had no children, he left his wife to his brother. 26The same thing happened to the second and third brother, right on down to the seventh. 27Finally, the woman died. 28Now then, at the resurrection, whose wife will she be of the seven, since all of them were married to her?"

29Jesus replied, "You are in error because you do not know the Scriptures or the power of God. 30At the resurrection people will neither marry nor be given in marriage; they will be like the angels in heaven. 31But about the resurrection of the dead — have you not read what God said to you, 32'I am the God of Abraham, the God of Isaac, and the God of Jacob'[d]? He is not the God of the dead but of the living."

33When the crowds heard this, they were astonished at his teaching.

The Greatest Commandment

34Hearing that Jesus had silenced the Sadducees, the Pharisees got together. 35One of them, an expert in the law, tested him with this question: 36"Teacher, which is the greatest commandment in the Law?"

37Jesus replied: "'Love the Lord your God

---

[a] 42 Psalm 118:22,23   [b] 44 Some manuscripts do not have verse 44.   [c] 17 A special tax levied on subject peoples, not on Roman citizens   [d] 32 Exodus 3:6

The Law of Solid Ground: Jesus' Character

Matthew 22:15–46

Each time Jesus faces some leadership tests, he proves his integrity by handling the situation expertly:

1. *The Pharisees attempt to trap him with the tax issue* (vv. 15–22).
   Should the Jews pay taxes to Caesar? Either expected answer would get Jesus in trouble, either with the Romans or the Jews. So Jesus answers the question with a question. He asks for a coin, then says: "Whose image is this? And whose inscription?" (Mt 22:20). The coin carried Caesar's image—so it should be surrendered to him. But the people were made in God's image—so they should surrender themselves to him.

2. *The Sadducees attempt to trap him with the marriage issue* (vv. 23–33).
   If a woman lost several husbands to premature death, whose wife would she be in heaven? Jesus explains there is no marriage in heaven, so it is a moot point. But then he poses his own question, proving from their own scriptures the existence of both a resurrection and a heaven.

3. *The Pharisees attempt to ask him an unanswerable question* (vv. 34–40).
   What was the greatest commandment? Surely Jesus wouldn't want to leave out any. Jesus summarizes the law with a single command: Love God and your neighbor. Then he poses an unanswerable question of his own, proving he knew the scriptures better than they did (vv. 41–46).

---

with all your heart and with all your soul and with all your mind.'[a] ³⁸This is the first and greatest commandment. ³⁹And the second is like it: 'Love your neighbor as yourself.'[b] ⁴⁰All the Law and the Prophets hang on these two commandments."

Whose Son Is the Messiah?

⁴¹While the Pharisees were gathered together, Jesus asked them, ⁴²"What do you think about the Messiah? Whose son is he?"

"The son of David," they replied.

⁴³He said to them, "How is it then that David, speaking by the Spirit, calls him 'Lord'? For he says,

⁴⁴"'The Lord said to my Lord:
    "Sit at my right hand
until I put your enemies
    under your feet."'[c]

⁴⁵If then David calls him 'Lord,' how can he be his son?" ⁴⁶No one could say a word in reply, and from that day on no one dared to ask him any more questions.

A Warning Against Hypocrisy

23 Then Jesus said to the crowds and to his disciples: ²"The teachers of the law and the Pharisees sit in Moses' seat. ³So you must be careful to do everything they tell you. But do not do what they do, for they do not practice what they preach. ⁴They tie up heavy, cumbersome loads and put them on other people's shoulders, but they themselves are not willing to lift a finger to move them.

⁵"Everything they do is done for people to see: They make their phylacteries[d] wide and the tassels on their garments long; ⁶they love the place of honor at banquets and the most important seats in the synagogues; ⁷they love to be greeted with respect in the marketplaces and to be called 'Rabbi' by others.

⁸"But you are not to be called 'Rabbi,' for you have one Teacher, and you are all brothers. ⁹And do not call anyone on earth 'father,' for you have one Father, and he is in heaven. ¹⁰Nor are you to be called instructors, for you have one Instructor, the Messiah. ¹¹The greatest among you will be your servant. ¹²For those who exalt themselves will be humbled, and those who humble themselves will be exalted.

Seven Woes on the Teachers of the Law and the Pharisees

¹³"Woe to you, teachers of the law and Pharisees, you hypocrites! You shut the door of the kingdom of heaven in people's faces. You your-

---

[a] 37 Deut. 6:5   [b] 39 Lev. 19:18   [c] 44 Psalm 110:1
[d] 5 That is, boxes containing Scripture verses, worn on forehead and arm

selves do not enter, nor will you let those enter who are trying to. [14]*a*

15"Woe to you, teachers of the law and Pharisees, you hypocrites! You travel over land and sea to win a single convert, and when you have succeeded, you make them twice as much a child of hell as you are.

16"Woe to you, blind guides! You say, 'If anyone swears by the temple, it means nothing; but anyone who swears by the gold of the temple is bound by that oath.' 17You blind fools! Which is greater: the gold, or the temple that makes the gold sacred? 18You also say, 'If anyone swears by the altar, it means nothing; but anyone who swears by the gift on the altar is bound by that oath.' 19You blind men! Which is greater: the gift, or the altar that makes the gift sacred? 20Therefore, anyone who swears by the altar swears by it and by everything on it. 21And anyone who swears by the temple swears by it and by the one who dwells in it. 22And anyone who swears by heaven swears by God's throne and by the one who sits on it.

23"Woe to you, teachers of the law and Pharisees, you hypocrites! You give a tenth of your spices — mint, dill and cumin. But you have neglected the more important matters of the law — justice, mercy and faithfulness. You should have practiced the latter, without neglecting the former. 24You blind guides! You strain out a gnat but swallow a camel.

25"Woe to you, teachers of the law and Pharisees, you hypocrites! You clean the outside of the cup and dish, but inside they are full of greed and self-indulgence. 26Blind Pharisee! First clean the inside of the cup and dish, and then the outside also will be clean.

27"Woe to you, teachers of the law and Pharisees, you hypocrites! You are like whitewashed tombs, which look beautiful on the outside but on the inside are full of the bones of the dead and everything unclean. 28In the same way, on the outside you appear to people as righteous but on the inside you are full of hypocrisy and wickedness.

29"Woe to you, teachers of the law and Pharisees, you hypocrites! You build tombs for the prophets and decorate the graves of the righteous. 30And you say, 'If we had lived in the days of our ancestors, we would not have taken part with them in shedding the blood of the prophets.' 31So you testify against yourselves that you are the descendants of those who murdered the prophets. 32Go ahead, then, and complete what your ancestors started!

The Law of Solid Ground: The Pharisees' Contrast

Matthew 23:13–32

Jesus instructed others to follow the Pharisees' words, but not their actions. Their confused priorities, two-faced behavior, impure motives and damaging leadership had lost them the trust of many common folk. Leaders must never forget: If people can't trust you, neither will they travel with you.

33"You snakes! You brood of vipers! How will you escape being condemned to hell? 34Therefore I am sending you prophets and sages and teachers. Some of them you will kill and crucify; others you will flog in your synagogues and pursue from town to town. 35And so upon you will come all the righteous blood that has been shed on earth, from the blood of righteous Abel to the blood of Zechariah son of Berekiah, whom you murdered between the temple and the altar. 36Truly I tell you, all this will come on this generation.

37"Jerusalem, Jerusalem, you who kill the prophets and stone those sent to you, how often I have longed to gather your children together, as a hen gathers her chicks under her wings, and you were not willing. 38Look, your house is left to you desolate. 39For I tell you, you will not see me again until you say, 'Blessed is he who comes in the name of the Lord.'*b*"

The Destruction of the Temple and Signs of the End Times

24 Jesus left the temple and was walking away when his disciples came up to him to call his attention to its buildings. 2"Do you see all these things?" he asked. "Truly I tell you, not one stone here will be left on another; every one will be thrown down."

3As Jesus was sitting on the Mount of Olives, the disciples came to him privately. "Tell us," they said, "when will this happen, and what will be the sign of your coming and of the end of the age?"

4Jesus answered: "Watch out that no one deceives you. 5For many will come in my name, claiming, 'I am the Messiah,' and will deceive

---

a 14 Some manuscripts include here words similar to Mark 12:40 and Luke 20:47.   *b 39* Psalm 118:26

many. [6]You will hear of wars and rumors of wars, but see to it that you are not alarmed. Such things must happen, but the end is still to come. [7]Nation will rise against nation, and kingdom against kingdom. There will be famines and earthquakes in various places. [8]All these are the beginning of birth pains.

[9]"Then you will be handed over to be persecuted and put to death, and you will be hated by all nations because of me. [10]At that time many will turn away from the faith and will betray and hate each other, [11]and many false prophets will appear and deceive many people. [12]Because of the increase of wickedness, the love of most will grow cold, [13]but the one who stands firm to the end will be saved. [14]And this gospel of the kingdom will be preached in the whole world as a testimony to all nations, and then the end will come.

[15]"So when you see standing in the holy place 'the abomination that causes desolation,'[a] spoken of through the prophet Daniel—let the reader understand— [16]then let those who are in Judea flee to the mountains. [17]Let no one on the housetop go down to take anything out of the house. [18]Let no one in the field go back to get their cloak. [19]How dreadful it will be in those days for pregnant women and nursing mothers! [20]Pray that your flight will not take place in winter or on the Sabbath. [21]For then there will be great distress, unequaled from the beginning of the world until now—and never to be equaled again.

[22]"If those days had not been cut short, no one would survive, but for the sake of the elect those days will be shortened. [23]At that time if anyone says to you, 'Look, here is the Messiah!' or, 'There he is!' do not believe it. [24]For false messiahs and false prophets will appear and perform great signs and wonders to deceive, if possible, even the elect. [25]See, I have told you ahead of time.

[26]"So if anyone tells you, 'There he is, out in the wilderness,' do not go out; or, 'Here he is, in the inner rooms,' do not believe it. [27]For as lightning that comes from the east is visible even in the west, so will be the coming of the Son of Man. [28]Wherever there is a carcass, there the vultures will gather.

[29]"Immediately after the distress of those days

"'the sun will be darkened,
    and the moon will not give its light;
the stars will fall from the sky,
    and the heavenly bodies will be shaken.'[b]

[30]"Then will appear the sign of the Son of Man in heaven. And then all the peoples of the

---

The Law of Navigation: Jesus Knew the Steps to Take into the Future

Matthew 24:1–44

Jesus instructed his disciples on how to prepare for the future and what they could expect to endure. The Master gained credibility by charting their course into the future. Few things help us more than leaders who can mentally walk their people into the future, providing both direction and hope.

---

earth[c] will mourn when they see the Son of Man coming on the clouds of heaven, with power and great glory.[d] [31]And he will send his angels with a loud trumpet call, and they will gather his elect from the four winds, from one end of the heavens to the other.

[32]"Now learn this lesson from the fig tree: As soon as its twigs get tender and its leaves come out, you know that summer is near. [33]Even so, when you see all these things, you know that it[e] is near, right at the door. [34]Truly I tell you, this generation will certainly not pass away until all these things have happened. [35]Heaven and earth will pass away, but my words will never pass away.

The Day and Hour Unknown

[36]"But about that day or hour no one knows, not even the angels in heaven, nor the Son,[f] but only the Father. [37]As it was in the days of Noah, so it will be at the coming of the Son of Man. [38]For in the days before the flood, people were eating and drinking, marrying and giving in marriage, up to the day Noah entered the ark; [39]and they knew nothing about what would happen until the flood came and took them all away. That is how it will be at the coming of the Son of Man. [40]Two men will be in the field; one will be taken and the other left. [41]Two women will be grinding with a hand mill; one will be taken and the other left.

[42]"Therefore keep watch, because you do not know on what day your Lord will come. [43]But understand this: If the owner of the house had

---

[a] 15 Daniel 9:27; 11:31; 12:11   [b] 29 Isaiah 13:10; 34:4
[c] 30 Or the tribes of the land   [d] 30 See Daniel 7:13-14.
[e] 33 Or he   [f] 36 Some manuscripts do not have nor the Son.

known at what time of night the thief was coming, he would have kept watch and would not have let his house be broken into. ⁴⁴So you also must be ready, because the Son of Man will come at an hour when you do not expect him.

⁴⁵"Who then is the faithful and wise servant, whom the master has put in charge of the servants in his household to give them their food at the proper time? ⁴⁶It will be good for that servant whose master finds him doing so when he returns. ⁴⁷Truly I tell you, he will put him in charge of all his possessions. ⁴⁸But suppose that servant is wicked and says to himself, 'My master is staying away a long time,' ⁴⁹and he then begins to beat his fellow servants and to eat and drink with drunkards. ⁵⁰The master of that servant will come on a day when he does not expect him and at an hour he is not aware of. ⁵¹He will cut him to pieces and assign him a place with the hypocrites, where there will be weeping and gnashing of teeth.

The Parable of the Ten Virgins

25 "At that time the kingdom of heaven will be like ten virgins who took their lamps and went out to meet the bridegroom. ²Five of them were foolish and five were wise. ³The foolish ones took their lamps but did not take any oil with them. ⁴The wise ones, however, took oil in jars along with their lamps. ⁵The bridegroom was a long time in coming, and they all became drowsy and fell asleep.

⁶"At midnight the cry rang out: 'Here's the bridegroom! Come out to meet him!'

⁷"Then all the virgins woke up and trimmed their lamps. ⁸The foolish ones said to the wise, 'Give us some of your oil; our lamps are going out.'

⁹"'No,' they replied, 'there may not be enough for both us and you. Instead, go to those who sell oil and buy some for yourselves.'

¹⁰"But while they were on their way to buy the oil, the bridegroom arrived. The virgins who were ready went in with him to the wedding banquet. And the door was shut.

¹¹"Later the others also came. 'Lord, Lord,' they said, 'open the door for us!'

¹²"But he replied, 'Truly I tell you, I don't know you.'

¹³"Therefore keep watch, because you do not know the day or the hour.

The Parable of the Bags of Gold

¹⁴"Again, it will be like a man going on a journey, who called his servants and entrusted his wealth to them. ¹⁵To one he gave five bags of gold, to another two bags, and to another one bag,ᵃ each according to his ability. Then he went on his journey. ¹⁶The man who had received five bags of gold went at once and put his money to work and gained five bags more. ¹⁷So also, the one with two bags of gold gained two more. ¹⁸But the man who had received one bag went off, dug a hole in the ground and hid his master's money.

¹⁹"After a long time the master of those servants returned and settled accounts with them. ²⁰The man who had received five bags of gold brought the other five. 'Master,' he said, 'you entrusted me with five bags of gold. See, I have gained five more.'

²¹"His master replied, 'Well done, good and faithful servant! You have been faithful with a few things; I will put you in charge of many things. Come and share your master's happiness!'

²²"The man with two bags of gold also came. 'Master,' he said, 'you entrusted me with two bags of gold; see, I have gained two more.'

²³"His master replied, 'Well done, good and faithful servant! You have been faithful with a few things; I will put you in charge of many things. Come and share your master's happiness!'

²⁴"Then the man who had received one bag of gold came. 'Master,' he said, 'I knew that you are a hard man, harvesting where you have not sown and gathering where you have not

---

ᵃ 15 Greek *five talents . . . two talents . . . one talent*; also throughout this parable; a talent was worth about 20 years of a day laborer's wage.

Preparation: The Man with the Plan Is the Man with the Power

Matthew 25:1–30

Charles de Gaulle once said, "History does not teach fatalism. . . . People get the history they deserve." Jesus taught two parables which illustrate this truth, both about people who diligently pursued a goal. Prepared leaders stand ready to meet the future. They don't react and are not easily surprised. This gives them power when it's time to move.

scattered seed. ²⁵So I was afraid and went out and hid your gold in the ground. See, here is what belongs to you.'

²⁶"His master replied, 'You wicked, lazy servant! So you knew that I harvest where I have not sown and gather where I have not scattered seed? ²⁷Well then, you should have put my money on deposit with the bankers, so that when I returned I would have received it back with interest.

²⁸"'So take the bag of gold from him and give it to the one who has ten bags. ²⁹For whoever has will be given more, and they will have an abundance. Whoever does not have, even what they have will be taken from them. ³⁰And throw that worthless servant outside, into the darkness, where there will be weeping and gnashing of teeth.'

The Sheep and the Goats

³¹"When the Son of Man comes in his glory, and all the angels with him, he will sit on his glorious throne. ³²All the nations will be gathered before him, and he will separate the people one from another as a shepherd separates the sheep from the goats. ³³He will put the sheep on his right and the goats on his left.

³⁴"Then the King will say to those on his right, 'Come, you who are blessed by my Father; take your inheritance, the kingdom prepared for you since the creation of the world. ³⁵For I was hungry and you gave me something to eat, I was thirsty and you gave me something to drink, I was a stranger and you invited me in, ³⁶I needed clothes and you clothed me, I was sick and you looked after me, I was in prison and you came to visit me.'

³⁷"Then the righteous will answer him, 'Lord, when did we see you hungry and feed you, or thirsty and give you something to drink? ³⁸When did we see you a stranger and invite you in, or needing clothes and clothe you? ³⁹When did we see you sick or in prison and go to visit you?'

⁴⁰"The King will reply, 'Truly I tell you, whatever you did for one of the least of these brothers and sisters of mine, you did for me.'

⁴¹"Then he will say to those on his left, 'Depart from me, you who are cursed, into the eternal fire prepared for the devil and his angels. ⁴²For I was hungry and you gave me nothing to eat, I was thirsty and you gave me nothing to drink, ⁴³I was a stranger and you did not invite me in, I needed clothes and you did not clothe me, I was sick and in prison and you did not look after me.'

⁴⁴"They also will answer, 'Lord, when did we see you hungry or thirsty or a stranger or needing clothes or sick or in prison, and did not help you?'

⁴⁵"He will reply, 'Truly I tell you, whatever you did not do for one of the least of these, you did not do for me.'

⁴⁶"Then they will go away to eternal punishment, but the righteous to eternal life."

The Plot Against Jesus

26 When Jesus had finished saying all these things, he said to his disciples, ²"As you know, the Passover is two days away — and the Son of Man will be handed over to be crucified."

³Then the chief priests and the elders of the people assembled in the palace of the high priest, whose name was Caiaphas, ⁴and they schemed to arrest Jesus secretly and kill him. ⁵"But not during the festival," they said, "or there may be a riot among the people."

Jesus Anointed at Bethany

⁶While Jesus was in Bethany in the home of Simon the Leper, ⁷a woman came to him with an alabaster jar of very expensive perfume, which she poured on his head as he was reclining at the table.

⁸When the disciples saw this, they were indignant. "Why this waste?" they asked. ⁹"This perfume could have been sold at a high price and the money given to the poor."

¹⁰Aware of this, Jesus said to them, "Why are you bothering this woman? She has done a beautiful thing to me. ¹¹The poor you will always have with you,^a but you will not always have me. ¹²When she poured this perfume on my body, she did it to prepare me for burial. ¹³Truly I tell you, wherever this gospel is preached throughout the world, what she has done will also be told, in memory of her."

Judas Agrees to Betray Jesus

¹⁴Then one of the Twelve — the one called Judas Iscariot — went to the chief priests ¹⁵and asked, "What are you willing to give me if I deliver him over to you?" So they counted out for him thirty pieces of silver. ¹⁶From then on Judas watched for an opportunity to hand him over.

The Last Supper

¹⁷On the first day of the Festival of Unleavened Bread, the disciples came to Jesus and

---

^a 11 See Deut. 15:11.

asked, "Where do you want us to make preparations for you to eat the Passover?"

¹⁸He replied, "Go into the city to a certain man and tell him, 'The Teacher says: My appointed time is near. I am going to celebrate the Passover with my disciples at your house.'" ¹⁹So the disciples did as Jesus had directed them and prepared the Passover.

²⁰When evening came, Jesus was reclining at the table with the Twelve. ²¹And while they were eating, he said, "Truly I tell you, one of you will betray me."

²²They were very sad and began to say to him one after the other, "Surely you don't mean me, Lord?"

²³Jesus replied, "The one who has dipped his hand into the bowl with me will betray me. ²⁴The Son of Man will go just as it is written about him. But woe to that man who betrays the Son of Man! It would be better for him if he had not been born."

²⁵Then Judas, the one who would betray him, said, "Surely you don't mean me, Rabbi?"

Jesus answered, "You have said so."

²⁶While they were eating, Jesus took bread, and when he had given thanks, he broke it and gave it to his disciples, saying, "Take and eat; this is my body."

²⁷Then he took a cup, and when he had given thanks, he gave it to them, saying, "Drink from it, all of you. ²⁸This is my blood of the*ᵃ* covenant, which is poured out for many for the forgiveness of sins. ²⁹I tell you, I will not drink from this fruit of the vine from now on until that day when I drink it new with you in my Father's kingdom."

³⁰When they had sung a hymn, they went out to the Mount of Olives.

Jesus Predicts Peter's Denial

³¹Then Jesus told them, "This very night you will all fall away on account of me, for it is written:

"'I will strike the shepherd,
    and the sheep of the flock will be
        scattered.'ᵇ

³²But after I have risen, I will go ahead of you into Galilee."

³³Peter replied, "Even if all fall away on account of you, I never will."

³⁴"Truly I tell you," Jesus answered, "this very night, before the rooster crows, you will disown me three times."

³⁵But Peter declared, "Even if I have to die with you, I will never disown you." And all the other disciples said the same.

Gethsemane

³⁶Then Jesus went with his disciples to a place called Gethsemane, and he said to them, "Sit here while I go over there and pray." ³⁷He took Peter and the two sons of Zebedee along with him, and he began to be sorrowful and troubled. ³⁸Then he said to them, "My soul is overwhelmed with sorrow to the point of death. Stay here and keep watch with me."

³⁹Going a little farther, he fell with his face to the ground and prayed, "My Father, if it is possible, may this cup be taken from me. Yet not as I will, but as you will."

⁴⁰Then he returned to his disciples and found them sleeping. "Couldn't you men keep watch with me for one hour?" he asked Peter. ⁴¹"Watch and pray so that you will not fall into temptation. The spirit is willing, but the flesh is weak."

⁴²He went away a second time and prayed, "My Father, if it is not possible for this cup to be taken away unless I drink it, may your will be done."

⁴³When he came back, he again found them sleeping, because their eyes were heavy. ⁴⁴So he left them and went away once more and prayed the third time, saying the same thing.

⁴⁵Then he returned to the disciples and said

The Law of Legacy:
Jesus Left a Memorial
to His Followers

Matthew 26:17–30

Leaders solidify their legacy when they add the following components:

1. *Tangible Elements*
   Jesus left the bread and the cup as symbols of his body and blood.

2. *Memorable Words*
   Jesus spoke simple words and phrases to be restated, year after year.

3. *Regular Events*
   Jesus instituted an event to be periodically celebrated.

ᵃ 28 Some manuscripts *the new*   ᵇ 31 Zech. 13:7

to them, "Are you still sleeping and resting? Look, the hour has come, and the Son of Man is delivered into the hands of sinners. [46]Rise! Let us go! Here comes my betrayer!"

Jesus Arrested

[47]While he was still speaking, Judas, one of the Twelve, arrived. With him was a large crowd armed with swords and clubs, sent from the chief priests and the elders of the people. [48]Now the betrayer had arranged a signal with them: "The one I kiss is the man; arrest him." [49]Going at once to Jesus, Judas said, "Greetings, Rabbi!" and kissed him.

[50]Jesus replied, "Do what you came for, friend."[a]

Then the men stepped forward, seized Jesus and arrested him. [51]With that, one of Jesus' companions reached for his sword, drew it out and struck the servant of the high priest, cutting off his ear.

[52]"Put your sword back in its place," Jesus said to him, "for all who draw the sword will die by the sword. [53]Do you think I cannot call on my Father, and he will at once put at my disposal more than twelve legions of angels? [54]But how then would the Scriptures be fulfilled that say it must happen in this way?"

[55]In that hour Jesus said to the crowd, "Am I leading a rebellion, that you have come out with swords and clubs to capture me? Every day I sat in the temple courts teaching, and you did not arrest me. [56]But this has all taken place that the writings of the prophets might be fulfilled." Then all the disciples deserted him and fled.

Jesus Before the Sanhedrin

[57]Those who had arrested Jesus took him to Caiaphas the high priest, where the teachers of the law and the elders had assembled. [58]But Peter followed him at a distance, right up to the courtyard of the high priest. He entered and sat down with the guards to see the outcome.

[59]The chief priests and the whole Sanhedrin were looking for false evidence against Jesus so that they could put him to death. [60]But they did not find any, though many false witnesses came forward.

Finally two came forward [61]and declared, "This fellow said, 'I am able to destroy the temple of God and rebuild it in three days.'"

[62]Then the high priest stood up and said to Jesus, "Are you not going to answer? What is this testimony that these men are bringing against you?" [63]But Jesus remained silent.

The high priest said to him, "I charge you under oath by the living God: Tell us if you are the Messiah, the Son of God."

[64]"You have said so," Jesus replied. "But I say to all of you: From now on you will see the Son of Man sitting at the right hand of the Mighty One and coming on the clouds of heaven."[b]

[65]Then the high priest tore his clothes and said, "He has spoken blasphemy! Why do we need any more witnesses? Look, now you have heard the blasphemy. [66]What do you think?"

"He is worthy of death," they answered.

[67]Then they spit in his face and struck him with their fists. Others slapped him [68]and said, "Prophesy to us, Messiah. Who hit you?"

Peter Disowns Jesus

[69]Now Peter was sitting out in the courtyard, and a servant girl came to him. "You also were with Jesus of Galilee," she said.

[70]But he denied it before them all. "I don't know what you're talking about," he said.

[71]Then he went out to the gateway, where another servant girl saw him and said to the people there, "This fellow was with Jesus of Nazareth."

[72]He denied it again, with an oath: "I don't know the man!"

[73]After a little while, those standing there went up to Peter and said, "Surely you are one of them; your accent gives you away."

[74]Then he began to call down curses, and he swore to them, "I don't know the man!"

Immediately a rooster crowed. [75]Then Peter remembered the word Jesus had spoken: "Before the rooster crows, you will disown me three times." And he went outside and wept bitterly.

Judas Hangs Himself

27 Early in the morning, all the chief priests and the elders of the people made their plans how to have Jesus executed. [2]So they bound him, led him away and handed him over to Pilate the governor.

[3]When Judas, who had betrayed him, saw that Jesus was condemned, he was seized with remorse and returned the thirty pieces of silver to the chief priests and the elders. [4]"I have sinned," he said, "for I have betrayed innocent blood."

"What is that to us?" they replied. "That's your responsibility."

[5]So Judas threw the money into the temple

---

[a] 50 Or "Why have you come, friend?"　　[b] 64 See Psalm 110:1; Daniel 7:13.

and left. Then he went away and hanged himself.

[6]The chief priests picked up the coins and said, "It is against the law to put this into the treasury, since it is blood money." [7]So they decided to use the money to buy the potter's field as a burial place for foreigners. [8]That is why it has been called the Field of Blood to this day. [9]Then what was spoken by Jeremiah the prophet was fulfilled: "They took the thirty pieces of silver, the price set on him by the people of Israel, [10]and they used them to buy the potter's field, as the Lord commanded me."[a]

Jesus Before Pilate

[11]Meanwhile Jesus stood before the governor, and the governor asked him, "Are you the king of the Jews?"

"You have said so," Jesus replied.

[12]When he was accused by the chief priests and the elders, he gave no answer. [13]Then Pilate asked him, "Don't you hear the testimony they are bringing against you?" [14]But Jesus made no reply, not even to a single charge—to the great amazement of the governor.

[15]Now it was the governor's custom at the festival to release a prisoner chosen by the crowd. [16]At that time they had a well-known prisoner whose name was Jesus[b] Barabbas. [17]So when the crowd had gathered, Pilate asked them, "Which one do you want me to release to you: Jesus Barabbas, or Jesus who is called the Messiah?" [18]For he knew it was out of self-interest that they had handed Jesus over to him.

[19]While Pilate was sitting on the judge's seat, his wife sent him this message: "Don't have anything to do with that innocent man, for I have suffered a great deal today in a dream because of him."

[20]But the chief priests and the elders persuaded the crowd to ask for Barabbas and to have Jesus executed.

[21]"Which of the two do you want me to release to you?" asked the governor.

"Barabbas," they answered.

[22]"What shall I do, then, with Jesus who is called the Messiah?" Pilate asked.

They all answered, "Crucify him!"

[23]"Why? What crime has he committed?" asked Pilate.

But they shouted all the louder, "Crucify him!"

[24]When Pilate saw that he was getting nowhere, but that instead an uproar was starting, he took water and washed his hands in front of the crowd. "I am innocent of this man's blood," he said. "It is your responsibility!"

[25]All the people answered, "His blood is on us and on our children!"

[26]Then he released Barabbas to them. But he had Jesus flogged, and handed him over to be crucified.

The Soldiers Mock Jesus

[27]Then the governor's soldiers took Jesus into the Praetorium and gathered the whole company of soldiers around him. [28]They stripped him and put a scarlet robe on him, [29]and then twisted together a crown of thorns and set it on his head. They put a staff in his right hand. Then they knelt in front of him and mocked him. "Hail, king of the Jews!" they said. [30]They spit on him, and took the staff and struck him on the head again and again. [31]After they had mocked him, they took off the robe and put his own clothes on him. Then they led him away to crucify him.

The Crucifixion of Jesus

[32]As they were going out, they met a man from Cyrene, named Simon, and they forced him to carry the cross. [33]They came to a place called Golgotha (which means "the place of the skull"). [34]There they offered Jesus wine to drink, mixed with gall; but after tasting it, he refused to drink it. [35]When they had crucified him, they divided up his clothes by casting lots. [36]And sitting down, they kept watch over him there. [37]Above his head they placed the written charge against him: THIS IS JESUS, THE KING OF THE JEWS.

[38]Two rebels were crucified with him, one on his right and one on his left. [39]Those who

---

[a] 10 See Zech. 11:12,13; Jer. 19:1-13; 32:6-9.   [b] 16 Many manuscripts do not have *Jesus*; also in verse 17.

The Law of Sacrifice: Jesus Gave Up His Life

Matthew 26:47—27:54

Jesus gave up his life so we could have ours back. He died like us so we could live like him. He not only pleased his Father, but received us as a bounty. This is the mark of a true leader. Leaders pay any price to get the job done.

21 QUALITIES

Matthew 27:11–31

PRESIDENT HARRY Truman was right when he said, "The buck stops here." Leaders cannot pass the buck. We cannot lead without taking responsibility. It comes with the territory.

Pontius Pilate, the Roman governor of Israel, gives us a sad example of a leader who failed to take responsibility. When Jesus appeared before him for judgment, he could find nothing wrong with him. Yet instead of judging him as innocent, he succumbed to the pressure of the crowd. Sensing they wanted to punish an innocent man, he gave them a choice: Barabbas or Jesus? When they wrongly chose Jesus as the more guilty man, Pilate walked over to a basin of water and tried to wash his hands of any responsibility for his decision. He pretended he could evade ownership of the consequences. Pilate committed the sin of omission and tried to get off on a legal technicality.

None of this surprised the Jews, since Pilate had a history of such behavior. He tended to withdraw whenever things heated up. Once he put the Roman eagle in the temple, prompting 5,000 Jews to march to his vacation home to demand he remove it. He called in the army and demanded they leave. When they refused, he threatened to cut off their heads. The Jews got down on their knees, in essence saying, "Go ahead!" Shocked by their moral conviction, he backed down. From that point on, the Jews knew this man lacked a backbone and would run from responsibility. He illustrates moral and political compromise.

Just why did Pilate "wash his hands" of responsibility?

1. *He had a problem with foundations* (v. 22).
   Pilate never forged the character to withstand adversity. Conflict paralyzed him.
2. *He had a problem with futility* (vv. 23–24).
   He perceived that no good would come from a right decision, so why waste time? Apathy proliferates when we sense that action seems useless.
3. *He had a problem with fear* (v. 24).
   Pilate felt preoccupied with survival. If he fought the Jews, he feared the loss of control, image, or position. His wife's warning added fuel to his fear.
4. *He had a problem with failure* (v. 24).
   Pilate knew a riot was brewing. The last time it happened, he failed to rise to the occasion and the Jews called his bluff. They knew he worried more about failure than they did.
5. *He had a problem with focus* (v. 24).
   Leaders cannot be neutral or passive over crucial decisions. Pilate picked up a basin and tried to wash his hands of the whole mess. No good leader does this.

For a positive example of responsibility, see p. 543.

passed by hurled insults at him, shaking their heads [40]and saying, "You who are going to destroy the temple and build it in three days, save yourself! Come down from the cross, if you are the Son of God!" [41]In the same way the chief priests, the teachers of the law and the elders mocked him. [42]"He saved others," they said, "but he can't save himself! He's the king of Israel! Let him come down now from the cross, and we will believe in him. [43]He trusts in God. Let God rescue him now if he wants him, for he said, 'I am the Son of God.'" [44]In the same way the rebels who were crucified with him also heaped insults on him.

The Death of Jesus

[45]From noon until three in the afternoon darkness came over all the land. [46]About three in the afternoon Jesus cried out in a loud voice, *"Eli, Eli,[a] lema sabachthani?"* (which means "My God, my God, why have you forsaken me?").[b]

[47]When some of those standing there heard this, they said, "He's calling Elijah."

[48]Immediately one of them ran and got a sponge. He filled it with wine vinegar, put it on a staff, and offered it to Jesus to drink. [49]The rest said, "Now leave him alone. Let's see if Elijah comes to save him."

[50]And when Jesus had cried out again in a loud voice, he gave up his spirit.

[51]At that moment the curtain of the temple was torn in two from top to bottom. The earth shook, the rocks split [52]and the tombs broke open. The bodies of many holy people who had died were raised to life. [53]They came out of the tombs after Jesus' resurrection and[c] went into the holy city and appeared to many people.

[54]When the centurion and those with him who were guarding Jesus saw the earthquake and all that had happened, they were terrified, and exclaimed, "Surely he was the Son of God!"

[55]Many women were there, watching from a distance. They had followed Jesus from Galilee to care for his needs. [56]Among them were Mary Magdalene, Mary the mother of James and Joseph,[d] and the mother of Zebedee's sons.

The Burial of Jesus

[57]As evening approached, there came a rich man from Arimathea, named Joseph, who had himself become a disciple of Jesus. [58]Going to Pilate, he asked for Jesus' body, and Pilate ordered that it be given to him. [59]Joseph took the body, wrapped it in a clean linen cloth, [60]and placed it in his own new tomb that he had cut out of the rock. He rolled a big stone in front of the entrance to the tomb and went away. [61]Mary Magdalene and the other Mary were sitting there opposite the tomb.

The Guard at the Tomb

[62]The next day, the one after Preparation Day, the chief priests and the Pharisees went to Pilate. [63]"Sir," they said, "we remember that while he was still alive that deceiver said, 'After three days I will rise again.' [64]So give the order for the tomb to be made secure until the third day. Otherwise, his disciples may come and steal the body and tell the people that he has been raised from the dead. This last deception will be worse than the first."

[65]"Take a guard," Pilate answered. "Go, make the tomb as secure as you know how." [66]So they went and made the tomb secure by putting a seal on the stone and posting the guard.

Jesus Has Risen

28 After the Sabbath, at dawn on the first day of the week, Mary Magdalene and the other Mary went to look at the tomb. [2]There was a violent earthquake, for an angel

---

[a] 46 Some manuscripts *Eloi, Eloi*   [b] 46 Psalm 22:1
[c] 53 Or *tombs, and after Jesus' resurrection they*   [d] 56 Greek *Joses,* a variant of *Joseph*

The Law of Victory: Jesus Defeated Our Greatest Enemy

Matthew 28:1–20

Jesus raised several people from the dead, but each case differed from his own resurrection. Those people would eventually die again. But Jesus rose from the dead, never to die again. He defeated mankind's greatest enemy: death. All other problems are problems because they kill us. Once Jesus defeated death, his followers could operate in total security.

No struggle is too big for God. No question is unanswerable. No problem is too difficult. The resurrection of Christ trumpeted good news from the graveyard! In spite of the black prospects, in spite of the big problems, in spite of the bad predictions—Jesus practiced the Law of Victory, decisively defeating even death itself.

21 LAWS

JESUS AND THE LAW OF LEGACY
A Leader's Lasting Value Is Measured by Succession

Matthew 28:16–20

JUST ABOUT anybody can make an organization look good for a moment—by launching a flashy new program or product, drawing crowds to a big event, or slashing the budget to boost the bottom line. But leaders who leave a legacy take a different approach. They lead with tomorrow as well as today in mind.

When all is said and done, your ability as a leader will be judged by how well your people and your organization did after you were gone. Your lasting value will be measured by succession.

■ ■ ■ ■ ■

To create a legacy, you need to be strategic and intentional. The following guidelines can help you get started:

1. *Decide ahead of time what you are willing to give up.*
   Being a leader has a price; being a leader who leaves a legacy has an even greater price. When you work to create a legacy, your life is no longer your own. That's why it's so important to know what you are willing to give up so that others can go up.

   What are you willing to give up? How much of your time? How much of your money? How many opportunities will you forgo? How many of your dreams are you willing to set aside to ensure that one or maybe two survive in the lives of others?

2. *Take the initiative to start the process.*
   If you want to create a legacy, you have to initiate the process—and there will be times when you'll have to fight for it. Jesus' followers had various agendas. Some, like Simon the Zealot, wanted him to lead a revolt against Rome. Others, like James and John, wanted positions of power (Mk 10:37). Even Peter tried to dissuade Jesus from the very act that would release the other disciples to follow in Jesus' footsteps (Mt 16:22).

3. *Know your goals with each person.*
   The process of creating a legacy relies primarily on people. It requires the selection of the right people and the right development process for each individual. Jesus carefully chose his legacy carriers. Scripture says he intentionally picked the twelve he wanted; he didn't take the first guys who showed up. And he didn't treat all of them the same. He had a specific development process for each person.

4. *Prepare to pass the baton well.*
   Once you have prepared your people, you need to prepare for the transition. There's a real art to preparing a successor, and it doesn't always go smoothly. Jesus had trouble handing the baton to his followers. He

appeared to them after his resurrection and gave them the Great Commission because some of them still didn't get it. Peter, James and John all returned to fishing *after they saw Jesus resurrected!* As you prepare to hand off to a successor, do everything you can to make for a smooth transition. And even then, plan to offer additional assistance without getting in the way.

Jesus' IDEA for Leaving a Legacy

Jesus faced the task of changing the lives of people thousands of years after him—and he succeeded. He did it without writing any books, building any schools, or founding any institutions. So if Jesus chose to deposit his legacy in people, we should learn his method and practice it as best we can. Consider Jesus' IDEA for working in the lives of people:

Instruction

Jesus constantly taught, most often with parables. More than half of the Gospels' content presents Jesus' teaching. The parable of the sower gives us insight into how Jesus worked. When the disciples asked him about the meaning of the parable, he explained it, revealing insightful truth cloaked in the story.

Demonstration

Educational philosophy today relies too heavily on instruction. If Jesus had taught the disciples and done nothing more, they never would have carried on his legacy. But Jesus shared his life with them.

Jesus' disciples went through three phases in their training:

- *Come and see.* Jesus invited them to observe him and his priorities. He invited them to evaluate him (and

themselves in light of what he was doing).
- *Come and follow Me.* Jesus asked for a greater level of commitment. The disciples were to do more than observe; they were to associate with him.
- *Come and be with Me.* This phase occupied most of Jesus' three years of ministry. He required the disciples' commitment and companionship. The Twelve were present with him as he taught, traveled, prayed, ate with "sinners," healed the sick, and raised the dead. They saw consistency between his teaching and his actions, and they learned the *how* and *why* of all he did.

Experience

After Jesus had modeled good leadership and taught spiritual truths, he didn't turn his men loose and move on. He gradually worked them into positions of independent leadership by giving them valuable experience. Jesus gave his followers an opportunity to practice what he had taught and to practice leadership.

Assessment

Jesus repeatedly evaluated the progress of his disciples. After the return of the seventy, he debriefed them, gave them instruction concerning priorities, and celebrated with them (Lk 10:17–24). Jesus also gave individual assessment to his disciples, including specific feedback concerning their character and their capabilities.

If you want to leave a legacy, you must look to people to carry it for you. Find the right people, and use the right preparation process for each of them. Only as you pour yourself into them will they be able to pour out themselves for others. No one can give what he does not have.

of the Lord came down from heaven and, going to the tomb, rolled back the stone and sat on it. [3]His appearance was like lightning, and his clothes were white as snow. [4]The guards were so afraid of him that they shook and became like dead men.

[5]The angel said to the women, "Do not be afraid, for I know that you are looking for Jesus, who was crucified. [6]He is not here; he has risen, just as he said. Come and see the place where he lay. [7]Then go quickly and tell his disciples: 'He has risen from the dead and is going ahead of you into Galilee. There you will see him.' Now I have told you."

[8]So the women hurried away from the tomb, afraid yet filled with joy, and ran to tell his disciples. [9]Suddenly Jesus met them. "Greetings," he said. They came to him, clasped his feet and worshiped him. [10]Then Jesus said to them, "Do not be afraid. Go and tell my brothers to go to Galilee; there they will see me."

The Guards' Report

[11]While the women were on their way, some of the guards went into the city and reported to the chief priests everything that had happened. [12]When the chief priests had met with the elders and devised a plan, they gave the soldiers a large sum of money, [13]telling them, "You are to say, 'His disciples came during the night and stole him away while we were asleep.' [14]If this report gets to the governor, we will satisfy him and keep you out of trouble." [15]So the soldiers took the money and did as they were instructed. And this story has been widely circulated among the Jews to this very day.

The Great Commission

[16]Then the eleven disciples went to Galilee, to the mountain where Jesus had told them to go. [17]When they saw him, they worshiped him; but some doubted. [18]Then Jesus came to them and said, "All authority in heaven and on earth has been given to me. [19]Therefore go and make disciples of all nations, baptizing them in the name of the Father and of the Son and of the Holy Spirit, [20]and teaching them to obey everything I have commanded you. And surely I am with you always, to the very end of the age."

INTRODUCTION TO
MARK

Jesus as a Servant-Leader

The book of Mark is the shortest of the four Gospels. Written during a time of acute persecution, it cuts straight to the point, discussing Jesus' identity, the role of suffering and the necessity of faith.

Mark, the author, was a disciple of Peter; therefore Peter's perspective appears repeatedly in the book. Mark paints a picture of Jesus as a Servant-Leader. He clearly and concisely portrays Christ as a compassionate model to follow. His fast-paced narrative describes the suffering Servant who engaged in consistent ministry to others through healing, teaching, feeding, encouraging and restoring the broken.

It makes sense that Mark might maintain such a focus, since he needed such encouragement himself. He traveled with Paul and Barnabas across Asia Minor on their first missionary journey, but sometime during their ministry, Mark grew frightened and left the team to return home. Later, when he wanted to try it again, Paul considered him young and cowardly and rejected his participation. Barnabas, however, took Mark under his wing and mentored this young, emerging leader. Years afterward, Paul wrote from prison and asked that Mark be sent to him, since "he is helpful to me in my ministry" (2Ti 4:11). Paul changed his opinion because Mark had grown into a responsible leader.

Mark sees Jesus as the Ultimate Leader, just as did Matthew. Mark's picture, however, portrays him not so much as the Messiah but as the model for all people. Jesus gave himself to others. He spent himself meeting physical needs (3:1–11); he spent time with his twelve staff members (3:13–14); he empowered those twelve for ministry (3:14–19); and he spent time teaching the people

God's Role in Mark

God's role is best seen in Jesus, the incarnation of God, and in the Holy Spirit, the inspiration of God. Jesus demonstrated what God looks like as a human. Through him we have a model to follow for our attitudes, our lifestyles, our conversations, our worldview and our relationships. Through the Holy Spirit, we have a divinely inspired biography of this incarnated God. Through their work, we have a picture of the authority God exercises over both the spiritual and the physical realms.

Leaders in Mark

Jesus, John the Baptist, Herod, Pontius Pilate, the chief priests in the Sanhedrin

Other People of Influence in Mark

The twelve disciples, the women who followed Jesus, the Pharisees

Lessons in Leadership

- Effective leadership requires no worldly credentials.
- Leaders who are change agents always transform the traditional paradigm.
- Healthy leaders are first servants.
- Effective leaders balance the need for solitude and socializing.

(3:23–29). More than anything, Mark teaches us that the Master considers relationships to be paramount. In this book we see Jesus embodying the Laws of Empowerment, Sacrifice, Connection, Priorities, Timing and Legacy.

- Good leaders provide security and confidence for their followers.
- The greater the leader, the greater the humility and sacrifice required.
- Principles serve effective leaders so leaders can effectively serve the people.

LEADERSHIP HIGHLIGHTS IN MARK

John the Baptist Prepares the Way

1 The beginning of the good news about Jesus the Messiah,[a] the Son of God,[b] [2]as it is written in Isaiah the prophet:

"I will send my messenger ahead of you,
    who will prepare your way"[c]—
[3]"a voice of one calling in the wilderness,
    'Prepare the way for the Lord,
    make straight paths for him.'"[d]

[4]And so John the Baptist appeared in the wilderness, preaching a baptism of repentance for the forgiveness of sins. [5]The whole Judean countryside and all the people of Jerusalem went out to him. Confessing their sins, they were baptized by him in the Jordan River. [6]John wore clothing made of camel's hair, with a leather belt around his waist, and he ate locusts and wild honey. [7]And this was his message: "After me comes the one more powerful than I, the straps of whose sandals I am not worthy to stoop down and untie. [8]I baptize you with[e] water, but he will baptize you with[e] the Holy Spirit."

The Baptism and Testing of Jesus

[9]At that time Jesus came from Nazareth in Galilee and was baptized by John in the Jordan. [10]Just as Jesus was coming up out of the water, he saw heaven being torn open and the Spirit descending on him like a dove. [11]And a voice came from heaven: "You are my Son, whom I love; with you I am well pleased."

[12]At once the Spirit sent him out into the wilderness, [13]and he was in the wilderness forty days, being tempted[f] by Satan. He was with the wild animals, and angels attended him.

Jesus Announces the Good News

[14]After John was put in prison, Jesus went into Galilee, proclaiming the good news of God. [15]"The time has come," he said. "The kingdom of God has come near. Repent and believe the good news!"

Jesus Calls His First Disciples

[16]As Jesus walked beside the Sea of Galilee, he saw Simon and his brother Andrew casting a net into the lake, for they were fishermen. [17]"Come, follow me," Jesus said, "and I will send you out to fish for people." [18]At once they left their nets and followed him.

[19]When he had gone a little farther, he saw James son of Zebedee and his brother John in a boat, preparing their nets. [20]Without delay he called them, and they left their father Zebedee in the boat with the hired men and followed him.

---

[a] 1 Or Jesus Christ. Messiah (Hebrew) and Christ (Greek) both mean Anointed One.   [b] 1 Some manuscripts do not have the Son of God.   [c] 2 Mal. 3:1   [d] 3 Isaiah 40:3   [e] 8 Or in   [f] 13 The Greek for tempted can also mean tested.

JOHN THE BAPTIST

Good Leaders Prepare the Way for Change
Mark 1:1–8

One of the marks of an excellent leader is how he or she brings about transformation in people and organizations. John the Baptist performed this role well as he prepared the Jewish people for Jesus. Since this Messiah would be very different from what everyone expected, John had to get the people ready for this radical shift.

A great word picture for the kind of person necessary to lead change comes from the airline industry. When people take their seats, airline flight attendants always look for leaders. As they announce the requirements for sitting in the exit row, they concisely explain the role of a leader:

1. You must be able to understand the instructions concerning the exit door.
2. You must be able to open the door.
3. You must be able to verbally guide others through the door.

Have you ever stopped to think that this is what is required when you lead others? You need to know what must happen. You must be able to pull it off. And you need to be able to take others with you.

PROFILE *in leadership*

Jesus Drives Out an Impure Spirit

²¹They went to Capernaum, and when the Sabbath came, Jesus went into the synagogue and began to teach. ²²The people were amazed at his teaching, because he taught them as one who had authority, not as the teachers of the law. ²³Just then a man in their synagogue who was possessed by an impure spirit cried out, ²⁴"What do you want with us, Jesus of Nazareth? Have you come to destroy us? I know who you are — the Holy One of God!"

²⁵"Be quiet!" said Jesus sternly. "Come out of him!" ²⁶The impure spirit shook the man violently and came out of him with a shriek.

²⁷The people were all so amazed that they asked each other, "What is this? A new teaching — and with authority! He even gives orders to impure spirits and they obey him." ²⁸News about him spread quickly over the whole region of Galilee.

Jesus Heals Many

²⁹As soon as they left the synagogue, they went with James and John to the home of Simon and Andrew. ³⁰Simon's mother-in-law was in bed with a fever, and they immediately told Jesus about her. ³¹So he went to her, took her hand and helped her up. The fever left her and she began to wait on them.

Marks of Leadership in Jesus' Ministry

Mark 1:16–35

Jesus clearly was a different sort of leader from the scribes and Pharisees of his day. Mark 1 reveals the following qualities in him:

1. *Competence:* He took responsibility to "make" them fishers of men (v. 17).

2. *Comprehension:* He had a thorough understanding of the scriptures (v. 22).

3. *Command:* He had authority and command of every situation (vv. 25–27).

4. *Compassion:* He served and healed the pain of others (vv. 30–31).

5. *Control:* He maintained organization and control in messy situations (v. 34).

6. *Communion:* He stayed renewed by connecting to the Source of his power (v. 35).

---

³²That evening after sunset the people brought to Jesus all the sick and demon-possessed. ³³The whole town gathered at the door, ³⁴and Jesus healed many who had various diseases. He also drove out many demons, but he would not let the demons speak because they knew who he was.

Jesus Prays in a Solitary Place

³⁵Very early in the morning, while it was still dark, Jesus got up, left the house and went off to a solitary place, where he prayed. ³⁶Simon and his companions went to look for him, ³⁷and when they found him, they exclaimed: "Everyone is looking for you!"

³⁸Jesus replied, "Let us go somewhere else — to the nearby villages — so I can preach there also. That is why I have come." ³⁹So he traveled throughout Galilee, preaching in their synagogues and driving out demons.

Jesus Heals a Man With Leprosy

⁴⁰A man with leprosy[a] came to him and begged him on his knees, "If you are willing, you can make me clean."

⁴¹Jesus was indignant.[b] He reached out his hand and touched the man. "I am willing," he said. "Be clean!" ⁴²Immediately the leprosy left him and he was cleansed.

⁴³Jesus sent him away at once with a strong warning: ⁴⁴"See that you don't tell this to anyone. But go, show yourself to the priest and offer the sacrifices that Moses commanded for your cleansing, as a testimony to them." ⁴⁵Instead he went out and began to talk freely, spreading the news. As a result, Jesus could no longer enter a town openly but stayed outside in lonely places. Yet the people still came to him from everywhere.

Jesus Forgives and Heals a Paralyzed Man

2 A few days later, when Jesus again entered Capernaum, the people heard that he had come home. ²They gathered in such large numbers that there was no room left, not even outside the door, and he preached the word to them. ³Some men came, bringing to him a paralyzed man, carried by four of them. ⁴Since they could not get him to Jesus because of the crowd, they made an opening in the roof above Jesus by digging through it and then lowered the mat the man was lying on. ⁵When Jesus saw their faith, he said to the paralyzed man, "Son, your sins are forgiven."

---

a 40 The Greek word traditionally translated *leprosy* was used for various diseases affecting the skin.   *b 41* Many manuscripts *Jesus was filled with compassion*

The Law of Priorities: Jesus Didn't Let Others Dictate His Agenda

Mark 1:32–38

Jesus often left the demands of his work to come apart and pray. He used this solitude to regain perspective and once more see the big picture. Watch the sequence of events detailed in this passage:

1. *The pressure is on.* The day is over, but the crowds have just begun to make demands (vv. 32–34).

2. *The paradox is obvious.* Jesus left in the middle of ministry time, with needs unmet (v. 35).

3. *The point is clear.* Jesus had to pause, leave the people, and replenish his own life (v. 35).

4. *The people are demanding.* Followers hunted for Jesus, reminding him how much they needed him (vv. 36–37).

5. *The purpose is declared.* His Father renewed his perspective and given direction (v. 38).

Jesus' priorities came from his heavenly Father, not from people. He always used the priorities he established to serve the people. So, how do you determine your own daily priorities?

⁶Now some teachers of the law were sitting there, thinking to themselves, ⁷"Why does this fellow talk like that? He's blaspheming! Who can forgive sins but God alone?"

⁸Immediately Jesus knew in his spirit that this was what they were thinking in their hearts, and he said to them, "Why are you thinking these things? ⁹Which is easier: to say to this paralyzed man, 'Your sins are forgiven,' or to say, 'Get up, take your mat and walk'? ¹⁰But I want you to know that the Son of Man has authority on earth to forgive sins." So he said to the man, ¹¹"I tell you, get up, take your mat and go home." ¹²He got up, took his mat and walked out in full view of them all. This amazed everyone and they praised God, saying, "We have never seen anything like this!"

Jesus Calls Levi and Eats With Sinners

¹³Once again Jesus went out beside the lake. A large crowd came to him, and he began to teach them. ¹⁴As he walked along, he saw Levi son of Alphaeus sitting at the tax collector's booth. "Follow me," Jesus told him, and Levi got up and followed him.

¹⁵While Jesus was having dinner at Levi's house, many tax collectors and sinners were eating with him and his disciples, for there were many who followed him. ¹⁶When the teachers of the law who were Pharisees saw him eating with the sinners and tax collectors, they asked his disciples: "Why does he eat with tax collectors and sinners?"

¹⁷On hearing this, Jesus said to them, "It is not the healthy who need a doctor, but the sick. I have not come to call the righteous, but sinners."

Jesus Questioned About Fasting

¹⁸Now John's disciples and the Pharisees were fasting. Some people came and asked Jesus, "How is it that John's disciples and the disciples of the Pharisees are fasting, but yours are not?"

The Law of Victory: The Four Men Got Their Friend to Jesus

Mark 2:1–12

Four men collected their paralyzed friend and attempted to take him to Jesus to be healed, but because of the large crowd, they could not reach Christ. So did that stop them? Absolutely not. They cut a hole in the roof and used a rope to let their paralyzed friend down through the opening.

Leaders who practice the Law of Victory don't allow obstacles to stop their progress. They determine to find a way to reach their goal and help their team win. Fulfilling a dream often does not come easy or within the realm of the conventional. In this case, practicing the Law of Victory forced the men to dare to do the difficult, the unorthodox, and the costly thing.

Team Building: Jesus Assembled a Team to Own a Vision

Mark 2:14–17

One could argue that Jesus constructed the most important team ever assembled. He chose specific individuals for specific roles. He chose the unlikely and developed them to reach their potential. And he chose an odd player—Matthew—to add to the mix.

Matthew was a hated tax collector, despised because he and his ilk seized money for the Roman government—traitors in the eyes of most Israelites. Jesus had the spiritual insight to choose those who were unloved and showed little promise. He saw Matthew's potential to become an apostle and a writer. Jesus never felt bound by human opinion or approval. He didn't judge by externals. He treated individuals based on their future potential, not present status.

In the same way, we must free ourselves from the boundaries that keep us from building a balanced team. Consider some questions we might learn from Jesus:

1. What positive qualities exist that may be seen as negative behavior?
2. Do the individuals show initiative, even if it has been misdirected?
3. Would these people add positive chemistry and unique value if placed on the team?
4. Are they hungry to become something more than what they are now?
5. Do they demonstrate passion that could be redirected?
6. Could they play a needed role on the team?

[19]Jesus answered, "How can the guests of the bridegroom fast while he is with them? They cannot, so long as they have him with them. [20]But the time will come when the bridegroom will be taken from them, and on that day they will fast.

[21]"No one sews a patch of unshrunk cloth on an old garment. Otherwise, the new piece will pull away from the old, making the tear worse. [22]And no one pours new wine into old wineskins. Otherwise, the wine will burst the skins, and both the wine and the wineskins will be ruined. No, they pour new wine into new wineskins."

Jesus Is Lord of the Sabbath

[23]One Sabbath Jesus was going through the grainfields, and as his disciples walked along, they began to pick some heads of grain. [24]The Pharisees said to him, "Look, why are they doing what is unlawful on the Sabbath?"

[25]He answered, "Have you never read what David did when he and his companions were hungry and in need? [26]In the days of Abiathar the high priest, he entered the house of God and ate the consecrated bread, which is lawful only for priests to eat. And he also gave some to his companions."

[27]Then he said to them, "The Sabbath was made for man, not man for the Sabbath. [28]So the Son of Man is Lord even of the Sabbath."

Jesus Heals on the Sabbath

3 Another time Jesus went into the synagogue, and a man with a shriveled hand was there. [2]Some of them were looking for a reason to accuse Jesus, so they watched him closely to see if he would heal him on the Sabbath. [3]Jesus said to the man with the shriveled hand, "Stand up in front of everyone."

[4]Then Jesus asked them, "Which is lawful on the Sabbath: to do good or to do evil, to save life or to kill?" But they remained silent.

[5]He looked around at them in anger and, deeply distressed at their stubborn hearts, said to the man, "Stretch out your hand." He stretched it out, and his hand was completely restored. [6]Then the Pharisees went out and began to plot with the Herodians how they might kill Jesus.

Crowds Follow Jesus

[7]Jesus withdrew with his disciples to the lake, and a large crowd from Galilee followed. [8]When they heard about all he was doing, many people came to him from Judea, Jerusalem, Idumea, and the regions across the Jordan and around Tyre and Sidon. [9]Because of the crowd he told his disciples to have a small boat ready for him, to keep the people from crowding him. [10]For he had healed many, so that those with diseases

were pushing forward to touch him. [11]Whenever the impure spirits saw him, they fell down before him and cried out, "You are the Son of God." [12]But he gave them strict orders not to tell others about him.

Jesus Appoints the Twelve

[13]Jesus went up on a mountainside and called to him those he wanted, and they came to him. [14]He appointed twelve[a] that they might be with him and that he might send them out to preach [15]and to have authority to drive out demons. [16]These are the twelve he appointed: Simon (to whom he gave the name Peter), [17]James son of Zebedee and his brother John (to them he gave the name Boanerges, which means "sons of thunder"), [18]Andrew, Philip, Bartholomew, Matthew, Thomas, James son of Alphaeus, Thaddaeus, Simon the Zealot [19]and Judas Iscariot, who betrayed him.

Jesus Accused by His Family and by Teachers of the Law

[20]Then Jesus entered a house, and again a crowd gathered, so that he and his disciples were not even able to eat. [21]When his family[b] heard

The Law of Empowerment: Jesus Gave Authority to His Team

Mark 3:13–19

Leadership teams must be chosen. Jesus deliberately chose all twelve members of his staff. He didn't call for a vote; he made the personnel decisions himself. Note what we learn about team building from Jesus' selection of the Twelve:

1. *Selection:* He handpicked them. He prayed all night about it (Lk 6:12).

2. *Motivation:* He selected the ones he personally wanted. There was chemistry.

3. *Connection:* He chose them to be with him. He modeled life in close proximity.

4. *Permission:* He released them and gave them specific assignments.

5. *Commission:* He empowered them and gave them authority to do their job.

about this, they went to take charge of him, for they said, "He is out of his mind."

[22]And the teachers of the law who came down from Jerusalem said, "He is possessed by Beelzebul! By the prince of demons he is driving out demons."

[23]So Jesus called them over to him and began to speak to them in parables: "How can Satan drive out Satan? [24]If a kingdom is divided against itself, that kingdom cannot stand. [25]If a house is divided against itself, that house cannot stand. [26]And if Satan opposes himself and is divided, he cannot stand; his end has come. [27]In fact, no one can enter a strong man's house without first tying him up. Then he can plunder the strong man's house. [28]Truly I tell you, people can be forgiven all their sins and every slander they utter, [29]but whoever blasphemes against the Holy Spirit will never be forgiven; they are guilty of an eternal sin."

[30]He said this because they were saying, "He has an impure spirit."

[31]Then Jesus' mother and brothers arrived. Standing outside, they sent someone in to call him. [32]A crowd was sitting around him, and they told him, "Your mother and brothers are outside looking for you."

[33]"Who are my mother and my brothers?" he asked.

[34]Then he looked at those seated in a circle around him and said, "Here are my mother and my brothers! [35]Whoever does God's will is my brother and sister and mother."

The Parable of the Sower

4 Again Jesus began to teach by the lake. The crowd that gathered around him was so large that he got into a boat and sat in it out on the lake, while all the people were along the shore at the water's edge. [2]He taught them many things by parables, and in his teaching said: [3]"Listen! A farmer went out to sow his seed. [4]As he was scattering the seed, some fell along the path, and the birds came and ate it up. [5]Some fell on rocky places, where it did not have much soil. It sprang up quickly, because the soil was shallow. [6]But when the sun came up, the plants were scorched, and they withered because they had no root. [7]Other seed fell among thorns, which grew up and choked the plants, so that they did not bear grain. [8]Still other seed fell on good soil. It came up, grew and produced a crop, some

---

[a] 14 Some manuscripts *twelve — designating them apostles —*
[b] 21 Or *his associates*

multiplying thirty, some sixty, some a hundred times."

⁹Then Jesus said, "Whoever has ears to hear, let them hear."

¹⁰When he was alone, the Twelve and the others around him asked him about the parables. ¹¹He told them, "The secret of the kingdom of God has been given to you. But to those on the outside everything is said in parables ¹²so that,

> "'they may be ever seeing but never
>   perceiving,
>   and ever hearing but never understanding;
> otherwise they might turn and be forgiven!'ᵃ"

¹³Then Jesus said to them, "Don't you understand this parable? How then will you understand any parable? ¹⁴The farmer sows the word. ¹⁵Some people are like seed along the path, where the word is sown. As soon as they hear it, Satan comes and takes away the word that was sown in them. ¹⁶Others, like seed sown on rocky places, hear the word and at once receive it with joy. ¹⁷But since they have no root, they last only a short time. When trouble or persecution comes because of the word, they quickly fall away. ¹⁸Still others, like seed sown among thorns, hear the word; ¹⁹but the worries of this life, the deceitfulness of wealth and the desires for other things come in and choke the word, making it unfruitful. ²⁰Others, like seed sown on good soil, hear the word, accept it, and produce a crop—some thirty, some sixty, some a hundred times what was sown."

A Lamp on a Stand

²¹He said to them, "Do you bring in a lamp to put it under a bowl or a bed? Instead, don't you put it on its stand? ²²For whatever is hidden is meant to be disclosed, and whatever is concealed is meant to be brought out into the open. ²³If anyone has ears to hear, let them hear."

²⁴"Consider carefully what you hear," he continued. "With the measure you use, it will be measured to you—and even more. ²⁵Whoever has will be given more; whoever does not have, even what they have will be taken from them."

The Parable of the Growing Seed

²⁶He also said, "This is what the kingdom of God is like. A man scatters seed on the ground. ²⁷Night and day, whether he sleeps or gets up, the seed sprouts and grows, though he does not know how. ²⁸All by itself the soil produces grain—first the stalk, then the head, then the full kernel in the head. ²⁹As soon as the grain is

---

The Principle of the Seed

Mark 4:2–20

Who is the sower in Jesus' parable? The sower is a person of influence, a leader, anyone who declares God's Word. The sower scatters a lot of seed, and only later determines the character of the soil. Note a few principles all leaders need to know about sowing seed:

1. A lot of seed must be scattered to produce a crop.

2. Not all soils produce, but we cannot reap if we do not sow.

3. We must continue sowing, because one day we will reap a harvest.

4. The soil that produces will multiply; we will reap more than we sow.

5. We will reap in proportion to what we have sown.

6. We cannot do anything about last year's harvest, but we can about this year's.

7. We must believe in the seed we sow, knowing that some will produce fruit.

8. Once we see fruit, all our effort seems worthwhile.

---

ripe, he puts the sickle to it, because the harvest has come."

The Parable of the Mustard Seed

³⁰Again he said, "What shall we say the kingdom of God is like, or what parable shall we use to describe it? ³¹It is like a mustard seed, which is the smallest of all seeds on earth. ³²Yet when planted, it grows and becomes the largest of all garden plants, with such big branches that the birds can perch in its shade."

³³With many similar parables Jesus spoke the word to them, as much as they could understand. ³⁴He did not say anything to them without using a parable. But when he was alone with his own disciples, he explained everything.

Jesus Calms the Storm

³⁵That day when evening came, he said to his disciples, "Let us go over to the other side."

ᵃ 12 Isaiah 6:9,10

[36]Leaving the crowd behind, they took him along, just as he was, in the boat. There were also other boats with him. [37]A furious squall came up, and the waves broke over the boat, so that it was nearly swamped. [38]Jesus was in the stern, sleeping on a cushion. The disciples woke him and said to him, "Teacher, don't you care if we drown?"

[39]He got up, rebuked the wind and said to the waves, "Quiet! Be still!" Then the wind died down and it was completely calm.

[40]He said to his disciples, "Why are you so afraid? Do you still have no faith?"

[41]They were terrified and asked each other, "Who is this? Even the wind and the waves obey him!"

Jesus Restores a Demon-Possessed Man

5 They went across the lake to the region of the Gerasenes.[a] [2]When Jesus got out of the boat, a man with an impure spirit came from the tombs to meet him. [3]This man lived in the tombs, and no one could bind him anymore,

---

The Principle of Resting and Caring

Mark 4:35–41

When a terrifying storm convinced the disciples they were about to die, they forgot one important factor: Jesus was in the boat and had told them they were going to the other side of the lake (Mk 4:35). His word always comes to pass.

When they finally awakened Jesus, he got up, rebuked the wind and the sea, and everything became completely calm. So long as the disciples assumed control of their situation, Jesus rested. But when they cast their care on him and released control to him, he cared for everything and they could rest.

This remains true for every leader today. While we must take responsibility, we are never to take control. Only God is big enough to take control. The principle works this way:

1. *We care . . . he rests.* God will allow us to mess up our situation.

2. *He cares . . . we rest.* When we release control to him, we find peace.

---

not even with a chain. [4]For he had often been chained hand and foot, but he tore the chains apart and broke the irons on his feet. No one was strong enough to subdue him. [5]Night and day among the tombs and in the hills he would cry out and cut himself with stones.

[6]When he saw Jesus from a distance, he ran and fell on his knees in front of him. [7]He shouted at the top of his voice, "What do you want with me, Jesus, Son of the Most High God? In God's name don't torture me!" [8]For Jesus had said to him, "Come out of this man, you impure spirit!"

[9]Then Jesus asked him, "What is your name?"

"My name is Legion," he replied, "for we are many." [10]And he begged Jesus again and again not to send them out of the area.

[11]A large herd of pigs was feeding on the nearby hillside. [12]The demons begged Jesus, "Send us among the pigs; allow us to go into them." [13]He gave them permission, and the impure spirits came out and went into the pigs. The herd, about two thousand in number, rushed down the steep bank into the lake and were drowned.

[14]Those tending the pigs ran off and reported this in the town and countryside, and the people went out to see what had happened. [15]When they came to Jesus, they saw the man who had been possessed by the legion of demons, sitting there, dressed and in his right mind; and they were afraid. [16]Those who had seen it told the people what had happened to the demon-possessed man—and told about the pigs as well. [17]Then the people began to plead with Jesus to leave their region.

[18]As Jesus was getting into the boat, the man who had been demon-possessed begged to go with him. [19]Jesus did not let him, but said, "Go home to your own people and tell them how much the Lord has done for you, and how he has had mercy on you." [20]So the man went away and began to tell in the Decapolis[b] how much Jesus had done for him. And all the people were amazed.

Jesus Raises a Dead Girl and Heals a Sick Woman

[21]When Jesus had again crossed over by boat to the other side of the lake, a large crowd gathered around him while he was by the lake. [22]Then one of the synagogue leaders, named Jairus, came, and when he saw Jesus, he fell at his

---

[a] 1 Some manuscripts *Gadarenes*; other manuscripts *Gergesenes*   [b] 20 That is, the Ten Cities

feet. ²³He pleaded earnestly with him, "My little daughter is dying. Please come and put your hands on her so that she will be healed and live." ²⁴So Jesus went with him.

A large crowd followed and pressed around him. ²⁵And a woman was there who had been subject to bleeding for twelve years. ²⁶She had suffered a great deal under the care of many doctors and had spent all she had, yet instead of getting better she grew worse. ²⁷When she heard about Jesus, she came up behind him in the crowd and touched his cloak, ²⁸because she thought, "If I just touch his clothes, I will be healed." ²⁹Immediately her bleeding stopped and she felt in her body that she was freed from her suffering.

³⁰At once Jesus realized that power had gone out from him. He turned around in the crowd and asked, "Who touched my clothes?"

³¹"You see the people crowding against you," his disciples answered, "and yet you can ask, 'Who touched me?'"

³²But Jesus kept looking around to see who had done it. ³³Then the woman, knowing what had happened to her, came and fell at his feet and, trembling with fear, told him the whole truth. ³⁴He said to her, "Daughter, your faith has healed you. Go in peace and be freed from your suffering."

³⁵While Jesus was still speaking, some people came from the house of Jairus, the synagogue leader. "Your daughter is dead," they said. "Why bother the teacher anymore?"

³⁶Overhearing[a] what they said, Jesus told him, "Don't be afraid; just believe."

³⁷He did not let anyone follow him except Peter, James and John the brother of James. ³⁸When they came to the home of the synagogue leader, Jesus saw a commotion, with people crying and wailing loudly. ³⁹He went in and said to them, "Why all this commotion and wailing? The child is not dead but asleep." ⁴⁰But they laughed at him.

After he put them all out, he took the child's father and mother and the disciples who were with him, and went in where the child was. ⁴¹He took her by the hand and said to her, "*Talitha koum!*" (which means "Little girl, I say to you, get up!"). ⁴²Immediately the girl stood up and began to walk around (she was twelve years old). At this they were completely astonished. ⁴³He gave strict orders not to let anyone know about this, and told them to give her something to eat.

A Prophet Without Honor

6 Jesus left there and went to his hometown, accompanied by his disciples. ²When the Sabbath came, he began to teach in the synagogue, and many who heard him were amazed.

"Where did this man get these things?" they

---

a 36 Or Ignoring

SIMON PETER

Privileged to See What Most Others Couldn't

Mark 5:35–43

PROFILE in leadership

As one of Jesus' most beloved and privileged leaders, the apostle Peter saw some astonishing things, things that others—not even most of the other twelve—ever had a chance to witness.

Mark records how Jesus allowed no one to follow him to the home of Jairus, a synagogue ruler whose daughter had just died from an illness, except Peter and the brothers James and John. For a reason not clearly spelled out in the Scripture, Jesus wanted only these three leaders with him when he performed one of his most amazing miracles.

No one could see what Peter saw that day without coming away profoundly changed and inspired. Peter had witnessed Jesus cast out demons and perform miracles of healing, and he had heard him teach with God-given authority. But on this remarkable day, Jesus gave Peter the privilege of seeing how he held power over life and death itself.

All who believe in the Lord Jesus Christ for their salvation have access to him at any time. But at special times, Jesus specifically calls his leaders—those with a unique call of service in ministry—to see and hear special things, things they alone have the privilege to witness. It is a special trust with unique responsibilities.

asked. "What's this wisdom that has been given him? What are these remarkable miracles he is performing? [3]Isn't this the carpenter? Isn't this Mary's son and the brother of James, Joseph,[a] Judas and Simon? Aren't his sisters here with us?" And they took offense at him.

[4]Jesus said to them, "A prophet is not without honor except in his own town, among his relatives and in his own home." [5]He could not do any miracles there, except lay his hands on a few sick people and heal them. [6]He was amazed at their lack of faith.

Jesus Sends Out the Twelve

Then Jesus went around teaching from village to village. [7]Calling the Twelve to him, he began to send them out two by two and gave them authority over impure spirits.

[8]These were his instructions: "Take nothing for the journey except a staff — no bread, no bag, no money in your belts. [9]Wear sandals but not an extra shirt. [10]Whenever you enter a house, stay there until you leave that town. [11]And if any place will not welcome you or listen to you, leave that place and shake the dust off your feet as a testimony against them."

[12]They went out and preached that people should repent. [13]They drove out many demons and anointed many sick people with oil and healed them.

John the Baptist Beheaded

[14]King Herod heard about this, for Jesus' name had become well known. Some were saying,[b] "John the Baptist has been raised from the dead, and that is why miraculous powers are at work in him."

[15]Others said, "He is Elijah."

And still others claimed, "He is a prophet, like one of the prophets of long ago."

[16]But when Herod heard this, he said, "John, whom I beheaded, has been raised from the dead!"

[17]For Herod himself had given orders to have John arrested, and he had him bound and put in prison. He did this because of Herodias, his brother Philip's wife, whom he had married. [18]For John had been saying to Herod, "It is not lawful for you to have your brother's wife." [19]So Herodias nursed a grudge against John and wanted to kill him. But she was not able to, [20]because Herod feared John and protected him, knowing him to be a righteous and holy man. When Herod heard John, he was greatly puzzled[c]; yet he liked to listen to him.

[21]Finally the opportune time came. On his birthday Herod gave a banquet for his high officials and military commanders and the leading men of Galilee. [22]When the daughter of[d] Herodias came in and danced, she pleased Herod and his dinner guests.

The king said to the girl, "Ask me for anything you want, and I'll give it to you." [23]And he promised her with an oath, "Whatever you ask I will give you, up to half my kingdom."

[24]She went out and said to her mother, "What shall I ask for?"

"The head of John the Baptist," she answered.

[25]At once the girl hurried in to the king with the request: "I want you to give me right now the head of John the Baptist on a platter."

[26]The king was greatly distressed, but because of his oaths and his dinner guests, he did not want to refuse her. [27]So he immediately sent an executioner with orders to bring John's head. The man went, beheaded John in the prison, [28]and brought back his head on a platter. He presented it to the girl, and she gave it to her mother. [29]On hearing of this, John's disciples came and took his body and laid it in a tomb.

Jesus Feeds the Five Thousand

[30]The apostles gathered around Jesus and reported to him all they had done and taught. [31]Then, because so many people were coming and going that they did not even have a chance to eat, he said to them, "Come with me by yourselves to a quiet place and get some rest."

[32]So they went away by themselves in a boat to a solitary place. [33]But many who saw them leaving recognized them and ran on foot from all the towns and got there ahead of them. [34]When Jesus landed and saw a large crowd, he had compassion on them, because they were like sheep without a shepherd. So he began teaching them many things.

[35]By this time it was late in the day, so his disciples came to him. "This is a remote place," they said, "and it's already very late. [36]Send the people away so that they can go to the surrounding countryside and villages and buy themselves something to eat."

[37]But he answered, "You give them something to eat."

They said to him, "That would take more than

---

[a] 3   Greek *Joses*, a variant of *Joseph*   [b] 14   Some early manuscripts *He was saying*   [c] 20   Some early manuscripts *he did many things*   [d] 22   Some early manuscripts *When his daughter*

Compassion: Love for People Moves Jesus to Lead

Mark 6:34

Jesus' leadership was empowered not by a sense of duty or obligation, or by a desire to build an image, but by compassion. Great leaders, like Jesus, build a deep love for people that moves them to do far more than obligation could ever induce. Do you deeply love those you lead?

half a year's wages[a]! Are we to go and spend that much on bread and give it to them to eat?"

[38] "How many loaves do you have?" he asked. "Go and see."

When they found out, they said, "Five — and two fish."

[39] Then Jesus directed them to have all the people sit down in groups on the green grass. [40] So they sat down in groups of hundreds and fifties. [41] Taking the five loaves and the two fish and looking up to heaven, he gave thanks and broke the loaves. Then he gave them to his disciples to distribute to the people. He also divided the two fish among them all. [42] They all ate and were satisfied, [43] and the disciples picked up twelve basketfuls of broken pieces of bread and fish. [44] The number of the men who had eaten was five thousand.

Jesus Walks on the Water

[45] Immediately Jesus made his disciples get into the boat and go on ahead of him to Bethsaida, while he dismissed the crowd. [46] After leaving them, he went up on a mountainside to pray.

[47] Later that night, the boat was in the middle of the lake, and he was alone on land. [48] He saw the disciples straining at the oars, because the wind was against them. Shortly before dawn he went out to them, walking on the lake. He was about to pass by them, [49] but when they saw him walking on the lake, they thought he was a ghost. They cried out, [50] because they all saw him and were terrified.

Immediately he spoke to them and said, "Take courage! It is I. Don't be afraid." [51] Then he climbed into the boat with them, and the wind died down. They were completely amazed, [52] for they had not understood about the loaves; their hearts were hardened.

[53] When they had crossed over, they landed at Gennesaret and anchored there. [54] As soon as they got out of the boat, people recognized Jesus. [55] They ran throughout that whole region and carried the sick on mats to wherever they heard he was. [56] And wherever he went — into villages, towns or countryside — they placed the sick in the marketplaces. They begged him to let them touch even the edge of his cloak, and all who touched it were healed.

That Which Defiles

7 The Pharisees and some of the teachers of the law who had come from Jerusalem gathered around Jesus [2] and saw some of his disciples eating food with hands that were defiled, that is, unwashed. [3] (The Pharisees and all the Jews do not eat unless they give their hands a ceremonial washing, holding to the tradition of the elders. [4] When they come from the marketplace they do not eat unless they wash. And they observe many other traditions, such as the washing of cups, pitchers and kettles.[b])

[5] So the Pharisees and teachers of the law asked Jesus, "Why don't your disciples live according to the tradition of the elders instead of eating their food with defiled hands?"

[6] He replied, "Isaiah was right when he prophesied about you hypocrites; as it is written:

"'These people honor me with their lips,
    but their hearts are far from me.
[7] They worship me in vain;
    their teachings are merely human rules.'[c]

[8] You have let go of the commands of God and are holding on to human traditions."

[9] And he continued, "You have a fine way of setting aside the commands of God in order to observe[d] your own traditions! [10] For Moses said, 'Honor your father and mother,'[e] and, 'Anyone who curses their father or mother is to be put to death.'[f] [11] But you say that if anyone declares that what might have been used to help their father or mother is Corban (that is, devoted to God) — [12] then you no longer let them do anything for their father or mother. [13] Thus you nullify the word of God by your tradition that you have handed down. And you do many things like that."

[14] Again Jesus called the crowd to him and said, "Listen to me, everyone, and understand

---

[a] 37 Greek *take two hundred denarii*   [b] 4 Some early manuscripts *pitchers, kettles and dining couches*   [c] 6,7 Isaiah 29:13   [d] 9 Some manuscripts *set up*   [e] 10 Exodus 20:12; Deut. 5:16   [f] 10 Exodus 21:17; Lev. 20:9

this. [15]Nothing outside a person can defile them by going into them. Rather, it is what comes out of a person that defiles them." [16] a

[17]After he had left the crowd and entered the house, his disciples asked him about this parable. [18]"Are you so dull?" he asked. "Don't you see that nothing that enters a person from the outside can defile them? [19]For it doesn't go into their heart but into their stomach, and then out of the body." (In saying this, Jesus declared all foods clean.)

[20]He went on: "What comes out of a person is what defiles them. [21]For it is from within, out of a person's heart, that evil thoughts come — sexual immorality, theft, murder, [22]adultery, greed, malice, deceit, lewdness, envy, slander, arrogance and folly. [23]All these evils come from inside and defile a person."

Jesus Honors a Syrophoenician Woman's Faith

[24]Jesus left that place and went to the vicinity of Tyre.[b] He entered a house and did not want anyone to know it; yet he could not keep his presence secret. [25]In fact, as soon as she heard about him, a woman whose little daughter was possessed by an impure spirit came and fell at his feet. [26]The woman was a Greek, born in Syrian Phoenicia. She begged Jesus to drive the demon out of her daughter.

[27]"First let the children eat all they want," he told her, "for it is not right to take the children's bread and toss it to the dogs."

[28]"Lord," she replied, "even the dogs under the table eat the children's crumbs."

[29]Then he told her, "For such a reply, you may go; the demon has left your daughter."

[30]She went home and found her child lying on the bed, and the demon gone.

Jesus Heals a Deaf and Mute Man

[31]Then Jesus left the vicinity of Tyre and went through Sidon, down to the Sea of Galilee and into the region of the Decapolis.[c] [32]There some people brought to him a man who was deaf and could hardly talk, and they begged Jesus to place his hand on him.

[33]After he took him aside, away from the crowd, Jesus put his fingers into the man's ears. Then he spit and touched the man's tongue. [34]He looked up to heaven and with a deep sigh said to him, *Ephphatha!*" (which means "Be opened!"). [35]At this, the man's ears were opened, his tongue was loosened and he began to speak plainly.

[36]Jesus commanded them not to tell anyone. But the more he did so, the more they kept talk-ing about it. [37]People were overwhelmed with amazement. "He has done everything well," they said. "He even makes the deaf hear and the mute speak."

Jesus Feeds the Four Thousand

8 During those days another large crowd gathered. Since they had nothing to eat, Jesus called his disciples to him and said, [2]"I have compassion for these people; they have already been with me three days and have nothing to eat. [3]If I send them home hungry, they will collapse on the way, because some of them have come a long distance."

[4]His disciples answered, "But where in this remote place can anyone get enough bread to feed them?"

[5]"How many loaves do you have?" Jesus asked.

"Seven," they replied.

[6]He told the crowd to sit down on the ground. When he had taken the seven loaves and given thanks, he broke them and gave them to his disciples to distribute to the people, and they did so. [7]They had a few small fish as well; he gave thanks for them also and told the disciples to distribute them. [8]The people ate and were satisfied. Afterward the disciples picked up seven basketfuls of broken pieces that were left over. [9]About four thousand were present. After he had sent them away, [10]he got into the boat with his disciples and went to the region of Dalmanutha.

[11]The Pharisees came and began to question Jesus. To test him, they asked him for a sign from heaven. [12]He sighed deeply and said, "Why does this generation ask for a sign? Truly I tell you, no sign will be given to it." [13]Then he left them, got back into the boat and crossed to the other side.

The Yeast of the Pharisees and Herod

[14]The disciples had forgotten to bring bread, except for one loaf they had with them in the boat. [15]"Be careful," Jesus warned them. "Watch out for the yeast of the Pharisees and that of Herod."

[16]They discussed this with one another and said, "It is because we have no bread."

[17]Aware of their discussion, Jesus asked them: "Why are you talking about having no bread?

---

a 16 Some manuscripts include here the words of 4:23.
b 24 Many early manuscripts *Tyre and Sidon*   *c 31* That is, the Ten Cities

Do you still not see or understand? Are your hearts hardened? [18]Do you have eyes but fail to see, and ears but fail to hear? And don't you remember? [19]When I broke the five loaves for the five thousand, how many basketfuls of pieces did you pick up?"

"Twelve," they replied.

[20]"And when I broke the seven loaves for the four thousand, how many basketfuls of pieces did you pick up?"

They answered, "Seven."

[21]He said to them, "Do you still not understand?"

Jesus Heals a Blind Man at Bethsaida

[22]They came to Bethsaida, and some people brought a blind man and begged Jesus to touch him. [23]He took the blind man by the hand and led him outside the village. When he had spit on the man's eyes and put his hands on him, Jesus asked, "Do you see anything?"

[24]He looked up and said, "I see people; they look like trees walking around."

[25]Once more Jesus put his hands on the man's eyes. Then his eyes were opened, his sight was restored, and he saw everything clearly. [26]Jesus sent him home, saying, "Don't even go into[a] the village."

Peter Declares That Jesus Is the Messiah

[27]Jesus and his disciples went on to the villages around Caesarea Philippi. On the way he asked them, "Who do people say I am?"

[28]They replied, "Some say John the Baptist; others say Elijah; and still others, one of the prophets."

[29]"But what about you?" he asked. "Who do you say I am?"

Peter answered, "You are the Messiah."

[30]Jesus warned them not to tell anyone about him.

Jesus Predicts His Death

[31]He then began to teach them that the Son of Man must suffer many things and be rejected by the elders, the chief priests and the teachers of the law, and that he must be killed and after three days rise again. [32]He spoke plainly about this, and Peter took him aside and began to rebuke him.

[33]But when Jesus turned and looked at his disciples, he rebuked Peter. "Get behind me, Satan!" he said. "You do not have in mind the concerns of God, but merely human concerns."

The Way of the Cross

[34]Then he called the crowd to him along with his disciples and said: "Whoever wants to be my disciple must deny themselves and take up their cross and follow me. [35]For whoever wants to save their life[b] will lose it, but whoever loses their life for me and for the gospel will save it. [36]What good is it for someone to gain the whole world, yet forfeit their soul? [37]Or what can anyone give in exchange for their soul? [38]If anyone is ashamed of me and my words in this adulterous and sinful generation, the Son of Man will be ashamed of them when he comes in his Father's glory with the holy angels."

Commitment: Moving from Displaying Care to Drawing Commitment

Mark 8:1–21

Leadership development always begins with showing concern for the emerging leader, then securing a foundation, and finally drawing commitment.

Jesus models this process in Mark 8: For the second time, Jesus fed thousands in a miraculous way (vv. 1–9), teaching the disciples that God can provide food. A deeper lesson came later when they recognized Jesus had performed the miracle to show them God would meet all their needs (vv. 17–21). Jesus also warned them about the "yeast of the Pharisees" and to guard against their attitude and perspective (vv. 14–15).

Jesus slowly moved his men from consumers to contributors. Jesus wanted to get emerging leaders to think about issues beyond themselves. Note the stages of his developmental process:

1. *Shepherd:* He met their immediate needs; he provided security.

2. *Equipper:* He trained them to serve; he provided opportunities.

3. *Developer:* He mentored them to lead others; he provided personal challenge.

---

a 26 Some manuscripts *go and tell anyone in*   *b 35* The Greek word means either *life* or *soul*; also in verses 36 and 37.

Vision: Jesus Based His Vision on His Values

Mark 8:31–33

While Peter sought comfort for his King, Jesus sought conquest for the kingdom. This teaches us that leaders must:

- build a vision off of their values
- correct others who drift from the vision
- help the team lay aside personal agendas to reach their vision
- pay the price to achieve their vision

9 And he said to them, "Truly I tell you, some who are standing here will not taste death before they see that the kingdom of God has come with power."

The Transfiguration

²After six days Jesus took Peter, James and John with him and led them up a high mountain, where they were all alone. There he was transfigured before them. ³His clothes became dazzling white, whiter than anyone in the world could bleach them. ⁴And there appeared before them Elijah and Moses, who were talking with Jesus.

⁵Peter said to Jesus, "Rabbi, it is good for us to be here. Let us put up three shelters — one for you, one for Moses and one for Elijah." ⁶(He did not know what to say, they were so frightened.)

⁷Then a cloud appeared and covered them, and a voice came from the cloud: "This is my Son, whom I love. Listen to him!"

⁸Suddenly, when they looked around, they no longer saw anyone with them except Jesus.

⁹As they were coming down the mountain, Jesus gave them orders not to tell anyone what they had seen until the Son of Man had risen from the dead. ¹⁰They kept the matter to themselves, discussing what "rising from the dead" meant.

¹¹And they asked him, "Why do the teachers of the law say that Elijah must come first?"

¹²Jesus replied, "To be sure, Elijah does come first, and restores all things. Why then is it written that the Son of Man must suffer much and be rejected? ¹³But I tell you, Elijah has come, and they have done to him everything they wished, just as it is written about him."

Jesus Heals a Boy Possessed by an Impure Spirit

¹⁴When they came to the other disciples, they saw a large crowd around them and the teachers

The Top Ten Leadership Principles of Jesus

Mark 8:34–38

The Gospels demonstrate beyond all doubt that Jesus really is the Ultimate Leader. No one has influenced people more than he. Although he never wrote a book or taught in a seminary, his movement continues to grow over two thousand years after he departed the earth. Consider ten leadership principles we see in his life, as recorded in the four Gospels:

1. Leadership is servanthood (Mt 20:25–28; Mk 8:35).

2. Let your purpose prioritize your life (Mt 6:33; Lk 19:10; Jn 17:4).

3. Live the life before you lead others (Lk 7:22–23; Jn 14:11).

4. Impact comes from relationships, not positions (Lk 9:6; Jn 4:5–30).

5. Leaders must replenish themselves (Mk 1:35–38; 6:31).

6. Great leaders call for great commitment (Mt 10:17; Mk 8:34–38).

7. Show security when handling tough issues (Mk 11:27–33; Lk 20:19–26).

8. Credibility comes by meeting needs and solving problems (Lk 5:12–15; 8:38–39).

9. Leaders must choose and develop their key people (Mk 3:14; Lk 10:1).

10. There is no success without a successor (Mt 28:20; Ac 1:8).

of the law arguing with them. 15As soon as all the people saw Jesus, they were overwhelmed with wonder and ran to greet him.

16"What are you arguing with them about?" he asked.

17A man in the crowd answered, "Teacher, I brought you my son, who is possessed by a spirit that has robbed him of speech. 18Whenever it seizes him, it throws him to the ground. He foams at the mouth, gnashes his teeth and becomes rigid. I asked your disciples to drive out the spirit, but they could not."

19"You unbelieving generation," Jesus replied, "how long shall I stay with you? How long shall I put up with you? Bring the boy to me."

20So they brought him. When the spirit saw Jesus, it immediately threw the boy into a convulsion. He fell to the ground and rolled around, foaming at the mouth.

21Jesus asked the boy's father, "How long has he been like this?"

"From childhood," he answered. 22"It has often thrown him into fire or water to kill him. But if you can do anything, take pity on us and help us."

23"'If you can'?" said Jesus. "Everything is possible for one who believes."

24Immediately the boy's father exclaimed, "I do believe; help me overcome my unbelief!"

25When Jesus saw that a crowd was running to the scene, he rebuked the impure spirit. "You deaf and mute spirit," he said, "I command you, come out of him and never enter him again."

26The spirit shrieked, convulsed him violently and came out. The boy looked so much like a corpse that many said, "He's dead." 27But Jesus took him by the hand and lifted him to his feet, and he stood up.

28After Jesus had gone indoors, his disciples asked him privately, "Why couldn't we drive it out?"

29He replied, "This kind can come out only by prayer.ᵃ"

Jesus Predicts His Death a Second Time

30They left that place and passed through Galilee. Jesus did not want anyone to know where they were, 31because he was teaching his disciples. He said to them, "The Son of Man is going to be delivered into the hands of men. They will kill him, and after three days he will rise." 32But they did not understand what he meant and were afraid to ask him about it.

33They came to Capernaum. When he was in the house, he asked them, "What were you arguing about on the road?" 34But they kept quiet because on the way they had argued about who was the greatest.

35Sitting down, Jesus called the Twelve and said, "Anyone who wants to be first must be the very last, and the servant of all."

36He took a little child whom he placed among them. Taking the child in his arms, he said to them, 37"Whoever welcomes one of these little children in my name welcomes me; and whoever welcomes me does not welcome me but the one who sent me."

Whoever Is Not Against Us Is for Us

38"Teacher," said John, "we saw someone driving out demons in your name and we told him to stop, because he was not one of us."

39"Do not stop him," Jesus said. "For no one who does a miracle in my name can in the next moment say anything bad about me, 40for whoever is not against us is for us. 41Truly I tell you, anyone who gives you a cup of water in my name because you belong to the Messiah will certainly not lose their reward.

Causing to Stumble

42"If anyone causes one of these little ones — those who believe in me — to stumble, it would be better for them if a large millstone were hung around their neck and they were thrown into the sea. 43If your hand causes you to stumble, cut it off. It is better for you to enter life maimed than with two hands to go into hell, where the fire never goes out. [44]ᵇ 45And if your foot causes you to stumble, cut it off. It is better for you to enter life crippled than to have two feet and be thrown into hell. [46]ᵇ 47And if your eye causes you to stumble, pluck it out. It is better for you to enter the kingdom of God with one eye than to have two eyes and be thrown into hell, 48where

"'the worms that eat them do not die,
and the fire is not quenched.'ᶜ

49Everyone will be salted with fire.

50"Salt is good, but if it loses its saltiness, how can you make it salty again? Have salt among yourselves, and be at peace with each other."

Divorce

10 Jesus then left that place and went into the region of Judea and across the Jordan. Again crowds of people came to him, and as was his custom, he taught them.

ᵃ 29 Some manuscripts *prayer and fasting*   ᵇ 44,46 Some manuscripts include here the words of verse 48.   ᶜ 48 Isaiah 66:24

[2]Some Pharisees came and tested him by asking, "Is it lawful for a man to divorce his wife?"

[3]"What did Moses command you?" he replied.

[4]They said, "Moses permitted a man to write a certificate of divorce and send her away."

[5]"It was because your hearts were hard that Moses wrote you this law," Jesus replied. [6]"But at the beginning of creation God 'made them male and female.'[a] [7]'For this reason a man will leave his father and mother and be united to his wife,[b] [8]and the two will become one flesh.'[c] So they are no longer two, but one flesh. [9]Therefore what God has joined together, let no one separate."

[10]When they were in the house again, the disciples asked Jesus about this. [11]He answered, "Anyone who divorces his wife and marries another woman commits adultery against her. [12]And if she divorces her husband and marries another man, she commits adultery."

The Little Children and Jesus

[13]People were bringing little children to Jesus for him to place his hands on them, but the disciples rebuked them. [14]When Jesus saw this, he was indignant. He said to them, "Let the little children come to me, and do not hinder them, for the kingdom of God belongs to such as these. [15]Truly I tell you, anyone who will not receive the kingdom of God like a little child will never enter it." [16]And he took the children in his arms, placed his hands on them and blessed them.

The Rich and the Kingdom of God

[17]As Jesus started on his way, a man ran up to him and fell on his knees before him. "Good teacher," he asked, "what must I do to inherit eternal life?"

[18]"Why do you call me good?" Jesus answered. "No one is good—except God alone. [19]You know the commandments: 'You shall not murder, you shall not commit adultery, you shall not steal, you shall not give false testimony, you shall not defraud, honor your father and mother.'[d]"

[20]"Teacher," he declared, "all these I have kept since I was a boy."

[21]Jesus looked at him and loved him. "One thing you lack," he said. "Go, sell everything you have and give to the poor, and you will have treasure in heaven. Then come, follow me."

[22]At this the man's face fell. He went away sad, because he had great wealth.

[23]Jesus looked around and said to his disciples, "How hard it is for the rich to enter the kingdom of God!"

The Law of Addition: The Way Up Is Down

Mark 9:33—10:16

When Jesus caught his disciples arguing about who among them was the greatest, they felt embarrassed—but Jesus didn't rebuke them for wanting to be great. He simply gave them an unexpected formula: Be a servant. Leaders add value by serving others.

Later, when the disciples asked about those who cast out demons in his name, Jesus said, "Whoever is not against us is for us" (Mk 9:40–41). A short time later, his disciples angered him again when they became more concerned with crowd control than with humility and service (10:13–16).

For Jesus, children presented the best example of the required attitude for servant leaders. Children exhibit humility, wonder, honesty, innocence, trust and dependence. Note four leadership lessons we glean from Mark 9 and 10:

1. The greater the leader, the greater the servant (9:35).

2. Leaders include others when they serve (9:40).

3. Any service rendered will be rewarded (9:41).

4. Servant leaders must become childlike (10:13–16).

---

[24]The disciples were amazed at his words. But Jesus said again, "Children, how hard it is[e] to enter the kingdom of God! [25]It is easier for a camel to go through the eye of a needle than for someone who is rich to enter the kingdom of God."

[26]The disciples were even more amazed, and said to each other, "Who then can be saved?"

[27]Jesus looked at them and said, "With man this is impossible, but not with God; all things are possible with God."

[28]Then Peter spoke up, "We have left everything to follow you!"

[29]"Truly I tell you," Jesus replied, "no one who

---

[a] 6 Gen. 1:27   [b] 7 Some early manuscripts do not have *and be united to his wife.*   [c] 8 Gen. 2:24   [d] 19 Exodus 20:12-16; Deut. 5:16-20   [e] 24 Some manuscripts *is for those who trust in riches*

has left home or brothers or sisters or mother or father or children or fields for me and the gospel ³⁰will fail to receive a hundred times as much in this present age: homes, brothers, sisters, mothers, children and fields — along with persecutions — and in the age to come eternal life. ³¹But many who are first will be last, and the last first."

Jesus Predicts His Death a Third Time

³²They were on their way up to Jerusalem, with Jesus leading the way, and the disciples were astonished, while those who followed were afraid. Again he took the Twelve aside and told them what was going to happen to him. ³³"We are going up to Jerusalem," he said, "and the Son of Man will be delivered over to the chief priests and the teachers of the law. They will condemn him to death and will hand him over to the Gentiles, ³⁴who will mock him and spit on him, flog him and kill him. Three days later he will rise."

The Request of James and John

³⁵Then James and John, the sons of Zebedee, came to him. "Teacher," they said, "we want you to do for us whatever we ask."

³⁶"What do you want me to do for you?" he asked.

³⁷They replied, "Let one of us sit at your right and the other at your left in your glory."

³⁸"You don't know what you are asking," Jesus said. "Can you drink the cup I drink or be baptized with the baptism I am baptized with?"

³⁹"We can," they answered.

Jesus said to them, "You will drink the cup I drink and be baptized with the baptism I am baptized with, ⁴⁰but to sit at my right or left is not for me to grant. These places belong to those for whom they have been prepared."

⁴¹When the ten heard about this, they became indignant with James and John. ⁴²Jesus called them together and said, "You know that those who are regarded as rulers of the Gentiles lord it over them, and their high officials exercise authority over them. ⁴³Not so with you. Instead, whoever wants to become great among you must be your servant, ⁴⁴and whoever wants to be first must be slave of all. ⁴⁵For even the Son of Man did not come to be served, but to serve, and to give his life as a ransom for many."

Blind Bartimaeus Receives His Sight

⁴⁶Then they came to Jericho. As Jesus and his disciples, together with a large crowd, were leaving the city, a blind man, Bartimaeus (which means "son of Timaeus"), was sitting by the roadside begging. ⁴⁷When he heard that it was Jesus of Nazareth, he began to shout, "Jesus, Son of David, have mercy on me!"

⁴⁸Many rebuked him and told him to be quiet, but he shouted all the more, "Son of David, have mercy on me!"

⁴⁹Jesus stopped and said, "Call him."

So they called to the blind man, "Cheer up! On your feet! He's calling you." ⁵⁰Throwing his cloak aside, he jumped to his feet and came to Jesus.

⁵¹"What do you want me to do for you?" Jesus asked him.

The blind man said, "Rabbi, I want to see."

⁵²"Go," said Jesus, "your faith has healed you." Immediately he received his sight and followed Jesus along the road.

Jesus Comes to Jerusalem as King

11 As they approached Jerusalem and came to Bethphage and Bethany at the Mount of Olives, Jesus sent two of his disciples, ²saying to them, "Go to the village ahead of you, and just as you enter it, you will find a colt tied there, which no one has ever ridden. Untie it and bring it here. ³If anyone asks you, 'Why are you doing this?' say, 'The Lord needs it and will send it back here shortly.'"

⁴They went and found a colt outside in the street, tied at a doorway. As they untied it, ⁵some people standing there asked, "What are you doing, untying that colt?" ⁶They answered as Jesus had told them to, and the people let them go. ⁷When they brought the colt to Jesus and threw their cloaks over it, he sat on it. ⁸Many people spread their cloaks on the road, while others spread branches they had cut in the fields. ⁹Those who went ahead and those who followed shouted,

"Hosanna!ᵃ"

"Blessed is he who comes in the name of the Lord!"ᵇ

¹⁰"Blessed is the coming kingdom of our father David!"

"Hosanna in the highest heaven!"

¹¹Jesus entered Jerusalem and went into the temple courts. He looked around at everything, but since it was already late, he went out to Bethany with the Twelve.

ᵃ 9 A Hebrew expression meaning "Save!" which became an exclamation of praise; also in verse 10   ᵇ 9 Psalm 118:25,26

Jesus Curses a Fig Tree and Clears the Temple Courts

[12] The next day as they were leaving Bethany, Jesus was hungry. [13] Seeing in the distance a fig tree in leaf, he went to find out if it had any fruit. When he reached it, he found nothing but leaves, because it was not the season for figs. [14] Then he said to the tree, "May no one ever eat fruit from you again." And his disciples heard him say it.

[15] On reaching Jerusalem, Jesus entered the temple courts and began driving out those who were buying and selling there. He overturned the tables of the money changers and the benches of those selling doves, [16] and would not allow anyone to carry merchandise through the temple courts. [17] And as he taught them, he said, "Is it not written: 'My house will be called a house of prayer for all nations'[a]? But you have made it 'a den of robbers.'[b]"

Security: Jesus Could Do the Unpopular

Mark 11:15–17

How could Jesus, so full of love, drive the money changers out of the temple? He felt secure in his identity and mission; he did not need consensus. Margaret Thatcher once rightly asked, "What great cause would have been fought and won under the banner, 'I stand for consensus'?"

[18] The chief priests and the teachers of the law heard this and began looking for a way to kill him, for they feared him, because the whole crowd was amazed at his teaching.

[19] When evening came, Jesus and his disciples[c] went out of the city.

[20] In the morning, as they went along, they saw the fig tree withered from the roots. [21] Peter remembered and said to Jesus, "Rabbi, look! The fig tree you cursed has withered!"

[22] "Have faith in God," Jesus answered. [23] "Truly[d] I tell you, if anyone says to this mountain, 'Go, throw yourself into the sea,' and does not doubt in their heart but believes that what they say will happen, it will be done for them. [24] Therefore I tell you, whatever you ask for in prayer, believe that you have received it, and it will be yours. [25] And when you stand praying, if you hold anything against anyone, forgive them, so that your Father in heaven may forgive you your sins." [26] [e]

The Authority of Jesus Questioned

[27] They arrived again in Jerusalem, and while Jesus was walking in the temple courts, the chief priests, the teachers of the law and the elders came to him. [28] "By what authority are you doing these things?" they asked. "And who gave you authority to do this?"

[29] Jesus replied, "I will ask you one question. Answer me, and I will tell you by what authority I am doing these things. [30] John's baptism — was it from heaven, or of human origin? Tell me!"

[31] They discussed it among themselves and said, "If we say, 'From heaven,' he will ask, 'Then why didn't you believe him?' [32] But if we say, 'Of human origin' . . . ." (They feared the people, for everyone held that John really was a prophet.)

[33] So they answered Jesus, "We don't know."

Jesus said, "Neither will I tell you by what authority I am doing these things."

The Parable of the Tenants

12 Jesus then began to speak to them in parables: "A man planted a vineyard. He put a wall around it, dug a pit for the winepress and built a watchtower. Then he rented the vineyard to some farmers and moved to another place. [2] At harvest time he sent a servant to the tenants to collect from them some of the fruit of the vineyard. [3] But they seized him, beat him and sent him away empty-handed. [4] Then he sent another servant to them; they struck this man on the head and treated him shamefully. [5] He sent still another, and that one they killed. He sent many others; some of them they beat, others they killed.

[6] "He had one left to send, a son, whom he loved. He sent him last of all, saying, 'They will respect my son.'

[7] "But the tenants said to one another, 'This is the heir. Come, let's kill him, and the inheritance will be ours.' [8] So they took him and killed him, and threw him out of the vineyard.

[9] "What then will the owner of the vineyard do? He will come and kill those tenants and give the vineyard to others. [10] Haven't you read this passage of Scripture:

---

[a] 17 Isaiah 56:7   [b] 17 Jer. 7:11   [c] 19 Some early manuscripts came, Jesus   [d] 22,23 Some early manuscripts "If you have faith in God," Jesus answered, [23] "truly   [e] 26 Some manuscripts include here words similar to Matt. 6:15.

"'The stone the builders rejected
   has become the cornerstone;
11 the Lord has done this,
   and it is marvelous in our eyes'[a]?"

12 Then the chief priests, the teachers of the law and the elders looked for a way to arrest him because they knew he had spoken the parable against them. But they were afraid of the crowd; so they left him and went away.

Paying the Imperial Tax to Caesar

13 Later they sent some of the Pharisees and Herodians to Jesus to catch him in his words. 14 They came to him and said, "Teacher, we know that you are a man of integrity. You aren't swayed by others, because you pay no attention to who they are; but you teach the way of God in accordance with the truth. Is it right to pay the imperial tax[b] to Caesar or not? 15 Should we pay or shouldn't we?"

But Jesus knew their hypocrisy. "Why are you trying to trap me?" he asked. "Bring me a denarius and let me look at it." 16 They brought the coin, and he asked them, "Whose image is this? And whose inscription?"

"Caesar's," they replied.

17 Then Jesus said to them, "Give back to Caesar what is Caesar's and to God what is God's."

And they were amazed at him.

Marriage at the Resurrection

18 Then the Sadducees, who say there is no resurrection, came to him with a question. 19 "Teacher," they said, "Moses wrote for us that if a man's brother dies and leaves a wife but no children, the man must marry the widow and raise up offspring for his brother. 20 Now there were seven brothers. The first one married and died without leaving any children. 21 The second one married the widow, but he also died, leaving no child. It was the same with the third. 22 In fact, none of the seven left any children. Last of all, the woman died too. 23 At the resurrection[c] whose wife will she be, since the seven were married to her?"

24 Jesus replied, "Are you not in error because you do not know the Scriptures or the power of God? 25 When the dead rise, they will neither marry nor be given in marriage; they will be like the angels in heaven. 26 Now about the dead rising—have you not read in the Book of Moses, in the account of the burning bush, how God said to him, 'I am the God of Abraham, the God of Isaac, and the God of Jacob'[d]? 27 He is not the God of the dead, but of the living. You are badly mistaken!"

The Greatest Commandment

28 One of the teachers of the law came and heard them debating. Noticing that Jesus had given them a good answer, he asked him, "Of all the commandments, which is the most important?"

29 "The most important one," answered Jesus, "is this: 'Hear, O Israel: The Lord our God, the Lord is one.[e] 30 Love the Lord your God with all your heart and with all your soul and with all your mind and with all your strength.'[f] 31 The second is this: 'Love your neighbor as yourself.'[g] There is no commandment greater than these."

32 "Well said, teacher," the man replied. "You are right in saying that God is one and there is no other but him. 33 To love him with all your heart, with all your understanding and with all your strength, and to love your neighbor as yourself is more important than all burnt offerings and sacrifices."

34 When Jesus saw that he had answered wisely, he said to him, "You are not far from the kingdom of God." And from then on no one dared ask him any more questions.

Jesus Reduces His Core Values to Two

Mark 12:28–34

Jesus declared that the entire law could be reduced to loving God with all our hearts and loving our neighbor as we love ourselves. This is the genius behind core values. Jesus summarized his vast kingdom using two simple phrases. Can you do that with your life and work?

Whose Son Is the Messiah?

35 While Jesus was teaching in the temple courts, he asked, "Why do the teachers of the law say that the Messiah is the son of David? 36 David himself, speaking by the Holy Spirit, declared:

"'The Lord said to my Lord:
   "Sit at my right hand
   until I put your enemies
   under your feet."'[h]

---

[a] 11 Psalm 118:22,23   [b] 14 A special tax levied on subject peoples, not on Roman citizens   [c] 23 Some manuscripts resurrection, when people rise from the dead,   [d] 26 Exodus 3:6   [e] 29 Or The Lord our God is one Lord   [f] 30 Deut. 6:4,5   [g] 31 Lev. 19:18   [h] 36 Psalm 110:1

[37]David himself calls him 'Lord.' How then can he be his son?"

The large crowd listened to him with delight.

Warning Against the Teachers of the Law

[38]As he taught, Jesus said, "Watch out for the teachers of the law. They like to walk around in flowing robes and be greeted with respect in the marketplaces, [39]and have the most important seats in the synagogues and the places of honor at banquets. [40]They devour widows' houses and for a show make lengthy prayers. These men will be punished most severely."

The Widow's Offering

[41]Jesus sat down opposite the place where the offerings were put and watched the crowd putting their money into the temple treasury. Many rich people threw in large amounts. [42]But a poor widow came and put in two very small copper coins, worth only a few cents.

[43]Calling his disciples to him, Jesus said, "Truly I tell you, this poor widow has put more into the treasury than all the others. [44]They all gave out of their wealth; but she, out of her poverty, put in everything — all she had to live on."

The Destruction of the Temple and Signs of the End Times

13 As Jesus was leaving the temple, one of his disciples said to him, "Look, Teacher! What massive stones! What magnificent buildings!"

[2]"Do you see all these great buildings?" replied Jesus. "Not one stone here will be left on another; every one will be thrown down."

[3]As Jesus was sitting on the Mount of Olives opposite the temple, Peter, James, John and Andrew asked him privately, [4]"Tell us, when will these things happen? And what will be the sign that they are all about to be fulfilled?"

[5]Jesus said to them: "Watch out that no one deceives you. [6]Many will come in my name, claiming, 'I am he,' and will deceive many. [7]When you hear of wars and rumors of wars, do not be alarmed. Such things must happen, but the end is still to come. [8]Nation will rise against nation, and kingdom against kingdom. There will be earthquakes in various places, and famines. These are the beginning of birth pains.

[9]"You must be on your guard. You will be handed over to the local councils and flogged in the synagogues. On account of me you will stand before governors and kings as witnesses to them. [10]And the gospel must first be preached to all nations. [11]Whenever you are arrested and brought to trial, do not worry beforehand about what to say. Just say whatever is given you at the time, for it is not you speaking, but the Holy Spirit.

[12]"Brother will betray brother to death, and a father his child. Children will rebel against their parents and have them put to death. [13]Everyone will hate you because of me, but the one who stands firm to the end will be saved.

[14]"When you see 'the abomination that causes desolation'[a] standing where it[b] does not belong — let the reader understand — then let those who are in Judea flee to the mountains. [15]Let no one on the housetop go down or enter the house to take anything out. [16]Let no one in the field go back to get their cloak. [17]How dreadful it will be in those days for pregnant women and nursing mothers! [18]Pray that this will not take place in winter, [19]because those will be days of distress unequaled from the beginning, when God created the world, until now — and never to be equaled again.

The Law of the Picture: Jesus Found a Model to Affirm

Mark 12:41–44

Once in a while, Jesus would use someone as a public model. For example, he affirmed the centurion for his faith, admonished the Pharisees for their pride, and commended a poor widow for her generosity.

One day Jesus spotted a destitute woman in the temple. Although she had almost nothing, she put two small coins into the treasury. Jesus singled her out and lauded her example. He even favorably compared her to the rich who gave out of their surplus. God considered her gift more noble than theirs!

Jesus was using the Law of the Picture. When you want to encourage certain behavior, find someone who is doing the right thing, and call attention to it. Affirm it. Like a shepherd hanging a bell around the neck of the sheep he wants the flock to follow, encourage others to observe the one doing right. Visual sermons yield far better results than verbal ones.

---

[a] 14 Daniel 9:27; 11:31; 12:11   [b] 14 Or he

²⁰"If the Lord had not cut short those days, no one would survive. But for the sake of the elect, whom he has chosen, he has shortened them. ²¹At that time if anyone says to you, 'Look, here is the Messiah!' or, 'Look, there he is!' do not believe it. ²²For false messiahs and false prophets will appear and perform signs and wonders to deceive, if possible, even the elect. ²³So be on your guard; I have told you everything ahead of time.

²⁴"But in those days, following that distress,

" 'the sun will be darkened,
      and the moon will not give its light;
²⁵ the stars will fall from the sky,
      and the heavenly bodies will be shaken.'ᵃ

²⁶"At that time people will see the Son of Man coming in clouds with great power and glory. ²⁷And he will send his angels and gather his elect from the four winds, from the ends of the earth to the ends of the heavens.

²⁸"Now learn this lesson from the fig tree: As soon as its twigs get tender and its leaves come out, you know that summer is near. ²⁹Even so, when you see these things happening, you know that itᵇ is near, right at the door. ³⁰Truly I tell you, this generation will certainly not pass away until all these things have happened. ³¹Heaven and earth will pass away, but my words will never pass away.

The Day and Hour Unknown

³²"But about that day or hour no one knows, not even the angels in heaven, nor the Son, but only the Father. ³³Be on guard! Be alert!ᶜ You do not know when that time will come. ³⁴It's like a man going away: He leaves his house and puts his servants in charge, each with their assigned task, and tells the one at the door to keep watch.

Vision: Jesus Called His Followers Back to the Original Goal

Mark 13:1-37

In his discourse on the end of time, Jesus paused to remind his men why he bothered to reveal such prophetic information. He declared that the gospel must be preached to the whole world—then the end would come. Jesus regularly called attention to the vision of God.

³⁵"Therefore keep watch because you do not know when the owner of the house will come back—whether in the evening, or at midnight, or when the rooster crows, or at dawn. ³⁶If he comes suddenly, do not let him find you sleeping. ³⁷What I say to you, I say to everyone: 'Watch!' "

Jesus Anointed at Bethany

14 Now the Passover and the Festival of Unleavened Bread were only two days away, and the chief priests and the teachers of the law were scheming to arrest Jesus secretly and kill him. ²"But not during the festival," they said, "or the people may riot."

³While he was in Bethany, reclining at the table in the home of Simon the Leper, a woman came with an alabaster jar of very expensive perfume, made of pure nard. She broke the jar and poured the perfume on his head.

⁴Some of those present were saying indignantly to one another, "Why this waste of perfume? ⁵It could have been sold for more than a year's wagesᵈ and the money given to the poor." And they rebuked her harshly.

⁶"Leave her alone," said Jesus. "Why are you bothering her? She has done a beautiful thing to me. ⁷The poor you will always have with you,ᵉ and you can help them any time you want. But you will not always have me. ⁸She did what she could. She poured perfume on my body beforehand to prepare for my burial. ⁹Truly I tell you, wherever the gospel is preached throughout the world, what she has done will also be told, in memory of her."

¹⁰Then Judas Iscariot, one of the Twelve, went to the chief priests to betray Jesus to them. ¹¹They were delighted to hear this and promised to give him money. So he watched for an opportunity to hand him over.

The Last Supper

¹²On the first day of the Festival of Unleavened Bread, when it was customary to sacrifice the Passover lamb, Jesus' disciples asked him, "Where do you want us to go and make preparations for you to eat the Passover?"

¹³So he sent two of his disciples, telling them, "Go into the city, and a man carrying a jar of water will meet you. Follow him. ¹⁴Say to the owner of the house he enters, 'The Teacher asks:

ᵃ 25 Isaiah 13:10; 34:4   ᵇ 29 Or he   ᶜ 33 Some manuscripts *alert and pray*   ᵈ 5 Greek *than three hundred denarii*   ᵉ 7 See Deut. 15:11.

Where is my guest room, where I may eat the Passover with my disciples?' ¹⁵He will show you a large room upstairs, furnished and ready. Make preparations for us there."

¹⁶The disciples left, went into the city and found things just as Jesus had told them. So they prepared the Passover.

¹⁷When evening came, Jesus arrived with the Twelve. ¹⁸While they were reclining at the table eating, he said, "Truly I tell you, one of you will betray me — one who is eating with me."

¹⁹They were saddened, and one by one they said to him, "Surely you don't mean me?"

²⁰"It is one of the Twelve," he replied, "one who dips bread into the bowl with me. ²¹The Son of Man will go just as it is written about him. But woe to that man who betrays the Son of Man! It would be better for him if he had not been born."

²²While they were eating, Jesus took bread, and when he had given thanks, he broke it and gave it to his disciples, saying, "Take it; this is my body."

²³Then he took a cup, and when he had given thanks, he gave it to them, and they all drank from it.

²⁴"This is my blood of the*ᵃ* covenant, which is poured out for many," he said to them. ²⁵"Truly I tell you, I will not drink again from the fruit of the vine until that day when I drink it new in the kingdom of God."

²⁶When they had sung a hymn, they went out to the Mount of Olives.

Jesus Predicts Peter's Denial

²⁷"You will all fall away," Jesus told them, "for it is written:

" 'I will strike the shepherd,
    and the sheep will be scattered.'ᵇ

²⁸But after I have risen, I will go ahead of you into Galilee."

²⁹Peter declared, "Even if all fall away, I will not."

³⁰"Truly I tell you," Jesus answered, "today — yes, tonight — before the rooster crows twiceᶜ you yourself will disown me three times."

³¹But Peter insisted emphatically, "Even if I have to die with you, I will never disown you." And all the others said the same.

Gethsemane

³²They went to a place called Gethsemane, and Jesus said to his disciples, "Sit here while I pray." ³³He took Peter, James and John along

with him, and he began to be deeply distressed and troubled. ³⁴"My soul is overwhelmed with sorrow to the point of death," he said to them. "Stay here and keep watch."

³⁵Going a little farther, he fell to the ground and prayed that if possible the hour might pass from him. ³⁶"Abba,ᵈ Father," he said, "everything is possible for you. Take this cup from me. Yet not what I will, but what you will."

³⁷Then he returned to his disciples and found them sleeping. "Simon," he said to Peter, "are you asleep? Couldn't you keep watch for one hour? ³⁸Watch and pray so that you will not fall into temptation. The spirit is willing, but the flesh is weak."

³⁹Once more he went away and prayed the same thing. ⁴⁰When he came back, he again found them sleeping, because their eyes were heavy. They did not know what to say to him.

⁴¹Returning the third time, he said to them, "Are you still sleeping and resting? Enough! The

---

ᵃ 24 Some manuscripts *the new*   ᵇ 27 Zech. 13:7
ᶜ 30 Some early manuscripts do not have *twice*.
ᵈ 36 Aramaic for *father*

Responsibility: Caring in the Midst of Crisis

Mark 14:32–42

Jesus must have endured his most difficult moments in the Garden of Gethsemane, just prior to his arrest, trial and crucifixion. The Gospels tell us he felt deeply distressed and troubled (Mk 14:33). He cried out and his sweat became like blood (Lk 22:44). In his time of dire need, however, his twelve followers drifted off to sleep. Twice he found them snoring. They had no idea how critical this night would be.

Instead of screaming at them in anguish, however, he encouraged them to pray for themselves (Mk 14:38). Even though he had every right to demand better performance, he felt compassion for them and gave them direction. He wanted them to stay protected from temptation. His sense of responsibility and concern overcame his preoccupation with the cross. His date with destiny did not overshadow his love and concern for his weak and sleepy staff. In the garden he provided us with the ultimate display of a leader's responsibility.

hour has come. Look, the Son of Man is delivered into the hands of sinners. [42]Rise! Let us go! Here comes my betrayer!"

Jesus Arrested

[43]Just as he was speaking, Judas, one of the Twelve, appeared. With him was a crowd armed with swords and clubs, sent from the chief priests, the teachers of the law, and the elders. [44]Now the betrayer had arranged a signal with them: "The one I kiss is the man; arrest him and lead him away under guard." [45]Going at once to Jesus, Judas said, "Rabbi!" and kissed him. [46]The men seized Jesus and arrested him. [47]Then one of those standing near drew his sword and struck the servant of the high priest, cutting off his ear.

[48]"Am I leading a rebellion," said Jesus, "that you have come out with swords and clubs to capture me? [49]Every day I was with you, teaching in the temple courts, and you did not arrest me. But the Scriptures must be fulfilled." [50]Then everyone deserted him and fled.

[51]A young man, wearing nothing but a linen garment, was following Jesus. When they seized him, [52]he fled naked, leaving his garment behind.

Jesus Before the Sanhedrin

[53]They took Jesus to the high priest, and all the chief priests, the elders and the teachers of the law came together. [54]Peter followed him at a distance, right into the courtyard of the high priest. There he sat with the guards and warmed himself at the fire.

[55]The chief priests and the whole Sanhedrin were looking for evidence against Jesus so that they could put him to death, but they did not find any. [56]Many testified falsely against him, but their statements did not agree.

[57]Then some stood up and gave this false testimony against him: [58]"We heard him say, 'I will destroy this temple made with human hands and in three days will build another, not made with hands.'" [59]Yet even then their testimony did not agree.

[60]Then the high priest stood up before them and asked Jesus, "Are you not going to answer? What is this testimony that these men are bringing against you?" [61]But Jesus remained silent and gave no answer.

Again the high priest asked him, "Are you the Messiah, the Son of the Blessed One?"

[62]"I am," said Jesus. "And you will see the Son of Man sitting at the right hand of the Mighty One and coming on the clouds of heaven."

[63]The high priest tore his clothes. "Why do we need any more witnesses?" he asked. [64]"You have heard the blasphemy. What do you think?"

They all condemned him as worthy of death. [65]Then some began to spit at him; they blindfolded him, struck him with their fists, and said, "Prophesy!" And the guards took him and beat him.

Peter Disowns Jesus

[66]While Peter was below in the courtyard, one of the servant girls of the high priest came by. [67]When she saw Peter warming himself, she looked closely at him.

"You also were with that Nazarene, Jesus," she said.

[68]But he denied it. "I don't know or understand what you're talking about," he said, and went out into the entryway.[a]

[69]When the servant girl saw him there, she said again to those standing around, "This fellow is one of them." [70]Again he denied it.

After a little while, those standing near said to Peter, "Surely you are one of them, for you are a Galilean."

[71]He began to call down curses, and he swore to them, "I don't know this man you're talking about."

[72]Immediately the rooster crowed the second time.[b] Then Peter remembered the word Jesus had spoken to him: "Before the rooster crows twice[c] you will disown me three times." And he broke down and wept.

Jesus Before Pilate

15 Very early in the morning, the chief priests, with the elders, the teachers of the law and the whole Sanhedrin, made their plans. So they bound Jesus, led him away and handed him over to Pilate.

[2]"Are you the king of the Jews?" asked Pilate.

"You have said so," Jesus replied.

[3]The chief priests accused him of many things. [4]So again Pilate asked him, "Aren't you going to answer? See how many things they are accusing you of."

[5]But Jesus still made no reply, and Pilate was amazed.

[6]Now it was the custom at the festival to release a prisoner whom the people requested. [7]A man called Barabbas was in prison with the insurrectionists who had committed murder in

---

[a] 68 Some early manuscripts *entryway and the rooster crowed*
[b] 72 Some early manuscripts do not have *the second time.*
[c] 72 Some early manuscripts do not have *twice.*

the uprising. [8]The crowd came up and asked Pilate to do for them what he usually did.

[9]"Do you want me to release to you the king of the Jews?" asked Pilate, [10]knowing it was out of self-interest that the chief priests had handed Jesus over to him. [11]But the chief priests stirred up the crowd to have Pilate release Barabbas instead.

[12]"What shall I do, then, with the one you call the king of the Jews?" Pilate asked them.

[13]"Crucify him!" they shouted.

[14]"Why? What crime has he committed?" asked Pilate.

But they shouted all the louder, "Crucify him!"

[15]Wanting to satisfy the crowd, Pilate released Barabbas to them. He had Jesus flogged, and handed him over to be crucified.

The Soldiers Mock Jesus

[16]The soldiers led Jesus away into the palace (that is, the Praetorium) and called together the whole company of soldiers. [17]They put a purple robe on him, then twisted together a crown of thorns and set it on him. [18]And they began to call out to him, "Hail, king of the Jews!" [19]Again and again they struck him on the head with a staff and spit on him. Falling on their knees, they paid homage to him. [20]And when they had mocked him, they took off the purple robe and put his own clothes on him. Then they led him out to crucify him.

The Crucifixion of Jesus

[21]A certain man from Cyrene, Simon, the father of Alexander and Rufus, was passing by on his way in from the country, and they forced him to carry the cross. [22]They brought Jesus to the place called Golgotha (which means "the place of the skull"). [23]Then they offered him wine mixed with myrrh, but he did not take it. [24]And they crucified him. Dividing up his clothes, they cast lots to see what each would get.

[25]It was nine in the morning when they crucified him. [26]The written notice of the charge against him read: THE KING OF THE JEWS.

[27]They crucified two rebels with him, one on his right and one on his left. [28][a] [29]Those who passed by hurled insults at him, shaking their heads and saying, "So! You who are going to destroy the temple and build it in three days, [30]come down from the cross and save yourself!" [31]In the same way the chief priests and the teachers of the law mocked him among themselves. "He saved others," they said, "but he can't save himself! [32]Let this Messiah, this king of Israel, come down now from the cross, that we

---

[a] 28 Some manuscripts include here words similar to Luke 22:37.

PONTIUS PILATE

A Leader Who Refused to Take Responsibility
Mark 15:1–15

PROFILE in leadership

Pontius Pilate, the governor of Judea, stood at a crossroads. The fate of the very Son of God rested in his hands. This same Jesus, who only a week before had performed miracles of healing and provision, now faced a mob demanding his death.

Pilate interrogated Jesus and found he had done nothing worthy of crucifixion. But instead of leading—instead of taking an unpopular stand and allowing this innocent man to go free—Pilate gave in to the outrage of an unruly crowd. He released a notorious criminal and sentenced this guiltless man to die an agonizing death on a cross. Pilate recognized the injustice. But with the mob looking on, Pilate "washed his hands" of Jesus' blood (Mt 27:24) and allowed him to be executed.

In a moment of supreme paradox, God used Pilate's refusal to lead and do what was right to carry out his own plan of salvation. In his providence, God saw into the heart of Pilate and knew that when push came to shove, this man would give in to the demands of the crowd.

When God calls his people to lead, when he calls us to make unpopular stands, we cannot "wash our hands" of the responsibility. Leaders will face moments when they have no choice but to stand up to the crowd and do what is right.

The Law of Sacrifice: Jesus Gave Up His Life to Gain the World

Mark 15:15–24

Anywhere worth going carries a price tag. Jesus chose to endure torture, mocking, humiliation and an excruciating death, even though he could have stopped it at any moment (Mt 26:53). The Leader of humankind, the Last Adam (1Co 15:45), decided that gaining the world was worth the pain of the cross.

may see and believe." Those crucified with him also heaped insults on him.

The Death of Jesus

³³At noon, darkness came over the whole land until three in the afternoon. ³⁴And at three in the afternoon Jesus cried out in a loud voice, *"Eloi, Eloi, lema sabachthani?"* (which means "My God, my God, why have you forsaken me?").ᵃ

³⁵When some of those standing near heard this, they said, "Listen, he's calling Elijah."

³⁶Someone ran, filled a sponge with wine vinegar, put it on a staff, and offered it to Jesus to drink. "Now leave him alone. Let's see if Elijah comes to take him down," he said.

³⁷With a loud cry, Jesus breathed his last.

³⁸The curtain of the temple was torn in two from top to bottom. ³⁹And when the centurion, who stood there in front of Jesus, saw how he died,ᵇ he said, "Surely this man was the Son of God!"

⁴⁰Some women were watching from a distance. Among them were Mary Magdalene, Mary the mother of James the younger and of Joseph,ᶜ and Salome. ⁴¹In Galilee these women had followed him and cared for his needs. Many other women who had come up with him to Jerusalem were also there.

The Burial of Jesus

⁴²It was Preparation Day (that is, the day before the Sabbath). So as evening approached, ⁴³Joseph of Arimathea, a prominent member of the Council, who was himself waiting for the kingdom of God, went boldly to Pilate and asked for Jesus' body. ⁴⁴Pilate was surprised to hear that he was already dead. Summoning the

centurion, he asked him if Jesus had already died. ⁴⁵When he learned from the centurion that it was so, he gave the body to Joseph. ⁴⁶So Joseph bought some linen cloth, took down the body, wrapped it in the linen, and placed it in a tomb cut out of rock. Then he rolled a stone against the entrance of the tomb. ⁴⁷Mary Magdalene and Mary the mother of Joseph saw where he was laid.

Jesus Has Risen

16 When the Sabbath was over, Mary Magdalene, Mary the mother of James, and Salome bought spices so that they might go to anoint Jesus' body. ²Very early on the first day of the week, just after sunrise, they were on their way to the tomb ³and they asked each other, "Who will roll the stone away from the entrance of the tomb?"

⁴But when they looked up, they saw that the stone, which was very large, had been rolled away. ⁵As they entered the tomb, they saw a

---

ᵃ 34 Psalm 22:1   ᵇ 39 Some manuscripts *saw that he died with such a cry*   ᶜ 40 Greek *Joses*, a variant of *Joseph*; also in verse 47

The Law of Victory: Jesus' Resurrection Surprised Everyone

Mark 16:1–7

Every Easter in churches around the world, Christians retell the story of Jesus' resurrection from the dead. From a leadership perspective, this event is the paramount illustration of the Law of Victory.

The disciples had lost their Teacher and Lord. The Jewish leaders had quieted their opposition. The common people had lost their hope of a revolution against Rome. Even the devil thought he had finally stopped this divine Leader and forced him to abort his mission (1Co 2:8).

What a surprise awaited that first Resurrection Sunday morning!

When Jesus rose from the dead, he gave his followers a potent hope to end every doubt about his kingdom. Jesus practiced the Law of Victory—and at least part of every leader's credibility comes from practicing this law (although no one can do it quite the way he did!).

young man dressed in a white robe sitting on the right side, and they were alarmed.

⁶"Don't be alarmed," he said. "You are looking for Jesus the Nazarene, who was crucified. He has risen! He is not here. See the place where they laid him. ⁷But go, tell his disciples and Peter, 'He is going ahead of you into Galilee. There you will see him, just as he told you.'"

⁸Trembling and bewildered, the women went out and fled from the tomb. They said nothing to anyone, because they were afraid.ᵃ

[The earliest manuscripts and some other ancient witnesses do not have verses 9–20.]

⁹When Jesus rose early on the first day of the week, he appeared first to Mary Magdalene, out of whom he had driven seven demons. ¹⁰She went and told those who had been with him and who were mourning and weeping. ¹¹When they heard that Jesus was alive and that she had seen him, they did not believe it.

¹²Afterward Jesus appeared in a different form to two of them while they were walking in the country.

¹³These returned and reported it to the rest; but they did not believe them either.

¹⁴Later Jesus appeared to the Eleven as they were eating; he rebuked them for their lack of faith and their stubborn refusal to believe those who had seen him after he had risen.

¹⁵He said to them, "Go into all the world and preach the gospel to all creation. ¹⁶Whoever believes and is baptized will be saved, but whoever does not believe will be condemned. ¹⁷And these signs will accompany those who believe: In my name they will drive out demons; they will speak in new tongues; ¹⁸they will pick up snakes with their hands; and when they drink deadly poison, it will not hurt them at all; they will place their hands on sick people, and they will get well."

¹⁹After the Lord Jesus had spoken to them, he was taken up into heaven and he sat at the right hand of God. ²⁰Then the disciples went out and preached everywhere, and the Lord worked with them and confirmed his word by the signs that accompanied it.

ᵃ 8 Some manuscripts have the following ending between verses 8 and 9, and one manuscript has it after verse 8 (omitting verses 9-20): Then they quickly reported all these instructions to those around Peter. After this, Jesus himself also sent out through them from east to west the sacred and imperishable proclamation of eternal salvation. Amen.

The Law of Legacy: Jesus Turned His Ministry Over to His Disciples

Mark 16:15–16

Before Jesus departed this world, he gathered his disciples and issued a final command. We call it the Great Commission. He told them to go and preach the gospel to every creature on earth. Just as he came to seek and save the lost, they were to continue his ministry and fulfill it.

Jesus' legacy remains to this day because he carefully laid a foundation. He trained twelve men to reproduce his ministry. He passed on transferable concepts that anyone could learn after he had gone. If he had failed to multiply himself in others, Christianity would have died long ago.

If we step back and look at Jesus' three-and-a-half-year ministry outlined in Mark, we can see him preparing to leave his legacy from the beginning:

1. He chose twelve potential leaders to mentor (3:13–19).

2. He spent the majority of his time with them (3:14).

3. He told them from the start that they, too, would be doing this (1:17).

4. He reproduced both his burden and his vision for people (6:7–13).

5. He allowed them to witness and even participate in his miracles (8:1–9).

6. He issued an imperative for them to go and do what he did (16:15–16).

7. He promised the credibility and provision they would need (16:17–18).

8. He worked with them, confirming their work and words (16:19–20).

INTRODUCTION TO
LUKE

Jesus as the Perfect Man

Luke is the only Gospel writer to record the events of Jesus' life in chronological order. Experts consider him to be one of the most accurate historians of his day, although by trade, he was a medical doctor. Rather than beginning his Gospel traditionally, he assures his readers that he founded his account on historically verifiable information and evidence—he wants to establish credibility for his message.

Luke portrays Jesus as the perfect Man. He recognizes Jesus' divinity, but wants to give his readers a picture of what a human life might look like if a man were to walk with God consistently. Jesus, once again, becomes the Ultimate Leader.

From Luke's vantage point, Jesus lives the perfect life of leadership and authority. He is the Man who, because he never sins, truly does take dominion over the earth and subdue it (Ge 1:26–28). The animals and fish obey him; the wind and the sea obey him; sick bodies obey him; fig trees obey him—even the dead obey him. Everywhere Jesus goes, he leads. Everywhere Jesus goes, he serves.

Luke also portrays Jesus as an equipping Leader. He focuses on the teaching ministry of Jesus, that he equips and empowers every hungry person who comes to him. Those who come to him already full and satisfied get nothing. Those who come to him starving receive everything needed. That's how Jesus leads. He compels no one to do anything, yet followers flock to him by the thousands. As you read through Luke, look especially for examples of the Laws of Empowerment, Navigation, Influence, Connection, Intuition and Explosive Growth.

God's Role in Luke

God reveals to us in Luke what a perfect leader looks like; he looks like Jesus. Instead of forcing others to follow or submit to his power, Jesus loves them into a desire to follow. He sets the standard for us in his exercise of authority over people, over the elements of nature, and even over the powers of his day. His serene and authoritative response to adverse circumstances shows us how we are to respond to our own difficult circumstances. His fulfillment of a divine purpose challenges us to pursue our own.

Jesus teaches us that a leader cannot pursue love and power simultaneously. Instead of pursuing power, Jesus pursues love—and in the end, he gets both. Today he holds more power and elicits more love than anyone in history.

Leaders in Luke

Jesus, John the Baptist, the Pharisees, Pilate, Herod

Other People of Influence in Luke

Mary, the centurion, the twelve disciples, the 72 followers, Zacchaeus

Lessons in Leadership

- Healthy leaders have nothing to prove, nothing to lose and nothing to hide.

- Wise leaders speak the truth, whatever the cost.
- Effective leaders provide incentives to their followers.
- Successful leaders discern, then develop, then delegate.
- Great leaders feel secure enough to express emotions and be vulnerable.

- The best leaders love the world, serve the many, but train the few.
- Good leaders practice repetition until others embrace the vision.
- The most powerful force in a leader's life is love for people.

LEADERSHIP HIGHLIGHTS IN LUKE

Introduction

1 Many have undertaken to draw up an account of the things that have been fulfilled[a] among us, [2]just as they were handed down to us by those who from the first were eyewitnesses and servants of the word. [3]With this in mind, since I myself have carefully investigated everything from the beginning, I too decided to write an orderly account for you, most excellent Theophilus, [4]so that you may know the certainty of the things you have been taught.

Credibility: Luke's Authority to Write About Jesus

Luke 1:1–4

Luke felt the need to establish his credibility as a biographer for Jesus. He wasn't one of the twelve disciples, an eyewitness of Christ, or even a theologian. So he opens his book by explaining why he chose to write Jesus' story. Good leaders recognize the need to establish their credibility.

The Birth of John the Baptist Foretold

[5]In the time of Herod king of Judea there was a priest named Zechariah, who belonged to the priestly division of Abijah; his wife Elizabeth was also a descendant of Aaron. [6]Both of them were righteous in the sight of God, observing all the Lord's commands and decrees blamelessly. [7]But they were childless because Elizabeth was not able to conceive, and they were both very old.

[8]Once when Zechariah's division was on duty and he was serving as priest before God, [9]he was chosen by lot, according to the custom of the priesthood, to go into the temple of the Lord and burn incense. [10]And when the time for the burning of incense came, all the assembled worshipers were praying outside.

[11]Then an angel of the Lord appeared to him, standing at the right side of the altar of incense. [12]When Zechariah saw him, he was startled and was gripped with fear. [13]But the angel said to him: "Do not be afraid, Zechariah; your prayer has been heard. Your wife Elizabeth will bear you a son, and you are to call him John. [14]He will be a joy and delight to you, and many will rejoice because of his birth, [15]for he will be great in the sight of the Lord. He is never to take wine or other fermented drink, and he will be filled with the Holy Spirit even before he is born. [16]He will bring back many of the people of Israel to the Lord their God. [17]And he will go on before the Lord, in the spirit and power of Elijah, to turn the hearts of the parents to their children and the disobedient to the wisdom of the righteous—to make ready a people prepared for the Lord."

[18]Zechariah asked the angel, "How can I be sure of this? I am an old man and my wife is well along in years."

[19]The angel said to him, "I am Gabriel. I stand in the presence of God, and I have been sent to speak to you and to tell you this good news. [20]And now you will be silent and not able to speak until the day this happens, because you did not believe my words, which will come true at their appointed time."

[21]Meanwhile, the people were waiting for Zechariah and wondering why he stayed so long in the temple. [22]When he came out, he could not speak to them. They realized he had seen a vision in the temple, for he kept making signs to them but remained unable to speak.

[23]When his time of service was completed, he returned home. [24]After this his wife Elizabeth became pregnant and for five months remained in seclusion. [25]"The Lord has done this for me," she said. "In these days he has shown his favor and taken away my disgrace among the people."

The Birth of Jesus Foretold

[26]In the sixth month of Elizabeth's pregnancy, God sent the angel Gabriel to Nazareth, a town in Galilee, [27]to a virgin pledged to be married to a man named Joseph, a descendant of David. The virgin's name was Mary. [28]The angel went to her and said, "Greetings, you who are highly favored! The Lord is with you."

[29]Mary was greatly troubled at his words and wondered what kind of greeting this might be. [30]But the angel said to her, "Do not be afraid, Mary; you have found favor with God. [31]You will conceive and give birth to a son, and you are to call him Jesus. [32]He will be great and will be called the Son of the Most High. The Lord God will give him the throne of his father David, [33]and he will reign over Jacob's descendants forever; his kingdom will never end."

[34]"How will this be," Mary asked the angel, "since I am a virgin?"

[35]The angel answered, "The Holy Spirit will come on you, and the power of the Most High will overshadow you. So the holy one to be born

---

[a] 1 Or been surely believed

will be called[a] the Son of God. [36]Even Elizabeth your relative is going to have a child in her old age, and she who was said to be unable to conceive is in her sixth month. [37]For no word from God will ever fail."

[38]"I am the Lord's servant," Mary answered. "May your word to me be fulfilled." Then the angel left her.

Mary Visits Elizabeth

[39]At that time Mary got ready and hurried to a town in the hill country of Judea, [40]where she entered Zechariah's home and greeted Elizabeth. [41]When Elizabeth heard Mary's greeting, the baby leaped in her womb, and Elizabeth was filled with the Holy Spirit. [42]In a loud voice she exclaimed: "Blessed are you among women, and blessed is the child you will bear! [43]But why am I so favored, that the mother of my Lord should come to me? [44]As soon as the sound of your greeting reached my ears, the baby in my womb leaped for joy. [45]Blessed is she who has believed that the Lord would fulfill his promises to her!"

Mary's Song

[46]And Mary said:

"My soul glorifies the Lord
[47]   and my spirit rejoices in God my Savior,

[48]for he has been mindful
        of the humble state of his servant.
From now on all generations will call me
        blessed,
[49]   for the Mighty One has done great things
        for me —
        holy is his name.
[50]His mercy extends to those who fear him,
        from generation to generation.
[51]He has performed mighty deeds with his
        arm;
        he has scattered those who are proud in
        their inmost thoughts.
[52]He has brought down rulers from their thrones
        but has lifted up the humble.
[53]He has filled the hungry with good things
        but has sent the rich away empty.
[54]He has helped his servant Israel,
        remembering to be merciful
[55]to Abraham and his descendants forever,
        just as he promised our ancestors."

[56]Mary stayed with Elizabeth for about three months and then returned home.

The Birth of John the Baptist

[57]When it was time for Elizabeth to have her baby, she gave birth to a son. [58]Her neighbors

---

[a] 35 Or So the child to be born will be called holy,

MARY — Chosen Vessel for God's Highest Purposes
Luke 1:26–38

PROFILE in leadership

Mary had to know that sooner or later, *somebody* would be chosen as the vessel of God's very highest purpose. She must have realized that *somebody* would be chosen to bring the Messiah into the world, that *somebody* would be most blessed among all women.

But she couldn't have known that, from the beginning of time, God had his eye on *her* as that somebody. He had prepared her for bearing, then rearing, the One who would be the Savior of the world.

This woman of faith responded with alarm when an angel of the Lord told her she had found favor with God and would give birth to the baby Jesus. "How will this be" she asked, "since I am a virgin?"

A legitimate question!

In short, the messenger answered, "With God, all things are possible. He has chosen you and honored you as the one to give birth to the Son of God."

And Mary's response? "I am the Lord's servant! May your word to me be fulfilled."

There may be times when we as leaders ask, "How can this be?" or wonder how God could do something through us. But wise leaders will respond the way Mary did: "I am your servant! May it be as you have said!"

and relatives heard that the Lord had shown her great mercy, and they shared her joy.

⁵⁹On the eighth day they came to circumcise the child, and they were going to name him after his father Zechariah, ⁶⁰but his mother spoke up and said, "No! He is to be called John."

⁶¹They said to her, "There is no one among your relatives who has that name."

⁶²Then they made signs to his father, to find out what he would like to name the child. ⁶³He asked for a writing tablet, and to everyone's astonishment he wrote, "His name is John." ⁶⁴Immediately his mouth was opened and his tongue set free, and he began to speak, praising God. ⁶⁵All the neighbors were filled with awe, and throughout the hill country of Judea people were talking about all these things. ⁶⁶Everyone who heard this wondered about it, asking, "What then is this child going to be?" For the Lord's hand was with him.

Zechariah's Song

⁶⁷His father Zechariah was filled with the Holy Spirit and prophesied:

⁶⁸"Praise be to the Lord, the God of Israel,
     because he has come to his people and
          redeemed them.
⁶⁹He has raised up a horn[a] of salvation for us
     in the house of his servant David
⁷⁰(as he said through his holy prophets of long
          ago),
⁷¹salvation from our enemies
     and from the hand of all who hate us —
⁷²to show mercy to our ancestors
     and to remember his holy covenant,
⁷³   the oath he swore to our father Abraham:
⁷⁴to rescue us from the hand of our enemies,
     and to enable us to serve him without fear
⁷⁵   in holiness and righteousness before him
          all our days.

⁷⁶And you, my child, will be called a prophet
          of the Most High;
     for you will go on before the Lord to
          prepare the way for him,
⁷⁷to give his people the knowledge of
          salvation
     through the forgiveness of their sins,
⁷⁸because of the tender mercy of our God,
     by which the rising sun will come to us
          from heaven
⁷⁹to shine on those living in darkness
     and in the shadow of death,
          to guide our feet into the path of peace."

⁸⁰And the child grew and became strong in spirit[b]; and he lived in the wilderness until he appeared publicly to Israel.

The Birth of Jesus

2 In those days Caesar Augustus issued a decree that a census should be taken of the entire Roman world. ²(This was the first census that took place while[c] Quirinius was governor of Syria.) ³And everyone went to their own town to register.

⁴So Joseph also went up from the town of Nazareth in Galilee to Judea, to Bethlehem the town of David, because he belonged to the house and line of David. ⁵He went there to register with Mary, who was pledged to be married to him and was expecting a child. ⁶While they were there, the time came for the baby to be born, ⁷and she gave birth to her firstborn, a son. She wrapped him in cloths and placed him in a manger, because there was no guest room available for them.

⁸And there were shepherds living out in the fields nearby, keeping watch over their flocks at night. ⁹An angel of the Lord appeared to them, and the glory of the Lord shone around them, and they were terrified. ¹⁰But the angel said to them, "Do not be afraid. I bring you good news that will cause great joy for all the people. ¹¹Today in the town of David a Savior has been born to you; he is the Messiah, the Lord. ¹²This will be a sign to you: You will find a baby wrapped in cloths and lying in a manger."

¹³Suddenly a great company of the heavenly host appeared with the angel, praising God and saying,

¹⁴"Glory to God in the highest heaven,
     and on earth peace to those on whom his
          favor rests."

¹⁵When the angels had left them and gone into heaven, the shepherds said to one another, "Let's go to Bethlehem and see this thing that has happened, which the Lord has told us about."

¹⁶So they hurried off and found Mary and Joseph, and the baby, who was lying in the manger. ¹⁷When they had seen him, they spread the word concerning what had been told them about this child, ¹⁸and all who heard it were amazed at what the shepherds said to them. ¹⁹But Mary treasured up all these things and pondered them in her heart. ²⁰The shepherds returned, glori-

---

ᵃ 69 Horn here symbolizes a strong king.   ᵇ 80 Or in the Spirit   ᶜ 2 Or This census took place before

fying and praising God for all the things they had heard and seen, which were just as they had been told.

²¹On the eighth day, when it was time to circumcise the child, he was named Jesus, the name the angel had given him before he was conceived.

Jesus Presented in the Temple

²²When the time came for the purification rites required by the Law of Moses, Joseph and Mary took him to Jerusalem to present him to the Lord ²³(as it is written in the Law of the Lord, "Every firstborn male is to be consecrated to the Lord"ᵃ), ²⁴and to offer a sacrifice in keeping with what is said in the Law of the Lord: "a pair of doves or two young pigeons."ᵇ

²⁵Now there was a man in Jerusalem called Simeon, who was righteous and devout. He was waiting for the consolation of Israel, and the Holy Spirit was on him. ²⁶It had been revealed to him by the Holy Spirit that he would not die before he had seen the Lord's Messiah. ²⁷Moved by the Spirit, he went into the temple courts. When the parents brought in the child Jesus to do for him what the custom of the Law required, ²⁸Simeon took him in his arms and praised God, saying:

²⁹"Sovereign Lord, as you have promised,
      you may now dismissᶜ your servant in
            peace.
³⁰For my eyes have seen your salvation,
³¹   which you have prepared in the sight of all
            nations:
³²a light for revelation to the Gentiles,
      and the glory of your people Israel."

³³The child's father and mother marveled at what was said about him. ³⁴Then Simeon blessed them and said to Mary, his mother: "This child is destined to cause the falling and rising of many in Israel, and to be a sign that will be spoken against, ³⁵so that the thoughts of many hearts will be revealed. And a sword will pierce your own soul too."

³⁶There was also a prophet, Anna, the daughter of Penuel, of the tribe of Asher. She was very old; she had lived with her husband seven years after her marriage, ³⁷and then was a widow until she was eighty-four.ᵈ She never left the temple but worshiped night and day, fasting and praying. ³⁸Coming up to them at that very moment, she gave thanks to God and spoke about the child to all who were looking forward to the redemption of Jerusalem.

³⁹When Joseph and Mary had done everything required by the Law of the Lord, they returned to Galilee to their own town of Nazareth. ⁴⁰And the child grew and became strong; he was filled with wisdom, and the grace of God was on him.

The Boy Jesus at the Temple

⁴¹Every year Jesus' parents went to Jerusalem for the Festival of the Passover. ⁴²When he was twelve years old, they went up to the festival, according to the custom. ⁴³After the festival was over, while his parents were returning home, the boy Jesus stayed behind in Jerusalem, but they were unaware of it. ⁴⁴Thinking he was in their company, they traveled on for a day. Then they began looking for him among their relatives and friends. ⁴⁵When they did not find him, they went back to Jerusalem to look for him. ⁴⁶After three days they found him in the temple courts, sitting among the teachers, listening to them and asking them questions. ⁴⁷Everyone who heard him was amazed at his understanding and his answers. ⁴⁸When his parents saw him, they were astonished. His mother said to him, "Son, why have you treated us like this? Your father and I have been anxiously searching for you."

⁴⁹"Why were you searching for me?" he asked. "Didn't you know I had to be in my Father's house?"ᵉ ⁵⁰But they did not understand what he was saying to them.

⁵¹Then he went down to Nazareth with them and was obedient to them. But his mother treasured all these things in her heart. ⁵²And Jesus grew in wisdom and stature, and in favor with God and man.

ᵃ 23 Exodus 13:2,12   ᵇ 24 Lev. 12:8   ᶜ 29 Or promised, / now dismiss   ᵈ 37 Or then had been a widow for eighty-four years.   ᵉ 49 Or be about my Father's business

Listening: Jesus Did This to Connect with People

Luke 2:42–52

Even at 12 years of age, Jesus was listening and asking questions. He never grew out of the habit. Before ministering to needy people or telling them about the kingdom, he took the time to listen. He knew that to connect with people's hearts, he had to use his ears.

John the Baptist Prepares the Way

3 In the fifteenth year of the reign of Tiberius Caesar — when Pontius Pilate was governor of Judea, Herod tetrarch of Galilee, his brother Philip tetrarch of Iturea and Traconitis, and Lysanias tetrarch of Abilene — [2] during the high-priesthood of Annas and Caiaphas, the word of God came to John son of Zechariah in the wilderness. [3] He went into all the country around the Jordan, preaching a baptism of repentance for the forgiveness of sins. [4] As it is written in the book of the words of Isaiah the prophet:

"A voice of one calling in the wilderness,
'Prepare the way for the Lord,
    make straight paths for him.
[5] Every valley shall be filled in,
    every mountain and hill made low.
The crooked roads shall become straight,
    the rough ways smooth.
[6] And all people will see God's salvation.'"[a]

[7] John said to the crowds coming out to be baptized by him, "You brood of vipers! Who warned you to flee from the coming wrath? [8] Produce fruit in keeping with repentance. And do not begin to say to yourselves, 'We have Abraham as our father.' For I tell you that out of these stones God can raise up children for Abraham. [9] The ax is already at the root of the trees, and every tree that does not produce good fruit will be cut down and thrown into the fire."

[10] "What should we do then?" the crowd asked.

[11] John answered, "Anyone who has two shirts should share with the one who has none, and anyone who has food should do the same."

[12] Even tax collectors came to be baptized. "Teacher," they asked, "what should we do?"

[13] "Don't collect any more than you are required to," he told them.

[14] Then some soldiers asked him, "And what should we do?"

He replied, "Don't extort money and don't accuse people falsely — be content with your pay."

[15] The people were waiting expectantly and were all wondering in their hearts if John might possibly be the Messiah. [16] John answered them all, "I baptize you with[b] water. But one who is more powerful than I will come, the straps of whose sandals I am not worthy to untie. He will baptize you with[b] the Holy Spirit and fire. [17] His winnowing fork is in his hand to clear his threshing floor and to gather the wheat into his barn, but he will burn up the chaff with unquenchable fire." [18] And with many other words John exhorted the people and proclaimed the good news to them.

[19] But when John rebuked Herod the tetrarch because of his marriage to Herodias, his brother's wife, and all the other evil things he had done, [20] Herod added this to them all: He locked John up in prison.

The Baptism and Genealogy of Jesus

[21] When all the people were being baptized, Jesus was baptized too. And as he was praying, heaven was opened [22] and the Holy Spirit descended on him in bodily form like a dove. And a voice came from heaven: "You are my Son, whom I love; with you I am well pleased."

[23] Now Jesus himself was about thirty years old when he began his ministry. He was the son, so it was thought, of Joseph,

the son of Heli, [24] the son of Matthat,
the son of Levi, the son of Melki,
the son of Jannai, the son of Joseph,
[25] the son of Mattathias, the son of Amos,
the son of Nahum, the son of Esli,
the son of Naggai, [26] the son of Maath,
the son of Mattathias, the son of Semein,
the son of Josek, the son of Joda,
[27] the son of Joanan, the son of Rhesa,
the son of Zerubbabel, the son of Shealtiel,
the son of Neri, [28] the son of Melki,
the son of Addi, the son of Cosam,
the son of Elmadam, the son of Er,
[29] the son of Joshua, the son of Eliezer,
the son of Jorim, the son of Matthat,
the son of Levi, [30] the son of Simeon,
the son of Judah, the son of Joseph,
the son of Jonam, the son of Eliakim,
[31] the son of Melea, the son of Menna,
the son of Mattatha, the son of Nathan,
the son of David, [32] the son of Jesse,
the son of Obed, the son of Boaz,
the son of Salmon,[c] the son of Nahshon,
[33] the son of Amminadab, the son of Ram,[d]
the son of Hezron, the son of Perez,
the son of Judah, [34] the son of Jacob,
the son of Isaac, the son of Abraham,
the son of Terah, the son of Nahor,
[35] the son of Serug, the son of Reu,
the son of Peleg, the son of Eber,
the son of Shelah, [36] the son of Cainan,
the son of Arphaxad, the son of Shem,

---

[a] 6 Isaiah 40:3-5   [b] 16 Or in   [c] 32 Some early manuscripts Sala   [d] 33 Some manuscripts Amminadab, the son of Admin, the son of Arni; other manuscripts vary widely.

21 QUALITIES

PASSION   John Served God with Gusto

Luke 3:2–22

THE BEST single word to describe John the Baptist might be the word "passion." John's passion began even before he was born. He leaped in his mother's womb when Mary spoke of her pregnancy (Lk 1:41). His passion for God grew so great, that before he began his public ministry, he lived alone in the desert, wearing camel's hair and a leather belt and eating locusts and wild honey (Mt 3:4). He was a radical and unafraid to let anyone know it.

John needed passion to fulfill his God-given calling. Every pioneer needs passion. Pioneers cannot be satisfied with mere maintenance, for they have nothing yet to maintain. They create from nothing. The common folk often view them as eccentric—but their passion attracts other pioneers.

What gave John *his* passion?

1. *He spent time in solitude.*
   Before John began his public ministry, he lived in the wilderness and spent much time with God. He boiled with the presence of God and could hardly stay quiet.
2. *He felt consumed with his mission.*
   John knew of Jesus' identity and his soon advent. John urgently tried to prepare the way for him.
3. *He possessed a magnetic temperament and wiring.*
   John is described as a voice crying out (Lk 3:4) and as an exhorter (3:18). Like a magnet, he repelled some and attracted others.
4. *He possessed a strong sense of justice.*

When people asked John what they should do, he told them to do justice (3:10–14). This hunger for justice drove him. He wouldn't sit still until he saw results.

5. *He saw things as black and white.*
   Like others with prophetic gifts, John saw most issues as either black or white. While this sounds narrow to most pastors or businesspersons, this is part of what gave John his passion.
6. *He felt dissatisfied with anything but action.*
   John was a doer. He didn't want people to merely talk about repentance and faith. He told the Pharisees they should bring forth fruit to prove their repentance.

Passion makes for an effective ministry. So how can you increase your passion?

1. *Take your temperature.* Get an honest assessment from coworkers: Are you passionate about what you do? You can't start a fire in your organization unless it first burns in you.
2. *Return to your first love.* Many leaders allow life to push them off track. Think back to when you first began your career. What drove you? What made you enthusiastic?
3. *Associate with people of passion.* Birds of a feather flock together. Hot coals stay hot when they remain in the fire. Find passionate people and let them rub off on you.

For a negative example of passion, see p. 389.

the son of Noah, the son of Lamech,
[37] the son of Methuselah, the son of Enoch,
the son of Jared, the son of Mahalalel,
the son of Kenan, [38] the son of Enosh,
the son of Seth, the son of Adam,
the son of God.

Jesus Is Tested in the Wilderness

4 Jesus, full of the Holy Spirit, left the Jordan and was led by the Spirit into the wilderness, [2] where for forty days he was tempted[a] by the devil. He ate nothing during those days, and at the end of them he was hungry.

[3] The devil said to him, "If you are the Son of God, tell this stone to become bread."

[4] Jesus answered, "It is written: 'Man shall not live on bread alone.'[b]"

[5] The devil led him up to a high place and showed him in an instant all the kingdoms of the world. [6] And he said to him, "I will give you all their authority and splendor; it has been given to me, and I can give it to anyone I want to. [7] If you worship me, it will all be yours."

The Role of the Wilderness

Luke 4:1–13

The role of the wilderness in the preparation of a leader cannot be overemphasized. Both Luke and Matthew record Jesus' time in the wilderness at the beginning of his ministry. Jesus spent 40 days alone, in a desert, abstaining from food and noise and distraction. Both Gospel writers tell us this was a time ordained by the Holy Spirit.

So what happens to leaders in this wilderness season? Luke gives us a hint:

1. We recognize that God will lead us into seasons of growth, not gratification.

2. We fight battles and overcome temptations to take shortcuts.

3. We learn discipline and the art of depending on God.

4. We are broken of self-sufficiency and self-promotion.

5. We solidify our sense of mission.

6. We gain perspective.

7. We are prepared to enter our vocation.

[8] Jesus answered, "It is written: 'Worship the Lord your God and serve him only.'[c]"

[9] The devil led him to Jerusalem and had him stand on the highest point of the temple. "If you are the Son of God," he said, "throw yourself down from here. [10] For it is written:

"'He will command his angels concerning you
    to guard you carefully;
[11] they will lift you up in their hands,
    so that you will not strike your foot
        against a stone.'[d]"

[12] Jesus answered, "It is said: 'Do not put the Lord your God to the test.'[e]"

[13] When the devil had finished all this tempting, he left him until an opportune time.

Jesus Rejected at Nazareth

[14] Jesus returned to Galilee in the power of the Spirit, and news about him spread through the whole countryside. [15] He was teaching in their synagogues, and everyone praised him.

[16] He went to Nazareth, where he had been brought up, and on the Sabbath day he went into the synagogue, as was his custom. He stood up to read, [17] and the scroll of the prophet Isaiah was handed to him. Unrolling it, he found the place where it is written:

[18] "The Spirit of the Lord is on me,
    because he has anointed me
    to proclaim good news to the poor.
He has sent me to proclaim freedom for the prisoners
    and recovery of sight for the blind,
to set the oppressed free,
[19]   to proclaim the year of the Lord's favor."[f]

[20] Then he rolled up the scroll, gave it back to the attendant and sat down. The eyes of everyone in the synagogue were fastened on him. [21] He began by saying to them, "Today this scripture is fulfilled in your hearing."

[22] All spoke well of him and were amazed at the gracious words that came from his lips. "Isn't this Joseph's son?" they asked.

[23] Jesus said to them, "Surely you will quote this proverb to me: 'Physician, heal yourself!' And you will tell me, 'Do here in your hometown what we have heard that you did in Capernaum.'"

---

[a] 2 The Greek for *tempted* can also mean *tested*.
[b] 4 Deut. 8:3   [c] 8 Deut. 6:13   [d] 11 Psalm 91:11,12
[e] 12 Deut. 6:16   [f] 19 Isaiah 61:1,2 (see Septuagint); Isaiah 58:6

Self-Discipline: Jesus Teaches That the First Person You Lead Is You

Luke 4:3–10

Jesus faced three major temptations during his 40 days in the desert. The enemy approached him and tried to entice him through the following temptations:

1. *Legitimate needs* (v. 3): He tried to get Jesus to act apart from God in order to meet his legitimate needs.

2. *Spiritual gifting* (vv. 6–7): He tried to urge Jesus to use his giftedness for self-profit or to draw a crowd.

3. *Personal worship* (vv. 9–10): He tried to convince Jesus to get ahead by linking up with a power other than God.

Jesus teaches every leader that the first person you lead is *you*. We earn the right to lead others when they see us lead well in our own lives.

²⁴"Truly I tell you," he continued, "no prophet is accepted in his hometown. ²⁵I assure you that there were many widows in Israel in Elijah's time, when the sky was shut for three and a half years and there was a severe famine throughout the land. ²⁶Yet Elijah was not sent to any of them, but to a widow in Zarephath in the region of Sidon. ²⁷And there were many in Israel with leprosy*a* in the time of Elisha the prophet, yet not one of them was cleansed — only Naaman the Syrian."

²⁸All the people in the synagogue were furious when they heard this. ²⁹They got up, drove him out of the town, and took him to the brow of the hill on which the town was built, in order to throw him off the cliff. ³⁰But he walked right through the crowd and went on his way.

Jesus Drives Out an Impure Spirit

³¹Then he went down to Capernaum, a town in Galilee, and on the Sabbath he taught the people. ³²They were amazed at his teaching, because his words had authority.

³³In the synagogue there was a man possessed by a demon, an impure spirit. He cried out at the top of his voice, ³⁴"Go away! What do you want with us, Jesus of Nazareth? Have you come to destroy us? I know who you are — the Holy One of God!"

³⁵"Be quiet!" Jesus said sternly. "Come out of him!" Then the demon threw the man down before them all and came out without injuring him.

³⁶All the people were amazed and said to each other, "What words these are! With authority and power he gives orders to impure spirits and they come out!" ³⁷And the news about him spread throughout the surrounding area.

Jesus Heals Many

³⁸Jesus left the synagogue and went to the home of Simon. Now Simon's mother-in-law was suffering from a high fever, and they asked Jesus to help her. ³⁹So he bent over her and rebuked the fever, and it left her. She got up at once and began to wait on them.

⁴⁰At sunset, the people brought to Jesus all who had various kinds of sickness, and laying his hands on each one, he healed them. ⁴¹Moreover, demons came out of many people, shouting, "You are the Son of God!" But he rebuked them and would not allow them to speak, because they knew he was the Messiah.

⁴²At daybreak, Jesus went out to a solitary place. The people were looking for him and when they came to where he was, they tried to keep him from leaving them. ⁴³But he said, "I must proclaim the good news of the kingdom of God to the other towns also, because that is why I was sent." ⁴⁴And he kept on preaching in the synagogues of Judea.

---

a 27 The Greek word traditionally translated *leprosy* was used for various diseases affecting the skin.

Focus: Jesus Won't Be Distracted from His Mission or Anointing

Luke 4:18–29

Jesus spoke from Isaiah 61 about his anointing (Lk 4:18). Even when his audience didn't like what he had to say (4:28–29), he moved on to the next town to continue his work. He would not let anything drain his anointing or distract him from his mission.

Jesus Calls His First Disciples

5 One day as Jesus was standing by the Lake of Gennesaret,[a] the people were crowding around him and listening to the word of God. [2]He saw at the water's edge two boats, left there by the fishermen, who were washing their nets. [3]He got into one of the boats, the one belonging to Simon, and asked him to put out a little from shore. Then he sat down and taught the people from the boat.

[4]When he had finished speaking, he said to Simon, "Put out into deep water, and let down the nets for a catch."

[5]Simon answered, "Master, we've worked hard all night and haven't caught anything. But because you say so, I will let down the nets."

[6]When they had done so, they caught such a large number of fish that their nets began to break. [7]So they signaled their partners in the other boat to come and help them, and they came and filled both boats so full that they began to sink.

[8]When Simon Peter saw this, he fell at Jesus' knees and said, "Go away from me, Lord; I am a sinful man!" [9]For he and all his companions were astonished at the catch of fish they had taken, [10]and so were James and John, the sons of Zebedee, Simon's partners.

Then Jesus said to Simon, "Don't be afraid; from now on you will fish for people." [11]So they

---

The Law of Buy-In: Jesus Builds a Team Before His Men Understand It All

Luke 5:1–11

The Law of Buy-In reminds us that people buy in to the leader before they buy in to the vision of that leader. Jesus directed three seasoned fishermen to let down their nets in a certain part of the lake in order to get a catch. Peter responded that they had fished hard all night, without catching anything. Yet he gave Jesus' word higher authority than his own experience.

This is crucial. Jesus' leadership drew a buy-in from professionals who felt certain they knew the fishing business better than he did. When Jesus' directions proved fruitful, they became willing to follow him anywhere. Even before they understood all the places they would be going, they left everything to follow him.

Communicating Vision: Jesus Shared a Compelling Vision

Luke 5:10

Jesus presented a compelling vision, using assuring terms ("Don't be afraid"), familiar pictures ("you will fish") and a challenging goal ("people"). He cast his vision in one sentence of 11 words! A vision that is short, sharp, and shaped to fit the people enables leaders to succeed.

---

pulled their boats up on shore, left everything and followed him.

Jesus Heals a Man With Leprosy

[12]While Jesus was in one of the towns, a man came along who was covered with leprosy.[b] When he saw Jesus, he fell with his face to the ground and begged him, "Lord, if you are willing, you can make me clean."

[13]Jesus reached out his hand and touched the man. "I am willing," he said. "Be clean!" And immediately the leprosy left him.

[14]Then Jesus ordered him, "Don't tell anyone, but go, show yourself to the priest and offer the sacrifices that Moses commanded for your cleansing, as a testimony to them."

[15]Yet the news about him spread all the more, so that crowds of people came to hear him and to be healed of their sicknesses. [16]But Jesus often withdrew to lonely places and prayed.

Jesus Forgives and Heals a Paralyzed Man

[17]One day Jesus was teaching, and Pharisees and teachers of the law were sitting there. They had come from every village of Galilee and from Judea and Jerusalem. And the power of the Lord was with Jesus to heal the sick. [18]Some men came carrying a paralyzed man on a mat and tried to take him into the house to lay him before Jesus. [19]When they could not find a way to do this because of the crowd, they went up on the roof and lowered him on his mat through the tiles into the middle of the crowd, right in front of Jesus.

---

[a] 1 That is, the Sea of Galilee   [b] 12 The Greek word traditionally translated *leprosy* was used for various diseases affecting the skin.

20When Jesus saw their faith, he said, "Friend, your sins are forgiven."

21The Pharisees and the teachers of the law began thinking to themselves, "Who is this fellow who speaks blasphemy? Who can forgive sins but God alone?"

22Jesus knew what they were thinking and asked, "Why are you thinking these things in your hearts? 23Which is easier: to say, 'Your sins are forgiven,' or to say, 'Get up and walk'? 24But I want you to know that the Son of Man has authority on earth to forgive sins." So he said to the paralyzed man, "I tell you, get up, take your mat and go home." 25Immediately he stood up in front of them, took what he had been lying on and went home praising God. 26Everyone was amazed and gave praise to God. They were filled with awe and said, "We have seen remarkable things today."

Jesus Calls Levi and Eats With Sinners

27After this, Jesus went out and saw a tax collector by the name of Levi sitting at his tax booth. "Follow me," Jesus said to him, 28and Levi got up, left everything and followed him.

29Then Levi held a great banquet for Jesus at his house, and a large crowd of tax collectors and others were eating with them. 30But the Pharisees and the teachers of the law who belonged to their sect complained to his disciples, "Why do you eat and drink with tax collectors and sinners?"

31Jesus answered them, "It is not the healthy who need a doctor, but the sick. 32I have not come to call the righteous, but sinners to repentance."

Jesus Questioned About Fasting

33They said to him, "John's disciples often fast and pray, and so do the disciples of the Pharisees, but yours go on eating and drinking."

34Jesus answered, "Can you make the friends of the bridegroom fast while he is with them? 35But the time will come when the bridegroom will be taken from them; in those days they will fast."

36He told them this parable: "No one tears a piece out of a new garment to patch an old one. Otherwise, they will have torn the new garment, and the patch from the new will not match the old. 37And no one pours new wine into old wineskins. Otherwise, the new wine will burst the skins; the wine will run out and the wineskins will be ruined. 38No, new wine must be poured into new wineskins. 39And no one after

---

The Law of Intuition: Jesus Saw Potential in Simon and Matthew

Luke 5:10–11, 27–28

Would any of us have picked Simon the fisherman or Matthew the tax collector to be on our team? The former spoke more than he thought; the latter took more than he gave. But Jesus saw them both as diamonds in the rough.

Jesus could see beyond the imperfections, and he put a "ten" on their foreheads instead of the "three" or "four" they deserved. Unstable Peter became a solid leader of the church at Jerusalem, while Matthew became one of the most generous people in the Gospels.

The Law of Intuition enables leaders to spot potential. Consider the biblical record . . .

1. Who would have chosen a stammering Moses to be a spokesman for God?

2. Who would have chosen a shepherd boy like David to be King of Israel?

3. Who would have chosen an uncouth John the Baptist to prepare the way for Jesus?

4. Who would have chosen a converted prostitute, Mary, to herald the resurrection?

---

drinking old wine wants the new, for they say, 'The old is better.'"

Jesus Is Lord of the Sabbath

6 One Sabbath Jesus was going through the grainfields, and his disciples began to pick some heads of grain, rub them in their hands and eat the kernels. 2Some of the Pharisees asked, "Why are you doing what is unlawful on the Sabbath?"

3Jesus answered them, "Have you never read what David did when he and his companions were hungry? 4He entered the house of God, and taking the consecrated bread, he ate what is lawful only for priests to eat. And he also gave some to his companions." 5Then Jesus said to them, "The Son of Man is Lord of the Sabbath."

6On another Sabbath he went into the synagogue and was teaching, and a man was there whose right hand was shriveled. 7The Pharisees and the teachers of the law were looking for a reason to accuse Jesus, so they watched him closely to see if he would heal on the Sabbath. ⁸But Jesus knew what they were thinking and said to the man with the shriveled hand, "Get up and stand in front of everyone." So he got up and stood there.

⁹Then Jesus said to them, "I ask you, which is lawful on the Sabbath: to do good or to do evil, to save life or to destroy it?"

¹⁰He looked around at them all, and then said to the man, "Stretch out your hand." He did so, and his hand was completely restored. ¹¹But the Pharisees and the teachers of the law were furious and began to discuss with one another what they might do to Jesus.

The Twelve Apostles

¹²One of those days Jesus went out to a mountainside to pray, and spent the night praying to God. ¹³When morning came, he called his disciples to him and chose twelve of them, whom he also designated apostles: ¹⁴Simon (whom he named Peter), his brother Andrew, James, John, Philip, Bartholomew, ¹⁵Matthew, Thomas, James son of Alphaeus, Simon who was called the Zealot, ¹⁶Judas son of James, and Judas Iscariot, who became a traitor.

Blessings and Woes

¹⁷He went down with them and stood on a level place. A large crowd of his disciples was there and a great number of people from all over Judea, from Jerusalem, and from the coastal region around Tyre and Sidon, ¹⁸who had come to hear him and to be healed of their diseases. Those troubled by impure spirits were cured, ¹⁹and the people all tried to touch him, because power was coming from him and healing them all.

²⁰Looking at his disciples, he said:

"Blessed are you who are poor,
    for yours is the kingdom of God.
²¹Blessed are you who hunger now,
    for you will be satisfied.
Blessed are you who weep now,
    for you will laugh.
²²Blessed are you when people hate you,
    when they exclude you and insult you
    and reject your name as evil,
        because of the Son of Man.

²³"Rejoice in that day and leap for joy, because great is your reward in heaven. For that is how their ancestors treated the prophets.

Mentoring: Jesus Spent the Majority of His Time with Twelve, Not Twelve Hundred

Luke 6:12–19

In less than one generation, the disciples of Jesus progressed from ignorant laborers to bold spiritual leaders in what is now the largest organization in the world. How could this transformation occur?

It happened because Jesus spent the bulk of his time with them. The Son of God invested the vast majority of his time with twelve, not twelve hundred. Jesus practiced the axiom: More time with less people equals greater kingdom impact.

Like all good mentors, Jesus provided:

1. *Handles:* He simplified truth into something his men could grasp, practice, and pass on to others. He took complex theology and made it usable.

2. *Roadmaps:* Roadmaps give you the big picture; they reveal where you are; they show you what roads to take; and they tell you what roads to avoid. Jesus did this consistently with the Twelve.

3. *Laboratories:* Labs are safe places for experimentation. Jesus didn't just lecture, he provided labs for his disciples to practice what they learned.

4. *Roots:* Jesus gave his followers a firm foundation and a sense of heritage. They sunk their roots into solid ground and were willing to die for him and his teaching.

5. *Wings:* Jesus empowered his men to soar beyond where he went himself (Jn 14:12). He pushed them and cheered them on in their victories.

Positive Attitude: Jesus' First Job Was to Change Their Perspective

Luke 6:20-23

What did Jesus do first when training his leaders? He transformed their perspective and attitude. He talked about the blessing of being poor, hungry, hated, insulted, or persecuted. Talk about a change of attitude! Effective training always begins with attitude and perspective, changing individuals from the inside out.

24 "But woe to you who are rich,
    for you have already received your
       comfort.
25 Woe to you who are well fed now,
    for you will go hungry.
Woe to you who laugh now,
    for you will mourn and weep.
26 Woe to you when everyone speaks well of
    you,
    for that is how their ancestors treated the
      false prophets.

Love for Enemies

27 "But to you who are listening I say: Love your enemies, do good to those who hate you, 28 bless those who curse you, pray for those who mistreat you. 29 If someone slaps you on one cheek, turn to them the other also. If someone takes your coat, do not withhold your shirt from them. 30 Give to everyone who asks you, and if anyone takes what belongs to you, do not demand it back. 31 Do to others as you would have them do to you.

32 "If you love those who love you, what credit is that to you? Even sinners love those who love them. 33 And if you do good to those who are good to you, what credit is that to you? Even sinners do that. 34 And if you lend to those from whom you expect repayment, what credit is that to you? Even sinners lend to sinners, expecting to be repaid in full. 35 But love your enemies, do good to them, and lend to them without expecting to get anything back. Then your reward will be great, and you will be children of the Most High, because he is kind to the ungrateful and wicked. 36 Be merciful, just as your Father is merciful.

Judging Others

37 "Do not judge, and you will not be judged. Do not condemn, and you will not be condemned. Forgive, and you will be forgiven. 38 Give, and it will be given to you. A good measure, pressed down, shaken together and running over, will be poured into your lap. For with the measure you use, it will be measured to you."

39 He also told them this parable: "Can the blind lead the blind? Will they not both fall into a pit? 40 The student is not above the teacher, but everyone who is fully trained will be like their teacher.

41 "Why do you look at the speck of sawdust in your brother's eye and pay no attention to the plank in your own eye? 42 How can you say to your brother, 'Brother, let me take the speck out of your eye,' when you yourself fail to see the plank in your own eye? You hypocrite, first take the plank out of your eye, and then you will see clearly to remove the speck from your brother's eye.

A Tree and Its Fruit

43 "No good tree bears bad fruit, nor does a bad tree bear good fruit. 44 Each tree is recognized by its own fruit. People do not pick figs from thornbushes, or grapes from briers. 45 A good man brings good things out of the good stored up in his heart, and an evil man brings evil things out of the evil stored up in his heart. For the mouth speaks what the heart is full of.

The Wise and Foolish Builders

46 "Why do you call me, 'Lord, Lord,' and do not do what I say? 47 As for everyone who comes to me and hears my words and puts them into practice, I will show you what they are like. 48 They are like a man building a house, who dug down deep and laid the foundation on rock. When a flood came, the torrent struck that house but could not shake it, because it was well built. 49 But the one who hears my words and does not put them into practice is like a man who built a house on the ground without a foundation. The moment the torrent struck that house, it collapsed and its destruction was complete."

The Faith of the Centurion

7 When Jesus had finished saying all this to the people who were listening, he entered Capernaum. 2 There a centurion's servant, whom his master valued highly, was sick and about to die. 3 The centurion heard of Jesus and sent some elders of the Jews to him, asking him to come and heal his servant. 4 When they came to Jesus, they pleaded earnestly with him, "This

man deserves to have you do this, [5]because he loves our nation and has built our synagogue." [6]So Jesus went with them.

He was not far from the house when the centurion sent friends to say to him: "Lord, don't trouble yourself, for I do not deserve to have you come under my roof. [7]That is why I did not even consider myself worthy to come to you. But say the word, and my servant will be healed. [8]For I myself am a man under authority, with soldiers under me. I tell this one, 'Go,' and he goes; and that one, 'Come,' and he comes. I say to my servant, 'Do this,' and he does it."

[9]When Jesus heard this, he was amazed at him, and turning to the crowd following him, he said, "I tell you, I have not found such great faith even in Israel." [10]Then the men who had been sent returned to the house and found the servant well.

Jesus Raises a Widow's Son

[11]Soon afterward, Jesus went to a town called Nain, and his disciples and a large crowd went along with him. [12]As he approached the town gate, a dead person was being carried out — the only son of his mother, and she was a widow. And a large crowd from the town was with her. [13]When the Lord saw her, his heart went out to her and he said, "Don't cry."

[14]Then he went up and touched the bier they were carrying him on, and the bearers stood still. He said, "Young man, I say to you, get up!" [15]The dead man sat up and began to talk, and Jesus gave him back to his mother.

[16]They were all filled with awe and praised God. "A great prophet has appeared among us," they said. "God has come to help his people." [17]This news about Jesus spread throughout Judea and the surrounding country.

Jesus and John the Baptist

[18]John's disciples told him about all these things. Calling two of them, [19]he sent them to the Lord to ask, "Are you the one who is to come, or should we expect someone else?"

[20]When the men came to Jesus, they said, "John the Baptist sent us to you to ask, 'Are you the one who is to come, or should we expect someone else?'"

[21]At that very time Jesus cured many who had diseases, sicknesses and evil spirits, and gave sight to many who were blind. [22]So he replied to the messengers, "Go back and report to John what you have seen and heard: The blind receive sight, the lame walk, those who have leprosy[a] are cleansed, the deaf hear, the dead are raised, and the good news is proclaimed to the poor. [23]Blessed is anyone who does not stumble on account of me."

---

[a] 22 The Greek word traditionally translated leprosy was used for various diseases affecting the skin.

JESUS PROFILE in leadership

The Perfect Man
Luke 7:1–17

There exists no better example of a godly leader than the Lord Jesus Christ. Every word he spoke, everything he did, served to model what godly leadership looks like. We see Jesus spending a day ministering, not to those who seemed by human standards to be most worthy, but to those who needed him most. He healed the sick and lame, cast out evil spirits, even raised the dead. And when he entered the home of one of the religious leaders of the day, he spent his time ministering to a lowly sinner.

All of those to whom Jesus ministered had one thing in common: They knew of their own need. They came to him with empty, outstretched hands, hoping he would show them compassion. And he did not disappoint their hope, for when the people saw Jesus' loving power in action, they glorified God and said, "A great prophet has appeared among us," and "God has come to help his people" (Lk 7:16).

Our world is full of needy people, overflowing with men and women who know they're missing out on something, bursting with hurting individuals who come to us with hands outstretched. As leaders for Christ, it is our job to reach out to the whole world so that those who admit their need have a chance to come to him.

²⁴After John's messengers left, Jesus began to speak to the crowd about John: "What did you go out into the wilderness to see? A reed swayed by the wind? ²⁵If not, what did you go out to see? A man dressed in fine clothes? No, those who wear expensive clothes and indulge in luxury are in palaces. ²⁶But what did you go out to see? A prophet? Yes, I tell you, and more than a prophet. ²⁷This is the one about whom it is written:

"'I will send my messenger ahead of you,
    who will prepare your way before you.'ᵃ

²⁸I tell you, among those born of women there is no one greater than John; yet the one who is least in the kingdom of God is greater than he."

²⁹(All the people, even the tax collectors, when they heard Jesus' words, acknowledged that God's way was right, because they had been baptized by John. ³⁰But the Pharisees and the experts in the law rejected God's purpose for themselves, because they had not been baptized by John.)

³¹Jesus went on to say, "To what, then, can I compare the people of this generation? What are they like? ³²They are like children sitting in the marketplace and calling out to each other:

"'We played the pipe for you,
    and you did not dance;
we sang a dirge,
    and you did not cry.'

³³For John the Baptist came neither eating bread nor drinking wine, and you say, 'He has a demon.' ³⁴The Son of Man came eating and drinking, and you say, 'Here is a glutton and a drunkard, a friend of tax collectors and sinners.' ³⁵But wisdom is proved right by all her children."

Jesus Anointed by a Sinful Woman

³⁶When one of the Pharisees invited Jesus to have dinner with him, he went to the Pharisee's house and reclined at the table. ³⁷A woman in that town who lived a sinful life learned that Jesus was eating at the Pharisee's house, so she came there with an alabaster jar of perfume. ³⁸As she stood behind him at his feet weeping, she began to wet his feet with her tears. Then she wiped them with her hair, kissed them and poured perfume on them.

³⁹When the Pharisee who had invited him saw this, he said to himself, "If this man were a prophet, he would know who is touching him and what kind of woman she is—that she is a sinner."

⁴⁰Jesus answered him, "Simon, I have something to tell you."

"Tell me, teacher," he said.

⁴¹"Two people owed money to a certain moneylender. One owed him five hundred denarii,ᵇ and the other fifty. ⁴²Neither of them had the money to pay him back, so he forgave the debts of both. Now which of them will love him more?"

⁴³Simon replied, "I suppose the one who had the bigger debt forgiven."

"You have judged correctly," Jesus said.

⁴⁴Then he turned toward the woman and said to Simon, "Do you see this woman? I came into your house. You did not give me any water for my feet, but she wet my feet with her tears and wiped them with her hair. ⁴⁵You did not give me a kiss, but this woman, from the time I entered, has not stopped kissing my feet. ⁴⁶You did not put oil on my head, but she has poured perfume on my feet. ⁴⁷Therefore, I tell you, her many sins have been forgiven—as her great love has shown. But whoever has been forgiven little loves little."

⁴⁸Then Jesus said to her, "Your sins are forgiven."

⁴⁹The other guests began to say among themselves, "Who is this who even forgives sins?"

⁵⁰Jesus said to the woman, "Your faith has saved you; go in peace."

The Parable of the Sower

8 After this, Jesus traveled about from one town and village to another, proclaiming the good news of the kingdom of God. The Twelve were with him, ²and also some women who had been cured of evil spirits and diseases: Mary (called Magdalene) from whom seven demons had come out; ³Joanna the wife of Chuza, the manager of Herod's household; Susanna; and many others. These women were helping to support them out of their own means.

⁴While a large crowd was gathering and people were coming to Jesus from town after town, he told this parable: ⁵"A farmer went out to sow his seed. As he was scattering the seed, some fell along the path; it was trampled on, and the birds ate it up. ⁶Some fell on rocky ground, and when it came up, the plants withered because they had no moisture. ⁷Other seed fell among thorns, which grew up with it and choked the plants. ⁸Still other seed fell on good soil. It came up and yielded a crop, a hundred times more than was sown."

ᵃ 27 Mal. 3:1   ᵇ 41 A denarius was the usual daily wage of a day laborer (see Matt. 20:2).

When he said this, he called out, "Whoever has ears to hear, let them hear."

[9]His disciples asked him what this parable meant. [10]He said, "The knowledge of the secrets of the kingdom of God has been given to you, but to others I speak in parables, so that,

> "'though seeing, they may not see;
> though hearing, they may not understand.'[a]

[11]"This is the meaning of the parable: The seed is the word of God. [12]Those along the path are the ones who hear, and then the devil comes and takes away the word from their hearts, so that they may not believe and be saved. [13]Those on the rocky ground are the ones who receive the word with joy when they hear it, but they have no root. They believe for a while, but in the time of testing they fall away. [14]The seed that fell among thorns stands for those who hear, but as they go on their way they are choked by life's worries, riches and pleasures, and they do not mature. [15]But the seed on good soil stands for those with a noble and good heart, who hear the word, retain it, and by persevering produce a crop.

A Lamp on a Stand

[16]"No one lights a lamp and hides it in a clay jar or puts it under a bed. Instead, they put it on a stand, so that those who come in can see the light. [17]For there is nothing hidden that will not be disclosed, and nothing concealed that will not be known or brought out into the open. [18]Therefore consider carefully how you listen. Whoever has will be given more; whoever does not have, even what they think they have will be taken from them."

Jesus' Mother and Brothers

[19]Now Jesus' mother and brothers came to see him, but they were not able to get near him because of the crowd. [20]Someone told him, "Your mother and brothers are standing outside, wanting to see you."

[21]He replied, "My mother and brothers are those who hear God's word and put it into practice."

Jesus Calms the Storm

[22]One day Jesus said to his disciples, "Let us go over to the other side of the lake." So they got into a boat and set out. [23]As they sailed, he fell asleep. A squall came down on the lake, so that the boat was being swamped, and they were in great danger.

[24]The disciples went and woke him, saying, "Master, Master, we're going to drown!"

He got up and rebuked the wind and the raging waters; the storm subsided, and all was calm. [25]"Where is your faith?" he asked his disciples.

In fear and amazement they asked one another, "Who is this? He commands even the winds and the water, and they obey him."

Jesus Restores a Demon-Possessed Man

[26]They sailed to the region of the Gerasenes,[b] which is across the lake from Galilee. [27]When Jesus stepped ashore, he was met by a demon-possessed man from the town. For a long time this man had not worn clothes or lived in a house, but had lived in the tombs.

---

[a] 10 Isaiah 6:9   [b] 26 Some manuscripts *Gadarenes*; other manuscripts *Gergesenes*; also in verse 37

The Law of Connection: Jesus Always Met Needs First

Luke 8:24—9:6

Jesus always approached people to meet their needs before he asked them to follow or obey him. After he delivered the demonized man in Gerasa, the man wanted to do something in return. Jesus told him to return to his hometown and spread the news of God's kingdom. The man acted as he did in response to a leader who practiced the Law of Connection. Gratitude nearly always follows grace. Look at the connection and response in these verses alone:

The Leader Connects	The People's Response
1. Jesus calmed the sea for his disciples (8:24).	1. They were sent out (9:1–6).
2. Jesus delivered the demonized man (8:33).	2. He was to preach at home (8:39).
3. Jesus healed the woman's blood disease (8:47).	3. She was to exhibit peace (8:48).
4. Jesus raised Jairus's daughter from the dead (8:54).	4. He was to feed and minister (8:55).

²⁸When he saw Jesus, he cried out and fell at his feet, shouting at the top of his voice, "What do you want with me, Jesus, Son of the Most High God? I beg you, don't torture me!" ²⁹For Jesus had commanded the impure spirit to come out of the man. Many times it had seized him, and though he was chained hand and foot and kept under guard, he had broken his chains and had been driven by the demon into solitary places.

³⁰Jesus asked him, "What is your name?"

"Legion," he replied, because many demons had gone into him. ³¹And they begged Jesus repeatedly not to order them to go into the Abyss.

³²A large herd of pigs was feeding there on the hillside. The demons begged Jesus to let them go into the pigs, and he gave them permission. ³³When the demons came out of the man, they went into the pigs, and the herd rushed down the steep bank into the lake and was drowned.

³⁴When those tending the pigs saw what had happened, they ran off and reported this in the town and countryside, ³⁵and the people went out to see what had happened. When they came to Jesus, they found the man from whom the demons had gone out, sitting at Jesus' feet, dressed and in his right mind; and they were afraid. ³⁶Those who had seen it told the people how the demon-possessed man had been cured.

³⁷Then all the people of the region of the Gerasenes asked Jesus to leave them, because they were overcome with fear. So he got into the boat and left.

³⁸The man from whom the demons had gone out begged to go with him, but Jesus sent him away, saying, ³⁹"Return home and tell how much God has done for you." So the man went away and told all over town how much Jesus had done for him.

Jesus Raises a Dead Girl and Heals a Sick Woman

⁴⁰Now when Jesus returned, a crowd welcomed him, for they were all expecting him. ⁴¹Then a man named Jairus, a synagogue leader, came and fell at Jesus' feet, pleading with him to come to his house ⁴²because his only daughter, a girl of about twelve, was dying.

As Jesus was on his way, the crowds almost crushed him. ⁴³And a woman was there who had been subject to bleeding for twelve years,[a] but no one could heal her. ⁴⁴She came up behind him and touched the edge of his cloak, and immediately her bleeding stopped. ⁴⁵"Who touched me?" Jesus asked.

---

[a] 43 Many manuscripts *years, and she had spent all she had on doctors*

Commitment: Solve Our Problems but Save Our Pigs

Luke 8:26–37

Jesus once met a man controlled by a legion of demons. The poor man had lost control and had to be chained and kept under guard. When Jesus cast the offending demons into some nearby pigs, the man instantly grew calm and whole.

Ironically, when the area's residents took one look at the man, they asked Jesus to depart. No doubt they felt pleased to see this man healed—but not at the expense of their livestock! They feared the demon-possessed man, but they feared even more a Jesus who took complete control over the situation. It's important to remember in any conflict: Jesus doesn't want to take sides; he wants to take over!

Often we resemble the Gadarenes, those who wanted Jesus to solve their problems but save their pigs. "We don't want to upset things or get radical," we say. "We want change . . . as long as it doesn't change us." But this is not Jesus' way.

Note several lessons this passage teaches us about leadership:

1. *Leadership means discomfort.*
   If you're going to be an effective leader, you must live outside of your comfort zone.

2. *Leadership means dissatisfaction.*
   God uses dissatisfaction as a tool to move us to greater things and higher ground.

3. *Leadership means disruption.*
   The status quo is never the goal of a leader. Disruption is our constant companion.

When they all denied it, Peter said, "Master, the people are crowding and pressing against you."

[46]But Jesus said, "Someone touched me; I know that power has gone out from me."

[47]Then the woman, seeing that she could not go unnoticed, came trembling and fell at his feet. In the presence of all the people, she told why she had touched him and how she had been instantly healed. [48]Then he said to her, "Daughter, your faith has healed you. Go in peace."

[49]While Jesus was still speaking, someone came from the house of Jairus, the synagogue leader. "Your daughter is dead," he said. "Don't bother the teacher anymore."

[50]Hearing this, Jesus said to Jairus, "Don't be afraid; just believe, and she will be healed."

[51]When he arrived at the house of Jairus, he did not let anyone go in with him except Peter, John and James, and the child's father and mother. [52]Meanwhile, all the people were wailing and mourning for her. "Stop wailing," Jesus said. "She is not dead but asleep."

[53]They laughed at him, knowing that she was dead. [54]But he took her by the hand and said, "My child, get up!" [55]Her spirit returned, and at once she stood up. Then Jesus told them to give her something to eat. [56]Her parents were astonished, but he ordered them not to tell anyone what had happened.

Jesus Sends Out the Twelve

9 When Jesus had called the Twelve together, he gave them power and authority to drive out all demons and to cure diseases, [2]and he sent them out to proclaim the kingdom of God and to heal the sick. [3]He told them: "Take nothing for the journey — no staff, no bag, no bread, no money, no extra shirt. [4]Whatever house you enter, stay there until you leave that town. [5]If people do not welcome you, leave their town and shake the dust off your feet as a testimony against them." [6]So they set out and went from village to village, proclaiming the good news and healing people everywhere.

[7]Now Herod the tetrarch heard about all that was going on. And he was perplexed because some were saying that John had been raised from the dead, [8]others that Elijah had appeared, and still others that one of the prophets of long ago had come back to life. [9]But Herod said, "I beheaded John. Who, then, is this I hear such things about?" And he tried to see him.

Delegation: Jesus Shared Both Responsibility and Authority

Luke 9:1–10

Jesus sent out his disciples, two by two, for some on-the-job training. Note how he got them ready for this ministry experience:

1. *Motivation:* He called them together (v. 1).
2. *Impartation:* He empowered them and gave them authority (v. 1).
3. *Delegation:* He sent them out to do a job (v. 2).
4. *Communication:* He gave them specific direction (vv. 3–5).
5. *Evaluation:* He held them accountable when they finished (v. 10).

If we are going to succeed in our mission (and live to tell about it), we must share the workload with a team. Jesus aimed to develop people as he shared the work. Consider three methods of distributing tasks among a team:

1. *Dumping:* Leaders unload a task, happy to relieve themselves of the burden. There is little to no preparation; the leaders focus on getting rid of a task. Major damage can be done to the people who receive the work.

2. *Delegating:* Leaders prepare ahead of time, then plan how to best give work away to the right people. Less damage results, but the leaders still focus on eliminating the task, not building the people.

3. *Developing:* This is the ultimate way to share work. Leaders prepare the people and the work, then focus on the training of the people. Both the leaders and the workers benefit.

Jesus Feeds the Five Thousand

[10]When the apostles returned, they reported to Jesus what they had done. Then he took them with him and they withdrew by themselves to a town called Bethsaida, [11]but the crowds learned about it and followed him. He welcomed them and spoke to them about the kingdom of God, and healed those who needed healing.

[12]Late in the afternoon the Twelve came to him and said, "Send the crowd away so they can go to the surrounding villages and countryside and find food and lodging, because we are in a remote place here."

[13]He replied, "You give them something to eat."

They answered, "We have only five loaves of bread and two fish — unless we go and buy food for all this crowd." [14](About five thousand men were there.)

But he said to his disciples, "Have them sit down in groups of about fifty each." [15]The disciples did so, and everyone sat down. [16]Taking the five loaves and the two fish and looking up to heaven, he gave thanks and broke them. Then he gave them to the disciples to distribute to the people. [17]They all ate and were satisfied, and the disciples picked up twelve basketfuls of broken pieces that were left over.

Generosity: A Candle Loses Nothing by Lighting Another

Luke 9:12–17

God likes win/win situations. We see this in the account of the feeding of the five thousand. Jesus took one basket of fish and bread, blessed it, and fed multitudes. Whoever gave up his lunch basket in the beginning received 12 times more at the end of the day. This is how generosity works.

Peter Declares That Jesus Is the Messiah

[18]Once when Jesus was praying in private and his disciples were with him, he asked them, "Who do the crowds say I am?"

[19]They replied, "Some say John the Baptist; others say Elijah; and still others, that one of the prophets of long ago has come back to life."

[20]"But what about you?" he asked. "Who do you say I am?"

Peter answered, "God's Messiah."

Jesus Predicts His Death

[21]Jesus strictly warned them not to tell this to anyone. [22]And he said, "The Son of Man must suffer many things and be rejected by the elders, the chief priests and the teachers of the law, and he must be killed and on the third day be raised to life."

[23]Then he said to them all: "Whoever wants to be my disciple must deny themselves and take up their cross daily and follow me. [24]For whoever wants to save their life will lose it, but whoever loses their life for me will save it. [25]What good is it for someone to gain the whole world, and yet lose or forfeit their very self? [26]Whoever is ashamed of me and my words, the Son of Man will be ashamed of them when he comes in his glory and in the glory of the Father and of the holy angels.

[27]"Truly I tell you, some who are standing here will not taste death before they see the kingdom of God."

The Transfiguration

[28]About eight days after Jesus said this, he took Peter, John and James with him and went up onto a mountain to pray. [29]As he was praying, the appearance of his face changed, and his clothes became as bright as a flash of lightning. [30]Two men, Moses and Elijah, appeared in glorious splendor, talking with Jesus. [31]They spoke about his departure,[a] which he was about to bring to fulfillment at Jerusalem. [32]Peter and his companions were very sleepy, but when they became fully awake, they saw his glory and the two men standing with him. [33]As the men were leaving Jesus, Peter said to him, "Master, it is good for us to be here. Let us put up three shelters — one for you, one for Moses and one for Elijah." (He did not know what he was saying.)

[34]While he was speaking, a cloud appeared and covered them, and they were afraid as they entered the cloud. [35]A voice came from the cloud, saying, "This is my Son, whom I have chosen; listen to him." [36]When the voice had spoken, they found that Jesus was alone. The disciples kept this to themselves and did not tell anyone at that time what they had seen.

Jesus Heals a Demon-Possessed Boy

[37]The next day, when they came down from the mountain, a large crowd met him. [38]A man in the crowd called out, "Teacher, I beg you to look at my son, for he is my only child. [39]A spirit

---

[a] 31 Greek *exodos*

The Law of the Inner Circle: Jesus Prepared Men to Represent Him

Luke 9:28–36

Three of Jesus' key men saw him transfigured on a mountain. He had specifically chosen these three to share the experience with him, one of several special times he arranged for Peter, James and John. While the other nine disciples waited at the foot of the mountain for their comrades to return, this "inner circle" witnessed a miracle.

Jesus, the ultimate Trainer and Mentor, did things this way to prepare some key players for future leadership. Watch how he did it. Jesus . . .

- selected a group of key men (v. 28)
- took them to a special place (v. 28)
- spent time praying with them (vv. 28–29)
- shared an unusual experience with them (vv. 30–31)
- provided a lasting memory for them (vv. 32–33)
- invested special time speaking with them (vv. 34–35)
- gave them a secret history with him that prepared them for the future (v. 36)

seizes him and he suddenly screams; it throws him into convulsions so that he foams at the mouth. It scarcely ever leaves him and is destroying him. [40]I begged your disciples to drive it out, but they could not."

[41]"You unbelieving and perverse generation," Jesus replied, "how long shall I stay with you and put up with you? Bring your son here."

[42]Even while the boy was coming, the demon threw him to the ground in a convulsion. But Jesus rebuked the impure spirit, healed the boy and gave him back to his father. [43]And they were all amazed at the greatness of God.

Jesus Predicts His Death a Second Time

While everyone was marveling at all that Jesus did, he said to his disciples, [44]"Listen carefully to what I am about to tell you: The Son of Man is going to be delivered into the hands of men." [45]But they did not understand what this meant. It was hidden from them, so that they did not grasp it, and they were afraid to ask him about it.

[46]An argument started among the disciples as to which of them would be the greatest. [47]Jesus, knowing their thoughts, took a little child and had him stand beside him. [48]Then he said to them, "Whoever welcomes this little child in my name welcomes me; and whoever welcomes me welcomes the one who sent me. For it is the one who is least among you all who is the greatest."

[49]"Master," said John, "we saw someone driving out demons in your name and we tried to stop him, because he is not one of us."

[50]"Do not stop him," Jesus said, "for whoever is not against you is for you."

Samaritan Opposition

[51]As the time approached for him to be taken up to heaven, Jesus resolutely set out for Jerusalem. [52]And he sent messengers on ahead, who went into a Samaritan village to get things ready for him; [53]but the people there did not welcome him, because he was heading for Jerusalem. [54]When the disciples James and John saw this, they asked, "Lord, do you want us to call fire down from heaven to destroy them[a]?" [55]But Jesus turned and rebuked them. [56]Then he and his disciples went to another village.

The Cost of Following Jesus

[57]As they were walking along the road, a man said to him, "I will follow you wherever you go."

[58]Jesus replied, "Foxes have dens and birds have nests, but the Son of Man has no place to lay his head."

[59]He said to another man, "Follow me."

[a] 54 Some manuscripts *them, just as Elijah did*

Focus: Jesus Resolved to Move Toward a Difficult Climax

Luke 9:51–56

Although Jesus saw the end coming, "He resolutely set out for Jerusalem" (Lk 9:51). His focus could be seen in his face (9:51–53) and in the arrangements to expedite his journey (9:52). Yet he never lost sight of the big picture (9:54–56). Jesus determined to reach his ultimate destination.

But he replied, "Lord, first let me go and bury my father."

⁶⁰Jesus said to him, "Let the dead bury their own dead, but you go and proclaim the kingdom of God."

⁶¹Still another said, "I will follow you, Lord; but first let me go back and say goodbye to my family."

⁶²Jesus replied, "No one who puts a hand to the plow and looks back is fit for service in the kingdom of God."

Jesus Sends Out the Seventy-Two

10 After this the Lord appointed seventy-two*a* others and sent them two by two ahead of him to every town and place where he was about to go. ²He told them, "The harvest is plentiful, but the workers are few. Ask the Lord of the harvest, therefore, to send out workers into his harvest field. ³Go! I am sending you out like lambs among wolves. ⁴Do not take a purse or bag or sandals; and do not greet anyone on the road.

⁵"When you enter a house, first say, 'Peace to this house.' ⁶If someone who promotes peace is there, your peace will rest on them; if not, it will return to you. ⁷Stay there, eating and drinking whatever they give you, for the worker deserves his wages. Do not move around from house to house.

⁸"When you enter a town and are welcomed, eat what is offered to you. ⁹Heal the sick who are there and tell them, 'The kingdom of God has come near to you.' ¹⁰But when you enter a town and are not welcomed, go into its streets and say, ¹¹'Even the dust of your town we wipe from our feet as a warning to you. Yet be sure of this: The kingdom of God has come near.' ¹²I tell you, it will be more bearable on that day for Sodom than for that town.

¹³"Woe to you, Chorazin! Woe to you, Bethsaida! For if the miracles that were performed in you had been performed in Tyre and Sidon, they would have repented long ago, sitting in sackcloth and ashes. ¹⁴But it will be more bearable for Tyre and Sidon at the judgment than for you. ¹⁵And you, Capernaum, will you be lifted to the heavens? No, you will go down to Hades.*b*

¹⁶"Whoever listens to you listens to me; whoever rejects you rejects me; but whoever rejects me rejects him who sent me."

¹⁷The seventy-two returned with joy and said, "Lord, even the demons submit to us in your name."

¹⁸He replied, "I saw Satan fall like lightning from heaven. ¹⁹I have given you authority to trample on snakes and scorpions and to overcome all the power of the enemy; nothing will harm you. ²⁰However, do not rejoice that the spirits submit to you, but rejoice that your names are written in heaven."

²¹At that time Jesus, full of joy through the Holy Spirit, said, "I praise you, Father, Lord of heaven and earth, because you have hidden these things from the wise and learned, and revealed them to little children. Yes, Father, for this is what you were pleased to do.

²²"All things have been committed to me by my Father. No one knows who the Son is except the Father, and no one knows who the Father is except the Son and those to whom the Son chooses to reveal him."

²³Then he turned to his disciples and said

---

a 1 Some manuscripts *seventy*; also in verse 17   *b* 15 That is, the realm of the dead

---

The Law of Explosive Growth: Jesus Expands His Training to Seventy

Luke 9:1—10:24

Some time after Jesus sent out his twelve, handpicked disciples for on-the-job training (Lk 9), he expanded his training to include 70 unnamed disciples who followed him (Lk 10). We have reason to believe both men and women made up this group of 70 trainees, and what they accomplished greatly multiplied Jesus' ministry in Judah.

Before they left, however, many felt apprehensive about being sent out—just look at the long briefing Jesus gave them. Also, after they returned, note their surprise at how well things went. Jesus expected a lot from them, but he also gave them a lot. This valuable team prepared each city for Jesus' coming and in return received valuable training from the experience.

The Law of Explosive Growth teaches that success is determined by *who* and *what* the leader teaches. To multiply his or her influence, the leader must teach other leaders and equip them with skills and principles to enable them to influence others. When a leader does this, he or she moves from addition to multiplication.

privately, "Blessed are the eyes that see what you see. [24]For I tell you that many prophets and kings wanted to see what you see but did not see it, and to hear what you hear but did not hear it."

The Parable of the Good Samaritan

[25]On one occasion an expert in the law stood up to test Jesus. "Teacher," he asked, "what must I do to inherit eternal life?"

[26]"What is written in the Law?" he replied. "How do you read it?"

[27]He answered, "'Love the Lord your God with all your heart and with all your soul and with all your strength and with all your mind'[a]; and, 'Love your neighbor as yourself.'[b]"

[28]"You have answered correctly," Jesus replied. "Do this and you will live."

The Law of Empowerment: Jesus Empowered His Team to Work

Luke 10:1–24

Jesus gave away his power to a team of 70 leaders and sent them out. Although they felt apprehensive about this first ministry tour, Jesus gave them everything they needed to succeed. Note how he equipped these leaders:

1. He appointed them and sent them out (v. 1).
2. He gave them a meaningful task to prepare cities for his arrival (v. 1).
3. He told them why their mission was so important (v. 2).
4. He calmed their fears with a long preparation speech (vv. 2–16).
5. He cautioned them about possible hardship (v. 3).
6. He issued explicit instructions about potential scenarios (vv. 4–11).
7. He imparted his convictions about their work (vv. 12–15).
8. He rejoiced with them as they returned (vv. 17–18).
9. He evaluated and debriefed them on their experience (vv. 19–20).
10. He prayed with them and affirmed their gifts and their future (vv. 21–24).

Evaluation and Debriefing: Jesus Helps His Team Interpret Results

Luke 10:17–20

When the 70 workers returned from their ministry trip, they reported to Jesus what had happened to them. They felt elated at the power that flowed through them and with the fruit they bore (Lk 10:17).

Jesus helped them to reflect on the results. He rejoiced with them and affirmed their authority over the enemy. He didn't stop there, however. He reminded them of the big picture and about what is really worth celebrating (10:20).

Practice doesn't make perfect; practice *with evaluation* makes perfect. In this passage, we see a master Mentor who evaluated what happened, guided the learning of his learners, and helped them assess the take-away value of their experience.

---

[29]But he wanted to justify himself, so he asked Jesus, "And who is my neighbor?"

[30]In reply Jesus said: "A man was going down from Jerusalem to Jericho, when he was attacked by robbers. They stripped him of his clothes, beat him and went away, leaving him half dead. [31]A priest happened to be going down the same road, and when he saw the man, he passed by on the other side. [32]So too, a Levite, when he came to the place and saw him, passed by on the other side. [33]But a Samaritan, as he traveled, came where the man was; and when he saw him, he took pity on him. [34]He went to him and bandaged his wounds, pouring on oil and wine. Then he put the man on his own donkey, brought him to an inn and took care of him. [35]The next day he took out two denarii[c] and gave them to the innkeeper. 'Look after him,' he said, 'and when I return, I will reimburse you for any extra expense you may have.'

[36]"Which of these three do you think was a neighbor to the man who fell into the hands of robbers?"

[37]The expert in the law replied, "The one who had mercy on him."

Jesus told him, "Go and do likewise."

---

[a] 27 Deut. 6:5   [b] 27 Lev. 19:18   [c] 35 A denarius was the usual daily wage of a day laborer (see Matt. 20:2).

At the Home of Martha and Mary

³⁸As Jesus and his disciples were on their way, he came to a village where a woman named Martha opened her home to him. ³⁹She had a sister called Mary, who sat at the Lord's feet listening to what he said. ⁴⁰But Martha was distracted by all the preparations that had to be made. She came to him and asked, "Lord, don't you care that my sister has left me to do the work by myself? Tell her to help me!"

⁴¹"Martha, Martha," the Lord answered, "you are worried and upset about many things, ⁴²but few things are needed—or indeed only one.^a Mary has chosen what is better, and it will not be taken away from her."

The Law of Priorities: Jesus Clarifies Priority One for Martha

Luke 10:38–42

When Martha became preoccupied with impressing her guests, Jesus clarified for her the most important activity. Jesus revealed to her that only "few things are needed—or indeed only one" (Lk 10:42). All through his ministry, Jesus helped people get clarity on the important things. It's the job of the leader.

Jesus' Teaching on Prayer

11 One day Jesus was praying in a certain place. When he finished, one of his disciples said to him, "Lord, teach us to pray, just as John taught his disciples."

²He said to them, "When you pray, say:

"'Father,^b
hallowed be your name,
your kingdom come.^c
³Give us each day our daily bread.
⁴Forgive us our sins,
   for we also forgive everyone who sins
      against us.^d
And lead us not into temptation.^e'"

⁵Then Jesus said to them, "Suppose you have a friend, and you go to him at midnight and say, 'Friend, lend me three loaves of bread; ⁶a friend of mine on a journey has come to me, and I have no food to offer him.' ⁷And suppose the one inside answers, 'Don't bother me. The door is already locked, and my children and I are in bed.

I can't get up and give you anything.' ⁸I tell you, even though he will not get up and give you the bread because of friendship, yet because of your shameless audacity^f he will surely get up and give you as much as you need.

⁹"So I say to you: Ask and it will be given to you; seek and you will find; knock and the door will be opened to you. ¹⁰For everyone who asks receives; the one who seeks finds; and to the one who knocks, the door will be opened.

¹¹"Which of you fathers, if your son asks for^g a fish, will give him a snake instead? ¹²Or if he asks for an egg, will give him a scorpion? ¹³If you then, though you are evil, know how to give good gifts to your children, how much more will your Father in heaven give the Holy Spirit to those who ask him!"

Jesus and Beelzebul

¹⁴Jesus was driving out a demon that was mute. When the demon left, the man who had been mute spoke, and the crowd was amazed. ¹⁵But some of them said, "By Beelzebul, the prince of demons, he is driving out demons." ¹⁶Others tested him by asking for a sign from heaven.

¹⁷Jesus knew their thoughts and said to them: "Any kingdom divided against itself will be ruined, and a house divided against itself will fall. ¹⁸If Satan is divided against himself, how can his kingdom stand? I say this because you claim that I drive out demons by Beelzebul. ¹⁹Now if I drive out demons by Beelzebul, by whom do your followers drive them out? So then, they will be your judges. ²⁰But if I drive out demons by the finger of God, then the kingdom of God has come upon you.

²¹"When a strong man, fully armed, guards his own house, his possessions are safe. ²²But when someone stronger attacks and overpowers him, he takes away the armor in which the man trusted and divides up his plunder.

²³"Whoever is not with me is against me, and whoever does not gather with me scatters.

²⁴"When an impure spirit comes out of a person, it goes through arid places seeking rest and does not find it. Then it says, 'I will return to the house I left.' ²⁵When it arrives, it finds the house

---

^a 42 Some manuscripts *but only one thing is needed*
^b 2 Some manuscripts *Our Father in heaven*   ^c 2 Some manuscripts *come. May your will be done on earth as it is in heaven.*   ^d 4 Greek *everyone who is indebted to us*
^e 4 Some manuscripts *temptation, but deliver us from the evil one*   ^f 8 Or *yet to preserve his good name*   ^g 11 Some manuscripts *for bread, will give him a stone? Or if he asks for*

Jesus Teaches Paternal Leadership and the Priority of Prayer

Luke 11:1–13

Jesus answered his disciples' request for instruction on prayer by giving them a model we call "the Lord's Prayer." In it, Jesus refers to God as "Father." On the heels of that prayer, he teaches about paternal leadership (Lk 11:5–13).

The wonderful father image suggests the strength and respect of a leader as well as the love and concern of a leader. Consider the ingredients of a healthy paternal leader in the home:

1. *His pattern for the family*
   He is to set an example for everyone else, to be a model.

2. *His provision for the family*
   He is to provide for others, insuring they have the resources they need.

3. *His protection for the family*
   He is to keep them from harm's way and make sure they are safe and secure.

4. *His prayer for the family*
   He is to pray for them to reach their potential and become all God intends them to be.

swept clean and put in order. ²⁶Then it goes and takes seven other spirits more wicked than itself, and they go in and live there. And the final condition of that person is worse than the first."

²⁷As Jesus was saying these things, a woman in the crowd called out, "Blessed is the mother who gave you birth and nursed you."

²⁸He replied, "Blessed rather are those who hear the word of God and obey it."

The Sign of Jonah

²⁹As the crowds increased, Jesus said, "This is a wicked generation. It asks for a sign, but none will be given it except the sign of Jonah. ³⁰For as Jonah was a sign to the Ninevites, so also will the Son of Man be to this generation. ³¹The Queen of the South will rise at the judgment with the people of this generation and condemn them, for she came from the ends of the earth to listen to Solomon's wisdom; and now something

greater than Solomon is here. ³²The men of Nineveh will stand up at the judgment with this generation and condemn it, for they repented at the preaching of Jonah; and now something greater than Jonah is here.

The Lamp of the Body

³³"No one lights a lamp and puts it in a place where it will be hidden, or under a bowl. Instead they put it on its stand, so that those who come in may see the light. ³⁴Your eye is the lamp of your body. When your eyes are healthy,[a] your whole body also is full of light. But when they are unhealthy,[b] your body also is full of darkness. ³⁵See to it, then, that the light within you is not darkness. ³⁶Therefore, if your whole body is full of light, and no part of it dark, it will be just as full of light as when a lamp shines its light on you."

Woes on the Pharisees and the Experts in the Law

³⁷When Jesus had finished speaking, a Pharisee invited him to eat with him; so he went in and reclined at the table. ³⁸But the Pharisee was surprised when he noticed that Jesus did not first wash before the meal.

³⁹Then the Lord said to him, "Now then, you Pharisees clean the outside of the cup and dish, but inside you are full of greed and wickedness. ⁴⁰You foolish people! Did not the one who made the outside make the inside also? ⁴¹But now as for what is inside you — be generous to the poor, and everything will be clean for you.

⁴²"Woe to you Pharisees, because you give God a tenth of your mint, rue and all other kinds of garden herbs, but you neglect justice and the love of God. You should have practiced the latter without leaving the former undone.

⁴³"Woe to you Pharisees, because you love the most important seats in the synagogues and respectful greetings in the marketplaces.

⁴⁴"Woe to you, because you are like unmarked graves, which people walk over without knowing it."

⁴⁵One of the experts in the law answered him, "Teacher, when you say these things, you insult us also."

⁴⁶Jesus replied, "And you experts in the law, woe to you, because you load people down with burdens they can hardly carry, and you yourselves will not lift one finger to help them.

---

[a] 34 The Greek for *healthy* here implies *generous*.   [b] 34 The Greek for *unhealthy* here implies *stingy*.

47"Woe to you, because you build tombs for the prophets, and it was your ancestors who killed them. 48So you testify that you approve of what your ancestors did; they killed the prophets, and you build their tombs. 49Because of this, God in his wisdom said, 'I will send them prophets and apostles, some of whom they will kill and others they will persecute.' 50Therefore this generation will be held responsible for the blood of all the prophets that has been shed since the beginning of the world, 51from the blood of Abel to the blood of Zechariah, who was killed between the altar and the sanctuary. Yes, I tell you, this generation will be held responsible for it all.

52"Woe to you experts in the law, because you have taken away the key to knowledge. You yourselves have not entered, and you have hindered those who were entering."

53When Jesus went outside, the Pharisees and the teachers of the law began to oppose him fiercely and to besiege him with questions, 54waiting to catch him in something he might say.

Warnings and Encouragements

12 Meanwhile, when a crowd of many thousands had gathered, so that they were trampling on one another, Jesus began to speak first to his disciples, saying: "Be*a* on your guard against the yeast of the Pharisees, which is hypocrisy. 2There is nothing concealed that will not be disclosed, or hidden that will not be made known. 3What you have said in the dark will be heard in the daylight, and what you have whispered in the ear in the inner rooms will be proclaimed from the roofs.

4"I tell you, my friends, do not be afraid of those who kill the body and after that can do no more. 5But I will show you whom you should fear: Fear him who, after your body has been killed, has authority to throw you into hell. Yes, I tell you, fear him. 6Are not five sparrows sold for two pennies? Yet not one of them is forgotten by God. 7Indeed, the very hairs of your head are all numbered. Don't be afraid; you are worth more than many sparrows.

8"I tell you, whoever publicly acknowledges me before others, the Son of Man will also acknowledge before the angels of God. 9But whoever disowns me before others will be disowned before the angels of God. 10And everyone who speaks a word against the Son of Man will be forgiven, but anyone who blasphemes against the Holy Spirit will not be forgiven.

11"When you are brought before synagogues, rulers and authorities, do not worry about how you will defend yourselves or what you will say, 12for the Holy Spirit will teach you at that time what you should say."

The Parable of the Rich Fool

13Someone in the crowd said to him, "Teacher, tell my brother to divide the inheritance with me."

14Jesus replied, "Man, who appointed me a judge or an arbiter between you?" 15Then he said to them, "Watch out! Be on your guard against all kinds of greed; life does not consist in an abundance of possessions."

16And he told them this parable: "The ground of a certain rich man yielded an abundant harvest. 17He thought to himself, 'What shall I do? I have no place to store my crops.'

18"Then he said, 'This is what I'll do. I will tear down my barns and build bigger ones, and there I will store my surplus grain. 19And I'll say to myself, "You have plenty of grain laid up for many years. Take life easy; eat, drink and be merry."'

20"But God said to him, 'You fool! This very night your life will be demanded from you. Then who will get what you have prepared for yourself?'

21"This is how it will be with whoever stores up things for themselves but is not rich toward God."

Do Not Worry

22Then Jesus said to his disciples: "Therefore I tell you, do not worry about your life, what you will eat; or about your body, what you will wear. 23For life is more than food, and the body more than clothes. 24Consider the ravens: They do not sow or reap, they have no storeroom or barn; yet God feeds them. And how much more valuable you are than birds! 25Who of you by worrying can add a single hour to your life*b*? 26Since you cannot do this very little thing, why do you worry about the rest?

27"Consider how the wild flowers grow. They do not labor or spin. Yet I tell you, not even Solomon in all his splendor was dressed like one of these. 28If that is how God clothes the grass of the field, which is here today, and tomorrow is thrown into the fire, how much more will he clothe you — you of little faith! 29And do not set your heart on what you will eat or drink; do not worry about it. 30For the pagan world runs after

a 1 Or speak to his disciples, saying: "First of all, be   b 25 Or single cubit to your height all such things, and your Father knows that you need them. [31]But seek his kingdom, and these things will be given to you as well.

[32]"Do not be afraid, little flock, for your Father has been pleased to give you the kingdom. [33]Sell your possessions and give to the poor. Provide purses for yourselves that will not wear out, a treasure in heaven that will never fail, where no thief comes near and no moth destroys. [34]For where your treasure is, there your heart will be also.

Watchfulness

[35]"Be dressed ready for service and keep your lamps burning, [36]like servants waiting for their master to return from a wedding banquet, so that when he comes and knocks they can immediately open the door for him. [37]It will be good for those servants whose master finds them watching when he comes. Truly I tell you, he will dress himself to serve, will have them recline at the table and will come and wait on them. [38]It will be good for those servants whose master finds them ready, even if he comes in the middle of the night or toward daybreak. [39]But understand this: If the owner of the house had known at what hour the thief was coming, he would not have let his house be broken into. [40]You also must be ready, because the Son of Man will come at an hour when you do not expect him."

[41]Peter asked, "Lord, are you telling this parable to us, or to everyone?"

[42]The Lord answered, "Who then is the faithful and wise manager, whom the master puts in charge of his servants to give them their food allowance at the proper time? [43]It will be good for that servant whom the master finds doing so when he returns. [44]Truly I tell you, he will put him in charge of all his possessions. [45]But suppose the servant says to himself, 'My master is taking a long time in coming,' and he then begins to beat the other servants, both men and women, and to eat and drink and get drunk. [46]The master of that servant will come on a day when he does not expect him and at an hour he is not aware of. He will cut him to pieces and assign him a place with the unbelievers.

[47]"The servant who knows the master's will and does not get ready or does not do what the master wants will be beaten with many blows. [48]But the one who does not know and does things deserving punishment will be beaten with few blows. From everyone who has been given much, much will be demanded; and from the one who has been entrusted with much, much more will be asked.

Not Peace but Division

[49]"I have come to bring fire on the earth, and how I wish it were already kindled! [50]But I have a baptism to undergo, and what constraint I am under until it is completed! [51]Do you think I came to bring peace on earth? No, I tell you, but division. [52]From now on there will be five in one family divided against each other, three against two and two against three. [53]They will be divided, father against son and son against father, mother against daughter and daughter against mother, mother-in-law against daughter-in-law and daughter-in-law against mother-in-law."

Interpreting the Times

[54]He said to the crowd: "When you see a cloud rising in the west, immediately you say, 'It's going to rain,' and it does. [55]And when the south

---

The Law of Navigation: Jesus Charts the Course for His Disciples

Luke 12:1–59

Jesus provided good instruction for his disciples on issues such as integrity, anxiety, convictions, problem solving, greed, jealousy, priorities and trusting God. Why these topics? Because Jesus intended to navigate life for his followers, to teach them how to live successfully.

If we were to condense the Lord's perspective on success in life, we might say that success involves:

- *Decisions*: We must know the truth and accept it.
- *Servanthood*: We must find a need and fill it.
- *Determination*: We must face a challenge and meet it.
- *Sacrifice*: We must lose our life to find it.
- *Preparation*: We must develop a plan and follow it.
- *Action*: We must discover God's will and obey it.
- *A gift*: We must find our talent and share it.
- *Durability*: We must be tenacious and finish well.

The Law of Navigation: Jesus Helps Listeners Interpret the Times

Luke 12:35–59

Like all good leaders, Jesus left his followers with a plan for the future and gave them some key tools, including:

1. *Lenses:* He modeled the right attitude to approach the future.

2. *A road map:* He warned them about rough roads ahead.

3. *A barometer:* He helped them interpret future conditions.

wind blows, you say, 'It's going to be hot,' and it is. [56]Hypocrites! You know how to interpret the appearance of the earth and the sky. How is it that you don't know how to interpret this present time?

[57]"Why don't you judge for yourselves what is right? [58]As you are going with your adversary to the magistrate, try hard to be reconciled on the way, or your adversary may drag you off to the judge, and the judge turn you over to the officer, and the officer throw you into prison. [59]I tell you, you will not get out until you have paid the last penny."

Repent or Perish

13 Now there were some present at that time who told Jesus about the Galileans whose blood Pilate had mixed with their sacrifices. [2]Jesus answered, "Do you think that these Galileans were worse sinners than all the other Galileans because they suffered this way? [3]I tell you, no! But unless you repent, you too will all perish. [4]Or those eighteen who died when the tower in Siloam fell on them—do you think they were more guilty than all the others living in Jerusalem? [5]I tell you, no! But unless you repent, you too will all perish."

[6]Then he told this parable: "A man had a fig tree growing in his vineyard, and he went to look for fruit on it but did not find any. [7]So he said to the man who took care of the vineyard, 'For three years now I've been coming to look for fruit on this fig tree and haven't found any. Cut it down! Why should it use up the soil?'

[8]"'Sir,' the man replied, 'leave it alone for one

more year, and I'll dig around it and fertilize it. [9]If it bears fruit next year, fine! If not, then cut it down.'"

Jesus Heals a Crippled Woman on the Sabbath

[10]On a Sabbath Jesus was teaching in one of the synagogues, [11]and a woman was there who had been crippled by a spirit for eighteen years. She was bent over and could not straighten up at all. [12]When Jesus saw her, he called her forward and said to her, "Woman, you are set free from your infirmity." [13]Then he put his hands on her, and immediately she straightened up and praised God.

[14]Indignant because Jesus had healed on the Sabbath, the synagogue leader said to the people, "There are six days for work. So come and be healed on those days, not on the Sabbath."

[15]The Lord answered him, "You hypocrites! Doesn't each of you on the Sabbath untie your ox or donkey from the stall and lead it out to give it water? [16]Then should not this woman, a daughter of Abraham, whom Satan has kept bound for eighteen long years, be set free on the Sabbath day from what bound her?"

[17]When he said this, all his opponents were humiliated, but the people were delighted with all the wonderful things he was doing.

The Parables of the Mustard Seed and the Yeast

[18]Then Jesus asked, "What is the kingdom of God like? What shall I compare it to? [19]It is like a mustard seed, which a man took and planted in his garden. It grew and became a tree, and the birds perched in its branches."

[20]Again he asked, "What shall I compare the kingdom of God to? [21]It is like yeast that a woman took and mixed into about sixty pounds[a] of flour until it worked all through the dough."

The Narrow Door

[22]Then Jesus went through the towns and villages, teaching as he made his way to Jerusalem. [23]Someone asked him, "Lord, are only a few people going to be saved?"

He said to them, [24]"Make every effort to enter through the narrow door, because many, I tell you, will try to enter and will not be able to. [25]Once the owner of the house gets up and closes the door, you will stand outside knocking and pleading, 'Sir, open the door for us.'

"But he will answer, 'I don't know you or where you come from.'

[a] 21 Or about 27 kilograms

26"Then you will say, 'We ate and drank with you, and you taught in our streets.'

27"But he will reply, 'I don't know you or where you come from. Away from me, all you evildoers!'

28"There will be weeping there, and gnashing of teeth, when you see Abraham, Isaac and Jacob and all the prophets in the kingdom of God, but you yourselves thrown out. 29People will come from east and west and north and south, and will take their places at the feast in the kingdom of God. 30Indeed there are those who are last who will be first, and first who will be last."

Jesus' Sorrow for Jerusalem

31At that time some Pharisees came to Jesus and said to him, "Leave this place and go somewhere else. Herod wants to kill you."

32He replied, "Go tell that fox, 'I will keep on driving out demons and healing people today and tomorrow, and on the third day I will reach my goal.' 33In any case, I must press on today and tomorrow and the next day — for surely no prophet can die outside Jerusalem!

34"Jerusalem, Jerusalem, you who kill the prophets and stone those sent to you, how often I have longed to gather your children together, as a hen gathers her chicks under her wings, and you were not willing. 35Look, your house is left to you desolate. I tell you, you will not see me again until you say, 'Blessed is he who comes in the name of the Lord.'*a*"

Jesus at a Pharisee's House

14 One Sabbath, when Jesus went to eat in the house of a prominent Pharisee, he was being carefully watched. 2There in front of him was a man suffering from abnormal swelling of his body. 3Jesus asked the Pharisees and experts in the law, "Is it lawful to heal on the Sabbath or not?" 4But they remained silent. So taking hold of the man, he healed him and sent him on his way.

5Then he asked them, "If one of you has a child*b* or an ox that falls into a well on the Sabbath day, will you not immediately pull it out?" 6And they had nothing to say.

7When he noticed how the guests picked the places of honor at the table, he told them this parable: 8"When someone invites you to a wedding feast, do not take the place of honor, for a person more distinguished than you may have been invited. 9If so, the host who invited both of you will come and say to you, 'Give this person your seat.' Then, humiliated, you will have to take the least important place. 10But when you are invited, take the lowest place, so that when your host comes, he will say to you, 'Friend, move up to a better place.' Then you will be honored in the presence of all the other guests. 11For all those who exalt themselves will be humbled, and those who humble themselves will be exalted."

12Then Jesus said to his host, "When you give a luncheon or dinner, do not invite your friends, your brothers or sisters, your relatives, or your rich neighbors; if you do, they may invite you back and so you will be repaid. 13But when you give a banquet, invite the poor, the crippled, the lame, the blind, 14and you will be blessed. Although they cannot repay you, you will be repaid at the resurrection of the righteous."

The Parable of the Great Banquet

15When one of those at the table with him heard this, he said to Jesus, "Blessed is the one who will eat at the feast in the kingdom of God."

16Jesus replied: "A certain man was preparing a great banquet and invited many guests. 17At the time of the banquet he sent his servant to tell those who had been invited, 'Come, for everything is now ready.'

18"But they all alike began to make excuses. The first said, 'I have just bought a field, and I must go and see it. Please excuse me.'

19"Another said, 'I have just bought five yoke of oxen, and I'm on my way to try them out. Please excuse me.'

20"Still another said, 'I just got married, so I can't come.'

21"The servant came back and reported this to his master. Then the owner of the house became angry and ordered his servant, 'Go out quickly into the streets and alleys of the town and bring in the poor, the crippled, the blind and the lame.'

22"'Sir,' the servant said, 'what you ordered has been done, but there is still room.'

23"Then the master told his servant, 'Go out to the roads and country lanes and compel them to come in, so that my house will be full. 24I tell you, not one of those who were invited will get a taste of my banquet.'"

The Cost of Being a Disciple

25Large crowds were traveling with Jesus, and turning to them he said: 26"If anyone comes to me and does not hate father and mother, wife

---

a 35 Psalm 118:26   *b* 5 Some manuscripts *donkey*

> ## Commitment: The Best Leaders Vote with Their Lives
>
> ### Luke 14:26–27
>
> Jesus gave himself wholly to his cause and to his men. Consequently, he could ask them to do the same. When leaders vote with their lives, their followers gain all kinds of security. Jesus' call for commitment both screened the uncommitted and attracted the committed.

and children, brothers and sisters — yes, even their own life — such a person cannot be my disciple. ²⁷And whoever does not carry their cross and follow me cannot be my disciple.

²⁸"Suppose one of you wants to build a tower. Won't you first sit down and estimate the cost to see if you have enough money to complete it? ²⁹For if you lay the foundation and are not able to finish it, everyone who sees it will ridicule you, ³⁰saying, 'This person began to build and wasn't able to finish.'

³¹"Or suppose a king is about to go to war against another king. Won't he first sit down and consider whether he is able with ten thousand men to oppose the one coming against him with twenty thousand? ³²If he is not able, he will send a delegation while the other is still a long way off and will ask for terms of peace. ³³In the same way, those of you who do not give up everything you have cannot be my disciples.

³⁴"Salt is good, but if it loses its saltiness, how

> ## The Law of Navigation: Count the Cost, Then Determine the Direction
>
> ### Luke 14:28–32
>
> In two small but wonderful parables, Jesus speaks about planning and preparation. He teaches listeners to count the cost before taking action, applauds evaluation before taking action and encourages damage prevention through preparation and negotiation. To calculate in this way is not a lack of faith, but foresight based on insight and hindsight.

can it be made salty again? ³⁵It is fit neither for the soil nor for the manure pile; it is thrown out.

"Whoever has ears to hear, let them hear."

The Parable of the Lost Sheep

15 Now the tax collectors and sinners were all gathering around to hear Jesus. ²But the Pharisees and the teachers of the law muttered, "This man welcomes sinners and eats with them."

³Then Jesus told them this parable: ⁴"Suppose one of you has a hundred sheep and loses one of them. Doesn't he leave the ninety-nine in the open country and go after the lost sheep until he finds it? ⁵And when he finds it, he joyfully puts it on his shoulders ⁶and goes home. Then he calls his friends and neighbors together and says, 'Rejoice with me; I have found my lost sheep.' ⁷I tell you that in the same way there will be more rejoicing in heaven over one sinner who repents than over ninety-nine righteous persons who do not need to repent.

The Parable of the Lost Coin

⁸"Or suppose a woman has ten silver coins[a] and loses one. Doesn't she light a lamp, sweep the house and search carefully until she finds it? ⁹And when she finds it, she calls her friends and neighbors together and says, 'Rejoice with me; I have found my lost coin.' ¹⁰In the same way, I tell you, there is rejoicing in the presence of the angels of God over one sinner who repents."

The Parable of the Lost Son

¹¹Jesus continued: "There was a man who had two sons. ¹²The younger one said to his father, 'Father, give me my share of the estate.' So he divided his property between them.

¹³"Not long after that, the younger son got together all he had, set off for a distant country and there squandered his wealth in wild living. ¹⁴After he had spent everything, there was a severe famine in that whole country, and he began to be in need. ¹⁵So he went and hired himself out to a citizen of that country, who sent him to his fields to feed pigs. ¹⁶He longed to fill his stomach with the pods that the pigs were eating, but no one gave him anything.

¹⁷"When he came to his senses, he said, 'How many of my father's hired servants have food to spare, and here I am starving to death! ¹⁸I will set out and go back to my father and say to him: Father, I have sinned against heaven and against

---

[a] 8 Greek *ten drachmas*, each worth about a day's wages

21 QUALITIES

COMPETENCE   A Necessary Step on the Road to Excellence

Luke 14:28–32

LABELING SOMEONE competent or incompetent may seem judgmental and narrow, yet all leaders must possess a level of competence that enables them to get the job done. The kingdom of God cannot do without competence.

Everyone knows that leaders must demonstrate a level of competence in order to gain the trust and respect of followers. No one chooses to follow an incompetent leader over a competent one, regardless of personality. Friendship is not synonymous with leadership; people can like you as a friend but not follow you as a leader. To the degree they feel you are incompetent to lead, they will distance themselves from your leadership.

Competence goes beyond words. It's the leader's ability to *say* it, *plan* it and *do* it in such a way that others know you know your business—and know that they want to follow you. Competence must be sought at every organizational level. Incompetence can be tolerated nowhere. John Gardner once wrote, "The society which scorns excellence in plumbing because plumbing is a humble activity and tolerates shoddiness in philosophy because it is an exalted activity will have neither good plumbing nor good philosophy. Neither its pipes nor its theories will hold water."

Jesus highlights the issue of competence in the two stories recounted in Luke 14. In both stories, what is missing is *competence*. The builder and the king in these stories lacked what it took to get the job done. Therefore the tower never got built and the war never was won. According to Jesus, competence requires three ingredients:

1. *Commitment*
   Jesus said our commitment to him must look like disdain for everyone else. We must pick up our cross and follow him.

2. *Resources*
   Jesus spoke about a builder calculating whether he had enough to finish a tower. Determine whether your resources, gifts, talents and abilities are available to do the job.

3. *Intelligence*
   Jesus spoke about a king seeking counsel to know whether he should go to battle. Part of competence is the insight to know what to do, when to do it, and how to do it.

The combination of these three components spells not only competence, but excellence. It's what makes people follow a leader. So—in what area are you most competent? Where do you excel? What makes others follow you?

For a positive example of competence, see p. 255.

you. ¹⁹I am no longer worthy to be called your son; make me like one of your hired servants.' ²⁰So he got up and went to his father.

"But while he was still a long way off, his father saw him and was filled with compassion for him; he ran to his son, threw his arms around him and kissed him.

²¹"The son said to him, 'Father, I have sinned against heaven and against you. I am no longer worthy to be called your son.'

²²"But the father said to his servants, 'Quick! Bring the best robe and put it on him. Put a ring on his finger and sandals on his feet. ²³Bring the fattened calf and kill it. Let's have a feast and celebrate. ²⁴For this son of mine was dead and is alive again; he was lost and is found.' So they began to celebrate.

²⁵"Meanwhile, the older son was in the field. When he came near the house, he heard mu-sic and dancing. ²⁶So he called one of the servants and asked him what was going on. ²⁷'Your brother has come,' he replied, 'and your father has killed the fattened calf because he has him back safe and sound.'

²⁸"The older brother became angry and refused to go in. So his father went out and pleaded with him. ²⁹But he answered his father, 'Look! All these years I've been slaving for you and never disobeyed your orders. Yet you never gave me even a young goat so I could celebrate with my friends. ³⁰But when this son of yours who has squandered your property with prostitutes comes home, you kill the fattened calf for him!'

³¹"'My son,' the father said, 'you are always with me, and everything I have is yours. ³²But we had to celebrate and be glad, because this brother of yours was dead and is alive again; he was lost and is found.'"

The Law of Priorities: Jesus Focused On the Lost

Luke 15:1–32

Luke 15 is often called the "lost chapter." In this passage, Jesus talks about the lost sheep, the lost coin and the lost son. The sheep got lost naturally; the coin got lost accidentally; and the son got lost willfully. In every case, someone went out to look for what got lost (Lk 15:4, 8, 20).

Jesus attempted to underscore God's passion to seek and save the lost. He would not be diverted from this paramount activity. Jesus believed he needed to underscore this priority because the scribes and Pharisees grumbled about how much time he spent with tax collectors and sinners. Instead of retreating and appeasing the wishes of the religious leaders, he reminded everyone of priority one. Jesus communicated his top priorities using these tools:

1. *Narrative*
   He told memorable stories illustrating his priorities.

2. *Repetition*
   He repeated three accounts that all underscored the priority.

3. *Familiarity*
   He spoke about familiar people and situations.

The Parable of the Shrewd Manager

16 Jesus told his disciples: "There was a rich man whose manager was accused of wasting his possessions. ²So he called him in and asked him, 'What is this I hear about you? Give an account of your management, because you cannot be manager any longer.'

³"The manager said to himself, 'What shall I do now? My master is taking away my job. I'm not strong enough to dig, and I'm ashamed to beg — ⁴I know what I'll do so that, when I lose my job here, people will welcome me into their houses.'

⁵"So he called in each one of his master's debtors. He asked the first, 'How much do you owe my master?'

⁶"'Nine hundred gallons*a* of olive oil,' he replied.

"The manager told him, 'Take your bill, sit down quickly, and make it four hundred and fifty.'

⁷"Then he asked the second, 'And how much do you owe?'

"'A thousand bushels*b* of wheat,' he replied.

"He told him, 'Take your bill and make it eight hundred.'

⁸"The master commended the dishonest manager because he had acted shrewdly. For the people of this world are more shrewd in dealing with their own kind than are the people of the light. ⁹I tell you, use worldly wealth to gain friends for yourselves, so that when it is gone, you will be welcomed into eternal dwellings.

a 6 Or about 3,000 liters   *b* 7 Or about 30 tons

10"Whoever can be trusted with very little can also be trusted with much, and whoever is dishonest with very little will also be dishonest with much. 11So if you have not been trustworthy in handling worldly wealth, who will trust you with true riches? 12And if you have not been trustworthy with someone else's property, who will give you property of your own?

13"No one can serve two masters. Either you will hate the one and love the other, or you will be devoted to the one and despise the other. You cannot serve both God and money."

14The Pharisees, who loved money, heard all this and were sneering at Jesus. 15He said to them, "You are the ones who justify yourselves in the eyes of others, but God knows your hearts. What people value highly is detestable in God's sight.

Additional Teachings

16"The Law and the Prophets were proclaimed until John. Since that time, the good news of the kingdom of God is being preached, and everyone is forcing their way into it. 17It is easier for heaven and earth to disappear than for the least stroke of a pen to drop out of the Law.

18"Anyone who divorces his wife and marries another woman commits adultery, and the man who marries a divorced woman commits adultery.

The Rich Man and Lazarus

19"There was a rich man who was dressed in purple and fine linen and lived in luxury every day. 20At his gate was laid a beggar named Lazarus, covered with sores 21and longing to eat what fell from the rich man's table. Even the dogs came and licked his sores.

22"The time came when the beggar died and the angels carried him to Abraham's side. The rich man also died and was buried. 23In Hades, where he was in torment, he looked up and saw Abraham far away, with Lazarus by his side. 24So he called to him, 'Father Abraham, have pity on me and send Lazarus to dip the tip of his finger in water and cool my tongue, because I am in agony in this fire.'

25"But Abraham replied, 'Son, remember that in your lifetime you received your good things, while Lazarus received bad things, but now he is comforted here and you are in agony. 26And besides all this, between us and you a great chasm has been set in place, so that those who want to go from here to you cannot, nor can anyone cross over from there to us.'

27"He answered, 'Then I beg you, father, send

Lessons from a Lousy Leader

Luke 16:1–13

Jesus' story of an unrighteous manager teaches us lessons about shrewd business and a few subtle truths about leadership. This lousy leader . . .

1. *Violated rule number one: Leadership is not to be used for personal benefit* (v. 1).
   He forgot that leadership is about giving, not getting. Leaders lose the right to be selfish.

2. *Learned that a leader cannot hide his heart* (vv. 1–2).
   Leadership rises or falls to the level of the leader's integrity. Leaders are vulnerable.

3. *Was proactive in facing problems* (v. 3).
   He surmised how he could address the problem. Good leaders aren't afraid to face reality.

4. *Understood the value of relationships* (v. 4).
   He utilized the relationships he had developed already. He received a return on his investment.

5. *Understood the nature of his influence* (vv. 4–5).
   Since leadership is influence, leaders know with whom they have influence—and they go there.

6. *Learned the keys to motivating others* (vv. 5–7).
   Everyone is motivated in different ways. He found ways to make friends and get results.

7. *Reminds us of the value of godly leadership* (vv. 8–10).
   In the end, his master praised his shrewdness; but Jesus has a deeper lesson for us.

Lazarus to my family, ²⁸for I have five brothers. Let him warn them, so that they will not also come to this place of torment.'

²⁹"Abraham replied, 'They have Moses and the Prophets; let them listen to them.'

³⁰"'No, father Abraham,' he said, 'but if someone from the dead goes to them, they will repent.'

³¹"He said to him, 'If they do not listen to Moses and the Prophets, they will not be convinced even if someone rises from the dead.'"

Sin, Faith, Duty

17 Jesus said to his disciples: "Things that cause people to stumble are bound to come, but woe to anyone through whom they come. ²It would be better for them to be thrown into the sea with a millstone tied around their neck than to cause one of these little ones to stumble. ³So watch yourselves.

"If your brother or sister*a* sins against you, rebuke them; and if they repent, forgive them. ⁴Even if they sin against you seven times in a day and seven times come back to you saying 'I repent,' you must forgive them."

⁵The apostles said to the Lord, "Increase our faith!"

⁶He replied, "If you have faith as small as a mustard seed, you can say to this mulberry tree, 'Be uprooted and planted in the sea,' and it will obey you.

⁷"Suppose one of you has a servant plowing or looking after the sheep. Will he say to the servant when he comes in from the field, 'Come along now and sit down to eat'? ⁸Won't he rather say, 'Prepare my supper, get yourself ready and wait on me while I eat and drink; after that you may eat and drink'? ⁹Will he thank the servant because he did what he was told to do? ¹⁰So you also, when you have done everything you were told to do, should say, 'We are unworthy servants; we have only done our duty.'"

Jesus Heals Ten Men With Leprosy

¹¹Now on his way to Jerusalem, Jesus traveled along the border between Samaria and Galilee. ¹²As he was going into a village, ten men who had leprosy*b* met him. They stood at a distance ¹³and called out in a loud voice, "Jesus, Master, have pity on us!"

¹⁴When he saw them, he said, "Go, show yourselves to the priests." And as they went, they were cleansed.

¹⁵One of them, when he saw he was healed, came back, praising God in a loud voice. ¹⁶He threw himself at Jesus' feet and thanked him — and he was a Samaritan.

¹⁷Jesus asked, "Were not all ten cleansed? Where are the other nine? ¹⁸Has no one returned to give praise to God except this foreigner?" ¹⁹Then he said to him, "Rise and go; your faith has made you well."

The Coming of the Kingdom of God

²⁰Once, on being asked by the Pharisees when the kingdom of God would come, Jesus replied, "The coming of the kingdom of God is not something that can be observed, ²¹nor will people say, 'Here it is,' or 'There it is,' because the kingdom of God is in your midst."*c*

²²Then he said to his disciples, "The time is coming when you will long to see one of the days of the Son of Man, but you will not see it. ²³People will tell you, 'There he is!' or 'Here he is!' Do not go running off after them. ²⁴For the Son of Man in his day*d* will be like the lightning, which flashes and lights up the sky from one end to the other. ²⁵But first he must suffer many things and be rejected by this generation.

²⁶"Just as it was in the days of Noah, so also will it be in the days of the Son of Man. ²⁷People were eating, drinking, marrying and being given in marriage up to the day Noah entered the ark. Then the flood came and destroyed them all.

²⁸"It was the same in the days of Lot. People were eating and drinking, buying and selling, planting and building. ²⁹But the day Lot left Sodom, fire and sulfur rained down from heaven and destroyed them all.

³⁰"It will be just like this on the day the Son of Man is revealed. ³¹On that day no one who is on the housetop, with possessions inside, should go down to get them. Likewise, no one in the field should go back for anything. ³²Remember Lot's wife! ³³Whoever tries to keep their life will lose it, and whoever loses their life will preserve it. ³⁴I tell you, on that night two people will be in one bed; one will be taken and the other left. ³⁵Two women will be grinding grain together; one will be taken and the other left." [36]*e*

³⁷"Where, Lord?" they asked.

He replied, "Where there is a dead body, there the vultures will gather."

---

a 3 The Greek word for *brother or sister* (*adelphos*) refers here to a fellow disciple, whether man or woman.   *b* 12 The Greek word traditionally translated *leprosy* was used for various diseases affecting the skin.   *c* 21 Or *is within you*   *d* 24 Some manuscripts do not have *in his day*.   *e* 36 Some manuscripts include here words similar to Matt. 24:40.

The Parable of the Persistent Widow

18 Then Jesus told his disciples a parable to show them that they should always pray and not give up. [2]He said: "In a certain town there was a judge who neither feared God nor cared what people thought. [3]And there was a widow in that town who kept coming to him with the plea, 'Grant me justice against my adversary.'

[4]"For some time he refused. But finally he said to himself, 'Even though I don't fear God or care what people think, [5]yet because this widow keeps bothering me, I will see that she gets justice, so that she won't eventually come and attack me!'"

[6]And the Lord said, "Listen to what the unjust judge says. [7]And will not God bring about justice for his chosen ones, who cry out to him day and night? Will he keep putting them off? [8]I tell you, he will see that they get justice, and quickly. However, when the Son of Man comes, will he find faith on the earth?"

The Parable of the Pharisee and the Tax Collector

[9]To some who were confident of their own righteousness and looked down on everyone else, Jesus told this parable: [10]"Two men went up to the temple to pray, one a Pharisee and the other a tax collector. [11]The Pharisee stood by himself and prayed: 'God, I thank you that I am not like other people — robbers, evildoers, adulterers — or even like this tax collector. [12]I fast twice a week and give a tenth of all I get.'

[13]"But the tax collector stood at a distance. He would not even look up to heaven, but beat his breast and said, 'God, have mercy on me, a sinner.'

[14]"I tell you that this man, rather than the other, went home justified before God. For all those who exalt themselves will be humbled, and those who humble themselves will be exalted."

The Little Children and Jesus

[15]People were also bringing babies to Jesus for him to place his hands on them. When the disciples saw this, they rebuked them. [16]But Jesus called the children to him and said, "Let the little children come to me, and do not hinder them, for the kingdom of God belongs to such as these. [17]Truly I tell you, anyone who will not receive the kingdom of God like a little child will never enter it."

The Rich and the Kingdom of God

[18]A certain ruler asked him, "Good teacher, what must I do to inherit eternal life?"

[19]"Why do you call me good?" Jesus answered. "No one is good — except God alone. [20]You know the commandments: 'You shall not commit adultery, you shall not murder, you shall not steal, you shall not give false testimony, honor your father and mother.'[a]"

[21]"All these I have kept since I was a boy," he said.

[22]When Jesus heard this, he said to him, "You still lack one thing. Sell everything you have and give to the poor, and you will have treasure in heaven. Then come, follow me."

[23]When he heard this, he became very sad, because he was very wealthy. [24]Jesus looked at him and said, "How hard it is for the rich to enter the kingdom of God! [25]Indeed, it is easier for a camel to go through the eye of a needle than for someone who is rich to enter the kingdom of God."

[26]Those who heard this asked, "Who then can be saved?"

[27]Jesus replied, "What is impossible with man is possible with God."

[28]Peter said to him, "We have left all we had to follow you!"

[29]"Truly I tell you," Jesus said to them, "no one who has left home or wife or brothers or

[a] 20 Exodus 20:12-16; Deut. 5:16-20

Commitment: The Rich Young Ruler Fails the Test

Luke 18:18–23

When a rich young man approached Jesus to ask about eternal life, the Lord gave him a radical imperative: Sell all you possess and give it to the poor, then come and follow me.

Jesus didn't say this to everyone. In fact, he said it only to his disciples. He knew this man needed the challenge, even though he refused to accept it. Only greed held him back from freedom. Even though he claimed to obey all the commands, he miserably failed at the first one: "You shall have no other gods before me" (Ex 20:3).

Jesus went straight to the central issue, preventing him from making a commitment he desperately needed to make. The man walked away, full of sadness. He clung to what he had instead of committing to what he could obtain.

sisters or parents or children for the sake of the kingdom of God [30]will fail to receive many times as much in this age, and in the age to come eternal life."

Jesus Predicts His Death a Third Time

[31]Jesus took the Twelve aside and told them, "We are going up to Jerusalem, and everything that is written by the prophets about the Son of Man will be fulfilled. [32]He will be delivered over to the Gentiles. They will mock him, insult him and spit on him; [33]they will flog him and kill him. On the third day he will rise again."

[34]The disciples did not understand any of this. Its meaning was hidden from them, and they did not know what he was talking about.

A Blind Beggar Receives His Sight

[35]As Jesus approached Jericho, a blind man was sitting by the roadside begging. [36]When he heard the crowd going by, he asked what was happening. [37]They told him, "Jesus of Nazareth is passing by."

[38]He called out, "Jesus, Son of David, have mercy on me!"

[39]Those who led the way rebuked him and told him to be quiet, but he shouted all the more, "Son of David, have mercy on me!"

[40]Jesus stopped and ordered the man to be brought to him. When he came near, Jesus asked him, [41]"What do you want me to do for you?"

"Lord, I want to see," he replied.

[42]Jesus said to him, "Receive your sight; your faith has healed you." [43]Immediately he received his sight and followed Jesus, praising God. When all the people saw it, they also praised God.

Zacchaeus the Tax Collector

19 Jesus entered Jericho and was passing through. [2]A man was there by the name of Zacchaeus; he was a chief tax collector and was wealthy. [3]He wanted to see who Jesus was, but because he was short he could not see over the crowd. [4]So he ran ahead and climbed a sycamore-fig tree to see him, since Jesus was coming that way.

[5]When Jesus reached the spot, he looked up and said to him, "Zacchaeus, come down immediately. I must stay at your house today." [6]So he came down at once and welcomed him gladly.

[7]All the people saw this and began to mutter, "He has gone to be the guest of a sinner."

[8]But Zacchaeus stood up and said to the Lord, "Look, Lord! Here and now I give half of my possessions to the poor, and if I have cheated anybody out of anything, I will pay back four times the amount."

[9]Jesus said to him, "Today salvation has come to this house, because this man, too, is a son of Abraham. [10]For the Son of Man came to seek and to save the lost."

The Parable of the Ten Minas

[11]While they were listening to this, he went on to tell them a parable, because he was near Jerusalem and the people thought that the kingdom of God was going to appear at once. [12]He said: "A man of noble birth went to a distant country to have himself appointed king and then to return. [13]So he called ten of his servants and gave them ten minas.[a] 'Put this money to work,' he said, 'until I come back.'

[14]"But his subjects hated him and sent a delegation after him to say, 'We don't want this man to be our king.'

[15]"He was made king, however, and returned home. Then he sent for the servants to whom he had given the money, in order to find out what they had gained with it.

[16]"The first one came and said, 'Sir, your mina has earned ten more.'

[17]"'Well done, my good servant!' his master replied. 'Because you have been trustworthy in a very small matter, take charge of ten cities.'

[18]"The second came and said, 'Sir, your mina has earned five more.'

[19]"His master answered, 'You take charge of five cities.'

[20]"Then another servant came and said, 'Sir, here is your mina; I have kept it laid away in a piece of cloth. [21]I was afraid of you, because you

---

[a] 13 A mina was about three months' wages.

The Law of Influence: Jesus Knew Influence Had a Ripple Effect

Luke 19:1–27

During his time with Jesus, Zacchaeus pledged to give half of his possessions to the poor and to repay those he had defrauded four times what he had taken. Immediately afterwards, Jesus declared that good stewards will be rewarded. God rewards good stewardship, multiplying the influence of godly leaders.

are a hard man. You take out what you did not put in and reap what you did not sow.'

22"His master replied, 'I will judge you by your own words, you wicked servant! You knew, did you, that I am a hard man, taking out what I did not put in, and reaping what I did not sow? 23Why then didn't you put my money on deposit, so that when I came back, I could have collected it with interest?'

24"Then he said to those standing by, 'Take his mina away from him and give it to the one who has ten minas.'

25"'Sir,' they said, 'he already has ten!'

26"He replied, 'I tell you that to everyone who has, more will be given, but as for the one who has nothing, even what they have will be taken away. 27But those enemies of mine who did not want me to be king over them — bring them here and kill them in front of me.'"

Jesus Comes to Jerusalem as King

28After Jesus had said this, he went on ahead, going up to Jerusalem. 29As he approached Bethphage and Bethany at the hill called the Mount of Olives, he sent two of his disciples, saying to them, 30"Go to the village ahead of you, and as you enter it, you will find a colt tied there, which

Stewardship: Leaders Are Brokers of Resources

Luke 19:11–26

Jesus told a story about a landowner who gave three men some funds to spend, save, or invest. Each did as he saw fit, and when the owner returned, he rewarded them according to how wisely they used their resources. Those who multiplied what had been entrusted to them received even more to use. The one who failed had even his little money taken away.

Our Lord wants us to remember that leaders are brokers of the resources they have been given. Those resources may include people, budget, time, wisdom and talents. When leaders broker those resources well, God rewards them and gives them even more to invest. When they fail, they lose what little they have.

This is a sobering truth, but one that leaders would do well to remember. Do you want more resources? If so, what are you doing with what you already have?

no one has ever ridden. Untie it and bring it here. 31If anyone asks you, 'Why are you untying it?' say, 'The Lord needs it.'"

32Those who were sent ahead went and found it just as he had told them. 33As they were untying the colt, its owners asked them, "Why are you untying the colt?"

34They replied, "The Lord needs it."

35They brought it to Jesus, threw their cloaks on the colt and put Jesus on it. 36As he went along, people spread their cloaks on the road.

37When he came near the place where the road goes down the Mount of Olives, the whole crowd of disciples began joyfully to praise God in loud voices for all the miracles they had seen:

38"Blessed is the king who comes in the name of the Lord!"[a]

"Peace in heaven and glory in the highest!"

39Some of the Pharisees in the crowd said to Jesus, "Teacher, rebuke your disciples!"

40"I tell you," he replied, "if they keep quiet, the stones will cry out."

41As he approached Jerusalem and saw the city, he wept over it 42and said, "If you, even you, had only known on this day what would bring you peace — but now it is hidden from your eyes. 43The days will come upon you when your enemies will build an embankment against you and encircle you and hem you in on every side. 44They will dash you to the ground, you and the children within your walls. They will not leave one stone on another, because you did not recognize the time of God's coming to you."

Jesus at the Temple

45When Jesus entered the temple courts, he began to drive out those who were selling. 46"It is written," he said to them, "'My house will be a house of prayer'[b]; but you have made it 'a den of robbers.'[c]"

47Every day he was teaching at the temple. But the chief priests, the teachers of the law and the leaders among the people were trying to kill him. 48Yet they could not find any way to do it, because all the people hung on his words.

The Authority of Jesus Questioned

20 One day as Jesus was teaching the people in the temple courts and proclaiming the good news, the chief priests and the teachers of the law, together with the elders, came up to

---

[a] 38 Psalm 118:26   [b] 46 Isaiah 56:7   [c] 46 Jer. 7:11

him. [2]"Tell us by what authority you are doing these things," they said. "Who gave you this authority?"

[3]He replied, "I will also ask you a question. Tell me: [4]John's baptism — was it from heaven, or of human origin?"

[5]They discussed it among themselves and said, "If we say, 'From heaven,' he will ask, 'Why didn't you believe him?' [6]But if we say, 'Of human origin,' all the people will stone us, because they are persuaded that John was a prophet."

[7]So they answered, "We don't know where it was from."

[8]Jesus said, "Neither will I tell you by what authority I am doing these things."

The Parable of the Tenants

[9]He went on to tell the people this parable: "A man planted a vineyard, rented it to some farmers and went away for a long time. [10]At harvest time he sent a servant to the tenants so they would give him some of the fruit of the vineyard. But the tenants beat him and sent him away empty-handed. [11]He sent another servant, but that one also they beat and treated shamefully and sent away empty-handed. [12]He sent still a third, and they wounded him and threw him out.

[13]"Then the owner of the vineyard said, 'What shall I do? I will send my son, whom I love; perhaps they will respect him.'

[14]"But when the tenants saw him, they talked the matter over. 'This is the heir,' they said. 'Let's kill him, and the inheritance will be ours.' [15]So they threw him out of the vineyard and killed him.

"What then will the owner of the vineyard do to them? [16]He will come and kill those tenants and give the vineyard to others."

When the people heard this, they said, "God forbid!"

[17]Jesus looked directly at them and asked, "Then what is the meaning of that which is written:

"'The stone the builders rejected
　has become the cornerstone'[a]?

[18]Everyone who falls on that stone will be broken to pieces; anyone on whom it falls will be crushed."

[19]The teachers of the law and the chief priests looked for a way to arrest him immediately, because they knew he had spoken this parable against them. But they were afraid of the people.

Paying Taxes to Caesar

[20]Keeping a close watch on him, they sent spies, who pretended to be sincere. They hoped to catch Jesus in something he said, so that they might hand him over to the power and authority of the governor. [21]So the spies questioned him: "Teacher, we know that you speak and teach what is right, and that you do not show partiality but teach the way of God in accordance with the truth. [22]Is it right for us to pay taxes to Caesar or not?"

[23]He saw through their duplicity and said to them, [24]"Show me a denarius. Whose image and inscription are on it?"

---

[a] 17 Psalm 118:22

The Law of Intuition: Jesus Discerned the Real Issue Was Surrender

Luke 20:19–26

One day the scribes sent spies to trap Jesus, asking about whether it was right to pay taxes to Caesar. They knew that if he said yes, they could label him a traitor. If he said no, they could report him to the Roman authorities. They thought they had a perfect plan to silence this radical leader.

In a classic reversal, Jesus turned the tables on them. Because he practiced the Law of Intuition, he was able to see past the facade they had erected. Taxes weren't the issue; surrender was the issue. So Jesus answered their question with another question. Whose image was on the coin they showed him? He meant that any object stamped with a person's image belongs to the individual pictured. This coin carried Caesar's image, so they were to surrender that coin to Caesar. On the other hand, God had stamped his image on *them*! They had been made in his image and should therefore surrender themselves to God.

What a memorable lesson! No wonder they became silent. This intuitive Leader answered their question by quickly getting to the real issue.

"Caesar's," they replied.

[25] He said to them, "Then give back to Caesar what is Caesar's, and to God what is God's."

[26] They were unable to trap him in what he had said there in public. And astonished by his answer, they became silent.

The Resurrection and Marriage

[27] Some of the Sadducees, who say there is no resurrection, came to Jesus with a question. [28] "Teacher," they said, "Moses wrote for us that if a man's brother dies and leaves a wife but no children, the man must marry the widow and raise up offspring for his brother. [29] Now there were seven brothers. The first one married a woman and died childless. [30] The second [31] and then the third married her, and in the same way the seven died, leaving no children. [32] Finally, the woman died too. [33] Now then, at the resurrection whose wife will she be, since the seven were married to her?"

[34] Jesus replied, "The people of this age marry and are given in marriage. [35] But those who are considered worthy of taking part in the age to come and in the resurrection from the dead will neither marry nor be given in marriage, [36] and they can no longer die; for they are like the angels. They are God's children, since they are children of the resurrection. [37] But in the account of the burning bush, even Moses showed that the dead rise, for he calls the Lord 'the God of Abraham, and the God of Isaac, and the God of Jacob.'[a] [38] He is not the God of the dead, but of the living, for to him all are alive."

[39] Some of the teachers of the law responded, "Well said, teacher!" [40] And no one dared to ask him any more questions.

Whose Son Is the Messiah?

[41] Then Jesus said to them, "Why is it said that the Messiah is the son of David? [42] David himself declares in the Book of Psalms:

"'The Lord said to my Lord:
  "Sit at my right hand
[43] until I make your enemies
  a footstool for your feet."'[b]

[44] David calls him 'Lord.' How then can he be his son?"

Warning Against the Teachers of the Law

[45] While all the people were listening, Jesus said to his disciples, [46] "Beware of the teachers of the law. They like to walk around in flowing robes and love to be greeted with respect in the marketplaces and have the most important seats in the synagogues and the places of honor at banquets. [47] They devour widows' houses and for a show make lengthy prayers. These men will be punished most severely."

The Widow's Offering

21 As Jesus looked up, he saw the rich putting their gifts into the temple treasury. [2] He also saw a poor widow put in two very small copper coins. [3] "Truly I tell you," he said, "this poor widow has put in more than all the others. [4] All these people gave their gifts out of their wealth; but she out of her poverty put in all she had to live on."

The Destruction of the Temple and Signs of the End Times

[5] Some of his disciples were remarking about how the temple was adorned with beautiful stones and with gifts dedicated to God. But Jesus said, [6] "As for what you see here, the time will come when not one stone will be left on another; every one of them will be thrown down."

[7] "Teacher," they asked, "when will these things happen? And what will be the sign that they are about to take place?"

[8] He replied: "Watch out that you are not deceived. For many will come in my name, claiming, 'I am he,' and, 'The time is near.' Do not follow them. [9] When you hear of wars and uprisings, do not be frightened. These things must happen first, but the end will not come right away."

[10] Then he said to them: "Nation will rise against nation, and kingdom against kingdom. [11] There will be great earthquakes, famines and pestilences in various places, and fearful events and great signs from heaven.

[12] "But before all this, they will seize you and persecute you. They will hand you over to synagogues and put you in prison, and you will be brought before kings and governors, and all on account of my name. [13] And so you will bear testimony to me. [14] But make up your mind not to worry beforehand how you will defend yourselves. [15] For I will give you words and wisdom that none of your adversaries will be able to resist or contradict. [16] You will be betrayed even by parents, brothers and sisters, relatives and friends, and they will put some of you to death. [17] Everyone will hate you because of me. [18] But not a hair of your head will perish. [19] Stand firm, and you will win life.

---

[a] 37 Exodus 3:6   [b] 43 Psalm 110:1

²⁰"When you see Jerusalem being surrounded by armies, you will know that its desolation is near. ²¹Then let those who are in Judea flee to the mountains, let those in the city get out, and let those in the country not enter the city. ²²For this is the time of punishment in fulfillment of all that has been written. ²³How dreadful it will be in those days for pregnant women and nursing mothers! There will be great distress in the land and wrath against this people. ²⁴They will fall by the sword and will be taken as prisoners to all the nations. Jerusalem will be trampled on by the Gentiles until the times of the Gentiles are fulfilled.

²⁵"There will be signs in the sun, moon and stars. On the earth, nations will be in anguish and perplexity at the roaring and tossing of the sea. ²⁶People will faint from terror, apprehensive of what is coming on the world, for the heavenly bodies will be shaken. ²⁷At that time they will see the Son of Man coming in a cloud with power and great glory. ²⁸When these things begin to take place, stand up and lift up your heads, because your redemption is drawing near."

²⁹He told them this parable: "Look at the fig tree and all the trees. ³⁰When they sprout leaves, you can see for yourselves and know that summer is near. ³¹Even so, when you see these things happening, you know that the kingdom of God is near.

³²"Truly I tell you, this generation will certainly not pass away until all these things have happened. ³³Heaven and earth will pass away, but my words will never pass away.

³⁴"Be careful, or your hearts will be weighed down with carousing, drunkenness and the anxieties of life, and that day will close on you suddenly like a trap. ³⁵For it will come on all those who live on the face of the whole earth. ³⁶Be always on the watch, and pray that you may be able to escape all that is about to happen, and that you may be able to stand before the Son of Man."

³⁷Each day Jesus was teaching at the temple, and each evening he went out to spend the night on the hill called the Mount of Olives, ³⁸and all the people came early in the morning to hear him at the temple.

Judas Agrees to Betray Jesus

22 Now the Festival of Unleavened Bread, called the Passover, was approaching, ²and the chief priests and the teachers of the law were looking for some way to get rid of Jesus, for they were afraid of the people. ³Then Satan entered Judas, called Iscariot, one of the Twelve. ⁴And Judas went to the chief priests and the officers of the temple guard and discussed with them how he might betray Jesus. ⁵They were delighted and agreed to give him money. ⁶He consented, and watched for an opportunity to hand Jesus over to them when no crowd was present.

The Last Supper

⁷Then came the day of Unleavened Bread on which the Passover lamb had to be sacrificed. ⁸Jesus sent Peter and John, saying, "Go and make preparations for us to eat the Passover."

⁹"Where do you want us to prepare for it?" they asked.

¹⁰He replied, "As you enter the city, a man carrying a jar of water will meet you. Follow him to the house that he enters, ¹¹and say to the owner of the house, 'The Teacher asks: Where is the guest room, where I may eat the Passover with my disciples?' ¹²He will show you a large room upstairs, all furnished. Make preparations there."

¹³They left and found things just as Jesus had told them. So they prepared the Passover.

¹⁴When the hour came, Jesus and his apostles reclined at the table. ¹⁵And he said to them,

---

The Law of Addition:
Judas Fails the Test
of Leadership

Luke 22:1–23

While Judas had accompanied Jesus for three-and-a-half years, enjoying the mentoring of Christ, he never learned the fundamentals of leadership. Luke 22 records Judas's betrayal of Jesus on the night of the Passover feast. Even though Jesus had served Judas supper, and even washed his feet (Jn 13:1–7), Judas missed the lesson on servanthood. He didn't add value in return. He joined the others in a discussion on who was the greatest (Lk 22:24), then left to betray Jesus, turning him over to the Jewish authorities.

That night Judas led the entire team of disciples in failing the test of Jesus' style of leadership: servanthood.

"I have eagerly desired to eat this Passover with you before I suffer. [16]For I tell you, I will not eat it again until it finds fulfillment in the kingdom of God."

[17]After taking the cup, he gave thanks and said, "Take this and divide it among you. [18]For I tell you I will not drink again from the fruit of the vine until the kingdom of God comes."

[19]And he took bread, gave thanks and broke it, and gave it to them, saying, "This is my body given for you; do this in remembrance of me."

[20]In the same way, after the supper he took the cup, saying, "This cup is the new covenant in my blood, which is poured out for you.[a] [21]But the hand of him who is going to betray me is with mine on the table. [22]The Son of Man will go as it has been decreed. But woe to that man who betrays him!" [23]They began to question among themselves which of them it might be who would do this.

[24]A dispute also arose among them as to which of them was considered to be greatest. [25]Jesus said to them, "The kings of the Gentiles lord it over them; and those who exercise authority over them call themselves Benefactors. [26]But you are not to be like that. Instead, the greatest among you should be like the youngest, and the one who rules like the one who serves. [27]For who is greater, the one who is at the table or the one who serves? Is it not the one who is at the table? But I am among you as one who serves. [28]You are those who have stood by me in my trials. [29]And I confer on you a kingdom, just as my Father conferred one on me, [30]so that you may eat and drink at my table in my kingdom and sit on thrones, judging the twelve tribes of Israel.

[31]"Simon, Simon, Satan has asked to sift all of you as wheat. [32]But I have prayed for you, Simon, that your faith may not fail. And when you have turned back, strengthen your brothers."

[33]But he replied, "Lord, I am ready to go with you to prison and to death."

[34]Jesus answered, "I tell you, Peter, before the rooster crows today, you will deny three times that you know me."

[35]Then Jesus asked them, "When I sent you without purse, bag or sandals, did you lack anything?"

"Nothing," they answered.

[36]He said to them, "But now if you have a purse, take it, and also a bag; and if you don't have a sword, sell your cloak and buy one. [37]It is written: 'And he was numbered with the transgressors'[b]; and I tell you that this must be ful-

filled in me. Yes, what is written about me is reaching its fulfillment."

[38]The disciples said, "See, Lord, here are two swords."

"That's enough!" he replied.

Jesus Prays on the Mount of Olives

[39]Jesus went out as usual to the Mount of Olives, and his disciples followed him. [40]On reaching the place, he said to them, "Pray that you will not fall into temptation." [41]He withdrew about a stone's throw beyond them, knelt down and prayed, [42]"Father, if you are willing, take this cup from me; yet not my will, but yours be done." [43]An angel from heaven appeared to him and strengthened him. [44]And being in anguish, he prayed more earnestly, and his sweat was like drops of blood falling to the ground.[c]

[45]When he rose from prayer and went back to the disciples, he found them asleep, exhausted from sorrow. [46]"Why are you sleeping?" he asked them. "Get up and pray so that you will not fall into temptation."

---

[a] 19,20 Some manuscripts do not have *given for you . . . poured out for you.*　[b] 37 Isaiah 53:12　[c] 43,44 Many early manuscripts do not have verses 43 and 44.

Leaders and Their Gethsemanes

Luke 22:39–46

At times all leaders feel alone, as when they pioneer new territory. Jesus endured one of his loneliest times in the Garden of Gethsemane. Just hours before he would be tried, tortured and crucified, every one of his team deserted him. His story in the garden provides us with one of the greatest examples in history of a leader's commitment.

Every leader who does something significant for God experiences a Gethsemane. What can we learn about this lonely season? Gethsemane is the place where . . .

1. spiritual battles occur (vv. 40–44).
2. loneliness is felt (v. 41).
3. honesty is expressed (vv. 41–42).
4. submission is required (v. 42).
5. strength is received (v. 43).

Jesus Arrested

⁴⁷While he was still speaking a crowd came up, and the man who was called Judas, one of the Twelve, was leading them. He approached Jesus to kiss him, ⁴⁸but Jesus asked him, "Judas, are you betraying the Son of Man with a kiss?"

⁴⁹When Jesus' followers saw what was going to happen, they said, "Lord, should we strike with our swords?" ⁵⁰And one of them struck the servant of the high priest, cutting off his right ear.

⁵¹But Jesus answered, "No more of this!" And he touched the man's ear and healed him.

⁵²Then Jesus said to the chief priests, the officers of the temple guard, and the elders, who had come for him, "Am I leading a rebellion, that you have come with swords and clubs? ⁵³Every day I was with you in the temple courts, and you did not lay a hand on me. But this is your hour—when darkness reigns."

Peter Disowns Jesus

⁵⁴Then seizing him, they led him away and took him into the house of the high priest. Peter followed at a distance. ⁵⁵And when some there had kindled a fire in the middle of the courtyard and had sat down together, Peter sat down with them. ⁵⁶A servant girl saw him seated there in the firelight. She looked closely at him and said, "This man was with him."

⁵⁷But he denied it. "Woman, I don't know him," he said.

⁵⁸A little later someone else saw him and said, "You also are one of them."

"Man, I am not!" Peter replied.

⁵⁹About an hour later another asserted, "Certainly this fellow was with him, for he is a Galilean."

⁶⁰Peter replied, "Man, I don't know what you're talking about!" Just as he was speaking, the rooster crowed. ⁶¹The Lord turned and looked straight at Peter. Then Peter remembered the word the Lord had spoken to him: "Before the rooster crows today, you will disown me three times." ⁶²And he went outside and wept bitterly.

The Guards Mock Jesus

⁶³The men who were guarding Jesus began mocking and beating him. ⁶⁴They blindfolded him and demanded, "Prophesy! Who hit you?" ⁶⁵And they said many other insulting things to him.

Jesus Before Pilate and Herod

⁶⁶At daybreak the council of the elders of the people, both the chief priests and the teachers of the law, met together, and Jesus was led before them. ⁶⁷"If you are the Messiah," they said, "tell us."

Jesus answered, "If I tell you, you will not believe me, ⁶⁸and if I asked you, you would not answer. ⁶⁹But from now on, the Son of Man will be seated at the right hand of the mighty God."

⁷⁰They all asked, "Are you then the Son of God?"

He replied, "You say that I am."

⁷¹Then they said, "Why do we need any more testimony? We have heard it from his own lips."

23 Then the whole assembly rose and led him off to Pilate. ²And they began to accuse him, saying, "We have found this man subverting our nation. He opposes payment of taxes to Caesar and claims to be Messiah, a king."

³So Pilate asked Jesus, "Are you the king of the Jews?"

"You have said so," Jesus replied.

⁴Then Pilate announced to the chief priests and the crowd, "I find no basis for a charge against this man."

⁵But they insisted, "He stirs up the people all over Judea by his teaching. He started in Galilee and has come all the way here."

⁶On hearing this, Pilate asked if the man was a Galilean. ⁷When he learned that Jesus was under Herod's jurisdiction, he sent him to Herod, who was also in Jerusalem at that time.

⁸When Herod saw Jesus, he was greatly pleased, because for a long time he had been wanting to see him. From what he had heard about him, he hoped to see him perform a sign of some sort. ⁹He plied him with many questions, but Jesus gave him no answer. ¹⁰The chief priests and the teachers of the law were standing there, vehemently accusing him. ¹¹Then Herod and his soldiers ridiculed and mocked him. Dressing him in an elegant robe, they sent him back to Pilate. ¹²That day Herod and Pilate became friends—before this they had been enemies.

¹³Pilate called together the chief priests, the rulers and the people, ¹⁴and said to them, "You brought me this man as one who was inciting the people to rebellion. I have examined him in your presence and have found no basis for your charges against him. ¹⁵Neither has Herod, for he sent him back to us; as you can see, he has done nothing to deserve death. ¹⁶Therefore, I will punish him and then release him." ^[17]^a

---

^a 17 Some manuscripts include here words similar to Matt. 27:15 and Mark 15:6.

21 QUALITIES

COMMITMENT Jesus Christ vs. Simon Peter

Luke 22:54–62

LUKE RECORDS a stark contrast between the commitment of two leaders, Jesus Christ and Simon Peter. While Jesus remained resolutely committed to his cause and his people in the face of betrayal and rejection, Simon Peter ran away. Although the big fisherman claimed he would never deny his Master, he did so three times before the night ended.

While Peter emphatically denied Christ around a little courtyard fire, that moment merely expressed the condition of his heart. His commitment level had already drained away in the Garden of Gethsemane. There he felt helpless, powerless to maintain the promise he had made (Mt 26:35).

When our commitment drains away, we follow the same progression as Peter:

Stage 1: His following became distant.

"Peter followed at a distance" (Lk 22:54). This is not what Jesus had in mind in Matthew 16:24. Peter is still following Christ, but incognito. He's no longer ready to die.

Stage 2: His fellowship became divided.

"Peter sat down with them" (22:55). Now the guilty disciple is mixing with an uncommitted crowd. He's a man without a country. He's torn between the apathetic and the committed.

Stage 3: His faith became deluded.

"But he denied it. 'Woman, I don't know him'" (22:57). His words now reveal his weakness, even among men and women who pose no immediate threat to him.

Stage 4: His fervor became denial.

"Peter replied, 'Man, I don't know what you're talking about!'" (22:60). Peter rejects any association with Jesus. His words no longer display apathy, but rejection.

Levels of Commitment

Jesus always related to people at the level of commitment they were ready to make. Note four levels of commitment in Jesus' disciples:

Level One: Come and See

This is the curiosity level (see Jn 1:35–51). At this stage Jesus' interaction is light and easy. When people are here, look for chemistry and faithfulness.

Level Two: Come and Follow

This is the commitment level (see Lk 5:1–11). Jesus' words now call for some commitment. The person is ready to be challenged. Look for hunger and teachability.

Level Three: Come and Surrender

This is the conviction level (see Mk 8:34–35). This step is appropriate only after deep relationship and mutual trust have developed. Look for initiative and determination.

Level Four: Come and Multiply

This is the commissioned level (see Mt 28:19–20). Here, Jesus calls his men to reproduce what he did with them. Look for leadership and people skills.

For a positive example of commitment, see p. 1301.

¹⁸But the whole crowd shouted, "Away with this man! Release Barabbas to us!" ¹⁹(Barabbas had been thrown into prison for an insurrection in the city, and for murder.)

²⁰Wanting to release Jesus, Pilate appealed to them again. ²¹But they kept shouting, "Crucify him! Crucify him!"

²²For the third time he spoke to them: "Why? What crime has this man committed? I have found in him no grounds for the death penalty. Therefore I will have him punished and then release him."

²³But with loud shouts they insistently demanded that he be crucified, and their shouts prevailed. ²⁴So Pilate decided to grant their demand. ²⁵He released the man who had been thrown into prison for insurrection and murder, the one they asked for, and surrendered Jesus to their will.

The Crucifixion of Jesus

²⁶As the soldiers led him away, they seized Simon from Cyrene, who was on his way in from the country, and put the cross on him and made him carry it behind Jesus. ²⁷A large number of people followed him, including women who mourned and wailed for him. ²⁸Jesus turned and said to them, "Daughters of Jerusalem, do not weep for me; weep for yourselves and for your children. ²⁹For the time will come when you will say, 'Blessed are the childless women, the wombs that never bore and the breasts that never nursed!' ³⁰Then

" 'they will say to the mountains, "Fall on us!"
and to the hills, "Cover us!" '[a]

³¹For if people do these things when the tree is green, what will happen when it is dry?"

³²Two other men, both criminals, were also led out with him to be executed. ³³When they came to the place called the Skull, they crucified him there, along with the criminals — one on his right, the other on his left. ³⁴Jesus said, "Father, forgive them, for they do not know what they are doing."[b] And they divided up his clothes by casting lots.

³⁵The people stood watching, and the rulers even sneered at him. They said, "He saved others; let him save himself if he is God's Messiah, the Chosen One."

³⁶The soldiers also came up and mocked him. They offered him wine vinegar ³⁷and said, "If you are the king of the Jews, save yourself."

³⁸There was a written notice above him, which read: THIS IS THE KING OF THE JEWS.

³⁹One of the criminals who hung there hurled

---

[a] 30 Hosea 10:8   [b] 34 Some early manuscripts do not have this sentence.

---

insults at him: "Aren't you the Messiah? Save yourself and us!"

⁴⁰But the other criminal rebuked him. "Don't you fear God," he said, "since you are under the same sentence? ⁴¹We are punished justly, for we are getting what our deeds deserve. But this man has done nothing wrong."

⁴²Then he said, "Jesus, remember me when you come into your kingdom.ᵃ"

⁴³Jesus answered him, "Truly I tell you, today you will be with me in paradise."

The Death of Jesus

⁴⁴It was now about noon, and darkness came over the whole land until three in the afternoon, ⁴⁵for the sun stopped shining. And the curtain of the temple was torn in two. ⁴⁶Jesus called out with a loud voice, "Father, into your hands I commit my spirit."ᵇ When he had said this, he breathed his last.

⁴⁷The centurion, seeing what had happened, praised God and said, "Surely this was a righteous man." ⁴⁸When all the people who had gathered to witness this sight saw what took place, they beat their breasts and went away. ⁴⁹But all those who knew him, including the women who had followed him from Galilee, stood at a distance, watching these things.

The Law of Sacrifice: Jesus Gave It All Up to Gain It All Back

Luke 23:1–47

Jesus stayed so committed to his mission that he allowed weaker men to seize him, arrest him, and crucify him. Jesus laid down his life, practicing the Law of Sacrifice. Leaders must give up to go up. Jesus paid the ultimate price because he knew what was coming.

The Burial of Jesus

⁵⁰Now there was a man named Joseph, a member of the Council, a good and upright man, ⁵¹who had not consented to their decision and action. He came from the Judean town of Arimathea, and he himself was waiting for the kingdom of God. ⁵²Going to Pilate, he asked for Jesus' body. ⁵³Then he took it down, wrapped it in linen cloth and placed it in a tomb cut in the rock, one in which no one had yet been laid. ⁵⁴It

was Preparation Day, and the Sabbath was about to begin.

⁵⁵The women who had come with Jesus from Galilee followed Joseph and saw the tomb and how his body was laid in it. ⁵⁶Then they went home and prepared spices and perfumes. But they rested on the Sabbath in obedience to the commandment.

Jesus Has Risen

24 On the first day of the week, very early in the morning, the women took the spices they had prepared and went to the tomb. ²They found the stone rolled away from the tomb, ³but when they entered, they did not find the body of the Lord Jesus. ⁴While they were wondering about this, suddenly two men in clothes that gleamed like lightning stood beside them. ⁵In their fright the women bowed down with their faces to the ground, but the men said to them, "Why do you look for the living among the dead? ⁶He is not here; he has risen! Remember how he told you, while he was still with you in Galilee: ⁷'The Son of Man must be delivered over to the hands of sinners, be crucified and on the third day be raised again.'" ⁸Then they remembered his words.

⁹When they came back from the tomb, they told all these things to the Eleven and to all the others. ¹⁰It was Mary Magdalene, Joanna, Mary the mother of James, and the others with them who told this to the apostles. ¹¹But they did not believe the women, because their words seemed to them like nonsense. ¹²Peter, however, got up and ran to the tomb. Bending over, he saw the strips of linen lying by themselves, and he went away, wondering to himself what had happened.

On the Road to Emmaus

¹³Now that same day two of them were going to a village called Emmaus, about seven milesᶜ from Jerusalem. ¹⁴They were talking with each other about everything that had happened. ¹⁵As they talked and discussed these things with each other, Jesus himself came up and walked along with them; ¹⁶but they were kept from recognizing him.

¹⁷He asked them, "What are you discussing together as you walk along?"

They stood still, their faces downcast. ¹⁸One of them, named Cleopas, asked him, "Are you the only one visiting Jerusalem who does not

---

ᵃ 42 Some manuscripts *come with your kingly power*
ᵇ 46 Psalm 31:5   ᶜ 13 Or about 11 kilometers

know the things that have happened there in these days?"

[19]"What things?" he asked.

"About Jesus of Nazareth," they replied. "He was a prophet, powerful in word and deed before God and all the people. [20]The chief priests and our rulers handed him over to be sentenced to death, and they crucified him; [21]but we had hoped that he was the one who was going to redeem Israel. And what is more, it is the third day since all this took place. [22]In addition, some of our women amazed us. They went to the tomb early this morning [23]but didn't find his body. They came and told us that they had seen a vision of angels, who said he was alive. [24]Then some of our companions went to the tomb and found it just as the women had said, but they did not see Jesus."

[25]He said to them, "How foolish you are, and how slow to believe all that the prophets have spoken! [26]Did not the Messiah have to suffer these things and then enter his glory?" [27]And beginning with Moses and all the Prophets, he explained to them what was said in all the Scriptures concerning himself.

[28]As they approached the village to which they were going, Jesus continued on as if he were going farther. [29]But they urged him strongly, "Stay with us, for it is nearly evening; the day is almost over." So he went in to stay with them.

[30]When he was at the table with them, he took bread, gave thanks, broke it and began to give it to them. [31]Then their eyes were opened and they recognized him, and he disappeared from their sight. [32]They asked each other, "Were not our hearts burning within us while he talked with us on the road and opened the Scriptures to us?"

[33]They got up and returned at once to Jerusalem. There they found the Eleven and those with them, assembled together [34]and saying, "It is true! The Lord has risen and has appeared to Simon." [35]Then the two told what had happened on the way, and how Jesus was recognized by them when he broke the bread.

Jesus Appears to the Disciples

[36]While they were still talking about this, Jesus himself stood among them and said to them, "Peace be with you."

[37]They were startled and frightened, thinking they saw a ghost. [38]He said to them, "Why

The Law of Intuition: Jesus Interprets Current Events

Luke 24:13–31

As two grieving men conversed about Jesus' crucifixion, they struggled to understand what it all meant. Jesus saw their confusion and could tell they needed someone to guide them. So he joined them and began to explain his resurrection in light of Scripture (Lk 24:27, 45). By the end of their time together, it all made sense.

Leaders interpret reality for their people. They see a bigger picture and have a leadership bias. They offer clear perspectve to those who need it. They understand current events and how they fit into the overall scheme of things. Remember: Who you are dictates what you see.

The Law of Empowerment: Jesus Turns His Work Over to His Trainees

Luke 24:46–49

Last words should always get our attention. Luke 24 records some of Jesus' last words to his disciples. He had trained them for more than three years. Now they were ready to go out as leaders and trainers themselves.

Jesus' work would have failed unless his followers had taken what he gave them and reproduced it in the lives of others. After his earthly ministry, Jesus trusted the future of his organization, the church, to former fishermen and tax collectors. Jesus employed at least twelve factors in empowering his followers:

1. *Vision* (Mt 4:19; Jn 4:35)
2. *Trust* (Mt 10:8)
3. *Commitment* (Mt 16:24; Jn 13:1)
4. *Launch* (Mt 28:18–20)
5. *Proximity* (Mk 3:14; Lk 8:1)
6. *Responsibility* (Mk 6:7)
7. *Initiative* (Lk 6:12–13)
8. *Knowledge* (Lk 8:9–10)
9. *Evaluation* (Lk 10:17–24)
10. *Example* (Jn 13:15)
11. *Friendship* (Jn 15:15)
12. *Power* (Jn 20:22; Ac 1:8)

are you troubled, and why do doubts rise in your minds? ³⁹Look at my hands and my feet. It is I myself! Touch me and see; a ghost does not have flesh and bones, as you see I have."

⁴⁰When he had said this, he showed them his hands and feet. ⁴¹And while they still did not believe it because of joy and amazement, he asked them, "Do you have anything here to eat?" ⁴²They gave him a piece of broiled fish, ⁴³and he took it and ate it in their presence.

⁴⁴He said to them, "This is what I told you while I was still with you: Everything must be fulfilled that is written about me in the Law of Moses, the Prophets and the Psalms."

⁴⁵Then he opened their minds so they could understand the Scriptures. ⁴⁶He told them, "This is what is written: The Messiah will suffer and rise from the dead on the third day, ⁴⁷and repentance for the forgiveness of sins will be preached in his name to all nations, beginning at Jerusalem. ⁴⁸You are witnesses of these things. ⁴⁹I am going to send you what my Father has promised; but stay in the city until you have been clothed with power from on high."

The Ascension of Jesus

⁵⁰When he had led them out to the vicinity of Bethany, he lifted up his hands and blessed them. ⁵¹While he was blessing them, he left them and was taken up into heaven. ⁵²Then they worshiped him and returned to Jerusalem with great joy. ⁵³And they stayed continually at the temple, praising God.

The Law of Victory: Jesus' Resurrection Brings Victory to the Hopeless

Luke 24:50–53

What a difference in the behavior of Jesus' disciples before the resurrection and after it! Just before, all they had was an executed Leader. They ran from everyone, hoping to save their own necks. Afterward, they became invincible. Leaders find a way for the team to win—something reflected in the team's morale.

INTRODUCTION TO
JOHN

Jesus as the Son of God

John's Gospel provides a wealth of material on Jesus' life and ministry not found in the Gospels of Matthew, Mark, or Luke. His work is considered the simplest yet most profound of the four Gospels. Only John is written from a divine perspective, in which Jesus is portrayed as the Son of God. "In the beginning was the Word," John writes, "and the Word was with God, and the Word was God. . . . The Word became flesh and made his dwelling among us" (1:1–2, 14).

John writes as a leader attempting to persuade his readers to believe in Jesus. He writes "that you may believe that Jesus is the Messiah, the Son of God, and that by believing you may have life in his name" (20:31). He tells certain stories from Jesus' life for a particular purpose and details many of Jesus' teachings concerning his identity.

Like the other Gospels, much of this book focuses on the final week of Jesus' life; in fact, almost half of it does so. We can learn much from this concentration.

For one thing, we see that the strength of one's leadership is magnified during one's most difficult times. Almost anyone can lead with momentum on his or her side, but it takes a true leader to lead with death staring you in the face. As John focuses on Jesus' critical climax, we see what a great leader does under pressure. We catch a glimpse of a Leader in the most stressful situation imaginable, yet one who displays more peace than ever before. He communicates vision more vividly than ever before. He assures his staff of his love and belief in them more than ever before. He speaks of the future and lays a track for his men to run on more clearly than ever

God's Role in John

If we had to distill this book and pull out just one divine message for leaders, it would be this: God grafts leaders into Jesus so that they might draw their strength and nourishment from Christ himself. In John 15, Jesus even describes himself as the "Vine" and us as the "branches."

No leader is an island. If we are to accomplish a divine mission, we must draw upon a divine power. God sustains and directs us as we lead. We must stay connected to him if we are to be competent for him. Because we see Jesus from God's perspective in this book, we can also see leadership from God's perspective. Jesus, the Ultimate Leader, labors to stay connected to the Father. He even says that he speaks only what he hears the Father speaking, and does only what he sees the Father doing (5:19–20). From a horizontal perspective, leadership is about initiating with people. But from a vertical perspective, it is about responding to God.

Leaders in John

Jesus, John the Baptist, chief priests, Pharisees, Pilate

Other People of Influence in John

The twelve disciples, Samaritan woman at the well, Mary Magdalene

before. And he prays more intensely than he ever has before.

Read this Gospel and see Jesus, not only as the King of kings, but as the Leader of leaders, who led under pressure better than anyone ever did before . . . or since.

LEADERSHIP HIGHLIGHTS IN JOHN

The Word Became Flesh

1 In the beginning was the Word, and the Word was with God, and the Word was God. ²He was with God in the beginning. ³Through him all things were made; without him nothing was made that has been made. ⁴In him was life, and that life was the light of all mankind. ⁵The light shines in the darkness, and the darkness has not overcome[a] it.

⁶There was a man sent from God whose name was John. ⁷He came as a witness to testify concerning that light, so that through him all might believe. ⁸He himself was not the light; he came only as a witness to the light.

⁹The true light that gives light to everyone was coming into the world. ¹⁰He was in the world, and though the world was made through him, the world did not recognize him. ¹¹He came to that which was his own, but his own did not receive him. ¹²Yet to all who did receive him, to those who believed in his name, he gave the right to become children of God— ¹³children born not of natural descent, nor of human decision or a husband's will, but born of God.

¹⁴The Word became flesh and made his dwelling among us. We have seen his glory, the glory of the one and only Son, who came from the Father, full of grace and truth.

Leadership Begins with Identity: Jesus Led from Who He Was

John 1:1, 14

The best leadership simply expresses who we are. Jesus led from who he was: God incarnate, the perfect expression of the Father. As he pursued his divine mission, he influenced others. Similarly, as we pursue who God called us to be, our leadership will be most natural and effective.

---

¹⁵(John testified concerning him. He cried out, saying, "This is the one I spoke about when I said, 'He who comes after me has surpassed me because he was before me.'") ¹⁶Out of his fullness we have all received grace in place of grace already given. ¹⁷For the law was given through Moses; grace and truth came through Jesus Christ. ¹⁸No one has ever seen God, but the one and only Son, who is himself God and[b] is in closest relationship with the Father, has made him known.

John the Baptist Denies Being the Messiah

¹⁹Now this was John's testimony when the Jewish leaders[c] in Jerusalem sent priests and Levites to ask him who he was. ²⁰He did not fail to confess, but confessed freely, "I am not the Messiah."

²¹They asked him, "Then who are you? Are you Elijah?"

He said, "I am not."

"Are you the Prophet?"

He answered, "No."

²²Finally they said, "Who are you? Give us an answer to take back to those who sent us. What do you say about yourself?"

²³John replied in the words of Isaiah the prophet, "I am the voice of one calling in the wilderness, 'Make straight the way for the Lord.'"[d]

²⁴Now the Pharisees who had been sent ²⁵questioned him, "Why then do you baptize if you are not the Messiah, nor Elijah, nor the Prophet?"

²⁶"I baptize with[e] water," John replied, "but among you stands one you do not know. ²⁷He is the one who comes after me, the straps of whose sandals I am not worthy to untie."

²⁸This all happened at Bethany on the other side of the Jordan, where John was baptizing.

John Testifies About Jesus

²⁹The next day John saw Jesus coming toward him and said, "Look, the Lamb of God, who takes away the sin of the world! ³⁰This is the one I meant when I said, 'A man who comes after me has surpassed me because he was before me.' ³¹I myself did not know him, but the reason I came baptizing with water was that he might be revealed to Israel."

³²Then John gave this testimony: "I saw the Spirit come down from heaven as a dove and remain on him. ³³And I myself did not know him, but the one who sent me to baptize with water told me, 'The man on whom you see the Spirit come down and remain is the one who will baptize with the Holy Spirit.' ³⁴I have seen and I testify that this is God's Chosen One."[f]

---

[a] 5 Or *understood*   [b] 18 Some manuscripts *but the only Son, who*   [c] 19 The Greek term traditionally translated *the Jews* (*hoi Ioudaioi*) refers here and elsewhere in John's Gospel to those Jewish leaders who opposed Jesus; also in 5:10, 15, 16; 7:1, 11, 13; 9:22; 18:14, 28, 36; 19:7, 12, 31, 38; 20:19.
[d] 23 Isaiah 40:3   [e] 26 Or *in*; also in verses 31 and 33 (twice)
[f] 34 See Isaiah 42:1; many manuscripts *is the Son of God.*

John's Disciples Follow Jesus

[35] The next day John was there again with two of his disciples. [36] When he saw Jesus passing by, he said, "Look, the Lamb of God!"

[37] When the two disciples heard him say this, they followed Jesus. [38] Turning around, Jesus saw them following and asked, "What do you want?"

They said, "Rabbi" (which means "Teacher"), "where are you staying?"

[39] "Come," he replied, "and you will see."

So they went and saw where he was staying, and they spent that day with him. It was about four in the afternoon.

[40] Andrew, Simon Peter's brother, was one of the two who heard what John had said and who had followed Jesus. [41] The first thing Andrew did was to find his brother Simon and tell him, "We have found the Messiah" (that is, the Christ). [42] And he brought him to Jesus.

Jesus looked at him and said, "You are Simon son of John. You will be called Cephas" (which, when translated, is Peter[a]).

Jesus Calls Philip and Nathanael

[43] The next day Jesus decided to leave for Galilee. Finding Philip, he said to him, "Follow me."

[44] Philip, like Andrew and Peter, was from the town of Bethsaida. [45] Philip found Nathanael and told him, "We have found the one Moses wrote about in the Law, and about whom the prophets also wrote — Jesus of Nazareth, the son of Joseph."

[46] "Nazareth! Can anything good come from there?" Nathanael asked.

"Come and see," said Philip.

[47] When Jesus saw Nathanael approaching, he said of him, "Here truly is an Israelite in whom there is no deceit."

[48] "How do you know me?" Nathanael asked.

Jesus answered, "I saw you while you were still under the fig tree before Philip called you."

[49] Then Nathanael declared, "Rabbi, you are the Son of God; you are the king of Israel."

[50] Jesus said, "You believe[b] because I told you I saw you under the fig tree. You will see greater things than that." [51] He then added, "Very truly I tell you,[c] you[c] will see 'heaven open, and the angels of God ascending and descending on'[d] the Son of Man."

Jesus Changes Water Into Wine

2 On the third day a wedding took place at Cana in Galilee. Jesus' mother was there, [2] and Jesus and his disciples had also been invited to the wedding. [3] When the wine was gone, Jesus' mother said to him, "They have no more wine."

[4] "Woman,[e] why do you involve me?" Jesus replied. "My hour has not yet come."

[5] His mother said to the servants, "Do whatever he tells you."

[6] Nearby stood six stone water jars, the kind used by the Jews for ceremonial washing, each holding from twenty to thirty gallons.[f]

[7] Jesus said to the servants, "Fill the jars with water"; so they filled them to the brim.

[8] Then he told them, "Now draw some out and take it to the master of the banquet."

They did so, [9] and the master of the banquet tasted the water that had been turned into wine. He did not realize where it had come from, though the servants who had drawn the water knew. Then he called the bridegroom aside [10] and said, "Everyone brings out the choice wine first and then the cheaper wine after the guests have had too much to drink; but you have saved the best till now."

[11] What Jesus did here in Cana of Galilee was the first of the signs through which he revealed his glory; and his disciples believed in him.

[12] After this he went down to Capernaum with his mother and brothers and his disciples. There they stayed for a few days.

Jesus Clears the Temple Courts

[13] When it was almost time for the Jewish Passover, Jesus went up to Jerusalem. [14] In the temple courts he found people selling cattle, sheep and doves, and others sitting at tables exchanging money. [15] So he made a whip out of cords, and drove all from the temple courts, both sheep and cattle; he scattered the coins of the money changers and overturned their tables. [16] To those who sold doves he said, "Get these out of here! Stop turning my Father's house into a market!" [17] His disciples remembered that it is written: "Zeal for your house will consume me."[g]

[18] The Jews then responded to him, "What sign can you show us to prove your authority to do all this?"

[19] Jesus answered them, "Destroy this temple, and I will raise it again in three days."

[20] They replied, "It has taken forty-six years

---

[a] 42 Cephas (Aramaic) and Peter (Greek) both mean rock.
[b] 50 Or Do you believe . . . ?   [c] 51 The Greek is plural.
[d] 51 Gen. 28:12   [e] 4 The Greek for Woman does not denote any disrespect.   [f] 6 Or from about 75 to about 115 liters
[g] 17 Psalm 69:9

The Law of Buy-In: The Disciples Embrace Jesus' Vision

John 2:11

The apostle John gives Jesus eight titles in his first chapter alone:

- the Word (v. 1)
- God (v. 1)
- Life (v. 4)
- Light (v. 7)
- Fullness (v. 16)
- Christ (v. 17)
- Lord (v. 23)
- Lamb of God (v. 29)

John 2 tells how Jesus' disciples embrace who he is after he performs his first miracle at the wedding in Cana (v. 11). They bought in to his identity before they bought in to his cause.

This is how the Law of Buy-In works. People buy in to the leader before they accept the vision. Once they believe in the leader, they generally go with the vision. Once the disciples recognized Jesus' identity, they felt ready to do whatever he called them to do. The leader's credibility precedes the leader's plan.

Courage: Jesus Did the Unpopular to Accomplish the Unforgettable

John 2:13–21

When Jesus threw the money changers out of the temple, everyone understood this loving "Shepherd" was dead serious about justice and righteousness. He could *lead* people because he didn't *need* people. His courage came from his sufficiency in his Father, which allowed him to carry out unpopular tasks and leave his unforgettable mark.

to build this temple, and you are going to raise it in three days?" [21]But the temple he had spoken of was his body. [22]After he was raised from the dead, his disciples recalled what he had said. Then they believed the scripture and the words that Jesus had spoken.

[23]Now while he was in Jerusalem at the Passover Festival, many people saw the signs he was performing and believed in his name.[a] [24]But Jesus would not entrust himself to them, for he knew all people. [25]He did not need any testimony about mankind, for he knew what was in each person.

Jesus Teaches Nicodemus

3 Now there was a Pharisee, a man named Nicodemus who was a member of the Jewish ruling council. [2]He came to Jesus at night and said, "Rabbi, we know that you are a teacher who has come from God. For no one could perform the signs you are doing if God were not with him."

[3]Jesus replied, "Very truly I tell you, no one can see the kingdom of God unless they are born again.[b]"

[4]"How can someone be born when they are old?" Nicodemus asked. "Surely they cannot enter a second time into their mother's womb to be born!"

[5]Jesus answered, "Very truly I tell you, no one can enter the kingdom of God unless they are born of water and the Spirit. [6]Flesh gives birth to flesh, but the Spirit[c] gives birth to spirit. [7]You should not be surprised at my saying, 'You[d] must be born again.' [8]The wind blows wherever it pleases. You hear its sound, but you cannot tell where it comes from or where it is going. So it is with everyone born of the Spirit."[e]

[9]"How can this be?" Nicodemus asked.

[10]"You are Israel's teacher," said Jesus, "and do you not understand these things? [11]Very truly I tell you, we speak of what we know, and we testify to what we have seen, but still you people do not accept our testimony. [12]I have spoken to you of earthly things and you do not believe; how then will you believe if I speak of heavenly things? [13]No one has ever gone into heaven except the one who came from heaven — the Son of Man.[f] [14]Just as Moses lifted up the snake in the wilderness, so the Son of Man must be lifted up,[g] [15]that everyone who believes may have eternal life in him."[h]

[16]For God so loved the world that he gave his

---

[a] 23 Or *in him*   [b] 3 The Greek for *again* also means *from above*; also in verse 7.   [c] 6 Or *but spirit*   [d] 7 The Greek is plural.   [e] 8 The Greek for *Spirit* is the same as that for *wind*. [f] 13 Some manuscripts *Man, who is in heaven*   [g] 14 The Greek for *lifted up* also means *exalted*.   [h] 15 Some interpreters end the quotation with verse 21.

New Testament Pictures of a Leader

John 2:13–22

While at times Jesus could act in ways that seemed harsh—as when he drove out the money changers and confronted the Jews—his short ministry also provides us with some crucial relational pictures of a leader. By looking at the entire record, we see both the tough and tender sides of Christ's leadership. Consider several of the New Testament's greatest pictures of leadership:

1. *Father and Child:* This is a warm and loving relationship in which the leader nurtures and respects his or her followers. "You know that we dealt with each of you as a father deals with his own children, encouraging, comforting and urging you to live lives worthy of God," says Paul (1Th 2:11–12).

2. *Husband and Wife:* This is a supportive, covenant relationship in which the leader shows love and commitment. "I am jealous for you with a godly jealousy. I promised you to one husband, to Christ," says Paul to the Corinthians (2Co 11:2).

3. *Head and Body:* This is a picture of the governing, protecting relationship in which the leader gives direction. "Speaking the truth in love," writes Paul, "we will grow to become in every respect the mature body of him who is the head, that is Christ. From him the whole body, joined and held together by every supporting ligament, grows and builds itself up in love, as each part does its work" (Eph 4:15–16).

4. *Vine and Branches:* This is a picture of the leader as a source of nourishment. The leader offers provision. "I am the vine; you are the branches," says Jesus. "If you remain in me and I in you, you will bear much fruit" (Jn 15:5).

5. *King and Citizens:* This is a picture of wisdom and influence. The leader guides the people. "You are no longer foreigners and strangers, but fellow citizens with God's people and also members of his household" (Eph 2:19).

6. *Potter and Clay:* This is a picture of responsibility and surrender. The leader develops the people. "Does not the potter have the right to make out of the same lump of clay some pottery for special purposes and some for common use?" (Ro 9:21).

7. *Vinedresser and Vineyard:* This is a picture of a farmer who prunes and cares for his own. The leader disciplines the people. "He cuts off every branch in me that bears no fruit, while every branch that does bear fruit he prunes so that it will be even more fruitful" (Jn 15:2).

8. *Captain and Army:* This is a picture of authority and training. The leader prepares the troops for battle. "Join with me in suffering, like a good soldier of Christ Jesus. No one serving as a soldier gets entangled in civilian affairs, but rather tries to please his commanding officer" (2Ti 2:3–4).

9. *Creator and Creature:* This is a picture of power and submission. The leader reproduces himself in others. "Put on the new self, which is being renewed in knowledge in the image of its Creator" (Col 3:10).

10. *Prophet and People:* This is a picture of anointing and spiritual power. The leader corrects and envisions. "After we had been there a number of days, a prophet named Agabus came down from Judea. Coming over to us, he . . . said, 'The Holy Spirit says . . .'" (Ac 21:10–11).

11. *Shepherd and Sheep:* This is a picture of warmth and beauty. The leader guides and protects his sheep. "I am the good shepherd. The good shepherd lays down his life for the sheep" (Jn 10:11).

12. *Priest and Worshipers:* This is a picture of godliness and spiritual intimacy. The leader connects people with God. "You are a chosen people, a royal priesthood, a holy nation, God's special possession, that you may declare the praises of him who called you out of darkness into his wonderful light" (1Pe 2:9).

As you read through Jesus' life and the rest of the New Testament, watch for these metaphors. They provide wonderful pictures of the kind of leadership roles God wants us to fulfill.

one and only Son, that whoever believes in him shall not perish but have eternal life. [17]For God did not send his Son into the world to condemn the world, but to save the world through him. [18]Whoever believes in him is not condemned, but whoever does not believe stands condemned already because they have not believed in the name of God's one and only Son. [19]This is the verdict: Light has come into the world, but people loved darkness instead of light because their deeds were evil. [20]Everyone who does evil hates the light, and will not come into the light for fear that their deeds will be exposed. [21]But whoever

Communication: Jesus Reduced His Message to One Memorable Phrase

John 3:16

In one verse of 25 words, Jesus explained the essence of his mission. Effective leaders know the importance of compressing their complex activities into an easily memorized sentence. This is a secret of good communication. Make it short! Make it simple! Make it significant! Make it sizzle!

lives by the truth comes into the light, so that it may be seen plainly that what they have done has been done in the sight of God.

John Testifies Again About Jesus

[22]After this, Jesus and his disciples went out into the Judean countryside, where he spent some time with them, and baptized. [23]Now John also was baptizing at Aenon near Salim, because there was plenty of water, and people were coming and being baptized. [24](This was before John was put in prison.) [25]An argument developed between some of John's disciples and a certain Jew over the matter of ceremonial washing. [26]They came to John and said to him, "Rabbi, that man who was with you on the other side of the Jordan — the one you testified about — look, he is baptizing, and everyone is going to him."

[27]To this John replied, "A person can receive only what is given them from heaven. [28]You yourselves can testify that I said, 'I am not the Messiah but am sent ahead of him.' [29]The bride belongs to the bridegroom. The friend who attends the bridegroom waits and listens for him, and is full of joy when he hears the bridegroom's voice. That joy is mine, and it is now complete. [30]He must become greater; I must become less."[a]

[31]The one who comes from above is above all; the one who is from the earth belongs to the

[a] 30 Some interpreters end the quotation with verse 36.

JESUS — God's Son, God's Leader

PROFILE in leadership

John 3:1–21

A Pharisee named Nicodemus recognized something special about Jesus, something that set him apart from the many other religious types he had met. Jesus seemed to possess a unique authority in everything he did or said. So this zealous leader rightly confessed to Jesus, "No one could perform the signs you are doing if God were not with him" (Jn 3:2). With that statement, Nicodemus showed how close he had come to understanding the true identity of Jesus Christ.

In his conversation with Nicodemus—and in the encounter with the Samaritan woman at the well and in a series of miracles and teachings that followed (Jn 4–6)—Jesus established himself in word and in deed as the One God had sent to be the Savior of the world.

While Nicodemus recognized that God had sent Jesus, there was much more to it than that. Christ wasn't just sent *of* God; he *was* God in the flesh, the Son of the true and living God.

Since none of us can claim Jesus' lofty heritage, none of us can exactly match the kind of leadership expressed by the Lord Jesus Christ when he walked the earth. But we can look to him as our model and example of perfect leadership, and rely on the Holy Spirit (as he did) to empower our leadership.

earth, and speaks as one from the earth. The one who comes from heaven is above all. [32]He testifies to what he has seen and heard, but no one accepts his testimony. [33]Whoever has accepted it has certified that God is truthful. [34]For the one whom God has sent speaks the words of God, for God[a] gives the Spirit without limit. [35]The Father loves the Son and has placed everything in his hands. [36]Whoever believes in the Son has eternal life, but whoever rejects the Son will not see life, for God's wrath remains on them.

Jesus Talks With a Samaritan Woman

4 Now Jesus learned that the Pharisees had heard that he was gaining and baptizing more disciples than John— [2]although in fact it was not Jesus who baptized, but his disciples. [3]So he left Judea and went back once more to Galilee.

[4]Now he had to go through Samaria. [5]So he came to a town in Samaria called Sychar, near the plot of ground Jacob had given to his son Joseph. [6]Jacob's well was there, and Jesus, tired as he was from the journey, sat down by the well. It was about noon.

[7]When a Samaritan woman came to draw water, Jesus said to her, "Will you give me a drink?" [8](His disciples had gone into the town to buy food.)

[9]The Samaritan woman said to him, "You are a Jew and I am a Samaritan woman. How can you ask me for a drink?" (For Jews do not associate with Samaritans.[b])

[10]Jesus answered her, "If you knew the gift of God and who it is that asks you for a drink, you would have asked him and he would have given you living water."

[11]"Sir," the woman said, "you have nothing to draw with and the well is deep. Where can you get this living water? [12]Are you greater than our father Jacob, who gave us the well and drank from it himself, as did also his sons and his livestock?"

[13]Jesus answered, "Everyone who drinks this water will be thirsty again, [14]but whoever drinks the water I give them will never thirst. Indeed, the water I give them will become in them a spring of water welling up to eternal life."

[15]The woman said to him, "Sir, give me this water so that I won't get thirsty and have to keep coming here to draw water."

[16]He told her, "Go, call your husband and come back."

[17]"I have no husband," she replied.

Jesus said to her, "You are right when you say you have no husband. [18]The fact is, you have had five husbands, and the man you now have is not your husband. What you have just said is quite true."

[19]"Sir," the woman said, "I can see that you are a prophet. [20]Our ancestors worshiped on this mountain, but you Jews claim that the place where we must worship is in Jerusalem."

[21]"Woman," Jesus replied, "believe me, a time is coming when you will worship the Father neither on this mountain nor in Jerusalem. [22]You Samaritans worship what you do not know; we worship what we do know, for salvation is from the Jews. [23]Yet a time is coming and has now come when the true worshipers will worship the Father in the Spirit and in truth, for they are the kind of worshipers the Father seeks. [24]God is spirit, and his worshipers must worship in the Spirit and in truth."

[25]The woman said, "I know that Messiah" (called Christ) "is coming. When he comes, he will explain everything to us."

[26]Then Jesus declared, "I, the one speaking to you—I am he."

The Disciples Rejoin Jesus

[27]Just then his disciples returned and were surprised to find him talking with a woman. But no one asked, "What do you want?" or "Why are you talking with her?"

[28]Then, leaving her water jar, the woman went back to the town and said to the people, [29]"Come, see a man who told me everything I ever did. Could this be the Messiah?" [30]They came out of the town and made their way toward him.

[31]Meanwhile his disciples urged him, "Rabbi, eat something."

[32]But he said to them, "I have food to eat that you know nothing about."

[33]Then his disciples said to each other, "Could someone have brought him food?"

[34]"My food," said Jesus, "is to do the will of him who sent me and to finish his work. [35]Don't you have a saying, 'It's still four months until harvest'? I tell you, open your eyes and look at the fields! They are ripe for harvest. [36]Even now the one who reaps draws a wage and harvests a crop for eternal life, so that the sower and the reaper may be glad together. [37]Thus the saying 'One sows and another reaps' is true. [38]I sent you to reap what you have not worked for. Others

---

[a] 34 Greek he   [b] 9 Or do not use dishes Samaritans have used

The Law of Connection: Jesus Connects with a Woman, Changes a City

John 4:1–26

We don't even know her name. Other Jews wouldn't even speak with her. Yet because Jesus was different, he spoke with this Samaritan woman—a snubbed gender within a despised race. Through this personal connection, God reached an entire city. We learn at least eight principles from Jesus' leadership in John 4:

1. *Leaders initiate the contact* (vv. 1–7).
   Jesus spoke first. He didn't isolate himself even from "undesirables."

2. *Leaders establish common ground* (vv. 7–8).
   He connected with her about a familiar interest: water.

3. *Leaders listen and allow others to speak* (v. 9).
   He knew people like to hear their own voices most of all.

4. *Leaders arouse interest* (vv. 10–15).
   Jesus built a verbal bridge by making her thirsty for something more than water.

5. *Leaders take others only so far as they are ready to go* (vv. 16–19).
   Jesus knew he mustn't go too far. He said enough to make her hungry for more.

6. *Leaders accept others where they are* (vv. 17–18).
   Jesus knew her lifestyle, but never condemned her for it.

7. *Leaders stick with the key issues* (vv. 20–24).
   He didn't allow her to get distracted. He wouldn't divert the focus from the real issue.

8. *Leaders communicate issues directly and simply* (vv. 25–26).
   Jesus revealed his identity in clear and simple terms.

have done the hard work, and you have reaped the benefits of their labor."

Many Samaritans Believe

³⁹Many of the Samaritans from that town believed in him because of the woman's testimony, "He told me everything I ever did." ⁴⁰So when the Samaritans came to him, they urged him to stay with them, and he stayed two days. ⁴¹And because of his words many more became believers.

⁴²They said to the woman, "We no longer believe just because of what you said; now we have heard for ourselves, and we know that this man really is the Savior of the world."

Jesus Heals an Official's Son

⁴³After the two days he left for Galilee. ⁴⁴(Now Jesus himself had pointed out that a prophet has no honor in his own country.) ⁴⁵When he arrived in Galilee, the Galileans welcomed him. They had seen all that he had done

in Jerusalem at the Passover Festival, for they also had been there.

⁴⁶Once more he visited Cana in Galilee, where he had turned the water into wine. And there was a certain royal official whose son lay sick at Capernaum. ⁴⁷When this man heard that Jesus had arrived in Galilee from Judea, he went to him and begged him to come and heal his son, who was close to death.

⁴⁸"Unless you people see signs and wonders," Jesus told him, "you will never believe."

⁴⁹The royal official said, "Sir, come down before my child dies."

⁵⁰"Go," Jesus replied, "your son will live."

The man took Jesus at his word and departed. ⁵¹While he was still on the way, his servants met him with the news that his boy was living. ⁵²When he inquired as to the time when his son got better, they said to him, "Yesterday, at one in the afternoon, the fever left him."

⁵³Then the father realized that this was the exact time at which Jesus had said to him, "Your

son will live." So he and his whole household believed.

[54]This was the second sign Jesus performed after coming from Judea to Galilee.

The Healing at the Pool

5 Some time later, Jesus went up to Jerusalem for one of the Jewish festivals. [2]Now there is in Jerusalem near the Sheep Gate a pool, which in Aramaic is called Bethesda[a] and which is surrounded by five covered colonnades. [3]Here a great number of disabled people used to lie — the blind, the lame, the paralyzed. [4][b] [5]One who was there had been an invalid for thirty-eight years. [6]When Jesus saw him lying there and learned that he had been in this condition for a long time, he asked him, "Do you want to get well?"

[7]"Sir," the invalid replied, "I have no one to help me into the pool when the water is stirred. While I am trying to get in, someone else goes down ahead of me."

[8]Then Jesus said to him, "Get up! Pick up your mat and walk." [9]At once the man was cured; he picked up his mat and walked.

The day on which this took place was a Sabbath, [10]and so the Jewish leaders said to the man who had been healed, "It is the Sabbath; the law forbids you to carry your mat."

[11]But he replied, "The man who made me well said to me, 'Pick up your mat and walk.'"

[12]So they asked him, "Who is this fellow who told you to pick it up and walk?"

[13]The man who was healed had no idea who it was, for Jesus had slipped away into the crowd that was there.

[14]Later Jesus found him at the temple and said to him, "See, you are well again. Stop sinning or something worse may happen to you." [15]The

man went away and told the Jewish leaders that it was Jesus who had made him well.

The Authority of the Son

[16]So, because Jesus was doing these things on the Sabbath, the Jewish leaders began to persecute him. [17]In his defense Jesus said to them, "My Father is always at his work to this very day, and I too am working." [18]For this reason they tried all the more to kill him; not only was he breaking the Sabbath, but he was even calling God his own Father, making himself equal with God.

[19]Jesus gave them this answer: "Very truly I tell you, the Son can do nothing by himself; he can do only what he sees his Father doing, because whatever the Father does the Son also does. [20]For the Father loves the Son and shows him all he does. Yes, and he will show him even greater works than these, so that you will be amazed. [21]For just as the Father raises the dead and gives them life, even so the Son gives life to whom he is pleased to give it. [22]Moreover, the Father judges no one, but has entrusted all judgment to the Son, [23]that all may honor the Son just as they honor the Father. Whoever does not honor the Son does not honor the Father, who sent him.

[24]"Very truly I tell you, whoever hears my word and believes him who sent me has eternal life and will not be judged but has crossed over from death to life. [25]Very truly I tell you, a time is coming and has now come when the dead will hear the voice of the Son of God and those who hear will live. [26]For as the Father has life in himself, so he has granted the Son also to have life in himself. [27]And he has given him authority to judge because he is the Son of Man.

[28]"Do not be amazed at this, for a time is coming when all who are in their graves will hear his voice [29]and come out — those who have done what is good will rise to live, and those who have done what is evil will rise to be condemned. [30]By myself I can do nothing; I judge only as I hear, and my judgment is just, for I seek not to please myself but him who sent me.

Testimonies About Jesus

[31]"If I testify about myself, my testimony is not true. [32]There is another who testifies in my

The Law of Solid Ground: Jesus' Credibility Came from Results

John 5:1–14

When the Jews confronted Jesus after he healed a man on the Sabbath, he replied that he was working only because his Father was working. In other words, Jesus' credibility came from results, not rhetoric. Leaders practice the Law of Solid Ground when their lives back up their words.

---

[a] 2 Some manuscripts *Bethzatha*; other manuscripts *Bethsaida*
[b] 3,4 Some manuscripts include here, wholly or in part, *paralyzed — and they waited for the moving of the waters.* [4]*From time to time an angel of the Lord would come down and stir up the waters. The first one into the pool after each such disturbance would be cured of whatever disease they had.*

favor, and I know that his testimony about me is true.

[33]"You have sent to John and he has testified to the truth. [34]Not that I accept human testimony; but I mention it that you may be saved. [35]John was a lamp that burned and gave light, and you chose for a time to enjoy his light.

[36]"I have testimony weightier than that of John. For the works that the Father has given me to finish — the very works that I am doing — testify that the Father has sent me. [37]And the Father who sent me has himself testified concerning me. You have never heard his voice nor seen his form, [38]nor does his word dwell in you, for you do not believe the one he sent. [39]You study[a] the Scriptures diligently because you think that in them you have eternal life. These are the very Scriptures that testify about me, [40]yet you refuse to come to me to have life.

[41]"I do not accept glory from human beings, [42]but I know you. I know that you do not have the love of God in your hearts. [43]I have come in my Father's name, and you do not accept me; but if someone else comes in his own name, you will accept him. [44]How can you believe since you accept glory from one another but do not seek the glory that comes from the only God[b]?

[45]"But do not think I will accuse you before the Father. Your accuser is Moses, on whom your hopes are set. [46]If you believed Moses, you would believe me, for he wrote about me. [47]But since you do not believe what he wrote, how are you going to believe what I say?"

Jesus Feeds the Five Thousand

6 Some time after this, Jesus crossed to the far shore of the Sea of Galilee (that is, the Sea of Tiberias), [2]and a great crowd of people followed him because they saw the signs he had performed by healing the sick. [3]Then Jesus went up on a mountainside and sat down with his disciples. [4]The Jewish Passover Festival was near.

[5]When Jesus looked up and saw a great crowd coming toward him, he said to Philip, "Where shall we buy bread for these people to eat?" [6]He asked this only to test him, for he already had in mind what he was going to do.

[7]Philip answered him, "It would take more than half a year's wages[c] to buy enough bread for each one to have a bite!"

[8]Another of his disciples, Andrew, Simon Peter's brother, spoke up, [9]"Here is a boy with five small barley loaves and two small fish, but how far will they go among so many?"

[10]Jesus said, "Have the people sit down."

There was plenty of grass in that place, and they sat down (about five thousand men were there). [11]Jesus then took the loaves, gave thanks, and distributed to those who were seated as much as they wanted. He did the same with the fish.

[12]When they had all had enough to eat, he said to his disciples, "Gather the pieces that are left over. Let nothing be wasted." [13]So they gathered them and filled twelve baskets with the pieces of the five barley loaves left over by those who had eaten.

[14]After the people saw the sign Jesus performed, they began to say, "Surely this is the Prophet who is to come into the world." [15]Jesus, knowing that they intended to come and make him king by force, withdrew again to a mountain by himself.

Jesus Walks on the Water

[16]When evening came, his disciples went down to the lake, [17]where they got into a boat and set off across the lake for Capernaum. By now it was dark, and Jesus had not yet joined them. [18]A strong wind was blowing and the waters grew rough. [19]When they had rowed about three or four miles,[d] they saw Jesus approaching the boat, walking on the water; and they were frightened. [20]But he said to them, "It is I; don't be afraid." [21]Then they were willing to take him into the boat, and immediately the boat reached the shore where they were heading.

[22]The next day the crowd that had stayed on the opposite shore of the lake realized that only one boat had been there, and that Jesus had not entered it with his disciples, but that they had gone away alone. [23]Then some boats from Tiberias landed near the place where the people had eaten the bread after the Lord had given thanks. [24]Once the crowd realized that neither Jesus nor his disciples were there, they got into the boats and went to Capernaum in search of Jesus.

Jesus the Bread of Life

[25]When they found him on the other side of the lake, they asked him, "Rabbi, when did you get here?"

[26]Jesus answered, "Very truly I tell you, you are looking for me, not because you saw the signs I performed but because you ate the loaves and had your fill. [27]Do not work for food that spoils, but for food that endures to eternal life,

---

[a] 39 Or [39]Study   [b] 44 Some early manuscripts the Only One
[c] 7 Greek take two hundred denarii   [d] 19 Or about 5 or
6 kilometers

The Law of Addition: A Lesson in Servanthood

John 6:3–14

As Jesus fed five thousand people with one small basket of food, the disciples learned another lesson in serving others. Jesus allowed the disciples to participate in this miracle; they served the food as it multiplied.

Through this experience, Jesus was beginning to reproduce his ministry in his followers. He taught that a pupil becomes like his teacher (Lk 6:40). When we add value by serving others it keeps adding to those under us. Author Frank Damazio notes how adding value occurs from Father, to Son, to leader:

From the Father	To the Son	To the Leader
My Father is working (Jn 5:17–19).	I myself am working (Jn 5:17; 9:4).	Leaders are to do the work (Ac 6:4; Eph 4:12).
The Father judges (Jn 8:16).	I judge (Jn 8:16).	Leaders must judge (1Co 6:1–6).
God is light (1Jn 1:5).	I am the light of the world (Jn 8:12; 12:46).	Leaders are light and are to walk in the light (Mt 5:14; 1Jn 1:7).
The Father teaches (Jn 8:28).	The Son teaches (Jn 8:28; Ac 1:1).	Leaders are teachers (Ac 5:42; 1Ti 3:2; 4:11).
The Father gave his Son (Jn 3:16).	The Son gave his life (Jn 10:11).	Leaders lay down their lives (1Jn 3:16).
The Father is perfect.	The Son is perfect.	Leaders are to be perfect and set the example (Mt 5:48; 1Co 3:18; Col 3:10).

which the Son of Man will give you. For on him God the Father has placed his seal of approval."

[28] Then they asked him, "What must we do to do the works God requires?"

[29] Jesus answered, "The work of God is this: to believe in the one he has sent."

[30] So they asked him, "What sign then will you give that we may see it and believe you? What will you do? [31] Our ancestors ate the manna in the wilderness; as it is written: 'He gave them bread from heaven to eat.'[a]"

[32] Jesus said to them, "Very truly I tell you, it is not Moses who has given you the bread from heaven, but it is my Father who gives you the true bread from heaven. [33] For the bread of God is the bread that comes down from heaven and gives life to the world."

[34] "Sir," they said, "always give us this bread."

[35] Then Jesus declared, "I am the bread of life. Whoever comes to me will never go hungry, and whoever believes in me will never be thirsty. [36] But as I told you, you have seen me and still you do not believe. [37] All those the Father gives me will come to me, and whoever comes to me I will never drive away. [38] For I have come down from heaven not to do my will but to do the will of him who sent me. [39] And this is the will of him who sent me, that I shall lose none of all those he has given me, but raise them up at the last day. [40] For my Father's will is that everyone who looks to the Son and believes in him shall have eternal life, and I will raise them up at the last day."

[41] At this the Jews there began to grumble about him because he said, "I am the bread that came down from heaven." [42] They said, "Is this not Jesus, the son of Joseph, whose father and mother we know? How can he now say, 'I came down from heaven'?"

[43] "Stop grumbling among yourselves," Jesus answered. [44] "No one can come to me unless the Father who sent me draws them, and I will raise them up at the last day. [45] It is written in the Prophets: 'They will all be taught by God.'[b] Everyone who has heard the Father and learned from him comes to me. [46] No one has seen the Father except the one who is from God; only he has seen the Father. [47] Very truly I tell you,

---

[a] 31 Exodus 16:4; Neh. 9:15; Psalm 78:24,25
[b] 45 Isaiah 54:13

the one who believes has eternal life. [48]I am the bread of life. [49]Your ancestors ate the manna in the wilderness, yet they died. [50]But here is the bread that comes down from heaven, which anyone may eat and not die. [51]I am the living bread that came down from heaven. Whoever eats this bread will live forever. This bread is my flesh, which I will give for the life of the world."

[52]Then the Jews began to argue sharply among themselves, "How can this man give us his flesh to eat?"

[53]Jesus said to them, "Very truly I tell you, unless you eat the flesh of the Son of Man and drink his blood, you have no life in you. [54]Whoever eats my flesh and drinks my blood has eternal life, and I will raise them up at the last day. [55]For my flesh is real food and my blood is real drink. [56]Whoever eats my flesh and drinks my blood remains in me, and I in them. [57]Just as the living Father sent me and I live because of the Father, so the one who feeds on me will live because of me. [58]This is the bread that came down from heaven. Your ancestors ate manna and died, but whoever feeds on this bread will live forever." [59]He said this while teaching in the synagogue in Capernaum.

Many Disciples Desert Jesus

[60]On hearing it, many of his disciples said, "This is a hard teaching. Who can accept it?"

[61]Aware that his disciples were grumbling about this, Jesus said to them, "Does this offend you? [62]Then what if you see the Son of Man ascend to where he was before! [63]The Spirit gives life; the flesh counts for nothing. The words I have spoken to you — they are full of the Spirit[a] and life. [64]Yet there are some of you who do not believe." For Jesus had known from the beginning which of them did not believe and who

would betray him. [65]He went on to say, "This is why I told you that no one can come to me unless the Father has enabled them."

[66]From this time many of his disciples turned back and no longer followed him.

[67]"You do not want to leave too, do you?" Jesus asked the Twelve.

[68]Simon Peter answered him, "Lord, to whom shall we go? You have the words of eternal life. [69]We have come to believe and to know that you are the Holy One of God."

[70]Then Jesus replied, "Have I not chosen you, the Twelve? Yet one of you is a devil!" [71](He meant Judas, the son of Simon Iscariot, who, though one of the Twelve, was later to betray him.)

Jesus Goes to the Festival of Tabernacles

7 After this, Jesus went around in Galilee. He did not want[b] to go about in Judea because the Jewish leaders there were looking for a way to kill him. [2]But when the Jewish Festival of Tabernacles was near, [3]Jesus' brothers said to him, "Leave Galilee and go to Judea, so that your disciples there may see the works you do. [4]No one who wants to become a public figure acts in secret. Since you are doing these things, show yourself to the world." [5]For even his own brothers did not believe in him.

[6]Therefore Jesus told them, "My time is not yet here; for you any time will do. [7]The world cannot hate you, but it hates me because I testify that its works are evil. [8]You go to the festival. I am not[c] going up to this festival, because my time has not yet fully come." [9]After he had said this, he stayed in Galilee.

[10]However, after his brothers had left for the festival, he went also, not publicly, but in secret. [11]Now at the festival the Jewish leaders were watching for Jesus and asking, "Where is he?"

[12]Among the crowds there was widespread whispering about him. Some said, "He is a good man."

Others replied, "No, he deceives the people." [13]But no one would say anything publicly about him for fear of the leaders.

Jesus Teaches at the Festival

[14]Not until halfway through the festival did Jesus go up to the temple courts and begin to teach. [15]The Jews there were amazed and asked, "How did this man get such learning without having been taught?"

Commitment: Jesus Clarified and Purified

John 6:41–65

Jesus never pursued huge crowds. In fact, he often had to find ways to escape them! To do so, Jesus clarified the level of commitment he expected from followers. Two things always happen when a leader calls for commitment: He clarifies where people stand, and he purifies the organization.

---

[a] 63 Or *are Spirit*; or *are spirit*   [b] 1 Some manuscripts *not have authority*   [c] 8 Some manuscripts *not yet*

[16]Jesus answered, "My teaching is not my own. It comes from the one who sent me. [17]Anyone who chooses to do the will of God will find out whether my teaching comes from God or whether I speak on my own. [18]Whoever speaks on their own does so to gain personal glory, but he who seeks the glory of the one who sent him is a man of truth; there is nothing false about him. [19]Has not Moses given you the law? Yet not one of you keeps the law. Why are you trying to kill me?"

[20]"You are demon-possessed," the crowd answered. "Who is trying to kill you?"

[21]Jesus said to them, "I did one miracle, and you are all amazed. [22]Yet, because Moses gave you circumcision (though actually it did not come from Moses, but from the patriarchs), you circumcise a boy on the Sabbath. [23]Now if a boy can be circumcised on the Sabbath so that the law of Moses may not be broken, why are you angry with me for healing a man's whole body on the Sabbath? [24]Stop judging by mere appearances, but instead judge correctly."

Division Over Who Jesus Is

[25]At that point some of the people of Jerusalem began to ask, "Isn't this the man they are trying to kill? [26]Here he is, speaking publicly, and they are not saying a word to him. Have the authorities really concluded that he is the Messiah? [27]But we know where this man is from; when the Messiah comes, no one will know where he is from."

[28]Then Jesus, still teaching in the temple courts, cried out, "Yes, you know me, and you know where I am from. I am not here on my own authority, but he who sent me is true. You do not know him, [29]but I know him because I am from him and he sent me."

[30]At this they tried to seize him, but no one laid a hand on him, because his hour had not yet come. [31]Still, many in the crowd believed in him. They said, "When the Messiah comes, will he perform more signs than this man?"

[32]The Pharisees heard the crowd whispering such things about him. Then the chief priests and the Pharisees sent temple guards to arrest him.

[33]Jesus said, "I am with you for only a short time, and then I am going to the one who sent me. [34]You will look for me, but you will not find me; and where I am, you cannot come."

[35]The Jews said to one another, "Where does this man intend to go that we cannot find him? Will he go where our people live scattered among the Greeks, and teach the Greeks? [36]What did he mean when he said, 'You will look for me, but you will not find me,' and 'Where I am, you cannot come'?"

[37]On the last and greatest day of the festival, Jesus stood and said in a loud voice, "Let anyone who is thirsty come to me and drink. [38]Whoever believes in me, as Scripture has said, rivers of living water will flow from within them."[a] [39]By this he meant the Spirit, whom those who believed in him were later to receive. Up to that time the Spirit had not been given, since Jesus had not yet been glorified.

[40]On hearing his words, some of the people said, "Surely this man is the Prophet."

[41]Others said, "He is the Messiah."

Still others asked, "How can the Messiah come from Galilee? [42]Does not Scripture say that the Messiah will come from David's descendants and from Bethlehem, the town where David lived?" [43]Thus the people were divided because of Jesus. [44]Some wanted to seize him, but no one laid a hand on him.

Unbelief of the Jewish Leaders

[45]Finally the temple guards went back to the chief priests and the Pharisees, who asked them, "Why didn't you bring him in?"

[46]"No one ever spoke the way this man does," the guards replied.

[47]"You mean he has deceived you also?" the Pharisees retorted. [48]"Have any of the rulers or of the Pharisees believed in him? [49]No! But this mob that knows nothing of the law — there is a curse on them."

[50]Nicodemus, who had gone to Jesus earlier and who was one of their own number, asked, [51]"Does our law condemn a man without first hearing him to find out what he has been doing?"

[52]They replied, "Are you from Galilee, too? Look into it, and you will find that a prophet does not come out of Galilee."

[The earliest manuscripts and many other ancient witnesses do not have John 7:53 — 8:11. A few manuscripts include these verses, wholly or in part, after John 7:36, John 21:25, Luke 21:38 or Luke 24:53.]

8 [53]*Then they all went home,* [1]*but Jesus went to the Mount of Olives.*

[2]*At dawn he appeared again in the temple courts, where all the people gathered around him, and he sat down to teach them.* [3]*The teachers of the law and the*

---

a 37,38 Or me. And let anyone drink [38]who believes in me." As Scripture has said, "Out of him (or them) will flow rivers of living water."

Pharisees brought in a woman caught in adultery. They made her stand before the group [4]and said to Jesus, "Teacher, this woman was caught in the act of adultery. [5]In the Law Moses commanded us to stone such women. Now what do you say?" [6]They were using this question as a trap, in order to have a basis for accusing him.

But Jesus bent down and started to write on the ground with his finger. [7]When they kept on questioning him, he straightened up and said to them, "Let any one of you who is without sin be the first to throw a stone at her." [8]Again he stooped down and wrote on the ground.

[9]At this, those who heard began to go away one at a time, the older ones first, until only Jesus was left, with the woman still standing there. [10]Jesus straightened up and asked her, "Woman, where are they? Has no one condemned you?"

[11]"No one, sir," she said.

"Then neither do I condemn you," Jesus declared. "Go now and leave your life of sin."

Dispute Over Jesus' Testimony

[12]When Jesus spoke again to the people, he said, "I am the light of the world. Whoever follows me will never walk in darkness, but will have the light of life."

[13]The Pharisees challenged him, "Here you are, appearing as your own witness; your testimony is not valid."

[14]Jesus answered, "Even if I testify on my own behalf, my testimony is valid, for I know where I came from and where I am going. But you have no idea where I come from or where I am going. [15]You judge by human standards; I pass judgment on no one. [16]But if I do judge, my decisions are true, because I am not alone. I stand with the Father, who sent me. [17]In your own Law it is written that the testimony of two witnesses is true. [18]I am one who testifies for myself; my other witness is the Father, who sent me."

[19]Then they asked him, "Where is your father?"

"You do not know me or my Father," Jesus replied. "If you knew me, you would know my Father also." [20]He spoke these words while teaching in the temple courts near the place where the offerings were put. Yet no one seized him, because his hour had not yet come.

Dispute Over Who Jesus Is

[21]Once more Jesus said to them, "I am going away, and you will look for me, and you will die in your sin. Where I go, you cannot come."

[22]This made the Jews ask, "Will he kill himself? Is that why he says, 'Where I go, you cannot come'?"

[23]But he continued, "You are from below; I am from above. You are of this world; I am not of this world. [24]I told you that you would die in your sins; if you do not believe that I am he, you will indeed die in your sins."

[25]"Who are you?" they asked.

"Just what I have been telling you from the beginning," Jesus replied. [26]"I have much to say in judgment of you. But he who sent me is trustworthy, and what I have heard from him I tell the world."

[27]They did not understand that he was telling them about his Father. [28]So Jesus said, "When you have lifted up[a] the Son of Man, then you will know that I am he and that I do nothing on my own but speak just what the Father has taught me. [29]The one who sent me is with me; he has not left me alone, for I always do what pleases him." [30]Even as he spoke, many believed in him.

Dispute Over Whose Children Jesus' Opponents Are

[31]To the Jews who had believed him, Jesus said, "If you hold to my teaching, you are really my disciples. [32]Then you will know the truth, and the truth will set you free."

[33]They answered him, "We are Abraham's descendants and have never been slaves of anyone. How can you say that we shall be set free?"

[34]Jesus replied, "Very truly I tell you, everyone who sins is a slave to sin. [35]Now a slave has no permanent place in the family, but a son belongs to it forever. [36]So if the Son sets you free, you will be free indeed. [37]I know that you are Abraham's descendants. Yet you are looking for a way to kill me, because you have no room for my word. [38]I am telling you what I have seen in the Father's presence, and you are doing what you have heard from your father.[b]"

[39]"Abraham is our father," they answered.

"If you were Abraham's children," said Jesus, "then you would[c] do what Abraham did. [40]As it is, you are looking for a way to kill me, a man who has told you the truth that I heard from God. Abraham did not do such things. [41]You are doing the works of your own father."

"We are not illegitimate children," they protested. "The only Father we have is God himself."

---

[a] 28 The Greek for lifted up also means exalted.   [b] 38 Or presence. Therefore do what you have heard from the Father.   [c] 39 Some early manuscripts "If you are Abraham's children," said Jesus, "then

21 QUALITIES

SERVANTHOOD   A Conflict Between Two Worldviews

John 8:1–59

JOHN 8 depicts one long showdown between two conflicting worldviews. It begins with the woman caught committing adultery (vv. 1–11), then moves to an argument between Jesus and the Pharisees about their fleshly judgment (vv. 12–30). Next, the Lord explains what it means to truly be born of Abraham (vv. 31–47). Finally, he debates the synagogue leaders about his identity (vv. 48–59).

The flawed worldview of the Jewish leaders contributed greatly to their continuing inability to understand Jesus. They sat in a place of power and feared being displaced. Jesus taught that leadership meant serving others; they sought titles and positions of honor. Jesus taught that leadership meant giving up rights; they took pride in their heritage as sons of Abraham. Jesus told them that their actions revealed their true father—and that's when they had had enough. This Jesus simply was too radical for them.

Still, they couldn't win a debate with him. He seemed to know the Scriptures better than they did! He was different from them—but much to their disappointment, he was right.

The Pharisees sought power and already competed with the Roman Empire for control of the masses. Not only did they have to deal with their own king, Herod, but they also needed to consider a Roman governor named Pontius Pilate. Consequently, they protected every bit of turf they could.

Does this sound like any leader you know? Someone who fights to maintain manmade traditions and rules? Someone blind to the needs of others and preoccupied with himself or herself? Such leaders stand in contrast to the servant leadership Jesus modeled.

Secular Leadership vs. Spiritual Leadership

Take a moment to contrast the world's leadership model with Jesus' model.

Issue	Secular Leadership	Spiritual Leadership
How to gain influence	Leverage power	Love people (Php 2:3–11)
How to possess confidence	Compete and win	Depend on God (2Co 3:4–6)
How to acquire authority	Claim your rights and position	Servanthood (Mt 20:20–28)
How to grow an organization	Demand of people	Develop people (Ac 19:8–10)
What vision drives you	Temporal gain	Eternal gain (Mt 6:31–33)
What is success	Overcoming the competition	Obeying the Lord (1Co 4:1–5)
The heart of leadership	The boss	A Father (1Co 4:15)

What does your leadership look like? Are you a Pharisee or a servant?

For a positive example of servanthood, see p. 359.

⁴²Jesus said to them, "If God were your Father, you would love me, for I have come here from God. I have not come on my own; God sent me. ⁴³Why is my language not clear to you? Because you are unable to hear what I say. ⁴⁴You belong to your father, the devil, and you want to carry out your father's desires. He was a murderer from the beginning, not holding to the truth, for there is no truth in him. When he lies, he speaks his native language, for he is a liar and the father of lies. ⁴⁵Yet because I tell the truth, you do not believe me! ⁴⁶Can any of you prove me guilty of sin? If I am telling the truth, why don't you believe me? ⁴⁷Whoever belongs to God hears what God says. The reason you do not hear is that you do not belong to God."

Jesus' Claims About Himself

⁴⁸The Jews answered him, "Aren't we right in saying that you are a Samaritan and demon-possessed?"

⁴⁹"I am not possessed by a demon," said Jesus, "but I honor my Father and you dishonor me. ⁵⁰I am not seeking glory for myself; but there is one who seeks it, and he is the judge. ⁵¹Very truly I tell you, whoever obeys my word will never see death."

⁵²At this they exclaimed, "Now we know that you are demon-possessed! Abraham died and so did the prophets, yet you say that whoever obeys your word will never taste death. ⁵³Are you greater than our father Abraham? He died, and so did the prophets. Who do you think you are?"

⁵⁴Jesus replied, "If I glorify myself, my glory means nothing. My Father, whom you claim as your God, is the one who glorifies me. ⁵⁵Though you do not know him, I know him. If I said I did not, I would be a liar like you, but I do know him and obey his word. ⁵⁶Your father Abraham rejoiced at the thought of seeing my day; he saw it and was glad."

⁵⁷"You are not yet fifty years old," they said to him, "and you have seen Abraham!"

⁵⁸"Very truly I tell you," Jesus answered, "before Abraham was born, I am!" ⁵⁹At this, they picked up stones to stone him, but Jesus hid himself, slipping away from the temple grounds.

Jesus Heals a Man Born Blind

9 As he went along, he saw a man blind from birth. ²His disciples asked him, "Rabbi, who sinned, this man or his parents, that he was born blind?"

³"Neither this man nor his parents sinned," said Jesus, "but this happened so that the works

Conflict Management: Confrontation Is the Way to Resolution

John 8:48–59

Many times Jesus had to confront opposition among the Pharisees, scribes and other Jewish leaders. Although Old Testament prophecies called him the "Prince of Peace," he decided on this day that there could be no peaceful agreement. Jesus stood toe-to-toe with his opponents and tackled the issue head-on—and things quickly got heated.

Sometimes, confrontation is the only way to resolution. What do we learn from Jesus about confrontation? Consider four steps to reach the heart of an issue:

1. Be clear and direct (vv. 48–49).
2. Don't draw attention to yourself (vv. 49–50).
3. Lay out the issue and ask for a decision (v. 51).
4. Trust God to justify and reveal the truth (vv. 52–54).

of God might be displayed in him. ⁴As long as it is day, we must do the works of him who sent me. Night is coming, when no one can work. ⁵While I am in the world, I am the light of the world."

⁶After saying this, he spit on the ground, made some mud with the saliva, and put it on the man's eyes. ⁷"Go," he told him, "wash in the Pool of Siloam" (this word means "Sent"). So the man went and washed, and came home seeing.

⁸His neighbors and those who had formerly seen him begging asked, "Isn't this the same man who used to sit and beg?" ⁹Some claimed that he was.

Others said, "No, he only looks like him."

But he himself insisted, "I am the man."

¹⁰"How then were your eyes opened?" they asked.

¹¹He replied, "The man they call Jesus made some mud and put it on my eyes. He told me to go to Siloam and wash. So I went and washed, and then I could see."

¹²"Where is this man?" they asked him.

"I don't know," he said.

The Pharisees Investigate the Healing

¹³They brought to the Pharisees the man who had been blind. ¹⁴Now the day on which Jesus had made the mud and opened the man's eyes was a Sabbath. ¹⁵Therefore the Pharisees also asked him how he had received his sight. "He put mud on my eyes," the man replied, "and I washed, and now I see."

¹⁶Some of the Pharisees said, "This man is not from God, for he does not keep the Sabbath."

But others asked, "How can a sinner perform such signs?" So they were divided.

¹⁷Then they turned again to the blind man, "What have you to say about him? It was your eyes he opened."

The man replied, "He is a prophet."

¹⁸They still did not believe that he had been blind and had received his sight until they sent for the man's parents. ¹⁹"Is this your son?" they asked. "Is this the one you say was born blind? How is it that now he can see?"

²⁰"We know he is our son," the parents answered, "and we know he was born blind. ²¹But how he can see now, or who opened his eyes, we don't know. Ask him. He is of age; he will speak for himself." ²²His parents said this because they were afraid of the Jewish leaders, who already had decided that anyone who acknowledged that Jesus was the Messiah would be put out of the synagogue. ²³That was why his parents said, "He is of age; ask him."

²⁴A second time they summoned the man who had been blind. "Give glory to God by telling the truth," they said. "We know this man is a sinner."

²⁵He replied, "Whether he is a sinner or not, I don't know. One thing I do know. I was blind but now I see!"

²⁶Then they asked him, "What did he do to you? How did he open your eyes?"

²⁷He answered, "I have told you already and you did not listen. Why do you want to hear it again? Do you want to become his disciples too?"

²⁸Then they hurled insults at him and said, "You are this fellow's disciple! We are disciples of Moses! ²⁹We know that God spoke to Moses, but as for this fellow, we don't even know where he comes from."

³⁰The man answered, "Now that is remarkable! You don't know where he comes from, yet he opened my eyes. ³¹We know that God does not listen to sinners. He listens to the godly person who does his will. ³²Nobody has ever heard of opening the eyes of a man born blind. ³³If this man were not from God, he could do nothing."

The Law of Victory: Jesus Heals a Blind Man and No One Can Deny It

John 9:1–34

By healing the blind man, Jesus silenced his opposition. When they questioned the man who was healed, he could only declare the result: "Whether he is a sinner or not, I don't know. One thing I do know. I was blind but now I see!" (Jn 9:25). Jesus practiced the Law of Victory.

---

³⁴To this they replied, "You were steeped in sin at birth; how dare you lecture us!" And they threw him out.

Spiritual Blindness

³⁵Jesus heard that they had thrown him out, and when he found him, he said, "Do you believe in the Son of Man?"

³⁶"Who is he, sir?" the man asked. "Tell me so that I may believe in him."

³⁷Jesus said, "You have now seen him; in fact, he is the one speaking with you."

³⁸Then the man said, "Lord, I believe," and he worshiped him.

³⁹Jesus said,ᵃ "For judgment I have come into this world, so that the blind will see and those who see will become blind."

⁴⁰Some Pharisees who were with him heard him say this and asked, "What? Are we blind too?"

⁴¹Jesus said, "If you were blind, you would not be guilty of sin; but now that you claim you can see, your guilt remains.

The Good Shepherd and His Sheep

10 "Very truly I tell you Pharisees, anyone who does not enter the sheep pen by the gate, but climbs in by some other way, is a thief and a robber. ²The one who enters by the gate is the shepherd of the sheep. ³The gatekeeper opens the gate for him, and the sheep listen to his voice. He calls his own sheep by name and leads them out. ⁴When he has brought out all his own, he goes on ahead of them, and his sheep follow him because they know his voice. ⁵But

---

ᵃ 38,39 Some early manuscripts do not have *Then the man said . . . ³⁹Jesus said.*

they will never follow a stranger; in fact, they will run away from him because they do not recognize a stranger's voice." [6]Jesus used this figure of speech, but the Pharisees did not understand what he was telling them.

[7]Therefore Jesus said again, "Very truly I tell you, I am the gate for the sheep. [8]All who have come before me are thieves and robbers, but the sheep have not listened to them. [9]I am the gate; whoever enters through me will be saved.[a] They will come in and go out, and find pasture. [10]The thief comes only to steal and kill and destroy; I have come that they may have life, and have it to the full.

[11]"I am the good shepherd. The good shepherd lays down his life for the sheep. [12]The hired hand is not the shepherd and does not own the sheep. So when he sees the wolf coming, he abandons the sheep and runs away. Then the wolf attacks the flock and scatters it. [13]The man runs away because he is a hired hand and cares nothing for the sheep.

[14]"I am the good shepherd; I know my sheep and my sheep know me— [15]just as the Father knows me and I know the Father—and I lay down my life for the sheep. [16]I have other sheep that are not of this sheep pen. I must bring them also. They too will listen to my voice, and there shall be one flock and one shepherd. [17]The reason my Father loves me is that I lay down my life—only to take it up again. [18]No one takes it from me, but I lay it down of my own accord. I have authority to lay it down and authority to take it up again. This command I received from my Father."

[19]The Jews who heard these words were again divided. [20]Many of them said, "He is demon-possessed and raving mad. Why listen to him?"

[21]But others said, "These are not the sayings of a man possessed by a demon. Can a demon open the eyes of the blind?"

Further Conflict Over Jesus' Claims

[22]Then came the Festival of Dedication[b] at Jerusalem. It was winter, [23]and Jesus was in the temple courts walking in Solomon's Colonnade. [24]The Jews who were there gathered around him, saying, "How long will you keep us in suspense? If you are the Messiah, tell us plainly."

[25]Jesus answered, "I did tell you, but you do not believe. The works I do in my Father's name testify about me, [26]but you do not believe because you are not my sheep. [27]My sheep listen to my voice; I know them, and they follow me.

---

[a] 9 Or kept safe   [b] 22 That is, Hanukkah

The Law of Connection: Jesus Relates Like a Shepherd to Sheep

John 10:1-16

Jesus describes himself as the Good Shepherd, a Leader who guides his people as a shepherd leads his sheep. The Old Testament prophets used this metaphor many times, from Moses (Nu 27:15–17) all the way to Ezekiel (Eze 34:1–10).

Everyone who wants to lead in the kingdom of God must develop certain heart qualifications. The image of the shepherd best captures the heart of a godly leader: Shepherds are tender, sincere, intimate, loving. They guide, correct, protect and feed. John contrasts the good shepherd with the hireling. A hireling receives pay for his job, but has no heart for it. He watches out for the sheep until he no longer benefits.

The Hireling	The Shepherd
1. Labors only for money (Mt 20:7)	1. Labors out of love
2. Has no heart for the sheep (Jn 10:13)	2. Has a heart for the sheep
3. Leaves when trouble comes (Jer 46:21)	3. Gives his life for sheep
4. Is unfaithful to his master (Jn 10:12)	4. Faithfully serves his master
5. Feeds himself, not the sheep (Eze 34:3)	5. Feeds the sheep
6. Neglects the sheep (Eze 34:3)	6. Tenderly cares for the sheep
7. Drives sheep hard and lacks mercy (Jer 23:2)	7. Leads the sheep wisely

²⁸I give them eternal life, and they shall never perish; no one will snatch them out of my hand. ²⁹My Father, who has given them to me, is greater than all[a]; no one can snatch them out of my Father's hand. ³⁰I and the Father are one."

³¹Again his Jewish opponents picked up stones to stone him, ³²but Jesus said to them, "I have shown you many good works from the Father. For which of these do you stone me?"

³³"We are not stoning you for any good work," they replied, "but for blasphemy, because you, a mere man, claim to be God."

³⁴Jesus answered them, "Is it not written in your Law, 'I have said you are "gods"'[b]? ³⁵If he called them 'gods,' to whom the word of God came—and Scripture cannot be set aside—³⁶what about the one whom the Father set apart as his very own and sent into the world? Why then do you accuse me of blasphemy because I said, 'I am God's Son'? ³⁷Do not believe me unless I do the works of my Father. ³⁸But if I do them, even though you do not believe me, believe the works, that you may know and understand that the Father is in me, and I in the Father." ³⁹Again they tried to seize him, but he escaped their grasp.

⁴⁰Then Jesus went back across the Jordan to the place where John had been baptizing in the early days. There he stayed, ⁴¹and many people came to him. They said, "Though John never performed a sign, all that John said about this man was true." ⁴²And in that place many believed in Jesus.

The Death of Lazarus

11 Now a man named Lazarus was sick. He was from Bethany, the village of Mary and her sister Martha. ²(This Mary, whose brother Lazarus now lay sick, was the same one who poured perfume on the Lord and wiped his feet with her hair.) ³So the sisters sent word to Jesus, "Lord, the one you love is sick."

⁴When he heard this, Jesus said, "This sickness will not end in death. No, it is for God's glory so that God's Son may be glorified through it." ⁵Now Jesus loved Martha and her sister and Lazarus. ⁶So when he heard that Lazarus was sick, he stayed where he was two more days, ⁷and then he said to his disciples, "Let us go back to Judea."

⁸"But Rabbi," they said, "a short while ago the Jews there tried to stone you, and yet you are going back?"

⁹Jesus answered, "Are there not twelve hours of daylight? Anyone who walks in the daytime

---

The Law of Timing: Jesus Timed His Visit to Lazarus and Won Big

John 11:1-6

When Jesus got word that one of his closest friends was near death, he waited two days before leaving to visit him. Why? Jesus knew the Law of Timing and waited until Lazarus died, then left for Bethany. When he raised his friend back to life, it got the attention of everyone in Jerusalem.

---

will not stumble, for they see by this world's light. ¹⁰It is when a person walks at night that they stumble, for they have no light."

¹¹After he had said this, he went on to tell them, "Our friend Lazarus has fallen asleep; but I am going there to wake him up."

¹²His disciples replied, "Lord, if he sleeps, he will get better." ¹³Jesus had been speaking of his death, but his disciples thought he meant natural sleep.

¹⁴So then he told them plainly, "Lazarus is dead, ¹⁵and for your sake I am glad I was not there, so that you may believe. But let us go to him."

¹⁶Then Thomas (also known as Didymus[c]) said to the rest of the disciples, "Let us also go, that we may die with him."

Jesus Comforts the Sisters of Lazarus

¹⁷On his arrival, Jesus found that Lazarus had already been in the tomb for four days. ¹⁸Now Bethany was less than two miles[d] from Jerusalem, ¹⁹and many Jews had come to Martha and Mary to comfort them in the loss of their brother. ²⁰When Martha heard that Jesus was coming, she went out to meet him, but Mary stayed at home.

²¹"Lord," Martha said to Jesus, "if you had been here, my brother would not have died. ²²But I know that even now God will give you whatever you ask."

²³Jesus said to her, "Your brother will rise again."

---

[a] 29 Many early manuscripts *What my Father has given me is greater than all*   [b] 34 Psalm 82:6   [c] 16 *Thomas* (Aramaic) and *Didymus* (Greek) both mean *twin*.   [d] 18 Or about 3 kilometers

²⁴Martha answered, "I know he will rise again in the resurrection at the last day."

²⁵Jesus said to her, "I am the resurrection and the life. The one who believes in me will live, even though they die; ²⁶and whoever lives by believing in me will never die. Do you believe this?"

²⁷"Yes, Lord," she replied, "I believe that you are the Messiah, the Son of God, who is to come into the world."

²⁸After she had said this, she went back and called her sister Mary aside. "The Teacher is here," she said, "and is asking for you." ²⁹When Mary heard this, she got up quickly and went to him. ³⁰Now Jesus had not yet entered the village, but was still at the place where Martha had met him. ³¹When the Jews who had been with Mary in the house, comforting her, noticed how quickly she got up and went out, they followed her, supposing she was going to the tomb to mourn there.

³²When Mary reached the place where Jesus was and saw him, she fell at his feet and said, "Lord, if you had been here, my brother would not have died."

³³When Jesus saw her weeping, and the Jews who had come along with her also weeping, he was deeply moved in spirit and troubled. ³⁴"Where have you laid him?" he asked.

"Come and see, Lord," they replied.

³⁵Jesus wept.

³⁶Then the Jews said, "See how he loved him!"

³⁷But some of them said, "Could not he who opened the eyes of the blind man have kept this man from dying?"

Jesus Raises Lazarus From the Dead

³⁸Jesus, once more deeply moved, came to the tomb. It was a cave with a stone laid across the entrance. ³⁹"Take away the stone," he said.

"But, Lord," said Martha, the sister of the dead man, "by this time there is a bad odor, for he has been there four days."

⁴⁰Then Jesus said, "Did I not tell you that if you believe, you will see the glory of God?"

⁴¹So they took away the stone. Then Jesus looked up and said, "Father, I thank you that you have heard me. ⁴²I knew that you always hear me, but I said this for the benefit of the people standing here, that they may believe that you sent me."

⁴³When he had said this, Jesus called in a loud voice, "Lazarus, come out!" ⁴⁴The dead man came out, his hands and feet wrapped with strips of linen, and a cloth around his face.

Jesus said to them, "Take off the grave clothes and let him go."

The Plot to Kill Jesus

⁴⁵Therefore many of the Jews who had come to visit Mary, and had seen what Jesus did, believed in him. ⁴⁶But some of them went to the Pharisees and told them what Jesus had done. ⁴⁷Then the chief priests and the Pharisees called a meeting of the Sanhedrin.

"What are we accomplishing?" they asked. "Here is this man performing many signs. ⁴⁸If we let him go on like this, everyone will believe in him, and then the Romans will come and take away both our temple and our nation."

⁴⁹Then one of them, named Caiaphas, who was high priest that year, spoke up, "You know nothing at all! ⁵⁰You do not realize that it is better for you that one man die for the people than that the whole nation perish."

⁵¹He did not say this on his own, but as high priest that year he prophesied that Jesus would die for the Jewish nation, ⁵²and not only for that nation but also for the scattered children of God, to bring them together and make them one. ⁵³So from that day on they plotted to take his life.

⁵⁴Therefore Jesus no longer moved about publicly among the people of Judea. Instead he withdrew to a region near the wilderness, to a village called Ephraim, where he stayed with his disciples.

⁵⁵When it was almost time for the Jewish Passover, many went up from the country to Jerusalem for their ceremonial cleansing before the Passover. ⁵⁶They kept looking for Jesus, and as they stood in the temple courts they asked one another, "What do you think? Isn't he coming to the festival at all?" ⁵⁷But the chief priests and the Pharisees had given orders that anyone who found out where Jesus was should report it so that they might arrest him.

Jesus Anointed at Bethany

12 Six days before the Passover, Jesus came to Bethany, where Lazarus lived, whom Jesus had raised from the dead. ²Here a dinner was given in Jesus' honor. Martha served, while Lazarus was among those reclining at the table with him. ³Then Mary took about a pint^a of pure nard, an expensive perfume; she poured it on Jesus' feet and wiped his feet with her hair. And the house was filled with the fragrance of the perfume.

---

^{a} 3 Or about 0.5 liter

⁴But one of his disciples, Judas Iscariot, who was later to betray him, objected, ⁵"Why wasn't this perfume sold and the money given to the poor? It was worth a year's wages.ᵃ" ⁶He did not say this because he cared about the poor but because he was a thief; as keeper of the money bag, he used to help himself to what was put into it.

⁷"Leave her alone," Jesus replied. "It was intended that she should save this perfume for the day of my burial. ⁸You will always have the poor among you,ᵇ but you will not always have me."

⁹Meanwhile a large crowd of Jews found out that Jesus was there and came, not only because of him but also to see Lazarus, whom he had raised from the dead. ¹⁰So the chief priests made plans to kill Lazarus as well, ¹¹for on account of him many of the Jews were going over to Jesus and believing in him.

Jesus Comes to Jerusalem as King

¹²The next day the great crowd that had come for the festival heard that Jesus was on his way to Jerusalem. ¹³They took palm branches and went out to meet him, shouting,

"Hosanna!ᶜ"

"Blessed is he who comes in the name of the Lord!"ᵈ

"Blessed is the king of Israel!"

¹⁴Jesus found a young donkey and sat on it, as it is written:

¹⁵"Do not be afraid, Daughter Zion;
    see, your king is coming,
    seated on a donkey's colt."ᵉ

¹⁶At first his disciples did not understand all this. Only after Jesus was glorified did they realize that these things had been written about him and that these things had been done to him.

¹⁷Now the crowd that was with him when he called Lazarus from the tomb and raised him from the dead continued to spread the word. ¹⁸Many people, because they had heard that he had performed this sign, went out to meet him. ¹⁹So the Pharisees said to one another, "See, this is getting us nowhere. Look how the whole world has gone after him!"

Jesus Predicts His Death

²⁰Now there were some Greeks among those who went up to worship at the festival. ²¹They came to Philip, who was from Bethsaida in Galilee, with a request. "Sir," they said, "we would like to see Jesus." ²²Philip went to tell Andrew; Andrew and Philip in turn told Jesus.

²³Jesus replied, "The hour has come for the Son of Man to be glorified. ²⁴Very truly I tell you, unless a kernel of wheat falls to the ground and dies, it remains only a single seed. But if it dies, it produces many seeds. ²⁵Anyone who loves their life will lose it, while anyone who hates their life in this world will keep it for eternal life. ²⁶Whoever serves me must follow me; and where I am, my servant also will be. My Father will honor the one who serves me.

²⁷"Now my soul is troubled, and what shall I say? 'Father, save me from this hour'? No, it was for this very reason I came to this hour. ²⁸Father, glorify your name!"

Then a voice came from heaven, "I have glorified it, and will glorify it again." ²⁹The crowd that was there and heard it said it had thundered; others said an angel had spoken to him.

³⁰Jesus said, "This voice was for your benefit, not mine. ³¹Now is the time for judgment on this world; now the prince of this world will be driven out. ³²And I, when I am lifted upᶠ from the earth, will draw all people to myself." ³³He said this to show the kind of death he was going to die.

³⁴The crowd spoke up, "We have heard from the Law that the Messiah will remain forever, so how can you say, 'The Son of Man must be lifted up'? Who is this 'Son of Man'?"

³⁵Then Jesus told them, "You are going to have the light just a little while longer. Walk while you have the light, before darkness over-

---

ᵃ 5 Greek *three hundred denarii*   ᵇ 8 See Deut. 15:11.
ᶜ 13 A Hebrew expression meaning "Save!" which became an exclamation of praise   ᵈ 13 Psalm 118:25,26
ᵉ 15 Zech. 9:9   ᶠ 32 The Greek for *lifted up* also means *exalted.*

The Law of Sacrifice: Jesus Gave Up to Go Up Permanently

John 12:24–33

Jesus compared his own death to a grain of wheat, falling to the earth, dying, and bearing much fruit (Jn 12:24). He then applied this law to us (12:25). Only when we give up our self-life and die can we really live. The greatest leaders willingly give up their lives for others.

takes you. Whoever walks in the dark does not know where they are going. [36]Believe in the light while you have the light, so that you may become children of light." When he had finished speaking, Jesus left and hid himself from them.

Belief and Unbelief Among the Jews

[37]Even after Jesus had performed so many signs in their presence, they still would not believe in him. [38]This was to fulfill the word of Isaiah the prophet:

"Lord, who has believed our message
    and to whom has the arm of the Lord been
        revealed?"[a]

[39]For this reason they could not believe, because, as Isaiah says elsewhere:

[40]"He has blinded their eyes
    and hardened their hearts,
so they can neither see with their eyes,
    nor understand with their hearts,
    nor turn — and I would heal them."[b]

[41]Isaiah said this because he saw Jesus' glory and spoke about him.

[42]Yet at the same time many even among the leaders believed in him. But because of the Pharisees they would not openly acknowledge their faith for fear they would be put out of the synagogue; [43]for they loved human praise more than praise from God.

[44]Then Jesus cried out, "Whoever believes in me does not believe in me only, but in the one who sent me. [45]The one who looks at me is seeing the one who sent me. [46]I have come into the world as a light, so that no one who believes in me should stay in darkness.

[47]"If anyone hears my words but does not keep them, I do not judge that person. For I did not come to judge the world, but to save the world. [48]There is a judge for the one who rejects me and does not accept my words; the very words I have spoken will condemn them at the last day. [49]For I did not speak on my own, but the Father who sent me commanded me to say all that I have spoken. [50]I know that his command leads to eternal life. So whatever I say is just what the Father has told me to say."

Jesus Washes His Disciples' Feet

13 It was just before the Passover Festival. Jesus knew that the hour had come for him to leave this world and go to the Father. Having loved his own who were in the world, he loved them to the end.

[2]The evening meal was in progress, and the devil had already prompted Judas, the son of Simon Iscariot, to betray Jesus. [3]Jesus knew that the Father had put all things under his power, and that he had come from God and was returning to God; [4]so he got up from the meal, took off his outer clothing, and wrapped a towel around his waist. [5]After that, he poured water into a basin and began to wash his disciples' feet, drying them with the towel that was wrapped around him.

[6]He came to Simon Peter, who said to him, "Lord, are you going to wash my feet?"

[7]Jesus replied, "You do not realize now what I am doing, but later you will understand."

[8]"No," said Peter, "you shall never wash my feet."

Jesus answered, "Unless I wash you, you have no part with me."

[9]"Then, Lord," Simon Peter replied, "not just my feet but my hands and my head as well!"

[10]Jesus answered, "Those who have had a bath need only to wash their feet; their whole body is clean. And you are clean, though not every one of you." [11]For he knew who was going to betray him, and that was why he said not every one was clean.

[12]When he had finished washing their feet, he put on his clothes and returned to his place. "Do you understand what I have done for you?" he asked them. [13]"You call me 'Teacher' and 'Lord,' and rightly so, for that is what I am. [14]Now that I, your Lord and Teacher, have washed your feet, you also should wash one another's feet. [15]I have set you an example that you should do as I have done for you. [16]Very truly I tell you, no servant is greater than his master, nor is a messenger greater than the one who sent him. [17]Now that you know these things, you will be blessed if you do them.

Jesus Predicts His Betrayal

[18]"I am not referring to all of you; I know those I have chosen. But this is to fulfill this passage of Scripture: 'He who shared my bread has turned[c] against me.'[d]

[19]"I am telling you now before it happens, so that when it does happen you will believe that I am who I am. [20]Very truly I tell you, whoever accepts anyone I send accepts me; and whoever accepts me accepts the one who sent me."

[21]After he had said this, Jesus was troubled in

---

[a] 38 Isaiah 53:1   [b] 40 Isaiah 6:10   [c] 18 Greek *has lifted up his heel*   [d] 18 Psalm 41:9

JESUS AND THE LAW OF ADDITION
A Visual Aid About Adding Value

John 13:1–17

WHEN YOU think of servanthood, do you envision it as an activity performed by relatively low-skilled people at the bottom of the flow chart? If you do, you have the wrong impression. Often we assume that if we serve, people will lower their view of us; that they will assume we possess the lowest position in the organization. But this is wrong. Think for a moment about the person who has served you more than anyone else in your life. Answers might vary, but most people will automatically respond, "My mother." Moms seem to be the greatest example of servanthood as they naturally serve the members of their family. Now here's another question: Do you have a lower view of your mother because she serves you, or a higher view of her? Most everyone would say a higher view. Why? Serving other people has exactly the opposite effect on them from what we think it will. People are drawn toward those who serve them sacrificially, not repelled by them. Service adds value to people. Servanthood is not about position or skill. It's about attitude. Leaders seek ways they can add value to others, and the primary way they do it is by serving them. In John 13, the Savior of the world exhibited that he was also the greatest Servant of all time. The story is familiar to many. When the disciples booked the upper room for the Passover feast, they forgot to secure the services of a servant to wash feet at the door. It was a custom to do this. Interestingly, as the disciples realized the servant was missing, none of them volunteered for the job. Instead, they argued over who was the greatest.

When Jesus saw this, he decided to make an object lesson out of it. So after supper, Jesus stripped down to a garment around his waist. He even looked the part of the servant! Then he took a basin of water and a towel and began washing his disciples' feet. As Jesus interacted with his men, several lessons about service and adding value arose.

Christlike Servant-Leaders . . .

1. *ARE motivated by love to serve others* (vv. 1–2).

Jesus' love was undeserved, unending, unconditional and unselfish. It was not the worthiness or the merits of the disciples that drove Jesus to serve them. He wasn't expressing gratitude, but grace. Love made him serve his disciples. Think about it: Jesus even washed the feet of Judas Iscariot, the man who would betray him and have him killed the next day.

2. *POSSESS a security that allows them to serve others* (v. 3).

Jesus knew who he was, and he was secure enough to get down on the floor and wash his disciples' feet. He didn't have to prove anything. In fact, he had nothing to prove, nothing to lose and nothing to hide. The insecure are into titles. The secure are into towels. Jesus' security enabled him to both stoop and stretch.

3. *INITIATE servant-leadership to others* (vv. 4–5).

Jesus didn't wait for someone to clarify protocol. He saw a need and met it. No one else had volunteered for the foot-washing job that night—so Jesus made an object lesson out of the event. He started something that he hoped would be passed down from those twelve disciples to others (see Jn 13:12–15). Foot washing will never be in vogue. It will be done by leaders who are willing to pioneer an act of humility and sacrifice.

4. *RECEIVE servant-ministry from others* (vv. 6–7).

A servant's heart exposes pride in others. Peter had a hard time letting Jesus serve him. He still possessed a worldly mindset that assumed that someone of Jesus' caliber should never stoop to wash feet. Sometimes leaders must learn to let others serve them. Because they become so used to serving others, it is difficult for them to relax and receive. In this instance, Jesus was asking Simon Peter to sit and allow the Master to serve him.

5. *WANT nothing to hinder their relationship with God* (vv. 8–9).

Peter moved from one extreme to the other. If Jesus was going to wash him, he didn't want to miss anything he might do. He wanted Jesus to wash his entire body. Simon Peter exhibits a great attitude here. If Jesus was giving away, he wanted to receive all that Jesus had to give; he didn't want anything to stand between him and his Lord.

6. *TEACH servanthood by their example* (vv. 12, 15).

Afterward, Jesus discussed the meaning of his foot washing. He reminded them that the Master and Lord had just washed their feet, so no position should prevent them from doing it for someone else. Jesus let them know that if the Master washed their feet, they ought to imitate him. His model was to be reproduced. In fact, his example was much more powerful than a lecture about the principles of service. Actions speak more loudly than words.

7. *LIVE a blessed life* (vv. 16–17).

Jesus reminded them they were blessed if they obeyed him in this lifestyle. The greatest blessing follows those who step out by faith and do the opposite of what the world is doing. God blesses those who "go countercultural" and serve people with no thought of getting something in return from them. The return comes in the form of God's blessing.

When leaders serve, they add value to the people who receive their service. This value might be as simple as feeling worthwhile or special. It could be that the value is a resource we put in people's hands or a word of encouragement we speak to them. Whatever it is, people always receive something and feel better about themselves because of their leader. A good habit for a leader is try to add value to everyone he or she meets; try to add something to their lives rather than take away. Seek to replenish and resource them to live the higher life God has called them to. This is what Jesus did, day in and day out. Whether he met up with a Samaritan woman as in John 4, or a tax collector like Matthew or Zacchaeus, or a prostitute like Mary Magdalene—Jesus served them and added value to them. Maybe that's why people think so highly of him. He served.

OUR APPLICATION Today . . .
Put others ahead of your agenda.
Develop the confidence and security to take risks.
Look for a need and take initiative.
Perform small acts anonymously.
Learn to walk slowly through the crowd.
Begin your day reflecting on the love you have for others in your life.
Develop a bias for action.

spirit and testified, "Very truly I tell you, one of you is going to betray me."

²²His disciples stared at one another, at a loss to know which of them he meant. ²³One of them, the disciple whom Jesus loved, was reclining next to him. ²⁴Simon Peter motioned to this disciple and said, "Ask him which one he means."

²⁵Leaning back against Jesus, he asked him, "Lord, who is it?"

²⁶Jesus answered, "It is the one to whom I will give this piece of bread when I have dipped it in the dish." Then, dipping the piece of bread, he gave it to Judas, the son of Simon Iscariot. ²⁷As soon as Judas took the bread, Satan entered into him.

So Jesus told him, "What you are about to do, do quickly." ²⁸But no one at the meal understood why Jesus said this to him. ²⁹Since Judas had charge of the money, some thought Jesus was telling him to buy what was needed for the festival, or to give something to the poor. ³⁰As soon as Judas had taken the bread, he went out. And it was night.

Jesus Predicts Peter's Denial

³¹When he was gone, Jesus said, "Now the Son of Man is glorified and God is glorified in him. ³²If God is glorified in him,ᵃ God will glorify the Son in himself, and will glorify him at once.

³³"My children, I will be with you only a little longer. You will look for me, and just as I told the Jews, so I tell you now: Where I am going, you cannot come.

³⁴"A new command I give you: Love one another. As I have loved you, so you must love one another. ³⁵By this everyone will know that you are my disciples, if you love one another."

³⁶Simon Peter asked him, "Lord, where are you going?"

Jesus replied, "Where I am going, you cannot follow now, but you will follow later."

³⁷Peter asked, "Lord, why can't I follow you now? I will lay down my life for you."

³⁸Then Jesus answered, "Will you really lay down your life for me? Very truly I tell you, before the rooster crows, you will disown me three times!

Jesus Comforts His Disciples

14 "Do not let your hearts be troubled. You believe in God*ᵇ*; believe also in me. ²My Father's house has many rooms; if that were not so, would I have told you that I am going there to prepare a place for you? ³And if I go and prepare a place for you, I will come back and take

you to be with me that you also may be where I am. ⁴You know the way to the place where I am going."

Jesus the Way to the Father

⁵Thomas said to him, "Lord, we don't know where you are going, so how can we know the way?"

⁶Jesus answered, "I am the way and the truth and the life. No one comes to the Father except through me. ⁷If you really know me, you will knowᶜ my Father as well. From now on, you do know him and have seen him."

⁸Philip said, "Lord, show us the Father and that will be enough for us."

⁹Jesus answered: "Don't you know me, Philip, even after I have been among you such a long time? Anyone who has seen me has seen the Father. How can you say, 'Show us the Father'? ¹⁰Don't you believe that I am in the Father, and that the Father is in me? The words I say to you I do not speak on my own authority. Rather, it is the Father, living in me, who is doing his work. ¹¹Believe me when I say that I am in the Father and the Father is in me; or at least believe on the evidence of the works themselves. ¹²Very truly I tell you, whoever believes in me will do the works I have been doing, and they will do even greater things than these, because I am going to the Father. ¹³And I will do whatever you ask in my name, so that the Father may be glorified in the Son. ¹⁴You may ask me for anything in my name, and I will do it.

Jesus Promises the Holy Spirit

¹⁵"If you love me, keep my commands. ¹⁶And I will ask the Father, and he will give you an-

---

ᵃ 32 Many early manuscripts do not have *If God is glorified in him.*   ᵇ 1 Or *Believe in God*   ᶜ 7 Some manuscripts *If you really knew me, you would know*

The Law of Navigation: Jesus Laid a Plan for the Future

John 14:1–31

Jesus practiced the Law of Navigation by looking to the future. He reminded his men that he would prepare a place for them (Jn 14:1–4) and that he was preparing them for a place (14:16–29). He laid plans for the Holy Spirit to finish the work he had begun.

The Law of Empowerment:
Jesus Had a Great IDEA to Equip Others

John 14:12

Jesus told his men that they would do greater works than he had done. How would this be possible? First, he would send the Holy Spirit to live in each of them. Second, he had already given so much of himself to equip them. The Law of Empowerment tells us that only secure leaders give their power to others. God prepared the disciples to reproduce their leadership in the lives of others. They were empowered by the Holy Spirit and equipped by the Lord Jesus. Talk about being ready to change the world!

How did Jesus mentor and reproduce his leadership in his disciples? Consider Jesus' IDEA of how to reproduce leadership in someone else:

Instruction
He verbally taught them. He constantly used daily routines to instruct them in leadership.

Demonstration
He modeled truth and let his men observe his life. He provided show-and-tell.

Experience
He let the disciples participate and apply the truths themselves. They got to practice.

Assessment
He debriefed their shared experience. He assessed their growth and gave them direction.

other advocate to help you and be with you forever — [17]the Spirit of truth. The world cannot accept him, because it neither sees him nor knows him. But you know him, for he lives with you and will be[a] in you. [18]I will not leave you as orphans; I will come to you. [19]Before long, the world will not see me anymore, but you will see me. Because I live, you also will live. [20]On that day you will realize that I am in my Father, and you are in me, and I am in you. [21]Whoever has my commands and keeps them is the one who loves me. The one who loves me will be loved by my Father, and I too will love them and show myself to them."

[22]Then Judas (not Judas Iscariot) said, "But, Lord, why do you intend to show yourself to us and not to the world?"

[23]Jesus replied, "Anyone who loves me will obey my teaching. My Father will love them, and we will come to them and make our home with them. [24]Anyone who does not love me will not obey my teaching. These words you hear are not my own; they belong to the Father who sent me.

[25]"All this I have spoken while still with you. [26]But the Advocate, the Holy Spirit, whom the Father will send in my name, will teach you all things and will remind you of everything I have said to you. [27]Peace I leave with you; my peace I give you. I do not give to you as the world gives.

Do not let your hearts be troubled and do not be afraid.

[28]"You heard me say, 'I am going away and I am coming back to you.' If you loved me, you would be glad that I am going to the Father, for the Father is greater than I. [29]I have told you now before it happens, so that when it does happen you will believe. [30]I will not say much more to you, for the prince of this world is coming. He has no hold over me, [31]but he comes so that the world may learn that I love the Father and do exactly what my Father has commanded me.

"Come now; let us leave.

The Vine and the Branches

15 "I am the true vine, and my Father is the gardener. [2]He cuts off every branch in me that bears no fruit, while every branch that does bear fruit he prunes[b] so that it will be even more fruitful. [3]You are already clean because of the word I have spoken to you. [4]Remain in me, as I also remain in you. No branch can bear fruit by itself; it must remain in the vine. Neither can you bear fruit unless you remain in me.

[5]"I am the vine; you are the branches. If you remain in me and I in you, you will bear much

---

a 17 Some early manuscripts *and is*   *b* 2 The Greek for *he prunes* also means *he cleans.*

fruit; apart from me you can do nothing. [6]If you do not remain in me, you are like a branch that is thrown away and withers; such branches are picked up, thrown into the fire and burned. [7]If you remain in me and my words remain in you, ask whatever you wish, and it will be done for you. [8]This is to my Father's glory, that you bear much fruit, showing yourselves to be my disciples.

[9]"As the Father has loved me, so have I loved you. Now remain in my love. [10]If you keep my commands, you will remain in my love, just as I have kept my Father's commands and remain in his love. [11]I have told you this so that my joy may be in you and that your joy may be complete. [12]My command is this: Love each other as I have loved you. [13]Greater love has no one than this: to lay down one's life for one's friends. [14]You are my friends if you do what I command. [15]I no longer call you servants, because a servant does not know his master's business. Instead, I have called you friends, for everything that I learned from my Father I have made known to you. [16]You did not choose me, but I chose you and appointed you so that you might go and bear fruit—fruit that will last—and so that whatever you ask in my name the Father will give you. [17]This is my command: Love each other.

The World Hates the Disciples

[18]"If the world hates you, keep in mind that it hated me first. [19]If you belonged to the world, it would love you as its own. As it is, you do not belong to the world, but I have chosen you out of the world. That is why the world hates you. [20]Remember what I told you: 'A servant is not greater than his master.'[a] If they persecuted me, they will persecute you also. If they obeyed my teaching, they will obey yours also. [21]They will treat you this way because of my name, for they do not know the one who sent me. [22]If I had not come and spoken to them, they would not be guilty of sin; but now they have no excuse for their sin. [23]Whoever hates me hates my Father as well. [24]If I had not done among them the works no one else did, they would not be guilty

[a] 20 John 13:16

Fruitfulness Is Fun!

John 15:1–16

Jesus taught his staff how to be fruitful so that their joy might be full (Jn 15:11). In other words, fruitfulness is fun! There is great joy in gaining the results God desires.

Jesus said that he chose us and appointed us in order to go and bear fruit (15:16). As leaders, our goal is not only to bear fruit, but to help others do the same. We must be more than faithful; we must be fruitful. We have great potential for fruitful leadership because of our . . .

1. *Source* (v. 1)
   Jesus is the true Vine. If we stay connected to him, we naturally bear fruit.

2. *Care* (v. 1)
   Our heavenly Father is the Vinedresser. He owns us and cares for us.

3. *Pruning* (v. 2)
   God removes anything that hinders our usefulness. He trims our weaknesses.

4. *Partnership* (v. 4)
   Our job isn't to artificially push fruit out, but to stay connected to the Vine.

5. *Promise* (v. 7)
   If we let his Word abide in us, he promises he will do what we ask.

6. *Purpose* (v. 8)
   God created us to glorify him by bearing much fruit.

7. *Obedience* (v. 10)
   Jesus gives only one condition to all this: We must obey God. We are to remain *in* him, receive *from* him, and reproduce *for* him.

of sin. As it is, they have seen, and yet they have hated both me and my Father. [25]But this is to fulfill what is written in their Law: 'They hated me without reason.'[a]

The Work of the Holy Spirit

[26]"When the Advocate comes, whom I will send to you from the Father—the Spirit of truth who goes out from the Father—he will testify about me. [27]And you also must testify, for you have been with me from the beginning.

16 "All this I have told you so that you will not fall away. [2]They will put you out of the synagogue; in fact, the time is coming when anyone who kills you will think they are offering a service to God. [3]They will do such things because they have not known the Father or me. [4]I have told you this, so that when their time comes you will remember that I warned you about them. I did not tell you this from the beginning because I was with you, [5]but now I am going to him who sent me. None of you asks me, 'Where are you going?' [6]Rather, you are filled with grief because I have said these things. [7]But very truly I tell you, it is for your good that I am going away. Unless I go away, the Advocate will not come to you; but if I go, I will send him to you. [8]When he comes, he will prove the world to be in the wrong about sin and righteousness and judgment: [9]about sin, because people do not believe in me; [10]about righteousness, because I am going to the Father, where you can see me no longer; [11]and about judgment, because the prince of this world now stands condemned.

[12]"I have much more to say to you, more than you can now bear. [13]But when he, the Spirit of truth, comes, he will guide you into all the truth. He will not speak on his own; he will speak only what he hears, and he will tell you what is yet to come. [14]He will glorify me because it is from me that he will receive what he will make known to you. [15]All that belongs to the Father is mine. That is why I said the Spirit will receive from me what he will make known to you."

The Disciples' Grief Will Turn to Joy

[16]Jesus went on to say, "In a little while you will see me no more, and then after a little while you will see me."

[17]At this, some of his disciples said to one another, "What does he mean by saying, 'In a little while you will see me no more, and then after a little while you will see me,' and 'Because I am going to the Father'?" [18]They kept asking,

"What does he mean by 'a little while'? We don't understand what he is saying."

[19]Jesus saw that they wanted to ask him about this, so he said to them, "Are you asking one another what I meant when I said, 'In a little while you will see me no more, and then after a little while you will see me'? [20]Very truly I tell you, you will weep and mourn while the world rejoices. You will grieve, but your grief will turn to joy. [21]A woman giving birth to a child has pain because her time has come; but when her baby is born she forgets the anguish because of her joy that a child is born into the world. [22]So with you: Now is your time of grief, but I will see you again and you will rejoice, and no one will take away your joy. [23]In that day you will no longer ask me anything. Very truly I tell you, my Father will give you whatever you ask in my name. [24]Until now you have not asked for anything in my name. Ask and you will receive, and your joy will be complete.

[25]"Though I have been speaking figuratively, a time is coming when I will no longer use this kind of language but will tell you plainly about my Father. [26]In that day you will ask in my name. I am not saying that I will ask the Father on your behalf. [27]No, the Father himself loves you because you have loved me and have believed that I came from God. [28]I came from the Father and entered the world; now I am leaving the world and going back to the Father."

[29]Then Jesus' disciples said, "Now you are speaking clearly and without figures of speech. [30]Now we can see that you know all things and that you do not even need to have anyone ask you questions. This makes us believe that you came from God."

[31]"Do you now believe?" Jesus replied. [32]"A time is coming and in fact has come when you will be scattered, each to your own home. You will leave me all alone. Yet I am not alone, for my Father is with me.

[33]"I have told you these things, so that in me you may have peace. In this world you will have trouble. But take heart! I have overcome the world."

Jesus Prays to Be Glorified

17 After Jesus said this, he looked toward heaven and prayed:

"Father, the hour has come. Glorify your Son, that your Son may glorify you. [2]For

---

[a] 25 Psalms 35:19; 69:4

you granted him authority over all people that he might give eternal life to all those you have given him. ³Now this is eternal life: that they know you, the only true God, and Jesus Christ, whom you have sent. ⁴I have brought you glory on earth by finishing the work you gave me to do. ⁵And now, Father, glorify me in your presence with the glory I had with you before the world began.

Jesus Prays for His Disciples

⁶"I have revealed you[a] to those whom you gave me out of the world. They were yours; you gave them to me and they have obeyed your word. ⁷Now they know that everything you have given me comes from you. ⁸For I gave them the words you gave me and they accepted them. They knew with certainty that I came from you, and they believed that you sent me. ⁹I pray for them. I am not praying for the world, but for those you have given me, for they are yours. ¹⁰All I have is yours, and all you have is mine. And glory has come to me through them. ¹¹I will remain in the world no longer, but they are still in the world,

and I am coming to you. Holy Father, protect them by the power of[b] your name, the name you gave me, so that they may be one as we are one. ¹²While I was with them, I protected them and kept them safe by[c] that name you gave me. None has been lost except the one doomed to destruction so that Scripture would be fulfilled.

¹³"I am coming to you now, but I say these things while I am still in the world, so that they may have the full measure of my joy within them. ¹⁴I have given them your word and the world has hated them, for they are not of the world any more than I am of the world. ¹⁵My prayer is not that you take them out of the world but that you protect them from the evil one. ¹⁶They are not of the world, even as I am not of it. ¹⁷Sanctify them by[d] the truth; your word is truth. ¹⁸As you sent me into the world, I have sent them into the world. ¹⁹For them I sanctify myself, that they too may be truly sanctified.

---

[a] 6 Greek *your name*   [b] 11 Or *Father, keep them faithful to*
[c] 12 Or *kept them faithful to*   [d] 17 Or *them to live in accordance with*

The Law of the Inner Circle: Leading When No One Sees

John 17:11–26

The majority of what we call Jesus' "high priestly prayer" concerns his inner circle. At the end of his life, he felt acutely aware that the success of his work depended chiefly on the twelve disciples he had trained. Observe what he prayed for:

1. Their faith (vv. 11–12)
2. Their fulfillment (v. 13)
3. Their future (vv. 14–15)
4. Their faithfulness (vv. 16–17)
5. Their fruitfulness (vv. 18–20)
6. Their fellowship (vv. 21–23)
7. Their sense of family (vv. 24–26)

When Jesus knew he had but twelve hours left to live, he didn't start big campaigns. He didn't try to change laws. He didn't even do any more public ministry. He spent the time *praying*.

Prayer is a chief task of the leader (Ac 6:4). The leadership we provide which no one sees may be more important than what we do in public. Followers think of leadership in terms of the visible. In reality, leadership is like an iceberg; most of it lies unseen.

A leader's prayer tells you a lot about the leader. It reveals his or her commitment and concerns. Prayer keeps the leader focused. It keeps a leader dependent on God. It sustains the leader's heart for people. If we are to lead people, we must pray for them.

Jesus Prays for All Believers

²⁰"My prayer is not for them alone. I pray also for those who will believe in me through their message, ²¹that all of them may be one, Father, just as you are in me and I am in you. May they also be in us so that the world may believe that you have sent me. ²²I have given them the glory that you gave me, that they may be one as we are one— ²³I in them and you in me—so that they may be brought to complete unity. Then the world will know that you sent me and have loved them even as you have loved me.

²⁴"Father, I want those you have given me to be with me where I am, and to see my glory, the glory you have given me because you loved me before the creation of the world.

²⁵"Righteous Father, though the world does not know you, I know you, and they know that you have sent me. ²⁶I have made you*a* known to them, and will continue to make you known in order that the love you have for me may be in them and that I myself may be in them."

Jesus Arrested

18 When he had finished praying, Jesus left with his disciples and crossed the Kidron Valley. On the other side there was a garden, and he and his disciples went into it.

²Now Judas, who betrayed him, knew the place, because Jesus had often met there with his disciples. ³So Judas came to the garden, guiding a detachment of soldiers and some officials from the chief priests and the Pharisees. They were carrying torches, lanterns and weapons.

⁴Jesus, knowing all that was going to happen to him, went out and asked them, "Who is it you want?"

⁵"Jesus of Nazareth," they replied.

"I am he," Jesus said. (And Judas the traitor was standing there with them.) ⁶When Jesus said, "I am he," they drew back and fell to the ground.

⁷Again he asked them, "Who is it you want?"

"Jesus of Nazareth," they said.

⁸Jesus answered, "I told you that I am he. If you are looking for me, then let these men go." ⁹This happened so that the words he had spoken would be fulfilled: "I have not lost one of those you gave me."*b*

¹⁰Then Simon Peter, who had a sword, drew it and struck the high priest's servant, cutting off his right ear. (The servant's name was Malchus.)

¹¹Jesus commanded Peter, "Put your sword away! Shall I not drink the cup the Father has given me?"

¹²Then the detachment of soldiers with its commander and the Jewish officials arrested Jesus. They bound him ¹³and brought him first to Annas, who was the father-in-law of Caiaphas, the high priest that year. ¹⁴Caiaphas was the one who had advised the Jewish leaders that it would be good if one man died for the people.

Peter's First Denial

¹⁵Simon Peter and another disciple were following Jesus. Because this disciple was known to the high priest, he went with Jesus into the high priest's courtyard, ¹⁶but Peter had to wait outside at the door. The other disciple, who was known to the high priest, came back, spoke to the servant girl on duty there and brought Peter in.

¹⁷"You aren't one of this man's disciples too, are you?" she asked Peter.

He replied, "I am not."

¹⁸It was cold, and the servants and officials stood around a fire they had made to keep warm. Peter also was standing with them, warming himself.

The High Priest Questions Jesus

¹⁹Meanwhile, the high priest questioned Jesus about his disciples and his teaching.

²⁰"I have spoken openly to the world," Jesus replied. "I always taught in synagogues or at the temple, where all the Jews come together. I said nothing in secret. ²¹Why question me? Ask those who heard me. Surely they know what I said."

²²When Jesus said this, one of the officials nearby slapped him in the face. "Is this the way you answer the high priest?" he demanded.

²³"If I said something wrong," Jesus replied, "testify as to what is wrong. But if I spoke the truth, why did you strike me?" ²⁴Then Annas sent him bound to Caiaphas the high priest.

Peter's Second and Third Denials

²⁵Meanwhile, Simon Peter was still standing there warming himself. So they asked him, "You aren't one of his disciples too, are you?"

He denied it, saying, "I am not."

²⁶One of the high priest's servants, a relative of the man whose ear Peter had cut off, challenged him, "Didn't I see you with him in the

---

a 26 Greek *your name*   *b 9* John 6:39

garden?" [27]Again Peter denied it, and at that moment a rooster began to crow.

Jesus Before Pilate

[28]Then the Jewish leaders took Jesus from Caiaphas to the palace of the Roman governor. By now it was early morning, and to avoid ceremonial uncleanness they did not enter the palace, because they wanted to be able to eat the Passover. [29]So Pilate came out to them and asked, "What charges are you bringing against this man?"

[30]"If he were not a criminal," they replied, "we would not have handed him over to you."

[31]Pilate said, "Take him yourselves and judge him by your own law."

"But we have no right to execute anyone," they objected. [32]This took place to fulfill what Jesus had said about the kind of death he was going to die.

[33]Pilate then went back inside the palace, summoned Jesus and asked him, "Are you the king of the Jews?"

[34]"Is that your own idea," Jesus asked, "or did others talk to you about me?"

[35]"Am I a Jew?" Pilate replied. "Your own people and chief priests handed you over to me. What is it you have done?"

[36]Jesus said, "My kingdom is not of this world. If it were, my servants would fight to prevent my arrest by the Jewish leaders. But now my kingdom is from another place."

[37]"You are a king, then!" said Pilate.

Jesus answered, "You say that I am a king. In fact, the reason I was born and came into the world is to testify to the truth. Everyone on the side of truth listens to me."

[38]"What is truth?" retorted Pilate. With this he went out again to the Jews gathered there and said, "I find no basis for a charge against him. [39]But it is your custom for me to release to you one prisoner at the time of the Passover. Do you want me to release 'the king of the Jews'?"

[40]They shouted back, "No, not him! Give us Barabbas!" Now Barabbas had taken part in an uprising.

Jesus Sentenced to Be Crucified

19 Then Pilate took Jesus and had him flogged. [2]The soldiers twisted together a crown of thorns and put it on his head. They clothed him in a purple robe [3]and went up to him again and again, saying, "Hail, king of the Jews!" And they slapped him in the face.

[4]Once more Pilate came out and said to the Jews gathered there, "Look, I am bringing him out to you to let you know that I find no basis for a charge against him." [5]When Jesus came out wearing the crown of thorns and the purple robe, Pilate said to them, "Here is the man!"

[6]As soon as the chief priests and their officials saw him, they shouted, "Crucify! Crucify!"

But Pilate answered, "You take him and crucify him. As for me, I find no basis for a charge against him."

[7]The Jewish leaders insisted, "We have a law, and according to that law he must die, because he claimed to be the Son of God."

[8]When Pilate heard this, he was even more afraid, [9]and he went back inside the palace. "Where do you come from?" he asked Jesus, but Jesus gave him no answer. [10]"Do you refuse to speak to me?" Pilate said. "Don't you realize I have power either to free you or to crucify you?"

[11]Jesus answered, "You would have no power over me if it were not given to you from above. Therefore the one who handed me over to you is guilty of a greater sin."

[12]From then on, Pilate tried to set Jesus free, but the Jewish leaders kept shouting, "If you let this man go, you are no friend of Caesar. Anyone who claims to be a king opposes Caesar."

[13]When Pilate heard this, he brought Jesus out and sat down on the judge's seat at a place known as the Stone Pavement (which in Aramaic is Gabbatha). [14]It was the day of Preparation of the Passover; it was about noon.

"Here is your king," Pilate said to the Jews.

[15]But they shouted, "Take him away! Take him away! Crucify him!"

"Shall I crucify your king?" Pilate asked.

"We have no king but Caesar," the chief priests answered.

[16]Finally Pilate handed him over to them to be crucified.

The Crucifixion of Jesus

So the soldiers took charge of Jesus. [17]Carrying his own cross, he went out to the place of the Skull (which in Aramaic is called Golgotha). [18]There they crucified him, and with him two others—one on each side and Jesus in the middle.

[19]Pilate had a notice prepared and fastened to the cross. It read: JESUS OF NAZARETH, THE KING OF THE JEWS. [20]Many of the Jews read this sign, for the place where Jesus was crucified was near the city, and the sign was written in Aramaic, Latin and Greek. [21]The chief priests of the Jews protested to Pilate, "Do not write 'The King of

the Jews,' but that this man claimed to be king of the Jews."

²²Pilate answered, "What I have written, I have written."

²³When the soldiers crucified Jesus, they took his clothes, dividing them into four shares, one for each of them, with the undergarment remaining. This garment was seamless, woven in one piece from top to bottom.

²⁴"Let's not tear it," they said to one another. "Let's decide by lot who will get it."

This happened that the scripture might be fulfilled that said,

"They divided my clothes among them
    and cast lots for my garment."[a]

So this is what the soldiers did.

²⁵Near the cross of Jesus stood his mother, his mother's sister, Mary the wife of Clopas, and Mary Magdalene. ²⁶When Jesus saw his mother there, and the disciple whom he loved standing nearby, he said to her, "Woman,[b] here is your son," ²⁷and to the disciple, "Here is your mother." From that time on, this disciple took her into his home.

The Death of Jesus

²⁸Later, knowing that everything had now been finished, and so that Scripture would be fulfilled, Jesus said, "I am thirsty." ²⁹A jar of wine vinegar was there, so they soaked a sponge in it, put the sponge on a stalk of the hyssop plant, and lifted it to Jesus' lips. ³⁰When he had received the drink, Jesus said, "It is finished." With that, he bowed his head and gave up his spirit.

³¹Now it was the day of Preparation, and the next day was to be a special Sabbath. Because the Jewish leaders did not want the bodies left on the crosses during the Sabbath, they asked Pilate to have the legs broken and the bodies taken down. ³²The soldiers therefore came and broke the legs of the first man who had been crucified with Jesus, and then those of the other. ³³But when they came to Jesus and found that he was already dead, they did not break his legs. ³⁴Instead, one of the soldiers pierced Jesus' side with a spear, bringing a sudden flow of blood and water. ³⁵The man who saw it has given testimony, and his testimony is true. He knows that he tells the truth, and he testifies so that you also may believe. ³⁶These things happened so that the scripture would be fulfilled: "Not one of his bones will be broken,"[c] ³⁷and, as another

---

The Law of the Picture: A Radical Leader Votes with His Life

John 19:30

Author Gary Wills talks about "the radical leader" in his book *Certain Trumpets*. Wills describes such leaders as people who vote with their life. Others follow them because they are ready to die for their cause. They are rare, but we see them throughout history. Jesus showed us he is the Ultimate Radical Leader by willingly giving up his life to accomplish his purpose. It was not easy for him; he felt pain just like anyone else. But his kind of abandonment to his cause challenges us to take notice and choose sides. The power of example is the greatest motivator there is.

---

scripture says, "They will look on the one they have pierced."[d]

The Burial of Jesus

³⁸Later, Joseph of Arimathea asked Pilate for the body of Jesus. Now Joseph was a disciple of Jesus, but secretly because he feared the Jewish leaders. With Pilate's permission, he came and took the body away. ³⁹He was accompanied by Nicodemus, the man who earlier had visited Jesus at night. Nicodemus brought a mixture of myrrh and aloes, about seventy-five pounds.[e] ⁴⁰Taking Jesus' body, the two of them wrapped it, with the spices, in strips of linen. This was in accordance with Jewish burial customs. ⁴¹At the place where Jesus was crucified, there was a garden, and in the garden a new tomb, in which no one had ever been laid. ⁴²Because it was the Jewish day of Preparation and since the tomb was nearby, they laid Jesus there.

The Empty Tomb

20 Early on the first day of the week, while it was still dark, Mary Magdalene went to the tomb and saw that the stone had been removed from the entrance. ²So she came running to Simon Peter and the other disciple, the one Jesus loved, and said, "They have taken the Lord

---

^a 24 Psalm 22:18   ^b 26 The Greek for *Woman* does not denote any disrespect.   ^c 36 Exodus 12:46; Num. 9:12; Psalm 34:20   ^d 37 Zech. 12:10   ^e 39 Or about 34 kilograms

out of the tomb, and we don't know where they have put him!"

³So Peter and the other disciple started for the tomb. ⁴Both were running, but the other disciple outran Peter and reached the tomb first. ⁵He bent over and looked in at the strips of linen lying there but did not go in. ⁶Then Simon Peter came along behind him and went straight into the tomb. He saw the strips of linen lying there, ⁷as well as the cloth that had been wrapped around Jesus' head. The cloth was still lying in its place, separate from the linen. ⁸Finally the other disciple, who had reached the tomb first, also went inside. He saw and believed. ⁹(They still did not understand from Scripture that Jesus had to rise from the dead.) ¹⁰Then the disciples went back to where they were staying.

Jesus Appears to Mary Magdalene

¹¹Now Mary stood outside the tomb crying. As she wept, she bent over to look into the tomb ¹²and saw two angels in white, seated where Jesus' body had been, one at the head and the other at the foot.

¹³They asked her, "Woman, why are you crying?"

"They have taken my Lord away," she said, "and I don't know where they have put him." ¹⁴At this, she turned around and saw Jesus standing there, but she did not realize that it was Jesus.

¹⁵He asked her, "Woman, why are you crying? Who is it you are looking for?"

Thinking he was the gardener, she said, "Sir, if you have carried him away, tell me where you have put him, and I will get him."

¹⁶Jesus said to her, "Mary."

She turned toward him and cried out in Aramaic, "Rabboni!" (which means "Teacher").

¹⁷Jesus said, "Do not hold on to me, for I have not yet ascended to the Father. Go instead to my brothers and tell them, 'I am ascending to my Father and your Father, to my God and your God.'"

¹⁸Mary Magdalene went to the disciples with the news: "I have seen the Lord!" And she told them that he had said these things to her.

The Law of Empowerment: Jesus Gave His Ministry Away

John 20:21–22

Many leaders say they intend to work themselves out of a job. That is exactly what Jesus did.

In John 20 Jesus puts his final touches on the empowerment of his twelve followers, then turns them loose. He gives them his peace (v. 21) and breathes on them to receive the power of the Holy Spirit (v. 22). This peace and power would enable them to serve supernaturally. Those men he mentored were now ready to be change agents.

How can we do the same? What steps can we take to mentor and empower others? Note some practical applications of the process Jesus modeled:

1. Pray for conviction and vision.

2. Select a person or group from your sphere of influence to mentor.

3. Spend two initial meetings together to discuss expectations and goals.

4. Cast vision to them for spiritual reproduction.

5. Ask for commitment.

6. Determine what tools or resources you will use together.

7. Prepare yourself and set goals for each meeting.

8. Meet regularly for a set time.

9. Discuss and apply the truths you learn together.

10. Invest yourself in the person, the process and the purpose.

11. Help them find a potential person to mentor.

12. Evaluate and launch them to try the process themselves.

Jesus Appears to His Disciples

[19]On the evening of that first day of the week, when the disciples were together, with the doors locked for fear of the Jewish leaders, Jesus came and stood among them and said, "Peace be with you!" [20]After he said this, he showed them his hands and side. The disciples were overjoyed when they saw the Lord.

[21]Again Jesus said, "Peace be with you! As the Father has sent me, I am sending you." [22]And with that he breathed on them and said, "Receive the Holy Spirit. [23]If you forgive anyone's sins, their sins are forgiven; if you do not forgive them, they are not forgiven."

Jesus Appears to Thomas

[24]Now Thomas (also known as Didymus[a]), one of the Twelve, was not with the disciples when Jesus came. [25]So the other disciples told him, "We have seen the Lord!"

But he said to them, "Unless I see the nail marks in his hands and put my finger where the nails were, and put my hand into his side, I will not believe."

[26]A week later his disciples were in the house again, and Thomas was with them. Though the doors were locked, Jesus came and stood among them and said, "Peace be with you!" [27]Then he said to Thomas, "Put your finger here; see my hands. Reach out your hand and put it into my side. Stop doubting and believe."

[28]Thomas said to him, "My Lord and my God!"

[29]Then Jesus told him, "Because you have seen me, you have believed; blessed are those who have not seen and yet have believed."

The Purpose of John's Gospel

[30]Jesus performed many other signs in the presence of his disciples, which are not recorded in this book. [31]But these are written that you may believe[b] that Jesus is the Messiah, the Son of God, and that by believing you may have life in his name.

Jesus and the Miraculous Catch of Fish

21 Afterward Jesus appeared again to his disciples, by the Sea of Galilee.[c] It happened this way: [2]Simon Peter, Thomas (also known as Didymus[a]), Nathanael from Cana in Galilee, the sons of Zebedee, and two other disciples were together. [3]"I'm going out to fish," Simon Peter told them, and they said, "We'll go with you." So they went out and got into the boat, but that night they caught nothing.

[4]Early in the morning, Jesus stood on the shore, but the disciples did not realize that it was Jesus.

[5]He called out to them, "Friends, haven't you any fish?"

"No," they answered.

[6]He said, "Throw your net on the right side of the boat and you will find some." When they did, they were unable to haul the net in because of the large number of fish.

[7]Then the disciple whom Jesus loved said to Peter, "It is the Lord!" As soon as Simon Peter heard him say, "It is the Lord," he wrapped his outer garment around him (for he had taken it off) and jumped into the water. [8]The other disciples followed in the boat, towing the net full of fish, for they were not far from shore, about a hundred yards.[d] [9]When they landed, they saw a fire of burning coals there with fish on it, and some bread.

[10]Jesus said to them, "Bring some of the fish you have just caught." [11]So Simon Peter climbed back into the boat and dragged the net ashore. It was full of large fish, 153, but even with so many the net was not torn. [12]Jesus said to them, "Come and have breakfast." None of the disciples dared ask him, "Who are you?" They knew it was the Lord. [13]Jesus came, took the bread and gave it to them, and did the same with the fish. [14]This was now the third time Jesus appeared to his disciples after he was raised from the dead.

Jesus Reinstates Peter

[15]When they had finished eating, Jesus said to Simon Peter, "Simon son of John, do you love me more than these?"

"Yes, Lord," he said, "you know that I love you."

Jesus said, "Feed my lambs."

[16]Again Jesus said, "Simon son of John, do you love me?"

He answered, "Yes, Lord, you know that I love you."

Jesus said, "Take care of my sheep."

[17]The third time he said to him, "Simon son of John, do you love me?"

Peter was hurt because Jesus asked him the third time, "Do you love me?" He said, "Lord, you know all things; you know that I love you."

Jesus said, "Feed my sheep. [18]Very truly I tell you, when you were younger you dressed

---

[a] 24,2 Thomas (Aramaic) and Didymus (Greek) both mean twin.   [b] 31 Or may continue to believe   [c] 1 Greek Tiberias   [d] 8 Or about 90 meters

Jesus and the 21 Irrefutable Laws of Leadership

John 20:30–31

The Gospels demonstrate that Jesus embodied each of the 21 Irrefutable Laws of Leadership:

1. **The Law of the Lid:** *Leadership ability determines a person's level of effectiveness.*
   - John 1:35–37—John the Baptist knew Jesus could lead his disciples further than he could.
   - John 6:66–68—Peter confessed the disciples had no better leader to whom to turn.

2. **The Law of Influence:** *The true measure of leadership is influence—nothing more, nothing less.*
   - Matthew 4:18–20—Jesus called his disciples, who left everything to follow him.
   - John 11:47–48—The Pharisees feared that if Jesus continued, everyone would follow him.

3. **The Law of Process:** *Leadership develops daily, not in a day.*
   - Luke 2:52—Jesus continued to grow in wisdom, stature and favor with God and men.
   - Hebrews 5:7–9—Although he was God's Son, Jesus grew and learned through suffering.

4. **The Law of Navigation:** *Anyone can steer the ship, but it takes a leader to chart the course.*
   - Matthew 10:1–23—Jesus gave specific direction in sending out his disciples.
   - Luke 14:25–35—Jesus taught the value of planning and calculating one's resources.

5. **The Law of the Picture:** *People do what people see.*
   - Matthew 10:24–25; John 15:5–20—Jesus taught followers soon look like their leader.
   - Matthew 14:22–33—When Jesus walked on water, Peter imitated him and attempted it.

6. **The Law of Solid Ground:** *Trust is the foundation of leadership.*
   - Matthew 17:24–27—To prevent offending anyone, Jesus paid even the smallest tax.
   - Matthew 22:15–46—Jesus debated enemies and answered questions with integrity.

7. **The Law of Respect:** *People naturally follow leaders stronger than themselves.*
   - Matthew 3:11–15—John the Baptist acknowledged Jesus' superiority over his ministry.
   - Matthew 8:5–10—A centurion sought out Jesus, knowing his authority over all things.

8. **The Law of Intuition:** *Leaders evaluate everything with a leadership bias.*
   - Matthew 9:35–38—Jesus saw the masses and discerned how to reach them.
   - Luke 5:1–11—Jesus saw Simon's leadership potential when he didn't see it himself.

9. **The Law of Magnetism:** *Who you are is who you attract.*
   - Mark 10:28–31—Peter reminded Jesus that he left everything, just as Christ did.
   - John 17:13–21—Jesus confessed the similarities and unity of the men God gave him.

10. **The Law of Connection:** *Leaders touch a heart before they ask for a hand.*
    - Luke 8:22—9:1—Jesus met the needs of his disciples, a demoniac and Jairus—then sent them out.
    - John 4:7–26—Jesus connected with a Samaritan woman right where she lived.

11. **The Law of the Inner Circle:** *A leader's potential is determined by those closest to him.*
   - Luke 9:1—10:42—Jesus sent out the Twelve and the 70, who multiplied his impact.
   - John 17:1–26—Jesus spent a night praying for the success of his inner circle.

12. **The Law of Empowerment:** *Only secure leaders give power to others.*
   - John 13:1–20—Jesus felt secure enough to wash feet and send men out to do the same.
   - Luke 10:1–24—Jesus gave his power away to the 70 so they could serve others.

13. **The Law of Addition:** *Leaders add value by serving others.*
   - John 13:1–17—Jesus washed his disciples' feet and gave an example of adding value.
   - Matthew 14:21–31—Jesus sought solitude but continued to serve others and meet needs.

14. **The Law of Buy-In:** *People buy in to the leader, then the vision.*
   - Luke 5:3–11—Jesus built his team before they understood the details of his vision.
   - Luke 9:57–62—Jesus confronted men who followed him before they knew his vision.

15. **The Law of Victory:** *Leaders find a way for the team to win.*
   - Matthew 14:13–33—Jesus found a way to feed the masses and saved his disciples on the ship.
   - Mark 16:1–20—Jesus' resurrection surprised everyone and restored their hope.

16. **The Law of the Big Mo:** *Momentum is a leader's best friend.*
   - Mark 1:40–45—Jesus' fame spread until he couldn't even enter a public place.
   - John 12:9–19—After Lazarus's resuscitation, it seemed the whole world sought Jesus.

17. **The Law of Priorities:** *Leaders understand that activity is not necessarily accomplishment.*
   - Mark 1:32–38—Jesus ministered all night, then got alone and decided to move on.
   - Luke 10:38–42—Jesus narrowed Martha's to-do list to one key priority.

18. **The Law of Sacrifice:** *A leader must give up to go up.*
   - Matthew 20:20–28—Jesus demonstrated that if you want to be great, you have to serve.
   - John 10:10–18—Jesus willingly laid down his life for his sheep.

19. **The Law of Timing:** *When to lead is as important as what to do and where to go.*
   - John 7:6–8—Jesus knew when his time had come to reveal the kingdom.
   - John 11:1–6—When Lazarus got sick, Jesus waited to visit him until after he had died.

20. **The Law of Explosive Growth:** *To add growth, lead followers; to multiply, lead leaders.*
   - Mark 16:15–20—Jesus trained and sent leaders, expecting them to reach the world.
   - John 14:12—Jesus prepared the Twelve to do greater works than he did.

21. **The Law of Legacy:** *A leader's lasting value is measured by succession.*
   - Acts 1:6–8—Jesus' most important words were his last ones to the next generation.
   - Acts 17:1–6—The apostles' reputation spread: They turned the world upside down.

The Law of Legacy: Success Without a Successor Is a Failure

John 21:15–17

Just before he left earth for heaven, Jesus invested significant time in Simon Peter. He wanted to help him recover from his sin the night he denied Jesus three times. Christ intended to call Peter to minister and lead.

Jesus knew that his time was short. Yet he asked Peter three times if he loved him. When Peter assured his Lord of his love, Christ called him to the natural response: "Feed my lambs" (Jn 21:15).

Love should motivate us to serve. In the same way the Father sent Jesus to save the lost sheep of Israel, Jesus called Peter to feed his lambs. Jesus made his legacy dependent on Peter and the other disciples who picked up the baton and ran with it.

yourself and went where you wanted; but when you are old you will stretch out your hands, and someone else will dress you and lead you where you do not want to go." [19]Jesus said this to indicate the kind of death by which Peter would glorify God. Then he said to him, "Follow me!"

[20]Peter turned and saw that the disciple whom Jesus loved was following them. (This was the one who had leaned back against Jesus at the supper and had said, "Lord, who is going to betray you?") [21]When Peter saw him, he asked, "Lord, what about him?"

[22]Jesus answered, "If I want him to remain alive until I return, what is that to you? You must follow me." [23]Because of this, the rumor spread among the believers that this disciple would not die. But Jesus did not say that he would not die; he only said, "If I want him to remain alive until I return, what is that to you?"

[24]This is the disciple who testifies to these things and who wrote them down. We know that his testimony is true.

[25]Jesus did many other things as well. If every one of them were written down, I suppose that even the whole world would not have room for the books that would be written.

INTRODUCTION TO ACTS

Followers of Jesus Transition into Leaders

Acts is a book of action! Notice, it's called "Acts," not "Reacts." It is about the initiative and action of the Holy Spirit in the lives of disciples who formerly were cowardly, unsure, and ignorant. Those men, who had learned to follow Jesus for three years, were now learning to lead!

In this sequel to his Gospel, Luke reports that those early disciples mobilized the church so effectively that they reached entire cities (9:35) and saturated whole countries with the gospel (19:10).

The action described in this book shows God empowering men and women who decide to stand for God with the Holy Spirit. They determine to be influencers. Despite their lack of human qualifications, they begin to penetrate their society. God accomplished this primarily through ordinary people with little in the way of education, political clout, or prestige (1Co 1:26).

The fisherman, Peter, becomes the leader of the church in Jerusalem. Philip becomes the first evangelist and missionary to cross-cultural groups. Stephen takes a stand against the false religious leaders of his day and becomes the first martyr. Barnabas and Paul establish the first equipping/sending church in Antioch, then lead the first mission team.

These leaders accomplish so much because they are governed by the priorities of God, incarnate the power of God, are motivated by the purposes of God, stay dependent on the provisions of God, and equip the people of God. Everyone gets involved in the task. Leaders equip followers and cheer on the church as she marches into the culture. Miracles break out. The community takes care of outstanding personal needs.

God's Role in Acts

God filled these ordinary people with his Spirit and bid them to influence the world. Miracles occurred as God confirmed his Word with signs following (Mk 16:17–18). Jesus personally appeared to Saul of Tarsus in order to call him to be an apostle (9:1–9). The Holy Spirit established this early church in purity so that he could empower it without limits. God entrusts his power to the pure. Note the sequence: first purity; then power; then proclamation; and finally, penetration.

Leaders in Acts

Peter and the original apostles, Gamaliel and the Sanhedrin, Stephen, Philip, Aquila and Priscilla, Paul, Barnabas, Herod, Agrippa, Festus, Apollos, Silas

Other People of Influence in Acts

The core of believers in the upper room, Lydia, Luke, Timothy, the Ephesian businessmen, the Antioch church family

Lessons in Leadership

- Holy Spirit power plus obedient leadership equals church growth.
- God raises up leaders in order to bring all people to himself.
- Leaders break down barriers and connect the familiar to the unfamiliar.

As you read through the book, note how many leaders emerge from within the church. Many are not apostles; we would consider most laypeople. Yet everyone seems committed to the vision of impacting the world for Christ.

- When the church adds more leaders, it adds more followers.
- There is no success without sacrifice.
- Momentum comes as a result of unity.
- Leaders start to thrive when they don't have to survive.

LEADERSHIP HIGHLIGHTS IN ACTS

Jesus Taken Up Into Heaven

1 In my former book, Theophilus, I wrote about all that Jesus began to do and to teach [2]until the day he was taken up to heaven, after giving instructions through the Holy Spirit to the apostles he had chosen. [3]After his suffering, he presented himself to them and gave many convincing proofs that he was alive. He appeared to them over a period of forty days and spoke about the kingdom of God. [4]On one occasion, while he was eating with them, he gave them this command: "Do not leave Jerusalem, but wait for the gift my Father promised, which you have heard me speak about. [5]For John baptized with[a] water, but in a few days you will be baptized with[a] the Holy Spirit."

[6]Then they gathered around him and asked him, "Lord, are you at this time going to restore the kingdom to Israel?"

[7]He said to them: "It is not for you to know the times or dates the Father has set by his own authority. [8]But you will receive power when the Holy Spirit comes on you; and you will be my witnesses in Jerusalem, and in all Judea and Samaria, and to the ends of the earth."

[9]After he said this, he was taken up before their very eyes, and a cloud hid him from their sight.

[10]They were looking intently up into the sky as he was going, when suddenly two men dressed in white stood beside them. [11]"Men of Galilee," they said, "why do you stand here looking into the sky? This same Jesus, who has been taken from you into heaven, will come back in the same way you have seen him go into heaven."

Matthias Chosen to Replace Judas

[12]Then the apostles returned to Jerusalem from the hill called the Mount of Olives, a Sabbath day's walk[b] from the city. [13]When they arrived, they went upstairs to the room where they were staying. Those present were Peter, John, James and Andrew; Philip and Thomas, Bartholomew and Matthew; James son of Alphaeus and Simon the Zealot, and Judas son of James. [14]They all joined together constantly in prayer, along with the women and Mary the mother of Jesus, and with his brothers.

[15]In those days Peter stood up among the believers (a group numbering about a hundred and twenty) [16]and said, "Brothers and sisters,[c] the

---

[a] 5 Or in   [b] 12 That is, about 5/8 mile or about 1 kilometer
[c] 16 The Greek word for *brothers and sisters* (*adelphoi*) refers here to believers, both men and women, as part of God's family; also in 6:3; 11:29; 12:17; 16:40; 18:18, 27; 21:7, 17; 28:14, 15.

Vision: Leaders Communicate Vision to Empower and Direct

Acts 1:4–8

The book of Acts begins with a bang. Jesus speaks his final words to his men before ascending to heaven. Even though they are now leaders, not merely followers, they ask Jesus when his kingdom would come (Ac 1:6). Jesus doesn't tell them, but instead communicates a vision about reaching the world (1:8). His men thought *defense*; Jesus wanted them to think *offense*.

Christ instructed them to stay in Jerusalem until they received the power they needed, then they were to go out, expanding little by little. They were to start with Jerusalem, then move to the rest of Judea, then expand to Samaria and ultimately to the ends of the earth. This was no man-made vision, but a God-given vision. Note the differences:

Man-Made Vision	God-Given Vision
1. Created based on human gifts and skills	1. Received as a revelation
2. Fulfilled by staying ahead of others	2. Fulfilled through obedience
3. Sees similar organizations as competitors	3. Sees similar organizations as complementary
4. Aims to grow the organization and generate revenue	4. Aims to serve people and advance God's rule
5. Stress may emerge both inwardly and outwardly	5. Accompanied by inward peace and outward opposition
6. May be dropped for something better	6. Compelling and captivating until fulfilled

Scripture had to be fulfilled in which the Holy Spirit spoke long ago through David concerning Judas, who served as guide for those who arrested Jesus. [17]He was one of our number and shared in our ministry."

[18](With the payment he received for his wickedness, Judas bought a field; there he fell headlong, his body burst open and all his intestines spilled out. [19]Everyone in Jerusalem heard about this, so they called that field in their language Akeldama, that is, Field of Blood.)

[20]"For," said Peter, "it is written in the Book of Psalms:

"'May his place be deserted;
    let there be no one to dwell in it,'[a]

and,

"'May another take his place of leadership.'[b]

[21]Therefore it is necessary to choose one of the men who have been with us the whole time the Lord Jesus was living among us, [22]beginning from John's baptism to the time when Jesus was taken up from us. For one of these must become a witness with us of his resurrection."

[23]So they nominated two men: Joseph called Barsabbas (also known as Justus) and Matthias. [24]Then they prayed, "Lord, you know everyone's heart. Show us which of these two you have chosen [25]to take over this apostolic ministry, which Judas left to go where he belongs." [26]Then they cast lots, and the lot fell to Matthias; so he was added to the eleven apostles.

The Holy Spirit Comes at Pentecost

2 When the day of Pentecost came, they were all together in one place. [2]Suddenly a sound like the blowing of a violent wind came from heaven and filled the whole house where they were sitting. [3]They saw what seemed to be tongues of fire that separated and came to rest on each of them. [4]All of them were filled with the Holy Spirit and began to speak in other tongues[c] as the Spirit enabled them.

Qualified Leaders Must Be Selected

Acts 1:20–26

The apostles chose Matthias to replace Judas, who betrayed Jesus and committed suicide soon afterward. Notice two things.

First, they didn't hold an election. Church eldership is never determined through a democracy in the New Testament. Leaders were chosen, not voted on.

Second, the apostles cast lots to discover God's choice for the position—a common method in biblical times to receive direction from the Lord. Today, Christians receive direction from the New Testament (2Ti 3:16; Titus 1:5–9) and from the witness of the Holy Spirit (Ro 8:14–16). Elders are leaders chosen by God and confirmed by the church.

The book of Acts makes 18 references to elders, ten relating directly to the ministry of a church elder. The various Greek words used to discuss leadership are most often translated by the terms "elder," "bishop," or "deacon." They all concern responsibility, spiritual oversight, inspection, service and ministry.

Empowerment: Leaders Must Be Empowered Before They Empower

Acts 2:1–4

Leaders can never empower anyone else until they are first supernaturally empowered themselves. The term "filled with the Holy Spirit" is used five times in Acts (2:4; 4:8, 31; 9:17; 13:9). Whenever someone is filled with the Holy Spirit, something happens. Empowered leaders express God's power, then empower others.

---

[5]Now there were staying in Jerusalem God-fearing Jews from every nation under heaven. [6]When they heard this sound, a crowd came together in bewilderment, because each one heard their own language being spoken. [7]Utterly amazed, they asked: "Aren't all these who are speaking Galileans? [8]Then how is it that each of us hears them in our native language? [9]Parthians, Medes and Elamites; residents of Mesopotamia, Judea and Cappadocia, Pontus and Asia,[d] [10]Phrygia and Pamphylia, Egypt and the parts of Libya near Cyrene; visitors from Rome

---

[a] 20 Psalm 69:25   [b] 20 Psalm 109:8   [c] 4 Or languages; also in verse 11   [d] 9 That is, the Roman province by that name

11(both Jews and converts to Judaism); Cretans and Arabs — we hear them declaring the wonders of God in our own tongues!" 12Amazed and perplexed, they asked one another, "What does this mean?"

13Some, however, made fun of them and said, "They have had too much wine."

Peter Addresses the Crowd

14Then Peter stood up with the Eleven, raised his voice and addressed the crowd: "Fellow Jews and all of you who live in Jerusalem, let me explain this to you; listen carefully to what I say. 15These people are not drunk, as you suppose. It's only nine in the morning! 16No, this is what was spoken by the prophet Joel:

17"'In the last days, God says,
     I will pour out my Spirit on all people.
Your sons and daughters will prophesy,
     your young men will see visions,
     your old men will dream dreams.
18Even on my servants, both men and women,
     I will pour out my Spirit in those days,
     and they will prophesy.
19I will show wonders in the heavens above
     and signs on the earth below,
     blood and fire and billows of smoke.
20The sun will be turned to darkness
     and the moon to blood
     before the coming of the great and
          glorious day of the Lord.
21And everyone who calls
     on the name of the Lord will be saved.'a

22"Fellow Israelites, listen to this: Jesus of Nazareth was a man accredited by God to you by miracles, wonders and signs, which God did among you through him, as you yourselves know. 23This man was handed over to you by God's deliberate plan and foreknowledge; and you, with the help of wicked men,b put him to death by nailing him to the cross. 24But God raised him from the dead, freeing him from the agony of death, because it was impossible for death to keep its hold on him. 25David said about him:

"'I saw the Lord always before me.
     Because he is at my right hand,
     I will not be shaken.
26Therefore my heart is glad and my tongue
          rejoices;
     my body also will rest in hope,
27because you will not abandon me to the
          realm of the dead,
     you will not let your holy one see decay.
28You have made known to me the paths of life;
     you will fill me with joy in your presence.'c

29"Fellow Israelites, I can tell you confidently that the patriarch David died and was buried, and his tomb is here to this day. 30But he was a prophet and knew that God had promised him on oath that he would place one of his descendants on his throne. 31Seeing what was to come, he spoke of the resurrection of the Messiah, that he was not abandoned to the realm of the dead, nor did his body see decay. 32God has raised this Jesus to life, and we are all witnesses of it. 33Exalted to the right hand of God, he has received from the Father the promised Holy Spirit and has poured out what you now see and hear. 34For David did not ascend to heaven, and yet he said,

"'The Lord said to my Lord:
     "Sit at my right hand
35until I make your enemies
     a footstool for your feet." 'd

36"Therefore let all Israel be assured of this: God has made this Jesus, whom you crucified, both Lord and Messiah."

37When the people heard this, they were cut to the heart and said to Peter and the other apostles, "Brothers, what shall we do?"

38Peter replied, "Repent and be baptized, every one of you, in the name of Jesus Christ for the forgiveness of your sins. And you will receive the gift of the Holy Spirit. 39The promise is for you and your children and for all who are far off — for all whom the Lord our God will call."

The Law of Magnetism: Passionate Leaders Are Magnetic for Others

Acts 2:7–21

When Peter stood up to preach, no doubt the crowd saw God-given power and purpose—but first they saw God-given passion. Passion made up for Peter's lack of natural gifts or education. When Peter became a magnet for others, three thousand people joined the church that day. Passion draws passion.

---

a 21 Joel 2:28-32   b 23 Or of those not having the law (that is, Gentiles)   c 28 Psalm 16:8-11 (see Septuagint)
d 35 Psalm 110:1

21 QUALITIES

CHARISMA   Peter Was a Magnet

Acts 2:1–41

ACTS 2 marks a pivotal point in the New Testament. One hundred twenty men and women become charter members of the church when it is born in an upper room somewhere in Jerusalem. Yet by the end of the chapter, it explodes into a body of more than three thousand members.

After the Holy Spirit falls on the believers (Ac 2:1–4), those visiting Jerusalem begin to wonder how these disciples of Jesus could speak so many languages (2:5–13). While some think the disciples are drunk, most just feel confused. Chaos seems to rule.

That's when Peter stands up and begins to speak. This same Peter, who ran in fear on the night of Jesus' trial, now speaks boldly. Within minutes, he has captivated everyone with his compelling words. The crowd gladly accepts his message. Why? He has charisma. Through a combination of God-given wiring and the gift of the Holy Spirit, this leader captures and motivates three thousand people to follow Christ.

What Are the Traits of a Charismatic Leader?

Most people think of charisma as something mystical, almost indefinable. They think it comes at birth or not at all. But that's not true. Charisma is the ability to draw people to you or your cause. Some people possess more of it naturally. Like other character traits, however, it can be learned. Notice what made Peter so charismatic (2:14–40):

1. *Confidence*
   Peter displayed poise and optimism as a buoyant communicator.
2. *Conviction*
   He knew where he was going and what he had to say. He spoke straight from his heart.
3. *Connection*
   He focused not on himself, but on others. He magnetically connected with his audience.
4. *Compassion*
   He exuded warmth and love. He gave the people practical answers to their needs.

By the end of his message, everyone asked, "What shall we do?" (2:37). They felt motivated and ready to act. God used Peter's charisma like a magnet.

How Can We Build Charisma?

How about you? Do you demonstrate charisma? To make yourself the kind of person who attracts others, build the following into your life:

1. *Love life.* Celebrate; don't complain. Enjoy the journey.
2. *Put a "10" on everyone's forehead.* Expect the best of people and treat them well.
3. *Give people hope.* Everyone looks for hope; leaders deal it out.
4. *Share yourself.* Be vulnerable and real. Share your heart, wisdom and resources.

For a negative example of charisma, see p. 441.

[40]With many other words he warned them; and he pleaded with them, "Save yourselves from this corrupt generation." [41]Those who accepted his message were baptized, and about three thousand were added to their number that day.

The Fellowship of the Believers

[42]They devoted themselves to the apostles' teaching and to fellowship, to the breaking of bread and to prayer. [43]Everyone was filled with awe at the many wonders and signs performed by the apostles. [44]All the believers were together and had everything in common. [45]They sold property and possessions to give to anyone who had need. [46]Every day they continued to meet together in the temple courts. They broke bread in their homes and ate together with glad and sincere hearts, [47]praising God and enjoying the favor of all the people. And the Lord added to their number daily those who were being saved.

Peter Heals a Lame Beggar

3 One day Peter and John were going up to the temple at the time of prayer — at three in the afternoon. [2]Now a man who was lame from birth was being carried to the temple gate called Beautiful, where he was put every day to beg from those going into the temple courts. [3]When he saw Peter and John about to enter, he asked them for money. [4]Peter looked straight at him,

as did John. Then Peter said, "Look at us!" [5]So the man gave them his attention, expecting to get something from them.

[6]Then Peter said, "Silver or gold I do not have, but what I do have I give you. In the name of Jesus Christ of Nazareth, walk." [7]Taking him by the right hand, he helped him up, and instantly the man's feet and ankles became strong. [8]He jumped to his feet and began to walk. Then he went with them into the temple courts, walking and jumping, and praising God. [9]When all the people saw him walking and praising God, [10]they recognized him as the same man who used to sit begging at the temple gate called Beautiful, and they were filled with wonder and amazement at what had happened to him.

Peter Speaks to the Onlookers

[11]While the man held on to Peter and John, all the people were astonished and came running to them in the place called Solomon's Colonnade. [12]When Peter saw this, he said to them: "Fellow Israelites, why does this surprise you? Why do you stare at us as if by our own power or godliness we had made this man walk? [13]The God of Abraham, Isaac and Jacob, the God of our fathers, has glorified his servant Jesus. You handed him over to be killed, and you disowned him before Pilate, though he had decided to let him go. [14]You disowned the Holy and Righteous One and asked that a murderer be released to

PETER

Most Improved Player and Turnaround Leader
Acts 3:1–26

PROFILE in leadership

The apostle Peter may be the greatest turnaround leader in the New Testament.

Peter—the same man who had promised to follow Jesus even if it meant death, but who cowered in fear when a mere servant girl identified him as one of the Lord's followers (Lk 22:56–57)—spoke the name of Christ with great power and authority and without fear of the consequences.

Peter knew the danger of preaching Jesus. He knew the hostility it could elicit. He knew that by doing the will of God and preaching he would be taking his life in his hands. Still, he had no choice. He *had* to preach. He *had* to speak the name of Jesus. As he told the authorities, he could do nothing else. After the things he had seen and heard—after the powerful touch he had received from the Holy Spirit of God—he felt *compelled* to preach the gospel (Ac 4:19–20).

So Peter preached . . . and the whole world turned upside down!

This is the kind of turnaround that occurs in the life of one touched by the Holy Spirit of God. When we have a genuine encounter with Jesus, when he transforms our hearts and minds and empowers us and emboldens us, we have no choice—we *must* preach the gospel, we *must* speak the Word of God.

Demonstration + Proclamation = Credibility

Acts 3:1–26

Immediately following Pentecost, the Christian movement picked up steam. Two leaders, Peter and John, encountered a lame man on their way to the temple. When the name of Jesus healed the man, they immediately gained credibility to share the gospel. In other words, once they walked the walk, they attracted an audience when they talked. Note how Acts 3 describes these early church leaders:

1. They faithfully did what they knew to do (v. 1).
2. They stopped and sensitively addressed needs (v. 3).
3. They had the courage to face problems (v. 4).
4. Others anticipated receiving solutions from them (v. 5).
5. They realistically admitted their lack of material resources (v. 6).
6. They fearlessly used their God-given authority (v. 6).
7. They generously gave away their spiritual resources (v. 6).
8. They solved practical problems (vv. 7–8).
9. They gained credibility through demonstration, not just proclamation (vv. 9–10).
10. Peter's demonstration gave him a platform and a convincing argument (vv. 11–26).

you. ¹⁵You killed the author of life, but God raised him from the dead. We are witnesses of this. ¹⁶By faith in the name of Jesus, this man whom you see and know was made strong. It is Jesus' name and the faith that comes through him that has completely healed him, as you can all see.

¹⁷"Now, fellow Israelites, I know that you acted in ignorance, as did your leaders. ¹⁸But this is how God fulfilled what he had foretold through all the prophets, saying that his Messiah would suffer. ¹⁹Repent, then, and turn to God, so that your sins may be wiped out, that times of refreshing may come from the Lord, ²⁰and that he may send the Messiah, who has been appointed for you—even Jesus. ²¹Heaven must receive him until the time comes for God to restore everything, as he promised long ago through his holy prophets. ²²For Moses said, 'The Lord your God will raise up for you a prophet like me from among your own people; you must listen to everything he tells you. ²³Anyone who does not listen to him will be completely cut off from their people.'ᵃ

²⁴"Indeed, beginning with Samuel, all the prophets who have spoken have foretold these days. ²⁵And you are heirs of the prophets and of the covenant God made with your fathers. He said to Abraham, 'Through your offspring all peoples on earth will be blessed.'ᵇ ²⁶When God raised up his servant, he sent him first to you to bless you by turning each of you from your wicked ways."

Peter and John Before the Sanhedrin

4 The priests and the captain of the temple guard and the Sadducees came up to Peter and John while they were speaking to the people. ²They were greatly disturbed because the apostles were teaching the people, proclaiming in Jesus the resurrection of the dead. ³They seized Peter and John and, because it was evening, they put them in jail until the next day. ⁴But many who heard the message believed; so the number of men who believed grew to about five thousand.

⁵The next day the rulers, the elders and the teachers of the law met in Jerusalem. ⁶Annas the high priest was there, and so were Caiaphas, John, Alexander and others of the high priest's family. ⁷They had Peter and John brought before them and began to question them: "By what power or what name did you do this?"

⁸Then Peter, filled with the Holy Spirit, said to them: "Rulers and elders of the people! ⁹If we are being called to account today for an act of kind-

---

ᵃ 23 Deut. 18:15,18,19   ᵇ 25 Gen. 22:18; 26:4

ness shown to a man who was lame and are being asked how he was healed, [10]then know this, you and all the people of Israel: It is by the name of Jesus Christ of Nazareth, whom you crucified but whom God raised from the dead, that this man stands before you healed. [11]Jesus is

> "'the stone you builders rejected,
>   which has become the cornerstone.'[a]

[12]Salvation is found in no one else, for there is no other name under heaven given to mankind by which we must be saved."

[13]When they saw the courage of Peter and John and realized that they were unschooled, ordinary men, they were astonished and they took note that these men had been with Jesus. [14]But since they could see the man who had been healed standing there with them, there was nothing they could say. [15]So they ordered them to withdraw from the Sanhedrin and then conferred together. [16]"What are we going to do with these men?" they asked. "Everyone living in Jerusalem knows they have performed a notable sign, and we cannot deny it. [17]But to stop this thing from spreading any further among the people, we must warn them to speak no longer to anyone in this name."

[18]Then they called them in again and commanded them not to speak or teach at all in the name of Jesus. [19]But Peter and John replied, "Which is right in God's eyes: to listen to you, or to him? You be the judges! [20]As for us, we cannot help speaking about what we have seen and heard."

[21]After further threats they let them go. They could not decide how to punish them, because all the people were praising God for what had happened. [22]For the man who was miraculously healed was over forty years old.

The Believers Pray

[23]On their release, Peter and John went back to their own people and reported all that the chief priests and the elders had said to them. [24]When they heard this, they raised their voices together in prayer to God. "Sovereign Lord,"

---

[a] 11 Psalm 118:22

Courage: One Person with Courage Is a Majority

Acts 4:10-13

In Acts 4 we see courage on display in the life of Peter and John. These two leaders were thrown in jail for preaching and for performing a miracle (vv. 1–4). When their captors ask about their ministry, Peter boldly asserts that the name of Jesus, not their own talent, had healed the man (v. 10). He also explains that salvation comes through no other name (v. 12). What accounted for his boldness? Not his education, but his experience with Jesus (v. 13).

Leadership requires courage. All leaders need courage to:

1. *Seek the truth*
   You never find yourself until you face the truth.

2. *Change*
   Courage is the power to let go of the familiar.

3. *Express convictions*
   Convictions help us to stand alone. The test of courage comes when we're in the minority.

4. *Overcome obstacles*
   Whatever you do, someone will think you're wrong. Expect trouble. Project courage.

5. *Learn and grow*
   You haven't learned until you step out, take a risk, and do something new.

6. *Take the high road*
   There is no traffic jam on the second mile.

7. *Lead others*
   Leadership is the expression of courage that compels others to do the right thing.

they said, "you made the heavens and the earth and the sea, and everything in them. ²⁵You spoke by the Holy Spirit through the mouth of your servant, our father David:

> "'Why do the nations rage
>   and the peoples plot in vain?
> ²⁶The kings of the earth rise up
>   and the rulers band together
> against the Lord
>   and against his anointed one.[a][b]

²⁷Indeed Herod and Pontius Pilate met together with the Gentiles and the people of Israel in this city to conspire against your holy servant Jesus, whom you anointed. ²⁸They did what your power and will had decided beforehand should happen. ²⁹Now, Lord, consider their threats and enable your servants to speak your word with great boldness. ³⁰Stretch out your hand to heal and perform signs and wonders through the name of your holy servant Jesus."

³¹After they prayed, the place where they were meeting was shaken. And they were all filled with the Holy Spirit and spoke the word of God boldly.

The Believers Share Their Possessions

³²All the believers were one in heart and mind. No one claimed that any of their possessions was their own, but they shared everything they had. ³³With great power the apostles continued to testify to the resurrection of the Lord Jesus. And God's grace was so powerfully at work in them all ³⁴that there were no needy persons among them. For from time to time those who owned land or houses sold them, brought the money from the sales ³⁵and put it at the apostles' feet, and it was distributed to anyone who had need.

³⁶Joseph, a Levite from Cyprus, whom the apostles called Barnabas (which means "son of encouragement"), ³⁷sold a field he owned and brought the money and put it at the apostles' feet.

Ananias and Sapphira

5 Now a man named Ananias, together with his wife Sapphira, also sold a piece of property. ²With his wife's full knowledge he kept back part of the money for himself, but brought the rest and put it at the apostles' feet.

³Then Peter said, "Ananias, how is it that Satan has so filled your heart that you have lied to the Holy Spirit and have kept for yourself some of the money you received for the land? ⁴Didn't

it belong to you before it was sold? And after it was sold, wasn't the money at your disposal? What made you think of doing such a thing? You have not lied just to human beings but to God."

⁵When Ananias heard this, he fell down and died. And great fear seized all who heard what had happened. ⁶Then some young men came forward, wrapped up his body, and carried him out and buried him.

⁷About three hours later his wife came in, not knowing what had happened. ⁸Peter asked her, "Tell me, is this the price you and Ananias got for the land?"

"Yes," she said, "that is the price."

⁹Peter said to her, "How could you conspire to test the Spirit of the Lord? Listen! The feet of the men who buried your husband are at the door, and they will carry you out also."

¹⁰At that moment she fell down at his feet and died. Then the young men came in and, finding her dead, carried her out and buried her beside her husband. ¹¹Great fear seized the whole church and all who heard about these events.

The Apostles Heal Many

¹²The apostles performed many signs and wonders among the people. And all the believers used to meet together in Solomon's Colonnade. ¹³No one else dared join them, even though they were highly regarded by the people. ¹⁴Nevertheless, more and more men and women believed in the Lord and were added to their number. ¹⁵As a result, people brought the sick into the streets and laid them on beds and mats so that at least Peter's shadow might fall on some of them as he passed by. ¹⁶Crowds gathered also from the towns around Jerusalem, bringing their sick and those tormented by impure spirits, and all of them were healed.

The Apostles Persecuted

¹⁷Then the high priest and all his associates, who were members of the party of the Sadducees, were filled with jealousy. ¹⁸They arrested the apostles and put them in the public jail. ¹⁹But during the night an angel of the Lord opened the doors of the jail and brought them out. ²⁰"Go, stand in the temple courts," he said, "and tell the people all about this new life."

²¹At daybreak they entered the temple courts, as they had been told, and began to teach the people.

---

^a 26 That is, Messiah or Christ   ^b 26 Psalm 2:1,2

GENEROSITY   Ananias and Sapphira Only Pretended

Acts 5:1–11

LEADERS GIVE of themselves liberally—at least, they did in the New Testament.

The whole church enjoyed unity and generosity, and it all started at the top. The example of the apostles spread a spirit of generosity throughout the whole church. Unfortunately, a couple of pretenders, Ananias and Sapphira, sold some land and gave part of the proceeds to the apostles, reporting that they had given *all* the money to the church. God revealed their deception to Peter and he called them on it. Their sin was not lack of generosity, but lack of honesty. They lied about what they had done. They wanted to be thought of as generous without paying the price.

God would have nothing to do with it. He surgically removed the spiritual cancer from the church by taking their lives. "Great fear seized the whole church and all who heard about these events," Luke says (Ac 5:11).

Let's look more closely at the problem and itemize it. Ananias and Sapphira . . .

1. Clung to their possessions.
2. Agreed to lie about their giving.
3. Pretended to be someone they were not.
4. Thought they could get by with appearing to be generous.
5. Felt more concerned with their image than their relationship to God.

Many leaders struggle with the same issues. Not only do we live in a materialistic world, but we buy into the world's economy. We think that if we grasp and cling to our possessions through our own cleverness, we will eventually "make it." God's economy is radically different. He is an extravagant Lord who gives generously to everyone with a need. He enjoys meeting the needs of his followers, directly or indirectly. He doesn't merely give of his resources, but of himself.

Building Generosity into Your Life

Nothing speaks to others more loudly or serves them better than a leader's generosity. Effective leaders gather for others, then give it away. Consider several ways to cultivate generosity in your own life:

1. Be grateful for whatever you have.
2. Put people first.
3. Don't allow greed to control you.
4. Regard money as a resource.
5. Develop the habit of giving.

Sometimes we hold on to our possessions because we fear we might run out—life seems scarce. But when we believe that giving is the way to live, we will produce more in the future—life seems abundant. This is the life Jesus had in mind for us (Jn 10:10).

For a positive example of generosity, see p. 309.

When the high priest and his associates arrived, they called together the Sanhedrin — the full assembly of the elders of Israel — and sent to the jail for the apostles. ²²But on arriving at the jail, the officers did not find them there. So they went back and reported, ²³"We found the jail securely locked, with the guards standing at the doors; but when we opened them, we found no one inside." ²⁴On hearing this report, the captain of the temple guard and the chief priests were at a loss, wondering what this might lead to.

²⁵Then someone came and said, "Look! The men you put in jail are standing in the temple courts teaching the people." ²⁶At that, the captain went with his officers and brought the apostles. They did not use force, because they feared that the people would stone them.

²⁷The apostles were brought in and made to appear before the Sanhedrin to be questioned by the high priest. ²⁸"We gave you strict orders not to teach in this name," he said. "Yet you have filled Jerusalem with your teaching and are determined to make us guilty of this man's blood."

²⁹Peter and the other apostles replied: "We must obey God rather than human beings!

³⁰The God of our ancestors raised Jesus from the dead — whom you killed by hanging him on a cross. ³¹God exalted him to his own right hand as Prince and Savior that he might bring Israel to repentance and forgive their sins. ³²We are witnesses of these things, and so is the Holy Spirit, whom God has given to those who obey him."

³³When they heard this, they were furious and wanted to put them to death. ³⁴But a Pharisee named Gamaliel, a teacher of the law, who was honored by all the people, stood up in the Sanhedrin and ordered that the men be put outside for a little while. ³⁵Then he addressed the Sanhedrin: "Men of Israel, consider carefully what you intend to do to these men. ³⁶Some time ago Theudas appeared, claiming to be somebody, and about four hundred men rallied to him. He was killed, all his followers were dispersed, and it all came to nothing. ³⁷After him, Judas the Galilean appeared in the days of the census and led a band of people in revolt. He too was killed, and all his followers were scattered. ³⁸Therefore, in the present case I advise you: Leave these men alone! Let them go! For if their purpose or activity is of human origin, it will fail. ³⁹But if it is from God, you will not be

Growth: Seven Signs of Leadership in the Early Church

Acts 5:1–42

The leadership of the early church produced growth naturally. The leaders didn't pursue growth, but practiced obedience, commitment, healthy relationships and faith. Growth was the natural result. This is a sign of healthy leadership. In Acts 5 we see the leadership ingredients that enable the church to grow:

1. *Purity* (vv. 1–11)
   The leaders didn't settle for anything less than integrity.

2. *Power* (vv. 12–16)
   The leaders modeled an attractive, supernatural power that met human needs.

3. *Persecution* (vv. 17–18)
   Opposition served to strengthen the leaders and their convictions.

4. *Proclamation* (vv. 19–28)
   The leaders eagerly communicated their message.

5. *Priorities* (vv. 29–32)
   The leaders clearly laid out their top priority, which made decisions easier.

6. *Praise* (v. 41)
   In the midst of adversity, leaders maintained an attitude of gratitude and praised God for everything.

7. *Perseverance* (v. 42)
   The leaders kept right on influencing others, living a life of conviction, not caution.

able to stop these men; you will only find yourselves fighting against God."

⁴⁰His speech persuaded them. They called the apostles in and had them flogged. Then they ordered them not to speak in the name of Jesus, and let them go.

⁴¹The apostles left the Sanhedrin, rejoicing because they had been counted worthy of suffering disgrace for the Name. ⁴²Day after day, in the temple courts and from house to house, they never stopped teaching and proclaiming the good news that Jesus is the Messiah.

The Choosing of the Seven

6 In those days when the number of disciples was increasing, the Hellenistic Jews*a* among them complained against the Hebraic Jews because their widows were being overlooked in the daily distribution of food. ²So the Twelve gathered all the disciples together and said, "It would not be right for us to neglect the ministry of the word of God in order to wait on tables. ³Brothers and sisters, choose seven men from among you who are known to be full of the Spirit and wisdom. We will turn this responsibility over to them ⁴and will give our attention to prayer and the ministry of the word."

⁵This proposal pleased the whole group. They chose Stephen, a man full of faith and of the Holy Spirit; also Philip, Procorus, Nicanor, Timon, Parmenas, and Nicolas from Antioch, a convert to Judaism. ⁶They presented these men to the apostles, who prayed and laid their hands on them.

⁷So the word of God spread. The number of disciples in Jerusalem increased rapidly, and a large number of priests became obedient to the faith.

Stephen Seized

⁸Now Stephen, a man full of God's grace and power, performed great wonders and signs among the people. ⁹Opposition arose, however, from members of the Synagogue of the Freedmen (as it was called) — Jews of Cyrene and Alexandria as well as the provinces of Cilicia and Asia — who began to argue with Stephen. ¹⁰But they could not stand up against the wisdom the Spirit gave him as he spoke.

¹¹Then they secretly persuaded some men to say, "We have heard Stephen speak blasphemous words against Moses and against God."

¹²So they stirred up the people and the elders and the teachers of the law. They seized Stephen and brought him before the Sanhedrin. ¹³They

---

ABCs of Leadership: Leaders Must Be Selected and Developed

Acts 6:3

Good leadership responds effectively to the need for more leaders and workers. Apparently, no one took a vote to determine the identity of these people. The leaders were chosen. The leadership of the early church practiced the ABCs of leadership. They:

Attracted leaders.
Believed in them.
Chose them.
Developed them.

The apostles had specific qualifications in mind for the leaders they wanted, and chose men who were . . .

1. *Known from their sphere of influence*— "choose . . . from among you."
2. *People who could serve on a team*—"seven men."
3. *Trusted among the people*—"known to be full of the Spirit."
4. *Empowered for the task*—"full of the Spirit."
5. *Competent and intelligent*—"full of . . . wisdom."
6. *Responsible*—"We will turn this responsibility over to them."

---

produced false witnesses, who testified, "This fellow never stops speaking against this holy place and against the law. ¹⁴For we have heard him say that this Jesus of Nazareth will destroy this place and change the customs Moses handed down to us."

¹⁵All who were sitting in the Sanhedrin looked intently at Stephen, and they saw that his face was like the face of an angel.

Stephen's Speech to the Sanhedrin

7 Then the high priest asked Stephen, "Are these charges true?"

²To this he replied: "Brothers and fathers, listen to me! The God of glory appeared to our

---

a 1 That is, Jews who had adopted the Greek language and culture

PETER AND THE LAW OF PRIORITIES
Leaders Understand That Activity Is Not Necessarily Accomplishment

Acts 6:1–7

LEADERS NEVER grow to the point where they no longer need to prioritize. Good leaders keep prioritizing, whether they're leading a small group, pastoring a church, running a small business, or leading a billion-dollar corporation.

The things that bring the greatest personal reward light the fires in a leader's life. Nothing energizes a person the way passion does. Tim Redmond admitted, "There are many things that will catch my eye, but there are only a few things that will catch my heart."

Take some time to reassess your leadership priorities. Are you spread out all over the place? Or are you focused on the few things that bring the highest reward? The greatest success comes only when you focus your people on what really matters.

Sharpening Your Focus by Expanding Your View

Maybe you're similar to Peter—he began full of passion, but lacking direction. The good news is that you already have half of the equation. The bad news is that if you don't know where you're going, you'll end up spinning your wheels—or worse, you could spend years heading in the wrong direction.

When you know where you should be headed, your priorities become clearer and your actions take on significance. The equation looks something like this:

Great Passion + Clear Mission = Focused Action

When the Grecian Jews came to Peter to voice their complaints, Peter recognized that he could further his mission by meeting their felt need. But he also understood that God had called *him* to focus on the people's *deepest* need—to hear the truth of God's Word. Instead of trying to do it all, he delegated the task of addressing the people's complaint to seven men competent to follow through. As a result, the church met both needs.

By examining Peter's situation, we learn a lot about remaining focused on priorities while still seeing the big picture. Peter demonstrated that when a need arises, focused leaders . . .

1. *Determine the validity of the need.*
Strong leaders quickly recognize when a course of action needs to be taken, and they promptly consider how to get the job done. Peter knew that the church could lose momentum if it didn't meet the Grecian Jews' request. Rather than trying to meet the need by himself (as many leaders do), he figured out another way to meet it.

How do you react when your people bring a genuine need before you? Do you stop what you're doing and immediately try to take care of it? Do you nod your head as if you're interested, then push it to the side and forget about it? Or, like Peter, do you step back, look at the big picture, and determine appropriate action according to your priorities?

2. *Look for a leadership opportunity.*

Even when a valid need doesn't fit your priorities, it may provide a learning opportunity for one of your people. Peter quickly recognized that he and the other disciples needed to continue teaching rather than hand out food. But he also recognized an opportunity to develop some emerging leaders.

Are your people one of your top priorities? Before you put something on a back burner, evaluate whether it fits the responsibilities of one or more of your people. The most effective leaders focus on only a few things; they trust their people to do the rest.

3. *Delegate the task to competent people.*

Leaders use delegation as a basic tool. Used the right way, it can take your efficiency to a whole new level. Peter and the disciples carefully chose a team of seven whom they deemed mature and capable to carry out the task.

It's always your responsibility to delegate to the right people. There's nothing worse than having to revisit a need because you assigned an incompetent person to the job. That decreases your efficiency and can damage your credibility. Before you delegate a task, make sure you know your people's skills and abilities.

4. *Publicly confirm and commission their people.*

Peter and the disciples set up their team for success. They not only made sure the seven men could meet the need, but also presented them to the people as worthy leaders. In doing so, they built trust and confidence in the men.

Is it more important to you to get things done or to get things done *right*? Many leaders hurriedly delegate a task just to check it off their to-do list. They falsely perceive delegation as a way of decreasing distractions instead of increasing effectiveness. But great leaders understand that their effectiveness depends on their people's success. Therefore they make it a priority to help them succeed.

Like all effective leaders, Peter understood the difference between activity and accomplishment. He viewed a need through the biggest lens first—his overall mission. Then he zoomed in on what needed to be done—first by him, then by others. As a result, Scripture says the number of Christians continually increased under his leadership.

The Pareto Principle

20 percent of your priorities will give you 80 percent of your production

IF

you spend your time, energy, money, and personnel on the top 20 percent of your priorities.

Priorities	Production
1	1
2	2
3	3
4	4
5	5
6	6
7	7
8	8
9	9
10	10

father Abraham while he was still in Mesopotamia, before he lived in Harran. ³'Leave your country and your people,' God said, 'and go to the land I will show you.'ᵃ

⁴"So he left the land of the Chaldeans and settled in Harran. After the death of his father, God sent him to this land where you are now living. ⁵He gave him no inheritance here, not even enough ground to set his foot on. But God promised him that he and his descendants after him would possess the land, even though at that time Abraham had no child. ⁶God spoke to him in this way: 'For four hundred years your descendants will be strangers in a country not their own, and they will be enslaved and mistreated. ⁷But I will punish the nation they serve as slaves,' God said, 'and afterward they will come out of that country and worship me in this place.'ᵇ ⁸Then he gave Abraham the covenant of circumcision. And Abraham became the father of Isaac and circumcised him eight days after his birth. Later Isaac became the father of Jacob, and Jacob became the father of the twelve patriarchs.

⁹"Because the patriarchs were jealous of Joseph, they sold him as a slave into Egypt. But God was with him ¹⁰and rescued him from all his troubles. He gave Joseph wisdom and enabled him to gain the goodwill of Pharaoh king of Egypt. So Pharaoh made him ruler over Egypt and all his palace.

¹¹"Then a famine struck all Egypt and Canaan, bringing great suffering, and our ancestors could not find food. ¹²When Jacob heard that there was grain in Egypt, he sent our forefathers on their first visit. ¹³On their second visit, Joseph told his brothers who he was, and Pharaoh learned about Joseph's family. ¹⁴After this, Joseph sent for his father Jacob and his whole family, seventy-five in all. ¹⁵Then Jacob went down to Egypt, where he and our ancestors died. ¹⁶Their bodies were brought back to Shechem and placed in the tomb that Abraham had bought from the sons of Hamor at Shechem for a certain sum of money.

¹⁷"As the time drew near for God to fulfill his promise to Abraham, the number of our people in Egypt had greatly increased. ¹⁸Then 'a new king, to whom Joseph meant nothing, came to power in Egypt.'ᶜ ¹⁹He dealt treacherously with our people and oppressed our ancestors by forcing them to throw out their newborn babies so that they would die.

²⁰"At that time Moses was born, and he was no ordinary child.ᵈ For three months he was cared for by his family. ²¹When he was placed outside, Pharaoh's daughter took him and brought him up as her own son. ²²Moses was educated in all the wisdom of the Egyptians and was powerful in speech and action.

²³"When Moses was forty years old, he decided to visit his own people, the Israelites. ²⁴He saw one of them being mistreated by an Egyptian, so he went to his defense and avenged him by killing the Egyptian. ²⁵Moses thought that his own people would realize that God was using him to rescue them, but they did not. ²⁶The next day Moses came upon two Israelites who were fighting. He tried to reconcile them by saying, 'Men, you are brothers; why do you want to hurt each other?'

²⁷"But the man who was mistreating the other pushed Moses aside and said, 'Who made you ruler and judge over us? ²⁸Are you thinking of killing me as you killed the Egyptian yesterday?'ᵉ ²⁹When Moses heard this, he fled to Midian, where he settled as a foreigner and had two sons.

³⁰"After forty years had passed, an angel appeared to Moses in the flames of a burning bush in the desert near Mount Sinai. ³¹When he saw this, he was amazed at the sight. As he went over to get a closer look, he heard the Lord say: ³²'I am the God of your fathers, the God of Abraham, Isaac and Jacob.'ᶠ Moses trembled with fear and did not dare to look.

³³"Then the Lord said to him, 'Take off your sandals, for the place where you are standing is holy ground. ³⁴I have indeed seen the oppression of my people in Egypt. I have heard their groaning and have come down to set them free. Now come, I will send you back to Egypt.'ᵍ

³⁵"This is the same Moses they had rejected with the words, 'Who made you ruler and judge?' He was sent to be their ruler and deliverer by God himself, through the angel who appeared to him in the bush. ³⁶He led them out of Egypt and performed wonders and signs in Egypt, at the Red Sea and for forty years in the wilderness.

³⁷"This is the Moses who told the Israelites, 'God will raise up for you a prophet like me from your own people.'ʰ ³⁸He was in the assembly in the wilderness, with the angel who spoke to him on Mount Sinai, and with our ancestors; and he received living words to pass on to us.

³⁹"But our ancestors refused to obey him. Instead, they rejected him and in their hearts

---

ᵃ 3 Gen. 12:1   ᵇ 7 Gen. 15:13,14   ᶜ 18 Exodus 1:8
ᵈ 20 Or was fair in the sight of God   ᵉ 28 Exodus 2:14
ᶠ 32 Exodus 3:6   ᵍ 34 Exodus 3:5,7,8,10   ʰ 37 Deut. 18:15

21 QUALITIES

COMMITMENT   Stephen Knew What to Stand For and Not Stand For

Acts 7:2–60

STEPHEN, THE first Christian martyr, had earned great influence among the people (Ac 6:8). Fearing the loss of their own influence, Jewish religious leaders seize this leader and bring him before the council.

In his defense, Stephen displays an unwavering commitment to his convictions. In the face of authorities with the power to execute him, he stands and expresses what he knows to be true, both about Christ and the religious leaders' stubborn hearts. This leads to his stoning (7:58–60). His straightforward manner leaves the religious leaders with no argument; they can only throw rocks. Yet even this doesn't shake him. He dies, gazing into heaven, asking God to forgive his murderers.

Where Did the Commitment Come From?

See the source of Stephen's commitment by considering his words and sensing his attitude:

1. He had the presence of God in his life (6:15).
2. He based his commitment on a biblical foundation (7:2–38).
3. He saw the error of past thinking (7:39–41).
4. He spotted the resistance of the religious leaders (7:51–53).
5. He kept his eyes on Jesus, the truth (7:55).
6. He maintained his perspective (7:60).

Commitment moves past the mind and emotions and goes straight to the will. The ancient Chinese said that the will of a man is like a cart pulled by two horses: the mind and the emotions. You must get both horses moving in the same direction to move the cart. Commitment results when your mind and emotions move forward, whatever the cost.

Leaders cannot expect followers to make commitments deeper than the ones they make. To develop commitment we must understand the following truths:

1. *Commitment starts in the heart.* Commitment precedes achievement. Look inside: where is your heart committed?
2. *Commitment is tested by action.* The only real measure of commitment is action. Talk is cheap; action is expensive.
3. *Commitment opens the door for accomplishment.* Once you commit yourself, all kinds of resources come your way to help you succeed.
4. *Commitment can be measured.* Leaders must evaluate their calendars and checkbooks to measure their commitment.
5. *Commitment enables a leader to make decisions.* Leaders must determine what's worth dying for, then make that the basis for decisions.
6. *Commitment flourishes with public accountability.* Go public with your commitments; then you'll have incentive to follow through.

For a negative example of commitment, see p. 1242.

turned back to Egypt. [40]They told Aaron, 'Make us gods who will go before us. As for this fellow Moses who led us out of Egypt—we don't know what has happened to him!'[a] [41]That was the time they made an idol in the form of a calf. They brought sacrifices to it and reveled in what their own hands had made. [42]But God turned away from them and gave them over to the worship of the sun, moon and stars. This agrees with what is written in the book of the prophets:

> "'Did you bring me sacrifices and offerings
>   forty years in the wilderness, people of
>   Israel?
> [43]You have taken up the tabernacle of Molek
>   and the star of your god Rephan,
>   the idols you made to worship.
> Therefore I will send you into exile'[b] beyond
>   Babylon.

[44]"Our ancestors had the tabernacle of the covenant law with them in the wilderness. It had been made as God directed Moses, according to the pattern he had seen. [45]After receiving the tabernacle, our ancestors under Joshua brought it with them when they took the land from the nations God drove out before them. It remained in the land until the time of David, [46]who enjoyed God's favor and asked that he might provide a dwelling place for the God of Jacob.[c] [47]But it was Solomon who built a house for him.

[48]"However, the Most High does not live in houses made by human hands. As the prophet says:

> [49]"'Heaven is my throne,
>   and the earth is my footstool.
> What kind of house will you build for me?
>   says the Lord.
> Or where will my resting place be?
> [50]Has not my hand made all these things?'[d]

[51]"You stiff-necked people! Your hearts and ears are still uncircumcised. You are just like your ancestors: You always resist the Holy Spirit! [52]Was there ever a prophet your ancestors did not persecute? They even killed those who predicted the coming of the Righteous One. And now you have betrayed and murdered him— [53]you who have received the law that was given through angels but have not obeyed it."

The Stoning of Stephen

[54]When the members of the Sanhedrin heard this, they were furious and gnashed their teeth at him. [55]But Stephen, full of the Holy Spirit, looked up to heaven and saw the glory of God,

and Jesus standing at the right hand of God. [56]"Look," he said, "I see heaven open and the Son of Man standing at the right hand of God."

[57]At this they covered their ears and, yelling at the top of their voices, they all rushed at him, [58]dragged him out of the city and began to stone him. Meanwhile, the witnesses laid their coats at the feet of a young man named Saul.

[59]While they were stoning him, Stephen prayed, "Lord Jesus, receive my spirit." [60]Then he fell on his knees and cried out, "Lord, do not hold this sin against them." When he had said this, he fell asleep.

8

And Saul approved of their killing him.

The Church Persecuted and Scattered

On that day a great persecution broke out against the church in Jerusalem, and all except the apostles were scattered throughout Judea and Samaria. [2]Godly men buried Stephen and mourned deeply for him. [3]But Saul began to destroy the church. Going from house to house, he dragged off both men and women and put them in prison.

Philip in Samaria

[4]Those who had been scattered preached the word wherever they went. [5]Philip went down to a city in Samaria and proclaimed the Messiah there. [6]When the crowds heard Philip and saw the signs he performed, they all paid close attention to what he said. [7]For with shrieks, impure spirits came out of many, and many who were paralyzed or lame were healed. [8]So there was great joy in that city.

Simon the Sorcerer

[9]Now for some time a man named Simon had practiced sorcery in the city and amazed all the people of Samaria. He boasted that he was someone great, [10]and all the people, both high and low, gave him their attention and exclaimed, "This man is rightly called the Great Power of God." [11]They followed him because he had amazed them for a long time with his sorcery. [12]But when they believed Philip as he proclaimed the good news of the kingdom of God and the name of Jesus Christ, they were baptized, both men and women. [13]Simon himself believed and was baptized. And he followed Philip everywhere, astonished by the great signs and miracles he saw.

---

[a] 40 Exodus 32:1   [b] 43 Amos 5:25-27 (see Septuagint)
[c] 46 Some early manuscripts the house of Jacob
[d] 50 Isaiah 66:1,2

[14]When the apostles in Jerusalem heard that Samaria had accepted the word of God, they sent Peter and John to Samaria. [15]When they arrived, they prayed for the new believers there that they might receive the Holy Spirit, [16]because the Holy Spirit had not yet come on any of them; they had simply been baptized in the name of the Lord Jesus. [17]Then Peter and John placed their hands on them, and they received the Holy Spirit.

[18]When Simon saw that the Spirit was given at the laying on of the apostles' hands, he offered them money [19]and said, "Give me also this ability so that everyone on whom I lay my hands may receive the Holy Spirit."

[20]Peter answered: "May your money perish with you, because you thought you could buy the gift of God with money! [21]You have no part or share in this ministry, because your heart is not right before God. [22]Repent of this wickedness and pray to the Lord in the hope that he may forgive you for having such a thought in your heart. [23]For I see that you are full of bitterness and captive to sin."

[24]Then Simon answered, "Pray to the Lord for me so that nothing you have said may happen to me."

[25]After they had further proclaimed the word of the Lord and testified about Jesus, Peter and John returned to Jerusalem, preaching the gospel in many Samaritan villages.

Philip and the Ethiopian

[26]Now an angel of the Lord said to Philip, "Go south to the road—the desert road—that goes down from Jerusalem to Gaza." [27]So he started out, and on his way he met an Ethiopian[a] eunuch, an important official in charge of all the treasury of the Kandake (which means "queen of the Ethiopians"). This man had gone to Jerusalem to worship, [28]and on his way home was sitting in his chariot reading the Book of Isaiah the prophet. [29]The Spirit told Philip, "Go to that chariot and stay near it."

[30]Then Philip ran up to the chariot and heard the man reading Isaiah the prophet. "Do you understand what you are reading?" Philip asked.

[31]"How can I," he said, "unless someone explains it to me?" So he invited Philip to come up and sit with him.

[32]This is the passage of Scripture the eunuch was reading:

"He was led like a sheep to the slaughter,
   and as a lamb before its shearer is silent,
      so he did not open his mouth.
[33]In his humiliation he was deprived of
      justice.
   Who can speak of his descendants?
   For his life was taken from the earth."[b]

---

[a] 27 That is, from the southern Nile region
[b] 33 Isaiah 53:7,8 (see Septuagint)

PHILIP

Ordinary Man, Extraordinary Results
Acts 8:5–8

PROFILE in leadership

It's amazing what can happen to and through an ordinary man when God pours a little hardship and the power of the Holy Spirit into the mix.

The believers of the Jerusalem church began fleeing the city in droves due to the waves of persecution they faced because of their testimony for Jesus Christ. But what the enemies of the faith meant for evil, God used for good, as the scattering believers carried with them the message of salvation through the Lord Jesus Christ.

Philip fled Jerusalem and headed toward Samaria, where his commitment to preaching the gospel led to the salvation of multitudes. When Philip performed miracles—casting out evil spirits and healing many—the people listened to Philip's words about the Messiah, who empowered him to perform these astonishing deeds.

One ordinary man, a little persecution, and a touch from the Spirit of God led to massive conversions in the city of Samaria. As Jesus had predicted, the gospel message made its way from Jerusalem into the outlying world (Ac 1:8).

Philip illustrates what one leader, with the empowerment of the Spirit of God and with the authority of Jesus Christ, can do to change the world.

³⁴The eunuch asked Philip, "Tell me, please, who is the prophet talking about, himself or someone else?" ³⁵Then Philip began with that very passage of Scripture and told him the good news about Jesus.

³⁶As they traveled along the road, they came to some water and the eunuch said, "Look, here is water. What can stand in the way of my being baptized?" [37]ᵃ ³⁸And he gave orders to stop the chariot. Then both Philip and the eunuch went down into the water and Philip baptized him. ³⁹When they came up out of the water, the Spirit of the Lord suddenly took Philip away, and the eunuch did not see him again, but went on his way rejoicing. ⁴⁰Philip, however, appeared at Azotus and traveled about, preaching the gospel in all the towns until he reached Caesarea.

Saul's Conversion

9 Meanwhile, Saul was still breathing out murderous threats against the Lord's disciples. He went to the high priest ²and asked him for letters to the synagogues in Damascus, so that if he found any there who belonged to the Way, whether men or women, he might take them as prisoners to Jerusalem. ³As he neared Damascus on his journey, suddenly a light from heaven flashed around him. ⁴He fell to the ground and heard a voice say to him, "Saul, Saul, why do you persecute me?"

⁵"Who are you, Lord?" Saul asked.

"I am Jesus, whom you are persecuting," he replied. ⁶"Now get up and go into the city, and you will be told what you must do."

⁷The men traveling with Saul stood there speechless; they heard the sound but did not see anyone. ⁸Saul got up from the ground, but when he opened his eyes he could see nothing. So they led him by the hand into Damascus. ⁹For three days he was blind, and did not eat or drink anything.

¹⁰In Damascus there was a disciple named Ananias. The Lord called to him in a vision, "Ananias!"

"Yes, Lord," he answered.

¹¹The Lord told him, "Go to the house of

ᵃ 37 Some manuscripts include here Philip said, "If you believe with all your heart, you may." The eunuch answered, "I believe that Jesus Christ is the Son of God."

Discernment: Leaders Read the Situation Before They Lead

Acts 8:26–40

Philip illustrates the importance of a leader who can adapt to a new situation and meet the need. Flexibility is the name of the game.

Philip had been preaching and praying for the sick in Samaria. While in the middle of revival, an angel spoke to him and told him to go south, to the Gaza road. Philip had to adjust his sails and redirect his course. On the road to Gaza, he read the situation. A significant official, the treasurer of Ethiopia, had stopped to read the Scriptures. Philip seized the opportunity to introduce the man to Christ.

How do leaders read similar situations? Spirit-filled leadership involves . . .

1. *Seeing your responsibilities* (v. 25).
   Philip was already doing what he knew to do.

2. *Surrendering your rights* (vv. 26–28).
   Philip didn't demand his own way, but remained flexible. He left a revival to go to a desert.

3. *Sensing your revelation* (vv. 29–30).
   Philip listened to the Spirit. God may speak through people, Scripture, or spiritual intuition.

4. *Sharing your relationship* (vv. 31–34).
   Philip approached the need from a relational perspective, not just a result perspective.

5. *Showing your relevance* (v. 35).
   Philip started where the Ethiopian eunuch was and connected with him there.

6. *Securing your response* (vv. 36–39).
   Philip led the man to a point of decision and saw results.

Judas on Straight Street and ask for a man from Tarsus named Saul, for he is praying. [12]In a vision he has seen a man named Ananias come and place his hands on him to restore his sight."

[13]"Lord," Ananias answered, "I have heard many reports about this man and all the harm he has done to your holy people in Jerusalem. [14]And he has come here with authority from the chief priests to arrest all who call on your name."

[15]But the Lord said to Ananias, "Go! This man is my chosen instrument to proclaim my name to the Gentiles and their kings and to the people of Israel. [16]I will show him how much he must suffer for my name."

[17]Then Ananias went to the house and entered it. Placing his hands on Saul, he said, "Brother Saul, the Lord — Jesus, who appeared to you on the road as you were coming here — has sent me so that you may see again and be filled with the Holy Spirit." [18]Immediately, something like scales fell from Saul's eyes, and he could see again. He got up and was baptized, [19]and after taking some food, he regained his strength.

Saul in Damascus and Jerusalem

Saul spent several days with the disciples in Damascus. [20]At once he began to preach in the synagogues that Jesus is the Son of God. [21]All those who heard him were astonished and asked, "Isn't he the man who raised havoc in Jerusalem among those who call on this name? And hasn't he come here to take them as prisoners to the chief priests?" [22]Yet Saul grew more and more powerful and baffled the Jews living in Damascus by proving that Jesus is the Messiah.

[23]After many days had gone by, there was a conspiracy among the Jews to kill him, [24]but Saul learned of their plan. Day and night they kept close watch on the city gates in order to kill him. [25]But his followers took him by night and lowered him in a basket through an opening in the wall.

[26]When he came to Jerusalem, he tried to join the disciples, but they were all afraid of him, not believing that he really was a disciple. [27]But Barnabas took him and brought him to the apostles. He told them how Saul on his journey had seen the Lord and that the Lord had spoken to him, and how in Damascus he had preached fearlessly in the name of Jesus. [28]So Saul stayed with them and moved about freely in Jerusalem, speaking boldly in the name of the Lord. [29]He talked and debated with the Hellenistic Jews,[a]

Leadership: Deliberate Selection vs. Democratic Election

Acts 9:1–20

Saul of Tarsus began his journey to becoming Paul the apostle on the road to Damascus. God knew Saul was perfectly suited for the task.

First, Paul was a Hebrew and a Pharisee. No one could accuse him of indifference or failure to set a standard. He had studied under Gamaliel, so no Jew would consider him ignorant of the Scriptures. He grew up in Tarsus, which gave him his Roman citizenship and acquainted him with the ways of the world. He was an articulate communicator, which made him perfect to write nearly two-thirds of the New Testament. He hotly pursued righteousness, a passion that helped him reach Asia Minor.

God appoints specific leaders to fulfill a mission; he doesn't hold a popular vote. If he had, no ancient believer would have voted for Saul. Instead, God saw Saul's qualities and called him to both follow Jesus and lead men.

---

but they tried to kill him. [30]When the believers learned of this, they took him down to Caesarea and sent him off to Tarsus.

[31]Then the church throughout Judea, Galilee and Samaria enjoyed a time of peace and was strengthened. Living in the fear of the Lord and encouraged by the Holy Spirit, it increased in numbers.

Aeneas and Dorcas

[32]As Peter traveled about the country, he went to visit the Lord's people who lived in Lydda. [33]There he found a man named Aeneas, who was paralyzed and had been bedridden for eight years. [34]"Aeneas," Peter said to him, "Jesus Christ heals you. Get up and roll up your mat." Immediately Aeneas got up. [35]All those who lived in Lydda and Sharon saw him and turned to the Lord.

[36]In Joppa there was a disciple named Tabitha (in Greek her name is Dorcas); she was always doing good and helping the poor. [37]About that

---

[a] 29 That is, Jews who had adopted the Greek language and culture

BARNABAS AND THE LAW OF EMPOWERMENT
Only Secure Leaders Give Power to Others

Acts 9:27

ONLY EMPOWERED people can reach their potential. When a leader can't or won't empower others, he creates barriers within the organization that people cannot overcome. If the barriers remain long enough, the people give up, or they move to another organization where they can maximize their potential.

If you want to be a successful leader, you have to become an empowerer. Theodore Roosevelt realized that "the best executive is one who has the sense enough to pick good men to do what he wants done, and the self-restraint enough to keep from meddling with them while they do it."

The truth is that the only way to make yourself indispensable is to make yourself dispensable. In other words, if you are able to continually empower others and help them develop so that they become capable of taking over your job, you will become so valuable to the organization that you become indispensable.

Can I Get a Lift?

Barnabas was definitely a lifter of people. It seems as though he let no opportunity escape to add value to others. And his greatest single contribution in terms of empowerment can be seen in his interaction with Paul.

1. *He believed in Paul before anyone else did.*

It's easy to give an opinion about a controversial person or subject after other leaders have given their support. It's something else to step up and speak before *anyone* else does. That's what Barnabas did. He didn't wait until the apostles endorsed Paul before believing in him. In fact, he believed in Paul while Peter and the others feared him.

To be an encouraging leader, you have to be willing to take chances on people. You have to look for the potential in them and encourage them to believe in themselves. And that can be risky, because they may not come through. But if they do, the payoff can be huge. You may be responsible for inspiring a new leader to achieve things he never thought possible. And leaders never forget the first person who believed in them.

2. *He endorsed Paul's leadership to other leaders.*

Scripture says that Barnabas took Paul "and brought him to the apostles. He told them how Saul on his journey had seen the Lord and that the Lord had spoken to him, and how in Damascus he had preached fearlessly in the name of Jesus" (Ac 9:27).

Can you imagine how things might have gone in Jerusalem in those days? Once Paul arrived in the city, word reached the apostles that he was claiming to be a supporter of Christ. They must have thought it was a trick. Here was the same man who had stood by and approved the stoning of Stephen, the first Christian martyr! Barnabas must have shown up at one of the apostles' gatherings with Paul in tow. An uncomfortable silence no doubt fell over the gathering as people realized the identity of Barnabas's companion. And then Barnabas told Paul's story. Paul didn't have to say a word. All the believers knew Barnabas. They knew his reputation, his integrity. That was all it took. Scripture records, "So Saul stayed with them and moved about freely in Jerusalem, speaking boldly in the name of the Lord" (Ac 9:28). The church had accepted Paul.

One of the best things you can do as an empowering leader is to sing your people's praises to others. When they're doing a good job, tell everyone. Be especially intentional about praising them to their friends and families. But also bring them before other leaders. Help them to make a connection on the strength of your credibility.

3. He empowered Paul to reach his potential.

The connection between Barnabas and Paul didn't end in Jerusalem. After Barnabas's endorsement enabled Paul to move freely throughout Jerusalem, teaching the people and debating the truth of Scripture, it wasn't long before Paul became an enemy of nonbelievers. The apostles wisely sent him back to Tarsus for his own safety.

But later, when Barnabas was assigned to help the church in Antioch, he found Paul and made him his companion. That action empowered Paul to take his first "assignment" as a leader, and it led to Paul's partnership with Barnabas as a missionary—the role for which God had destined him.

To be an empowering leader, you must do more than believe in emerging leaders. You need to take steps to help them *become* the leaders they have the potential to be. You must invest in them if you want to empower them to become their best.

Empowering people takes a personal investment. It requires energy and time. But it's worth the price. If you do it right, you will have the privilege of seeing someone move up to a higher level. And as an added bonus, when you empower others you create power in your organization.

time she became sick and died, and her body was washed and placed in an upstairs room. ³⁸Lydda was near Joppa; so when the disciples heard that Peter was in Lydda, they sent two men to him and urged him, "Please come at once!"

³⁹Peter went with them, and when he arrived he was taken upstairs to the room. All the widows stood around him, crying and showing him the robes and other clothing that Dorcas had made while she was still with them.

⁴⁰Peter sent them all out of the room; then he got down on his knees and prayed. Turning toward the dead woman, he said, "Tabitha, get up." She opened her eyes, and seeing Peter she sat up. ⁴¹He took her by the hand and helped her to her feet. Then he called for the believers, especially the widows, and presented her to them alive. ⁴²This became known all over Joppa, and many people believed in the Lord. ⁴³Peter stayed in Joppa for some time with a tanner named Simon.

Cornelius Calls for Peter

10 At Caesarea there was a man named Cornelius, a centurion in what was known as the Italian Regiment. ²He and all his family were devout and God-fearing; he gave generously to those in need and prayed to God regularly. ³One day at about three in the afternoon he had a vision. He distinctly saw an angel of God, who came to him and said, "Cornelius!"

⁴Cornelius stared at him in fear. "What is it, Lord?" he asked.

The angel answered, "Your prayers and gifts to the poor have come up as a memorial offering before God. ⁵Now send men to Joppa to bring back a man named Simon who is called Peter. ⁶He is staying with Simon the tanner, whose house is by the sea."

⁷When the angel who spoke to him had gone, Cornelius called two of his servants and a devout soldier who was one of his attendants. ⁸He told them everything that had happened and sent them to Joppa.

Peter's Vision

⁹About noon the following day as they were on their journey and approaching the city, Peter went up on the roof to pray. ¹⁰He became hungry and wanted something to eat, and while the meal was being prepared, he fell into a trance. ¹¹He saw heaven opened and something like a large sheet being let down to earth by its four corners. ¹²It contained all kinds of four-footed animals, as well as reptiles and birds. ¹³Then a voice told him, "Get up, Peter. Kill and eat."

¹⁴"Surely not, Lord!" Peter replied. "I have never eaten anything impure or unclean."

¹⁵The voice spoke to him a second time, "Do not call anything impure that God has made clean."

¹⁶This happened three times, and immediately the sheet was taken back to heaven.

¹⁷While Peter was wondering about the meaning of the vision, the men sent by Cornelius found out where Simon's house was and stopped at the gate. ¹⁸They called out, asking if Simon who was known as Peter was staying there.

¹⁹While Peter was still thinking about the vision, the Spirit said to him, "Simon, three*ᵃ* men are looking for you. ²⁰So get up and go downstairs. Do not hesitate to go with them, for I have sent them."

²¹Peter went down and said to the men, "I'm the one you're looking for. Why have you come?"

²²The men replied, "We have come from Cornelius the centurion. He is a righteous and God-fearing man, who is respected by all the Jewish people. A holy angel told him to ask you to come to his house so that he could hear what you have to say." ²³Then Peter invited the men into the house to be his guests.

Peter at Cornelius's House

The next day Peter started out with them, and some of the believers from Joppa went along. ²⁴The following day he arrived in Caesarea. Cornelius was expecting them and had called together his relatives and close friends. ²⁵As Peter entered the house, Cornelius met him and fell at his feet in reverence. ²⁶But Peter made him get up. "Stand up," he said, "I am only a man myself."

²⁷While talking with him, Peter went inside and found a large gathering of people. ²⁸He said to them: "You are well aware that it is against our law for a Jew to associate with or visit a Gentile. But God has shown me that I should not call anyone impure or unclean. ²⁹So when I was sent for, I came without raising any objection. May I ask why you sent for me?"

³⁰Cornelius answered: "Three days ago I was in my house praying at this hour, at three in the afternoon. Suddenly a man in shining clothes stood before me ³¹and said, 'Cornelius, God has heard your prayer and remembered your gifts to the poor. ³²Send to Joppa for Simon who is called Peter. He is a guest in the home of Simon the tanner, who lives by the sea.' ³³So I sent

---

ᵃ 19 One early manuscript *two*; other manuscripts do not have the number.

for you immediately, and it was good of you to come. Now we are all here in the presence of God to listen to everything the Lord has commanded you to tell us."

³⁴Then Peter began to speak: "I now realize how true it is that God does not show favoritism ³⁵but accepts from every nation the one who fears him and does what is right. ³⁶You know the message God sent to the people of Israel, announcing the good news of peace through Jesus Christ, who is Lord of all. ³⁷You know what has happened throughout the province of Judea, beginning in Galilee after the baptism that John preached — ³⁸how God anointed Jesus of Nazareth with the Holy Spirit and power, and how he went around doing good and healing all who were under the power of the devil, because God was with him.

Cornelius: Peter's Paradigm Expands

Acts 10:1–35

Missiologists would have called him ethnocentric. While the apostle Peter knew that Jesus told him to go into all the world and preach the gospel, he still had trouble speaking with a Roman centurion named Cornelius. So God provided fresh vision for him. Author Steve Moore notes the sequence of God's vision-building work:

1. *Supernatural Revelation* (vv. 9–16)
   God expands Peter's horizons and helps him out of the box—education that led to new conviction.

2. *Supernatural Invitation* (vv. 17–23)
   God sends associates of Cornelius to invite Peter to enter a new scope of ministry to Gentiles—exposure that led to a new compassion.

3. *Supernatural Confirmation* (vv. 24–35)
   God confirmed this enlarged vision with a receptive Cornelius and signs following his conversion—an experience that led to new commitment.

When God wants to draw new obedience from his servants, he almost always communicates fresh vision. This is exactly what Peter got.

³⁹"We are witnesses of everything he did in the country of the Jews and in Jerusalem. They killed him by hanging him on a cross, ⁴⁰but God raised him from the dead on the third day and caused him to be seen. ⁴¹He was not seen by all the people, but by witnesses whom God had already chosen — by us who ate and drank with him after he rose from the dead. ⁴²He commanded us to preach to the people and to testify that he is the one whom God appointed as judge of the living and the dead. ⁴³All the prophets testify about him that everyone who believes in him receives forgiveness of sins through his name."

⁴⁴While Peter was still speaking these words, the Holy Spirit came on all who heard the message. ⁴⁵The circumcised believers who had come with Peter were astonished that the gift of the Holy Spirit had been poured out even on Gentiles. ⁴⁶For they heard them speaking in tongues*ᵃ* and praising God.

Then Peter said, ⁴⁷"Surely no one can stand in the way of their being baptized with water. They have received the Holy Spirit just as we have." ⁴⁸So he ordered that they be baptized in the name of Jesus Christ. Then they asked Peter to stay with them for a few days.

Peter Explains His Actions

11 The apostles and the believers throughout Judea heard that the Gentiles also had received the word of God. ²So when Peter went up to Jerusalem, the circumcised believers criticized him ³and said, "You went into the house of uncircumcised men and ate with them."

⁴Starting from the beginning, Peter told them the whole story: ⁵"I was in the city of Joppa praying, and in a trance I saw a vision. I saw something like a large sheet being let down from heaven by its four corners, and it came down to where I was. ⁶I looked into it and saw four-footed animals of the earth, wild beasts, reptiles and birds. ⁷Then I heard a voice telling me, 'Get up, Peter. Kill and eat.'

⁸"I replied, 'Surely not, Lord! Nothing impure or unclean has ever entered my mouth.'

⁹"The voice spoke from heaven a second time, 'Do not call anything impure that God has made clean.' ¹⁰This happened three times, and then it was all pulled up to heaven again.

¹¹"Right then three men who had been sent to me from Caesarea stopped at the house where I was staying. ¹²The Spirit told me to have no

---

ᵃ 46 *Or other languages*

hesitation about going with them. These six brothers also went with me, and we entered the man's house. [13]He told us how he had seen an angel appear in his house and say, 'Send to Joppa for Simon who is called Peter. [14]He will bring you a message through which you and all your household will be saved.'

[15]"As I began to speak, the Holy Spirit came on them as he had come on us at the beginning. [16]Then I remembered what the Lord had said: 'John baptized with[a] water, but you will be baptized with[a] the Holy Spirit.' [17]So if God gave them the same gift he gave us who believed in the Lord Jesus Christ, who was I to think that I could stand in God's way?"

[18]When they heard this, they had no further objections and praised God, saying, "So then, even to Gentiles God has granted repentance that leads to life."

Teachability: Peter's New Market Accepted by Church Leaders

Acts 11:1–18

Jesus must have been serious when he told the church to go to the Gentiles! Peter reported to his peers how God had led him to a whole new audience. By the time they heard the story, they glorified God for the new ministry. They remained teachable. The moment you stop learning, you stop leading.

The Church in Antioch

[19]Now those who had been scattered by the persecution that broke out when Stephen was killed traveled as far as Phoenicia, Cyprus and Antioch, spreading the word only among Jews. [20]Some of them, however, men from Cyprus and Cyrene, went to Antioch and began to speak to Greeks also, telling them the good news about the Lord Jesus. [21]The Lord's hand was with them, and a great number of people believed and turned to the Lord.

[22]News of this reached the church in Jerusalem, and they sent Barnabas to Antioch. [23]When he arrived and saw what the grace of God had done, he was glad and encouraged them all to remain true to the Lord with all their hearts. [24]He was a good man, full of the Holy Spirit

and faith, and a great number of people were brought to the Lord.

[25]Then Barnabas went to Tarsus to look for Saul, [26]and when he found him, he brought him to Antioch. So for a whole year Barnabas and Saul met with the church and taught great numbers of people. The disciples were called Christians first at Antioch.

[27]During this time some prophets came down from Jerusalem to Antioch. [28]One of them, named Agabus, stood up and through the Spirit predicted that a severe famine would spread over the entire Roman world. (This happened during the reign of Claudius.) [29]The disciples, as each one was able, decided to provide help for the brothers and sisters living in Judea. [30]This they did, sending their gift to the elders by Barnabas and Saul.

Peter's Miraculous Escape From Prison

12 It was about this time that King Herod arrested some who belonged to the church, intending to persecute them. [2]He had James, the brother of John, put to death with the sword. [3]When he saw that this met with approval among the Jews, he proceeded to seize Peter also. This happened during the Festival of Unleavened Bread. [4]After arresting him, he put him in prison, handing him over to be guarded by four squads of four soldiers each. Herod intended to bring him out for public trial after the Passover.

[5]So Peter was kept in prison, but the church was earnestly praying to God for him.

[6]The night before Herod was to bring him to trial, Peter was sleeping between two soldiers, bound with two chains, and sentries stood guard at the entrance. [7]Suddenly an angel of the Lord appeared and a light shone in the cell. He struck Peter on the side and woke him up. "Quick, get up!" he said, and the chains fell off Peter's wrists.

[8]Then the angel said to him, "Put on your clothes and sandals." And Peter did so. "Wrap your cloak around you and follow me," the angel told him. [9]Peter followed him out of the prison, but he had no idea that what the angel was doing was really happening; he thought he was seeing a vision. [10]They passed the first and second guards and came to the iron gate leading to the city. It opened for them by itself, and they went through it. When they had walked the length of one street, suddenly the angel left him.

[11]Then Peter came to himself and said, "Now I know without a doubt that the Lord has sent

---

[a] 16 Or in

Servanthood: No Task Too Small

Acts 11:22–24

If any early church leader could be called a servant, it is Barnabas. He took initiative and did whatever it took to raise morale, men, or money. He led with clarity and example by becoming a servant. He considered no task too small. What allowed Barnabas to demonstrate such a lifestyle? He had . . .

1. *Nothing to prove.*
   Barnabas didn't have to play games. He never sought the limelight. When he mentored Paul, he happily let the emerging apostle rise above him. Barnabas didn't feel the need to project his self-worth or prove himself to anyone.

2. *Nothing to lose.*
   Barnabas didn't have to guard his reputation or fear that he would lose popularity. He came to serve, not to be served. This enabled him to focus on giving, not getting. As a servant, he had no rights to lose.

3. *Nothing to hide.*
   Barnabas didn't maintain a façade or image. He remained authentic, vulnerable, and transparent. He could rejoice with others' victories (Ac 11:23) and never wondered about his own fame.

If God called you to be another Barnabas to another Paul—if you knew that this new, emerging leader would soon overshadow you—would you accept the call? In other words, are you a servant? You must love your people more than your position.

---

his angel and rescued me from Herod's clutches and from everything the Jewish people were hoping would happen."

¹²When this had dawned on him, he went to the house of Mary the mother of John, also called Mark, where many people had gathered and were praying. ¹³Peter knocked at the outer entrance, and a servant named Rhoda came to answer the door. ¹⁴When she recognized Peter's voice, she was so overjoyed she ran back without opening it and exclaimed, "Peter is at the door!"

¹⁵"You're out of your mind," they told her. When she kept insisting that it was so, they said, "It must be his angel."

¹⁶But Peter kept on knocking, and when they opened the door and saw him, they were astonished. ¹⁷Peter motioned with his hand for them to be quiet and described how the Lord had brought him out of prison. "Tell James and the other brothers and sisters about this," he said, and then he left for another place.

¹⁸In the morning, there was no small commotion among the soldiers as to what had become of Peter. ¹⁹After Herod had a thorough search made for him and did not find him, he cross-examined the guards and ordered that they be executed.

Herod's Death

Then Herod went from Judea to Caesarea and stayed there. ²⁰He had been quarreling with the people of Tyre and Sidon; they now joined together and sought an audience with him. After securing the support of Blastus, a trusted personal servant of the king, they asked for peace, because they depended on the king's country for their food supply.

²¹On the appointed day Herod, wearing his royal robes, sat on his throne and delivered a public address to the people. ²²They shouted, "This is the voice of a god, not of a man." ²³Immediately, because Herod did not give praise to God, an angel of the Lord struck him down, and he was eaten by worms and died.

²⁴But the word of God continued to spread and flourish.

Barnabas and Saul Sent Off

²⁵When Barnabas and Saul had finished their mission, they returned from[a] Jerusalem, taking with them John, also called Mark. ¹³ ¹Now in the church at Antioch there were prophets and teachers: Barnabas, Simeon called Niger, Lucius of Cyrene, Manaen (who had

---

ᵃ 25 Some manuscripts *to*

21 QUALITIES

CHARACTER   Herod Lacked It and Lost Everything

Acts 12:1–23

EGO DROVE King Herod of Paul's day, just as it had driven his father and grandfather. They all desperately lacked character.

Herod was the surname of a family of rulers who held power by permission of the Roman Empire. Herod the Great ruled at the time of Jesus' birth; he's the one who killed all the male babies in Bethlehem. Herod Antipas ordered the beheading of John the Baptist. The Herod in Acts 12 is Herod Agrippa I, the grandson of Herod the Great.

Herod's lack of character provides us with many examples of what *not* to do as a leader:

1. *He mistreated his own citizens* (v. 1).
   He unjustly ordered the arrests of Jewish believers in order to harass them.
2. *He executed innocent people* (v. 2).
   He had James killed by the sword, although he had committed no crime.
3. *He made decisions based on popularity* (v. 3).
   When he saw it pleased the Jews to kill James, he had Peter arrested, too.
4. *He acted irrationally in difficult times* (v. 19).
   He killed the 16 guards who had been on duty at the time of Peter's prison escape.
5. *He harbored anger toward others* (v. 20).
   He remained angry toward outside ethnic groups and looked for ways to get even.

6. *He sought power out of insecurity* (v. 20).
   He enjoyed controlling others and especially loved having people at his mercy.
7. *He projected an infallible image* (vv. 21–22).
   He loved wearing his royal garb and being worshiped.
8. *He was blinded by his ego* (v. 23).
   He lived in an unreal world and couldn't see how his ego sabotaged his leadership.

How Do We Avoid Herod's Trap?

To improve your character and build a solid foundation for your own leadership, you must:

1. *Search for the cracks.*
   Look at the major areas of your life. Identify where you're weak or have taken shortcuts.
2. *Look for patterns.*
   Do any weaknesses remain? Patterns can help you diagnose character flaws.
3. *Face the music.*
   Character repair begins when you face your flaws and apologize to those you've wronged.
4. *Stay teachable and rebuild.*
   Once you face your past, create a plan to build inward strength.

For a positive example of character, see p. 1007.

been brought up with Herod the tetrarch) and Saul. ²While they were worshiping the Lord and fasting, the Holy Spirit said, "Set apart for me Barnabas and Saul for the work to which I have called them." ³So after they had fasted and prayed, they placed their hands on them and sent them off.

On Cyprus

⁴The two of them, sent on their way by the Holy Spirit, went down to Seleucia and sailed from there to Cyprus. ⁵When they arrived at Salamis, they proclaimed the word of God in the Jewish synagogues. John was with them as their helper.

⁶They traveled through the whole island until they came to Paphos. There they met a Jewish sorcerer and false prophet named Bar-Jesus, ⁷who was an attendant of the proconsul, Sergius Paulus. The proconsul, an intelligent man, sent for Barnabas and Saul because he wanted to hear the word of God. ⁸But Elymas the sorcerer (for that is what his name means) opposed them and tried to turn the proconsul from the faith. ⁹Then Saul, who was also called Paul, filled with the Holy Spirit, looked straight at Elymas and said, ¹⁰"You are a child of the devil and an enemy of everything that is right! You are full of all kinds of deceit and trickery. Will you never stop perverting the right ways of the Lord? ¹¹Now the hand of the Lord is against you. You are going to be blind for a time, not even able to see the light of the sun."

Immediately mist and darkness came over him, and he groped about, seeking someone to lead him by the hand. ¹²When the proconsul saw what had happened, he believed, for he was amazed at the teaching about the Lord.

In Pisidian Antioch

¹³From Paphos, Paul and his companions sailed to Perga in Pamphylia, where John left them to return to Jerusalem. ¹⁴From Perga they went on to Pisidian Antioch. On the Sabbath they entered the synagogue and sat down. ¹⁵After the reading from the Law and the Prophets, the leaders of the synagogue sent word to them, saying, "Brothers, if you have a word of exhortation for the people, please speak."

¹⁶Standing up, Paul motioned with his hand

The Law of Explosive Growth: Antioch Sends Out Leaders

Acts 13:1–3

By the middle of the book of Acts, three churches have sent out leaders: Cyprus, Cyrene and Jerusalem. Unfortunately, those endeavors seem to be isolated events. By Acts 13, God's attention shifts to the church in Antioch. Why? Because it remains committed to global impact, busy about raising up leaders to become international change agents. Jerusalem ceases to be the center of God's activity. In fact, it becomes a needy church, requiring the help of churches in Asia and Greece.

Antioch thrives because of its vision to send out leaders. It sends out its leaders as a team, members with complementary gifts and shared vision. This enables them to connect with people and produce results almost everywhere they go.

God does his work by sending out teams of leaders. Jesus sent out his team of twelve (Lk 9:1–6), and the pattern continued in Acts. Most of these leadership teams came from the church in Antioch:

1. Peter and John (Ac 3)
2. Philip, Peter, John (Ac 8)
3. Peter and certain others (Ac 10)
4. Men from Cyprus and Cyrene (Ac 11)
5. Paul and Barnabas (Ac 13; 14)
6. Judas, Silas, Paul (Ac 15)
7. Barnabas and Mark (Ac 15)
8. Timothy, Paul, Silas (Ac 16)
9. Paul, Aquila, Priscilla (Ac 18)
10. Timothy and Erastus (Ac 19)

and said: "Fellow Israelites and you Gentiles who worship God, listen to me! [17] The God of the people of Israel chose our ancestors; he made the people prosper during their stay in Egypt; with mighty power he led them out of that country; [18] for about forty years he endured their conduct[a] in the wilderness; [19] and he overthrew seven nations in Canaan, giving their land to his people as their inheritance. [20] All this took about 450 years.

"After this, God gave them judges until the time of Samuel the prophet. [21] Then the people asked for a king, and he gave them Saul son of Kish, of the tribe of Benjamin, who ruled forty years. [22] After removing Saul, he made David their king. God testified concerning him: 'I have found David son of Jesse, a man after my own heart; he will do everything I want him to do.'

[23] "From this man's descendants God has brought to Israel the Savior Jesus, as he promised. [24] Before the coming of Jesus, John preached repentance and baptism to all the people of Israel. [25] As John was completing his work, he said: 'Who do you suppose I am? I am not the one you are looking for. But there is one coming after me whose sandals I am not worthy to untie.'

[26] "Fellow children of Abraham and you God-fearing Gentiles, it is to us that this message of salvation has been sent. [27] The people of Jerusalem and their rulers did not recognize Jesus, yet in condemning him they fulfilled the words of the prophets that are read every Sabbath. [28] Though they found no proper ground for a death sentence, they asked Pilate to have him executed. [29] When they had carried out all that was written about him, they took him down from the cross and laid him in a tomb. [30] But God raised him from the dead, [31] and for many days he was seen by those who had traveled with him from Galilee to Jerusalem. They are now his witnesses to our people.

[32] "We tell you the good news: What God promised our ancestors [33] he has fulfilled for us, their children, by raising up Jesus. As it is written in the second Psalm:

"'You are my son;
    today I have become your father.'[b]

[34] God raised him from the dead so that he will never be subject to decay. As God has said,

"'I will give you the holy and sure blessings
    promised to David.'[c]

[35] So it is also stated elsewhere:

"'You will not let your holy one see decay.'[d]

[36] "Now when David had served God's purpose in his own generation, he fell asleep; he was buried with his ancestors and his body decayed. [37] But the one whom God raised from the dead did not see decay.

[38] "Therefore, my friends, I want you to know that through Jesus the forgiveness of sins is proclaimed to you. [39] Through him everyone who believes is set free from every sin, a justification you were not able to obtain under the law of Moses. [40] Take care that what the prophets have said does not happen to you:

[41] "'Look, you scoffers,
    wonder and perish,
for I am going to do something in your days
    that you would never believe,
    even if someone told you.'[e]"

[42] As Paul and Barnabas were leaving the synagogue, the people invited them to speak further about these things on the next Sabbath. [43] When the congregation was dismissed, many of the Jews and devout converts to Judaism followed Paul and Barnabas, who talked with them and urged them to continue in the grace of God.

[44] On the next Sabbath almost the whole city gathered to hear the word of the Lord. [45] When the Jews saw the crowds, they were filled with jealousy. They began to contradict what Paul was saying and heaped abuse on him.

[46] Then Paul and Barnabas answered them boldly: "We had to speak the word of God to you first. Since you reject it and do not consider yourselves worthy of eternal life, we now turn to the Gentiles. [47] For this is what the Lord has commanded us:

"'I have made you[f] a light for the Gentiles,
    that you[f] may bring salvation to the ends
        of the earth.'[g]"

[48] When the Gentiles heard this, they were glad and honored the word of the Lord; and all who were appointed for eternal life believed.

[49] The word of the Lord spread through the whole region. [50] But the Jewish leaders incited the God-fearing women of high standing and the leading men of the city. They stirred up persecution against Paul and Barnabas, and expelled them from their region. [51] So they shook the dust off their feet as a warning to them and

---

[a] 18 Some manuscripts *he cared for them*   [b] 33 Psalm 2:7
[c] 34 Isaiah 55:3   [d] 35 Psalm 16:10 (see Septuagint)
[e] 41 Hab. 1:5   [f] 47 The Greek is singular.   [g] 47 Isaiah 49:6

went to Iconium. ⁵²And the disciples were filled with joy and with the Holy Spirit.

In Iconium

14 At Iconium Paul and Barnabas went as usual into the Jewish synagogue. There they spoke so effectively that a great number of Jews and Greeks believed. ²But the Jews who refused to believe stirred up the other Gentiles and poisoned their minds against the brothers. ³So Paul and Barnabas spent considerable time there, speaking boldly for the Lord, who confirmed the message of his grace by enabling them to perform signs and wonders. ⁴The people of the city were divided; some sided with the Jews, others with the apostles. ⁵There was a plot afoot among both Gentiles and Jews, together with their leaders, to mistreat them and stone them. ⁶But they found out about it and fled to the Lycaonian cities of Lystra and Derbe and to the surrounding country, ⁷where they continued to preach the gospel.

In Lystra and Derbe

⁸In Lystra there sat a man who was lame. He had been that way from birth and had never walked. ⁹He listened to Paul as he was speaking. Paul looked directly at him, saw that he had faith to be healed ¹⁰and called out, "Stand up on your feet!" At that, the man jumped up and began to walk.

¹¹When the crowd saw what Paul had done, they shouted in the Lycaonian language, "The gods have come down to us in human form!" ¹²Barnabas they called Zeus, and Paul they called Hermes because he was the chief speaker. ¹³The priest of Zeus, whose temple was just outside the city, brought bulls and wreaths to the city gates because he and the crowd wanted to offer sacrifices to them.

¹⁴But when the apostles Barnabas and Paul heard of this, they tore their clothes and rushed out into the crowd, shouting: ¹⁵"Friends, why are you doing this? We too are only human, like you. We are bringing you good news, telling you to turn from these worthless things to the living God, who made the heavens and the earth and the sea and everything in them. ¹⁶In the past, he let all nations go their own way. ¹⁷Yet he has not left himself without testimony: He has shown kindness by giving you rain from heaven and crops in their seasons; he provides you with plenty of food and fills your hearts with joy." ¹⁸Even with these words, they had difficulty keeping the crowd from sacrificing to them.

¹⁹Then some Jews came from Antioch and Iconium and won the crowd over. They stoned Paul and dragged him outside the city, thinking he was dead. ²⁰But after the disciples had gathered around him, he got up and went back into the city. The next day he and Barnabas left for Derbe.

The Return to Antioch in Syria

²¹They preached the gospel in that city and won a large number of disciples. Then they returned to Lystra, Iconium and Antioch, ²²strengthening the disciples and encouraging them to remain true to the faith. "We must go through many hardships to enter the kingdom of God," they said. ²³Paul and Barnabas appointed elders^a for them in each church and, with prayer and fasting, committed them to the Lord, in whom they had put their trust. ²⁴After going through Pisidia, they came into Pamphylia, ²⁵and when they had preached the word in Perga, they went down to Attalia.

²⁶From Attalia they sailed back to Antioch, where they had been committed to the grace of God for the work they had now completed. ²⁷On arriving there, they gathered the church together and reported all that God had done through them and how he had opened a door of faith to the Gentiles. ²⁸And they stayed there a long time with the disciples.

The Council at Jerusalem

15 Certain people came down from Judea to Antioch and were teaching the believers: "Unless you are circumcised, according to the custom taught by Moses, you cannot be saved."

---

^a 23 Or *Barnabas ordained elders*; or *Barnabas had elders elected*

Accountability: The Team Remains Accountable to the Church

Acts 14:26–28

Although leaders do not require a formal position to make a difference, God rarely calls them to act alone. He usually calls them to be a part of a team to be sent out by an organization, such as a local church. Some leaders send; others go. Both are to support the other.

²This brought Paul and Barnabas into sharp dispute and debate with them. So Paul and Barnabas were appointed, along with some other believers, to go up to Jerusalem to see the apostles and elders about this question. ³The church sent them on their way, and as they traveled through Phoenicia and Samaria, they told how the Gentiles had been converted. This news made all the believers very glad. ⁴When they came to Jerusalem, they were welcomed by the church and the apostles and elders, to whom they reported everything God had done through them.

⁵Then some of the believers who belonged to the party of the Pharisees stood up and said, "The Gentiles must be circumcised and required to keep the law of Moses."

⁶The apostles and elders met to consider this question. ⁷After much discussion, Peter got up and addressed them: "Brothers, you know that some time ago God made a choice among you that the Gentiles might hear from my lips the message of the gospel and believe. ⁸God, who knows the heart, showed that he accepted them by giving the Holy Spirit to them, just as he did to us. ⁹He did not discriminate between us and them, for he purified their hearts by faith. ¹⁰Now then, why do you try to test God by putting on the necks of Gentiles a yoke that neither we nor our ancestors have been able to bear? ¹¹No! We believe it is through the grace of our Lord Jesus that we are saved, just as they are."

¹²The whole assembly became silent as they listened to Barnabas and Paul telling about the signs and wonders God had done among the Gentiles through them. ¹³When they finished, James spoke up. "Brothers," he said, "listen to me. ¹⁴Simon[a] has described to us how God first

---

The Law of Intuition: Peter Proposes a Major Shift from the Old

Acts 15:7-11

Peter's suggested change to the way the church does things amounts to a paradigm shift in both thought and belief. He persuades leaders to change by convincingly communicating what God is doing. Peter sees the need for change before others do. His perception, coupled with his credibility, keeps the church moving forward.

---

intervened to choose a people for his name from the Gentiles. ¹⁵The words of the prophets are in agreement with this, as it is written:

¹⁶"'After this I will return
    and rebuild David's fallen tent.
  Its ruins I will rebuild,
    and I will restore it,
¹⁷that the rest of mankind may seek the Lord,
    even all the Gentiles who bear my name,
  says the Lord, who does these things'[b] —
¹⁸   things known from long ago.'[c]

¹⁹"It is my judgment, therefore, that we should not make it difficult for the Gentiles who are turning to God. ²⁰Instead we should write to them, telling them to abstain from food polluted by idols, from sexual immorality, from the meat of strangled animals and from blood. ²¹For the law of Moses has been preached in every city from the earliest times and is read in the synagogues on every Sabbath."

The Council's Letter to Gentile Believers

²²Then the apostles and elders, with the whole church, decided to choose some of their own men and send them to Antioch with Paul and Barnabas. They chose Judas (called Barsabbas) and Silas, men who were leaders among the believers. ²³With them they sent the following letter:

The apostles and elders, your brothers,

To the Gentile believers in Antioch, Syria and Cilicia:

Greetings.

²⁴We have heard that some went out from us without our authorization and disturbed you, troubling your minds by what they said. ²⁵So we all agreed to choose some men and send them to you with our dear friends Barnabas and Paul— ²⁶men who have risked their lives for the name of our Lord Jesus Christ. ²⁷Therefore we are sending Judas and Silas to confirm by word of mouth what we are writing. ²⁸It seemed good to the Holy Spirit and to us not to burden you with anything beyond the following requirements: ²⁹You are to abstain from food sacrificed to idols, from blood, from the meat of strangled animals

---

[a] 14 Greek *Simeon*, a variant of *Simon*; that is, Peter   [b] 17 Amos 9:11,12 (see Septuagint)   [c] 17,18 Some manuscripts *things'* — / [18]*the Lord's work is known to him from long ago*

The Law of Influence: The Council Impacts the Gentiles

Acts 15:22–29

Through one document the Jerusalem church liberated Christians everywhere of terrible burdens and potential guilt laid on them by Jewish law. They exercised their influence and changed the course of church history. Power isn't always evil. The Jerusalem Council exercised positive influence on its generation; so can we.

and from sexual immorality. You will do well to avoid these things.

Farewell.

³⁰So the men were sent off and went down to Antioch, where they gathered the church together and delivered the letter. ³¹The people read it and were glad for its encouraging message. ³²Judas and Silas, who themselves were prophets, said much to encourage and strengthen the believers. ³³After spending some time there, they were sent off by the believers with the blessing of peace to return to those who had sent them. [34]ᵃ ³⁵But Paul and Barnabas remained in Antioch, where they and many others taught and preached the word of the Lord.

Disagreement Between Paul and Barnabas

³⁶Some time later Paul said to Barnabas, "Let us go back and visit the believers in all the towns where we preached the word of the Lord and see how they are doing." ³⁷Barnabas wanted to take John, also called Mark, with them, ³⁸but Paul did not think it wise to take him, because he had deserted them in Pamphylia and had not continued with them in the work. ³⁹They had such a sharp disagreement that they parted company. Barnabas took Mark and sailed for Cyprus, ⁴⁰but Paul chose Silas and left, commended by the believers to the grace of the Lord. ⁴¹He went through Syria and Cilicia, strengthening the churches.

Timothy Joins Paul and Silas

16 Paul came to Derbe and then to Lystra, where a disciple named Timothy lived, whose mother was Jewish and a believer but

whose father was a Greek. ²The believers at Lystra and Iconium spoke well of him. ³Paul wanted to take him along on the journey, so he circumcised him because of the Jews who lived in that area, for they all knew that his father was a Greek. ⁴As they traveled from town to town, they delivered the decisions reached by the apostles and elders in Jerusalem for the people to obey. ⁵So the churches were strengthened in the faith and grew daily in numbers.

Paul's Vision of the Man of Macedonia

⁶Paul and his companions traveled throughout the region of Phrygia and Galatia, having been kept by the Holy Spirit from preaching the word in the province of Asia. ⁷When they came to the border of Mysia, they tried to enter Bithynia, but the Spirit of Jesus would not allow them to. ⁸So they passed by Mysia and went down to Troas. ⁹During the night Paul had a vision of a man of Macedonia standing and begging him, "Come over to Macedonia and help us." ¹⁰After Paul had seen the vision, we got ready at once to leave for Macedonia, concluding that God had called us to preach the gospel to them.

Lydia's Conversion in Philippi

¹¹From Troas we put out to sea and sailed straight for Samothrace, and the next day we went on to Neapolis. ¹²From there we traveled to Philippi, a Roman colony and the leading city of that districtᵇ of Macedonia. And we stayed there several days.

¹³On the Sabbath we went outside the city gate to the river, where we expected to find a place of prayer. We sat down and began to speak to the women who had gathered there. ¹⁴One of those listening was a woman from the city of Thyatira named Lydia, a dealer in purple cloth. She was a worshiper of God. The Lord opened her heart to respond to Paul's message. ¹⁵When she and the members of her household were baptized, she invited us to her home. "If you consider me a believer in the Lord," she said, "come and stay at my house." And she persuaded us.

Paul and Silas in Prison

¹⁶Once when we were going to the place of prayer, we were met by a female slave who had a spirit by which she predicted the future. She

---

ᵃ 34 Some manuscripts include here *But Silas decided to remain there.*   ᵇ 12 The text and meaning of the Greek for *the leading city of that district* are uncertain.

Recruiting Volunteers

Acts 15:32–35

Organizations staffed by volunteers require the most leadership of any group. Such organizations must have good leaders, because their volunteers' only incentive comes through the vision of the leadership. The organization gives no salary, no retirement benefits, no perks.

The fact is, only a small percentage of volunteers do the work. In most churches, about 20 percent of the members do 80 percent of the ministry. Why is this? Why don't more people serve?

1. *No one has asked them.*
   Hesitant to infringe on someone else's territory, they wait to serve until they're asked.

2. *They have a fear of responsibility.*
   Afraid that duties may force them to become overcommitted, they hesitate to do anything.

3. *They suffer from past burnout.*
   Having gone from "pillars" to "pew-sitters," they feel the need to rest and be fed.

4. *They're intimidated by present workers.*
   "Pillars" unwilling to exchange power for fresh ideas keep others idle.

5. *They are ignorant of the biblical paradigm for ministry.*
   Many churches don't model the priesthood of the believer or the truth of Ephesians 4:11–12.

6. *They have a preoccupation with their personal agenda and busyness.*
   Most people play defense with their calendar and the ultimate loses to the immediate.

7. *They feel untrained, ill equipped, and ungifted.*
   Many people mistakenly believe that only trained or gifted people can serve and, since they have no training or special gifts, they don't qualify.

8. *They're unaware of the options available.*
   Most leaders wrongly assume that people know the vast opportunities that exist.

9. *They don't "own" the cause.*
   Many would sign up for a ministry if they could only catch a vision for the big picture.

10. *They are selfish, lazy, and indifferent.*
    Some don't get involved simply because they don't care for anything but themselves.

So what can be done to mobilize volunteers? Try the following:

1. Schedule ministry interviews with new people to explain the opportunities.

2. Offer training for every position. Model servanthood.

3. Match ministry opportunities with spiritual gifts.

4. Constantly publicize available ministry options.

5. Make ministry involvement part of membership.

6. Create several entry-level positions for the new, apprehensive person.

7. Teach and cast vision on the priesthood of the believer—everyone has a gift to use.

8. Develop realistic commitment blocks for people to share the load.

9. Rotate as many ministry positions as possible to make room for new people.

10. Constantly applaud ordinary servants who make a difference.

Discernment: Paul Changed His Plans as He Discerned the Needs

Acts 16:1–13

All leaders need discernment. Paul had it and he used it to select new leaders, to size up what to say in a courtroom, and to know where to go next on his missionary trips.

As Paul's team traveled through Asia, he must have been listening to the Holy Spirit in his quiet times. God prevented him from speaking any more in Asia and compelled him to move on. Next, the Spirit forbade Paul to minister in Mysia and Bithynia. In Troas, he had a vision in which a man begged him to visit Macedonia.

Such was the dynamic leadership of God. Discerning leaders usually share some common traits. They are:

- good listeners
- intuitive or perceptive
- well networked
- flexible
- optimistic

earned a great deal of money for her owners by fortune-telling. [17]She followed Paul and the rest of us, shouting, "These men are servants of the Most High God, who are telling you the way to be saved." [18]She kept this up for many days. Finally Paul became so annoyed that he turned around and said to the spirit, "In the name of Jesus Christ I command you to come out of her!" At that moment the spirit left her.

[19]When her owners realized that their hope of making money was gone, they seized Paul and Silas and dragged them into the marketplace to face the authorities. [20]They brought them before the magistrates and said, "These men are Jews, and are throwing our city into an uproar [21]by advocating customs unlawful for us Romans to accept or practice."

[22]The crowd joined in the attack against Paul and Silas, and the magistrates ordered them to be stripped and beaten with rods. [23]After they had been severely flogged, they were thrown into prison, and the jailer was commanded to guard them carefully. [24]When he received these orders, he put them in the inner cell and fastened their feet in the stocks.

[25]About midnight Paul and Silas were praying and singing hymns to God, and the other prisoners were listening to them. [26]Suddenly there was such a violent earthquake that the foundations of the prison were shaken. At once all the prison doors flew open, and everyone's chains came loose. [27]The jailer woke up, and when he saw the prison doors open, he drew his sword and was about to kill himself because he thought the prisoners had escaped. [28]But Paul shouted, "Don't harm yourself! We are all here!"

[29]The jailer called for lights, rushed in and fell trembling before Paul and Silas. [30]He then brought them out and asked, "Sirs, what must I do to be saved?"

[31]They replied, "Believe in the Lord Jesus, and you will be saved — you and your household." [32]Then they spoke the word of the Lord to him and to all the others in his house. [33]At that hour of the night the jailer took them and washed their wounds; then immediately he and all his household were baptized. [34]The jailer brought them into his house and set a meal before them; he was filled with joy because he had come to believe in God — he and his whole household.

[35]When it was daylight, the magistrates sent their officers to the jailer with the order: "Release those men." [36]The jailer told Paul, "The magistrates have ordered that you and Silas be released. Now you can leave. Go in peace."

[37]But Paul said to the officers: "They beat us publicly without a trial, even though we are Roman citizens, and threw us into prison. And now do they want to get rid of us quietly? No! Let them come themselves and escort us out."

[38]The officers reported this to the magistrates, and when they heard that Paul and Silas were Roman citizens, they were alarmed. [39]They came to appease them and escorted them from the prison, requesting them to leave the city. [40]After Paul and Silas came out of the prison, they went to Lydia's house, where they met with the brothers and sisters and encouraged them. Then they left.

In Thessalonica

17 When Paul and his companions had passed through Amphipolis and Apollonia, they came to Thessalonica, where there was a Jewish synagogue. [2]As was his custom, Paul went into the synagogue, and on three Sabbath days he reasoned with them from the Scriptures, [3]explaining and proving that the Messiah had to suffer and rise from the dead. "This

Jesus I am proclaiming to you is the Messiah," he said. [4]Some of the Jews were persuaded and joined Paul and Silas, as did a large number of God-fearing Greeks and quite a few prominent women.

[5]But other Jews were jealous; so they rounded up some bad characters from the marketplace, formed a mob and started a riot in the city. They rushed to Jason's house in search of Paul and Silas in order to bring them out to the crowd.[a] [6]But when they did not find them, they dragged Jason and some other believers before the city officials, shouting: "These men who have caused trouble all over the world have now come here, [7]and Jason has welcomed them into his house. They are all defying Caesar's decrees, saying that there is another king, one called Jesus." [8]When they heard this, the crowd and the city officials were thrown into turmoil. [9]Then they made Jason and the others post bond and let them go.

In Berea

[10]As soon as it was night, the believers sent Paul and Silas away to Berea. On arriving there, they went to the Jewish synagogue. [11]Now the Berean Jews were of more noble character than those in Thessalonica, for they received the message with great eagerness and examined the Scriptures every day to see if what Paul said was true. [12]As a result, many of them believed, as did also a number of prominent Greek women and many Greek men.

[13]But when the Jews in Thessalonica learned that Paul was preaching the word of God at Berea, some of them went there too, agitating the crowds and stirring them up. [14]The believers immediately sent Paul to the coast, but Silas and Timothy stayed at Berea. [15]Those who escorted Paul brought him to Athens and then left with instructions for Silas and Timothy to join him as soon as possible.

In Athens

[16]While Paul was waiting for them in Athens, he was greatly distressed to see that the city was full of idols. [17]So he reasoned in the synagogue with both Jews and God-fearing Greeks, as well as in the marketplace day by day with those who happened to be there. [18]A group of Epicurean and Stoic philosophers began to debate with him. Some of them asked, "What is this babbler trying to say?" Others remarked, "He seems to be advocating foreign gods." They said this because Paul was preaching the good news about Jesus and the resurrection. [19]Then they took him and brought him to a meeting of the Areopagus, where they said to him, "May we know what this new teaching is that you are presenting? [20]You are bringing some strange ideas to our ears, and we would like to know what they mean." [21](All the Athenians and the foreigners who lived there spent their time doing nothing but talking about and listening to the latest ideas.)

[22]Paul then stood up in the meeting of the Areopagus and said: "People of Athens! I see that in every way you are very religious. [23]For as I walked around and looked carefully at your objects of worship, I even found an altar with this inscription: TO AN UNKNOWN GOD. So you are ignorant of the very thing you worship—and this is what I am going to proclaim to you.

[24]"The God who made the world and everything in it is the Lord of heaven and earth and does not live in temples built by human hands. [25]And he is not served by human hands, as if he needed anything. Rather, he himself gives everyone life and breath and everything else. [26]From one man he made all the nations, that they should inhabit the whole earth; and he marked out their appointed times in history and the boundaries of their lands. [27]God did this so that they would seek him and perhaps reach out for him and find him, though he is not far from any one of us. [28]'For in him we live and move and have our being.'[b] As some of your own poets have said, 'We are his offspring.'[c]

[29]"Therefore since we are God's offspring, we should not think that the divine being is like gold or silver or stone—an image made by human design and skill. [30]In the past God overlooked such ignorance, but now he commands all people everywhere to repent. [31]For he has set a day when he will judge the world with justice by the man he has appointed. He has given proof of this to everyone by raising him from the dead."

[32]When they heard about the resurrection of the dead, some of them sneered, but others said, "We want to hear you again on this subject." [33]At that, Paul left the Council. [34]Some of the people became followers of Paul and believed. Among them was Dionysius, a member of the Areopagus, also a woman named Damaris, and a number of others.

---

[a] 5 Or *the assembly of the people*   [b] 28 From the Cretan philosopher Epimenides   [c] 28 From the Cilician Stoic philosopher Aratus

The Law of Connection: Paul Was Effective in Athens

Acts 17:22–34

Peter, Stephen and Paul all practiced the Law of Connection in the four sermons that Luke records (Ac 2:14–36; 7:2–53; 13:16–41; 17:22–31). The one Paul delivered in Acts 17 is a masterpiece. He connected brilliantly with people from a different culture, showing he understood both Greek society and human needs. Read his message and watch a master communicator in action:

1. He began with affirmation (v. 22).
2. He bridged his subject with the familiar (v. 23).
3. He enlarged their vision of God (vv. 24–25).
4. He used inclusive language (v. 26).
5. He gave them encouragement and hope (v. 27).
6. He identified with some of their own poets (v. 28).
7. He gave them specific action steps (vv. 29–31).

Effective leaders *connect* before they *expect*. Only when Paul had built relational bridges with the people, did he issue a clear call to repent. Connection precedes decision. And what happened? According to the text, everyone acted. Some sneered at Paul; others said they wanted to hear more; and others followed immediately (vv. 32–34).

In Corinth

18 After this, Paul left Athens and went to Corinth. ²There he met a Jew named Aquila, a native of Pontus, who had recently come from Italy with his wife Priscilla, because Claudius had ordered all Jews to leave Rome. Paul went to see them, ³and because he was a tentmaker as they were, he stayed and worked with them. ⁴Every Sabbath he reasoned in the synagogue, trying to persuade Jews and Greeks.

⁵When Silas and Timothy came from Macedonia, Paul devoted himself exclusively to preaching, testifying to the Jews that Jesus was the Messiah. ⁶But when they opposed Paul and became abusive, he shook out his clothes in protest and said to them, "Your blood be on your own heads! I am innocent of it. From now on I will go to the Gentiles."

⁷Then Paul left the synagogue and went next door to the house of Titius Justus, a worshiper of God. ⁸Crispus, the synagogue leader, and his entire household believed in the Lord; and many of the Corinthians who heard Paul believed and were baptized.

⁹One night the Lord spoke to Paul in a vision: "Do not be afraid; keep on speaking, do not be silent. ¹⁰For I am with you, and no one is going to attack and harm you, because I have many people in this city." ¹¹So Paul stayed in Corinth

for a year and a half, teaching them the word of God.

¹²While Gallio was proconsul of Achaia, the Jews of Corinth made a united attack on Paul and brought him to the place of judgment. ¹³"This man," they charged, "is persuading the people to worship God in ways contrary to the law."

¹⁴Just as Paul was about to speak, Gallio said to them, "If you Jews were making a complaint about some misdemeanor or serious crime, it would be reasonable for me to listen to you. ¹⁵But since it involves questions about words and names and your own law — settle the matter yourselves. I will not be a judge of such things." ¹⁶So he drove them off. ¹⁷Then the crowd there turned on Sosthenes the synagogue leader and beat him in front of the proconsul; and Gallio showed no concern whatever.

Priscilla, Aquila and Apollos

¹⁸Paul stayed on in Corinth for some time. Then he left the brothers and sisters and sailed for Syria, accompanied by Priscilla and Aquila. Before he sailed, he had his hair cut off at Cenchreae because of a vow he had taken. ¹⁹They arrived at Ephesus, where Paul left Priscilla and Aquila. He himself went into the synagogue and reasoned with the Jews. ²⁰When they asked

him to spend more time with them, he declined. [21]But as he left, he promised, "I will come back if it is God's will." Then he set sail from Ephesus. [22]When he landed at Caesarea, he went up to Jerusalem and greeted the church and then went down to Antioch.

[23]After spending some time in Antioch, Paul set out from there and traveled from place to place throughout the region of Galatia and Phrygia, strengthening all the disciples.

[24]Meanwhile a Jew named Apollos, a native of Alexandria, came to Ephesus. He was a learned man, with a thorough knowledge of the Scriptures. [25]He had been instructed in the way of the Lord, and he spoke with great fervor[a] and taught about Jesus accurately, though he knew only the baptism of John. [26]He began to speak boldly in the synagogue. When Priscilla and Aquila heard him, they invited him to their home and explained to him the way of God more adequately.

[27]When Apollos wanted to go to Achaia, the brothers and sisters encouraged him and wrote to the disciples there to welcome him. When he arrived, he was a great help to those who by grace had believed. [28]For he vigorously refuted his Jewish opponents in public debate, proving from the Scriptures that Jesus was the Messiah.

Paul in Ephesus

19 While Apollos was at Corinth, Paul took the road through the interior and arrived at Ephesus. There he found some disciples [2]and asked them, "Did you receive the Holy Spirit when[b] you believed?"

They answered, "No, we have not even heard that there is a Holy Spirit."

[3]So Paul asked, "Then what baptism did you receive?"

"John's baptism," they replied.

[4]Paul said, "John's baptism was a baptism of repentance. He told the people to believe in the one coming after him, that is, in Jesus." [5]On hearing this, they were baptized in the name of the Lord Jesus. [6]When Paul placed his hands on them, the Holy Spirit came on them, and they spoke in tongues[c] and prophesied. [7]There were about twelve men in all.

[8]Paul entered the synagogue and spoke boldly

---

[a] 25 Or with fervor in the Spirit   [b] 2 Or after   [c] 6 Or other languages

---

AQUILA AND PRISCILLA

PROFILE in leadership

Leaders Who Trained More Leaders
Acts 18:24–28

Leadership doesn't mean just getting others to follow; it also means equipping and preparing leaders to guide God's people. The account of Aquila, his wife Priscilla, the apostle Paul and Apollos illustrates this principle.

Aquila and Priscilla—who, like Paul, were Jewish believers and tentmakers—had fled to Corinth from Rome when the Emperor Claudius ordered all Jews to leave the city. When Paul arrived in Corinth, he stayed with this couple and evidently taught them a great deal about the things of God. They took the teaching seriously, for when they traveled to Ephesus, they instructed a minister named Apollos about the gospel of Jesus Christ.

Apollos had heard and believed a portion of the Christian message and with great eloquence was vigorously teaching what he knew. But when Aquila and Priscilla heard him preach, they realized he hadn't heard the complete message, so they took him aside and explained the gospel more fully. After that, Apollos could preach with even greater effectiveness.

When we come to Christ for salvation, God calls us to "go and make disciples" (Mt 28:19). Similarly, when God calls us to leadership, he directs us to help equip others to lead more effectively.

21 QUALITIES

THE BOOK of Acts portrays Apollos as an excellent teacher. God greatly used him in a number of cultures, and he became known as the apostle's right-hand man.

What most impresses about Apollos, however, is his teachability. He never thought he had learned so much that he couldn't improve his game. Luke points out several facts about this man:

1. He came from a cultured city (v. 24).
2. He was an educated man (v. 24).
3. He knew the Scriptures well (v. 24).
4. He'd been taught the Christian faith (v. 25).
5. He had an obvious gift (v. 25).
6. He taught truth accurately (v. 25).
7. He taught truth passionately (v. 26).

Church history tells us that Apollos was such a good teacher that most people would rather have listened to him than to the apostle Paul. That's quite a feather in his cap! This might cause us to assume he had everything together. Yet Apollos "knew only the baptism of John" (18:25). He understood repentance. He understood what it meant to surrender to God. But he wasn't familiar with the deeper truths of discipleship or the Spirit-filled life. So Aquila and Priscilla mentored him by taking the time to listen, evaluate, relate and explain "the way of God" (18:26).

Leaders face the danger of contentment with the status quo. After all, if a leader already possesses influence and has achieved a level of respect, why should he or she keep growing?

1. Your growth determines who you are.
2. Who you are determines who you attract.
3. Who you attract determines the success of your organization.

Leaders must remain teachable. Consider five guidelines to cultivate a teachable attitude:

1. *Cure your destination disease.*
   Lack of teachability is rooted in achievement. If you stop growing, you stop leading.
2. *Overcome your success.*
   Success often hinders teachability. Look not at past trophies, but future goals.
3. *Swear off shortcuts.*
   Everything valuable has a price. The longest distance between two points is a shortcut.
4. *Trade in your pride.*
   Admit you don't know everything, even though you do know some things.
5. *Never pay the price twice for the same mistake.*
   Growth means you'll make mistakes, but you must learn from each of them.

For a negative example of teachability, see p. 1013.

there for three months, arguing persuasively about the kingdom of God. [9]But some of them became obstinate; they refused to believe and publicly maligned the Way. So Paul left them. He took the disciples with him and had discussions daily in the lecture hall of Tyrannus. [10]This went on for two years, so that all the Jews and Greeks who lived in the province of Asia heard the word of the Lord.

[11]God did extraordinary miracles through Paul, [12]so that even handkerchiefs and aprons that had touched him were taken to the sick, and their illnesses were cured and the evil spirits left them.

[13]Some Jews who went around driving out evil spirits tried to invoke the name of the Lord Jesus over those who were demon-possessed. They would say, "In the name of the Jesus whom Paul preaches, I command you to come out." [14]Seven sons of Sceva, a Jewish chief priest, were doing this. [15]One day the evil spirit answered them, "Jesus I know, and Paul I know about, but who are you?" [16]Then the man who had the evil spirit jumped on them and overpowered them all. He gave them such a beating that they ran out of the house naked and bleeding.

[17]When this became known to the Jews and Greeks living in Ephesus, they were all seized with fear, and the name of the Lord Jesus was held in high honor. [18]Many of those who believed now came and openly confessed what they had done. [19]A number who had practiced sorcery brought their scrolls together and burned them publicly. When they calculated the value of the scrolls, the total came to fifty thousand drachmas.[a] [20]In this way the word of the Lord spread widely and grew in power.

[21]After all this had happened, Paul decided[b] to go to Jerusalem, passing through Macedonia and Achaia. "After I have been there," he said, "I must visit Rome also." [22]He sent two of his helpers, Timothy and Erastus, to Macedonia, while he stayed in the province of Asia a little longer.

---

[a] 19 A drachma was a silver coin worth about a day's wages.
[b] 21 Or *decided in the Spirit*

The Law of Explosive Growth: Paul's Mini Seminary Reaches Asia

Acts 19:8–10

Paul began a miniature seminary in Ephesus to teach students the ins and outs of the gospel. For two years he rounded up young men and trained them in the lecture hall of Tyrannus. No doubt the education included practical application—with plenty of hands-on experience—for Luke says that everyone in Asia Minor heard the word of the Lord during those two years (Ac 19:10)!

As he mentored students, Paul remained committed to the people, to the process, and to the purpose. His training always resulted in Great Commission activities. Paul committed himself to developing leaders. Consider how we can do the same as we develop others:

1. Know yourself; be familiar with your strengths and weaknesses.
2. Know the person you wish to develop.
3. Clearly define the goals and assignments.
4. Teach the "why" behind the assignments.
5. Discuss their growth process as you go.
6. Spend relational time with them.
7. Allow them to watch you serve and lead.
8. Give them the resources you need.
9. Encourage them to journal during the process.
10. Hold them accountable for their work.
11. Give them the freedom to fail.
12. Evaluate and affirm regularly.

The Riot in Ephesus

[23] About that time there arose a great disturbance about the Way. [24] A silversmith named Demetrius, who made silver shrines of Artemis, brought in a lot of business for the craftsmen there. [25] He called them together, along with the workers in related trades, and said: "You know, my friends, that we receive a good income from this business. [26] And you see and hear how this fellow Paul has convinced and led astray large numbers of people here in Ephesus and in practically the whole province of Asia. He says that gods made by human hands are no gods at all. [27] There is danger not only that our trade will lose its good name, but also that the temple of the great goddess Artemis will be discredited; and the goddess herself, who is worshiped throughout the province of Asia and the world, will be robbed of her divine majesty."

[28] When they heard this, they were furious and began shouting: "Great is Artemis of the Ephesians!" [29] Soon the whole city was in an uproar. The people seized Gaius and Aristarchus, Paul's traveling companions from Macedonia, and all of them rushed into the theater together. [30] Paul wanted to appear before the crowd, but the disciples would not let him. [31] Even some of the officials of the province, friends of Paul, sent him a message begging him not to venture into the theater.

[32] The assembly was in confusion: Some were shouting one thing, some another. Most of the people did not even know why they were there. [33] The Jews in the crowd pushed Alexander to the front, and they shouted instructions to him. He motioned for silence in order to make a defense before the people. [34] But when they realized he was a Jew, they all shouted in unison for about two hours: "Great is Artemis of the Ephesians!"

[35] The city clerk quieted the crowd and said: "Fellow Ephesians, doesn't all the world know that the city of Ephesus is the guardian of the temple of the great Artemis and of her image, which fell from heaven? [36] Therefore, since these facts are undeniable, you ought to calm down and not do anything rash. [37] You have brought these men here, though they have neither robbed temples nor blasphemed our goddess. [38] If, then, Demetrius and his fellow craftsmen have a grievance against anybody, the courts are open and there are proconsuls. They can press charges. [39] If there is anything further you want to bring up, it must be settled in a legal assembly. [40] As it is, we are in danger of being charged with rioting because of what happened today. In that case we would not be able to account for this commotion, since there is no reason for it." [41] After he had said this, he dismissed the assembly.

Through Macedonia and Greece

20 When the uproar had ended, Paul sent for the disciples and, after encouraging them, said goodbye and set out for Macedonia. [2] He traveled through that area, speaking many words of encouragement to the people, and finally arrived in Greece, [3] where he stayed three months. Because some Jews had plotted against him just as he was about to sail for Syria, he decided to go back through Macedonia. [4] He was accompanied by Sopater son of Pyrrhus from Berea, Aristarchus and Secundus from Thessalonica, Gaius from Derbe, Timothy also, and Tychicus and Trophimus from the province of Asia. [5] These men went on ahead and waited for us at Troas. [6] But we sailed from Philippi after the Festival of Unleavened Bread, and five days later joined the others at Troas, where we stayed seven days.

Eutychus Raised From the Dead at Troas

[7] On the first day of the week we came together to break bread. Paul spoke to the people and, because he intended to leave the next day, kept on talking until midnight. [8] There were many lamps in the upstairs room where we were meeting. [9] Seated in a window was a young man named Eutychus, who was sinking into a deep sleep as Paul talked on and on. When he was sound asleep, he fell to the ground from the third story and was picked up dead. [10] Paul went down, threw himself on the young man and put his arms around him. "Don't be alarmed," he said. "He's alive!" [11] Then he went upstairs again and broke bread and ate. After talking until daylight, he left. [12] The people took the young man home alive and were greatly comforted.

Paul's Farewell to the Ephesian Elders

[13] We went on ahead to the ship and sailed for Assos, where we were going to take Paul aboard. He had made this arrangement because he was going there on foot. [14] When he met us at Assos, we took him aboard and went on to Mitylene. [15] The next day we set sail from there and arrived off Chios. The day after that we crossed over to Samos, and on the following day arrived at Miletus. [16] Paul had decided to sail past Ephesus to

avoid spending time in the province of Asia, for he was in a hurry to reach Jerusalem, if possible, by the day of Pentecost.

[17]From Miletus, Paul sent to Ephesus for the elders of the church. [18]When they arrived, he said to them: "You know how I lived the whole time I was with you, from the first day I came into the province of Asia. [19]I served the Lord with great humility and with tears and in the midst of severe testing by the plots of my Jewish opponents. [20]You know that I have not hesitated to preach anything that would be helpful to you but have taught you publicly and from house to house. [21]I have declared to both Jews and Greeks that they must turn to God in repentance and have faith in our Lord Jesus.

[22]"And now, compelled by the Spirit, I am going to Jerusalem, not knowing what will happen to me there. [23]I only know that in every city the Holy Spirit warns me that prison and hardships are facing me. [24]However, I consider my life worth nothing to me; my only aim is to finish the race and complete the task the Lord Jesus has given me — the task of testifying to the good news of God's grace.

[25]"Now I know that none of you among whom I have gone about preaching the kingdom will ever see me again. [26]Therefore, I declare to you today that I am innocent of the blood of any of you. [27]For I have not hesitated to proclaim to you the whole will of God. [28]Keep watch over yourselves and all the flock of which the Holy Spirit has made you overseers. Be shepherds of the church of God,[a] which he bought with his own blood.[b] [29]I know that after I leave, savage wolves will come in among you and will not spare the flock. [30]Even from your own number men will arise and distort the truth in order to draw away disciples after them. [31]So be on your guard! Remember that for three years I never stopped warning each of you night and day with tears.

[32]"Now I commit you to God and to the word of his grace, which can build you up and give you an inheritance among all those who are sanctified. [33]I have not coveted anyone's silver or gold or clothing. [34]You yourselves know that these hands of mine have supplied my own needs and the needs of my companions. [35]In everything I did, I showed you that by this kind of hard work we must help the weak, remembering the words the Lord Jesus himself said: 'It is more blessed to give than to receive.'"

[36]When Paul had finished speaking, he knelt down with all of them and prayed. [37]They all wept as they embraced him and kissed him. [38]What grieved them most was his statement that they would never see his face again. Then they accompanied him to the ship.

On to Jerusalem

21 After we had torn ourselves away from them, we put out to sea and sailed straight to Kos. The next day we went to Rhodes and from there to Patara. [2]We found a ship crossing over to Phoenicia, went on board and set sail. [3]After sighting Cyprus and passing to

---

[a] 28 Many manuscripts *of the Lord*　　[b] 28 Or *with the blood of his own Son.*

Paul: The Heart of an Effective Leader

Acts 20:18–24

Who you are comes before what you do. Leadership is "being" before "doing." As Paul spoke to the Ephesians, he described the ingredients of an effective leader. Paul led from his soul. He made tough calls, yet shed tears in front of his people. One thing is sure: Leadership begins with the heart. Paul had a heart that was . . .

1. *Consistent*—he lived steadily while moving among them (v. 18).
2. *Contrite*—he acted humbly and willingly showed his weakness (v. 19).
3. *Courageous*—he didn't shrink from doing the right thing (v. 20).
4. *Convictional*—he communicated his convictions boldly (v. 21).
5. *Committed*—he left for Jerusalem, willing to die for Jesus (vv. 22–23).
6. *Captivated*—he showed that a surrendered man doesn't have to survive (v. 24).

the south of it, we sailed on to Syria. We landed at Tyre, where our ship was to unload its cargo. [4]We sought out the disciples there and stayed with them seven days. Through the Spirit they urged Paul not to go on to Jerusalem. [5]When it was time to leave, we left and continued on our way. All of them, including wives and children, accompanied us out of the city, and there on the beach we knelt to pray. [6]After saying goodbye to each other, we went aboard the ship, and they returned home.

[7]We continued our voyage from Tyre and landed at Ptolemais, where we greeted the brothers and sisters and stayed with them for a day. [8]Leaving the next day, we reached Caesarea and stayed at the house of Philip the evangelist, one of the Seven. [9]He had four unmarried daughters who prophesied.

[10]After we had been there a number of days, a prophet named Agabus came down from Judea. [11]Coming over to us, he took Paul's belt, tied his own hands and feet with it and said, "The Holy Spirit says, 'In this way the Jewish leaders in Jerusalem will bind the owner of this belt and will hand him over to the Gentiles.'"

[12]When we heard this, we and the people there pleaded with Paul not to go up to Jerusalem. [13]Then Paul answered, "Why are you weeping and breaking my heart? I am ready not only to be bound, but also to die in Jerusalem for the name of the Lord Jesus." [14]When he would not be dissuaded, we gave up and said, "The Lord's will be done."

[15]After this, we started on our way up to Jerusalem. [16]Some of the disciples from Caesarea accompanied us and brought us to the home of Mnason, where we were to stay. He was a man from Cyprus and one of the early disciples.

Paul's Arrival at Jerusalem

[17]When we arrived at Jerusalem, the brothers and sisters received us warmly. [18]The next day Paul and the rest of us went to see James, and all the elders were present. [19]Paul greeted them and reported in detail what God had done among the Gentiles through his ministry.

[20]When they heard this, they praised God. Then they said to Paul: "You see, brother, how many thousands of Jews have believed, and all of them are zealous for the law. [21]They have been informed that you teach all the Jews who live among the Gentiles to turn away from Moses, telling them not to circumcise their children or live according to our customs. [22]What shall we do? They will certainly hear that you have come,

[23]so do what we tell you. There are four men with us who have made a vow. [24]Take these men, join in their purification rites and pay their expenses, so that they can have their heads shaved. Then everyone will know there is no truth in these reports about you, but that you yourself are living in obedience to the law. [25]As for the Gentile believers, we have written to them our decision that they should abstain from food sacrificed to idols, from blood, from the meat of strangled animals and from sexual immorality."

[26]The next day Paul took the men and purified himself along with them. Then he went to the temple to give notice of the date when the days of purification would end and the offering would be made for each of them.

Paul Arrested

[27]When the seven days were nearly over, some Jews from the province of Asia saw Paul at the temple. They stirred up the whole crowd and seized him, [28]shouting, "Fellow Israelites, help us! This is the man who teaches everyone everywhere against our people and our law and this place. And besides, he has brought Greeks into the temple and defiled this holy place." [29](They had previously seen Trophimus the Ephesian in the city with Paul and assumed that Paul had brought him into the temple.)

[30]The whole city was aroused, and the people came running from all directions. Seizing Paul, they dragged him from the temple, and immediately the gates were shut. [31]While they were trying to kill him, news reached the commander of the Roman troops that the whole city of Jerusalem was in an uproar. [32]He at once took some officers and soldiers and ran down to the crowd. When the rioters saw the commander and his soldiers, they stopped beating Paul.

[33]The commander came up and arrested him and ordered him to be bound with two chains. Then he asked who he was and what he had done. [34]Some in the crowd shouted one thing and some another, and since the commander could not get at the truth because of the uproar, he ordered that Paul be taken into the barracks. [35]When Paul reached the steps, the violence of the mob was so great he had to be carried by the soldiers. [36]The crowd that followed kept shouting, "Get rid of him!"

Paul Speaks to the Crowd

[37]As the soldiers were about to take Paul into the barracks, he asked the commander, "May I say something to you?"

"Do you speak Greek?" he replied. [38]"Aren't you the Egyptian who started a revolt and led four thousand terrorists out into the wilderness some time ago?"

[39]Paul answered, "I am a Jew, from Tarsus in Cilicia, a citizen of no ordinary city. Please let me speak to the people."

[40]After receiving the commander's permission, Paul stood on the steps and motioned to the crowd. When they were all silent, he said to them in Aramaic[a]: [1]"Brothers and fathers, listen now to my defense."

22

[2]When they heard him speak to them in Aramaic, they became very quiet.

Then Paul said: [3]"I am a Jew, born in Tarsus of Cilicia, but brought up in this city. I studied under Gamaliel and was thoroughly trained in the law of our ancestors. I was just as zealous for God as any of you are today. [4]I persecuted the followers of this Way to their death, arresting both men and women and throwing them into prison, [5]as the high priest and all the Council can themselves testify. I even obtained letters from them to their associates in Damascus, and went there to bring these people as prisoners to Jerusalem to be punished.

[6]"About noon as I came near Damascus, suddenly a bright light from heaven flashed around me. [7]I fell to the ground and heard a voice say to me, 'Saul! Saul! Why do you persecute me?'

[8]"'Who are you, Lord?' I asked.

"'I am Jesus of Nazareth, whom you are persecuting,' he replied. [9]My companions saw the light, but they did not understand the voice of him who was speaking to me.

[10]"'What shall I do, Lord?' I asked.

"'Get up,' the Lord said, 'and go into Damascus. There you will be told all that you have been assigned to do.' [11]My companions led me by the hand into Damascus, because the brilliance of the light had blinded me.

[12]"A man named Ananias came to see me. He was a devout observer of the law and highly respected by all the Jews living there. [13]He stood beside me and said, 'Brother Saul, receive your sight!' And at that very moment I was able to see him.

[14]"Then he said: 'The God of our ancestors has chosen you to know his will and to see the Righteous One and to hear words from his mouth. [15]You will be his witness to all people of what you have seen and heard. [16]And now what are you waiting for? Get up, be baptized and wash your sins away, calling on his name.'

[17]"When I returned to Jerusalem and was praying at the temple, I fell into a trance [18]and saw the Lord speaking to me. 'Quick!' he said. 'Leave Jerusalem immediately, because the people here will not accept your testimony about me.'

[19]"'Lord,' I replied, 'these people know that I went from one synagogue to another to imprison and beat those who believe in you. [20]And when the blood of your martyr[b] Stephen was shed, I stood there giving my approval and guarding the clothes of those who were killing him.'

[21]"Then the Lord said to me, 'Go; I will send you far away to the Gentiles.'"

Paul the Roman Citizen

[22]The crowd listened to Paul until he said this. Then they raised their voices and shouted, "Rid the earth of him! He's not fit to live!"

[23]As they were shouting and throwing off their cloaks and flinging dust into the air, [24]the commander ordered that Paul be taken into the

---

[a] 40 Or possibly *Hebrew*; also in 22:2   [b] 20 Or *witness*

Communication: Paul Adapts, Shares His Story to Persuade

Acts 22:1–21; 26:4–23

Three times the book of Acts recounts Paul's conversion. Twice he tells his story before government rulers. In both settings he adapts his story and emphasizes a facet that meets the needs of his audience.

Effective leaders know not only *what* to say, but *how* to say it in order to most powerfully impact their listeners. When they speak, they take into account impact, not image. They evaluate their audience and communicate in a way that best connects with their listeners, then they help them to make practical applications to their message.

Try a little exercise. Read Paul's testimony in Acts 22 and 26, with an eye toward comparing and contrasting his accounts. What differences do you note? What similarities? Why would he emphasize one thing to one audience and another to a second audience? What do you learn from Paul about effectively shaping your message to different groups?

barracks. He directed that he be flogged and interrogated in order to find out why the people were shouting at him like this. ²⁵As they stretched him out to flog him, Paul said to the centurion standing there, "Is it legal for you to flog a Roman citizen who hasn't even been found guilty?"

²⁶When the centurion heard this, he went to the commander and reported it. "What are you going to do?" he asked. "This man is a Roman citizen."

²⁷The commander went to Paul and asked, "Tell me, are you a Roman citizen?"

"Yes, I am," he answered.

²⁸Then the commander said, "I had to pay a lot of money for my citizenship."

"But I was born a citizen," Paul replied.

²⁹Those who were about to interrogate him withdrew immediately. The commander himself was alarmed when he realized that he had put Paul, a Roman citizen, in chains.

Paul Before the Sanhedrin

³⁰The commander wanted to find out exactly why Paul was being accused by the Jews. So the next day he released him and ordered the chief priests and all the members of the Sanhedrin to assemble. Then he brought Paul and had him stand before them.

23 Paul looked straight at the Sanhedrin and said, "My brothers, I have fulfilled my duty to God in all good conscience to this day." ²At this the high priest Ananias ordered those standing near Paul to strike him on the mouth. ³Then Paul said to him, "God will strike you, you whitewashed wall! You sit there to judge me according to the law, yet you yourself violate the law by commanding that I be struck!"

⁴Those who were standing near Paul said, "How dare you insult God's high priest!"

⁵Paul replied, "Brothers, I did not realize that he was the high priest; for it is written: 'Do not speak evil about the ruler of your people.'ᵃ"

⁶Then Paul, knowing that some of them were Sadducees and the others Pharisees, called out in the Sanhedrin, "My brothers, I am a Pharisee, descended from Pharisees. I stand on trial because of the hope of the resurrection of the dead." ⁷When he said this, a dispute broke out between the Pharisees and the Sadducees, and the assembly was divided. ⁸(The Sadducees say that there is no resurrection, and that there are neither angels nor spirits, but the Pharisees believe all these things.)

⁹There was a great uproar, and some of the teachers of the law who were Pharisees stood up and argued vigorously. "We find nothing wrong with this man," they said. "What if a spirit or an angel has spoken to him?" ¹⁰The dispute became so violent that the commander was afraid Paul would be torn to pieces by them. He ordered the troops to go down and take him away from them by force and bring him into the barracks.

¹¹The following night the Lord stood near Paul and said, "Take courage! As you have testified about me in Jerusalem, so you must also testify in Rome."

The Plot to Kill Paul

¹²The next morning some Jews formed a conspiracy and bound themselves with an oath not to eat or drink until they had killed Paul. ¹³More than forty men were involved in this plot. ¹⁴They went to the chief priests and the elders and said, "We have taken a solemn oath not to eat anything until we have killed Paul. ¹⁵Now then, you and the Sanhedrin petition the commander to bring him before you on the pretext of wanting more accurate information about his case. We are ready to kill him before he gets here."

¹⁶But when the son of Paul's sister heard of this plot, he went into the barracks and told Paul.

¹⁷Then Paul called one of the centurions and said, "Take this young man to the commander; he has something to tell him." ¹⁸So he took him to the commander.

The centurion said, "Paul, the prisoner, sent for me and asked me to bring this young man to you because he has something to tell you."

¹⁹The commander took the young man by the hand, drew him aside and asked, "What is it you want to tell me?"

²⁰He said: "Some Jews have agreed to ask you to bring Paul before the Sanhedrin tomorrow on the pretext of wanting more accurate information about him. ²¹Don't give in to them, because more than forty of them are waiting in ambush for him. They have taken an oath not to eat or drink until they have killed him. They are ready now, waiting for your consent to their request."

²²The commander dismissed the young man with this warning: "Don't tell anyone that you have reported this to me."

Paul Transferred to Caesarea

²³Then he called two of his centurions and ordered them, "Get ready a detachment of two hundred soldiers, seventy horsemen and two

---

ᵃ 5 Exodus 22:28

hundred spearmen[a] to go to Caesarea at nine tonight. ²⁴Provide horses for Paul so that he may be taken safely to Governor Felix."

²⁵He wrote a letter as follows:

²⁶Claudius Lysias,

To His Excellency, Governor Felix:

Greetings.

²⁷This man was seized by the Jews and they were about to kill him, but I came with my troops and rescued him, for I had learned that he is a Roman citizen. ²⁸I wanted to know why they were accusing him, so I brought him to their Sanhedrin. ²⁹I found that the accusation had to do with questions about their law, but there was no charge against him that deserved death or imprisonment. ³⁰When I was informed of a plot to be carried out against the man, I sent him to you at once. I also ordered his accusers to present to you their case against him.

³¹So the soldiers, carrying out their orders, took Paul with them during the night and brought him as far as Antipatris. ³²The next day they let the cavalry go on with him, while they returned to the barracks. ³³When the cavalry arrived in Caesarea, they delivered the letter to the governor and handed Paul over to him. ³⁴The governor read the letter and asked what province he was from. Learning that he was from Cilicia, ³⁵he said, "I will hear your case when your accusers get here." Then he ordered that Paul be kept under guard in Herod's palace.

Paul's Trial Before Felix

24 Five days later the high priest Ananias went down to Caesarea with some of the elders and a lawyer named Tertullus, and they brought their charges against Paul before the governor. ²When Paul was called in, Tertullus presented his case before Felix: "We have enjoyed a long period of peace under you, and your foresight has brought about reforms in this nation. ³Everywhere and in every way, most excellent Felix, we acknowledge this with profound gratitude. ⁴But in order not to weary you further, I would request that you be kind enough to hear us briefly.

⁵"We have found this man to be a troublemaker, stirring up riots among the Jews all over the world. He is a ringleader of the Nazarene sect ⁶and even tried to desecrate the temple; so we seized him. [7][b] ⁸By examining him yourself you will be able to learn the truth about all these charges we are bringing against him."

⁹The other Jews joined in the accusation, asserting that these things were true.

¹⁰When the governor motioned for him to speak, Paul replied: "I know that for a number of years you have been a judge over this nation; so I gladly make my defense. ¹¹You can easily verify that no more than twelve days ago I went up to Jerusalem to worship. ¹²My accusers did not find me arguing with anyone at the temple, or stirring up a crowd in the synagogues or anywhere else in the city. ¹³And they cannot prove to you the charges they are now making against me. ¹⁴However, I admit that I worship the God of our ancestors as a follower of the Way, which they call a sect. I believe everything that is in accordance with the Law and that is written in the Prophets, ¹⁵and I have the same hope in God as these men themselves have, that there will be a resurrection of both the righteous and the wicked. ¹⁶So I strive always to keep my conscience clear before God and man.

¹⁷"After an absence of several years, I came to Jerusalem to bring my people gifts for the poor and to present offerings. ¹⁸I was ceremonially clean when they found me in the temple courts doing this. There was no crowd with me, nor was I involved in any disturbance. ¹⁹But there are some Jews from the province of Asia, who ought to be here before you and bring charges if they have anything against me. ²⁰Or these who are here should state what crime they found in me when I stood before the Sanhedrin — ²¹unless it was this one thing I shouted as I stood in their presence: 'It is concerning the resurrection of the dead that I am on trial before you today.' "

²²Then Felix, who was well acquainted with the Way, adjourned the proceedings. "When Lysias the commander comes," he said, "I will decide your case." ²³He ordered the centurion to keep Paul under guard but to give him some freedom and permit his friends to take care of his needs.

²⁴Several days later Felix came with his wife Drusilla, who was Jewish. He sent for Paul and listened to him as he spoke about faith in Christ Jesus. ²⁵As Paul talked about righteousness, self-

---

[a] 23 The meaning of the Greek for this word is uncertain.
[b] 6-8 Some manuscripts include here *him, and we would have judged him in accordance with our law. ⁷But the commander Lysias came and took him from us with much violence, ⁸ordering his accusers to come before you.*

control and the judgment to come, Felix was afraid and said, "That's enough for now! You may leave. When I find it convenient, I will send for you." ²⁶At the same time he was hoping that Paul would offer him a bribe, so he sent for him frequently and talked with him.

²⁷When two years had passed, Felix was succeeded by Porcius Festus, but because Felix wanted to grant a favor to the Jews, he left Paul in prison.

Paul's Trial Before Festus

25 Three days after arriving in the province, Festus went up from Caesarea to Jerusalem, ²where the chief priests and the Jewish leaders appeared before him and presented the charges against Paul. ³They requested Festus, as a favor to them, to have Paul transferred to Jerusalem, for they were preparing an ambush to kill him along the way. ⁴Festus answered, "Paul is being held at Caesarea, and I myself am going there soon. ⁵Let some of your leaders come with me, and if the man has done anything wrong, they can press charges against him there."

⁶After spending eight or ten days with them, Festus went down to Caesarea. The next day he convened the court and ordered that Paul be brought before him. ⁷When Paul came in, the Jews who had come down from Jerusalem stood around him. They brought many serious charges against him, but they could not prove them.

⁸Then Paul made his defense: "I have done nothing wrong against the Jewish law or against the temple or against Caesar."

⁹Festus, wishing to do the Jews a favor, said to Paul, "Are you willing to go up to Jerusalem and stand trial before me there on these charges?"

¹⁰Paul answered: "I am now standing before Caesar's court, where I ought to be tried. I have not done any wrong to the Jews, as you yourself know very well. ¹¹If, however, I am guilty of doing anything deserving death, I do not refuse to die. But if the charges brought against me by these Jews are not true, no one has the right to hand me over to them. I appeal to Caesar!"

¹²After Festus had conferred with his council, he declared: "You have appealed to Caesar. To Caesar you will go!"

Festus Consults King Agrippa

¹³A few days later King Agrippa and Bernice arrived at Caesarea to pay their respects to

---

FELIX, FESTUS AND AGRIPPA

PROFILE *in leadership*

Leaders on Power Trips
Acts 23:23—26:32

Appearing before two powerful men—the Roman governor Festus and the king Agrippa—stood a raggedly dressed man in shackles. Yet Paul, who sat in prison for more than two years and who faced a possible death sentence, spoke boldly of the risen Christ.

Festus had inherited the case from his predecessor, Felix, who held Paul on unofficial charges of inciting riots among Jews and encouraging rebellion against Rome. Both Festus and Felix took more interest in gaining favor with the Jews than with doing what was right. When Festus told the visiting King Agrippa of the "Paul problem," the king gave the apostle a hearing. Paul took the opportunity to present the gospel, but when he told Agrippa of his experiences with Christ, it was like nothing Festus had ever heard.

Both governmental leaders had the chance to turn to Christ that day. But neither accepted the invitation. Why not? Apparently their positions of power and leadership meant more to them than the condition of their souls.

Godly leaders know that the pursuit of a deeper knowledge of (and obedience to) Jesus takes precedence over everything else, including the acquisition or protection of power. Power not only corrupts, it also dissipates—unlike the sterling character we can acquire through submission to Christ.

Festus. ¹⁴Since they were spending many days there, Festus discussed Paul's case with the king. He said: "There is a man here whom Felix left as a prisoner. ¹⁵When I went to Jerusalem, the chief priests and the elders of the Jews brought charges against him and asked that he be condemned.

¹⁶"I told them that it is not the Roman custom to hand over anyone before they have faced their accusers and have had an opportunity to defend themselves against the charges. ¹⁷When they came here with me, I did not delay the case, but convened the court the next day and ordered the man to be brought in. ¹⁸When his accusers got up to speak, they did not charge him with any of the crimes I had expected. ¹⁹Instead, they had some points of dispute with him about their own religion and about a dead man named Jesus who Paul claimed was alive. ²⁰I was at a loss how to investigate such matters; so I asked if he would be willing to go to Jerusalem and stand trial there on these charges. ²¹But when Paul made his appeal to be held over for the Emperor's decision, I ordered him held until I could send him to Caesar."

²²Then Agrippa said to Festus, "I would like to hear this man myself."

He replied, "Tomorrow you will hear him."

Paul Before Agrippa

²³The next day Agrippa and Bernice came with great pomp and entered the audience room with the high-ranking military officers and the prominent men of the city. At the command of Festus, Paul was brought in. ²⁴Festus said: "King Agrippa, and all who are present with us, you see this man! The whole Jewish community has petitioned me about him in Jerusalem and here in Caesarea, shouting that he ought not to live any longer. ²⁵I found he had done nothing deserving of death, but because he made his appeal to the Emperor I decided to send him to Rome. ²⁶But I have nothing definite to write to His Majesty about him. Therefore I have brought him before all of you, and especially before you, King Agrippa, so that as a result of this investigation I may have something to write. ²⁷For I think it is unreasonable to send a prisoner on to Rome without specifying the charges against him."

26 Then Agrippa said to Paul, "You have permission to speak for yourself."

So Paul motioned with his hand and began his defense: ²"King Agrippa, I consider myself fortunate to stand before you today as I make my defense against all the accusations of the Jews, ³and especially so because you are well acquainted with all the Jewish customs and con-

PAUL

The Most Influential Leader of the Early Church
Acts 26:1–23

PROFILE in leadership

From the very beginning, the apostle Paul's life in Christ greatly influenced everyone around him.

This persecutor-turned-apostle stood before kings, governors and the religious power structures of the day. His enemies accused him, imprisoned him, beat him, and threatened him with death. He traveled untold thousands of miles and even survived a shipwreck. Through all of this, Paul never failed to vigorously and courageously defend and preach the gospel of Jesus Christ.

Paul didn't become an influential leader because of his eloquence or because he possessed some special talent withheld from everyone else. Paul gained influence because, regardless of his circumstances—whether he sat in shackles during another interrogation, whether he lay in a cold prison cell, or whether he roamed free to do his work—he stayed committed to one thing: preaching the name of Jesus.

Without question, Paul became the most influential leader of the early church. We continue to feel his influence to this day.

By the world's standards—then *and* today—Paul must have appeared a fanatic. But all he did was obey God's call to influence the world around him. Wise leaders today would do well to follow Paul's example by purposefully taking the Word of God both to the body of Christ and to the unbelieving world.

troversies. Therefore, I beg you to listen to me patiently.

4"The Jewish people all know the way I have lived ever since I was a child, from the beginning of my life in my own country, and also in Jerusalem. 5They have known me for a long time and can testify, if they are willing, that I conformed to the strictest sect of our religion, living as a Pharisee. 6And now it is because of my hope in what God has promised our ancestors that I am on trial today. 7This is the promise our twelve tribes are hoping to see fulfilled as they earnestly serve God day and night. King Agrippa, it is because of this hope that these Jews are accusing me. 8Why should any of you consider it incredible that God raises the dead?

9"I too was convinced that I ought to do all that was possible to oppose the name of Jesus of Nazareth. 10And that is just what I did in Jerusalem. On the authority of the chief priests I put many of the Lord's people in prison, and when they were put to death, I cast my vote against

them. 11Many a time I went from one synagogue to another to have them punished, and I tried to force them to blaspheme. I was so obsessed with persecuting them that I even hunted them down in foreign cities.

12"On one of these journeys I was going to Damascus with the authority and commission of the chief priests. 13About noon, King Agrippa, as I was on the road, I saw a light from heaven, brighter than the sun, blazing around me and my companions. 14We all fell to the ground, and I heard a voice saying to me in Aramaic,[a] 'Saul, Saul, why do you persecute me? It is hard for you to kick against the goads.'

15"Then I asked, 'Who are you, Lord?'

"'I am Jesus, whom you are persecuting,' the Lord replied. 16'Now get up and stand on your feet. I have appeared to you to appoint you as a servant and as a witness of what you have seen and will see of me. 17I will rescue you from your

a 14 Or Hebrew

Persuasion: Leaders Speak to Transform, Not Merely Inform

Acts 26:1–29

In one of his most compelling court speeches, Paul addressed King Agrippa. As you read this chapter, try to sense Paul's strategy. Paul believed the best defense is a good offense and nearly converted King Agrippa. Observe how this leader attempted to persuade his audience:

1. He appeared relaxed, yet used animated gestures (v. 1).

2. He humbly thanked the king for allowing him to speak (v. 2).

3. He affirmed the king's knowledge and expertise (v. 3).

4. He admitted his life was an open book (v. 4).

5. He reminded them of his strict past (vv. 5–8).

6. He identified with their opposition to the life he now embraced (vv. 9–11).

7. He used a narrative to defend his changed life (vv. 12–18).

8. He described his motives as pure and constructive (v. 18).

9. He conceded that he was obeying a divine vision (vv. 19–20).

10. He explained that his obedience to God caused his trouble (v. 21).

11. He illustrated God's favor on his life (v. 22).

12. He affirmed that he preached the Scripture (vv. 22–23).

13. He challenged them with reasonable and verifiable facts (v. 25).

14. He admitted the king knew these facts (v. 26).

15. He confronted the king directly with a question (v. 27).

16. He pled with them to obey God (v. 29).

own people and from the Gentiles. I am sending you to them [18]to open their eyes and turn them from darkness to light, and from the power of Satan to God, so that they may receive forgiveness of sins and a place among those who are sanctified by faith in me.'

[19]"So then, King Agrippa, I was not disobedient to the vision from heaven. [20]First to those in Damascus, then to those in Jerusalem and in all Judea, and then to the Gentiles, I preached that they should repent and turn to God and demonstrate their repentance by their deeds. [21]That is why some Jews seized me in the temple courts and tried to kill me. [22]But God has helped me to this very day; so I stand here and testify to small and great alike. I am saying nothing beyond what the prophets and Moses said would happen— [23]that the Messiah would suffer and, as the first to rise from the dead, would bring the message of light to his own people and to the Gentiles."

[24]At this point Festus interrupted Paul's defense. "You are out of your mind, Paul!" he shouted. "Your great learning is driving you insane."

[25]"I am not insane, most excellent Festus," Paul replied. "What I am saying is true and reasonable. [26]The king is familiar with these things, and I can speak freely to him. I am convinced that none of this has escaped his notice, because it was not done in a corner. [27]King Agrippa, do you believe the prophets? I know you do."

[28]Then Agrippa said to Paul, "Do you think that in such a short time you can persuade me to be a Christian?"

[29]Paul replied, "Short time or long—I pray to God that not only you but all who are listening to me today may become what I am, except for these chains."

[30]The king rose, and with him the governor and Bernice and those sitting with them. [31]After they left the room, they began saying to one another, "This man is not doing anything that deserves death or imprisonment." [32]Agrippa said to Festus, "This man could have been set free if he had not appealed to Caesar."

Paul Sails for Rome

27 When it was decided that we would sail for Italy, Paul and some other prisoners were handed over to a centurion named Julius, who belonged to the Imperial Regiment. [2]We boarded a ship from Adramyttium about to sail for ports along the coast of the province of Asia, and we put out to sea. Aristarchus, a Macedonian from Thessalonica, was with us.

[3]The next day we landed at Sidon; and Julius, in kindness to Paul, allowed him to go to his friends so they might provide for his needs. [4]From there we put out to sea again and passed to the lee of Cyprus because the winds were against us. [5]When we had sailed across the open sea off the coast of Cilicia and Pamphylia, we landed at Myra in Lycia. [6]There the centurion found an Alexandrian ship sailing for Italy and put us on board. [7]We made slow headway for many days and had difficulty arriving off Cnidus. When the wind did not allow us to hold our course, we sailed to the lee of Crete, opposite Salmone. [8]We moved along the coast with difficulty and came to a place called Fair Havens, near the town of Lasea.

[9]Much time had been lost, and sailing had already become dangerous because by now it was after the Day of Atonement.[a] So Paul warned them, [10]"Men, I can see that our voyage is going to be disastrous and bring great loss to ship

---

Vision: Paul's Vision Led to His Victory

Acts 26:12–29

Paul's vision on the road to Damascus became the captivating force behind his success. The apostle teaches us the power of a vision. God's vision for Paul accomplished a number of things:

1. *It stopped him* (vv. 12–15).
   Vision allows us to see ourselves. We see things not as they are, but as we are.

2. *It sent him* (vv. 16–18).
   Vision allows us to see others. We feel compelled to act.

3. *It strengthened him* (vv. 20–23).
   Vision enables us to continue despite struggle and lack of resources.

4. *It stretched him* (vv. 24–29).
   Vision gave him conviction to stand, confidence to speak, and compassion to share.

5. *It satisfied him* (v. 19).
   Obedience to this vision motivated Paul to act. It fulfilled him.

---

[a] 9 That is, Yom Kippur

and cargo, and to our own lives also." [11]But the centurion, instead of listening to what Paul said, followed the advice of the pilot and of the owner of the ship. [12]Since the harbor was unsuitable to winter in, the majority decided that we should sail on, hoping to reach Phoenix and winter there. This was a harbor in Crete, facing both southwest and northwest.

The Storm

[13]When a gentle south wind began to blow, they saw their opportunity; so they weighed anchor and sailed along the shore of Crete. [14]Before very long, a wind of hurricane force, called the Northeaster, swept down from the island. [15]The ship was caught by the storm and could not head into the wind; so we gave way to it and were driven along. [16]As we passed to the lee of a small island called Cauda, we were hardly able to make the lifeboat secure, [17]so the men hoisted it aboard. Then they passed ropes under the ship itself to hold it together. Because they were afraid they would run aground on the sandbars of Syrtis, they lowered the sea anchor[a] and let the ship be driven along. [18]We took such a violent battering from the storm that the next day they began to throw the cargo overboard. [19]On the third day, they threw the ship's tackle overboard with their own hands. [20]When neither sun nor stars appeared for many days and the storm continued raging, we finally gave up all hope of being saved.

---

[a] 17 Or the sails

The Law of Influence: An Inmate Takes Command

Acts 27:1–44

As an inmate on a virtual prison ship, Paul began with no influence (Ac 27:11). By the end of the voyage, however, everyone was listening to him, including the centurion. Note how this leader gained his influence:

1. *He built trust* (v. 3).
   Julius allowed Paul special privileges, noting his trustworthiness.

2. *He took initiative* (vv. 9–10).
   With no position or permission, Paul stepped in and took action.

3. *He possessed good judgment* (v. 10).
   Paul's speech revealed wisdom and experience.

4. *He spoke with authority and credibility* (v. 21).
   Paul unashamedly reminded the crew he had been right earlier.

5. *He was optimistic and confident* (vv. 22–24).
   Paul spoke boldly.

6. *He gave encouragement* (v. 25).
   Paul gave hope for survival and rescue.

7. *He was honest* (v. 26).
   Paul candidly told the crew they would face problems.

8. *He didn't compromise on absolutes* (vv. 27–32).
   Paul wouldn't drift from God-given instructions.

9. *He stayed focused* (vv. 33–34).
   Paul focused on objectives, not obstacles.

10. *He led by example* (vv. 35–38).
    Paul led by modeling the right attitude.

11. *He ultimately succeeded* (vv. 39–44).
    Paul eventually accomplished what he set out to do.

²¹After they had gone a long time without food, Paul stood up before them and said: "Men, you should have taken my advice not to sail from Crete; then you would have spared yourselves this damage and loss. ²²But now I urge you to keep up your courage, because not one of you will be lost; only the ship will be destroyed. ²³Last night an angel of the God to whom I belong and whom I serve stood beside me ²⁴and said, 'Do not be afraid, Paul. You must stand trial before Caesar; and God has graciously given you the lives of all who sail with you.' ²⁵So keep up your courage, men, for I have faith in God that it will happen just as he told me. ²⁶Nevertheless, we must run aground on some island."

The Shipwreck

²⁷On the fourteenth night we were still being driven across the Adriatic^a Sea, when about midnight the sailors sensed they were approaching land. ²⁸They took soundings and found that the water was a hundred and twenty feet^b deep. A short time later they took soundings again and found it was ninety feet^c deep. ²⁹Fearing that we would be dashed against the rocks, they dropped four anchors from the stern and prayed for daylight. ³⁰In an attempt to escape from the ship, the sailors let the lifeboat down into the sea, pretending they were going to lower some anchors from the bow. ³¹Then Paul said to the centurion and the soldiers, "Unless these men stay with the ship, you cannot be saved." ³²So the soldiers cut the ropes that held the lifeboat and let it drift away.

³³Just before dawn Paul urged them all to eat. "For the last fourteen days," he said, "you have been in constant suspense and have gone without food—you haven't eaten anything. ³⁴Now I urge you to take some food. You need it to survive. Not one of you will lose a single hair from his head." ³⁵After he said this, he took some bread and gave thanks to God in front of them all. Then he broke it and began to eat. ³⁶They were all encouraged and ate some food themselves. ³⁷Altogether there were 276 of us on board. ³⁸When they had eaten as much as they wanted, they lightened the ship by throwing the grain into the sea.

³⁹When daylight came, they did not recognize the land, but they saw a bay with a sandy beach, where they decided to run the ship aground if they could. ⁴⁰Cutting loose the anchors, they left them in the sea and at the same time untied the ropes that held the rudders. Then they hoisted the foresail to the wind and made for the beach. ⁴¹But the ship struck a sandbar and ran aground. The bow stuck fast and would not move, and the stern was broken to pieces by the pounding of the surf.

⁴²The soldiers planned to kill the prisoners to prevent any of them from swimming away and escaping. ⁴³But the centurion wanted to spare Paul's life and kept them from carrying out their plan. He ordered those who could swim to jump overboard first and get to land. ⁴⁴The rest were to get there on planks or on other pieces of the ship. In this way everyone reached land safely.

Paul Ashore on Malta

28 Once safely on shore, we found out that the island was called Malta. ²The islanders showed us unusual kindness. They built a fire and welcomed us all because it was raining and cold. ³Paul gathered a pile of brushwood and, as he put it on the fire, a viper, driven out by the heat, fastened itself on his hand. ⁴When the islanders saw the snake hanging from his hand, they said to each other, "This man must be a murderer; for though he escaped from the sea, the goddess Justice has not allowed him to live." ⁵But Paul shook the snake off into the fire and suffered no ill effects. ⁶The people expected him to swell up or suddenly fall dead; but after waiting a long time and seeing nothing unusual happen to him, they changed their minds and said he was a god.

⁷There was an estate nearby that belonged to Publius, the chief official of the island. He welcomed us to his home and showed us generous hospitality for three days. ⁸His father was sick in bed, suffering from fever and dysentery. Paul

---

^{a} 27 In ancient times the name referred to an area extending well south of Italy. ^{b} 28 Or about 37 meters ^{c} 28 Or about 27 meters

---

The Law of Solid Ground: Paul Earned the Right to Be Heard

Acts 28:3–6

When Paul continued living after a snake bit him, the locals proclaimed him a god (Ac 28:6). Credibility comes in one of two ways: Someone can loan you theirs, or you can get it from the life you live. People attach credibility to leaders who get the job done.

went in to see him and, after prayer, placed his hands on him and healed him. [9]When this had happened, the rest of the sick on the island came and were cured. [10]They honored us in many ways; and when we were ready to sail, they furnished us with the supplies we needed.

Paul's Arrival at Rome

[11]After three months we put out to sea in a ship that had wintered in the island—it was an Alexandrian ship with the figurehead of the twin gods Castor and Pollux. [12]We put in at Syracuse and stayed there three days. [13]From there we set sail and arrived at Rhegium. The next day the south wind came up, and on the following day we reached Puteoli. [14]There we found some brothers and sisters who invited us to spend a week with them. And so we came to Rome. [15]The brothers and sisters there had heard that we were coming, and they traveled as far as the Forum of Appius and the Three Taverns to meet us. At the sight of these people Paul thanked God and was encouraged. [16]When we got to Rome, Paul was allowed to live by himself, with a soldier to guard him.

Paul Preaches at Rome Under Guard

[17]Three days later he called together the local Jewish leaders. When they had assembled, Paul said to them: "My brothers, although I have done nothing against our people or against the customs of our ancestors, I was arrested in Jerusalem and handed over to the Romans. [18]They examined me and wanted to release me, because I was not guilty of any crime deserving death. [19]The Jews objected, so I was compelled to make an appeal to Caesar. I certainly did not intend to bring any charge against my own people. [20]For this reason I have asked to see you and talk with you. It is because of the hope of Israel that I am bound with this chain."

[21]They replied, "We have not received any letters from Judea concerning you, and none of our people who have come from there has reported or said anything bad about you. [22]But we want to hear what your views are, for we know that people everywhere are talking against this sect."

[23]They arranged to meet Paul on a certain day, and came in even larger numbers to the place where he was staying. He witnessed to them from morning till evening, explaining about the kingdom of God, and from the Law of Moses and from the Prophets he tried to persuade them about Jesus. [24]Some were convinced by what he said, but others would not believe. [25]They disagreed among themselves and began to leave after Paul had made this final statement: "The Holy Spirit spoke the truth to your ancestors when he said through Isaiah the prophet:

[26]"'Go to this people and say,
"You will be ever hearing but never
    understanding;
you will be ever seeing but never
    perceiving."
[27]For this people's heart has become calloused;
    they hardly hear with their ears,
    and they have closed their eyes.
Otherwise they might see with their eyes,
    hear with their ears,
    understand with their hearts
and turn, and I would heal them.'[a]

[28]"Therefore I want you to know that God's salvation has been sent to the Gentiles, and they will listen!" [29][b]

[30]For two whole years Paul stayed there in his own rented house and welcomed all who came to see him. [31]He proclaimed the kingdom of God and taught about the Lord Jesus Christ— with all boldness and without hindrance!

---

[a] 27 Isaiah 6:9,10 (see Septuagint)   [b] 29 Some manuscripts include here *After he said this, the Jews left, arguing vigorously among themselves.*

INTRODUCTION TO ROMANS

God's Solution for the Human Dilemma

The book of Romans offers the most systematic teaching in the Bible about the human dilemma and God's solution for it. Written by the apostle Paul about AD 57, Romans lays out the major themes of sin, salvation, redemption, justification, grace and reconciliation.

Because Paul is such an outstanding teaching-leader, he communicates with purpose. No one could miss his objectives. He doesn't attempt merely to *inform*, but to *transform* this church (12:1–2), even though he had never visited it. With his words he endeavored to influence the believers in the most influential city in the world. Consider his classic methods for doing so.

First, Paul influences by building rapport. The first 17 verses of chapter one prepare the reader for all the apostle intends to write. He affirms and tells his readers how much he looks forward to meeting them, since he's heard so much about them.

Second, Paul influences by creating a dilemma relevant to everyone. He reminds the people how God spoke through creation and the human conscience. He discusses the predicament of sin and its universal impact on mankind. He then moves to God's gift of righteousness that we receive by faith. He contrasts how man tries to make everything right on his own, but never succeeds.

Third, Paul influences by proposing potential questions and objections, then by responding to them. He often brings up a question as though the reader had thought of it—then he rationally answers the question.

Fourth, Paul influences by providing feasible steps for the reader to take toward God. Everyone can do what Paul suggests. His plan is manageable and understandable.

God's Role in Romans

Because Paul is so convinced that real change happens from the inside out, God plays a huge role in this book. Paul argues that if we want to think like God, we must renew our minds and present our bodies to him as living sacrifices. We must trust him to revolutionize our lives and transform them as only he can.

God orchestrates the metamorphosis inside the believer. In that sense, spiritual leadership is about leading others to Christ to allow him to do the necessary work inside of them. Hence, Christian leadership cooperates with God's initiative to transform men and women, one life at a time.

Leaders in Romans

Paul, Phoebe, Aquila, Priscilla, the host of others listed in Romans 16

Other People of Influence in Romans

Tertius, Erastus, the host of others listed in Romans 16

Lessons in Leadership

- Leaders increase their effectiveness when they improve their ability to communicate.
- The most consistent leaders are led by their own values, beliefs and convictions.
- Great leaders communicate both passion and substance.

In the final five chapters of this book, Paul supplies practical applications of all he has taught. Chapters 1–11 concern doctrine, while chapters 12–16 highlight duty.

Finally, Paul influences by affirming his love for the people and thanks many of them by name. He encourages the church to follow those he names as models of the life he has challenged them to live.

- Great leaders connect with both the head and heart.
- Lasting leaders motivate through grace and relationship, not guilt and religious ritual.
- People want to follow leaders who offer hope and direction.
- Spiritual leaders work to change people from the inside out, not the outside in.

LEADERSHIP HIGHLIGHTS IN ROMANS

1

Paul, a servant of Christ Jesus, called to be an apostle and set apart for the gospel of God — [2]the gospel he promised beforehand through his prophets in the Holy Scriptures [3]regarding his Son, who as to his earthly life[a] was a descendant of David, [4]and who through the Spirit of holiness was appointed the Son of God in power[b] by his resurrection from the dead: Jesus Christ our Lord. [5]Through him we received grace and apostleship to call all the Gentiles to the obedience that comes from[c] faith for his name's sake. [6]And you also are among those Gentiles who are called to belong to Jesus Christ.

[7]To all in Rome who are loved by God and called to be his holy people:

Grace and peace to you from God our Father and from the Lord Jesus Christ.

Paul's Longing to Visit Rome

[8]First, I thank my God through Jesus Christ for all of you, because your faith is being reported all over the world. [9]God, whom I serve in my spirit in preaching the gospel of his Son, is my witness how constantly I remember you [10]in my prayers at all times; and I pray that now at last by God's will the way may be opened for me to come to you.

[11]I long to see you so that I may impart to you some spiritual gift to make you strong — [12]that is, that you and I may be mutually encouraged by each other's faith. [13]I do not want you to be unaware, brothers and sisters,[d] that I planned many times to come to you (but have been prevented from doing so until now) in order that I might have a harvest among you, just as I have had among the other Gentiles.

[14]I am obligated both to Greeks and non-Greeks, both to the wise and the foolish. [15]That is why I am so eager to preach the gospel also to you who are in Rome.

[16]For I am not ashamed of the gospel, because it is the power of God that brings salvation to everyone who believes: first to the Jew, then to the Gentile. [17]For in the gospel the righteousness of God is revealed — a righteousness that is by faith from first to last,[e] just as it is written: "The righteous will live by faith."[f]

God's Wrath Against Sinful Humanity

[18]The wrath of God is being revealed from heaven against all the godlessness and wickedness of people, who suppress the truth by their wickedness, [19]since what may be known about

---

[a] 3 Or *who according to the flesh*   [b] 4 Or *was declared with power to be the Son of God*   [c] 5 Or *that is*   [d] 13 The Greek word for *brothers and sisters* (*adelphoi*) refers here to believers, both men and women, as part of God's family; also in 7:1, 4; 8:12, 29; 10:1; 11:25; 12:1; 15:14, 30; 16:14, 17.   [e] 17 Or *is from faith to faith*   [f] 17 Hab. 2:4

PAUL

PROFILE in leadership

Genius with a Pen
Romans 1:1-7

Anyone writing a set of instructions ought to communicate the steps for completing a certain task with simplicity, clarity and power. That is exactly what the apostle Paul has done in his letter to the Romans.

The book systematically presents the Good News of salvation through Christ. It starts by explaining God's wrath on humankind for its sinfulness, then works its way through the grace of God as demonstrated through the atoning sacrifice of the Lord Jesus, and finishes by describing the kind of life those whom God has made "not guilty" should live. Along the way it anticipates and answers objections, provides vital encouragement and hope, and offers enough theological meat to keep thoughtful believers chewing for centuries.

Paul communicates with clarity and power what all leaders in the body of Christ need to keep on declaring to the world. All of us—from the greatest to the least—are sinners who deserve God's eternal judgment. But God has lavished his grace on every one of us through the person of his Son, Jesus Christ—and the key to accessing that grace is faith.

Paul left us a great many gifts of the faith, but none is greater than the message of Romans. We should rather have no bread than have no Romans.

The Attitude of a Leader

Romans 1:1, 14–16

Paul begins Romans by profiling himself as a servant of the Lord Jesus. Before he is an apostle or a preacher of the gospel, he is a servant. This is the most comprehensive picture of leadership in the New Testament. Paul uses the Greek word *doulos*, which most often signifies a servant who has willingly and legally bonded himself to a master (Ro 1:1; Php 1:1; Titus 1:1).

The Old Testament gives the Hebrew background for this concept (Dt 15:1–23). When it came time for a master to release a slave, that slave had two options: accept his freedom, or remain and serve the master by choice. To stay as a love-slave made him far more useful, since he served willingly. Note how Paul describes this servant attitude:

1. **"I am obligated"** (v. 14).
   This literally meant he had a debt to pay. Notice it wasn't a debt he had to the Lord, but to people! He owed those who hadn't heard the gospel.

2. **"I am so eager"** (v. 15).
   The word literally means he was burning inside. He passionately gave himself to the cause by choice. His enthusiasm came in response to God's grace.

3. **"I am not ashamed"** (v. 16).
   Why not? Because although he was a despised minority within a despised minority, his message brought God's power to save everyone.

God is plain to them, because God has made it plain to them. [20]For since the creation of the world God's invisible qualities—his eternal power and divine nature—have been clearly seen, being understood from what has been made, so that people are without excuse.

[21]For although they knew God, they neither glorified him as God nor gave thanks to him, but their thinking became futile and their foolish hearts were darkened. [22]Although they claimed to be wise, they became fools [23]and exchanged the glory of the immortal God for images made to look like a mortal human being and birds and animals and reptiles.

[24]Therefore God gave them over in the sinful desires of their hearts to sexual impurity for the degrading of their bodies with one another. [25]They exchanged the truth about God for a lie, and worshiped and served created things rather than the Creator—who is forever praised. Amen.

[26]Because of this, God gave them over to shameful lusts. Even their women exchanged natural sexual relations for unnatural ones. [27]In the same way the men also abandoned natural relations with women and were inflamed with lust for one another. Men committed shameful acts with other men, and received in themselves the due penalty for their error.

[28]Furthermore, just as they did not think it worthwhile to retain the knowledge of God, so God gave them over to a depraved mind, so that they do what ought not to be done. [29]They have become filled with every kind of wickedness, evil, greed and depravity. They are full of envy, murder, strife, deceit and malice. They are gossips, [30]slanderers, God-haters, insolent, arrogant and boastful; they invent ways of doing evil; they disobey their parents; [31]they have no understanding, no fidelity, no love, no mercy. [32]Although they know God's righteous decree that those who do such things deserve death, they not only continue to do these very things but also approve of those who practice them.

God's Righteous Judgment

2 You, therefore, have no excuse, you who pass judgment on someone else, for at whatever point you judge another, you are condemning yourself, because you who pass judgment do the same things. [2]Now we know that God's judgment against those who do such things is based on truth. [3]So when you, a mere human being, pass judgment on them and yet do the same things, do you think you will escape God's judgment? [4]Or do you show contempt for the riches of his kindness, forbearance and patience, not realizing that God's kindness is intended to lead you to repentance?

[5]But because of your stubbornness and your unrepentant heart, you are storing up wrath against yourself for the day of God's wrath, when his righteous judgment will be revealed. [6]God "will repay each person according to what they have done."[a] [7]To those who by persistence in doing good seek glory, honor and immortality, he will give eternal life. [8]But for those who are self-seeking and who reject the truth and follow evil, there will be wrath and anger. [9]There will be trouble and distress for every human being who does evil: first for the Jew, then for the Gentile; [10]but glory, honor and peace for everyone who does good: first for the Jew, then for the Gentile. [11]For God does not show favoritism.

[12]All who sin apart from the law will also perish apart from the law, and all who sin under the law will be judged by the law. [13]For it is not those who hear the law who are righteous in God's sight, but it is those who obey the law who will be declared righteous. [14](Indeed, when Gentiles, who do not have the law, do by nature things required by the law, they are a law for themselves, even though they do not have the law. [15]They show that the requirements of the law are written on their hearts, their consciences also bearing witness, and their thoughts sometimes accusing them and at other times even defending them.) [16]This will take place on the day when God judges people's secrets through Jesus Christ, as my gospel declares.

The Jews and the Law

[17]Now you, if you call yourself a Jew; if you rely on the law and boast in God; [18]if you know his will and approve of what is superior because you are instructed by the law; [19]if you are convinced that you are a guide for the blind, a light for those who are in the dark, [20]an instructor of the foolish, a teacher of little children, because you have in the law the embodiment of knowledge and truth— [21]you, then, who teach others, do you not teach yourself? You who preach against stealing, do you steal? [22]You who say that people should not commit adultery, do you commit adultery? You who abhor idols, do you rob temples? [23]You who boast in the law, do you dishonor God by breaking the law? [24]As it is written: "God's name is blasphemed among the Gentiles because of you."[b]

[25]Circumcision has value if you observe the law, but if you break the law, you have become as though you had not been circumcised. [26]So then, if those who are not circumcised keep the law's requirements, will they not be regarded as though they were circumcised? [27]The one who is not circumcised physically and yet obeys the law will condemn you who, even though you have the[c] written code and circumcision, are a lawbreaker.

[28]A person is not a Jew who is one only outwardly, nor is circumcision merely outward and physical. [29]No, a person is a Jew who is one inwardly; and circumcision is circumcision of the heart, by the Spirit, not by the written code. Such a person's praise is not from other people, but from God.

Problem Solving: Paul Addresses Man's Number One Dilemma

Romans 1:17—2:29

After Paul addresses mankind's ultimate problem—God's judgment for our sinful, imperfect condition—he masterfully offers the remedy for it. He knows that leaders gain an audience when they solve problems. Problem solving is the fastest way to gain leadership.

God's Faithfulness

3 What advantage, then, is there in being a Jew, or what value is there in circumcision? [2]Much in every way! First of all, the Jews have been entrusted with the very words of God.

[3]What if some were unfaithful? Will their unfaithfulness nullify God's faithfulness? [4]Not at all! Let God be true, and every human being a liar. As it is written:

"So that you may be proved right when you
    speak
and prevail when you judge."[d]

[5]But if our unrighteousness brings out God's righteousness more clearly, what shall we say? That God is unjust in bringing his wrath on us? (I am using a human argument.) [6]Certainly not! If that were so, how could God judge the world? [7]Someone might argue, "If my falsehood enhances God's truthfulness and so increases his glory, why am I still condemned as a sinner?"

---

[a] 6 Psalm 62:12; Prov. 24:12   [b] 24 Isaiah 52:5 (see Septuagint); Ezek. 36:20,22   [c] 27 Or who, by means of a   [d] 4 Psalm 51:4

[8]Why not say — as some slanderously claim that we say — "Let us do evil that good may result"? Their condemnation is just!

No One Is Righteous

[9]What shall we conclude then? Do we have any advantage? Not at all! For we have already made the charge that Jews and Gentiles alike are all under the power of sin. [10]As it is written:

"There is no one righteous, not even one;
[11]   there is no one who understands;
        there is no one who seeks God.
[12]All have turned away,
        they have together become worthless;
    there is no one who does good,
        not even one."[a]
[13]"Their throats are open graves;
        their tongues practice deceit."[b]
"The poison of vipers is on their lips."[c]
[14]   "Their mouths are full of cursing and
        bitterness."[d]
[15]"Their feet are swift to shed blood;
[16]   ruin and misery mark their ways,
[17]and the way of peace they do not know."[e]
[18]   "There is no fear of God before their eyes."[f]

[19]Now we know that whatever the law says, it says to those who are under the law, so that every mouth may be silenced and the whole world held accountable to God. [20]Therefore no one will be declared righteous in God's sight by the works of the law; rather, through the law we become conscious of our sin.

Righteousness Through Faith

[21]But now apart from the law the righteousness of God has been made known, to which the Law and the Prophets testify. [22]This righteousness is given through faith in[g] Jesus Christ to all who believe. There is no difference between Jew and Gentile, [23]for all have sinned and fall short of the glory of God, [24]and all are justified freely by his grace through the redemption that came by Christ Jesus. [25]God presented Christ as a sacrifice of atonement,[h] through the shedding of his blood — to be received by faith. He did this to demonstrate his righteousness, because in his forbearance he had left the sins committed beforehand unpunished — [26]he did it to demonstrate his righteousness at the present time, so as to be just and the one who justifies those who have faith in Jesus.

[27]Where, then, is boasting? It is excluded. Because of what law? The law that requires works? No, because of the law that requires faith. [28]For

Discernment: The Leader as a Doctor

Romans 3:21–26

Paul gives us a new picture of leadership: the leader as spiritual doctor. Leaders must match problems with solutions. Their understanding must be broad and general, but also deep and personal. Although doctors have graduated from medical school, to be relevant they must examine their patients. Only then can they suggest prescriptions.

we maintain that a person is justified by faith apart from the works of the law. [29]Or is God the God of Jews only? Is he not the God of Gentiles too? Yes, of Gentiles too, [30]since there is only one God, who will justify the circumcised by faith and the uncircumcised through that same faith. [31]Do we, then, nullify the law by this faith? Not at all! Rather, we uphold the law.

Abraham Justified by Faith

4 What then shall we say that Abraham, our forefather according to the flesh, discovered in this matter? [2]If, in fact, Abraham was justified by works, he had something to boast about — but not before God. [3]What does Scripture say? "Abraham believed God, and it was credited to him as righteousness."[i]

[4]Now to the one who works, wages are not credited as a gift but as an obligation. [5]However, to the one who does not work but trusts God who justifies the ungodly, their faith is credited as righteousness. [6]David says the same thing when he speaks of the blessedness of the one to whom God credits righteousness apart from works:

[7]"Blessed are those
        whose transgressions are forgiven,
        whose sins are covered.
[8]Blessed is the one
        whose sin the Lord will never count
        against them."[j]

---

[a] 12 Psalms 14:1-3; 53:1-3; Eccles. 7:20   [b] 13 Psalm 5:9
[c] 13 Psalm 140:3   [d] 14 Psalm 10:7 (see Septuagint)
[e] 17 Isaiah 59:7,8   [f] 18 Psalm 36:1   [g] 22 Or through the faithfulness of   [h] 25 The Greek for sacrifice of atonement refers to the atonement cover on the ark of the covenant (see Lev. 16:15,16).   [i] 3 Gen. 15:6; also in verse 22
[j] 8 Psalm 32:1,2

⁹Is this blessedness only for the circumcised, or also for the uncircumcised? We have been saying that Abraham's faith was credited to him as righteousness. ¹⁰Under what circumstances was it credited? Was it after he was circumcised, or before? It was not after, but before! ¹¹And he received circumcision as a sign, a seal of the righteousness that he had by faith while he was still uncircumcised. So then, he is the father of all who believe but have not been circumcised, in order that righteousness might be credited to them. ¹²And he is then also the father of the circumcised who not only are circumcised but who also follow in the footsteps of the faith that our father Abraham had before he was circumcised.

¹³It was not through the law that Abraham and his offspring received the promise that he would be heir of the world, but through the righteousness that comes by faith. ¹⁴For if those who depend on the law are heirs, faith means nothing and the promise is worthless, ¹⁵because the law brings wrath. And where there is no law there is no transgression.

¹⁶Therefore, the promise comes by faith, so that it may be by grace and may be guaranteed to all Abraham's offspring — not only to those who are of the law but also to those who have the faith of Abraham. He is the father of us all. ¹⁷As it is written: "I have made you a father of many nations."[a] He is our father in the sight of God, in whom he believed — the God who gives life to the dead and calls into being things that were not.

¹⁸Against all hope, Abraham in hope believed and so became the father of many nations, just as it had been said to him, "So shall your offspring be."[b] ¹⁹Without weakening in his faith, he faced the fact that his body was as good as dead — since he was about a hundred years old — and that Sarah's womb was also dead. ²⁰Yet he did not waver through unbelief regarding the prom-

ise of God, but was strengthened in his faith and gave glory to God, ²¹being fully persuaded that God had power to do what he had promised. ²²This is why "it was credited to him as righteousness." ²³The words "it was credited to him" were written not for him alone, ²⁴but also for us, to whom God will credit righteousness — for us who believe in him who raised Jesus our Lord from the dead. ²⁵He was delivered over to death for our sins and was raised to life for our justification.

Peace and Hope

5 Therefore, since we have been justified through faith, we[c] have peace with God through our Lord Jesus Christ, ²through whom we have gained access by faith into this grace in which we now stand. And we[d] boast in the hope of the glory of God. ³Not only so, but we[d] also glory in our sufferings, because we know that suffering produces perseverance; ⁴perseverance, character; and character, hope. ⁵And hope does not put us to shame, because God's love has been poured out into our hearts through the Holy Spirit, who has been given to us.

⁶You see, at just the right time, when we were still powerless, Christ died for the ungodly. ⁷Very rarely will anyone die for a righteous person, though for a good person someone might possibly dare to die. ⁸But God demonstrates his own love for us in this: While we were still sinners, Christ died for us.

⁹Since we have now been justified by his blood, how much more shall we be saved from God's wrath through him! ¹⁰For if, while we were God's enemies, we were reconciled to him through the death of his Son, how much more, having been reconciled, shall we be saved through his life! ¹¹Not only is this so, but we also boast in God through our Lord Jesus Christ, through whom we have now received reconciliation.

Death Through Adam, Life Through Christ

¹²Therefore, just as sin entered the world through one man, and death through sin, and in this way death came to all people, because all sinned —

¹³To be sure, sin was in the world before the law was given, but sin is not charged against anyone's account where there is no law. ¹⁴Nevertheless, death reigned from the time of Adam to the time of Moses, even over those who did not

Vision: The Leader as an Artist

Romans 4:1–22

Communicators know the value of pictures. Paul paints a picture of the life he promotes, illustrating the life of faith using individuals such as Abraham, Sarah and David. People need a point for their heads and a picture for their hearts.

---

[a] 17 Gen. 17:5   [b] 18 Gen. 15:5   [c] 1 Many manuscripts let us   [d] 2,3 Or let us

sin by breaking a command, as did Adam, who is a pattern of the one to come.

[15]But the gift is not like the trespass. For if the many died by the trespass of the one man, how much more did God's grace and the gift that came by the grace of the one man, Jesus Christ, overflow to the many! [16]Nor can the gift of God be compared with the result of one man's sin: The judgment followed one sin and brought condemnation, but the gift followed many trespasses and brought justification. [17]For if, by the trespass of the one man, death reigned through that one man, how much more will those who receive God's abundant provision of grace and of the gift of righteousness reign in life through the one man, Jesus Christ!

[18]Consequently, just as one trespass resulted in condemnation for all people, so also one righteous act resulted in justification and life for all people. [19]For just as through the disobedience of the one man the many were made sinners, so also through the obedience of the one man the many will be made righteous.

[20]The law was brought in so that the trespass might increase. But where sin increased, grace increased all the more, [21]so that, just as sin reigned in death, so also grace might reign through righteousness to bring eternal life through Jesus Christ our Lord.

Dead to Sin, Alive in Christ

6 What shall we say, then? Shall we go on sinning so that grace may increase? [2]By no means! We are those who have died to sin; how can we live in it any longer? [3]Or don't you know that all of us who were baptized into Christ Jesus were baptized into his death? [4]We were therefore buried with him through baptism into death in order that, just as Christ was raised from the dead through the glory of the Father, we too may live a new life.

[5]For if we have been united with him in a death like his, we will certainly also be united with him in a resurrection like his. [6]For we know that our old self was crucified with him so that the body ruled by sin might be done

---

The Law of Empowerment:
God Changes Us from the Inside Out

Romans 5:12–21

God's leadership is transformational. Paul carefully compares and contrasts Adam's work with Christ's and shows the fundamental changes God makes in us. He radically and permanently changes his people from the inside out.

God never demands conduct that he doesn't first empower his followers to achieve. Romans provides a virtual survey of New Testament theology and of God's empowering leadership:

1. *He liberates.*
   He frees us from the chains, stains and pains of the past.

2. *He elevates.*
   He embraces us and lifts us up to reign with him.

3. *He educates.*
   He gives us wise counsel and future direction.

4. *He compensates.*
   He fills areas where we are weak or lack competence.

5. *He motivates.*
   He is our source of vision, hope and purpose.

6. *He regenerates.*
   He transforms us to live on a higher level by his supernatural resources.

7. *He activates.*
   He commissions us to obey and move forward in his cause.

away with,[a] that we should no longer be slaves to sin — [7]because anyone who has died has been set free from sin.

[8]Now if we died with Christ, we believe that we will also live with him. [9]For we know that since Christ was raised from the dead, he cannot die again; death no longer has mastery over him. [10]The death he died, he died to sin once for all; but the life he lives, he lives to God.

[11]In the same way, count yourselves dead to sin but alive to God in Christ Jesus. [12]Therefore do not let sin reign in your mortal body so that you obey its evil desires. [13]Do not offer any part of yourself to sin as an instrument of wickedness, but rather offer yourselves to God as those who have been brought from death to life; and offer every part of yourself to him as an instrument of righteousness. [14]For sin shall no longer be your master, because you are not under the law, but under grace.

Slaves to Righteousness

[15]What then? Shall we sin because we are not under the law but under grace? By no means! [16]Don't you know that when you offer yourselves to someone as obedient slaves, you are slaves of the one you obey — whether you are slaves to sin, which leads to death, or to obedience, which leads to righteousness? [17]But thanks be to God that, though you used to be slaves to sin, you have come to obey from your heart the pattern of teaching that has now claimed your allegiance. [18]You have been set free from sin and have become slaves to righteousness.

[19]I am using an example from everyday life because of your human limitations. Just as you used to offer yourselves as slaves to impurity and to ever-increasing wickedness, so now offer yourselves as slaves to righteousness leading to holiness. [20]When you were slaves to sin, you were free from the control of righteousness. [21]What benefit did you reap at that time from the things you are now ashamed of? Those things result in death! [22]But now that you have been set free from sin and have become slaves of God, the benefit you reap leads to holiness, and the result is eternal life. [23]For the wages of sin is death, but the gift of God is eternal life in[b] Christ Jesus our Lord.

Released From the Law, Bound to Christ

7 Do you not know, brothers and sisters — for I am speaking to those who know the law — that the law has authority over someone only as long as that person lives? [2]For example, by law a married woman is bound to her husband as long as he is alive, but if her husband dies, she is released from the law that binds her to him. [3]So then, if she has sexual relations with another man while her husband is still alive, she is called an adulteress. But if her husband dies, she is released from that law and is not an adulteress if she marries another man.

[4]So, my brothers and sisters, you also died to the law through the body of Christ, that you might belong to another, to him who was raised from the dead, in order that we might bear fruit for God. [5]For when we were in the realm of the flesh,[c] the sinful passions aroused by the law were at work in us, so that we bore fruit for death. [6]But now, by dying to what once bound

---

[a] 6 Or be rendered powerless   [b] 23 Or through   [c] 5 In contexts like this, the Greek word for flesh (sarx) refers to the sinful state of human beings, often presented as a power in opposition to the Spirit.

Communicating Vision: Paul Delivers a Clear Image of Our Need

Romans 6:1—7:6

Knowing that his readers would need pictures to catch the revolutionary truth of the gospel, Paul uses the vivid images of water baptism, dead bodies and slavery to explain God's message.

Paul sums up his point in Romans 6:23 and in Romans 7 moves to a marriage analogy. The first six verses remind us that the dead are no longer bound to sin. Although none of us started well, we can all finish well, thanks to God. He remains committed to our welfare.

These chapters are the final ones dedicated to helping us see humankind's need. Because of our fallen human state, everybody has three fundamental needs:

1. *To believe:* All human hearts need to have faith in something or Someone.

2. *To belong:* All human hearts need to experience community and family.

3. *To become:* All human hearts need to grow, stretch, and reach their potential.

us, we have been released from the law so that we serve in the new way of the Spirit, and not in the old way of the written code.

The Law and Sin

[7]What shall we say, then? Is the law sinful? Certainly not! Nevertheless, I would not have known what sin was had it not been for the law. For I would not have known what coveting really was if the law had not said, "You shall not covet."[a] [8]But sin, seizing the opportunity afforded by the commandment, produced in me every kind of coveting. For apart from the law, sin was dead. [9]Once I was alive apart from the law; but when the commandment came, sin sprang to life and I died. [10]I found that the very commandment that was intended to bring life actually brought death. [11]For sin, seizing the opportunity afforded by the commandment, deceived me, and through the commandment put me to death. [12]So then, the law is holy, and the commandment is holy, righteous and good.

[13]Did that which is good, then, become death to me? By no means! Nevertheless, in order that sin might be recognized as sin, it used what is good to bring about my death, so that through the commandment sin might become utterly sinful.

[14]We know that the law is spiritual; but I am unspiritual, sold as a slave to sin. [15]I do not understand what I do. For what I want to do I do not do, but what I hate I do. [16]And if I do what I do not want to do, I agree that the law is good. [17]As it is, it is no longer I myself who do it, but it is sin living in me. [18]For I know that good itself does not dwell in me, that is, in my sinful nature.[b] For I have the desire to do what is good, but I cannot carry it out. [19]For I do not do the good I want to do, but the evil I do not want to do — this I keep on doing. [20]Now if I do what I do not want to do, it is no longer I who do it, but it is sin living in me that does it.

[21]So I find this law at work: Although I want to do good, evil is right there with me. [22]For in my inner being I delight in God's law; [23]but I see another law at work in me, waging war against the law of my mind and making me a prisoner of the law of sin at work within me. [24]What a wretched man I am! Who will rescue me from this body that is subject to death? [25]Thanks be to God, who delivers me through Jesus Christ our Lord!

So then, I myself in my mind am a slave to God's law, but in my sinful nature[c] a slave to the law of sin.

Identification: Paul Identifies with the Struggles of His Listeners

Romans 7:14–25

Paul identifies with the struggles of common men and women. He knows we all can feel trapped (Ro 7:14); confused (7:15); eager to do what is right (7:18); unable to follow through (7:18); an inward war (7:21–23); and frustration (7:24). Good leaders do not seek to impress, but to identify.

Life Through the Spirit

8 Therefore, there is now no condemnation for those who are in Christ Jesus, [2]because through Christ Jesus the law of the Spirit who gives life has set you[d] free from the law of sin and death. [3]For what the law was powerless to do because it was weakened by the flesh,[e] God did by sending his own Son in the likeness of sinful flesh to be a sin offering.[f] And so he condemned sin in the flesh, [4]in order that the righteous requirement of the law might be fully met in us, who do not live according to the flesh but according to the Spirit.

[5]Those who live according to the flesh have their minds set on what the flesh desires; but those who live in accordance with the Spirit have their minds set on what the Spirit desires. [6]The mind governed by the flesh is death, but the mind governed by the Spirit is life and peace. [7]The mind governed by the flesh is hostile to God; it does not submit to God's law, nor can it do so. [8]Those who are in the realm of the flesh cannot please God.

[9]You, however, are not in the realm of the flesh but are in the realm of the Spirit, if indeed the Spirit of God lives in you. And if anyone does not have the Spirit of Christ, they do not belong to Christ. [10]But if Christ is in you, then even though your body is subject to death because of sin, the Spirit gives life[g] because of righteousness. [11]And if the Spirit of him who

---

[a] 7 Exodus 20:17; Deut. 5:21   [b] 18 Or my flesh   [c] 25 Or in the flesh   [d] 2 The Greek is singular; some manuscripts me   [e] 3 In contexts like this, the Greek word for flesh (sarx) refers to the sinful state of human beings, often presented as a power in opposition to the Spirit; also in verses 4-13.   [f] 3 Or flesh, for sin   [g] 10 Or you, your body is dead because of sin, yet your spirit is alive

raised Jesus from the dead is living in you, he who raised Christ from the dead will also give life to your mortal bodies because of[a] his Spirit who lives in you.

¹²Therefore, brothers and sisters, we have an obligation—but it is not to the flesh, to live according to it. ¹³For if you live according to the flesh, you will die; but if by the Spirit you put to death the misdeeds of the body, you will live.

¹⁴For those who are led by the Spirit of God are the children of God. ¹⁵The Spirit you received does not make you slaves, so that you live in fear again; rather, the Spirit you received brought about your adoption to sonship.[b] And by him we cry, *"Abba,[c] Father."* ¹⁶The Spirit himself testifies with our spirit that we are God's children. ¹⁷Now if we are children, then we are heirs—heirs of God and co-heirs with Christ, if indeed we share in his sufferings in order that we may also share in his glory.

Present Suffering and Future Glory

¹⁸I consider that our present sufferings are not worth comparing with the glory that will be revealed in us. ¹⁹For the creation waits in eager expectation for the children of God to be revealed. ²⁰For the creation was subjected to frustration, not by its own choice, but by the will of the one who subjected it, in hope ²¹that[d] the creation itself will be liberated from its bondage to decay and brought into the freedom and glory of the children of God.

²²We know that the whole creation has been groaning as in the pains of childbirth right up to the present time. ²³Not only so, but we ourselves, who have the firstfruits of the Spirit, groan inwardly as we wait eagerly for our adoption to sonship, the redemption of our bodies. ²⁴For in this hope we were saved. But hope that is seen is no hope at all. Who hopes for what they already have? ²⁵But if we hope for what we do not yet have, we wait for it patiently.

²⁶In the same way, the Spirit helps us in our weakness. We do not know what we ought to pray for, but the Spirit himself intercedes for us through wordless groans. ²⁷And he who searches our hearts knows the mind of the Spirit, because the Spirit intercedes for God's people in accordance with the will of God.

²⁸And we know that in all things God works for the good of those who love him, who[e] have been called according to his purpose. ²⁹For those God foreknew he also predestined to be conformed to the image of his Son, that he might be the firstborn among many brothers and sisters. ³⁰And those he predestined, he also called; those he called, he also justified; those he justified, he also glorified.

More Than Conquerors

³¹What, then, shall we say in response to these things? If God is for us, who can be against us? ³²He who did not spare his own Son, but gave him up for us all—how will he not also, along with him, graciously give us all things? ³³Who will bring any charge against those whom God has chosen? It is God who justifies. ³⁴Who then

---

[a] 11 Some manuscripts *bodies through*   [b] 15 The Greek word for *adoption to sonship* is a term referring to the full legal standing of an adopted male heir in Roman culture; also in verse 23.   [c] 15 Aramaic for *father*   [d] 20,21 Or *subjected it in hope.* ²¹*For*   [e] 28 Or *that all things work together for good to those who love God, who;* or *that in all things God works together with those who love him to bring about what is good—with those who*

The Law of Navigation: Paul Describes the Spirit-Filled Life

Romans 8:1–39

After declaring that the law of the Spirit of life has set us free from the law of sin and death, Paul navigates the Spirit-filled life. He is the under-navigator, directing us to the Holy Spirit, the ultimate navigator.

This reveals the difference between Christian mentoring and the world's mentoring. Christian mentors do not build a reliance on themselves, but point their protégés to God. The life Paul navigates is a life of liberty (Ro 8:1–8), hope (8:9–15) and power (8:26–39). Observe how the Holy Spirit navigates life for us:

1. *He intercedes and groans for us* (Ro 8:22–23,26–27).

2. *He directs and testifies to us* (Jn 16:13; Ac 20:22–23; Ro 8:14).

3. *He empowers and anoints for service* (Ac 1:8; Ro 8:28–37; 1Jn 2:27).

4. *He searches and enables us to discern* (Ro 8:26–27; 1Co 2:9–15).

5. *He confirms and bears witness with us* (Ro 8:14–16; 1Jn 5:5–9).

is the one who condemns? No one. Christ Jesus who died—more than that, who was raised to life—is at the right hand of God and is also interceding for us. [35]Who shall separate us from the love of Christ? Shall trouble or hardship or persecution or famine or nakedness or danger or sword? [36]As it is written:

> "For your sake we face death all day long;
>   we are considered as sheep to be
>   slaughtered."[a]

[37]No, in all these things we are more than conquerors through him who loved us. [38]For I am convinced that neither death nor life, neither angels nor demons,[b] neither the present nor the future, nor any powers, [39]neither height nor depth, nor anything else in all creation, will be able to separate us from the love of God that is in Christ Jesus our Lord.

The Law of Intuition: Paul Intuitively Knew the Remedy

Romans 8:12–39

Paul intuitively knew both man's fundamental sickness and the cure. He explained the proof (Ro 8:14), the problems (8:18–25), the privilege (8:26–30), and the promise (8:31–39) of the Spirit-filled lifestyle. When leaders face problems, they automatically measure them and begin solving them using the Law of Intuition.

Paul's Anguish Over Israel

9 I speak the truth in Christ—I am not lying, my conscience confirms it through the Holy Spirit— [2]I have great sorrow and unceasing anguish in my heart. [3]For I could wish that I myself were cursed and cut off from Christ for the sake of my people, those of my own race, [4]the people of Israel. Theirs is the adoption to sonship; theirs the divine glory, the covenants, the receiving of the law, the temple worship and the promises. [5]Theirs are the patriarchs, and from them is traced the human ancestry of the Messiah, who is God over all, forever praised![c] Amen.

God's Sovereign Choice

[6]It is not as though God's word had failed. For not all who are descended from Israel are Israel.

[7]Nor because they are his descendants are they all Abraham's children. On the contrary, "It is through Isaac that your offspring will be reckoned."[d] [8]In other words, it is not the children by physical descent who are God's children, but it is the children of the promise who are regarded as Abraham's offspring. [9]For this was how the promise was stated: "At the appointed time I will return, and Sarah will have a son."[e]

[10]Not only that, but Rebekah's children were conceived at the same time by our father Isaac. [11]Yet, before the twins were born or had done anything good or bad—in order that God's purpose in election might stand: [12]not by works but by him who calls—she was told, "The older will serve the younger."[f] [13]Just as it is written: "Jacob I loved, but Esau I hated."[g]

[14]What then shall we say? Is God unjust? Not at all! [15]For he says to Moses,

> "I will have mercy on whom I have mercy,
>   and I will have compassion on whom I
>   have compassion."[h]

[16]It does not, therefore, depend on human desire or effort, but on God's mercy. [17]For Scripture says to Pharaoh: "I raised you up for this very purpose, that I might display my power in you and that my name might be proclaimed in all the earth."[i] [18]Therefore God has mercy on whom he wants to have mercy, and he hardens whom he wants to harden.

[19]One of you will say to me: "Then why does God still blame us? For who is able to resist his will?" [20]But who are you, a human being, to talk back to God? "Shall what is formed say to the one who formed it, 'Why did you make me like this?'"[j] [21]Does not the potter have the right to make out of the same lump of clay some pottery for special purposes and some for common use?

[22]What if God, although choosing to show his wrath and make his power known, bore with great patience the objects of his wrath—prepared for destruction? [23]What if he did this to make the riches of his glory known to the objects of his mercy, whom he prepared in advance for glory— [24]even us, whom he also called, not only from the Jews but also from the Gentiles? [25]As he says in Hosea:

---

[a] 36 Psalm 44:22   [b] 38 Or nor heavenly rulers   [c] 5 Or Messiah, who is over all. God be forever praised! Or Messiah. God who is over all be forever praised!   [d] 7 Gen. 21:12   [e] 9 Gen. 18:10,14   [f] 12 Gen. 25:23   [g] 13 Mal. 1:2,3   [h] 15 Exodus 33:19   [i] 17 Exodus 9:16   [j] 20 Isaiah 29:16; 45:9

"I will call them 'my people' who are not my
        people;
    and I will call her 'my loved one' who is
        not my loved one,"[a]

²⁶and,

"In the very place where it was said to them,
    'You are not my people,'
    there they will be called 'children of the
        living God.'"[b]

²⁷Isaiah cries out concerning Israel:

"Though the number of the Israelites be like
        the sand by the sea,
    only the remnant will be saved.
²⁸For the Lord will carry out
    his sentence on earth with speed and
        finality."[c]

²⁹It is just as Isaiah said previously:

"Unless the Lord Almighty
    had left us descendants,
we would have become like Sodom,
    we would have been like Gomorrah."[d]

Israel's Unbelief

³⁰What then shall we say? That the Gentiles,
who did not pursue righteousness, have obtained it, a righteousness that is by faith; ³¹but
the people of Israel, who pursued the law as the
way of righteousness, have not attained their
goal. ³²Why not? Because they pursued it not by
faith but as if it were by works. They stumbled
over the stumbling stone. ³³As it is written:

"See, I lay in Zion a stone that causes people
        to stumble
    and a rock that makes them fall,
    and the one who believes in him will
        never be put to shame."[e]

10 Brothers and sisters, my heart's desire
and prayer to God for the Israelites is
that they may be saved. ²For I can testify about
them that they are zealous for God, but their
zeal is not based on knowledge. ³Since they did
not know the righteousness of God and sought
to establish their own, they did not submit to
God's righteousness. ⁴Christ is the culmination
of the law so that there may be righteousness for
everyone who believes.

⁵Moses writes this about the righteousness that
is by the law: "The person who does these things
will live by them."[f] ⁶But the righteousness that is
by faith says: "Do not say in your heart, 'Who will
ascend into heaven?'"[g] (that is, to bring Christ

down) ⁷"or 'Who will descend into the deep?'"[h]
(that is, to bring Christ up from the dead). ⁸But
what does it say? "The word is near you; it is in
your mouth and in your heart,"[i] that is, the message concerning faith that we proclaim: ⁹If you
declare with your mouth, "Jesus is Lord," and believe in your heart that God raised him from the
dead, you will be saved. ¹⁰For it is with your heart
that you believe and are justified, and it is with
your mouth that you profess your faith and are
saved. ¹¹As Scripture says, "Anyone who believes
in him will never be put to shame."[j] ¹²For there
is no difference between Jew and Gentile—the
same Lord is Lord of all and richly blesses all who
call on him, ¹³for, "Everyone who calls on the
name of the Lord will be saved."[k]

¹⁴How, then, can they call on the one they
have not believed in? And how can they believe
in the one of whom they have not heard? And
how can they hear without someone preaching
to them? ¹⁵And how can anyone preach unless
they are sent? As it is written: "How beautiful
are the feet of those who bring good news!"[l]

¹⁶But not all the Israelites accepted the good
news. For Isaiah says, "Lord, who has believed
our message?"[m] ¹⁷Consequently, faith comes
from hearing the message, and the message is
heard through the word about Christ. ¹⁸But I
ask: Did they not hear? Of course they did:

"Their voice has gone out into all the earth,
    their words to the ends of the world."[n]

¹⁹Again I ask: Did Israel not understand? First,
Moses says,

"I will make you envious by those who are
        not a nation;
    I will make you angry by a nation that has
        no understanding."[o]

²⁰And Isaiah boldly says,

"I was found by those who did not seek me;
    I revealed myself to those who did not ask
        for me."[p]

²¹But concerning Israel he says,

"All day long I have held out my hands
    to a disobedient and obstinate people."[q]

---

[a] 25 Hosea 2:23   [b] 26 Hosea 1:10   [c] 28 Isaiah 10:22,23
(see Septuagint)   [d] 29 Isaiah 1:9   [e] 33 Isaiah 8:14; 28:16
[f] 5 Lev. 18:5   [g] 6 Deut. 30:12   [h] 7 Deut. 30:13
[i] 8 Deut. 30:14   [j] 11 Isaiah 28:16 (see Septuagint)
[k] 13 Joel 2:32   [l] 15 Isaiah 52:7   [m] 16 Isaiah 53:1
[n] 18 Psalm 19:4   [o] 19 Deut. 32:21   [p] 20 Isaiah 65:1
[q] 21 Isaiah 65:2

> "May their table become a snare and a trap,
>   a stumbling block and a retribution for
>   them.
> [10] May their eyes be darkened so they cannot
>   see,
>   and their backs be bent forever."[d]

Ingrafted Branches

[11] Again I ask: Did they stumble so as to fall beyond recovery? Not at all! Rather, because of their transgression, salvation has come to the Gentiles to make Israel envious. [12] But if their transgression means riches for the world, and their loss means riches for the Gentiles, how much greater riches will their full inclusion bring!

[13] I am talking to you Gentiles. Inasmuch as I am the apostle to the Gentiles, I take pride in my ministry [14] in the hope that I may somehow arouse my own people to envy and save some of them. [15] For if their rejection brought reconciliation to the world, what will their acceptance be but life from the dead? [16] If the part of the dough offered as firstfruits is holy, then the whole batch is holy; if the root is holy, so are the branches.

[17] If some of the branches have been broken off, and you, though a wild olive shoot, have been grafted in among the others and now share in the nourishing sap from the olive root, [18] do not consider yourself to be superior to those other branches. If you do, consider this: You do not support the root, but the root supports you. [19] You will say then, "Branches were broken off so that I could be grafted in." [20] Granted. But they were broken off because of unbelief, and you stand by faith. Do not be arrogant, but tremble. [21] For if God did not spare the natural branches, he will not spare you either.

[22] Consider therefore the kindness and sternness of God: sternness to those who fell, but kindness to you, provided that you continue in his kindness. Otherwise, you also will be cut off. [23] And if they do not persist in unbelief, they will be grafted in, for God is able to graft them in again. [24] After all, if you were cut out of an olive tree that is wild by nature, and contrary to nature were grafted into a cultivated olive tree, how much more readily will these, the natural branches, be grafted into their own olive tree!

All Israel Will Be Saved

[25] I do not want you to be ignorant of this mystery, brothers and sisters, so that you may

---

The Law of Victory: Paul Communicates What to Do to Be Saved

Romans 10:8–17

In his earlier days, Paul believed personal victory came through self-righteousness. By the time he wrote to the Romans, he understood that the only way to gain victory came through God's righteousness.

How can one be saved from God's just condemnation? Paul explains his answer in Romans 10: "that if you declare with your mouth, 'Jesus is Lord,' and believe in your heart that God raised him from the dead, you will be saved," he says (v. 9).

In a sense, this chapter provides the climax to the dilemma building through the book's first nine chapters. Only after thoroughly explaining the problem does the apostle lay out the plan to find and experience victory. Leaders always progress toward solutions.

The Remnant of Israel

11 I ask then: Did God reject his people? By no means! I am an Israelite myself, a descendant of Abraham, from the tribe of Benjamin. [2] God did not reject his people, whom he foreknew. Don't you know what Scripture says in the passage about Elijah — how he appealed to God against Israel: [3] "Lord, they have killed your prophets and torn down your altars; I am the only one left, and they are trying to kill me"[a]? [4] And what was God's answer to him? "I have reserved for myself seven thousand who have not bowed the knee to Baal."[b] [5] So too, at the present time there is a remnant chosen by grace. [6] And if by grace, then it cannot be based on works; if it were, grace would no longer be grace.

[7] What then? What the people of Israel sought so earnestly they did not obtain. The elect among them did, but the others were hardened, [8] as it is written:

> "God gave them a spirit of stupor,
>   eyes that could not see
>   and ears that could not hear,
>   to this very day."[c]

[9] And David says:

---

[a] 3 1 Kings 19:10,14   [b] 4 1 Kings 19:18   [c] 8 Deut. 29:4; Isaiah 29:10   [d] 10 Psalm 69:22,23

not be conceited: Israel has experienced a hardening in part until the full number of the Gentiles has come in, [26]and in this way[a] all Israel will be saved. As it is written:

"The deliverer will come from Zion;
    he will turn godlessness away from Jacob.
[27] And this is[b] my covenant with them
    when I take away their sins."[c]

[28]As far as the gospel is concerned, they are enemies for your sake; but as far as election is concerned, they are loved on account of the patriarchs, [29]for God's gifts and his call are irrevocable. [30]Just as you who were at one time disobedient to God have now received mercy as a result of their disobedience, [31]so they too have now become disobedient in order that they too may now[d] receive mercy as a result of God's mercy to you. [32]For God has bound everyone over to disobedience so that he may have mercy on them all.

Doxology

[33]Oh, the depth of the riches of the wisdom
    and[e] knowledge of God!
    How unsearchable his judgments,
    and his paths beyond tracing out!
[34]"Who has known the mind of the Lord?
    Or who has been his counselor?"[f]
[35]"Who has ever given to God,
    that God should repay them?"[g]
[36]For from him and through him and for him
    are all things.
    To him be the glory forever! Amen.

A Living Sacrifice

12 Therefore, I urge you, brothers and sisters, in view of God's mercy, to offer your bodies as a living sacrifice, holy and pleasing to God—this is your true and proper worship. [2]Do not conform to the pattern of this world, but be transformed by the renewing of your mind. Then you will be able to test and approve what God's will is—his good, pleasing and perfect will.

Humble Service in the Body of Christ

[3]For by the grace given me I say to every one of you: Do not think of yourself more highly than you ought, but rather think of yourself with sober judgment, in accordance with the faith God has distributed to each of you. [4]For just as each of us has one body with many members, and these members do not all have the same function, [5]so in Christ we, though many,

---

The Law of Connection: Paul Touches Hearts, Then Asks for Response

Romans 12:1–2

After climbing an enormous theological hill, Paul shifts gears in Romans 12. The first eleven chapters provide a basis for our belief, but from chapter twelve to the end of the book, the apostle supplies a basis for our behavior. First doctrine; then duty. This is how Paul always attempted to connect with his listeners.

Paul pleads with his friends, based on God's mercy, to lovingly surrender themselves to the Lord. He urges them to respond in four ways:

1. *Presentation:* We are to present our bodies to God as living sacrifices (v. 1).
2. *Separation:* We are to avoid conforming to the world's ways (v. 2).
3. *Transformation:* We are to renew our minds and thus change our lives (v. 2).
4. *Demonstration:* We are to prove we belong to God by doing his will (v. 2).

Paul argues that these four acts provide the logical response to God's grace. He knew this was a tall request, but he spent 11 chapters building a foundation for the "big ask." Leaders who connect touch hearts in a big way, then ask for a big response.

---

form one body, and each member belongs to all the others. [6]We have different gifts, according to the grace given to each of us. If your gift is prophesying, then prophesy in accordance with your[h] faith; [7]if it is serving, then serve; if it is teaching, then teach; [8]if it is to encourage, then give encouragement; if it is giving, then give generously; if it is to lead,[i] do it diligently; if it is to show mercy, do it cheerfully.

Love in Action

[9]Love must be sincere. Hate what is evil; cling to what is good. [10]Be devoted to one another

---

[a] 26 Or *and so*   [b] 27 Or *will be*   [c] 27 Isaiah 59:20,21; 27:9 (see Septuagint); Jer. 31:33,34   [d] 31 Some manuscripts do not have *now.*   [e] 33 Or *riches and the wisdom and the*   [f] 34 Isaiah 40:13   [g] 35 Job 41:11   [h] 6 Or *the*   [i] 8 Or *to provide for others*

in love. Honor one another above yourselves. [11]Never be lacking in zeal, but keep your spiritual fervor, serving the Lord. [12]Be joyful in hope, patient in affliction, faithful in prayer. [13]Share with the Lord's people who are in need. Practice hospitality.

[14]Bless those who persecute you; bless and do not curse. [15]Rejoice with those who rejoice; mourn with those who mourn. [16]Live in harmony with one another. Do not be proud, but be willing to associate with people of low position.[a] Do not be conceited.

[17]Do not repay anyone evil for evil. Be careful to do what is right in the eyes of everyone. [18]If it is possible, as far as it depends on you, live at peace with everyone. [19]Do not take revenge, my dear friends, but leave room for God's wrath, for it is written: "It is mine to avenge; I will repay,"[b] says the Lord. [20]On the contrary:

"If your enemy is hungry, feed him;
    if he is thirsty, give him something to
        drink.
In doing this, you will heap burning coals on
        his head."[c]

[21]Do not be overcome by evil, but overcome evil with good.

Submission to Governing Authorities

13 Let everyone be subject to the governing authorities, for there is no authority except that which God has established. The authorities that exist have been established by God. [2]Consequently, whoever rebels against the authority is rebelling against what God has instituted, and those who do so will bring judgment on themselves. [3]For rulers hold no terror for those who do right, but for those who do wrong. Do you want to be free from fear of the one in authority? Then do what is right and you will be commended. [4]For the one in authority is God's servant for your good. But if you do wrong, be afraid, for rulers do not bear the sword for no reason. They are God's servants, agents of wrath to bring punishment on the wrongdoer. [5]Therefore, it is necessary to submit to the authorities, not only because of possible punishment but also as a matter of conscience.

[6]This is also why you pay taxes, for the authorities are God's servants, who give their full time to governing. [7]Give to everyone what you owe them: If you owe taxes, pay taxes; if revenue, then revenue; if respect, then respect; if honor, then honor.

Love Fulfills the Law

[8]Let no debt remain outstanding, except the continuing debt to love one another, for whoever loves others has fulfilled the law. [9]The commandments, "You shall not commit adultery," "You shall not murder," "You shall not steal," "You shall not covet,"[d] and whatever other command there may be, are summed up in this one command: "Love your neighbor as yourself."[e]

Leaders Are Brokers of Gifts

Romans 12:6–8

Paul describes seven spiritual gifts, distributed to different members in the body of Christ. Like any good leader, he recognizes his role as a broker of gifts, talents and resources. He urges everyone to discover, develop, and distribute his or her gift.

Every resource God provides should be in use. Every believer is a steward of the abilities he or she has been given. Every leader is a manager whose goal should be to maximize everyone's gift.

The list of gifts in Romans 12 is not exhaustive. They are commonly called "motivational gifts," which means they are central to our lives, the hub of the wheel around which our particular set of gifts revolve. Paul's list includes:

1. *Gift of Prophecy:* to challenge others by declaring God's truth and calling for action.

2. *Gift of Service or Ministry:* to serve others and meet their needs.

3. *Gift of Teaching:* to explain truth so that others can understand and apply it.

4. *Gift of Exhortation:* to encourage, strengthen and inspire others to be their best.

5. *Gift of Giving:* to generously share what God has given.

6. *Gift of Leadership:* to govern and oversee others so that the group moves forward.

7. *Gift of Mercy:* to empathize with, cheer and show compassion to those who hurt.

---

[a] 16 Or *willing to do menial work*   [b] 19 Deut. 32:35
[c] 20 Prov. 25:21,22   [d] 9 Exodus 20:13-15,17; Deut. 5:17-19,21
[e] 9 Lev. 19:18

Relationships: If You Get Along, They Will Go Along

Romans 12:9–21

Many leaders commit the error of separating leadership from relationships. This happens when a person steps into a position of leadership and assumes that everyone will follow his or her ideas because of his or her position. Some leaders wrongly believe that their knowledge alone qualifies them to lead others.

People don't care how much you know until they know how much you care. We cannot separate leadership from relationships. Leaders help themselves by developing good relational skills. Paul instructs us how to lead through relationships:

1. *Avoid hypocrisy*—be sincere and genuine (v. 9).

2. *Be loyal to colleagues*—treat others like brothers or sisters (v. 10).

3. *Give preference to others*—honor the desires of others above your own (v. 10).

4. *Be hospitable*—look for ways to meet the needs of others (v. 13).

5. *Return good for evil*—act, don't react, when others hurt you (v. 14).

6. *Identify with others*—treat others' needs or victories as your own (v. 15).

7. *Be open-minded toward others*—seek to connect with anyone you speak to (v. 16).

8. *Treat everyone with respect*—this is a compliment to any person (v. 17).

9. *Do everything possible to keep peace*—choose wisely which hills to die on (v. 18).

10. *Remove revenge from your life*—let God judge others; you love them (vv. 19–21).

The Authority Test: Submitting to God-Given Authority

Romans 13:1–7

Paul gets very practical in how to apply our beliefs to our lives by challenging us to submit to God-given authorities. For children, this means parents; for adults, this means leaders in government, the workplace and the church.

Why should we so submit? Is it because these leaders are the smartest, most reliable individuals on earth? No. God simply provides us with an authority test. Before we will ever become leaders of integrity, we must learn to follow other leaders, regardless of differences. In fact, the acid test of character comes when we disagree with legitimate authorities. When we refuse to demand our own way and instead submit to others, our hearts are right. This is when God can trust us to lead others.

[10]Love does no harm to a neighbor. Therefore love is the fulfillment of the law.

The Day Is Near

[11]And do this, understanding the present time: The hour has already come for you to wake up from your slumber, because our salvation is nearer now than when we first believed. [12]The night is nearly over; the day is almost here. So let us put aside the deeds of darkness and put on the armor of light. [13]Let us behave decently, as in the daytime, not in carousing and drunkenness, not in sexual immorality and debauchery, not in dissension and jealousy. [14]Rather, clothe yourselves with the Lord Jesus Christ, and do not think about how to gratify the desires of the flesh.[a]

The Weak and the Strong

14 Accept the one whose faith is weak, without quarreling over disputable matters. [2]One person's faith allows them to eat anything, but another, whose faith is weak, eats only vegeta-

---

[a] 14 In contexts like this, the Greek word for *flesh* (*sarx*) refers to the sinful state of human beings, often presented as a power in opposition to the Spirit.

bles. ³The one who eats everything must not treat with contempt the one who does not, and the one who does not eat everything must not judge the one who does, for God has accepted them. ⁴Who are you to judge someone else's servant? To their own master, servants stand or fall. And they will stand, for the Lord is able to make them stand.

⁵One person considers one day more sacred than another; another considers every day alike. Each of them should be fully convinced in their own mind. ⁶Whoever regards one day as special does so to the Lord. Whoever eats meat does so to the Lord, for they give thanks to God; and whoever abstains does so to the Lord and gives thanks to God. ⁷For none of us lives for ourselves alone, and none of us dies for ourselves alone. ⁸If we live, we live for the Lord; and if we die, we die for the Lord. So, whether we live or die, we belong to the Lord. ⁹For this very reason, Christ died and returned to life so that he might be the Lord of both the dead and the living.

¹⁰You, then, why do you judge your brother or sister*a*? Or why do you treat them with contempt? For we will all stand before God's judgment seat. ¹¹It is written:

> "'As surely as I live,' says the Lord,
> 'every knee will bow before me;
> every tongue will acknowledge
> God.'"*b*

¹²So then, each of us will give an account of ourselves to God.

¹³Therefore let us stop passing judgment on one another. Instead, make up your mind not to put any stumbling block or obstacle in the way of a brother or sister. ¹⁴I am convinced, being fully persuaded in the Lord Jesus, that nothing is unclean in itself. But if anyone regards something as unclean, then for that person it is unclean. ¹⁵If your brother or sister is distressed because of what you eat, you are no longer acting in love. Do not by your eating destroy someone for whom Christ died. ¹⁶Therefore do not let what you know is good be spoken of as evil. ¹⁷For the kingdom of God is not a matter of eating and drinking, but of righteousness, peace and joy in the Holy Spirit, ¹⁸because anyone who

---

a 10 The Greek word for *brother or sister* (*adelphos*) refers here to a believer, whether man or woman, as part of God's family; also in verses 13, 15 and 21.   *b 11* Isaiah 45:23

The Values and Conscience of a Leader

Romans 14:1-23

How are we to respond to others who hold values different from our own? That's the issue of Romans 14. Paul speaks in this passage not of eternal issues or absolute truths, but about "gray areas"—subjects that are questionable and maybe even fuzzy. Christians can differ on these issues and still be part of the same organization. On these issues, no scripture declares an unequivocal right or wrong. Note Paul's counsel for situations like this:

1. Be open, not condescending (vv. 1–3).
2. Remember that everyone answers to the Lord, not to you (v. 4).
3. Cling to your own convictions (v. 5).
4. Whatever your values, your motive should be to please God (vv. 6–9).
5. You are ultimately accountable to the Lord (vv. 10–12).
6. Do not cause anyone to stumble (v. 13).
7. Don't let others impose their values on you, and vice versa (v. 14).
8. Make love your highest aim (v. 15).
9. Major on the majors and minor on the minors (vv. 16–18).
10. Pursue peace and adding value to people (v. 19).
11. Don't destroy anyone by imposing your values on them (vv. 20–22).
12. Anything is wrong that is not done out of personal faith (v. 23).

serves Christ in this way is pleasing to God and receives human approval.

[19]Let us therefore make every effort to do what leads to peace and to mutual edification. [20]Do not destroy the work of God for the sake of food. All food is clean, but it is wrong for a person to eat anything that causes someone else to stumble. [21]It is better not to eat meat or drink wine or to do anything else that will cause your brother or sister to fall.

[22]So whatever you believe about these things keep between yourself and God. Blessed is the one who does not condemn himself by what he approves. [23]But whoever has doubts is condemned if they eat, because their eating is not from faith; and everything that does not come from faith is sin.[a]

15 We who are strong ought to bear with the failings of the weak and not to please ourselves. [2]Each of us should please our neighbors for their good, to build them up. [3]For even Christ did not please himself but, as it is written: "The insults of those who insult you have fallen on me."[b] [4]For everything that was written in the past was written to teach us, so that through the endurance taught in the Scriptures and the encouragement they provide we might have hope.

[5]May the God who gives endurance and encouragement give you the same attitude of mind toward each other that Christ Jesus had, [6]so that with one mind and one voice you may glorify the God and Father of our Lord Jesus Christ.

[7]Accept one another, then, just as Christ accepted you, in order to bring praise to God. [8]For I tell you that Christ has become a servant of the Jews[c] on behalf of God's truth, so that the promises made to the patriarchs might be confirmed [9]and, moreover, that the Gentiles might glorify God for his mercy. As it is written:

"Therefore I will praise you among the
    Gentiles;
  I will sing the praises of your name."[d]

[10]Again, it says,

"Rejoice, you Gentiles, with his people."[e]

[11]And again,

"Praise the Lord, all you Gentiles;
  let all the peoples extol him."[f]

[12]And again, Isaiah says,

"The Root of Jesse will spring up,
  one who will arise to rule over the nations;
  in him the Gentiles will hope."[g]

Servanthood: Leaders Lose the Right to Be Selfish

Romans 15:1–6

How can leaders increasingly gain a servant's heart? This passage serves as another reminder that leadership is about serving others, not wielding power. Notice how Paul describes a servant:

1. *Denies self*—we are to please others, not ourselves (v. 1).

2. *Develops others*—we are to add value to others (v. 2).

3. *Accepts mistreatment*—we are to forgive wrongs (v. 3).

4. *Imitates Christ*—we are to look to Jesus as our model (v. 3).

5. *Takes the attitude of a student*—we are to remain teachable (v. 4).

6. *Pursues the harmony of relationships*—we are to pursue unity and peace (vv. 5–6).

[13]May the God of hope fill you with all joy and peace as you trust in him, so that you may overflow with hope by the power of the Holy Spirit.

Paul the Minister to the Gentiles

[14]I myself am convinced, my brothers and sisters, that you yourselves are full of goodness, filled with knowledge and competent to instruct one another. [15]Yet I have written you quite boldly on some points to remind you of them again, because of the grace God gave me [16]to be a minister of Christ Jesus to the Gentiles. He gave me the priestly duty of proclaiming the gospel of God, so that the Gentiles might become an offering acceptable to God, sanctified by the Holy Spirit.

[17]Therefore I glory in Christ Jesus in my service to God. [18]I will not venture to speak of anything except what Christ has accomplished through me in leading the Gentiles to obey God by what I have said and done — [19]by the power

---

[a] 23 Some manuscripts place 16:25-27 here; others after 15:33.
[b] 3 Psalm 69:9   [c] 8 Greek *circumcision*
[d] 9 2 Samuel 22:50; Psalm 18:49   [e] 10 Deut. 32:43
[f] 11 Psalm 117:1   [g] 12 Isaiah 11:10 (see Septuagint)

of signs and wonders, through the power of the Spirit of God. So from Jerusalem all the way around to Illyricum, I have fully proclaimed the gospel of Christ. [20]It has always been my ambition to preach the gospel where Christ was not known, so that I would not be building on someone else's foundation. [21]Rather, as it is written:

Relationships: Paul Affirms His Colleagues by Name

Romans 16:1–21

Paul sent his personal greetings to a variety of individuals in Rome. Perhaps this was Paul's way of establishing credibility with his readers, since he had never visited Rome. In any case, we see the warm, relational approach this tough leader practiced.

Note that the first few people Paul greets are women: Phoebe, Priscilla, Mary. Many pillars of the early church were faithful ladies who ministered and gave strong leadership. Jesus' life began with a woman named Mary and ended at his resurrection with a woman at the tomb. Recall several significant women in the New Testament:

1. Anna (Lk 2:36–38)
2. Bernice (Ac 25:13)
3. Candace (Ac 8:27)
4. Chloe (1Co 1:11)
5. Claudia (2Ti 4:21)
6. Damaris (Ac 17:34)
7. Dorcas (Ac 9:36–41)
8. Drusilla (Ac 24:24)
9. Elizabeth (Lk 1:5, 13)
10. Eunice (2Ti 1:5)
11. Herodias (Mt 14:3–10)
12. Joanna (Lk 8:3)
13. Lois (2Ti 1:5)
14. Lydia (Ac 16:14)
15. Martha, Mary (Lk 10:38–42)
16. Mary, the mother of Jesus (Lk 1:26–56)
17. Mary Magdalene (Mt 27:61)
18. Phoebe (Ro 16:1–2)
19. Priscilla (Ac 18:2, 18)
20. Salome (Mt 20:20–26)
21. Sapphira (Ac 5:1)
22. Susanna (Lk 8:3)

"Those who were not told about him will see,
    and those who have not heard will
        understand."[a]

[22]This is why I have often been hindered from coming to you.

Paul's Plan to Visit Rome

[23]But now that there is no more place for me to work in these regions, and since I have been longing for many years to visit you, [24]I plan to do so when I go to Spain. I hope to see you while passing through and to have you assist me on my journey there, after I have enjoyed your company for a while. [25]Now, however, I am on my way to Jerusalem in the service of the Lord's people there. [26]For Macedonia and Achaia were pleased to make a contribution for the poor among the Lord's people in Jerusalem. [27]They were pleased to do it, and indeed they owe it to them. For if the Gentiles have shared in the Jews' spiritual blessings, they owe it to the Jews to share with them their material blessings. [28]So after I have completed this task and have made sure that they have received this contribution, I will go to Spain and visit you on the way. [29]I know that when I come to you, I will come in the full measure of the blessing of Christ.

[30]I urge you, brothers and sisters, by our Lord Jesus Christ and by the love of the Spirit, to join me in my struggle by praying to God for me. [31]Pray that I may be kept safe from the unbelievers in Judea and that the contribution I take to Jerusalem may be favorably received by the Lord's people there, [32]so that I may come to you with joy, by God's will, and in your company be refreshed. [33]The God of peace be with you all. Amen.

Personal Greetings

16 I commend to you our sister Phoebe, a deacon[b,c] of the church in Cenchreae. [2]I ask you to receive her in the Lord in a way worthy of his people and to give her any help she may need from you, for she has been the benefactor of many people, including me.

[3]Greet Priscilla[d] and Aquila, my co-workers in Christ Jesus. [4]They risked their lives for me. Not only I but all the churches of the Gentiles are grateful to them.

---

[a] 21 Isaiah 52:15 (see Septuagint)   [b] 1 Or *servant*   [c] 1 The word *deacon* refers here to a Christian designated to serve with the overseers/elders of the church in a variety of ways; similarly in Phil. 1:1 and 1 Tim. 3:8,12.   [d] 3 Greek *Prisca*, a variant of *Priscilla*

5 Greet also the church that meets at their house.

Greet my dear friend Epenetus, who was the first convert to Christ in the province of Asia. 6 Greet Mary, who worked very hard for you. 7 Greet Andronicus and Junia, my fellow Jews who have been in prison with me. They are outstanding among[a] the apostles, and they were in Christ before I was.

8 Greet Ampliatus, my dear friend in the Lord. 9 Greet Urbanus, our co-worker in Christ, and my dear friend Stachys.

10 Greet Apelles, whose fidelity to Christ has stood the test.

Greet those who belong to the household of Aristobulus.

11 Greet Herodion, my fellow Jew.

Greet those in the household of Narcissus who are in the Lord.

12 Greet Tryphena and Tryphosa, those women who work hard in the Lord.

Greet my dear friend Persis, another woman who has worked very hard in the Lord.

13 Greet Rufus, chosen in the Lord, and his mother, who has been a mother to me, too.

14 Greet Asyncritus, Phlegon, Hermes, Patrobas, Hermas and the other brothers and sisters with them.

15 Greet Philologus, Julia, Nereus and his sister, and Olympas and all the Lord's people who are with them.

16 Greet one another with a holy kiss.

All the churches of Christ send greetings.

17 I urge you, brothers and sisters, to watch out for those who cause divisions and put obstacles in your way that are contrary to the teaching you have learned. Keep away from them. 18 For such people are not serving our Lord Christ, but their own appetites. By smooth talk and flattery they deceive the minds of naive people. 19 Everyone has heard about your obedience, so I rejoice because of you; but I want you to be wise about what is good, and innocent about what is evil.

20 The God of peace will soon crush Satan under your feet.

The grace of our Lord Jesus be with you.

21 Timothy, my co-worker, sends his greetings to you, as do Lucius, Jason and Sosipater, my fellow Jews.

22 I, Tertius, who wrote down this letter, greet you in the Lord.

23 Gaius, whose hospitality I and the whole church here enjoy, sends you his greetings.

Erastus, who is the city's director of public works, and our brother Quartus send you their greetings. [24] b

25 Now to him who is able to establish you in accordance with my gospel, the message I proclaim about Jesus Christ, in keeping with the revelation of the mystery hidden for long ages past, 26 but now revealed and made known through the prophetic writings by the command of the eternal God, so that all the Gentiles might come to the obedience that comes from[c] faith — 27 to the only wise God be glory forever through Jesus Christ! Amen.

a 7 Or are esteemed by   b 24 Some manuscripts include here May the grace of our Lord Jesus Christ be with all of you. Amen. c 26 Or that is

INTRODUCTION TO
1 CORINTHIANS

Leaders Must Take Risks and Overcome Fear

The two books to the Corinthian church teach us much about leadership. Various scholars agree that Paul actually wrote four letters to Corinth; our Bibles have letters two and four. While Paul appointed leaders for this church, he also led this body through his letters. He provided wise direction and needed confrontation, without ignoring their need for ministry to the heart.

The city of Corinth became a strategic center for Paul and even influenced his missionary endeavors. In order to impact this key, wealthy, commercial port, he planted the church with the help of Aquila and Priscilla (Ac 18:1–17).

First Corinthians teaches us that leaders must take risks and overcome fear. By definition, leaders initiate. They take risks. Paul stood for his convictions even when he stood alone. He confronted sin without help from others. He attempted new methods and strategies no one else was using. When rejected in his attempt to preach Christ in the synagogue, he began to equip others in the house of Titus Justus next door. Imagine the fear! He taught right next to where the Jewish religious leaders could arrest him. The Lord appeared to him in a vision and encouraged him to "not be afraid" and to continue teaching, for God had "many people in this city" (Ac 18:9–10).

Second, we learn that the best leaders invest time in building other leaders. While in Corinth, Paul started one of the first underground seminaries. So far as we can tell, he taught leaders in the afternoon when they were on a "siesta" from their workplace, just as he did in Ephesus. Most would go home to rest each afternoon, but Paul equipped leaders willing to give up their personal time to gain some tools to plant a church or evangelize the lost.

God's Role in 1 Corinthians

God used the words and personality of the apostle Paul to both encourage and correct the Corinthian church. God used Paul's educated mind to confound the wise and educated, the apostle's Jewish background to identify and convince the Hebrews, and his Roman political and social background to reach the Gentiles. First Corinthians 9 tells us that Paul became all things to all people for the purpose of reaching as many as possible.

Leaders in 1 Corinthians

Paul, Apollos, Aquila, Priscilla, Timothy, Crispus, Sosthenes

Other People of Influence in 1 Corinthians

Stephanas, the church members who abused their spiritual gifts and caused division

Lessons in Leadership

- Leaders must find their identity in Christ, not in people.
- Confrontation and criticism go with the leader's territory.
- Corporate purity and security result when a leader courageously deals with problems.
- Good leaders create a unified corporate atmosphere.

Third, leaders must be both tough and tender. Paul waded through several difficult issues in the Corinthian letters, beautifully balancing love and discipline. Call him a "velvet-covered brick!" In the end, his gentle wisdom helped resolve the sticky issues.

- Effective leaders find a place for every member to serve effectively.
- It is a leader's job to keep the main thing the main thing.

LEADERSHIP HIGHLIGHTS IN 1 CORINTHIANS

1 Paul, called to be an apostle of Christ Jesus by the will of God, and our brother Sosthenes,

[2] To the church of God in Corinth, to those sanctified in Christ Jesus and called to be his holy people, together with all those everywhere who call on the name of our Lord Jesus Christ — their Lord and ours:

[3] Grace and peace to you from God our Father and the Lord Jesus Christ.

Thanksgiving

[4] I always thank my God for you because of his grace given you in Christ Jesus. [5] For in him you have been enriched in every way — with all kinds of speech and with all knowledge — [6] God thus confirming our testimony about Christ among you. [7] Therefore you do not lack any spiritual gift as you eagerly wait for our Lord Jesus Christ to be revealed. [8] He will also keep you firm to the end, so that you will be blameless on the day of our Lord Jesus Christ. [9] God is faithful, who has called you into fellowship with his Son, Jesus Christ our Lord.

A Church Divided Over Leaders

[10] I appeal to you, brothers and sisters,[a] in the name of our Lord Jesus Christ, that all of you agree with one another in what you say and that there be no divisions among you, but that you be perfectly united in mind and thought. [11] My brothers and sisters, some from Chloe's household have informed me that there are quarrels among you. [12] What I mean is this: One of you says, "I follow Paul"; another, "I follow Apollos"; another, "I follow Cephas[b]"; still another, "I follow Christ."

[13] Is Christ divided? Was Paul crucified for you? Were you baptized in the name of Paul? [14] I thank God that I did not baptize any of you except Crispus and Gaius, [15] so no one can say that you were baptized in my name. [16] (Yes, I also baptized the household of Stephanas; beyond that, I don't remember if I baptized anyone else.) [17] For Christ did not send me to baptize, but to preach the gospel — not with wisdom and eloquence, lest the cross of Christ be emptied of its power.

Christ Crucified Is God's Power and Wisdom

[18] For the message of the cross is foolishness to those who are perishing, but to us who are being saved it is the power of God. [19] For it is written:

> "I will destroy the wisdom of the wise;
>   the intelligence of the intelligent I will
>   frustrate."[c]

---

[a] 10 The Greek word for *brothers and sisters* (*adelphoi*) refers here to believers, both men and women, as part of God's family; also in verses 11 and 26; and in 2:1; 3:1; 4:6; 6:8; 7:24, 29; 10:1; 11:33; 12:1; 14:6, 20, 26, 39; 15:1, 6, 50, 58; 16:15, 20.   [b] 12 That is, Peter   [c] 19 Isaiah 29:14

PAUL
PROFILE in leadership

The Velvet-Covered Brick
1 Corinthians 1:1–2

As the human founder of the Corinthian church (Ac 18:1–17), Paul had a really big task before him.

Paul loved his Corinthian brothers and sisters in Christ. But when he received reports that divisions, immorality and pride had crept their way into the church, he knew he had to speak up and confront the sin that some members of the church had grown proud of.

Paul felt grieved—perhaps even angered—over the reports he received about his Corinthian colleagues. We can see in his letter the anguish he felt over what had been going on in the church, but we also read of an overriding sense of love and concern for these dear friends, the ones he had referred to as "those sanctified in Christ Jesus and called to be his holy people" (1Co 1:2).

It was as if Paul were hitting the Corinthian church on the head with a velvet-covered brick—the brick being his condemnation of their sin, the velvet being his love for those whom God had set apart for good works.

It isn't always easy to speak correction to those we know are clearly in the wrong. But the Lord uses strong leaders to correct his people, courageous leaders who can speak the truth in love. May each of us whom God has called be that kind of leader.

The 101% Principle

1 Corinthians 1:4–10

The church at Corinth provided Paul with one of his greatest challenges. In this letter, he was forced to confront several problems. This was a *defiled* church—some members had committed sexual immorality and drunkenness. It was a *divided* church—at least four groups competed for leadership. It was a *disgraced* church—its problems became known throughout the community. Paul's letter could have become one long, verbal spanking.

Instead, Paul saw this church's potential, despite its problems. He practiced "The 101% Principle"—find the 1 percent you can affirm, and give it 100 percent of your attention. As the old saying goes, you catch more bees with honey than with vinegar.

While Paul knew he must confront the issues, he began his letter with words of appreciation (1Co 1:1–9). Leadership rule #1 is this: Affirmation comes before confrontation. Although Corinth had some problem people, Paul still saw the good in them:

1. They were enriched by God (vv. 4–8).

2. They had fellowship with God (v. 9).

3. They could make positive, right decisions (v. 10).

Good leaders look for the good in people and affirm it. Only then do they address the problem.

---

²⁰Where is the wise person? Where is the teacher of the law? Where is the philosopher of this age? Has not God made foolish the wisdom of the world? ²¹For since in the wisdom of God the world through its wisdom did not know him, God was pleased through the foolishness of what was preached to save those who believe. ²²Jews demand signs and Greeks look for wisdom, ²³but we preach Christ crucified: a stumbling block to Jews and foolishness to Gentiles, ²⁴but to those whom God has called, both Jews and Greeks, Christ the power of God and the wisdom of God. ²⁵For the foolishness of God is wiser than human wisdom, and the weakness of God is stronger than human strength.

²⁶Brothers and sisters, think of what you were when you were called. Not many of you were wise by human standards; not many were influential; not many were of noble birth. ²⁷But God chose the foolish things of the world to shame the wise; God chose the weak things of the world to shame the strong. ²⁸God chose the lowly things of this world and the despised things — and the things that are not — to nullify the things that are, ²⁹so that no one may boast before him. ³⁰It is because of him that you are in Christ Jesus, who has become for us wisdom from God — that is, our righteousness, holiness and redemption. ³¹Therefore, as it is written: "Let the one who boasts boast in the Lord."*ᵃ*

2 And so it was with me, brothers and sisters. When I came to you, I did not come with eloquence or human wisdom as I proclaimed to you the testimony about God.*ᵇ* ²For I resolved to know nothing while I was with you except Jesus Christ and him crucified. ³I came to you in weakness with great fear and trembling. ⁴My message and my preaching were not with wise and persuasive words, but with a demonstration

Responsibility: Leaders Assume Responsibility to Build Community

1 Corinthians 1:10

Good things happen when leaders take responsibility for creating an organization's atmosphere and culture. They create:

1. *A sense of destiny*: We are here by God's design to do his work.

2. *A sense of family*: We are in this together.

3. *A militant spirit*: We must get the job done at any cost.

ᵃ 31 Jer. 9:24   *ᵇ 1* Some manuscripts *proclaimed to you God's mystery*

of the Spirit's power, [5]so that your faith might not rest on human wisdom, but on God's power.

God's Wisdom Revealed by the Spirit

[6]We do, however, speak a message of wisdom among the mature, but not the wisdom of this age or of the rulers of this age, who are coming to nothing. [7]No, we declare God's wisdom, a mystery that has been hidden and that God destined for our glory before time began. [8]None of the rulers of this age understood it, for if they had, they would not have crucified the Lord of glory. [9]However, as it is written:

"What no eye has seen,
    what no ear has heard,
and what no human mind has conceived"[a] —
    the things God has prepared for those
        who love him —

[10]these are the things God has revealed to us by his Spirit.

The Spirit searches all things, even the deep things of God. [11]For who knows a person's thoughts except their own spirit within them? In the same way no one knows the thoughts of God except the Spirit of God. [12]What we have received is not the spirit of the world, but the Spirit who is from God, so that we may understand what God has freely given us. [13]This is what we speak, not in words taught us by hu-man wisdom but in words taught by the Spirit, explaining spiritual realities with Spirit-taught words.[b] [14]The person without the Spirit does not accept the things that come from the Spirit of God but considers them foolishness, and cannot understand them because they are discerned only through the Spirit. [15]The person with the Spirit makes judgments about all things, but such a person is not subject to merely human judgments, [16]for,

"Who has known the mind of the Lord
    so as to instruct him?"[c]

But we have the mind of Christ.

The Church and Its Leaders

3 Brothers and sisters, I could not address you as people who live by the Spirit but as people who are still worldly—mere infants in Christ. [2]I gave you milk, not solid food, for you were not yet ready for it. Indeed, you are still not ready. [3]You are still worldly. For since there is jealousy and quarreling among you, are you not worldly? Are you not acting like mere humans? [4]For when one says, "I follow Paul," and another, "I follow Apollos," are you not mere human beings? [5]What, after all, is Apollos? And what is Paul?

---

[a] 9 Isaiah 64:4   [b] 13 Or Spirit, interpreting spiritual truths to those who are spiritual   [c] 16 Isaiah 40:13

The Glory Factor

1 Corinthians 1:18—2:5

It is natural for leaders to want a bit of glory. Most leaders enjoy the limelight and feel it is only human to want their ego stroked from time to time. Paul resisted this tendency to pursue the glory that only God deserves. He focused on the superiority of God's wisdom and teaches leaders some valuable truths about:

1. *The perception of God's wisdom*—it seems to be foolishness (1:18).

2. *The permanence of God's wisdom*—it is infinite (1:19–20).

3. *The power of God's wisdom*—it can do what ours cannot (1:21–25).

4. *The paradox of God's wisdom*—it is backwards (1:26–28).

5. *The purpose of God's wisdom*—it ensures he gets the glory (1:29–31).

Paul concludes that leaders must respond in humility, seek dependence on God, and not seek the glory he alone deserves. He draws three conclusions about his leadership:

1. *I renounce human values*—I will think the way God thinks (2:1–2).

2. *I renounce human strength*—I'll be weak and seek his strength (2:3).

3. *I renounce human wisdom*—I'll ask for God's wisdom and favor (2:4–5).

Only servants, through whom you came to believe — as the Lord has assigned to each his task. [6]I planted the seed, Apollos watered it, but God has been making it grow. [7]So neither the one who plants nor the one who waters is anything, but only God, who makes things grow. [8]The one who plants and the one who waters have one purpose, and they will each be rewarded according to their own labor. [9]For we are co-workers in God's service; you are God's field, God's building.

[10]By the grace God has given me, I laid a foundation as a wise builder, and someone else is building on it. But each one should build with care. [11]For no one can lay any foundation other than the one already laid, which is Jesus Christ. [12]If anyone builds on this foundation using gold, silver, costly stones, wood, hay or straw, [13]their work will be shown for what it is, because the Day will bring it to light. It will be revealed with fire, and the fire will test the quality of each person's work. [14]If what has been built survives, the builder will receive a reward. [15]If it is burned up, the builder will suffer loss but yet will be saved — even though only as one escaping through the flames.

[16]Don't you know that you yourselves are God's temple and that God's Spirit dwells in your midst? [17]If anyone destroys God's temple, God will destroy that person; for God's temple is sacred, and you together are that temple.

[18]Do not deceive yourselves. If any of you think you are wise by the standards of this age, you should become "fools" so that you may become wise. [19]For the wisdom of this world is foolishness in God's sight. As it is written: "He catches the wise in their craftiness"[a]; [20]and again, "The Lord knows that the thoughts of the wise are futile."[b] [21]So then, no more boasting about human leaders! All things are yours, [22]whether Paul or Apollos or Cephas[c] or the world or life or death or the present or the future — all are yours, [23]and you are of Christ, and Christ is of God.

The Nature of True Apostleship

4 This, then, is how you ought to regard us: as servants of Christ and as those entrusted with the mysteries God has revealed. [2]Now it is required that those who have been given a trust must prove faithful. [3]I care very little if I am judged by you or by any human court; indeed, I do not even judge myself. [4]My conscience is clear, but that does not make me innocent. It is the Lord who judges me. [5]Therefore judge nothing before the appointed time; wait until the Lord comes. He will bring to light what is hidden in darkness and will expose the motives of the heart. At that time each will receive their praise from God.

[6]Now, brothers and sisters, I have applied these things to myself and Apollos for your benefit, so that you may learn from us the meaning of the saying, "Do not go beyond what is written." Then

---

[a] 19 Job 5:13   [b] 20 Psalm 94:11   [c] 22 That is, Peter

The Law of Process: Three Pictures of Growth

1 Corinthians 3:1–23

Paul, the pioneer and leader of the Corinthian church, had trouble hiding his disappointment. The members of this church were acting like babies rather than adults (1Co 3:1–3). No doubt he had to remind himself that leadership development is a process, not an event.

Paul desperately wanted competent leaders to rise up within the church, leaders who were healthy, strong, and able to make decisions without his help. Paul gave them three pictures to illustrate how God wanted them to grow:

1. *The church is a family*—the goal is maturity (vv. 1–4).
   It is natural for children to grow physically as they age. This should also be true spiritually. The marks of maturity are what you eat (vv. 1–2), what you do (v. 3), and what you say (v. 4).

2. *The church is a field*—the goal is fruitfulness (vv. 5–9).
   It doesn't matter who planted or who watered; the point is, are the plants growing? Fruit includes the results of your work, the response of your people, and the reward of your fulfillment.

3. *The church is a building*—the goal is quality (vv. 9–23).
   We are like a building. The measure of a good structure is quality. This includes the right foundation (vv. 9–11), the right materials (vv. 12–17), and the right motives (vv. 18–23).

Accountability: Leaders Are Servants with a Sacred Trust

1 Corinthians 4:1–5

Paul viewed himself as a servant-leader with a sacred trust (1Co 4:1) to which he needed to stay faithful (4:2). Neither the opinions of others or his own would sway him (4:3). Leaders are to serve people, but obey God, proving faithful to their sacred trust.

you will not be puffed up in being a follower of one of us over against the other. ⁷For who makes you different from anyone else? What do you have that you did not receive? And if you did receive it, why do you boast as though you did not?

⁸Already you have all you want! Already you have become rich! You have begun to reign — and that without us! How I wish that you really had begun to reign so that we also might reign with you! ⁹For it seems to me that God has put us apostles on display at the end of the procession, like those condemned to die in the arena. We have been made a spectacle to the whole universe, to angels as well as to human beings. ¹⁰We are fools for Christ, but you are so wise in Christ! We are weak, but you are strong! You are honored, we are dishonored! ¹¹To this very hour we go hungry and thirsty, we are in rags, we are brutally treated, we are homeless. ¹²We work hard with our own hands. When we are cursed, we bless; when we are persecuted, we endure it; ¹³when we are slandered, we answer kindly. We have become the scum of the earth, the garbage of the world — right up to this moment.

Paul's Appeal and Warning

¹⁴I am writing this not to shame you but to warn you as my dear children. ¹⁵Even if you had ten thousand guardians in Christ, you do not have many fathers, for in Christ Jesus I became your father through the gospel. ¹⁶Therefore I urge you to imitate me. ¹⁷For this reason I have sent to you Timothy, my son whom I love, who is faithful in the Lord. He will remind you of my way of life

The Law of the Picture: Leadership Is Caught More Than Taught

1 Corinthians 4:9–21

The greatest missing ingredient in Christian leaders today is credibility. Paul tests his level of credibility with his Corinthian followers by reminding them of how he had modeled what was right. Now he pleads with them to imitate him as a father in the Lord. He understood the Law of the Picture: People do what people see.

Leaders add infinite weight to their words by embodying the principles they teach. Paul was able to scold the erring people and sternly correct them because he never asked them to do something he hadn't already done. Listen to him:

1. His leadership was on display and open for ridicule (v. 9).

2. He was willing to play the fool in order to model a surrendered life (v. 10).

3. He endured mocking from others, but didn't waver (v. 10).

4. He sacrificed luxuries that others enjoyed (v. 11).

5. He worked hard and didn't retaliate against opposition (vv. 12–13).

6. He saw his role as a father, living an exemplary life for his children (vv. 14–15).

7. He urged his followers to imitate his life (v. 16).

8. He sent Timothy to help them live up to godly standards (vv. 17–18).

9. He warned them of his own coming (v. 19).

10. He reminded them that God's kingdom was not about talk, but power (v. 20).

in Christ Jesus, which agrees with what I teach everywhere in every church.

[18]Some of you have become arrogant, as if I were not coming to you. [19]But I will come to you very soon, if the Lord is willing, and then I will find out not only how these arrogant people are talking, but what power they have. [20]For the kingdom of God is not a matter of talk but of power. [21]What do you prefer? Shall I come to you with a rod of discipline, or shall I come in love and with a gentle spirit?

Dealing With a Case of Incest

5 It is actually reported that there is sexual immorality among you, and of a kind that even pagans do not tolerate: A man is sleeping with his father's wife. [2]And you are proud! Shouldn't you rather have gone into mourning and have put out of your fellowship the man who has been doing this? [3]For my part, even though I am not physically present, I am with you in spirit. As one who is present with you in this way, I have already passed judgment in the name of our Lord Jesus on the one who has been doing this. [4]So when you are assembled and I

How Do Leaders Confront?

1 Corinthians 5:1–2

Once Paul had identified the sin that plagued the church, as well as what should be done about it, he encouraged the leaders to confront this erring man. Most of us avoid confrontation; only a sadistic person likes it. So, how do we confront in a healthy and effective manner? Try to follow these steps:

1. Address the issue immediately and personally.
2. Confront with the right spirit.
3. Start on a positive note.
4. Outline the problem.
5. Encourage a response.
6. Show that you understand the other person's position.
7. Explain why the action is damaging.
8. Indicate the desired action.
9. Reiterate the positive strengths of the person.
10. Put the issue in the past.

am with you in spirit, and the power of our Lord Jesus is present, [5]hand this man over to Satan for the destruction of the flesh,[a,b] so that his spirit may be saved on the day of the Lord.

[6]Your boasting is not good. Don't you know that a little yeast leavens the whole batch of dough? [7]Get rid of the old yeast, so that you may be a new unleavened batch—as you really are. For Christ, our Passover lamb, has been sacrificed. [8]Therefore let us keep the Festival, not with the old bread leavened with malice and wickedness, but with the unleavened bread of sincerity and truth.

[9]I wrote to you in my letter not to associate with sexually immoral people— [10]not at all meaning the people of this world who are immoral, or the greedy and swindlers, or idolaters. In that case you would have to leave this world. [11]But now I am writing to you that you must not associate with anyone who claims to be a brother or sister[c] but is sexually immoral or greedy, an idolater or slanderer, a drunkard or swindler. Do not even eat with such people.

[12]What business is it of mine to judge those outside the church? Are you not to judge those inside? [13]God will judge those outside. "Expel the wicked person from among you."[d]

Lawsuits Among Believers

6 If any of you has a dispute with another, do you dare to take it before the ungodly for judgment instead of before the Lord's people? [2]Or do you not know that the Lord's people will judge the world? And if you are to judge the world, are you not competent to judge trivial cases? [3]Do you not know that we will judge angels? How much more the things of this life! [4]Therefore, if you have disputes about such matters, do you ask for a ruling from those whose way of life is scorned in the church? [5]I say this to shame you. Is it possible that there is nobody among you wise enough to judge a dispute between believers? [6]But instead, one brother takes another to court—and this in front of unbelievers!

[7]The very fact that you have lawsuits among you means you have been completely defeated already. Why not rather be wronged? Why not rather be cheated? [8]Instead, you yourselves cheat and do wrong, and you do this to your brothers and sisters. [9]Or do you not know that wrongdoers

---

[a] 5 In contexts like this, the Greek word for *flesh* (*sarx*) refers to the sinful state of human beings, often presented as a power in opposition to the Spirit.   [b] 5 Or *of his body*   [c] 11 The Greek word for *brother or sister* (*adelphos*) refers here to a believer, whether man or woman, as part of God's family; also in 8:11, 13.   [d] 13 Deut. 13:5; 17:7; 19:19; 21:21; 22:21,24; 24:7

Confrontation Results in Purity and Security

1 Corinthians 5:1–13

Paul had to confront the problems the Corinthians faced, the first one over the issue of incest in the church (1Co 5:1). Unfortunately, the leaders failed to deal with this sin; many felt proud of what they should be ashamed of, and vice versa (5:2). Paul therefore instructs leaders in how to deal with a member who deliberately rebels against a life of obedience to the Lord (5:2–13). This standard does not apply to outsiders, but to those who call themselves brothers (5:9–11). We learn from 2 Corinthians that the leaders followed Paul's instruction, bringing both purity and security to the church.

Why is confrontation so difficult? We often misunderstand its purpose. Our goal should not be to punish or excommunicate, but to restore. Confrontation is a redemptive act of leadership. So what are the goals of healthy confrontation?

1. *Clarification:* I will get a better understanding of the person and what happened.

2. *Change:* I hope to get improvement from it (and it may be me!).

3. *Relationship:* I will likely deepen my relationship with this person.

4. *Purity:* As word gets out, the organization will be purified and sobered.

5. *Respect:* The organization will likely raise the members' level of respect for the leadership.

6. *Security:* People feel safe knowing leaders are strong enough to take a stand.

---

will not inherit the kingdom of God? Do not be deceived: Neither the sexually immoral nor idolaters nor adulterers nor men who have sex with men[a] [10]nor thieves nor the greedy nor drunkards nor slanderers nor swindlers will inherit the kingdom of God. [11]And that is what some of you were. But you were washed, you were sanctified, you were justified in the name of the Lord Jesus Christ and by the Spirit of our God.

Sexual Immorality

[12]"I have the right to do anything," you say — but not everything is beneficial. "I have the right to do anything" — but I will not be mastered by anything. [13]You say, "Food for the stomach and the stomach for food, and God will destroy them both." The body, however, is not meant for sexual immorality but for the Lord, and the Lord for the body. [14]By his power God raised the Lord from the dead, and he will raise us also. [15]Do you not know that your bodies are members of Christ himself? Shall I then take the members of Christ and unite them with a prostitute? Never! [16]Do you not know that he who unites himself with a prostitute is one with her in body? For it is said, "The two will become one flesh."[b] [17]But whoever is united with the Lord is one with him in spirit.[c]

[18]Flee from sexual immorality. All other sins a person commits are outside the body, but whoever sins sexually, sins against their own body.

Self-Discipline: Leaders Remove Stumbling Blocks

1 Corinthians 6:1–20

Paul believed all things were lawful for the obedient Christian. Yet while he remained free of legalism and bondage, he had the self-discipline to refuse anything that would hinder him from fulfilling his call. Paul knew that the first person a leader must lead is himself.

---

[19]Do you not know that your bodies are temples of the Holy Spirit, who is in you, whom you have received from God? You are not your own; [20]you were bought at a price. Therefore honor God with your bodies.

Concerning Married Life

7 Now for the matters you wrote about: "It is good for a man not to have sexual relations with a woman." [2]But since sexual immorality is occurring, each man should have sexual relations with his own wife, and each woman with her own

---

[a] 9 The words *men who have sex with men* translate two Greek words that refer to the passive and active participants in homosexual acts.   [b] 16 Gen. 2:24   [c] 17 Or *in the Spirit*

husband. ³The husband should fulfill his marital duty to his wife, and likewise the wife to her husband. ⁴The wife does not have authority over her own body but yields it to her husband. In the same way, the husband does not have authority over his own body but yields it to his wife. ⁵Do not deprive each other except perhaps by mutual consent and for a time, so that you may devote yourselves to prayer. Then come together again so that Satan will not tempt you because of your lack of self-control. ⁶I say this as a concession, not as a command. ⁷I wish that all of you were as I am. But each of you has your own gift from God; one has this gift, another has that.

⁸Now to the unmarried[a] and the widows I say: It is good for them to stay unmarried, as I do. ⁹But if they cannot control themselves, they should marry, for it is better to marry than to burn with passion.

¹⁰To the married I give this command (not I, but the Lord): A wife must not separate from her husband. ¹¹But if she does, she must remain unmarried or else be reconciled to her husband. And a husband must not divorce his wife.

¹²To the rest I say this (I, not the Lord): If any brother has a wife who is not a believer and she is willing to live with him, he must not divorce her. ¹³And if a woman has a husband who is not a believer and he is willing to live with her, she must not divorce him. ¹⁴For the unbelieving husband has been sanctified through his wife, and the unbelieving wife has been sanctified through her believing husband. Otherwise your children would be unclean, but as it is, they are holy.

¹⁵But if the unbeliever leaves, let it be so. The brother or the sister is not bound in such circumstances; God has called us to live in peace. ¹⁶How do you know, wife, whether you will save your husband? Or, how do you know, husband, whether you will save your wife?

Concerning Change of Status

¹⁷Nevertheless, each person should live as a believer in whatever situation the Lord has assigned to them, just as God has called them. This is the rule I lay down in all the churches. ¹⁸Was a man already circumcised when he was called? He should not become uncircumcised. Was a man uncircumcised when he was called? He should not be circumcised. ¹⁹Circumcision is nothing and uncircumcision is nothing. Keeping God's commands is what counts. ²⁰Each person should remain in the situation they were in when God called them.

²¹Were you a slave when you were called? Don't let it trouble you—although if you can gain your freedom, do so. ²²For the one who was a slave when called to faith in the Lord is the Lord's freed person; similarly, the one who was free when called is Christ's slave. ²³You were bought at a price; do not become slaves of human beings. ²⁴Brothers and sisters, each person, as responsible to God, should remain in the situation they were in when God called them.

Concerning the Unmarried

²⁵Now about virgins: I have no command from the Lord, but I give a judgment as one who by the Lord's mercy is trustworthy. ²⁶Because of the present crisis, I think that it is good for a man to remain as he is. ²⁷Are you pledged to a woman? Do not seek to be released. Are you free from such a commitment? Do not look for a wife. ²⁸But if you do marry, you have not sinned; and if a virgin marries, she has not sinned. But those who marry will face many troubles in this life, and I want to spare you this.

²⁹What I mean, brothers and sisters, is that the time is short. From now on those who have wives should live as if they do not; ³⁰those who mourn, as if they did not; those who are happy, as if they were not; those who buy something, as if it were not theirs to keep; ³¹those who use the things of the world, as if not engrossed in them. For this world in its present form is passing away.

³²I would like you to be free from concern. An unmarried man is concerned about the Lord's affairs—how he can please the Lord. ³³But a married man is concerned about the affairs of this world—how he can please his wife— ³⁴and his interests are divided. An unmarried woman or virgin is concerned about the Lord's affairs: Her aim is to be devoted to the Lord in both body and spirit. But a married woman is concerned about the affairs of this world—how she can please her husband. ³⁵I am saying this for your own good, not to restrict you, but that you may live in a right way in undivided devotion to the Lord.

³⁶If anyone is worried that he might not be acting honorably toward the virgin he is engaged to, and if his passions are too strong[b] and he feels he ought to marry, he should do as he wants. He is not sinning. They should get married. ³⁷But the man who has settled the matter in his own mind, who is under no compulsion but has control over his own will, and who has made up his mind not to marry the virgin—this man also does the right thing. ³⁸So then, he who

---

[a] 8 Or widowers   [b] 36 Or if she is getting beyond the usual age for marriage

marries the virgin does right, but he who does not marry her does better.[a]

[39]A woman is bound to her husband as long as he lives. But if her husband dies, she is free to marry anyone she wishes, but he must belong to the Lord. [40]In my judgment, she is happier if she stays as she is—and I think that I too have the Spirit of God.

Concerning Food Sacrificed to Idols

8 Now about food sacrificed to idols: We know that "We all possess knowledge." But knowledge puffs up while love builds up. [2]Those who think they know something do not yet know as they ought to know. [3]But whoever loves God is known by God.[b]

[4]So then, about eating food sacrificed to idols: We know that "An idol is nothing at all in the world" and that "There is no God but one." [5]For even if there are so-called gods, whether in heaven or on earth (as indeed there are many "gods" and many "lords"), [6]yet for us there is but one God, the Father, from whom all things came and for whom we live; and there is but one Lord, Jesus Christ, through whom all things came and through whom we live.

[7]But not everyone possesses this knowledge. Some people are still so accustomed to idols that when they eat sacrificial food they think of it as having been sacrificed to a god, and since their conscience is weak, it is defiled. [8]But food does not bring us near to God; we are no worse if we do not eat, and no better if we do.

[9]Be careful, however, that the exercise of your rights does not become a stumbling block to the weak. [10]For if someone with a weak conscience sees you, with all your knowledge, eating in an idol's temple, won't that person be emboldened to eat what is sacrificed to idols? [11]So this weak brother

The Law of Sacrifice: Freedom Plus Responsibility

1 Corinthians 8:9–13

The hot issue in Paul's day was meat sacrificed to idols. Today, it may be personal freedoms such as drinking, clothing fashions, or topics of conversation. Spiritual leaders live free from legalism, but also set aside personal preferences when dealing with a sensitive conscience. Leaders always put others first.

or sister, for whom Christ died, is destroyed by your knowledge. [12]When you sin against them in this way and wound their weak conscience, you sin against Christ. [13]Therefore, if what I eat causes my brother or sister to fall into sin, I will never eat meat again, so that I will not cause them to fall.

Paul's Rights as an Apostle

9 Am I not free? Am I not an apostle? Have I not seen Jesus our Lord? Are you not the result of my work in the Lord? [2]Even though I may not be an apostle to others, surely I am to you! For you are the seal of my apostleship in the Lord.

[3]This is my defense to those who sit in judgment on me. [4]Don't we have the right to food and drink? [5]Don't we have the right to take a believing wife along with us, as do the other apostles and the Lord's brothers and Cephas[c]? [6]Or is it only I and Barnabas who lack the right to not work for a living?

[7]Who serves as a soldier at his own expense? Who plants a vineyard and does not eat its grapes? Who tends a flock and does not drink the milk? [8]Do I say this merely on human authority? Doesn't the Law say the same thing? [9]For it is written in the Law of Moses: "Do not muzzle an ox while it is treading out the grain."[d] Is it about oxen that God is concerned? [10]Surely he says this for us, doesn't he? Yes, this was written for us, because whoever plows and threshes should be able to do so in the hope of sharing in the harvest. [11]If we have sown spiritual seed among you, is it too much if we reap a material harvest from you? [12]If others have this right of support from you, shouldn't we have it all the more?

But we did not use this right. On the contrary, we put up with anything rather than hinder the gospel of Christ.

[13]Don't you know that those who serve in the temple get their food from the temple, and that those who serve at the altar share in what is offered on the altar? [14]In the same way, the Lord

---

[a] 36-38 Or [36]If anyone thinks he is not treating his daughter properly, and if she is getting along in years (or if her passions are too strong), and he feels she ought to marry, he should do as he wants. He is not sinning. He should let her get married. [37]But the man who has settled the matter in his own mind, who is under no compulsion but has control over his own will, and who has made up his mind to keep the virgin unmarried—this man also does the right thing. [38]So then, he who gives his virgin in marriage does right, but he who does not give her in marriage does better.   [b] 2,3 An early manuscript and another ancient witness think they have knowledge do not know as they ought to know. [3]But whoever loves truly knows.   [c] 5 That is, Peter   [d] 9 Deut. 25:4

The Law of Sacrifice: What Paul Gave Up

1 Corinthians 9:5–15

Paul was a leader who surrendered the rights he could have legally held on to—and this is what made him effective. Consider what this leader gave up:

1. He was a man who gave up his right to a wife (v. 5).
2. He was a soldier who gave up his right to a salary (v. 7).
3. He was a vineyard worker who gave up his right to eat his grapes (v. 7).
4. He was a shepherd who gave up his right to drink the sheep's milk (v. 7).
5. He was an ox who gave up his right to eat grain (vv. 9–10).
6. He was a plowman who gave up his right to the harvest (v. 10).
7. He was a temple worker who gave up his right to its food (vv. 13–14).
8. He was a preacher who gave up his right to an offering (vv. 14–15).

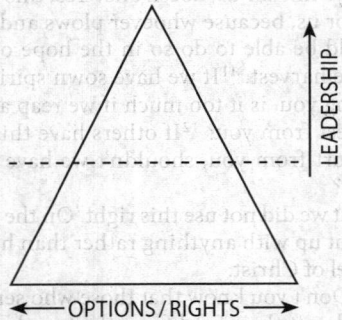

THE LEADERSHIP TRIANGLE

This pyramid diagrams how biblical leadership works. As leaders grow up, they give up options. Contrary to the world's thinking, they willingly surrender their rights when they reach the top.

has commanded that those who preach the gospel should receive their living from the gospel.

¹⁵But I have not used any of these rights. And I am not writing this in the hope that you will do such things for me, for I would rather die than allow anyone to deprive me of this boast.

¹⁶For when I preach the gospel, I cannot boast, since I am compelled to preach. Woe to me if I do not preach the gospel! ¹⁷If I preach voluntarily, I have a reward; if not voluntarily, I am simply discharging the trust committed to me. ¹⁸What then is my reward? Just this: that in preaching the gospel I may offer it free of charge, and so not make full use of my rights as a preacher of the gospel.

Paul's Use of His Freedom

¹⁹Though I am free and belong to no one, I have made myself a slave to everyone, to win as many as possible. ²⁰To the Jews I became like a Jew, to win the Jews. To those under the law I became like one under the law (though I myself am not under the law), so as to win those under the law. ²¹To those not having the law I became like one not having the law (though I am not free from God's law but am under Christ's law), so as

The Law of Addition: Paul Added Value Before He Gave Direction

1 Corinthians 9:19–21

In 1 Corinthians 9:19–21, Paul talks about becoming like a Jew so he could reach the Jews, and like a person without the law so he could reach those who were without the law. In fact, he said he became all things to all men so that he could save them. His point? He advocated practicing the law of addition: first add value to others; move toward them before you ask them to take a step.

The Law of Intuition: Leaders Read Accurately, Lead Accordingly

1 Corinthians 9:19–23

Leaders always read their situation, then lead their situation. Paul refused to cling to his past as a Pharisee or to his rights as an apostle (1Co 9:7–18), but he laid both aside because they often got in the way of leading Gentiles. The goal is always more important than the role.

Passion: Paul's Energy for Serving Others

1 Corinthians 9:19–27

Paul was a leader who possessed both passion (1Co 9:19–23) and discipline (9:24–27).
The reason? He felt consumed with his mission. Note some truths about his leadership:

1. *Paul's passion exceeded his position* (v. 19). His position: I am free from all men. His passion: I have become a slave to all men.

2. *Paul's passion exceeded his personal preferences* (vv. 20–22). He insists on fulfilling his mission. Compassion drove him, not compromise.

3. *Paul was high on people, low on procedure* (v. 22). Paul knew what was worth dying for and what wasn't. He valued people over procedure.

4. *Paul remained fixed on his mission and flexible in his methods* (v. 23). Paul remained flexible because he kept his mission in sharp focus. He committed himself to God and his goal.

Self-Discipline: Running for Eternal Rewards

1 Corinthians 9:24–27

Paul, the leader, challenges his readers to run the Christian life with focus (1Co 9:24), train (9:25), compete with passion (9:26), fight with purpose (9:26), and master their flesh (9:27). Paul asks, If athletes work to get a trophy, why not we who receive eternal rewards?

passed through the sea. ²They were all baptized into Moses in the cloud and in the sea. ³They all ate the same spiritual food ⁴and drank the same spiritual drink; for they drank from the spiritual rock that accompanied them, and that rock was Christ. ⁵Nevertheless, God was not pleased with most of them; their bodies were scattered in the wilderness.

⁶Now these things occurred as examples to keep us from setting our hearts on evil things as they did. ⁷Do not be idolaters, as some of them were; as it is written: "The people sat down to eat and drink and got up to indulge in revelry."[a] ⁸We should not commit sexual immorality, as some of them did—and in one day twenty-three thousand of them died. ⁹We should not test Christ,[b] as some of them did—and were killed by snakes. ¹⁰And do not grumble, as some of them did—and were killed by the destroying angel.

¹¹These things happened to them as examples and were written down as warnings for us, on whom the culmination of the ages has come. ¹²So, if you think you are standing firm, be careful that you don't fall! ¹³No temptation[c] has overtaken you except what is common to mankind. And God is faithful; he will not let you be tempted[c] beyond what you can bear. But when you are tempted,[c] he will also provide a way out so that you can endure it.

Idol Feasts and the Lord's Supper

¹⁴Therefore, my dear friends, flee from idolatry. ¹⁵I speak to sensible people; judge for yourselves what I say. ¹⁶Is not the cup of thanksgiving for which we give thanks a participation in the blood of Christ? And is not the bread that

to win those not having the law. ²²To the weak I became weak, to win the weak. I have become all things to all people so that by all possible means I might save some. ²³I do all this for the sake of the gospel, that I may share in its blessings.

The Need for Self-Discipline

²⁴Do you not know that in a race all the runners run, but only one gets the prize? Run in such a way as to get the prize. ²⁵Everyone who competes in the games goes into strict training. They do it to get a crown that will not last, but we do it to get a crown that will last forever. ²⁶Therefore I do not run like someone running aimlessly; I do not fight like a boxer beating the air. ²⁷No, I strike a blow to my body and make it my slave so that after I have preached to others, I myself will not be disqualified for the prize.

Warnings From Israel's History

10 For I do not want you to be ignorant of the fact, brothers and sisters, that our ancestors were all under the cloud and that they all

---

[a] 7 Exodus 32:6   [b] 9 Some manuscripts *test the Lord*
[c] 13 The Greek for *temptation* and *tempted* can also mean *testing* and *tested*.

Teachability: Leaders Learn from the Past

1 Corinthians 10:1–13

Paul reminds us of Israel's patriarchs, whose disobedience forced them to wander through the wilderness for 40 years. The first generation had the opportunity to enter the promised land (1Co 10:1–5), but never made it. These things were recorded as examples for us! We are to remain teachable and learn from the past.

we break a participation in the body of Christ? [17]Because there is one loaf, we, who are many, are one body, for we all share the one loaf.

[18]Consider the people of Israel: Do not those who eat the sacrifices participate in the altar? [19]Do I mean then that food sacrificed to an idol is anything, or that an idol is anything? [20]No, but the sacrifices of pagans are offered to demons, not to God, and I do not want you to be participants with demons. [21]You cannot drink the cup of the Lord and the cup of demons too; you cannot have a part in both the Lord's table and the table of demons. [22]Are we trying to arouse the Lord's jealousy? Are we stronger than he?

The Believer's Freedom

[23]"I have the right to do anything," you say—but not everything is beneficial. "I have the right to do anything"—but not everything is constructive. [24]No one should seek their own good, but the good of others.

[25]Eat anything sold in the meat market without raising questions of conscience, [26]for, "The earth is the Lord's, and everything in it."[a]

[27]If an unbeliever invites you to a meal and you want to go, eat whatever is put before you without raising questions of conscience. [28]But if someone says to you, "This has been offered in sacrifice," then do not eat it, both for the sake of the one who told you and for the sake of conscience. [29]I am referring to the other person's conscience, not yours. For why is my freedom being judged by another's conscience? [30]If I take part in the meal with thankfulness, why am I denounced because of something I thank God for?

[31]So whether you eat or drink or whatever you do, do it all for the glory of God. [32]Do not cause anyone to stumble, whether Jews, Greeks or the church of God— [33]even as I try to please everyone in every way. For I am not seeking my own good but the good of many, so that they may be saved. **11** [1]Follow my example, as I follow the example of Christ.

[a] 26 Psalm 24:1

Decision Making in the Gray Areas

1 Corinthians 10:24–33

Leaders regularly face choices that affect not only their own lives, but many others. What's more, many of these decisions have no clear answer; they do not appear black and white, but gray. So how does a leader make good decisions in the gray areas? Paul describes a system for making tough decisions:

1. *Prioritize God's people* (vv. 24–30).
   Put others first. The term *others* describes a person unlike you, one with whom you are likely to disagree. Leaders must choose what is best for others, not what appeals to their own tastes. Ask yourself: Who will benefit most from this decision, me or others?

2. *Pursue God's glory* (v. 31).
   Does the decision glorify God or someone else? Paul would agree with the shorter catechism: The chief end of man is to glorify God and to enjoy him forever. Ask yourself: Does this decision give people a better picture of who God is?

3. *Perceive God's purpose* (vv. 32–33).
   The ultimate purpose for our being on earth is to bring others to Christ. We must always move toward fulfilling this mission. Ask yourself: Will this decision please God and fulfill his purposes?

On Covering the Head in Worship

²I praise you for remembering me in everything and for holding to the traditions just as I passed them on to you. ³But I want you to realize that the head of every man is Christ, and the head of the woman is man,ᵃ and the head of Christ is God. ⁴Every man who prays or prophesies with his head covered dishonors his head. ⁵But every woman who prays or prophesies with her head uncovered dishonors her head—it is the same as having her head shaved. ⁶For if a woman does not cover her head, she might as well have her hair cut off; but if it is a disgrace for a woman to have her hair cut off or her head shaved, then she should cover her head.

⁷A man ought not to cover his head,ᵇ since he is the image and glory of God; but woman is the glory of man. ⁸For man did not come from woman, but woman from man; ⁹neither was man created for woman, but woman for man. ¹⁰It is for this reason that a woman ought to have authority over her ownᶜ head, because of the angels. ¹¹Nevertheless, in the Lord woman is not independent of man, nor is man independent of woman. ¹²For as woman came from man, so also man is born of woman. But everything comes from God.

¹³Judge for yourselves: Is it proper for a woman to pray to God with her head uncovered? ¹⁴Does not the very nature of things teach you that if a man has long hair, it is a disgrace to him, ¹⁵but that if a woman has long hair, it is her glory? For long hair is given to her as a covering. ¹⁶If anyone wants to be contentious about this, we have no other practice—nor do the churches of God.

Correcting an Abuse of the Lord's Supper

¹⁷In the following directives I have no praise for you, for your meetings do more harm than good. ¹⁸In the first place, I hear that when you come together as a church, there are divisions among you, and to some extent I believe it. ¹⁹No doubt there have to be differences among you to show which of you have God's approval. ²⁰So then, when you come together, it is not the Lord's Supper you eat, ²¹for when you are eating, some of you go ahead with your own private suppers. As a result, one person remains hungry and another gets drunk. ²²Don't you have homes to eat and drink in? Or do you despise the church of God by humiliating those who have nothing? What shall I say to you? Shall I praise you? Certainly not in this matter!

²³For I received from the Lord what I also passed on to you: The Lord Jesus, on the night he was betrayed, took bread, ²⁴and when he had given thanks, he broke it and said, "This is my body, which is for you; do this in remembrance of me." ²⁵In the same way, after supper he took the cup, saying, "This cup is the new covenant in my blood; do this, whenever you drink it, in remembrance of me." ²⁶For whenever you eat this bread and drink this cup, you proclaim the Lord's death until he comes.

²⁷So then, whoever eats the bread or drinks the cup of the Lord in an unworthy manner will be guilty of sinning against the body and blood of the Lord. ²⁸Everyone ought to examine themselves before they eat of the bread and drink from the cup. ²⁹For those who eat and drink without discerning the body of Christ eat and drink judgment on themselves. ³⁰That is why many among you are weak and sick, and a number of you have fallen asleep. ³¹But if we were more discerning with regard to ourselves, we would not come under such judgment. ³²Nevertheless, when we are judged in this way by the Lord, we are being disciplined so that we will not be finally condemned with the world.

³³So then, my brothers and sisters, when you gather to eat, you should all eat together. ³⁴Anyone who is hungry should eat something at home, so that when you meet together it may not result in judgment.

And when I come I will give further directions.

Concerning Spiritual Gifts

12 Now about the gifts of the Spirit, brothers and sisters, I do not want you to be uninformed. ²You know that when you were pagans, somehow or other you were influenced and led astray to mute idols. ³Therefore I want you to know that no one who is speaking by the Spirit of God says, "Jesus be cursed," and no one can say, "Jesus is Lord," except by the Holy Spirit.

⁴There are different kinds of gifts, but the same Spirit distributes them. ⁵There are different kinds of service, but the same Lord. ⁶There are different kinds of working, but in all of them and in everyone it is the same God at work. ⁷Now to each one the manifestation of the

---

ᵃ 3 Or of the wife is her husband   ᵇ 4-7 Or ⁴Every man who prays or prophesies with long hair dishonors his head. ⁵But every woman who prays or prophesies with no covering of hair dishonors her head—she is just like one of the "shorn women." ⁶If a woman has no covering, let her be for now with short hair; but since it is a disgrace for a woman to have her hair shorn or shaved, she should grow it again. ⁷A man ought not to have long hair   ᶜ 10 Or have a sign of authority on her

Team Building: Leaders Are Brokers of Gifts

1 Corinthians 12:4–31

Leaders aren't supposed to do all the work of the church, but are to effectively broker the talent on their team. Good teams use every gift and enjoy both unity and diversity. Consider Paul's philosophy of team building:

1. The team possesses a variety of gifts or positions, but pursues the same goal and God (vv. 4–6).
2. Everyone has a contribution to make which benefits the team (v. 7).
3. God is the source of each gift, so he deserves the glory (vv. 8–10).
4. God chooses who has what gifts, so we must not compete or compare (v. 11).
5. Team members are to function like the organs and muscles in a body (vv. 12–14).
6. No team member is less important than another; all are necessary (vv. 15–21).
7. Sometimes, the players who seem less important are actually more important (vv. 22–24).
8. God's goal is team harmony and mutual care (vv. 25–26).
9. Although members are equally important, they are meant to be diverse (vv. 27–28).
10. We should not compete with each other, but complete each other (vv. 29–31).

Spirit is given for the common good. ⁸To one there is given through the Spirit a message of wisdom, to another a message of knowledge by means of the same Spirit, ⁹to another faith by the same Spirit, to another gifts of healing by that one Spirit, ¹⁰to another miraculous powers, to another prophecy, to another distinguishing between spirits, to another speaking in different kinds of tongues,*ᵃ* and to still another the interpretation of tongues.*ᵃ* ¹¹All these are the work of one and the same Spirit, and he distributes them to each one, just as he determines.

Unity and Diversity in the Body

¹²Just as a body, though one, has many parts, but all its many parts form one body, so it is with Christ. ¹³For we were all baptized by*ᵇ* one Spirit so as to form one body — whether Jews or Gentiles, slave or free — and we were all given the one Spirit to drink. ¹⁴Even so the body is not made up of one part but of many.

¹⁵Now if the foot should say, "Because I am not a hand, I do not belong to the body," it would not for that reason stop being part of the body. ¹⁶And if the ear should say, "Because I am not an eye, I do not belong to the body," it would not for that reason stop being part of the body. ¹⁷If the whole body were an eye, where would the sense of hearing be? If the whole body were an ear, where would the sense of smell be? ¹⁸But

in fact God has placed the parts in the body, every one of them, just as he wanted them to be. ¹⁹If they were all one part, where would the body be? ²⁰As it is, there are many parts, but one body.

²¹The eye cannot say to the hand, "I don't need you!" And the head cannot say to the feet, "I don't need you!" ²²On the contrary, those parts of the body that seem to be weaker are indispensable, ²³and the parts that we think are less honorable we treat with special honor. And the parts that are unpresentable are treated with special modesty, ²⁴while our presentable parts

---

ᵃ 10 Or *languages*; also in verse 28   *ᵇ 13* Or *with*; or *in*

Leaders Who Celebrate Diversity Accomplish More

1 Corinthians 12:14–31

Leaders must build a team spirit that celebrates diversity. Teams must share a common goal, but not the same gifts. Teams mature when the leader insists on diversity and celebrates what everyone does together. Former UCLA basketball coach John Wooden said, "Individuals win trophies, but teams win championships."

need no special treatment. But God has put the body together, giving greater honor to the parts that lacked it, 25so that there should be no division in the body, but that its parts should have equal concern for each other. 26If one part suffers, every part suffers with it; if one part is honored, every part rejoices with it.

27Now you are the body of Christ, and each one of you is a part of it. 28And God has placed in the church first of all apostles, second prophets, third teachers, then miracles, then gifts of healing, of helping, of guidance, and of different kinds of tongues. 29Are all apostles? Are all prophets? Are all teachers? Do all work miracles? 30Do all have gifts of healing? Do all speak in tongues*a*? Do all interpret? 31Now eagerly desire the greater gifts.

Love Is Indispensable

And yet I will show you the most excellent way.

13 If I speak in the tongues*b* of men or of angels, but do not have love, I am only a resounding gong or a clanging cymbal. 2If I have the gift of prophecy and can fathom all mysteries and all knowledge, and if I have a faith that can move mountains, but do not have love, I am nothing. 3If I give all I possess to the poor and

give over my body to hardship that I may boast,*c* but do not have love, I gain nothing.

4Love is patient, love is kind. It does not envy, it does not boast, it is not proud. 5It does not dishonor others, it is not self-seeking, it is not easily angered, it keeps no record of wrongs. 6Love does not delight in evil but rejoices with the truth. 7It always protects, always trusts, always hopes, always perseveres.

8Love never fails. But where there are prophecies, they will cease; where there are tongues, they will be stilled; where there is knowledge, it will pass away. 9For we know in part and we prophesy in part, 10but when completeness comes, what is in part disappears. 11When I was a child, I talked like a child, I thought like a child, I reasoned like a child. When I became a man, I put the ways of childhood behind me. 12For now we see only a reflection as in a mirror; then we shall see face to face. Now I know in part; then I shall know fully, even as I am fully known.

13And now these three remain: faith, hope and love. But the greatest of these is love.

---

a 30 Or *other languages*   *b 1* Or *languages*   *c 3* Some manuscripts *body to the flames*

Love: The Foundation for Every Act of a Leader

1 Corinthians 13:4–7

Have you ever pondered why Paul took an entire chapter of the Bible to discuss the supremacy of love? In the early church, leaders modeled love to their churches. In turn, the churches modeled it to the rest of the world. They lived by the watchwords in 1 Corinthians 13:4–7. Love was the foundation and motive for the leaders' actions. They were first love-slaves and served the people. While leaders indeed possessed great gifts, their gifts took second place to serving others out of love. Consider how the early leaders lived out this passage:

1. Timothy and Erastus served the church and Paul (Ac 19:22).

2. Phoebe served the church in Cenchrea (Ro 16:1).

3. Aquila and Priscilla risked death to serve Paul and the Gentiles (Ro 16:3–4).

4. Stephanas's family devoted themselves to serving the saints (1Co 16:15).

5. The apostles served the Corinthian church (2Co 3:3).

6. Titus served the church in Corinth (2Co 8:16–17).

7. Paul ministered to the needs of the saints at Jerusalem (2Co 8:18–19).

8. Epaphroditus served Paul in prison (Php 2:25–30).

9. Epaphras served the Colossian church (Col 1:7).

10. Onesiphorus served Paul in Ephesus (2Ti 1:16–18).

Intelligibility in Worship

14 Follow the way of love and eagerly desire gifts of the Spirit, especially prophecy. [2]For anyone who speaks in a tongue[a] does not speak to people but to God. Indeed, no one understands them; they utter mysteries by the Spirit. [3]But the one who prophesies speaks to people for their strengthening, encouraging and comfort. [4]Anyone who speaks in a tongue edifies themselves, but the one who prophesies edifies the church. [5]I would like every one of you to speak in tongues,[b] but I would rather have you prophesy. The one who prophesies is greater than the one who speaks in tongues,[b] unless someone interprets, so that the church may be edified.

[6]Now, brothers and sisters, if I come to you and speak in tongues, what good will I be to you, unless I bring you some revelation or knowledge or prophecy or word of instruction? [7]Even in the case of lifeless things that make sounds, such as the pipe or harp, how will anyone know what tune is being played unless there is a distinction in the notes? [8]Again, if the trumpet does not sound a clear call, who will get ready for battle? [9]So it is with you. Unless you speak intelligible words with your tongue, how will anyone know what you are saying? You will just be speaking into the air. [10]Undoubtedly there are all sorts of languages in the world, yet none of them is without meaning. [11]If then I do not grasp the meaning of what someone is saying, I am a foreigner to the speaker, and the speaker is a foreigner to me. [12]So it is with you. Since you are eager for gifts of the Spirit, try to excel in those that build up the church.

[13]For this reason the one who speaks in a tongue should pray that they may interpret what they say. [14]For if I pray in a tongue, my spirit prays, but my mind is unfruitful. [15]So what shall I do? I will pray with my spirit, but I will also pray with my understanding; I will sing with my spirit, but I will also sing with my understanding. [16]Otherwise when you are praising God in the Spirit, how can someone else, who is now put in the position of an inquirer,[c] say "Amen" to your thanksgiving, since they do not know what you are saying? [17]You are giving thanks well enough, but no one else is edified.

[18]I thank God that I speak in tongues more than all of you. [19]But in the church I would rather speak five intelligible words to instruct others than ten thousand words in a tongue.

[20]Brothers and sisters, stop thinking like children. In regard to evil be infants, but in your thinking be adults. [21]In the Law it is written:

"With other tongues
and through the lips of foreigners
I will speak to this people,
but even then they will not listen to me,
says the Lord."[d]

[22]Tongues, then, are a sign, not for believers but for unbelievers; prophecy, however, is not for unbelievers but for believers. [23]So if the whole church comes together and everyone speaks in tongues, and inquirers or unbelievers come in, will they not say that you are out of your mind? [24]But if an unbeliever or an inquirer comes in while everyone is prophesying, they are convicted of sin and are brought under judgment by all, [25]as the secrets of their hearts are laid bare. So they will fall down and worship God, exclaiming, "God is really among you!"

Good Order in Worship

[26]What then shall we say, brothers and sisters? When you come together, each of you has a hymn, or a word of instruction, a revelation, a tongue or an interpretation. Everything must be done so that the church may be built up. [27]If anyone speaks in a tongue, two — or at the most three — should speak, one at a time, and someone must interpret. [28]If there is no interpreter, the speaker should keep quiet in the church and speak to himself and to God.

[29]Two or three prophets should speak, and the others should weigh carefully what is said. [30]And if a revelation comes to someone who is sitting down, the first speaker should stop. [31]For you can all prophesy in turn so that everyone may be instructed and encouraged. [32]The spirits of prophets are subject to the control of prophets. [33]For God is not a God of disorder but of peace — as in all the congregations of the Lord's people.

[34]Women[e] should remain silent in the churches. They are not allowed to speak, but must be in submission, as the law says. [35]If they want to inquire about something, they should ask their own husbands at home; for it is disgraceful for a woman to speak in the church.[f]

---

[a] 2 Or *in another language*; also in verses 4, 13, 14, 19, 26 and 27   [b] 5 Or *in other languages*; also in verses 6, 18, 22, 23 and 39   [c] 16 The Greek word for *inquirer* is a technical term for someone not fully initiated into a religion; also in verses 23 and 24.   [d] 21 Isaiah 28:11,12   [e] 33,34 Or *peace. As in all the congregations of the Lord's people,* [34]*women*   [f] 34,35 In a few manuscripts these verses come after verse 40.

Organization: Leaders Organize So They Don't Have to Agonize

1 Corinthians 14:1–40

Paul wrote to bring order to a church in chaos. The Corinthians were abusing their gifts and calling attention to themselves rather than to Christ. As a leader, Paul had to change this. In fact, 1 Corinthians 14:40 urges them to do everything "in a fitting and orderly way." What can we learn about organization from this chapter?

1. Identify and pursue your top priorities (v. 1).

2. Seek to practice what will benefit the most people (vv. 2–12).

3. Communicate clearly (vv. 7–8).

4. See things through the eyes of the outsider (vv. 23–25).

5. Order activities simply for the purpose of adding value to others (vv. 26–33).

6. Make sure everything is done in an appropriate manner (v. 40).

³⁶Or did the word of God originate with you? Or are you the only people it has reached? ³⁷If anyone thinks they are a prophet or otherwise gifted by the Spirit, let them acknowledge that what I am writing to you is the Lord's command. ³⁸But if anyone ignores this, they will themselves be ignored.ᵃ

³⁹Therefore, my brothers and sisters, be eager to prophesy, and do not forbid speaking in tongues. ⁴⁰But everything should be done in a fitting and orderly way.

The Resurrection of Christ

15 Now, brothers and sisters, I want to remind you of the gospel I preached to you, which you received and on which you have taken your stand. ²By this gospel you are saved, if you hold firmly to the word I preached to you. Otherwise, you have believed in vain.

³For what I received I passed on to you as of first importanceᵇ: that Christ died for our sins according to the Scriptures, ⁴that he was buried, that he was raised on the third day according to the Scriptures, ⁵and that he appeared to

Cephas,ᶜ and then to the Twelve. ⁶After that, he appeared to more than five hundred of the brothers and sisters at the same time, most of whom are still living, though some have fallen asleep. ⁷Then he appeared to James, then to all the apostles, ⁸and last of all he appeared to me also, as to one abnormally born.

⁹For I am the least of the apostles and do not even deserve to be called an apostle, because I persecuted the church of God. ¹⁰But by the grace of God I am what I am, and his grace to me was not without effect. No, I worked harder than all of them — yet not I, but the grace of God that was with me. ¹¹Whether, then, it is I or they, this is what we preach, and this is what you believed.

The Resurrection of the Dead

¹²But if it is preached that Christ has been raised from the dead, how can some of you say that there is no resurrection of the dead? ¹³If there is no resurrection of the dead, then not even Christ has been raised. ¹⁴And if Christ has not been raised, our preaching is useless and so is your faith. ¹⁵More than that, we are then found to be false witnesses about God, for we have testified about God that he raised Christ from the dead. But he did not raise him if in fact the dead are not raised. ¹⁶For if the dead are not raised, then Christ has not been raised either. ¹⁷And if Christ has not been raised, your faith is futile; you are still in your sins. ¹⁸Then those also who have fallen asleep in Christ are lost. ¹⁹If only for this life we have hope in Christ, we are of all people most to be pitied.

²⁰But Christ has indeed been raised from the dead, the firstfruits of those who have fallen asleep. ²¹For since death came through a man, the resurrection of the dead comes also through a man. ²²For as in Adam all die, so in Christ all will be made alive. ²³But each in turn: Christ, the firstfruits; then, when he comes, those who belong to him. ²⁴Then the end will come, when he hands over the kingdom to God the Father after he has destroyed all dominion, authority and power. ²⁵For he must reign until he has put all his enemies under his feet. ²⁶The last enemy to be destroyed is death. ²⁷For he "has put everything under his feet."ᵈ Now when it says that "everything" has been put under him, it is clear that this does not include God himself, who put everything under Christ. ²⁸When he has done

---

ᵃ 38 Some manuscripts *But anyone who is ignorant of this will be ignorant*   ᵇ 3 Or *you at the first*   ᶜ 5 That is, Peter   ᵈ 27 Psalm 8:6

this, then the Son himself will be made subject to him who put everything under him, so that God may be all in all.

²⁹Now if there is no resurrection, what will those do who are baptized for the dead? If the dead are not raised at all, why are people baptized for them? ³⁰And as for us, why do we endanger ourselves every hour? ³¹I face death every day—yes, just as surely as I boast about you in Christ Jesus our Lord. ³²If I fought wild beasts in Ephesus with no more than human hopes, what have I gained? If the dead are not raised,

"Let us eat and drink,
    for tomorrow we die."ᵃ

³³Do not be misled: "Bad company corrupts good character."ᵇ ³⁴Come back to your senses as you ought, and stop sinning; for there are some who are ignorant of God—I say this to your shame.

The Resurrection Body

³⁵But someone will ask, "How are the dead raised? With what kind of body will they come?" ³⁶How foolish! What you sow does not come to life unless it dies. ³⁷When you sow, you do not plant the body that will be, but just a seed, perhaps of wheat or of something else. ³⁸But God gives it a body as he has determined, and to each kind of seed he gives its own body. ³⁹Not all flesh is the same: People have one kind of flesh, animals have another, birds another and fish another. ⁴⁰There are also heavenly bodies and there are earthly bodies; but the splendor of the heavenly bodies is one kind, and the splendor of the earthly bodies is another. ⁴¹The sun has one kind of splendor, the moon another and the stars another; and star differs from star in splendor.

The Law of Victory: Paul Closes with Hope and Victory

1 Corinthians 15:1–9, 57–58

Like any good leader, Paul closes his letter by reminding his friends of the absolute victory of their cause. Paul fuels their convictions to stay the course and fulfill their mission (1Co 15:57–58). Leaders find a way for the team to win, then use past victories to build future ones.

---

⁴²So will it be with the resurrection of the dead. The body that is sown is perishable, it is raised imperishable; ⁴³it is sown in dishonor, it is raised in glory; it is sown in weakness, it is raised in power; ⁴⁴it is sown a natural body, it is raised a spiritual body.

If there is a natural body, there is also a spiritual body. ⁴⁵So it is written: "The first man Adam became a living being"ᶜ; the last Adam, a life-giving spirit. ⁴⁶The spiritual did not come first, but the natural, and after that the spiritual. ⁴⁷The first man was of the dust of the earth; the second man is of heaven. ⁴⁸As was the earthly man, so are those who are of the earth; and as is the heavenly man, so also are those who are of heaven. ⁴⁹And just as we have borne the image of the earthly man, so shall weᵈ bear the image of the heavenly man.

⁵⁰I declare to you, brothers and sisters, that flesh and blood cannot inherit the kingdom of God, nor does the perishable inherit the imperishable. ⁵¹Listen, I tell you a mystery: We will not all sleep, but we will all be changed— ⁵²in a flash, in the twinkling of an eye, at the last trumpet. For the trumpet will sound, the dead will be raised imperishable, and we will be changed. ⁵³For the perishable must clothe itself with the imperishable, and the mortal with immortality. ⁵⁴When the perishable has been clothed with the imperishable, and the mortal with immortality, then the saying that is written will come true: "Death has been swallowed up in victory."ᵉ

⁵⁵ "Where, O death, is your victory?
    Where, O death, is your sting?"ᶠ

⁵⁶The sting of death is sin, and the power of sin is the law. ⁵⁷But thanks be to God! He gives us the victory through our Lord Jesus Christ.

⁵⁸Therefore, my dear brothers and sisters, stand firm. Let nothing move you. Always give yourselves fully to the work of the Lord, because you know that your labor in the Lord is not in vain.

The Collection for the Lord's People

16 Now about the collection for the Lord's people: Do what I told the Galatian churches to do. ²On the first day of every week, each one of you should set aside a sum of money in keeping with your income, saving it up, so

---

ᵃ 32 Isaiah 22:13   ᵇ 33 From the Greek poet Menander
ᶜ 45 Gen. 2:7   ᵈ 49 Some early manuscripts *so let us*
ᵉ 54 Isaiah 25:8   ᶠ 55 Hosea 13:14

that when I come no collections will have to be made. [3]Then, when I arrive, I will give letters of introduction to the men you approve and send them with your gift to Jerusalem. [4]If it seems advisable for me to go also, they will accompany me.

Personal Requests

[5]After I go through Macedonia, I will come to you — for I will be going through Macedonia. [6]Perhaps I will stay with you for a while, or even spend the winter, so that you can help me on my journey, wherever I go. [7]For I do not want to see you now and make only a passing visit; I hope to spend some time with you, if the Lord permits. [8]But I will stay on at Ephesus until Pentecost, [9]because a great door for effective work has opened to me, and there are many who oppose me.

[10]When Timothy comes, see to it that he has nothing to fear while he is with you, for he is carrying on the work of the Lord, just as I am. [11]No one, then, should treat him with contempt. Send him on his way in peace so that he may return to me. I am expecting him along with the brothers.

[12]Now about our brother Apollos: I strongly urged him to go to you with the brothers. He was quite unwilling to go now, but he will go when he has the opportunity.

[13]Be on your guard; stand firm in the faith; be courageous; be strong. [14]Do everything in love.

[15]You know that the household of Stephanas were the first converts in Achaia, and they have devoted themselves to the service of the Lord's people. I urge you, brothers and sisters, [16]to submit to such people and to everyone who joins in the work and labors at it. [17]I was glad when Stephanas, Fortunatus and Achaicus arrived, because they have supplied what was lacking from you. [18]For they refreshed my spirit and yours also. Such men deserve recognition.

Final Greetings

[19]The churches in the province of Asia send you greetings. Aquila and Priscilla[a] greet you warmly in the Lord, and so does the church that meets at their house. [20]All the brothers and sisters here send you greetings. Greet one another with a holy kiss.

[21]I, Paul, write this greeting in my own hand. [22]If anyone does not love the Lord, let that person be cursed! Come, Lord[b]! [23]The grace of the Lord Jesus be with you. [24]My love to all of you in Christ Jesus. Amen.[c]

---

[a] 19 Greek *Prisca*, a variant of *Priscilla*   [b] 22 The Greek for *Come, Lord* reproduces an Aramaic expression (*Marana tha*) used by early Christians.   [c] 24 Some manuscripts do not have *Amen*.

The Law of Navigation: The Strategy to Reach Asia Minor

1 Corinthians 16:5–9

Paul had a plan to reach the major cities of his day. In a conversational manner, he describes his plan to start in Macedonia, then move south to Corinth and finally visit Asia Minor and the major port city of Ephesus, where "a great door for effective work [had] opened" to him (1Co 16:9).

Effective leaders don't drift from one place to another. Paul had a divine plan to impact major cities that would in turn influence those who visited these cities. He focused on the large metropolitan areas, knowing that well-trained followers would bring God's message to the smaller towns and villages in the region.

Leaders can do anything, but they can't do everything. Paul did not spend his energies haphazardly, but charted the course to reach the Roman Empire in his lifetime.

What kind of plan do you have?

INTRODUCTION TO
2 CORINTHIANS

Leadership Amidst a Difficult Situation

Like its counterpart, 1 Corinthians, this letter was written by the apostle Paul to the believers in Corinth, a strategic port city with great influence and exposure to the rest of the Roman Empire. The fact that Paul selected Corinth as a site for a church plant shows his leadership intuition. Cities like Corinth, Ephesus, Athens and Rome all provided great exposure for a new movement.

Scholars believe the book of 2 Corinthians was actually Paul's fourth letter to the church. The letter provides a marvelous case study of leadership amidst a difficult situation. For a moment, step into Paul's sandals and try to feel what he faced.

First, he had to defend his leadership and authority in the face of false teachers who undermined his leadership. If you've led anything, you know this is a tough call to make. How much should you defend yourself? When does it become too much so that people think you're simply projecting your self-worth?

Second, the church was fragmenting and dividing over personalities and theological issues. The church in Corinth gave Paul one of his greatest challenges. Its members were spiritually immature and carnal (3:1–3). Paul made a valiant effort to bring the people together and produce a culture of cooperation. In the process, he teaches us how leaders must take responsibility to foster an environment of teamwork and unity.

Third, the Corinthians struggled with moral compromise and upholding basic behavioral standards. Even the leaders looked out for themselves and failed to catch any vision for leadership. Paul had to correct immorality, idolatry and carnality. He wanted to receive an offering

God's Role in 2 Corinthians

God must have approved of Paul's defense of his leadership and his argument that he did not receive his power from man, but from the Lord. God gave Paul the strength and the language to articulate some of the most difficult claims any leader will have to communicate. God furnishes Paul with the power to argue and defend himself; the power to correct laxity among the Corinthians; and the power to persuade the people to repent of their selfishness.

Leaders in 2 Corinthians

Paul, the Corinthian church leaders, Titus

Other People of Influence in 2 Corinthians

False apostles (teachers)

Lessons in Leadership

- When defending your leadership, check your motives; pure motives are essential.
- When followers doubt your authority and direction, always go back to the basics.
- If you lead with a clear conscience, you can defend your actions with deep passion.

for the church in Jerusalem, but he realized he first had to offer a theological discourse on the benefits of giving.

Second Corinthians is the most personal of all of Paul's church letters. Like an outraged father, he pleads, rebukes, and weeps with the people, sharing his heart and vision for their future.

- There is no success without sacrifice.
- It is easier to follow a leader who acknowledges he/she is following God.
- When all else fails, remember the original vision God gave you.
- Leaders should invest in people like a farmer plants seed—with expectancy.

LEADERSHIP HIGHLIGHTS IN 2 CORINTHIANS

Paul, an apostle of Christ Jesus by the will of God, and Timothy our brother,

To the church of God in Corinth, together with all his holy people throughout Achaia:

[2] Grace and peace to you from God our Father and the Lord Jesus Christ.

Praise to the God of All Comfort

[3] Praise be to the God and Father of our Lord Jesus Christ, the Father of compassion and the God of all comfort, [4] who comforts us in all our troubles, so that we can comfort those in any trouble with the comfort we ourselves receive from God. [5] For just as we share abundantly in the sufferings of Christ, so also our comfort abounds through Christ. [6] If we are distressed, it is for your comfort and salvation; if we are comforted, it is for your comfort, which produces in you patient endurance of the same sufferings we suffer. [7] And our hope for you is firm, because we know that just as you share in our sufferings, so also you share in our comfort.

[8] We do not want you to be uninformed, brothers and sisters, [a] about the troubles we experienced in the province of Asia. We were under great pressure, far beyond our ability to endure, so that we despaired of life itself. [9] Indeed, we felt we had received the sentence of death. But this happened that we might not rely on ourselves but on God, who raises the dead. [10] He has delivered us from such a deadly peril, and he will deliver us again. On him we have set our hope that he will continue to deliver us, [11] as you help us by your prayers. Then many will give thanks on our behalf for the gracious favor granted us in answer to the prayers of many.

Paul's Change of Plans

[12] Now this is our boast: Our conscience testifies that we have conducted ourselves in the world, and especially in our relations with you, with integrity[b] and godly sincerity. We have done so, relying not on worldly wisdom but on God's grace. [13] For we do not write you anything you cannot read or understand. And I hope that, [14] as you have understood us in part, you will come to understand fully that you can boast of us just as we will boast of you in the day of the Lord Jesus.

[15] Because I was confident of this, I wanted to visit you first so that you might benefit twice. [16] I wanted to visit you on my way to Macedonia and to come back to you from Macedonia, and then to have you send me on my way to Judea. [17] Was I fickle when I intended to do this?

---

[a] 8 The Greek word for *brothers and sisters* (*adelphoi*) refers here to believers, both men and women, as part of God's family; also in 8:1; 13:11.　　[b] 12 Many manuscripts *holiness*

The Law of Empowerment:
Our Comfort Allows Us to Comfort Others

2 Corinthians 1:2–4

God promises to comfort us in our troubles, then asks us to share that comfort with others. Remember, we can't give away what we don't possess. We are to pass on what God gives to us. We don't receive as an end in itself, but as a means to an end. We are to empower others with the power God gives us. Leaders who empower others offer these gifts:

1. *Accountability*—They help others keep their commitments to God.

2. *Affirmation*—They speak words of support and encouragement.

3. *Assessment*—They evaluate others' progress, offering an objective perspective.

4. *Advice*—They offer words of wise counsel and direction.

5. *Admonishment*—They lend words of caution, rebuke, or correction.

6. *Assets*—They give tangible resources to help their people reach their goals.

7. *Acceptance*—They provide unconditional love, regardless of the recipients' identity.

8. *Application*—They help others find places to apply and practice what they learn.

Communication: When Plans Change, Leaders Overcommunicate

2 Corinthians 1:12–17

When Paul had to change his travel plans, some of the Corinthians used it against him, accusing him of indecision and weakness. This would not have bothered Paul, except that it affected people's view of his message; they considered it fickle, as well. To explain his position, Paul openly communicated with the church, explaining his change of plans.

Paul knew leaders must be flexible, not fickle. Yet when plans change, people need more communication. Leaders maintain integrity when they overcommunicate and calmly assure their people that they are still making progress.

Or do I make my plans in a worldly manner so that in the same breath I say both "Yes, yes" and "No, no"?

[18]But as surely as God is faithful, our message to you is not "Yes" and "No." [19]For the Son of God, Jesus Christ, who was preached among you by us — by me and Silas[a] and Timothy — was not "Yes" and "No," but in him it has always been "Yes." [20]For no matter how many promises God has made, they are "Yes" in Christ. And so through him the "Amen" is spoken by us to the glory of God. [21]Now it is God who makes both us and you stand firm in Christ. He anointed us, [22]set his seal of ownership on us, and put his Spirit in our hearts as a deposit, guaranteeing what is to come.

[23]I call God as my witness — and I stake my life on it — that it was in order to spare you that I did not return to Corinth. [24]Not that we lord it over your faith, but we work with you for your joy, because it is by faith you stand firm. [1]So I made up my mind that I would not make another painful visit to you. [2]For if I grieve you, who is left to make me glad but you whom I have grieved? [3]I wrote as I did, so that when I came I would not be distressed by those who should have made me rejoice. I had confidence in all of you, that you would all share my joy. [4]For I wrote you out of great distress and anguish of heart and with many tears, not to grieve you but to let you know the depth of my love for you.

Forgiveness for the Offender

[5]If anyone has caused grief, he has not so much grieved me as he has grieved all of you to some extent — not to put it too severely. [6]The punishment inflicted on him by the majority is sufficient. [7]Now instead, you ought to forgive and comfort him, so that he will not be overwhelmed by excessive sorrow. [8]I urge you, therefore, to reaffirm your love for him. [9]Another reason I wrote you was to see if you would stand the test and be obedient in everything. [10]Anyone you forgive, I also forgive. And what I have

---

[a] 19 Greek *Silvanus*, a variant of *Silas*

Follow-Up and Confrontation

2 Corinthians 2:6–8

It has been said that 2 Corinthians was written with a pen dipped in tears. In chapter 2, Paul has to follow up on the confrontation he first brought up in 1 Corinthians 5. The church had responded well to his advice, and now Paul encourages them to reaffirm their love for their erring brother (2Co 2:6–8).

Paul knew that follow-up has to take place after confrontation. The organization and leadership must live up to their values. When the confrontation is done well, the follow-up can be especially warm and personal. Compare the differences between Paul's two letters to the Corinthians:

1 Corinthians	**2 Corinthians**
1. Very objective content and character	1. Very subjective character
2. Practical in its approach	2. Personal in its approach
3. Deliberate church instruction	3. Personal life and experience
4. Gives insight into the church ministry	4. Gives insight into Paul's life

forgiven — if there was anything to forgive — I have forgiven in the sight of Christ for your sake, [11]in order that Satan might not outwit us. For we are not unaware of his schemes.

Ministers of the New Covenant

[12]Now when I went to Troas to preach the gospel of Christ and found that the Lord had opened a door for me, [13]I still had no peace of mind, because I did not find my brother Titus there. So I said goodbye to them and went on to Macedonia.

[14]But thanks be to God, who always leads us as captives in Christ's triumphal procession and uses us to spread the aroma of the knowledge of him everywhere. [15]For we are to God the pleasing aroma of Christ among those who are being saved and those who are perishing. [16]To the one we are an aroma that brings death; to the other, an aroma that brings life. And who is equal to such a task? [17]Unlike so many, we do not peddle the word of God for profit. On the contrary, in Christ we speak before God with sincerity, as those sent from God.

3 Are we beginning to commend ourselves again? Or do we need, like some people, letters of recommendation to you or from you? [2]You yourselves are our letter, written on our hearts, known and read by everyone. [3]You show that you are a letter from Christ, the result of our ministry, written not with ink but with the Spirit of the living God, not on tablets of stone but on tablets of human hearts.

[4]Such confidence we have through Christ before God. [5]Not that we are competent in ourselves to claim anything for ourselves, but our competence comes from God. [6]He has made us competent as ministers of a new covenant — not of the letter but of the Spirit; for the letter kills, but the Spirit gives life.

The Greater Glory of the New Covenant

[7]Now if the ministry that brought death, which was engraved in letters on stone, came with glory, so that the Israelites could not look steadily at the face of Moses because of its glory, transitory though it was, [8]will not the ministry of the Spirit be even more glorious? [9]If the ministry that brought condemnation was glorious, how much more glorious is the ministry that brings righteousness! [10]For what was glorious has no glory now in comparison with the surpassing glory. [11]And if what was transitory came with glory, how much greater is the glory of that which lasts!

[12]Therefore, since we have such a hope, we

PAUL — Faithful Follow-Up Friend

PROFILE in leadership

2 Corinthians 3:1–6

Sometimes godly leaders have to humble themselves and seek reconciliation with those they lead—even when they've done nothing wrong.

Following the apostle Paul's first letter to the Corinthian Christians, there arose a faction within the church who took offense at his words. These "false teachers" swayed the people against Paul, questioning his credentials and authority.

Paul sent his coworker, Titus, to deal with the situation. After the Corinthians' hearts turned back to Paul, he wrote them again to follow up and remind them of his love for them. Though his beloved friends had at one point turned against him—questioning his character, his speech, his conduct, even his appearance—the apostle gently and humbly reminded them of his God-ordained credentials and of his motivation for speaking to them.

Paul tells the Corinthians that he found no joy in correcting them, that his heart broke as he wrote strong words of correction (2Co 2:4). He tells them that he wrote nothing that wasn't motivated out of love and concern for their relationship with Christ.

Through this second letter, Paul provides a terrific example for all leaders. He demonstrates the kind of humility that motivates leaders to go out of their way to say that whatever they felt compelled to do—no matter how harsh their actions may have seemed—came from a heart of love and compassion.

Humility: It Is Easier to Follow a Leader Who Follows God

2 Corinthians 3:4–6

Paul could have taken great pride in his accomplishments, but instead threw away his trophies (Php 3:4–7). He explained that his competency came from God, not himself. Let your people notice your achievements on their own. They will follow a leader more easily who humbly follows God.

are very bold. ¹³We are not like Moses, who would put a veil over his face to prevent the Israelites from seeing the end of what was passing away. ¹⁴But their minds were made dull, for to this day the same veil remains when the old covenant is read. It has not been removed, because only in Christ is it taken away. ¹⁵Even to this day when Moses is read, a veil covers their hearts. ¹⁶But whenever anyone turns to the Lord, the veil is taken away. ¹⁷Now the Lord is the Spirit, and where the Spirit of the Lord is, there is freedom. ¹⁸And we all, who with unveiled faces contemplate[a] the Lord's glory, are being transformed into his image with ever-increasing glory, which comes from the Lord, who is the Spirit.

Present Weakness and Resurrection Life

4 Therefore, since through God's mercy we have this ministry, we do not lose heart. ²Rather, we have renounced secret and shameful ways; we do not use deception, nor do we distort the word of God. On the contrary, by setting forth the truth plainly we commend ourselves to everyone's conscience in the sight of God. ³And even if our gospel is veiled, it is veiled to those who are perishing. ⁴The god of this age has blinded the minds of unbelievers, so that they cannot see the light of the gospel that displays the glory of Christ, who is the image of God. ⁵For what we preach is not ourselves, but Jesus Christ as Lord, and ourselves as your servants for Jesus' sake. ⁶For God, who said, "Let light shine out of darkness,"[b] made his light shine in our hearts to give us the light of the knowledge of God's glory displayed in the face of Christ.

⁷But we have this treasure in jars of clay to show that this all-surpassing power is from God and not from us. ⁸We are hard pressed on every side, but not crushed; perplexed, but not in despair; ⁹persecuted, but not abandoned; struck down, but not destroyed. ¹⁰We always carry around in our body the death of Jesus, so that the life of Jesus may also be revealed in our body. ¹¹For we who are alive are always being given over to death for Jesus' sake, so that his life may also be revealed in our mortal body. ¹²So then, death is at work in us, but life is at work in you.

a 18 Or reflect   *b 6 Gen. 1:3*

The Law of Sacrifice: Leaders Surrender to Stick with the Mission

2 Corinthians 4:7–12

Paul regularly had to give up to go up. In fact, Paul said, "I face death every day" (1Co 15:31). The apostle made all kinds of sacrifices so he could stick with his God-given mission. Each time Paul gave up something, he moved forward and honored God.

Note how Paul gave up to go up:

What Paul Gave Up:

1. Health and comfort. He felt hard-pressed (v. 8).
2. Calm and certainty. He felt perplexed (v. 8).
3. Peace and acceptance. He was persecuted (v. 9).
4. Strength and poise. He was struck down (v. 9).
5. His own life. He bore the marks of Christ's death (v. 10).

How Paul Went Up:

1. He was never crushed (v. 8).
2. He never fell into despair (v. 8).
3. He was never forsaken (v. 9).
4. He was never destroyed (v. 9).
5. He received the life of Jesus (v. 10).

[13]It is written: "I believed; therefore I have spoken."[a] Since we have that same spirit of[b] faith, we also believe and therefore speak, [14]because we know that the one who raised the Lord Jesus from the dead will also raise us with Jesus and present us with you to himself. [15]All this is for your benefit, so that the grace that is reaching more and more people may cause thanksgiving to overflow to the glory of God.

[16]Therefore we do not lose heart. Though outwardly we are wasting away, yet inwardly we are being renewed day by day. [17]For our light and momentary troubles are achieving for us an eternal glory that far outweighs them all. [18]So we fix our eyes not on what is seen, but on what is unseen, since what is seen is temporary, but what is unseen is eternal.

Awaiting the New Body

5 For we know that if the earthly tent we live in is destroyed, we have a building from God, an eternal house in heaven, not built by human hands. [2]Meanwhile we groan, longing to be clothed instead with our heavenly dwelling, [3]because when we are clothed, we will not be found naked. [4]For while we are in this tent, we groan and are burdened, because we do not wish to be unclothed but to be clothed instead with our heavenly dwelling, so that what is mortal may be swallowed up by life. [5]Now the one who has fashioned us for this very purpose is God, who has given us the Spirit as a deposit, guaranteeing what is to come.

[6]Therefore we are always confident and know that as long as we are at home in the body we are away from the Lord. [7]For we live by faith, not by

---

[a] 13 Psalm 116:10 (see Septuagint)   [b] 13 Or *Spirit-given*

Perspective: Leaders Paint the Big Picture for Others

2 Corinthians 4:16–18

Success has less to do with gifts than with perspective. Paul tells us: Never lose heart (2Co 4:16); progress isn't always visible (4:16); our struggles develop us (4:17); we must fix our eyes on the invisible (4:18); the importance of the eternal realm far exceeds the visible one (4:18).

Reward vs. Inheritance: What a Leader Can Expect from His Labor

2 Corinthians 5:10

Every spiritual leader needs to remember that we will all face the judgment seat of Christ. This event is not the Great White Throne judgment, mentioned in the book of Revelation, for that judgment concerns sin, and every Christian already has passed through that judgment based on Jesus' work on the cross. At the judgment seat of Christ, we will be rewarded or admonished for the labor we give after our conversion. Paul mentions the testing of our work (1Co 3:12–15; Eph 6:8). Note the difference between inheritance and rewards:

Inheritance	Reward
1. Based on Jesus' merits	1. Based on our service
2. Given freely by God's grace	2. Given in proportion to our work
3. The condition: being a son or daughter	3. The condition: being a laborer
4. Salvation based on birthright	4. Blessing based on obedience
5. We must have faith in Christ	5. We must be faithful to him
6. Secure	6. Pending

Faithful leaders can expect their inheritance to include both the gift of salvation and the blessing of a reward for their spiritual leadership. The Bible teaches that rewards in heaven will be handed out justly, but not equally. Our degree of faithfulness determines our heavenly reward and responsibility (Lk 19:11–26).

sight. [8]We are confident, I say, and would prefer to be away from the body and at home with the Lord. [9]So we make it our goal to please him, whether we are at home in the body or away from it. [10]For we must all appear before the judgment seat of Christ, so that each of us may receive what is due us for the things done while in the body, whether good or bad.

The Ministry of Reconciliation

[11]Since, then, we know what it is to fear the Lord, we try to persuade others. What we are is plain to God, and I hope it is also plain to your conscience. [12]We are not trying to commend ourselves to you again, but are giving you an opportunity to take pride in us, so that you can answer those who take pride in what is seen rather than in what is in the heart. [13]If we are "out of our mind," as some say, it is for God; if we are in our right mind, it is for you. [14]For Christ's love compels us, because we are convinced that one died for all, and therefore all died. [15]And he died for all, that those who live should no longer live for themselves but for him who died for them and was raised again.

[16]So from now on we regard no one from a worldly point of view. Though we once regarded Christ in this way, we do so no longer. [17]Therefore, if anyone is in Christ, the new creation has come:[a] The old has gone, the new is here! [18]All this is from God, who reconciled us to himself through Christ and gave us the ministry of reconciliation: [19]that God was reconciling the world to himself in Christ, not counting people's sins against them. And he has committed to us the message of reconciliation. [20]We are therefore Christ's ambassadors, as though God were making his appeal through us. We implore you on Christ's behalf: Be reconciled to God. [21]God made him who had no sin to be sin[b] for us, so that in him we might become the righteousness of God.

6 As God's co-workers we urge you not to receive God's grace in vain. [2]For he says,

"In the time of my favor I heard you,
    and in the day of salvation I helped you."[c]

I tell you, now is the time of God's favor, now is the day of salvation.

Paul's Hardships

[3]We put no stumbling block in anyone's path, so that our ministry will not be discredited. [4]Rather, as servants of God we commend ourselves in every way: in great endurance; in troubles, hardships and distresses; [5]in beatings, imprisonments and riots; in hard work, sleepless nights and hunger; [6]in purity, understanding, patience and kindness; in the Holy Spirit and in sincere love; [7]in truthful speech and in the power of God; with weapons of righteousness in the right hand and in the left; [8]through glory and dishonor, bad report and good report; genuine, yet regarded as impostors; [9]known, yet regarded as unknown; dying, and yet we live on; beaten, and yet not killed; [10]sorrowful, yet always rejoicing; poor, yet making many rich; having nothing, and yet possessing everything.

[11]We have spoken freely to you, Corinthians, and opened wide our hearts to you. [12]We are not withholding our affection from you, but you are withholding yours from us. [13]As a fair exchange — I speak as to my children — open wide your hearts also.

Warning Against Idolatry

[14]Do not be yoked together with unbelievers. For what do righteousness and wickedness have

---

[a] 17 Or *Christ, that person is a new creation.*   [b] 21 Or *be a sin offering*   [c] 2 Isaiah 49:8

Partnerships: They Make or Break the Leader

2 Corinthians 6:14–18

Healthy leaders often partner with others to reach their goals. In fact, we live in an age of partnerships, both in the corporate world and in the church. Paul reminds us that there is nothing more dangerous to a leader than an unhealthy or destructive partnership. Note several signs of a bad partnership:

1. The parties don't share the same values.

2. The parties don't agree on the goal.

3. One or both parties must compromise their convictions.

4. One party selfishly demands that the other surrender.

5. One party benefits and the other loses.

Good partnerships do not foster codependence or independence, but interdependence. Every party feels secure, is stretched, and enjoys synergy. The partnership multiplies the productivity of both parties.

in common? Or what fellowship can light have with darkness? [15]What harmony is there between Christ and Belial[a]? Or what does a believer have in common with an unbeliever? [16]What agreement is there between the temple of God and idols? For we are the temple of the living God. As God has said:

"I will live with them
  and walk among them,
and I will be their God,
  and they will be my people."[b]

[17]Therefore,

"Come out from them
  and be separate,
                    says the Lord.
Touch no unclean thing,
  and I will receive you."[c]

[18]And,

"I will be a Father to you,
  and you will be my sons and
    daughters,
        says the Lord Almighty."[d]

7 Therefore, since we have these promises, dear friends, let us purify ourselves from everything that contaminates body and spirit, perfecting holiness out of reverence for God.

Paul's Joy Over the Church's Repentance

[2]Make room for us in your hearts. We have wronged no one, we have corrupted no one, we have exploited no one. [3]I do not say this to condemn you; I have said before that you have such a place in our hearts that we would live or die with you. [4]I have spoken to you with great frankness; I take great pride in you. I am greatly encouraged; in all our troubles my joy knows no bounds.

[5]For when we came into Macedonia, we had no rest, but we were harassed at every turn—conflicts on the outside, fears within. [6]But God, who comforts the downcast, comforted us by the coming of Titus, [7]and not only by his coming but also by the comfort you had given him. He told us about your longing for me, your deep sorrow, your ardent concern for me, so that my joy was greater than ever.

[8]Even if I caused you sorrow by my letter, I do not regret it. Though I did regret it—I see that my letter hurt you, but only for a little while—[9]yet now I am happy, not because you were made sorry, but because your sorrow led you to repentance. For you became sorrowful as God intended and so were not harmed in any way by us.

---

[a] 15 Greek *Beliar*, a variant of *Belial*   [b] 16 Lev. 26:12; Jer. 32:38; Ezek. 37:27   [c] 17 Isaiah 52:11; Ezek. 20:34,41
[d] 18 2 Samuel 7:14; 7:8

TITUS

Troubleshooter in Corinth
2 Corinthians 7:2–16

PROFILE in leadership

The Corinthian church had a big problem, and the apostle Paul had the right man to deal with it. Paul sent a young gentile by the name of Titus to visit the Corinthians. Titus was, in effect, the apostle's "troubleshooter."

When Titus arrived in Corinth, he found a church that had, by and large, rejected the teaching and authority of Paul. His previous letter to them had contained some honest, accurate, and hard words concerning divisions, pride and sexual immorality among them, and it didn't receive a warm welcome. Although Paul had written from a heart of love and concern, false teachers undermined his authority by portraying him as arrogant, unqualified to teach, and dishonest.

Young Titus traveled to Corinth, dealt with the problem, and returned to Paul with news that many of the Corinthian Christians had repented and accepted Paul's authority as their leader sent from God. The Bible doesn't describe exactly what Titus did to correct the situation in Corinth, but it is clear that he returned to Paul with good news.

The body of Christ needs leaders who have the patience and perceptivity to look into a troubled situation, discern the problem, then do what it takes to correct the difficulty. In short, the church needs "troubleshooters" in order to grow and maintain its spiritual health.

The Tough and Tender Leader

2 Corinthians 7:8–13

In his previous letter to the church, Paul played the role of the tough leader. He instigated conflict. In this letter, he speaks more from a personal viewpoint, more from his heart. He exudes tenderness.

In this passage, the apostle discusses how he caused the Corinthians sorrow, but distinguishes between good sorrow and bad sorrow. Every leader will find this distinction profitable to understand. Consider the differences:

Bad Sorrow	Good Sorrow
1. Pain goes on indefinitely	1. Pain is temporary
2. Example: Judas (Mt 27:3–5)	2. Example: Peter (Lk 22:54–62)
3. Leads to regret and death	3. Leads to repentance and life
4. Suffering based on selfishness	4. Suffering based on God's will

Leaders should never seek revenge or desire to hurt someone just to vindicate their action. The pain they bring should have the constructive purpose of repentance and recovery.

[10]Godly sorrow brings repentance that leads to salvation and leaves no regret, but worldly sorrow brings death. [11]See what this godly sorrow has produced in you: what earnestness, what eagerness to clear yourselves, what indignation, what alarm, what longing, what concern, what readiness to see justice done. At every point you have proved yourselves to be innocent in this matter. [12]So even though I wrote to you, it was neither on account of the one who did the wrong nor on account of the injured party, but rather that before God you could see for yourselves how devoted to us you are. [13]By all this we are encouraged.

In addition to our own encouragement, we were especially delighted to see how happy Titus was, because his spirit has been refreshed by all of you. [14]I had boasted to him about you, and you have not embarrassed me. But just as everything we said to you was true, so our boasting about you to Titus has proved to be true as well. [15]And his affection for you is all the greater when he remembers that you were all obedient, receiving him with fear and trembling. [16]I am glad I can have complete confidence in you.

The Collection for the Lord's People

8 And now, brothers and sisters, we want you to know about the grace that God has given the Macedonian churches. [2]In the midst of a very severe trial, their overflowing joy and their extreme poverty welled up in rich generosity. [3]For I testify that they gave as much as they were able, and even beyond their ability. Entirely on their own, [4]they urgently pleaded with us for the privilege of sharing in this service to the Lord's people. [5]And they exceeded our expectations: They gave themselves first of all to the Lord, and then by the will of God also to us. [6]So we urged Titus, just as he had earlier made a beginning, to bring also to completion this act of grace on your part. [7]But since you excel in everything—in faith, in speech, in knowledge, in complete earnestness and in the love we have kindled in you[a]—see that you also excel in this grace of giving.

[8]I am not commanding you, but I want to test the sincerity of your love by comparing it with

---

[a] 7 Some manuscripts *and in your love for us*

Generosity: Leaders Can't Love Without Giving

2 Corinthians 8:2–5

Paul encouraged generosity among the Corinthians by bragging on the poverty-stricken church in Macedonia, proving that liberality has nothing to do with feeling comfortable (2Co 8:2), having abundance (8:2), calculating what one can afford (8:3), or being coerced (8:4). Effective leaders are generous with themselves.

the earnestness of others. [9]For you know the grace of our Lord Jesus Christ, that though he was rich, yet for your sake he became poor, so that you through his poverty might become rich.

[10]And here is my judgment about what is best for you in this matter. Last year you were the first not only to give but also to have the desire to do so. [11]Now finish the work, so that your eager willingness to do it may be matched by your completion of it, according to your means. [12]For if the willingness is there, the gift is acceptable according to what one has, not according to what one does not have.

[13]Our desire is not that others might be relieved while you are hard pressed, but that there might be equality. [14]At the present time your plenty will supply what they need, so that in turn their plenty will supply what you need. The goal is equality, [15]as it is written: "The one who gathered much did not have too much, and the one who gathered little did not have too little."[a]

Titus Sent to Receive the Collection

[16]Thanks be to God, who put into the heart of Titus the same concern I have for you. [17]For Titus not only welcomed our appeal, but he is coming to you with much enthusiasm and on his own initiative. [18]And we are sending along with him the brother who is praised by all the churches for his service to the gospel. [19]What is more, he was chosen by the churches to accompany us as we carry the offering, which we administer in order to honor the Lord himself and to show our eagerness to help. [20]We want to avoid any criticism of the way we administer this liberal gift. [21]For we are taking pains to do what is right, not only in the eyes of the Lord but also in the eyes of man.

[22]In addition, we are sending with them our brother who has often proved to us in many ways that he is zealous, and now even more so because of his great confidence in you. [23]As for Titus, he is my partner and co-worker among you; as for our brothers, they are representatives of the churches and an honor to Christ. [24]Therefore show these men the proof of your love and the reason for our pride in you, so that the churches can see it.

9 There is no need for me to write to you about this service to the Lord's people. [2]For I know your eagerness to help, and I have been boasting about it to the Macedonians, telling them that since last year you in Achaia were ready to give; and your enthusiasm has stirred most of them to action. [3]But I am sending the broth-

ers in order that our boasting about you in this matter should not prove hollow, but that you may be ready, as I said you would be. [4]For if any Macedonians come with me and find you unprepared, we — not to say anything about you — would be ashamed of having been so confident. [5]So I thought it necessary to urge the brothers to visit you in advance and finish the arrangements for the generous gift you had promised. Then it will be ready as a generous gift, not as one grudgingly given.

Generosity Encouraged

[6]Remember this: Whoever sows sparingly will also reap sparingly, and whoever sows generously will also reap generously. [7]Each of you should give what you have decided in your heart to give, not reluctantly or under compulsion, for God loves a cheerful giver. [8]And God is able to bless you abundantly, so that in all things at all times, having all that you need, you will abound in every good work. [9]As it is written:

"They have freely scattered their gifts to the poor;
    their righteousness endures forever."[b]

[10]Now he who supplies seed to the sower and bread for food will also supply and increase your store of seed and will enlarge the harvest of your righteousness. [11]You will be enriched in every way so that you can be generous on every occasion, and through us your generosity will result in thanksgiving to God.

[12]This service that you perform is not only supplying the needs of the Lord's people but is also overflowing in many expressions of thanks to God. [13]Because of the service by which you have proved yourselves, others will praise God for the obedience that accompanies your confession of the gospel of Christ, and for your generosity in sharing with them and with everyone else. [14]And in their prayers for you their hearts will go out to you, because of the surpassing grace God has given you. [15]Thanks be to God for his indescribable gift!

Paul's Defense of His Ministry

10 By the humility and gentleness of Christ, I appeal to you — I, Paul, who am "timid" when face to face with you, but "bold" toward you when away! [2]I beg you that when I come I may not have to be as bold as I expect to be toward some people who think that we live by the

---

[a] 15 Exodus 16:18   [b] 9 Psalm 112:9

Stewardship: Leaders Invest Resources Like Farmers Sow Seed

2 Corinthians 9:6–11

Paul uses dozens of metaphors throughout this book. In this passage, he compares stewardship to farming. In trying to encourage the Corinthian church to give generously to their brothers and sisters in Jerusalem, he instructs the church to view its resources as a farmer views sowing seed. A good farmer liberally sows seed, trying to ensure a good fall harvest. The more he sows, the more he reaps. You can't harvest if you haven't planted.

Some leaders, like the Corinthians, find it hard to invest resources because they seem so deficient—feeling their commodities are about to run out. Good leaders see the same resources as sufficient seed to be sown—knowing the harvest will come and more will be created. We must guard life against poverty; we should give our life because it is plentiful. Consider the differences:

Deficiency Perspective	Sufficiency Perspective
1. Defense	1. Offense
2. Maintain	2. Create
3. Escape loss	3. Pursue vision
4. Gifts contained	4. Gifts released
5. Reactive	5. Proactive
6. Guard and protect	6. Risk and seize opportunity
7. Stagnation	7. Multiplication
8. Paralyzed: Hold on!	8. Dynamic: Let go!
9. Narrow and closed	9. Wide and open
10. Thinks win/lose	10. Thinks win/win

standards of this world. ³For though we live in the world, we do not wage war as the world does. ⁴The weapons we fight with are not the weapons of the world. On the contrary, they have divine power to demolish strongholds. ⁵We demolish arguments and every pretension that sets itself up against the knowledge of God, and we take captive every thought to make it obedient to Christ. ⁶And we will be ready to punish every act of disobedience, once your obedience is complete.

⁷You are judging by appearances.*a* If anyone is confident that they belong to Christ, they should consider again that we belong to Christ just as much as they do. ⁸So even if I boast somewhat freely about the authority the Lord gave us for building you up rather than tearing you down, I will not be ashamed of it. ⁹I do not want to seem to be trying to frighten you with my letters. ¹⁰For some say, "His letters are weighty and forceful, but in person he is unimpressive and his speaking amounts to nothing." ¹¹Such people should realize that what we are in our letters when we are absent, we will be in our actions when we are present.

¹²We do not dare to classify or compare ourselves with some who commend themselves. When they measure themselves by themselves and compare themselves with themselves, they are not wise. ¹³We, however, will not boast beyond proper limits, but will confine our boasting to the sphere of service God himself has assigned to us, a sphere that also includes you. ¹⁴We are not going too far in our boasting, as would be the case if we had not come to you, for we did get as far as you with the gospel of Christ. ¹⁵Neither do we go beyond our limits by boasting of work done by others. Our hope is that, as your faith continues to grow, our sphere of activity among you will greatly expand, ¹⁶so that we can preach the gospel in the regions beyond you. For we do not want to boast about work already done in someone else's territory. ¹⁷But, "Let the one who boasts boast in the Lord."*b* ¹⁸For it is not the one who commends himself who is approved, but the one whom the Lord commends.

a 7 Or Look at the obvious facts   b 17 Jer. 9:24

Paul and the False Apostles

11 I hope you will put up with me in a little foolishness. Yes, please put up with me! ²I am jealous for you with a godly jealousy. I promised you to one husband, to Christ, so that I might present you as a pure virgin to him. ³But I am afraid that just as Eve was deceived by the serpent's cunning, your minds may somehow be led astray from your sincere and pure devotion to Christ. ⁴For if someone comes to you and preaches a Jesus other than the Jesus we preached, or if you receive a different spirit from the Spirit you received, or a different gospel from the one you accepted, you put up with it easily enough.

⁵I do not think I am in the least inferior to those "super-apostles."*a* ⁶I may indeed be untrained as a speaker, but I do have knowledge. We have made this perfectly clear to you in every way. ⁷Was it a sin for me to lower myself in order to elevate you by preaching the gospel of God to you free of charge? ⁸I robbed other churches by receiving support from them so as to serve you. ⁹And when I was with you and needed something, I was not a burden to anyone, for the brothers who came from Macedonia supplied what I needed. I have kept myself from being a burden to you in any way, and will continue to do so. ¹⁰As surely as the truth of Christ is in me, nobody in the regions of Achaia will stop this boasting of mine. ¹¹Why? Because I do not love you? God knows I do!

¹²And I will keep on doing what I am doing in order to cut the ground from under those who want an opportunity to be considered equal with us in the things they boast about. ¹³For such people are false apostles, deceitful workers, masquerading as apostles of Christ. ¹⁴And no wonder, for Satan himself masquerades as an angel of light. ¹⁵It is not surprising, then, if his servants also masquerade as servants of righteousness. Their end will be what their actions deserve.

Paul Boasts About His Sufferings

¹⁶I repeat: Let no one take me for a fool. But if you do, then tolerate me just as you would a fool, so that I may do a little boasting. ¹⁷In this self-

---

a 5 Or to the most eminent apostles

The Law of Solid Ground: Paul Answers His Critics

2 Corinthians 10:1—11:33

Paul felt embarrassed to defend his ministry and leadership, but he believed he had to do so. He had lost his credibility in the eyes of many Corinthians, and good leaders know that is the one thing they must not lose. When leaders surrender their credibility, they lose the right to lead.

Still, the price of leadership is criticism. Aristotle said, "Criticism is something you can avoid easily—by saying nothing, doing nothing, and being nothing." Paul handled his criticism by reviewing his track record and reminding the people of his commitment to them. Paul attacked the problem head-on. Sometimes this is right, while at other times it's best to wait. Ponder the following list of ten ways to handle criticism successfully:

1. Understand the difference between constructive and destructive criticism.

2. Don't take yourself too seriously.

3. Look beyond the criticism and see the critic. Do *you* constantly criticize?

4. Watch your own attitude toward the critic.

5. Recognize that good people (even Jesus!) get criticized.

6. Stay in shape—physically, emotionally and spiritually.

7. Don't just see the critic; see the crowd: Are many criticizing you?

8. Don't get defensive. Wait for a time to prove them wrong.

9. Try to learn a principle. Thank the critic for what you learn.

10. Concentrate on your mission; change your mistake.

confident boasting I am not talking as the Lord would, but as a fool. [18]Since many are boasting in the way the world does, I too will boast. [19]You gladly put up with fools since you are so wise! [20]In fact, you even put up with anyone who enslaves you or exploits you or takes advantage of you or puts on airs or slaps you in the face. [21]To my shame I admit that we were too weak for that!

Whatever anyone else dares to boast about — I am speaking as a fool — I also dare to boast about. [22]Are they Hebrews? So am I. Are they Israelites? So am I. Are they Abraham's descendants? So am I. [23]Are they servants of Christ? (I am out of my mind to talk like this.) I am more. I have worked much harder, been in prison more frequently, been flogged more severely, and been exposed to death again and again. [24]Five times I received from the Jews the forty lashes minus one. [25]Three times I was beaten with rods, once I was pelted with stones, three times I was shipwrecked, I spent a night and a day in the open sea, [26]I have been constantly on the move. I have been in danger from rivers, in danger from bandits, in danger from my fellow Jews, in danger from Gentiles; in danger in the city, in danger in the country, in danger at sea; and in danger from false believers. [27]I have labored and toiled and have often gone without sleep; I have known hunger and thirst and have often gone without food; I have been cold and naked. [28]Besides everything else, I face daily the pressure of my concern for all the churches. [29]Who is weak, and I do not feel weak? Who is led into sin, and I do not inwardly burn?

[30]If I must boast, I will boast of the things that show my weakness. [31]The God and Father of the Lord Jesus, who is to be praised forever, knows that I am not lying. [32]In Damascus the governor under King Aretas had the city of the Damascenes guarded in order to arrest me. [33]But I was lowered in a basket from a window in the wall and slipped through his hands.

Paul's Vision and His Thorn

12 I must go on boasting. Although there is nothing to be gained, I will go on to visions and revelations from the Lord. [2]I know a man in Christ who fourteen years ago was caught up to the third heaven. Whether it was in the body or out of the body I do not know — God knows. [3]And I know that this man — whether in the body or apart from the body I do not know, but God knows — [4]was caught up to paradise and heard inexpressible things, things that no

one is permitted to tell. [5]I will boast about a man like that, but I will not boast about myself, except about my weaknesses. [6]Even if I should choose to boast, I would not be a fool, because I would be speaking the truth. But I refrain, so no one will think more of me than is warranted by what I do or say, [7]or because of these surpassingly great revelations. Therefore, in order to keep me from becoming conceited, I was given a thorn in my flesh, a messenger of Satan, to torment me. [8]Three times I pleaded with the Lord to take it away from me. [9]But he said to me, "My grace is sufficient for you, for my power is made perfect in weakness." Therefore I will boast all the more gladly about my weaknesses, so that Christ's power may rest on me. [10]That is why, for Christ's sake, I delight in weaknesses, in insults, in hardships, in persecutions, in difficulties. For when I am weak, then I am strong.

Paul's Concern for the Corinthians

[11]I have made a fool of myself, but you drove me to it. I ought to have been commended by you, for I am not in the least inferior to the "super-apostles,"[a] even though I am nothing. [12]I persevered in demonstrating among you the marks of a true apostle, including signs, wonders and miracles. [13]How were you inferior to the other churches, except that I was never a burden to you? Forgive me this wrong!

[14]Now I am ready to visit you for the third time, and I will not be a burden to you, because what I want is not your possessions but you. After all, children should not have to save up for their parents, but parents for their children. [15]So I will very gladly spend for you everything I have and expend myself as well. If I love you

---

[a] 11 Or *the most eminent apostles*

Vision: Paul's Vision and Thorn

2 Corinthians 12:7–9

Paul linked an extraordinary vision with an exasperating thorn. God gave Paul a motivating vista of heaven, but also some opposition to keep him humble. God gave him the grace and power to overcome the thorn, but didn't take it away. Visions make leaders passionate; thorns keep them authentic.

The Law of Intuition: Paul Relished His Weaknesses

2 Corinthians 12:7–10

Instead of getting angry at his thorn and the way it slowed him down, Paul relished how weak it made him. Why? It kept him in close dependence on the power of God (2Co 12:10).

Paul understood that the weaker he was, the stronger God became within him. When there is less of you as *a* leader, there is more of God as *the* Leader. Only a wise leader can understand this paradox.

Paul practiced the Law of Intuition. What did Paul's leadership intuition enable him to understand? He recognized that . . .

1. The opposition was not from God (v. 7).
2. He must seek God's answer to this problem (v. 8).
3. God's answer was grace (v. 9).
4. Grace is perfected in his imperfections (v. 9).
5. He should boast about his weaknesses, not brag on his strength (v. 9).
6. The tougher his problems, the greater the grace (v. 10).

more, will you love me less? [16]Be that as it may, I have not been a burden to you. Yet, crafty fellow that I am, I caught you by trickery! [17]Did I exploit you through any of the men I sent to you? [18]I urged Titus to go to you and I sent our brother with him. Titus did not exploit you, did he? Did we not walk in the same footsteps by the same Spirit?

[19]Have you been thinking all along that we have been defending ourselves to you? We have been speaking in the sight of God as those in Christ; and everything we do, dear friends, is for your strengthening. [20]For I am afraid that when I come I may not find you as I want you to be, and you may not find me as you want me to be. I fear that there may be discord, jealousy, fits of rage, selfish ambition, slander, gossip, ar-

rogance and disorder. [21]I am afraid that when I come again my God will humble me before you, and I will be grieved over many who have sinned earlier and have not repented of the impurity, sexual sin and debauchery in which they have indulged.

Final Warnings

13 This will be my third visit to you. "Every matter must be established by the testimony of two or three witnesses."[a] [2]I already gave you a warning when I was with you the second time. I now repeat it while absent: On my return I will not spare those who sinned earlier or any of the others, [3]since you are demanding proof that Christ is speaking through me. He is not weak in dealing with you, but is powerful among you. [4]For to be sure, he was crucified in weakness, yet he lives by God's power. Likewise, we are weak in him, yet by God's power we will live with him in our dealing with you.

[5]Examine yourselves to see whether you are in the faith; test yourselves. Do you not realize that Christ Jesus is in you—unless, of course, you fail the test? [6]And I trust that you will discover that we have not failed the test. [7]Now we pray to God that you will not do anything wrong—not so that people will see that we have stood the test but so that you will do what is right even though we may seem to have failed. [8]For we cannot do anything against the truth, but only for the truth. [9]We are glad whenever we are weak but you are strong; and our prayer is that you may be fully restored. [10]This is why I write these things when I am absent, that when I come I may not have to be harsh in my use of authority—the authority the Lord gave me for building you up, not for tearing you down.

Final Greetings

[11]Finally, brothers and sisters, rejoice! Strive for full restoration, encourage one another, be of one mind, live in peace. And the God of love and peace will be with you.

[12]Greet one another with a holy kiss. [13]All God's people here send their greetings.

[14]May the grace of the Lord Jesus Christ, and the love of God, and the fellowship of the Holy Spirit be with you all.

---

[a] 1 Deut. 19:15

INTRODUCTION TO
GALATIANS

How God Saves Mankind

O nly in the book of Galatians does Paul fail to affirm anything or anyone as he begins his letter. After a brief salutation, the apostle jumps right in and contends with the erring Galatian believers.

This letter contains the most emphatic statement of salvation apart from the law to be found in Scripture. It is the only letter in which Paul develops a lengthy allegory to explain how God saves mankind. It provides us with a tremendous case study of a leader who must lead an erring group of followers back to God's original plan and purpose.

First, it teaches us that leaders worth their salt will confront those who drift from the vision. A drifting team member dilutes the organization, the vision, the momentum and the resources. Effective leaders always seek to maintain focus on their organization's primary mission. Paul defends both his own leadership and the original mission he declared. He takes a stand. He determines to help the Galatians walk by faith.

Second, healthy leaders motivate rather than manipulate. Paul argues against the idea that people must work to earn their salvation. He wants the Galatians to live free. How much more mercenary it would have been to push them toward a "works theology!" Paul could have benefited from this as the leader who won them to Christ. Instead, he calls them to grace, where they cannot be manipulated by anyone. He has enough integrity to keep a clear conscience and to build trust with others.

Third, we learn that leaders communicate best when they speak the truth in love. Paul addresses these hard issues out of his love for the Galatians. He will not compromise his message, but neither does he burn any

God's Role in Galatians

God speaks through Paul and calls the Galatians back to the original gospel. Like the words of an Old Testament prophet, Paul's words cut deep with truth at the very point of his readers' need. People naturally tend to think they must earn God's approval. Something inside of us feels drawn to achieve. We like to merit what we possess, like a trophy.

But God knows the downside of that empty theology. First, no one is good enough to merit heaven. Second, our own labor and leadership grows stronger when we cannot earn it, because grace, not guilt, is our motivation; love, not law, drives us to act. Leaders who lead in an environment of grace always obtain superior results.

Leaders in Galatians
Paul, Abraham, Sarah, the false teachers

Other People of Influence in Galatians
The members of the Galatian church, Hagar, Ishmael, Isaac

Lessons in Leadership
- Integrity builds trust and trust builds relationships.
- Leaders know what they'll stand for and won't stand for.
- Effective leaders aren't afraid to confront when necessary.
- Spiritual leaders lead from the inside out.

relational bridges. No one can question his deep compassion for those he corrects. He never minces words, either in his admonition or his affirmation. As you read through this book, observe how Paul incarnates each of these lessons. Allow him to mentor you.

LEADERSHIP HIGHLIGHTS IN GALATIANS

1 Paul, an apostle — sent not from men nor by a man, but by Jesus Christ and God the Father, who raised him from the dead — [2]and all the brothers and sisters[a] with me,

To the churches in Galatia:

[3]Grace and peace to you from God our Father and the Lord Jesus Christ, [4]who gave himself for our sins to rescue us from the present evil age, according to the will of our God and Father, [5]to whom be glory for ever and ever. Amen.

No Other Gospel

[6]I am astonished that you are so quickly deserting the one who called you to live in the grace of Christ and are turning to a different gospel — [7]which is really no gospel at all. Evidently some people are throwing you into confusion and are trying to pervert the gospel of Christ. [8]But even if we or an angel from heaven should preach a gospel other than the one we preached to you, let them be under God's curse! [9]As we have already said, so now I say again: If anybody is preaching to you a gospel other than what you accepted, let them be under God's curse!

[10]Am I now trying to win the approval of human beings, or of God? Or am I trying to please people? If I were still trying to please people, I would not be a servant of Christ.

The Law of Influence: Paul Exercises Emotional Authority

Galatians 1:6–10

Paul challenges the direction of the Galatian church, accusing it of embracing a different gospel. The apostle risks his leadership by exercising his emotional authority. This is the acid test of the Law of Influence. A leader discovers his or her level of influence when he or she must confront an erring group's direction.

Paul Called by God

[11]I want you to know, brothers and sisters, that the gospel I preached is not of human origin. [12]I did not receive it from any man, nor was I taught it; rather, I received it by revelation from Jesus Christ.

[13]For you have heard of my previous way of life in Judaism, how intensely I persecuted the church of God and tried to destroy it. [14]I was advancing in Judaism beyond many of my own age among my people and was extremely zealous for the traditions of my fathers. [15]But when God, who set me apart from my mother's womb and called me by his grace, was pleased [16]to reveal his Son in me so that I might preach him among the Gentiles, my immediate response was not to consult any human being. [17]I did not go up to Jerusalem to see those who were apostles before I was, but I went into Arabia. Later I returned to Damascus.

[18]Then after three years, I went up to Jerusalem to get acquainted with Cephas[b] and stayed with him fifteen days. [19]I saw none of the other apostles — only James, the Lord's brother. [20]I assure you before God that what I am writing you is no lie.

[21]Then I went to Syria and Cilicia. [22]I was personally unknown to the churches of Judea that are in Christ. [23]They only heard the report: "The man who formerly persecuted us is now preaching the faith he once tried to destroy." [24]And they praised God because of me.

Paul Accepted by the Apostles

2 Then after fourteen years, I went up again to Jerusalem, this time with Barnabas. I took Titus along also. [2]I went in response to a revelation and, meeting privately with those esteemed as leaders, I presented to them the gospel that I preach among the Gentiles. I wanted to be sure I was not running and had not been running my race in vain. [3]Yet not even Titus, who was with me, was compelled to be circumcised, even though he was a Greek. [4]This matter arose because some false believers had infiltrated our ranks to spy on the freedom we have in Christ Jesus and to make us slaves. [5]We did not give in to them for a moment, so that the truth of the gospel might be preserved for you.

[6]As for those who were held in high esteem — whatever they were makes no difference to me; God does not show favoritism — they added nothing to my message. [7]On the contrary, they recognized that I had been entrusted with the task of preaching the gospel to the uncircumcised,[c] just as Peter had been to the circumcised.[d] [8]For God, who was at work in Peter as an apostle to the circumcised, was also at work

---

[a] 2 The Greek word for *brothers and sisters* (*adelphoi*) refers here to believers, both men and women, as part of God's family; also in verse 11; and in 3:15; 4:12, 28, 31; 5:11, 13; 6:1, 18.
[b] 18 That is, Peter   [c] 7 That is, Gentiles   [d] 7 That is, Jews; also in verses 8 and 9

in me as an apostle to the Gentiles. [9]James, Cephas[a] and John, those esteemed as pillars, gave me and Barnabas the right hand of fellowship when they recognized the grace given to me. They agreed that we should go to the Gentiles, and they to the circumcised. [10]All they asked was that we should continue to remember the poor, the very thing I had been eager to do all along.

Paul Opposes Cephas

[11]When Cephas came to Antioch, I opposed him to his face, because he stood condemned. [12]For before certain men came from James, he used to eat with the Gentiles. But when they arrived, he began to draw back and separate himself from the Gentiles because he was afraid of those who belonged to the circumcision group. [13]The other Jews joined him in his hypocrisy, so that by their hypocrisy even Barnabas was led astray.

[14]When I saw that they were not acting in line with the truth of the gospel, I said to Cephas in front of them all, "You are a Jew, yet you live like a Gentile and not like a Jew. How is it, then, that you force Gentiles to follow Jewish customs?

[15]"We who are Jews by birth and not sinful Gentiles [16]know that a person is not justified by the works of the law, but by faith in Jesus Christ. So we, too, have put our faith in Christ Jesus that we may be justified by faith in[b] Christ and not by the works of the law, because by the works of the law no one will be justified.

[17]"But if, in seeking to be justified in Christ, we Jews find ourselves also among the sinners, doesn't that mean that Christ promotes sin? Absolutely not! [18]If I rebuild what I destroyed, then I really would be a lawbreaker.

[19]"For through the law I died to the law so that I might live for God. [20]I have been crucified with Christ and I no longer live, but Christ lives in me. The life I now live in the body, I live by faith in the Son of God, who loved me and gave himself for me. [21]I do not set aside the grace of God, for if righteousness could be gained through the law, Christ died for nothing!"[c]

Faith or Works of the Law

3 You foolish Galatians! Who has bewitched you? Before your very eyes Jesus Christ was clearly portrayed as crucified. [2]I would like to learn just one thing from you: Did you receive the Spirit by the works of the law, or by believing what you heard? [3]Are you so foolish? After beginning by means of the Spirit, are you now trying to finish by means of the flesh?[d] [4]Have you experienced[e] so much in vain — if it really was in vain? [5]So again I ask, does God give you his Spirit and work miracles among you by the works of the law, or by your believing what you heard? [6]So also Abraham "believed God, and it was credited to him as righteousness."[f]

[7]Understand, then, that those who have faith are children of Abraham. [8]Scripture foresaw that God would justify the Gentiles by faith, and announced the gospel in advance to Abraham: "All nations will be blessed through you."[g] [9]So those who rely on faith are blessed along with Abraham, the man of faith.

[10]For all who rely on the works of the law are under a curse, as it is written: "Cursed is everyone who does not continue to do everything

---

The Law of Solid Ground: How Leaders Gain Trust

Galatians 2:1–10

It seems Paul constantly had to defend his leadership with some churches. He felt compelled to proclaim his trustworthiness with the churches in both Corinth and Galatia. He earned their trust by . . .

1. Investing his time in learning from God (v. 1).
2. Associating with a trusted leader (v. 1).
3. Submitting to respected leaders and sharing his journey (v. 2).
4. Asserting that even the leaders didn't correct his team (vv. 3, 6).
5. Standing up to those who opposed God's truth (vv. 4–5).
6. Putting no confidence in people's infallibility, but trusting in God (v. 6).
7. Affirming that even the leaders fully endorse him (vv. 7–9).
8. Cooperating with the present leaders and honoring their requests (v. 10).

---

[a] 9 That is, Peter; also in verses 11 and 14   [b] 16 Or but through the faithfulness of . . . justified on the basis of the faithfulness of   [c] 21 Some interpreters end the quotation after verse 14.   [d] 3 In contexts like this, the Greek word for flesh (sarx) refers to the sinful state of human beings, often presented as a power in opposition to the Spirit.   [e] 4 Or suffered   [f] 6 Gen. 15:6   [g] 8 Gen. 12:3; 18:18; 22:18

Confrontation: Paul Exhibits Integrity with Peter

Galatians 2:11–21

Paul's integrity drove him to stand up to Peter, his fellow leader, in front of several Jewish and Gentile believers. He criticized Peter's hypocrisy and demanded that all Christian leaders remain consistent, regardless of the company they keep.

Paul teaches us how to critique someone. Consider his checklist:

1. *Check your motive.* Your goal should be to help, not humiliate.
2. *Make sure the issue is worthy of criticism.* Does it really matter?
3. *Be specific.* Don't drop hints, but clearly name the problem.
4. *Don't undermine the person's self-confidence or identity.* Make it obvious that you value the person.
5. *Don't compare people.* Use realistic standards to measure conduct.
6. *Be creative or don't criticize.* Find ways to reach a solution.
7. *Don't attack the person.* Critique the problem, not the person.
8. *Do not postpone needed criticism.* If the issue is big, act now.
9. *Look at yourself looking at others.* Take the log out of your own eye.
10. *End criticism with encouragement.* Finish on a positive note.

---

written in the Book of the Law."[a] [11]Clearly no one who relies on the law is justified before God, because "the righteous will live by faith."[b] [12]The law is not based on faith; on the contrary, it says, "The person who does these things will live by them."[c] [13]Christ redeemed us from the curse of the law by becoming a curse for us, for it is written: "Cursed is everyone who is hung on a pole."[d] [14]He redeemed us in order that the blessing given to Abraham might come to the Gentiles through Christ Jesus, so that by faith we might receive the promise of the Spirit.

The Law and the Promise

[15]Brothers and sisters, let me take an example from everyday life. Just as no one can set aside or add to a human covenant that has been duly established, so it is in this case. [16]The promises were spoken to Abraham and to his seed. Scripture does not say "and to seeds," meaning many people, but "and to your seed,"[e] meaning one person, who is Christ. [17]What I mean is this: The law, introduced 430 years later, does not set aside the covenant previously established by God and thus do away with the promise. [18]For if the inheritance depends on the law, then it no longer depends on the promise; but God in his grace gave it to Abraham through a promise. [19]Why, then, was the law given at all? It was

added because of transgressions until the Seed to whom the promise referred had come. The law was given through angels and entrusted to a mediator. [20]A mediator, however, implies more than one party; but God is one.

[21]Is the law, therefore, opposed to the promises of God? Absolutely not! For if a law had been given that could impart life, then righteousness would certainly have come by the law. [22]But Scripture has locked up everything under the control of sin, so that what was promised, being given through faith in Jesus Christ, might be given to those who believe.

Children of God

[23]Before the coming of this faith,[f] we were held in custody under the law, locked up until the faith that was to come would be revealed. [24]So the law was our guardian until Christ came that we might be justified by faith. [25]Now that this faith has come, we are no longer under a guardian.

[26]So in Christ Jesus you are all children of God through faith, [27]for all of you who were baptized into Christ have clothed yourselves with Christ. [28]There is neither Jew nor Gentile,

---

[a] 10 Deut. 27:26   [b] 11 Hab. 2:4   [c] 12 Lev. 18:5
[d] 13 Deut. 21:23   [e] 16 Gen. 12:7; 13:15; 24:7   [f] 22,23 Or
through the faithfulness of Jesus . . . [23]*Before faith came*

neither slave nor free, nor is there male and female, for you are all one in Christ Jesus. [29]If you belong to Christ, then you are Abraham's seed, and heirs according to the promise.

4 What I am saying is that as long as an heir is underage, he is no different from a slave, although he owns the whole estate. [2]The heir is subject to guardians and trustees until the time set by his father. [3]So also, when we were underage, we were in slavery under the elemental spiritual forces[a] of the world. [4]But when the set time had fully come, God sent his Son, born of a woman, born under the law, [5]to redeem those under the law, that we might receive adoption to sonship.[b] [6]Because you are his sons, God sent the Spirit of his Son into our hearts, the Spirit who calls out, "Abba,[c] Father." [7]So you are no longer a slave, but God's child; and since you are his child, God has made you also an heir.

Paul's Concern for the Galatians

[8]Formerly, when you did not know God, you were slaves to those who by nature are not gods.

[9]But now that you know God—or rather are known by God—how is it that you are turning back to those weak and miserable forces[d]? Do you wish to be enslaved by them all over again? [10]You are observing special days and months and seasons and years! [11]I fear for you, that somehow I have wasted my efforts on you.

[12]I plead with you, brothers and sisters, become like me, for I became like you. You did me no wrong. [13]As you know, it was because of an illness that I first preached the gospel to you, [14]and even though my illness was a trial to you, you did not treat me with contempt or scorn. Instead, you welcomed me as if I were an angel of God, as if I were Christ Jesus himself. [15]Where, then, is your blessing of me now? I can testify that, if you could have done so, you would have torn out your eyes and given them to me. [16]Have I now become your enemy by telling you the truth?

---

[a] 3 Or under the basic principles   [b] 5 The Greek word for adoption to sonship is a legal term referring to the full legal standing of an adopted male heir in Roman culture.   [c] 6 Aramaic for Father   [d] 9 Or principles

---

The Law of Connection: Paul Illustrates and Invites

Galatians 3:6—4:31

To make plain his teaching on grace, Paul uses stories and allegories. To drive home the truth, he uses an illustration of Abraham (Gal 3:6–29); an Old Testament scripture (3:10–14); an illustration of a son and a slave (4:1–7); and an allegory of Sarah and Hagar (4:21–31). Paul knew just how to connect with his audience. He painted familiar pictures to connect them with unfamiliar truths.

Paul also knew how to connect with a difficult group of people. Although they are living in error and it might feel tempting to focus on their foolishness (3:1), instead the apostle invites them into the experience of discovery.

Consider the "Ten Commandments of Handling Difficult People":

1. *Use the 101% Principle.* Find the 1 percent you agree on and give it 100 percent of your attention.

2. *Love people more than policies, but love truth more than people.*

3. *Give others the benefit of the doubt.*

4. *Learn to be flexible where you can.*

5. *Check your own attitude.*

6. *Don't overreact to conflict and disagreement.*

7. *Welcome the conflict.* Make it a learning experience.

8. *Provide an escape for the person in conflict.* Let them maintain their dignity.

9. *Take a risk.* Give people a second chance.

10. *Take the high road.* Be generous and believe the best about others.

[17]Those people are zealous to win you over, but for no good. What they want is to alienate you from us, so that you may have zeal for them. [18]It is fine to be zealous, provided the purpose is good, and to be so always, not just when I am with you. [19]My dear children, for whom I am again in the pains of childbirth until Christ is formed in you, [20]how I wish I could be with you now and change my tone, because I am perplexed about you!

Hagar and Sarah

[21]Tell me, you who want to be under the law, are you not aware of what the law says? [22]For it is written that Abraham had two sons, one by the slave woman and the other by the free woman. [23]His son by the slave woman was born according to the flesh, but his son by the free woman was born as the result of a divine promise.

[24]These things are being taken figuratively: The women represent two covenants. One covenant is from Mount Sinai and bears children who are to be slaves: This is Hagar. [25]Now Hagar stands for Mount Sinai in Arabia and corresponds to the present city of Jerusalem, because she is in slavery with her children. [26]But the Jerusalem that is above is free, and she is our mother. [27]For it is written:

"Be glad, barren woman,
    you who never bore a child;

shout for joy and cry aloud,
    you who were never in labor;
because more are the children of the desolate
        woman
    than of her who has a husband."[a]

[28]Now you, brothers and sisters, like Isaac, are children of promise. [29]At that time the son born according to the flesh persecuted the son born by the power of the Spirit. It is the same now. [30]But what does Scripture say? "Get rid of the slave woman and her son, for the slave woman's son will never share in the inheritance with the free woman's son."[b] [31]Therefore, brothers and sisters, we are not children of the slave woman, but of the free woman.

Freedom in Christ

5 It is for freedom that Christ has set us free. Stand firm, then, and do not let yourselves be burdened again by a yoke of slavery.

[2]Mark my words! I, Paul, tell you that if you let yourselves be circumcised, Christ will be of no value to you at all. [3]Again I declare to every man who lets himself be circumcised that he is obligated to obey the whole law. [4]You who are trying to be justified by the law have been alienated from Christ; you have fallen away from grace. [5]For through the Spirit we eagerly await

---

[a] 27 Isaiah 54:1   [b] 30 Gen. 21:10

PROFILE in leadership

PAUL — Navigator and Corrector
Galatians 4:8–20

The apostle Paul knew that, in his role as a leader of the Galatian Christians, God had called him to navigate the church. But more than that, Paul knew what to navigate his fellow Christians *toward*.

False teachers were trying to convince the Galatians to rely on their own works for salvation instead of the grace God had poured out on them in the person of Jesus. This Paul could not ignore.

Something within each of us tempts us to believe that we need to add something to God's perfect plan of salvation—to believe that, without our own efforts, we just aren't going to make it into the kingdom of heaven. This remains just as true today as it was in the days of the first-century church.

Paul attempted to correct the errant course the Galatians had chosen by pointing out that no one can add anything to what Jesus already has accomplished on the cross. No one can do a single thing to make themselves "more acceptable" to God.

To navigate means to make course corrections, to steer *toward* something. Godly leaders know they are to navigate their people to one thing only: the Lord Jesus Christ who died for their sins on the cross.

by faith the righteousness for which we hope. [6]For in Christ Jesus neither circumcision nor uncircumcision has any value. The only thing that counts is faith expressing itself through love.

[7]You were running a good race. Who cut in on you to keep you from obeying the truth? [8]That kind of persuasion does not come from the one who calls you. [9]"A little yeast works through the whole batch of dough." [10]I am confident in the Lord that you will take no other view. The one who is throwing you into confusion, whoever that may be, will have to pay the penalty. [11]Brothers and sisters, if I am still preaching circumcision, why am I still being persecuted? In that case the offense of the cross has been abolished. [12]As for those agitators, I wish they would go the whole way and emasculate themselves!

Life by the Spirit

[13]You, my brothers and sisters, were called to be free. But do not use your freedom to indulge the flesh[a]; rather, serve one another humbly in love. [14]For the entire law is fulfilled in keeping this one command: "Love your neighbor as yourself."[b] [15]If you bite and devour each other, watch out or you will be destroyed by each other.

The Law of Empowerment: Paul Gives Power to Act

Galatians 5:13–15

When leaders empower their followers, they give them the freedom to act—and trust that they will do so responsibly. Paul released the Galatians to become all God intended them to be. They felt free and empowered by God's Spirit and Paul's leadership. As a secure leader, Paul freely gave power to others.

[16]So I say, walk by the Spirit, and you will not gratify the desires of the flesh. [17]For the flesh desires what is contrary to the Spirit, and the Spirit what is contrary to the flesh. They are in conflict with each other, so that you are not to do whatever[c] you want. [18]But if you are led by the Spirit, you are not under the law.

[19]The acts of the flesh are obvious: sexual immorality, impurity and debauchery; [20]idolatry and witchcraft; hatred, discord, jealousy, fits of rage, selfish ambition, dissensions, factions [21]and envy; drunkenness, orgies, and the like. I warn you, as I did before, that those who live like this will not inherit the kingdom of God.

[22]But the fruit of the Spirit is love, joy, peace, forbearance, kindness, goodness, faithfulness, [23]gentleness and self-control. Against such things there is no law. [24]Those who belong to Christ Jesus have crucified the flesh with its passions and desires. [25]Since we live by the Spirit, let us keep in step with the Spirit. [26]Let us not become conceited, provoking and envying each other.

---

[a] 13 In contexts like this, the Greek word for *flesh* (*sarx*) refers to the sinful state of human beings, often presented as a power in opposition to the Spirit; also in verses 16, 17, 19 and 24; and in 6:8.   [b] 14 Lev. 19:18   [c] 17 Or *you do not do what*

Leadership Qualities and the Fruit of the Spirit

Galatians 5:22–23

Probably the most memorable verses in this book are those that list the "fruit of the Spirit." Fruit results from planted seeds. When seeds grow, they bear fruit. Fruit represents outward, visible behavior. Every leader should embrace this marvelous list of inward qualities. Evaluate yourself against them:

1. *Love:* Is my leadership motivated by love for people?
2. *Joy:* Do I exhibit an unshakable joy, regardless of circumstances?
3. *Peace:* Do people see my inward peace and take courage?
4. *Forbearance:* Do I wait patiently for results as I develop people or goals?
5. *Kindness:* Am I caring and understanding toward everyone I meet?
6. *Goodness:* Do I want the best for others and the organization?
7. *Faithfulness:* Have I kept my commitments to the mission?
8. *Gentleness:* Is my strength under control? Can I be both tough and tender?
9. *Self-Control:* Am I disciplined to make progress toward my goals?

Doing Good to All

6 Brothers and sisters, if someone is caught in a sin, you who live by the Spirit should restore that person gently. But watch yourselves, or you also may be tempted. ²Carry each other's burdens, and in this way you will fulfill the law of Christ. ³If anyone thinks they are something when they are not, they deceive themselves. ⁴Each one should test their own actions. Then they can take pride in themselves alone, without comparing themselves to someone else, ⁵for each one should carry their own load. ⁶Nevertheless, the one who receives instruction in the word should share all good things with their instructor.

Responsibility: If You Won't Carry the Ball, You Can't Lead the Team

Galatians 6:1–6

Responsibility must start at the top. Leaders are to restore those who've failed, guard against their own sin, help bear others' burdens, and stay humble (Gal 6:1–3). This attitude should then bleed down through the ranks (6:4–6). Shoulders that bear responsibility leave no room for chips.

---

⁷Do not be deceived: God cannot be mocked. A man reaps what he sows. ⁸Whoever sows to please their flesh, from the flesh will reap destruction; whoever sows to please the Spirit, from the Spirit will reap eternal life. ⁹Let us not become weary in doing good, for at the proper time we will reap a harvest if we do not give up. ¹⁰Therefore, as we have opportunity, let us do good to all people, especially to those who belong to the family of believers.

Not Circumcision but the New Creation

¹¹See what large letters I use as I write to you with my own hand!

¹²Those who want to impress people by means of the flesh are trying to compel you to be circumcised. The only reason they do this is to avoid being persecuted for the cross of Christ. ¹³Not even those who are circumcised keep the law, yet they want you to be circumcised that they may boast about your circumcision in the flesh. ¹⁴May I never boast except in the cross of our Lord Jesus Christ, through which[a] the world has been crucified to me, and I to the world. ¹⁵Neither circumcision nor uncircumcision means anything; what counts is the new creation. ¹⁶Peace and mercy to all who follow this rule — to[b] the Israel of God.

¹⁷From now on, let no one cause me trouble, for I bear on my body the marks of Jesus.

¹⁸The grace of our Lord Jesus Christ be with your spirit, brothers and sisters. Amen.

---

[a] 14 Or *whom*   [b] 16 Or *rule and to*

Accountability: Leaders Need Alarm Bells

Galatians 6:7–10

We can't pull a fast one on God. He sees all and cannot be deceived. He notices our shortcuts and also our efforts when we do well. To ensure that we live by this truth, seek others to hold you accountable and act as your "alarm bells." Invite others to ask you tough questions, such as the following:

1. Is my personal walk with God up-to-date?
2. Am I keeping my priorities straight?
3. Am I asking myself the hard questions?
4. Am I accountable to someone in authority?
5. Am I sensitive to what God is saying to the whole body of Christ?
6. Am I over-concerned with building my image?
7. Do I put more stock in "events" rather than "process"?
8. Am I a loner in my leadership and personal life?
9. Am I aware and honest about my weaknesses?
10. Is my calling constantly before me?

INTRODUCTION TO EPHESIANS

The Whole Panorama of God's Redemptive Work

Some consider this epistle to be the most profound work in the Bible. The apostle Paul wrote Ephesians while in prison. In it he covers the whole panorama of God's redemptive work—from before the foundation of the world to its consummation in the fullness of Christ. Clearly, Paul casts a huge vision for followers of Jesus.

Paul describes his vision in the first half of the letter, paving the way for application in the second half. Once someone catches Paul's vision, the only logical response is to "live a life worthy of the calling you have received" (4:1).

What can we learn about leadership from this grand work?

First, Ephesians classically illustrates a leader who first casts a vision for the big picture before he calls the people to act. Paul knew that his readers would better obey when they simply responded to a huge initiative from God.

Second, Paul uses the metaphor of a human body to help leaders and followers better understand the church. He calls Christ the "head," while he calls followers the "body." What a wonderful picture of leadership! Just as a "head" cannot accomplish anything apart from the hands, feet, eyes, ears, etc., so a leader cannot accomplish any goal without each part of the team contributing to the whole. In the same way that Jesus enables us to act on his vision for the world, so the leader enables the followers to act on the organizational vision.

Third, Paul recognizes the diversity of the body of Christ and calls for unity in the midst of variety. Good leaders always do this. There may be one goal or vision, but a variety of gifts must be tapped to accomplish it.

God's Role in Ephesians

Paul and God work hand in hand; both play a leadership role. God is the Head Coach who furnishes church members with a position of authority, then provides them with gifts and positions. Paul follows God's leadership as an assistant coach, equipping the people to use their gifts in service. He instructs the people to find their calling and pursue it. Finally, both God and Paul equip the reader to engage in battle. God provides the armor, Paul the instructions to use it.

Leaders in Ephesians

Paul, Timothy, the apostles, prophets, evangelists, pastor-teachers

Other People of Influence in Ephesians

Tychicus

Lessons in Leadership

- Leaders touch a heart before they ask for a hand.
- The primary role of the leader is to equip people to use their gifts.
- Authority must always accompany responsibility.
- Leaders raise the bar and call followers to a high standard.
- Leaders celebrate diversity while they work for unity.
- Leaders understand that belief precedes behavior.

Paul attempts to build a team out of disparate believers: pastors, teachers, apostles, prophets and evangelists. Any good coach wants every player to flourish. This can happen only when tasks match abilities. Players must find their correct positions.

Finally, Paul warns of hardship. He doesn't want to scare his readers, but to prepare them for battle. He soberly tells them what to expect in the coming spiritual warfare. This, too, is good leadership.

- A person's influence must flow from his or her identity.
- Leaders avoid living in denial, but define reality.

LEADERSHIP HIGHLIGHTS IN EPHESIANS

1 Paul, an apostle of Christ Jesus by the will of God,

To God's holy people in Ephesus,[a] the faithful in Christ Jesus:

[2]Grace and peace to you from God our Father and the Lord Jesus Christ.

Praise for Spiritual Blessings in Christ

[3]Praise be to the God and Father of our Lord Jesus Christ, who has blessed us in the heavenly realms with every spiritual blessing in Christ. [4]For he chose us in him before the creation of the world to be holy and blameless in his sight. In love [5]he[b] predestined us for adoption to sonship[c] through Jesus Christ, in accordance with his pleasure and will — [6]to the praise of his glorious grace, which he has freely given us in the One he loves. [7]In him we have redemption through his blood, the forgiveness of sins, in accordance with the riches of God's grace [8]that he lavished on us. With all wisdom and understanding, [9]he[d] made known to us the mystery of his will according to his good pleasure, which he purposed in Christ, [10]to be put into effect when the times reach their fulfillment — to bring unity to all things in heaven and on earth under Christ.

[11]In him we were also chosen,[e] having been predestined according to the plan of him who works out everything in conformity with the purpose of his will, [12]in order that we, who were the first to put our hope in Christ, might be for the praise of his glory. [13]And you also were included in Christ when you heard the message of truth, the gospel of your salvation. When you believed, you were marked in him with a seal, the promised Holy Spirit, [14]who is a deposit guaranteeing our inheritance until the redemption of those who are God's possession — to the praise of his glory.

Thanksgiving and Prayer

[15]For this reason, ever since I heard about your faith in the Lord Jesus and your love for all God's people, [16]I have not stopped giving thanks for you, remembering you in my prayers. [17]I keep asking that the God of our Lord Jesus Christ, the glorious Father, may give you the Spirit[f] of wisdom and revelation, so that you may know him better. [18]I pray that the eyes of your heart may be enlightened in order that you may know the hope to which he has called you, the riches of his glorious inheritance in his holy people, [19]and his incomparably great power for us who believe. That power is the same as the mighty strength [20]he exerted when he raised Christ from the dead and seated him at his right hand in the heavenly realms, [21]far above all rule and authority, power and dominion, and every name that is invoked, not only in the present age but also in the one to come. [22]And God placed all things under his feet and appointed him to be head over everything for the church, [23]which is his body, the fullness of him who fills everything in every way.

The Law of Empowerment: Influence Flows from Identity

Ephesians 1:15–23

Paul prays that God will reveal to his readers the riches of their inheritance (hope, calling, glory and power). Then he reminds them they are Christ's body. Power, influence and confidence all come from a strong sense of identity. Are you secure in your identity? Does your influence reflect this strength?

Made Alive in Christ

2 As for you, you were dead in your transgressions and sins, [2]in which you used to live when you followed the ways of this world and

---

The Law of Connection: Empowerment Precedes Imperative

Ephesians 1:1–14

Because Paul believes he needs to give before he asks, he reminds us of our choice position in Christ: chosen (Eph 1:4); predestined (1:5); accepted (1:6); redeemed (1:7); informed (1:9); heirs (1:11); and sealed (1:13). He declares what God has done for us before demanding we do anything for him.

---

[a] 1 Some early manuscripts do not have *in Ephesus.*
[b] 4,5 Or *sight in love.* [5]*He*   [c] 5 The Greek word for *adoption to sonship* is a legal term referring to the full legal standing of an adopted male heir in Roman culture.   [d] 8,9 Or *us with all wisdom and understanding.* [9]*And he*   [e] 11 Or *were made heirs*   [f] 17 Or *a spirit*

of the ruler of the kingdom of the air, the spirit who is now at work in those who are disobedient. ³All of us also lived among them at one time, gratifying the cravings of our flesh[a] and following its desires and thoughts. Like the rest, we were by nature deserving of wrath. ⁴But because of his great love for us, God, who is rich in mercy, ⁵made us alive with Christ even when we were dead in transgressions — it is by grace you have been saved. ⁶And God raised us up with Christ and seated us with him in the heavenly realms in Christ Jesus, ⁷in order that in the coming ages he might show the incomparable riches of his grace, expressed in his kindness to us in Christ Jesus. ⁸For it is by grace you have been saved, through faith — and this is not from yourselves, it is the gift of God — ⁹not by works, so that no one can boast. ¹⁰For we are God's handiwork, created in Christ Jesus to do good works, which God prepared in advance for us to do.

Jew and Gentile Reconciled Through Christ

¹¹Therefore, remember that formerly you who are Gentiles by birth and called "uncircumcised" by those who call themselves "the circumcision" (which is done in the body by human hands) — ¹²remember that at that time you were separate from Christ, excluded from citizenship in Israel and foreigners to the covenants of the promise, without hope and without God in the world. ¹³But now in Christ Jesus you who once were far away have been brought near by the blood of Christ.

¹⁴For he himself is our peace, who has made the two groups one and has destroyed the barrier, the dividing wall of hostility, ¹⁵by setting aside in his flesh the law with its commands and regulations. His purpose was to create in himself one new humanity out of the two, thus making peace, ¹⁶and in one body to reconcile both of them to God through the cross, by which he put to death their hostility. ¹⁷He came and preached peace to you who were far away and peace to those who were near. ¹⁸For through him we both have access to the Father by one Spirit.

¹⁹Consequently, you are no longer foreigners and strangers, but fellow citizens with God's people and also members of his household, ²⁰built on the foundation of the apostles and prophets, with Christ Jesus himself as the chief cornerstone. ²¹In him the whole building is joined together and rises to become a holy temple in the Lord. ²²And in him you too are being built together to become a dwelling in which God lives by his Spirit.

---

[a] 3 In contexts like this, the Greek word for *flesh* (*sarx*) refers to the sinful state of human beings, often presented as a power in opposition to the Spirit.

Communicating Vision:
Paul Remembers Who They Were and Are

Ephesians 2:1–10

Paul took time to reflect on our past failures and God's present redemption. He insists that God not only raised Jesus up and sat him in heavenly places above all authority (Eph 2:20–21), but he did the same for us (2:4–6). We must identify with Christ in his life, death, resurrection and *ascension*. We have been *raised* with Christ. No wonder Paul could lead with such boldness! He lived and led off of this paramount truth.

What must we do to experience the same kind of authority in Christ? Paul gives his answer:

1. *Renew your perspective* (Col 3:1–3).
   We must think like God thinks. We must see ourselves as he does and fix our minds on him. We must base our life on this position rather than our experience.

2. *Release your past* (Gal 2:20).
   We must let go of old patterns. We will never lead in an empowering way if we hold on to our old self, our old baggage, our old citizenship. We must die to the past.

3. *Remember your purpose* (Eph 1:3–12).
   We drift when we lose sight of why God left us on earth. Our goal is to participate in God's redemptive plan for the world. If we embrace purpose, we gain power.

Equipping: Paul Gives the Tools to Do the Job

Ephesians 2:8–22

Paul provides some tools for his readers to live in the way God intends for them to live. He informs them they are saved by grace (Eph 2:8–9) and created to do good works (2:10). Then he equips them for these good works with divine tools, explaining how they have been delivered from darkness and transformed into new persons (2:14–16) and a new building (2:19–22).

Paul labored hard to unleash the church and prepare its members for service. If we pursue the same goal, we must embrace the following assumptions:

1. Everyone wants to feel worthwhile.
2. Everyone needs and responds to encouragement.
3. People buy into the leader before they buy into the plan.
4. Most people don't know how to be successful.
5. People are naturally motivated.
6. Most people will move once they receive permission and equipping.

God's Marvelous Plan for the Gentiles

3 For this reason I, Paul, the prisoner of Christ Jesus for the sake of you Gentiles—

² Surely you have heard about the administration of God's grace that was given to me for you, ³ that is, the mystery made known to me by revelation, as I have already written briefly. ⁴ In reading this, then, you will be able to understand my insight into the mystery of Christ, ⁵ which was not made known to people in other generations as it has now been revealed by the Spirit to God's holy apostles and prophets. ⁶ This mystery is that through the gospel the Gentiles are heirs together with Israel, members together of one body, and sharers together in the promise in Christ Jesus.

⁷ I became a servant of this gospel by the gift of God's grace given me through the working of his power. ⁸ Although I am less than the least of all the Lord's people, this grace was given me: to preach to the Gentiles the boundless riches of Christ, ⁹ and to make plain to everyone the ad-

ministration of this mystery, which for ages past was kept hidden in God, who created all things. ¹⁰ His intent was that now, through the church, the manifold wisdom of God should be made known to the rulers and authorities in the heavenly realms, ¹¹ according to his eternal purpose that he accomplished in Christ Jesus our Lord. ¹² In him and through faith in him we may approach God with freedom and confidence. ¹³ I ask you, therefore, not to be discouraged because of my sufferings for you, which are your glory.

A Prayer for the Ephesians

¹⁴ For this reason I kneel before the Father, ¹⁵ from whom every family[a] in heaven and on earth derives its name. ¹⁶ I pray that out of his glorious riches he may strengthen you with power through his Spirit in your inner being, ¹⁷ so that Christ may dwell in your hearts through faith. And I pray that you, being rooted and established in love, ¹⁸ may have power, together with all the Lord's holy people, to grasp how wide and long and high and deep is the love of Christ, ¹⁹ and to know this love that surpasses knowledge—that you may be filled to the measure of all the fullness of God.

²⁰ Now to him who is able to do immeasurably more than all we ask or imagine, according to his power that is at work within us, ²¹ to him be glory in the church and in Christ Jesus throughout all generations, for ever and ever! Amen.

Unity and Maturity in the Body of Christ

4 As a prisoner for the Lord, then, I urge you to live a life worthy of the calling you have

---

[a] 15 The Greek for *family* (*patria*) is derived from the Greek for *father* (*pater*).

Passion: Paul Teaches Them to Take This Life and Love It

Ephesians 3:14–21

Paul prays passionately that his readers comprehend the love of God (Eph 3:14, 18), experience the love of Christ (3:19), and be filled with God (3:19). Then he declares God is able to do exceedingly, abundantly, above all we ask or think (3:20)! Passion is the first step to achievement.

received. ²Be completely humble and gentle; be patient, bearing with one another in love. ³Make every effort to keep the unity of the Spirit through the bond of peace. ⁴There is one body and one Spirit, just as you were called to one hope when you were called; ⁵one Lord, one faith, one baptism; ⁶one God and Father of all, who is over all and through all and in all.

PAUL AND TIMOTHY

PROFILE in leadership

A Model for Equipping
Ephesians 3:1–7

By themselves, not even the best accountants or financial advisers can create wealth for their clients. All they can do is give advice concerning the accumulation of financial reserves. The rest is up to the recipients of that advice.

The same is true for leaders who wish to see others access the riches of heaven. The lives and ministries of the apostle Paul and Timothy—the young leader of the church at Ephesus—demonstrate this principle.

On their own, neither Paul nor Timothy could equip the Ephesians to please God. But they knew how to direct their charges to the ultimate source of ultimate power: the Holy Spirit and the Word of God.

Paul exhorts the Ephesian Christians to take full advantage of all the resources and power God has made available to them. The apostle knows that all believers have at their disposal immeasurable wealth and power, infinite resources sufficient to equip every believer for the spiritual fight ahead.

Godly leaders have at their disposal the same kind of power Paul describes here. Leaders are responsible to direct other believers to the place where they can be enriched and equipped so they can serve God and do battle for the kingdom.

Team Building: Paul Builds Unity Amidst Diversity

Ephesians 4:1–8

The apostle Paul labored to foster unity amidst a diverse population—in other words, he worked at team building.

He reminds the Ephesians of the attitude of the individual players (Eph 4:1–3), then discusses the attitude of the corporate body (3:4–6). Paul insists there is one body, one Spirit, one hope, one Lord, one faith, one baptism and one God and Father. He says each player has been given some grace and some gifts. He calls the church a temple, a bride, a mystery, an army and a body.

Think of Paul as a coach, building his team. How do we build a diverse group into a unified team? Ask the following questions:

1. Am I building people, or building my kingdom and using people?
2. Do I care enough to confront people when it will make a difference?
3. Am I listening with more than my ears?
4. Am I asking the right questions to develop the right relationships?
5. What are the major strengths of each individual?
6. Have I placed a high priority on their jobs?
7. Have I shown the value they will receive from this work?
8. Are their goals compatible with mine?

⁷But to each one of us grace has been given as Christ apportioned it. ⁸This is why itᵃ says:

"When he ascended on high,
   he took many captives
   and gave gifts to his people."ᵇ

⁹(What does "he ascended" mean except that he also descended to the lower, earthly regionsᶜ? ¹⁰He who descended is the very one who ascended higher than all the heavens, in order to fill the whole universe.) ¹¹So Christ himself gave the apostles, the prophets, the evangelists, the pastors and teachers, ¹²to equip his people for works of service, so that the body of Christ may be built up ¹³until we all reach unity in the faith and in the knowledge of the Son of God and become mature, attaining to the whole measure of the fullness of Christ.

¹⁴Then we will no longer be infants, tossed back and forth by the waves, and blown here and there by every wind of teaching and by the cunning and craftiness of people in their deceitful scheming. ¹⁵Instead, speaking the truth in love, we will grow to become in every respect the mature body of him who is the head, that is, Christ. ¹⁶From him the whole body, joined and held together by every supporting ligament, grows and builds itself up in love, as each part does its work.

Instructions for Christian Living

¹⁷So I tell you this, and insist on it in the Lord, that you must no longer live as the Gentiles do, in the futility of their thinking. ¹⁸They are darkened in their understanding and separated from the life of God because of the ignorance that is in them due to the hardening of their hearts. ¹⁹Having lost all sensitivity, they have given themselves over to sensuality so as to indulge in every kind of impurity, and they are full of greed.

²⁰That, however, is not the way of life you learned ²¹when you heard about Christ and were

---

ᵃ 8 Or *God*   ᵇ 8 Psalm 68:18   ᶜ 9 Or *the depths of the earth*

Five Leadership Roles in the Church

Ephesians 4:11–16

God gave at least five types of leaders to the church: apostles, prophets, evangelists, pastors and teachers. They exist to complete the members' growth and to equip them to serve (Eph 4:12–16). Their roles vary:

1. *Apostle*: One sent forth to pioneer and establish new works and new leaders.

2. *Prophet*: One who speaks forth God's Word to inspire, correct, and motivate.

3. *Evangelist*: One who shares Christ with outsiders and trains others to do so.

4. *Pastor*: One who shepherds, guides, and guards God's people as they serve.

5. *Teacher*: One who trains God's people in the truth and teaches others to do so.

When the church fills these five offices, ordinary people get equipped for ministry. Ask yourself the following questions:

1. What eternally significant growth occurs in the lives of those I lead (vv. 11–13)?

2. Do our people understand that my role is to equip them to serve (v. 12)?

3. How are our followers serving and ministering (v. 12)?

4. Do our people know that involvement in service is essential to growth (v. 12)?

5. Do our people grow spiritually mature as a result of their ministry involvement (v. 13)?

6. Do our people's lifestyles reflect Christ's character (v. 13)?

7. What percentage of our people's faith and involvement is easily shaken (v. 14)?

8. Do our people build up one another (vv. 15–16)?

Equipping: The Leader's Job

Ephesians 4:12–16

Equipping is a tough job, much harder than shepherding. The leader is to equip others for ministry. Paul explains the goal for the shepherd (Eph 4:12) and the goal of the sheep (4:13), then describes the result (4:14–16).

If leaders wish to equip their people, they must give them certain gifts:

1. I must CARE for them (Communication, Affirmation, Recognition and Example).

2. I must work *on* their weaknesses, but work *out* their strengths.

3. I must give them myself (time, energy and focus).

4. I must give them ownership of the ministry.

5. I must become a resource person (atmosphere, training, support, tools).

6. I must make expectations clear.

7. I must eliminate unnecessary burdens.

8. I must catch them doing something good, then reward them.

taught in him in accordance with the truth that is in Jesus. [22]You were taught, with regard to your former way of life, to put off your old self, which is being corrupted by its deceitful desires; [23]to be made new in the attitude of your minds; [24]and to put on the new self, created to be like God in true righteousness and holiness.

[25]Therefore each of you must put off falsehood and speak truthfully to your neighbor, for we are all members of one body. [26]"In your anger do not sin"[a]: Do not let the sun go down while you are still angry, [27]and do not give the devil a foothold. [28]Anyone who has been stealing must steal no longer, but must work, doing something useful with their own hands, that they may have something to share with those in need.

[29]Do not let any unwholesome talk come out of your mouths, but only what is helpful for building others up according to their needs, that it may benefit those who listen. [30]And do not grieve the Holy Spirit of God, with whom you were sealed for the day of redemption. [31]Get rid of all bitterness, rage and anger, brawling and slander, along with every form of malice. [32]Be kind and compassionate to one another, forgiving each other, just as in Christ God forgave you.

5 [1]Follow God's example, therefore, as dearly loved children [2]and walk in the way of love, just as Christ loved us and gave himself up for us as a fragrant offering and sacrifice to God.

[3]But among you there must not be even a hint of sexual immorality, or of any kind of impuri-ty, or of greed, because these are improper for God's holy people. [4]Nor should there be obscenity, foolish talk or coarse joking, which are out of place, but rather thanksgiving. [5]For of this you can be sure: No immoral, impure or greedy person—such a person is an idolater—has any inheritance in the kingdom of Christ and of God.[b] [6]Let no one deceive you with empty words, for because of such things God's wrath comes on those who are disobedient. [7]Therefore do not be partners with them.

[8]For you were once darkness, but now you are light in the Lord. Live as children of light [9](for the fruit of the light consists in all goodness, righteousness and truth) [10]and find out what pleases the Lord. [11]Have nothing to do with the fruitless deeds of darkness, but rather expose them. [12]It is shameful even to mention what the disobedient do in secret. [13]But everything exposed by the light becomes visible—and everything that is illuminated becomes a light. [14]This is why it is said:

"Wake up, sleeper,
    rise from the dead,
    and Christ will shine on you."

[15]Be very careful, then, how you live—not as unwise but as wise, [16]making the most of every opportunity, because the days are evil. [17]Therefore

---

[a] 26 Psalm 4:4 (see Septuagint)   [b] 5 Or *kingdom of the Messiah and God*

The Law of Priorities: Redeem Your Time

Ephesians 5:15–17

Because activity is not necessarily accomplishment, Paul advises us to: analyze our lifestyles (Eph 5:15); utilize the present (5:16); and prioritize what is important (5:17). While every leader, every day, gets the same amount of time, not every leader gets the same results.

do not be foolish, but understand what the Lord's will is. [18]Do not get drunk on wine, which leads to debauchery. Instead, be filled with the Spirit, [19]speaking to one another with psalms, hymns, and songs from the Spirit. Sing and make music from your heart to the Lord, [20]always giving thanks to God the Father for everything, in the name of our Lord Jesus Christ.

Instructions for Christian Households

[21]Submit to one another out of reverence for Christ.

[22]Wives, submit yourselves to your own husbands as you do to the Lord. [23]For the husband is the head of the wife as Christ is the head of the church, his body, of which he is the Savior. [24]Now as the church submits to Christ, so also wives should submit to their husbands in everything.

[25]Husbands, love your wives, just as Christ loved the church and gave himself up for her [26]to make her holy, cleansing[a] her by the washing with water through the word, [27]and to present her to himself as a radiant church, without stain or wrinkle or any other blemish, but holy and blameless. [28]In this same way, husbands ought to love their wives as their own bodies. He who loves his wife loves himself. [29]After all, no one ever hated their own body, but they feed and care for their body, just as Christ does the church— [30]for we are members of his body. [31]"For this reason a man will leave his father and mother and be united to his wife, and the two will become one flesh."[b] [32]This is a profound mystery—but I am talking about Christ and the church. [33]However, each one of you also must love his wife as he loves himself, and the wife must respect her husband.

[a] 26 Or *having cleansed*   [b] 31 Gen. 2:24

Leadership in the Home

Ephesians 5:21–33

Contrary to what many teach, leadership in the home is not about power or control. Paul asks for mutual submission (Eph 5:21) and calls husbands to be Christ-figures (5:23–25). And how did Christ lead the church? He provided, taught, wept, healed, and died on a cross. Spiritual leadership means giving up yourself for someone else (5:25). It means assuming responsibility for the health and development of your relationships. Evaluate your home leadership in each of the following categories:

1. *Initiative*
   Do I give direction and take responsibility for my primary relationships?

2. *Intimacy*
   Do I experience intimacy with God and others through open conversation?

3. *Influence*
   Do I exercise biblical influence by encouraging and developing others?

4. *Integrity*
   Do I lead an honest life, unashamed of who I am when no one is looking?

5. *Identity*
   Am I secure in who I am in Christ? Or am I defensive?

6. *Inner Character*
   Do I exhibit the fruit of the Spirit in my life, including self-discipline?

6 Children, obey your parents in the Lord, for this is right. [2]"Honor your father and mother" — which is the first commandment with a promise — [3]"so that it may go well with you and that you may enjoy long life on the earth."[a]

[4]Fathers,[b] do not exasperate your children; instead, bring them up in the training and instruction of the Lord.

Work Ethic: You're Not Working for People

Ephesians 6:5–9

The principles Paul taught to owners and slaves apply today to employees and employers. He twice states the important principle: We are not to be people pleasers (Eph 6:6). We aren't to work while others watch, then slack off when alone. We are to render service as though we are working for God, who watches at all times (6:7). Not only does God watch, but he rewards anything good we do (6:8).

People may forget how fast you did your last job, but they will remember how well you did it. Ultimately, we all work for ourselves and for God.

[5]Slaves, obey your earthly masters with respect and fear, and with sincerity of heart, just as you would obey Christ. [6]Obey them not only to win their favor when their eye is on you, but as slaves of Christ, doing the will of God from your heart. [7]Serve wholeheartedly, as if you were serving the Lord, not people, [8]because you know that the Lord will reward each one for whatever good they do, whether they are slave or free.

[9]And masters, treat your slaves in the same way. Do not threaten them, since you know that he who is both their Master and yours is in heaven, and there is no favoritism with him.

The Armor of God

[10]Finally, be strong in the Lord and in his mighty power. [11]Put on the full armor of God, so that you can take your stand against the devil's schemes. [12]For our struggle is not against flesh and blood, but against the rulers, against the authorities, against the powers of this dark world and against the spiritual forces of evil in the heavenly realms. [13]Therefore put on the full armor of God, so that when the day of evil comes, you may be able to stand your ground, and after you have done everything, to stand. [14]Stand firm then, with the belt of truth buckled around your waist, with the breastplate of

[a] 3 Deut. 5:16   [b] 4 Or *Parents*

The Law of Intuition: Paul Understood How to Defeat the Enemy

Ephesians 6:10–20

Like any good leader, Paul issues a warning at the end of his letter about the tough times his people will face. They are up against Satan himself (Eph 6:12), an enemy who will do everything to stop their progress.

Instead of moping about the situation, however, Paul lays out a specific plan for his Ephesian friends. They are not to approach this fight in their own strength, but remember that only God can defeat the enemy (6:10). As a Warrior, God fills a role his people desperately need. He serves as their Protector, Defender, Deliverer, Provider and Guide. God gives his army every supply needed to win.

Paul then instructs his readers to put on the whole armor of God, in order to stand and prevail (6:11–17). Serving as an officer under God, Paul issues the orders for the troops. When leaders practice the Law of Intuition, they provide their people with . . .

1. A strategy to win (vv. 11–12).

2. Knowledge of the opposition (v. 12).

3. The resources they need (v. 13).

4. A plan for how to use them (vv. 14–17).

5. Detailed communication (vv. 14–20).

righteousness in place, [15]and with your feet fitted with the readiness that comes from the gospel of peace. [16]In addition to all this, take up the shield of faith, with which you can extinguish all the flaming arrows of the evil one. [17]Take the helmet of salvation and the sword of the Spirit, which is the word of God.

[18]And pray in the Spirit on all occasions with all kinds of prayers and requests. With this in mind, be alert and always keep on praying for all the Lord's people. [19]Pray also for me, that whenever I speak, words may be given me so that I will fearlessly make known the mystery of the gospel, [20]for which I am an ambassador in chains. Pray that I may declare it fearlessly, as I should.

Final Greetings

[21]Tychicus, the dear brother and faithful servant in the Lord, will tell you everything, so that you also may know how I am and what I am doing. [22]I am sending him to you for this very purpose, that you may know how we are, and that he may encourage you.

[23]Peace to the brothers and sisters,[a] and love with faith from God the Father and the Lord Jesus Christ. [24]Grace to all who love our Lord Jesus Christ with an undying love.[b]

---

[a] 23 The Greek word for brothers and sisters (adelphoi) refers here to believers, both men and women, as part of God's family.
[b] 24 Or Grace and immortality to all who love our Lord Jesus Christ.

INTRODUCTION TO
PHILIPPIANS

For the Progress of the Gospel

This letter proves that even while the apostle Paul sat in a foul Roman prison, he never lost his passion, his sense of mission, his sense of direction, or his command of the situation. While Paul remained an inmate of Rome, he couldn't plant new churches as he felt called to do. Instead, he sat in chains, attached to a Praetorian guard, awaiting a trial that he thought could end his life (1:21). Yet even in the midst of all of this, he never abandoned his role of leadership.

In chapter one, he speaks of his unchanging mission. He remains on track, even in prison. He insists that his circumstances have actually turned out for the progress of the gospel. No matter where he ends up, Paul uses his location as a platform to accomplish the mission.

The apostle also models for us an incredible attitude toward adversity. He mentions that he can't choose between life or death; to him, both seem positive options. Finally, he decides he will continue to live, knowing he can be more useful to the cause while alive.

In chapter two, he discusses the servant's heart of a leader, illustrating with the humility Christ displayed in coming to earth. Jesus didn't insist on the prerogatives of deity, but instead emptied himself and assumed the position of a man, taking the form of a bondservant, becoming mortal and dying—even a terrible kind of death: crucifixion. Paul claims that all effective leaders must live such a selfless life.

In chapter three, Paul discusses priorities, goal setting and perseverance. He reminds the reader of his trophies. Then he discards them, treating them like trash compared to the priority of knowing Christ and fulfilling his priorities. He speaks of the thing he's set his mind to

God's Role in Philippians

God's heart shows up vividly in this book. God can be seen in people who, although they find themselves in positions of adversity, nevertheless display attitudes of conquest, joy, peace and ministry. This is the supernatural leader, empowered by God to live out his values and vision in a fallen world.

God is the source of Paul's joy, his peace, his conquering spirit and his heart for ministry, even when he is an inmate and in need of someone to minister to him. God enables us to remain leaders who are "on mission" no matter where we find ourselves.

Leaders in Philippians
Paul, Epaphroditus, Timothy, the Philippian church elders

Other People of Influence in Philippians
Euodia, Syntyche

Lessons in Leadership
- Leaders either surrender to a cause or they surrender to their circumstances.
- Only secure leaders will stoop and stretch.
- A leader's attitude at the beginning of a task will affect its outcome more than anything else.

do, forgetting what lies behind him and looking forward to what lies ahead. He persists, pressing on toward the goal until he has obtained it.

In his final chapter, Paul concludes with words of rejoicing. He urges his readers to maintain tough minds, fixing on what is right and profitable. Discipline, contentment and focus are all key. Paul thanks the members of the Philippian church for their partnership and affirms his love for them—a fitting close to a warm, personal exhortation from a model leader.

- Leaders can do anything, but they can't do everything.
- One cannot be a great leader without being a great servant.

LEADERSHIP HIGHLIGHTS IN PHILIPPIANS

1 Paul and Timothy, servants of Christ Jesus,

To all God's holy people in Christ Jesus at Philippi, together with the overseers and deacons[a]:

[2]Grace and peace to you from God our Father and the Lord Jesus Christ.

Thanksgiving and Prayer

[3]I thank my God every time I remember you. [4]In all my prayers for all of you, I always pray with joy [5]because of your partnership in the gospel from the first day until now, [6]being confident of this, that he who began a good work in you will carry it on to completion until the day of Christ Jesus.

[7]It is right for me to feel this way about all of you, since I have you in my heart and, whether I am in chains or defending and confirming the gospel, all of you share in God's grace with me. [8]God can testify how I long for all of you with the affection of Christ Jesus.

[9]And this is my prayer: that your love may abound more and more in knowledge and depth of insight, [10]so that you may be able to discern what is best and may be pure and blameless for the day of Christ, [11]filled with the fruit of righteousness that comes through Jesus Christ — to the glory and praise of God.

Encouragement: Leaders Connect When They Encourage

Philippians 1:3–11

Paul never issues some worn-out, generic brand of encouragement. His words speak to specific needs, express specific love for particular people, and communicate a specific hope for their future. Encouragement ought to be given sincerely, personally, specifically, publicly, and frequently.

Paul's Chains Advance the Gospel

[12]Now I want you to know, brothers and sisters,[b] that what has happened to me has actually served to advance the gospel. [13]As a result, it has become clear throughout the whole palace guard[c] and to everyone else that I am in chains for Christ. [14]And because of my chains, most of the brothers and sisters have become confident in the Lord and dare all the more to proclaim the gospel without fear.

[15]It is true that some preach Christ out of envy and rivalry, but others out of goodwill. [16]The latter do so out of love, knowing that I am put here for the defense of the gospel. [17]The former preach Christ out of selfish ambition, not sincerely, supposing that they can stir up trouble for me while I am in chains. [18]But what does it matter? The important thing is that in every way, whether from false motives or true, Christ is preached. And because of this I rejoice.

Yes, and I will continue to rejoice, [19]for I know that through your prayers and God's provision of the Spirit of Jesus Christ what has happened

[a] 1 The word *deacons* refers here to Christians designated to serve with the overseers/elders of the church in a variety of ways; similarly in Romans 16:1 and 1 Tim. 3:8,12.   [b] 12 The Greek word for *brothers and sisters* (*adelphoi*) refers here to believers, both men and women, as part of God's family; also in verse 14; and in 3:1, 13, 17; 4:1, 8, 21.   [c] 13 Or *whole palace*

Positive Attitude: Paul's Attitude Determined His Altitude

Philippians 1:12–18

A personal sense of purpose works in two ways. First, we work on it. Then, it works on us.

Once Paul had determined his life mission, that purpose daily improved his attitude. In prisons, shipwrecks, beatings, through trials and debates, Paul kept on smiling because of his strong sense of purpose. He understood that leaders can either surrender to their circumstances, or they can surrender to a cause that is so great, their circumstances won't matter.

When we surrender to our circumstances, we have good days and bad days. We are at the mercy of what happens to us. When we surrender to a cause or purpose, we have good days wherever we go; the purpose never dies. Paul's attitude helped his purpose go forward, then his purpose helped his attitude go forward! His attitude helped him conclude that it didn't matter what happened to him or others—so long as the mission continued.

Purpose: Paul Stayed on Mission, Even in Prison

Philippians 1:12–18

Paul might have been forgiven had he chosen to take a little sabbatical as he sat in prison, awaiting his trial. Yet he used even this opportunity to advance the gospel (Php 1:12).

Paul was a leader who never drifted from his mission. He determined to leave his mark wherever he went. George Washington Carver wrote, "No individual has any right to come into the world and go out of it without leaving behind him distinct and legitimate reasons for having passed through it."

How did Paul's sense of purpose keep him in the battle as he sat in prison? What did he learn behind bars? Consider the following:

1. A purpose will motivate you.
2. A purpose will keep your priorities straight.
3. A purpose will develop your potential.
4. A purpose will give you power to live in the present.
5. A purpose will help you evaluate your progress.

to me will turn out for my deliverance.ᵃ ²⁰I eagerly expect and hope that I will in no way be ashamed, but will have sufficient courage so that now as always Christ will be exalted in my body, whether by life or by death. ²¹For to me, to live is Christ and to die is gain. ²²If I am to go on living in the body, this will mean fruitful labor for me. Yet what shall I choose? I do not know! ²³I am torn between the two: I desire to depart and be with Christ, which is better by far; ²⁴but it is more necessary for you that I remain in the body. ²⁵Convinced of this, I know that I will remain, and I will continue with all of you for your progress and joy in the faith, ²⁶so that through my being with you again your boasting in Christ Jesus will abound on account of me.

Life Worthy of the Gospel

²⁷Whatever happens, conduct yourselves in a manner worthy of the gospel of Christ. Then, whether I come and see you or only hear about you in my absence, I will know that you stand firm in the one Spirit,ᵇ striving together as one for the faith of the gospel ²⁸without being frightened in any way by those who oppose you. This is a sign to them that they will be destroyed, but that you will be saved — and that by God. ²⁹For it has been granted to you on behalf of Christ not only to believe in him, but also to suffer for him, ³⁰since you are going through the same struggle you saw I had, and now hear that I still have.

Imitating Christ's Humility

2 Therefore if you have any encouragement from being united with Christ, if any comfort from his love, if any common sharing in the Spirit, if any tenderness and compassion, ²then make my joy complete by being like-minded, having the same love, being one in spirit and of one mind. ³Do nothing out of selfish ambition or vain conceit. Rather, in humility value others above yourselves, ⁴not looking to your own

---

ᵃ 19 Or *vindication*; or *salvation*   ᵇ 27 Or *in one spirit*

The Law of Sacrifice: Jesus' Six Steps of Servanthood

Philippians 2:2–11

Paul used Jesus as the ultimate example of servant leadership. After urging his audience to humble themselves and live selflessly (Php 2:2–4), he reminds them of Christ's incarnation. Here the Ultimate Leader made the ultimate sacrifice. He left the glories of heaven and the highest position in heaven, not only to join his creation, but to take on the lowest form of the creation.

Jesus stepped through six levels as he moved downward toward us. In his leadership he practiced the Law of Sacrifice:

Level One: He gave up his divine form (v. 6).

Level Two: He emptied himself of any rights (v. 7).

Level Three: He became a man (v. 7).

Level Four: He became a servant (v. 7).

Level Five: He was obedient to the point of death (v. 8).

Level Six: He died a terrible kind of death (v. 8).

interests but each of you to the interests of the others.

⁵In your relationships with one another, have the same mindset as Christ Jesus:

⁶Who, being in very nature*ᵃ* God,
    did not consider equality with God
        something to be used to his own
        advantage;
⁷rather, he made himself nothing
    by taking the very nature*ᵇ* of a servant,
    being made in human likeness.
⁸And being found in appearance as a man,
    he humbled himself
    by becoming obedient to death —
        even death on a cross!

⁹Therefore God exalted him to the highest
        place
    and gave him the name that is above every
        name,
¹⁰that at the name of Jesus every knee should
        bow,
    in heaven and on earth and under the
        earth,

¹¹and every tongue acknowledge that Jesus
        Christ is Lord,
    to the glory of God the Father.

Do Everything Without Grumbling

¹²Therefore, my dear friends, as you have always obeyed — not only in my presence, but now much more in my absence — continue to work out your salvation with fear and trembling, ¹³for it is God who works in you to will and to act in order to fulfill his good purpose.

¹⁴Do everything without grumbling or arguing, ¹⁵so that you may become blameless and pure, "children of God without fault in a warped and crooked generation."*ᶜ* Then you will shine among them like stars in the sky ¹⁶as you hold firmly to the word of life. And then I will be able to boast on the day of Christ that I did not run or labor in vain. ¹⁷But even if I am being poured out like a drink offering on the sacrifice and service coming from your faith, I am glad and rejoice with all of you. ¹⁸So you too should be glad and rejoice with me.

ᵃ 6 Or in the form of   *ᵇ 7 Or the form*   *ᶜ 15 Deut. 32:5*

EPAPHRODITUS

A Leader Who Didn't Make a Name for Himself

Philippians 2:25–30

PROFILE in leadership

Several leaders in the Bible qualify as "nobodies." They never became famous, like Moses or David or Paul, but remained obscure, even though they played a vital role in the kingdom. Epaphroditus was such a man.

Epaphroditus is mentioned only in Philippians. No books were ever written about him, to him, or by him. We know of no statues or memorials erected to him. He was a "nobody" who became a "somebody" to Paul. He ran all the way from Philippi to Rome to join Paul in prison and minister to him. He also carried this letter back home to the Philippians. Note how Paul describes him:

1. *A People Lover*
   Paul calls him a minister. He feels distressed that the Philippians might worry about him when he became sick (vv. 25–26).
2. *A Risk Taker*
   Paul calls him a fellow soldier. He keeps on risking his life when most would have pampered themselves (vv. 25, 30).
3. *A Tireless Worker*
   Paul calls him a fellow worker. We know little about his illness, except that it was tied to his hard work (vv. 25, 27).
4. *A Servant-Leader*
   Paul calls him a messenger. Paul tells the church to give him a hero's welcome (vv. 25, 29). He both led and served as he became a spokesman for the church.

21 QUALITIES

FOCUS Letting Go of Nice Things That Don't Matter

Philippians 3:5–9

PAUL'S ABSOLUTE focus gave him an absolute willingness to let go of nice things that didn't matter. Note some items that he discarded:

1. *His heritage:* a Hebrew of the Hebrews (v. 5)
2. *His pure lineage:* from the tribe of Benjamin (v. 5)
3. *His former legalism:* a strict Pharisee (v. 5)
4. *His past zeal:* a persecutor of the church (v. 6)
5. *His self-righteousness:* a blameless life (v. 6)

Paul so narrowed his focus that he discarded not only the things he once counted as gain, but he counted everything as garbage for the sake of obtaining Christ! He would lose it all if that allowed him to gain intimacy with Christ (Php 3:8–9).

Leaders who change the world have this kind of sharp focus. Think about the leaders of the Bible and the focus they had to bring about revolutionary change:

1. Abraham left his homeland, wealth, and friends for a new land because he focused on an unseen kingdom.
2. Joseph had strength to endure hardship and prisons because his dream focused on the greatness of God.
3. Moses could turn his back on Egypt because he focused on God's plan.
4. Stephen preached an unpopular message and died a martyr because of his focus.

5. Paul gave everything up and said, "This one thing I do."
6. Jesus told Martha, "Only one thing is necessary."

What does it take to gain the focus required to become a truly effective leader? The keys are *priorities* and *concentration*. A leader who knows his priorities but lacks concentration knows what to do, but never gets it done. A leader with concentration but no priorities has excellence without progress. But when leaders harness both, they gain the potential to achieve great things.

People base their decisions on a variety of things:

1. *The Ultimate:* first things first.
2. *The Urgent:* loud things first.
3. *The Unpleasant:* hard things first.
4. *The Unfinished:* last things first.
5. *The Unfulfilling:* dull things first.

Paul exemplifies a leader who focused on the ultimate every day. How about you? To get back on track with your focus, work on these items:

1. *Work on yourself.* You are your greatest asset or worst liability.
2. *Work on your priorities.* Fight for the important ones.
3. *Work in your strengths.* You can reach your potential if you do.
4. *Work with your colleagues.* You can't be effective alone.

For a negative example of focus, see p. 781.

Timothy and Epaphroditus

[19]I hope in the Lord Jesus to send Timothy to you soon, that I also may be cheered when I receive news about you. [20]I have no one else like him, who will show genuine concern for your welfare. [21]For everyone looks out for their own interests, not those of Jesus Christ. [22]But you know that Timothy has proved himself, because as a son with his father he has served with me in the work of the gospel. [23]I hope, therefore, to send him as soon as I see how things go with me. [24]And I am confident in the Lord that I myself will come soon.

[25]But I think it is necessary to send back to you Epaphroditus, my brother, co-worker and fellow soldier, who is also your messenger, whom you sent to take care of my needs. [26]For he longs for all of you and is distressed because you heard he was ill. [27]Indeed he was ill, and almost died. But God had mercy on him, and not on him only but also on me, to spare me sorrow upon sorrow. [28]Therefore I am all the more eager to send him, so that when you see him again you may be glad and I may have less anxiety. [29]So then, welcome him in the Lord with great joy, and honor people like him, [30]because he almost died for the work of Christ. He risked his life to make up for the help you yourselves could not give me.

No Confidence in the Flesh

3 Further, my brothers and sisters, rejoice in the Lord! It is no trouble for me to write the same things to you again, and it is a safeguard for you. [2]Watch out for those dogs, those evildoers, those mutilators of the flesh. [3]For it is we who are the circumcision, we who serve God by his Spirit, who boast in Christ Jesus, and who put no confidence in the flesh — [4]though I myself have reasons for such confidence.

If someone else thinks they have reasons to put confidence in the flesh, I have more: [5]circumcised on the eighth day, of the people of Israel, of the tribe of Benjamin, a Hebrew of Hebrews; in regard to the law, a Pharisee; [6]as for zeal, persecuting the church; as for righteousness based on the law, faultless.

[7]But whatever were gains to me I now consider loss for the sake of Christ. [8]What is more, I consider everything a loss because of the surpassing worth of knowing Christ Jesus my Lord, for whose sake I have lost all things. I consider them garbage, that I may gain Christ [9]and be found in him, not having a righteousness of my own that comes from the law, but that which is through faith in[a] Christ — the righteousness that comes from God on the basis of faith. [10]I want to know Christ — yes, to know the power of his resurrection and participation in his sufferings, becoming like him in his death, [11]and so, somehow, attaining to the resurrection from the dead.

[12]Not that I have already obtained all this, or have already arrived at my goal, but I press on to take hold of that for which Christ Jesus took hold of me. [13]Brothers and sisters, I do not consider myself yet to have taken hold of it. But one

---

[a] 9 Or through the faithfulness of

The Law of Priorities: Paul Narrowed His Activities

Philippians 3:7–14

Paul openly communicated his priorities. All the trophies and culture of his past he counted as rubbish, in order to gain Christ. He wanted to know Christ, experience his power, share in and complete his sufferings, and ultimately be conformed to his death (Php 3:10–11). He did all of this for the purpose of attaining the resurrection.

Here is a man on a mission. Paul narrowed his wedge and his focus to the essentials. What was his secret?

1. *He discerned what hindered him* (vv. 7–8).
   Paul had to let go of all the things he once cherished, considering them distractions to grace.

2. *He discovered what he wanted* (vv. 9–11).
   Paul wanted God's righteousness, not his own. Christ became his solitary pursuit.

3. *He determined how to get it* (vv. 12–14).
   With single-minded passion, Paul forgot the past and pursued the prize of his call.

How about you? Have you narrowed your focus? What is your "one thing"? Can you list your priorities on one hand? What are you pursuing?

thing I do: Forgetting what is behind and straining toward what is ahead, ¹⁴I press on toward the goal to win the prize for which God has called me heavenward in Christ Jesus.

Following Paul's Example

¹⁵All of us, then, who are mature should take such a view of things. And if on some point you think differently, that too God will make clear to you. ¹⁶Only let us live up to what we have already attained.

¹⁷Join together in following my example, brothers and sisters, and just as you have us as a model, keep your eyes on those who live as we do. ¹⁸For, as I have often told you before and now tell you again even with tears, many live as enemies of the cross of Christ. ¹⁹Their destiny is destruction, their god is their stomach, and their glory is in their shame. Their mind is set on earthly things. ²⁰But our citizenship is in heaven. And we eagerly await a Savior from there, the Lord Jesus Christ, ²¹who, by the power that enables him to bring everything under his control, will transform our lowly bodies so that they will be like his glorious body.

Closing Appeal for Steadfastness and Unity

4 Therefore, my brothers and sisters, you whom I love and long for, my joy and crown, stand firm in the Lord in this way, dear friends! ²I plead with Euodia and I plead with Syntyche

Teamwork: Petty Differences Can Prevent Victory

Philippians 4:2–3

Paul knows the importance of teamwork, so he encourages two women who have been quarreling to make peace.

Euodia and Syntyche, members of the Philippian church, had by their disharmony created some division. Paul uses them as examples to launch into an entire chapter on peace. He doesn't ask these women to act uniformly, but rather to be of the same mind. The word he uses connotes harmony. Singing in harmony doesn't mean singing in unison. Players *should* play different positions on a team. Harmony means their efforts complement the efforts of others, rather than conflict with them.

Self-Discipline: Paul Mastered What Would Help Him

Philippians 4:1–19

Philippians 4 provides a call to discipline. Paul declares that the goal of peace and fulfillment runs through the path of self-discipline. The apostle elaborates on three disciplines that help leaders stay aligned with their mission:

1. *Govern your actions* (vv. 1–5).
   Paul pleads with his friends to stand firm. Live in harmony. Display self-control.

2. *Guard your attitudes* (vv. 6–9).
   He says to replace worry with prayer and to think on the positive things that edify.

3. *Give your assets* (vv. 10–19).
   Nothing purifies more than sharing resources and trusting God to meet your needs.

to be of the same mind in the Lord. ³Yes, and I ask you, my true companion, help these women since they have contended at my side in the cause of the gospel, along with Clement and the rest of my co-workers, whose names are in the book of life.

Final Exhortations

⁴Rejoice in the Lord always. I will say it again: Rejoice! ⁵Let your gentleness be evident to all. The Lord is near. ⁶Do not be anxious about anything, but in every situation, by prayer and petition, with thanksgiving, present your requests to God. ⁷And the peace of God, which transcends all understanding, will guard your hearts and your minds in Christ Jesus.

⁸Finally, brothers and sisters, whatever is true, whatever is noble, whatever is right, whatever is pure, whatever is lovely, whatever is admirable — if anything is excellent or praiseworthy — think about such things. ⁹Whatever you have learned or received or heard from me, or seen in me — put it into practice. And the God of peace will be with you.

Thanks for Their Gifts

¹⁰I rejoiced greatly in the Lord that at last you renewed your concern for me. Indeed, you were concerned, but you had no opportunity to

show it. [11]I am not saying this because I am in need, for I have learned to be content whatever the circumstances. [12]I know what it is to be in need, and I know what it is to have plenty. I have learned the secret of being content in any and every situation, whether well fed or hungry, whether living in plenty or in want. [13]I can do all this through him who gives me strength.

Positive Attitude: Paul Had the Mind to Make It

Philippians 4:11–13

Paul maintained a positive attitude even on rotten days. He teaches us that:

1. Attitude has little to do with circumstances (v. 11).
2. Attitudes can change, just like circumstances (v. 12).
3. Attitudes can be improved, if we learn the secret (v. 12).
4. Attitudes have a source for their strength (v. 13).

---

[14]Yet it was good of you to share in my troubles. [15]Moreover, as you Philippians know, in the early days of your acquaintance with the gospel, when I set out from Macedonia, not one church shared with me in the matter of giving and receiving, except you only; [16]for even when I was in Thessalonica, you sent me aid more than once when I was in need. [17]Not that I desire your gifts; what I desire is that more be credited to your account. [18]I have received full payment and have more than enough. I am amply supplied, now that I have received from Epaphroditus the gifts you sent. They are a fragrant offering, an acceptable sacrifice, pleasing to God. [19]And my God will meet all your needs according to the riches of his glory in Christ Jesus.

[20]To our God and Father be glory for ever and ever. Amen.

Final Greetings

[21]Greet all God's people in Christ Jesus. The brothers and sisters who are with me send greetings. [22]All God's people here send you greetings, especially those who belong to Caesar's household.

[23]The grace of the Lord Jesus Christ be with your spirit. Amen.[a]

---

[a] 23 Some manuscripts do not have *Amen*.

PAUL   A Leader Who Couldn't Be Stopped

Philippians 4:4–13

PROFILE in leadership

The apostle Paul was a man who truly practiced what he preached.

Paul challenged the Philippian believers to rejoice because of their relationship with Jesus Christ, to cast aside all worry because he cared about them, and to focus their minds on the things of God (Php 4:4–8). He encouraged them to put into practice the things he had taught them, and he reminded them that the true and living God would be with them to empower them to do those things.

Paul was the kind of leader who could say such things with great conviction and authority—even while sitting in prison—because he practiced them daily. He depended upon and felt grateful to the God he served, and he focused his heart on serving God by making the preaching of the gospel of Jesus Christ his prime activity.

With a mind and heart like that, Paul truly became an unstoppable leader. As he so rightly stated, "I can do *all* this through him who gives me strength" (4:13, emphasis added).

Paul, the man who willingly endured incredible suffering, persecution and want during the course of his missionary journeys, demonstrated a state of heart and mind that made him God's kind of leader. *Anyone* who adopts a similar attitude and heart can become a similar unstoppable kind of leader.

Introduction to COLOSSIANS

Knowing God and Making Him Known

The apostle Paul wrote the book of Colossians from prison to a group of believers in Colosse. It may well remind you of Ephesians, since about a quarter of the message of Ephesians is found in Colossians. Paul clearly believed that everyone needed to embrace a few fundamental building blocks.

What makes this book unique, however, and especially helpful to leaders, is that Paul wrote it in response to heresy. Some false teachers were making their way through the church, indoctrinating believers with a combination of Jewish and Hellenistic beliefs that troubled and confused these new Christians. Paul stepped in to rescue the church from cultic doctrine and restore believers to the business of knowing God and making him known.

Paul's leadership training course begins with courage. He does not shrink from addressing trouble and making the tough call. His love for people doesn't cause him to become a people-pleaser. Quite the opposite, it prompts him to want the best for them, even if it means speaking corrective words.

It follows, then, that Paul teaches a second leadership lesson. He sets a standard for excellence and articulates it repeatedly. He raises the bar, teaching that Jesus is not only a wonderful Savior, but the preeminent Lord, Creator and Master of everything. He is, in fact, our all in all (1:15–17). "Excellence" is Paul's description of Jesus and what he calls for from fellow believers.

Finally, in order to prevent the Colossians from feeling overwhelmed by this high calling, Paul teaches them the Law of Process. In the second chapter, he urges them to continue growing in Christ, just as they have been rooted in him. Maturity is a process, not an event.

God's Role in Colossians

God appears in this book as the cosmic Christ, superior to every other deity and armed with truths greater than any doctrine or philosophy in the world. Colossians 2 teaches that "in Christ all the fullness of the Deity lives in bodily form" (v. 9), and we "in Christ . . . have been brought to fullness. He is the head over every power and authority" (v. 10). Consequently, God not only is our Leader, but he also is our source of power, our wisdom for decision making, our peace in the midst of stress, and our love for those who seem unlovable. His supernatural leadership resources us with every tool we need to imitate Jesus.

Leaders in Colossians

Paul, Barnabas, Aristarchus

Other People of Influence in Colossians

Justus, the gnostic (heretical) teachers in Colosse

Lessons in Leadership

- Christ is the center of all complete leadership.
- To be a lifelong leader, you must be a lifelong learner.
- Leaders can't simultaneously pursue pleasing God and pleasing people.

In the final two chapters, the apostle lays out a game plan for growth which addresses the Christian's thought life, relationships, solitude, work ethic and family. Colossians remains a basic training manual for us today.

- Excellence is not an accident; it happens when leaders call for it.
- Leadership begins on the inside; it starts with "being," not "doing."

LEADERSHIP HIGHLIGHTS IN COLOSSIANS

1 Paul, an apostle of Christ Jesus by the will of God, and Timothy our brother,

²To God's holy people in Colossae, the faithful brothers and sisters*a* in Christ:

Grace and peace to you from God our Father.*b*

Thanksgiving and Prayer

³We always thank God, the Father of our Lord Jesus Christ, when we pray for you, ⁴because we have heard of your faith in Christ Jesus and of the love you have for all God's people— ⁵the faith and love that spring from the hope stored up for you in heaven and about which you have already heard in the true message of the gospel ⁶that has come to you. In the same way, the gospel is bearing fruit and growing throughout the whole world—just as it has been doing among you since the day you heard it and truly understood God's grace. ⁷You learned it from Epaphras, our dear fellow servant,*c* who is a faithful minister of Christ on our*d* behalf, ⁸and who also told us of your love in the Spirit.

⁹For this reason, since the day we heard about you, we have not stopped praying for you. We continually ask God to fill you with the knowledge of his will through all the wisdom and understanding that the Spirit gives,*e* ¹⁰so that you may live a life worthy of the Lord and please him in every way: bearing fruit in every good work, growing in the knowledge of God, ¹¹being strengthened with all power according to his glorious might so that you may have great endurance and patience, ¹²and giving joyful thanks to the Father, who has qualified you*f* to share in the inheritance of his holy people in the kingdom of light. ¹³For he has rescued us from the dominion of darkness and brought us into the kingdom of the Son he loves, ¹⁴in whom we have redemption, the forgiveness of sins.

The Supremacy of the Son of God

¹⁵The Son is the image of the invisible God, the firstborn over all creation. ¹⁶For in him all things were created: things in heaven and on earth, visible and invisible, whether thrones or powers or rulers or authorities; all things have been created through him and for him. ¹⁷He is before all things, and in him all things hold together. ¹⁸And he is the head of the body, the church; he is the beginning and the firstborn from among the dead, so that in everything he might have the supremacy. ¹⁹For God was pleased to have all his fullness dwell in him, ²⁰and through him to reconcile to himself all things, whether things on earth or things in heaven, by making peace through his blood, shed on the cross.

The Law of Respect: Jesus Is Superior to Everyone

Colossians 1:13–20

Although Paul clearly was a strong leader, he constantly declared his submission to the leadership of Christ.

At the very beginning of his letter to the Colossians, Paul paints a picture of Jesus' supremacy over every authority on earth. Our Lord rescues, redeems, and transforms. He is the image of the invisible God, who created everything, including other leaders and authorities. Christ takes priority among every created thing as the "firstborn from among the dead" (Col 1:18). Paul argues Jesus' supremacy based on the Law of Respect.

²¹Once you were alienated from God and were enemies in your minds because of*g* your evil behavior. ²²But now he has reconciled you by Christ's physical body through death to present you holy in his sight, without blemish and free from accusation— ²³if you continue

Teachability: Paul Encouraged Readers to Be Lifelong Learners

Colossians 1:4–10

Although the Colossians already understood saving knowledge (Col 1:4–7), their leader wanted them to know how to apply that knowledge. These are two different things. Teachability begins with knowledge (1:9), moves to understanding (1:9), then results in application (1:10). You are teachable if you're changing.

---

a 2 The Greek word for *brothers and sisters* (*adelphoi*) refers here to believers, both men and women, as part of God's family; also in 4:15.　*b* 2 Some manuscripts *Father and the Lord Jesus Christ*　*c* 7 Or *slave*　*d* 7 Some manuscripts *your*　*e* 9 Or *all spiritual wisdom and understanding*　*f* 12 Some manuscripts *us*　*g* 21 Or *minds, as shown by*

in your faith, established and firm, and do not move from the hope held out in the gospel. This is the gospel that you heard and that has been proclaimed to every creature under heaven, and of which I, Paul, have become a servant.

Paul's Labor for the Church

²⁴Now I rejoice in what I am suffering for you, and I fill up in my flesh what is still lacking in regard to Christ's afflictions, for the sake of his body, which is the church. ²⁵I have become its servant by the commission God gave me to present to you the word of God in its fullness— ²⁶the mystery that has been kept hidden for ages and generations, but is now disclosed to the Lord's people. ²⁷To them God has chosen to make known among the Gentiles the glorious riches of this mystery, which is Christ in you, the hope of glory. ²⁸He is the one we proclaim, admonishing and teaching everyone with all wisdom, so that we may present everyone fully mature in Christ. ²⁹To this end I strenuously contend with all the energy Christ so powerfully works in me.

2 I want you to know how hard I am contending for you and for those at Laodicea, and for all who have not met me personally. ²My goal is that they may be encouraged in heart and united in love, so that they may have the full riches of complete understanding, in order that they may know the mystery of God, namely, Christ, ³in whom are hidden all the treasures of wisdom and knowledge. ⁴I tell you this so that no one

may deceive you by fine-sounding arguments. ⁵For though I am absent from you in body, I am present with you in spirit and delight to see how disciplined you are and how firm your faith in Christ is.

Spiritual Fullness in Christ

⁶So then, just as you received Christ Jesus as Lord, continue to live your lives in him, ⁷rooted and built up in him, strengthened in the faith as you were taught, and overflowing with thankfulness.

⁸See to it that no one takes you captive through hollow and deceptive philosophy, which depends on human tradition and the elemental spiritual forces[a] of this world rather than on Christ.

⁹For in Christ all the fullness of the Deity lives in bodily form, ¹⁰and in Christ you have been brought to fullness. He is the head over every power and authority. ¹¹In him you were also circumcised with a circumcision not performed by human hands. Your whole self ruled by the flesh[b] was put off when you were circumcised by[c] Christ, ¹²having been buried with him in baptism, in which you were also raised with him through your faith in the working of God, who raised him from the dead.

---

[a] 8 Or *the basic principles*; also in verse 20   [b] 11 In contexts like this, the Greek word for *flesh* (*sarx*) refers to the sinful state of human beings, often presented as a power in opposition to the Spirit; also in verse 13.   [c] 11 Or *put off in the circumcision of*

The Law of Addition: Paul Was a Provider for People

Colossians 1:28–29

Paul longed to present everyone complete in Christ. In Colossians 1:28–29 he speaks not of adding anything to Christ's redemptive work, but rather he declares his intention to equip others to realize their God-given potential. He did part of his equipping through letters like this one.

The apostle says his goal is to preach, warn, and teach, so that listeners become complete in Christ. What does this mean? Part of it, no doubt, means that those he taught could reproduce themselves in others. Paul was an equipping leader with a heart to develop others. He practiced the Law of Addition: Leaders add value to others by serving them. Paul was a *provider* for the people in his life. Providers are:

Purposeful: They approach others with a purpose: to add value.
Relational: They are warm and inviting and work at relationships.
Objective: They assess strengths and weaknesses objectively.
Vulnerable: They model self-disclosure and honesty.
Incarnational: They are examples of what they teach.
Dependable: They are consistent and responsible for their promises.
Empowering: They give power away and facilitate growth in others.
Resourceful: They use every tool they have to grow people.

[13]When you were dead in your sins and in the uncircumcision of your flesh, God made you[a] alive with Christ. He forgave us all our sins, [14]having canceled the charge of our legal indebtedness, which stood against us and condemned us; he has taken it away, nailing it to the cross. [15]And having disarmed the powers and authorities, he made a public spectacle of them, triumphing over them by the cross.[b]

Freedom From Human Rules

[16]Therefore do not let anyone judge you by what you eat or drink, or with regard to a religious festival, a New Moon celebration or a Sabbath day. [17]These are a shadow of the things that were to come; the reality, however, is found in Christ. [18]Do not let anyone who delights in false humility and the worship of angels disqualify you. Such a person also goes into great detail about what they have seen; they are puffed up with idle notions by their unspiritual mind. [19]They have lost connection with the head, from whom the whole body, supported and held together by its ligaments and sinews, grows as God causes it to grow.

[20]Since you died with Christ to the elemental spiritual forces of this world, why, as though you still belonged to the world, do you submit to its rules: [21]"Do not handle! Do not taste! Do not touch!"? [22]These rules, which have to do with things that are all destined to perish with use, are based on merely human commands and teachings. [23]Such regulations indeed have an appearance of wisdom, with their self-imposed worship, their false humility and their harsh treatment of the body, but they lack any value in restraining sensual indulgence.

Living as Those Made Alive in Christ

3 Since, then, you have been raised with Christ, set your hearts on things above, where Christ is, seated at the right hand of God. [2]Set your minds on things above, not on earthly things. [3]For you died, and your life is now hidden with Christ in God. [4]When Christ, who is your[c] life, appears, then you also will appear with him in glory.

[5]Put to death, therefore, whatever belongs to your earthly nature: sexual immorality, impurity, lust, evil desires and greed, which is idolatry. [6]Because of these, the wrath of God is coming.[d] [7]You used to walk in these ways, in the life you

---

The Law of Victory: Jesus Defeats Death, Provides Weapons

Colossians 2:10–15

Jesus not only provides us the weapons we need for victory (Col 2:10–14), but he also disarms the enemy, thus assuring our success (2:15). Christ ensures us of victory by providing the resources we need, by removing hindrances, by stripping the enemy of his own devices, and by publicly declaring victory.

The Law of Process: Growth Is Not an Event

Colossians 2:1–7

Spiritual growth doesn't "just happen," any more than climbing a mountain "just happens." You don't wander up a mountain and surprise yourself when you reach the top. Growth results from hard work.

Paul compares maturing a person to growing a plant (Col 2:6–7). When you take seed, soil, sunshine and water and put them together, you don't get a plant overnight. You need time. Paul knows that the Colossians' roots won't grow deep overnight. So he reminds them of what must happen for growth to occur:

1. *Labor* (v. 1)—Someone has to work.
2. *Stretching* (v. 2)—You have to stretch for more.
3. *Learning* (vv. 2–3)—Knowledge must be consumed.
4. *Focus* (v. 4)—You cannot drift or get distracted.
5. *Accountability* (v. 5)—Growth accelerates when someone watches.
6. *Building on the past* (v. 6)—Growth always uses past truth.
7. *Application* (v. 6)—Growth solidifies when you practice what you know.
8. *Gratitude* (v. 7)—Give joyful thanksgiving for past blessings.

---

[a] 13 Some manuscripts *us*   [b] 15 Or *them in him*
[c] 4 Some manuscripts *our*   [d] 6 Some early manuscripts *coming on those who are disobedient*

once lived. [8]But now you must also rid yourselves of all such things as these: anger, rage, malice, slander, and filthy language from your lips. [9]Do not lie to each other, since you have taken off your old self with its practices [10]and have put on the new self, which is being renewed in knowledge in the image of its Creator. [11]Here there is no Gentile or Jew, circumcised or uncircumcised, barbarian, Scythian, slave or free, but Christ is all, and is in all.

[12]Therefore, as God's chosen people, holy and dearly loved, clothe yourselves with compassion, kindness, humility, gentleness and patience. [13]Bear with each other and forgive one another if any of you has a grievance against someone. Forgive as the Lord forgave you. [14]And over all these virtues put on love, which binds them all together in perfect unity.

[15]Let the peace of Christ rule in your hearts, since as members of one body you were called to peace. And be thankful. [16]Let the message of Christ dwell among you richly as you teach and admonish one another with all wisdom through psalms, hymns, and songs from the Spirit, singing to God with gratitude in your hearts. [17]And whatever you do, whether in word or deed, do it all in the name of the Lord Jesus, giving thanks to God the Father through him.

Instructions for Christian Households

[18]Wives, submit yourselves to your husbands, as is fitting in the Lord.

[19]Husbands, love your wives and do not be harsh with them.

[20]Children, obey your parents in everything, for this pleases the Lord.

[21]Fathers,[a] do not embitter your children, or they will become discouraged.

[22]Slaves, obey your earthly masters in everything; and do it, not only when their eye is on you and to curry their favor, but with sincerity of heart and reverence for the Lord. [23]Whatever you do, work at it with all your heart, as working for the Lord, not for human masters, [24]since you know that you will receive an inheritance from the Lord as a reward. It is the Lord Christ you are serving. [25]Anyone who does wrong will be repaid for their wrongs, and there is no favoritism.

4 Masters, provide your slaves with what is right and fair, because you know that you also have a Master in heaven.

Further Instructions

[2]Devote yourselves to prayer, being watchful and thankful. [3]And pray for us, too, that God may open a door for our message, so that we may proclaim the mystery of Christ, for which I am in chains. [4]Pray that I may proclaim it clearly, as I should. [5]Be wise in the way you act toward outsiders; make the most of every opportunity. [6]Let your conversation be always full of grace, seasoned with salt, so that you may know how to answer everyone.

Final Greetings

[7]Tychicus will tell you all the news about me. He is a dear brother, a faithful minister and fellow servant[b] in the Lord. [8]I am sending him to you for the express purpose that you may know about our[c] circumstances and that he may encourage your hearts. [9]He is coming with Onesimus, our faithful and dear brother, who is one of you. They will tell you everything that is happening here. [10]My fellow prisoner Aristarchus sends you

---

Self-Discipline: The Battle Begins in the Mind

Colossians 3:1–14

The battle begins in the mind. Paul argues that since we have a new position, we need to get a new perspective (Col 3:1). Permanent change and improvement always happen from the inside out. Consider Paul's prescription for self-discipline:

1. *Remember your identity* (v. 1).
   We must focus first on our position in Christ. It all starts there.

2. *Renew your thought life* (v. 2).
   We must focus our minds on things above. We must raise new internal standards.

3. *Recognize your old life is dead* (vv. 3–7).
   Change doesn't happen if we maintain any way to return to old patterns.

4. *Release past habits* (vv. 8–11).
   We must put off the old, like taking off a worn-out set of clothes.

5. *Replace them with new ones* (vv. 12–14).
   We get rid of old habits only when we substitute new habits for them.

---

[a] 21 Or *Parents*   [b] 7 Or *slave*; also in verse 12   [c] 8 Some manuscripts *that he may know about your*

his greetings, as does Mark, the cousin of Barnabas. (You have received instructions about him; if he comes to you, welcome him.) [11]Jesus, who is called Justus, also sends greetings. These are the only Jews[a] among my co-workers for the kingdom of God, and they have proved a comfort to me. [12]Epaphras, who is one of you and a servant of Christ Jesus, sends greetings. He is always wrestling in prayer for you, that you may stand firm in all the will of God, mature and fully assured. [13]I vouch for him that he is working hard for you and for those at Laodicea and Hierapolis. [14]Our dear friend Luke, the doctor, and Demas send greetings. [15]Give my greetings to the brothers and sisters at Laodicea, and to Nympha and the church in her house.

[16]After this letter has been read to you, see that it is also read in the church of the Laodiceans and that you in turn read the letter from Laodicea.

[17]Tell Archippus: "See to it that you complete the ministry you have received in the Lord."

[18]I, Paul, write this greeting in my own hand. Remember my chains. Grace be with you.

---

[a] 11 Greek *only ones of the circumcision group*

You Can't Divorce Leadership from Relationships

Colossians 3:18—4:6

Paul spends a lot of time in Colossians discussing relationships, a paramount concern for leaders. Leadership is about relationships. Consider three levels of leadership:

1. Leaders can *impress* others from a distance.
   This requires the will of the leader. The leader must determine to perform excellently.

2. Leaders can *influence* others if they get a bit closer.
   This requires the will of the followers. They must choose to emulate the leader.

3. Leaders can *impact* others only in close relationship.
   This requires both the will of the leader and the follower. It occurs when intimacy and trust develop.

Paul begins his instruction on relationships with the home (Col 3:18–21). Then he moves outward to colleagues, to masters and slaves (3:22—4:4). Finally, he addresses relationships with outsiders (4:5–6).

God has placed everyone within a chain of care. Leaders are to connect with followers, from parenting, to supervising, to evangelizing. These circles of relationship serve as proving grounds, each giving credibility to the next. When we lead well in the home, we gain credibility to be heard in the marketplace. If it doesn't work at home, don't export it! Success is gaining the respect of those who know us best.

INTRODUCTION TO
1 THESSALONIANS

The Basics of the Christian Life

The apostle Paul planted the church of Thessalonica during his second missionary journey. Thessalonica was yet another of those key, port cities where multitudes interacted and engaged in commerce. Unfortunately, the Jews harassed Paul and ran him out of town shortly after he started this infant church. He wrote the letters we call 1 and 2 Thessalonians almost immediately after leaving town in order to equip those young believers in the basics of the Christian life. In these letters he assumes his rightful role as leader of the church family and answers questions, solves problems, and casts vision for the ultimate plan of God on earth.

Paul demonstrates that you must lead differently based on who your followers are and the context in which they live. The spiritually young Thessalonians needed to hear things that Paul didn't have to say to others. They had caught only a glimpse of Paul's message, so he had to teach them big-picture perspectives on Christ's return and the end of the age. Paul discerned how this people needed to be led. He customized his leadership to the needs of Thessalonica.

Paul also demonstrated a leader's follow-through. Since he had to leave town prematurely, he sent Timothy (one of his team members) back to Thessalonica to check on the church's growth and spiritual health. Paul consistently developed a plan to continue making progress in his church planting efforts, but he also determined to finish what he started. He dispatched team members to follow up; identified and equipped local leaders; and wrote letters and corresponded with his young churches to answer specific questions.

Paul understood the necessity of mentoring leaders.

God's Role in 1 Thessalonians

God used Paul as a church pioneer, but he also took on a greater role to the young believers, safeguarding them while few or no experienced shepherds existed to lead them. Paul had to trust God to do what the apostle could not, given the little time he had in town. God worked on the people's hearts and used Paul's brief letters to disciple them and ready them for what lay ahead.

Leaders in 1 Thessalonians

Paul, church leaders in Thessalonica

Other People of Influence in 1 Thessalonians

Silas, Silvanus, Timothy

Lessons in Leadership

- The more a leader loves the people, the easier it is to lead the people.
- A bright and promising future motivates faster than a fond and memorable past.
- Leaders must tailor their approach to the needs of the people.
- Leaders who last mentor a second generation of leaders.
- People can live with a tough today if they believe a terrific tomorrow is coming.

He selected key leaders in Thessalonica and encouraged them all to follow him, to observe and remember his lifestyle (1:5–6). In chapter 2 he even takes it a step further when his mentoring becomes parental. "We were like young children among you, just as a nursing mother cares for her children," he writes. "So we cared for you. Because we loved you so much, we were delighted to share with you not only the gospel of God but our lives as well . . . For you know that we dealt with each of you as a father deals with his own children, encouraging, comforting and urging you to live lives worthy of God" (vv. 7–8, 11–12). He gave his "children" more than mere lectures. He mentored like a parent.

LEADERSHIP HIGHLIGHTS IN 1 THESSALONIANS

EQUIPPING: Paul Develops Leaders in Mentoring Relationships (1:5–8)	**page 1433**
THE LAW OF CONNECTION: Paul Mentors His Children (2:7–12)	**page 1434**
THE LAW OF THE INNER CIRCLE: Paul's Team Represented Him (3:2–10)	**page 1435**
VISION: Paul Was a Futurist (4:13—5:11)	**page 1436**

1 Paul, Silas[a] and Timothy,

To the church of the Thessalonians in God the Father and the Lord Jesus Christ:

Grace and peace to you.

Thanksgiving for the Thessalonians' Faith

2 We always thank God for all of you and continually mention you in our prayers. 3 We remember before our God and Father your work produced by faith, your labor prompted by love, and your endurance inspired by hope in our Lord Jesus Christ.

4 For we know, brothers and sisters[b] loved by God, that he has chosen you, 5 because our gospel came to you not simply with words but also with power, with the Holy Spirit and deep conviction. You know how we lived among you for your sake. 6 You became imitators of us and of the Lord, for you welcomed the message in the midst of severe suffering with the joy given by the Holy Spirit. 7 And so you became a model to all the believers in Macedonia and Achaia. 8 The Lord's message rang out from you not only in Macedonia and Achaia — your faith in God has become known everywhere. Therefore we do not need to say anything about it, 9 for they themselves report what kind of reception you gave us. They tell how you turned to God from idols to serve the living and true God, 10 and to wait for his Son from heaven, whom he raised from the dead — Jesus, who rescues us from the coming wrath.

Paul's Ministry in Thessalonica

2 You know, brothers and sisters, that our visit to you was not without results. 2 We had previously suffered and been treated outrageously in Philippi, as you know, but with the help of our God we dared to tell you his gospel in the face of strong opposition. 3 For the appeal we make does not spring from error or impure motives, nor are we trying to trick you. 4 On the contrary, we speak as those approved by God to be entrusted with the gospel. We are not trying to please people but God, who tests our hearts. 5 You know we never used flattery, nor did we put on a mask to cover up greed — God is our witness. 6 We were not looking for praise from people, not from you or anyone else, even though as apostles of Christ we could have asserted our authority. 7 Instead, we were like young children[c] among you.

Just as a nursing mother cares for her children, 8 so we cared for you. Because we loved you so much, we were delighted to share with you not only the gospel of God but our lives as well. 9 Surely you remember, brothers and sisters, our toil and hardship; we worked night and day in order not to be a burden to anyone while we preached the gospel of God to you. 10 You are witnesses, and so is God, of how holy, righteous and blameless we were among you who believed.

---

[a] 1 Greek *Silvanus*, a variant of *Silas*   [b] 4 The Greek word for *brothers and sisters* (*adelphoi*) refers here to believers, both men and women, as part of God's family; also in 2:1, 9, 14, 17; 3:7; 4:1, 10, 13; 5:1, 4, 12, 14, 25, 27.   [c] 7 Some manuscripts *were gentle*

Equipping: Paul Developed Leaders in Mentoring Relationships

1 Thessalonians 1:5–8

Because Paul was forced to leave Thessalonica shortly after he planted a church there, he developed many of its leaders through the mail. The apostle wrote 1 and 2 Thessalonians to disciple and train those who had recently chosen to follow Christ. Paul tried to work himself out of a job through this training, equipping other leaders. The apostle reminds us how good training works:

1. Training involves not only words, but also demonstration (v. 5).
2. Training transforms others when done with conviction (v. 5).
3. Training is remembered when the life of the trainer supports the message (v. 5).
4. Training is incarnated when the follower imitates the teacher (v. 6).
5. Training is relevant when done in the midst of problems (v. 6).
6. Training is complete when the trainee becomes a trainer (vv. 7–8).
7. Training has been reproduced when the original trainer has no need to say more (v. 8).

The Law of Connection: Paul Mentors His Children

1 Thessalonians 2:7–12

Although Paul had met with this young church only on three Sabbaths, he longed for them like a parent longs for a child. As Paul mentored his "children," he developed a parental, coaching relationship with them. Note how he describes this relationship:

1. We were like a gentle, nurturing mother to you (v. 7).
2. We shared not only the good news, but also our very lives (v. 8).
3. We worked hard not to burden you with our needs (v. 9).
4. We strove to be an example while among you (v. 10).
5. We dealt with you as a father deals with his children (v. 11).
6. We encouraged you to live up to your potential as God's children (v. 12).

Relationships grow strong when those involved share common experiences (vv. 17–20); continual encouragement (vv. 2, 6–7, 9); concerned expressions (vv. 1, 3–5); and challenging expectations (vv. 8, 10–13). Good relationships both comfort and stretch.

[11] For you know that we dealt with each of you as a father deals with his own children, [12] encouraging, comforting and urging you to live lives worthy of God, who calls you into his kingdom and glory.

[13] And we also thank God continually because, when you received the word of God, which you heard from us, you accepted it not as a human word, but as it actually is, the word of God, which is indeed at work in you who believe. [14] For you, brothers and sisters, became imitators of God's churches in Judea, which are in Christ Jesus: You suffered from your own people the same things those churches suffered from the Jews [15] who killed the Lord Jesus and the prophets and also drove us out. They displease God and are hostile to everyone [16] in their effort to keep us from speaking to the Gentiles so that they may be saved. In this way they always heap up their sins to the limit. The wrath of God has come upon them at last.[a]

Paul's Longing to See the Thessalonians

[17] But, brothers and sisters, when we were orphaned by being separated from you for a short time (in person, not in thought), out of our intense longing we made every effort to see you. [18] For we wanted to come to you—certainly I, Paul, did, again and again—but Satan blocked our way. [19] For what is our hope, our joy, or the crown in which we will glory in the presence of our Lord Jesus when he comes? Is it not you? [20] Indeed, you are our glory and joy.

3 So when we could stand it no longer, we thought it best to be left by ourselves in Athens. [2] We sent Timothy, who is our brother and co-worker in God's service in spreading the gospel of Christ, to strengthen and encourage you in your faith, [3] so that no one would be unsettled by these trials. For you know quite well that we are destined for them. [4] In fact, when we were with you, we kept telling you that we would be persecuted. And it turned out that way, as you well know. [5] For this reason, when I could stand it no longer, I sent to find out about your faith. I was afraid that in some way the tempter had

---

[a] 16 Or *them fully*

Accountability: Paul Sent Timothy to Support and Report

1 Thessalonians 3:1–10

Leaders understand the power of accountability for the purposes of support and challenge. Accountability provides a *cure* for situations like the one Paul encountered in Thessalonica, where the Jews ran him out of town after only three weeks of work. CURE stands for the four gifts of accountability: Correction, Updates, Reminders and Encouragement.

tempted you and that our labors might have been in vain.

Timothy's Encouraging Report

[6]But Timothy has just now come to us from you and has brought good news about your faith and love. He has told us that you always have pleasant memories of us and that you long to see us, just as we also long to see you. [7]Therefore, brothers and sisters, in all our distress and persecution we were encouraged about you because of your faith. [8]For now we really live, since you are standing firm in the Lord. [9]How can we thank God enough for you in return for all the joy we have in the presence of our God because of you? [10]Night and day we pray most earnestly that we may see you again and supply what is lacking in your faith.

[11]Now may our God and Father himself and our Lord Jesus clear the way for us to come to you. [12]May the Lord make your love increase and overflow for each other and for everyone else, just as ours does for you. [13]May he strengthen your hearts so that you will be blameless and holy in the presence of our God and Father when our Lord Jesus comes with all his holy ones.

Living to Please God

4 As for other matters, brothers and sisters, we instructed you how to live in order to please God, as in fact you are living. Now we ask you and urge you in the Lord Jesus to do this more and more. [2]For you know what instructions we gave you by the authority of the Lord Jesus.

[3]It is God's will that you should be sanctified: that you should avoid sexual immorality; [4]that each of you should learn to control your own body[a] in a way that is holy and honorable, [5]not in passionate lust like the pagans, who do not know God; [6]and that in this matter no one should wrong or take advantage of a brother or sister.[b] The Lord will punish all those who commit such sins, as we told you and warned you before. [7]For God did not call us to be impure, but to live a holy life. [8]Therefore, anyone who rejects this instruction does not reject a human being but God, the very God who gives you his Holy Spirit.

[9]Now about your love for one another we do not need to write to you, for you yourselves have been taught by God to love each other. [10]And in fact, you do love all of God's family throughout Macedonia. Yet we urge you, brothers and sisters, to do so more and more, [11]and to make it your ambition to lead a quiet life: You should mind your own business and work with your hands, just as we told you, [12]so that your daily life may win the respect of outsiders and so that you will not be dependent on anybody.

Believers Who Have Died

[13]Brothers and sisters, we do not want you to be uninformed about those who sleep in death, so that you do not grieve like the rest of mankind, who have no hope. [14]For we believe that Jesus died and rose again, and so we believe that God will bring with Jesus those who have fallen asleep in him. [15]According to the Lord's word, we tell you that we who are still alive, who are left until the coming of the Lord, will certainly not precede those who have fallen asleep. [16]For the Lord himself will come down from heaven,

---

The Law of the Inner Circle: Paul's Team Represented Him

1 Thessalonians 3:2–10

Paul found it difficult to send Timothy to Thessalonica; he would rather have returned himself. If he had, however, he might have been killed. The religious leaders remained on the lookout for him, ever since they ran him out of town. So Paul sent one of his key players, Timothy, a member of Paul's inner circle.

Paul's potential multiplied because of individuals like Timothy. Timothy did just what Paul would have done had he been present:

1. *Provide*—He gave them strength and encouragement (v. 2).

2. *Protect*—He worked to rescue those who might fall away (v. 3).

3. *Preserve*—He fought to ensure their work had not been in vain (vv. 4–5).

4. *Promote*—He motivated them and cheered them on to grow (vv. 6–7).

5. *Present*—He reported to Paul how their faith had flourished (vv. 6–8).

6. *Pray*—He led the way in praying for what they still lacked (vv. 9–10).

---

[a] 4 Or *learn to live with your own wife*; or *learn to acquire a wife*   [b] 6 The Greek word for *brother or sister (adelphos)* refers here to a believer, whether man or woman, as part of God's family.

The Law of Solid Ground: Paul Built Respect

1 Thessalonians 4:11–12

If the Thessalonians were to win their city for Christ, they would have to commit themselves to excellence. They needed to lead a peaceful life, pay their bills, and work with integrity. When we gain the respect of others by leading our own lives well, we gain the opportunity to lead others.

with a loud command, with the voice of the archangel and with the trumpet call of God, and the dead in Christ will rise first. [17] After that, we who are still alive and are left will be caught up together with them in the clouds to meet the Lord in the air. And so we will be with the Lord forever. [18] Therefore encourage one another with these words.

The Day of the Lord

5 Now, brothers and sisters, about times and dates we do not need to write to you, [2] for you know very well that the day of the Lord will come like a thief in the night. [3] While people are saying, "Peace and safety," destruction will come on them suddenly, as labor pains on a pregnant woman, and they will not escape.

[4] But you, brothers and sisters, are not in darkness so that this day should surprise you like a thief. [5] You are all children of the light and children of the day. We do not belong to the night or to the darkness. [6] So then, let us not be like others, who are asleep, but let us be awake and sober. [7] For those who sleep, sleep at night, and those who get drunk, get drunk at night. [8] But since we belong to the day, let us be sober, putting on faith and love as a breastplate, and the hope of salvation as a helmet. [9] For God did not appoint us to suffer wrath but to receive salvation through our Lord Jesus Christ. [10] He died for us so that, whether we are awake or asleep, we may live together with him. [11] Therefore encourage one another and build each other up, just as in fact you are doing.

Final Instructions

[12] Now we ask you, brothers and sisters, to acknowledge those who work hard among you, who care for you in the Lord and who admonish you. [13] Hold them in the highest regard in love because of their work. Live in peace with each other. [14] And we urge you, brothers and sisters, warn those who are idle and disruptive, encourage the disheartened, help the weak, be patient with everyone. [15] Make sure that nobody pays back wrong for wrong, but always strive to do what is good for each other and for everyone else.

[16] Rejoice always, [17] pray continually, [18] give thanks in all circumstances; for this is God's will for you in Christ Jesus.

[19] Do not quench the Spirit. [20] Do not treat prophecies with contempt [21] but test them all; hold on to what is good, [22] reject every kind of evil.

[23] May God himself, the God of peace, sanctify you through and through. May your whole spirit, soul and body be kept blameless at the coming of our Lord Jesus Christ. [24] The one who calls you is faithful, and he will do it.

[25] Brothers and sisters, pray for us. [26] Greet all God's people with a holy kiss. [27] I charge you before the Lord to have this letter read to all the brothers and sisters.

[28] The grace of our Lord Jesus Christ be with you.

Vision: Paul Was a Futurist

1 Thessalonians 4:13—5:11

As he closes his letter, Paul turns his attention to the future and the day of the Lord. Every leader can count on Christ's return as the one certain future event. Because of this, Paul casts vision for the future and communicates his convictions about this great event.

Like all good leaders, Paul understood the power of vision. He purposely closed this letter with encouraging words that would motivate his readers for years to come. He knew that when there is no hope for the future, there is no power in the present. By communicating his vision, Paul accomplished the following:

1. Comfort for those who had lost loved ones (4:13–15).
2. Assurance for those who believe (4:16–18).
3. Warning for those who might forget (5:1–5).
4. Direction for those who needed it (5:6–11).

INTRODUCTION TO
2 THESSALONIANS

Do the basics well and you can build your life from that foundation. In short, that was Paul's message in his second letter to the Thessalonians.

The apostle wanted his friends to develop a life of integrity and trustworthiness for others to see, and he didn't much care if they lacked "razzle-dazzle" or polish. He just wanted to know: Were you faithful to the commitments you made? Did you keep your word? Are you loving and warm when you interact with others? Can you refrain from gossip and sarcasm? Do others trust you? Is your work ethic solid?

Such questions deserved high priority among the young church members of Thessalonica, for they had become preoccupied that they might be living in the last days. Christ could return at any moment! Consequently, they began to wonder, *Why even bother working? Why bother paying off debts? Why try to invest in relationships for the long haul? We probably won't be around long anyway!* Paul recognized this unhealthy perspective and, while he agreed they should get ready for Christ's return, they also must prepare for a marathon, not a sprint. Paul challenged them to think about the future and to anticipate serving and influencing others for years to come.

To put it succinctly, some of the Thessalonians had grown lazy. They didn't prepare for tomorrow, nor did they care much about who or what they might leave behind when they left. Jesus was coming back and they simply wanted to *go*. Paul argued, "You don't get ready for Christ's return by packing suitcases and waiting on a hillside, but by staying busy obeying God and serving your fellowman. When Jesus comes back, he wants to find his people working, not idle."

Develop a Life of Integrity

God's Role in 2 Thessalonians

God uses this book to spank and chastise his people. It is parental in nature and, while it does encourage the reader, it also corrects wrong patterns of thought and behavior. God uses Paul to speak as a father and mother, just as he did in his first letter to the Thessalonians (2:7–11). This time, the letter challenges believers to build some discipline into their lives: find work, avoid gossip, refrain from being a busybody. God used this letter to "disciple" the young Thessalonians, even though Paul lived miles away.

Leaders in 2 Thessalonians

Paul, the man of sin

Other People of Influence in 2 Thessalonians

Undisciplined believers in the church

Lessons in Leadership

- Even followers who catch your vision need midcourse corrections and reminders.
- Leaders must communicate confidence and assurance.
- Good leaders practice reverse gossip: They applaud/affirm individuals behind their backs.
- Leaders who show the way succeed faster than ones who simply share the way.

God still has a message here for leaders today. First, we can never allow ourselves to slip into ruts where we become physically or mentally idle. Second, we should always strive for excellence in everything we do. We honor God when we excel above mediocrity. Leadership really is about excelling beyond the crowd. Otherwise, are we really leading anyone?

As you read this book, allow the Lord to train and admonish you to push for improvement and excellence. Press beyond good enough and go the second mile (Mt 5:41).

LEADERSHIP HIGHLIGHTS IN 2 THESSALONIANS

ENCOURAGEMENT: Paul Knew How to Boast About His People (1:3–6)	page 1439
THE MAN of Lawlessness (2:1–11)	page 1440
PAUL: A Different Kind of Leader (2:13–17)	page 1440
THE LAW OF BUY-IN: Examples Beat Exhortation (3:6–13)	page 1441

1

Paul, Silas[a] and Timothy,

To the church of the Thessalonians in God our Father and the Lord Jesus Christ:

[2]Grace and peace to you from God the Father and the Lord Jesus Christ.

Thanksgiving and Prayer

[3]We ought always to thank God for you, brothers and sisters,[b] and rightly so, because your faith is growing more and more, and the love all of you have for one another is increasing. [4]Therefore, among God's churches we boast about your perseverance and faith in all the persecutions and trials you are enduring.

[5]All this is evidence that God's judgment is right, and as a result you will be counted worthy of the kingdom of God, for which you are

---

Encouragement: Paul Knew How to Boast About His People

2 Thessalonians 1:3–6

Encouragement is the oxygen of the soul; everyone needs it and they perform better when they get it. Paul understood this fact, so in this letter he tells his friends how much he boasts about them all over Asia.

Good leaders liberally hand out encouragement. It costs little to affirm others, yet pays great dividends. In this text Paul capitalizes on the power of encouragement and teaches us a few things along the way. Encouragement should be . . .

1. *Personal* (v. 3).
   He told them personally how much he believed in them.

2. *Pointed* (v. 4).
   He told them specifically what he appreciated about them.

3. *Public* (v. 4).
   He told all his other churches how much he thought of the Thessalonians.

4. *Purposeful* (vv. 5–6).
   He had a goal he was shooting for in their lives—their motivation and vindication.

---

suffering. [6]God is just: He will pay back trouble to those who trouble you [7]and give relief to you who are troubled, and to us as well. This will happen when the Lord Jesus is revealed from heaven in blazing fire with his powerful angels. [8]He will punish those who do not know God and do not obey the gospel of our Lord Jesus. [9]They will be punished with everlasting destruction and shut out from the presence of the Lord and from the glory of his might [10]on the day he comes to be glorified in his holy people and to be marveled at among all those who have believed. This includes you, because you believed our testimony to you.

[11]With this in mind, we constantly pray for you, that our God may make you worthy of his calling, and that by his power he may bring to fruition your every desire for goodness and your every deed prompted by faith. [12]We pray this so that the name of our Lord Jesus may be glorified in you, and you in him, according to the grace of our God and the Lord Jesus Christ.[c]

The Man of Lawlessness

2

Concerning the coming of our Lord Jesus Christ and our being gathered to him, we ask you, brothers and sisters, [2]not to become easily unsettled or alarmed by the teaching allegedly from us — whether by a prophecy or by word of mouth or by letter — asserting that the day of the Lord has already come. [3]Don't let anyone deceive you in any way, for that day will not come until the rebellion occurs and the man of lawlessness[d] is revealed, the man doomed to destruction. [4]He will oppose and will exalt himself over everything that is called God or is worshiped, so that he sets himself up in God's temple, proclaiming himself to be God.

[5]Don't you remember that when I was with you I used to tell you these things? [6]And now you know what is holding him back, so that he may be revealed at the proper time. [7]For the secret power of lawlessness is already at work; but the one who now holds it back will continue to do so till he is taken out of the way. [8]And then the lawless one will be revealed, whom the Lord Jesus will overthrow with the breath of his

---

[a] 1 Greek *Silvanus*, a variant of *Silas*   [b] 3 The Greek word for *brothers and sisters* (*adelphoi*) refers here to believers, both men and women, as part of God's family; also in 2:1, 13, 15; 3:1, 6, 13.   [c] 12 Or *God and Lord, Jesus Christ*   [d] 3 Some manuscripts *sin*

mouth and destroy by the splendor of his coming. [9]The coming of the lawless one will be in accordance with how Satan works. He will use all sorts of displays of power through signs and wonders that serve the lie, [10]and all the ways that wickedness deceives those who are perishing. They perish because they refused to love the truth and so be saved. [11]For this reason God sends them a powerful delusion so that they will believe the lie [12]and so that all will be condemned who have not believed the truth but have delighted in wickedness.

Stand Firm

[13]But we ought always to thank God for you, brothers and sisters loved by the Lord, because

The Man of Lawlessness

2 Thessalonians 2:1–11

The "man of lawlessness" (or the "man doomed to destruction," 2Th 2:3) will be an extremely influential leader with international fame. He will be powerful and prideful, and will usurp a divine place in the world. Other biblical texts call him the "antichrist" or the "beast."

This evil leader reminds us that it is possible to be a great leader, but not a good one. God calls his leaders to be both great and good. Note why both great and good leadership is necessary:

Great Leadership	Good Leadership
1. Has to do with our competence	1. Has to do with our character
2. Makes us effective in our work	2. Makes our work constructive
3. Enables our cause to progress	3. Enables us to choose the right cause
4. Means we have good heads	4. Means we have good hearts
5. Ensures our skills will influence	5. Ensures our service will impact

PAUL

A Different Kind of Leader

2 Thessalonians 2:13–17

PROFILE in leadership

Godly leaders tend to have a strong passion and a deep optimism about the future. This attitude springs from their sense of purpose and from the assurance of their ultimate destination.

The apostle Paul was just such a leader.

Paul led a Thessalonian church full of young believers who expected the soon and imminent return of Christ. Add to this expectation the persecution and hardship the church faced, and you might expect to find great confusion and anxiety. It got to the point where many of the Thessalonians not only stopped working, but also attempted to thwart others from doing so.

Paul knew he needed to speak some sense to these erring brothers and correct some misperceptions about the second coming of Jesus. He told them that Christ wouldn't return until certain things had taken place, events that had not yet transpired. He also instructed them to continue working as though Christ would not return for a very long time.

Effective leaders have reason for Paul's kind of passion and optimism. They know that if Jesus returns tomorrow, all believers will share in the joy of being with him in person. On the other hand, they know that if he tarries, believers have all the more time to work to bring others to him. Who could ask for a better no-lose situation?

God chose you as firstfruits[a] to be saved through the sanctifying work of the Spirit and through belief in the truth. [14]He called you to this through our gospel, that you might share in the glory of our Lord Jesus Christ.

[15]So then, brothers and sisters, stand firm and hold fast to the teachings[b] we passed on to you, whether by word of mouth or by letter.

[16]May our Lord Jesus Christ himself and God our Father, who loved us and by his grace gave us eternal encouragement and good hope, [17]encourage your hearts and strengthen you in every good deed and word.

Request for Prayer

3 As for other matters, brothers and sisters, pray for us that the message of the Lord may spread rapidly and be honored, just as it was with you. [2]And pray that we may be delivered from wicked and evil people, for not everyone has faith. [3]But the Lord is faithful, and he will strengthen you and protect you from the evil one. [4]We have confidence in the Lord that you are doing and will continue to do the things we command. [5]May the Lord direct your hearts into God's love and Christ's perseverance.

Warning Against Idleness

[6]In the name of the Lord Jesus Christ, we command you, brothers and sisters, to keep away from every believer who is idle and disruptive and does not live according to the teaching[c] you received from us. [7]For you yourselves know how you ought to follow our example. We were not idle when we were with you, [8]nor did we eat anyone's food without paying for it. On the contrary, we worked night and day, laboring and toiling so that we would not be a burden to any of you. [9]We did this, not because we do not have the right to such help, but in order to offer ourselves as a model for you to imitate. [10]For even when we were with you, we gave you this rule: "The one who is unwilling to work shall not eat."

[11]We hear that some among you are idle and disruptive. They are not busy; they are busybodies. [12]Such people we command and urge in the Lord Jesus Christ to settle down and earn the food they eat. [13]And as for you, brothers and sisters, never tire of doing what is good.

[14]Take special note of anyone who does not obey our instruction in this letter. Do not associate with them, in order that they may feel ashamed. [15]Yet do not regard them as an enemy, but warn them as you would a fellow believer.

Final Greetings

[16]Now may the Lord of peace himself give you peace at all times and in every way. The Lord be with all of you.

[17]I, Paul, write this greeting in my own hand, which is the distinguishing mark in all my letters. This is how I write.

[18]The grace of our Lord Jesus Christ be with you all.

---

[a] 13 Some manuscripts *because from the beginning God chose you*   [b] 15 Or *traditions*   [c] 6 Or *tradition*

The Law of Buy-In: Examples Beat Exhortation

2 Thessalonians 3:6–13

Paul wanted desperately to challenge the Thessalonians regarding their lifestyle. He instinctively knew the Law of Buy-In—that people buy in to the leader before they buy in to his words. Consequently, he reminds them of the model that he and Silas left them. He knows that example is always stronger than exhortation. So, before he exhorts them to work hard, he reminds them of how hard his team had worked while among them (2Th 3:7–8). Consider Paul's argument:

The Issue	Paul's Example	Paul's Exhortation
1. Discipline	1. We're not undisciplined (v. 7)	1. Some are undisciplined (vv. 11–12)
2. Work	2. We worked hard (v. 8)	2. No work, no food (v. 10)
3. Burdens	3. We weren't a burden (vv. 8–9)	3. Don't be a burden (vv. 11–13)

INTRODUCTION TO
1 TIMOTHY

A Leadership Training Manual

The book of 1 Timothy amounts to a leadership training manual. Written by the apostle Paul to his young apprentice, Timothy, it contains not only good instruction for emerging leaders, but also lists the qualifications of a leader.

Paul and Timothy provide the clearest mentoring relationship in Scripture of any since Elijah and Elisha. Their story begins in Acts 16:1–3, when Timothy joined Paul in Lystra. Paul invested in him for a long time, taking him on short-term mission trips, letting him preach, leaving him to pastor a young church, and writing instructional letters to him while apart. Paul would do anything for his young protégé. Note how Paul developed Timothy as a leader.

First, we spot the *Principle of Purposeful Pursuit*. Paul proactively identified a young leader he could develop. He had been to Lystra and seen Timothy. His antennas were up. He insisted his team go back to challenge and invite the young man to join them.

Second, we see the *Principle of Proven Potential*. Paul did his homework on Timothy. He recognized him as a diamond in the rough. He watched Timothy prove himself in his hometown while growing up, and he knew Timothy's family and the spiritual stock he came from.

Third, Paul demonstrated the *Principle of Practical Patience*. Paul patiently selected and mentored Timothy. He was careful not to act prematurely and even advised his student not to "hasty in the laying on of hands" (5:22). He believed his team had acted too quickly in letting John Mark travel with them (Ac 12:25), and he didn't want to pick fruit too early.

God's Role in 1 Timothy

God plays out his role in 1 Timothy as the One who develops leaders who develop other leaders. Our Lord is the Master Developer who raised up Paul the apostle to equip Timothy to equip his church in Ephesus. God revealed to Timothy the fundamental principles and guidelines for church leadership, and the qualifications for overseers and their code of conduct. Through this book God speaks very personally to Timothy and every spiritual leader.

Leaders in 1 Timothy

Paul, Timothy, elders

Other People of Influence in 1 Timothy

Hymenaeus, Alexander, deacons

Lessons in Leadership

- Leaders must live by a higher standard than followers.
- Leaders are not mass produced, but must be mentored one at a time.
- Leaders must celebrate diversity, but confront deviancy.
- The greatest contribution a leader can make is to develop more leaders.
- Young leaders can influence by their example, if nothing else.
- A leader's integrity will directly affect his/her influence.

Fourth, notice the *Principle of the Participatory Process*. Paul recognized that he was but one participant in a long line of contributors in Timothy's life. In his second letter, Paul reminds Timothy of his other mentors, including his mother and grandmother. Timothy had a strong heritage before Paul came along; Paul simply played his role in the process.

Finally, we see the *Principle of Passion and Pricetags*. Paul made clear the price of leadership in both of his letters to Timothy. After Paul found Timothy in Lystra, a mob dragged the apostle out of the city, stoned him, and left him for dead. When he recovered, he returned, grabbed Timothy, and finished his work there. This kind of passion for leadership drove Paul to reproduce leaders like Timothy.

LEADERSHIP HIGHLIGHTS IN 1 TIMOTHY

LEADERSHIP by Objective (1:1–2)	page 1444
QUALIFICATIONS of Spiritual Leaders (3:1–13)	page 1445
THE QUALITIES of a Spiritual Leader (3:2–13)	page 1446
TIMOTHY: An Unlikely Leader (4:12)	page 1447
THE LAW OF THE PICTURE: The Most Important Lesson About Influence (4:12–16)	page 1448
THE LAW OF EMPOWERMENT: Timothy Was to Equip Elders (5:17–22)	page 1449
MOTIVE CHECK: Why You Do Something Determines What You Do (6:3–10, 17–19)	page 1450

1 Paul, an apostle of Christ Jesus by the command of God our Savior and of Christ Jesus our hope,

²To Timothy my true son in the faith:

Grace, mercy and peace from God the Father and Christ Jesus our Lord.

Timothy Charged to Oppose False Teachers

³As I urged you when I went into Macedonia, stay there in Ephesus so that you may command certain people not to teach false doctrines any longer ⁴or to devote themselves to myths and endless genealogies. Such things promote controversial speculations rather than advancing God's work — which is by faith. ⁵The goal of this command is love, which comes from a pure heart and a good conscience and a sincere faith. ⁶Some have departed from these and have turned to meaningless talk. ⁷They want to be teachers of the law, but they do not know what they are talking about or what they so confidently affirm.

⁸We know that the law is good if one uses it properly. ⁹We also know that the law is made not for the righteous but for lawbreakers and rebels, the ungodly and sinful, the unholy and irreligious, for those who kill their fathers or mothers, for murderers, ¹⁰for the sexually immoral, for those practicing homosexuality, for slave traders and liars and perjurers — and for whatever else is contrary to the sound doctrine ¹¹that conforms to the gospel concerning the glory of the blessed God, which he entrusted to me.

The Lord's Grace to Paul

¹²I thank Christ Jesus our Lord, who has given me strength, that he considered me trustworthy,

---

Humility:
Paul Never Forgot
Where He Came From

1 Timothy 1:12–17

While we know Paul as the greatest evangelist in history, he knew that, left to himself, he was the worst sinner (1Ti 1:15). God chose him because of his weakness, so that the Lord could display his great patience and grace in him. The more leaders mature, the more humble they become.

Leadership by Objective

1 Timothy 1:1–2

Paul wrote this book as a training manual for young Timothy and sent it to the young leader as he attempted to pastor an intimidating church in Ephesus. Paul issues five charges for Timothy:

1. *First charge:* Wage the good warfare (1:18–20).

2. *Second charge:* Conduct yourself worthy of God's house (3:14–15).

3. *Third charge:* Do not neglect your gift (4:11–16).

4. *Fourth charge:* Observe these things without prejudice (5:21).

5. *Fifth charge:* Guard what is committed to you (6:20–21).

Paul communicates his purpose on several occasions. He declares it in 1 Timothy 1:5. Paul believed in management by objective. He was quick to share his bottom line goals with his team and encouraged them to meet those objectives in the manner that suited them best. He considered the mission, not the methods, sacred. He teaches us that:

1. *Leaders manage goals.* They let people choose their own methods.

2. *Leaders create atmosphere.* They let people own their style.

3. *Leaders determine budget.* They give ownership of how money is spent.

4. *Leaders choose priorities.* They share activities with gifted people.

5. *Leaders train the team.* They freely give away the credit for victories.

appointing me to his service. [13]Even though I was once a blasphemer and a persecutor and a violent man, I was shown mercy because I acted in ignorance and unbelief. [14]The grace of our Lord was poured out on me abundantly, along with the faith and love that are in Christ Jesus. [15]Here is a trustworthy saying that deserves full acceptance: Christ Jesus came into the world to save sinners — of whom I am the worst. [16]But for that very reason I was shown mercy so that in me, the worst of sinners, Christ Jesus might display his immense patience as an example for those who would believe in him and receive eternal life. [17]Now to the King eternal, immortal, invisible, the only God, be honor and glory for ever and ever. Amen.

The Charge to Timothy Renewed

[18]Timothy, my son, I am giving you this command in keeping with the prophecies once made about you, so that by recalling them you may fight the battle well, [19]holding on to faith and a good conscience, which some have rejected and so have suffered shipwreck with regard to the faith. [20]Among them are Hymenaeus and Alexander, whom I have handed over to Satan to be taught not to blaspheme.

Instructions on Worship

2 I urge, then, first of all, that petitions, prayers, intercession and thanksgiving be made for all people — [2]for kings and all those in authority, that we may live peaceful and quiet lives in all godliness and holiness. [3]This is good, and pleases God our Savior, [4]who wants all people to be saved and to come to a knowledge of the truth.

Leaders Need Prayer Partners

1 Timothy 2:1–4

When we pray for God to change leaders, we affect them and everyone who follows them. Praying for our leaders results in an atmosphere conducive to the spreading of the gospel. Every leader ought to be proactive, recruiting and equipping a team of prayer partners, who will pray for their protection, wisdom and strength.

---

[5]For there is one God and one mediator between God and mankind, the man Christ Jesus, [6]who gave himself as a ransom for all people. This has now been witnessed to at the proper time. [7]And for this purpose I was appointed a herald and an apostle — I am telling the truth, I am not lying — and a true and faithful teacher of the Gentiles.

[8]Therefore I want the men everywhere to pray, lifting up holy hands without anger or disputing. [9]I also want the women to dress modestly, with decency and propriety, adorning themselves, not with elaborate hairstyles or gold or pearls or expensive clothes, [10]but with good deeds, appropriate for women who profess to worship God.

[11]A woman[a] should learn in quietness and full submission. [12]I do not permit a woman to teach or to assume authority over a man;[b] she

---

[a] 11 Or wife; also in verse 12   [b] 12 Or over her husband

---

Qualifications of Spiritual Leaders

1 Timothy 3:1–13

In Paul's list of qualifications for church leaders, 1 Timothy 3:10 is key: "They must first be tested." Every leader should be tested before given an official position. The preparation of a leader is crucial to their success. Frank Damazio outlines Paul's logic concerning leadership:

Leader's Salvation	Leader's Call	Leader's Preparation	Leader's Position
Leadership is planted as a seed.	Leadership begins to sprout.	Leadership is tested as a plant.	Leadership matures and bears fruit.

Paul gave this list of qualifications for two reasons: first, to provide guidelines for churches to select leaders; second, to give church leaders a checkpoint for their own spiritual lives. Paul reminds us that if anyone aspires to be a leader, he aspires to a noble task. To have the gifts and qualities and not take on leadership positions may be disobedience. The desire, however, must be accompanied by discipline.

must be quiet. [13]For Adam was formed first, then Eve. [14]And Adam was not the one deceived; it was the woman who was deceived and became a sinner. [15]But women[a] will be saved through childbearing — if they continue in faith, love and holiness with propriety.

Qualifications for Overseers and Deacons

3 Here is a trustworthy saying: Whoever aspires to be an overseer desires a noble task. [2]Now the overseer is to be above reproach, faithful to his wife, temperate, self-controlled, respectable, hospitable, able to teach, [3]not given to drunkenness, not violent but gentle, not quarrelsome, not a lover of money. [4]He must manage his own family well and see that his children obey him, and he must do so in a manner worthy of full[b] respect. [5](If anyone does not know how to manage his own family, how can he take care of God's church?) [6]He must not be a recent convert, or he may become conceited and fall under the same judgment as the devil. [7]He must also have a good reputation with outsiders, so that he will not fall into disgrace and into the devil's trap.

[8]In the same way, deacons[c] are to be worthy of respect, sincere, not indulging in much wine, and not pursuing dishonest gain. [9]They must keep hold of the deep truths of the faith with a clear conscience. [10]They must first be tested; and then if there is nothing against them, let them serve as deacons.

[11]In the same way, the women[d] are to be worthy of respect, not malicious talkers but temperate and trustworthy in everything.

[12]A deacon must be faithful to his wife and must manage his children and his household well. [13]Those who have served well gain an excellent standing and great assurance in their faith in Christ Jesus.

Reasons for Paul's Instructions

[14]Although I hope to come to you soon, I am writing you these instructions so that, [15]if I am delayed, you will know how people ought to conduct themselves in God's household, which is the church of the living God, the pillar and foundation of the truth. [16]Beyond all question, the mystery from which true godliness springs is great:

---

[a] 15 Greek *she*   [b] 4 Or *him with proper*   [c] 8 The word *deacons* refers here to Christians designated to serve with the overseers/elders of the church in a variety of ways; similarly in verse 12; and in Romans 16:1 and Phil. 1:1.   [d] 11 Possibly deacons' wives or women who are deacons

---

The Qualities of a Spiritual Leader

1 Timothy 3:2–13

What sort of qualifications must church leaders possess? Paul lists the following traits:

1. *Blameless* (v. 2)—Question: Am I quick to improve those areas that can damage my integrity?

2. *Husband of one wife* (v. 2)—Question: Am I loving my wife as Christ loved the church?

3. *Temperate, sober-minded, of good behavior* (v. 2)—Question: Am I master of myself, that I may be a servant to many?

4. *Hospitable* (v. 2)—Question: Do I exhibit a warm and welcoming spirit?

5. *Able to teach* (v. 2)—Question: Do I consistently help others learn and become better disciples?

6. *Not given to wine* (v. 3)—Question: Am I sober, watchful, and diligent, so that I do not damage those who watch me?

7. *Not violent, not quarrelsome* (v. 3)—Question: Do I have an approachable disposition that brings peace and healing?

8. *Not greedy, not covetous* (v. 3)—Question: Am I allowing my leadership to be controlled by the rich?

9. *Rules his own house well* (vv. 4–5)—Question: Do I manage my own family before I try to manage the church?

10. *Not a novice* (v. 6)—Question: Am I a seasoned, solid example for both insiders and outsiders?

He appeared in the flesh,
     was vindicated by the Spirit,[a]
was seen by angels,
     was preached among the nations,
was believed on in the world,
     was taken up in glory.

4 The Spirit clearly says that in later times some will abandon the faith and follow deceiving spirits and things taught by demons. [2]Such teachings come through hypocritical liars, whose consciences have been seared as with a hot iron. [3]They forbid people to marry and order them to abstain from certain foods, which

---

The Law of Solid Ground: Timothy Must Earn Trust

1 Timothy 4:1–16

Every spiritual leader faces at least two important duties. First, they must confront those who fall away from the faith (1Ti 4:1–6). Second, they must discipline themselves for godliness (4:7–16). When leaders fulfill these two duties, they practice the Law of Solid Ground and earn the trust of others.

God created to be received with thanksgiving by those who believe and who know the truth. [4]For everything God created is good, and nothing is to be rejected if it is received with thanksgiving, [5]because it is consecrated by the word of God and prayer.

[6]If you point these things out to the brothers and sisters,[b] you will be a good minister of Christ Jesus, nourished on the truths of the faith and of the good teaching that you have followed. [7]Have nothing to do with godless myths and old wives' tales; rather, train yourself to be godly. [8]For physical training is of some value, but godliness has value for all things, holding promise for both the present life and the life to come. [9]This is a trustworthy saying that deserves full acceptance. [10]That is why we labor and strive, because we have put our hope in the living God, who is the Savior of all people, and especially of those who believe.

[11]Command and teach these things. [12]Don't let anyone look down on you because you are young, but set an example for the believers in speech, in conduct, in love, in faith and in purity. [13]Until I come, devote yourself to the public reading of Scripture, to preaching and to

---

[a] 16 Or *vindicated in spirit*   [b] 6 The Greek word for *brothers and sisters (adelphoi)* refers here to believers, both men and women, as part of God's family.

TIMOTHY

An Unlikely Leader
1 Timothy 4:12

PROFILE in leadership

Nothing can make someone more unlikely—even unwilling—to lead than feelings of inadequacy.

Timothy, the young protégé of the apostle Paul, must have felt much as Moses did when God called him to lead Israel out of Egyptian captivity. Moses felt inadequate for the task, and likely so did Timothy.

We can identify any number of reasons that Timothy might have felt unfit to accept his assignment as pastor of the Ephesian church. He was too young and too inexperienced, and the church seemed too large for a first pastoral assignment. Besides, how could he take over for the church's founder, Paul? Would anyone take him seriously?

"Never mind all that," Paul tells him in his letter. "If you follow my instructions, you will be more than able to do the job. Don't let anyone look down on you because of your relative youth and inexperience. Rather, be the kind of example of godliness that won't allow anyone to treat you with anything but respect."

God doesn't necessarily choose leaders based on their natural talent or ability. Neither does he always choose them based on their age and experience. As Paul tells Timothy, God chooses leaders based on their availability, not their ability; on their willingness to walk in obedience to him, not their experience.

The Law of the Picture: The Most Important Lesson About Influence

1 Timothy 4:12–16

How could Timothy prevent anyone from looking down on him because of his youth? He could do it by being an example; this would ensure his effectiveness (1Ti 4:15–16). The more you walk, the less you have to talk. Live the life in front of the ones you seek to influence. Our leadership is more caught than taught. People would rather see a sermon than hear one.

teaching. ¹⁴Do not neglect your gift, which was given you through prophecy when the body of elders laid their hands on you.

¹⁵Be diligent in these matters; give yourself wholly to them, so that everyone may see your progress. ¹⁶Watch your life and doctrine closely. Persevere in them, because if you do, you will save both yourself and your hearers.

Widows, Elders and Slaves

5 Do not rebuke an older man harshly, but exhort him as if he were your father. Treat younger men as brothers, ²older women as mothers, and younger women as sisters, with absolute purity.

³Give proper recognition to those widows who are really in need. ⁴But if a widow has children or grandchildren, these should learn first of all to put their religion into practice by caring for their own family and so repaying their parents and grandparents, for this is pleasing to God. ⁵The widow who is really in need and left all alone puts her hope in God and continues night and day to pray and to ask God for help. ⁶But the widow who lives for pleasure is dead even while she lives. ⁷Give the people these instructions, so that no one may be open to blame. ⁸Anyone who does not provide for their relatives, and especially for their own household, has denied the faith and is worse than an unbeliever.

⁹No widow may be put on the list of widows unless she is over sixty, has been faithful to her husband, ¹⁰and is well known for her good deeds, such as bringing up children, showing hospitality, washing the feet of the Lord's people, helping those in trouble and devoting herself to all kinds of good deeds.

¹¹As for younger widows, do not put them on such a list. For when their sensual desires overcome their dedication to Christ, they want to marry. ¹²Thus they bring judgment on themselves, because they have broken their first pledge. ¹³Besides, they get into the habit of being idle and going about from house to house. And not only do they become idlers, but also busybodies who talk nonsense, saying things they ought not to. ¹⁴So I counsel younger widows to marry, to have children, to manage their homes and to give the enemy no opportunity for slander. ¹⁵Some have in fact already turned away to follow Satan.

¹⁶If any woman who is a believer has widows in her care, she should continue to help them and not let the church be burdened with them, so that the church can help those widows who are really in need.

¹⁷The elders who direct the affairs of the church well are worthy of double honor, especially those whose work is preaching and teaching. ¹⁸For Scripture says, "Do not muzzle an ox while

The Law of Priorities: Leadership Begins at Home, Then Goes Public

1 Timothy 5:8

In the midst of all his teaching about how believers are to relate to one another in the church, Paul prioritizes Timothy's leadership as a pastor. If anyone doesn't provide for his own home, the apostle declares, he cannot expect to provide for the church with any integrity (1Ti 5:8).

Leadership starts at home. If it doesn't work at home, don't export it. Pastors, especially, must heed this warning. Leadership works best when it is prioritized as follows:

1. I am first a *person*. I must prioritize my own relationship with God.

2. Second, I am a *partner*. I must prioritize my relationship with my spouse.

3. Third, I am a *parent*. I must prioritize my relationship with my children.

4. Fourth, I am a *pastor*. I must prioritize my relationship with my ministry.

it is treading out the grain,"[a] and "The worker deserves his wages."[b] [19]Do not entertain an accusation against an elder unless it is brought by two or three witnesses. [20]But those elders who are sinning you are to reprove before everyone, so that the others may take warning. [21]I charge you, in the sight of God and Christ Jesus and the elect angels, to keep these instructions without partiality, and to do nothing out of favoritism.

[22]Do not be hasty in the laying on of hands, and do not share in the sins of others. Keep yourself pure.

[23]Stop drinking only water, and use a little wine because of your stomach and your frequent illnesses.

[24]The sins of some are obvious, reaching the place of judgment ahead of them; the sins of others trail behind them. [25]In the same way, good deeds are obvious, and even those that are not obvious cannot remain hidden forever.

6 All who are under the yoke of slavery should consider their masters worthy of full respect, so that God's name and our teaching may

---

The Law of Empowerment: Timothy Was to Equip Elders

1 Timothy 5:17–22

Leaders are crucial to any organization. Mistakes made at the leadership level impact everyone. As the senior pastor, Timothy was to identify, prepare, and affirm his church leaders. He was to honor those who served well (1Ti 5:17–18), correct those in error (5:19–21), and prepare those who were called, patiently and carefully (5:22). Nothing should be done in haste.

Consider the steps Paul endorsed concerning the establishment of leaders in the church:

1. *Identification:* Identify those with character, gifts and influence.

2. *Separation:* Set them apart for the work of their calling.

3. *Preparation:* Equip them with the tools and experiences they need.

4. *Recognition:* Allow the church to affirm their calling.

5. *Ordination:* Lay hands on them and ordain them for the work.

---

not be slandered. [2]Those who have believing masters should not show them disrespect just because they are fellow believers. Instead, they should serve them even better because their masters are dear to them as fellow believers and are devoted to the welfare[c] of their slaves.

False Teachers and the Love of Money

These are the things you are to teach and insist on. [3]If anyone teaches otherwise and does not agree to the sound instruction of our Lord Jesus Christ and to godly teaching, [4]they are conceited and understand nothing. They have an unhealthy interest in controversies and quarrels about words that result in envy, strife, malicious talk, evil suspicions [5]and constant friction between people of corrupt mind, who have been robbed of the truth and who think that godliness is a means to financial gain.

[6]But godliness with contentment is great gain. [7]For we brought nothing into the world, and we can take nothing out of it. [8]But if we have food and clothing, we will be content with that. [9]Those who want to get rich fall into temptation and a trap and into many foolish and harmful desires that plunge people into ruin and destruction. [10]For the love of money is a root of all kinds of evil. Some people, eager for money, have wandered from the faith and pierced themselves with many griefs.

Final Charge to Timothy

[11]But you, man of God, flee from all this, and pursue righteousness, godliness, faith, love, endurance and gentleness. [12]Fight the good fight of the faith. Take hold of the eternal life to which you were called when you made your good confession in the presence of many witnesses. [13]In the sight of God, who gives life to everything, and of Christ Jesus, who while testifying before Pontius Pilate made the good confession, I charge you [14]to keep this command without spot or blame until the appearing of our Lord Jesus Christ, [15]which God will bring about in his own time — God, the blessed and only Ruler, the King of kings and Lord of lords, [16]who alone is immortal and who lives in unapproachable light, whom no one has seen or can see. To him be honor and might forever. Amen.

[17]Command those who are rich in this present world not to be arrogant nor to put their hope in wealth, which is so uncertain, but to put their hope in God, who richly provides us with

---

[a] 18 Deut. 25:4   [b] 18 Luke 10:7   [c] 2 Or *and benefit from the service*

everything for our enjoyment. ¹⁸Command them to do good, to be rich in good deeds, and to be generous and willing to share. ¹⁹In this way they will lay up treasure for themselves as a firm foundation for the coming age, so that they may take hold of the life that is truly life.

²⁰Timothy, guard what has been entrusted to your care. Turn away from godless chatter and the opposing ideas of what is falsely called knowledge, ²¹which some have professed and in so doing have departed from the faith.

Grace be with you all.

Motive Check: Why You Do Something Determines What You Do

1 Timothy 6:3–10, 17–19

Because our motives eventually determine our direction, Paul taught that right motives were even more important for the leader than right moves. Note Paul's teaching on motives:

1. *The evidence of wrong motives* (v. 3)
   The leader's doctrine drifts and the teaching does not produce godliness.

2. *The nature of wrong motives* (vv. 4–5)
   The proud leader stirs division and pursues personal gain.

3. *The results of wrong motives* (vv. 9–10)
   The leader falls into temptation, wanders from the faith, and destroys himself or herself.

So how are we to watch our motives? What key principles should we keep in mind?

1. Trouble comes when leadership performs for the wrong reasons.

2. Spiritual leadership brings rewards, so long as the rewards don't control us.

3. Prosperity is everything God gives you above food and covering.

4. We must be content with God's provision and placement.

5. We must remain dissatisfied with our own fruitfulness and pursuit of God.

6. Wrong motives can lead to wrong moves, and even disqualify us for leadership.

INTRODUCTION TO
2 TIMOTHY

You can often tell what is important to a man by listening to his last words. Deathbed statements and confessions have furnished the themes of movies and books for decades. David Livingston uttered his last words in prayer for the tribes he tried to reach in Africa. Jesus' last words make up the Great Commission. And we read the apostle Paul's last words in 2 Timothy.

This epistle is the last extant book written by the great first-century leader. In it he communicates several crucial issues with his spiritual son Timothy, the young pastor of the church in Ephesus. Paul had been his mentor and discipler. This letter contains the apostle's final lessons for his protégé.

Paul exhorts Timothy to stir up his leadership gifts. Timothy, young and timid, at times felt overwhelmed by his leadership role. Paul reminds Timothy of the day he laid his hands on him and commissioned him for ministry. Now Timothy needs to fan into flame those God-given gifts and use them without fear or shame.

Paul also motivates Timothy with word pictures. In chapter two alone the apostle uses seven leadership metaphors: teacher, soldier, athlete, farmer, worker, vessel and servant. These pictures portray a leader who is generous, disciplined, patient, rugged, tenacious, pure, hardworking, and sacrificial.

Paul also mentors his young leader in how to face difficult times. He reviews with him the culture around him and warns him of coming opposition. He describes the gospel as a trust to be preserved, a tool to be proven, and a treasure to be prized. Timothy is to advance this gospel beyond where Paul has taken it.

Finally, Paul challenges Timothy to carry on his

God's Role in 2 Timothy

God made sure that Paul spoke to the heart of a leader, not merely to the head. While the book contains practical instructions for the mind and challenging exhortations for the will, God delivers through Paul's pen words that fly straight to the heart and the emotions of Timothy.

Any leader can receive valuable encouragement from this letter. It calls leaders to lead out of their souls and their convictions, to stand for what is right even when no one else does, to finish well, regardless of the moral failure of the world. God speaks very personally and mentors us to be his kind of leaders—good ones and not evil, great ones instead of miserable.

Leaders in 2 Timothy
Paul, Timothy

Other People of Influence in 2 Timothy
Demas, Crescens, Carpus, Titus, Luke, John Mark, Alexander

Lessons in Leadership
- We are most effective when we lead in the area of our gifts.
- Leaders are to equip and develop other leaders who will do the same.
- Leaders set the standard for excellence, morality, productivity and atmosphere.

legacy. He speaks as a mentor, particularly at the end of his book, and charges him to lead with conviction, to preach the gospel just as he had received it, and to reproduce other leaders to be as faithful as he has been. This kind of labor will bring a heavenly crown of reward.

- The pathway to effective leadership is uphill with lots of hurdles along the way.
- Leaders must consciously work to finish well.
- Spiritual leaders who finish well will be rewarded richly.

LEADERSHIP HIGHLIGHTS IN 2 TIMOTHY

1 Paul, an apostle of Christ Jesus by the will of God, in keeping with the promise of life that is in Christ Jesus,

²To Timothy, my dear son:

Grace, mercy and peace from God the Father and Christ Jesus our Lord.

Thanksgiving

³I thank God, whom I serve, as my ancestors did, with a clear conscience, as night and day I constantly remember you in my prayers. ⁴Recalling your tears, I long to see you, so that I may be filled with joy. ⁵I am reminded of your sincere faith, which first lived in your grandmother Lois and in your mother Eunice and, I am persuaded, now lives in you also.

Appeal for Loyalty to Paul and the Gospel

⁶For this reason I remind you to fan into flame the gift of God, which is in you through the laying on of my hands. ⁷For the Spirit God gave us does not make us timid, but gives us power, love and self-discipline. ⁸So do not be ashamed of the testimony about our Lord or of me his prisoner. Rather, join with me in suf-

fering for the gospel, by the power of God. ⁹He has saved us and called us to a holy life — not because of anything we have done but because of his own purpose and grace. This grace was given us in Christ Jesus before the beginning of time, ¹⁰but it has now been revealed through the appearing of our Savior, Christ Jesus, who has destroyed death and has brought life and immortality to light through the gospel. ¹¹And of this gospel I was appointed a herald and an apostle and a teacher. ¹²That is why I am suffering as I am. Yet this is no cause for shame, because I know whom I have believed, and am convinced that he is able to guard what I have entrusted to him until that day.

¹³What you heard from me, keep as the pattern of sound teaching, with faith and love in Christ Jesus. ¹⁴Guard the good deposit that was entrusted to you — guard it with the help of the Holy Spirit who lives in us.

Examples of Disloyalty and Loyalty

¹⁵You know that everyone in the province of Asia has deserted me, including Phygelus and Hermogenes.

¹⁶May the Lord show mercy to the household of Onesiphorus, because he often refreshed me and was not ashamed of my chains. ¹⁷On the contrary, when he was in Rome, he searched hard for me until he found me. ¹⁸May the Lord grant that he will find mercy from the Lord on that day! You know very well in how many ways he helped me in Ephesus.

The Appeal Renewed

2 You then, my son, be strong in the grace that is in Christ Jesus. ²And the things you have heard me say in the presence of many witnesses entrust to reliable people who will also be qualified to teach others. ³Join with me in suffering, like a good soldier of Christ Jesus. ⁴No one serving as a soldier gets entangled in civilian affairs, but rather tries to please his commanding officer. ⁵Similarly, anyone who competes as an athlete does not receive the victor's crown except by competing according to the rules. ⁶The hardworking farmer should be the first to receive a share of the crops. ⁷Reflect on what I am saying, for the Lord will give you insight into all this.

⁸Remember Jesus Christ, raised from the dead, descended from David. This is my gospel, ⁹for which I am suffering even to the point of being chained like a criminal. But God's word is not chained. ¹⁰Therefore I endure everything for the sake of the elect, that they too may obtain

---

Gifts: We Are Most Effective When We Lead from Our Gifts

2 Timothy 1:5–7

Our leadership will always be most natural, most effective and most influential when we lead from our gifts and strengths. Then it won't be forced, feel awkward, seem artificial, or copy someone else. Effective leadership occurs when we lead from our own identity. Paul believed Timothy's leadership would grow strong when he remembered three truths:

1. *His secure heritage* (v. 5)
   Paul reminded Timothy of the spiritual foundation his family gave him.

2. *His spiritual gift* (v. 6)
   Paul reminded Timothy to stir up the gifts inside him and lead from those gifts.

3. *His solid conviction* (v. 7)
   Paul reminded Timothy that God didn't give him fear, but the tools to do the job.

PAUL AND THE LAW OF EXPLOSIVE GROWTH
To Add Growth, Lead Followers—To Multiply, Lead Leaders

2 Timothy 2:1

LEADERS WHO develop followers grow their organization only one person at a time. But leaders who develop leaders multiply their growth, because for every leader they develop, they also receive all of that leader's followers. Add ten followers to your organization, and you have the power of ten people. Add ten leaders to your organization, and you have the power of ten leaders times all the followers and leaders *they* influence. That's the difference between addition and multiplication. It's like growing your organization by teams instead of by individuals.

■　　■　　■　　■　　■

Paul was a master of explosive growth. He dedicated himself to people and activities that would impact the world. His strategy remains as effective today as it was two thousand years ago. To promote explosive growth . . .

1. *Attract and equip people.*

Everywhere Paul went, he gathered listeners and taught them. Paul would enter a town and begin teaching—for days, months, and sometimes years. No matter where he went, he continually equipped as many people as possible.

2. *Find and mentor emerging leaders.*

Paul mentored too many leaders to count. Some of them, such as Silas, came to him already possessing influence and leadership skills (Ac 15:22). Others were homegrown, such as Timothy (1Ti 1:2). But no matter their background, Paul took them with him as he worked, preached, and led. Then he turned them loose, giving them responsibility and authority.

3. *Create new organizations.*

Paul didn't hoard the leaders he developed. He raised up leaders to multiply and extend his influence. And he did it with a strategy—he planted churches. Wherever he traveled, he left a church with leaders to carry on the ministry.

4. *Engage in the ongoing development of leaders.*

Paul visited the leaders in his churches to follow up with them, encourage them, and give them direction. Paul's second missionary journey began with the following suggestion: "Let us go back and visit the believers in all the towns where we preached the word of the Lord and see how they are doing" (Ac 15:36).

You can achieve a large vision only through explosive growth. Anything less will leave you far short of your dreams. But becoming an explosive-growth leader requires more than a change in the way you work; it requires a change in the way you think.

Leaders Who Gather Followers vs. Leaders Who Develop Leaders

Consider seven major differences between leaders who gather followers and leaders who develop other leaders:

1. *Leaders who gather followers need to be needed; leaders who develop leaders want to be succeeded.*

Many who desire to lead followers do so because followers stroke their egos. They feel indispensable. But leaders who develop leaders work to make themselves dispensable. They don't want a following, but a legacy.

2. *Leaders who gather followers focus on people's weaknesses; leaders who develop leaders focus on their strengths.*

Ineffective leaders focus on their followers' weaknesses, sometimes out of misunderstanding the way development and encouragement work, other times because of insecurity—they want to keep their followers off-balance. But strong leaders focus on their people's strengths because they know that is the key to developing people.

3. *Leaders who gather followers focus on the bottom 20 percent; leaders who develop leaders focus on the top 20 percent.*

Explosive-growth leaders focus on the best in their leaders; they also focus on the best potential leaders. In contrast, leaders of followers usually give their attention to the loudest and most difficult people, the ones who take and take, giving nothing in return.

4. *Leaders who gather followers treat everyone the same; leaders who develop leaders treat people as individuals.*

When Paul went on his missionary journeys, he didn't try to take everybody with him. Nor did he give everyone an equal chance to oversee the churches he started. He treated each person he encountered according to his gifts, calling, and willingness to grow.

5. *Leaders who gather followers spend their time; leaders who develop leaders invest their time.*

Everywhere Paul went, he took companions. He considered the time he spent with them an investment. And if he didn't see a return—as in the case of John Mark (Ac 13:13)—Paul felt reluctant to keep investing in them (15:37–40). Think of your work with emerging leaders as an opportunity to invest in them.

6. *Leaders who gather followers ask for little commitment; leaders who develop leaders ask for great commitment.*

Following a leader takes commitment. But it's nothing compared to the commitment of a follower who is asked to lead others. As you ask people to step up to leadership, don't treat your request lightly. Let them know to what you are asking them to commit. Acquaint them with the sacrifice and the service that come with leadership.

7. *Leaders who gather followers impact this generation; leaders who develop leaders impact future generations.*

People who lead followers impact only the individuals whose lives they touch personally. But people who develop and lead leaders extend their reach.

It takes a good leader to gather a group of followers and lead them to achieve a worthy goal. But it takes a great leader to lead other leaders—and that's the only kind of leader who can take an organization to the highest level and achieve explosive growth.

The Law of Empowerment: God Gives Us What We Need to Lead

2 Timothy 1:7–8

God always gives us what we need to lead. Paul reminded Timothy that God didn't give him the timidity he felt; that came either from Timothy's own baggage or from the pit of hell itself. Instead, God equipped him with love, power and a sound mind. All leaders need these three fundamental tools:

Love: The relational ingredient that enables us to attract and connect with others.
Power: The courage and competence to get the job done.
Sound mind: The perspective and wisdom to grasp a vision and take the right steps.

Because God has so equipped us, he instructs us to "not be ashamed . . . join with me in suffering" (2Ti 1:8). God gave Timothy (and us!) everything needed to accomplish the job. He empowers us before he ever expects from us. He gives before he demands. We receive his competence before we receive his commands.

the salvation that is in Christ Jesus, with eternal glory.

¹¹Here is a trustworthy saying:

If we died with him,
    we will also live with him;
¹²if we endure,
    we will also reign with him.
If we disown him,
    he will also disown us;
¹³if we are faithless,
    he remains faithful,
    for he cannot disown himself.

Dealing With False Teachers

¹⁴Keep reminding God's people of these things. Warn them before God against quarreling about words; it is of no value, and only ruins those who listen. ¹⁵Do your best to present yourself to God as one approved, a worker who does not need to be ashamed and who correctly handles the word of truth. ¹⁶Avoid godless chatter, because those who indulge in it will become more and more ungodly. ¹⁷Their teaching will

spread like gangrene. Among them are Hymenaeus and Philetus, ¹⁸who have departed from the truth. They say that the resurrection has already taken place, and they destroy the faith of some. ¹⁹Nevertheless, God's solid foundation stands firm, sealed with this inscription: "The Lord knows those who are his," and, "Everyone who confesses the name of the Lord must turn away from wickedness."

²⁰In a large house there are articles not only of gold and silver, but also of wood and clay; some are for special purposes and some for common use. ²¹Those who cleanse themselves from the latter will be instruments for special purposes, made holy, useful to the Master and prepared to do any good work.

²²Flee the evil desires of youth and pursue righteousness, faith, love and peace, along with those who call on the Lord out of a pure heart. ²³Don't have anything to do with foolish and stupid arguments, because you know they produce quarrels. ²⁴And the Lord's servant must not be quarrelsome but must be kind to everyone, able to teach, not resentful. ²⁵Opponents must be gently instructed, in the hope that God will grant

Portraits of a Leader

2 Timothy 2:2–26

Paul was a master at using metaphors to illustrate what a leader should look like. Right after he encourages Timothy to be strong (2Ti 2:1), he gives him seven snapshots of what he meant:

1. *A teacher* (v. 2)
   A leader is to be reproductive.

2. *A soldier* (vv. 3–4)
   A leader is to be loyal.

3. *An athlete* (v. 5)
   A leader is to be disciplined.

4. *A farmer* (vv. 6–7)
   A leader is to be a hard worker.

5. *A worker* (vv. 15–19)
   A leader is to be diligent.

6. *A vessel* (vv. 20–22)
   A leader is to be pure.

7. *A servant* (vv. 23–26)
   A leader is to be submissive.

Courage: The Process of Taking a Stand

2 Timothy 2:22—3:17

Paul knew how important it was to encourage Timothy, for the young leader would have to take a stand in many tough situations. So he charged him to take courage and do what was right in difficult times.

Courage is the first essential quality for effective leadership. Leaders initiate and take a stand even when no one else travels with them. Paul prepares Timothy for this act with his words:

1. *There is something to prevent* (2:22–23).
   Leaders must flee temptations, such as pleasure and power, that ruin their personal lives.

2. *There are some things to pursue* (2:22).
   Leaders must chase after qualities that will build their character and integrity.

3. *There are some things to portray* (2:24–26).
   Leaders must model right attitudes so that others will want to submit to God.

4. *There are some things to perceive* (3:1–9).
   Leaders must read the times and take responsibility to hold firm to what is right.

5. *There is something to pronounce* (3:10–17).
   Leaders must hold forth God's Word and use it as a standard for training.

---

them repentance leading them to a knowledge of the truth, [26]and that they will come to their senses and escape from the trap of the devil, who has taken them captive to do his will.

3 But mark this: There will be terrible times in the last days. [2]People will be lovers of themselves, lovers of money, boastful, proud, abusive, disobedient to their parents, ungrateful, unholy, [3]without love, unforgiving, slanderous, without self-control, brutal, not lovers of the good, [4]treacherous, rash, conceited, lovers of pleasure rather than lovers of God— [5]having a form of godliness but denying its power. Have nothing to do with such people.

[6]They are the kind who worm their way into homes and gain control over gullible women, who are loaded down with sins and are swayed by all kinds of evil desires, [7]always learning but never able to come to a knowledge of the truth. [8]Just as Jannes and Jambres opposed Moses, so also these teachers oppose the truth. They are men of depraved minds, who, as far as the faith is concerned, are rejected. [9]But they will not get very far because, as in the case of those men, their folly will be clear to everyone.

A Final Charge to Timothy

[10]You, however, know all about my teaching, my way of life, my purpose, faith, patience, love, endurance, [11]persecutions, sufferings — what kinds of things happened to me in Antioch, Iconium and Lystra, the persecutions I endured. Yet the Lord rescued me from all of them. [12]In fact, everyone who wants to live a godly life in Christ Jesus will be persecuted, [13]while evildoers and impostors will go from bad to worse, deceiving and being deceived. [14]But as for you, continue in what you have learned and have become convinced of, because you know those from whom you learned it, [15]and how from infancy you have known the Holy Scriptures, which are able to make you wise for salvation through faith in Christ Jesus. [16]All Scripture is God-breathed and is useful for teaching, rebuking, correcting

The Law of Sacrifice: Timothy Must Give Up to Go Up

2 Timothy 3:10–17

Paul called Timothy to surrender many of the comforts he could have enjoyed as a pastor. Paul teaches us how to handle sacrifices by addressing our *example* as a leader (2Ti 3:10–13), our *experience* as a leader (3:14–15), and our *equipping* as a leader (3:16–17).

The Word of God: An Equipping Tool

2 Timothy 3:16–17

The Scripture is a thorough equipping tool, providing doctrine, reproof, correction and instruction, so that everyone may be equipped for every good work (2Ti 3:16–17). Using Scripture, the leader is to lay the foundation, provide direction, confront others when they err, correct their behavior, and help them progress again.

and training in righteousness, [17]so that the servant of God[a] may be thoroughly equipped for every good work.

4 In the presence of God and of Christ Jesus, who will judge the living and the dead, and in view of his appearing and his kingdom, I give you this charge: [2]Preach the word; be prepared in season and out of season; correct, rebuke and encourage — with great patience and careful instruction. [3]For the time will come when people will not put up with sound doctrine. Instead, to suit their own desires, they will gather around them a great number of teachers to say what

The Law of Priorities: Timothy's Three Priorities

2 Timothy 4:1–8

Paul's last written communication reveals a sense of urgency. He wastes no words; every one of them counts. More than any other passage, this text tells us what is most important to Paul, the leader. He challenges Timothy with three priorities:

1. *Preach the Word* (vv. 1–2).
   Timothy must keep the message alive, teaching urgently, persistently, and with conviction.

2. *Do the work* (vv. 3–5).
   Timothy was to do the work of an evangelist, fulfilling his call, reaching his potential.

3. *Run the race* (vv. 6–8).
   Timothy was to emulate Paul, who finished his course and won the prize.

their itching ears want to hear. [4]They will turn their ears away from the truth and turn aside to myths. [5]But you, keep your head in all situations, endure hardship, do the work of an evangelist, discharge all the duties of your ministry.

[6]For I am already being poured out like a drink offering, and the time for my departure is near. [7]I have fought the good fight, I have finished the race, I have kept the faith. [8]Now there is in store for me the crown of righteousness, which the Lord, the righteous Judge, will award to me on that day — and not only to me, but also to all who have longed for his appearing.

Personal Remarks

[9]Do your best to come to me quickly, [10]for Demas, because he loved this world, has deserted me and has gone to Thessalonica. Crescens has gone to Galatia, and Titus to Dalmatia. [11]Only Luke is with me. Get Mark and bring him with you, because he is helpful to me in my ministry. [12]I sent Tychicus to Ephesus. [13]When you come, bring the cloak that I left with Carpus at Troas, and my scrolls, especially the parchments.

[14]Alexander the metalworker did me a great deal of harm. The Lord will repay him for what he has done. [15]You too should be on your guard against him, because he strongly opposed our message.

[16]At my first defense, no one came to my support, but everyone deserted me. May it not be held against them. [17]But the Lord stood at my side and gave me strength, so that through me the message might be fully proclaimed and all the Gentiles might hear it. And I was delivered from the lion's mouth. [18]The Lord will rescue me from every evil attack and will bring me safely to his heavenly kingdom. To him be glory for ever and ever. Amen.

[a] 17 Or *that you, a man of God,*

The Law of Legacy

2 Timothy 4:6–8

Paul's deathbed was no place of sorrow. He had planted churches, mentored leaders, established doctrine, and written epistles. The only thing left was his homecoming. Paul saw life as a race to be won, a battle to be fought, and a trust to be kept (2Ti 4:7). His crown awaited him.

Mentoring: Paul and Timothy Both Fulfill the Call

2 Timothy 4:9–21

From many of the leaders in whom Paul invested, he also needed an investment in return. He acknowledges he needs Timothy (2Ti 4:9), Mark (4:11) and the books of Carpus (4:13). Paul poured his life into every one of them and received from every one of them.

Final Greetings

[19]Greet Priscilla[a] and Aquila and the household of Onesiphorus. [20]Erastus stayed in Corinth, and I left Trophimus sick in Miletus. [21]Do your best to get here before winter. Eubulus greets you, and so do Pudens, Linus, Claudia and all the brothers and sisters.[b]

[22]The Lord be with your spirit. Grace be with you all.

[a] 19 Greek *Prisca*, a variant of *Priscilla*   [b] 21 The Greek word for *brothers and sisters* (*adelphoi*) refers here to believers, both men and women, as part of God's family.

INTRODUCTION TO TITUS

Instruction on Leadership Qualifications

The epistle of Titus is the third book in a row written by Paul the apostle to a young leader he was mentoring. Titus joined Paul's ministry team and traveled with him through Asia Minor. Paul believed in Titus and called him a "true son" in the faith (1:4). The apostle trusted him with the toughest of assignments, often sending him to troubled churches so that he could iron out problems and correct leadership errors.

Paul's mentoring relationship to Titus often gets lost in the shadow of Timothy or other team members in the book of Acts. Titus's name never appears in Acts and shows up in only three of Paul's other letters. The little information we have indicates that Titus became one of Paul's closest and most trusted apprentices and colleagues. The apostle describes Titus as having the same "concern" for the Corinthian church that he does (2Co 8:16–17), and the young man even goes to Corinth to appeal to the church on *his own initiative*. Clearly, Paul and Titus seem cut from the same cloth. Paul chose his men well.

Many apt descriptions come to mind for Titus. First, he was a *trusted son*. When Paul traveled to Jerusalem to fight for salvation by grace through faith alone, he took Titus with him. This young man became Paul's prime exhibit of a Gentile convert worthy of full acceptance by the church, apart from the ritual of circumcision.

Second, Titus was a *troubleshooter*. Like Paul, Titus was a tough, bottom-line decision maker. In fact, Paul wrote this letter to Titus while the young leader completed a special assignment in Crete. He had been sent there to resolve some problems and prepare a set of leaders in the

God's Role in Titus

God has used this book in the lives of many leaders throughout history. Through it he has provided instruction on leadership qualifications, the mentoring roles of older saints to younger ones, principles for dealing with false teachers, and the relationship between sound doctrine and lifestyle. God teaches us it is possible for a strong leader to reproduce himself in another strong leader and thereby extend his accomplishments. Titus provides a terrific example of the Law of the Inner Circle. Paul accomplished more and was able to follow up on work he'd started because he could send Titus as an extension of himself.

Leaders in Titus
Paul, Titus, elders

Other People of Influence in Titus
Zenas, Apollos, older saints of the church in Crete

Lessons in Leadership
- The quickest way to gain leadership is to solve problems.
- Leaders must be both tough and tender, knowing how to confront and resolve conflict.
- Leaders must not only prepare other leaders, but also furnish guiding principles by which to lead.

church (1:5), like a secretary of state dispatched to troubled nations on missions of diplomacy.

Third, Titus was a *task-oriented specialist*. Paul sent him on a number of special assignments that required a specialist. The apostle sent Titus to Corinth to collect an offering for the needy in Jerusalem. On another occasion, Paul sent him back to Corinth to confront some messy situations and opponents of Paul's teaching. In Crete he needed to organize and establish church leaders in each city.

Finally, Titus was a *teachable servant*. He demonstrated himself to be a meek and willing learner under Paul's tutelage. He remained subordinate to Paul; we have no record of him questioning Paul's judgment or demands. This servant-leader proved valuable in reaching Asia Minor, since he was a Gentile himself.

- Elders are to assume the role of mentors to the younger generation.
- Positions of authority require leaders to model an appropriate lifestyle.

LEADERSHIP HIGHLIGHTS IN TITUS

THE LAW OF EXPLOSIVE GROWTH: Titus's Job Was to Prepare Leaders (1:5)	page 1462
PROBLEM SOLVING: Titus, the Man to Look For (1:10–14)	page 1463
THE LAW OF EMPOWERMENT: Elders Are to Mentor and Model for Young Leaders (2:1–7)	page 1464
LEADER DEVELOPMENT: From Shepherding to Developing (2:15)	page 1465

1 Paul, a servant of God and an apostle of Jesus Christ to further the faith of God's elect and their knowledge of the truth that leads to godliness— [2]in the hope of eternal life, which God, who does not lie, promised before the beginning of time, [3]and which now at his appointed season he has brought to light through the preaching entrusted to me by the command of God our Savior,

[4]To Titus, my true son in our common faith:

Grace and peace from God the Father and Christ Jesus our Savior.

Appointing Elders Who Love What Is Good

[5]The reason I left you in Crete was that you might put in order what was left unfinished and appoint[a] elders in every town, as I directed you. [6]An elder must be blameless, faithful to his wife, a man whose children believe[b] and are not open to the charge of being wild and disobedient. [7]Since an overseer manages God's household, he must be blameless—not overbearing, not quick-tempered, not given to drunkenness, not violent, not pursuing dishonest gain. [8]Rather, he must be hospitable, one who loves what is good, who is self-controlled, upright, holy and disciplined. [9]He must hold firmly to the trustworthy message as it has been taught, so that he can encourage others by sound doctrine and refute those who oppose it.

Rebuking Those Who Fail to Do Good

[10]For there are many rebellious people, full of meaningless talk and deception, especially those of the circumcision group. [11]They must be silenced, because they are disrupting whole households by teaching things they ought not to teach—and that for the sake of dishonest gain. [12]One of Crete's own prophets has said it: "Cretans are always liars, evil brutes, lazy gluttons."[c] [13]This saying is true. Therefore rebuke them sharply, so that they will be sound in the faith [14]and will pay no attention to Jewish myths or to the merely human commands of those who

---

[a] 5 Or *ordain*   [b] 6 Or *children are trustworthy*   [c] 12 From the Cretan philosopher Epimenides

---

The Law of Explosive Growth:
Titus's Job Was to Prepare Leaders

Titus 1:5

Paul left Titus in Crete to do two things: organize the people and appoint leaders. The new converts in Crete had experienced the power of God. Now they needed strong leadership to preserve what God had done.

Titus was a leader of leaders whom Paul trusted to solve problems in the most difficult of places. Paul knew that every church needs a leader to establish order and to develop a team of elders. This was Titus's job, and it remains the job of leaders today. Consider the following method of accomplishing this important task:

1. *Choose the men.*
   How creative am I at finding new people to invest in?

2. *Cultivate the models.*
   How am I doing at turning my people into examples?

3. *Create the ministries.*
   How am I at creating ministry opportunities for these leaders?

4. *Construct the management.*
   How am I at monitoring them along the way?

5. *Communicate the mindset.*
   How am I at constantly keeping the vision alive?

6. *Celebrate the mentoring.*
   How do I encourage and celebrate growth?

21 QUALITIES

PROBLEM SOLVING   Titus, the Man to Look For

Titus 1:10–14

WHILE TIMOTHY had a shepherd's heart and a tendency toward timidity, Titus was the man to call upon when a church had a problem. The apostle Paul sent Titus to both Corinth and Crete to organize the chaos and establish leaders. Titus later returned to Corinth to organize the offering Paul wanted to collect for the church in Jerusalem. Still later, when conflict arose between the Corinthian church and Paul, Titus took the initiative and negotiated with the church until he achieved peace. Paul trusted him more than anyone else to solve problems and make peace among the people.

Problem solving is the fastest way to gain leadership. Left alone, things go awry. Left alone, people go astray. Left alone, plans go amiss. When someone steps forward with solutions, he or she catches the attention of others. The man with the plan is the man with the power. Consider the characteristics of good problem solvers.

1. *They anticipate problems.*
   Titus anticipated problems in Corinth and prevented a possible church split.
2. *They accept the truth.*
   Titus was always honest with Paul and the troubled churches he led. He faced reality.
3. *They see the big picture.*
   Titus knew how to deal with the church in Crete, due to his larger perspective.
4. *They handle one thing at a time.*
   Titus took the initiative and dealt with one major conflict at a time.

5. *They don't give up a major goal when they're down.*
   Titus tenaciously addressed the conflicts in Corinth until he solved them.

When you face a problem, how do you react? Do you ignore it and hope it will go away? Do you feel paralyzed or powerless? Do you tend to give up after one attempt at a solution? The ability to solve problems comes from experience in facing and overcoming obstacles. If you never try, fail, and try again, you'll never master the difficulty. To improve your problem-solving skills, do the following:

1. *Look for trouble.*
   Don't avoid problems; attack them. Use caution, but find them and take them to someone with experience in that area. We learn to solve problems by pursuing them.
2. *Develop a method.*
   Come up with a system. Take time to discover the real issue; find out what others have done; have your team study options; prioritize solutions and try one.
3. *Surround yourself with problem solvers.*
   Find others who complement your weaknesses, especially if you aren't a good problem solver. Diverse thinking allows you to solve a variety of problems.

For a negative example of problem solving, see p. 20.

Character: Qualifications for Church Leadership

Titus 1:5–9

What qualities should church leaders possess? Paul outlines for Titus a list similar to the one he gave Timothy. Note that most of the traits he mentions deal with personal character, not techniques, gifts, or skills. Note what Paul considered most important:

1. *Personal life:* blameless, not self-willed, not quick-tempered, not violent, soberminded, holy, self-controlled.

2. *Family life:* husband of one wife, with faithful children.

3. *Social life:* hospitable, not accused of dissipation, not given to wine.

4. *Financial life:* a steward of God, not greedy for money.

5. *Professional life:* not accused of insubordination, a lover of what is good, just, holding fast the faithful word, able to exhort and convict those who contradict.

reject the truth. [15]To the pure, all things are pure, but to those who are corrupted and do not believe, nothing is pure. In fact, both their minds and consciences are corrupted. [16]They claim to know God, but by their actions they deny him. They are detestable, disobedient and unfit for doing anything good.

Doing Good for the Sake of the Gospel

2 You, however, must teach what is appropriate to sound doctrine. [2]Teach the older men to be temperate, worthy of respect, self-controlled, and sound in faith, in love and in endurance.

[3]Likewise, teach the older women to be reverent in the way they live, not to be slanderers or addicted to much wine, but to teach what is good. [4]Then they can urge the younger women to love their husbands and children, [5]to be self-controlled and pure, to be busy at home, to be kind, and to be subject to their husbands, so that no one will malign the word of God.

[6]Similarly, encourage the young men to be self-controlled. [7]In everything set them an example by doing what is good. In your teaching show integrity, seriousness [8]and soundness of speech that cannot be condemned, so that those who oppose you may be ashamed because they have nothing bad to say about us.

[9]Teach slaves to be subject to their masters in everything, to try to please them, not to talk back to them, [10]and not to steal from them, but to show that they can be fully trusted, so that in every way they will make the teaching about God our Savior attractive.

The Law of Empowerment: Elders Are to Mentor and Model for Young Leaders

Titus 2:1–7

Paul helps us to see four levels of leadership development. He himself represented the first level. He charged Titus as the second level. Titus was to teach older men and women, representing the third level. Finally, Titus was also to teach the young men and women, representing the fourth level. Each level was to model leadership, and to mentor and empower others in leadership. This is the pattern throughout Scripture:

1. Abraham and Lot
2. Jacob and Joseph
3. Jethro and Moses
4. Moses and Joshua
5. Naomi and Ruth
6. Eli and Samuel
7. Jonathan and David
8. David and Mephibosheth
9. Nathan and David
10. Elijah and Elisha
11. Elijah and the prophets
12. Elizabeth and Mary
13. John the Baptist and disciples
14. Barnabas and Saul
15. Barnabas and Mark
16. Paul and Silas
17. Paul and Timothy
18. Paul and Philemon
19. Paul and Aquila
20. Paul and Julius
21. Jesus and the Twelve

Leader Development: From Shepherding to Developing

Titus 2:15

Paul modeled more than mere nurturing of his young disciple, Titus; the apostle developed him as a leader. He focused not merely on meeting immediate needs, but on producing a leader who could go on meeting needs without Paul's help.

Paul had a passion for developing leaders such as Timothy and Titus. Consider the necessary progression for growing beyond mere shepherding, to equipping and developing:

Shepherding	Equipping	Developing
1. Care	1. Train for ministry	1. Train for personal growth
2. Immediate-need focus	2. Task focus	2. Person focus
3. Need-oriented	3. Skill-oriented	3. Character-oriented
4. Masses	4. Many	4. Few
5. Maintenance	5. Addition	5. Multiplication
6. Feel better	6. Unleashing	6. Empowering
7. Immediate	7. Short-term	7. Long-term
8. Nurture	8. Teaching	8. Mentoring
9. What is the problem?	9. What do I need?	9. What do they need?
10. They begin to walk	10. They walk the first mile	10. They walk the second mile

[11] For the grace of God has appeared that offers salvation to all people. [12] It teaches us to say "No" to ungodliness and worldly passions, and to live self-controlled, upright and godly lives in this present age, [13] while we wait for the blessed hope — the appearing of the glory of our great God and Savior, Jesus Christ, [14] who gave himself for us to redeem us from all wickedness and to purify for himself a people that are his very own, eager to do what is good.

[15] These, then, are the things you should teach. Encourage and rebuke with all authority. Do not let anyone despise you.

Saved in Order to Do Good

3 Remind the people to be subject to rulers and authorities, to be obedient, to be ready to do whatever is good, [2] to slander no one, to be peaceable and considerate, and always to be gentle toward everyone.

[3] At one time we too were foolish, disobedient, deceived and enslaved by all kinds of passions and pleasures. We lived in malice and envy, being hated and hating one another. [4] But when the kindness and love of God our Savior appeared, [5] he saved us, not because of righteous things we had done, but because of his mercy. He saved us through the washing of rebirth and renewal by the Holy Spirit, [6] whom he poured out on us generously through Jesus Christ our Savior, [7] so that,

having been justified by his grace, we might become heirs having the hope of eternal life. [8] This is a trustworthy saying. And I want you to stress these things, so that those who have trusted in God may be careful to devote themselves to doing what is good. These things are excellent and profitable for everyone.

[9] But avoid foolish controversies and genealogies and arguments and quarrels about the law, because these are unprofitable and useless. [10] Warn a divisive person once, and then warn them a second time. After that, have nothing to do with them. [11] You may be sure that such

Authority and Submission: Everyone Is Responsible to Someone

Titus 3:1–2

Everyone and everything exists in submission to someone else. Even in the home, God has called parents to assume responsibility for the health and growth of the family. Those in authority do not necessarily have greater intelligence or gifts, but they do have greater responsibility.

people are warped and sinful; they are self-condemned.

Final Remarks

¹²As soon as I send Artemas or Tychicus to you, do your best to come to me at Nicopolis, because I have decided to winter there. ¹³Do everything you can to help Zenas the lawyer and Apollos on their way and see that they have everything they need. ¹⁴Our people must learn to devote themselves to doing what is good, in order to provide for urgent needs and not live unproductive lives.

¹⁵Everyone with me sends you greetings. Greet those who love us in the faith.

Grace be with you all.

INTRODUCTION TO PHILEMON

A Case Study in Healthy Confrontation

The letter from Paul to his friend Philemon reveals a warm, touching side to the apostle's personality and leadership style.

Philemon was a friend of Paul's who helped start the Colossian church in his own home. Some time after Paul left, one of Philemon's slaves, Onesimus, ran away. Interestingly, Paul does not deliver a discourse against slavery, but instead teaches on how we are to relate to each other in Christ. He suggests that a completely new frame of reference, brotherhood, should transform all earthly relationships. Consequently, Paul leads Philemon as a brother, avoiding compulsion. Paul leads Onesimus not as a slave, but as a brother who has learned to want to do what is right. In this letter we see Paul act as a mentor to Philemon and to Onesimus in their relationship to one another.

Yet what a heavy issue to discuss through the mail! Philemon had a legal right to punish Onesimus for running away. However, as God would have it, Onesimus found Paul in prison and joined him there to talk. During those discussions, no doubt, Paul led him to the Lord. At this point, the issue got sticky, for Onesimus was not merely a runaway slave, but a brother in Christ. Paul challenged Philemon to receive Onesimus back as a brother—clearly, a lot to ask. Philemon must have felt confused, angry, and perhaps even thought about ignoring the request and giving Paul the silent treatment.

Paul made this option nearly impossible, however. The apostle wrote with such heart and grace that Philemon couldn't help but respond in kind. This letter stands as a case study in healthy confrontation, the act every leader must master. All leaders *will* face conflict. Difficult

God's Role in Philemon

Some have wondered why the Lord included this personal letter in Scripture. After all, it doesn't address general issues facing everyone. Yet a number of reasons suggest why God wanted this letter in the Bible.

First, it teaches us about healthy leadership and relationships within the church. Second, at the time Paul wrote, the master-slave relationship posed a problem for the whole church. Even today in employer-employee relationships, we are to relate to believers in a way distinct from the unbelieving world. Finally, God provides a snapshot of the personal side of a leader practicing healthy confrontation.

Leaders in Philemon

Paul, Timothy, Philemon

Other People of Influence in Philemon

Onesimus, Apphia, Archippus

Lessons in Leadership

- Good leaders always initiate confrontation.
- Managing conflict goes with the leader's territory.
- Leadership is relationships.
- Spiritual leaders motivate others as brothers and sisters, not through compulsion.

people and circumstances *will* arise. Leaders must recognize that conflict is *natural*: It occurs simply because of human differences. Conflict is also *neutral*: In itself, it is neither destructive nor constructive. And conflict is *normal*: It happens to all of us.

Paul seemed to understand all this. He addressed the problem through this letter written from prison, then sent it with great confidence to Philemon through a messenger—none other than Onesimus himself.

LEADERSHIP HIGHLIGHTS IN PHILEMON

THE LAW OF CONNECTION: Paul Connects, Then Asks for Help (4–22)	**page 1469**
PROBLEM SOLVING: Healthy Confrontation and Resolution (8–10)	**page 1470**

¹Paul, a prisoner of Christ Jesus, and Timothy our brother,

To Philemon our dear friend and fellow worker— ²also to Apphia our sister and Archippus our fellow soldier—and to the church that meets in your home:

³Grace and peace to you[a] from God our Father and the Lord Jesus Christ.

Thanksgiving and Prayer

⁴I always thank my God as I remember you in my prayers, ⁵because I hear about your love for all his holy people and your faith in the Lord Jesus. ⁶I pray that your partnership with us in the faith may be effective in deepening your understanding of every good thing we share for the sake of Christ. ⁷Your love has given me great joy and encouragement, because you, brother, have refreshed the hearts of the Lord's people.

Paul's Plea for Onesimus

⁸Therefore, although in Christ I could be bold and order you to do what you ought to do, ⁹yet I prefer to appeal to you on the basis of love. It is as none other than Paul—an old man and now also a prisoner of Christ Jesus— ¹⁰that I appeal to you for my son Onesimus,[b] who became my son while I was in chains. ¹¹Formerly he was useless to you, but now he has become useful both to you and to me.

¹²I am sending him—who is my very heart— back to you. ¹³I would have liked to keep him with me so that he could take your place in helping me while I am in chains for the gospel. ¹⁴But I did not want to do anything without your consent, so that any favor you do would not seem forced but would be voluntary. ¹⁵Perhaps the reason he was separated from you for a little while was that you might have him back forever— ¹⁶no longer as a slave, but better than a slave, as a dear brother. He is very dear to me but even dearer to you, both as a fellow man and as a brother in the Lord.

¹⁷So if you consider me a partner, welcome him as you would welcome me. ¹⁸If he has done you any wrong or owes you anything, charge it

---

[a] 3 The Greek is plural; also in verses 22 and 25; elsewhere in this letter "you" is singular.   [b] 10 Onesimus means useful.

The Law of Connection: Paul Connects, Then Asks for Help

Philemon 4–22

In the very personal letter of Philemon, Paul asks his friend to do something very difficult: graciously receive back a runaway slave. Before he confronts Philemon, Paul connects by walking through the following stages of conflict management:

1. *The compliment stage* (vv. 4–7)
   Paul affirmed Philemon and reminded him of his love. Good leaders begin confrontation with affirmation. They focus on positive qualities.

2. *The compromise stage* (vv. 8–13)
   Before his appeal, Paul concedes the present status of the slave, Onesimus. Good leaders own some responsibility for the conflict and recognize their differences.

3. *The choice stage* (v. 14)
   Paul sought the consent of Philemon to send back Onesimus. He laid out the challenge to receive him. In this stage, leaders clearly articulate the decision in front of both parties.

4. *The challenge stage* (vv. 15–20)
   Paul challenged Philemon to do what was right. He committed to steps he'd take to make things right, but issued a challenge to Philemon to respond and take the high road.

5. *The confidence stage* (vv. 21–22)
   Paul expressed confidence in Philemon that he would, indeed, do what was right in the sight of God. Paul believed the best about his friend and communicated his love for him.

to me. ¹⁹I, Paul, am writing this with my own hand. I will pay it back — not to mention that you owe me your very self. ²⁰I do wish, brother, that I may have some benefit from you in the Lord; refresh my heart in Christ. ²¹Confident of your obedience, I write to you, knowing that you will do even more than I ask.

²²And one thing more: Prepare a guest room for me, because I hope to be restored to you in answer to your prayers.

²³Epaphras, my fellow prisoner in Christ Jesus, sends you greetings. ²⁴And so do Mark, Aristarchus, Demas and Luke, my fellow workers.

²⁵The grace of the Lord Jesus Christ be with your spirit.

When Leaders Are Challenged to Do the Difficult

Philemon 21

Would Philemon forgive or erect emotional walls against Paul? He had done nothing wrong; in fact, *he* had been wronged. Fortunately, Philemon acted instead of reacting. Church history tells us Philemon responded with grace, received Onesimus back, and enabled him not only to participate in the church, but later to become a bishop!

Problem Solving: Healthy Confrontation and Resolution

Philemon 8–10

The best way to solve many problems is to confront them. Sometimes those problems are people. Paul took great pains to confront Philemon about Onesimus. Consider these steps for confronting someone:

1. *Pray through your own anger.* Don't let emotion lead you. Wait until you can be objective.

2. *Initiate the contact.* Don't wait for the other person. God calls us to make things right.

3. *Begin with affirmation.* Encourage first, then receive permission to talk candidly.

4. *Admit you have a problem.* Don't say it's the other person's problem; admit you are struggling.

5. *Bring up the issue and explain you don't understand what's happened.* Aim to clarify.

6. *Let the person respond.* After you lay out the issue, let the individual speak from his or her angle.

7. *Narrow the focus.* Identify and prioritize the issues. Go after one change at a time.

8. *Establish forgiveness and repentance, if needed.* Don't stop until change occurs.

9. *Compromise on opinions, not on principles.* Be flexible with everything except truth.

10. *Pray and affirm your love as you close.* Never let the person doubt God's love or yours.

INTRODUCTION TO HEBREWS

A Solid Foundation for Faith in Christ

Like Romans, the book of Hebrews addresses both doctrine and duty in the Christian's life. An unnamed author wrote the book to Jewish believers who needed a solid foundation for their faith in Jesus as the Messiah. They needed to learn that their new lifestyle didn't require circumcision, sacrifices, or other Old Testament traditions. This book provides a radical apologetic on Christianity.

Three profound leadership truths jump off the pages of this great book. First, the writer is not merely a teacher, but a leader attempting to convince Jewish believers to shift to new paradigms and to live in the freedom of grace. Every leader is a teacher in one sense, helping others to learn the ways of the organization and prepare for their job. But not every teacher is a leader! While no one can positively identify the author, one thing is clear: It was written by a strong, compelling leader determined to help his people change the way they thought and acted. New paradigms had to be embraced and fresh vision had to be cast to explain the superiority of the new paradigms.

Second, the book portrays Jesus not only as a wonderful Savior, but also as a superior Leader. Several times the book speaks of the superiority of Christ as compared to other Old Covenant leaders (Moses, Joshua, angels). The book can be divided into three sections. The first section talks about the superiority of Christ's Person (1:1—4:13); the second talks about the superiority of Christ's work (4:14—10:18); the third discusses the superiority of the Christian lifestyle (10:19—13:25). Hence, the book proclaims Jesus to be a superior Leader with a superior life.

Third, the book clearly develops the power of vision. Effective leadership always operates off of a compel-

God's Role in Hebrews

God uses the book of Hebrews to build a bridge between the Old and New Testaments. Hebrews quotes a wide variety of Old Testament passages to present a strong case for Jesus' superiority over everything that came before him. God speaks clearly of the Person and work of Christ, and in this book provides us with a clear discourse on the need for a new covenant and why faith is so central to his kingdom. God acts as both an Apologist and a Visionary, convincing readers to change and move with him as he ushers in an age of grace.

Leaders in Hebrews

The writer, Moses, Joshua, Melchizedek, Hebrew patriarchs, Jesus

Other People of Influence in Hebrews

The Old Testament Israelites, the high priests

Lessons in Leadership

- As both God and man, Jesus had authority to lead.
- Leaders gain credibility when they suffer with those they lead.
- Good leaders build a sense of urgency, destiny and family.
- Leaders earn their right to be heard by serving others.

ling vision. Throughout the 13 chapters of Hebrews, the writer paints pictures of a better life, contrasting it with the old one. In the famous "Hall of Faith" (11:1–40), we see a number of patriarchs living by faith and energized by a vision: "All these people were still living by faith when they died. They did not receive the things promised; they only saw them and welcomed them from a distance (11:13). The entire book communicates a huge vision and a preferred future.

- Effective leaders build a convincing case for why their people should change.
- Productive leaders communicate the superiority and the benefits of their ideas.
- Faith and vision are not options to good leadership, but necessities.
- Christ's leadership and covenant are superior to any before or since.

LEADERSHIP HIGHLIGHTS IN HEBREWS

God's Final Word: His Son

1 In the past God spoke to our ancestors through the prophets at many times and in various ways, [2]but in these last days he has spoken to us by his Son, whom he appointed heir of all things, and through whom also he made the universe. [3]The Son is the radiance of God's glory and the exact representation of his being, sustaining all things by his powerful word. After he had provided purification for sins, he sat down at the right hand of the Majesty in heaven. [4]So he became as much superior to the angels as the name he has inherited is superior to theirs.

The Son Superior to Angels

[5]For to which of the angels did God ever say,

"You are my Son;
today I have become your Father"[a]?

Or again,

"I will be his Father,
and he will be my Son"[b]?

[6]And again, when God brings his firstborn into the world, he says,

"Let all God's angels worship him."[c]

[7]In speaking of the angels he says,

"He makes his angels spirits,
and his servants flames of fire."[d]

[8]But about the Son he says,

"Your throne, O God, will last for ever and
ever;
a scepter of justice will be the scepter of
your kingdom.
[9]You have loved righteousness and hated
wickedness;
therefore God, your God, has set you
above your companions
by anointing you with the oil of joy."[e]

[10]He also says,

"In the beginning, Lord, you laid the
foundations of the earth,
and the heavens are the work of your
hands.
[11]They will perish, but you remain;
they will all wear out like a garment.
[12]You will roll them up like a robe;
like a garment they will be changed.
But you remain the same,
and your years will never end."[f]

The Law of Respect: Jesus Is the Superior Leader

Hebrews 1:3–12

Hebrews paints Jesus as the ultimate revelation of God, superior to the prophets or the angels. Jesus is the exact representation of God (Heb 1:3) and has a position above everyone (1:5–12). Jesus displayed his strength in creation and salvation. He is the strongest Leader and even the angels follow him.

---

[13]To which of the angels did God ever say,

"Sit at my right hand
until I make your enemies
a footstool for your feet"[g]?

[14]Are not all angels ministering spirits sent to serve those who will inherit salvation?

Warning to Pay Attention

2 We must pay the most careful attention, therefore, to what we have heard, so that we do not drift away. [2]For since the message spoken through angels was binding, and every violation and disobedience received its just punishment, [3]how shall we escape if we ignore so great a salvation? This salvation, which was first announced by the Lord, was confirmed to us by those who heard him. [4]God also testified to it by signs, wonders and various miracles, and by gifts of the Holy Spirit distributed according to his will.

Jesus Made Fully Human

[5]It is not to angels that he has subjected the world to come, about which we are speaking. [6]But there is a place where someone has testified:

"What is mankind that you are mindful of
them,
a son of man that you care for him?
[7]You made them a little[h] lower than the
angels;
you crowned them with glory and honor
[8] and put everything under their feet."[i,j]

---

[a] 5 Psalm 2:7 [b] 5 2 Samuel 7:14; 1 Chron. 17:13
[c] 6 Deut. 32:43 (see Dead Sea Scrolls and Septuagint)
[d] 7 Psalm 104:4 [e] 9 Psalm 45:6,7 [f] 12 Psalm 102:25-27
[g] 13 Psalm 110:1 [h] 7 Or them for a little while
[i] 6-8 Psalm 8:4-6 [j] 7,8 Or *You made him a little lower than the angels;/ you crowned him with glory and honor/* [8] *and put everything under his feet.*

In putting everything under them,[a] God left nothing that is not subject to them.[a] Yet at present we do not see everything subject to them.[a] [9]But we do see Jesus, who was made lower than the angels for a little while, now crowned with glory and honor because he suffered death, so that by the grace of God he might taste death for everyone.

[10]In bringing many sons and daughters to glory, it was fitting that God, for whom and through whom everything exists, should make the pioneer of their salvation perfect through what he suffered. [11]Both the one who makes people holy and those who are made holy are of the same family. So Jesus is not ashamed to call them brothers and sisters.[b] [12]He says,

"I will declare your name to my brothers and sisters;
in the assembly I will sing your praises."[c]

The Law of Sacrifice: Jesus Became Like Us So We Could Be Like Him

Hebrews 2:1–18

Jesus is the ultimate example of a leader who paid the price to get the job done. Consider how Christ practiced the Law of Sacrifice:

1. He was made lower than the angels, even though they worshiped him (v. 9).

2. He tasted death for everyone, even though he is the immortal God (v. 9).

3. He suffered for us, even though he is the omnipotent Savior (v. 10).

4. He calls us brothers, even though he is the Creator of us all (vv. 11–13).

5. He shared our humanity, even though he is the unlimited, perfect Spirit (v. 14).

Why did Jesus go through all this sacrifice? Verses 17 and 18 give the answer:

1. That he could be merciful to us in our humanity.

2. That he could empathize with our temptations.

3. That he could deliver us from our sufferings.

[13]And again,

"I will put my trust in him."[d]

And again he says,

"Here am I, and the children God has given me."[e]

[14]Since the children have flesh and blood, he too shared in their humanity so that by his death he might break the power of him who holds the power of death—that is, the devil— [15]and free those who all their lives were held in slavery by their fear of death. [16]For surely it is not angels he helps, but Abraham's descendants. [17]For this reason he had to be made like them,[f] fully human in every way, in order that he might become a merciful and faithful high priest in service to God, and that he might make atonement for the sins of the people. [18]Because he himself suffered when he was tempted, he is able to help those who are being tempted.

Jesus Greater Than Moses

3 Therefore, holy brothers and sisters, who share in the heavenly calling, fix your thoughts on Jesus, whom we acknowledge as our apostle and high priest. [2]He was faithful to the one who appointed him, just as Moses was faithful in all God's house. [3]Jesus has been found worthy of greater honor than Moses, just as the builder of a house has greater honor than the house itself. [4]For every house is built by someone, but God is the builder of everything. [5]"Moses was faithful as a servant in all God's house,"[g] bearing witness to what would be spoken by God in the future. [6]But Christ is faithful as the Son over God's house. And we are his house, if indeed we hold firmly to our confidence and the hope in which we glory.

Warning Against Unbelief

[7]So, as the Holy Spirit says:

"Today, if you hear his voice,
[8]   do not harden your hearts
as you did in the rebellion,
     during the time of testing in the wilderness,
[9]where your ancestors tested and tried me,
     though for forty years they saw what I did.

---

[a] 8 Or him   [b] 11 The Greek word for brothers and sisters (adelphoi) refers here to believers, both men and women, as part of God's family; also in verse 12; and in 3:1, 12; 10:19; 13:22.   [c] 12 Psalm 22:22   [d] 13 Isaiah 8:17
[e] 13 Isaiah 8:18   [f] 17 Or like his brothers   [g] 5 Num. 12:7

The Law of Respect: Jesus Is Superior to Moses

Hebrews 3:2–5

By comparing Jesus' priesthood to Moses and the old covenant, once again the writer attempts to demonstrate Christ's superiority to Moses, knowing that people naturally follow the strongest leader. They followed Moses, but if Jesus is measurably superior to Moses, then perhaps he deserves a look. Consider the unequaled leadership of Jesus:

Moses' Priesthood	Jesus' Priesthood
1. Faithful to God (v. 2)	1. Faithful to God (v. 2)
2. Honor and glory (v. 3)	2. More honor and glory (v. 3)
3. The house (vv. 3–4)	3. The builder of the house (vv. 3–4)
4. A servant (v. 5)	4. A Son (v. 5)
5. Testimony to truth (v. 5)	5. The Truth (v. 5)

10 That is why I was angry with that generation;
I said, 'Their hearts are always going astray,
and they have not known my ways.'
11 So I declared on oath in my anger,
'They shall never enter my rest.' "*a*

12 See to it, brothers and sisters, that none of you has a sinful, unbelieving heart that turns away from the living God. 13 But encourage one another daily, as long as it is called "Today," so that none of you may be hardened by sin's deceitfulness. 14 We have come to share in Christ, if indeed we hold our original conviction firmly to the very end. 15 As has just been said:

"Today, if you hear his voice,
do not harden your hearts
as you did in the rebellion."*b*

16 Who were they who heard and rebelled? Were they not all those Moses led out of Egypt? 17 And with whom was he angry for forty years? Was it not with those who sinned, whose bodies perished in the wilderness? 18 And to whom did God swear that they would never enter his rest if not to those who disobeyed? 19 So we see that they were not able to enter, because of their unbelief.

A Sabbath-Rest for the People of God

4 Therefore, since the promise of entering his rest still stands, let us be careful that none of you be found to have fallen short of it. 2 For we also have had the good news proclaimed to us, just as they did; but the message they heard was of no value to them, because they did not share the faith of those who obeyed.*c* 3 Now we who have believed enter that rest, just as God has said,

"So I declared on oath in my anger,
'They shall never enter my rest.' "*d*

And yet his works have been finished since the creation of the world. 4 For somewhere he has spoken about the seventh day in these words: "On the seventh day God rested from all his works."*e* 5 And again in the passage above he says, "They shall never enter my rest."

6 Therefore since it still remains for some to enter that rest, and since those who formerly had the good news proclaimed to them did not go in because of their disobedience, 7 God again set a certain day, calling it "Today." This he did when a long time later he spoke through David, as in the passage already quoted:

"Today, if you hear his voice,
do not harden your hearts."*b*

8 For if Joshua had given them rest, God would not have spoken later about another day. 9 There remains, then, a Sabbath-rest for the people of God; 10 for anyone who enters God's rest also rests from their works,*f* just as God did from his. 11 Let us, therefore, make every effort to enter that rest, so that no one will perish by following their example of disobedience.

12 For the word of God is alive and active.

---

a 11 Psalm 95:7-11   *b* 15,7 Psalm 95:7,8   *c* 2 Some manuscripts *because those who heard did not combine it with faith*   *d* 3 Psalm 95:11; also in verse 5   *e* 4 Gen. 2:2   *f* 10 Or *labor*

Sharper than any double-edged sword, it penetrates even to dividing soul and spirit, joints and marrow; it judges the thoughts and attitudes of the heart. [13]Nothing in all creation is hidden from God's sight. Everything is uncovered and laid bare before the eyes of him to whom we must give account.

Jesus the Great High Priest

[14]Therefore, since we have a great high priest who has ascended into heaven,[a] Jesus the Son of God, let us hold firmly to the faith we profess. [15]For we do not have a high priest who is unable to empathize with our weaknesses, but we have one who has been tempted in every way, just as we are—yet he did not sin. [16]Let us then approach God's throne of grace with confidence, so that we may receive mercy and find grace to help us in our time of need.

Servanthood: Jesus Earns His Right to Be Followed

Hebrews 4:1–16

We face no temptation that Jesus did not face. He earned his right to be followed by enduring every temptation, without succumbing to any of them. The Servant Jesus worked to identify with us, but he didn't stop there. We can put our confidence in him because he serves us with his sympathy and his salvation.

5 Every high priest is selected from among the people and is appointed to represent the people in matters related to God, to offer gifts and sacrifices for sins. [2]He is able to deal gently with those who are ignorant and are going astray, since he himself is subject to weakness. [3]This is why he has to offer sacrifices for his own sins, as well as for the sins of the people. [4]And no one takes this honor on himself, but he receives it when called by God, just as Aaron was.

[5]In the same way, Christ did not take on himself the glory of becoming a high priest. But God said to him,

"You are my Son;
today I have become your Father."[b]

[6]And he says in another place,

"You are a priest forever,
in the order of Melchizedek."[c]

[7]During the days of Jesus' life on earth, he offered up prayers and petitions with fervent cries and tears to the one who could save him from death, and he was heard because of his reverent submission. [8]Son though he was, he learned obedience from what he suffered [9]and, once made perfect, he became the source of eternal salvation for all who obey him [10]and was designated by God to be high priest in the order of Melchizedek.

Teachability: Even Jesus Learned Obedience

Hebrews 5:8

Although Hebrews describes Jesus as the superior Leader and perfect High Priest, he learned obedience through the things he suffered. Luke 2:52 tells us Jesus increased in wisdom, stature and favor with God and man. This growth didn't stop at age 12. All good leaders learn from their experiences, especially suffering.

Warning Against Falling Away

[11]We have much to say about this, but it is hard to make it clear to you because you no longer try to understand. [12]In fact, though by this time you ought to be teachers, you need someone to teach you the elementary truths of God's word all over again. You need milk, not solid food! [13]Anyone who lives on milk, being still an infant, is not acquainted with the teaching about righteousness. [14]But solid food is for the mature, who by constant use have trained themselves to distinguish good from evil.

6 Therefore let us move beyond the elementary teachings about Christ and be taken forward to maturity, not laying again the foundation of repentance from acts that lead to death,[d] and of faith in God, [2]instruction about cleansing rites,[e] the laying on of hands, the resurrection of the dead, and eternal judgment. [3]And God permitting, we will do so.

[4]It is impossible for those who have once been enlightened, who have tasted the heavenly gift, who have shared in the Holy Spirit, [5]who have tasted the goodness of the word of God and the

---

[a] 14 Greek has gone through the heavens   [b] 5 Psalm 2:7
[c] 6 Psalm 110:4   [d] 1 Or from useless rituals   [e] 2 Or about baptisms

powers of the coming age [6]and who have fallen[a] away, to be brought back to repentance. To their loss they are crucifying the Son of God all over again and subjecting him to public disgrace. [7]Land that drinks in the rain often falling on it and that produces a crop useful to those for whom it is farmed receives the blessing of God. [8]But land that produces thorns and thistles is worthless and is in danger of being cursed. In the end it will be burned.

[9]Even though we speak like this, dear friends, we are convinced of better things in your case — the things that have to do with salvation. [10]God is not unjust; he will not forget your work and the love you have shown him as you have helped his people and continue to help them. [11]We want each of you to show this same diligence to the very end, so that what you hope for may be fully realized. [12]We do not want you to become lazy, but to imitate those who through faith and patience inherit what has been promised.

The Certainty of God's Promise

[13]When God made his promise to Abraham, since there was no one greater for him to swear by, he swore by himself, [14]saying, "I will surely bless you and give you many descendants."[b] [15]And so after waiting patiently, Abraham received what was promised.

[16]People swear by someone greater than themselves, and the oath confirms what is said and puts an end to all argument. [17]Because God wanted to make the unchanging nature of his purpose very clear to the heirs of what was promised, he confirmed it with an oath. [18]God did this so that, by two unchangeable things in which it is impossible for God to lie, we who have fled to take hold of the hope set before us may be greatly encouraged. [19]We have this hope as an anchor for the soul, firm and secure. It

---

The Law of Solid Ground: God Swore by Himself

Hebrews 6:13–18

When God made a promise to Abraham, both took an oath. God not only kept his promise, but could find no better way to communicate his good faith than to use his own name. Leaders whose word is as good as a bond personify both integrity and trustworthiness.

The Law of Navigation: Jesus Is Our Forerunner

Hebrews 4:14–16; 6:19–20

Aforerunner was a small boat that navigated its way through dark waters, connecting a rope from the mother ship to the shore so the ship could dock without damage. Jesus is our forerunner, navigating unsafe waters ahead of us. He makes it possible for all his followers to make it home safely.

---

enters the inner sanctuary behind the curtain, [20]where our forerunner, Jesus, has entered on our behalf. He has become a high priest forever, in the order of Melchizedek.

Melchizedek the Priest

7 This Melchizedek was king of Salem and priest of God Most High. He met Abraham returning from the defeat of the kings and blessed him, [2]and Abraham gave him a tenth of everything. First, the name Melchizedek means "king of righteousness"; then also, "king of Salem" means "king of peace." [3]Without father or mother, without genealogy, without beginning of days or end of life, resembling the Son of God, he remains a priest forever.

[4]Just think how great he was: Even the patriarch Abraham gave him a tenth of the plunder! [5]Now the law requires the descendants of Levi who become priests to collect a tenth from the people — that is, from their fellow Israelites — even though they also are descended from Abraham. [6]This man, however, did not trace his descent from Levi, yet he collected a tenth from Abraham and blessed him who had the promises. [7]And without doubt the lesser is blessed by the greater. [8]In the one case, the tenth is collected by people who die; but in the other case, by him who is declared to be living. [9]One might even say that Levi, who collects the tenth, paid the tenth through Abraham, [10]because when Melchizedek met Abraham, Levi was still in the body of his ancestor.

Jesus Like Melchizedek

[11]If perfection could have been attained through the Levitical priesthood — and indeed

---

[a] 6 Or age, [6]if they fall　　[b] 14 Gen. 22:17

the law given to the people established that priesthood — why was there still need for another priest to come, one in the order of Melchizedek, not in the order of Aaron? [12]For when the priesthood is changed, the law must be changed also. [13]He of whom these things are said belonged to a different tribe, and no one from that tribe has ever served at the altar. [14]For it is clear that our Lord descended from Judah, and in regard to that tribe Moses said nothing about priests. [15]And what we have said is even more clear if another priest like Melchizedek appears, [16]one who has become a priest not on the basis of a regulation as to his ancestry but on the basis of the power of an indestructible life. [17]For it is declared:

> "You are a priest forever,
>   in the order of Melchizedek."[a]

[18]The former regulation is set aside because it was weak and useless [19](for the law made nothing perfect), and a better hope is introduced, by which we draw near to God.

[20]And it was not without an oath! Others became priests without any oath, [21]but he became a priest with an oath when God said to him:

> "The Lord has sworn
>   and will not change his mind:
>   'You are a priest forever.'"[a]

[22]Because of this oath, Jesus has become the guarantor of a better covenant.

[23]Now there have been many of those priests, since death prevented them from continuing in office; [24]but because Jesus lives forever, he has a permanent priesthood. [25]Therefore he is able to save completely[b] those who come to God through him, because he always lives to intercede for them.

[26]Such a high priest truly meets our need — one who is holy, blameless, pure, set apart from sinners, exalted above the heavens. [27]Unlike the other high priests, he does not need to offer sacrifices day after day, first for his own sins, and then for the sins of the people. He sacrificed for their sins once for all when he offered himself. [28]For the law appoints as high priests men in all their weakness; but the oath, which came after the law, appointed the Son, who has been made perfect forever.

The High Priest of a New Covenant

8 Now the main point of what we are saying is this: We do have such a high priest, who sat down at the right hand of the throne of the

Communication: Melchizedek Is a Metaphor for Christ

Hebrews 7:1–22

If leaders fail to communicate with others, they travel alone. The writer to the Hebrews provides a picture of Christ's superiority by comparing Jesus to Melchizedek. Good communicators give a picture of something familiar to explain something unfamiliar. Melchizedek supplied a powerful metaphor because, like Christ . . .

1. *His leadership was universal, not national.* He wasn't limited to a priesthood in a single country.

2. *His leadership was superior, not mediocre.* He is pictured as a superior and respected leader to whom even Abraham gave a tithe.

3. *His leadership was based on righteousness, not selfishness.* This king's name meant "righteousness over Salem (peace)."

4. *His leadership was personal, not hereditary.* He didn't lead because he was born into the right family or had the right genes.

5. *His leadership is eternal, not temporary.* He abides as a priest perpetually, just like Christ.

Majesty in heaven, [2]and who serves in the sanctuary, the true tabernacle set up by the Lord, not by a mere human being.

[3]Every high priest is appointed to offer both gifts and sacrifices, and so it was necessary for this one also to have something to offer. [4]If he were on earth, he would not be a priest, for there are already priests who offer the gifts prescribed by the law. [5]They serve at a sanctuary that is a copy and shadow of what is in heaven. This is why Moses was warned when he was about to build the tabernacle: "See to it that you make everything according to the pattern shown you on the mountain."[c] [6]But in fact the ministry Jesus has received is as superior to theirs as the covenant of which he is mediator is superior to the

old one, since the new covenant is established on better promises.

⁷For if there had been nothing wrong with that first covenant, no place would have been sought for another. ⁸But God found fault with the people and said[a]:

"The days are coming, declares the Lord,
when I will make a new covenant
with the people of Israel
and with the people of Judah.
⁹It will not be like the covenant
I made with their ancestors
when I took them by the hand
to lead them out of Egypt,
because they did not remain faithful to my
covenant,
and I turned away from them,
declares the Lord.
¹⁰This is the covenant I will establish with the
people of Israel
after that time, declares the Lord.
I will put my laws in their minds
and write them on their hearts.
I will be their God,
and they will be my people.
¹¹No longer will they teach their neighbor,
or say to one another, 'Know the Lord,'
because they will all know me,
from the least of them to the greatest.
¹²For I will forgive their wickedness
and will remember their sins no more."[b]

¹³By calling this covenant "new," he has made the first one obsolete; and what is obsolete and outdated will soon disappear.

Worship in the Earthly Tabernacle

9 Now the first covenant had regulations for worship and also an earthly sanctuary. ²A tabernacle was set up. In its first room were the lampstand and the table with its consecrated bread; this was called the Holy Place. ³Behind the second curtain was a room called the Most Holy Place, ⁴which had the golden altar of incense and the gold-covered ark of the covenant. This ark contained the gold jar of manna, Aaron's staff that had budded, and the stone tablets of the covenant. ⁵Above the ark were the cherubim of the Glory, overshadowing the atonement cover. But we cannot discuss these things in detail now.

⁶When everything had been arranged like this, the priests entered regularly into the outer room to carry on their ministry. ⁷But only the high priest entered the inner room, and that only once a year, and never without blood, which he offered for himself and for the sins the people had committed in ignorance. ⁸The Holy Spirit was showing by this that the way into the Most Holy Place had not yet been disclosed as long as the first tabernacle was still functioning. ⁹This is an illustration for the present time, indicating that the gifts and sacrifices being offered were not able to clear the conscience of the worshiper. ¹⁰They are only a matter of food and drink and various ceremonial washings — external regulations applying until the time of the new order.

The Blood of Christ

¹¹But when Christ came as high priest of the good things that are now already here,[c] he went through the greater and more perfect tabernacle that is not made with human hands, that is to say, is not a part of this creation. ¹²He did not enter by means of the blood of goats and calves; but he entered the Most Holy Place once for all by his own blood, thus obtaining[d] eternal redemption. ¹³The blood of goats and bulls and the ashes of a heifer sprinkled on those who are ceremonially unclean sanctify them so that they are outwardly clean. ¹⁴How much more, then, will the blood of Christ, who through the eternal Spirit offered himself unblemished to God, cleanse our consciences from acts that lead to death,[e] so that we may serve the living God!

¹⁵For this reason Christ is the mediator of a new covenant, that those who are called may receive the promised eternal inheritance — now that he has died as a ransom to set them free from the sins committed under the first covenant.

¹⁶In the case of a will,[f] it is necessary to prove the death of the one who made it, ¹⁷because a will is in force only when somebody has died; it never takes effect while the one who made it is living. ¹⁸This is why even the first covenant was not put into effect without blood. ¹⁹When Moses had proclaimed every command of the law to all the people, he took the blood of calves, together with water, scarlet wool and branches of hyssop, and sprinkled the scroll and all the people. ²⁰He said, "This is the blood of the covenant, which God has commanded you to keep."[g] ²¹In the same way, he sprinkled with the blood both the tabernacle and everything used

---

[a] 8 Some manuscripts may be translated *fault and said to the people.* [b] 12 Jer. 31:31-34 [c] 11 Some early manuscripts *are to come* [d] 12 Or *blood, having obtained* [e] 14 Or *from useless rituals* [f] 16 Same Greek word as *covenant*; also in verse 17 [g] 20 Exodus 24:8

in its ceremonies. ²²In fact, the law requires that nearly everything be cleansed with blood, and without the shedding of blood there is no forgiveness.

²³It was necessary, then, for the copies of the heavenly things to be purified with these sacrifices, but the heavenly things themselves with better sacrifices than these. ²⁴For Christ did not enter a sanctuary made with human hands that was only a copy of the true one; he entered heaven itself, now to appear for us in God's presence. ²⁵Nor did he enter heaven to offer himself again and again, the way the high priest enters the Most Holy Place every year with blood that is not his own. ²⁶Otherwise Christ would have had to suffer many times since the creation of the world. But he has appeared once for all at the culmination of the ages to do away with sin by the sacrifice of himself. ²⁷Just as people are destined to die once, and after that to face judgment, ²⁸so Christ was sacrificed once to take away the sins of many; and he will appear a second time, not to bear sin, but to bring salvation to those who are waiting for him.

The Law of Connection: God Connects with the Head and Heart

Hebrews 8:1—9:28

The new covenant is a better ministry, established by a better Mediator, and established on better promises (Heb 8:6). God will write his law on the heart, not just on a stone tablet. By this point, the writer has convinced readers at both the head and the heart level—thus making the connection.

Christ's Sacrifice Once for All

10 The law is only a shadow of the good things that are coming—not the realities themselves. For this reason it can never, by the same sacrifices repeated endlessly year after year, make perfect those who draw near to worship. ²Otherwise, would they not have stopped being offered? For the worshipers would have been cleansed once for all, and would no longer have felt guilty for their sins. ³But those sacrifices are an annual reminder of sins. ⁴It is impossible for the blood of bulls and goats to take away sins.

⁵Therefore, when Christ came into the world, he said:

"Sacrifice and offering you did not desire,
    but a body you prepared for me;
⁶with burnt offerings and sin offerings
    you were not pleased.
⁷Then I said, 'Here I am—it is written about
        me in the scroll—
    I have come to do your will, my God.'"[a]

⁸First he said, "Sacrifices and offerings, burnt offerings and sin offerings you did not desire, nor were you pleased with them"—though they were offered in accordance with the law. ⁹Then he said, "Here I am, I have come to do your will." He sets aside the first to establish the second. ¹⁰And by that will, we have been made holy through the sacrifice of the body of Jesus Christ once for all.

¹¹Day after day every priest stands and performs his religious duties; again and again he offers the same sacrifices, which can never take away sins. ¹²But when this priest had offered for all time one sacrifice for sins, he sat down at the right hand of God, ¹³and since that time he waits for his enemies to be made his footstool. ¹⁴For by one sacrifice he has made perfect forever those who are being made holy.

¹⁵The Holy Spirit also testifies to us about this. First he says:

¹⁶"This is the covenant I will make with
        them
    after that time, says the Lord.
I will put my laws in their hearts,
    and I will write them on their minds."[b]

¹⁷Then he adds:

"Their sins and lawless acts
    I will remember no more."[c]

¹⁸And where these have been forgiven, sacrifice for sin is no longer necessary.

A Call to Persevere in Faith

¹⁹Therefore, brothers and sisters, since we have confidence to enter the Most Holy Place by the blood of Jesus, ²⁰by a new and living way opened for us through the curtain, that is, his body, ²¹and since we have a great priest over the house of God, ²²let us draw near to God with a sincere heart and with the full assurance that faith brings, having our hearts sprinkled to

[a] 7 Psalm 40:6-8 (see Septuagint)   [b] 16 Jer. 31:33   [c] 17 Jer. 31:34

cleanse us from a guilty conscience and having our bodies washed with pure water. ²³Let us hold unswervingly to the hope we profess, for he who promised is faithful. ²⁴And let us consider how we may spur one another on toward love and good deeds, ²⁵not giving up meeting together, as some are in the habit of doing, but encouraging one another — and all the more as you see the Day approaching.

²⁶If we deliberately keep on sinning after we have received the knowledge of the truth, no sacrifice for sins is left, ²⁷but only a fearful expectation of judgment and of raging fire that will consume the enemies of God. ²⁸Anyone who rejected the law of Moses died without mercy on the testimony of two or three witnesses. ²⁹How much more severely do you think someone deserves to be punished who has trampled the Son of God underfoot, who has treated as an unholy thing the blood of the covenant that sanctified them, and who has insulted the Spirit of grace? ³⁰For we know him who said, "It is mine to avenge; I will repay,"ᵃ and again, "The Lord will judge his people."ᵇ ³¹It is a dreadful thing to fall into the hands of the living God.

³²Remember those earlier days after you had received the light, when you endured in a great conflict full of suffering. ³³Sometimes you were publicly exposed to insult and persecution; at other times you stood side by side with those who were so treated. ³⁴You suffered along with those in prison and joyfully accepted the confiscation of your property, because you knew that you yourselves had better and lasting possessions. ³⁵So do not throw away your confidence; it will be richly rewarded.

³⁶You need to persevere so that when you

The Law of Process: Perseverance Is Essential to Finish Well

Hebrews 10:19–39

Every leader should aim to finish well. We need to persevere because confidence will be rewarded; obedience will be recognized; shrinking back will be regretted; and Christ's return will be celebrated. Our journey is not a sprint, but a marathon. We must pace ourselves and endure to the end.

---

have done the will of God, you will receive what he has promised. ³⁷For,

"In just a little while,
    he who is coming will come
    and will not delay."ᶜ

³⁸And,

"But my righteousᵈ one will live by faith.
    And I take no pleasure
    in the one who shrinks back."ᵉ

³⁹But we do not belong to those who shrink back and are destroyed, but to those who have faith and are saved.

Faith in Action

11 Now faith is confidence in what we hope for and assurance about what we do not see. ²This is what the ancients were commended for.

³By faith we understand that the universe was formed at God's command, so that what is seen was not made out of what was visible.

⁴By faith Abel brought God a better offering than Cain did. By faith he was commended as righteous, when God spoke well of his offerings. And by faith Abel still speaks, even though he is dead.

⁵By faith Enoch was taken from this life, so that he did not experience death: "He could not be found, because God had taken him away."ᶠ For before he was taken, he was commended as one who pleased God. ⁶And without faith it is impossible to please God, because anyone who comes to him must believe that he exists and that he rewards those who earnestly seek him.

⁷By faith Noah, when warned about things not yet seen, in holy fear built an ark to save his family. By his faith he condemned the world and became heir of the righteousness that is in keeping with faith.

⁸By faith Abraham, when called to go to a place he would later receive as his inheritance, obeyed and went, even though he did not know where he was going. ⁹By faith he made his home in the promised land like a stranger in a foreign country; he lived in tents, as did Isaac and Jacob, who were heirs with him of the same promise. ¹⁰For he was looking forward to the city with foundations, whose architect and builder is God. ¹¹And by faith even Sarah, who was past

---

ᵃ 30 Deut. 32:35   ᵇ 30 Deut. 32:36; Psalm 135:14
ᶜ 37 Isaiah 26:20; Hab. 2:3   ᵈ 38 Some early manuscripts But the righteous   ᵉ 38 Hab. 2:4 (see Septuagint)   ᶠ 5 Gen. 5:24

childbearing age, was enabled to bear children because she[a] considered him faithful who had made the promise. [12]And so from this one man, and he as good as dead, came descendants as numerous as the stars in the sky and as countless as the sand on the seashore.

[13]All these people were still living by faith when they died. They did not receive the things promised; they only saw them and welcomed them from a distance, admitting that they were foreigners and strangers on earth. [14]People who say such things show that they are looking for a country of their own. [15]If they had been thinking of the country they had left, they would have had opportunity to return. [16]Instead, they were longing for a better country — a heavenly one. Therefore God is not ashamed to be called their God, for he has prepared a city for them.

[17]By faith Abraham, when God tested him, offered Isaac as a sacrifice. He who had embraced the promises was about to sacrifice his one and only son, [18]even though God had said to him, "It is through Isaac that your offspring will be reckoned."[b] [19]Abraham reasoned that God could even raise the dead, and so in a manner of speaking he did receive Isaac back from death.

[20]By faith Isaac blessed Jacob and Esau in regard to their future.

[21]By faith Jacob, when he was dying, blessed each of Joseph's sons, and worshiped as he leaned on the top of his staff.

[22]By faith Joseph, when his end was near, spoke about the exodus of the Israelites from Egypt and gave instructions concerning the burial of his bones.

[23]By faith Moses' parents hid him for three months after he was born, because they saw he was no ordinary child, and they were not afraid of the king's edict.

[24]By faith Moses, when he had grown up, refused to be known as the son of Pharaoh's daughter. [25]He chose to be mistreated along with the people of God rather than to enjoy the fleeting pleasures of sin. [26]He regarded disgrace for the sake of Christ as of greater value than the treasures of Egypt, because he was looking ahead to his reward. [27]By faith he left Egypt, not fearing the king's anger; he persevered because he saw him who is invisible. [28]By faith he kept the Passover and the application of blood, so that the destroyer of the firstborn would not touch the firstborn of Israel.

[29]By faith the people passed through the Red Sea as on dry land; but when the Egyptians tried to do so, they were drowned.

[30]By faith the walls of Jericho fell, after the army had marched around them for seven days. [31]By faith the prostitute Rahab, because she

a 11 Or By faith Abraham, even though he was too old to have children — and Sarah herself was not able to conceive — was enabled to become a father because he   b 18 Gen. 21:12

Vision: Seeing the Invisible Future

Hebrews 11:1–32

Hebrews 11 is often called the "Hall of Faith" because it enshrines men and women of faith who triumphed in their own lifetimes. The passage summarizes an initial list of heroes with a word about vision (Heb 11:13).

It is almost impossible to separate faith and vision. These leaders died in faith, and although they didn't receive the tangible fulfillment of God's promises, they did see them from a distance. Their journey was all about vision, about seeing the invisible future. Leaders live by vision. These ancient men and women of faith continue to lead the way because of their:

1. *Vision:* They saw the promises afar off. These leaders had power for today because they had a vision for tomorrow.

2. *Confidence:* They were assured of the promises. They remained optimistic because they wanted to make a legacy more than a living.

3. *Hunger:* They embraced the promises. They had ownership of what only their descendants would enjoy.

4. *Resolve:* They confessed they were strangers and pilgrims. They made up their minds. Their dreams, not their memories, consumed them.

welcomed the spies, was not killed with those who were disobedient.[a]

[32] And what more shall I say? I do not have time to tell about Gideon, Barak, Samson and Jephthah, about David and Samuel and the prophets, [33] who through faith conquered kingdoms, administered justice, and gained what was promised; who shut the mouths of lions, [34] quenched the fury of the flames, and escaped the edge of the sword; whose weakness was turned to strength; and who became powerful in battle and routed foreign armies. [35] Women received back their dead, raised to life again. There were others who were tortured, refusing to be released so that they might gain an even better resurrection. [36] Some faced jeers and flogging, and even chains and imprisonment. [37] They were put to death by stoning;[b] they were sawed in two; they were killed by the sword. They went about in sheepskins and goatskins, destitute, persecuted and mistreated— [38] the world was not worthy of them. They wandered in deserts and mountains, living in caves and in holes in the ground.

[39] These were all commended for their faith, yet none of them received what had been promised, [40] since God had planned something better for us so that only together with us would they be made perfect.

12 Therefore, since we are surrounded by such a great cloud of witnesses, let us throw off everything that hinders and the sin that so easily entangles. And let us run with perseverance the race marked out for us, [2] fixing our eyes on Jesus, the pioneer and perfecter of faith. For the joy set before him he endured the cross, scorning its shame, and sat down at the right hand of the throne of God. [3] Consider him who endured such opposition from sinners, so that you will not grow weary and lose heart.

God Disciplines His Children

[4] In your struggle against sin, you have not yet resisted to the point of shedding your blood. [5] And have you completely forgotten this word of encouragement that addresses you as a father addresses his son? It says,

> "My son, do not make light of the Lord's
> discipline,
> and do not lose heart when he rebukes
> you,
> [6] because the Lord disciplines the one he
> loves,
> and he chastens everyone he accepts as
> his son."[c]

---

[a] 31 Or *unbelieving*   [b] 37 Some early manuscripts *stoning; they were put to the test;*   [c] 5,6 Prov. 3:11,12 (see Septuagint)

The Law of Sacrifice: Moses Gave Up the Riches of Egypt

Hebrews 11:23–29

Moses exemplified the Law of Sacrifice as well as any leader. Moses understood that life is full of tradeoffs. He made some tradeoffs that looked ridiculous to the Egyptians—but his choices later paid great dividends. He became one of the greatest leaders in Israel's history because he settled his priorities and willingly gave up pleasure for purpose.

Consider what Moses gave up and received in return. Notice that the first four all appear negative, but the last four confirm he made the right decision. The payoff came *after* the sacrifice.

Gave Up	Received
1. Being called son of Pharaoh's daughter	1. Called a Hebrew
2. Pleasures of sin	2. Ill treatment of God's people
3. Treasures of Egypt	3. Reproach of Christ
4. Life in Egypt	4. Life in the wilderness
5. Losing his firstborn son	5. Keeping his firstborn son
6. Divine plagues	6. Divine protection
7. Drowning in the Red Sea	7. Walking through the Red Sea
8. A life outside of God's purposes	8. Fulfilling God's purpose for his life

Passion: Run with Passion, Purpose and Perspective

Hebrews 12:1–3

Hebrews 12 develops the theme of endurance. The first three verses teach us that the key to persistence is passion.

All the men and women of faith in Hebrews 11 "made it" because they felt passionate about their cause. The writer compares our lives to a race and tries to convince us that we must run with endurance if we plan to finish well.

The text also suggests that if the key to persistence is passion, then the key to passion is purpose. We must run with purpose, not aimlessly.

And the key to purpose? Perspective. The writer of Hebrews admonishes us to consider three things that will help us to finish well:

1. *Consider them* (v. 1).
   Since a great cloud of witnesses has gone before us, we must get serious about finishing well.

2. *Consider ourselves* (v. 1).
   It is now our turn to run the race and watch for pitfalls. We must lay aside every encumbrance that would prevent us from finishing well.

3. *Consider Jesus* (vv. 2–3).
   Jesus ran his own race and endured hardship by fixing his eyes on the rewards; we must follow his example.

[7]Endure hardship as discipline; God is treating you as his children. For what children are not disciplined by their father? [8]If you are not disciplined—and everyone undergoes discipline—then you are not legitimate, not true sons and daughters at all. [9]Moreover, we have all had human fathers who disciplined us and we respected them for it. How much more should we submit to the Father of spirits and live! [10]They disciplined us for a little while as they thought best; but God disciplines us for our good, in order that we may share in his holiness. [11]No discipline seems pleasant at the time, but painful. Later on, however, it produces a harvest of righteousness and peace for those who have been trained by it.

[12]Therefore, strengthen your feeble arms and weak knees. [13]"Make level paths for your feet,"[a] so that the lame may not be disabled, but rather healed.

Warning and Encouragement

[14]Make every effort to live in peace with everyone and to be holy; without holiness no one will see the Lord. [15]See to it that no one falls short of the grace of God and that no bitter root grows up to cause trouble and defile many. [16]See that no one is sexually immoral, or is godless like Esau, who for a single meal sold his inher-

Self-Discipline: You Must Lead Yourself Before You Can Lead Others

Hebrews 12:5–13

People follow leaders primarily because they see a life they believe they can trust and one they want to emulate. We are to welcome God's discipline and respond with self-discipline. Once we yield both to God's discipline (Heb 12:5–11) and our own (12:12–13), we produce a life worth following.

itance rights as the oldest son. [17]Afterward, as you know, when he wanted to inherit this blessing, he was rejected. Even though he sought the blessing with tears, he could not change what he had done.

The Mountain of Fear and the Mountain of Joy

[18]You have not come to a mountain that can be touched and that is burning with fire; to darkness, gloom and storm; [19]to a trumpet blast

---

[a] 13 Prov. 4:26

or to such a voice speaking words that those who heard it begged that no further word be spoken to them, [20]because they could not bear what was commanded: "If even an animal touches the mountain, it must be stoned to death."[a] [21]The sight was so terrifying that Moses said, "I am trembling with fear."[b]

[22]But you have come to Mount Zion, to the city of the living God, the heavenly Jerusalem. You have come to thousands upon thousands of angels in joyful assembly, [23]to the church of the firstborn, whose names are written in heaven. You have come to God, the Judge of all, to the spirits of the righteous made perfect, [24]to Jesus the mediator of a new covenant, and to the sprinkled blood that speaks a better word than the blood of Abel.

[25]See to it that you do not refuse him who speaks. If they did not escape when they refused him who warned them on earth, how much less will we, if we turn away from him who warns us from heaven? [26]At that time his voice shook the earth, but now he has promised, "Once more I will shake not only the earth but also the heavens."[c] [27]The words "once more" indicate the removing of what can be shaken — that is, created things — so that what cannot be shaken may remain.

[28]Therefore, since we are receiving a kingdom that cannot be shaken, let us be thankful, and so worship God acceptably with reverence and awe, [29]for our "God is a consuming fire."[d]

Concluding Exhortations

13 Keep on loving one another as brothers and sisters. [2]Do not forget to show hospitality to strangers, for by so doing some people have shown hospitality to angels without knowing it. [3]Continue to remember those in prison as if you were together with them in prison, and those who are mistreated as if you yourselves were suffering.

[4]Marriage should be honored by all, and the marriage bed kept pure, for God will judge the adulterer and all the sexually immoral. [5]Keep your lives free from the love of money and be content with what you have, because God has said,

"Never will I leave you;
never will I forsake you."[e]

[6]So we say with confidence,

"The Lord is my helper; I will not be afraid.
What can mere mortals do to me?"[f]

[7]Remember your leaders, who spoke the word of God to you. Consider the outcome of their way of life and imitate their faith. [8]Jesus Christ is the same yesterday and today and forever.

[9]Do not be carried away by all kinds of strange teachings. It is good for our hearts to be strengthened by grace, not by eating ceremonial foods, which is of no benefit to those who do so. [10]We have an altar from which those who minister at the tabernacle have no right to eat.

[11]The high priest carries the blood of animals into the Most Holy Place as a sin offering, but the bodies are burned outside the camp. [12]And so Jesus also suffered outside the city gate to make the people holy through his own blood. [13]Let us, then, go to him outside the camp, bearing the disgrace he bore. [14]For here we do not have an enduring city, but we are looking for the city that is to come.

---

[a] 20 Exodus 19:12,13   [b] 21 See Deut. 9:19.
[c] 26 Haggai 2:6   [d] 29 Deut. 4:24   [e] 5 Deut. 31:6
[f] 6 Psalm 118:6,7

Leadership Models: God Can Do for You What He Did for Them

Hebrews 13:7–8

Although verses 7 and 8 of Hebrews 13 are rarely tied together, they should be, for verse 7 furnishes the context for the truth of verse 8.

The writer of Hebrews tells us to remember the leaders from yesterday, think about their lives, and imitate their faith. Then he reminds us that Jesus Christ is the same yesterday, today and forever. In other words, what God did for those leaders in years gone by, he can do for you and me! The same great things he accomplished through their leadership—like liberating a nation or building a temple or equipping other leaders—he would like to do through us today.

When you read of any great leader in the Bible, just remember it was God who worked through them. And the same God who led through them wants to lead through you! God is in the business of not only saving lives, but also leading leaders.

¹⁵Through Jesus, therefore, let us continually offer to God a sacrifice of praise — the fruit of lips that openly profess his name. ¹⁶And do not forget to do good and to share with others, for with such sacrifices God is pleased.

¹⁷Have confidence in your leaders and submit to their authority, because they keep watch over you as those who must give an account. Do this

Accountability: Leaders Are Stewards of Their Resources

Hebrews 13:17

Why should believers obey their leaders? Because their leaders watch out for their souls and must give account to God. Leaders are stewards of everyone who follows them. God has placed leaders in "middle management" under his leadership. When their life ends, they will answer for how responsibly they tended to his divine vision and values.

so that their work will be a joy, not a burden, for that would be of no benefit to you.

¹⁸Pray for us. We are sure that we have a clear conscience and desire to live honorably in every way. ¹⁹I particularly urge you to pray so that I may be restored to you soon.

Benediction and Final Greetings

²⁰Now may the God of peace, who through the blood of the eternal covenant brought back from the dead our Lord Jesus, that great Shepherd of the sheep, ²¹equip you with everything good for doing his will, and may he work in us what is pleasing to him, through Jesus Christ, to whom be glory for ever and ever. Amen.

²²Brothers and sisters, I urge you to bear with my word of exhortation, for in fact I have written to you quite briefly.

²³I want you to know that our brother Timothy has been released. If he arrives soon, I will come with him to see you.

²⁴Greet all your leaders and all the Lord's people. Those from Italy send you their greetings.

²⁵Grace be with you all.

INTRODUCTION TO JAMES

Translating Faith into Obedience

James is the kind of book you ought to read standing up. It contains a ringing call for action, a plea for vital Christianity and a faith that demonstrates itself not in mere words, but in lifestyle. James is one of the most practical books of the Bible, teaching that faith without corresponding action is dead.

If James were leading an organization and you were his employee, you would feel the heat of this leader. He would motivate you with words like:

"Don't tell me about your accomplishments; show me!"

"The more you walk the walk, the less you have to talk!"

"Let's put some shoe leather on our core values!"

In this short book of five chapters, James addresses temptation, hypocrisy, prejudice, how to deal with problems, deception, discipline, controlling the tongue, recognizing godly wisdom, conflict, humility, priorities, patience and faith. In essence, we have a transcribed sermon delivered to Jewish Christians all over the Roman Empire.

James models a leadership weary of sterile mission statements framed on a wall. He cares nothing for the set of core values the subcommittee wrote down last year if they were only words on paper that got filed away. He is an activist who labels as "self-deceived" those who say they are committed to do something but never do it.

James also models a leadership that errs on the side of pragmatism. Because he doesn't want anyone to miss "practicing what they preach," he suggests several ideas on how to flesh out the mission of Christ—from feeding and clothing the poor, to providing good seating at

God's Role in James

God speaks to leaders in this book about real-life situations. This book especially helps the leader who gets caught up in an idealistic vision and never gets to his to-do list. God calls us to translate our faith into obedience.

Every leader should read this brief book with the goal of personal faithfulness to God and to his or her leadership position. After reading this book, you will sense a leader's passion and conviction about justice. You will also observe a wise leader communicating perspective to erring followers. And you will be challenged to pay the price to practice what you preach.

Leaders in James

James, teachers, church elders

Other People of Influence in James

Rich people, Old Testament prophets, Job

Lessons in Leadership

- The more you walk, the less you have to talk.
- Integrity occurs when words and actions match.
- Leaders will be judged more strictly than followers.
- If you can bridle your tongue, you can discipline any part of your life.

church services for the poor, to controlling your speech, to praying for the sick and those in need. He intuitively knows that leadership integrity exists only when our words and actions meet.

James also furnishes us with the best common-sense wisdom regarding life on earth. He strongly advocates humility in the sight of God and encourages us to pray when we don't know what to do next. He possesses a divine perspective that enables a follower to trust him more easily. James maintains a big-picture view of eternity while incarnating his beliefs in a pair of overalls.

- Leadership motives must be pure; mercy and justice are healthy motivators.
- Leaders are to humble themselves and let God exalt them in due time.

LEADERSHIP HIGHLIGHTS IN JAMES

1 James, a servant of God and of the Lord Jesus Christ,

To the twelve tribes scattered among the nations:

Greetings.

Trials and Temptations

[2]Consider it pure joy, my brothers and sisters,[a] whenever you face trials of many kinds, [3]because you know that the testing of your faith produces perseverance. [4]Let perseverance finish its work so that you may be mature and complete, not lacking anything. [5]If any of you lacks wisdom, you should ask God, who gives generously to all without finding fault, and it will be given to you. [6]But when you ask, you must believe and not doubt, because the one who doubts is like a wave of the sea, blown and tossed by the wind. [7]That person should not expect to receive anything from the Lord. [8]Such a person is double-minded and unstable in all they do.

[9]Believers in humble circumstances ought to take pride in their high position. [10]But the rich should take pride in their humiliation — since they will pass away like a wild flower. [11]For the sun rises with scorching heat and withers the plant; its blossom falls and its beauty is destroyed. In the same way, the rich will fade away even while they go about their business.

[12]Blessed is the one who perseveres under trial because, having stood the test, that person will receive the crown of life that the Lord has promised to those who love him.

[13]When tempted, no one should say, "God is tempting me." For God cannot be tempted by evil, nor does he tempt anyone; [14]but each person is tempted when they are dragged away by their own evil desire and enticed. [15]Then, after desire has conceived, it gives birth to sin; and sin, when it is full-grown, gives birth to death.

[16]Don't be deceived, my dear brothers and sisters. [17]Every good and perfect gift is from above, coming down from the Father of the heavenly lights, who does not change like shifting shadows. [18]He chose to give us birth through the word of truth, that we might be a kind of firstfruits of all he created.

Listening and Doing

[19]My dear brothers and sisters, take note of this: Everyone should be quick to listen, slow to speak and slow to become angry, [20]because human anger does not produce the righteousness that God desires. [21]Therefore, get rid of all moral filth and the evil that is so prevalent and

---

[a] 2 The Greek word for *brothers and sisters* (*adelphoi*) refers here to believers, both men and women, as part of God's family; also in verses 16 and 19; and in 2:1, 5, 14; 3:10, 12; 4:11; 5:7, 9, 10, 12, 19.

Problem Solving:
Leaders Must Maintain Perspective with Problems

James 1:1-8

James is vitally concerned with big-picture living. After his brief greeting, he jumps into how to handle problems. Because leadership depends to a large degree on problem solving, James remains relevant to every leader. He teaches us to approach problems with:

1. *Contemplation* (vv. 2–4)
   We can find joy in the midst of problems only when we recognize their purpose and results. The key is perspective. Leaders must think correctly about problems and see that their followers grow stronger through them.

2. *Supplication* (v. 5)
   God gives us trials in such a way that we lack nothing in the end. James says, however, that if we do lack wisdom, we should ask God for it. It is no sign of weakness for a leader to pray for wisdom when facing problems.

3. *Expectation* (vv. 6–8)
   If we do ask God for wisdom, we must ask in faith, expecting his answer. Once leaders gain perspective and trust God for wisdom, the only thing left to do is to anticipate solutions and exude optimism.

Listening: To Connect with Hearts, Use Your Ears

James 1:19

Good leaders motivate others by their listening skills. We are to: avoid prejudicial first impressions; become less self-centered; withhold initial criticism; stay calm; listen with empathy; be active listeners; clarify what we hear; and recognize the healing power of listening. Then we are to act on what we hear (Jas 1:22)!

humbly accept the word planted in you, which can save you.

²²Do not merely listen to the word, and so deceive yourselves. Do what it says. ²³Anyone who listens to the word but does not do what it says is like someone who looks at his face in a mirror ²⁴and, after looking at himself, goes away and immediately forgets what he looks like. ²⁵But whoever looks intently into the perfect law that gives freedom, and continues in it — not forgetting what they have heard, but doing it — they will be blessed in what they do.

²⁶Those who consider themselves religious and yet do not keep a tight rein on their tongues deceive themselves, and their religion is worthless. ²⁷Religion that God our Father accepts as pure and faultless is this: to look after orphans

The Law of Solid Ground: Hypocritical Leaders Sabotage Themselves

James 1:22–26

If a man thinks himself to be religious, but doesn't bridle his tongue, he deceives himself. His religion is worthless. Why? Because when he thinks one way, but talks another way, he becomes double-minded.

The Greek word translated "doubt" is taken from the same root as the word "double." A leader who thinks one way, but whose words stand in contrast to his mindset, will fail. The power of his mind and the power of his words neutralize each other. Such a leader fails to practice the Law of Solid Ground and will eventually sabotage himself.

and widows in their distress and to keep oneself from being polluted by the world.

Favoritism Forbidden

2 My brothers and sisters, believers in our glorious Lord Jesus Christ must not show favoritism. ²Suppose a man comes into your meeting wearing a gold ring and fine clothes, and a poor man in filthy old clothes also comes in. ³If you

Relationships: Leaders Must Love out of a Decision, Not a Reaction

James 2:1–9

Relationships and leadership cannot be divorced. Further, leaders must learn to relate to people based on a decision, not a reaction. We must love people regardless of what they can give in return.

James 2 begins by talking about the sin of partiality. Leaders must not treat a rich man well and a poor man poorly. Love must be given unconditionally. Does this mean we treat everyone the same? Not at all. We must relate to each individual based on his or her inward gifts, not outward gifts. Leaders must identify talents and gifts in others, then place the individuals in suitable positions to encourage the use of their gifts. Note the diagram below.

The Issue	My Response
1. Loving people	1. I love them based on an unconditional decision.
2. Positions and tasks	2. I place them according to their giftedness.
3. Recognition	3. I recognize everyone's value and contribution.
4. Affirmation	4. I base it on the need of the person.

show special attention to the man wearing fine clothes and say, "Here's a good seat for you," but say to the poor man, "You stand there" or "Sit on the floor by my feet," [4]have you not discriminated among yourselves and become judges with evil thoughts?

[5]Listen, my dear brothers and sisters: Has not God chosen those who are poor in the eyes of the world to be rich in faith and to inherit the kingdom he promised those who love him? [6]But you have dishonored the poor. Is it not the rich who are exploiting you? Are they not the ones

---

The Law of Addition:
The Measure of Our Commitment Is Action

James 2:1–26

James reminds us that we are called to serve others. The measuring stick of our commitment is not our lip service, but our life. Leaders must act on their values; action is the gauge, not mere words or thoughts. The Law of Addition reminds us: If you want to add value to others as a leader, don't just say something, serve.

James proceeds to give us six pictures and six principles to back up his teaching:

Picture One: The rich and the poor (vv. 1–4)
  Selfish motives prevent a servant's ministry.
Picture Two: The legalist (vv. 9–13)
  Following rules cannot save us, but following Jesus can.
Picture Three: The hypocrite (vv. 14–17)
  A lifestyle that costs nothing is worth nothing.
Picture Four: The foolish man (vv. 18–19)
  A faith that's only in my head is dead.
Picture Five: Abraham (vv. 21–23)
  Faith justifies the leader; works justify the faith.
Picture Six: Rahab (vv. 25–26)
  A worthless past is resolved by a present that works.

JAMES
Brother of Jesus, Leader of Men
James 2:24, 26

PROFILE in leadership

If you were trying to find an apple tree, you would look for a tall, woody plant with a fairly sturdy trunk, beautiful green foliage, and of course, apples. Certain kinds of trees produce certain kinds of fruit.

It's like that with faith in God. James tells us that if we are looking for someone with saving faith, we should look for a person who voices belief in the works of Jesus Christ *and* whose actions back up his or her words. That is the governing principle of James's epistle, which describes religion that is practical, that produces change, and that works. Without those works, James tells us, such a person's faith isn't the genuine article.

James doesn't mean that our good works save us. He knew there is nothing we can do or say to add to what Christ has already done on the cross. Rather, he means that we recognize genuine, saving faith by the works it produces in the life of the believer.

Godly leaders challenge us to embrace a faith beyond mere mental assent, more than emotionalism, more than words. They challenge us to examine our faith and determine if it is producing the kind of fruit James tells us it should.

who are dragging you into court? ⁷Are they not the ones who are blaspheming the noble name of him to whom you belong?

⁸If you really keep the royal law found in Scripture, "Love your neighbor as yourself,"ᵃ you are doing right. ⁹But if you show favoritism, you sin and are convicted by the law as lawbreakers. ¹⁰For whoever keeps the whole law and yet stumbles at just one point is guilty of breaking all of it. ¹¹For he who said, "You shall not commit adultery,"ᵇ also said, "You shall not murder."ᶜ If you do not commit adultery but do commit murder, you have become a lawbreaker.

¹²Speak and act as those who are going to be judged by the law that gives freedom, ¹³because judgment without mercy will be shown to anyone who has not been merciful. Mercy triumphs over judgment.

Faith and Deeds

¹⁴What good is it, my brothers and sisters, if someone claims to have faith but has no deeds? Can such faith save them? ¹⁵Suppose a brother or a sister is without clothes and daily food. ¹⁶If one of you says to them, "Go in peace; keep warm and well fed," but does nothing about their physical needs, what good is it? ¹⁷In the same way, faith by itself, if it is not accompanied by action, is dead.

¹⁸But someone will say, "You have faith; I have deeds."

Show me your faith without deeds, and I will show you my faith by my deeds. ¹⁹You believe that there is one God. Good! Even the demons believe that — and shudder.

²⁰You foolish person, do you want evidence that faith without deeds is uselessᵈ? ²¹Was not our father Abraham considered righteous for what he did when he offered his son Isaac on the altar? ²²You see that his faith and his actions were working together, and his faith was made complete by what he did. ²³And the scripture was fulfilled that says, "Abraham believed God, and it was credited to him as righteousness,"ᵉ and he was called God's friend. ²⁴You see that a person is considered righteous by what they do and not by faith alone.

²⁵In the same way, was not even Rahab the prostitute considered righteous for what she did when she gave lodging to the spies and sent them off in a different direction? ²⁶As the body without the spirit is dead, so faith without deeds is dead.

Taming the Tongue

3 Not many of you should become teachers, my fellow believers, because you know that we who teach will be judged more strictly. ²We all stumble in many ways. Anyone who is never at fault in what they say is perfect, able to keep their whole body in check.

³When we put bits into the mouths of horses to make them obey us, we can turn the whole animal. ⁴Or take ships as an example. Although they are so large and are driven by strong winds, they are steered by a very small rudder wherever the pilot wants to go. ⁵Likewise, the tongue is a small part of the body, but it makes great boasts. Consider what a great forest is set on fire by a small spark. ⁶The tongue also is a fire, a world of evil among the parts of the body. It corrupts the whole body, sets the whole course of one's life on fire, and is itself set on fire by hell.

⁷All kinds of animals, birds, reptiles and sea creatures are being tamed and have been tamed

---

ᵃ 8 Lev. 19:18　　ᵇ 11 Exodus 20:14; Deut. 5:18　ᶜ 11 Exodus 20:13; Deut. 5:17　ᵈ 20 Some early manuscripts *dead*　ᵉ 23 Gen. 15:6

Accountability: Leaders Will Endure a Stricter Judgment

James 3:1

James informs us that leaders and teachers will receive a stricter judgment than other believers when they stand before God. Why? Because of their greater influence.

When a follower makes a mistake, he affects only himself and perhaps his family. When a leader makes a mistake, he affects the many who follow.

When the real leader speaks, people listen. This can be both good news and bad news, depending on whether the leader's words are worth listening to! God promises that those in positions of influence will give account for how they use that influence.

In one sense, God will be a spiritual accountant, the heavenly C.P.A., calling leaders to answer for how they used the resources he gave them. At the judgment seat of Christ we will be required to give an account for what we did with our lives and our influence.

by mankind, [8]but no human being can tame the tongue. It is a restless evil, full of deadly poison.

[9]With the tongue we praise our Lord and Father, and with it we curse human beings, who have been made in God's likeness. [10]Out of the same mouth come praise and cursing. My brothers and sisters, this should not be. [11]Can both fresh water and salt water flow from the same spring? [12]My brothers and sisters, can a fig tree bear olives, or a grapevine bear figs? Neither can a salt spring produce fresh water.

Two Kinds of Wisdom

[13]Who is wise and understanding among you? Let them show it by their good life, by deeds done in the humility that comes from wisdom. [14]But if you harbor bitter envy and selfish

---

Self-Discipline: If You Can Tame the Tongue, You Can Tame Anything

James 3:1–18

What power our words contain! James focuses on the little muscle inside our mouths, called the tongue, a little thing that dispenses both blessing and cursing. Leaders must pay close attention, for they communicate often and carry great influence when they speak. James lists four functions of the tongue:

1. *Function One: to gauge* (vv. 1–2)
   The tongue is a spiritual meter. If we can bridle it, we can bridle the whole body. It becomes the gauge for our maturity. Our faith will never register higher than our words.

2. *Function Two: to guide* (vv. 3–5)
   The tongue is like a horse's bit, a ship's rudder, or kindling wood. It starts things in motion. If we can control it, we can guide our lives, just as a bit directs a horse or a rudder steers a ship.

3. *Function Three: to gird* (vv. 6–8)
   The tongue is powerful. Like a huge fire, it can ruin or bless our entire lives. This power was meant to send us down the right path, not to kill us.

4. *Function Four: to guard* (vv. 9–18)
   The tongue can reveal what sort of wisdom we harbor inside. A good tongue protects our integrity. James asks: Is yours a good guard or a bad one? Does it create peace or reveal hypocrisy?

The Law of Intuition: Godly Wisdom vs. Worldly Wisdom

James 3:13–18

James speaks of two kinds of wisdom: the wisdom from above and the wisdom from below. Good leadership intuition always springs from the wisdom from above. Notice the following differences.

Wisdom from Above	Wisdom from Below
1. Gentle and generous	1. Selfishly ambitious and jealous
2. Speaks the truth	2. Speaks lies and deceives
3. Pure and organized	3. Disorderly and demonic
4. Results in peace	4. Results in disharmony
5. Reasonable	5. Self-centered
6. The fruit of love and mercy	6. The fruit of strife and competition

ambition in your hearts, do not boast about it or deny the truth. [15]Such "wisdom" does not come down from heaven but is earthly, unspiritual, demonic. [16]For where you have envy and selfish ambition, there you find disorder and every evil practice.

[17]But the wisdom that comes from heaven is first of all pure; then peace-loving, considerate, submissive, full of mercy and good fruit, impartial and sincere. [18]Peacemakers who sow in peace reap a harvest of righteousness.

Submit Yourselves to God

4 What causes fights and quarrels among you? Don't they come from your desires that battle within you? [2]You desire but do not have, so you kill. You covet but you cannot get what you want, so you quarrel and fight. You do not have because you do not ask God. [3]When you ask, you do not receive, because you ask with wrong motives, that you may spend what you get on your pleasures.

[4]You adulterous people,[a] don't you know that friendship with the world means enmity against God? Therefore, anyone who chooses to be a friend of the world becomes an enemy of God. [5]Or do you think Scripture says without

reason that he jealously longs for the spirit he has caused to dwell in us[b]? [6]But he gives us more grace. That is why Scripture says:

"God opposes the proud
    but shows favor to the humble."[c]

[7]Submit yourselves, then, to God. Resist the devil, and he will flee from you. [8]Come near to God and he will come near to you. Wash your hands, you sinners, and purify your hearts, you double-minded. [9]Grieve, mourn and wail. Change your laughter to mourning and your joy to gloom. [10]Humble yourselves before the Lord, and he will lift you up.

[11]Brothers and sisters, do not slander one another. Anyone who speaks against a brother or sister[d] or judges them speaks against the law and judges it. When you judge the law, you are not keeping it, but sitting in judgment on it. [12]There is only one Lawgiver and Judge, the one who is

---

[a] 4 An allusion to covenant unfaithfulness; see Hosea 3:1.
[b] 5 Or that the spirit he caused to dwell in us envies intensely; or that the Spirit he caused to dwell in us longs jealously
[c] 6 Prov. 3:34   [d] 11 The Greek word for brother or sister (adelphos) refers here to a believer, whether man or woman, as part of God's family.

Problem Solving: The Reason, Results and Remedy for Problems

James 4:1–10

James gives a lot of attention to problem solving. He begins by asking a question: What is the source of conflict among his readers? On their own they could not resolve their divisions and quarrels. When James steps in, he cuts through the fat and spells out the reason and the remedy for their problems.

Good leaders discern the root of problems quickly and offer practical solutions. Most of the time they find people problems:

1. *The reason for our problems: Hedonism* (vv. 1–3)
   James offers the answer to his own question. The source of their problems? Their own self-centered search for pleasure. The Greek term he uses is the root word for "hedonism." Like symptoms of a disease, their emotions revealed selfish goals: lust, envy, quarreling and fighting.

2. *The results of our problems: Hostility* (vv. 4–6)
   Hedonism always leads to hostility. Because the people got so caught up in their own pursuits, they became hostile toward others and God. They were like adulterers who so badly wanted self-fulfillment, they forgot their marriage.

3. *The remedy to our problems: Humility* (vv. 7–10)
   Since God opposes the proud but helps the humble, the solution lies in asking humbly for God's grace. These people hadn't asked for anyone's help (v. 2). Most of the time humility brings both peace and solutions.

able to save and destroy. But you — who are you to judge your neighbor?

Boasting About Tomorrow

¹³Now listen, you who say, "Today or tomorrow we will go to this or that city, spend a year there, carry on business and make money." ¹⁴Why, you do not even know what will happen tomorrow. What is your life? You are a mist that appears for a little while and then vanishes. ¹⁵Instead, you ought to say, "If it is the Lord's will, we will live and do this or that." ¹⁶As it is, you boast in your arrogant schemes. All such boasting is evil. ¹⁷If anyone, then, knows the good they ought to do and doesn't do it, it is sin for them.

Warning to Rich Oppressors

5 Now listen, you rich people, weep and wail because of the misery that is coming on you. ²Your wealth has rotted, and moths have eaten your clothes. ³Your gold and silver are corroded. Their corrosion will testify against you and eat your flesh like fire. You have hoarded wealth in the last days. ⁴Look! The wages you failed to pay the workers who mowed your fields are crying out against you. The cries of the harvesters have reached the ears of the Lord Almighty. ⁵You have lived on earth in luxury and self-indul-

gence. You have fattened yourselves in the day of slaughter.ᵃ ⁶You have condemned and murdered the innocent one, who was not opposing you.

Patience in Suffering

⁷Be patient, then, brothers and sisters, until the Lord's coming. See how the farmer waits for the land to yield its valuable crop, patiently waiting for the autumn and spring rains. ⁸You too, be patient and stand firm, because the Lord's coming is near. ⁹Don't grumble against one another, brothers and sisters, or you will be judged. The Judge is standing at the door!

¹⁰Brothers and sisters, as an example of patience in the face of suffering, take the proph-

---

ᵃ 5 Or yourselves as in a day of feasting

The Law of Process: We Mature Like a Seed Awaiting Harvest

James 5:7–8

James calls us to be patient, just like a farmer who patiently waits for his harvest. The farmer knows that if he picks the corn too early, he will miss out on some of the grain.

So it is with us. The Law of Process reminds us that our leadership development is a process, not an event. We grow daily, not in a day. Not only do we wait on Jesus to return, but he waits on us to grow! He is not only preparing a place for us, but us for a place.

If the metaphor of the farmer doesn't do the trick for us, James supplies two more images. He reminds us of two further examples of patience: the prophets and Job (Jas 5:11–12). Regardless of the image, the key is to focus on the fruit or the result that will surely come in the end.

Prayer Partners: The Leader as an Intercessor

James 5:13–20

Not only do leaders need prayer partners, but leaders are prayer partners for the needy. James calls us to identify the problem, intercede for others, and intervene in the process.

James 5:14, in particular, speaks to leaders. Prayer is a significant function that leaders are to perform. (Peter echoes this instruction in Acts 6:4.)

Consider what James calls leaders to do:

1. *Identify*
   Leaders are to identify the problems, then identify *with* the problems. They are to come to the aid of those in need, whether they suffer from sickness, suffering, or sin.

2. *Intercede*
   Leaders are to pray for those in need. This involves anointing the person with oil, laying hands on him or her, and praying for restoration.

3. *Intervene*
   Leaders are to throw themselves in the direction of their prayers. In addition to prayer, they should do anything they can to aid in the restoration for which they so earnestly pray.

ets who spoke in the name of the Lord. [11]As you know, we count as blessed those who have persevered. You have heard of Job's perseverance and have seen what the Lord finally brought about. The Lord is full of compassion and mercy.

[12]Above all, my brothers and sisters, do not swear—not by heaven or by earth or by anything else. All you need to say is a simple "Yes" or "No." Otherwise you will be condemned.

The Prayer of Faith

[13]Is anyone among you in trouble? Let them pray. Is anyone happy? Let them sing songs of praise. [14]Is anyone among you sick? Let them call the elders of the church to pray over them and anoint them with oil in the name of the Lord. [15]And the prayer offered in faith will make the sick person well; the Lord will raise them up. If they have sinned, they will be forgiven. [16]Therefore confess your sins to each other and pray for each other so that you may be healed. The prayer of a righteous person is powerful and effective.

[17]Elijah was a human being, even as we are. He prayed earnestly that it would not rain, and it did not rain on the land for three and a half years. [18]Again he prayed, and the heavens gave rain, and the earth produced its crops.

[19]My brothers and sisters, if one of you should wander from the truth and someone should bring that person back, [20]remember this: Whoever turns a sinner from the error of their way will save them from death and cover over a multitude of sins.

INTRODUCTION TO
1 PETER

Lessons and Principles for Leaders

Simon Peter, one of Jesus' own disciples, wrote 1 and 2 Peter to encourage believers who had fallen prey to the persecution of the Roman Empire. He sent his letter to all five provinces of Asia Minor.

As a recipient of persecution for taking a stand himself, Peter could speak with credibility and conviction. Acts 5 describes how he suffered for his faith; Acts 12 reports his imprisonment. Eventually, the Romans crucified Peter upside down. Tradition says he told his executors that he felt unworthy to die in the same manner as his Lord, so they hung him upside down instead of right side up.

Peter filled his letter with lessons and principles for leaders; Jesus had groomed him to be a leader. Peter began his journey as a crude, brash, outspoken, but influential individual. By the time Jesus sent the Holy Spirit upon his church as reported in Acts 2, Peter had become wise, winsome, convictional, and even more influential. Consider some of the lessons he learned along the way.

First, *find your security in the Lord*. Peter didn't embrace this lesson at first. He consistently projected his self-worth and drew his value from the attention others gave him. He teaches that "once you were not a people, but now you are the people of God." He drives home that God chose us to be a royal priesthood (2:9–10).

Second, *leaders must recognize that suffering and opposition come with the territory*. Peter writes to Christians who have begun to suffer opposition for their convictions. By the time he wrote, Peter had suffered opposition for many years. He knew what it meant to be rebuked, beaten, arrested, imprisoned, and mocked. Yet in a classic response to the authorities, Peter said, "We must obey God rather than human beings" (Ac 5:29).

God's Role in 1 Peter

God plays the role of encourager. Leaders can come away from this book knowing that they are not alone in their sacrifice and suffering. Their cause has not gone unnoticed, so long as it lies within the boundaries of the kingdom of God.

God exhorts leaders to be holy and humble; to be patient and persistent; and to be servants and shepherds. The book unflinchingly depicts the harsh realities of life. Leadership can be a thankless job. But any leader can receive hope and strength from the insights and instructions God provides. When we humble ourselves, we receive God's power.

Leaders in 1 Peter

Peter, elders and undershepherds, government authorities

Other People of Influence in 1 Peter

Husbands and wives

Lessons in Leadership

- If leaders will humble themselves, God will exalt them.
- A leader's identity must be found in Christ, not in the corporate ladder.
- Opposition and struggle are part of the leadership territory.

Third, *your highest call is to use your gifts to serve and shepherd others.* In 1 Peter 4, Peter tells us to identify our spiritual gifts and use them to serve others. As we do this, we glorify God. In chapter five, he challenges leaders to "be shepherds of God's flock that is under your care" (v. 2). To Peter, it doesn't get any better than this.

Finally, *strive for holiness and humility.* Peter addresses both the holy lifestyle (chs. 1; 2) and the humble lifestyle (chs. 3–5). These are high but elusive aims for leaders who battle with ego. Peter's own struggle and victory in these two areas drove him to call others to the same standard.

- Leaders who practice holiness and humility receive God's hope and help.
- Spiritual leaders are to be models, ministers, mentors and managers.

LEADERSHIP HIGHLIGHTS IN 1 PETER

1 Peter, an apostle of Jesus Christ,

To God's elect, exiles scattered throughout the provinces of Pontus, Galatia, Cappadocia, Asia and Bithynia, ²who have been chosen according to the foreknowledge of God the Father, through the sanctifying work of the Spirit, to be obedient to Jesus Christ and sprinkled with his blood:

Grace and peace be yours in abundance.

Praise to God for a Living Hope

³Praise be to the God and Father of our Lord Jesus Christ! In his great mercy he has given us new birth into a living hope through the resurrection of Jesus Christ from the dead, ⁴and into an inheritance that can never perish, spoil or fade. This inheritance is kept in heaven for you, ⁵who through faith are shielded by God's power until the coming of the salvation that is ready to be revealed in the last time. ⁶In all this you greatly rejoice, though now for a little while you may have had to suffer grief in all kinds of trials. ⁷These have come so that the proven genuineness of your faith — of greater worth than gold, which perishes even though refined by fire — may result in praise, glory and honor when Jesus Christ is revealed. ⁸Though you have not seen him, you love him; and even though you do not see him now, you believe in him and are filled with an inexpressible and glorious joy, ⁹for you are receiving the end result of your faith, the salvation of your souls.

¹⁰Concerning this salvation, the prophets, who spoke of the grace that was to come to you, searched intently and with the greatest care, ¹¹trying to find out the time and circumstances to which the Spirit of Christ in them was pointing when he predicted the sufferings of the Messiah and the glories that would follow. ¹²It was revealed to them that they were not serving themselves but you, when they spoke of the things that have now been told you by those who have preached the gospel to you by the Holy Spirit sent from heaven. Even angels long to look into these things.

Be Holy

¹³Therefore, with minds that are alert and fully sober, set your hope on the grace to be brought to you when Jesus Christ is revealed at his coming. ¹⁴As obedient children, do not conform to the evil desires you had when you lived in ignorance. ¹⁵But just as he who called you is holy, so be holy in all you do; ¹⁶for it is written: "Be holy, because I am holy."ᵃ

¹⁷Since you call on a Father who judges each person's work impartially, live out your time as foreigners here in reverent fear. ¹⁸For you know

---

ᵃ 16 Lev. 11:44,45; 19:2

PETER — A Leader Who Learned from His Failure

1 Peter 1:1–5

PROFILE in leadership

No New Testament leader realized more deeply his own fallibility than the apostle Peter.

At the moment of truth, Peter—the same one who stepped out of a boat to walk on water when Jesus called him (Mt 14:27–30); the same one who identified Jesus as the Christ (Mt 16:13–20); the same one who witnessed the transfiguration (Mt 17:1–8)—miserably failed his Lord, denying him three times on the night of his arrest.

Yet this man, in the face of incredible persecution and opposition, got up off the ground to do incredible things for Christ's church. Now he writes to Jewish Christians enduring intense persecution for their faith, encouraging them to persevere through their suffering by remembering that their reward awaits them.

This is not the brash, impetuous, emotional Peter who traveled with Jesus during his earthly ministry. This is a Peter who has matured in his faith, a man who has learned from his failures—and who, most of all, has been filled with the Holy Spirit of God.

Effective leaders walk by the power of the Holy Spirit. They realize that all of us—even those with the best of intentions—are prone to fail when we walk in our own strength and not in the empowerment of the Spirit.

Leadership Is Built on the Foundation of Focus and Self-Discipline

1 Peter 1:13–16

Focus and self-discipline provide the foundation for solid leadership. Peter learned this lesson the hard way. Over three and a half tough years, God transformed Peter from an impetuous, loud influence to a thoughtful, humble leader. Consider the marching orders Peter gives leaders:

1. *Gird your minds* (v. 13).
   Just as men would gird their loins so their robes wouldn't get caught on obstructions as they walked, so we are to gird the loins of our minds. We must remain focused and sober.

2. *Guard your hearts* (v. 14).
   Leaders must prevent old patterns from penetrating their hearts. Peter specifically warns against former lusts, which would not only distract them, but might also destroy their leadership.

3. *Guide your lifestyle* (vv. 15–16).
   Leaders must pursue holiness—and the only way to attain it is to embrace the model Christ gave. Since God is holy, we must copy what we see him doing.

that it was not with perishable things such as silver or gold that you were redeemed from the empty way of life handed down to you from your ancestors, [19]but with the precious blood of Christ, a lamb without blemish or defect. [20]He was chosen before the creation of the world, but was revealed in these last times for your sake. [21]Through him you believe in God, who raised him from the dead and glorified him, and so your faith and hope are in God.

[22]Now that you have purified yourselves by obeying the truth so that you have sincere love for each other, love one another deeply, from the heart.[a] [23]For you have been born again, not of perishable seed, but of imperishable, through the living and enduring word of God. [24]For,

"All people are like grass,
    and all their glory is like the flowers of the field;
the grass withers and the flowers fall,
[25]   but the word of the Lord endures forever."[b]

And this is the word that was preached to you.

2 Therefore, rid yourselves of all malice and all deceit, hypocrisy, envy, and slander of every kind. [2]Like newborn babies, crave pure spiritual milk, so that by it you may grow up in your salvation, [3]now that you have tasted that the Lord is good.

The Living Stone and a Chosen People

[4]As you come to him, the living Stone — rejected by humans but chosen by God and pre-

cious to him — [5]you also, like living stones, are being built into a spiritual house[c] to be a holy priesthood, offering spiritual sacrifices acceptable to God through Jesus Christ. [6]For in Scripture it says:

"See, I lay a stone in Zion,
    a chosen and precious cornerstone,
and the one who trusts in him
    will never be put to shame."[d]

[7]Now to you who believe, this stone is precious. But to those who do not believe,

"The stone the builders rejected
    has become the cornerstone,"[e]

[8]and,

"A stone that causes people to stumble
    and a rock that makes them fall."[f]

They stumble because they disobey the message — which is also what they were destined for.

[9]But you are a chosen people, a royal priesthood, a holy nation, God's special possession, that you may declare the praises of him who called you out of darkness into his wonderful light. [10]Once you were not a people, but now you are the people of God; once you had not received mercy, but now you have received mercy.

---

[a] 22 Some early manuscripts *from a pure heart*
[b] 25 Isaiah 40:6-8 (see Septuagint)   [c] 5 Or *into a temple of the Spirit*   [d] 6 Isaiah 28:16   [e] 7 Psalm 118:22
[f] 8 Isaiah 8:14

God's Twofold Call

1 Peter 2:9-10

Every leader in the body of Christ is to serve in response to a divine calling. Five times Peter brings up the issue of calling (1Pe 1:15; 2:9, 21; 3:9; 5:10).

God's call is twofold and is confirmed in two ways. There is a general calling he offers to everyone; anyone who responds to him is considered the "called" (Isa 6:8). But a second call is more specific. This call is given to individuals who are meant to serve in a particular role (Ac 9:3–6). This calling is confirmed both by an inward witness of the heart and an outward recognition by the body of Christ.

What is your calling? How is your call recognized by others?

Living Godly Lives in a Pagan Society

[11]Dear friends, I urge you, as foreigners and exiles, to abstain from sinful desires, which wage war against your soul. [12]Live such good lives among the pagans that, though they accuse you of doing wrong, they may see your good deeds and glorify God on the day he visits us.

[13]Submit yourselves for the Lord's sake to every human authority: whether to the emperor, as the supreme authority, [14]or to governors, who are sent by him to punish those who do wrong and to commend those who do right. [15]For it is God's will that by doing good you should silence the ignorant talk of foolish people. [16]Live as free people, but do not use your freedom as a cover-up for evil; live as God's slaves. [17]Show proper respect to everyone, love the family of believers, fear God, honor the emperor.

[18]Slaves, in reverent fear of God submit yourselves to your masters, not only to those who are good and considerate, but also to those who are harsh. [19]For it is commendable if someone bears up under the pain of unjust suffering because they are conscious of God. [20]But how is it to your credit if you receive a beating for doing wrong and endure it? But if you suffer for doing good and you endure it, this is commendable before God. [21]To this you were called, because Christ suffered for you, leaving you an example, that you should follow in his steps.

[22] "He committed no sin,
    and no deceit was found in his mouth."[a]

[23]When they hurled their insults at him, he did not retaliate; when he suffered, he made no threats. Instead, he entrusted himself to him who judges justly. [24]"He himself bore our sins" in his body on the cross, so that we might die to sins and live for righteousness; "by his wounds you have been healed." [25]For "you were like sheep going astray,"[b] but now you have returned to the Shepherd and Overseer of your souls.

3 Wives, in the same way submit yourselves to your own husbands so that, if any of them do not believe the word, they may be won over

---

[a] 22 Isaiah 53:9   [b] 24,25 Isaiah 53:4,5,6 (see Septuagint)

The Law of Sacrifice: Christ Is Our Model for Leadership

1 Peter 2:13-18

Peter calls everyone to respect and submit to authorities, regardless of how the authorities might treat their subjects. He reminds us that no one occupies a leadership position without God's sanction.

To illustrate his point, he brings up Christ's leadership (1Pe 2:21–23). Jesus suffered unjustly and endured it without complaint. Just as our Lord sacrificed so much in heading toward the cross, we are to practice the Law of Sacrifice, giving up the pleasures and comforts we might normally enjoy. Consider how Jesus practiced this law:

What Happened to Him	His Sacrificial Response
1. Insults and mockery	1. Didn't retaliate, but kept silent
2. Suffered through beating	2. Made no threats
3. Accused falsely	3. No deceit was in his mouth
4. Carried our sin	4. Entrusted himself to the Father

without words by the behavior of their wives, [2]when they see the purity and reverence of your lives. [3]Your beauty should not come from outward adornment, such as elaborate hairstyles and the wearing of gold jewelry or fine clothes. [4]Rather, it should be that of your inner self, the unfading beauty of a gentle and quiet spirit, which is of great worth in God's sight. [5]For this is the way the holy women of the past who put their hope in God used to adorn themselves. They submitted themselves to their own husbands, [6]like Sarah, who obeyed Abraham and called him her lord. You are her daughters if you do what is right and do not give way to fear.

[7]Husbands, in the same way be considerate as you live with your wives, and treat them with respect as the weaker partner and as heirs with you of the gracious gift of life, so that nothing will hinder your prayers.

Suffering for Doing Good

[8]Finally, all of you, be like-minded, be sympathetic, love one another, be compassionate and humble. [9]Do not repay evil with evil or insult with insult. On the contrary, repay evil with blessing, because to this you were called so that you may inherit a blessing. [10]For,

"Whoever would love life
    and see good days
must keep their tongue from evil
    and their lips from deceitful speech.
[11]They must turn from evil and do good;
    they must seek peace and pursue it.
[12]For the eyes of the Lord are on the righteous
    and his ears are attentive to their prayer,
but the face of the Lord is against those who
    do evil."[a]

[13]Who is going to harm you if you are eager to do good? [14]But even if you should suffer for what is right, you are blessed. "Do not fear their threats[b]; do not be frightened."[c] [15]But in your hearts revere Christ as Lord. Always be prepared to give an answer to everyone who asks you to give the reason for the hope that you have. But do this with gentleness and respect, [16]keeping a clear conscience, so that those who speak maliciously against your good behavior in Christ may be ashamed of their slander. [17]For it is better, if it is God's will, to suffer for doing good than for doing evil. [18]For Christ also suffered once for sins, the righteous for the unrighteous, to bring you to God. He was put to death in the body but made alive in the Spirit. [19]After being

---

Leadership in the Home

1 Peter 3:1-7

No home can thrive without functioning according to sound leadership principles.

Peter first challenges wives to submit to their husbands, even those who do not submit to Christ. This is the principle of authority and submission. It shows up most pointedly when you disagree with the leader. When the wife submits even though she opposes her husband's decision, she gives a powerful witness to Christ and brings a special honor to him.

Husbands are called to live with their wives in an understanding way. They are to honor their wives and model submission and service. They are to initiate blessing, rather than retaliate when things go wrong.

Spiritual leaders assume responsibility for the health of their relationships. This means they set the tone. They must initiate what they want others to do.

---

made alive,[d] he went and made proclamation to the imprisoned spirits— [20]to those who were disobedient long ago when God waited patiently in the days of Noah while the ark was being built. In it only a few people, eight in all, were saved through water, [21]and this water symbolizes baptism that now saves you also—not the removal of dirt from the body but the pledge of a clear conscience toward God.[e] It saves you by the resurrection of Jesus Christ, [22]who has gone into heaven and is at God's right hand—with angels, authorities and powers in submission to him.

Living for God

4 Therefore, since Christ suffered in his body, arm yourselves also with the same attitude, because whoever suffers in the body is done with sin. [2]As a result, they do not live the rest of their earthly lives for evil human desires, but rather for the will of God. [3]For you have spent enough time in the past doing what pagans choose to do—living in debauchery, lust, drunkenness, orgies, carousing and detestable idolatry. [4]They

---

[a] 12 Psalm 34:12-16   [b] 14 Or fear what they fear
[c] 14 Isaiah 8:12   [d] 18,19 Or but made alive in the spirit, [19]in which also   [e] 21 Or but an appeal to God for a clear conscience

are surprised that you do not join them in their reckless, wild living, and they heap abuse on you. [5]But they will have to give account to him who is ready to judge the living and the dead. [6]For this is the reason the gospel was preached even to those who are now dead, so that they might be judged according to human standards in regard to the body, but live according to God in regard to the spirit.

[7]The end of all things is near. Therefore be alert and of sober mind so that you may pray. [8]Above all, love each other deeply, because love covers over a multitude of sins. [9]Offer hospitality to one another without grumbling. [10]Each of you should use whatever gift you have received to serve others, as faithful stewards of God's grace in its various forms. [11]If anyone speaks, they should do so as one who speaks the very words of God. If anyone serves, they should do so with the strength God provides, so that in all things God may be praised through Jesus Christ. To him be the glory and the power for ever and ever. Amen.

Suffering for Being a Christian

[12]Dear friends, do not be surprised at the fiery ordeal that has come on you to test you, as though something strange were happening to you. [13]But rejoice inasmuch as you participate in the sufferings of Christ, so that you may be overjoyed when his glory is revealed. [14]If you are insulted because of the name of Christ, you are blessed, for the Spirit of glory and of God rests on you. [15]If you suffer, it should not be as a murderer or thief or any other kind of criminal, or even as a meddler. [16]However, if you suffer as a Christian, do not be ashamed, but praise God that you bear that name. [17]For it is time for judgment to begin with God's household; and if it begins with us, what will the outcome be for those who do not obey the gospel of God? [18]And,

"If it is hard for the righteous to be saved,
what will become of the ungodly and the sinner?"[a]

[19]So then, those who suffer according to God's will should commit themselves to their faithful Creator and continue to do good.

[a] 18 Prov. 11:31 (see Septuagint)

Spiritual Gifts: We Lead Best When We Lead from Our Gifts

1 Peter 4:10–11

In this passage, Peter encourages us to make five observations about our spiritual gifts:

1. Every one of us has at least one spiritual gift (v. 10).

2. Spiritual gifts are intended to serve people, not bolster our reputations (v. 10).

3. We use our gifts as stewards, not owners (v. 10).

4. God is the source and the sustainer of every gift (v. 11).

5. We are to employ our gifts as though we were serving the Lord (v. 11).

Three disappointments result when we fail to use our gifts properly:

1. We are disobedient.

2. The Body of Christ suffers.

3. God is not glorified.

Leadership Motive Check

1 Peter 5:1–4

At the end of his first letter, Peter furnishes a motive check for leaders. Note that he calls us to: lead and serve voluntarily, not for selfish gain; eagerly do God's will, not to get ahead; serve as an example, not as a lord. Take the following motive check:

1. When you lead, do you remember the example of Christ's sufferings? (v. 1).

2. When you shepherd, do you do it out of a sense of obligation, or privilege? (v. 2).

3. When you serve, are you motivated by the will of God, or men? (v. 2).

4. When you minister, are you driven by personal gain, or godly passion? (v. 2).

5. When influencing others, does your life example speak clearly? (v. 3).

6. When sacrificing, can you wait for the ultimate reward, or must you see an immediate payback? (v. 3).

To the Elders and the Flock

5 To the elders among you, I appeal as a fellow elder and a witness of Christ's sufferings who also will share in the glory to be revealed: [2] Be shepherds of God's flock that is under your care, watching over them — not because you must, but because you are willing, as God wants you to be; not pursuing dishonest gain, but eager to serve; [3] not lording it over those entrusted to you, but being examples to the flock. [4] And when the Chief Shepherd appears, you will receive the crown of glory that will never fade away.

[5] In the same way, you who are younger, submit yourselves to your elders. All of you, clothe yourselves with humility toward one another, because,

> "God opposes the proud
>   but shows favor to the humble."[a]

[6] Humble yourselves, therefore, under God's mighty hand, that he may lift you up in due time. [7] Cast all your anxiety on him because he cares for you.

[8] Be alert and of sober mind. Your enemy the devil prowls around like a roaring lion looking for someone to devour. [9] Resist him, standing firm in the faith, because you know that the family of believers throughout the world is undergoing the same kind of sufferings.

[10] And the God of all grace, who called you to his eternal glory in Christ, after you have suffered a little while, will himself restore you and make you strong, firm and steadfast. [11] To him be the power for ever and ever. Amen.

Final Greetings

[12] With the help of Silas,[b] whom I regard as a faithful brother, I have written to you briefly, encouraging you and testifying that this is the true grace of God. Stand fast in it.

[13] She who is in Babylon, chosen together with you, sends you her greetings, and so does my son Mark. [14] Greet one another with a kiss of love.

Peace to all of you who are in Christ.

---

[a] 5 Prov. 3:34   [b] 12 Greek *Silvanus*, a variant of *Silas*

The Law of Sacrifice: Leaders Humble Themselves to Be Exalted

1 Peter 5:5–7

To the degree that we display pride, God removes his grace from us. The leader is to humble himself by casting all his cares on God (1Pe 5:7). Only then does God promise to exalt the leader. What do you find yourself doing these days—humbling yourself, or feeding your pride?

The Role of Spiritual Leaders

1 Peter 5:1–4

Peter closes his book by addressing the church elders and encouraging them to lead well, according to a whole new paradigm of leadership. He urges them to follow Christ, not only as their suffering Savior, but as their example of leadership. A leader is called to be . . .

1. *A minister to the people* (v. 2).
   Peter exhorts them to shepherd their flock, serving them before being served.

2. *A mentor of the people* (vv. 2–3).
   Peter asks them to eagerly invest in the flock, not as lords, but as examples.

3. *A manager of the people* (vv. 2–3).
   Peter calls them to exercise oversight over those entrusted to their care.

4. *A model for the people* (v. 3).
   Peter tells them to be examples to the flock, demonstrating how to live.

INTRODUCTION TO 2 PETER

Confronting Problems of Opposition

Knowledge of Simon Peter's personal biography helps us understand why his words carry so much weight. Peter was Christ's most outspoken disciple, a natural leader who frequently erred on the side of impulsiveness and presumption. More than once during Jesus' days on earth, Peter stuck his foot in his mouth.

Despite this, God greatly used him. Peter maintained his personality while the Holy Spirit groomed him as a leader. From the crucifixion of Jesus until the day of Pentecost, Peter went through some radical changes. Later, he deepened as a trustworthy apostle and church leader in Jerusalem.

Peter's writings come out of his own life failures. He provides an example of how God must break leaders in the area of their strengths. Peter took great pride in his courage. He boasted that although the other disciples might deny Jesus, he never would. Christ had to declare to him that he would fail in his commitment three times before the rooster crowed. Peter wept bitterly after his failure, but God was working on him, building him into a leader others could trust. Peter wrote of the leadership lessons he learned and the qualities he developed along the way. Note some of the lessons and qualities he addresses in this book:

1. *Character in the midst of low morals.* Peter strongly advocated living out of character. For years, he had lived off of impulse and emotion. Later, he discovered the importance of demonstrating character, especially in his day of moral laxity. In chapter one he lists the ingredients leaders must possess in this area.

2. *Initiative in the midst of poor models.* Peter never lacked initiative, but he had to learn how to curb his

God's Role in 2 Peter

God uses this book to confront the problems of internal opposition to the gospel. Peter raises his trusted voice to address the issues church leaders must face. His humanity makes him believable, and his humility makes him approachable.

God dealt with spiritual counterfeits through Peter, who understood the necessity of taking a stand for what is right. Leaders can take comfort in this book, written by a man who wasn't afraid to get back up after he had fallen.

Leaders in 2 Peter
Peter, prophets

Other People of Influence in 2 Peter
False teachers, lawless men

Lessons in Leadership
- Leadership is built on the foundation of character, not gifts or charisma.
- A leader's motive will determine his movement and mindset.
- If you don't stand for something, you will fall for anything.
- Effective leaders see both the big picture and the little process.

enthusiasm. He was a "ready, fire, aim" sort of leader who learned to take better aim before firing. Religious leaders in Peter's day were slow to believe in Jesus, so he confronted them about their lethargic ways. He also lived in a day filled with false teachers quick to mislead Christians. In chapters one and two, Peter confronts them both.

3. *Risk in the midst of increasing martyrdom.* When Peter erred, he did so on the side of risk. In his day, torture and executions multiplied. Over the years, he identified which issues were worth dying for and which weren't. When he determined his priorities, he risked his life for them. He calls for this kind of conviction in chapters two and three.

4. *Faith in the midst of fearful masses.* After failing in his own faith during Jesus' trial, Peter came back strong and began calling others to an unshakable faith. In the final chapter, Peter speaks of Christ's return and our need to trust him completely until that day. The Romans martyred Peter for his faith in the late 60s AD.

LEADERSHIP HIGHLIGHTS IN 2 PETER

THE LAW OF EMPOWERMENT: God Gave Us All We Need in a Seed (1:1–8)	page 1507
THE LAW OF PROCESS: Leadership Begins with Eight Characteristics (1:5–11)	page 1508
COURAGE: Leaders Stand for What Is True (2:1–6)	page 1509

1
Simon Peter, a servant and apostle of Jesus Christ,

To those who through the righteousness of our God and Savior Jesus Christ have received a faith as precious as ours:

²Grace and peace be yours in abundance through the knowledge of God and of Jesus our Lord.

Confirming One's Calling and Election

³His divine power has given us everything we need for a godly life through our knowledge of him who called us by his own glory and goodness. ⁴Through these he has given us his very great and precious promises, so that through them you may participate in the divine nature, having escaped the corruption in the world caused by evil desires.

⁵For this very reason, make every effort to add to your faith goodness; and to goodness, knowledge; ⁶and to knowledge, self-control; and to self-control, perseverance; and to perseverance, godliness; ⁷and to godliness, mutual affection; and to mutual affection, love. ⁸For if you possess these qualities in increasing measure, they will keep you from being ineffective and unproductive in your knowledge of our Lord Jesus Christ. ⁹But whoever does not have them is nearsighted and blind, forgetting that they have been cleansed from their past sins.

¹⁰Therefore, my brothers and sisters,[a] make every effort to confirm your calling and election. For if you do these things, you will never stumble, ¹¹and you will receive a rich welcome into the eternal kingdom of our Lord and Savior Jesus Christ.

Prophecy of Scripture

¹²So I will always remind you of these things, even though you know them and are firmly established in the truth you now have. ¹³I think it is right to refresh your memory as long as I live in the tent of this body, ¹⁴because I know that I will soon put it aside, as our Lord Jesus Christ has made clear to me. ¹⁵And I will make every effort to see that after my departure you will always be able to remember these things.

¹⁶For we did not follow cleverly devised stories when we told you about the coming of our Lord Jesus Christ in power, but we were eyewitnesses of his majesty. ¹⁷He received honor and glory from God the Father when the voice came to him from the Majestic Glory, saying, "This is my Son, whom I love; with him I am well pleased."[b] ¹⁸We ourselves heard this voice that came from heaven when we were with him on the sacred mountain.

¹⁹We also have the prophetic message as something completely reliable, and you will do well to pay attention to it, as to a light shining in a dark place, until the day dawns and the morning star rises in your hearts. ²⁰Above all, you must understand that no prophecy of Scripture came about by the prophet's own interpretation

---

[a] 10 The Greek word for *brothers and sisters* (*adelphoi*) refers here to believers, both men and women, as part of God's family.
[b] 17 Matt. 17:5; Mark 9:7; Luke 9:35

The Law of Empowerment:
God Gave Us All We Need in a Seed

2 Peter 1:1–8

Second Peter emphasizes God's empowerment of his people. Like all good leaders, God equips us with everything we need to do what he calls us to do.

Peter tells us that God granted to us "everything we need for a godly life" (2Pe 1:3). God's divine power has granted us his divine nature (1:3), and we participate in this divine nature by laying hold of his divine promises (1:4). We cooperate with him by developing ourselves. We exercise our new nature by being diligent. We are to add virtue to our faith, then knowledge, self-control, perseverance, godliness, brotherly kindness, and finally love. When we have gone through this sequence of character development, the divine nature has matured in us (1:2–8).

Jesus said the process works like a seed (Mt 13:31–32). The seed is planted and, although it is entirely present, it is very small. As it grows, it becomes large and helpful. Seeds are complete, but undeveloped.

In the same way, God has planted within us all we need, but these resources require time and growth before they become visible to others.

The Law of Process: Leadership Begins with Eight Characteristics

2 Peter 1:5–11

Peter gives us a ladder to climb that leads to maturity, demonstrating that he believed in the Law of Process. Spiritual leadership happens daily, not in a day. Peter selects choice words to describe the sequence of our process. We are to diligently add . . .

1. *Faith:* the foundation on which we grow spiritually.

2. *Virtue:* a life of strong character and discipline.

3. *Knowledge:* an understanding of what God thinks and values.

4. *Self-control:* the ability to lead oneself before leading others.

5. *Perseverance:* the ability to patiently stick to what is right.

6. *Godliness:* a Spirit-filled, Spirit-led lifestyle that reflects the Lord.

7. *Brotherly kindness:* a lifestyle that is warm, relational, and caring.

8. *Love:* the highest quality that enables a leader to sacrificially give to others.

The Law of Solid Ground: Peter's Credible Leadership

2 Peter 1:16–18

Every leader must remember that people subconsciously ask the question: *Why should I listen to you?* Peter reminds his audience that he was an eyewitness of the power and life of Jesus. He saw Christ on the Mount of Transfiguration and heard the voice of God. This gives his words more weight.

of things. ²¹For prophecy never had its origin in the human will, but prophets, though human, spoke from God as they were carried along by the Holy Spirit.

False Teachers and Their Destruction

2 But there were also false prophets among the people, just as there will be false teachers among you. They will secretly introduce destructive heresies, even denying the sovereign Lord who bought them — bringing swift destruction on themselves. ²Many will follow their depraved conduct and will bring the way of truth into disrepute. ³In their greed these teachers will exploit you with fabricated stories. Their condemnation has long been hanging over them, and their destruction has not been sleeping.

⁴For if God did not spare angels when they sinned, but sent them to hell,[a] putting them in chains of darkness[b] to be held for judgment; ⁵if he did not spare the ancient world when he brought the flood on its ungodly people, but protected Noah, a preacher of righteousness, and seven others; ⁶if he condemned the cities of Sodom and Gomorrah by burning them to ashes, and made them an example of what is going to happen to the ungodly; ⁷and if he rescued Lot, a righteous man, who was distressed by the depraved conduct of the lawless ⁸(for that righteous man, living among them day after day, was tormented in his righteous soul by the lawless deeds he saw and heard) — ⁹if this is so, then the Lord knows how to rescue the godly from trials and to hold the unrighteous for punishment on the day of judgment. ¹⁰This is especially true of those who follow the corrupt desire of the flesh[c] and despise authority.

Bold and arrogant, they are not afraid to heap abuse on celestial beings; ¹¹yet even angels, although they are stronger and more powerful, do not heap abuse on such beings when bringing judgment on them from[d] the Lord. ¹²But these people blaspheme in matters they do not understand. They are like unreasoning animals, creatures of instinct, born only to be caught and destroyed, and like animals they too will perish.

¹³They will be paid back with harm for the harm they have done. Their idea of pleasure is to carouse in broad daylight. They are blots and blemishes, reveling in their pleasures while they feast with you.[e] ¹⁴With eyes full of adultery, they

---

[a] 4 Greek *Tartarus*   [b] 4 Some manuscripts *in gloomy dungeons*   [c] 10 In contexts like this, the Greek word for *flesh* (*sarx*) refers to the sinful state of human beings, often presented as a power in opposition to the Spirit; also in verse 18.
[d] 11 Many manuscripts *beings in the presence of*   [e] 13 Some manuscripts *in their love feasts*

Courage: Leaders Stand for What Is True

2 Peter 2:1–6

Peter earnestly warns his readers about false teachers. He describes in detail their destructive beliefs, their lust for power, their denial of Christ's deity, their greed, and their perverted sensuality. These false leaders exploit God's people. Therefore, God has chosen to punish them and rescue those who stand for what is right.

Peter illustrates his point by contrasting self-appointed leaders with godly leaders:

1. *The fall of the angels:* God cast them into prison to preserve the godly (v. 4).
2. *The days of Noah:* God sent the flood, but rescued Noah (v. 5).
3. *The destruction of Sodom:* God destroyed the city, but spared Lot (v. 6).

It is never easy to take a courageous stand; there is always a price. It always seems cheaper to . . .

1. *Stand for what is easy:* Some leaders look for the easy road and take it.
2. *Stand for what is popular:* Some leaders check the pulse of the majority.
3. *Stand for what is comfortable:* Some leaders choose what fits them best.
4. *Stand for what is convenient:* Some leaders do what fits their calendar.
5. *Stand for what is beneficial:* Some leaders stand for what profits them.
6. *Stand for what is wrong:* Some leaders simply stand for the wrong issues.

---

never stop sinning; they seduce the unstable; they are experts in greed — an accursed brood! [15]They have left the straight way and wandered off to follow the way of Balaam son of Bezer,[a] who loved the wages of wickedness. [16]But he was rebuked for his wrongdoing by a donkey — an animal without speech — who spoke with a human voice and restrained the prophet's madness.

[17]These people are springs without water and mists driven by a storm. Blackest darkness is reserved for them. [18]For they mouth empty, boastful words and, by appealing to the lustful desires of the flesh, they entice people who are just escaping from those who live in error. [19]They promise them freedom, while they themselves are slaves of depravity — for "people are slaves to whatever has mastered them." [20]If they have escaped the corruption of the world by knowing our Lord and Savior Jesus Christ and are again entangled in it and are overcome, they are worse off at the end than they were at the beginning. [21]It would have been better for them not to have known the way of righteousness, than to have known it and then to turn their backs on the sacred command that was passed on to them. [22]Of them the proverbs are true: "A dog returns to its vomit,"[b] and, "A sow that is washed returns to her wallowing in the mud."

The Day of the Lord

3 Dear friends, this is now my second letter to you. I have written both of them as reminders to stimulate you to wholesome thinking. [2]I want you to recall the words spoken in the past by the holy prophets and the command given by our Lord and Savior through your apostles.

[3]Above all, you must understand that in the last days scoffers will come, scoffing and following their own evil desires. [4]They will say, "Where is this 'coming' he promised? Ever since our ancestors died, everything goes on as it has since the beginning of creation." [5]But they deliberately forget that long ago by God's word the heavens came into being and the earth was formed out of water and by water. [6]By these waters also the world of that time was deluged and destroyed. [7]By the same word the present heavens and earth are reserved for fire, being kept for the day of judgment and destruction of the ungodly.

[8]But do not forget this one thing, dear friends: With the Lord a day is like a thousand years, and a thousand years are like a day. [9]The Lord is not slow in keeping his promise, as some understand slowness. Instead he is patient with you, not wanting anyone to perish, but everyone to come to repentance.

---

[a] 15 Greek *Bosor*   [b] 22 Prov. 26:11

The Law of Priorities: Leaders Recognize How to Steward Resources

2 Peter 3:8–13

Peter teaches us five lessons about our stewardship of resources:

1. God sees the big picture (v. 8).

2. God patiently and actively waits for the results he desires (v. 9).

3. Because God could end this world at any time, we should live wisely (vv. 10–11).

4. We should prioritize the things that will hasten his return (v. 12).

5. We should seek to align our priorities with his priorities (v. 13).

[10]But the day of the Lord will come like a thief. The heavens will disappear with a roar; the elements will be destroyed by fire, and the earth and everything done in it will be laid bare.[a]

[11]Since everything will be destroyed in this way, what kind of people ought you to be? You ought to live holy and godly lives [12]as you look forward to the day of God and speed its coming.[b] That day will bring about the destruction of the heavens by fire, and the elements will melt in the heat. [13]But in keeping with his promise we are looking forward to a new heaven and a new earth, where righteousness dwells.

[14]So then, dear friends, since you are looking forward to this, make every effort to be found spotless, blameless and at peace with him. [15]Bear in mind that our Lord's patience means salvation, just as our dear brother Paul also wrote you with the wisdom that God gave him. [16]He writes the same way in all his letters, speaking in them of these matters. His letters contain some things that are hard to understand, which ignorant and unstable people distort, as they do the other Scriptures, to their own destruction.

[17]Therefore, dear friends, since you have been forewarned, be on your guard so that you may not be carried away by the error of the lawless and fall from your secure position. [18]But grow in the grace and knowledge of our Lord and Savior Jesus Christ. To him be glory both now and forever! Amen.

---

[a] 10 Some manuscripts *be burned up*   [b] 12 Or *as you wait eagerly for the day of God to come*

The Law of Timing: Peter Calls Leaders to See the Big Picture

2 Peter 3:8–9

God looks at time differently than we do. Jesus waits patiently to return because he wants to harvest every soul he can (2Pe 3:9). Leaders must combine the ability to wait for results with the ability to seize the day. Leaders must both wait and watch.

INTRODUCTION TO THE
EPISTLES OF JOHN

Life... Light... Love

John was the youngest of the twelve disciples whom Jesus chose to follow him, one of the "sons of thunder," along with his brother, James. In the beginning, he displayed a lot of selfishness and anger, constantly looking for ways to get ahead or gain a favored position. But soon, Jesus began to mold him as a leader.

Jesus' transforming ministry and model eventually turned John into the disciple "whom Jesus loved" (Jn 13:23). John slowly learned to trust Jesus, while earning Jesus' trust. For example, John leaned his head on Jesus' lap during the Last Supper; he couldn't get close enough to him. Even at the cross, John was the only one of the Twelve to remain near the Master. While he stood at the foot of Jesus' cross, he risked crucifixion himself. He knelt right next to Mary, the mother of Jesus. In fact, Jesus spoke one of his last words to John as he hung from the cross: "Here is your mother" (Jn 19:27). In doing this, Jesus fulfilled a Jewish custom. As the firstborn son, it was his responsibility to make sure his parents were cared for. His mother needed someone to care for her needs— and Jesus chose John for this crucial job.

Church history tells us that John stuck to that commission. While all the other apostles fanned out to preach the gospel, John remained with Mary until her death. Why? Trust. Jesus had commanded John to watch his mother. John had become a trusted leader, full of integrity.

John wrote three small letters to the early church, touching upon several fundamental themes: maintaining honesty and integrity; living by our authority as children of God; relating to others with love and compassion;

God's Role in the Epistles of John

John describes God, the original Leader, as the source of life, light and love. God takes the initiative on each one. "We love because he first loved us" (1Jn 4:19). "God is light; in him there is no darkness at all.... If we walk in the light, as he is in the light, we have fellowship with one another" (1:5, 7). "Whoever has the Son has life; whoever does not have the Son of God does not have life" (5:12). God models each of the characteristics he desires for us to develop, just as any good leader does.

Leaders in the Epistles of John
John

Other People of Influence in the Epistles of John
The elect lady (2Jn), deceivers, Gaius (3Jn), Diotrephes (3Jn)

Lessons in Leadership
- Leaders need not attempt great things, but good things done with great love.
- There must be no disparity between our words and our actions.
- The power of any leader comes from the authority God gives him or her.
- Godly leaders must be sources of love, light and life.

internalizing and applying the truth we say we believe; and holding fast the values we first embraced as disciples.

Three key words appear throughout the letters: *life, light,* and *love.* These are the qualities that Jesus Christ, the Leader of leaders, embodies for his people. They are also the qualities a good leader breathes into his or her organization. Effective leaders *love* their people and relate to them well. They shed *light* on issues and the decisions that need to be made. And they push *life* into the organization by their presence, their skills and their character.

LEADERSHIP HIGHLIGHTS IN THE EPISTLES OF JOHN

THE LAW OF CONNECTION: Love Is the Gauge for Spiritual Leaders (1Jn 2:7–11)	**page 1514**
THE LAW OF PROCESS: Three Stages of Maturity (1Jn 2:12–14)	**page 1514**
JOHN: A Leader Motivated by Love (1Jn 3:16–18)	**page 1515**
THE LAW OF EMPOWERMENT: Love Casts Out Fear (1Jn 4:17–21)	**page 1517**
VALUES: Leaders Must Cherish Truth More Than Anything (2Jn 1–4)	**page 1519**
INITIATIVE: Leaders Are to Host the People in Their Lives (3Jn 3–12)	**page 1520**

The Incarnation of the Word of Life

1 That which was from the beginning, which we have heard, which we have seen with our eyes, which we have looked at and our hands have touched—this we proclaim concerning the Word of life. ²The life appeared; we have seen it and testify to it, and we proclaim to you the eternal life, which was with the Father and has appeared to us. ³We proclaim to you what we have seen and heard, so that you also may have fellowship with us. And our fellowship is with the Father and with his Son, Jesus Christ. ⁴We write this to make our*a* joy complete.

Light and Darkness, Sin and Forgiveness

⁵This is the message we have heard from him and declare to you: God is light; in him there is no darkness at all. ⁶If we claim to have fellowship with him and yet walk in the darkness, we lie and do not live out the truth. ⁷But if we walk in the light, as he is in the light, we have fellowship with one another, and the blood of Jesus, his Son, purifies us from all*b* sin.

⁸If we claim to be without sin, we deceive ourselves and the truth is not in us. ⁹If we confess our sins, he is faithful and just and will forgive us our sins and purify us from all unrighteousness. ¹⁰If we claim we have not sinned, we make him out to be a liar and his word is not in us.

2 My dear children, I write this to you so that you will not sin. But if anybody does sin, we have an advocate with the Father—Jesus Christ, the Righteous One. ²He is the atoning sacrifice for our sins, and not only for ours but also for the sins of the whole world.

Love and Hatred for Fellow Believers

³We know that we have come to know him if we keep his commands. ⁴Whoever says, "I know him," but does not do what he commands is a liar, and the truth is not in that person. ⁵But if anyone obeys his word, love for God*c* is truly made complete in them. This is how we know we are in him: ⁶Whoever claims to live in him must live as Jesus did.

⁷Dear friends, I am not writing you a new command but an old one, which you have had since the beginning. This old command is the message you have heard. ⁸Yet I am writing you a new command; its truth is seen in him and in you, because the darkness is passing and the true light is already shining.

⁹Anyone who claims to be in the light but hates a brother or sister*d* is still in the darkness. ¹⁰Anyone who loves their brother and sister*e* lives

---

---

in the light, and there is nothing in them to make them stumble. ¹¹But anyone who hates a brother or sister is in the darkness and walks around in the darkness. They do not know where they are going, because the darkness has blinded them.

Reasons for Writing

¹²I am writing to you, dear children,
    because your sins have been forgiven on
        account of his name.
¹³I am writing to you, fathers,
    because you know him who is from the
        beginning.
I am writing to you, young men,
    because you have overcome the evil one.

¹⁴I write to you, dear children,
    because you know the Father.
I write to you, fathers,
    because you know him who is from the
        beginning.

---

a 4 Some manuscripts *your*   *b 7* Or *every*   *c 5* Or *word, God's love*   *d 9* The Greek word for *brother or sister* (*adelphos*) refers here to a believer, whether man or woman, as part of God's family; also in verse 11; and in 3:15, 17; 4:20; 5:16.
e 10 The Greek word for *brother and sister* (*adelphos*) refers here to a believer, whether man or woman, as part of God's family; also in 3:10; 4:20, 21.

I write to you, young men,
because you are strong,
and the word of God lives in you,
and you have overcome the evil one.

On Not Loving the World

[15]Do not love the world or anything in the world. If anyone loves the world, love for the Father[a] is not in them. [16]For everything in the world—the lust of the flesh, the lust of the eyes, and the pride of life—comes not from the Father but from the world. [17]The world and its desires pass away, but whoever does the will of God lives forever.

Warnings Against Denying the Son

[18]Dear children, this is the last hour; and as you have heard that the antichrist is coming, even now many antichrists have come. This is how we know it is the last hour. [19]They went out from us, but they did not really belong to us. For if they had belonged to us, they would have remained with us; but their going showed that none of them belonged to us. [20]But you have an anointing from the Holy One, and all of you know the truth.[b] [21]I do not write to you because you do not know the truth, but because you do know it and because no lie comes from the truth. [22]Who is the liar? It is whoever denies that Jesus is the Christ. Such a person is the antichrist—denying the Father and the Son. [23]No one who denies the Son has the Father; whoever acknowledges the Son has the Father also. [24]As for you, see that what you have heard from the beginning remains in you. If it does, you also will remain in the Son and in the Father. [25]And this is what he promised us—eternal life.

The Law of Connection: Love Is the Gauge for Spiritual Leaders

1 John 2:7–11

John's greatest theme is love. Church history tells us that as a very old and mature believer, he had to be carried in on a stretcher to give his last public message—an encouragement for believers to love each other. John knew how to connect with people by letting them know how much he cared for them.

Love is the highest motivation for a leader to connect with people. If you don't love them, don't try to lead them. For John, love and relationship provided the gauge for spiritual leadership. A spiritual leader assumes responsibility for the health and development of his or her relationships. John calls leaders back to the basics:

- We must love the Lord.
- We must love the truth.
- We must love our calling.
- We must love the people.

[26]I am writing these things to you about those who are trying to lead you astray. [27]As for you, the anointing you received from him remains in you, and you do not need anyone to teach you.

[a] 15 Or world, the Father's love   [b] 20 Some manuscripts and you know all things

---

The Law of Process: Three Stages of Maturity

1 John 2:12–14

John illustrates the Law of Process by speaking to three different groups: children, young men and fathers. He does not write to believers at differing chronological stages, however, but to those in differing spiritual stages. Each stage faces fundamentally different issues. So says the Law of Process.

As we grow toward mature leadership and influence, we will pass through various phases and have to settle various issues along the way. Remember, leadership development doesn't happen in a day, but daily. Consider the issues in each of the stages:

Stage	Issue
1. Little children	1. Getting right with God and forgiven of sins
2. Young men	2. Waging spiritual warfare and defeating opposition
3. Fathers	3. Intimacy with God

But as his anointing teaches you about all things and as that anointing is real, not counterfeit — just as it has taught you, remain in him.

God's Children and Sin

[28]And now, dear children, continue in him, so that when he appears we may be confident and unashamed before him at his coming.

[29]If you know that he is righteous, you know that everyone who does what is right has been born of him.

3 See what great love the Father has lavished on us, that we should be called children of God! And that is what we are! The reason the world does not know us is that it did not know him. [2]Dear friends, now we are children of God, and what we will be has not yet been made known. But we know that when Christ appears,[a] we shall be like him, for we shall see him as he is. [3]All who have this hope in him purify themselves, just as he is pure.

[4]Everyone who sins breaks the law; in fact, sin is lawlessness. [5]But you know that he appeared so that he might take away our sins. And in him is no sin. [6]No one who lives in him keeps on sinning. No one who continues to sin has either seen him or known him.

[7]Dear children, do not let anyone lead you astray. The one who does what is right is righteous, just as he is righteous. [8]The one who does what is sinful is of the devil, because the devil has been sinning from the beginning. The reason the Son of God appeared was to destroy the devil's work. [9]No one who is born of God will continue to sin, because God's seed remains in them; they cannot go on sinning, because they have been born of God. [10]This is how we know who the children of God are and who the children of the devil are: Anyone who does not do what is right is not God's child, nor is anyone who does not love their brother and sister.

More on Love and Hatred

[11]For this is the message you heard from the beginning: We should love one another. [12]Do not be like Cain, who belonged to the evil one and murdered his brother. And why did he murder him? Because his own actions were evil and his brother's were righteous. [13]Do not be surprised, my brothers and sisters,[b] if the world hates you. [14]We know that we have passed from death to life, because we love each other. Anyone who does not love remains in death. [15]Anyone who hates a brother or sister is a murderer, and you know that no murderer has eternal life residing in him.

[16]This is how we know what love is: Jesus Christ laid down his life for us. And we ought

---

[a] 2 Or *when it is made known*   [b] 13 The Greek word for *brothers and sisters (adelphoi)* refers here to believers, both men and women, as part of God's family; also in verse 16.

---

to lay down our lives for our brothers and sisters. [17]If anyone has material possessions and sees a brother or sister in need but has no pity on them, how can the love of God be in that person? [18]Dear children, let us not love with words or speech but with actions and in truth.

[19]This is how we know that we belong to the truth and how we set our hearts at rest in his presence: [20]If our hearts condemn us, we know that God is greater than our hearts, and he knows everything. [21]Dear friends, if our hearts do not condemn us, we have confidence before God [22]and receive from him anything we ask, because we keep his commands and do what pleases him. [23]And this is his command: to believe in the name of his Son, Jesus Christ, and to love one another as he commanded us. [24]The one who keeps God's commands lives in him, and he in them. And this is how we know that he lives in us: We know it by the Spirit he gave us.

On Denying the Incarnation

4 Dear friends, do not believe every spirit, but test the spirits to see whether they are from God, because many false prophets have gone out into the world. [2]This is how you can recognize the Spirit of God: Every spirit that acknowledges that Jesus Christ has come in the flesh is from God, [3]but every spirit that does not acknowledge Jesus is not from God. This is the spirit of the antichrist, which you have heard is coming and even now is already in the world.

[4]You, dear children, are from God and have overcome them, because the one who is in you is greater than the one who is in the world. [5]They are from the world and therefore speak from the viewpoint of the world, and the world listens to them. [6]We are from God, and whoever knows God listens to us; but whoever is not from God does not listen to us. This is how we recognize the Spirit[a] of truth and the spirit of falsehood.

God's Love and Ours

[7]Dear friends, let us love one another, for love comes from God. Everyone who loves has been born of God and knows God. [8]Whoever does not love does not know God, because God is love. [9]This is how God showed his love among us: He sent his one and only Son into the world that we might live through him. [10]This is love: not that we loved God, but that he loved us and sent his Son as an atoning sacrifice for our sins. [11]Dear friends, since God so loved us, we also ought to love one another. [12]No one has ever

The Law of Intuition: Leaders Must Discern the Spirit of Behavior

1 John 4:1–8

Leaders are to read the spirit behind a person's behavior to sense how ready he or she may be to contribute to the team. Leaders look for a spirit that: confesses Christ as Lord (1Jn 4:1–3); agrees with and believes the truth (4:5–6); and loves others (4:7–8).

seen God; but if we love one another, God lives in us and his love is made complete in us.

[13]This is how we know that we live in him and he in us: He has given us of his Spirit. [14]And we have seen and testify that the Father has sent his Son to be the Savior of the world. [15]If anyone acknowledges that Jesus is the Son of God, God lives in them and they in God. [16]And so we know and rely on the love God has for us.

God is love. Whoever lives in love lives in God, and God in them. [17]This is how love is made complete among us so that we will have confidence on the day of judgment: In this world we are like Jesus. [18]There is no fear in love. But perfect love drives out fear, because fear has to do with punishment. The one who fears is not made perfect in love.

[19]We love because he first loved us. [20]Whoever claims to love God yet hates a brother or sister is a liar. For whoever does not love their brother and sister, whom they have seen, cannot love God, whom they have not seen. [21]And he has given us this command: Anyone who loves God must also love their brother and sister.

Faith in the Incarnate Son of God

5 Everyone who believes that Jesus is the Christ is born of God, and everyone who loves the father loves his child as well. [2]This is how we know that we love the children of God: by loving God and carrying out his commands. [3]In fact, this is love for God: to keep his commands. And his commands are not burdensome, [4]for everyone born of God overcomes the world. This is the victory that has overcome the world, even our faith. [5]Who is it that overcomes the world? Only the one who believes that Jesus is the Son of God.

[a] 6 Or *spirit*

The Law of Empowerment: Love Casts Out Fear

1 John 4:17–21

When God perfects his love in us, we need not fear or feel insecure. We remain secure in his grace. We don't fear punishment or judgment. We are free to love others (1Jn 4:19).

Only these sorts of leaders empower others. The Law of Empowerment reminds us that only secure leaders give power away. Insecure leaders focus on themselves and feel consumed with how they look and whether people like them. The love of God is the only source of absolute security—and all of us can have it. Consider what John teaches us about living secure in Christ:

1. Embracing God's love gives confidence (v. 17).
2. Leaders can incarnate God's security and peace even in this life (v. 17).
3. Enjoying God's love eliminates fear and insecurity (v. 18).
4. We can love others only because God has given us his love (v. 19).
5. Leaders must allow God to empower them with his love before leading others (v. 19).
6. Our love for others is a sign that we love God (v. 20).
7. If I can't get along with people, I can't get along with God (vv. 20–21).

The Law of Victory: God Provides Victory to All of Us

1 John 5:1–21

As the Ultimate Leader, God practices the Law of Victory and allows each of his people to share in his victory. He found a way for the team to win! Consider how God practices this law and takes us to a new level:

1. His people receive a new birth (v. 1).
2. His people receive a lighter load (v. 3).
3. His people overcome the world (v. 4).
4. His people gain a victorious faith (vv. 4–5).
5. His people receive an inward confirmation (vv. 10–11).
6. His people receive a new life (v. 12).
7. His people gain answers to prayer (vv. 14–15).
8. His people receive protection (v. 18).
9. His people gain wisdom and understanding (v. 20).
10. His people receive a new position (v. 20).

[6]This is the one who came by water and blood — Jesus Christ. He did not come by water only, but by water and blood. And it is the Spirit who testifies, because the Spirit is the truth. [7]For there are three that testify: [8]the[a] Spirit, the water and the blood; and the three are in agreement. [9]We accept human testimony, but God's testimony is greater because it is the testimony of God, which he has given about his Son. [10]Whoever believes in the Son of God accepts this testimony. Whoever does not believe God has made him out to be a liar, because they have not believed the testimony God has given about his Son. [11]And this is the testimony: God has given us eternal life, and this life is in his Son. [12]Whoever has the Son has life; whoever does not have the Son of God does not have life.

Concluding Affirmations

[13]I write these things to you who believe in the name of the Son of God so that you may know that you have eternal life. [14]This is the confidence we have in approaching God: that if we ask anything according to his will, he hears us. [15]And if we know that he hears us — whatever we ask — we know that we have what we asked of him.

---

[a] 7,8 Late manuscripts of the Vulgate *testify in heaven: the Father, the Word and the Holy Spirit, and these three are one.* [8]*And there are three that testify on earth: the* (not found in any Greek manuscript before the fourteenth century)

[16]If you see any brother or sister commit a sin that does not lead to death, you should pray and God will give them life. I refer to those whose sin does not lead to death. There is a sin that leads to death. I am not saying that you should pray about that. [17]All wrongdoing is sin, and there is sin that does not lead to death.

[18]We know that anyone born of God does not continue to sin; the One who was born of God keeps them safe, and the evil one cannot harm them. [19]We know that we are children of God, and that the whole world is under the control of the evil one. [20]We know also that the Son of God has come and has given us understanding, so that we may know him who is true. And we are in him who is true by being in his Son Jesus Christ. He is the true God and eternal life.

[21]Dear children, keep yourselves from idols.

2 JOHN

The Second Epistle

¹The elder,

To the lady chosen by God and to her children, whom I love in the truth — and not I only, but also all who know the truth — ²because of the truth, which lives in us and will be with us forever:

³Grace, mercy and peace from God the Father and from Jesus Christ, the Father's Son, will be with us in truth and love.

⁴It has given me great joy to find some of your children walking in the truth, just as the Father commanded us. ⁵And now, dear lady, I am not writing you a new command but one we have had from the beginning. I ask that we love one another. ⁶And this is love: that we walk in obedience to his commands. As you have heard from the beginning, his command is that you walk in love.

⁷I say this because many deceivers, who do not acknowledge Jesus Christ as coming in the flesh, have gone out into the world. Any such person is the deceiver and the antichrist. ⁸Watch out that you do not lose what we*a* have worked for, but that you may be rewarded fully. ⁹Anyone who runs ahead and does not continue in the teaching of Christ does not have God; whoever continues in the teaching has both the Father and the Son. ¹⁰If anyone comes to you and does not bring this teaching, do not take them into your house or welcome them. ¹¹Anyone who welcomes them shares in their wicked work.

¹²I have much to write to you, but I do not want to use paper and ink. Instead, I hope to visit you and talk with you face to face, so that our joy may be complete.

¹³The children of your sister, who is chosen by God, send their greetings.

a 8 Some manuscripts *you*

Values: Leaders Must Cherish Truth More Than Anything

2 John 1–4

Leaders need to examine their professional relationships in light of their organization's vision. Energy follows when the leader's personal beliefs align with the organization's values. When leaders eliminate hypocrisy and deception from their organizations, liberty and power prevail. John uses the word "truth" five times in this short letter to underscore the necessity of integrity.

Leaders must value truth more than anything else. When truth presides in an organization, several benefits result:

1. Trust is evident among staff.

2. The leader has less mental clutter.

3. People feel the freedom to be transparent.

4. The leader has credibility when he or she speaks.

3 JOHN

The Third Epistle

¹The elder,

To my dear friend Gaius, whom I love in the truth.

²Dear friend, I pray that you may enjoy good health and that all may go well with you, even as your soul is getting along well. ³It gave me great joy when some believers came and testified about your faithfulness to the truth, telling how you continue to walk in it. ⁴I have no greater joy than to hear that my children are walking in the truth.

⁵Dear friend, you are faithful in what you are doing for the brothers and sisters,ᵃ even though they are strangers to you. ⁶They have told the church about your love. Please send them on their way in a manner that honors God. ⁷It was for the sake of the Name that they went out, receiving no help from the pagans. ⁸We ought therefore to show hospitality to such people so that we may work together for the truth.

⁹I wrote to the church, but Diotrephes, who loves to be first, will not welcome us. ¹⁰So when I come, I will call attention to what he is doing, spreading malicious nonsense about us. Not satisfied with that, he even refuses to welcome other believers. He also stops those who want to do so and puts them out of the church.

¹¹Dear friend, do not imitate what is evil but what is good. Anyone who does what is good is from God. Anyone who does what is evil has not seen God. ¹²Demetrius is well spoken of by everyone — and even by the truth itself. We also speak well of him, and you know that our testimony is true.

¹³I have much to write you, but I do not want to do so with pen and ink. ¹⁴I hope to see you soon, and we will talk face to face.

Peace to you. The friends here send their greetings. Greet the friends there by name.

ᵃ 5 The Greek word for *brothers and sisters* (*adelphoi*) refers here to believers, both men and women, as part of God's family.

Initiative: Leaders Are to Host the People in Their Lives

3 John 3–12

While 1 John is about God's life and 2 John is about God's truth, 3 John is about God's way. Jesus said, "I am the way and the truth and the life" (Jn 14:6).

In his last letter, John uses the picture of a host. Hosts take initiative with their guests. They do what is right by others, make them feel comfortable, give direction to conversation, and provide for others. Leaders, like hosts, don't react; they act. They go first and risk whether the other person will respond positively. It is part of being a leader.

Interestingly, John distinguishes between *going* first and *wanting* to be first. He brings up Diotrephes, "who loves to be first" (3Jn 9). Diotrephes wanted to be first, but not necessarily go first in serving others. Here we see the difference between a "guest" and a "host." Consider what this letter teaches us about the leader as "host." Leaders take initiative . . .

- in their lifestyle (vv. 3–4)
- with others, especially strangers (vv. 5–6)
- in owning responsibility (vv. 7–8)
- in doing good, by acting and not reacting (v. 11)
- in modeling for others (v. 12)

INTRODUCTION TO JUDE

Correcting Error in the Church

Like James, Jude was the half brother of Jesus. He struggled early on with Jesus' ministry, but after the Lord's resurrection he became a radical spokesman for the kingdom of God. This brief letter exhibits his commitment to radical faith and obedience.

Jude wrote his letter to correct error in the early church. An early form of gnosticism had begun to trouble God's people, and many unstable believers had drifted from their original faith in Jesus Christ. Jude confronts the issue head-on and uses no fewer than three powerful illustrations to remind the people that God cannot put up with those who depart from their original mission and adopt some alien lifestyle.

Jude teaches leaders how to confront those who meander from the vision. He is direct, yet rational. He is convictional, yet compassionate. He reminds his readers of past incidents and the outcome of such drifting. He mentions the journey from Egypt into the promised land, the fallen angels who failed to believe, and the citizens of Sodom and Gomorrah who indulged in self-serving lifestyles. Jude has backbone!

Jude also teaches leaders how to communicate values. Every organization has values, whether they talk about them or not. Jude urges his readers to "contend for the faith" (v. 3). He communicates simply and with great humility, making an example of Michael, the archangel, who contended with Satan, but who spoke only in the authority and power of Jesus' name.

At the end of the book, Jude teaches leaders how to motivate others to act. He creates a sense of urgency and a sense of destiny in his readers with the examples he chooses. In closing his epistle, he speaks of Enoch, the

God's Role in Jude

God plays the role of the Chief Executive Officer, for whom Jude is speaking. Jude sees God as the righteous Judge who will execute justice; as the One who saved the Hebrews out of Egypt; and as the Protector who is able to keep us from stumbling en route to heaven.

Jude speaks on behalf of God with prophetic boldness. He clearly represents God, who is both merciful and just and who gives to all what they deserve. Jude acts and talks like an Old Testament prophet, calling the Lord's people back to the changeless God who is victorious in the end, the God who will include his people in his victory if they choose to remain true to his vision and values.

Leaders in Jude
Jude, Enoch

Other People of Influence in Jude
False teachers (proto-gnostics)

Lessons in Leadership
- Leaders must use pictures to capture the hearts of their people.
- Leaders must express certainty when possible, but clarity at all times.
- Effective leaders don't demand, but exhort, appeal, and urge others to act.

man who walked with God until God took him home. He persuasively reminds his readers of God's promise to execute justice for all. He inspires and instructs us by listing six action steps that, if followed, will please the Lord, then prays a benediction of victory.

> ■ People need both negative and positive reinforcement.

LEADERSHIP HIGHLIGHTS IN JUDE

[1]Jude, a servant of Jesus Christ and a brother of James,

To those who have been called, who are loved in God the Father and kept for[a] Jesus Christ:

[2]Mercy, peace and love be yours in abundance.

The Sin and Doom of Ungodly People

[3]Dear friends, although I was very eager to write to you about the salvation we share, I felt compelled to write and urge you to contend for the faith that was once for all entrusted to God's holy people. [4]For certain individuals whose condemnation was written about[b] long ago have secretly slipped in among you. They are ungodly people, who pervert the grace of our God into a license for immorality and deny Jesus Christ our only Sovereign and Lord.

[5]Though you already know all this, I want to remind you that the Lord[c] at one time delivered his people out of Egypt, but later destroyed those who did not believe. [6]And the angels who

---

Vision: Jude Uses Three Powerful Pictures

Jude 5–7

Jude uses three powerful pictures to illustrate the importance of staying true to God's vision. He knew people could seize only what they could see. Therefore, Jude gives his readers a *point* for their head and some *pictures* for their heart.

He makes his point in verse 4: We must remain true to the message we have been given; we must keep the faith. Then he furnishes pictures to illustrate this point:

1. The Jews in the wilderness were destroyed due to unbelief (v. 5).
2. The fallen angels were imprisoned due to disobedience (v. 6).
3. Sodom and Gomorrah were burned due to immorality and rebellion (v. 7).

This repetition proved to be a powerful tool to drive home his point. Effective leaders are good communicators who know how to illustrate their point to make it both memorable and transformational.

Confrontation: Jude Admonishes People to Do Right

Jude 3–4

Confrontation is a necessary evil. No one enjoys it, but it must be done in order to rectify, purify, and unify the organization. When leaders refuse to confront wrongs, the atmosphere can become lethargic and unfocused. When leaders don't stand for something, their people will fall for anything.

---

did not keep their positions of authority but abandoned their proper dwelling—these he has kept in darkness, bound with everlasting chains for judgment on the great Day. [7]In a similar way, Sodom and Gomorrah and the surrounding towns gave themselves up to sexual immorality and perversion. They serve as an example of those who suffer the punishment of eternal fire.

[8]In the very same way, on the strength of their dreams these ungodly people pollute their own bodies, reject authority and heap abuse on celestial beings. [9]But even the archangel Michael, when he was disputing with the devil about the body of Moses, did not himself dare to condemn him for slander but said, "The Lord rebuke you!"[d] [10]Yet these people slander whatever

---

[a] 1 Or by; or in   [b] 4 Or individuals who were marked out for condemnation   [c] 5 Some early manuscripts Jesus   [d] 9 Jude is alluding to the Jewish Testament of Moses (approximately the first century A.D.).

Humility: Leaders Know Authority Comes from God, Not from Within

Jude 9

Even Michael the archangel did not combat the enemy on his own authority, but spoke in the name of the Lord. Mature leaders swallow their egos and recognize God as their power source. They walk confidently in his authority, but never assume credit for it. Faith enables them to stretch, while humility enables them to stoop.

Empowerment: People Need Positive and Negative Reinforcement

Jude 14–16

Jude uses the word "ungodly" to guide his readers into a lifestyle pleasing to God. Like all good leaders, Jude understands the need for both positive and negative reinforcement. He empowers his readers to do what is right by sharing the rewards of righteous living and the consequences of unrighteous living. Note both sides of this motivational coin:

Positive Reinforcement	**Negative Reinforcement**
1. Enoch's prophecy of the Lord's return	1. The Lord's judgment against the ungodly
2. The apostles' writings about Christ	2. The last days will produce selfish people
3. God's judgment will bless the godly	3. God's judgment will punish the wicked

they do not understand, and the very things they do understand by instinct—as irrational animals do—will destroy them.

[11]Woe to them! They have taken the way of Cain; they have rushed for profit into Balaam's error; they have been destroyed in Korah's rebellion.

[12]These people are blemishes at your love feasts, eating with you without the slightest qualm—shepherds who feed only themselves. They are clouds without rain, blown along by the wind; autumn trees, without fruit and uprooted—twice dead. [13]They are wild waves of the sea, foaming up their shame; wandering stars, for whom blackest darkness has been reserved forever.

[14]Enoch, the seventh from Adam, prophesied about them: "See, the Lord is coming with thousands upon thousands of his holy ones [15]to judge everyone, and to convict all of them of all the ungodly acts they have committed in their ungodliness, and of all the defiant words ungodly sinners have spoken against him."[a] [16]These people are grumblers and faultfinders; they follow their own evil desires; they boast about themselves and flatter others for their own advantage.

A Call to Persevere

[17]But, dear friends, remember what the apostles of our Lord Jesus Christ foretold. [18]They said to you, "In the last times there will be scoffers who will follow their own ungodly desires." [19]These are the people who divide you, who follow mere natural instincts and do not have the Spirit.

[20]But you, dear friends, by building your-

selves up in your most holy faith and praying in the Holy Spirit, [21]keep yourselves in God's love as you wait for the mercy of our Lord Jesus Christ to bring you to eternal life.

[22]Be merciful to those who doubt; [23]save others by snatching them from the fire; to others show mercy, mixed with fear—hating even the clothing stained by corrupted flesh.[b]

Doxology

[24]To him who is able to keep you from stumbling and to present you before his glorious presence without fault and with great joy— [25]to the only God our Savior be glory, majesty, power and authority, through Jesus Christ our Lord, before all ages, now and forevermore! Amen.

[a] 14,15 From the Jewish First Book of Enoch (approximately the first century B.C.)   [b] 22,23 The Greek manuscripts of these verses vary at several points.

Communication: Good Leaders Provide Action Steps

Jude 17–23

Jude doesn't close his message with mere information, but offers points of application. Jude challenges his readers to pray in the Spirit (v. 20), remain in the love of God (v. 21), have compassion on doubters (v. 22), and snatch others out of their sin (v. 23). Effective leaders give both information and application.

INTRODUCTION TO
REVELATION

The Revealing of Jesus to the World

The book of Revelation differs from every other New Testament book. It contains not only a message for the first-century church, to whom it was written, but also to the church through the ages, particularly those living in the "end times" who will see Christ return to earth.

The apostle John, the author of this unique book, wrote five books in the New Testament. This was his last, written just before his death. The name "Revelation" comes from the main event of the book: the revealing of Jesus to the world's inhabitants in the final days. So what does this prophetic book have to say about leadership?

First, it is a book about *vision*. God gave John a vision about the final events of world history. In the midst of this grand vision John teaches us how to live and perceive life in light of the revelation. Vision drives all good leaders; throughout the book we see its power to change lives.

Second, it is a book about *virtue*. The book revolves around the final conflict between good and evil, God and Satan. Consequently, we see the centrality of God's character and virtue, as he ensures that right makes might and that virtue triumphs. Good leaders continue to stand for what is right, despite occasionally losing battles.

Third, it is a book about a *verdict*. Leaders must draw tough conclusions somewhere along the way. They can research, hold focus groups, and survey the needs of a culture—but sooner or later, they must issue a verdict about what they perceive to be true. Leaders make decisions. This book is about the verdict God and his people make, a verdict that influences the whole world.

Fourth, it is a book about *vigor*. John and the saints throughout history display passion, energy and deep convictions. This book teaches leaders that logic alone

God's Role in Revelation

God is the Ultimate Leader, the One who provides the vision to John and the One who implements the vision, defeating his enemies as the Captain of heaven's army. God is also the coming Judge who will sit before the world's population, assessing what each individual has done with his or her life. Finally, God is the King of kings, the Sovereign Lord who gives a clear picture of his ultimate control and dominion.

Leaders in Revelation

John, Jesus—the Lamb of God, the dragon, the angels (or messengers) of the seven churches in Asia

Other People of Influence in Revelation

The two witnesses, the remnant of Israel (144,000 individuals)

Lessons in Leadership

- A leader can be seen in four pictures: a shepherd, a seer, a soldier and a servant.
- Effective leaders assess their people and furnish them with a plan for improvement.
- Vision is the driving force behind all of heaven's activities.
- Leaders find a way to bring victory to their people.

accomplishes little. Success comes with passionate commitment and radical obedience.

Finally, it is a book about *victory*. Revelation vividly portrays the imminent showdown between God and Satan. God is the Ultimate Leader while Satan is the temporary influence—the "god of this age," as Paul put it (2Co 4:4). Although Satan's influence is real, he has no chance in the final struggle. The Ultimate Leader practices the Law of Victory.

- Leadership is about transformation, not mere information.
- A leader's victory always comes at a high cost.
- In the end, great leaders give God all the glory.

LEADERSHIP HIGHLIGHTS IN REVELATION

JOHN: A Visionary Leader Who Refused to Die Until Done (1:1–2)	**page 1527**
PERSPECTIVE: The Leader Must Define Reality (3:1–22)	**page 1531**
THE LAW OF SACRIFICE: Jesus Served First, Now Is Exalted (5:11–14)	**page 1533**
PROBLEM SOLVING: Jesus Resolves Earth's Conflict at Its Root (19:1–21)	**page 1543**
THE LAW OF VICTORY: Jesus Reigns After Defeating the Enemy for Good (22:12–16)	**page 1545**

Prologue

1 The revelation from Jesus Christ, which God gave him to show his servants what must soon take place. He made it known by sending his angel to his servant John, [2]who testifies to everything he saw—that is, the word of God and the testimony of Jesus Christ. [3]Blessed is the one who reads aloud the words of this prophecy, and blessed are those who hear it and take to heart what is written in it, because the time is near.

Greetings and Doxology

[4]John,

To the seven churches in the province of Asia:

Grace and peace to you from him who is, and who was, and who is to come, and from the seven spirits[a] before his throne, [5]and from Jesus Christ, who is the faithful witness, the firstborn from the dead, and the ruler of the kings of the earth.

To him who loves us and has freed us from our sins by his blood, [6]and has made us to be a kingdom and priests to serve his God and Father—to him be glory and power for ever and ever! Amen.

[7]"Look, he is coming with the clouds,"[b]
    and "every eye will see him,
        even those who pierced him";
    and all peoples on earth "will mourn
        because of him."[c]
                    So shall it be! Amen.

[8]"I am the Alpha and the Omega," says the Lord God, "who is, and who was, and who is to come, the Almighty."

John's Vision of Christ

[9]I, John, your brother and companion in the suffering and kingdom and patient endurance that are ours in Jesus, was on the island of Patmos because of the word of God and the testimony of Jesus. [10]On the Lord's Day I was in the Spirit, and I heard behind me a loud voice like a trumpet, [11]which said: "Write on a scroll what you see and send it to the seven churches: to Ephesus, Smyrna, Pergamum, Thyatira, Sardis, Philadelphia and Laodicea."

[12]I turned around to see the voice that was speaking to me. And when I turned I saw seven golden lampstands, [13]and among the lampstands was someone like a son of man,[d] dressed in a robe reaching down to his feet and with a golden sash around his chest. [14]The hair on his head was white like wool, as white as snow, and

---

[a] 4 That is, the sevenfold Spirit   [b] 7 Daniel 7:13
[c] 7 Zech. 12:10   [d] 13 See Daniel 7:13.

JOHN

A Visionary Leader Who Refused to Die Until Done

Revelation 1:1–2

PROFILE in leadership

The apostle John lived an amazing life of service to Christ. Not only was he numbered among the original twelve apostles, but Jesus included him in his "inner circle" during his earthly ministry. John walked closely with the Lord and even witnessed Jesus' transfiguration (Lk 9:28–36). Later—following Jesus' death, resurrection and ascension—John became a respected leader in the church at Jerusalem (Ac 4:1–12). He also wrote the Gospel and three New Testament epistles that bear his name.

John enjoyed a life full of service to Christ, but before he died, God would give him one more assignment: prophet. During the latter part of John's life, as he sat in exile on the rocky and remote island of Patmos, he penned the book of Revelation, a prophecy detailing the final conflict between good and evil.

John adopted the attitude and mindset of a truly godly leader. He devoted himself to doing what God had assigned to him, right up to the very end of his life. John knew that God had called him to a lifetime of service. And he saw his own life—his own body—as expendable for the purpose of serving the Lord Jesus Christ.

Wise leaders keep in mind that each day God gives them is to be used for his glory and the benefit of his people.

Vision: What You See Is What You Get

Revelation 1:9–20

While John worships God on the island of Patmos, Jesus speaks to him; but when he turns to hear the voice, he "sees" a vision (Rev 1:12). For the remainder of the book, John describes the vision that drove him to write and encourage others.

Vision always drives leaders, especially when they believe God is its source. Note the qualities of a divine vision:

1. It is not discovered or created, but revealed.

2. It doesn't compete with others, but completes others.

3. It is captivating, not optional. I cannot get it out of my mind.

4. Its goal is not to make money, but to meet needs.

5. Its success depends not on staying ahead of others, but on serving others.

6. It stops me before it drives me to act.

7. Its fulfillment doesn't rest on staying ahead of others, but on simple obedience.

8. Its purpose is not to feed my ego, but to glorify God.

---

his eyes were like blazing fire. ¹⁵His feet were like bronze glowing in a furnace, and his voice was like the sound of rushing waters. ¹⁶In his right hand he held seven stars, and coming out of his mouth was a sharp, double-edged sword. His face was like the sun shining in all its brilliance.

¹⁷When I saw him, I fell at his feet as though dead. Then he placed his right hand on me and said: "Do not be afraid. I am the First and the Last. ¹⁸I am the Living One; I was dead, and now look, I am alive for ever and ever! And I hold the keys of death and Hades.

¹⁹"Write, therefore, what you have seen, what is now and what will take place later. ²⁰The mystery of the seven stars that you saw in my right hand and of the seven golden lampstands is this: The seven stars are the angels[a] of the seven churches, and the seven lampstands are the seven churches.

To the Church in Ephesus

2 "To the angel[b] of the church in Ephesus write:

These are the words of him who holds the seven stars in his right hand and walks among the seven golden lampstands. ²I know your deeds, your hard work and your perseverance. I know that you cannot tolerate wicked people, that you have test-

ed those who claim to be apostles but are not, and have found them false. ³You have persevered and have endured hardships for my name, and have not grown weary.

⁴Yet I hold this against you: You have forsaken the love you had at first. ⁵Consider how far you have fallen! Repent and do the things you did at first. If you do not repent, I will come to you and remove your lampstand from its place. ⁶But you have this in your favor: You hate the practices of the Nicolaitans, which I also hate.

⁷Whoever has ears, let them hear what the Spirit says to the churches. To the one who is victorious, I will give the right to eat from the tree of life, which is in the paradise of God.

To the Church in Smyrna

⁸"To the angel of the church in Smyrna write:

These are the words of him who is the First and the Last, who died and came to life again. ⁹I know your afflictions and your poverty—yet you are rich! I know about the slander of those who say they are Jews and are not, but are a synagogue of Satan. ¹⁰Do not be afraid of what you are

---

^a 20 Or *messengers*   ^b 1 Or *messenger*; also in verses 8, 12 and 18

Priorities: Church Leaders Left Their First Love
Revelation 2:1–7

The church at Ephesus provides a classic illustration of leaders who failed to practice the Law of Priorities. Leaders can't merely stay busy; they must stay busy with the right activities. They don't just do things right; they do the right things.

The Ephesian leaders kept their people busy (Rev 2:2–3) and the Lord commends them for their labor, but somehow they had left their first priority, which was to love God. Their work *for* God had actually distracted them *from* God! They had busy hands, crowded calendars, full heads—but empty hearts.

What does God say about the remedy for their situation? In one sentence it is this: Remember and repent, or I will return and remove your light (2:5). This is good advice for any leader who has drifted from the top priorities:

1. *Reflect:* Think back and remember the original vision and goals.

2. *Repent:* Decide to change. List what you must discard and prioritize.

3. *Restore:* Begin to restore one top priority at a time, each week.

4. *Recognize:* Remember that God holds us accountable. He rewards fruit, not activity.

---

about to suffer. I tell you, the devil will put some of you in prison to test you, and you will suffer persecution for ten days. Be faithful, even to the point of death, and I will give you life as your victor's crown.

[11] Whoever has ears, let them hear what the Spirit says to the churches. The one who is victorious will not be hurt at all by the second death.

To the Church in Pergamum

[12] "To the angel of the church in Pergamum write:

These are the words of him who has the sharp, double-edged sword. [13] I know where you live—where Satan has his throne. Yet you remain true to my name. You did not renounce your faith in me, not even in the days of Antipas, my faithful witness, who was put to death in your city—where Satan lives.

[14] Nevertheless, I have a few things against you: There are some among you who hold to the teaching of Balaam, who taught Balak to entice the Israelites to sin so that they ate food sacrificed to idols and committed sexual immorality. [15] Likewise, you also have those who hold to the teaching of the Nicolaitans. [16] Repent therefore! Otherwise, I will soon come to you and will fight against them with the sword of my mouth.

[17] Whoever has ears, let them hear what the Spirit says to the churches. To the one who is victorious, I will give some of the hidden manna. I will also give that person a white stone with a new name written on it, known only to the one who receives it.

To the Church in Thyatira

[18] "To the angel of the church in Thyatira write:

These are the words of the Son of God, whose eyes are like blazing fire and whose feet are like burnished bronze. [19] I know your deeds, your love and faith, your service and perseverance, and that you are now doing more than you did at first.

The Law of Connection: Jesus Puts Compassion Before Correction
Revelation 2:1–29

Jesus lets each church know he understands their situation. He affirms their positive qualities—he touches their hearts—then voices concern over an area that needs attention. Finally, he beseeches them to listen. He consistently shows compassion before he corrects. Leaders touch a heart before they ask for a hand.

Encouragement: Jesus Affirms the Church at Smyrna

Revelation 2:8–11

Jesus encourages the hard-pressed church at Smyrna to stand firm and to keep doing what its members know to be right. He reminds them of the reward that awaits them and that their trouble will be temporary. People get emotionally low, they grow weary, and they become doubtful and insecure. They need a leader's encouragement.

[20]Nevertheless, I have this against you: You tolerate that woman Jezebel, who calls herself a prophet. By her teaching she misleads my servants into sexual immorality and the eating of food sacrificed to idols. [21]I have given her time to repent of her immorality, but she is unwilling. [22]So I will cast her on a bed of suffering, and I will make those who commit adultery with her suffer intensely, unless they repent of her ways. [23]I will strike her children dead. Then all the churches will know that I am he who searches hearts and minds, and I will repay each of you according to your deeds.

[24]Now I say to the rest of you in Thyatira, to you who do not hold to her teaching and have not learned Satan's so-called deep secrets, 'I will not impose any other burden on you, [25]except to hold on to what you have until I come.'

[26]To the one who is victorious and does my will to the end, I will give authority over the nations— [27]that one 'will rule them with an iron scepter and will dash them to pieces like pottery'[a]—just as I have received authority from my Father. [28]I will also give that one the morning star. [29]Whoever has ears, let them hear what the Spirit says to the churches.

To the Church in Sardis

3 "To the angel[b] of the church in Sardis write:

These are the words of him who holds the seven spirits[c] of God and the seven stars. I know your deeds; you have a rep-

utation of being alive, but you are dead. [2]Wake up! Strengthen what remains and is about to die, for I have found your deeds unfinished in the sight of my God. [3]Remember, therefore, what you have received and heard; hold it fast, and repent. But if you do not wake up, I will come like a thief, and you will not know at what time I will come to you.

[4]Yet you have a few people in Sardis who have not soiled their clothes. They will walk with me, dressed in white, for they are worthy. [5]The one who is victorious will, like them, be dressed in white. I will never blot out the name of that person from the book of life, but will acknowledge that name before my Father and his angels. [6]Whoever has ears, let them hear what the Spirit says to the churches.

To the Church in Philadelphia

[7]"To the angel of the church in Philadelphia write:

These are the words of him who is holy and true, who holds the key of David. What he opens no one can shut, and what he shuts no one can open. [8]I know your deeds. See, I have placed before you an open door that no one can shut. I know that you have little strength, yet you have kept my word and have not denied my name. [9]I will make those who are of the synagogue of Satan, who claim to be Jews though they are not, but are liars—I will make them come and fall down at your feet and acknowledge that I have loved you. [10]Since you have kept my command to endure patiently, I will also keep you from the hour of trial that is going to come on the whole world to test the inhabitants of the earth.

[11]I am coming soon. Hold on to what you have, so that no one will take your crown. [12]The one who is victorious I will make a pillar in the temple of my God. Never again will they leave it. I will write on them the name of my God and the name of the city of my God, the new Jerusalem, which is coming down out of heaven from my God; and I will also write on them my new name. [13]Whoever has ears, let them hear what the Spirit says to the churches.

---

[a] 27 Psalm 2:9   [b] 1 Or *messenger*; also in verses 7 and 14
[c] 1 That is, the sevenfold Spirit

Perspective: The Leader Must Define Reality

Revelation 3:1–22

John, writing for Jesus, sends a message to the churches of Sardis, Philadelphia and Laodicea. In each case, he calls attention to something that has escaped their attention.

Call these words midcourse corrections. Call them healthy accountability. Or just call them sound wisdom. In any case, these three churches illustrate the truth that a leader must define reality. See how Jesus does this:

Church	Reality Check	Action Step
1. Sardis	1. Fell asleep on the job	1. Wake up and repent
2. Philadelphia	2. Little power but big opportunity	2. Don't give up
3. Laodicea	3. Deceived; blind to their condition	3. Change your priorities

Leaders must stay on top of what is happening in their organization. They must discern what keeps their people from moving to the next level. They must confront mediocrity and give steps to correct it. They must never feel satisfied with the status quo.

To the Church in Laodicea

¹⁴"To the angel of the church in Laodicea write:

These are the words of the Amen, the faithful and true witness, the ruler of God's creation. ¹⁵I know your deeds, that you are neither cold nor hot. I wish you were either one or the other! ¹⁶So, because you are lukewarm—neither hot nor cold—I am about to spit you out of my mouth. ¹⁷You say, 'I am rich; I have acquired wealth and do not need a thing.' But you do not realize that you are wretched, pitiful, poor, blind and naked. ¹⁸I counsel you to buy from me gold refined in the fire, so you can become rich; and white clothes to wear, so you can cover your shameful nakedness; and salve to put on your eyes, so you can see.

¹⁹Those whom I love I rebuke and discipline. So be earnest and repent. ²⁰Here I am! I stand at the door and knock. If anyone hears my voice and opens the door, I will come in and eat with that person, and they with me.

²¹To the one who is victorious, I will give the right to sit with me on my throne, just as I was victorious and sat down with my Father on his throne. ²²Whoever has ears, let them hear what the Spirit says to the churches."

The Throne in Heaven

4 After this I looked, and there before me was a door standing open in heaven. And the voice I had first heard speaking to me like a trumpet said, "Come up here, and I will show you what must take place after this." ²At once I was in the Spirit, and there before me was a throne in heaven with someone sitting on it. ³And the one who sat there had the appearance of jasper and ruby. A rainbow that shone like an emerald encircled the throne. ⁴Surrounding the throne were twenty-four other thrones, and seated on them were twenty-four elders. They were dressed in white and had crowns of gold on their heads. ⁵From the throne came flashes of lightning, rumblings and peals of thunder. In front of the throne, seven lamps were blazing. These are the seven spirits*a* of God. ⁶Also in front of the throne there was what looked like a sea of glass, clear as crystal.

In the center, around the throne, were four living creatures, and they were covered with eyes, in front and in back. ⁷The first living creature was like a lion, the second was like an ox, the third had a face like a man, the fourth was like a flying eagle. ⁸Each of the four living creatures had six wings and was covered with eyes all around, even under its wings. Day and night they never stop saying:

"'Holy, holy, holy
    is the Lord God Almighty,'*b*
who was, and is, and is to come."

⁹Whenever the living creatures give glory, honor and thanks to him who sits on the throne and

---

a 5 That is, the sevenfold Spirit   *b* 8 Isaiah 6:3

God's Nature Is Organization, Not Chaos

Revelation 4:1–11

John's description of heaven reminds us that we serve a God of order and harmony, not of chaos or anarchy. John paints a portrait of form, structure, harmony, precision and dignity. God's acts never result in disarray. "God is not a God of disorder but of peace" (1Co 14:33).

who lives for ever and ever, [10]the twenty-four elders fall down before him who sits on the throne and worship him who lives for ever and ever. They lay their crowns before the throne and say:

[11]"You are worthy, our Lord and God,
    to receive glory and honor and power,
  for you created all things,
    and by your will they were created
    and have their being."

The Scroll and the Lamb

5 Then I saw in the right hand of him who sat on the throne a scroll with writing on both sides and sealed with seven seals. [2]And I saw a mighty angel proclaiming in a loud voice, "Who is worthy to break the seals and open the scroll?" [3]But no one in heaven or on earth or under the earth could open the scroll or even look inside it. [4]I wept and wept because no one was found who was worthy to open the scroll or look inside. [5]Then one of the elders said to me, "Do not weep! See, the Lion of the tribe of Judah, the Root of David, has triumphed. He is able to open the scroll and its seven seals."

[6]Then I saw a Lamb, looking as if it had been slain, standing at the center of the throne, encircled by the four living creatures and the elders. The Lamb had seven horns and seven eyes, which are the seven spirits[a] of God sent out into all the earth. [7]He went and took the scroll from the right hand of him who sat on the throne. [8]And when he had taken it, the four living creatures and the twenty-four elders fell down before the Lamb. Each one had a harp and they were holding golden bowls full of incense, which are the prayers of God's people. [9]And they sang a new song, saying:

"You are worthy to take the scroll
    and to open its seals,

because you were slain,
    and with your blood you purchased for God
    persons from every tribe and language
      and people and nation.
[10]You have made them to be a kingdom and
      priests to serve our God,
    and they will reign[b] on the earth."

[11]Then I looked and heard the voice of many angels, numbering thousands upon thousands, and ten thousand times ten thousand. They encircled the throne and the living creatures and the elders. [12]In a loud voice they were saying:

"Worthy is the Lamb, who was slain,
    to receive power and wealth and wisdom
      and strength
    and honor and glory and praise!"

[13]Then I heard every creature in heaven and on earth and under the earth and on the sea, and all that is in them, saying:

"To him who sits on the throne and to the
      Lamb
    be praise and honor and glory and power,
      for ever and ever!"

[14]The four living creatures said, "Amen," and the elders fell down and worshiped.

The Seals

6 I watched as the Lamb opened the first of the seven seals. Then I heard one of the four living creatures say in a voice like thunder, "Come!" [2]I looked, and there before me was a white horse! Its rider held a bow, and he was given a crown, and he rode out as a conqueror bent on conquest.

[3]When the Lamb opened the second seal, I heard the second living creature say, "Come!" [4]Then another horse came out, a fiery red one. Its rider was given power to take peace from the earth and to make people kill each other. To him was given a large sword.

[5]When the Lamb opened the third seal, I heard the third living creature say, "Come!" I looked, and there before me was a black horse! Its rider was holding a pair of scales in his hand. [6]Then I heard what sounded like a voice among the four living creatures, saying, "Two pounds[c] of wheat for a day's wages,[d] and six pounds[e] of barley for a day's wages,[d] and do not damage the oil and the wine!"

[7]When the Lamb opened the fourth seal, I heard the voice of the fourth living creature say,

---

[a] 6 That is, the sevenfold Spirit   [b] 10 Some manuscripts they reign   [c] 6 Or about 1 kilogram   [d] 6 Greek a denarius   [e] 6 Or about 3 kilograms

The Law of Sacrifice: Jesus Served First, Now Is Exalted

Revelation 5:11–14

The leader's job is to sacrifice; God's job is to promote. If we will stoop down, he will raise up. This message is given in other New Testament books (Jas 4:10; 1Pe 5:6), but is never clearer than here.

The Lamb of God, who came to be slaughtered, now sits on a throne far above every other leader (Rev 5:11–14). Paul predicted this in Philippians 2:9.

The rule of thumb seems to be: The lower you go, the higher you grow. We lower; God lifts. Jesus is the ultimate example of this leadership law. Yet many others in history have also obeyed this law. Reflect for a moment on a few biblical illustrations:

Leader	His Sacrifice	The Result
1. Abraham	1. Security, rich land, success	1. Became father of nations
2. Moses	2. Royal position in Egypt	2. Became deliverer of Israel
3. Jesus' disciples	3. Everything they had	3. Leaders of the church
4. Apostle Paul	4. Leader among Pharisees	4. Greatest apostle in history
5. Jesus Christ	5. His divine rights and his life	5. Ruler of the universe

Question: What have you given up to go up?

"Come!" [8]I looked, and there before me was a pale horse! Its rider was named Death, and Hades was following close behind him. They were given power over a fourth of the earth to kill by sword, famine and plague, and by the wild beasts of the earth.

[9]When he opened the fifth seal, I saw under the altar the souls of those who had been slain because of the word of God and the testimony they had maintained. [10]They called out in a loud voice, "How long, Sovereign Lord, holy and true, until you judge the inhabitants of the earth and avenge our blood?" [11]Then each of them was given a white robe, and they were told to wait a little longer, until the full number of their fellow servants, their brothers and sisters,[a] were killed just as they had been.

[12]I watched as he opened the sixth seal. There was a great earthquake. The sun turned black like sackcloth made of goat hair, the whole moon turned blood red, [13]and the stars in the sky fell to earth, as figs drop from a fig tree when shaken by a strong wind. [14]The heavens receded like a scroll being rolled up, and every mountain and island was removed from its place.

[15]Then the kings of the earth, the princes, the generals, the rich, the mighty, and everyone else, both slave and free, hid in caves and among the rocks of the mountains. [16]They called to the mountains and the rocks, "Fall on us and hide

us[b] from the face of him who sits on the throne and from the wrath of the Lamb! [17]For the great day of their[c] wrath has come, and who can withstand it?"

144,000 Sealed

7 After this I saw four angels standing at the four corners of the earth, holding back the four winds of the earth to prevent any wind from blowing on the land or on the sea or on any tree. [2]Then I saw another angel coming up from the east, having the seal of the living God. He called out in a loud voice to the four angels who had been given power to harm the land and the sea: [3]"Do not harm the land or the sea or the trees until we put a seal on the foreheads of the servants of our God." [4]Then I heard the number of those who were sealed: 144,000 from all the tribes of Israel.

[5]From the tribe of Judah 12,000 were sealed,
from the tribe of Reuben 12,000,
from the tribe of Gad 12,000,
[6]from the tribe of Asher 12,000,
from the tribe of Naphtali 12,000,
from the tribe of Manasseh 12,000,

[a] 11 The Greek word for *brothers and sisters* (*adelphoi*) refers here to believers, both men and women, as part of God's family; also in 12:10; 19:10.   [b] 16 See Hosea 10:8.   [c] 17 Some manuscripts *his*

[7] from the tribe of Simeon 12,000,
   from the tribe of Levi 12,000,
   from the tribe of Issachar 12,000,
[8] from the tribe of Zebulun 12,000,
   from the tribe of Joseph 12,000,
   from the tribe of Benjamin 12,000.

The Great Multitude in White Robes

[9] After this I looked, and there before me was a great multitude that no one could count, from every nation, tribe, people and language, standing before the throne and before the Lamb. They were wearing white robes and were holding palm branches in their hands. [10] And they cried out in a loud voice:

"Salvation belongs to our God,
who sits on the throne,
and to the Lamb."

[11] All the angels were standing around the throne and around the elders and the four living creatures. They fell down on their faces before the throne and worshiped God, [12] saying:

"Amen!
Praise and glory
and wisdom and thanks and honor
and power and strength
be to our God for ever and ever.
Amen!"

[13] Then one of the elders asked me, "These in white robes — who are they, and where did they come from?"

[14] I answered, "Sir, you know."

And he said, "These are they who have come out of the great tribulation; they have washed their robes and made them white in the blood of the Lamb. [15] Therefore,

Commitment: When Leaders Are Tested, Commitment Is Revealed

Revelation 7:4–17

Tribulation always tests a leader's commitment level. Trouble doesn't always make a leader become committed, but it does reveal his or her commitment. Unless leaders remain committed, they will be tempted to hesitate or withdraw in tough times. This is why leaders must begin with commitment, before they are tested.

"they are before the throne of God
and serve him day and night in his temple;
and he who sits on the throne
will shelter them with his presence.
[16] 'Never again will they hunger;
never again will they thirst.
The sun will not beat down on them,'[a]
nor any scorching heat.
[17] For the Lamb at the center of the throne
will be their shepherd;
'he will lead them to springs of living water.'[a]
'And God will wipe away every tear from
their eyes.'[b]"

The Seventh Seal and the Golden Censer

8 When he opened the seventh seal, there was silence in heaven for about half an hour.

[2] And I saw the seven angels who stand before God, and seven trumpets were given to them.

[3] Another angel, who had a golden censer, came and stood at the altar. He was given much incense to offer, with the prayers of all God's people, on the golden altar in front of the throne. [4] The smoke of the incense, together with the prayers of God's people, went up before God from the angel's hand. [5] Then the angel took the censer, filled it with fire from the altar, and hurled it on the earth; and there came peals of thunder, rumblings, flashes of lightning and an earthquake.

The Trumpets

[6] Then the seven angels who had the seven trumpets prepared to sound them.

[7] The first angel sounded his trumpet, and there came hail and fire mixed with blood, and it was hurled down on the earth. A third of the earth was burned up, a third of the trees were burned up, and all the green grass was burned up.

[8] The second angel sounded his trumpet, and something like a huge mountain, all ablaze, was thrown into the sea. A third of the sea turned into blood, [9] a third of the living creatures in the sea died, and a third of the ships were destroyed.

[10] The third angel sounded his trumpet, and a great star, blazing like a torch, fell from the sky on a third of the rivers and on the springs of water — [11] the name of the star is Wormwood.[c] A third of the waters turned bitter, and many people died from the waters that had become bitter.

[12] The fourth angel sounded his trumpet, and a third of the sun was struck, a third of the moon, and a third of the stars, so that a third of

---

[a] 16,17 Isaiah 49:10   [b] 17 Isaiah 25:8   [c] 11 Wormwood is a bitter substance.

them turned dark. A third of the day was without light, and also a third of the night.

[13] As I watched, I heard an eagle that was flying in midair call out in a loud voice: "Woe! Woe! Woe to the inhabitants of the earth, because of the trumpet blasts about to be sounded by the other three angels!"

9 The fifth angel sounded his trumpet, and I saw a star that had fallen from the sky to the earth. The star was given the key to the shaft of the Abyss. [2] When he opened the Abyss, smoke rose from it like the smoke from a gigantic furnace. The sun and sky were darkened by the smoke from the Abyss. [3] And out of the smoke locusts came down on the earth and were given power like that of scorpions of the earth. [4] They were told not to harm the grass of the earth or any plant or tree, but only those people who did not have the seal of God on their foreheads. [5] They were not allowed to kill them but only to torture them for five months. And the agony they suffered was like that of the sting of a scorpion when it strikes. [6] During those days people will seek death but will not find it; they will long to die, but death will elude them.

[7] The locusts looked like horses prepared for battle. On their heads they wore something like crowns of gold, and their faces resembled human faces. [8] Their hair was like women's hair, and their teeth were like lions' teeth. [9] They had breastplates like breastplates of iron, and the sound of their wings was like the thundering of many horses and chariots rushing into battle. [10] They had tails with stingers, like scorpions, and in their tails they had power to torment people for five months. [11] They had as king over them the angel of the Abyss, whose name in Hebrew is Abaddon and in Greek is Apollyon (that is, Destroyer).

[12] The first woe is past; two other woes are yet to come.

[13] The sixth angel sounded his trumpet, and I heard a voice coming from the four horns of the golden altar that is before God. [14] It said to the sixth angel who had the trumpet, "Release the four angels who are bound at the great river Euphrates." [15] And the four angels who had been kept ready for this very hour and day and month and year were released to kill a third of mankind. [16] The number of the mounted troops was twice ten thousand times ten thousand. I heard their number.

[17] The horses and riders I saw in my vision looked like this: Their breastplates were fiery red, dark blue, and yellow as sulfur. The heads of the horses resembled the heads of lions, and out of their mouths came fire, smoke and sulfur. [18] A third of mankind was killed by the three plagues of fire, smoke and sulfur that came out of their mouths. [19] The power of the horses was in their mouths and in their tails; for their tails were like snakes, having heads with which they inflict injury.

[20] The rest of mankind who were not killed by these plagues still did not repent of the work of their hands; they did not stop worshiping demons, and idols of gold, silver, bronze, stone and wood—idols that cannot see or hear or walk. [21] Nor did they repent of their murders, their magic arts, their sexual immorality or their thefts.

The Angel and the Little Scroll

10 Then I saw another mighty angel coming down from heaven. He was robed in a cloud, with a rainbow above his head; his face was like the sun, and his legs were like fiery pillars. [2] He was holding a little scroll, which lay open in his hand. He planted his right foot on the sea and his left foot on the land, [3] and he gave a loud shout like the roar of a lion. When he shouted, the voices of the seven thunders spoke. [4] And when the seven thunders spoke, I was about to write; but I heard a voice from heaven say, "Seal up what the seven thunders have said and do not write it down."

[5] Then the angel I had seen standing on the sea and on the land raised his right hand to heaven. [6] And he swore by him who lives for ever and ever, who created the heavens and all that is in them, the earth and all that is in it, and the sea and all that is in it, and said, "There will be no more delay! [7] But in the days when the seventh angel is about to sound his trumpet, the mystery of God will be accomplished, just as he announced to his servants the prophets."

[8] Then the voice that I had heard from heaven spoke to me once more: "Go, take the scroll that lies open in the hand of the angel who is standing on the sea and on the land."

[9] So I went to the angel and asked him to give me the little scroll. He said to me, "Take it and eat it. It will turn your stomach sour, but 'in your mouth it will be as sweet as honey.'[a]" [10] I took the little scroll from the angel's hand and ate it. It tasted as sweet as honey in my mouth, but when I had eaten it, my stomach turned sour. [11] Then I was told, "You must prophesy again about many peoples, nations, languages and kings."

---

[a] 9 Ezek. 3:3

The Two Witnesses

11 I was given a reed like a measuring rod and was told, "Go and measure the temple of God and the altar, with its worshipers. ²But exclude the outer court; do not measure it, because it has been given to the Gentiles. They will trample on the holy city for 42 months. ³And I will appoint my two witnesses, and they will prophesy for 1,260 days, clothed in sackcloth." ⁴They are "the two olive trees" and the two lampstands, and "they stand before the Lord of the earth."ᵃ ⁵If anyone tries to harm them, fire comes from their mouths and devours their enemies. This is how anyone who wants to harm them must die. ⁶They have power to shut up the heavens so that it will not rain during the time they are prophesying; and they have power to turn the waters into blood and to strike the earth with every kind of plague as often as they want.

⁷Now when they have finished their testimony, the beast that comes up from the Abyss will attack them, and overpower and kill them. ⁸Their bodies will lie in the public square of the great city— which is figuratively called Sodom and Egypt— where also their Lord was crucified. ⁹For three and a half days some from every people, tribe, language and nation will gaze on their bodies and refuse them burial. ¹⁰The inhabitants of the earth will gloat over them and will celebrate by sending each other gifts, because these two prophets had tormented those who live on the earth.

¹¹But after the three and a half days the breathᵇ of life from God entered them, and they stood on their feet, and terror struck those who saw them. ¹²Then they heard a loud voice from heaven saying to them, "Come up here." And they went up to heaven in a cloud, while their enemies looked on.

¹³At that very hour there was a severe earthquake and a tenth of the city collapsed. Seven thousand people were killed in the earthquake, and the survivors were terrified and gave glory to the God of heaven.

¹⁴The second woe has passed; the third woe is coming soon.

The Seventh Trumpet

¹⁵The seventh angel sounded his trumpet, and there were loud voices in heaven, which said:

> "The kingdom of the world has become
>   the kingdom of our Lord and of his
>   Messiah,
>   and he will reign for ever and ever."

¹⁶And the twenty-four elders, who were seated on their thrones before God, fell on their faces and worshiped God, ¹⁷saying:

> "We give thanks to you, Lord God Almighty,
>   the One who is and who was,
> because you have taken your great power
>   and have begun to reign.
> ¹⁸The nations were angry,
>   and your wrath has come.
> The time has come for judging the dead,
>   and for rewarding your servants the
>   prophets
> and your people who revere your name,
>   both great and small—
> and for destroying those who destroy the
>   earth."

¹⁹Then God's temple in heaven was opened, and within his temple was seen the ark of his covenant. And there came flashes of lightning,

---

The Law of Navigation: God Raises Up Leaders to Correct and Direct

Revelation 11:3–13

John describes two remarkable "witnesses" whom God will raise up as leaders during the Great Tribulation. Notice how John portrays these two end-times leaders:

1. They are given power over people and nature (vv. 3, 6).
2. They speak for the cause of righteousness (v. 3).
3. They are burdened for the world's condition (v. 3).
4. They are a source of light and hope (v. 4).
5. They are given divine protection (v. 5).
6. They eventually die for their cause (v. 7).
7. They and their cause ultimately succeed (vv. 11–12).

Why will God raise up these leaders? Because the world will always need someone to practice the Law of Navigation. The spiritual vacuum in the world will call for leaders to correct and direct the people back to God. God will raise up these two leaders to chart the course for everyone. How does your leadership stack up to theirs?

ᵃ 4 See Zech. 4:3,11,14.   ᵇ 11 Or *Spirit* (see Ezek. 37:5,14)

rumblings, peals of thunder, an earthquake and a severe hailstorm.

The Woman and the Dragon

12 A great sign appeared in heaven: a woman clothed with the sun, with the moon under her feet and a crown of twelve stars on her head. [2]She was pregnant and cried out in pain as she was about to give birth. [3]Then another sign appeared in heaven: an enormous red dragon with seven heads and ten horns and seven crowns on its heads. [4]Its tail swept a third of the stars out of the sky and flung them to the earth. The dragon stood in front of the woman who was about to give birth, so that it might devour her child the moment he was born. [5]She gave birth to a son, a male child, who "will rule all the nations with an iron scepter."[a] And her child was snatched up to God and to his throne. [6]The woman fled into the wilderness to a place prepared for her by God, where she might be taken care of for 1,260 days.

[7]Then war broke out in heaven. Michael and his angels fought against the dragon, and the dragon and his angels fought back. [8]But he was not strong enough, and they lost their place in heaven. [9]The great dragon was hurled down—that ancient serpent called the devil, or Satan, who leads the whole world astray. He was hurled to the earth, and his angels with him.

[10]Then I heard a loud voice in heaven say:

"Now have come the salvation and the power
  and the kingdom of our God,
  and the authority of his Messiah.
For the accuser of our brothers and sisters,
  who accuses them before our God day and
    night,
  has been hurled down.
[11]They triumphed over him
  by the blood of the Lamb
  and by the word of their testimony;
they did not love their lives so much
  as to shrink from death.
[12]Therefore rejoice, you heavens
  and you who dwell in them!
But woe to the earth and the sea,
  because the devil has gone down to you!
He is filled with fury,
  because he knows that his time is short."

[13]When the dragon saw that he had been hurled to the earth, he pursued the woman who had given birth to the male child. [14]The woman was given the two wings of a great eagle, so that she might fly to the place prepared for her in the wilderness, where she would be taken care of for a time, times

---

The Law of Victory: Godly Leadership Won't Succeed Without a Fight

Revelation 12:7–12

In order for leaders to find a way for the team to win, there must be a contest. In Revelation 12, we read about the ultimate contest between the forces of good and the forces of evil. The hosts of heaven take on the dragon and his angels. Good eventually wins out through the blood of Christ and the testimony of the believers (Rev 12:11).

The truth for leaders? First, victory rarely comes without a fight. There is no success without sacrifice; there is a cost to every crown. The good news is, anything worth achieving is worth the battle. Second, victory rarely comes without a team effort. Michael didn't fight alone (12:7). The saints didn't overcome the enemy alone (12:11). God designed us to win in community. Third, victory should never come without a celebration. The heavens rejoice at the victory of the Lamb (12:12). The greater the victory, the bigger the celebration!

---

and half a time, out of the serpent's reach. [15]Then from his mouth the serpent spewed water like a river, to overtake the woman and sweep her away with the torrent. [16]But the earth helped the woman by opening its mouth and swallowing the river that the dragon had spewed out of his mouth. [17]Then the dragon was enraged at the woman and went off to wage war against the rest of her offspring—those who keep God's commands and hold fast their testimony about Jesus.

The Beast out of the Sea

13 The dragon[b] stood on the shore of the sea. And I saw a beast coming out of the sea. It had ten horns and seven heads, with ten crowns on its horns, and on each head a blasphemous name. [2]The beast I saw resembled a leopard, but had feet like those of a bear and a mouth like that of a lion. The dragon gave the beast his power and his throne and great authority. [3]One of the heads of the beast seemed to have had a fatal wound, but the fatal wound had been healed. The whole world was filled with wonder and followed the beast. [4]People worshiped the dragon

---

[a] 5 Psalm 2:9   [b] 1 Some manuscripts *And I*

because he had given authority to the beast, and they also worshiped the beast and asked, "Who is like the beast? Who can wage war against it?"

⁵The beast was given a mouth to utter proud words and blasphemies and to exercise its authority for forty-two months. ⁶It opened its mouth to blaspheme God, and to slander his name and his dwelling place and those who live in heaven. ⁷It was given power to wage war against God's holy people and to conquer them. And it was given authority over every tribe, people, language and nation. ⁸All inhabitants of the earth will worship the beast — all whose names have not been written in the Lamb's book of life, the Lamb who was slain from the creation of the world.ᵃ

⁹Whoever has ears, let them hear.

¹⁰ "If anyone is to go into captivity,
     into captivity they will go.
If anyone is to be killedᵇ with the sword,
     with the sword they will be killed."ᶜ

This calls for patient endurance and faithfulness on the part of God's people.

The Beast out of the Earth

¹¹Then I saw a second beast, coming out of the earth. It had two horns like a lamb, but it spoke like a dragon. ¹²It exercised all the authority of the first beast on its behalf, and made the earth and its inhabitants worship the first beast, whose fatal wound had been healed. ¹³And it performed great signs, even causing fire to come down from heaven to the earth in full view of the people. ¹⁴Because of the signs it was given power to perform on behalf of the first beast, it deceived the inhabitants of the earth. It ordered them to set up an image in honor of the beast who was wounded by the sword and yet lived. ¹⁵The second beast was given power to give breath to the image of the first beast, so that the image could speak and cause all who refused to worship the image to be killed. ¹⁶It also forced all people, great and small, rich and poor, free and slave, to receive a mark on their right hands or on their foreheads, ¹⁷so that they could not buy or sell unless they had the mark, which is the name of the beast or the number of its name.

¹⁸This calls for wisdom. Let the person who has insight calculate the number of the beast, for it is the number of a man.ᵈ That number is 666.

The Lamb and the 144,000

14 Then I looked, and there before me was the Lamb, standing on Mount Zion, and with him 144,000 who had his name and his Fa-

---

The Law of Buy-In: Passion Draws People, Even to the Wrong Causes

Revelation 13:1–18

The Beast demonstrates that leaders can have a passion for evil. This man builds a large following despite his immoral vision. This illustrates the awesome power of passion. People flock to passionate leaders, even when their cause is wrong. When people are attracted to the leader, they buy in to his vision.

---

ther's name written on their foreheads. ²And I heard a sound from heaven like the roar of rushing waters and like a loud peal of thunder. The sound I heard was like that of harpists playing their harps. ³And they sang a new song before the throne and before the four living creatures and the elders. No one could learn the song except the 144,000 who had been redeemed from the earth. ⁴These are those who did not defile themselves with women, for they remained virgins. They follow the Lamb wherever he goes. They were purchased from among mankind and offered as firstfruits to God and the Lamb. ⁵No lie was found in their mouths; they are blameless.

The Three Angels

⁶Then I saw another angel flying in midair, and he had the eternal gospel to proclaim to those who live on the earth — to every nation, tribe, language and people. ⁷He said in a loud voice, "Fear God and give him glory, because the hour of his judgment has come. Worship him who made the heavens, the earth, the sea and the springs of water."

⁸A second angel followed and said, " 'Fallen! Fallen is Babylon the Great,'ᵉ which made all the nations drink the maddening wine of her adulteries."

⁹A third angel followed them and said in a loud voice: "If anyone worships the beast and its image and receives its mark on their forehead or on their hand, ¹⁰they, too, will drink the wine of God's fury, which has been poured full strength into the cup of his wrath. They will be tormented

---

ᵃ 8 Or *written from the creation of the world in the book of life belonging to the Lamb who was slain*   ᵇ 10 Some manuscripts *anyone kills*   ᶜ 10 Jer. 15:2   ᵈ 18 Or *is humanity's number*   ᵉ 8 Isaiah 21:9

with burning sulfur in the presence of the holy angels and of the Lamb. [11]And the smoke of their torment will rise for ever and ever. There will be no rest day or night for those who worship the beast and its image, or for anyone who receives the mark of its name." [12]This calls for patient endurance on the part of the people of God who keep his commands and remain faithful to Jesus.

[13]Then I heard a voice from heaven say, "Write this: Blessed are the dead who die in the Lord from now on."

"Yes," says the Spirit, "they will rest from their labor, for their deeds will follow them."

Harvesting the Earth and Trampling the Winepress

[14]I looked, and there before me was a white cloud, and seated on the cloud was one like a son of man[a] with a crown of gold on his head and a sharp sickle in his hand. [15]Then another angel came out of the temple and called in a loud voice to him who was sitting on the cloud, "Take your sickle and reap, because the time to reap has come, for the harvest of the earth is ripe." [16]So he who was seated on the cloud swung his sickle over the earth, and the earth was harvested.

[17]Another angel came out of the temple in heaven, and he too had a sharp sickle. [18]Still another angel, who had charge of the fire, came from the altar and called in a loud voice to him who had the sharp sickle, "Take your sharp sickle and gather the clusters of grapes from the earth's vine, because its grapes are ripe." [19]The angel swung his sickle on the earth, gathered its grapes and threw them into the great winepress of God's wrath. [20]They were trampled in the winepress outside the city, and blood flowed out of the press, rising as high as the horses' bridles for a distance of 1,600 stadia.[b]

Seven Angels With Seven Plagues

15 I saw in heaven another great and marvelous sign: seven angels with the seven last plagues—last, because with them God's wrath is completed. [2]And I saw what looked like a sea of glass glowing with fire and, standing beside the sea, those who had been victorious over the beast and its image and over the number of its name. They held harps given them by God [3]and sang the song of God's servant Moses and of the Lamb:

"Great and marvelous are your deeds,
     Lord God Almighty.
Just and true are your ways,
     King of the nations.[c]

[4]Who will not fear you, Lord,
     and bring glory to your name?
For you alone are holy.
All nations will come
     and worship before you,
for your righteous acts have been revealed."[d]

[5]After this I looked, and I saw in heaven the temple—that is, the tabernacle of the covenant law—and it was opened. [6]Out of the temple came the seven angels with the seven plagues. They were dressed in clean, shining linen and wore golden sashes around their chests. [7]Then one of the four living creatures gave to the seven angels seven golden bowls filled with the wrath of God, who lives for ever and ever. [8]And the temple was filled with smoke from the glory of God and from his power, and no one could enter the temple until the seven plagues of the seven angels were completed.

The Seven Bowls of God's Wrath

16 Then I heard a loud voice from the temple saying to the seven angels, "Go, pour out the seven bowls of God's wrath on the earth."

[2]The first angel went and poured out his bowl on the land, and ugly, festering sores broke out on the people who had the mark of the beast and worshiped its image.

[3]The second angel poured out his bowl on the sea, and it turned into blood like that of a dead person, and every living thing in the sea died.

[4]The third angel poured out his bowl on the rivers and springs of water, and they became blood. [5]Then I heard the angel in charge of the waters say:

"You are just in these judgments, O Holy One,
     you who are and who were;
[6]for they have shed the blood of your holy
          people and your prophets,
     and you have given them blood to drink
          as they deserve."

[7]And I heard the altar respond:

"Yes, Lord God Almighty,
     true and just are your judgments."

[8]The fourth angel poured out his bowl on the sun, and the sun was allowed to scorch people with fire. [9]They were seared by the intense heat and they cursed the name of God, who had

---

[a] 14 See Daniel 7:13.   [b] 20 That is, about 180 miles or about 300 kilometers   [c] 3 Some manuscripts ages   [d] 3,4 Phrases in this song are drawn from Psalm 111:2,3; Deut. 32:4; Jer. 10:7; Psalms 86:9; 98:2.

control over these plagues, but they refused to repent and glorify him.

[10]The fifth angel poured out his bowl on the throne of the beast, and its kingdom was plunged into darkness. People gnawed their tongues in agony [11]and cursed the God of heaven because of their pains and their sores, but they refused to repent of what they had done.

[12]The sixth angel poured out his bowl on the great river Euphrates, and its water was dried up to prepare the way for the kings from the East. [13]Then I saw three impure spirits that looked like frogs; they came out of the mouth of the dragon, out of the mouth of the beast and out of the mouth of the false prophet. [14]They are demonic spirits that perform signs, and they go out to the kings of the whole world, to gather them for the battle on the great day of God Almighty.

[15]"Look, I come like a thief! Blessed is the one who stays awake and remains clothed, so as not to go naked and be shamefully exposed."

[16]Then they gathered the kings together to the place that in Hebrew is called Armageddon.

[17]The seventh angel poured out his bowl into the air, and out of the temple came a loud voice from the throne, saying, "It is done!" [18]Then there came flashes of lightning, rumblings, peals of thunder and a severe earthquake. No earthquake like it has ever occurred since mankind has been on earth, so tremendous was the quake. [19]The great city split into three parts, and the cities of the nations collapsed. God remembered Babylon the Great and gave her the cup filled with the wine of the fury of his wrath. [20]Every island fled away and the mountains could not be found. [21]From the sky huge hailstones, each weighing about a hundred pounds,[a] fell on

people. And they cursed God on account of the plague of hail, because the plague was so terrible.

Babylon, the Prostitute on the Beast

17 One of the seven angels who had the seven bowls came and said to me, "Come, I will show you the punishment of the great prostitute, who sits by many waters. [2]With her the kings of the earth committed adultery, and the inhabitants of the earth were intoxicated with the wine of her adulteries."

[3]Then the angel carried me away in the Spirit into a wilderness. There I saw a woman sitting on a scarlet beast that was covered with blasphemous names and had seven heads and ten horns. [4]The woman was dressed in purple and scarlet, and was glittering with gold, precious stones and pearls. She held a golden cup in her hand, filled with abominable things and the filth of her adulteries. [5]The name written on her forehead was a mystery:

BABYLON THE GREAT
THE MOTHER OF PROSTITUTES
AND OF THE ABOMINATIONS OF THE EARTH.

[6]I saw that the woman was drunk with the blood of God's holy people, the blood of those who bore testimony to Jesus.

When I saw her, I was greatly astonished. [7]Then the angel said to me: "Why are you astonished? I will explain to you the mystery of the woman and of the beast she rides, which has the seven heads and ten horns. [8]The beast, which you saw, once was, now is not, and yet will come up out of the Abyss and go to its destruction. The inhabitants of the earth whose names have not been written in the book of life from the creation of the world will be astonished when they see the beast, because it once was, now is not, and yet will come.

[9]"This calls for a mind with wisdom. The seven heads are seven hills on which the woman sits. [10]They are also seven kings. Five have fallen, one is, the other has not yet come; but when he does come, he must remain for only a little while. [11]The beast who once was, and now is not, is an eighth king. He belongs to the seven and is going to his destruction.

[12]"The ten horns you saw are ten kings who have not yet received a kingdom, but who for one hour will receive authority as kings along with the beast. [13]They have one purpose and will give their power and authority to the beast. [14]They will wage war against the Lamb, but the Lamb will triumph over them because he is Lord

Justice: The Ultimate Leader Executes Justice for All

Revelation 14:1—16:21

Healthy leaders hunger for justice, not only in their organizations, but in the public arena. Here we see Jesus executing justice on the earth. As the Ultimate Leader, Christ feels motivated to provide justice to everyone. How about you? Are you doing anything to influence your world for the cause of justice?

[a] 21 Or about 45 kilograms

of lords and King of kings — and with him will be his called, chosen and faithful followers."

¹⁵Then the angel said to me, "The waters you saw, where the prostitute sits, are peoples, multitudes, nations and languages. ¹⁶The beast and the ten horns you saw will hate the prostitute. They will bring her to ruin and leave her naked; they will eat her flesh and burn her with fire. ¹⁷For God has put it into their hearts to accomplish his purpose by agreeing to hand over to the beast their royal authority, until God's words are fulfilled. ¹⁸The woman you saw is the great city that rules over the kings of the earth."

Lament Over Fallen Babylon

18 After this I saw another angel coming down from heaven. He had great authority, and the earth was illuminated by his splendor. ²With a mighty voice he shouted:

"'Fallen! Fallen is Babylon the Great!'ᵃ
  She has become a dwelling for demons
and a haunt for every impure spirit,
  a haunt for every unclean bird,
  a haunt for every unclean and detestable
    animal.
³For all the nations have drunk
  the maddening wine of her adulteries.
The kings of the earth committed adultery
    with her,
  and the merchants of the earth grew rich
    from her excessive luxuries."

Warning to Escape Babylon's Judgment

⁴Then I heard another voice from heaven say:

"'Come out of her, my people,'ᵇ
  so that you will not share in her sins,
  so that you will not receive any of her
    plagues;
⁵for her sins are piled up to heaven,
  and God has remembered her crimes.
⁶Give back to her as she has given;
  pay her back double for what she has done.
  Pour her a double portion from her own
    cup.
⁷Give her as much torment and grief
  as the glory and luxury she gave herself.
In her heart she boasts,
  'I sit enthroned as queen.
I am not a widow;ᶜ
  I will never mourn.'
⁸Therefore in one day her plagues will
    overtake her:
  death, mourning and famine.
She will be consumed by fire,
  for mighty is the Lord God who judges her.

Threefold Woe Over Babylon's Fall

⁹"When the kings of the earth who committed adultery with her and shared her luxury see the smoke of her burning, they will weep and mourn over her. ¹⁰Terrified at her torment, they will stand far off and cry:

"'Woe! Woe to you, great city,
  you mighty city of Babylon!
In one hour your doom has come!'

¹¹"The merchants of the earth will weep and mourn over her because no one buys their cargoes anymore — ¹²cargoes of gold, silver, precious stones and pearls; fine linen, purple, silk and scarlet cloth; every sort of citron wood, and articles of every kind made of ivory, costly wood, bronze, iron and marble; ¹³cargoes of cinnamon and spice, of incense, myrrh and frankincense, of wine and olive oil, of fine flour and wheat; cattle and sheep; horses and carriages; and human beings sold as slaves.

¹⁴"They will say, 'The fruit you longed for is gone from you. All your luxury and splendor have vanished, never to be recovered.' ¹⁵The merchants who sold these things and gained their wealth from her will stand far off, terrified at her torment. They will weep and mourn ¹⁶and cry out:

"'Woe! Woe to you, great city,
  dressed in fine linen, purple and scarlet,
  and glittering with gold, precious stones
    and pearls!
¹⁷In one hour such great wealth has been
    brought to ruin!'

"Every sea captain, and all who travel by ship, the sailors, and all who earn their living from the sea, will stand far off. ¹⁸When they see the smoke of her burning, they will exclaim, 'Was there ever a city like this great city?' ¹⁹They will throw dust on their heads, and with weeping and mourning cry out:

"'Woe! Woe to you, great city,
  where all who had ships on the sea
    became rich through her wealth!
In one hour she has been brought to ruin!'

²⁰"Rejoice over her, you heavens!
  Rejoice, you people of God!
  Rejoice, apostles and prophets!
For God has judged her
  with the judgment she imposed on you."

The Finality of Babylon's Doom

²¹Then a mighty angel picked up a boulder

ᵃ 2 Isaiah 21:9   ᵇ 4 Jer. 51:45   ᶜ 7 See Isaiah 47:7,8.

the size of a large millstone and threw it into the sea, and said:

"With such violence
    the great city of Babylon will be thrown
      down,
    never to be found again.
22 The music of harpists and musicians, pipers
      and trumpeters,
    will never be heard in you again.
No worker of any trade
    will ever be found in you again.
The sound of a millstone
    will never be heard in you again.
23 The light of a lamp
    will never shine in you again.
The voice of bridegroom and bride
    will never be heard in you again.
Your merchants were the world's important
      people.
By your magic spell all the nations were
      led astray.
24 In her was found the blood of prophets and
      of God's holy people,
    of all who have been slaughtered on the
      earth."

Threefold Hallelujah Over Babylon's Fall

19 After this I heard what sounded like the roar of a great multitude in heaven shouting:

"Hallelujah!
Salvation and glory and power belong to our
    God,
2   for true and just are his judgments.
He has condemned the great prostitute
    who corrupted the earth by her adulteries.
He has avenged on her the blood of his
      servants."

3 And again they shouted:

"Hallelujah!
The smoke from her goes up for ever and
      ever."

4 The twenty-four elders and the four living creatures fell down and worshiped God, who was seated on the throne. And they cried:

"Amen, Hallelujah!"

5 Then a voice came from the throne, saying:

"Praise our God,
    all you his servants,
you who fear him,
    both great and small!"

6 Then I heard what sounded like a great multitude, like the roar of rushing waters and like loud peals of thunder, shouting:

"Hallelujah!
    For our Lord God Almighty reigns.
7 Let us rejoice and be glad
    and give him glory!
For the wedding of the Lamb has come,
    and his bride has made herself ready.
8 Fine linen, bright and clean,
    was given her to wear."
(Fine linen stands for the righteous acts of God's holy people.)

9 Then the angel said to me, "Write this: Blessed are those who are invited to the wedding supper of the Lamb!" And he added, "These are the true words of God."

10 At this I fell at his feet to worship him. But he said to me, "Don't do that! I am a fellow servant with you and with your brothers and sisters who hold to the testimony of Jesus. Worship God! For it is the Spirit of prophecy who bears testimony to Jesus."

The Heavenly Warrior Defeats the Beast

11 I saw heaven standing open and there before me was a white horse, whose rider is called Faithful and True. With justice he judges and wages war. 12 His eyes are like blazing fire, and on his head are many crowns. He has a name written on him that no one knows but he himself. 13 He is dressed in a robe dipped in blood, and his name is the Word of God. 14 The armies of heaven were following him, riding on white horses and dressed in fine linen, white and clean. 15 Coming out of his mouth is a sharp sword with which to strike down the nations. "He will rule them with an iron scepter."[a] He treads the winepress of the fury of the wrath of God Almighty. 16 On his robe and on his thigh he has this name written:

KING OF KINGS AND LORD OF LORDS.

17 And I saw an angel standing in the sun, who cried in a loud voice to all the birds flying in midair, "Come, gather together for the great supper of God, 18 so that you may eat the flesh of kings, generals, and the mighty, of horses and their riders, and the flesh of all people, free and slave, great and small."

19 Then I saw the beast and the kings of the earth and their armies gathered together to wage

a 15 Psalm 2:9

war against the rider on the horse and his army. [20]But the beast was captured, and with it the false prophet who had performed the signs on its behalf. With these signs he had deluded those who had received the mark of the beast and worshiped its image. The two of them were thrown alive into the fiery lake of burning sulfur. [21]The rest were killed with the sword coming out of the mouth of the rider on the horse, and all the birds gorged themselves on their flesh.

The Thousand Years

20 And I saw an angel coming down out of heaven, having the key to the Abyss and holding in his hand a great chain. [2]He seized the dragon, that ancient serpent, who is the devil, or Satan, and bound him for a thousand years. [3]He threw him into the Abyss, and locked and sealed it over him, to keep him from deceiving the nations anymore until the thousand years were ended. After that, he must be set free for a short time.

[4]I saw thrones on which were seated those who had been given authority to judge. And I saw the souls of those who had been beheaded because of their testimony about Jesus and because of the word of God. They[a] had not worshiped the beast or its image and had not received its mark on their foreheads or their hands. They came to life and reigned with Christ a thousand years. [5](The rest of the dead did not come to life until the thousand years were ended.) This is the first resurrection. [6]Blessed and holy are those who share in the first resurrection. The second death has no power over them, but they will be priests of God and of Christ and will reign with him for a thousand years.

The Judgment of Satan

[7]When the thousand years are over, Satan will be released from his prison [8]and will go out to deceive the nations in the four corners of the earth — Gog and Magog — and to gather them for battle. In number they are like the sand on the seashore. [9]They marched across the breadth of the earth and surrounded the camp of God's people, the city he loves. But fire came down from heaven and devoured them. [10]And the devil, who deceived them, was thrown into the lake of burning sulfur, where the beast and the false prophet had been thrown. They will be tormented day and night for ever and ever.

The Judgment of the Dead

[11]Then I saw a great white throne and him who was seated on it. The earth and the heavens fled from his presence, and there was no place for them. [12]And I saw the dead, great and small, standing before the throne, and books were opened. Another book was opened, which is the book of life. The dead were judged according to what they had done as recorded in the books. [13]The sea gave up the dead that were in it, and death and Hades gave up the dead that were in them, and each person was judged according to what they had done. [14]Then death and Hades were thrown into the lake of fire. The lake of fire is the second death. [15]Anyone whose name was not found written in the book of life was thrown into the lake of fire.

---

[a] 4 Or God; I also saw those who

Problem Solving: Jesus Resolves Earth's Conflict at Its Root

Revelation 19:1–21

Jesus will take decisive action to resolve the world conflict raging during the Great Tribulation. Four times heavenly voices shout "Hallelujah!" to celebrate the end of the problems that prevailed on the earth for seven long years.

Like any effective leader, Jesus didn't merely put a bandage on the problem; he solved it permanently. Take note of how efficiently the King of kings has and will take care of man's root problems:

Our Greatest Problem	Why?	How Christ Solved It
1. Our greatest flaw: sin.	1. It leads to death.	1. He died for our sin.
2. Our greatest defeat: death.	2. It severs us from God.	2. He eliminated death.
3. Our greatest emotion: fear.	3. We fear dying.	3. He rose from the dead.
4. Our greatest enemy: Satan.	4. He destroys us.	4. He will cast him into hell.

A New Heaven and a New Earth

21 Then I saw "a new heaven and a new earth,"[a] for the first heaven and the first earth had passed away, and there was no longer any sea. [2]I saw the Holy City, the new Jerusalem, coming down out of heaven from God, prepared as a bride beautifully dressed for her husband. [3]And I heard a loud voice from the throne saying, "Look! God's dwelling place is now among the people, and he will dwell with them. They will be his people, and God himself will be with them and be their God. [4]'He will wipe every tear from their eyes. There will be no more death'[b] or mourning or crying or pain, for the old order of things has passed away."

[5]He who was seated on the throne said, "I am making everything new!" Then he said, "Write this down, for these words are trustworthy and true."

[6]He said to me: "It is done. I am the Alpha and the Omega, the Beginning and the End. To the thirsty I will give water without cost from the spring of the water of life. [7]Those who are victorious will inherit all this, and I will be their God and they will be my children. [8]But the cowardly, the unbelieving, the vile, the murderers, the sexually immoral, those who practice magic arts, the idolaters and all liars — they will be consigned to the fiery lake of burning sulfur. This is the second death."

The New Jerusalem, the Bride of the Lamb

[9]One of the seven angels who had the seven bowls full of the seven last plagues came and said to me, "Come, I will show you the bride, the wife of the Lamb." [10]And he carried me away in the Spirit to a mountain great and high, and showed me the Holy City, Jerusalem, coming down out of heaven from God. [11]It shone with the glory of God, and its brilliance was like that of a very precious jewel, like a jasper, clear as crystal. [12]It had a great, high wall with twelve gates, and with twelve angels at the gates. On the gates were written the names of the twelve tribes of Israel. [13]There were three gates on the east, three on the north, three on the south and three on the west. [14]The wall of the city had twelve foundations, and on them were the names of the twelve apostles of the Lamb.

[15]The angel who talked with me had a measuring rod of gold to measure the city, its gates and its walls. [16]The city was laid out like a square, as long as it was wide. He measured the city with the rod and found it to be 12,000

> ## Vision: The Ultimate Leader Reveals His Person and Plan
> ### *Revelation 21:1–7*
>
> The vision of Christ for a new heaven and earth is creative (Rev 21:1–2), an improvement on the present (21:3), meets needs (21:4), and offers a permanent solution (21:6). Vision is an informed bridge to a better tomorrow. Jesus restores what we lost in the Garden of Eden.

stadia[c] in length, and as wide and high as it is long. [17]The angel measured the wall using human measurement, and it was 144 cubits[d] thick.[e] [18]The wall was made of jasper, and the city of pure gold, as pure as glass. [19]The foundations of the city walls were decorated with every kind of precious stone. The first foundation was jasper, the second sapphire, the third agate, the fourth emerald, [20]the fifth onyx, the sixth ruby, the seventh chrysolite, the eighth beryl, the ninth topaz, the tenth turquoise, the eleventh jacinth, and the twelfth amethyst.[f] [21]The twelve gates were twelve pearls, each gate made of a single pearl. The great street of the city was of gold, as pure as transparent glass.

[22]I did not see a temple in the city, because the Lord God Almighty and the Lamb are its temple. [23]The city does not need the sun or the moon to shine on it, for the glory of God gives it light, and the Lamb is its lamp. [24]The nations will walk by its light, and the kings of the earth will bring their splendor into it. [25]On no day will its gates ever be shut, for there will be no night there. [26]The glory and honor of the nations will be brought into it. [27]Nothing impure will ever enter it, nor will anyone who does what is shameful or deceitful, but only those whose names are written in the Lamb's book of life.

Eden Restored

22 Then the angel showed me the river of the water of life, as clear as crystal, flowing from the throne of God and of the Lamb [2]down the middle of the great street of the city. On each side of the river stood the tree of life,

---

[a] 1 Isaiah 65:17   [b] 4 Isaiah 25:8   [c] 16 That is, about 1,400 miles or about 2,200 kilometers   [d] 17 That is, about 200 feet or about 65 meters   [e] 17 Or *high*   [f] 20 The precise identification of some of these precious stones is uncertain.

bearing twelve crops of fruit, yielding its fruit every month. And the leaves of the tree are for the healing of the nations. ³No longer will there be any curse. The throne of God and of the Lamb will be in the city, and his servants will serve him. ⁴They will see his face, and his name will be on their foreheads. ⁵There will be no more night. They will not need the light of a lamp or the light of the sun, for the Lord God will give them light. And they will reign for ever and ever.

John and the Angel

⁶The angel said to me, "These words are trustworthy and true. The Lord, the God who inspires the prophets, sent his angel to show his servants the things that must soon take place."

⁷"Look, I am coming soon! Blessed is the one who keeps the words of the prophecy written in this scroll."

⁸I, John, am the one who heard and saw these things. And when I had heard and seen them, I fell down to worship at the feet of the angel who had been showing them to me. ⁹But he said to me, "Don't do that! I am a fellow servant with you and with your fellow prophets and with all who keep the words of this scroll. Worship God!"

¹⁰Then he told me, "Do not seal up the words of the prophecy of this scroll, because the time is near. ¹¹Let the one who does wrong continue to do wrong; let the vile person continue to be vile; let the one who does right continue to do right; and let the holy person continue to be holy."

Epilogue: Invitation and Warning

¹²"Look, I am coming soon! My reward is with me, and I will give to each person according to what they have done. ¹³I am the Alpha and the Omega, the First and the Last, the Beginning and the End.

¹⁴"Blessed are those who wash their robes, that they may have the right to the tree of life and may go through the gates into the city. ¹⁵Outside are the dogs, those who practice magic arts, the sexually immoral, the murderers, the idolaters and everyone who loves and practices falsehood.

¹⁶"I, Jesus, have sent my angel to give you[a] this testimony for the churches. I am the Root and the Offspring of David, and the bright Morning Star."

¹⁷The Spirit and the bride say, "Come!" And let the one who hears say, "Come!" Let the one who is thirsty come; and let the one who wishes take the free gift of the water of life.

¹⁸I warn everyone who hears the words of the prophecy of this scroll: If anyone adds anything to them, God will add to that person the plagues described in this scroll. ¹⁹And if anyone takes words away from this scroll of prophecy, God will take away from that person any share in the tree of life and in the Holy City, which are described in this scroll.

²⁰He who testifies to these things says, "Yes, I am coming soon."

Amen. Come, Lord Jesus.

²¹The grace of the Lord Jesus be with God's people. Amen.

---

a 16 The Greek is plural.

The Law of Victory: Jesus Reigns After Defeating the Enemy for Good

Revelation 22:12–16

You can almost hear John gasp as he describes the conditions of the Holy City, with its crystal clear river, its streets of transparent gold, and its splendid trees.

Christ has practiced the Law of Victory for the final time, finding a way for his people to win. He shares his victory, like a rich man shares his inheritance with his family. There is great *consolation*, great *celebration*, and great *confirmation* in this victory, as the Ultimate Leader keeps the promise of victory he made through the Old Testament prophets. The final book of the Bible refers to this victorious Leader by several names:

1. Faithful witness (1:5)
2. Firstborn from the dead (1:5)
3. Ruler of the kings (1:5)
4. Alpha and Omega (1:8)
5. Lion of the tribe of Judah (5:5)
6. The root of David (5:5)
7. The Lamb (17:14)
8. The Word of God (19:13)
9. King of kings (19:16)
10. Lord of lords (19:16)

TABLE OF WEIGHTS AND MEASURES

Biblical Unit	Approximate American Equivalent	Approximate Metric Equivalent
WEIGHTS		
talent (60 minas)	75 pounds	34 kilograms
mina (50 shekels)	1 1/4 pounds	560 grams
shekel (2 bekas)	2/5 ounce	11.5 grams
pim (2/3 shekel)	1/4 ounce	7.8 grams
beka (10 gerahs)	1/5 ounce	5.7 grams
gerah	1/50 ounce	0.6 gram
daric	1/3 ounce	8.4 grams
LENGTH		
cubit	18 inches	45 centimeters
span	9 inches	23 centimeters
handbreadth	3 inches	7.5 centimeters
stadion (pl. stadia)	600 feet	183 meters
CAPACITY		
Dry Measure		
cor [homer] (10 ephahs)	6 bushels	220 liters
lethek (5 ephahs)	3 bushels	110 liters
ephah (10 omers)	3/5 bushel	22 liters
seah (1/3 ephah)	7 quarts	7.5 liters
omer (1/10 ephah)	2 quarts	2 liters
cab (1/18 ephah)	1 quart	1 liter
Liquid Measure		
bath (1 ephah)	6 gallons	22 liters
hin (1/6 bath)	1 gallon	3.8 liters
log (1/72 bath)	1/3 quart	0.3 liter

The figures of the table are calculated on the basis of a shekel equaling 11.5 grams, a cubit equaling 18 inches and an ephah equaling 22 liters. The quart referred to is either a dry quart (slightly larger than a liter) or a liquid quart (slightly smaller than a liter), whichever is applicable. The ton referred to in the footnotes is the American ton of 2,000 pounds. These weights are calculated relative to the particular commodity involved. Accordingly, the same measure of capacity in the text may be converted into different weights in the footnotes.

This table is based upon the best available information, but it is not intended to be mathematically precise; like the measurement equivalents in the footnotes, it merely gives approximate amounts and distances. Weights and measures differed somewhat at various times and places in the ancient world. There is uncertainty particularly about the ephah and the bath; further discoveries may shed more light on these units of capacity.

LEADERSHIP LAWS

The main article for each of the 21 Laws of Leadership is set in boldface color type.

Jesus and the 21 Irrefutable Laws of Leadership . . . . . . **John 20:30–31**

The Law of the Picture

The Law of Solid Ground

The Law of Respect

The Law of Intuition

LEADERSHIP QUALITIES

Both positive and negative examples for each of the 21 Indispensable Qualities of a Leader are set in boldface color type.

Servanthood

Teachability

Vision

LEADERSHIP ISSUES

Results in Purity and
Security. . . . . *1 Corinthians 5:1–13*
Follow-Up . . . . *2 Corinthians 2:6–8*
Paul with Peter . . . . *Galatians 2:11–21*
Jude Admonishes People. . . . . *Jude 3–4*
See also Conflict

Control

Leaders Know Difference . . . . *Proverbs 21:1*

Convictions

Don't Allow Compromise. . . . . . . *Joshua 7:1—8:29*
Consequences of
Compromise . . . . *1 Kings 13:11–24*
One Is a Majority . . . . *1 Kings 17:1*
Daring Courage . . . . *Isaiah 63:11–14*
Defeat into Dividends . . . . *Jeremiah 20:1–18*
Don't Drop. . . . . *Hosea 14:9*

Correction

God Rebukes for Questioning . . . . *Job 38:1–7*

Credibility

Regardless of Age . . . . *Joshua 14:6–15*
Not About Position. . . . . *Proverbs 17:2*
Luke's Authority. . . . . *Luke 1:1–4*
Demonstration + Proclamation. . . . . . . *Acts 3:1–26*

Criticism

Criticism and
Confrontation Come . . . . *Numbers 12:3–14*

Cycles

Organizational . . . . *Judges 2:1–6*

Decision Making

Sowing and Reaping. . . . . *Leviticus 26:3–39*
Joshua Distributes Land . . . . . . *Joshua 13:1—19:51*
Jephthah's Poor Choice . . . . *Judges 11:1–31*
Intuition and Decision
Making. . . . . *2 Samuel 6:1—7:17*
Poor Skills Lead to
Disaster. . . . . *Jeremiah 40:5—41:2*
Jeremiah Makes
Tough Call. . . . . *Jeremiah 42:1—43:13*
In the Gray Areas . . . . *1 Corinthians 10:24–33*

Delegation

Broker Human Resources. . . *1 Chronicles 18:14–17*
Jesus Shared Responsibility . . . . *Luke 9:1–10*

Destiny

Born to Lead . . . . *Genesis 1:26–31*
Purpose and Passion . . . . . . *Deuteronomy 4:32–40*

Direction

Pillar and Cloud . . . . *Exodus 13:21*
Know Way to Show Way . . . . *Psalm 119:1–176*

Discipline

Moral Failure. . . . . *Proverbs 5:3–23*
God Punishes, Rewards. . . . . . . *Jeremiah 30:10–22*
God's Method . . . . *Nahum 2:13*

Emotions

Burnout . . . . *1 Kings 19:1–3*
Leader and Stress . . . . *Psalm 23:1–6*

Encouragement

Affirm Qualities
in Others . . . . *Song of Songs 1:10–15*
Leaders Connect. . . . . *Philippians 1:3–11*
Paul Knew How . . . . *2 Thessalonians 1:3–6*
Jesus Affirms Smyrna . . . . *Revelation 2:8–11*

Equipping

Aaron Equips Moses . . . . *Exodus 5:1—12:37*
Fruitfulness Is Fun. . . . . *John 15:1–6*
Tools to Do Job . . . . *Ephesians 2:8–22*
The Leader's Job . . . . *Ephesians 4:12–16*
Paul Was Provider . . . . *Colossians 1:28–29*
The Word of God . . . . *2 Timothy 3:16–17*

Ethics

Absolute Leader in a
Relative World. . . . . *Psalm 18:1–34*
Reflect God's Values . . . . *Isaiah 58:1–14*
Efficiency - Ethics = Emptiness. . . *Amos 1:1—2:16*
Not Working for People. . . . . *Ephesians 6:5–9*

Evaluation

Round Two of Census . . . . *Numbers 26:1–63*
God Looks at Heart . . . . *Ezekiel 11:1–13*

Man-Appointed Leadership

Mentoring

Mercy

Modeling

Motivation

Motives

Needs

Organization

Partnership

Perception

Perspective

Persuasion

PROFILES IN LEADERSHIP

Aaron
Cost of Leadership . . . . *Leviticus 7:33–35*

Abednego
Courage Fueled by Faith . . . .*Daniel 3:16–18*

Abigail
Law of Connection. . . . . *1 Samuel 25:1–42*

Abimelek
Self-Promotion . . . .*Judges 9:1–57*

Abraham
Went the Distance . . . . *Genesis 12:1—25:11*

Absalom
Tragic Case . . . . *2 Samuel 16:1—18:18*

Achan
Ripple Effect of Sin. . . . .*Joshua 7:1–25*

Adam
Drops the Ball . . . .*Genesis 3:6–19*

Agrippa
Power Trip . . . .*Acts 23:23—26:32*

Amnon
No Self-Discipline. . . . .*1 Chronicles 3:1*

Amos
Prophet of Wrath and Mercy . . . .*Amos 4:1–12*

Aquila
Trained More Leaders . . . .*Acts 18:24–28*

Asa
Difficulty of
Finishing Well. . . . . *2 Chronicles 15:1—16:13*

Athaliah
Pursuing Power. . . . .*2 Chronicles 22:10—23:15*

Bad Leaders
Refuse Warnings. . . . .*Jeremiah 36:1—40:16*

Balaam
Good but Not Godly . . . .*Numbers 22:5—24:25*

Boaz
Model of Kindness . . . .*Ruth 2:4–17*

Caleb
Brave Heart . . . .*Joshua 14:10–12*

Daniel
Sought Understanding. . . . .*Daniel 8:15, 17, 27*

David
Leader After God's Heart . . . . . . *1 Samuel 16:1–13*
Partnership with Jonathan . . *1 Samuel 19:1—23:18*
Heart of Great King . . . . *2 Samuel 4:5–12*
Assumes Blame. . . . .*1 Chronicles 21:1–17*
Trusting in God . . . .*Psalm 40:1–17*

Elijah
Standing Alone . . . .*1 Kings 17:1—18:40*

Elisha
Prophet with Heart . . . .*2 Kings 4:1–44*

Epaphroditus
Didn't Make a Name . . . . *Philippians 2:25–30*

Esther
Protected Messianic Line . . . .*Esther 2:1–17*

Eve
Learned from Failure. . . . . *Genesis 4:1—5:5*

Ezekiel
Zealous for the Lord. . . . . *Ezekiel 6:7, 10, 13–14*

Ezra
Doing the Right Thing . . . .*Ezra 7:6–10*

Felix
Power Trip . . . .*Acts 23:23—26:32*

Festus
Power Trip . . . .*Acts 23:23—26:32*

WINNING WITH PEOPLE

A faith-based leader who desires to lead in a way that pleases God cannot separate healthy leadership from healthy relationships. Relationships are the currency of God's kingdom. In the book *Winning with People* there are several "people principles" that have helped leaders connect with people over the centuries. They are timeless and universal. Here are some biblical examples of each principle:

1. The Lens Principle: Who we are determines how we see others.
Example: Nabal (1 Samuel 25:1–42)

2. The Mirror Principle: The first person we must examine is ourselves.
Example: David (2 Samuel 12)

3. The Pain Principle: Hurting people hurt people and are easily hurt by them.
Example: King Saul (1 Samuel 18:6–29)

4. The Hammer Principle: Never use a hammer to swat a fly off of someone's head.
Example: Rehoboam (2 Chronicles 10:1–17)

5. The Elevator Principle: We can lift people up or take them down in our relationships.
Example: Jonah and the people of Nineveh (Jonah 4:1–11)

6. The Big Picture Principle: The entire population of the world, with one minor exception, is composed of others.
Example: Nebuchadnezzar and the Babylonian empire (Daniel 4:1–37)

7. The Exchange Principle: Instead of putting others in their place, we must put ourselves in their place.
Example: Abigail and David's army (1 Samuel 25:18–35)

8. The Learning Principle: Each person we meet has the potential to teach us something.
Example: Naaman and his servant (2 Kings 5:1–14)

9. The Charisma Principle: People are interested in the person who is interested in them.
Example: Jonathan (1 Samuel 18:1–4; 20:1–42)

10. The Number 10 Principle: Believing the best in people usually brings the best out of people.
Example: Barnabas and John Mark (Acts 15:36–39; 2 Timothy 4:11)

11. The Confrontation Principle: Caring for people should precede confronting people.
Example: Nathan and David (2 Samuel 12)

12. The Bedrock Principle: Trust is the foundation of any relationship.
Example: Mordecai and Esther (Esther 4:6–17)

13. The Situation Principle: Never let the situation mean more than the relationship.
Example: Joseph and his brothers (Genesis 42:1–28; 45:1–15)

14. The Bob Principle: When Bob has a problem with everyone, Bob is usually the problem.
Example: Herod and the people of Israel (Acts 12:1–23)

15. *The Approachability Principle: Being at ease with ourselves helps others be at ease with us.*
Example: Daniel in Babylon and Persia (Daniel 2:1–28; 5:13–14)

16. *The Foxhole Principle: When preparing for battle, dig a foxhole big enough for a friend.*
Example: Solomon (Ecclesiastes 4:9–12)

17. *The Gardening Principle: All relationships need cultivation.*
Example: Joseph, Potiphar and Pharaoh (Genesis 39:1—41:16)

18. *The 101 Percent Principle: Find the 1% we agree on and give it 100% of our effort.*
Example: Paul in Athens (Acts 17:22–31)

19. *The Patience Principle: The journey with others is slower than the journey alone.*
Example: Moses and the people of Israel (Exodus 17:1–7; 32:1–35)

20. *The Celebration Principle: The true test of relationships is not only how loyal we are when friends fail, but how thrilled we are when they succeed.*
Example: Barnabas and Saul (Acts 9:22–28; 13:1–52)

21. *The High Road Principle: We go to a higher level when we treat others better than they treat us.*
Example: Abraham and Lot (Genesis 13:7–18) / David and King Saul (1 Samuel 24:1–22)

22. *The Boomerang Principle: When we help others, we help ourselves.*
Example: Nehemiah (Nehemiah 1–5)

23. *The Friendship Principle: All things being equal, people will work with people they like; all things not being equal, they still will.*
Example: David's mighty men (1 Samuel 22:1—23:29)

24. *The Partnership Principle: Working together increases the odds of winning together.*
Example: Paul, Julius and the stormy journey (Acts 27)

25. *The Satisfaction Principle: In great relationships, the joy of being together is enough.*
Example: Jesus and the twelve disciples (John 15:9–17)

25 WAYS TO WIN WITH PEOPLE

by John C. Maxwell and Les Parrott III

Biblical Examples

1. Start with Yourself—King Solomon (1 Kings 3:5–14)
2. Practice the 30-Second Rule (encourage them during the first 30 seconds)—Jesus and Simon Peter (John 1:42)
3. Let People Know You Need Them—Paul (Galatians 4:13–15; 2 Timothy 4:11)
4. Create a Memory and Visit It Often—Joshua (Joshua 4:1–7)
5. Compliment People in Front of People—John the Baptist (John 1:29–31)
6. Give Others a Reputation to Uphold—Jesus and Nathaniel (John 1:45–48)
7. Say the Right Words at the Right Time—Mordecai to Esther (Esther 4:13–14)
8. Encourage the Dream of Others—Naomi and Ruth (Ruth 3:1–6)
9. Pass the Credit On to Others—David and his men (1 Samuel 30:21–31)
10. Offer Your Very Best—Epaphroditus (Philippians 2:25–30)
11. Share a Secret with Someone—Mary and Elizabeth (Luke 1:39–45)
12. Mine the Gold of Good Intentions—Abigail and David (1 Samuel 25:23–35)
13. Keep Your Eyes Off the Mirror—Joseph and His Brothers (Genesis 50:18–20)
14. Do for Others What They Can't Do for Themselves—Joseph (Genesis 41)
15. Listen with Your Heart—Barnabas and John Mark (Acts 15:36–41)
16. Find the Keys to Their Heart—Nehemiah and builders (Nehemiah 2:17–18)
17. Be the First to Help—Barnabas and Saul (Acts 9:26–27)
18. Add Value to People—Rebekah and Abraham (Genesis 24:10–27)
19. Remember a Person's Story—David, Jonathan and Mephibosheth (1 Samuel 9:1–13)
20. Tell a Good Story—Paul (Acts 26:1–29)
21. Give With No Strings Attached—Jonathan (1 Samuel 18:1–4)
22. Learn Your Mailman's Name—Paul (Romans 16:3–15)
23. Point Out People's Strengths—Peter and Paul (2 Peter 3:14–16)
24. Write Notes of Encouragement—Paul and his epistles (Philippians, 2 Timothy)
25. Help People Win—Deborah and Barak (Judges 4:4–5)

Say the Right Words at the Right Time

Esther 4:13–14—Mordecai and Esther

Mordecai was a cousin and mentor to Esther the queen. During her reign, Haman, the prime minister, turned against the Hebrews. It was a critical time in Jewish history.

I. The Moment Was Frightening

Haman planned to commit genocide against the Jews. He hated them. If he got his way, every Hebrew in Persia would die, including Esther the queen. It was a sobering moment.

Therefore, Mordecai's words were honest. They awakened Esther to reality. Because of the circumstances, Mordecai was brutally honest. He defined the situation for Esther. His clarity was an attempt to awaken the hero inside her.

II. The Issue Was National in Scope

Mordecai informed Esther twice that every Jew was in danger. This was a huge crisis, national in scope. He wanted to make sure she recognized how important this issue was.

Therefore, Mordecai's words were personal. They lit a fire in Esther's heart. Because the issue was so big, Mordecai knew it would be easy for Esther to think she couldn't make a difference. He spoke into her life and ministered to her true self.

III. The Opportunity Was Risky

Esther reminded Mordecai that if she entered the throne room in the palace, she could be killed. It was all too risky—she might die either way: by acting or not acting.

Therefore, Mordecai's words were bold. They provided Esther courage to act. Recognizing the risk involved, Mordecai knew his words had to be bold; he had to call Esther out and offer a challenge that would match the need of the hour.

IV. The Need Was Confusing

It all happened so fast, it was difficult for Esther to draw the conclusion that she had to act. Wouldn't her position as queen keep her safe? Or, could Haman take her life, too?

Therefore, Mordecai's words were visionary. They gave Esther perspective. In her confusion, Mordecai knew he had to give Esther a sense of destiny. He connected this challenge to her divine calling in life. He gave her God's perspective on the crisis.

Question: How do we intuitively know what to say and when?

Add Value to People

Genesis 24:10–27—Rebekah and Abraham's Servant

Abraham sent his servant out to find a wife for his son Isaac. It was a monumental task. The servant decided to choose a woman based on this principle. He wanted to find a woman who would add value to him on his journey. Such a woman would make a good life partner for Isaac. You might call this the Rebekah Principle. Rebekah went the extra mile. Her generosity stands in stark contrast to the prevailing attitudes today. Her life seemed to say: I'll do what you ask me to do, then I'm going to do something more. Today, people seem to say: I'm going to do the least that is expected of me, and I'm going to get the most out of it. To be more like Rebekah, we need to keep in mind that:

We Can't Be Generous and Legalistic at the Same Time

She did more than what was required or expected. Her generous spirit was unusual. Her actions were opposite those of the Pharisees whose religion could be measured with a yardstick. In the end, legalism always leaves people feeling miserable. It becomes either unbearably arrogant or incurably insecure. Rebekah teaches us: Don't keep score, just keep giving.

Question: Why do we begin life generous but become legalistic over time?

You Cannot Walk the Second Mile Until You've Walked the First

It's easy for people to talk about the great and generous things they intend to do in the future. But if they're not being generous with what they have now, it is unlikely they will suddenly change in the future. Rebekah started her serving by first doing what was asked of her. Only when she finished that did she take care of the camels. Rebekah teaches us: We will become what we are becoming right now.

Question: What is more difficult about walking the "first mile" than the "second mile"?

Extra Blessings Result from Extra Effort
How easy it would have been for Rebekah to lower her jar, give the stranger a drink and continue on to her home. That would have been both fair and nice. It also would have been convenient. Before she offered to be generous, she must have considered the time and effort it would take; that team of camels might have taken a couple of hours to care for, carrying buckets of water back and forth.

Question: Why do we simply do the expected instead of the unexpected?

When We Give Generously, the Impact of Our Generosity Often Outlives Us
In the moment of giving, you cannot imagine how your actions might impact the lives of others in the future. Rebekah had no idea that her generosity that day opened the door for a marriage to Isaac, and she became part of the line of Christ! Because generously adding value to others is rare, the impact of that generosity lingers long after we're gone. Sometimes it outlives us both now and in eternity.

Question: Why is a generous spirit critical to adding value to people?

Do for Others What They Cannot Do for Themselves

Genesis 41—Joseph and Pharaoh
Joseph was a prison inmate until Pharaoh needed what he had to offer. Joseph moved from prisoner to prime minister in Egypt because he did for Pharaoh what the leader could not do for himself. His gift made him indispensable.

What's interesting is that we all have gifts to offer others. God has placed inside of us strengths we are to use to benefit others. Everyone has something we all need. So, here is the question:

Why Don't We Do for Others What They Cannot Do for Themselves?
1. Fear and intimidation: We're afraid we won't measure up.
Joseph was not intimidated from using his God-given gifts in the palace. Frequently we don't step out because we're afraid of failure. What if we can't do it? The fear of not measuring up to perfection has kept many gifted people idle when they should have acted. Joseph overcame this fear by believing that the value he added if he was right far outweighed the price he'd pay if he was wrong. His life was on the line, but he ventured out to offer wisdom to Pharaoh, who desperately needed it.

2. Pride and ego: We're too self-centered with our resources.
Joseph was able to maintain perspective by crediting God for his ability. Often we are afraid of giving away "too much." After all, it's our intellectual property! Joseph overcame this obstacle by declaring he didn't have the ability to interpret the Pharaoh's dream, but God did. He was well aware that this endowment really wasn't his. He was stewarding a gift from God, and it was to be used to advance his fame.

3. Greed with our time: We keep score on how much we give.
Joseph offered a relevant service without asking for payment or recognition. Too many of us give to others, but with strings attached. We keep score along the way, and stop giving the moment we feel we're being used. We're busy people, too busy to be too generous. This attitude limits our value because our focus is on what we're giving up, not what the other person is gaining. Joseph gave his gift away without a thought of asking for payment. In return, he was surprised by being named prime minister of Egypt.

4. Scarcity mindset: We stop at doing the bare minimum for others.
Joseph not only diagnosed the problem but he prescribed a solution as well. Sometimes when we give what others need, we stop at doing only what they've asked. We dare not be extravagant. Joseph shocked everyone when he gave not only a supernatural interpretation of the dream but a solution on how to handle the situation.

5. Lack of vision: We don't see how our action could make any difference.
Joseph saw God's hand in Pharaoh's dream and in the significance of his response. Too often, we don't do more for others because we just don't believe it will make much difference. We say we're just adding a "drop in the bucket." Joseph may have had no idea how much he was changing history, but it's a good thing he chose to risk and offer what he had.

Offer Your Very Best

Philippians 2:25–30—Epaphroditus

Epaphroditus would be considered one of the "nobodies" in scripture. He never wrote a book in the Bible, nor is he mentioned anywhere else. He has never had a statue erected in his honor or become famous for his accomplishments. However, Paul called Epaphroditus a hero. In this passage, Paul uses five terms to describe him:

1. A brother
2. A co-worker
3. A fellow soldier
4. A messenger
5. A caregiver

Epaphroditus made four decisions which each allowed him to give his very best:

1. He was a people lover.
Paul called him a caregiver. He longed for them (v. 26). He felt distressed, not by his own sickness, but because the Philippians might worry about him when he was sick.

Question: Do you long for people?

2. He was a risk taker.
Paul called him a soldier. He risked his life for the sake of Christ (v. 30). He ran all the way from Philippi to Rome to meet Paul in prison, and he almost lost his life in the process.

Question: Do you play it safe?

3. He was a tireless worker.
Paul called him a worker, the word Jesus used in Matthew 9:37 when he described them as rare. All we know of his sickness was that it was due to his hard work for Christ.

Question: Do you work tirelessly?

4. He was a servant-leader.
Paul called him a caregiver and a messenger: a servant who is a leader. He was a pioneer. He did the work no one else would do. Paul said to hold men like him in high regard.

Question: Do you lead the way in some area of service? Do you excel?

In my book, *A Talent Is Never Enough*, I communicate that while talent is important, there are millions of talented people who have ability but never get to use it and never reach their potential because they lack the characteristics that separate successful people from unsuccessful people. Those who neglect to make right choices to release and maximize their talent continually under-perform. These choices may be as simple as being punctual, giving effort, showing patience, or being unselfish. None of these choices require talent but they sure enhance talent. Below is a list of those choices and characteristics that enhance a person's talent and advance them in life, along with biblical examples of men and women who illustrate the characteristic.

1. Belief lifts your talent.
Consider young David, in 1 Samuel 17. He visited his brothers in the battlefield as they faced the Philistine army. Goliath was the Philistine champion, a giant who taunted the army of Israel day after day. No one in Israel believed they could face this nine-foot-tall giant and beat him. That is, until a young teenager named David entered the scene. He believed his God was bigger than the giant, and he believed his God-given ability to defeat enemies—demonstrated as he tended sheep and slew a lion and a bear—were enough to take on the giant. He was right. His belief enabled him to use his talent from God and show the world what a miracle looks like.

2. Passion energizes your talent.
Consider Elijah, in 1 Kings 18. This prophet confronted 850 false prophets on top of Mount Carmel. He was outnumbered greatly, but one man with passion can defeat several hundred men who are no more than curious. Elijah was fed up with the apathy of his own people and wanted to prove to them that the Lord was the true God and deserved their commitment. Elijah's passion enabled him to confront the false prophets, call down fire from heaven, and direct the people back to God. The fire from heaven was a picture of the fire already burning inside of Elijah. It allowed him to bring everyone to a point of decision—and cure them of apathy.

3. Initiative activates your talent.
Consider Paul, in Acts 9 and 27. Three times in the book of Acts we read of his conversion to faith in Christ. Each of the accounts not only reminds us of the sovereignty of God, but of the power of initiative. Paul went directly to Damascus, where he had planned to arrest and imprison followers of Christ, but now he wanted to begin ministering to them immediately! He wanted to preach of his marvelous conversion and start helping the world find Christ as well. In addition, Acts 27 is a vivid account of Paul's initiative. He was a prisoner on board a ship, with no rights or authority. But he took initiative when the ship and crew encountered a storm and saved the day.

4. Focus directs your talent.
Consider Noah, in Genesis 6. You remember the story. Noah was confronted by God and told to build an ark—a huge vessel that could preserve him and his family during the flood that was coming. Noah had likely never even see rain and probably never built a boat before. Yet

he stayed on task for 120 years. No doubt he withstood criticism and was the brunt of jokes as he prepared for the flood. Can you imagine the focus Noah must have possessed? Staying true to God's instructions despite all kinds of opposition enabled him to use his abilities and succeed in sparing the human race. You and I are the beneficiaries of his great focus.

5. Preparation positions your talent.
Consider Moses, in Exodus 2–4. He grew up in Pharaoh's palace in Egypt and was given the benefits of all the education and resources he needed to succeed in his adult life—except for one small ingredient. God had to prepare his heart. Moses killed an Egyptian who was beating a Hebrew slave (Exodus 2:12). God sent Moses into the wilderness for forty years where he could prepare him for the job of leading the Hebrews out of slavery in Egypt and into Canaan. Think about it. God took forty years to get this man ready for his mission; the job was too big for a novice. God made sure Moses' head, hands and heart were ready before turning him loose.

6. Practice sharpens your talent.
Consider Daniel, in Daniel 2, 4, 5, 6, 8 and 10. Daniel was a young man when his country was overtaken by the Babylonians. While in a foreign land, he never left the practices that made him such a sharp young leader. One of his gifts was the ability to interpret dreams and visions. All through his years he had the opportunity to practice using this gift—and practice made perfect. One king after another needed his talent, and Daniel was always ready. Late in his adult years, Daniel was called in to help a king who didn't even know him. Fortunately he wasn't rusty, and because of his sharp talent he attracted still another king to his great God.

7. Perseverance sustains your talent.
Consider Joseph, in Genesis 41. Joseph was given a dream from God as a young man. He was gifted to be a leader, and one day he'd have the opportunity to play that role. What he didn't know was there would be incredible obstacles to face along the way. His brothers were jealous of him and treated him abusively. Later they sold him into slavery. He served in Egypt until Potiphar's wife tried to seduce him. When he refused to violate her marriage, she blackmailed him and had him thrown in prison. Soon he was forgotten. Joseph eventually got to use his talent to lead when Pharaoh needed it, but only after persevering through severe hardship. What would have made most people bitter simply made Joseph better.

8. Courage tests your talent.
Consider Deborah, in Judges 4. This woman possessed amazing talent to plan strategy and lead the people of Israel. In her story, however, she faced an intimidating enemy in the army of Canaan. They were ruthless, possessing 900 iron chariots. They seemed invincible. Deborah recognized, however, that this was the number problem to be solved for the oppressed Israelites—so she called for Barak, the commander of Israel's army, and gave him a plan to defeat the Canaanites. Even Barak, a soldier, feared facing them, and refused to do so unless Deborah went with him! This was the ultimate test for her: Do you trust your plan enough to use it in the face of a bigger enemy? She did, and her talent helped set her people free.

9. Teachability expands your talent.
Consider Simon Peter, in Acts 10. Peter was a talented preacher. He was the one who preached the first sermon as the church was launched in Acts 2. He spoke all over Jerusalem and clearly was the "senior" leader, and spokesman for the gospel in the first eight chapters of the book

of Acts. However, in Acts 10, God challenges Peter with a new insight—that the gospel was meant for the Gentiles too, not just the Jews. Peter had a difficult time embracing this idea, but thankfully, his teachable spirit opened a door for him to take the gospel (and his talent) to those outside the Jewish faith, and a whole new ministry was born.

10. Character protects your talent.
Consider Samuel, in 1 Samuel 3. Beginning from his boyhood working under Eli, young Samuel was a person of strong character. He was honest and forthright in all of his relationships, from the lowliest to the kings of Israel. Consequently his influence was great, and his career spanned two generations. In 1 Samuel 3:19–20 we read how everyone looked to him, from one end of the nation to the other. Samuel's talent was perfect for the job of a prophet and priest, but his character kept him in the game long enough to become the most influential man in Israel. Eli, his mentor, was removed from office because he failed at home. Saul, the first king, was removed from office because he failed at work. Samuel's talent outlived them because of his character.

11. Relationships influence your talent.
Consider Rehoboam, in 1 Kings 12. He was appointed king following his father Solomon. There was every reason why his reign would succeed, just as his father and grandfather's reigns had succeeded. Sadly, that's where this truth about relationships enters the scene. Relationships can make or break a person. In Rehoboam's case, they broke him. He had both good people and not-so-good people around him, and he chose to listen to the wrong crowd. Afterward, he made some devastating decisions that ruined his reign. The nation of Israel split and was never the same again. Rehoboam's talent was sufficient—but was affected negatively by his relationships.

12. Responsibility strengthens your talent.
Consider Gideon, in Judges 6–7. Gideon was the runt in his family, belonged to a runt family within his tribe, and many would argue that the tribe was the runt tribe within a runt country, Israel. In other words, he was the least likely to accomplish anything. But he did. Once the angel of the Lord cast a vision for defeating the oppressive Midianites, Gideon stepped up and took responsibility. In fact, it was his sense of ownership of this problem that attracted so many men to fight with him. He actually recruited too many troops and had to cut back the volume. His talent got discovered only when he demonstrated responsibility enough to use it.

13. Teamwork multiplies your talent.
Consider Nehemiah, in Nehemiah 2–3. Nehemiah saw the need to rebuild the wall around Israel's capital city of Jerusalem. However, he wasn't a builder by trade, he was a cupbearer to a foreign king. Once he decided to act, however, he attracted others by expressing the need for resources and people to participate in the solution. After all, people support what they help create. Nehemiah shrewdly cast vision to the folks that lived within the city, who had the most to gain by a strong wall protecting Jerusalem. He harnessed their time, gifts and energy and built the wall in 52 days. He soon became governor because he was a great broker of not only his own talent but that of others too.

THE 360 DEGREE LEADER

Nehemiah (Book of Nehemiah)

Nehemiah is the perfect case study of a 360 degree leader, because he began his leadership journey without a leadership position. He was a cupbearer to King Artaxerxes. He tasted food and wine for a living. He didn't really lead anyone. He was a foreigner in captivity. It would have been easier for him to remain secure in the palace and not attempt any leadership. Had he stayed where he was, no one would have thought less of him for not trying to influence the situation in Jerusalem.

LEADERSHIP SEQUENCE

Phase One: He led himself first (Nehemiah 1)
Phase Two: He led King Artaxerxes (Nehemiah 2)
Phase Three: He led his countrymen (Nehemiah 3–5)
Phase Four: He led as governor (Nehemiah 5–13)

KEY INGREDIENTS

Discipline / Responsibility
Excellence / Respect
Service / Perspective
Vision / Integrity / Planning

Leading Himself

The first person Nehemiah led was himself (Nehemiah 1:4–11):

a. He remained sensitive to the needs of others, mourning the disgrace of Jerusalem (1:4).
b. He exercised self-discipline, fasting for days before doing anything else (1:4).
c. He practiced intimacy with God, praying for days about the circumstances (1:4).
d. He experienced worship, declaring the lordship of God over all things (1:5).
e. He was emotionally secure, confessing Israel's sins as though they were his own (1:6).
f. He acted honestly and with integrity, admitting to his own selfish attitude (1:7).
g. He was well versed in the scriptures, reminding God of his covenant (1:8–9).
h. He acted on his faith, boldly asking God to tend to his request for help (1:10–11).

Someone has said, "Discipline yourself so someone else doesn't have to." That's a great truth. When people demonstrate self-discipline, they win the respect of others. Regardless of their title (or lack thereof), they have the ear of people who can see that their life is in order. In reality, true leadership begins here—not when you gain a position but when you gain control of yourself and can grow beyond the reputation that others have given you. This is step one for a 360 degree leader.

Leading Up

Once Nehemiah had practiced self-leadership, he practiced leading up, with regard to King Artaxerxes (Nehemiah 2:1–9):

a. He faithfully executed his job with excellence and a good attitude (2:1).
b. He interacted with the king with total respect and submission (2:3a).
c. He spoke in a straightforward manner; he wasn't a "yes man" (2:3b).
d. He offered not just a concern but a solution to the problem (2:5).
e. He had done his homework creatively and asked for what he wanted (2:7–8a).
f. He added so much value that the king gave him more than he asked for (2:8b–9).

This passage is a clinic on "leading up." Nehemiah approached the king with humility and respect, and his comments were backed by his excellent work under the king in the past.

Without these ingredients, attempting to lead up with your overseer is often futile. Leading up involves the use of personal power instead of positional power.

Leading Across

Next, Nehemiah practiced leading laterally, with regard to colleagues (Nehemiah 2:11–20; 4:13–23; 5:1–13):

a. He took initiative and met them where they were, in the rubble (2:11).
b. He patiently did his homework on the need (2:12–15).
c. He remained silent until he was prepared (2:16).
d. He identified the need they all faced and embraced it (2:17a).
e. He provided a relevant solution to meet the need (2:17b).
f. His vision included divine support and government support (2:18).
g. He took the heat of opposition and responded on behalf of the people (2:19–20).
h. He offered people God's perspective on their situation (4:13–14).
i. He developed a plan for facing adversity, staying unified and making progress (4:16–23).
j. He took a stand for justice, even when it didn't directly benefit him (5:6–13).
k. He incarnated a spirit of service; his motivation was other-centered (5:6–13).

Once again, this requires a leader to rely more on leveraging personal power rather than positional power. The key ingredients for "leading across" are (1) taking initiative to serve and (2) perspective. Nehemiah saw something others didn't see and he offered himself as part of the solution. He took initiative when no one else did. Trust is deepened when we offer a big-picture perspective and take initiative to serve outside the realm of our own benefits. And leadership always operates on the basis of trust.

Leading Down

Finally, Nehemiah led down, as the people made him governor of Judah (Nehemiah 5–13):

a. He led without reproach, refusing to indulge in leadership privileges (5:14–15).
b. He continued practicing what he preached, with a solid work ethic (5:16).
c. He was inclusive, allowing common workers to enjoy access to him (5:17–18).
d. He refused to get distracted from his mission and priorities (6:2–4).
e. He refused to be bullied or bought by special interest groups (6:10–13).
f. He built a solid team around him (7:1–3).
g. He took a census to assess the population (7:5).
h. His work led to the recovery of the scriptures and spiritual renewal (chapters 8–9).
i. He restored order to people's lives and, consequently, hope (chapters 11–13).

If you consistently lead yourself well, win the heart of your supervisor through excellent work and connect with others well—eventually you'll be given an opportunity to lead down. Others will be willing to serve under your care. This was certainly the case with Nehemiah. The cupbearer became a governor. Did he earn this? You bet he did, but the people gave him this title.

In Nehemiah's case, I don't get the impression that a position was his goal, however. His concern was connecting with others and getting a job done well. It was about relationships and results. He was not pursuing more responsibility, a corner office or a bigger name badge. We are most fit for a promotion when we aren't seeking one. We are only seeking the benefit of others. 360 degree leaders seek the good of the whole, and in the process receive positions and recognition from others. This was certainly true of Nehemiah.

Paul (Acts 27)

The apostle Paul is a New Testament example of a 360 degree leader. More than once Paul found himself a prison inmate. Yet, this never stopped him from influencing the authorities around him. He was able to lead with no title or position. In Acts 27, Paul was escorted along with a group of prisoners to Rome. At the beginning of the journey on board the ship, no one listened to him. By the end of the trip, everyone, including the captain, was not only listening, but following his directions. What were the phases of Paul's 360 degree leadership?

Paul Led Himself

    a. He spent disciplined time with God and heard his voice (27:23–25).

    b. He modeled prayer and faith for others (27:35).

    c. He maintained perspective in a life-threatening situation (27:18–22).

Paul Led Up

    a. He drew special consideration from Julius, the ship's leader (27:3).

    b. He provided hope and encouragement to the hopeless centurion (27:21–26).

    c. He furnished a plan to the soldiers who worked on the ship (27:31–32).

Paul Led Across

    a. He exhorted the passengers to eat and strengthen themselves (27:33).

    b. He gave them vision that they would survive, unhurt if obedient (27:34).

    c. He led by example both spiritually and physically (27:35–36).

Paul Led Down

    a. By the end of the trip, Paul led the crew and passengers to a safe arrival (27:41–44).

    b. By the end of the trip, Paul was leading everyone, including the centurion (27:42–43).

THE DIFFERENCE MAKER

Biblical Examples

Our attitude makes the difference in our life more than just about anything else. All things being equal, the person with a positive, healthy attitude will prevail over the person who may have skill but a lousy attitude. Attitude cannot replace talent, but it's the difference between two talented people. Below is a biblical treatment of "The Difference Maker."

1. Where Did You Get Your Attitude?

Our attitude is an inward feeling expressed in our outward behavior. It comes from our personality, our environment, the impact of others, our self image, our exposure to growth opportunities, our association with others, our beliefs, and our choices.

2. What Your Attitude Cannot Do for You

Case Study: Moses, who led the people of Israel to the Jordan River, but wasn't allowed to cross, despite being a godly leader. Why? His earlier disobedience prevented him. Even though he modeled a great attitude most of the time, it didn't get him across the river.

Case Study: Joshua, who returned from spying out the promised land with a positive attitude about conquering it, wasn't able to persuade the people to go at that time. This was the people's disobedience.

3. What Your Attitude Can Do for You

Case Study: Joseph, whose great attitude kept him steady despite being beat up and thrown into a pit by his brothers, sold into slavery, blackmailed by Potiphar's wife, and forgotten by fellow inmates in prison. What kept Joseph from giving up on his journey from the pit to the prison to the palace? He maintained a positive, hopeful attitude, believing that each step was not an end, but merely a bend in the road.

4. How to Make Your Attitude Your Greatest Asset

Case Study: Ruth. Ruth was an outsider who remained positive and hopeful despite losing her husband early in their marriage. Her mother in law insisted she go home and find a new husband, but she refused to take matters into her own hands and stayed with Naomi and looked after her. Her consistently attractive demeanor drew Boaz to her, and he later asked her to marry him. She became a part of the line of Christ.

Five Big Attitude Obstacles

5. Discouragement

Case Study: Elijah. This great prophet went from conquering the false prophets of Baal to the worst days of his career within a matter of days. Why? Discouragement. He went from victory to defeat quickly and ran from a woman name Jezebel because he felt he was the only one left who was faithful to God. In fact, it took God to restore his perspective.

6. Change

Case Study: Daniel. This young man was removed from his familiar surroundings and taken captive by the Babylonians and the Persians. He was forced to adapt to a new culture and way of life. Talk about change! But Daniel negotiated the changes in his life and maintained his principles. He later became the most influential man in the nation.

7. Problems
Case Study: Job. The story of Job is the story of a man who faced the worst of problems. In a short time, he lost his land, his livestock, his possessions and even his children. To make matters worse, his friends began to throw their theories at him as to why he was going through such a tough time; surely he must have done something wrong to deserve this! But Job's attitude stayed steady and hopeful and was rewarded by God in the end.

8. Fear
Case Study: David. Do you remember this teenager who fought Goliath and won? Consider the fact that he did it in the face of hundreds of frightened soldiers. Fear surrounded him in the camp, but David saw only one thing: Goliath was a man defiling God himself. He knew God was bigger than the giant and defeated him with a stone and a good attitude.

9. Failure
Case Study: Barnabas. Some scholars believe that Barnabas was the Barsabas who was passed over to replace Judas Iscariot as the twelfth apostle. If so, he didn't grumble and go home. He assumed his ministry was to promote others, and he did so, by giving his money generously, and his time to mentor young leaders, not the least of whom was Paul, the greatest apostle in history. Barnabas took failure and turned it into success.

The Difference Maker in Your Life Can Help You Make a Difference in Others
Case Study: Paul. This man faced all kinds of opposition, including the kinds that would have defeated most people. But Paul told the Philippians that he had learned the secret of contentment in any circumstance. He had been ridiculed, tortured, beaten, and left for dead, but he continued joyfully serving his Lord. This has given millions of others the confidence to do the same throughout history as they read what Paul wrote in the New Testament.

ETHICS 101

Ethics cannot be categorized in our lives. People try to use one set of ethics for their professional life, another for their spiritual life and still another at home with their family. This gets them into trouble. Ethics is ethics. If we desire to be ethical, we live by one standard across the board. In other words, there is no such thing as business ethics. This is the heart of *Ethics 101*. When leaders find a standard of values to govern their lives, they can be ethical wherever they go. I believe the Scriptures teach that one standard is "The Golden Rule." This rule is simple: Do to others what you would have them do to you (Matthew 7:12). When personal convenience or getting results or winning or rationalizing our decisions or revenge is more important to us than doing what is right, we will act unethically when the going gets tough. This is what happened to one of the greatest leaders in Scripture: King David. He and one of his soldiers, a man named Uriah, provide a study in contrast concerning ethics.

Uriah: A Man of Influence Who Possessed Ethics

King David failed as a leader in 2 Samuel 11. He committed adultery with Bathsheba, his most famous sin. The story has been circulated worldwide in history, and even movies have been made about it. It was the worst of times for David.

There is a man, however, who emerged during this episode whose ethics shone brightly and clearly, in stark contrast to David's. It was Uriah, the husband of Bathsheba. After David slept with Uriah's wife and she became pregnant, the king sent for Uriah to return home for a few days. David's hope was that Uriah would spend some time with his wife, and later believe that it was his child in her womb. David planned to deceive his way out of trouble by simply getting Uriah to enjoy a day or two at home.

But alas, that was easier said than done. Uriah proved to be a better man than David on this day. He refused to spend time with his wife. His conscience wouldn't let him. His ethics were too clear and strong for him to do such a thing. We learn from both Uriah and David about situational ethics:

1. Uriah's ethics compelled him to submit to Joab, his authority and commanding officer, even when he didn't understand his orders (11:6–7).

2. Uriah's ethics caused him to sleep with the king's servants instead of in his own home, choosing humility instead of exercising his personal rights (11:8–9).

3. Uriah's ethics prevented him from enjoying the pleasures of intimacy with his wife when his fellow soldiers were sacrificing their lives on the battlefield (11:10–11).

4. Uriah's ethics were motivated by his faith in God and his sense of justice. He could not rest while the ark of God's covenant remained in temporary shelters (11:11).

5. Uriah's ethics enabled him to obey the king without questioning the situation (11:12).

6. Uriah's ethics remained even when he was drunk, as he remained with the servants instead of returning home. A drunk Uriah was a better man than a sober David (11:13).

7. Uriah's ethics kept him from reading or altering the letter he carried back to his commander, a letter that contained his own death sentence (11:14–15).

The Role of Convictions

Uriah's ethics were born out of his personal convictions. He wouldn't have been breaking any law by spending time at home; in fact, he would have been obeying his king. But Uriah's convictions guided him in what was right and wrong. For ethics to have any staying power, they must be birthed from personal convictions. In fact, the strongest ethics come out of:

1. Generosity (My ethics must revolve around giving myself away.)

2. Justice (My ethics must revolve around a desire for justice for all.)

3. Excellence (My ethics must revolve around setting a standard above average.)

4. Service (My ethics must revolve around adding value to other people.)

5. Convictions (My ethics must revolve around a firm inward compass.)

If my ethics are not borne out of my convictions, they may shift and change with the tide of the culture or with what is convenient for me. When I form my ethics out of spiritual convictions, they are unchanging. I have a standard that is transcendent beyond my personal preferences.

What Are Convictions?

A conviction is a strong belief that so governs your decisions that you are willing to die for it. History of full of leaders who changed the world because of their convictions. The Scripture tells how Joseph's convictions enabled him to say no to sexual pleasure, how Daniel's convictions led him to civil disobedience in Babylon, and how Elijah's convictions led to a showdown on Mount Carmel against the prophets of Baal.

Convictions are a strong inward compass. Ethics result from this inward compass. They show us our true north. They go on vivid display when we're under pressure. Someone has said that humans are like tea. Our colors show up when we get into hot water. Many people never develop convictions because they make them appear narrow and intolerant. Convictions are stronger than ideas or feelings. In fact, we might list it this way:

1. Idea—A thought or concept which is usually attractive because it is novel or because it's yours.

2. Opinion—An idea you feel emotionally tied to, but which might change as your emotions change.

3. Belief—A strong inclination not only tied to emotions but based upon thoughtful reflection.

4. Commitment—A decision to embrace a belief or principle based on your emotions, mind and will.

5. Conviction—A strong belief that so governs your decisions that you are willing to die for it.

Convictions Come in Our Life When . . .

1. We decide on a truth source from which we will live.

We have chosen to follow the Scriptures as our truth source. The Judeo-Christian ethic can be found in both the Old and New Testaments.

2. We choose to apply that truth source to our daily life.
A truth source only works if we do. If it is only theory, it won't have any power over us when we need it to guide us during tough times.

3. We expose ourselves to a relevant need or crisis.
Convictions rarely form in a vacuum of safety and security. When we choose to put ourselves in view of needs and crisis, we begin to feel the need to respond.

4. We choose what's worth living and dying for.
We cannot determine convictions when we're in the middle of the crisis. They must be decided in quietness when we take the time to determine what's worth living for.

5. We determine our life mission and values.
Once we know our passion and the contribution we want to make in life, we can determine values. These values begin to direct what become our convictions.

6. Our identity is secure and we like the person we've become.
Almost everyone who embraces firm convictions also has a healthy self esteem. We must be secure in who we are and embrace that identity.

Building Convictions into Your Life

1. Summarize and meditate on major principles from Scripture.
2. Repeatedly expose yourself to needs around you.
3. Interview people who possess deep convictions.
4. Determine your life mission and values.
5. Make an all-out commitment to a habit for a set time.
6. Identify why you do what you do; adjust your motives.
7. Get someone to hold you accountable to your convictions.

THINKING FOR A CHANGE

Change your thinking and you can change your life. That's the premise of the book *Thinking for a Change*. Very few people really take the time and effort to think deeply about life or work or faith. This book tries to lead you into a habit of thinking well. It's work but it's worth it. Below are listed some biblical case studies of those who mastered or failed to master the various kinds of thinking habits and how this impacted their life. It was often true: Before God could change the world he had to change the thinking of an individual.

Eleven Thinking Skills Every Successful Person Needs

1. Acquire the wisdom of big-picture thinking.
Case Study: King Jehoram in 2 Kings 3. This king of Israel was in dire straits. The Moabites, with a much larger army than his, planned to conquer him. As he marched his allies across the desert, they ran out of water. When they groaned to Elisha that they needed water, God replied through the prophet: I will give you your water, but this is a small request; I will also give the Moabites into your hands. King Jehoram saw the immediate need but took his eyes off the ultimate solution. He failed to see the big picture.

2. Unleash the potential of focused thinking.
Case Study: The Syrophoenician woman in Mark 7. She was an outsider who came to Jesus with a request and wouldn't be denied. She persistently asked him to heal her daughter. At first, however, Jesus refused to respond. Despite this, she stayed focused and tried a different angle. When Jesus said he came to the Jews first as God's children, she replied that even the dogs get scraps from the children's table. She was right on target. Her focused and determined thinking moved Jesus to meet her need.

3. Discover the joy of creative thinking.
Case Study: Nehemiah in Nehemiah 2–4. Nehemiah led the way in rebuilding the wall of Jerusalem. He did it because of his shrewd, creative thinking. He mobilized the citizens by selling his vision for the value of a new wall. He stationed workers to build the wall across from their own homes so incentive would be high to do a good job. He planned how to encourage when they discouraged, and he protected the workers by using an armed rotation of soldiers until the job was finished.

4. Recognize the importance of realistic thinking.
Case Study: Abraham in Genesis 18. Abraham was interested in sparing the city of Sodom, where his nephew lived. His first proposal was a bit optimistic as he negotiated with God about how many righteous people lived in the city. Over time, Abraham grew more realistic about the state of the citizens and finally arrived at a realistic conclusion. His realism may have spared Lot and his family.

5. Release the power of strategic thinking.
Case Study: Joseph in Genesis 50. Joseph endured a difficult life, beginning with mistreatment by his brothers in Canaan. When he assumed leadership of food supply management in Egypt, and his brothers needed him, they were naturally fearful. This was Joseph's chance to get revenge. But Joseph recognized what was happening, and told them that what they

meant for evil, God meant for good, to spare the children of Israel and preserve their future. Fortunately, Joseph saw things from a strategic perspective.

6. Feel the energy of possibility thinking.
Case Study: Peter in Acts 10. Simon Peter was praying on a rooftop when God gave him an unusual vision. The vision expanded Peter's thinking so he would be open to sharing the gospel with Gentile people. Peter was so entrenched in his current paradigm he pushed back. This new thought was foreign to him. God finally convinced Peter that his goal was to reach the nations, and he needed to see new possibilities. This led to Peter's visit to Cornelius and a new world of ministry.

7. Embrace the lessons of reflective thinking.
Case Study: Jonah, in Jonah 4. This prophet whined about the outcome of his work and God's grace toward the citizens of Nineveh. Jonah lamented the situation rather than learn from it. He was so caught up in himself that he failed to reflect on what had happened. He only saw one angle and only lived in the moment. This forced God to use an object lesson to give him proper perspective in the end.

8. Question the acceptance of popular thinking.
Case Study: Shadrach, Meshach and Abednego in Daniel 3. This classic story illustrates how a handful of individuals can change a nation. The king had erected a statue of himself and instructed everyone to bow down to it. If they refused, they would die. Shadrach, Meshach and Abednego questioned the popular thinking of the day and forced everyone—including the king—to rethink his law. While everyone else just flowed with the crowd, these three thought on their own.

9. Encourage the participation of shared thinking.
Case Study: The elders in Acts 15. In this chapter we read about the Council of Jerusalem, where a huge debate took place among the Jewish leaders of the early church. In this council, the church leaders including Paul, Barnabas and Simon Peter interacted over whether the Gentiles must keep the Law of Moses, and specifically, whether they must practice circumcision. It was not until the key leaders shared their thoughts and a healthy debate ensued that they came to a unified decision.

10. Experience the satisfaction of unselfish thinking.
Case Study: Barnabas in Acts 1, 9, 11, 13 and 14. Barnabas (if indeed he was the same person as Barsabas, who wasn't chosen to replace Judas Iscariot) didn't cease to stay involved. He continued seeking, supporting, and serving people wherever he went. Barnabas's agenda revolved around others. His unselfish thinking moved him to give his money, possessions and time liberally; it enabled him to mentor potential leaders in the church, and ultimately it led to his becoming an apostle after all (Acts 14:14).

11. Enjoy the return of bottom-line thinking.
Case Study: The apostles in Acts 6. This chapter details the first conflict in the early church, where some people felt they were being neglected in the ministry. The widows at some tables were being overlooked. The twelve apostles gathered the congregation together and communicated some healthy, bottom-line thinking: It would not be wise for the key leaders to serve tables and neglect teaching and prayer. In this text, it is interesting to note that apparently the apostles didn't even have to pray about this issue. They recognized the value of bottom-line results and pursued them.

Romans 13:11–14:
Paul's Challenge Can Be Summarized in Three Words:

1. Awaken.
He tells us wake up! The night is almost gone. Now is the time to get up and act! Today matters.

2. Abandon.
He tells us to lay aside the undisciplined patterns of the flesh, and he even cites examples!

3. Adorn.
Finally, he tells us to "put on" Christ. We know he's inside you; now adorn yourself with him.

Today Mattered to People in the Scriptures

Today mattered to Lot (Genesis 19:15–16).
Lot learned the hard way that today matters when he hesitated, and the angels had to seize him and his wife and remove them from Sodom. He failed to build disciplines that would enable him to do what he needed to do, when he needed to do it.

Today mattered to Joshua (Joshua 24:14–15).
Joshua's final speech was a challenge to make today matter. He laid the decision before the people: "Choose for yourselves this day whom you will serve . . . But as for me and my household, we will serve the Lord." Making today matter is a daily choice.

Today mattered to Esther (Esther 4:13–14).
Esther longed to sit still and do nothing, but Mordecai wouldn't let her. The fate of God's people hung in the balance. Mordecai shocked her when he said, "Who knows but that you have come to your royal position for such a time as this?" He pushed Esther to seize the day, and she did.

Today mattered to Nehemiah (Nehemiah 4:16–23).
Nehemiah learned that today matters as he and his builders faced opposition when they constructed the wall around Jerusalem. They worked through the night with a sword in one hand and a brick in the other. Life was a battle. Every moment counted.

Today mattered to David (Psalm 118:24).
David sang, "The Lord has done it this very day; let us rejoice today and be glad." Later he wrote: "Today, if you hear his voice, do not harden your hearts." David was very aware of the significance of today. He worked to see the value of each day and he helped others do the same.

Today mattered to Solomon (Ecclesiastes 3:1–14).
Solomon wrote that God has made everything appropriate in its time. There is a time for everything under the sun. He realized in the end of the book of Ecclesiastes that we must make the most of each day in the sight of God.

Today mattered to Mary (Luke 1:26–30).
Mary learned something from the angel who announced she would give birth to the Christ child. God had been watching her. She had lived a life of discipline and discretion. She prepared herself to be used greatly, in private moments when there was no glamour. She found favor with God.

Today mattered to Paul (1 Corinthians 9:24–27).
Paul compared life to a race. He threw off any weight that would entangle him or slow him down. He made the most of his pursuit of the prize. We all know that runners don't wander. They head straight for the finish. He reminds us of this in Philippians 3:7–14.

Today mattered to Jesus (Matthew 6:34).
Finally, our Master, Jesus Christ, would tell us: Today matters. In the Sermon on the Mount, He tells us to seek first his kingdom, and all the other needs we have will be added to us. Following that challenge, he reminds us not to worry about tomorrow—each day has enough trouble of its own. Just focus on today.

Just for Today . . .

In the book *Today Matters* there is a list of twelve commitments we should make each day of our lives. Here is the list, with a biblical foundation for each one:

1. Just for today, I will choose and display the right attitudes.
Foundation: Philippians 2:3–8

2. Just for today, I will determine and act on important priorities.
Foundation: Ephesians 5:15–17

3. Just for today, I will know and follow healthy guidelines.
Foundation: 1 Corinthians 6:19–20

4. Just for today, I will communicate with and care for my family.
Foundation: 1 Timothy 5:8

5. Just for today, I will practice and develop good thinking.
Foundation: Proverbs 4:5–9

6. Just for today, I will make and keep proper commitments.
Foundation: Philippians 3:12–14

7. Just for today, I will earn and properly manage my finances.
Foundation: Ecclesiastes 5:10–20

8. Just for today, I will deepen and live out my faith.
Foundation: Colossians 2:6–7

9. Just for today, I will initiate and invest in solid relationships.
Foundation: Colossians 3:12–24

10. Just for today, I will plan for and model generosity.
Foundation: Proverbs 11:24–28

11. Just for today, I will embrace and practice good values.
Foundation: Psalm 119:33–40

12. Just for today, I will seek and experience improvements.
Foundation: 1 Peter 2:1–3

moment testify to the Jews that God will always raise up sufficient leadership for each crisis that emerges.

Esther joined the company of such illustrious deliverers as Joseph, who kept his people alive during the famine in Egypt; Moses, who led Israel out of slavery; Samson and David, who delivered the Hebrews from the Philistines; and Gideon, who delivered the people from the hand of the Midianites.

Esther tells the story of an ordinary person who fulfills an extraordinary leadership challenge in an unlikely context. She is a Jew in a foreign land and a woman in a male-dominated world—a minority within a minority. But God raised her up at exactly the right time.

Lessons in Leadership

- The first step a leader takes may be alone and at great risk.
- God is at work behind the scenes whenever you act on his Word.
- Every leader needs mentors.
- Great leaders act on behalf of their people and serve them.
- Timing is everything.

LEADERSHIP HIGHLIGHTS IN ESTHER

Queen Vashti Deposed

1 This is what happened during the time of Xerxes,[a] the Xerxes who ruled over 127 provinces stretching from India to Cush[b]: [2]At that time King Xerxes reigned from his royal throne in the citadel of Susa, [3]and in the third year of his reign he gave a banquet for all his nobles and officials. The military leaders of Persia and Media, the princes, and the nobles of the provinces were present.

[4]For a full 180 days he displayed the vast wealth of his kingdom and the splendor and glory of his majesty. [5]When these days were over, the king gave a banquet, lasting seven days, in the enclosed garden of the king's palace, for all the people from the least to the greatest who were in the citadel of Susa. [6]The garden had hangings of white and blue linen, fastened with cords of white linen and purple material to silver rings on marble pillars. There were couches of gold and silver on a mosaic pavement of porphyry, marble, mother-of-pearl and other costly stones. [7]Wine was served in goblets of gold, each one different from the other, and the royal wine was abundant, in keeping with the king's liberality. [8]By the king's command each guest was allowed to drink with no restrictions, for the king instructed all the wine stewards to serve each man what he wished.

[9]Queen Vashti also gave a banquet for the women in the royal palace of King Xerxes.

[10]On the seventh day, when King Xerxes was in high spirits from wine, he commanded the seven eunuchs who served him — Mehuman, Biztha, Harbona, Bigtha, Abagtha, Zethar and Karkas — [11]to bring before him Queen Vashti, wearing her royal crown, in order to display her beauty to the people and nobles, for she was lovely to look at. [12]But when the attendants delivered the king's command, Queen Vashti refused to come. Then the king became furious and burned with anger.

[13]Since it was customary for the king to consult experts in matters of law and justice, he spoke with the wise men who understood the times [14]and were closest to the king — Karshena, Shethar, Admatha, Tarshish, Meres, Marsena and Memukan, the seven nobles of Persia and Media who had special access to the king and were highest in the kingdom.

[15]"According to law, what must be done to Queen Vashti?" he asked. "She has not obeyed the command of King Xerxes that the eunuchs have taken to her."

[16]Then Memukan replied in the presence of the king and the nobles, "Queen Vashti has done wrong, not only against the king but also against all the nobles and the peoples of all the provinces of King Xerxes. [17]For the queen's conduct will become known to all the women, and so they will despise their husbands and say, 'King Xerxes commanded Queen Vashti to be brought before him, but she would not come.' [18]This very day the Persian and Median women of the nobility who have heard about the queen's conduct will respond to all the king's nobles in the same way. There will be no end of disrespect and discord.

[19]"Therefore, if it pleases the king, let him issue a royal decree and let it be written in the laws of Persia and Media, which cannot be repealed, that Vashti is never again to enter the presence of King Xerxes. Also let the king give her royal position to someone else who is better than she. [20]Then when the king's edict is proclaimed throughout all his vast realm, all the women will respect their husbands, from the least to the greatest."

[21]The king and his nobles were pleased with this advice, so the king did as Memukan proposed. [22]He sent dispatches to all parts of the kingdom, to each province in its own script and to each people in their own language, proclaiming that every man should be ruler over his own household, using his native tongue.

Esther Made Queen

2 Later when King Xerxes' fury had subsided, he remembered Vashti and what she had done and what he had decreed about her. [2]Then the king's personal attendants proposed, "Let a search be made for beautiful young virgins for

---

The Law of Influence

Esther 1:12

When Queen Vashti refused to be put on display, King Xerxes grew angry. At the counsel of his advisors, he removed her from office, opening the door for Esther to take her spot. Esther serves as a marvelous illustration of how God uses one person's influence to accomplish his plans!

---

[a] 1 Hebrew *Ahasuerus*; here and throughout Esther
[b] 1 That is, the upper Nile region

Lessons in Leadership

- Trustworthy leaders must have pure motives.
- Commitment separates the doers from the dreamers.
- Vision is essential: You can't seize what you can't see.
- Leaders must be faithful over time and flexible with their schedules.
- Leadership and responsibility must be shared according to giftedness.
- Leaders must understand their resources before they plan their journey.
- Leaders must be secure enough to handle conflict, criticism, and confrontation.

LEADERSHIP HIGHLIGHTS IN NUMBERS

INTRODUCTION TO NUMBERS

Israel's Leaders Implement the Laws

While the book of Leviticus records the ceremonial laws of Israel, the book of Numbers tells how Israel's leaders implemented those laws.

Numbers describes how the people of Israel learn to function as a camp. It tells how God sets in order their religious, civil, and military economies in preparation for the worshiping, conquering, and journeying that lay ahead.

Like the rest of the Bible, Numbers bluntly records the mistakes as well as the successes of both leaders and followers. Primary among its leadership lessons: Leaders without faith and vision stifle the potential of the group they lead.

The sin of unbelief breaks out repeatedly in the book of Numbers. Temporal and self-protective perspectives multiply. The prophet Balaam, for example, willingly discards his principles for personal profit. Korah loses sight of God's established chain of care and rebels against Israel's God-given leaders. Ten of the spies sent into Canaan come back fearful, discouraging the nation from moving ahead and accomplishing its goal of possessing the promised land.

On the other hand, Numbers also furnishes a picture of healthy, effective leadership. Eleazar, the son of Aaron, assumes the position of high priest after his father's death. He successfully fulfills the role, thanks to godly mentors and role models who support him. And despite their impatience with the Israelites, Moses, Aaron, Joshua and Caleb all demonstrate godly convictions and principle-centered leadership. Their kind of leadership provides the positive lessons of the book.

God's Role in Numbers

God must exercise both the "rod" and the "staff" as he leads his people through the wilderness. The first generation never made it into the promised land, due to their lack of vision, their unbelief and their disobedience. They suffered the rod of punishment. The second generation did make it in, guided by clear instructions from on high and the divine staff of visionary leaders. The book divides naturally into these two stories.

The book's title comes from two censuses God instructed his leaders to take, thus splitting the book into two logical parts. The first census took place near Sinai at the beginning, just prior to the wilderness journey. The second occurred near the Jordan, almost 40 years later, in preparation for entering the promised land.

Near the end, disobedience prevented even Moses from entering the land, and God called on Joshua, Moses' apprentice, to succeed him as leader of Israel.

Leaders in Numbers

Moses, Aaron, Joshua, Balaam, Eleazar, the seventy elders

Other People of Influence in Numbers

Caleb, Korah, Dathan, Abiram, the ten spies, Gad, Reuben, Zelophehad's daughters

they have lied, they have put them with their own possessions. [12]That is why the Israelites cannot stand against their enemies; they turn their backs and run because they have been made liable to destruction. I will not be with you anymore unless you destroy whatever among you is devoted to destruction.

[13]"Go, consecrate the people. Tell them, 'Consecrate yourselves in preparation for tomorrow; for this is what the LORD, the God of Israel, says: There are devoted things among you, Israel. You cannot stand against your enemies until you remove them.

[14]"'In the morning, present yourselves tribe by tribe. The tribe the LORD chooses shall come forward clan by clan; the clan the LORD chooses shall come forward family by family; and the family the LORD chooses shall come forward man by man. [15]Whoever is caught with the devoted things shall be destroyed by fire, along with all that belongs to him. He has violated the covenant of the LORD and has done an outrageous thing in Israel!'"

[16]Early the next morning Joshua had Israel come forward by tribes, and Judah was chosen. [17]The clans of Judah came forward, and the Zerahites were chosen. He had the clan of the Zerahites come forward by families, and Zimri was chosen. [18]Joshua had his family come forward man by man, and Achan son of Karmi, the son of Zimri, the son of Zerah, of the tribe of Judah, was chosen.

[19]Then Joshua said to Achan, "My son, give glory to the LORD, the God of Israel, and honor him. Tell me what you have done; do not hide it from me."

[20]Achan replied, "It is true! I have sinned against the LORD, the God of Israel. This is what I have done: [21]When I saw in the plunder a beautiful robe from Babylonia,[a] two hundred shekels[b] of silver and a bar of gold weighing fifty shekels,[c] I coveted them and took them. They are hidden in the ground inside my tent, with the silver underneath."

[22]So Joshua sent messengers, and they ran to the tent, and there it was, hidden in his tent, with the silver underneath. [23]They took the things from the tent, brought them to Joshua and all the Israelites and spread them out before the LORD.

[24]Then Joshua, together with all Israel, took Achan son of Zerah, the silver, the robe, the gold bar, his sons and daughters, his cattle, donkeys and sheep, his tent and all that he had, to the Valley of Achor. [25]Joshua said, "Why have you

---

[a] 21 Hebrew Shinar   [b] 21 That is, about 5 pounds or about 2.3 kilograms   [c] 21 That is, about 1 1/4 pounds or about 575 grams

---

ACHAN

The Ripple Effect of Sin
Joshua 7:1–25

PROFILE in leadership

Things had been going so well. And then, suddenly—*this*!

After an incredible victory over Jericho, an Israelite foot soldier named Achan chose to disobey some clear directives regarding treasures captured in war. Joshua told his men that all the spoils taken from Jericho were to be considered "devoted things," belonging in God's treasury. Achan defied Joshua's orders, taking some valuables and hiding them under his family's tent.

Joshua, unaware of Achan's sin, sent a small contingent of soldiers against Ai—and the confident Israelites suffered a major rout. Joshua immediately recognized that something must be very wrong. He sought God's face for answers and eventually identified Achan as the culprit. In an act of severe judgment, the guilty man, his entire family, their livestock and possessions were all destroyed. By this fearsome act, Joshua determined to follow God and to remove those who would stand in the way of God's work.

The story of Achan illustrates the principle that leaders may become vulnerable following a major success. Although it can be very difficult, leaders must take the appropriate steps to remove those who block God's blessing and work. When a team member like Achan compromises a core value, the ripple effect of his or her action can hurt many others. Godly leaders must stop the ripple before it becomes a flood.

Joshua Practices the Law of Victory

Joshua 6:1-20

Perhaps the most memorable of Joshua's many victories came in the destruction of Jericho. But what a strange story it is!

Try to picture how absurd God's military strategy must have seemed to real men of war. March around Jericho 13 times in one week, blow some trumpets—and that's it? No weapons? No fighting? No plan of attack? No doubt, the residents of Jericho laughed heartily at the weeklong entertainment provided by the dizzy Hebrew army circling their walls.

Yet Joshua was committed to doing whatever it took to gain victory, and if God said shout, then the general would discard his swords and spears and wholeheartedly go with the absurd. Consider 10 things to really like about Joshua:

1. **He made obedience his first priority.**

2. **He never waited to see what the crowd wanted to do.**

3. **He made decisions from an eternal perspective, not a temporary one.**

4. **He acted decisively.**

5. **He deeply appreciated the past without worshiping it.**

6. **He valued results more than image and reputation.**

7. **He knew that to influence others, he had to stand up and be counted.**

8. **He never wavered from his understanding of what was right.**

9. **He trusted his God more than his gift.**

10. **He made glorifying God his ultimate objective.**

27So the LORD was with Joshua, and his fame spread throughout the land.

Achan's Sin

7 But the Israelites were unfaithful in regard to the devoted things[a]; Achan son of Karmi, the son of Zimri,[b] the son of Zerah, of the tribe of Judah, took some of them. So the LORD's anger burned against Israel.

2Now Joshua sent men from Jericho to Ai, which is near Beth Aven to the east of Bethel, and told them, "Go up and spy out the region." So the men went up and spied out Ai.

3When they returned to Joshua, they said, "Not all the army will have to go up against Ai. Send two or three thousand men to take it and do not weary the whole army, for only a few people live there." 4So about three thousand went up; but they were routed by the men of Ai, 5who killed about thirty-six of them. They chased the Israelites from the city gate as far as the stone quarries and struck them down on the slopes. At this the hearts of the people melted in fear and became like water.

6Then Joshua tore his clothes and fell face-down to the ground before the ark of the LORD, remaining there till evening. The elders of Israel did the same, and sprinkled dust on their heads. 7And Joshua said, "Alas, Sovereign LORD, why did you ever bring this people across the Jordan to deliver us into the hands of the Amorites to destroy us? If only we had been content to stay on the other side of the Jordan! 8Pardon your servant, Lord. What can I say, now that Israel has been routed by its enemies? 9The Canaanites and the other people of the country will hear about this and they will surround us and wipe out our name from the earth. What then will you do for your own great name?"

10The LORD said to Joshua, "Stand up! What are you doing down on your face? 11Israel has sinned; they have violated my covenant, which I commanded them to keep. They have taken some of the devoted things; they have stolen,

---

a 1 The Hebrew term refers to the irrevocable giving over of things or persons to the LORD, often by totally destroying them; also in verses 11, 12, 13 and 15.   b 1 See Septuagint and 1 Chron. 2:6; Hebrew Zabdi; also in verses 17 and 18.